ST/LIB/SER.B/A.92 (Part II)

Index to Proceedings of the General Assembly

Seventy-eighth session — 2023/2024
Part II — Index to Speeches

Dag Hammarskjöld Library New York, 2025 United Nations

DAG HAMMARSKJÖLD LIBRARY
Bibliographical Series, No. A. 92 (Part II)

ST/LIB/SER.B/A.92 (Part II)

UNITED NATIONS PUBLICATION
Sales No. E.25.I.3

ISBN 978-92-1-003465-4
eISBN 978-92-1-107146-7
ISSN 0082-8157

Printed at the United Nations, New York

CONTENTS

Part I

Introduction iii
Abbreviations iv
Sessional information v
Check-list of meetings vii
Agenda xi
Other matters included in the Index xxii
Subject index 1
List of documents 210
Supplements to Official Records 223
Reports of the Main and procedural committees 227
List of resolutions 233

Part II

Introduction iii
Abbreviations Iv
Index to speeches
Corporate names/countries 1
Speakers 253
Subjects 528

INTRODUCTION

The *Index to Proceedings of the General Assembly* is a bibliographic guide to the proceedings and documentation of the General Assembly. This issue covers the seventy-eighth session of the Assembly including its Main and ad hoc committees. The Index is prepared by the Dag Hammarskjöld Library, Department of Global Communications, as one of the products of the United Nations Bibliographic Information System (UNBIS).

ARRANGEMENT OF THE INDEX

Part I consists of the following sections:

Sessional information, listing officers, and providing information on the rules of procedure and on the republication of the resolutions and decisions;

Check-list of meetings, listing the plenary meetings of the Assembly and the meetings of the Main Committees;

Agenda, listing items considered by and brought before the General Assembly together with the subject headings under which they appear in the Subject index;

Subject index, providing topical access to General Assembly documentation arranged alphabetically by agenda subjects and listing documents submitted under each agenda item, the meetings at which the items were considered and the action taken on each item;

List of documents, listing documents issued in connection with the session and providing information on the republication of provisional documents in the printed *Supplements to Official Records;*

Reports of the Main and procedural committees, providing a listing by subject of the reports on the items discussed in the committees;

Resolutions adopted during the seventy-eighth session, indicating the number and title of each resolution, the meeting number and date, the agenda item number, and the vote where appropriate;

Part II (*Index to speeches*) is subdivided into three sections: corporate names/countries, speakers and subjects.

Speakers' names are based on information found in United Nations documents. To submit a name correction, please send an e-mail to Library-ny@un.org

DOCUMENTATION OF THE GENERAL ASSEMBLY

The symbols of the documents of the General Assembly begin with A/-, followed by the session number and an indication of the type of document or Main Committee to which they apply. The number following indicates the number of the document issued in that specific series.

For example: A/78/34 is the thirty-fourth in the series of main documents of the seventy-eighth session; A/INF/78/3 is the third in the information series; A/C.5/78/L.20 is the twentieth in the series of limited distribution documents of the Fifth Committee.

In the series of main documents of the General Assembly's seventy-eighth session, the symbols A/78/1 to A/78/56 are the *Supplements* to the *Official Records of the General Assembly* for that session.

Meeting records are numbered in a similar way. Thus the verbatim record of the first plenary meeting of the seventy-eighth session of the General Assembly bears the symbol A/78/PV.1, while the summary record of the fifteenth meeting of the Third Committee bears the symbol A/C.3/78/SR.15.

In accordance with criteria approved by the General Assembly for the provision of meeting records of United Nations bodies, the verbatim records of the plenary meetings and of the First Committee, as well as the summary records of the other Committees are issued in only one form, as *Official Records of the General Assembly.*

Resolutions adopted by the General Assembly, first issued separately, are collected in a printed *Supplement* to the *Official Records* of each session.

ABBREVIATIONS

Add.	Addendum, addenda
A.I.	Agenda item
Corr.	Corrigendum; corrigenda
ECOSOC	Economic and Social Council
ESCWA	Economic and Social Commission for Western Asia
FAO	Food and Agricultural Organization
GAOR	*Official Records of the General Assembly*
IAEA	International Atomic Energy Agency
ITU	International Telecommunication Union
No.	Number
para., paras.	Paragraph(s)
Rev.	Revision
sess.	Session
Suppl.	Supplement
UN	United Nations
UNCTAD	United Nations Conference on Trade and Development
UNDP	United Nations Development Programme
UNEP	United Nations Environment Programme
UNESCO	United Nations Educational, Scientific and Cultural Organization
UNFPA	United Nations Population Fund
UN-HABITAT	United Nations Settlement Programme
UNHCR	United Nations High Commissioner for Refugees
UNICEF	United Nations Children's Fund
UNIDO	United Nations Industrial Development Organization
UNITAR	United Nations Institute for Training and Research
UNOPS	United Nations Office for Project Services
UNRWA	United Nations Relief and Works Agency for Palestine Refugees in the Near East
UN-Women	UN Entity for Gender Equality and the Empowerment of Women
Vol.	Volume

(personal capacity)
NEW CALEDONIA QUESTION (Agenda item 58)
Wateou, Naïa - A/C.4/78/SR.5
SLAVERY—MEMORIALS (Agenda item 118)
King, Yolanda - A/78/PV.64
UN. INTERNATIONAL COURT OF JUSTICE—REPORTS (Agenda item 73)
Chindawongse, Suriya - A/C.6/78/SR.26
WESTERN SAHARA QUESTION (Agenda item 58)
Adda, M'Rabih - A/C.4/78/SR.5
Adjissa, Youcef - A/C.4/78/SR.5
Aly, Ahmed - A/C.4/78/SR.4
Assor Sydney, Solomon - A/C.4/78/SR.6
Basinet, Cynthia - A/C.4/78/SR.4
Belmeddah, Nor Eddine - A/C.4/78/SR.5
Boulon, Malaainin - A/C.4/78/SR.5
Boussif Hammou, Limam - A/C.4/78/SR.5
Breid Eleil, Hamadi - A/C.4/78/SR.5
Chrif, Moulay Brahim - A/C.4/78/SR.5
Debeche, Smail - A/C.4/78/SR.4
Déniz Verona, Palmira - A/C.4/78/SR.4
El Ahmadi, Brahim - A/C.4/78/SR.6
El Ouali, Zine El Aabidine - A/C.4/78/SR.6
Esparza Machín, Rafael - A/C.4/78/SR.5
Hamudi, Malika - A/C.4/78/SR.5
Jiménez Martín, María Inés - A/C.4/78/SR.4
Lenz, Janet - A/C.4/78/SR.5
Lygeros, Nikos - A/C.4/78/SR.5
Mohamed, El Fadel Bua Da - A/C.4/78/SR.6
Mohamed, Mahfud - A/C.4/78/SR.6
Molina García Alcañiz, Mar - A/C.4/78/SR.4
Ouakli, Mohamed - A/C.4/78/SR.5
Pace, Giulia - A/C.4/78/SR.4
Perino, Romina - A/C.4/78/SR.6
Ramírez Marrero, Carmelo - A/C.4/78/SR.4
Roios, Ana - A/C.4/78/SR.4
Shaibata, Mrabih Rabou - A/C.4/78/SR.5
Souvi, Mouhidine - A/C.4/78/SR.5
Taleb Aomar, Boullah - A/C.4/78/SR.5
Tate, El Moustapha - A/C.4/78/SR.5
Taualumru, Chejuna - A/C.4/78/SR.5
Tessouh, Miloud - A/C.4/78/SR.5
Vucic, Mihajlo - A/C.4/78/SR.4

Accountability, Coherence and Transparency (ACT) Group
UN. GENERAL ASSEMBLY—WORK PROGRAMME (Agenda item 120)
Tammsaar, Rein (Estonia) - A/78/PV.32
UN. SECURITY COUNCIL—REPORTS (Agenda item 26)
Vinhas, Rui (Portugal) - A/78/PV.93
UN RESOLUTIONS—IMPLEMENTATION (Agenda item 119)
Tammsaar, Rein (Estonia) - A/78/PV.32

Advancing Health Equity (Organization)
RACIAL DISCRIMINATION—ELIMINATION (Agenda item 69a)
Blackstock, Uché - A/78/PV.63

Advisory Committee on the United Nations Programme of Assistance in the Teaching, Study, Dissemination and Wider Appreciation of International Law. Chair
INTERNATIONAL LAW—TRAINING PROGRAMMES (Agenda item 78)
Agyeman, Harold Adlai (Ghana) - A/C.6/78/SR.21

Advisory Committee on the United Nations Programme of Assistance in the Teaching, Study, Dissemination and Wider Appreciation of International Law. Secretary
INTERNATIONAL LAW—TRAINING PROGRAMMES (Agenda item 78)
Pallek, Markus - A/C.6/78/SR.21

Afghanistan
HUMAN RIGHTS (Agenda item 71)
Faiq, Naseer Ahmed - A/C.3/78/SR.16
HUMAN RIGHTS—AFGHANISTAN (Agenda item 71c)
Faiq, Naseer Ahmed - A/C.3/78/SR.26; A/C.3/78/SR.34
UN HIGH COMMISSIONER FOR REFUGEES—REPORTS (Agenda item 60)
Faiq, Naseer Ahmed - A/C.3/78/SR.44; A/C.3/78/SR.45
WOMEN'S ADVANCEMENT (Agenda item 25a)
Faiq, Naseer Ahmed - A/C.3/78/SR.10
WOMEN'S ADVANCEMENT—CONFERENCES (Agenda item 25b)
Faiq, Naseer Ahmed - A/C.3/78/SR.10

Africa Centre for Strategic Intelligence (Senegal)
WESTERN SAHARA QUESTION (Agenda item 58)
Aidara, Abdoul Latif - A/C.4/78/SR.5

African Forum for Research and Studies in Human Rights
WESTERN SAHARA QUESTION (Agenda item 58)
Ezaoui, Khadija - A/C.4/78/SR.5

African Institute for Peacebuilding and Conflict Transformation
WESTERN SAHARA QUESTION (Agenda item 58)
Gain, Mohammed Ahmed - A/C.4/78/SR.6

African Union
UN. SECURITY COUNCIL—MEMBERSHIP (Agenda item 121)
Kpukumu, Sulay-Manah J. (Sierra Leone) - A/78/PV.34
Sowa, Amara Sheikh Mohammed (Sierra Leone) - A/78/PV.104

Agency for the Prohibition of Nuclear Weapons in Latin America and the Caribbean

NUCLEAR-WEAPON-FREE ZONES (Agenda item 99cc)
Damico, Flávio Soares - A/C.1/78/PV.11

Albania

CRIMES AGAINST HUMANITY (Agenda item 80)
Laboti, Shkëlqim - A/C.6/78/SR.11; A/C.6/78/SR.45
ELECTION VERIFICATION—UN (Agenda item 71b)
Lamce, Enian - A/C.3/78/SR.50
HUMAN RIGHTS—AFGHANISTAN (Agenda item 71c)
Lamce, Enian - A/C.3/78/SR.26; A/C.3/78/SR.34
HUMAN RIGHTS—RUSSIAN FEDERATION (Agenda item 71c)
Lamce, Enian - A/C.3/78/SR.37
HUMAN RIGHTS—TERRITORIES OCCUPIED BY ISRAEL (Agenda item 71c)
Lamce, Enian - A/C.3/78/SR.35
HUMAN RIGHTS—UKRAINE (Agenda item 71c)
Lamce, Enian - A/C.3/78/SR.26; A/C.3/78/SR.37
HUMAN RIGHTS ACTIVISTS (Agenda item 71b)
Lamce, Enian - A/C.3/78/SR.26
INTERNATIONAL RESIDUAL MECHANISM FOR CRIMINAL TRIBUNALS (Agenda item 126)
Stastoli, Andris - A/78/PV.19
MINORITIES (Agenda item 71b)
Lamce, Enian - A/C.3/78/SR.39
RACIAL DISCRIMINATION—ELIMINATION (Agenda item 69a)
Lamce, Enian - A/C.3/78/SR.47
RESPONSIBILITY TO PROTECT (Agenda item 129)
Janina, Suela - A/78/PV.96
RIGHTS OF THE CHILD (Agenda item 67)
Lamce, Enian - A/C.3/78/SR.11
TERRORISM (Agenda item 109)
Spasse, Arian - A/C.6/78/SR.4
UKRAINE—POLITICAL CONDITIONS (Agenda item 62)
Spasse, Arian - A/78/PV.57
UN—BUDGET (2024) (Agenda item 134)
Prizreni, Ingrit - A/C.5/78/SR.34
UN. GENERAL ASSEMBLY (78TH SESS. : 2023-2024). 1ST COMMITTEE—GENERAL DEBATE (Agenda item 8)
Bekteshi, Etrit - A/C.1/78/PV.6
UN. GENERAL ASSEMBLY (78TH SESS. : 2023-2024). 2ND COMMITTEE—GENERAL DEBATE (Agenda item 8)
Kapisyzi, Arb - A/C.2/78/SR.5
VETO (Agenda item 63)
Janina, Suela - A/78/PV.69; A/78/PV.79
Spasse, Arian - A/78/PV.3

Albania (continued)

WOMEN'S ADVANCEMENT (Agenda item 25a)
Lamce, Enian - A/C.3/78/SR.9
WOMEN'S ADVANCEMENT—CONFERENCES (Agenda item 25b)
Lamce, Enian - A/C.3/78/SR.9
YOUTH (Agenda item 24b)
Delija, Marsela - A/C.3/78/SR.3
Kasmi, Aldi - A/C.3/78/SR.3

Albania. President

UN. GENERAL ASSEMBLY (78TH SESS. : 2023-2024)—GENERAL DEBATE (Agenda item 8)
Begaj, Bajram - A/78/PV.9
UN. GENERAL ASSEMBLY (78TH SESS. : 2023-2024)—SPECIAL STATEMENTS
Begaj, Bajram - A/78/PV.9

Algeria

AGEING PERSONS (Agenda item 24b)
Samai, Rahma - A/C.3/78/SR.3
ARMS RACE—OUTER SPACE (Agenda item 97a)
Lebbaz, Larbi Abdelfattah - A/C.1/78/PV.17
BIOLOGICAL WEAPONS—TREATIES (Agenda item 106)
Lebbaz, Larbi Abdelfattah - A/C.1/78/PV.15
CHEMICAL WEAPONS—TREATIES (Agenda item 99l)
Lebbaz, Larbi Abdelfattah - A/C.1/78/PV.15
COMMODITIES (Agenda item 16d)
Latrous, Mohamed-Esseghir - A/C.2/78/SR.14
CONVENTIONAL WEAPONS—TREATIES (Agenda item 103)
Lebbaz, Larbi Abdelfattah - A/C.1/78/PV.19
CRIME PREVENTION (Agenda item 107)
Hassani, Billel - A/C.3/78/SR.6
CRIMES AGAINST HUMANITY (Agenda item 80)
Bouchedoub, Mohamed Faiz - A/C.6/78/SR.11; A/C.6/78/SR.39; A/C.6/78/SR.41; A/C.6/78/SR.43; A/C.6/78/SR.45
CUBA—UNITED STATES (Agenda item 38)
Bendjama, Amar - A/78/PV.24
CYBERCRIME (Agenda item 108)
Hassani, Billel - A/C.3/78/SR.6
DISARMAMENT—GENERAL AND COMPLETE (Agenda item 99)
Lebbaz, Larbi Abdelfattah - A/C.1/78/PV.19; A/C.1/78/PV.30
DISARMAMENT AGREEMENTS—OUTER SPACE (Agenda item 97c)
Lebbaz, Larbi Abdelfattah - A/C.1/78/PV.17
DISPLACED PERSONS (Agenda item 71b)
Sahraoui, Ahmed - A/C.3/78/SR.49
ECONOMIC SANCTIONS—INTERNATIONAL RELATIONS (Agenda item 28)
Bendjama, Amar - A/78/PV.90

Algeria (continued)

ELECTION VERIFICATION—UN (Agenda item 71b)
Hassani, Billel - A/C.3/78/SR.50
EMERGENCY ASSISTANCE (Agenda item 72a)
Samai, Rahma - A/78/PV.47
FOOD SECURITY (Agenda item 23a)
Latrous, Mohamed-Esseghir - A/C.2/78/SR.17
HEALTH (Agenda item 125)
Hassani, Billel - A/78/PV.41
Sahraoui, Ahmed - A/78/PV.16
HUMAN RIGHTS (Agenda item 71)
Hassani, Billel - A/C.3/78/SR.16; A/C.3/78/SR.27
HUMAN RIGHTS—ERITREA (Agenda item 71c)
Hassani, Billel - A/C.3/78/SR.36
HUMAN RIGHTS—INTERNATIONAL INSTRUMENTS (Agenda item 71a)
Hassani, Billel - A/C.3/78/SR.17
HUMAN RIGHTS—TERRITORIES OCCUPIED BY ISRAEL (Agenda item 71c)
Hassani, Billel - A/C.3/78/SR.27
Yahiaoui, Dahmane - A/C.3/78/SR.35
IAEA—REPORTS (Agenda item 89)
Bendjama, Amar - A/78/PV.30
INFORMATION (Agenda item 53)
Merabet, Ismaïl - A/C.4/78/SR.13
INFORMATION—INTERNATIONAL SECURITY (Agenda item 94)
Lebbaz, Larbi Abdelfattah - A/C.1/78/PV.21
INTERNATIONAL JURISDICTION (Agenda item 84)
Bouchedoub, Mohamed Faiz - A/C.6/78/SR.13
LANDMINES—TREATIES (Agenda item 99m)
Lebbaz, Larbi Abdelfattah - A/C.1/78/PV.19
MEDITERRANEAN REGION—REGIONAL SECURITY (Agenda item 104)
Lebbaz, Larbi Abdelfattah - A/C.1/78/PV.22
MIDDLE EAST—NUCLEAR-WEAPON-FREE ZONES (Agenda item 95)
Lebbaz, Larbi Abdelfattah - A/C.1/78/PV.14; A/C.1/78/PV.22
MULTILATERALISM—DISARMAMENT (Agenda item 99r)
Lebbaz, Larbi Abdelfattah - A/C.1/78/PV.22
NUCLEAR DISARMAMENT (Agenda item 99b)
Lebbaz, Larbi Abdelfattah - A/C.1/78/PV.14
NUCLEAR NON-PROLIFERATION—INTERNATIONAL OBLIGATIONS (Agenda item 99w)
Lebbaz, Larbi Abdelfattah - A/C.1/78/PV.14
NUCLEAR WEAPON TESTS—TREATIES (Agenda item 105)
Lebbaz, Larbi Abdelfattah - A/C.1/78/PV.14
OUTER SPACE—CONFIDENCE-BUILDING MEASURES (Agenda item 99v)
Lebbaz, Larbi Abdelfattah - A/C.1/78/PV.17
OUTER SPACE—PRINCIPLES (Agenda item 97d)
Lebbaz, Larbi Abdelfattah - A/C.1/78/PV.17

Algeria (continued)

PALESTINE QUESTION (Agenda item 35)
Gaouaoui, Nacim - A/78/PV.40
PALESTINIANS—ASSISTANCE (Agenda item 72b)
Samai, Rahma - A/78/PV.47
PEACE (Agenda item 14)
Alem, Mohammed Walid - A/78/PV.77
Merabet, Ismaïl - A/78/PV.82
PEACE—REGIONAL CENTRE—AFRICA (Agenda item 100b)
Lebbaz, Larbi Abdelfattah - A/C.1/78/PV.23
PEACEBUILDING (Agenda item 61)
Gaouaoui, Nacim - A/78/PV.100
PEACEKEEPING OPERATIONS (Agenda item 51)
Bendjama, Amar - A/C.4/78/SR.19
PERSONS WITH DISABILITIES—HUMAN RIGHTS (Agenda item 71a)
Samai, Rahma - A/C.3/78/SR.38; A/C.3/78/SR.51
POVERTY—INTERNATIONAL DECADES (Agenda item 21a)
Latrous, Mohamed-Esseghir - A/C.2/78/SR.17
RACIAL DISCRIMINATION—ELIMINATION (Agenda item 69a)
Hassani, Billel - A/C.3/78/SR.42; A/C.3/78/SR.47
RACIAL DISCRIMINATION—PROGRAMMES OF ACTION (Agenda item 69b)
Hassani, Billel - A/C.3/78/SR.42
RIGHT TO DEVELOPMENT (Agenda item 71b)
Hassani, Billel - A/C.3/78/SR.20
RIGHTS OF THE CHILD (Agenda item 67)
Samai, Rahma - A/C.3/78/SR.11; A/C.3/78/SR.12; A/C.3/78/SR.14
RULE OF LAW (Agenda item 83)
Bouchedoub, Mohamed Faiz - A/C.6/78/SR.18
RURAL POVERTY (Agenda item 21b)
Latrous, Mohamed-Esseghir - A/C.2/78/SR.17
RURAL WOMEN (Agenda item 25a)
Samai, Rahma - A/C.3/78/SR.9; A/C.3/78/SR.49
SELF-DETERMINATION OF PEOPLES (Agenda item 70)
Hassani, Billel - A/C.3/78/SR.42; A/C.3/78/SR.43
SMALL ARMS—ILLICIT TRAFFIC (Agenda item 99p)
Lebbaz, Larbi Abdelfattah - A/C.1/78/PV.19
SMALL ARMS—ILLICIT TRAFFIC—ASSISTANCE (Agenda item 99n)
Lebbaz, Larbi Abdelfattah - A/C.1/78/PV.19
SOCIAL CONDITIONS (Agenda item 24b)
Samai, Rahma - A/C.3/78/SR.3
SOCIAL DEVELOPMENT (Agenda item 24)
Samai, Rahma - A/C.3/78/SR.3
SPECIAL POLITICAL MISSIONS (Agenda item 52)
Alem, Mohammed Walid - A/C.4/78/SR.21
SUSTAINABLE DEVELOPMENT (Agenda item 18)
Latrous, Mohamed-Esseghir - A/C.2/78/SR.14
Merabet, Ismaïl - A/C.2/78/SR.15; A/C.2/78/SR.25

Algeria (continued)

TERRITORIES OCCUPIED BY ISRAEL—HUMAN RIGHTS (Agenda item 50)
Sahraoui, Ahmed - A/C.4/78/SR.24
TERRITORIES OCCUPIED BY ISRAEL—NATURAL RESOURCES (Agenda item 59)
Merabet, Ismaïl - A/C.2/78/SR.19
TERRORISM (Agenda item 109)
Gaouaoui, Nacim - A/C.6/78/SR.4
TORTURE AND OTHER CRUEL TREATMENT (Agenda item 71a)
Hassani, Billel - A/C.3/78/SR.18
UN—BUDGET (2024) (Agenda item 134)
Gadouri, Hakim - A/C.5/78/SR.33
Kara, Kamel - A/C.5/78/SR.5
UN—HUMAN RESOURCES MANAGEMENT (Agenda item 139)
Gadouri, Hakim - A/C.5/78/SR.27
UN—PROGRAMME PLANNING (Agenda item 135)
Kara, Kamel - A/C.5/78/SR.5
UN. GENERAL ASSEMBLY (78TH SESS. : 2023-2024)—GENERAL DEBATE—RIGHT OF REPLY (Agenda item 8)
Bendjama, Amar - A/78/PV.14
UN. GENERAL ASSEMBLY (78TH SESS. : 2023-2024). 1ST COMMITTEE—GENERAL DEBATE (Agenda item 8)
Lebbaz, Larbi Abdelfattah - A/C.1/78/PV.8
UN. GENERAL ASSEMBLY (78TH SESS. : 2023-2024). 2ND COMMITTEE—GENERAL DEBATE (Agenda item 8)
Latrous, Mohamed-Esseghir - A/C.2/78/SR.6
UN. HUMAN RIGHTS COUNCIL—REPORTS (Agenda item 66)
Hassani, Billel - A/78/PV.28; A/C.3/78/SR.46
Samai, Rahma - A/C.3/78/SR.46
UN. INTERNATIONAL LAW COMMISSION—REPORTS (Agenda item 79)
Bouchedoub, Mohamed Faiz - A/C.6/78/SR.28
UN. PEACEBUILDING COMMISSION—REPORTS (Agenda item 27)
Gaouaoui, Nacim - A/78/PV.100
UN. PEACEBUILDING FUND—REPORTS (Agenda item 111)
Gaouaoui, Nacim - A/78/PV.100
UN. SECURITY COUNCIL—MEMBERSHIP (Agenda item 121)
Bendjama, Amar - A/78/PV.35
UN CHARTER—REPORTS (Agenda item 82)
Bouchedoub, Mohamed Faiz - A/C.6/78/SR.34
UN HIGH COMMISSIONER FOR REFUGEES—REPORTS (Agenda item 60)
Sahraoui, Ahmed - A/C.3/78/SR.45
Samai, Rahma - A/C.3/78/SR.44
UNRWA—ACTIVITIES (Agenda item 49)
Bendjama, Amar - A/C.4/78/SR.22
Sahraoui, Ahmed - A/C.4/78/SR.23
VETO (Agenda item 63)
Gaouaoui, Nacim - A/78/PV.51; A/78/PV.66
Sahraoui, Ahmed - A/78/PV.59; A/78/PV.74

Algeria (continued)

WEAPONS—OUTER SPACE (Agenda item 97b)
Lebbaz, Larbi Abdelfattah - A/C.1/78/PV.17
WESTERN SAHARA QUESTION (Agenda item 58)
Bendjama, Amar - A/C.4/78/SR.9
Koudri, Toufik Laid - A/C.4/78/SR.5
Sahel, Makhlouf - A/C.4/78/SR.5
WOMEN'S ADVANCEMENT (Agenda item 25a)
Samai, Rahma - A/C.3/78/SR.7; A/C.3/78/SR.9
WOMEN'S ADVANCEMENT—CONFERENCES (Agenda item 25b)
Samai, Rahma - A/C.3/78/SR.7; A/C.3/78/SR.9; A/C.3/78/SR.51

Algeria. President

UN. GENERAL ASSEMBLY (78TH SESS. : 2023-2024)—GENERAL DEBATE (Agenda item 8)
Tebboune, Abdelmadjid - A/78/PV.5
UN. GENERAL ASSEMBLY (78TH SESS. : 2023-2024)—SPECIAL STATEMENTS
Tebboune, Abdelmadjid - A/78/PV.5

Algerian Youth Academy (Organization)

WESTERN SAHARA QUESTION (Agenda item 58)
Bouaziz, Samir - A/C.4/78/SR.5

Alliance of Small Island States

2030 AGENDA—PROGRAMME IMPLEMENTATION (Agenda item 18a)
Lautasi, Isaia (Samoa) - A/C.2/78/SR.12
CLIMATE (Agenda item 18d)
Lautasi, Isaia (Samoa) - A/C.2/78/SR.12
DEVELOPMENT FINANCE (Agenda item 16b)
Bartley, Matilda (Samoa) - A/C.2/78/SR.8
DISASTER PREVENTION (Agenda item 18c)
Lautasi, Isaia (Samoa) - A/C.2/78/SR.12
EXTERNAL DEBT (Agenda item 16c)
Bartley, Matilda (Samoa) - A/C.2/78/SR.8
FOOD SECURITY (Agenda item 23a)
Lautasi, Isaia (Samoa) - A/C.2/78/SR.16
INTERNATIONAL TRADE (Agenda item 16a)
Bartley, Matilda (Samoa) - A/C.2/78/SR.8
LANDLOCKED DEVELOPING COUNTRIES—CONFERENCES (Agenda item 20b)
Bartley, Matilda (Samoa) - A/C.2/78/SR.7
LAW OF THE SEA (Agenda item 75a)
Bartley, Matilda (Samoa) - A/78/PV.43
LEAST DEVELOPED COUNTRIES—CONFERENCES (Agenda item 20a)
Bartley, Matilda (Samoa) - A/C.2/78/SR.7

Alliance of Small Island States (continued)

MACROECONOMIC POLICY (Agenda item 16)
Bartley, Matilda (Samoa) - A/C.2/78/SR.8
MARINE ECOSYSTEMS—BIOLOGICAL DIVERSITY (Agenda item 75c)
Bartley, Matilda (Samoa) - A/78/PV.43; A/78/PV.73
Luteru, Fatumanava-o-Upolu III Pa'olelei (Samoa) - A/78/PV.103
MILLENNIUM SUMMIT—CONFERENCES (Agenda item 117)
Lautasi, Isaia (Samoa) - A/78/PV.102
Luteru, Fatumanava-o-Upolu III Pa'olelei (Samoa) - A/78/PV.53
POVERTY—INTERNATIONAL DECADES (Agenda item 21a)
Lautasi, Isaia (Samoa) - A/C.2/78/SR.16
RURAL POVERTY (Agenda item 21b)
Lautasi, Isaia (Samoa) - A/C.2/78/SR.16
SMALL ISLAND DEVELOPING STATES—PROGRAMMES OF ACTION (Agenda item 18b)
Bartley, Matilda (Samoa) - A/C.2/78/SR.22
Luteru, Fatumanava-o-Upolu III Pa'olelei (Samoa) - A/78/PV.100; A/78/PV.103
STRADDLING FISH STOCKS (Agenda item 75b)
Bartley, Matilda (Samoa) - A/78/PV.43
SUSTAINABLE DEVELOPMENT (Agenda item 18)
Lautasi, Isaia (Samoa) - A/C.2/78/SR.12
UN. GENERAL ASSEMBLY (78TH SESS. : 2023-2024). 2ND COMMITTEE—GENERAL DEBATE (Agenda item 8)
Bartley, Matilda (Samoa) - A/C.2/78/SR.2
UN. INTERNATIONAL LAW COMMISSION—REPORTS (Agenda item 79)
Luteru, Fatumanava-o-Upolu III Pa'olelei (Samoa) - A/C.6/78/SR.27
UN CONFERENCES (Agenda item 13)
Lautasi, Isaia (Samoa) - A/78/PV.102
Luteru, Fatumanava-o-Upolu III Pa'olelei (Samoa) - A/78/PV.53

Amazones Pacific (Organization)

FRENCH POLYNESIA QUESTION (Agenda item 58)
Labrousse, Lou - A/C.4/78/SR.3

American Association of Jurists

WESTERN SAHARA QUESTION (Agenda item 58)
Ramos, Vanessa - A/C.4/78/SR.5

Andorra

MULTILINGUALISM (Agenda item 124)
Font Vilagines, Meritxell - A/78/PV.107
RIGHTS OF THE CHILD (Agenda item 67)
Font Vilagines, Meritxell - A/C.3/78/SR.14

Andorra (continued)

UN. GENERAL ASSEMBLY (78TH SESS. : 2023-2024). 2ND COMMITTEE—GENERAL DEBATE (Agenda item 8)
Kallis Baldrich, Guillem - A/C.2/78/SR.4
VETO (Agenda item 63)
Vives Balmaña, Elisenda - A/78/PV.75
WOMEN'S ADVANCEMENT (Agenda item 25a)
Vives Balmaña, Elisenda - A/C.3/78/SR.10
WOMEN'S ADVANCEMENT—CONFERENCES (Agenda item 25b)
Vives Balmaña, Elisenda - A/C.3/78/SR.10

Andorra. Head of Government

UN. GENERAL ASSEMBLY (78TH SESS. : 2023-2024)—GENERAL DEBATE (Agenda item 8)
Espot Zamora, Xavier - A/78/PV.10
UN. GENERAL ASSEMBLY (78TH SESS. : 2023-2024)—SPECIAL STATEMENTS
Espot Zamora, Xavier - A/78/PV.10

Angola

AFRICA—DEVELOPMENT (Agenda item 65b)
Cruz, Francisco José da - A/78/PV.18
CHEMICAL WEAPONS—TREATIES (Agenda item 99l)
Luemba, Mateus Pedro - A/C.1/78/PV.15
CLIMATE (Agenda item 18d)
Luemba, Mateus Pedro - A/C.2/78/SR.13
CUBA—UNITED STATES (Agenda item 38)
Cruz, Francisco José da - A/78/PV.24
DECOLONIZATION (Agenda item 58)
Luemba, Mateus Pedro - A/C.4/78/SR.6
DEVELOPMENT FINANCE (Agenda item 16b)
Cruz, Francisco José da - A/C.2/78/SR.9
DISASTER PREVENTION (Agenda item 18c)
Luemba, Mateus Pedro - A/C.2/78/SR.13
EXTERNAL DEBT (Agenda item 16c)
Cruz, Francisco José da - A/C.2/78/SR.9
FALKLAND ISLANDS (MALVINAS) QUESTION (Agenda item 42)
Luemba, Mateus Pedro - A/C.4/78/SR.6
FOOD SECURITY (Agenda item 23a)
Luemba, Mateus Pedro - A/C.2/78/SR.16
HUMAN RIGHTS (Agenda item 71)
Luemba, Mateus Pedro - A/C.3/78/SR.28
INFORMATION TECHNOLOGY—DEVELOPMENT (Agenda item 15)
Cruz, Francisco José da - A/C.2/78/SR.10
LANDLOCKED DEVELOPING COUNTRIES—CONFERENCES (Agenda item 20b)
Cruz, Francisco José da - A/C.2/78/SR.7
LANDMINES—TREATIES (Agenda item 99m)
Luemba, Mateus Pedro - A/C.1/78/PV.19

Angola (continued)

LEAST DEVELOPED COUNTRIES—CONFERENCES (Agenda item 20a)
Cruz, Francisco José da - A/C.2/78/SR.7
MINE CLEARANCE (Agenda item 46)
Luemba, Mateus Pedro - A/C.4/78/SR.10
PEACE (Agenda item 14)
Luemba, Mateus Pedro - A/78/PV.82
POVERTY—INTERNATIONAL DECADES (Agenda item 21a)
Luemba, Mateus Pedro - A/C.2/78/SR.16
RACIAL DISCRIMINATION—ELIMINATION (Agenda item 69a)
Luemba, Mateus Pedro - A/78/PV.50
RULE OF LAW (Agenda item 83)
Luemba, Mateus Pedro - A/C.6/78/SR.19
RURAL POVERTY (Agenda item 21b)
Luemba, Mateus Pedro - A/C.2/78/SR.16
SCIENCE AND TECHNOLOGY—DEVELOPMENT (Agenda item 19a)
Cruz, Francisco José da - A/C.2/78/SR.10
SPECIAL POLITICAL MISSIONS (Agenda item 52)
Cruz, Francisco José da - A/C.4/78/SR.21
TRAFFIC SAFETY (Agenda item 12)
Cruz, Francisco José da - A/78/PV.92
UN—BUDGET (2024) (Agenda item 134)
Luemba, Mateus Pedro - A/C.5/78/SR.5; A/C.5/78/SR.33
UN—PROGRAMME PLANNING (Agenda item 135)
Luemba, Mateus Pedro - A/C.5/78/SR.5
UN. ECONOMIC AND SOCIAL COUNCIL—REPORTS (Agenda item 9)
Cruz, Francisco José da - A/78/PV.48
UN. GENERAL ASSEMBLY (78TH SESS. : 2023-2024). 1ST COMMITTEE—GENERAL DEBATE (Agenda item 8)
Cruz, Francisco José da - A/C.1/78/PV.9
UN. GENERAL ASSEMBLY (78TH SESS. : 2023-2024). 2ND COMMITTEE—GENERAL DEBATE (Agenda item 8)
Cruz, Francisco José da - A/C.2/78/SR.3
UN. SECRETARY-GENERAL—REPORTS (Agenda item 110)
Cruz, Francisco José da - A/78/PV.55
UN. SECURITY COUNCIL—MEMBERSHIP (Agenda item 121)
Luemba, Mateus Pedro - A/78/PV.36
UN. SECURITY COUNCIL—REPORTS (Agenda item 26)
Cruz, Francisco José da - A/78/PV.94
WEAPONS OF MASS DESTRUCTION—TERRORISM (Agenda item 99s)
Luemba, Mateus Pedro - A/C.1/78/PV.15
WESTERN SAHARA QUESTION (Agenda item 58)
Luemba, Mateus Pedro - A/C.4/78/SR.6

Angola. President

UN. GENERAL ASSEMBLY (78TH SESS. : 2023-2024)—GENERAL DEBATE (Agenda item 8)
Lourenço, João Manuel Gonçalves - A/78/PV.6
UN. GENERAL ASSEMBLY (78TH SESS. : 2023-2024)—SPECIAL STATEMENTS
Lourenço, João Manuel Gonçalves - A/78/PV.6

Antigua and Barbuda

BRITISH VIRGIN ISLANDS QUESTION (Agenda item 58)
Thomas, Glentis - A/C.4/78/SR.9
SMALL ISLAND DEVELOPING STATES—PROGRAMMES OF ACTION (Agenda item 18b)
Webson, Walton Alfonso - A/78/PV.100; A/78/PV.103
WESTERN SAHARA QUESTION (Agenda item 58)
Thomas, Glentis - A/C.4/78/SR.9

Antigua and Barbuda. Prime Minister

UN. GENERAL ASSEMBLY (78TH SESS. : 2023-2024)—GENERAL DEBATE (Agenda item 8)
Browne, Gaston Alphonso - A/78/PV.10
UN. GENERAL ASSEMBLY (78TH SESS. : 2023-2024)—SPECIAL STATEMENTS
Browne, Gaston Alphonso - A/78/PV.10

Argentina

AGEING PERSONS (Agenda item 24b)
Squeff, María del Carmen - A/C.3/78/SR.1; A/C.3/78/SR.2; A/C.3/78/SR.49
ARMS RACE—OUTER SPACE (Agenda item 97a)
Guerra, Hugo Emmanuel - A/C.1/78/PV.16
ARMS TRANSFERS—TREATIES (Agenda item 99x)
Guerra, Hugo Emmanuel - A/C.1/78/PV.18
COMMODITIES (Agenda item 16d)
Nicolino, Sebastián Lucas - A/C.2/78/SR.14
CONVENTIONAL WEAPONS (Agenda item 99u)
Guerra, Hugo Emmanuel - A/C.1/78/PV.18
CONVENTIONAL WEAPONS—TREATIES (Agenda item 103)
Guerra, Hugo Emmanuel - A/C.1/78/PV.18
CRIMES AGAINST HUMANITY (Agenda item 80)
López Ferrucci, Mariano Javier - A/C.6/78/SR.38
Mainero, Martín Juan - A/C.6/78/SR.10; A/C.6/78/SR.40; A/C.6/78/SR.41; A/C.6/78/SR.43; A/C.6/78/SR.44; A/C.6/78/SR.45
CUBA—UNITED STATES (Agenda item 38)
Squeff, María del Carmen - A/78/PV.24
DECOLONIZATION (Agenda item 58)
Alvarez, Maximiliano Javier - A/C.4/78/SR.9
DECOLONIZATION—UN SYSTEM (Agenda item 56)
Alvarez, Maximiliano Javier - A/C.4/78/SR.9

Argentina (continued)

DISAPPEARANCE OF PERSONS (Agenda item 71b)
Oddone, Fabián - A/C.3/78/SR.22
Squeff, María del Carmen - A/C.3/78/SR.50
DISARMAMENT—GENERAL AND COMPLETE (Agenda item 99)
Guerra, Hugo Emmanuel - A/C.1/78/PV.18; A/C.1/78/PV.28
DISARMAMENT AGREEMENTS—OUTER SPACE (Agenda item 97c)
Guerra, Hugo Emmanuel - A/C.1/78/PV.27
ELECTION VERIFICATION—UN (Agenda item 71b)
González, María Florencia - A/C.3/78/SR.50
FALKLAND ISLANDS (MALVINAS) QUESTION (Agenda item 42)
Alvarez, Maximiliano Javier - A/C.4/78/SR.2; A/C.4/78/SR.6; A/C.4/78/SR.7; A/C.4/78/SR.8; A/C.4/78/SR.9
Carmona, Guillermo - A/C.4/78/SR.7
FAMILY (Agenda item 24b)
Squeff, María del Carmen - A/C.3/78/SR.2
HEALTH (Agenda item 125)
Nicolino, Sebastián Lucas - A/78/PV.16
HUMAN RIGHTS (Agenda item 71)
Escobar, Luciano Hernán - A/C.3/78/SR.16
HUMAN RIGHTS—INTERNATIONAL INSTRUMENTS (Agenda item 71a)
González, María Florencia - A/C.3/78/SR.24
HUMAN RIGHTS—SYRIAN ARAB REPUBLIC (Agenda item 71c)
González, María Florencia - A/C.3/78/SR.54
HUMAN RIGHTS ADVANCEMENT (Agenda item 71b)
González, María Florencia - A/C.3/78/SR.24
IAEA—REPORTS (Agenda item 89)
Squeff, María del Carmen - A/78/PV.29
INFORMATION (Agenda item 53)
Alvarez, Maximiliano Javier - A/C.4/78/SR.13
INTERNATIONAL CRIMINAL COURT—REPORTS (Agenda item 74)
Squeff, María del Carmen - A/78/PV.22
INTERNATIONAL JURISDICTION (Agenda item 84)
Mainero, Martín Juan - A/C.6/78/SR.12
LAW OF THE SEA (Agenda item 75a)
Mainero, Martín Juan - A/78/PV.44
Squeff, María del Carmen - A/78/PV.44
MARINE ECOSYSTEMS—BIOLOGICAL DIVERSITY (Agenda item 75c)
Mainero, Martín Juan - A/78/PV.44
Squeff, María del Carmen - A/78/PV.44
MERCENARIES (Agenda item 70)
Escobar, Luciano Hernán - A/C.3/78/SR.48
MIDDLE EAST SITUATION (Agenda item 34)
Squeff, María del Carmen - A/78/PV.40
MILLENNIUM SUMMIT—CONFERENCES (Agenda item 117)
Squeff, María del Carmen - A/78/PV.15

Argentina (continued)

NON-NUCLEAR-WEAPON STATES—SECURITY (Agenda item 96)
Squeff, María del Carmen - A/C.1/78/PV.13
NON-SELF-GOVERNING TERRITORIES—ECONOMIC INTERESTS (Agenda item 55)
Alvarez, Maximiliano Javier - A/C.4/78/SR.9
NUCLEAR DISARMAMENT (Agenda item 99b)
Squeff, María del Carmen - A/C.1/78/PV.13
NUCLEAR DISARMAMENT—VERIFICATION (Agenda item 99ee)
Squeff, María del Carmen - A/C.1/78/PV.13
NUCLEAR WEAPON TESTS—TREATIES (Agenda item 105)
Squeff, María del Carmen - A/C.1/78/PV.13
NUCLEAR WEAPONS—ELIMINATION (Agenda item 99z)
Guerra, Hugo Emmanuel - A/C.1/78/PV.26
NUCLEAR WEAPONS—TREATIES (Agenda item 99ff)
Guerra, Hugo Emmanuel - A/C.1/78/PV.26
ORGANIZATION OF IBERO-AMERICAN STATES FOR EDUCATION, SCIENCE AND CULTURE—OBSERVER STATUS (Agenda item 171)
Mainero, Martín Juan - A/C.6/78/SR.36
Squeff, María del Carmen - A/C.6/78/SR.14
OUTER SPACE—PEACEFUL USES—INTERNATIONAL COOPERATION (Agenda item 48)
Alvarez, Maximiliano Javier - A/C.4/78/SR.15
OUTER SPACE—PRINCIPLES (Agenda item 97d)
Guerra, Hugo Emmanuel - A/C.1/78/PV.16; A/C.1/78/PV.27
PALESTINE QUESTION (Agenda item 35)
Squeff, María del Carmen - A/78/PV.39
PEACE (Agenda item 14)
Oddone, Fabián - A/78/PV.62; A/78/PV.82
RACIAL DISCRIMINATION—ELIMINATION (Agenda item 69a)
Escobar, Luciano Hernán - A/78/PV.103
RADIATION EFFECTS (Agenda item 47)
Alvarez, Maximiliano Javier - A/C.4/78/SR.11
RESPONSIBILITY TO PROTECT (Agenda item 129)
Lagorio, Ricardo E. - A/78/PV.96
RIGHT TO DEVELOPMENT (Agenda item 71b)
Escobar, Luciano Hernán - A/C.3/78/SR.48
RIGHT TO THE TRUTH (Agenda item 71b)
Oddone, Fabián - A/C.3/78/SR.22
RIGHTS OF THE CHILD (Agenda item 67)
González, María Florencia - A/C.3/78/SR.11
RULE OF LAW (Agenda item 83)
Mainero, Martín Juan - A/C.6/78/SR.16
SELF-DETERMINATION OF PEOPLES (Agenda item 70)
Alvarez, Maximiliano Javier - A/C.3/78/SR.49
González, María Florencia - A/C.3/78/SR.56

Argentina (continued)

SMALL ARMS—ILLICIT TRAFFIC—ASSISTANCE (Agenda item 99n)
Guerra, Hugo Emmanuel - A/C.1/78/PV.18
SOCIAL DEVELOPMENT (Agenda item 24)
Squeff, María del Carmen - A/C.3/78/SR.2
STRADDLING FISH STOCKS (Agenda item 75b)
Mainero, Martín Juan - A/78/PV.44
Squeff, María del Carmen - A/78/PV.44
SUSTAINABLE DEVELOPMENT (Agenda item 18)
Nicolino, Sebastián Lucas - A/C.2/78/SR.14; A/C.2/78/SR.25
TERRORISM (Agenda item 109)
Mainero, Martín Juan - A/C.6/78/SR.1
TORTURE AND OTHER CRUEL TREATMENT (Agenda item 71a)
González, María Florencia - A/C.3/78/SR.18
TREATIES (Agenda item 87)
Mainero, Martín Juan - A/C.6/78/SR.20
UKRAINE—POLITICAL CONDITIONS (Agenda item 62)
Mainero, Martín Juan - A/78/PV.58
UN—BUDGET (2024) (Agenda item 134)
Cosentino, Leandro Carlos - A/C.5/78/SR.26/PartII; A/C.5/78/SR.33
UN. GENERAL ASSEMBLY—WORK PROGRAMME (Agenda item 120)
Squeff, María del Carmen - A/78/PV.33
UN. GENERAL ASSEMBLY (78TH SESS. : 2023-2024). 1ST COMMITTEE—GENERAL DEBATE (Agenda item 8)
Guerra, Hugo Emmanuel - A/C.1/78/PV.5
UN. GENERAL ASSEMBLY (78TH SESS. : 2023-2024). 2ND COMMITTEE—GENERAL DEBATE (Agenda item 8)
Nicolino, Sebastián Lucas - A/C.2/78/SR.2
Oddone, Fabián - A/C.2/78/SR.3
UN. HUMAN RIGHTS COUNCIL—REPORTS (Agenda item 66)
Escobar, Luciano Hernán - A/C.3/78/SR.46
Squeff, María del Carmen - A/78/PV.23
UN. INTERNATIONAL COURT OF JUSTICE—REPORTS (Agenda item 73)
Herrera, Gabriel - A/78/PV.20
UN. INTERNATIONAL LAW COMMISSION—REPORTS (Agenda item 79)
Herrera, Gabriel - A/C.6/78/SR.28
Mainero, Martín Juan - A/C.6/78/SR.30; A/C.6/78/SR.37
UN. SECURITY COUNCIL—MEMBERSHIP (Agenda item 121)
Oddone, Fabián - A/78/PV.35
UN. SECURITY COUNCIL—REPORTS (Agenda item 26)
Lagorio, Ricardo E. - A/78/PV.93
UN CONFERENCES (Agenda item 13)
Squeff, María del Carmen - A/78/PV.15

Argentina (continued)

UN RESOLUTIONS—IMPLEMENTATION (Agenda item 119)
Squeff, María del Carmen - A/78/PV.33
UNRWA—ACTIVITIES (Agenda item 49)
Squeff, María del Carmen - A/C.4/78/SR.23
VETO (Agenda item 63)
Lagorio, Ricardo E. - A/78/PV.67; A/78/PV.69; A/78/PV.71; A/78/PV.78
WOMEN'S ADVANCEMENT (Agenda item 25a)
Oddone, Fabián - A/C.3/78/SR.8
WOMEN'S ADVANCEMENT—CONFERENCES (Agenda item 25b)
Oddone, Fabián - A/C.3/78/SR.8

Argentina. President

UN. GENERAL ASSEMBLY (78TH SESS. : 2023-2024)—GENERAL DEBATE (Agenda item 8)
Fernández, Alberto - A/78/PV.5
UN. GENERAL ASSEMBLY (78TH SESS. : 2023-2024)—SPECIAL STATEMENTS
Fernández, Alberto - A/78/PV.5

Armenia

ARMS TRANSFERS—TREATIES (Agenda item 99x)
Grigoryan, Andranik - A/C.1/78/PV.28
CLIMATE (Agenda item 18d)
Babikyan, Araksya - A/C.2/78/SR.15
CRIMES AGAINST HUMANITY (Agenda item 80)
Galstyan, Tigran - A/C.6/78/SR.11
Margaryan, Mher - A/C.6/78/SR.11
Melikyan, Varduhi - A/C.6/78/SR.41
Sarvarian, Arman - A/C.6/78/SR.39
DISARMAMENT—GENERAL AND COMPLETE (Agenda item 99)
Grigoryan, Andranik - A/C.1/78/PV.24
DISARMAMENT-DEVELOPMENT LINK (Agenda item 99d)
Grigoryan, Andranik - A/C.1/78/PV.29
HUMAN RIGHTS (Agenda item 71)
Hakobyan, Aram - A/C.3/78/SR.16
HUMAN RIGHTS—REPORTS (Agenda item 71c)
Hakobyan, Aram - A/C.3/78/SR.25
HUMAN RIGHTS ADVANCEMENT (Agenda item 71b)
Hakobyan, Aram - A/C.3/78/SR.24
IAEA—REPORTS (Agenda item 89)
Galstyan, Tigran - A/78/PV.29
INFORMATION TECHNOLOGY—DEVELOPMENT (Agenda item 15)
Babikyan, Araksya - A/C.2/78/SR.10
LANDLOCKED DEVELOPING COUNTRIES—CONFERENCES (Agenda item 20b)
Babikyan, Araksya - A/C.2/78/SR.7

Armenia (continued)

LANDMINES—TREATIES (Agenda item 99m)
Grigoryan, Andranik - A/C.1/78/PV.19
LEAST DEVELOPED COUNTRIES—CONFERENCES (Agenda item 20a)
Babikyan, Araksya - A/C.2/78/SR.7
MERCENARIES (Agenda item 70)
Hakobyan, Aram - A/C.3/78/SR.42
MULTILATERALISM—DISARMAMENT (Agenda item 99r)
Grigoryan, Andranik - A/C.1/78/PV.22; A/C.1/78/PV.29
NUCLEAR WEAPONS USE—UN. INTERNATIONAL COURT OF JUSTICE OPINION (Agenda item 99k)
Grigoryan, Andranik - A/C.1/78/PV.29
ORGANIZATION FOR DEMOCRACY AND ECONOMIC DEVELOPMENT - GUAM (Agenda item 32)
Margaryan, Mher - A/78/PV.85
PEACE (Agenda item 14)
Margaryan, Mher - A/78/PV.82
PEACE—REGIONAL CENTRES (Agenda item 100f)
Grigoryan, Andranik - A/C.1/78/PV.29
RACIAL DISCRIMINATION—ELIMINATION (Agenda item 69a)
Hakobyan, Aram - A/C.3/78/SR.42
RACIAL DISCRIMINATION—PROGRAMMES OF ACTION (Agenda item 69b)
Hakobyan, Aram - A/C.3/78/SR.42
RESPONSIBILITY TO PROTECT (Agenda item 129)
Margaryan, Mher - A/78/PV.96
RIGHT TO DEVELOPMENT (Agenda item 71b)
Hakobyan, Aram - A/C.3/78/SR.48
RIGHTS OF THE CHILD (Agenda item 67)
Hakobyan, Aram - A/C.3/78/SR.11; A/C.3/78/SR.13; A/C.3/78/SR.14
RULE OF LAW (Agenda item 83)
Galstyan, Tigran - A/C.6/78/SR.18
SCIENCE AND TECHNOLOGY—DEVELOPMENT (Agenda item 19a)
Babikyan, Araksya - A/C.2/78/SR.10
SUSTAINABLE DEVELOPMENT (Agenda item 18)
Babikyan, Araksya - A/C.2/78/SR.15
TERRORISM (Agenda item 109)
Galstyan, Tigran - A/C.6/78/SR.5
UN. GENERAL ASSEMBLY (78TH SESS. : 2023-2024)—GENERAL DEBATE (Agenda item 8)
Mirzoyan, Ararat - A/78/PV.13
UN. GENERAL ASSEMBLY (78TH SESS. : 2023-2024)—GENERAL DEBATE—RIGHT OF REPLY (Agenda item 8)
Galstyan, Tigran - A/78/PV.14

Armenia (continued)

UN. GENERAL ASSEMBLY (78TH SESS. : 2023-2024). 1ST COMMITTEE—GENERAL DEBATE (Agenda item 8)
Grigoryan, Andranik - A/C.1/78/PV.7; A/C.1/78/PV.8
Margaryan, Mher - A/C.1/78/PV.4
UN. GENERAL ASSEMBLY (78TH SESS. : 2023-2024). 2ND COMMITTEE—GENERAL DEBATE (Agenda item 8)
Babikyan, Araksya - A/C.2/78/SR.5
Galstyan, Tigran - A/C.2/78/SR.3
UN. INTERNATIONAL COURT OF JUSTICE—REPORTS (Agenda item 73)
Margaryan, Mher - A/78/PV.28
UN. INTERNATIONAL LAW COMMISSION—REPORTS (Agenda item 79)
Sarvarian, Arman - A/C.6/78/SR.27; A/C.6/78/SR.30
UN. SECRETARY-GENERAL—REPORTS (Agenda item 110)
Margaryan, Mher - A/78/PV.54
UN HIGH COMMISSIONER FOR REFUGEES—REPORTS (Agenda item 60)
Hakobyan, Aram - A/C.3/78/SR.44; A/C.3/78/SR.45
WEAPONS OF MASS DESTRUCTION—TERRORISM (Agenda item 99s)
Grigoryan, Andranik - A/C.1/78/PV.29
WOMEN'S ADVANCEMENT (Agenda item 25a)
Hakobyan, Aram - A/C.3/78/SR.8; A/C.3/78/SR.10
WOMEN'S ADVANCEMENT—CONFERENCES (Agenda item 25b)
Hakobyan, Aram - A/C.3/78/SR.8; A/C.3/78/SR.10

Arms Control Association (Washington, D.C.)

DISARMAMENT—GENERAL AND COMPLETE (Agenda item 99)
Kuramitsu, Shizuka - A/78/PV.105

ASEAN

2030 AGENDA—PROGRAMME IMPLEMENTATION (Agenda item 18a)
Lora-Santos, Leila Castillon (Philippines) - A/C.2/78/SR.12
AGEING PERSONS (Agenda item 24b)
Dang, Hoang Giang (Viet Nam) - A/C.3/78/SR.1
ARMS RACE—OUTER SPACE (Agenda item 97a)
Muhamad, Ahmad Faisal (Malaysia) - A/C.1/78/PV.16
ARMS TRANSFERS—TREATIES (Agenda item 99x)
Mao, Tithiarun (Cambodia) - A/C.1/78/PV.17
BIOLOGICAL DIVERSITY—TREATIES (Agenda item 18f)
Lora-Santos, Leila Castillon (Philippines) - A/C.2/78/SR.12

ASEAN (continued)

BIOLOGICAL WEAPONS—TREATIES (Agenda item 106)
Vongnorkeo, Anouparb (Lao People's Democratic Republic) - A/C.1/78/PV.14
CHEMICAL WEAPONS—TREATIES (Agenda item 99l)
Vongnorkeo, Anouparb (Lao People's Democratic Republic) - A/C.1/78/PV.14
CONVENTIONAL WEAPONS (Agenda item 99u)
Mao, Tithiarun (Cambodia) - A/C.1/78/PV.17
CONVENTIONAL WEAPONS—TREATIES (Agenda item 103)
Mao, Tithiarun (Cambodia) - A/C.1/78/PV.17
CRIME PREVENTION (Agenda item 107)
Gafoor, Burhan (Singapore) - A/C.3/78/SR.5
CUBA—UNITED STATES (Agenda item 38)
Gafoor, Burhan (Singapore) - A/78/PV.24
CYBERCRIME (Agenda item 108)
Gafoor, Burhan (Singapore) - A/C.3/78/SR.5
DEVELOPMENT FINANCE (Agenda item 16b)
Nasir, Arrmanatha Christiawan (Indonesia) - A/C.2/78/SR.8
DISARMAMENT—GENERAL AND COMPLETE (Agenda item 99)
Philakone, Khamphinh (Lao People's Democratic Republic) - A/78/PV.105
Vongnorkeo, Anouparb (Lao People's Democratic Republic) - A/C.1/78/PV.14
DISARMAMENT AGREEMENTS—OUTER SPACE (Agenda item 97c)
Muhamad, Ahmad Faisal (Malaysia) - A/C.1/78/PV.16
DISASTER PREVENTION (Agenda item 18c)
Lora-Santos, Leila Castillon (Philippines) - A/C.2/78/SR.12
ECONOMIC COOPERATION AMONG DEVELOPING COUNTRIES (Agenda item 22b)
Chindawongse, Suriya (Thailand) - A/C.2/78/SR.18
EMERGENCY ASSISTANCE (Agenda item 72a)
Nasir, Arrmanatha Christiawan (Indonesia) - A/78/PV.46
FOOD SECURITY (Agenda item 23a)
Dang, Hoang Giang (Viet Nam) - A/C.2/78/SR.16
HUMAN RIGHTS—INTERNATIONAL INSTRUMENTS (Agenda item 71a)
Muhamad, Ahmad Faisal (Malaysia) - A/C.3/78/SR.24
HUMAN RIGHTS ADVANCEMENT (Agenda item 71b)
Muhamad, Ahmad Faisal (Malaysia) - A/C.3/78/SR.24
HUMANITARIAN ASSISTANCE (Agenda item 72)
Nasir, Arrmanatha Christiawan (Indonesia) - A/78/PV.46

ASEAN (continued)

INFORMATION (Agenda item 53)
Nguyen, Hoang Nguyen (Viet Nam) - A/C.4/78/SR.12
INFORMATION—INTERNATIONAL SECURITY (Agenda item 94)
Chindawongse, Suriya (Thailand) - A/C.1/78/PV.20
INTERNATIONAL LAW—TRAINING PROGRAMMES (Agenda item 78)
Seah, Mark (Singapore) - A/C.6/78/SR.21
INTERNATIONAL TRADE (Agenda item 16a)
Nasir, Arrmanatha Christiawan (Indonesia) - A/C.2/78/SR.8
INVESTMENT PROMOTION (Agenda item 16g)
Nasir, Arrmanatha Christiawan (Indonesia) - A/C.2/78/SR.8
LANDLOCKED DEVELOPING COUNTRIES—CONFERENCES (Agenda item 20b)
Vongnorkeo, Anouparb (Lao People's Democratic Republic) - A/C.2/78/SR.7
LANDMINES—TREATIES (Agenda item 99m)
Mao, Tithiarun (Cambodia) - A/C.1/78/PV.17
LEAST DEVELOPED COUNTRIES—CONFERENCES (Agenda item 20a)
Vongnorkeo, Anouparb (Lao People's Democratic Republic) - A/C.2/78/SR.7
MACROECONOMIC POLICY (Agenda item 16)
Nasir, Arrmanatha Christiawan (Indonesia) - A/C.2/78/SR.8
NUCLEAR DISARMAMENT (Agenda item 99b)
Dang, Hoang Giang (Viet Nam) - A/C.1/78/PV.11
NUCLEAR NON-PROLIFERATION (Agenda item 99o)
Dang, Hoang Giang (Viet Nam) - A/C.1/78/PV.11
NUCLEAR NON-PROLIFERATION—INTERNATIONAL OBLIGATIONS (Agenda item 99w)
Dang, Hoang Giang (Viet Nam) - A/C.1/78/PV.11
NUCLEAR WEAPON TESTS—TREATIES (Agenda item 105)
Dang, Hoang Giang (Viet Nam) - A/C.1/78/PV.11
NUCLEAR WEAPONS—TREATIES (Agenda item 99ff)
Dang, Hoang Giang (Viet Nam) - A/C.1/78/PV.11
OPERATIONAL ACTIVITIES—UN SYSTEM (Agenda item 22a)
Chindawongse, Suriya (Thailand) - A/C.2/78/SR.18
OUTER SPACE—CONFIDENCE-BUILDING MEASURES (Agenda item 99v)
Muhamad, Ahmad Faisal (Malaysia) - A/C.1/78/PV.16
OUTER SPACE—PEACEFUL USES—INTERNATIONAL COOPERATION (Agenda item 48)
Nguyen, Hoang Nguyen (Viet Nam) - A/C.4/78/SR.15

ASEAN (continued)

OUTER SPACE—PRINCIPLES (Agenda item 97d)
Muhamad, Ahmad Faisal (Malaysia) - A/C.1/78/PV.16
PALESTINIANS—ASSISTANCE (Agenda item 72b)
Nasir, Arrmanatha Christiawan (Indonesia) - A/78/PV.46
PEACE (Agenda item 14)
Sulaiman, Noor Qamar (Brunei Darussalam) - A/78/PV.76
PEACEKEEPING OPERATIONS (Agenda item 51)
Nasir, Arrmanatha Christiawan (Indonesia) - A/C.4/78/SR.18
PERSONS WITH DISABILITIES (Agenda item 24b)
Dang, Hoang Giang (Viet Nam) - A/C.3/78/SR.1
POVERTY—INTERNATIONAL DECADES (Agenda item 21a)
Dang, Hoang Giang (Viet Nam) - A/C.2/78/SR.16
RIGHTS OF THE CHILD (Agenda item 67)
Prabowo, Hari (Indonesia) - A/C.3/78/SR.11
RULE OF LAW (Agenda item 83)
Arumpac-Marte, Azela Guerrero (Philippines) - A/C.6/78/SR.15
RURAL POVERTY (Agenda item 21b)
Dang, Hoang Giang (Viet Nam) - A/C.2/78/SR.16
SCIENCE AND TECHNOLOGY—DEVELOPMENT (Agenda item 19a)
Muhamad, Ahmad Faisal (Malaysia) - A/C.2/78/SR.10
SMALL ARMS—ILLICIT TRAFFIC (Agenda item 99p)
Mao, Tithiarun (Cambodia) - A/C.1/78/PV.17
SMALL ARMS—ILLICIT TRAFFIC—ASSISTANCE (Agenda item 99n)
Mao, Tithiarun (Cambodia) - A/C.1/78/PV.17
SOCIAL CONDITIONS (Agenda item 24b)
Dang, Hoang Giang (Viet Nam) - A/C.3/78/SR.1
SOCIAL DEVELOPMENT (Agenda item 24)
Dang, Hoang Giang (Viet Nam) - A/C.3/78/SR.1
SOUTH-EAST ASIA—NUCLEAR-WEAPON-FREE ZONES (Agenda item 99y)
Dang, Hoang Giang (Viet Nam) - A/C.1/78/PV.11
Nasir, Arrmanatha Christiawan (Indonesia) - A/C.1/78/PV.30
Zakaria, Izzat Hayati (Brunei Darussalam) - A/C.1/78/PV.22
SPECIAL POLITICAL MISSIONS (Agenda item 52)
Nasir, Arrmanatha Christiawan (Indonesia) - A/C.4/78/SR.21
SUSTAINABLE DEVELOPMENT (Agenda item 18)
Lora-Santos, Leila Castillon (Philippines) - A/C.2/78/SR.12
TERRORISM (Agenda item 109)
Eat, Sophea (Cambodia) - A/C.6/78/SR.1

ASEAN (continued)

UN—BUDGET (2024) (Agenda item 134)
Chak Yong, Mok (Singapore) - A/C.5/78/SR.12
Chua, Li Si Felicia (Singapore) - A/C.5/78/SR.33
Lagdameo, Antonio Manuel Revilla (Philippines) - A/C.5/78/SR.13
Seah, Mark (Singapore) - A/C.5/78/SR.3
Tam, Noelle (Singapore) - A/C.5/78/SR.11
Valles, Marivil Villa (Philippines) - A/C.5/78/SR.5
UN—FINANCIAL SITUATION (Agenda item 136)
Gafoor, Burhan (Singapore) - A/C.5/78/SR.38
Seah, Mark (Singapore) - A/C.5/78/SR.6
UN—HUMAN RESOURCES MANAGEMENT (Agenda item 139)
Lora-Santos, Leila Castillon (Philippines) - A/C.5/78/SR.27
UN—PROGRAMME PLANNING (Agenda item 135)
Valles, Marivil Villa (Philippines) - A/C.5/78/SR.5
UN. CONFERENCE ON DISARMAMENT—REPORTS (Agenda item 101a)
Seah, Mark (Singapore) - A/C.1/78/PV.22
UN. DISARMAMENT COMMISSION—REPORTS (Agenda item 101b)
Seah, Mark (Singapore) - A/C.1/78/PV.22
UN. GENERAL ASSEMBLY—WORK PROGRAMME (Agenda item 120)
Omar, Khairi (Malaysia) - A/78/PV.32
UN. GENERAL ASSEMBLY (78TH SESS. : 2023-2024)—OFFICERS (Agenda item 5)
Gafoor, Burhan (Singapore) - A/C.5/78/SR.1
UN. GENERAL ASSEMBLY (78TH SESS. : 2023-2024). 1ST COMMITTEE—GENERAL DEBATE (Agenda item 8)
Peñaranda, Ariel Rodelas (Philippines) - A/C.1/78/PV.2
UN. GENERAL ASSEMBLY (78TH SESS. : 2023-2024). 2ND COMMITTEE—GENERAL DEBATE (Agenda item 8)
Prabowo, Hari (Indonesia) - A/C.2/78/SR.2
UN. GENERAL ASSEMBLY (78TH SESS. : 2023-2024). 5TH COMMITTEE—WORK ORGANIZATION (Agenda item 7)
Gafoor, Burhan (Singapore) - A/C.5/78/SR.27
UN RESOLUTIONS—IMPLEMENTATION (Agenda item 119)
Omar, Khairi (Malaysia) - A/78/PV.32
WEAPONS—OUTER SPACE (Agenda item 97b)
Muhamad, Ahmad Faisal (Malaysia) - A/C.1/78/PV.16
WOMEN'S ADVANCEMENT (Agenda item 25a)
Vichankaiyakij, Vathayudh (Thailand) - A/C.3/78/SR.8

ASEAN (continued)

WOMEN'S ADVANCEMENT—CONFERENCES (Agenda item 25b)
Vichankaiyakij, Vathayudh (Thailand) - A/C.3/78/SR.8

Asociación Canaria de Juristas por la Paz y los Derechos Humanos

WESTERN SAHARA QUESTION (Agenda item 58)
Travieso Darias, María Dolores - A/C.4/78/SR.4

Asociación Canaria de Mujeres Tejiendo Futuro

WESTERN SAHARA QUESTION (Agenda item 58)
Travieso Hernández, Victoria - A/C.4/78/SR.4

Asociación Canaria de Solidaridad con el Pueblo Saharaui

WESTERN SAHARA QUESTION (Agenda item 58)
Hernández González, Leticia María - A/C.4/78/SR.4

Asociación Colombiana de Amistad con el Pueblo Saharaui

WESTERN SAHARA QUESTION (Agenda item 58)
Angola Mejía, Nassoli Bibiana - A/C.4/78/SR.4

Asociación Ecuatoriana de Amistad con el Pueblo Saharaui

WESTERN SAHARA QUESTION (Agenda item 58)
Vega, Pablo de la - A/C.4/78/SR.4

Asociación Siembra Canaria

WESTERN SAHARA QUESTION (Agenda item 58)
Ramírez Galindo, Sergio - A/C.4/78/SR.4

Association 193 (French Polynesia)

FRENCH POLYNESIA QUESTION (Agenda item 58)
Normand, Lena - A/C.4/78/SR.3

Association algérienne de soutien au peuple sahraoui

WESTERN SAHARA QUESTION (Agenda item 58)
Bouamama, Zoheir - A/C.4/78/SR.4

Association de foot ball Otemanu, Bora Bora

FRENCH POLYNESIA QUESTION (Agenda item 58)
Jordan, Rudolph - A/C.4/78/SR.3

Association for the Freedom of Women Sequestered in the Tindouf Camps

WESTERN SAHARA QUESTION (Agenda item 58)
Hmyene, Touria - A/C.4/78/SR.6

Association for the Support of the Moroccan Autonomy Initiative

WESTERN SAHARA QUESTION (Agenda item 58)
Bendriss, Khalid - A/C.4/78/SR.6

Association Moruroa e Tatou (French Polynesia)

FRENCH POLYNESIA QUESTION (Agenda item 58)
Puarai, Tevaearai - A/C.4/78/SR.3

Association Na Papa e Vaù (French Polynesia)

FRENCH POLYNESIA QUESTION (Agenda item 58)
Temauri, Vainui - A/C.4/78/SR.3

Association Rotary International à Boujdour

WESTERN SAHARA QUESTION (Agenda item 58)
Edabadda, Mohamed - A/C.4/78/SR.5

Association sahraouie contre l'impunité dans les camps de Tindouf

WESTERN SAHARA QUESTION (Agenda item 58)
Zrug, Lemaadla Mohamed Salem - A/C.4/78/SR.6

Association Tamariki Teavaroa

FRENCH POLYNESIA QUESTION (Agenda item 58)
Homai, François - A/C.4/78/SR.3

Association Te Utuafare No Mahaena

FRENCH POLYNESIA QUESTION (Agenda item 58)
Tarahu, Frangelica - A/C.4/78/SR.3

Association Tumu Ra'i Fenua

FRENCH POLYNESIA QUESTION (Agenda item 58)
Tiatoa, Sylvana - A/C.4/78/SR.3

Association Vaihau

FRENCH POLYNESIA QUESTION (Agenda item 58)
Vaianui, Marania - A/C.4/78/SR.3

Australia

ARMED CONFLICTS PREVENTION (Agenda item 31a)
Hutchison, Alexandra - A/78/PV.72
ARMS RACE—OUTER SPACE (Agenda item 97a)
Lia, Alex - A/C.1/78/PV.16
ARMS TRANSFERS—TREATIES (Agenda item 99x)
Carr, Michelle - A/C.1/78/PV.19
BIOLOGICAL WEAPONS—TREATIES (Agenda item 106)
Hill, Ruth - A/C.1/78/PV.14
CHEMICAL WEAPONS—TREATIES (Agenda item 99l)
Hill, Ruth - A/C.1/78/PV.14
CLIMATE (Agenda item 18d)
Larsen, James - A/C.2/78/SR.15
CLIMATE CHANGE (Agenda item 71b)
Kim, Yunei - A/C.3/78/SR.29
CLUSTER MUNITIONS (Agenda item 99dd)
Carr, Michelle - A/C.1/78/PV.19
CRIME PREVENTION (Agenda item 107)
Lukabyo, Emma Jane Mutesi - A/C.3/78/SR.56
CRIMES AGAINST HUMANITY (Agenda item 80)
Hutchison, Alexandra - A/C.6/78/SR.38; A/C.6/78/SR.41; A/C.6/78/SR.42; A/C.6/78/SR.43; A/C.6/78/SR.44; A/C.6/78/SR.45
DECOLONIZATION—UN SYSTEM (Agenda item 56)
Volkov, Alice - A/C.4/78/SR.9
DISARMAMENT—GENERAL AND COMPLETE (Agenda item 99)
Carr, Michelle - A/C.1/78/PV.19; A/C.1/78/PV.28
Della-porta, Demi Heather See - A/C.1/78/PV.30
Larsen, James - A/78/PV.106
DISARMAMENT AGREEMENTS—OUTER SPACE (Agenda item 97c)
Della-porta, Demi Heather See - A/C.1/78/PV.27
DISASTER PREVENTION (Agenda item 18c)
Prosser, Amy - A/C.2/78/SR.23
DISASTER VICTIMS (Agenda item 86)
Hutchison, Alexandra - A/C.6/78/SR.5
ECONOMIC SANCTIONS—INTERNATIONAL RELATIONS (Agenda item 28)
Bryant, Rebecca Suzanne - A/78/PV.89
ELECTION VERIFICATION—UN (Agenda item 71b)
Hamer, David - A/C.3/78/SR.50
EMERGENCY ASSISTANCE (Agenda item 72a)
Larsen, James - A/78/PV.46
HEALTH (Agenda item 125)
Kim, Yunei - A/78/PV.48
Larsen, James - A/78/PV.16
Pullela, Shilpa Kadambari - A/78/PV.41
HIV/AIDS—DECLARATIONS (Agenda item 10)
Larsen, James - A/78/PV.91

Australia (continued)

HUMAN RIGHTS (Agenda item 71)
Kim, Yunei - A/C.3/78/SR.16
HUMAN RIGHTS—AFGHANISTAN (Agenda item 71c)
Larsen, James - A/C.3/78/SR.34
HUMAN RIGHTS—DEMOCRATIC PEOPLE'S REPUBLIC OF KOREA (Agenda item 71c)
Kim, Yunei - A/C.3/78/SR.33
HUMAN RIGHTS—INTERNATIONAL INSTRUMENTS (Agenda item 71a)
Larsen, James - A/C.3/78/SR.25
HUMAN RIGHTS—IRAN (ISLAMIC REPUBLIC OF) (Agenda item 71c)
Hamer, David - A/C.3/78/SR.53
Kim, Yunei - A/C.3/78/SR.34
HUMAN RIGHTS—MYANMAR (Agenda item 71c)
Pullela, Shilpa Kadambari - A/C.3/78/SR.33
HUMAN RIGHTS—REPORTS (Agenda item 71c)
Larsen, James - A/C.3/78/SR.25
HUMAN RIGHTS—RUSSIAN FEDERATION (Agenda item 71c)
Kim, Yunei - A/C.3/78/SR.37
HUMAN RIGHTS—SYRIAN ARAB REPUBLIC (Agenda item 71c)
Larsen, James - A/C.3/78/SR.34
HUMAN RIGHTS—TERRITORIES OCCUPIED BY ISRAEL (Agenda item 71c)
Pullela, Shilpa Kadambari - A/C.3/78/SR.35
HUMAN RIGHTS—UKRAINE (Agenda item 71c)
Kim, Yunei - A/C.3/78/SR.37
IAEA—REPORTS (Agenda item 89)
Della-porta, Demi Heather See - A/78/PV.30
INDIGENOUS PEOPLES (Agenda item 68a)
Larsen, James - A/78/PV.107; A/C.3/78/SR.15
INDIGENOUS PEOPLES—CONFERENCES (Agenda item 68b)
Larsen, James - A/C.3/78/SR.15
INFORMATION (Agenda item 53)
Bryant, Rebecca Suzanne - A/C.4/78/SR.14
INFORMATION—INTERNATIONAL SECURITY (Agenda item 94)
Lukabyo, Emma Jane Mutesi - A/C.1/78/PV.20; A/C.1/78/PV.29
INTERNATIONAL CRIMINAL COURT—REPORTS (Agenda item 74)
Larsen, James - A/78/PV.22
LANDMINES—TREATIES (Agenda item 99m)
Carr, Michelle - A/C.1/78/PV.19
LAW OF THE SEA (Agenda item 75a)
Dundon, Nick - A/78/PV.48
Larsen, James - A/78/PV.43
MARINE ECOSYSTEMS—BIOLOGICAL DIVERSITY (Agenda item 75c)
Larsen, James - A/78/PV.43
MILLENNIUM SUMMIT—CONFERENCES (Agenda item 117)
Larsen, James - A/78/PV.15

Australia (continued)

MINE CLEARANCE (Agenda item 46)
Larsen, James - A/C.4/78/SR.10
NUCLEAR DISARMAMENT (Agenda item 99b)
Gorely, Amanda Louise - A/C.1/78/PV.11
Larsen, James - A/C.1/78/PV.12
NUCLEAR DISARMAMENT—VERIFICATION (Agenda item 99ee)
Larsen, James - A/C.1/78/PV.12
NUCLEAR NON-PROLIFERATION—INTERNATIONAL OBLIGATIONS (Agenda item 99w)
Gorely, Amanda Louise - A/C.1/78/PV.11
Larsen, James - A/C.1/78/PV.12
NUCLEAR WEAPON TESTS—TREATIES (Agenda item 105)
Gorely, Amanda Louise - A/C.1/78/PV.11
Larsen, James - A/C.1/78/PV.12
ORGANIZATION FOR DEMOCRACY AND ECONOMIC DEVELOPMENT - GUAM (Agenda item 32)
Larsen, James - A/78/PV.85
OUTER SPACE—PRINCIPLES (Agenda item 97d)
Lia, Alex - A/C.1/78/PV.16
PEACE (Agenda item 14)
Bryant, Rebecca Suzanne - A/78/PV.62
Kim, Yunei - A/78/PV.88
PEACEKEEPING OPERATIONS (Agenda item 51)
Larsen, James - A/C.4/78/SR.18
PERSONS WITH DISABILITIES—HUMAN RIGHTS (Agenda item 71a)
Bryant, Rebecca Suzanne - A/C.3/78/SR.38
RACIAL DISCRIMINATION—ELIMINATION (Agenda item 69a)
Kim, Yunei - A/C.3/78/SR.47
Larsen, James - A/C.3/78/SR.47
RELIGIOUS INTOLERANCE (Agenda item 71b)
Bryant, Rebecca Suzanne - A/C.3/78/SR.38
RESPONSIBILITY TO PROTECT (Agenda item 129)
Larsen, James - A/78/PV.96
RIGHTS OF THE CHILD (Agenda item 67)
Kelson, Matthew - A/C.3/78/SR.55
Mitchell, Rob - A/C.3/78/SR.13
RURAL WOMEN (Agenda item 25a)
Kim, Yunei - A/C.3/78/SR.49
SEXUAL ORIENTATION (Agenda item 71b)
Hamer, David - A/C.3/78/SR.39
SLAVERY (Agenda item 71a)
Hamer, David - A/C.3/78/SR.21
SMALL ARMS—ILLICIT TRAFFIC—ASSISTANCE (Agenda item 99n)
Carr, Michelle - A/C.1/78/PV.19
SMALL ISLAND DEVELOPING STATES—PROGRAMMES OF ACTION (Agenda item 18b)
Larsen, James - A/C.2/78/SR.15
Reynolds, Gregory Edward Ivor - A/78/PV.103

Australia (continued)

STRADDLING FISH STOCKS (Agenda item 75b)
Larsen, James - A/78/PV.43
SUSTAINABLE DEVELOPMENT (Agenda item 18)
Larsen, James - A/78/PV.107; A/C.2/78/SR.15
Linton, Sarah Joy - A/C.2/78/SR.24
TERRITORIES OCCUPIED BY ISRAEL—NATURAL RESOURCES (Agenda item 59)
Bryant, Rebecca Suzanne - A/C.2/78/SR.19
TERRORISM (Agenda item 109)
Biggs, Ian - A/C.6/78/SR.1
TRAFFICKING IN PERSONS (Agenda item 71b)
Kelson, Matthew - A/C.3/78/SR.23
UKRAINE—POLITICAL CONDITIONS (Agenda item 62)
Larsen, James - A/78/PV.57
UN—ADMINISTRATION (Agenda item 132)
Jones, Alexandra - A/C.5/78/SR.26/PartII
UN—BUDGET (2024) (Agenda item 134)
Jones, Alexandra - A/C.5/78/SR.26/PartII
UN—PROGRAMME PLANNING (Agenda item 135)
Della-porta, Demi Heather See - A/C.1/78/PV.10
UN. CONFERENCE ON DISARMAMENT—REPORTS (Agenda item 101a)
Della-porta, Demi Heather See - A/C.1/78/PV.24
UN. GENERAL ASSEMBLY—WORK PROGRAMME (Agenda item 120)
Della-porta, Demi Heather See - A/C.1/78/PV.10
Hutchison, Alexandra - A/C.6/78/SR.36
Van Bronswijk, Sarah - A/78/PV.32
UN. GENERAL ASSEMBLY (78TH SESS. : 2023-2024)—GENERAL DEBATE (Agenda item 8)
Wong, Penny - A/78/PV.11
UN. GENERAL ASSEMBLY (78TH SESS. : 2023-2024)—OFFICERS (Agenda item 5)
Larsen, James - A/C.5/78/SR.1
UN. GENERAL ASSEMBLY (78TH SESS. : 2023-2024). 1ST COMMITTEE—GENERAL DEBATE (Agenda item 8)
Wood, Vanessa - A/C.1/78/PV.3; A/C.1/78/PV.5
UN. GENERAL ASSEMBLY (78TH SESS. : 2023-2024). 2ND COMMITTEE—GENERAL DEBATE (Agenda item 8)
Larsen, James - A/C.2/78/SR.2
UN. GENERAL ASSEMBLY (78TH SESS. : 2023-2024). 5TH COMMITTEE—WORK ORGANIZATION (Agenda item 7)
Jones, Alexandra - A/C.5/78/SR.27
UN. HUMAN RIGHTS COUNCIL—REPORTS (Agenda item 66)
Pullela, Shilpa Kadambari - A/C.3/78/SR.46
UN. INTERNATIONAL COURT OF JUSTICE—REPORTS (Agenda item 73)
Hutchison, Alexandra - A/C.6/78/SR.26
McCarthy, Adam - A/78/PV.20

Australia (continued)

UN. INTERNATIONAL LAW COMMISSION—REPORTS (Agenda item 79)
Mason, Naomi - A/C.6/78/SR.29
McCarthy, Adam - A/C.6/78/SR.23
UN. SECURITY COUNCIL—MEMBERSHIP (Agenda item 121)
Bryant, Rebecca Suzanne - A/78/PV.35
UN CONFERENCES (Agenda item 13)
Larsen, James - A/78/PV.15
UN RESOLUTIONS—IMPLEMENTATION (Agenda item 119)
Van Bronswijk, Sarah - A/78/PV.32
VETO (Agenda item 63)
Bryant, Rebecca Suzanne - A/78/PV.74
Larsen, James - A/78/PV.51; A/78/PV.59; A/78/PV.68; A/78/PV.78
WEAPONS—OUTER SPACE (Agenda item 97b)
Della-porta, Demi Heather See - A/C.1/78/PV.27
WEAPONS OF MASS DESTRUCTION—TERRORISM (Agenda item 99s)
Hill, Ruth - A/C.1/78/PV.14
WOMEN'S ADVANCEMENT (Agenda item 25a)
Mitchell, Rob - A/C.3/78/SR.7
WOMEN'S ADVANCEMENT—CONFERENCES (Agenda item 25b)
Mitchell, Rob - A/C.3/78/SR.7
YOUTH (Agenda item 24b)
Kane, Imogen - A/C.3/78/SR.3

Austria

AGEING PERSONS (Agenda item 24b)
Hardwick, Nicola Ann - A/C.3/78/SR.1
ARMED CONFLICTS PREVENTION (Agenda item 31a)
Pretterhofer, Stefan - A/78/PV.72
ARMS RACE—OUTER SPACE (Agenda item 97a)
Bilgeri, Andreas - A/C.1/78/PV.16
BIOLOGICAL WEAPONS—TREATIES (Agenda item 106)
Woergoetter, Caroline - A/C.1/78/PV.15
CHEMICAL WEAPONS—TREATIES (Agenda item 99l)
Woergoetter, Caroline - A/C.1/78/PV.15
CLUSTER MUNITIONS (Agenda item 99dd)
Kmentt, Alexander - A/C.1/78/PV.18
CONVENTIONAL WEAPONS—TREATIES (Agenda item 103)
Kmentt, Alexander - A/C.1/78/PV.18
CRIMES AGAINST HUMANITY (Agenda item 80)
Gorke, Maximilian - A/C.6/78/SR.9; A/C.6/78/SR.38; A/C.6/78/SR.40; A/C.6/78/SR.41; A/C.6/78/SR.43; A/C.6/78/SR.44; A/C.6/78/SR.45

Austria (continued)

DISARMAMENT—GENERAL AND COMPLETE (Agenda item 99)
Edtmayer, Matthias - A/C.1/78/PV.27; A/C.1/78/PV.30
Kmentt, Alexander - A/C.1/78/PV.18
Pretterhofer, Stefan - A/78/PV.105
FISSIONABLE MATERIALS—TREATIES (Agenda item 99a)
Edtmayer, Matthias - A/C.1/78/PV.26
FREEDOM OF EXPRESSION (Agenda item 71b)
Soyka, Juliane - A/C.3/78/SR.19
HUMAN RIGHTS (Agenda item 71)
Pretterhofer, Stefan - A/C.3/78/SR.16
HUMAN RIGHTS—AFGHANISTAN (Agenda item 71c)
Hardwick, Nicola Ann - A/C.3/78/SR.34
HUMAN RIGHTS—INTERNATIONAL INSTRUMENTS (Agenda item 71a)
Pretterhofer, Stefan - A/C.3/78/SR.24
HUMAN RIGHTS—PROGRAMMES OF ACTION (Agenda item 71d)
Pretterhofer, Stefan - A/C.3/78/SR.24
HUMAN RIGHTS—TERRITORIES OCCUPIED BY ISRAEL (Agenda item 71c)
Pretterhofer, Stefan - A/C.3/78/SR.35
HUMAN RIGHTS ACTIVISTS (Agenda item 71b)
Mahidi, Mourad - A/C.3/78/SR.19
HUMAN RIGHTS ADVANCEMENT (Agenda item 71b)
Soyka, Juliane - A/C.3/78/SR.52
IAEA—REPORTS (Agenda item 89)
Pretterhofer, Stefan - A/78/PV.30
LANDMINES—TREATIES (Agenda item 99m)
Kmentt, Alexander - A/C.1/78/PV.18
MIGRANTS—PROTECTION (Agenda item 71b)
Hardwick, Nicola Ann - A/C.3/78/SR.56
MINORITIES (Agenda item 71b)
Hardwick, Nicola Ann - A/C.3/78/SR.39; A/C.3/78/SR.52
NUCLEAR DISARMAMENT (Agenda item 99b)
Kmentt, Alexander - A/C.1/78/PV.12
NUCLEAR NON-PROLIFERATION—INTERNATIONAL OBLIGATIONS (Agenda item 99w)
Kmentt, Alexander - A/C.1/78/PV.12
NUCLEAR WEAPON TESTS—TREATIES (Agenda item 105)
Kmentt, Alexander - A/C.1/78/PV.12
NUCLEAR WEAPONS—ELIMINATION (Agenda item 99z)
Edtmayer, Matthias - A/C.1/78/PV.25
NUCLEAR WEAPONS—HUMANITARIAN CONSEQUENCES (Agenda item 99bb)
Edtmayer, Matthias - A/C.1/78/PV.25
Kmentt, Alexander - A/C.1/78/PV.12

Austria (continued)

NUCLEAR WEAPONS—TREATIES (Agenda item 99ff)
Edtmayer, Matthias - A/C.1/78/PV.25
Kmentt, Alexander - A/C.1/78/PV.12
OUTER SPACE—CONFIDENCE-BUILDING MEASURES (Agenda item 99v)
Bilgeri, Andreas - A/C.1/78/PV.16
OUTER SPACE—PRINCIPLES (Agenda item 97d)
Bilgeri, Andreas - A/C.1/78/PV.16
PEACEKEEPING OPERATIONS (Agenda item 51)
Marschik, Alexander - A/C.4/78/SR.19
RACIAL DISCRIMINATION—ELIMINATION (Agenda item 69a)
Pretterhofer, Stefan - A/C.3/78/SR.47
RIGHT OF ASSEMBLY (Agenda item 71b)
Mahidi, Mourad - A/C.3/78/SR.19
RIGHT TO PRIVACY (Agenda item 71b)
Soyka, Juliane - A/C.3/78/SR.21
SMALL ARMS—ILLICIT TRAFFIC (Agenda item 99p)
Kmentt, Alexander - A/C.1/78/PV.18
SMALL ARMS—ILLICIT TRAFFIC—ASSISTANCE (Agenda item 99n)
Kmentt, Alexander - A/C.1/78/PV.18
UKRAINE—POLITICAL CONDITIONS (Agenda item 62)
Marschik, Nikolaus - A/78/PV.56
UN. CONFERENCE ON DISARMAMENT—REPORTS (Agenda item 101a)
Kmentt, Alexander - A/C.1/78/PV.23
UN. GENERAL ASSEMBLY (78TH SESS. : 2023-2024)—GENERAL DEBATE (Agenda item 8)
Schallenberg, Alexander - A/78/PV.9
UN. GENERAL ASSEMBLY (78TH SESS. : 2023-2024). 1ST COMMITTEE—GENERAL DEBATE (Agenda item 8)
Marschik, Alexander - A/C.1/78/PV.4
UN. INTERNATIONAL LAW COMMISSION—REPORTS (Agenda item 79)
Bühler, Konrad G. - A/C.6/78/SR.24
Gorke, Maximilian - A/C.6/78/SR.31
Pretterhofer, Stefan - A/C.6/78/SR.29
UN. SECURITY COUNCIL—REPORTS (Agenda item 26)
Pretterhofer, Stefan - A/78/PV.93
UN COMMISSION ON INTERNATIONAL TRADE LAW—REPORTS (Agenda item 77)
Gorke, Maximilian - A/C.6/78/SR.14; A/C.6/78/SR.37
VETO (Agenda item 63)
Marschik, Alexander - A/78/PV.51; A/78/PV.69; A/78/PV.70; A/78/PV.79
Pretterhofer, Stefan - A/78/PV.3
WESTERN SAHARA QUESTION (Agenda item 58)
Troch, Harald - A/C.4/78/SR.5

Austria (continued)

YOUTH (Agenda item 24b)
Huber, Marvin - A/C.3/78/SR.2

Autonomy for the Sahara Coalition (Organization)

WESTERN SAHARA QUESTION (Agenda item 58)
Abugamel, Firas - A/C.4/78/SR.4
Besnard, Jérôme - A/C.4/78/SR.5

Azerbaijan

CENTRAL ASIA—ZONES OF PEACE (Agenda item 64)
Ahangari, Narmin - A/78/PV.85
CLIMATE (Agenda item 18d)
Bayramli-Hamidova, Nigar - A/C.2/78/SR.13
CRIMES AGAINST HUMANITY (Agenda item 80)
Musayev, Tofig - A/C.6/78/SR.11
CULTURE—DEVELOPMENT (Agenda item 19b)
Ahmadova, Billur - A/C.2/78/SR.11
DISARMAMENT—GENERAL AND COMPLETE (Agenda item 99)
Gurbanov, Ilgar - A/C.1/78/PV.24
HUMAN RIGHTS (Agenda item 71)
Ahangari, Narmin - A/C.3/78/SR.25
HUMAN RIGHTS—INTERNATIONAL INSTRUMENTS (Agenda item 71a)
Ahangari, Narmin - A/C.3/78/SR.25
HUMAN RIGHTS—UKRAINE (Agenda item 71c)
Ahangari, Narmin - A/C.3/78/SR.53
HUMAN RIGHTS ADVANCEMENT (Agenda item 71b)
Ahangari, Narmin - A/C.3/78/SR.25
INFORMATION TECHNOLOGY—DEVELOPMENT (Agenda item 15)
Ahmadova, Billur - A/C.2/78/SR.11
LANDLOCKED DEVELOPING COUNTRIES—CONFERENCES (Agenda item 20b)
Ahmadova, Billur - A/C.2/78/SR.7
LANDMINES—TREATIES (Agenda item 99m)
Gurbanov, Ilgar - A/C.1/78/PV.19
LEAST DEVELOPED COUNTRIES—CONFERENCES (Agenda item 20a)
Ahmadova, Billur - A/C.2/78/SR.7
MACROECONOMIC POLICY (Agenda item 16)
Bayramli-Hamidova, Nigar - A/C.2/78/SR.9
MINORITIES (Agenda item 71b)
Ahangari, Narmin - A/C.3/78/SR.25
MULTILATERALISM—DISARMAMENT (Agenda item 99r)
Gurbanov, Ilgar - A/C.1/78/PV.23
PEACE (Agenda item 14)
Musayev, Tofig - A/78/PV.82

Azerbaijan (continued)

RACIAL DISCRIMINATION—ELIMINATION (Agenda item 69a)
Ahangari, Narmin - A/C.3/78/SR.41; A/C.3/78/SR.43
RACIAL DISCRIMINATION—PROGRAMMES OF ACTION (Agenda item 69b)
Ahangari, Narmin - A/C.3/78/SR.41; A/C.3/78/SR.43
RESPONSIBILITY TO PROTECT (Agenda item 129)
Gusman, Vadim - A/78/PV.97
RIGHTS OF THE CHILD (Agenda item 67)
Ahangari, Narmin - A/C.3/78/SR.11; A/C.3/78/SR.13; A/C.3/78/SR.14
RULE OF LAW (Agenda item 83)
Musayev, Tofig - A/C.6/78/SR.19
RURAL WOMEN (Agenda item 25a)
Ahangari, Narmin - A/C.3/78/SR.10
SUSTAINABLE DEVELOPMENT (Agenda item 18)
Bayramli-Hamidova, Nigar - A/C.2/78/SR.13; A/C.2/78/SR.15
SUSTAINABLE ENERGY (Agenda item 18h)
Bayramli-Hamidova, Nigar - A/C.2/78/SR.13
TERRORISM (Agenda item 109)
Musayev, Tofig - A/C.6/78/SR.4; A/C.6/78/SR.5
UN. GENERAL ASSEMBLY (78TH SESS. : 2023-2024)—GENERAL DEBATE (Agenda item 8)
Bayramov, Jeyhun - A/78/PV.12
UN. GENERAL ASSEMBLY (78TH SESS. : 2023-2024)—GENERAL DEBATE—RIGHT OF REPLY (Agenda item 8)
Musayev, Tofig - A/78/PV.14
UN. GENERAL ASSEMBLY (78TH SESS. : 2023-2024). 1ST COMMITTEE—GENERAL DEBATE (Agenda item 8)
Gurbanov, Ilgar - A/C.1/78/PV.7; A/C.1/78/PV.8
Musayev, Tofig - A/C.1/78/PV.7
UN. GENERAL ASSEMBLY (78TH SESS. : 2023-2024). 2ND COMMITTEE—GENERAL DEBATE (Agenda item 8)
Bayramli-Hamidova, Nigar - A/C.2/78/SR.4; A/C.2/78/SR.5
UN. INTERNATIONAL COURT OF JUSTICE—REPORTS (Agenda item 73)
Musayev, Tofig - A/78/PV.27; A/78/PV.28
UN CONFERENCES (Agenda item 13)
Aliyev, Yashar T. - A/78/PV.37
UN HIGH COMMISSIONER FOR REFUGEES—REPORTS (Agenda item 60)
Ahangari, Narmin - A/C.3/78/SR.44; A/C.3/78/SR.45
WOMEN'S ADVANCEMENT (Agenda item 25a)
Ahangari, Narmin - A/C.3/78/SR.10
WOMEN'S ADVANCEMENT—CONFERENCES (Agenda item 25b)
Ahangari, Narmin - A/C.3/78/SR.10

Bahamas

DEVELOPMENT FINANCE (Agenda item 16b)
Mott, T'Sean - A/C.2/78/SR.11
EXTERNAL DEBT (Agenda item 16c)
Mott, T'Sean - A/C.2/78/SR.11
EXTERNAL DEBT—HUMAN RIGHTS (Agenda item 71b)
DeGregory, Kelli - A/C.3/78/SR.32
SMALL ISLAND DEVELOPING STATES—PROGRAMMES OF ACTION (Agenda item 18b)
Mott, T'Sean - A/78/PV.100
TAXATION (Agenda item 16h)
Mott, T'Sean - A/C.2/78/SR.11; A/C.2/78/SR.25
UN—BUDGET (2024) (Agenda item 134)
DeGregory, Kelli - A/C.5/78/SR.23
UN. GENERAL ASSEMBLY (78TH SESS. : 2023-2024)—GENERAL DEBATE (Agenda item 8)
Mitchell, Frederick A. - A/78/PV.11
UN. HUMAN RIGHTS COUNCIL—REPORTS (Agenda item 66)
DeGregory, Kelli - A/C.3/78/SR.46

Bahrain

ADMINISTRATION OF JUSTICE—HUMAN RIGHTS (Agenda item 71b)
Alhammadi, Hessa - A/C.3/78/SR.25
AGEING PERSONS (Agenda item 24b)
Alhammadi, Hessa - A/C.3/78/SR.3
DECOLONIZATION (Agenda item 58)
Aljalahma, Shaikha - A/C.4/78/SR.7
FOOD SECURITY (Agenda item 23a)
Alsindi, Yusuf Khaled - A/C.2/78/SR.17
INFORMATION—INTERNATIONAL SECURITY (Agenda item 94)
Janahi, Balqees - A/C.1/78/PV.21
INFORMATION TECHNOLOGY—DEVELOPMENT (Agenda item 15)
Alatawi, Innas Abdulrahman - A/C.2/78/SR.10
MIDDLE EAST—NUCLEAR-WEAPON-FREE ZONES (Agenda item 95)
Janahi, Balqees - A/C.1/78/PV.14
NATIONAL INSTITUTIONS—HUMAN RIGHTS (Agenda item 71b)
Alhammadi, Hessa - A/C.3/78/SR.25
NUCLEAR DISARMAMENT (Agenda item 99b)
Janahi, Balqees - A/C.1/78/PV.14
NUCLEAR NON-PROLIFERATION—INTERNATIONAL OBLIGATIONS (Agenda item 99w)
Janahi, Balqees - A/C.1/78/PV.14
OUTER SPACE—PEACEFUL USES—INTERNATIONAL COOPERATION (Agenda item 48)
Aljalahma, Shaikha - A/C.4/78/SR.17
PALESTINE QUESTION (Agenda item 35)
Alrowaiei, Jamal Fares - A/78/PV.40
PEACE (Agenda item 14)
Alrowaiei, Jamal Fares - A/78/PV.76

Bahrain (continued)

PERSONS WITH DISABILITIES (Agenda item 24b)
Alhammadi, Hessa - A/C.3/78/SR.3
POVERTY—INTERNATIONAL DECADES (Agenda item 21a)
Alsindi, Yusuf Khaled - A/C.2/78/SR.17
RELIGIOUS INTOLERANCE (Agenda item 71b)
Alhammadi, Hessa - A/C.3/78/SR.25
RIGHTS OF THE CHILD (Agenda item 67)
Alabbasi, Amina Abdulaziz - A/C.3/78/SR.14
RURAL POVERTY (Agenda item 21b)
Alsindi, Yusuf Khaled - A/C.2/78/SR.17
SOCIAL DEVELOPMENT (Agenda item 24)
Alhammadi, Hessa - A/C.3/78/SR.3
SPORTS—OLYMPIC GAMES (Agenda item 11)
Alrowaiei, Jamal Fares - A/78/PV.38
SUSTAINABLE DEVELOPMENT (Agenda item 18)
Al Fadhel, Noura Abdul Rahman - A/C.2/78/SR.13
TERRITORIES OCCUPIED BY ISRAEL—HUMAN RIGHTS (Agenda item 50)
Aljalahma, Shaikha - A/C.4/78/SR.25
TERRITORIES OCCUPIED BY ISRAEL—NATURAL RESOURCES (Agenda item 59)
Al Bin Khalil, Maryam - A/C.2/78/SR.19
TERRORISM (Agenda item 109)
Almarzooqi, Hazem Abdulqader Khalifa Abdulla - A/C.6/78/SR.4
UN. GENERAL ASSEMBLY (78TH SESS. : 2023-2024)—GENERAL DEBATE (Agenda item 8)
Al Zayani, Abdul Latif bin Rashid - A/78/PV.11
UN. GENERAL ASSEMBLY (78TH SESS. : 2023-2024). 1ST COMMITTEE—GENERAL DEBATE (Agenda item 8)
Alrowaiei, Jamal Fares - A/C.1/78/PV.9
UN. GENERAL ASSEMBLY (78TH SESS. : 2023-2024). 2ND COMMITTEE—GENERAL DEBATE (Agenda item 8)
Alatawi, Innas Abdulrahman - A/C.2/78/SR.5
VETO (Agenda item 63)
Alrowaiei, Jamal Fares - A/78/PV.67; A/78/PV.75
WESTERN SAHARA QUESTION (Agenda item 58)
Aljalahma, Shaikha - A/C.4/78/SR.7
WOMEN'S ADVANCEMENT (Agenda item 25a)
Alabbasi, Amina Abdulaziz - A/C.3/78/SR.9
WOMEN'S ADVANCEMENT—CONFERENCES (Agenda item 25b)
Alabbasi, Amina Abdulaziz - A/C.3/78/SR.9
YOUTH (Agenda item 24b)
Alhammadi, Hessa - A/C.3/78/SR.3

Baku Initiative Group

FRENCH POLYNESIA QUESTION (Agenda item 58)
Tokoragi, Ella - A/C.4/78/SR.3

Banco de Alimentos

WESTERN SAHARA QUESTION (Agenda item 58)
Díaz de la Vega García, Pedro - A/C.4/78/SR.5

Bangladesh

AGEING PERSONS (Agenda item 24b)
Abdullah, Md Showeb - A/C.3/78/SR.1
ARMS RACE—OUTER SPACE (Agenda item 97a)
Muhith, Muhammad A. - A/C.1/78/PV.16
ARMS TRANSFERS—TREATIES (Agenda item 99x)
Shatil, Toufiq Islam - A/C.1/78/PV.18
BIOLOGICAL WEAPONS—TREATIES (Agenda item 106)
Muhith, Muhammad A. - A/C.1/78/PV.15
CHEMICAL WEAPONS—TREATIES (Agenda item 99l)
Muhith, Muhammad A. - A/C.1/78/PV.15
CLIMATE CHANGE (Agenda item 71b)
Abdullah, Md Showeb - A/C.3/78/SR.29
CRIMES AGAINST HUMANITY (Agenda item 80)
Muhith, Muhammad A. - A/C.6/78/SR.10
DECOLONIZATION (Agenda item 58)
Shatil, Toufiq Islam - A/C.4/78/SR.2
DEVELOPMENT FINANCE (Agenda item 16b)
Hossain, Faruk - A/C.2/78/SR.9
DISASTER VICTIMS (Agenda item 86)
Uddin, Nasir - A/C.6/78/SR.6
DISPLACED PERSONS (Agenda item 71b)
Abdullah, Md Showeb - A/C.3/78/SR.32
FOOD SECURITY (Agenda item 23a)
Hossain, Faruk - A/C.2/78/SR.17
FREEDOM OF EXPRESSION (Agenda item 71b)
Monica, Mosammat Shahanara - A/C.3/78/SR.19
HUMAN RIGHTS (Agenda item 71)
Monica, Mosammat Shahanara - A/C.3/78/SR.16
HUMAN RIGHTS—INTERNATIONAL INSTRUMENTS (Agenda item 71a)
Muhith, Muhammad A. - A/C.3/78/SR.25
HUMAN RIGHTS—MYANMAR (Agenda item 71c)
Monica, Mosammat Shahanara - A/C.3/78/SR.33; A/C.3/78/SR.53
Muhith, Muhammad A. - A/C.3/78/SR.25
HUMAN RIGHTS—TERRITORIES OCCUPIED BY ISRAEL (Agenda item 71c)
Abdullah, Md Showeb - A/C.3/78/SR.35
Monica, Mosammat Shahanara - A/C.3/78/SR.35

Bangladesh (continued)

HUMAN RIGHTS ACTIVISTS (Agenda item 71b)
Monica, Mosammat Shahanara - A/C.3/78/SR.19
IAEA—REPORTS (Agenda item 89)
Abdullah, Md Showeb - A/78/PV.29
INDIGENOUS PEOPLES (Agenda item 68a)
Abdullah, Md Showeb - A/C.3/78/SR.15
INDIGENOUS PEOPLES—CONFERENCES (Agenda item 68b)
Abdullah, Md Showeb - A/C.3/78/SR.15
INFORMATION (Agenda item 53)
Muhith, Muhammad A. - A/C.4/78/SR.13
INFORMATION—INTERNATIONAL SECURITY (Agenda item 94)
Muhith, Muhammad A. - A/C.1/78/PV.20
INFORMATION TECHNOLOGY—DEVELOPMENT (Agenda item 15)
Hossain, Faruk - A/C.2/78/SR.10
INTERNATIONAL CRIMINAL COURT—REPORTS (Agenda item 74)
Muhith, Muhammad A. - A/78/PV.21
LANDLOCKED DEVELOPING COUNTRIES—CONFERENCES (Agenda item 20b)
Molla, Md Rafiqul Alam - A/C.2/78/SR.7
LANDMINES—TREATIES (Agenda item 99m)
Shatil, Toufiq Islam - A/C.1/78/PV.18
LAW OF THE SEA (Agenda item 75a)
Uddin, Nasir - A/78/PV.43
LEAST DEVELOPED COUNTRIES—CONFERENCES (Agenda item 20a)
Molla, Md Rafiqul Alam - A/C.2/78/SR.7
MACROECONOMIC POLICY (Agenda item 16)
Hossain, Faruk - A/C.2/78/SR.9
MARINE ECOSYSTEMS—BIOLOGICAL DIVERSITY (Agenda item 75c)
Uddin, Nasir - A/78/PV.43
MIGRANT WORKERS (Agenda item 71a)
Abdullah, Md Showeb - A/C.3/78/SR.23
MIGRANTS—PROTECTION (Agenda item 71b)
Abdullah, Md Showeb - A/C.3/78/SR.23
MINE CLEARANCE (Agenda item 46)
Shatil, Toufiq Islam - A/C.4/78/SR.10
MULTILATERALISM—DISARMAMENT (Agenda item 99r)
Molla, Md Rafiqul Alam - A/C.1/78/PV.21
NATURAL FIBRES (Agenda item 23b)
Hossain, Faruk - A/C.2/78/SR.23
NUCLEAR DISARMAMENT (Agenda item 99b)
Molla, Md Rafiqul Alam - A/C.1/78/PV.12
NUCLEAR NON-PROLIFERATION—INTERNATIONAL OBLIGATIONS (Agenda item 99w)
Molla, Md Rafiqul Alam - A/C.1/78/PV.12
NUCLEAR WEAPONS—TREATIES (Agenda item 99ff)
Molla, Md Rafiqul Alam - A/C.1/78/PV.12

Bangladesh (continued)

OUTER SPACE—PEACEFUL USES—INTERNATIONAL COOPERATION (Agenda item 48)
Shatil, Toufiq Islam - A/C.4/78/SR.15
OUTER SPACE—PRINCIPLES (Agenda item 97d)
Muhith, Muhammad A. - A/C.1/78/PV.16
PALESTINE QUESTION (Agenda item 35)
Muhith, Muhammad A. - A/78/PV.40
PEACE (Agenda item 14)
Muhith, Muhammad A. - A/78/PV.76
PEACEKEEPING OPERATIONS (Agenda item 51)
Muhith, Muhammad A. - A/C.4/78/SR.19
PEACEKEEPING OPERATIONS—CRIMINAL LIABILITY (Agenda item 76)
Muhith, Muhammad A. - A/C.6/78/SR.8
PERSONS WITH DISABILITIES—HUMAN RIGHTS (Agenda item 71a)
Monica, Mosammat Shahanara - A/C.3/78/SR.38
POVERTY—HUMAN RIGHTS (Agenda item 71b)
Abdullah, Md Showeb - A/C.3/78/SR.30
POVERTY—INTERNATIONAL DECADES (Agenda item 21a)
Hossain, Faruk - A/C.2/78/SR.17
RACIAL DISCRIMINATION—ELIMINATION (Agenda item 69a)
Muhith, Muhammad A. - A/C.3/78/SR.43
RACIAL DISCRIMINATION—PROGRAMMES OF ACTION (Agenda item 69b)
Muhith, Muhammad A. - A/C.3/78/SR.43
RADIATION EFFECTS (Agenda item 47)
Molla, Md Rafiqul Alam - A/C.4/78/SR.11
RELIGIOUS INTOLERANCE (Agenda item 71b)
Monica, Mosammat Shahanara - A/C.3/78/SR.38
RESPONSIBILITY TO PROTECT (Agenda item 129)
Shatil, Toufiq Islam - A/78/PV.99
RIGHT OF ASSEMBLY (Agenda item 71b)
Monica, Mosammat Shahanara - A/C.3/78/SR.19
RIGHT TO DEVELOPMENT (Agenda item 71b)
Monica, Mosammat Shahanara - A/C.3/78/SR.20
RIGHT TO DRINKING WATER (Agenda item 71b)
Abdullah, Md Showeb - A/C.3/78/SR.28
RIGHT TO EDUCATION (Agenda item 71b)
Abdullah, Md Showeb - A/C.3/78/SR.27
RIGHT TO HEALTH (Agenda item 71b)
Abdullah, Md Showeb - A/C.3/78/SR.39
RIGHT TO HOUSING (Agenda item 71b)
Abdullah, Md Showeb - A/C.3/78/SR.30
RIGHTS OF THE CHILD (Agenda item 67)
Abdullah, Md Showeb - A/C.3/78/SR.13
Monica, Mosammat Shahanara - A/C.3/78/SR.11; A/C.3/78/SR.12
RURAL POVERTY (Agenda item 21b)
Hossain, Faruk - A/C.2/78/SR.17

Bangladesh (continued)

SELF-DETERMINATION OF PEOPLES (Agenda item 70)
Monica, Mosammat Shahanara - A/C.3/78/SR.49
Muhith, Muhammad A. - A/C.3/78/SR.43
SMALL ARMS—ILLICIT TRAFFIC (Agenda item 99p)
Shatil, Toufiq Islam - A/C.1/78/PV.18
SMALL ARMS—ILLICIT TRAFFIC—ASSISTANCE (Agenda item 99n)
Shatil, Toufiq Islam - A/C.1/78/PV.18
SOCIAL CONDITIONS (Agenda item 24b)
Shatil, Toufiq Islam - A/C.3/78/SR.3
SOCIAL DEVELOPMENT (Agenda item 24)
Shatil, Toufiq Islam - A/C.3/78/SR.3
SPECIAL POLITICAL MISSIONS (Agenda item 52)
Shatil, Toufiq Islam - A/C.4/78/SR.21
STRADDLING FISH STOCKS (Agenda item 75b)
Uddin, Nasir - A/78/PV.43
SUSTAINABLE DEVELOPMENT (Agenda item 18)
Muhith, Muhammad A. - A/C.2/78/SR.15
TERRITORIES OCCUPIED BY ISRAEL—HUMAN RIGHTS (Agenda item 50)
Shatil, Toufiq Islam - A/C.4/78/SR.24
TERRITORIES OCCUPIED BY ISRAEL—NATURAL RESOURCES (Agenda item 59)
Prince, Gomar Faruk Khandakar - A/C.2/78/SR.19
TERRORISM (Agenda item 109)
Shatil, Toufiq Islam - A/C.6/78/SR.1
UN—BUDGET (2024) (Agenda item 134)
Farhan, Fahmid - A/C.5/78/SR.3
Muhith, Muhammad A. - A/C.5/78/SR.5
UN—PROGRAMME PLANNING (Agenda item 135)
Muhith, Muhammad A. - A/C.5/78/SR.5
UN. CONFERENCE ON DISARMAMENT—REPORTS (Agenda item 101a)
Molla, Md Rafiqul Alam - A/C.1/78/PV.23
UN. DISARMAMENT COMMISSION—REPORTS (Agenda item 101b)
Molla, Md Rafiqul Alam - A/C.1/78/PV.23
UN. GENERAL ASSEMBLY—WORK PROGRAMME (Agenda item 120)
Molla, Md Rafiqul Alam - A/78/PV.33
UN. GENERAL ASSEMBLY (78TH SESS. : 2023-2024)—OFFICERS (Agenda item 5)
Muhith, Muhammad A. - A/C.2/78/SR.26
Shatil, Toufiq Islam - A/C.5/78/SR.1
UN. GENERAL ASSEMBLY (78TH SESS. : 2023-2024). 1ST COMMITTEE—GENERAL DEBATE (Agenda item 8)
Shatil, Toufiq Islam - A/C.1/78/PV.3
UN. GENERAL ASSEMBLY (78TH SESS. : 2023-2024). 2ND COMMITTEE—GENERAL DEBATE (Agenda item 8)
Shatil, Toufiq Islam - A/C.2/78/SR.6

Bangladesh (continued)

UN. GENERAL ASSEMBLY (78TH SESS. : 2023-2024). 5TH COMMITTEE—WORK ORGANIZATION (Agenda item 7)
Muhith, Muhammad A. - A/C.5/78/SR.35
UN. HUMAN RIGHTS COUNCIL—REPORTS (Agenda item 66)
Monica, Mosammat Shahanara - A/C.3/78/SR.46
UN. INTERNATIONAL COURT OF JUSTICE—REPORTS (Agenda item 73)
Muhith, Muhammad A. - A/78/PV.27
UN. INTERNATIONAL LAW COMMISSION—REPORTS (Agenda item 79)
Uddin, Nasir - A/C.6/78/SR.24
UN. SECURITY COUNCIL—MEMBERSHIP (Agenda item 121)
Molla, Md Rafiqul Alam - A/78/PV.35
UN CONFERENCES (Agenda item 13)
Muhith, Muhammad A. - A/78/PV.107
UN HIGH COMMISSIONER FOR REFUGEES—REPORTS (Agenda item 60)
Monica, Mosammat Shahanara - A/C.3/78/SR.44; A/C.3/78/SR.45
UN RESOLUTIONS—IMPLEMENTATION (Agenda item 119)
Molla, Md Rafiqul Alam - A/78/PV.33
UNRWA—ACTIVITIES (Agenda item 49)
Muhith, Muhammad A. - A/C.4/78/SR.23
VETO (Agenda item 63)
Farhan, Fahmid - A/78/PV.61
Muhith, Muhammad A. - A/78/PV.52; A/78/PV.67; A/78/PV.71; A/78/PV.75
WEAPONS OF MASS DESTRUCTION—TERRORISM (Agenda item 99s)
Muhith, Muhammad A. - A/C.1/78/PV.15
WOMEN'S ADVANCEMENT (Agenda item 25a)
Monica, Mosammat Shahanara - A/C.3/78/SR.7; A/C.3/78/SR.10
WOMEN'S ADVANCEMENT—CONFERENCES (Agenda item 25b)
Monica, Mosammat Shahanara - A/C.3/78/SR.7; A/C.3/78/SR.10

Bangladesh. Prime Minister

UN. GENERAL ASSEMBLY (78TH SESS. : 2023-2024)—GENERAL DEBATE (Agenda item 8)
Hasina, Sheikh - A/78/PV.10
UN. GENERAL ASSEMBLY (78TH SESS. : 2023-2024)—SPECIAL STATEMENTS
Hasina, Sheikh - A/78/PV.10

Barbados

CUBA—UNITED STATES (Agenda item 38)
Jackman, François - A/78/PV.26

Barbados. Prime Minister

UN. GENERAL ASSEMBLY (78TH SESS. : 2023-2024)—GENERAL DEBATE (Agenda item 8)
Mottley, Mia Amor - A/78/PV.10
UN. GENERAL ASSEMBLY (78TH SESS. : 2023-2024)—SPECIAL STATEMENTS
Mottley, Mia Amor - A/78/PV.10

Belarus

2030 AGENDA—PROGRAMME IMPLEMENTATION (Agenda item 18a)
Pisarevich, Vadim - A/C.2/78/SR.13
AGEING PERSONS (Agenda item 24b)
Mozgovaya, Ekaterina - A/C.3/78/SR.2
BIOLOGICAL WEAPONS—TREATIES (Agenda item 106)
Makarevich, Siarhei - A/C.1/78/PV.15
CHEMICAL WEAPONS—TREATIES (Agenda item 99l)
Makarevich, Siarhei - A/C.1/78/PV.15
CRIME PREVENTION (Agenda item 107)
Pilipenko, Igor - A/C.3/78/SR.50
Velichko, Irina - A/C.3/78/SR.5
CRIMES AGAINST HUMANITY (Agenda item 80)
Evseenko, Pavel - A/C.6/78/SR.10
CUBA—UNITED STATES (Agenda item 38)
Evseenko, Pavel - A/78/PV.24
CYBERCRIME (Agenda item 108)
Velichko, Irina - A/C.3/78/SR.5
DEVELOPMENT COOPERATION—MIDDLE-INCOME COUNTRIES (Agenda item 19c)
Kavaleuskaya, Alena - A/C.2/78/SR.10
ECONOMIC SANCTIONS—INTERNATIONAL RELATIONS (Agenda item 28)
Rybakov, Valentin - A/78/PV.89
ELECTION VERIFICATION—UN (Agenda item 71b)
Mozgovaya, Ekaterina - A/78/PV.50; A/C.3/78/SR.50
EMERGENCY ASSISTANCE (Agenda item 72a)
Kavaleuskaya, Alena - A/78/PV.47
FAMILY (Agenda item 24b)
Mozgovaya, Ekaterina - A/C.3/78/SR.49
FOOD SECURITY (Agenda item 23a)
Kavaleuskaya, Alena - A/C.2/78/SR.25
Pisarevich, Vadim - A/C.2/78/SR.16
HEALTH (Agenda item 125)
Mozgovaya, Ekaterina - A/78/PV.16
Pilipenko, Igor - A/78/PV.48
HIV/AIDS—DECLARATIONS (Agenda item 10)
Mozgovaya, Ekaterina - A/78/PV.91
HUMAN RIGHTS (Agenda item 71)
Pilipenko, Igor - A/C.3/78/SR.16
HUMAN RIGHTS—BURUNDI (Agenda item 71c)
Tozik, Artsiom - A/C.3/78/SR.36

Belarus (continued)

HUMAN RIGHTS—DEMOCRATIC PEOPLE'S REPUBLIC OF KOREA (Agenda item 71c)
Pilipenko, Igor - A/78/PV.50; A/C.3/78/SR.53
Tozik, Artsiom - A/C.3/78/SR.33
HUMAN RIGHTS—ERITREA (Agenda item 71c)
Tozik, Artsiom - A/C.3/78/SR.36
HUMAN RIGHTS—ETHIOPIA (Agenda item 71c)
Tozik, Artsiom - A/C.3/78/SR.36
HUMAN RIGHTS—IRAN (ISLAMIC REPUBLIC OF) (Agenda item 71c)
Pilipenko, Igor - A/78/PV.50; A/C.3/78/SR.53
Tozik, Artsiom - A/C.3/78/SR.34
HUMAN RIGHTS—MYANMAR (Agenda item 71c)
Pilipenko, Igor - A/78/PV.50; A/C.3/78/SR.53
Tozik, Artsiom - A/C.3/78/SR.33
HUMAN RIGHTS—REPORTS (Agenda item 71c)
Kryvaltsevich, Aliaksei - A/C.3/78/SR.24
Pilipenko, Igor - A/78/PV.50
HUMAN RIGHTS—RUSSIAN FEDERATION (Agenda item 71c)
Mozgovaya, Ekaterina - A/C.3/78/SR.37
HUMAN RIGHTS—SYRIAN ARAB REPUBLIC (Agenda item 71c)
Pilipenko, Igor - A/78/PV.50; A/C.3/78/SR.54
Tozik, Artsiom - A/C.3/78/SR.34
HUMAN RIGHTS—UKRAINE (Agenda item 71c)
Pilipenko, Igor - A/78/PV.50
HUMAN RIGHTS ADVANCEMENT (Agenda item 71b)
Kryvaltsevich, Aliaksei - A/C.3/78/SR.24
IAEA—REPORTS (Agenda item 89)
Kavaleuskaya, Alena - A/78/PV.29; A/78/PV.30
INTERNATIONAL JURISDICTION (Agenda item 84)
Evseenko, Pavel - A/C.6/78/SR.12
INTERNATIONAL TRADE (Agenda item 16a)
Kavaleuskaya, Alena - A/C.2/78/SR.9; A/C.2/78/SR.22; A/C.2/78/SR.24
MILLENNIUM SUMMIT—CONFERENCES (Agenda item 117)
Evseenko, Pavel - A/78/PV.15
NON-CITIZENS—DEPORTATION (Agenda item 81)
Evseenko, Pavel - A/C.6/78/SR.34
OPERATIONAL ACTIVITIES—UN SYSTEM (Agenda item 22a)
Pisarevich, Vadim - A/C.2/78/SR.18
PERSONS WITH DISABILITIES (Agenda item 24b)
Mozgovaya, Ekaterina - A/C.3/78/SR.2
PERSONS WITH DISABILITIES—HUMAN RIGHTS (Agenda item 71a)
Tozik, Artsiom - A/C.3/78/SR.38

Belarus (continued)

POVERTY—INTERNATIONAL DECADES (Agenda item 21a)
Pisarevich, Vadim - A/C.2/78/SR.16
RACIAL DISCRIMINATION—ELIMINATION (Agenda item 69a)
Pilipenko, Igor - A/78/PV.50
Tozik, Artsiom - A/C.3/78/SR.40
RACIAL DISCRIMINATION—PROGRAMMES OF ACTION (Agenda item 69b)
Tozik, Artsiom - A/C.3/78/SR.40
RESPONSIBILITY OF INTERNATIONAL ORGANIZATIONS (Agenda item 85)
Evseenko, Pavel - A/C.6/78/SR.19
RIGHT TO DEVELOPMENT (Agenda item 71b)
Pisarevich, Vadim - A/C.3/78/SR.20
RIGHT TO FOOD (Agenda item 71b)
Kryvaltsevich, Aliaksei - A/C.3/78/SR.30
Pilipenko, Igor - A/C.3/78/SR.48
RIGHT TO HEALTH (Agenda item 71b)
Tozik, Artsiom - A/C.3/78/SR.39
RIGHTS OF THE CHILD (Agenda item 67)
Velichko, Irina - A/C.3/78/SR.11; A/C.3/78/SR.12
RULE OF LAW (Agenda item 83)
Evseenko, Pavel - A/C.6/78/SR.16
RURAL POVERTY (Agenda item 21b)
Pisarevich, Vadim - A/C.2/78/SR.16
SANCTIONS—INTERNATIONAL RELATIONS (Agenda item 71b)
Kryvaltsevich, Aliaksei - A/C.3/78/SR.28
Pilipenko, Igor - A/C.3/78/SR.48
SOCIAL CONDITIONS (Agenda item 24b)
Mozgovaya, Ekaterina - A/78/PV.57; A/C.3/78/SR.2
SOCIAL DEVELOPMENT—CONFERENCES (Agenda item 24a)
Mozgovaya, Ekaterina - A/C.3/78/SR.2
SPORTS—OLYMPIC GAMES (Agenda item 11)
Mozgovaya, Ekaterina - A/78/PV.38
SUSTAINABLE DEVELOPMENT (Agenda item 18)
Pisarevich, Vadim - A/C.2/78/SR.13
TRAFFICKING IN PERSONS (Agenda item 71b)
Kryvaltsevich, Aliaksei - A/C.3/78/SR.23
TREATIES (Agenda item 87)
Evseenko, Pavel - A/C.6/78/SR.20
UN—BUDGET (2024) (Agenda item 134)
Evseenko, Pavel - A/C.5/78/SR.26/PartII; A/C.5/78/SR.34
UN—PROGRAMME PLANNING (Agenda item 135)
Evseenko, Pavel - A/78/PV.50(Resumption1)
UN. COMMITTEE ON RELATIONS WITH THE HOST COUNTRY—REPORTS (Agenda item 161)
Shaev, Evgeny - A/C.6/78/SR.35

Belarus (continued)

UN. GENERAL ASSEMBLY (78TH SESS. : 2023-2024)—GENERAL DEBATE (Agenda item 8)
Aleinik, Sergei - A/78/PV.13
UN. GENERAL ASSEMBLY (78TH SESS. : 2023-2024). 1ST COMMITTEE—GENERAL DEBATE (Agenda item 8)
Pavlov, Vasiliy - A/C.1/78/PV.5
UN. HUMAN RIGHTS COUNCIL—REPORTS (Agenda item 66)
Pilipenko, Igor - A/78/PV.23
UN. INTERNATIONAL LAW COMMISSION—REPORTS (Agenda item 79)
Evseenko, Pavel - A/C.6/78/SR.31
Popkov, Andrei N. - A/C.6/78/SR.24; A/C.6/78/SR.28
UN. SECRETARY-GENERAL—REPORTS (Agenda item 110)
Mozgovaya, Ekaterina - A/78/PV.55
UN. SECURITY COUNCIL—MEMBERSHIP (Agenda item 121)
Makarevich, Siarhei - A/78/PV.36
UN CHARTER—REPORTS (Agenda item 82)
Evseenko, Pavel - A/C.6/78/SR.22
UN COMMISSION ON INTERNATIONAL TRADE LAW—REPORTS (Agenda item 77)
Evseenko, Pavel - A/C.6/78/SR.14
UN CONFERENCES (Agenda item 13)
Evseenko, Pavel - A/78/PV.15
UN HIGH COMMISSIONER FOR REFUGEES—REPORTS (Agenda item 60)
Pilipenko, Igor - A/C.3/78/SR.44
WEAPONS OF MASS DESTRUCTION (Agenda item 93)
Makarevich, Siarhei - A/C.1/78/PV.29
WOMEN'S ADVANCEMENT (Agenda item 25a)
Velichko, Irina - A/C.3/78/SR.8
WOMEN'S ADVANCEMENT—CONFERENCES (Agenda item 25b)
Velichko, Irina - A/C.3/78/SR.8

Belgium

ARMED CONFLICTS PREVENTION (Agenda item 31a)
Cardon De Lichtbuer, Christophe Alain C. - A/78/PV.72
CRIMES AGAINST HUMANITY (Agenda item 80)
Grandjean, Laurence - A/C.6/78/SR.9
Raes, Elisa de - A/C.6/78/SR.38; A/C.6/78/SR.45
DISAPPEARANCE OF PERSONS (Agenda item 71b)
Bauwens, Gilles - A/C.3/78/SR.22
FREEDOM OF EXPRESSION (Agenda item 71b)
Bauwens, Gilles - A/C.3/78/SR.19
HEALTH (Agenda item 125)
Bouthé, Marc Gerard C. - A/78/PV.77

Belgium (continued)

HUMAN RIGHTS—INTERNATIONAL INSTRUMENTS (Agenda item 71a)
Kridelka, Philippe - A/C.3/78/SR.25
INTERNATIONAL CRIMINAL COURT—REPORTS (Agenda item 74)
Lagatie, Karl - A/78/PV.22
LAW OF THE SEA (Agenda item 75a)
Lagatie, Karl - A/78/PV.43
MARINE ECOSYSTEMS—BIOLOGICAL DIVERSITY (Agenda item 75c)
Lagatie, Karl - A/78/PV.43; A/78/PV.103
NATIONAL INSTITUTIONS—HUMAN RIGHTS (Agenda item 71b)
Kridelka, Philippe - A/C.3/78/SR.25
PALESTINIANS—ASSISTANCE (Agenda item 72b)
Kridelka, Philippe - A/78/PV.46
RACIAL DISCRIMINATION—ELIMINATION (Agenda item 69a)
Bauwens, Gilles - A/C.3/78/SR.40
Willekens, Vincent - A/C.3/78/SR.41
RACIAL DISCRIMINATION—PROGRAMMES OF ACTION (Agenda item 69b)
Bauwens, Gilles - A/C.3/78/SR.40
Willekens, Vincent - A/C.3/78/SR.41
RELIGIOUS INTOLERANCE (Agenda item 71b)
Bauwens, Gilles - A/C.3/78/SR.38
RIGHT OF ASSEMBLY (Agenda item 71b)
Kridelka, Philippe - A/C.3/78/SR.19
RIGHTS OF THE CHILD (Agenda item 67)
Bauwens, Gilles - A/C.3/78/SR.11
SEXUAL ORIENTATION (Agenda item 71b)
Bauwens, Gilles - A/C.3/78/SR.39
SOCIAL CONDITIONS (Agenda item 24b)
Kridelka, Philippe - A/78/PV.101
STRADDLING FISH STOCKS (Agenda item 75b)
Lagatie, Karl - A/78/PV.43
SUMMARY EXECUTIONS (Agenda item 71b)
Bauwens, Gilles - A/C.3/78/SR.31
TERRORISM—HUMAN RIGHTS (Agenda item 71b)
Bauwens, Gilles - A/C.3/78/SR.31
TREATIES (Agenda item 87)
Raes, Elisa de - A/C.6/78/SR.20
UKRAINE—POLITICAL CONDITIONS (Agenda item 62)
Maesschalck, Filip de - A/78/PV.57
UN. GENERAL ASSEMBLY (78TH SESS. : 2023-2024). 1ST COMMITTEE—GENERAL DEBATE (Agenda item 8)
Kridelka, Philippe - A/C.1/78/PV.8
UN. INTERNATIONAL COURT OF JUSTICE—REPORTS (Agenda item 73)
Raes, Elisa de - A/78/PV.27
VETO (Agenda item 63)
Bouthé, Marc Gerard C. - A/78/PV.67
Kridelka, Philippe - A/78/PV.59; A/78/PV.68
Lagatie, Karl - A/78/PV.51; A/78/PV.75

Belgium (continued)

WOMEN'S ADVANCEMENT (Agenda item 25a)
Bauwens, Gilles - A/C.3/78/SR.7; A/C.3/78/SR.8
WOMEN'S ADVANCEMENT—CONFERENCES (Agenda item 25b)
Bauwens, Gilles - A/C.3/78/SR.7; A/C.3/78/SR.8
YOUTH (Agenda item 24b)
Muaku, Samuel - A/C.3/78/SR.3
Quinet, Manon - A/C.3/78/SR.3

Belgium. Prime Minister

UN. GENERAL ASSEMBLY (78TH SESS. : 2023-2024)—GENERAL DEBATE (Agenda item 8)
De Croo, Alexander - A/78/PV.7
UN. GENERAL ASSEMBLY (78TH SESS. : 2023-2024)—SPECIAL STATEMENTS
De Croo, Alexander - A/78/PV.7

Belize

CUBA—UNITED STATES (Agenda item 38)
Fuller, Carlos C. - A/78/PV.26
MARINE ECOSYSTEMS—BIOLOGICAL DIVERSITY (Agenda item 75c)
Fuller, Carlos C. - A/78/PV.103
UN. GENERAL ASSEMBLY (78TH SESS. : 2023-2024)—GENERAL DEBATE (Agenda item 8)
Courtenay, Eamon - A/78/PV.13
UN. GENERAL ASSEMBLY (78TH SESS. : 2023-2024)—GENERAL DEBATE—RIGHT OF REPLY (Agenda item 8)
Fuller, Carlos C. - A/78/PV.14

Benin

UN. GENERAL ASSEMBLY (78TH SESS. : 2023-2024)—GENERAL DEBATE (Agenda item 8)
Araba, Marc Hermanne Gninadoou - A/78/PV.14
WESTERN SAHARA QUESTION (Agenda item 58)
Biaou, Maurille Firmin - A/C.4/78/SR.8

Bhutan

UN. ECONOMIC AND SOCIAL COUNCIL—REPORTS (Agenda item 9)
Nidup, Dorji - A/78/PV.48
UN. GENERAL ASSEMBLY (78TH SESS. : 2023-2024)—GENERAL DEBATE (Agenda item 8)
Dorji, Tandi - A/78/PV.14

Bolivia (Plurinational State of)

ARMS RACE—OUTER SPACE (Agenda item 97a)
Muñoz Ponce, Tatiana Bárbara - A/C.1/78/PV.17

Bolivia (Plurinational State of) (continued)
BIOLOGICAL DIVERSITY—TREATIES (Agenda item 18f)
Pary Rodríguez, Diego - A/C.2/78/SR.13
CLIMATE (Agenda item 18d)
Pary Rodríguez, Diego - A/C.2/78/SR.13
CRIMES AGAINST HUMANITY (Agenda item 80)
Ríos, Carmen Rosa - A/C.6/78/SR.10; A/C.6/78/SR.45
CUBA—UNITED STATES (Agenda item 38)
Pary Rodríguez, Diego - A/78/PV.26
DECOLONIZATION (Agenda item 58)
Pary Rodríguez, Diego - A/C.4/78/SR.2
DISARMAMENT AGREEMENTS—OUTER SPACE (Agenda item 97c)
Muñoz Ponce, Tatiana Bárbara - A/C.1/78/PV.17
ECONOMIC SANCTIONS—INTERNATIONAL RELATIONS (Agenda item 28)
Pary Rodríguez, Diego - A/78/PV.90
FALKLAND ISLANDS (MALVINAS) QUESTION (Agenda item 42)
Pary Rodríguez, Diego - A/C.4/78/SR.2
FOOD SECURITY (Agenda item 23a)
Zambrana Flores, Carlos Iván - A/C.2/78/SR.16
HUMAN RIGHTS—INTERNATIONAL INSTRUMENTS (Agenda item 71a)
Pary Rodríguez, Diego - A/C.3/78/SR.26
INDIGENOUS PEOPLES (Agenda item 68a)
Caldera Gutiérrez, Fiorella - A/C.3/78/SR.48
Pary Rodríguez, Diego - A/C.3/78/SR.15
INDIGENOUS PEOPLES—CONFERENCES (Agenda item 68b)
Pary Rodríguez, Diego - A/C.3/78/SR.15
INFORMATION (Agenda item 53)
Ríos, Carmen Rosa - A/C.4/78/SR.14
INFORMATION TECHNOLOGY—DEVELOPMENT (Agenda item 15)
Pary Rodríguez, Diego - A/C.2/78/SR.11
INTERNATIONAL LAW—TRAINING PROGRAMMES (Agenda item 78)
Ríos, Carmen Rosa - A/C.6/78/SR.22
MILLENNIUM SUMMIT—CONFERENCES (Agenda item 117)
Pary Rodríguez, Diego - A/78/PV.15
NUCLEAR DISARMAMENT (Agenda item 99b)
Muñoz Ponce, Tatiana Bárbara - A/C.1/78/PV.13
NUCLEAR NON-PROLIFERATION—INTERNATIONAL OBLIGATIONS (Agenda item 99w)
Muñoz Ponce, Tatiana Bárbara - A/C.1/78/PV.13
NUCLEAR WEAPON TESTS—TREATIES (Agenda item 105)
Muñoz Ponce, Tatiana Bárbara - A/C.1/78/PV.13
OUTER SPACE—CONFIDENCE-BUILDING MEASURES (Agenda item 99v)
Muñoz Ponce, Tatiana Bárbara - A/C.1/78/PV.17
PALESTINIANS—ASSISTANCE (Agenda item 72b)
Zambrana Flores, Carlos Iván - A/78/PV.47

Bolivia (Plurinational State of) (continued)
PEACEKEEPING OPERATIONS (Agenda item 51)
Choque Rosario, Dem Mijael - A/C.4/78/SR.20
POVERTY—INTERNATIONAL DECADES (Agenda item 21a)
Zambrana Flores, Carlos Iván - A/C.2/78/SR.16
RACIAL DISCRIMINATION—ELIMINATION (Agenda item 69a)
Caldera Gutiérrez, Fiorella - A/C.3/78/SR.42
RACIAL DISCRIMINATION—PROGRAMMES OF ACTION (Agenda item 69b)
Caldera Gutiérrez, Fiorella - A/C.3/78/SR.42
RULE OF LAW (Agenda item 83)
Ríos, Carmen Rosa - A/C.6/78/SR.17
RURAL POVERTY (Agenda item 21b)
Zambrana Flores, Carlos Iván - A/C.2/78/SR.16
SELF-DETERMINATION OF PEOPLES (Agenda item 70)
Caldera Gutiérrez, Fiorella - A/C.3/78/SR.42
SUSTAINABLE DEVELOPMENT (Agenda item 18)
Pary Rodríguez, Diego - A/C.2/78/SR.13
SUSTAINABLE ENERGY (Agenda item 18h)
Pary Rodríguez, Diego - A/C.2/78/SR.13
TAXATION (Agenda item 16h)
Muñoz Ponce, Tatiana Bárbara - A/C.2/78/SR.25
TERRITORIES OCCUPIED BY ISRAEL—HUMAN RIGHTS (Agenda item 50)
Ríos, Carmen Rosa - A/C.4/78/SR.25
TERRITORIES OCCUPIED BY ISRAEL—NATURAL RESOURCES (Agenda item 59)
Pary Rodríguez, Diego - A/C.2/78/SR.19
TERRORISM (Agenda item 109)
Pary Rodríguez, Diego - A/C.6/78/SR.3
UN—BUDGET (2024) (Agenda item 134)
Bayley Angeleri, Roberto - A/C.5/78/SR.28
Muñoz Ponce, Tatiana Bárbara - A/C.5/78/SR.26/PartII
UN—PROGRAMME PLANNING (Agenda item 135)
Muñoz Ponce, Tatiana Bárbara - A/78/PV.50(Resumption1); A/C.5/78/SR.24
UN. GENERAL ASSEMBLY (78TH SESS. : 2023-2024). 1ST COMMITTEE—GENERAL DEBATE (Agenda item 8)
Pary Rodríguez, Diego - A/C.1/78/PV.4
UN. GENERAL ASSEMBLY (78TH SESS. : 2023-2024). 2ND COMMITTEE—GENERAL DEBATE (Agenda item 8)
Pary Rodríguez, Diego - A/C.2/78/SR.4
UN. HUMAN RIGHTS COUNCIL—REPORTS (Agenda item 66)
Caldera Gutiérrez, Fiorella - A/78/PV.28
UN. INTERNATIONAL COURT OF JUSTICE—REPORTS (Agenda item 73)
Ríos, Carmen Rosa - A/78/PV.27
UN. SECURITY COUNCIL—MEMBERSHIP (Agenda item 121)
Pary Rodríguez, Diego - A/78/PV.36

Bolivia (Plurinational State of) (continued)

UN. SECURITY COUNCIL—REPORTS (Agenda item 26)
Pary Rodríguez, Diego - A/78/PV.94
UN CHARTER—REPORTS (Agenda item 82)
Ríos, Carmen Rosa - A/C.6/78/SR.34
UN CONFERENCES (Agenda item 13)
Muñoz Ponce, Tatiana Bárbara - A/78/PV.107
Pary Rodríguez, Diego - A/78/PV.15
VETO (Agenda item 63)
Pary Rodríguez, Diego - A/78/PV.60
Ríos, Carmen Rosa - A/78/PV.79
WEAPONS—OUTER SPACE (Agenda item 97b)
Muñoz Ponce, Tatiana Bárbara - A/C.1/78/PV.17
WESTERN SAHARA QUESTION (Agenda item 58)
Pary Rodríguez, Diego - A/C.4/78/SR.2

Bolivia (Plurinational State of). President

UN. GENERAL ASSEMBLY (78TH SESS. : 2023-2024)—GENERAL DEBATE (Agenda item 8)
Arce Catacora, Luis Alberto - A/78/PV.5
UN. GENERAL ASSEMBLY (78TH SESS. : 2023-2024)—SPECIAL STATEMENTS
Arce Catacora, Luis Alberto - A/78/PV.5

Bosnia and Herzegovina. Presidency. Chair

UN. GENERAL ASSEMBLY (78TH SESS. : 2023-2024)—GENERAL DEBATE (Agenda item 8)
Komsic, Zeljko - A/78/PV.6
UN. GENERAL ASSEMBLY (78TH SESS. : 2023-2024)—SPECIAL STATEMENTS
Komsic, Zeljko - A/78/PV.6

Botswana

DECOLONIZATION (Agenda item 58)
Mokhawa, Gladys - A/C.4/78/SR.8
DIAMONDS—FUELLING CONFLICT (Agenda item 30)
Badubi, Ronald Seabo - A/78/PV.65
RULE OF LAW (Agenda item 83)
Mokhawa, Gladys - A/C.6/78/SR.18
UN—BUDGET (2024) (Agenda item 134)
Mokhawa, Gladys - A/C.5/78/SR.5
UN—PROGRAMME PLANNING (Agenda item 135)
Mokhawa, Gladys - A/C.5/78/SR.5
UN. GENERAL ASSEMBLY (78TH SESS. : 2023-2024). 1ST COMMITTEE—GENERAL DEBATE (Agenda item 8)
Mokhawa, Gladys - A/C.1/78/PV.7
UN. GENERAL ASSEMBLY (78TH SESS. : 2023-2024). 2ND COMMITTEE—GENERAL DEBATE (Agenda item 8)
Mokhawa, Gladys - A/C.2/78/SR.5

Botswana (continued)

UN. GENERAL ASSEMBLY (78TH SESS. : 2023-2024). 5TH COMMITTEE—WORK ORGANIZATION (Agenda item 7)
Mokhawa, Gladys - A/C.5/78/SR.40
WESTERN SAHARA QUESTION (Agenda item 58)
Mokhawa, Gladys - A/C.4/78/SR.8

Botswana. President

UN. GENERAL ASSEMBLY (78TH SESS. : 2023-2024)—GENERAL DEBATE (Agenda item 8)
Masisi, Mokgweetsi Eric Keabetswe - A/78/PV.7
UN. GENERAL ASSEMBLY (78TH SESS. : 2023-2024)—SPECIAL STATEMENTS
Masisi, Mokgweetsi Eric Keabetswe - A/78/PV.7

Brazil

AGEING PERSONS (Agenda item 24b)
Dias, João Henrique Nascimento - A/C.3/78/SR.1
ARMS RACE—OUTER SPACE (Agenda item 97a)
Damico, Flávio Soares - A/C.1/78/PV.17
Szatmari, Roberto Wazima - A/C.1/78/PV.27
ARMS TRANSFERS—TREATIES (Agenda item 99x)
Damico, Flávio Soares - A/C.1/78/PV.19
BIOLOGICAL DIVERSITY—TREATIES (Agenda item 18f)
Kloss, Emerson Coraiola Yinde - A/C.2/78/SR.13
BIOLOGICAL WEAPONS—TREATIES (Agenda item 106)
Damico, Flávio Soares - A/C.1/78/PV.15
CHEMICAL WEAPONS—TREATIES (Agenda item 99l)
Damico, Flávio Soares - A/C.1/78/PV.15
CLIMATE (Agenda item 18d)
Kloss, Emerson Coraiola Yinde - A/C.2/78/SR.13
CLUSTER MUNITIONS (Agenda item 99dd)
Szatmari, Roberto Wazima - A/C.1/78/PV.28
COMMODITIES (Agenda item 16d)
Dubeux, Rafael - A/C.2/78/SR.14
CRIME PREVENTION (Agenda item 107)
Dias, João Henrique Nascimento - A/C.3/78/SR.5
CRIMES AGAINST HUMANITY (Agenda item 80)
Braoios, Victor Silveira - A/C.6/78/SR.9; A/C.6/78/SR.38; A/C.6/78/SR.40; A/C.6/78/SR.43
Sloboda, Pedro Muniz Pinto - A/C.6/78/SR.41; A/C.6/78/SR.44; A/C.6/78/SR.45
CUBA—UNITED STATES (Agenda item 38)
Danese, Sérgio França - A/78/PV.26
CYBERCRIME (Agenda item 108)
Dias, João Henrique Nascimento - A/C.3/78/SR.5
DEVELOPMENT FINANCE—CONFERENCES (Agenda item 17)
Bayer, Guilherme Marquardt - A/78/PV.90

Brazil (continued)

DISARMAMENT—GENERAL AND COMPLETE (Agenda item 99)
Damico, Flávio Soares - A/C.1/78/PV.19
Szatmari, Roberto Wazima - A/C.1/78/PV.28; A/C.1/78/PV.30
DISARMAMENT AGREEMENTS—OUTER SPACE (Agenda item 97c)
Szatmari, Roberto Wazima - A/C.1/78/PV.27
DISASTER VICTIMS (Agenda item 86)
Sloboda, Pedro Muniz Pinto - A/C.6/78/SR.5
ECONOMIC SANCTIONS—INTERNATIONAL RELATIONS (Agenda item 28)
Danese, Sérgio França - A/78/PV.89
ELECTION VERIFICATION—UN (Agenda item 71b)
Balbino, Viviane Rios - A/C.3/78/SR.50
FAMILY (Agenda item 24b)
Dias, João Henrique Nascimento - A/C.3/78/SR.2
FISSIONABLE MATERIALS—TREATIES (Agenda item 99a)
Szatmari, Roberto Wazima - A/C.1/78/PV.26
FOOD SECURITY (Agenda item 23a)
Santos, Luiz Felipe Rosa dos - A/C.2/78/SR.17
FREEDOM OF EXPRESSION (Agenda item 71b)
Paranhos, Pedro Barreto Da Rocha - A/C.3/78/SR.19
HEALTH (Agenda item 125)
Gomes, Elaine Cristina Pereira - A/78/PV.102
HIV/AIDS—DECLARATIONS (Agenda item 10)
Danese, Sérgio França - A/78/PV.91
HUMAN RIGHTS—IRAN (ISLAMIC REPUBLIC OF) (Agenda item 71c)
Balbino, Viviane Rios - A/C.3/78/SR.53
HUMAN RIGHTS—SYRIAN ARAB REPUBLIC (Agenda item 71c)
Balbino, Viviane Rios - A/C.3/78/SR.54
Moretti, Norberto - A/C.3/78/SR.34
HUMAN RIGHTS—TERRITORIES OCCUPIED BY ISRAEL (Agenda item 71c)
Paranhos, Pedro Barreto Da Rocha - A/C.3/78/SR.35
HUMAN RIGHTS ACTIVISTS (Agenda item 71b)
Paranhos, Pedro Barreto Da Rocha - A/C.3/78/SR.19
INDIGENOUS PEOPLES (Agenda item 68a)
Balbino, Viviane Rios - A/C.3/78/SR.48
Gomes, Elaine Cristina Pereira - A/C.3/78/SR.15
INDIGENOUS PEOPLES—CONFERENCES (Agenda item 68b)
Gomes, Elaine Cristina Pereira - A/C.3/78/SR.15
INFORMATION—INTERNATIONAL SECURITY (Agenda item 94)
Damico, Flávio Soares - A/C.1/78/PV.21
Szatmari, Roberto Wazima - A/C.1/78/PV.29

Brazil (continued)

INTERNATIONAL CRIMINAL COURT—REPORTS (Agenda item 74)
Pinto, Alessandro De Rezende - A/78/PV.22; A/78/PV.25
INTERNATIONAL JURISDICTION (Agenda item 84)
Sloboda, Pedro Muniz Pinto - A/C.6/78/SR.12
INTERNATIONAL RESIDUAL MECHANISM FOR CRIMINAL TRIBUNALS (Agenda item 126)
Braoios, Victor Silveira - A/78/PV.19
LANDMINES—TREATIES (Agenda item 99m)
Damico, Flávio Soares - A/C.1/78/PV.19
LEPROSY (Agenda item 71b)
Gomes, Elaine Cristina Pereira - A/C.3/78/SR.17
MULTILATERALISM—DISARMAMENT (Agenda item 99r)
Damico, Flávio Soares - A/C.1/78/PV.22
NON-CITIZENS—DEPORTATION (Agenda item 81)
Braoios, Victor Silveira - A/C.6/78/SR.34
NUCLEAR DISARMAMENT (Agenda item 99b)
Damico, Flávio Soares - A/C.1/78/PV.13
NUCLEAR DISARMAMENT—VERIFICATION (Agenda item 99ee)
Damico, Flávio Soares - A/C.1/78/PV.12
NUCLEAR NON-PROLIFERATION—INTERNATIONAL OBLIGATIONS (Agenda item 99w)
Damico, Flávio Soares - A/C.1/78/PV.13
NUCLEAR WEAPONS—ELIMINATION (Agenda item 99z)
Szatmari, Roberto Wazima - A/C.1/78/PV.26
NUCLEAR WEAPONS—TREATIES (Agenda item 99ff)
Damico, Flávio Soares - A/C.1/78/PV.13
ORGANIZATION FOR DEMOCRACY AND ECONOMIC DEVELOPMENT - GUAM (Agenda item 32)
Danese, Sérgio França - A/78/PV.85
OUTER SPACE—CONFIDENCE-BUILDING MEASURES (Agenda item 99v)
Damico, Flávio Soares - A/C.1/78/PV.17
Szatmari, Roberto Wazima - A/C.1/78/PV.27
OUTER SPACE—PEACEFUL USES—INTERNATIONAL COOPERATION (Agenda item 48)
Campos, Erika Helena - A/C.4/78/SR.16
OUTER SPACE—PRINCIPLES (Agenda item 97d)
Szatmari, Roberto Wazima - A/C.1/78/PV.27
PEACE (Agenda item 14)
Danese, Sérgio França - A/78/PV.82
Gomes, Elaine Cristina Pereira - A/78/PV.62
PEACEKEEPING OPERATIONS (Agenda item 51)
Campos, Erika Helena - A/C.4/78/SR.20
PEACEKEEPING OPERATIONS—CRIMINAL LIABILITY (Agenda item 76)
Braoios, Victor Silveira - A/C.6/78/SR.8

Brazil (continued)

PERSONS WITH DISABILITIES—HUMAN RIGHTS (Agenda item 71a)
Gomes, Elaine Cristina Pereira - A/C.3/78/SR.38
POVERTY—HUMAN RIGHTS (Agenda item 71b)
Dias, João Henrique Nascimento - A/C.3/78/SR.30
POVERTY—INTERNATIONAL DECADES (Agenda item 21a)
Santos, Luiz Felipe Rosa dos - A/C.2/78/SR.17
RACIAL DISCRIMINATION—ELIMINATION (Agenda item 69a)
Gomes, Elaine Cristina Pereira - A/C.3/78/SR.40; A/C.3/78/SR.41; A/C.3/78/SR.42
Moretti, Norberto - A/78/PV.103
RACIAL DISCRIMINATION—PROGRAMMES OF ACTION (Agenda item 69b)
Balbino, Viviane Rios - A/C.3/78/SR.56
Gomes, Elaine Cristina Pereira - A/C.3/78/SR.40; A/C.3/78/SR.41; A/C.3/78/SR.42
RESPONSIBILITY TO PROTECT (Agenda item 129)
Sloboda, Pedro Muniz Pinto - A/78/PV.96
RIGHT TO DEVELOPMENT (Agenda item 71b)
Paranhos, Pedro Barreto Da Rocha - A/C.3/78/SR.20
RIGHT TO FOOD (Agenda item 71b)
Dias, João Henrique Nascimento - A/C.3/78/SR.30
RIGHT TO HEALTH (Agenda item 71b)
Leite, Patricia Soares - A/C.3/78/SR.39
RIGHT TO HOUSING (Agenda item 71b)
Dias, João Henrique Nascimento - A/C.3/78/SR.30
RIGHT TO PRIVACY (Agenda item 71b)
Dias, João Henrique Nascimento - A/C.3/78/SR.21
RIGHTS OF THE CHILD (Agenda item 67)
Gomes, Elaine Cristina Pereira - A/C.3/78/SR.11; A/C.3/78/SR.12
RULE OF LAW (Agenda item 83)
Braoios, Victor Silveira - A/C.6/78/SR.16
RURAL POVERTY (Agenda item 21b)
Santos, Luiz Felipe Rosa dos - A/C.2/78/SR.17
SEXUAL ORIENTATION (Agenda item 71b)
Leite, Patricia Soares - A/C.3/78/SR.39
SOCIAL CONDITIONS (Agenda item 24b)
Dias, João Henrique Nascimento - A/C.3/78/SR.2
SUSTAINABLE DEVELOPMENT (Agenda item 18)
Dubeux, Rafael - A/C.2/78/SR.14
SUSTAINABLE ENERGY (Agenda item 18h)
Kloss, Emerson Coraiola Yinde - A/C.2/78/SR.13
TERRORISM (Agenda item 109)
Braoios, Victor Silveira - A/C.6/78/SR.1
TORTURE AND OTHER CRUEL TREATMENT (Agenda item 71a)
Gomes, Elaine Cristina Pereira - A/C.3/78/SR.18
UKRAINE—POLITICAL CONDITIONS (Agenda item 62)
Danese, Sérgio França - A/78/PV.58

Brazil (continued)

UN. CONFERENCE ON DISARMAMENT—REPORTS (Agenda item 101a)
Damico, Flávio Soares - A/C.1/78/PV.24
UN. GENERAL ASSEMBLY (78TH SESS. : 2023-2024). 1ST COMMITTEE—GENERAL DEBATE (Agenda item 8)
Damico, Flávio Soares - A/C.1/78/PV.9
Moretti, Norberto - A/C.1/78/PV.8
UN. GENERAL ASSEMBLY (78TH SESS. : 2023-2024). 2ND COMMITTEE—GENERAL DEBATE (Agenda item 8)
Moretti, Norberto - A/C.2/78/SR.4
UN. INTERNATIONAL COURT OF JUSTICE—REPORTS (Agenda item 73)
Braoios, Victor Silveira - A/78/PV.27
UN. INTERNATIONAL LAW COMMISSION—REPORTS (Agenda item 79)
Bernandes, Rafael - A/C.6/78/SR.29; A/C.6/78/SR.31
Sloboda, Pedro Muniz Pinto - A/C.6/78/SR.23
UN. SECURITY COUNCIL—MEMBERSHIP (Agenda item 121)
Moretti, Norberto - A/78/PV.35
UN. SECURITY COUNCIL—REPORTS (Agenda item 26)
Danese, Sérgio França - A/78/PV.93
VETO (Agenda item 63)
Danese, Sérgio França - A/78/PV.51; A/78/PV.60; A/78/PV.67; A/78/PV.69; A/78/PV.70; A/78/PV.75; A/78/PV.78
Moretti, Norberto - A/78/PV.3
WEAPONS—OUTER SPACE (Agenda item 97b)
Szatmari, Roberto Wazima - A/C.1/78/PV.27
WOMEN'S ADVANCEMENT (Agenda item 25a)
Balbino, Viviane Rios - A/C.3/78/SR.9
Leite, Patricia Soares - A/C.3/78/SR.7
WOMEN'S ADVANCEMENT—CONFERENCES (Agenda item 25b)
Balbino, Viviane Rios - A/C.3/78/SR.9
Leite, Patricia Soares - A/C.3/78/SR.7

Brazil. President

UN. GENERAL ASSEMBLY (78TH SESS. : 2023-2024)—GENERAL DEBATE (Agenda item 8)
Silva, Luiz Inácio Lula da - A/78/PV.4
UN. GENERAL ASSEMBLY (78TH SESS. : 2023-2024)—SPECIAL STATEMENTS
Silva, Luiz Inácio Lula da - A/78/PV.4

British Virgin Islands

BRITISH VIRGIN ISLANDS QUESTION (Agenda item 58)
Wheatley, Natalio - A/C.4/78/SR.3

Brunei Darussalam

EMERGENCY ASSISTANCE (Agenda item 72a)
Lee, Kok Ting - A/78/PV.47
INFORMATION TECHNOLOGY—DEVELOPMENT (Agenda item 15)
Pg Ibrahim, Dk Nur Maseleiana Rahimah - A/C.2/78/SR.10
PALESTINIANS—ASSISTANCE (Agenda item 72b)
Lee, Kok Ting - A/78/PV.47
RIGHT TO HEALTH (Agenda item 71b)
Wafiuddin, Illyana - A/C.3/78/SR.26
RIGHTS OF THE CHILD (Agenda item 67)
Sulaiman, Muhamad Syukri - A/C.3/78/SR.13
RULE OF LAW (Agenda item 83)
Sahrip, Nazihah Mohd - A/C.6/78/SR.18
SUSTAINABLE DEVELOPMENT (Agenda item 18)
Haji Zaini, Hajah Razan Dzafirah Binti - A/C.2/78/SR.13
TERRITORIES OCCUPIED BY ISRAEL—HUMAN RIGHTS (Agenda item 50)
Hamzah, Fatin Hilyati Haji - A/C.4/78/SR.24
UN. GENERAL ASSEMBLY (78TH SESS. : 2023-2024)—GENERAL DEBATE (Agenda item 8)
Yusof, Dato Erywan Pehin - A/78/PV.13
UN. GENERAL ASSEMBLY (78TH SESS. : 2023-2024). 1ST COMMITTEE—GENERAL DEBATE (Agenda item 8)
Sah, Hermy Ahmad - A/C.1/78/PV.7
VETO (Agenda item 63)
Sulaiman, Noor Qamar - A/78/PV.60

Bulgaria

ARMED CONFLICTS PREVENTION (Agenda item 31a)
Stoeva, Lachezara - A/78/PV.72
CRIMES AGAINST HUMANITY (Agenda item 80)
Beshkova, Krassimira - A/C.6/78/SR.45
FISSIONABLE MATERIALS—TREATIES (Agenda item 99a)
Stoeva, Lachezara - A/C.1/78/PV.12
HUMAN RIGHTS—RUSSIAN FEDERATION (Agenda item 71c)
Dimitrov, Svetozar Angelov - A/C.3/78/SR.37
HUMAN RIGHTS—TERRITORIES OCCUPIED BY ISRAEL (Agenda item 71c)
Dimitrov, Svetozar Angelov - A/C.3/78/SR.35
MIGRANTS—PROTECTION (Agenda item 71b)
Dimitrov, Svetozar Angelov - A/C.3/78/SR.56
NUCLEAR DISARMAMENT (Agenda item 99b)
Stoeva, Lachezara - A/C.1/78/PV.12
NUCLEAR NON-PROLIFERATION—INTERNATIONAL OBLIGATIONS (Agenda item 99w)
Stoeva, Lachezara - A/C.1/78/PV.12

Bulgaria (continued)

NUCLEAR WEAPON TESTS—TREATIES (Agenda item 105)
Stoeva, Lachezara - A/C.1/78/PV.12
RIGHTS OF THE CHILD (Agenda item 67)
Stoeva, Lachezara - A/C.3/78/SR.12
UKRAINE—POLITICAL CONDITIONS (Agenda item 62)
Stoeva, Lachezara - A/78/PV.57
UN. GENERAL ASSEMBLY (78TH SESS. : 2023-2024). 1ST COMMITTEE—GENERAL DEBATE (Agenda item 8)
Stoeva, Lachezara - A/C.1/78/PV.5
UN. INTERNATIONAL LAW COMMISSION—REPORTS (Agenda item 79)
Dramova, Dimana - A/C.6/78/SR.28
VETO (Agenda item 63)
Beshkova, Krassimira - A/78/PV.68
Stoeva, Lachezara - A/78/PV.3; A/78/PV.70; A/78/PV.78
WOMEN'S ADVANCEMENT (Agenda item 25a)
Stoeva, Lachezara - A/C.3/78/SR.9
WOMEN'S ADVANCEMENT—CONFERENCES (Agenda item 25b)
Stoeva, Lachezara - A/C.3/78/SR.9
YOUTH (Agenda item 24b)
Garelova, Tsvetelina - A/C.3/78/SR.2
Savova, Victoria - A/C.3/78/SR.2

Bulgaria. President

UN. GENERAL ASSEMBLY (78TH SESS. : 2023-2024)—GENERAL DEBATE (Agenda item 8)
Radev, Rumen - A/78/PV.6
UN. GENERAL ASSEMBLY (78TH SESS. : 2023-2024)—SPECIAL STATEMENTS
Radev, Rumen - A/78/PV.6

Burkina Faso

CRIMES AGAINST HUMANITY (Agenda item 80)
Ganou, Oumarou - A/C.6/78/SR.10
DECOLONIZATION (Agenda item 58)
Ganou, Oumarou - A/C.4/78/SR.7
DISASTER VICTIMS (Agenda item 86)
Lompo, Boulmonli Léonard - A/C.6/78/SR.6
ECONOMIC COOPERATION AMONG DEVELOPING COUNTRIES (Agenda item 22b)
Bokoum, Mahamadou - A/C.2/78/SR.18
EXTERNAL DEBT (Agenda item 16c)
Bokoum, Mahamadou - A/C.2/78/SR.9
FOOD SECURITY (Agenda item 23a)
Bokoum, Mahamadou - A/C.2/78/SR.16
HUMAN RIGHTS—INTERNATIONAL INSTRUMENTS (Agenda item 71a)
Ouattara Cisse, Aminata - A/C.3/78/SR.25
IAEA—REPORTS (Agenda item 89)
Ganou, Oumarou - A/78/PV.30

Burkina Faso (continued)

INFORMATION (Agenda item 53)
Ouattara Cisse, Aminata - A/C.4/78/SR.13
INFORMATION TECHNOLOGY—DEVELOPMENT (Agenda item 15)
Barro, Braima - A/C.2/78/SR.10
INTERNATIONAL CRIMINAL COURT—REPORTS (Agenda item 74)
Ganou, Oumarou - A/78/PV.22
INTERNATIONAL JURISDICTION (Agenda item 84)
Ganou, Oumarou - A/C.6/78/SR.13
INTERNATIONAL LAW—TRAINING PROGRAMMES (Agenda item 78)
Ganou, Oumarou - A/C.6/78/SR.21
LANDMINES—TREATIES (Agenda item 99m)
Ganou, Oumarou - A/C.1/78/PV.18
MACROECONOMIC POLICY (Agenda item 16)
Bokoum, Mahamadou - A/C.2/78/SR.9
NUCLEAR DISARMAMENT (Agenda item 99b)
Ganou, Oumarou - A/C.1/78/PV.12
OPERATIONAL ACTIVITIES—UN SYSTEM (Agenda item 22a)
Bokoum, Mahamadou - A/C.2/78/SR.18
PEACEKEEPING OPERATIONS (Agenda item 51)
Savadogo, Halidou - A/C.4/78/SR.20
PEACEKEEPING OPERATIONS—CRIMINAL LIABILITY (Agenda item 76)
Ganou, Oumarou - A/C.6/78/SR.8
POVERTY—INTERNATIONAL DECADES (Agenda item 21a)
Bokoum, Mahamadou - A/C.2/78/SR.16
RIGHTS OF THE CHILD (Agenda item 67)
Ouattara, Isaac Alassane - A/C.3/78/SR.13
RULE OF LAW (Agenda item 83)
Ganou, Oumarou - A/C.6/78/SR.17
RURAL POVERTY (Agenda item 21b)
Bokoum, Mahamadou - A/C.2/78/SR.16
RURAL WOMEN (Agenda item 25a)
Niamba Congo, Salamata Odette - A/C.3/78/SR.49
SCIENCE AND TECHNOLOGY—DEVELOPMENT (Agenda item 19a)
Barro, Braima - A/C.2/78/SR.10
SMALL ARMS—ILLICIT TRAFFIC (Agenda item 99p)
Ganou, Oumarou - A/C.1/78/PV.18
SOCIAL CONDITIONS (Agenda item 24b)
Niamba Congo, Salamata Odette - A/C.3/78/SR.2
SUSTAINABLE DEVELOPMENT (Agenda item 18)
Dipama, Abdoul Karim - A/C.2/78/SR.13
TERRORISM (Agenda item 109)
Ouattara Cisse, Aminata - A/C.6/78/SR.2
TERRORISM—HUMAN RIGHTS (Agenda item 71b)
Ouattara Cisse, Aminata - A/C.3/78/SR.25

Burkina Faso (continued)

UN. GENERAL ASSEMBLY (78TH SESS. : 2023-2024)—GENERAL DEBATE (Agenda item 8)
Bazie, Bassolma - A/78/PV.13
UN. GENERAL ASSEMBLY (78TH SESS. : 2023-2024). 1ST COMMITTEE—GENERAL DEBATE (Agenda item 8)
Ganou, Oumarou - A/C.1/78/PV.6
UN HIGH COMMISSIONER FOR REFUGEES—REPORTS (Agenda item 60)
Ganou, Oumarou - A/C.3/78/SR.44
WESTERN SAHARA QUESTION (Agenda item 58)
Ganou, Oumarou - A/C.4/78/SR.7
WOMEN'S ADVANCEMENT (Agenda item 25a)
Ganou, Oumarou - A/C.3/78/SR.9
WOMEN'S ADVANCEMENT—CONFERENCES (Agenda item 25b)
Ganou, Oumarou - A/C.3/78/SR.9

Burundi

DISARMAMENT—GENERAL AND COMPLETE (Agenda item 99)
Maniratanga, Zéphyrin - A/78/PV.105
DISPLACED PERSONS (Agenda item 71b)
Sibomana, Landry - A/C.3/78/SR.49
HUMAN RIGHTS—BURUNDI (Agenda item 71c)
Maniratanga, Zéphyrin - A/C.3/78/SR.36
HUMAN RIGHTS—DEMOCRATIC PEOPLE'S REPUBLIC OF KOREA (Agenda item 71c)
Sibomana, Landry - A/C.3/78/SR.33
HUMAN RIGHTS—ERITREA (Agenda item 71c)
Sibomana, Landry - A/C.3/78/SR.36
HUMAN RIGHTS—REPORTS (Agenda item 71c)
Sibomana, Landry - A/C.3/78/SR.37
HUMAN RIGHTS—SYRIAN ARAB REPUBLIC (Agenda item 71c)
Sibomana, Landry - A/C.3/78/SR.54
WESTERN SAHARA QUESTION (Agenda item 58)
Sibomana, Landry - A/C.4/78/SR.8

Burundi. President

UN. GENERAL ASSEMBLY (78TH SESS. : 2023-2024)—GENERAL DEBATE (Agenda item 8)
Ndayishimiye, Évariste - A/78/PV.8
UN. GENERAL ASSEMBLY (78TH SESS. : 2023-2024)—SPECIAL STATEMENTS
Ndayishimiye, Évariste - A/78/PV.8

Cabo Verde

DISARMAMENT—GENERAL AND COMPLETE (Agenda item 99)
Romualdo, Tania Serafim Yvonne - A/78/PV.106
FOOD SECURITY (Agenda item 23a)
Romualdo, Tania Serafim Yvonne - A/C.2/78/SR.17
HIV/AIDS—DECLARATIONS (Agenda item 10)
Romualdo, Tania Serafim Yvonne - A/78/PV.91
POVERTY—INTERNATIONAL DECADES (Agenda item 21a)
Romualdo, Tania Serafim Yvonne - A/C.2/78/SR.17
RURAL POVERTY (Agenda item 21b)
Romualdo, Tania Serafim Yvonne - A/C.2/78/SR.17
TERRORISM (Agenda item 109)
Romualdo, Tania Serafim Yvonne - A/C.6/78/SR.5
UN. GENERAL ASSEMBLY (78TH SESS. : 2023-2024). 1ST COMMITTEE—GENERAL DEBATE (Agenda item 8)
Romualdo, Tania Serafim Yvonne - A/C.1/78/PV.9
WOMEN'S ADVANCEMENT (Agenda item 25a)
Romualdo, Tania Serafim Yvonne - A/C.3/78/SR.9
WOMEN'S ADVANCEMENT—CONFERENCES (Agenda item 25b)
Romualdo, Tania Serafim Yvonne - A/C.3/78/SR.9
YOUTH (Agenda item 24b)
Romualdo, Tania Serafim Yvonne - A/C.3/78/SR.55

Cabo Verde. Prime Minister

UN. GENERAL ASSEMBLY (78TH SESS. : 2023-2024)—GENERAL DEBATE (Agenda item 8)
Silva, José Ulisses Correia e - A/78/PV.12
UN. GENERAL ASSEMBLY (78TH SESS. : 2023-2024)—SPECIAL STATEMENTS
Silva, José Ulisses Correia e - A/78/PV.12

Cambodia

CUBA—UNITED STATES (Agenda item 38)
Eat, Sophea - A/78/PV.24
HUMAN RIGHTS ADVANCEMENT (Agenda item 71b)
Eat, Sophea - A/C.3/78/SR.26
MACROECONOMIC POLICY (Agenda item 16)
Heng, Somoly - A/C.2/78/SR.9
PEACE (Agenda item 14)
Mao, Tithiarun - A/78/PV.76
PEACEKEEPING OPERATIONS (Agenda item 51)
Mao, Tithiarun - A/C.4/78/SR.20
SANCTIONS—INTERNATIONAL RELATIONS (Agenda item 71b)
Eat, Sophea - A/C.3/78/SR.26
TAXATION (Agenda item 16h)
Heng, Somoly - A/C.2/78/SR.9
UN—BUDGET (2024) (Agenda item 134)
Eat, Sophea - A/C.5/78/SR.16

Cambodia (continued)

UN. GENERAL ASSEMBLY (78TH SESS. : 2023-2024). 1ST COMMITTEE—GENERAL DEBATE (Agenda item 8)
Eat, Sophea - A/C.1/78/PV.3
UN. GENERAL ASSEMBLY (78TH SESS. : 2023-2024). 2ND COMMITTEE—GENERAL DEBATE (Agenda item 8)
Eat, Sophea - A/C.2/78/SR.5
UN. SECURITY COUNCIL—MEMBERSHIP (Agenda item 121)
Mao, Tithiarun - A/78/PV.36
VETO (Agenda item 63)
Mao, Tithiarun - A/78/PV.75

Cambodia. Prime Minister

UN. GENERAL ASSEMBLY (78TH SESS. : 2023-2024)—GENERAL DEBATE (Agenda item 8)
Hun, Manet - A/78/PV.11
UN. GENERAL ASSEMBLY (78TH SESS. : 2023-2024)—SPECIAL STATEMENTS
Hun, Manet - A/78/PV.11

Cameroon

ADMINISTRATION OF JUSTICE (Agenda item 144)
Nyanid, Zacharie Serge Raoul - A/C.6/78/SR.9
AFRICA—DEVELOPMENT (Agenda item 65b)
Tommo Monthe, Michel - A/78/PV.18
AFRICA—SUSTAINABLE DEVELOPMENT—PARTNERSHIP (Agenda item 65a)
Tommo Monthe, Michel - A/78/PV.18
CLIMATE (Agenda item 18d)
Banaken Elel, Nelly - A/C.2/78/SR.13
CRIMES AGAINST HUMANITY (Agenda item 80)
Nyanid, Zacharie Serge Raoul - A/C.6/78/SR.10; A/C.6/78/SR.39; A/C.6/78/SR.40; A/C.6/78/SR.41; A/C.6/78/SR.42; A/C.6/78/SR.43; A/C.6/78/SR.44; A/C.6/78/SR.47
CYBERCRIME (Agenda item 108)
Banaken Elel, Nelly - A/C.3/78/SR.5
DEMOCRACY (Agenda item 71b)
Wainwel, Gwedji Doris - A/C.3/78/SR.28
DEVELOPMENT FINANCE (Agenda item 16b)
Banaken Elel, Nelly - A/C.2/78/SR.9
DISARMAMENT—GENERAL AND COMPLETE (Agenda item 99)
Nyanid, Zacharie Serge Raoul - A/C.1/78/PV.30
DISASTER VICTIMS (Agenda item 86)
Nyanid, Zacharie Serge Raoul - A/C.6/78/SR.6
DISPLACED PERSONS (Agenda item 71b)
Banaken Elel, Nelly - A/C.3/78/SR.32
FAMILY (Agenda item 24b)
Banaken Elel, Nelly - A/C.3/78/SR.2
FOOD SECURITY (Agenda item 23a)
Etoundi Ayissi, Joseph - A/C.2/78/SR.16

Cameroon (continued)

HUMAN RIGHTS (Agenda item 71)
Wainwel, Gwedji Doris - A/C.3/78/SR.16
HUMAN RIGHTS—BURUNDI (Agenda item 71c)
Banaken Elel, Nelly - A/C.3/78/SR.36
HUMAN RIGHTS—CENTRAL AFRICAN REPUBLIC (Agenda item 71c)
Banaken Elel, Nelly - A/C.3/78/SR.33
HUMAN RIGHTS—DEMOCRATIC PEOPLE'S REPUBLIC OF KOREA (Agenda item 71c)
Banaken Elel, Nelly - A/C.3/78/SR.33
HUMAN RIGHTS—ERITREA (Agenda item 71c)
Banaken Elel, Nelly - A/C.3/78/SR.36
HUMAN RIGHTS—ETHIOPIA (Agenda item 71c)
Banaken Elel, Nelly - A/C.3/78/SR.36
HUMAN RIGHTS—INTERNATIONAL INSTRUMENTS (Agenda item 71a)
Banaken Elel, Nelly - A/C.3/78/SR.17; A/C.3/78/SR.25
HUMAN RIGHTS ADVANCEMENT (Agenda item 71b)
Banaken Elel, Nelly - A/C.3/78/SR.25
HUMAN RIGHTS INSTITUTIONS—CENTRAL AFRICA (Agenda item 71b)
Tommo Monthe, Michel - A/C.3/78/SR.56
INDIGENOUS PEOPLES (Agenda item 68a)
Wainwel, Gwedji Doris - A/C.3/78/SR.15
INDIGENOUS PEOPLES—CONFERENCES (Agenda item 68b)
Wainwel, Gwedji Doris - A/C.3/78/SR.15
INFORMATION (Agenda item 53)
Ngouambe Wouaga, Jean Luc - A/C.4/78/SR.14
INTERNATIONAL JURISDICTION (Agenda item 84)
Nyanid, Zacharie Serge Raoul - A/C.6/78/SR.12; A/C.6/78/SR.37
INTERNATIONAL LAW—TRAINING PROGRAMMES (Agenda item 78)
Nyanid, Zacharie Serge Raoul - A/C.6/78/SR.21
INTERNATIONAL TRADE (Agenda item 16a)
Banaken Elel, Nelly - A/C.2/78/SR.9
LAW OF THE SEA (Agenda item 75a)
Tommo Monthe, Michel - A/78/PV.44
MARINE ECOSYSTEMS—BIOLOGICAL DIVERSITY (Agenda item 75c)
Tommo Monthe, Michel - A/78/PV.44
MIGRANTS—PROTECTION (Agenda item 71b)
Wainwel, Gwedji Doris - A/C.3/78/SR.23
MINE CLEARANCE (Agenda item 46)
Ondo Ebang, William - A/C.4/78/SR.10
MINORITIES (Agenda item 71b)
Ahidjo, Ahidjo - A/C.3/78/SR.39
NON-CITIZENS—DEPORTATION (Agenda item 81)
Nyanid, Zacharie Serge Raoul - A/C.6/78/SR.34

Cameroon (continued)

OPERATIONAL ACTIVITIES—UN SYSTEM (Agenda item 22a)
Etoundi Ayissi, Joseph - A/C.2/78/SR.18
OUTER SPACE—PEACEFUL USES—INTERNATIONAL COOPERATION (Agenda item 48)
Ahidjo, Ahidjo - A/C.4/78/SR.16
PEACEKEEPING OPERATIONS (Agenda item 51)
Tommo Monthe, Michel - A/C.4/78/SR.20
PEACEKEEPING OPERATIONS—CRIMINAL LIABILITY (Agenda item 76)
Nyanid, Zacharie Serge Raoul - A/C.6/78/SR.9
POVERTY—HUMAN RIGHTS (Agenda item 71b)
Banaken Elel, Nelly - A/C.3/78/SR.30
POVERTY—INTERNATIONAL DECADES (Agenda item 21a)
Etoundi Ayissi, Joseph - A/C.2/78/SR.16
RACIAL DISCRIMINATION—ELIMINATION (Agenda item 69a)
Banaken Elel, Nelly - A/C.3/78/SR.40; A/C.3/78/SR.42
Mezang Akamba, Serge Pamphile - A/C.3/78/SR.41
RACIAL DISCRIMINATION—PROGRAMMES OF ACTION (Agenda item 69b)
Banaken Elel, Nelly - A/C.3/78/SR.40; A/C.3/78/SR.42
Mezang Akamba, Serge Pamphile - A/C.3/78/SR.41
RADIATION EFFECTS (Agenda item 47)
Ondo Ebang, William - A/C.4/78/SR.11
RESPONSIBILITY OF INTERNATIONAL ORGANIZATIONS (Agenda item 85)
Nyanid, Zacharie Serge Raoul - A/C.6/78/SR.19
RIGHT TO CULTURE (Agenda item 71b)
Wainwel, Gwedji Doris - A/C.3/78/SR.27
RIGHT TO DEVELOPMENT (Agenda item 71b)
Banaken Elel, Nelly - A/C.3/78/SR.20
RIGHT TO DRINKING WATER (Agenda item 71b)
Banaken Elel, Nelly - A/C.3/78/SR.50
RIGHT TO EDUCATION (Agenda item 71b)
Wainwel, Gwedji Doris - A/C.3/78/SR.27
RIGHT TO FOOD (Agenda item 71b)
Banaken Elel, Nelly - A/C.3/78/SR.30
RIGHT TO HEALTH (Agenda item 71b)
Ahidjo, Ahidjo - A/C.3/78/SR.39
RIGHT TO HOUSING (Agenda item 71b)
Banaken Elel, Nelly - A/C.3/78/SR.30
RIGHTS OF THE CHILD (Agenda item 67)
Banaken Elel, Nelly - A/C.3/78/SR.12; A/C.3/78/SR.55
RULE OF LAW (Agenda item 83)
Nyanid, Zacharie Serge Raoul - A/C.6/78/SR.16
RURAL POVERTY (Agenda item 21b)
Etoundi Ayissi, Joseph - A/C.2/78/SR.16
SOLIDARITY (Agenda item 71b)
Banaken Elel, Nelly - A/C.3/78/SR.32

Cameroon (continued)

STRADDLING FISH STOCKS (Agenda item 75b)
Tommo Monthe, Michel - A/78/PV.44
SUSTAINABLE DEVELOPMENT (Agenda item 18)
Mezang Akamba, Serge Pamphile - A/C.2/78/SR.24; A/C.2/78/SR.25
TAXATION (Agenda item 16h)
Mezang Akamba, Serge Pamphile - A/C.2/78/SR.25
TERRORISM (Agenda item 109)
Nyanid, Zacharie Serge Raoul - A/C.6/78/SR.2
TRANSNATIONAL CORPORATIONS—HUMAN RIGHTS (Agenda item 71b)
Wainwel, Gwedji Doris - A/C.3/78/SR.21
TREATIES (Agenda item 87)
Nyanid, Zacharie Serge Raoul - A/C.6/78/SR.20
UN—BUDGET (2024) (Agenda item 134)
Tommo Monthe, Michel - A/C.5/78/SR.22
UN. GENERAL ASSEMBLY (78TH SESS. : 2023-2024)—GENERAL DEBATE (Agenda item 8)
Mbella Mbella, Lejeune - A/78/PV.14
UN. GENERAL ASSEMBLY (78TH SESS. : 2023-2024). 1ST COMMITTEE—GENERAL DEBATE (Agenda item 8)
Babo, Paul David - A/C.1/78/PV.8
UN. GENERAL ASSEMBLY (78TH SESS. : 2023-2024). 2ND COMMITTEE—GENERAL DEBATE (Agenda item 8)
Banaken Elel, Nelly - A/C.2/78/SR.4
UN. GENERAL ASSEMBLY (78TH SESS. : 2023-2024). PRESIDENT (Agenda item 4)
Yang, Philémon - A/78/PV.87
UN. HUMAN RIGHTS COMMITTEE—REPORTS (Agenda item 71a)
Banaken Elel, Nelly - A/C.3/78/SR.17
UN. HUMAN RIGHTS COUNCIL—REPORTS (Agenda item 66)
Banaken Elel, Nelly - A/C.3/78/SR.46
Tommo Monthe, Michel - A/78/PV.23
UN. INTERNATIONAL LAW COMMISSION—REPORTS (Agenda item 79)
Nyanid, Zacharie Serge Raoul - A/C.6/78/SR.25; A/C.6/78/SR.30; A/C.6/78/SR.33; A/C.6/78/SR.37
UN HIGH COMMISSIONER FOR REFUGEES—REPORTS (Agenda item 60)
Banaken Elel, Nelly - A/C.3/78/SR.44; A/C.3/78/SR.45
UN RESOLUTIONS—IMPLEMENTATION (Agenda item 119)
Banaken Elel, Nelly - A/78/PV.103
WESTERN SAHARA QUESTION (Agenda item 58)
Tommo Monthe, Michel - A/C.4/78/SR.8
WOMEN'S ADVANCEMENT (Agenda item 25a)
Banaken Elel, Nelly - A/C.3/78/SR.8

Cameroon (continued)

WOMEN'S ADVANCEMENT—CONFERENCES (Agenda item 25b)
Banaken Elel, Nelly - A/C.3/78/SR.8

Canada

ADMINISTRATION OF JUSTICE (Agenda item 144)
Mead, Kevin Timothy - A/C.6/78/SR.9
ARMED CONFLICTS PREVENTION (Agenda item 31a)
Rae, Robert - A/78/PV.72
ARMS RACE—OUTER SPACE (Agenda item 97a)
Milligan, Ashlyn - A/C.1/78/PV.17
ARMS TRANSFERS—TREATIES (Agenda item 99x)
Svadjian, Méliné - A/C.1/78/PV.19
BIOLOGICAL DIVERSITY—TREATIES (Agenda item 18f)
Natale, Giuliana - A/C.2/78/SR.15
BIOLOGICAL WEAPONS—TREATIES (Agenda item 106)
Tomlinson, Bryan - A/C.1/78/PV.15
CENTRAL ASIA—ZONES OF PEACE (Agenda item 64)
Mead, Kevin Timothy - A/78/PV.85
CHEMICAL WEAPONS—TREATIES (Agenda item 99l)
Tomlinson, Bryan - A/C.1/78/PV.15
CLIMATE (Agenda item 18d)
Natale, Giuliana - A/C.2/78/SR.15
CLUSTER MUNITIONS (Agenda item 99dd)
Svadjian, Méliné - A/C.1/78/PV.19
CRIME PREVENTION (Agenda item 107)
Baur, Lianna Maureen - A/C.3/78/SR.51
CRIMES AGAINST HUMANITY (Agenda item 80)
Bourdon, Sarah - A/C.6/78/SR.44
Mead, Kevin Timothy - A/C.6/78/SR.38; A/C.6/78/SR.40; A/C.6/78/SR.42; A/C.6/78/SR.43
DEVELOPMENT FINANCE (Agenda item 16b)
Ong, Shirley - A/C.2/78/SR.8
DEVELOPMENT FINANCE—CONFERENCES (Agenda item 17)
Maillé, Béatrice - A/C.2/78/SR.25
Ong, Shirley - A/78/PV.90
DISARMAMENT—GENERAL AND COMPLETE (Agenda item 99)
Fetz, Thomas - A/C.1/78/PV.23; A/C.1/78/PV.30
Svadjian, Méliné - A/C.1/78/PV.19
Tomlinson, Bryan - A/C.1/78/PV.15
DISARMAMENT AGREEMENTS—OUTER SPACE (Agenda item 97c)
Fetz, Thomas - A/C.1/78/PV.27
Milligan, Ashlyn - A/C.1/78/PV.17
EMERGENCY ASSISTANCE (Agenda item 72a)
Ong, Shirley - A/78/PV.46; A/78/PV.47

Canada (continued)

FISSIONABLE MATERIALS—TREATIES (Agenda item 99a)
Fetz, Thomas - A/C.1/78/PV.13; A/C.1/78/PV.25
FREEDOM OF EXPRESSION (Agenda item 71b)
Wallenius, Devyn Lyn - A/C.3/78/SR.19
HEALTH (Agenda item 125)
Castonguay, Marie-Eve - A/78/PV.64
Wallenius, Devyn Lyn - A/78/PV.48
HUMAN RIGHTS (Agenda item 71)
Arbeiter, Richard - A/C.3/78/SR.16
HUMAN RIGHTS—AFGHANISTAN (Agenda item 71c)
Arbeiter, Richard - A/C.3/78/SR.26
Maillé, Béatrice - A/C.3/78/SR.34
HUMAN RIGHTS—IRAN (ISLAMIC REPUBLIC OF) (Agenda item 71c)
Arbeiter, Richard - A/C.3/78/SR.26; A/C.3/78/SR.53; A/C.3/78/SR.54
Rae, Robert - A/C.3/78/SR.34
HUMAN RIGHTS—MYANMAR (Agenda item 71c)
Rae, Robert - A/C.3/78/SR.33
HUMAN RIGHTS—SYRIAN ARAB REPUBLIC (Agenda item 71c)
Wallenius, Devyn Lyn - A/C.3/78/SR.54
HUMAN RIGHTS—UKRAINE (Agenda item 71c)
Rae, Robert - A/C.3/78/SR.37
HUMAN RIGHTS ACTIVISTS (Agenda item 71b)
Wallenius, Devyn Lyn - A/C.3/78/SR.19
HUMAN RIGHTS ADVANCEMENT (Agenda item 71b)
Morin, Cassandra - A/C.3/78/SR.48
HUMAN RIGHTS INSTITUTIONS—CENTRAL AFRICA (Agenda item 71b)
Wallenius, Devyn Lyn - A/C.3/78/SR.56
INDIGENOUS PEOPLES (Agenda item 68a)
Gort, Michael Christian - A/78/PV.107
Morin, Cassandra - A/C.3/78/SR.48
Rae, Robert - A/C.3/78/SR.15
INDIGENOUS PEOPLES—CONFERENCES (Agenda item 68b)
Rae, Robert - A/C.3/78/SR.15
INFORMATION (Agenda item 53)
Turnbull, Andrea Megan - A/C.4/78/SR.14
INFORMATION—INTERNATIONAL SECURITY (Agenda item 94)
Berard Cadieux, Xavier - A/C.1/78/PV.20
INTERNATIONAL CRIMINAL COURT—REPORTS (Agenda item 74)
Maillé, Béatrice - A/78/PV.21
Rae, Robert - A/78/PV.22
INTERNATIONAL JURISDICTION (Agenda item 84)
Agnello, Alexander - A/C.6/78/SR.12
LANDMINES—TREATIES (Agenda item 99m)
Svadjian, Méliné - A/C.1/78/PV.19

Canada (continued)

LAW OF THE SEA (Agenda item 75a)
Kessel, Alan - A/78/PV.43
MARINE ECOSYSTEMS—BIOLOGICAL DIVERSITY (Agenda item 75c)
Kessel, Alan - A/78/PV.43
NUCLEAR DISARMAMENT (Agenda item 99b)
Fetz, Thomas - A/C.1/78/PV.13
NUCLEAR DISARMAMENT—TREATY COMPLIANCE (Agenda item 99q)
Fetz, Thomas - A/C.1/78/PV.26
NUCLEAR NON-PROLIFERATION—INTERNATIONAL OBLIGATIONS (Agenda item 99w)
Fetz, Thomas - A/C.1/78/PV.13
NUCLEAR WEAPON TESTS—TREATIES (Agenda item 105)
Fetz, Thomas - A/C.1/78/PV.13
OUTER SPACE—CONFIDENCE-BUILDING MEASURES (Agenda item 99v)
Milligan, Ashlyn - A/C.1/78/PV.17
OUTER SPACE—PEACEFUL USES—INTERNATIONAL COOPERATION (Agenda item 48)
Pacey-Parker, Sarah - A/C.4/78/SR.16
OUTER SPACE—PRINCIPLES (Agenda item 97d)
Milligan, Ashlyn - A/C.1/78/PV.17
PEACE (Agenda item 14)
Hirji, Hussein - A/78/PV.62
PERSONS WITH DISABILITIES—HUMAN RIGHTS (Agenda item 71a)
Tudor-Bezies, Elizabeth - A/C.3/78/SR.38; A/C.3/78/SR.51
RACIAL DISCRIMINATION—ELIMINATION (Agenda item 69a)
Tudor-Bezies, Elizabeth - A/C.3/78/SR.42
Wallenius, Devyn Lyn - A/C.3/78/SR.47
RACIAL DISCRIMINATION—PROGRAMMES OF ACTION (Agenda item 69b)
Tudor-Bezies, Elizabeth - A/C.3/78/SR.42
RADIATION EFFECTS (Agenda item 47)
Hirji, Hussein - A/C.4/78/SR.11
RELIGIOUS INTOLERANCE (Agenda item 71b)
Greenhalgh, Bronwyn - A/C.3/78/SR.38
RIGHT TO DEVELOPMENT (Agenda item 71b)
Wallenius, Devyn Lyn - A/C.3/78/SR.48
RIGHTS OF THE CHILD (Agenda item 67)
Baur, Lianna Maureen - A/C.3/78/SR.55
Klaise, Inara - A/C.3/78/SR.55
RULE OF LAW (Agenda item 83)
Agnello, Alexander - A/C.6/78/SR.15
SEXUAL ORIENTATION (Agenda item 71b)
Arbeiter, Richard - A/C.3/78/SR.26
Morin, Cassandra - A/C.3/78/SR.39
SOCIAL DEVELOPMENT (Agenda item 24)
Wallenius, Devyn Lyn - A/C.3/78/SR.47
SPECIAL POLITICAL MISSIONS (Agenda item 52)
Oliveira, Sasha - A/C.4/78/SR.21

Canada (continued)

STRADDLING FISH STOCKS (Agenda item 75b)
Kessel, Alan - A/78/PV.43
SUSTAINABLE DEVELOPMENT (Agenda item 18)
Natale, Giuliana - A/C.2/78/SR.15
TAXATION (Agenda item 16h)
Ong, Shirley - A/C.2/78/SR.8
TERRITORIES OCCUPIED BY ISRAEL—HUMAN RIGHTS (Agenda item 50)
Rae, Robert - A/78/PV.45
TERRITORIES OCCUPIED BY ISRAEL—NATURAL RESOURCES (Agenda item 59)
Arbeiter, Richard - A/C.2/78/SR.20
TORTURE AND OTHER CRUEL TREATMENT (Agenda item 71a)
Klaise, Inara - A/C.3/78/SR.18
UKRAINE—POLITICAL CONDITIONS (Agenda item 62)
Rae, Robert - A/78/PV.57
UN—BUDGET (2024) (Agenda item 134)
Tan, Jonathan Necaster - A/C.5/78/SR.26/PartII
UN. CONFERENCE ON DISARMAMENT—REPORTS (Agenda item 101a)
Fetz, Thomas - A/C.1/78/PV.23
UN. GENERAL ASSEMBLY (78TH SESS. : 2023-2024)—GENERAL DEBATE (Agenda item 8)
Rae, Robert - A/78/PV.14
UN. GENERAL ASSEMBLY (78TH SESS. : 2023-2024). 1ST COMMITTEE—GENERAL DEBATE (Agenda item 8)
Norton, Leslie - A/C.1/78/PV.3
UN. GENERAL ASSEMBLY (78TH SESS. : 2023-2024). 5TH COMMITTEE—WORK ORGANIZATION (Agenda item 7)
Arbeiter, Richard - A/C.5/78/SR.35
UN. INTERNATIONAL LAW COMMISSION—REPORTS (Agenda item 79)
Kessel, Alan - A/C.6/78/SR.25
Mead, Kevin Timothy - A/C.6/78/SR.30
UN COMMISSION ON INTERNATIONAL TRADE LAW—REPORTS (Agenda item 77)
Mead, Kevin Timothy - A/C.6/78/SR.14
UN HIGH COMMISSIONER FOR REFUGEES—REPORTS (Agenda item 60)
Klaise, Inara - A/C.3/78/SR.51
Rae, Robert - A/C.3/78/SR.44
UNRWA—ACTIVITIES (Agenda item 49)
Arbeiter, Richard - A/C.4/78/SR.26
VETO (Agenda item 63)
Arbeiter, Richard - A/78/PV.3; A/78/PV.52
Rae, Robert - A/78/PV.66; A/78/PV.69; A/78/PV.79
WEAPONS—OUTER SPACE (Agenda item 97b)
Fetz, Thomas - A/C.1/78/PV.27
WOMEN'S ADVANCEMENT (Agenda item 25a)
Arbeiter, Richard - A/C.3/78/SR.8

Canada (continued)

WOMEN'S ADVANCEMENT (Agenda item 25a)
Baur, Lianna Maureen - A/C.3/78/SR.7
WOMEN'S ADVANCEMENT—CONFERENCES (Agenda item 25b)
Arbeiter, Richard - A/C.3/78/SR.8
Baur, Lianna Maureen - A/C.3/78/SR.7; A/C.3/78/SR.51
YOUTH (Agenda item 24b)
Tudor-Bezies, Elizabeth - A/C.3/78/SR.55

Capitol Hill Prayer Partners (Organization : United States)

WESTERN SAHARA QUESTION (Agenda item 58)
Eads, Vivian - A/C.4/78/SR.4

Caribbean Community

2030 AGENDA—PROGRAMME IMPLEMENTATION (Agenda item 18a)
Wallace, Brian Christopher Manley (Jamaica) - A/C.2/78/SR.12
BIOLOGICAL WEAPONS—TREATIES (Agenda item 106)
Wallace, Brian Christopher Manley (Jamaica) - A/C.1/78/PV.14
CHEMICAL WEAPONS—TREATIES (Agenda item 99l)
Wallace, Brian Christopher Manley (Jamaica) - A/C.1/78/PV.14
CLIMATE (Agenda item 18d)
Wallace, Brian Christopher Manley (Jamaica) - A/C.2/78/SR.12
CRIME PREVENTION (Agenda item 107)
Wallace, Brian Christopher Manley (Jamaica) - A/C.3/78/SR.5
CUBA—UNITED STATES (Agenda item 38)
Rambally, Menissa (Saint Lucia) - A/78/PV.24
CYBERCRIME (Agenda item 108)
Wallace, Brian Christopher Manley (Jamaica) - A/C.3/78/SR.5
DEVELOPMENT FINANCE (Agenda item 16b)
Wallace, Brian Christopher Manley (Jamaica) - A/C.2/78/SR.8
DISARMAMENT-DEVELOPMENT LINK (Agenda item 99d)
Wallace, Brian Christopher Manley (Jamaica) - A/C.1/78/PV.21
DISASTER VICTIMS (Agenda item 86)
Wallace, Brian Christopher Manley (Jamaica) - A/C.6/78/SR.5
FOOD SECURITY (Agenda item 23a)
Wallace, Brian Christopher Manley (Jamaica) - A/C.2/78/SR.16
GLOBALIZATION—INTERDEPENDENCE (Agenda item 19)
Wallace, Brian Christopher Manley (Jamaica) - A/C.2/78/SR.10

Caribbean Community (continued)

HUMAN RIGHTS—PROGRAMMES OF ACTION (Agenda item 71d)
Wallace, Brian Christopher Manley (Jamaica) - A/C.3/78/SR.24
HUMAN RIGHTS ADVANCEMENT (Agenda item 71b)
Wallace, Brian Christopher Manley (Jamaica) - A/C.3/78/SR.24
INDIGENOUS PEOPLES (Agenda item 68a)
Wallace, Brian Christopher Manley (Jamaica) - A/C.3/78/SR.15
INDIGENOUS PEOPLES—CONFERENCES (Agenda item 68b)
Wallace, Brian Christopher Manley (Jamaica) - A/C.3/78/SR.15
INFORMATION (Agenda item 53)
Wallace, Brian Christopher Manley (Jamaica) - A/C.4/78/SR.12
INFORMATION—INTERNATIONAL SECURITY (Agenda item 94)
Wallace, Brian Christopher Manley (Jamaica) - A/C.1/78/PV.21
INFORMATION TECHNOLOGY—DEVELOPMENT (Agenda item 15)
Wallace, Brian Christopher Manley (Jamaica) - A/C.2/78/SR.10
INTERNATIONAL TRADE (Agenda item 16a)
Wallace, Brian Christopher Manley (Jamaica) - A/C.2/78/SR.8
MACROECONOMIC POLICY (Agenda item 16)
Wallace, Brian Christopher Manley (Jamaica) - A/C.2/78/SR.8
MARINE ECOSYSTEMS—BIOLOGICAL DIVERSITY (Agenda item 75c)
Fuller, Carlos C. (Belize) - A/78/PV.73
Williams, Mutryce (Saint Kitts and Nevis) - A/78/PV.103
NUCLEAR DISARMAMENT (Agenda item 99b)
Fuller, Carlos C. (Belize) - A/C.1/78/PV.11
NUCLEAR NON-PROLIFERATION—INTERNATIONAL OBLIGATIONS (Agenda item 99w)
Fuller, Carlos C. (Belize) - A/C.1/78/PV.11
NUCLEAR WEAPONS—HUMANITARIAN CONSEQUENCES (Agenda item 99bb)
Fuller, Carlos C. (Belize) - A/C.1/78/PV.11
NUCLEAR WEAPONS—TREATIES (Agenda item 99ff)
Fuller, Carlos C. (Belize) - A/C.1/78/PV.11
NUCLEAR-WEAPON-FREE ZONES (Agenda item 99cc)
Fuller, Carlos C. (Belize) - A/C.1/78/PV.11
OPERATIONAL ACTIVITIES—UN SYSTEM (Agenda item 22a)
Wallace, Brian Christopher Manley (Jamaica) - A/C.2/78/SR.18

Caribbean Community (continued)

PALESTINE QUESTION (Agenda item 35)
Wallace, Brian Christopher Manley (Jamaica) - A/78/PV.39
PEACE—REGIONAL CENTRE—LATIN AMERICA AND THE CARIBBEAN (Agenda item 100c)
Moxey, Matthew (Bahamas) - A/C.1/78/PV.22
PEACEKEEPING OPERATIONS (Agenda item 51)
Douglas, Craig Barrington (Jamaica) - A/C.4/78/SR.18
POVERTY—INTERNATIONAL DECADES (Agenda item 21a)
Wallace, Brian Christopher Manley (Jamaica) - A/C.2/78/SR.16
RACIAL DISCRIMINATION—ELIMINATION (Agenda item 69a)
Rodrigue, Antonio (Haiti) - A/78/PV.63
Wallace, Brian Christopher Manley (Jamaica) - A/C.3/78/SR.40
RACIAL DISCRIMINATION—PROGRAMMES OF ACTION (Agenda item 69b)
Wallace, Brian Christopher Manley (Jamaica) - A/C.3/78/SR.40
RIGHTS OF THE CHILD (Agenda item 67)
Wallace, Brian Christopher Manley (Jamaica) - A/C.3/78/SR.12
RURAL POVERTY (Agenda item 21b)
Wallace, Brian Christopher Manley (Jamaica) - A/C.2/78/SR.16
SCIENCE AND TECHNOLOGY—DEVELOPMENT (Agenda item 19a)
Wallace, Brian Christopher Manley (Jamaica) - A/C.2/78/SR.10
SLAVERY—MEMORIALS (Agenda item 118)
Rodrigue, Antonio (Haiti) - A/78/PV.64
SMALL ARMS—ILLICIT TRAFFIC (Agenda item 99p)
Douglas, Craig Barrington (Jamaica) - A/C.1/78/PV.18
SMALL ARMS—ILLICIT TRAFFIC—ASSISTANCE (Agenda item 99n)
Douglas, Craig Barrington (Jamaica) - A/C.1/78/PV.18
SMALL ISLAND DEVELOPING STATES—PROGRAMMES OF ACTION (Agenda item 18b)
Habet, Orlando (Belize) - A/78/PV.100
Wallace, Brian Christopher Manley (Jamaica) - A/C.2/78/SR.12
Williams, Mutryce (Saint Kitts and Nevis) - A/78/PV.103
SOCIAL CONDITIONS (Agenda item 24b)
Wallace, Brian Christopher Manley (Jamaica) - A/C.3/78/SR.1
SUSTAINABLE DEVELOPMENT (Agenda item 18)
Wallace, Brian Christopher Manley (Jamaica) - A/C.2/78/SR.12
UN—BUDGET (2024) (Agenda item 134)
Wallace, Brian Christopher Manley (Jamaica) - A/C.5/78/SR.13

Caribbean Community (continued)

UN—BUDGET (2024) (Agenda item 134)
Walters, Iyeeka Latoy (Jamaica) - A/C.5/78/SR.18
UN. CONFERENCE ON DISARMAMENT—REPORTS (Agenda item 101a)
Moxey, Matthew (Bahamas) - A/C.1/78/PV.22
UN. DISARMAMENT COMMISSION—REPORTS (Agenda item 101b)
Moxey, Matthew (Bahamas) - A/C.1/78/PV.22
UN. GENERAL ASSEMBLY (78TH SESS. : 2023-2024). 1ST COMMITTEE—GENERAL DEBATE (Agenda item 8)
Wallace, Brian Christopher Manley (Jamaica) - A/C.1/78/PV.2
UN. GENERAL ASSEMBLY (78TH SESS. : 2023-2024). 2ND COMMITTEE—GENERAL DEBATE (Agenda item 8)
Wallace, Brian Christopher Manley (Jamaica) - A/C.2/78/SR.2
UN. SECURITY COUNCIL—MEMBERSHIP (Agenda item 121)
Rambally, Menissa (Saint Lucia) - A/78/PV.34
WEAPONS OF MASS DESTRUCTION—TERRORISM (Agenda item 99s)
Wallace, Brian Christopher Manley (Jamaica) - A/C.1/78/PV.14
WOMEN'S ADVANCEMENT (Agenda item 25a)
Wallace, Brian Christopher Manley (Jamaica) - A/C.3/78/SR.8
WOMEN'S ADVANCEMENT—CONFERENCES (Agenda item 25b)
Wallace, Brian Christopher Manley (Jamaica) - A/C.3/78/SR.8

Cenacolo (Organization)

WESTERN SAHARA QUESTION (Agenda item 58)
Stame Cervone, Anna Maria - A/C.4/78/SR.4

Central African Republic

HUMAN RIGHTS—CENTRAL AFRICAN REPUBLIC (Agenda item 71c)
Nzessioue, Marius Aristide Hoja - A/C.3/78/SR.33
RIGHTS OF THE CHILD (Agenda item 67)
Lenanguy Brinz, Yannick-Michel - A/C.3/78/SR.13
WESTERN SAHARA QUESTION (Agenda item 58)
Sepe, Tobie - A/C.4/78/SR.6
WOMEN'S ADVANCEMENT (Agenda item 25a)
Lenanguy Brinz, Yannick-Michel - A/C.3/78/SR.9
WOMEN'S ADVANCEMENT—CONFERENCES (Agenda item 25b)
Lenanguy Brinz, Yannick-Michel - A/C.3/78/SR.9
YOUTH (Agenda item 24b)
Lenanguy Brinz, Yannick-Michel - A/C.3/78/SR.3

Central African Republic. President

UN. GENERAL ASSEMBLY (78TH SESS. : 2023-2024)—GENERAL DEBATE (Agenda item 8)
Touadera, Faustin Archange - A/78/PV.8
UN. GENERAL ASSEMBLY (78TH SESS. : 2023-2024)—SPECIAL STATEMENTS
Touadera, Faustin Archange - A/78/PV.8

Centre Africain de recherche pour la paix et le développement durable (Organization)

WESTERN SAHARA QUESTION (Agenda item 58)
Tamekamta, Zozime Alphonse - A/C.4/78/SR.4

Centre de jeunes adolescents de Vaiare Moorea (Organization)

FRENCH POLYNESIA QUESTION (Agenda item 58)
Hoiore, Tevaipaea - A/C.4/78/SR.3

Centre de la paix pour les études politiques et stratégiques

WESTERN SAHARA QUESTION (Agenda item 58)
Ennass, Bahi Larbi - A/C.4/78/SR.5

Chad

UN. GENERAL ASSEMBLY (78TH SESS. : 2023-2024)—GENERAL DEBATE (Agenda item 8)
Annadif, Mahamat Saleh - A/78/PV.9

Chile

ARMS RACE—OUTER SPACE (Agenda item 97a)
Vidal Mercado, Jorge Andrés - A/C.1/78/PV.16
BIOLOGICAL WEAPONS—TREATIES (Agenda item 106)
Vidal Mercado, Jorge Andrés - A/C.1/78/PV.14
CHEMICAL WEAPONS—TREATIES (Agenda item 99l)
Vidal Mercado, Jorge Andrés - A/C.1/78/PV.14
CLIMATE CHANGE (Agenda item 71b)
Fernández Carter, Catalina - A/C.3/78/SR.29
CONVENTIONAL WEAPONS (Agenda item 99u)
Vidal Mercado, Jorge Andrés - A/C.1/78/PV.18
CRIMES AGAINST HUMANITY (Agenda item 80)
Hernández Chávez, José Juan - A/C.6/78/SR.11; A/C.6/78/SR.38; A/C.6/78/SR.41; A/C.6/78/SR.45
CUBA—UNITED STATES (Agenda item 38)
Narváez Ojeda, Paula - A/78/PV.26
DISAPPEARANCE OF PERSONS (Agenda item 71b)
Fernández Carter, Catalina - A/C.3/78/SR.22

Chile (continued)

DISARMAMENT—GENERAL AND COMPLETE (Agenda item 99)
Vidal Mercado, Jorge Andrés - A/C.1/78/PV.18; A/C.1/78/PV.23
DISARMAMENT—YOUTH (Agenda item 99gg)
Vidal Mercado, Jorge Andrés - A/C.1/78/PV.20
ELECTION VERIFICATION—UN (Agenda item 71b)
Nishihara, Carmen - A/C.3/78/SR.50
ENVIRONMENT (Agenda item 71b)
Fernández Carter, Catalina - A/C.3/78/SR.29
FALKLAND ISLANDS (MALVINAS) QUESTION (Agenda item 42)
Ruidíaz, René - A/C.4/78/SR.7
HAZARDOUS WASTES (Agenda item 71b)
Fernández Carter, Catalina - A/C.3/78/SR.29
HUMAN RIGHTS (Agenda item 71)
Perdomo, María Paula - A/C.3/78/SR.16
HUMAN RIGHTS—INTERNATIONAL INSTRUMENTS (Agenda item 71a)
Fernández Carter, Catalina - A/C.3/78/SR.25
HUMAN RIGHTS—TERRITORIES OCCUPIED BY ISRAEL (Agenda item 71c)
Nishihara, Carmen - A/C.3/78/SR.35
HUMAN RIGHTS ACTIVISTS (Agenda item 71b)
Fernández Carter, Catalina - A/C.3/78/SR.19
HUMAN RIGHTS ADVANCEMENT (Agenda item 71b)
Fernández Carter, Catalina - A/C.3/78/SR.25
IAEA—REPORTS (Agenda item 89)
Narváez Ojeda, Paula - A/78/PV.29
INFORMATION—INTERNATIONAL SECURITY (Agenda item 94)
Vidal Mercado, Jorge Andrés - A/C.1/78/PV.20
INTERNATIONAL CRIMINAL COURT—REPORTS (Agenda item 74)
Narváez Ojeda, Paula - A/78/PV.21
INTERNATIONAL LAW—TRAINING PROGRAMMES (Agenda item 78)
Hernández Chávez, José Juan - A/C.6/78/SR.22
JUDICIAL INDEPENDENCE (Agenda item 71b)
Fernández Carter, Catalina - A/C.3/78/SR.31
LAW OF THE SEA (Agenda item 75a)
Narváez Ojeda, Paula - A/78/PV.43
MARINE ECOSYSTEMS—BIOLOGICAL DIVERSITY (Agenda item 75c)
Narváez Ojeda, Paula - A/78/PV.43
MERCENARIES (Agenda item 70)
Nishihara, Carmen - A/C.3/78/SR.48
MIGRANTS—PROTECTION (Agenda item 71b)
Fernández Carter, Catalina - A/C.3/78/SR.23
MILLENNIUM SUMMIT—CONFERENCES (Agenda item 117)
Narváez Ojeda, Paula - A/78/PV.15

Chile (continued)

NON-CITIZENS—DEPORTATION (Agenda item 81)
Hernández Chávez, José Juan - A/C.6/78/SR.34
NUCLEAR DISARMAMENT (Agenda item 99b)
Vidal Mercado, Jorge Andrés - A/C.1/78/PV.12
NUCLEAR NON-PROLIFERATION—INTERNATIONAL OBLIGATIONS (Agenda item 99w)
Vidal Mercado, Jorge Andrés - A/C.1/78/PV.12
NUCLEAR WEAPON TESTS—TREATIES (Agenda item 105)
Vidal Mercado, Jorge Andrés - A/C.1/78/PV.12
NUCLEAR WEAPONS—TREATIES (Agenda item 99ff)
Vidal Mercado, Jorge Andrés - A/C.1/78/PV.12
OUTER SPACE—PRINCIPLES (Agenda item 97d)
Vidal Mercado, Jorge Andrés - A/C.1/78/PV.16
PALESTINE QUESTION (Agenda item 35)
Narváez Ojeda, Paula - A/78/PV.40
PERSONS WITH DISABILITIES—HUMAN RIGHTS (Agenda item 71a)
Zalaquett, Ignacia - A/C.3/78/SR.38
POVERTY—HUMAN RIGHTS (Agenda item 71b)
Nishihara, Carmen - A/C.3/78/SR.30
RIGHT TO DEVELOPMENT (Agenda item 71b)
Nishihara, Carmen - A/C.3/78/SR.48
RIGHT TO HEALTH (Agenda item 71b)
Ruidíaz, René - A/C.3/78/SR.39
RIGHT TO HOUSING (Agenda item 71b)
Nishihara, Carmen - A/C.3/78/SR.30
RIGHT TO THE TRUTH (Agenda item 71b)
Fernández Carter, Catalina - A/C.3/78/SR.22
RIGHTS OF THE CHILD (Agenda item 67)
Perdomo, María Paula - A/C.3/78/SR.55
RULE OF LAW (Agenda item 83)
Hernández Chávez, José Juan - A/C.6/78/SR.18
SANCTIONS—INTERNATIONAL RELATIONS (Agenda item 71b)
Nishihara, Carmen - A/C.3/78/SR.48
SEXUAL ORIENTATION (Agenda item 71b)
Ruidíaz, René - A/C.3/78/SR.39
SLAVERY (Agenda item 71a)
Fernández Carter, Catalina - A/C.3/78/SR.21
SMALL ARMS—ILLICIT TRAFFIC (Agenda item 99p)
Vidal Mercado, Jorge Andrés - A/C.1/78/PV.18
SOCIAL DEVELOPMENT—CONFERENCES (Agenda item 24a)
Perdomo, María Paula - A/C.3/78/SR.4
STRADDLING FISH STOCKS (Agenda item 75b)
Narváez Ojeda, Paula - A/78/PV.43
SUMMARY EXECUTIONS (Agenda item 71b)
Fernández Carter, Catalina - A/C.3/78/SR.31

Chile (continued)

SUSTAINABLE DEVELOPMENT (Agenda item 18)
González Carrillo, Montserrat - A/C.2/78/SR.25
TAXATION (Agenda item 16h)
Ruidíaz, René - A/C.2/78/SR.25
TORTURE AND OTHER CRUEL TREATMENT (Agenda item 71a)
Fernández Carter, Catalina - A/C.3/78/SR.18
UKRAINE—POLITICAL CONDITIONS (Agenda item 62)
Narváez Ojeda, Paula - A/78/PV.57
UN—BUDGET (2024) (Agenda item 134)
González Sese, José Antonio - A/C.5/78/SR.12
UN—PROGRAMME PLANNING (Agenda item 135)
Vidal Mercado, Jorge Andrés - A/C.1/78/PV.10
UN. GENERAL ASSEMBLY—WORK PROGRAMME (Agenda item 120)
Vidal Mercado, Jorge Andrés - A/C.1/78/PV.10
UN. GENERAL ASSEMBLY (78TH SESS. : 2023-2024). 1ST COMMITTEE—GENERAL DEBATE (Agenda item 8)
Vidal Mercado, Jorge Andrés - A/C.1/78/PV.5
UN. GENERAL ASSEMBLY (78TH SESS. : 2023-2024). 2ND COMMITTEE—GENERAL DEBATE (Agenda item 8)
González Carrillo, Montserrat - A/C.2/78/SR.5
UN. HUMAN RIGHTS COUNCIL—REPORTS (Agenda item 66)
Nishihara, Carmen - A/C.3/78/SR.46
UN. INTERNATIONAL COURT OF JUSTICE—REPORTS (Agenda item 73)
Hernández Chávez, José Juan - A/78/PV.27
Poblete Troncoso, Moisés - A/78/PV.20
UN. INTERNATIONAL LAW COMMISSION—REPORTS (Agenda item 79)
Hernández Chávez, José Juan - A/C.6/78/SR.29; A/C.6/78/SR.31
Troncoso, Claudio - A/C.6/78/SR.24
UN. SECURITY COUNCIL—MEMBERSHIP (Agenda item 121)
Vidal Mercado, Jorge Andrés - A/78/PV.35
UN. SECURITY COUNCIL—REPORTS (Agenda item 26)
Vidal Mercado, Jorge Andrés - A/78/PV.93
UN COMMISSION ON INTERNATIONAL TRADE LAW—REPORTS (Agenda item 77)
Hernández Chávez, José Juan - A/C.6/78/SR.14
UN CONFERENCES (Agenda item 13)
Narváez Ojeda, Paula - A/78/PV.15
UN RESOLUTIONS—IMPLEMENTATION (Agenda item 119)
Garrido Melo, Claudio Ernesto - A/78/PV.103
UNRWA—ACTIVITIES (Agenda item 49)
Garrido Melo, Claudio Ernesto - A/C.4/78/SR.23
VETO (Agenda item 63)
Garrido Melo, Claudio Ernesto - A/78/PV.60; A/78/PV.74
Narváez Ojeda, Paula - A/78/PV.51; A/78/PV.66; A/78/PV.68

Chile (continued)

VETO (Agenda item 63)
Vidal Mercado, Jorge Andrés - A/78/PV.70; A/78/PV.78
WOMEN'S ADVANCEMENT (Agenda item 25a)
Garrido Melo, Claudio Ernesto - A/C.3/78/SR.8
Perdomo, María Paula - A/C.3/78/SR.7
WOMEN'S ADVANCEMENT—CONFERENCES (Agenda item 25b)
Garrido Melo, Claudio Ernesto - A/C.3/78/SR.8
Perdomo, María Paula - A/C.3/78/SR.7

Chile. President

UN. GENERAL ASSEMBLY (78TH SESS. : 2023-2024)—GENERAL DEBATE (Agenda item 8)
Boric Font, Gabriel - A/78/PV.7
UN. GENERAL ASSEMBLY (78TH SESS. : 2023-2024)—SPECIAL STATEMENTS
Boric Font, Gabriel - A/78/PV.7

China

ADMINISTRATION OF JUSTICE (Agenda item 144)
Ma, Yanbo - A/C.6/78/SR.9
AFRICA—DEVELOPMENT (Agenda item 65b)
Dai, Bing - A/78/PV.18
AFRICA—SUSTAINABLE DEVELOPMENT—PARTNERSHIP (Agenda item 65a)
Dai, Bing - A/78/PV.18
ALBINISM (Agenda item 71b)
Wang, Zixu - A/C.3/78/SR.27
ARMED CONFLICTS PREVENTION (Agenda item 31a)
Niu, Xiaoqiang - A/78/PV.72
ARMS RACE—OUTER SPACE (Agenda item 97a)
Shen, Jian - A/C.1/78/PV.17; A/C.1/78/PV.27
BIOLOGICAL DIVERSITY—TREATIES (Agenda item 18f)
Guo, Jingnan - A/C.2/78/SR.13
Liu, Liqun - A/C.2/78/SR.25
BIOLOGICAL WEAPONS—TREATIES (Agenda item 106)
Sun, Yiliang - A/C.1/78/PV.15
CENTRAL ASIA—ZONES OF PEACE (Agenda item 64)
Wang, Zixu - A/78/PV.85
CHEMICAL WEAPONS—TREATIES (Agenda item 99l)
Sun, Yiliang - A/C.1/78/PV.15
Zhang, Qian - A/C.1/78/PV.26
CLIMATE (Agenda item 18d)
Guo, Jingnan - A/C.2/78/SR.13
Liu, Liqun - A/C.2/78/SR.25
CLIMATE CHANGE (Agenda item 71b)
Liu, Luoge - A/C.3/78/SR.29
CRIME PREVENTION (Agenda item 107)
Liu, Han - A/C.3/78/SR.5

China (continued)

CRIMES AGAINST HUMANITY (Agenda item 80)
Geng, Shuang - A/C.6/78/SR.10
Li, Linlin - A/C.6/78/SR.38; A/C.6/78/SR.40
Ma, Yanbo - A/C.6/78/SR.42; A/C.6/78/SR.43; A/C.6/78/SR.44; A/C.6/78/SR.45
CUBA—UNITED STATES (Agenda item 38)
Dai, Bing - A/78/PV.24
CYBERCRIME (Agenda item 108)
Liu, Han - A/C.3/78/SR.5
DECOLONIZATION (Agenda item 58)
Geng, Shuang - A/C.4/78/SR.8
DEMOCRACY (Agenda item 71b)
Yang, Fan - A/C.3/78/SR.28
DISAPPEARANCE OF PERSONS (Agenda item 71b)
Zhang, Qiuruo - A/C.3/78/SR.22
DISARMAMENT—GENERAL AND COMPLETE (Agenda item 99)
Lai, Haiyang - A/C.1/78/PV.21
Ren, Hongyan - A/78/PV.105
Shen, Jian - A/C.1/78/PV.19; A/C.1/78/PV.20; A/C.1/78/PV.23; A/C.1/78/PV.30
Sun, Yiliang - A/C.1/78/PV.26
Zhang, Junjie - A/C.1/78/PV.28
DISARMAMENT AGREEMENTS—OUTER SPACE (Agenda item 97c)
Shen, Jian - A/C.1/78/PV.17; A/C.1/78/PV.27
Zhang, Junjie - A/C.1/78/PV.27
DISASTER VICTIMS (Agenda item 86)
Zhao, Yanrui - A/C.6/78/SR.6
DISPLACED PERSONS (Agenda item 71b)
Yang, Fan - A/C.3/78/SR.32
ECONOMIC COOPERATION AMONG DEVELOPING COUNTRIES (Agenda item 22b)
Dai, Bing - A/C.2/78/SR.18
ECONOMIC SANCTIONS—INTERNATIONAL RELATIONS (Agenda item 28)
Geng, Shuang - A/78/PV.89
ELECTION VERIFICATION—UN (Agenda item 71b)
Wang, Zixu - A/C.3/78/SR.50
EMERGENCY ASSISTANCE (Agenda item 72a)
Dai, Bing - A/78/PV.46
ENVIRONMENT (Agenda item 71b)
Liu, Luoge - A/C.3/78/SR.29
EXTERNAL DEBT (Agenda item 16c)
Hua, Chenghang - A/C.2/78/SR.9
EXTERNAL DEBT—HUMAN RIGHTS (Agenda item 71b)
Yang, Fan - A/C.3/78/SR.32
FALKLAND ISLANDS (MALVINAS) QUESTION (Agenda item 42)
Geng, Shuang - A/C.4/78/SR.8
FISSIONABLE MATERIALS—TREATIES (Agenda item 99a)
Sun, Yiliang - A/C.1/78/PV.13; A/C.1/78/PV.26
FOOD SECURITY (Agenda item 23a)
Cao, Liwen - A/C.2/78/SR.16

China (continued)

FREEDOM OF EXPRESSION (Agenda item 71b)
Zhang, Tianhao - A/C.3/78/SR.19
HEALTH (Agenda item 125)
Dai, Bing - A/78/PV.48
Zhang, Sisi - A/78/PV.41
Zhang, Tianhao - A/78/PV.16
HIV/AIDS—DECLARATIONS (Agenda item 10)
Li, Nan - A/78/PV.91
HUMAN RIGHTS (Agenda item 71)
Dai, Bing - A/C.3/78/SR.16
Yang, Xiaokun - A/C.3/78/SR.27
HUMAN RIGHTS—AFGHANISTAN (Agenda item 71c)
Chen, Jiawen - A/C.3/78/SR.34
HUMAN RIGHTS—BURUNDI (Agenda item 71c)
Liu, Luoge - A/C.3/78/SR.36
HUMAN RIGHTS—CENTRAL AFRICAN REPUBLIC (Agenda item 71c)
Chen, Jiawen - A/C.3/78/SR.33
HUMAN RIGHTS—DEMOCRATIC PEOPLE'S REPUBLIC OF KOREA (Agenda item 71c)
Chen, Jiawen - A/C.3/78/SR.33
Zhang, Sisi - A/78/PV.50; A/C.3/78/SR.53
HUMAN RIGHTS—ERITREA (Agenda item 71c)
Liu, Luoge - A/C.3/78/SR.36
HUMAN RIGHTS—ETHIOPIA (Agenda item 71c)
Mao, Yizong - A/C.3/78/SR.36
HUMAN RIGHTS—INTERNATIONAL INSTRUMENTS (Agenda item 71a)
La, Haozhao - A/C.3/78/SR.17
HUMAN RIGHTS—IRAN (ISLAMIC REPUBLIC OF) (Agenda item 71c)
Chen, Jiawen - A/C.3/78/SR.34
Zhang, Sisi - A/78/PV.50; A/C.3/78/SR.53
HUMAN RIGHTS—MYANMAR (Agenda item 71c)
Chen, Jiawen - A/C.3/78/SR.33
Zhang, Sisi - A/78/PV.50; A/C.3/78/SR.53
HUMAN RIGHTS—REPORTS (Agenda item 71c)
Dai, Bing - A/C.3/78/SR.25
Zhang, Jun - A/C.3/78/SR.24; A/C.3/78/SR.27
Zhang, Sisi - A/78/PV.50; A/C.3/78/SR.18
HUMAN RIGHTS—RUSSIAN FEDERATION (Agenda item 71c)
Yang, Xiaokun - A/C.3/78/SR.37
HUMAN RIGHTS—SOMALIA (Agenda item 71c)
Yang, Fan - A/C.3/78/SR.35
HUMAN RIGHTS—SYRIAN ARAB REPUBLIC (Agenda item 71c)
Chen, Jiawen - A/C.3/78/SR.34
Zhang, Sisi - A/78/PV.50; A/C.3/78/SR.54

China (continued)

HUMAN RIGHTS—TERRITORIES OCCUPIED BY ISRAEL (Agenda item 71c)
Yang, Xiaokun - A/C.3/78/SR.35
Zhang, Jun - A/C.3/78/SR.24
HUMAN RIGHTS—UKRAINE (Agenda item 71c)
Chen, Jiawen - A/C.3/78/SR.37
Zhang, Sisi - A/78/PV.50; A/C.3/78/SR.53
HUMAN RIGHTS ACTIVISTS (Agenda item 71b)
Zhang, Sisi - A/C.3/78/SR.56
HUMAN RIGHTS ADVANCEMENT (Agenda item 71b)
Zhang, Jun - A/C.3/78/SR.24
Zhang, Sisi - A/C.3/78/SR.18
IAEA—REPORTS (Agenda item 89)
Liu, Zhao - A/78/PV.30
INDIGENOUS PEOPLES (Agenda item 68a)
Zhang, Sisi - A/C.3/78/SR.15
INDIGENOUS PEOPLES—CONFERENCES (Agenda item 68b)
Zhang, Sisi - A/C.3/78/SR.15
INFORMATION—INTERNATIONAL SECURITY (Agenda item 94)
Li, Nan - A/C.1/78/PV.29
Shen, Jian - A/C.1/78/PV.20
INFORMATION TECHNOLOGY—DEVELOPMENT (Agenda item 15)
Zhao, Haibo - A/C.2/78/SR.10
INTERNATIONAL CRIMINAL COURT—REPORTS (Agenda item 74)
Ma, Xinmin - A/78/PV.21
INTERNATIONAL JURISDICTION (Agenda item 84)
Li, Linlin - A/C.6/78/SR.12
INTERNATIONAL LAW—TRAINING PROGRAMMES (Agenda item 78)
Ma, Yanbo - A/C.6/78/SR.21
INTERNATIONAL TRADE (Agenda item 16a)
Hua, Chenghang - A/C.2/78/SR.9
JUDICIAL INDEPENDENCE (Agenda item 71b)
Zhang, Qiuruo - A/C.3/78/SR.31
LANDLOCKED DEVELOPING COUNTRIES—CONFERENCES (Agenda item 20b)
Wang, Hongbo - A/C.2/78/SR.7
LANDMINES—TREATIES (Agenda item 99m)
Shen, Jian - A/C.1/78/PV.19
LAW OF THE SEA (Agenda item 75a)
Geng, Shuang - A/78/PV.43
Li, Linlin - A/78/PV.44
LEAST DEVELOPED COUNTRIES—CONFERENCES (Agenda item 20a)
Wang, Hongbo - A/C.2/78/SR.7
LEPROSY (Agenda item 71b)
La, Haozhao - A/C.3/78/SR.17
MACROECONOMIC POLICY (Agenda item 16)
Hua, Chenghang - A/C.2/78/SR.9

China (continued)

MARINE ECOSYSTEMS—BIOLOGICAL DIVERSITY (Agenda item 75c)
Geng, Shuang - A/78/PV.43
Li, Linlin - A/78/PV.44
MIGRANTS—PROTECTION (Agenda item 71b)
Zhang, Qiuruo - A/C.3/78/SR.23
MINE CLEARANCE (Agenda item 46)
Wang, Zhenjiang - A/C.4/78/SR.10
MINORITIES (Agenda item 71b)
Liu, Luoge - A/C.3/78/SR.39
MULTILINGUALISM (Agenda item 124)
Jiang, Hua - A/78/PV.108
NUCLEAR DISARMAMENT (Agenda item 99b)
Sun, Yiliang - A/C.1/78/PV.11; A/C.1/78/PV.13
Wu, Jianjian - A/C.1/78/PV.13
NUCLEAR NON-PROLIFERATION (Agenda item 99o)
Sun, Yiliang - A/C.1/78/PV.13
NUCLEAR WEAPON TESTS—TREATIES (Agenda item 105)
Sun, Yiliang - A/C.1/78/PV.26
NUCLEAR WEAPONS—ELIMINATION (Agenda item 99z)
Sun, Yiliang - A/C.1/78/PV.26
NUCLEAR WEAPONS—TREATIES (Agenda item 99ff)
Sun, Yiliang - A/C.1/78/PV.26
OPERATIONAL ACTIVITIES—UN SYSTEM (Agenda item 22a)
Dai, Bing - A/C.2/78/SR.18
OUTER SPACE—CONFIDENCE-BUILDING MEASURES (Agenda item 99v)
Shen, Jian - A/C.1/78/PV.17; A/C.1/78/PV.27
OUTER SPACE—PEACEFUL USES—INTERNATIONAL COOPERATION (Agenda item 48)
Ma, Yuanchun - A/C.4/78/SR.16
OUTER SPACE—PRINCIPLES (Agenda item 97d)
Shen, Jian - A/C.1/78/PV.17; A/C.1/78/PV.27
Zhang, Junjie - A/C.1/78/PV.27
PALESTINIANS—ASSISTANCE (Agenda item 72b)
Dai, Bing - A/78/PV.46
PEACE (Agenda item 14)
Dai, Bing - A/78/PV.76
Fu, Cong - A/78/PV.82; A/78/PV.88
PEACEKEEPING OPERATIONS—CRIMINAL LIABILITY (Agenda item 76)
Wang, Yuanjie - A/C.6/78/SR.8
PERSONNEL QUESTIONS—UN SYSTEM (Agenda item 142)
Guo, Ke - A/C.5/78/SR.10
PERSONS WITH DISABILITIES—HUMAN RIGHTS (Agenda item 71a)
Chen, Jiawen - A/C.3/78/SR.38
POVERTY—HUMAN RIGHTS (Agenda item 71b)
Liu, Luoge - A/C.3/78/SR.30

China (continued)

POVERTY—INTERNATIONAL DECADES (Agenda item 21a)
Cao, Liwen - A/C.2/78/SR.16
RACIAL DISCRIMINATION—ELIMINATION (Agenda item 69a)
Dai, Bing - A/C.3/78/SR.40
Liu, Luoge - A/C.3/78/SR.41
Mao, Yizong - A/C.3/78/SR.41
Xing, Jisheng - A/C.3/78/SR.47
Zhang, Sisi - A/78/PV.50; A/C.3/78/SR.41; A/C.3/78/SR.42
RACIAL DISCRIMINATION—PROGRAMMES OF ACTION (Agenda item 69b)
Dai, Bing - A/C.3/78/SR.40
Liu, Luoge - A/C.3/78/SR.40; A/C.3/78/SR.41
Mao, Yizong - A/C.3/78/SR.41
Zhang, Sisi - A/C.3/78/SR.41; A/C.3/78/SR.42
RADIATION EFFECTS (Agenda item 47)
Ling, Feng - A/C.4/78/SR.11
RELIGIOUS INTOLERANCE (Agenda item 71b)
Chen, Jiawen - A/C.3/78/SR.38
RESPONSIBILITY TO PROTECT (Agenda item 129)
Sun, Zhiqiang - A/78/PV.97
RIGHT OF ASSEMBLY (Agenda item 71b)
Zhang, Tianhao - A/C.3/78/SR.19
RIGHT TO CULTURE (Agenda item 71b)
Wang, Zixu - A/C.3/78/SR.27
RIGHT TO DEVELOPMENT (Agenda item 71b)
Wang, Zixu - A/C.3/78/SR.20
RIGHT TO DRINKING WATER (Agenda item 71b)
Yang, Xiaokun - A/C.3/78/SR.28
RIGHT TO EDUCATION (Agenda item 71b)
Wang, Zixu - A/C.3/78/SR.27
RIGHT TO FOOD (Agenda item 71b)
Liu, Luoge - A/C.3/78/SR.30
RIGHT TO HEALTH (Agenda item 71b)
Liu, Luoge - A/C.3/78/SR.39
RIGHT TO HOUSING (Agenda item 71b)
Liu, Luoge - A/C.3/78/SR.30
RIGHT TO PRIVACY (Agenda item 71b)
Zhang, Tianhao - A/C.3/78/SR.21
RIGHTS OF THE CHILD (Agenda item 67)
La, Haozhao - A/C.3/78/SR.11; A/C.3/78/SR.12
RULE OF LAW (Agenda item 83)
Li, Linlin - A/C.6/78/SR.16
RURAL POVERTY (Agenda item 21b)
Cao, Liwen - A/C.2/78/SR.16
Liu, Liqun - A/C.2/78/SR.22
SANCTIONS—INTERNATIONAL RELATIONS (Agenda item 71b)
Yang, Xiaokun - A/C.3/78/SR.28
Zhang, Jun - A/C.3/78/SR.24
SCIENCE AND TECHNOLOGY—DEVELOPMENT (Agenda item 19a)
Zhao, Haibo - A/C.2/78/SR.10

China (continued)

SELF-DETERMINATION OF PEOPLES (Agenda item 70)
Dai, Bing - A/C.3/78/SR.40
SLAVERY (Agenda item 71a)
Zhang, Tianhao - A/C.3/78/SR.21
SMALL ARMS—ILLICIT TRAFFIC (Agenda item 99p)
Shen, Jian - A/C.1/78/PV.19
SMALL ARMS—ILLICIT TRAFFIC—ASSISTANCE (Agenda item 99n)
Shen, Jian - A/C.1/78/PV.19
SOCIAL DEVELOPMENT (Agenda item 24)
Dai, Bing - A/C.3/78/SR.2
SOLIDARITY (Agenda item 71b)
Yang, Fan - A/C.3/78/SR.32
SOUTH-EAST ASIA—NUCLEAR-WEAPON-FREE ZONES (Agenda item 99y)
Shen, Jian - A/C.1/78/PV.30
SPORTS—OLYMPIC GAMES (Agenda item 11)
Dai, Bing - A/78/PV.38
STRADDLING FISH STOCKS (Agenda item 75b)
Geng, Shuang - A/78/PV.43
Li, Linlin - A/78/PV.44
SUMMARY EXECUTIONS (Agenda item 71b)
Zhang, Qiuruo - A/C.3/78/SR.31
SUSTAINABLE DEVELOPMENT (Agenda item 18)
Cao, Liwen - A/C.2/78/SR.24
Guo, Jingnan - A/C.2/78/SR.13
SUSTAINABLE ENERGY (Agenda item 18h)
Guo, Jingnan - A/C.2/78/SR.13
TERRITORIES OCCUPIED BY ISRAEL—HUMAN RIGHTS (Agenda item 50)
Geng, Shuang - A/C.4/78/SR.25
TERRITORIES OCCUPIED BY ISRAEL—NATURAL RESOURCES (Agenda item 59)
Cao, Liwen - A/C.2/78/SR.19
TERRORISM (Agenda item 109)
Geng, Shuang - A/C.6/78/SR.3
TERRORISM—HUMAN RIGHTS (Agenda item 71b)
Zhang, Qiuruo - A/C.3/78/SR.31
TORTURE AND OTHER CRUEL TREATMENT (Agenda item 71a)
La, Haozhao - A/C.3/78/SR.18
TRAFFICKING IN PERSONS (Agenda item 71b)
Liu, Luoge - A/C.3/78/SR.23
TRANSNATIONAL CORPORATIONS—HUMAN RIGHTS (Agenda item 71b)
Zhang, Tianhao - A/C.3/78/SR.21
TREATIES (Agenda item 87)
Zhao, Yanrui - A/C.6/78/SR.20
UKRAINE—POLITICAL CONDITIONS (Agenda item 62)
Fu, Cong - A/78/PV.99
UN—BUDGET (2024) (Agenda item 134)
Chen, Yuanhang - A/C.5/78/SR.3

China (continued)

UN—BUDGET (2024) (Agenda item 134)
Han, Jin - A/C.5/78/SR.28
Jiang, Hua - A/C.5/78/SR.5; A/C.5/78/SR.33; A/C.5/78/SR.34
UN—FINANCIAL REPORTS (Agenda item 131)
Guo, Zhiqi - A/C.5/78/SR.14
UN—FINANCIAL SITUATION (Agenda item 136)
Guo, Zhiqi - A/C.5/78/SR.6
UN—HUMAN RESOURCES MANAGEMENT (Agenda item 139)
Guo, Ke - A/C.5/78/SR.25
UN—PROGRAMME PLANNING (Agenda item 135)
Jiang, Hua - A/C.5/78/SR.5
Zhang, Sisi - A/78/PV.50(Resumption1)
UN. COMMITTEE ON RELATIONS WITH THE HOST COUNTRY—REPORTS (Agenda item 161)
Li, Linlin - A/C.6/78/SR.35
UN. CONFERENCE ON DISARMAMENT—REPORTS (Agenda item 101a)
Shen, Jian - A/C.1/78/PV.23
UN. GENERAL ASSEMBLY (78TH SESS. : 2023-2024)—AGENDA (Agenda item 7)
Liang, Hengzhu - A/BUR/78/SR.2
UN. GENERAL ASSEMBLY (78TH SESS. : 2023-2024)—GENERAL DEBATE—RIGHT OF REPLY (Agenda item 8)
Li, Linlin - A/78/PV.13
UN. GENERAL ASSEMBLY (78TH SESS. : 2023-2024)—OFFICERS (Agenda item 5)
Dai, Bing - A/C.5/78/SR.1
UN. GENERAL ASSEMBLY (78TH SESS. : 2023-2024). 1ST COMMITTEE—GENERAL DEBATE (Agenda item 8)
Li, Nan - A/C.1/78/PV.6
Sun, Xiaobo - A/C.1/78/PV.5
Sun, Yiliang - A/C.1/78/PV.5
UN. GENERAL ASSEMBLY (78TH SESS. : 2023-2024). 2ND COMMITTEE—GENERAL DEBATE (Agenda item 8)
Geng, Shuang - A/C.2/78/SR.4
UN. GENERAL ASSEMBLY (78TH SESS. : 2023-2024). 5TH COMMITTEE—WORK ORGANIZATION (Agenda item 7)
Dai, Bing - A/C.5/78/SR.35
Jiang, Hua - A/C.5/78/SR.26/PartII; A/C.5/78/SR.27; A/C.5/78/SR.34
UN. HUMAN RIGHTS COUNCIL—REPORTS (Agenda item 66)
Zhang, Sisi - A/C.3/78/SR.46
UN. INTERNATIONAL COURT OF JUSTICE—REPORTS (Agenda item 73)
Ma, Xinmin - A/78/PV.20
UN. INTERNATIONAL LAW COMMISSION—REPORTS (Agenda item 79)
Li, Linlin - A/C.6/78/SR.37
Ma, Xinmin - A/C.6/78/SR.27; A/C.6/78/SR.29

China (continued)

UN. SECURITY COUNCIL—MEMBERSHIP (Agenda item 121)
Dai, Bing - A/78/PV.104
Zhang, Jun - A/78/PV.35
UN CHARTER—REPORTS (Agenda item 82)
Geng, Shuang - A/C.6/78/SR.33
UN COMMISSION ON INTERNATIONAL TRADE LAW—REPORTS (Agenda item 77)
Zhao, Yanrui - A/C.6/78/SR.14
UN CONFERENCES (Agenda item 13)
Fu, Cong - A/78/PV.97
UN HIGH COMMISSIONER FOR REFUGEES—REPORTS (Agenda item 60)
Zhang, Sisi - A/C.3/78/SR.44
UNRWA—ACTIVITIES (Agenda item 49)
Geng, Shuang - A/C.4/78/SR.23
VETO (Agenda item 63)
Dai, Bing - A/78/PV.66
Fu, Cong - A/78/PV.75; A/78/PV.78
Geng, Shuang - A/78/PV.51; A/78/PV.60; A/78/PV.68
WEAPONS—OUTER SPACE (Agenda item 97b)
Shen, Jian - A/C.1/78/PV.17
WOMEN'S ADVANCEMENT (Agenda item 25a)
Le, Shuang - A/C.3/78/SR.7
Shuang, Le - A/C.3/78/SR.8
WOMEN'S ADVANCEMENT—CONFERENCES (Agenda item 25b)
Le, Shuang - A/C.3/78/SR.7
Shuang, Le - A/C.3/78/SR.8

China. Vice-President

UN. GENERAL ASSEMBLY (78TH SESS. : 2023-2024)—GENERAL DEBATE (Agenda item 8)
Han, Zheng - A/78/PV.9
UN. GENERAL ASSEMBLY (78TH SESS. : 2023-2024)—SPECIAL STATEMENTS
Han, Zheng - A/78/PV.9

Classical Conversations Foundation

WESTERN SAHARA QUESTION (Agenda item 58)
Dail, Elizabeth - A/C.4/78/SR.4

Coalition for Addressing Sea-level Rise and its Existential Threat

MILLENNIUM SUMMIT—CONFERENCES (Agenda item 117)
Falefou, Tapugao (Tuvalu) - A/78/PV.53
Zahneisen, Thomas (Germany) - A/78/PV.102
UN CONFERENCES (Agenda item 13)
Falefou, Tapugao (Tuvalu) - A/78/PV.53
Zahneisen, Thomas (Germany) - A/78/PV.102

Collective of Saharawi Human Rights Defenders

WESTERN SAHARA QUESTION (Agenda item 58)
Fall, Ahmed Mohamed - A/C.4/78/SR.5

Collective Security Treaty Organization

RACIAL DISCRIMINATION—ELIMINATION (Agenda item 69a)
Pilipenko, Igor (Belarus) - A/C.3/78/SR.47

Colombia

2030 AGENDA—PROGRAMME IMPLEMENTATION (Agenda item 18a)
Ríos Serna, Manuela - A/C.2/78/SR.12
BIOLOGICAL WEAPONS—TREATIES (Agenda item 106)
Quintero Correa, Nohra María - A/C.1/78/PV.16
CENTRAL ASIA—ZONES OF PEACE (Agenda item 64)
Solano Ramírez, Lucía Teresa - A/78/PV.85
CHEMICAL WEAPONS—TREATIES (Agenda item 99l)
Quintero Correa, Nohra María - A/C.1/78/PV.16
CLIMATE (Agenda item 18d)
Ríos Serna, Manuela - A/C.2/78/SR.12
Solano Ramírez, Lucía Teresa - A/C.2/78/SR.25
CLIMATE CHANGE (Agenda item 71b)
Orduz Durán, Jessica Beatriz - A/C.3/78/SR.29
COASTAL ZONE MANAGEMENT (Agenda item 18j)
Ríos Serna, Manuela - A/C.2/78/SR.23
COMMODITIES (Agenda item 16d)
Tickner, Arlene Beth - A/C.2/78/SR.14
CONVENTIONAL WEAPONS (Agenda item 99u)
Quintero Correa, Nohra María - A/C.1/78/PV.18
CRIME PREVENTION (Agenda item 107)
Paredes Campaña, Jairo Andrés - A/C.3/78/SR.56
Zalabata Torres, Leonor - A/C.3/78/SR.5
CRIMES AGAINST HUMANITY (Agenda item 80)
Solano Ramírez, Lucía Teresa - A/C.6/78/SR.10; A/C.6/78/SR.39; A/C.6/78/SR.40; A/C.6/78/SR.41; A/C.6/78/SR.42; A/C.6/78/SR.43; A/C.6/78/SR.44; A/C.6/78/SR.45
CUBA—UNITED STATES (Agenda item 38)
Zalabata Torres, Leonor - A/78/PV.24
CYBERCRIME (Agenda item 108)
Zalabata Torres, Leonor - A/C.3/78/SR.5
DEVELOPMENT COOPERATION—MIDDLE-INCOME COUNTRIES (Agenda item 19c)
Murillo Ferrer, Jorge Adrián - A/C.2/78/SR.23
Ríos Serna, Manuela - A/C.2/78/SR.10
DEVELOPMENT FINANCE (Agenda item 16b)
Tickner, Arlene Beth - A/C.2/78/SR.8
DISAPPEARANCE OF PERSONS (Agenda item 71b)
Paredes Campaña, Jairo Andrés - A/C.3/78/SR.22

Colombia (continued)

DISARMAMENT—GENERAL AND COMPLETE (Agenda item 99)
Quintero Correa, Nohra María - A/C.1/78/PV.18
DISASTER PREVENTION (Agenda item 18c)
Ríos Serna, Manuela - A/C.2/78/SR.12
DISASTER VICTIMS (Agenda item 86)
Solano Ramírez, Lucía Teresa - A/C.6/78/SR.5
Zalabata Torres, Leonor - A/C.6/78/SR.5
DISPLACED PERSONS (Agenda item 71b)
Tickner, Arlene Beth - A/C.3/78/SR.32
ECONOMIC SANCTIONS—INTERNATIONAL RELATIONS (Agenda item 28)
Zalabata Torres, Leonor - A/78/PV.90
ELECTION VERIFICATION—UN (Agenda item 71b)
Sánchez García, Nathalia - A/C.3/78/SR.50
ENVIRONMENT (Agenda item 71b)
Orduz Durán, Jessica Beatriz - A/C.3/78/SR.29
EXTERNAL DEBT (Agenda item 16c)
Murillo Ferrer, Jorge Adrián - A/C.2/78/SR.25
Tickner, Arlene Beth - A/C.2/78/SR.8
FALKLAND ISLANDS (MALVINAS) QUESTION (Agenda item 42)
Zalabata Torres, Leonor - A/C.4/78/SR.7
FREEDOM OF EXPRESSION (Agenda item 71b)
Tickner, Arlene Beth - A/C.3/78/SR.19
HEALTH (Agenda item 125)
Tickner, Arlene Beth - A/78/PV.48
HIV/AIDS—DECLARATIONS (Agenda item 10)
Méndez Bocanegra, Rodrigo Andrés - A/78/PV.91
HUMAN RIGHTS (Agenda item 71)
Sánchez García, Nathalia - A/C.3/78/SR.16
HUMAN RIGHTS—INTERNATIONAL INSTRUMENTS (Agenda item 71a)
Orduz Durán, Jessica Beatriz - A/C.3/78/SR.24
HUMAN RIGHTS ACTIVISTS (Agenda item 71b)
Sánchez García, Nathalia - A/C.3/78/SR.19
IAEA—REPORTS (Agenda item 89)
Zalabata Torres, Leonor - A/78/PV.29
INDIGENOUS PEOPLES (Agenda item 68a)
Méndez Bocanegra, Rodrigo Andrés - A/C.3/78/SR.15
Zalabata Torres, Leonor - A/C.3/78/SR.15; A/C.3/78/SR.48
INDIGENOUS PEOPLES—CONFERENCES (Agenda item 68b)
Méndez Bocanegra, Rodrigo Andrés - A/C.3/78/SR.15
Zalabata Torres, Leonor - A/C.3/78/SR.15
INFORMATION—INTERNATIONAL SECURITY (Agenda item 94)
Quintero Correa, Nohra María - A/C.1/78/PV.21
INTERNATIONAL CRIMINAL COURT—REPORTS (Agenda item 74)
Solano Ramírez, Lucía Teresa - A/78/PV.21

Colombia (continued)

INTERNATIONAL LAW—TRAINING PROGRAMMES (Agenda item 78)
Botero, Stephanie - A/C.6/78/SR.21
INTERNATIONAL TRADE (Agenda item 16a)
Murillo Ferrer, Jorge Adrián - A/C.2/78/SR.22
INVESTMENT PROMOTION (Agenda item 16g)
Murillo Ferrer, Jorge Adrián - A/C.2/78/SR.23
JUDICIAL INDEPENDENCE (Agenda item 71b)
Sánchez García, Nathalia - A/C.3/78/SR.31
LANDMINES—TREATIES (Agenda item 99m)
Quintero Correa, Nohra María - A/C.1/78/PV.18; A/C.1/78/PV.28
MILLENNIUM SUMMIT—CONFERENCES (Agenda item 117)
Zalabata Torres, Leonor - A/78/PV.15
NON-CITIZENS—DEPORTATION (Agenda item 81)
Solano Ramírez, Lucía Teresa - A/C.6/78/SR.34
NUCLEAR DISARMAMENT (Agenda item 99b)
Quintero Correa, Nohra María - A/C.1/78/PV.14
NUCLEAR NON-PROLIFERATION—INTERNATIONAL OBLIGATIONS (Agenda item 99w)
Quintero Correa, Nohra María - A/C.1/78/PV.14
NUCLEAR WEAPONS—ELIMINATION (Agenda item 99z)
Quintero Correa, Nohra María - A/C.1/78/PV.26
PALESTINE QUESTION (Agenda item 35)
Zalabata Torres, Leonor - A/78/PV.40
PALESTINIANS—ASSISTANCE (Agenda item 72b)
Sánchez García, Nathalia - A/78/PV.46
PEACEBUILDING (Agenda item 61)
Zalabata Torres, Leonor - A/78/PV.100
PERSONS WITH DISABILITIES—HUMAN RIGHTS (Agenda item 71a)
Sánchez García, Nathalia - A/C.3/78/SR.51
RACIAL DISCRIMINATION—ELIMINATION (Agenda item 69a)
Orduz Durán, Jessica Beatriz - A/C.3/78/SR.42
Zalabata Torres, Leonor - A/78/PV.103; A/C.3/78/SR.41
RACIAL DISCRIMINATION—PROGRAMMES OF ACTION (Agenda item 69b)
Orduz Durán, Jessica Beatriz - A/C.3/78/SR.42
Zalabata Torres, Leonor - A/C.3/78/SR.41
RELIGIOUS INTOLERANCE (Agenda item 71b)
Orduz Durán, Jessica Beatriz - A/C.3/78/SR.38
RESPONSIBILITY OF INTERNATIONAL ORGANIZATIONS (Agenda item 85)
Botero, Stephanie - A/C.6/78/SR.19
RIGHT OF ASSEMBLY (Agenda item 71b)
Tickner, Arlene Beth - A/C.3/78/SR.19
RIGHT TO THE TRUTH (Agenda item 71b)
Paredes Campaña, Jairo Andrés - A/C.3/78/SR.22

Colombia (continued)

RIGHTS OF THE CHILD (Agenda item 67)
Orduz Durán, Jessica Beatriz - A/C.3/78/SR.11
Zalabata Torres, Leonor - A/C.3/78/SR.12
RULE OF LAW (Agenda item 83)
Solano Ramírez, Lucía Teresa - A/C.6/78/SR.16
RURAL WOMEN (Agenda item 25a)
Sánchez García, Nathalia - A/C.3/78/SR.7; A/C.3/78/SR.49
SCIENCE AND TECHNOLOGY—DEVELOPMENT (Agenda item 19a)
Ríos Serna, Manuela - A/C.2/78/SR.10
SMALL ARMS—ILLICIT TRAFFIC (Agenda item 99p)
Quintero Correa, Nohra María - A/C.1/78/PV.18; A/C.1/78/PV.28
SMALL ARMS—ILLICIT TRAFFIC—ASSISTANCE (Agenda item 99n)
Quintero Correa, Nohra María - A/C.1/78/PV.18
SMALL ISLAND DEVELOPING STATES—PROGRAMMES OF ACTION (Agenda item 18b)
Murillo Ferrer, Jorge Adrián - A/C.2/78/SR.22
Zalabata Torres, Leonor - A/78/PV.103
SOCIAL DEVELOPMENT (Agenda item 24)
Zalabata Torres, Leonor - A/C.3/78/SR.2
SPECIAL POLITICAL MISSIONS (Agenda item 52)
Zalabata Torres, Leonor - A/C.4/78/SR.21
SUMMARY EXECUTIONS (Agenda item 71b)
Sánchez García, Nathalia - A/C.3/78/SR.31
SUSTAINABLE DEVELOPMENT (Agenda item 18)
Ríos Serna, Manuela - A/C.2/78/SR.12; A/C.2/78/SR.22; A/C.2/78/SR.24
Tickner, Arlene Beth - A/C.2/78/SR.14
SUSTAINABLE ENERGY (Agenda item 18h)
Ríos Serna, Manuela - A/C.2/78/SR.23
TAXATION (Agenda item 16h)
Murillo Ferrer, Jorge Adrián - A/C.2/78/SR.25
Tickner, Arlene Beth - A/C.2/78/SR.8
TREATIES (Agenda item 87)
Botero, Stephanie - A/C.6/78/SR.20
UN—BUDGET (2024) (Agenda item 134)
Zalabata Torres, Leonor - A/C.5/78/SR.4; A/C.5/78/SR.18
UN—PROGRAMME PLANNING (Agenda item 135)
Quintero Correa, Nohra María - A/C.1/78/PV.10
UN. GENERAL ASSEMBLY—WORK PROGRAMME (Agenda item 120)
Quintero Correa, Nohra María - A/C.1/78/PV.10
UN. GENERAL ASSEMBLY (78TH SESS. : 2023-2024). 1ST COMMITTEE—GENERAL DEBATE (Agenda item 8)
Zalabata Torres, Leonor - A/C.1/78/PV.7
UN. GENERAL ASSEMBLY (78TH SESS. : 2023-2024). 1ST COMMITTEE—WORK ORGANIZATION (Agenda item 7)
Quintero Correa, Nohra María - A/C.1/78/PV.28; A/C.1/78/PV.30

Colombia (continued)

UN. GENERAL ASSEMBLY (78TH SESS. : 2023-2024). 2ND COMMITTEE—GENERAL DEBATE (Agenda item 8)
Zalabata Torres, Leonor - A/C.2/78/SR.3
UN. HUMAN RIGHTS COUNCIL—REPORTS (Agenda item 66)
Sánchez García, Nathalia - A/78/PV.28
UN. INTERNATIONAL COURT OF JUSTICE—REPORTS (Agenda item 73)
Solano Ramírez, Lucía Teresa - A/C.6/78/SR.26
UN. INTERNATIONAL LAW COMMISSION—REPORTS (Agenda item 79)
Solano Ramírez, Lucía Teresa - A/C.6/78/SR.27; A/C.6/78/SR.30; A/C.6/78/SR.33
UN. PEACEBUILDING COMMISSION—REPORTS (Agenda item 27)
Zalabata Torres, Leonor - A/78/PV.100
UN. PEACEBUILDING FUND—REPORTS (Agenda item 111)
Zalabata Torres, Leonor - A/78/PV.100
UN. SECURITY COUNCIL—MEMBERSHIP (Agenda item 121)
Zalabata Torres, Leonor - A/78/PV.34
UN. SECURITY COUNCIL—REPORTS (Agenda item 26)
Zalabata Torres, Leonor - A/78/PV.93
UN CONFERENCES (Agenda item 13)
Zalabata Torres, Leonor - A/78/PV.15
UN HIGH COMMISSIONER FOR REFUGEES—REPORTS (Agenda item 60)
Sánchez García, Nathalia - A/C.3/78/SR.44
UNRWA—ACTIVITIES (Agenda item 49)
Zalabata Torres, Leonor - A/C.4/78/SR.23
VETO (Agenda item 63)
Taylor Jay, Elizabeth - A/78/PV.74
Zalabata Torres, Leonor - A/78/PV.61; A/78/PV.67; A/78/PV.68; A/78/PV.71; A/78/PV.79
WOMEN MIGRANT WORKERS (Agenda item 25a)
Sánchez García, Nathalia - A/C.3/78/SR.7; A/C.3/78/SR.49
WOMEN'S ADVANCEMENT (Agenda item 25a)
Sánchez García, Nathalia - A/C.3/78/SR.7
Zalabata Torres, Leonor - A/C.3/78/SR.8
WOMEN'S ADVANCEMENT—CONFERENCES (Agenda item 25b)
Sánchez García, Nathalia - A/C.3/78/SR.7
Zalabata Torres, Leonor - A/C.3/78/SR.8
YOUTH (Agenda item 24b)
Méndez Bocanegra, Rodrigo Andrés - A/C.3/78/SR.55

Colombia. President

UN. GENERAL ASSEMBLY (78TH SESS. : 2023-2024)—GENERAL DEBATE (Agenda item 8)
Petro Urrego, Gustavo - A/78/PV.4

Colombia. President (continued)

UN. GENERAL ASSEMBLY (78TH SESS. : 2023-2024)—SPECIAL STATEMENTS
Petro Urrego, Gustavo - A/78/PV.4

Colombia. Vice-President

RACIAL DISCRIMINATION—ELIMINATION (Agenda item 69a)
Márquez Mina, Francia - A/78/PV.103
UN. GENERAL ASSEMBLY (78TH SESS. : 2023-2024)—SPECIAL STATEMENTS
Márquez Mina, Francia - A/78/PV.103

Columbia University (New York)

COMMODITIES (Agenda item 16d)
Stiglitz, Joseph E. - A/C.2/78/SR.14
SUSTAINABLE DEVELOPMENT (Agenda item 18)
Stiglitz, Joseph E. - A/C.2/78/SR.14

Common Fund for Commodities

COMMODITIES (Agenda item 16d)
Belal, Mohammed - A/C.2/78/SR.14
SUSTAINABLE DEVELOPMENT (Agenda item 18)
Belal, Mohammed - A/C.2/78/SR.14

Community of Latin American and Caribbean States

DECOLONIZATION (Agenda item 58)
King, Inga Rhonda (Saint Vincent and the Grenadines) - A/C.4/78/SR.7
DISARMAMENT—GENERAL AND COMPLETE (Agenda item 99)
Flores, Mary Elizabeth (Honduras) - A/78/PV.105
DISASTER VICTIMS (Agenda item 86)
Mark, Hayley-Ann (Saint Vincent and the Grenadines) - A/C.6/78/SR.5
FALKLAND ISLANDS (MALVINAS) QUESTION (Agenda item 42)
King, Inga Rhonda (Saint Vincent and the Grenadines) - A/C.4/78/SR.7
INTERNATIONAL JURISDICTION (Agenda item 84)
Mark, Hayley-Ann (Saint Vincent and the Grenadines) - A/C.6/78/SR.12
INTERNATIONAL LAW—TRAINING PROGRAMMES (Agenda item 78)
Mark, Hayley-Ann (Saint Vincent and the Grenadines) - A/C.6/78/SR.21
NON-SELF-GOVERNING TERRITORIES—REPORTS (Agenda item 54)
King, Inga Rhonda (Saint Vincent and the Grenadines) - A/C.4/78/SR.7
PEACEKEEPING OPERATIONS—CRIMINAL LIABILITY (Agenda item 76)
Mark, Hayley-Ann (Saint Vincent and the Grenadines) - A/C.6/78/SR.8

Community of Latin American and Caribbean States (continued)

TERRORISM (Agenda item 109)
Mark, Hayley-Ann (Saint Vincent and the Grenadines) - A/C.6/78/SR.2
TREATIES (Agenda item 87)
Mark, Hayley-Ann (Saint Vincent and the Grenadines) - A/C.6/78/SR.20
TURKS AND CAICOS ISLANDS QUESTION (Agenda item 58)
King, Inga Rhonda (Saint Vincent and the Grenadines) - A/C.4/78/SR.7
UN. GENERAL ASSEMBLY (78TH SESS. : 2023-2024). 1ST COMMITTEE—GENERAL DEBATE (Agenda item 8)
Miguel, Nedra P. (Saint Vincent and the Grenadines) - A/C.1/78/PV.3
UN CHARTER—REPORTS (Agenda item 82)
Dunbar, Ed (Saint Vincent and the Grenadines) - A/C.6/78/SR.22
WESTERN SAHARA QUESTION (Agenda item 58)
King, Inga Rhonda (Saint Vincent and the Grenadines) - A/C.4/78/SR.7

Comoros

DECOLONIZATION (Agenda item 58)
Oussein, Kadim - A/C.4/78/SR.9
NUCLEAR DISARMAMENT (Agenda item 99b)
Oussein, Kadim - A/C.1/78/PV.13
NUCLEAR WEAPONS—TREATIES (Agenda item 99ff)
Oussein, Kadim - A/C.1/78/PV.13
WESTERN SAHARA QUESTION (Agenda item 58)
Oussein, Kadim - A/C.4/78/SR.9

Comoros. President

UN. GENERAL ASSEMBLY (78TH SESS. : 2023-2024)—GENERAL DEBATE (Agenda item 8)
Assoumani, Azali - A/78/PV.7
UN. GENERAL ASSEMBLY (78TH SESS. : 2023-2024)—SPECIAL STATEMENTS
Assoumani, Azali - A/78/PV.7

Comunidade dos Países de Língua Portuguesa

CRIMES AGAINST HUMANITY (Agenda item 80)
Soares, Dionísio Da Costa Babo (Timor-Leste) - A/C.6/78/SR.45
HUMAN RIGHTS (Agenda item 71)
Cruz, Francisco José da (Angola) - A/C.3/78/SR.24

Comunidade dos Países de Língua Portuguesa (continued)

HUMAN RIGHTS—INTERNATIONAL INSTRUMENTS (Agenda item 71a)
Cruz, Francisco José da (Angola) - A/C.3/78/SR.24
INFORMATION (Agenda item 53)
Cruz, Francisco José da (Angola) - A/C.4/78/SR.12
MULTILINGUALISM (Agenda item 124)
Romualdo, Tania Serafim Yvonne (Cabo Verde) - A/78/PV.107
UN. INTERNATIONAL COURT OF JUSTICE—REPORTS (Agenda item 73)
Cruz, Francisco José da (Angola) - A/78/PV.27

Congo

CUBA—UNITED STATES (Agenda item 38)
Gabi, Emery - A/78/PV.26
DECOLONIZATION (Agenda item 58)
Manzeri Ngondo, Jean Claude - A/C.4/78/SR.7
ECONOMIC COOPERATION AMONG DEVELOPING COUNTRIES (Agenda item 22b)
Gabi, Emery - A/C.2/78/SR.18
HUMAN RIGHTS INSTITUTIONS—CENTRAL AFRICA (Agenda item 71b)
Ahoue Itoua Lekegny, Patience - A/C.3/78/SR.56
INFORMATION (Agenda item 53)
Manzeri Ngondo, Jean Claude - A/C.4/78/SR.13
PEACEKEEPING OPERATIONS—CRIMINAL LIABILITY (Agenda item 76)
Douckaga Nzengui, Nicaise Servais - A/C.6/78/SR.9
POVERTY—INTERNATIONAL DECADES (Agenda item 21a)
Gabi, Emery - A/C.2/78/SR.17
RIGHTS OF THE CHILD (Agenda item 67)
Ahoue Itoua Lekegny, Patience - A/C.3/78/SR.13
RULE OF LAW (Agenda item 83)
Douckaga Nzengui, Nicaise Servais - A/C.6/78/SR.19
RURAL POVERTY (Agenda item 21b)
Gabi, Emery - A/C.2/78/SR.17
TERRORISM (Agenda item 109)
Makayat-Safouesse, Lazare - A/C.6/78/SR.4
UN. GENERAL ASSEMBLY (78TH SESS. : 2023-2024). 1ST COMMITTEE—GENERAL DEBATE (Agenda item 8)
Douckaga Nzengui, Nicaise Servais - A/C.1/78/PV.7
UN. GENERAL ASSEMBLY (78TH SESS. : 2023-2024). 2ND COMMITTEE—GENERAL DEBATE (Agenda item 8)
Makayat-Safouesse, Lazare - A/C.2/78/SR.4
WOMEN'S ADVANCEMENT (Agenda item 25a)
Pulchérie, Mayel Camille Asnayde - A/C.3/78/SR.9
WOMEN'S ADVANCEMENT—CONFERENCES (Agenda item 25b)
Pulchérie, Mayel Camille Asnayde - A/C.3/78/SR.9

Congo. President

UN. GENERAL ASSEMBLY (78TH SESS. : 2023-2024)—GENERAL DEBATE (Agenda item 8)
Sassou N'Guesso, Denis - A/78/PV.8
UN. GENERAL ASSEMBLY (78TH SESS. : 2023-2024)—SPECIAL STATEMENTS
Sassou N'Guesso, Denis - A/78/PV.8

Coordinating Bureau of the Non-Aligned Countries

ARMS RACE—OUTER SPACE (Agenda item 97a)
Sirie, Mochammad Iqbal (Indonesia) - A/C.1/78/PV.16
ARMS TRANSFERS—TREATIES (Agenda item 99x)
Kristanti, Maria Benedicta Diah (Indonesia) - A/C.1/78/PV.17
BIOLOGICAL WEAPONS—TREATIES (Agenda item 106)
Aron, Andy (Indonesia) - A/C.1/78/PV.14
CHEMICAL WEAPONS—TREATIES (Agenda item 99l)
Aron, Andy (Indonesia) - A/C.1/78/PV.14
CONVENTIONAL WEAPONS (Agenda item 99u)
Kristanti, Maria Benedicta Diah (Indonesia) - A/C.1/78/PV.17
CONVENTIONAL WEAPONS—TREATIES (Agenda item 103)
Kristanti, Maria Benedicta Diah (Indonesia) - A/C.1/78/PV.17
CUBA—UNITED STATES (Agenda item 38)
Aliyev, Yashar T. (Azerbaijan) - A/78/PV.24
DEMOCRACY (Agenda item 71b)
Novruz, Leyla (Azerbaijan) - A/C.3/78/SR.28
DISARMAMENT—GENERAL AND COMPLETE (Agenda item 99)
Kristanti, Maria Benedicta Diah (Indonesia) - A/C.1/78/PV.17
DISARMAMENT—UN. GENERAL ASSEMBLY (4TH SPECIAL SESS. ON DISARMAMENT : xxxx) (Agenda item 99h)
Sirie, Mochammad Iqbal (Indonesia) - A/C.1/78/PV.22
DISARMAMENT AGREEMENTS—ENVIRONMENT (Agenda item 99j)
Sirie, Mochammad Iqbal (Indonesia) - A/C.1/78/PV.20
DISARMAMENT-DEVELOPMENT LINK (Agenda item 99d)
Sirie, Mochammad Iqbal (Indonesia) - A/C.1/78/PV.20
ECONOMIC SANCTIONS—INTERNATIONAL RELATIONS (Agenda item 28)
Kwoba, Godfrey (Uganda) - A/78/PV.89
HUMAN RIGHTS—INTERNATIONAL INSTRUMENTS (Agenda item 71a)
Novruz, Leyla (Azerbaijan) - A/C.3/78/SR.33

Coordinating Bureau of the Non-Aligned Countries (continued)

HUMAN RIGHTS—REPORTS (Agenda item 71c)
Novruz, Leyla (Azerbaijan) - A/C.3/78/SR.53
HUMAN RIGHTS—TERRITORIES OCCUPIED BY ISRAEL (Agenda item 71c)
Novruz, Leyla (Azerbaijan) - A/C.3/78/SR.35
HUMAN RIGHTS ADVANCEMENT (Agenda item 71b)
González Behmaras, Alejandro (Cuba) - A/C.3/78/SR.48
INDIAN OCEAN—ZONES OF PEACE (Agenda item 91)
Sirie, Mochammad Iqbal (Indonesia) - A/C.1/78/PV.21
INFORMATION—INTERNATIONAL SECURITY (Agenda item 94)
Sirie, Mochammad Iqbal (Indonesia) - A/C.1/78/PV.20
INTERNATIONAL JURISDICTION (Agenda item 84)
Heidari, Bahram (Iran (Islamic Republic of)) - A/C.6/78/SR.12
INTERNATIONAL LAW—TRAINING PROGRAMMES (Agenda item 78)
Heidari, Bahram (Iran (Islamic Republic of)) - A/C.6/78/SR.21
LANDMINES—TREATIES (Agenda item 99m)
Kristanti, Maria Benedicta Diah (Indonesia) - A/C.1/78/PV.17
MIDDLE EAST—NUCLEAR-WEAPON-FREE ZONES (Agenda item 95)
Dhanutirto, Mariska Dwianti (Indonesia) - A/C.1/78/PV.11
Sirie, Mochammad Iqbal (Indonesia) - A/C.1/78/PV.21
MULTILATERALISM—DISARMAMENT (Agenda item 99r)
Sirie, Mochammad Iqbal (Indonesia) - A/C.1/78/PV.20
NUCLEAR DISARMAMENT (Agenda item 99b)
Dhanutirto, Mariska Dwianti (Indonesia) - A/C.1/78/PV.11
NUCLEAR DISARMAMENT—CONFERENCES (Agenda item 99aa)
Dhanutirto, Mariska Dwianti (Indonesia) - A/C.1/78/PV.11
NUCLEAR NON-PROLIFERATION—INTERNATIONAL OBLIGATIONS (Agenda item 99w)
Dhanutirto, Mariska Dwianti (Indonesia) - A/C.1/78/PV.11
NUCLEAR WEAPONS—TREATIES (Agenda item 99ff)
Dhanutirto, Mariska Dwianti (Indonesia) - A/C.1/78/PV.11
OUTER SPACE—CONFIDENCE-BUILDING MEASURES (Agenda item 99v)
Sirie, Mochammad Iqbal (Indonesia) - A/C.1/78/PV.16

Coordinating Bureau of the Non-Aligned Countries (continued)

PEACE—REGIONAL CENTRES (Agenda item 100f)
Sirie, Mochammad Iqbal (Indonesia) - A/C.1/78/PV.22
PEACEKEEPING OPERATIONS (Agenda item 51)
El Ouazzani, Mouna Chahdi (Morocco) - A/C.4/78/SR.18
PEACEKEEPING OPERATIONS—CRIMINAL LIABILITY (Agenda item 76)
Aref, Yahya (Iran (Islamic Republic of)) - A/C.6/78/SR.8
RACIAL DISCRIMINATION—ELIMINATION (Agenda item 69a)
Novruz, Leyla (Azerbaijan) - A/C.3/78/SR.41
RACIAL DISCRIMINATION—PROGRAMMES OF ACTION (Agenda item 69b)
Novruz, Leyla (Azerbaijan) - A/C.3/78/SR.41
RAISI, SEYYED EBRAHIM (IRAN (ISLAMIC REPUBLID OF). PRESIDENT)—TRIBUTES
Kwoba, Godfrey (Uganda) - A/78/PV.83
RIGHT TO DEVELOPMENT (Agenda item 71b)
González Behmaras, Alejandro (Cuba) - A/C.3/78/SR.48
Novruz, Leyla (Azerbaijan) - A/C.3/78/SR.20
RIGHT TO FOOD (Agenda item 71b)
Novruz, Leyla (Azerbaijan) - A/C.3/78/SR.30
RULE OF LAW (Agenda item 83)
Heidari, Bahram (Iran (Islamic Republic of)) - A/C.6/78/SR.15
SANCTIONS—INTERNATIONAL RELATIONS (Agenda item 71b)
González Behmaras, Alejandro (Cuba) - A/C.3/78/SR.48
Novruz, Leyla (Azerbaijan) - A/C.3/78/SR.28
SMALL ARMS—ILLICIT TRAFFIC (Agenda item 99p)
Kristanti, Maria Benedicta Diah (Indonesia) - A/C.1/78/PV.17
SMALL ARMS—ILLICIT TRAFFIC—ASSISTANCE (Agenda item 99n)
Kristanti, Maria Benedicta Diah (Indonesia) - A/C.1/78/PV.17
SOLIDARITY (Agenda item 71b)
Novruz, Leyla (Azerbaijan) - A/C.3/78/SR.32
SPECIAL POLITICAL MISSIONS (Agenda item 52)
El Ouazzani, Mouna Chahdi (Morocco) - A/C.4/78/SR.21
TERRORISM (Agenda item 109)
Ershadi, Zahra (Iran (Islamic Republic of)) - A/C.6/78/SR.1
UN. COMMITTEE ON RELATIONS WITH THE HOST COUNTRY—REPORTS (Agenda item 161)
Aref, Yahya (Iran (Islamic Republic of)) - A/C.6/78/SR.35

Coordinating Bureau of the Non-Aligned Countries (continued)

UN. DISARMAMENT COMMISSION—REPORTS (Agenda item 101b)
Sirie, Mochammad Iqbal (Indonesia) - A/C.1/78/PV.22
UN. GENERAL ASSEMBLY—WORK PROGRAMME (Agenda item 120)
Bendjama, Amar (Algeria) - A/78/PV.32
UN. GENERAL ASSEMBLY (78TH SESS. : 2023-2024). 1ST COMMITTEE—GENERAL DEBATE (Agenda item 8)
Nasir, Armanatha Christiawan (Indonesia) - A/C.1/78/PV.2
UN. INTERNATIONAL COURT OF JUSTICE—REPORTS (Agenda item 73)
Musayev, Tofig (Azerbaijan) - A/78/PV.27
UN CHARTER—REPORTS (Agenda item 82)
Ershadi, Zahra (Iran (Islamic Republic of)) - A/C.6/78/SR.22
UN RESOLUTIONS—IMPLEMENTATION (Agenda item 119)
Bendjama, Amar (Algeria) - A/78/PV.32
UNRWA—ACTIVITIES (Agenda item 49)
Alizada, Kamal (Azerbaijan) - A/C.4/78/SR.23
VETO (Agenda item 63)
Kwoba, Godfrey (Uganda) - A/78/PV.74
WEAPONS—OUTER SPACE (Agenda item 97b)
Sirie, Mochammad Iqbal (Indonesia) - A/C.1/78/PV.16
WEAPONS OF MASS DESTRUCTION—TERRORISM (Agenda item 99s)
Aron, Andy (Indonesia) - A/C.1/78/PV.14

Coordinating Committee for International Staff Unions and Associations of the United Nations System

PERSONNEL QUESTIONS—UN SYSTEM (Agenda item 142)
Meynet, Nathalie - A/C.5/78/SR.10

Corporación Líderes Unidos para Servir (Organization)

WESTERN SAHARA QUESTION (Agenda item 58)
Teatin Rosas, Alfa Maritza - A/C.4/78/SR.4

Costa Rica

AGEING PERSONS (Agenda item 24b)
Chan Valverde, Maritza - A/C.3/78/SR.3
ARMED CONFLICTS PREVENTION (Agenda item 31a)
Chan Valverde, Maritza - A/78/PV.72
ARMS RACE—OUTER SPACE (Agenda item 97a)
Chan Valverde, Maritza - A/C.1/78/PV.16
BIOLOGICAL DIVERSITY—TREATIES (Agenda item 18f)
Chan Valverde, Maritza - A/C.2/78/SR.13

Costa Rica (continued)

CLIMATE (Agenda item 18d)
Chan Valverde, Maritza - A/C.2/78/SR.13
Zamora Zumbado, Leticia María - A/C.2/78/SR.25
CLIMATE CHANGE (Agenda item 71b)
Zavala Porras, Daniel Andrés - A/C.3/78/SR.29
COMMODITIES (Agenda item 16d)
Pizarro-Viales, Laura Raquel - A/C.2/78/SR.14
CONVENTIONAL WEAPONS (Agenda item 99u)
Chan Valverde, Maritza - A/C.1/78/PV.18
CRIME PREVENTION (Agenda item 107)
Zavala Porras, Daniel Andrés - A/C.3/78/SR.6
CRIMES AGAINST HUMANITY (Agenda item 80)
Chan Valverde, Maritza - A/C.6/78/SR.10
CYBERCRIME (Agenda item 108)
Zavala Porras, Daniel Andrés - A/C.3/78/SR.6
DECOLONIZATION (Agenda item 58)
Chan Valverde, Maritza - A/C.4/78/SR.7
DEVELOPMENT COOPERATION—MIDDLE-INCOME COUNTRIES (Agenda item 19c)
Zamora Zumbado, Leticia María - A/C.2/78/SR.11
DEVELOPMENT FINANCE (Agenda item 16b)
Zamora Zumbado, Leticia María - A/C.2/78/SR.9
DISARMAMENT—GENERAL AND COMPLETE (Agenda item 99)
Chan Valverde, Maritza - A/C.1/78/PV.18
DISARMAMENT AGREEMENTS—OUTER SPACE (Agenda item 97c)
Ávila Becerril, Ana Maricela - A/C.1/78/PV.27
Chan Valverde, Maritza - A/C.1/78/PV.16
DISASTER PREVENTION (Agenda item 18c)
Chan Valverde, Maritza - A/C.2/78/SR.13
ELECTION VERIFICATION—UN (Agenda item 71b)
Pizarro-Viales, Laura Raquel - A/C.3/78/SR.50
ENVIRONMENT (Agenda item 71b)
Chan Valverde, Maritza - A/C.3/78/SR.26
Zavala Porras, Daniel Andrés - A/C.3/78/SR.29
EXTERNAL DEBT (Agenda item 16c)
Zamora Zumbado, Leticia María - A/C.2/78/SR.9
FALKLAND ISLANDS (MALVINAS) QUESTION (Agenda item 42)
Chan Valverde, Maritza - A/C.4/78/SR.7
FOOD SECURITY (Agenda item 23a)
Chan Valverde, Maritza - A/C.2/78/SR.17
HUMAN RIGHTS—INTERNATIONAL INSTRUMENTS (Agenda item 71a)
Chan Valverde, Maritza - A/C.3/78/SR.26
IAEA—REPORTS (Agenda item 89)
Chan Valverde, Maritza - A/78/PV.29
INFORMATION (Agenda item 53)
Chan Valverde, Maritza - A/C.4/78/SR.13
INFORMATION—INTERNATIONAL SECURITY (Agenda item 94)
Ávila Becerril, Ana Maricela - A/C.1/78/PV.21

Costa Rica (continued)

INFORMATION TECHNOLOGY—DEVELOPMENT (Agenda item 15)
Zamora Zumbado, Leticia María - A/C.2/78/SR.11
INTERNATIONAL CRIMINAL COURT—REPORTS (Agenda item 74)
Chan Valverde, Maritza - A/78/PV.21
INTERNATIONAL JURISDICTION (Agenda item 84)
Ramírez Baca, Gustavo Adolfo - A/C.6/78/SR.12
LAW OF THE SEA (Agenda item 75a)
Chan Valverde, Maritza - A/78/PV.44
MARINE ECOSYSTEMS—BIOLOGICAL DIVERSITY (Agenda item 75c)
Chan Valverde, Maritza - A/78/PV.44
MIGRANTS—PROTECTION (Agenda item 71b)
Chan Valverde, Maritza - A/C.3/78/SR.26
MILLENNIUM SUMMIT—CONFERENCES (Agenda item 117)
Chan Valverde, Maritza - A/78/PV.102
NUCLEAR DISARMAMENT (Agenda item 99b)
Chan Valverde, Maritza - A/C.1/78/PV.13
NUCLEAR NON-PROLIFERATION—INTERNATIONAL OBLIGATIONS (Agenda item 99w)
Chan Valverde, Maritza - A/C.1/78/PV.13
NUCLEAR WEAPONS—ELIMINATION (Agenda item 99z)
Ávila Becerril, Ana Maricela - A/C.1/78/PV.26
NUCLEAR WEAPONS—TREATIES (Agenda item 99ff)
Chan Valverde, Maritza - A/C.1/78/PV.13
OUTER SPACE—CONFIDENCE-BUILDING MEASURES (Agenda item 99v)
Chan Valverde, Maritza - A/C.1/78/PV.16
OUTER SPACE—PEACEFUL USES—INTERNATIONAL COOPERATION (Agenda item 48)
Chan Valverde, Maritza - A/C.4/78/SR.16
OUTER SPACE—PRINCIPLES (Agenda item 97d)
Ávila Becerril, Ana Maricela - A/C.1/78/PV.27
Chan Valverde, Maritza - A/C.1/78/PV.16
POVERTY—INTERNATIONAL DECADES (Agenda item 21a)
Chan Valverde, Maritza - A/C.2/78/SR.17
RACIAL DISCRIMINATION—ELIMINATION (Agenda item 69a)
Chan Valverde, Maritza - A/C.3/78/SR.42
RACIAL DISCRIMINATION—PROGRAMMES OF ACTION (Agenda item 69b)
Chan Valverde, Maritza - A/C.3/78/SR.42
RESPONSIBILITY TO PROTECT (Agenda item 129)
Chan Valverde, Maritza - A/78/PV.96
RIGHT TO DEVELOPMENT (Agenda item 71b)
Pizarro-Viales, Laura Raquel - A/C.3/78/SR.48
RIGHTS OF THE CHILD (Agenda item 67)
Zavala Porras, Daniel Andrés - A/C.3/78/SR.14

Costa Rica (continued)

RULE OF LAW (Agenda item 83)
Chan Valverde, Maritza - A/C.6/78/SR.16
RURAL POVERTY (Agenda item 21b)
Chan Valverde, Maritza - A/C.2/78/SR.17
SCIENCE AND TECHNOLOGY—DEVELOPMENT (Agenda item 19a)
Zamora Zumbado, Leticia María - A/C.2/78/SR.11
SMALL ARMS—ILLICIT TRAFFIC (Agenda item 99p)
Chan Valverde, Maritza - A/C.1/78/PV.18
SMALL ARMS—ILLICIT TRAFFIC—ASSISTANCE (Agenda item 99n)
Chan Valverde, Maritza - A/C.1/78/PV.18
SOCIAL CONDITIONS (Agenda item 24b)
Chan Valverde, Maritza - A/C.3/78/SR.3
SOCIAL DEVELOPMENT (Agenda item 24)
Chan Valverde, Maritza - A/C.3/78/SR.3
SOCIAL DEVELOPMENT—CONFERENCES (Agenda item 24a)
Chan Valverde, Maritza - A/C.3/78/SR.3
STRADDLING FISH STOCKS (Agenda item 75b)
Chan Valverde, Maritza - A/78/PV.44
SUSTAINABLE DEVELOPMENT (Agenda item 18)
Pizarro-Viales, Laura Raquel - A/C.2/78/SR.14
TERRORISM (Agenda item 109)
Ramírez Baca, Gustavo Adolfo - A/C.6/78/SR.2
UKRAINE—POLITICAL CONDITIONS (Agenda item 62)
Chan Valverde, Maritza - A/78/PV.57
UN—BUDGET (2024) (Agenda item 134)
Chan Valverde, Maritza - A/C.5/78/SR.5
Videche Guevara, Carlos Manuel - A/C.5/78/SR.23
UN—PROGRAMME PLANNING (Agenda item 135)
Chan Valverde, Maritza - A/C.1/78/PV.10; A/C.5/78/SR.5
UN. GENERAL ASSEMBLY—WORK PROGRAMME (Agenda item 120)
Chan Valverde, Maritza - A/78/PV.32; A/C.1/78/PV.10; A/C.6/78/SR.36
UN. GENERAL ASSEMBLY (78TH SESS. : 2023-2024)—GENERAL DEBATE (Agenda item 8)
André Tinoco, Arnoldo - A/78/PV.11
UN. GENERAL ASSEMBLY (78TH SESS. : 2023-2024)—OFFICERS (Agenda item 5)
Chan Valverde, Maritza - A/C.1/78/PV.31
UN. GENERAL ASSEMBLY (78TH SESS. : 2023-2024). 1ST COMMITTEE—GENERAL DEBATE (Agenda item 8)
Chan Valverde, Maritza - A/C.1/78/PV.8
UN. GENERAL ASSEMBLY (78TH SESS. : 2023-2024). 2ND COMMITTEE—GENERAL DEBATE (Agenda item 8)
Zamora Zumbado, Leticia María - A/C.2/78/SR.2; A/C.2/78/SR.5

Costa Rica (continued)

UN. GENERAL ASSEMBLY (78TH SESS. : 2023-2024). 5TH COMMITTEE—WORK ORGANIZATION (Agenda item 7)
Videche Guevara, Carlos Manuel - A/C.5/78/SR.27
UN. HUMAN RIGHTS COMMITTEE—REPORTS (Agenda item 71a)
Zavala Porras, Daniel Andrés - A/C.3/78/SR.17
UN. HUMAN RIGHTS COUNCIL—REPORTS (Agenda item 66)
Chan Valverde, Maritza - A/78/PV.23
Zavala Porras, Daniel Andrés - A/C.3/78/SR.46
UN. INTERNATIONAL COURT OF JUSTICE—REPORTS (Agenda item 73)
Chan Valverde, Maritza - A/78/PV.27
UN. SECRETARY-GENERAL—REPORTS (Agenda item 110)
Chan Valverde, Maritza - A/78/PV.54
UN. SECURITY COUNCIL—MEMBERSHIP (Agenda item 121)
Chan Valverde, Maritza - A/78/PV.34
UN. SECURITY COUNCIL—REPORTS (Agenda item 26)
Videche Guevara, Carlos Manuel - A/78/PV.94
UN CONFERENCES (Agenda item 13)
Chan Valverde, Maritza - A/78/PV.102
UN RESOLUTIONS—IMPLEMENTATION (Agenda item 119)
Chan Valverde, Maritza - A/78/PV.32
VETO (Agenda item 63)
Chan Valverde, Maritza - A/78/PV.3; A/78/PV.66; A/78/PV.70; A/78/PV.74; A/78/PV.78
Videche Guevara, Carlos Manuel - A/78/PV.59; A/78/PV.68
WEAPONS—OUTER SPACE (Agenda item 97b)
Ávila Becerril, Ana Maricela - A/C.1/78/PV.27
WESTERN SAHARA QUESTION (Agenda item 58)
Chan Valverde, Maritza - A/C.4/78/SR.7
WOMEN'S ADVANCEMENT (Agenda item 25a)
Zavala Porras, Daniel Andrés - A/C.3/78/SR.7; A/C.3/78/SR.10
WOMEN'S ADVANCEMENT—CONFERENCES (Agenda item 25b)
Zavala Porras, Daniel Andrés - A/C.3/78/SR.7; A/C.3/78/SR.10
YOUTH (Agenda item 24b)
Zavala Porras, Daniel Andrés - A/C.3/78/SR.55

Côte d'Ivoire

ARMS TRANSFERS—TREATIES (Agenda item 99x)
Moriko, Tiémoko - A/C.1/78/PV.18
CLIMATE (Agenda item 18d)
Moriko, Tiémoko - A/C.2/78/SR.15
CONVENTIONAL WEAPONS (Agenda item 99u)
Moriko, Tiémoko - A/C.1/78/PV.18

Côte d'Ivoire (continued)

CONVENTIONAL WEAPONS—TREATIES (Agenda item 103)
Moriko, Tiémoko - A/C.1/78/PV.18
DECOLONIZATION (Agenda item 58)
Moriko, Tiémoko - A/C.4/78/SR.2
DESERTIFICATION—TREATIES (Agenda item 18e)
Moriko, Tiémoko - A/C.2/78/SR.15
DEVELOPMENT FINANCE (Agenda item 16b)
Ipo, Gbolié Desiré Wulfran - A/C.2/78/SR.9
HUMAN RIGHTS—INTERNATIONAL INSTRUMENTS (Agenda item 71a)
Moriko, Tiémoko - A/C.3/78/SR.26
HUMAN RIGHTS ACTIVISTS (Agenda item 71b)
Kouakou, Kouadjo Michel - A/C.3/78/SR.19
INFORMATION (Agenda item 53)
Ipo, Gbolié Desiré Wulfran - A/C.4/78/SR.13
INFORMATION—INTERNATIONAL SECURITY (Agenda item 94)
Moriko, Tiémoko - A/C.1/78/PV.20
INTERNATIONAL JURISDICTION (Agenda item 84)
Moriko, Tiémoko - A/C.6/78/SR.13
MACROECONOMIC POLICY (Agenda item 16)
Ipo, Gbolié Desiré Wulfran - A/C.2/78/SR.9
NATIONAL INSTITUTIONS—HUMAN RIGHTS (Agenda item 71b)
Moriko, Tiémoko - A/C.3/78/SR.26
NUCLEAR DISARMAMENT (Agenda item 99b)
Moriko, Tiémoko - A/C.1/78/PV.12
NUCLEAR NON-PROLIFERATION—INTERNATIONAL OBLIGATIONS (Agenda item 99w)
Moriko, Tiémoko - A/C.1/78/PV.12
NUCLEAR WEAPON TESTS—TREATIES (Agenda item 105)
Moriko, Tiémoko - A/C.1/78/PV.12
NUCLEAR WEAPONS—HUMANITARIAN CONSEQUENCES (Agenda item 99bb)
Moriko, Tiémoko - A/C.1/78/PV.12
NUCLEAR WEAPONS—TREATIES (Agenda item 99ff)
Moriko, Tiémoko - A/C.1/78/PV.12
PEACEKEEPING OPERATIONS (Agenda item 51)
Moriko, Tiémoko - A/C.4/78/SR.19
RACIAL DISCRIMINATION—ELIMINATION (Agenda item 69a)
Moriko, Tiémoko - A/C.3/78/SR.42
RACIAL DISCRIMINATION—PROGRAMMES OF ACTION (Agenda item 69b)
Moriko, Tiémoko - A/C.3/78/SR.42
RESPONSIBILITY TO PROTECT (Agenda item 129)
Moriko, Tiémoko - A/78/PV.97

Côte d'Ivoire (continued)

RIGHTS OF THE CHILD (Agenda item 67)
Kouakou, Kouadjo Michel - A/C.3/78/SR.11
Moriko, Tiémoko - A/C.3/78/SR.14
SMALL ARMS—ILLICIT TRAFFIC—ASSISTANCE (Agenda item 99n)
Moriko, Tiémoko - A/C.1/78/PV.18
SOCIAL DEVELOPMENT (Agenda item 24)
Moriko, Tiémoko - A/C.3/78/SR.3
SUSTAINABLE DEVELOPMENT (Agenda item 18)
Moriko, Tiémoko - A/C.2/78/SR.15
TERRORISM (Agenda item 109)
Moriko, Tiémoko - A/C.6/78/SR.3
UN. GENERAL ASSEMBLY (78TH SESS. : 2023-2024). 1ST COMMITTEE—GENERAL DEBATE (Agenda item 8)
Moriko, Tiémoko - A/C.1/78/PV.4
UN. GENERAL ASSEMBLY (78TH SESS. : 2023-2024). 2ND COMMITTEE—GENERAL DEBATE (Agenda item 8)
Moriko, Tiémoko - A/C.2/78/SR.4
UN. INTERNATIONAL LAW COMMISSION—REPORTS (Agenda item 79)
Moriko, Tiémoko - A/C.6/78/SR.28; A/C.6/78/SR.30
WEAPONS OF MASS DESTRUCTION—TERRORISM (Agenda item 99s)
Moriko, Tiémoko - A/C.1/78/PV.12
WESTERN SAHARA QUESTION (Agenda item 58)
Moriko, Tiémoko - A/C.4/78/SR.2
WOMEN'S ADVANCEMENT (Agenda item 25a)
Moriko, Tiémoko - A/C.3/78/SR.10
WOMEN'S ADVANCEMENT—CONFERENCES (Agenda item 25b)
Moriko, Tiémoko - A/C.3/78/SR.10

Côte d'Ivoire. Vice-President

UN. GENERAL ASSEMBLY (78TH SESS. : 2023-2024)—GENERAL DEBATE (Agenda item 8)
Kone, Tiémoko Meyliet - A/78/PV.9
UN. GENERAL ASSEMBLY (78TH SESS. : 2023-2024)—SPECIAL STATEMENTS
Kone, Tiémoko Meyliet - A/78/PV.9

Council of Europe

UN. INTERNATIONAL LAW COMMISSION—REPORTS (Agenda item 79)
Gómez Heredero, Ana - A/C.6/78/SR.28

Croatia

ARMED CONFLICTS PREVENTION (Agenda item 31a)
Ćurić Hrvatinić, Hrvoje - A/78/PV.72
CLIMATE CHANGE (Agenda item 71b)
Šukurica, Alen - A/C.3/78/SR.29

Croatia (continued)

DISAPPEARANCE OF PERSONS (Agenda item 71b)
Andrić, Katarina - A/C.3/78/SR.22
DISASTER VICTIMS (Agenda item 86)
Papac, Kristijan - A/C.6/78/SR.6
ENVIRONMENT (Agenda item 71b)
Šukurica, Alen - A/C.3/78/SR.29
HUMAN RIGHTS—AFGHANISTAN (Agenda item 71c)
Koncul, Ivana - A/C.3/78/SR.34
HUMAN RIGHTS—SYRIAN ARAB REPUBLIC (Agenda item 71c)
Koncul, Ivana - A/C.3/78/SR.34
LANDMINES—TREATIES (Agenda item 99m)
Glasenhardt, Blanka - A/C.1/78/PV.19
RESPONSIBILITY TO PROTECT (Agenda item 129)
Simonovic, Ivan - A/78/PV.96
RIGHT TO DRINKING WATER (Agenda item 71b)
Šukurica, Alen - A/C.3/78/SR.28
RIGHT TO HOUSING (Agenda item 71b)
Šukurica, Alen - A/C.3/78/SR.30
RIGHTS OF THE CHILD (Agenda item 67)
Andrić, Katarina - A/C.3/78/SR.11
UKRAINE—POLITICAL CONDITIONS (Agenda item 62)
Grlić-Radman, Gordan - A/78/PV.56
UN. GENERAL ASSEMBLY (78TH SESS. : 2023-2024). 1ST COMMITTEE—GENERAL DEBATE (Agenda item 8)
Glasenhardt, Blanka - A/C.1/78/PV.7
UN. HUMAN RIGHTS COUNCIL—REPORTS (Agenda item 66)
Simonovic, Ivan - A/78/PV.28
UN. INTERNATIONAL LAW COMMISSION—REPORTS (Agenda item 79)
Mesarek, Gordana Vidovic - A/C.6/78/SR.27
UN. PEACEBUILDING COMMISSION—REPORTS (Agenda item 27)
Simonovic, Ivan - A/78/PV.100
UN. SECRETARY-GENERAL—REPORTS (Agenda item 110)
Simonovic, Ivan - A/78/PV.55
VETO (Agenda item 63)
Ćurić Hrvatinić, Hrvoje - A/78/PV.69
WOMEN'S ADVANCEMENT (Agenda item 25a)
Koncul, Ivana - A/C.3/78/SR.7
WOMEN'S ADVANCEMENT—CONFERENCES (Agenda item 25b)
Koncul, Ivana - A/C.3/78/SR.7

Croatia. President

UN. GENERAL ASSEMBLY (78TH SESS. : 2023-2024)—GENERAL DEBATE (Agenda item 8)
Milanovic, Zoran - A/78/PV.6

Croatia. President (continued)

UN. GENERAL ASSEMBLY (78TH SESS. : 2023-2024)—SPECIAL STATEMENTS
Milanovic, Zoran - A/78/PV.6

Cuba

ADMINISTRATION OF JUSTICE (Agenda item 144)
Carral Castelo, Arianna - A/C.6/78/SR.9
AGEING PERSONS (Agenda item 24b)
García Hernández, Martha - A/C.3/78/SR.3
González Behmaras, Alejandro - A/C.3/78/SR.1
ARMED CONFLICTS PREVENTION (Agenda item 31a)
González Behmaras, Alejandro - A/78/PV.72
ARMS RACE—OUTER SPACE (Agenda item 97a)
Gómez Sardiñas, Yiliam - A/C.1/78/PV.17
Romero López, Rosanis - A/C.1/78/PV.27
ARMS TRANSFERS—TREATIES (Agenda item 99x)
Garcia Moré, Yohan Yuniet - A/C.1/78/PV.28
Gómez Sardiñas, Yiliam - A/C.1/78/PV.19
BIOLOGICAL WEAPONS—TREATIES (Agenda item 106)
Thomas Ramírez, Vilma - A/C.1/78/PV.15
CHEMICAL WEAPONS—TREATIES (Agenda item 99l)
Romero López, Rosanis - A/C.1/78/PV.26
Thomas Ramírez, Vilma - A/C.1/78/PV.15
CONVENTIONAL WEAPONS (Agenda item 99u)
Garcia Moré, Yohan Yuniet - A/C.1/78/PV.28
Gómez Sardiñas, Yiliam - A/C.1/78/PV.19
CONVENTIONAL WEAPONS—TREATIES (Agenda item 103)
Gómez Sardiñas, Yiliam - A/C.1/78/PV.19
CRIME PREVENTION (Agenda item 107)
Valido Martínez, Yoangel - A/C.3/78/SR.5
CRIMES AGAINST HUMANITY (Agenda item 80)
Carral Castelo, Arianna - A/C.6/78/SR.39; A/C.6/78/SR.40
Peñalver Portal, Gerardo - A/C.6/78/SR.10
CUBA—UNITED STATES (Agenda item 38)
Rodríguez Parrilla, Bruno Eduardo - A/78/PV.26
Romero Puentes, Yusnier - A/78/PV.26
CYBERCRIME (Agenda item 108)
Valido Martínez, Yoangel - A/C.3/78/SR.5
DECOLONIZATION (Agenda item 58)
Fernández Palacios, Yumirka - A/C.4/78/SR.8
Romero Puentes, Yusnier - A/C.4/78/SR.2
DEMOCRACY (Agenda item 71b)
González Behmaras, Alejandro - A/C.3/78/SR.48
Lamigueiro Cañedo, Ivette - A/C.3/78/SR.28
Valido Martínez, Yoangel - A/C.3/78/SR.28
DEVELOPMENT FINANCE (Agenda item 16b)
Guevara Rodríguez, Adiel - A/C.2/78/SR.8

Cuba (continued)

DISARMAMENT—GENERAL AND COMPLETE (Agenda item 99)
Gómez Sardiñas, Yiliam - A/C.1/78/PV.19
Romero López, Rosanis - A/C.1/78/PV.30
DISARMAMENT AGREEMENTS—ENVIRONMENT (Agenda item 99j)
Romero López, Rosanis - A/C.1/78/PV.28
DISARMAMENT AGREEMENTS—OUTER SPACE (Agenda item 97c)
Gómez Sardiñas, Yiliam - A/C.1/78/PV.17
Romero López, Rosanis - A/C.1/78/PV.27
DISARMAMENT-DEVELOPMENT LINK (Agenda item 99d)
Romero López, Rosanis - A/C.1/78/PV.28
DISASTER VICTIMS (Agenda item 86)
Carral Castelo, Arianna - A/C.6/78/SR.6
DISPLACED PERSONS (Agenda item 71b)
González Behmaras, Alejandro - A/78/PV.50; A/C.3/78/SR.49
ECONOMIC SANCTIONS—INTERNATIONAL RELATIONS (Agenda item 28)
Rodríguez Perdomo, Elio - A/78/PV.89
EMERGENCY ASSISTANCE (Agenda item 72a)
González Behmaras, Alejandro - A/78/PV.47
ENVIRONMENT (Agenda item 71b)
García Hernández, Martha - A/C.3/78/SR.29
EXTERNAL DEBT (Agenda item 16c)
Guevara Rodríguez, Adiel - A/C.2/78/SR.8
EXTERNAL DEBT—HUMAN RIGHTS (Agenda item 71b)
García Hernández, Martha - A/C.3/78/SR.32
FALKLAND ISLANDS (MALVINAS) QUESTION (Agenda item 42)
Romero Puentes, Yusnier - A/C.4/78/SR.2
FISSIONABLE MATERIALS—TREATIES (Agenda item 99a)
Romero López, Rosanis - A/C.1/78/PV.26
HEALTH (Agenda item 125)
González Behmaras, Alejandro - A/78/PV.16; A/78/PV.48; A/78/PV.77
Peñalver Portal, Gerardo - A/78/PV.41
Valido Martínez, Yoangel - A/78/PV.102
HIV/AIDS—DECLARATIONS (Agenda item 10)
Romero Puentes, Yusnier - A/78/PV.91
HUMAN RIGHTS (Agenda item 71)
Gala López, Yuri - A/C.3/78/SR.16
González Behmaras, Alejandro - A/C.3/78/SR.25
HUMAN RIGHTS—BURUNDI (Agenda item 71c)
González Behmaras, Alejandro - A/C.3/78/SR.36
HUMAN RIGHTS—DEMOCRATIC PEOPLE'S REPUBLIC OF KOREA (Agenda item 71c)
González Behmaras, Alejandro - A/78/PV.50; A/C.3/78/SR.53
Valido Martínez, Yoangel - A/C.3/78/SR.33
HUMAN RIGHTS—ERITREA (Agenda item 71c)
González Behmaras, Alejandro - A/C.3/78/SR.36

Cuba (continued)

HUMAN RIGHTS—ETHIOPIA (Agenda item 71c)
González Behmaras, Alejandro - A/C.3/78/SR.36
HUMAN RIGHTS—INTERNATIONAL INSTRUMENTS (Agenda item 71a)
Romero Puentes, Yusnier - A/C.3/78/SR.25
HUMAN RIGHTS—IRAN (ISLAMIC REPUBLIC OF) (Agenda item 71c)
González Behmaras, Alejandro - A/78/PV.50; A/C.3/78/SR.34; A/C.3/78/SR.53
HUMAN RIGHTS—REPORTS (Agenda item 71c)
González Behmaras, Alejandro - A/78/PV.50; A/C.3/78/SR.18
HUMAN RIGHTS—SYRIAN ARAB REPUBLIC (Agenda item 71c)
González Behmaras, Alejandro - A/78/PV.50; A/C.3/78/SR.34; A/C.3/78/SR.54
HUMAN RIGHTS—TERRITORIES OCCUPIED BY ISRAEL (Agenda item 71c)
González Behmaras, Alejandro - A/C.3/78/SR.35
HUMAN RIGHTS ADVANCEMENT (Agenda item 71b)
González Behmaras, Alejandro - A/C.3/78/SR.48
IAEA—REPORTS (Agenda item 89)
Peñalver Portal, Gerardo - A/78/PV.30
INDIGENOUS PEOPLES (Agenda item 68a)
Lamigueiro Cañedo, Ivette - A/C.3/78/SR.15
INDIGENOUS PEOPLES—CONFERENCES (Agenda item 68b)
Lamigueiro Cañedo, Ivette - A/C.3/78/SR.15
INFORMATION—INTERNATIONAL SECURITY (Agenda item 94)
Gómez Sardiñas, Yiliam - A/C.1/78/PV.20
Romero López, Rosanis - A/C.1/78/PV.28; A/C.1/78/PV.29
INTERNATIONAL CRIMINAL COURT—REPORTS (Agenda item 74)
Silva Walker, Eva Yelina - A/78/PV.22
INTERNATIONAL JURISDICTION (Agenda item 84)
Carral Castelo, Arianna - A/C.6/78/SR.12
INTERNATIONAL TRADE (Agenda item 16a)
Guevara Rodríguez, Adiel - A/C.2/78/SR.8
Romero Puentes, Yusnier - A/C.2/78/SR.24
LANDMINES—TREATIES (Agenda item 99m)
Garcia Moré, Yohan Yuniet - A/C.1/78/PV.28
MACROECONOMIC POLICY (Agenda item 16)
Guevara Rodríguez, Adiel - A/C.2/78/SR.8
MERCENARIES (Agenda item 70)
González Behmaras, Alejandro - A/C.3/78/SR.42; A/C.3/78/SR.48
MIDDLE EAST—NUCLEAR-WEAPON-FREE ZONES (Agenda item 95)
Peñalver Portal, Gerardo - A/C.1/78/PV.11
MIGRANTS—PROTECTION (Agenda item 71b)
Valido Martínez, Yoangel - A/C.3/78/SR.23

Cuba (continued)

MILLENNIUM SUMMIT—CONFERENCES (Agenda item 117)
Peñalver Portal, Gerardo - A/78/PV.15
MULTILATERALISM—DISARMAMENT (Agenda item 99r)
Gómez Sardiñas, Yiliam - A/C.1/78/PV.20; A/C.1/78/PV.21
Romero López, Rosanis - A/C.1/78/PV.28
NON-CITIZENS—DEPORTATION (Agenda item 81)
Mora Fonseca, Vladimir - A/C.6/78/SR.34
NON-NUCLEAR-WEAPON STATES—SECURITY (Agenda item 96)
Gómez Sardiñas, Yiliam - A/C.1/78/PV.25
NUCLEAR DISARMAMENT (Agenda item 99b)
Gómez Sardiñas, Yiliam - A/C.1/78/PV.25
Peñalver Portal, Gerardo - A/C.1/78/PV.11
NUCLEAR DISARMAMENT—CONFERENCES (Agenda item 99aa)
Gómez Sardiñas, Yiliam - A/C.1/78/PV.25
NUCLEAR NON-PROLIFERATION (Agenda item 99o)
Gómez Sardiñas, Yiliam - A/C.1/78/PV.25
NUCLEAR NON-PROLIFERATION—INTERNATIONAL OBLIGATIONS (Agenda item 99w)
Peñalver Portal, Gerardo - A/C.1/78/PV.11
NUCLEAR WEAPONS—HUMANITARIAN CONSEQUENCES (Agenda item 99bb)
Gómez Sardiñas, Yiliam - A/C.1/78/PV.25
NUCLEAR WEAPONS—TREATIES (Agenda item 99ff)
Gómez Sardiñas, Yiliam - A/C.1/78/PV.25
Peñalver Portal, Gerardo - A/C.1/78/PV.11
NUCLEAR WEAPONS USE—UN. INTERNATIONAL COURT OF JUSTICE OPINION (Agenda item 99k)
Gómez Sardiñas, Yiliam - A/C.1/78/PV.25
NUCLEAR-WEAPON-FREE ZONE—SOUTHERN HEMISPHERE (Agenda item 99i)
Gómez Sardiñas, Yiliam - A/C.1/78/PV.25
NUCLEAR-WEAPON-FREE ZONES (Agenda item 99cc)
Gómez Sardiñas, Yiliam - A/C.1/78/PV.25
OUTER SPACE—CONFIDENCE-BUILDING MEASURES (Agenda item 99v)
Gómez Sardiñas, Yiliam - A/C.1/78/PV.17
Romero López, Rosanis - A/C.1/78/PV.27
OUTER SPACE—PEACEFUL USES—INTERNATIONAL COOPERATION (Agenda item 48)
Fernández Palacios, Yumirka - A/C.4/78/SR.15
OUTER SPACE—PRINCIPLES (Agenda item 97d)
Romero López, Rosanis - A/C.1/78/PV.27
PALESTINE QUESTION (Agenda item 35)
Romero Puentes, Yusnier - A/78/PV.40
PALESTINIANS—ASSISTANCE (Agenda item 72b)
González Behmaras, Alejandro - A/78/PV.47

Cuba (continued)

PEACE (Agenda item 14)
Soberón Guzmán, Ernesto - A/78/PV.76; A/78/PV.82
PEACEBUILDING (Agenda item 61)
Gala López, Yuri - A/78/PV.100
PEACEKEEPING OPERATIONS (Agenda item 51)
Sánchez Fuentes, Jorge Sain - A/C.4/78/SR.18
PEACEKEEPING OPERATIONS—CRIMINAL LIABILITY (Agenda item 76)
Carral Castelo, Arianna - A/C.6/78/SR.8
PERSONS WITH DISABILITIES (Agenda item 24b)
García Hernández, Martha - A/C.3/78/SR.3
POVERTY—HUMAN RIGHTS (Agenda item 71b)
Lamigueiro Cañedo, Ivette - A/C.3/78/SR.30
RACIAL DISCRIMINATION—ELIMINATION (Agenda item 69a)
González Behmaras, Alejandro - A/78/PV.50; A/C.3/78/SR.42; A/C.3/78/SR.47
Padilla González, Cristian - A/78/PV.103
Valido Martínez, Yoangel - A/C.3/78/SR.41
RACIAL DISCRIMINATION—PROGRAMMES OF ACTION (Agenda item 69b)
González Behmaras, Alejandro - A/C.3/78/SR.42; A/C.3/78/SR.56
Valido Martínez, Yoangel - A/C.3/78/SR.41
RADIATION EFFECTS (Agenda item 47)
Rolle Hernández, Gretel - A/C.4/78/SR.11
RELIGIOUS INTOLERANCE (Agenda item 71b)
González Behmaras, Alejandro - A/C.3/78/SR.38
RESPONSIBILITY OF INTERNATIONAL ORGANIZATIONS (Agenda item 85)
Mora Fonseca, Vladimir - A/C.6/78/SR.19
RESPONSIBILITY TO PROTECT (Agenda item 129)
Romero Puentes, Yusnier - A/78/PV.96
RIGHT TO CULTURE (Agenda item 71b)
Valido Martínez, Yoangel - A/C.3/78/SR.27
RIGHT TO DEVELOPMENT (Agenda item 71b)
González Behmaras, Alejandro - A/C.3/78/SR.20
RIGHT TO EDUCATION (Agenda item 71b)
Valido Martínez, Yoangel - A/C.3/78/SR.27
RIGHT TO FOOD (Agenda item 71b)
García Hernández, Martha - A/C.3/78/SR.30
González Behmaras, Alejandro - A/C.3/78/SR.48
RIGHT TO HEALTH (Agenda item 71b)
Valido Martínez, Yoangel - A/C.3/78/SR.39
RIGHTS OF THE CHILD (Agenda item 67)
Armas García, Mercedes de - A/C.3/78/SR.12
González Behmaras, Alejandro - A/C.3/78/SR.55
RULE OF LAW (Agenda item 83)
Mora Fonseca, Vladimir - A/C.6/78/SR.16
SANCTIONS—INTERNATIONAL RELATIONS (Agenda item 71b)
González Behmaras, Alejandro - A/C.3/78/SR.48
Lamigueiro Cañedo, Ivette - A/C.3/78/SR.28
Romero Puentes, Yusnier - A/C.3/78/SR.25

Cuba (continued)

SELF-DETERMINATION OF PEOPLES (Agenda item 70)
González Behmaras, Alejandro - A/78/PV.50; A/C.3/78/SR.42; A/C.3/78/SR.49
SEXUAL ORIENTATION (Agenda item 71b)
Valido Martínez, Yoangel - A/C.3/78/SR.39
SMALL ARMS—ILLICIT TRAFFIC (Agenda item 99p)
Gómez Sardiñas, Yiliam - A/C.1/78/PV.19
SMALL ARMS—ILLICIT TRAFFIC—ASSISTANCE (Agenda item 99n)
Gómez Sardiñas, Yiliam - A/C.1/78/PV.19
SOCIAL DEVELOPMENT—CONFERENCES (Agenda item 24a)
García Hernández, Martha - A/C.3/78/SR.3
SOLIDARITY (Agenda item 71b)
Lamigueiro Cañedo, Ivette - A/C.3/78/SR.32
TERRITORIES OCCUPIED BY ISRAEL—HUMAN RIGHTS (Agenda item 50)
Fernández Palacios, Yumirka - A/C.4/78/SR.24
Romero Puentes, Yusnier - A/C.4/78/SR.26
TERRITORIES OCCUPIED BY ISRAEL—NATURAL RESOURCES (Agenda item 59)
Peñalver Portal, Gerardo - A/C.2/78/SR.19
TERRORISM (Agenda item 109)
Peñalver Portal, Gerardo - A/C.6/78/SR.2
TERRORISM—HUMAN RIGHTS (Agenda item 71b)
González Behmaras, Alejandro - A/C.3/78/SR.31
TREATIES (Agenda item 87)
Mora Fonseca, Vladimir - A/C.6/78/SR.20
UKRAINE—POLITICAL CONDITIONS (Agenda item 62)
Fernández Palacios, Yumirka - A/78/PV.99
UN—BUDGET (2024) (Agenda item 134)
Tur de la Concepción, Richard - A/78/PV.50(Resumption1); A/C.5/78/SR.3; A/C.5/78/SR.26/PartII; A/C.5/78/SR.34
UN—PROGRAMME PLANNING (Agenda item 135)
Hernández Morera, Diosdado de Jesús - A/C.5/78/SR.24
Romero López, Rosanis - A/C.1/78/PV.10
Tur de la Concepción, Richard - A/78/PV.50(Resumption1)
UN. COMMITTEE ON RELATIONS WITH THE HOST COUNTRY—REPORTS (Agenda item 161)
Gala López, Yuri - A/C.6/78/SR.35
UN. CONFERENCE ON DISARMAMENT—REPORTS (Agenda item 101a)
Thomas Ramírez, Vilma - A/C.1/78/PV.23
UN. DISARMAMENT COMMISSION—REPORTS (Agenda item 101b)
Thomas Ramírez, Vilma - A/C.1/78/PV.23
UN. GENERAL ASSEMBLY—WORK PROGRAMME (Agenda item 120)
Romero López, Rosanis - A/C.1/78/PV.10
San Román Valdés, Jorge - A/78/PV.32

Cuba (continued)

UN. GENERAL ASSEMBLY (78TH SESS. : 2023-2024). 1ST COMMITTEE—GENERAL DEBATE (Agenda item 8)
Gala López, Yuri - A/C.1/78/PV.6
UN. HUMAN RIGHTS COUNCIL—REPORTS (Agenda item 66)
González Behmaras, Alejandro - A/78/PV.28; A/C.3/78/SR.46; A/C.3/78/SR.51
UN. INTERNATIONAL COURT OF JUSTICE—REPORTS (Agenda item 73)
Carral Castelo, Arianna - A/78/PV.27
UN. INTERNATIONAL LAW COMMISSION—REPORTS (Agenda item 79)
Mora Fonseca, Vladimir - A/C.6/78/SR.25
Silva Walker, Eva Yelina - A/C.6/78/SR.29; A/C.6/78/SR.32
UN. PEACEBUILDING COMMISSION—REPORTS (Agenda item 27)
Gala López, Yuri - A/78/PV.100
UN. PEACEBUILDING FUND—REPORTS (Agenda item 111)
Gala López, Yuri - A/78/PV.100
UN. SECRETARY-GENERAL—REPORTS (Agenda item 110)
Romero Puentes, Yusnier - A/78/PV.55
UN. SECURITY COUNCIL—MEMBERSHIP (Agenda item 121)
Romero Puentes, Yusnier - A/78/PV.36
UN. SECURITY COUNCIL—REPORTS (Agenda item 26)
Gala López, Yuri - A/78/PV.93
UN CHARTER—REPORTS (Agenda item 82)
Mora Fonseca, Vladimir - A/C.6/78/SR.22
UN COMMISSION ON INTERNATIONAL TRADE LAW—REPORTS (Agenda item 77)
Mora Fonseca, Vladimir - A/C.6/78/SR.14
UN CONFERENCES (Agenda item 13)
Pedroso Cuesta, Pedro Luis - A/78/PV.52
Peñalver Portal, Gerardo - A/78/PV.15
UN RESOLUTIONS—IMPLEMENTATION (Agenda item 119)
Padilla González, Cristian - A/78/PV.103
San Román Valdés, Jorge - A/78/PV.32
UN SYSTEM—STRENGTHENING (Agenda item 122)
Padilla González, Cristian - A/78/PV.99
UNRWA—ACTIVITIES (Agenda item 49)
Romero Puentes, Yusnier - A/C.4/78/SR.23; A/C.4/78/SR.26
VETO (Agenda item 63)
Gala López, Yuri - A/78/PV.70
Peñalver Portal, Gerardo - A/78/PV.51; A/78/PV.60
Soberón Guzmán, Ernesto - A/78/PV.67; A/78/PV.69; A/78/PV.74
WEAPONS—OUTER SPACE (Agenda item 97b)
Romero López, Rosanis - A/C.1/78/PV.27
WESTERN SAHARA QUESTION (Agenda item 58)
Romero Puentes, Yusnier - A/C.4/78/SR.2

Cuba (continued)

WOMEN'S ADVANCEMENT (Agenda item 25a)
García Hernández, Martha - A/C.3/78/SR.7; A/C.3/78/SR.9
González Behmaras, Alejandro - A/C.3/78/SR.7
WOMEN'S ADVANCEMENT—CONFERENCES (Agenda item 25b)
García Hernández, Martha - A/C.3/78/SR.7; A/C.3/78/SR.9
González Behmaras, Alejandro - A/C.3/78/SR.7
YOUTH (Agenda item 24b)
García Hernández, Martha - A/C.3/78/SR.3

Cuba. President

UN. GENERAL ASSEMBLY (78TH SESS. : 2023-2024)—GENERAL DEBATE (Agenda item 8)
Díaz-Canel Bermúdez, Miguel - A/78/PV.4
UN. GENERAL ASSEMBLY (78TH SESS. : 2023-2024)—SPECIAL STATEMENTS
Díaz-Canel Bermúdez, Miguel - A/78/PV.4

Cyprus

CRIME PREVENTION (Agenda item 107)
Demosthenous, Ioanna - A/C.3/78/SR.5
CRIMES AGAINST HUMANITY (Agenda item 80)
Pittakis, Theodoulos - A/C.6/78/SR.39; A/C.6/78/SR.41; A/C.6/78/SR.45
HUMAN RIGHTS (Agenda item 71)
Michaelidou, Gabriella - A/C.3/78/SR.24
HUMAN RIGHTS—REPORTS (Agenda item 71c)
Demosthenous, Ioanna - A/C.3/78/SR.25
INFORMATION (Agenda item 53)
Demosthenous, Ioanna - A/C.4/78/SR.14
INTERNATIONAL CRIMINAL COURT—REPORTS (Agenda item 74)
Pittakis, Theodoulos - A/78/PV.22
PEACEKEEPING OPERATIONS (Agenda item 51)
Panteli, Rona Marie - A/C.4/78/SR.20
SUMMARY EXECUTIONS (Agenda item 71b)
Demosthenous, Ioanna - A/C.3/78/SR.31
UN—BUDGET (2024) (Agenda item 134)
Demosthenous, Ioanna - A/C.5/78/SR.3
UN. COMMITTEE ON RELATIONS WITH THE HOST COUNTRY—REPORTS (Agenda item 161)
Pittakis, Theodoulos - A/C.6/78/SR.37
UN. INTERNATIONAL COURT OF JUSTICE—REPORTS (Agenda item 73)
Pittakis, Theodoulos - A/78/PV.28
UN. INTERNATIONAL LAW COMMISSION—REPORTS (Agenda item 79)
Pittakis, Theodoulos - A/C.6/78/SR.28
WOMEN'S ADVANCEMENT (Agenda item 25a)
Hadjichrysanthou, Andreas - A/C.3/78/SR.8

Cyprus (continued)

WOMEN'S ADVANCEMENT—CONFERENCES (Agenda item 25b)
Hadjichrysanthou, Andreas - A/C.3/78/SR.8
YOUTH (Agenda item 24b)
Demosthenous, Ioanna - A/C.3/78/SR.55

Cyprus. President

UN. GENERAL ASSEMBLY (78TH SESS. : 2023-2024)—GENERAL DEBATE (Agenda item 8)
Christodoulides, Nikos - A/78/PV.6
UN. GENERAL ASSEMBLY (78TH SESS. : 2023-2024)—SPECIAL STATEMENTS
Christodoulides, Nikos - A/78/PV.6

Czechia

ARMED CONFLICTS PREVENTION (Agenda item 31a)
Kulhánek, Jakub - A/78/PV.72
ARMS RACE—OUTER SPACE (Agenda item 97a)
Štěpánek, Jaroslav - A/C.1/78/PV.16
BIOLOGICAL WEAPONS—TREATIES (Agenda item 106)
Štěpánek, Jaroslav - A/C.1/78/PV.14
CHEMICAL WEAPONS—TREATIES (Agenda item 99l)
Štěpánek, Jaroslav - A/C.1/78/PV.14
FISSIONABLE MATERIALS—TREATIES (Agenda item 99a)
Štěpánek, Jaroslav - A/C.1/78/PV.12
FREEDOM OF EXPRESSION (Agenda item 71b)
Kulhánek, Jakub - A/C.3/78/SR.19
HUMAN RIGHTS—AFGHANISTAN (Agenda item 71c)
Kulhánek, Jakub - A/C.3/78/SR.24
HUMAN RIGHTS—BELARUS (Agenda item 71c)
Kaminek, Jan - A/C.3/78/SR.37
HUMAN RIGHTS—DEMOCRATIC PEOPLE'S REPUBLIC OF KOREA (Agenda item 71c)
Kaminek, Jan - A/C.3/78/SR.33
HUMAN RIGHTS—MYANMAR (Agenda item 71c)
Kaminek, Jan - A/C.3/78/SR.33
HUMAN RIGHTS—REPORTS (Agenda item 71c)
Kulhánek, Jakub - A/C.3/78/SR.24
HUMAN RIGHTS—RUSSIAN FEDERATION (Agenda item 71c)
Kaminek, Jan - A/C.3/78/SR.37
HUMAN RIGHTS—TERRITORIES OCCUPIED BY ISRAEL (Agenda item 71c)
Kulhánek, Jakub - A/C.3/78/SR.35
HUMAN RIGHTS—UKRAINE (Agenda item 71c)
Kaminek, Jan - A/C.3/78/SR.37
Kulhánek, Jakub - A/C.3/78/SR.24

Czechia (continued)

HUMAN RIGHTS ACTIVISTS (Agenda item 71b)
Kulhánek, Jakub - A/C.3/78/SR.19
HUMAN RIGHTS ADVANCEMENT (Agenda item 71b)
Kulhánek, Jakub - A/C.3/78/SR.52
INTERNATIONAL CRIMINAL COURT—REPORTS (Agenda item 74)
Kafková, Eva Anna - A/78/PV.22
INTERNATIONAL JURISDICTION (Agenda item 84)
Zukal, Marek - A/C.6/78/SR.12
NUCLEAR DISARMAMENT (Agenda item 99b)
Štěpánek, Jaroslav - A/C.1/78/PV.12
NUCLEAR NON-PROLIFERATION—INTERNATIONAL OBLIGATIONS (Agenda item 99w)
Štěpánek, Jaroslav - A/C.1/78/PV.12
NUCLEAR WEAPON TESTS—TREATIES (Agenda item 105)
Štěpánek, Jaroslav - A/C.1/78/PV.12
OUTER SPACE—PRINCIPLES (Agenda item 97d)
Štěpánek, Jaroslav - A/C.1/78/PV.16
RIGHT OF ASSEMBLY (Agenda item 71b)
Kulhánek, Jakub - A/C.3/78/SR.19
SOCIAL CONDITIONS (Agenda item 24b)
Hellerová, Zuzana - A/C.3/78/SR.2
UKRAINE—POLITICAL CONDITIONS (Agenda item 62)
Marian, Jan - A/78/PV.56
UN. GENERAL ASSEMBLY (78TH SESS. : 2023-2024). 1ST COMMITTEE—GENERAL DEBATE (Agenda item 8)
Stromsiková, Veronika - A/C.1/78/PV.3
UN. INTERNATIONAL LAW COMMISSION—REPORTS (Agenda item 79)
Smolek, Martin - A/C.6/78/SR.25
Zukal, Marek - A/C.6/78/SR.29; A/C.6/78/SR.31
VETO (Agenda item 63)
Kulhánek, Jakub - A/78/PV.3; A/78/PV.67; A/78/PV.69; A/78/PV.78
YOUTH (Agenda item 24b)
Bulvasová, Kristýna - A/C.3/78/SR.2

Czechia. President

UN. GENERAL ASSEMBLY (78TH SESS. : 2023-2024)—GENERAL DEBATE (Agenda item 8)
Pavel, Petr - A/78/PV.5
UN. GENERAL ASSEMBLY (78TH SESS. : 2023-2024)—SPECIAL STATEMENTS
Pavel, Petr - A/78/PV.5

Democratic People's Republic of Korea

ARMED CONFLICTS PREVENTION (Agenda item 31a)
Kim, Song - A/78/PV.72

Democratic People's Republic of Korea (continued)

ARMS RACE—OUTER SPACE (Agenda item 97a)
Kim, In Chol - A/C.1/78/PV.17
CUBA—UNITED STATES (Agenda item 38)
Kim, Song - A/78/PV.24
DISAPPEARANCE OF PERSONS (Agenda item 71b)
Kim, Nam Hyok - A/C.3/78/SR.22
DISARMAMENT—GENERAL AND COMPLETE (Agenda item 99)
Kim, In Chol - A/C.1/78/PV.19; A/C.1/78/PV.21
FOOD SECURITY (Agenda item 23a)
Jo, Tong Hyon - A/C.2/78/SR.16
HUMAN RIGHTS (Agenda item 71)
Kim, Nam Hyok - A/C.3/78/SR.16
HUMAN RIGHTS—BURUNDI (Agenda item 71c)
Kim, Nam Hyok - A/C.3/78/SR.36
HUMAN RIGHTS—DEMOCRATIC PEOPLE'S REPUBLIC OF KOREA (Agenda item 71c)
Kim, Nam Hyok - A/78/PV.50; A/C.3/78/SR.18; A/C.3/78/SR.27
Kim, Song - A/C.3/78/SR.53
HUMAN RIGHTS—ERITREA (Agenda item 71c)
Kim, Nam Hyok - A/C.3/78/SR.36
HUMAN RIGHTS—IRAN (ISLAMIC REPUBLIC OF) (Agenda item 71c)
Kim, Nam Hyok - A/C.3/78/SR.34; A/C.3/78/SR.53
HUMAN RIGHTS—REPORTS (Agenda item 71c)
Kim, Nam Hyok - A/C.3/78/SR.25
Kim, Song - A/C.3/78/SR.25
HUMAN RIGHTS—RUSSIAN FEDERATION (Agenda item 71c)
Kim, Nam Hyok - A/C.3/78/SR.37
HUMAN RIGHTS—SYRIAN ARAB REPUBLIC (Agenda item 71c)
Kim, Nam Hyok - A/C.3/78/SR.34; A/C.3/78/SR.54
HUMAN RIGHTS—TERRITORIES OCCUPIED BY ISRAEL (Agenda item 71c)
Kim, Nam Hyok - A/C.3/78/SR.35
HUMAN RIGHTS—UKRAINE (Agenda item 71c)
Kim, Nam Hyok - A/C.3/78/SR.53
IAEA—REPORTS (Agenda item 89)
Kim, Song - A/78/PV.29
INFORMATION (Agenda item 53)
Kim, In Chol - A/C.4/78/SR.12
MULTILATERALISM—DISARMAMENT (Agenda item 99r)
Kim, In Chol - A/C.1/78/PV.22; A/C.1/78/PV.23
NUCLEAR DISARMAMENT (Agenda item 99b)
Kim, In Chol - A/C.1/78/PV.13
Kim, Song - A/C.1/78/PV.11
NUCLEAR DISARMAMENT—TREATY COMPLIANCE (Agenda item 99q)
Kim, In Chol - A/C.1/78/PV.26

Democratic People's Republic of Korea (continued)

NUCLEAR WEAPON TESTS—TREATIES (Agenda item 105)
Kim, In Chol - A/C.1/78/PV.26
NUCLEAR WEAPONS—ELIMINATION (Agenda item 99z)
Kim, In Chol - A/C.1/78/PV.25; A/C.1/78/PV.26
OUTER SPACE—PEACEFUL USES—INTERNATIONAL COOPERATION (Agenda item 48)
Kim, In Chol - A/C.4/78/SR.17
Kim, Song - A/C.4/78/SR.15
PEACEKEEPING OPERATIONS (Agenda item 51)
Kim, In Chol - A/C.4/78/SR.19
POVERTY—INTERNATIONAL DECADES (Agenda item 21a)
Jo, Tong Hyon - A/C.2/78/SR.16
RACIAL DISCRIMINATION—ELIMINATION (Agenda item 69a)
Kim, Nam Hyok - A/78/PV.50; A/C.3/78/SR.47
RESPONSIBILITY TO PROTECT (Agenda item 129)
Kim, Song - A/78/PV.96
RIGHT TO THE TRUTH (Agenda item 71b)
Kim, Nam Hyok - A/C.3/78/SR.22
RIGHTS OF THE CHILD (Agenda item 67)
Kim, Nam Hyok - A/C.3/78/SR.13
RURAL POVERTY (Agenda item 21b)
Jo, Tong Hyon - A/C.2/78/SR.16
SUSTAINABLE DEVELOPMENT (Agenda item 18)
Jo, Tong Hyon - A/C.2/78/SR.13
TERRITORIES OCCUPIED BY ISRAEL—HUMAN RIGHTS (Agenda item 50)
Kim, In Chol - A/C.4/78/SR.24; A/C.4/78/SR.26
TERRORISM (Agenda item 109)
Kim, Song - A/C.6/78/SR.3
UKRAINE—POLITICAL CONDITIONS (Agenda item 62)
Kim, Nam Hyok - A/78/PV.56; A/78/PV.58
UN—BUDGET (2024) (Agenda item 134)
Kim, Nam Hyok - A/78/PV.73; A/C.5/78/SR.26/PartII; A/C.5/78/SR.34
UN—PROGRAMME PLANNING (Agenda item 135)
Kim, In Chol - A/C.5/78/SR.24
Kim, Nam Hyok - A/78/PV.50(Resumption1)
UN. GENERAL ASSEMBLY (78TH SESS. : 2023-2024)—GENERAL DEBATE (Agenda item 8)
Kim, Song - A/78/PV.14
UN. GENERAL ASSEMBLY (78TH SESS. : 2023-2024)—GENERAL DEBATE—RIGHT OF REPLY (Agenda item 8)
Kim, Song - A/78/PV.14
UN. GENERAL ASSEMBLY (78TH SESS. : 2023-2024). 1ST COMMITTEE—GENERAL DEBATE (Agenda item 8)
Kim, In Chol - A/C.1/78/PV.2; A/C.1/78/PV.4; A/C.1/78/PV.5; A/C.1/78/PV.7; A/C.1/78/PV.8
Kim, Song - A/C.1/78/PV.7

Democratic People's Republic of Korea (continued)

UN. GENERAL ASSEMBLY (78TH SESS. : 2023-2024). 2ND COMMITTEE—GENERAL DEBATE (Agenda item 8)
Kim, Song - A/C.2/78/SR.3
UN. HUMAN RIGHTS COUNCIL—REPORTS (Agenda item 66)
Kim, Nam Hyok - A/C.3/78/SR.46
UN. SECURITY COUNCIL—MEMBERSHIP (Agenda item 121)
Kim, Song - A/78/PV.36
UN CHARTER—REPORTS (Agenda item 82)
Kim, In Chol - A/C.6/78/SR.33; A/C.6/78/SR.34
UN HIGH COMMISSIONER FOR REFUGEES—REPORTS (Agenda item 60)
Kim, Nam Hyok - A/C.3/78/SR.45
VETO (Agenda item 63)
Kim, Song - A/78/PV.3; A/78/PV.51; A/78/PV.60; A/78/PV.67; A/78/PV.68; A/78/PV.71; A/78/PV.75
WOMEN'S ADVANCEMENT (Agenda item 25a)
Kim, Song - A/C.3/78/SR.9
WOMEN'S ADVANCEMENT—CONFERENCES (Agenda item 25b)
Kim, Song - A/C.3/78/SR.9

Democratic Republic of the Congo

DECOLONIZATION (Agenda item 58)
Mukongo Ngay, Zénon - A/C.4/78/SR.9
INTERNATIONAL CRIMINAL COURT—REPORTS (Agenda item 74)
Mukongo Ngay, Zénon - A/78/PV.22
NUCLEAR NON-PROLIFERATION—INTERNATIONAL OBLIGATIONS (Agenda item 99w)
Liolocha, Victoria Lieta - A/C.1/78/PV.13
NUCLEAR WEAPONS—HUMANITARIAN CONSEQUENCES (Agenda item 99bb)
Liolocha, Victoria Lieta - A/C.1/78/PV.13
NUCLEAR WEAPONS—TREATIES (Agenda item 99ff)
Liolocha, Victoria Lieta - A/C.1/78/PV.13
PEACE (Agenda item 14)
Mukongo Ngay, Zénon - A/78/PV.82
PEACEKEEPING OPERATIONS (Agenda item 51)
Mukongo Ngay, Zénon - A/C.4/78/SR.20
RIGHTS OF THE CHILD (Agenda item 67)
Ahuka Lutundul, Claudy - A/C.3/78/SR.14
UN. INTERNATIONAL COURT OF JUSTICE—REPORTS (Agenda item 73)
Mukongo Ngay, Zénon - A/78/PV.28
WESTERN SAHARA QUESTION (Agenda item 58)
Mukongo Ngay, Zénon - A/C.4/78/SR.9

Democratic Republic of the Congo. President

UN. GENERAL ASSEMBLY (78TH SESS. : 2023-2024)—GENERAL DEBATE (Agenda item 8)
Tshisekedi Tshilombo, Félix Antoine - A/78/PV.7

Democratic Republic of the Congo. President (continued)

UN. GENERAL ASSEMBLY (78TH SESS. : 2023-2024)—SPECIAL STATEMENTS
Tshisekedi Tshilombo, Félix Antoine - A/78/PV.7

Denmark

CRIMES AGAINST HUMANITY (Agenda item 80)
Laursen, Erik - A/C.6/78/SR.41
DISASTER VICTIMS (Agenda item 86)
Laursen, Erik - A/C.6/78/SR.5
ELECTION VERIFICATION—UN (Agenda item 71b)
Scheuer, Emil Fischer-Nielsen - A/C.3/78/SR.50
HUMAN RIGHTS ADVANCEMENT (Agenda item 71b)
Rendtorff-Smith, Sara - A/C.3/78/SR.52
INDIGENOUS PEOPLES (Agenda item 68a)
Lassen, Christina Markus - A/C.3/78/SR.15
INDIGENOUS PEOPLES—CONFERENCES (Agenda item 68b)
Lassen, Christina Markus - A/C.3/78/SR.15
INTERNATIONAL LAW—TRAINING PROGRAMMES (Agenda item 78)
Laursen, Erik - A/C.6/78/SR.21
PEACEBUILDING (Agenda item 61)
Laursen, Erik - A/78/PV.100
RULE OF LAW (Agenda item 83)
Laursen, Erik - A/C.6/78/SR.15
TERRORISM (Agenda item 109)
Laursen, Erik - A/C.6/78/SR.1
TORTURE AND OTHER CRUEL TREATMENT (Agenda item 71a)
Lassen, Christina Markus - A/C.3/78/SR.18
TREATIES (Agenda item 87)
Byth-Visholm, Sebastian - A/C.6/78/SR.20
UKRAINE—POLITICAL CONDITIONS (Agenda item 62)
Zilmer-Johns, Lisbet - A/78/PV.56
UN. GENERAL ASSEMBLY (78TH SESS. : 2023-2024)—GENERAL DEBATE (Agenda item 8)
Jørgensen, Dan - A/78/PV.9
UN. GENERAL ASSEMBLY (78TH SESS. : 2023-2024). 1ST COMMITTEE—GENERAL DEBATE (Agenda item 8)
Laursen, Erik - A/C.1/78/PV.2
UN. INTERNATIONAL COURT OF JUSTICE—REPORTS (Agenda item 73)
Pasternak Jørgensen, Vibeke - A/78/PV.20
UN. INTERNATIONAL LAW COMMISSION—REPORTS (Agenda item 79)
Byth-Visholm, Sebastian - A/C.6/78/SR.30
Laursen, Erik - A/C.6/78/SR.29
Pasternak Jørgensen, Vibeke - A/C.6/78/SR.23
UN. PEACEBUILDING COMMISSION—REPORTS (Agenda item 27)
Laursen, Erik - A/78/PV.100

Denmark (continued)

UN. PEACEBUILDING FUND—REPORTS (Agenda item 111)
Laursen, Erik - A/78/PV.100
UN. SECURITY COUNCIL—MEMBERSHIP (Agenda item 121)
Laursen, Erik - A/78/PV.34
UN HIGH COMMISSIONER FOR REFUGEES—REPORTS (Agenda item 60)
Lassen, Christina Markus - A/C.3/78/SR.44
Laursen, Erik - A/C.3/78/SR.51
Rasmussen, Lea - A/C.3/78/SR.44
UNRWA—ACTIVITIES (Agenda item 49)
Lassen, Christina Markus - A/C.4/78/SR.22
VETO (Agenda item 63)
Lassen, Christina Markus - A/78/PV.3; A/78/PV.78
Laursen, Erik - A/78/PV.70
YOUTH (Agenda item 24b)
Andersen, Julie Juel - A/C.3/78/SR.55
Blasius, Jacob - A/C.3/78/SR.3
Zade Iseni, Cecilia - A/C.3/78/SR.3

Derechos Humanos sin Fronteras (Organization : Peru)

WESTERN SAHARA QUESTION (Agenda item 58)
Moraga Duque, Juan Carlos - A/C.4/78/SR.5

Djibouti

CRIMES AGAINST HUMANITY (Agenda item 80)
Moussa, Moussa Mohamed - A/C.6/78/SR.11
ELECTION VERIFICATION—UN (Agenda item 71b)
Moussa, Youssouf Aden - A/78/PV.50
HUMAN RIGHTS INSTITUTIONS—CENTRAL AFRICA (Agenda item 71b)
Moussa, Youssouf Aden - A/C.3/78/SR.56
INFORMATION—INTERNATIONAL SECURITY (Agenda item 94)
Assoweh, Zeinab Ismaël - A/C.1/78/PV.29
RULE OF LAW (Agenda item 83)
Moussa, Moussa Mohamed - A/C.6/78/SR.17
SOCIAL CONDITIONS (Agenda item 24b)
Moussa, Youssouf Aden - A/78/PV.101
TERRORISM (Agenda item 109)
Moussa, Moussa Mohamed - A/C.6/78/SR.4
UN. GENERAL ASSEMBLY (78TH SESS. : 2023-2024)—AGENDA (Agenda item 7)
Moussa, Youssouf Aden - A/BUR/78/SR.2
UN. GENERAL ASSEMBLY (78TH SESS. : 2023-2024)—GENERAL DEBATE (Agenda item 8)
Youssouf, Mahamoud Ali - A/78/PV.13
UN. GENERAL ASSEMBLY (78TH SESS. : 2023-2024). 1ST COMMITTEE—GENERAL DEBATE (Agenda item 8)
Assoweh, Zeinab Ismaël - A/C.1/78/PV.8

Djibouti (continued)

UN. INTERNATIONAL LAW COMMISSION—REPORTS (Agenda item 79)
Moussa, Moussa Mohamed - A/C.6/78/SR.30
WESTERN SAHARA QUESTION (Agenda item 58)
Moussa, Youssouf Aden - A/C.4/78/SR.8
WOMEN'S ADVANCEMENT—CONFERENCES (Agenda item 25b)
Moussa, Youssouf Aden - A/C.3/78/SR.51
YOUTH (Agenda item 24b)
Moussa, Youssouf Aden - A/C.3/78/SR.55

Dominica

CUBA—UNITED STATES (Agenda item 38)
Darroux, Kelver Dwight - A/78/PV.24

Dominica. President

UN. GENERAL ASSEMBLY (78TH SESS. : 2023-2024)—GENERAL DEBATE (Agenda item 8)
Savarin, Charles Angelo - A/78/PV.8
UN. GENERAL ASSEMBLY (78TH SESS. : 2023-2024)—SPECIAL STATEMENTS
Savarin, Charles Angelo - A/78/PV.8

Dominican Republic

AGEING PERSONS (Agenda item 24b)
Andújar, Luz del Carmen - A/C.3/78/SR.1; A/C.3/78/SR.3
CLIMATE CHANGE (Agenda item 71b)
Andújar, Luz del Carmen - A/C.3/78/SR.29
CRIME PREVENTION (Agenda item 107)
Cedano, Joan Margarita - A/C.3/78/SR.6
CRIMES AGAINST HUMANITY (Agenda item 80)
Rodríguez Torres, Radhafil - A/C.6/78/SR.11
CYBERCRIME (Agenda item 108)
Cedano, Joan Margarita - A/C.3/78/SR.6
ELECTION VERIFICATION—UN (Agenda item 71b)
Andújar, Luz del Carmen - A/C.3/78/SR.50
ENVIRONMENT (Agenda item 71b)
Andújar, Luz del Carmen - A/C.3/78/SR.29
FALKLAND ISLANDS (MALVINAS) QUESTION (Agenda item 42)
Blanco Conde, José Alfonso - A/C.4/78/SR.7
HEALTH (Agenda item 125)
Matos Menéndez, Gala - A/78/PV.16
HUMAN RIGHTS—AFGHANISTAN (Agenda item 71c)
Andújar, Luz del Carmen - A/C.3/78/SR.34
HUMAN RIGHTS ADVANCEMENT (Agenda item 71b)
Cedano, Joan Margarita - A/C.3/78/SR.26
INFORMATION (Agenda item 53)
Cedano, Joan Margarita - A/C.4/78/SR.13
INFORMATION TECHNOLOGY—DEVELOPMENT (Agenda item 15)
Rubio, Celina - A/C.2/78/SR.10

Dominican Republic (continued)

PEACEKEEPING OPERATIONS (Agenda item 51)
Blanco Conde, José Alfonso - A/C.4/78/SR.20
PERSONS WITH DISABILITIES (Agenda item 24b)
Andújar, Luz del Carmen - A/C.3/78/SR.3
PERSONS WITH DISABILITIES—HUMAN RIGHTS (Agenda item 71a)
Matos Menéndez, Gala - A/C.3/78/SR.38
RIGHT TO EDUCATION (Agenda item 71b)
Matos Menéndez, Gala - A/C.3/78/SR.27
RIGHT TO FOOD (Agenda item 71b)
Andújar, Luz del Carmen - A/C.3/78/SR.30
RIGHT TO HEALTH (Agenda item 71b)
Matos Menéndez, Gala - A/C.3/78/SR.39
RIGHTS OF THE CHILD (Agenda item 67)
Matos Menéndez, Gala - A/C.3/78/SR.11; A/C.3/78/SR.13
RULE OF LAW (Agenda item 83)
Cedano, Joan Margarita - A/C.6/78/SR.18
SOCIAL CONDITIONS (Agenda item 24b)
Matos Menéndez, Gala - A/C.3/78/SR.51
SOCIAL DEVELOPMENT (Agenda item 24)
Andújar, Luz del Carmen - A/C.3/78/SR.3
TERRORISM (Agenda item 109)
Blanco Conde, José Alfonso - A/C.6/78/SR.4
TORTURE AND OTHER CRUEL TREATMENT (Agenda item 71a)
Andújar, Luz del Carmen - A/C.3/78/SR.18
TRAFFICKING IN PERSONS (Agenda item 71b)
Andújar, Luz del Carmen - A/C.3/78/SR.23
UN. GENERAL ASSEMBLY (78TH SESS. : 2023-2024). 1ST COMMITTEE—GENERAL DEBATE (Agenda item 8)
Luna, Madelin Esther - A/C.1/78/PV.9
UN. GENERAL ASSEMBLY (78TH SESS. : 2023-2024). 2ND COMMITTEE—GENERAL DEBATE (Agenda item 8)
Blanco Conde, José Alfonso - A/C.2/78/SR.3
LaRue, Claudia M. - A/C.2/78/SR.2
UN. HUMAN RIGHTS COUNCIL—REPORTS (Agenda item 66)
Andújar, Luz del Carmen - A/C.3/78/SR.46
Cedano, Joan Margarita - A/78/PV.28
VETO (Agenda item 63)
Hidalgo, Melanie - A/78/PV.3
WESTERN SAHARA QUESTION (Agenda item 58)
Blanco Conde, José Alfonso - A/C.4/78/SR.7
WOMEN'S ADVANCEMENT (Agenda item 25a)
Blanco Conde, José Alfonso - A/78/PV.88; A/C.3/78/SR.7
Cedano, Joan Margarita - A/C.3/78/SR.9
WOMEN'S ADVANCEMENT—CONFERENCES (Agenda item 25b)
Blanco Conde, José Alfonso - A/C.3/78/SR.7
Cedano, Joan Margarita - A/C.3/78/SR.9

Dominican Republic (continued)

YOUTH (Agenda item 24b)
Andújar, Luz del Carmen - A/C.3/78/SR.3; A/C.3/78/SR.55

Dominican Republic. President

UN. GENERAL ASSEMBLY (78TH SESS. : 2023-2024)—GENERAL DEBATE (Agenda item 8)
Abinader Corona, Luis Rodolfo - A/78/PV.7
UN. GENERAL ASSEMBLY (78TH SESS. : 2023-2024)—SPECIAL STATEMENTS
Abinader Corona, Luis Rodolfo - A/78/PV.7

Economic Community of Central African States

HUMAN RIGHTS INSTITUTIONS—CENTRAL AFRICA (Agenda item 71b)
Banaken Elel, Nelly (Cameroon) - A/C.3/78/SR.56

Ecuador

AGEING PERSONS (Agenda item 24b)
Méndez Gruezo, Elizabeth - A/C.3/78/SR.2
BIOLOGICAL DIVERSITY—TREATIES (Agenda item 18f)
Barba Bustos, Irina Alexandra - A/C.2/78/SR.13
CLIMATE (Agenda item 18d)
Barba Bustos, Irina Alexandra - A/C.2/78/SR.13
CRIME PREVENTION (Agenda item 107)
Bravo, Karina - A/C.3/78/SR.5
CRIMES AGAINST HUMANITY (Agenda item 80)
Escobar Ullauri, Pablo - A/C.6/78/SR.38
CYBERCRIME (Agenda item 108)
Bravo, Karina - A/C.3/78/SR.5
DECOLONIZATION (Agenda item 58)
Montalvo Sosa, Andrés Efren - A/C.4/78/SR.7
DISASTER PREVENTION (Agenda item 18c)
Barba Bustos, Irina Alexandra - A/C.2/78/SR.13
DISASTER VICTIMS (Agenda item 86)
Escobar Ullauri, Pablo - A/C.6/78/SR.6
FALKLAND ISLANDS (MALVINAS) QUESTION (Agenda item 42)
Montalvo Sosa, Andrés Efren - A/C.4/78/SR.7
FOOD SECURITY (Agenda item 23a)
Barba Bustos, Irina Alexandra - A/C.2/78/SR.17
HUMAN RIGHTS—INTERNATIONAL INSTRUMENTS (Agenda item 71a)
Montalvo Sosa, Andrés Efren - A/C.3/78/SR.26
IAEA—REPORTS (Agenda item 89)
Montalvo Sosa, Andrés Efren - A/78/PV.29
INDIGENOUS PEOPLES (Agenda item 68a)
Pérez Loose, Hernán - A/C.3/78/SR.15
INDIGENOUS PEOPLES—CONFERENCES (Agenda item 68b)
Pérez Loose, Hernán - A/C.3/78/SR.15
INTERNATIONAL CRIMINAL COURT—REPORTS (Agenda item 74)
Escobar Ullauri, Pablo - A/78/PV.21

Ecuador (continued)

MIGRANTS—PROTECTION (Agenda item 71b)
Montalvo Sosa, Andrés Efren - A/C.3/78/SR.26
NON-CITIZENS—DEPORTATION (Agenda item 81)
Escobar Ullauri, Pablo - A/C.6/78/SR.34
PEACE (Agenda item 14)
Montalvo Sosa, Andrés Efren - A/78/PV.77
POVERTY—INTERNATIONAL DECADES (Agenda item 21a)
Barba Bustos, Irina Alexandra - A/C.2/78/SR.17
RIGHTS OF THE CHILD (Agenda item 67)
Méndez Gruezo, Elizabeth - A/C.3/78/SR.13
RULE OF LAW (Agenda item 83)
Escobar Ullauri, Pablo - A/C.6/78/SR.16
RURAL POVERTY (Agenda item 21b)
Barba Bustos, Irina Alexandra - A/C.2/78/SR.17
SOCIAL CONDITIONS (Agenda item 24b)
Méndez Gruezo, Elizabeth - A/C.3/78/SR.2
TERRORISM (Agenda item 109)
Escobar Ullauri, Pablo - A/C.6/78/SR.1
UKRAINE—POLITICAL CONDITIONS (Agenda item 62)
De la Gasca LopezDomínguez, José Javier - A/78/PV.58
UN. GENERAL ASSEMBLY—WORK PROGRAMME (Agenda item 120)
Fiallo Karolys, Andrés Fernando - A/78/PV.32
UN. GENERAL ASSEMBLY (78TH SESS. : 2023-2024). 1ST COMMITTEE—GENERAL DEBATE (Agenda item 8)
Montalvo Sosa, Andrés Efren - A/C.1/78/PV.5
UN. GENERAL ASSEMBLY (78TH SESS. : 2023-2024). 2ND COMMITTEE—GENERAL DEBATE (Agenda item 8)
Montalvo Sosa, Andrés Efren - A/C.2/78/SR.5
UN. HUMAN RIGHTS COUNCIL—REPORTS (Agenda item 66)
Méndez Gruezo, Elizabeth - A/C.3/78/SR.46
UN. INTERNATIONAL COURT OF JUSTICE—REPORTS (Agenda item 73)
Escobar Ullauri, Pablo - A/78/PV.27; A/C.6/78/SR.26
UN. INTERNATIONAL LAW COMMISSION—REPORTS (Agenda item 79)
Escobar Ullauri, Pablo - A/C.6/78/SR.24; A/C.6/78/SR.31
UN. SECURITY COUNCIL—MEMBERSHIP (Agenda item 121)
Montalvo Sosa, Andrés Efren - A/78/PV.36
UN COMMISSION ON INTERNATIONAL TRADE LAW—REPORTS (Agenda item 77)
Escobar Ullauri, Pablo - A/C.6/78/SR.14
UN RESOLUTIONS—IMPLEMENTATION (Agenda item 119)
Fiallo Karolys, Andrés Fernando - A/78/PV.32
VETO (Agenda item 63)
De la Gasca LopezDomínguez, José Javier - A/78/PV.60; A/78/PV.67; A/78/PV.71; A/78/PV.75; A/78/PV.78
Pérez Loose, Hernán - A/78/PV.3

Ecuador (continued)

VETO (Agenda item 63)
Sánchez Izquierdo, Mónica - A/78/PV.68
WESTERN SAHARA QUESTION (Agenda item 58)
Montalvo Sosa, Andrés Efren - A/C.4/78/SR.7
WOMEN'S ADVANCEMENT (Agenda item 25a)
Méndez Gruezo, Elizabeth - A/C.3/78/SR.9
WOMEN'S ADVANCEMENT—CONFERENCES (Agenda item 25b)
Méndez Gruezo, Elizabeth - A/C.3/78/SR.9
YOUTH (Agenda item 24b)
Méndez Gruezo, Elizabeth - A/C.3/78/SR.2

Ecuador. President

UN. GENERAL ASSEMBLY (78TH SESS. : 2023-2024)—GENERAL DEBATE (Agenda item 8)
Lasso Mendoza, Guillermo - A/78/PV.6
UN. GENERAL ASSEMBLY (78TH SESS. : 2023-2024)—SPECIAL STATEMENTS
Lasso Mendoza, Guillermo - A/78/PV.6

Egypt

2030 AGENDA—PROGRAMME IMPLEMENTATION (Agenda item 18a)
Abdelaal, Ahmed Magdy Mohamed Rashad - A/C.2/78/SR.12
ADMINISTRATION OF JUSTICE (Agenda item 144)
Roshdy, Hussein Ossama Hussein Abdelrhman - A/C.5/78/SR.15
AFRICA—NUCLEAR-WEAPON-FREE ZONES (Agenda item 92)
Ahmed, Amr Essameldin Sadek - A/C.1/78/PV.25
AGEING PERSONS (Agenda item 24b)
Mostafa Rizk, Heba - A/C.3/78/SR.2
ARMS RACE—OUTER SPACE (Agenda item 97a)
Hegazy, Abdelrhman Mohamed Farid - A/C.1/78/PV.16
ARMS TRANSFERS—TREATIES (Agenda item 99x)
Hegazy, Abdelrhman Mohamed Farid - A/C.1/78/PV.18; A/C.1/78/PV.28
BIOLOGICAL DIVERSITY—TREATIES (Agenda item 18f)
Abdelaal, Ahmed Magdy Mohamed Rashad - A/C.2/78/SR.12
BIOLOGICAL WEAPONS—TREATIES (Agenda item 106)
Ahmed, Amr Essameldin Sadek - A/C.1/78/PV.14
CHEMICAL WEAPONS—TREATIES (Agenda item 99l)
Ahmed, Amr Essameldin Sadek - A/C.1/78/PV.14; A/C.1/78/PV.26
CLIMATE (Agenda item 18d)
Abdelaal, Ahmed Magdy Mohamed Rashad - A/C.2/78/SR.12

Egypt (continued)

CLUSTER MUNITIONS (Agenda item 99dd)
Hegazy, Abdelrhman Mohamed Farid - A/C.1/78/PV.28
CONVENTIONAL WEAPONS (Agenda item 99u)
Hegazy, Abdelrhman Mohamed Farid - A/C.1/78/PV.18; A/C.1/78/PV.28
CRIME PREVENTION (Agenda item 107)
Mostafa Rizk, Heba - A/C.3/78/SR.6; A/C.3/78/SR.56
CRIMES AGAINST HUMANITY (Agenda item 80)
Elhomosany, Mohamed Kamal Ali - A/C.6/78/SR.10
Nouh, Amr Mohamed Mosaad - A/C.6/78/SR.43; A/C.6/78/SR.47
Roshdy, Hussein Ossama Hussein Abdelrhman - A/C.6/78/SR.39; A/C.6/78/SR.41; A/C.6/78/SR.42; A/C.6/78/SR.44
CUBA—UNITED STATES (Agenda item 38)
Elshandawily, Ahmed - A/78/PV.26
CYBERCRIME (Agenda item 108)
Mostafa Rizk, Heba - A/C.3/78/SR.6
DEVELOPMENT FINANCE (Agenda item 16b)
Abdelaal, Ahmed Magdy Mohamed Rashad - A/C.2/78/SR.9
DISARMAMENT—GENERAL AND COMPLETE (Agenda item 99)
Ahmed, Amr Essameldin Sadek - A/C.1/78/PV.23; A/C.1/78/PV.30
Hegazy, Abdelrhman Mohamed Farid - A/C.1/78/PV.18; A/C.1/78/PV.28
DISARMAMENT—UN. GENERAL ASSEMBLY (4TH SPECIAL SESS. ON DISARMAMENT : xxxx) (Agenda item 99h)
Ahmed, Amr Essameldin Sadek - A/C.1/78/PV.23
DISARMAMENT AGREEMENTS—OUTER SPACE (Agenda item 97c)
Hegazy, Abdelrhman Mohamed Farid - A/C.1/78/PV.16; A/C.1/78/PV.27
DISASTER VICTIMS (Agenda item 86)
Nouh, Amr Mohamed Mosaad - A/C.6/78/SR.6
ELECTION VERIFICATION—UN (Agenda item 71b)
Mostafa Rizk, Heba - A/78/PV.50; A/C.3/78/SR.50
EXTERNAL DEBT (Agenda item 16c)
Abdelaal, Ahmed Magdy Mohamed Rashad - A/C.2/78/SR.9
Elsaeed, Sherine Mohamed Eissa Ahmed - A/C.2/78/SR.8
FAMILY (Agenda item 24b)
Mostafa Rizk, Heba - A/C.3/78/SR.2
FISSIONABLE MATERIALS—TREATIES (Agenda item 99a)
Ahmed, Amr Essameldin Sadek - A/C.1/78/PV.25; A/C.1/78/PV.26
FREEDOM OF EXPRESSION (Agenda item 71b)
Mostafa Rizk, Heba - A/C.3/78/SR.19
HEALTH (Agenda item 125)
Elshandawily, Ahmed - A/78/PV.16

Egypt (continued)

HEALTH (Agenda item 125)
Mohamed, Mohamed Omar Elfarouk Hassan - A/78/PV.41; A/78/PV.77
Mostafa Rizk, Heba - A/78/PV.48
HUMAN RIGHTS (Agenda item 71)
Mostafa Rizk, Heba - A/C.3/78/SR.16
HUMAN RIGHTS—BURUNDI (Agenda item 71c)
Eldahshan, Wael Mahmoud Abdelaziz - A/C.3/78/SR.36
HUMAN RIGHTS—REPORTS (Agenda item 71c)
Mostafa Rizk, Heba - A/C.3/78/SR.26
HUMAN RIGHTS—TERRITORIES OCCUPIED BY ISRAEL (Agenda item 71c)
Eldahshan, Wael Mahmoud Abdelaziz - A/C.3/78/SR.35
HUMAN RIGHTS ACTIVISTS (Agenda item 71b)
Mostafa Rizk, Heba - A/C.3/78/SR.56
HUMAN RIGHTS ADVANCEMENT (Agenda item 71b)
Mostafa Rizk, Heba - A/C.3/78/SR.52
IAEA—REPORTS (Agenda item 89)
Ahmed, Amr Essameldin Sadek - A/78/PV.30
INFORMATION (Agenda item 53)
Elshandawily, Ahmed - A/C.4/78/SR.12
INFORMATION—INTERNATIONAL SECURITY (Agenda item 94)
Hegazy, Abdelrhman Mohamed Farid - A/C.1/78/PV.20; A/C.1/78/PV.29
INTERNATIONAL JURISDICTION (Agenda item 84)
Roshdy, Hussein Ossama Hussein Abdelrhman - A/C.6/78/SR.12
INTERNATIONAL LAW—TRAINING PROGRAMMES (Agenda item 78)
Nouh, Amr Mohamed Mosaad - A/C.6/78/SR.21
LANDMINES—TREATIES (Agenda item 99m)
Hegazy, Abdelrhman Mohamed Farid - A/C.1/78/PV.28
MIDDLE EAST—NUCLEAR PROLIFERATION (Agenda item 102)
Ahmed, Amr Essameldin Sadek - A/C.1/78/PV.11; A/C.1/78/PV.25
MIDDLE EAST—NUCLEAR-WEAPON-FREE ZONES (Agenda item 95)
Ahmed, Amr Essameldin Sadek - A/C.1/78/PV.11; A/C.1/78/PV.14; A/C.1/78/PV.21; A/C.1/78/PV.25
MIDDLE EAST SITUATION (Agenda item 34)
Abdelkhalek, Osama Mahmoud - A/78/PV.40
MIGRANTS—PROTECTION (Agenda item 71b)
Mohamed, Mohamed Omar Elfarouk Hassan - A/C.3/78/SR.23; A/C.3/78/SR.56
MILLENNIUM SUMMIT—CONFERENCES (Agenda item 117)
Abdelkhalek, Osama Mahmoud - A/78/PV.15

Egypt (continued)

NUCLEAR DISARMAMENT (Agenda item 99b)
Ahmed, Amr Essameldin Sadek - A/C.1/78/PV.11
NUCLEAR DISARMAMENT—CONFERENCES (Agenda item 99aa)
Ahmed, Amr Essameldin Sadek - A/C.1/78/PV.25
NUCLEAR DISARMAMENT—TREATY COMPLIANCE (Agenda item 99q)
Ahmed, Amr Essameldin Sadek - A/C.1/78/PV.11; A/C.1/78/PV.25
NUCLEAR NON-PROLIFERATION—INTERNATIONAL OBLIGATIONS (Agenda item 99w)
Ahmed, Amr Essameldin Sadek - A/C.1/78/PV.11
NUCLEAR WEAPON TESTS—TREATIES (Agenda item 105)
Ahmed, Amr Essameldin Sadek - A/C.1/78/PV.26
OUTER SPACE—CONFIDENCE-BUILDING MEASURES (Agenda item 99v)
Hegazy, Abdelrhman Mohamed Farid - A/C.1/78/PV.16
OUTER SPACE—PRINCIPLES (Agenda item 97d)
Hegazy, Abdelrhman Mohamed Farid - A/C.1/78/PV.16; A/C.1/78/PV.27
PALESTINE QUESTION (Agenda item 35)
Abdelkhalek, Osama Mahmoud - A/78/PV.39
PEACE (Agenda item 14)
Abdelkhalek, Osama Mahmoud - A/78/PV.76; A/78/PV.82
Elshandawily, Ahmed - A/78/PV.62
PEACEBUILDING (Agenda item 61)
Abdelkhalek, Osama Mahmoud - A/78/PV.100
PEACEKEEPING OPERATIONS (Agenda item 51)
Eldahshan, Wael Mahmoud Abdelaziz - A/C.4/78/SR.18
PEACEKEEPING OPERATIONS—CRIMINAL LIABILITY (Agenda item 76)
Nouh, Amr Mohamed Mosaad - A/C.6/78/SR.8
RACIAL DISCRIMINATION—ELIMINATION (Agenda item 69a)
Mostafa Rizk, Heba - A/78/PV.50; A/78/PV.103; A/C.3/78/SR.43; A/C.3/78/SR.47
RACIAL DISCRIMINATION—PROGRAMMES OF ACTION (Agenda item 69b)
Mostafa Rizk, Heba - A/C.3/78/SR.43
RADIOACTIVE WASTES MANAGEMENT (Agenda item 99e)
Ahmed, Amr Essameldin Sadek - A/C.1/78/PV.25
RELIGIOUS INTOLERANCE (Agenda item 71b)
Mostafa Rizk, Heba - A/C.3/78/SR.18; A/C.3/78/SR.26
RESPONSIBILITY OF INTERNATIONAL ORGANIZATIONS (Agenda item 85)
Roshdy, Hussein Ossama Hussein Abdelrhman - A/C.6/78/SR.19
RESPONSIBILITY TO PROTECT (Agenda item 129)
Mostafa Rizk, Heba - A/78/PV.97

Egypt (continued)

RIGHT TO DEVELOPMENT (Agenda item 71b)
Mostafa Rizk, Heba - A/C.3/78/SR.20; A/C.3/78/SR.26; A/C.3/78/SR.48
RIGHT TO DRINKING WATER (Agenda item 71b)
Eldahshan, Wael Mahmoud Abdelaziz - A/C.3/78/SR.28
RIGHT TO EDUCATION (Agenda item 71b)
Mohamed, Mohamed Omar Elfarouk Hassan - A/C.3/78/SR.27
RIGHT TO HEALTH (Agenda item 71b)
Mohamed, Mohamed Omar Elfarouk Hassan - A/C.3/78/SR.39
RIGHTS OF THE CHILD (Agenda item 67)
Eldahshan, Wael Mahmoud Abdelaziz - A/C.3/78/SR.11
Mohamed, Mohamed Omar Elfarouk Hassan - A/C.3/78/SR.11; A/C.3/78/SR.12; A/C.3/78/SR.55
RULE OF LAW (Agenda item 83)
Nouh, Amr Mohamed Mosaad - A/C.6/78/SR.16
RURAL WOMEN (Agenda item 25a)
Mostafa Rizk, Heba - A/C.3/78/SR.10; A/C.3/78/SR.49
SELF-DETERMINATION OF PEOPLES (Agenda item 70)
Mostafa Rizk, Heba - A/78/PV.50; A/C.3/78/SR.43
SMALL ARMS—ILLICIT TRAFFIC (Agenda item 99p)
Hegazy, Abdelrhman Mohamed Farid - A/C.1/78/PV.18; A/C.1/78/PV.28
SMALL ARMS—ILLICIT TRAFFIC—ASSISTANCE (Agenda item 99n)
Hegazy, Abdelrhman Mohamed Farid - A/C.1/78/PV.18
SOCIAL CONDITIONS (Agenda item 24b)
Mohamed, Mohamed Omar Elfarouk Hassan - A/C.3/78/SR.51
Mostafa Rizk, Heba - A/78/PV.57; A/C.3/78/SR.2
SPECIAL POLITICAL MISSIONS (Agenda item 52)
Eldahshan, Wael Mahmoud Abdelaziz - A/C.4/78/SR.21
SPORTS—OLYMPIC GAMES (Agenda item 11)
Hassan, Khaled Aly Awadalla - A/78/PV.38
SUSTAINABLE DEVELOPMENT (Agenda item 18)
Abdelaal, Ahmed Magdy Mohamed Rashad - A/C.2/78/SR.12; A/C.2/78/SR.24
TERRITORIES OCCUPIED BY ISRAEL—HUMAN RIGHTS (Agenda item 50)
Elshandawily, Ahmed - A/C.4/78/SR.24
TERRITORIES OCCUPIED BY ISRAEL—NATURAL RESOURCES (Agenda item 59)
Abdelaal, Ahmed Magdy Mohamed Rashad - A/C.2/78/SR.19
TERRORISM (Agenda item 109)
Elhomosany, Mohamed Kamal Ali - A/C.6/78/SR.2

Egypt (continued)

TERRORISM—HUMAN RIGHTS (Agenda item 71b)
Eldahshan, Wael Mahmoud Abdelaziz - A/C.3/78/SR.31
TORTURE AND OTHER CRUEL TREATMENT (Agenda item 71a)
Eldahshan, Wael Mahmoud Abdelaziz - A/C.3/78/SR.18
TRAFFICKING IN PERSONS (Agenda item 71b)
Mohamed, Mohamed Omar Elfarouk Hassan - A/C.3/78/SR.23
UN. CONFERENCE ON DISARMAMENT—REPORTS (Agenda item 101a)
Ahmed, Amr Essameldin Sadek - A/C.1/78/PV.23
UN. DISARMAMENT COMMISSION—REPORTS (Agenda item 101b)
Ahmed, Amr Essameldin Sadek - A/C.1/78/PV.23
UN. GENERAL ASSEMBLY—WORK PROGRAMME (Agenda item 120)
Abdelkhalek, Osama Mahmoud - A/78/PV.32
Nouh, Amr Mohamed Mosaad - A/C.6/78/SR.36
UN. GENERAL ASSEMBLY (78TH SESS. : 2023-2024)—GENERAL DEBATE (Agenda item 8)
Selim, Sameh Hassan Shokry - A/78/PV.12
UN. GENERAL ASSEMBLY (78TH SESS. : 2023-2024). 1ST COMMITTEE—GENERAL DEBATE (Agenda item 8)
Ahmed, Amr Essameldin Sadek - A/C.1/78/PV.3
UN. GENERAL ASSEMBLY (78TH SESS. : 2023-2024). 1ST COMMITTEE—WORK ORGANIZATION (Agenda item 7)
Ahmed, Amr Essameldin Sadek - A/C.1/78/PV.26; A/C.1/78/PV.30
UN. GENERAL ASSEMBLY (78TH SESS. : 2023-2024). 2ND COMMITTEE—GENERAL DEBATE (Agenda item 8)
Abdelkhalek, Osama Mahmoud - A/C.2/78/SR.2
UN. GENERAL ASSEMBLY (78TH SESS. : 2023-2024). 5TH COMMITTEE—WORK ORGANIZATION (Agenda item 7)
Roshdy, Hussein Ossama Hussein Abdelrhman - A/C.5/78/SR.26/PartII; A/C.5/78/SR.40
UN. HUMAN RIGHTS COUNCIL—REPORTS (Agenda item 66)
Mostafa Rizk, Heba - A/78/PV.28; A/C.3/78/SR.46
UN. INTERNATIONAL COURT OF JUSTICE—REPORTS (Agenda item 73)
Roshdy, Hussein Ossama Hussein Abdelrhman - A/78/PV.28
UN. PEACEBUILDING COMMISSION—REPORTS (Agenda item 27)
Abdelkhalek, Osama Mahmoud - A/78/PV.100
UN. PEACEBUILDING FUND—REPORTS (Agenda item 111)
Abdelkhalek, Osama Mahmoud - A/78/PV.100

Egypt (continued)

UN. SECURITY COUNCIL—MEMBERSHIP (Agenda item 121)
Abdelkhalek, Osama Mahmoud - A/78/PV.35
UN CHARTER—REPORTS (Agenda item 82)
Attelb, Abdullah Ibrahim Abdelhamud Alsayed - A/C.6/78/SR.34
UN COMMISSION ON INTERNATIONAL TRADE LAW—REPORTS (Agenda item 77)
Attelb, Abdullah Ibrahim Abdelhamud Alsayed - A/C.6/78/SR.14
UN CONFERENCES (Agenda item 13)
Abdelkhalek, Osama Mahmoud - A/78/PV.15
UN HIGH COMMISSIONER FOR REFUGEES—REPORTS (Agenda item 60)
Mohamed, Mohamed Omar Elfarouk Hassan - A/C.3/78/SR.44
UN RESOLUTIONS—IMPLEMENTATION (Agenda item 119)
Abdelkhalek, Osama Mahmoud - A/78/PV.32
Mohamed, Mohamed Omar Elfarouk Hassan - A/78/PV.108
UN YOUTH OFFICE—REPORTS (Agenda item 130)
Mohamed, Mohamed Omar Elfarouk Hassan - A/78/PV.102
UNRWA—ACTIVITIES (Agenda item 49)
Elshandawily, Ahmed - A/C.4/78/SR.22
VETO (Agenda item 63)
Abdelkhalek, Osama Mahmoud - A/78/PV.52; A/78/PV.60; A/78/PV.66; A/78/PV.70; A/78/PV.74
WEAPONS OF MASS DESTRUCTION—TERRORISM (Agenda item 99s)
Ahmed, Amr Essameldin Sadek - A/C.1/78/PV.14
WOMEN MIGRANT WORKERS (Agenda item 25a)
Mohamed, Mohamed Omar Elfarouk Hassan - A/C.3/78/SR.49
WOMEN'S ADVANCEMENT (Agenda item 25a)
Mostafa Rizk, Heba - A/C.3/78/SR.10
WOMEN'S ADVANCEMENT—CONFERENCES (Agenda item 25b)
Mostafa Rizk, Heba - A/C.3/78/SR.10
YOUTH (Agenda item 24b)
Mohamed, Mohamed Omar Elfarouk Hassan - A/C.3/78/SR.55

El Salvador

AGEING PERSONS (Agenda item 24b)
González López, Egriselda Aracely - A/C.3/78/SR.1
CLIMATE (Agenda item 18d)
González López, Egriselda Aracely - A/C.2/78/SR.13
CONVENTIONAL WEAPONS (Agenda item 99u)
Rodríguez Acosta, Julia Elizabeth - A/C.1/78/PV.18

El Salvador (continued)

CRIMES AGAINST HUMANITY (Agenda item 80)
Flores Soto, Ligia Lorena - A/C.6/78/SR.10; A/C.6/78/SR.39; A/C.6/78/SR.40; A/C.6/78/SR.42; A/C.6/78/SR.43; A/C.6/78/SR.45
DECOLONIZATION (Agenda item 58)
González López, Egriselda Aracely - A/C.4/78/SR.2
DEVELOPMENT FINANCE (Agenda item 16b)
González López, Egriselda Aracely - A/C.2/78/SR.8
DISARMAMENT—GENERAL AND COMPLETE (Agenda item 99)
Rodríguez Acosta, Julia Elizabeth - A/C.1/78/PV.18
DISARMAMENT AGREEMENTS—OUTER SPACE (Agenda item 97c)
Rodríguez Acosta, Julia Elizabeth - A/C.1/78/PV.27
ECONOMIC COOPERATION AMONG DEVELOPING COUNTRIES (Agenda item 22b)
González López, Egriselda Aracely - A/C.2/78/SR.18
FALKLAND ISLANDS (MALVINAS) QUESTION (Agenda item 42)
González López, Egriselda Aracely - A/C.4/78/SR.2
FOOD SECURITY (Agenda item 23a)
Barahona Figueroa, Andrea Alejandra - A/C.2/78/SR.16
HUMAN RIGHTS—INTERNATIONAL INSTRUMENTS (Agenda item 71a)
Sorto Rosales, Mayra Lisseth - A/C.3/78/SR.17
IAEA—REPORTS (Agenda item 89)
González López, Egriselda Aracely - A/78/PV.29
INFORMATION (Agenda item 53)
González López, Egriselda Aracely - A/C.4/78/SR.13
INFORMATION—INTERNATIONAL SECURITY (Agenda item 94)
González López, Egriselda Aracely - A/C.1/78/PV.20
INTERNATIONAL CRIMINAL COURT—REPORTS (Agenda item 74)
González López, Egriselda Aracely - A/78/PV.25
INTERNATIONAL JURISDICTION (Agenda item 84)
Flores Soto, Ligia Lorena - A/C.6/78/SR.13
INTERNATIONAL LAW—TRAINING PROGRAMMES (Agenda item 78)
González López, Egriselda Aracely - A/C.6/78/SR.21
LAW OF THE SEA (Agenda item 75a)
Flores Soto, Ligia Lorena - A/78/PV.44
MACROECONOMIC POLICY (Agenda item 16)
González López, Egriselda Aracely - A/C.2/78/SR.8

El Salvador (continued)

MARINE ECOSYSTEMS—BIOLOGICAL DIVERSITY (Agenda item 75c)
Flores Soto, Ligia Lorena - A/78/PV.44
MIGRANT WORKERS (Agenda item 71a)
Sorto Rosales, Mayra Lisseth - A/C.3/78/SR.23
MIGRANTS—PROTECTION (Agenda item 71b)
Segura Aragón, Carlos Efraín - A/C.3/78/SR.23
Sorto Rosales, Mayra Lisseth - A/C.3/78/SR.56
MILLENNIUM SUMMIT—CONFERENCES (Agenda item 117)
Flores Soto, Ligia Lorena - A/78/PV.53
MINE CLEARANCE (Agenda item 46)
González López, Egriselda Aracely - A/C.4/78/SR.10
NON-CITIZENS—DEPORTATION (Agenda item 81)
Flores Soto, Ligia Lorena - A/C.6/78/SR.34; A/C.6/78/SR.37
NUCLEAR DISARMAMENT (Agenda item 99b)
Segura Aragón, Carlos Efraín - A/C.1/78/PV.12
NUCLEAR NON-PROLIFERATION—INTERNATIONAL OBLIGATIONS (Agenda item 99w)
Segura Aragón, Carlos Efraín - A/C.1/78/PV.12
NUCLEAR WEAPONS—TREATIES (Agenda item 99ff)
Segura Aragón, Carlos Efraín - A/C.1/78/PV.12
NUCLEAR-WEAPON-FREE ZONES (Agenda item 99cc)
Segura Aragón, Carlos Efraín - A/C.1/78/PV.12
OPERATIONAL ACTIVITIES—UN SYSTEM (Agenda item 22a)
González López, Egriselda Aracely - A/C.2/78/SR.18
OUTER SPACE—PEACEFUL USES—INTERNATIONAL COOPERATION (Agenda item 48)
Baños Müller, Liliana Verónica - A/C.4/78/SR.16
OUTER SPACE—PRINCIPLES (Agenda item 97d)
Rodríguez Acosta, Julia Elizabeth - A/C.1/78/PV.27
PEACEBUILDING (Agenda item 61)
González López, Egriselda Aracely - A/78/PV.100
PEACEKEEPING OPERATIONS (Agenda item 51)
González López, Egriselda Aracely - A/C.4/78/SR.19
PEACEKEEPING OPERATIONS—CRIMINAL LIABILITY (Agenda item 76)
González López, Egriselda Aracely - A/C.6/78/SR.8
PERSONS WITH DISABILITIES—HUMAN RIGHTS (Agenda item 71a)
Segura Aragón, Carlos Efraín - A/C.3/78/SR.38
POVERTY—INTERNATIONAL DECADES (Agenda item 21a)
Barahona Figueroa, Andrea Alejandra - A/C.2/78/SR.16

El Salvador (continued)

RESPONSIBILITY OF INTERNATIONAL ORGANIZATIONS (Agenda item 85)
Flores Soto, Ligia Lorena - A/C.6/78/SR.19
RIGHT TO EDUCATION (Agenda item 71b)
González López, Egriselda Aracely - A/C.3/78/SR.27
RIGHT TO FOOD (Agenda item 71b)
Amaya Garay, Sofía Alejandra - A/C.3/78/SR.30
RIGHT TO HEALTH (Agenda item 71b)
Segura Aragón, Carlos Efraín - A/C.3/78/SR.39
RIGHT TO HOUSING (Agenda item 71b)
Amaya Garay, Sofía Alejandra - A/C.3/78/SR.30
RIGHTS OF THE CHILD (Agenda item 67)
Segura Aragón, Carlos Efraín - A/C.3/78/SR.12
Sorto Rosales, Mayra Lisseth - A/C.3/78/SR.55
RULE OF LAW (Agenda item 83)
Flores Soto, Ligia Lorena - A/C.6/78/SR.18
RURAL POVERTY (Agenda item 21b)
Barahona Figueroa, Andrea Alejandra - A/C.2/78/SR.16
SCIENCE AND TECHNOLOGY—DEVELOPMENT (Agenda item 19a)
Mira Ramírez, Walter José - A/C.2/78/SR.10
SMALL ARMS—ILLICIT TRAFFIC (Agenda item 99p)
Rodríguez Acosta, Julia Elizabeth - A/C.1/78/PV.18
SMALL ARMS—ILLICIT TRAFFIC—ASSISTANCE (Agenda item 99n)
Rodríguez Acosta, Julia Elizabeth - A/C.1/78/PV.18
SPECIAL POLITICAL MISSIONS (Agenda item 52)
González López, Egriselda Aracely - A/C.4/78/SR.21
STRADDLING FISH STOCKS (Agenda item 75b)
Flores Soto, Ligia Lorena - A/78/PV.44
SUSTAINABLE DEVELOPMENT (Agenda item 18)
Segura Aragón, Carlos Efraín - A/C.2/78/SR.22
TERRORISM (Agenda item 109)
González López, Egriselda Aracely - A/C.6/78/SR.2
TREATIES (Agenda item 87)
Flores Soto, Ligia Lorena - A/C.6/78/SR.20
UN—BUDGET (2024) (Agenda item 134)
González López, Egriselda Aracely - A/C.5/78/SR.5
Herrera García, Edilma America - A/C.5/78/SR.18
UN—PROGRAMME PLANNING (Agenda item 135)
González López, Egriselda Aracely - A/C.1/78/PV.10; A/C.5/78/SR.5
UN. GENERAL ASSEMBLY—WORK PROGRAMME (Agenda item 120)
González López, Egriselda Aracely - A/78/PV.32; A/C.1/78/PV.10
Sorto Rosales, Mayra Lisseth - A/C.3/78/SR.56

El Salvador (continued)

UN. GENERAL ASSEMBLY (78TH SESS. : 2023-2024)—OFFICERS (Agenda item 5)
González López, Egriselda Aracely - A/C.5/78/SR.39
UN. HUMAN RIGHTS COUNCIL—REPORTS (Agenda item 66)
González López, Egriselda Aracely - A/C.3/78/SR.46
UN. INTERNATIONAL COURT OF JUSTICE—REPORTS (Agenda item 73)
Flores Soto, Ligia Lorena - A/C.6/78/SR.26
UN. INTERNATIONAL LAW COMMISSION—REPORTS (Agenda item 79)
Flores Soto, Ligia Lorena - A/C.6/78/SR.28; A/C.6/78/SR.29; A/C.6/78/SR.33
UN. PEACEBUILDING COMMISSION—REPORTS (Agenda item 27)
González López, Egriselda Aracely - A/78/PV.100
UN. PEACEBUILDING FUND—REPORTS (Agenda item 111)
González López, Egriselda Aracely - A/78/PV.100
UN. SECURITY COUNCIL—MEMBERSHIP (Agenda item 121)
Segura Aragón, Carlos Efraín - A/78/PV.36
UN. SECURITY COUNCIL—REPORTS (Agenda item 26)
González López, Egriselda Aracely - A/78/PV.93
UN CHARTER—REPORTS (Agenda item 82)
Flores Soto, Ligia Lorena - A/C.6/78/SR.22
UN COMMISSION ON INTERNATIONAL TRADE LAW—REPORTS (Agenda item 77)
Flores Soto, Ligia Lorena - A/C.6/78/SR.14
UN CONFERENCES (Agenda item 13)
Flores Soto, Ligia Lorena - A/78/PV.53
UN RESOLUTIONS—IMPLEMENTATION (Agenda item 119)
González López, Egriselda Aracely - A/78/PV.32
UNRWA—ACTIVITIES (Agenda item 49)
González López, Egriselda Aracely - A/C.4/78/SR.23
VETO (Agenda item 63)
Baños Müller, Liliana Verónica - A/78/PV.79
González López, Egriselda Aracely - A/78/PV.3; A/78/PV.67
Rodríguez Acosta, Julia Elizabeth - A/78/PV.68
Segura Aragón, Carlos Efraín - A/78/PV.61
WESTERN SAHARA QUESTION (Agenda item 58)
González López, Egriselda Aracely - A/C.4/78/SR.2
YOUTH (Agenda item 24b)
Cordero Vargas, Mariana - A/C.3/78/SR.55

El Salvador. President

UN. GENERAL ASSEMBLY (78TH SESS. : 2023-2024)—GENERAL DEBATE (Agenda item 8)
Bukele, Nayib Armando - A/78/PV.5

El Salvador. President (continued)

UN. GENERAL ASSEMBLY (78TH SESS. : 2023-2024)—SPECIAL STATEMENTS
Bukele, Nayib Armando - A/78/PV.5

Episcopal Church (Colombia)

WESTERN SAHARA QUESTION (Agenda item 58)
Guevara Rodríguez, Carlos Eduardo - A/C.4/78/SR.4

Equatorial Guinea

BIOLOGICAL WEAPONS—TREATIES (Agenda item 106)
Edu Mbasogo, Marcial - A/C.1/78/PV.15
CHEMICAL WEAPONS—TREATIES (Agenda item 99l)
Edu Mbasogo, Marcial - A/C.1/78/PV.15
CLUSTER MUNITIONS (Agenda item 99dd)
Edu Mbasogo, Marcial - A/C.1/78/PV.19
CONFIDENCE-BUILDING MEASURES (Agenda item 99t)
Edu Mbasogo, Marcial - A/C.1/78/PV.22
CONFIDENCE-BUILDING MEASURES—REGIONAL PROGRAMMES (Agenda item 100e)
Edu Mbasogo, Marcial - A/C.1/78/PV.29
CRIMES AGAINST HUMANITY (Agenda item 80)
Nze Mansogo, Estela Mercedes - A/C.6/78/SR.45
DECOLONIZATION (Agenda item 58)
Edjo Memba, Juan De Dios - A/C.4/78/SR.7
DISASTER VICTIMS (Agenda item 86)
Nze Mansogo, Estela Mercedes - A/C.6/78/SR.6
ECONOMIC SANCTIONS—INTERNATIONAL RELATIONS (Agenda item 28)
Ndong Mba, Anatolio - A/78/PV.90
HUMAN RIGHTS (Agenda item 71)
Mangue, Victoriana Mbasogo - A/C.3/78/SR.28
INTERNATIONAL LAW—TRAINING PROGRAMMES (Agenda item 78)
Nze Mansogo, Estela Mercedes - A/C.6/78/SR.22
LANDMINES—TREATIES (Agenda item 99m)
Edu Mbasogo, Marcial - A/C.1/78/PV.19
MULTILATERALISM—DISARMAMENT (Agenda item 99r)
Edu Mbasogo, Marcial - A/C.1/78/PV.22
NUCLEAR WEAPONS—ELIMINATION (Agenda item 99z)
Edu Mbasogo, Marcial - A/C.1/78/PV.25
RACIAL DISCRIMINATION—ELIMINATION (Agenda item 69a)
Ndong Mba, Anatolio - A/78/PV.63
RESPONSIBILITY OF INTERNATIONAL ORGANIZATIONS (Agenda item 85)
Nze Mansogo, Estela Mercedes - A/C.6/78/SR.19
RESPONSIBILITY TO PROTECT (Agenda item 129)
Ndong Mba, Anatolio - A/78/PV.97
RULE OF LAW (Agenda item 83)
Nze Mansogo, Estela Mercedes - A/C.6/78/SR.18

Equatorial Guinea (continued)

SLAVERY—MEMORIALS (Agenda item 118)
Ndong Mba, Anatolio - A/78/PV.64
SMALL ARMS—ILLICIT TRAFFIC (Agenda item 99p)
Edu Mbasogo, Marcial - A/C.1/78/PV.19
TERRORISM (Agenda item 109)
Ndong Mba, Anatolio - A/C.6/78/SR.2
UN. GENERAL ASSEMBLY (78TH SESS. : 2023-2024). 1ST COMMITTEE—GENERAL DEBATE (Agenda item 8)
Ndong Mba, Anatolio - A/C.1/78/PV.9
UN. INTERNATIONAL COURT OF JUSTICE—REPORTS (Agenda item 73)
Nze Mansogo, Estela Mercedes - A/78/PV.28
UN CHARTER—REPORTS (Agenda item 82)
Nze Mansogo, Estela Mercedes - A/C.6/78/SR.33
WEAPONS OF MASS DESTRUCTION—TERRORISM (Agenda item 99s)
Edu Mbasogo, Marcial - A/C.1/78/PV.15
WESTERN SAHARA QUESTION (Agenda item 58)
Edjo Memba, Juan De Dios - A/C.4/78/SR.7

Equatorial Guinea. Vice-President

UN. GENERAL ASSEMBLY (78TH SESS. : 2023-2024)—GENERAL DEBATE (Agenda item 8)
Nguema Obiang Mangue, Teodoro - A/78/PV.9
UN. GENERAL ASSEMBLY (78TH SESS. : 2023-2024)—SPECIAL STATEMENTS
Nguema Obiang Mangue, Teodoro - A/78/PV.9

Erblaw (Organization)

WESTERN SAHARA QUESTION (Agenda item 58)
Erb, Sherry - A/C.4/78/SR.5

Eritrea

ADMINISTRATION OF JUSTICE (Agenda item 144)
Giorgio, Amanuel - A/C.6/78/SR.9
ARMED CONFLICTS PREVENTION (Agenda item 31a)
Giorgio, Amanuel - A/78/PV.73
CRIME PREVENTION (Agenda item 107)
Gebrekidan, Zebib - A/C.3/78/SR.6
CRIMES AGAINST HUMANITY (Agenda item 80)
Essaias, Meron Habte - A/C.6/78/SR.10; A/C.6/78/SR.38; A/C.6/78/SR.41; A/C.6/78/SR.45; A/C.6/78/SR.47
CYBERCRIME (Agenda item 108)
Gebrekidan, Zebib - A/C.3/78/SR.6
ECONOMIC SANCTIONS—INTERNATIONAL RELATIONS (Agenda item 28)
Tesfamariam, Sophia - A/78/PV.90
HUMAN RIGHTS (Agenda item 71)
Gebrekidan, Zebib - A/C.3/78/SR.28

Eritrea (continued)

HUMAN RIGHTS—BURUNDI (Agenda item 71c)
Tesfamariam, Sophia - A/C.3/78/SR.36
HUMAN RIGHTS—DEMOCRATIC PEOPLE'S REPUBLIC OF KOREA (Agenda item 71c)
Gebrekidan, Zebib - A/C.3/78/SR.33
HUMAN RIGHTS—ERITREA (Agenda item 71c)
Tesfamariam, Sophia - A/C.3/78/SR.36
HUMAN RIGHTS—IRAN (ISLAMIC REPUBLIC OF) (Agenda item 71c)
Gebrekidan, Zebib - A/C.3/78/SR.53
HUMAN RIGHTS—RUSSIAN FEDERATION (Agenda item 71c)
Gebrekidan, Zebib - A/C.3/78/SR.37
HUMAN RIGHTS—SYRIAN ARAB REPUBLIC (Agenda item 71c)
Gebrekidan, Zebib - A/C.3/78/SR.34
INTERNATIONAL JURISDICTION (Agenda item 84)
Essaias, Meron Habte - A/C.6/78/SR.13
INTERNATIONAL LAW—TRAINING PROGRAMMES (Agenda item 78)
Essaias, Meron Habte - A/C.6/78/SR.21
LANDLOCKED DEVELOPING COUNTRIES—CONFERENCES (Agenda item 20b)
Ibrahim, Ahmed Saeed - A/C.2/78/SR.7
LEAST DEVELOPED COUNTRIES—CONFERENCES (Agenda item 20a)
Ibrahim, Ahmed Saeed - A/C.2/78/SR.7
RACIAL DISCRIMINATION—ELIMINATION (Agenda item 69a)
Gebrekidan, Zebib - A/C.3/78/SR.41; A/C.3/78/SR.43
RACIAL DISCRIMINATION—PROGRAMMES OF ACTION (Agenda item 69b)
Gebrekidan, Zebib - A/C.3/78/SR.41; A/C.3/78/SR.43
RIGHT TO CULTURE (Agenda item 71b)
Gebrekidan, Zebib - A/C.3/78/SR.27
RULE OF LAW (Agenda item 83)
Giorgio, Amanuel - A/C.6/78/SR.17
SANCTIONS—INTERNATIONAL RELATIONS (Agenda item 71b)
Gebrekidan, Zebib - A/C.3/78/SR.28
SUSTAINABLE DEVELOPMENT (Agenda item 18)
Ibrahim, Ahmed Saeed - A/C.2/78/SR.15
TERRORISM (Agenda item 109)
Giorgio, Amanuel - A/C.6/78/SR.3
UN—BUDGET (2024) (Agenda item 134)
Hadgu, Daniel Abraham - A/C.5/78/SR.26/PartII; A/C.5/78/SR.34
UN—PROGRAMME PLANNING (Agenda item 135)
Hadgu, Daniel Abraham - A/78/PV.50(Resumption1)

Eritrea (continued)

UN. GENERAL ASSEMBLY (78TH SESS. : 2023-2024)—GENERAL DEBATE (Agenda item 8)
Mohammed, Osman Saleh - A/78/PV.13
UN. GENERAL ASSEMBLY (78TH SESS. : 2023-2024). 1ST COMMITTEE—GENERAL DEBATE (Agenda item 8)
Tesfamariam, Sophia - A/C.1/78/PV.9
UN. GENERAL ASSEMBLY (78TH SESS. : 2023-2024). 2ND COMMITTEE—GENERAL DEBATE (Agenda item 8)
Tesfamariam, Sophia - A/C.2/78/SR.4
UN. HUMAN RIGHTS COUNCIL—REPORTS (Agenda item 66)
Gebrekidan, Zebib - A/C.3/78/SR.51
UN. INTERNATIONAL COURT OF JUSTICE—REPORTS (Agenda item 73)
Essaias, Meron Habte - A/C.6/78/SR.26
UN. INTERNATIONAL LAW COMMISSION—REPORTS (Agenda item 79)
Essaias, Meron Habte - A/C.6/78/SR.30
UN CHARTER—REPORTS (Agenda item 82)
Giorgio, Amanuel - A/C.6/78/SR.33
WOMEN'S ADVANCEMENT (Agenda item 25a)
Gebrekidan, Zebib - A/C.3/78/SR.10
WOMEN'S ADVANCEMENT—CONFERENCES (Agenda item 25b)
Gebrekidan, Zebib - A/C.3/78/SR.10

Escuela de Gobierno y Políticas Públicas Norberto Bobbio (Paraguay)

WESTERN SAHARA QUESTION (Agenda item 58)
Giménez, Francisco Javier - A/C.4/78/SR.5

Estonia

FREEDOM OF EXPRESSION (Agenda item 71b)
Tammsaar, Rein - A/C.3/78/SR.26
HUMAN RIGHTS—REPORTS (Agenda item 71c)
Tammsaar, Rein - A/C.3/78/SR.26
HUMAN RIGHTS—UKRAINE (Agenda item 71c)
Tammsaar, Rein - A/C.3/78/SR.26
INFORMATION—INTERNATIONAL SECURITY (Agenda item 94)
Varem, Mattias - A/C.1/78/PV.20
INTERNATIONAL CRIMINAL COURT—REPORTS (Agenda item 74)
Tammsaar, Rein - A/78/PV.21
REGIONAL DISARMAMENT (Agenda item 99f)
Varem, Mattias - A/C.1/78/PV.22
RIGHTS OF THE CHILD (Agenda item 67)
Tammsaar, Rein - A/C.3/78/SR.11

Estonia (continued)

SEXUAL ORIENTATION (Agenda item 71b)
Tammsaar, Rein - A/C.3/78/SR.26
UKRAINE—POLITICAL CONDITIONS (Agenda item 62)
Tammsaar, Rein - A/78/PV.58
UN. GENERAL ASSEMBLY (78TH SESS. : 2023-2024). 1ST COMMITTEE—GENERAL DEBATE (Agenda item 8)
Tammsaar, Rein - A/C.1/78/PV.6
UN. INTERNATIONAL LAW COMMISSION—REPORTS (Agenda item 79)
Kaeval, Kristel - A/C.6/78/SR.29; A/C.6/78/SR.33
Veski, Kerli - A/C.6/78/SR.24
UN. SECURITY COUNCIL—MEMBERSHIP (Agenda item 121)
Tammsaar, Rein - A/78/PV.36
UN CONFERENCES (Agenda item 13)
Tammsaar, Rein - A/78/PV.47
VETO (Agenda item 63)
Tammsaar, Rein - A/78/PV.70; A/78/PV.78
WOMEN'S ADVANCEMENT (Agenda item 25a)
Tammsaar, Rein - A/C.3/78/SR.7
WOMEN'S ADVANCEMENT—CONFERENCES (Agenda item 25b)
Tammsaar, Rein - A/C.3/78/SR.7
YOUTH (Agenda item 24b)
Tornius, Hanna-Stiina - A/C.3/78/SR.2

Estonia. President

UN. GENERAL ASSEMBLY (78TH SESS. : 2023-2024)—GENERAL DEBATE (Agenda item 8)
Karis, Alar - A/78/PV.7
UN. GENERAL ASSEMBLY (78TH SESS. : 2023-2024)—SPECIAL STATEMENTS
Karis, Alar - A/78/PV.7

Eswatini

UN. GENERAL ASSEMBLY (78TH SESS. : 2023-2024)—GENERAL DEBATE (Agenda item 8)
Mswati III, King of Eswatini, 1968- - A/78/PV.7
UN. GENERAL ASSEMBLY (78TH SESS. : 2023-2024)—SPECIAL STATEMENTS
Mswati III, King of Eswatini, 1968- - A/78/PV.7
UN. GENERAL ASSEMBLY (78TH SESS. : 2023-2024). 1ST COMMITTEE—GENERAL DEBATE (Agenda item 8)
Mbingo, Mduduzi Kieth Kenneth - A/C.1/78/PV.8

Ethiopia

AFRICA—NUCLEAR-WEAPON-FREE ZONES (Agenda item 92)
Getahun, Kedir - A/C.1/78/PV.13
CLIMATE (Agenda item 18d)
Shiferaw, Girum Getachew - A/C.2/78/SR.15

Ethiopia (continued)

CRIMES AGAINST HUMANITY (Agenda item 80)
Dabesa, Kurabachew Tirfesa - A/C.6/78/SR.39; A/C.6/78/SR.41; A/C.6/78/SR.42
Minale, Lemlem Fiseha - A/C.6/78/SR.11
CUBA—UNITED STATES (Agenda item 38)
Anulo, Semalign Kebede - A/78/PV.24
DECOLONIZATION (Agenda item 58)
Kassaye, Yoseph - A/C.4/78/SR.8
DESERTIFICATION—TREATIES (Agenda item 18e)
Shiferaw, Girum Getachew - A/C.2/78/SR.15
DEVELOPMENT FINANCE (Agenda item 16b)
Muktar, Anwar - A/C.2/78/SR.11
DISASTER PREVENTION (Agenda item 18c)
Shiferaw, Girum Getachew - A/C.2/78/SR.15
DISASTER VICTIMS (Agenda item 86)
Alemayehu, Betelihem Taye - A/C.6/78/SR.6
ELECTION VERIFICATION—UN (Agenda item 71b)
Dabesa, Kurabachew Tirfesa - A/C.3/78/SR.50
FOOD SECURITY (Agenda item 23a)
Kindeya, Tsigabu Girmay - A/C.2/78/SR.17
HUMAN RIGHTS—ETHIOPIA (Agenda item 71c)
Sabo, Tesfaye Yilma - A/C.3/78/SR.36
HUMAN RIGHTS ADVANCEMENT (Agenda item 71b)
Chala, Samuel Isa - A/C.3/78/SR.25
INFORMATION (Agenda item 53)
Kassaye, Yoseph - A/C.4/78/SR.8
INFORMATION—INTERNATIONAL SECURITY (Agenda item 94)
Getahun, Kedir - A/C.1/78/PV.20
INFORMATION TECHNOLOGY—DEVELOPMENT (Agenda item 15)
Muktar, Anwar - A/C.2/78/SR.11
INTERNATIONAL JURISDICTION (Agenda item 84)
Alemayehu, Betelihem Taye - A/C.6/78/SR.13
INTERNATIONAL LAW—TRAINING PROGRAMMES (Agenda item 78)
Alemayehu, Betelihem Taye - A/C.6/78/SR.21
INTERNATIONAL TRADE (Agenda item 16a)
Muktar, Anwar - A/C.2/78/SR.11
LANDLOCKED DEVELOPING COUNTRIES—CONFERENCES (Agenda item 20b)
Abebe, Leulseged Tadese - A/C.2/78/SR.7
LEAST DEVELOPED COUNTRIES—CONFERENCES (Agenda item 20a)
Abebe, Leulseged Tadese - A/C.2/78/SR.7
NUCLEAR DISARMAMENT (Agenda item 99b)
Getahun, Kedir - A/C.1/78/PV.13

Ethiopia (continued)

NUCLEAR NON-PROLIFERATION—INTERNATIONAL OBLIGATIONS (Agenda item 99w)
Getahun, Kedir - A/C.1/78/PV.13
OUTER SPACE—PEACEFUL USES—INTERNATIONAL COOPERATION (Agenda item 48)
Kassaye, Yoseph - A/C.4/78/SR.8
Temesgen, Tenna Misgana - A/C.4/78/SR.16
PEACEKEEPING OPERATIONS (Agenda item 51)
Kassaye, Yoseph - A/C.4/78/SR.8
PEACEKEEPING OPERATIONS—CRIMINAL LIABILITY (Agenda item 76)
Alemayehu, Betelihem Taye - A/C.6/78/SR.9
POVERTY—INTERNATIONAL DECADES (Agenda item 21a)
Kindeya, Tsigabu Girmay - A/C.2/78/SR.17
RESPONSIBILITY OF INTERNATIONAL ORGANIZATIONS (Agenda item 85)
Alemayehu, Betelihem Taye - A/C.6/78/SR.19
RIGHTS OF THE CHILD (Agenda item 67)
Chala, Samuel Isa - A/C.3/78/SR.13
RULE OF LAW (Agenda item 83)
Alemayehu, Betelihem Taye - A/C.6/78/SR.18
RURAL POVERTY (Agenda item 21b)
Kindeya, Tsigabu Girmay - A/C.2/78/SR.17
RURAL WOMEN (Agenda item 25a)
Arega, Elleni Henok - A/C.3/78/SR.10
SCIENCE AND TECHNOLOGY—DEVELOPMENT (Agenda item 19a)
Muktar, Anwar - A/C.2/78/SR.11
SPECIAL POLITICAL MISSIONS (Agenda item 52)
Kassaye, Yoseph - A/C.4/78/SR.8
SUSTAINABLE ENERGY (Agenda item 18h)
Shiferaw, Girum Getachew - A/C.2/78/SR.15
TERRORISM (Agenda item 109)
Alemayehu, Betelihem Taye - A/C.6/78/SR.4
UN. GENERAL ASSEMBLY (78TH SESS. : 2023-2024). 1ST COMMITTEE—GENERAL DEBATE (Agenda item 8)
Abebe, Leulseged Tadese - A/C.1/78/PV.8
UN. GENERAL ASSEMBLY (78TH SESS. : 2023-2024). 2ND COMMITTEE—GENERAL DEBATE (Agenda item 8)
Abebe, Leulseged Tadese - A/C.2/78/SR.2
Sabo, Tesfaye Yilma - A/C.2/78/SR.2
UN. SECURITY COUNCIL—MEMBERSHIP (Agenda item 121)
Anulo, Semalign Kebede - A/78/PV.36
UN HIGH COMMISSIONER FOR REFUGEES—REPORTS (Agenda item 60)
Worku, Hirut Habtamu - A/C.3/78/SR.45
WESTERN SAHARA QUESTION (Agenda item 58)
Kassaye, Yoseph - A/C.4/78/SR.8
WOMEN'S ADVANCEMENT (Agenda item 25a)
Arega, Elleni Henok - A/C.3/78/SR.10

Ethiopia (continued)
WOMEN'S ADVANCEMENT—CONFERENCES (Agenda item 25b)
Arega, Elleni Henok - A/C.3/78/SR.10

Ethiopia. Deputy Prime Minister
UN. GENERAL ASSEMBLY (78TH SESS. : 2023-2024)—GENERAL DEBATE (Agenda item 8)
Hassen, Demeke Mekonnen - A/78/PV.12
UN. GENERAL ASSEMBLY (78TH SESS. : 2023-2024)—SPECIAL STATEMENTS
Hassen, Demeke Mekonnen - A/78/PV.12

European Conference of Support and Solidarity with the Saharawi People
WESTERN SAHARA QUESTION (Agenda item 58)
Salvia, Fabio - A/C.4/78/SR.4

European Council. President
UN. GENERAL ASSEMBLY (78TH SESS. : 2023-2024)—GENERAL DEBATE (Agenda item 8)
Michel, Charles - A/78/PV.8

European Public Law Organization
RULE OF LAW (Agenda item 83)
Melchionna, Luca - A/C.6/78/SR.19

European Union
ADMINISTRATION OF JUSTICE (Agenda item 144)
Popan, Simona - A/C.6/78/SR.9
AFRICA—DEVELOPMENT (Agenda item 65b)
Samson, Hedda - A/78/PV.18
AFRICA—SUSTAINABLE DEVELOPMENT—PARTNERSHIP (Agenda item 65a)
Maesschalck, Filip de (Belgium) - A/78/PV.57
Samson, Hedda - A/78/PV.18
AGEING PERSONS (Agenda item 24b)
Schuller, Simone - A/C.3/78/SR.1
ALBINISM (Agenda item 71b)
Greffine, Venise Catherine - A/C.3/78/SR.27
ARMED CONFLICTS PREVENTION (Agenda item 31a)
Samson, Hedda - A/78/PV.72
ARMS RACE—OUTER SPACE (Agenda item 97a)
Claeys, Carine - A/C.1/78/PV.16
ARMS TRANSFERS—TREATIES (Agenda item 99x)
Karczmarz, Michał - A/C.1/78/PV.18; A/C.1/78/PV.19
BIOLOGICAL DIVERSITY—TREATIES (Agenda item 18f)
Gambert, Sylvain - A/C.2/78/SR.25

European Union (continued)
BIOLOGICAL WEAPONS—TREATIES (Agenda item 106)
Claeys, Carine - A/C.1/78/PV.14
CENTRAL ASIA—ZONES OF PEACE (Agenda item 64)
Lagatie, Karl (Belgium) - A/78/PV.85
CHEMICAL WEAPONS—TREATIES (Agenda item 99l)
Claeys, Carine - A/C.1/78/PV.14
Hansen, Steen Malthe - A/C.1/78/PV.15
CLIMATE (Agenda item 18d)
Kaspar, Martin - A/C.2/78/SR.25
CLIMATE CHANGE (Agenda item 71b)
Szelivanov, Julia - A/C.3/78/SR.29
COASTAL ZONE MANAGEMENT (Agenda item 18j)
Gambert, Sylvain - A/C.2/78/SR.23
COMMODITIES (Agenda item 16d)
Pougin de La Maisonneuve, Axel - A/C.2/78/SR.14
CONVENTIONAL WEAPONS—TREATIES (Agenda item 103)
Karczmarz, Michał - A/C.1/78/PV.18
CRIME PREVENTION (Agenda item 107)
Alonso Giganto, Ana María (Spain) - A/C.3/78/SR.50
Samson, Hedda - A/C.3/78/SR.5
Schuller, Simone - A/C.3/78/SR.5
CRIMES AGAINST HUMANITY (Agenda item 80)
Jaiteh, Amadou (Gambia) - A/C.6/78/SR.9
Popan, Simona - A/C.6/78/SR.9; A/C.6/78/SR.38; A/C.6/78/SR.39; A/C.6/78/SR.41; A/C.6/78/SR.43; A/C.6/78/SR.44; A/C.6/78/SR.45
CUBA—UNITED STATES (Agenda item 38)
Jiménez de la Hoz, Ana (Spain) - A/78/PV.26
CYBERCRIME (Agenda item 108)
Schuller, Simone - A/C.3/78/SR.5
DEVELOPMENT FINANCE—CONFERENCES (Agenda item 17)
Kaiser, Annette Karoline (Germany) - A/78/PV.90
Pougin de La Maisonneuve, Axel - A/C.2/78/SR.25
DIAMONDS—FUELLING CONFLICT (Agenda item 30)
Curran, Clayton - A/78/PV.65
DISAPPEARANCE OF PERSONS (Agenda item 71b)
Szelivanov, Julia - A/C.3/78/SR.22
DISARMAMENT—GENERAL AND COMPLETE (Agenda item 99)
Hansen, Steen Malthe - A/78/PV.105
Karczmarz, Michał - A/C.1/78/PV.18; A/C.1/78/PV.21
Sánchez de Lerín García-Ovies, Ignacio (Spain) - A/C.1/78/PV.30
DISARMAMENT AGREEMENTS—OUTER SPACE (Agenda item 97c)
Sánchez de Lerín García-Ovies, Ignacio (Spain) - A/C.1/78/PV.27
DISASTER VICTIMS (Agenda item 86)
Ramopoulos, Thomas - A/C.6/78/SR.5

European Union (continued)
DISPLACED PERSONS (Agenda item 71b)
McCauley, Natalie - A/C.3/78/SR.32
ECONOMIC SANCTIONS—INTERNATIONAL RELATIONS (Agenda item 28)
Popan, Simona - A/78/PV.89
ELECTION VERIFICATION—UN (Agenda item 71b)
Jiménez de la Hoz, Ana (Spain) - A/C.3/78/SR.50
EMERGENCY ASSISTANCE (Agenda item 72a)
Jiménez de la Hoz, Ana (Spain) - A/78/PV.46; A/78/PV.47
ENVIRONMENT (Agenda item 71b)
Szelivanov, Julia - A/C.3/78/SR.29
FAMILY (Agenda item 24b)
Alonso Giganto, Ana María (Spain) - A/C.3/78/SR.49
FOOD SECURITY (Agenda item 23a)
Barbotte, Daphné - A/C.2/78/SR.25
FREEDOM OF EXPRESSION (Agenda item 71b)
Nyman, Klas - A/C.3/78/SR.19
HEALTH (Agenda item 125)
Alonso Giganto, Ana María (Spain) - A/78/PV.48
Bouthé, Marc Gerard C. (Belgium) - A/78/PV.77
Gaal, Miklos (Hungary) - A/78/PV.102
Jiménez de la Hoz, Ana (Spain) - A/78/PV.16
Korac, Sofija (United States) - A/78/PV.77
Maesschalck, Filip de (Belgium) - A/78/PV.64
Satuli, Tiina - A/78/PV.41
HUMAN RIGHTS (Agenda item 71)
Carlé, Hanne - A/C.3/78/SR.16
HUMAN RIGHTS—AFGHANISTAN (Agenda item 71c)
Schuller, Simone - A/C.3/78/SR.34
Skoog, Olof - A/C.3/78/SR.24
HUMAN RIGHTS—BELARUS (Agenda item 71c)
Clifford, Katarina - A/C.3/78/SR.37
Skoog, Olof - A/C.3/78/SR.24
HUMAN RIGHTS—BURUNDI (Agenda item 71c)
Nyman, Klas - A/C.3/78/SR.36
HUMAN RIGHTS—CENTRAL AFRICAN REPUBLIC (Agenda item 71c)
Nyman, Klas - A/C.3/78/SR.33
HUMAN RIGHTS—DEMOCRATIC PEOPLE'S REPUBLIC OF KOREA (Agenda item 71c)
Bellmont Roldán, Xavier (Spain) - A/C.3/78/SR.53
Nyman, Klas - A/C.3/78/SR.33
Skoog, Olof - A/C.3/78/SR.24
HUMAN RIGHTS—ERITREA (Agenda item 71c)
Nyman, Klas - A/C.3/78/SR.36
HUMAN RIGHTS—ETHIOPIA (Agenda item 71c)
Nyman, Klas - A/C.3/78/SR.36

European Union (continued)
HUMAN RIGHTS—INTERNATIONAL INSTRUMENTS (Agenda item 71a)
Keogh, Briana - A/C.3/78/SR.17
Skoog, Olof - A/C.3/78/SR.24
HUMAN RIGHTS—IRAN (ISLAMIC REPUBLIC OF) (Agenda item 71c)
Bellmont Roldán, Xavier (Spain) - A/C.3/78/SR.53
Schuller, Simone - A/C.3/78/SR.34
HUMAN RIGHTS—MYANMAR (Agenda item 71c)
Alwasil, Abdulaziz M.O. (Saudi Arabia) - A/C.3/78/SR.53
Carlé, Hanne - A/C.3/78/SR.33
García Rico, Lucía (Spain) - A/C.3/78/SR.53
Skoog, Olof - A/C.3/78/SR.24
HUMAN RIGHTS—RUSSIAN FEDERATION (Agenda item 71c)
Clifford, Katarina - A/C.3/78/SR.37
Skoog, Olof - A/C.3/78/SR.24
HUMAN RIGHTS—SOMALIA (Agenda item 71c)
Nyman, Klas - A/C.3/78/SR.35
HUMAN RIGHTS—SYRIAN ARAB REPUBLIC (Agenda item 71c)
García Rico, Lucía (Spain) - A/C.3/78/SR.54
Schuller, Simone - A/C.3/78/SR.34
Skoog, Olof - A/C.3/78/SR.24
HUMAN RIGHTS—TERRITORIES OCCUPIED BY ISRAEL (Agenda item 71c)
Carlsson Szlezak, Teresa - A/C.3/78/SR.35
HUMAN RIGHTS—UKRAINE (Agenda item 71c)
Bellmont Roldán, Xavier (Spain) - A/C.3/78/SR.53
Clifford, Katarina - A/C.3/78/SR.37
Skoog, Olof - A/C.3/78/SR.24
HUMAN RIGHTS ACTIVISTS (Agenda item 71b)
Bellmont Roldán, Xavier (Spain) - A/C.3/78/SR.56
Carlé, Hanne - A/C.3/78/SR.19
HUMAN RIGHTS ADVANCEMENT (Agenda item 71b)
Carlé, Hanne - A/C.3/78/SR.18
Mythen, Fergal Tomas (Ireland) - A/C.3/78/SR.24
Skoog, Olof - A/C.3/78/SR.24
HUMAN RIGHTS INSTITUTIONS—CENTRAL AFRICA (Agenda item 71b)
Alonso Giganto, Ana María (Spain) - A/C.3/78/SR.56
HUMANITARIAN ASSISTANCE (Agenda item 72)
Popowski, Maciej - A/78/PV.46
IAEA—REPORTS (Agenda item 89)
Samson, Hedda - A/78/PV.29
INDIGENOUS PEOPLES (Agenda item 68a)
Nyman, Klas - A/C.3/78/SR.15
Samson, Hedda - A/C.3/78/SR.15

European Union (continued)

INDIGENOUS PEOPLES—CONFERENCES (Agenda item 68b)
Nyman, Klas - A/C.3/78/SR.15
Samson, Hedda - A/C.3/78/SR.15
INFORMATION (Agenda item 53)
Ladois, Jean-Noël - A/C.4/78/SR.12
INFORMATION—INTERNATIONAL SECURITY (Agenda item 94)
Karczmarz, Michał - A/C.1/78/PV.20
Sánchez de Lerín García-Ovies, Ignacio (Spain) - A/C.1/78/PV.29
INFORMATION TECHNOLOGY—DEVELOPMENT (Agenda item 15)
Bologa, Anda - A/C.2/78/SR.23
INTERNATIONAL CRIMINAL COURT—REPORTS (Agenda item 74)
Marquardt, Stephan - A/78/PV.21
INTERNATIONAL JURISDICTION (Agenda item 84)
Popan, Simona - A/C.6/78/SR.12
INTERNATIONAL LAW—TRAINING PROGRAMMES (Agenda item 78)
Popan, Simona - A/C.6/78/SR.21
INTERNATIONAL RESIDUAL MECHANISM FOR CRIMINAL TRIBUNALS (Agenda item 126)
Popan, Simona - A/78/PV.19
INTERNATIONAL TRADE (Agenda item 16a)
Martín Couce, Adrián (Spain) - A/C.2/78/SR.22; A/C.2/78/SR.24
JUDICIAL INDEPENDENCE (Agenda item 71b)
Keogh, Briana - A/C.3/78/SR.31
LANDMINES—TREATIES (Agenda item 99m)
Karczmarz, Michał - A/C.1/78/PV.18
LAW OF THE SEA (Agenda item 75a)
Ramopoulos, Thomas - A/78/PV.43
LEPROSY (Agenda item 71b)
Keogh, Briana - A/C.3/78/SR.17
MARINE ECOSYSTEMS—BIOLOGICAL DIVERSITY (Agenda item 75c)
Raes, Elisa de (Belgium) - A/78/PV.73
Ramopoulos, Thomas - A/78/PV.43
Vittay, Melinda (Hungary) - A/78/PV.103
MEDITERRANEAN REGION—REGIONAL SECURITY (Agenda item 104)
Sánchez de Lerín García-Ovies, Ignacio (Spain) - A/C.1/78/PV.29
MERCENARIES (Agenda item 70)
Nyman, Klas - A/C.3/78/SR.42
MIDDLE EAST—NUCLEAR-WEAPON-FREE ZONES (Agenda item 95)
Sánchez de Lerín García-Ovies, Ignacio (Spain) - A/C.1/78/PV.26
MIDDLE EAST SITUATION (Agenda item 34)
Jiménez de la Hoz, Ana (Spain) - A/78/PV.40
MIGRANT WORKERS (Agenda item 71a)
Szelivanov, Julia - A/C.3/78/SR.23

European Union (continued)

MIGRANTS—PROTECTION (Agenda item 71b)
Alonso Giganto, Ana María (Spain) - A/C.3/78/SR.56
Szelivanov, Julia - A/C.3/78/SR.23
MILLENNIUM SUMMIT—CONFERENCES (Agenda item 117)
Jiménez de la Hoz, Ana (Spain) - A/78/PV.15
Samson, Hedda - A/78/PV.102
MINE CLEARANCE (Agenda item 46)
Samson, Hedda - A/C.4/78/SR.10
Szczerski, Krzysztof (Poland) - A/C.4/78/SR.10
MINORITIES (Agenda item 71b)
Greffine, Venise Catherine - A/C.3/78/SR.39
MULTILATERALISM—DISARMAMENT (Agenda item 99r)
Karczmarz, Michał - A/C.1/78/PV.22
NUCLEAR DISARMAMENT (Agenda item 99b)
Hansen, Steen Malthe - A/C.1/78/PV.11; A/C.1/78/PV.13
NUCLEAR NON-PROLIFERATION—INTERNATIONAL OBLIGATIONS (Agenda item 99w)
Hansen, Steen Malthe - A/C.1/78/PV.11
NUCLEAR WEAPON TESTS—TREATIES (Agenda item 105)
Hansen, Steen Malthe - A/C.1/78/PV.11
OPERATIONAL ACTIVITIES—UN SYSTEM (Agenda item 22a)
Kaspar, Martin - A/C.2/78/SR.22
ORGANIZATION FOR DEMOCRACY AND ECONOMIC DEVELOPMENT - GUAM (Agenda item 32)
Lambrinidis, Stavros - A/78/PV.85
OUTER SPACE—CONFIDENCE-BUILDING MEASURES (Agenda item 99v)
Claeys, Carine - A/C.1/78/PV.16
OUTER SPACE—PEACEFUL USES—INTERNATIONAL COOPERATION (Agenda item 48)
Hansen, Steen Malthe - A/C.4/78/SR.15
OUTER SPACE—PRINCIPLES (Agenda item 97d)
Claeys, Carine - A/C.1/78/PV.16
PEACE (Agenda item 14)
Bellmont Roldán, Xavier (Spain) - A/78/PV.48
Lagatie, Karl (Belgium) - A/78/PV.62
Samson, Hedda - A/78/PV.76
PEACEBUILDING (Agenda item 61)
Tolstoi, Natalie - A/78/PV.100
PEACEKEEPING OPERATIONS (Agenda item 51)
Coppola, Antonio Gaetano - A/C.4/78/SR.18
PEACEKEEPING OPERATIONS—CRIMINAL LIABILITY (Agenda item 76)
Mead, Kevin Timothy (Canada) - A/C.6/78/SR.37
Ramopoulos, Thomas - A/C.6/78/SR.8
PERSONS WITH DISABILITIES—HUMAN RIGHTS (Agenda item 71a)
Nyman, Klas - A/C.3/78/SR.38
Schuller, Simone - A/C.3/78/SR.18

European Union (continued)

POVERTY—HUMAN RIGHTS (Agenda item 71b)
Szelivanov, Julia - A/C.3/78/SR.30
POVERTY—INTERNATIONAL DECADES (Agenda item 21a)
Woźniak, Agata Magdalena - A/C.2/78/SR.25
RACIAL DISCRIMINATION—ELIMINATION (Agenda item 69a)
Bellmont Roldán, Xavier (Spain) - A/78/PV.50; A/C.3/78/SR.47
Greffine, Venise Catherine - A/C.3/78/SR.41
Kridelka, Philippe (Belgium) - A/78/PV.63
Nyman, Klas - A/C.3/78/SR.40; A/C.3/78/SR.42
RACIAL DISCRIMINATION—PROGRAMMES OF ACTION (Agenda item 69b)
Bellmont Roldán, Xavier (Spain) - A/C.3/78/SR.56
Greffine, Venise Catherine - A/C.3/78/SR.41
Nyman, Klas - A/C.3/78/SR.40; A/C.3/78/SR.42
RADIATION EFFECTS (Agenda item 47)
Hansen, Steen Malthe - A/C.4/78/SR.11
RELIGIOUS INTOLERANCE (Agenda item 71b)
Jiménez de la Hoz, Ana (Spain) - A/C.3/78/SR.52
Nyman, Klas - A/C.3/78/SR.38
RESPONSIBILITY OF INTERNATIONAL ORGANIZATIONS (Agenda item 85)
Popan, Simona - A/C.6/78/SR.19
RESPONSIBILITY TO PROTECT (Agenda item 129)
Samson, Hedda - A/78/PV.96
RIGHT OF ASSEMBLY (Agenda item 71b)
Carlé, Hanne - A/C.3/78/SR.19
RIGHT TO CULTURE (Agenda item 71b)
Greffine, Venise Catherine - A/C.3/78/SR.27
RIGHT TO DEVELOPMENT (Agenda item 71b)
Alonso Giganto, Ana María (Spain) - A/C.3/78/SR.48
Carlsson Szlezak, Teresa - A/C.3/78/SR.20
RIGHT TO DRINKING WATER (Agenda item 71b)
Szelivanov, Julia - A/C.3/78/SR.28
RIGHT TO EDUCATION (Agenda item 71b)
Keogh, Briana - A/C.3/78/SR.27
RIGHT TO FOOD (Agenda item 71b)
Skoog, Olof - A/C.3/78/SR.24
Szelivanov, Julia - A/C.3/78/SR.30
RIGHT TO HEALTH (Agenda item 71b)
Greffine, Venise Catherine - A/C.3/78/SR.39
RIGHT TO HOUSING (Agenda item 71b)
Szelivanov, Julia - A/C.3/78/SR.30
RIGHT TO PRIVACY (Agenda item 71b)
Szelivanov, Julia - A/C.3/78/SR.21
RIGHTS OF THE CHILD (Agenda item 67)
Alonso Giganto, Ana María (Spain) - A/C.3/78/SR.55
Clifford, Katarina - A/C.3/78/SR.11
Keogh, Briana - A/C.3/78/SR.12
Schuller, Simone - A/C.3/78/SR.11; A/C.3/78/SR.12

European Union (continued)

RULE OF LAW (Agenda item 83)
Popan, Simona - A/C.6/78/SR.15
RURAL POVERTY (Agenda item 21b)
Martín Couce, Adrián (Spain) - A/C.2/78/SR.22
RURAL WOMEN (Agenda item 25a)
Alonso Giganto, Ana María (Spain) - A/C.3/78/SR.49
SANCTIONS—INTERNATIONAL RELATIONS (Agenda item 71b)
Alonso Giganto, Ana María (Spain) - A/C.3/78/SR.48
SEXUAL ORIENTATION (Agenda item 71b)
Greffine, Venise Catherine - A/C.3/78/SR.39
SLAVERY (Agenda item 71a)
Szelivanov, Julia - A/C.3/78/SR.21
SMALL ARMS—ILLICIT TRAFFIC (Agenda item 99p)
Karczmarz, Michał - A/C.1/78/PV.18
SMALL ARMS—ILLICIT TRAFFIC—ASSISTANCE (Agenda item 99n)
Karczmarz, Michał - A/C.1/78/PV.18
SMALL ISLAND DEVELOPING STATES—PROGRAMMES OF ACTION (Agenda item 18b)
Kaspar, Martin - A/C.2/78/SR.22
Lorenzen, Emma Siemens (Denmark) - A/78/PV.103
SOCIAL CONDITIONS (Agenda item 24b)
Kókai, Anita (Hungary) - A/78/PV.101
Mogyorósi, Bálint (Hungary) - A/78/PV.57
SOCIAL DEVELOPMENT (Agenda item 24)
Tariello, Giulia - A/C.3/78/SR.1
SOCIAL DEVELOPMENT—CONFERENCES (Agenda item 24a)
Alonso Giganto, Ana María (Spain) - A/C.3/78/SR.55
SPORTS—OLYMPIC GAMES (Agenda item 11)
Curran, Clayton - A/78/PV.38
STRADDLING FISH STOCKS (Agenda item 75b)
Ramopoulos, Thomas - A/78/PV.43
SUMMARY EXECUTIONS (Agenda item 71b)
Carlé, Hanne - A/C.3/78/SR.31
SUSTAINABLE DEVELOPMENT (Agenda item 18)
Gaal, Miklos (Hungary) - A/78/PV.107
Gambert, Sylvain - A/C.2/78/SR.22
Martín Couce, Adrián (Spain) - A/C.2/78/SR.24
Pougin de La Maisonneuve, Axel - A/C.2/78/SR.14
Tholin, Isadora Jahanfar (Sweden) - A/C.2/78/SR.24
SUSTAINABLE ENERGY (Agenda item 18h)
Kaspar, Martin - A/C.2/78/SR.23
TAXATION (Agenda item 16h)
Martín Couce, Adrián (Spain) - A/C.2/78/SR.25
TERRITORIES OCCUPIED BY ISRAEL—HUMAN RIGHTS (Agenda item 50)
Angarón Bolea, María del Mar (Spain) - A/C.4/78/SR.26
Clune, Mary - A/C.4/78/SR.24

European Union (continued)

TERRITORIES OCCUPIED BY ISRAEL—NATURAL RESOURCES (Agenda item 59)
Lavalle Merchán, Jesús María (Spain) - A/C.2/78/SR.21
TERRORISM (Agenda item 109)
Ramopoulos, Thomas - A/C.6/78/SR.1
TERRORISM—HUMAN RIGHTS (Agenda item 71b)
Carlé, Hanne - A/C.3/78/SR.31
TORTURE AND OTHER CRUEL TREATMENT (Agenda item 71a)
Nyman, Klas - A/C.3/78/SR.18
TRAFFICKING IN PERSONS (Agenda item 71b)
Szelivanov, Julia - A/C.3/78/SR.23
TRANSNATIONAL CORPORATIONS—HUMAN RIGHTS (Agenda item 71b)
Szelivanov, Julia - A/C.3/78/SR.21
UKRAINE—POLITICAL CONDITIONS (Agenda item 62)
Lambrinidis, Stavros - A/78/PV.57
UN—BUDGET (2024) (Agenda item 134)
Bogaerts, Basiel (Belgium) - A/C.5/78/SR.34
Camelli, Thibault - A/C.5/78/SR.3
Jiménez de la Hoz, Ana (Spain) - A/C.5/78/SR.26/PartII
Samson, Hedda - A/C.5/78/SR.5
UN—FINANCIAL SITUATION (Agenda item 136)
Camelli, Thibault - A/C.5/78/SR.38
UN—PROGRAMME PLANNING (Agenda item 135)
Samson, Hedda - A/C.5/78/SR.5
Viñayo Fernández, Sofía (Spain) - A/C.5/78/SR.24
UN. COMMITTEE ON RELATIONS WITH THE HOST COUNTRY—REPORTS (Agenda item 161)
Popan, Simona - A/C.6/78/SR.35
UN. CONFERENCE ON DISARMAMENT—REPORTS (Agenda item 101a)
Karczmarz, Michał - A/C.1/78/PV.22
Sánchez de Lerín García-Ovies, Ignacio (Spain) - A/C.1/78/PV.29
UN. DISARMAMENT COMMISSION—REPORTS (Agenda item 101b)
Karczmarz, Michał - A/C.1/78/PV.22
UN. GENERAL ASSEMBLY—WORK PROGRAMME (Agenda item 120)
Linton, Sarah Joy (Australia) - A/C.2/78/SR.25
Samson, Hedda - A/78/PV.32
UN. GENERAL ASSEMBLY (78TH SESS. : 2023-2024)—OFFICERS (Agenda item 5)
Samson, Hedda - A/C.5/78/SR.1
UN. GENERAL ASSEMBLY (78TH SESS. : 2023-2024). 1ST COMMITTEE—GENERAL DEBATE (Agenda item 8)
Hansen, Steen Malthe - A/C.1/78/PV.4
Skoog, Olof - A/C.1/78/PV.2

European Union (continued)

UN. GENERAL ASSEMBLY (78TH SESS. : 2023-2024). 2ND COMMITTEE—GENERAL DEBATE (Agenda item 8)
Skoog, Olof - A/C.2/78/SR.2
UN. GENERAL ASSEMBLY (78TH SESS. : 2023-2024). 5TH COMMITTEE—WORK ORGANIZATION (Agenda item 7)
Camelli, Thibault - A/C.5/78/SR.27; A/C.5/78/SR.34; A/C.5/78/SR.35
Gaber-Wennholz, Basma - A/C.5/78/SR.26/PartII
Samson, Hedda - A/C.5/78/SR.40
UN. HUMAN RIGHTS COMMITTEE—REPORTS (Agenda item 71a)
Keogh, Briana - A/C.3/78/SR.17
UN. HUMAN RIGHTS COUNCIL—REPORTS (Agenda item 66)
Alonso Giganto, Ana María (Spain) - A/C.3/78/SR.51
Clifford, Katarina - A/78/PV.23
UN. INTERNATIONAL COURT OF JUSTICE—REPORTS (Agenda item 73)
Hoffmeister, Frank - A/78/PV.20
UN. INTERNATIONAL LAW COMMISSION—REPORTS (Agenda item 79)
Bouquet, André - A/C.6/78/SR.28
Hoffmeister, Frank - A/C.6/78/SR.28
Marquardt, Stephan - A/C.6/78/SR.23
Ramopoulos, Thomas - A/C.6/78/SR.23; A/C.6/78/SR.30
UN. PEACEBUILDING COMMISSION—REPORTS (Agenda item 27)
Tolstoi, Natalie - A/78/PV.100
UN. PEACEBUILDING FUND—REPORTS (Agenda item 111)
Tolstoi, Natalie - A/78/PV.100
UN CHARTER—REPORTS (Agenda item 82)
Popan, Simona - A/C.6/78/SR.22
UN COMMISSION ON INTERNATIONAL TRADE LAW—REPORTS (Agenda item 77)
Ramopoulos, Thomas - A/C.6/78/SR.14
UN CONFERENCES (Agenda item 13)
Jiménez de la Hoz, Ana (Spain) - A/78/PV.15
Lázár, Lilla (Hungary) - A/78/PV.107
Samson, Hedda - A/78/PV.102
UN HIGH COMMISSIONER FOR REFUGEES—REPORTS (Agenda item 60)
García Rico, Lucía (Spain) - A/C.3/78/SR.48
Skoog, Olof - A/C.3/78/SR.44
UN INTERIM FORCE IN LEBANON—FINANCING (Agenda item 156b)
Bogaerts, Basiel (Belgium) - A/C.5/78/SR.40
UN RESOLUTIONS—IMPLEMENTATION (Agenda item 119)
Samson, Hedda - A/78/PV.32
UN SYSTEM—STRENGTHENING (Agenda item 122)
Horváth, Zsuzsanna (Hungary) - A/78/PV.98
UN YOUTH OFFICE—REPORTS (Agenda item 130)
Samson, Hedda - A/78/PV.102

European Union (continued)

UNRWA—ACTIVITIES (Agenda item 49)
Clune, Mary - A/C.4/78/SR.22
VETO (Agenda item 63)
Lambrinidis, Stavros - A/78/PV.59; A/78/PV.66; A/78/PV.68
Samson, Hedda - A/78/PV.78
Skoog, Olof - A/78/PV.3
WEAPONS—OUTER SPACE (Agenda item 97b)
Claeys, Carine - A/C.1/78/PV.16
Sánchez de Lerín García-Ovies, Ignacio (Spain) - A/C.1/78/PV.27
WEAPONS OF MASS DESTRUCTION—TERRORISM (Agenda item 99s)
Claeys, Carine - A/C.1/78/PV.14
WESTERN SAHARA QUESTION (Agenda item 58)
Gómez Aoiz, Elena (Spain) - A/C.4/78/SR.9
WOMEN MIGRANT WORKERS (Agenda item 25a)
Alonso Giganto, Ana María (Spain) - A/C.3/78/SR.49
WOMEN'S ADVANCEMENT (Agenda item 25a)
Carlé, Hanne - A/C.3/78/SR.7
Samson, Hedda - A/C.3/78/SR.7
WOMEN'S ADVANCEMENT—CONFERENCES (Agenda item 25b)
Carlé, Hanne - A/C.3/78/SR.7
Samson, Hedda - A/C.3/78/SR.7
YOUTH (Agenda item 24b)
Svana, Lukas - A/C.3/78/SR.1
Tariello, Giulia - A/C.3/78/SR.1

FAO

FOOD SECURITY (Agenda item 23a)
Villarreal, Marcela - A/C.2/78/SR.16
RURAL POVERTY (Agenda item 21b)
Davis, Benjamin - A/C.2/78/SR.16
RURAL WOMEN (Agenda item 25a)
Ngirwa-Mpesha, Doris - A/C.3/78/SR.10
STORMS (Agenda item 18i)
Li, Lifeng - A/C.2/78/SR.12
WOMEN'S ADVANCEMENT (Agenda item 25a)
Ngirwa-Mpesha, Doris - A/C.3/78/SR.10
WOMEN'S ADVANCEMENT—CONFERENCES (Agenda item 25b)
Ngirwa-Mpesha, Doris - A/C.3/78/SR.10

Federación de Periodistas del Perú

WESTERN SAHARA QUESTION (Agenda item 58)
Sánchez Serra, Ricardo - A/C.4/78/SR.4

Federación Estatal de Instituciones Solidarias con el Pueblo Saharaui

WESTERN SAHARA QUESTION (Agenda item 58)
Sosa Guerra, Sibisse - A/C.4/78/SR.4

Fédération mondiale des amis du Sahara marocain

WESTERN SAHARA QUESTION (Agenda item 58)
Moctar, El Hadji - A/C.4/78/SR.5

Federation of International Civil Servants' Associations

PERSONNEL QUESTIONS—UN SYSTEM (Agenda item 142)
Quinn-Maguire, Tanya - A/C.5/78/SR.10

Fiji

FRENCH POLYNESIA QUESTION (Agenda item 58)
Tarakinikini, Filipo - A/C.4/78/SR.3
MILLENNIUM SUMMIT—CONFERENCES (Agenda item 117)
May, Vueti Kosoniu - A/78/PV.102
SMALL ISLAND DEVELOPING STATES—PROGRAMMES OF ACTION (Agenda item 18b)
May, Vueti Kosoniu - A/78/PV.103
UN CONFERENCES (Agenda item 13)
May, Vueti Kosoniu - A/78/PV.102

Fiji. Prime Minister

UN. GENERAL ASSEMBLY (78TH SESS. : 2023-2024)—GENERAL DEBATE (Agenda item 8)
Rabuka, Sitiveni Ligamamada - A/78/PV.10
UN. GENERAL ASSEMBLY (78TH SESS. : 2023-2024)—SPECIAL STATEMENTS
Rabuka, Sitiveni Ligamamada - A/78/PV.10

Finland

ARMS TRANSFERS—TREATIES (Agenda item 99x)
Voionmaa, Lauri - A/C.1/78/PV.19
CRIMES AGAINST HUMANITY (Agenda item 80)
Lemmetty, Elina - A/C.6/78/SR.39
DISARMAMENT—GENERAL AND COMPLETE (Agenda item 99)
Voionmaa, Lauri - A/C.1/78/PV.19
HUMAN RIGHTS—UKRAINE (Agenda item 71c)
Kalkku, Elina - A/C.3/78/SR.37
INTERNATIONAL CRIMINAL COURT—REPORTS (Agenda item 74)
Kalkku, Elina - A/78/PV.21
LANDMINES—TREATIES (Agenda item 99m)
Voionmaa, Lauri - A/C.1/78/PV.19

Finland (continued)

NUCLEAR DISARMAMENT (Agenda item 99b)
Viinanen, Jarmo Veli Tapio - A/C.1/78/PV.12
NUCLEAR NON-PROLIFERATION—INTERNATIONAL OBLIGATIONS (Agenda item 99w)
Viinanen, Jarmo Veli Tapio - A/C.1/78/PV.12
PERSONS WITH DISABILITIES—HUMAN RIGHTS (Agenda item 71a)
Kalkku, Elina - A/C.3/78/SR.38
RESPONSIBILITY OF INTERNATIONAL ORGANIZATIONS (Agenda item 85)
Laukkanen, Virpi - A/C.6/78/SR.19
UKRAINE—POLITICAL CONDITIONS (Agenda item 62)
Tierala, Lauri - A/78/PV.56
UN. GENERAL ASSEMBLY (78TH SESS. : 2023-2024). 1ST COMMITTEE—GENERAL DEBATE (Agenda item 8)
Hyvärinen, Outi - A/C.1/78/PV.4
VETO (Agenda item 63)
Kalkku, Elina - A/78/PV.68
WOMEN'S ADVANCEMENT (Agenda item 25a)
Voionmaa, Lauri - A/C.3/78/SR.10
WOMEN'S ADVANCEMENT—CONFERENCES (Agenda item 25b)
Voionmaa, Lauri - A/C.3/78/SR.10
YOUTH (Agenda item 24b)
Pättikangas, Paula - A/C.3/78/SR.3

Finland. President

UN. GENERAL ASSEMBLY (78TH SESS. : 2023-2024)—GENERAL DEBATE (Agenda item 8)
Niinistö, Sauli - A/78/PV.6
UN. GENERAL ASSEMBLY (78TH SESS. : 2023-2024)—SPECIAL STATEMENTS
Niinistö, Sauli - A/78/PV.6

Fondation France Maroc

WESTERN SAHARA QUESTION (Agenda item 58)
Seillan, Hubert - A/C.4/78/SR.5

Fondazione Proclade Internazionale - Onlus

WESTERN SAHARA QUESTION (Agenda item 58)
Ramírez Soler, Henry - A/C.4/78/SR.4

Foreign Policy and Global Health Initiative

HEALTH (Agenda item 125)
Schalkwyk, Marthinus van (South Africa) - A/78/PV.77

Forum Canario-Saharaui

WESTERN SAHARA QUESTION (Agenda item 58)
Ortiz Palacio, Ignacio - A/C.4/78/SR.4

France

ARMED CONFLICTS PREVENTION (Agenda item 31a)
Dime-Labille, Diarra - A/78/PV.72
ARMS RACE—OUTER SPACE (Agenda item 97a)
Petit, Camille - A/C.1/78/PV.17
ARMS TRANSFERS—TREATIES (Agenda item 99x)
Petit, Camille - A/C.1/78/PV.18
BIOLOGICAL WEAPONS—TREATIES (Agenda item 106)
Petit, Camille - A/C.1/78/PV.15
CHEMICAL WEAPONS—TREATIES (Agenda item 99l)
Petit, Camille - A/C.1/78/PV.15
CLIMATE (Agenda item 18d)
Segovia, Lisa Isabelle - A/C.2/78/SR.25
CLUSTER MUNITIONS (Agenda item 99dd)
Petit, Camille - A/C.1/78/PV.18
CONVENTIONAL WEAPONS (Agenda item 99u)
Petit, Camille - A/C.1/78/PV.18
CONVENTIONAL WEAPONS—TREATIES (Agenda item 103)
Petit, Camille - A/C.1/78/PV.18
CRIMES AGAINST HUMANITY (Agenda item 80)
Dime-Labille, Diarra - A/C.6/78/SR.38; A/C.6/78/SR.40; A/C.6/78/SR.44
Wavrin, Hugo - A/C.6/78/SR.11; A/C.6/78/SR.42; A/C.6/78/SR.43
DISAPPEARANCE OF PERSONS (Agenda item 71b)
Dumas, Anouk - A/C.3/78/SR.22
DISARMAMENT—GENERAL AND COMPLETE (Agenda item 99)
Petit, Camille - A/C.1/78/PV.18; A/C.1/78/PV.26; A/C.1/78/PV.30
DISARMAMENT AGREEMENTS—OUTER SPACE (Agenda item 97c)
Petit, Camille - A/C.1/78/PV.17
ELECTION VERIFICATION—UN (Agenda item 71b)
Freudenreich, Anne - A/C.3/78/SR.50
EMERGENCY ASSISTANCE (Agenda item 72a)
Dime-Labille, Diarra - A/78/PV.47
FREEDOM OF EXPRESSION (Agenda item 71b)
Freudenreich, Anne - A/C.3/78/SR.19
FRENCH POLYNESIA QUESTION (Agenda item 58)
Chailloux, Steve - A/C.4/78/SR.3
Le Gayic, Tematai - A/C.4/78/SR.3
Rivière, Nicolas de - A/C.4/78/SR.3
HUMAN RIGHTS (Agenda item 71)
Dime-Labille, Diarra - A/C.3/78/SR.16
HUMAN RIGHTS—AFGHANISTAN (Agenda item 71c)
Froment, Lucas - A/C.3/78/SR.34

France (continued)

HUMAN RIGHTS—AFGHANISTAN (Agenda item 71c)
Lebédel-Delumeau, Eric - A/C.3/78/SR.25
HUMAN RIGHTS—MYANMAR (Agenda item 71c)
Froment, Lucas - A/C.3/78/SR.33
HUMAN RIGHTS—REPORTS (Agenda item 71c)
Lebédel-Delumeau, Eric - A/C.3/78/SR.25
HUMAN RIGHTS—RUSSIAN FEDERATION (Agenda item 71c)
Martinet, Philippe - A/C.3/78/SR.37
HUMAN RIGHTS—SYRIAN ARAB REPUBLIC (Agenda item 71c)
Lebédel-Delumeau, Eric - A/C.3/78/SR.25
HUMAN RIGHTS—UKRAINE (Agenda item 71c)
Lamy, Jean - A/C.3/78/SR.37
Lebédel-Delumeau, Eric - A/C.3/78/SR.25
HUMAN RIGHTS ACTIVISTS (Agenda item 71b)
Freudenreich, Anne - A/C.3/78/SR.19
INFORMATION—INTERNATIONAL SECURITY (Agenda item 94)
Petit, Camille - A/C.1/78/PV.21; A/C.1/78/PV.28
INTERNATIONAL CRIMINAL COURT—REPORTS (Agenda item 74)
Dime-Labille, Diarra - A/78/PV.21
INTERNATIONAL LAW—TRAINING PROGRAMMES (Agenda item 78)
Dime-Labille, Diarra - A/C.6/78/SR.21
INTERNATIONAL RESIDUAL MECHANISM FOR CRIMINAL TRIBUNALS (Agenda item 126)
Dime-Labille, Diarra - A/78/PV.19
LANDMINES—TREATIES (Agenda item 99m)
Petit, Camille - A/C.1/78/PV.18; A/C.1/78/PV.19
LAW OF THE SEA (Agenda item 75a)
Broadhurst Estival, Nathalie - A/78/PV.48
Dime-Labille, Diarra - A/78/PV.44
MARINE ECOSYSTEMS—BIOLOGICAL DIVERSITY (Agenda item 75c)
Dime-Labille, Diarra - A/78/PV.44
MEDITERRANEAN REGION—REGIONAL SECURITY (Agenda item 104)
Petit, Camille - A/C.1/78/PV.25
MIDDLE EAST—NUCLEAR-WEAPON-FREE ZONES (Agenda item 95)
Petit, Camille - A/C.1/78/PV.25
MULTILATERALISM—DISARMAMENT (Agenda item 99r)
Petit, Camille - A/C.1/78/PV.22
NEW CALEDONIA QUESTION (Agenda item 58)
Rivière, Nicolas de - A/C.4/78/SR.7
NUCLEAR DISARMAMENT (Agenda item 99b)
Petit, Camille - A/C.1/78/PV.11

France (continued)

NUCLEAR NON-PROLIFERATION—INTERNATIONAL OBLIGATIONS (Agenda item 99w)
Petit, Camille - A/C.1/78/PV.11
NUCLEAR WEAPONS—ELIMINATION (Agenda item 99z)
Petit, Camille - A/C.1/78/PV.26
OUTER SPACE—CONFIDENCE-BUILDING MEASURES (Agenda item 99v)
Petit, Camille - A/C.1/78/PV.17
OUTER SPACE—PRINCIPLES (Agenda item 97d)
Petit, Camille - A/C.1/78/PV.17
PALESTINIANS—ASSISTANCE (Agenda item 72b)
Dime-Labille, Diarra - A/78/PV.47
POVERTY—HUMAN RIGHTS (Agenda item 71b)
Lebédel-Delumeau, Eric - A/C.3/78/SR.30
RACIAL DISCRIMINATION—ELIMINATION (Agenda item 69a)
Wagner, Julie - A/C.3/78/SR.41
RACIAL DISCRIMINATION—PROGRAMMES OF ACTION (Agenda item 69b)
Wagner, Julie - A/C.3/78/SR.41
RIGHTS OF THE CHILD (Agenda item 67)
Dime-Labille, Diarra - A/C.3/78/SR.13
Freudenreich, Anne - A/C.3/78/SR.11
SEXUAL ORIENTATION (Agenda item 71b)
Freudenreich, Anne - A/C.3/78/SR.39
SMALL ARMS—ILLICIT TRAFFIC (Agenda item 99p)
Petit, Camille - A/C.1/78/PV.18
SMALL ARMS—ILLICIT TRAFFIC—ASSISTANCE (Agenda item 99n)
Petit, Camille - A/C.1/78/PV.18
SPORTS—OLYMPIC GAMES (Agenda item 11)
Estanguet, Tony - A/78/PV.38
Richard, Olivier-Gabriel - A/78/PV.38
STRADDLING FISH STOCKS (Agenda item 75b)
Dime-Labille, Diarra - A/78/PV.44
SUSTAINABLE DEVELOPMENT (Agenda item 18)
Broadhurst Estival, Nathalie - A/78/PV.103
TRANSNATIONAL CORPORATIONS—HUMAN RIGHTS (Agenda item 71b)
Lamy, Jean - A/C.3/78/SR.21
UKRAINE—POLITICAL CONDITIONS (Agenda item 62)
Séjourné, Stéphane - A/78/PV.56
UN—PROGRAMME PLANNING (Agenda item 135)
Semon, Alizée - A/C.1/78/PV.10
UN. CONFERENCE ON DISARMAMENT—REPORTS (Agenda item 101a)
Petit, Camille - A/C.1/78/PV.22

France (continued)

UN. GENERAL ASSEMBLY—WORK PROGRAMME (Agenda item 120)
Semon, Alizée - A/C.1/78/PV.10
Wavrin, Hugo - A/78/PV.33
UN. GENERAL ASSEMBLY (78TH SESS. : 2023-2024)—AGENDA (Agenda item 7)
Dime-Labille, Diarra - A/BUR/78/SR.2
UN. GENERAL ASSEMBLY (78TH SESS. : 2023-2024)—GENERAL DEBATE (Agenda item 8)
Colonna, Catherine - A/78/PV.9
UN. GENERAL ASSEMBLY (78TH SESS. : 2023-2024). 1ST COMMITTEE—GENERAL DEBATE (Agenda item 8)
Petit, Camille - A/C.1/78/PV.8
UN. INTERNATIONAL COURT OF JUSTICE—REPORTS (Agenda item 73)
Colas, Diego - A/78/PV.20
UN. INTERNATIONAL LAW COMMISSION—REPORTS (Agenda item 79)
Colas, Diego - A/C.6/78/SR.23
Thiéry, Charline - A/C.6/78/SR.29; A/C.6/78/SR.31
UN. SECURITY COUNCIL—MEMBERSHIP (Agenda item 121)
Rivière, Nicolas de - A/78/PV.35
UN COMMISSION ON INTERNATIONAL TRADE LAW—REPORTS (Agenda item 77)
Tabuteau-Mangels, Aurélie - A/C.6/78/SR.14
UN RESOLUTIONS—IMPLEMENTATION (Agenda item 119)
Wavrin, Hugo - A/78/PV.33
VETO (Agenda item 63)
Dime-Labille, Diarra - A/78/PV.70
Jaraud-Darnault, Isis Marie Doriane - A/78/PV.66
Rivière, Nicolas de - A/78/PV.51; A/78/PV.60; A/78/PV.68; A/78/PV.74; A/78/PV.78
WOMEN'S ADVANCEMENT (Agenda item 25a)
LeClerc, Emmanuel - A/C.3/78/SR.9
WOMEN'S ADVANCEMENT—CONFERENCES (Agenda item 25b)
LeClerc, Emmanuel - A/C.3/78/SR.9
YOUTH (Agenda item 24b)
Wagner, Julie - A/C.3/78/SR.55

French Polynesia

FRENCH POLYNESIA QUESTION (Agenda item 58)
Brotherson, Moetai - A/C.4/78/SR.3
Brown, Tahia - A/C.4/78/SR.3
Cross, Valentina - A/C.4/78/SR.3
Flores, Bruno - A/C.4/78/SR.3
Flores, Rachelle - A/C.4/78/SR.3
Géros, Antony - A/C.4/78/SR.3
Hamblin, Ueva - A/C.4/78/SR.3
Hauata Ah-Min, Maite - A/C.4/78/SR.3
Homai, Odette - A/C.4/78/SR.3
Kohumoetini, Hina - A/C.4/78/SR.3
Kohumoetini, Marielle - A/C.4/78/SR.3

French Polynesia (continued)

FRENCH POLYNESIA QUESTION (Agenda item 58)
Loussan, Cliff - A/C.4/78/SR.3
Maamaatuaiahutapu, Maurea - A/C.4/78/SR.3
Salmon, Allen - A/C.4/78/SR.3
Tapati, Tafai - A/C.4/78/SR.3
Temaru, Oscar Manutahi - A/C.4/78/SR.3
Teremate, Ruben - A/C.4/78/SR.3
Terou, Pierre - A/C.4/78/SR.3
Tuheiava, Richard Ariihau - A/C.4/78/SR.3
Vaianui, Jeanne - A/C.4/78/SR.3
Vanaa, Elise - A/C.4/78/SR.3

Frente Polisario

WESTERN SAHARA QUESTION (Agenda item 58)
Omar, Sidi - A/C.4/78/SR.4

Friends of the Comprehensive Nuclear Test-Ban Treaty

DISARMAMENT—GENERAL AND COMPLETE (Agenda item 99)
Yamazaki, Kazuyuki (Japan) - A/78/PV.105

Front de libération nationale kanak et socialiste (New Caledonia)

NEW CALEDONIA QUESTION (Agenda item 58)
Tingal, Magalie - A/C.4/78/SR.5

Fundación Canaria de Apoyo a los Trastornos del Neurodesarrollo

WESTERN SAHARA QUESTION (Agenda item 58)
Fortea Sevilla, María del Sol - A/C.4/78/SR.4

Fundación Universitaria Compensa (Colombia)

WESTERN SAHARA QUESTION (Agenda item 58)
Córdoba Heredia, Alexandra - A/C.4/78/SR.4

Gabon

CUBA—UNITED STATES (Agenda item 38)
Koumba Pambo, Aurélie Flore - A/78/PV.26
DECOLONIZATION (Agenda item 58)
Ayoune, Lia Berthiana Bouanga - A/C.4/78/SR.9
RACIAL DISCRIMINATION—ELIMINATION (Agenda item 69a)
Biang, Michel Xavier - A/C.3/78/SR.42
RACIAL DISCRIMINATION—PROGRAMMES OF ACTION (Agenda item 69b)
Biang, Michel Xavier - A/C.3/78/SR.42
UN. GENERAL ASSEMBLY (78TH SESS. : 2023-2024). 1ST COMMITTEE—GENERAL DEBATE (Agenda item 8)
Koumba Pambo, Aurélie Flore - A/C.1/78/PV.9

Gabon (continued)

UN HIGH COMMISSIONER FOR REFUGEES—REPORTS (Agenda item 60)
Biang, Michel Xavier - A/C.3/78/SR.45
WESTERN SAHARA QUESTION (Agenda item 58)
Ayoune, Lia Berthiana Bouanga - A/C.4/78/SR.9

Gabon. Prime Minister

UN. GENERAL ASSEMBLY (78TH SESS. : 2023-2024)—GENERAL DEBATE (Agenda item 8)
Ndong Sima, Raymond - A/78/PV.10
UN. GENERAL ASSEMBLY (78TH SESS. : 2023-2024)—SPECIAL STATEMENTS
Ndong Sima, Raymond - A/78/PV.10

Gambia

CRIMES AGAINST HUMANITY (Agenda item 80)
Jaiteh, Amadou - A/C.6/78/SR.45; A/C.6/78/SR.47
INDIGENOUS PEOPLES (Agenda item 68a)
Sillah, Aminata - A/C.3/78/SR.48
PEACEKEEPING OPERATIONS (Agenda item 51)
Badjie, Isatou - A/C.4/78/SR.19
RURAL WOMEN (Agenda item 25a)
Jaiteh, Amadou - A/C.3/78/SR.49
SUSTAINABLE DEVELOPMENT (Agenda item 18)
Dibba, Lamin B. - A/C.2/78/SR.24
WESTERN SAHARA QUESTION (Agenda item 58)
Badjie, Isatou - A/C.4/78/SR.6
WOMEN MIGRANT WORKERS (Agenda item 25a)
Jaiteh, Amadou - A/C.3/78/SR.49

Gambia. Vice-President

UN. GENERAL ASSEMBLY (78TH SESS. : 2023-2024)—GENERAL DEBATE (Agenda item 8)
Jallow, Mohammed - A/78/PV.9
UN. GENERAL ASSEMBLY (78TH SESS. : 2023-2024)—SPECIAL STATEMENTS
Jallow, Mohammed - A/78/PV.9

George Washington University (Washington, D.C.)

DISARMAMENT—GENERAL AND COMPLETE (Agenda item 99)
Squassoni, Sharon A. - A/78/PV.105

Georgia

ARMED CONFLICTS PREVENTION (Agenda item 31a)
Abesadze, David - A/78/PV.72
CRIME PREVENTION (Agenda item 107)
Lortkipanidze, Ekaterine - A/C.3/78/SR.6

Georgia (continued)

CRIMES AGAINST HUMANITY (Agenda item 80)
Abesadze, David - A/C.6/78/SR.44
DISPLACED PERSONS (Agenda item 71b)
Lortkipanidze, Ekaterine - A/C.3/78/SR.32
HIV/AIDS—DECLARATIONS (Agenda item 10)
Abesadze, David - A/78/PV.91
HUMAN RIGHTS (Agenda item 71)
Lortkipanidze, Ekaterine - A/C.3/78/SR.16
HUMAN RIGHTS—RUSSIAN FEDERATION (Agenda item 71c)
Lortkipanidze, Ekaterine - A/C.3/78/SR.37
HUMAN RIGHTS—UKRAINE (Agenda item 71c)
Abesadze, David - A/C.3/78/SR.53
Lortkipanidze, Ekaterine - A/C.3/78/SR.37
HUMAN RIGHTS ACTIVISTS (Agenda item 71b)
Lortkipanidze, Ekaterine - A/C.3/78/SR.19
INTERNATIONAL CRIMINAL COURT—REPORTS (Agenda item 74)
Abesadze, David - A/78/PV.22
MULTILATERALISM—DISARMAMENT (Agenda item 99r)
Dvali, Akaki - A/C.1/78/PV.22
ORGANIZATION FOR DEMOCRACY AND ECONOMIC DEVELOPMENT - GUAM (Agenda item 32)
Bakradze, David - A/78/PV.85
PERSONS WITH DISABILITIES—HUMAN RIGHTS (Agenda item 71a)
Lortkipanidze, Ekaterine - A/C.3/78/SR.38
RACIAL DISCRIMINATION—ELIMINATION (Agenda item 69a)
Lortkipanidze, Ekaterine - A/C.3/78/SR.42
RACIAL DISCRIMINATION—PROGRAMMES OF ACTION (Agenda item 69b)
Lortkipanidze, Ekaterine - A/C.3/78/SR.42
RESPONSIBILITY TO PROTECT (Agenda item 129)
Pipia, Temur - A/78/PV.97; A/78/PV.99
RIGHTS OF THE CHILD (Agenda item 67)
Lortkipanidze, Ekaterine - A/C.3/78/SR.11; A/C.3/78/SR.13
RULE OF LAW (Agenda item 83)
Kupradze, Sopio - A/C.6/78/SR.18
SEXUAL ORIENTATION (Agenda item 71b)
Lortkipanidze, Ekaterine - A/C.3/78/SR.39
TERRORISM (Agenda item 109)
Kupradze, Sopio - A/C.6/78/SR.4
TORTURE AND OTHER CRUEL TREATMENT (Agenda item 71a)
Lortkipanidze, Ekaterine - A/C.3/78/SR.18
UKRAINE—POLITICAL CONDITIONS (Agenda item 62)
Darsalia, Lasha - A/78/PV.56

Georgia (continued)

UN. GENERAL ASSEMBLY (78TH SESS. : 2023-2024). 1ST COMMITTEE—GENERAL DEBATE (Agenda item 8)
Bakradze, David - A/C.1/78/PV.7
Dvali, Akaki - A/C.1/78/PV.8
UN. GENERAL ASSEMBLY (78TH SESS. : 2023-2024). 2ND COMMITTEE—GENERAL DEBATE (Agenda item 8)
Abesadze, David - A/C.2/78/SR.3
UN. HUMAN RIGHTS COUNCIL—REPORTS (Agenda item 66)
Abesadze, David - A/78/PV.23
UN. INTERNATIONAL COURT OF JUSTICE—REPORTS (Agenda item 73)
Bakradze, David - A/78/PV.28
UN CHARTER—REPORTS (Agenda item 82)
Kupradze, Sopio - A/C.6/78/SR.22
UN HIGH COMMISSIONER FOR REFUGEES—REPORTS (Agenda item 60)
Abesadze, David - A/C.3/78/SR.45
VETO (Agenda item 63)
Abesadze, David - A/78/PV.71
WOMEN'S ADVANCEMENT (Agenda item 25a)
Lortkipanidze, Ekaterine - A/C.3/78/SR.9
WOMEN'S ADVANCEMENT—CONFERENCES (Agenda item 25b)
Lortkipanidze, Ekaterine - A/C.3/78/SR.9

Georgia. Prime Minister

UN. GENERAL ASSEMBLY (78TH SESS. : 2023-2024)—GENERAL DEBATE (Agenda item 8)
Garibashvili, Irakli - A/78/PV.11
UN. GENERAL ASSEMBLY (78TH SESS. : 2023-2024)—SPECIAL STATEMENTS
Garibashvili, Irakli - A/78/PV.11

Germany

ARMED CONFLICTS PREVENTION (Agenda item 31a)
Geisler, Michael Alexander - A/78/PV.72
ARMS RACE—OUTER SPACE (Agenda item 97a)
Himmler, Benjamin - A/C.1/78/PV.16
ARMS TRANSFERS—TREATIES (Agenda item 99x)
Göbel, Thomas - A/C.1/78/PV.18
BIOLOGICAL WEAPONS—TREATIES (Agenda item 106)
Himmler, Benjamin - A/C.1/78/PV.14
CHEMICAL WEAPONS—TREATIES (Agenda item 99l)
Himmler, Benjamin - A/C.1/78/PV.14
CLIMATE CHANGE (Agenda item 71b)
Wennholz, Philipp Alexander - A/C.3/78/SR.29
CONVENTIONAL WEAPONS (Agenda item 99u)
Göbel, Thomas - A/C.1/78/PV.18; A/C.1/78/PV.28

Germany (continued)

CRIMES AGAINST HUMANITY (Agenda item 80)
Craemer, Cathrine - A/C.6/78/SR.45
Hasenau, Michael - A/C.6/78/SR.9; A/C.6/78/SR.38
DISARMAMENT—GENERAL AND COMPLETE (Agenda item 99)
Göbel, Thomas - A/C.1/78/PV.18
DISARMAMENT AGREEMENTS—OUTER SPACE (Agenda item 97c)
Himmler, Benjamin - A/C.1/78/PV.16
DISASTER VICTIMS (Agenda item 86)
Hasenau, Michael - A/C.6/78/SR.5
HUMAN RIGHTS (Agenda item 71)
Drescher, Daniel - A/C.3/78/SR.16
HUMAN RIGHTS—AFGHANISTAN (Agenda item 71c)
Drescher, Daniel - A/C.3/78/SR.34
HUMAN RIGHTS—IRAN (ISLAMIC REPUBLIC OF) (Agenda item 71c)
Drescher, Daniel - A/C.3/78/SR.34
HUMAN RIGHTS—MYANMAR (Agenda item 71c)
Geisler, Michael Alexander - A/C.3/78/SR.33
HUMAN RIGHTS—RUSSIAN FEDERATION (Agenda item 71c)
Drescher, Daniel - A/C.3/78/SR.37
HUMAN RIGHTS—SYRIAN ARAB REPUBLIC (Agenda item 71c)
Drescher, Daniel - A/C.3/78/SR.34
HUMAN RIGHTS—TERRITORIES OCCUPIED BY ISRAEL (Agenda item 71c)
Zahneisen, Thomas - A/C.3/78/SR.35
HUMAN RIGHTS—UKRAINE (Agenda item 71c)
Drescher, Daniel - A/C.3/78/SR.37
HUMAN RIGHTS ACTIVISTS (Agenda item 71b)
Drescher, Daniel - A/C.3/78/SR.19
HUMAN RIGHTS ADVANCEMENT (Agenda item 71b)
Leendertse, Antje - A/C.3/78/SR.26
INTERNATIONAL CRIMINAL COURT—REPORTS (Agenda item 74)
Hasenau, Michael - A/78/PV.22
INTERNATIONAL JURISDICTION (Agenda item 84)
Hasenau, Michael - A/C.6/78/SR.12
INTERNATIONAL RESIDUAL MECHANISM FOR CRIMINAL TRIBUNALS (Agenda item 126)
Hasenau, Michael - A/78/PV.19
LANDMINES—TREATIES (Agenda item 99m)
Göbel, Thomas - A/C.1/78/PV.18
LAW OF THE SEA (Agenda item 75a)
Freiin von Uslar-Gleichen, Tania - A/78/PV.43
MARINE ECOSYSTEMS—BIOLOGICAL DIVERSITY (Agenda item 75c)
Freiin von Uslar-Gleichen, Tania - A/78/PV.43

Germany (continued)

NATIONAL INSTITUTIONS—HUMAN RIGHTS (Agenda item 71b)
Drescher, Daniel - A/C.3/78/SR.49
NUCLEAR DISARMAMENT (Agenda item 99b)
Himmler, Benjamin - A/C.1/78/PV.11
NUCLEAR NON-PROLIFERATION—INTERNATIONAL OBLIGATIONS (Agenda item 99w)
Himmler, Benjamin - A/C.1/78/PV.11
NUCLEAR WEAPON TESTS—TREATIES (Agenda item 105)
Himmler, Benjamin - A/C.1/78/PV.11
OUTER SPACE—CONFIDENCE-BUILDING MEASURES (Agenda item 99v)
Himmler, Benjamin - A/C.1/78/PV.16
OUTER SPACE—PRINCIPLES (Agenda item 97d)
Himmler, Benjamin - A/C.1/78/PV.16
PEACE (Agenda item 14)
Leendertse, Antje - A/78/PV.82
PEACEBUILDING (Agenda item 61)
Geisler, Michael Alexander - A/78/PV.100
PEACEKEEPING OPERATIONS (Agenda item 51)
Geisler, Michael Alexander - A/C.4/78/SR.20
RACIAL DISCRIMINATION—ELIMINATION (Agenda item 69a)
Ludwig, Annette - A/C.3/78/SR.41
RACIAL DISCRIMINATION—PROGRAMMES OF ACTION (Agenda item 69b)
Ludwig, Annette - A/C.3/78/SR.41
RESPONSIBILITY TO PROTECT (Agenda item 129)
Wennholz, Philipp Alexander - A/78/PV.97
RIGHT TO DRINKING WATER (Agenda item 71b)
Wennholz, Philipp Alexander - A/C.3/78/SR.28
SELF-DETERMINATION OF PEOPLES (Agenda item 70)
Geisler, Michael Alexander - A/C.3/78/SR.49
SEXUAL ORIENTATION (Agenda item 71b)
Krabatsch, Ann-Jasmin - A/C.3/78/SR.39
SMALL ARMS—ILLICIT TRAFFIC (Agenda item 99p)
Göbel, Thomas - A/C.1/78/PV.18
STRADDLING FISH STOCKS (Agenda item 75b)
Freiin von Uslar-Gleichen, Tania - A/78/PV.43
TERRITORIES OCCUPIED BY ISRAEL—NATURAL RESOURCES (Agenda item 59)
Roeder-Messell, Ernst Heinrich - A/C.2/78/SR.21
UKRAINE—POLITICAL CONDITIONS (Agenda item 62)
Baerbock, Annalena - A/78/PV.56
UN. GENERAL ASSEMBLY (78TH SESS. : 2023-2024). 1ST COMMITTEE—GENERAL DEBATE (Agenda item 8)
Göbel, Thomas - A/C.1/78/PV.5

Germany (continued)

UN. INTERNATIONAL COURT OF JUSTICE—REPORTS (Agenda item 73)
Freiin von Uslar-Gleichen, Tania - A/78/PV.20
UN. INTERNATIONAL LAW COMMISSION—REPORTS (Agenda item 79)
Freiin von Uslar-Gleichen, Tania - A/C.6/78/SR.24
Hasenau, Michael - A/C.6/78/SR.29; A/C.6/78/SR.31
UN. PEACEBUILDING COMMISSION—REPORTS (Agenda item 27)
Geisler, Michael Alexander - A/78/PV.100
UN. PEACEBUILDING FUND—REPORTS (Agenda item 111)
Geisler, Michael Alexander - A/78/PV.100
UN. SECURITY COUNCIL—REPORTS (Agenda item 26)
Alscher, Daniel Friedrich - A/78/PV.93
UN HIGH COMMISSIONER FOR REFUGEES—REPORTS (Agenda item 60)
Lasota, Josephine - A/C.3/78/SR.45
VETO (Agenda item 63)
Geisler, Michael Alexander - A/78/PV.52
Hasenau, Michael - A/78/PV.70
Leendertse, Antje - A/78/PV.68; A/78/PV.78
Saadi, Samy Sofian - A/78/PV.3
WOMEN'S ADVANCEMENT (Agenda item 25a)
Ludwig, Annette - A/C.3/78/SR.8
WOMEN'S ADVANCEMENT—CONFERENCES (Agenda item 25b)
Ludwig, Annette - A/C.3/78/SR.8
YOUTH (Agenda item 24b)
Essig, Ilka - A/C.3/78/SR.3
Töpfer, Lew - A/C.3/78/SR.3

Germany. Chancellor

UN. GENERAL ASSEMBLY (78TH SESS. : 2023-2024)—GENERAL DEBATE (Agenda item 8)
Scholz, Olaf - A/78/PV.5
UN. GENERAL ASSEMBLY (78TH SESS. : 2023-2024)—SPECIAL STATEMENTS
Scholz, Olaf - A/78/PV.5

Ghana

CRIME PREVENTION (Agenda item 107)
Anyanah, Bismark - A/C.3/78/SR.6
CRIMES AGAINST HUMANITY (Agenda item 80)
Korbieh, Solomon - A/C.6/78/SR.45
CYBERCRIME (Agenda item 108)
Anyanah, Bismark - A/C.3/78/SR.6
DECOLONIZATION (Agenda item 58)
Nyarku, Felix Akom - A/C.4/78/SR.8
DISARMAMENT—GENERAL AND COMPLETE (Agenda item 99)
Kesse Antwi, Linda - A/78/PV.106; A/C.1/78/PV.30

Ghana (continued)

FISSIONABLE MATERIALS—TREATIES (Agenda item 99a)
Kesse Antwi, Linda - A/C.1/78/PV.12
HUMAN RIGHTS—INTERNATIONAL INSTRUMENTS (Agenda item 71a)
Williams, Edna Stephanie - A/C.3/78/SR.26
NATIONAL INSTITUTIONS—HUMAN RIGHTS (Agenda item 71b)
Williams, Edna Stephanie - A/C.3/78/SR.26
NUCLEAR DISARMAMENT (Agenda item 99b)
Kesse Antwi, Linda - A/C.1/78/PV.12
NUCLEAR NON-PROLIFERATION—INTERNATIONAL OBLIGATIONS (Agenda item 99w)
Kesse Antwi, Linda - A/C.1/78/PV.12
PEACE (Agenda item 14)
Barnor, Nana Akua - A/78/PV.82
PEACEKEEPING OPERATIONS—CRIMINAL LIABILITY (Agenda item 76)
Hackman, Khalilah - A/C.6/78/SR.8
RESPONSIBILITY TO PROTECT (Agenda item 129)
Barnor, Nana Akua - A/78/PV.99
RIGHTS OF THE CHILD (Agenda item 67)
Corquaye, Ama Anima - A/C.3/78/SR.14
RULE OF LAW (Agenda item 83)
Hackman, Khalilah - A/C.6/78/SR.17
SUSTAINABLE DEVELOPMENT (Agenda item 18)
Oppong-Ntiri, Carolyn - A/78/PV.88
TERRORISM (Agenda item 109)
Hackman, Khalilah - A/C.6/78/SR.2
UKRAINE—POLITICAL CONDITIONS (Agenda item 62)
Kesse Antwi, Linda - A/78/PV.99
UN. GENERAL ASSEMBLY (78TH SESS. : 2023-2024). 1ST COMMITTEE—GENERAL DEBATE (Agenda item 8)
Kesse Antwi, Linda - A/C.1/78/PV.5
UN. GENERAL ASSEMBLY (78TH SESS. : 2023-2024). 2ND COMMITTEE—GENERAL DEBATE (Agenda item 8)
Abudu-Birresborn, Jeswuni - A/C.2/78/SR.3
VETO (Agenda item 63)
Agyeman, Harold Adlai - A/78/PV.75; A/78/PV.78

Ghana. President

UN. GENERAL ASSEMBLY (78TH SESS. : 2023-2024)—GENERAL DEBATE (Agenda item 8)
Akufo-Addo, Nana Addo Dankwa - A/78/PV.6
UN. GENERAL ASSEMBLY (78TH SESS. : 2023-2024)—SPECIAL STATEMENTS
Akufo-Addo, Nana Addo Dankwa - A/78/PV.6

Gibraltar

GIBRALTAR QUESTION (Agenda item 58)
Garcia, Joseph - A/C.4/78/SR.13

Global Directives (Organization)

WESTERN SAHARA QUESTION (Agenda item 58)
Thomas, Kathleen - A/C.4/78/SR.5

Greece

ARMS RACE—OUTER SPACE (Agenda item 97a)
Papathanasiou, Artemis - A/C.1/78/PV.17
ARMS TRANSFERS—TREATIES (Agenda item 99x)
Christoglou, Konstantinos - A/C.1/78/PV.19
CLIMATE CHANGE (Agenda item 71b)
Kastanas, Elias - A/C.3/78/SR.29
CONVENTIONAL WEAPONS (Agenda item 99u)
Christoglou, Konstantinos - A/C.1/78/PV.19
DISARMAMENT—GENERAL AND COMPLETE (Agenda item 99)
Christoglou, Konstantinos - A/C.1/78/PV.19
FREEDOM OF EXPRESSION (Agenda item 71b)
Alexandridou, Alexandra - A/C.3/78/SR.19
HUMAN RIGHTS (Agenda item 71)
Alexandridou, Alexandra - A/C.3/78/SR.16
HUMAN RIGHTS—INTERNATIONAL INSTRUMENTS (Agenda item 71a)
Sekeris, Evangelos C. - A/C.3/78/SR.25
HUMAN RIGHTS ADVANCEMENT (Agenda item 71b)
Sekeris, Evangelos C. - A/C.3/78/SR.52
INFORMATION (Agenda item 53)
Sekeris, Evangelos C. - A/C.4/78/SR.13
INFORMATION—INTERNATIONAL SECURITY (Agenda item 94)
Christoglou, Konstantinos - A/C.1/78/PV.20
INTERNATIONAL CRIMINAL COURT—REPORTS (Agenda item 74)
Stavridi, Zinovia Chaido - A/78/PV.21
MEDITERRANEAN REGION—REGIONAL SECURITY (Agenda item 104)
Christoglou, Konstantinos - A/C.1/78/PV.22
MULTILATERALISM—DISARMAMENT (Agenda item 99r)
Christoglou, Konstantinos - A/C.1/78/PV.22
NUCLEAR DISARMAMENT (Agenda item 99b)
Margaris, Pantelis - A/C.1/78/PV.11
NUCLEAR NON-PROLIFERATION—INTERNATIONAL OBLIGATIONS (Agenda item 99w)
Margaris, Pantelis - A/C.1/78/PV.11
NUCLEAR WEAPON TESTS—TREATIES (Agenda item 105)
Margaris, Pantelis - A/C.1/78/PV.11
OUTER SPACE—PRINCIPLES (Agenda item 97d)
Papathanasiou, Artemis - A/C.1/78/PV.17
PEACE (Agenda item 14)
Sekeris, Evangelos C. - A/78/PV.82

Greece (continued)

PERSONS WITH DISABILITIES—HUMAN RIGHTS (Agenda item 71a)
Retalis, Michail - A/C.3/78/SR.38
RELIGIOUS INTOLERANCE (Agenda item 71b)
Retalis, Michail - A/C.3/78/SR.38
RESPONSIBILITY TO PROTECT (Agenda item 129)
Sekeris, Evangelos C. - A/78/PV.97
RIGHTS OF THE CHILD (Agenda item 67)
Alexandridou, Alexandra - A/C.3/78/SR.11
SMALL ARMS—ILLICIT TRAFFIC—ASSISTANCE (Agenda item 99n)
Christoglou, Konstantinos - A/C.1/78/PV.19
SPORTS—OLYMPIC GAMES (Agenda item 11)
Sekeris, Evangelos C. - A/78/PV.38
TRAFFICKING IN PERSONS (Agenda item 71b)
Kastanas, Elias - A/C.3/78/SR.23
UKRAINE—POLITICAL CONDITIONS (Agenda item 62)
Lampridis, Spyridon - A/78/PV.56
UN. GENERAL ASSEMBLY (78TH SESS. : 2023-2024). 1ST COMMITTEE—GENERAL DEBATE (Agenda item 8)
Sekeris, Evangelos C. - A/C.1/78/PV.4
UN. GENERAL ASSEMBLY (78TH SESS. : 2023-2024). 2ND COMMITTEE—GENERAL DEBATE (Agenda item 8)
Sekeris, Evangelos C. - A/C.2/78/SR.4
UN. INTERNATIONAL COURT OF JUSTICE—REPORTS (Agenda item 73)
Stellakatos-Loverdos, Michael - A/78/PV.28
UN. INTERNATIONAL LAW COMMISSION—REPORTS (Agenda item 79)
Stavridi, Zinovia Chaido - A/C.6/78/SR.27
Stellakatos-Loverdos, Michael - A/C.6/78/SR.30; A/C.6/78/SR.32
UN HIGH COMMISSIONER FOR REFUGEES—REPORTS (Agenda item 60)
Retalis, Michail - A/C.3/78/SR.44
VETO (Agenda item 63)
Sekeris, Evangelos C. - A/78/PV.52; A/78/PV.69
WOMEN'S ADVANCEMENT (Agenda item 25a)
Alexandridou, Alexandra - A/C.3/78/SR.7
WOMEN'S ADVANCEMENT—CONFERENCES (Agenda item 25b)
Alexandridou, Alexandra - A/C.3/78/SR.7

Greece. Prime Minister

UN. GENERAL ASSEMBLY (78TH SESS. : 2023-2024)—GENERAL DEBATE (Agenda item 8)
Mitsotakis, Kyriakos - A/78/PV.9
UN. GENERAL ASSEMBLY (78TH SESS. : 2023-2024)—SPECIAL STATEMENTS
Mitsotakis, Kyriakos - A/78/PV.9

Grenada. Prime Minister

UN. GENERAL ASSEMBLY (78TH SESS. : 2023-2024)—GENERAL DEBATE (Agenda item 8)
Mitchell, Dickon - A/78/PV.11
UN. GENERAL ASSEMBLY (78TH SESS. : 2023-2024)—SPECIAL STATEMENTS
Mitchell, Dickon - A/78/PV.11

Group of 77

2030 AGENDA—PROGRAMME IMPLEMENTATION (Agenda item 18a)
Téllez Alonso, Frank (Cuba) - A/C.2/78/SR.12
Torres Seara, Dalia Marlen (Cuba) - A/C.2/78/SR.21
ADMINISTRATION OF JUSTICE (Agenda item 144)
Hernández Morera, Diosdado de Jesús (Cuba) - A/C.5/78/SR.15
AFRICA—DEVELOPMENT (Agenda item 65b)
Kwoba, Godfrey (Uganda) - A/78/PV.57
AFRICA—SUSTAINABLE DEVELOPMENT—PARTNERSHIP (Agenda item 65a)
Kwoba, Godfrey (Uganda) - A/78/PV.57
AGEING PERSONS (Agenda item 24b)
González Behmaras, Alejandro (Cuba) - A/C.3/78/SR.1; A/C.3/78/SR.49
BIOLOGICAL DIVERSITY—TREATIES (Agenda item 18f)
Torres Seara, Dalia Marlen (Cuba) - A/C.2/78/SR.21
CLIMATE (Agenda item 18d)
Téllez Alonso, Frank (Cuba) - A/C.2/78/SR.12
Torres Seara, Dalia Marlen (Cuba) - A/C.2/78/SR.21
COMMODITIES (Agenda item 16d)
Guevara Rodríguez, Adiel (Cuba) - A/C.2/78/SR.14
Torres Seara, Dalia Marlen (Cuba) - A/C.2/78/SR.21
CONFERENCE AND MEETING SERVICES (Agenda item 137)
Tur de la Concepción, Richard (Cuba) - A/C.5/78/SR.7
CUBA—UNITED STATES (Agenda item 38)
Kwoba, Godfrey (Uganda) - A/78/PV.24
CULTURE—DEVELOPMENT (Agenda item 19b)
Torres Seara, Dalia Marlen (Cuba) - A/C.2/78/SR.21
DESERTIFICATION—TREATIES (Agenda item 18e)
Torres Seara, Dalia Marlen (Cuba) - A/C.2/78/SR.21
DEVELOPMENT COOPERATION—MIDDLE-INCOME COUNTRIES (Agenda item 19c)
Torres Seara, Dalia Marlen (Cuba) - A/C.2/78/SR.21

Group of 77 (continued)

DEVELOPMENT EDUCATION (Agenda item 18g)
Torres Seara, Dalia Marlen (Cuba) - A/C.2/78/SR.21
DEVELOPMENT FINANCE (Agenda item 16b)
Torres Seara, Dalia Marlen (Cuba) - A/C.2/78/SR.8; A/C.2/78/SR.21
DEVELOPMENT FINANCE—CONFERENCES (Agenda item 17)
Torres Seara, Dalia Marlen (Cuba) - A/C.2/78/SR.21
DISASTER PREVENTION (Agenda item 18c)
Torres Seara, Dalia Marlen (Cuba) - A/C.2/78/SR.21
ECONOMIC COOPERATION AMONG DEVELOPING COUNTRIES (Agenda item 22b)
Guevara Rodríguez, Adiel (Cuba) - A/C.2/78/SR.18
Torres Seara, Dalia Marlen (Cuba) - A/C.2/78/SR.21
ECONOMIC SANCTIONS—INTERNATIONAL RELATIONS (Agenda item 28)
Kwoba, Godfrey (Uganda) - A/78/PV.89
EMERGENCY ASSISTANCE (Agenda item 72a)
González Behmaras, Alejandro (Cuba) - A/78/PV.46
EXTERNAL DEBT (Agenda item 16c)
Torres Seara, Dalia Marlen (Cuba) - A/C.2/78/SR.8; A/C.2/78/SR.21
FAMILY (Agenda item 24b)
González Behmaras, Alejandro (Cuba) - A/C.3/78/SR.1; A/C.3/78/SR.49
FINANCIAL FLOWS (Agenda item 16f)
Torres Seara, Dalia Marlen (Cuba) - A/C.2/78/SR.21
FINANCIAL INCLUSION (Agenda item 16e)
Torres Seara, Dalia Marlen (Cuba) - A/C.2/78/SR.21
FOOD SECURITY (Agenda item 23a)
Guevara Rodríguez, Adiel (Cuba) - A/C.2/78/SR.16
Torres Seara, Dalia Marlen (Cuba) - A/C.2/78/SR.21
GLOBALIZATION—INTERDEPENDENCE (Agenda item 19)
Guevara Rodríguez, Adiel (Cuba) - A/C.2/78/SR.10
HEALTH (Agenda item 125)
González Behmaras, Alejandro (Cuba) - A/78/PV.16
Muhumuza, Duncan Laki (Uganda) - A/78/PV.77
INFORMATION (Agenda item 53)
Peñalver Portal, Gerardo (Cuba) - A/C.4/78/SR.13
Romero Puentes, Yusnier (Cuba) - A/C.4/78/SR.12

Group of 77 (continued)

INFORMATION TECHNOLOGY—DEVELOPMENT (Agenda item 15)
Guevara Rodríguez, Adiel (Cuba) - A/C.2/78/SR.10
Torres Seara, Dalia Marlen (Cuba) - A/C.2/78/SR.21
INTERNATIONAL LAW—TRAINING PROGRAMMES (Agenda item 78)
Carral Castelo, Arianna (Cuba) - A/C.6/78/SR.21
INTERNATIONAL RESIDUAL MECHANISM FOR CRIMINAL TRIBUNALS—FINANCING (Agenda item 145)
Hernández Morera, Diosdado de Jesús (Cuba) - A/C.5/78/SR.20
INTERNATIONAL TRADE (Agenda item 16a)
Torres Seara, Dalia Marlen (Cuba) - A/C.2/78/SR.8; A/C.2/78/SR.21
INVESTMENT PROMOTION (Agenda item 16g)
Torres Seara, Dalia Marlen (Cuba) - A/C.2/78/SR.21
JOINT INSPECTION UNIT (Agenda item 141)
Ainomuhisha, Medard (Uganda) - A/C.5/78/SR.29
LANDLOCKED DEVELOPING COUNTRIES—CONFERENCES (Agenda item 20b)
Kwoba, Godfrey (Uganda) - A/78/PV.98
Téllez Alonso, Frank (Cuba) - A/C.2/78/SR.7
Torres Seara, Dalia Marlen (Cuba) - A/C.2/78/SR.21
LAW OF THE SEA (Agenda item 75a)
Peñalver Portal, Gerardo (Cuba) - A/78/PV.43
LEAST DEVELOPED COUNTRIES—CONFERENCES (Agenda item 20a)
Téllez Alonso, Frank (Cuba) - A/C.2/78/SR.7
Torres Seara, Dalia Marlen (Cuba) - A/C.2/78/SR.21
MARINE ECOSYSTEMS—BIOLOGICAL DIVERSITY (Agenda item 75c)
Ikondere, Marvin (Uganda) - A/78/PV.73
Peñalver Portal, Gerardo (Cuba) - A/78/PV.43
MILLENNIUM SUMMIT—CONFERENCES (Agenda item 117)
Peñalver Portal, Gerardo (Cuba) - A/78/PV.15
OPERATIONAL ACTIVITIES—UN SYSTEM (Agenda item 22a)
Guevara Rodríguez, Adiel (Cuba) - A/C.2/78/SR.18
Torres Seara, Dalia Marlen (Cuba) - A/C.2/78/SR.21
PEACEKEEPING OPERATIONS—FINANCING (Agenda item 146)
Ainomuhisha, Medard (Uganda) - A/C.5/78/SR.35; A/C.5/78/SR.36
PERSONNEL QUESTIONS—UN SYSTEM (Agenda item 142)
Tur de la Concepción, Richard (Cuba) - A/C.5/78/SR.10

Group of 77 (continued)

POVERTY—INTERNATIONAL DECADES (Agenda item 21a)
Guevara Rodríguez, Adiel (Cuba) - A/C.2/78/SR.16
Torres Seara, Dalia Marlen (Cuba) - A/C.2/78/SR.21
RACIAL DISCRIMINATION—ELIMINATION (Agenda item 69a)
Navarro Barro, Nadieska (Cuba) - A/C.3/78/SR.40
RACIAL DISCRIMINATION—PROGRAMMES OF ACTION (Agenda item 69b)
González Behmaras, Alejandro (Cuba) - A/C.3/78/SR.56
Navarro Barro, Nadieska (Cuba) - A/C.3/78/SR.40
RURAL POVERTY (Agenda item 21b)
Guevara Rodríguez, Adiel (Cuba) - A/C.2/78/SR.16
Torres Seara, Dalia Marlen (Cuba) - A/C.2/78/SR.21
SCIENCE AND TECHNOLOGY—DEVELOPMENT (Agenda item 19a)
Guevara Rodríguez, Adiel (Cuba) - A/C.2/78/SR.10
Torres Seara, Dalia Marlen (Cuba) - A/C.2/78/SR.21
SMALL ISLAND DEVELOPING STATES—PROGRAMMES OF ACTION (Agenda item 18b)
Kwoba, Godfrey (Uganda) - A/78/PV.100
Téllez Alonso, Frank (Cuba) - A/C.2/78/SR.12
Torres Seara, Dalia Marlen (Cuba) - A/C.2/78/SR.21
SOCIAL CONDITIONS (Agenda item 24b)
González Behmaras, Alejandro (Cuba) - A/C.3/78/SR.1
Nabeta, Celia Kafureka (Uganda) - A/78/PV.101
SOCIAL DEVELOPMENT (Agenda item 24)
González Behmaras, Alejandro (Cuba) - A/C.3/78/SR.1
SOCIAL DEVELOPMENT—CONFERENCES (Agenda item 24a)
González Behmaras, Alejandro (Cuba) - A/C.3/78/SR.55
STORMS (Agenda item 18i)
Kwoba, Godfrey (Uganda) - A/78/PV.98
Torres Seara, Dalia Marlen (Cuba) - A/C.2/78/SR.21
STRADDLING FISH STOCKS (Agenda item 75b)
Peñalver Portal, Gerardo (Cuba) - A/78/PV.43
SUSTAINABLE DEVELOPMENT (Agenda item 18)
Guevara Rodríguez, Adiel (Cuba) - A/C.2/78/SR.14
Téllez Alonso, Frank (Cuba) - A/C.2/78/SR.12; A/C.2/78/SR.21
SUSTAINABLE ENERGY (Agenda item 18h)
Torres Seara, Dalia Marlen (Cuba) - A/C.2/78/SR.21
TERRITORIES OCCUPIED BY ISRAEL—NATURAL RESOURCES (Agenda item 59)
Romero Puentes, Yusnier (Cuba) - A/C.2/78/SR.19

Group of 77 (continued)

TERRITORIES OCCUPIED BY ISRAEL—NATURAL RESOURCES (Agenda item 59)
Téllez Alonso, Frank (Cuba) - A/C.2/78/SR.21
UN—ADMINISTRATION (Agenda item 132)
Ainomuhisha, Medard (Uganda) - A/C.5/78/SR.29; A/C.5/78/SR.32
Tur de la Concepción, Richard (Cuba) - A/C.5/78/SR.2
UN—BUDGET (2023) (Agenda item 133)
Tur de la Concepción, Richard (Cuba) - A/C.5/78/SR.4; A/C.5/78/SR.9
UN—BUDGET (2024) (Agenda item 134)
Ainomuhisha, Medard (Uganda) - A/C.5/78/SR.33
Gala López, Yuri (Cuba) - A/C.5/78/SR.5
Hernández Morera, Diosdado de Jesús (Cuba) - A/C.5/78/SR.14; A/C.5/78/SR.16; A/C.5/78/SR.17; A/C.5/78/SR.18; A/C.5/78/SR.19; A/C.5/78/SR.21; A/C.5/78/SR.22
Tur de la Concepción, Richard (Cuba) - A/C.5/78/SR.2; A/C.5/78/SR.9; A/C.5/78/SR.11; A/C.5/78/SR.12; A/C.5/78/SR.13; A/C.5/78/SR.26/PartII
UN—BUDGET CONTRIBUTIONS (Agenda item 138)
Tur de la Concepción, Richard (Cuba) - A/C.5/78/SR.1
UN—FINANCIAL REPORTS (Agenda item 131)
Ainomuhisha, Medard (Uganda) - A/C.5/78/SR.35
Tur de la Concepción, Richard (Cuba) - A/C.5/78/SR.14
UN—FINANCIAL SITUATION (Agenda item 136)
Ainomuhisha, Medard (Uganda) - A/C.5/78/SR.38
Tur de la Concepción, Richard (Cuba) - A/C.5/78/SR.6
UN—HUMAN RESOURCES MANAGEMENT (Agenda item 139)
Ainomuhisha, Medard (Uganda) - A/C.5/78/SR.27
Hernández Morera, Diosdado de Jesús (Cuba) - A/C.5/78/SR.25
UN—PROGRAMME PLANNING (Agenda item 135)
Gala López, Yuri (Cuba) - A/C.5/78/SR.5
UN. ECONOMIC AND SOCIAL COUNCIL—REPORTS (Agenda item 9)
Nidup, Dorji (Bhutan) - A/78/PV.48
UN. ETHICS OFFICE—REPORTS (Agenda item 140)
Tur de la Concepción, Richard (Cuba) - A/C.5/78/SR.2
UN. GENERAL ASSEMBLY (78TH SESS. : 2023-2024)—OFFICERS (Agenda item 5)
Tur de la Concepción, Richard (Cuba) - A/C.5/78/SR.1
UN. GENERAL ASSEMBLY (78TH SESS. : 2023-2024). 2ND COMMITTEE—GENERAL DEBATE (Agenda item 8)
Téllez Alonso, Frank (Cuba) - A/C.2/78/SR.2

Group of 77 (continued)

UN. GENERAL ASSEMBLY (78TH SESS. : 2023-2024). 5TH COMMITTEE—WORK ORGANIZATION (Agenda item 7)
Ainomuhisha, Medard (Uganda) - A/C.5/78/SR.27; A/C.5/78/SR.34; A/C.5/78/SR.35; A/C.5/78/SR.40
Tur de la Concepción, Richard (Cuba) - A/C.5/78/SR.26/PartII
UN. OFFICE OF INTERNAL OVERSIGHT SERVICES—REPORTS (Agenda item 143)
Tur de la Concepción, Richard (Cuba) - A/C.5/78/SR.2
UN CONFERENCES (Agenda item 13)
Peñalver Portal, Gerardo (Cuba) - A/78/PV.15
UN INTERIM FORCE IN LEBANON—FINANCING (Agenda item 156b)
Ainomuhisha, Medard (Uganda) - A/C.5/78/SR.40

Group of Arab States

AL-SABAH, NAWAF AL-AHMAD AL-JABER (KUWAIT. AMIR)—TRIBUTES
Abdelkhalek, Osama Mahmoud (Egypt) - A/78/PV.50(Resumption1)
ARMS RACE—OUTER SPACE (Agenda item 97a)
Alqaisi, Sultan Natheir Mustafa (Jordan) - A/C.1/78/PV.16; A/C.1/78/PV.17
BIOLOGICAL WEAPONS—TREATIES (Agenda item 106)
Alqaisi, Sultan Natheir Mustafa (Jordan) - A/C.1/78/PV.14
CHEMICAL WEAPONS—TREATIES (Agenda item 99l)
Alqaisi, Sultan Natheir Mustafa (Jordan) - A/C.1/78/PV.14
CONVENTIONAL WEAPONS (Agenda item 99u)
Alqaisi, Sultan Natheir Mustafa (Jordan) - A/C.1/78/PV.28
CRIMES AGAINST HUMANITY (Agenda item 80)
Alwasil, Abdulaziz M.O. (Saudi Arabia) - A/C.6/78/SR.38
DISARMAMENT—GENERAL AND COMPLETE (Agenda item 99)
Aldahhak, Koussay Abduljabbar (Syrian Arab Republic) - A/78/PV.105
Alqaisi, Sultan Natheir Mustafa (Jordan) - A/C.1/78/PV.19; A/C.1/78/PV.21; A/C.1/78/PV.23
DISARMAMENT—UN. GENERAL ASSEMBLY (4TH SPECIAL SESS. ON DISARMAMENT : xxxx) (Agenda item 99h)
Alqaisi, Sultan Natheir Mustafa (Jordan) - A/C.1/78/PV.22
DISARMAMENT AGREEMENTS—OUTER SPACE (Agenda item 97c)
Alqaisi, Sultan Natheir Mustafa (Jordan) - A/C.1/78/PV.16

Group of Arab States (continued)

DISARMAMENT-DEVELOPMENT LINK (Agenda item 99d)
Alqaisi, Sultan Natheir Mustafa (Jordan) - A/C.1/78/PV.20
EMERGENCY ASSISTANCE (Agenda item 72a)
Abdelkhalek, Osama Mahmoud (Egypt) - A/78/PV.46
HUMAN RIGHTS—INTERNATIONAL INSTRUMENTS (Agenda item 71a)
Al-halique, Katherine Anas Ahmad (Jordan) - A/C.3/78/SR.24
HUMAN RIGHTS—TERRITORIES OCCUPIED BY ISRAEL (Agenda item 71c)
Al-halique, Katherine Anas Ahmad (Jordan) - A/C.3/78/SR.24
INFORMATION—INTERNATIONAL SECURITY (Agenda item 94)
Alqaisi, Sultan Natheir Mustafa (Jordan) - A/C.1/78/PV.20
MIDDLE EAST—NUCLEAR PROLIFERATION (Agenda item 102)
Hmoud, Mahmoud Daifallah Mahmoud (Jordan) - A/C.1/78/PV.11
MIDDLE EAST—NUCLEAR-WEAPON-FREE ZONES (Agenda item 95)
Alqaisi, Sultan Natheir Mustafa (Jordan) - A/C.1/78/PV.14; A/C.1/78/PV.21
Hmoud, Mahmoud Daifallah Mahmoud (Jordan) - A/C.1/78/PV.11
MULTILATERALISM—DISARMAMENT (Agenda item 99r)
Alqaisi, Sultan Natheir Mustafa (Jordan) - A/C.1/78/PV.20; A/C.1/78/PV.21
NUCLEAR DISARMAMENT (Agenda item 99b)
Hmoud, Mahmoud Daifallah Mahmoud (Jordan) - A/C.1/78/PV.11
NUCLEAR NON-PROLIFERATION—INTERNATIONAL OBLIGATIONS (Agenda item 99w)
Hmoud, Mahmoud Daifallah Mahmoud (Jordan) - A/C.1/78/PV.11
NUCLEAR WEAPON TESTS—TREATIES (Agenda item 105)
Hmoud, Mahmoud Daifallah Mahmoud (Jordan) - A/C.1/78/PV.11
NUCLEAR WEAPONS—TREATIES (Agenda item 99ff)
Hmoud, Mahmoud Daifallah Mahmoud (Jordan) - A/C.1/78/PV.11
OUTER SPACE—CONFIDENCE-BUILDING MEASURES (Agenda item 99v)
Alqaisi, Sultan Natheir Mustafa (Jordan) - A/C.1/78/PV.16
OUTER SPACE—PRINCIPLES (Agenda item 97d)
Alqaisi, Sultan Natheir Mustafa (Jordan) - A/C.1/78/PV.16
PALESTINIANS—ASSISTANCE (Agenda item 72b)
Abdelkhalek, Osama Mahmoud (Egypt) - A/78/PV.46

Group of Arab States (continued)

RULE OF LAW (Agenda item 83)
Bisharat, Nadien Isam Fraih (Jordan) - A/C.6/78/SR.15
SMALL ARMS—ILLICIT TRAFFIC (Agenda item 99p)
Alqaisi, Sultan Natheir Mustafa (Jordan) - A/C.1/78/PV.28
SUSTAINABLE DEVELOPMENT (Agenda item 18)
Etomzini, Intisar M. KH (Libya) - A/C.2/78/SR.22
TERRITORIES OCCUPIED BY ISRAEL—HUMAN RIGHTS (Agenda item 50)
Alwasil, Abdulaziz M.O. (Saudi Arabia) - A/C.4/78/SR.24
TERRITORIES OCCUPIED BY ISRAEL—NATURAL RESOURCES (Agenda item 59)
Al-halique, Katherine Anas Ahmad (Jordan) - A/C.2/78/SR.19
UN. CONFERENCE ON DISARMAMENT—REPORTS (Agenda item 101a)
Alqaisi, Sultan Natheir Mustafa (Jordan) - A/C.1/78/PV.22
UN. DISARMAMENT COMMISSION—REPORTS (Agenda item 101b)
Alqaisi, Sultan Natheir Mustafa (Jordan) - A/C.1/78/PV.22
UN. GENERAL ASSEMBLY (78TH SESS. : 2023-2024). 1ST COMMITTEE—GENERAL DEBATE (Agenda item 8)
Hmoud, Mahmoud Daifallah Mahmoud (Jordan) - A/C.1/78/PV.2
UN. INTERNATIONAL COURT OF JUSTICE—REPORTS (Agenda item 73)
Bisharat, Nadien Isam Fraih (Jordan) - A/78/PV.27
UN. SECRETARY-GENERAL—REPORTS (Agenda item 110)
Ladeb, Tarek (Tunisia) - A/78/PV.55
UN. SECURITY COUNCIL—MEMBERSHIP (Agenda item 121)
Alrowaiei, Jamal Fares (Bahrain) - A/78/PV.34; A/78/PV.104
UNRWA—ACTIVITIES (Agenda item 49)
Alwasil, Abdulaziz M.O. (Saudi Arabia) - A/C.4/78/SR.22
VETO (Agenda item 63)
Abushahab, Mohamed Issa (United Arab Emirates) - A/78/PV.74
Al-Saadi, Abdullah Ali Fadhel (Yemen) - A/78/PV.59
Alrowaiei, Jamal Fares (Bahrain) - A/78/PV.51
Alwasil, Abdulaziz M.O. (Saudi Arabia) - A/78/PV.66

Group of Four

UN. SECURITY COUNCIL—MEMBERSHIP (Agenda item 121)
Danese, Sérgio França (Brazil) - A/78/PV.104
Leendertse, Antje (Germany) - A/78/PV.34

Group of Friends for Disaster Risk Reduction

2030 AGENDA—PROGRAMME IMPLEMENTATION (Agenda item 18a)
Macchiavello, Julissa (Peru) - A/C.2/78/SR.12
DISASTER PREVENTION (Agenda item 18c)
Macchiavello, Julissa (Peru) - A/C.2/78/SR.12
SUSTAINABLE DEVELOPMENT (Agenda item 18)
Macchiavello, Julissa (Peru) - A/C.2/78/SR.12

Group of Friends in Defence of the Charter of the United Nations

2030 AGENDA—PROGRAMME IMPLEMENTATION (Agenda item 18a)
Pérez Ayestarán, Joaquín Alberto (Venezuela (Bolivarian Republic of)) - A/C.2/78/SR.12
CLIMATE (Agenda item 18d)
Pérez Ayestarán, Joaquín Alberto (Venezuela (Bolivarian Republic of)) - A/C.2/78/SR.12
CRIME PREVENTION (Agenda item 107)
Poveda Brito, Robert Alexander (Venezuela (Bolivarian Republic of)) - A/C.3/78/SR.50
CUBA—UNITED STATES (Agenda item 38)
Tesfamariam, Sophia (Eritrea) - A/78/PV.24
DECOLONIZATION (Agenda item 58)
Pérez Ayestarán, Joaquín Alberto (Venezuela (Bolivarian Republic of)) - A/C.4/78/SR.2
DEVELOPMENT FINANCE (Agenda item 16b)
Pérez Ayestarán, Joaquín Alberto (Venezuela (Bolivarian Republic of)) - A/C.2/78/SR.8
ECONOMIC SANCTIONS—INTERNATIONAL RELATIONS (Agenda item 28)
Gil Pinto, Yvan (Venezuela (Bolivarian Republic of)) - A/78/PV.89
EMERGENCY ASSISTANCE (Agenda item 72a)
Castillo, William (Venezuela (Bolivarian Republic of)) - A/78/PV.46
FOOD SECURITY (Agenda item 23a)
Marín Sevilla, Asbina (Venezuela (Bolivarian Republic of)) - A/C.2/78/SR.16
GLOBALIZATION—INTERDEPENDENCE (Agenda item 19)
Pérez Ayestarán, Joaquín Alberto (Venezuela (Bolivarian Republic of)) - A/C.2/78/SR.10
HEALTH (Agenda item 125)
Pérez Ayestarán, Joaquín Alberto (Venezuela (Bolivarian Republic of)) - A/78/PV.16; A/78/PV.41
HUMAN RIGHTS (Agenda item 71)
Pérez Ayestarán, Joaquín Alberto (Venezuela (Bolivarian Republic of)) - A/C.3/78/SR.24
Poveda Brito, Robert Alexander (Venezuela (Bolivarian Republic of)) - A/C.3/78/SR.16
HUMAN RIGHTS—DEMOCRATIC PEOPLE'S REPUBLIC OF KOREA (Agenda item 71c)
Poveda Brito, Robert Alexander (Venezuela (Bolivarian Republic of)) - A/C.3/78/SR.53

Group of Friends in Defence of the Charter of the United Nations (continued)

HUMAN RIGHTS—IRAN (ISLAMIC REPUBLIC OF) (Agenda item 71c)
Poveda Brito, Robert Alexander (Venezuela (Bolivarian Republic of)) - A/C.3/78/SR.53
HUMAN RIGHTS—REPORTS (Agenda item 71c)
Pérez Ayestarán, Joaquín Alberto (Venezuela (Bolivarian Republic of)) - A/C.3/78/SR.24
HUMAN RIGHTS—SYRIAN ARAB REPUBLIC (Agenda item 71c)
Poveda Brito, Robert Alexander (Venezuela (Bolivarian Republic of)) - A/C.3/78/SR.54
HUMAN RIGHTS—UKRAINE (Agenda item 71c)
Poveda Brito, Robert Alexander (Venezuela (Bolivarian Republic of)) - A/C.3/78/SR.53
INFORMATION (Agenda item 53)
Pérez Ayestarán, Joaquín Alberto (Venezuela (Bolivarian Republic of)) - A/C.4/78/SR.12
INTERNATIONAL TRADE (Agenda item 16a)
Pérez Ayestarán, Joaquín Alberto (Venezuela (Bolivarian Republic of)) - A/C.2/78/SR.8
INVESTMENT PROMOTION (Agenda item 16g)
Pérez Ayestarán, Joaquín Alberto (Venezuela (Bolivarian Republic of)) - A/C.2/78/SR.8
MACROECONOMIC POLICY (Agenda item 16)
Pérez Ayestarán, Joaquín Alberto (Venezuela (Bolivarian Republic of)) - A/C.2/78/SR.8
MILLENNIUM SUMMIT—CONFERENCES (Agenda item 117)
Pérez Ayestarán, Joaquín Alberto (Venezuela (Bolivarian Republic of)) - A/78/PV.15
PALESTINIANS—ASSISTANCE (Agenda item 72b)
Castillo, William (Venezuela (Bolivarian Republic of)) - A/78/PV.46
PEACE (Agenda item 14)
Moncada Acosta, Samuel R. (Venezuela (Bolivarian Republic of)) - A/78/PV.76
POVERTY—INTERNATIONAL DECADES (Agenda item 21a)
Marín Sevilla, Asbina (Venezuela (Bolivarian Republic of)) - A/C.2/78/SR.16
RACIAL DISCRIMINATION—ELIMINATION (Agenda item 69a)
Altarsha, Elie (Syrian Arab Republic) - A/C.3/78/SR.40
RACIAL DISCRIMINATION—PROGRAMMES OF ACTION (Agenda item 69b)
Altarsha, Elie (Syrian Arab Republic) - A/C.3/78/SR.40
RESPONSIBILITY TO PROTECT (Agenda item 129)
Reyes Hernández, Jorge Arturo (Venezuela (Bolivarian Republic of)) - A/78/PV.96

Group of Friends in Defence of the Charter of the United Nations (continued)

RIGHT TO DEVELOPMENT (Agenda item 71b)
Pérez Ayestarán, Joaquín Alberto (Venezuela (Bolivarian Republic of)) - A/C.3/78/SR.20
RULE OF LAW (Agenda item 83)
Pérez Ayestarán, Joaquín Alberto (Venezuela (Bolivarian Republic of)) - A/C.6/78/SR.15
RURAL POVERTY (Agenda item 21b)
Marín Sevilla, Asbina (Venezuela (Bolivarian Republic of)) - A/C.2/78/SR.16
SANCTIONS—INTERNATIONAL RELATIONS (Agenda item 71b)
Poveda Brito, Robert Alexander (Venezuela (Bolivarian Republic of)) - A/C.3/78/SR.28; A/C.3/78/SR.48
SUSTAINABLE DEVELOPMENT (Agenda item 18)
Pérez Ayestarán, Joaquín Alberto (Venezuela (Bolivarian Republic of)) - A/C.2/78/SR.12
TERRORISM (Agenda item 109)
Pérez Ayestarán, Joaquín Alberto (Venezuela (Bolivarian Republic of)) - A/C.6/78/SR.2
UN. COMMITTEE ON RELATIONS WITH THE HOST COUNTRY—REPORTS (Agenda item 161)
Pérez Ayestarán, Joaquín Alberto (Venezuela (Bolivarian Republic of)) - A/C.6/78/SR.35
UN. HUMAN RIGHTS COUNCIL—REPORTS (Agenda item 66)
Pérez Ayestarán, Joaquín Alberto (Venezuela (Bolivarian Republic of)) - A/78/PV.23
UN. SECRETARY-GENERAL—REPORTS (Agenda item 110)
Pérez Ayestarán, Joaquín Alberto (Venezuela (Bolivarian Republic of)) - A/78/PV.55
UN CHARTER—REPORTS (Agenda item 82)
Guerra Sansonetti, Jhon (Venezuela (Bolivarian Republic of)) - A/C.6/78/SR.22
UN CONFERENCES (Agenda item 13)
Pérez Ayestarán, Joaquín Alberto (Venezuela (Bolivarian Republic of)) - A/78/PV.15
UN HIGH COMMISSIONER FOR REFUGEES—REPORTS (Agenda item 60)
Poveda Brito, Robert Alexander (Venezuela (Bolivarian Republic of)) - A/C.3/78/SR.44
UNRWA—ACTIVITIES (Agenda item 49)
Pérez Ayestarán, Joaquín Alberto (Venezuela (Bolivarian Republic of)) - A/C.4/78/SR.23
VETO (Agenda item 63)
Marín Sevilla, Asbina (Venezuela (Bolivarian Republic of)) - A/78/PV.66
Pérez Ayestarán, Joaquín Alberto (Venezuela (Bolivarian Republic of)) - A/78/PV.3; A/78/PV.59

Group of Friends of Indigenous Peoples

INDIGENOUS PEOPLES (Agenda item 68a)
Buenrostro Massieu, Alicia (Mexico) - A/C.3/78/SR.15

Group of Friends of Indigenous Peoples (continued)

INDIGENOUS PEOPLES—CONFERENCES (Agenda item 68b)
Buenrostro Massieu, Alicia (Mexico) - A/C.3/78/SR.15

Group of Friends of Older Persons

AGEING PERSONS (Agenda item 24b)
Narváez Ojeda, Paula (Chile) - A/C.3/78/SR.1

Group of Friends of the Family

FAMILY (Agenda item 24b)
Evseenko, Pavel (Belarus) - A/C.3/78/SR.1

Group of Friends of the Responsibility to Protect

RESPONSIBILITY TO PROTECT (Agenda item 129)
Simonovic, Ivan (Croatia) - A/78/PV.96
UN. SECRETARY-GENERAL—REPORTS (Agenda item 110)
Rodríguez Mancia, Carla María (Guatemala) - A/78/PV.54

Group of Friends of the Rule of Law

RULE OF LAW (Agenda item 83)
Marschik, Alexander (Austria) - A/C.6/78/SR.15

Group of Friends of the United Nations Voluntary Fund for Victims of Torture

TORTURE AND OTHER CRUEL TREATMENT (Agenda item 71a)
Macchiavello, Julissa (Peru) - A/C.3/78/SR.24

Group of Landlocked Developing Countries

2030 AGENDA—PROGRAMME IMPLEMENTATION (Agenda item 18a)
Motsumi, Lorato (Botswana) - A/C.2/78/SR.12
COMMODITIES (Agenda item 16d)
Mmalane, Katlego Boase (Botswana) - A/C.2/78/SR.8
Mokhawa, Gladys (Botswana) - A/C.2/78/SR.14
DEVELOPMENT FINANCE (Agenda item 16b)
Mmalane, Katlego Boase (Botswana) - A/C.2/78/SR.8
ECONOMIC COOPERATION AMONG DEVELOPING COUNTRIES (Agenda item 22b)
Motsumi, Lorato (Botswana) - A/C.2/78/SR.18
FOOD SECURITY (Agenda item 23a)
Mokhawa, Gladys (Botswana) - A/C.2/78/SR.16
INFORMATION TECHNOLOGY—DEVELOPMENT (Agenda item 15)
Motsumi, Lorato (Botswana) - A/C.2/78/SR.10
INVESTMENT PROMOTION (Agenda item 16g)
Mmalane, Katlego Boase (Botswana) - A/C.2/78/SR.8

Group of Landlocked Developing Countries (continued)

LANDLOCKED DEVELOPING COUNTRIES—CONFERENCES (Agenda item 20b)
Mokhawa, Gladys (Botswana) - A/C.2/78/SR.7
LEAST DEVELOPED COUNTRIES—CONFERENCES (Agenda item 20a)
Mokhawa, Gladys (Botswana) - A/C.2/78/SR.7
MACROECONOMIC POLICY (Agenda item 16)
Mmalane, Katlego Boase (Botswana) - A/C.2/78/SR.8
OPERATIONAL ACTIVITIES—UN SYSTEM (Agenda item 22a)
Motsumi, Lorato (Botswana) - A/C.2/78/SR.18
POVERTY—INTERNATIONAL DECADES (Agenda item 21a)
Mokhawa, Gladys (Botswana) - A/C.2/78/SR.16
RURAL POVERTY (Agenda item 21b)
Mokhawa, Gladys (Botswana) - A/C.2/78/SR.16
SCIENCE AND TECHNOLOGY—DEVELOPMENT (Agenda item 19a)
Motsumi, Lorato (Botswana) - A/C.2/78/SR.10
SUSTAINABLE DEVELOPMENT (Agenda item 18)
Mokhawa, Gladys (Botswana) - A/C.2/78/SR.14
Motsumi, Lorato (Botswana) - A/C.2/78/SR.12
UN. GENERAL ASSEMBLY (78TH SESS. : 2023-2024). 2ND COMMITTEE—GENERAL DEBATE (Agenda item 8)
Mokhawa, Gladys (Botswana) - A/C.2/78/SR.2

Group of Least Developed Countries

2030 AGENDA—PROGRAMME IMPLEMENTATION (Agenda item 18a)
Adhikari, Pramita (Nepal) - A/C.2/78/SR.12
DEVELOPMENT FINANCE (Agenda item 16b)
Ray, Kaushal Kishor (Nepal) - A/C.2/78/SR.8
ECONOMIC COOPERATION AMONG DEVELOPING COUNTRIES (Agenda item 22b)
Ray, Kaushal Kishor (Nepal) - A/C.2/78/SR.18
FOOD SECURITY (Agenda item 23a)
Adhikari, Pramita (Nepal) - A/C.2/78/SR.16
INFORMATION TECHNOLOGY—DEVELOPMENT (Agenda item 15)
Dhungel, Purushottam (Nepal) - A/C.2/78/SR.10
INTERNATIONAL TRADE (Agenda item 16a)
Ray, Kaushal Kishor (Nepal) - A/C.2/78/SR.8
INVESTMENT PROMOTION (Agenda item 16g)
Ray, Kaushal Kishor (Nepal) - A/C.2/78/SR.8
LANDLOCKED DEVELOPING COUNTRIES—CONFERENCES (Agenda item 20b)
Ray, Kaushal Kishor (Nepal) - A/C.2/78/SR.7
LEAST DEVELOPED COUNTRIES—CONFERENCES (Agenda item 20a)
Ray, Kaushal Kishor (Nepal) - A/C.2/78/SR.7

Group of Least Developed Countries (continued)

OPERATIONAL ACTIVITIES—UN SYSTEM (Agenda item 22a)
Ray, Kaushal Kishor (Nepal) - A/C.2/78/SR.18
POVERTY—INTERNATIONAL DECADES (Agenda item 21a)
Adhikari, Pramita (Nepal) - A/C.2/78/SR.16
RURAL POVERTY (Agenda item 21b)
Adhikari, Pramita (Nepal) - A/C.2/78/SR.16
SCIENCE AND TECHNOLOGY—DEVELOPMENT (Agenda item 19a)
Dhungel, Purushottam (Nepal) - A/C.2/78/SR.10
SUSTAINABLE DEVELOPMENT (Agenda item 18)
Adhikari, Pramita (Nepal) - A/C.2/78/SR.12
UN. GENERAL ASSEMBLY (78TH SESS. : 2023-2024). 2ND COMMITTEE—GENERAL DEBATE (Agenda item 8)
Thapa, Lok Bahadur (Nepal) - A/C.2/78/SR.2

Groupe des ambassadeurs francophones

MULTILINGUALISM (Agenda item 124)
Banza, Serge Ngoy (Democratic Republic of the Congo) - A/78/PV.107
PEACEKEEPING OPERATIONS (Agenda item 51)
Abdillahi, Elaye Yacin (Djibouti) - A/C.4/78/SR.18

Grupo de Amigos del Español en las Naciones Unidas

INFORMATION (Agenda item 53)
Thomas Ramírez, Vilma (Cuba) - A/C.4/78/SR.12
MULTILINGUALISM (Agenda item 124)
Cedano, Joan Margarita (Dominican Republic) - A/78/PV.107

Guam

GUAM QUESTION (Agenda item 58)
Won Pat-Borja, Melvin - A/C.4/78/SR.3

Guatemala

AGEING PERSONS (Agenda item 24b)
Rodríguez Mancia, Carla María - A/C.3/78/SR.1
ARMS TRANSFERS—TREATIES (Agenda item 99x)
Rodríguez Mancia, Carla María - A/C.1/78/PV.18
COMMODITIES (Agenda item 16d)
Rodríguez Mancia, Carla María - A/C.2/78/SR.14
CONVENTIONAL WEAPONS (Agenda item 99u)
Rodríguez Mancia, Carla María - A/C.1/78/PV.18
CRIME PREVENTION (Agenda item 107)
Rodríguez Mancia, Carla María - A/C.3/78/SR.5
CRIMES AGAINST HUMANITY (Agenda item 80)
Leal Matta, Edgar Daniel - A/C.6/78/SR.45; A/C.6/78/SR.46
Rodríguez Mancia, Carla María - A/C.6/78/SR.9

Guatemala (continued)

CYBERCRIME (Agenda item 108)
Rodríguez Mancia, Carla María - A/C.3/78/SR.5
DISASTER VICTIMS (Agenda item 86)
Rodríguez Mancia, Carla María - A/C.6/78/SR.5
FALKLAND ISLANDS (MALVINAS) QUESTION (Agenda item 42)
Benard Estrada, Juan Antonio - A/C.4/78/SR.6
FOOD SECURITY (Agenda item 23a)
Rodríguez Mancia, Carla María - A/C.2/78/SR.17
HEALTH (Agenda item 125)
Del Águila-Castillo, María José - A/78/PV.16
HUMAN RIGHTS—TERRITORIES OCCUPIED BY ISRAEL (Agenda item 71c)
Del Águila-Castillo, María José - A/C.3/78/SR.35
IAEA—REPORTS (Agenda item 89)
Rodríguez Mancia, Carla María - A/78/PV.29
INDIGENOUS PEOPLES (Agenda item 68a)
Rodríguez Mancia, Carla María - A/78/PV.107; A/C.3/78/SR.15
INDIGENOUS PEOPLES—CONFERENCES (Agenda item 68b)
Rodríguez Mancia, Carla María - A/C.3/78/SR.15
INFORMATION—INTERNATIONAL SECURITY (Agenda item 94)
Rodríguez Mancia, Carla María - A/C.1/78/PV.20
INTERNATIONAL CRIMINAL COURT—REPORTS (Agenda item 74)
Rodríguez Mancia, Carla María - A/78/PV.21
LANDMINES—TREATIES (Agenda item 99m)
Rodríguez Mancia, Carla María - A/C.1/78/PV.18
LAW OF THE SEA (Agenda item 75a)
Rodríguez Mancia, Carla María - A/78/PV.43
MARINE ECOSYSTEMS—BIOLOGICAL DIVERSITY (Agenda item 75c)
Rodríguez Mancia, Carla María - A/78/PV.43
MULTILINGUALISM (Agenda item 124)
Rodríguez Mancia, Carla María - A/78/PV.107
PEACE (Agenda item 14)
Leal Matta, Edgar Daniel - A/78/PV.82
PEACEKEEPING OPERATIONS (Agenda item 51)
Benard Estrada, Juan Antonio - A/C.4/78/SR.19
PERSONS WITH DISABILITIES (Agenda item 24b)
Rodríguez Mancia, Carla María - A/C.3/78/SR.1
POVERTY—INTERNATIONAL DECADES (Agenda item 21a)
Rodríguez Mancia, Carla María - A/C.2/78/SR.17
RACIAL DISCRIMINATION—ELIMINATION (Agenda item 69a)
Cruz Morataya, Andrea Flor de María - A/C.3/78/SR.41
RACIAL DISCRIMINATION—PROGRAMMES OF ACTION (Agenda item 69b)
Cruz Morataya, Andrea Flor de María - A/C.3/78/SR.41
RESPONSIBILITY TO PROTECT (Agenda item 129)
Rodríguez Mancia, Carla María - A/78/PV.96

Guatemala (continued)

RIGHTS OF THE CHILD (Agenda item 67)
Rodríguez Mancia, Carla María - A/C.3/78/SR.11
RULE OF LAW (Agenda item 83)
Rodríguez Mancia, Carla María - A/C.6/78/SR.15
RURAL POVERTY (Agenda item 21b)
Rodríguez Mancia, Carla María - A/C.2/78/SR.17
SMALL ARMS—ILLICIT TRAFFIC (Agenda item 99p)
Rodríguez Mancia, Carla María - A/C.1/78/PV.18
SOCIAL CONDITIONS (Agenda item 24b)
Rodríguez Mancia, Carla María - A/C.3/78/SR.1
STRADDLING FISH STOCKS (Agenda item 75b)
Rodríguez Mancia, Carla María - A/78/PV.43
SUSTAINABLE DEVELOPMENT (Agenda item 18)
Rodríguez Mancia, Carla María - A/C.2/78/SR.14
TERRORISM (Agenda item 109)
Rodríguez Mancia, Carla María - A/C.6/78/SR.1
UKRAINE—POLITICAL CONDITIONS (Agenda item 62)
Rodríguez Mancia, Carla María - A/78/PV.58
UN. GENERAL ASSEMBLY (78TH SESS. : 2023-2024)—GENERAL DEBATE—RIGHT OF REPLY (Agenda item 8)
Búcaro Flores, Mario Adolfo - A/78/PV.13
Leal Matta, Edgar Daniel - A/78/PV.14
UN. GENERAL ASSEMBLY (78TH SESS. : 2023-2024). 1ST COMMITTEE—GENERAL DEBATE (Agenda item 8)
Rodríguez Mancia, Carla María - A/C.1/78/PV.5
UN. GENERAL ASSEMBLY (78TH SESS. : 2023-2024). 2ND COMMITTEE—GENERAL DEBATE (Agenda item 8)
Rodríguez Mancia, Carla María - A/C.2/78/SR.5
UN. INTERNATIONAL COURT OF JUSTICE—REPORTS (Agenda item 73)
Búcaro Flores, Mario Adolfo - A/78/PV.20
UN. INTERNATIONAL LAW COMMISSION—REPORTS (Agenda item 79)
Briz Gutiérrez, José Alberto - A/C.6/78/SR.27
Leal Matta, Edgar Daniel - A/C.6/78/SR.30; A/C.6/78/SR.32
UN HIGH COMMISSIONER FOR REFUGEES—REPORTS (Agenda item 60)
Rodríguez Mancia, Carla María - A/C.3/78/SR.48
VETO (Agenda item 63)
Del Águila-Castillo, María José - A/78/PV.74; A/78/PV.78
Rodríguez Mancia, Carla María - A/78/PV.3; A/78/PV.68; A/78/PV.70
WESTERN SAHARA QUESTION (Agenda item 58)
Benard Estrada, Juan Antonio - A/C.4/78/SR.6
WOMEN'S ADVANCEMENT (Agenda item 25a)
Rodríguez Mancia, Carla María - A/C.3/78/SR.8
WOMEN'S ADVANCEMENT—CONFERENCES (Agenda item 25b)
Rodríguez Mancia, Carla María - A/C.3/78/SR.8

Guatemala (continued)

YOUTH (Agenda item 24b)
Rodríguez Mancia, Carla María - A/C.3/78/SR.1

Guatemala. President

MULTILATERALISM
Arévalo de León, César Bernardo - A/78/PV.84
UN. GENERAL ASSEMBLY (78TH SESS. : 2023-2024)—GENERAL DEBATE (Agenda item 8)
Giammattei Falla, Alejandro - A/78/PV.4
UN. GENERAL ASSEMBLY (78TH SESS. : 2023-2024)—SPECIAL STATEMENTS
Arévalo de León, César Bernardo - A/78/PV.84
Giammattei Falla, Alejandro - A/78/PV.4

Guinea

ECONOMIC COOPERATION AMONG DEVELOPING COUNTRIES (Agenda item 22b)
Zoumanigui, Paul Goa - A/C.2/78/SR.18
INTERNATIONAL LAW—TRAINING PROGRAMMES (Agenda item 78)
Condé, N'Nagbé - A/C.6/78/SR.21
OPERATIONAL ACTIVITIES—UN SYSTEM (Agenda item 22a)
Zoumanigui, Paul Goa - A/C.2/78/SR.18
PEACEKEEPING OPERATIONS—CRIMINAL LIABILITY (Agenda item 76)
Camara, Mohamed Nassir - A/C.6/78/SR.9
RIGHTS OF THE CHILD (Agenda item 67)
Konaté, Sékou - A/C.3/78/SR.13
RULE OF LAW (Agenda item 83)
Camara, Mohamed Nassir - A/C.6/78/SR.18
UN. GENERAL ASSEMBLY (78TH SESS. : 2023-2024). 1ST COMMITTEE—GENERAL DEBATE (Agenda item 8)
Diallo, Oumou - A/C.1/78/PV.6
WESTERN SAHARA QUESTION (Agenda item 58)
Zoumanigui, Paul Goa - A/C.4/78/SR.8

Guinea. President

UN. GENERAL ASSEMBLY (78TH SESS. : 2023-2024)—GENERAL DEBATE (Agenda item 8)
Doumbouya, Mamadi - A/78/PV.8
UN. GENERAL ASSEMBLY (78TH SESS. : 2023-2024)—SPECIAL STATEMENTS
Doumbouya, Mamadi - A/78/PV.8

Guinea-Bissau

WESTERN SAHARA QUESTION (Agenda item 58)
Mendes, Francisco - A/C.4/78/SR.8

Guinea-Bissau. President

UN. GENERAL ASSEMBLY (78TH SESS. : 2023-2024)—GENERAL DEBATE (Agenda item 8)
Embaló, Úmaro Sissoco - A/78/PV.9
UN. GENERAL ASSEMBLY (78TH SESS. : 2023-2024)—SPECIAL STATEMENTS
Embaló, Úmaro Sissoco - A/78/PV.9

Gulf Cooperation Council

AL-SABAH, NAWAF AL-AHMAD AL-JABER (KUWAIT. AMIR)—TRIBUTES
Al-Thani, Alya Ahmed S.A. (Qatar) - A/78/PV.50(Resumption1)
ELECTION VERIFICATION—UN (Agenda item 71b)
Al Rawahi, Abdulhalim Mubarak Saloom (Oman) - A/C.3/78/SR.50
Al-thani, Almaha Mubarak F.J. (Qatar) - A/78/PV.50
EMERGENCY ASSISTANCE (Agenda item 72a)
Al-Thani, Abdulrahman Abdulaziz F.A. (Qatar) - A/78/PV.47
HEALTH (Agenda item 125)
Al Rubkhi, Khalid Saleh Said (Oman) - A/78/PV.16
Al-thani, Almaha Mubarak F.J. (Qatar) - A/78/PV.48
HUMAN RIGHTS—TERRITORIES OCCUPIED BY ISRAEL (Agenda item 71c)
Al Jaradi, Heba Khalid (Oman) - A/C.3/78/SR.35
HUMAN RIGHTS ACTIVISTS (Agenda item 71b)
Al Jaradi, Heba Khalid (Oman) - A/C.3/78/SR.19
MIGRANTS—PROTECTION (Agenda item 71b)
Al-Sinani, Nashwa Hilal (Oman) - A/C.3/78/SR.23
MILLENNIUM SUMMIT—CONFERENCES (Agenda item 117)
Al-Hassan, Mohamed (Oman) - A/78/PV.15
PALESTINE QUESTION (Agenda item 35)
Al Rubkhi, Khalid Saleh Said (Oman) - A/78/PV.39
PERSONS WITH DISABILITIES—HUMAN RIGHTS (Agenda item 71a)
Al Rawahi, Abdulhalim Mubarak Saloom (Oman) - A/C.3/78/SR.51
RAISI, SEYYED EBRAHIM (IRAN (ISLAMIC REPUBLID OF). PRESIDENT)—TRIBUTES
Al-Thani, Alya Ahmed S.A. (Qatar) - A/78/PV.83
RELIGIOUS INTOLERANCE (Agenda item 71b)
Al Rubkhi, Khalid Saleh Said (Oman) - A/C.3/78/SR.26
RIGHT TO DEVELOPMENT (Agenda item 71b)
Al Rubkhi, Khalid Saleh Said (Oman) - A/C.3/78/SR.26

Gulf Cooperation Council (continued)

RURAL WOMEN (Agenda item 25a)
Al Rawahi, Abdulhalim Mubarak Saloom (Oman) - A/C.3/78/SR.49
TERRITORIES OCCUPIED BY ISRAEL—HUMAN RIGHTS (Agenda item 50)
Al Rashdi, Amal (Oman) - A/C.4/78/SR.24
TERRITORIES OCCUPIED BY ISRAEL—NATURAL RESOURCES (Agenda item 59)
Al Rubkhi, Khalid Saleh Said (Oman) - A/C.2/78/SR.19
TERRORISM—HUMAN RIGHTS (Agenda item 71b)
Al Rubkhi, Khalid Saleh Said (Oman) - A/C.3/78/SR.26
UKRAINE—POLITICAL CONDITIONS (Agenda item 62)
Al-Thani, Alya Ahmed S.A. (Qatar) - A/78/PV.57
UN—BUDGET (2024) (Agenda item 134)
Al-Sharji, Saud (Oman) - A/C.5/78/SR.13
UN—HUMAN RESOURCES MANAGEMENT (Agenda item 139)
Alnasr, Mohammed Khalifa H. (Qatar) - A/C.5/78/SR.27
UN. GENERAL ASSEMBLY (78TH SESS. : 2023-2024)—OFFICERS (Agenda item 5)
Al-Hassan, Mohamed (Oman) - A/C.5/78/SR.1
UN. GENERAL ASSEMBLY (78TH SESS. : 2023-2024). 5TH COMMITTEE—WORK ORGANIZATION (Agenda item 7)
Alnasr, Mohammed Khalifa H. (Qatar) - A/C.5/78/SR.27
UN CONFERENCES (Agenda item 13)
Al-Hassan, Mohamed (Oman) - A/78/PV.15
UN HIGH COMMISSIONER FOR REFUGEES—REPORTS (Agenda item 60)
Al Jaradi, Heba Khalid (Oman) - A/C.3/78/SR.44
Al Rawahi, Abdulhalim Mubarak Saloom (Oman) - A/C.3/78/SR.51
UNRWA—ACTIVITIES (Agenda item 49)
Al Busaidi, Ahmed Hamood Faisal (Oman) - A/C.4/78/SR.22
VETO (Agenda item 63)
Al-Thani, Alya Ahmed S.A. (Qatar) - A/78/PV.59
WOMEN'S ADVANCEMENT (Agenda item 25a)
Al Jaradi, Heba Khalid (Oman) - A/C.3/78/SR.7
WOMEN'S ADVANCEMENT—CONFERENCES (Agenda item 25b)
Al Jaradi, Heba Khalid (Oman) - A/C.3/78/SR.7

Guyana

CLIMATE (Agenda item 18d)
Alkins, Royston - A/C.2/78/SR.15
CUBA—UNITED STATES (Agenda item 38)
Rodrigues-Birkett, Carolyn - A/78/PV.24
DECOLONIZATION (Agenda item 58)
Rodrigues-Birkett, Carolyn - A/C.4/78/SR.7
DEVELOPMENT FINANCE (Agenda item 16b)
Doimen, Tash van - A/C.2/78/SR.9

Guyana (continued)

DEVELOPMENT FINANCE—CONFERENCES (Agenda item 17)
Doimen, Tash van - A/C.2/78/SR.9
DISASTER PREVENTION (Agenda item 18c)
Alkins, Royston - A/C.2/78/SR.15
FOOD SECURITY (Agenda item 23a)
Alkins, Royston - A/C.2/78/SR.17
GLOBALIZATION—INTERDEPENDENCE (Agenda item 19)
Rodrigues-Birkett, Carolyn - A/C.2/78/SR.10
INDIGENOUS PEOPLES (Agenda item 68a)
Hazlewood, Abosede - A/C.3/78/SR.15
INDIGENOUS PEOPLES—CONFERENCES (Agenda item 68b)
Hazlewood, Abosede - A/C.3/78/SR.15
INTERNATIONAL TRADE (Agenda item 16a)
Doimen, Tash van - A/C.2/78/SR.9
NON-SELF-GOVERNING TERRITORIES—REPORTS (Agenda item 54)
Rodrigues-Birkett, Carolyn - A/C.4/78/SR.7
PALESTINE QUESTION (Agenda item 35)
Rodrigues-Birkett, Carolyn - A/78/PV.39
POVERTY—INTERNATIONAL DECADES (Agenda item 21a)
Alkins, Royston - A/C.2/78/SR.17
RIGHTS OF THE CHILD (Agenda item 67)
Hazlewood, Abosede - A/C.3/78/SR.13
RULE OF LAW (Agenda item 83)
Daw, Texine Wonda - A/C.6/78/SR.18
RURAL POVERTY (Agenda item 21b)
Alkins, Royston - A/C.2/78/SR.17
RURAL WOMEN (Agenda item 25a)
Rodrigues-Birkett, Carolyn - A/C.3/78/SR.10
SCIENCE AND TECHNOLOGY—DEVELOPMENT (Agenda item 19a)
Rodrigues-Birkett, Carolyn - A/C.2/78/SR.10
SMALL ISLAND DEVELOPING STATES—PROGRAMMES OF ACTION (Agenda item 18b)
Alkins, Royston - A/C.2/78/SR.15
SPORTS—OLYMPIC GAMES (Agenda item 11)
Alkins, Royston - A/78/PV.38
SUSTAINABLE DEVELOPMENT (Agenda item 18)
Alkins, Royston - A/C.2/78/SR.15
SUSTAINABLE ENERGY (Agenda item 18h)
Alkins, Royston - A/C.2/78/SR.15
TERRITORIES OCCUPIED BY ISRAEL—NATURAL RESOURCES (Agenda item 59)
Rodrigues-Birkett, Carolyn - A/C.2/78/SR.19
UKRAINE—POLITICAL CONDITIONS (Agenda item 62)
Rodrigues-Birkett, Carolyn - A/78/PV.58
UN—FINANCIAL SITUATION (Agenda item 136)
Edwards, Marissa Audra Faith - A/C.5/78/SR.6

Guyana (continued)

UN. GENERAL ASSEMBLY (78TH SESS. : 2023-2024)—GENERAL DEBATE—RIGHT OF REPLY (Agenda item 8)
Rodrigues-Birkett, Carolyn - A/78/PV.14
UN. GENERAL ASSEMBLY (78TH SESS. : 2023-2024). 1ST COMMITTEE—GENERAL DEBATE (Agenda item 8)
Rodrigues-Birkett, Carolyn - A/C.1/78/PV.3
UN. GENERAL ASSEMBLY (78TH SESS. : 2023-2024). 2ND COMMITTEE—GENERAL DEBATE (Agenda item 8)
Rodrigues-Birkett, Carolyn - A/C.2/78/SR.5
UN. INTERNATIONAL COURT OF JUSTICE—REPORTS (Agenda item 73)
Rodrigues-Birkett, Carolyn - A/78/PV.28
UN. SECURITY COUNCIL—MEMBERSHIP (Agenda item 121)
Rodrigues-Birkett, Carolyn - A/78/PV.36
UN YOUTH OFFICE—REPORTS (Agenda item 130)
Parmanand, Sosheena Foranda - A/78/PV.102
VETO (Agenda item 63)
Persaud, Trishala Simantini - A/78/PV.75
Rodrigues-Birkett, Carolyn - A/78/PV.61
WESTERN SAHARA QUESTION (Agenda item 58)
Rodrigues-Birkett, Carolyn - A/C.4/78/SR.7
WOMEN'S ADVANCEMENT (Agenda item 25a)
Rodrigues-Birkett, Carolyn - A/C.3/78/SR.10
WOMEN'S ADVANCEMENT—CONFERENCES (Agenda item 25b)
Rodrigues-Birkett, Carolyn - A/C.3/78/SR.10

Guyana. President

UN. GENERAL ASSEMBLY (78TH SESS. : 2023-2024)—GENERAL DEBATE (Agenda item 8)
Ali, Mohamed Irfaan - A/78/PV.6
UN. GENERAL ASSEMBLY (78TH SESS. : 2023-2024)—SPECIAL STATEMENTS
Ali, Mohamed Irfaan - A/78/PV.6

Haiti

CRIMES AGAINST HUMANITY (Agenda item 80)
Panier, Wisnique - A/C.6/78/SR.11; A/C.6/78/SR.45
DISASTER VICTIMS (Agenda item 86)
Panier, Wisnique - A/C.6/78/SR.6
FOOD SECURITY (Agenda item 23a)
Vilmenay Joseph, Linouse - A/C.2/78/SR.17
HIV/AIDS—DECLARATIONS (Agenda item 10)
Gaspard, Fritzner - A/78/PV.91
INFORMATION (Agenda item 53)
Pierre, Christopher - A/C.4/78/SR.13
INTERNATIONAL LAW—TRAINING PROGRAMMES (Agenda item 78)
Panier, Wisnique - A/C.6/78/SR.22

Haiti (continued)

PEACEKEEPING OPERATIONS (Agenda item 51)
Pierre, Christopher - A/C.4/78/SR.20
PEACEKEEPING OPERATIONS—CRIMINAL LIABILITY (Agenda item 76)
Panier, Wisnique - A/C.6/78/SR.9
POVERTY—INTERNATIONAL DECADES (Agenda item 21a)
Vilmenay Joseph, Linouse - A/C.2/78/SR.17
RIGHTS OF THE CHILD (Agenda item 67)
Pierre Fabre, Celine - A/C.3/78/SR.14
RURAL POVERTY (Agenda item 21b)
Vilmenay Joseph, Linouse - A/C.2/78/SR.17
SLAVERY—MEMORIALS (Agenda item 118)
Rodrigue, Antonio - A/78/PV.64
SOCIAL DEVELOPMENT (Agenda item 24)
Pierre Fabre, Celine - A/C.3/78/SR.4
SPECIAL POLITICAL MISSIONS (Agenda item 52)
Pierre, Christopher - A/C.4/78/SR.21
TERRORISM (Agenda item 109)
Panier, Wisnique - A/C.6/78/SR.4
UN—BUDGET (2024) (Agenda item 134)
Betor, Guensy - A/C.5/78/SR.4
Rodrigue, Antonio - A/C.5/78/SR.18
UN—BUDGET CONTRIBUTIONS (Agenda item 138)
Betor, Guensy - A/C.5/78/SR.1
UN. GENERAL ASSEMBLY (78TH SESS. : 2023-2024). 1ST COMMITTEE—GENERAL DEBATE (Agenda item 8)
Pierre, Wislyne - A/C.1/78/PV.8
UN. GENERAL ASSEMBLY (78TH SESS. : 2023-2024). 2ND COMMITTEE—GENERAL DEBATE (Agenda item 8)
Vilmenay Joseph, Linouse - A/C.2/78/SR.5
WOMEN'S ADVANCEMENT (Agenda item 25a)
Célestin, Miousemine - A/C.3/78/SR.10
WOMEN'S ADVANCEMENT—CONFERENCES (Agenda item 25b)
Célestin, Miousemine - A/C.3/78/SR.10

Haiti. Prime Minister

UN. GENERAL ASSEMBLY (78TH SESS. : 2023-2024)—GENERAL DEBATE (Agenda item 8)
Henry, Ariel - A/78/PV.11
UN. GENERAL ASSEMBLY (78TH SESS. : 2023-2024)—SPECIAL STATEMENTS
Henry, Ariel - A/78/PV.11

Hispafrica Aprican (Organization)

WESTERN SAHARA QUESTION (Agenda item 58)
Yahya, Alamine - A/C.4/78/SR.6

Holy See

ARMS RACE—OUTER SPACE (Agenda item 97a)
Caccia, Gabriele Giordano - A/C.1/78/PV.17
CRIME PREVENTION (Agenda item 107)
Murphy, Robert David - A/C.3/78/SR.6
CRIMES AGAINST HUMANITY (Agenda item 80)
Caccia, Gabriele Giordano - A/C.6/78/SR.11; A/C.6/78/SR.39; A/C.6/78/SR.41; A/C.6/78/SR.45
Murphy, Robert David - A/C.6/78/SR.43; A/C.6/78/SR.44
CYBERCRIME (Agenda item 108)
Murphy, Robert David - A/C.3/78/SR.6
DEVELOPMENT EDUCATION (Agenda item 18g)
Caccia, Gabriele Giordano - A/C.2/78/SR.15
DISARMAMENT—GENERAL AND COMPLETE (Agenda item 99)
Caccia, Gabriele Giordano - A/78/PV.106
ELECTION VERIFICATION—UN (Agenda item 71b)
Murphy, Robert David - A/C.3/78/SR.50
FAMILY (Agenda item 24b)
Murphy, Robert David - A/C.3/78/SR.4
HEALTH (Agenda item 125)
Murphy, Robert David - A/78/PV.48
HUMAN RIGHTS (Agenda item 71)
Caccia, Gabriele Giordano - A/C.3/78/SR.27
HUMAN RIGHTS ACTIVISTS (Agenda item 71b)
Murphy, Robert David - A/C.3/78/SR.56
HUMAN RIGHTS ADVANCEMENT (Agenda item 71b)
Murphy, Robert David - A/C.3/78/SR.52
INDIGENOUS PEOPLES (Agenda item 68a)
Caccia, Gabriele Giordano - A/C.3/78/SR.15
Murphy, Robert David - A/C.3/78/SR.48
INDIGENOUS PEOPLES—CONFERENCES (Agenda item 68b)
Caccia, Gabriele Giordano - A/C.3/78/SR.15
INFORMATION—INTERNATIONAL SECURITY (Agenda item 94)
Caccia, Gabriele Giordano - A/C.1/78/PV.21
LANDLOCKED DEVELOPING COUNTRIES—CONFERENCES (Agenda item 20b)
Murphy, Robert David - A/C.2/78/SR.7
LEAST DEVELOPED COUNTRIES—CONFERENCES (Agenda item 20a)
Murphy, Robert David - A/C.2/78/SR.7
MIGRANTS—PROTECTION (Agenda item 71b)
Murphy, Robert David - A/C.3/78/SR.56
NON-CITIZENS—DEPORTATION (Agenda item 81)
Caccia, Gabriele Giordano - A/C.6/78/SR.34
NUCLEAR DISARMAMENT (Agenda item 99b)
Caccia, Gabriele Giordano - A/C.1/78/PV.14

Holy See (continued)

NUCLEAR NON-PROLIFERATION—INTERNATIONAL OBLIGATIONS (Agenda item 99w)
Caccia, Gabriele Giordano - A/C.1/78/PV.14
OUTER SPACE—CONFIDENCE-BUILDING MEASURES (Agenda item 99v)
Caccia, Gabriele Giordano - A/C.1/78/PV.17
OUTER SPACE—PEACEFUL USES—INTERNATIONAL COOPERATION (Agenda item 48)
Caccia, Gabriele Giordano - A/C.4/78/SR.17
OUTER SPACE—PRINCIPLES (Agenda item 97d)
Caccia, Gabriele Giordano - A/C.1/78/PV.17
PEACEKEEPING OPERATIONS (Agenda item 51)
Quirighetti, Giuseppe - A/C.4/78/SR.20
PERSONS WITH DISABILITIES—HUMAN RIGHTS (Agenda item 71a)
Murphy, Robert David - A/C.3/78/SR.51
POVERTY—INTERNATIONAL DECADES (Agenda item 21a)
Caccia, Gabriele Giordano - A/C.2/78/SR.18
RACIAL DISCRIMINATION—ELIMINATION (Agenda item 69a)
Caccia, Gabriele Giordano - A/78/PV.63; A/C.3/78/SR.43
RACIAL DISCRIMINATION—PROGRAMMES OF ACTION (Agenda item 69b)
Caccia, Gabriele Giordano - A/C.3/78/SR.43
RADIATION EFFECTS (Agenda item 47)
Caccia, Gabriele Giordano - A/C.4/78/SR.11
RIGHTS OF THE CHILD (Agenda item 67)
Murphy, Robert David - A/C.3/78/SR.14; A/C.3/78/SR.55
RULE OF LAW (Agenda item 83)
Caccia, Gabriele Giordano - A/C.6/78/SR.19
SMALL ARMS—ILLICIT TRAFFIC—ASSISTANCE (Agenda item 99n)
Caccia, Gabriele Giordano - A/C.1/78/PV.20
SOCIAL CONDITIONS (Agenda item 24b)
Murphy, Robert David - A/C.3/78/SR.4
SOCIAL DEVELOPMENT (Agenda item 24)
Murphy, Robert David - A/C.3/78/SR.4
SUSTAINABLE DEVELOPMENT (Agenda item 18)
Caccia, Gabriele Giordano - A/C.2/78/SR.15
Murphy, Robert David - A/C.2/78/SR.25
TERRORISM (Agenda item 109)
Murphy, Robert David - A/C.6/78/SR.5
UN. GENERAL ASSEMBLY (78TH SESS. : 2023-2024)—GENERAL DEBATE (Agenda item 8)
Gallagher, Paul Richard - A/78/PV.14
UN. GENERAL ASSEMBLY (78TH SESS. : 2023-2024). 1ST COMMITTEE—GENERAL DEBATE (Agenda item 8)
Caccia, Gabriele Giordano - A/C.1/78/PV.9

Holy See (continued)

UN. GENERAL ASSEMBLY (78TH SESS. : 2023-2024). 2ND COMMITTEE—GENERAL DEBATE (Agenda item 8)
Murphy, Robert David - A/C.2/78/SR.6
UN. INTERNATIONAL LAW COMMISSION—REPORTS (Agenda item 79)
Caccia, Gabriele Giordano - A/C.6/78/SR.28; A/C.6/78/SR.30; A/C.6/78/SR.33
UN HIGH COMMISSIONER FOR REFUGEES—REPORTS (Agenda item 60)
Murphy, Robert David - A/C.3/78/SR.51
UNRWA—ACTIVITIES (Agenda item 49)
Caccia, Gabriele Giordano - A/C.4/78/SR.23
WOMEN'S ADVANCEMENT (Agenda item 25a)
Murphy, Robert David - A/C.3/78/SR.10
WOMEN'S ADVANCEMENT—CONFERENCES (Agenda item 25b)
Murphy, Robert David - A/C.3/78/SR.10
YOUTH (Agenda item 24b)
Murphy, Robert David - A/C.3/78/SR.4; A/C.3/78/SR.55

Honduras

CRIME PREVENTION (Agenda item 107)
Espinoza Madrid, Noemí Ruth - A/78/PV.50(Resumption1)
DECOLONIZATION (Agenda item 58)
Rivera Reyes, Isabella Regina - A/C.4/78/SR.2
ECONOMIC SANCTIONS—INTERNATIONAL RELATIONS (Agenda item 28)
Flores, Ramón Emilio - A/78/PV.90
FALKLAND ISLANDS (MALVINAS) QUESTION (Agenda item 42)
Rivera Reyes, Isabella Regina - A/C.4/78/SR.2
IAEA—REPORTS (Agenda item 89)
Flores, Ramón Emilio - A/78/PV.29
SOCIAL CONDITIONS (Agenda item 24b)
Rivera Reyes, Isabella Regina - A/C.3/78/SR.2
SOCIAL DEVELOPMENT (Agenda item 24)
Rivera Reyes, Isabella Regina - A/C.3/78/SR.2
TERRORISM (Agenda item 109)
Rivera Reyes, Isabella Regina - A/C.6/78/SR.2
UN. GENERAL ASSEMBLY (78TH SESS. : 2023-2024). 1ST COMMITTEE—GENERAL DEBATE (Agenda item 8)
Flores, Ramón Emilio - A/C.1/78/PV.4
UN. GENERAL ASSEMBLY (78TH SESS. : 2023-2024). 2ND COMMITTEE—GENERAL DEBATE (Agenda item 8)
Flores, Ramón Emilio - A/C.2/78/SR.3
UN. INTERNATIONAL COURT OF JUSTICE—REPORTS (Agenda item 73)
Rivera Reyes, Isabella Regina - A/78/PV.27

Honduras. President

UN. GENERAL ASSEMBLY (78TH SESS. : 2023-2024)—GENERAL DEBATE (Agenda item 8)
Castro Sarmiento, Iris Xiomara - A/78/PV.6
UN. GENERAL ASSEMBLY (78TH SESS. : 2023-2024)—SPECIAL STATEMENTS
Castro Sarmiento, Iris Xiomara - A/78/PV.6

Hungary

AFRICA—DEVELOPMENT (Agenda item 65b)
Atanaszov, Anna Mária - A/78/PV.57
AFRICA—SUSTAINABLE DEVELOPMENT—PARTNERSHIP (Agenda item 65a)
Atanaszov, Anna Mária - A/78/PV.57
ARMED CONFLICTS PREVENTION (Agenda item 31a)
Svercsok, Szabolcs - A/78/PV.72
BIOLOGICAL WEAPONS—TREATIES (Agenda item 106)
Talpai, Tamás - A/C.1/78/PV.15
CRIME PREVENTION (Agenda item 107)
Ivanyi, Balint - A/C.3/78/SR.51
CRIMES AGAINST HUMANITY (Agenda item 80)
Vittay, Melinda - A/C.6/78/SR.9; A/C.6/78/SR.38; A/C.6/78/SR.40; A/C.6/78/SR.45
DISARMAMENT—GENERAL AND COMPLETE (Agenda item 99)
Svercsok, Szabolcs - A/C.1/78/PV.26
ELECTION VERIFICATION—UN (Agenda item 71b)
Mogyorósi, Bálint - A/C.3/78/SR.50
EMERGENCY ASSISTANCE (Agenda item 72a)
Ivanyi, Balint - A/78/PV.47
FISSIONABLE MATERIALS—TREATIES (Agenda item 99a)
Talpai, Tamás - A/C.1/78/PV.13
FREEDOM OF EXPRESSION (Agenda item 71b)
Horváth, Zsuzsanna - A/C.3/78/SR.19
HEALTH (Agenda item 125)
Gaal, Miklos - A/78/PV.16
HUMAN RIGHTS—TERRITORIES OCCUPIED BY ISRAEL (Agenda item 71c)
Kókai, Anita - A/C.3/78/SR.35
INDIGENOUS PEOPLES (Agenda item 68a)
Mogyorósi, Bálint - A/C.3/78/SR.48
INTERNATIONAL JURISDICTION (Agenda item 84)
Vittay, Melinda - A/C.6/78/SR.12
MIGRANTS—PROTECTION (Agenda item 71b)
Pongor, Magdolna - A/C.3/78/SR.56
MILLENNIUM SUMMIT—CONFERENCES (Agenda item 117)
Horváth, Zsuzsanna - A/78/PV.15
MINORITIES (Agenda item 71b)
Mogyorósi, Bálint - A/C.3/78/SR.39

Hungary (continued)

NUCLEAR DISARMAMENT (Agenda item 99b)
Talpai, Tamás - A/C.1/78/PV.13
NUCLEAR DISARMAMENT—VERIFICATION (Agenda item 99ee)
Talpai, Tamás - A/C.1/78/PV.13
NUCLEAR NON-PROLIFERATION—INTERNATIONAL OBLIGATIONS (Agenda item 99w)
Talpai, Tamás - A/C.1/78/PV.13
PEACE (Agenda item 14)
Horváth, Zsuzsanna - A/78/PV.82
PERSONS WITH DISABILITIES—HUMAN RIGHTS (Agenda item 71a)
Pongor, Magdolna - A/C.3/78/SR.38
RACIAL DISCRIMINATION—ELIMINATION (Agenda item 69a)
Mogyorósi, Bálint - A/78/PV.103
RELIGIOUS INTOLERANCE (Agenda item 71b)
Mogyorósi, Bálint - A/C.3/78/SR.38
RESPONSIBILITY TO PROTECT (Agenda item 129)
Vittay, Melinda - A/78/PV.96
SPORTS—OLYMPIC GAMES (Agenda item 11)
Horváth, Zsuzsanna - A/78/PV.97
UN. GENERAL ASSEMBLY (78TH SESS. : 2023-2024). 1ST COMMITTEE—GENERAL DEBATE (Agenda item 8)
Balázs, Szilvia - A/C.1/78/PV.5
UN. INTERNATIONAL LAW COMMISSION—REPORTS (Agenda item 79)
Csergő, Csongor - A/C.6/78/SR.24
Vittay, Melinda - A/C.6/78/SR.31
UN CONFERENCES (Agenda item 13)
Horváth, Zsuzsanna - A/78/PV.15
UN HIGH COMMISSIONER FOR REFUGEES—REPORTS (Agenda item 60)
Ivanyi, Balint - A/C.3/78/SR.51; A/C.3/78/SR.54
VETO (Agenda item 63)
Kókai, Anita - A/78/PV.52
Svercsok, Szabolcs - A/78/PV.79
Szijjártó, Péter - A/78/PV.59
WOMEN MIGRANT WORKERS (Agenda item 25a)
Pongor, Magdolna - A/C.3/78/SR.49
WOMEN'S ADVANCEMENT (Agenda item 25a)
Pongor, Magdolna - A/C.3/78/SR.10
WOMEN'S ADVANCEMENT—CONFERENCES (Agenda item 25b)
Pongor, Magdolna - A/C.3/78/SR.10
YOUTH (Agenda item 24b)
Offenbächer, Csenge - A/C.3/78/SR.3
Pongor, Magdolna - A/C.3/78/SR.55

Hungary. President

UN. GENERAL ASSEMBLY (78TH SESS. : 2023-2024)—GENERAL DEBATE (Agenda item 8)
Novák, Katalin - A/78/PV.4
UN. GENERAL ASSEMBLY (78TH SESS. : 2023-2024)—SPECIAL STATEMENTS
Novák, Katalin - A/78/PV.4

Hurria - Saharawi Solidarity Association

WESTERN SAHARA QUESTION (Agenda item 58)
Bongini, Asia - A/C.4/78/SR.5

IAEA

DISARMAMENT—GENERAL AND COMPLETE (Agenda item 99)
Okeke, Vivian Nwunaku Rose - A/78/PV.105
NUCLEAR DISARMAMENT (Agenda item 99b)
Okeke, Vivian Nwunaku Rose - A/C.1/78/PV.13

IAEA. Director General

IAEA—REPORTS (Agenda item 89)
Grossi, Rafael Mariano - A/78/PV.29

ICAN France (Organization)

FRENCH POLYNESIA QUESTION (Agenda item 58)
Morgant-Cross, Hinamoeura - A/C.4/78/SR.3

Iceland

CRIMES AGAINST HUMANITY (Agenda item 80)
Karlsdóttir, Helga Hronn - A/C.6/78/SR.44; A/C.6/78/SR.45
Sverrisdóttir, Anna Pála - A/C.6/78/SR.41; A/C.6/78/SR.46; A/C.6/78/SR.47
HUMAN RIGHTS—AFGHANISTAN (Agenda item 71c)
Kolsöe, Ragnheidur - A/C.3/78/SR.34
HUMAN RIGHTS—ETHIOPIA (Agenda item 71c)
Kolsöe, Ragnheidur - A/C.3/78/SR.36
HUMAN RIGHTS—IRAN (ISLAMIC REPUBLIC OF) (Agenda item 71c)
Kolsöe, Ragnheidur - A/C.3/78/SR.34
HUMAN RIGHTS—MYANMAR (Agenda item 71c)
Kolsöe, Ragnheidur - A/C.3/78/SR.33
HUMAN RIGHTS ACTIVISTS (Agenda item 71b)
Valtýsson, Jörundur - A/C.3/78/SR.26
LAW OF THE SEA (Agenda item 75a)
Valtýsson, Jörundur - A/78/PV.44
MARINE ECOSYSTEMS—BIOLOGICAL DIVERSITY (Agenda item 75c)
Valtýsson, Jörundur - A/78/PV.44

Iceland (continued)

PEACE (Agenda item 14)
Valtýsson, Jörundur - A/78/PV.62
RIGHTS OF THE CHILD (Agenda item 67)
Valtýsson, Jörundur - A/C.3/78/SR.14
SEXUAL ORIENTATION (Agenda item 71b)
Óskarsson, Thórdur Aegir - A/C.3/78/SR.39
Valtýsson, Jörundur - A/C.3/78/SR.26
STRADDLING FISH STOCKS (Agenda item 75b)
Valtýsson, Jörundur - A/78/PV.44
UN—BUDGET (2024) (Agenda item 134)
Thorbjörnsdóttir, Guðrún - A/C.5/78/SR.26/PartII
UN. GENERAL ASSEMBLY (78TH SESS. : 2023-2024)—GENERAL DEBATE (Agenda item 8)
Gylfadóttir, Thórdís Kolbrún Reykfjörd - A/78/PV.12
UN. GENERAL ASSEMBLY (78TH SESS. : 2023-2024). 1ST COMMITTEE—GENERAL DEBATE (Agenda item 8)
Valtýsson, Jörundur - A/C.1/78/PV.7
UN. HUMAN RIGHTS COUNCIL—REPORTS (Agenda item 66)
Valtýsson, Jörundur - A/78/PV.23
UN COMMISSION ON INTERNATIONAL TRADE LAW—REPORTS (Agenda item 77)
Valtýsson, Jörundur - A/C.6/78/SR.14
VETO (Agenda item 63)
Valtýsson, Jörundur - A/78/PV.61
WOMEN'S ADVANCEMENT (Agenda item 25a)
Valtýsson, Jörundur - A/C.3/78/SR.10
WOMEN'S ADVANCEMENT—CONFERENCES (Agenda item 25b)
Valtýsson, Jörundur - A/C.3/78/SR.10

Independent International Commission of Inquiry on the Syrian Arab Republic

HUMAN RIGHTS—SYRIAN ARAB REPUBLIC (Agenda item 71c)
Megally, Hanny - A/C.3/78/SR.34
Pinheiro, Paulo Sérgio de M.S. - A/C.3/78/SR.34

India

AFRICA—DEVELOPMENT (Agenda item 65b)
Parihar, Rajesh - A/78/PV.18
AFRICA—SUSTAINABLE DEVELOPMENT—PARTNERSHIP (Agenda item 65a)
Parihar, Rajesh - A/78/PV.18
AGEING PERSONS (Agenda item 24b)
Sonkar, Suman - A/C.3/78/SR.1
ARMS TRANSFERS—TREATIES (Agenda item 99x)
Bedi, Anmol Sher Singh - A/C.1/78/PV.28
BIOLOGICAL WEAPONS—TREATIES (Agenda item 106)
Kamboj, Ruchira - A/C.1/78/PV.15

India (continued)

CHEMICAL WEAPONS—TREATIES (Agenda item 99l)
Kamboj, Ruchira - A/C.1/78/PV.15
Ray, Anupam - A/C.1/78/PV.26
CLIMATE (Agenda item 18d)
Gahlot, Petal - A/C.2/78/SR.13
COMMODITIES (Agenda item 16d)
Gahlot, Petal - A/C.2/78/SR.14
CONVENTIONAL ARMS—REGIONAL PROGRAMMES (Agenda item 99g)
Bedi, Anmol Sher Singh - A/C.1/78/PV.29
CONVENTIONAL WEAPONS (Agenda item 99u)
Parihar, Rajesh - A/C.1/78/PV.19
CONVENTIONAL WEAPONS—TREATIES (Agenda item 103)
Parihar, Rajesh - A/C.1/78/PV.19
CRIMES AGAINST HUMANITY (Agenda item 80)
Bhat, Kajal - A/C.6/78/SR.10; A/C.6/78/SR.11; A/C.6/78/SR.38; A/C.6/78/SR.40; A/C.6/78/SR.42; A/C.6/78/SR.43; A/C.6/78/SR.44; A/C.6/78/SR.47
DECOLONIZATION (Agenda item 58)
Birdi, Nitish - A/C.4/78/SR.7
DEVELOPMENT FINANCE—CONFERENCES (Agenda item 17)
Gahlot, Petal - A/C.2/78/SR.9
DISARMAMENT—GENERAL AND COMPLETE (Agenda item 99)
Kulkarni, Maitrey - A/C.1/78/PV.30
Parihar, Rajesh - A/C.1/78/PV.19
Ray, Anupam - A/C.1/78/PV.26; A/C.1/78/PV.28
DISARMAMENT—UN. GENERAL ASSEMBLY (4TH SPECIAL SESS. ON DISARMAMENT : xxxx) (Agenda item 99h)
Bedi, Anmol Sher Singh - A/C.1/78/PV.23
DISARMAMENT AGREEMENTS—OUTER SPACE (Agenda item 97c)
Kulkarni, Maitrey - A/C.1/78/PV.27
ECONOMIC COOPERATION AMONG DEVELOPING COUNTRIES (Agenda item 22b)
Gahlot, Petal - A/C.2/78/SR.18
EXTERNAL DEBT (Agenda item 16c)
Gahlot, Petal - A/C.2/78/SR.9
FISSIONABLE MATERIALS—TREATIES (Agenda item 99a)
Kulkarni, Maitrey - A/C.1/78/PV.25
FOOD SECURITY (Agenda item 23a)
Gahlot, Petal - A/C.2/78/SR.16
FREEDOM OF EXPRESSION (Agenda item 71b)
Sonkar, Suman - A/C.3/78/SR.19
HEALTH (Agenda item 125)
Gahlot, Petal - A/78/PV.77
HIV/AIDS—DECLARATIONS (Agenda item 10)
Patel, Yojna - A/78/PV.91
HUMAN RIGHTS (Agenda item 71)
Sonkar, Suman - A/C.3/78/SR.16

India (continued)

HUMAN RIGHTS—INTERNATIONAL INSTRUMENTS (Agenda item 71a)
Sonkar, Suman - A/C.3/78/SR.26
HUMAN RIGHTS—REPORTS (Agenda item 71c)
Parihar, Rajesh - A/C.3/78/SR.25
HUMAN RIGHTS ACTIVISTS (Agenda item 71b)
Sonkar, Suman - A/C.3/78/SR.19
HUMAN RIGHTS ADVANCEMENT (Agenda item 71b)
Sonkar, Suman - A/C.3/78/SR.26
INDIGENOUS PEOPLES (Agenda item 68a)
Sonkar, Suman - A/C.3/78/SR.15
INDIGENOUS PEOPLES—CONFERENCES (Agenda item 68b)
Sonkar, Suman - A/C.3/78/SR.15
INFORMATION (Agenda item 53)
Birdi, Nitish - A/C.4/78/SR.12
INFORMATION—INTERNATIONAL SECURITY (Agenda item 94)
Bedi, Anmol Sher Singh - A/C.1/78/PV.21
Parihar, Rajesh - A/C.1/78/PV.29
INFORMATION TECHNOLOGY—DEVELOPMENT (Agenda item 15)
Gahlot, Petal - A/C.2/78/SR.10
INTERNATIONAL JURISDICTION (Agenda item 84)
Bhat, Kajal - A/C.6/78/SR.13
INTERNATIONAL PARLIAMENTARIANS' CONGRESS—OBSERVER STATUS (Agenda item 170)
Bhat, Kajal - A/C.6/78/SR.14
INTERNATIONAL TRADE (Agenda item 16a)
Gahlot, Petal - A/C.2/78/SR.9; A/C.2/78/SR.22
LANDLOCKED DEVELOPING COUNTRIES—CONFERENCES (Agenda item 20b)
Gahlot, Petal - A/C.2/78/SR.7
LANDMINES—TREATIES (Agenda item 99m)
Bedi, Anmol Sher Singh - A/C.1/78/PV.28
Parihar, Rajesh - A/C.1/78/PV.19
LAW OF THE SEA (Agenda item 75a)
Bhat, Kajal - A/78/PV.43
LEAST DEVELOPED COUNTRIES—CONFERENCES (Agenda item 20a)
Gahlot, Petal - A/C.2/78/SR.7
MARINE ECOSYSTEMS—BIOLOGICAL DIVERSITY (Agenda item 75c)
Bhat, Kajal - A/78/PV.43
MIDDLE EAST—NUCLEAR PROLIFERATION (Agenda item 102)
Kulkarni, Maitrey - A/C.1/78/PV.25
MINORITIES (Agenda item 71b)
Sonkar, Suman - A/C.3/78/SR.39
NATIONAL INSTITUTIONS—HUMAN RIGHTS (Agenda item 71b)
Sonkar, Suman - A/C.3/78/SR.26

India (continued)

NUCLEAR DISARMAMENT (Agenda item 99b)
Ray, Anupam - A/C.1/78/PV.13
NUCLEAR NON-PROLIFERATION (Agenda item 99o)
Ray, Anupam - A/C.1/78/PV.13
NUCLEAR WEAPONS—ELIMINATION (Agenda item 99z)
Ray, Anupam - A/C.1/78/PV.26
NUCLEAR WEAPONS—HUMANITARIAN CONSEQUENCES (Agenda item 99bb)
Kulkarni, Maitrey - A/C.1/78/PV.25
NUCLEAR WEAPONS—TREATIES (Agenda item 99ff)
Kulkarni, Maitrey - A/C.1/78/PV.25
NUCLEAR WEAPONS USE—TREATIES (Agenda item 100a)
Ray, Anupam - A/C.1/78/PV.13
NUCLEAR WEAPONS USE—UN. INTERNATIONAL COURT OF JUSTICE OPINION (Agenda item 99k)
Kulkarni, Maitrey - A/C.1/78/PV.25
OPERATIONAL ACTIVITIES—UN SYSTEM (Agenda item 22a)
Gahlot, Petal - A/C.2/78/SR.18
OUTER SPACE—PEACEFUL USES—INTERNATIONAL COOPERATION (Agenda item 48)
Birdi, Nitish - A/C.4/78/SR.16
OUTER SPACE—PRINCIPLES (Agenda item 97d)
Kulkarni, Maitrey - A/C.1/78/PV.27
PALESTINE QUESTION (Agenda item 35)
Kamboj, Ruchira - A/78/PV.39
PEACE (Agenda item 14)
Kamboj, Ruchira - A/78/PV.62; A/78/PV.76
PEACEBUILDING (Agenda item 61)
Bhalla, Ashish - A/78/PV.101
PEACEKEEPING OPERATIONS (Agenda item 51)
Bhalla, Ashish - A/C.4/78/SR.20
PEACEKEEPING OPERATIONS—CRIMINAL LIABILITY (Agenda item 76)
Bhat, Kajal - A/C.6/78/SR.8
POVERTY—INTERNATIONAL DECADES (Agenda item 21a)
Gahlot, Petal - A/C.2/78/SR.16
RACIAL DISCRIMINATION—ELIMINATION (Agenda item 69a)
Sonkar, Suman - A/C.3/78/SR.41
RACIAL DISCRIMINATION—PROGRAMMES OF ACTION (Agenda item 69b)
Sonkar, Suman - A/C.3/78/SR.41
RELIGIOUS INTOLERANCE (Agenda item 71b)
Sonkar, Suman - A/C.3/78/SR.38
RESPONSIBILITY TO PROTECT (Agenda item 129)
Bhat, Kajal - A/78/PV.97

India (continued)

RIGHT TO CULTURE (Agenda item 71b)
Sonkar, Suman - A/C.3/78/SR.27
RIGHTS OF THE CHILD (Agenda item 67)
Sonkar, Suman - A/C.3/78/SR.11; A/C.3/78/SR.13
RULE OF LAW (Agenda item 83)
Bhat, Kajal - A/C.6/78/SR.18
RURAL POVERTY (Agenda item 21b)
Gahlot, Petal - A/C.2/78/SR.16
SCIENCE AND TECHNOLOGY—DEVELOPMENT (Agenda item 19a)
Gahlot, Petal - A/C.2/78/SR.10
SCIENCE AND TECHNOLOGY—INTERNATIONAL SECURITY (Agenda item 98)
Bedi, Anmol Sher Singh - A/C.1/78/PV.21
SELF-DETERMINATION OF PEOPLES (Agenda item 70)
Sonkar, Suman - A/C.3/78/SR.41; A/C.3/78/SR.56
SMALL ISLAND DEVELOPING STATES—PROGRAMMES OF ACTION (Agenda item 18b)
Gahlot, Petal - A/C.2/78/SR.13
SOCIAL CONDITIONS (Agenda item 24b)
Kamboj, Ruchira - A/78/PV.57
Sonkar, Suman - A/C.3/78/SR.3
SOCIAL DEVELOPMENT (Agenda item 24)
Sonkar, Suman - A/C.3/78/SR.3
SOUTH-EAST ASIA—NUCLEAR-WEAPON-FREE ZONES (Agenda item 99y)
Kulkarni, Maitrey - A/C.1/78/PV.30
SPECIAL POLITICAL MISSIONS (Agenda item 52)
Birdi, Nitish - A/C.4/78/SR.21
STRADDLING FISH STOCKS (Agenda item 75b)
Bhat, Kajal - A/78/PV.43
SUMMARY EXECUTIONS (Agenda item 71b)
Sonkar, Suman - A/C.3/78/SR.31
SUSTAINABLE DEVELOPMENT (Agenda item 18)
Gahlot, Petal - A/C.2/78/SR.13; A/C.2/78/SR.14
SUSTAINABLE ENERGY (Agenda item 18h)
Gahlot, Petal - A/C.2/78/SR.13
TERRORISM (Agenda item 109)
Bhat, Kajal - A/C.6/78/SR.2; A/C.6/78/SR.4
TERRORISM—HUMAN RIGHTS (Agenda item 71b)
Sonkar, Suman - A/C.3/78/SR.31
TORTURE AND OTHER CRUEL TREATMENT (Agenda item 71a)
Sonkar, Suman - A/C.3/78/SR.18
TRAFFICKING IN PERSONS (Agenda item 71b)
Parihar, Rajesh - A/C.3/78/SR.23
UKRAINE—POLITICAL CONDITIONS (Agenda item 62)
Kamboj, Ruchira - A/78/PV.57
UN. CONFERENCE ON DISARMAMENT—REPORTS (Agenda item 101a)
Bedi, Anmol Sher Singh - A/C.1/78/PV.23

India (continued)

UN. DISARMAMENT COMMISSION—REPORTS (Agenda item 101b)
Bedi, Anmol Sher Singh - A/C.1/78/PV.23
UN. GENERAL ASSEMBLY—WORK PROGRAMME (Agenda item 120)
Mathur, Pratik - A/78/PV.33
UN. GENERAL ASSEMBLY (78TH SESS. : 2023-2024)—GENERAL DEBATE (Agenda item 8)
Jaishankar, Subrahmanyam - A/78/PV.14
UN. GENERAL ASSEMBLY (78TH SESS. : 2023-2024)—GENERAL DEBATE—RIGHT OF REPLY (Agenda item 8)
Gahlot, Petal - A/78/PV.11
UN. GENERAL ASSEMBLY (78TH SESS. : 2023-2024). 1ST COMMITTEE—GENERAL DEBATE (Agenda item 8)
Ray, Anupam - A/C.1/78/PV.6
UN. GENERAL ASSEMBLY (78TH SESS. : 2023-2024). 2ND COMMITTEE—GENERAL DEBATE (Agenda item 8)
Gahlot, Petal - A/C.2/78/SR.4
UN. HUMAN RIGHTS COUNCIL—REPORTS (Agenda item 66)
Sonkar, Suman - A/78/PV.28
UN. INTERNATIONAL COURT OF JUSTICE—REPORTS (Agenda item 73)
Bhat, Kajal - A/78/PV.27
UN. INTERNATIONAL LAW COMMISSION—REPORTS (Agenda item 79)
Bhat, Kajal - A/C.6/78/SR.30; A/C.6/78/SR.32; A/C.6/78/SR.37
Sekhar, Uma - A/C.6/78/SR.25
UN. PEACEBUILDING COMMISSION—REPORTS (Agenda item 27)
Bhalla, Ashish - A/78/PV.101
UN. PEACEBUILDING FUND—REPORTS (Agenda item 111)
Bhalla, Ashish - A/78/PV.101
UN. SECURITY COUNCIL—MEMBERSHIP (Agenda item 121)
Kamboj, Ruchira - A/78/PV.35
Patel, Yojna - A/78/PV.104
UN. SECURITY COUNCIL—REPORTS (Agenda item 26)
Mathur, Pratik - A/78/PV.94
UN CHARTER—REPORTS (Agenda item 82)
Bhat, Kajal - A/C.6/78/SR.33
UN COMMISSION ON INTERNATIONAL TRADE LAW—REPORTS (Agenda item 77)
Bhat, Kajal - A/C.6/78/SR.14
UN HIGH COMMISSIONER FOR REFUGEES—REPORTS (Agenda item 60)
Sonkar, Suman - A/C.3/78/SR.45
UN RESOLUTIONS—IMPLEMENTATION (Agenda item 119)
Mathur, Pratik - A/78/PV.33

India (continued)

UN YOUTH OFFICE—REPORTS (Agenda item 130)
Patel, Yojna - A/78/PV.102
VETO (Agenda item 63)
Kamboj, Ruchira - A/78/PV.52; A/78/PV.59; A/78/PV.67; A/78/PV.70; A/78/PV.74
WEAPONS—OUTER SPACE (Agenda item 97b)
Kulkarni, Maitrey - A/C.1/78/PV.27
WEAPONS OF MASS DESTRUCTION—TERRORISM (Agenda item 99s)
Kamboj, Ruchira - A/C.1/78/PV.15
WOMEN'S ADVANCEMENT (Agenda item 25a)
Sonkar, Suman - A/C.3/78/SR.7; A/C.3/78/SR.9
WOMEN'S ADVANCEMENT—CONFERENCES (Agenda item 25b)
Sonkar, Suman - A/C.3/78/SR.7; A/C.3/78/SR.9

Indonesia

AGEING PERSONS (Agenda item 24b)
Imanuel, Fnu - A/C.3/78/SR.1
ARMS RACE—OUTER SPACE (Agenda item 97a)
Sinaga, Liandra Jean - A/C.1/78/PV.16
ARMS TRANSFERS—TREATIES (Agenda item 99x)
Sirie, Mochammad Iqbal - A/C.1/78/PV.28
BIOLOGICAL WEAPONS—TREATIES (Agenda item 106)
Kristanti, Maria Benedicta Diah - A/C.1/78/PV.14
CHEMICAL WEAPONS—TREATIES (Agenda item 99l)
Kristanti, Maria Benedicta Diah - A/C.1/78/PV.14
CLIMATE (Agenda item 18d)
Prabowo, Hari - A/C.2/78/SR.15
CLIMATE CHANGE (Agenda item 71b)
Pella, Blandina Ruth Viditha Adeleide - A/C.3/78/SR.29
COMMODITIES (Agenda item 16d)
Tharyat, Tri - A/C.2/78/SR.14
CONVENTIONAL WEAPONS (Agenda item 99u)
Sirie, Mochammad Iqbal - A/C.1/78/PV.18; A/C.1/78/PV.28
CRIME PREVENTION (Agenda item 107)
Pella, Blandina Ruth Viditha Adeleide - A/C.3/78/SR.6; A/C.3/78/SR.56
CRIMES AGAINST HUMANITY (Agenda item 80)
Aron, Andy - A/C.6/78/SR.11; A/C.6/78/SR.38; A/C.6/78/SR.39; A/C.6/78/SR.42
Sandiori, Sherley Mega - A/C.6/78/SR.44; A/C.6/78/SR.45
CUBA—UNITED STATES (Agenda item 38)
Nasir, Arrmanatha Christiawan - A/78/PV.26

Indonesia (continued)

CYBERCRIME (Agenda item 108)
Pella, Blandina Ruth Viditha Adeleide - A/C.3/78/SR.6
DECOLONIZATION (Agenda item 58)
Dhanutirto, Mariska Dwianti - A/C.4/78/SR.7
DEVELOPMENT COOPERATION—MIDDLE-INCOME COUNTRIES (Agenda item 19c)
Prabowo, Hari - A/C.2/78/SR.11
DEVELOPMENT FINANCE (Agenda item 16b)
Prabowo, Hari - A/C.2/78/SR.9
DEVELOPMENT FINANCE—CONFERENCES (Agenda item 17)
Irawati Mamesah, Febrian - A/78/PV.90
DISARMAMENT—GENERAL AND COMPLETE (Agenda item 99)
Kristanti, Maria Benedicta Diah - A/C.1/78/PV.30
Sirie, Mochammad Iqbal - A/C.1/78/PV.28
DISARMAMENT—UN. GENERAL ASSEMBLY (4TH SPECIAL SESS. ON DISARMAMENT : xxxx) (Agenda item 99h)
Sirie, Mochammad Iqbal - A/C.1/78/PV.22
DISARMAMENT AGREEMENTS—OUTER SPACE (Agenda item 97c)
Kristanti, Maria Benedicta Diah - A/C.1/78/PV.27
Sinaga, Liandra Jean - A/C.1/78/PV.16
DISASTER PREVENTION (Agenda item 18c)
Prabowo, Hari - A/C.2/78/SR.15
DISASTER VICTIMS (Agenda item 86)
Aron, Andy - A/C.6/78/SR.5; A/C.6/78/SR.36
DISPLACED PERSONS (Agenda item 71b)
Khairunsyah, Aidil - A/C.3/78/SR.32
ECONOMIC COOPERATION AMONG DEVELOPING COUNTRIES (Agenda item 22b)
Prabowo, Hari - A/C.2/78/SR.18
ECONOMIC SANCTIONS—INTERNATIONAL RELATIONS (Agenda item 28)
Irawati Mamesah, Febrian - A/78/PV.90
ELECTION VERIFICATION—UN (Agenda item 71b)
Dhanutirto, Mariska Dwianti - A/C.3/78/SR.50
ENVIRONMENT (Agenda item 71b)
Meizura, Novia - A/C.3/78/SR.29
FISSIONABLE MATERIALS—TREATIES (Agenda item 99a)
Kristanti, Maria Benedicta Diah - A/C.1/78/PV.26
FOOD SECURITY (Agenda item 23a)
Prabowo, Hari - A/C.2/78/SR.17
HEALTH (Agenda item 125)
Imanuel, Fnu - A/78/PV.102
Pella, Blandina Ruth Viditha Adeleide - A/78/PV.48
Prabowo, Hari - A/78/PV.16; A/78/PV.41
HUMAN RIGHTS—AFGHANISTAN (Agenda item 71c)
Khairunsyah, Aidil - A/C.3/78/SR.34

Indonesia (continued)

HUMAN RIGHTS—INTERNATIONAL INSTRUMENTS (Agenda item 71a)
Aron, Andy - A/C.3/78/SR.26
HUMAN RIGHTS—MYANMAR (Agenda item 71c)
Dhanutirto, Mariska Dwianti - A/C.3/78/SR.53
Khairunsyah, Aidil - A/C.3/78/SR.33
HUMAN RIGHTS—TERRITORIES OCCUPIED BY ISRAEL (Agenda item 71c)
Khairunsyah, Aidil - A/C.3/78/SR.35
HUMAN RIGHTS ACTIVISTS (Agenda item 71b)
Imanuel, Fnu - A/C.3/78/SR.56
Pella, Blandina Ruth Viditha Adeleide - A/C.3/78/SR.19
HUMAN RIGHTS ADVANCEMENT (Agenda item 71b)
Pella, Blandina Ruth Viditha Adeleide - A/C.3/78/SR.52
IAEA—REPORTS (Agenda item 89)
Dhanutirto, Mariska Dwianti - A/78/PV.29
INDIGENOUS PEOPLES (Agenda item 68a)
Dhanutirto, Mariska Dwianti - A/C.3/78/SR.48
Pella, Blandina Ruth Viditha Adeleide - A/C.3/78/SR.17
INFORMATION—INTERNATIONAL SECURITY (Agenda item 94)
Sirie, Mochammad Iqbal - A/C.1/78/PV.20; A/C.1/78/PV.29
INFORMATION TECHNOLOGY—DEVELOPMENT (Agenda item 15)
Prabowo, Hari - A/C.2/78/SR.11
INVESTMENT PROMOTION (Agenda item 16g)
Prabowo, Hari - A/C.2/78/SR.9
JUDICIAL INDEPENDENCE (Agenda item 71b)
Sandiori, Sherley Mega - A/C.3/78/SR.31
LAW OF THE SEA (Agenda item 75a)
Prabowo, Hari - A/78/PV.44
MACROECONOMIC POLICY (Agenda item 16)
Prabowo, Hari - A/C.2/78/SR.9; A/C.2/78/SR.25
MARINE ECOSYSTEMS—BIOLOGICAL DIVERSITY (Agenda item 75c)
Prabowo, Hari - A/78/PV.44
NUCLEAR DISARMAMENT (Agenda item 99b)
Aron, Andy - A/C.1/78/PV.11
NUCLEAR NON-PROLIFERATION—INTERNATIONAL OBLIGATIONS (Agenda item 99w)
Aron, Andy - A/C.1/78/PV.11
NUCLEAR WEAPON TESTS—TREATIES (Agenda item 105)
Aron, Andy - A/C.1/78/PV.11
NUCLEAR WEAPONS—ELIMINATION (Agenda item 99z)
Kristanti, Maria Benedicta Diah - A/C.1/78/PV.26

Indonesia (continued)

NUCLEAR WEAPONS—TREATIES (Agenda item 99ff)
Aron, Andy - A/C.1/78/PV.11
OPERATIONAL ACTIVITIES—UN SYSTEM (Agenda item 22a)
Prabowo, Hari - A/C.2/78/SR.18
OUTER SPACE—CONFIDENCE-BUILDING MEASURES (Agenda item 99v)
Sinaga, Liandra Jean - A/C.1/78/PV.16
OUTER SPACE—PRINCIPLES (Agenda item 97d)
Kristanti, Maria Benedicta Diah - A/C.1/78/PV.27
Sinaga, Liandra Jean - A/C.1/78/PV.16
PALESTINE QUESTION (Agenda item 35)
Marsudi, Retno Lestari Priansari - A/78/PV.39
PEACE (Agenda item 14)
Dhanutirto, Mariska Dwianti - A/78/PV.76
Nasir, Arrmanatha Christiawan - A/78/PV.62
Prabowo, Hari - A/78/PV.82
PERSONS WITH DISABILITIES (Agenda item 24b)
Imanuel, Fnu - A/C.3/78/SR.3
PERSONS WITH DISABILITIES—HUMAN RIGHTS (Agenda item 71a)
Imanuel, Fnu - A/C.3/78/SR.51
POVERTY—HUMAN RIGHTS (Agenda item 71b)
Meizura, Novia - A/C.3/78/SR.30
POVERTY—INTERNATIONAL DECADES (Agenda item 21a)
Prabowo, Hari - A/C.2/78/SR.17
RACIAL DISCRIMINATION—ELIMINATION (Agenda item 69a)
Dhanutirto, Mariska Dwianti - A/C.3/78/SR.42; A/C.3/78/SR.47
RACIAL DISCRIMINATION—PROGRAMMES OF ACTION (Agenda item 69b)
Dhanutirto, Mariska Dwianti - A/C.3/78/SR.42
RELIGIOUS INTOLERANCE (Agenda item 71b)
Khairunsyah, Aidil - A/C.3/78/SR.38
RESPONSIBILITY TO PROTECT (Agenda item 129)
Prabowo, Hari - A/78/PV.96
RIGHT TO DEVELOPMENT (Agenda item 71b)
Imanuel, Fnu - A/C.3/78/SR.20
RIGHT TO EDUCATION (Agenda item 71b)
Meizura, Novia - A/C.3/78/SR.27
RIGHT TO THE TRUTH (Agenda item 71b)
Meizura, Novia - A/C.3/78/SR.22
RIGHTS OF THE CHILD (Agenda item 67)
Imanuel, Fnu - A/C.3/78/SR.55
RULE OF LAW (Agenda item 83)
Aron, Andy - A/C.6/78/SR.18
RURAL POVERTY (Agenda item 21b)
Prabowo, Hari - A/C.2/78/SR.17
RURAL WOMEN (Agenda item 25a)
Imanuel, Fnu - A/C.3/78/SR.49

Indonesia (continued)

SELF-DETERMINATION OF PEOPLES (Agenda item 70)
Dhanutirto, Mariska Dwianti - A/C.3/78/SR.42; A/C.3/78/SR.49
SMALL ARMS—ILLICIT TRAFFIC (Agenda item 99p)
Sirie, Mochammad Iqbal - A/C.1/78/PV.18
SMALL ARMS—ILLICIT TRAFFIC—ASSISTANCE (Agenda item 99n)
Sirie, Mochammad Iqbal - A/C.1/78/PV.18
SOCIAL CONDITIONS (Agenda item 24b)
Imanuel, Fnu - A/C.3/78/SR.3; A/C.3/78/SR.51
SOCIAL DEVELOPMENT (Agenda item 24)
Imanuel, Fnu - A/C.3/78/SR.3
SOUTH-EAST ASIA—NUCLEAR-WEAPON-FREE ZONES (Agenda item 99y)
Sirie, Mochammad Iqbal - A/C.1/78/PV.21
STRADDLING FISH STOCKS (Agenda item 75b)
Prabowo, Hari - A/78/PV.44
SUSTAINABLE DEVELOPMENT (Agenda item 18)
Imanuel, Fnu - A/C.2/78/SR.24
Prabowo, Hari - A/C.2/78/SR.15
Tharyat, Tri - A/C.2/78/SR.14
TAXATION (Agenda item 16h)
Imanuel, Fnu - A/C.2/78/SR.25
Prabowo, Hari - A/C.2/78/SR.9
TERRITORIES OCCUPIED BY ISRAEL—HUMAN RIGHTS (Agenda item 50)
Dhanutirto, Mariska Dwianti - A/C.4/78/SR.24
TERRITORIES OCCUPIED BY ISRAEL—NATURAL RESOURCES (Agenda item 59)
Prabowo, Hari - A/C.2/78/SR.19
TERRORISM (Agenda item 109)
Prabowo, Hari - A/C.6/78/SR.2
UKRAINE—POLITICAL CONDITIONS (Agenda item 62)
Prabowo, Hari - A/78/PV.57
UN. DISARMAMENT COMMISSION—REPORTS (Agenda item 101b)
Sirie, Mochammad Iqbal - A/C.1/78/PV.22
UN. GENERAL ASSEMBLY—WORK PROGRAMME (Agenda item 120)
Aron, Andy - A/78/PV.32
UN. GENERAL ASSEMBLY (78TH SESS. : 2023-2024)—GENERAL DEBATE (Agenda item 8)
Marsudi, Retno Lestari Priansari - A/78/PV.12
UN. GENERAL ASSEMBLY (78TH SESS. : 2023-2024). 1ST COMMITTEE—GENERAL DEBATE (Agenda item 8)
Nasir, Arrmanatha Christiawan - A/C.1/78/PV.3
UN. GENERAL ASSEMBLY (78TH SESS. : 2023-2024). 5TH COMMITTEE—WORK ORGANIZATION (Agenda item 7)
Ratnamurti, Karina - A/C.5/78/SR.35
Wardhana, Yochpy Ihsan - A/C.5/78/SR.26/PartII

Indonesia (continued)

UN. HUMAN RIGHTS COUNCIL—REPORTS (Agenda item 66)
Dhanutirto, Mariska Dwianti - A/78/PV.28
UN. INTERNATIONAL COURT OF JUSTICE—REPORTS (Agenda item 73)
Nasir, Arrmanatha Christiawan - A/78/PV.28
UN. INTERNATIONAL LAW COMMISSION—REPORTS (Agenda item 79)
Aron, Andy - A/C.6/78/SR.30
Sandiori, Sherley Mega - A/C.6/78/SR.27
UN. SECRETARY-GENERAL—REPORTS (Agenda item 110)
Nasir, Arrmanatha Christiawan - A/78/PV.54
UN. SECURITY COUNCIL—MEMBERSHIP (Agenda item 121)
Nasir, Arrmanatha Christiawan - A/78/PV.35
UN. SECURITY COUNCIL—REPORTS (Agenda item 26)
Dhanutirto, Mariska Dwianti - A/78/PV.93
UN HIGH COMMISSIONER FOR REFUGEES—REPORTS (Agenda item 60)
Khairunsyah, Aidil - A/C.3/78/SR.44
UN RESOLUTIONS—IMPLEMENTATION (Agenda item 119)
Aron, Andy - A/78/PV.32
UNRWA—ACTIVITIES (Agenda item 49)
Dhanutirto, Mariska Dwianti - A/C.4/78/SR.22
Nasir, Arrmanatha Christiawan - A/C.4/78/SR.26
VETO (Agenda item 63)
Dhanutirto, Mariska Dwianti - A/78/PV.70; A/78/PV.78
Nasir, Arrmanatha Christiawan - A/78/PV.52
Prabowo, Hari - A/78/PV.60; A/78/PV.67; A/78/PV.75
WEAPONS—OUTER SPACE (Agenda item 97b)
Sinaga, Liandra Jean - A/C.1/78/PV.16
WOMEN'S ADVANCEMENT (Agenda item 25a)
Prabowo, Hari - A/C.3/78/SR.10
WOMEN'S ADVANCEMENT—CONFERENCES (Agenda item 25b)
Prabowo, Hari - A/C.3/78/SR.10
YOUTH (Agenda item 24b)
Imanuel, Fnu - A/C.3/78/SR.55

Institut sahélien de recherche et d'analyse pour la transformation des conflits

WESTERN SAHARA QUESTION (Agenda item 58)
Sidibe, Souleymane Satigui - A/C.4/78/SR.5

International Association of Jurists for Western Sahara

WESTERN SAHARA QUESTION (Agenda item 58)
González Sánchez, José Luis - A/C.4/78/SR.4

International Civil Service Commission

PERSONNEL QUESTIONS—UN SYSTEM (Agenda item 142)
Djacta, Larbi - A/C.5/78/SR.10

International Committee of the Red Cross

HUMANITARIAN ASSISTANCE (Agenda item 72)
Courtois, Laetitia - A/78/PV.47
INTERNATIONAL JURISDICTION (Agenda item 84)
Apraxine, Pierre - A/C.6/78/SR.13
TERRORISM (Agenda item 109)
Apraxine, Pierre - A/C.6/78/SR.5
TORTURE AND OTHER CRUEL TREATMENT (Agenda item 71a)
Mabe, Brady Michael - A/C.3/78/SR.18
UN. GENERAL ASSEMBLY (78TH SESS. : 2023-2024). 1ST COMMITTEE—GENERAL DEBATE (Agenda item 8)
Gisel, Laurent - A/C.1/78/PV.9

International Criminal Court. President

INTERNATIONAL CRIMINAL COURT—REPORTS (Agenda item 74)
Hofmański, Piotr - A/78/PV.21

International Development Law Organization

RULE OF LAW (Agenda item 83)
Brinkman, Henk-Jan - A/C.6/78/SR.19

International Federation of Red Cross and Red Crescent Societies

DISASTER PREVENTION (Agenda item 18c)
Aultman, Kallie - A/C.2/78/SR.15
DISASTER VICTIMS (Agenda item 86)
Aultman, Kallie - A/C.6/78/SR.7
HUMAN RIGHTS (Agenda item 71)
Aultman, Kallie - A/C.3/78/SR.28
HUMANITARIAN ASSISTANCE (Agenda item 72)
Aultman, Kallie - A/78/PV.47
UN HIGH COMMISSIONER FOR REFUGEES—REPORTS (Agenda item 60)
Chasi, Victoria - A/C.3/78/SR.45

International Institute for Democracy and Electoral Assistance

HUMAN RIGHTS—MYANMAR (Agenda item 71c)
Sourek, Amanda Pirutti - A/C.3/78/SR.33

International Law Chambers (United Kingdom)

WESTERN SAHARA QUESTION (Agenda item 58)
Rosemarine, Andrew M. - A/C.4/78/SR.5

International Olympic Committee

SPORTS—OLYMPIC GAMES (Agenda item 11)
Bach, Thomas - A/78/PV.38

International Renewable Energy Agency

LANDLOCKED DEVELOPING COUNTRIES—CONFERENCES (Agenda item 20b)
Biya, Alain Wilfried - A/C.2/78/SR.7
LEAST DEVELOPED COUNTRIES—CONFERENCES (Agenda item 20a)
Biya, Alain Wilfried - A/C.2/78/SR.7
SUSTAINABLE ENERGY (Agenda item 18h)
Biya, Alain Wilfried - A/C.2/78/SR.15

International Residual Mechanism for Criminal Tribunals. President

INTERNATIONAL RESIDUAL MECHANISM FOR CRIMINAL TRIBUNALS (Agenda item 126)
Gatti Santana, Graciela Susana - A/78/PV.19

International Seabed Authority. Secretary-General

LAW OF THE SEA (Agenda item 75a)
Lodge, Michael - A/78/PV.44
MARINE ECOSYSTEMS—BIOLOGICAL DIVERSITY (Agenda item 75c)
Lodge, Michael - A/78/PV.44
STRADDLING FISH STOCKS (Agenda item 75b)
Lodge, Michael - A/78/PV.44

International Tribunal for the Law of the Sea. President

LAW OF THE SEA (Agenda item 75a)
Heidar, Tomas H. - A/78/PV.44
MARINE ECOSYSTEMS—BIOLOGICAL DIVERSITY (Agenda item 75c)
Heidar, Tomas H. - A/78/PV.44
STRADDLING FISH STOCKS (Agenda item 75b)
Heidar, Tomas H. - A/78/PV.44

International Union for Conservation of Nature and Natural Resources

ENVIRONMENT (Agenda item 71b)
Sandström Jaffe, Sofie - A/C.3/78/SR.29

International Youth Organization for Ibero-America

HUMAN RIGHTS (Agenda item 71)
Valle Blanco, Daniel del - A/C.3/78/SR.28
RIGHT TO CULTURE (Agenda item 71b)
Rando Ibáñez, Alicia - A/C.3/78/SR.27
RIGHT TO EDUCATION (Agenda item 71b)
Valle Blanco, Daniel del - A/C.3/78/SR.27

International, Impartial and Independent Mechanism to Assist in the Investigation and Prosecution of Persons Responsible for the Most Serious Crimes under International Law Committed in the Syrian Arab Republic since March 2011

ARMED CONFLICTS PREVENTION (Agenda item 31a)
Marchi-Uhel, Catherine - A/78/PV.72

Iran (Islamic Republic of)

AGEING PERSONS (Agenda item 24b)
Arab Bafrani, Fatemeh - A/C.3/78/SR.2
ARMED CONFLICTS PREVENTION (Agenda item 31a)
Aref, Yahya - A/78/PV.72
ARMS RACE—OUTER SPACE (Agenda item 97a)
Eshragh Jahromi, Asadollah - A/C.1/78/PV.17
Ghorbanpour Najafabadi, Mohammad - A/C.1/78/PV.16; A/C.1/78/PV.17
ARMS TRANSFERS—TREATIES (Agenda item 99x)
Ghorbanpour Najafabadi, Mohammad - A/C.1/78/PV.28
BIOLOGICAL WEAPONS—TREATIES (Agenda item 106)
Eshragh Jahromi, Asadollah - A/C.1/78/PV.15
Ghorbanpour Najafabadi, Mohammad - A/C.1/78/PV.14; A/C.1/78/PV.15
CHEMICAL WEAPONS—TREATIES (Agenda item 99l)
Eshragh Jahromi, Asadollah - A/C.1/78/PV.15
Ghorbanpour Najafabadi, Mohammad - A/C.1/78/PV.14; A/C.1/78/PV.15; A/C.1/78/PV.26
CLIMATE (Agenda item 18d)
Jalili, Tahereh - A/C.2/78/SR.13
CLUSTER MUNITIONS (Agenda item 99dd)
Ghorbanpour Najafabadi, Mohammad - A/C.1/78/PV.28
COASTAL ZONE MANAGEMENT (Agenda item 18j)
Momeni, Javad - A/C.2/78/SR.23
CONVENTIONAL WEAPONS (Agenda item 99u)
Ghorbanpour Najafabadi, Mohammad - A/C.1/78/PV.28
CRIME PREVENTION (Agenda item 107)
Arab Bafrani, Fatemeh - A/C.3/78/SR.5; A/C.3/78/SR.51; A/C.3/78/SR.56
CRIMES AGAINST HUMANITY (Agenda item 80)
Aref, Yahya - A/C.6/78/SR.38; A/C.6/78/SR.40; A/C.6/78/SR.42; A/C.6/78/SR.43; A/C.6/78/SR.44; A/C.6/78/SR.45; A/C.6/78/SR.47
Heidari, Bahram - A/C.6/78/SR.10
CUBA—UNITED STATES (Agenda item 38)
Sahraei, Mohammad Reza - A/78/PV.26
CYBERCRIME (Agenda item 108)
Arab Bafrani, Fatemeh - A/C.3/78/SR.5
DECOLONIZATION (Agenda item 58)
Ghelich, Vahid - A/C.4/78/SR.7; A/C.4/78/SR.9
Sahraei, Mohammad Reza - A/C.4/78/SR.8
DEMOCRACY (Agenda item 71b)
Arab Bafrani, Fatemeh - A/C.3/78/SR.28

Iran (Islamic Republic of) (continued)

DESERTIFICATION—TREATIES (Agenda item 18e)
Jalili, Tahereh - A/C.2/78/SR.13
DEVELOPMENT FINANCE (Agenda item 16b)
Teymourpour, Nooshin - A/C.2/78/SR.8
DISARMAMENT—GENERAL AND COMPLETE (Agenda item 99)
Eshragh Jahromi, Asadollah - A/C.1/78/PV.19
Ghorbanpour Najafabadi, Mohammad - A/C.1/78/PV.19; A/C.1/78/PV.21; A/C.1/78/PV.24; A/C.1/78/PV.28; A/C.1/78/PV.30
Jalil Iravani, Amir Saeid - A/78/PV.106
Rahimi Majd, Hassan - A/78/PV.106
DISARMAMENT AGREEMENTS—OUTER SPACE (Agenda item 97c)
Eshragh Jahromi, Asadollah - A/C.1/78/PV.17
DISASTER PREVENTION (Agenda item 18c)
Jalili, Tahereh - A/C.2/78/SR.13
DISASTER VICTIMS (Agenda item 86)
Heidari, Bahram - A/C.6/78/SR.5
ECONOMIC SANCTIONS—INTERNATIONAL RELATIONS (Agenda item 28)
Najafi, Reza - A/78/PV.89
ELECTION VERIFICATION—UN (Agenda item 71b)
Arab Bafrani, Fatemeh - A/C.3/78/SR.50
EMERGENCY ASSISTANCE (Agenda item 72a)
Ershadi, Zahra - A/78/PV.46
FAMILY (Agenda item 24b)
Arab Bafrani, Fatemeh - A/C.3/78/SR.2
FISSIONABLE MATERIALS—TREATIES (Agenda item 99a)
Ghorbanpour Najafabadi, Mohammad - A/C.1/78/PV.25; A/C.1/78/PV.26
FOOD SECURITY (Agenda item 23a)
Jalili, Tahereh - A/C.2/78/SR.16
FREEDOM OF EXPRESSION (Agenda item 71b)
Arab Bafrani, Fatemeh - A/C.3/78/SR.19
HEALTH (Agenda item 125)
Arab Bafrani, Fatemeh - A/78/PV.48
Ershadi, Zahra - A/78/PV.16
Ghafouri, Mojtaba - A/78/PV.77
HIV/AIDS—DECLARATIONS (Agenda item 10)
Ghafouri, Mojtaba - A/78/PV.91
HUMAN RIGHTS (Agenda item 71)
Arab Bafrani, Fatemeh - A/C.3/78/SR.16
HUMAN RIGHTS—DEMOCRATIC PEOPLE'S REPUBLIC OF KOREA (Agenda item 71c)
Arab Bafrani, Fatemeh - A/C.3/78/SR.33; A/C.3/78/SR.53
HUMAN RIGHTS—ERITREA (Agenda item 71c)
Ghanei, Mohsen - A/C.3/78/SR.36

Iran (Islamic Republic of) (continued)

HUMAN RIGHTS—INTERNATIONAL INSTRUMENTS (Agenda item 71a)
Arab Bafrani, Fatemeh - A/C.3/78/SR.25
HUMAN RIGHTS—IRAN (ISLAMIC REPUBLIC OF) (Agenda item 71c)
Arab Bafrani, Fatemeh - A/78/PV.50; A/C.3/78/SR.18; A/C.3/78/SR.27; A/C.3/78/SR.34; A/C.3/78/SR.54
Ershadi, Zahra - A/C.3/78/SR.53
Ghanei, Mohsen - A/C.3/78/SR.34
HUMAN RIGHTS—MYANMAR (Agenda item 71c)
Arab Bafrani, Fatemeh - A/C.3/78/SR.33
HUMAN RIGHTS—REPORTS (Agenda item 71c)
Arab Bafrani, Fatemeh - A/C.3/78/SR.18; A/C.3/78/SR.25
Ghanei, Mohsen - A/C.3/78/SR.37
HUMAN RIGHTS—SYRIAN ARAB REPUBLIC (Agenda item 71c)
Arab Bafrani, Fatemeh - A/C.3/78/SR.34; A/C.3/78/SR.54
HUMAN RIGHTS—TERRITORIES OCCUPIED BY ISRAEL (Agenda item 71c)
Arab Bafrani, Fatemeh - A/C.3/78/SR.27; A/C.3/78/SR.35
HUMAN RIGHTS—UKRAINE (Agenda item 71c)
Arab Bafrani, Fatemeh - A/C.3/78/SR.53
HUMAN RIGHTS ACTIVISTS (Agenda item 71b)
Arab Bafrani, Fatemeh - A/C.3/78/SR.56
HUMAN RIGHTS ADVANCEMENT (Agenda item 71b)
Arab Bafrani, Fatemeh - A/C.3/78/SR.52
IAEA—REPORTS (Agenda item 89)
Ghorbanpour Najafabadi, Mohammad - A/78/PV.30
Jalil Iravani, Amir Saeid - A/78/PV.29
INDIGENOUS PEOPLES (Agenda item 68a)
Arab Bafrani, Fatemeh - A/C.3/78/SR.15; A/C.3/78/SR.48
INDIGENOUS PEOPLES—CONFERENCES (Agenda item 68b)
Arab Bafrani, Fatemeh - A/C.3/78/SR.15
INFORMATION (Agenda item 53)
Ghelich, Vahid - A/C.4/78/SR.13
Sahraei, Mohammad Reza - A/C.4/78/SR.13
INFORMATION—INTERNATIONAL SECURITY (Agenda item 94)
Ghorbanpour Najafabadi, Mohammad - A/C.1/78/PV.20; A/C.1/78/PV.29
INFORMATION TECHNOLOGY—DEVELOPMENT (Agenda item 15)
Jalili, Tahereh - A/C.2/78/SR.10
INTERNATIONAL CRIMINAL COURT—REPORTS (Agenda item 74)
Mousavi, Seyed Ali - A/78/PV.21
INTERNATIONAL JURISDICTION (Agenda item 84)
Heidari, Bahram - A/C.6/78/SR.12

Iran (Islamic Republic of) (continued)

INTERNATIONAL TRADE (Agenda item 16a)
Teymourpour, Nooshin - A/C.2/78/SR.8
LANDMINES—TREATIES (Agenda item 99m)
Ghorbanpour Najafabadi, Mohammad - A/C.1/78/PV.28
LAW OF THE SEA (Agenda item 75a)
Aref, Yahya - A/78/PV.44
Ershadi, Zahra - A/78/PV.43
MARINE ECOSYSTEMS—BIOLOGICAL DIVERSITY (Agenda item 75c)
Aref, Yahya - A/78/PV.44
Ershadi, Zahra - A/78/PV.43
MEDITERRANEAN REGION—REGIONAL SECURITY (Agenda item 104)
Ghorbanpour Najafabadi, Mohammad - A/C.1/78/PV.29
MIDDLE EAST—NUCLEAR PROLIFERATION (Agenda item 102)
Ghorbanpour Najafabadi, Mohammad - A/C.1/78/PV.13; A/C.1/78/PV.26
MIDDLE EAST—NUCLEAR-WEAPON-FREE ZONES (Agenda item 95)
Ghorbanpour Najafabadi, Mohammad - A/C.1/78/PV.12; A/C.1/78/PV.22; A/C.1/78/PV.26
MILLENNIUM SUMMIT—CONFERENCES (Agenda item 117)
Ghafouri, Mojtaba - A/78/PV.102
Momeni, Javad - A/78/PV.15
MINE CLEARANCE (Agenda item 46)
Sahraei, Mohammad Reza - A/C.4/78/SR.10
MULTILATERALISM—DISARMAMENT (Agenda item 99r)
Ghorbanpour Najafabadi, Mohammad - A/C.1/78/PV.22
NON-CITIZENS—DEPORTATION (Agenda item 81)
Fallah Assadi, Mahdad - A/C.6/78/SR.34
NUCLEAR DISARMAMENT (Agenda item 99b)
Ghorbanpour Najafabadi, Mohammad - A/C.1/78/PV.11; A/C.1/78/PV.12
NUCLEAR DISARMAMENT—TREATY COMPLIANCE (Agenda item 99q)
Ghorbanpour Najafabadi, Mohammad - A/C.1/78/PV.26
NUCLEAR DISARMAMENT—VERIFICATION (Agenda item 99ee)
Ghorbanpour Najafabadi, Mohammad - A/C.1/78/PV.26
NUCLEAR NON-PROLIFERATION—INTERNATIONAL OBLIGATIONS (Agenda item 99w)
Ghorbanpour Najafabadi, Mohammad - A/C.1/78/PV.12
NUCLEAR WEAPON TESTS—TREATIES (Agenda item 105)
Ghorbanpour Najafabadi, Mohammad - A/C.1/78/PV.26

Iran (Islamic Republic of) (continued)

NUCLEAR WEAPONS—ELIMINATION (Agenda item 99z)
Ghorbanpour Najafabadi, Mohammad - A/C.1/78/PV.25
NUCLEAR WEAPONS USE—TREATIES (Agenda item 100a)
Ghorbanpour Najafabadi, Mohammad - A/C.1/78/PV.26
OUTER SPACE—CONFIDENCE-BUILDING MEASURES (Agenda item 99v)
Ghorbanpour Najafabadi, Mohammad - A/C.1/78/PV.27
OUTER SPACE—PEACEFUL USES—INTERNATIONAL COOPERATION (Agenda item 48)
Sahraei, Mohammad Reza - A/C.4/78/SR.15
OUTER SPACE—PRINCIPLES (Agenda item 97d)
Eshragh Jahromi, Asadollah - A/C.1/78/PV.17
Ghorbanpour Najafabadi, Mohammad - A/C.1/78/PV.27
PALESTINE QUESTION (Agenda item 35)
Jalil Iravani, Amir Saeid - A/78/PV.40
PALESTINIANS—ASSISTANCE (Agenda item 72b)
Ershadi, Zahra - A/78/PV.46
PEACE (Agenda item 14)
Jalil Iravani, Amir Saeid - A/78/PV.62; A/78/PV.82
PEACEKEEPING OPERATIONS (Agenda item 51)
Sahraei, Mohammad Reza - A/C.4/78/SR.20
PEACEKEEPING OPERATIONS—CRIMINAL LIABILITY (Agenda item 76)
Heidari, Bahram - A/C.6/78/SR.8
PERSONS WITH DISABILITIES—HUMAN RIGHTS (Agenda item 71a)
Arab Bafrani, Fatemeh - A/C.3/78/SR.38; A/C.3/78/SR.51
POVERTY—INTERNATIONAL DECADES (Agenda item 21a)
Jalili, Tahereh - A/C.2/78/SR.16
RACIAL DISCRIMINATION—ELIMINATION (Agenda item 69a)
Arab Bafrani, Fatemeh - A/78/PV.103; A/C.3/78/SR.41
Ghanei, Mohsen - A/C.3/78/SR.40
RACIAL DISCRIMINATION—PROGRAMMES OF ACTION (Agenda item 69b)
Arab Bafrani, Fatemeh - A/C.3/78/SR.41
Ghanei, Mohsen - A/C.3/78/SR.40
RADIATION EFFECTS (Agenda item 47)
Sahraei, Mohammad Reza - A/C.4/78/SR.11
RAISI, SEYYED EBRAHIM (IRAN (ISLAMIC REPUBLID OF). PRESIDENT)—TRIBUTES
Jalil Iravani, Amir Saeid - A/78/PV.83
RELIGIOUS INTOLERANCE (Agenda item 71b)
Arab Bafrani, Fatemeh - A/C.3/78/SR.38

Iran (Islamic Republic of) (continued)

RESPONSIBILITY OF INTERNATIONAL ORGANIZATIONS (Agenda item 85)
Fallah Assadi, Mahdad - A/C.6/78/SR.37
Heidari, Bahram - A/C.6/78/SR.19
RESPONSIBILITY TO PROTECT (Agenda item 129)
Ghafouri, Mojtaba - A/78/PV.99
RIGHT TO DEVELOPMENT (Agenda item 71b)
Arab Bafrani, Fatemeh - A/C.3/78/SR.20
RIGHT TO FOOD (Agenda item 71b)
Arab Bafrani, Fatemeh - A/C.3/78/SR.30
RIGHTS OF THE CHILD (Agenda item 67)
Arab Bafrani, Fatemeh - A/C.3/78/SR.11; A/C.3/78/SR.12; A/C.3/78/SR.55
RULE OF LAW (Agenda item 83)
Heidari, Bahram - A/C.6/78/SR.16
RURAL POVERTY (Agenda item 21b)
Jalili, Tahereh - A/C.2/78/SR.16
RURAL WOMEN (Agenda item 25a)
Arab Bafrani, Fatemeh - A/C.3/78/SR.49
SANCTIONS—INTERNATIONAL RELATIONS (Agenda item 71b)
Arab Bafrani, Fatemeh - A/C.3/78/SR.25; A/C.3/78/SR.28
SCIENCE AND TECHNOLOGY—DEVELOPMENT (Agenda item 19a)
Jalili, Tahereh - A/C.2/78/SR.10
SCIENCE AND TECHNOLOGY—INTERNATIONAL SECURITY (Agenda item 98)
Ghorbanpour Najafabadi, Mohammad - A/C.1/78/PV.29
SELF-DETERMINATION OF PEOPLES (Agenda item 70)
Arab Bafrani, Fatemeh - A/C.3/78/SR.49
Ghanei, Mohsen - A/C.3/78/SR.40
SMALL ARMS—ILLICIT TRAFFIC—ASSISTANCE (Agenda item 99n)
Ghorbanpour Najafabadi, Mohammad - A/C.1/78/PV.28
SOCIAL CONDITIONS (Agenda item 24b)
Arab Bafrani, Fatemeh - A/C.3/78/SR.51
STORMS (Agenda item 18i)
Momeni, Javad - A/C.2/78/SR.22
STRADDLING FISH STOCKS (Agenda item 75b)
Aref, Yahya - A/78/PV.44
Ershadi, Zahra - A/78/PV.43
SUSTAINABLE DEVELOPMENT (Agenda item 18)
Ghafouri, Mojtaba - A/C.2/78/SR.24
Jalili, Tahereh - A/C.2/78/SR.13
Momeni, Javad - A/C.2/78/SR.21; A/C.2/78/SR.22
TERRITORIES OCCUPIED BY ISRAEL—HUMAN RIGHTS (Agenda item 50)
Baghaei Hamaneh, Esmaeil - A/C.4/78/SR.25
Ghelich, Vahid - A/C.4/78/SR.25; A/C.4/78/SR.26
TERRITORIES OCCUPIED BY ISRAEL—NATURAL RESOURCES (Agenda item 59)
Jalili, Tahereh - A/C.2/78/SR.19

Iran (Islamic Republic of) (continued)

TERRITORIES OCCUPIED BY ISRAEL—NATURAL RESOURCES (Agenda item 59)
Momeni, Javad - A/C.2/78/SR.21
TERRORISM (Agenda item 109)
Heidari, Bahram - A/C.6/78/SR.1
TORTURE AND OTHER CRUEL TREATMENT (Agenda item 71a)
Arab Bafrani, Fatemeh - A/C.3/78/SR.18
UKRAINE—POLITICAL CONDITIONS (Agenda item 62)
Ghadirkhomi, Payman - A/78/PV.58
Ghafouri, Mojtaba - A/78/PV.99
UN—BUDGET (2024) (Agenda item 134)
Amrollahi, Mohammad Taghi - A/78/PV.73; A/C.5/78/SR.3; A/C.5/78/SR.26/PartII; A/C.5/78/SR.28; A/C.5/78/SR.34
UN—PROGRAMME PLANNING (Agenda item 135)
Amrollahi, Mohammad Taghi - A/78/PV.50(Resumption1); A/C.5/78/SR.24
UN. COMMITTEE FOR PROGRAMME AND COORDINATION—MEMBERS (Agenda item 114a)
Alshahin, Essam - A/78/PV.37
Ghadirkhomi, Payman - A/78/PV.37
UN. COMMITTEE ON RELATIONS WITH THE HOST COUNTRY—REPORTS (Agenda item 161)
Ershadi, Zahra - A/C.6/78/SR.35
UN. CONFERENCE ON DISARMAMENT—REPORTS (Agenda item 101a)
Ghorbanpour Najafabadi, Mohammad - A/C.1/78/PV.23
UN. GENERAL ASSEMBLY (78TH SESS. : 2023-2024)—GENERAL DEBATE—RIGHT OF REPLY (Agenda item 8)
Ghadirkhomi, Payman - A/78/PV.13
Karimi Magham, Ali - A/78/PV.11
UN. GENERAL ASSEMBLY (78TH SESS. : 2023-2024). 1ST COMMITTEE—GENERAL DEBATE (Agenda item 8)
Ghorbanpour Najafabadi, Mohammad - A/C.1/78/PV.2; A/C.1/78/PV.3; A/C.1/78/PV.6; A/C.1/78/PV.7; A/C.1/78/PV.8; A/C.1/78/PV.9
UN. GENERAL ASSEMBLY (78TH SESS. : 2023-2024). 2ND COMMITTEE—GENERAL DEBATE (Agenda item 8)
Momeni, Javad - A/C.2/78/SR.2; A/C.2/78/SR.3
UN. GENERAL ASSEMBLY (78TH SESS. : 2023-2024). CREDENTIALS COMMITTEE—REPORTS (Agenda item 3b)
Ghadirkhomi, Payman - A/78/PV.48
UN. HUMAN RIGHTS COUNCIL—REPORTS (Agenda item 66)
Arab Bafrani, Fatemeh - A/78/PV.23; A/C.3/78/SR.46; A/C.3/78/SR.51
UN. INTERNATIONAL COURT OF JUSTICE—REPORTS (Agenda item 73)
Fallah Assadi, Mahdad - A/78/PV.28
Mousavi, Seyed Ali - A/78/PV.20; A/C.6/78/SR.26

Iran (Islamic Republic of) (continued)

UN. INTERNATIONAL LAW COMMISSION—REPORTS (Agenda item 79)
Baghaei Hamaneh, Esmaeil - A/C.6/78/SR.33
Fallah Assadi, Mahdad - A/C.6/78/SR.29; A/C.6/78/SR.31
Mousavi, Seyed Ali - A/C.6/78/SR.24
UN. SECURITY COUNCIL—MEMBERSHIP (Agenda item 121)
Karimi Magham, Ali - A/78/PV.35
UN CHARTER—REPORTS (Agenda item 82)
Fallah Assadi, Mahdad - A/C.6/78/SR.34
UN COMMISSION ON INTERNATIONAL TRADE LAW—REPORTS (Agenda item 77)
Heidari, Bahram - A/C.6/78/SR.14
UN CONFERENCES (Agenda item 13)
Ghafouri, Mojtaba - A/78/PV.102
Momeni, Javad - A/78/PV.15
UN HIGH COMMISSIONER FOR REFUGEES—REPORTS (Agenda item 60)
Arab Bafrani, Fatemeh - A/C.3/78/SR.44; A/C.3/78/SR.51
UN RESOLUTIONS—IMPLEMENTATION (Agenda item 119)
Arab Bafrani, Fatemeh - A/78/PV.103
UN SYSTEM—STRENGTHENING (Agenda item 122)
Ghafouri, Mojtaba - A/78/PV.99
UNRWA—ACTIVITIES (Agenda item 49)
Ghelich, Vahid - A/C.4/78/SR.22
VETO (Agenda item 63)
Ghadirkhomi, Payman - A/78/PV.69
Jalil Iravani, Amir Saeid - A/78/PV.51; A/78/PV.59; A/78/PV.66; A/78/PV.74
Rahimi Majd, Hassan - A/78/PV.78
WEAPONS—OUTER SPACE (Agenda item 97b)
Eshragh Jahromi, Asadollah - A/C.1/78/PV.17
Ghorbanpour Najafabadi, Mohammad - A/C.1/78/PV.27
WESTERN SAHARA QUESTION (Agenda item 58)
Ghelich, Vahid - A/C.4/78/SR.7
WOMEN MIGRANT WORKERS (Agenda item 25a)
Arab Bafrani, Fatemeh - A/C.3/78/SR.49
WOMEN'S ADVANCEMENT (Agenda item 25a)
Arab Bafrani, Fatemeh - A/C.3/78/SR.8
Azad, Farzaneh Baniasad - A/C.3/78/SR.10
Ghafouri, Mojtaba - A/78/PV.88
WOMEN'S ADVANCEMENT—CONFERENCES (Agenda item 25b)
Arab Bafrani, Fatemeh - A/C.3/78/SR.8; A/C.3/78/SR.51
Azad, Farzaneh Baniasad - A/C.3/78/SR.10
YOUTH (Agenda item 24b)
Arab Bafrani, Fatemeh - A/C.3/78/SR.2; A/C.3/78/SR.55

Iran (Islamic Republic of). President

UN. GENERAL ASSEMBLY (78TH SESS. : 2023-2024)—GENERAL DEBATE (Agenda item 8)
Raisi, Seyyed Ebrahim - A/78/PV.5
UN. GENERAL ASSEMBLY (78TH SESS. : 2023-2024)—SPECIAL STATEMENTS
Raisi, Seyyed Ebrahim - A/78/PV.5

Iraq

CLIMATE (Agenda item 18d)
Jasim, Saber Ahmed - A/C.2/78/SR.13
CLUSTER MUNITIONS (Agenda item 99dd)
Al-Sadar, Hamzah - A/C.1/78/PV.18
COMMODITIES (Agenda item 16d)
Al-Niami, Mustafa - A/C.2/78/SR.9
CONVENTIONAL WEAPONS (Agenda item 99u)
Al-Sadar, Hamzah - A/C.1/78/PV.18
CRIMES AGAINST HUMANITY (Agenda item 80)
Al-Fatlawi, Abbas Kadhom Obaid - A/C.6/78/SR.38
Al-Hasani, Haider - A/C.6/78/SR.11
DECOLONIZATION (Agenda item 58)
Al-Fatlawi, Abbas Kadhom Obaid - A/C.4/78/SR.8
DESERTIFICATION—TREATIES (Agenda item 18e)
Jasim, Saber Ahmed - A/C.2/78/SR.13
DISAPPEARANCE OF PERSONS (Agenda item 71b)
Al-Khaqani, Hassan Jabbar - A/C.3/78/SR.22
DISARMAMENT—GENERAL AND COMPLETE (Agenda item 99)
Al-Sadar, Hamzah - A/C.1/78/PV.19
Al-Taie, Sarmad Muwafaq Mohammed - A/C.1/78/PV.24; A/C.1/78/PV.30
DISPLACED PERSONS (Agenda item 71b)
Yaseen, Safaa - A/C.3/78/SR.32
FAMILY (Agenda item 24b)
Al-Khaqani, Hassan Jabbar - A/C.3/78/SR.4
FINANCIAL FLOWS (Agenda item 16f)
Al-Niami, Mustafa - A/C.2/78/SR.9
HEALTH (Agenda item 125)
Al-Musawi, Ali Rida Abdulmohsin Hasan - A/78/PV.48
HUMAN RIGHTS (Agenda item 71)
Al-Khaqani, Hassan Jabbar - A/C.3/78/SR.16
HUMAN RIGHTS—TERRITORIES OCCUPIED BY ISRAEL (Agenda item 71c)
Abdullateef, Mohammed Ayad - A/C.3/78/SR.35
Al-Khaqani, Hassan Jabbar - A/C.3/78/SR.35
HUMAN RIGHTS ACTIVISTS (Agenda item 71b)
Abdullateef, Mohammed Ayad - A/C.3/78/SR.56
HUMAN RIGHTS ADVANCEMENT (Agenda item 71b)
Raed Dawood Al-Saadi, Amna - A/C.3/78/SR.18
IAEA—REPORTS (Agenda item 89)
Marzooq, Mohammed Sahib - A/78/PV.29
INFORMATION (Agenda item 53)
Alsammak, Uday Qais Mahdi - A/C.4/78/SR.13

Iraq (continued)

INFORMATION—INTERNATIONAL SECURITY (Agenda item 94)
Saadi, Abu Alhakam Adnan Sadek - A/C.1/78/PV.20
INTERNATIONAL TRADE (Agenda item 16a)
Al-Niami, Mustafa - A/C.2/78/SR.9
LANDMINES—TREATIES (Agenda item 99m)
Al-Sadar, Hamzah - A/C.1/78/PV.18
MACROECONOMIC POLICY (Agenda item 16)
Al-Niami, Mustafa - A/C.2/78/SR.9
MERCENARIES (Agenda item 70)
Abdullateef, Mohammed Ayad - A/C.3/78/SR.42
MIDDLE EAST—NUCLEAR-WEAPON-FREE ZONES (Agenda item 95)
Al-Taie, Sarmad Muwafaq Mohammed - A/C.1/78/PV.22
MINE CLEARANCE (Agenda item 46)
Al-Saed, Saadoon - A/C.4/78/SR.10
MINORITIES (Agenda item 71b)
Yaseen, Safaa - A/C.3/78/SR.39
MULTILATERALISM—DISARMAMENT (Agenda item 99r)
Al-Taie, Sarmad Muwafaq Mohammed - A/C.1/78/PV.22
NUCLEAR DISARMAMENT (Agenda item 99b)
Salih, Muthanna - A/C.1/78/PV.12
NUCLEAR NON-PROLIFERATION—INTERNATIONAL OBLIGATIONS (Agenda item 99w)
Salih, Muthanna - A/C.1/78/PV.12
OUTER SPACE—PEACEFUL USES—INTERNATIONAL COOPERATION (Agenda item 48)
Alsammak, Uday Qais Mahdi - A/C.4/78/SR.15
PALESTINIANS—ASSISTANCE (Agenda item 72b)
Al-Khaqani, Hassan Jabbar - A/78/PV.47
PEACE (Agenda item 14)
Al-Fatlawi, Abbas Kadhom Obaid - A/78/PV.62
PEACEKEEPING OPERATIONS (Agenda item 51)
Al-Dahlaki, Hasanain Hadi Hasan - A/C.4/78/SR.20
PEACEKEEPING OPERATIONS—CRIMINAL LIABILITY (Agenda item 76)
Al-Hasani, Haider - A/C.6/78/SR.9
PERSONS WITH DISABILITIES—HUMAN RIGHTS (Agenda item 71a)
Al-Khaqani, Hassan Jabbar - A/C.3/78/SR.51
RACIAL DISCRIMINATION—ELIMINATION (Agenda item 69a)
Yaseen, Safaa - A/C.3/78/SR.41
RACIAL DISCRIMINATION—PROGRAMMES OF ACTION (Agenda item 69b)
Yaseen, Safaa - A/C.3/78/SR.41
RADIATION EFFECTS (Agenda item 47)
Al-Saed, Saadoon - A/C.4/78/SR.11
RELIGIOUS INTOLERANCE (Agenda item 71b)
Abdullateef, Mohammed Ayad - A/C.3/78/SR.38

Iraq (continued)

RIGHT TO DRINKING WATER (Agenda item 71b)
Al-Khaqani, Hassan Jabbar - A/C.3/78/SR.28
RIGHTS OF THE CHILD (Agenda item 67)
Abdullateef, Mohammed Ayad - A/C.3/78/SR.55
RURAL WOMEN (Agenda item 25a)
Al-Khaqani, Hassan Jabbar - A/C.3/78/SR.49
SELF-DETERMINATION OF PEOPLES (Agenda item 70)
Yaseen, Safaa - A/C.3/78/SR.41
SOCIAL DEVELOPMENT (Agenda item 24)
Al-Khaqani, Hassan Jabbar - A/C.3/78/SR.4
SPECIAL POLITICAL MISSIONS (Agenda item 52)
Al-Dahlaki, Hasanain Hadi Hasan - A/C.4/78/SR.21
STORMS (Agenda item 18i)
Jasim, Saber Ahmed - A/C.2/78/SR.13
SUSTAINABLE DEVELOPMENT (Agenda item 18)
Al-khalidi, Hasan Badri Mhalhal - A/C.2/78/SR.15; A/C.2/78/SR.24
SUSTAINABLE ENERGY (Agenda item 18h)
Jasim, Saber Ahmed - A/C.2/78/SR.13
TERRITORIES OCCUPIED BY ISRAEL—HUMAN RIGHTS (Agenda item 50)
Al-Dahlaki, Hasanain Hadi Hasan - A/C.4/78/SR.25
TERRITORIES OCCUPIED BY ISRAEL—NATURAL RESOURCES (Agenda item 59)
Al-khalidi, Hasan Badri Mhalhal - A/C.2/78/SR.19
TERRORISM (Agenda item 109)
Al-Zubaidi, Zaid Mohammed Hussein Abed - A/C.6/78/SR.4
UN—BUDGET (2024) (Agenda item 134)
Al-Fatlawi, Abbas Kadhom Obaid - A/C.5/78/SR.3
UN. GENERAL ASSEMBLY (78TH SESS. : 2023-2024)—OFFICERS (Agenda item 5)
Albu-Mohammed, Ahmed Kamil Rahif - A/C.5/78/SR.1
UN. GENERAL ASSEMBLY (78TH SESS. : 2023-2024). 1ST COMMITTEE—GENERAL DEBATE (Agenda item 8)
Al-Fatlawi, Abbas Kadhom Obaid - A/C.1/78/PV.6
UN. GENERAL ASSEMBLY (78TH SESS. : 2023-2024). 2ND COMMITTEE—GENERAL DEBATE (Agenda item 8)
Al-khalidi, Hasan Badri Mhalhal - A/C.2/78/SR.3
UN. HUMAN RIGHTS COUNCIL—REPORTS (Agenda item 66)
Abdullateef, Mohammed Ayad - A/C.3/78/SR.46
UN HIGH COMMISSIONER FOR REFUGEES—REPORTS (Agenda item 60)
Al-Musawi, Ali Rida Abdulmohsin Hasan - A/C.3/78/SR.45
UNRWA—ACTIVITIES (Agenda item 49)
Al-Dahlaki, Hasanain Hadi Hasan - A/C.4/78/SR.23

Iraq (continued)

VETO (Agenda item 63)
Al-Fatlawi, Abbas Kadhom Obaid - A/78/PV.61
Al-Khaqani, Hassan Jabbar - A/78/PV.67
WOMEN MIGRANT WORKERS (Agenda item 25a)
Al-Khaqani, Hassan Jabbar - A/C.3/78/SR.49
WOMEN'S ADVANCEMENT (Agenda item 25a)
Raed Dawood Al-Saadi, Amna - A/C.3/78/SR.9
WOMEN'S ADVANCEMENT—CONFERENCES (Agenda item 25b)
Al-Khaqani, Hassan Jabbar - A/C.3/78/SR.51
Raed Dawood Al-Saadi, Amna - A/C.3/78/SR.9
YOUTH (Agenda item 24b)
Abdullateef, Mohammed Ayad - A/C.3/78/SR.55
Al-Khaqani, Hassan Jabbar - A/C.3/78/SR.4

Iraq. Prime Minister

UN. GENERAL ASSEMBLY (78TH SESS. : 2023-2024)—GENERAL DEBATE (Agenda item 8)
Al Sudani, Mohammed Shia' - A/78/PV.10
UN. GENERAL ASSEMBLY (78TH SESS. : 2023-2024)—SPECIAL STATEMENTS
Al Sudani, Mohammed Shia' - A/78/PV.10

Ireland

ARMED CONFLICTS PREVENTION (Agenda item 31a)
Kirk, James - A/78/PV.72
ARMS RACE—OUTER SPACE (Agenda item 97a)
Robinson, Jason - A/C.1/78/PV.17
ARMS TRANSFERS—TREATIES (Agenda item 99x)
Udom, Caoimhe - A/C.1/78/PV.18
BIOLOGICAL WEAPONS—TREATIES (Agenda item 106)
Udom, Caoimhe - A/C.1/78/PV.15
CHEMICAL WEAPONS—TREATIES (Agenda item 99l)
Udom, Caoimhe - A/C.1/78/PV.15
CLUSTER MUNITIONS (Agenda item 99dd)
Udom, Caoimhe - A/C.1/78/PV.18
CONVENTIONAL WEAPONS (Agenda item 99u)
Udom, Caoimhe - A/C.1/78/PV.18
CONVENTIONAL WEAPONS—TREATIES (Agenda item 103)
Udom, Caoimhe - A/C.1/78/PV.18
CRIMES AGAINST HUMANITY (Agenda item 80)
Kirk, James - A/C.6/78/SR.10; A/C.6/78/SR.38; A/C.6/78/SR.39; A/C.6/78/SR.42; A/C.6/78/SR.43; A/C.6/78/SR.45
DISARMAMENT—GENERAL AND COMPLETE (Agenda item 99)
Doyle, Ciaran James - A/C.1/78/PV.22

Ireland (continued)

DISARMAMENT AGREEMENTS—OUTER SPACE (Agenda item 97c)
Robinson, Jason - A/C.1/78/PV.17
DISASTER VICTIMS (Agenda item 86)
Kirk, James - A/C.6/78/SR.6
FREEDOM OF EXPRESSION (Agenda item 71b)
Landy, Caoimhe - A/C.3/78/SR.19
HIV/AIDS—DECLARATIONS (Agenda item 10)
Cronin, Donal - A/78/PV.91
HUMAN RIGHTS (Agenda item 71)
Broderick, Fiona - A/C.3/78/SR.16
HUMAN RIGHTS—AFGHANISTAN (Agenda item 71c)
Broderick, Fiona - A/C.3/78/SR.34
HUMAN RIGHTS—DEMOCRATIC PEOPLE'S REPUBLIC OF KOREA (Agenda item 71c)
Digney, Leanne - A/C.3/78/SR.33
HUMAN RIGHTS—IRAN (ISLAMIC REPUBLIC OF) (Agenda item 71c)
Broderick, Fiona - A/C.3/78/SR.34
HUMAN RIGHTS—MYANMAR (Agenda item 71c)
Swan, Ellen - A/C.3/78/SR.33
HUMAN RIGHTS—RUSSIAN FEDERATION (Agenda item 71c)
Mc Bean, Keith - A/C.3/78/SR.37
HUMAN RIGHTS—SYRIAN ARAB REPUBLIC (Agenda item 71c)
Broderick, Fiona - A/C.3/78/SR.34
Mc Bean, Keith - A/C.3/78/SR.54
HUMAN RIGHTS—TERRITORIES OCCUPIED BY ISRAEL (Agenda item 71c)
Mc Bean, Keith - A/C.3/78/SR.35
HUMAN RIGHTS—UKRAINE (Agenda item 71c)
Mc Bean, Keith - A/C.3/78/SR.37
HUMAN RIGHTS ACTIVISTS (Agenda item 71b)
Swan, Ellen - A/C.3/78/SR.19
HUMAN RIGHTS ADVANCEMENT (Agenda item 71b)
Leonard, Roisin - A/C.3/78/SR.18
INTERNATIONAL CRIMINAL COURT—REPORTS (Agenda item 74)
Kirk, James - A/78/PV.22
INTERNATIONAL JURISDICTION (Agenda item 84)
Kirk, James - A/C.6/78/SR.12
INTERNATIONAL LAW—TRAINING PROGRAMMES (Agenda item 78)
Kirk, James - A/C.6/78/SR.22
LANDMINES—TREATIES (Agenda item 99m)
Udom, Caoimhe - A/C.1/78/PV.18
NUCLEAR DISARMAMENT (Agenda item 99b)
Duffy, Patrick - A/C.1/78/PV.12

Ireland (continued)

NUCLEAR NON-PROLIFERATION—INTERNATIONAL OBLIGATIONS (Agenda item 99w)
Duffy, Patrick - A/C.1/78/PV.12
NUCLEAR WEAPON TESTS—TREATIES (Agenda item 105)
Duffy, Patrick - A/C.1/78/PV.12
NUCLEAR WEAPONS—ELIMINATION (Agenda item 99z)
Doyle, Ciaran James - A/C.1/78/PV.26
NUCLEAR WEAPONS—TREATIES (Agenda item 99ff)
Duffy, Patrick - A/C.1/78/PV.12
OUTER SPACE—CONFIDENCE-BUILDING MEASURES (Agenda item 99v)
Robinson, Jason - A/C.1/78/PV.17
OUTER SPACE—PRINCIPLES (Agenda item 97d)
Robinson, Jason - A/C.1/78/PV.17
PERSONS WITH DISABILITIES—HUMAN RIGHTS (Agenda item 71a)
Swan, Ellen - A/C.3/78/SR.38
RACIAL DISCRIMINATION—ELIMINATION (Agenda item 69a)
Swan, Ellen - A/C.3/78/SR.41
RACIAL DISCRIMINATION—PROGRAMMES OF ACTION (Agenda item 69b)
Swan, Ellen - A/C.3/78/SR.41
RELIGIOUS INTOLERANCE (Agenda item 71b)
Landy, Caoimhe - A/C.3/78/SR.38
RIGHTS OF THE CHILD (Agenda item 67)
Leonard, Roisin - A/C.3/78/SR.13
SEXUAL ORIENTATION (Agenda item 71b)
Swan, Ellen - A/C.3/78/SR.39
SOCIAL DEVELOPMENT (Agenda item 24)
O'Sullivan, Alicia - A/C.3/78/SR.2
TERRORISM—HUMAN RIGHTS (Agenda item 71b)
Leonard, Roisin - A/C.3/78/SR.18; A/C.3/78/SR.31
TRAFFICKING IN PERSONS (Agenda item 71b)
Digney, Leanne - A/C.3/78/SR.23
TRANSNATIONAL CORPORATIONS—HUMAN RIGHTS (Agenda item 71b)
Leonard, Roisin - A/C.3/78/SR.21
UKRAINE—POLITICAL CONDITIONS (Agenda item 62)
Fleming, Seán - A/78/PV.56
UN. GENERAL ASSEMBLY (78TH SESS. : 2023-2024). 1ST COMMITTEE—GENERAL DEBATE (Agenda item 8)
White, Noel - A/C.1/78/PV.6
UN. INTERNATIONAL COURT OF JUSTICE—REPORTS (Agenda item 73)
Kirk, James - A/78/PV.27
UN. INTERNATIONAL LAW COMMISSION—REPORTS (Agenda item 79)
Kirk, James - A/C.6/78/SR.29; A/C.6/78/SR.31
Smyth, Declan - A/C.6/78/SR.25

Ireland (continued)

UN. SECURITY COUNCIL—MEMBERSHIP (Agenda item 121)
Mythen, Fergal Tomas - A/78/PV.35
VETO (Agenda item 63)
Mc Bean, Keith - A/78/PV.59
Mythen, Fergal Tomas - A/78/PV.3; A/78/PV.51; A/78/PV.67; A/78/PV.74; A/78/PV.78
WOMEN'S ADVANCEMENT (Agenda item 25a)
Mc Bean, Keith - A/C.3/78/SR.9
WOMEN'S ADVANCEMENT—CONFERENCES (Agenda item 25b)
Mc Bean, Keith - A/C.3/78/SR.9
YOUTH (Agenda item 24b)
Broderick, Fiona - A/C.3/78/SR.55
Naeem, Mohammad - A/C.3/78/SR.2

Ireland. Prime Minister

UN. GENERAL ASSEMBLY (78TH SESS. : 2023-2024)—GENERAL DEBATE (Agenda item 8)
Varadkar, Leo - A/78/PV.11
UN. GENERAL ASSEMBLY (78TH SESS. : 2023-2024)—SPECIAL STATEMENTS
Varadkar, Leo - A/78/PV.11

Israel

ADMINISTRATION OF JUSTICE (Agenda item 144)
Brash, Zoe - A/C.5/78/SR.15
AGEING PERSONS (Agenda item 24b)
Aviel, Shir - A/C.3/78/SR.2
Shaked, Or - A/C.3/78/SR.1
ARMS RACE—OUTER SPACE (Agenda item 97a)
Kalmar, Nimrod - A/C.1/78/PV.17
Maayan, Michal - A/C.1/78/PV.16
Sharoni, Benjamin - A/C.1/78/PV.27
ARMS TRANSFERS—TREATIES (Agenda item 99x)
Sharoni, Benjamin - A/C.1/78/PV.19; A/C.1/78/PV.28
BIOLOGICAL WEAPONS—TREATIES (Agenda item 106)
Maayan, Michal - A/C.1/78/PV.15
CHEMICAL WEAPONS—TREATIES (Agenda item 99l)
Maayan, Michal - A/C.1/78/PV.15
Sharoni, Benjamin - A/C.1/78/PV.26
CONVENTIONAL WEAPONS—TREATIES (Agenda item 103)
Sharoni, Benjamin - A/C.1/78/PV.19
CRIME PREVENTION (Agenda item 107)
Mimran Rosenberg, Avital - A/C.3/78/SR.5
CRIMES AGAINST HUMANITY (Agenda item 80)
Cappon, Noam - A/C.6/78/SR.10; A/C.6/78/SR.11; A/C.6/78/SR.38

Israel (continued)

CRIMES AGAINST HUMANITY (Agenda item 80)
Heumann, Amit - A/C.6/78/SR.42; A/C.6/78/SR.44; A/C.6/78/SR.45
DECOLONIZATION (Agenda item 58)
Shapir Ben Naftaly, Reut - A/C.4/78/SR.7; A/C.4/78/SR.8
DISARMAMENT—GENERAL AND COMPLETE (Agenda item 99)
Shapir Ben Naftaly, Reut - A/78/PV.106
Sharoni, Benjamin - A/C.1/78/PV.19; A/C.1/78/PV.24; A/C.1/78/PV.28
DISASTER VICTIMS (Agenda item 86)
Cappon, Noam - A/C.6/78/SR.5
Rubinshtein, Yarden - A/C.6/78/SR.7
FISSIONABLE MATERIALS—TREATIES (Agenda item 99a)
Sharoni, Benjamin - A/C.1/78/PV.26
HEALTH (Agenda item 125)
Ben Naftaly, Emil - A/78/PV.77
Cappon, Noam - A/78/PV.41
HUMAN RIGHTS (Agenda item 71)
Erdan, Gilad Menashe - A/C.3/78/SR.16
Mimran Rosenberg, Avital - A/C.3/78/SR.25
HUMAN RIGHTS—IRAN (ISLAMIC REPUBLIC OF) (Agenda item 71c)
Aviel, Shir - A/C.3/78/SR.34
Mimran Rosenberg, Avital - A/C.3/78/SR.53
HUMAN RIGHTS—SYRIAN ARAB REPUBLIC (Agenda item 71c)
Aviel, Shir - A/C.3/78/SR.34
Shaked, Or - A/C.3/78/SR.54
HUMAN RIGHTS—TERRITORIES OCCUPIED BY ISRAEL (Agenda item 71c)
Erdan, Gilad Menashe - A/C.3/78/SR.35
Shaked, Or - A/C.3/78/SR.27
HUMAN RIGHTS—UKRAINE (Agenda item 71c)
Mimran Rosenberg, Avital - A/C.3/78/SR.37
HUMAN RIGHTS ACTIVISTS (Agenda item 71b)
Mimran Rosenberg, Avital - A/C.3/78/SR.19
HUMAN RIGHTS ADVANCEMENT (Agenda item 71b)
Mimran Rosenberg, Avital - A/C.3/78/SR.52
IAEA—REPORTS (Agenda item 89)
Kalmar, Nimrod - A/78/PV.30
INDIGENOUS PEOPLES (Agenda item 68a)
Mimran Rosenberg, Avital - A/C.3/78/SR.17
INFORMATION (Agenda item 53)
Maayan, Michal - A/C.4/78/SR.13
Shapir Ben Naftaly, Reut - A/C.4/78/SR.14
INFORMATION—INTERNATIONAL SECURITY (Agenda item 94)
Sharoni, Benjamin - A/C.1/78/PV.21; A/C.1/78/PV.29
INTERNATIONAL CRIMINAL COURT—REPORTS (Agenda item 74)
Cappon, Noam - A/78/PV.25

Israel (continued)

INTERNATIONAL JURISDICTION (Agenda item 84)
Rubinshtein, Yarden - A/C.6/78/SR.12; A/C.6/78/SR.13
MEDITERRANEAN REGION—REGIONAL SECURITY (Agenda item 104)
Sharoni, Benjamin - A/C.1/78/PV.29
MIDDLE EAST—NUCLEAR PROLIFERATION (Agenda item 102)
Sharoni, Benjamin - A/C.1/78/PV.26
MIDDLE EAST—NUCLEAR-WEAPON-FREE ZONES (Agenda item 95)
Maayan, Michal - A/C.1/78/PV.12
Sharoni, Benjamin - A/C.1/78/PV.26
MINORITIES (Agenda item 71b)
Aviel, Shir - A/C.3/78/SR.39
MULTILATERALISM—DISARMAMENT (Agenda item 99r)
Sharoni, Benjamin - A/C.1/78/PV.23
NUCLEAR DISARMAMENT (Agenda item 99b)
Maayan, Michal - A/C.1/78/PV.11; A/C.1/78/PV.12; A/C.1/78/PV.13; A/C.1/78/PV.14
NUCLEAR NON-PROLIFERATION—INTERNATIONAL OBLIGATIONS (Agenda item 99w)
Maayan, Michal - A/C.1/78/PV.12
NUCLEAR WEAPONS—TREATIES (Agenda item 99ff)
Sharoni, Benjamin - A/C.1/78/PV.26
ORGANIZATION FOR DEMOCRACY AND ECONOMIC DEVELOPMENT - GUAM (Agenda item 32)
Kalmar, Nimrod - A/78/PV.85
OUTER SPACE—CONFIDENCE-BUILDING MEASURES (Agenda item 99v)
Sharoni, Benjamin - A/C.1/78/PV.27
OUTER SPACE—PEACEFUL USES—INTERNATIONAL COOPERATION (Agenda item 48)
Kedar, Gershon - A/C.4/78/SR.16
PALESTINE QUESTION (Agenda item 35)
Shapir Ben Naftaly, Reut - A/78/PV.39
PEACE (Agenda item 14)
Mimran Rosenberg, Avital - A/78/PV.77
PEACEKEEPING OPERATIONS (Agenda item 51)
Kedar, Gershon - A/C.4/78/SR.19; A/C.4/78/SR.20
PEACEKEEPING OPERATIONS—FINANCING (Agenda item 146)
Brash, Zoe - A/C.5/78/SR.35
PERSONS WITH DISABILITIES (Agenda item 24b)
Aviel, Shir - A/C.3/78/SR.2
PERSONS WITH DISABILITIES—HUMAN RIGHTS (Agenda item 71a)
Shaked, Or - A/C.3/78/SR.38
POVERTY—HUMAN RIGHTS (Agenda item 71b)
Shaked, Or - A/C.3/78/SR.30

Israel (continued)

RACIAL DISCRIMINATION—ELIMINATION (Agenda item 69a)
Mimran Rosenberg, Avital - A/C.3/78/SR.41; A/C.3/78/SR.47
Shapir Ben Naftaly, Reut - A/78/PV.103
RACIAL DISCRIMINATION—PROGRAMMES OF ACTION (Agenda item 69b)
Mimran Rosenberg, Avital - A/C.3/78/SR.41; A/C.3/78/SR.56
RELIGIOUS INTOLERANCE (Agenda item 71b)
Mimran Rosenberg, Avital - A/C.3/78/SR.38
RIGHT TO EDUCATION (Agenda item 71b)
Shaked, Or - A/C.3/78/SR.27
RIGHT TO FOOD (Agenda item 71b)
Mimran Rosenberg, Avital - A/C.3/78/SR.30
RIGHT TO HOUSING (Agenda item 71b)
Mimran Rosenberg, Avital - A/C.3/78/SR.30
RIGHTS OF THE CHILD (Agenda item 67)
Carmeli, Mor - A/C.3/78/SR.12
Mimran Rosenberg, Avital - A/C.3/78/SR.11; A/C.3/78/SR.55
Rodkin, Boaz - A/C.3/78/SR.13
RULE OF LAW (Agenda item 83)
Cappon, Noam - A/C.6/78/SR.19
SELF-DETERMINATION OF PEOPLES (Agenda item 70)
Mimran Rosenberg, Avital - A/C.3/78/SR.42; A/C.3/78/SR.49
SMALL ARMS—ILLICIT TRAFFIC (Agenda item 99p)
Sharoni, Benjamin - A/C.1/78/PV.28
STORMS (Agenda item 18i)
Ben Naftaly, Emil - A/C.2/78/SR.22
SUSTAINABLE DEVELOPMENT (Agenda item 18)
Barak, Noga - A/C.2/78/SR.24
Ben Naftaly, Emil - A/C.2/78/SR.15; A/C.2/78/SR.21; A/C.2/78/SR.22
TAXATION (Agenda item 16h)
Silverberg, Peter Andrew - A/C.2/78/SR.25
TERRITORIES OCCUPIED BY ISRAEL—HUMAN RIGHTS (Agenda item 50)
Kedar, Gershon - A/C.4/78/SR.25
TERRITORIES OCCUPIED BY ISRAEL—NATURAL RESOURCES (Agenda item 59)
Ben Naftaly, Emil - A/C.2/78/SR.19; A/C.2/78/SR.20; A/C.2/78/SR.21
TERRORISM (Agenda item 109)
Cappon, Noam - A/C.6/78/SR.1; A/C.6/78/SR.5
TERRORISM—HUMAN RIGHTS (Agenda item 71b)
Carmeli, Mor - A/C.3/78/SR.26
TORTURE AND OTHER CRUEL TREATMENT (Agenda item 71a)
Aviel, Shir - A/C.3/78/SR.18
UKRAINE—POLITICAL CONDITIONS (Agenda item 62)
Erdan, Gilad Menashe - A/78/PV.58

Israel (continued)

UN—BUDGET (2024) (Agenda item 134)
Zilbergeld, Sherry - A/78/PV.50(Resumption1); A/C.5/78/SR.5; A/C.5/78/SR.26/PartII
UN—PROGRAMME PLANNING (Agenda item 135)
Zilbergeld, Sherry - A/C.5/78/SR.5
UN. ECONOMIC AND SOCIAL COUNCIL—REPORTS (Agenda item 9)
Ben Naftaly, Emil - A/78/PV.33
UN. GENERAL ASSEMBLY—WORK PROGRAMME (Agenda item 120)
Ben Naftaly, Emil - A/78/PV.33
UN. GENERAL ASSEMBLY (78TH SESS. : 2023-2024)—OFFICERS (Agenda item 5)
Zilbergeld, Sherry - A/C.5/78/SR.1
UN. GENERAL ASSEMBLY (78TH SESS. : 2023-2024). 1ST COMMITTEE—GENERAL DEBATE (Agenda item 8)
Erdan, Gilad Menashe - A/C.1/78/PV.7
Maayan, Michal - A/C.1/78/PV.6; A/C.1/78/PV.7; A/C.1/78/PV.8; A/C.1/78/PV.9
UN. GENERAL ASSEMBLY (78TH SESS. : 2023-2024). 2ND COMMITTEE—GENERAL DEBATE (Agenda item 8)
Miller, Brett Jonathan - A/C.2/78/SR.3
UN. HUMAN RIGHTS COUNCIL—REPORTS (Agenda item 66)
Mimran Rosenberg, Avital - A/C.3/78/SR.51
UN. INTERNATIONAL COURT OF JUSTICE—REPORTS (Agenda item 73)
Cappon, Noam - A/78/PV.28
UN. INTERNATIONAL LAW COMMISSION—REPORTS (Agenda item 79)
Cappon, Noam - A/C.6/78/SR.24
Rubinshtein, Yarden - A/C.6/78/SR.28; A/C.6/78/SR.31; A/C.6/78/SR.33
UN INTERIM FORCE IN LEBANON—FINANCING (Agenda item 156b)
Cappon, Noam - A/78/PV.95
Zilbergeld, Sherry - A/C.5/78/SR.40
UN RESOLUTIONS—IMPLEMENTATION (Agenda item 119)
Ben Naftaly, Emil - A/78/PV.33
UNRWA—ACTIVITIES (Agenda item 49)
Kedar, Gershon - A/C.4/78/SR.23; A/C.4/78/SR.26
Shapir Ben Naftaly, Reut - A/C.4/78/SR.22
VETO (Agenda item 63)
Erdan, Gilad Menashe - A/78/PV.51; A/78/PV.59; A/78/PV.66; A/78/PV.74
Miller, Brett Jonathan - A/78/PV.69; A/78/PV.79
WOMEN'S ADVANCEMENT (Agenda item 25a)
Aviel, Shir - A/C.3/78/SR.8
WOMEN'S ADVANCEMENT—CONFERENCES (Agenda item 25b)
Aviel, Shir - A/C.3/78/SR.8
YOUTH (Agenda item 24b)
Aviel, Shir - A/C.3/78/SR.2
Carmeli, Mor - A/C.3/78/SR.55

Israel. Prime Minister

UN. GENERAL ASSEMBLY (78TH SESS. : 2023-2024)—GENERAL DEBATE (Agenda item 8)
Netanyahu, Benjamin - A/78/PV.10
UN. GENERAL ASSEMBLY (78TH SESS. : 2023-2024)—SPECIAL STATEMENTS
Netanyahu, Benjamin - A/78/PV.10

Italy

ARMS RACE—OUTER SPACE (Agenda item 97a)
Bencini, Leonardo - A/C.1/78/PV.17
ARMS TRANSFERS—TREATIES (Agenda item 99x)
Gai, Elena - A/C.1/78/PV.19
BIOLOGICAL WEAPONS—TREATIES (Agenda item 106)
Bencini, Leonardo - A/C.1/78/PV.15
CHEMICAL WEAPONS—TREATIES (Agenda item 99l)
Bencini, Leonardo - A/C.1/78/PV.15
CLIMATE CHANGE (Agenda item 71b)
Di Capua, Giacomo - A/C.3/78/SR.29
CLUSTER MUNITIONS (Agenda item 99dd)
Gai, Elena - A/C.1/78/PV.19
CONVENTIONAL WEAPONS—TREATIES (Agenda item 103)
Gai, Elena - A/C.1/78/PV.19
CRIME PREVENTION (Agenda item 107)
Franz, Silvio - A/C.3/78/SR.5
Greco, Gianluca - A/C.3/78/SR.56
Massari, Maurizio - A/78/PV.63
CRIMES AGAINST HUMANITY (Agenda item 80)
Franz, Silvio - A/C.6/78/SR.43
Milano, Enrico - A/C.6/78/SR.11; A/C.6/78/SR.38; A/C.6/78/SR.40; A/C.6/78/SR.41; A/C.6/78/SR.44; A/C.6/78/SR.45
DISARMAMENT—GENERAL AND COMPLETE (Agenda item 99)
Gai, Elena - A/C.1/78/PV.19
DISARMAMENT AGREEMENTS—OUTER SPACE (Agenda item 97c)
Bencini, Leonardo - A/C.1/78/PV.17
DISASTER VICTIMS (Agenda item 86)
Massari, Maurizio - A/C.6/78/SR.5
FOOD SECURITY (Agenda item 23a)
Massari, Maurizio - A/C.2/78/SR.16
HUMAN RIGHTS (Agenda item 71)
Tonon, Daniela - A/C.3/78/SR.16
HUMAN RIGHTS—INTERNATIONAL INSTRUMENTS (Agenda item 71a)
Greco, Gianluca - A/C.3/78/SR.25
HUMAN RIGHTS—TERRITORIES OCCUPIED BY ISRAEL (Agenda item 71c)
Greco, Gianluca - A/C.3/78/SR.35
HUMAN RIGHTS ADVANCEMENT (Agenda item 71b)
Greco, Gianluca - A/C.3/78/SR.25

Italy (continued)

INFORMATION—INTERNATIONAL SECURITY (Agenda item 94)
Bencini, Leonardo - A/C.1/78/PV.21
INTERNATIONAL CRIMINAL COURT—REPORTS (Agenda item 74)
Massari, Maurizio - A/78/PV.22
LANDMINES—TREATIES (Agenda item 99m)
Gai, Elena - A/C.1/78/PV.19
NUCLEAR DISARMAMENT (Agenda item 99b)
Bencini, Leonardo - A/C.1/78/PV.13
NUCLEAR NON-PROLIFERATION—INTERNATIONAL OBLIGATIONS (Agenda item 99w)
Bencini, Leonardo - A/C.1/78/PV.13
NUCLEAR WEAPON TESTS—TREATIES (Agenda item 105)
Bencini, Leonardo - A/C.1/78/PV.13
OUTER SPACE—CONFIDENCE-BUILDING MEASURES (Agenda item 99v)
Bencini, Leonardo - A/C.1/78/PV.17
OUTER SPACE—PRINCIPLES (Agenda item 97d)
Bencini, Leonardo - A/C.1/78/PV.17
PEACEBUILDING (Agenda item 61)
Martin Topranin, Pietro de - A/78/PV.100
PERSONS WITH DISABILITIES (Agenda item 24b)
Tonon, Daniela - A/C.3/78/SR.2
POVERTY—INTERNATIONAL DECADES (Agenda item 21a)
Massari, Maurizio - A/C.2/78/SR.16
RIGHT TO EDUCATION (Agenda item 71b)
Napolitano, Annarita - A/C.3/78/SR.27
RIGHTS OF THE CHILD (Agenda item 67)
Di Capua, Giacomo - A/C.3/78/SR.11
Tonon, Daniela - A/C.3/78/SR.13
RURAL POVERTY (Agenda item 21b)
Massari, Maurizio - A/C.2/78/SR.16
RURAL WOMEN (Agenda item 25a)
Napolitano, Annarita - A/C.3/78/SR.7
SOCIAL CONDITIONS (Agenda item 24b)
Tonon, Daniela - A/C.3/78/SR.2
UKRAINE—POLITICAL CONDITIONS (Agenda item 62)
Greco, Gianluca - A/78/PV.57
UN. CONFERENCE ON DISARMAMENT—REPORTS (Agenda item 101a)
Bencini, Leonardo - A/C.1/78/PV.23
UN. GENERAL ASSEMBLY (78TH SESS. : 2023-2024). 1ST COMMITTEE—GENERAL DEBATE (Agenda item 8)
Bencini, Leonardo - A/C.1/78/PV.4
UN. GENERAL ASSEMBLY (78TH SESS. : 2023-2024). 2ND COMMITTEE—GENERAL DEBATE (Agenda item 8)
Massari, Maurizio - A/C.2/78/SR.6
UN. INTERNATIONAL COURT OF JUSTICE—REPORTS (Agenda item 73)
Zanini, Stefano - A/78/PV.20

Italy (continued)

UN. INTERNATIONAL LAW COMMISSION—REPORTS (Agenda item 79)
Ferrara, Walter - A/C.6/78/SR.29; A/C.6/78/SR.31
Zanini, Stefano - A/C.6/78/SR.23
UN. PEACEBUILDING COMMISSION—REPORTS (Agenda item 27)
Martin Topranin, Pietro de - A/78/PV.100
UN. PEACEBUILDING FUND—REPORTS (Agenda item 111)
Martin Topranin, Pietro de - A/78/PV.100
UN COMMISSION ON INTERNATIONAL TRADE LAW—REPORTS (Agenda item 77)
Milano, Enrico - A/C.6/78/SR.14
VETO (Agenda item 63)
Greco, Gianluca - A/78/PV.3
Jovanovic, Nikola - A/78/PV.78
Massari, Maurizio - A/78/PV.52; A/78/PV.68; A/78/PV.71
WEAPONS OF MASS DESTRUCTION—TERRORISM (Agenda item 99s)
Bencini, Leonardo - A/C.1/78/PV.15
WOMEN'S ADVANCEMENT (Agenda item 25a)
Napolitano, Annarita - A/C.3/78/SR.9
Tonon, Daniela - A/C.3/78/SR.9
WOMEN'S ADVANCEMENT—CONFERENCES (Agenda item 25b)
Napolitano, Annarita - A/C.3/78/SR.9
Tonon, Daniela - A/C.3/78/SR.9
YOUTH (Agenda item 24b)
Di Capua, Giacomo - A/C.3/78/SR.2
Tonon, Daniela - A/C.3/78/SR.2

Italy. Council of Ministers. President

UN. GENERAL ASSEMBLY (78TH SESS. : 2023-2024)—GENERAL DEBATE (Agenda item 8)
Meloni, Giorgia - A/78/PV.7
UN. GENERAL ASSEMBLY (78TH SESS. : 2023-2024)—SPECIAL STATEMENTS
Meloni, Giorgia - A/78/PV.7

Italy. President

MULTILATERALISM
Mattarella, Sergio - A/78/PV.81
UN. GENERAL ASSEMBLY (78TH SESS. : 2023-2024)—SPECIAL STATEMENTS
Mattarella, Sergio - A/78/PV.81

ITU

INFORMATION TECHNOLOGY—DEVELOPMENT (Agenda item 15)
Wynhoven, Ursula - A/C.2/78/SR.11

Jamaica

CUBA—UNITED STATES (Agenda item 38)
Wallace, Brian Christopher Manley - A/78/PV.26

Jamaica (continued)

HUMAN RIGHTS ADVANCEMENT (Agenda item 71b)
DaCosta, Yanique Nissan - A/C.3/78/SR.52
LAW OF THE SEA (Agenda item 75a)
Douglas, Craig Barrington - A/78/PV.44
MARINE ECOSYSTEMS—BIOLOGICAL DIVERSITY (Agenda item 75c)
Douglas, Craig Barrington - A/78/PV.44
STRADDLING FISH STOCKS (Agenda item 75b)
Douglas, Craig Barrington - A/78/PV.44
SUSTAINABLE DEVELOPMENT (Agenda item 18)
Denton-Watts, Cyeth Cylonia Allison - A/C.2/78/SR.24
UN. GENERAL ASSEMBLY (78TH SESS. : 2023-2024)—GENERAL DEBATE (Agenda item 8)
Johnson Smith, Kamina - A/78/PV.14
UN. INTERNATIONAL LAW COMMISSION—REPORTS (Agenda item 79)
Bailey, Claudine - A/C.6/78/SR.28; A/C.6/78/SR.33

Japan

ARMED CONFLICTS PREVENTION (Agenda item 31a)
Shino, Mitsuko - A/78/PV.72
ARMS RACE—OUTER SPACE (Agenda item 97a)
Ogasawara, Ichiro - A/C.1/78/PV.17
BIOLOGICAL WEAPONS—TREATIES (Agenda item 106)
Ogasawara, Ichiro - A/C.1/78/PV.15
CHEMICAL WEAPONS—TREATIES (Agenda item 99l)
Ogasawara, Ichiro - A/C.1/78/PV.15
CLUSTER MUNITIONS (Agenda item 99dd)
Ogasawara, Ichiro - A/C.1/78/PV.18
COASTAL ZONE MANAGEMENT (Agenda item 18j)
Nishigori, Naofumi - A/C.2/78/SR.23
CONVENTIONAL WEAPONS (Agenda item 99u)
Ogasawara, Ichiro - A/C.1/78/PV.18
CONVENTIONAL WEAPONS—TREATIES (Agenda item 103)
Ogasawara, Ichiro - A/C.1/78/PV.18
CRIME PREVENTION (Agenda item 107)
Ono, Sho - A/C.3/78/SR.6
CRIMES AGAINST HUMANITY (Agenda item 80)
Urano, Hibiki - A/C.6/78/SR.44
Yamashita, Yuhei - A/C.6/78/SR.39; A/C.6/78/SR.40; A/C.6/78/SR.42; A/C.6/78/SR.43
CYBERCRIME (Agenda item 108)
Ono, Sho - A/C.3/78/SR.6
DISAPPEARANCE OF PERSONS (Agenda item 71b)
Miyamoto, Sogaku - A/C.3/78/SR.22

Japan (continued)

DISARMAMENT—GENERAL AND COMPLETE (Agenda item 99)
Namekawa, Hirochika - A/C.1/78/PV.28; A/C.1/78/PV.30
Ogasawara, Ichiro - A/C.1/78/PV.18
DISARMAMENT AGREEMENTS—OUTER SPACE (Agenda item 97c)
Namekawa, Hirochika - A/C.1/78/PV.27
Ogasawara, Ichiro - A/C.1/78/PV.17
ELECTION VERIFICATION—UN (Agenda item 71b)
Ono, Sho - A/C.3/78/SR.50
EMERGENCY ASSISTANCE (Agenda item 72a)
Miyamoto, Sogaku - A/78/PV.46
ENVIRONMENT (Agenda item 71b)
Ono, Sho - A/C.3/78/SR.29
HEALTH (Agenda item 125)
Iriya, Takayuki - A/78/PV.77
Kita, Yosuke - A/78/PV.48
Nakagawa, Shu - A/78/PV.16
HIV/AIDS—DECLARATIONS (Agenda item 10)
Kitada, Tetsuo - A/78/PV.91
HUMAN RIGHTS (Agenda item 71)
Ono, Sho - A/C.3/78/SR.27
Yamanaka, Osamu - A/C.3/78/SR.16
HUMAN RIGHTS—AFGHANISTAN (Agenda item 71c)
Ono, Sho - A/C.3/78/SR.26
Tonai, Akihiro - A/C.3/78/SR.34
HUMAN RIGHTS—DEMOCRATIC PEOPLE'S REPUBLIC OF KOREA (Agenda item 71c)
Ono, Sho - A/C.3/78/SR.53
Yamanaka, Osamu - A/C.3/78/SR.33
HUMAN RIGHTS—MYANMAR (Agenda item 71c)
Ono, Sho - A/C.3/78/SR.26
Yamanaka, Osamu - A/C.3/78/SR.33
HUMAN RIGHTS—TERRITORIES OCCUPIED BY ISRAEL (Agenda item 71c)
Shino, Mitsuko - A/C.3/78/SR.35
HUMAN RIGHTS—UKRAINE (Agenda item 71c)
Ono, Sho - A/C.3/78/SR.26; A/C.3/78/SR.37
HUMAN RIGHTS ADVANCEMENT (Agenda item 71b)
Ono, Sho - A/C.3/78/SR.18
HUMAN RIGHTS INSTITUTIONS—CENTRAL AFRICA (Agenda item 71b)
Ono, Sho - A/C.3/78/SR.56
IAEA—REPORTS (Agenda item 89)
Ishikane, Kimihiro - A/78/PV.29
Kusano, Yuta - A/78/PV.30
INFORMATION (Agenda item 53)
Yoshida, Aya - A/C.4/78/SR.13
INFORMATION—INTERNATIONAL SECURITY (Agenda item 94)
Namekawa, Hirochika - A/C.1/78/PV.29
Ogasawara, Ichiro - A/C.1/78/PV.20

Japan (continued)

INTERNATIONAL CRIMINAL COURT—REPORTS (Agenda item 74)
Tokunaga, Fumie - A/78/PV.22
INTERNATIONAL RESIDUAL MECHANISM FOR CRIMINAL TRIBUNALS (Agenda item 126)
Nagano, Shunsuke - A/78/PV.19
LANDMINES—TREATIES (Agenda item 99m)
Ogasawara, Ichiro - A/C.1/78/PV.18
LAW OF THE SEA (Agenda item 75a)
Nagano, Shunsuke - A/78/PV.44
Sorimachi, Masayuki - A/78/PV.44
LEPROSY (Agenda item 71b)
Kamiya, Masako - A/C.3/78/SR.17
MARINE ECOSYSTEMS—BIOLOGICAL DIVERSITY (Agenda item 75c)
Nagano, Shunsuke - A/78/PV.44
Sorimachi, Masayuki - A/78/PV.44
MILLENNIUM SUMMIT—CONFERENCES (Agenda item 117)
Yamanaka, Osamu - A/78/PV.15
MINE CLEARANCE (Agenda item 46)
Ono, Sho - A/C.4/78/SR.10
MINORITIES (Agenda item 71b)
Akita, Mio - A/C.3/78/SR.39
MULTILINGUALISM (Agenda item 124)
Minegishi, Shunsuke - A/78/PV.108
NUCLEAR DISARMAMENT (Agenda item 99b)
Ogasawara, Ichiro - A/C.1/78/PV.12
NUCLEAR NON-PROLIFERATION—INTERNATIONAL OBLIGATIONS (Agenda item 99w)
Ogasawara, Ichiro - A/C.1/78/PV.12
NUCLEAR WEAPONS—ELIMINATION (Agenda item 99z)
Ogasawara, Ichiro - A/C.1/78/PV.12; A/C.1/78/PV.25; A/C.1/78/PV.26
NUCLEAR WEAPONS—HUMANITARIAN CONSEQUENCES (Agenda item 99bb)
Ogasawara, Ichiro - A/C.1/78/PV.26
NUCLEAR WEAPONS—TREATIES (Agenda item 99ff)
Ogasawara, Ichiro - A/C.1/78/PV.26
ORGANIZATION FOR DEMOCRACY AND ECONOMIC DEVELOPMENT - GUAM (Agenda item 32)
Shino, Mitsuko - A/78/PV.85
OUTER SPACE—CONFIDENCE-BUILDING MEASURES (Agenda item 99v)
Ogasawara, Ichiro - A/C.1/78/PV.17
OUTER SPACE—PEACEFUL USES—INTERNATIONAL COOPERATION (Agenda item 48)
Kusano, Yuta - A/C.4/78/SR.16
OUTER SPACE—PRINCIPLES (Agenda item 97d)
Ogasawara, Ichiro - A/C.1/78/PV.17
PALESTINIANS—ASSISTANCE (Agenda item 72b)
Miyamoto, Sogaku - A/78/PV.46
PEACE (Agenda item 14)
Ono, Sho - A/78/PV.88

Japan (continued)

PEACEBUILDING (Agenda item 61)
Shino, Mitsuko - A/78/PV.100
PEACEKEEPING OPERATIONS (Agenda item 51)
Hamamoto, Yukiya - A/C.4/78/SR.20
PERSONNEL QUESTIONS—UN SYSTEM (Agenda item 142)
Kawasaki, Yuta - A/C.5/78/SR.10
PERSONS WITH DISABILITIES (Agenda item 24b)
Kamiya, Masako - A/C.3/78/SR.3
RACIAL DISCRIMINATION—ELIMINATION (Agenda item 69a)
Ono, Sho - A/C.3/78/SR.47
RACIAL DISCRIMINATION—PROGRAMMES OF ACTION (Agenda item 69b)
Ono, Sho - A/C.3/78/SR.56
RADIATION EFFECTS (Agenda item 47)
Washino, Yurie - A/C.4/78/SR.11
RIGHT TO DRINKING WATER (Agenda item 71b)
Ono, Sho - A/C.3/78/SR.28
RIGHT TO FOOD (Agenda item 71b)
Ono, Sho - A/C.3/78/SR.30; A/C.3/78/SR.48
RIGHT TO THE TRUTH (Agenda item 71b)
Miyamoto, Sogaku - A/C.3/78/SR.22
RIGHTS OF THE CHILD (Agenda item 67)
Kamiya, Masako - A/C.3/78/SR.13
Ono, Sho - A/C.3/78/SR.11
RULE OF LAW (Agenda item 83)
Nagano, Shunsuke - A/C.6/78/SR.18
SEXUAL ORIENTATION (Agenda item 71b)
Akita, Mio - A/C.3/78/SR.39
SLAVERY (Agenda item 71a)
Tonai, Akihiro - A/C.3/78/SR.21
SMALL ARMS—ILLICIT TRAFFIC (Agenda item 99p)
Nagai, Nana - A/C.1/78/PV.27
Ogasawara, Ichiro - A/C.1/78/PV.18
SOCIAL DEVELOPMENT (Agenda item 24)
Kamiya, Masako - A/C.3/78/SR.3
Ono, Sho - A/C.3/78/SR.47
SPECIAL POLITICAL MISSIONS (Agenda item 52)
Washino, Yurie - A/C.4/78/SR.21
SPORTS—OLYMPIC GAMES (Agenda item 11)
Ishikane, Kimihiro - A/78/PV.38
STRADDLING FISH STOCKS (Agenda item 75b)
Nagano, Shunsuke - A/78/PV.44
Sorimachi, Masayuki - A/78/PV.44
TAXATION (Agenda item 16h)
Nishigori, Naofumi - A/C.2/78/SR.8; A/C.2/78/SR.25
TERRITORIES OCCUPIED BY ISRAEL—HUMAN RIGHTS (Agenda item 50)
Nishiyama, Akira - A/C.4/78/SR.25

Japan (continued)

UKRAINE—POLITICAL CONDITIONS (Agenda item 62)
Tsuji, Kiyoto - A/78/PV.56
UN—BUDGET (2024) (Agenda item 134)
Abo, Ai - A/C.5/78/SR.3
Fujinuma, Atsuyuki - A/C.5/78/SR.33
Ishikane, Kimihiro - A/C.5/78/SR.5
UN—BUDGET CONTRIBUTIONS (Agenda item 138)
Wakabayashi, Sato - A/C.5/78/SR.1
UN—FINANCIAL SITUATION (Agenda item 136)
Abo, Ai - A/C.5/78/SR.6
UN—PROGRAMME PLANNING (Agenda item 135)
Ishikane, Kimihiro - A/C.5/78/SR.5
Kusano, Yuta - A/C.1/78/PV.10
UN. GENERAL ASSEMBLY—WORK PROGRAMME (Agenda item 120)
Kusano, Yuta - A/C.1/78/PV.10
Yoshida, Aya - A/78/PV.32
UN. GENERAL ASSEMBLY (78TH SESS. : 2023-2024)—GENERAL DEBATE—RIGHT OF REPLY (Agenda item 8)
Shino, Mitsuko - A/78/PV.11; A/78/PV.14
UN. GENERAL ASSEMBLY (78TH SESS. : 2023-2024)—OFFICERS (Agenda item 5)
Yamanaka, Osamu - A/C.5/78/SR.1
UN. GENERAL ASSEMBLY (78TH SESS. : 2023-2024). 1ST COMMITTEE—GENERAL DEBATE (Agenda item 8)
Ogasawara, Ichiro - A/C.1/78/PV.5; A/C.1/78/PV.6; A/C.1/78/PV.7
UN. GENERAL ASSEMBLY (78TH SESS. : 2023-2024). 2ND COMMITTEE—GENERAL DEBATE (Agenda item 8)
Yamanaka, Osamu - A/C.2/78/SR.4
UN. GENERAL ASSEMBLY (78TH SESS. : 2023-2024). 5TH COMMITTEE—WORK ORGANIZATION (Agenda item 7)
Abo, Ai - A/C.5/78/SR.40
Fujinuma, Atsuyuki - A/C.5/78/SR.26/PartII
Kawasaki, Yuta - A/C.5/78/SR.34
Yamanaka, Osamu - A/C.5/78/SR.27; A/C.5/78/SR.35
UN. INTERNATIONAL COURT OF JUSTICE—REPORTS (Agenda item 73)
Mikanagi, Tomohiro - A/78/PV.20
UN. INTERNATIONAL LAW COMMISSION—REPORTS (Agenda item 79)
Maeda, Gensaku - A/C.6/78/SR.30; A/C.6/78/SR.32
Nagano, Shunsuke - A/C.6/78/SR.28
UN. PEACEBUILDING COMMISSION—REPORTS (Agenda item 27)
Shino, Mitsuko - A/78/PV.100
UN. PEACEBUILDING FUND—REPORTS (Agenda item 111)
Shino, Mitsuko - A/78/PV.100
UN. SECURITY COUNCIL—MEMBERSHIP (Agenda item 121)
Ishikane, Kimihiro - A/78/PV.35

Japan (continued)

UN. SECURITY COUNCIL—MEMBERSHIP (Agenda item 121)
Nagano, Shunsuke - A/78/PV.36
Shino, Mitsuko - A/78/PV.104
UN COMMISSION ON INTERNATIONAL TRADE LAW—REPORTS (Agenda item 77)
Nagano, Shunsuke - A/C.6/78/SR.14
UN CONFERENCES (Agenda item 13)
Yamanaka, Osamu - A/78/PV.15
UN HIGH COMMISSIONER FOR REFUGEES—REPORTS (Agenda item 60)
Miyamoto, Sogaku - A/C.3/78/SR.45
UN RESOLUTIONS—IMPLEMENTATION (Agenda item 119)
Yoshida, Aya - A/78/PV.32
UNRWA—ACTIVITIES (Agenda item 49)
Nishiyama, Akira - A/C.4/78/SR.23
VETO (Agenda item 63)
Ishikane, Kimihiro - A/78/PV.3
Shino, Mitsuko - A/78/PV.52; A/78/PV.67; A/78/PV.70
Yamazaki, Kazuyuki - A/78/PV.68; A/78/PV.75; A/78/PV.78
WOMEN'S ADVANCEMENT (Agenda item 25a)
Akita, Mio - A/C.3/78/SR.7
Kamiya, Masako - A/C.3/78/SR.10
WOMEN'S ADVANCEMENT—CONFERENCES (Agenda item 25b)
Akita, Mio - A/C.3/78/SR.7
Kamiya, Masako - A/C.3/78/SR.10
YOUTH (Agenda item 24b)
Ono, Sho - A/C.3/78/SR.55

Japan. Prime Minister

UN. GENERAL ASSEMBLY (78TH SESS. : 2023-2024)—GENERAL DEBATE (Agenda item 8)
Kishida, Fumio - A/78/PV.5
UN. GENERAL ASSEMBLY (78TH SESS. : 2023-2024)—SPECIAL STATEMENTS
Kishida, Fumio - A/78/PV.5

Joint Inspection Unit

JOINT INSPECTION UNIT (Agenda item 141)
Cronin, Eileen A. - A/C.5/78/SR.27; A/C.5/78/SR.29
UN—ADMINISTRATION (Agenda item 132)
Cronin, Eileen A. - A/C.5/78/SR.29

Joint Inspection Unit. Chair

JOINT INSPECTION UNIT (Agenda item 141)
Fernández Opazo, Carolina María - A/C.5/78/SR.27

Jordan

CRIME PREVENTION (Agenda item 107)
Habashneh, Ahmad Samir Fahim - A/C.3/78/SR.5

Jordan (continued)

CRIMES AGAINST HUMANITY (Agenda item 80)
Bisharat, Nadien Isam Fraih - A/C.6/78/SR.38; A/C.6/78/SR.40; A/C.6/78/SR.41; A/C.6/78/SR.44; A/C.6/78/SR.45
Habashneh, Ahmad Samir Fahim - A/C.6/78/SR.10
CYBERCRIME (Agenda item 108)
Habashneh, Ahmad Samir Fahim - A/C.3/78/SR.5
DISARMAMENT—GENERAL AND COMPLETE (Agenda item 99)
Alqaisi, Sultan Natheir Mustafa - A/C.1/78/PV.19; A/C.1/78/PV.23
HUMAN RIGHTS—TERRITORIES OCCUPIED BY ISRAEL (Agenda item 71c)
Al-halique, Katherine Anas Ahmad - A/C.3/78/SR.35
PALESTINE QUESTION (Agenda item 35)
Hmoud, Mahmoud Daifallah Mahmoud - A/78/PV.39
PEACEKEEPING OPERATIONS (Agenda item 51)
Habashneh, Ahmad Samir Fahim - A/C.4/78/SR.20
RACIAL DISCRIMINATION—ELIMINATION (Agenda item 69a)
Al-halique, Katherine Anas Ahmad - A/C.3/78/SR.42
RACIAL DISCRIMINATION—PROGRAMMES OF ACTION (Agenda item 69b)
Al-halique, Katherine Anas Ahmad - A/C.3/78/SR.42
RESPONSIBILITY TO PROTECT (Agenda item 129)
Alqaisi, Sultan Natheir Mustafa - A/78/PV.96
SUSTAINABLE DEVELOPMENT (Agenda item 18)
Alqudah, Mohammad Abdel Rahman Hasan - A/C.2/78/SR.24
TERRITORIES OCCUPIED BY ISRAEL—HUMAN RIGHTS (Agenda item 50)
Habashneh, Ahmad Samir Fahim - A/C.4/78/SR.25
TERRORISM (Agenda item 109)
Habashneh, Ahmad Samir Fahim - A/C.6/78/SR.2
UKRAINE—POLITICAL CONDITIONS (Agenda item 62)
Hmoud, Mahmoud Daifallah Mahmoud - A/78/PV.99
UN. GENERAL ASSEMBLY (78TH SESS. : 2023-2024)—GENERAL DEBATE (Agenda item 8)
Abdullah II, King of Jordan, 1962- - A/78/PV.4
UN. GENERAL ASSEMBLY (78TH SESS. : 2023-2024)—SPECIAL STATEMENTS
Abdullah II, King of Jordan, 1962- - A/78/PV.4
UN. GENERAL ASSEMBLY (78TH SESS. : 2023-2024). 1ST COMMITTEE—GENERAL DEBATE (Agenda item 8)
Alqaisi, Sultan Natheir Mustafa - A/C.1/78/PV.5
UN. GENERAL ASSEMBLY (78TH SESS. : 2023-2024). 2ND COMMITTEE—GENERAL DEBATE (Agenda item 8)
Al-halique, Katherine Anas Ahmad - A/C.2/78/SR.3

Jordan (continued)

UN HIGH COMMISSIONER FOR REFUGEES—REPORTS (Agenda item 60)
Al-halique, Katherine Anas Ahmad - A/C.3/78/SR.44
UNRWA—ACTIVITIES (Agenda item 49)
Habashneh, Ahmad Samir Fahim - A/C.4/78/SR.22
VETO (Agenda item 63)
Alqaisi, Sultan Natheir Mustafa - A/78/PV.67
Habashneh, Ahmad Samir Fahim - A/78/PV.61
Hmoud, Mahmoud Daifallah Mahmoud - A/78/PV.52; A/78/PV.75
WESTERN SAHARA QUESTION (Agenda item 58)
Habashneh, Ahmad Samir Fahim - A/C.4/78/SR.7

Juntos por Guía (Firm : Spain)

WESTERN SAHARA QUESTION (Agenda item 58)
Suárez Moreno, Sergio Agustín - A/C.4/78/SR.4

Justice Action Coalition

RULE OF LAW (Agenda item 83)
Tahzib-Lie, Bahia (Netherlands (Kingdom of the)) - A/C.6/78/SR.15

Kazakhstan

AGEING PERSONS (Agenda item 24b)
Bakytbekkyzy, Anel - A/C.3/78/SR.2
ARMS RACE—OUTER SPACE (Agenda item 97a)
Rakhmetullin, Akan - A/C.1/78/PV.16
BIOLOGICAL WEAPONS—TREATIES (Agenda item 106)
Omarov, Arsen - A/C.1/78/PV.15
CHEMICAL WEAPONS—TREATIES (Agenda item 99l)
Omarov, Arsen - A/C.1/78/PV.15
DISARMAMENT—GENERAL AND COMPLETE (Agenda item 99)
Syrymbet, Zhangeldy - A/C.1/78/PV.12
Umarov, Kairat - A/78/PV.105
HUMAN RIGHTS—INTERNATIONAL INSTRUMENTS (Agenda item 71a)
Islamuly, Amirbek - A/C.3/78/SR.25
HUMAN RIGHTS—IRAN (ISLAMIC REPUBLIC OF) (Agenda item 71c)
Islamuly, Amirbek - A/C.3/78/SR.53
HUMAN RIGHTS ADVANCEMENT (Agenda item 71b)
Islamuly, Amirbek - A/C.3/78/SR.25
IAEA—REPORTS (Agenda item 89)
Syrymbet, Zhangeldy - A/78/PV.30
LANDLOCKED DEVELOPING COUNTRIES—CONFERENCES (Agenda item 20b)
Kerimkulov, Bauyrzhan - A/C.2/78/SR.7
LEAST DEVELOPED COUNTRIES—CONFERENCES (Agenda item 20a)
Kerimkulov, Bauyrzhan - A/C.2/78/SR.7

Kazakhstan (continued)

NUCLEAR DISARMAMENT (Agenda item 99b)
Syrymbet, Zhangeldy - A/C.1/78/PV.12
NUCLEAR NON-PROLIFERATION—INTERNATIONAL OBLIGATIONS (Agenda item 99w)
Syrymbet, Zhangeldy - A/C.1/78/PV.12
NUCLEAR WEAPON TESTS—TREATIES (Agenda item 105)
Syrymbet, Zhangeldy - A/C.1/78/PV.12
OUTER SPACE—CONFIDENCE-BUILDING MEASURES (Agenda item 99v)
Rakhmetullin, Akan - A/C.1/78/PV.16
REGIONAL DISARMAMENT (Agenda item 99f)
Nurken, Azat - A/C.1/78/PV.21
RIGHTS OF THE CHILD (Agenda item 67)
Bakytbekkyzy, Anel - A/C.3/78/SR.13
SOCIAL DEVELOPMENT (Agenda item 24)
Bakytbekkyzy, Anel - A/C.3/78/SR.2
SUSTAINABLE DEVELOPMENT (Agenda item 18)
Kerimkulov, Bauyrzhan - A/C.2/78/SR.21
UN. DISARMAMENT COMMISSION—REPORTS (Agenda item 101b)
Zhangarayev, Nurmukhamed - A/C.1/78/PV.29
UN. GENERAL ASSEMBLY (78TH SESS. : 2023-2024). 1ST COMMITTEE—GENERAL DEBATE (Agenda item 8)
Baissuanov, Arman - A/C.1/78/PV.5
UN. GENERAL ASSEMBLY (78TH SESS. : 2023-2024). 2ND COMMITTEE—GENERAL DEBATE (Agenda item 8)
Kerimkulov, Bauyrzhan - A/C.2/78/SR.5
UN CONFERENCES (Agenda item 13)
Rakhmetullin, Akan - A/78/PV.48
WOMEN'S ADVANCEMENT (Agenda item 25a)
Gazizulina, Zhanna - A/C.3/78/SR.9
WOMEN'S ADVANCEMENT—CONFERENCES (Agenda item 25b)
Gazizulina, Zhanna - A/C.3/78/SR.9
YOUTH (Agenda item 24b)
Bakytbekkyzy, Anel - A/C.3/78/SR.2

Kazakhstan. President

UN. GENERAL ASSEMBLY (78TH SESS. : 2023-2024)—GENERAL DEBATE (Agenda item 8)
Tokayev, Kassym-Jomart - A/78/PV.5
UN. GENERAL ASSEMBLY (78TH SESS. : 2023-2024)—SPECIAL STATEMENTS
Tokayev, Kassym-Jomart - A/78/PV.5

Kea Consulting (Organization)

FRENCH POLYNESIA QUESTION (Agenda item 58)
Chong, Mickaël - A/C.4/78/SR.3

Kenya

BIOLOGICAL DIVERSITY—TREATIES (Agenda item 18f)
Kenga, Emmanuel Kingi - A/C.2/78/SR.13
CLIMATE (Agenda item 18d)
Kenga, Emmanuel Kingi - A/C.2/78/SR.13
CRIMES AGAINST HUMANITY (Agenda item 80)
Nyakoe, Catherine Nyaboke - A/C.6/78/SR.11; A/C.6/78/SR.43; A/C.6/78/SR.44; A/C.6/78/SR.47
CUBA—UNITED STATES (Agenda item 38)
Kinyungu, Njambi - A/78/PV.24
DEVELOPMENT FINANCE (Agenda item 16b)
Nzumbu, Christine - A/C.2/78/SR.9
DISASTER PREVENTION (Agenda item 18c)
Kenga, Emmanuel Kingi - A/C.2/78/SR.13
DISASTER VICTIMS (Agenda item 86)
Nyakoe, Catherine Nyaboke - A/C.6/78/SR.6
ECONOMIC COOPERATION AMONG DEVELOPING COUNTRIES (Agenda item 22b)
Abbas, Swabri Ali - A/C.2/78/SR.18
EXTERNAL DEBT (Agenda item 16c)
Nzumbu, Christine - A/C.2/78/SR.9
FOOD SECURITY (Agenda item 23a)
Nzumbu, Christine - A/C.2/78/SR.16
INFORMATION—INTERNATIONAL SECURITY (Agenda item 94)
Muigai, Stephanie Ngonyo - A/C.1/78/PV.20
INTERNATIONAL CRIMINAL COURT—REPORTS (Agenda item 74)
Waweru, James Ndiragu - A/78/PV.21
INTERNATIONAL JURISDICTION (Agenda item 84)
Nyakoe, Catherine Nyaboke - A/C.6/78/SR.13
INTERNATIONAL LAW—TRAINING PROGRAMMES (Agenda item 78)
Nyakoe, Catherine Nyaboke - A/C.6/78/SR.22
NUCLEAR DISARMAMENT (Agenda item 99b)
Ndung'u, Gideon Kinuthia - A/C.1/78/PV.12
OPERATIONAL ACTIVITIES—UN SYSTEM (Agenda item 22a)
Abbas, Swabri Ali - A/C.2/78/SR.18
PEACEBUILDING (Agenda item 61)
Kiboino, Michael Kapkiai - A/78/PV.100
PEACEKEEPING OPERATIONS (Agenda item 51)
Kiboino, Michael Kapkiai - A/C.4/78/SR.20
PEACEKEEPING OPERATIONS—CRIMINAL LIABILITY (Agenda item 76)
Ngungu, Edith Kaki - A/C.6/78/SR.9
POVERTY—INTERNATIONAL DECADES (Agenda item 21a)
Nzumbu, Christine - A/C.2/78/SR.16
RACIAL DISCRIMINATION—ELIMINATION (Agenda item 69a)
Kinyungu, Njambi - A/C.3/78/SR.40

Kenya (continued)

RACIAL DISCRIMINATION—PROGRAMMES OF ACTION (Agenda item 69b)
Kinyungu, Njambi - A/C.3/78/SR.40
RIGHT TO EDUCATION (Agenda item 71b)
Kariuki, Kamau - A/C.3/78/SR.27
RULE OF LAW (Agenda item 83)
Nyakoe, Catherine Nyaboke - A/C.6/78/SR.18
RURAL POVERTY (Agenda item 21b)
Nzumbu, Christine - A/C.2/78/SR.16
SUSTAINABLE ENERGY (Agenda item 18h)
Kenga, Emmanuel Kingi - A/C.2/78/SR.13
TAXATION (Agenda item 16h)
Nzumbu, Christine - A/C.2/78/SR.9
TERRORISM (Agenda item 109)
Kiboino, Michael Kapkiai - A/C.6/78/SR.4
UKRAINE—POLITICAL CONDITIONS (Agenda item 62)
Kimani, Martin - A/78/PV.57
UN—BUDGET (2024) (Agenda item 134)
Kinyungu, Njambi - A/C.5/78/SR.5; A/C.5/78/SR.11
UN—PROGRAMME PLANNING (Agenda item 135)
Kinyungu, Njambi - A/C.5/78/SR.5
UN. GENERAL ASSEMBLY (78TH SESS. : 2023-2024). 1ST COMMITTEE—GENERAL DEBATE (Agenda item 8)
Kiboino, Michael Kapkiai - A/C.1/78/PV.8
UN. GENERAL ASSEMBLY (78TH SESS. : 2023-2024). 2ND COMMITTEE—GENERAL DEBATE (Agenda item 8)
Onyoni-Mogaka, Catherine Bonareri - A/C.2/78/SR.4
UN. INTERNATIONAL LAW COMMISSION—REPORTS (Agenda item 79)
Waweru, James Ndiragu - A/C.6/78/SR.33
UN. PEACEBUILDING COMMISSION—REPORTS (Agenda item 27)
Kiboino, Michael Kapkiai - A/78/PV.100
UN. PEACEBUILDING FUND—REPORTS (Agenda item 111)
Kiboino, Michael Kapkiai - A/78/PV.100
UN. SECURITY COUNCIL—MEMBERSHIP (Agenda item 121)
Kiboino, Michael Kapkiai - A/78/PV.36
VETO (Agenda item 63)
Kiboino, Michael Kapkiai - A/78/PV.3; A/78/PV.52
Kimani, Martin - A/78/PV.60; A/78/PV.69; A/78/PV.70; A/78/PV.75
WOMEN'S ADVANCEMENT (Agenda item 25a)
Onyoni-Mogaka, Catherine Bonareri - A/C.3/78/SR.8
WOMEN'S ADVANCEMENT—CONFERENCES (Agenda item 25b)
Onyoni-Mogaka, Catherine Bonareri - A/C.3/78/SR.8

Kenya. President

UN. GENERAL ASSEMBLY (78TH SESS. : 2023-2024)—GENERAL DEBATE (Agenda item 8)
Ruto, William Samoei - A/78/PV.8
UN. GENERAL ASSEMBLY (78TH SESS. : 2023-2024)—SPECIAL STATEMENTS
Ruto, William Samoei - A/78/PV.8

Kiribati

DECOLONIZATION (Agenda item 58)
Tito, Teburoro - A/C.4/78/SR.8
DISARMAMENT—GENERAL AND COMPLETE (Agenda item 99)
Ciobanu, Christian Niculae - A/C.1/78/PV.13
Tito, Teburoro - A/78/PV.106; A/C.1/78/PV.25
NUCLEAR DISARMAMENT (Agenda item 99b)
Ciobanu, Christian Niculae - A/C.1/78/PV.13
NUCLEAR WEAPONS—HUMANITARIAN CONSEQUENCES (Agenda item 99bb)
Ciobanu, Christian Niculae - A/C.1/78/PV.13
RESPONSIBILITY TO PROTECT (Agenda item 129)
Tito, Teburoro - A/78/PV.97
UN. GENERAL ASSEMBLY (78TH SESS. : 2023-2024). 1ST COMMITTEE—GENERAL DEBATE (Agenda item 8)
Tito, Teburoro - A/C.1/78/PV.8
WESTERN SAHARA QUESTION (Agenda item 58)
Tito, Teburoro - A/C.4/78/SR.8

Kiribati. President

UN. GENERAL ASSEMBLY (78TH SESS. : 2023-2024)—GENERAL DEBATE (Agenda item 8)
Maamau, Taneti - A/78/PV.8
UN. GENERAL ASSEMBLY (78TH SESS. : 2023-2024)—SPECIAL STATEMENTS
Maamau, Taneti - A/78/PV.8

Kuwait

AGEING PERSONS (Agenda item 24b)
Al Mulla, Wafiqah - A/C.3/78/SR.3
AL-SABAH, NAWAF AL-AHMAD AL-JABER (KUWAIT. AMIR)—TRIBUTES
Albanai, Tareq M.A.M. - A/78/PV.50(Resumption1)
CRIMES AGAINST HUMANITY (Agenda item 80)
Alenezi, Faisal G. - A/C.6/78/SR.11
DECOLONIZATION (Agenda item 58)
Alenezi, Faisal G. - A/C.4/78/SR.8
DISARMAMENT—GENERAL AND COMPLETE (Agenda item 99)
Alsharhan, Reem - A/C.1/78/PV.24
EMERGENCY ASSISTANCE (Agenda item 72a)
Alajmi, Fahad M. - A/78/PV.47

Kuwait (continued)

FAMILY (Agenda item 24b)
Al Mulla, Wafiqah - A/C.3/78/SR.3
FOOD SECURITY (Agenda item 23a)
Almezyad, Fatma - A/C.2/78/SR.17
HEALTH (Agenda item 125)
Albanai, Tareq M.A.M. - A/78/PV.41
HUMAN RIGHTS—TERRITORIES OCCUPIED BY ISRAEL (Agenda item 71c)
Al Mulla, Wafiqah - A/C.3/78/SR.35
HUMAN RIGHTS ADVANCEMENT (Agenda item 71b)
Al-Dikaan, Ahmed Khaled Ghanem - A/C.3/78/SR.26
IAEA—REPORTS (Agenda item 89)
Alsaeedi, Abdulaziz - A/78/PV.29
INFORMATION TECHNOLOGY—DEVELOPMENT (Agenda item 15)
Alkhuraibet, Ali - A/C.2/78/SR.10
LAW OF THE SEA (Agenda item 75a)
Alajmi, Fahad M. - A/78/PV.44
MARINE ECOSYSTEMS—BIOLOGICAL DIVERSITY (Agenda item 75c)
Alajmi, Fahad M. - A/78/PV.44
MIDDLE EAST—NUCLEAR-WEAPON-FREE ZONES (Agenda item 95)
Basheer, Manar - A/C.1/78/PV.23
MULTILATERALISM—DISARMAMENT (Agenda item 99r)
Al-Murad, Mariam - A/C.1/78/PV.21
PALESTINE QUESTION (Agenda item 35)
Alenezi, Faisal G. - A/78/PV.40
PALESTINIANS—ASSISTANCE (Agenda item 72b)
Alajmi, Fahad M. - A/78/PV.47
PEACE (Agenda item 14)
Albanai, Tareq M.A.M. - A/78/PV.62
PERSONS WITH DISABILITIES—HUMAN RIGHTS (Agenda item 71a)
Al Mulla, Wafiqah - A/C.3/78/SR.51
POVERTY—INTERNATIONAL DECADES (Agenda item 21a)
Almezyad, Fatma - A/C.2/78/SR.17
RACIAL DISCRIMINATION—ELIMINATION (Agenda item 69a)
Al Munaifi, Shahad - A/C.3/78/SR.41
RACIAL DISCRIMINATION—PROGRAMMES OF ACTION (Agenda item 69b)
Al Munaifi, Shahad - A/C.3/78/SR.41
RIGHTS OF THE CHILD (Agenda item 67)
Al Munaifi, Shahad - A/C.3/78/SR.12
RULE OF LAW (Agenda item 83)
Alharbi, Saoud Abdullah - A/C.6/78/SR.19
RURAL POVERTY (Agenda item 21b)
Almezyad, Fatma - A/C.2/78/SR.17
SELF-DETERMINATION OF PEOPLES (Agenda item 70)
Al Munaifi, Shahad - A/C.3/78/SR.41
SOCIAL DEVELOPMENT (Agenda item 24)
Al Mulla, Wafiqah - A/C.3/78/SR.3

Kuwait (continued)

STRADDLING FISH STOCKS (Agenda item 75b)
Alajmi, Fahad M. - A/78/PV.44
SUSTAINABLE DEVELOPMENT (Agenda item 18)
Alkhuraibet, Ali - A/C.2/78/SR.13
TERRITORIES OCCUPIED BY ISRAEL—HUMAN RIGHTS (Agenda item 50)
Alajmi, Fahad M. - A/C.4/78/SR.25
TERRITORIES OCCUPIED BY ISRAEL—NATURAL RESOURCES (Agenda item 59)
Almezyad, Fatma - A/C.2/78/SR.19
UN—BUDGET (2024) (Agenda item 134)
Alenezi, Faisal G. - A/C.5/78/SR.3
UN. ECONOMIC AND SOCIAL COUNCIL—REPORTS (Agenda item 9)
Al-Kandari, Ismail Abdullah - A/78/PV.33
UN. GENERAL ASSEMBLY (78TH SESS. : 2023-2024). 1ST COMMITTEE—GENERAL DEBATE (Agenda item 8)
Alajmi, Fahad M. - A/C.1/78/PV.9
UN. GENERAL ASSEMBLY (78TH SESS. : 2023-2024). 2ND COMMITTEE—GENERAL DEBATE (Agenda item 8)
Aldehani, Bader A. - A/C.2/78/SR.5
UN. HUMAN RIGHTS COUNCIL—REPORTS (Agenda item 66)
AlSabah, Khaled S. - A/78/PV.23
UN COMMISSION ON INTERNATIONAL TRADE LAW—REPORTS (Agenda item 77)
Alenezi, Faisal G. - A/C.6/78/SR.14
UN HIGH COMMISSIONER FOR REFUGEES—REPORTS (Agenda item 60)
Al-Dikaan, Ahmed Khaled Ghanem - A/C.3/78/SR.45
UNRWA—ACTIVITIES (Agenda item 49)
Abushaibah, Shayea - A/C.4/78/SR.22
WESTERN SAHARA QUESTION (Agenda item 58)
Alenezi, Faisal G. - A/C.4/78/SR.8
WOMEN'S ADVANCEMENT (Agenda item 25a)
Al Mulla, Wafiqah - A/C.3/78/SR.7; A/C.3/78/SR.8
WOMEN'S ADVANCEMENT—CONFERENCES (Agenda item 25b)
Al Mulla, Wafiqah - A/C.3/78/SR.7; A/C.3/78/SR.8

Kuwait. Prime Minister

UN. GENERAL ASSEMBLY (78TH SESS. : 2023-2024)—GENERAL DEBATE (Agenda item 8)
Al-Sabah, Ahmad Nawaf Al-Ahmad - A/78/PV.9
UN. GENERAL ASSEMBLY (78TH SESS. : 2023-2024)—SPECIAL STATEMENTS
Al-Sabah, Ahmad Nawaf Al-Ahmad - A/78/PV.9

Kyrgyzstan

PERSONS WITH DISABILITIES (Agenda item 24b)
Kasymalieva, Aida - A/C.3/78/SR.3
SOCIAL CONDITIONS (Agenda item 24b)
Kasymalieva, Aida - A/C.3/78/SR.3
SOCIAL DEVELOPMENT (Agenda item 24)
Kasymalieva, Aida - A/C.3/78/SR.3
UN. GENERAL ASSEMBLY (78TH SESS. : 2023-2024). 1ST COMMITTEE—GENERAL DEBATE (Agenda item 8)
Utebaev, Meder - A/C.1/78/PV.9
UN. GENERAL ASSEMBLY (78TH SESS. : 2023-2024). 2ND COMMITTEE—GENERAL DEBATE (Agenda item 8)
Kasymalieva, Aida - A/C.2/78/SR.6
WOMEN'S ADVANCEMENT (Agenda item 25a)
Kasymalieva, Aida - A/C.3/78/SR.9
WOMEN'S ADVANCEMENT—CONFERENCES (Agenda item 25b)
Kasymalieva, Aida - A/C.3/78/SR.9

Kyrgyzstan. President

UN. GENERAL ASSEMBLY (78TH SESS. : 2023-2024)—GENERAL DEBATE (Agenda item 8)
Zhaparov, Sadyr - A/78/PV.5
UN. GENERAL ASSEMBLY (78TH SESS. : 2023-2024)—SPECIAL STATEMENTS
Zhaparov, Sadyr - A/78/PV.5

L.69 Group

UN. SECURITY COUNCIL—MEMBERSHIP (Agenda item 121)
King, Inga Rhonda (Saint Vincent and the Grenadines) - A/78/PV.104
Miguel, Nedra P. (Saint Vincent and the Grenadines) - A/78/PV.34

Lao People's Democratic Republic

CLUSTER MUNITIONS (Agenda item 99dd)
Souliyong, So Inxay - A/C.1/78/PV.19
CUBA—UNITED STATES (Agenda item 38)
Vongnorkeo, Anouparb - A/78/PV.24
ECONOMIC SANCTIONS—INTERNATIONAL RELATIONS (Agenda item 28)
Vongnorkeo, Anouparb - A/78/PV.90
HUMAN RIGHTS—DEMOCRATIC PEOPLE'S REPUBLIC OF KOREA (Agenda item 71c)
Sengdara, Xayfhong - A/C.3/78/SR.33
HUMAN RIGHTS—INTERNATIONAL INSTRUMENTS (Agenda item 71a)
Sengdara, Xayfhong - A/C.3/78/SR.25
HUMAN RIGHTS ADVANCEMENT (Agenda item 71b)
Sengdara, Xayfhong - A/C.3/78/SR.25
LANDMINES—TREATIES (Agenda item 99m)
Souliyong, So Inxay - A/C.1/78/PV.19

Lao People's Democratic Republic (continued)

MIGRANT WORKERS (Agenda item 71a)
Meunluang, Veomanee - A/C.3/78/SR.23
MINE CLEARANCE (Agenda item 46)
Souliyong, So Inxay - A/C.4/78/SR.10
NUCLEAR DISARMAMENT (Agenda item 99b)
Vongnorkeo, Anouparb - A/C.1/78/PV.13
NUCLEAR NON-PROLIFERATION—INTERNATIONAL OBLIGATIONS (Agenda item 99w)
Vongnorkeo, Anouparb - A/C.1/78/PV.13
NUCLEAR WEAPON TESTS—TREATIES (Agenda item 105)
Vongnorkeo, Anouparb - A/C.1/78/PV.13
OPERATIONAL ACTIVITIES—UN SYSTEM (Agenda item 22a)
Thaphanya, Natthakith - A/C.2/78/SR.18
PALESTINE QUESTION (Agenda item 35)
Vongnorkeo, Anouparb - A/78/PV.40
PERSONS WITH DISABILITIES (Agenda item 24b)
Vongnorkeo, Anouparb - A/C.3/78/SR.4
REGIONAL DISARMAMENT (Agenda item 99f)
Vongnorkeo, Anouparb - A/C.1/78/PV.13
RELIGIOUS INTOLERANCE (Agenda item 71b)
Meunluang, Veomanee - A/C.3/78/SR.38
RIGHTS OF THE CHILD (Agenda item 67)
Meunluang, Veomanee - A/C.3/78/SR.13
RULE OF LAW (Agenda item 83)
Vannasin, Soudchai - A/C.6/78/SR.18
SCIENCE AND TECHNOLOGY—DEVELOPMENT (Agenda item 19a)
Xaiyavong, Thanouphet - A/C.2/78/SR.11
SMALL ARMS—ILLICIT TRAFFIC (Agenda item 99p)
Souliyong, So Inxay - A/C.1/78/PV.19
SMALL ARMS—ILLICIT TRAFFIC—ASSISTANCE (Agenda item 99n)
Souliyong, So Inxay - A/C.1/78/PV.19
SOCIAL DEVELOPMENT (Agenda item 24)
Vongnorkeo, Anouparb - A/C.3/78/SR.4
SOUTH-EAST ASIA—NUCLEAR-WEAPON-FREE ZONES (Agenda item 99y)
Vongnorkeo, Anouparb - A/C.1/78/PV.13
SUSTAINABLE DEVELOPMENT (Agenda item 18)
Xaiyavong, Thanouphet - A/C.2/78/SR.15
TERRORISM (Agenda item 109)
Seneduangdeth, Vilayluck - A/C.6/78/SR.4
UN. GENERAL ASSEMBLY (78TH SESS. : 2023-2024). 1ST COMMITTEE—GENERAL DEBATE (Agenda item 8)
Vongnorkeo, Anouparb - A/C.1/78/PV.6
UN. GENERAL ASSEMBLY (78TH SESS. : 2023-2024). 2ND COMMITTEE—GENERAL DEBATE (Agenda item 8)
Vongnorkeo, Anouparb - A/C.2/78/SR.6

Lao People's Democratic Republic (continued)

UN. SECURITY COUNCIL—MEMBERSHIP (Agenda item 121)
Khousakoun, Phetvanxay - A/78/PV.36
WOMEN'S ADVANCEMENT (Agenda item 25a)
Seneduangdeth, Vilayluck - A/C.3/78/SR.9
WOMEN'S ADVANCEMENT—CONFERENCES (Agenda item 25b)
Seneduangdeth, Vilayluck - A/C.3/78/SR.9

Lao People's Democratic Republic. Deputy Prime Minister

UN. GENERAL ASSEMBLY (78TH SESS. : 2023-2024)—GENERAL DEBATE (Agenda item 8)
Kommasith, Saleumxay - A/78/PV.12
UN. GENERAL ASSEMBLY (78TH SESS. : 2023-2024)—SPECIAL STATEMENTS
Kommasith, Saleumxay - A/78/PV.12

Latvia

AFRICA—DEVELOPMENT (Agenda item 65b)
Ilgis, Olegs - A/78/PV.18
AFRICA—SUSTAINABLE DEVELOPMENT—PARTNERSHIP (Agenda item 65a)
Ilgis, Olegs - A/78/PV.18
ARMED CONFLICTS PREVENTION (Agenda item 31a)
Pavļuta-Deslandes, Sanita - A/78/PV.72
CRIME PREVENTION (Agenda item 107)
Ilgis, Olegs - A/C.3/78/SR.51
CRIMES AGAINST HUMANITY (Agenda item 80)
Cupika-Mavrina, Elvira - A/C.6/78/SR.9; A/C.6/78/SR.38; A/C.6/78/SR.39; A/C.6/78/SR.41
DISARMAMENT—GENERAL AND COMPLETE (Agenda item 99)
Filipsons, Peteris - A/C.1/78/PV.30
HUMAN RIGHTS ADVANCEMENT (Agenda item 71b)
Pavļuta-Deslandes, Sanita - A/C.3/78/SR.18
INFORMATION (Agenda item 53)
Pavļuta-Deslandes, Sanita - A/C.4/78/SR.13
INTERNATIONAL RESIDUAL MECHANISM FOR CRIMINAL TRIBUNALS (Agenda item 126)
Pavļuta-Deslandes, Sanita - A/78/PV.19
RESPONSIBILITY TO PROTECT (Agenda item 129)
Pavļuta-Deslandes, Sanita - A/78/PV.96
RIGHT OF ASSEMBLY (Agenda item 71b)
Pavļuta-Deslandes, Sanita - A/C.3/78/SR.19
RULE OF LAW (Agenda item 83)
Ilgis, Olegs - A/C.6/78/SR.15
TERRORISM (Agenda item 109)
Cupika-Mavrina, Elvira - A/C.6/78/SR.1
UKRAINE—POLITICAL CONDITIONS (Agenda item 62)
Brusbārdis, Reinis - A/78/PV.56

Latvia (continued)

UN. GENERAL ASSEMBLY (78TH SESS. : 2023-2024)—OFFICERS (Agenda item 5)
Pavļuta-Deslandes, Sanita - A/C.4/78/SR.28
UN. GENERAL ASSEMBLY (78TH SESS. : 2023-2024). 1ST COMMITTEE—GENERAL DEBATE (Agenda item 8)
Pavļuta-Deslandes, Sanita - A/C.1/78/PV.3
UN. HUMAN RIGHTS COUNCIL—REPORTS (Agenda item 66)
Burbergs, Māris - A/C.3/78/SR.46
UN. INTERNATIONAL LAW COMMISSION—REPORTS (Agenda item 79)
Cupika-Mavrina, Elvira - A/C.6/78/SR.28
WOMEN'S ADVANCEMENT (Agenda item 25a)
Pavļuta-Deslandes, Sanita - A/C.3/78/SR.7
WOMEN'S ADVANCEMENT—CONFERENCES (Agenda item 25b)
Pavļuta-Deslandes, Sanita - A/C.3/78/SR.7

Latvia. President

UN. GENERAL ASSEMBLY (78TH SESS. : 2023-2024)—GENERAL DEBATE (Agenda item 8)
Rinkevics, Edgars - A/78/PV.6
UN. GENERAL ASSEMBLY (78TH SESS. : 2023-2024)—SPECIAL STATEMENTS
Rinkevics, Edgars - A/78/PV.6

League of Arab States

INFORMATION (Agenda item 53)
Elardja Flitti, Nasria - A/C.4/78/SR.14
SELF-DETERMINATION OF PEOPLES (Agenda item 70)
Abdallah, Amina Mohamed - A/C.3/78/SR.43
TERRITORIES OCCUPIED BY ISRAEL—HUMAN RIGHTS (Agenda item 50)
Elardja Flitti, Nasria - A/C.4/78/SR.25
TERRITORIES OCCUPIED BY ISRAEL—NATURAL RESOURCES (Agenda item 59)
Al-Amri, Islam Abdullah Hassan - A/C.2/78/SR.20
UN. GENERAL ASSEMBLY (78TH SESS. : 2023-2024). 1ST COMMITTEE—GENERAL DEBATE (Agenda item 8)
Abdelaziz, Maged Abdelfattah - A/C.1/78/PV.9
UNRWA—ACTIVITIES (Agenda item 49)
Elardja Flitti, Nasria - A/C.4/78/SR.23
VETO (Agenda item 63)
Abdelaziz, Maged Abdelfattah - A/78/PV.61

Lebanon

CRIMES AGAINST HUMANITY (Agenda item 80)
Hitti, Youssef - A/C.6/78/SR.11; A/C.6/78/SR.39; A/C.6/78/SR.41; A/C.6/78/SR.43; A/C.6/78/SR.44
DISASTER VICTIMS (Agenda item 86)
Hitti, Youssef - A/C.6/78/SR.6

Lebanon (continued)

DISPLACED PERSONS (Agenda item 71b)
Zoghbi, Rawa - A/C.3/78/SR.32
HUMAN RIGHTS—INTERNATIONAL INSTRUMENTS (Agenda item 71a)
Hachem, Hadi - A/C.3/78/SR.24
HUMAN RIGHTS—TERRITORIES OCCUPIED BY ISRAEL (Agenda item 71c)
Hachem, Hadi - A/C.3/78/SR.24
Zoghbi, Rawa - A/C.3/78/SR.35
HUMAN RIGHTS ADVANCEMENT (Agenda item 71b)
Zoghbi, Rawa - A/C.3/78/SR.52
INTERNATIONAL LAW—TRAINING PROGRAMMES (Agenda item 78)
Hitti, Youssef - A/C.6/78/SR.22
MIDDLE EAST SITUATION (Agenda item 34)
Hachem, Hadi - A/78/PV.40
PEACEKEEPING OPERATIONS (Agenda item 51)
Hachem, Hadi - A/C.4/78/SR.20
Jardali, Mohammad Ali - A/C.4/78/SR.20
RIGHTS OF THE CHILD (Agenda item 67)
Zoghbi, Rawa - A/C.3/78/SR.11
RULE OF LAW (Agenda item 83)
Hitti, Youssef - A/C.6/78/SR.19
SUSTAINABLE DEVELOPMENT (Agenda item 18)
Hachem, Hadi - A/C.2/78/SR.21
TERRITORIES OCCUPIED BY ISRAEL—HUMAN RIGHTS (Agenda item 50)
Jardali, Mohammad Ali - A/C.4/78/SR.25
TERRORISM (Agenda item 109)
Hitti, Youssef - A/C.6/78/SR.2
UN. GENERAL ASSEMBLY—WORK PROGRAMME (Agenda item 120)
Zoghbi, Rawa - A/C.3/78/SR.56
UN. GENERAL ASSEMBLY (78TH SESS. : 2023-2024). 1ST COMMITTEE—GENERAL DEBATE (Agenda item 8)
Hachem, Hadi - A/C.1/78/PV.6
UN. GENERAL ASSEMBLY (78TH SESS. : 2023-2024). 2ND COMMITTEE—GENERAL DEBATE (Agenda item 8)
Zoghbi, Rawa - A/C.2/78/SR.5
UN. INTERNATIONAL COURT OF JUSTICE—REPORTS (Agenda item 73)
Hitti, Youssef - A/78/PV.27; A/C.6/78/SR.26
UN. INTERNATIONAL LAW COMMISSION—REPORTS (Agenda item 79)
Hitti, Youssef - A/C.6/78/SR.28; A/C.6/78/SR.37
UN HIGH COMMISSIONER FOR REFUGEES—REPORTS (Agenda item 60)
Hachem, Hadi - A/C.3/78/SR.44
UNRWA—ACTIVITIES (Agenda item 49)
Jardali, Mohammad Ali - A/C.4/78/SR.22; A/C.4/78/SR.23
VETO (Agenda item 63)
Hachem, Hadi - A/78/PV.71; A/78/PV.75

Lebanon (continued)

WOMEN'S ADVANCEMENT (Agenda item 25a)
Zoghbi, Rawa - A/C.3/78/SR.8
WOMEN'S ADVANCEMENT—CONFERENCES (Agenda item 25b)
Zoghbi, Rawa - A/C.3/78/SR.8

Lebanon. Prime Minister

UN. GENERAL ASSEMBLY (78TH SESS. : 2023-2024)—GENERAL DEBATE (Agenda item 8)
Najib Azmi Mikati, Mohammad - A/78/PV.7
UN. GENERAL ASSEMBLY (78TH SESS. : 2023-2024)—SPECIAL STATEMENTS
Najib Azmi Mikati, Mohammad - A/78/PV.7

Lesotho

ARMS TRANSFERS—TREATIES (Agenda item 99x)
Nena, Matete - A/C.1/78/PV.19
DECOLONIZATION (Agenda item 58)
Nena, Matete - A/C.4/78/SR.8
DISARMAMENT—GENERAL AND COMPLETE (Agenda item 99)
Nena, Matete - A/C.1/78/PV.19
DISPLACED PERSONS (Agenda item 71b)
Nena, Matete - A/C.3/78/SR.32
EXTERNAL DEBT—HUMAN RIGHTS (Agenda item 71b)
Nena, Matete - A/C.3/78/SR.32
FOOD SECURITY (Agenda item 23a)
Nena, Matete - A/C.2/78/SR.17
HUMAN RIGHTS (Agenda item 71)
Lelisa, Nthabiseng Matlhohonolofatso - A/C.3/78/SR.28
HUMAN RIGHTS—INTERNATIONAL INSTRUMENTS (Agenda item 71a)
Lelisa, Nthabiseng Matlhohonolofatso - A/C.3/78/SR.28
JUDICIAL INDEPENDENCE (Agenda item 71b)
Lelisa, Nthabiseng Matlhohonolofatso - A/C.3/78/SR.31
LANDLOCKED DEVELOPING COUNTRIES—CONFERENCES (Agenda item 20b)
Monyane, Nkopane Raseeng - A/C.2/78/SR.7
LEAST DEVELOPED COUNTRIES—CONFERENCES (Agenda item 20a)
Monyane, Nkopane Raseeng - A/C.2/78/SR.7
PERSONS WITH DISABILITIES—HUMAN RIGHTS (Agenda item 71a)
Lelisa, Nthabiseng Matlhohonolofatso - A/C.3/78/SR.38
POVERTY—INTERNATIONAL DECADES (Agenda item 21a)
Nena, Matete - A/C.2/78/SR.17

Lesotho (continued)

RACIAL DISCRIMINATION—ELIMINATION (Agenda item 69a)
Lelisa, Nthabiseng Matlhohonolofatso - A/C.3/78/SR.40
RACIAL DISCRIMINATION—PROGRAMMES OF ACTION (Agenda item 69b)
Lelisa, Nthabiseng Matlhohonolofatso - A/C.3/78/SR.40
RIGHT TO FOOD (Agenda item 71b)
Nena, Matete - A/C.3/78/SR.30
RIGHT TO HEALTH (Agenda item 71b)
Lelisa, Nthabiseng Matlhohonolofatso - A/C.3/78/SR.39
RIGHTS OF THE CHILD (Agenda item 67)
Nena, Matete - A/C.3/78/SR.13
RURAL POVERTY (Agenda item 21b)
Nena, Matete - A/C.2/78/SR.17
SMALL ARMS—ILLICIT TRAFFIC (Agenda item 99p)
Nena, Matete - A/C.1/78/PV.19
SMALL ARMS—ILLICIT TRAFFIC—ASSISTANCE (Agenda item 99n)
Nena, Matete - A/C.1/78/PV.19
SOLIDARITY (Agenda item 71b)
Nena, Matete - A/C.3/78/SR.32
UN—BUDGET (2024) (Agenda item 134)
Nena, Matete - A/C.5/78/SR.5
UN—PROGRAMME PLANNING (Agenda item 135)
Nena, Matete - A/C.5/78/SR.5
UN. GENERAL ASSEMBLY (78TH SESS. : 2023-2024). 1ST COMMITTEE—GENERAL DEBATE (Agenda item 8)
Nena, Matete - A/C.1/78/PV.6
UN. GENERAL ASSEMBLY (78TH SESS. : 2023-2024). 2ND COMMITTEE—GENERAL DEBATE (Agenda item 8)
Nena, Matete - A/C.2/78/SR.3
WESTERN SAHARA QUESTION (Agenda item 58)
Nena, Matete - A/C.4/78/SR.8
WOMEN'S ADVANCEMENT (Agenda item 25a)
Nena, Matete - A/C.3/78/SR.10
WOMEN'S ADVANCEMENT—CONFERENCES (Agenda item 25b)
Nena, Matete - A/C.3/78/SR.10

Lesotho. Prime Minister

UN. GENERAL ASSEMBLY (78TH SESS. : 2023-2024)—GENERAL DEBATE (Agenda item 8)
Matekane, Ntsokoane Samuel - A/78/PV.11
UN. GENERAL ASSEMBLY (78TH SESS. : 2023-2024)—SPECIAL STATEMENTS
Matekane, Ntsokoane Samuel - A/78/PV.11

LGBTI Core Group

SEXUAL ORIENTATION (Agenda item 71b)
Maes, Olivier (Luxembourg) - A/C.3/78/SR.24
Squeff, María del Carmen (Argentina) - A/C.3/78/SR.39

Liberia

ELECTION VERIFICATION—UN (Agenda item 71b)
Gbai, Tangbae Kortemah - A/C.3/78/SR.50
WESTERN SAHARA QUESTION (Agenda item 58)
Fyneah, Sarah Safyn - A/C.4/78/SR.8

Liberia. President

UN. GENERAL ASSEMBLY (78TH SESS. : 2023-2024)—GENERAL DEBATE (Agenda item 8)
Weah, George Manneh - A/78/PV.7
UN. GENERAL ASSEMBLY (78TH SESS. : 2023-2024)—SPECIAL STATEMENTS
Weah, George Manneh - A/78/PV.7

Libya

AFRICA—DEVELOPMENT (Agenda item 65b)
Suweed, Mohamed - A/78/PV.18
AFRICA—SUSTAINABLE DEVELOPMENT—PARTNERSHIP (Agenda item 65a)
Suweed, Mohamed - A/78/PV.18
CRIMES AGAINST HUMANITY (Agenda item 80)
Shibl, Maruan Naserdien Ali - A/C.6/78/SR.11
ELECTION VERIFICATION—UN (Agenda item 71b)
Hamed, Ashraf A.O. - A/C.3/78/SR.50
HUMAN RIGHTS—TERRITORIES OCCUPIED BY ISRAEL (Agenda item 71c)
Hamed, Ashraf A.O. - A/C.3/78/SR.35
PALESTINE QUESTION (Agenda item 35)
Habib, Hanan M.M. - A/78/PV.40
RIGHTS OF THE CHILD (Agenda item 67)
Hamed, Ashraf A.O. - A/C.3/78/SR.55
RURAL WOMEN (Agenda item 25a)
Hamed, Ashraf A.O. - A/C.3/78/SR.49
SPORTS—OLYMPIC GAMES (Agenda item 11)
El-Sonni, Taher M. - A/78/PV.80
TERRITORIES OCCUPIED BY ISRAEL—HUMAN RIGHTS (Agenda item 50)
Hamed, Ashraf A.O. - A/C.4/78/SR.25
TERRITORIES OCCUPIED BY ISRAEL—NATURAL RESOURCES (Agenda item 59)
Ghawar, Samir - A/C.2/78/SR.19
UN. GENERAL ASSEMBLY (78TH SESS. : 2023-2024)—GENERAL DEBATE (Agenda item 8)
Elzuni, Fatalla AF - A/78/PV.7

Libya (continued)

UN. GENERAL ASSEMBLY (78TH SESS. : 2023-2024). 1ST COMMITTEE—GENERAL DEBATE (Agenda item 8)
Ben Zitun, Esam - A/C.1/78/PV.7
UN HIGH COMMISSIONER FOR REFUGEES—REPORTS (Agenda item 60)
Elsonni, Taher M.T. - A/C.3/78/SR.48
WOMEN MIGRANT WORKERS (Agenda item 25a)
Hamed, Ashraf A.O. - A/C.3/78/SR.49
YOUTH (Agenda item 24b)
Hamed, Ashraf A.O. - A/C.3/78/SR.55

Liechtenstein

ARMED CONFLICTS PREVENTION (Agenda item 31a)
Wenaweser, Christian - A/78/PV.72
CLIMATE CHANGE (Agenda item 71b)
Alcaraz Romero De Tejada, Leticia - A/C.3/78/SR.29
CRIMES AGAINST HUMANITY (Agenda item 80)
Hasler, Merhaba - A/C.6/78/SR.9; A/C.6/78/SR.40
ELECTION VERIFICATION—UN (Agenda item 71b)
Oehri, Noah - A/C.3/78/SR.50
ENVIRONMENT (Agenda item 71b)
Oehri, Noah - A/C.3/78/SR.24
HIV/AIDS—DECLARATIONS (Agenda item 10)
Oehri, Noah - A/78/PV.91
HUMAN RIGHTS (Agenda item 71)
Wenaweser, Christian - A/C.3/78/SR.16
HUMAN RIGHTS—AFGHANISTAN (Agenda item 71c)
Oehri, Noah - A/C.3/78/SR.34
HUMAN RIGHTS—BELARUS (Agenda item 71c)
Oehri, Noah - A/C.3/78/SR.37
HUMAN RIGHTS—INTERNATIONAL INSTRUMENTS (Agenda item 71a)
Oehri, Noah - A/C.3/78/SR.24
HUMAN RIGHTS—MYANMAR (Agenda item 71c)
Oehri, Myriam - A/C.3/78/SR.53
Oehri, Noah - A/C.3/78/SR.33
HUMAN RIGHTS—RUSSIAN FEDERATION (Agenda item 71c)
Oehri, Noah - A/C.3/78/SR.37
HUMAN RIGHTS—UKRAINE (Agenda item 71c)
Meidert, Michael Sebastian - A/C.3/78/SR.37
INTERNATIONAL CRIMINAL COURT—REPORTS (Agenda item 74)
Wenaweser, Christian - A/78/PV.22
INTERNATIONAL JURISDICTION (Agenda item 84)
Hasler, Merhaba - A/C.6/78/SR.12

Liechtenstein (continued)

JUDICIAL INDEPENDENCE (Agenda item 71b)
Oehri, Noah - A/C.3/78/SR.31
RACIAL DISCRIMINATION—ELIMINATION (Agenda item 69a)
Oehri, Noah - A/C.3/78/SR.47
RIGHT TO DEVELOPMENT (Agenda item 71b)
Oehri, Noah - A/C.3/78/SR.48
RIGHTS OF THE CHILD (Agenda item 67)
Oehri, Noah - A/C.3/78/SR.11
RULE OF LAW (Agenda item 83)
Oehri, Myriam - A/C.6/78/SR.15
SELF-DETERMINATION OF PEOPLES (Agenda item 70)
Edbrooke, Matthew David - A/C.3/78/SR.40
SLAVERY (Agenda item 71a)
Oehri, Noah - A/C.3/78/SR.21
TAXATION (Agenda item 16h)
Oehri, Noah - A/C.2/78/SR.25
TERRITORIES OCCUPIED BY ISRAEL—HUMAN RIGHTS (Agenda item 50)
Oehri, Myriam - A/C.4/78/SR.26
UKRAINE—POLITICAL CONDITIONS (Agenda item 62)
Oehri, Myriam - A/78/PV.57
UN. GENERAL ASSEMBLY (78TH SESS. : 2023-2024)—GENERAL DEBATE (Agenda item 8)
Hasler, Dominique - A/78/PV.9
UN. GENERAL ASSEMBLY (78TH SESS. : 2023-2024). 1ST COMMITTEE—GENERAL DEBATE (Agenda item 8)
Oehri, Myriam - A/C.1/78/PV.3
UN. HUMAN RIGHTS COUNCIL—REPORTS (Agenda item 66)
Oehri, Myriam - A/78/PV.23
Oehri, Noah - A/C.3/78/SR.51
UN. INTERNATIONAL COURT OF JUSTICE—REPORTS (Agenda item 73)
Oehri, Myriam - A/78/PV.27
UN. INTERNATIONAL LAW COMMISSION—REPORTS (Agenda item 79)
Alavi, Sina - A/C.6/78/SR.23
UN. SECURITY COUNCIL—MEMBERSHIP (Agenda item 121)
Wenaweser, Christian - A/78/PV.34
UN. SECURITY COUNCIL—REPORTS (Agenda item 26)
Wenaweser, Christian - A/78/PV.93
UNRWA—ACTIVITIES (Agenda item 49)
Oehri, Myriam - A/C.4/78/SR.26
VETO (Agenda item 63)
Oehri, Myriam - A/78/PV.51; A/78/PV.66; A/78/PV.75
Wenaweser, Christian - A/78/PV.3; A/78/PV.59; A/78/PV.70
WOMEN'S ADVANCEMENT (Agenda item 25a)
Oehri, Noah - A/C.3/78/SR.8

Liechtenstein (continued)

WOMEN'S ADVANCEMENT—CONFERENCES (Agenda item 25b)
Oehri, Noah - A/C.3/78/SR.8

Ligue Sahara pour la démocratie et les droits de l'homme

WESTERN SAHARA QUESTION (Agenda item 58)
El Baihi, Hammada - A/C.4/78/SR.6

Like-Minded Group of Supporters of Middle-Income Countries

DEVELOPMENT COOPERATION—MIDDLE-INCOME COUNTRIES (Agenda item 19c)
Hamdouni, Meryem (Morocco) - A/C.2/78/SR.10
DEVELOPMENT FINANCE (Agenda item 16b)
Hamdouni, Meryem (Morocco) - A/C.2/78/SR.8
EXTERNAL DEBT (Agenda item 16c)
Hamdouni, Meryem (Morocco) - A/C.2/78/SR.8
UN. GENERAL ASSEMBLY (78TH SESS. : 2023-2024). 2ND COMMITTEE—GENERAL DEBATE (Agenda item 8)
Hilale, Omar (Morocco) - A/C.2/78/SR.2

Lithuania

CRIME PREVENTION (Agenda item 107)
Vest, Dangirutė - A/C.3/78/SR.51
HUMAN RIGHTS—BELARUS (Agenda item 71c)
Bimbaitė, Monika - A/C.3/78/SR.37
IAEA—REPORTS (Agenda item 89)
Rosinas, Robertas - A/78/PV.30
INTERNATIONAL JURISDICTION (Agenda item 84)
Paulauskas, Rytis - A/C.6/78/SR.12
INTERNATIONAL TRADE (Agenda item 16a)
Malinauskas, Andrius - A/C.2/78/SR.24
NUCLEAR DISARMAMENT (Agenda item 99b)
Geleževičienė, Giedrė - A/C.1/78/PV.13
ORGANIZATION FOR DEMOCRACY AND ECONOMIC DEVELOPMENT - GUAM (Agenda item 32)
Paulauskas, Rytis - A/78/PV.85
RELIGIOUS INTOLERANCE (Agenda item 71b)
Bimbaitė, Monika - A/C.3/78/SR.38
SUSTAINABLE DEVELOPMENT (Agenda item 18)
Paulauskas, Rytis - A/C.2/78/SR.15; A/C.2/78/SR.22
UKRAINE—POLITICAL CONDITIONS (Agenda item 62)
Landsbergis, Gabrielius - A/78/PV.56

Lithuania (continued)

UN. GENERAL ASSEMBLY (78TH SESS. : 2023-2024). 1ST COMMITTEE—GENERAL DEBATE (Agenda item 8)
Jievaltas, Arūnas - A/C.1/78/PV.5
UN. INTERNATIONAL COURT OF JUSTICE—REPORTS (Agenda item 73)
Paulauskas, Rytis - A/78/PV.27
VETO (Agenda item 63)
Paulauskas, Rytis - A/78/PV.68

Lithuania. President

UN. GENERAL ASSEMBLY (78TH SESS. : 2023-2024)—GENERAL DEBATE (Agenda item 8)
Nausėda, Gitanas - A/78/PV.6
UN. GENERAL ASSEMBLY (78TH SESS. : 2023-2024)—SPECIAL STATEMENTS
Nausėda, Gitanas - A/78/PV.6

Luxembourg

ARMED CONFLICTS PREVENTION (Agenda item 31a)
Maes, Olivier - A/78/PV.72
CRIME PREVENTION (Agenda item 107)
Wald, Julien - A/C.3/78/SR.6
CYBERCRIME (Agenda item 108)
Wald, Julien - A/C.3/78/SR.6
ENVIRONMENT (Agenda item 71b)
Vlokhoven, Flore van - A/C.3/78/SR.29
FREEDOM OF EXPRESSION (Agenda item 71b)
Toschi, Stéphanie - A/C.3/78/SR.19
HUMAN RIGHTS—AFGHANISTAN (Agenda item 71c)
Gordet, Levina Christine Margaux - A/C.3/78/SR.34
HUMAN RIGHTS—BELARUS (Agenda item 71c)
Folmer, Sophie - A/C.3/78/SR.37
HUMAN RIGHTS—ETHIOPIA (Agenda item 71c)
Gordet, Levina Christine Margaux - A/C.3/78/SR.36
HUMAN RIGHTS—MYANMAR (Agenda item 71c)
Toschi, Stéphanie - A/C.3/78/SR.33
HUMAN RIGHTS—RUSSIAN FEDERATION (Agenda item 71c)
Maes, Olivier - A/C.3/78/SR.37
HUMAN RIGHTS—SYRIAN ARAB REPUBLIC (Agenda item 71c)
Folmer, Sophie - A/C.3/78/SR.34
INTERNATIONAL CRIMINAL COURT—REPORTS (Agenda item 74)
Germeaux, Alain - A/78/PV.21
MIGRANTS—PROTECTION (Agenda item 71b)
Folmer, Sophie - A/C.3/78/SR.23

Luxembourg (continued)

PERSONS WITH DISABILITIES—HUMAN RIGHTS (Agenda item 71a)
Dostert, Anne Françoise - A/C.3/78/SR.38
RIGHT TO EDUCATION (Agenda item 71b)
Vlokhoven, Flore van - A/C.3/78/SR.27
RIGHT TO PRIVACY (Agenda item 71b)
Wald, Julien - A/C.3/78/SR.21
RIGHTS OF THE CHILD (Agenda item 67)
Lepage, Natasha - A/C.3/78/SR.12
Maes, Olivier - A/C.3/78/SR.11
Wald, Julien - A/C.3/78/SR.11; A/C.3/78/SR.12
SEXUAL ORIENTATION (Agenda item 71b)
Toschi, Stéphanie - A/C.3/78/SR.39
TORTURE AND OTHER CRUEL TREATMENT (Agenda item 71a)
Lepage, Natasha - A/C.3/78/SR.18
TRAFFICKING IN PERSONS (Agenda item 71b)
Folmer, Sophie - A/C.3/78/SR.23
UN. INTERNATIONAL COURT OF JUSTICE—REPORTS (Agenda item 73)
Germeaux, Alain - A/78/PV.27
UN. SECURITY COUNCIL—MEMBERSHIP (Agenda item 121)
Maes, Olivier - A/78/PV.34
VETO (Agenda item 63)
Maes, Olivier - A/78/PV.52; A/78/PV.60; A/78/PV.67; A/78/PV.70; A/78/PV.78
WOMEN'S ADVANCEMENT (Agenda item 25a)
Lepage, Natasha - A/C.3/78/SR.8
WOMEN'S ADVANCEMENT—CONFERENCES (Agenda item 25b)
Lepage, Natasha - A/C.3/78/SR.8

Luxembourg. Deputy Prime Minister

UKRAINE—POLITICAL CONDITIONS (Agenda item 62)
Bettel, Xavier - A/78/PV.56
UN. GENERAL ASSEMBLY (78TH SESS. : 2023-2024)—SPECIAL STATEMENTS
Bettel, Xavier - A/78/PV.56

Luxembourg. Prime Minister

UN. GENERAL ASSEMBLY (78TH SESS. : 2023-2024)—GENERAL DEBATE (Agenda item 8)
Bettel, Xavier - A/78/PV.10
UN. GENERAL ASSEMBLY (78TH SESS. : 2023-2024)—SPECIAL STATEMENTS
Bettel, Xavier - A/78/PV.10

Malawi

ALBINISM (Agenda item 71b)
Chimbiri-Molande, Agnes Mary - A/C.3/78/SR.47
FOOD SECURITY (Agenda item 23a)
Chivundu, Renata - A/C.2/78/SR.17

Malawi (continued)

INFORMATION TECHNOLOGY—DEVELOPMENT (Agenda item 15)
Chivundu, Renata - A/C.2/78/SR.10
POVERTY—INTERNATIONAL DECADES (Agenda item 21a)
Chivundu, Renata - A/C.2/78/SR.17
RIGHTS OF THE CHILD (Agenda item 67)
Nyirongo, Bertha Mkaka - A/C.3/78/SR.13
RURAL POVERTY (Agenda item 21b)
Chivundu, Renata - A/C.2/78/SR.17
SOCIAL DEVELOPMENT (Agenda item 24)
Chimbiri-Molande, Agnes Mary - A/C.3/78/SR.47
TERRORISM (Agenda item 109)
Namangale, Clement Amamai Dima - A/C.6/78/SR.5
UN. GENERAL ASSEMBLY (78TH SESS. : 2023-2024). 2ND COMMITTEE—GENERAL DEBATE (Agenda item 8)
Chimbiri-Molande, Agnes Mary - A/C.2/78/SR.6

Malawi. President

UN. GENERAL ASSEMBLY (78TH SESS. : 2023-2024)—GENERAL DEBATE (Agenda item 8)
Chakwera, Lazarus McCarthy - A/78/PV.8
UN. GENERAL ASSEMBLY (78TH SESS. : 2023-2024)—SPECIAL STATEMENTS
Chakwera, Lazarus McCarthy - A/78/PV.8

Malaysia

AGEING PERSONS (Agenda item 24b)
Escopper Zumilla, Michael Jawa - A/C.3/78/SR.49
Muhamad, Ahmad Faisal - A/C.3/78/SR.2
Rahman, Siti Adibah Abdul - A/C.3/78/SR.1
ARMS RACE—OUTER SPACE (Agenda item 97a)
Muhamad, Ahmad Faisal - A/C.1/78/PV.16
ARMS TRANSFERS—TREATIES (Agenda item 99x)
Noordin, Shamsuri - A/C.1/78/PV.18
BIOLOGICAL DIVERSITY—TREATIES (Agenda item 18f)
Zulasri Bin Rosdi, Muhammad - A/C.2/78/SR.15
BIOLOGICAL WEAPONS—TREATIES (Agenda item 106)
Sivamohan, Shivanand - A/C.1/78/PV.14
CHEMICAL WEAPONS—TREATIES (Agenda item 99l)
Sivamohan, Shivanand - A/C.1/78/PV.14; A/C.1/78/PV.26
CLIMATE (Agenda item 18d)
Zulasri Bin Rosdi, Muhammad - A/C.2/78/SR.15
CLIMATE CHANGE (Agenda item 71b)
Escopper Zumilla, Michael Jawa - A/C.3/78/SR.29
COMMODITIES (Agenda item 16d)
Adnan, Yang Aishah Binti - A/C.2/78/SR.14
CONVENTIONAL WEAPONS (Agenda item 99u)
Noordin, Shamsuri - A/C.1/78/PV.18

Malaysia (continued)

CRIME PREVENTION (Agenda item 107)
Rizal, Nizhan Faraz Bin - A/C.3/78/SR.5
CRIMES AGAINST HUMANITY (Agenda item 80)
Abd Karim, Nur Azura Binti - A/C.6/78/SR.10
Rizal, Nizhan Faraz Bin - A/C.6/78/SR.46
CUBA—UNITED STATES (Agenda item 38)
Omar, Khairi - A/78/PV.24
CYBERCRIME (Agenda item 108)
Rizal, Nizhan Faraz Bin - A/C.3/78/SR.5
DEMOCRACY (Agenda item 71b)
Escopper Zumilla, Michael Jawa - A/C.3/78/SR.28
DEVELOPMENT FINANCE (Agenda item 16b)
Adnan, Yang Aishah Binti - A/C.2/78/SR.9
DISARMAMENT AGREEMENTS—OUTER SPACE (Agenda item 97c)
Sivamohan, Shivanand - A/C.1/78/PV.27
DISASTER PREVENTION (Agenda item 18c)
Zulasri Bin Rosdi, Muhammad - A/C.2/78/SR.15
DISASTER VICTIMS (Agenda item 86)
Abd Karim, Nur Azura Binti - A/C.6/78/SR.6
ECONOMIC SANCTIONS—INTERNATIONAL RELATIONS (Agenda item 28)
Abd Karim, Sofian Akmal Bin - A/78/PV.89
ELECTION VERIFICATION—UN (Agenda item 71b)
Rizal, Nizhan Faraz Bin - A/78/PV.50; A/C.3/78/SR.50
ENVIRONMENT (Agenda item 71b)
Escopper Zumilla, Michael Jawa - A/C.3/78/SR.29
EXTERNAL DEBT (Agenda item 16c)
Adnan, Yang Aishah Binti - A/C.2/78/SR.9
FOOD SECURITY (Agenda item 23a)
Zulasri Bin Rosdi, Muhammad - A/C.2/78/SR.17
HEALTH (Agenda item 125)
Zin Zawawi, Nordiana Binti - A/78/PV.77
HUMAN RIGHTS (Agenda item 71)
Muhamad, Ahmad Faisal - A/C.3/78/SR.16
HUMAN RIGHTS—AFGHANISTAN (Agenda item 71c)
Escopper Zumilla, Michael Jawa - A/C.3/78/SR.34
HUMAN RIGHTS—INTERNATIONAL INSTRUMENTS (Agenda item 71a)
Escopper Zumilla, Michael Jawa - A/C.3/78/SR.17
Rizal, Nizhan Faraz Bin - A/C.3/78/SR.24
HUMAN RIGHTS—MYANMAR (Agenda item 71c)
Escopper Zumilla, Michael Jawa - A/C.3/78/SR.33
Rizal, Nizhan Faraz Bin - A/C.3/78/SR.24; A/C.3/78/SR.53
HUMAN RIGHTS—PROGRAMMES OF ACTION (Agenda item 71d)
Rizal, Nizhan Faraz Bin - A/C.3/78/SR.24
HUMAN RIGHTS—TERRITORIES OCCUPIED BY ISRAEL (Agenda item 71c)
Escopper Zumilla, Michael Jawa - A/C.3/78/SR.35

Malaysia (continued)

HUMAN RIGHTS ACTIVISTS (Agenda item 71b)
Rizal, Nizhan Faraz Bin - A/C.3/78/SR.56
HUMAN RIGHTS ADVANCEMENT (Agenda item 71b)
Rizal, Nizhan Faraz Bin - A/C.3/78/SR.24
IAEA—REPORTS (Agenda item 89)
Muhamad, Ahmad Faisal - A/78/PV.29
INDIGENOUS PEOPLES (Agenda item 68a)
Escopper Zumilla, Michael Jawa - A/C.3/78/SR.48
Rahman, Siti Adibah Abdul - A/C.3/78/SR.15
INDIGENOUS PEOPLES—CONFERENCES (Agenda item 68b)
Rahman, Siti Adibah Abdul - A/C.3/78/SR.15
INFORMATION (Agenda item 53)
Sabarudin, Mohamad Shahir - A/C.4/78/SR.13
INFORMATION—INTERNATIONAL SECURITY (Agenda item 94)
Sivamohan, Shivanand - A/C.1/78/PV.20; A/C.1/78/PV.29
INTERNATIONAL LAW—TRAINING PROGRAMMES (Agenda item 78)
Abd Karim, Nur Azura Binti - A/C.6/78/SR.21
INTERNATIONAL TRADE (Agenda item 16a)
Adnan, Yang Aishah Binti - A/C.2/78/SR.9
INVESTMENT PROMOTION (Agenda item 16g)
Adnan, Yang Aishah Binti - A/C.2/78/SR.9
LANDLOCKED DEVELOPING COUNTRIES—CONFERENCES (Agenda item 20b)
Zulasri Bin Rosdi, Muhammad - A/C.2/78/SR.7
LEAST DEVELOPED COUNTRIES—CONFERENCES (Agenda item 20a)
Zulasri Bin Rosdi, Muhammad - A/C.2/78/SR.7
MIDDLE EAST—NUCLEAR-WEAPON-FREE ZONES (Agenda item 95)
Sivamohan, Shivanand - A/C.1/78/PV.22
MIGRANT WORKERS (Agenda item 71a)
Escopper Zumilla, Michael Jawa - A/C.3/78/SR.23
MIGRANTS—PROTECTION (Agenda item 71b)
Escopper Zumilla, Michael Jawa - A/C.3/78/SR.23
MINORITIES (Agenda item 71b)
Escopper Zumilla, Michael Jawa - A/C.3/78/SR.52
MULTILATERALISM—DISARMAMENT (Agenda item 99r)
Sivamohan, Shivanand - A/C.1/78/PV.22
NON-CITIZENS—DEPORTATION (Agenda item 81)
Abd Karim, Nur Azura Binti - A/C.6/78/SR.34
NUCLEAR DISARMAMENT (Agenda item 99b)
Muhamad, Ahmad Faisal - A/C.1/78/PV.11
NUCLEAR NON-PROLIFERATION—INTERNATIONAL OBLIGATIONS (Agenda item 99w)
Muhamad, Ahmad Faisal - A/C.1/78/PV.11

Malaysia (continued)

NUCLEAR WEAPON TESTS—TREATIES (Agenda item 105)
Muhamad, Ahmad Faisal - A/C.1/78/PV.11
NUCLEAR WEAPONS—ELIMINATION (Agenda item 99z)
Sivamohan, Shivanand - A/C.1/78/PV.25
NUCLEAR WEAPONS—TREATIES (Agenda item 99ff)
Muhamad, Ahmad Faisal - A/C.1/78/PV.11
NUCLEAR WEAPONS USE—UN. INTERNATIONAL COURT OF JUSTICE OPINION (Agenda item 99k)
Muhamad, Ahmad Faisal - A/C.1/78/PV.11
Sivamohan, Shivanand - A/C.1/78/PV.25
OPERATIONAL ACTIVITIES—UN SYSTEM (Agenda item 22a)
Zulasri Bin Rosdi, Muhammad - A/C.2/78/SR.18
OUTER SPACE—CONFIDENCE-BUILDING MEASURES (Agenda item 99v)
Muhamad, Ahmad Faisal - A/C.1/78/PV.16
OUTER SPACE—PEACEFUL USES—INTERNATIONAL COOPERATION (Agenda item 48)
Nordin, Hana Binti - A/C.4/78/SR.15
OUTER SPACE—PRINCIPLES (Agenda item 97d)
Muhamad, Ahmad Faisal - A/C.1/78/PV.16
Sivamohan, Shivanand - A/C.1/78/PV.27
PALESTINE QUESTION (Agenda item 35)
Abdul Kadir, Zambry - A/78/PV.39
PEACE (Agenda item 14)
Muhamad, Ahmad Faisal - A/78/PV.62
Zin Zawawi, Nordiana Binti - A/78/PV.77
PEACEKEEPING OPERATIONS (Agenda item 51)
Noordin, Shamsuri - A/C.4/78/SR.19
PEACEKEEPING OPERATIONS—CRIMINAL LIABILITY (Agenda item 76)
Abd Karim, Nur Azura Binti - A/C.6/78/SR.8
PERSONS WITH DISABILITIES—HUMAN RIGHTS (Agenda item 71a)
Escopper Zumilla, Michael Jawa - A/C.3/78/SR.38; A/C.3/78/SR.51
POVERTY—HUMAN RIGHTS (Agenda item 71b)
Escopper Zumilla, Michael Jawa - A/C.3/78/SR.30
POVERTY—INTERNATIONAL DECADES (Agenda item 21a)
Zulasri Bin Rosdi, Muhammad - A/C.2/78/SR.17
RACIAL DISCRIMINATION—ELIMINATION (Agenda item 69a)
Rizal, Nizhan Faraz Bin - A/C.3/78/SR.41; A/C.3/78/SR.47
RACIAL DISCRIMINATION—PROGRAMMES OF ACTION (Agenda item 69b)
Escopper Zumilla, Michael Jawa - A/C.3/78/SR.40
Rizal, Nizhan Faraz Bin - A/C.3/78/SR.41
RIGHT TO CULTURE (Agenda item 71b)
Escopper Zumilla, Michael Jawa - A/C.3/78/SR.27

Malaysia (continued)

RIGHT TO DEVELOPMENT (Agenda item 71b)
Escopper Zumilla, Michael Jawa - A/C.3/78/SR.20
RIGHT TO EDUCATION (Agenda item 71b)
Escopper Zumilla, Michael Jawa - A/C.3/78/SR.27
RIGHT TO FOOD (Agenda item 71b)
Escopper Zumilla, Michael Jawa - A/C.3/78/SR.30
RIGHT TO HOUSING (Agenda item 71b)
Escopper Zumilla, Michael Jawa - A/C.3/78/SR.30
RIGHT TO PRIVACY (Agenda item 71b)
Escopper Zumilla, Michael Jawa - A/C.3/78/SR.21
RIGHTS OF THE CHILD (Agenda item 67)
Dolah, Rizzal - A/C.3/78/SR.11; A/C.3/78/SR.12
Rizal, Nizhan Faraz Bin - A/C.3/78/SR.11; A/C.3/78/SR.55
Ruslan, Muhammad Ammar Rafiq - A/C.3/78/SR.11
RULE OF LAW (Agenda item 83)
Abd Karim, Nur Azura Binti - A/C.6/78/SR.19
RURAL POVERTY (Agenda item 21b)
Zulasri Bin Rosdi, Muhammad - A/C.2/78/SR.17
RURAL WOMEN (Agenda item 25a)
Escopper Zumilla, Michael Jawa - A/C.3/78/SR.49
SANCTIONS—INTERNATIONAL RELATIONS (Agenda item 71b)
Escopper Zumilla, Michael Jawa - A/C.3/78/SR.28
SELF-DETERMINATION OF PEOPLES (Agenda item 70)
Rizal, Nizhan Faraz Bin - A/C.3/78/SR.49
SMALL ARMS—ILLICIT TRAFFIC (Agenda item 99p)
Noordin, Shamsuri - A/C.1/78/PV.18
SMALL ARMS—ILLICIT TRAFFIC—ASSISTANCE (Agenda item 99n)
Noordin, Shamsuri - A/C.1/78/PV.18
SOCIAL CONDITIONS (Agenda item 24b)
Escopper Zumilla, Michael Jawa - A/C.3/78/SR.51
Muhamad, Ahmad Faisal - A/C.3/78/SR.2
SOUTH-EAST ASIA—NUCLEAR-WEAPON-FREE ZONES (Agenda item 99y)
Muhamad, Ahmad Faisal - A/C.1/78/PV.11
Sivamohan, Shivanand - A/C.1/78/PV.22; A/C.1/78/PV.30
SUSTAINABLE DEVELOPMENT (Agenda item 18)
Adnan, Yang Aishah Binti - A/C.2/78/SR.14
TERRITORIES OCCUPIED BY ISRAEL—HUMAN RIGHTS (Agenda item 50)
Muhamad, Ahmad Faisal - A/C.4/78/SR.24
TERRITORIES OCCUPIED BY ISRAEL—NATURAL RESOURCES (Agenda item 59)
Adnan, Yang Aishah Binti - A/C.2/78/SR.19
TERRORISM (Agenda item 109)
Omar, Khairi - A/C.6/78/SR.4
TRAFFICKING IN PERSONS (Agenda item 71b)
Escopper Zumilla, Michael Jawa - A/C.3/78/SR.23
TREATIES (Agenda item 87)
Abd Karim, Nur Azura Binti - A/C.6/78/SR.20

Malaysia (continued)

UN. CONFERENCE ON DISARMAMENT—REPORTS (Agenda item 101a)
Sivamohan, Shivanand - A/C.1/78/PV.23
UN. DISARMAMENT COMMISSION—REPORTS (Agenda item 101b)
Sivamohan, Shivanand - A/C.1/78/PV.23
UN. GENERAL ASSEMBLY (78TH SESS. : 2023-2024). 1ST COMMITTEE—GENERAL DEBATE (Agenda item 8)
Muhamad, Ahmad Faisal - A/C.1/78/PV.4
UN. GENERAL ASSEMBLY (78TH SESS. : 2023-2024). 2ND COMMITTEE—GENERAL DEBATE (Agenda item 8)
Adnan, Yang Aishah Binti - A/C.2/78/SR.5
UN. HUMAN RIGHTS COUNCIL—REPORTS (Agenda item 66)
Rizal, Nizhan Faraz Bin - A/78/PV.23
UN. INTERNATIONAL COURT OF JUSTICE—REPORTS (Agenda item 73)
Omar, Khairi - A/78/PV.27
UN. INTERNATIONAL LAW COMMISSION—REPORTS (Agenda item 79)
Abd Karim, Nur Azura Binti - A/C.6/78/SR.30; A/C.6/78/SR.32
Omar, Khairi - A/C.6/78/SR.27
UN. SECRETARY-GENERAL—REPORTS (Agenda item 110)
Zin Zawawi, Nordiana Binti - A/78/PV.55
UN. SECURITY COUNCIL—MEMBERSHIP (Agenda item 121)
Abd Karim, Sofian Akmal Bin - A/78/PV.35
UN. SECURITY COUNCIL—REPORTS (Agenda item 26)
Zin Zawawi, Nordiana Binti - A/78/PV.93
UN COMMISSION ON INTERNATIONAL TRADE LAW—REPORTS (Agenda item 77)
Abd Karim, Nur Azura Binti - A/C.6/78/SR.14
UN HIGH COMMISSIONER FOR REFUGEES—REPORTS (Agenda item 60)
Escopper Zumilla, Michael Jawa - A/C.3/78/SR.44; A/C.3/78/SR.51
UN RESOLUTIONS—IMPLEMENTATION (Agenda item 119)
Abd Karim, Sofian Akmal Bin - A/78/PV.108
UNRWA—ACTIVITIES (Agenda item 49)
Sabarudin, Mohamad Shahir - A/C.4/78/SR.22
VETO (Agenda item 63)
Abd Karim, Sofian Akmal Bin - A/78/PV.51
Muhamad, Ahmad Faisal - A/78/PV.59; A/78/PV.70; A/78/PV.74
Rizal, Nizhan Faraz Bin - A/78/PV.66
Sivamohan, Shivanand - A/78/PV.69
WOMEN MIGRANT WORKERS (Agenda item 25a)
Escopper Zumilla, Michael Jawa - A/C.3/78/SR.49
WOMEN'S ADVANCEMENT (Agenda item 25a)
Rahman, Siti Adibah Abdul - A/C.3/78/SR.7
Ruslan, Muhammad Ammar Rafiq - A/C.3/78/SR.8

Malaysia (continued)

WOMEN'S ADVANCEMENT—CONFERENCES (Agenda item 25b)
Rahman, Siti Adibah Abdul - A/C.3/78/SR.7
Ruslan, Muhammad Ammar Rafiq - A/C.3/78/SR.8
YOUTH (Agenda item 24b)
Escopper Zumilla, Michael Jawa - A/C.3/78/SR.55

Malaysia. Prime Minister

UN. GENERAL ASSEMBLY (78TH SESS. : 2023-2024)—GENERAL DEBATE (Agenda item 8)
Ibrahim, Anwar - A/78/PV.10
UN. GENERAL ASSEMBLY (78TH SESS. : 2023-2024)—SPECIAL STATEMENTS
Ibrahim, Anwar - A/78/PV.10

Maldives

CLIMATE (Agenda item 18d)
Hameed, Hala - A/C.2/78/SR.13
CLIMATE CHANGE (Agenda item 71b)
Hameed, Hala - A/C.3/78/SR.29
EMERGENCY ASSISTANCE (Agenda item 72a)
Khadeeja, Aufiyau - A/78/PV.46
EXTERNAL DEBT (Agenda item 16c)
Zuhuree, Ibrahim - A/C.2/78/SR.9
FOOD SECURITY (Agenda item 23a)
Nashwa, Fathimath - A/C.2/78/SR.16
HUMAN RIGHTS ADVANCEMENT (Agenda item 71b)
Zuhuree, Ibrahim - A/C.3/78/SR.25
INTERNATIONAL TRADE (Agenda item 16a)
Zuhuree, Ibrahim - A/C.2/78/SR.9
LANDLOCKED DEVELOPING COUNTRIES—CONFERENCES (Agenda item 20b)
Shamun, Amr Danyal - A/C.2/78/SR.7
LAW OF THE SEA (Agenda item 75a)
Shamun, Amr Danyal - A/78/PV.43
LEAST DEVELOPED COUNTRIES—CONFERENCES (Agenda item 20a)
Shamun, Amr Danyal - A/C.2/78/SR.7
MARINE ECOSYSTEMS—BIOLOGICAL DIVERSITY (Agenda item 75c)
Shamun, Amr Danyal - A/78/PV.43
PALESTINE QUESTION (Agenda item 35)
Zuhuree, Ibrahim - A/78/PV.39
PALESTINIANS—ASSISTANCE (Agenda item 72b)
Khadeeja, Aufiyau - A/78/PV.46
PERSONS WITH DISABILITIES—HUMAN RIGHTS (Agenda item 71a)
Khadeeja, Aufiyau - A/C.3/78/SR.38
POVERTY—INTERNATIONAL DECADES (Agenda item 21a)
Nashwa, Fathimath - A/C.2/78/SR.16
RIGHT TO EDUCATION (Agenda item 71b)
Hameed, Hala - A/C.3/78/SR.27

Maldives (continued)

RIGHT TO HEALTH (Agenda item 71b)
Khadeeja, Aufiyau - A/C.3/78/SR.39
RIGHTS OF THE CHILD (Agenda item 67)
Hameed, Hala - A/C.3/78/SR.13
RULE OF LAW (Agenda item 83)
Zuhuree, Ibrahim - A/C.6/78/SR.17
RURAL POVERTY (Agenda item 21b)
Nashwa, Fathimath - A/C.2/78/SR.16
SMALL ISLAND DEVELOPING STATES—PROGRAMMES OF ACTION (Agenda item 18b)
Hameed, Hala - A/C.2/78/SR.13
Mohamed, Ali Naseer - A/78/PV.100
SOCIAL CONDITIONS (Agenda item 24b)
Khadeeja, Aufiyau - A/C.3/78/SR.3
SOCIAL DEVELOPMENT (Agenda item 24)
Khadeeja, Aufiyau - A/C.3/78/SR.3
STRADDLING FISH STOCKS (Agenda item 75b)
Shamun, Amr Danyal - A/78/PV.43
SUSTAINABLE DEVELOPMENT (Agenda item 18)
Hameed, Hala - A/C.2/78/SR.13
TERRITORIES OCCUPIED BY ISRAEL—NATURAL RESOURCES (Agenda item 59)
Hameed, Hala - A/C.2/78/SR.19
TERRORISM (Agenda item 109)
Guraisha, Aminath - A/C.6/78/SR.2
UN. ECONOMIC AND SOCIAL COUNCIL—REPORTS (Agenda item 9)
Nashwa, Fathimath - A/78/PV.33
UN. GENERAL ASSEMBLY—WORK PROGRAMME (Agenda item 120)
Guraisha, Aminath - A/78/PV.32
UN. GENERAL ASSEMBLY (78TH SESS. : 2023-2024)—GENERAL DEBATE (Agenda item 8)
Khaleel, Ahmed - A/78/PV.14
UN. GENERAL ASSEMBLY (78TH SESS. : 2023-2024). 1ST COMMITTEE—GENERAL DEBATE (Agenda item 8)
Guraisha, Aminath - A/C.1/78/PV.5
UN. GENERAL ASSEMBLY (78TH SESS. : 2023-2024). 2ND COMMITTEE—GENERAL DEBATE (Agenda item 8)
Hussain, Thilmeeza - A/C.2/78/SR.3
UN. HUMAN RIGHTS COUNCIL—REPORTS (Agenda item 66)
Hameed, Hala - A/78/PV.23
UN. SECURITY COUNCIL—MEMBERSHIP (Agenda item 121)
Zuhuree, Ibrahim - A/78/PV.34
UN RESOLUTIONS—IMPLEMENTATION (Agenda item 119)
Guraisha, Aminath - A/78/PV.32
UNRWA—ACTIVITIES (Agenda item 49)
Zuhuree, Ibrahim - A/C.4/78/SR.22
VETO (Agenda item 63)
Ahmed, Ali Haidar - A/78/PV.74
Mohamed, Ali Naseer - A/78/PV.60
Zuhuree, Ibrahim - A/78/PV.52

Maldives (continued)

WOMEN'S ADVANCEMENT (Agenda item 25a)
Khadeeja, Aufiyau - A/C.3/78/SR.9
WOMEN'S ADVANCEMENT—CONFERENCES (Agenda item 25b)
Khadeeja, Aufiyau - A/C.3/78/SR.9
YOUTH (Agenda item 24b)
Khadeeja, Aufiyau - A/C.3/78/SR.3

Mali

CRIME PREVENTION (Agenda item 107)
Dabo N'diaye, Djeneba - A/C.3/78/SR.6
CRIMES AGAINST HUMANITY (Agenda item 80)
Dabo N'diaye, Djeneba - A/C.6/78/SR.39; A/C.6/78/SR.42; A/C.6/78/SR.47
Konfourou, Issa - A/C.6/78/SR.11
ELECTION VERIFICATION—UN (Agenda item 71b)
Dabo N'diaye, Djeneba - A/78/PV.50
FOOD SECURITY (Agenda item 23a)
Coulibaly, Kanisson - A/C.2/78/SR.17
HUMAN RIGHTS—BURUNDI (Agenda item 71c)
Maiga, Aissata Ibrahim - A/C.3/78/SR.36
HUMAN RIGHTS—ERITREA (Agenda item 71c)
Dabo N'diaye, Djeneba - A/C.3/78/SR.36
HUMAN RIGHTS—ETHIOPIA (Agenda item 71c)
Dabo N'diaye, Djeneba - A/C.3/78/SR.36
HUMAN RIGHTS—INTERNATIONAL INSTRUMENTS (Agenda item 71a)
Maiga, Aissata Ibrahim - A/C.3/78/SR.26
HUMAN RIGHTS ACTIVISTS (Agenda item 71b)
Dabo N'diaye, Djeneba - A/C.3/78/SR.56
HUMAN RIGHTS INSTITUTIONS—CENTRAL AFRICA (Agenda item 71b)
Dabo N'diaye, Djeneba - A/C.3/78/SR.56
INTERNATIONAL CRIMINAL COURT—REPORTS (Agenda item 74)
Konfourou, Issa - A/78/PV.22
INTERNATIONAL JURISDICTION (Agenda item 84)
Konfourou, Issa - A/C.6/78/SR.13
PERSONS WITH DISABILITIES—HUMAN RIGHTS (Agenda item 71a)
Dabo N'diaye, Djeneba - A/C.3/78/SR.38; A/C.3/78/SR.51
POVERTY—INTERNATIONAL DECADES (Agenda item 21a)
Coulibaly, Kanisson - A/C.2/78/SR.17
RIGHT TO CULTURE (Agenda item 71b)
Dabo N'diaye, Djeneba - A/C.3/78/SR.27
RIGHT TO DEVELOPMENT (Agenda item 71b)
Dabo N'diaye, Djeneba - A/C.3/78/SR.20

Mali (continued)

RIGHT TO DRINKING WATER (Agenda item 71b)
Dabo N'diaye, Djeneba - A/C.3/78/SR.50
RIGHT TO EDUCATION (Agenda item 71b)
Dabo N'diaye, Djeneba - A/C.3/78/SR.27
RIGHTS OF THE CHILD (Agenda item 67)
Dabo N'diaye, Djeneba - A/C.3/78/SR.14; A/C.3/78/SR.55
RURAL POVERTY (Agenda item 21b)
Coulibaly, Kanisson - A/C.2/78/SR.17
SANCTIONS—INTERNATIONAL RELATIONS (Agenda item 71b)
Maiga, Aissata Ibrahim - A/C.3/78/SR.26
SOCIAL CONDITIONS (Agenda item 24b)
Dabo N'diaye, Djeneba - A/C.3/78/SR.4
SOCIAL DEVELOPMENT (Agenda item 24)
Dabo N'diaye, Djeneba - A/C.3/78/SR.4
TERRORISM (Agenda item 109)
Konfourou, Issa - A/C.6/78/SR.4
UN. GENERAL ASSEMBLY (78TH SESS. : 2023-2024)—GENERAL DEBATE (Agenda item 8)
Diop, Abdoulaye - A/78/PV.13
UN. HUMAN RIGHTS COUNCIL—REPORTS (Agenda item 66)
Dabo N'diaye, Djeneba - A/78/PV.28
UN MULTIDIMENSIONAL INTEGRATED STABILIZATION MISSION IN MALI—FINANCING (Agenda item 155)
Sissoko, Aboubacar - A/C.5/78/SR.36
VETO (Agenda item 63)
Konfourou, Issa - A/78/PV.3; A/78/PV.69
WOMEN'S ADVANCEMENT (Agenda item 25a)
Dabo N'diaye, Djeneba - A/C.3/78/SR.10
WOMEN'S ADVANCEMENT—CONFERENCES (Agenda item 25b)
Dabo N'diaye, Djeneba - A/C.3/78/SR.10
YOUTH (Agenda item 24b)
Dabo N'diaye, Djeneba - A/C.3/78/SR.55

Malta

AGEING PERSONS (Agenda item 24b)
Gabriele, Emma de - A/C.3/78/SR.1
CLIMATE CHANGE (Agenda item 71b)
Micallef, Justine - A/C.3/78/SR.29
CRIMES AGAINST HUMANITY (Agenda item 80)
Kuymizakis, Adam - A/C.6/78/SR.40
Siman, Augustina - A/C.6/78/SR.10; A/C.6/78/SR.47
HUMAN RIGHTS—AFGHANISTAN (Agenda item 71c)
Micallef, Justine - A/C.3/78/SR.34
HUMAN RIGHTS—SYRIAN ARAB REPUBLIC (Agenda item 71c)
Micallef, Justine - A/C.3/78/SR.34
INTERNATIONAL CRIMINAL COURT—REPORTS (Agenda item 74)
Kuymizakis, Adam - A/78/PV.22

Malta (continued)

INTERNATIONAL RESIDUAL MECHANISM FOR CRIMINAL TRIBUNALS (Agenda item 126)
Kuymizakis, Adam - A/78/PV.19
PERSONS WITH DISABILITIES—HUMAN RIGHTS (Agenda item 71a)
Aquilina, Cara Borg - A/C.3/78/SR.38
RACIAL DISCRIMINATION—ELIMINATION (Agenda item 69a)
Aquilina, Cara Borg - A/C.3/78/SR.41
RACIAL DISCRIMINATION—PROGRAMMES OF ACTION (Agenda item 69b)
Aquilina, Cara Borg - A/C.3/78/SR.41
RESPONSIBILITY TO PROTECT (Agenda item 129)
De Bono Sant Cassia, Andrea - A/78/PV.99
RIGHTS OF THE CHILD (Agenda item 67)
Kuymizakis, Adam - A/C.3/78/SR.11
SEXUAL ORIENTATION (Agenda item 71b)
Kuymizakis, Adam - A/C.3/78/SR.39
SOCIAL CONDITIONS (Agenda item 24b)
Gabriele, Emma de - A/C.3/78/SR.3
TRAFFICKING IN PERSONS (Agenda item 71b)
Micallef, Justine - A/C.3/78/SR.23
UKRAINE—POLITICAL CONDITIONS (Agenda item 62)
Kuymizakis, Adam - A/78/PV.58
UN. GENERAL ASSEMBLY (78TH SESS. : 2023-2024). 1ST COMMITTEE—GENERAL DEBATE (Agenda item 8)
Kuymizakis, Adam - A/C.1/78/PV.3
UN. GENERAL ASSEMBLY (78TH SESS. : 2023-2024). 2ND COMMITTEE—GENERAL DEBATE (Agenda item 8)
Kuymizakis, Adam - A/C.2/78/SR.3
UN. INTERNATIONAL COURT OF JUSTICE—REPORTS (Agenda item 73)
Kuymizakis, Adam - A/78/PV.27
UN. INTERNATIONAL LAW COMMISSION—REPORTS (Agenda item 79)
Frazier, Vanessa - A/C.6/78/SR.27
UN. SECURITY COUNCIL—MEMBERSHIP (Agenda item 121)
Frazier, Vanessa - A/78/PV.35
UN YOUTH OFFICE—REPORTS (Agenda item 130)
Gatt, Francesca Maria - A/78/PV.102
VETO (Agenda item 63)
Camilleri, Darren - A/78/PV.78
Frazier, Vanessa - A/78/PV.3; A/78/PV.51; A/78/PV.59
Kuymizakis, Adam - A/78/PV.66; A/78/PV.68; A/78/PV.70; A/78/PV.75
WOMEN'S ADVANCEMENT (Agenda item 25a)
Gabriele, Emma de - A/C.3/78/SR.7
WOMEN'S ADVANCEMENT—CONFERENCES (Agenda item 25b)
Gabriele, Emma de - A/C.3/78/SR.7

Malta (continued)

YOUTH (Agenda item 24b)
Gabriele, Emma de - A/C.3/78/SR.3
Micallef, Justine - A/C.3/78/SR.55

Malta. Prime Minister

UN. GENERAL ASSEMBLY (78TH SESS. : 2023-2024)—GENERAL DEBATE (Agenda item 8)
Abela, Robert - A/78/PV.10
UN. GENERAL ASSEMBLY (78TH SESS. : 2023-2024)—SPECIAL STATEMENTS
Abela, Robert - A/78/PV.10

Maohi Protestant Church (French Polynesia)

FRENCH POLYNESIA QUESTION (Agenda item 58)
Neuffer, Philippe - A/C.4/78/SR.3
Neuffer, Tetuanuiahuuraiterai - A/C.4/78/SR.3
Pihaatae, François - A/C.4/78/SR.3

Marshall Islands

CLIMATE CHANGE (Agenda item 71b)
Kabua, Amatlain Elizabeth - A/C.3/78/SR.29
DISARMAMENT—GENERAL AND COMPLETE (Agenda item 99)
Kabua, Amatlain Elizabeth - A/C.1/78/PV.26
Silk, John M. - A/78/PV.105
HUMAN RIGHTS—DEMOCRATIC PEOPLE'S REPUBLIC OF KOREA (Agenda item 71c)
Kabua, Amatlain Elizabeth - A/C.3/78/SR.33
HUMAN RIGHTS—MYANMAR (Agenda item 71c)
Kabua, Amatlain Elizabeth - A/C.3/78/SR.33
RESPONSIBILITY TO PROTECT (Agenda item 129)
Silk, John M. - A/78/PV.97

Marshall Islands. President

UN. GENERAL ASSEMBLY (78TH SESS. : 2023-2024)—GENERAL DEBATE (Agenda item 8)
Kabua, David - A/78/PV.7
UN. GENERAL ASSEMBLY (78TH SESS. : 2023-2024)—SPECIAL STATEMENTS
Kabua, David - A/78/PV.7

Mauritania

CLIMATE (Agenda item 18d)
Soumaré, Boukary - A/C.2/78/SR.15
CONVENTIONAL WEAPONS (Agenda item 99u)
Mohamedou, El Hadj Lehbib - A/C.1/78/PV.19
DISARMAMENT—GENERAL AND COMPLETE (Agenda item 99)
Laghdaf, Sidi Mohamed - A/78/PV.105
ELECTION VERIFICATION—UN (Agenda item 71b)
Guera, Soueda El - A/78/PV.50

Mauritania (continued)

HUMAN RIGHTS—TERRITORIES OCCUPIED BY ISRAEL (Agenda item 71c)
Guera, Soueda El - A/C.3/78/SR.35
INTERNATIONAL LAW—TRAINING PROGRAMMES (Agenda item 78)
Sao, Mariam - A/C.6/78/SR.22
LANDMINES—TREATIES (Agenda item 99m)
Mohamedou, El Hadj Lehbib - A/C.1/78/PV.19
PEACE (Agenda item 14)
Laghdaf, Sidi Mohamed - A/78/PV.76
RULE OF LAW (Agenda item 83)
Sao, Mariam - A/C.6/78/SR.16
RURAL WOMEN (Agenda item 25a)
Guera, Soueda El - A/C.3/78/SR.49
SMALL ARMS—ILLICIT TRAFFIC (Agenda item 99p)
Mohamedou, El Hadj Lehbib - A/C.1/78/PV.19
SMALL ARMS—ILLICIT TRAFFIC—ASSISTANCE (Agenda item 99n)
Mohamedou, El Hadj Lehbib - A/C.1/78/PV.19
SUSTAINABLE DEVELOPMENT (Agenda item 18)
Soumaré, Boukary - A/C.2/78/SR.15
TERRITORIES OCCUPIED BY ISRAEL—NATURAL RESOURCES (Agenda item 59)
Laghdaf, Sidi Mohamed - A/C.2/78/SR.19
TERRORISM (Agenda item 109)
Sao, Mariam - A/C.6/78/SR.5
UN. GENERAL ASSEMBLY (78TH SESS. : 2023-2024). 1ST COMMITTEE—GENERAL DEBATE (Agenda item 8)
Mohamedou, Mohamed Mahmoud Ould - A/C.1/78/PV.8

Mauritania. President

UN. GENERAL ASSEMBLY (78TH SESS. : 2023-2024)—GENERAL DEBATE (Agenda item 8)
El Ghazouani, Mohamed Ould Cheikh - A/78/PV.7
UN. GENERAL ASSEMBLY (78TH SESS. : 2023-2024)—SPECIAL STATEMENTS
El Ghazouani, Mohamed Ould Cheikh - A/78/PV.7

Mauritius

VETO (Agenda item 63)
Koonjul, Jagdish - A/78/PV.61
Segobin Maulloo, Vandana - A/78/PV.67; A/78/PV.75

Mauritius. Prime Minister

UN. GENERAL ASSEMBLY (78TH SESS. : 2023-2024)—GENERAL DEBATE (Agenda item 8)
Jugnauth, Pravind Kumar - A/78/PV.10
UN. GENERAL ASSEMBLY (78TH SESS. : 2023-2024)—SPECIAL STATEMENTS
Jugnauth, Pravind Kumar - A/78/PV.10

Melanesian Spearhead Group

DECOLONIZATION (Agenda item 58)
Sarufa, Fred (Papua New Guinea) - A/C.4/78/SR.6
NEW CALEDONIA QUESTION (Agenda item 58)
Sarufa, Fred (Papua New Guinea) - A/C.4/78/SR.6

MERCOSUR (Organization)

FALKLAND ISLANDS (MALVINAS) QUESTION (Agenda item 42)
Danese, Sérgio França (Brazil) - A/C.4/78/SR.2

Mexico

ADMINISTRATION OF JUSTICE (Agenda item 144)
Jiménez Alegría, Natalia - A/C.6/78/SR.9
AGEING PERSONS (Agenda item 24b)
Santa Ana Vara, Alma Esperanza - A/C.3/78/SR.1; A/C.3/78/SR.2
ARMS RACE—OUTER SPACE (Agenda item 97a)
Fausto, Braulio - A/C.1/78/PV.17
BIOLOGICAL WEAPONS—TREATIES (Agenda item 106)
Yarahuán Dodero, Santiago - A/C.1/78/PV.14
CENTRAL ASIA—ZONES OF PEACE (Agenda item 64)
Reza Bautista, Mauricio - A/78/PV.85
CHEMICAL WEAPONS—TREATIES (Agenda item 99l)
Yarahuán Dodero, Santiago - A/C.1/78/PV.14
CLIMATE (Agenda item 18d)
Curzio Vila, Elena - A/C.2/78/SR.13
CLUSTER MUNITIONS (Agenda item 99dd)
Sánchez Kiesslich, Eduardo Alcibiades - A/C.1/78/PV.18
COASTAL ZONE MANAGEMENT (Agenda item 18j)
Curzio Vila, Elena - A/C.2/78/SR.23
COMMODITIES (Agenda item 16d)
Reta Haddad, Rodolfo - A/C.2/78/SR.9
Robledo López, Carmen - A/C.2/78/SR.14
CONVENTIONAL WEAPONS (Agenda item 99u)
Sánchez Kiesslich, Eduardo Alcibiades - A/C.1/78/PV.18
CRIME PREVENTION (Agenda item 107)
Reza Bautista, Mauricio - A/C.3/78/SR.5
CRIMES AGAINST HUMANITY (Agenda item 80)
Buenrostro Massieu, Alicia - A/C.6/78/SR.10; A/C.6/78/SR.45
Delgado Fernández, Sergio Emanuel - A/C.6/78/SR.44
Jiménez Alegría, Natalia - A/C.6/78/SR.38; A/C.6/78/SR.40; A/C.6/78/SR.47
Pérez Manríquez, Alfredo Uriel - A/C.6/78/SR.41; A/C.6/78/SR.43
CUBA—UNITED STATES (Agenda item 38)
Buenrostro Massieu, Alicia - A/78/PV.24

Mexico (continued)

CULTURE—DEVELOPMENT (Agenda item 19b)
Curzio Vila, Elena - A/C.2/78/SR.10
CYBERCRIME (Agenda item 108)
Reza Bautista, Mauricio - A/C.3/78/SR.5
DECOLONIZATION (Agenda item 58)
Cisneros Chávez, José de Jesús - A/C.4/78/SR.2
DEVELOPMENT FINANCE (Agenda item 16b)
Reta Haddad, Rodolfo - A/C.2/78/SR.9
DEVELOPMENT FINANCE—CONFERENCES (Agenda item 17)
Mendoza Elguea, Sylvia Paola - A/78/PV.90
DISAPPEARANCE OF PERSONS (Agenda item 71b)
Buenrostro Massieu, Alicia - A/C.3/78/SR.22
DISARMAMENT—GENERAL AND COMPLETE (Agenda item 99)
Sánchez Kiesslich, Eduardo Alcibiades - A/C.1/78/PV.18; A/C.1/78/PV.30
Vasconcelos y Cruz, Héctor Enrique - A/78/PV.105
DISARMAMENT AGREEMENTS—OUTER SPACE (Agenda item 97c)
Fausto, Braulio - A/C.1/78/PV.17
Sánchez Kiesslich, Eduardo Alcibiades - A/C.1/78/PV.27
DISASTER VICTIMS (Agenda item 86)
Jiménez Alegría, Natalia - A/C.6/78/SR.6
ECONOMIC COOPERATION AMONG DEVELOPING COUNTRIES (Agenda item 22b)
Robledo López, Carmen - A/C.2/78/SR.18
ECONOMIC SANCTIONS—INTERNATIONAL RELATIONS (Agenda item 28)
Buenrostro Massieu, Alicia - A/78/PV.89
ELECTION VERIFICATION—UN (Agenda item 71b)
Santa Ana Vara, Alma Esperanza - A/C.3/78/SR.50
ENVIRONMENT (Agenda item 71b)
Riveroll Usabiaga, Renata - A/C.3/78/SR.29
EXTERNAL DEBT (Agenda item 16c)
Reta Haddad, Rodolfo - A/C.2/78/SR.9
FALKLAND ISLANDS (MALVINAS) QUESTION (Agenda item 42)
Cisneros Chávez, José de Jesús - A/C.4/78/SR.2
FAMILY (Agenda item 24b)
Reyna Barrón, María Fernanda - A/C.3/78/SR.49
FISSIONABLE MATERIALS—TREATIES (Agenda item 99a)
Sánchez Kiesslich, Eduardo Alcibiades - A/C.1/78/PV.26
FOOD SECURITY (Agenda item 23a)
Vásquez Solano, Leonel - A/C.2/78/SR.16
FREEDOM OF EXPRESSION (Agenda item 71b)
Riveroll Usabiaga, Renata - A/C.3/78/SR.19
HEALTH (Agenda item 125)
Buenrostro Massieu, Alicia - A/78/PV.48
Mendoza Elguea, Sylvia Paola - A/78/PV.64
Quinto González, Jatnael - A/78/PV.102

Mexico (continued)

HIV/AIDS—DECLARATIONS (Agenda item 10)
Mendoza Elguea, Sylvia Paola - A/78/PV.91
HUMAN RIGHTS (Agenda item 71)
Elizondo Belden, Luis Gerardo - A/C.3/78/SR.16
HUMAN RIGHTS—UKRAINE (Agenda item 71c)
Mendoza Elguea, Sylvia Paola - A/C.3/78/SR.53
HUMAN RIGHTS ACTIVISTS (Agenda item 71b)
Elizondo Belden, Luis Gerardo - A/C.3/78/SR.19
HUMAN RIGHTS ADVANCEMENT (Agenda item 71b)
Elizondo Belden, Luis Gerardo - A/C.3/78/SR.24; A/C.3/78/SR.52
IAEA—REPORTS (Agenda item 89)
Buenrostro Massieu, Alicia - A/78/PV.29
INDIGENOUS PEOPLES (Agenda item 68a)
Buenrostro Massieu, Alicia - A/78/PV.107
Vásquez Solano, Leonel - A/C.3/78/SR.15
INDIGENOUS PEOPLES—CONFERENCES (Agenda item 68b)
Vásquez Solano, Leonel - A/C.3/78/SR.15
INFORMATION (Agenda item 53)
Cisneros Chávez, José de Jesús - A/C.4/78/SR.12
Guzik Duno, Aline - A/C.4/78/SR.14
INFORMATION—INTERNATIONAL SECURITY (Agenda item 94)
Fausto, Braulio - A/C.1/78/PV.20
Sánchez Kiesslich, Eduardo Alcibiades - A/C.1/78/PV.29
INFORMATION TECHNOLOGY—DEVELOPMENT (Agenda item 15)
Curzio Vila, Elena - A/C.2/78/SR.10
INTERNATIONAL CRIMINAL COURT—REPORTS (Agenda item 74)
Buenrostro Massieu, Alicia - A/78/PV.22
INTERNATIONAL JURISDICTION (Agenda item 84)
Arrocha Olabuenaga, Pablo Adrián - A/C.6/78/SR.12
INTERNATIONAL LAW—TRAINING PROGRAMMES (Agenda item 78)
Delgado Fernández, Sergio Emanuel - A/C.6/78/SR.21
LAW OF THE SEA (Agenda item 75a)
Buenrostro Massieu, Alicia - A/78/PV.44
MARINE ECOSYSTEMS—BIOLOGICAL DIVERSITY (Agenda item 75c)
Buenrostro Massieu, Alicia - A/78/PV.44
MIGRANT WORKERS (Agenda item 71a)
Gil Rojas, Elia Lizette - A/C.3/78/SR.23
MIGRANTS—PROTECTION (Agenda item 71b)
Gil Rojas, Elia Lizette - A/C.3/78/SR.23
Mendoza Elguea, Sylvia Paola - A/C.3/78/SR.56
MULTILATERALISM—DISARMAMENT (Agenda item 99r)
Flores Troche, Manuel - A/C.1/78/PV.22

Mexico (continued)

NON-CITIZENS—DEPORTATION (Agenda item 81)
Jiménez Alegría, Natalia - A/C.6/78/SR.34
NUCLEAR DISARMAMENT (Agenda item 99b)
Sánchez Kiesslich, Eduardo Alcibiades - A/C.1/78/PV.12
NUCLEAR DISARMAMENT—TREATY COMPLIANCE (Agenda item 99q)
Sánchez Kiesslich, Eduardo Alcibiades - A/C.1/78/PV.12
NUCLEAR NON-PROLIFERATION—INTERNATIONAL OBLIGATIONS (Agenda item 99w)
Sánchez Kiesslich, Eduardo Alcibiades - A/C.1/78/PV.12
NUCLEAR WEAPON TESTS—TREATIES (Agenda item 105)
Sánchez Kiesslich, Eduardo Alcibiades - A/C.1/78/PV.12; A/C.1/78/PV.25
NUCLEAR WEAPONS—ELIMINATION (Agenda item 99z)
Sánchez Kiesslich, Eduardo Alcibiades - A/C.1/78/PV.26
NUCLEAR WEAPONS—TREATIES (Agenda item 99ff)
Sánchez Kiesslich, Eduardo Alcibiades - A/C.1/78/PV.11; A/C.1/78/PV.12
NUCLEAR WEAPONS USE—TREATIES (Agenda item 100a)
Sánchez Kiesslich, Eduardo Alcibiades - A/C.1/78/PV.25
OPERATIONAL ACTIVITIES—UN SYSTEM (Agenda item 22a)
Robledo López, Carmen - A/C.2/78/SR.18
OUTER SPACE—PRINCIPLES (Agenda item 97d)
Sánchez Kiesslich, Eduardo Alcibiades - A/C.1/78/PV.27
PALESTINE QUESTION (Agenda item 35)
Ochoa Martínez, Enrique Javier - A/78/PV.40
PEACE (Agenda item 14)
Curzio Vila, Elena - A/78/PV.76
Elizondo Belden, Luis Gerardo - A/78/PV.62
Vasconcelos y Cruz, Héctor Enrique - A/78/PV.82
PEACEBUILDING (Agenda item 61)
Cisneros Chávez, José de Jesús - A/78/PV.100
PEACEKEEPING OPERATIONS (Agenda item 51)
Cisneros Chávez, José de Jesús - A/C.4/78/SR.18
PEACEKEEPING OPERATIONS—CRIMINAL LIABILITY (Agenda item 76)
Jiménez Alegría, Natalia - A/C.6/78/SR.8
PERSONNEL QUESTIONS—UN SYSTEM (Agenda item 142)
Velázquez Castillo, Jesús - A/C.5/78/SR.10
PERSONS WITH DISABILITIES—HUMAN RIGHTS (Agenda item 71a)
Buenrostro Massieu, Alicia - A/C.3/78/SR.51
Reza Bautista, Mauricio - A/C.3/78/SR.38

Mexico (continued)

POVERTY—INTERNATIONAL DECADES (Agenda item 21a)
Vásquez Solano, Leonel - A/C.2/78/SR.16
RACIAL DISCRIMINATION—ELIMINATION (Agenda item 69a)
Elizondo Belden, Luis Gerardo - A/C.3/78/SR.40
Mendoza Elguea, Sylvia Paola - A/78/PV.103
Riveroll Usabiaga, Renata - A/C.3/78/SR.42
RACIAL DISCRIMINATION—PROGRAMMES OF ACTION (Agenda item 69b)
Elizondo Belden, Luis Gerardo - A/C.3/78/SR.40
Riveroll Usabiaga, Renata - A/C.3/78/SR.42
RESPONSIBILITY OF INTERNATIONAL ORGANIZATIONS (Agenda item 85)
Delgado Fernández, Sergio Emanuel - A/C.6/78/SR.19
RESPONSIBILITY TO PROTECT (Agenda item 129)
Vasconcelos y Cruz, Héctor Enrique - A/78/PV.96
RIGHT TO DEVELOPMENT (Agenda item 71b)
Santa Ana Vara, Alma Esperanza - A/C.3/78/SR.48
RIGHT TO HEALTH (Agenda item 71b)
Mendoza Elguea, Sylvia Paola - A/C.3/78/SR.39
RIGHTS OF THE CHILD (Agenda item 67)
Reza Bautista, Mauricio - A/C.3/78/SR.11; A/C.3/78/SR.12
Yarahuán Dodero, Santiago - A/C.3/78/SR.12
RULE OF LAW (Agenda item 83)
Jiménez Alegría, Natalia - A/C.6/78/SR.18
RURAL POVERTY (Agenda item 21b)
Mendoza Elguea, Sylvia Paola - A/C.2/78/SR.22
Vásquez Solano, Leonel - A/C.2/78/SR.16
RURAL WOMEN (Agenda item 25a)
Santa Ana Vara, Alma Esperanza - A/C.3/78/SR.49
SCIENCE AND TECHNOLOGY—DEVELOPMENT (Agenda item 19a)
Curzio Vila, Elena - A/C.2/78/SR.10
SEXUAL ORIENTATION (Agenda item 71b)
Pedraza Calleja, Rodrigo - A/C.3/78/SR.39
SMALL ARMS—ILLICIT TRAFFIC—ASSISTANCE (Agenda item 99n)
Sánchez Kiesslich, Eduardo Alcibiades - A/C.1/78/PV.18
SOCIAL CONDITIONS (Agenda item 24b)
Santa Ana Vara, Alma Esperanza - A/C.3/78/SR.2; A/C.3/78/SR.47
SOCIAL DEVELOPMENT—CONFERENCES (Agenda item 24a)
Santa Ana Vara, Alma Esperanza - A/C.3/78/SR.55
SPECIAL POLITICAL MISSIONS (Agenda item 52)
Buenrostro Massieu, Alicia - A/C.4/78/SR.21
STRADDLING FISH STOCKS (Agenda item 75b)
Buenrostro Massieu, Alicia - A/78/PV.44
SUMMARY EXECUTIONS (Agenda item 71b)
Riveroll Usabiaga, Renata - A/C.3/78/SR.31

Mexico (continued)

SUSTAINABLE DEVELOPMENT (Agenda item 18)
Buenrostro Massieu, Alicia - A/78/PV.107; A/C.2/78/SR.24
Robledo López, Carmen - A/C.2/78/SR.14
TERRORISM (Agenda item 109)
Jiménez Alegría, Natalia - A/C.6/78/SR.1
TERRORISM—HUMAN RIGHTS (Agenda item 71b)
Elizondo Belden, Luis Gerardo - A/C.3/78/SR.31; A/C.3/78/SR.51
TORTURE AND OTHER CRUEL TREATMENT (Agenda item 71a)
Buenrostro Massieu, Alicia - A/C.3/78/SR.18
TREATIES (Agenda item 87)
Arrocha Olabuenaga, Pablo Adrián - A/C.6/78/SR.20
UKRAINE—POLITICAL CONDITIONS (Agenda item 62)
Buenrostro Massieu, Alicia - A/78/PV.57
Vasconcelos y Cruz, Héctor Enrique - A/78/PV.99
UN—BUDGET (2024) (Agenda item 134)
Buenrostro Massieu, Alicia - A/C.5/78/SR.5
Velázquez Castillo, Jesús - A/C.5/78/SR.3; A/C.5/78/SR.33
UN—PROGRAMME PLANNING (Agenda item 135)
Buenrostro Massieu, Alicia - A/C.5/78/SR.5
Sánchez Kiesslich, Eduardo Alcibiades - A/C.1/78/PV.10
UN. CONFERENCE ON DISARMAMENT—REPORTS (Agenda item 101a)
Sánchez Kiesslich, Eduardo Alcibiades - A/C.1/78/PV.22; A/C.1/78/PV.29
UN. DISARMAMENT COMMISSION—REPORTS (Agenda item 101b)
Sánchez Kiesslich, Eduardo Alcibiades - A/C.1/78/PV.22
UN. GENERAL ASSEMBLY—WORK PROGRAMME (Agenda item 120)
Basulto Alvarez, Alejandrina - A/C.2/78/SR.25
Buenrostro Massieu, Alicia - A/78/PV.33
Sánchez Kiesslich, Eduardo Alcibiades - A/C.1/78/PV.10
UN. GENERAL ASSEMBLY (78TH SESS. : 2023-2024)—GENERAL DEBATE (Agenda item 8)
Bárcena Ibarra, Alicia - A/78/PV.12
UN. GENERAL ASSEMBLY (78TH SESS. : 2023-2024)—OFFICERS (Agenda item 5)
Velázquez Castillo, Jesús - A/C.5/78/SR.1
UN. GENERAL ASSEMBLY (78TH SESS. : 2023-2024). 1ST COMMITTEE—GENERAL DEBATE (Agenda item 8)
Buenrostro Massieu, Alicia - A/C.1/78/PV.2
UN. GENERAL ASSEMBLY (78TH SESS. : 2023-2024). 2ND COMMITTEE—GENERAL DEBATE (Agenda item 8)
Buenrostro Massieu, Alicia - A/C.2/78/SR.3
Mendoza Elguea, Sylvia Paola - A/C.2/78/SR.2

Mexico (continued)

UN. GENERAL ASSEMBLY (78TH SESS. : 2023-2024). 5TH COMMITTEE—WORK ORGANIZATION (Agenda item 7)
Velázquez Castillo, Jesús - A/C.5/78/SR.27; A/C.5/78/SR.35
UN. HUMAN RIGHTS COMMITTEE—REPORTS (Agenda item 71a)
Riveroll Usabiaga, Renata - A/C.3/78/SR.17
UN. HUMAN RIGHTS COUNCIL—REPORTS (Agenda item 66)
Elizondo Belden, Luis Gerardo - A/78/PV.23
UN. INTERNATIONAL COURT OF JUSTICE—REPORTS (Agenda item 73)
Celorio Alcántara, Alexandro - A/78/PV.20
UN. INTERNATIONAL LAW COMMISSION—REPORTS (Agenda item 79)
Arrocha Olabuenaga, Pablo Adrián - A/C.6/78/SR.29; A/C.6/78/SR.37
Jiménez Alegría, Natalia - A/78/PV.45; A/C.6/78/SR.32
Reyes Moncayo, Miguel Ángel - A/C.6/78/SR.25
UN. PEACEBUILDING COMMISSION—REPORTS (Agenda item 27)
Cisneros Chávez, José de Jesús - A/78/PV.100
UN. PEACEBUILDING FUND—REPORTS (Agenda item 111)
Cisneros Chávez, José de Jesús - A/78/PV.100
UN. SECURITY COUNCIL—MEMBERSHIP (Agenda item 121)
Buenrostro Massieu, Alicia - A/78/PV.34
UN. SECURITY COUNCIL—REPORTS (Agenda item 26)
Buenrostro Massieu, Alicia - A/78/PV.93
UN CHARTER—REPORTS (Agenda item 82)
Arrocha Olabuenaga, Pablo Adrián - A/C.6/78/SR.22
UN COMMISSION ON INTERNATIONAL TRADE LAW—REPORTS (Agenda item 77)
Sánchez Cordero Dávila, Jorge A. - A/C.6/78/SR.14
UN CONFERENCES (Agenda item 13)
Curzio Vila, Elena - A/78/PV.63
UN HIGH COMMISSIONER FOR REFUGEES—REPORTS (Agenda item 60)
Mendoza Elguea, Sylvia Paola - A/C.3/78/SR.44
UN RESOLUTIONS—IMPLEMENTATION (Agenda item 119)
Buenrostro Massieu, Alicia - A/78/PV.33
Reyna Barrón, María Fernanda - A/78/PV.108
UN SYSTEM—STRENGTHENING (Agenda item 122)
Mendoza Elguea, Sylvia Paola - A/78/PV.99
UNRWA—ACTIVITIES (Agenda item 49)
Robledo López, Carmen - A/C.4/78/SR.22
VETO (Agenda item 63)
Buenrostro Massieu, Alicia - A/78/PV.71
Jiménez Alegría, Natalia - A/78/PV.52
Ochoa Martínez, Enrique Javier - A/78/PV.3
Vasconcelos y Cruz, Héctor Enrique - A/78/PV.60; A/78/PV.67; A/78/PV.68; A/78/PV.75; A/78/PV.78

Mexico (continued)

WEAPONS—OUTER SPACE (Agenda item 97b)
Sánchez Kiesslich, Eduardo Alcibiades - A/C.1/78/PV.27
WESTERN SAHARA QUESTION (Agenda item 58)
Cisneros Chávez, José de Jesús - A/C.4/78/SR.2
El Mekaoui, Amina - A/C.4/78/SR.5
WOMEN MIGRANT WORKERS (Agenda item 25a)
Díaz Corona, Meigan - A/C.3/78/SR.49
WOMEN'S ADVANCEMENT (Agenda item 25a)
Escobar Vargas, Pamela - A/C.3/78/SR.8
Santa Ana Vara, Alma Esperanza - A/C.3/78/SR.7
WOMEN'S ADVANCEMENT—CONFERENCES (Agenda item 25b)
Escobar Vargas, Pamela - A/C.3/78/SR.8
Santa Ana Vara, Alma Esperanza - A/C.3/78/SR.7; A/C.3/78/SR.51
YOUTH (Agenda item 24b)
Santa Ana Vara, Alma Esperanza - A/C.3/78/SR.2

Micronesia (Federated States of)

BIOLOGICAL DIVERSITY—TREATIES (Agenda item 18f)
Welles, Kenneth - A/C.2/78/SR.15
DISASTER PREVENTION (Agenda item 18c)
Welles, Kenneth - A/C.2/78/SR.15
DISASTER VICTIMS (Agenda item 86)
Lippwe, Jeem - A/C.6/78/SR.6
ELECTION VERIFICATION—UN (Agenda item 71b)
Welles, Kenneth - A/C.3/78/SR.50
HUMAN RIGHTS—TERRITORIES OCCUPIED BY ISRAEL (Agenda item 71c)
Welles, Kenneth - A/C.3/78/SR.35
INDIGENOUS PEOPLES (Agenda item 68a)
Welles, Kenneth - A/C.3/78/SR.15
INDIGENOUS PEOPLES—CONFERENCES (Agenda item 68b)
Welles, Kenneth - A/C.3/78/SR.15
LAW OF THE SEA (Agenda item 75a)
Lippwe, Jeem - A/78/PV.44
MARINE ECOSYSTEMS—BIOLOGICAL DIVERSITY (Agenda item 75c)
Lippwe, Jeem - A/78/PV.44
RIGHTS OF THE CHILD (Agenda item 67)
Lippwe, Jeem - A/C.3/78/SR.13
SMALL ISLAND DEVELOPING STATES—PROGRAMMES OF ACTION (Agenda item 18b)
Welles, Kenneth - A/C.2/78/SR.15
STRADDLING FISH STOCKS (Agenda item 75b)
Lippwe, Jeem - A/78/PV.44

Micronesia (Federated States of) (continued)

UN. GENERAL ASSEMBLY (78TH SESS. : 2023-2024). 1ST COMMITTEE—WORK ORGANIZATION (Agenda item 7)
Zvachula, Martin - A/C.1/78/PV.30
UN. INTERNATIONAL LAW COMMISSION—REPORTS (Agenda item 79)
Lippwe, Jeem - A/C.6/78/SR.27
WOMEN'S ADVANCEMENT (Agenda item 25a)
Lippwe, Jeem - A/C.3/78/SR.10
WOMEN'S ADVANCEMENT—CONFERENCES (Agenda item 25b)
Lippwe, Jeem - A/C.3/78/SR.10

Micronesia (Federated States of). President

UN. GENERAL ASSEMBLY (78TH SESS. : 2023-2024)—GENERAL DEBATE (Agenda item 8)
Simina, Wesley - A/78/PV.8
UN. GENERAL ASSEMBLY (78TH SESS. : 2023-2024)—SPECIAL STATEMENTS
Simina, Wesley - A/78/PV.8

Monaco

CLIMATE (Agenda item 18d)
Du Sault, Serena - A/C.2/78/SR.15
DISASTER PREVENTION (Agenda item 18c)
Du Sault, Serena - A/C.2/78/SR.15
LAW OF THE SEA (Agenda item 75a)
Botto, Florian - A/78/PV.43
MARINE ECOSYSTEMS—BIOLOGICAL DIVERSITY (Agenda item 75c)
Botto, Florian - A/78/PV.43
RIGHTS OF THE CHILD (Agenda item 67)
Beuzit, Léa - A/C.3/78/SR.14
SPORTS—OLYMPIC GAMES (Agenda item 11)
Le Son, Daphné Brigitte Marie - A/78/PV.38
STRADDLING FISH STOCKS (Agenda item 75b)
Botto, Florian - A/78/PV.43
SUSTAINABLE DEVELOPMENT (Agenda item 18)
Du Sault, Serena - A/C.2/78/SR.15
SUSTAINABLE ENERGY (Agenda item 18h)
Du Sault, Serena - A/C.2/78/SR.15
UN. GENERAL ASSEMBLY (78TH SESS. : 2023-2024)—GENERAL DEBATE (Agenda item 8)
Albert II, Prince of Monaco, 1958- - A/78/PV.7
UN. GENERAL ASSEMBLY (78TH SESS. : 2023-2024)—SPECIAL STATEMENTS
Albert II, Prince of Monaco, 1958- - A/78/PV.7
YOUTH (Agenda item 24b)
Calem-Sangiorgio, Alyson - A/C.3/78/SR.3

Mongolia

AGEING PERSONS (Agenda item 24b)
Vorshilov, Enkhbold - A/C.3/78/SR.2
CLIMATE (Agenda item 18d)
Vorshilov, Enkhbold - A/C.2/78/SR.13
DESERTIFICATION—TREATIES (Agenda item 18e)
Vorshilov, Enkhbold - A/C.2/78/SR.13
EXTERNAL DEBT (Agenda item 16c)
Vorshilov, Enkhbold - A/C.2/78/SR.9
INTERNATIONAL CRIMINAL COURT—REPORTS (Agenda item 74)
Damdin, Erdenebal Suren - A/78/PV.21
LANDLOCKED DEVELOPING COUNTRIES—CONFERENCES (Agenda item 20b)
Ulziibayar, Vangansuren - A/C.2/78/SR.7
LEAST DEVELOPED COUNTRIES—CONFERENCES (Agenda item 20a)
Ulziibayar, Vangansuren - A/C.2/78/SR.7
PEACEKEEPING OPERATIONS (Agenda item 51)
Vorshilov, Enkhbold - A/C.4/78/SR.19
RURAL WOMEN (Agenda item 25a)
Vorshilov, Enkhbold - A/C.3/78/SR.49
SOCIAL CONDITIONS (Agenda item 24b)
Ulziibayar, Vangansuren - A/C.3/78/SR.47
Vorshilov, Enkhbold - A/C.3/78/SR.2
TERRORISM (Agenda item 109)
Vorshilov, Enkhbold - A/C.6/78/SR.2
UN. GENERAL ASSEMBLY—WORK PROGRAMME (Agenda item 120)
Vorshilov, Enkhbold - A/78/PV.32
UN. GENERAL ASSEMBLY (78TH SESS. : 2023-2024). 1ST COMMITTEE—GENERAL DEBATE (Agenda item 8)
Vorshilov, Enkhbold - A/C.1/78/PV.6
UN. GENERAL ASSEMBLY (78TH SESS. : 2023-2024). 2ND COMMITTEE—GENERAL DEBATE (Agenda item 8)
Vorshilov, Enkhbold - A/C.2/78/SR.3
UN. SECURITY COUNCIL—MEMBERSHIP (Agenda item 121)
Vorshilov, Enkhbold - A/78/PV.35
UN CONFERENCES (Agenda item 13)
Ulziibayar, Vangansuren - A/78/PV.91
UN RESOLUTIONS—IMPLEMENTATION (Agenda item 119)
Vorshilov, Enkhbold - A/78/PV.32
YOUTH (Agenda item 24b)
Vorshilov, Enkhbold - A/C.3/78/SR.2

Mongolia. President

UN. GENERAL ASSEMBLY (78TH SESS. : 2023-2024)—GENERAL DEBATE (Agenda item 8)
Khurelsukh, Ukhnaa - A/78/PV.7
UN. GENERAL ASSEMBLY (78TH SESS. : 2023-2024)—SPECIAL STATEMENTS
Khurelsukh, Ukhnaa - A/78/PV.7

Montenegro

ELECTION VERIFICATION—UN (Agenda item 71b)
Bubanja, Jovana - A/C.3/78/SR.50
HUMAN RIGHTS—RUSSIAN FEDERATION (Agenda item 71c)
Bubanja, Jovana - A/C.3/78/SR.37
HUMAN RIGHTS—UKRAINE (Agenda item 71c)
Bubanja, Jovana - A/C.3/78/SR.37
PEACE (Agenda item 14)
Sabanovic, Damir - A/78/PV.82
UKRAINE—POLITICAL CONDITIONS (Agenda item 62)
Sabanovic, Damir - A/78/PV.58

Montenegro. President

UN. GENERAL ASSEMBLY (78TH SESS. : 2023-2024)—GENERAL DEBATE (Agenda item 8)
Milatović, Jakov - A/78/PV.8
UN. GENERAL ASSEMBLY (78TH SESS. : 2023-2024)—SPECIAL STATEMENTS
Milatović, Jakov - A/78/PV.8

Moroccan Jordanian Friendship Association

WESTERN SAHARA QUESTION (Agenda item 58)
Alkhalaileh, Fawaz - A/C.4/78/SR.4

Morocco

AGEING PERSONS (Agenda item 24b)
Moutchou, Majda - A/C.3/78/SR.1
CLIMATE (Agenda item 18d)
Ouatiki, Assia - A/C.2/78/SR.13
CLIMATE CHANGE (Agenda item 71b)
Alaoui, Rabia - A/C.3/78/SR.29
COASTAL ZONE MANAGEMENT (Agenda item 18j)
El Hilali, Meriem - A/C.2/78/SR.23
CRIME PREVENTION (Agenda item 107)
Bouchikhi, Hanaa - A/C.3/78/SR.6
CRIMES AGAINST HUMANITY (Agenda item 80)
Lahsaini, Khalid - A/C.6/78/SR.39; A/C.6/78/SR.41
CYBERCRIME (Agenda item 108)
Bouchikhi, Hanaa - A/C.3/78/SR.6
DISAPPEARANCE OF PERSONS (Agenda item 71b)
Bouchikhi, Hanaa - A/C.3/78/SR.22
DISASTER VICTIMS (Agenda item 86)
Lasri, El Hassan - A/C.6/78/SR.6
DISPLACED PERSONS (Agenda item 71b)
Elhamriti, Soufiane - A/C.3/78/SR.32
ECONOMIC COOPERATION AMONG DEVELOPING COUNTRIES (Agenda item 22b)
Ouatiki, Assia - A/C.2/78/SR.18

Morocco (continued)

EMERGENCY ASSISTANCE (Agenda item 72a)
Kadiri, Omar - A/78/PV.47
HAZARDOUS WASTES (Agenda item 71b)
Chaouki, Naser-Allah - A/C.3/78/SR.29
HUMAN RIGHTS (Agenda item 71)
Bouchikhi, Hanaa - A/C.3/78/SR.16
HUMAN RIGHTS—CENTRAL AFRICAN REPUBLIC (Agenda item 71c)
Kadiri, Omar - A/C.3/78/SR.33
HUMAN RIGHTS—INTERNATIONAL INSTRUMENTS (Agenda item 71a)
Moutchou, Majda - A/C.3/78/SR.27
HUMAN RIGHTS—TERRITORIES OCCUPIED BY ISRAEL (Agenda item 71c)
Moutchou, Majda - A/C.3/78/SR.27
IAEA—REPORTS (Agenda item 89)
Kadiri, Omar - A/78/PV.29
INFORMATION (Agenda item 53)
El Mezouaghi, Youssef - A/C.4/78/SR.13
INTERNATIONAL JURISDICTION (Agenda item 84)
Lahsaini, Khalid - A/C.6/78/SR.13
MIGRANTS—PROTECTION (Agenda item 71b)
Ouafi, Sara - A/C.3/78/SR.23
OPERATIONAL ACTIVITIES—UN SYSTEM (Agenda item 22a)
Ouatiki, Assia - A/C.2/78/SR.18
PALESTINE QUESTION (Agenda item 35)
Kadiri, Omar - A/78/PV.39
PALESTINIANS—ASSISTANCE (Agenda item 72b)
Kadiri, Omar - A/78/PV.47
PEACE (Agenda item 14)
Kadri, Taha - A/78/PV.76
PEACEBUILDING (Agenda item 61)
Hilale, Omar - A/78/PV.100
PEACEKEEPING OPERATIONS (Agenda item 51)
El Ouazzani, Mouna Chahdi - A/C.4/78/SR.20
RELIGIOUS INTOLERANCE (Agenda item 71b)
Bouchikhi, Hanaa - A/C.3/78/SR.38
RESPONSIBILITY TO PROTECT (Agenda item 129)
Bouchikhi, Hanaa - A/78/PV.96
RIGHT TO DRINKING WATER (Agenda item 71b)
Alaoui, Rabia - A/C.3/78/SR.28
RIGHT TO EDUCATION (Agenda item 71b)
Alaoui, Rabia - A/C.3/78/SR.27
RIGHT TO FOOD (Agenda item 71b)
Chaouki, Naser-Allah - A/C.3/78/SR.30
RIGHTS OF THE CHILD (Agenda item 67)
Lyazidi, Naima - A/C.3/78/SR.14
Moutchou, Majda - A/C.3/78/SR.11; A/C.3/78/SR.12
RULE OF LAW (Agenda item 83)
Bouziane, Zineb - A/C.6/78/SR.19

Morocco (continued)

SELF-DETERMINATION OF PEOPLES (Agenda item 70)
Moutchou, Majda - A/C.3/78/SR.43
SOCIAL CONDITIONS (Agenda item 24b)
Hilale, Omar - A/78/PV.101
SOCIAL DEVELOPMENT (Agenda item 24)
Moutchou, Majda - A/C.3/78/SR.1
SPORTS—OLYMPIC GAMES (Agenda item 11)
Hilale, Omar - A/78/PV.38
SUMMARY EXECUTIONS (Agenda item 71b)
Bouchikhi, Hanaa - A/C.3/78/SR.31
SUSTAINABLE DEVELOPMENT (Agenda item 18)
Ouatiki, Assia - A/C.2/78/SR.13
SUSTAINABLE ENERGY (Agenda item 18h)
Ouatiki, Assia - A/C.2/78/SR.13
TERRITORIES OCCUPIED BY ISRAEL—HUMAN RIGHTS (Agenda item 50)
Jerboui, Hind - A/C.4/78/SR.25
TERRORISM (Agenda item 109)
Lasri, El Hassan - A/C.6/78/SR.4
TERRORISM—HUMAN RIGHTS (Agenda item 71b)
Bouchikhi, Hanaa - A/C.3/78/SR.31
TORTURE AND OTHER CRUEL TREATMENT (Agenda item 71a)
Chabi, Amine - A/C.3/78/SR.18
TRAFFIC SAFETY (Agenda item 12)
Bouchikhi, Hanaa - A/78/PV.92
TRAFFICKING IN PERSONS (Agenda item 71b)
Alaoui, Rabia - A/C.3/78/SR.23
UN—BUDGET (2024) (Agenda item 134)
Boutaqa, Soufiane - A/C.5/78/SR.33
Hilale, Omar - A/C.5/78/SR.5
UN—FINANCIAL SITUATION (Agenda item 136)
Bouazzaoui, Chaimae - A/C.5/78/SR.6
UN—PROGRAMME PLANNING (Agenda item 135)
Hilale, Omar - A/C.5/78/SR.5
UN. GENERAL ASSEMBLY—WORK PROGRAMME (Agenda item 120)
Benziane, Imane - A/78/PV.32
UN. GENERAL ASSEMBLY (78TH SESS. : 2023-2024)—GENERAL DEBATE (Agenda item 8)
Hilale, Omar - A/78/PV.14
UN. GENERAL ASSEMBLY (78TH SESS. : 2023-2024)—GENERAL DEBATE—RIGHT OF REPLY (Agenda item 8)
Hilale, Omar - A/78/PV.14
UN. GENERAL ASSEMBLY (78TH SESS. : 2023-2024). 1ST COMMITTEE—GENERAL DEBATE (Agenda item 8)
Yousfi, Salim - A/C.1/78/PV.3

Morocco (continued)

UN. GENERAL ASSEMBLY (78TH SESS. : 2023-2024). 2ND COMMITTEE—GENERAL DEBATE (Agenda item 8)
Hamdouni, Meryem - A/C.2/78/SR.4
UN. HUMAN RIGHTS COUNCIL—REPORTS (Agenda item 66)
Bouchikhi, Hanaa - A/C.3/78/SR.46
Kadiri, Omar - A/78/PV.28
UN. INTERNATIONAL LAW COMMISSION—REPORTS (Agenda item 79)
Lahsaini, Khalid - A/C.6/78/SR.37
UN. PEACEBUILDING COMMISSION—REPORTS (Agenda item 27)
Hilale, Omar - A/78/PV.100
UN. PEACEBUILDING FUND—REPORTS (Agenda item 111)
Hilale, Omar - A/78/PV.100
UN. SECURITY COUNCIL—MEMBERSHIP (Agenda item 121)
Kadiri, Omar - A/78/PV.34
UN COMMISSION ON INTERNATIONAL TRADE LAW—REPORTS (Agenda item 77)
Bouziane, Zineb - A/C.6/78/SR.14
UN HIGH COMMISSIONER FOR REFUGEES—REPORTS (Agenda item 60)
Bouchikhi, Hanaa - A/C.3/78/SR.45
Elhamriti, Soufiane - A/C.3/78/SR.44
UN RESOLUTIONS—IMPLEMENTATION (Agenda item 119)
Benziane, Imane - A/78/PV.32
UNRWA—ACTIVITIES (Agenda item 49)
El Ouazzani, Mouna Chahdi - A/C.4/78/SR.22
Jerboui, Hind - A/C.4/78/SR.23
VETO (Agenda item 63)
Hilale, Omar - A/78/PV.52; A/78/PV.61; A/78/PV.66
Kadiri, Omar - A/78/PV.69
Kadri, Taha - A/78/PV.75
Yousfi, Salim - A/78/PV.79
WESTERN SAHARA QUESTION (Agenda item 58)
Dahi, Leila - A/C.4/78/SR.4
Hilale, Omar - A/C.4/78/SR.9
Kadiri, Omar - A/C.4/78/SR.4; A/C.4/78/SR.5
Laariche, Hayat - A/C.4/78/SR.4
WOMEN'S ADVANCEMENT (Agenda item 25a)
Iraqui, Abla - A/C.3/78/SR.9
WOMEN'S ADVANCEMENT—CONFERENCES (Agenda item 25b)
Iraqui, Abla - A/C.3/78/SR.9
YOUTH (Agenda item 24b)
Chaquki, Naser-Allah - A/C.3/78/SR.3
Skali, Abla - A/C.3/78/SR.3

Mozambique

ADMINISTRATION OF JUSTICE (Agenda item 144)
Saranga, Geraldo - A/C.6/78/SR.9

Mozambique (continued)

CRIMES AGAINST HUMANITY (Agenda item 80)
Saranga, Geraldo - A/C.6/78/SR.11
DECOLONIZATION (Agenda item 58)
Buanahagi, Tarcísio Baltazar - A/C.4/78/SR.8
DISASTER PREVENTION (Agenda item 18c)
Abdala, Paulina Feliciano Francisco - A/C.2/78/SR.15
ECONOMIC COOPERATION AMONG DEVELOPING COUNTRIES (Agenda item 22b)
Abdala, Paulina Feliciano Francisco - A/C.2/78/SR.18
FALKLAND ISLANDS (MALVINAS) QUESTION (Agenda item 42)
Buanahagi, Tarcísio Baltazar - A/C.4/78/SR.8
FOOD SECURITY (Agenda item 23a)
Maure, Adnito - A/C.2/78/SR.17
INTERNATIONAL JURISDICTION (Agenda item 84)
Saranga, Geraldo - A/C.6/78/SR.13
PEACEKEEPING OPERATIONS (Agenda item 51)
Efson, Gladys Evangelina - A/C.4/78/SR.20
POVERTY—INTERNATIONAL DECADES (Agenda item 21a)
Maure, Adnito - A/C.2/78/SR.17
RIGHT TO DEVELOPMENT (Agenda item 71b)
Raivoso, Ilda - A/C.3/78/SR.26
RULE OF LAW (Agenda item 83)
Saranga, Geraldo - A/C.6/78/SR.18
RURAL POVERTY (Agenda item 21b)
Maure, Adnito - A/C.2/78/SR.17
SELF-DETERMINATION OF PEOPLES (Agenda item 70)
Serage, Bruno Bernardo - A/C.3/78/SR.42
TERRORISM (Agenda item 109)
Saranga, Geraldo - A/C.6/78/SR.4
UN—BUDGET (2024) (Agenda item 134)
Kumanga, Martins Mariano - A/C.5/78/SR.5
UN—PROGRAMME PLANNING (Agenda item 135)
Kumanga, Martins Mariano - A/C.5/78/SR.5
UN. GENERAL ASSEMBLY (78TH SESS. : 2023-2024). 1ST COMMITTEE—GENERAL DEBATE (Agenda item 8)
Fernandes, Domingos Estêvão - A/C.1/78/PV.9
UN. SECURITY COUNCIL—REPORTS (Agenda item 26)
Afonso, Pedro Comissário - A/78/PV.94
UN HIGH COMMISSIONER FOR REFUGEES—REPORTS (Agenda item 60)
Serage, Bruno Bernardo - A/C.3/78/SR.45
VETO (Agenda item 63)
Afonso, Pedro Comissário - A/78/PV.75
WESTERN SAHARA QUESTION (Agenda item 58)
Buanahagi, Tarcísio Baltazar - A/C.4/78/SR.8

Mozambique. President

UN. GENERAL ASSEMBLY (78TH SESS. : 2023-2024)—GENERAL DEBATE (Agenda item 8)
Nyusi, Filipe Jacinto - A/78/PV.5
UN. GENERAL ASSEMBLY (78TH SESS. : 2023-2024)—SPECIAL STATEMENTS
Nyusi, Filipe Jacinto - A/78/PV.5

Myanmar

BIOLOGICAL WEAPONS—TREATIES (Agenda item 106)
Tun, Kyaw Moe - A/C.1/78/PV.16
CHEMICAL WEAPONS—TREATIES (Agenda item 99l)
Tun, Kyaw Moe - A/C.1/78/PV.16
CRIME PREVENTION (Agenda item 107)
Tun, Kyaw Moe - A/C.3/78/SR.6
CRIMES AGAINST HUMANITY (Agenda item 80)
Tun, Kyaw Moe - A/C.6/78/SR.11
DISAPPEARANCE OF PERSONS (Agenda item 71b)
Tun, Kyaw Moe - A/C.3/78/SR.22
DISPLACED PERSONS (Agenda item 71b)
Tun, Kyaw Moe - A/C.3/78/SR.32
EMERGENCY ASSISTANCE (Agenda item 72a)
Tun, Kyaw Moe - A/78/PV.47
FOOD SECURITY (Agenda item 23a)
Tun, Kyaw Moe - A/C.2/78/SR.17
FREEDOM OF EXPRESSION (Agenda item 71b)
Tun, Kyaw Moe - A/C.3/78/SR.19
HUMAN RIGHTS (Agenda item 71)
Tun, Kyaw Moe - A/C.3/78/SR.16
HUMAN RIGHTS—MYANMAR (Agenda item 71c)
Tun, Kyaw Moe - A/C.3/78/SR.27; A/C.3/78/SR.33; A/C.3/78/SR.53
HUMAN RIGHTS ACTIVISTS (Agenda item 71b)
Tun, Kyaw Moe - A/C.3/78/SR.19
IAEA—REPORTS (Agenda item 89)
Tun, Kyaw Moe - A/78/PV.29
INFORMATION (Agenda item 53)
Tun, Kyaw Moe - A/C.4/78/SR.14
INTERNATIONAL CRIMINAL COURT—REPORTS (Agenda item 74)
Tun, Kyaw Moe - A/78/PV.22
INTERNATIONAL JURISDICTION (Agenda item 84)
Tun, Kyaw Moe - A/C.6/78/SR.13
LANDLOCKED DEVELOPING COUNTRIES—CONFERENCES (Agenda item 20b)
Tun, Kyaw Moe - A/C.2/78/SR.7
LEAST DEVELOPED COUNTRIES—CONFERENCES (Agenda item 20a)
Tun, Kyaw Moe - A/C.2/78/SR.7

Myanmar (continued)

MACROECONOMIC POLICY (Agenda item 16)
Tun, Kyaw Moe - A/C.2/78/SR.9
MINE CLEARANCE (Agenda item 46)
Tun, Kyaw Moe - A/C.4/78/SR.10
NUCLEAR DISARMAMENT (Agenda item 99b)
Tun, Kyaw Moe - A/C.1/78/PV.14
NUCLEAR NON-PROLIFERATION—INTERNATIONAL OBLIGATIONS (Agenda item 99w)
Tun, Kyaw Moe - A/C.1/78/PV.14
NUCLEAR WEAPON TESTS—TREATIES (Agenda item 105)
Tun, Kyaw Moe - A/C.1/78/PV.14
PEACE (Agenda item 14)
Tun, Kyaw Moe - A/78/PV.76
PERSONS WITH DISABILITIES—HUMAN RIGHTS (Agenda item 71a)
Tun, Kyaw Moe - A/C.3/78/SR.38
POVERTY—INTERNATIONAL DECADES (Agenda item 21a)
Tun, Kyaw Moe - A/C.2/78/SR.17
RESPONSIBILITY TO PROTECT (Agenda item 129)
Tun, Kyaw Moe - A/78/PV.96
RIGHTS OF THE CHILD (Agenda item 67)
Tun, Kyaw Moe - A/C.3/78/SR.14
RULE OF LAW (Agenda item 83)
Tun, Kyaw Moe - A/C.6/78/SR.18
RURAL POVERTY (Agenda item 21b)
Tun, Kyaw Moe - A/C.2/78/SR.17
SOCIAL CONDITIONS (Agenda item 24b)
Tun, Kyaw Moe - A/C.3/78/SR.3
SUMMARY EXECUTIONS (Agenda item 71b)
Tun, Kyaw Moe - A/C.3/78/SR.31
SUSTAINABLE DEVELOPMENT (Agenda item 18)
Tun, Kyaw Moe - A/C.2/78/SR.15
TORTURE AND OTHER CRUEL TREATMENT (Agenda item 71a)
Tun, Kyaw Moe - A/C.3/78/SR.18
UN—BUDGET (2024) (Agenda item 134)
Tun, Kyaw Moe - A/C.5/78/SR.5
UN—PROGRAMME PLANNING (Agenda item 135)
Tun, Kyaw Moe - A/C.5/78/SR.5
UN. GENERAL ASSEMBLY (78TH SESS. : 2023-2024). 1ST COMMITTEE—GENERAL DEBATE (Agenda item 8)
Tun, Kyaw Moe - A/C.1/78/PV.7
UN. GENERAL ASSEMBLY (78TH SESS. : 2023-2024). 2ND COMMITTEE—GENERAL DEBATE (Agenda item 8)
Tun, Kyaw Moe - A/C.2/78/SR.5
UN. HUMAN RIGHTS COUNCIL—REPORTS (Agenda item 66)
Tun, Kyaw Moe - A/78/PV.23; A/C.3/78/SR.46

Myanmar (continued)

UN. INTERNATIONAL COURT OF JUSTICE—REPORTS (Agenda item 73)
Tun, Kyaw Moe - A/78/PV.28
UN. SECRETARY-GENERAL—REPORTS (Agenda item 110)
Tun, Kyaw Moe - A/78/PV.55
UN. SECURITY COUNCIL—REPORTS (Agenda item 26)
Tun, Kyaw Moe - A/78/PV.93
UN HIGH COMMISSIONER FOR REFUGEES—REPORTS (Agenda item 60)
Tun, Kyaw Moe - A/C.3/78/SR.45
WOMEN'S ADVANCEMENT (Agenda item 25a)
Tun, Kyaw Moe - A/C.3/78/SR.10
WOMEN'S ADVANCEMENT—CONFERENCES (Agenda item 25b)
Tun, Kyaw Moe - A/C.3/78/SR.10

Namibia

AFRICA—DEVELOPMENT (Agenda item 65b)
Gertze, Neville Melvin - A/78/PV.18
AFRICA—SUSTAINABLE DEVELOPMENT—PARTNERSHIP (Agenda item 65a)
Gertze, Neville Melvin - A/78/PV.18
AGEING PERSONS (Agenda item 24b)
Gertze, Neville Melvin - A/C.3/78/SR.2
CUBA—UNITED STATES (Agenda item 38)
Gantana, Audrey Fay - A/78/PV.24
DECOLONIZATION (Agenda item 58)
Gertze, Neville Melvin - A/C.4/78/SR.7
DEVELOPMENT COOPERATION—MIDDLE-INCOME COUNTRIES (Agenda item 19c)
Gantana, Audrey Fay - A/C.2/78/SR.10
DEVELOPMENT FINANCE (Agenda item 16b)
Naanda, Anne - A/C.2/78/SR.9
FOOD SECURITY (Agenda item 23a)
Gertze, Neville Melvin - A/C.2/78/SR.16
GEINGOB, HAGE GOTTFRIED (NAMIBIA. PRESIDENT)—TRIBUTES
Gertze, Neville Melvin - A/78/PV.55
HEALTH (Agenda item 125)
Gertze, Neville Melvin - A/78/PV.41
Kuzee, Helena Ndapewa - A/78/PV.16
HIV/AIDS—DECLARATIONS (Agenda item 10)
Kuzee, Helena Ndapewa - A/78/PV.91
HUMAN RIGHTS—TERRITORIES OCCUPIED BY ISRAEL (Agenda item 71c)
Iileka, Nekwayahelalia - A/C.3/78/SR.35
IAEA—REPORTS (Agenda item 89)
Gertze, Neville Melvin - A/78/PV.30
INFORMATION (Agenda item 53)
Kuzee, Helena Ndapewa - A/C.4/78/SR.14
INTERNATIONAL TRADE (Agenda item 16a)
Naanda, Anne - A/C.2/78/SR.9

Namibia (continued)

MACROECONOMIC POLICY (Agenda item 16)
Naanda, Anne - A/C.2/78/SR.9
NUCLEAR DISARMAMENT (Agenda item 99b)
Kuzee, Helena Ndapewa - A/C.1/78/PV.14
PALESTINE QUESTION (Agenda item 35)
Gertze, Neville Melvin - A/78/PV.39
PEACE (Agenda item 14)
Gertze, Neville Melvin - A/78/PV.82
POVERTY—INTERNATIONAL DECADES (Agenda item 21a)
Gertze, Neville Melvin - A/C.2/78/SR.16
RACIAL DISCRIMINATION—ELIMINATION (Agenda item 69a)
Ashipala, Sevelina - A/C.3/78/SR.40
RACIAL DISCRIMINATION—PROGRAMMES OF ACTION (Agenda item 69b)
Ashipala, Sevelina - A/C.3/78/SR.40
RIGHTS OF THE CHILD (Agenda item 67)
Iileka, Nekwayahelalia - A/C.3/78/SR.13
RURAL POVERTY (Agenda item 21b)
Gertze, Neville Melvin - A/C.2/78/SR.16
SELF-DETERMINATION OF PEOPLES (Agenda item 70)
Ashipala, Sevelina - A/C.3/78/SR.40
SOCIAL CONDITIONS (Agenda item 24b)
Gertze, Neville Melvin - A/C.3/78/SR.2
SOCIAL DEVELOPMENT (Agenda item 24)
Gertze, Neville Melvin - A/C.3/78/SR.2
SUSTAINABLE DEVELOPMENT (Agenda item 18)
Gertze, Neville Melvin - A/C.2/78/SR.13
TERRITORIES OCCUPIED BY ISRAEL—HUMAN RIGHTS (Agenda item 50)
Gertze, Neville Melvin - A/C.4/78/SR.26
TERRITORIES OCCUPIED BY ISRAEL—NATURAL RESOURCES (Agenda item 59)
Gertze, Neville Melvin - A/C.2/78/SR.19
UN. GENERAL ASSEMBLY (78TH SESS. : 2023-2024). 1ST COMMITTEE—GENERAL DEBATE (Agenda item 8)
Kuzee, Helena Ndapewa - A/C.1/78/PV.8
UN. GENERAL ASSEMBLY (78TH SESS. : 2023-2024). 2ND COMMITTEE—GENERAL DEBATE (Agenda item 8)
Gertze, Neville Melvin - A/C.2/78/SR.4
VETO (Agenda item 63)
Gertze, Neville Melvin - A/78/PV.60
Kuzee, Helena Ndapewa - A/78/PV.52
WESTERN SAHARA QUESTION (Agenda item 58)
Gertze, Neville Melvin - A/C.4/78/SR.7
WOMEN'S ADVANCEMENT (Agenda item 25a)
Kuzee, Helena Ndapewa - A/C.3/78/SR.9
WOMEN'S ADVANCEMENT—CONFERENCES (Agenda item 25b)
Kuzee, Helena Ndapewa - A/C.3/78/SR.9

Namibia (continued)

YOUTH (Agenda item 24b)
Gertze, Neville Melvin - A/C.3/78/SR.2

Namibia. President

UN. GENERAL ASSEMBLY (78TH SESS. : 2023-2024)—GENERAL DEBATE (Agenda item 8)
Geingob, Hage Gottfried - A/78/PV.6
UN. GENERAL ASSEMBLY (78TH SESS. : 2023-2024)—SPECIAL STATEMENTS
Geingob, Hage Gottfried - A/78/PV.6

Nauru

HUMAN RIGHTS—TERRITORIES OCCUPIED BY ISRAEL (Agenda item 71c)
Dongobir, Josie-Ann - A/C.3/78/SR.35
LAW OF THE SEA (Agenda item 75a)
Adire, Anastasia Francilia - A/78/PV.44
MARINE ECOSYSTEMS—BIOLOGICAL DIVERSITY (Agenda item 75c)
Adire, Anastasia Francilia - A/78/PV.44
STRADDLING FISH STOCKS (Agenda item 75b)
Adire, Anastasia Francilia - A/78/PV.44
UN. GENERAL ASSEMBLY (78TH SESS. : 2023-2024). 2ND COMMITTEE—GENERAL DEBATE (Agenda item 8)
Tsiode, Branessa - A/C.2/78/SR.6

Nauru. President

UN. GENERAL ASSEMBLY (78TH SESS. : 2023-2024)—GENERAL DEBATE (Agenda item 8)
Kun, Russ - A/78/PV.9
UN. GENERAL ASSEMBLY (78TH SESS. : 2023-2024)—SPECIAL STATEMENTS
Kun, Russ - A/78/PV.9

Nepal

BIOLOGICAL WEAPONS—TREATIES (Agenda item 106)
Gohiwar Aryal, Indira - A/C.1/78/PV.15
CHEMICAL WEAPONS—TREATIES (Agenda item 99l)
Gohiwar Aryal, Indira - A/C.1/78/PV.15
DECOLONIZATION (Agenda item 58)
Ray, Kaushal Kishor - A/C.4/78/SR.6
DISASTER VICTIMS (Agenda item 86)
Thapa, Lok Bahadur - A/C.6/78/SR.6
FALKLAND ISLANDS (MALVINAS) QUESTION (Agenda item 42)
Ray, Kaushal Kishor - A/C.4/78/SR.6
HUMAN RIGHTS—INTERNATIONAL INSTRUMENTS (Agenda item 71a)
Ray, Kaushal Kishor - A/C.3/78/SR.25
HUMAN RIGHTS ADVANCEMENT (Agenda item 71b)
Ray, Kaushal Kishor - A/C.3/78/SR.25

Nepal (continued)

INDIGENOUS PEOPLES (Agenda item 68a)
Rai, Pratigya - A/C.3/78/SR.15
INDIGENOUS PEOPLES—CONFERENCES (Agenda item 68b)
Rai, Pratigya - A/C.3/78/SR.15
INFORMATION (Agenda item 53)
Ray, Kaushal Kishor - A/C.4/78/SR.13
LANDLOCKED DEVELOPING COUNTRIES—CONFERENCES (Agenda item 20b)
Ray, Kaushal Kishor - A/C.2/78/SR.7
LEAST DEVELOPED COUNTRIES—CONFERENCES (Agenda item 20a)
Ray, Kaushal Kishor - A/C.2/78/SR.7
NUCLEAR DISARMAMENT (Agenda item 99b)
Gohiwar Aryal, Indira - A/C.1/78/PV.13
NUCLEAR NON-PROLIFERATION—INTERNATIONAL OBLIGATIONS (Agenda item 99w)
Gohiwar Aryal, Indira - A/C.1/78/PV.13
PEACE—REGIONAL CENTRE—ASIA AND THE PACIFIC (Agenda item 100d)
Gohiwar Aryal, Indira - A/C.1/78/PV.23
PEACE—REGIONAL CENTRES (Agenda item 100f)
Gohiwar Aryal, Indira - A/C.1/78/PV.23
PEACEKEEPING OPERATIONS (Agenda item 51)
Ray, Kaushal Kishor - A/C.4/78/SR.19
PEACEKEEPING OPERATIONS—CRIMINAL LIABILITY (Agenda item 76)
Charmakar, Ramesh Kumar - A/C.6/78/SR.8
RIGHTS OF THE CHILD (Agenda item 67)
Aryal, Krishna - A/C.3/78/SR.12
RULE OF LAW (Agenda item 83)
Ray, Kaushal Kishor - A/C.6/78/SR.17
SOCIAL CONDITIONS (Agenda item 24b)
Thapa, Lok Bahadur - A/C.3/78/SR.2
TERRITORIES OCCUPIED BY ISRAEL—HUMAN RIGHTS (Agenda item 50)
Ray, Kaushal Kishor - A/78/PV.45
TERRORISM (Agenda item 109)
Thapa, Lok Bahadur - A/C.6/78/SR.2
UN. CONFERENCE ON DISARMAMENT—REPORTS (Agenda item 101a)
Gohiwar Aryal, Indira - A/C.1/78/PV.23
UN. DISARMAMENT COMMISSION—REPORTS (Agenda item 101b)
Gohiwar Aryal, Indira - A/C.1/78/PV.23
UN. GENERAL ASSEMBLY (78TH SESS. : 2023-2024). 1ST COMMITTEE—GENERAL DEBATE (Agenda item 8)
Thapa, Lok Bahadur - A/C.1/78/PV.5
UN. GENERAL ASSEMBLY (78TH SESS. : 2023-2024). 2ND COMMITTEE—GENERAL DEBATE (Agenda item 8)
Thapa, Lok Bahadur - A/C.2/78/SR.2
WESTERN SAHARA QUESTION (Agenda item 58)
Ray, Kaushal Kishor - A/C.4/78/SR.6

Nepal (continued)

WOMEN'S ADVANCEMENT (Agenda item 25a)
Aryal, Krishna - A/C.3/78/SR.7
Uprety, Prathma - A/C.3/78/SR.9
WOMEN'S ADVANCEMENT—CONFERENCES (Agenda item 25b)
Aryal, Krishna - A/C.3/78/SR.7
Uprety, Prathma - A/C.3/78/SR.9
YOUTH (Agenda item 24b)
Thapa, Lok Bahadur - A/C.3/78/SR.2

Nepal. Prime Minister

UN. GENERAL ASSEMBLY (78TH SESS. : 2023-2024)—GENERAL DEBATE (Agenda item 8)
Dahal, Pushpa Kamal - A/78/PV.9
UN. GENERAL ASSEMBLY (78TH SESS. : 2023-2024)—SPECIAL STATEMENTS
Dahal, Pushpa Kamal - A/78/PV.9

Netherlands (Kingdom of the)

ADMINISTRATION OF JUSTICE (Agenda item 144)
Made, Angelique van der - A/C.6/78/SR.9
ARMED CONFLICTS PREVENTION (Agenda item 31a)
Brandt, Yoka - A/78/PV.72
ARMS RACE—OUTER SPACE (Agenda item 97a)
Bosch, Robert in den - A/C.1/78/PV.16
ARMS TRANSFERS—TREATIES (Agenda item 99x)
Bosch, Robert in den - A/C.1/78/PV.18
BIOLOGICAL WEAPONS—TREATIES (Agenda item 106)
Bosch, Robert in den - A/C.1/78/PV.14
CHEMICAL WEAPONS—TREATIES (Agenda item 99l)
Bosch, Robert in den - A/C.1/78/PV.14; A/C.1/78/PV.15
CLUSTER MUNITIONS (Agenda item 99dd)
Bosch, Robert in den - A/C.1/78/PV.18
CRIMES AGAINST HUMANITY (Agenda item 80)
Ensing, Janine - A/C.6/78/SR.38; A/C.6/78/SR.40; A/C.6/78/SR.41
Made, Angelique van der - A/C.6/78/SR.10
Riep, Elisabeth - A/C.6/78/SR.43; A/C.6/78/SR.44
Theeuwen, Wieteke Elisabeth Christina - A/C.6/78/SR.41
DISARMAMENT—GENERAL AND COMPLETE (Agenda item 99)
Bosch, Robert in den - A/C.1/78/PV.18
DISARMAMENT AGREEMENTS—OUTER SPACE (Agenda item 97c)
Bosch, Robert in den - A/C.1/78/PV.16
DISASTER VICTIMS (Agenda item 86)
Theeuwen, Wieteke Elisabeth Christina - A/C.6/78/SR.5

Netherlands (Kingdom of the) (continued)

ELECTION VERIFICATION—UN (Agenda item 71b)
Reichwein, Mark - A/78/PV.50; A/C.3/78/SR.50
FREEDOM OF EXPRESSION (Agenda item 71b)
Reichwein, Mark - A/C.3/78/SR.19
HIV/AIDS—DECLARATIONS (Agenda item 10)
Tahzib-Lie, Bahia - A/78/PV.91
HUMAN RIGHTS (Agenda item 71)
Lasseur, Katja - A/C.3/78/SR.16
HUMAN RIGHTS—AFGHANISTAN (Agenda item 71c)
Vogel, Robin Maria de - A/C.3/78/SR.34
HUMAN RIGHTS—BELARUS (Agenda item 71c)
Tunen, Maarten van - A/C.3/78/SR.37
HUMAN RIGHTS—ETHIOPIA (Agenda item 71c)
Leede, Iris Mariken de - A/C.3/78/SR.36
HUMAN RIGHTS—IRAN (ISLAMIC REPUBLIC OF) (Agenda item 71c)
Tahzib-Lie, Bahia - A/C.3/78/SR.34
HUMAN RIGHTS—MYANMAR (Agenda item 71c)
Tunen, Maarten van - A/C.3/78/SR.33
HUMAN RIGHTS—RUSSIAN FEDERATION (Agenda item 71c)
Lasseur, Katja - A/C.3/78/SR.37
HUMAN RIGHTS—SYRIAN ARAB REPUBLIC (Agenda item 71c)
Vogel, Robin Maria de - A/C.3/78/SR.34
HUMAN RIGHTS—UKRAINE (Agenda item 71c)
Lasseur, Katja - A/C.3/78/SR.37
HUMAN RIGHTS ACTIVISTS (Agenda item 71b)
Brandt, Yoka - A/C.3/78/SR.19
IAEA—REPORTS (Agenda item 89)
Tahzib-Lie, Bahia - A/78/PV.30
INFORMATION—INTERNATIONAL SECURITY (Agenda item 94)
Bosch, Robert in den - A/C.1/78/PV.20
INTERNATIONAL CRIMINAL COURT—REPORTS (Agenda item 74)
Brandt, Yoka - A/78/PV.21
INTERNATIONAL JURISDICTION (Agenda item 84)
Jacobs, Mats - A/C.6/78/SR.12
LANDMINES—TREATIES (Agenda item 99m)
Bosch, Robert in den - A/C.1/78/PV.18
NON-CITIZENS—DEPORTATION (Agenda item 81)
Theeuwen, Wieteke Elisabeth Christina - A/C.6/78/SR.34
NUCLEAR DISARMAMENT (Agenda item 99b)
Bosch, Robert in den - A/C.1/78/PV.11

Netherlands (Kingdom of the) (continued)

NUCLEAR DISARMAMENT—CONFERENCES (Agenda item 99aa)
Bosch, Robert in den - A/C.1/78/PV.26
NUCLEAR DISARMAMENT—VERIFICATION (Agenda item 99ee)
Bosch, Robert in den - A/C.1/78/PV.11
NUCLEAR NON-PROLIFERATION—INTERNATIONAL OBLIGATIONS (Agenda item 99w)
Bosch, Robert in den - A/C.1/78/PV.11
OUTER SPACE—PRINCIPLES (Agenda item 97d)
Bosch, Robert in den - A/C.1/78/PV.16
PEACEKEEPING OPERATIONS—CRIMINAL LIABILITY (Agenda item 76)
Made, Angelique van der - A/C.6/78/SR.8
RELIGIOUS INTOLERANCE (Agenda item 71b)
Tusscher, Berendina ten - A/C.3/78/SR.38
RESPONSIBILITY OF INTERNATIONAL ORGANIZATIONS (Agenda item 85)
Theeuwen, Wieteke Elisabeth Christina - A/C.6/78/SR.19
RESPONSIBILITY TO PROTECT (Agenda item 129)
Brandt, Yoka - A/78/PV.96
SEXUAL ORIENTATION (Agenda item 71b)
Reichwein, Mark - A/C.3/78/SR.39
UKRAINE—POLITICAL CONDITIONS (Agenda item 62)
Bruins Slot, Hanke Gerdina Johannette - A/78/PV.56
UN. CONFERENCE ON DISARMAMENT—REPORTS (Agenda item 101a)
Bosch, Robert in den - A/C.1/78/PV.23
UN. GENERAL ASSEMBLY (78TH SESS. : 2023-2024). 1ST COMMITTEE—GENERAL DEBATE (Agenda item 8)
Bosch, Robert in den - A/C.1/78/PV.3
UN. HUMAN RIGHTS COUNCIL—REPORTS (Agenda item 66)
Lasseur, Katja - A/C.3/78/SR.46
UN. INTERNATIONAL COURT OF JUSTICE—REPORTS (Agenda item 73)
Lefeber, René - A/78/PV.20; A/C.6/78/SR.26
UN. INTERNATIONAL LAW COMMISSION—REPORTS (Agenda item 79)
Egmond, Liselot Francesca - A/C.6/78/SR.31
Lefeber, René - A/C.6/78/SR.24
Theeuwen, Wieteke Elisabeth Christina - A/C.6/78/SR.28
UN YOUTH OFFICE—REPORTS (Agenda item 130)
Sar, Minke van der - A/78/PV.102
UNRWA—ACTIVITIES (Agenda item 49)
Brandt, Yoka - A/C.4/78/SR.22
VETO (Agenda item 63)
Brandt, Yoka - A/78/PV.3
Tahzib-Lie, Bahia - A/78/PV.70

Netherlands (Kingdom of the) (continued)

WOMEN'S ADVANCEMENT (Agenda item 25a)
Korteweg, Chantal - A/C.3/78/SR.9
Tahzib-Lie, Bahia - A/C.3/78/SR.7
WOMEN'S ADVANCEMENT—CONFERENCES (Agenda item 25b)
Korteweg, Chantal - A/C.3/78/SR.9
Tahzib-Lie, Bahia - A/C.3/78/SR.7
YOUTH (Agenda item 24b)
Lasseur, Katja - A/C.3/78/SR.55

Netherlands (Kingdom of the). Prime Minister

UN. GENERAL ASSEMBLY (78TH SESS. : 2023-2024)—GENERAL DEBATE (Agenda item 8)
Rutte, Mark - A/78/PV.10
UN. GENERAL ASSEMBLY (78TH SESS. : 2023-2024)—SPECIAL STATEMENTS
Rutte, Mark - A/78/PV.10

New Agenda Coalition

UN. GENERAL ASSEMBLY (78TH SESS. : 2023-2024). 1ST COMMITTEE—GENERAL DEBATE (Agenda item 8)
Sánchez Kiesslich, Eduardo Alcibiades (Mexico) - A/C.1/78/PV.4

New Caledonia

NEW CALEDONIA QUESTION (Agenda item 58)
Darras, Amandine - A/C.4/78/SR.5
Falaeo, Veylma - A/C.4/78/SR.3
Forrest, Mickaël - A/C.4/78/SR.3
Trenyiwa, Karyl - A/C.4/78/SR.5
Wamytan, Roch - A/C.4/78/SR.5

New Zealand

ARMED CONFLICTS PREVENTION (Agenda item 31a)
Pringle, Rachael - A/78/PV.72
ARMS RACE—OUTER SPACE (Agenda item 97a)
Clutterbuck, Nicholas - A/C.1/78/PV.17
ARMS TRANSFERS—TREATIES (Agenda item 99x)
De Schot, Jikita - A/C.1/78/PV.19
BIOLOGICAL WEAPONS—TREATIES (Agenda item 106)
De Schot, Jikita - A/C.1/78/PV.15
CHEMICAL WEAPONS—TREATIES (Agenda item 99l)
De Schot, Jikita - A/C.1/78/PV.15
CLUSTER MUNITIONS (Agenda item 99dd)
De Schot, Jikita - A/C.1/78/PV.19
CONVENTIONAL WEAPONS—TREATIES (Agenda item 103)
De Schot, Jikita - A/C.1/78/PV.19

New Zealand (continued)

CRIMES AGAINST HUMANITY (Agenda item 80)
Janah, Naushyn - A/C.6/78/SR.39; A/C.6/78/SR.40; A/C.6/78/SR.42; A/C.6/78/SR.44
Russell, Zoe - A/C.6/78/SR.9
DISARMAMENT—GENERAL AND COMPLETE (Agenda item 99)
Clutterbuck, Nicholas - A/C.1/78/PV.11
De Schot, Jikita - A/C.1/78/PV.19; A/C.1/78/PV.30
DISARMAMENT AGREEMENTS—OUTER SPACE (Agenda item 97c)
Clutterbuck, Nicholas - A/C.1/78/PV.17
Nam, Christine - A/C.1/78/PV.27
EMERGENCY ASSISTANCE (Agenda item 72a)
Fepuleai, Justin Peter - A/78/PV.46
FISSIONABLE MATERIALS—TREATIES (Agenda item 99a)
Nam, Christine - A/C.1/78/PV.26
HEALTH (Agenda item 125)
Schaare, Ben - A/78/PV.77
HUMAN RIGHTS (Agenda item 71)
Fepuleai, Justin Peter - A/C.3/78/SR.16
HUMAN RIGHTS ACTIVISTS (Agenda item 71b)
Buist-Catherwood, Emily - A/C.3/78/SR.56
IAEA—REPORTS (Agenda item 89)
Nam, Christine - A/78/PV.30
INDIGENOUS PEOPLES (Agenda item 68a)
Carrell, Leah - A/C.3/78/SR.15
INDIGENOUS PEOPLES—CONFERENCES (Agenda item 68b)
Carrell, Leah - A/C.3/78/SR.15
INFORMATION—INTERNATIONAL SECURITY (Agenda item 94)
Nam, Christine - A/C.1/78/PV.20
INTERNATIONAL CRIMINAL COURT—REPORTS (Agenda item 74)
Fepuleai, Justin Peter - A/78/PV.22
INTERNATIONAL RESIDUAL MECHANISM FOR CRIMINAL TRIBUNALS (Agenda item 126)
Schwalger, Carolyn - A/78/PV.19
LANDMINES—TREATIES (Agenda item 99m)
De Schot, Jikita - A/C.1/78/PV.19
NUCLEAR DISARMAMENT (Agenda item 99b)
Clutterbuck, Nicholas - A/C.1/78/PV.11
NUCLEAR DISARMAMENT—TREATY COMPLIANCE (Agenda item 99q)
Clutterbuck, Nicholas - A/C.1/78/PV.11
Nam, Christine - A/C.1/78/PV.25
NUCLEAR NON-PROLIFERATION—INTERNATIONAL OBLIGATIONS (Agenda item 99w)
Clutterbuck, Nicholas - A/C.1/78/PV.11
NUCLEAR WEAPON TESTS—TREATIES (Agenda item 105)
Clutterbuck, Nicholas - A/C.1/78/PV.11
NUCLEAR WEAPONS—ELIMINATION (Agenda item 99z)
Nam, Christine - A/C.1/78/PV.26

New Zealand (continued)

NUCLEAR WEAPONS—HUMANITARIAN CONSEQUENCES (Agenda item 99bb)
Clutterbuck, Nicholas - A/C.1/78/PV.11
NUCLEAR WEAPONS—TREATIES (Agenda item 99ff)
Clutterbuck, Nicholas - A/C.1/78/PV.11
NUCLEAR-WEAPON-FREE ZONE—SOUTHERN HEMISPHERE (Agenda item 99i)
Clutterbuck, Nicholas - A/C.1/78/PV.11
Nam, Christine - A/C.1/78/PV.25
NUCLEAR-WEAPON-FREE ZONES (Agenda item 99cc)
Clutterbuck, Nicholas - A/C.1/78/PV.11
OUTER SPACE—CONFIDENCE-BUILDING MEASURES (Agenda item 99v)
Clutterbuck, Nicholas - A/C.1/78/PV.17
OUTER SPACE—PRINCIPLES (Agenda item 97d)
Clutterbuck, Nicholas - A/C.1/78/PV.17
PALESTINIANS—ASSISTANCE (Agenda item 72b)
Fepuleai, Justin Peter - A/78/PV.46
PEACE (Agenda item 14)
Fepuleai, Justin Peter - A/78/PV.62
PEACEKEEPING OPERATIONS—CRIMINAL LIABILITY (Agenda item 76)
Russell, Zoe - A/C.6/78/SR.8
PERSONS WITH DISABILITIES—HUMAN RIGHTS (Agenda item 71a)
Buist-Catherwood, Emily - A/C.3/78/SR.18; A/C.3/78/SR.51
Fruean, Tausala - A/C.3/78/SR.38
RACIAL DISCRIMINATION—ELIMINATION (Agenda item 69a)
Buist-Catherwood, Emily - A/C.3/78/SR.47
RIGHT TO DEVELOPMENT (Agenda item 71b)
Buist-Catherwood, Emily - A/C.3/78/SR.48
RURAL WOMEN (Agenda item 25a)
Fruean, Tausala - A/C.3/78/SR.49
SOCIAL CONDITIONS (Agenda item 24b)
Buist-Catherwood, Emily - A/C.3/78/SR.51
TAXATION (Agenda item 16h)
Pringle, Rachael - A/C.2/78/SR.25
TREATIES (Agenda item 87)
Janah, Naushyn - A/C.6/78/SR.20
UKRAINE—POLITICAL CONDITIONS (Agenda item 62)
Buist-Catherwood, Emily - A/78/PV.58
UN—BUDGET (2024) (Agenda item 134)
Hardie, Alexandra - A/C.5/78/SR.26/PartII
UN. GENERAL ASSEMBLY (78TH SESS. : 2023-2024)—GENERAL DEBATE (Agenda item 8)
Mahuta, Nanaia - A/78/PV.12
UN. GENERAL ASSEMBLY (78TH SESS. : 2023-2024). 1ST COMMITTEE—GENERAL DEBATE (Agenda item 8)
Schwalger, Carolyn - A/C.1/78/PV.3

New Zealand (continued)

UN. INTERNATIONAL LAW COMMISSION—REPORTS (Agenda item 79)
Janah, Naushyn - A/C.6/78/SR.25
VETO (Agenda item 63)
Fepuleai, Justin Peter - A/78/PV.68
Schwalger, Carolyn - A/78/PV.51; A/78/PV.60; A/78/PV.70; A/78/PV.75; A/78/PV.78
WEAPONS—OUTER SPACE (Agenda item 97b)
Nam, Christine - A/C.1/78/PV.27
WOMEN'S ADVANCEMENT (Agenda item 25a)
Tieman, Connor - A/C.3/78/SR.8
WOMEN'S ADVANCEMENT—CONFERENCES (Agenda item 25b)
Tieman, Connor - A/C.3/78/SR.8

New Zealand. Deputy Prime Minister

UN. GENERAL ASSEMBLY (78TH SESS. : 2023-2024)—SPECIAL STATEMENTS
Peters, Winston - A/78/PV.66
VETO (Agenda item 63)
Peters, Winston - A/78/PV.66

Nicaragua

AGEING PERSONS (Agenda item 24b)
Pichardo Urbina, Eleane Yaoska - A/C.3/78/SR.4
ARMED CONFLICTS PREVENTION (Agenda item 31a)
Pichardo Urbina, Eleane Yaoska - A/78/PV.72
CHEMICAL WEAPONS—TREATIES (Agenda item 99l)
Jiménez, Jasser - A/C.1/78/PV.26
CLIMATE (Agenda item 18d)
Jiménez, Jasser - A/C.2/78/SR.13
CRIME PREVENTION (Agenda item 107)
Pichardo Urbina, Eleane Yaoska - A/C.3/78/SR.6
CRIMES AGAINST HUMANITY (Agenda item 80)
Llano, Alina J. - A/C.6/78/SR.45
CUBA—UNITED STATES (Agenda item 38)
Hermida Castillo, Jaime - A/78/PV.26
CYBERCRIME (Agenda item 108)
Pichardo Urbina, Eleane Yaoska - A/C.3/78/SR.6
DEVELOPMENT FINANCE (Agenda item 16b)
Hermida Castillo, Jaime - A/C.2/78/SR.9
DISPLACED PERSONS (Agenda item 71b)
Jiménez, Jasser - A/C.3/78/SR.49
ECONOMIC COOPERATION AMONG DEVELOPING COUNTRIES (Agenda item 22b)
Gutiérrez Tórrez, Lisandra Marina - A/C.2/78/SR.18
ECONOMIC SANCTIONS—INTERNATIONAL RELATIONS (Agenda item 28)
Palacios, Iván Lara - A/78/PV.89
EMERGENCY ASSISTANCE (Agenda item 72a)
Ochoa Espinales, Olimpia Raquel - A/78/PV.47

Nicaragua (continued)

FALKLAND ISLANDS (MALVINAS) QUESTION (Agenda item 42)
Hermida Castillo, Jaime - A/C.4/78/SR.6
HEALTH (Agenda item 125)
Jiménez, Jasser - A/78/PV.16
Llano, Alina J. - A/78/PV.48
HUMAN RIGHTS—BURUNDI (Agenda item 71c)
Pichardo Urbina, Eleane Yaoska - A/C.3/78/SR.36
HUMAN RIGHTS—DEMOCRATIC PEOPLE'S REPUBLIC OF KOREA (Agenda item 71c)
Ochoa Espinales, Olimpia Raquel - A/78/PV.50
Pichardo Urbina, Eleane Yaoska - A/C.3/78/SR.33; A/C.3/78/SR.53
HUMAN RIGHTS—ERITREA (Agenda item 71c)
Pichardo Urbina, Eleane Yaoska - A/C.3/78/SR.36
HUMAN RIGHTS—ETHIOPIA (Agenda item 71c)
Pichardo Urbina, Eleane Yaoska - A/C.3/78/SR.36
HUMAN RIGHTS—IRAN (ISLAMIC REPUBLIC OF) (Agenda item 71c)
Pichardo Urbina, Eleane Yaoska - A/C.3/78/SR.34; A/C.3/78/SR.53
HUMAN RIGHTS—REPORTS (Agenda item 71c)
Hermida Castillo, Jaime - A/C.3/78/SR.26
Ochoa Espinales, Olimpia Raquel - A/78/PV.50
HUMAN RIGHTS—RUSSIAN FEDERATION (Agenda item 71c)
Pichardo Urbina, Eleane Yaoska - A/C.3/78/SR.37
HUMAN RIGHTS—SYRIAN ARAB REPUBLIC (Agenda item 71c)
Pichardo Urbina, Eleane Yaoska - A/C.3/78/SR.34; A/C.3/78/SR.54
HUMAN RIGHTS ADVANCEMENT (Agenda item 71b)
Hermida Castillo, Jaime - A/C.3/78/SR.26
INDIGENOUS PEOPLES (Agenda item 68a)
Hermida Castillo, Jaime - A/C.3/78/SR.15
INDIGENOUS PEOPLES—CONFERENCES (Agenda item 68b)
Hermida Castillo, Jaime - A/C.3/78/SR.15
INFORMATION—INTERNATIONAL SECURITY (Agenda item 94)
Jiménez, Jasser - A/C.1/78/PV.29
INTERNATIONAL TRADE (Agenda item 16a)
Hermida Castillo, Jaime - A/C.2/78/SR.9
MACROECONOMIC POLICY (Agenda item 16)
Hermida Castillo, Jaime - A/C.2/78/SR.9
MARINE ECOSYSTEMS—BIOLOGICAL DIVERSITY (Agenda item 75c)
Llano, Alina J. - A/78/PV.73
MILLENNIUM SUMMIT—CONFERENCES (Agenda item 117)
Jiménez, Jasser - A/78/PV.15
PALESTINE QUESTION (Agenda item 35)
Pichardo Urbina, Eleane Yaoska - A/78/PV.40

Nicaragua (continued)

PEACE (Agenda item 14)
Pichardo Urbina, Eleane Yaoska - A/78/PV.76; A/78/PV.82
PERSONS WITH DISABILITIES (Agenda item 24b)
Pichardo Urbina, Eleane Yaoska - A/C.3/78/SR.4
POVERTY—INTERNATIONAL DECADES (Agenda item 21a)
Gutiérrez Tórrez, Lisandra Marina - A/C.2/78/SR.17
RACIAL DISCRIMINATION—ELIMINATION (Agenda item 69a)
Ochoa Espinales, Olimpia Raquel - A/78/PV.50
Pichardo Urbina, Eleane Yaoska - A/C.3/78/SR.42; A/C.3/78/SR.47
RACIAL DISCRIMINATION—PROGRAMMES OF ACTION (Agenda item 69b)
Pichardo Urbina, Eleane Yaoska - A/C.3/78/SR.42
RESPONSIBILITY TO PROTECT (Agenda item 129)
Pichardo Urbina, Eleane Yaoska - A/78/PV.96
RIGHT TO DEVELOPMENT (Agenda item 71b)
Pichardo Urbina, Eleane Yaoska - A/C.3/78/SR.20
RIGHTS OF THE CHILD (Agenda item 67)
Hermida Castillo, Jaime - A/C.3/78/SR.13
RULE OF LAW (Agenda item 83)
Hermida Castillo, Jaime - A/C.6/78/SR.16
RURAL POVERTY (Agenda item 21b)
Gutiérrez Tórrez, Lisandra Marina - A/C.2/78/SR.17
RURAL WOMEN (Agenda item 25a)
Jiménez, Jasser - A/C.3/78/SR.49
SANCTIONS—INTERNATIONAL RELATIONS (Agenda item 71b)
Hermida Castillo, Jaime - A/C.3/78/SR.26
Pichardo Urbina, Eleane Yaoska - A/C.3/78/SR.28
SELF-DETERMINATION OF PEOPLES (Agenda item 70)
Pichardo Urbina, Eleane Yaoska - A/C.3/78/SR.42
SOCIAL CONDITIONS (Agenda item 24b)
Pichardo Urbina, Eleane Yaoska - A/C.3/78/SR.4
SOCIAL DEVELOPMENT (Agenda item 24)
Pichardo Urbina, Eleane Yaoska - A/C.3/78/SR.4
SUSTAINABLE DEVELOPMENT (Agenda item 18)
Jiménez, Jasser - A/C.2/78/SR.13
TERRORISM (Agenda item 109)
Llano, Alina J. - A/C.6/78/SR.5
TORTURE AND OTHER CRUEL TREATMENT (Agenda item 71a)
Pichardo Urbina, Eleane Yaoska - A/C.3/78/SR.18
UN—BUDGET (2024) (Agenda item 134)
Llano, Alina J. - A/78/PV.73; A/C.5/78/SR.28; A/C.5/78/SR.34
Ochoa Espinales, Olimpia Raquel - A/C.5/78/SR.26/PartII

Nicaragua (continued)

UN—PROGRAMME PLANNING (Agenda item 135)
Ochoa Espinales, Olimpia Raquel - A/78/PV.50(Resumption1); A/C.5/78/SR.24
UN. GENERAL ASSEMBLY (78TH SESS. : 2023-2024)—GENERAL DEBATE (Agenda item 8)
Moncada Colindres, Denis Ronaldo - A/78/PV.14
UN. GENERAL ASSEMBLY (78TH SESS. : 2023-2024). 1ST COMMITTEE—GENERAL DEBATE (Agenda item 8)
Jiménez, Jasser - A/C.1/78/PV.8
UN. GENERAL ASSEMBLY (78TH SESS. : 2023-2024). 2ND COMMITTEE—GENERAL DEBATE (Agenda item 8)
Jiménez, Jasser - A/C.2/78/SR.4
UN. HUMAN RIGHTS COUNCIL—REPORTS (Agenda item 66)
Jiménez, Jasser - A/78/PV.23
Pichardo Urbina, Eleane Yaoska - A/C.3/78/SR.46; A/C.3/78/SR.51
UN. INTERNATIONAL COURT OF JUSTICE—REPORTS (Agenda item 73)
Hermida Castillo, Jaime - A/78/PV.28
UN CHARTER—REPORTS (Agenda item 82)
Llano, Alina J. - A/C.6/78/SR.34
UN CONFERENCES (Agenda item 13)
Jiménez, Jasser - A/78/PV.15
VETO (Agenda item 63)
Hermida Castillo, Jaime - A/78/PV.60; A/78/PV.75
Pichardo Urbina, Eleane Yaoska - A/78/PV.69
WESTERN SAHARA QUESTION (Agenda item 58)
Hermida Castillo, Jaime - A/C.4/78/SR.6
WOMEN'S ADVANCEMENT (Agenda item 25a)
Pichardo Urbina, Eleane Yaoska - A/C.3/78/SR.9
WOMEN'S ADVANCEMENT—CONFERENCES (Agenda item 25b)
Pichardo Urbina, Eleane Yaoska - A/C.3/78/SR.9
YOUTH (Agenda item 24b)
Pichardo Urbina, Eleane Yaoska - A/C.3/78/SR.4

Niger

ELECTION VERIFICATION—UN (Agenda item 71b)
Seydou, Abdoul Fadh Mahamadou - A/78/PV.50; A/C.3/78/SR.50
FOOD SECURITY (Agenda item 23a)
Moussa, Mahaman - A/C.2/78/SR.17
HUMAN RIGHTS ACTIVISTS (Agenda item 71b)
Seydou, Abdoul Fadh Mahamadou - A/C.3/78/SR.56
HUMAN RIGHTS ADVANCEMENT (Agenda item 71b)
Seydou, Abdoul Fadh Mahamadou - A/C.3/78/SR.52
MINORITIES (Agenda item 71b)
Seydou, Abdoul Fadh Mahamadou - A/C.3/78/SR.52

Niger (continued)

PERSONS WITH DISABILITIES—HUMAN RIGHTS (Agenda item 71a)
Seydou, Abdoul Fadh Mahamadou - A/C.3/78/SR.51
POVERTY—INTERNATIONAL DECADES (Agenda item 21a)
Moussa, Mahaman - A/C.2/78/SR.17
RIGHTS OF THE CHILD (Agenda item 67)
Seydou, Abdoul Fadh Mahamadou - A/C.3/78/SR.55
RURAL POVERTY (Agenda item 21b)
Moussa, Mahaman - A/C.2/78/SR.17
RURAL WOMEN (Agenda item 25a)
Seydou, Abdoul Fadh Mahamadou - A/C.3/78/SR.49
SANCTIONS—INTERNATIONAL RELATIONS (Agenda item 71b)
Seydou, Abdoul Fadh Mahamadou - A/C.3/78/SR.48
SUSTAINABLE DEVELOPMENT (Agenda item 18)
Moussa, Mahaman - A/C.2/78/SR.24
TERRORISM (Agenda item 109)
Ousman, Samadou - A/C.6/78/SR.4
WOMEN MIGRANT WORKERS (Agenda item 25a)
Seydou, Abdoul Fadh Mahamadou - A/C.3/78/SR.49
WOMEN'S ADVANCEMENT—CONFERENCES (Agenda item 25b)
Seydou, Abdoul Fadh Mahamadou - A/C.3/78/SR.51
YOUTH (Agenda item 24b)
Seydou, Abdoul Fadh Mahamadou - A/C.3/78/SR.55

Nigeria

AGEING PERSONS (Agenda item 24b)
Asaju, Bola - A/C.3/78/SR.1
ARMS RACE—OUTER SPACE (Agenda item 97a)
Mahmud, Mohammed Lawal - A/C.1/78/PV.17
ARMS TRANSFERS—TREATIES (Agenda item 99x)
Mahmud, Mohammed Lawal - A/C.1/78/PV.19
CRIME PREVENTION (Agenda item 107)
Marwa, Mohammed Buba - A/C.3/78/SR.5
CRIMES AGAINST HUMANITY (Agenda item 80)
Ajayi, Eniola Olaitan - A/C.6/78/SR.11
Dakwak, Gloria - A/C.6/78/SR.38; A/C.6/78/SR.40; A/C.6/78/SR.41; A/C.6/78/SR.44; A/C.6/78/SR.45; A/C.6/78/SR.47
DEVELOPMENT FINANCE (Agenda item 16b)
Gana Alkali, Baba - A/C.2/78/SR.9
DISARMAMENT—GENERAL AND COMPLETE (Agenda item 99)
Endoni, Syndoph Paebi - A/78/PV.106
DISASTER VICTIMS (Agenda item 86)
Dakwak, Gloria - A/C.6/78/SR.6
ECONOMIC COOPERATION AMONG DEVELOPING COUNTRIES (Agenda item 22b)
Dagari, Rabiu - A/C.2/78/SR.18

Nigeria (continued)

ELECTION VERIFICATION—UN (Agenda item 71b)
Asaju, Bola - A/78/PV.50; A/C.3/78/SR.50
EXTERNAL DEBT (Agenda item 16c)
Gana Alkali, Baba - A/C.2/78/SR.9
FOOD SECURITY (Agenda item 23a)
Maitafsir, Musa Garba - A/C.2/78/SR.17
GLOBALIZATION—INTERDEPENDENCE (Agenda item 19)
Adenopo, Adeyinka A. - A/C.2/78/SR.10
HUMAN RIGHTS—ERITREA (Agenda item 71c)
Asaju, Bola - A/C.3/78/SR.36
HUMAN RIGHTS—INTERNATIONAL INSTRUMENTS (Agenda item 71a)
Asaju, Bola - A/C.3/78/SR.25
HUMAN RIGHTS ACTIVISTS (Agenda item 71b)
Asaju, Bola - A/C.3/78/SR.56
HUMAN RIGHTS ADVANCEMENT (Agenda item 71b)
Asaju, Bola - A/C.3/78/SR.52
HUMAN RIGHTS INSTITUTIONS—CENTRAL AFRICA (Agenda item 71b)
Asaju, Bola - A/C.3/78/SR.56
IAEA—REPORTS (Agenda item 89)
Mahmud, Mohammed Lawal - A/78/PV.30
INTERNATIONAL JURISDICTION (Agenda item 84)
Ajayi, Eniola Olaitan - A/C.6/78/SR.13
INTERNATIONAL LAW—TRAINING PROGRAMMES (Agenda item 78)
Olisa, Janet - A/C.6/78/SR.22
NUCLEAR DISARMAMENT (Agenda item 99b)
Ajayi, Eniola Olaitan - A/C.1/78/PV.13
NUCLEAR NON-PROLIFERATION—INTERNATIONAL OBLIGATIONS (Agenda item 99w)
Ajayi, Eniola Olaitan - A/C.1/78/PV.13
NUCLEAR WEAPONS—TREATIES (Agenda item 99ff)
Ajayi, Eniola Olaitan - A/C.1/78/PV.13
OPERATIONAL ACTIVITIES—UN SYSTEM (Agenda item 22a)
Dagari, Rabiu - A/C.2/78/SR.18
OUTER SPACE—PRINCIPLES (Agenda item 97d)
Mahmud, Mohammed Lawal - A/C.1/78/PV.17
PEACE (Agenda item 14)
Endoni, Syndoph Paebi - A/78/PV.82
PEACEKEEPING OPERATIONS—CRIMINAL LIABILITY (Agenda item 76)
Dakwak, Gloria - A/C.6/78/SR.9
PERSONS WITH DISABILITIES—HUMAN RIGHTS (Agenda item 71a)
Asaju, Bola - A/C.3/78/SR.51
POVERTY—INTERNATIONAL DECADES (Agenda item 21a)
Maitafsir, Musa Garba - A/C.2/78/SR.17

Nigeria (continued)

RACIAL DISCRIMINATION—ELIMINATION (Agenda item 69a)
Asaju, Bola - A/78/PV.63; A/78/PV.103; A/C.3/78/SR.41; A/C.3/78/SR.47
RACIAL DISCRIMINATION—PROGRAMMES OF ACTION (Agenda item 69b)
Asaju, Bola - A/C.3/78/SR.41
RESPONSIBILITY TO PROTECT (Agenda item 129)
Endoni, Syndoph Paebi - A/78/PV.97
RIGHTS OF THE CHILD (Agenda item 67)
Asaju, Bola - A/C.3/78/SR.11; A/C.3/78/SR.13; A/C.3/78/SR.55
RULE OF LAW (Agenda item 83)
Ajayi, Eniola Olaitan - A/C.6/78/SR.17
RURAL POVERTY (Agenda item 21b)
Maitafsir, Musa Garba - A/C.2/78/SR.17
RURAL WOMEN (Agenda item 25a)
Asaju, Bola - A/C.3/78/SR.49
SCIENCE AND TECHNOLOGY—DEVELOPMENT (Agenda item 19a)
Adenopo, Adeyinka A. - A/C.2/78/SR.10
SLAVERY—MEMORIALS (Agenda item 118)
Asaju, Bola - A/78/PV.64
SMALL ARMS—ILLICIT TRAFFIC (Agenda item 99p)
Mahmud, Mohammed Lawal - A/C.1/78/PV.19
SOCIAL CONDITIONS (Agenda item 24b)
Asaju, Bola - A/C.3/78/SR.3; A/C.3/78/SR.51
SOCIAL DEVELOPMENT (Agenda item 24)
Asaju, Bola - A/C.3/78/SR.3
SOCIAL DEVELOPMENT—CONFERENCES (Agenda item 24a)
Asaju, Bola - A/C.3/78/SR.3
SUSTAINABLE DEVELOPMENT (Agenda item 18)
Anyaegbu, Ezekwesiri David - A/C.2/78/SR.24
Edokpa, George Ehidiamen - A/C.2/78/SR.13
TAXATION (Agenda item 16h)
Gana Alkali, Baba - A/C.2/78/SR.9
Muhammad Bande, Tijjani - A/C.2/78/SR.25
TERRORISM (Agenda item 109)
Dakwak, Gloria - A/C.6/78/SR.2
TREATIES (Agenda item 87)
Ajileye, Abimbola - A/C.6/78/SR.20
UN—BUDGET (2024) (Agenda item 134)
Shehu, Muktar - A/C.5/78/SR.33
UN. GENERAL ASSEMBLY (78TH SESS. : 2023-2024). 1ST COMMITTEE—GENERAL DEBATE (Agenda item 8)
Mahmud, Mohammed Lawal - A/C.1/78/PV.8
UN. GENERAL ASSEMBLY (78TH SESS. : 2023-2024). 2ND COMMITTEE—GENERAL DEBATE (Agenda item 8)
Muhammad Bande, Tijjani - A/C.2/78/SR.2
UN. HUMAN RIGHTS COUNCIL—REPORTS (Agenda item 66)
Asaju, Bola - A/C.3/78/SR.46

Nigeria (continued)

UN. SECURITY COUNCIL—MEMBERSHIP (Agenda item 121)
Lamuwa, Adamu Ibrahim - A/78/PV.36
UN CHARTER—REPORTS (Agenda item 82)
Dakwak, Gloria - A/C.6/78/SR.34
UN HIGH COMMISSIONER FOR REFUGEES—REPORTS (Agenda item 60)
Asaju, Bola - A/C.3/78/SR.44
Umar, Mujahid Ahmed - A/C.3/78/SR.45
VETO (Agenda item 63)
Asaju, Bola - A/78/PV.67
Dakwak, Gloria - A/78/PV.70
WEAPONS—OUTER SPACE (Agenda item 97b)
Mahmud, Mohammed Lawal - A/C.1/78/PV.17
WOMEN'S ADVANCEMENT (Agenda item 25a)
Kwarra, Nasir Isa - A/C.3/78/SR.9
WOMEN'S ADVANCEMENT—CONFERENCES (Agenda item 25b)
Kwarra, Nasir Isa - A/C.3/78/SR.9
YOUTH (Agenda item 24b)
Asaju, Bola - A/C.3/78/SR.55

Nigeria. President

UN. GENERAL ASSEMBLY (78TH SESS. : 2023-2024)—GENERAL DEBATE (Agenda item 8)
Tinubu, Bola Ahmed - A/78/PV.5
UN. GENERAL ASSEMBLY (78TH SESS. : 2023-2024)—SPECIAL STATEMENTS
Tinubu, Bola Ahmed - A/78/PV.5

North Macedonia

ELECTION VERIFICATION—UN (Agenda item 71b)
Danailov Frčkoski, Ljubomir - A/C.3/78/SR.50
HUMAN RIGHTS—INTERNATIONAL INSTRUMENTS (Agenda item 71a)
Danailov Frčkoski, Ljubomir - A/C.3/78/SR.17
UKRAINE—POLITICAL CONDITIONS (Agenda item 62)
Osmani, Bujar - A/78/PV.56
VETO (Agenda item 63)
Danailov Frčkoski, Ljubomir - A/78/PV.69
Uzunovski, Dushko - A/78/PV.79
WOMEN'S ADVANCEMENT (Agenda item 25a)
Danailov Frčkoski, Ljubomir - A/C.3/78/SR.7
WOMEN'S ADVANCEMENT—CONFERENCES (Agenda item 25b)
Danailov Frčkoski, Ljubomir - A/C.3/78/SR.7

North Macedonia. President

UN. GENERAL ASSEMBLY (78TH SESS. : 2023-2024)—GENERAL DEBATE (Agenda item 8)
Pendarovski, Stevo - A/78/PV.10

North Macedonia. President (continued)

UN. GENERAL ASSEMBLY (78TH SESS. : 2023-2024)—SPECIAL STATEMENTS
Pendarovski, Stevo - A/78/PV.10

Norway

ARMS RACE—OUTER SPACE (Agenda item 97a)
Sæter, William - A/C.1/78/PV.17
ARMS TRANSFERS—TREATIES (Agenda item 99x)
Andersen, Tor Henrik - A/C.1/78/PV.19
BIOLOGICAL WEAPONS—TREATIES (Agenda item 106)
Hunskaar, Maria - A/C.1/78/PV.15
CHEMICAL WEAPONS—TREATIES (Agenda item 99l)
Hunskaar, Maria - A/C.1/78/PV.15
CLUSTER MUNITIONS (Agenda item 99dd)
Andersen, Tor Henrik - A/C.1/78/PV.19
CRIMES AGAINST HUMANITY (Agenda item 80)
Bierling, Mirjam - A/C.6/78/SR.43
DEVELOPMENT FINANCE (Agenda item 16b)
Lovold, Andreas - A/C.2/78/SR.11
DISARMAMENT—GENERAL AND COMPLETE (Agenda item 99)
Andersen, Tor Henrik - A/C.1/78/PV.19; A/C.1/78/PV.30
Brattested, Merete Fjeld - A/78/PV.105
Hunskaar, Maria - A/C.1/78/PV.15
DISPLACED PERSONS (Agenda item 71b)
Ramboll, Unni - A/C.3/78/SR.32; A/C.3/78/SR.49
EMERGENCY ASSISTANCE (Agenda item 72a)
Lovold, Andreas - A/78/PV.46
FINANCIAL FLOWS (Agenda item 16f)
Lovold, Andreas - A/C.2/78/SR.11
FREEDOM OF EXPRESSION (Agenda item 71b)
Berg, Kristin Soennesyn - A/C.3/78/SR.19
HUMAN RIGHTS—AFGHANISTAN (Agenda item 71c)
Dale, Katrine Ørnehaug - A/C.3/78/SR.34
HUMAN RIGHTS—INTERNATIONAL INSTRUMENTS (Agenda item 71a)
Lovold, Andreas - A/C.3/78/SR.24
HUMAN RIGHTS—IRAN (ISLAMIC REPUBLIC OF) (Agenda item 71c)
Holter, Sigrun Stigen - A/C.3/78/SR.34
HUMAN RIGHTS—TERRITORIES OCCUPIED BY ISRAEL (Agenda item 71c)
Dale, Katrine Ørnehaug - A/C.3/78/SR.35
HUMAN RIGHTS ACTIVISTS (Agenda item 71b)
Brattested, Merete Fjeld - A/C.3/78/SR.19
Dale, Katrine Ørnehaug - A/C.3/78/SR.56
Lovold, Andreas - A/C.3/78/SR.24

Norway (continued)

LANDMINES—TREATIES (Agenda item 99m)
Andersen, Tor Henrik - A/C.1/78/PV.19
LAW OF THE SEA (Agenda item 75a)
Lovold, Andreas - A/78/PV.43
MARINE ECOSYSTEMS—BIOLOGICAL DIVERSITY (Agenda item 75c)
Lovold, Andreas - A/78/PV.43
MINE CLEARANCE (Agenda item 46)
Ramboll, Unni - A/C.4/78/SR.10
NUCLEAR DISARMAMENT (Agenda item 99b)
Osmundsen, Jorn - A/C.1/78/PV.13
NUCLEAR DISARMAMENT—VERIFICATION (Agenda item 99ee)
Osmundsen, Jorn - A/C.1/78/PV.12; A/C.1/78/PV.13
NUCLEAR NON-PROLIFERATION—INTERNATIONAL OBLIGATIONS (Agenda item 99w)
Osmundsen, Jorn - A/C.1/78/PV.13
NUCLEAR WEAPON TESTS—TREATIES (Agenda item 105)
Osmundsen, Jorn - A/C.1/78/PV.13
OUTER SPACE—CONFIDENCE-BUILDING MEASURES (Agenda item 99v)
Sæter, William - A/C.1/78/PV.17
OUTER SPACE—PRINCIPLES (Agenda item 97d)
Sæter, William - A/C.1/78/PV.17
PALESTINE QUESTION (Agenda item 35)
Brattested, Merete Fjeld - A/78/PV.40
PEACE (Agenda item 14)
Dale, Katrine Ørnehaug - A/78/PV.88
PEACEKEEPING OPERATIONS (Agenda item 51)
Lovold, Andreas - A/C.4/78/SR.19
PEACEKEEPING OPERATIONS—CRIMINAL LIABILITY (Agenda item 76)
Holm, Tor Tanke - A/C.6/78/SR.8
SOCIAL CONDITIONS (Agenda item 24b)
Jensen, Jørgen Reymert - A/C.3/78/SR.2
STRADDLING FISH STOCKS (Agenda item 75b)
Lovold, Andreas - A/78/PV.43
SUSTAINABLE DEVELOPMENT (Agenda item 18)
Kristmoen, Rina Lise - A/C.2/78/SR.24
TAXATION (Agenda item 16h)
Brattested, Merete Fjeld - A/C.2/78/SR.25
Lovold, Andreas - A/C.2/78/SR.11
UN—BUDGET (2024) (Agenda item 134)
Dalin, Inga - A/C.5/78/SR.33
UN. GENERAL ASSEMBLY (78TH SESS. : 2023-2024)—GENERAL DEBATE (Agenda item 8)
Tvinnereim, Anne Beathe - A/78/PV.13
UN. GENERAL ASSEMBLY (78TH SESS. : 2023-2024)—OFFICERS (Agenda item 5)
Brattested, Merete Fjeld - A/C.5/78/SR.1

Norway (continued)

UN. GENERAL ASSEMBLY (78TH SESS. : 2023-2024). 1ST COMMITTEE—GENERAL DEBATE (Agenda item 8)
Brattested, Merete Fjeld - A/C.1/78/PV.3
UN. GENERAL ASSEMBLY (78TH SESS. : 2023-2024). 2ND COMMITTEE—GENERAL DEBATE (Agenda item 8)
Brattested, Merete Fjeld - A/C.2/78/SR.4
UN. SECURITY COUNCIL—REPORTS (Agenda item 26)
Lovold, Andreas - A/78/PV.93
UNRWA—ACTIVITIES (Agenda item 49)
Lovold, Andreas - A/C.4/78/SR.22
VETO (Agenda item 63)
Brattested, Merete Fjeld - A/78/PV.51; A/78/PV.60
Havn, Anne Melangen - A/78/PV.75
Lovold, Andreas - A/78/PV.67; A/78/PV.68
WEAPONS OF MASS DESTRUCTION—TERRORISM (Agenda item 99s)
Hunskaar, Maria - A/C.1/78/PV.15
WOMEN'S ADVANCEMENT (Agenda item 25a)
Brattested, Merete Fjeld - A/C.3/78/SR.8
Vaeroyvik, Vilde - A/C.3/78/SR.7
WOMEN'S ADVANCEMENT—CONFERENCES (Agenda item 25b)
Brattested, Merete Fjeld - A/C.3/78/SR.8
Vaeroyvik, Vilde - A/C.3/78/SR.7
YOUTH (Agenda item 24b)
Stokke, Kristine Meek - A/C.3/78/SR.2

Observatoire du sud pour le développement territorial (Organization)

WESTERN SAHARA QUESTION (Agenda item 58)
Essalek, Hanane - A/C.4/78/SR.6

Observatorio Asturiano de Derechos Humanos para el Sáhara Occidental (Spain)

WESTERN SAHARA QUESTION (Agenda item 58)
Arbesu Sancho, Gemma - A/C.4/78/SR.4

Observatorio de Derechos Humanos de Castilla La Mancha para el Sáhara Occidental (Spain)

WESTERN SAHARA QUESTION (Agenda item 58)
Crespo Aguilar, Juan Ramón - A/C.4/78/SR.4

Oman

CRIME PREVENTION (Agenda item 107)
Al-Sinani, Nashwa Hilal - A/C.3/78/SR.6
HUMAN RIGHTS (Agenda item 71)
Al Jaradi, Heba Khalid - A/C.3/78/SR.27
HUMAN RIGHTS—TERRITORIES OCCUPIED BY ISRAEL (Agenda item 71c)
Al Jaradi, Heba Khalid - A/C.3/78/SR.27

Oman (continued)

IAEA—REPORTS (Agenda item 89)
Al Rubkhi, Khalid Saleh Said - A/78/PV.30
INFORMATION (Agenda item 53)
Al Rashdi, Amal - A/C.4/78/SR.13
OUTER SPACE—PEACEFUL USES—INTERNATIONAL COOPERATION (Agenda item 48)
Al Rashdi, Amal - A/C.4/78/SR.16
PEACE (Agenda item 14)
Al Rubkhi, Khalid Saleh Said - A/78/PV.62; A/78/PV.82
RIGHTS OF THE CHILD (Agenda item 67)
Al Jaradi, Heba Khalid - A/C.3/78/SR.14
Al Rawahi, Abdulhalim Mubarak Saloom - A/C.3/78/SR.55
RULE OF LAW (Agenda item 83)
Al-Ajmi, Mohammed - A/C.6/78/SR.18
SUSTAINABLE DEVELOPMENT (Agenda item 18)
Al Haddabi, Alya Nasser Saif - A/C.2/78/SR.15
TERRORISM (Agenda item 109)
Al Shehhi, Mohammed Ali Ahmed - A/C.6/78/SR.2
UN. GENERAL ASSEMBLY (78TH SESS. : 2023-2024)—GENERAL DEBATE (Agenda item 8)
AlBusaidi, Sayyid Badr Bin Hamad bin Hamood - A/78/PV.13
UN. GENERAL ASSEMBLY (78TH SESS. : 2023-2024). 1ST COMMITTEE—GENERAL DEBATE (Agenda item 8)
Al Rubkhi, Khalid Saleh Said - A/C.1/78/PV.6
UN. GENERAL ASSEMBLY (78TH SESS. : 2023-2024). 2ND COMMITTEE—GENERAL DEBATE (Agenda item 8)
Al Rawahi, Abdulhalim Mubarak Saloom - A/C.2/78/SR.6
UN. INTERNATIONAL COURT OF JUSTICE—REPORTS (Agenda item 73)
Al Shehhi, Mohammed Ali Ahmed - A/78/PV.27
UN. SECURITY COUNCIL—REPORTS (Agenda item 26)
Al Shehhi, Mohammed Ali Ahmed - A/78/PV.94
VETO (Agenda item 63)
Al-Hassan, Mohamed - A/78/PV.74
WOMEN'S ADVANCEMENT (Agenda item 25a)
Al Rubkhi, Khalid Saleh Said - A/C.3/78/SR.10
WOMEN'S ADVANCEMENT—CONFERENCES (Agenda item 25b)
Al Rubkhi, Khalid Saleh Said - A/C.3/78/SR.10
YOUTH (Agenda item 24b)
Al Rawahi, Abdulhalim Mubarak Saloom - A/C.3/78/SR.55

On Purpose Group (Organization)

WESTERN SAHARA QUESTION (Agenda item 58)
Goebel, Suzanne - A/C.4/78/SR.4

Organisation for the Prohibition of Chemical Weapons

CHEMICAL WEAPONS—TREATIES (Agenda item 99l)
Li, Hong - A/C.1/78/PV.16

Organisation internationale de la Francophonie

INFORMATION (Agenda item 53)
Nkalwo, Joseph Léa - A/C.4/78/SR.14
PEACEKEEPING OPERATIONS (Agenda item 51)
Kontoleontos, Ifigeneia - A/C.4/78/SR.20

Organisation of Islamic Cooperation

CUBA—UNITED STATES (Agenda item 38)
Laghdaf, Sidi Mohamed (Mauritania) - A/78/PV.24
HUMAN RIGHTS—INTERNATIONAL INSTRUMENTS (Agenda item 71a)
Abdelkhalek, Osama Mahmoud (Egypt) - A/C.3/78/SR.24
HUMAN RIGHTS—MYANMAR (Agenda item 71c)
Alwasil, Abdulaziz M.O. (Saudi Arabia) - A/C.3/78/SR.53
HUMAN RIGHTS—TERRITORIES OCCUPIED BY ISRAEL (Agenda item 71c)
Abdelkhalek, Osama Mahmoud (Egypt) - A/C.3/78/SR.24
PEACE (Agenda item 14)
Akram, Munir (Pakistan) - A/78/PV.62
RAISI, SEYYED EBRAHIM (IRAN (ISLAMIC REPUBLID OF). PRESIDENT)—TRIBUTES
Akram, Munir (Pakistan) - A/78/PV.83
RELIGIOUS INTOLERANCE (Agenda item 71b)
Abdelkhalek, Osama Mahmoud (Egypt) - A/C.3/78/SR.24
Mostafa Rizk, Heba (Egypt) - A/C.3/78/SR.52
SELF-DETERMINATION OF PEOPLES (Agenda item 70)
Mostafa Rizk, Heba (Egypt) - A/C.3/78/SR.49
TERRORISM (Agenda item 109)
Felemban, Khalid (Saudi Arabia) - A/C.6/78/SR.1
UN. INTERNATIONAL COURT OF JUSTICE—REPORTS (Agenda item 73)
Laghdaf, Sidi Mohamed (Mauritania) - A/78/PV.27
VETO (Agenda item 63)
Akram, Munir (Pakistan) - A/78/PV.59

Oxfam America

COMMODITIES (Agenda item 16d)
Mutasah, Tawanda - A/C.2/78/SR.14
SUSTAINABLE DEVELOPMENT (Agenda item 18)
Mutasah, Tawanda - A/C.2/78/SR.14

Pacific Islands Forum

LAW OF THE SEA (Agenda item 75a)
Vaea, Darlene Atuamua Hakeifalehaakili (Tonga) - A/78/PV.43

Pacific Islands Forum (continued)

MARINE ECOSYSTEMS—BIOLOGICAL DIVERSITY (Agenda item 75c)
Vaea, Darlene Atuamua Hakeifalehaakili (Tonga) - A/78/PV.43
Vea, Jeanett (Tonga) - A/78/PV.103
MILLENNIUM SUMMIT—CONFERENCES (Agenda item 117)
May, Vueti Kosoniu (Fiji) - A/78/PV.102
Va'inga Tone, Viliami (Tonga) - A/78/PV.53
SMALL ISLAND DEVELOPING STATES—PROGRAMMES OF ACTION (Agenda item 18b)
Vaea, Darlene Atuamua Hakeifalehaakili (Tonga) - A/C.2/78/SR.22
STRADDLING FISH STOCKS (Agenda item 75b)
Vaea, Darlene Atuamua Hakeifalehaakili (Tonga) - A/78/PV.43
UN. INTERNATIONAL LAW COMMISSION—REPORTS (Agenda item 79)
Ali-Harm, Agnes (Fiji) - A/C.6/78/SR.23
UN CONFERENCES (Agenda item 13)
May, Vueti Kosoniu (Fiji) - A/78/PV.102
Va'inga Tone, Viliami (Tonga) - A/78/PV.53

Pacific Small Island Developing States

MARINE ECOSYSTEMS—BIOLOGICAL DIVERSITY (Agenda item 75c)
Wells, Majorie May (Vanuatu) - A/78/PV.103
William, Sanlan (Vanuatu) - A/78/PV.73

Pakistan

ARMS RACE—OUTER SPACE (Agenda item 97a)
Sarwani, Gul Qaiser - A/C.1/78/PV.16
ARMS TRANSFERS—TREATIES (Agenda item 99x)
Ahmed, Husham - A/C.1/78/PV.19
BIOLOGICAL WEAPONS—TREATIES (Agenda item 106)
Gohar, Sarfaraz Ahmed - A/C.1/78/PV.15
CHEMICAL WEAPONS—TREATIES (Agenda item 99l)
Gohar, Sarfaraz Ahmed - A/C.1/78/PV.15
CLUSTER MUNITIONS (Agenda item 99dd)
Sarwani, Gul Qaiser - A/C.1/78/PV.28
CONFIDENCE-BUILDING MEASURES (Agenda item 99t)
Ahmed, Husham - A/C.1/78/PV.21
CONVENTIONAL ARMS—REGIONAL PROGRAMMES (Agenda item 99g)
Ahmed, Husham - A/C.1/78/PV.21
CONVENTIONAL WEAPONS—TREATIES (Agenda item 103)
Ahmed, Husham - A/C.1/78/PV.19
CRIME PREVENTION (Agenda item 107)
Khan, Mohammad Aamir - A/C.3/78/SR.5
CRIMES AGAINST HUMANITY (Agenda item 80)
Ijaz, Rabia - A/C.6/78/SR.10; A/C.6/78/SR.11

Pakistan (continued)

CRIMES AGAINST HUMANITY (Agenda item 80)
Syed, Ansar Hussain Shah - A/C.6/78/SR.39; A/C.6/78/SR.41; A/C.6/78/SR.42; A/C.6/78/SR.44
CUBA—UNITED STATES (Agenda item 38)
Jadoon, Usman Iqbal - A/78/PV.26
CYBERCRIME (Agenda item 108)
Khan, Mohammad Aamir - A/C.3/78/SR.5
DECOLONIZATION (Agenda item 58)
Akram, Munir - A/C.4/78/SR.2
Khan, Naeem Sabir - A/C.4/78/SR.7
DEVELOPMENT FINANCE (Agenda item 16b)
Shafique, Umar - A/C.2/78/SR.9
DISAPPEARANCE OF PERSONS (Agenda item 71b)
Qureshi, Hadeeqa - A/C.3/78/SR.22
DISARMAMENT—GENERAL AND COMPLETE (Agenda item 99)
Ahmed, Husham - A/C.1/78/PV.19; A/C.1/78/PV.20
Gohar, Sarfaraz Ahmed - A/C.1/78/PV.30
Sarwani, Gul Qaiser - A/C.1/78/PV.26; A/C.1/78/PV.28
DISARMAMENT—UN. GENERAL ASSEMBLY (4TH SPECIAL SESS. ON DISARMAMENT : xxxx) (Agenda item 99h)
Sarwani, Gul Qaiser - A/C.1/78/PV.23
DISARMAMENT AGREEMENTS—OUTER SPACE (Agenda item 97c)
Gohar, Sarfaraz Ahmed - A/C.1/78/PV.27
DISASTER VICTIMS (Agenda item 86)
Ijaz, Rabia - A/C.6/78/SR.6
ECONOMIC COOPERATION AMONG DEVELOPING COUNTRIES (Agenda item 22b)
Sharif, Shahsawar - A/C.2/78/SR.18
ELECTION VERIFICATION—UN (Agenda item 71b)
Qureshi, Hadeeqa - A/C.3/78/SR.50
Saleem, Saima - A/78/PV.50
EMERGENCY ASSISTANCE (Agenda item 72a)
Jadoon, Usman Iqbal - A/78/PV.46
EXTERNAL DEBT (Agenda item 16c)
Shafique, Umar - A/C.2/78/SR.9
FINANCIAL FLOWS (Agenda item 16f)
Shafique, Umar - A/C.2/78/SR.9
FISSIONABLE MATERIALS—TREATIES (Agenda item 99a)
Ahmed, Husham - A/C.1/78/PV.25
Jadoon, Usman Iqbal - A/C.1/78/PV.12
FOOD SECURITY (Agenda item 23a)
Javaid, Hafiza Humaira - A/C.2/78/SR.17
FREEDOM OF EXPRESSION (Agenda item 71b)
Qureshi, Hadeeqa - A/C.3/78/SR.19
HEALTH (Agenda item 125)
Jadoon, Usman Iqbal - A/78/PV.41
HUMAN RIGHTS (Agenda item 71)
Khan, Mohammad Aamir - A/C.3/78/SR.16

Pakistan (continued)

HUMAN RIGHTS—AFGHANISTAN (Agenda item 71c)
Ajmal, Muhammad Jawad - A/C.3/78/SR.34
HUMAN RIGHTS—ERITREA (Agenda item 71c)
Qureshi, Hadeeqa - A/C.3/78/SR.36
HUMAN RIGHTS—IRAN (ISLAMIC REPUBLIC OF) (Agenda item 71c)
Qureshi, Hadeeqa - A/C.3/78/SR.53
Saleem, Saima - A/C.3/78/SR.34
HUMAN RIGHTS—REPORTS (Agenda item 71c)
Akram, Munir - A/C.3/78/SR.24
Saleem, Saima - A/C.3/78/SR.25
HUMAN RIGHTS—TERRITORIES OCCUPIED BY ISRAEL (Agenda item 71c)
Akram, Munir - A/C.3/78/SR.24
Qureshi, Hadeeqa - A/C.3/78/SR.35
HUMAN RIGHTS ACTIVISTS (Agenda item 71b)
Kanwal, Tehreem - A/C.3/78/SR.19
IAEA—REPORTS (Agenda item 89)
Akram, Munir - A/78/PV.29
INFORMATION (Agenda item 53)
Jadoon, Usman Iqbal - A/C.4/78/SR.12
INFORMATION—INTERNATIONAL SECURITY (Agenda item 94)
Ahmed, Husham - A/C.1/78/PV.20
Sarwani, Gul Qaiser - A/C.1/78/PV.29
INFORMATION TECHNOLOGY—DEVELOPMENT (Agenda item 15)
Shafique, Umar - A/C.2/78/SR.10
INTERNATIONAL JURISDICTION (Agenda item 84)
Jadoon, Usman Iqbal - A/C.6/78/SR.12
INTERNATIONAL LAW—TRAINING PROGRAMMES (Agenda item 78)
Khokhar, Adeel Mumtaz - A/C.6/78/SR.21
INTERNATIONAL PARLIAMENTARIANS' CONGRESS—OBSERVER STATUS (Agenda item 170)
Akram, Munir - A/C.6/78/SR.14
LANDMINES—TREATIES (Agenda item 99m)
Sarwani, Gul Qaiser - A/C.1/78/PV.28
LAW OF THE SEA (Agenda item 75a)
Jadoon, Usman Iqbal - A/78/PV.44
MARINE ECOSYSTEMS—BIOLOGICAL DIVERSITY (Agenda item 75c)
Jadoon, Usman Iqbal - A/78/PV.44
MIDDLE EAST—NUCLEAR PROLIFERATION (Agenda item 102)
Sarwani, Gul Qaiser - A/C.1/78/PV.26
MIGRANTS—PROTECTION (Agenda item 71b)
Qureshi, Hadeeqa - A/C.3/78/SR.23
MILLENNIUM SUMMIT—CONFERENCES (Agenda item 117)
Akram, Munir - A/78/PV.15
MINORITIES (Agenda item 71b)
Qureshi, Hadeeqa - A/C.3/78/SR.39

Pakistan (continued)

NON-NUCLEAR-WEAPON STATES—SECURITY (Agenda item 96)
Jadoon, Usman Iqbal - A/C.1/78/PV.12
NUCLEAR DISARMAMENT (Agenda item 99b)
Jadoon, Usman Iqbal - A/C.1/78/PV.12
Sarwani, Gul Qaiser - A/C.1/78/PV.26
NUCLEAR DISARMAMENT—TREATY COMPLIANCE (Agenda item 99q)
Sarwani, Gul Qaiser - A/C.1/78/PV.26
NUCLEAR NON-PROLIFERATION (Agenda item 99o)
Ahmed, Husham - A/C.1/78/PV.25
NUCLEAR NON-PROLIFERATION—INTERNATIONAL OBLIGATIONS (Agenda item 99w)
Sarwani, Gul Qaiser - A/C.1/78/PV.26
NUCLEAR WEAPON TESTS—TREATIES (Agenda item 105)
Sarwani, Gul Qaiser - A/C.1/78/PV.26
NUCLEAR WEAPONS—ELIMINATION (Agenda item 99z)
Sarwani, Gul Qaiser - A/C.1/78/PV.26
NUCLEAR WEAPONS—HUMANITARIAN CONSEQUENCES (Agenda item 99bb)
Ahmed, Husham - A/C.1/78/PV.25
NUCLEAR WEAPONS—TREATIES (Agenda item 99ff)
Sarwani, Gul Qaiser - A/C.1/78/PV.26
NUCLEAR WEAPONS USE—TREATIES (Agenda item 100a)
Ahmed, Husham - A/C.1/78/PV.25
NUCLEAR WEAPONS USE—UN. INTERNATIONAL COURT OF JUSTICE OPINION (Agenda item 99k)
Sarwani, Gul Qaiser - A/C.1/78/PV.26
NUCLEAR-WEAPON-FREE ZONES (Agenda item 99cc)
Ahmed, Husham - A/C.1/78/PV.25
OPERATIONAL ACTIVITIES—UN SYSTEM (Agenda item 22a)
Sharif, Shahsawar - A/C.2/78/SR.18
OUTER SPACE—CONFIDENCE-BUILDING MEASURES (Agenda item 99v)
Sarwani, Gul Qaiser - A/C.1/78/PV.16
OUTER SPACE—PEACEFUL USES—INTERNATIONAL COOPERATION (Agenda item 48)
Khan, Naeem Sabir - A/C.4/78/SR.15
OUTER SPACE—PRINCIPLES (Agenda item 97d)
Gohar, Sarfaraz Ahmed - A/C.1/78/PV.27
Sarwani, Gul Qaiser - A/C.1/78/PV.16
PALESTINE QUESTION (Agenda item 35)
Jadoon, Usman Iqbal - A/78/PV.39
PALESTINIANS—ASSISTANCE (Agenda item 72b)
Jadoon, Usman Iqbal - A/78/PV.46
PEACE (Agenda item 14)
Akram, Munir - A/78/PV.48; A/78/PV.76; A/78/PV.82

Pakistan (continued)

PEACEKEEPING OPERATIONS (Agenda item 51)
Akram, Munir - A/C.4/78/SR.18
PEACEKEEPING OPERATIONS—CRIMINAL LIABILITY (Agenda item 76)
Ijaz, Rabia - A/C.6/78/SR.8
POVERTY—HUMAN RIGHTS (Agenda item 71b)
Qureshi, Hadeeqa - A/C.3/78/SR.30
POVERTY—INTERNATIONAL DECADES (Agenda item 21a)
Javaid, Hafiza Humaira - A/C.2/78/SR.17
RACIAL DISCRIMINATION—ELIMINATION (Agenda item 69a)
Ijaz, Rabia - A/C.3/78/SR.41
Qureshi, Hadeeqa - A/C.3/78/SR.41
RACIAL DISCRIMINATION—PROGRAMMES OF ACTION (Agenda item 69b)
Ijaz, Rabia - A/C.3/78/SR.41
Qureshi, Hadeeqa - A/C.3/78/SR.41
RADIATION EFFECTS (Agenda item 47)
Khan, Naeem Sabir - A/C.4/78/SR.11
REGIONAL DISARMAMENT (Agenda item 99f)
Ahmed, Husham - A/C.1/78/PV.21
RELIGIOUS INTOLERANCE (Agenda item 71b)
Akram, Munir - A/C.3/78/SR.24
Ijaz, Rabia - A/C.3/78/SR.38
RESPONSIBILITY TO PROTECT (Agenda item 129)
Akram, Munir - A/78/PV.97
Ijaz, Rabia - A/78/PV.97
RIGHT OF ASSEMBLY (Agenda item 71b)
Kanwal, Tehreem - A/C.3/78/SR.19
RIGHT TO DEVELOPMENT (Agenda item 71b)
Jadoon, Usman Iqbal - A/C.3/78/SR.20
RIGHT TO FOOD (Agenda item 71b)
Qureshi, Hadeeqa - A/C.3/78/SR.30
RIGHTS OF THE CHILD (Agenda item 67)
Ijaz, Rabia - A/C.3/78/SR.11
Qureshi, Hadeeqa - A/C.3/78/SR.11; A/C.3/78/SR.14
Saleem, Saima - A/C.3/78/SR.13
RULE OF LAW (Agenda item 83)
Akram, Munir - A/C.6/78/SR.16
RURAL POVERTY (Agenda item 21b)
Javaid, Hafiza Humaira - A/C.2/78/SR.17
SCIENCE AND TECHNOLOGY—DEVELOPMENT (Agenda item 19a)
Shafique, Umar - A/C.2/78/SR.10
SELF-DETERMINATION OF PEOPLES (Agenda item 70)
Akram, Munir - A/C.3/78/SR.40; A/C.3/78/SR.56
SOCIAL CONDITIONS (Agenda item 24b)
Akram, Munir - A/C.3/78/SR.2
Majeed, Aleena - A/78/PV.57
SOCIAL DEVELOPMENT (Agenda item 24)
Akram, Munir - A/C.3/78/SR.2

Pakistan (continued)

STRADDLING FISH STOCKS (Agenda item 75b)
Jadoon, Usman Iqbal - A/78/PV.44
SUMMARY EXECUTIONS (Agenda item 71b)
Qureshi, Hadeeqa - A/C.3/78/SR.31
SUSTAINABLE DEVELOPMENT (Agenda item 18)
Javaid, Hafiza Humaira - A/C.2/78/SR.13
TERRITORIES OCCUPIED BY ISRAEL—NATURAL RESOURCES (Agenda item 59)
Jadoon, Usman Iqbal - A/C.2/78/SR.19; A/C.2/78/SR.21
TERRORISM (Agenda item 109)
Ajmal, Muhammad Jawad - A/C.6/78/SR.4
Akram, Munir - A/C.6/78/SR.2
TERRORISM—HUMAN RIGHTS (Agenda item 71b)
Qureshi, Hadeeqa - A/C.3/78/SR.31
TORTURE AND OTHER CRUEL TREATMENT (Agenda item 71a)
Kanwal, Tehreem - A/C.3/78/SR.18
TRAFFICKING IN PERSONS (Agenda item 71b)
Qureshi, Hadeeqa - A/C.3/78/SR.23
TRANSNATIONAL CORPORATIONS—HUMAN RIGHTS (Agenda item 71b)
Qureshi, Hadeeqa - A/C.3/78/SR.21
UN. CONFERENCE ON DISARMAMENT—REPORTS (Agenda item 101a)
Sarwani, Gul Qaiser - A/C.1/78/PV.23
UN. GENERAL ASSEMBLY—WORK PROGRAMME (Agenda item 120)
Akram, Munir - A/78/PV.32
UN. GENERAL ASSEMBLY (78TH SESS. : 2023-2024)—GENERAL DEBATE—RIGHT OF REPLY (Agenda item 8)
Saleem, Saima - A/78/PV.11
UN. GENERAL ASSEMBLY (78TH SESS. : 2023-2024). 1ST COMMITTEE—GENERAL DEBATE (Agenda item 8)
Hashmi, Khalil Ur Rahman - A/C.1/78/PV.6
Siddique, Umer - A/C.1/78/PV.6
UN. GENERAL ASSEMBLY (78TH SESS. : 2023-2024). 2ND COMMITTEE—GENERAL DEBATE (Agenda item 8)
Akram, Munir - A/C.2/78/SR.2
Majeed, Aleena - A/C.2/78/SR.2
UN. HUMAN RIGHTS COUNCIL—REPORTS (Agenda item 66)
Akram, Munir - A/78/PV.23
Qureshi, Hadeeqa - A/78/PV.28
UN. INTERNATIONAL COURT OF JUSTICE—REPORTS (Agenda item 73)
Akram, Munir - A/78/PV.27
UN. SECRETARY-GENERAL—REPORTS (Agenda item 110)
Akram, Munir - A/78/PV.55

Pakistan (continued)

UN. SECURITY COUNCIL—MEMBERSHIP (Agenda item 121)
Akram, Munir - A/78/PV.35
Jadoon, Usman Iqbal - A/78/PV.104
UN. SECURITY COUNCIL—REPORTS (Agenda item 26)
Akram, Munir - A/78/PV.93
UN CHARTER—REPORTS (Agenda item 82)
Ijaz, Rabia - A/C.6/78/SR.22
UN COMMISSION ON INTERNATIONAL TRADE LAW—REPORTS (Agenda item 77)
Khokhar, Adeel Mumtaz - A/C.6/78/SR.14
UN CONFERENCES (Agenda item 13)
Akram, Munir - A/78/PV.15
UN HIGH COMMISSIONER FOR REFUGEES—REPORTS (Agenda item 60)
Jadoon, Usman Iqbal - A/C.3/78/SR.44
Qureshi, Hadeeqa - A/C.3/78/SR.44
Saleem, Saima - A/C.3/78/SR.45
UN RESOLUTIONS—IMPLEMENTATION (Agenda item 119)
Akram, Munir - A/78/PV.32
UNRWA—ACTIVITIES (Agenda item 49)
Akram, Munir - A/C.4/78/SR.22
VETO (Agenda item 63)
Akram, Munir - A/78/PV.67; A/78/PV.74; A/78/PV.78
Jadoon, Usman Iqbal - A/78/PV.51
WOMEN'S ADVANCEMENT (Agenda item 25a)
Akram, Munir - A/C.3/78/SR.8
Kanwal, Tehreem - A/C.3/78/SR.7
WOMEN'S ADVANCEMENT—CONFERENCES (Agenda item 25b)
Akram, Munir - A/C.3/78/SR.8
Kanwal, Tehreem - A/C.3/78/SR.7

Pakistan. Prime Minister

UN. GENERAL ASSEMBLY (78TH SESS. : 2023-2024)—GENERAL DEBATE (Agenda item 8)
Kakar, Anwaar-ul-Haq - A/78/PV.10
UN. GENERAL ASSEMBLY (78TH SESS. : 2023-2024)—SPECIAL STATEMENTS
Kakar, Anwaar-ul-Haq - A/78/PV.10

Palau

MILLENNIUM SUMMIT—CONFERENCES (Agenda item 117)
Sisior, Gwendalyn - A/78/PV.102
SMALL ISLAND DEVELOPING STATES—PROGRAMMES OF ACTION (Agenda item 18b)
Seid, Ilana Victorya - A/78/PV.100
UN CONFERENCES (Agenda item 13)
Sisior, Gwendalyn - A/78/PV.102

Palau. President

UN. GENERAL ASSEMBLY (78TH SESS. : 2023-2024)—GENERAL DEBATE (Agenda item 8)
Whipps, Surangel S. - A/78/PV.5
UN. GENERAL ASSEMBLY (78TH SESS. : 2023-2024)—SPECIAL STATEMENTS
Whipps, Surangel S. - A/78/PV.5

Palestinian Moroccan Friendship Society

WESTERN SAHARA QUESTION (Agenda item 58)
Aljabari, Ziad - A/C.4/78/SR.4

Panama

CLIMATE (Agenda item 18d)
Thompson Ramírez, Marilyn del Carmen - A/C.2/78/SR.13
FALKLAND ISLANDS (MALVINAS) QUESTION (Agenda item 42)
Pinto Berrío, Harry Eduardo - A/C.4/78/SR.7
FOOD SECURITY (Agenda item 23a)
Concepción Jaramillo, Markova - A/C.2/78/SR.16
HIV/AIDS—DECLARATIONS (Agenda item 10)
Abad Garcia, Jienevit Juset - A/78/PV.91
INDIGENOUS PEOPLES (Agenda item 68a)
Luque Nuñez, Linda del Carmen - A/C.3/78/SR.15
INDIGENOUS PEOPLES—CONFERENCES (Agenda item 68b)
Luque Nuñez, Linda del Carmen - A/C.3/78/SR.15
MIGRANTS—PROTECTION (Agenda item 71b)
Concepción Jaramillo, Markova - A/C.3/78/SR.23
NUCLEAR WEAPON TESTS—TREATIES (Agenda item 105)
Veliz Rodríguez, Aris Anel - A/C.1/78/PV.25
NUCLEAR WEAPONS—ELIMINATION (Agenda item 99z)
Veliz Rodríguez, Aris Anel - A/C.1/78/PV.25
NUCLEAR WEAPONS—TREATIES (Agenda item 99ff)
Veliz Rodríguez, Aris Anel - A/C.1/78/PV.25
NUCLEAR-WEAPON-FREE ZONES (Agenda item 99cc)
Veliz Rodríguez, Aris Anel - A/C.1/78/PV.25
PEACE (Agenda item 14)
Cano Franco, Zoraya del Carmen - A/78/PV.82
POVERTY—INTERNATIONAL DECADES (Agenda item 21a)
Concepción Jaramillo, Markova - A/C.2/78/SR.16
RACIAL DISCRIMINATION—ELIMINATION (Agenda item 69a)
Salerno Vega, James Azel - A/C.3/78/SR.40
RACIAL DISCRIMINATION—PROGRAMMES OF ACTION (Agenda item 69b)
Salerno Vega, James Azel - A/C.3/78/SR.40
RURAL POVERTY (Agenda item 21b)
Concepción Jaramillo, Markova - A/C.2/78/SR.16

Panama (continued)

SPORTS—OLYMPIC GAMES (Agenda item 11)
Salerno Vega, James Azel - A/78/PV.38
SUSTAINABLE ENERGY (Agenda item 18h)
Thompson Ramírez, Marilyn del Carmen - A/C.2/78/SR.13
TAXATION (Agenda item 16h)
Concepción Jaramillo, Markova - A/C.2/78/SR.25
UN. GENERAL ASSEMBLY (78TH SESS. : 2023-2024). 1ST COMMITTEE—GENERAL DEBATE (Agenda item 8)
Veliz Rodríguez, Aris Anel - A/C.1/78/PV.7
UN. GENERAL ASSEMBLY (78TH SESS. : 2023-2024). 2ND COMMITTEE—GENERAL DEBATE (Agenda item 8)
Thompson Ramírez, Marilyn del Carmen - A/C.2/78/SR.3
UN. SECURITY COUNCIL—MEMBERSHIP (Agenda item 121)
Concepción Jaramillo, Markova - A/78/PV.36
VETO (Agenda item 63)
Cano Franco, Zoraya del Carmen - A/78/PV.69
WOMEN'S ADVANCEMENT (Agenda item 25a)
Luque Nuñez, Linda del Carmen - A/C.3/78/SR.10
WOMEN'S ADVANCEMENT—CONFERENCES (Agenda item 25b)
Luque Nuñez, Linda del Carmen - A/C.3/78/SR.10

Panama. President

UN. GENERAL ASSEMBLY (78TH SESS. : 2023-2024)—GENERAL DEBATE (Agenda item 8)
Cortizo Cohen, Laurentino - A/78/PV.5
UN. GENERAL ASSEMBLY (78TH SESS. : 2023-2024)—SPECIAL STATEMENTS
Cortizo Cohen, Laurentino - A/78/PV.5

Papua New Guinea

FRENCH POLYNESIA QUESTION (Agenda item 58)
Sarufa, Fred - A/C.4/78/SR.6
NEW CALEDONIA QUESTION (Agenda item 58)
Sarufa, Fred - A/C.4/78/SR.3
RIGHTS OF THE CHILD (Agenda item 67)
Mokono, Anna Konara - A/C.3/78/SR.14
UN. INTERNATIONAL LAW COMMISSION—REPORTS (Agenda item 79)
Sarufa, Fred - A/C.6/78/SR.27
WESTERN SAHARA QUESTION (Agenda item 58)
Sarufa, Fred - A/C.4/78/SR.6
WOMEN'S ADVANCEMENT (Agenda item 25a)
Rai, Max - A/C.3/78/SR.10
WOMEN'S ADVANCEMENT—CONFERENCES (Agenda item 25b)
Rai, Max - A/C.3/78/SR.10

Papua New Guinea. Deputy Prime Minister

UN. GENERAL ASSEMBLY (78TH SESS. : 2023-2024)—GENERAL DEBATE (Agenda item 8)
Rosso, John - A/78/PV.12
UN. GENERAL ASSEMBLY (78TH SESS. : 2023-2024)—SPECIAL STATEMENTS
Rosso, John - A/78/PV.12

Paraguay

ARMS RACE—OUTER SPACE (Agenda item 97a)
Sanabria Duarte, Viviana Rocio - A/C.1/78/PV.17
DECOLONIZATION (Agenda item 58)
Pereira Sosa, José Eduardo - A/C.4/78/SR.7
FALKLAND ISLANDS (MALVINAS) QUESTION (Agenda item 42)
Pereira Sosa, José Eduardo - A/C.4/78/SR.7
IAEA—REPORTS (Agenda item 89)
Sanabria de Montiel, María Gloria Beatriz - A/78/PV.30
INDIGENOUS PEOPLES (Agenda item 68a)
Pereira Sosa, José Eduardo - A/C.3/78/SR.15
INDIGENOUS PEOPLES—CONFERENCES (Agenda item 68b)
Pereira Sosa, José Eduardo - A/C.3/78/SR.15
INTERNATIONAL CRIMINAL COURT—REPORTS (Agenda item 74)
Pereira Sosa, José Eduardo - A/78/PV.22
INTERNATIONAL LAW—TRAINING PROGRAMMES (Agenda item 78)
Giret Soto, David Antonio - A/C.6/78/SR.22
LANDLOCKED DEVELOPING COUNTRIES—CONFERENCES (Agenda item 20b)
Pereira Sosa, José Eduardo - A/C.2/78/SR.7
LEAST DEVELOPED COUNTRIES—CONFERENCES (Agenda item 20a)
Pereira Sosa, José Eduardo - A/C.2/78/SR.7
OUTER SPACE—CONFIDENCE-BUILDING MEASURES (Agenda item 99v)
Sanabria Duarte, Viviana Rocio - A/C.1/78/PV.17
RIGHTS OF THE CHILD (Agenda item 67)
Candia Ibarra, Miguel Ricardo - A/C.3/78/SR.14
RULE OF LAW (Agenda item 83)
Giret Soto, David Antonio - A/C.6/78/SR.18
SOCIAL CONDITIONS (Agenda item 24b)
Pereira Sosa, José Eduardo - A/C.3/78/SR.3
SOCIAL DEVELOPMENT (Agenda item 24)
Pereira Sosa, José Eduardo - A/C.3/78/SR.3
TERRORISM (Agenda item 109)
Pereira Sosa, José Eduardo - A/C.6/78/SR.5
UKRAINE—POLITICAL CONDITIONS (Agenda item 62)
Pereira Sosa, José Eduardo - A/78/PV.58
UN. GENERAL ASSEMBLY (78TH SESS. : 2023-2024). 1ST COMMITTEE—GENERAL DEBATE (Agenda item 8)
Pereira Sosa, José Eduardo - A/C.1/78/PV.9

Paraguay (continued)

UN. GENERAL ASSEMBLY (78TH SESS. : 2023-2024). 2ND COMMITTEE—GENERAL DEBATE (Agenda item 8)
Pereira Sosa, José Eduardo - A/C.2/78/SR.3
UN. HUMAN RIGHTS COMMITTEE—REPORTS (Agenda item 71a)
Candia Ibarra, Miguel Ricardo - A/C.3/78/SR.17
UN. INTERNATIONAL COURT OF JUSTICE—REPORTS (Agenda item 73)
Giret Soto, David Antonio - A/78/PV.27
WESTERN SAHARA QUESTION (Agenda item 58)
Pereira Sosa, José Eduardo - A/C.4/78/SR.7
WOMEN'S ADVANCEMENT (Agenda item 25a)
González Cabello Maldonado, Stephania Mercedes - A/C.3/78/SR.9
WOMEN'S ADVANCEMENT—CONFERENCES (Agenda item 25b)
González Cabello Maldonado, Stephania Mercedes - A/C.3/78/SR.9

Paraguay. President

UN. GENERAL ASSEMBLY (78TH SESS. : 2023-2024)—GENERAL DEBATE (Agenda item 8)
Peña Palacios, Santiago - A/78/PV.5
UN. GENERAL ASSEMBLY (78TH SESS. : 2023-2024)—SPECIAL STATEMENTS
Peña Palacios, Santiago - A/78/PV.5

Peru

CRIMES AGAINST HUMANITY (Agenda item 80)
Falconi, Alessandra - A/C.6/78/SR.10
CUBA—UNITED STATES (Agenda item 38)
Ugarelli, Luis F. - A/78/PV.26
DECOLONIZATION (Agenda item 58)
Ugarelli, Luis F. - A/C.4/78/SR.7
DISASTER VICTIMS (Agenda item 86)
Falconi, Alessandra - A/C.6/78/SR.6
ELECTION VERIFICATION—UN (Agenda item 71b)
Rojas, Eder - A/C.3/78/SR.50
FALKLAND ISLANDS (MALVINAS) QUESTION (Agenda item 42)
Ugarelli, Luis F. - A/C.4/78/SR.7
FOOD SECURITY (Agenda item 23a)
Napurí Pita, Andrés - A/C.2/78/SR.17
HUMAN RIGHTS—DEMOCRATIC PEOPLE'S REPUBLIC OF KOREA (Agenda item 71c)
Rojas, Eder - A/C.3/78/SR.33
HUMAN RIGHTS—SYRIAN ARAB REPUBLIC (Agenda item 71c)
Rojas, Eder - A/C.3/78/SR.54
INDIGENOUS PEOPLES (Agenda item 68a)
Rojas, Eder - A/C.3/78/SR.15

Peru (continued)

INDIGENOUS PEOPLES—CONFERENCES (Agenda item 68b)
Rojas, Eder - A/C.3/78/SR.15
INTERNATIONAL CRIMINAL COURT—REPORTS (Agenda item 74)
García Toma, Victor Óscar Shiyin - A/78/PV.21
PEACE (Agenda item 14)
Rojas, Eder - A/78/PV.62
Vegas Torres, Juan Pablo - A/78/PV.82
PEACEBUILDING (Agenda item 61)
García Toma, Victor Óscar Shiyin - A/78/PV.100
PEACEKEEPING OPERATIONS (Agenda item 51)
Llosa, Luis Felipe - A/C.4/78/SR.19
PERSONS WITH DISABILITIES (Agenda item 24b)
Rojas, Eder - A/C.3/78/SR.4
POVERTY—HUMAN RIGHTS (Agenda item 71b)
Pedroza, David - A/C.3/78/SR.30
POVERTY—INTERNATIONAL DECADES (Agenda item 21a)
Napurí Pita, Andrés - A/C.2/78/SR.17
RULE OF LAW (Agenda item 83)
Falconi, Alessandra - A/C.6/78/SR.16
RURAL POVERTY (Agenda item 21b)
Napurí Pita, Andrés - A/C.2/78/SR.17
SEXUAL ORIENTATION (Agenda item 71b)
Pedroza, David - A/C.3/78/SR.39
SOCIAL CONDITIONS (Agenda item 24b)
Rojas, Eder - A/C.3/78/SR.4
Ugarelli, Luis F. - A/C.3/78/SR.51
SOCIAL DEVELOPMENT (Agenda item 24)
Rojas, Eder - A/C.3/78/SR.4
SPECIAL POLITICAL MISSIONS (Agenda item 52)
Ugarelli, Luis F. - A/C.4/78/SR.21
SUSTAINABLE DEVELOPMENT (Agenda item 18)
Napurí Pita, Andrés - A/C.2/78/SR.24
TERRORISM (Agenda item 109)
Falconi, Alessandra - A/C.6/78/SR.4
UKRAINE—POLITICAL CONDITIONS (Agenda item 62)
Ugarelli, Luis F. - A/78/PV.58
UN. GENERAL ASSEMBLY (78TH SESS. : 2023-2024). 1ST COMMITTEE—GENERAL DEBATE (Agenda item 8)
Salas de los Ríos, Javier Leonardo - A/C.1/78/PV.7
UN. GENERAL ASSEMBLY (78TH SESS. : 2023-2024). 2ND COMMITTEE—GENERAL DEBATE (Agenda item 8)
Napurí Pita, Andrés - A/C.2/78/SR.5
UN. HUMAN RIGHTS COUNCIL—REPORTS (Agenda item 66)
Pedroza, David - A/C.3/78/SR.46
UN. INTERNATIONAL COURT OF JUSTICE—REPORTS (Agenda item 73)
Ugarelli, Luis F. - A/78/PV.27

Peru (continued)

UN. INTERNATIONAL LAW COMMISSION—REPORTS (Agenda item 79)
Falconi, Alessandra - A/C.6/78/SR.25; A/C.6/78/SR.32
UN. PEACEBUILDING COMMISSION—REPORTS (Agenda item 27)
García Toma, Victor Óscar Shiyin - A/78/PV.100
UN. PEACEBUILDING FUND—REPORTS (Agenda item 111)
García Toma, Victor Óscar Shiyin - A/78/PV.100
UN CONFERENCES (Agenda item 13)
García Toma, Victor Óscar Shiyin - A/78/PV.47
WESTERN SAHARA QUESTION (Agenda item 58)
Ugarelli, Luis F. - A/C.4/78/SR.7

Peru. President

UN. GENERAL ASSEMBLY (78TH SESS. : 2023-2024)—GENERAL DEBATE (Agenda item 8)
Boluarte Zegarra, Dina Ercilia - A/78/PV.5
UN. GENERAL ASSEMBLY (78TH SESS. : 2023-2024)—SPECIAL STATEMENTS
Boluarte Zegarra, Dina Ercilia - A/78/PV.5

Philippines

AGEING PERSONS (Agenda item 24b)
Fangco, Maria Roseny Baltazar - A/C.3/78/SR.1
ARMS RACE—OUTER SPACE (Agenda item 97a)
Lipana, Diane Shayne Dela Fuente - A/C.1/78/PV.16
BIOLOGICAL WEAPONS—TREATIES (Agenda item 106)
Lipana, Diane Shayne Dela Fuente - A/C.1/78/PV.14
CHEMICAL WEAPONS—TREATIES (Agenda item 99l)
Lipana, Diane Shayne Dela Fuente - A/C.1/78/PV.14
CONVENTIONAL WEAPONS (Agenda item 99u)
Reyes, Narciso - A/C.1/78/PV.18
CRIMES AGAINST HUMANITY (Agenda item 80)
Arumpac-Marte, Azela Guerrero - A/C.6/78/SR.11; A/C.6/78/SR.40; A/C.6/78/SR.42
Lora-Santos, Leila Castillon - A/C.6/78/SR.38
CUBA—UNITED STATES (Agenda item 38)
Lagdameo, Antonio Manuel Revilla - A/78/PV.26
CULTURE—DEVELOPMENT (Agenda item 19b)
Bregala, Dennis Borromeo - A/C.2/78/SR.11
DEVELOPMENT COOPERATION—MIDDLE-INCOME COUNTRIES (Agenda item 19c)
Bregala, Dennis Borromeo - A/C.2/78/SR.11

Philippines (continued)

DISARMAMENT—GENERAL AND COMPLETE (Agenda item 99)
Lipana, Diane Shayne Dela Fuente - A/78/PV.105; A/C.1/78/PV.20
DISARMAMENT AGREEMENTS—ENVIRONMENT (Agenda item 99j)
Lipana, Diane Shayne Dela Fuente - A/C.1/78/PV.20
DISARMAMENT AGREEMENTS—OUTER SPACE (Agenda item 97c)
Lipana, Diane Shayne Dela Fuente - A/C.1/78/PV.27
DISARMAMENT-DEVELOPMENT LINK (Agenda item 99d)
Lipana, Diane Shayne Dela Fuente - A/C.1/78/PV.20
DISASTER VICTIMS (Agenda item 86)
Lagdameo, Antonio Manuel Revilla - A/C.6/78/SR.5
EMERGENCY ASSISTANCE (Agenda item 72a)
Fangco, Maria Roseny Baltazar - A/78/PV.46
FISSIONABLE MATERIALS—TREATIES (Agenda item 99a)
Reyes, Narciso - A/C.1/78/PV.12
FOOD SECURITY (Agenda item 23a)
Beriana, Charlene Aravejo - A/C.2/78/SR.16
HEALTH (Agenda item 125)
Lora-Santos, Leila Castillon - A/78/PV.48
HIV/AIDS—DECLARATIONS (Agenda item 10)
Lagdameo, Antonio Manuel Revilla - A/78/PV.91
HUMAN RIGHTS—DEMOCRATIC PEOPLE'S REPUBLIC OF KOREA (Agenda item 71c)
Guevarra-de Dios, Nadine Bobadilla - A/C.3/78/SR.53
HUMAN RIGHTS ADVANCEMENT (Agenda item 71b)
Fangco, Maria Roseny Baltazar - A/C.3/78/SR.24
IAEA—REPORTS (Agenda item 89)
Lagdameo, Antonio Manuel Revilla - A/78/PV.30
INDIGENOUS PEOPLES (Agenda item 68a)
Navarrete, Angelica Saldivar - A/C.3/78/SR.15
INDIGENOUS PEOPLES—CONFERENCES (Agenda item 68b)
Navarrete, Angelica Saldivar - A/C.3/78/SR.15
INFORMATION—INTERNATIONAL SECURITY (Agenda item 94)
Lipana, Diane Shayne Dela Fuente - A/C.1/78/PV.20; A/C.1/78/PV.29
INTERNATIONAL CRIMINAL COURT—REPORTS (Agenda item 74)
Lagdameo, Antonio Manuel Revilla - A/78/PV.22
INTERNATIONAL JURISDICTION (Agenda item 84)
Arumpac-Marte, Azela Guerrero - A/C.6/78/SR.13
INTERNATIONAL LAW—TRAINING PROGRAMMES (Agenda item 78)
Arumpac-Marte, Azela Guerrero - A/C.6/78/SR.21

Philippines (continued)

LAW OF THE SEA (Agenda item 75a)
Arumpac-Marte, Azela Guerrero - A/78/PV.44
Peñaranda, Ariel Rodelas - A/78/PV.43
MARINE ECOSYSTEMS—BIOLOGICAL DIVERSITY (Agenda item 75c)
Arumpac-Marte, Azela Guerrero - A/78/PV.44
Peñaranda, Ariel Rodelas - A/78/PV.43
MIGRANTS—PROTECTION (Agenda item 71b)
Fangco, Maria Roseny Baltazar - A/C.3/78/SR.24
MULTILATERALISM—DISARMAMENT (Agenda item 99r)
Gomez, Jan Michael - A/C.1/78/PV.22
NON-CITIZENS—DEPORTATION (Agenda item 81)
Arumpac-Marte, Azela Guerrero - A/C.6/78/SR.34
NUCLEAR DISARMAMENT (Agenda item 99b)
Reyes, Narciso - A/C.1/78/PV.12
NUCLEAR NON-PROLIFERATION—INTERNATIONAL OBLIGATIONS (Agenda item 99w)
Reyes, Narciso - A/C.1/78/PV.12
NUCLEAR WEAPON TESTS—TREATIES (Agenda item 105)
Reyes, Narciso - A/C.1/78/PV.12
NUCLEAR WEAPONS—TREATIES (Agenda item 99ff)
Reyes, Narciso - A/C.1/78/PV.12
OUTER SPACE—CONFIDENCE-BUILDING MEASURES (Agenda item 99v)
Lipana, Diane Shayne Dela Fuente - A/C.1/78/PV.16
OUTER SPACE—PEACEFUL USES—INTERNATIONAL COOPERATION (Agenda item 48)
Novicio, Noel Mangaoang - A/C.4/78/SR.17
OUTER SPACE—PRINCIPLES (Agenda item 97d)
Lipana, Diane Shayne Dela Fuente - A/C.1/78/PV.16; A/C.1/78/PV.27
PALESTINE QUESTION (Agenda item 35)
Peñaranda, Ariel Rodelas - A/78/PV.39
PEACE (Agenda item 14)
Lagdameo, Antonio Manuel Revilla - A/78/PV.76
PEACEKEEPING OPERATIONS (Agenda item 51)
Novicio, Noel Mangaoang - A/C.4/78/SR.20
POVERTY—INTERNATIONAL DECADES (Agenda item 21a)
Beriana, Charlene Aravejo - A/C.2/78/SR.16
RESPONSIBILITY TO PROTECT (Agenda item 129)
Arumpac-Marte, Azela Guerrero - A/78/PV.99
RIGHTS OF THE CHILD (Agenda item 67)
Fangco, Maria Roseny Baltazar - A/C.3/78/SR.11
Guevarra-de Dios, Nadine Bobadilla - A/C.3/78/SR.12
RULE OF LAW (Agenda item 83)
Arumpac-Marte, Azela Guerrero - A/C.6/78/SR.16
RURAL POVERTY (Agenda item 21b)
Beriana, Charlene Aravejo - A/C.2/78/SR.16

Philippines (continued)

SCIENCE AND TECHNOLOGY—DEVELOPMENT (Agenda item 19a)
Bregala, Dennis Borromeo - A/C.2/78/SR.11
SMALL ARMS—ILLICIT TRAFFIC (Agenda item 99p)
Reyes, Narciso - A/C.1/78/PV.18
SMALL ARMS—ILLICIT TRAFFIC—ASSISTANCE (Agenda item 99n)
Reyes, Narciso - A/C.1/78/PV.18
SOCIAL CONDITIONS (Agenda item 24b)
Lagdameo, Antonio Manuel Revilla - A/C.3/78/SR.2
SOUTH-EAST ASIA—NUCLEAR-WEAPON-FREE ZONES (Agenda item 99y)
Gomez, Jan Michael - A/C.1/78/PV.22
Reyes, Narciso - A/C.1/78/PV.12
STRADDLING FISH STOCKS (Agenda item 75b)
Arumpac-Marte, Azela Guerrero - A/78/PV.44
Peñaranda, Ariel Rodelas - A/78/PV.43
TERRORISM (Agenda item 109)
Peñaranda, Ariel Rodelas - A/C.6/78/SR.2
TREATIES (Agenda item 87)
Arumpac-Marte, Azela Guerrero - A/C.6/78/SR.20
UN—BUDGET (2024) (Agenda item 134)
Valles, Marivil Villa - A/C.5/78/SR.33
UN. CONFERENCE ON DISARMAMENT—REPORTS (Agenda item 101a)
Gomez, Jan Michael - A/C.1/78/PV.22
Lipana, Diane Shayne Dela Fuente - A/C.1/78/PV.29
UN. DISARMAMENT COMMISSION—REPORTS (Agenda item 101b)
Gomez, Jan Michael - A/C.1/78/PV.22
UN. GENERAL ASSEMBLY—WORK PROGRAMME (Agenda item 120)
Lagdameo, Antonio Manuel Revilla - A/78/PV.32
UN. GENERAL ASSEMBLY (78TH SESS. : 2023-2024)—GENERAL DEBATE (Agenda item 8)
Manalo, Enrique A. - A/78/PV.12
UN. GENERAL ASSEMBLY (78TH SESS. : 2023-2024)—OFFICERS (Agenda item 5)
Peñaranda, Ariel Rodelas - A/C.5/78/SR.1
UN. GENERAL ASSEMBLY (78TH SESS. : 2023-2024). 1ST COMMITTEE—GENERAL DEBATE (Agenda item 8)
Peñaranda, Ariel Rodelas - A/C.1/78/PV.3
UN. GENERAL ASSEMBLY (78TH SESS. : 2023-2024). 1ST COMMITTEE—WORK ORGANIZATION (Agenda item 7)
Lipana, Diane Shayne Dela Fuente - A/C.1/78/PV.29
UN. GENERAL ASSEMBLY (78TH SESS. : 2023-2024). 2ND COMMITTEE—GENERAL DEBATE (Agenda item 8)
Lora-Santos, Leila Castillon - A/C.2/78/SR.3
UN. INTERNATIONAL COURT OF JUSTICE—REPORTS (Agenda item 73)
Lagdameo, Antonio Manuel Revilla - A/78/PV.28

Philippines (continued)

UN. INTERNATIONAL LAW COMMISSION—REPORTS (Agenda item 79)
Arumpac-Marte, Azela Guerrero - A/C.6/78/SR.28; A/C.6/78/SR.30
Peñaranda, Ariel Rodelas - A/C.6/78/SR.32
UN. SECURITY COUNCIL—MEMBERSHIP (Agenda item 121)
Lagdameo, Antonio Manuel Revilla - A/78/PV.35
UN CHARTER—REPORTS (Agenda item 82)
Arumpac-Marte, Azela Guerrero - A/C.6/78/SR.33
UN COMMISSION ON INTERNATIONAL TRADE LAW—REPORTS (Agenda item 77)
Arumpac-Marte, Azela Guerrero - A/C.6/78/SR.14
UN RESOLUTIONS—IMPLEMENTATION (Agenda item 119)
Lagdameo, Antonio Manuel Revilla - A/78/PV.32
UNRWA—ACTIVITIES (Agenda item 49)
Novicio, Noel Mangaoang - A/C.4/78/SR.23
VETO (Agenda item 63)
Lagdameo, Antonio Manuel Revilla - A/78/PV.70
WEAPONS OF MASS DESTRUCTION—TERRORISM (Agenda item 99s)
Lipana, Diane Shayne Dela Fuente - A/C.1/78/PV.14
WOMEN MIGRANT WORKERS (Agenda item 25a)
Lagdameo, Antonio Manuel Revilla - A/C.3/78/SR.49
WOMEN'S ADVANCEMENT (Agenda item 25a)
Peñaranda, Ariel Rodelas - A/C.3/78/SR.8
WOMEN'S ADVANCEMENT—CONFERENCES (Agenda item 25b)
Peñaranda, Ariel Rodelas - A/C.3/78/SR.8

Plataforma Latinoamericana y Caribeña de Solidaridad con el Pueblo Saharaui (Organization)

WESTERN SAHARA QUESTION (Agenda item 58)
Botero Martínez, José Leonar - A/C.4/78/SR.4

Poland

AFRICA—DEVELOPMENT (Agenda item 65b)
Sakowicz, Mateusz - A/78/PV.18
AFRICA—SUSTAINABLE DEVELOPMENT—PARTNERSHIP (Agenda item 65a)
Sakowicz, Mateusz - A/78/PV.18
CHEMICAL WEAPONS—TREATIES (Agenda item 99l)
Szczerski, Krzysztof - A/C.1/78/PV.26
COMMODITIES (Agenda item 16d)
Skoczek, Joanna Sylwia - A/C.2/78/SR.14
CONVENTIONAL ARMS—REGIONAL PROGRAMMES (Agenda item 99g)
Joniec, Katarzyna - A/C.1/78/PV.29
CRIME PREVENTION (Agenda item 107)
Skoczek, Joanna Sylwia - A/C.3/78/SR.50

Poland (continued)

CRIMES AGAINST HUMANITY (Agenda item 80)
Domagała, Przemysław - A/C.6/78/SR.45
Górzyńska, Marzena - A/C.6/78/SR.44
Szczerski, Krzysztof - A/C.6/78/SR.10
CYBERCRIME (Agenda item 108)
Stadnicka, Małgorzata - A/C.3/78/SR.5
DISARMAMENT—GENERAL AND COMPLETE (Agenda item 99)
Joniec, Katarzyna - A/C.1/78/PV.28
EMERGENCY ASSISTANCE (Agenda item 72a)
Skoczek, Joanna Sylwia - A/78/PV.46
FREEDOM OF EXPRESSION (Agenda item 71b)
Skoczek, Joanna Sylwia - A/C.3/78/SR.19
HIV/AIDS—DECLARATIONS (Agenda item 10)
Szczerski, Krzysztof - A/78/PV.91
HUMAN RIGHTS—BELARUS (Agenda item 71c)
Szczerski, Krzysztof - A/C.3/78/SR.37
HUMAN RIGHTS—RUSSIAN FEDERATION (Agenda item 71c)
Szczerski, Krzysztof - A/C.3/78/SR.37
HUMAN RIGHTS—UKRAINE (Agenda item 71c)
Skoczek, Joanna Sylwia - A/C.3/78/SR.37
HUMAN RIGHTS ACTIVISTS (Agenda item 71b)
Skoczek, Joanna Sylwia - A/C.3/78/SR.19
INTERNATIONAL CRIMINAL COURT—REPORTS (Agenda item 74)
Szczerski, Krzysztof - A/78/PV.22
MINE CLEARANCE (Agenda item 46)
Szczerski, Krzysztof - A/C.4/78/SR.10
NUCLEAR DISARMAMENT (Agenda item 99b)
Dzwonek, Piotr - A/C.1/78/PV.13
NUCLEAR NON-PROLIFERATION—INTERNATIONAL OBLIGATIONS (Agenda item 99w)
Dzwonek, Piotr - A/C.1/78/PV.13
PALESTINIANS—ASSISTANCE (Agenda item 72b)
Skoczek, Joanna Sylwia - A/78/PV.46
PEACEBUILDING (Agenda item 61)
Szczerski, Krzysztof - A/78/PV.100
PEACEKEEPING OPERATIONS (Agenda item 51)
Sakowicz, Mateusz - A/C.4/78/SR.19
PERSONS WITH DISABILITIES—HUMAN RIGHTS (Agenda item 71a)
Lula, Iwona Anna - A/C.3/78/SR.38
Skoczek, Joanna Sylwia - A/C.3/78/SR.18; A/C.3/78/SR.51
RELIGIOUS INTOLERANCE (Agenda item 71b)
Skoczek, Joanna Sylwia - A/C.3/78/SR.38

Poland (continued)

RESPONSIBILITY TO PROTECT (Agenda item 129)
Szczerski, Krzysztof - A/78/PV.96
RIGHTS OF THE CHILD (Agenda item 67)
Domańska, Anna - A/C.3/78/SR.11
Lula, Iwona Anna - A/C.3/78/SR.11
Stadnicka, Małgorzata - A/C.3/78/SR.11
Szczerski, Krzysztof - A/C.3/78/SR.11
SOCIAL CONDITIONS (Agenda item 24b)
Stadnicka, Małgorzata - A/C.3/78/SR.2
SOCIAL DEVELOPMENT (Agenda item 24)
Lula, Iwona Anna - A/C.3/78/SR.1
SUSTAINABLE DEVELOPMENT (Agenda item 18)
Skoczek, Joanna Sylwia - A/C.2/78/SR.14
TERRITORIES OCCUPIED BY ISRAEL—HUMAN RIGHTS (Agenda item 50)
Szczerski, Krzysztof - A/C.4/78/SR.26
UKRAINE—POLITICAL CONDITIONS (Agenda item 62)
Sikorski, Radoslaw - A/78/PV.56
UN. GENERAL ASSEMBLY (78TH SESS. : 2023-2024). 1ST COMMITTEE—GENERAL DEBATE (Agenda item 8)
Sawicz, Jacek - A/C.1/78/PV.5
UN. GENERAL ASSEMBLY (78TH SESS. : 2023-2024). 2ND COMMITTEE—GENERAL DEBATE (Agenda item 8)
Sakowicz, Mateusz - A/C.2/78/SR.4
UN. INTERNATIONAL LAW COMMISSION—REPORTS (Agenda item 79)
Majszyk, Slawomir - A/C.6/78/SR.24
Padło-Pękala, Katarzyna - A/C.6/78/SR.29; A/C.6/78/SR.31
UN. PEACEBUILDING COMMISSION—REPORTS (Agenda item 27)
Szczerski, Krzysztof - A/78/PV.100
UN. PEACEBUILDING FUND—REPORTS (Agenda item 111)
Szczerski, Krzysztof - A/78/PV.100
UN. SECURITY COUNCIL—REPORTS (Agenda item 26)
Szczerski, Krzysztof - A/78/PV.93
UN HIGH COMMISSIONER FOR REFUGEES—REPORTS (Agenda item 60)
Skoczek, Joanna Sylwia - A/C.3/78/SR.44
VETO (Agenda item 63)
Szczerski, Krzysztof - A/78/PV.68; A/78/PV.78
WESTERN SAHARA QUESTION (Agenda item 58)
Szczerski, Krzysztof - A/C.4/78/SR.6
WOMEN'S ADVANCEMENT (Agenda item 25a)
Lula, Iwona Anna - A/C.3/78/SR.7
WOMEN'S ADVANCEMENT—CONFERENCES (Agenda item 25b)
Lula, Iwona Anna - A/C.3/78/SR.7
YOUTH (Agenda item 24b)
Lula, Iwona Anna - A/C.3/78/SR.55
Stadnicka, Małgorzata - A/C.3/78/SR.2

Poland. President

UN. GENERAL ASSEMBLY (78TH SESS. : 2023-2024)—GENERAL DEBATE (Agenda item 8)
Duda, Andrzej - A/78/PV.4
UN. GENERAL ASSEMBLY (78TH SESS. : 2023-2024)—SPECIAL STATEMENTS
Duda, Andrzej - A/78/PV.4

Portugal

AGEING PERSONS (Agenda item 24b)
Guerra, Stefano Venancio - A/C.3/78/SR.1
Zacarias, Ana Paula - A/C.3/78/SR.2
CRIMES AGAINST HUMANITY (Agenda item 80)
Carvalho, Sergio Amaral Alves de - A/C.6/78/SR.38; A/C.6/78/SR.40; A/C.6/78/SR.45
Kowalski, Mateus - A/C.6/78/SR.42; A/C.6/78/SR.43; A/C.6/78/SR.44
Zacarias, Ana Paula - A/C.6/78/SR.10
DISASTER VICTIMS (Agenda item 86)
Matos, Ines - A/C.6/78/SR.5
HUMAN RIGHTS (Agenda item 71)
Marinho, Joana Almeida - A/C.3/78/SR.25
Zacarias, Ana Paula - A/C.3/78/SR.16
HUMAN RIGHTS—INTERNATIONAL INSTRUMENTS (Agenda item 71a)
Silva, Miguel Alegre - A/C.3/78/SR.17
INFORMATION (Agenda item 53)
Aranda, Jorge Eduardo Ferreira Silva - A/C.4/78/SR.13
INTERNATIONAL LAW—TRAINING PROGRAMMES (Agenda item 78)
Matos, Ines - A/C.6/78/SR.21
LEPROSY (Agenda item 71b)
Zacarias, Ana Paula - A/C.3/78/SR.17
MIGRANTS—PROTECTION (Agenda item 71b)
Guerra, Stefano Venancio - A/C.3/78/SR.23
PEACEKEEPING OPERATIONS (Agenda item 51)
Zacarias, Ana Paula - A/C.4/78/SR.19
PEACEKEEPING OPERATIONS—CRIMINAL LIABILITY (Agenda item 76)
Carvalho, Sergio Amaral Alves de - A/C.6/78/SR.8
RACIAL DISCRIMINATION—ELIMINATION (Agenda item 69a)
Marinho, Joana Almeida - A/C.3/78/SR.41
RACIAL DISCRIMINATION—PROGRAMMES OF ACTION (Agenda item 69b)
Marinho, Joana Almeida - A/C.3/78/SR.41
RESPONSIBILITY OF INTERNATIONAL ORGANIZATIONS (Agenda item 85)
Carvalho, Sergio Amaral Alves de - A/C.6/78/SR.19
RIGHT TO EDUCATION (Agenda item 71b)
Guerra, Stefano Venancio - A/C.3/78/SR.27
RIGHTS OF THE CHILD (Agenda item 67)
Marinho, Joana Almeida - A/C.3/78/SR.11

Portugal (continued)

SEXUAL ORIENTATION (Agenda item 71b)
Marinho, Joana Almeida - A/C.3/78/SR.39
SMALL ISLAND DEVELOPING STATES—PROGRAMMES OF ACTION (Agenda item 18b)
Lages, Afonso - A/78/PV.103
Oliveira, Vitorino Alberto Melo Gomes - A/78/PV.100
SOCIAL CONDITIONS (Agenda item 24b)
Zacarias, Ana Paula - A/78/PV.57; A/C.3/78/SR.2
SOCIAL DEVELOPMENT (Agenda item 24)
Zacarias, Ana Paula - A/C.3/78/SR.2
UKRAINE—POLITICAL CONDITIONS (Agenda item 62)
Carreiras, Helena - A/78/PV.56
UN. GENERAL ASSEMBLY—WORK PROGRAMME (Agenda item 120)
Aranda, Jorge Eduardo Ferreira Silva - A/78/PV.33
Carvalho, Sergio Amaral Alves de - A/C.6/78/SR.36
UN. GENERAL ASSEMBLY (78TH SESS. : 2023-2024)—OFFICERS (Agenda item 5)
Aranda, Jorge Eduardo Ferreira Silva - A/C.6/78/SR.48
UN. GENERAL ASSEMBLY (78TH SESS. : 2023-2024). 1ST COMMITTEE—GENERAL DEBATE (Agenda item 8)
Zacarias, Ana Paula - A/C.1/78/PV.4
UN. GENERAL ASSEMBLY (78TH SESS. : 2023-2024). 2ND COMMITTEE—GENERAL DEBATE (Agenda item 8)
Zacarias, Ana Paula - A/C.2/78/SR.4
UN. INTERNATIONAL LAW COMMISSION—REPORTS (Agenda item 79)
Carvalho, Sergio Amaral Alves de - A/C.6/78/SR.29; A/C.6/78/SR.31
Kowalski, Mateus - A/C.6/78/SR.24
UN HIGH COMMISSIONER FOR REFUGEES—REPORTS (Agenda item 60)
Marinho, Joana Almeida - A/C.3/78/SR.44
UN RESOLUTIONS—IMPLEMENTATION (Agenda item 119)
Aranda, Jorge Eduardo Ferreira Silva - A/78/PV.33
UN YOUTH OFFICE—REPORTS (Agenda item 130)
Aranda, Jorge Eduardo Ferreira Silva - A/78/PV.102
VETO (Agenda item 63)
Aranda, Jorge Eduardo Ferreira Silva - A/78/PV.52; A/78/PV.68; A/78/PV.70
Zacarias, Ana Paula - A/78/PV.3; A/78/PV.61; A/78/PV.67; A/78/PV.74; A/78/PV.78
WESTERN SAHARA QUESTION (Agenda item 58)
Pureza, José Manuel - A/C.4/78/SR.5
YOUTH (Agenda item 24b)
Zacarias, Ana Paula - A/C.3/78/SR.2

Portugal. President
UN. GENERAL ASSEMBLY (78TH SESS. : 2023-2024)—GENERAL DEBATE (Agenda item 8)
Sousa, Marcelo Rebelo de - A/78/PV.4
UN. GENERAL ASSEMBLY (78TH SESS. : 2023-2024)—SPECIAL STATEMENTS
Sousa, Marcelo Rebelo de - A/78/PV.4

Preparatory Commission for the Comprehensive Nuclear Test-Ban Treaty Organization
NUCLEAR WEAPON TESTS—TREATIES (Agenda item 105)
Rosemberg Guerrero, José - A/C.1/78/PV.13

Preparatory Commission for the Comprehensive Nuclear Test-Ban Treaty Organization. Executive Secretary
DISARMAMENT—GENERAL AND COMPLETE (Agenda item 99)
Floyd, Robert - A/78/PV.105

Qatar
2030 AGENDA—PROGRAMME IMPLEMENTATION (Agenda item 18a)
Al-Kuwari, Shaheen - A/C.2/78/SR.12
ARMED CONFLICTS PREVENTION (Agenda item 31a)
Alnesf, Sharifa Yousef A.S. - A/78/PV.72
BIOLOGICAL WEAPONS—TREATIES (Agenda item 106)
Al-Mehaizza, Essa Abdulla - A/C.1/78/PV.15
CHEMICAL WEAPONS—TREATIES (Agenda item 99l)
Al-Mehaizza, Essa Abdulla - A/C.1/78/PV.15
CONFERENCE AND MEETING SERVICES (Agenda item 137)
Alnasr, Mohammed Khalifa H. - A/C.5/78/SR.7
CRIMES AGAINST HUMANITY (Agenda item 80)
Al-Kaabi, Soud Abdulaziz - A/C.6/78/SR.10; A/C.6/78/SR.39
Al-Marri, Rashid Ali - A/C.6/78/SR.40; A/C.6/78/SR.43
DECOLONIZATION (Agenda item 58)
Al-thani, Jassim Abdulaziz J.A. - A/C.4/78/SR.2
FAMILY (Agenda item 24b)
Al-Thani, Alya Ahmed S.A. - A/C.3/78/SR.3
FOOD SECURITY (Agenda item 23a)
Al-Khayareen, Abdulla Ghanim - A/C.2/78/SR.16
HUMAN RIGHTS (Agenda item 71)
Al-Buainain, Hemyan Hassan Nasser - A/C.3/78/SR.16
HUMAN RIGHTS—SYRIAN ARAB REPUBLIC (Agenda item 71c)
Al-Maawda, Jassim Sayyar - A/C.3/78/SR.54
HUMAN RIGHTS—TERRITORIES OCCUPIED BY ISRAEL (Agenda item 71c)
Al-thani, Almaha Mubarak F.J. - A/C.3/78/SR.24
HUMAN RIGHTS—UKRAINE (Agenda item 71c)
Al-thani, Almaha Mubarak F.J. - A/C.3/78/SR.53
HUMAN RIGHTS ADVANCEMENT (Agenda item 71b)
Al-thani, Almaha Mubarak F.J. - A/C.3/78/SR.24

Qatar (continued)
HUMAN RIGHTS INSTITUTIONS—SOUTHWEST ASIA AND ARAB COUNTRIES (Agenda item 71b)
Al-Thani, Alya Ahmed S.A. - A/C.3/78/SR.50
INFORMATION (Agenda item 53)
Al-Thani, Alya Ahmed S.A. - A/C.4/78/SR.14
LANDLOCKED DEVELOPING COUNTRIES—CONFERENCES (Agenda item 20b)
Al-naama, Talal Abdulaziz - A/C.2/78/SR.7
LEAST DEVELOPED COUNTRIES—CONFERENCES (Agenda item 20a)
Al-naama, Talal Abdulaziz - A/C.2/78/SR.7
MIDDLE EAST—NUCLEAR-WEAPON-FREE ZONES (Agenda item 95)
Al-Safran, Hussain Mohammed - A/C.1/78/PV.12
NUCLEAR DISARMAMENT (Agenda item 99b)
Al-Safran, Hussain Mohammed - A/C.1/78/PV.12
NUCLEAR NON-PROLIFERATION—INTERNATIONAL OBLIGATIONS (Agenda item 99w)
Al-Safran, Hussain Mohammed - A/C.1/78/PV.12
PALESTINE QUESTION (Agenda item 35)
Al-Thani, Alya Ahmed S.A. - A/78/PV.39
PEACE (Agenda item 14)
Al-thani, Almaha Mubarak F.J. - A/78/PV.76
PERSONS WITH DISABILITIES (Agenda item 24b)
Al-Thani, Alya Ahmed S.A. - A/C.3/78/SR.3
PERSONS WITH DISABILITIES—HUMAN RIGHTS (Agenda item 71a)
Al Khayarin, Saleh Mohammed - A/C.3/78/SR.51
Al-thani, Almaha Mubarak F.J. - A/C.3/78/SR.24
POVERTY—INTERNATIONAL DECADES (Agenda item 21a)
Al-Khayareen, Abdulla Ghanim - A/C.2/78/SR.16
RIGHTS OF THE CHILD (Agenda item 67)
Al-Buainain, Hemyan Hassan Nasser - A/C.3/78/SR.11
Al-thani, Almaha Mubarak F.J. - A/C.3/78/SR.12
RULE OF LAW (Agenda item 83)
Al-Kaabi, Soud Abdulaziz - A/C.6/78/SR.16
RURAL POVERTY (Agenda item 21b)
Al-Khayareen, Abdulla Ghanim - A/C.2/78/SR.16
SPORTS—OLYMPIC GAMES (Agenda item 11)
Alnesf, Sharifa Yousef A.S. - A/78/PV.38
SUSTAINABLE DEVELOPMENT (Agenda item 18)
Al-Kuwari, Shaheen - A/C.2/78/SR.12
Al-naama, Talal Abdulaziz - A/C.2/78/SR.24
TERRITORIES OCCUPIED BY ISRAEL—HUMAN RIGHTS (Agenda item 50)
Al-thani, Jassim Abdulaziz J.A. - A/C.4/78/SR.25
TERRITORIES OCCUPIED BY ISRAEL—NATURAL RESOURCES (Agenda item 59)
Al-naama, Talal Abdulaziz - A/C.2/78/SR.19
TERRORISM (Agenda item 109)
Almansouri, Ali Ahmad M.A. - A/C.6/78/SR.2

Qatar (continued)

UKRAINE—POLITICAL CONDITIONS (Agenda item 62)
Al-Thani, Abdulrahman Abdulaziz F.A. - A/78/PV.99
UN—BUDGET (2024) (Agenda item 134)
Al-Thani, Alya Ahmed S.A. - A/C.5/78/SR.5
Alnasr, Mohammed Khalifa H. - A/C.5/78/SR.26/PartII
UN—PROGRAMME PLANNING (Agenda item 135)
Al-Thani, Alya Ahmed S.A. - A/C.5/78/SR.5
Alnasr, Mohammed Khalifa H. - A/C.5/78/SR.24
UN. GENERAL ASSEMBLY—WORK PROGRAMME (Agenda item 120)
Al-Thani, Hamad bin Abdulrahman - A/78/PV.33
UN. GENERAL ASSEMBLY (78TH SESS. : 2023-2024). 1ST COMMITTEE—GENERAL DEBATE (Agenda item 8)
Al-Thani, Abdulrahman Abdulaziz F.A. - A/C.1/78/PV.3
UN. GENERAL ASSEMBLY (78TH SESS. : 2023-2024). 2ND COMMITTEE—GENERAL DEBATE (Agenda item 8)
Al-naama, Talal Abdulaziz - A/C.2/78/SR.2
UN. HUMAN RIGHTS COUNCIL—REPORTS (Agenda item 66)
Al-thani, Almaha Mubarak F.J. - A/78/PV.23
UN. SECURITY COUNCIL—MEMBERSHIP (Agenda item 121)
Alnesf, Sharifa Yousef A.S. - A/78/PV.36
UN CHARTER—REPORTS (Agenda item 82)
Al-Marri, Rashid Ali - A/C.6/78/SR.22
UN HIGH COMMISSIONER FOR REFUGEES—REPORTS (Agenda item 60)
Al Khayarin, Saleh Mohammed - A/C.3/78/SR.45
UN RESOLUTIONS—IMPLEMENTATION (Agenda item 119)
Al-Thani, Hamad bin Abdulrahman - A/78/PV.33
UNRWA—ACTIVITIES (Agenda item 49)
Al-thani, Jassim Abdulaziz J.A. - A/C.4/78/SR.22
VETO (Agenda item 63)
Al-Maawda, Jassim Sayyar - A/78/PV.70
Al-Thani, Alya Ahmed S.A. - A/78/PV.66; A/78/PV.75
WEAPONS OF MASS DESTRUCTION—TERRORISM (Agenda item 99s)
Al-Mehaizza, Essa Abdulla - A/C.1/78/PV.15
WESTERN SAHARA QUESTION (Agenda item 58)
Al-thani, Jassim Abdulaziz J.A. - A/C.4/78/SR.2
WOMEN'S ADVANCEMENT (Agenda item 25a)
Al-Buainain, Hemyan Hassan Nasser - A/C.3/78/SR.7
Al-Thani, Alya Ahmed S.A. - A/C.3/78/SR.8
WOMEN'S ADVANCEMENT—CONFERENCES (Agenda item 25b)
Al-Buainain, Hemyan Hassan Nasser - A/C.3/78/SR.7

Qatar (continued)

WOMEN'S ADVANCEMENT—CONFERENCES (Agenda item 25b)
Al-Thani, Alya Ahmed S.A. - A/C.3/78/SR.8
YOUTH (Agenda item 24b)
Al-Thani, Alya Ahmed S.A. - A/C.3/78/SR.3

Qatar. Amir

UN. GENERAL ASSEMBLY (78TH SESS. : 2023-2024)—GENERAL DEBATE (Agenda item 8)
Al-Thani, Sheikh Tamim bin Hamad - A/78/PV.4
UN. GENERAL ASSEMBLY (78TH SESS. : 2023-2024)—SPECIAL STATEMENTS
Al-Thani, Sheikh Tamim bin Hamad - A/78/PV.4

Republic of Korea

ARMS RACE—OUTER SPACE (Agenda item 97a)
Kim, Sunghoon - A/C.1/78/PV.17
Yoon, Seong-mee - A/C.1/78/PV.17
ARMS TRANSFERS—TREATIES (Agenda item 99x)
Yoon, Seong-mee - A/C.1/78/PV.18
BIOLOGICAL WEAPONS—TREATIES (Agenda item 106)
Yoon, Seong-mee - A/C.1/78/PV.15
CHEMICAL WEAPONS—TREATIES (Agenda item 99l)
Yoon, Seong-mee - A/C.1/78/PV.15
CONVENTIONAL WEAPONS (Agenda item 99u)
Yoon, Seong-mee - A/C.1/78/PV.18
CONVENTIONAL WEAPONS—TREATIES (Agenda item 103)
Yoon, Seong-mee - A/C.1/78/PV.18
CRIMES AGAINST HUMANITY (Agenda item 80)
Song, Miyoung - A/C.6/78/SR.38; A/C.6/78/SR.39; A/C.6/78/SR.41; A/C.6/78/SR.43; A/C.6/78/SR.44
DISARMAMENT—GENERAL AND COMPLETE (Agenda item 99)
Kim, Sunghoon - A/C.1/78/PV.28
Yoon, Seong-mee - A/C.1/78/PV.18; A/C.1/78/PV.19
DISARMAMENT—YOUTH (Agenda item 99gg)
Lee, Hyun Goo - A/C.1/78/PV.21; A/C.1/78/PV.28
DISARMAMENT AGREEMENTS—OUTER SPACE (Agenda item 97c)
Yoon, Seong-mee - A/C.1/78/PV.17
DISARMAMENT-DEVELOPMENT LINK (Agenda item 99d)
Kim, Sunghoon - A/C.1/78/PV.28
HUMAN RIGHTS (Agenda item 71)
Song, Hye-ryoung - A/C.3/78/SR.27
HUMAN RIGHTS—AFGHANISTAN (Agenda item 71c)
Song, Hye-ryoung - A/C.3/78/SR.34
HUMAN RIGHTS—DEMOCRATIC PEOPLE'S REPUBLIC OF KOREA (Agenda item 71c)
Hwang, Joonkook - A/C.3/78/SR.26; A/C.3/78/SR.53

Republic of Korea (continued)

HUMAN RIGHTS—DEMOCRATIC PEOPLE'S REPUBLIC OF KOREA (Agenda item 71c)
Lee, Shin-wha - A/C.3/78/SR.33
Song, Hye-ryoung - A/C.3/78/SR.27
HUMAN RIGHTS—MYANMAR (Agenda item 71c)
Kim, Yong Yi - A/C.3/78/SR.33
IAEA—REPORTS (Agenda item 89)
Kim, Sunghoon - A/78/PV.30
INFORMATION (Agenda item 53)
Jung, Jae Hyuk - A/C.4/78/SR.12; A/C.4/78/SR.13
INFORMATION—INTERNATIONAL SECURITY (Agenda item 94)
Lee, Hyun Goo - A/C.1/78/PV.21; A/C.1/78/PV.29
INTERNATIONAL CRIMINAL COURT—REPORTS (Agenda item 74)
Choi, Taeeun - A/78/PV.22
LANDMINES—TREATIES (Agenda item 99m)
Kim, Sunghoon - A/C.1/78/PV.28
NUCLEAR DISARMAMENT (Agenda item 99b)
Kim, Sunghoon - A/C.1/78/PV.12; A/C.1/78/PV.13
NUCLEAR NON-PROLIFERATION—INTERNATIONAL OBLIGATIONS (Agenda item 99w)
Kim, Sunghoon - A/C.1/78/PV.12
NUCLEAR WEAPON TESTS—TREATIES (Agenda item 105)
Kim, Sunghoon - A/C.1/78/PV.12
NUCLEAR WEAPONS—ELIMINATION (Agenda item 99z)
Kim, Sangjin - A/C.1/78/PV.26
OUTER SPACE—CONFIDENCE-BUILDING MEASURES (Agenda item 99v)
Yoon, Seong-mee - A/C.1/78/PV.17
OUTER SPACE—PEACEFUL USES—INTERNATIONAL COOPERATION (Agenda item 48)
Lee, Hyun Goo - A/C.4/78/SR.17
OUTER SPACE—PRINCIPLES (Agenda item 97d)
Yoon, Seong-mee - A/C.1/78/PV.17
PEACEBUILDING (Agenda item 61)
Park, Jeewon - A/78/PV.101
PEACEKEEPING OPERATIONS (Agenda item 51)
Hwang, Won - A/C.4/78/SR.20
PERSONS WITH DISABILITIES—HUMAN RIGHTS (Agenda item 71a)
Lee, Yeseung - A/C.3/78/SR.38
RESPONSIBILITY TO PROTECT (Agenda item 129)
Kim, Hyunsoo - A/78/PV.97
RULE OF LAW (Agenda item 83)
Kim, Hyunsoo - A/C.6/78/SR.18
SMALL ARMS—ILLICIT TRAFFIC (Agenda item 99p)
Yoon, Seong-mee - A/C.1/78/PV.18
SMALL ARMS—ILLICIT TRAFFIC—ASSISTANCE (Agenda item 99n)
Yoon, Seong-mee - A/C.1/78/PV.18

Republic of Korea (continued)

TAXATION (Agenda item 16h)
Cho, Seong-Jun - A/C.2/78/SR.25
TERRORISM (Agenda item 109)
Kim, Hyunsoo - A/C.6/78/SR.4
TERRORISM—HUMAN RIGHTS (Agenda item 71b)
Lee, Yeseung - A/C.3/78/SR.31
UKRAINE—POLITICAL CONDITIONS (Agenda item 62)
Hong, Sung Hun - A/78/PV.58
Kim, Sangjin - A/78/PV.58
UN. CONFERENCE ON DISARMAMENT—REPORTS (Agenda item 101a)
Yoon, Seong-mee - A/C.1/78/PV.23
UN. DISARMAMENT COMMISSION—REPORTS (Agenda item 101b)
Yoon, Seong-mee - A/C.1/78/PV.23
UN. GENERAL ASSEMBLY (78TH SESS. : 2023-2024)—GENERAL DEBATE—RIGHT OF REPLY (Agenda item 8)
Kim, Sangjin - A/78/PV.14
UN. GENERAL ASSEMBLY (78TH SESS. : 2023-2024)—OFFICERS (Agenda item 5)
Seong, Woong - A/C.5/78/SR.1
UN. GENERAL ASSEMBLY (78TH SESS. : 2023-2024). 1ST COMMITTEE—GENERAL DEBATE (Agenda item 8)
Hwang, Joonkook - A/C.1/78/PV.2
Kim, Sunghoon - A/C.1/78/PV.2; A/C.1/78/PV.7
UN. GENERAL ASSEMBLY (78TH SESS. : 2023-2024). 2ND COMMITTEE—GENERAL DEBATE (Agenda item 8)
Cho, Hyunwoo - A/C.2/78/SR.4
UN. GENERAL ASSEMBLY (78TH SESS. : 2023-2024). 5TH COMMITTEE—WORK ORGANIZATION (Agenda item 7)
Seong, Woong - A/C.5/78/SR.27; A/C.5/78/SR.35
UN. HUMAN RIGHTS COUNCIL—REPORTS (Agenda item 66)
Song, Hye-ryoung - A/C.3/78/SR.46
UN. INTERNATIONAL LAW COMMISSION—REPORTS (Agenda item 79)
Lee, Young Ju - A/C.6/78/SR.28; A/C.6/78/SR.30; A/C.6/78/SR.31
UN. PEACEBUILDING COMMISSION—REPORTS (Agenda item 27)
Park, Jeewon - A/78/PV.101
UN. PEACEBUILDING FUND—REPORTS (Agenda item 111)
Park, Jeewon - A/78/PV.101
UN. SECURITY COUNCIL—MEMBERSHIP (Agenda item 121)
Hwang, Joonkook - A/78/PV.35
UN CHARTER—REPORTS (Agenda item 82)
Kim, Hyunsoo - A/C.6/78/SR.33; A/C.6/78/SR.34
UN COMMISSION ON INTERNATIONAL TRADE LAW—REPORTS (Agenda item 77)
Choi, Taeeun - A/C.6/78/SR.14

Republic of Korea (continued)

UN HIGH COMMISSIONER FOR REFUGEES—REPORTS (Agenda item 60)
Kim, Sangjin - A/C.3/78/SR.45
Song, Hye-ryoung - A/C.3/78/SR.45
VETO (Agenda item 63)
Cho, Hyunwoo - A/78/PV.70
Hwang, Joonkook - A/78/PV.3; A/78/PV.68
Kim, Sangjin - A/78/PV.51; A/78/PV.60; A/78/PV.66; A/78/PV.75
Kim, Sunghoon - A/78/PV.68
Lee, Hyun Goo - A/78/PV.79
Tak, Minsoo - A/78/PV.71

Republic of Korea. President

UN. GENERAL ASSEMBLY (78TH SESS. : 2023-2024)—GENERAL DEBATE (Agenda item 8)
Yoon, Suk Yeol - A/78/PV.6
UN. GENERAL ASSEMBLY (78TH SESS. : 2023-2024)—SPECIAL STATEMENTS
Yoon, Suk Yeol - A/78/PV.6

Republic of Moldova

HUMAN RIGHTS (Agenda item 71)
Leuca, Gheorghe - A/C.3/78/SR.25
SANCTIONS—INTERNATIONAL RELATIONS (Agenda item 71b)
Leuca, Gheorghe - A/C.3/78/SR.25
SUSTAINABLE DEVELOPMENT (Agenda item 18)
Nipomici, Galina - A/C.2/78/SR.24
UKRAINE—POLITICAL CONDITIONS (Agenda item 62)
Leuca, Gheorghe - A/78/PV.57
UN. GENERAL ASSEMBLY (78TH SESS. : 2023-2024). 1ST COMMITTEE—GENERAL DEBATE (Agenda item 8)
Nipomici, Galina - A/C.1/78/PV.6
UN. GENERAL ASSEMBLY (78TH SESS. : 2023-2024). 2ND COMMITTEE—GENERAL DEBATE (Agenda item 8)
Nipomici, Galina - A/C.2/78/SR.4

Republic of Moldova. President

UN. GENERAL ASSEMBLY (78TH SESS. : 2023-2024)—GENERAL DEBATE (Agenda item 8)
Sandu, Maia - A/78/PV.7
UN. GENERAL ASSEMBLY (78TH SESS. : 2023-2024)—SPECIAL STATEMENTS
Sandu, Maia - A/78/PV.7

Rescue and Relief International (Organization)

WESTERN SAHARA QUESTION (Agenda item 58)
DiCianni, Amanda - A/C.4/78/SR.4

Rete Saharawi (Organization)

WESTERN SAHARA QUESTION (Agenda item 58)
Mezzetti, Andrea - A/C.4/78/SR.5

Review Conference of the State Parties to the Convention on the Prohibition of the Development, Production and Stockpiling of Bacteriological (Biological) and Toxin Weapons and on Their Destruction. President

BIOLOGICAL WEAPONS—TREATIES (Agenda item 106)
Bencini, Leonardo (Italy) - A/C.1/78/PV.14

RMOL Network (Organization)

WESTERN SAHARA QUESTION (Agenda item 58)
Santosa, Teguh - A/C.4/78/SR.4

Roberto Gym (Organization)

FRENCH POLYNESIA QUESTION (Agenda item 58)
Cowan, Mike - A/C.4/78/SR.3

Romania

AFRICA—DEVELOPMENT (Agenda item 65b)
Horosanu, Gabriela-Cornelia - A/78/PV.18
AFRICA—SUSTAINABLE DEVELOPMENT—PARTNERSHIP (Agenda item 65a)
Horosanu, Gabriela-Cornelia - A/78/PV.18
ARMS TRANSFERS—TREATIES (Agenda item 99x)
Mocanu, Andreea - A/C.1/78/PV.19
CRIMES AGAINST HUMANITY (Agenda item 80)
Lungu, Alis - A/C.6/78/SR.11; A/C.6/78/SR.38; A/C.6/78/SR.42; A/C.6/78/SR.43; A/C.6/78/SR.44; A/C.6/78/SR.45; A/C.6/78/SR.47
Mocanu, Andreea - A/C.6/78/SR.40
FREEDOM OF EXPRESSION (Agenda item 71b)
Drăghia, Alexandru - A/C.3/78/SR.19
HUMAN RIGHTS (Agenda item 71)
Feruță, Cornel - A/C.3/78/SR.16
HUMAN RIGHTS—INTERNATIONAL INSTRUMENTS (Agenda item 71a)
Mihail, Ioana-Cristina - A/C.3/78/SR.25
HUMAN RIGHTS—TERRITORIES OCCUPIED BY ISRAEL (Agenda item 71c)
Mocanu, Andreea - A/C.3/78/SR.35
HUMAN RIGHTS—UKRAINE (Agenda item 71c)
Mihail, Ioana-Cristina - A/C.3/78/SR.25; A/C.3/78/SR.37
HUMAN RIGHTS ADVANCEMENT (Agenda item 71b)
Mihail, Ioana-Cristina - A/C.3/78/SR.18
INFORMATION (Agenda item 53)
Mocanu, Andreea - A/C.4/78/SR.12; A/C.4/78/SR.13

Romania (continued)

INTERNATIONAL CRIMINAL COURT—REPORTS (Agenda item 74)
Feruță, Cornel - A/78/PV.21
Orosan, Alina - A/78/PV.21
PEACEKEEPING OPERATIONS (Agenda item 51)
Mocanu, Andreea - A/C.4/78/SR.19
RACIAL DISCRIMINATION—ELIMINATION (Agenda item 69a)
Mihail, Ioana-Cristina - A/C.3/78/SR.41
RACIAL DISCRIMINATION—PROGRAMMES OF ACTION (Agenda item 69b)
Mihail, Ioana-Cristina - A/C.3/78/SR.41
RIGHT TO EDUCATION (Agenda item 71b)
Mihail, Ioana-Cristina - A/C.3/78/SR.27
RIGHT TO FOOD (Agenda item 71b)
Mihail, Ioana-Cristina - A/C.3/78/SR.30
RIGHTS OF THE CHILD (Agenda item 67)
Feruță, Cornel - A/C.3/78/SR.13
Mihail, Ioana-Cristina - A/C.3/78/SR.11
RULE OF LAW (Agenda item 83)
Feruță, Cornel - A/C.6/78/SR.18
RURAL WOMEN (Agenda item 25a)
Mihail, Ioana-Cristina - A/C.3/78/SR.7
SOCIAL DEVELOPMENT (Agenda item 24)
Lazaruc, Ana Maria - A/C.3/78/SR.3
TRAFFICKING IN PERSONS (Agenda item 71b)
Mihail, Ioana-Cristina - A/C.3/78/SR.23
UKRAINE—POLITICAL CONDITIONS (Agenda item 62)
Hristea, Traian - A/78/PV.56
UN. GENERAL ASSEMBLY (78TH SESS. : 2023-2024)—AGENDA (Agenda item 7)
Mocanu, Andreea - A/BUR/78/SR.2
UN. GENERAL ASSEMBLY (78TH SESS. : 2023-2024). 1ST COMMITTEE—GENERAL DEBATE (Agenda item 8)
Feruță, Cornel - A/C.1/78/PV.5
UN. GENERAL ASSEMBLY (78TH SESS. : 2023-2024). 2ND COMMITTEE—GENERAL DEBATE (Agenda item 8)
Feruță, Cornel - A/C.2/78/SR.3
UN. INTERNATIONAL COURT OF JUSTICE—REPORTS (Agenda item 73)
Orosan, Alina - A/78/PV.20
UN. INTERNATIONAL LAW COMMISSION—REPORTS (Agenda item 79)
Orosan, Alina - A/C.6/78/SR.25; A/C.6/78/SR.29; A/C.6/78/SR.31
UN. SECURITY COUNCIL—REPORTS (Agenda item 26)
Horosanu, Gabriela-Cornelia - A/78/PV.94
UN HIGH COMMISSIONER FOR REFUGEES—REPORTS (Agenda item 60)
Feruță, Cornel - A/C.3/78/SR.44
Mihail, Ioana-Cristina - A/C.3/78/SR.45
VETO (Agenda item 63)
Feruță, Cornel - A/78/PV.3; A/78/PV.67; A/78/PV.69; A/78/PV.70; A/78/PV.79
WOMEN'S ADVANCEMENT (Agenda item 25a)
Feruță, Cornel - A/C.3/78/SR.9
WOMEN'S ADVANCEMENT—CONFERENCES (Agenda item 25b)
Feruță, Cornel - A/C.3/78/SR.9
YOUTH (Agenda item 24b)
Drăghia, Alexandru - A/C.3/78/SR.3

Romania. President

UN. GENERAL ASSEMBLY (78TH SESS. : 2023-2024)—GENERAL DEBATE (Agenda item 8)
Iohannis, Klaus Werner - A/78/PV.6
UN. GENERAL ASSEMBLY (78TH SESS. : 2023-2024)—SPECIAL STATEMENTS
Iohannis, Klaus Werner - A/78/PV.6

Russian Federation

AFRICA—DEVELOPMENT (Agenda item 65b)
Chumakov, Dmitry S. - A/78/PV.57
Meschchanov, Boris A. - A/78/PV.18
AFRICA—SUSTAINABLE DEVELOPMENT—PARTNERSHIP (Agenda item 65a)
Chumakov, Dmitry S. - A/78/PV.57
Meschchanov, Boris A. - A/78/PV.18
AGEING PERSONS (Agenda item 24b)
Kashaev, Roman G. - A/C.3/78/SR.2; A/C.3/78/SR.49
Kuzmenkov, Stepan Y. - A/C.3/78/SR.1
ARMED CONFLICTS PREVENTION (Agenda item 31a)
Skachkov, Evgeny A. - A/78/PV.73
ARMS RACE—OUTER SPACE (Agenda item 97a)
Vorontsov, Konstantin - A/C.1/78/PV.16
ARMS TRANSFERS—TREATIES (Agenda item 99x)
Belousov, Andrey I. - A/C.1/78/PV.19
BIOLOGICAL WEAPONS—TREATIES (Agenda item 106)
Vorontsov, Konstantin - A/C.1/78/PV.14; A/C.1/78/PV.15; A/C.1/78/PV.16
CENTRAL ASIA—ZONES OF PEACE (Agenda item 64)
Bulgaru, Dmitrii I. - A/78/PV.85
CHEMICAL WEAPONS—TREATIES (Agenda item 99l)
Belousov, Andrey I. - A/C.1/78/PV.26
Vorontsov, Konstantin - A/C.1/78/PV.14; A/C.1/78/PV.15
CLIMATE (Agenda item 18d)
Meschchanov, Boris A. - A/C.2/78/SR.25
Uskov, Vladimir - A/C.2/78/SR.15
CLIMATE CHANGE (Agenda item 71b)
Kuzmenkov, Stepan Y. - A/C.3/78/SR.29
CLUSTER MUNITIONS (Agenda item 99dd)
Belousov, Andrey I. - A/C.1/78/PV.28

Russian Federation (continued)

CONFERENCE AND MEETING SERVICES (Agenda item 137)
Devyatkin, Daniil A. - A/C.5/78/SR.7
CONVENTIONAL WEAPONS—TREATIES (Agenda item 103)
Belousov, Andrey I. - A/C.1/78/PV.19
CRIME PREVENTION (Agenda item 107)
Bulgaru, Dmitrii I. - A/C.3/78/SR.6; A/C.3/78/SR.56
Devyatkin, Daniil A. - A/78/PV.50(Resumption1)
Kashaev, Roman G. - A/C.3/78/SR.51
Kuzmenkov, Stepan Y. - A/78/PV.50
Leonidchenko, Sergey A. - A/C.3/78/SR.5
CRIMES AGAINST HUMANITY (Agenda item 80)
Skachkov, Evgeny A. - A/C.6/78/SR.11; A/C.6/78/SR.39; A/C.6/78/SR.41; A/C.6/78/SR.42; A/C.6/78/SR.43; A/C.6/78/SR.44; A/C.6/78/SR.45; A/C.6/78/SR.47
CUBA—UNITED STATES (Agenda item 38)
Nebenzia, Vasilii - A/78/PV.24
CYBERCRIME (Agenda item 108)
Leonidchenko, Sergey A. - A/C.3/78/SR.5
DECOLONIZATION (Agenda item 58)
Ilichev, Petr - A/C.4/78/SR.2
DEMOCRACY (Agenda item 71b)
Kuzmenkov, Stepan Y. - A/C.3/78/SR.28
DEVELOPMENT COOPERATION—MIDDLE-INCOME COUNTRIES (Agenda item 19c)
Aristov, Dmitry S. - A/C.2/78/SR.10
DEVELOPMENT FINANCE (Agenda item 16b)
Kardash, Viktoriia E. - A/C.2/78/SR.9
DEVELOPMENT FINANCE—CONFERENCES (Agenda item 17)
Fondukov, Pavel A. - A/78/PV.90
DIAMONDS—FUELLING CONFLICT (Agenda item 30)
Repkin, Alexander V. - A/78/PV.65
DISARMAMENT—GENERAL AND COMPLETE (Agenda item 99)
Belousov, Andrey I. - A/C.1/78/PV.19; A/C.1/78/PV.23; A/C.1/78/PV.24; A/C.1/78/PV.28; A/C.1/78/PV.30
Glukhov, Dmitry - A/78/PV.106
DISARMAMENT AGREEMENTS—OUTER SPACE (Agenda item 97c)
Belousov, Andrey I. - A/C.1/78/PV.27
Vorontsov, Konstantin - A/C.1/78/PV.16; A/C.1/78/PV.17
DISASTER VICTIMS (Agenda item 86)
Antonova, Anna V. - A/C.6/78/SR.6
DISPLACED PERSONS (Agenda item 71b)
Kashaev, Roman G. - A/C.3/78/SR.49
Kuzmenkov, Stepan Y. - A/C.3/78/SR.32
ECONOMIC COOPERATION AMONG DEVELOPING COUNTRIES (Agenda item 22b)
Meschchanov, Boris A. - A/C.2/78/SR.18
ECONOMIC SANCTIONS—INTERNATIONAL RELATIONS (Agenda item 28)
Nebenzia, Vasilii - A/78/PV.89

Russian Federation (continued)

ELECTION VERIFICATION—UN (Agenda item 71b)
Kashaev, Roman G. - A/C.3/78/SR.50
EMERGENCY ASSISTANCE (Agenda item 72a)
Chumakov, Dmitry S. - A/78/PV.46; A/78/PV.47
ENVIRONMENT (Agenda item 71b)
Kuzmenkov, Stepan Y. - A/C.3/78/SR.29
EXTERNAL DEBT—HUMAN RIGHTS (Agenda item 71b)
Kuzmenkov, Stepan Y. - A/C.3/78/SR.32
FALKLAND ISLANDS (MALVINAS) QUESTION (Agenda item 42)
Ilichev, Petr - A/C.4/78/SR.2
FAMILY (Agenda item 24b)
Kashaev, Roman G. - A/C.3/78/SR.2
FOOD SECURITY (Agenda item 23a)
Aristov, Dmitry S. - A/C.2/78/SR.17
Meschchanov, Boris A. - A/C.2/78/SR.25
FREEDOM OF EXPRESSION (Agenda item 71b)
Kuzmenkov, Stepan Y. - A/C.3/78/SR.19
HEALTH (Agenda item 125)
Bulgaru, Dmitrii I. - A/78/PV.48
Chumakov, Dmitry S. - A/78/PV.16; A/78/PV.64; A/78/PV.77
Kardash, Viktoriia E. - A/78/PV.102
Meschchanov, Boris A. - A/78/PV.41
Zabolotskaya, Maria V. - A/78/PV.48
HIV/AIDS—DECLARATIONS (Agenda item 10)
Aristov, Dmitry S. - A/78/PV.91
HUMAN RIGHTS (Agenda item 71)
Viktorov, Evgeny - A/C.3/78/SR.16
HUMAN RIGHTS—AFGHANISTAN (Agenda item 71c)
Kuzmenkov, Stepan Y. - A/C.3/78/SR.34
HUMAN RIGHTS—BURUNDI (Agenda item 71c)
Kondratev, Sergei V. - A/C.3/78/SR.36
HUMAN RIGHTS—CENTRAL AFRICAN REPUBLIC (Agenda item 71c)
Kuzmenkov, Stepan Y. - A/C.3/78/SR.33
HUMAN RIGHTS—DEMOCRATIC PEOPLE'S REPUBLIC OF KOREA (Agenda item 71c)
Kuzmenkov, Stepan Y. - A/C.3/78/SR.33; A/C.3/78/SR.53
Zabolotskaya, Maria V. - A/78/PV.50
HUMAN RIGHTS—ERITREA (Agenda item 71c)
Kondratev, Sergei V. - A/C.3/78/SR.36
HUMAN RIGHTS—ETHIOPIA (Agenda item 71c)
Kondratev, Sergei V. - A/C.3/78/SR.36
HUMAN RIGHTS—INTERNATIONAL INSTRUMENTS (Agenda item 71a)
Kuzmenkov, Stepan Y. - A/C.3/78/SR.17; A/C.3/78/SR.25

Russian Federation (continued)

HUMAN RIGHTS—IRAN (ISLAMIC REPUBLIC OF) (Agenda item 71c)
Kuzmenkov, Stepan Y. - A/C.3/78/SR.34; A/C.3/78/SR.53
Zabolotskaya, Maria V. - A/78/PV.50
HUMAN RIGHTS—MYANMAR (Agenda item 71c)
Kashaev, Roman G. - A/C.3/78/SR.33
Kuzmenkov, Stepan Y. - A/C.3/78/SR.53
Zabolotskaya, Maria V. - A/78/PV.50
HUMAN RIGHTS—REPORTS (Agenda item 71c)
Zabolotskaya, Maria V. - A/78/PV.50
HUMAN RIGHTS—SOMALIA (Agenda item 71c)
Kuzmenkov, Stepan Y. - A/C.3/78/SR.35
HUMAN RIGHTS—SYRIAN ARAB REPUBLIC (Agenda item 71c)
Kuzmenkov, Stepan Y. - A/C.3/78/SR.34; A/C.3/78/SR.54
Zabolotskaya, Maria V. - A/78/PV.50
HUMAN RIGHTS—TERRITORIES OCCUPIED BY ISRAEL (Agenda item 71c)
Kuzmenkov, Stepan Y. - A/C.3/78/SR.27; A/C.3/78/SR.35
HUMAN RIGHTS—UKRAINE (Agenda item 71c)
Zabolotskaya, Maria V. - A/78/PV.50; A/C.3/78/SR.53
IAEA—REPORTS (Agenda item 89)
Eremin, Sergey - A/78/PV.30
INDIGENOUS PEOPLES (Agenda item 68a)
Kuzmenkov, Stepan Y. - A/C.3/78/SR.15
INDIGENOUS PEOPLES—CONFERENCES (Agenda item 68b)
Kuzmenkov, Stepan Y. - A/C.3/78/SR.15
INFORMATION (Agenda item 53)
Strzhizhovskiy, Fedor K. - A/C.4/78/SR.12; A/C.4/78/SR.13; A/C.4/78/SR.14
INFORMATION—INTERNATIONAL SECURITY (Agenda item 94)
Belousov, Andrey I. - A/C.1/78/PV.21; A/C.1/78/PV.28; A/C.1/78/PV.29
INFORMATION TECHNOLOGY—DEVELOPMENT (Agenda item 15)
Aristov, Dmitry S. - A/C.2/78/SR.10
INTERNATIONAL CRIMINAL COURT—REPORTS (Agenda item 74)
Zabolotskaya, Maria V. - A/78/PV.21; A/78/PV.25
INTERNATIONAL JURISDICTION (Agenda item 84)
Proskuryakov, Alexander S. - A/C.6/78/SR.12
INTERNATIONAL LAW—TRAINING PROGRAMMES (Agenda item 78)
Skachkov, Evgeny A. - A/C.6/78/SR.21
INTERNATIONAL RESIDUAL MECHANISM FOR CRIMINAL TRIBUNALS (Agenda item 126)
Zabolotskaya, Maria V. - A/78/PV.19

Russian Federation (continued)

INTERNATIONAL TRADE (Agenda item 16a)
Chumakov, Dmitry S. - A/C.2/78/SR.24
Kardash, Viktoriia E. - A/C.2/78/SR.9
Meschchanov, Boris A. - A/C.2/78/SR.22; A/C.2/78/SR.24
JUDICIAL INDEPENDENCE (Agenda item 71b)
Kuzmenkov, Stepan Y. - A/C.3/78/SR.31
LANDLOCKED DEVELOPING COUNTRIES—CONFERENCES (Agenda item 20b)
Chumakov, Dmitry S. - A/78/PV.107
Kardash, Viktoriia E. - A/C.2/78/SR.7
LANDMINES—TREATIES (Agenda item 99m)
Belousov, Andrey I. - A/C.1/78/PV.19
LAW OF THE SEA (Agenda item 75a)
Proskuryakov, Alexander S. - A/78/PV.44
LEAST DEVELOPED COUNTRIES—CONFERENCES (Agenda item 20a)
Kardash, Viktoriia E. - A/C.2/78/SR.7
MACROECONOMIC POLICY (Agenda item 16)
Kardash, Viktoriia E. - A/C.2/78/SR.25
MARINE ECOSYSTEMS—BIOLOGICAL DIVERSITY (Agenda item 75c)
Antonova, Anna V. - A/78/PV.73; A/78/PV.103
Proskuryakov, Alexander S. - A/78/PV.44
MEDITERRANEAN REGION—REGIONAL SECURITY (Agenda item 104)
Belousov, Andrey I. - A/C.1/78/PV.29
MIGRANTS—PROTECTION (Agenda item 71b)
Kuzmenkov, Stepan Y. - A/C.3/78/SR.23
MILLENNIUM SUMMIT—CONFERENCES (Agenda item 117)
Chumakov, Dmitry S. - A/78/PV.15; A/78/PV.53; A/78/PV.107
Kardash, Viktoriia E. - A/78/PV.102
MINE CLEARANCE (Agenda item 46)
Evstigneeva, Anna M. - A/C.4/78/SR.10
MINORITIES (Agenda item 71b)
Kuzmenkov, Stepan Y. - A/C.3/78/SR.39
MULTILATERALISM—DISARMAMENT (Agenda item 99r)
Belousov, Andrey I. - A/C.1/78/PV.22
MULTILINGUALISM (Agenda item 124)
Devyatkin, Daniil A. - A/78/PV.107
NON-CITIZENS—DEPORTATION (Agenda item 81)
Antonova, Anna V. - A/C.6/78/SR.34
NUCLEAR DISARMAMENT (Agenda item 99b)
Vorontsov, Konstantin - A/C.1/78/PV.11; A/C.1/78/PV.12; A/C.1/78/PV.13
NUCLEAR DISARMAMENT—VERIFICATION (Agenda item 99ee)
Belousov, Andrey I. - A/C.1/78/PV.25
NUCLEAR NON-PROLIFERATION—INTERNATIONAL OBLIGATIONS (Agenda item 99w)
Vorontsov, Konstantin - A/C.1/78/PV.12

Russian Federation (continued)

NUCLEAR WEAPON TESTS—TREATIES (Agenda item 105)
Belousov, Andrey I. - A/C.1/78/PV.26
Vorontsov, Konstantin - A/C.1/78/PV.12
NUCLEAR WEAPONS—ELIMINATION (Agenda item 99z)
Belousov, Andrey I. - A/C.1/78/PV.25
OPERATIONAL ACTIVITIES—UN SYSTEM (Agenda item 22a)
Meschchanov, Boris A. - A/C.2/78/SR.18
ORGANIZATION FOR DEMOCRACY AND ECONOMIC DEVELOPMENT - GUAM (Agenda item 32)
Zabolotskaya, Maria V. - A/78/PV.85
OUTER SPACE—CONFIDENCE-BUILDING MEASURES (Agenda item 99v)
Belousov, Andrey I. - A/C.1/78/PV.27
Vorontsov, Konstantin - A/C.1/78/PV.16; A/C.1/78/PV.17
OUTER SPACE—PEACEFUL USES—INTERNATIONAL COOPERATION (Agenda item 48)
Belousko, Sergey - A/C.4/78/SR.15; A/C.4/78/SR.16; A/C.4/78/SR.17
OUTER SPACE—PRINCIPLES (Agenda item 97d)
Belousov, Andrey I. - A/C.1/78/PV.27
PALESTINE QUESTION (Agenda item 35)
Chumakov, Dmitry S. - A/78/PV.40
PEACE (Agenda item 14)
Nebenzia, Vasilii - A/78/PV.82
Zabolotskaya, Maria V. - A/78/PV.48; A/78/PV.62; A/78/PV.76
PEACEBUILDING (Agenda item 61)
Agaronova, Gloriya A. - A/78/PV.101
PEACEKEEPING OPERATIONS (Agenda item 51)
Evstigneeva, Anna M. - A/C.4/78/SR.20
PEACEKEEPING OPERATIONS—CRIMINAL LIABILITY (Agenda item 76)
Antonova, Anna V. - A/C.6/78/SR.8
PERSONS WITH DISABILITIES—HUMAN RIGHTS (Agenda item 71a)
Kondratev, Sergei V. - A/C.3/78/SR.38
Mazaeva, Viktoriia - A/C.3/78/SR.51
POVERTY—HUMAN RIGHTS (Agenda item 71b)
Kuzmenkov, Stepan Y. - A/C.3/78/SR.30
POVERTY—INTERNATIONAL DECADES (Agenda item 21a)
Aristov, Dmitry S. - A/C.2/78/SR.17
RACIAL DISCRIMINATION—ELIMINATION (Agenda item 69a)
Kondratev, Sergei V. - A/C.3/78/SR.41
Kuzmenkov, Stepan Y. - A/C.3/78/SR.40; A/C.3/78/SR.42
Lukiantsev, Grigory Y. - A/C.3/78/SR.47
Zabolotskaya, Maria V. - A/78/PV.50
RACIAL DISCRIMINATION—PROGRAMMES OF ACTION (Agenda item 69b)
Kondratev, Sergei V. - A/C.3/78/SR.41

Russian Federation (continued)

RACIAL DISCRIMINATION—PROGRAMMES OF ACTION (Agenda item 69b)
Kuzmenkov, Stepan Y. - A/C.3/78/SR.40; A/C.3/78/SR.42
RELIGIOUS INTOLERANCE (Agenda item 71b)
Kondratev, Sergei V. - A/C.3/78/SR.38
RESPONSIBILITY OF INTERNATIONAL ORGANIZATIONS (Agenda item 85)
Antonova, Anna V. - A/C.6/78/SR.19
RESPONSIBILITY TO PROTECT (Agenda item 129)
Leonidchenko, Sergey A. - A/78/PV.97; A/78/PV.99
RIGHT OF ASSEMBLY (Agenda item 71b)
Kuzmenkov, Stepan Y. - A/C.3/78/SR.19
RIGHT TO CULTURE (Agenda item 71b)
Kuzmenkov, Stepan Y. - A/C.3/78/SR.27
RIGHT TO DEVELOPMENT (Agenda item 71b)
Zabolotskaya, Maria V. - A/C.3/78/SR.20
RIGHT TO DRINKING WATER (Agenda item 71b)
Kuzmenkov, Stepan Y. - A/C.3/78/SR.28
RIGHT TO EDUCATION (Agenda item 71b)
Kuzmenkov, Stepan Y. - A/C.3/78/SR.27
RIGHT TO FOOD (Agenda item 71b)
Kuzmenkov, Stepan Y. - A/C.3/78/SR.30
RIGHT TO HEALTH (Agenda item 71b)
Kuzmenkov, Stepan Y. - A/C.3/78/SR.39
RIGHT TO HOUSING (Agenda item 71b)
Kuzmenkov, Stepan Y. - A/C.3/78/SR.30
RIGHT TO PRIVACY (Agenda item 71b)
Kuzmenkov, Stepan Y. - A/C.3/78/SR.21
RIGHTS OF THE CHILD (Agenda item 67)
Kashaev, Roman G. - A/C.3/78/SR.55
Kuzmenkov, Stepan Y. - A/C.3/78/SR.11; A/C.3/78/SR.12
RULE OF LAW (Agenda item 83)
Proskuryakov, Alexander S. - A/C.6/78/SR.17; A/C.6/78/SR.19
RURAL POVERTY (Agenda item 21b)
Aristov, Dmitry S. - A/C.2/78/SR.17
SANCTIONS—INTERNATIONAL RELATIONS (Agenda item 71b)
Kuzmenkov, Stepan Y. - A/C.3/78/SR.28
SCIENCE AND TECHNOLOGY—DEVELOPMENT (Agenda item 19a)
Aristov, Dmitry S. - A/C.2/78/SR.10
SELF-DETERMINATION OF PEOPLES (Agenda item 70)
Kuzmenkov, Stepan Y. - A/C.3/78/SR.40
SLAVERY (Agenda item 71a)
Kuzmenkov, Stepan Y. - A/C.3/78/SR.21
SMALL ARMS—ILLICIT TRAFFIC—ASSISTANCE (Agenda item 99n)
Belousov, Andrey I. - A/C.1/78/PV.19
SMALL ISLAND DEVELOPING STATES—PROGRAMMES OF ACTION (Agenda item 18b)
Meschchanov, Boris A. - A/78/PV.100

Russian Federation (continued)

SOCIAL CONDITIONS (Agenda item 24b)
Chumakov, Dmitry S. - A/78/PV.57
Kashaev, Roman G. - A/C.3/78/SR.2
Mazaeva, Viktoriia - A/78/PV.101
SOCIAL DEVELOPMENT (Agenda item 24)
Kashaev, Roman G. - A/C.3/78/SR.2
SOLIDARITY (Agenda item 71b)
Kuzmenkov, Stepan Y. - A/C.3/78/SR.32
SPECIAL POLITICAL MISSIONS (Agenda item 52)
Evstigneeva, Anna M. - A/C.4/78/SR.21
SPORTS—OLYMPIC GAMES (Agenda item 11)
Kondratev, Sergei V. - A/78/PV.97
Zabolotskaya, Maria V. - A/78/PV.38
STRADDLING FISH STOCKS (Agenda item 75b)
Proskuryakov, Alexander S. - A/78/PV.44
SUBSIDIARY ORGANS—APPOINTMENTS (Agenda item 115)
Chumakov, Dmitry S. - A/78/PV.60
SUMMARY EXECUTIONS (Agenda item 71b)
Kuzmenkov, Stepan Y. - A/C.3/78/SR.31
SUSTAINABLE DEVELOPMENT (Agenda item 18)
Chumakov, Dmitry S. - A/78/PV.107; A/C.2/78/SR.24
Uskov, Vladimir - A/C.2/78/SR.15
SUSTAINABLE ENERGY (Agenda item 18h)
Meschchanov, Boris A. - A/C.2/78/SR.23
Uskov, Vladimir - A/C.2/78/SR.15
TAXATION (Agenda item 16h)
Kardash, Viktoriia E. - A/C.2/78/SR.9
Meschchanov, Boris A. - A/C.2/78/SR.25
TERRITORIES OCCUPIED BY ISRAEL—HUMAN RIGHTS (Agenda item 50)
Polyanskiy, Dmitry A. - A/C.4/78/SR.25
TERRITORIES OCCUPIED BY ISRAEL—NATURAL RESOURCES (Agenda item 59)
Meschchanov, Boris A. - A/C.2/78/SR.20
TERRORISM (Agenda item 109)
Mikhaylov, Oleg O. - A/C.6/78/SR.2
TERRORISM—HUMAN RIGHTS (Agenda item 71b)
Kuzmenkov, Stepan Y. - A/C.3/78/SR.31
TORTURE AND OTHER CRUEL TREATMENT (Agenda item 71a)
Kuzmenkov, Stepan Y. - A/C.3/78/SR.18
TRAFFIC SAFETY (Agenda item 12)
Chumakov, Dmitry S. - A/78/PV.92
TRAFFICKING IN PERSONS (Agenda item 71b)
Kuzmenkov, Stepan Y. - A/C.3/78/SR.23
TRANSNATIONAL CORPORATIONS—HUMAN RIGHTS (Agenda item 71b)
Kuzmenkov, Stepan Y. - A/C.3/78/SR.21
UKRAINE—POLITICAL CONDITIONS (Agenda item 62)
Nebenzia, Vasilii - A/78/PV.56
Polyanskiy, Dmitry A. - A/78/PV.99

Russian Federation (continued)

UN—ADMINISTRATION (Agenda item 132)
Chumakov, Dmitry S. - A/C.5/78/SR.32
Laputin, Vadim - A/C.5/78/SR.2
UN—BUDGET (2023) (Agenda item 133)
Chumakov, Dmitry S. - A/C.5/78/SR.26/PartII
UN—BUDGET (2024) (Agenda item 134)
Chumakov, Dmitry S. - A/C.5/78/SR.5; A/C.5/78/SR.26/PartII; A/C.5/78/SR.34
Devyatkin, Daniil A. - A/78/PV.50(Resumption1); A/C.5/78/SR.9
Laputin, Vadim - A/78/PV.73; A/C.5/78/SR.23; A/C.5/78/SR.28
UN—BUDGET CONTRIBUTIONS (Agenda item 138)
Alyakin, Dmitry S. - A/78/PV.16; A/C.5/78/SR.2
Laputin, Vadim - A/C.5/78/SR.1
UN—FINANCIAL SITUATION (Agenda item 136)
Lysikov, Andrei - A/C.5/78/SR.38
UN—HUMAN RESOURCES MANAGEMENT (Agenda item 139)
Chumakov, Dmitry S. - A/C.5/78/SR.34
Laputin, Vadim - A/C.5/78/SR.27
UN—PROGRAMME PLANNING (Agenda item 135)
Chumakov, Dmitry S. - A/C.5/78/SR.5; A/C.5/78/SR.24
Devyatkin, Daniil A. - A/78/PV.50(Resumption1)
Vorontsov, Konstantin - A/C.1/78/PV.10
UN. COMMITTEE ON RELATIONS WITH THE HOST COUNTRY—REPORTS (Agenda item 161)
Proskuryakov, Alexander S. - A/C.6/78/SR.35
UN. CONFERENCE ON DISARMAMENT—REPORTS (Agenda item 101a)
Belousov, Andrey I. - A/C.1/78/PV.23; A/C.1/78/PV.24; A/C.1/78/PV.29
UN. ECONOMIC AND SOCIAL COUNCIL—REPORTS (Agenda item 9)
Chumakov, Dmitry S. - A/78/PV.33
UN. ETHICS OFFICE—REPORTS (Agenda item 140)
Fonina, Svetlana F. - A/C.5/78/SR.2
UN. GENERAL ASSEMBLY—WORK PROGRAMME (Agenda item 120)
Antonova, Anna V. - A/C.6/78/SR.36
Gilmutdinova, Dina Anisovna - A/78/PV.33
Vorontsov, Konstantin - A/C.1/78/PV.10
UN. GENERAL ASSEMBLY (78TH SESS. : 2023-2024)—AGENDA (Agenda item 7)
Leonidchenko, Sergey A. - A/BUR/78/SR.2
Zabolotskaya, Maria V. - A/78/PV.2; A/BUR/78/SR.1
UN. GENERAL ASSEMBLY (78TH SESS. : 2023-2024)—GENERAL DEBATE (Agenda item 8)
Lavrov, Sergei Viktorovich - A/78/PV.12
UN. GENERAL ASSEMBLY (78TH SESS. : 2023-2024)—OFFICERS (Agenda item 5)
Chumakov, Dmitry S. - A/C.5/78/SR.1
Shulgin, Egor S. - A/C.4/78/SR.28

Russian Federation (continued)

UN. GENERAL ASSEMBLY (78TH SESS. : 2023-2024). 1ST COMMITTEE—GENERAL DEBATE (Agenda item 8)
Vorontsov, Konstantin - A/C.1/78/PV.2; A/C.1/78/PV.3; A/C.1/78/PV.4; A/C.1/78/PV.5; A/C.1/78/PV.6; A/C.1/78/PV.7; A/C.1/78/PV.8
UN. GENERAL ASSEMBLY (78TH SESS. : 2023-2024). 1ST COMMITTEE—WORK ORGANIZATION (Agenda item 7)
Belousov, Andrey I. - A/C.1/78/PV.27; A/C.1/78/PV.28; A/C.1/78/PV.30
Glukhov, Dmitry - A/C.1/78/PV.1
UN. GENERAL ASSEMBLY (78TH SESS. : 2023-2024). 2ND COMMITTEE—GENERAL DEBATE (Agenda item 8)
Chumakov, Dmitry S. - A/C.2/78/SR.5
Meschchanov, Boris A. - A/C.2/78/SR.2
UN. GENERAL ASSEMBLY (78TH SESS. : 2023-2024). 5TH COMMITTEE—WORK ORGANIZATION (Agenda item 7)
Laputin, Vadim - A/C.5/78/SR.27; A/C.5/78/SR.35
UN. HUMAN RIGHTS COMMITTEE—REPORTS (Agenda item 71a)
Kuzmenkov, Stepan Y. - A/C.3/78/SR.17
UN. HUMAN RIGHTS COUNCIL—REPORTS (Agenda item 66)
Kondratev, Sergei V. - A/C.3/78/SR.46
UN. INTERNATIONAL COURT OF JUSTICE—REPORTS (Agenda item 73)
Zabolotskaya, Maria V. - A/78/PV.28
UN. INTERNATIONAL LAW COMMISSION—REPORTS (Agenda item 79)
Melikbekyan, Elena A. - A/C.6/78/SR.30
Musikhin, Maxim V. - A/C.6/78/SR.26
Skachkov, Evgeny A. - A/C.6/78/SR.32
UN. OFFICE OF INTERNAL OVERSIGHT SERVICES—REPORTS (Agenda item 143)
Laputin, Vadim - A/C.5/78/SR.2
UN. PEACEBUILDING COMMISSION—REPORTS (Agenda item 27)
Agaronova, Gloriya A. - A/78/PV.101
UN. PEACEBUILDING FUND—REPORTS (Agenda item 111)
Agaronova, Gloriya A. - A/78/PV.101
UN. SECURITY COUNCIL—MEMBERSHIP (Agenda item 121)
Polyanskiy, Dmitry A. - A/78/PV.36; A/78/PV.104
UN CHARTER—REPORTS (Agenda item 82)
Skachkov, Evgeny A. - A/C.6/78/SR.22
UN COMMISSION ON INTERNATIONAL TRADE LAW—REPORTS (Agenda item 77)
Skachkov, Evgeny A. - A/C.6/78/SR.14
UN CONFERENCES (Agenda item 13)
Chumakov, Dmitry S. - A/78/PV.15; A/78/PV.33; A/78/PV.53; A/78/PV.107
Kardash, Viktoriia E. - A/78/PV.102
UN HIGH COMMISSIONER FOR REFUGEES—REPORTS (Agenda item 60)
Kashaev, Roman G. - A/C.3/78/SR.48
Surkov, Vladimir - A/C.3/78/SR.44

Russian Federation (continued)

UN RESOLUTIONS—IMPLEMENTATION (Agenda item 119)
Gilmutdinova, Dina Anisovna - A/78/PV.33
Mazaeva, Viktoriia - A/78/PV.103
UN SYSTEM—STRENGTHENING (Agenda item 122)
Chumakov, Dmitry S. - A/78/PV.98
Meschchanov, Boris A. - A/78/PV.99
UN YOUTH OFFICE—REPORTS (Agenda item 130)
Mazaeva, Viktoriia - A/78/PV.102
UNRWA—ACTIVITIES (Agenda item 49)
Chumakov, Dmitry S. - A/C.4/78/SR.23
VETO (Agenda item 63)
Evstigneeva, Anna M. - A/78/PV.51
Nebenzia, Vasilii - A/78/PV.3; A/78/PV.68; A/78/PV.75; A/78/PV.78
Polyanskiy, Dmitry A. - A/78/PV.61; A/78/PV.66; A/78/PV.70
WEAPONS—OUTER SPACE (Agenda item 97b)
Belousov, Andrey I. - A/C.1/78/PV.27
Vorontsov, Konstantin - A/C.1/78/PV.16; A/C.1/78/PV.17
WEAPONS OF MASS DESTRUCTION—TERRORISM (Agenda item 99s)
Vorontsov, Konstantin - A/C.1/78/PV.15
WOMEN'S ADVANCEMENT (Agenda item 25a)
Kuzmenkov, Stepan Y. - A/C.3/78/SR.7; A/C.3/78/SR.8
WOMEN'S ADVANCEMENT—CONFERENCES (Agenda item 25b)
Kuzmenkov, Stepan Y. - A/C.3/78/SR.7; A/C.3/78/SR.8
Vorobiev, Dmitry V. - A/C.3/78/SR.51
YOUTH (Agenda item 24b)
Kashaev, Roman G. - A/C.3/78/SR.2
Mazaeva, Viktoriia - A/C.3/78/SR.55

Rwanda

CRIMES AGAINST HUMANITY (Agenda item 80)
Shehata, Kyrollos - A/C.6/78/SR.39
HUMAN RIGHTS (Agenda item 71)
Umulisa, Flavia - A/C.3/78/SR.16
HUMAN RIGHTS—REPORTS (Agenda item 71c)
Vmulisa, Flavia - A/C.3/78/SR.24
HUMAN RIGHTS INSTITUTIONS—CENTRAL AFRICA (Agenda item 71b)
Umulisa, Flavia - A/C.3/78/SR.56
INTERNATIONAL RESIDUAL MECHANISM FOR CRIMINAL TRIBUNALS (Agenda item 126)
Kayinamura, Robert - A/78/PV.19
INTERNATIONAL RESIDUAL MECHANISM FOR CRIMINAL TRIBUNALS—FINANCING (Agenda item 145)
Uzabumwana Tona, Yannick - A/C.5/78/SR.20

Rwanda (continued)

PEACE (Agenda item 14)
Rwamucyo, Ernest - A/78/PV.82
PEACEKEEPING OPERATIONS (Agenda item 51)
Mutabazi, Deo - A/C.4/78/SR.20
RESPONSIBILITY TO PROTECT (Agenda item 129)
Sesonga, Fred - A/78/PV.99
RIGHTS OF THE CHILD (Agenda item 67)
Vmulisa, Flavia - A/C.3/78/SR.11
SOCIAL CONDITIONS (Agenda item 24b)
Umulisa, Flavia - A/C.3/78/SR.2
WOMEN'S ADVANCEMENT (Agenda item 25a)
Umulisa, Flavia - A/C.3/78/SR.8
WOMEN'S ADVANCEMENT—CONFERENCES (Agenda item 25b)
Umulisa, Flavia - A/C.3/78/SR.8
YOUTH (Agenda item 24b)
Umulisa, Flavia - A/C.3/78/SR.2

Rwanda. President

UN. GENERAL ASSEMBLY (78TH SESS. : 2023-2024)—GENERAL DEBATE (Agenda item 8)
Kagame, Paul - A/78/PV.6
UN. GENERAL ASSEMBLY (78TH SESS. : 2023-2024)—SPECIAL STATEMENTS
Kagame, Paul - A/78/PV.6

Safety and Security Instructional Services

WESTERN SAHARA QUESTION (Agenda item 58)
Mason, Michelle - A/C.4/78/SR.4

Sahrawi Association in the USA

WESTERN SAHARA QUESTION (Agenda item 58)
Sid Ahmed, Mula Ihfid - A/C.4/78/SR.5

Saint Kitts and Nevis. Prime Minister

UN. GENERAL ASSEMBLY (78TH SESS. : 2023-2024)—GENERAL DEBATE (Agenda item 8)
Drew, Terrance Micheal - A/78/PV.12
UN. GENERAL ASSEMBLY (78TH SESS. : 2023-2024)—SPECIAL STATEMENTS
Drew, Terrance Micheal - A/78/PV.12

Saint Lucia

BRITISH VIRGIN ISLANDS QUESTION (Agenda item 58)
Henry, Carlton Ronnie - A/C.4/78/SR.7
CUBA—UNITED STATES (Agenda item 38)
Rambally, Menissa - A/78/PV.24
DECOLONIZATION (Agenda item 58)
Henry, Carlton Ronnie - A/C.4/78/SR.7

Saint Lucia (continued)

FALKLAND ISLANDS (MALVINAS) QUESTION (Agenda item 42)
Henry, Carlton Ronnie - A/C.4/78/SR.7
WESTERN SAHARA QUESTION (Agenda item 58)
Henry, Carlton Ronnie - A/C.4/78/SR.7

Saint Lucia. Prime Minister

UN. GENERAL ASSEMBLY (78TH SESS. : 2023-2024)—GENERAL DEBATE (Agenda item 8)
Pierre, Philip Joseph - A/78/PV.10
UN. GENERAL ASSEMBLY (78TH SESS. : 2023-2024)—SPECIAL STATEMENTS
Pierre, Philip Joseph - A/78/PV.10

Saint Vincent and the Grenadines

CUBA—UNITED STATES (Agenda item 38)
King, Inga Rhonda - A/78/PV.24
DECOLONIZATION (Agenda item 58)
Andrews, Lasana - A/C.4/78/SR.8
ECONOMIC SANCTIONS—INTERNATIONAL RELATIONS (Agenda item 28)
King, Inga Rhonda - A/78/PV.90
FALKLAND ISLANDS (MALVINAS) QUESTION (Agenda item 42)
Andrews, Lasana - A/C.4/78/SR.8
PEACE (Agenda item 14)
Andrews, Lasana - A/78/PV.82
WESTERN SAHARA QUESTION (Agenda item 58)
Andrews, Lasana - A/C.4/78/SR.8

Saint Vincent and the Grenadines. Prime Minister

UN. GENERAL ASSEMBLY (78TH SESS. : 2023-2024)—GENERAL DEBATE (Agenda item 8)
Gonsalves, Ralph E. - A/78/PV.12
UN. GENERAL ASSEMBLY (78TH SESS. : 2023-2024)—SPECIAL STATEMENTS
Gonsalves, Ralph E. - A/78/PV.12

Samoa. Prime Minister

UN. GENERAL ASSEMBLY (78TH SESS. : 2023-2024)—GENERAL DEBATE (Agenda item 8)
Mataafa, Fiame Naomi - A/78/PV.12
UN. GENERAL ASSEMBLY (78TH SESS. : 2023-2024)—SPECIAL STATEMENTS
Mataafa, Fiame Naomi - A/78/PV.12

San Marino

RIGHTS OF THE CHILD (Agenda item 67)
Arona, Sofia - A/C.3/78/SR.14

San Marino (continued)

UN. GENERAL ASSEMBLY (78TH SESS. : 2023-2024)—GENERAL DEBATE (Agenda item 8)
Beleffi, Damiano - A/78/PV.14
UN. GENERAL ASSEMBLY (78TH SESS. : 2023-2024). 1ST COMMITTEE—GENERAL DEBATE (Agenda item 8)
Bartolini, Natasia - A/C.1/78/PV.6
UN. GENERAL ASSEMBLY (78TH SESS. : 2023-2024). 2ND COMMITTEE—GENERAL DEBATE (Agenda item 8)
Beleffi, Damiano - A/C.2/78/SR.4
UN. SECURITY COUNCIL—MEMBERSHIP (Agenda item 121)
Beleffi, Damiano - A/78/PV.35
VETO (Agenda item 63)
Beleffi, Damiano - A/78/PV.61; A/78/PV.75

Sao Tome and Principe. Prime Minister

UN. GENERAL ASSEMBLY (78TH SESS. : 2023-2024)—GENERAL DEBATE (Agenda item 8)
Trovoada, Patrice Emery - A/78/PV.7
UN. GENERAL ASSEMBLY (78TH SESS. : 2023-2024)—SPECIAL STATEMENTS
Trovoada, Patrice Emery - A/78/PV.7

Saudi Arabia

ARMS RACE—OUTER SPACE (Agenda item 97a)
Moharram, Wajdi Hassan M. - A/C.1/78/PV.16
CENTRAL ASIA—ZONES OF PEACE (Agenda item 64)
Alomair, Reem Fahad O. - A/78/PV.85
CONVENTIONAL WEAPONS (Agenda item 99u)
Bin Shafi, Mohammed - A/C.1/78/PV.19
Moharram, Wajdi Hassan M. - A/C.1/78/PV.28
CRIMES AGAINST HUMANITY (Agenda item 80)
Alabdali, Ali - A/C.6/78/SR.42
Alamri, Hassan Mohammed A. - A/C.6/78/SR.11
Yankssar, Ahlam - A/C.6/78/SR.38
CYBERCRIME (Agenda item 108)
Shaker, Mohammed Amin - A/C.3/78/SR.5
DECOLONIZATION (Agenda item 58)
Alamri, Hassan Mohammed A. - A/C.4/78/SR.7
DEVELOPMENT COOPERATION—MIDDLE-INCOME COUNTRIES (Agenda item 19c)
Shaker, Mohammed Amin - A/C.2/78/SR.10
DISARMAMENT—GENERAL AND COMPLETE (Agenda item 99)
Moharram, Wajdi Hassan M. - A/C.1/78/PV.21; A/C.1/78/PV.23; A/C.1/78/PV.30
DISASTER VICTIMS (Agenda item 86)
Yankssar, Ahlam - A/C.6/78/SR.6
EMERGENCY ASSISTANCE (Agenda item 72a)
Alwasil, Abdulaziz M.O. - A/78/PV.46

Saudi Arabia (continued)

FINANCIAL FLOWS (Agenda item 16f)
Alomair, Reem Fahad O. - A/C.2/78/SR.9
FOOD SECURITY (Agenda item 23a)
Bakhsh, Khalid - A/C.2/78/SR.17
HEALTH (Agenda item 125)
Alwasil, Abdulaziz M.O. - A/78/PV.97
Mousa, Sulafa - A/78/PV.41
HUMAN RIGHTS (Agenda item 71)
Mousa, Sulafa - A/C.3/78/SR.16
HUMAN RIGHTS—INTERNATIONAL INSTRUMENTS (Agenda item 71a)
Alwasil, Abdulaziz M.O. - A/C.3/78/SR.26
HUMAN RIGHTS—MYANMAR (Agenda item 71c)
Mousa, Sulafa - A/C.3/78/SR.33
HUMAN RIGHTS—REPORTS (Agenda item 71c)
Alwasil, Abdulaziz M.O. - A/C.3/78/SR.26
HUMAN RIGHTS—TERRITORIES OCCUPIED BY ISRAEL (Agenda item 71c)
Mousa, Sulafa - A/C.3/78/SR.35
HUMAN RIGHTS ADVANCEMENT (Agenda item 71b)
Bin Jadid, Faisal Fahad M. - A/C.3/78/SR.18
INFORMATION (Agenda item 53)
Alaklabi, Faisal Saeed M. - A/C.4/78/SR.13
INFORMATION TECHNOLOGY—DEVELOPMENT (Agenda item 15)
Shaker, Mohammed Amin - A/C.2/78/SR.10
INTERNATIONAL JURISDICTION (Agenda item 84)
Alwasil, Abdulaziz M.O. - A/C.6/78/SR.13
INTERNATIONAL TRADE (Agenda item 16a)
Alomair, Reem Fahad O. - A/C.2/78/SR.9
MACROECONOMIC POLICY (Agenda item 16)
Alomair, Reem Fahad O. - A/C.2/78/SR.9
MINE CLEARANCE (Agenda item 46)
Abaalala, Majed - A/C.4/78/SR.10
MULTILATERALISM—DISARMAMENT (Agenda item 99r)
Moharram, Wajdi Hassan M. - A/C.1/78/PV.21
NUCLEAR DISARMAMENT (Agenda item 99b)
Alibrahim, Faisal - A/C.1/78/PV.13
OUTER SPACE—CONFIDENCE-BUILDING MEASURES (Agenda item 99v)
Moharram, Wajdi Hassan M. - A/C.1/78/PV.16
OUTER SPACE—PEACEFUL USES—INTERNATIONAL COOPERATION (Agenda item 48)
Al Kahtani, Fayee Fahad M. - A/C.4/78/SR.16
PALESTINE QUESTION (Agenda item 35)
Alwasil, Abdulaziz M.O. - A/78/PV.40
PALESTINIANS—ASSISTANCE (Agenda item 72b)
Alwasil, Abdulaziz M.O. - A/78/PV.46
PEACE (Agenda item 14)
Alwasil, Abdulaziz M.O. - A/78/PV.62; A/78/PV.77; A/78/PV.82

Saudi Arabia (continued)

PERSONS WITH DISABILITIES (Agenda item 24b)
Bin Jadid, Faisal Fahad M. - A/C.3/78/SR.2
POVERTY—INTERNATIONAL DECADES (Agenda item 21a)
Bakhsh, Khalid - A/C.2/78/SR.17
RACIAL DISCRIMINATION—ELIMINATION (Agenda item 69a)
Albadr, Saleh - A/C.3/78/SR.41
RACIAL DISCRIMINATION—PROGRAMMES OF ACTION (Agenda item 69b)
Albadr, Saleh - A/C.3/78/SR.41
RELIGIOUS INTOLERANCE (Agenda item 71b)
Bin Jadid, Faisal Fahad M. - A/C.3/78/SR.38
RIGHT TO DEVELOPMENT (Agenda item 71b)
Al Mandil, Mishal - A/C.3/78/SR.20
Alwasil, Abdulaziz M.O. - A/C.3/78/SR.26
RIGHT TO DRINKING WATER (Agenda item 71b)
Bin Jadid, Faisal Fahad M. - A/C.3/78/SR.50
RIGHTS OF THE CHILD (Agenda item 67)
Al Mandil, Mishal - A/C.3/78/SR.12
Bin Jadid, Faisal Fahad M. - A/C.3/78/SR.55
Mousa, Sulafa - A/C.3/78/SR.11
RULE OF LAW (Agenda item 83)
Almhawas, Ibtihal - A/C.6/78/SR.18
RURAL POVERTY (Agenda item 21b)
Bakhsh, Khalid - A/C.2/78/SR.17
SELF-DETERMINATION OF PEOPLES (Agenda item 70)
Albadr, Saleh - A/C.3/78/SR.41
SMALL ARMS—ILLICIT TRAFFIC (Agenda item 99p)
Bin Shafi, Mohammed - A/C.1/78/PV.19
SOCIAL DEVELOPMENT (Agenda item 24)
Bin Jadid, Faisal Fahad M. - A/C.3/78/SR.2
SUSTAINABLE DEVELOPMENT (Agenda item 18)
Al Shehri, Muhammad - A/C.2/78/SR.15
Alomair, Reem Fahad O. - A/C.2/78/SR.24
TERRITORIES OCCUPIED BY ISRAEL—HUMAN RIGHTS (Agenda item 50)
Al Kahtani, Fayee Fahad M. - A/C.4/78/SR.25
TERRITORIES OCCUPIED BY ISRAEL—NATURAL RESOURCES (Agenda item 59)
Al-Saud, Prince of Saudi Arabia - A/C.2/78/SR.19
TERRORISM (Agenda item 109)
Alodaib, Khalid Nasser A. - A/C.6/78/SR.4
TORTURE AND OTHER CRUEL TREATMENT (Agenda item 71a)
Albadr, Saleh - A/C.3/78/SR.18
UN—BUDGET (2024) (Agenda item 134)
AlRasheed, Mohammed Abdullah - A/C.5/78/SR.13
Alwasil, Abdulaziz M.O. - A/C.5/78/SR.5
UN—FINANCIAL SITUATION (Agenda item 136)
Alshaikh, Hayfaa Abdullatif A. - A/C.5/78/SR.38

Saudi Arabia (continued)

UN—PROGRAMME PLANNING (Agenda item 135)
Alwasil, Abdulaziz M.O. - A/C.5/78/SR.5
UN. GENERAL ASSEMBLY (78TH SESS. : 2023-2024)—GENERAL DEBATE (Agenda item 8)
Al-Saud, Prince of Saudi Arabia - A/78/PV.13
UN. GENERAL ASSEMBLY (78TH SESS. : 2023-2024)—SPECIAL STATEMENTS
Al-Saud, Prince of Saudi Arabia - A/78/PV.13
UN. GENERAL ASSEMBLY (78TH SESS. : 2023-2024). 1ST COMMITTEE—GENERAL DEBATE (Agenda item 8)
Moharram, Wajdi Hassan M. - A/C.1/78/PV.6
UN. GENERAL ASSEMBLY (78TH SESS. : 2023-2024). 2ND COMMITTEE—GENERAL DEBATE (Agenda item 8)
Alomair, Reem Fahad O. - A/C.2/78/SR.4
UN. HUMAN RIGHTS COUNCIL—REPORTS (Agenda item 66)
Alwasil, Abdulaziz M.O. - A/78/PV.23
Bin Jadid, Faisal Fahad M. - A/C.3/78/SR.46
UN. INTERNATIONAL LAW COMMISSION—REPORTS (Agenda item 79)
Yankssar, Ahlam - A/C.6/78/SR.37
UN. SECURITY COUNCIL—MEMBERSHIP (Agenda item 121)
Alwasil, Abdulaziz M.O. - A/78/PV.36
UN CHARTER—REPORTS (Agenda item 82)
Almuaithir, Nouf - A/C.6/78/SR.33
UN HIGH COMMISSIONER FOR REFUGEES—REPORTS (Agenda item 60)
Shaman, Ali - A/C.3/78/SR.44
UN SYSTEM—STRENGTHENING (Agenda item 122)
Alamri, Hassan Mohammed A. - A/78/PV.99
UNRWA—ACTIVITIES (Agenda item 49)
Alamri, Hassan Mohammed A. - A/C.4/78/SR.23
VETO (Agenda item 63)
Alwasil, Abdulaziz M.O. - A/78/PV.60; A/78/PV.75
WESTERN SAHARA QUESTION (Agenda item 58)
Alamri, Hassan Mohammed A. - A/C.4/78/SR.7
WOMEN'S ADVANCEMENT (Agenda item 25a)
Mousa, Sulafa - A/C.3/78/SR.8
WOMEN'S ADVANCEMENT—CONFERENCES (Agenda item 25b)
Mousa, Sulafa - A/C.3/78/SR.8
YOUTH (Agenda item 24b)
Bin Jadid, Faisal Fahad M. - A/C.3/78/SR.2
Mousa, Sulafa - A/C.3/78/SR.55

Secretariat of the Convention on Biological Diversity. Deputy Executive Secretary

BIOLOGICAL DIVERSITY—TREATIES (Agenda item 18f)
Cooper, David - A/C.2/78/SR.12

Secretariat of the Convention to Combat Desertification. Deputy Executive Secretary

DESERTIFICATION—TREATIES (Agenda item 18e)
Meza Murillo, Andrea - A/C.2/78/SR.12

Secretariat of the United Nations Framework Convention on Climate Change. Technology and Capacity-Building Programme. Director

CLIMATE (Agenda item 18d)
Violetti, Daniele - A/C.2/78/SR.12

Senegal

ARMS TRANSFERS—TREATIES (Agenda item 99x)
Diack, Papa Samba - A/C.1/78/PV.18
CONVENTIONAL WEAPONS (Agenda item 99u)
Diack, Papa Samba - A/C.1/78/PV.18
CRIMES AGAINST HUMANITY (Agenda item 80)
Ndoye, Abdou - A/C.6/78/SR.10
ELECTION VERIFICATION—UN (Agenda item 71b)
Niasse, Samba Thiam - A/C.3/78/SR.50
FOOD SECURITY (Agenda item 23a)
Dioum, Assane - A/C.2/78/SR.18
HUMAN RIGHTS ACTIVISTS (Agenda item 71b)
Niasse, Samba Thiam - A/C.3/78/SR.56
HUMAN RIGHTS ADVANCEMENT (Agenda item 71b)
Niasse, Samba Thiam - A/C.3/78/SR.52
INDIGENOUS PEOPLES (Agenda item 68a)
Ndiaye, Mamadou Mounsir - A/C.3/78/SR.48
INFORMATION (Agenda item 53)
Niane, Adja Binta - A/C.4/78/SR.12
INTERNATIONAL CRIMINAL COURT—REPORTS (Agenda item 74)
Niang, Cheikh - A/78/PV.22
INTERNATIONAL JURISDICTION (Agenda item 84)
Ndoye, Abdou - A/C.6/78/SR.12
INTERNATIONAL LAW—TRAINING PROGRAMMES (Agenda item 78)
Diome, Diamane - A/C.6/78/SR.21
NUCLEAR DISARMAMENT (Agenda item 99b)
Diack, Papa Samba - A/C.1/78/PV.12
PALESTINE QUESTION (Agenda item 35)
Gueye, Cheikh Mohamadou Bamba - A/78/PV.40
PEACEKEEPING OPERATIONS (Agenda item 51)
Ndiaye, Joseph Dominique Ngor - A/C.4/78/SR.19
PEACEKEEPING OPERATIONS—CRIMINAL LIABILITY (Agenda item 76)
Ndoye, Abdou - A/C.6/78/SR.8
PERSONS WITH DISABILITIES—HUMAN RIGHTS (Agenda item 71a)
Niasse, Samba Thiam - A/C.3/78/SR.51

Senegal (continued)

RACIAL DISCRIMINATION—ELIMINATION (Agenda item 69a)
Ndiaye, Mamadou Mounsir - A/C.3/78/SR.47
RIGHT TO DRINKING WATER (Agenda item 71b)
Niasse, Samba Thiam - A/C.3/78/SR.50
RIGHTS OF THE CHILD (Agenda item 67)
Niasse, Samba Thiam - A/C.3/78/SR.14; A/C.3/78/SR.55
RULE OF LAW (Agenda item 83)
Ndoye, Abdou - A/C.6/78/SR.18
RURAL WOMEN (Agenda item 25a)
Diouf, Aminata - A/C.3/78/SR.49
SOCIAL CONDITIONS (Agenda item 24b)
Niasse, Samba Thiam - A/C.3/78/SR.51
SPORTS—OLYMPIC GAMES (Agenda item 11)
Niasse, Samba Thiam - A/78/PV.38
SUSTAINABLE DEVELOPMENT (Agenda item 18)
Gueye, Mamadou Soule - A/C.2/78/SR.24
TERRITORIES OCCUPIED BY ISRAEL—HUMAN RIGHTS (Agenda item 50)
Niang, Cheikh - A/C.4/78/SR.24
TERRITORIES OCCUPIED BY ISRAEL—NATURAL RESOURCES (Agenda item 59)
Dioum, Assane - A/C.2/78/SR.19
TERRORISM (Agenda item 109)
Diome, Diamane - A/C.6/78/SR.1
UN. GENERAL ASSEMBLY (78TH SESS. : 2023-2024)—AGENDA (Agenda item 7)
Niang, Cheikh - A/BUR/78/SR.1
UN. GENERAL ASSEMBLY (78TH SESS. : 2023-2024). 1ST COMMITTEE—GENERAL DEBATE (Agenda item 8)
Ndiaye, Ndeye Fatou - A/C.1/78/PV.8
UN. GENERAL ASSEMBLY (78TH SESS. : 2023-2024). 2ND COMMITTEE—GENERAL DEBATE (Agenda item 8)
Ndoye, Abdou - A/C.2/78/SR.3
UN. INTERNATIONAL COURT OF JUSTICE—REPORTS (Agenda item 73)
Ndoye, Abdou - A/78/PV.27
UN. INTERNATIONAL LAW COMMISSION—REPORTS (Agenda item 79)
Gueye, Cheikh Mohamadou Bamba - A/C.6/78/SR.29
UN. SECURITY COUNCIL—MEMBERSHIP (Agenda item 121)
Diome, Diamane - A/78/PV.35
UNRWA—ACTIVITIES (Agenda item 49)
Diome, Diamane - A/C.4/78/SR.23
VETO (Agenda item 63)
Gueye, Cheikh Mohamadou Bamba - A/78/PV.79
Ndoye, Abdou - A/78/PV.61; A/78/PV.67
WESTERN SAHARA QUESTION (Agenda item 58)
Diome, Diamane - A/C.4/78/SR.7

Senegal (continued)

WOMEN MIGRANT WORKERS (Agenda item 25a)
Diouf, Aminata - A/C.3/78/SR.49
WOMEN'S ADVANCEMENT (Agenda item 25a)
Diouf, Aminata - A/C.3/78/SR.10
WOMEN'S ADVANCEMENT—CONFERENCES (Agenda item 25b)
Diouf, Aminata - A/C.3/78/SR.10
YOUTH (Agenda item 24b)
Niasse, Samba Thiam - A/C.3/78/SR.55

Senegal. President

UN. GENERAL ASSEMBLY (78TH SESS. : 2023-2024)—GENERAL DEBATE (Agenda item 8)
Sall, Macky - A/78/PV.5
UN. GENERAL ASSEMBLY (78TH SESS. : 2023-2024)—SPECIAL STATEMENTS
Sall, Macky - A/78/PV.5

Serbia

DECOLONIZATION (Agenda item 58)
Vujačić, Dušan - A/C.4/78/SR.8
FALKLAND ISLANDS (MALVINAS) QUESTION (Agenda item 42)
Vujačić, Dušan - A/C.4/78/SR.8
FOOD SECURITY (Agenda item 23a)
Mart, Saša - A/C.2/78/SR.17
HUMAN RIGHTS—INTERNATIONAL INSTRUMENTS (Agenda item 71a)
Radović, Branislav - A/C.3/78/SR.27
INTERNATIONAL RESIDUAL MECHANISM FOR CRIMINAL TRIBUNALS (Agenda item 126)
Buden, Radmila - A/78/PV.19
INVESTMENT PROMOTION (Agenda item 16g)
Mart, Saša - A/C.2/78/SR.9
MACROECONOMIC POLICY (Agenda item 16)
Mart, Saša - A/C.2/78/SR.9
MIGRANTS—PROTECTION (Agenda item 71b)
Radović, Branislav - A/C.3/78/SR.27
PEACEKEEPING OPERATIONS (Agenda item 51)
Radović, Branislav - A/C.4/78/SR.20
POVERTY—INTERNATIONAL DECADES (Agenda item 21a)
Mart, Saša - A/C.2/78/SR.17
RURAL POVERTY (Agenda item 21b)
Mart, Saša - A/C.2/78/SR.17
SCIENCE AND TECHNOLOGY—DEVELOPMENT (Agenda item 19a)
Mart, Saša - A/C.2/78/SR.11
UN. GENERAL ASSEMBLY (78TH SESS. : 2023-2024). 2ND COMMITTEE—GENERAL DEBATE (Agenda item 8)
Vujačić, Dušan - A/C.2/78/SR.5

Serbia (continued)

UN HIGH COMMISSIONER FOR REFUGEES—REPORTS (Agenda item 60)
Radović, Branislav - A/C.3/78/SR.45
YOUTH (Agenda item 24b)
Marjanović, Tamara - A/C.3/78/SR.3
Matković, Mihajlo - A/C.3/78/SR.3

Serbia. President

PEACE (Agenda item 14)
Vučić, Aleksandar - A/78/PV.82
UN. GENERAL ASSEMBLY (78TH SESS. : 2023-2024)—GENERAL DEBATE (Agenda item 8)
Vučić, Aleksandar - A/78/PV.8
UN. GENERAL ASSEMBLY (78TH SESS. : 2023-2024)—SPECIAL STATEMENTS
Vučić, Aleksandar - A/78/PV.8; A/78/PV.82

Seychelles

SMALL ISLAND DEVELOPING STATES—PROGRAMMES OF ACTION (Agenda item 18b)
Madeleine, Ian Dereck Joseph - A/78/PV.103

Seychelles. President

UN. GENERAL ASSEMBLY (78TH SESS. : 2023-2024)—GENERAL DEBATE (Agenda item 8)
Ramkalawan, Wavel - A/78/PV.6
UN. GENERAL ASSEMBLY (78TH SESS. : 2023-2024)—SPECIAL STATEMENTS
Ramkalawan, Wavel - A/78/PV.6

Sierra Leone

AFRICA—DEVELOPMENT (Agenda item 65b)
Kanu, Michael Imran - A/78/PV.18
AFRICA—SUSTAINABLE DEVELOPMENT—PARTNERSHIP (Agenda item 65a)
Kanu, Michael Imran - A/78/PV.18
CRIME PREVENTION (Agenda item 107)
Yajah, Christian Fayia - A/C.3/78/SR.6
CRIMES AGAINST HUMANITY (Agenda item 80)
Kamanda, George Shadrack - A/C.6/78/SR.44; A/C.6/78/SR.45
Kamara, Abass Salieu - A/C.6/78/SR.38; A/C.6/78/SR.41; A/C.6/78/SR.42
Kebe, Hawanatu - A/C.6/78/SR.43
Sowa, Amara Sheikh Mohammed - A/C.6/78/SR.11
CYBERCRIME (Agenda item 108)
Yajah, Christian Fayia - A/C.3/78/SR.6
DECOLONIZATION (Agenda item 58)
Alghali, Francess Piagie - A/C.4/78/SR.7
DISASTER VICTIMS (Agenda item 86)
Kebe, Hawanatu - A/C.6/78/SR.6
EXTERNAL DEBT (Agenda item 16c)
Sowa, Amara Sheikh Mohammed - A/C.2/78/SR.9
FINANCIAL FLOWS (Agenda item 16f)
Sowa, Amara Sheikh Mohammed - A/C.2/78/SR.9

Sierra Leone (continued)

FOOD SECURITY (Agenda item 23a)
George, Alan Ebun - A/C.2/78/SR.17
HUMAN RIGHTS ADVANCEMENT (Agenda item 71b)
Kanu, Michael Imran - A/C.3/78/SR.25
INFORMATION TECHNOLOGY—DEVELOPMENT (Agenda item 15)
Alghali, Francess Piagie - A/C.2/78/SR.11
INTERNATIONAL JURISDICTION (Agenda item 84)
Kanu, Michael Imran - A/C.6/78/SR.13
LANDLOCKED DEVELOPING COUNTRIES—CONFERENCES (Agenda item 20b)
Sanusi, Zainu-Deen - A/C.2/78/SR.7
LEAST DEVELOPED COUNTRIES—CONFERENCES (Agenda item 20a)
Sanusi, Zainu-Deen - A/C.2/78/SR.7
MACROECONOMIC POLICY (Agenda item 16)
Sowa, Amara Sheikh Mohammed - A/C.2/78/SR.9
PALESTINE QUESTION (Agenda item 35)
Baimarro, Karen Jean - A/78/PV.40
PEACE (Agenda item 14)
Kanu, Michael Imran - A/78/PV.82
PEACEKEEPING OPERATIONS (Agenda item 51)
Sowa, Amara Sheikh Mohammed - A/C.4/78/SR.19
PEACEKEEPING OPERATIONS—CRIMINAL LIABILITY (Agenda item 76)
Sowa, Amara Sheikh Mohammed - A/C.6/78/SR.8
POVERTY—INTERNATIONAL DECADES (Agenda item 21a)
George, Alan Ebun - A/C.2/78/SR.17
RACIAL DISCRIMINATION—ELIMINATION (Agenda item 69a)
Sowa, Amara Sheikh Mohammed - A/C.3/78/SR.42
RACIAL DISCRIMINATION—PROGRAMMES OF ACTION (Agenda item 69b)
Sowa, Amara Sheikh Mohammed - A/C.3/78/SR.42
RIGHTS OF THE CHILD (Agenda item 67)
Alghali, Francess Piagie - A/C.3/78/SR.13
RULE OF LAW (Agenda item 83)
Kebe, Hawanatu - A/C.6/78/SR.19
RURAL POVERTY (Agenda item 21b)
George, Alan Ebun - A/C.2/78/SR.17
SCIENCE AND TECHNOLOGY—DEVELOPMENT (Agenda item 19a)
Alghali, Francess Piagie - A/C.2/78/SR.11
SPECIAL POLITICAL MISSIONS (Agenda item 52)
Baimarro, Karen Jean - A/C.4/78/SR.21
SUSTAINABLE DEVELOPMENT (Agenda item 18)
Sowa, Amara Sheikh Mohammed - A/C.2/78/SR.13
TERRORISM (Agenda item 109)
Kanu, Michael Imran - A/C.6/78/SR.3
UN—BUDGET (2024) (Agenda item 134)
Yajah, Christian Fayia - A/C.5/78/SR.33

Sierra Leone (continued)

UN. GENERAL ASSEMBLY (78TH SESS. : 2023-2024). 1ST COMMITTEE—GENERAL DEBATE (Agenda item 8)
Alghali, Francess Piagie - A/C.1/78/PV.7
UN. GENERAL ASSEMBLY (78TH SESS. : 2023-2024). 2ND COMMITTEE—GENERAL DEBATE (Agenda item 8)
Kanu, Michael Imran - A/C.2/78/SR.3
UN. INTERNATIONAL LAW COMMISSION—REPORTS (Agenda item 79)
George, Alan Ebun - A/C.6/78/SR.32
Kebe, Hawanatu - A/C.6/78/SR.27
UNRWA—ACTIVITIES (Agenda item 49)
Kanu, Michael Imran - A/C.4/78/SR.23
VETO (Agenda item 63)
Baimarro, Karen Jean - A/78/PV.61
Kanu, Michael Imran - A/78/PV.3
Sowa, Amara Sheikh Mohammed - A/78/PV.52; A/78/PV.67; A/78/PV.75
WESTERN SAHARA QUESTION (Agenda item 58)
Alghali, Francess Piagie - A/C.4/78/SR.7
WOMEN'S ADVANCEMENT (Agenda item 25a)
Senesi, Roselynn Finda - A/C.3/78/SR.9
WOMEN'S ADVANCEMENT—CONFERENCES (Agenda item 25b)
Senesi, Roselynn Finda - A/C.3/78/SR.9

Sierra Leone. President

UN. GENERAL ASSEMBLY (78TH SESS. : 2023-2024)—GENERAL DEBATE (Agenda item 8)
Bio, Julius Maada - A/78/PV.7
UN. GENERAL ASSEMBLY (78TH SESS. : 2023-2024)—SPECIAL STATEMENTS
Bio, Julius Maada - A/78/PV.7

Singapore

AGEING PERSONS (Agenda item 24b)
Choong, Brandon - A/C.3/78/SR.2
CENTRAL ASIA—ZONES OF PEACE (Agenda item 64)
Rajandran, Dhivya - A/78/PV.85
CLIMATE (Agenda item 18d)
Yuan Fang, Yeo - A/C.2/78/SR.13
CLUSTER MUNITIONS (Agenda item 99dd)
Jiamin, Liu - A/C.1/78/PV.28
CONVENTIONAL WEAPONS (Agenda item 99u)
Jiamin, Liu - A/C.1/78/PV.18
CONVENTIONAL WEAPONS—TREATIES (Agenda item 103)
Jiamin, Liu - A/C.1/78/PV.18
CRIME PREVENTION (Agenda item 107)
Jesudason, Joshua E. - A/C.3/78/SR.5

Singapore (continued)
CRIMES AGAINST HUMANITY (Agenda item 80)
Khng, Nathaniel - A/C.6/78/SR.9; A/C.6/78/SR.39; A/C.6/78/SR.41; A/C.6/78/SR.42; A/C.6/78/SR.43; A/C.6/78/SR.44; A/C.6/78/SR.45; A/C.6/78/SR.47
CYBERCRIME (Agenda item 108)
Jesudason, Joshua E. - A/C.3/78/SR.5
DISARMAMENT AGREEMENTS—OUTER SPACE (Agenda item 97c)
Low, Si Tong Berenice - A/C.1/78/PV.27
DISASTER VICTIMS (Agenda item 86)
Tan, Scott - A/C.6/78/SR.6
ELECTION VERIFICATION—UN (Agenda item 71b)
Rajandran, Dhivya - A/C.3/78/SR.50
EMERGENCY ASSISTANCE (Agenda item 72a)
Chak Yong, Mok - A/78/PV.46
FAMILY (Agenda item 24b)
Choong, Brandon - A/C.3/78/SR.2
HEALTH (Agenda item 125)
Rajandran, Dhivya - A/78/PV.48
HUMAN RIGHTS—DEMOCRATIC PEOPLE'S REPUBLIC OF KOREA (Agenda item 71c)
Gafoor, Burhan - A/C.3/78/SR.53
HUMAN RIGHTS—IRAN (ISLAMIC REPUBLIC OF) (Agenda item 71c)
Rajandran, Dhivya - A/C.3/78/SR.53
HUMAN RIGHTS—MYANMAR (Agenda item 71c)
Gafoor, Burhan - A/C.3/78/SR.53
HUMAN RIGHTS—SYRIAN ARAB REPUBLIC (Agenda item 71c)
Rajandran, Dhivya - A/C.3/78/SR.54
HUMAN RIGHTS—UKRAINE (Agenda item 71c)
Rajandran, Dhivya - A/C.3/78/SR.53
HUMAN RIGHTS ADVANCEMENT (Agenda item 71b)
Gafoor, Burhan - A/C.3/78/SR.24
Rajandran, Dhivya - A/C.3/78/SR.52
IAEA—REPORTS (Agenda item 89)
Lim, Jessie - A/78/PV.29
INFORMATION TECHNOLOGY—DEVELOPMENT (Agenda item 15)
Ching, Martha - A/C.2/78/SR.10
INTERNATIONAL JURISDICTION (Agenda item 84)
Tan, Scott - A/C.6/78/SR.13
INTERNATIONAL LAW—TRAINING PROGRAMMES (Agenda item 78)
Seah, Mark - A/C.6/78/SR.21
INTERNATIONAL TRADE (Agenda item 16a)
Tan, Jason Han Wei - A/C.2/78/SR.24
LANDMINES—TREATIES (Agenda item 99m)
Jiamin, Liu - A/C.1/78/PV.18; A/C.1/78/PV.28
LAW OF THE SEA (Agenda item 75a)
Gafoor, Burhan - A/78/PV.43

Singapore (continued)
MARINE ECOSYSTEMS—BIOLOGICAL DIVERSITY (Agenda item 75c)
Gafoor, Burhan - A/78/PV.43
Seah, Mark - A/78/PV.73
NON-CITIZENS—DEPORTATION (Agenda item 81)
Tan, Scott - A/C.6/78/SR.34
NUCLEAR DISARMAMENT (Agenda item 99b)
Lim, Jessie - A/C.1/78/PV.12
NUCLEAR NON-PROLIFERATION—INTERNATIONAL OBLIGATIONS (Agenda item 99w)
Lim, Jessie - A/C.1/78/PV.12
NUCLEAR WEAPON TESTS—TREATIES (Agenda item 105)
Lim, Jessie - A/C.1/78/PV.12
NUCLEAR WEAPONS—TREATIES (Agenda item 99ff)
Liu, Lu - A/C.1/78/PV.26
OUTER SPACE—PEACEFUL USES—INTERNATIONAL COOPERATION (Agenda item 48)
Lim, Luo You Clarice - A/C.4/78/SR.16
OUTER SPACE—PRINCIPLES (Agenda item 97d)
Low, Si Tong Berenice - A/C.1/78/PV.27
PALESTINIANS—ASSISTANCE (Agenda item 72b)
Chak Yong, Mok - A/78/PV.46
PEACE (Agenda item 14)
Gafoor, Burhan - A/78/PV.62
Khng, Nathaniel - A/78/PV.82
Tan, Jason Han Wei - A/78/PV.76
PEACEKEEPING OPERATIONS (Agenda item 51)
Nadarajah, Vicnesh - A/C.4/78/SR.20
PERSONS WITH DISABILITIES (Agenda item 24b)
Choong, Brandon - A/C.3/78/SR.2
RACIAL DISCRIMINATION—ELIMINATION (Agenda item 69a)
Rajandran, Dhivya - A/C.3/78/SR.47
RESPONSIBILITY OF INTERNATIONAL ORGANIZATIONS (Agenda item 85)
Khng, Nathaniel - A/C.6/78/SR.19
RESPONSIBILITY TO PROTECT (Agenda item 129)
Seah, Mark - A/78/PV.97
RIGHTS OF THE CHILD (Agenda item 67)
Rajandran, Dhivya - A/C.3/78/SR.55
Teo, Bernice Yi Lin - A/C.3/78/SR.13
RULE OF LAW (Agenda item 83)
Seah, Mark - A/C.6/78/SR.15
SCIENCE AND TECHNOLOGY—DEVELOPMENT (Agenda item 19a)
Ching, Martha - A/C.2/78/SR.10
SMALL ARMS—ILLICIT TRAFFIC (Agenda item 99p)
Jiamin, Liu - A/C.1/78/PV.18

Singapore (continued)

SMALL ARMS—ILLICIT TRAFFIC—ASSISTANCE (Agenda item 99n)
Jiamin, Liu - A/C.1/78/PV.18
SOUTH-EAST ASIA—NUCLEAR-WEAPON-FREE ZONES (Agenda item 99y)
Gafoor, Burhan - A/C.1/78/PV.30
Lim, Jessie - A/C.1/78/PV.12
SPORTS—OLYMPIC GAMES (Agenda item 11)
Tam, Noelle - A/78/PV.38
STRADDLING FISH STOCKS (Agenda item 75b)
Gafoor, Burhan - A/78/PV.43
SUSTAINABLE DEVELOPMENT (Agenda item 18)
Luo, Phoebe - A/C.2/78/SR.24
SUSTAINABLE ENERGY (Agenda item 18h)
Yuan Fang, Yeo - A/C.2/78/SR.13
TAXATION (Agenda item 16h)
Luo, Phoebe - A/C.2/78/SR.25
TERRORISM (Agenda item 109)
Gafoor, Burhan - A/C.6/78/SR.1
TREATIES (Agenda item 87)
Khng, Nathaniel - A/C.6/78/SR.20
UKRAINE—POLITICAL CONDITIONS (Agenda item 62)
Gafoor, Burhan - A/78/PV.57
UN—FINANCIAL SITUATION (Agenda item 136)
Gafoor, Burhan - A/C.5/78/SR.38
UN. COMMITTEE ON RELATIONS WITH THE HOST COUNTRY—REPORTS (Agenda item 161)
Gafoor, Burhan - A/C.6/78/SR.35
UN. GENERAL ASSEMBLY—WORK PROGRAMME (Agenda item 120)
Seah, Mark - A/78/PV.32
UN. GENERAL ASSEMBLY (78TH SESS. : 2023-2024)—GENERAL DEBATE (Agenda item 8)
Balakrishnan, Vivian - A/78/PV.11
UN. GENERAL ASSEMBLY (78TH SESS. : 2023-2024). 1ST COMMITTEE—GENERAL DEBATE (Agenda item 8)
Low, Si Tong Berenice - A/C.1/78/PV.3
UN. GENERAL ASSEMBLY (78TH SESS. : 2023-2024). 1ST COMMITTEE—WORK ORGANIZATION (Agenda item 7)
Gafoor, Burhan - A/C.1/78/PV.30
UN. GENERAL ASSEMBLY (78TH SESS. : 2023-2024). 2ND COMMITTEE—GENERAL DEBATE (Agenda item 8)
Tan, Jason Han Wei - A/C.2/78/SR.4
UN. INTERNATIONAL COURT OF JUSTICE—REPORTS (Agenda item 73)
Gafoor, Burhan - A/78/PV.27
UN. INTERNATIONAL LAW COMMISSION—REPORTS (Agenda item 79)
Hong, Daphne Fan Sin - A/C.6/78/SR.23

Singapore (continued)

UN. INTERNATIONAL LAW COMMISSION—REPORTS (Agenda item 79)
Khng, Nathaniel - A/C.6/78/SR.37
Tan, Scott - A/C.6/78/SR.29; A/C.6/78/SR.31
UN. SECURITY COUNCIL—MEMBERSHIP (Agenda item 121)
Gafoor, Burhan - A/78/PV.34
Ganesh, Vivek - A/78/PV.104
UN. SECURITY COUNCIL—REPORTS (Agenda item 26)
Gafoor, Burhan - A/78/PV.93
UN COMMISSION ON INTERNATIONAL TRADE LAW—REPORTS (Agenda item 77)
Tan, Scott - A/C.6/78/SR.14
UN HIGH COMMISSIONER FOR REFUGEES—REPORTS (Agenda item 60)
Rajandran, Dhivya - A/C.3/78/SR.51
UN RESOLUTIONS—IMPLEMENTATION (Agenda item 119)
Seah, Mark - A/78/PV.32
VETO (Agenda item 63)
Gafoor, Burhan - A/78/PV.59; A/78/PV.68
Seah, Mark - A/78/PV.70
WOMEN'S ADVANCEMENT (Agenda item 25a)
Chong, Charis - A/C.3/78/SR.8
WOMEN'S ADVANCEMENT—CONFERENCES (Agenda item 25b)
Chong, Charis - A/C.3/78/SR.8
YOUTH (Agenda item 24b)
Choong, Brandon - A/C.3/78/SR.2

Sistema de la Integración Centroamericana

AGEING PERSONS (Agenda item 24b)
González López, Egriselda Aracely (El Salvador) - A/C.3/78/SR.1
CUBA—UNITED STATES (Agenda item 38)
González López, Egriselda Aracely (El Salvador) - A/78/PV.24
DECOLONIZATION (Agenda item 58)
González López, Egriselda Aracely (El Salvador) - A/C.4/78/SR.6
DISASTER VICTIMS (Agenda item 86)
González López, Egriselda Aracely (El Salvador) - A/C.6/78/SR.5
FALKLAND ISLANDS (MALVINAS) QUESTION (Agenda item 42)
González López, Egriselda Aracely (El Salvador) - A/C.4/78/SR.6
INDIGENOUS PEOPLES (Agenda item 68a)
González López, Egriselda Aracely (El Salvador) - A/C.3/78/SR.15
INDIGENOUS PEOPLES—CONFERENCES (Agenda item 68b)
González López, Egriselda Aracely (El Salvador) - A/C.3/78/SR.15
MIGRANTS—PROTECTION (Agenda item 71b)
Sorto Rosales, Mayra Lisseth (El Salvador) - A/C.3/78/SR.24

Sistema de la Integración Centroamericana (continued)

PERSONS WITH DISABILITIES (Agenda item 24b)
González López, Egriselda Aracely (El Salvador) - A/C.3/78/SR.1
RACIAL DISCRIMINATION—ELIMINATION (Agenda item 69a)
González López, Egriselda Aracely (El Salvador) - A/C.3/78/SR.40
RACIAL DISCRIMINATION—PROGRAMMES OF ACTION (Agenda item 69b)
González López, Egriselda Aracely (El Salvador) - A/C.3/78/SR.40
RIGHTS OF THE CHILD (Agenda item 67)
González López, Egriselda Aracely (El Salvador) - A/C.3/78/SR.11
SOCIAL CONDITIONS (Agenda item 24b)
González López, Egriselda Aracely (El Salvador) - A/C.3/78/SR.1
SUSTAINABLE DEVELOPMENT (Agenda item 18)
Barahona Figueroa, Andrea Alejandra (El Salvador) - A/C.2/78/SR.22
UN. GENERAL ASSEMBLY (78TH SESS. : 2023-2024). 1ST COMMITTEE—GENERAL DEBATE (Agenda item 8)
González López, Egriselda Aracely (El Salvador) - A/C.1/78/PV.2
WOMEN'S ADVANCEMENT (Agenda item 25a)
González López, Egriselda Aracely (El Salvador) - A/C.3/78/SR.8
WOMEN'S ADVANCEMENT—CONFERENCES (Agenda item 25b)
González López, Egriselda Aracely (El Salvador) - A/C.3/78/SR.8
YOUTH (Agenda item 24b)
González López, Egriselda Aracely (El Salvador) - A/C.3/78/SR.1

Slovakia

AGEING PERSONS (Agenda item 24b)
Beblavý, Pavol - A/C.3/78/SR.2
Grünwald, Tomáš - A/C.3/78/SR.1
ARMED CONFLICTS PREVENTION (Agenda item 31a)
Košuth, Matus - A/78/PV.72
CRIMES AGAINST HUMANITY (Agenda item 80)
Košuth, Matus - A/C.6/78/SR.10; A/C.6/78/SR.39; A/C.6/78/SR.40; A/C.6/78/SR.42; A/C.6/78/SR.45
FREEDOM OF EXPRESSION (Agenda item 71b)
Košuth, Matus - A/C.3/78/SR.19
HUMAN RIGHTS (Agenda item 71)
Grünwald, Tomáš - A/C.3/78/SR.16
HUMAN RIGHTS—BELARUS (Agenda item 71c)
Grünwald, Tomáš - A/C.3/78/SR.24

Slovakia (continued)

HUMAN RIGHTS—IRAN (ISLAMIC REPUBLIC OF) (Agenda item 71c)
Grünwald, Tomáš - A/C.3/78/SR.24
HUMAN RIGHTS—RUSSIAN FEDERATION (Agenda item 71c)
Grünwald, Tomáš - A/C.3/78/SR.24
HUMAN RIGHTS—TERRITORIES OCCUPIED BY ISRAEL (Agenda item 71c)
Grünwald, Tomáš - A/C.3/78/SR.24
HUMAN RIGHTS—UKRAINE (Agenda item 71c)
Grünwald, Tomáš - A/C.3/78/SR.24
INDIGENOUS PEOPLES (Agenda item 68a)
Grünwald, Tomáš - A/C.3/78/SR.48
INTERNATIONAL CRIMINAL COURT—REPORTS (Agenda item 74)
Klanduch, Peter - A/78/PV.21
MINORITIES (Agenda item 71b)
Grünwald, Tomáš - A/C.3/78/SR.39
PEACE (Agenda item 14)
Galbavý, Richard - A/78/PV.82
RIGHTS OF THE CHILD (Agenda item 67)
Beblavý, Pavol - A/C.3/78/SR.12
SOCIAL CONDITIONS (Agenda item 24b)
Beblavý, Pavol - A/C.3/78/SR.2
UKRAINE—POLITICAL CONDITIONS (Agenda item 62)
Galbavý, Richard - A/78/PV.57
UN. GENERAL ASSEMBLY (78TH SESS. : 2023-2024). 1ST COMMITTEE—GENERAL DEBATE (Agenda item 8)
Chatrnúch, Róbert - A/C.1/78/PV.4
UN. INTERNATIONAL LAW COMMISSION—REPORTS (Agenda item 79)
Klanduch, Peter - A/C.6/78/SR.25; A/C.6/78/SR.29
Košuth, Matus - A/C.6/78/SR.31
UN YOUTH OFFICE—REPORTS (Agenda item 130)
Grünwald, Tomáš - A/78/PV.102
YOUTH (Agenda item 24b)
Beblavý, Pavol - A/C.3/78/SR.2
Grünwald, Tomáš - A/C.3/78/SR.2

Slovakia. President

UN. GENERAL ASSEMBLY (78TH SESS. : 2023-2024)—GENERAL DEBATE (Agenda item 8)
Caputová, Zuzana - A/78/PV.6
UN. GENERAL ASSEMBLY (78TH SESS. : 2023-2024)—SPECIAL STATEMENTS
Caputová, Zuzana - A/78/PV.6

Slovenia

AGEING PERSONS (Agenda item 24b)
Malovrh, Bostjan - A/C.3/78/SR.1
ARMS TRANSFERS—TREATIES (Agenda item 99x)
Ponikvar Velázquez, Jasna - A/C.1/78/PV.19

Slovenia (continued)

CLUSTER MUNITIONS (Agenda item 99dd)
Ponikvar Velázquez, Jasna - A/C.1/78/PV.19
CRIMES AGAINST HUMANITY (Agenda item 80)
Šebenik, Nataša - A/C.6/78/SR.10
DISARMAMENT—GENERAL AND COMPLETE (Agenda item 99)
Ponikvar Velázquez, Jasna - A/C.1/78/PV.19
ENVIRONMENT (Agenda item 71b)
Zitko, Andrej - A/C.3/78/SR.29
HUMAN RIGHTS (Agenda item 71)
Zitko, Andrej - A/C.3/78/SR.16
HUMAN RIGHTS ACTIVISTS (Agenda item 71b)
Zitko, Andrej - A/C.3/78/SR.19
INTERNATIONAL CRIMINAL COURT—REPORTS (Agenda item 74)
Malovrh, Bostjan - A/78/PV.22
INTERNATIONAL JURISDICTION (Agenda item 84)
Šebenik, Nataša - A/C.6/78/SR.12
LANDMINES—TREATIES (Agenda item 99m)
Ponikvar Velázquez, Jasna - A/C.1/78/PV.19
NUCLEAR DISARMAMENT (Agenda item 99b)
Jerman, Bostjan - A/C.1/78/PV.14
NUCLEAR DISARMAMENT—VERIFICATION (Agenda item 99ee)
Jerman, Bostjan - A/C.1/78/PV.14
NUCLEAR NON-PROLIFERATION—INTERNATIONAL OBLIGATIONS (Agenda item 99w)
Jerman, Bostjan - A/C.1/78/PV.14
NUCLEAR WEAPON TESTS—TREATIES (Agenda item 105)
Jerman, Bostjan - A/C.1/78/PV.14
RACIAL DISCRIMINATION—ELIMINATION (Agenda item 69a)
Zitko, Andrej - A/C.3/78/SR.47
RESPONSIBILITY TO PROTECT (Agenda item 129)
Jurecko, Sasa - A/78/PV.97
RIGHTS OF THE CHILD (Agenda item 67)
Šmidt, Arina - A/C.3/78/SR.11
RULE OF LAW (Agenda item 83)
Šebenik, Nataša - A/C.6/78/SR.16
UN. CONFERENCE ON DISARMAMENT—REPORTS (Agenda item 101a)
Jerman, Bostjan - A/C.1/78/PV.23
UN. GENERAL ASSEMBLY—WORK PROGRAMME (Agenda item 120)
Malovrh, Bostjan - A/78/PV.33
UN. GENERAL ASSEMBLY (78TH SESS. : 2023-2024). 1ST COMMITTEE—GENERAL DEBATE (Agenda item 8)
Malovrh, Bostjan - A/C.1/78/PV.6
UN. INTERNATIONAL COURT OF JUSTICE—REPORTS (Agenda item 73)
Rakovec, Marko - A/78/PV.20

Slovenia (continued)

UN. INTERNATIONAL LAW COMMISSION—REPORTS (Agenda item 79)
Rakovec, Marko - A/C.6/78/SR.27
Šinigoj, Miha - A/C.6/78/SR.29; A/C.6/78/SR.31
UN. SECURITY COUNCIL—MEMBERSHIP (Agenda item 121)
Malovrh, Bostjan - A/78/PV.35
UN RESOLUTIONS—IMPLEMENTATION (Agenda item 119)
Malovrh, Bostjan - A/78/PV.33
UNRWA—ACTIVITIES (Agenda item 49)
Malovrh, Bostjan - A/C.4/78/SR.22
VETO (Agenda item 63)
Jurecko, Sasa - A/78/PV.70; A/78/PV.79
Malovrh, Bostjan - A/78/PV.3; A/78/PV.51; A/78/PV.60; A/78/PV.67; A/78/PV.69; A/78/PV.74
WOMEN'S ADVANCEMENT (Agenda item 25a)
Ponikvar, Ursa - A/C.3/78/SR.7
WOMEN'S ADVANCEMENT—CONFERENCES (Agenda item 25b)
Ponikvar, Ursa - A/C.3/78/SR.7
YOUTH (Agenda item 24b)
Šmidt, Arina - A/C.3/78/SR.1

Slovenia. Deputy Prime Minister

UKRAINE—POLITICAL CONDITIONS (Agenda item 62)
Fajon, Tanja - A/78/PV.56
UN. GENERAL ASSEMBLY (78TH SESS. : 2023-2024)—SPECIAL STATEMENTS
Fajon, Tanja - A/78/PV.56

Slovenia. President

UN. GENERAL ASSEMBLY (78TH SESS. : 2023-2024)—GENERAL DEBATE (Agenda item 8)
Pirc Musar, Nataša - A/78/PV.4
UN. GENERAL ASSEMBLY (78TH SESS. : 2023-2024)—SPECIAL STATEMENTS
Pirc Musar, Nataša - A/78/PV.4

Sociedad Peruana de Derecho Internacional

WESTERN SAHARA QUESTION (Agenda item 58)
Rodríguez Mackay, Miguel Ángel - A/C.4/78/SR.4

Solomon Islands

CUBA—UNITED STATES (Agenda item 38)
Indu, Fiona - A/78/PV.26
FRENCH POLYNESIA QUESTION (Agenda item 58)
Waetara, Jane Mugafalu Kabui - A/C.4/78/SR.3

Solomon Islands. Prime Minister

UN. GENERAL ASSEMBLY (78TH SESS. : 2023-2024)—GENERAL DEBATE (Agenda item 8)
Sogavare, Manasseh - A/78/PV.11
UN. GENERAL ASSEMBLY (78TH SESS. : 2023-2024)—SPECIAL STATEMENTS
Sogavare, Manasseh - A/78/PV.11

Somalia. Prime Minister

UN. GENERAL ASSEMBLY (78TH SESS. : 2023-2024)—GENERAL DEBATE (Agenda item 8)
Barre, Hamza Abdi - A/78/PV.12
UN. GENERAL ASSEMBLY (78TH SESS. : 2023-2024)—SPECIAL STATEMENTS
Barre, Hamza Abdi - A/78/PV.12

South Africa

AFRICA—DEVELOPMENT (Agenda item 65b)
Joyini, Mathu - A/78/PV.18
AFRICA—SUSTAINABLE DEVELOPMENT—PARTNERSHIP (Agenda item 65a)
Joyini, Mathu - A/78/PV.18
AGEING PERSONS (Agenda item 24b)
Makgati, Penelope Ramatsobane - A/C.3/78/SR.2
ARMS TRANSFERS—TREATIES (Agenda item 99x)
Lagardien, Yaseen - A/C.1/78/PV.18
BIOLOGICAL WEAPONS—TREATIES (Agenda item 106)
Mahomed, Shuaib - A/C.1/78/PV.14
CHEMICAL WEAPONS—TREATIES (Agenda item 99l)
Mahomed, Shuaib - A/C.1/78/PV.14
CONVENTIONAL WEAPONS (Agenda item 99u)
Lagardien, Yaseen - A/C.1/78/PV.18
CRIME PREVENTION (Agenda item 107)
Sekonyana, Ngako Elphus - A/C.3/78/SR.5
CRIMES AGAINST HUMANITY (Agenda item 80)
Joyini, Mathu - A/C.6/78/SR.10
Motsepe, Keke Mantsho - A/C.6/78/SR.39; A/C.6/78/SR.40; A/C.6/78/SR.42; A/C.6/78/SR.45
CUBA—UNITED STATES (Agenda item 38)
Joyini, Mathu - A/78/PV.24
CYBERCRIME (Agenda item 108)
Sekonyana, Ngako Elphus - A/C.3/78/SR.5
DEVELOPMENT FINANCE (Agenda item 16b)
Seedat, Ahmed Hoosen - A/C.2/78/SR.11
DISARMAMENT—GENERAL AND COMPLETE (Agenda item 99)
Lagardien, Yaseen - A/C.1/78/PV.28
DISASTER PREVENTION (Agenda item 18c)
Mandla, Bulelani - A/C.2/78/SR.15
DISASTER VICTIMS (Agenda item 86)
Motsepe, Keke Mantsho - A/C.6/78/SR.6

South Africa (continued)

ECONOMIC COOPERATION AMONG DEVELOPING COUNTRIES (Agenda item 22b)
Mandla, Bulelani - A/C.2/78/SR.18
ECONOMIC SANCTIONS—INTERNATIONAL RELATIONS (Agenda item 28)
Schalkwyk, Marthinus van - A/78/PV.89
ELECTION VERIFICATION—UN (Agenda item 71b)
Passmoor, Jonathan David - A/C.3/78/SR.50
FINANCIAL FLOWS (Agenda item 16f)
Seedat, Ahmed Hoosen - A/C.2/78/SR.11
FOOD SECURITY (Agenda item 23a)
Mandla, Bulelani - A/C.2/78/SR.17
HEALTH (Agenda item 125)
Passmoor, Jonathan David - A/78/PV.41
Schalkwyk, Marthinus van - A/78/PV.16
HIV/AIDS—DECLARATIONS (Agenda item 10)
Schalkwyk, Marthinus van - A/78/PV.91
HUMAN RIGHTS—INTERNATIONAL INSTRUMENTS (Agenda item 71a)
Joyini, Mathu - A/C.3/78/SR.24
HUMAN RIGHTS—PROGRAMMES OF ACTION (Agenda item 71d)
Joyini, Mathu - A/C.3/78/SR.24
HUMAN RIGHTS—TERRITORIES OCCUPIED BY ISRAEL (Agenda item 71c)
Passmoor, Jonathan David - A/C.3/78/SR.35
IAEA—REPORTS (Agenda item 89)
Joyini, Mathu - A/78/PV.29
INFORMATION (Agenda item 53)
Schalkwyk, Marthinus van - A/C.4/78/SR.14
INFORMATION—INTERNATIONAL SECURITY (Agenda item 94)
Lagardien, Yaseen - A/C.1/78/PV.20; A/C.1/78/PV.29
INFORMATION TECHNOLOGY—DEVELOPMENT (Agenda item 15)
Mpama, Sibusiso Qetello - A/C.2/78/SR.11
INTERNATIONAL LAW—TRAINING PROGRAMMES (Agenda item 78)
Motsepe, Keke Mantsho - A/C.6/78/SR.21
INTERNATIONAL TRADE (Agenda item 16a)
Seedat, Ahmed Hoosen - A/C.2/78/SR.11
MACROECONOMIC POLICY (Agenda item 16)
Seedat, Ahmed Hoosen - A/C.2/78/SR.11
MIGRANTS—PROTECTION (Agenda item 71b)
Diedricks, Meryl Michelle - A/C.3/78/SR.23
MILLENNIUM SUMMIT—CONFERENCES (Agenda item 117)
Joyini, Mathu - A/78/PV.15
NON-CITIZENS—DEPORTATION (Agenda item 81)
Motsepe, Keke Mantsho - A/C.6/78/SR.34

South Africa (continued)
NUCLEAR DISARMAMENT (Agenda item 99b)
Saran, Sherina - A/C.1/78/PV.11
NUCLEAR NON-PROLIFERATION—INTERNATIONAL OBLIGATIONS (Agenda item 99w)
Saran, Sherina - A/C.1/78/PV.11
NUCLEAR WEAPON TESTS—TREATIES (Agenda item 105)
Saran, Sherina - A/C.1/78/PV.11
NUCLEAR WEAPONS—ELIMINATION (Agenda item 99z)
Schalkwyk, Marthinus van - A/C.1/78/PV.25
NUCLEAR WEAPONS—TREATIES (Agenda item 99ff)
Saran, Sherina - A/C.1/78/PV.11
NUCLEAR-WEAPON-FREE ZONES (Agenda item 99cc)
Saran, Sherina - A/C.1/78/PV.11
OPERATIONAL ACTIVITIES—UN SYSTEM (Agenda item 22a)
Mandla, Bulelani - A/C.2/78/SR.18
OUTER SPACE—PEACEFUL USES—INTERNATIONAL COOPERATION (Agenda item 48)
Mabeba, Bernard - A/C.4/78/SR.16
PALESTINE QUESTION (Agenda item 35)
Joyini, Mathu - A/78/PV.39
PEACEBUILDING (Agenda item 61)
Schalkwyk, Marthinus van - A/78/PV.100
PEACEKEEPING OPERATIONS (Agenda item 51)
Mabeba, Bernard - A/C.4/78/SR.20
PEACEKEEPING OPERATIONS—CRIMINAL LIABILITY (Agenda item 76)
Motsepe, Keke Mantsho - A/C.6/78/SR.8
POVERTY—INTERNATIONAL DECADES (Agenda item 21a)
Mandla, Bulelani - A/C.2/78/SR.17
RACIAL DISCRIMINATION—ELIMINATION (Agenda item 69a)
Joyini, Mathu - A/C.3/78/SR.40
Passmoor, Jonathan David - A/C.3/78/SR.47
Schalkwyk, Marthinus van - A/78/PV.63; A/78/PV.103
RACIAL DISCRIMINATION—PROGRAMMES OF ACTION (Agenda item 69b)
Joyini, Mathu - A/C.3/78/SR.40
Passmoor, Jonathan David - A/C.3/78/SR.40; A/C.3/78/SR.56
RESPONSIBILITY TO PROTECT (Agenda item 129)
Passmoor, Jonathan David - A/78/PV.96
RIGHT TO DEVELOPMENT (Agenda item 71b)
Passmoor, Jonathan David - A/C.3/78/SR.20
RIGHT TO HEALTH (Agenda item 71b)
Sekonyana, Ngako Elphus - A/C.3/78/SR.39
RIGHTS OF THE CHILD (Agenda item 67)
Makwati, Babalwa - A/C.3/78/SR.12
Schalkwyk, Marthinus van - A/C.3/78/SR.12

South Africa (continued)
RULE OF LAW (Agenda item 83)
Motsepe, Keke Mantsho - A/C.6/78/SR.16
RURAL POVERTY (Agenda item 21b)
Mandla, Bulelani - A/C.2/78/SR.17
SANCTIONS—INTERNATIONAL RELATIONS (Agenda item 71b)
Passmoor, Jonathan David - A/C.3/78/SR.28
SCIENCE AND TECHNOLOGY—DEVELOPMENT (Agenda item 19a)
Mpama, Sibusiso Qetello - A/C.2/78/SR.11
SELF-DETERMINATION OF PEOPLES (Agenda item 70)
Passmoor, Jonathan David - A/C.3/78/SR.43; A/C.3/78/SR.49
SEXUAL ORIENTATION (Agenda item 71b)
Passmoor, Jonathan David - A/C.3/78/SR.39
SMALL ARMS—ILLICIT TRAFFIC (Agenda item 99p)
Lagardien, Yaseen - A/C.1/78/PV.18
SMALL ARMS—ILLICIT TRAFFIC—ASSISTANCE (Agenda item 99n)
Lagardien, Yaseen - A/C.1/78/PV.18
SOCIAL CONDITIONS (Agenda item 24b)
Makgati, Penelope Ramatsobane - A/C.3/78/SR.2
SOCIAL DEVELOPMENT (Agenda item 24)
Makgati, Penelope Ramatsobane - A/C.3/78/SR.2
SPECIAL POLITICAL MISSIONS (Agenda item 52)
Schalkwyk, Marthinus van - A/C.4/78/SR.21
TAXATION (Agenda item 16h)
Joyini, Mathu - A/C.2/78/SR.25
TERRITORIES OCCUPIED BY ISRAEL—HUMAN RIGHTS (Agenda item 50)
Schalkwyk, Marthinus van - A/C.4/78/SR.25
TERRITORIES OCCUPIED BY ISRAEL—NATURAL RESOURCES (Agenda item 59)
Schalkwyk, Marthinus van - A/C.2/78/SR.19
TERRORISM (Agenda item 109)
Motsepe, Keke Mantsho - A/C.6/78/SR.2
TERRORISM—HUMAN RIGHTS (Agenda item 71b)
Passmoor, Jonathan David - A/C.3/78/SR.31
TREATIES (Agenda item 87)
Motsepe, Keke Mantsho - A/C.6/78/SR.20
UKRAINE—POLITICAL CONDITIONS (Agenda item 62)
Schalkwyk, Marthinus van - A/78/PV.99
UN—BUDGET (2024) (Agenda item 134)
Joyini, Mathu - A/C.5/78/SR.5
UN—PROGRAMME PLANNING (Agenda item 135)
Joyini, Mathu - A/C.5/78/SR.5
UN. CONFERENCE ON DISARMAMENT—REPORTS (Agenda item 101a)
Mahomed, Shuaib - A/C.1/78/PV.22
UN. DISARMAMENT COMMISSION—REPORTS (Agenda item 101b)
Mahomed, Shuaib - A/C.1/78/PV.22

South Africa (continued)

UN. GENERAL ASSEMBLY—WORK PROGRAMME (Agenda item 120)
Schalkwyk, Marthinus van - A/78/PV.32
UN. GENERAL ASSEMBLY (78TH SESS. : 2023-2024). 1ST COMMITTEE—GENERAL DEBATE (Agenda item 8)
Joyini, Mathu - A/C.1/78/PV.2
UN. GENERAL ASSEMBLY (78TH SESS. : 2023-2024). 2ND COMMITTEE—GENERAL DEBATE (Agenda item 8)
Schalkwyk, Marthinus van - A/C.2/78/SR.3
UN. HUMAN RIGHTS COUNCIL—REPORTS (Agenda item 66)
Mngomezulu, Portia Lindiwe - A/C.3/78/SR.46
Schalkwyk, Marthinus van - A/78/PV.28
UN. INTERNATIONAL LAW COMMISSION—REPORTS (Agenda item 79)
Motsepe, Keke Mantsho - A/C.6/78/SR.25; A/C.6/78/SR.29; A/C.6/78/SR.31
UN. PEACEBUILDING COMMISSION—REPORTS (Agenda item 27)
Schalkwyk, Marthinus van - A/78/PV.100
UN. PEACEBUILDING FUND—REPORTS (Agenda item 111)
Schalkwyk, Marthinus van - A/78/PV.100
UN. SECRETARY-GENERAL—REPORTS (Agenda item 110)
Lagardien, Yaseen - A/78/PV.55
UN. SECURITY COUNCIL—MEMBERSHIP (Agenda item 121)
Passmoor, Jonathan David - A/78/PV.34
UN. SECURITY COUNCIL—REPORTS (Agenda item 26)
Joyini, Mathu - A/78/PV.93
UN COMMISSION ON INTERNATIONAL TRADE LAW—REPORTS (Agenda item 77)
Motsepe, Keke Mantsho - A/C.6/78/SR.14
UN CONFERENCES (Agenda item 13)
Joyini, Mathu - A/78/PV.15
Sithole, Tiyani Raymond - A/78/PV.33
UN HIGH COMMISSIONER FOR REFUGEES—REPORTS (Agenda item 60)
Moruke, Cathy - A/C.3/78/SR.44
UN RESOLUTIONS—IMPLEMENTATION (Agenda item 119)
Schalkwyk, Marthinus van - A/78/PV.32
UN YOUTH OFFICE—REPORTS (Agenda item 130)
Makgati, Penelope Ramatsobane - A/78/PV.102
UNRWA—ACTIVITIES (Agenda item 49)
Schalkwyk, Marthinus van - A/C.4/78/SR.22; A/C.4/78/SR.23; A/C.4/78/SR.26
VETO (Agenda item 63)
Joyini, Mathu - A/78/PV.60; A/78/PV.67
Schalkwyk, Marthinus van - A/78/PV.3; A/78/PV.51; A/78/PV.68; A/78/PV.70; A/78/PV.74
WESTERN SAHARA QUESTION (Agenda item 58)
Schalkwyk, Marthinus van - A/C.4/78/SR.6

South Africa (continued)

WOMEN'S ADVANCEMENT (Agenda item 25a)
Passmoor, Jonathan David - A/C.3/78/SR.8
WOMEN'S ADVANCEMENT—CONFERENCES (Agenda item 25b)
Passmoor, Jonathan David - A/C.3/78/SR.8

South Africa. President

UN. GENERAL ASSEMBLY (78TH SESS. : 2023-2024)—GENERAL DEBATE (Agenda item 8)
Ramaphosa, Matamela Cyril - A/78/PV.4
UN. GENERAL ASSEMBLY (78TH SESS. : 2023-2024)—SPECIAL STATEMENTS
Ramaphosa, Matamela Cyril - A/78/PV.4

South Sudan

HUMAN RIGHTS—ERITREA (Agenda item 71c)
Adeng, Cecilia A.M. - A/C.3/78/SR.36

South Sudan. President

UN. GENERAL ASSEMBLY (78TH SESS. : 2023-2024)—GENERAL DEBATE (Agenda item 8)
Kiir Mayardit, Slava - A/78/PV.8
UN. GENERAL ASSEMBLY (78TH SESS. : 2023-2024)—SPECIAL STATEMENTS
Kiir Mayardit, Slava - A/78/PV.8

Southern African Development Community

ECONOMIC SANCTIONS—INTERNATIONAL RELATIONS (Agenda item 28)
Cruz, Francisco José da (Angola) - A/78/PV.89
RACIAL DISCRIMINATION—ELIMINATION (Agenda item 69a)
Cruz, Francisco José da (Angola) - A/C.3/78/SR.40
RACIAL DISCRIMINATION—PROGRAMMES OF ACTION (Agenda item 69b)
Cruz, Francisco José da (Angola) - A/C.3/78/SR.40
RIGHTS OF THE CHILD (Agenda item 67)
Cruz, Francisco José da (Angola) - A/C.3/78/SR.11
Luemba, Mateus Pedro (Angola) - A/C.3/78/SR.55
SANCTIONS—INTERNATIONAL RELATIONS (Agenda item 71b)
Cruz, Francisco José da (Angola) - A/C.3/78/SR.26

Sovereign Order of Malta

AGEING PERSONS (Agenda item 24b)
Beresford-Hill, Paul - A/C.3/78/SR.1
CLIMATE CHANGE (Agenda item 71b)
Tripptrap, Ravi Christian - A/C.3/78/SR.29
CRIME PREVENTION (Agenda item 107)
Maenpaa, Conor C. - A/C.3/78/SR.6

Sovereign Order of Malta (continued)

CYBERCRIME (Agenda item 108)
Maenpaa, Conor C. - A/C.3/78/SR.6
DEMOCRACY (Agenda item 71b)
Scalabrini-McKellar, Tobias - A/C.3/78/SR.28
DISAPPEARANCE OF PERSONS (Agenda item 71b)
O'Hara Rusckowski, Deborah - A/C.3/78/SR.22
ENVIRONMENT (Agenda item 71b)
Rosario-Blackett, Marissa del - A/C.3/78/SR.29
FREEDOM OF EXPRESSION (Agenda item 71b)
McGuire, Peter Davidson - A/C.3/78/SR.19
HUMAN RIGHTS (Agenda item 71)
Muñoz, Zachary N. - A/C.3/78/SR.28
Scalabrini-McKellar, Tobias - A/C.3/78/SR.16
INDIGENOUS PEOPLES (Agenda item 68a)
Rosario-Blackett, Marissa del - A/C.3/78/SR.17
JUDICIAL INDEPENDENCE (Agenda item 71b)
Muñoz, Zachary N. - A/C.3/78/SR.31
LEPROSY (Agenda item 71b)
Muñoz, Zachary N. - A/C.3/78/SR.17
MIGRANT WORKERS (Agenda item 71a)
McGuire, Peter Davidson - A/C.3/78/SR.23
MIGRANTS—PROTECTION (Agenda item 71b)
Greenwood, James Harrison - A/C.3/78/SR.23
MINORITIES (Agenda item 71b)
Rosario-Blackett, Marissa del - A/C.3/78/SR.39
PERSONS WITH DISABILITIES—HUMAN RIGHTS (Agenda item 71a)
Arditi di Castelvetere Manzo, Fiamma - A/C.3/78/SR.38
POVERTY—HUMAN RIGHTS (Agenda item 71b)
Scalabrini-McKellar, Tobias - A/C.3/78/SR.30
RACIAL DISCRIMINATION—ELIMINATION (Agenda item 69a)
Tegoni, Nicola - A/C.3/78/SR.40
RELIGIOUS INTOLERANCE (Agenda item 71b)
Muñoz, Zachary N. - A/C.3/78/SR.38
RIGHT TO DRINKING WATER (Agenda item 71b)
Lucii, Costanza - A/C.3/78/SR.28
RIGHT TO FOOD (Agenda item 71b)
Rosario-Blackett, Marissa del - A/C.3/78/SR.30
RIGHT TO HEALTH (Agenda item 71b)
Espiritu, Michael - A/C.3/78/SR.39
RIGHT TO HOUSING (Agenda item 71b)
Lucii, Costanza - A/C.3/78/SR.30
RIGHTS OF THE CHILD (Agenda item 67)
Espiritu, Michael - A/C.3/78/SR.14
Muñoz, Zachary N. - A/C.3/78/SR.11
RURAL WOMEN (Agenda item 25a)
Lucii, Costanza - A/C.3/78/SR.10
SANCTIONS—INTERNATIONAL RELATIONS (Agenda item 71b)
Muñoz, Zachary N. - A/C.3/78/SR.28

Sovereign Order of Malta (continued)

SOCIAL CONDITIONS (Agenda item 24b)
Schönburg, Laetitia - A/C.3/78/SR.4
SOCIAL DEVELOPMENT (Agenda item 24)
Schönburg, Laetitia - A/C.3/78/SR.4
SOLIDARITY (Agenda item 71b)
Buckley, James E. - A/C.3/78/SR.32
SUMMARY EXECUTIONS (Agenda item 71b)
McGuire, Peter Davidson - A/C.3/78/SR.31
TERRORISM—HUMAN RIGHTS (Agenda item 71b)
Espiritu, Michael - A/C.3/78/SR.31
TORTURE AND OTHER CRUEL TREATMENT (Agenda item 71a)
Greenwood, James Harrison - A/C.3/78/SR.18
TRAFFICKING IN PERSONS (Agenda item 71b)
O'Hara Rusckowski, Deborah - A/C.3/78/SR.23
UN HIGH COMMISSIONER FOR REFUGEES—REPORTS (Agenda item 60)
Rosario-Blackett, Marissa del - A/C.3/78/SR.44
WOMEN'S ADVANCEMENT (Agenda item 25a)
Buckley, James E. - A/C.3/78/SR.7
Lucii, Costanza - A/C.3/78/SR.7; A/C.3/78/SR.10
WOMEN'S ADVANCEMENT—CONFERENCES (Agenda item 25b)
Buckley, James E. - A/C.3/78/SR.7
Lucii, Costanza - A/C.3/78/SR.7; A/C.3/78/SR.10

Spain

AFRICA—NUCLEAR-WEAPON-FREE ZONES (Agenda item 92)
Sánchez de Lerín García-Ovies, Ignacio - A/C.1/78/PV.25
ARMS RACE—OUTER SPACE (Agenda item 97a)
Rosario Vela, Manuel Jesús del - A/C.1/78/PV.17
ARMS TRANSFERS—TREATIES (Agenda item 99x)
Rosario Vela, Manuel Jesús del - A/C.1/78/PV.19
BIOLOGICAL WEAPONS—TREATIES (Agenda item 106)
Rosario Vela, Manuel Jesús del - A/C.1/78/PV.15
CHEMICAL WEAPONS—TREATIES (Agenda item 99l)
Rosario Vela, Manuel Jesús del - A/C.1/78/PV.15
CLUSTER MUNITIONS (Agenda item 99dd)
Rosario Vela, Manuel Jesús del - A/C.1/78/PV.19
CONVENTIONAL WEAPONS (Agenda item 99u)
Rosario Vela, Manuel Jesús del - A/C.1/78/PV.19
CRIMES AGAINST HUMANITY (Agenda item 80)
Jiménez de la Hoz, Ana - A/C.6/78/SR.45
DEVELOPMENT FINANCE (Agenda item 16b)
Martín Couce, Adrián - A/C.2/78/SR.9

Spain (continued)

DEVELOPMENT FINANCE—CONFERENCES (Agenda item 17)
Jiménez de la Hoz, Ana - A/C.2/78/SR.25
DISARMAMENT—GENERAL AND COMPLETE (Agenda item 99)
Rosario Vela, Manuel Jesús del - A/C.1/78/PV.19
DISPLACED PERSONS (Agenda item 71b)
Bellmont Roldán, Xavier - A/C.3/78/SR.49
ENVIRONMENT (Agenda item 71b)
Cantero Talavera, Francisco Javier - A/C.3/78/SR.29
EXTERNAL DEBT (Agenda item 16c)
Martín Couce, Adrián - A/C.2/78/SR.9
GIBRALTAR QUESTION (Agenda item 58)
Gómez Aoiz, Elena - A/C.4/78/SR.2; A/C.4/78/SR.8
Jiménez de la Hoz, Ana - A/C.4/78/SR.2
HUMAN RIGHTS—AFGHANISTAN (Agenda item 71c)
Alonso Giganto, Ana María - A/C.3/78/SR.34
HUMAN RIGHTS ACTIVISTS (Agenda item 71b)
Bellmont Roldán, Xavier - A/C.3/78/SR.19
INFORMATION (Agenda item 53)
Rodríguez Gómez-Aller, Juan - A/C.4/78/SR.12
LANDMINES—TREATIES (Agenda item 99m)
Rosario Vela, Manuel Jesús del - A/C.1/78/PV.19
NUCLEAR DISARMAMENT (Agenda item 99b)
Rosario Vela, Manuel Jesús del - A/C.1/78/PV.12
NUCLEAR NON-PROLIFERATION—INTERNATIONAL OBLIGATIONS (Agenda item 99w)
Rosario Vela, Manuel Jesús del - A/C.1/78/PV.12
NUCLEAR WEAPON TESTS—TREATIES (Agenda item 105)
Rosario Vela, Manuel Jesús del - A/C.1/78/PV.12
OUTER SPACE—CONFIDENCE-BUILDING MEASURES (Agenda item 99v)
Rosario Vela, Manuel Jesús del - A/C.1/78/PV.17
OUTER SPACE—PRINCIPLES (Agenda item 97d)
Rosario Vela, Manuel Jesús del - A/C.1/78/PV.17
RIGHT TO DRINKING WATER (Agenda item 71b)
Bellmont Roldán, Xavier - A/C.3/78/SR.28; A/C.3/78/SR.50
SELF-DETERMINATION OF PEOPLES (Agenda item 70)
Bellmont Roldán, Xavier - A/C.3/78/SR.56
SEXUAL ORIENTATION (Agenda item 71b)
Alonso Giganto, Ana María - A/C.3/78/SR.39
SOCIAL CONDITIONS (Agenda item 24b)
Alonso Giganto, Ana María - A/C.3/78/SR.3
Jiménez de la Hoz, Ana - A/C.3/78/SR.51
SOCIAL DEVELOPMENT (Agenda item 24)
Alonso Giganto, Ana María - A/C.3/78/SR.3
UKRAINE—POLITICAL CONDITIONS (Agenda item 62)
Albares Bueno, José Manuel - A/78/PV.56

Spain (continued)

UN. GENERAL ASSEMBLY (78TH SESS. : 2023-2024). 1ST COMMITTEE—GENERAL DEBATE (Agenda item 8)
Jiménez de la Hoz, Ana - A/C.1/78/PV.8
UN. GENERAL ASSEMBLY (78TH SESS. : 2023-2024). 2ND COMMITTEE—GENERAL DEBATE (Agenda item 8)
Jiménez de la Hoz, Ana - A/C.2/78/SR.5
UN. INTERNATIONAL LAW COMMISSION—REPORTS (Agenda item 79)
Solà Pardell, Oriol - A/C.6/78/SR.27
UN. SECURITY COUNCIL—MEMBERSHIP (Agenda item 121)
Jiménez de la Hoz, Ana - A/78/PV.36
VETO (Agenda item 63)
Gómez Hernández, Héctor José - A/78/PV.60; A/78/PV.67; A/78/PV.69; A/78/PV.75; A/78/PV.79
Jiménez de la Hoz, Ana - A/78/PV.52; A/78/PV.71
WEAPONS OF MASS DESTRUCTION—TERRORISM (Agenda item 99s)
Rosario Vela, Manuel Jesús del - A/C.1/78/PV.15
WOMEN'S ADVANCEMENT (Agenda item 25a)
Alonso Giganto, Ana María - A/C.3/78/SR.7; A/C.3/78/SR.9
WOMEN'S ADVANCEMENT—CONFERENCES (Agenda item 25b)
Alonso Giganto, Ana María - A/C.3/78/SR.7; A/C.3/78/SR.9

Spain. President

UN. GENERAL ASSEMBLY (78TH SESS. : 2023-2024)—GENERAL DEBATE (Agenda item 8)
Sánchez, Pedro - A/78/PV.7
UN. GENERAL ASSEMBLY (78TH SESS. : 2023-2024)—SPECIAL STATEMENTS
Sánchez, Pedro - A/78/PV.7

Sri Lanka

ARMS RACE—OUTER SPACE (Agenda item 97a)
Gunaratna, Pahala Rallage Sanathana Sugeeshwara - A/C.1/78/PV.27
Pieris, Peter Mohan Maithri - A/C.1/78/PV.16
BIOLOGICAL WEAPONS—TREATIES (Agenda item 106)
Pieris, Peter Mohan Maithri - A/C.1/78/PV.14
CHEMICAL WEAPONS—TREATIES (Agenda item 99l)
Pieris, Peter Mohan Maithri - A/C.1/78/PV.14
CONVENTIONAL WEAPONS (Agenda item 99u)
Pieris, Peter Mohan Maithri - A/C.1/78/PV.18
CRIMES AGAINST HUMANITY (Agenda item 80)
Pieris, Peter Mohan Maithri - A/C.6/78/SR.10; A/C.6/78/SR.39; A/C.6/78/SR.42; A/C.6/78/SR.43; A/C.6/78/SR.44; A/C.6/78/SR.47

Sri Lanka (continued)

CUBA—UNITED STATES (Agenda item 38)
Pieris, Peter Mohan Maithri - A/78/PV.26
DISARMAMENT—GENERAL AND COMPLETE (Agenda item 99)
Pieris, Peter Mohan Maithri - A/78/PV.105
DISARMAMENT AGREEMENTS—OUTER SPACE (Agenda item 97c)
Gunaratna, Pahala Rallage Sanathana Sugeeshwara - A/C.1/78/PV.27
DISASTER VICTIMS (Agenda item 86)
Pieris, Peter Mohan Maithri - A/C.6/78/SR.5
ECONOMIC COOPERATION AMONG DEVELOPING COUNTRIES (Agenda item 22b)
Pieris, Peter Mohan Maithri - A/C.2/78/SR.18
HEALTH (Agenda item 125)
Weerasekara, Weerasekarage Chathura Ramyajith - A/78/PV.48
HUMAN RIGHTS—IRAN (ISLAMIC REPUBLIC OF) (Agenda item 71c)
Gunaratna, Pahala Rallage Sanathana Sugeeshwara - A/C.3/78/SR.34
HUMAN RIGHTS—RUSSIAN FEDERATION (Agenda item 71c)
Gunaratna, Pahala Rallage Sanathana Sugeeshwara - A/C.3/78/SR.37
IAEA—REPORTS (Agenda item 89)
Pieris, Peter Mohan Maithri - A/78/PV.30
INFORMATION (Agenda item 53)
Pieris, Peter Mohan Maithri - A/C.4/78/SR.13
INFORMATION—INTERNATIONAL SECURITY (Agenda item 94)
Pieris, Peter Mohan Maithri - A/C.1/78/PV.20
INTERNATIONAL JURISDICTION (Agenda item 84)
Pieris, Peter Mohan Maithri - A/C.6/78/SR.12
MINE CLEARANCE (Agenda item 46)
Pieris, Peter Mohan Maithri - A/C.4/78/SR.10
NUCLEAR DISARMAMENT (Agenda item 99b)
Pieris, Peter Mohan Maithri - A/C.1/78/PV.11
NUCLEAR NON-PROLIFERATION—INTERNATIONAL OBLIGATIONS (Agenda item 99w)
Pieris, Peter Mohan Maithri - A/C.1/78/PV.11
NUCLEAR WEAPONS—TREATIES (Agenda item 99ff)
Pieris, Peter Mohan Maithri - A/C.1/78/PV.11
OUTER SPACE—CONFIDENCE-BUILDING MEASURES (Agenda item 99v)
Gunaratna, Pahala Rallage Sanathana Sugeeshwara - A/C.1/78/PV.27
Pieris, Peter Mohan Maithri - A/C.1/78/PV.16
OUTER SPACE—PEACEFUL USES—INTERNATIONAL COOPERATION (Agenda item 48)
Pieris, Peter Mohan Maithri - A/C.4/78/SR.15
OUTER SPACE—PRINCIPLES (Agenda item 97d)
Gunaratna, Pahala Rallage Sanathana Sugeeshwara - A/C.1/78/PV.27
PEACE (Agenda item 14)
Pieris, Peter Mohan Maithri - A/78/PV.76

Sri Lanka (continued)

PEACEKEEPING OPERATIONS (Agenda item 51)
Pieris, Peter Mohan Maithri - A/C.4/78/SR.18
RACIAL DISCRIMINATION—ELIMINATION (Agenda item 69a)
Gunaratna, Pahala Rallage Sanathana Sugeeshwara - A/C.3/78/SR.47
Pieris, Peter Mohan Maithri - A/C.3/78/SR.42
RACIAL DISCRIMINATION—PROGRAMMES OF ACTION (Agenda item 69b)
Pieris, Peter Mohan Maithri - A/C.3/78/SR.42
RADIATION EFFECTS (Agenda item 47)
Pieris, Peter Mohan Maithri - A/C.4/78/SR.11
RIGHTS OF THE CHILD (Agenda item 67)
Pieris, Peter Mohan Maithri - A/C.3/78/SR.13
RULE OF LAW (Agenda item 83)
Pieris, Peter Mohan Maithri - A/C.6/78/SR.16
SCIENCE AND TECHNOLOGY—DEVELOPMENT (Agenda item 19a)
Gunaratna, Pahala Rallage Sanathana Sugeeshwara - A/C.2/78/SR.11
SMALL ARMS—ILLICIT TRAFFIC (Agenda item 99p)
Pieris, Peter Mohan Maithri - A/C.1/78/PV.18
SMALL ARMS—ILLICIT TRAFFIC—ASSISTANCE (Agenda item 99n)
Pieris, Peter Mohan Maithri - A/C.1/78/PV.18
SOCIAL CONDITIONS (Agenda item 24b)
Gunaratna, Pahala Rallage Sanathana Sugeeshwara - A/C.3/78/SR.2
SOCIAL DEVELOPMENT (Agenda item 24)
Gunaratna, Pahala Rallage Sanathana Sugeeshwara - A/C.3/78/SR.2
TERRORISM (Agenda item 109)
Pieris, Peter Mohan Maithri - A/C.6/78/SR.1
UN. GENERAL ASSEMBLY—WORK PROGRAMME (Agenda item 120)
Pieris, Peter Mohan Maithri - A/78/PV.33
UN. GENERAL ASSEMBLY (78TH SESS. : 2023-2024)—AGENDA (Agenda item 7)
Pieris, Peter Mohan Maithri - A/78/PV.2
UN. GENERAL ASSEMBLY (78TH SESS. : 2023-2024). 1ST COMMITTEE—GENERAL DEBATE (Agenda item 8)
Pieris, Peter Mohan Maithri - A/C.1/78/PV.4
UN. GENERAL ASSEMBLY (78TH SESS. : 2023-2024). 2ND COMMITTEE—GENERAL DEBATE (Agenda item 8)
Pieris, Peter Mohan Maithri - A/C.2/78/SR.4
UN. SECURITY COUNCIL—MEMBERSHIP (Agenda item 121)
Pieris, Peter Mohan Maithri - A/78/PV.104
UN RESOLUTIONS—IMPLEMENTATION (Agenda item 119)
Pieris, Peter Mohan Maithri - A/78/PV.33
UNRWA—ACTIVITIES (Agenda item 49)
Pieris, Peter Mohan Maithri - A/C.4/78/SR.22
VETO (Agenda item 63)
Pieris, Peter Mohan Maithri - A/78/PV.61; A/78/PV.71

Sri Lanka (continued)

WEAPONS—OUTER SPACE (Agenda item 97b)
Gunaratna, Pahala Rallage Sanathana Sugeeshwara - A/C.1/78/PV.27
WEAPONS OF MASS DESTRUCTION—TERRORISM (Agenda item 99s)
Pieris, Peter Mohan Maithri - A/C.1/78/PV.14
WOMEN'S ADVANCEMENT (Agenda item 25a)
Pieris, Peter Mohan Maithri - A/C.3/78/SR.9
WOMEN'S ADVANCEMENT—CONFERENCES (Agenda item 25b)
Pieris, Peter Mohan Maithri - A/C.3/78/SR.9

Sri Lanka. President

UN. GENERAL ASSEMBLY (78TH SESS. : 2023-2024)—GENERAL DEBATE (Agenda item 8)
Wickremesinghe, Ranil - A/78/PV.8
UN. GENERAL ASSEMBLY (78TH SESS. : 2023-2024)—SPECIAL STATEMENTS
Wickremesinghe, Ranil - A/78/PV.8

State of Palestine

ARMS RACE—OUTER SPACE (Agenda item 97a)
Kasabri, Qais Z.F. - A/C.1/78/PV.16
BIOLOGICAL WEAPONS—TREATIES (Agenda item 106)
Kasabri, Qais Z.F. - A/C.1/78/PV.14
CHEMICAL WEAPONS—TREATIES (Agenda item 99l)
Kasabri, Qais Z.F. - A/C.1/78/PV.14
CRIMES AGAINST HUMANITY (Agenda item 80)
Bamya, Majed - A/C.6/78/SR.11
Sayej, Loureen O.A. - A/C.6/78/SR.39; A/C.6/78/SR.41; A/C.6/78/SR.43; A/C.6/78/SR.44; A/C.6/78/SR.45
DISARMAMENT—GENERAL AND COMPLETE (Agenda item 99)
Kasabri, Qais Z.F. - A/C.1/78/PV.23; A/C.1/78/PV.24
DISASTER VICTIMS (Agenda item 86)
Sayej, Loureen O.A. - A/C.6/78/SR.7
ECONOMIC SANCTIONS—INTERNATIONAL RELATIONS (Agenda item 28)
Abdelhady-Nasser, Feda - A/78/PV.90
EMERGENCY ASSISTANCE (Agenda item 72a)
Abushawesh, Sahar - A/78/PV.47
HUMAN RIGHTS (Agenda item 71)
Bamya, Majed - A/C.3/78/SR.16
Salem, Sahar K.H. - A/C.3/78/SR.26
HUMAN RIGHTS—TERRITORIES OCCUPIED BY ISRAEL (Agenda item 71c)
Salem, Sahar K.H. - A/C.3/78/SR.35
INFORMATION (Agenda item 53)
Bamya, Majed - A/C.4/78/SR.14

State of Palestine (continued)

INTERNATIONAL CRIMINAL COURT—REPORTS (Agenda item 74)
Bamya, Majed - A/78/PV.25
INTERNATIONAL JURISDICTION (Agenda item 84)
Sayej, Loureen O.A. - A/C.6/78/SR.13
PALESTINE QUESTION (Agenda item 35)
Mansour, Riyad H. - A/78/PV.39
PALESTINIANS—ASSISTANCE (Agenda item 72b)
Abushawesh, Sahar - A/78/PV.47
POVERTY—HUMAN RIGHTS (Agenda item 71b)
Salem, Sahar K.H. - A/C.3/78/SR.30
RIGHTS OF THE CHILD (Agenda item 67)
Salem, Sahar K.H. - A/C.3/78/SR.11; A/C.3/78/SR.14
RULE OF LAW (Agenda item 83)
Sayej, Loureen O.A. - A/C.6/78/SR.19
SELF-DETERMINATION OF PEOPLES (Agenda item 70)
Salem, Sahar K.H. - A/C.3/78/SR.49
SOLIDARITY (Agenda item 71b)
Salem, Sahar K.H. - A/C.3/78/SR.32
SUSTAINABLE DEVELOPMENT (Agenda item 18)
Abushawesh, Sahar - A/C.2/78/SR.22
Nasser-Abushawesh, Sahar - A/C.2/78/SR.15
TERRITORIES OCCUPIED BY ISRAEL—HUMAN RIGHTS (Agenda item 50)
Abdelhady-Nasser, Feda - A/C.4/78/SR.24; A/C.4/78/SR.25
Mansour, Riyad H. - A/C.4/78/SR.26
TERRITORIES OCCUPIED BY ISRAEL—NATURAL RESOURCES (Agenda item 59)
Abushawesh, Sahar - A/C.2/78/SR.21
Nasser-Abushawesh, Sahar - A/C.2/78/SR.19; A/C.2/78/SR.20
TERRORISM (Agenda item 109)
Bamya, Majed - A/C.6/78/SR.5
UN. GENERAL ASSEMBLY (78TH SESS. : 2023-2024). 1ST COMMITTEE—GENERAL DEBATE (Agenda item 8)
Bamya, Majed - A/C.1/78/PV.7; A/C.1/78/PV.8
Kasabri, Qais Z.F. - A/C.1/78/PV.9
UN. INTERNATIONAL COURT OF JUSTICE—REPORTS (Agenda item 73)
Mansour, Riyad H. - A/78/PV.28
UN. INTERNATIONAL LAW COMMISSION—REPORTS (Agenda item 79)
Sayej, Loureen O.A. - A/C.6/78/SR.28; A/C.6/78/SR.33
UN CHARTER—REPORTS (Agenda item 82)
Sayej, Loureen O.A. - A/C.6/78/SR.34
UNRWA—ACTIVITIES (Agenda item 49)
Abdelhady-Nasser, Feda - A/C.4/78/SR.22
Mansour, Riyad H. - A/C.4/78/SR.26
VETO (Agenda item 63)
Mansour, Riyad H. - A/78/PV.51; A/78/PV.59; A/78/PV.66; A/78/PV.74

State of Palestine. President
UN. GENERAL ASSEMBLY (78TH SESS. : 2023-2024)—GENERAL DEBATE (Agenda item 8)
Abbas, Mahmoud - A/78/PV.8
UN. GENERAL ASSEMBLY (78TH SESS. : 2023-2024)—SPECIAL STATEMENTS
Abbas, Mahmoud - A/78/PV.8

Sudan
ARMED CONFLICTS PREVENTION (Agenda item 31a)
Mohamed, Abuzied Shamseldin Ahmed - A/78/PV.72
CRIMES AGAINST HUMANITY (Agenda item 80)
Mohammed, Ammar Mohammed Mahmoud - A/C.6/78/SR.39
ECONOMIC SANCTIONS—INTERNATIONAL RELATIONS (Agenda item 28)
Mohamed, Abuzied Shamseldin Ahmed - A/78/PV.90
ELECTION VERIFICATION—UN (Agenda item 71b)
Idres, Nusaiba Hashim Mohamed Ali - A/C.3/78/SR.50
HUMAN RIGHTS—ERITREA (Agenda item 71c)
Bakhit, Badreldeen Bakhit Musa - A/C.3/78/SR.36
HUMAN RIGHTS—INTERNATIONAL INSTRUMENTS (Agenda item 71a)
Idres, Nusaiba Hashim Mohamed Ali - A/C.3/78/SR.26
HUMAN RIGHTS—TERRITORIES OCCUPIED BY ISRAEL (Agenda item 71c)
Idres, Nusaiba Hashim Mohamed Ali - A/C.3/78/SR.35
INFORMATION (Agenda item 53)
Mohamed, Abuzied Shamseldin Ahmed - A/C.4/78/SR.13
INTERNATIONAL JURISDICTION (Agenda item 84)
Mohammed, Ammar Mohammed Mahmoud - A/C.6/78/SR.12
INTERNATIONAL LAW—TRAINING PROGRAMMES (Agenda item 78)
Mohammed, Ammar Mohammed Mahmoud - A/C.6/78/SR.21
MINE CLEARANCE (Agenda item 46)
Mohamed, Abuzied Shamseldin Ahmed - A/C.4/78/SR.10
PEACEKEEPING OPERATIONS (Agenda item 51)
Mohamed, Abuzied Shamseldin Ahmed - A/C.4/78/SR.19
PEACEKEEPING OPERATIONS—CRIMINAL LIABILITY (Agenda item 76)
Mohammed, Ammar Mohammed Mahmoud - A/C.6/78/SR.8
RACIAL DISCRIMINATION—ELIMINATION (Agenda item 69a)
Idres, Nusaiba Hashim Mohamed Ali - A/C.3/78/SR.47

Sudan (continued)
RESPONSIBILITY TO PROTECT (Agenda item 129)
Mohammed, Ammar Mohammed Mahmoud - A/78/PV.99
RULE OF LAW (Agenda item 83)
Mohammed, Ammar Mohammed Mahmoud - A/C.6/78/SR.16
SPECIAL POLITICAL MISSIONS (Agenda item 52)
Mohamed, Abuzied Shamseldin Ahmed - A/C.4/78/SR.21
TERRITORIES OCCUPIED BY ISRAEL—HUMAN RIGHTS (Agenda item 50)
Mohamed, Abuzied Shamseldin Ahmed - A/C.4/78/SR.24
TERRORISM (Agenda item 109)
Mohammed, Ammar Mohammed Mahmoud - A/C.6/78/SR.2
UN—BUDGET (2024) (Agenda item 134)
Bakhit, Badreldeen Bakhit Musa - A/78/PV.50(Resumption1); A/C.5/78/SR.4; A/C.5/78/SR.23; A/C.5/78/SR.26/PartII
UN. COMMITTEE ON RELATIONS WITH THE HOST COUNTRY—REPORTS (Agenda item 161)
Idres, Nusaiba Hashim Mohamed Ali - A/C.6/78/SR.35
UN. GENERAL ASSEMBLY (78TH SESS. : 2023-2024). 1ST COMMITTEE—GENERAL DEBATE (Agenda item 8)
Mohamed, Faisal Abdelazim Salim - A/C.1/78/PV.5
UN. GENERAL ASSEMBLY (78TH SESS. : 2023-2024). 2ND COMMITTEE—GENERAL DEBATE (Agenda item 8)
Abuhaj, Hiba Jafaar Abubakr - A/C.2/78/SR.5
UN. HUMAN RIGHTS COUNCIL—REPORTS (Agenda item 66)
Idres, Nusaiba Hashim Mohamed Ali - A/C.3/78/SR.51
UN. INTERNATIONAL COURT OF JUSTICE—REPORTS (Agenda item 73)
Mohamed, Al-Harith Idriss al-Harith - A/78/PV.28
UN CHARTER—REPORTS (Agenda item 82)
Mohammed, Ammar Mohammed Mahmoud - A/C.6/78/SR.22
UN HIGH COMMISSIONER FOR REFUGEES—REPORTS (Agenda item 60)
Idres, Nusaiba Hashim Mohamed Ali - A/C.3/78/SR.44
UNRWA—ACTIVITIES (Agenda item 49)
Mohamed, Abuzied Shamseldin Ahmed - A/C.4/78/SR.23
VETO (Agenda item 63)
Mohamed, Abuzied Shamseldin Ahmed - A/78/PV.79

Sudan. President

UN. GENERAL ASSEMBLY (78TH SESS. : 2023-2024)—GENERAL DEBATE (Agenda item 8)
Al-Burhan, Abdel-Fattah Al-Burhan Abdelrahman - A/78/PV.9
UN. GENERAL ASSEMBLY (78TH SESS. : 2023-2024)—SPECIAL STATEMENTS
Al-Burhan, Abdel-Fattah Al-Burhan Abdelrahman - A/78/PV.9

Suriname

PEACE (Agenda item 14)
Sitaldin, Sunil A. - A/78/PV.76

Suriname. President

UN. GENERAL ASSEMBLY (78TH SESS. : 2023-2024)—GENERAL DEBATE (Agenda item 8)
Santokhi, Chandrikapersad - A/78/PV.6
UN. GENERAL ASSEMBLY (78TH SESS. : 2023-2024)—SPECIAL STATEMENTS
Santokhi, Chandrikapersad - A/78/PV.6

Sweden

ARMS RACE—OUTER SPACE (Agenda item 97a)
Escaig, Benjamin - A/C.1/78/PV.16
CRIMES AGAINST HUMANITY (Agenda item 80)
Fielding, Julia - A/C.6/78/SR.9
Janfalk, Disa - A/C.6/78/SR.38
DISARMAMENT AGREEMENTS—OUTER SPACE (Agenda item 97c)
Escaig, Benjamin - A/C.1/78/PV.16
EMERGENCY ASSISTANCE (Agenda item 72a)
Uexküll, Andreas von - A/78/PV.46
FREEDOM OF EXPRESSION (Agenda item 71b)
Schlyter, Charlotta - A/C.3/78/SR.19
HUMAN RIGHTS—INTERNATIONAL INSTRUMENTS (Agenda item 71a)
Eneström, Anna-Karin - A/C.3/78/SR.26
HUMAN RIGHTS—RUSSIAN FEDERATION (Agenda item 71c)
Uexküll, Andreas von - A/C.3/78/SR.37
INTERNATIONAL JURISDICTION (Agenda item 84)
Fielding, Julia - A/C.6/78/SR.12
NUCLEAR DISARMAMENT (Agenda item 99b)
Escaig, Benjamin - A/C.1/78/PV.11
NUCLEAR DISARMAMENT—VERIFICATION (Agenda item 99ee)
Escaig, Benjamin - A/C.1/78/PV.11
NUCLEAR NON-PROLIFERATION—INTERNATIONAL OBLIGATIONS (Agenda item 99w)
Escaig, Benjamin - A/C.1/78/PV.11

Sweden (continued)

NUCLEAR WEAPON TESTS—TREATIES (Agenda item 105)
Escaig, Benjamin - A/C.1/78/PV.11
OUTER SPACE—CONFIDENCE-BUILDING MEASURES (Agenda item 99v)
Escaig, Benjamin - A/C.1/78/PV.16
OUTER SPACE—PRINCIPLES (Agenda item 97d)
Escaig, Benjamin - A/C.1/78/PV.16
RACIAL DISCRIMINATION—ELIMINATION (Agenda item 69a)
Eneström, Anna-Karin - A/C.3/78/SR.47
SUMMARY EXECUTIONS (Agenda item 71b)
Uexküll, Andreas von - A/C.3/78/SR.31
UN. GENERAL ASSEMBLY (78TH SESS. : 2023-2024)—GENERAL DEBATE (Agenda item 8)
Billström, Tobias - A/78/PV.11
UN. GENERAL ASSEMBLY (78TH SESS. : 2023-2024). 1ST COMMITTEE—GENERAL DEBATE (Agenda item 8)
Nilsson, Ann-Sofie - A/C.1/78/PV.4

Switzerland

2030 AGENDA—PROGRAMME IMPLEMENTATION (Agenda item 18a)
Allet, Alexandra - A/C.2/78/SR.22
ADMINISTRATION OF JUSTICE (Agenda item 144)
Rathe, Fanny Elizabeth - A/C.6/78/SR.9
Schmied, Gina Andrea - A/C.5/78/SR.15
ARMED CONFLICTS PREVENTION (Agenda item 31a)
Baeriswyl, Pascale - A/78/PV.72
ARMS RACE—OUTER SPACE (Agenda item 97a)
Masmejean, Laurent - A/C.1/78/PV.17
BIOLOGICAL DIVERSITY—TREATIES (Agenda item 18f)
Allet, Alexandra - A/C.2/78/SR.25
BIOLOGICAL WEAPONS—TREATIES (Agenda item 106)
Thoeni, Julien - A/C.1/78/PV.15
CENTRAL ASIA—ZONES OF PEACE (Agenda item 64)
Hauri, Adrian - A/78/PV.85
CHEMICAL WEAPONS—TREATIES (Agenda item 99l)
Thoeni, Julien - A/C.1/78/PV.15
CLIMATE CHANGE (Agenda item 71b)
Hubatka, Pascal - A/C.3/78/SR.29
CLUSTER MUNITIONS (Agenda item 99dd)
Haegen, Laurin van der - A/C.1/78/PV.19
CONFERENCE AND MEETING SERVICES (Agenda item 137)
Danese, Aurora Maria - A/C.5/78/SR.7
CONVENTIONAL WEAPONS (Agenda item 99u)
Haegen, Laurin van der - A/C.1/78/PV.19

Switzerland (continued)

CONVENTIONAL WEAPONS—TREATIES (Agenda item 103)
Haegen, Laurin van der - A/C.1/78/PV.19
CRIMES AGAINST HUMANITY (Agenda item 80)
Rathe, Fanny Elizabeth - A/C.6/78/SR.10; A/C.6/78/SR.38; A/C.6/78/SR.40; A/C.6/78/SR.42; A/C.6/78/SR.43; A/C.6/78/SR.44; A/C.6/78/SR.45
DISARMAMENT—GENERAL AND COMPLETE (Agenda item 99)
Haegen, Laurin van der - A/C.1/78/PV.19
DISARMAMENT AGREEMENTS—OUTER SPACE (Agenda item 97c)
Anderegg, Julius - A/C.1/78/PV.27
DISASTER VICTIMS (Agenda item 86)
Chanda, Riccarda - A/C.6/78/SR.6
DISPLACED PERSONS (Agenda item 71b)
Desigis, Lucia Piera Giovanna - A/C.3/78/SR.32; A/C.3/78/SR.49
EMERGENCY ASSISTANCE (Agenda item 72a)
Desigis, Lucia Piera Giovanna - A/78/PV.47
Stillhart, Dominik - A/78/PV.46
ENVIRONMENT (Agenda item 71b)
Wagner, Valérie - A/C.3/78/SR.29
FINANCIAL FLOWS (Agenda item 16f)
Pauli, Aurore N'zassa Julianne - A/C.2/78/SR.23
FREEDOM OF EXPRESSION (Agenda item 71b)
Wagner, Valérie - A/C.3/78/SR.19
HEALTH (Agenda item 125)
Birrer, Jacqueline - A/78/PV.16; A/78/PV.48; A/78/PV.77
HIV/AIDS—DECLARATIONS (Agenda item 10)
Birrer, Jacqueline - A/78/PV.91
HUMAN RIGHTS (Agenda item 71)
Baeriswyl, Pascale - A/C.3/78/SR.16
HUMAN RIGHTS—AFGHANISTAN (Agenda item 71c)
Wagner, Valérie - A/C.3/78/SR.34
HUMAN RIGHTS—BELARUS (Agenda item 71c)
Segessemann, Tim - A/C.3/78/SR.37
HUMAN RIGHTS—DEMOCRATIC PEOPLE'S REPUBLIC OF KOREA (Agenda item 71c)
Hubatka, Pascal - A/C.3/78/SR.33
HUMAN RIGHTS—ETHIOPIA (Agenda item 71c)
Fontana, Barbara - A/C.3/78/SR.36
HUMAN RIGHTS—INTERNATIONAL INSTRUMENTS (Agenda item 71a)
Wagner, Valérie - A/C.3/78/SR.24
HUMAN RIGHTS—IRAN (ISLAMIC REPUBLIC OF) (Agenda item 71c)
Fontana, Barbara - A/C.3/78/SR.34
HUMAN RIGHTS—MYANMAR (Agenda item 71c)
Hubatka, Pascal - A/C.3/78/SR.33

Switzerland (continued)

HUMAN RIGHTS—RUSSIAN FEDERATION (Agenda item 71c)
Segessemann, Tim - A/C.3/78/SR.37
HUMAN RIGHTS—SOMALIA (Agenda item 71c)
Segessemann, Tim - A/C.3/78/SR.35
HUMAN RIGHTS—SYRIAN ARAB REPUBLIC (Agenda item 71c)
Hubatka, Pascal - A/C.3/78/SR.34
HUMAN RIGHTS—UKRAINE (Agenda item 71c)
Segessemann, Tim - A/C.3/78/SR.37
HUMAN RIGHTS ACTIVISTS (Agenda item 71b)
Wagner, Valérie - A/C.3/78/SR.19
HUMAN RIGHTS ADVANCEMENT (Agenda item 71b)
Wagner, Valérie - A/C.3/78/SR.24
INFORMATION—INTERNATIONAL SECURITY (Agenda item 94)
Anderegg, Julius - A/C.1/78/PV.29
Haegen, Laurin van der - A/C.1/78/PV.20
INFORMATION TECHNOLOGY—DEVELOPMENT (Agenda item 15)
Schlaepfer, Christian - A/C.2/78/SR.23
INTERNATIONAL CRIMINAL COURT—REPORTS (Agenda item 74)
Chanda, Riccarda - A/78/PV.22
INTERNATIONAL TRADE (Agenda item 16a)
Schlaepfer, Christian - A/C.2/78/SR.24
JOINT INSPECTION UNIT (Agenda item 141)
Danese, Aurora Maria - A/C.5/78/SR.29
LANDMINES—TREATIES (Agenda item 99m)
Haegen, Laurin van der - A/C.1/78/PV.19
MIDDLE EAST—NUCLEAR PROLIFERATION (Agenda item 102)
Anderegg, Julius - A/C.1/78/PV.26
MIGRANTS—PROTECTION (Agenda item 71b)
Allet, Alexandra - A/C.3/78/SR.23
MINORITIES (Agenda item 71b)
Eugster, Manuel - A/C.3/78/SR.39
NUCLEAR DISARMAMENT (Agenda item 99b)
Thoeni, Julien - A/C.1/78/PV.12
NUCLEAR DISARMAMENT—CONFERENCES (Agenda item 99aa)
Anderegg, Julius - A/C.1/78/PV.26
NUCLEAR DISARMAMENT—TREATY COMPLIANCE (Agenda item 99q)
Anderegg, Julius - A/C.1/78/PV.26
NUCLEAR NON-PROLIFERATION—INTERNATIONAL OBLIGATIONS (Agenda item 99w)
Thoeni, Julien - A/C.1/78/PV.12
NUCLEAR WEAPON TESTS—TREATIES (Agenda item 105)
Thoeni, Julien - A/C.1/78/PV.12

Switzerland (continued)

NUCLEAR WEAPONS—ELIMINATION (Agenda item 99z)
Anderegg, Julius - A/C.1/78/PV.26
NUCLEAR WEAPONS—TREATIES (Agenda item 99ff)
Anderegg, Julius - A/C.1/78/PV.26
OUTER SPACE—PEACEFUL USES—INTERNATIONAL COOPERATION (Agenda item 48)
Archinard, Natália - A/C.4/78/SR.16
OUTER SPACE—PRINCIPLES (Agenda item 97d)
Masmejean, Laurent - A/C.1/78/PV.17
PEACE (Agenda item 14)
Wagner, Valérie - A/78/PV.62; A/78/PV.88
PEACEKEEPING OPERATIONS (Agenda item 51)
Stritt, Marc-Alain - A/C.4/78/SR.19
PEACEKEEPING OPERATIONS—FINANCING (Agenda item 146)
Schmied, Gina Andrea - A/C.5/78/SR.35
PERSONNEL QUESTIONS—UN SYSTEM (Agenda item 142)
Schmied, Gina Andrea - A/C.5/78/SR.10
RACIAL DISCRIMINATION—ELIMINATION (Agenda item 69a)
Maric, Martina - A/C.3/78/SR.47
RESPONSIBILITY TO PROTECT (Agenda item 129)
Baeriswyl, Pascale - A/78/PV.96
RIGHT OF ASSEMBLY (Agenda item 71b)
Wagner, Valérie - A/C.3/78/SR.19
RIGHT TO THE TRUTH (Agenda item 71b)
Bless, Adrian - A/C.3/78/SR.22
RIGHTS OF THE CHILD (Agenda item 67)
Stricker, Julia - A/C.3/78/SR.11
Wagner, Valérie - A/C.3/78/SR.12
RULE OF LAW (Agenda item 83)
Zerbe, Yannick - A/C.6/78/SR.16
SOCIAL CONDITIONS (Agenda item 24b)
Berchtold, Aneschka - A/C.3/78/SR.3
SOCIAL DEVELOPMENT (Agenda item 24)
Wagner, Valérie - A/C.3/78/SR.3
SPECIAL POLITICAL MISSIONS (Agenda item 52)
Hauri, Adrian - A/C.4/78/SR.21
SUSTAINABLE DEVELOPMENT (Agenda item 18)
Schlaepfer, Christian - A/C.2/78/SR.24
TAXATION (Agenda item 16h)
Frey, Benjamin Jay - A/C.2/78/SR.25
TERRITORIES OCCUPIED BY ISRAEL—HUMAN RIGHTS (Agenda item 50)
Carpenter, Christoph - A/C.4/78/SR.26
TERRORISM—HUMAN RIGHTS (Agenda item 71b)
Maric, Martina - A/C.3/78/SR.51
Wägli, Christian - A/C.3/78/SR.31
TRAFFICKING IN PERSONS (Agenda item 71b)
Wagner, Valérie - A/C.3/78/SR.23

Switzerland (continued)

TRANSNATIONAL CORPORATIONS—HUMAN RIGHTS (Agenda item 71b)
Bless, Adrian - A/C.3/78/SR.21
TREATIES (Agenda item 87)
Rathe, Fanny Elizabeth - A/C.6/78/SR.20
UKRAINE—POLITICAL CONDITIONS (Agenda item 62)
Cassis, Ignazio - A/78/PV.56
UN—ADMINISTRATION (Agenda item 132)
Danese, Aurora Maria - A/C.5/78/SR.29
Schmied, Gina Andrea - A/C.5/78/SR.2
UN—BUDGET (2024) (Agenda item 134)
Baeriswyl, Pascale - A/C.5/78/SR.5; A/C.5/78/SR.14
Danese, Aurora Maria - A/C.5/78/SR.26/PartII
Schmied, Gina Andrea - A/C.5/78/SR.26/PartII; A/C.5/78/SR.28; A/C.5/78/SR.33
UN—FINANCIAL SITUATION (Agenda item 136)
Schmied, Gina Andrea - A/C.5/78/SR.6
UN—HUMAN RESOURCES MANAGEMENT (Agenda item 139)
Schmied, Gina Andrea - A/C.5/78/SR.27
UN—PROGRAMME PLANNING (Agenda item 135)
Baeriswyl, Pascale - A/C.5/78/SR.5
Schmied, Gina Andrea - A/C.5/78/SR.24
Thoeni, Julien - A/C.1/78/PV.10
UN. CONFERENCE ON DISARMAMENT—REPORTS (Agenda item 101a)
Greve, Silvia - A/C.1/78/PV.23
UN. GENERAL ASSEMBLY—WORK PROGRAMME (Agenda item 120)
Thoeni, Julien - A/C.1/78/PV.10
UN. GENERAL ASSEMBLY (78TH SESS. : 2023-2024)—OFFICERS (Agenda item 5)
Chanda, Riccarda - A/C.5/78/SR.1
UN. GENERAL ASSEMBLY (78TH SESS. : 2023-2024). 1ST COMMITTEE—GENERAL DEBATE (Agenda item 8)
Thoeni, Julien - A/C.1/78/PV.3
UN. GENERAL ASSEMBLY (78TH SESS. : 2023-2024). 2ND COMMITTEE—GENERAL DEBATE (Agenda item 8)
Hauri, Adrian - A/C.2/78/SR.2
UN. HUMAN RIGHTS COUNCIL—REPORTS (Agenda item 66)
Chanda, Riccarda - A/78/PV.23
Fontana, Barbara - A/C.3/78/SR.46
UN. INTERNATIONAL COURT OF JUSTICE—REPORTS (Agenda item 73)
Perrez, Franz - A/78/PV.20
UN. INTERNATIONAL LAW COMMISSION—REPORTS (Agenda item 79)
Rathe, Fanny Elizabeth - A/C.6/78/SR.24
UN. OFFICE OF INTERNAL OVERSIGHT SERVICES—REPORTS (Agenda item 143)
Schmied, Gina Andrea - A/C.5/78/SR.2

Switzerland (continued)

UN. SECURITY COUNCIL—MEMBERSHIP (Agenda item 121)
Baeriswyl, Pascale - A/78/PV.34
UN HIGH COMMISSIONER FOR REFUGEES—REPORTS (Agenda item 60)
Hauri, Adrian - A/C.3/78/SR.44
UNRWA—ACTIVITIES (Agenda item 49)
Carpenter, Christoph - A/C.4/78/SR.26
VETO (Agenda item 63)
Baeriswyl, Pascale - A/78/PV.3; A/78/PV.70; A/78/PV.78
Chanda, Riccarda - A/78/PV.60; A/78/PV.66; A/78/PV.68
Hauri, Adrian - A/78/PV.51; A/78/PV.75
WEAPONS—OUTER SPACE (Agenda item 97b)
Anderegg, Julius - A/C.1/78/PV.27
Masmejean, Laurent - A/C.1/78/PV.17
WOMEN'S ADVANCEMENT (Agenda item 25a)
Maric, Martina - A/C.3/78/SR.7
Wagner, Valérie - A/C.3/78/SR.8
WOMEN'S ADVANCEMENT—CONFERENCES (Agenda item 25b)
Maric, Martina - A/C.3/78/SR.7
Wagner, Valérie - A/C.3/78/SR.8
YOUTH (Agenda item 24b)
Berchtold, Aneschka - A/C.3/78/SR.3

Switzerland. President

UN. GENERAL ASSEMBLY (78TH SESS. : 2023-2024)—GENERAL DEBATE (Agenda item 8)
Berset, Alain - A/78/PV.4
UN. GENERAL ASSEMBLY (78TH SESS. : 2023-2024)—SPECIAL STATEMENTS
Berset, Alain - A/78/PV.4

Syrian Arab Republic

AGEING PERSONS (Agenda item 24b)
Altarsha, Elie - A/C.3/78/SR.1
ALBINISM (Agenda item 71b)
Altarsha, Elie - A/C.3/78/SR.27
ARMED CONFLICTS PREVENTION (Agenda item 31a)
Khaddour, Mhd. Riyad - A/78/PV.73
ARMS RACE—OUTER SPACE (Agenda item 97a)
Al Ashkar, Adib - A/C.1/78/PV.17
ARMS TRANSFERS—TREATIES (Agenda item 99x)
Al Ashkar, Adib - A/C.1/78/PV.28
BIOLOGICAL WEAPONS—TREATIES (Agenda item 106)
Al Ashkar, Adib - A/C.1/78/PV.15
CHEMICAL WEAPONS—TREATIES (Agenda item 99l)
Al Ashkar, Adib - A/C.1/78/PV.14; A/C.1/78/PV.15
Mustafa, Marah - A/C.1/78/PV.26

Syrian Arab Republic (continued)

CONVENTIONAL WEAPONS (Agenda item 99u)
Al Ashkar, Adib - A/C.1/78/PV.28
CRIME PREVENTION (Agenda item 107)
Altarsha, Elie - A/C.3/78/SR.6; A/C.3/78/SR.51
CRIMES AGAINST HUMANITY (Agenda item 80)
Khaddour, Mhd. Riyad - A/C.6/78/SR.11; A/C.6/78/SR.39; A/C.6/78/SR.40; A/C.6/78/SR.41; A/C.6/78/SR.42; A/C.6/78/SR.46
CUBA—UNITED STATES (Agenda item 38)
Altarsha, Elie - A/78/PV.24
DECOLONIZATION (Agenda item 58)
Baghdadi, Mohannad - A/C.4/78/SR.7
DISAPPEARANCE OF PERSONS (Agenda item 71b)
Altarsha, Elie - A/C.3/78/SR.22
DISARMAMENT—GENERAL AND COMPLETE (Agenda item 99)
Al Ashkar, Adib - A/C.1/78/PV.23; A/C.1/78/PV.30
DISASTER VICTIMS (Agenda item 86)
Khaddour, Mhd. Riyad - A/C.6/78/SR.6
DISPLACED PERSONS (Agenda item 71b)
Altarsha, Elie - A/C.3/78/SR.49
ECONOMIC SANCTIONS—INTERNATIONAL RELATIONS (Agenda item 28)
Aldahhak, Koussay Abduljabbar - A/78/PV.89
ELECTION VERIFICATION—UN (Agenda item 71b)
Altarsha, Elie - A/C.3/78/SR.50
EXTERNAL DEBT—HUMAN RIGHTS (Agenda item 71b)
Altarsha, Elie - A/C.3/78/SR.32
FREEDOM OF EXPRESSION (Agenda item 71b)
Altarsha, Elie - A/C.3/78/SR.19
HEALTH (Agenda item 125)
Al Nahhas, Wissam - A/78/PV.77
Altarsha, Elie - A/78/PV.41
Baghdadi, Mohannad - A/78/PV.16
Nayyal, Mhd. Majd - A/78/PV.48
HUMAN RIGHTS (Agenda item 71)
Altarsha, Elie - A/C.3/78/SR.16; A/C.3/78/SR.25
HUMAN RIGHTS—DEMOCRATIC PEOPLE'S REPUBLIC OF KOREA (Agenda item 71c)
Al Nahhas, Wissam - A/78/PV.50
Altarsha, Elie - A/C.3/78/SR.33; A/C.3/78/SR.53
HUMAN RIGHTS—ERITREA (Agenda item 71c)
Altarsha, Elie - A/C.3/78/SR.36
HUMAN RIGHTS—IRAN (ISLAMIC REPUBLIC OF) (Agenda item 71c)
Altarsha, Elie - A/C.3/78/SR.34; A/C.3/78/SR.53
HUMAN RIGHTS—REPORTS (Agenda item 71c)
Altarsha, Elie - A/C.3/78/SR.25
HUMAN RIGHTS—RUSSIAN FEDERATION (Agenda item 71c)
Altarsha, Elie - A/C.3/78/SR.37

Syrian Arab Republic (continued)

HUMAN RIGHTS—SYRIAN ARAB REPUBLIC (Agenda item 71c)
Al Nahhas, Wissam - A/78/PV.50
Altarsha, Elie - A/C.3/78/SR.34; A/C.3/78/SR.54
HUMAN RIGHTS—TERRITORIES OCCUPIED BY ISRAEL (Agenda item 71c)
Altarsha, Elie - A/C.3/78/SR.35
HUMAN RIGHTS—UKRAINE (Agenda item 71c)
Altarsha, Elie - A/C.3/78/SR.53
HUMAN RIGHTS ACTIVISTS (Agenda item 71b)
Altarsha, Elie - A/C.3/78/SR.56
HUMAN RIGHTS ADVANCEMENT (Agenda item 71b)
Altarsha, Elie - A/C.3/78/SR.52
IAEA—REPORTS (Agenda item 89)
Al Ashkar, Adib - A/78/PV.29; A/78/PV.30
INDIGENOUS PEOPLES (Agenda item 68a)
Altarsha, Elie - A/C.3/78/SR.15
INDIGENOUS PEOPLES—CONFERENCES (Agenda item 68b)
Altarsha, Elie - A/C.3/78/SR.15
INFORMATION—INTERNATIONAL SECURITY (Agenda item 94)
Al Ashkar, Adib - A/C.1/78/PV.29
INTERNATIONAL CRIMINAL COURT—REPORTS (Agenda item 74)
Khaddour, Mhd. Riyad - A/78/PV.21; A/78/PV.25
INTERNATIONAL JURISDICTION (Agenda item 84)
Khaddour, Mhd. Riyad - A/C.6/78/SR.12; A/C.6/78/SR.13
INTERNATIONAL TRADE (Agenda item 16a)
Al Nahhas, Wissam - A/C.2/78/SR.8
Altarsha, Elie - A/C.2/78/SR.24
LAW OF THE SEA (Agenda item 75a)
Khaddour, Mhd. Riyad - A/78/PV.44
MARINE ECOSYSTEMS—BIOLOGICAL DIVERSITY (Agenda item 75c)
Khaddour, Mhd. Riyad - A/78/PV.44
MEDITERRANEAN REGION—REGIONAL SECURITY (Agenda item 104)
Al Ashkar, Adib - A/C.1/78/PV.29
MIDDLE EAST—NUCLEAR PROLIFERATION (Agenda item 102)
Al Ashkar, Adib - A/C.1/78/PV.13; A/C.1/78/PV.26
MIDDLE EAST—NUCLEAR-WEAPON-FREE ZONES (Agenda item 95)
Al Ashkar, Adib - A/C.1/78/PV.15; A/C.1/78/PV.21; A/C.1/78/PV.22; A/C.1/78/PV.26
MIDDLE EAST SITUATION (Agenda item 34)
Dandy, Alhakam - A/78/PV.40
MIGRANTS—PROTECTION (Agenda item 71b)
Altarsha, Elie - A/C.3/78/SR.23

Syrian Arab Republic (continued)

MILLENNIUM SUMMIT—CONFERENCES (Agenda item 117)
Dandy, Alhakam - A/78/PV.15
MINE CLEARANCE (Agenda item 46)
Mustafa, Marah - A/C.4/78/SR.10
NUCLEAR DISARMAMENT (Agenda item 99b)
Al Ashkar, Adib - A/C.1/78/PV.11; A/C.1/78/PV.14
PEACE (Agenda item 14)
Aldahhak, Koussay Abduljabbar - A/78/PV.82
Alnwelati, Mohammad Feras - A/78/PV.62
PEACEKEEPING OPERATIONS (Agenda item 51)
Baghdadi, Mohannad - A/C.4/78/SR.19
PERSONS WITH DISABILITIES—HUMAN RIGHTS (Agenda item 71a)
Altarsha, Elie - A/C.3/78/SR.38; A/C.3/78/SR.51
POVERTY—HUMAN RIGHTS (Agenda item 71b)
Altarsha, Elie - A/C.3/78/SR.30
RACIAL DISCRIMINATION—ELIMINATION (Agenda item 69a)
Al Nahhas, Wissam - A/78/PV.50
Altarsha, Elie - A/78/PV.103; A/C.3/78/SR.47
RESPONSIBILITY TO PROTECT (Agenda item 129)
Alshahin, Essam - A/78/PV.99
RIGHT TO DEVELOPMENT (Agenda item 71b)
Altarsha, Elie - A/C.3/78/SR.20
RIGHT TO EDUCATION (Agenda item 71b)
Altarsha, Elie - A/C.3/78/SR.27
RIGHT TO FOOD (Agenda item 71b)
Altarsha, Elie - A/C.3/78/SR.30
RIGHT TO HEALTH (Agenda item 71b)
Altarsha, Elie - A/C.3/78/SR.39
RIGHT TO PRIVACY (Agenda item 71b)
Altarsha, Elie - A/C.3/78/SR.21
RIGHTS OF THE CHILD (Agenda item 67)
Altarsha, Elie - A/C.3/78/SR.11; A/C.3/78/SR.12; A/C.3/78/SR.13; A/C.3/78/SR.55
RULE OF LAW (Agenda item 83)
Khaddour, Mhd. Riyad - A/C.6/78/SR.18; A/C.6/78/SR.37
RURAL WOMEN (Agenda item 25a)
Altarsha, Elie - A/C.3/78/SR.49
SANCTIONS—INTERNATIONAL RELATIONS (Agenda item 71b)
Alnwelati, Mohammad Feras - A/C.3/78/SR.28
SELF-DETERMINATION OF PEOPLES (Agenda item 70)
Altarsha, Elie - A/C.3/78/SR.42; A/C.3/78/SR.49
SOCIAL DEVELOPMENT (Agenda item 24)
Altarsha, Elie - A/C.3/78/SR.3
SPORTS—OLYMPIC GAMES (Agenda item 11)
Mustafa, Marah - A/78/PV.38
STRADDLING FISH STOCKS (Agenda item 75b)
Khaddour, Mhd. Riyad - A/78/PV.44

Syrian Arab Republic (continued)

SUSTAINABLE DEVELOPMENT (Agenda item 18)
Al Nahhas, Wissam - A/C.2/78/SR.13; A/C.2/78/SR.22; A/C.2/78/SR.24
TERRITORIES OCCUPIED BY ISRAEL—HUMAN RIGHTS (Agenda item 50)
Baghdadi, Mohannad - A/C.4/78/SR.25; A/C.4/78/SR.26
TERRITORIES OCCUPIED BY ISRAEL—NATURAL RESOURCES (Agenda item 59)
Al Nahhas, Wissam - A/C.2/78/SR.19; A/C.2/78/SR.21
TERRORISM (Agenda item 109)
Khaddour, Mhd. Riyad - A/C.6/78/SR.3
TERRORISM—HUMAN RIGHTS (Agenda item 71b)
Altarsha, Elie - A/C.3/78/SR.31
TORTURE AND OTHER CRUEL TREATMENT (Agenda item 71a)
Altarsha, Elie - A/C.3/78/SR.18
TRAFFICKING IN PERSONS (Agenda item 71b)
Altarsha, Elie - A/C.3/78/SR.23
UKRAINE—POLITICAL CONDITIONS (Agenda item 62)
Aldahhak, Koussay Abduljabbar - A/78/PV.58
Mustafa, Marah - A/78/PV.99
UN—BUDGET (2024) (Agenda item 134)
Al-mansour, Osama - A/78/PV.73; A/C.5/78/SR.3; A/C.5/78/SR.5; A/C.5/78/SR.26/PartII; A/C.5/78/SR.28; A/C.5/78/SR.34
UN—PROGRAMME PLANNING (Agenda item 135)
Al-mansour, Osama - A/78/PV.50(Resumption1); A/C.5/78/SR.5; A/C.5/78/SR.24
UN. COMMITTEE ON RELATIONS WITH THE HOST COUNTRY—REPORTS (Agenda item 161)
Khaddour, Mhd. Riyad - A/C.6/78/SR.35
UN. GENERAL ASSEMBLY (78TH SESS. : 2023-2024)—GENERAL DEBATE (Agenda item 8)
Sabbagh, Bassam - A/78/PV.14
UN. GENERAL ASSEMBLY (78TH SESS. : 2023-2024). 1ST COMMITTEE—GENERAL DEBATE (Agenda item 8)
Al Ashkar, Adib - A/C.1/78/PV.3; A/C.1/78/PV.4; A/C.1/78/PV.5; A/C.1/78/PV.6; A/C.1/78/PV.7; A/C.1/78/PV.8
UN. GENERAL ASSEMBLY (78TH SESS. : 2023-2024). 2ND COMMITTEE—GENERAL DEBATE (Agenda item 8)
Al Nahhas, Wissam - A/C.2/78/SR.3
UN. HUMAN RIGHTS COUNCIL—REPORTS (Agenda item 66)
Altarsha, Elie - A/C.3/78/SR.46; A/C.3/78/SR.51
UN. SECURITY COUNCIL—MEMBERSHIP (Agenda item 121)
Khaddour, Mhd. Riyad - A/78/PV.36

Syrian Arab Republic (continued)

UN. SECURITY COUNCIL—REPORTS (Agenda item 26)
Alshahin, Essam - A/78/PV.93
UN CHARTER—REPORTS (Agenda item 82)
Khaddour, Mhd. Riyad - A/C.6/78/SR.22
UN CONFERENCES (Agenda item 13)
Dandy, Alhakam - A/78/PV.15
UN DISENGAGEMENT OBSERVER FORCE—FINANCING (Agenda item 156a)
Al-mansour, Osama - A/C.5/78/SR.35
UN HIGH COMMISSIONER FOR REFUGEES—REPORTS (Agenda item 60)
Alnwelati, Mohammad Feras - A/C.3/78/SR.45
Altarsha, Elie - A/C.3/78/SR.44
UNRWA—ACTIVITIES (Agenda item 49)
Baghdadi, Mohannad - A/C.4/78/SR.23; A/C.4/78/SR.26
VETO (Agenda item 63)
Al Ashkar, Adib - A/78/PV.78
Aldahhak, Koussay Abduljabbar - A/78/PV.60; A/78/PV.67; A/78/PV.75
Dandy, Alhakam - A/78/PV.52; A/78/PV.68
WEAPONS OF MASS DESTRUCTION—TERRORISM (Agenda item 99s)
Al Ashkar, Adib - A/C.1/78/PV.15
WESTERN SAHARA QUESTION (Agenda item 58)
Baghdadi, Mohannad - A/C.4/78/SR.7
WOMEN'S ADVANCEMENT (Agenda item 25a)
Altarsha, Elie - A/C.3/78/SR.7; A/C.3/78/SR.9
WOMEN'S ADVANCEMENT—CONFERENCES (Agenda item 25b)
Altarsha, Elie - A/C.3/78/SR.7; A/C.3/78/SR.9

Tajikistan

FAMILY (Agenda item 24b)
Gulov, Golibjon - A/C.3/78/SR.2
FOOD SECURITY (Agenda item 23a)
Hasanova, Tahmina - A/C.2/78/SR.17
HUMAN RIGHTS—INTERNATIONAL INSTRUMENTS (Agenda item 71a)
Gulov, Golibjon - A/C.3/78/SR.26
PERSONS WITH DISABILITIES (Agenda item 24b)
Gulov, Golibjon - A/C.3/78/SR.2
POVERTY—INTERNATIONAL DECADES (Agenda item 21a)
Hasanova, Tahmina - A/C.2/78/SR.17
RURAL POVERTY (Agenda item 21b)
Hasanova, Tahmina - A/C.2/78/SR.17
SOCIAL DEVELOPMENT (Agenda item 24)
Gulov, Golibjon - A/C.3/78/SR.2
SUSTAINABLE DEVELOPMENT (Agenda item 18)
Hasanova, Tahmina - A/C.2/78/SR.15

Tajikistan (continued)

UN. GENERAL ASSEMBLY (78TH SESS. : 2023-2024). 1ST COMMITTEE—GENERAL DEBATE (Agenda item 8)
Bobozoda, Amriyo - A/C.1/78/PV.7
UN. GENERAL ASSEMBLY (78TH SESS. : 2023-2024). 2ND COMMITTEE—GENERAL DEBATE (Agenda item 8)
Hasanova, Tahmina - A/C.2/78/SR.3
UN CONFERENCES (Agenda item 13)
Hikmat, Jonibek Ismoil - A/78/PV.77
YOUTH (Agenda item 24b)
Gulov, Golibjon - A/C.3/78/SR.2

Tajikistan. President

UN. GENERAL ASSEMBLY (78TH SESS. : 2023-2024)—GENERAL DEBATE (Agenda item 8)
Rahmon, Emomali - A/78/PV.6
UN. GENERAL ASSEMBLY (78TH SESS. : 2023-2024)—SPECIAL STATEMENTS
Rahmon, Emomali - A/78/PV.6

Teach the Children International (Organization)

WESTERN SAHARA QUESTION (Agenda item 58)
Huff, Nancy - A/C.4/78/SR.4

Thailand

AFRICA—NUCLEAR-WEAPON-FREE ZONES (Agenda item 92)
Khundee, Wichayaporn - A/C.1/78/PV.26
AFRICA—SUSTAINABLE DEVELOPMENT—PARTNERSHIP (Agenda item 65a)
Chindawongse, Suriya - A/78/PV.18
BIOLOGICAL WEAPONS—TREATIES (Agenda item 106)
Khundee, Wichayaporn - A/C.1/78/PV.15
CHEMICAL WEAPONS—TREATIES (Agenda item 99l)
Khundee, Wichayaporn - A/C.1/78/PV.15
CLIMATE (Agenda item 18d)
Phuaknuem, Kanok - A/C.2/78/SR.13
CONVENTIONAL WEAPONS (Agenda item 99u)
Khundee, Wichayaporn - A/C.1/78/PV.18
CRIME PREVENTION (Agenda item 107)
Hsieh, Nichamon May - A/C.3/78/SR.5
CRIMES AGAINST HUMANITY (Agenda item 80)
Hanlumyuang, Thararut - A/C.6/78/SR.10
Jantarasombat, Panpailin - A/C.6/78/SR.42; A/C.6/78/SR.43
CYBERCRIME (Agenda item 108)
Hsieh, Nichamon May - A/C.3/78/SR.5
DEVELOPMENT FINANCE (Agenda item 16b)
Sapkul, Louismongkol - A/C.2/78/SR.9

Thailand (continued)

DISARMAMENT—GENERAL AND COMPLETE (Agenda item 99)
Khundee, Wichayaporn - A/C.1/78/PV.26
DISASTER PREVENTION (Agenda item 18c)
Phuaknuem, Kanok - A/C.2/78/SR.13
DISASTER VICTIMS (Agenda item 86)
Hanlumyuang, Thararut - A/C.6/78/SR.6
ECONOMIC COOPERATION AMONG DEVELOPING COUNTRIES (Agenda item 22b)
Suwantra, Maes - A/C.2/78/SR.18
FOOD SECURITY (Agenda item 23a)
Sangkhapreecha, Kantapon - A/C.2/78/SR.16
HEALTH (Agenda item 125)
Chindawongse, Suriya - A/78/PV.41
HIV/AIDS—DECLARATIONS (Agenda item 10)
Chaivaivid, Cherdchai - A/78/PV.91
HUMAN RIGHTS—MYANMAR (Agenda item 71c)
Chindawongse, Suriya - A/C.3/78/SR.33; A/C.3/78/SR.53
HUMAN RIGHTS ADVANCEMENT (Agenda item 71b)
Chindawongse, Suriya - A/C.3/78/SR.25
INFORMATION (Agenda item 53)
Norapoompipat, Sorawut - A/C.4/78/SR.12
INFORMATION—INTERNATIONAL SECURITY (Agenda item 94)
Hanlumyuang, Thararut - A/C.1/78/PV.20
INTERNATIONAL JURISDICTION (Agenda item 84)
Chindawongse, Suriya - A/C.6/78/SR.12
INTERNATIONAL LAW—TRAINING PROGRAMMES (Agenda item 78)
Sresthabutr, Hataipat - A/C.6/78/SR.21
INTERNATIONAL TRADE (Agenda item 16a)
Sapkul, Louismongkol - A/C.2/78/SR.9
LANDMINES—TREATIES (Agenda item 99m)
Khundee, Wichayaporn - A/C.1/78/PV.18
MINE CLEARANCE (Agenda item 46)
Jeranukosol, Natsaran - A/C.4/78/SR.10
NUCLEAR DISARMAMENT (Agenda item 99b)
Chindawongse, Suriya - A/C.1/78/PV.13
NUCLEAR NON-PROLIFERATION—INTERNATIONAL OBLIGATIONS (Agenda item 99w)
Chindawongse, Suriya - A/C.1/78/PV.13
NUCLEAR WEAPON TESTS—TREATIES (Agenda item 105)
Chindawongse, Suriya - A/C.1/78/PV.13
NUCLEAR WEAPONS—TREATIES (Agenda item 99ff)
Chindawongse, Suriya - A/C.1/78/PV.13
NUCLEAR WEAPONS USE—TREATIES (Agenda item 100a)
Khundee, Wichayaporn - A/C.1/78/PV.26

Thailand (continued)

OPERATIONAL ACTIVITIES—UN SYSTEM (Agenda item 22a)
Suwantra, Maes - A/C.2/78/SR.18
OUTER SPACE—PEACEFUL USES—INTERNATIONAL COOPERATION (Agenda item 48)
Vichankaiyakij, Vathayudh - A/C.4/78/SR.15
PEACE (Agenda item 14)
Vichankaiyakij, Vathayudh - A/78/PV.76; A/78/PV.82
PEACEKEEPING OPERATIONS (Agenda item 51)
Hanlumyuang, Thararut - A/C.4/78/SR.18
POVERTY—INTERNATIONAL DECADES (Agenda item 21a)
Sangkhapreecha, Kantapon - A/C.2/78/SR.16
RIGHT TO HEALTH (Agenda item 71b)
Chindawongse, Suriya - A/C.3/78/SR.25
RIGHTS OF THE CHILD (Agenda item 67)
Treedara, Jakarin - A/C.3/78/SR.11
RULE OF LAW (Agenda item 83)
Chindawongse, Suriya - A/C.6/78/SR.16
RURAL POVERTY (Agenda item 21b)
Sangkhapreecha, Kantapon - A/C.2/78/SR.16
SOUTH-EAST ASIA—NUCLEAR-WEAPON-FREE ZONES (Agenda item 99y)
Chindawongse, Suriya - A/C.1/78/PV.13
TERRORISM (Agenda item 109)
Vichankaiyakij, Vathayudh - A/C.6/78/SR.2
UKRAINE—POLITICAL CONDITIONS (Agenda item 62)
Chindawongse, Suriya - A/78/PV.58
UN—BUDGET (2024) (Agenda item 134)
Suwwannikha, Surat - A/C.5/78/SR.12
UN. ECONOMIC AND SOCIAL COUNCIL—REPORTS (Agenda item 9)
Chindawongse, Suriya - A/78/PV.33
UN. GENERAL ASSEMBLY—WORK PROGRAMME (Agenda item 120)
Chindawongse, Suriya - A/78/PV.32
UN. GENERAL ASSEMBLY (78TH SESS. : 2023-2024)—OFFICERS (Agenda item 5)
Vichankaiyakij, Vathayudh - A/C.5/78/SR.1
UN. GENERAL ASSEMBLY (78TH SESS. : 2023-2024). 1ST COMMITTEE—GENERAL DEBATE (Agenda item 8)
Chindawongse, Suriya - A/C.1/78/PV.3
UN. GENERAL ASSEMBLY (78TH SESS. : 2023-2024). 2ND COMMITTEE—GENERAL DEBATE (Agenda item 8)
Chindawongse, Suriya - A/C.2/78/SR.3
UN. INTERNATIONAL COURT OF JUSTICE—REPORTS (Agenda item 73)
Tang, Suphanvasa Chotikajan - A/C.6/78/SR.26
UN. INTERNATIONAL LAW COMMISSION—REPORTS (Agenda item 79)
Jantarasombat, Panpailin - A/C.6/78/SR.30; A/C.6/78/SR.31
Tang, Suphanvasa Chotikajan - A/C.6/78/SR.25

Thailand (continued)

UN. SECURITY COUNCIL—MEMBERSHIP (Agenda item 121)
Chindawongse, Suriya - A/78/PV.34
UN COMMISSION ON INTERNATIONAL TRADE LAW—REPORTS (Agenda item 77)
Nachom, Yaninee - A/C.6/78/SR.14
UN CONFERENCES (Agenda item 13)
Chindawongse, Suriya - A/78/PV.33
UN HIGH COMMISSIONER FOR REFUGEES—REPORTS (Agenda item 60)
Vichankaiyakij, Vathayudh - A/C.3/78/SR.44
UN RESOLUTIONS—IMPLEMENTATION (Agenda item 119)
Chindawongse, Suriya - A/78/PV.32
UNRWA—ACTIVITIES (Agenda item 49)
Chindawongse, Suriya - A/C.4/78/SR.22
VETO (Agenda item 63)
Chindawongse, Suriya - A/78/PV.51; A/78/PV.60; A/78/PV.75
Vichankaiyakij, Vathayudh - A/78/PV.67
WOMEN'S ADVANCEMENT (Agenda item 25a)
Diloknawarit, Ornwara - A/C.3/78/SR.8
WOMEN'S ADVANCEMENT—CONFERENCES (Agenda item 25b)
Diloknawarit, Ornwara - A/C.3/78/SR.8
YOUTH (Agenda item 24b)
Akanitvong, Pataschol - A/C.3/78/SR.2
Juntree, Paranut - A/C.3/78/SR.2

Thailand. Prime Minister

UN. GENERAL ASSEMBLY (78TH SESS. : 2023-2024)—GENERAL DEBATE (Agenda item 8)
Thavisin, Srettha - A/78/PV.10
UN. GENERAL ASSEMBLY (78TH SESS. : 2023-2024)—SPECIAL STATEMENTS
Thavisin, Srettha - A/78/PV.10

Timor-Leste

BIOLOGICAL DIVERSITY—TREATIES (Agenda item 18f)
Nunes, Karlito - A/C.2/78/SR.15
CUBA—UNITED STATES (Agenda item 38)
Nunes, Karlito - A/78/PV.26
DECOLONIZATION (Agenda item 58)
Nunes, Karlito - A/C.4/78/SR.2
DEVELOPMENT FINANCE—CONFERENCES (Agenda item 17)
Soares, Dionísio Da Costa Babo - A/78/PV.90
ECONOMIC SANCTIONS—INTERNATIONAL RELATIONS (Agenda item 28)
Soares, Dionísio Da Costa Babo - A/78/PV.90
FALKLAND ISLANDS (MALVINAS) QUESTION (Agenda item 42)
Nunes, Karlito - A/C.4/78/SR.2
FOOD SECURITY (Agenda item 23a)
Barros, Sebastiana - A/C.2/78/SR.18

Timor-Leste (continued)

GIBRALTAR QUESTION (Agenda item 58)
Nunes, Karlito - A/C.4/78/SR.2
HUMAN RIGHTS—MYANMAR (Agenda item 71c)
Nunes, Karlito - A/C.3/78/SR.25
HUMAN RIGHTS ADVANCEMENT (Agenda item 71b)
Nunes, Karlito - A/C.3/78/SR.25
INFORMATION—INTERNATIONAL SECURITY (Agenda item 94)
Sousa, Ivens Gusmao de - A/C.1/78/PV.20
LANDLOCKED DEVELOPING COUNTRIES—CONFERENCES (Agenda item 20b)
Nunes, Karlito - A/C.2/78/SR.7
LEAST DEVELOPED COUNTRIES—CONFERENCES (Agenda item 20a)
Nunes, Karlito - A/C.2/78/SR.7
MILLENNIUM SUMMIT—CONFERENCES (Agenda item 117)
Soares, Dionísio Da Costa Babo - A/78/PV.102
NUCLEAR DISARMAMENT (Agenda item 99b)
Sousa, Ivens Gusmao de - A/C.1/78/PV.13
NUCLEAR NON-PROLIFERATION—INTERNATIONAL OBLIGATIONS (Agenda item 99w)
Sousa, Ivens Gusmao de - A/C.1/78/PV.13
NUCLEAR WEAPONS—TREATIES (Agenda item 99ff)
Sousa, Ivens Gusmao de - A/C.1/78/PV.13
PEACE (Agenda item 14)
Soares, Dionísio Da Costa Babo - A/78/PV.77
PEACEBUILDING (Agenda item 61)
Chaves, Joaquim José Costa - A/78/PV.101
PEACEKEEPING OPERATIONS (Agenda item 51)
Chaves, Joaquim José Costa - A/C.4/78/SR.19
PERSONS WITH DISABILITIES—HUMAN RIGHTS (Agenda item 71a)
Sousa, Maria Lourdes de - A/C.3/78/SR.38
POVERTY—INTERNATIONAL DECADES (Agenda item 21a)
Barros, Sebastiana - A/C.2/78/SR.18
RACIAL DISCRIMINATION—PROGRAMMES OF ACTION (Agenda item 69b)
Sousa, Maria Lourdes de - A/C.3/78/SR.40
RESPONSIBILITY TO PROTECT (Agenda item 129)
Soares, Dionísio Da Costa Babo - A/78/PV.96
RIGHTS OF THE CHILD (Agenda item 67)
Nunes, Karlito - A/C.3/78/SR.13
SMALL ARMS—ILLICIT TRAFFIC (Agenda item 99p)
Alves, Nuno Moniz - A/C.1/78/PV.18
SMALL ARMS—ILLICIT TRAFFIC—ASSISTANCE (Agenda item 99n)
Alves, Nuno Moniz - A/C.1/78/PV.18
SUSTAINABLE DEVELOPMENT (Agenda item 18)
Nunes, Karlito - A/C.2/78/SR.15

Timor-Leste (continued)

UN. GENERAL ASSEMBLY (78TH SESS. : 2023-2024). 1ST COMMITTEE—GENERAL DEBATE (Agenda item 8)
Sousa, Ivens Gusmao de - A/C.1/78/PV.5
UN. GENERAL ASSEMBLY (78TH SESS. : 2023-2024). 2ND COMMITTEE—GENERAL DEBATE (Agenda item 8)
Nunes, Karlito - A/C.2/78/SR.4
UN. PEACEBUILDING COMMISSION—REPORTS (Agenda item 27)
Chaves, Joaquim José Costa - A/78/PV.101
UN. PEACEBUILDING FUND—REPORTS (Agenda item 111)
Chaves, Joaquim José Costa - A/78/PV.101
UN. SECURITY COUNCIL—REPORTS (Agenda item 26)
Soares, Dionísio Da Costa Babo - A/78/PV.94
UN CONFERENCES (Agenda item 13)
Soares, Dionísio Da Costa Babo - A/78/PV.102
VETO (Agenda item 63)
Soares, Dionísio Da Costa Babo - A/78/PV.67
WESTERN SAHARA QUESTION (Agenda item 58)
Nunes, Karlito - A/C.4/78/SR.2
WOMEN'S ADVANCEMENT (Agenda item 25a)
Nunes, Karlito - A/C.3/78/SR.10
WOMEN'S ADVANCEMENT—CONFERENCES (Agenda item 25b)
Nunes, Karlito - A/C.3/78/SR.10

Timor-Leste. President

UN. GENERAL ASSEMBLY (78TH SESS. : 2023-2024)—GENERAL DEBATE (Agenda item 8)
Ramos-Horta, José - A/78/PV.8
UN. GENERAL ASSEMBLY (78TH SESS. : 2023-2024)—SPECIAL STATEMENTS
Ramos-Horta, José - A/78/PV.8

Togo

ARMS TRANSFERS—TREATIES (Agenda item 99x)
Tchalare, Abd-el Kader Yasmin - A/C.1/78/PV.19
FOOD SECURITY (Agenda item 23a)
Debataba, Yawa - A/C.2/78/SR.17
HUMAN RIGHTS—INTERNATIONAL INSTRUMENTS (Agenda item 71a)
Baka, Sondou - A/C.3/78/SR.26
HUMAN RIGHTS ADVANCEMENT (Agenda item 71b)
Baka, Sondou - A/C.3/78/SR.26
INFORMATION—INTERNATIONAL SECURITY (Agenda item 94)
Tchalare, Abd-el Kader Yasmin - A/C.1/78/PV.21
INTERNATIONAL JURISDICTION (Agenda item 84)
Ouro-bodi, Tchakpide - A/C.6/78/SR.13

Togo (continued)

NUCLEAR DISARMAMENT (Agenda item 99b)
Ouro-Tagba, Tawfic - A/C.1/78/PV.12
NUCLEAR NON-PROLIFERATION—INTERNATIONAL OBLIGATIONS (Agenda item 99w)
Ouro-Tagba, Tawfic - A/C.1/78/PV.12
NUCLEAR WEAPON TESTS—TREATIES (Agenda item 105)
Ouro-Tagba, Tawfic - A/C.1/78/PV.12
PEACE (Agenda item 14)
Akakpo, Koffi - A/78/PV.76
PEACEKEEPING OPERATIONS (Agenda item 51)
Medzinyuie, Edem Kodzovi - A/C.4/78/SR.18
POVERTY—INTERNATIONAL DECADES (Agenda item 21a)
Debataba, Yawa - A/C.2/78/SR.17
RACIAL DISCRIMINATION—ELIMINATION (Agenda item 69a)
Tchalare, Abd-el Kader Yasmin - A/78/PV.103
RURAL POVERTY (Agenda item 21b)
Debataba, Yawa - A/C.2/78/SR.17
SMALL ARMS—ILLICIT TRAFFIC (Agenda item 99p)
Tchalare, Abd-el Kader Yasmin - A/C.1/78/PV.19
SMALL ARMS—ILLICIT TRAFFIC—ASSISTANCE (Agenda item 99n)
Tchalare, Abd-el Kader Yasmin - A/C.1/78/PV.19
TERRORISM (Agenda item 109)
Ouro-bodi, Tchakpide - A/C.6/78/SR.4
UN. GENERAL ASSEMBLY (78TH SESS. : 2023-2024)—GENERAL DEBATE (Agenda item 8)
Dussey, Robert - A/78/PV.9
UN SYSTEM—STRENGTHENING (Agenda item 122)
Akakpo, Koffi - A/78/PV.99
WESTERN SAHARA QUESTION (Agenda item 58)
Akakpo, Koffi - A/C.4/78/SR.6

Tonga

DISASTER VICTIMS (Agenda item 86)
Vea, Jeanett - A/C.6/78/SR.6
SMALL ISLAND DEVELOPING STATES—PROGRAMMES OF ACTION (Agenda item 18b)
Va'inga Tone, Viliami - A/78/PV.100
UN. GENERAL ASSEMBLY (78TH SESS. : 2023-2024). 2ND COMMITTEE—GENERAL DEBATE (Agenda item 8)
Vea, Jeanett - A/C.2/78/SR.6
UN. INTERNATIONAL LAW COMMISSION—REPORTS (Agenda item 79)
Va'inga Tone, Viliami - A/C.6/78/SR.28

Tonga. Prime Minister

UN. GENERAL ASSEMBLY (78TH SESS. : 2023-2024)—GENERAL DEBATE (Agenda item 8)
Sovaleni, Siaosi 'Ofakivahafolau - A/78/PV.11
UN. GENERAL ASSEMBLY (78TH SESS. : 2023-2024)—SPECIAL STATEMENTS
Sovaleni, Siaosi 'Ofakivahafolau - A/78/PV.11

Trinidad and Tobago

CUBA—UNITED STATES (Agenda item 38)
Barman, Ordell Cedric - A/78/PV.24
DEVELOPMENT FINANCE (Agenda item 16b)
Budhu, Vladamir - A/C.2/78/SR.9
DEVELOPMENT FINANCE—CONFERENCES (Agenda item 17)
Budhu, Vladamir - A/C.2/78/SR.9
INTERNATIONAL CRIMINAL COURT—REPORTS (Agenda item 74)
Abraham, Devita - A/78/PV.22
MACROECONOMIC POLICY (Agenda item 16)
Budhu, Vladamir - A/C.2/78/SR.9
TAXATION (Agenda item 16h)
Budhu, Vladamir - A/C.2/78/SR.9
UN. GENERAL ASSEMBLY (78TH SESS. : 2023-2024). 2ND COMMITTEE—GENERAL DEBATE (Agenda item 8)
Budhu, Vladamir - A/C.2/78/SR.5

Trinidad and Tobago. Prime Minister

UN. GENERAL ASSEMBLY (78TH SESS. : 2023-2024)—GENERAL DEBATE (Agenda item 8)
Rowley, Keith - A/78/PV.9
UN. GENERAL ASSEMBLY (78TH SESS. : 2023-2024)—SPECIAL STATEMENTS
Rowley, Keith - A/78/PV.9

Tunisia

CRIMES AGAINST HUMANITY (Agenda item 80)
Ben Lagha, Adel - A/C.6/78/SR.10; A/C.6/78/SR.39
HUMAN RIGHTS—INTERNATIONAL INSTRUMENTS (Agenda item 71a)
Bessadok, Marwa Jabou - A/C.3/78/SR.26
HUMAN RIGHTS—TERRITORIES OCCUPIED BY ISRAEL (Agenda item 71c)
Bessadok, Marwa Jabou - A/C.3/78/SR.35
PALESTINE QUESTION (Agenda item 35)
Ladeb, Tarek - A/78/PV.40
PEACE (Agenda item 14)
Ladeb, Tarek - A/78/PV.62; A/78/PV.82
PEACEKEEPING OPERATIONS (Agenda item 51)
Salah, Yassine - A/C.4/78/SR.19

Tunisia (continued)

RACIAL DISCRIMINATION—ELIMINATION (Agenda item 69a)
Bessadok, Marwa Jabou - A/78/PV.103
RIGHTS OF THE CHILD (Agenda item 67)
Bessadok, Marwa Jabou - A/C.3/78/SR.13
RULE OF LAW (Agenda item 83)
Ben Lagha, Adel - A/C.6/78/SR.18
TERRITORIES OCCUPIED BY ISRAEL—HUMAN RIGHTS (Agenda item 50)
Salah, Yassine - A/C.4/78/SR.24
TERRORISM (Agenda item 109)
Ben Lagha, Adel - A/C.6/78/SR.3
UN. GENERAL ASSEMBLY—WORK PROGRAMME (Agenda item 120)
Bessadok, Marwa Jabou - A/C.3/78/SR.56
UN. GENERAL ASSEMBLY (78TH SESS. : 2023-2024)—GENERAL DEBATE (Agenda item 8)
Ammar, Nabil - A/78/PV.12
UN. GENERAL ASSEMBLY (78TH SESS. : 2023-2024). 1ST COMMITTEE—GENERAL DEBATE (Agenda item 8)
Cherif, Ali - A/C.1/78/PV.4
UN. GENERAL ASSEMBLY (78TH SESS. : 2023-2024). 2ND COMMITTEE—GENERAL DEBATE (Agenda item 8)
Chelbi, Kaouthar - A/C.2/78/SR.4
UNRWA—ACTIVITIES (Agenda item 49)
Salah, Yassine - A/C.4/78/SR.22
VETO (Agenda item 63)
Ben Lagha, Adel - A/78/PV.60
Ladeb, Tarek - A/78/PV.67; A/78/PV.74
WOMEN'S ADVANCEMENT (Agenda item 25a)
Bessadok, Marwa Jabou - A/C.3/78/SR.8
WOMEN'S ADVANCEMENT—CONFERENCES (Agenda item 25b)
Bessadok, Marwa Jabou - A/C.3/78/SR.8

Türkiye

AGEING PERSONS (Agenda item 24b)
Güven, Fikriye Asli - A/C.3/78/SR.3
ARMED CONFLICTS PREVENTION (Agenda item 31a)
Özgür, Ceren Hande - A/78/PV.72
ARMS TRANSFERS—TREATIES (Agenda item 99x)
Çetin, Ahmet Erman - A/C.1/78/PV.18
CENTRAL ASIA—ZONES OF PEACE (Agenda item 64)
Tanriöver, Emre - A/78/PV.85
CHEMICAL WEAPONS—TREATIES (Agenda item 99l)
Çetin, Ahmet Erman - A/C.1/78/PV.26
CLIMATE (Agenda item 18d)
İstemil Aydil, Alara - A/C.2/78/SR.15
COASTAL ZONE MANAGEMENT (Agenda item 18j)
Demir, İlknur - A/C.2/78/SR.23

Türkiye (continued)

COASTAL ZONE MANAGEMENT (Agenda item 18j)
İstemil Aydil, Alara - A/78/PV.49
CONVENTIONAL WEAPONS (Agenda item 99u)
Çetin, Ahmet Erman - A/C.1/78/PV.18
CONVENTIONAL WEAPONS—TREATIES (Agenda item 103)
Çetin, Ahmet Erman - A/C.1/78/PV.18
CRIME PREVENTION (Agenda item 107)
Aydil, İsmail - A/C.3/78/SR.6
CRIMES AGAINST HUMANITY (Agenda item 80)
Güç, Eda - A/C.6/78/SR.11
Seymenoğlu, Melek Dilsen - A/C.6/78/SR.39; A/C.6/78/SR.41
Sirmen, Vedia - A/C.6/78/SR.44
Uraz, Onur - A/C.6/78/SR.42; A/C.6/78/SR.43
CYBERCRIME (Agenda item 108)
Aydil, İsmail - A/C.3/78/SR.6
DEVELOPMENT FINANCE—CONFERENCES (Agenda item 17)
İstemil Aydil, Alara - A/78/PV.90
DISARMAMENT—GENERAL AND COMPLETE (Agenda item 99)
Çetin, Ahmet Erman - A/C.1/78/PV.28
DISARMAMENT AGREEMENTS—OUTER SPACE (Agenda item 97c)
Çetin, Ahmet Erman - A/C.1/78/PV.27
EMERGENCY ASSISTANCE (Agenda item 72a)
Akbulut, Mustafa Kemal - A/78/PV.46
FOOD SECURITY (Agenda item 23a)
Demir, İlknur - A/C.2/78/SR.17
HUMAN RIGHTS—AFGHANISTAN (Agenda item 71c)
Aydil, İsmail - A/C.3/78/SR.26
HUMAN RIGHTS—INTERNATIONAL INSTRUMENTS (Agenda item 71a)
Aydil, İsmail - A/C.3/78/SR.26
HUMAN RIGHTS—REPORTS (Agenda item 71c)
Aydil, İsmail - A/C.3/78/SR.25
HUMAN RIGHTS—SYRIAN ARAB REPUBLIC (Agenda item 71c)
Aydil, İsmail - A/C.3/78/SR.26; A/C.3/78/SR.54
HUMAN RIGHTS—TERRITORIES OCCUPIED BY ISRAEL (Agenda item 71c)
Aydil, İsmail - A/C.3/78/SR.35
HUMAN RIGHTS—UKRAINE (Agenda item 71c)
Aydil, İsmail - A/C.3/78/SR.26
INTERNATIONAL JURISDICTION (Agenda item 84)
Güç, Eda - A/C.6/78/SR.13
LANDLOCKED DEVELOPING COUNTRIES—CONFERENCES (Agenda item 20b)
Ekren, Kemal Onur - A/C.2/78/SR.7
LANDMINES—TREATIES (Agenda item 99m)
Çetin, Ahmet Erman - A/C.1/78/PV.18

Türkiye (continued)

LAW OF THE SEA (Agenda item 75a)
Çetin, Ahmet Erman - A/78/PV.44
LEAST DEVELOPED COUNTRIES—CONFERENCES (Agenda item 20a)
Ekren, Kemal Onur - A/C.2/78/SR.7
MARINE ECOSYSTEMS—BIOLOGICAL DIVERSITY (Agenda item 75c)
Çetin, Ahmet Erman - A/78/PV.44
MILLENNIUM SUMMIT—CONFERENCES (Agenda item 117)
Çetin, Ahmet Erman - A/78/PV.102
MINORITIES (Agenda item 71b)
Aydil, İsmail - A/C.3/78/SR.39; A/C.3/78/SR.52
NUCLEAR DISARMAMENT (Agenda item 99b)
Çetin, Ahmet Erman - A/C.1/78/PV.13
NUCLEAR NON-PROLIFERATION—INTERNATIONAL OBLIGATIONS (Agenda item 99w)
Çetin, Ahmet Erman - A/C.1/78/PV.13
NUCLEAR WEAPON TESTS—TREATIES (Agenda item 105)
Çetin, Ahmet Erman - A/C.1/78/PV.13
PALESTINE QUESTION (Agenda item 35)
Güven, Fikriye Asli - A/78/PV.39
PALESTINIANS—ASSISTANCE (Agenda item 72b)
Akbulut, Mustafa Kemal - A/78/PV.46
PEACE (Agenda item 14)
Güven, Fikriye Asli - A/78/PV.62
POVERTY—INTERNATIONAL DECADES (Agenda item 21a)
Demir, İlknur - A/C.2/78/SR.17
RACIAL DISCRIMINATION—ELIMINATION (Agenda item 69a)
Aydil, İsmail - A/C.3/78/SR.42
RACIAL DISCRIMINATION—PROGRAMMES OF ACTION (Agenda item 69b)
Aydil, İsmail - A/C.3/78/SR.42
RESPONSIBILITY TO PROTECT (Agenda item 129)
Güç, Eda - A/78/PV.97
RIGHT TO DRINKING WATER (Agenda item 71b)
Aydil, İsmail - A/C.3/78/SR.28; A/C.3/78/SR.50
RIGHTS OF THE CHILD (Agenda item 67)
Aydil, İsmail - A/C.3/78/SR.14
RURAL POVERTY (Agenda item 21b)
Demir, İlknur - A/C.2/78/SR.17
SMALL ARMS—ILLICIT TRAFFIC (Agenda item 99p)
Çetin, Ahmet Erman - A/C.1/78/PV.18
SMALL ARMS—ILLICIT TRAFFIC—ASSISTANCE (Agenda item 99n)
Çetin, Ahmet Erman - A/C.1/78/PV.18
SMALL ISLAND DEVELOPING STATES—PROGRAMMES OF ACTION (Agenda item 18b)
İstemil Aydil, Alara - A/C.2/78/SR.15
Karatepe, Merve - A/78/PV.100

Türkiye (continued)

SOCIAL CONDITIONS (Agenda item 24b)
Aydil, İsmail - A/78/PV.101
Güven, Fikriye Asli - A/C.3/78/SR.3
SOCIAL DEVELOPMENT (Agenda item 24)
Güven, Fikriye Asli - A/C.3/78/SR.3
STORMS (Agenda item 18i)
İstemil Aydil, Alara - A/C.2/78/SR.15
STRADDLING FISH STOCKS (Agenda item 75b)
Çetin, Ahmet Erman - A/78/PV.44
SUSTAINABLE DEVELOPMENT (Agenda item 18)
Aydil, İsmail - A/78/PV.107
İstemil Aydil, Alara - A/C.2/78/SR.15; A/C.2/78/SR.22
SUSTAINABLE ENERGY (Agenda item 18h)
İstemil Aydil, Alara - A/C.2/78/SR.15
TAXATION (Agenda item 16h)
Güven, Fikriye Asli - A/C.2/78/SR.25
TERRITORIES OCCUPIED BY ISRAEL—HUMAN RIGHTS (Agenda item 50)
Sezer, Alper - A/C.4/78/SR.24
TERRITORIES OCCUPIED BY ISRAEL—NATURAL RESOURCES (Agenda item 59)
Ekren, Kemal Onur - A/C.2/78/SR.19
Özgür, Ceren Hande - A/C.2/78/SR.21
TERRORISM (Agenda item 109)
Ekren, Kemal Onur - A/C.6/78/SR.3
TORTURE AND OTHER CRUEL TREATMENT (Agenda item 71a)
Tanriöven, Enes - A/C.3/78/SR.18
UKRAINE—POLITICAL CONDITIONS (Agenda item 62)
Önal, Sedat - A/78/PV.57
UN—BUDGET (2024) (Agenda item 134)
Aras, Nisan Su - A/C.5/78/SR.3; A/C.5/78/SR.5
UN—PROGRAMME PLANNING (Agenda item 135)
Aras, Nisan Su - A/C.5/78/SR.5
UN. GENERAL ASSEMBLY (78TH SESS. : 2023-2024). 1ST COMMITTEE—GENERAL DEBATE (Agenda item 8)
Çetin, Ahmet Erman - A/C.1/78/PV.7
UN. GENERAL ASSEMBLY (78TH SESS. : 2023-2024). 2ND COMMITTEE—GENERAL DEBATE (Agenda item 8)
İstemil Aydil, Alara - A/C.2/78/SR.6
UN. INTERNATIONAL LAW COMMISSION—REPORTS (Agenda item 79)
Esener, Kaan - A/C.6/78/SR.27
Güç, Eda - A/C.6/78/SR.33
Tansu-Seckin, Cagla - A/C.6/78/SR.30
UN. SECURITY COUNCIL—MEMBERSHIP (Agenda item 121)
Önal, Sedat - A/78/PV.35
UN CONFERENCES (Agenda item 13)
Çetin, Ahmet Erman - A/78/PV.102
UN HIGH COMMISSIONER FOR REFUGEES—REPORTS (Agenda item 60)
Aydil, İsmail - A/C.3/78/SR.45

Türkiye (continued)

UN SYSTEM—STRENGTHENING (Agenda item 122)
İstemil Aydil, Alara - A/78/PV.99
UNRWA—ACTIVITIES (Agenda item 49)
Özgür, Ceren Hande - A/C.4/78/SR.22
VETO (Agenda item 63)
Ekren, Kemal Onur - A/78/PV.70
Güven, Fikriye Asli - A/78/PV.51; A/78/PV.60; A/78/PV.67
Yildiz, Ahmet - A/78/PV.74
WOMEN'S ADVANCEMENT (Agenda item 25a)
Aydil, İsmail - A/C.3/78/SR.10
WOMEN'S ADVANCEMENT—CONFERENCES (Agenda item 25b)
Aydil, İsmail - A/C.3/78/SR.10
YOUTH (Agenda item 24b)
Güven, Fikriye Asli - A/C.3/78/SR.3

Türkiye. President

UN. GENERAL ASSEMBLY (78TH SESS. : 2023-2024)—GENERAL DEBATE (Agenda item 8)
Erdogan, Recep Tayyip - A/78/PV.4
UN. GENERAL ASSEMBLY (78TH SESS. : 2023-2024)—SPECIAL STATEMENTS
Erdogan, Recep Tayyip - A/78/PV.4

Turkmenistan

PEACE (Agenda item 14)
Ataeva, Aksoltan T. - A/78/PV.63
SPORTS—OLYMPIC GAMES (Agenda item 11)
Ataeva, Aksoltan T. - A/78/PV.107
SUSTAINABLE DEVELOPMENT (Agenda item 18)
Ataeva, Aksoltan T. - A/C.2/78/SR.22; A/C.2/78/SR.23
UN. GENERAL ASSEMBLY (78TH SESS. : 2023-2024). 2ND COMMITTEE—GENERAL DEBATE (Agenda item 8)
Eyeberdiyev, Ata - A/C.2/78/SR.3

Turkmenistan. President

UN. GENERAL ASSEMBLY (78TH SESS. : 2023-2024)—GENERAL DEBATE (Agenda item 8)
Berdimuhamedov, Serdar - A/78/PV.4
UN. GENERAL ASSEMBLY (78TH SESS. : 2023-2024)—SPECIAL STATEMENTS
Berdimuhamedov, Serdar - A/78/PV.4

Tuvalu

MILLENNIUM SUMMIT—CONFERENCES (Agenda item 117)
Navoti, Selema K. - A/78/PV.102
UN CONFERENCES (Agenda item 13)
Navoti, Selema K. - A/78/PV.102

Tuvalu. Prime Minister

UN. GENERAL ASSEMBLY (78TH SESS. : 2023-2024)—GENERAL DEBATE (Agenda item 8)
Natano, Kausea - A/78/PV.11
UN. GENERAL ASSEMBLY (78TH SESS. : 2023-2024)—SPECIAL STATEMENTS
Natano, Kausea - A/78/PV.11

Uganda

ADMINISTRATION OF JUSTICE (Agenda item 144)
Muhumuza, Duncan Laki - A/C.6/78/SR.9
CRIMES AGAINST HUMANITY (Agenda item 80)
Ikondere, Marvin - A/C.6/78/SR.47
DECOLONIZATION (Agenda item 58)
Kwoba, Godfrey - A/C.4/78/SR.8
ELECTION VERIFICATION—UN (Agenda item 71b)
Gurhan, Amina - A/C.3/78/SR.50
HIV/AIDS—DECLARATIONS (Agenda item 10)
Muhumuza, Duncan Laki - A/78/PV.91
HUMAN RIGHTS (Agenda item 71)
Kwoba, Godfrey - A/C.3/78/SR.28
INDIGENOUS PEOPLES (Agenda item 68a)
Nabeta, Celia Kafureka - A/C.3/78/SR.17
INTERNATIONAL CRIMINAL COURT—REPORTS (Agenda item 74)
Muhumuza, Duncan Laki - A/78/PV.21
INTERNATIONAL JURISDICTION (Agenda item 84)
Ikondere, Marvin - A/C.6/78/SR.12
INTERNATIONAL LAW—TRAINING PROGRAMMES (Agenda item 78)
Ikondere, Marvin - A/C.6/78/SR.22
PEACE (Agenda item 14)
Gurhan, Amina - A/78/PV.62
RIGHT TO DEVELOPMENT (Agenda item 71b)
Kwoba, Godfrey - A/C.3/78/SR.28
RIGHTS OF THE CHILD (Agenda item 67)
Nabeta, Celia Kafureka - A/C.3/78/SR.13
RULE OF LAW (Agenda item 83)
Muhumuza, Duncan Laki - A/C.6/78/SR.18
SEXUAL ORIENTATION (Agenda item 71b)
Nabeta, Celia Kafureka - A/C.3/78/SR.27
TERRORISM (Agenda item 109)
Ikondere, Marvin - A/C.6/78/SR.4
UN—BUDGET (2024) (Agenda item 134)
Ainomuhisha, Medard - A/C.5/78/SR.33
UN. GENERAL ASSEMBLY (78TH SESS. : 2023-2024). 1ST COMMITTEE—GENERAL DEBATE (Agenda item 8)
Isabirye, Haruna Bazirondere - A/C.1/78/PV.6
UN. INTERNATIONAL COURT OF JUSTICE—MEMBERS (Agenda item 113c)
Muhumuza, Duncan Laki - A/78/PV.31

Uganda (continued)

UN. INTERNATIONAL LAW COMMISSION—REPORTS (Agenda item 79)
Ikondere, Marvin - A/C.6/78/SR.27; A/C.6/78/SR.32
UN COMMISSION ON INTERNATIONAL TRADE LAW—REPORTS (Agenda item 77)
Ikondere, Marvin - A/C.6/78/SR.14
UN HIGH COMMISSIONER FOR REFUGEES—REPORTS (Agenda item 60)
Gurhan, Amina - A/C.3/78/SR.45
VETO (Agenda item 63)
Muhumuza, Duncan Laki - A/78/PV.60
WOMEN'S ADVANCEMENT (Agenda item 25a)
Nabeta, Celia Kafureka - A/C.3/78/SR.9
WOMEN'S ADVANCEMENT—CONFERENCES (Agenda item 25b)
Nabeta, Celia Kafureka - A/C.3/78/SR.9

Uganda. Vice-President

UN. GENERAL ASSEMBLY (78TH SESS. : 2023-2024)—GENERAL DEBATE (Agenda item 8)
Alupo, Jessica - A/78/PV.9
UN. GENERAL ASSEMBLY (78TH SESS. : 2023-2024)—SPECIAL STATEMENTS
Alupo, Jessica - A/78/PV.9

Ukraine

ARMED CONFLICTS PREVENTION (Agenda item 31a)
Kyslytsya, Sergiy - A/78/PV.72
BIOLOGICAL WEAPONS—TREATIES (Agenda item 106)
Zlenko, Anatoli M. - A/C.1/78/PV.15
CHEMICAL WEAPONS—TREATIES (Agenda item 99l)
Zlenko, Anatoli M. - A/C.1/78/PV.14; A/C.1/78/PV.15
CLIMATE (Agenda item 18d)
Leschenko, Volodymyr - A/C.2/78/SR.13
CRIME PREVENTION (Agenda item 107)
Tokarska, Anastasiia - A/C.3/78/SR.51
CRIMES AGAINST HUMANITY (Agenda item 80)
Prytula, Mykola - A/C.6/78/SR.45
DISAPPEARANCE OF PERSONS (Agenda item 71b)
Mudrenko, Nataliia - A/C.3/78/SR.22
DISARMAMENT—GENERAL AND COMPLETE (Agenda item 99)
Hayovyshyn, Khrystyna - A/78/PV.106
Zlenko, Anatoli M. - A/C.1/78/PV.15
DISPLACED PERSONS (Agenda item 71b)
Zlenko, Anatoli M. - A/C.3/78/SR.32
EMERGENCY ASSISTANCE (Agenda item 72a)
Hayovyshyn, Khrystyna - A/78/PV.47

Ukraine (continued)

FOOD SECURITY (Agenda item 23a)
Leschenko, Volodymyr - A/C.2/78/SR.16; A/C.2/78/SR.25
FREEDOM OF EXPRESSION (Agenda item 71b)
Tokarska, Anastasiia - A/C.3/78/SR.19
HEALTH (Agenda item 125)
Dvornyk, Serhii - A/78/PV.77
HUMAN RIGHTS (Agenda item 71)
Mudrenko, Nataliia - A/C.3/78/SR.16
HUMAN RIGHTS—BELARUS (Agenda item 71c)
Mudrenko, Nataliia - A/C.3/78/SR.37
HUMAN RIGHTS—INTERNATIONAL INSTRUMENTS (Agenda item 71a)
Mudrenko, Nataliia - A/C.3/78/SR.25
HUMAN RIGHTS—RUSSIAN FEDERATION (Agenda item 71c)
Mudrenko, Nataliia - A/C.3/78/SR.37
HUMAN RIGHTS—UKRAINE (Agenda item 71c)
Kyslytsya, Sergiy - A/78/PV.50; A/C.3/78/SR.53
Mudrenko, Nataliia - A/C.3/78/SR.18; A/C.3/78/SR.25; A/C.3/78/SR.37
Tokarska, Anastasiia - A/C.3/78/SR.27
IAEA—REPORTS (Agenda item 89)
Zlenko, Anatolii - A/78/PV.30
INDIGENOUS PEOPLES (Agenda item 68a)
Tokarska, Anastasiia - A/C.3/78/SR.15
INDIGENOUS PEOPLES—CONFERENCES (Agenda item 68b)
Tokarska, Anastasiia - A/C.3/78/SR.15
INFORMATION (Agenda item 53)
Tokarska, Anastasiia - A/C.4/78/SR.14
INTERNATIONAL CRIMINAL COURT—REPORTS (Agenda item 74)
Prytula, Mykola - A/78/PV.22
JUDICIAL INDEPENDENCE (Agenda item 71b)
Mudrenko, Nataliia - A/C.3/78/SR.31
MINE CLEARANCE (Agenda item 46)
Zlenko, Anatolii - A/C.4/78/SR.10
NUCLEAR DISARMAMENT (Agenda item 99b)
Zlenko, Anatoli M. - A/C.1/78/PV.12; A/C.1/78/PV.13
NUCLEAR NON-PROLIFERATION—INTERNATIONAL OBLIGATIONS (Agenda item 99w)
Zlenko, Anatoli M. - A/C.1/78/PV.12
NUCLEAR WEAPON TESTS—TREATIES (Agenda item 105)
Zlenko, Anatoli M. - A/C.1/78/PV.12
ORGANIZATION FOR DEMOCRACY AND ECONOMIC DEVELOPMENT - GUAM (Agenda item 32)
Hayovyshyn, Khrystyna - A/78/PV.85
PEACE (Agenda item 14)
Tokarska, Anastasiia - A/78/PV.48

Ukraine (continued)

PERSONS WITH DISABILITIES—HUMAN RIGHTS (Agenda item 71a)
Tokarska, Anastasiia - A/C.3/78/SR.38
POVERTY—INTERNATIONAL DECADES (Agenda item 21a)
Leschenko, Volodymyr - A/C.2/78/SR.16
RACIAL DISCRIMINATION—ELIMINATION (Agenda item 69a)
Mudrenko, Nataliia - A/78/PV.50; A/C.3/78/SR.41; A/C.3/78/SR.47
Tokarska, Anastasiia - A/C.3/78/SR.41
RACIAL DISCRIMINATION—PROGRAMMES OF ACTION (Agenda item 69b)
Mudrenko, Nataliia - A/C.3/78/SR.41
Tokarska, Anastasiia - A/C.3/78/SR.41
RELIGIOUS INTOLERANCE (Agenda item 71b)
Mudrenko, Nataliia - A/78/PV.50
RESPONSIBILITY TO PROTECT (Agenda item 129)
Kyslytsya, Sergiy - A/78/PV.99
RIGHT TO CULTURE (Agenda item 71b)
Tokarska, Anastasiia - A/C.3/78/SR.27
RIGHT TO EDUCATION (Agenda item 71b)
Prytula, Mykola - A/C.3/78/SR.27
RIGHT TO FOOD (Agenda item 71b)
Tokarska, Anastasiia - A/C.3/78/SR.30
RIGHT TO HOUSING (Agenda item 71b)
Tokarska, Anastasiia - A/C.3/78/SR.30
RIGHT TO THE TRUTH (Agenda item 71b)
Mudrenko, Nataliia - A/C.3/78/SR.22
RIGHTS OF THE CHILD (Agenda item 67)
Mudrenko, Nataliia - A/C.3/78/SR.11; A/C.3/78/SR.12
RURAL POVERTY (Agenda item 21b)
Leschenko, Volodymyr - A/C.2/78/SR.16
SEXUAL ORIENTATION (Agenda item 71b)
Tokarska, Anastasiia - A/C.3/78/SR.39
SOCIAL CONDITIONS (Agenda item 24b)
Popadiuk, Mykola - A/C.3/78/SR.3
SPORTS—OLYMPIC GAMES (Agenda item 11)
Tokarska, Anastasiia - A/78/PV.38
SUMMARY EXECUTIONS (Agenda item 71b)
Tokarska, Anastasiia - A/C.3/78/SR.31
SUSTAINABLE DEVELOPMENT (Agenda item 18)
Leschenko, Volodymyr - A/C.2/78/SR.13
TERRORISM (Agenda item 109)
Prytula, Mykola - A/C.6/78/SR.1
TERRORISM—HUMAN RIGHTS (Agenda item 71b)
Mudrenko, Nataliia - A/C.3/78/SR.31
TORTURE AND OTHER CRUEL TREATMENT (Agenda item 71a)
Mudrenko, Nataliia - A/C.3/78/SR.18
TRAFFIC SAFETY (Agenda item 12)
Leschenko, Volodymyr - A/78/PV.92

Ukraine (continued)

TRAFFICKING IN PERSONS (Agenda item 71b)
Tokarska, Anastasiia - A/C.3/78/SR.23
UKRAINE—POLITICAL CONDITIONS (Agenda item 62)
Kuleba, Dmytro - A/78/PV.56
Kyslytsya, Sergiy - A/78/PV.58; A/78/PV.99
UN. GENERAL ASSEMBLY—WORK PROGRAMME (Agenda item 120)
Prytula, Mykola - A/78/PV.33
UN. GENERAL ASSEMBLY (78TH SESS. : 2023-2024)—AGENDA (Agenda item 7)
Hayovyshyn, Khrystyna - A/78/PV.2
UN. GENERAL ASSEMBLY (78TH SESS. : 2023-2024). 1ST COMMITTEE—GENERAL DEBATE (Agenda item 8)
Hayovyshyn, Khrystyna - A/C.1/78/PV.4
Zlenko, Anatolii - A/C.1/78/PV.3
UN. GENERAL ASSEMBLY (78TH SESS. : 2023-2024). 2ND COMMITTEE—GENERAL DEBATE (Agenda item 8)
Leschenko, Volodymyr - A/C.2/78/SR.3
UN. HUMAN RIGHTS COUNCIL—REPORTS (Agenda item 66)
Mudrenko, Nataliia - A/C.3/78/SR.46
UN. INTERNATIONAL COURT OF JUSTICE—REPORTS (Agenda item 73)
Korynevych, Anton - A/78/PV.20
UN. INTERNATIONAL LAW COMMISSION—REPORTS (Agenda item 79)
Korynevych, Anton - A/C.6/78/SR.25
UN. SECURITY COUNCIL—MEMBERSHIP (Agenda item 121)
Dvornyk, Serhii - A/78/PV.36
UN. SECURITY COUNCIL—REPORTS (Agenda item 26)
Kyslytsya, Sergiy - A/78/PV.93
UN HIGH COMMISSIONER FOR REFUGEES—REPORTS (Agenda item 60)
Kyslytsya, Sergiy - A/C.3/78/SR.48
Mudrenko, Nataliia - A/78/PV.50; A/C.3/78/SR.44; A/C.3/78/SR.45
UN RESOLUTIONS—IMPLEMENTATION (Agenda item 119)
Prytula, Mykola - A/78/PV.33
VETO (Agenda item 63)
Dvornyk, Serhii - A/78/PV.71
Hayovyshyn, Khrystyna - A/78/PV.68
Zlenko, Anatoli M. - A/78/PV.79
Zlenko, Anatolii - A/78/PV.3
WOMEN'S ADVANCEMENT (Agenda item 25a)
Tokarska, Anastasiia - A/C.3/78/SR.9
WOMEN'S ADVANCEMENT—CONFERENCES (Agenda item 25b)
Tokarska, Anastasiia - A/C.3/78/SR.9
YOUTH (Agenda item 24b)
Demchenko, Kyrylo - A/C.3/78/SR.3
Popadiuk, Mykola - A/C.3/78/SR.3

Ukraine. President

UN. GENERAL ASSEMBLY (78TH SESS. : 2023-2024)—GENERAL DEBATE (Agenda item 8)
Zelenskyy, Volodymyr - A/78/PV.4
UN. GENERAL ASSEMBLY (78TH SESS. : 2023-2024)—SPECIAL STATEMENTS
Zelenskyy, Volodymyr - A/78/PV.4

UN. Advisory Committee on Administrative and Budgetary Questions. Chair

CONFERENCE AND MEETING SERVICES (Agenda item 137)
Bachar Bong, Abdallah - A/C.5/78/SR.7
PERSONNEL QUESTIONS—UN SYSTEM (Agenda item 142)
Bachar Bong, Abdallah - A/C.5/78/SR.10
UN—ADMINISTRATION (Agenda item 132)
Bachar Bong, Abdallah - A/C.5/78/SR.32
UN—BUDGET (2023) (Agenda item 133)
Bachar Bong, Abdallah - A/C.5/78/SR.9
UN—BUDGET (2024) (Agenda item 134)
Bachar Bong, Abdallah - A/C.5/78/SR.5; A/C.5/78/SR.9; A/C.5/78/SR.14; A/C.5/78/SR.16; A/C.5/78/SR.17; A/C.5/78/SR.19; A/C.5/78/SR.21; A/C.5/78/SR.23; A/C.5/78/SR.24; A/C.5/78/SR.28; A/C.5/78/SR.30; A/C.5/78/SR.33
UN—FINANCIAL REPORTS (Agenda item 131)
Bachar Bong, Abdallah - A/C.5/78/SR.14

UN. Advisory Committee on Administrative and Budgetary Questions. Vice-Chair

ADMINISTRATION OF JUSTICE (Agenda item 144)
Ruas, Juliana Gaspar - A/C.5/78/SR.15
INTERNATIONAL RESIDUAL MECHANISM FOR CRIMINAL TRIBUNALS—FINANCING (Agenda item 145)
Chmielewski, Jakub - A/C.5/78/SR.20
Ruas, Juliana Gaspar - A/C.5/78/SR.25
PERSONNEL QUESTIONS—UN SYSTEM (Agenda item 142)
Al-Kumaim, Amjad Qaid Ahmed - A/C.5/78/SR.27
UN—ADMINISTRATION (Agenda item 132)
Chmielewski, Jakub - A/C.5/78/SR.29
UN—BUDGET (2024) (Agenda item 134)
Al-Kumaim, Amjad Qaid Ahmed - A/C.5/78/SR.4; A/C.5/78/SR.13; A/C.5/78/SR.22
Brennen-Haylock, Sharon - A/C.5/78/SR.31
Chmielewski, Jakub - A/C.5/78/SR.3; A/C.5/78/SR.11; A/C.5/78/SR.12
Ruas, Juliana Gaspar - A/C.5/78/SR.2; A/C.5/78/SR.18; A/C.5/78/SR.25
UN—HUMAN RESOURCES MANAGEMENT (Agenda item 139)
Al-Kumaim, Amjad Qaid Ahmed - A/C.5/78/SR.27
Ruas, Juliana Gaspar - A/C.5/78/SR.25

UN. Advisory Committee on Administrative and Budgetary Questions. Vice-Chair (continued)

UN MULTIDIMENSIONAL INTEGRATED STABILIZATION MISSION IN MALI—FINANCING (Agenda item 155)
Chmielewski, Jakub - A/C.5/78/SR.20

UN. Assistant Secretary-General for Economic Development

DEVELOPMENT COOPERATION—MIDDLE-INCOME COUNTRIES (Agenda item 19c)
Hanif, Navid - A/C.2/78/SR.10

UN. Assistant Secretary-General for Europe, Central Asia and the Americas

SPECIAL POLITICAL MISSIONS (Agenda item 52)
Jenca, Miroslav - A/C.4/78/SR.21

UN. Assistant Secretary-General for Human Resources Management

PERSONNEL QUESTIONS—UN SYSTEM (Agenda item 142)
López, Martha Helena - A/C.5/78/SR.27
UN—HUMAN RESOURCES MANAGEMENT (Agenda item 139)
López, Martha Helena - A/C.5/78/SR.25; A/C.5/78/SR.27

UN. Assistant Secretary-General for Human Rights

DISAPPEARANCE OF PERSONS (Agenda item 71b)
Brands Kehris, Ilze - A/C.3/78/SR.18
HUMAN RIGHTS—DEMOCRATIC PEOPLE'S REPUBLIC OF KOREA (Agenda item 71c)
Brands Kehris, Ilze - A/C.3/78/SR.18
HUMAN RIGHTS—IRAN (ISLAMIC REPUBLIC OF) (Agenda item 71c)
Brands Kehris, Ilze - A/C.3/78/SR.18
HUMAN RIGHTS—MYANMAR (Agenda item 71c)
Brands Kehris, Ilze - A/C.3/78/SR.18
HUMAN RIGHTS—UKRAINE (Agenda item 71c)
Brands Kehris, Ilze - A/C.3/78/SR.18
HUMAN RIGHTS ADVANCEMENT (Agenda item 71b)
Brands Kehris, Ilze - A/C.3/78/SR.18
HUMAN RIGHTS INSTITUTIONS—CENTRAL AFRICA (Agenda item 71b)
Brands Kehris, Ilze - A/C.3/78/SR.18
HUMAN RIGHTS INSTITUTIONS—SOUTHWEST ASIA AND ARAB COUNTRIES (Agenda item 71b)
Brands Kehris, Ilze - A/C.3/78/SR.18
MIGRANTS—PROTECTION (Agenda item 71b)
Brands Kehris, Ilze - A/C.3/78/SR.18

UN. Assistant Secretary-General for Human Rights (continued)

MINORITIES (Agenda item 71b)
Brands Kehris, Ilze - A/C.3/78/SR.18
NATIONAL INSTITUTIONS—HUMAN RIGHTS (Agenda item 71b)
Brands Kehris, Ilze - A/C.3/78/SR.18
RACIAL DISCRIMINATION—ELIMINATION (Agenda item 69a)
Brands Kehris, Ilze - A/78/PV.63; A/C.3/78/SR.40
RACIAL DISCRIMINATION—PROGRAMMES OF ACTION (Agenda item 69b)
Brands Kehris, Ilze - A/C.3/78/SR.40
RELIGIOUS INTOLERANCE (Agenda item 71b)
Brands Kehris, Ilze - A/C.3/78/SR.18
RIGHT TO DEVELOPMENT (Agenda item 71b)
Brands Kehris, Ilze - A/C.3/78/SR.18
SELF-DETERMINATION OF PEOPLES (Agenda item 70)
Brands Kehris, Ilze - A/C.3/78/SR.40
SLAVERY (Agenda item 71a)
Brands Kehris, Ilze - A/C.3/78/SR.18
TERRITORIES OCCUPIED BY ISRAEL—HUMAN RIGHTS (Agenda item 50)
Brands Kehris, Ilze - A/C.4/78/SR.24
TERRORISM—HUMAN RIGHTS (Agenda item 71b)
Brands Kehris, Ilze - A/C.3/78/SR.18
TORTURE AND OTHER CRUEL TREATMENT (Agenda item 71a)
Brands Kehris, Ilze - A/C.3/78/SR.18

UN. Assistant Secretary-General for Internal Oversight Services

PEACEKEEPING OPERATIONS—FINANCING (Agenda item 146)
Swanson, Benjamin Gordon Robert - A/C.5/78/SR.35
UN MISSION IN SOUTH SUDAN—FINANCING (Agenda item 157)
Swanson, Benjamin Gordon Robert - A/C.5/78/SR.36

UN. Assistant Secretary-General for Middle East, Asia and the Pacific

ELECTION VERIFICATION—UN (Agenda item 71b)
Khiari, Mohamed Khaled - A/C.3/78/SR.18
HUMAN RIGHTS—MYANMAR (Agenda item 71c)
Khiari, Mohamed Khaled - A/C.3/78/SR.33

UN. Assistant Secretary-General for Rule of Law and Security Institutions

MINE CLEARANCE (Agenda item 46)
Zouev, Alexandre - A/C.4/78/SR.10

UN. Assistant Secretary-General for Rule of Law and Security Institutions (continued)

PEACEKEEPING OPERATIONS (Agenda item 51)
Zouev, Alexandre - A/C.4/78/SR.18

UN. Assistant Secretary-General for Supply Chain Management

PEACEKEEPING OPERATIONS—FINANCING (Agenda item 146)
Berg, AnneMarie van den - A/C.5/78/SR.35
UN—ADMINISTRATION (Agenda item 132)
Berg, AnneMarie van den - A/C.5/78/SR.32

UN. Board of Auditors. Audit Operations Committee. Chair

UN—BUDGET (2024) (Agenda item 134)
Hu, Xuewen - A/C.5/78/SR.9
UN—FINANCIAL REPORTS (Agenda item 131)
Hu, Xuewen - A/C.5/78/SR.35

UN. Committee against Torture. Chair

TORTURE AND OTHER CRUEL TREATMENT (Agenda item 71a)
Heller, Claude - A/C.3/78/SR.18

UN. Committee for Programme and Coordination. Vice-Chair

UN—PROGRAMME PLANNING (Agenda item 135)
Jerboui, Hind (Morocco) - A/C.5/78/SR.5

UN. Committee on Conferences. Chair

CONFERENCE AND MEETING SERVICES (Agenda item 137)
Abo, Ai (Japan) - A/C.5/78/SR.7

UN. Committee on Contributions. Chair

UN—BUDGET CONTRIBUTIONS (Agenda item 138)
Greiver, Bernardo - A/C.5/78/SR.1

UN. Committee on Economic, Social and Cultural Rights. Chair

HUMAN RIGHTS—INTERNATIONAL INSTRUMENTS (Agenda item 71a)
Craciunean-Tatu, Laura-Maria (Romania) - A/C.3/78/SR.17

UN. Committee on Enforced Disappearances. Rapporteur

DISAPPEARANCE OF PERSONS (Agenda item 71b)
Albán Alencastro, Juan Pablo - A/C.3/78/SR.22

UN. Committee on Information. Vice-Chair

INFORMATION (Agenda item 53)
Baños Müller, Liliana Verónica (El Salvador) - A/C.4/78/SR.12

UN. Committee on Relations with the Host Country

UN. COMMITTEE ON RELATIONS WITH THE HOST COUNTRY—REPORTS (Agenda item 161)
Hadjichrysanthou, Andreas (Cyprus) - A/C.6/78/SR.35

UN. Committee on the Elimination of Discrimination against Women. Chair

WOMEN'S ADVANCEMENT (Agenda item 25a)
Peláez Narváez, Ana - A/C.3/78/SR.7
WOMEN'S ADVANCEMENT—CONFERENCES (Agenda item 25b)
Peláez Narváez, Ana - A/C.3/78/SR.7

UN. Committee on the Elimination of Racial Discrimination. Chair

RACIAL DISCRIMINATION—ELIMINATION (Agenda item 69a)
Shepherd, Verene - A/78/PV.63; A/C.3/78/SR.41

UN. Committee on the Exercise of the Inalienable Rights of the Palestinian People. Vice-Chair

PALESTINE QUESTION (Agenda item 35)
Muhamad, Ahmad Faisal (Malaysia) - A/78/PV.39

UN. Committee on the Peaceful Uses of Outer Space. Chair

OUTER SPACE—PEACEFUL USES—INTERNATIONAL COOPERATION (Agenda item 48)
Sharaf, Omran (United Arab Emirates) - A/C.4/78/SR.15

UN. Committee on the Protection of the Rights of All Migrant Workers and Members of Their Families. Chair

MIGRANT WORKERS (Agenda item 71a)
Corzo Sosa, Edgar - A/C.3/78/SR.23

UN. Committee on the Rights of Persons with Disabilities. Chair

PERSONS WITH DISABILITIES—HUMAN RIGHTS (Agenda item 71a)
Fefoame, Gertrude Oforiwa - A/C.3/78/SR.38

UN. Committee on the Rights of the Child. Chair

RIGHTS OF THE CHILD (Agenda item 67)
Skelton, Ann Marie (South Africa) - A/C.3/78/SR.12

UN. Conference on Disarmament. President

UN. CONFERENCE ON DISARMAMENT—REPORTS (Agenda item 101a)
Szűcs, Margit (Hungary) - A/C.1/78/PV.24

UN. Controller

AU-UN HYBRID OPERATION IN DARFUR—FINANCING (Agenda item 159)
Ramanathan, Chandramouli - A/C.5/78/SR.35
PEACEKEEPING OPERATIONS—FINANCING (Agenda item 146)
Ramanathan, Chandramouli - A/C.5/78/SR.35; A/C.5/78/SR.36
UN—BUDGET (2023) (Agenda item 133)
Ramanathan, Chandramouli - A/C.5/78/SR.9
UN—BUDGET (2024) (Agenda item 134)
Ramanathan, Chandramouli - A/C.5/78/SR.2; A/C.5/78/SR.4; A/C.5/78/SR.11; A/C.5/78/SR.16; A/C.5/78/SR.26/PartII; A/C.5/78/SR.28; A/C.5/78/SR.30; A/C.5/78/SR.33
UN—BUDGET CONTRIBUTIONS (Agenda item 138)
Ramanathan, Chandramouli - A/C.5/78/SR.1
UN—FINANCIAL REPORTS (Agenda item 131)
Ramanathan, Chandramouli - A/C.5/78/SR.35
UN—FINANCIAL SITUATION (Agenda item 136)
Ramanathan, Chandramouli - A/C.5/78/SR.6
UN. GENERAL ASSEMBLY (78TH SESS. : 2023-2024). 5TH COMMITTEE—WORK ORGANIZATION (Agenda item 7)
Ramanathan, Chandramouli - A/C.5/78/SR.26/PartII; A/C.5/78/SR.40
UN. SUPPORT OFFICE IN SOMALIA—FINANCING (Agenda item 160)
Ramanathan, Chandramouli - A/C.5/78/SR.35
UN DISENGAGEMENT OBSERVER FORCE—FINANCING (Agenda item 156a)
Ramanathan, Chandramouli - A/C.5/78/SR.35
UN INTERIM ADMINISTRATION MISSION IN KOSOVO—FINANCING (Agenda item 153)
Ramanathan, Chandramouli - A/C.5/78/SR.35
UN INTERIM FORCE IN LEBANON—FINANCING (Agenda item 156b)
Ramanathan, Chandramouli - A/C.5/78/SR.35
UN MISSION FOR THE REFERENDUM IN WESTERN SAHARA—FINANCING (Agenda item 158)
Ramanathan, Chandramouli - A/C.5/78/SR.35
UN MISSION IN SOUTH SUDAN—FINANCING (Agenda item 157)
Ramanathan, Chandramouli - A/C.5/78/SR.36
UN MULTIDIMENSIONAL INTEGRATED STABILIZATION MISSION IN MALI—FINANCING (Agenda item 155)
Ramanathan, Chandramouli - A/C.5/78/SR.36

UN. Controller (continued)

UN MULTIDIMENSIONAL INTEGRATED STABILIZATION MISSION IN THE CENTRAL AFRICAN REPUBLIC—FINANCING (Agenda item 148)
Ramanathan, Chandramouli - A/C.5/78/SR.35
UN ORGANIZATION STABILIZATION MISSION IN THE DEMOCRATIC REPUBLIC OF THE CONGO—FINANCING (Agenda item 151)
Ramanathan, Chandramouli - A/C.5/78/SR.35
UN PEACEKEEPING FORCE IN CYPRUS—FINANCING (Agenda item 150)
Ramanathan, Chandramouli - A/C.5/78/SR.35
UN SECURITY FORCE FOR ABYEI—FINANCING (Agenda item 147)
Ramanathan, Chandramouli - A/C.5/78/SR.36

UN. Department for General Assembly and Conference Management

AFRICA—DEVELOPMENT (Agenda item 65b)
Nakano, Kenji - A/78/PV.57
DEVELOPMENT FINANCE—CONFERENCES (Agenda item 17)
Buyanover, Gal - A/78/PV.69
HEALTH (Agenda item 125)
Sharma, Sangeeta - A/78/PV.16
LANDLOCKED DEVELOPING COUNTRIES—CONFERENCES (Agenda item 20b)
Miranda, Ruth de - A/78/PV.80
LAW OF THE SEA (Agenda item 75a)
Nakano, Kenji - A/78/PV.44
MARINE ECOSYSTEMS—BIOLOGICAL DIVERSITY (Agenda item 75c)
Nakano, Kenji - A/78/PV.44; A/78/PV.103
MILLENNIUM SUMMIT—CONFERENCES (Agenda item 117)
Miranda, Ruth de - A/78/PV.102
MULTILINGUALISM (Agenda item 124)
Nakano, Kenji - A/78/PV.107
PEACE (Agenda item 14)
Emelina-Sarte, Svetlana - A/78/PV.77
Nakano, Kenji - A/78/PV.82
Sharma, Sangeeta - A/78/PV.62
SMALL ISLAND DEVELOPING STATES—PROGRAMMES OF ACTION (Agenda item 18b)
Nakano, Kenji - A/78/PV.103
Sharma, Sangeeta - A/78/PV.100
SOCIAL CONDITIONS (Agenda item 24b)
Sharma, Sangeeta - A/78/PV.101
STRADDLING FISH STOCKS (Agenda item 75b)
Nakano, Kenji - A/78/PV.44
UN CONFERENCES (Agenda item 13)
Miranda, Ruth de - A/78/PV.102

UN. Department of Economic and Social Affairs. Development Policy Analysis Division. Director

INTERNATIONAL TRADE (Agenda item 16a)
Mukherjee, Shantanu - A/C.2/78/SR.8

UN. Department of Economic and Social Affairs. Division for Inclusive Social Development. Officer-in-Charge

AGEING PERSONS (Agenda item 24b)
Wilmoth, John - A/C.3/78/SR.1
FAMILY (Agenda item 24b)
Wilmoth, John - A/C.3/78/SR.1
PERSONS WITH DISABILITIES (Agenda item 24b)
Wilmoth, John - A/C.3/78/SR.1
POVERTY—INTERNATIONAL DECADES (Agenda item 21a)
Wilmoth, John - A/C.2/78/SR.16
SOCIAL CONDITIONS (Agenda item 24b)
Wilmoth, John - A/C.3/78/SR.1
SOCIAL DEVELOPMENT—CONFERENCES (Agenda item 24a)
Wilmoth, John - A/C.3/78/SR.1
YOUTH (Agenda item 24b)
Wilmoth, John - A/C.3/78/SR.1

UN. Department of Economic and Social Affairs. Division for Sustainable Development Goals. Officer-in-Charge

2030 AGENDA—PROGRAMME IMPLEMENTATION (Agenda item 18a)
Tahtinen, Lotta - A/C.2/78/SR.12
SMALL ISLAND DEVELOPING STATES—PROGRAMMES OF ACTION (Agenda item 18b)
Tahtinen, Lotta - A/C.2/78/SR.12
SUSTAINABLE DEVELOPMENT (Agenda item 18)
Tahtinen, Lotta - A/C.2/78/SR.12
SUSTAINABLE ENERGY (Agenda item 18h)
Tahtinen, Lotta - A/C.2/78/SR.12

UN. Department of Economic and Social Affairs. Financing for Sustainable Development Office. Policy Analysis and Development Branch. Chief

DEVELOPMENT FINANCE (Agenda item 16b)
Spiegel, Shari - A/C.2/78/SR.8
DEVELOPMENT FINANCE—CONFERENCES (Agenda item 17)
Spiegel, Shari - A/C.2/78/SR.8
FINANCIAL FLOWS (Agenda item 16f)
Spiegel, Shari - A/C.2/78/SR.8
TAXATION (Agenda item 16h)
Spiegel, Shari - A/C.2/78/SR.8

UN. Department of Economic and Social Affairs. Financing for Sustainable Development Office. Strategic Engagement and Policy Integration Branch. Chief

COMMODITIES (Agenda item 16d)
Parra-Lancourt, Mariangela - A/C.2/78/SR.14
SUSTAINABLE DEVELOPMENT (Agenda item 18)
Parra-Lancourt, Mariangela - A/C.2/78/SR.14

UN. Department of Economic and Social Affairs. Office of Intergovernmental Support and Coordination for Sustainable Development. Director

OPERATIONAL ACTIVITIES—UN SYSTEM (Agenda item 22a)
Pierre, Neil - A/C.2/78/SR.18

UN. Department of Management Strategy, Policy and Compliance. Business Transformation and Accountability Division

UN—ADMINISTRATION (Agenda item 132)
Summersgill, Kevin - A/C.5/78/SR.29

UN. Department of Management Strategy, Policy and Compliance. Office of Human Resources. Administrative Law Division. Director

PEACEKEEPING OPERATIONS (Agenda item 51)
Thanabalasingam, Aruna - A/C.4/78/SR.18

UN. Department of Management Strategy, Policy and Compliance. Office of Programme Planning, Finance and Budget. Finance Division. Director

INTERNATIONAL RESIDUAL MECHANISM FOR CRIMINAL TRIBUNALS—FINANCING (Agenda item 145)
Costa, Maria - A/C.5/78/SR.20; A/C.5/78/SR.25
UN—BUDGET (2024) (Agenda item 134)
Costa, Maria - A/C.5/78/SR.3; A/C.5/78/SR.12; A/C.5/78/SR.14; A/C.5/78/SR.18; A/C.5/78/SR.21; A/C.5/78/SR.22; A/C.5/78/SR.24; A/C.5/78/SR.25; A/C.5/78/SR.31
UN—FINANCIAL REPORTS (Agenda item 131)
Costa, Maria - A/C.5/78/SR.14
UN MULTIDIMENSIONAL INTEGRATED STABILIZATION MISSION IN MALI—FINANCING (Agenda item 155)
Costa, Maria - A/C.5/78/SR.20

UN. Department of Operational Support. Division of Administration. Director

UN—BUDGET (2024) (Agenda item 134)
Carey, Patrick - A/C.5/78/SR.11

UN. Deputy Secretary-General

HIV/AIDS—DECLARATIONS (Agenda item 10)
Mohammed, Amina J. - A/78/PV.91

UN. Deputy Secretary-General (continued)

RULE OF LAW (Agenda item 83)
Mohammed, Amina J. - A/C.6/78/SR.16
UN SYSTEM—STRENGTHENING (Agenda item 122)
Mohammed, Amina J. - A/78/PV.1

UN. Deputy to the High Representative for Disarmament Affairs

DISARMAMENT—GENERAL AND COMPLETE (Agenda item 99)
Ebo, Adedeji - A/78/PV.105; A/C.1/78/PV.11

UN. Disarmament Commission. Chair

UN. DISARMAMENT COMMISSION—REPORTS (Agenda item 101b)
Rakhmetullin, Akan (Kazakhstan) - A/C.1/78/PV.24

UN. Division for Ocean Affairs and the Law of the Sea

INTERNATIONAL LAW—TRAINING PROGRAMMES (Agenda item 78)
Hicuburundi, Alice - A/C.6/78/SR.21

UN. Economic and Social Council. President

COMMODITIES (Agenda item 16d)
Narváez Ojeda, Paula (Chile) - A/C.2/78/SR.14
SUSTAINABLE DEVELOPMENT (Agenda item 18)
Narváez Ojeda, Paula (Chile) - A/C.2/78/SR.14
UN. ECONOMIC AND SOCIAL COUNCIL—REPORTS (Agenda item 9)
Stoeva, Lachezara (Bulgaria) - A/78/PV.33

UN. Enterprise Resource Planning Solution Division. Director

UN—BUDGET (2024) (Agenda item 134)
Korithiwada, Sunitha - A/C.5/78/SR.19

UN. ESCWA. Division for Emerging and Conflict-related Issues. Director

TERRITORIES OCCUPIED BY ISRAEL—NATURAL RESOURCES (Agenda item 59)
Alami, Tarik - A/C.2/78/SR.19

UN. Ethics Office. Director

UN. ETHICS OFFICE—REPORTS (Agenda item 140)
Armstrong, Elia Yi - A/C.5/78/SR.2

UN. Executive Office of the Secretary-General. Sustainable Development Unit. Deputy Director

PERSONS WITH DISABILITIES—HUMAN RIGHTS (Agenda item 71a)
Blanco Rothe, Lara - A/C.3/78/SR.18

UN. General Assembly. 1st Committee. Chair

UN. GENERAL ASSEMBLY (78TH SESS. : 2023-2024). 1ST COMMITTEE—GENERAL DEBATE (Agenda item 8)
Paulauskas, Rytis (Lithuania) - A/C.1/78/PV.2; A/C.1/78/PV.7
UN. GENERAL ASSEMBLY (78TH SESS. : 2023-2024). 1ST COMMITTEE—WORK ORGANIZATION (Agenda item 7)
Paulauskas, Rytis (Lithuania) - A/C.1/78/PV.1; A/C.1/78/PV.30

UN. General Assembly. 1st Committee. Rapporteur

AFRICA—NUCLEAR-WEAPON-FREE ZONES (Agenda item 92)
Balouji, Heidar Ali (Iran (Islamic Republic of)) - A/78/PV.42
ARMS RACE—OUTER SPACE (Agenda item 97a)
Balouji, Heidar Ali (Iran (Islamic Republic of)) - A/78/PV.42
BIOLOGICAL WEAPONS—TREATIES (Agenda item 106)
Balouji, Heidar Ali (Iran (Islamic Republic of)) - A/78/PV.42
CONVENTIONAL WEAPONS—TREATIES (Agenda item 103)
Balouji, Heidar Ali (Iran (Islamic Republic of)) - A/78/PV.42
DISARMAMENT—GENERAL AND COMPLETE (Agenda item 99)
Balouji, Heidar Ali (Iran (Islamic Republic of)) - A/78/PV.42
DISARMAMENT—UN. GENERAL ASSEMBLY (10TH SPECIAL SESS. : 1978) (Agenda item 101)
Balouji, Heidar Ali (Iran (Islamic Republic of)) - A/78/PV.42
DISARMAMENT—UN. GENERAL ASSEMBLY (12TH SPECIAL SESS. : 1982) (Agenda item 100)
Balouji, Heidar Ali (Iran (Islamic Republic of)) - A/78/PV.42
DISARMAMENT AGREEMENTS—OUTER SPACE (Agenda item 97c)
Balouji, Heidar Ali (Iran (Islamic Republic of)) - A/78/PV.42
INDIAN OCEAN—ZONES OF PEACE (Agenda item 91)
Balouji, Heidar Ali (Iran (Islamic Republic of)) - A/78/PV.42
INFORMATION—INTERNATIONAL SECURITY (Agenda item 94)
Balouji, Heidar Ali (Iran (Islamic Republic of)) - A/78/PV.42
MEDITERRANEAN REGION—REGIONAL SECURITY (Agenda item 104)
Balouji, Heidar Ali (Iran (Islamic Republic of)) - A/78/PV.42

UN. General Assembly. 1st Committee. Rapporteur (continued)

MIDDLE EAST—NUCLEAR PROLIFERATION (Agenda item 102)
Balouji, Heidar Ali (Iran (Islamic Republic of)) - A/78/PV.42
MIDDLE EAST—NUCLEAR-WEAPON-FREE ZONES (Agenda item 95)
Balouji, Heidar Ali (Iran (Islamic Republic of)) - A/78/PV.42
MILITARY BUDGETS (Agenda item 90)
Balouji, Heidar Ali (Iran (Islamic Republic of)) - A/78/PV.42
NON-NUCLEAR-WEAPON STATES—SECURITY (Agenda item 96)
Balouji, Heidar Ali (Iran (Islamic Republic of)) - A/78/PV.42
NUCLEAR WEAPON TESTS—TREATIES (Agenda item 105)
Balouji, Heidar Ali (Iran (Islamic Republic of)) - A/78/PV.42
OUTER SPACE—PRINCIPLES (Agenda item 97d)
Balouji, Heidar Ali (Iran (Islamic Republic of)) - A/78/PV.42
SCIENCE AND TECHNOLOGY—INTERNATIONAL SECURITY (Agenda item 98)
Balouji, Heidar Ali (Iran (Islamic Republic of)) - A/78/PV.42
UN—PROGRAMME PLANNING (Agenda item 135)
Balouji, Heidar Ali (Iran (Islamic Republic of)) - A/78/PV.42
UN. GENERAL ASSEMBLY—WORK PROGRAMME (Agenda item 120)
Balouji, Heidar Ali (Iran (Islamic Republic of)) - A/78/PV.42
WEAPONS—OUTER SPACE (Agenda item 97b)
Balouji, Heidar Ali (Iran (Islamic Republic of)) - A/78/PV.42
WEAPONS OF MASS DESTRUCTION (Agenda item 93)
Balouji, Heidar Ali (Iran (Islamic Republic of)) - A/78/PV.42

UN. General Assembly. 2nd Committee. Chair

COMMODITIES (Agenda item 16d)
Amorín, Carlos Daniel (Uruguay) - A/C.2/78/SR.14
SUSTAINABLE DEVELOPMENT (Agenda item 18)
Amorín, Carlos Daniel (Uruguay) - A/C.2/78/SR.14
UN—PROGRAMME PLANNING (Agenda item 135)
Amorín, Carlos Daniel (Uruguay) - A/C.2/78/SR.1
UN. GENERAL ASSEMBLY (78TH SESS. : 2023-2024). 2ND COMMITTEE—GENERAL DEBATE (Agenda item 8)
Amorín, Carlos Daniel (Uruguay) - A/C.2/78/SR.2

UN. General Assembly. 2nd Committee. Chair (continued)

UN. GENERAL ASSEMBLY (78TH SESS. : 2023-2024). 2ND COMMITTEE—WORK ORGANIZATION (Agenda item 7)
Amorín, Carlos Daniel (Uruguay) - A/C.2/78/SR.1; A/C.2/78/SR.25

UN. General Assembly. 2nd Committee. Rapporteur

2030 AGENDA—PROGRAMME IMPLEMENTATION (Agenda item 18a)
Gatev, Ivaylo (Bulgaria) - A/78/PV.49
BIOLOGICAL DIVERSITY—TREATIES (Agenda item 18f)
Gatev, Ivaylo (Bulgaria) - A/78/PV.49
CLIMATE (Agenda item 18d)
Gatev, Ivaylo (Bulgaria) - A/78/PV.49
COASTAL ZONE MANAGEMENT (Agenda item 18j)
Gatev, Ivaylo (Bulgaria) - A/78/PV.49
COMMODITIES (Agenda item 16d)
Gatev, Ivaylo (Bulgaria) - A/78/PV.49
CULTURE—DEVELOPMENT (Agenda item 19b)
Gatev, Ivaylo (Bulgaria) - A/78/PV.49
DESERTIFICATION—TREATIES (Agenda item 18e)
Gatev, Ivaylo (Bulgaria) - A/78/PV.49
DEVELOPMENT COOPERATION—MIDDLE-INCOME COUNTRIES (Agenda item 19c)
Gatev, Ivaylo (Bulgaria) - A/78/PV.49
DEVELOPMENT EDUCATION (Agenda item 18g)
Gatev, Ivaylo (Bulgaria) - A/78/PV.49
DEVELOPMENT FINANCE (Agenda item 16b)
Gatev, Ivaylo (Bulgaria) - A/78/PV.49
DEVELOPMENT FINANCE—CONFERENCES (Agenda item 17)
Gatev, Ivaylo (Bulgaria) - A/78/PV.49
DISASTER PREVENTION (Agenda item 18c)
Gatev, Ivaylo (Bulgaria) - A/78/PV.49
ECONOMIC COOPERATION AMONG DEVELOPING COUNTRIES (Agenda item 22b)
Gatev, Ivaylo (Bulgaria) - A/78/PV.49
EXTERNAL DEBT (Agenda item 16c)
Gatev, Ivaylo (Bulgaria) - A/78/PV.49
FINANCIAL FLOWS (Agenda item 16f)
Gatev, Ivaylo (Bulgaria) - A/78/PV.49
FINANCIAL INCLUSION (Agenda item 16e)
Gatev, Ivaylo (Bulgaria) - A/78/PV.49
FOOD SECURITY (Agenda item 23a)
Gatev, Ivaylo (Bulgaria) - A/78/PV.49
GLOBALIZATION—INTERDEPENDENCE (Agenda item 19)
Gatev, Ivaylo (Bulgaria) - A/78/PV.49

UN. General Assembly. 2nd Committee. Rapporteur (continued)

INFORMATION TECHNOLOGY—DEVELOPMENT (Agenda item 15)
Gatev, Ivaylo (Bulgaria) - A/78/PV.49
INTERNATIONAL TRADE (Agenda item 16a)
Gatev, Ivaylo (Bulgaria) - A/78/PV.49
INVESTMENT PROMOTION (Agenda item 16g)
Gatev, Ivaylo (Bulgaria) - A/78/PV.49
LANDLOCKED DEVELOPING COUNTRIES—CONFERENCES (Agenda item 20b)
Gatev, Ivaylo (Bulgaria) - A/78/PV.49
LEAST DEVELOPED COUNTRIES—CONFERENCES (Agenda item 20a)
Gatev, Ivaylo (Bulgaria) - A/78/PV.49
MACROECONOMIC POLICY (Agenda item 16)
Gatev, Ivaylo (Bulgaria) - A/78/PV.49
NATURAL FIBRES (Agenda item 23b)
Gatev, Ivaylo (Bulgaria) - A/78/PV.49
OPERATIONAL ACTIVITIES—DEVELOPMENT (Agenda item 22)
Gatev, Ivaylo (Bulgaria) - A/78/PV.49
OPERATIONAL ACTIVITIES—UN SYSTEM (Agenda item 22a)
Gatev, Ivaylo (Bulgaria) - A/78/PV.49
POVERTY—INTERNATIONAL DECADES (Agenda item 21a)
Gatev, Ivaylo (Bulgaria) - A/78/PV.49
POVERTY MITIGATION (Agenda item 21)
Gatev, Ivaylo (Bulgaria) - A/78/PV.49
RURAL POVERTY (Agenda item 21b)
Gatev, Ivaylo (Bulgaria) - A/78/PV.49
SCIENCE AND TECHNOLOGY—DEVELOPMENT (Agenda item 19a)
Gatev, Ivaylo (Bulgaria) - A/78/PV.49
SMALL ISLAND DEVELOPING STATES—PROGRAMMES OF ACTION (Agenda item 18b)
Gatev, Ivaylo (Bulgaria) - A/78/PV.49
STORMS (Agenda item 18i)
Gatev, Ivaylo (Bulgaria) - A/78/PV.49
SUSTAINABLE DEVELOPMENT (Agenda item 18)
Gatev, Ivaylo (Bulgaria) - A/78/PV.49
SUSTAINABLE ENERGY (Agenda item 18h)
Gatev, Ivaylo (Bulgaria) - A/78/PV.49
TAXATION (Agenda item 16h)
Gatev, Ivaylo (Bulgaria) - A/78/PV.49
TERRITORIES OCCUPIED BY ISRAEL—NATURAL RESOURCES (Agenda item 59)
Gatev, Ivaylo (Bulgaria) - A/78/PV.49
UN—PROGRAMME PLANNING (Agenda item 135)
Gatev, Ivaylo (Bulgaria) - A/78/PV.49
UN. GENERAL ASSEMBLY—WORK PROGRAMME (Agenda item 120)
Gatev, Ivaylo (Bulgaria) - A/78/PV.49

UN. General Assembly. 2nd Committee. Secretary

COASTAL ZONE MANAGEMENT (Agenda item 18j)
Herity, Emer - A/C.2/78/SR.23
SUSTAINABLE DEVELOPMENT (Agenda item 18)
Herity, Emer - A/C.2/78/SR.24

UN. General Assembly. 3rd Committee. Chair

UN. GENERAL ASSEMBLY (78TH SESS. : 2023-2024)—OFFICERS (Agenda item 5)
Marschik, Alexander (Austria) - A/C.3/78/SR.57

UN. General Assembly. 3rd Committee. Rapporteur

CRIME PREVENTION (Agenda item 107)
Poveda Brito, Robert Alexander (Venezuela (Bolivarian Republic of)) - A/78/PV.50
CYBERCRIME (Agenda item 108)
Poveda Brito, Robert Alexander (Venezuela (Bolivarian Republic of)) - A/78/PV.50
HUMAN RIGHTS (Agenda item 71)
Poveda Brito, Robert Alexander (Venezuela (Bolivarian Republic of)) - A/78/PV.50
HUMAN RIGHTS—INTERNATIONAL INSTRUMENTS (Agenda item 71a)
Poveda Brito, Robert Alexander (Venezuela (Bolivarian Republic of)) - A/78/PV.50
HUMAN RIGHTS—PROGRAMMES OF ACTION (Agenda item 71d)
Poveda Brito, Robert Alexander (Venezuela (Bolivarian Republic of)) - A/78/PV.50
HUMAN RIGHTS—REPORTS (Agenda item 71c)
Poveda Brito, Robert Alexander (Venezuela (Bolivarian Republic of)) - A/78/PV.50
HUMAN RIGHTS ADVANCEMENT (Agenda item 71b)
Poveda Brito, Robert Alexander (Venezuela (Bolivarian Republic of)) - A/78/PV.50
INDIGENOUS PEOPLES (Agenda item 68a)
Poveda Brito, Robert Alexander (Venezuela (Bolivarian Republic of)) - A/78/PV.50
INDIGENOUS PEOPLES—CONFERENCES (Agenda item 68b)
Poveda Brito, Robert Alexander (Venezuela (Bolivarian Republic of)) - A/78/PV.50
RACIAL DISCRIMINATION—ELIMINATION (Agenda item 69a)
Poveda Brito, Robert Alexander (Venezuela (Bolivarian Republic of)) - A/78/PV.50
RACIAL DISCRIMINATION—PROGRAMMES OF ACTION (Agenda item 69b)
Poveda Brito, Robert Alexander (Venezuela (Bolivarian Republic of)) - A/78/PV.50
RIGHTS OF THE CHILD (Agenda item 67)
Poveda Brito, Robert Alexander (Venezuela (Bolivarian Republic of)) - A/78/PV.50

UN. General Assembly. 3rd Committee. Rapporteur (continued)

SELF-DETERMINATION OF PEOPLES (Agenda item 70)
Poveda Brito, Robert Alexander (Venezuela (Bolivarian Republic of)) - A/78/PV.50
SOCIAL CONDITIONS (Agenda item 24b)
Poveda Brito, Robert Alexander (Venezuela (Bolivarian Republic of)) - A/78/PV.50
SOCIAL DEVELOPMENT (Agenda item 24)
Poveda Brito, Robert Alexander (Venezuela (Bolivarian Republic of)) - A/78/PV.50
SOCIAL DEVELOPMENT—CONFERENCES (Agenda item 24a)
Poveda Brito, Robert Alexander (Venezuela (Bolivarian Republic of)) - A/78/PV.50
UN—PROGRAMME PLANNING (Agenda item 135)
Poveda Brito, Robert Alexander (Venezuela (Bolivarian Republic of)) - A/78/PV.50
UN. GENERAL ASSEMBLY—WORK PROGRAMME (Agenda item 120)
Poveda Brito, Robert Alexander (Venezuela (Bolivarian Republic of)) - A/78/PV.50
UN. HUMAN RIGHTS COUNCIL—REPORTS (Agenda item 66)
Poveda Brito, Robert Alexander (Venezuela (Bolivarian Republic of)) - A/78/PV.50
UN HIGH COMMISSIONER FOR REFUGEES—REPORTS (Agenda item 60)
Poveda Brito, Robert Alexander (Venezuela (Bolivarian Republic of)) - A/78/PV.50
WOMEN'S ADVANCEMENT (Agenda item 25a)
Poveda Brito, Robert Alexander (Venezuela (Bolivarian Republic of)) - A/78/PV.50
WOMEN'S ADVANCEMENT—CONFERENCES (Agenda item 25b)
Poveda Brito, Robert Alexander (Venezuela (Bolivarian Republic of)) - A/78/PV.50

UN. General Assembly. 3rd Committee. Secretary

CRIME PREVENTION (Agenda item 107)
Mahmassani, Ziad - A/C.3/78/SR.47
WOMEN'S ADVANCEMENT—CONFERENCES (Agenda item 25b)
Mahmassani, Ziad - A/C.3/78/SR.51

UN. General Assembly. 5th Committee. Chair

SUBSIDIARY ORGANS—APPOINTMENTS (Agenda item 115)
Abdelkhalek, Osama Mahmoud (Egypt) - A/C.5/78/SR.8
UN—FINANCIAL SITUATION (Agenda item 136)
Abdelkhalek, Osama Mahmoud (Egypt) - A/C.5/78/SR.38

UN. General Assembly. 5th Committee. Chair (continued)

UN. ADVISORY COMMITTEE ON ADMINISTRATIVE AND BUDGETARY QUESTIONS—MEMBERS (Agenda item 115a)
Abdelkhalek, Osama Mahmoud (Egypt) - A/C.5/78/SR.8
UN. BOARD OF AUDITORS—MEMBERS (Agenda item 115d)
Abdelkhalek, Osama Mahmoud (Egypt) - A/C.5/78/SR.8
UN. COMMITTEE ON CONTRIBUTIONS—MEMBERS (Agenda item 115b)
Abdelkhalek, Osama Mahmoud (Egypt) - A/C.5/78/SR.8
UN. GENERAL ASSEMBLY (78TH SESS. : 2023-2024). 5TH COMMITTEE—WORK ORGANIZATION (Agenda item 7)
Abdelkhalek, Osama Mahmoud (Egypt) - A/C.5/78/SR.35
UN. INDEPENDENT AUDIT ADVISORY COMMITTEE—MEMBERS (Agenda item 115e)
Abdelkhalek, Osama Mahmoud (Egypt) - A/C.5/78/SR.8
UN. INVESTMENTS COMMITTEE—MEMBERS (Agenda item 115c)
Abdelkhalek, Osama Mahmoud (Egypt) - A/C.5/78/SR.8

UN. General Assembly. 5th Committee. Rapporteur

ADMINISTRATION OF JUSTICE (Agenda item 144)
Hartog, Laurens Thomas den (Netherlands (Kingdom of the)) - A/78/PV.50(Resumption1)
AU-UN HYBRID OPERATION IN DARFUR—FINANCING (Agenda item 159)
Hartog, Laurens Thomas den (Netherlands (Kingdom of the)) - A/78/PV.95
CONFERENCE AND MEETING SERVICES (Agenda item 137)
Hartog, Laurens Thomas den (Netherlands (Kingdom of the)) - A/78/PV.50(Resumption1)
INTERNATIONAL RESIDUAL MECHANISM FOR CRIMINAL TRIBUNALS—FINANCING (Agenda item 145)
Hartog, Laurens Thomas den (Netherlands (Kingdom of the)) - A/78/PV.50(Resumption1)
JOINT INSPECTION UNIT (Agenda item 141)
Hartog, Laurens Thomas den (Netherlands (Kingdom of the)) - A/78/PV.73
PEACEKEEPING OPERATIONS—FINANCING (Agenda item 146)
Hartog, Laurens Thomas den (Netherlands (Kingdom of the)) - A/78/PV.95
UN—ADMINISTRATION (Agenda item 132)
Hartog, Laurens Thomas den (Netherlands (Kingdom of the)) - A/78/PV.50(Resumption1); A/78/PV.73; A/78/PV.95

UN. General Assembly. 5th Committee. Rapporteur (continued)

UN—BUDGET (2023) (Agenda item 133)
Hartog, Laurens Thomas den (Netherlands (Kingdom of the)) - A/78/PV.50(Resumption1)
UN—BUDGET (2024) (Agenda item 134)
Hartog, Laurens Thomas den (Netherlands (Kingdom of the)) - A/78/PV.50(Resumption1); A/78/PV.73
UN—FINANCIAL REPORTS (Agenda item 131)
Hartog, Laurens Thomas den (Netherlands (Kingdom of the)) - A/78/PV.50(Resumption1); A/78/PV.95
UN—HUMAN RESOURCES MANAGEMENT (Agenda item 139)
Hartog, Laurens Thomas den (Netherlands (Kingdom of the)) - A/78/PV.73; A/78/PV.95
UN—PROGRAMME PLANNING (Agenda item 135)
Hartog, Laurens Thomas den (Netherlands (Kingdom of the)) - A/78/PV.50(Resumption1)
UN. ETHICS OFFICE—REPORTS (Agenda item 140)
Hartog, Laurens Thomas den (Netherlands (Kingdom of the)) - A/78/PV.50(Resumption1)
UN. OFFICE OF INTERNAL OVERSIGHT SERVICES—REPORTS (Agenda item 143)
Hartog, Laurens Thomas den (Netherlands (Kingdom of the)) - A/78/PV.50(Resumption1)
UN. SUPPORT OFFICE IN SOMALIA—FINANCING (Agenda item 160)
Hartog, Laurens Thomas den (Netherlands (Kingdom of the)) - A/78/PV.95
UN DISENGAGEMENT OBSERVER FORCE—FINANCING (Agenda item 156a)
Hartog, Laurens Thomas den (Netherlands (Kingdom of the)) - A/78/PV.95
UN INTERIM ADMINISTRATION MISSION IN KOSOVO—FINANCING (Agenda item 153)
Hartog, Laurens Thomas den (Netherlands (Kingdom of the)) - A/78/PV.95
UN INTERIM FORCE IN LEBANON—FINANCING (Agenda item 156b)
Hartog, Laurens Thomas den (Netherlands (Kingdom of the)) - A/78/PV.95
UN MISSION FOR THE REFERENDUM IN WESTERN SAHARA—FINANCING (Agenda item 158)
Hartog, Laurens Thomas den (Netherlands (Kingdom of the)) - A/78/PV.95
UN MISSION IN LIBERIA—FINANCING (Agenda item 154)
Hartog, Laurens Thomas den (Netherlands (Kingdom of the)) - A/78/PV.95
UN MISSION IN SOUTH SUDAN—FINANCING (Agenda item 157)
Hartog, Laurens Thomas den (Netherlands (Kingdom of the)) - A/78/PV.95

UN. General Assembly. 5th Committee. Rapporteur (continued)

UN MULTIDIMENSIONAL INTEGRATED STABILIZATION MISSION IN MALI—FINANCING (Agenda item 155)
Hartog, Laurens Thomas den (Netherlands (Kingdom of the)) - A/78/PV.50(Resumption1); A/78/PV.95
UN MULTIDIMENSIONAL INTEGRATED STABILIZATION MISSION IN THE CENTRAL AFRICAN REPUBLIC—FINANCING (Agenda item 148)
Hartog, Laurens Thomas den (Netherlands (Kingdom of the)) - A/78/PV.95
UN OPERATION IN CÔTE D'IVOIRE—FINANCING (Agenda item 149)
Hartog, Laurens Thomas den (Netherlands (Kingdom of the)) - A/78/PV.95
UN ORGANIZATION STABILIZATION MISSION IN THE DEMOCRATIC REPUBLIC OF THE CONGO—FINANCING (Agenda item 151)
Hartog, Laurens Thomas den (Netherlands (Kingdom of the)) - A/78/PV.95
UN PEACEKEEPING FORCE IN CYPRUS—FINANCING (Agenda item 150)
Hartog, Laurens Thomas den (Netherlands (Kingdom of the)) - A/78/PV.95
UN SECURITY FORCE FOR ABYEI—FINANCING (Agenda item 147)
Hartog, Laurens Thomas den (Netherlands (Kingdom of the)) - A/78/PV.95

UN. General Assembly. 6th Committee. Bureau

ADMINISTRATION OF JUSTICE (Agenda item 144)
Vittay, Melinda (Hungary) - A/C.6/78/SR.37
INTERNATIONAL JURISDICTION (Agenda item 84)
Raojee, Vreeshini (Mauritius) - A/C.6/78/SR.37
INTERNATIONAL LAW—TRAINING PROGRAMMES (Agenda item 78)
Hackman, Khalilah (Ghana) - A/C.6/78/SR.37
NON-CITIZENS—DEPORTATION (Agenda item 81)
Panier, Wisnique (Haiti) - A/C.6/78/SR.37
PEACEKEEPING OPERATIONS—CRIMINAL LIABILITY (Agenda item 76)
Uddin, Nasir (Bangladesh) - A/C.6/78/SR.37
RESPONSIBILITY OF INTERNATIONAL ORGANIZATIONS (Agenda item 85)
Sloboda, Pedro Muniz Pinto (Brazil) - A/C.6/78/SR.37
RULE OF LAW (Agenda item 83)
Jiménez Alegría, Natalia (Mexico) - A/C.6/78/SR.37
TERRORISM (Agenda item 109)
Maillé, Béatrice (Canada) - A/C.6/78/SR.37
TREATIES (Agenda item 87)
Khng, Nathaniel (Singapore) - A/C.6/78/SR.37

UN. General Assembly. 6th Committee. Bureau (continued)

UN. INTERNATIONAL LAW COMMISSION—REPORTS (Agenda item 79)
Košuth, Matus (Slovakia) - A/C.6/78/SR.37
Solano Ramírez, Lucía Teresa (Colombia) - A/C.6/78/SR.37
UN CHARTER—REPORTS (Agenda item 82)
Nouh, Amr Mohamed Mosaad (Egypt) - A/C.6/78/SR.37
UN COMMISSION ON INTERNATIONAL TRADE LAW—REPORTS (Agenda item 77)
Flores Soto, Ligia Lorena (El Salvador) - A/C.6/78/SR.37
Gorke, Maximilian (Austria) - A/C.6/78/SR.37
Khng, Nathaniel (Singapore) - A/C.6/78/SR.37

UN. General Assembly. 6th Committee. Rapporteur

BOAO FORUM FOR ASIA—OBSERVER STATUS (Agenda item 169)
Moussa, Moussa Mohamed (Djibouti) - A/78/PV.45
COMMUNITY OF DEMOCRACIES—OBSERVER STATUS (Agenda item 164)
Moussa, Moussa Mohamed (Djibouti) - A/78/PV.45
COOPERATION COUNCIL OF TURKIC-SPEAKING STATES—OBSERVER STATUS (Agenda item 162)
Moussa, Moussa Mohamed (Djibouti) - A/78/PV.45
DISASTER VICTIMS (Agenda item 86)
Moussa, Moussa Mohamed (Djibouti) - A/78/PV.45
EURASIAN ECONOMIC UNION—OBSERVER STATUS (Agenda item 163)
Moussa, Moussa Mohamed (Djibouti) - A/78/PV.45
GLOBAL ENVIRONMENT FACILITY—OBSERVER STATUS (Agenda item 166)
Moussa, Moussa Mohamed (Djibouti) - A/78/PV.45
INTERNATIONAL JURISDICTION (Agenda item 84)
Moussa, Moussa Mohamed (Djibouti) - A/78/PV.45
INTERNATIONAL LAW—TRAINING PROGRAMMES (Agenda item 78)
Moussa, Moussa Mohamed (Djibouti) - A/78/PV.45
INTERNATIONAL ORGANIZATION OF EMPLOYERS—OBSERVER STATUS (Agenda item 167)
Moussa, Moussa Mohamed (Djibouti) - A/78/PV.45
INTERNATIONAL PARLIAMENTARIANS' CONGRESS—OBSERVER STATUS (Agenda item 170)
Moussa, Moussa Mohamed (Djibouti) - A/78/PV.45
INTERNATIONAL TRADE UNION CONFEDERATION—OBSERVER STATUS (Agenda item 168)
Moussa, Moussa Mohamed (Djibouti) - A/78/PV.45
NON-CITIZENS—DEPORTATION (Agenda item 81)
Moussa, Moussa Mohamed (Djibouti) - A/78/PV.45
ORGANIZATION OF IBERO-AMERICAN STATES FOR EDUCATION, SCIENCE AND CULTURE—OBSERVER STATUS (Agenda item 171)
Moussa, Moussa Mohamed (Djibouti) - A/78/PV.45

UN. General Assembly. 6th Committee. Rapporteur (continued)

PEACEKEEPING OPERATIONS—CRIMINAL LIABILITY (Agenda item 76)
Moussa, Moussa Mohamed (Djibouti) - A/78/PV.45
RAMSAR CONVENTION SECRETARIAT—OBSERVER STATUS (Agenda item 165)
Moussa, Moussa Mohamed (Djibouti) - A/78/PV.45
RESPONSIBILITY OF INTERNATIONAL ORGANIZATIONS (Agenda item 85)
Moussa, Moussa Mohamed (Djibouti) - A/78/PV.45
RULE OF LAW (Agenda item 83)
Moussa, Moussa Mohamed (Djibouti) - A/78/PV.45
TERRORISM (Agenda item 109)
Moussa, Moussa Mohamed (Djibouti) - A/78/PV.45
TREATIES (Agenda item 87)
Moussa, Moussa Mohamed (Djibouti) - A/78/PV.45
UN—PROGRAMME PLANNING (Agenda item 135)
Moussa, Moussa Mohamed (Djibouti) - A/78/PV.45
UN. COMMITTEE ON RELATIONS WITH THE HOST COUNTRY—REPORTS (Agenda item 161)
Moussa, Moussa Mohamed (Djibouti) - A/78/PV.45
UN. GENERAL ASSEMBLY—WORK PROGRAMME (Agenda item 120)
Moussa, Moussa Mohamed (Djibouti) - A/78/PV.45
UN. INTERNATIONAL LAW COMMISSION—REPORTS (Agenda item 79)
Moussa, Moussa Mohamed (Djibouti) - A/78/PV.45
UN CHARTER—REPORTS (Agenda item 82)
Moussa, Moussa Mohamed (Djibouti) - A/78/PV.45
UN COMMISSION ON INTERNATIONAL TRADE LAW—REPORTS (Agenda item 77)
Moussa, Moussa Mohamed (Djibouti) - A/78/PV.45

UN. General Assembly. 6th Committee. Working Group on Measures to Eliminate International Terrorism. Chair

TERRORISM (Agenda item 109)
Perera, Amrith Rohan (Sri Lanka) - A/C.6/78/SR.36

UN. General Assembly. 6th Committee. Working Group on Protection of Persons in the Event of Disasters. Chair

DISASTER VICTIMS (Agenda item 86)
Lagdameo, Antonio Manuel Revilla (Philippines) - A/C.6/78/SR.36

UN. General Assembly. Ad Hoc Working Group on the Revitalization of the General Assembly. Co-Chair

UN. GENERAL ASSEMBLY—WORK PROGRAMME (Agenda item 120)
Feruță, Cornel (Romania) - A/78/PV.33
UN RESOLUTIONS—IMPLEMENTATION (Agenda item 119)
Feruță, Cornel (Romania) - A/78/PV.33

UN. General Assembly. Credentials Committee. Chair

UN. GENERAL ASSEMBLY (78TH SESS. : 2023-2024). CREDENTIALS COMMITTEE—REPORTS (Agenda item 3b)
Waetara, Jane Mugafalu Kabui (Solomon Islands) - A/78/PV.48

UN. General Assembly. President

AFRICA—DEVELOPMENT (Agenda item 65b)
Francis, Dennis (Trinidad and Tobago) - A/78/PV.18
AFRICA—SUSTAINABLE DEVELOPMENT—PARTNERSHIP (Agenda item 65a)
Francis, Dennis (Trinidad and Tobago) - A/78/PV.18
AL-SABAH, NAWAF AL-AHMAD AL-JABER (KUWAIT. AMIR)—TRIBUTES
Francis, Dennis (Trinidad and Tobago) - A/78/PV.50(Resumption1)
DISARMAMENT—GENERAL AND COMPLETE (Agenda item 99)
Francis, Dennis (Trinidad and Tobago) - A/78/PV.105
GEINGOB, HAGE GOTTFRIED (NAMIBIA. PRESIDENT)—TRIBUTES
Francis, Dennis (Trinidad and Tobago) - A/78/PV.55
INTERNATIONAL CRIMINAL COURT—REPORTS (Agenda item 74)
Francis, Dennis (Trinidad and Tobago) - A/78/PV.21
LAW OF THE SEA (Agenda item 75a)
Francis, Dennis (Trinidad and Tobago) - A/78/PV.43
MARINE ECOSYSTEMS—BIOLOGICAL DIVERSITY (Agenda item 75c)
Francis, Dennis (Trinidad and Tobago) - A/78/PV.43
MILLENNIUM SUMMIT—CONFERENCES (Agenda item 117)
Francis, Dennis (Trinidad and Tobago) - A/78/PV.53; A/78/PV.102
MULTILATERALISM
Francis, Dennis (Trinidad and Tobago) - A/78/PV.81; A/78/PV.84
ORGANIZATION FOR DEMOCRACY AND ECONOMIC DEVELOPMENT - GUAM (Agenda item 32)
Francis, Dennis (Trinidad and Tobago) - A/78/PV.85
PALESTINE QUESTION (Agenda item 35)
Francis, Dennis (Trinidad and Tobago) - A/78/PV.39
RACIAL DISCRIMINATION—ELIMINATION (Agenda item 69a)
Francis, Dennis (Trinidad and Tobago) - A/78/PV.63
RAISI, SEYYED EBRAHIM (IRAN (ISLAMIC REPUBLID OF). PRESIDENT)—TRIBUTES
Francis, Dennis (Trinidad and Tobago) - A/78/PV.83

UN. General Assembly. President (continued)

SLAVERY—MEMORIALS (Agenda item 118)
Francis, Dennis (Trinidad and Tobago) - A/78/PV.64
SMALL ISLAND DEVELOPING STATES—PROGRAMMES OF ACTION (Agenda item 18b)
Francis, Dennis (Trinidad and Tobago) - A/78/PV.103
SPORTS—OLYMPIC GAMES (Agenda item 11)
Francis, Dennis (Trinidad and Tobago) - A/78/PV.93
STRADDLING FISH STOCKS (Agenda item 75b)
Francis, Dennis (Trinidad and Tobago) - A/78/PV.43
UKRAINE—POLITICAL CONDITIONS (Agenda item 62)
Francis, Dennis (Trinidad and Tobago) - A/78/PV.56
UN. GENERAL ASSEMBLY—PRESIDENT-ELECT—OATH OF OFFICE
Yang, Philémon (Cameroon) - A/78/PV.109
UN. GENERAL ASSEMBLY—WORK PROGRAMME (Agenda item 120)
Francis, Dennis (Trinidad and Tobago) - A/78/PV.32
UN. GENERAL ASSEMBLY (78TH SESS. : 2023-2024)—AGENDA (Agenda item 7)
Francis, Dennis (Trinidad and Tobago) - A/78/PV.1
UN. GENERAL ASSEMBLY (78TH SESS. : 2023-2024)—CLOSING
Francis, Dennis (Trinidad and Tobago) - A/78/PV.109
UN. GENERAL ASSEMBLY (78TH SESS. : 2023-2024)—GENERAL DEBATE (Agenda item 8)
Francis, Dennis (Trinidad and Tobago) - A/78/PV.4; A/78/PV.14
UN. GENERAL ASSEMBLY (78TH SESS. : 2023-2024). 1ST COMMITTEE—GENERAL DEBATE (Agenda item 8)
Francis, Dennis (Trinidad and Tobago) - A/C.1/78/PV.2
UN. GENERAL ASSEMBLY (78TH SESS. : 2023-2024). 2ND COMMITTEE—WORK ORGANIZATION (Agenda item 7)
Francis, Dennis (Trinidad and Tobago) - A/C.2/78/SR.12
UN. GENERAL ASSEMBLY (78TH SESS. : 2023-2024). 3RD COMMITTEE—WORK ORGANIZATION (Agenda item 7)
Francis, Dennis (Trinidad and Tobago) - A/C.3/78/SR.17
UN. GENERAL ASSEMBLY (78TH SESS. : 2023-2024). 4TH COMMITTEE—WORK ORGANIZATION (Agenda item 7)
Francis, Dennis (Trinidad and Tobago) - A/C.4/78/SR.2

UN. General Assembly. President (continued)

UN. GENERAL ASSEMBLY (78TH SESS. : 2023-2024). 5TH COMMITTEE—WORK ORGANIZATION (Agenda item 7)
Francis, Dennis (Trinidad and Tobago) - A/C.5/78/SR.4
UN. GENERAL ASSEMBLY (78TH SESS. : 2023-2024). 6TH COMMITTEE—WORK ORGANIZATION (Agenda item 7)
Francis, Dennis (Trinidad and Tobago) - A/C.6/78/SR.12
UN. GENERAL ASSEMBLY (78TH SESS. : 2023-2024). PRESIDENT (Agenda item 4)
Francis, Dennis (Trinidad and Tobago) - A/78/PV.87
UN. HUMAN RIGHTS COUNCIL—MEMBERS (Agenda item 114c)
Francis, Dennis (Trinidad and Tobago) - A/78/PV.17
UN. HUMAN RIGHTS COUNCIL—REPORTS (Agenda item 66)
Francis, Dennis (Trinidad and Tobago) - A/78/PV.23
UN. INTERNATIONAL COURT OF JUSTICE—REPORTS (Agenda item 73)
Francis, Dennis (Trinidad and Tobago) - A/78/PV.20
UN. SECURITY COUNCIL—MEMBERS (Agenda item 113a)
Francis, Dennis (Trinidad and Tobago) - A/78/PV.86
UN. SECURITY COUNCIL—MEMBERSHIP (Agenda item 121)
Francis, Dennis (Trinidad and Tobago) - A/78/PV.34; A/78/PV.104
UN. SECURITY COUNCIL—REPORTS (Agenda item 26)
Francis, Dennis (Trinidad and Tobago) - A/78/PV.93
UN CONFERENCES (Agenda item 13)
Francis, Dennis (Trinidad and Tobago) - A/78/PV.53; A/78/PV.102
UN RESOLUTIONS—IMPLEMENTATION (Agenda item 119)
Francis, Dennis (Trinidad and Tobago) - A/78/PV.32
VETO (Agenda item 63)
Francis, Dennis (Trinidad and Tobago) - A/78/PV.3; A/78/PV.59; A/78/PV.66; A/78/PV.68; A/78/PV.70

UN. General Assembly. Special Political and Decolonization Committee (4th Committee). Chair

OUTER SPACE—PEACEFUL USES—INTERNATIONAL COOPERATION (Agenda item 48)
Joyini, Mathu (South Africa) - A/C.4/78/SR.15
UN. GENERAL ASSEMBLY (78TH SESS. : 2023-2024). 4TH COMMITTEE—WORK ORGANIZATION (Agenda item 7)
Joyini, Mathu (South Africa) - A/C.4/78/SR.1

UN. General Assembly. Special Political and Decolonization Committee (4th Committee). Chair (continued)

UNRWA—ACTIVITIES (Agenda item 49)
Joyini, Mathu (South Africa) - A/C.4/78/SR.22

UN. General Assembly. Special Political and Decolonization Committee (4th Committee). Rapporteur

DECOLONIZATION (Agenda item 58)
Dhanutirto, Mariska Dwianti (Indonesia) - A/78/PV.45
DECOLONIZATION—UN SYSTEM (Agenda item 56)
Dhanutirto, Mariska Dwianti (Indonesia) - A/78/PV.45
INFORMATION (Agenda item 53)
Dhanutirto, Mariska Dwianti (Indonesia) - A/78/PV.45
MINE CLEARANCE (Agenda item 46)
Dhanutirto, Mariska Dwianti (Indonesia) - A/78/PV.45
NON-SELF-GOVERNING TERRITORIES—ECONOMIC INTERESTS (Agenda item 55)
Dhanutirto, Mariska Dwianti (Indonesia) - A/78/PV.45
NON-SELF-GOVERNING TERRITORIES—FELLOWSHIPS (Agenda item 57)
Dhanutirto, Mariska Dwianti (Indonesia) - A/78/PV.45
NON-SELF-GOVERNING TERRITORIES—REPORTS (Agenda item 54)
Dhanutirto, Mariska Dwianti (Indonesia) - A/78/PV.45
OUTER SPACE—PEACEFUL USES—INTERNATIONAL COOPERATION (Agenda item 48)
Dhanutirto, Mariska Dwianti (Indonesia) - A/78/PV.45
PEACEKEEPING OPERATIONS (Agenda item 51)
Dhanutirto, Mariska Dwianti (Indonesia) - A/78/PV.45
RADIATION EFFECTS (Agenda item 47)
Dhanutirto, Mariska Dwianti (Indonesia) - A/78/PV.45
SPECIAL POLITICAL MISSIONS (Agenda item 52)
Dhanutirto, Mariska Dwianti (Indonesia) - A/78/PV.45
TERRITORIES OCCUPIED BY ISRAEL—HUMAN RIGHTS (Agenda item 50)
Dhanutirto, Mariska Dwianti (Indonesia) - A/78/PV.45
UN—PROGRAMME PLANNING (Agenda item 135)
Dhanutirto, Mariska Dwianti (Indonesia) - A/78/PV.45
UN. GENERAL ASSEMBLY—WORK PROGRAMME (Agenda item 120)
Dhanutirto, Mariska Dwianti (Indonesia) - A/78/PV.45

UN. General Assembly. Special Political and Decolonization Committee (4th Committee). Rapporteur (continued)

UNRWA—ACTIVITIES (Agenda item 49)
Dhanutirto, Mariska Dwianti (Indonesia) - A/78/PV.45

UN. General Assembly. Special Political and Decolonization Committee (4th Committee). Working Group on International Cooperation in the Peaceful Uses of Outer Space. Chair

OUTER SPACE—PEACEFUL USES—INTERNATIONAL COOPERATION (Agenda item 48)
Sharaf, Omran (United Arab Emirates) - A/C.4/78/SR.17

UN. General Assembly. Vice-President

HIV/AIDS—DECLARATIONS (Agenda item 10)
Valtýsson, Jörundur (Iceland) - A/78/PV.91
SPORTS—OLYMPIC GAMES (Agenda item 11)
Pieris, Peter Mohan Maithri (Sri Lanka) - A/78/PV.38
VETO (Agenda item 63)
Muhamad, Ahmad Faisal (Malaysia) - A/78/PV.78
Niang, Cheikh (Senegal) - A/78/PV.51

UN. Group of African States

2030 AGENDA—PROGRAMME IMPLEMENTATION (Agenda item 18a)
Ladeb, Tarek (Tunisia) - A/C.2/78/SR.12
ADMINISTRATION OF JUSTICE (Agenda item 144)
Ikondere, Marvin (Uganda) - A/C.6/78/SR.9
AFRICA—DEVELOPMENT (Agenda item 65b)
Ladeb, Tarek (Tunisia) - A/78/PV.18
Mokhawa, Gladys (Botswana) - A/78/PV.57
AFRICA—NUCLEAR-WEAPON-FREE ZONES (Agenda item 92)
Mahmud, Mohammed Lawal (Nigeria) - A/C.1/78/PV.11
AFRICA—SUSTAINABLE DEVELOPMENT—PARTNERSHIP (Agenda item 65a)
Ladeb, Tarek (Tunisia) - A/78/PV.18
Mokhawa, Gladys (Botswana) - A/78/PV.57
AL-SABAH, NAWAF AL-AHMAD AL-JABER (KUWAIT. AMIR)—TRIBUTES
Boma, Regina Chama (Zambia) - A/78/PV.50(Resumption1)
ARMS RACE—OUTER SPACE (Agenda item 97a)
Mahmud, Mohammed Lawal (Nigeria) - A/C.1/78/PV.16
CONVENTIONAL WEAPONS (Agenda item 99u)
Mahmud, Mohammed Lawal (Nigeria) - A/C.1/78/PV.17
CRIMES AGAINST HUMANITY (Agenda item 80)
Muhumuza, Duncan Laki (Uganda) - A/C.6/78/SR.9; A/C.6/78/SR.38

UN. Group of African States (continued)

CUBA—UNITED STATES (Agenda item 38)
Milambo, Chola (Zambia) - A/78/PV.24
DISARMAMENT—GENERAL AND COMPLETE (Agenda item 99)
Makiza, Maurice Gatien (Congo) - A/78/PV.105
DISARMAMENT AGREEMENTS—OUTER SPACE (Agenda item 97c)
Mahmud, Mohammed Lawal (Nigeria) - A/C.1/78/PV.16
DISASTER VICTIMS (Agenda item 86)
Ikondere, Marvin (Uganda) - A/C.6/78/SR.5
ECONOMIC SANCTIONS—INTERNATIONAL RELATIONS (Agenda item 28)
Imohe, Uhimwen Robert (Nigeria) - A/78/PV.89
EXTERNAL DEBT (Agenda item 16c)
Ladeb, Tarek (Tunisia) - A/C.2/78/SR.9
FINANCIAL FLOWS (Agenda item 16f)
Ladeb, Tarek (Tunisia) - A/C.2/78/SR.9
GEINGOB, HAGE GOTTFRIED (NAMIBIA. PRESIDENT)—TRIBUTES
Mokhawa, Gladys (Botswana) - A/78/PV.55
HUMAN RIGHTS—BURUNDI (Agenda item 71c)
Milambo, Chola (Zambia) - A/C.3/78/SR.36
HUMAN RIGHTS—ERITREA (Agenda item 71c)
Milambo, Chola (Zambia) - A/C.3/78/SR.36
HUMAN RIGHTS—ETHIOPIA (Agenda item 71c)
Milambo, Chola (Zambia) - A/C.3/78/SR.36
INTERNATIONAL JURISDICTION (Agenda item 84)
Ikondere, Marvin (Uganda) - A/C.6/78/SR.12
INTERNATIONAL LAW—TRAINING PROGRAMMES (Agenda item 78)
Ikondere, Marvin (Uganda) - A/C.6/78/SR.21
INTERNATIONAL RESIDUAL MECHANISM FOR CRIMINAL TRIBUNALS—FINANCING (Agenda item 145)
Minale, Lemlem Fiseha (Ethiopia) - A/C.5/78/SR.20
INTERNATIONAL TRADE (Agenda item 16a)
Ladeb, Tarek (Tunisia) - A/C.2/78/SR.9
MACROECONOMIC POLICY (Agenda item 16)
Ladeb, Tarek (Tunisia) - A/C.2/78/SR.9
MIDDLE EAST—NUCLEAR-WEAPON-FREE ZONES (Agenda item 95)
Mahmud, Mohammed Lawal (Nigeria) - A/C.1/78/PV.11
MULTILINGUALISM (Agenda item 124)
Kattanga, Hussein A. (United Republic of Tanzania) - A/78/PV.97
NUCLEAR DISARMAMENT (Agenda item 99b)
Mahmud, Mohammed Lawal (Nigeria) - A/C.1/78/PV.11

UN. Group of African States (continued)

NUCLEAR NON-PROLIFERATION—INTERNATIONAL OBLIGATIONS (Agenda item 99w)
Mahmud, Mohammed Lawal (Nigeria) - A/C.1/78/PV.11
NUCLEAR WEAPON TESTS—TREATIES (Agenda item 105)
Mahmud, Mohammed Lawal (Nigeria) - A/C.1/78/PV.11
NUCLEAR WEAPONS—HUMANITARIAN CONSEQUENCES (Agenda item 99bb)
Mahmud, Mohammed Lawal (Nigeria) - A/C.1/78/PV.11
NUCLEAR WEAPONS—TREATIES (Agenda item 99ff)
Mahmud, Mohammed Lawal (Nigeria) - A/C.1/78/PV.11
OUTER SPACE—CONFIDENCE-BUILDING MEASURES (Agenda item 99v)
Mahmud, Mohammed Lawal (Nigeria) - A/C.1/78/PV.16
PEACEKEEPING OPERATIONS—CRIMINAL LIABILITY (Agenda item 76)
Ikondere, Marvin (Uganda) - A/C.6/78/SR.8
PEACEKEEPING OPERATIONS—FINANCING (Agenda item 146)
Minale, Lemlem Fiseha (Ethiopia) - A/C.5/78/SR.36
Sibomana, Landry (Burundi) - A/C.5/78/SR.35
PERSONNEL QUESTIONS—UN SYSTEM (Agenda item 142)
Mwasota, Joseph Aron (United Republic of Tanzania) - A/C.5/78/SR.10
RACIAL DISCRIMINATION—ELIMINATION (Agenda item 69a)
Banaken Elel, Nelly (Cameroon) - A/78/PV.103
Ladeb, Tarek (Tunisia) - A/C.3/78/SR.40
Nabeta, Celia Kafureka (Uganda) - A/78/PV.63
RACIAL DISCRIMINATION—PROGRAMMES OF ACTION (Agenda item 69b)
Ladeb, Tarek (Tunisia) - A/C.3/78/SR.40
RAISI, SEYYED EBRAHIM (IRAN (ISLAMIC REPUBLID OF). PRESIDENT)—TRIBUTES
Maniratanga, Zéphyrin (Burundi) - A/78/PV.83
RIGHT TO DEVELOPMENT (Agenda item 71b)
Ladeb, Tarek (Tunisia) - A/C.3/78/SR.20
RIGHTS OF THE CHILD (Agenda item 67)
Banaken Elel, Nelly (Cameroon) - A/C.3/78/SR.55
Ladeb, Tarek (Tunisia) - A/C.3/78/SR.12
RULE OF LAW (Agenda item 83)
Ikondere, Marvin (Uganda) - A/C.6/78/SR.16
SLAVERY—MEMORIALS (Agenda item 118)
Gurhan, Amina (Uganda) - A/78/PV.64
SMALL ARMS—ILLICIT TRAFFIC (Agenda item 99p)
Mahmud, Mohammed Lawal (Nigeria) - A/C.1/78/PV.17

UN. Group of African States (continued)

SMALL ARMS—ILLICIT TRAFFIC—ASSISTANCE (Agenda item 99n)
Mahmud, Mohammed Lawal (Nigeria) - A/C.1/78/PV.17
SOCIAL CONDITIONS (Agenda item 24b)
Ladeb, Tarek (Tunisia) - A/C.3/78/SR.2
SOCIAL DEVELOPMENT (Agenda item 24)
Andriamiarisoa, Vero Henintsoa (Madagascar) - A/C.3/78/SR.47
SUSTAINABLE DEVELOPMENT (Agenda item 18)
Ladeb, Tarek (Tunisia) - A/C.2/78/SR.12
TAXATION (Agenda item 16h)
Ladeb, Tarek (Tunisia) - A/C.2/78/SR.9
Muhammad Bande, Tijjani (Nigeria) - A/C.2/78/SR.25
TERRORISM (Agenda item 109)
Ikondere, Marvin (Uganda) - A/C.6/78/SR.1
UN—BUDGET (2024) (Agenda item 134)
Lamuwa, Adamu Ibrahim (Nigeria) - A/C.5/78/SR.13
Minale, Lemlem Fiseha (Ethiopia) - A/C.5/78/SR.3; A/C.5/78/SR.11; A/C.5/78/SR.12; A/C.5/78/SR.22; A/C.5/78/SR.23; A/C.5/78/SR.33
Sabo, Tesfaye Yilma (Ethiopia) - A/C.5/78/SR.5; A/C.5/78/SR.14
UN—FINANCIAL SITUATION (Agenda item 136)
Osei, Rita (Ghana) - A/C.5/78/SR.6
UN—HUMAN RESOURCES MANAGEMENT (Agenda item 139)
Minale, Lemlem Fiseha (Ethiopia) - A/C.5/78/SR.27
UN—PROGRAMME PLANNING (Agenda item 135)
Sabo, Tesfaye Yilma (Ethiopia) - A/C.5/78/SR.5
UN. GENERAL ASSEMBLY (78TH SESS. : 2023-2024)—OFFICERS (Agenda item 5)
Ladeb, Tarek (Tunisia) - A/C.5/78/SR.1
UN. GENERAL ASSEMBLY (78TH SESS. : 2023-2024). 1ST COMMITTEE—GENERAL DEBATE (Agenda item 8)
Muhammad Bande, Tijjani (Nigeria) - A/C.1/78/PV.3
UN. GENERAL ASSEMBLY (78TH SESS. : 2023-2024). 2ND COMMITTEE—GENERAL DEBATE (Agenda item 8)
Muhammad Bande, Tijjani (Nigeria) - A/C.2/78/SR.2
UN. GENERAL ASSEMBLY (78TH SESS. : 2023-2024). 5TH COMMITTEE—WORK ORGANIZATION (Agenda item 7)
Minale, Lemlem Fiseha (Ethiopia) - A/C.5/78/SR.26/PartII; A/C.5/78/SR.34; A/C.5/78/SR.35; A/C.5/78/SR.40
UN. GENERAL ASSEMBLY (78TH SESS. : 2023-2024). PRESIDENT (Agenda item 4)
Tommo Monthe, Michel (Cameroon) - A/78/PV.87

UN. Group of African States (continued)

UN. HUMAN RIGHTS COUNCIL—REPORTS (Agenda item 66)
Milambo, Chola (Zambia) - A/C.3/78/SR.51
UN. INTERNATIONAL LAW COMMISSION—REPORTS (Agenda item 79)
Kanu, Michael Imran (Sierra Leone) - A/C.6/78/SR.23
UN CHARTER—REPORTS (Agenda item 82)
Ikondere, Marvin (Uganda) - A/C.6/78/SR.22
UN CONFERENCES (Agenda item 13)
Milambo, Chola (Zambia) - A/78/PV.33
UN HIGH COMMISSIONER FOR REFUGEES—REPORTS (Agenda item 60)
Banaken Elel, Nelly (Cameroon) - A/C.3/78/SR.44
Ossebi Iyolo, Isis (Congo) - A/C.3/78/SR.54
WEAPONS—OUTER SPACE (Agenda item 97b)
Mahmud, Mohammed Lawal (Nigeria) - A/C.1/78/PV.16
WOMEN'S ADVANCEMENT (Agenda item 25a)
Arega, Elleni Henok (Ethiopia) - A/C.3/78/SR.7
WOMEN'S ADVANCEMENT—CONFERENCES (Agenda item 25b)
Arega, Elleni Henok (Ethiopia) - A/C.3/78/SR.7

UN. Group of Asia-Pacific States

AL-SABAH, NAWAF AL-AHMAD AL-JABER (KUWAIT. AMIR)—TRIBUTES
Eyeberdiyev, Ata (Turkmenistan) - A/78/PV.50(Resumption1)
GEINGOB, HAGE GOTTFRIED (NAMIBIA. PRESIDENT)—TRIBUTES
Abushahab, Mohamed Issa (United Arab Emirates) - A/78/PV.55
RACIAL DISCRIMINATION—ELIMINATION (Agenda item 69a)
Alrowaiei, Jamal Fares (Bahrain) - A/78/PV.63
RAISI, SEYYED EBRAHIM (IRAN (ISLAMIC REPUBLID OF). PRESIDENT)—TRIBUTES
Wells, Majorie May (Vanuatu) - A/78/PV.83
SLAVERY—MEMORIALS (Agenda item 118)
Alalaiwat, Suma Sameer (Bahrain) - A/78/PV.64
UN. GENERAL ASSEMBLY (78TH SESS. : 2023-2024). PRESIDENT (Agenda item 4)
Al-Saadi, Abdullah Ali Fadhel (Yemen) - A/78/PV.87

UN. Group of Latin American and Caribbean States

GEINGOB, HAGE GOTTFRIED (NAMIBIA. PRESIDENT)—TRIBUTES
González López, Egriselda Aracely (El Salvador) - A/78/PV.55
RACIAL DISCRIMINATION—ELIMINATION (Agenda item 69a)
Rodríguez Mancia, Carla María (Guatemala) - A/78/PV.63

UN. Group of Latin American and Caribbean States (continued)

RAISI, SEYYED EBRAHIM (IRAN (ISLAMIC REPUBLID OF). PRESIDENT)—TRIBUTES
Rodrigue, Antonio (Haiti) - A/78/PV.83
RIGHTS OF THE CHILD (Agenda item 67)
Alonso Giganto, Ana María (Spain) - A/C.3/78/SR.55
Riva Grela, Juan José (Uruguay) - A/C.3/78/SR.55
SLAVERY—MEMORIALS (Agenda item 118)
Rodríguez Mancia, Carla María (Guatemala) - A/78/PV.64

UN. Group of Western European and Other States

AL-SABAH, NAWAF AL-AHMAD AL-JABER (KUWAIT. AMIR)—TRIBUTES
Uexküll, Andreas von (Sweden) - A/78/PV.50(Resumption1)
GEINGOB, HAGE GOTTFRIED (NAMIBIA. PRESIDENT)—TRIBUTES
Güven, Fikriye Asli (Türkiye) - A/78/PV.55
RACIAL DISCRIMINATION—ELIMINATION (Agenda item 69a)
Leendertse, Antje (Germany) - A/78/PV.63
SLAVERY—MEMORIALS (Agenda item 118)
Zahneisen, Thomas (Germany) - A/78/PV.64
UN. GENERAL ASSEMBLY (78TH SESS. : 2023-2024). PRESIDENT (Agenda item 4)
Marschik, Alexander (Austria) - A/78/PV.87

UN. High Representative for Disarmament Affairs

UN. GENERAL ASSEMBLY (78TH SESS. : 2023-2024). 1ST COMMITTEE—GENERAL DEBATE (Agenda item 8)
Nakamitsu, Izumi - A/C.1/78/PV.2

UN. High Representative of the Secretary-General for the Least Developed Countries, Landlocked Developing Countries and Small Island Developing States

LANDLOCKED DEVELOPING COUNTRIES—CONFERENCES (Agenda item 20b)
Fatima, Rabab - A/C.2/78/SR.7
LEAST DEVELOPED COUNTRIES—CONFERENCES (Agenda item 20a)
Fatima, Rabab - A/C.2/78/SR.7

UN. Human Rights Committee. Chair

UN. HUMAN RIGHTS COMMITTEE—REPORTS (Agenda item 71a)
Abdo Rocholl, Tania María (Paraguay) - A/C.3/78/SR.17

UN. Human Rights Council. Ad Hoc Committee on the Elaboration of Complementary International Standards. Chair

RACIAL DISCRIMINATION—ELIMINATION (Agenda item 69a)
Hassan, Kadra Ahmed - A/C.3/78/SR.41

UN. Human Rights Council. Expert Mechanism on the Right to Development. Chair

RIGHT TO DEVELOPMENT (Agenda item 71b)
Valiña, Liliana - A/C.3/78/SR.20

UN. Human Rights Council. Group of Independent Eminent Experts on the Implementation of the Durban Declaration and Programme of Action. Chair

RACIAL DISCRIMINATION—PROGRAMMES OF ACTION (Agenda item 69b)
Suchocka, Hanna - A/C.3/78/SR.40

UN. Human Rights Council. Independent Expert on Human Rights and International Solidarity

SOLIDARITY (Agenda item 71b)
Okafor, Obiora Chinedu - A/C.3/78/SR.32

UN. Human Rights Council. Independent Expert on Protection against Violence and Discrimination based on Sexual Orientation and Gender Identity

SEXUAL ORIENTATION (Agenda item 71b)
Madrigal-Borloz, Victor - A/C.3/78/SR.39

UN. Human Rights Council. Independent Expert on the Effects of Foreign Debt and Other Related International Financial Obligations of States on the Full Enjoyment of All Human Rights, particularly Economic, Social and Cultural Rights

EXTERNAL DEBT—HUMAN RIGHTS (Agenda item 71b)
Waris, Attiya - A/C.3/78/SR.32

UN. Human Rights Council. Independent Expert on the Enjoyment of All Human Rights by Older Persons

AGEING PERSONS (Agenda item 24b)
Mahler, Claudia - A/C.3/78/SR.1

UN. Human Rights Council. Independent Expert on the Enjoyment of Human Rights by Persons with Albinism

ALBINISM (Agenda item 71b)
Miti-Drummond, Muluka-Anne - A/C.3/78/SR.27

UN. Human Rights Council. Independent Expert on the Promotion of a Democratic and Equitable International Order

DEMOCRACY (Agenda item 71b)
Sewanyana, Livingstone - A/C.3/78/SR.28

UN. Human Rights Council. Independent Expert on the Situation of Human Rights in Somalia

HUMAN RIGHTS—SOMALIA (Agenda item 71c)
Dyfan, Isha - A/C.3/78/SR.35

UN. Human Rights Council. Independent Expert on the Situation of Human Rights in the Central African Republic

HUMAN RIGHTS—CENTRAL AFRICAN REPUBLIC (Agenda item 71c)
Agbetse, Yao - A/C.3/78/SR.33

UN. Human Rights Council. Independent International Commission of Inquiry on the Occupied Palestinian Territory, including East Jerusalem, and Israel. Chair

HUMAN RIGHTS—TERRITORIES OCCUPIED BY ISRAEL (Agenda item 71c)
Pillay, Navanethem - A/C.3/78/SR.35

UN. Human Rights Council. Independent International Commission of Inquiry to Investigate All Alleged Violations of Human Rights in the Context of the Russian Federation's Aggression against Ukraine. Chair

HUMAN RIGHTS—UKRAINE (Agenda item 71c)
Møse, Erik - A/C.3/78/SR.37

UN. Human Rights Council. Intergovernmental Working Group on the Effective Implementation of the Durban Declaration and Programme of Action. Chair

RACIAL DISCRIMINATION—PROGRAMMES OF ACTION (Agenda item 69b)
Rwakazina, Marie Chantal - A/C.3/78/SR.40

UN. Human Rights Council. President

UN. HUMAN RIGHTS COUNCIL—REPORTS (Agenda item 66)
Bálek, Václav (Czechia) - A/78/PV.23; A/C.3/78/SR.46

UN. Human Rights Council. Special Rapporteur in the Field of Cultural Rights

RIGHT TO CULTURE (Agenda item 71b)
Xanthaki, Alexandra - A/C.3/78/SR.27

UN. Human Rights Council. Special Rapporteur on Adequate Housing as a Component of the Right to an Adequate Standard of Living

RIGHT TO HOUSING (Agenda item 71b)
Rajagopal, Balakrishnan - A/C.3/78/SR.30

UN. Human Rights Council. Special Rapporteur on Contemporary Forms of Racism, Racial Discrimination, Xenophobia and Related Intolerance

RACIAL DISCRIMINATION—ELIMINATION (Agenda item 69a)
K.P., Ashwini - A/C.3/78/SR.41

UN. Human Rights Council. Special Rapporteur on Contemporary Forms of Slavery

SLAVERY (Agenda item 71a)
Obokata, Tomoya - A/C.3/78/SR.21

UN. Human Rights Council. Special Rapporteur on Extrajudicial, Summary or Arbitrary Executions

SUMMARY EXECUTIONS (Agenda item 71b)
Tidball-Binz, Morris - A/C.3/78/SR.31

UN. Human Rights Council. Special Rapporteur on Extreme Poverty and Human Rights

POVERTY—HUMAN RIGHTS (Agenda item 71b)
Schutter, Olivier de - A/C.3/78/SR.30

UN. Human Rights Council. Special Rapporteur on Freedom of Religion or Belief

RELIGIOUS INTOLERANCE (Agenda item 71b)
Ghanea, Nazila - A/C.3/78/SR.38

UN. Human Rights Council. Special Rapporteur on Minority Issues

MINORITIES (Agenda item 71b)
Varennes, Fernand de - A/C.3/78/SR.39

UN. Human Rights Council. Special Rapporteur on Rights of Indigenous Peoples

INDIGENOUS PEOPLES (Agenda item 68a)
Cali Tzay, José Francisco - A/C.3/78/SR.15

UN. Human Rights Council. Special Rapporteur on the Elimination of Discrimination against Persons Affected by Leprosy (Hansen's disease) and Their Family Members

LEPROSY (Agenda item 71b)
Cruz, Alice - A/C.3/78/SR.17

UN. Human Rights Council. Special Rapporteur on the Human Right to a Clean, Healthy and Sustainable Environment

ENVIRONMENT (Agenda item 71b)
Boyd, David Richard - A/C.3/78/SR.29

UN. Human Rights Council. Special Rapporteur on the Human Right to Safe Drinking Water and Sanitation

HUMAN RIGHTS—TERRITORIES OCCUPIED BY ISRAEL (Agenda item 71c)
Arrojo Agudo, Pedro - A/C.3/78/SR.28
RIGHT TO DRINKING WATER (Agenda item 71b)
Arrojo Agudo, Pedro - A/C.3/78/SR.28

UN. Human Rights Council. Special Rapporteur on the Human Rights of Internally Displaced Persons

DISPLACED PERSONS (Agenda item 71b)
Gaviria Betancur, Paula - A/C.3/78/SR.32

UN. Human Rights Council. Special Rapporteur on the Human Rights of Migrants

MIGRANTS—PROTECTION (Agenda item 71b)
González Morales, Felipe - A/C.3/78/SR.23

UN. Human Rights Council. Special Rapporteur on the Implications for Human Rights of the Environmentally Sound Management and Disposal of Hazardous Substances and Wastes

HAZARDOUS WASTES (Agenda item 71b)
Orellana, Marcos - A/C.3/78/SR.29

UN. Human Rights Council. Special Rapporteur on the Independence of Judges and Lawyers

JUDICIAL INDEPENDENCE (Agenda item 71b)
Satterthwaite, Margaret L. - A/C.3/78/SR.31

UN. Human Rights Council. Special Rapporteur on the Negative Impact of Unilateral Coercive Measures on the Enjoyment of Human Rights

SANCTIONS—INTERNATIONAL RELATIONS (Agenda item 71b)
Douhan, Alena - A/C.3/78/SR.28

UN. Human Rights Council. Special Rapporteur on the Promotion and Protection of Human Rights and Fundamental Freedoms while Countering Terrorism

TERRORISM—HUMAN RIGHTS (Agenda item 71b)
Ní Aoláin, Fionnuala - A/C.3/78/SR.31

UN. Human Rights Council. Special Rapporteur on the Promotion and Protection of Human Rights in the Context of Climate Change

CLIMATE CHANGE (Agenda item 71b)
Fry, Ian - A/C.3/78/SR.29

UN. Human Rights Council. Special Rapporteur on the Promotion and Protection of the Right to Freedom of Opinion and Expression

FREEDOM OF EXPRESSION (Agenda item 71b)
Khan, Irene - A/C.3/78/SR.19

UN. Human Rights Council. Special Rapporteur on the Promotion of Truth, Justice, Reparation and Guarantees of Non-Recurrence

RIGHT TO THE TRUTH (Agenda item 71b)
Salvioli, Fabián - A/C.3/78/SR.22

UN. Human Rights Council. Special Rapporteur on the Right of Everyone to the Enjoyment of the Highest Attainable Standard of Physical and Mental Health

RIGHT TO HEALTH (Agenda item 71b)
Mofokeng, Tlaleng - A/C.3/78/SR.39

UN. Human Rights Council. Special Rapporteur on the Right to Development

RIGHT TO DEVELOPMENT (Agenda item 71b)
Deva, Surya - A/C.3/78/SR.20

UN. Human Rights Council. Special Rapporteur on the Right to Education

RIGHT TO EDUCATION (Agenda item 71b)
Shaheed, Farida - A/C.3/78/SR.27

UN. Human Rights Council. Special Rapporteur on the Right to Food

RIGHT TO FOOD (Agenda item 71b)
Fakhri, Michael - A/C.3/78/SR.30

UN. Human Rights Council. Special Rapporteur on the Right to Privacy

RIGHT TO PRIVACY (Agenda item 71b)
Brian Nougrères, Ana - A/C.3/78/SR.21

UN. Human Rights Council. Special Rapporteur on the Rights of Persons with Disabilities

PERSONS WITH DISABILITIES—HUMAN RIGHTS (Agenda item 71a)
Quinn, Gerard - A/C.3/78/SR.38

UN. Human Rights Council. Special Rapporteur on the Rights to Freedom of Peaceful Assembly and of Association

RIGHT OF ASSEMBLY (Agenda item 71b)
Voulé, Clément Nyaletsossi - A/C.3/78/SR.19

UN. Human Rights Council. Special Rapporteur on the Sale, Sexual Exploitation and Sexual Abuse of Children

RIGHTS OF THE CHILD (Agenda item 67)
Singhateh, Mama Fatima - A/C.3/78/SR.12

UN. Human Rights Council. Special Rapporteur on the Situation of Human Rights Defenders

HUMAN RIGHTS ACTIVISTS (Agenda item 71b)
Lawlor, Mary - A/C.3/78/SR.19

UN. Human Rights Council. Special Rapporteur on the Situation of Human Rights in Afghanistan

HUMAN RIGHTS—AFGHANISTAN (Agenda item 71c)
Bennett, Richard - A/C.3/78/SR.34

UN. Human Rights Council. Special Rapporteur on the Situation of Human Rights in Belarus

HUMAN RIGHTS—BELARUS (Agenda item 71c)
Marin, Anaïs - A/C.3/78/SR.37

UN. Human Rights Council. Special Rapporteur on the Situation of Human Rights in Burundi

HUMAN RIGHTS—BURUNDI (Agenda item 71c)
Zongo, Fortuné Gaétan - A/C.3/78/SR.36

UN. Human Rights Council. Special Rapporteur on the Situation of Human Rights in Eritrea

HUMAN RIGHTS—ERITREA (Agenda item 71c)
Babiker, Mohamed Abdelsalam - A/C.3/78/SR.36

UN. Human Rights Council. Special Rapporteur on the Situation of Human Rights in Myanmar

HUMAN RIGHTS—MYANMAR (Agenda item 71c)
Andrews, Thomas H. - A/C.3/78/SR.33

UN. Human Rights Council. Special Rapporteur on the Situation of Human Rights in the Democratic People's Republic of Korea

HUMAN RIGHTS—DEMOCRATIC PEOPLE'S REPUBLIC OF KOREA (Agenda item 71c)
Salmón, Elizabeth - A/C.3/78/SR.33

UN. Human Rights Council. Special Rapporteur on the Situation of Human Rights in the Islamic Republic of Iran

HUMAN RIGHTS—IRAN (ISLAMIC REPUBLIC OF) (Agenda item 71c)
Rehman, Javaid - A/C.3/78/SR.34

UN. Human Rights Council. Special Rapporteur on the Situation of Human Rights in the Palestinian Territories Occupied since 1967

HUMAN RIGHTS—TERRITORIES OCCUPIED BY ISRAEL (Agenda item 71c)
Albanese, Francesca - A/C.3/78/SR.35

UN. Human Rights Council. Special Rapporteur on the Situation of Human Rights in the Russian Federation

HUMAN RIGHTS—RUSSIAN FEDERATION (Agenda item 71c)
Katzarova, Mariana - A/C.3/78/SR.37

UN. Human Rights Council. Special Rapporteur on Torture and Other Cruel, Inhuman or Degrading Treatment or Punishment

TORTURE AND OTHER CRUEL TREATMENT (Agenda item 71a)
Edwards, Alice Jill - A/C.3/78/SR.18

UN. Human Rights Council. Special Rapporteur on Trafficking in Persons, Especially in Women and Children

TRAFFICKING IN PERSONS (Agenda item 71b)
Mullally, Siobhán - A/C.3/78/SR.23

UN. Human Rights Council. Special Rapporteur on Violence against Women and Girls, its Causes and its Consequences

WOMEN'S ADVANCEMENT (Agenda item 25a)
Alsalem, Reem - A/C.3/78/SR.7
WOMEN'S ADVANCEMENT—CONFERENCES (Agenda item 25b)
Alsalem, Reem - A/C.3/78/SR.7

UN. Human Rights Council. Working Group of Experts on People of African Descent. Chair

RACIAL DISCRIMINATION—ELIMINATION (Agenda item 69a)
Reynolds, Barbara G. - A/C.3/78/SR.42

UN. Human Rights Council. Working Group on Discrimination against Women and Girls. Chair

WOMEN'S ADVANCEMENT (Agenda item 25a)
Estrada-Tanck, Dorothy - A/C.3/78/SR.7
WOMEN'S ADVANCEMENT—CONFERENCES (Agenda item 25b)
Estrada-Tanck, Dorothy - A/C.3/78/SR.7

UN. Human Rights Council. Working Group on Enforced or Involuntary Disappearances. Chair

DISAPPEARANCE OF PERSONS (Agenda item 71b)
Baldé, Aua - A/C.3/78/SR.22

UN. Human Rights Council. Working Group on the Issue of Human Rights and Transnational Corporations and Other Business Enterprises. Chair

TRANSNATIONAL CORPORATIONS—HUMAN RIGHTS (Agenda item 71b)
Olawuyi, Damilola - A/C.3/78/SR.21

UN. Human Rights Council. Working Group on the Right to Development. Chair

RIGHT TO DEVELOPMENT (Agenda item 71b)
Akram, Zamir - A/C.3/78/SR.20

UN. Human Rights Council. Working Group on the Use of Mercenaries as a Means of Violating Human Rights and Impeding the Exercise of the Right of Peoples to Self-Determination

MERCENARIES (Agenda item 70)
MacLeod, Sorcha - A/C.3/78/SR.42

UN. Independent Audit Advisory Committee. Chair

UN—ADMINISTRATION (Agenda item 132)
Vanker, Imran - A/C.5/78/SR.2

UN. Independent Investigative Mechanism for Myanmar. Head

HUMAN RIGHTS—MYANMAR (Agenda item 71c)
Koumjian, Nicholas - A/C.3/78/SR.33

UN. International Commission of Human Rights Experts on Ethiopia

HUMAN RIGHTS—ETHIOPIA (Agenda item 71c)
Ratner, Steven R. - A/C.3/78/SR.36

UN. International Commission of Human Rights Experts on Ethiopia. Chair

HUMAN RIGHTS—ETHIOPIA (Agenda item 71c)
Othman, Mohamed Chande - A/C.3/78/SR.36

UN. International Court of Justice. President

UN. INTERNATIONAL COURT OF JUSTICE—REPORTS (Agenda item 73)
Donoghue, Joan E. - A/78/PV.20; A/C.6/78/SR.26

UN. International Law Commission. Chair

UN. INTERNATIONAL LAW COMMISSION—REPORTS (Agenda item 79)
Oral, Nilufer - A/C.6/78/SR.23; A/C.6/78/SR.33
Teles, Patricia Galvao - A/C.6/78/SR.23; A/C.6/78/SR.33

UN. International Law Commission. Special Rapporteur on General Principles of Law

UN. INTERNATIONAL LAW COMMISSION—REPORTS (Agenda item 79)
Vázquez-Bermúdez, Marcelo - A/C.6/78/SR.28

UN. International Law Commission. Special Rapporteur on Subsidiary Means for the Determination of Rules of International Law

UN. INTERNATIONAL LAW COMMISSION—REPORTS (Agenda item 79)
Jalloh, Charles - A/C.6/78/SR.33

UN. International Law Commission. Study Group on Sea-level Rise in Relation to International Law. Co-Chair

UN. INTERNATIONAL LAW COMMISSION—REPORTS (Agenda item 79)
Aurescu, Bogdan Lucian - A/C.6/78/SR.28

UN. Legal Counsel

INTERNATIONAL LAW—TRAINING PROGRAMMES (Agenda item 78)
Soares, João Miguel Ferreira de Serpa - A/C.6/78/SR.21

UN. Office for Disarmament Affairs (Mar. 2007-). Regional Disarmament Branch. Chief

PEACE—REGIONAL CENTRES (Agenda item 100f)
Day, Radha - A/C.1/78/PV.23

UN. Office of Legal Affairs. Codification Division. Director

UN CHARTER—REPORTS (Agenda item 82)
Llewellyn, Huw - A/C.6/78/SR.22

UN. Office of the Administration of Justice. Executive Director

ADMINISTRATION OF JUSTICE (Agenda item 144)
Frankson-Wallace, Alayne - A/C.5/78/SR.15

UN. Open-ended Working Group on Conventional Ammunition. Chair

CONVENTIONAL WEAPONS (Agenda item 99u)
Wittke, Albrecht von (Germany) - A/C.1/78/PV.18

UN. Open-ended Working Group on Security of and in the Use of Information and Communications Technologies 2021-2025. Chair

INFORMATION—INTERNATIONAL SECURITY (Agenda item 94)
Gafoor, Burhan (Singapore) - A/C.1/78/PV.21

UN. Peacebuilding Commission. Chair

UN. PEACEBUILDING COMMISSION—REPORTS (Agenda item 27)
Danese, Sérgio França (Brazil) - A/78/PV.100
UN. SECRETARY-GENERAL—REPORTS (Agenda item 110)
Danese, Sérgio França (Brazil) - A/78/PV.54

UN. Permanent Forum on People of African Descent

RACIAL DISCRIMINATION—ELIMINATION (Agenda item 69a)
Soomer, June - A/78/PV.63

UN. Permanent Forum on People of African Descent. Chair

RACIAL DISCRIMINATION—PROGRAMMES OF ACTION (Agenda item 69b)
Campbell Barr, Epsy - A/C.3/78/SR.42

UN. Programme Planning and Budget Division. Director

UN—BUDGET (2024) (Agenda item 134)
Huisman, Johannes - A/C.5/78/SR.9; A/C.5/78/SR.23

UN. Secretary-General

AL-SABAH, NAWAF AL-AHMAD AL-JABER (KUWAIT. AMIR)—TRIBUTES
Guterres, António, 1949- - A/78/PV.50(Resumption1)
GEINGOB, HAGE GOTTFRIED (NAMIBIA. PRESIDENT)—TRIBUTES
Guterres, António, 1949- - A/78/PV.55
MULTILATERALISM
Guterres, António, 1949- - A/78/PV.81
PEACE (Agenda item 14)
Guterres, António, 1949- - A/78/PV.62
RAISI, SEYYED EBRAHIM (IRAN (ISLAMIC REPUBLID OF). PRESIDENT)—TRIBUTES
Guterres, António, 1949- - A/78/PV.83
UN—BUDGET (2024) (Agenda item 134)
Guterres, António, 1949- - A/C.5/78/SR.5
UN—PROGRAMME PLANNING (Agenda item 135)
Guterres, António, 1949- - A/C.5/78/SR.5
UN. GENERAL ASSEMBLY (78TH SESS. : 2023-2024)—CLOSING
Guterres, António, 1949- - A/78/PV.109
UN. GENERAL ASSEMBLY (78TH SESS. : 2023-2024). PRESIDENT (Agenda item 4)
Guterres, António, 1949- - A/78/PV.87
UN. SECRETARY-GENERAL—REPORTS (Agenda item 110)
Guterres, António, 1949- - A/78/PV.4; A/78/PV.54

UN. Security Council. President

UN. SECURITY COUNCIL—REPORTS (Agenda item 26)
Hwang, Joonkook (Republic of Korea) - A/78/PV.93

UN. Security Council Practices and Charter Research Branch

UN CHARTER—REPORTS (Agenda item 82)
Montejo, Blanca - A/C.6/78/SR.22

UN. Special Adviser for Addressing Racism in the Workplace

UN—BUDGET (2024) (Agenda item 134)
Gumbi, Mojankunyane - A/C.5/78/SR.13

UN. Special Adviser to the Secretary-General on the Responsibility to Protect

RESPONSIBILITY TO PROTECT (Agenda item 129)
Bleeker, Mô - A/78/PV.96

UN. Special Committee of 24. Chair

DECOLONIZATION (Agenda item 58)
Rambally, Menissa (Saint Lucia) - A/C.4/78/SR.2
DECOLONIZATION—UN SYSTEM (Agenda item 56)
Rambally, Menissa (Saint Lucia) - A/C.4/78/SR.2
NON-SELF-GOVERNING TERRITORIES—ECONOMIC INTERESTS (Agenda item 55)
Rambally, Menissa (Saint Lucia) - A/C.4/78/SR.2
NON-SELF-GOVERNING TERRITORIES—FELLOWSHIPS (Agenda item 57)
Rambally, Menissa (Saint Lucia) - A/C.4/78/SR.2
NON-SELF-GOVERNING TERRITORIES—REPORTS (Agenda item 54)
Rambally, Menissa (Saint Lucia) - A/C.4/78/SR.2

UN. Special Committee of 24. Vice-Chair

DECOLONIZATION (Agenda item 58)
Nasir, Armanatha Christiawan (Indonesia) - A/C.4/78/SR.2
DECOLONIZATION—UN SYSTEM (Agenda item 56)
Nasir, Armanatha Christiawan (Indonesia) - A/C.4/78/SR.2
NON-SELF-GOVERNING TERRITORIES—ECONOMIC INTERESTS (Agenda item 55)
Nasir, Armanatha Christiawan (Indonesia) - A/C.4/78/SR.2
NON-SELF-GOVERNING TERRITORIES—FELLOWSHIPS (Agenda item 57)
Nasir, Armanatha Christiawan (Indonesia) - A/C.4/78/SR.2
NON-SELF-GOVERNING TERRITORIES—REPORTS (Agenda item 54)
Nasir, Armanatha Christiawan (Indonesia) - A/C.4/78/SR.2

UN. Special Committee on Peacekeeping Operations. Rapporteur
PEACEKEEPING OPERATIONS (Agenda item 51)
Eldahshan, Wael Mahmoud Abdelaziz (Egypt) - A/C.4/78/SR.27

UN. Special Committee on the Charter of the United Nations and on the Strengthening of the Role of the Organization. Chair
UN CHARTER—REPORTS (Agenda item 82)
Maniratanga, Zéphyrin (Burundi) - A/C.6/78/SR.22

UN. Special Committee to Investigate Israeli Practices affecting the Human Rights of the Palestinian People and Other Arabs of the Occupied Territories. Chair
TERRITORIES OCCUPIED BY ISRAEL—HUMAN RIGHTS (Agenda item 50)
Pieris, Peter Mohan Maithri (Sri Lanka) - A/C.4/78/SR.24

UN. Special Representative of the Secretary-General for Children and Armed Conflict
RIGHTS OF THE CHILD (Agenda item 67)
Gamba, Virginia - A/C.3/78/SR.11

UN. Special Representative of the Secretary-General for Disaster Risk Reduction
DISASTER PREVENTION (Agenda item 18c)
Mizutori, Mami - A/C.2/78/SR.12

UN. Special Representative of the Secretary-General on Violence against Children
RIGHTS OF THE CHILD (Agenda item 67)
Maalla M'jid, Najat - A/C.3/78/SR.11

UN. Statistics Division. Director
SUSTAINABLE DEVELOPMENT (Agenda item 18)
Min, Yongyi - A/C.2/78/SR.12

UN. Subcommittee on Prevention of Torture and Other Cruel, Inhuman or Degrading Treatment or Punishment. Chair
TORTURE AND OTHER CRUEL TREATMENT (Agenda item 71a)
Jabbour, Suzanne - A/C.3/78/SR.18

UN. Under-Secretary-General and Chef de Cabinet
RACIAL DISCRIMINATION—ELIMINATION (Agenda item 69a)
Rattray, Courtenay - A/78/PV.63
SLAVERY—MEMORIALS (Agenda item 118)
Rattray, Courtenay - A/78/PV.64

UN. Under-Secretary-General for Economic and Social Affairs
SOCIAL DEVELOPMENT (Agenda item 24)
Li, Junhua - A/C.3/78/SR.1
UN. GENERAL ASSEMBLY (78TH SESS. : 2023-2024). 2ND COMMITTEE—GENERAL DEBATE (Agenda item 8)
Li, Junhua - A/C.2/78/SR.2
UN. GENERAL ASSEMBLY (78TH SESS. : 2023-2024). 2ND COMMITTEE—WORK ORGANIZATION (Agenda item 7)
Li, Junhua - A/C.2/78/SR.25

UN. Under-Secretary-General for General Assembly and Conference Management
CONFERENCE AND MEETING SERVICES (Agenda item 137)
Abelian, Movses - A/C.5/78/SR.7

UN. Under-Secretary-General for Global Communications
INFORMATION (Agenda item 53)
Fleming, Melissa - A/C.4/78/SR.12

UN. Under-Secretary-General for Internal Oversight Services
UN—ADMINISTRATION (Agenda item 132)
Ndiaye, Fatoumata - A/C.5/78/SR.2; A/C.5/78/SR.32
UN—BUDGET (2024) (Agenda item 134)
Ndiaye, Fatoumata - A/C.5/78/SR.11
UN. OFFICE OF INTERNAL OVERSIGHT SERVICES—REPORTS (Agenda item 143)
Ndiaye, Fatoumata - A/C.5/78/SR.2

UN. Under-Secretary-General for Management Strategy, Policy and Compliance
PERSONNEL QUESTIONS—UN SYSTEM (Agenda item 142)
Pollard, Catherine - A/C.5/78/SR.10
UN—BUDGET (2024) (Agenda item 134)
Pollard, Catherine - A/C.5/78/SR.5; A/C.5/78/SR.13; A/C.5/78/SR.33
UN—FINANCIAL SITUATION (Agenda item 136)
Pollard, Catherine - A/C.5/78/SR.4; A/C.5/78/SR.6; A/C.5/78/SR.37; A/C.5/78/SR.38
UN—PROGRAMME PLANNING (Agenda item 135)
Pollard, Catherine - A/C.5/78/SR.5

UN. Under-Secretary-General for Operational Support
PEACEKEEPING OPERATIONS (Agenda item 51)
Khare, Atul - A/C.4/78/SR.18
SPECIAL POLITICAL MISSIONS (Agenda item 52)
Khare, Atul - A/C.4/78/SR.21
UN—BUDGET (2024) (Agenda item 134)
Khare, Atul - A/C.5/78/SR.17

UN. Working Group on the Financing of the United Nations Relief and Works Agency for Palestine Refugees in the Near East. Rapporteur

UNRWA—ACTIVITIES (Agenda item 49)
Havn, Anne Melangen (Norway) - A/C.4/78/SR.22

UN Commission on International Trade Law. Chair

UN COMMISSION ON INTERNATIONAL TRADE LAW—REPORTS (Agenda item 77)
Sabo, Kathryn - A/C.6/78/SR.13; A/C.6/78/SR.14

UN Commission on International Trade Law. Secretary

UN COMMISSION ON INTERNATIONAL TRADE LAW—REPORTS (Agenda item 77)
Joubin-Bret, Anna - A/C.6/78/SR.13

UN High Commissioner for Human Rights

HUMAN RIGHTS (Agenda item 71)
Türk, Volker - A/C.3/78/SR.16

UN High Commissioner for Refugees

UN HIGH COMMISSIONER FOR REFUGEES—REPORTS (Agenda item 60)
Grandi, Filippo - A/C.3/78/SR.44

UN Institute for Disarmament Research. Director

DISARMAMENT—UN. GENERAL ASSEMBLY (12TH SPECIAL SESS. : 1982) (Agenda item 100)
Geiss, Robin - A/C.1/78/PV.24

UN International Civil Servants Federation

PERSONNEL QUESTIONS—UN SYSTEM (Agenda item 142)
Esposito, Karin - A/C.5/78/SR.10

UN Joint Staff Pension Board. Chair

UN—BUDGET (2024) (Agenda item 134)
Van Houtte, Annick - A/C.5/78/SR.9

UN Office for Partnerships. Executive Director

UN—BUDGET (2023) (Agenda item 133)
Hou, Annemarie - A/C.5/78/SR.4

UN Office for South-South Cooperation. Director

ECONOMIC COOPERATION AMONG DEVELOPING COUNTRIES (Agenda item 22b)
Wang, Xiaojun Grace - A/C.2/78/SR.18

UN Office on Drugs and Crime. New York Office

CRIME PREVENTION (Agenda item 107)
Schantz, Delphine - A/C.3/78/SR.5

UN Office on Drugs and Crime. New York Office (continued)

CYBERCRIME (Agenda item 108)
Schantz, Delphine - A/C.3/78/SR.5

UN Ombudsman

ADMINISTRATION OF JUSTICE (Agenda item 144)
Dodson, Shireen L. - A/C.5/78/SR.15

UN Regional Centre for Peace and Disarmament in Africa. Director

PEACE—REGIONAL CENTRE—AFRICA (Agenda item 100b)
Yabouri, Anselme - A/C.1/78/PV.23

UN Regional Centre for Peace and Disarmament in Asia and the Pacific. Director

PEACE—REGIONAL CENTRE—ASIA AND THE PACIFIC (Agenda item 100d)
Basu Ray, Deepayan - A/C.1/78/PV.23

UN Regional Centre for Peace, Disarmament and Development in Latin America and the Caribbean. Director

PEACE—REGIONAL CENTRE—LATIN AMERICA AND THE CARIBBEAN (Agenda item 100c)
Urruela Arenales, María Soledad - A/C.1/78/PV.23

UN Scientific Committee on the Effects of Atomic Radiation. Chair

RADIATION EFFECTS (Agenda item 47)
Chen, Jing (Canada) - A/C.4/78/SR.11

UN Staff Union

UN—HUMAN RESOURCES MANAGEMENT (Agenda item 139)
Johnson, Laura - A/C.5/78/SR.27

UN System Chief Executives Board for Coordination

JOINT INSPECTION UNIT (Agenda item 141)
Pietracci, Federica - A/C.5/78/SR.27; A/C.5/78/SR.29
UN—ADMINISTRATION (Agenda item 132)
Pietracci, Federica - A/C.5/78/SR.29

UN-HABITAT

SOCIAL DEVELOPMENT (Agenda item 24)
Williams, Christopher - A/C.3/78/SR.1

UN-Women

RURAL WOMEN (Agenda item 25a)
Seymour, Daniel - A/C.3/78/SR.7

UN-Women (continued)

WOMEN MIGRANT WORKERS (Agenda item 25a)
Seymour, Daniel - A/C.3/78/SR.7
WOMEN'S ADVANCEMENT—CONFERENCES (Agenda item 25b)
Seymour, Daniel - A/C.3/78/SR.7

UNCTAD

COMMODITIES (Agenda item 16d)
Martínez Badillo, Juan José - A/C.2/78/SR.14
Shirotori, Miho - A/C.2/78/SR.8; A/C.2/78/SR.14
EXTERNAL DEBT (Agenda item 16c)
Hawkins, Penelope - A/C.2/78/SR.8
FINANCIAL FLOWS (Agenda item 16f)
Nastav, Bojan - A/C.2/78/SR.8
INFORMATION TECHNOLOGY—DEVELOPMENT (Agenda item 15)
González Sanz, Angel - A/C.2/78/SR.10
INTERNATIONAL TRADE (Agenda item 16a)
Hashmi, Khalil Ur Rahman - A/C.2/78/SR.8
Shirotori, Miho - A/C.2/78/SR.8
INVESTMENT PROMOTION (Agenda item 16g)
Bolwijn, Richard - A/C.2/78/SR.8
SCIENCE AND TECHNOLOGY—DEVELOPMENT (Agenda item 19a)
González Sanz, Angel - A/C.2/78/SR.10
SUSTAINABLE DEVELOPMENT (Agenda item 18)
Martínez Badillo, Juan José - A/C.2/78/SR.14
Shirotori, Miho - A/C.2/78/SR.14

UNDP

SUSTAINABLE DEVELOPMENT (Agenda item 18)
Al-Hammal, Ahmad - A/C.2/78/SR.12
Živković, Ivana - A/C.2/78/SR.12

UNEP

COASTAL ZONE MANAGEMENT (Agenda item 18j)
Noronha, Ligia - A/C.2/78/SR.12

UNESCO

CULTURE—DEVELOPMENT (Agenda item 19b)
Minchenberg, Eliot - A/C.2/78/SR.10
DEVELOPMENT EDUCATION (Agenda item 18g)
Minchenberg, Eliot - A/C.2/78/SR.12
RIGHT TO CULTURE (Agenda item 71b)
Zadra, Estelle - A/C.3/78/SR.27
RIGHT TO EDUCATION (Agenda item 71b)
Gray, Lily - A/C.3/78/SR.27

UNICEF

RIGHTS OF THE CHILD (Agenda item 67)
Fontaine, Manuel - A/C.3/78/SR.11

UNIDO

DEVELOPMENT FINANCE (Agenda item 16b)
Klose, Christoph - A/C.2/78/SR.11
FOOD SECURITY (Agenda item 23a)
Miljkovicova, Adriana - A/C.2/78/SR.18
MACROECONOMIC POLICY (Agenda item 16)
Klose, Christoph - A/C.2/78/SR.11
POVERTY—INTERNATIONAL DECADES (Agenda item 21a)
Miljkovicova, Adriana - A/C.2/78/SR.18
SUSTAINABLE ENERGY (Agenda item 18h)
Bredel, Ralf - A/C.2/78/SR.15

Union chrétienne des jeunes gens de Polynésie

FRENCH POLYNESIA QUESTION (Agenda item 58)
Tairua, Tiare Maohi - A/C.4/78/SR.3

United Arab Emirates

CLIMATE (Agenda item 18d)
Hassan, Tariq Ahmed - A/C.2/78/SR.13
CRIMES AGAINST HUMANITY (Agenda item 80)
Tantawy, Myan Medhat Anwar - A/C.6/78/SR.41
DECOLONIZATION (Agenda item 58)
Al-Ali, Maryam - A/C.4/78/SR.7
Matar, Shahd Jamal Yousuf - A/C.4/78/SR.8
Mohammad, Fatema Yousuf Ibrahim - A/C.4/78/SR.7; A/C.4/78/SR.9
DIAMONDS—FUELLING CONFLICT (Agenda item 30)
Abushahab, Mohamed Issa - A/78/PV.65
DISASTER VICTIMS (Agenda item 86)
Al Blooshi, Ahmed Ali - A/C.6/78/SR.7
EMERGENCY ASSISTANCE (Agenda item 72a)
Alolama, Mohd Abdulrahman Mohamed Jalil Sultan - A/78/PV.47
FOOD SECURITY (Agenda item 23a)
Almahmoud, Ahmed Abdelrahman Ahmed - A/C.2/78/SR.16
HUMAN RIGHTS (Agenda item 71)
Alameri, Reem Mohamed - A/C.3/78/SR.16
HUMAN RIGHTS—INTERNATIONAL INSTRUMENTS (Agenda item 71a)
Alameri, Reem Mohamed - A/C.3/78/SR.25
HUMAN RIGHTS ACTIVISTS (Agenda item 71b)
Alameri, Reem Mohamed - A/C.3/78/SR.19
HUMAN RIGHTS ADVANCEMENT (Agenda item 71b)
Alameri, Reem Mohamed - A/C.3/78/SR.25

United Arab Emirates (continued)

INTERNATIONAL JURISDICTION (Agenda item 84)
Al Blooshi, Ahmed Ali - A/C.6/78/SR.13
LAW OF THE SEA (Agenda item 75a)
Azzam, Rashed Jamal Ibrahim Ibrahim - A/78/PV.44
MARINE ECOSYSTEMS—BIOLOGICAL DIVERSITY (Agenda item 75c)
Azzam, Rashed Jamal Ibrahim Ibrahim - A/78/PV.44
MIDDLE EAST—NUCLEAR-WEAPON-FREE ZONES (Agenda item 95)
Alemad, Ahmed - A/C.1/78/PV.22
MULTILATERALISM—DISARMAMENT (Agenda item 99r)
Alemad, Ahmed - A/C.1/78/PV.22
NUCLEAR DISARMAMENT (Agenda item 99b)
Alnuaimi, Hessa - A/C.1/78/PV.14
NUCLEAR NON-PROLIFERATION—INTERNATIONAL OBLIGATIONS (Agenda item 99w)
Alnuaimi, Hessa - A/C.1/78/PV.14
OUTER SPACE—PEACEFUL USES—INTERNATIONAL COOPERATION (Agenda item 48)
Al Qasim, Ibrahim - A/C.4/78/SR.16
PALESTINE QUESTION (Agenda item 35)
Abushahab, Mohamed Issa - A/78/PV.40
PALESTINIANS—ASSISTANCE (Agenda item 72b)
Alolama, Mohd Abdulrahman Mohamed Jalil Sultan - A/78/PV.47
PEACE (Agenda item 14)
Abushahab, Mohamed Issa - A/78/PV.76; A/78/PV.82
PERSONS WITH DISABILITIES (Agenda item 24b)
Alseyabi, Eman - A/C.3/78/SR.3
POVERTY—INTERNATIONAL DECADES (Agenda item 21a)
Almahmoud, Ahmed Abdelrahman Ahmed - A/C.2/78/SR.16
RACIAL DISCRIMINATION—ELIMINATION (Agenda item 69a)
Al Dhanani, Nouf Abdulla - A/C.3/78/SR.41
RACIAL DISCRIMINATION—PROGRAMMES OF ACTION (Agenda item 69b)
Al Dhanani, Nouf Abdulla - A/C.3/78/SR.41
RESPONSIBILITY TO PROTECT (Agenda item 129)
Abushahab, Mohamed Issa - A/78/PV.97
RIGHTS OF THE CHILD (Agenda item 67)
Abdalrhman, Fatma Mohammad - A/C.3/78/SR.13
RULE OF LAW (Agenda item 83)
Al Marzooqi, Tahreer - A/C.6/78/SR.19
RURAL POVERTY (Agenda item 21b)
Almahmoud, Ahmed Abdelrahman Ahmed - A/C.2/78/SR.16
SOCIAL CONDITIONS (Agenda item 24b)
Alseyabi, Eman - A/C.3/78/SR.3
SOCIAL DEVELOPMENT (Agenda item 24)
Alseyabi, Eman - A/C.3/78/SR.3

United Arab Emirates (continued)

SPECIAL POLITICAL MISSIONS (Agenda item 52)
Al-Ali, Maryam - A/C.4/78/SR.21
SPORTS—OLYMPIC GAMES (Agenda item 11)
Alawadhi, Sarah Ebrahim Abdulla Beddah - A/78/PV.38
STRADDLING FISH STOCKS (Agenda item 75b)
Azzam, Rashed Jamal Ibrahim Ibrahim - A/78/PV.44
SUSTAINABLE DEVELOPMENT (Agenda item 18)
Abushahab, Mohamed Issa - A/78/PV.107
SUSTAINABLE ENERGY (Agenda item 18h)
Hassan, Tariq Ahmed - A/C.2/78/SR.13
TERRITORIES OCCUPIED BY ISRAEL—HUMAN RIGHTS (Agenda item 50)
Al-Ali, Maryam - A/C.4/78/SR.25
TERRITORIES OCCUPIED BY ISRAEL—NATURAL RESOURCES (Agenda item 59)
Al Hammadi, Asma Hassan Mohamed - A/C.2/78/SR.19
TERRORISM (Agenda item 109)
Al Marzooqi, Tahreer - A/C.6/78/SR.4
UN. GENERAL ASSEMBLY (78TH SESS. : 2023-2024)—GENERAL DEBATE (Agenda item 8)
Al Hashimy, Reem Ebrahim - A/78/PV.13
UN. GENERAL ASSEMBLY (78TH SESS. : 2023-2024)—GENERAL DEBATE—RIGHT OF REPLY (Agenda item 8)
Matar, Shahd Jamal Yousuf - A/78/PV.13
UN. GENERAL ASSEMBLY (78TH SESS. : 2023-2024)—OFFICERS (Agenda item 5)
Al-Khaabi, Najla - A/C.5/78/SR.1
UN. GENERAL ASSEMBLY (78TH SESS. : 2023-2024). 1ST COMMITTEE—GENERAL DEBATE (Agenda item 8)
Shaheen, Ghasaq Yousif - A/C.1/78/PV.4
UN. GENERAL ASSEMBLY (78TH SESS. : 2023-2024). 2ND COMMITTEE—GENERAL DEBATE (Agenda item 8)
Bastaki, Mohammad Yousuf Abdulla Mohammad - A/C.2/78/SR.4
UN. INTERNATIONAL COURT OF JUSTICE—REPORTS (Agenda item 73)
Alshamsi, Khaula Ali Khamis Obaid - A/78/PV.28
UN. SECURITY COUNCIL—REPORTS (Agenda item 26)
Shaheen, Ghasaq Yousif - A/78/PV.93
UNRWA—ACTIVITIES (Agenda item 49)
Al Nahyan, Zayed bin Sultan - A/C.4/78/SR.23
VETO (Agenda item 63)
Abushahab, Mohamed Issa - A/78/PV.61; A/78/PV.67; A/78/PV.78
Al-Ali, Mohamed Essa Saif Boausaibah - A/78/PV.71
Matar, Shahd Jamal Yousuf - A/78/PV.69
Nusseibeh, Lana Zaki - A/78/PV.52

United Arab Emirates (continued)

VETO (Agenda item 63)
Shaheen, Ghasaq Yousif - A/78/PV.3
WESTERN SAHARA QUESTION (Agenda item 58)
Al-Ali, Maryam - A/C.4/78/SR.7
WOMEN'S ADVANCEMENT (Agenda item 25a)
Al Hebsi, Jawaher Abdulla - A/C.3/78/SR.9
Nusseibeh, Lana Zaki - A/C.3/78/SR.8
WOMEN'S ADVANCEMENT—CONFERENCES (Agenda item 25b)
Al Hebsi, Jawaher Abdulla - A/C.3/78/SR.9
Nusseibeh, Lana Zaki - A/C.3/78/SR.8
YOUTH (Agenda item 24b)
Alshamsi, Mohamed - A/C.3/78/SR.3

United Kingdom

ADMINISTRATION OF JUSTICE (Agenda item 144)
Lito, Melina - A/C.6/78/SR.9
AFRICA—DEVELOPMENT (Agenda item 65b)
Young, Archie - A/78/PV.57
AFRICA—SUSTAINABLE DEVELOPMENT—PARTNERSHIP (Agenda item 65a)
Young, Archie - A/78/PV.57
ARMED CONFLICTS PREVENTION (Agenda item 31a)
Sylvester, Timothy James - A/78/PV.72
ARMS RACE—OUTER SPACE (Agenda item 97a)
Liddle, Aidan Thomas - A/C.1/78/PV.16
ARMS TRANSFERS—TREATIES (Agenda item 99x)
Saggese, Eleonora - A/C.1/78/PV.19
BIOLOGICAL WEAPONS—TREATIES (Agenda item 106)
Floyd, Ian - A/C.1/78/PV.15
CHEMICAL WEAPONS—TREATIES (Agenda item 99l)
Floyd, Ian - A/C.1/78/PV.15
CLIMATE (Agenda item 18d)
Fidoe, Nicholas - A/C.2/78/SR.25
CLUSTER MUNITIONS (Agenda item 99dd)
Saggese, Eleonora - A/C.1/78/PV.19
COMMODITIES (Agenda item 16d)
Sowah, Malcolm - A/C.2/78/SR.23
CRIME PREVENTION (Agenda item 107)
Reyes, Gaia - A/C.3/78/SR.51
CRIMES AGAINST HUMANITY (Agenda item 80)
Hollis, Jonathan Samuel - A/C.6/78/SR.10; A/C.6/78/SR.45
McIntyre, Colin Roger - A/C.6/78/SR.39
Woodifield, Mungo - A/C.6/78/SR.40; A/C.6/78/SR.42; A/C.6/78/SR.43; A/C.6/78/SR.44
DECOLONIZATION (Agenda item 58)
Meyrick, Phoebe - A/C.4/78/SR.9
Woodifield, Mungo - A/C.4/78/SR.8

United Kingdom (continued)

DECOLONIZATION—UN SYSTEM (Agenda item 56)
Meyrick, Phoebe - A/C.4/78/SR.9
DEVELOPMENT FINANCE (Agenda item 16b)
Dix, Laura Gabrielle - A/C.2/78/SR.9
DEVELOPMENT FINANCE—CONFERENCES (Agenda item 17)
Boyd-Lee, Katherine Suzanne Jenkins - A/78/PV.90
DIAMONDS—FUELLING CONFLICT (Agenda item 30)
Kriss, Benjamin - A/78/PV.65
DISARMAMENT—GENERAL AND COMPLETE (Agenda item 99)
Floyd, Ian - A/C.1/78/PV.26
Saggese, Eleonora - A/C.1/78/PV.19
DISARMAMENT—UN. GENERAL ASSEMBLY (4TH SPECIAL SESS. ON DISARMAMENT : xxxx) (Agenda item 99h)
Floyd, Ian - A/C.1/78/PV.23
DISASTER VICTIMS (Agenda item 86)
Hollis, Jonathan Samuel - A/C.6/78/SR.6
ECONOMIC SANCTIONS—INTERNATIONAL RELATIONS (Agenda item 28)
Young, Archie - A/78/PV.90
ELECTION VERIFICATION—UN (Agenda item 71b)
White, Megan Marie - A/C.3/78/SR.50
EMERGENCY ASSISTANCE (Agenda item 72a)
Kariuki, James - A/78/PV.46
EXTERNAL DEBT (Agenda item 16c)
Dix, Laura Gabrielle - A/C.2/78/SR.9
FALKLAND ISLANDS (MALVINAS) QUESTION (Agenda item 42)
Meyrick, Phoebe - A/C.4/78/SR.2; A/C.4/78/SR.6; A/C.4/78/SR.7; A/C.4/78/SR.8; A/C.4/78/SR.9
Woodifield, Mungo - A/C.4/78/SR.8
FAMILY (Agenda item 24b)
White, Megan Marie - A/C.3/78/SR.49
FOOD SECURITY (Agenda item 23a)
Kelsey, Alistair Robert Steven - A/C.2/78/SR.25
FREEDOM OF EXPRESSION (Agenda item 71b)
Devereaux, Brendan - A/C.3/78/SR.19
GIBRALTAR QUESTION (Agenda item 58)
Meyrick, Phoebe - A/C.4/78/SR.2
Woodifield, Mungo - A/C.4/78/SR.8
HEALTH (Agenda item 125)
Reyes, Gaia - A/78/PV.102
Sowah, Malcolm - A/78/PV.48; A/78/PV.77
Woodroffe, Tom - A/78/PV.16
HIV/AIDS—DECLARATIONS (Agenda item 10)
Sowah, Malcolm - A/78/PV.91
HUMAN RIGHTS (Agenda item 71)
Sylvester, Timothy James - A/C.3/78/SR.16

United Kingdom (continued)

HUMAN RIGHTS—AFGHANISTAN (Agenda item 71c)
White, Megan Marie - A/C.3/78/SR.34
HUMAN RIGHTS—BELARUS (Agenda item 71c)
Rosen, Katie - A/C.3/78/SR.37
HUMAN RIGHTS—CENTRAL AFRICAN REPUBLIC (Agenda item 71c)
Devereaux, Brendan - A/C.3/78/SR.33
HUMAN RIGHTS—DEMOCRATIC PEOPLE'S REPUBLIC OF KOREA (Agenda item 71c)
Devereaux, Brendan - A/C.3/78/SR.33; A/C.3/78/SR.53
HUMAN RIGHTS—ETHIOPIA (Agenda item 71c)
Devereaux, Brendan - A/C.3/78/SR.36
HUMAN RIGHTS—IRAN (ISLAMIC REPUBLIC OF) (Agenda item 71c)
Sylvester, Timothy James - A/C.3/78/SR.34
HUMAN RIGHTS—MYANMAR (Agenda item 71c)
Devereaux, Brendan - A/C.3/78/SR.53
Lundy, Phoebe - A/C.3/78/SR.33
HUMAN RIGHTS—REPORTS (Agenda item 71c)
Kariuki, James - A/C.3/78/SR.26
HUMAN RIGHTS—RUSSIAN FEDERATION (Agenda item 71c)
Croker, Richard - A/C.3/78/SR.24
Sylvester, Timothy James - A/C.3/78/SR.37
HUMAN RIGHTS—SOMALIA (Agenda item 71c)
Lundy, Phoebe - A/C.3/78/SR.35
HUMAN RIGHTS—SYRIAN ARAB REPUBLIC (Agenda item 71c)
Sylvester, Timothy James - A/C.3/78/SR.54
White, Megan Marie - A/C.3/78/SR.34
HUMAN RIGHTS—TERRITORIES OCCUPIED BY ISRAEL (Agenda item 71c)
Croker, Richard - A/C.3/78/SR.24; A/C.3/78/SR.35
HUMAN RIGHTS—UKRAINE (Agenda item 71c)
Croker, Richard - A/C.3/78/SR.24
Sylvester, Timothy James - A/C.3/78/SR.37; A/C.3/78/SR.53
HUMAN RIGHTS ACTIVISTS (Agenda item 71b)
Devereaux, Brendan - A/C.3/78/SR.19
HUMAN RIGHTS ADVANCEMENT (Agenda item 71b)
Callaghan-Pace, Laura Frances - A/C.3/78/SR.52
Croker, Richard - A/C.3/78/SR.18; A/C.3/78/SR.24
Sigley, Andrew - A/C.3/78/SR.52
HUMAN RIGHTS INSTITUTIONS—CENTRAL AFRICA (Agenda item 71b)
Lundy, Phoebe - A/C.3/78/SR.56
IAEA—REPORTS (Agenda item 89)
Jones, Katherine Sarah - A/78/PV.30
INDIGENOUS PEOPLES (Agenda item 68a)
Sylvester, Timothy James - A/C.3/78/SR.48

United Kingdom (continued)

INFORMATION (Agenda item 53)
Woodifield, Mungo - A/C.4/78/SR.14
INFORMATION—INTERNATIONAL SECURITY (Agenda item 94)
Page, Elizabeth Louise - A/C.1/78/PV.20
INFORMATION TECHNOLOGY—DEVELOPMENT (Agenda item 15)
Kelsey, Alistair Robert Steven - A/C.2/78/SR.23
INTERNATIONAL CRIMINAL COURT—REPORTS (Agenda item 74)
Hollis, Jonathan Samuel - A/78/PV.22
INTERNATIONAL JURISDICTION (Agenda item 84)
Hollis, Jonathan Samuel - A/C.6/78/SR.12
INTERNATIONAL LAW—TRAINING PROGRAMMES (Agenda item 78)
Lito, Melina - A/C.6/78/SR.21
INTERNATIONAL RESIDUAL MECHANISM FOR CRIMINAL TRIBUNALS (Agenda item 126)
Hollis, Jonathan Samuel - A/78/PV.19
INTERNATIONAL TRADE (Agenda item 16a)
Baric, Ana - A/C.2/78/SR.22
Kelsey, Alistair Robert Steven - A/C.2/78/SR.24
INVESTMENT PROMOTION (Agenda item 16g)
Sowah, Malcolm - A/C.2/78/SR.23
LANDMINES—TREATIES (Agenda item 99m)
Saggese, Eleonora - A/C.1/78/PV.19
LAW OF THE SEA (Agenda item 75a)
Pickens, Andrew - A/78/PV.48
Woodward, Barbara - A/78/PV.44
MARINE ECOSYSTEMS—BIOLOGICAL DIVERSITY (Agenda item 75c)
Woodward, Barbara - A/78/PV.44
MERCENARIES (Agenda item 70)
Kumaria, Sacha - A/C.3/78/SR.48
MIDDLE EAST SITUATION (Agenda item 34)
Eckersley, Fergus - A/78/PV.40
MIGRANTS—PROTECTION (Agenda item 71b)
Devereaux, Brendan - A/C.3/78/SR.56
MILLENNIUM SUMMIT—CONFERENCES (Agenda item 117)
Fidoe, Nicholas - A/78/PV.102
Woodroffe, Tom - A/78/PV.15
MULTILATERALISM—DISARMAMENT (Agenda item 99r)
Liddle, Aidan Thomas - A/C.1/78/PV.21
MULTILINGUALISM (Agenda item 124)
Sigley, Andrew - A/78/PV.108
NON-CITIZENS—DEPORTATION (Agenda item 81)
Lito, Melina - A/C.6/78/SR.34
NON-SELF-GOVERNING TERRITORIES—ECONOMIC INTERESTS (Agenda item 55)
Meyrick, Phoebe - A/C.4/78/SR.9

United Kingdom (continued)

NON-SELF-GOVERNING TERRITORIES—REPORTS (Agenda item 54)
Meyrick, Phoebe - A/C.4/78/SR.9
NUCLEAR DISARMAMENT (Agenda item 99b)
Liddle, Aidan Thomas - A/C.1/78/PV.13
NUCLEAR DISARMAMENT—VERIFICATION (Agenda item 99ee)
Liddle, Aidan Thomas - A/C.1/78/PV.13
NUCLEAR NON-PROLIFERATION—INTERNATIONAL OBLIGATIONS (Agenda item 99w)
Liddle, Aidan Thomas - A/C.1/78/PV.13
NUCLEAR WEAPON TESTS—TREATIES (Agenda item 105)
Liddle, Aidan Thomas - A/C.1/78/PV.13
ORGANIZATION FOR DEMOCRACY AND ECONOMIC DEVELOPMENT - GUAM (Agenda item 32)
Alldridge, Rebecca - A/78/PV.85
OUTER SPACE—PEACEFUL USES—INTERNATIONAL COOPERATION (Agenda item 48)
Croker, Richard - A/C.4/78/SR.17
OUTER SPACE—PRINCIPLES (Agenda item 97d)
Liddle, Aidan Thomas - A/C.1/78/PV.16; A/C.1/78/PV.27
PEACE (Agenda item 14)
Kariuki, James - A/78/PV.62
PEACEBUILDING (Agenda item 61)
Weld-Blundell, Stacy John - A/78/PV.101
PEACEKEEPING OPERATIONS—CRIMINAL LIABILITY (Agenda item 76)
Hollis, Jonathan Samuel - A/C.6/78/SR.8
RACIAL DISCRIMINATION—PROGRAMMES OF ACTION (Agenda item 69b)
Lundy, Phoebe - A/C.3/78/SR.56
RELIGIOUS INTOLERANCE (Agenda item 71b)
Manzare, Max - A/C.3/78/SR.38
RESPONSIBILITY OF INTERNATIONAL ORGANIZATIONS (Agenda item 85)
Hollis, Jonathan Samuel - A/C.6/78/SR.19
RESPONSIBILITY TO PROTECT (Agenda item 129)
Hollis, Jonathan Samuel - A/78/PV.97
RIGHT OF ASSEMBLY (Agenda item 71b)
Devereaux, Brendan - A/C.3/78/SR.19
RIGHT TO DEVELOPMENT (Agenda item 71b)
Lundy, Phoebe - A/C.3/78/SR.48
RIGHT TO FOOD (Agenda item 71b)
Kumaria, Sacha - A/C.3/78/SR.48
RIGHTS OF THE CHILD (Agenda item 67)
Reyes, Gaia - A/C.3/78/SR.55
RULE OF LAW (Agenda item 83)
Lito, Melina - A/C.6/78/SR.16
SANCTIONS—INTERNATIONAL RELATIONS (Agenda item 71b)
Lundy, Phoebe - A/C.3/78/SR.48

United Kingdom (continued)

SCIENCE AND TECHNOLOGY—DEVELOPMENT (Agenda item 19a)
Baric, Ana - A/C.2/78/SR.22
SELF-DETERMINATION OF PEOPLES (Agenda item 70)
Eckersley, Fergus - A/C.3/78/SR.49
SEXUAL ORIENTATION (Agenda item 71b)
White, Megan Marie - A/C.3/78/SR.39
SLAVERY (Agenda item 71a)
Manzare, Max - A/C.3/78/SR.21
SMALL ISLAND DEVELOPING STATES—PROGRAMMES OF ACTION (Agenda item 18b)
Baric, Ana - A/C.2/78/SR.22
Soomro, Tara - A/78/PV.103
SOCIAL DEVELOPMENT (Agenda item 24)
Devereaux, Brendan - A/C.3/78/SR.47
STRADDLING FISH STOCKS (Agenda item 75b)
Woodward, Barbara - A/78/PV.44
SUMMARY EXECUTIONS (Agenda item 71b)
Sylvester, Timothy James - A/C.3/78/SR.31
SUSTAINABLE DEVELOPMENT (Agenda item 18)
Croker, Richard - A/C.2/78/SR.24
Kelsey, Alistair Robert Steven - A/C.2/78/SR.24
Soomro, Tara - A/78/PV.107
SUSTAINABLE ENERGY (Agenda item 18h)
Fidoe, Nicholas - A/C.2/78/SR.23
TAXATION (Agenda item 16h)
Croker, Richard - A/C.2/78/SR.25
TERRITORIES OCCUPIED BY ISRAEL—HUMAN RIGHTS (Agenda item 50)
Croker, Richard - A/C.4/78/SR.26
TERRITORIES OCCUPIED BY ISRAEL—NATURAL RESOURCES (Agenda item 59)
Kelsey, Alistair Robert Steven - A/C.2/78/SR.21
Wood, Grace Louise - A/C.2/78/SR.19
TERRORISM (Agenda item 109)
Clark, Joel - A/C.6/78/SR.1
TREATIES (Agenda item 87)
Lito, Melina - A/C.6/78/SR.20
UKRAINE—POLITICAL CONDITIONS (Agenda item 62)
Cameron, David - A/78/PV.56
UN—BUDGET (2024) (Agenda item 134)
Capek, Hannah Rose - A/C.5/78/SR.26/PartII
Cottam, Paul Arthur - A/C.5/78/SR.33
Staples, James - A/C.5/78/SR.5
UN—FINANCIAL SITUATION (Agenda item 136)
Cottam, Paul Arthur - A/C.5/78/SR.6
Williams, Ian - A/C.5/78/SR.38
UN—PROGRAMME PLANNING (Agenda item 135)
Liddle, Aidan Thomas - A/C.1/78/PV.10
Staples, James - A/C.5/78/SR.5
UN. CONFERENCE ON DISARMAMENT—REPORTS (Agenda item 101a)
Floyd, Ian - A/C.1/78/PV.23

United Kingdom (continued)

UN. GENERAL ASSEMBLY—WORK PROGRAMME (Agenda item 120)
Liddle, Aidan Thomas - A/C.1/78/PV.10
UN. GENERAL ASSEMBLY (78TH SESS. : 2023-2024)—OFFICERS (Agenda item 5)
Kariuki, James - A/C.5/78/SR.1
UN. GENERAL ASSEMBLY (78TH SESS. : 2023-2024). 1ST COMMITTEE—GENERAL DEBATE (Agenda item 8)
Liddle, Aidan Thomas - A/C.1/78/PV.4
UN. GENERAL ASSEMBLY (78TH SESS. : 2023-2024). 2ND COMMITTEE—GENERAL DEBATE (Agenda item 8)
Kariuki, James - A/C.2/78/SR.5
UN. GENERAL ASSEMBLY (78TH SESS. : 2023-2024). 5TH COMMITTEE—WORK ORGANIZATION (Agenda item 7)
Kariuki, James - A/C.5/78/SR.35
Staples, James - A/C.5/78/SR.26/PartII
Young, Archie - A/C.5/78/SR.27; A/C.5/78/SR.34; A/C.5/78/SR.40
UN. HUMAN RIGHTS COUNCIL—REPORTS (Agenda item 66)
Manzare, Max - A/C.3/78/SR.46
UN. INTERNATIONAL COURT OF JUSTICE—REPORTS (Agenda item 73)
Langrish, Sally - A/78/PV.20
UN. INTERNATIONAL LAW COMMISSION—REPORTS (Agenda item 79)
Hollis, Jonathan Samuel - A/C.6/78/SR.37
Janeczko, Frazer - A/C.6/78/SR.29; A/C.6/78/SR.31
Langrish, Sally - A/C.6/78/SR.23
UN. PEACEBUILDING COMMISSION—REPORTS (Agenda item 27)
Weld-Blundell, Stacy John - A/78/PV.101
UN. PEACEBUILDING FUND—REPORTS (Agenda item 111)
Weld-Blundell, Stacy John - A/78/PV.101
UN. SECURITY COUNCIL—MEMBERSHIP (Agenda item 121)
Kariuki, James - A/78/PV.34
UN CHARTER—REPORTS (Agenda item 82)
Lito, Melina - A/C.6/78/SR.22
UN COMMISSION ON INTERNATIONAL TRADE LAW—REPORTS (Agenda item 77)
Lito, Melina - A/C.6/78/SR.14
UN CONFERENCES (Agenda item 13)
Fidoe, Nicholas - A/78/PV.102
Woodroffe, Tom - A/78/PV.15
UN SYSTEM—STRENGTHENING (Agenda item 122)
Reyes, Gaia - A/78/PV.99
UNRWA—ACTIVITIES (Agenda item 49)
Croker, Richard - A/C.4/78/SR.26
Gibbon, James - A/C.4/78/SR.23
VETO (Agenda item 63)
Eckersley, Fergus - A/78/PV.3
Kariuki, James - A/78/PV.75
Woodward, Barbara - A/78/PV.59; A/78/PV.67; A/78/PV.68; A/78/PV.78

United Kingdom (continued)

VETO (Agenda item 63)
Young, Archie - A/78/PV.51; A/78/PV.71
WEAPONS—OUTER SPACE (Agenda item 97b)
Liddle, Aidan Thomas - A/C.1/78/PV.16
WOMEN'S ADVANCEMENT (Agenda item 25a)
White, Megan Marie - A/C.3/78/SR.8
WOMEN'S ADVANCEMENT—CONFERENCES (Agenda item 25b)
Reyes, Gaia - A/C.3/78/SR.51
White, Megan Marie - A/C.3/78/SR.8

United Kingdom. Deputy Prime Minister

UN. GENERAL ASSEMBLY (78TH SESS. : 2023-2024)—GENERAL DEBATE (Agenda item 8)
Dowden, Oliver - A/78/PV.11
UN. GENERAL ASSEMBLY (78TH SESS. : 2023-2024)—SPECIAL STATEMENTS
Dowden, Oliver - A/78/PV.11

United Republic of Tanzania

ALBINISM (Agenda item 71b)
Tambwe, Zuleikha Rutha - A/C.3/78/SR.27
CUBA—UNITED STATES (Agenda item 38)
Mwasota, Joseph Aron - A/78/PV.24
DIAMONDS—FUELLING CONFLICT (Agenda item 30)
Kattanga, Hussein A. - A/78/PV.65
ELECTION VERIFICATION—UN (Agenda item 71b)
Tambwe, Zuleikha Rutha - A/C.3/78/SR.50
FOOD SECURITY (Agenda item 23a)
Kattanga, Hussein A. - A/C.2/78/SR.17
HUMAN RIGHTS—REPORTS (Agenda item 71c)
Tambwe, Zuleikha Rutha - A/C.3/78/SR.26
INDIGENOUS PEOPLES (Agenda item 68a)
Malebo, Hamisi - A/C.3/78/SR.15
INDIGENOUS PEOPLES—CONFERENCES (Agenda item 68b)
Malebo, Hamisi - A/C.3/78/SR.15
INTERNATIONAL JURISDICTION (Agenda item 84)
Kattanga, Hussein A. - A/C.6/78/SR.13
INTERNATIONAL LAW—TRAINING PROGRAMMES (Agenda item 78)
Mwasota, Joseph Aron - A/C.6/78/SR.22
INTERNATIONAL RESIDUAL MECHANISM FOR CRIMINAL TRIBUNALS (Agenda item 126)
Mwasota, Joseph Aron - A/78/PV.19
INTERNATIONAL RESIDUAL MECHANISM FOR CRIMINAL TRIBUNALS—FINANCING (Agenda item 145)
Suleiman, Suleiman Haji - A/C.5/78/SR.20
PEACE (Agenda item 14)
Kattanga, Hussein A. - A/78/PV.82

United Republic of Tanzania (continued)

POVERTY—INTERNATIONAL DECADES (Agenda item 21a)
Kattanga, Hussein A. - A/C.2/78/SR.17
RIGHTS OF THE CHILD (Agenda item 67)
Tambwe, Zuleikha Rutha - A/C.3/78/SR.14
RURAL POVERTY (Agenda item 21b)
Kattanga, Hussein A. - A/C.2/78/SR.17
SOCIAL CONDITIONS (Agenda item 24b)
Kattanga, Hussein A. - A/C.3/78/SR.3
SOCIAL DEVELOPMENT (Agenda item 24)
Kattanga, Hussein A. - A/C.3/78/SR.3
SUSTAINABLE DEVELOPMENT (Agenda item 18)
Kattanga, Hussein A. - A/C.2/78/SR.15
SUSTAINABLE ENERGY (Agenda item 18h)
Kattanga, Hussein A. - A/C.2/78/SR.15
UN. GENERAL ASSEMBLY (78TH SESS. : 2023-2024). 1ST COMMITTEE—GENERAL DEBATE (Agenda item 8)
Kattanga, Hussein A. - A/C.1/78/PV.5
UN. GENERAL ASSEMBLY (78TH SESS. : 2023-2024). 2ND COMMITTEE—GENERAL DEBATE (Agenda item 8)
Kattanga, Hussein A. - A/C.2/78/SR.5
WOMEN'S ADVANCEMENT (Agenda item 25a)
Kattanga, Hussein A. - A/C.3/78/SR.10
WOMEN'S ADVANCEMENT—CONFERENCES (Agenda item 25b)
Kattanga, Hussein A. - A/C.3/78/SR.10
YOUTH (Agenda item 24b)
Kattanga, Hussein A. - A/C.3/78/SR.3

United Republic of Tanzania. Vice-President

UN. GENERAL ASSEMBLY (78TH SESS. : 2023-2024)—GENERAL DEBATE (Agenda item 8)
Mpango, Philip Isdor - A/78/PV.9
UN. GENERAL ASSEMBLY (78TH SESS. : 2023-2024)—SPECIAL STATEMENTS
Mpango, Philip Isdor - A/78/PV.9

United States

ADMINISTRATION OF JUSTICE (Agenda item 144)
Patton, Dorothy - A/C.6/78/SR.9
AFRICA—SUSTAINABLE DEVELOPMENT—PARTNERSHIP (Agenda item 65a)
Fogarty, Daniel - A/78/PV.57
AGEING PERSONS (Agenda item 24b)
Lang, Dylan - A/C.3/78/SR.1
AL-SABAH, NAWAF AL-AHMAD AL-JABER (KUWAIT. AMIR)—TRIBUTES
Lu, Christopher P. - A/78/PV.50(Resumption1)
AMERICAN SAMOA QUESTION (Agenda item 58)
Kris, Robert - A/C.4/78/SR.7

United States (continued)

ARMED CONFLICTS PREVENTION (Agenda item 31a)
Sullivan, Stephanie - A/78/PV.72
ARMS RACE—OUTER SPACE (Agenda item 97a)
Turner, Bruce - A/C.1/78/PV.17
BIOLOGICAL DIVERSITY—TREATIES (Agenda item 18f)
Lawrence, Jason N. - A/C.2/78/SR.25
BIOLOGICAL WEAPONS—TREATIES (Agenda item 106)
Turner, Bruce - A/C.1/78/PV.15; A/C.1/78/PV.16
CENTRAL ASIA—ZONES OF PEACE (Agenda item 64)
Madinger, Sean - A/78/PV.85
CHEMICAL WEAPONS—TREATIES (Agenda item 99l)
Turner, Bruce - A/C.1/78/PV.15; A/C.1/78/PV.26
CLIMATE (Agenda item 18d)
Henzel, Christopher - A/C.2/78/SR.15
Lawrence, Jason N. - A/C.2/78/SR.25
CLIMATE CHANGE (Agenda item 71b)
Worthe, Jeffrey - A/C.3/78/SR.29
CLUSTER MUNITIONS (Agenda item 99dd)
Turner, Bruce - A/C.1/78/PV.28
COASTAL ZONE MANAGEMENT (Agenda item 18j)
Kroeker-Maus, Faith - A/C.2/78/SR.23
COMMODITIES (Agenda item 16d)
Lawrence, Jason N. - A/C.2/78/SR.23
CONVENTIONAL ARMS—REGIONAL PROGRAMMES (Agenda item 99g)
Turner, Bruce - A/C.1/78/PV.29
CONVENTIONAL WEAPONS (Agenda item 99u)
Storsve, Alison - A/C.1/78/PV.19; A/C.1/78/PV.28
CRIME PREVENTION (Agenda item 107)
Eyrich, Kara - A/C.3/78/SR.47
Johnson, Timothy J. - A/C.3/78/SR.56
Merron, Eric - A/C.3/78/SR.5
CRIMES AGAINST HUMANITY (Agenda item 80)
Genoversa-Wong, Bridget - A/C.6/78/SR.41; A/C.6/78/SR.43
Ghaus, Hawa - A/C.6/78/SR.40; A/C.6/78/SR.44
Simonoff, Mark - A/C.6/78/SR.9; A/C.6/78/SR.38; A/C.6/78/SR.45
CUBA—UNITED STATES (Agenda item 38)
Folmsbee, Paul - A/78/PV.26
CULTURE—DEVELOPMENT (Agenda item 19b)
Kroeker-Maus, Faith - A/C.2/78/SR.23
CYBERCRIME (Agenda item 108)
Heartney, Edward - A/C.3/78/SR.5
Merron, Eric - A/C.3/78/SR.5
DECOLONIZATION (Agenda item 58)
Kris, Robert - A/C.4/78/SR.7
DEMOCRACY (Agenda item 71b)
Merron, Eric - A/C.3/78/SR.48

United States (continued)

DESERTIFICATION—TREATIES (Agenda item 18e)
Kroeker-Maus, Faith - A/C.2/78/SR.23
DEVELOPMENT COOPERATION—MIDDLE-INCOME COUNTRIES (Agenda item 19c)
Kroeker-Maus, Faith - A/C.2/78/SR.23
DEVELOPMENT EDUCATION (Agenda item 18g)
Sharma, Deeksha - A/C.2/78/SR.22
DEVELOPMENT FINANCE (Agenda item 16b)
Armbruster, Thomas - A/C.2/78/SR.21
Hamilton, Jim - A/C.2/78/SR.22
DEVELOPMENT FINANCE—CONFERENCES (Agenda item 17)
Marks, Rose Ann - A/78/PV.90; A/C.2/78/SR.25
DIAMONDS—FUELLING CONFLICT (Agenda item 30)
Lelek, Julia - A/78/PV.65
DISAPPEARANCE OF PERSONS (Agenda item 71b)
Heartney, Edward - A/C.3/78/SR.22
Johnson, Timothy J. - A/C.3/78/SR.50
DISARMAMENT—GENERAL AND COMPLETE (Agenda item 99)
Sharp, Matthew - A/78/PV.105
Storsve, Alison - A/C.1/78/PV.19; A/C.1/78/PV.28
Turner, Bruce - A/C.1/78/PV.15; A/C.1/78/PV.26; A/C.1/78/PV.30
DISARMAMENT AGREEMENTS—ENVIRONMENT (Agenda item 99j)
Turner, Bruce - A/C.1/78/PV.29
DISARMAMENT AGREEMENTS—OUTER SPACE (Agenda item 97c)
Turner, Bruce - A/C.1/78/PV.17; A/C.1/78/PV.27
DISARMAMENT-DEVELOPMENT LINK (Agenda item 99d)
Turner, Bruce - A/C.1/78/PV.29
DISASTER PREVENTION (Agenda item 18c)
Armbruster, Thomas - A/C.2/78/SR.21
Kroeker-Maus, Faith - A/C.2/78/SR.23
DISASTER VICTIMS (Agenda item 86)
Grosso, Elizabeth Maryanne - A/C.6/78/SR.5
DISPLACED PERSONS (Agenda item 71b)
McGlothlin, Cameron - A/C.3/78/SR.32
ECONOMIC COOPERATION AMONG DEVELOPING COUNTRIES (Agenda item 22b)
Armbruster, Thomas - A/C.2/78/SR.21
Marks, Rose Ann - A/C.2/78/SR.25
ECONOMIC SANCTIONS—INTERNATIONAL RELATIONS (Agenda item 28)
Heartney, Edward - A/78/PV.90
ELECTION VERIFICATION—UN (Agenda item 71b)
Korac, Sofija - A/78/PV.50
Millard, Elisabeth I. - A/C.3/78/SR.50
EMERGENCY ASSISTANCE (Agenda item 72a)
Carty, Lisa A. - A/78/PV.46

United States (continued)

ENVIRONMENT (Agenda item 71b)
Lang, Dylan - A/C.3/78/SR.29
EXTERNAL DEBT (Agenda item 16c)
Hamilton, Jim - A/C.2/78/SR.25
FAMILY (Agenda item 24b)
Lang, Dylan - A/C.3/78/SR.49
FINANCIAL FLOWS (Agenda item 16f)
Armbruster, Thomas - A/C.2/78/SR.21
Lawrence, Jason N. - A/C.2/78/SR.23
FINANCIAL INCLUSION (Agenda item 16e)
Macarena Apud, Maria - A/C.2/78/SR.22
FISSIONABLE MATERIALS—TREATIES (Agenda item 99a)
Turner, Bruce - A/C.1/78/PV.25
FOOD SECURITY (Agenda item 23a)
Armbruster, Thomas - A/C.2/78/SR.21
Kroeker-Maus, Faith - A/C.2/78/SR.25
Leonard, Mary Beth - A/C.2/78/SR.17
Torres Small, Xochitl - A/78/PV.77
FREEDOM OF EXPRESSION (Agenda item 71b)
Billingsley, Kelly - A/C.3/78/SR.19
GEINGOB, HAGE GOTTFRIED (NAMIBIA. PRESIDENT)—TRIBUTES
Thomas-Greenfield, Linda - A/78/PV.55
GUAM QUESTION (Agenda item 58)
Kris, Robert - A/C.4/78/SR.7
HEALTH (Agenda item 125)
Carty, Lisa A. - A/78/PV.16; A/78/PV.48
Eyrich, Kara - A/78/PV.48
Korac, Sofija - A/78/PV.77
Shrier, Jonathan - A/78/PV.102
HIV/AIDS—DECLARATIONS (Agenda item 10)
Heartney, Edward - A/78/PV.91
HUMAN RIGHTS (Agenda item 71)
Shrier, Jonathan - A/C.3/78/SR.16
HUMAN RIGHTS—AFGHANISTAN (Agenda item 71c)
Johnson, Timothy J. - A/C.3/78/SR.34
Shrier, Jonathan - A/C.3/78/SR.25
HUMAN RIGHTS—BELARUS (Agenda item 71c)
Millard, Elisabeth I. - A/C.3/78/SR.37
Shrier, Jonathan - A/C.3/78/SR.25
HUMAN RIGHTS—BURUNDI (Agenda item 71c)
Leonard, Mary Beth - A/C.3/78/SR.36
HUMAN RIGHTS—CENTRAL AFRICAN REPUBLIC (Agenda item 71c)
Leonard, Mary Beth - A/C.3/78/SR.33
HUMAN RIGHTS—DEMOCRATIC PEOPLE'S REPUBLIC OF KOREA (Agenda item 71c)
Armbruster, Thomas - A/C.3/78/SR.33
Eyrich, Kara - A/C.3/78/SR.53
Shrier, Jonathan - A/C.3/78/SR.25
HUMAN RIGHTS—ERITREA (Agenda item 71c)
Leonard, Mary Beth - A/C.3/78/SR.36

United States (continued)

HUMAN RIGHTS—ETHIOPIA (Agenda item 71c)
Leonard, Mary Beth - A/C.3/78/SR.36
HUMAN RIGHTS—INTERNATIONAL INSTRUMENTS (Agenda item 71a)
Korac, Sofija - A/C.3/78/SR.47
HUMAN RIGHTS—IRAN (ISLAMIC REPUBLIC OF) (Agenda item 71c)
Carty, Lisa A. - A/C.3/78/SR.34
Henzel, Christopher - A/C.3/78/SR.53
HUMAN RIGHTS—MYANMAR (Agenda item 71c)
Armbruster, Thomas - A/C.3/78/SR.33
HUMAN RIGHTS—REPORTS (Agenda item 71c)
Heartney, Edward - A/C.3/78/SR.18
Shrier, Jonathan - A/C.3/78/SR.25
HUMAN RIGHTS—RUSSIAN FEDERATION (Agenda item 71c)
Millard, Elisabeth I. - A/C.3/78/SR.37
Shrier, Jonathan - A/C.3/78/SR.25
HUMAN RIGHTS—SOMALIA (Agenda item 71c)
Leonard, Mary Beth - A/C.3/78/SR.35
HUMAN RIGHTS—SYRIAN ARAB REPUBLIC (Agenda item 71c)
Carty, Lisa A. - A/C.3/78/SR.54
Henzel, Christopher - A/C.3/78/SR.34
Shrier, Jonathan - A/C.3/78/SR.25
HUMAN RIGHTS—TERRITORIES OCCUPIED BY ISRAEL (Agenda item 71c)
Shrier, Jonathan - A/C.3/78/SR.35
HUMAN RIGHTS—UKRAINE (Agenda item 71c)
Millard, Elisabeth I. - A/C.3/78/SR.37
HUMAN RIGHTS ACTIVISTS (Agenda item 71b)
Eyrich, Kara - A/C.3/78/SR.56
Murphy, Daniel - A/C.3/78/SR.19
HUMAN RIGHTS ADVANCEMENT (Agenda item 71b)
Eyrich, Kara - A/C.3/78/SR.52
Merron, Eric - A/C.3/78/SR.48
Vasović, Angela - A/C.3/78/SR.52
HUMAN RIGHTS INSTITUTIONS—CENTRAL AFRICA (Agenda item 71b)
Lang, Dylan - A/C.3/78/SR.56
INDIGENOUS PEOPLES (Agenda item 68a)
Murphy, Daniel - A/C.3/78/SR.15
Shrier, Jonathan - A/78/PV.107; A/C.3/78/SR.15
INDIGENOUS PEOPLES—CONFERENCES (Agenda item 68b)
Murphy, Daniel - A/C.3/78/SR.15
Shrier, Jonathan - A/C.3/78/SR.15
INFORMATION—INTERNATIONAL SECURITY (Agenda item 94)
Turner, Bruce - A/C.1/78/PV.21
INFORMATION TECHNOLOGY—DEVELOPMENT (Agenda item 15)
Lawrence, Jason N. - A/C.2/78/SR.23

United States (continued)

INTERNATIONAL CRIMINAL COURT—REPORTS (Agenda item 74)
Smyre, Calvin - A/78/PV.22
INTERNATIONAL JURISDICTION (Agenda item 84)
Grosso, Elizabeth Maryanne - A/C.6/78/SR.12
INTERNATIONAL LAW—TRAINING PROGRAMMES (Agenda item 78)
Patton, Dorothy - A/C.6/78/SR.21
INTERNATIONAL PARLIAMENTARIANS' CONGRESS—OBSERVER STATUS (Agenda item 170)
Patton, Dorothy - A/C.6/78/SR.14
INTERNATIONAL RESIDUAL MECHANISM FOR CRIMINAL TRIBUNALS (Agenda item 126)
Lu, Christopher P. - A/78/PV.19
INTERNATIONAL TRADE (Agenda item 16a)
Armbruster, Thomas - A/C.2/78/SR.21
Lawrence, Jason N. - A/C.2/78/SR.22; A/C.2/78/SR.24
INVESTMENT PROMOTION (Agenda item 16g)
Lawrence, Jason N. - A/C.2/78/SR.23
JUDICIAL INDEPENDENCE (Agenda item 71b)
Breen, Patrick - A/C.3/78/SR.31
LANDLOCKED DEVELOPING COUNTRIES—CONFERENCES (Agenda item 20b)
Armbruster, Thomas - A/C.2/78/SR.7
Kroeker-Maus, Faith - A/C.2/78/SR.23
LAW OF THE SEA (Agenda item 75a)
Armbruster, Thomas - A/78/PV.44
LEAST DEVELOPED COUNTRIES—CONFERENCES (Agenda item 20a)
Armbruster, Thomas - A/C.2/78/SR.7
Kroeker-Maus, Faith - A/C.2/78/SR.23
MARINE ECOSYSTEMS—BIOLOGICAL DIVERSITY (Agenda item 75c)
Armbruster, Thomas - A/78/PV.44
MEDITERRANEAN REGION—REGIONAL SECURITY (Agenda item 104)
Turner, Bruce - A/C.1/78/PV.29
MERCENARIES (Agenda item 70)
Merron, Eric - A/C.3/78/SR.48
MIDDLE EAST—NUCLEAR PROLIFERATION (Agenda item 102)
Turner, Bruce - A/C.1/78/PV.26
MIDDLE EAST—NUCLEAR-WEAPON-FREE ZONES (Agenda item 95)
Turner, Bruce - A/C.1/78/PV.25
MIGRANTS—PROTECTION (Agenda item 71b)
Johnson, Timothy J. - A/C.3/78/SR.56
McGlothlin, Cameron - A/C.3/78/SR.23
MILLENNIUM SUMMIT—CONFERENCES (Agenda item 117)
Carty, Lisa A. - A/78/PV.15
Pell, Herbert - A/78/PV.102

United States (continued)
MINORITIES (Agenda item 71b)
Lang, Dylan - A/C.3/78/SR.39
MULTILINGUALISM (Agenda item 124)
Stetter, Elizabeth - A/78/PV.108
NATURAL FIBRES (Agenda item 23b)
Kroeker-Maus, Faith - A/C.2/78/SR.23
NON-CITIZENS—DEPORTATION (Agenda item 81)
Grosso, Elizabeth Maryanne - A/C.6/78/SR.34
NON-SELF-GOVERNING TERRITORIES—REPORTS (Agenda item 54)
Boluda, Miguel - A/C.4/78/SR.9
NUCLEAR DISARMAMENT (Agenda item 99b)
Turner, Bruce - A/C.1/78/PV.13
NUCLEAR DISARMAMENT—TREATY COMPLIANCE (Agenda item 99q)
Turner, Bruce - A/C.1/78/PV.25
NUCLEAR NON-PROLIFERATION—INTERNATIONAL OBLIGATIONS (Agenda item 99w)
Turner, Bruce - A/C.1/78/PV.13
NUCLEAR WEAPONS—ELIMINATION (Agenda item 99z)
Storsve, Alison - A/C.1/78/PV.25
NUCLEAR WEAPONS—HUMANITARIAN CONSEQUENCES (Agenda item 99bb)
Turner, Bruce - A/C.1/78/PV.25
NUCLEAR-WEAPON-FREE ZONE—SOUTHERN HEMISPHERE (Agenda item 99i)
Turner, Bruce - A/C.1/78/PV.25; A/C.1/78/PV.26
NUCLEAR-WEAPON-FREE ZONES (Agenda item 99cc)
Turner, Bruce - A/C.1/78/PV.25
OUTER SPACE—CONFIDENCE-BUILDING MEASURES (Agenda item 99v)
Turner, Bruce - A/C.1/78/PV.17
OUTER SPACE—PEACEFUL USES—INTERNATIONAL COOPERATION (Agenda item 48)
Poling, Caitlin - A/C.4/78/SR.16
OUTER SPACE—PRINCIPLES (Agenda item 97d)
Turner, Bruce - A/C.1/78/PV.17; A/C.1/78/PV.27
PALESTINE QUESTION (Agenda item 35)
Henzel, Christopher - A/78/PV.40
PALESTINIANS—ASSISTANCE (Agenda item 72b)
Carty, Lisa A. - A/78/PV.46
PEACE (Agenda item 14)
Breen, Patrick - A/78/PV.48
Eyrich, Kara - A/78/PV.62
Fogarty, Daniel - A/78/PV.88
PEACEBUILDING (Agenda item 61)
Shrier, Jonathan - A/78/PV.101
PEACEKEEPING OPERATIONS—CRIMINAL LIABILITY (Agenda item 76)
Patton, Dorothy - A/C.6/78/SR.8
PERSONS WITH DISABILITIES—HUMAN RIGHTS (Agenda item 71a)
Breen, Patrick - A/C.3/78/SR.38
Lang, Dylan - A/C.3/78/SR.51

United States (continued)
POVERTY—INTERNATIONAL DECADES (Agenda item 21a)
Leonard, Mary Beth - A/C.2/78/SR.17
Marks, Rose Ann - A/C.2/78/SR.25
RACIAL DISCRIMINATION—ELIMINATION (Agenda item 69a)
Breen, Patrick - A/C.3/78/SR.40
Carty, Lisa A. - A/C.3/78/SR.47
Heartney, Edward - A/78/PV.103
Johnson, Timothy J. - A/C.3/78/SR.41
Korac, Sofija - A/78/PV.50
Lang, Dylan - A/C.3/78/SR.42
Murphy, Daniel - A/C.3/78/SR.41; A/C.3/78/SR.42
Smyre, Calvin - A/C.3/78/SR.41
Thomas-Greenfield, Linda - A/78/PV.63
RACIAL DISCRIMINATION—PROGRAMMES OF ACTION (Agenda item 69b)
Breen, Patrick - A/C.3/78/SR.40
Johnson, Timothy J. - A/C.3/78/SR.41; A/C.3/78/SR.56
Lang, Dylan - A/C.3/78/SR.42
Murphy, Daniel - A/C.3/78/SR.41
Smyre, Calvin - A/C.3/78/SR.41
REGIONAL DISARMAMENT (Agenda item 99f)
Turner, Bruce - A/C.1/78/PV.22
RELIGIOUS INTOLERANCE (Agenda item 71b)
Eyrich, Kara - A/C.3/78/SR.38; A/C.3/78/SR.52
RESPONSIBILITY OF INTERNATIONAL ORGANIZATIONS (Agenda item 85)
Grosso, Elizabeth Maryanne - A/C.6/78/SR.19
RESPONSIBILITY TO PROTECT (Agenda item 129)
Shrier, Jonathan - A/78/PV.97
RIGHT OF ASSEMBLY (Agenda item 71b)
Brzeski, Jessica - A/C.3/78/SR.19
RIGHT TO CULTURE (Agenda item 71b)
Brzeski, Jessica - A/C.3/78/SR.27
RIGHT TO DEVELOPMENT (Agenda item 71b)
Korac, Sofija - A/C.3/78/SR.47
Merron, Eric - A/C.3/78/SR.48
RIGHT TO DRINKING WATER (Agenda item 71b)
Johnson, Timothy J. - A/C.3/78/SR.50
Worthe, Jeffrey - A/C.3/78/SR.28
RIGHT TO EDUCATION (Agenda item 71b)
Korac, Sofija - A/C.3/78/SR.47
Lang, Dylan - A/C.3/78/SR.27
RIGHT TO FOOD (Agenda item 71b)
Merron, Eric - A/C.3/78/SR.48
RIGHT TO HEALTH (Agenda item 71b)
Lang, Dylan - A/C.3/78/SR.39
RIGHT TO HOUSING (Agenda item 71b)
Breen, Patrick - A/C.3/78/SR.30
RIGHT TO PRIVACY (Agenda item 71b)
Merron, Eric - A/C.3/78/SR.21
RIGHTS OF THE CHILD (Agenda item 67)
Keller, Janet - A/C.3/78/SR.12
Lang, Dylan - A/C.3/78/SR.11; A/C.3/78/SR.55

United States (continued)

RIGHTS OF THE CHILD (Agenda item 67)
Shrier, Jonathan - A/C.3/78/SR.13
RULE OF LAW (Agenda item 83)
Grosso, Elizabeth Maryanne - A/C.6/78/SR.16
RURAL POVERTY (Agenda item 21b)
Lawrence, Jason N. - A/C.2/78/SR.22
Leonard, Mary Beth - A/C.2/78/SR.17
RURAL WOMEN (Agenda item 25a)
Korac, Sofija - A/C.3/78/SR.49
SANCTIONS—INTERNATIONAL RELATIONS (Agenda item 71b)
Merron, Eric - A/C.3/78/SR.48
SCIENCE AND TECHNOLOGY—DEVELOPMENT (Agenda item 19a)
Lawrence, Jason N. - A/C.2/78/SR.22
SCIENCE AND TECHNOLOGY—INTERNATIONAL SECURITY (Agenda item 98)
Turner, Bruce - A/C.1/78/PV.29
SELF-DETERMINATION OF PEOPLES (Agenda item 70)
Johnson, Timothy J. - A/C.3/78/SR.56
Shrier, Jonathan - A/C.3/78/SR.49
SEXUAL ORIENTATION (Agenda item 71b)
Lang, Dylan - A/C.3/78/SR.39
SLAVERY (Agenda item 71a)
Smyre, Calvin - A/C.3/78/SR.21
SLAVERY—MEMORIALS (Agenda item 118)
Carty, Lisa A. - A/78/PV.64
SMALL ISLAND DEVELOPING STATES—PROGRAMMES OF ACTION (Agenda item 18b)
Aiello, Jack - A/78/PV.100
Heartney, Edward - A/78/PV.103
Marks, Rose Ann - A/C.2/78/SR.22
SOCIAL CONDITIONS (Agenda item 24b)
Breen, Patrick - A/C.3/78/SR.51
SOCIAL DEVELOPMENT (Agenda item 24)
Brzeski, Jessica - A/C.3/78/SR.47
SOCIAL DEVELOPMENT—CONFERENCES (Agenda item 24a)
Lang, Dylan - A/C.3/78/SR.55
SOUTH-EAST ASIA—NUCLEAR-WEAPON-FREE ZONES (Agenda item 99y)
Turner, Bruce - A/C.1/78/PV.30
SPORTS—OLYMPIC GAMES (Agenda item 11)
Elkon, Nicole - A/78/PV.38
STRADDLING FISH STOCKS (Agenda item 75b)
Armbruster, Thomas - A/78/PV.44
SUMMARY EXECUTIONS (Agenda item 71b)
Billingsley, Kelly - A/C.3/78/SR.31
SUSTAINABLE DEVELOPMENT (Agenda item 18)
Armbruster, Thomas - A/C.2/78/SR.21
Henzel, Christopher - A/C.2/78/SR.15
Keane, Shane - A/C.2/78/SR.22
Korac, Sofija - A/C.3/78/SR.47
Marks, Rose Ann - A/C.2/78/SR.22
Shrier, Jonathan - A/78/PV.107
Udell, Isabel - A/C.2/78/SR.22; A/C.2/78/SR.24

United States (continued)

SUSTAINABLE ENERGY (Agenda item 18h)
Kroeker-Maus, Faith - A/C.2/78/SR.23
TAXATION (Agenda item 16h)
Aiello, Jack - A/C.2/78/SR.9
Marks, Rose Ann - A/C.2/78/SR.25
TERRITORIES OCCUPIED BY ISRAEL—HUMAN RIGHTS (Agenda item 50)
Kelley, John - A/C.4/78/SR.26
Kris, Robert - A/C.4/78/SR.26
Wood, Robert A. - A/C.4/78/SR.25
TERRITORIES OCCUPIED BY ISRAEL—NATURAL RESOURCES (Agenda item 59)
Armbruster, Thomas - A/C.2/78/SR.21
Weinstein, Andrew - A/C.2/78/SR.19
TERRORISM (Agenda item 109)
Patton, Dorothy - A/C.6/78/SR.1
TERRORISM—HUMAN RIGHTS (Agenda item 71b)
Johnson, Timothy J. - A/C.3/78/SR.51
Murphy, Daniel - A/C.3/78/SR.31
TORTURE AND OTHER CRUEL TREATMENT (Agenda item 71a)
Eyrich, Kara - A/C.3/78/SR.18
Merron, Eric - A/C.3/78/SR.18
TRAFFICKING IN PERSONS (Agenda item 71b)
McGlothlin, Cameron - A/C.3/78/SR.23
TRANSNATIONAL CORPORATIONS—HUMAN RIGHTS (Agenda item 71b)
Weinstein, Andrew - A/C.3/78/SR.21
TREATIES (Agenda item 87)
Patton, Dorothy - A/C.6/78/SR.20
UKRAINE—POLITICAL CONDITIONS (Agenda item 62)
Thomas-Greenfield, Linda - A/78/PV.56
UN—BUDGET (2024) (Agenda item 134)
Lu, Christopher P. - A/C.5/78/SR.5; A/C.5/78/SR.26/PartII
UN—FINANCIAL SITUATION (Agenda item 136)
Hanna, Paul - A/C.5/78/SR.6
UN—PROGRAMME PLANNING (Agenda item 135)
Lu, Christopher P. - A/C.5/78/SR.5
Storsve, Alison - A/C.1/78/PV.10
UN. COMMITTEE ON RELATIONS WITH THE HOST COUNTRY—REPORTS (Agenda item 161)
Patton, Dorothy - A/C.6/78/SR.35
UN. CONFERENCE ON DISARMAMENT—REPORTS (Agenda item 101a)
Turner, Bruce - A/C.1/78/PV.23
UN. GENERAL ASSEMBLY—WORK PROGRAMME (Agenda item 120)
Adelman, Dylan - A/78/PV.33
Storsve, Alison - A/C.1/78/PV.10
UN. GENERAL ASSEMBLY (78TH SESS. : 2023-2024)—OFFICERS (Agenda item 5)
Lu, Christopher P. - A/C.5/78/SR.1

United States (continued)

UN. GENERAL ASSEMBLY (78TH SESS. : 2023-2024)—VICE-PRESIDENTS (Agenda item 6)
Carty, Lisa A. - A/78/PV.87
UN. GENERAL ASSEMBLY (78TH SESS. : 2023-2024). 1ST COMMITTEE—GENERAL DEBATE (Agenda item 8)
Jenkins, Bonnie D. - A/C.1/78/PV.2
Stewart, Mallory - A/C.1/78/PV.4
Turner, Bruce - A/C.1/78/PV.5; A/C.1/78/PV.6; A/C.1/78/PV.7
UN. GENERAL ASSEMBLY (78TH SESS. : 2023-2024). 1ST COMMITTEE—WORK ORGANIZATION (Agenda item 7)
Knight, Stephen B. - A/C.1/78/PV.1
Storsve, Alison - A/C.1/78/PV.27
Turner, Bruce - A/C.1/78/PV.30
UN. GENERAL ASSEMBLY (78TH SESS. : 2023-2024). 2ND COMMITTEE—GENERAL DEBATE (Agenda item 8)
Carty, Lisa A. - A/C.2/78/SR.3
UN. GENERAL ASSEMBLY (78TH SESS. : 2023-2024). 5TH COMMITTEE—WORK ORGANIZATION (Agenda item 7)
Lu, Christopher P. - A/C.5/78/SR.26/PartII; A/C.5/78/SR.27; A/C.5/78/SR.34; A/C.5/78/SR.35; A/C.5/78/SR.40
UN. GENERAL ASSEMBLY (78TH SESS. : 2023-2024). PRESIDENT (Agenda item 4)
Carty, Lisa A. - A/78/PV.87
UN. HUMAN RIGHTS COMMITTEE—REPORTS (Agenda item 71a)
Breen, Patrick - A/C.3/78/SR.17
UN. HUMAN RIGHTS COUNCIL—REPORTS (Agenda item 66)
Johnson, Timothy J. - A/C.3/78/SR.46; A/C.3/78/SR.51
UN. INTERNATIONAL COURT OF JUSTICE—REPORTS (Agenda item 73)
Visek, Richard - A/78/PV.20
UN. INTERNATIONAL LAW COMMISSION—REPORTS (Agenda item 79)
Thornton, Nicole - A/C.6/78/SR.29; A/C.6/78/SR.31
Visek, Richard - A/C.6/78/SR.24
UN. PEACEBUILDING COMMISSION—REPORTS (Agenda item 27)
Shrier, Jonathan - A/78/PV.101
UN. PEACEBUILDING FUND—REPORTS (Agenda item 111)
Shrier, Jonathan - A/78/PV.101
UN. SECURITY COUNCIL—MEMBERSHIP (Agenda item 121)
Thomas-Greenfield, Linda - A/78/PV.34
UN CHARTER—REPORTS (Agenda item 82)
Patton, Dorothy - A/C.6/78/SR.22
UN COMMISSION ON INTERNATIONAL TRADE LAW—REPORTS (Agenda item 77)
Grosso, Elizabeth Maryanne - A/C.6/78/SR.14
UN CONFERENCES (Agenda item 13)
Carty, Lisa A. - A/78/PV.15

United States (continued)

UN CONFERENCES (Agenda item 13)
Heartney, Edward - A/78/PV.107
Pell, Herbert - A/78/PV.102
Thomas-Greenfield, Linda - A/78/PV.63
UN HIGH COMMISSIONER FOR REFUGEES—REPORTS (Agenda item 60)
Breen, Patrick - A/C.3/78/SR.44
Shrier, Jonathan - A/C.3/78/SR.45
UN INTERIM FORCE IN LEBANON—FINANCING (Agenda item 156b)
Lu, Christopher P. - A/C.5/78/SR.40
UN RESOLUTIONS—IMPLEMENTATION (Agenda item 119)
Adelman, Dylan - A/78/PV.33
UN SYSTEM—STRENGTHENING (Agenda item 122)
Adelman, Dylan - A/78/PV.99
UNITED STATES VIRGIN ISLANDS QUESTION (Agenda item 58)
Kris, Robert - A/C.4/78/SR.7
UNRWA—ACTIVITIES (Agenda item 49)
Kelley, John - A/C.4/78/SR.26
Lu, Christopher P. - A/C.4/78/SR.23
VETO (Agenda item 63)
Wood, Robert A. - A/78/PV.3; A/78/PV.51; A/78/PV.59; A/78/PV.66; A/78/PV.69; A/78/PV.70; A/78/PV.74; A/78/PV.78
WEAPONS—OUTER SPACE (Agenda item 97b)
Turner, Bruce - A/C.1/78/PV.17; A/C.1/78/PV.27
WEAPONS OF MASS DESTRUCTION (Agenda item 93)
Turner, Bruce - A/C.1/78/PV.29
WOMEN'S ADVANCEMENT (Agenda item 25a)
Breen, Patrick - A/C.3/78/SR.7
Carty, Lisa A. - A/C.3/78/SR.9
Keller, Janet - A/C.3/78/SR.7
Millard, Elisabeth I. - A/C.3/78/SR.7
WOMEN'S ADVANCEMENT—CONFERENCES (Agenda item 25b)
Breen, Patrick - A/C.3/78/SR.7
Carty, Lisa A. - A/C.3/78/SR.9
Keller, Janet - A/C.3/78/SR.7
Lang, Dylan - A/C.3/78/SR.51
Millard, Elisabeth I. - A/C.3/78/SR.7
YOUTH (Agenda item 24b)
Lang, Dylan - A/C.3/78/SR.55

United States. President

UN. GENERAL ASSEMBLY (78TH SESS. : 2023-2024)—GENERAL DEBATE (Agenda item 8)
Biden, Joseph R. - A/78/PV.4
UN. GENERAL ASSEMBLY (78TH SESS. : 2023-2024)—SPECIAL STATEMENTS
Biden, Joseph R. - A/78/PV.4

Uniting for Consensus Group
UN. SECURITY COUNCIL—MEMBERSHIP (Agenda item 121)
Massari, Maurizio (Italy) - A/78/PV.34; A/78/PV.104

Universidad Autónoma de Campeche (Mexico)
WESTERN SAHARA QUESTION (Agenda item 58)
Israel Herrera, José - A/C.4/78/SR.5

Universidad de la Tierra (Mexico)
WESTERN SAHARA QUESTION (Agenda item 58)
Naranjo Lizano, Verónica Elizabeth - A/C.4/78/SR.5

Universidad Nacional Autónoma de México
WESTERN SAHARA QUESTION (Agenda item 58)
Ordóñez, Andrés - A/C.4/78/SR.5

Universidad Pablo de Olavide (Spain)
WESTERN SAHARA QUESTION (Agenda item 58)
Gómez Justo, Juan Carlos - A/C.4/78/SR.4

Université de Caen
WESTERN SAHARA QUESTION (Agenda item 58)
Boutin, Christophe - A/C.4/78/SR.5

Université nationale du Rwanda
WESTERN SAHARA QUESTION (Agenda item 58)
Aboui, Ismael Buchanan - A/C.4/78/SR.4

University of Las Palmas
WESTERN SAHARA QUESTION (Agenda item 58)
Vidal Garrido, Manuel - A/C.4/78/SR.4

University of Massachusetts at Amherst
COMMODITIES (Agenda item 16d)
Pickbourn, Lynda - A/C.2/78/SR.14
SUSTAINABLE DEVELOPMENT (Agenda item 18)
Pickbourn, Lynda - A/C.2/78/SR.14
UN. GENERAL ASSEMBLY (78TH SESS. : 2023-2024). 2ND COMMITTEE—GENERAL DEBATE (Agenda item 8)
Ghosh, Jayati - A/C.2/78/SR.2

University of Oxford
COMMODITIES (Agenda item 16d)
Lebdioui, Amir - A/C.2/78/SR.14

University of Oxford (continued)
SUSTAINABLE DEVELOPMENT (Agenda item 18)
Lebdioui, Amir - A/C.2/78/SR.14

University of the West Indies
SLAVERY—MEMORIALS (Agenda item 118)
Beckles, Hilary - A/78/PV.64

UNRWA
UNRWA—ACTIVITIES (Agenda item 49)
Gunnarsdóttir, Greta - A/C.4/78/SR.22

Uruguay
ADMINISTRATION OF JUSTICE—HUMAN RIGHTS (Agenda item 71b)
Machado Mouriño, Felipe - A/C.3/78/SR.28
CAPITAL PUNISHMENT (Agenda item 71b)
Machado Mouriño, Felipe - A/C.3/78/SR.28
CONVENTIONAL WEAPONS (Agenda item 99u)
Eustathiou de los Santos, Matías Andrés - A/C.1/78/PV.18
CRIME PREVENTION (Agenda item 107)
González Hernández, Gabriela Lilián - A/C.3/78/SR.6
CRIMES AGAINST HUMANITY (Agenda item 80)
Katz Pavlotzky, Alejandro Leonel - A/C.6/78/SR.11; A/C.6/78/SR.45
CYBERCRIME (Agenda item 108)
González Hernández, Gabriela Lilián - A/C.3/78/SR.6
DECOLONIZATION (Agenda item 58)
Amorín, Carlos Daniel - A/C.4/78/SR.2
FALKLAND ISLANDS (MALVINAS) QUESTION (Agenda item 42)
Amorín, Carlos Daniel - A/C.4/78/SR.2
FAMILY (Agenda item 24b)
Riva Grela, Juan José - A/C.3/78/SR.49
HUMAN RIGHTS (Agenda item 71)
Machado Mouriño, Felipe - A/C.3/78/SR.28
HUMAN RIGHTS ADVANCEMENT (Agenda item 71b)
Riva Grela, Juan José - A/C.3/78/SR.52
IAEA—REPORTS (Agenda item 89)
Eustathiou de los Santos, Matías Andrés - A/78/PV.30
INFORMATION—INTERNATIONAL SECURITY (Agenda item 94)
Eustathiou de los Santos, Matías Andrés - A/C.1/78/PV.20
MULTILATERALISM—DISARMAMENT (Agenda item 99r)
Eustathiou de los Santos, Matías Andrés - A/C.1/78/PV.21
NUCLEAR DISARMAMENT (Agenda item 99b)
Eustathiou de los Santos, Matías Andrés - A/C.1/78/PV.12

Uruguay (continued)

PEACEKEEPING OPERATIONS (Agenda item 51)
Amorín, Carlos Daniel - A/C.4/78/SR.19
RESPONSIBILITY TO PROTECT (Agenda item 129)
Beretta Tassano, María Noel - A/78/PV.97
RIGHTS OF THE CHILD (Agenda item 67)
Amorín, Carlos Daniel - A/C.3/78/SR.13
RULE OF LAW (Agenda item 83)
Katz Pavlotzky, Alejandro Leonel - A/C.6/78/SR.18
SEXUAL ORIENTATION (Agenda item 71b)
Riva Grela, Juan José - A/C.3/78/SR.39
SMALL ARMS—ILLICIT TRAFFIC (Agenda item 99p)
Eustathiou de los Santos, Matías Andrés - A/C.1/78/PV.18
SUMMARY EXECUTIONS (Agenda item 71b)
Machado Mouriño, Felipe - A/C.3/78/SR.28
SUSTAINABLE DEVELOPMENT (Agenda item 18)
Romero Veiga, Stefany - A/C.2/78/SR.25
TERRORISM (Agenda item 109)
Katz Pavlotzky, Alejandro Leonel - A/C.6/78/SR.4
UN—BUDGET (2024) (Agenda item 134)
Machado Mouriño, Felipe - A/C.5/78/SR.21
UN—PROGRAMME PLANNING (Agenda item 135)
Eustathiou de los Santos, Matías Andrés - A/C.1/78/PV.10
UN. GENERAL ASSEMBLY—WORK PROGRAMME (Agenda item 120)
Eustathiou de los Santos, Matías Andrés - A/C.1/78/PV.10
UN. GENERAL ASSEMBLY (78TH SESS. : 2023-2024)—OFFICERS (Agenda item 5)
González Hernández, Gabriela Lilián - A/C.5/78/SR.1
UN. GENERAL ASSEMBLY (78TH SESS. : 2023-2024). 1ST COMMITTEE—GENERAL DEBATE (Agenda item 8)
González Hernández, Gabriela Lilián - A/C.1/78/PV.4
UN. GENERAL ASSEMBLY (78TH SESS. : 2023-2024). 2ND COMMITTEE—GENERAL DEBATE (Agenda item 8)
Romero Veiga, Stefany - A/C.2/78/SR.5
UN. GENERAL ASSEMBLY (78TH SESS. : 2023-2024). 5TH COMMITTEE—WORK ORGANIZATION (Agenda item 7)
Machado Mouriño, Felipe - A/C.5/78/SR.27; A/C.5/78/SR.35; A/C.5/78/SR.40
VETO (Agenda item 63)
Amorín, Carlos Daniel - A/78/PV.61; A/78/PV.75; A/78/PV.78
Beretta Tassano, María Noel - A/78/PV.69

Uruguay (continued)

WOMEN'S ADVANCEMENT (Agenda item 25a)
González Hernández, Gabriela Lilián - A/C.3/78/SR.10
WOMEN'S ADVANCEMENT—CONFERENCES (Agenda item 25b)
González Hernández, Gabriela Lilián - A/C.3/78/SR.10
YOUTH (Agenda item 24b)
Riva Grela, Juan José - A/C.3/78/SR.55

Uruguay. President

UN. GENERAL ASSEMBLY (78TH SESS. : 2023-2024)—GENERAL DEBATE (Agenda item 8)
Lacalle Pou, Luis - A/78/PV.5
UN. GENERAL ASSEMBLY (78TH SESS. : 2023-2024)—SPECIAL STATEMENTS
Lacalle Pou, Luis - A/78/PV.5

Uzbekistan

CENTRAL ASIA—ZONES OF PEACE (Agenda item 64)
Lapasov, Ulugbek - A/78/PV.85
SUSTAINABLE DEVELOPMENT (Agenda item 18)
Eshkobilov, Oybek - A/C.2/78/SR.22
Lapasov, Ulugbek - A/78/PV.57; A/78/PV.103
UN. GENERAL ASSEMBLY (78TH SESS. : 2023-2024). 2ND COMMITTEE—GENERAL DEBATE (Agenda item 8)
Lapasov, Ulugbek - A/C.2/78/SR.6

Uzbekistan. President

UN. GENERAL ASSEMBLY (78TH SESS. : 2023-2024)—GENERAL DEBATE (Agenda item 8)
Mirziyoyev, Shavkat - A/78/PV.4
UN. GENERAL ASSEMBLY (78TH SESS. : 2023-2024)—SPECIAL STATEMENTS
Mirziyoyev, Shavkat - A/78/PV.4

Vanuatu

UN. GENERAL ASSEMBLY (78TH SESS. : 2023-2024)—GENERAL DEBATE (Agenda item 8)
Tevi, Odo - A/78/PV.14
UN. GENERAL ASSEMBLY (78TH SESS. : 2023-2024). 1ST COMMITTEE—GENERAL DEBATE (Agenda item 8)
William, Sanlan - A/C.1/78/PV.8

Venezuela (Bolivarian Republic of)

AFRICA—DEVELOPMENT (Agenda item 65b)
Pérez Ayestarán, Joaquín Alberto - A/78/PV.18
AFRICA—SUSTAINABLE DEVELOPMENT—PARTNERSHIP (Agenda item 65a)
Pérez Ayestarán, Joaquín Alberto - A/78/PV.18

Venezuela (Bolivarian Republic of) (continued)

ARMED CONFLICTS PREVENTION (Agenda item 31a)
Poveda Brito, Robert Alexander - A/78/PV.72
CENTRAL ASIA—ZONES OF PEACE (Agenda item 64)
Solorzano Cavalieri, Isis Amahl Gabriela - A/78/PV.85
COASTAL ZONE MANAGEMENT (Agenda item 18j)
Marín Sevilla, Asbina - A/78/PV.49; A/C.2/78/SR.23
CRIME PREVENTION (Agenda item 107)
Poveda Brito, Robert Alexander - A/C.3/78/SR.6
CUBA—UNITED STATES (Agenda item 38)
Pérez Ayestarán, Joaquín Alberto - A/78/PV.24
CYBERCRIME (Agenda item 108)
Poveda Brito, Robert Alexander - A/C.3/78/SR.6
DECOLONIZATION (Agenda item 58)
Pérez Ayestarán, Joaquín Alberto - A/C.4/78/SR.2
ECONOMIC SANCTIONS—INTERNATIONAL RELATIONS (Agenda item 28)
Gil Pinto, Yvan - A/78/PV.89
Ron Martínez, Carlos - A/78/PV.90
FALKLAND ISLANDS (MALVINAS) QUESTION (Agenda item 42)
Pérez Ayestarán, Joaquín Alberto - A/C.4/78/SR.2
FRENCH POLYNESIA QUESTION (Agenda item 58)
Pérez Ayestarán, Joaquín Alberto - A/C.4/78/SR.2
HUMAN RIGHTS—BURUNDI (Agenda item 71c)
Poveda Brito, Robert Alexander - A/C.3/78/SR.36
HUMAN RIGHTS—DEMOCRATIC PEOPLE'S REPUBLIC OF KOREA (Agenda item 71c)
Poveda Brito, Robert Alexander - A/78/PV.50; A/C.3/78/SR.33; A/C.3/78/SR.53
HUMAN RIGHTS—ERITREA (Agenda item 71c)
Poveda Brito, Robert Alexander - A/C.3/78/SR.36
HUMAN RIGHTS—ETHIOPIA (Agenda item 71c)
Poveda Brito, Robert Alexander - A/C.3/78/SR.36
HUMAN RIGHTS—IRAN (ISLAMIC REPUBLIC OF) (Agenda item 71c)
Poveda Brito, Robert Alexander - A/C.3/78/SR.34
HUMAN RIGHTS—REPORTS (Agenda item 71c)
Poveda Brito, Robert Alexander - A/78/PV.50; A/C.3/78/SR.25; A/C.3/78/SR.37
HUMAN RIGHTS—SYRIAN ARAB REPUBLIC (Agenda item 71c)
Poveda Brito, Robert Alexander - A/C.3/78/SR.34
HUMAN RIGHTS—TERRITORIES OCCUPIED BY ISRAEL (Agenda item 71c)
Poveda Brito, Robert Alexander - A/C.3/78/SR.35
INDIGENOUS PEOPLES (Agenda item 68a)
Poveda Brito, Robert Alexander - A/C.3/78/SR.17

Venezuela (Bolivarian Republic of) (continued)

INTERNATIONAL CRIMINAL COURT—REPORTS (Agenda item 74)
Pérez Ayestarán, Joaquín Alberto - A/78/PV.25
INTERNATIONAL TRADE (Agenda item 16a)
Marín Sevilla, Asbina - A/C.2/78/SR.9; A/C.2/78/SR.24
LAW OF THE SEA (Agenda item 75a)
Pérez Ayestarán, Joaquín Alberto - A/78/PV.44
MACROECONOMIC POLICY (Agenda item 16)
Marín Sevilla, Asbina - A/C.2/78/SR.9
MARINE ECOSYSTEMS—BIOLOGICAL DIVERSITY (Agenda item 75c)
Pérez Ayestarán, Joaquín Alberto - A/78/PV.44
MIGRANTS—PROTECTION (Agenda item 71b)
Poveda Brito, Robert Alexander - A/C.3/78/SR.23
NEW CALEDONIA QUESTION (Agenda item 58)
Pérez Ayestarán, Joaquín Alberto - A/C.4/78/SR.2
PALESTINE QUESTION (Agenda item 35)
Moncada Acosta, Samuel R. - A/78/PV.39
PEACE (Agenda item 14)
Reyes Hernández, Jorge Arturo - A/78/PV.82
RACIAL DISCRIMINATION—ELIMINATION (Agenda item 69a)
Poveda Brito, Robert Alexander - A/78/PV.50; A/C.3/78/SR.47
SANCTIONS—INTERNATIONAL RELATIONS (Agenda item 71b)
Poveda Brito, Robert Alexander - A/C.3/78/SR.28
SOLIDARITY (Agenda item 71b)
Poveda Brito, Robert Alexander - A/C.3/78/SR.32
STRADDLING FISH STOCKS (Agenda item 75b)
Pérez Ayestarán, Joaquín Alberto - A/78/PV.44
TERRITORIES OCCUPIED BY ISRAEL—HUMAN RIGHTS (Agenda item 50)
Pérez Ayestarán, Joaquín Alberto - A/C.4/78/SR.24
TERRITORIES OCCUPIED BY ISRAEL—NATURAL RESOURCES (Agenda item 59)
Marín Sevilla, Asbina - A/C.2/78/SR.19
UKRAINE—POLITICAL CONDITIONS (Agenda item 62)
Pérez Ayestarán, Joaquín Alberto - A/78/PV.58
UN—BUDGET (2024) (Agenda item 134)
Bayley Angeleri, Roberto - A/C.5/78/SR.34
UN—PROGRAMME PLANNING (Agenda item 135)
Bayley Angeleri, Roberto - A/78/PV.50(Resumption1)
UN. GENERAL ASSEMBLY (78TH SESS. : 2023-2024)—GENERAL DEBATE (Agenda item 8)
Gil Pinto, Yvan - A/78/PV.13

Venezuela (Bolivarian Republic of) (continued)

UN. GENERAL ASSEMBLY (78TH SESS. : 2023-2024). 1ST COMMITTEE—GENERAL DEBATE (Agenda item 8)
Pérez Ayestarán, Joaquín Alberto - A/C.1/78/PV.7
UN. GENERAL ASSEMBLY (78TH SESS. : 2023-2024). 2ND COMMITTEE—GENERAL DEBATE (Agenda item 8)
Marín Sevilla, Asbina - A/C.2/78/SR.5
UN. SECURITY COUNCIL—MEMBERSHIP (Agenda item 121)
Pérez Ayestarán, Joaquín Alberto - A/78/PV.35
UN SYSTEM—STRENGTHENING (Agenda item 122)
Pérez Ayestarán, Joaquín Alberto - A/78/PV.107
VETO (Agenda item 63)
Moncada Acosta, Samuel R. - A/78/PV.75
Pérez Ayestarán, Joaquín Alberto - A/78/PV.59
WESTERN SAHARA QUESTION (Agenda item 58)
Pérez Ayestarán, Joaquín Alberto - A/C.4/78/SR.2

Viet Nam

CONVENTIONAL WEAPONS (Agenda item 99u)
Mai, Ngan Ha - A/C.1/78/PV.18
CRIMES AGAINST HUMANITY (Agenda item 80)
Nguyen, Thi Ngoc Ha - A/C.6/78/SR.10
CUBA—UNITED STATES (Agenda item 38)
Dang, Hoang Giang - A/78/PV.24
DECOLONIZATION (Agenda item 58)
Nguyen, Hoang Nguyen - A/C.4/78/SR.2
DEVELOPMENT FINANCE—CONFERENCES (Agenda item 17)
Nguyen, Hoang Nguyen - A/78/PV.90
DISASTER VICTIMS (Agenda item 86)
Nguyen, Thi Hong Quyen - A/C.6/78/SR.6
FOOD SECURITY (Agenda item 23a)
Nguyen, Hoang Nguyen - A/C.2/78/SR.16
FREEDOM OF EXPRESSION (Agenda item 71b)
Dang, Tran Nam Trung - A/C.3/78/SR.19
HUMAN RIGHTS ADVANCEMENT (Agenda item 71b)
Dang, Hoang Giang - A/C.3/78/SR.24
IAEA—REPORTS (Agenda item 89)
Dang, Hoang Giang - A/78/PV.30
INFORMATION—INTERNATIONAL SECURITY (Agenda item 94)
Mai, Ngan Ha - A/C.1/78/PV.29
INTERNATIONAL JURISDICTION (Agenda item 84)
Pham, Nha - A/C.6/78/SR.13
INTERNATIONAL LAW—TRAINING PROGRAMMES (Agenda item 78)
Tran, Thi Phuong Ha - A/C.6/78/SR.21

Viet Nam (continued)

LANDMINES—TREATIES (Agenda item 99m)
Mai, Ngan Ha - A/C.1/78/PV.18
LAW OF THE SEA (Agenda item 75a)
Dang, Hoang Giang - A/78/PV.43
MARINE ECOSYSTEMS—BIOLOGICAL DIVERSITY (Agenda item 75c)
Dang, Hoang Giang - A/78/PV.43
NUCLEAR DISARMAMENT (Agenda item 99b)
Tran, Thi Thanh Hai - A/C.1/78/PV.13
NUCLEAR NON-PROLIFERATION—INTERNATIONAL OBLIGATIONS (Agenda item 99w)
Tran, Thi Thanh Hai - A/C.1/78/PV.13
NUCLEAR WEAPON TESTS—TREATIES (Agenda item 105)
Tran, Thi Thanh Hai - A/C.1/78/PV.13
OPERATIONAL ACTIVITIES—UN SYSTEM (Agenda item 22a)
Nguyen, Hoang Nguyen - A/C.2/78/SR.18
PALESTINE QUESTION (Agenda item 35)
Dang, Hoang Giang - A/78/PV.40
PEACE (Agenda item 14)
Dang, Hoang Giang - A/78/PV.64; A/78/PV.82
PEACEKEEPING OPERATIONS (Agenda item 51)
Nguyen, Hoang Nguyen - A/C.4/78/SR.19
PEACEKEEPING OPERATIONS—CRIMINAL LIABILITY (Agenda item 76)
Nguyen, Thi Ngoc Ha - A/C.6/78/SR.9
POVERTY—INTERNATIONAL DECADES (Agenda item 21a)
Nguyen, Hoang Nguyen - A/C.2/78/SR.16
RESPONSIBILITY OF INTERNATIONAL ORGANIZATIONS (Agenda item 85)
Tran, Thi Phuong Ha - A/C.6/78/SR.19
RIGHTS OF THE CHILD (Agenda item 67)
Dang, Tran Nam Trung - A/C.3/78/SR.12
RULE OF LAW (Agenda item 83)
Dang, Hoang Giang - A/C.6/78/SR.16
RURAL POVERTY (Agenda item 21b)
Nguyen, Hoang Nguyen - A/C.2/78/SR.16
SMALL ARMS—ILLICIT TRAFFIC—ASSISTANCE (Agenda item 99n)
Mai, Ngan Ha - A/C.1/78/PV.18
SOCIAL DEVELOPMENT (Agenda item 24)
Thoa Le, Thi Minh - A/C.3/78/SR.3
SOUTH-EAST ASIA—NUCLEAR-WEAPON-FREE ZONES (Agenda item 99y)
Tran, Thi Thanh Hai - A/C.1/78/PV.13
STRADDLING FISH STOCKS (Agenda item 75b)
Dang, Hoang Giang - A/78/PV.43
SUSTAINABLE DEVELOPMENT (Agenda item 18)
Nguyen, Hoang Nguyen - A/C.2/78/SR.13
SUSTAINABLE ENERGY (Agenda item 18h)
Nguyen, Hoang Nguyen - A/C.2/78/SR.13
TERRORISM (Agenda item 109)
Nguyen, Hong Nhat - A/C.6/78/SR.2

Viet Nam (continued)

UN. GENERAL ASSEMBLY—WORK PROGRAMME (Agenda item 120)
Thoa Le, Thi Minh - A/78/PV.32
UN. GENERAL ASSEMBLY (78TH SESS. : 2023-2024). 1ST COMMITTEE—GENERAL DEBATE (Agenda item 8)
Dang, Hoang Giang - A/C.1/78/PV.6
UN. GENERAL ASSEMBLY (78TH SESS. : 2023-2024). 2ND COMMITTEE—GENERAL DEBATE (Agenda item 8)
Nguyen, Hoang Nguyen - A/C.2/78/SR.4
UN. GENERAL ASSEMBLY (78TH SESS. : 2023-2024). 5TH COMMITTEE—WORK ORGANIZATION (Agenda item 7)
Pham, Cao Cuong - A/C.5/78/SR.26/PartII; A/C.5/78/SR.40
UN. INTERNATIONAL COURT OF JUSTICE—REPORTS (Agenda item 73)
Thoa Le, Thi Minh - A/78/PV.27
UN. INTERNATIONAL LAW COMMISSION—REPORTS (Agenda item 79)
Le, Duc Hanh - A/C.6/78/SR.25; A/C.6/78/SR.28
UN. SECURITY COUNCIL—MEMBERSHIP (Agenda item 121)
Nguyen, Hoang Nguyen - A/78/PV.35
UN COMMISSION ON INTERNATIONAL TRADE LAW—REPORTS (Agenda item 77)
Tran, Thi Phuong Ha - A/C.6/78/SR.14
UN RESOLUTIONS—IMPLEMENTATION (Agenda item 119)
Thoa Le, Thi Minh - A/78/PV.32
UN SYSTEM—STRENGTHENING (Agenda item 122)
Nguyen, Hoang Nguyen - A/78/PV.99
UNRWA—ACTIVITIES (Agenda item 49)
Nguyen, Hoang Nguyen - A/C.4/78/SR.23
VETO (Agenda item 63)
Dang, Hoang Giang - A/78/PV.61
WOMEN'S ADVANCEMENT (Agenda item 25a)
Thoa Le, Thi Minh - A/C.3/78/SR.8
WOMEN'S ADVANCEMENT—CONFERENCES (Agenda item 25b)
Thoa Le, Thi Minh - A/C.3/78/SR.8

Viet Nam. Prime Minister

UN. GENERAL ASSEMBLY (78TH SESS. : 2023-2024)—GENERAL DEBATE (Agenda item 8)
Pham, Minh Chinh - A/78/PV.11
UN. GENERAL ASSEMBLY (78TH SESS. : 2023-2024)—SPECIAL STATEMENTS
Pham, Minh Chinh - A/78/PV.11

Visegrad Group

UN. INTERNATIONAL COURT OF JUSTICE—REPORTS (Agenda item 73)
Ruffer, Emil (Czechia) - A/78/PV.20

Women Investment Network (Zambia)

WESTERN SAHARA QUESTION (Agenda item 58)
Njapau-Efrati, Grace - A/C.4/78/SR.5

World Action for Refugees (Norway)

WESTERN SAHARA QUESTION (Agenda item 58)
Cameron, Eric - A/C.4/78/SR.5

World Humanitarian Drive (Organization : United Kingdom)

WESTERN SAHARA QUESTION (Agenda item 58)
Syedibrahim, Abdul Basith Pattinathar K. - A/C.4/78/SR.5

World Tourism Organization

CLIMATE (Agenda item 18d)
Urosevic, Zoritsa - A/C.2/78/SR.12

Yemen

ARMS RACE—OUTER SPACE (Agenda item 97a)
Al-Dobhany, Marwan Ali Noman - A/C.1/78/PV.16
CRIMES AGAINST HUMANITY (Agenda item 80)
Balobaid, Ali Mabkhot Salem - A/C.6/78/SR.11
DISPLACED PERSONS (Agenda item 71b)
Al-mashehari, Sarah Ahmed Ahmed - A/C.3/78/SR.32
ELECTION VERIFICATION—UN (Agenda item 71b)
Al-mashehari, Sarah Ahmed Ahmed - A/78/PV.50; A/C.3/78/SR.50
FAMILY (Agenda item 24b)
Al-mashehari, Sarah Ahmed Ahmed - A/C.3/78/SR.2
FOOD SECURITY (Agenda item 23a)
Al-barati, Abdulrahman Hasan Yahya - A/C.2/78/SR.17
HUMAN RIGHTS—INTERNATIONAL INSTRUMENTS (Agenda item 71a)
Balobaid, Ali Mabkhot Salem - A/C.3/78/SR.28
HUMAN RIGHTS—TERRITORIES OCCUPIED BY ISRAEL (Agenda item 71c)
Al-mashehari, Sarah Ahmed Ahmed - A/C.3/78/SR.35
HUMAN RIGHTS ACTIVISTS (Agenda item 71b)
Al-mashehari, Sarah Ahmed Ahmed - A/C.3/78/SR.19
INFORMATION (Agenda item 53)
Al-mashehari, Sarah Ahmed Ahmed - A/C.4/78/SR.14
MINE CLEARANCE (Agenda item 46)
Al-mashehari, Sarah Ahmed Ahmed - A/C.4/78/SR.10
PALESTINE QUESTION (Agenda item 35)
Al-Saadi, Abdullah Ali Fadhel - A/78/PV.40

Yemen (continued)

PERSONS WITH DISABILITIES—HUMAN RIGHTS (Agenda item 71a)
Al-mashehari, Sarah Ahmed Ahmed - A/C.3/78/SR.51
POVERTY—INTERNATIONAL DECADES (Agenda item 21a)
Al-barati, Abdulrahman Hasan Yahya - A/C.2/78/SR.17
RIGHTS OF THE CHILD (Agenda item 67)
Al-mashehari, Sarah Ahmed Ahmed - A/C.3/78/SR.55
Balobaid, Ali Mabkhot Salem - A/C.3/78/SR.11; A/C.3/78/SR.14
RURAL POVERTY (Agenda item 21b)
Al-barati, Abdulrahman Hasan Yahya - A/C.2/78/SR.17
RURAL WOMEN (Agenda item 25a)
Al-mashehari, Sarah Ahmed Ahmed - A/C.3/78/SR.49
SELF-DETERMINATION OF PEOPLES (Agenda item 70)
Balobaid, Ali Mabkhot Salem - A/C.3/78/SR.43
SPECIAL POLITICAL MISSIONS (Agenda item 52)
Al-mashehari, Sarah Ahmed Ahmed - A/C.4/78/SR.21
SUSTAINABLE DEVELOPMENT (Agenda item 18)
Al-barati, Abdulrahman Hasan Yahya - A/C.2/78/SR.24; A/C.2/78/SR.25
TERRITORIES OCCUPIED BY ISRAEL—HUMAN RIGHTS (Agenda item 50)
Al-mashehari, Sarah Ahmed Ahmed - A/C.4/78/SR.24
TERRITORIES OCCUPIED BY ISRAEL—NATURAL RESOURCES (Agenda item 59)
Al-barati, Abdulrahman Hasan Yahya - A/C.2/78/SR.19
TERRORISM (Agenda item 109)
Balobaid, Ali Mabkhot Salem - A/C.6/78/SR.4
UN. GENERAL ASSEMBLY (78TH SESS. : 2023-2024). 1ST COMMITTEE—GENERAL DEBATE (Agenda item 8)
Al-Dobhany, Marwan Ali Noman - A/C.1/78/PV.4
UN. GENERAL ASSEMBLY (78TH SESS. : 2023-2024). 2ND COMMITTEE—GENERAL DEBATE (Agenda item 8)
Al-barati, Abdulrahman Hasan Yahya - A/C.2/78/SR.6
UN HIGH COMMISSIONER FOR REFUGEES—REPORTS (Agenda item 60)
Balobaid, Ali Mabkhot Salem - A/C.3/78/SR.45
UN SYSTEM—STRENGTHENING (Agenda item 122)
Al-Dobhany, Marwan Ali Noman - A/78/PV.99
UNRWA—ACTIVITIES (Agenda item 49)
Al-mashehari, Sarah Ahmed Ahmed - A/C.4/78/SR.23
VETO (Agenda item 63)
Al-Dobhany, Marwan Ali Noman - A/78/PV.75

Yemen (continued)

WOMEN'S ADVANCEMENT (Agenda item 25a)
Al-mashehari, Sarah Ahmed Ahmed - A/C.3/78/SR.8
WOMEN'S ADVANCEMENT—CONFERENCES (Agenda item 25b)
Al-mashehari, Sarah Ahmed Ahmed - A/C.3/78/SR.8
YOUTH (Agenda item 24b)
Al-mashehari, Sarah Ahmed Ahmed - A/C.3/78/SR.2; A/C.3/78/SR.55

Yemen. Presidential Leadership Council. President

UN. GENERAL ASSEMBLY (78TH SESS. : 2023-2024)—GENERAL DEBATE (Agenda item 8)
Al-Alimi, Rashad Mohammed - A/78/PV.8
UN. GENERAL ASSEMBLY (78TH SESS. : 2023-2024)—SPECIAL STATEMENTS
Al-Alimi, Rashad Mohammed - A/78/PV.8

Zambia

ARMS RACE—OUTER SPACE (Agenda item 97a)
Musonda, Oliver - A/C.1/78/PV.17
CLIMATE (Agenda item 18d)
Milambo, Chola - A/C.2/78/SR.15
COMMODITIES (Agenda item 16d)
Milambo, Chola - A/C.2/78/SR.14
DEVELOPMENT FINANCE (Agenda item 16b)
Boma, Regina Chama - A/C.2/78/SR.9
FOOD SECURITY (Agenda item 23a)
Mungandi, Lubasi - A/C.2/78/SR.17
HUMAN RIGHTS—INTERNATIONAL INSTRUMENTS (Agenda item 71a)
Milambo, Chola - A/C.3/78/SR.26
HUMAN RIGHTS ADVANCEMENT (Agenda item 71b)
Milambo, Chola - A/C.3/78/SR.26
INFORMATION TECHNOLOGY—DEVELOPMENT (Agenda item 15)
Milambo, Chola - A/C.2/78/SR.11
INTERNATIONAL TRADE (Agenda item 16a)
Boma, Regina Chama - A/C.2/78/SR.9
LANDLOCKED DEVELOPING COUNTRIES—CONFERENCES (Agenda item 20b)
Chanda, Theresah Chipulu Luswili - A/C.2/78/SR.7
LEAST DEVELOPED COUNTRIES—CONFERENCES (Agenda item 20a)
Chanda, Theresah Chipulu Luswili - A/C.2/78/SR.7
NUCLEAR DISARMAMENT (Agenda item 99b)
Milambo, Chola - A/C.1/78/PV.14
OUTER SPACE—PEACEFUL USES—INTERNATIONAL COOPERATION (Agenda item 48)
Mungandi, Lubasi - A/C.4/78/SR.16

Zambia (continued)

POVERTY—INTERNATIONAL DECADES (Agenda item 21a)
Mungandi, Lubasi - A/C.2/78/SR.17
RIGHTS OF THE CHILD (Agenda item 67)
Milambo, Chola - A/C.3/78/SR.13
RULE OF LAW (Agenda item 83)
Muzumbwe-Katongo, Miyoba - A/C.6/78/SR.18
RURAL POVERTY (Agenda item 21b)
Mungandi, Lubasi - A/C.2/78/SR.17
SCIENCE AND TECHNOLOGY—DEVELOPMENT (Agenda item 19a)
Milambo, Chola - A/C.2/78/SR.11
SUSTAINABLE DEVELOPMENT (Agenda item 18)
Milambo, Chola - A/C.2/78/SR.14; A/C.2/78/SR.15
SUSTAINABLE ENERGY (Agenda item 18h)
Milambo, Chola - A/C.2/78/SR.15
TAXATION (Agenda item 16h)
Boma, Regina Chama - A/C.2/78/SR.9
UN—FINANCIAL SITUATION (Agenda item 136)
Sakala, Rose - A/C.5/78/SR.6
UN. GENERAL ASSEMBLY (78TH SESS. : 2023-2024)—GENERAL DEBATE (Agenda item 8)
Kakubo, Stanley - A/78/PV.14
UN. GENERAL ASSEMBLY (78TH SESS. : 2023-2024). 1ST COMMITTEE—GENERAL DEBATE (Agenda item 8)
Boma, Regina Chama - A/C.1/78/PV.8
UN. GENERAL ASSEMBLY (78TH SESS. : 2023-2024). 2ND COMMITTEE—GENERAL DEBATE (Agenda item 8)
Milambo, Chola - A/C.2/78/SR.6
UN. INTERNATIONAL COURT OF JUSTICE—REPORTS (Agenda item 73)
Milambo, Chola - A/78/PV.28
WEAPONS—OUTER SPACE (Agenda item 97b)
Musonda, Oliver - A/C.1/78/PV.17
WOMEN'S ADVANCEMENT (Agenda item 25a)
Milambo, Chola - A/C.3/78/SR.10
WOMEN'S ADVANCEMENT—CONFERENCES (Agenda item 25b)
Milambo, Chola - A/C.3/78/SR.10
YOUTH (Agenda item 24b)
Siamalambwa, Bentry - A/C.3/78/SR.55

Zimbabwe

CLIMATE (Agenda item 18d)
Rupende, Tapiwa Roy - A/C.2/78/SR.13
COMMODITIES (Agenda item 16d)
Rupende, Tapiwa Roy - A/C.2/78/SR.14
CUBA—UNITED STATES (Agenda item 38)
Rupende, Tapiwa Roy - A/78/PV.24
DIAMONDS—FUELLING CONFLICT (Agenda item 30)
Chimbindi, Albert Ranganai - A/78/PV.65

Zimbabwe (continued)

ECONOMIC SANCTIONS—INTERNATIONAL RELATIONS (Agenda item 28)
Chimbindi, Albert Ranganai - A/78/PV.90
EXTERNAL DEBT (Agenda item 16c)
Rupende, Tapiwa Roy - A/C.2/78/SR.9
HEALTH (Agenda item 125)
Manyanga, Garikai - A/78/PV.16
HIV/AIDS—DECLARATIONS (Agenda item 10)
Chimbindi, Albert Ranganai - A/78/PV.91
HUMAN RIGHTS (Agenda item 71)
Manyanga, Garikai - A/C.3/78/SR.27
HUMAN RIGHTS—DEMOCRATIC PEOPLE'S REPUBLIC OF KOREA (Agenda item 71c)
Manyanga, Garikai - A/C.3/78/SR.33
HUMAN RIGHTS—ETHIOPIA (Agenda item 71c)
Manyanga, Garikai - A/C.3/78/SR.36
HUMAN RIGHTS—REPORTS (Agenda item 71c)
Manyanga, Garikai - A/C.3/78/SR.27
INTERNATIONAL TRADE (Agenda item 16a)
Rupende, Tapiwa Roy - A/C.2/78/SR.9; A/C.2/78/SR.24
LANDLOCKED DEVELOPING COUNTRIES—CONFERENCES (Agenda item 20b)
Rupende, Tapiwa Roy - A/C.2/78/SR.7
LEAST DEVELOPED COUNTRIES—CONFERENCES (Agenda item 20a)
Rupende, Tapiwa Roy - A/C.2/78/SR.7
MACROECONOMIC POLICY (Agenda item 16)
Rupende, Tapiwa Roy - A/C.2/78/SR.9
MILLENNIUM SUMMIT—CONFERENCES (Agenda item 117)
Nyagura, Petronella - A/78/PV.15
RACIAL DISCRIMINATION—ELIMINATION (Agenda item 69a)
Chimbindi, Albert Ranganai - A/78/PV.50
RIGHT TO DEVELOPMENT (Agenda item 71b)
Manyanga, Garikai - A/C.3/78/SR.20
SANCTIONS—INTERNATIONAL RELATIONS (Agenda item 71b)
Manyanga, Garikai - A/C.3/78/SR.28
SUSTAINABLE DEVELOPMENT (Agenda item 18)
Rupende, Tapiwa Roy - A/C.2/78/SR.13; A/C.2/78/SR.14
UN. GENERAL ASSEMBLY (78TH SESS. : 2023-2024). 2ND COMMITTEE—GENERAL DEBATE (Agenda item 8)
Rupende, Tapiwa Roy - A/C.2/78/SR.5
UN. SECURITY COUNCIL—MEMBERSHIP (Agenda item 121)
Kadyautumbe, Darlington Mashoko - A/78/PV.35
UN CONFERENCES (Agenda item 13)
Nyagura, Petronella - A/78/PV.15

Zimbabwe (continued)

WESTERN SAHARA QUESTION (Agenda item 58)
Mawire, Tirivavi - A/C.4/78/SR.8

Zimbabwe. President

UN. GENERAL ASSEMBLY (78TH SESS. : 2023-2024)—GENERAL DEBATE (Agenda item 8)
Mnangagwa, Emmerson Dambudzo - A/78/PV.8
UN. GENERAL ASSEMBLY (78TH SESS. : 2023-2024)—SPECIAL STATEMENTS
Mnangagwa, Emmerson Dambudzo - A/78/PV.8

Abaalala, Majed (Saudi Arabia)
MINE CLEARANCE (Agenda item 46)
A/C.4/78/SR.10

Abad Garcia, Jienevit Juset (Panama)
HIV/AIDS—DECLARATIONS (Agenda item 10)
A/78/PV.91

Abbas, Mahmoud (State of Palestine. President)
UN. GENERAL ASSEMBLY (78TH SESS. : 2023-2024)—GENERAL DEBATE (Agenda item 8)
A/78/PV.8
UN. GENERAL ASSEMBLY (78TH SESS. : 2023-2024)—SPECIAL STATEMENTS
A/78/PV.8

Abbas, Swabri Ali (Kenya)
ECONOMIC COOPERATION AMONG DEVELOPING COUNTRIES (Agenda item 22b)
A/C.2/78/SR.18
OPERATIONAL ACTIVITIES—UN SYSTEM (Agenda item 22a)
A/C.2/78/SR.18

Abd Karim, Nur Azura Binti (Malaysia)
CRIMES AGAINST HUMANITY (Agenda item 80)
A/C.6/78/SR.10
DISASTER VICTIMS (Agenda item 86)
A/C.6/78/SR.6
INTERNATIONAL LAW—TRAINING PROGRAMMES (Agenda item 78)
A/C.6/78/SR.21
NON-CITIZENS—DEPORTATION (Agenda item 81)
A/C.6/78/SR.34
PEACEKEEPING OPERATIONS—CRIMINAL LIABILITY (Agenda item 76)
A/C.6/78/SR.8
RULE OF LAW (Agenda item 83)
A/C.6/78/SR.19
TREATIES (Agenda item 87)
A/C.6/78/SR.20
UN. INTERNATIONAL LAW COMMISSION—REPORTS (Agenda item 79)
A/C.6/78/SR.30; A/C.6/78/SR.32
UN COMMISSION ON INTERNATIONAL TRADE LAW—REPORTS (Agenda item 77)
A/C.6/78/SR.14

Abd Karim, Sofian Akmal Bin (Malaysia)
ECONOMIC SANCTIONS—INTERNATIONAL RELATIONS (Agenda item 28)
A/78/PV.89
UN. SECURITY COUNCIL—MEMBERSHIP (Agenda item 121)
A/78/PV.35
UN RESOLUTIONS—IMPLEMENTATION (Agenda item 119)
A/78/PV.108
VETO (Agenda item 63)
A/78/PV.51

Abdala, Paulina Feliciano Francisco (Mozambique)
DISASTER PREVENTION (Agenda item 18c)
A/C.2/78/SR.15
ECONOMIC COOPERATION AMONG DEVELOPING COUNTRIES (Agenda item 22b)
A/C.2/78/SR.18

Abdallah, Amina Mohamed (League of Arab States)
SELF-DETERMINATION OF PEOPLES (Agenda item 70)
A/C.3/78/SR.43

Abdalrhman, Fatma Mohammad (United Arab Emirates)
RIGHTS OF THE CHILD (Agenda item 67)
A/C.3/78/SR.13

Abdelaal, Ahmed Magdy Mohamed Rashad (Egypt)
2030 AGENDA—PROGRAMME IMPLEMENTATION (Agenda item 18a)
A/C.2/78/SR.12
BIOLOGICAL DIVERSITY—TREATIES (Agenda item 18f)
A/C.2/78/SR.12
CLIMATE (Agenda item 18d)
A/C.2/78/SR.12
DEVELOPMENT FINANCE (Agenda item 16b)
A/C.2/78/SR.9
EXTERNAL DEBT (Agenda item 16c)
A/C.2/78/SR.9
SUSTAINABLE DEVELOPMENT (Agenda item 18)
A/C.2/78/SR.12; A/C.2/78/SR.24
TERRITORIES OCCUPIED BY ISRAEL—NATURAL RESOURCES (Agenda item 59)
A/C.2/78/SR.19

Abdelaziz, Maged Abdelfattah (League of Arab States)
UN. GENERAL ASSEMBLY (78TH SESS. : 2023-2024). 1ST COMMITTEE—GENERAL DEBATE (Agenda item 8)
A/C.1/78/PV.9
VETO (Agenda item 63)
A/78/PV.61

Abdelhady-Nasser, Feda (State of Palestine)
ECONOMIC SANCTIONS—INTERNATIONAL RELATIONS (Agenda item 28)
A/78/PV.90
TERRITORIES OCCUPIED BY ISRAEL—HUMAN RIGHTS (Agenda item 50)
A/C.4/78/SR.24; A/C.4/78/SR.25
UNRWA—ACTIVITIES (Agenda item 49)
A/C.4/78/SR.22

Abdelkhalek, Osama Mahmoud (Egypt)
MIDDLE EAST SITUATION (Agenda item 34)
A/78/PV.40

Abdelkhalek, Osama Mahmoud (Egypt) (continued)

MILLENNIUM SUMMIT—CONFERENCES (Agenda item 117)
A/78/PV.15
PALESTINE QUESTION (Agenda item 35)
A/78/PV.39
PEACE (Agenda item 14)
A/78/PV.76; A/78/PV.82
PEACEBUILDING (Agenda item 61)
A/78/PV.100
UN. GENERAL ASSEMBLY—WORK PROGRAMME (Agenda item 120)
A/78/PV.32
UN. GENERAL ASSEMBLY (78TH SESS. : 2023-2024). 2ND COMMITTEE—GENERAL DEBATE (Agenda item 8)
A/C.2/78/SR.2
UN. PEACEBUILDING COMMISSION—REPORTS (Agenda item 27)
A/78/PV.100
UN. PEACEBUILDING FUND—REPORTS (Agenda item 111)
A/78/PV.100
UN. SECURITY COUNCIL—MEMBERSHIP (Agenda item 121)
A/78/PV.35
UN CONFERENCES (Agenda item 13)
A/78/PV.15
UN RESOLUTIONS—IMPLEMENTATION (Agenda item 119)
A/78/PV.32
VETO (Agenda item 63)
A/78/PV.52; A/78/PV.60; A/78/PV.66; A/78/PV.70; A/78/PV.74

Abdelkhalek, Osama Mahmoud (Egypt) (Group of Arab States)

AL-SABAH, NAWAF AL-AHMAD AL-JABER (KUWAIT. AMIR)—TRIBUTES
A/78/PV.50(Resumption1)
EMERGENCY ASSISTANCE (Agenda item 72a)
A/78/PV.46
PALESTINIANS—ASSISTANCE (Agenda item 72b)
A/78/PV.46

Abdelkhalek, Osama Mahmoud (Egypt) (Organisation of Islamic Cooperation)

HUMAN RIGHTS—INTERNATIONAL INSTRUMENTS (Agenda item 71a)
A/C.3/78/SR.24
HUMAN RIGHTS—TERRITORIES OCCUPIED BY ISRAEL (Agenda item 71c)
A/C.3/78/SR.24
RELIGIOUS INTOLERANCE (Agenda item 71b)
A/C.3/78/SR.24

Abdelkhalek, Osama Mahmoud (Egypt) (UN. General Assembly. 5th Committee. Chair)

SUBSIDIARY ORGANS—APPOINTMENTS (Agenda item 115)
A/C.5/78/SR.8

Abdelkhalek, Osama Mahmoud (Egypt) (UN. General Assembly. 5th Committee. Chair) (continued)

UN—FINANCIAL SITUATION (Agenda item 136)
A/C.5/78/SR.38
UN. ADVISORY COMMITTEE ON ADMINISTRATIVE AND BUDGETARY QUESTIONS—MEMBERS (Agenda item 115a)
A/C.5/78/SR.8
UN. BOARD OF AUDITORS—MEMBERS (Agenda item 115d)
A/C.5/78/SR.8
UN. COMMITTEE ON CONTRIBUTIONS—MEMBERS (Agenda item 115b)
A/C.5/78/SR.8
UN. GENERAL ASSEMBLY (78TH SESS. : 2023-2024). 5TH COMMITTEE—WORK ORGANIZATION (Agenda item 7)
A/C.5/78/SR.35
UN. INDEPENDENT AUDIT ADVISORY COMMITTEE—MEMBERS (Agenda item 115e)
A/C.5/78/SR.8
UN. INVESTMENTS COMMITTEE—MEMBERS (Agenda item 115c)
A/C.5/78/SR.8

Abdillahi, Elaye Yacin (Djibouti) (Groupe des ambassadeurs francophones)

PEACEKEEPING OPERATIONS (Agenda item 51)
A/C.4/78/SR.18

Abdo Rocholl, Tania María (Paraguay) (UN. Human Rights Committee. Chair)

UN. HUMAN RIGHTS COMMITTEE—REPORTS (Agenda item 71a)
A/C.3/78/SR.17

Abdul Kadir, Zambry (Malaysia)

PALESTINE QUESTION (Agenda item 35)
A/78/PV.39

Abdullah, Md Showeb (Bangladesh)

AGEING PERSONS (Agenda item 24b)
A/C.3/78/SR.1
CLIMATE CHANGE (Agenda item 71b)
A/C.3/78/SR.29
DISPLACED PERSONS (Agenda item 71b)
A/C.3/78/SR.32
HUMAN RIGHTS—TERRITORIES OCCUPIED BY ISRAEL (Agenda item 71c)
A/C.3/78/SR.35
IAEA—REPORTS (Agenda item 89)
A/78/PV.29
INDIGENOUS PEOPLES (Agenda item 68a)
A/C.3/78/SR.15
INDIGENOUS PEOPLES—CONFERENCES (Agenda item 68b)
A/C.3/78/SR.15
MIGRANT WORKERS (Agenda item 71a)
A/C.3/78/SR.23
MIGRANTS—PROTECTION (Agenda item 71b)
A/C.3/78/SR.23

Abdullah, Md Showeb (Bangladesh) (continued)

POVERTY—HUMAN RIGHTS (Agenda item 71b)
A/C.3/78/SR.30
RIGHT TO DRINKING WATER (Agenda item 71b)
A/C.3/78/SR.28
RIGHT TO EDUCATION (Agenda item 71b)
A/C.3/78/SR.27
RIGHT TO HEALTH (Agenda item 71b)
A/C.3/78/SR.39
RIGHT TO HOUSING (Agenda item 71b)
A/C.3/78/SR.30
RIGHTS OF THE CHILD (Agenda item 67)
A/C.3/78/SR.13

Abdullah II, King of Jordan, 1962- (Jordan)

UN. GENERAL ASSEMBLY (78TH SESS. : 2023-2024)—GENERAL DEBATE (Agenda item 8)
A/78/PV.4
UN. GENERAL ASSEMBLY (78TH SESS. : 2023-2024)—SPECIAL STATEMENTS
A/78/PV.4

Abdullateef, Mohammed Ayad (Iraq)

HUMAN RIGHTS—TERRITORIES OCCUPIED BY ISRAEL (Agenda item 71c)
A/C.3/78/SR.35
HUMAN RIGHTS ACTIVISTS (Agenda item 71b)
A/C.3/78/SR.56
MERCENARIES (Agenda item 70)
A/C.3/78/SR.42
RELIGIOUS INTOLERANCE (Agenda item 71b)
A/C.3/78/SR.38
RIGHTS OF THE CHILD (Agenda item 67)
A/C.3/78/SR.55
UN. HUMAN RIGHTS COUNCIL—REPORTS (Agenda item 66)
A/C.3/78/SR.46
YOUTH (Agenda item 24b)
A/C.3/78/SR.55

Abebe, Leulseged Tadese (Ethiopia)

LANDLOCKED DEVELOPING COUNTRIES—CONFERENCES (Agenda item 20b)
A/C.2/78/SR.7
LEAST DEVELOPED COUNTRIES—CONFERENCES (Agenda item 20a)
A/C.2/78/SR.7
UN. GENERAL ASSEMBLY (78TH SESS. : 2023-2024). 1ST COMMITTEE—GENERAL DEBATE (Agenda item 8)
A/C.1/78/PV.8
UN. GENERAL ASSEMBLY (78TH SESS. : 2023-2024). 2ND COMMITTEE—GENERAL DEBATE (Agenda item 8)
A/C.2/78/SR.2

Abela, Robert (Malta. Prime Minister)

UN. GENERAL ASSEMBLY (78TH SESS. : 2023-2024)—GENERAL DEBATE (Agenda item 8)
A/78/PV.10

Abela, Robert (Malta. Prime Minister) (continued)

UN. GENERAL ASSEMBLY (78TH SESS. : 2023-2024)—SPECIAL STATEMENTS
A/78/PV.10

Abelian, Movses (UN. Under-Secretary-General for General Assembly and Conference Management)

CONFERENCE AND MEETING SERVICES (Agenda item 137)
A/C.5/78/SR.7

Abesadze, David (Georgia)

ARMED CONFLICTS PREVENTION (Agenda item 31a)
A/78/PV.72
CRIMES AGAINST HUMANITY (Agenda item 80)
A/C.6/78/SR.44
HIV/AIDS—DECLARATIONS (Agenda item 10)
A/78/PV.91
HUMAN RIGHTS—UKRAINE (Agenda item 71c)
A/C.3/78/SR.53
INTERNATIONAL CRIMINAL COURT—REPORTS (Agenda item 74)
A/78/PV.22
UN. GENERAL ASSEMBLY (78TH SESS. : 2023-2024). 2ND COMMITTEE—GENERAL DEBATE (Agenda item 8)
A/C.2/78/SR.3
UN. HUMAN RIGHTS COUNCIL—REPORTS (Agenda item 66)
A/78/PV.23
UN HIGH COMMISSIONER FOR REFUGEES—REPORTS (Agenda item 60)
A/C.3/78/SR.45
VETO (Agenda item 63)
A/78/PV.71

Abinader Corona, Luis Rodolfo (Dominican Republic. President)

UN. GENERAL ASSEMBLY (78TH SESS. : 2023-2024)—GENERAL DEBATE (Agenda item 8)
A/78/PV.7
UN. GENERAL ASSEMBLY (78TH SESS. : 2023-2024)—SPECIAL STATEMENTS
A/78/PV.7

Abo, Ai (Japan)

UN—BUDGET (2024) (Agenda item 134)
A/C.5/78/SR.3
UN—FINANCIAL SITUATION (Agenda item 136)
A/C.5/78/SR.6
UN. GENERAL ASSEMBLY (78TH SESS. : 2023-2024). 5TH COMMITTEE—WORK ORGANIZATION (Agenda item 7)
A/C.5/78/SR.40

Abo, Ai (Japan) (UN. Committee on Conferences. Chair)

CONFERENCE AND MEETING SERVICES (Agenda item 137)
A/C.5/78/SR.7

Aboui, Ismael Buchanan (Université nationale du Rwanda)

WESTERN SAHARA QUESTION (Agenda item 58)
A/C.4/78/SR.4

Abraham, Devita (Trinidad and Tobago)

INTERNATIONAL CRIMINAL COURT—REPORTS (Agenda item 74)
A/78/PV.22

Abudu-Birresborn, Jeswuni (Ghana)

UN. GENERAL ASSEMBLY (78TH SESS. : 2023-2024). 2ND COMMITTEE—GENERAL DEBATE (Agenda item 8)
A/C.2/78/SR.3

Abugamel, Firas (Autonomy for the Sahara Coalition (Organization))

WESTERN SAHARA QUESTION (Agenda item 58)
A/C.4/78/SR.4

Abuhaj, Hiba Jafaar Abubakr (Sudan)

UN. GENERAL ASSEMBLY (78TH SESS. : 2023-2024). 2ND COMMITTEE—GENERAL DEBATE (Agenda item 8)
A/C.2/78/SR.5

Abushahab, Mohamed Issa (United Arab Emirates)

DIAMONDS—FUELLING CONFLICT (Agenda item 30)
A/78/PV.65
PALESTINE QUESTION (Agenda item 35)
A/78/PV.40
PEACE (Agenda item 14)
A/78/PV.76; A/78/PV.82
RESPONSIBILITY TO PROTECT (Agenda item 129)
A/78/PV.97
SUSTAINABLE DEVELOPMENT (Agenda item 18)
A/78/PV.107
VETO (Agenda item 63)
A/78/PV.61; A/78/PV.67; A/78/PV.78

Abushahab, Mohamed Issa (United Arab Emirates) (Group of Arab States)

VETO (Agenda item 63)
A/78/PV.74

Abushahab, Mohamed Issa (United Arab Emirates) (UN. Group of Asia-Pacific States)

GEINGOB, HAGE GOTTFRIED (NAMIBIA. PRESIDENT)—TRIBUTES
A/78/PV.55

Abushaibah, Shayea (Kuwait)

UNRWA—ACTIVITIES (Agenda item 49)
A/C.4/78/SR.22

Abushawesh, Sahar (State of Palestine)

EMERGENCY ASSISTANCE (Agenda item 72a)
A/78/PV.47
PALESTINIANS—ASSISTANCE (Agenda item 72b)
A/78/PV.47
SUSTAINABLE DEVELOPMENT (Agenda item 18)
A/C.2/78/SR.22
TERRITORIES OCCUPIED BY ISRAEL—NATURAL RESOURCES (Agenda item 59)
A/C.2/78/SR.21

Adda, M'Rabih ((personal capacity))

WESTERN SAHARA QUESTION (Agenda item 58)
A/C.4/78/SR.5

Adelman, Dylan (United States)

UN. GENERAL ASSEMBLY—WORK PROGRAMME (Agenda item 120)
A/78/PV.33
UN RESOLUTIONS—IMPLEMENTATION (Agenda item 119)
A/78/PV.33
UN SYSTEM—STRENGTHENING (Agenda item 122)
A/78/PV.99

Adeng, Cecilia A.M. (South Sudan)

HUMAN RIGHTS—ERITREA (Agenda item 71c)
A/C.3/78/SR.36

Adenopo, Adeyinka A. (Nigeria)

GLOBALIZATION—INTERDEPENDENCE (Agenda item 19)
A/C.2/78/SR.10
SCIENCE AND TECHNOLOGY—DEVELOPMENT (Agenda item 19a)
A/C.2/78/SR.10

Adhikari, Pramita (Nepal) (Group of Least Developed Countries)

2030 AGENDA—PROGRAMME IMPLEMENTATION (Agenda item 18a)
A/C.2/78/SR.12
FOOD SECURITY (Agenda item 23a)
A/C.2/78/SR.16
POVERTY—INTERNATIONAL DECADES (Agenda item 21a)
A/C.2/78/SR.16
RURAL POVERTY (Agenda item 21b)
A/C.2/78/SR.16
SUSTAINABLE DEVELOPMENT (Agenda item 18)
A/C.2/78/SR.12

Adire, Anastasia Francilia (Nauru)

LAW OF THE SEA (Agenda item 75a)
A/78/PV.44

Adire, Anastasia Francilia (Nauru) (continued)

MARINE ECOSYSTEMS—BIOLOGICAL DIVERSITY (Agenda item 75c)
A/78/PV.44
STRADDLING FISH STOCKS (Agenda item 75b)
A/78/PV.44

Adjissa, Youcef ((personal capacity))

WESTERN SAHARA QUESTION (Agenda item 58)
A/C.4/78/SR.5

Adnan, Yang Aishah Binti (Malaysia)

COMMODITIES (Agenda item 16d)
A/C.2/78/SR.14
DEVELOPMENT FINANCE (Agenda item 16b)
A/C.2/78/SR.9
EXTERNAL DEBT (Agenda item 16c)
A/C.2/78/SR.9
INTERNATIONAL TRADE (Agenda item 16a)
A/C.2/78/SR.9
INVESTMENT PROMOTION (Agenda item 16g)
A/C.2/78/SR.9
SUSTAINABLE DEVELOPMENT (Agenda item 18)
A/C.2/78/SR.14
TERRITORIES OCCUPIED BY ISRAEL—NATURAL RESOURCES (Agenda item 59)
A/C.2/78/SR.19
UN. GENERAL ASSEMBLY (78TH SESS. : 2023-2024). 2ND COMMITTEE—GENERAL DEBATE (Agenda item 8)
A/C.2/78/SR.5

Afonso, Pedro Comissário (Mozambique)

UN. SECURITY COUNCIL—REPORTS (Agenda item 26)
A/78/PV.94
VETO (Agenda item 63)
A/78/PV.75

Agaronova, Gloriya A. (Russian Federation)

PEACEBUILDING (Agenda item 61)
A/78/PV.101
UN. PEACEBUILDING COMMISSION—REPORTS (Agenda item 27)
A/78/PV.101
UN. PEACEBUILDING FUND—REPORTS (Agenda item 111)
A/78/PV.101

Agbetse, Yao (UN. Human Rights Council. Independent Expert on the Situation of Human Rights in the Central African Republic)

HUMAN RIGHTS—CENTRAL AFRICAN REPUBLIC (Agenda item 71c)
A/C.3/78/SR.33

Agnello, Alexander (Canada)

INTERNATIONAL JURISDICTION (Agenda item 84)
A/C.6/78/SR.12

Agnello, Alexander (Canada) (continued)

RULE OF LAW (Agenda item 83)
A/C.6/78/SR.15

Agyeman, Harold Adlai (Ghana)

VETO (Agenda item 63)
A/78/PV.75; A/78/PV.78

Agyeman, Harold Adlai (Ghana) (Advisory Committee on the United Nations Programme of Assistance in the Teaching, Study, Dissemination and Wider Appreciation of International Law. Chair)

INTERNATIONAL LAW—TRAINING PROGRAMMES (Agenda item 78)
A/C.6/78/SR.21

Ahangari, Narmin (Azerbaijan)

CENTRAL ASIA—ZONES OF PEACE (Agenda item 64)
A/78/PV.85
HUMAN RIGHTS (Agenda item 71)
A/C.3/78/SR.25
HUMAN RIGHTS—INTERNATIONAL INSTRUMENTS (Agenda item 71a)
A/C.3/78/SR.25
HUMAN RIGHTS—UKRAINE (Agenda item 71c)
A/C.3/78/SR.53
HUMAN RIGHTS ADVANCEMENT (Agenda item 71b)
A/C.3/78/SR.25
MINORITIES (Agenda item 71b)
A/C.3/78/SR.25
RACIAL DISCRIMINATION—ELIMINATION (Agenda item 69a)
A/C.3/78/SR.41; A/C.3/78/SR.43
RACIAL DISCRIMINATION—PROGRAMMES OF ACTION (Agenda item 69b)
A/C.3/78/SR.41; A/C.3/78/SR.43
RIGHTS OF THE CHILD (Agenda item 67)
A/C.3/78/SR.11; A/C.3/78/SR.13; A/C.3/78/SR.14
RURAL WOMEN (Agenda item 25a)
A/C.3/78/SR.10
UN HIGH COMMISSIONER FOR REFUGEES—REPORTS (Agenda item 60)
A/C.3/78/SR.44; A/C.3/78/SR.45
WOMEN'S ADVANCEMENT (Agenda item 25a)
A/C.3/78/SR.10
WOMEN'S ADVANCEMENT—CONFERENCES (Agenda item 25b)
A/C.3/78/SR.10

Ahidjo, Ahidjo (Cameroon)

MINORITIES (Agenda item 71b)
A/C.3/78/SR.39
OUTER SPACE—PEACEFUL USES—INTERNATIONAL COOPERATION (Agenda item 48)
A/C.4/78/SR.16
RIGHT TO HEALTH (Agenda item 71b)
A/C.3/78/SR.39

Ahmadova, Billur (Azerbaijan)

CULTURE—DEVELOPMENT (Agenda item 19b)
A/C.2/78/SR.11
INFORMATION TECHNOLOGY—DEVELOPMENT (Agenda item 15)
A/C.2/78/SR.11
LANDLOCKED DEVELOPING COUNTRIES—CONFERENCES (Agenda item 20b)
A/C.2/78/SR.7
LEAST DEVELOPED COUNTRIES—CONFERENCES (Agenda item 20a)
A/C.2/78/SR.7

Ahmed, Ali Haidar (Maldives)

VETO (Agenda item 63)
A/78/PV.74

Ahmed, Amr Essameldin Sadek (Egypt)

AFRICA—NUCLEAR-WEAPON-FREE ZONES (Agenda item 92)
A/C.1/78/PV.25
BIOLOGICAL WEAPONS—TREATIES (Agenda item 106)
A/C.1/78/PV.14
CHEMICAL WEAPONS—TREATIES (Agenda item 99l)
A/C.1/78/PV.14; A/C.1/78/PV.26
DISARMAMENT—GENERAL AND COMPLETE (Agenda item 99)
A/C.1/78/PV.23; A/C.1/78/PV.30
DISARMAMENT—UN. GENERAL ASSEMBLY (4TH SPECIAL SESS. ON DISARMAMENT : xxxx) (Agenda item 99h)
A/C.1/78/PV.23
FISSIONABLE MATERIALS—TREATIES (Agenda item 99a)
A/C.1/78/PV.25; A/C.1/78/PV.26
IAEA—REPORTS (Agenda item 89)
A/78/PV.30
MIDDLE EAST—NUCLEAR PROLIFERATION (Agenda item 102)
A/C.1/78/PV.11; A/C.1/78/PV.25
MIDDLE EAST—NUCLEAR-WEAPON-FREE ZONES (Agenda item 95)
A/C.1/78/PV.11; A/C.1/78/PV.14; A/C.1/78/PV.21; A/C.1/78/PV.25
NUCLEAR DISARMAMENT (Agenda item 99b)
A/C.1/78/PV.11
NUCLEAR DISARMAMENT—CONFERENCES (Agenda item 99aa)
A/C.1/78/PV.25
NUCLEAR DISARMAMENT—TREATY COMPLIANCE (Agenda item 99q)
A/C.1/78/PV.11; A/C.1/78/PV.25
NUCLEAR NON-PROLIFERATION—INTERNATIONAL OBLIGATIONS (Agenda item 99w)
A/C.1/78/PV.11
NUCLEAR WEAPON TESTS—TREATIES (Agenda item 105)
A/C.1/78/PV.26

Ahmed, Amr Essameldin Sadek (Egypt) (continued)

RADIOACTIVE WASTES MANAGEMENT (Agenda item 99e)
A/C.1/78/PV.25
UN. CONFERENCE ON DISARMAMENT—REPORTS (Agenda item 101a)
A/C.1/78/PV.23
UN. DISARMAMENT COMMISSION—REPORTS (Agenda item 101b)
A/C.1/78/PV.23
UN. GENERAL ASSEMBLY (78TH SESS. : 2023-2024). 1ST COMMITTEE—GENERAL DEBATE (Agenda item 8)
A/C.1/78/PV.3
UN. GENERAL ASSEMBLY (78TH SESS. : 2023-2024). 1ST COMMITTEE—WORK ORGANIZATION (Agenda item 7)
A/C.1/78/PV.26; A/C.1/78/PV.30
WEAPONS OF MASS DESTRUCTION—TERRORISM (Agenda item 99s)
A/C.1/78/PV.14

Ahmed, Husham (Pakistan)

ARMS TRANSFERS—TREATIES (Agenda item 99x)
A/C.1/78/PV.19
CONFIDENCE-BUILDING MEASURES (Agenda item 99t)
A/C.1/78/PV.21
CONVENTIONAL ARMS—REGIONAL PROGRAMMES (Agenda item 99g)
A/C.1/78/PV.21
CONVENTIONAL WEAPONS—TREATIES (Agenda item 103)
A/C.1/78/PV.19
DISARMAMENT—GENERAL AND COMPLETE (Agenda item 99)
A/C.1/78/PV.19; A/C.1/78/PV.20
FISSIONABLE MATERIALS—TREATIES (Agenda item 99a)
A/C.1/78/PV.25
INFORMATION—INTERNATIONAL SECURITY (Agenda item 94)
A/C.1/78/PV.20
NUCLEAR NON-PROLIFERATION (Agenda item 99o)
A/C.1/78/PV.25
NUCLEAR WEAPONS—HUMANITARIAN CONSEQUENCES (Agenda item 99bb)
A/C.1/78/PV.25
NUCLEAR WEAPONS USE—TREATIES (Agenda item 100a)
A/C.1/78/PV.25
NUCLEAR-WEAPON-FREE ZONES (Agenda item 99cc)
A/C.1/78/PV.25
REGIONAL DISARMAMENT (Agenda item 99f)
A/C.1/78/PV.21

Ahoue Itoua Lekegny, Patience (Congo)

HUMAN RIGHTS INSTITUTIONS—CENTRAL AFRICA (Agenda item 71b)
A/C.3/78/SR.56
RIGHTS OF THE CHILD (Agenda item 67)
A/C.3/78/SR.13

Ahuka Lutundul, Claudy (Democratic Republic of the Congo)

RIGHTS OF THE CHILD (Agenda item 67)
A/C.3/78/SR.14

Aidara, Abdoul Latif (Africa Centre for Strategic Intelligence (Senegal))

WESTERN SAHARA QUESTION (Agenda item 58)
A/C.4/78/SR.5

Aiello, Jack (United States)

SMALL ISLAND DEVELOPING STATES—PROGRAMMES OF ACTION (Agenda item 18b)
A/78/PV.100
TAXATION (Agenda item 16h)
A/C.2/78/SR.9

Ainomuhisha, Medard (Uganda)

UN—BUDGET (2024) (Agenda item 134)
A/C.5/78/SR.33

Ainomuhisha, Medard (Uganda) (Group of 77)

JOINT INSPECTION UNIT (Agenda item 141)
A/C.5/78/SR.29
PEACEKEEPING OPERATIONS—FINANCING (Agenda item 146)
A/C.5/78/SR.35; A/C.5/78/SR.36
UN—ADMINISTRATION (Agenda item 132)
A/C.5/78/SR.29; A/C.5/78/SR.32
UN—BUDGET (2024) (Agenda item 134)
A/C.5/78/SR.33
UN—FINANCIAL REPORTS (Agenda item 131)
A/C.5/78/SR.35
UN—FINANCIAL SITUATION (Agenda item 136)
A/C.5/78/SR.38
UN—HUMAN RESOURCES MANAGEMENT (Agenda item 139)
A/C.5/78/SR.27
UN. GENERAL ASSEMBLY (78TH SESS. : 2023-2024). 5TH COMMITTEE—WORK ORGANIZATION (Agenda item 7)
A/C.5/78/SR.27; A/C.5/78/SR.34; A/C.5/78/SR.35; A/C.5/78/SR.40
UN INTERIM FORCE IN LEBANON—FINANCING (Agenda item 156b)
A/C.5/78/SR.40

Ajayi, Eniola Olaitan (Nigeria)

CRIMES AGAINST HUMANITY (Agenda item 80)
A/C.6/78/SR.11
INTERNATIONAL JURISDICTION (Agenda item 84)
A/C.6/78/SR.13

Ajayi, Eniola Olaitan (Nigeria) (continued)

NUCLEAR DISARMAMENT (Agenda item 99b)
A/C.1/78/PV.13
NUCLEAR NON-PROLIFERATION—INTERNATIONAL OBLIGATIONS (Agenda item 99w)
A/C.1/78/PV.13
NUCLEAR WEAPONS—TREATIES (Agenda item 99ff)
A/C.1/78/PV.13
RULE OF LAW (Agenda item 83)
A/C.6/78/SR.17

Ajileye, Abimbola (Nigeria)

TREATIES (Agenda item 87)
A/C.6/78/SR.20

Ajmal, Muhammad Jawad (Pakistan)

HUMAN RIGHTS—AFGHANISTAN (Agenda item 71c)
A/C.3/78/SR.34
TERRORISM (Agenda item 109)
A/C.6/78/SR.4

Akakpo, Koffi (Togo)

PEACE (Agenda item 14)
A/78/PV.76
UN SYSTEM—STRENGTHENING (Agenda item 122)
A/78/PV.99
WESTERN SAHARA QUESTION (Agenda item 58)
A/C.4/78/SR.6

Akanitvong, Pataschol (Thailand)

YOUTH (Agenda item 24b)
A/C.3/78/SR.2

Akbulut, Mustafa Kemal (Türkiye)

EMERGENCY ASSISTANCE (Agenda item 72a)
A/78/PV.46
PALESTINIANS—ASSISTANCE (Agenda item 72b)
A/78/PV.46

Akita, Mio (Japan)

MINORITIES (Agenda item 71b)
A/C.3/78/SR.39
SEXUAL ORIENTATION (Agenda item 71b)
A/C.3/78/SR.39
WOMEN'S ADVANCEMENT (Agenda item 25a)
A/C.3/78/SR.7
WOMEN'S ADVANCEMENT—CONFERENCES (Agenda item 25b)
A/C.3/78/SR.7

Akram, Munir (Pakistan)

DECOLONIZATION (Agenda item 58)
A/C.4/78/SR.2
HUMAN RIGHTS—REPORTS (Agenda item 71c)
A/C.3/78/SR.24
HUMAN RIGHTS—TERRITORIES OCCUPIED BY ISRAEL (Agenda item 71c)
A/C.3/78/SR.24

Akram, Munir (Pakistan) (continued)

IAEA—REPORTS (Agenda item 89)
A/78/PV.29
INTERNATIONAL PARLIAMENTARIANS' CONGRESS—OBSERVER STATUS (Agenda item 170)
A/C.6/78/SR.14
MILLENNIUM SUMMIT—CONFERENCES (Agenda item 117)
A/78/PV.15
PEACE (Agenda item 14)
A/78/PV.48; A/78/PV.76; A/78/PV.82
PEACEKEEPING OPERATIONS (Agenda item 51)
A/C.4/78/SR.18
RELIGIOUS INTOLERANCE (Agenda item 71b)
A/C.3/78/SR.24
RESPONSIBILITY TO PROTECT (Agenda item 129)
A/78/PV.97
RULE OF LAW (Agenda item 83)
A/C.6/78/SR.16
SELF-DETERMINATION OF PEOPLES (Agenda item 70)
A/C.3/78/SR.40; A/C.3/78/SR.56
SOCIAL CONDITIONS (Agenda item 24b)
A/C.3/78/SR.2
SOCIAL DEVELOPMENT (Agenda item 24)
A/C.3/78/SR.2
TERRORISM (Agenda item 109)
A/C.6/78/SR.2
UN. GENERAL ASSEMBLY—WORK PROGRAMME (Agenda item 120)
A/78/PV.32
UN. GENERAL ASSEMBLY (78TH SESS. : 2023-2024). 2ND COMMITTEE—GENERAL DEBATE (Agenda item 8)
A/C.2/78/SR.2
UN. HUMAN RIGHTS COUNCIL—REPORTS (Agenda item 66)
A/78/PV.23
UN. INTERNATIONAL COURT OF JUSTICE—REPORTS (Agenda item 73)
A/78/PV.27
UN. SECRETARY-GENERAL—REPORTS (Agenda item 110)
A/78/PV.55
UN. SECURITY COUNCIL—MEMBERSHIP (Agenda item 121)
A/78/PV.35
UN. SECURITY COUNCIL—REPORTS (Agenda item 26)
A/78/PV.93
UN CONFERENCES (Agenda item 13)
A/78/PV.15
UN RESOLUTIONS—IMPLEMENTATION (Agenda item 119)
A/78/PV.32
UNRWA—ACTIVITIES (Agenda item 49)
A/C.4/78/SR.22
VETO (Agenda item 63)
A/78/PV.67; A/78/PV.74; A/78/PV.78
WOMEN'S ADVANCEMENT (Agenda item 25a)
A/C.3/78/SR.8

Akram, Munir (Pakistan) (continued)

WOMEN'S ADVANCEMENT—CONFERENCES (Agenda item 25b)
A/C.3/78/SR.8

Akram, Munir (Pakistan) (Organisation of Islamic Cooperation)

PEACE (Agenda item 14)
A/78/PV.62
RAISI, SEYYED EBRAHIM (IRAN (ISLAMIC REPUBLID OF). PRESIDENT)—TRIBUTES
A/78/PV.83
VETO (Agenda item 63)
A/78/PV.59

Akram, Zamir (UN. Human Rights Council. Working Group on the Right to Development. Chair)

RIGHT TO DEVELOPMENT (Agenda item 71b)
A/C.3/78/SR.20

Akufo-Addo, Nana Addo Dankwa (Ghana. President)

UN. GENERAL ASSEMBLY (78TH SESS. : 2023-2024)—GENERAL DEBATE (Agenda item 8)
A/78/PV.6
UN. GENERAL ASSEMBLY (78TH SESS. : 2023-2024)—SPECIAL STATEMENTS
A/78/PV.6

Al Ashkar, Adib (Syrian Arab Republic)

ARMS RACE—OUTER SPACE (Agenda item 97a)
A/C.1/78/PV.17
ARMS TRANSFERS—TREATIES (Agenda item 99x)
A/C.1/78/PV.28
BIOLOGICAL WEAPONS—TREATIES (Agenda item 106)
A/C.1/78/PV.15
CHEMICAL WEAPONS—TREATIES (Agenda item 99l)
A/C.1/78/PV.14; A/C.1/78/PV.15
CONVENTIONAL WEAPONS (Agenda item 99u)
A/C.1/78/PV.28
DISARMAMENT—GENERAL AND COMPLETE (Agenda item 99)
A/C.1/78/PV.23; A/C.1/78/PV.30
IAEA—REPORTS (Agenda item 89)
A/78/PV.29; A/78/PV.30
INFORMATION—INTERNATIONAL SECURITY (Agenda item 94)
A/C.1/78/PV.29
MEDITERRANEAN REGION—REGIONAL SECURITY (Agenda item 104)
A/C.1/78/PV.29
MIDDLE EAST—NUCLEAR PROLIFERATION (Agenda item 102)
A/C.1/78/PV.13; A/C.1/78/PV.26
MIDDLE EAST—NUCLEAR-WEAPON-FREE ZONES (Agenda item 95)
A/C.1/78/PV.15; A/C.1/78/PV.21; A/C.1/78/PV.22; A/C.1/78/PV.26
NUCLEAR DISARMAMENT (Agenda item 99b)
A/C.1/78/PV.11; A/C.1/78/PV.14

Al Ashkar, Adib (Syrian Arab Republic) (continued)

UN. GENERAL ASSEMBLY (78TH SESS. : 2023-2024). 1ST COMMITTEE—GENERAL DEBATE (Agenda item 8)
A/C.1/78/PV.3; A/C.1/78/PV.4; A/C.1/78/PV.5; A/C.1/78/PV.6; A/C.1/78/PV.7; A/C.1/78/PV.8
VETO (Agenda item 63)
A/78/PV.78
WEAPONS OF MASS DESTRUCTION—TERRORISM (Agenda item 99s)
A/C.1/78/PV.15

Al Bin Khalil, Maryam (Bahrain)

TERRITORIES OCCUPIED BY ISRAEL—NATURAL RESOURCES (Agenda item 59)
A/C.2/78/SR.19

Al Blooshi, Ahmed Ali (United Arab Emirates)

DISASTER VICTIMS (Agenda item 86)
A/C.6/78/SR.7
INTERNATIONAL JURISDICTION (Agenda item 84)
A/C.6/78/SR.13

Al Busaidi, Ahmed Hamood Faisal (Oman) (Gulf Cooperation Council)

UNRWA—ACTIVITIES (Agenda item 49)
A/C.4/78/SR.22

Al Dhanani, Nouf Abdulla (United Arab Emirates)

RACIAL DISCRIMINATION—ELIMINATION (Agenda item 69a)
A/C.3/78/SR.41
RACIAL DISCRIMINATION—PROGRAMMES OF ACTION (Agenda item 69b)
A/C.3/78/SR.41

Al Fadhel, Noura Abdul Rahman (Bahrain)

SUSTAINABLE DEVELOPMENT (Agenda item 18)
A/C.2/78/SR.13

Al Haddabi, Alya Nasser Saif (Oman)

SUSTAINABLE DEVELOPMENT (Agenda item 18)
A/C.2/78/SR.15

Al Hammadi, Asma Hassan Mohamed (United Arab Emirates)

TERRITORIES OCCUPIED BY ISRAEL—NATURAL RESOURCES (Agenda item 59)
A/C.2/78/SR.19

Al Hashimy, Reem Ebrahim (United Arab Emirates)

UN. GENERAL ASSEMBLY (78TH SESS. : 2023-2024)—GENERAL DEBATE (Agenda item 8)
A/78/PV.13

Al Hebsi, Jawaher Abdulla (United Arab Emirates)

WOMEN'S ADVANCEMENT (Agenda item 25a)
A/C.3/78/SR.9
WOMEN'S ADVANCEMENT—CONFERENCES (Agenda item 25b)
A/C.3/78/SR.9

Al Jaradi, Heba Khalid (Oman)

HUMAN RIGHTS (Agenda item 71)
A/C.3/78/SR.27
HUMAN RIGHTS—TERRITORIES OCCUPIED BY ISRAEL (Agenda item 71c)
A/C.3/78/SR.27
RIGHTS OF THE CHILD (Agenda item 67)
A/C.3/78/SR.14

Al Jaradi, Heba Khalid (Oman) (Gulf Cooperation Council)

HUMAN RIGHTS—TERRITORIES OCCUPIED BY ISRAEL (Agenda item 71c)
A/C.3/78/SR.35
HUMAN RIGHTS ACTIVISTS (Agenda item 71b)
A/C.3/78/SR.19
UN HIGH COMMISSIONER FOR REFUGEES—REPORTS (Agenda item 60)
A/C.3/78/SR.44
WOMEN'S ADVANCEMENT (Agenda item 25a)
A/C.3/78/SR.7
WOMEN'S ADVANCEMENT—CONFERENCES (Agenda item 25b)
A/C.3/78/SR.7

Al Kahtani, Fayee Fahad M. (Saudi Arabia)

OUTER SPACE—PEACEFUL USES—INTERNATIONAL COOPERATION (Agenda item 48)
A/C.4/78/SR.16
TERRITORIES OCCUPIED BY ISRAEL—HUMAN RIGHTS (Agenda item 50)
A/C.4/78/SR.25

Al Khayarin, Saleh Mohammed (Qatar)

PERSONS WITH DISABILITIES—HUMAN RIGHTS (Agenda item 71a)
A/C.3/78/SR.51
UN HIGH COMMISSIONER FOR REFUGEES—REPORTS (Agenda item 60)
A/C.3/78/SR.45

Al Mandil, Mishal (Saudi Arabia)

RIGHT TO DEVELOPMENT (Agenda item 71b)
A/C.3/78/SR.20
RIGHTS OF THE CHILD (Agenda item 67)
A/C.3/78/SR.12

Al Marzooqi, Tahreer (United Arab Emirates)

RULE OF LAW (Agenda item 83)
A/C.6/78/SR.19
TERRORISM (Agenda item 109)
A/C.6/78/SR.4

Al Mulla, Wafiqah (Kuwait)
AGEING PERSONS (Agenda item 24b)
A/C.3/78/SR.3
FAMILY (Agenda item 24b)
A/C.3/78/SR.3
HUMAN RIGHTS—TERRITORIES OCCUPIED BY ISRAEL (Agenda item 71c)
A/C.3/78/SR.35
PERSONS WITH DISABILITIES—HUMAN RIGHTS (Agenda item 71a)
A/C.3/78/SR.51
SOCIAL DEVELOPMENT (Agenda item 24)
A/C.3/78/SR.3
WOMEN'S ADVANCEMENT (Agenda item 25a)
A/C.3/78/SR.7; A/C.3/78/SR.8
WOMEN'S ADVANCEMENT—CONFERENCES (Agenda item 25b)
A/C.3/78/SR.7; A/C.3/78/SR.8

Al Munaifi, Shahad (Kuwait)
RACIAL DISCRIMINATION—ELIMINATION (Agenda item 69a)
A/C.3/78/SR.41
RACIAL DISCRIMINATION—PROGRAMMES OF ACTION (Agenda item 69b)
A/C.3/78/SR.41
RIGHTS OF THE CHILD (Agenda item 67)
A/C.3/78/SR.12
SELF-DETERMINATION OF PEOPLES (Agenda item 70)
A/C.3/78/SR.41

Al Nahhas, Wissam (Syrian Arab Republic)
HEALTH (Agenda item 125)
A/78/PV.77
HUMAN RIGHTS—DEMOCRATIC PEOPLE'S REPUBLIC OF KOREA (Agenda item 71c)
A/78/PV.50
HUMAN RIGHTS—SYRIAN ARAB REPUBLIC (Agenda item 71c)
A/78/PV.50
INTERNATIONAL TRADE (Agenda item 16a)
A/C.2/78/SR.8
RACIAL DISCRIMINATION—ELIMINATION (Agenda item 69a)
A/78/PV.50
SUSTAINABLE DEVELOPMENT (Agenda item 18)
A/C.2/78/SR.13; A/C.2/78/SR.22; A/C.2/78/SR.24
TERRITORIES OCCUPIED BY ISRAEL—NATURAL RESOURCES (Agenda item 59)
A/C.2/78/SR.19; A/C.2/78/SR.21
UN. GENERAL ASSEMBLY (78TH SESS. : 2023-2024). 2ND COMMITTEE—GENERAL DEBATE (Agenda item 8)
A/C.2/78/SR.3

Al Nahyan, Zayed bin Sultan (United Arab Emirates)
UNRWA—ACTIVITIES (Agenda item 49)
A/C.4/78/SR.23

Al Qasim, Ibrahim (United Arab Emirates)
OUTER SPACE—PEACEFUL USES—INTERNATIONAL COOPERATION (Agenda item 48)
A/C.4/78/SR.16

Al Rashdi, Amal (Oman)
INFORMATION (Agenda item 53)
A/C.4/78/SR.13
OUTER SPACE—PEACEFUL USES—INTERNATIONAL COOPERATION (Agenda item 48)
A/C.4/78/SR.16

Al Rashdi, Amal (Oman) (Gulf Cooperation Council)
TERRITORIES OCCUPIED BY ISRAEL—HUMAN RIGHTS (Agenda item 50)
A/C.4/78/SR.24

Al Rawahi, Abdulhalim Mubarak Saloom (Oman)
RIGHTS OF THE CHILD (Agenda item 67)
A/C.3/78/SR.55
UN. GENERAL ASSEMBLY (78TH SESS. : 2023-2024). 2ND COMMITTEE—GENERAL DEBATE (Agenda item 8)
A/C.2/78/SR.6
YOUTH (Agenda item 24b)
A/C.3/78/SR.55

Al Rawahi, Abdulhalim Mubarak Saloom (Oman) (Gulf Cooperation Council)
ELECTION VERIFICATION—UN (Agenda item 71b)
A/C.3/78/SR.50
PERSONS WITH DISABILITIES—HUMAN RIGHTS (Agenda item 71a)
A/C.3/78/SR.51
RURAL WOMEN (Agenda item 25a)
A/C.3/78/SR.49
UN HIGH COMMISSIONER FOR REFUGEES—REPORTS (Agenda item 60)
A/C.3/78/SR.51

Al Rubkhi, Khalid Saleh Said (Oman)
IAEA—REPORTS (Agenda item 89)
A/78/PV.30
PEACE (Agenda item 14)
A/78/PV.62; A/78/PV.82
UN. GENERAL ASSEMBLY (78TH SESS. : 2023-2024). 1ST COMMITTEE—GENERAL DEBATE (Agenda item 8)
A/C.1/78/PV.6
WOMEN'S ADVANCEMENT (Agenda item 25a)
A/C.3/78/SR.10
WOMEN'S ADVANCEMENT—CONFERENCES (Agenda item 25b)
A/C.3/78/SR.10

Al Rubkhi, Khalid Saleh Said (Oman) (Gulf Cooperation Council)

HEALTH (Agenda item 125)
A/78/PV.16
PALESTINE QUESTION (Agenda item 35)
A/78/PV.39
RELIGIOUS INTOLERANCE (Agenda item 71b)
A/C.3/78/SR.26
RIGHT TO DEVELOPMENT (Agenda item 71b)
A/C.3/78/SR.26
TERRITORIES OCCUPIED BY ISRAEL—NATURAL RESOURCES (Agenda item 59)
A/C.2/78/SR.19
TERRORISM—HUMAN RIGHTS (Agenda item 71b)
A/C.3/78/SR.26

Al Shehhi, Mohammed Ali Ahmed (Oman)

TERRORISM (Agenda item 109)
A/C.6/78/SR.2
UN. INTERNATIONAL COURT OF JUSTICE—REPORTS (Agenda item 73)
A/78/PV.27
UN. SECURITY COUNCIL—REPORTS (Agenda item 26)
A/78/PV.94

Al Shehri, Muhammad (Saudi Arabia)

SUSTAINABLE DEVELOPMENT (Agenda item 18)
A/C.2/78/SR.15

Al Sudani, Mohammed Shia' (Iraq. Prime Minister)

UN. GENERAL ASSEMBLY (78TH SESS. : 2023-2024)—GENERAL DEBATE (Agenda item 8)
A/78/PV.10
UN. GENERAL ASSEMBLY (78TH SESS. : 2023-2024)—SPECIAL STATEMENTS
A/78/PV.10

Al Zayani, Abdul Latif bin Rashid (Bahrain)

UN. GENERAL ASSEMBLY (78TH SESS. : 2023-2024)—GENERAL DEBATE (Agenda item 8)
A/78/PV.11

Al-Ajmi, Mohammed (Oman)

RULE OF LAW (Agenda item 83)
A/C.6/78/SR.18

Al-Ali, Maryam (United Arab Emirates)

DECOLONIZATION (Agenda item 58)
A/C.4/78/SR.7
SPECIAL POLITICAL MISSIONS (Agenda item 52)
A/C.4/78/SR.21
TERRITORIES OCCUPIED BY ISRAEL—HUMAN RIGHTS (Agenda item 50)
A/C.4/78/SR.25
WESTERN SAHARA QUESTION (Agenda item 58)
A/C.4/78/SR.7

Al-Ali, Mohamed Essa Saif Boausaibah (United Arab Emirates)

VETO (Agenda item 63)
A/78/PV.71

Al-Alimi, Rashad Mohammed (Yemen. Presidential Leadership Council. President)

UN. GENERAL ASSEMBLY (78TH SESS. : 2023-2024)—GENERAL DEBATE (Agenda item 8)
A/78/PV.8
UN. GENERAL ASSEMBLY (78TH SESS. : 2023-2024)—SPECIAL STATEMENTS
A/78/PV.8

Al-Amri, Islam Abdullah Hassan (League of Arab States)

TERRITORIES OCCUPIED BY ISRAEL—NATURAL RESOURCES (Agenda item 59)
A/C.2/78/SR.20

Al-barati, Abdulrahman Hasan Yahya (Yemen)

FOOD SECURITY (Agenda item 23a)
A/C.2/78/SR.17
POVERTY—INTERNATIONAL DECADES (Agenda item 21a)
A/C.2/78/SR.17
RURAL POVERTY (Agenda item 21b)
A/C.2/78/SR.17
SUSTAINABLE DEVELOPMENT (Agenda item 18)
A/C.2/78/SR.24; A/C.2/78/SR.25
TERRITORIES OCCUPIED BY ISRAEL—NATURAL RESOURCES (Agenda item 59)
A/C.2/78/SR.19
UN. GENERAL ASSEMBLY (78TH SESS. : 2023-2024). 2ND COMMITTEE—GENERAL DEBATE (Agenda item 8)
A/C.2/78/SR.6

Al-Buainain, Hemyan Hassan Nasser (Qatar)

HUMAN RIGHTS (Agenda item 71)
A/C.3/78/SR.16
RIGHTS OF THE CHILD (Agenda item 67)
A/C.3/78/SR.11
WOMEN'S ADVANCEMENT (Agenda item 25a)
A/C.3/78/SR.7
WOMEN'S ADVANCEMENT—CONFERENCES (Agenda item 25b)
A/C.3/78/SR.7

Al-Burhan, Abdel-Fattah Al-Burhan Abdelrahman (Sudan. President)

UN. GENERAL ASSEMBLY (78TH SESS. : 2023-2024)—GENERAL DEBATE (Agenda item 8)
A/78/PV.9
UN. GENERAL ASSEMBLY (78TH SESS. : 2023-2024)—SPECIAL STATEMENTS
A/78/PV.9

Al-Dahlaki, Hasanain Hadi Hasan (Iraq)
PEACEKEEPING OPERATIONS (Agenda item 51)
A/C.4/78/SR.20
SPECIAL POLITICAL MISSIONS (Agenda item 52)
A/C.4/78/SR.21
TERRITORIES OCCUPIED BY ISRAEL—HUMAN RIGHTS (Agenda item 50)
A/C.4/78/SR.25
UNRWA—ACTIVITIES (Agenda item 49)
A/C.4/78/SR.23

Al-Dikaan, Ahmed Khaled Ghanem (Kuwait)
HUMAN RIGHTS ADVANCEMENT (Agenda item 71b)
A/C.3/78/SR.26
UN HIGH COMMISSIONER FOR REFUGEES—REPORTS (Agenda item 60)
A/C.3/78/SR.45

Al-Dobhany, Marwan Ali Noman (Yemen)
ARMS RACE—OUTER SPACE (Agenda item 97a)
A/C.1/78/PV.16
UN. GENERAL ASSEMBLY (78TH SESS. : 2023-2024). 1ST COMMITTEE—GENERAL DEBATE (Agenda item 8)
A/C.1/78/PV.4
UN SYSTEM—STRENGTHENING (Agenda item 122)
A/78/PV.99
VETO (Agenda item 63)
A/78/PV.75

Al-Fatlawi, Abbas Kadhom Obaid (Iraq)
CRIMES AGAINST HUMANITY (Agenda item 80)
A/C.6/78/SR.38
DECOLONIZATION (Agenda item 58)
A/C.4/78/SR.8
PEACE (Agenda item 14)
A/78/PV.62
UN—BUDGET (2024) (Agenda item 134)
A/C.5/78/SR.3
UN. GENERAL ASSEMBLY (78TH SESS. : 2023-2024). 1ST COMMITTEE—GENERAL DEBATE (Agenda item 8)
A/C.1/78/PV.6
VETO (Agenda item 63)
A/78/PV.61

Al-halique, Katherine Anas Ahmad (Jordan)
HUMAN RIGHTS—TERRITORIES OCCUPIED BY ISRAEL (Agenda item 71c)
A/C.3/78/SR.35
RACIAL DISCRIMINATION—ELIMINATION (Agenda item 69a)
A/C.3/78/SR.42
RACIAL DISCRIMINATION—PROGRAMMES OF ACTION (Agenda item 69b)
A/C.3/78/SR.42

Al-halique, Katherine Anas Ahmad (Jordan) (continued)
UN. GENERAL ASSEMBLY (78TH SESS. : 2023-2024). 2ND COMMITTEE—GENERAL DEBATE (Agenda item 8)
A/C.2/78/SR.3
UN HIGH COMMISSIONER FOR REFUGEES—REPORTS (Agenda item 60)
A/C.3/78/SR.44

Al-halique, Katherine Anas Ahmad (Jordan) (Group of Arab States)
HUMAN RIGHTS—INTERNATIONAL INSTRUMENTS (Agenda item 71a)
A/C.3/78/SR.24
HUMAN RIGHTS—TERRITORIES OCCUPIED BY ISRAEL (Agenda item 71c)
A/C.3/78/SR.24
TERRITORIES OCCUPIED BY ISRAEL—NATURAL RESOURCES (Agenda item 59)
A/C.2/78/SR.19

Al-Hammal, Ahmad (UNDP)
SUSTAINABLE DEVELOPMENT (Agenda item 18)
A/C.2/78/SR.12

Al-Hasani, Haider (Iraq)
CRIMES AGAINST HUMANITY (Agenda item 80)
A/C.6/78/SR.11
PEACEKEEPING OPERATIONS—CRIMINAL LIABILITY (Agenda item 76)
A/C.6/78/SR.9

Al-Hassan, Mohamed (Oman)
VETO (Agenda item 63)
A/78/PV.74

Al-Hassan, Mohamed (Oman) (Gulf Cooperation Council)
MILLENNIUM SUMMIT—CONFERENCES (Agenda item 117)
A/78/PV.15
UN. GENERAL ASSEMBLY (78TH SESS. : 2023-2024)—OFFICERS (Agenda item 5)
A/C.5/78/SR.1
UN CONFERENCES (Agenda item 13)
A/78/PV.15

Al-Kaabi, Soud Abdulaziz (Qatar)
CRIMES AGAINST HUMANITY (Agenda item 80)
A/C.6/78/SR.10; A/C.6/78/SR.39
RULE OF LAW (Agenda item 83)
A/C.6/78/SR.16

Al-Kandari, Ismail Abdullah (Kuwait)
UN. ECONOMIC AND SOCIAL COUNCIL—REPORTS (Agenda item 9)
A/78/PV.33

Al-Khaabi, Najla (United Arab Emirates)

UN. GENERAL ASSEMBLY (78TH SESS. : 2023-2024)—OFFICERS (Agenda item 5)
A/C.5/78/SR.1

Al-khalidi, Hasan Badri Mhalhal (Iraq)

SUSTAINABLE DEVELOPMENT (Agenda item 18)
A/C.2/78/SR.15; A/C.2/78/SR.24
TERRITORIES OCCUPIED BY ISRAEL—NATURAL RESOURCES (Agenda item 59)
A/C.2/78/SR.19
UN. GENERAL ASSEMBLY (78TH SESS. : 2023-2024). 2ND COMMITTEE—GENERAL DEBATE (Agenda item 8)
A/C.2/78/SR.3

Al-Khaqani, Hassan Jabbar (Iraq)

DISAPPEARANCE OF PERSONS (Agenda item 71b)
A/C.3/78/SR.22
FAMILY (Agenda item 24b)
A/C.3/78/SR.4
HUMAN RIGHTS (Agenda item 71)
A/C.3/78/SR.16
HUMAN RIGHTS—TERRITORIES OCCUPIED BY ISRAEL (Agenda item 71c)
A/C.3/78/SR.35
PALESTINIANS—ASSISTANCE (Agenda item 72b)
A/78/PV.47
PERSONS WITH DISABILITIES—HUMAN RIGHTS (Agenda item 71a)
A/C.3/78/SR.51
RIGHT TO DRINKING WATER (Agenda item 71b)
A/C.3/78/SR.28
RURAL WOMEN (Agenda item 25a)
A/C.3/78/SR.49
SOCIAL DEVELOPMENT (Agenda item 24)
A/C.3/78/SR.4
VETO (Agenda item 63)
A/78/PV.67
WOMEN MIGRANT WORKERS (Agenda item 25a)
A/C.3/78/SR.49
WOMEN'S ADVANCEMENT—CONFERENCES (Agenda item 25b)
A/C.3/78/SR.51
YOUTH (Agenda item 24b)
A/C.3/78/SR.4

Al-Khayareen, Abdulla Ghanim (Qatar)

FOOD SECURITY (Agenda item 23a)
A/C.2/78/SR.16
POVERTY—INTERNATIONAL DECADES (Agenda item 21a)
A/C.2/78/SR.16
RURAL POVERTY (Agenda item 21b)
A/C.2/78/SR.16

Al-Kumaim, Amjad Qaid Ahmed (UN. Advisory Committee on Administrative and Budgetary Questions. Vice-Chair)

PERSONNEL QUESTIONS—UN SYSTEM (Agenda item 142)
A/C.5/78/SR.27
UN—BUDGET (2024) (Agenda item 134)
A/C.5/78/SR.4; A/C.5/78/SR.13; A/C.5/78/SR.22
UN—HUMAN RESOURCES MANAGEMENT (Agenda item 139)
A/C.5/78/SR.27

Al-Kuwari, Shaheen (Qatar)

2030 AGENDA—PROGRAMME IMPLEMENTATION (Agenda item 18a)
A/C.2/78/SR.12
SUSTAINABLE DEVELOPMENT (Agenda item 18)
A/C.2/78/SR.12

Al-Maawda, Jassim Sayyar (Qatar)

HUMAN RIGHTS—SYRIAN ARAB REPUBLIC (Agenda item 71c)
A/C.3/78/SR.54
VETO (Agenda item 63)
A/78/PV.70

Al-mansour, Osama (Syrian Arab Republic)

UN—BUDGET (2024) (Agenda item 134)
A/78/PV.73; A/C.5/78/SR.3; A/C.5/78/SR.5; A/C.5/78/SR.26/PartII; A/C.5/78/SR.28; A/C.5/78/SR.34
UN—PROGRAMME PLANNING (Agenda item 135)
A/78/PV.50(Resumption1); A/C.5/78/SR.5; A/C.5/78/SR.24
UN DISENGAGEMENT OBSERVER FORCE—FINANCING (Agenda item 156a)
A/C.5/78/SR.35

Al-Marri, Rashid Ali (Qatar)

CRIMES AGAINST HUMANITY (Agenda item 80)
A/C.6/78/SR.40; A/C.6/78/SR.43
UN CHARTER—REPORTS (Agenda item 82)
A/C.6/78/SR.22

Al-mashehari, Sarah Ahmed Ahmed (Yemen)

DISPLACED PERSONS (Agenda item 71b)
A/C.3/78/SR.32
ELECTION VERIFICATION—UN (Agenda item 71b)
A/78/PV.50; A/C.3/78/SR.50
FAMILY (Agenda item 24b)
A/C.3/78/SR.2
HUMAN RIGHTS—TERRITORIES OCCUPIED BY ISRAEL (Agenda item 71c)
A/C.3/78/SR.35
HUMAN RIGHTS ACTIVISTS (Agenda item 71b)
A/C.3/78/SR.19
INFORMATION (Agenda item 53)
A/C.4/78/SR.14
MINE CLEARANCE (Agenda item 46)
A/C.4/78/SR.10

Al-mashehari, Sarah Ahmed Ahmed (Yemen) (continued)

PERSONS WITH DISABILITIES—HUMAN RIGHTS (Agenda item 71a)
A/C.3/78/SR.51
RIGHTS OF THE CHILD (Agenda item 67)
A/C.3/78/SR.55
RURAL WOMEN (Agenda item 25a)
A/C.3/78/SR.49
SPECIAL POLITICAL MISSIONS (Agenda item 52)
A/C.4/78/SR.21
TERRITORIES OCCUPIED BY ISRAEL—HUMAN RIGHTS (Agenda item 50)
A/C.4/78/SR.24
UNRWA—ACTIVITIES (Agenda item 49)
A/C.4/78/SR.23
WOMEN'S ADVANCEMENT (Agenda item 25a)
A/C.3/78/SR.8
WOMEN'S ADVANCEMENT—CONFERENCES (Agenda item 25b)
A/C.3/78/SR.8
YOUTH (Agenda item 24b)
A/C.3/78/SR.2; A/C.3/78/SR.55

Al-Mehaizza, Essa Abdulla (Qatar)

BIOLOGICAL WEAPONS—TREATIES (Agenda item 106)
A/C.1/78/PV.15
CHEMICAL WEAPONS—TREATIES (Agenda item 99l)
A/C.1/78/PV.15
WEAPONS OF MASS DESTRUCTION—TERRORISM (Agenda item 99s)
A/C.1/78/PV.15

Al-Murad, Mariam (Kuwait)

MULTILATERALISM—DISARMAMENT (Agenda item 99r)
A/C.1/78/PV.21

Al-Musawi, Ali Rida Abdulmohsin Hasan (Iraq)

HEALTH (Agenda item 125)
A/78/PV.48
UN HIGH COMMISSIONER FOR REFUGEES—REPORTS (Agenda item 60)
A/C.3/78/SR.45

Al-naama, Talal Abdulaziz (Qatar)

LANDLOCKED DEVELOPING COUNTRIES—CONFERENCES (Agenda item 20b)
A/C.2/78/SR.7
LEAST DEVELOPED COUNTRIES—CONFERENCES (Agenda item 20a)
A/C.2/78/SR.7
SUSTAINABLE DEVELOPMENT (Agenda item 18)
A/C.2/78/SR.24
TERRITORIES OCCUPIED BY ISRAEL—NATURAL RESOURCES (Agenda item 59)
A/C.2/78/SR.19

Al-naama, Talal Abdulaziz (Qatar) (continued)

UN. GENERAL ASSEMBLY (78TH SESS. : 2023-2024). 2ND COMMITTEE—GENERAL DEBATE (Agenda item 8)
A/C.2/78/SR.2

Al-Niami, Mustafa (Iraq)

COMMODITIES (Agenda item 16d)
A/C.2/78/SR.9
FINANCIAL FLOWS (Agenda item 16f)
A/C.2/78/SR.9
INTERNATIONAL TRADE (Agenda item 16a)
A/C.2/78/SR.9
MACROECONOMIC POLICY (Agenda item 16)
A/C.2/78/SR.9

Al-Saadi, Abdullah Ali Fadhel (Yemen)

PALESTINE QUESTION (Agenda item 35)
A/78/PV.40

Al-Saadi, Abdullah Ali Fadhel (Yemen) (Group of Arab States)

VETO (Agenda item 63)
A/78/PV.59

Al-Saadi, Abdullah Ali Fadhel (Yemen) (UN. Group of Asia-Pacific States)

UN. GENERAL ASSEMBLY (78TH SESS. : 2023-2024). PRESIDENT (Agenda item 4)
A/78/PV.87

Al-Sabah, Ahmad Nawaf Al-Ahmad (Kuwait. Prime Minister)

UN. GENERAL ASSEMBLY (78TH SESS. : 2023-2024)—GENERAL DEBATE (Agenda item 8)
A/78/PV.9
UN. GENERAL ASSEMBLY (78TH SESS. : 2023-2024)—SPECIAL STATEMENTS
A/78/PV.9

Al-Sadar, Hamzah (Iraq)

CLUSTER MUNITIONS (Agenda item 99dd)
A/C.1/78/PV.18
CONVENTIONAL WEAPONS (Agenda item 99u)
A/C.1/78/PV.18
DISARMAMENT—GENERAL AND COMPLETE (Agenda item 99)
A/C.1/78/PV.19
LANDMINES—TREATIES (Agenda item 99m)
A/C.1/78/PV.18

Al-Saed, Saadoon (Iraq)

MINE CLEARANCE (Agenda item 46)
A/C.4/78/SR.10
RADIATION EFFECTS (Agenda item 47)
A/C.4/78/SR.11

Al-Safran, Hussain Mohammed (Qatar)

MIDDLE EAST—NUCLEAR-WEAPON-FREE ZONES (Agenda item 95)
A/C.1/78/PV.12
NUCLEAR DISARMAMENT (Agenda item 99b)
A/C.1/78/PV.12
NUCLEAR NON-PROLIFERATION—INTERNATIONAL OBLIGATIONS (Agenda item 99w)
A/C.1/78/PV.12

Al-Saud, Prince of Saudi Arabia (Saudi Arabia)

TERRITORIES OCCUPIED BY ISRAEL—NATURAL RESOURCES (Agenda item 59)
A/C.2/78/SR.19
UN. GENERAL ASSEMBLY (78TH SESS. : 2023-2024)—GENERAL DEBATE (Agenda item 8)
A/78/PV.13
UN. GENERAL ASSEMBLY (78TH SESS. : 2023-2024)—SPECIAL STATEMENTS
A/78/PV.13

Al-Sharji, Saud (Oman) (Gulf Cooperation Council)

UN—BUDGET (2024) (Agenda item 134)
A/C.5/78/SR.13

Al-Sinani, Nashwa Hilal (Oman)

CRIME PREVENTION (Agenda item 107)
A/C.3/78/SR.6

Al-Sinani, Nashwa Hilal (Oman) (Gulf Cooperation Council)

MIGRANTS—PROTECTION (Agenda item 71b)
A/C.3/78/SR.23

Al-Taie, Sarmad Muwafaq Mohammed (Iraq)

DISARMAMENT—GENERAL AND COMPLETE (Agenda item 99)
A/C.1/78/PV.24; A/C.1/78/PV.30
MIDDLE EAST—NUCLEAR-WEAPON-FREE ZONES (Agenda item 95)
A/C.1/78/PV.22
MULTILATERALISM—DISARMAMENT (Agenda item 99r)
A/C.1/78/PV.22

Al-Thani, Abdulrahman Abdulaziz F.A. (Qatar)

UKRAINE—POLITICAL CONDITIONS (Agenda item 62)
A/78/PV.99
UN. GENERAL ASSEMBLY (78TH SESS. : 2023-2024). 1ST COMMITTEE—GENERAL DEBATE (Agenda item 8)
A/C.1/78/PV.3

Al-Thani, Abdulrahman Abdulaziz F.A. (Qatar) (Gulf Cooperation Council)

EMERGENCY ASSISTANCE (Agenda item 72a)
A/78/PV.47

Al-thani, Almaha Mubarak F.J. (Qatar)

HUMAN RIGHTS—TERRITORIES OCCUPIED BY ISRAEL (Agenda item 71c)
A/C.3/78/SR.24
HUMAN RIGHTS—UKRAINE (Agenda item 71c)
A/C.3/78/SR.53
HUMAN RIGHTS ADVANCEMENT (Agenda item 71b)
A/C.3/78/SR.24
PEACE (Agenda item 14)
A/78/PV.76
PERSONS WITH DISABILITIES—HUMAN RIGHTS (Agenda item 71a)
A/C.3/78/SR.24
RIGHTS OF THE CHILD (Agenda item 67)
A/C.3/78/SR.12
UN. HUMAN RIGHTS COUNCIL—REPORTS (Agenda item 66)
A/78/PV.23

Al-thani, Almaha Mubarak F.J. (Qatar) (Gulf Cooperation Council)

ELECTION VERIFICATION—UN (Agenda item 71b)
A/78/PV.50
HEALTH (Agenda item 125)
A/78/PV.48

Al-Thani, Alya Ahmed S.A. (Qatar)

FAMILY (Agenda item 24b)
A/C.3/78/SR.3
HUMAN RIGHTS INSTITUTIONS—SOUTHWEST ASIA AND ARAB COUNTRIES (Agenda item 71b)
A/C.3/78/SR.50
INFORMATION (Agenda item 53)
A/C.4/78/SR.14
PALESTINE QUESTION (Agenda item 35)
A/78/PV.39
PERSONS WITH DISABILITIES (Agenda item 24b)
A/C.3/78/SR.3
UN—BUDGET (2024) (Agenda item 134)
A/C.5/78/SR.5
UN—PROGRAMME PLANNING (Agenda item 135)
A/C.5/78/SR.5
VETO (Agenda item 63)
A/78/PV.66; A/78/PV.75
WOMEN'S ADVANCEMENT (Agenda item 25a)
A/C.3/78/SR.8
WOMEN'S ADVANCEMENT—CONFERENCES (Agenda item 25b)
A/C.3/78/SR.8
YOUTH (Agenda item 24b)
A/C.3/78/SR.3

Al-Thani, Alya Ahmed S.A. (Qatar) (Gulf Cooperation Council)

AL-SABAH, NAWAF AL-AHMAD AL-JABER (KUWAIT. AMIR)—TRIBUTES
A/78/PV.50(Resumption1)

Al-Thani, Alya Ahmed S.A. (Qatar) (Gulf Cooperation Council) (continued)

RAISI, SEYYED EBRAHIM (IRAN (ISLAMIC REPUBLID OF). PRESIDENT)—TRIBUTES
A/78/PV.83
UKRAINE—POLITICAL CONDITIONS (Agenda item 62)
A/78/PV.57
VETO (Agenda item 63)
A/78/PV.59

Al-Thani, Hamad bin Abdulrahman (Qatar)

UN. GENERAL ASSEMBLY—WORK PROGRAMME (Agenda item 120)
A/78/PV.33
UN RESOLUTIONS—IMPLEMENTATION (Agenda item 119)
A/78/PV.33

Al-thani, Jassim Abdulaziz J.A. (Qatar)

DECOLONIZATION (Agenda item 58)
A/C.4/78/SR.2
TERRITORIES OCCUPIED BY ISRAEL—HUMAN RIGHTS (Agenda item 50)
A/C.4/78/SR.25
UNRWA—ACTIVITIES (Agenda item 49)
A/C.4/78/SR.22
WESTERN SAHARA QUESTION (Agenda item 58)
A/C.4/78/SR.2

Al-Thani, Sheikh Tamim bin Hamad (Qatar. Amir)

UN. GENERAL ASSEMBLY (78TH SESS. : 2023-2024)—GENERAL DEBATE (Agenda item 8)
A/78/PV.4
UN. GENERAL ASSEMBLY (78TH SESS. : 2023-2024)—SPECIAL STATEMENTS
A/78/PV.4

Al-Zubaidi, Zaid Mohammed Hussein Abed (Iraq)

TERRORISM (Agenda item 109)
A/C.6/78/SR.4

Alabbasi, Amina Abdulaziz (Bahrain)

RIGHTS OF THE CHILD (Agenda item 67)
A/C.3/78/SR.14
WOMEN'S ADVANCEMENT (Agenda item 25a)
A/C.3/78/SR.9
WOMEN'S ADVANCEMENT—CONFERENCES (Agenda item 25b)
A/C.3/78/SR.9

Alabdali, Ali (Saudi Arabia)

CRIMES AGAINST HUMANITY (Agenda item 80)
A/C.6/78/SR.42

Alajmi, Fahad M. (Kuwait)

EMERGENCY ASSISTANCE (Agenda item 72a)
A/78/PV.47
LAW OF THE SEA (Agenda item 75a)
A/78/PV.44

Alajmi, Fahad M. (Kuwait) (continued)

MARINE ECOSYSTEMS—BIOLOGICAL DIVERSITY (Agenda item 75c)
A/78/PV.44
PALESTINIANS—ASSISTANCE (Agenda item 72b)
A/78/PV.47
STRADDLING FISH STOCKS (Agenda item 75b)
A/78/PV.44
TERRITORIES OCCUPIED BY ISRAEL—HUMAN RIGHTS (Agenda item 50)
A/C.4/78/SR.25
UN. GENERAL ASSEMBLY (78TH SESS. : 2023-2024). 1ST COMMITTEE—GENERAL DEBATE (Agenda item 8)
A/C.1/78/PV.9

Alaklabi, Faisal Saeed M. (Saudi Arabia)

INFORMATION (Agenda item 53)
A/C.4/78/SR.13

Alalaiwat, Suma Sameer (Bahrain) (UN. Group of Asia-Pacific States)

SLAVERY—MEMORIALS (Agenda item 118)
A/78/PV.64

Alameri, Reem Mohamed (United Arab Emirates)

HUMAN RIGHTS (Agenda item 71)
A/C.3/78/SR.16
HUMAN RIGHTS—INTERNATIONAL INSTRUMENTS (Agenda item 71a)
A/C.3/78/SR.25
HUMAN RIGHTS ACTIVISTS (Agenda item 71b)
A/C.3/78/SR.19
HUMAN RIGHTS ADVANCEMENT (Agenda item 71b)
A/C.3/78/SR.25

Alami, Tarik (UN. ESCWA. Division for Emerging and Conflict-related Issues. Director)

TERRITORIES OCCUPIED BY ISRAEL—NATURAL RESOURCES (Agenda item 59)
A/C.2/78/SR.19

Alamri, Hassan Mohammed A. (Saudi Arabia)

CRIMES AGAINST HUMANITY (Agenda item 80)
A/C.6/78/SR.11
DECOLONIZATION (Agenda item 58)
A/C.4/78/SR.7
UN SYSTEM—STRENGTHENING (Agenda item 122)
A/78/PV.99
UNRWA—ACTIVITIES (Agenda item 49)
A/C.4/78/SR.23
WESTERN SAHARA QUESTION (Agenda item 58)
A/C.4/78/SR.7

Alaoui, Rabia (Morocco)

CLIMATE CHANGE (Agenda item 71b)
A/C.3/78/SR.29
RIGHT TO DRINKING WATER (Agenda item 71b)
A/C.3/78/SR.28

Alaoui, Rabia (Morocco) (continued)
RIGHT TO EDUCATION (Agenda item 71b)
A/C.3/78/SR.27
TRAFFICKING IN PERSONS (Agenda item 71b)
A/C.3/78/SR.23

Alatawi, Innas Abdulrahman (Bahrain)
INFORMATION TECHNOLOGY—DEVELOPMENT (Agenda item 15)
A/C.2/78/SR.10
UN. GENERAL ASSEMBLY (78TH SESS. : 2023-2024). 2ND COMMITTEE—GENERAL DEBATE (Agenda item 8)
A/C.2/78/SR.5

Alavi, Sina (Liechtenstein)
UN. INTERNATIONAL LAW COMMISSION—REPORTS (Agenda item 79)
A/C.6/78/SR.23

Alawadhi, Sarah Ebrahim Abdulla Beddah (United Arab Emirates)
SPORTS—OLYMPIC GAMES (Agenda item 11)
A/78/PV.38

Albadr, Saleh (Saudi Arabia)
RACIAL DISCRIMINATION—ELIMINATION (Agenda item 69a)
A/C.3/78/SR.41
RACIAL DISCRIMINATION—PROGRAMMES OF ACTION (Agenda item 69b)
A/C.3/78/SR.41
SELF-DETERMINATION OF PEOPLES (Agenda item 70)
A/C.3/78/SR.41
TORTURE AND OTHER CRUEL TREATMENT (Agenda item 71a)
A/C.3/78/SR.18

Albán Alencastro, Juan Pablo (UN. Committee on Enforced Disappearances. Rapporteur)
DISAPPEARANCE OF PERSONS (Agenda item 71b)
A/C.3/78/SR.22

Albanai, Tareq M.A.M. (Kuwait)
AL-SABAH, NAWAF AL-AHMAD AL-JABER (KUWAIT. AMIR)—TRIBUTES
A/78/PV.50(Resumption1)
HEALTH (Agenda item 125)
A/78/PV.41
PEACE (Agenda item 14)
A/78/PV.62

Albanese, Francesca (UN. Human Rights Council. Special Rapporteur on the Situation of Human Rights in the Palestinian Territories Occupied since 1967)
HUMAN RIGHTS—TERRITORIES OCCUPIED BY ISRAEL (Agenda item 71c)
A/C.3/78/SR.35

Albares Bueno, José Manuel (Spain)
UKRAINE—POLITICAL CONDITIONS (Agenda item 62)
A/78/PV.56

Albert II, Prince of Monaco, 1958- (Monaco)
UN. GENERAL ASSEMBLY (78TH SESS. : 2023-2024)—GENERAL DEBATE (Agenda item 8)
A/78/PV.7
UN. GENERAL ASSEMBLY (78TH SESS. : 2023-2024)—SPECIAL STATEMENTS
A/78/PV.7

Albu-Mohammed, Ahmed Kamil Rahif (Iraq)
UN. GENERAL ASSEMBLY (78TH SESS. : 2023-2024)—OFFICERS (Agenda item 5)
A/C.5/78/SR.1

AlBusaidi, Sayyid Badr Bin Hamad bin Hamood (Oman)
UN. GENERAL ASSEMBLY (78TH SESS. : 2023-2024)—GENERAL DEBATE (Agenda item 8)
A/78/PV.13

Alcaraz Romero De Tejada, Leticia (Liechtenstein)
CLIMATE CHANGE (Agenda item 71b)
A/C.3/78/SR.29

Aldahhak, Koussay Abduljabbar (Syrian Arab Republic)
ECONOMIC SANCTIONS—INTERNATIONAL RELATIONS (Agenda item 28)
A/78/PV.89
PEACE (Agenda item 14)
A/78/PV.82
UKRAINE—POLITICAL CONDITIONS (Agenda item 62)
A/78/PV.58
VETO (Agenda item 63)
A/78/PV.60; A/78/PV.67; A/78/PV.75

Aldahhak, Koussay Abduljabbar (Syrian Arab Republic) (Group of Arab States)
DISARMAMENT—GENERAL AND COMPLETE (Agenda item 99)
A/78/PV.105

Aldehani, Bader A. (Kuwait)

UN. GENERAL ASSEMBLY (78TH SESS. : 2023-2024). 2ND COMMITTEE—GENERAL DEBATE (Agenda item 8)
A/C.2/78/SR.5

Aleinik, Sergei (Belarus)

UN. GENERAL ASSEMBLY (78TH SESS. : 2023-2024)—GENERAL DEBATE (Agenda item 8)
A/78/PV.13

Alem, Mohammed Walid (Algeria)

PEACE (Agenda item 14)
A/78/PV.77
SPECIAL POLITICAL MISSIONS (Agenda item 52)
A/C.4/78/SR.21

Alemad, Ahmed (United Arab Emirates)

MIDDLE EAST—NUCLEAR-WEAPON-FREE ZONES (Agenda item 95)
A/C.1/78/PV.22
MULTILATERALISM—DISARMAMENT (Agenda item 99r)
A/C.1/78/PV.22

Alemayehu, Betelihem Taye (Ethiopia)

DISASTER VICTIMS (Agenda item 86)
A/C.6/78/SR.6
INTERNATIONAL JURISDICTION (Agenda item 84)
A/C.6/78/SR.13
INTERNATIONAL LAW—TRAINING PROGRAMMES (Agenda item 78)
A/C.6/78/SR.21
PEACEKEEPING OPERATIONS—CRIMINAL LIABILITY (Agenda item 76)
A/C.6/78/SR.9
RESPONSIBILITY OF INTERNATIONAL ORGANIZATIONS (Agenda item 85)
A/C.6/78/SR.19
RULE OF LAW (Agenda item 83)
A/C.6/78/SR.18
TERRORISM (Agenda item 109)
A/C.6/78/SR.4

Alenezi, Faisal G. (Kuwait)

CRIMES AGAINST HUMANITY (Agenda item 80)
A/C.6/78/SR.11
DECOLONIZATION (Agenda item 58)
A/C.4/78/SR.8
PALESTINE QUESTION (Agenda item 35)
A/78/PV.40
UN—BUDGET (2024) (Agenda item 134)
A/C.5/78/SR.3
UN COMMISSION ON INTERNATIONAL TRADE LAW—REPORTS (Agenda item 77)
A/C.6/78/SR.14
WESTERN SAHARA QUESTION (Agenda item 58)
A/C.4/78/SR.8

Alexandridou, Alexandra (Greece)

FREEDOM OF EXPRESSION (Agenda item 71b)
A/C.3/78/SR.19
HUMAN RIGHTS (Agenda item 71)
A/C.3/78/SR.16
RIGHTS OF THE CHILD (Agenda item 67)
A/C.3/78/SR.11
WOMEN'S ADVANCEMENT (Agenda item 25a)
A/C.3/78/SR.7
WOMEN'S ADVANCEMENT—CONFERENCES (Agenda item 25b)
A/C.3/78/SR.7

Alghali, Francess Piagie (Sierra Leone)

DECOLONIZATION (Agenda item 58)
A/C.4/78/SR.7
INFORMATION TECHNOLOGY—DEVELOPMENT (Agenda item 15)
A/C.2/78/SR.11
RIGHTS OF THE CHILD (Agenda item 67)
A/C.3/78/SR.13
SCIENCE AND TECHNOLOGY—DEVELOPMENT (Agenda item 19a)
A/C.2/78/SR.11
UN. GENERAL ASSEMBLY (78TH SESS. : 2023-2024). 1ST COMMITTEE—GENERAL DEBATE (Agenda item 8)
A/C.1/78/PV.7
WESTERN SAHARA QUESTION (Agenda item 58)
A/C.4/78/SR.7

Alhammadi, Hessa (Bahrain)

ADMINISTRATION OF JUSTICE—HUMAN RIGHTS (Agenda item 71b)
A/C.3/78/SR.25
AGEING PERSONS (Agenda item 24b)
A/C.3/78/SR.3
NATIONAL INSTITUTIONS—HUMAN RIGHTS (Agenda item 71b)
A/C.3/78/SR.25
PERSONS WITH DISABILITIES (Agenda item 24b)
A/C.3/78/SR.3
RELIGIOUS INTOLERANCE (Agenda item 71b)
A/C.3/78/SR.25
SOCIAL DEVELOPMENT (Agenda item 24)
A/C.3/78/SR.3
YOUTH (Agenda item 24b)
A/C.3/78/SR.3

Alharbi, Saoud Abdullah (Kuwait)

RULE OF LAW (Agenda item 83)
A/C.6/78/SR.19

Ali, Mohamed Irfaan (Guyana. President)

UN. GENERAL ASSEMBLY (78TH SESS. : 2023-2024)—GENERAL DEBATE (Agenda item 8)
A/78/PV.6
UN. GENERAL ASSEMBLY (78TH SESS. : 2023-2024)—SPECIAL STATEMENTS
A/78/PV.6

Ali-Harm, Agnes (Fiji) (Pacific Islands Forum)
UN. INTERNATIONAL LAW COMMISSION—REPORTS (Agenda item 79)
A/C.6/78/SR.23

Alibrahim, Faisal (Saudi Arabia)
NUCLEAR DISARMAMENT (Agenda item 99b)
A/C.1/78/PV.13

Aliyev, Yashar T. (Azerbaijan)
UN CONFERENCES (Agenda item 13)
A/78/PV.37

Aliyev, Yashar T. (Azerbaijan) (Coordinating Bureau of the Non-Aligned Countries)
CUBA—UNITED STATES (Agenda item 38)
A/78/PV.24

Alizada, Kamal (Azerbaijan) (Coordinating Bureau of the Non-Aligned Countries)
UNRWA—ACTIVITIES (Agenda item 49)
A/C.4/78/SR.23

Aljabari, Ziad (Palestinian Moroccan Friendship Society)
WESTERN SAHARA QUESTION (Agenda item 58)
A/C.4/78/SR.4

Aljalahma, Shaikha (Bahrain)
DECOLONIZATION (Agenda item 58)
A/C.4/78/SR.7
OUTER SPACE—PEACEFUL USES—INTERNATIONAL COOPERATION (Agenda item 48)
A/C.4/78/SR.17
TERRITORIES OCCUPIED BY ISRAEL—HUMAN RIGHTS (Agenda item 50)
A/C.4/78/SR.25
WESTERN SAHARA QUESTION (Agenda item 58)
A/C.4/78/SR.7

Alkhalaileh, Fawaz (Moroccan Jordanian Friendship Association)
WESTERN SAHARA QUESTION (Agenda item 58)
A/C.4/78/SR.4

Alkhuraibet, Ali (Kuwait)
INFORMATION TECHNOLOGY—DEVELOPMENT (Agenda item 15)
A/C.2/78/SR.10
SUSTAINABLE DEVELOPMENT (Agenda item 18)
A/C.2/78/SR.13

Alkins, Royston (Guyana)
CLIMATE (Agenda item 18d)
A/C.2/78/SR.15
DISASTER PREVENTION (Agenda item 18c)
A/C.2/78/SR.15
FOOD SECURITY (Agenda item 23a)
A/C.2/78/SR.17

Alkins, Royston (Guyana) (continued)
POVERTY—INTERNATIONAL DECADES (Agenda item 21a)
A/C.2/78/SR.17
RURAL POVERTY (Agenda item 21b)
A/C.2/78/SR.17
SMALL ISLAND DEVELOPING STATES—PROGRAMMES OF ACTION (Agenda item 18b)
A/C.2/78/SR.15
SPORTS—OLYMPIC GAMES (Agenda item 11)
A/78/PV.38
SUSTAINABLE DEVELOPMENT (Agenda item 18)
A/C.2/78/SR.15
SUSTAINABLE ENERGY (Agenda item 18h)
A/C.2/78/SR.15

Alldridge, Rebecca (United Kingdom)
ORGANIZATION FOR DEMOCRACY AND ECONOMIC DEVELOPMENT - GUAM (Agenda item 32)
A/78/PV.85

Allet, Alexandra (Switzerland)
2030 AGENDA—PROGRAMME IMPLEMENTATION (Agenda item 18a)
A/C.2/78/SR.22
BIOLOGICAL DIVERSITY—TREATIES (Agenda item 18f)
A/C.2/78/SR.25
MIGRANTS—PROTECTION (Agenda item 71b)
A/C.3/78/SR.23

Almahmoud, Ahmed Abdelrahman Ahmed (United Arab Emirates)
FOOD SECURITY (Agenda item 23a)
A/C.2/78/SR.16
POVERTY—INTERNATIONAL DECADES (Agenda item 21a)
A/C.2/78/SR.16
RURAL POVERTY (Agenda item 21b)
A/C.2/78/SR.16

Almansouri, Ali Ahmad M.A. (Qatar)
TERRORISM (Agenda item 109)
A/C.6/78/SR.2

Almarzooqi, Hazem Abdulqader Khalifa Abdulla (Bahrain)
TERRORISM (Agenda item 109)
A/C.6/78/SR.4

Almezyad, Fatma (Kuwait)
FOOD SECURITY (Agenda item 23a)
A/C.2/78/SR.17
POVERTY—INTERNATIONAL DECADES (Agenda item 21a)
A/C.2/78/SR.17
RURAL POVERTY (Agenda item 21b)
A/C.2/78/SR.17

Almezyad, Fatma (Kuwait) (continued)
TERRITORIES OCCUPIED BY ISRAEL—NATURAL RESOURCES (Agenda item 59)
A/C.2/78/SR.19

Almhawas, Ibtihal (Saudi Arabia)
RULE OF LAW (Agenda item 83)
A/C.6/78/SR.18

Almuaithir, Nouf (Saudi Arabia)
UN CHARTER—REPORTS (Agenda item 82)
A/C.6/78/SR.33

Alnasr, Mohammed Khalifa H. (Qatar)
CONFERENCE AND MEETING SERVICES (Agenda item 137)
A/C.5/78/SR.7
UN—BUDGET (2024) (Agenda item 134)
A/C.5/78/SR.26/PartII
UN—PROGRAMME PLANNING (Agenda item 135)
A/C.5/78/SR.24

Alnasr, Mohammed Khalifa H. (Qatar) (Gulf Cooperation Council)
UN—HUMAN RESOURCES MANAGEMENT (Agenda item 139)
A/C.5/78/SR.27
UN. GENERAL ASSEMBLY (78TH SESS. : 2023-2024). 5TH COMMITTEE—WORK ORGANIZATION (Agenda item 7)
A/C.5/78/SR.27

Alnesf, Sharifa Yousef A.S. (Qatar)
ARMED CONFLICTS PREVENTION (Agenda item 31a)
A/78/PV.72
SPORTS—OLYMPIC GAMES (Agenda item 11)
A/78/PV.38
UN. SECURITY COUNCIL—MEMBERSHIP (Agenda item 121)
A/78/PV.36

Alnuaimi, Hessa (United Arab Emirates)
NUCLEAR DISARMAMENT (Agenda item 99b)
A/C.1/78/PV.14
NUCLEAR NON-PROLIFERATION—INTERNATIONAL OBLIGATIONS (Agenda item 99w)
A/C.1/78/PV.14

Alnwelati, Mohammad Feras (Syrian Arab Republic)
PEACE (Agenda item 14)
A/78/PV.62
SANCTIONS—INTERNATIONAL RELATIONS (Agenda item 71b)
A/C.3/78/SR.28
UN HIGH COMMISSIONER FOR REFUGEES—REPORTS (Agenda item 60)
A/C.3/78/SR.45

Alodaib, Khalid Nasser A. (Saudi Arabia)
TERRORISM (Agenda item 109)
A/C.6/78/SR.4

Alolama, Mohd Abdulrahman Mohamed Jalil Sultan (United Arab Emirates)
EMERGENCY ASSISTANCE (Agenda item 72a)
A/78/PV.47
PALESTINIANS—ASSISTANCE (Agenda item 72b)
A/78/PV.47

Alomair, Reem Fahad O. (Saudi Arabia)
CENTRAL ASIA—ZONES OF PEACE (Agenda item 64)
A/78/PV.85
FINANCIAL FLOWS (Agenda item 16f)
A/C.2/78/SR.9
INTERNATIONAL TRADE (Agenda item 16a)
A/C.2/78/SR.9
MACROECONOMIC POLICY (Agenda item 16)
A/C.2/78/SR.9
SUSTAINABLE DEVELOPMENT (Agenda item 18)
A/C.2/78/SR.24
UN. GENERAL ASSEMBLY (78TH SESS. : 2023-2024). 2ND COMMITTEE—GENERAL DEBATE (Agenda item 8)
A/C.2/78/SR.4

Alonso Giganto, Ana María (Spain)
HUMAN RIGHTS—AFGHANISTAN (Agenda item 71c)
A/C.3/78/SR.34
SEXUAL ORIENTATION (Agenda item 71b)
A/C.3/78/SR.39
SOCIAL CONDITIONS (Agenda item 24b)
A/C.3/78/SR.3
SOCIAL DEVELOPMENT (Agenda item 24)
A/C.3/78/SR.3
WOMEN'S ADVANCEMENT (Agenda item 25a)
A/C.3/78/SR.7; A/C.3/78/SR.9
WOMEN'S ADVANCEMENT—CONFERENCES (Agenda item 25b)
A/C.3/78/SR.7; A/C.3/78/SR.9

Alonso Giganto, Ana María (Spain) (European Union)
CRIME PREVENTION (Agenda item 107)
A/C.3/78/SR.50
FAMILY (Agenda item 24b)
A/C.3/78/SR.49
HEALTH (Agenda item 125)
A/78/PV.48
HUMAN RIGHTS INSTITUTIONS—CENTRAL AFRICA (Agenda item 71b)
A/C.3/78/SR.56
MIGRANTS—PROTECTION (Agenda item 71b)
A/C.3/78/SR.56
RIGHT TO DEVELOPMENT (Agenda item 71b)
A/C.3/78/SR.48
RIGHTS OF THE CHILD (Agenda item 67)
A/C.3/78/SR.55

Alonso Giganto, Ana María (Spain) (European Union) (continued)

RURAL WOMEN (Agenda item 25a)
A/C.3/78/SR.49
SANCTIONS—INTERNATIONAL RELATIONS (Agenda item 71b)
A/C.3/78/SR.48
SOCIAL DEVELOPMENT—CONFERENCES (Agenda item 24a)
A/C.3/78/SR.55
UN. HUMAN RIGHTS COUNCIL—REPORTS (Agenda item 66)
A/C.3/78/SR.51
WOMEN MIGRANT WORKERS (Agenda item 25a)
A/C.3/78/SR.49

Alonso Giganto, Ana María (Spain) (UN. Group of Latin American and Caribbean States)

RIGHTS OF THE CHILD (Agenda item 67)
A/C.3/78/SR.55

Alqaisi, Sultan Natheir Mustafa (Jordan)

DISARMAMENT—GENERAL AND COMPLETE (Agenda item 99)
A/C.1/78/PV.19; A/C.1/78/PV.23
RESPONSIBILITY TO PROTECT (Agenda item 129)
A/78/PV.96
UN. GENERAL ASSEMBLY (78TH SESS. : 2023-2024). 1ST COMMITTEE—GENERAL DEBATE (Agenda item 8)
A/C.1/78/PV.5
VETO (Agenda item 63)
A/78/PV.67

Alqaisi, Sultan Natheir Mustafa (Jordan) (Group of Arab States)

ARMS RACE—OUTER SPACE (Agenda item 97a)
A/C.1/78/PV.16; A/C.1/78/PV.17
BIOLOGICAL WEAPONS—TREATIES (Agenda item 106)
A/C.1/78/PV.14
CHEMICAL WEAPONS—TREATIES (Agenda item 99l)
A/C.1/78/PV.14
CONVENTIONAL WEAPONS (Agenda item 99u)
A/C.1/78/PV.28
DISARMAMENT—GENERAL AND COMPLETE (Agenda item 99)
A/C.1/78/PV.19; A/C.1/78/PV.21; A/C.1/78/PV.23
DISARMAMENT—UN. GENERAL ASSEMBLY (4TH SPECIAL SESS. ON DISARMAMENT : xxxx) (Agenda item 99h)
A/C.1/78/PV.22
DISARMAMENT AGREEMENTS—OUTER SPACE (Agenda item 97c)
A/C.1/78/PV.16
DISARMAMENT-DEVELOPMENT LINK (Agenda item 99d)
A/C.1/78/PV.20

Alqaisi, Sultan Natheir Mustafa (Jordan) (Group of Arab States) (continued)

INFORMATION—INTERNATIONAL SECURITY (Agenda item 94)
A/C.1/78/PV.20
MIDDLE EAST—NUCLEAR-WEAPON-FREE ZONES (Agenda item 95)
A/C.1/78/PV.14; A/C.1/78/PV.21
MULTILATERALISM—DISARMAMENT (Agenda item 99r)
A/C.1/78/PV.20; A/C.1/78/PV.21
OUTER SPACE—CONFIDENCE-BUILDING MEASURES (Agenda item 99v)
A/C.1/78/PV.16
OUTER SPACE—PRINCIPLES (Agenda item 97d)
A/C.1/78/PV.16
SMALL ARMS—ILLICIT TRAFFIC (Agenda item 99p)
A/C.1/78/PV.28
UN. CONFERENCE ON DISARMAMENT—REPORTS (Agenda item 101a)
A/C.1/78/PV.22
UN. DISARMAMENT COMMISSION—REPORTS (Agenda item 101b)
A/C.1/78/PV.22

Alqudah, Mohammad Abdel Rahman Hasan (Jordan)

SUSTAINABLE DEVELOPMENT (Agenda item 18)
A/C.2/78/SR.24

AlRasheed, Mohammed Abdullah (Saudi Arabia)

UN—BUDGET (2024) (Agenda item 134)
A/C.5/78/SR.13

Alrowaiei, Jamal Fares (Bahrain)

PALESTINE QUESTION (Agenda item 35)
A/78/PV.40
PEACE (Agenda item 14)
A/78/PV.76
SPORTS—OLYMPIC GAMES (Agenda item 11)
A/78/PV.38
UN. GENERAL ASSEMBLY (78TH SESS. : 2023-2024). 1ST COMMITTEE—GENERAL DEBATE (Agenda item 8)
A/C.1/78/PV.9
VETO (Agenda item 63)
A/78/PV.67; A/78/PV.75

Alrowaiei, Jamal Fares (Bahrain) (Group of Arab States)

UN. SECURITY COUNCIL—MEMBERSHIP (Agenda item 121)
A/78/PV.34; A/78/PV.104
VETO (Agenda item 63)
A/78/PV.51

Alrowaiei, Jamal Fares (Bahrain) (UN. Group of Asia-Pacific States)

RACIAL DISCRIMINATION—ELIMINATION (Agenda item 69a)
A/78/PV.63

AlSabah, Khaled S. (Kuwait)

UN. HUMAN RIGHTS COUNCIL—REPORTS (Agenda item 66)
A/78/PV.23

Alsaeedi, Abdulaziz (Kuwait)

IAEA—REPORTS (Agenda item 89)
A/78/PV.29

Alsalem, Reem (UN. Human Rights Council. Special Rapporteur on Violence against Women and Girls, its Causes and its Consequences)

WOMEN'S ADVANCEMENT (Agenda item 25a)
A/C.3/78/SR.7
WOMEN'S ADVANCEMENT—CONFERENCES (Agenda item 25b)
A/C.3/78/SR.7

Alsammak, Uday Qais Mahdi (Iraq)

INFORMATION (Agenda item 53)
A/C.4/78/SR.13
OUTER SPACE—PEACEFUL USES—INTERNATIONAL COOPERATION (Agenda item 48)
A/C.4/78/SR.15

Alscher, Daniel Friedrich (Germany)

UN. SECURITY COUNCIL—REPORTS (Agenda item 26)
A/78/PV.93

Alseyabi, Eman (United Arab Emirates)

PERSONS WITH DISABILITIES (Agenda item 24b)
A/C.3/78/SR.3
SOCIAL CONDITIONS (Agenda item 24b)
A/C.3/78/SR.3
SOCIAL DEVELOPMENT (Agenda item 24)
A/C.3/78/SR.3

Alshahin, Essam (Iran (Islamic Republic of))

UN. COMMITTEE FOR PROGRAMME AND COORDINATION—MEMBERS (Agenda item 114a)
A/78/PV.37

Alshahin, Essam (Syrian Arab Republic)

RESPONSIBILITY TO PROTECT (Agenda item 129)
A/78/PV.99
UN. SECURITY COUNCIL—REPORTS (Agenda item 26)
A/78/PV.93

Alshaikh, Hayfaa Abdullatif A. (Saudi Arabia)

UN—FINANCIAL SITUATION (Agenda item 136)
A/C.5/78/SR.38

Alshamsi, Khaula Ali Khamis Obaid (United Arab Emirates)

UN. INTERNATIONAL COURT OF JUSTICE—REPORTS (Agenda item 73)
A/78/PV.28

Alshamsi, Mohamed (United Arab Emirates)

YOUTH (Agenda item 24b)
A/C.3/78/SR.3

Alsharhan, Reem (Kuwait)

DISARMAMENT—GENERAL AND COMPLETE (Agenda item 99)
A/C.1/78/PV.24

Alsindi, Yusuf Khaled (Bahrain)

FOOD SECURITY (Agenda item 23a)
A/C.2/78/SR.17
POVERTY—INTERNATIONAL DECADES (Agenda item 21a)
A/C.2/78/SR.17
RURAL POVERTY (Agenda item 21b)
A/C.2/78/SR.17

Altarsha, Elie (Syrian Arab Republic)

AGEING PERSONS (Agenda item 24b)
A/C.3/78/SR.1
ALBINISM (Agenda item 71b)
A/C.3/78/SR.27
CRIME PREVENTION (Agenda item 107)
A/C.3/78/SR.6; A/C.3/78/SR.51
CUBA—UNITED STATES (Agenda item 38)
A/78/PV.24
DISAPPEARANCE OF PERSONS (Agenda item 71b)
A/C.3/78/SR.22
DISPLACED PERSONS (Agenda item 71b)
A/C.3/78/SR.49
ELECTION VERIFICATION—UN (Agenda item 71b)
A/C.3/78/SR.50
EXTERNAL DEBT—HUMAN RIGHTS (Agenda item 71b)
A/C.3/78/SR.32
FREEDOM OF EXPRESSION (Agenda item 71b)
A/C.3/78/SR.19
HEALTH (Agenda item 125)
A/78/PV.41
HUMAN RIGHTS (Agenda item 71)
A/C.3/78/SR.16; A/C.3/78/SR.25
HUMAN RIGHTS—DEMOCRATIC PEOPLE'S REPUBLIC OF KOREA (Agenda item 71c)
A/C.3/78/SR.33; A/C.3/78/SR.53
HUMAN RIGHTS—ERITREA (Agenda item 71c)
A/C.3/78/SR.36
HUMAN RIGHTS—IRAN (ISLAMIC REPUBLIC OF) (Agenda item 71c)
A/C.3/78/SR.34; A/C.3/78/SR.53
HUMAN RIGHTS—REPORTS (Agenda item 71c)
A/C.3/78/SR.25

Altarsha, Elie (Syrian Arab Republic) (continued)

HUMAN RIGHTS—RUSSIAN FEDERATION (Agenda item 71c)
A/C.3/78/SR.37
HUMAN RIGHTS—SYRIAN ARAB REPUBLIC (Agenda item 71c)
A/C.3/78/SR.34; A/C.3/78/SR.54
HUMAN RIGHTS—TERRITORIES OCCUPIED BY ISRAEL (Agenda item 71c)
A/C.3/78/SR.35
HUMAN RIGHTS—UKRAINE (Agenda item 71c)
A/C.3/78/SR.53
HUMAN RIGHTS ACTIVISTS (Agenda item 71b)
A/C.3/78/SR.56
HUMAN RIGHTS ADVANCEMENT (Agenda item 71b)
A/C.3/78/SR.52
INDIGENOUS PEOPLES (Agenda item 68a)
A/C.3/78/SR.15
INDIGENOUS PEOPLES—CONFERENCES (Agenda item 68b)
A/C.3/78/SR.15
INTERNATIONAL TRADE (Agenda item 16a)
A/C.2/78/SR.24
MIGRANTS—PROTECTION (Agenda item 71b)
A/C.3/78/SR.23
PERSONS WITH DISABILITIES—HUMAN RIGHTS (Agenda item 71a)
A/C.3/78/SR.38; A/C.3/78/SR.51
POVERTY—HUMAN RIGHTS (Agenda item 71b)
A/C.3/78/SR.30
RACIAL DISCRIMINATION—ELIMINATION (Agenda item 69a)
A/78/PV.103; A/C.3/78/SR.47
RIGHT TO DEVELOPMENT (Agenda item 71b)
A/C.3/78/SR.20
RIGHT TO EDUCATION (Agenda item 71b)
A/C.3/78/SR.27
RIGHT TO FOOD (Agenda item 71b)
A/C.3/78/SR.30
RIGHT TO HEALTH (Agenda item 71b)
A/C.3/78/SR.39
RIGHT TO PRIVACY (Agenda item 71b)
A/C.3/78/SR.21
RIGHTS OF THE CHILD (Agenda item 67)
A/C.3/78/SR.11; A/C.3/78/SR.12; A/C.3/78/SR.13; A/C.3/78/SR.55
RURAL WOMEN (Agenda item 25a)
A/C.3/78/SR.49
SELF-DETERMINATION OF PEOPLES (Agenda item 70)
A/C.3/78/SR.42; A/C.3/78/SR.49
SOCIAL DEVELOPMENT (Agenda item 24)
A/C.3/78/SR.3
TERRORISM—HUMAN RIGHTS (Agenda item 71b)
A/C.3/78/SR.31
TORTURE AND OTHER CRUEL TREATMENT (Agenda item 71a)
A/C.3/78/SR.18
TRAFFICKING IN PERSONS (Agenda item 71b)
A/C.3/78/SR.23

Altarsha, Elie (Syrian Arab Republic) (continued)

UN. HUMAN RIGHTS COUNCIL—REPORTS (Agenda item 66)
A/C.3/78/SR.46; A/C.3/78/SR.51
UN HIGH COMMISSIONER FOR REFUGEES—REPORTS (Agenda item 60)
A/C.3/78/SR.44
WOMEN'S ADVANCEMENT (Agenda item 25a)
A/C.3/78/SR.7; A/C.3/78/SR.9
WOMEN'S ADVANCEMENT—CONFERENCES (Agenda item 25b)
A/C.3/78/SR.7; A/C.3/78/SR.9

Altarsha, Elie (Syrian Arab Republic) (Group of Friends in Defence of the Charter of the United Nations)

RACIAL DISCRIMINATION—ELIMINATION (Agenda item 69a)
A/C.3/78/SR.40
RACIAL DISCRIMINATION—PROGRAMMES OF ACTION (Agenda item 69b)
A/C.3/78/SR.40

Alupo, Jessica (Uganda. Vice-President)

UN. GENERAL ASSEMBLY (78TH SESS. : 2023-2024)—GENERAL DEBATE (Agenda item 8)
A/78/PV.9
UN. GENERAL ASSEMBLY (78TH SESS. : 2023-2024)—SPECIAL STATEMENTS
A/78/PV.9

Alvarez, Maximiliano Javier (Argentina)

DECOLONIZATION (Agenda item 58)
A/C.4/78/SR.9
DECOLONIZATION—UN SYSTEM (Agenda item 56)
A/C.4/78/SR.9
FALKLAND ISLANDS (MALVINAS) QUESTION (Agenda item 42)
A/C.4/78/SR.2; A/C.4/78/SR.6; A/C.4/78/SR.7; A/C.4/78/SR.8; A/C.4/78/SR.9
INFORMATION (Agenda item 53)
A/C.4/78/SR.13
NON-SELF-GOVERNING TERRITORIES—ECONOMIC INTERESTS (Agenda item 55)
A/C.4/78/SR.9
OUTER SPACE—PEACEFUL USES—INTERNATIONAL COOPERATION (Agenda item 48)
A/C.4/78/SR.15
RADIATION EFFECTS (Agenda item 47)
A/C.4/78/SR.11
SELF-DETERMINATION OF PEOPLES (Agenda item 70)
A/C.3/78/SR.49

Alves, Nuno Moniz (Timor-Leste)

SMALL ARMS—ILLICIT TRAFFIC (Agenda item 99p)
A/C.1/78/PV.18

Alves, Nuno Moniz (Timor-Leste) (continued)
SMALL ARMS—ILLICIT TRAFFIC—ASSISTANCE (Agenda item 99n)
A/C.1/78/PV.18

Alwasil, Abdulaziz M.O. (Saudi Arabia)
EMERGENCY ASSISTANCE (Agenda item 72a)
A/78/PV.46
HEALTH (Agenda item 125)
A/78/PV.97
HUMAN RIGHTS—INTERNATIONAL INSTRUMENTS (Agenda item 71a)
A/C.3/78/SR.26
HUMAN RIGHTS—REPORTS (Agenda item 71c)
A/C.3/78/SR.26
INTERNATIONAL JURISDICTION (Agenda item 84)
A/C.6/78/SR.13
PALESTINE QUESTION (Agenda item 35)
A/78/PV.40
PALESTINIANS—ASSISTANCE (Agenda item 72b)
A/78/PV.46
PEACE (Agenda item 14)
A/78/PV.62; A/78/PV.77; A/78/PV.82
RIGHT TO DEVELOPMENT (Agenda item 71b)
A/C.3/78/SR.26
UN—BUDGET (2024) (Agenda item 134)
A/C.5/78/SR.5
UN—PROGRAMME PLANNING (Agenda item 135)
A/C.5/78/SR.5
UN. HUMAN RIGHTS COUNCIL—REPORTS (Agenda item 66)
A/78/PV.23
UN. SECURITY COUNCIL—MEMBERSHIP (Agenda item 121)
A/78/PV.36
VETO (Agenda item 63)
A/78/PV.60; A/78/PV.75

Alwasil, Abdulaziz M.O. (Saudi Arabia) (European Union)
HUMAN RIGHTS—MYANMAR (Agenda item 71c)
A/C.3/78/SR.53

Alwasil, Abdulaziz M.O. (Saudi Arabia) (Group of Arab States)
CRIMES AGAINST HUMANITY (Agenda item 80)
A/C.6/78/SR.38
TERRITORIES OCCUPIED BY ISRAEL—HUMAN RIGHTS (Agenda item 50)
A/C.4/78/SR.24
UNRWA—ACTIVITIES (Agenda item 49)
A/C.4/78/SR.22
VETO (Agenda item 63)
A/78/PV.66

Alwasil, Abdulaziz M.O. (Saudi Arabia) (Organisation of Islamic Cooperation)
HUMAN RIGHTS—MYANMAR (Agenda item 71c)
A/C.3/78/SR.53

Aly, Ahmed ((personal capacity))
WESTERN SAHARA QUESTION (Agenda item 58)
A/C.4/78/SR.4

Alyakin, Dmitry S. (Russian Federation)
UN—BUDGET CONTRIBUTIONS (Agenda item 138)
A/78/PV.16; A/C.5/78/SR.2

Amaya Garay, Sofía Alejandra (El Salvador)
RIGHT TO FOOD (Agenda item 71b)
A/C.3/78/SR.30
RIGHT TO HOUSING (Agenda item 71b)
A/C.3/78/SR.30

Ammar, Nabil (Tunisia)
UN. GENERAL ASSEMBLY (78TH SESS. : 2023-2024)—GENERAL DEBATE (Agenda item 8)
A/78/PV.12

Amorín, Carlos Daniel (Uruguay)
DECOLONIZATION (Agenda item 58)
A/C.4/78/SR.2
FALKLAND ISLANDS (MALVINAS) QUESTION (Agenda item 42)
A/C.4/78/SR.2
PEACEKEEPING OPERATIONS (Agenda item 51)
A/C.4/78/SR.19
RIGHTS OF THE CHILD (Agenda item 67)
A/C.3/78/SR.13
VETO (Agenda item 63)
A/78/PV.61; A/78/PV.75; A/78/PV.78

Amorín, Carlos Daniel (Uruguay) (UN. General Assembly. 2nd Committee. Chair)
COMMODITIES (Agenda item 16d)
A/C.2/78/SR.14
SUSTAINABLE DEVELOPMENT (Agenda item 18)
A/C.2/78/SR.14
UN—PROGRAMME PLANNING (Agenda item 135)
A/C.2/78/SR.1
UN. GENERAL ASSEMBLY (78TH SESS. : 2023-2024). 2ND COMMITTEE—GENERAL DEBATE (Agenda item 8)
A/C.2/78/SR.2
UN. GENERAL ASSEMBLY (78TH SESS. : 2023-2024). 2ND COMMITTEE—WORK ORGANIZATION (Agenda item 7)
A/C.2/78/SR.1; A/C.2/78/SR.25

Amrollahi, Mohammad Taghi (Iran (Islamic Republic of))
UN—BUDGET (2024) (Agenda item 134)
A/78/PV.73; A/C.5/78/SR.3; A/C.5/78/SR.26/PartII; A/C.5/78/SR.28; A/C.5/78/SR.34
UN—PROGRAMME PLANNING (Agenda item 135)
A/78/PV.50(Resumption1); A/C.5/78/SR.24

Anderegg, Julius (Switzerland)
DISARMAMENT AGREEMENTS—OUTER SPACE (Agenda item 97c)
A/C.1/78/PV.27
INFORMATION—INTERNATIONAL SECURITY (Agenda item 94)
A/C.1/78/PV.29
MIDDLE EAST—NUCLEAR PROLIFERATION (Agenda item 102)
A/C.1/78/PV.26
NUCLEAR DISARMAMENT—CONFERENCES (Agenda item 99aa)
A/C.1/78/PV.26
NUCLEAR DISARMAMENT—TREATY COMPLIANCE (Agenda item 99q)
A/C.1/78/PV.26
NUCLEAR WEAPONS—ELIMINATION (Agenda item 99z)
A/C.1/78/PV.26
NUCLEAR WEAPONS—TREATIES (Agenda item 99ff)
A/C.1/78/PV.26
WEAPONS—OUTER SPACE (Agenda item 97b)
A/C.1/78/PV.27

Andersen, Julie Juel (Denmark)
YOUTH (Agenda item 24b)
A/C.3/78/SR.55

Andersen, Tor Henrik (Norway)
ARMS TRANSFERS—TREATIES (Agenda item 99x)
A/C.1/78/PV.19
CLUSTER MUNITIONS (Agenda item 99dd)
A/C.1/78/PV.19
DISARMAMENT—GENERAL AND COMPLETE (Agenda item 99)
A/C.1/78/PV.19; A/C.1/78/PV.30
LANDMINES—TREATIES (Agenda item 99m)
A/C.1/78/PV.19

André Tinoco, Arnoldo (Costa Rica)
UN. GENERAL ASSEMBLY (78TH SESS. : 2023-2024)—GENERAL DEBATE (Agenda item 8)
A/78/PV.11

Andrews, Lasana (Saint Vincent and the Grenadines)
DECOLONIZATION (Agenda item 58)
A/C.4/78/SR.8
FALKLAND ISLANDS (MALVINAS) QUESTION (Agenda item 42)
A/C.4/78/SR.8
PEACE (Agenda item 14)
A/78/PV.82
WESTERN SAHARA QUESTION (Agenda item 58)
A/C.4/78/SR.8

Andrews, Thomas H. (UN. Human Rights Council. Special Rapporteur on the Situation of Human Rights in Myanmar)
HUMAN RIGHTS—MYANMAR (Agenda item 71c)
A/C.3/78/SR.33

Andriamiarisoa, Vero Henintsoa (Madagascar) (UN. Group of African States)
SOCIAL DEVELOPMENT (Agenda item 24)
A/C.3/78/SR.47

Andrić, Katarina (Croatia)
DISAPPEARANCE OF PERSONS (Agenda item 71b)
A/C.3/78/SR.22
RIGHTS OF THE CHILD (Agenda item 67)
A/C.3/78/SR.11

Andújar, Luz del Carmen (Dominican Republic)
AGEING PERSONS (Agenda item 24b)
A/C.3/78/SR.1; A/C.3/78/SR.3
CLIMATE CHANGE (Agenda item 71b)
A/C.3/78/SR.29
ELECTION VERIFICATION—UN (Agenda item 71b)
A/C.3/78/SR.50
ENVIRONMENT (Agenda item 71b)
A/C.3/78/SR.29
HUMAN RIGHTS—AFGHANISTAN (Agenda item 71c)
A/C.3/78/SR.34
PERSONS WITH DISABILITIES (Agenda item 24b)
A/C.3/78/SR.3
RIGHT TO FOOD (Agenda item 71b)
A/C.3/78/SR.30
SOCIAL DEVELOPMENT (Agenda item 24)
A/C.3/78/SR.3
TORTURE AND OTHER CRUEL TREATMENT (Agenda item 71a)
A/C.3/78/SR.18
TRAFFICKING IN PERSONS (Agenda item 71b)
A/C.3/78/SR.23
UN. HUMAN RIGHTS COUNCIL—REPORTS (Agenda item 66)
A/C.3/78/SR.46
YOUTH (Agenda item 24b)
A/C.3/78/SR.3; A/C.3/78/SR.55

Angarón Bolea, María del Mar (Spain) (European Union)
TERRITORIES OCCUPIED BY ISRAEL—HUMAN RIGHTS (Agenda item 50)
A/C.4/78/SR.26

Angola Mejía, Nassoli Bibiana (Asociación Colombiana de Amistad con el Pueblo Saharaui)
WESTERN SAHARA QUESTION (Agenda item 58)
A/C.4/78/SR.4

Annadif, Mahamat Saleh (Chad)

UN. GENERAL ASSEMBLY (78TH SESS. : 2023-2024)—GENERAL DEBATE (Agenda item 8)
A/78/PV.9

Antonova, Anna V. (Russian Federation)

DISASTER VICTIMS (Agenda item 86)
A/C.6/78/SR.6
MARINE ECOSYSTEMS—BIOLOGICAL DIVERSITY (Agenda item 75c)
A/78/PV.73; A/78/PV.103
NON-CITIZENS—DEPORTATION (Agenda item 81)
A/C.6/78/SR.34
PEACEKEEPING OPERATIONS—CRIMINAL LIABILITY (Agenda item 76)
A/C.6/78/SR.8
RESPONSIBILITY OF INTERNATIONAL ORGANIZATIONS (Agenda item 85)
A/C.6/78/SR.19
UN. GENERAL ASSEMBLY—WORK PROGRAMME (Agenda item 120)
A/C.6/78/SR.36

Anulo, Semalign Kebede (Ethiopia)

CUBA—UNITED STATES (Agenda item 38)
A/78/PV.24
UN. SECURITY COUNCIL—MEMBERSHIP (Agenda item 121)
A/78/PV.36

Anyaegbu, Ezekwesiri David (Nigeria)

SUSTAINABLE DEVELOPMENT (Agenda item 18)
A/C.2/78/SR.24

Anyanah, Bismark (Ghana)

CRIME PREVENTION (Agenda item 107)
A/C.3/78/SR.6
CYBERCRIME (Agenda item 108)
A/C.3/78/SR.6

Apraxine, Pierre (International Committee of the Red Cross)

INTERNATIONAL JURISDICTION (Agenda item 84)
A/C.6/78/SR.13
TERRORISM (Agenda item 109)
A/C.6/78/SR.5

Aquilina, Cara Borg (Malta)

PERSONS WITH DISABILITIES—HUMAN RIGHTS (Agenda item 71a)
A/C.3/78/SR.38
RACIAL DISCRIMINATION—ELIMINATION (Agenda item 69a)
A/C.3/78/SR.41
RACIAL DISCRIMINATION—PROGRAMMES OF ACTION (Agenda item 69b)
A/C.3/78/SR.41

Arab Bafrani, Fatemeh (Iran (Islamic Republic of))

AGEING PERSONS (Agenda item 24b)
A/C.3/78/SR.2
CRIME PREVENTION (Agenda item 107)
A/C.3/78/SR.5; A/C.3/78/SR.51; A/C.3/78/SR.56
CYBERCRIME (Agenda item 108)
A/C.3/78/SR.5
DEMOCRACY (Agenda item 71b)
A/C.3/78/SR.28
ELECTION VERIFICATION—UN (Agenda item 71b)
A/C.3/78/SR.50
FAMILY (Agenda item 24b)
A/C.3/78/SR.2
FREEDOM OF EXPRESSION (Agenda item 71b)
A/C.3/78/SR.19
HEALTH (Agenda item 125)
A/78/PV.48
HUMAN RIGHTS (Agenda item 71)
A/C.3/78/SR.16
HUMAN RIGHTS—DEMOCRATIC PEOPLE'S REPUBLIC OF KOREA (Agenda item 71c)
A/C.3/78/SR.33; A/C.3/78/SR.53
HUMAN RIGHTS—INTERNATIONAL INSTRUMENTS (Agenda item 71a)
A/C.3/78/SR.25
HUMAN RIGHTS—IRAN (ISLAMIC REPUBLIC OF) (Agenda item 71c)
A/78/PV.50; A/C.3/78/SR.18; A/C.3/78/SR.27; A/C.3/78/SR.34; A/C.3/78/SR.54
HUMAN RIGHTS—MYANMAR (Agenda item 71c)
A/C.3/78/SR.33
HUMAN RIGHTS—REPORTS (Agenda item 71c)
A/C.3/78/SR.18; A/C.3/78/SR.25
HUMAN RIGHTS—SYRIAN ARAB REPUBLIC (Agenda item 71c)
A/C.3/78/SR.34; A/C.3/78/SR.54
HUMAN RIGHTS—TERRITORIES OCCUPIED BY ISRAEL (Agenda item 71c)
A/C.3/78/SR.27; A/C.3/78/SR.35
HUMAN RIGHTS—UKRAINE (Agenda item 71c)
A/C.3/78/SR.53
HUMAN RIGHTS ACTIVISTS (Agenda item 71b)
A/C.3/78/SR.56
HUMAN RIGHTS ADVANCEMENT (Agenda item 71b)
A/C.3/78/SR.52
INDIGENOUS PEOPLES (Agenda item 68a)
A/C.3/78/SR.15; A/C.3/78/SR.48
INDIGENOUS PEOPLES—CONFERENCES (Agenda item 68b)
A/C.3/78/SR.15
PERSONS WITH DISABILITIES—HUMAN RIGHTS (Agenda item 71a)
A/C.3/78/SR.38; A/C.3/78/SR.51
RACIAL DISCRIMINATION—ELIMINATION (Agenda item 69a)
A/78/PV.103; A/C.3/78/SR.41
RACIAL DISCRIMINATION—PROGRAMMES OF ACTION (Agenda item 69b)
A/C.3/78/SR.41

Arab Bafrani, Fatemeh (Iran (Islamic Republic of)) (continued)

RELIGIOUS INTOLERANCE (Agenda item 71b)
A/C.3/78/SR.38
RIGHT TO DEVELOPMENT (Agenda item 71b)
A/C.3/78/SR.20
RIGHT TO FOOD (Agenda item 71b)
A/C.3/78/SR.30
RIGHTS OF THE CHILD (Agenda item 67)
A/C.3/78/SR.11; A/C.3/78/SR.12; A/C.3/78/SR.55
RURAL WOMEN (Agenda item 25a)
A/C.3/78/SR.49
SANCTIONS—INTERNATIONAL RELATIONS (Agenda item 71b)
A/C.3/78/SR.25; A/C.3/78/SR.28
SELF-DETERMINATION OF PEOPLES (Agenda item 70)
A/C.3/78/SR.49
SOCIAL CONDITIONS (Agenda item 24b)
A/C.3/78/SR.51
TORTURE AND OTHER CRUEL TREATMENT (Agenda item 71a)
A/C.3/78/SR.18
UN. HUMAN RIGHTS COUNCIL—REPORTS (Agenda item 66)
A/78/PV.23; A/C.3/78/SR.46; A/C.3/78/SR.51
UN HIGH COMMISSIONER FOR REFUGEES—REPORTS (Agenda item 60)
A/C.3/78/SR.44; A/C.3/78/SR.51
UN RESOLUTIONS—IMPLEMENTATION (Agenda item 119)
A/78/PV.103
WOMEN MIGRANT WORKERS (Agenda item 25a)
A/C.3/78/SR.49
WOMEN'S ADVANCEMENT (Agenda item 25a)
A/C.3/78/SR.8
WOMEN'S ADVANCEMENT—CONFERENCES (Agenda item 25b)
A/C.3/78/SR.8; A/C.3/78/SR.51
YOUTH (Agenda item 24b)
A/C.3/78/SR.2; A/C.3/78/SR.55

Araba, Marc Hermanne Gninadoou (Benin)

UN. GENERAL ASSEMBLY (78TH SESS. : 2023-2024)—GENERAL DEBATE (Agenda item 8)
A/78/PV.14

Aranda, Jorge Eduardo Ferreira Silva (Portugal)

INFORMATION (Agenda item 53)
A/C.4/78/SR.13
UN. GENERAL ASSEMBLY—WORK PROGRAMME (Agenda item 120)
A/78/PV.33
UN. GENERAL ASSEMBLY (78TH SESS. : 2023-2024)—OFFICERS (Agenda item 5)
A/C.6/78/SR.48
UN RESOLUTIONS—IMPLEMENTATION (Agenda item 119)
A/78/PV.33
UN YOUTH OFFICE—REPORTS (Agenda item 130)
A/78/PV.102

Aranda, Jorge Eduardo Ferreira Silva (Portugal) (continued)

VETO (Agenda item 63)
A/78/PV.52; A/78/PV.68; A/78/PV.70

Aras, Nisan Su (Türkiye)

UN—BUDGET (2024) (Agenda item 134)
A/C.5/78/SR.3; A/C.5/78/SR.5
UN—PROGRAMME PLANNING (Agenda item 135)
A/C.5/78/SR.5

Arbeiter, Richard (Canada)

HUMAN RIGHTS (Agenda item 71)
A/C.3/78/SR.16
HUMAN RIGHTS—AFGHANISTAN (Agenda item 71c)
A/C.3/78/SR.26
HUMAN RIGHTS—IRAN (ISLAMIC REPUBLIC OF) (Agenda item 71c)
A/C.3/78/SR.26; A/C.3/78/SR.53; A/C.3/78/SR.54
SEXUAL ORIENTATION (Agenda item 71b)
A/C.3/78/SR.26
TERRITORIES OCCUPIED BY ISRAEL—NATURAL RESOURCES (Agenda item 59)
A/C.2/78/SR.20
UN. GENERAL ASSEMBLY (78TH SESS. : 2023-2024). 5TH COMMITTEE—WORK ORGANIZATION (Agenda item 7)
A/C.5/78/SR.35
UNRWA—ACTIVITIES (Agenda item 49)
A/C.4/78/SR.26
VETO (Agenda item 63)
A/78/PV.3; A/78/PV.52
WOMEN'S ADVANCEMENT (Agenda item 25a)
A/C.3/78/SR.8
WOMEN'S ADVANCEMENT—CONFERENCES (Agenda item 25b)
A/C.3/78/SR.8

Arbesu Sancho, Gemma (Observatorio Asturiano de Derechos Humanos para el Sáhara Occidental (Spain))

WESTERN SAHARA QUESTION (Agenda item 58)
A/C.4/78/SR.4

Arce Catacora, Luis Alberto (Bolivia (Plurinational State of). President)

UN. GENERAL ASSEMBLY (78TH SESS. : 2023-2024)—GENERAL DEBATE (Agenda item 8)
A/78/PV.5
UN. GENERAL ASSEMBLY (78TH SESS. : 2023-2024)—SPECIAL STATEMENTS
A/78/PV.5

Archinard, Natália (Switzerland)

OUTER SPACE—PEACEFUL USES—INTERNATIONAL COOPERATION (Agenda item 48)
A/C.4/78/SR.16

Arditi di Castelvetere Manzo, Fiamma (Sovereign Order of Malta)

PERSONS WITH DISABILITIES—HUMAN RIGHTS (Agenda item 71a)
A/C.3/78/SR.38

Aref, Yahya (Iran (Islamic Republic of))

ARMED CONFLICTS PREVENTION (Agenda item 31a)
A/78/PV.72
CRIMES AGAINST HUMANITY (Agenda item 80)
A/C.6/78/SR.38; A/C.6/78/SR.40; A/C.6/78/SR.42; A/C.6/78/SR.43; A/C.6/78/SR.44; A/C.6/78/SR.45; A/C.6/78/SR.47
LAW OF THE SEA (Agenda item 75a)
A/78/PV.44
MARINE ECOSYSTEMS—BIOLOGICAL DIVERSITY (Agenda item 75c)
A/78/PV.44
STRADDLING FISH STOCKS (Agenda item 75b)
A/78/PV.44

Aref, Yahya (Iran (Islamic Republic of)) (Coordinating Bureau of the Non-Aligned Countries)

PEACEKEEPING OPERATIONS—CRIMINAL LIABILITY (Agenda item 76)
A/C.6/78/SR.8
UN. COMMITTEE ON RELATIONS WITH THE HOST COUNTRY—REPORTS (Agenda item 161)
A/C.6/78/SR.35

Arega, Elleni Henok (Ethiopia)

RURAL WOMEN (Agenda item 25a)
A/C.3/78/SR.10
WOMEN'S ADVANCEMENT (Agenda item 25a)
A/C.3/78/SR.10
WOMEN'S ADVANCEMENT—CONFERENCES (Agenda item 25b)
A/C.3/78/SR.10

Arega, Elleni Henok (Ethiopia) (UN. Group of African States)

WOMEN'S ADVANCEMENT (Agenda item 25a)
A/C.3/78/SR.7
WOMEN'S ADVANCEMENT—CONFERENCES (Agenda item 25b)
A/C.3/78/SR.7

Arévalo de León, César Bernardo (Guatemala. President)

MULTILATERALISM
A/78/PV.84
UN. GENERAL ASSEMBLY (78TH SESS. : 2023-2024)—SPECIAL STATEMENTS
A/78/PV.84

Aristov, Dmitry S. (Russian Federation)

DEVELOPMENT COOPERATION—MIDDLE-INCOME COUNTRIES (Agenda item 19c)
A/C.2/78/SR.10

Aristov, Dmitry S. (Russian Federation) (continued)

FOOD SECURITY (Agenda item 23a)
A/C.2/78/SR.17
HIV/AIDS—DECLARATIONS (Agenda item 10)
A/78/PV.91
INFORMATION TECHNOLOGY—DEVELOPMENT (Agenda item 15)
A/C.2/78/SR.10
POVERTY—INTERNATIONAL DECADES (Agenda item 21a)
A/C.2/78/SR.17
RURAL POVERTY (Agenda item 21b)
A/C.2/78/SR.17
SCIENCE AND TECHNOLOGY—DEVELOPMENT (Agenda item 19a)
A/C.2/78/SR.10

Armas García, Mercedes de (Cuba)

RIGHTS OF THE CHILD (Agenda item 67)
A/C.3/78/SR.12

Armbruster, Thomas (United States)

DEVELOPMENT FINANCE (Agenda item 16b)
A/C.2/78/SR.21
DISASTER PREVENTION (Agenda item 18c)
A/C.2/78/SR.21
ECONOMIC COOPERATION AMONG DEVELOPING COUNTRIES (Agenda item 22b)
A/C.2/78/SR.21
FINANCIAL FLOWS (Agenda item 16f)
A/C.2/78/SR.21
FOOD SECURITY (Agenda item 23a)
A/C.2/78/SR.21
HUMAN RIGHTS—DEMOCRATIC PEOPLE'S REPUBLIC OF KOREA (Agenda item 71c)
A/C.3/78/SR.33
HUMAN RIGHTS—MYANMAR (Agenda item 71c)
A/C.3/78/SR.33
INTERNATIONAL TRADE (Agenda item 16a)
A/C.2/78/SR.21
LANDLOCKED DEVELOPING COUNTRIES—CONFERENCES (Agenda item 20b)
A/C.2/78/SR.7
LAW OF THE SEA (Agenda item 75a)
A/78/PV.44
LEAST DEVELOPED COUNTRIES—CONFERENCES (Agenda item 20a)
A/C.2/78/SR.7
MARINE ECOSYSTEMS—BIOLOGICAL DIVERSITY (Agenda item 75c)
A/78/PV.44
STRADDLING FISH STOCKS (Agenda item 75b)
A/78/PV.44
SUSTAINABLE DEVELOPMENT (Agenda item 18)
A/C.2/78/SR.21
TERRITORIES OCCUPIED BY ISRAEL—NATURAL RESOURCES (Agenda item 59)
A/C.2/78/SR.21

Armstrong, Elia Yi (UN. Ethics Office. Director)

UN. ETHICS OFFICE—REPORTS (Agenda item 140)
A/C.5/78/SR.2

Aron, Andy (Indonesia)

CRIMES AGAINST HUMANITY (Agenda item 80)
A/C.6/78/SR.11; A/C.6/78/SR.38; A/C.6/78/SR.39; A/C.6/78/SR.42
DISASTER VICTIMS (Agenda item 86)
A/C.6/78/SR.5; A/C.6/78/SR.36
HUMAN RIGHTS—INTERNATIONAL INSTRUMENTS (Agenda item 71a)
A/C.3/78/SR.26
NUCLEAR DISARMAMENT (Agenda item 99b)
A/C.1/78/PV.11
NUCLEAR NON-PROLIFERATION—INTERNATIONAL OBLIGATIONS (Agenda item 99w)
A/C.1/78/PV.11
NUCLEAR WEAPON TESTS—TREATIES (Agenda item 105)
A/C.1/78/PV.11
NUCLEAR WEAPONS—TREATIES (Agenda item 99ff)
A/C.1/78/PV.11
RULE OF LAW (Agenda item 83)
A/C.6/78/SR.18
UN. GENERAL ASSEMBLY—WORK PROGRAMME (Agenda item 120)
A/78/PV.32
UN. INTERNATIONAL LAW COMMISSION—REPORTS (Agenda item 79)
A/C.6/78/SR.30
UN RESOLUTIONS—IMPLEMENTATION (Agenda item 119)
A/78/PV.32

Aron, Andy (Indonesia) (Coordinating Bureau of the Non-Aligned Countries)

BIOLOGICAL WEAPONS—TREATIES (Agenda item 106)
A/C.1/78/PV.14
CHEMICAL WEAPONS—TREATIES (Agenda item 99l)
A/C.1/78/PV.14
WEAPONS OF MASS DESTRUCTION—TERRORISM (Agenda item 99s)
A/C.1/78/PV.14

Arona, Sofia (San Marino)

RIGHTS OF THE CHILD (Agenda item 67)
A/C.3/78/SR.14

Arrocha Olabuenaga, Pablo Adrián (Mexico)

INTERNATIONAL JURISDICTION (Agenda item 84)
A/C.6/78/SR.12
TREATIES (Agenda item 87)
A/C.6/78/SR.20

Arrocha Olabuenaga, Pablo Adrián (Mexico) (continued)

UN. INTERNATIONAL LAW COMMISSION—REPORTS (Agenda item 79)
A/C.6/78/SR.29; A/C.6/78/SR.37
UN CHARTER—REPORTS (Agenda item 82)
A/C.6/78/SR.22

Arrojo Agudo, Pedro (UN. Human Rights Council. Special Rapporteur on the Human Right to Safe Drinking Water and Sanitation)

HUMAN RIGHTS—TERRITORIES OCCUPIED BY ISRAEL (Agenda item 71c)
A/C.3/78/SR.28
RIGHT TO DRINKING WATER (Agenda item 71b)
A/C.3/78/SR.28

Arumpac-Marte, Azela Guerrero (Philippines)

CRIMES AGAINST HUMANITY (Agenda item 80)
A/C.6/78/SR.11; A/C.6/78/SR.40; A/C.6/78/SR.42
INTERNATIONAL JURISDICTION (Agenda item 84)
A/C.6/78/SR.13
INTERNATIONAL LAW—TRAINING PROGRAMMES (Agenda item 78)
A/C.6/78/SR.21
LAW OF THE SEA (Agenda item 75a)
A/78/PV.44
MARINE ECOSYSTEMS—BIOLOGICAL DIVERSITY (Agenda item 75c)
A/78/PV.44
NON-CITIZENS—DEPORTATION (Agenda item 81)
A/C.6/78/SR.34
RESPONSIBILITY TO PROTECT (Agenda item 129)
A/78/PV.99
RULE OF LAW (Agenda item 83)
A/C.6/78/SR.16
STRADDLING FISH STOCKS (Agenda item 75b)
A/78/PV.44
TREATIES (Agenda item 87)
A/C.6/78/SR.20
UN. INTERNATIONAL LAW COMMISSION—REPORTS (Agenda item 79)
A/C.6/78/SR.28; A/C.6/78/SR.30
UN CHARTER—REPORTS (Agenda item 82)
A/C.6/78/SR.33
UN COMMISSION ON INTERNATIONAL TRADE LAW—REPORTS (Agenda item 77)
A/C.6/78/SR.14

Arumpac-Marte, Azela Guerrero (Philippines) (ASEAN)

RULE OF LAW (Agenda item 83)
A/C.6/78/SR.15

Aryal, Krishna (Nepal)

RIGHTS OF THE CHILD (Agenda item 67)
A/C.3/78/SR.12
WOMEN'S ADVANCEMENT (Agenda item 25a)
A/C.3/78/SR.7

Aryal, Krishna (Nepal) (continued)
WOMEN'S ADVANCEMENT—CONFERENCES (Agenda item 25b)
A/C.3/78/SR.7

Asaju, Bola (Nigeria)
AGEING PERSONS (Agenda item 24b)
A/C.3/78/SR.1
ELECTION VERIFICATION—UN (Agenda item 71b)
A/78/PV.50; A/C.3/78/SR.50
HUMAN RIGHTS—ERITREA (Agenda item 71c)
A/C.3/78/SR.36
HUMAN RIGHTS—INTERNATIONAL INSTRUMENTS (Agenda item 71a)
A/C.3/78/SR.25
HUMAN RIGHTS ACTIVISTS (Agenda item 71b)
A/C.3/78/SR.56
HUMAN RIGHTS ADVANCEMENT (Agenda item 71b)
A/C.3/78/SR.52
HUMAN RIGHTS INSTITUTIONS—CENTRAL AFRICA (Agenda item 71b)
A/C.3/78/SR.56
PERSONS WITH DISABILITIES—HUMAN RIGHTS (Agenda item 71a)
A/C.3/78/SR.51
RACIAL DISCRIMINATION—ELIMINATION (Agenda item 69a)
A/78/PV.63; A/78/PV.103; A/C.3/78/SR.41; A/C.3/78/SR.47
RACIAL DISCRIMINATION—PROGRAMMES OF ACTION (Agenda item 69b)
A/C.3/78/SR.41
RIGHTS OF THE CHILD (Agenda item 67)
A/C.3/78/SR.11; A/C.3/78/SR.13; A/C.3/78/SR.55
RURAL WOMEN (Agenda item 25a)
A/C.3/78/SR.49
SLAVERY—MEMORIALS (Agenda item 118)
A/78/PV.64
SOCIAL CONDITIONS (Agenda item 24b)
A/C.3/78/SR.3; A/C.3/78/SR.51
SOCIAL DEVELOPMENT (Agenda item 24)
A/C.3/78/SR.3
SOCIAL DEVELOPMENT—CONFERENCES (Agenda item 24a)
A/C.3/78/SR.3
UN. HUMAN RIGHTS COUNCIL—REPORTS (Agenda item 66)
A/C.3/78/SR.46
UN HIGH COMMISSIONER FOR REFUGEES—REPORTS (Agenda item 60)
A/C.3/78/SR.44
VETO (Agenda item 63)
A/78/PV.67
YOUTH (Agenda item 24b)
A/C.3/78/SR.55

Ashipala, Sevelina (Namibia)
RACIAL DISCRIMINATION—ELIMINATION (Agenda item 69a)
A/C.3/78/SR.40

Ashipala, Sevelina (Namibia) (continued)
RACIAL DISCRIMINATION—PROGRAMMES OF ACTION (Agenda item 69b)
A/C.3/78/SR.40
SELF-DETERMINATION OF PEOPLES (Agenda item 70)
A/C.3/78/SR.40

Assor Sydney, Solomon ((personal capacity))
WESTERN SAHARA QUESTION (Agenda item 58)
A/C.4/78/SR.6

Assoumani, Azali (Comoros. President)
UN. GENERAL ASSEMBLY (78TH SESS. : 2023-2024)—GENERAL DEBATE (Agenda item 8)
A/78/PV.7
UN. GENERAL ASSEMBLY (78TH SESS. : 2023-2024)—SPECIAL STATEMENTS
A/78/PV.7

Assoweh, Zeinab Ismaël (Djibouti)
INFORMATION—INTERNATIONAL SECURITY (Agenda item 94)
A/C.1/78/PV.29
UN. GENERAL ASSEMBLY (78TH SESS. : 2023-2024). 1ST COMMITTEE—GENERAL DEBATE (Agenda item 8)
A/C.1/78/PV.8

Ataeva, Aksoltan T. (Turkmenistan)
PEACE (Agenda item 14)
A/78/PV.63
SPORTS—OLYMPIC GAMES (Agenda item 11)
A/78/PV.107
SUSTAINABLE DEVELOPMENT (Agenda item 18)
A/C.2/78/SR.22; A/C.2/78/SR.23

Atanaszov, Anna Mária (Hungary)
AFRICA—DEVELOPMENT (Agenda item 65b)
A/78/PV.57
AFRICA—SUSTAINABLE DEVELOPMENT—PARTNERSHIP (Agenda item 65a)
A/78/PV.57

Atteib, Abdullah Ibrahim Abdelhamud Alsayed (Egypt)
UN CHARTER—REPORTS (Agenda item 82)
A/C.6/78/SR.34
UN COMMISSION ON INTERNATIONAL TRADE LAW—REPORTS (Agenda item 77)
A/C.6/78/SR.14

Aultman, Kallie (International Federation of Red Cross and Red Crescent Societies)
DISASTER PREVENTION (Agenda item 18c)
A/C.2/78/SR.15
DISASTER VICTIMS (Agenda item 86)
A/C.6/78/SR.7
HUMAN RIGHTS (Agenda item 71)
A/C.3/78/SR.28

Aultman, Kallie (International Federation of Red Cross and Red Crescent Societies) (continued)

HUMANITARIAN ASSISTANCE (Agenda item 72)
A/78/PV.47

Aurescu, Bogdan Lucian (UN. International Law Commission. Study Group on Sea-level Rise in Relation to International Law. Co-Chair)

UN. INTERNATIONAL LAW COMMISSION—REPORTS (Agenda item 79)
A/C.6/78/SR.28

Aviel, Shir (Israel)

AGEING PERSONS (Agenda item 24b)
A/C.3/78/SR.2
HUMAN RIGHTS—IRAN (ISLAMIC REPUBLIC OF) (Agenda item 71c)
A/C.3/78/SR.34
HUMAN RIGHTS—SYRIAN ARAB REPUBLIC (Agenda item 71c)
A/C.3/78/SR.34
MINORITIES (Agenda item 71b)
A/C.3/78/SR.39
PERSONS WITH DISABILITIES (Agenda item 24b)
A/C.3/78/SR.2
TORTURE AND OTHER CRUEL TREATMENT (Agenda item 71a)
A/C.3/78/SR.18
WOMEN'S ADVANCEMENT (Agenda item 25a)
A/C.3/78/SR.8
WOMEN'S ADVANCEMENT—CONFERENCES (Agenda item 25b)
A/C.3/78/SR.8
YOUTH (Agenda item 24b)
A/C.3/78/SR.2

Ávila Becerril, Ana Maricela (Costa Rica)

DISARMAMENT AGREEMENTS—OUTER SPACE (Agenda item 97c)
A/C.1/78/PV.27
INFORMATION—INTERNATIONAL SECURITY (Agenda item 94)
A/C.1/78/PV.21
NUCLEAR WEAPONS—ELIMINATION (Agenda item 99z)
A/C.1/78/PV.26
OUTER SPACE—PRINCIPLES (Agenda item 97d)
A/C.1/78/PV.27
WEAPONS—OUTER SPACE (Agenda item 97b)
A/C.1/78/PV.27

Aydil, İsmail (Türkiye)

CRIME PREVENTION (Agenda item 107)
A/C.3/78/SR.6
CYBERCRIME (Agenda item 108)
A/C.3/78/SR.6
HUMAN RIGHTS—AFGHANISTAN (Agenda item 71c)
A/C.3/78/SR.26

Aydil, İsmail (Türkiye) (continued)

HUMAN RIGHTS—INTERNATIONAL INSTRUMENTS (Agenda item 71a)
A/C.3/78/SR.26
HUMAN RIGHTS—REPORTS (Agenda item 71c)
A/C.3/78/SR.25
HUMAN RIGHTS—SYRIAN ARAB REPUBLIC (Agenda item 71c)
A/C.3/78/SR.26; A/C.3/78/SR.54
HUMAN RIGHTS—TERRITORIES OCCUPIED BY ISRAEL (Agenda item 71c)
A/C.3/78/SR.35
HUMAN RIGHTS—UKRAINE (Agenda item 71c)
A/C.3/78/SR.26
MINORITIES (Agenda item 71b)
A/C.3/78/SR.39; A/C.3/78/SR.52
RACIAL DISCRIMINATION—ELIMINATION (Agenda item 69a)
A/C.3/78/SR.42
RACIAL DISCRIMINATION—PROGRAMMES OF ACTION (Agenda item 69b)
A/C.3/78/SR.42
RIGHT TO DRINKING WATER (Agenda item 71b)
A/C.3/78/SR.28; A/C.3/78/SR.50
RIGHTS OF THE CHILD (Agenda item 67)
A/C.3/78/SR.14
SOCIAL CONDITIONS (Agenda item 24b)
A/78/PV.101
SUSTAINABLE DEVELOPMENT (Agenda item 18)
A/78/PV.107
UN HIGH COMMISSIONER FOR REFUGEES—REPORTS (Agenda item 60)
A/C.3/78/SR.45
WOMEN'S ADVANCEMENT (Agenda item 25a)
A/C.3/78/SR.10
WOMEN'S ADVANCEMENT—CONFERENCES (Agenda item 25b)
A/C.3/78/SR.10

Ayoune, Lia Berthiana Bouanga (Gabon)

DECOLONIZATION (Agenda item 58)
A/C.4/78/SR.9
WESTERN SAHARA QUESTION (Agenda item 58)
A/C.4/78/SR.9

Azad, Farzaneh Baniasad (Iran (Islamic Republic of))

WOMEN'S ADVANCEMENT (Agenda item 25a)
A/C.3/78/SR.10
WOMEN'S ADVANCEMENT—CONFERENCES (Agenda item 25b)
A/C.3/78/SR.10

Azzam, Rashed Jamal Ibrahim Ibrahim (United Arab Emirates)

LAW OF THE SEA (Agenda item 75a)
A/78/PV.44
MARINE ECOSYSTEMS—BIOLOGICAL DIVERSITY (Agenda item 75c)
A/78/PV.44

Azzam, Rashed Jamal Ibrahim Ibrahim (United Arab Emirates) (continued)

STRADDLING FISH STOCKS (Agenda item 75b)
A/78/PV.44

Babiker, Mohamed Abdelsalam (UN. Human Rights Council. Special Rapporteur on the Situation of Human Rights in Eritrea)

HUMAN RIGHTS—ERITREA (Agenda item 71c)
A/C.3/78/SR.36

Babikyan, Araksya (Armenia)

CLIMATE (Agenda item 18d)
A/C.2/78/SR.15
INFORMATION TECHNOLOGY—DEVELOPMENT (Agenda item 15)
A/C.2/78/SR.10
LANDLOCKED DEVELOPING COUNTRIES—CONFERENCES (Agenda item 20b)
A/C.2/78/SR.7
LEAST DEVELOPED COUNTRIES—CONFERENCES (Agenda item 20a)
A/C.2/78/SR.7
SCIENCE AND TECHNOLOGY—DEVELOPMENT (Agenda item 19a)
A/C.2/78/SR.10
SUSTAINABLE DEVELOPMENT (Agenda item 18)
A/C.2/78/SR.15
UN. GENERAL ASSEMBLY (78TH SESS. : 2023-2024). 2ND COMMITTEE—GENERAL DEBATE (Agenda item 8)
A/C.2/78/SR.5

Babo, Paul David (Cameroon)

UN. GENERAL ASSEMBLY (78TH SESS. : 2023-2024). 1ST COMMITTEE—GENERAL DEBATE (Agenda item 8)
A/C.1/78/PV.8

Bach, Thomas (International Olympic Committee)

SPORTS—OLYMPIC GAMES (Agenda item 11)
A/78/PV.38

Bachar Bong, Abdallah (UN. Advisory Committee on Administrative and Budgetary Questions. Chair)

CONFERENCE AND MEETING SERVICES (Agenda item 137)
A/C.5/78/SR.7
PERSONNEL QUESTIONS—UN SYSTEM (Agenda item 142)
A/C.5/78/SR.10
UN—ADMINISTRATION (Agenda item 132)
A/C.5/78/SR.32
UN—BUDGET (2023) (Agenda item 133)
A/C.5/78/SR.9
UN—BUDGET (2024) (Agenda item 134)
A/C.5/78/SR.5; A/C.5/78/SR.9; A/C.5/78/SR.14; A/C.5/78/SR.16; A/C.5/78/SR.17; A/C.5/78/SR.19; A/C.5/78/SR.21; A/C.5/78/SR.23; A/C.5/78/SR.24; A/C.5/78/SR.28; A/C.5/78/SR.30; A/C.5/78/SR.33

Bachar Bong, Abdallah (UN. Advisory Committee on Administrative and Budgetary Questions. Chair) (continued)

UN—FINANCIAL REPORTS (Agenda item 131)
A/C.5/78/SR.14

Badjie, Isatou (Gambia)

PEACEKEEPING OPERATIONS (Agenda item 51)
A/C.4/78/SR.19
WESTERN SAHARA QUESTION (Agenda item 58)
A/C.4/78/SR.6

Badubi, Ronald Seabo (Botswana)

DIAMONDS—FUELLING CONFLICT (Agenda item 30)
A/78/PV.65

Baerbock, Annalena (Germany)

UKRAINE—POLITICAL CONDITIONS (Agenda item 62)
A/78/PV.56

Baeriswyl, Pascale (Switzerland)

ARMED CONFLICTS PREVENTION (Agenda item 31a)
A/78/PV.72
HUMAN RIGHTS (Agenda item 71)
A/C.3/78/SR.16
RESPONSIBILITY TO PROTECT (Agenda item 129)
A/78/PV.96
UN—BUDGET (2024) (Agenda item 134)
A/C.5/78/SR.5; A/C.5/78/SR.14
UN—PROGRAMME PLANNING (Agenda item 135)
A/C.5/78/SR.5
UN. SECURITY COUNCIL—MEMBERSHIP (Agenda item 121)
A/78/PV.34
VETO (Agenda item 63)
A/78/PV.3; A/78/PV.70; A/78/PV.78

Baghaei Hamaneh, Esmaeil (Iran (Islamic Republic of))

TERRITORIES OCCUPIED BY ISRAEL—HUMAN RIGHTS (Agenda item 50)
A/C.4/78/SR.25
UN. INTERNATIONAL LAW COMMISSION—REPORTS (Agenda item 79)
A/C.6/78/SR.33

Baghdadi, Mohannad (Syrian Arab Republic)

DECOLONIZATION (Agenda item 58)
A/C.4/78/SR.7
HEALTH (Agenda item 125)
A/78/PV.16
PEACEKEEPING OPERATIONS (Agenda item 51)
A/C.4/78/SR.19
TERRITORIES OCCUPIED BY ISRAEL—HUMAN RIGHTS (Agenda item 50)
A/C.4/78/SR.25; A/C.4/78/SR.26
UNRWA—ACTIVITIES (Agenda item 49)
A/C.4/78/SR.23; A/C.4/78/SR.26

Baghdadi, Mohannad (Syrian Arab Republic) (continued)
WESTERN SAHARA QUESTION (Agenda item 58)
A/C.4/78/SR.7

Bailey, Claudine (Jamaica)
UN. INTERNATIONAL LAW COMMISSION—REPORTS (Agenda item 79)
A/C.6/78/SR.28; A/C.6/78/SR.33

Baimarro, Karen Jean (Sierra Leone)
PALESTINE QUESTION (Agenda item 35)
A/78/PV.40
SPECIAL POLITICAL MISSIONS (Agenda item 52)
A/C.4/78/SR.21
VETO (Agenda item 63)
A/78/PV.61

Baissuanov, Arman (Kazakhstan)
UN. GENERAL ASSEMBLY (78TH SESS. : 2023-2024). 1ST COMMITTEE—GENERAL DEBATE (Agenda item 8)
A/C.1/78/PV.5

Baka, Sondou (Togo)
HUMAN RIGHTS—INTERNATIONAL INSTRUMENTS (Agenda item 71a)
A/C.3/78/SR.26
HUMAN RIGHTS ADVANCEMENT (Agenda item 71b)
A/C.3/78/SR.26

Bakhit, Badreldeen Bakhit Musa (Sudan)
HUMAN RIGHTS—ERITREA (Agenda item 71c)
A/C.3/78/SR.36
UN—BUDGET (2024) (Agenda item 134)
A/78/PV.50(Resumption1); A/C.5/78/SR.4; A/C.5/78/SR.23; A/C.5/78/SR.26/PartII

Bakhsh, Khalid (Saudi Arabia)
FOOD SECURITY (Agenda item 23a)
A/C.2/78/SR.17
POVERTY—INTERNATIONAL DECADES (Agenda item 21a)
A/C.2/78/SR.17
RURAL POVERTY (Agenda item 21b)
A/C.2/78/SR.17

Bakradze, David (Georgia)
ORGANIZATION FOR DEMOCRACY AND ECONOMIC DEVELOPMENT - GUAM (Agenda item 32)
A/78/PV.85
UN. GENERAL ASSEMBLY (78TH SESS. : 2023-2024). 1ST COMMITTEE—GENERAL DEBATE (Agenda item 8)
A/C.1/78/PV.7
UN. INTERNATIONAL COURT OF JUSTICE—REPORTS (Agenda item 73)
A/78/PV.28

Bakytbekkyzy, Anel (Kazakhstan)
AGEING PERSONS (Agenda item 24b)
A/C.3/78/SR.2
RIGHTS OF THE CHILD (Agenda item 67)
A/C.3/78/SR.13
SOCIAL DEVELOPMENT (Agenda item 24)
A/C.3/78/SR.2
YOUTH (Agenda item 24b)
A/C.3/78/SR.2

Balakrishnan, Vivian (Singapore)
UN. GENERAL ASSEMBLY (78TH SESS. : 2023-2024)—GENERAL DEBATE (Agenda item 8)
A/78/PV.11

Balázs, Szilvia (Hungary)
UN. GENERAL ASSEMBLY (78TH SESS. : 2023-2024). 1ST COMMITTEE—GENERAL DEBATE (Agenda item 8)
A/C.1/78/PV.5

Balbino, Viviane Rios (Brazil)
ELECTION VERIFICATION—UN (Agenda item 71b)
A/C.3/78/SR.50
HUMAN RIGHTS—IRAN (ISLAMIC REPUBLIC OF) (Agenda item 71c)
A/C.3/78/SR.53
HUMAN RIGHTS—SYRIAN ARAB REPUBLIC (Agenda item 71c)
A/C.3/78/SR.54
INDIGENOUS PEOPLES (Agenda item 68a)
A/C.3/78/SR.48
RACIAL DISCRIMINATION—PROGRAMMES OF ACTION (Agenda item 69b)
A/C.3/78/SR.56
WOMEN'S ADVANCEMENT (Agenda item 25a)
A/C.3/78/SR.9
WOMEN'S ADVANCEMENT—CONFERENCES (Agenda item 25b)
A/C.3/78/SR.9

Baldé, Aua (UN. Human Rights Council. Working Group on Enforced or Involuntary Disappearances. Chair)
DISAPPEARANCE OF PERSONS (Agenda item 71b)
A/C.3/78/SR.22

Bálek, Václav (Czechia) (UN. Human Rights Council. President)
UN. HUMAN RIGHTS COUNCIL—REPORTS (Agenda item 66)
A/78/PV.23; A/C.3/78/SR.46

Balobaid, Ali Mabkhot Salem (Yemen)
CRIMES AGAINST HUMANITY (Agenda item 80)
A/C.6/78/SR.11

Balobaid, Ali Mabkhot Salem (Yemen) (continued)

HUMAN RIGHTS—INTERNATIONAL INSTRUMENTS (Agenda item 71a)
A/C.3/78/SR.28
RIGHTS OF THE CHILD (Agenda item 67)
A/C.3/78/SR.11; A/C.3/78/SR.14
SELF-DETERMINATION OF PEOPLES (Agenda item 70)
A/C.3/78/SR.43
TERRORISM (Agenda item 109)
A/C.6/78/SR.4
UN HIGH COMMISSIONER FOR REFUGEES—REPORTS (Agenda item 60)
A/C.3/78/SR.45

Balouji, Heidar Ali (Iran (Islamic Republic of)) (UN. General Assembly. 1st Committee. Rapporteur)

AFRICA—NUCLEAR-WEAPON-FREE ZONES (Agenda item 92)
A/78/PV.42
ARMS RACE—OUTER SPACE (Agenda item 97a)
A/78/PV.42
BIOLOGICAL WEAPONS—TREATIES (Agenda item 106)
A/78/PV.42
CONVENTIONAL WEAPONS—TREATIES (Agenda item 103)
A/78/PV.42
DISARMAMENT—GENERAL AND COMPLETE (Agenda item 99)
A/78/PV.42
DISARMAMENT—UN. GENERAL ASSEMBLY (10TH SPECIAL SESS. : 1978) (Agenda item 101)
A/78/PV.42
DISARMAMENT—UN. GENERAL ASSEMBLY (12TH SPECIAL SESS. : 1982) (Agenda item 100)
A/78/PV.42
DISARMAMENT AGREEMENTS—OUTER SPACE (Agenda item 97c)
A/78/PV.42
INDIAN OCEAN—ZONES OF PEACE (Agenda item 91)
A/78/PV.42
INFORMATION—INTERNATIONAL SECURITY (Agenda item 94)
A/78/PV.42
MEDITERRANEAN REGION—REGIONAL SECURITY (Agenda item 104)
A/78/PV.42
MIDDLE EAST—NUCLEAR PROLIFERATION (Agenda item 102)
A/78/PV.42
MIDDLE EAST—NUCLEAR-WEAPON-FREE ZONES (Agenda item 95)
A/78/PV.42
MILITARY BUDGETS (Agenda item 90)
A/78/PV.42
NON-NUCLEAR-WEAPON STATES—SECURITY (Agenda item 96)
A/78/PV.42

Balouji, Heidar Ali (Iran (Islamic Republic of)) (UN. General Assembly. 1st Committee. Rapporteur) (continued)

NUCLEAR WEAPON TESTS—TREATIES (Agenda item 105)
A/78/PV.42
OUTER SPACE—PRINCIPLES (Agenda item 97d)
A/78/PV.42
SCIENCE AND TECHNOLOGY—INTERNATIONAL SECURITY (Agenda item 98)
A/78/PV.42
UN—PROGRAMME PLANNING (Agenda item 135)
A/78/PV.42
UN. GENERAL ASSEMBLY—WORK PROGRAMME (Agenda item 120)
A/78/PV.42
WEAPONS—OUTER SPACE (Agenda item 97b)
A/78/PV.42
WEAPONS OF MASS DESTRUCTION (Agenda item 93)
A/78/PV.42

Bamya, Majed (State of Palestine)

CRIMES AGAINST HUMANITY (Agenda item 80)
A/C.6/78/SR.11
HUMAN RIGHTS (Agenda item 71)
A/C.3/78/SR.16
INFORMATION (Agenda item 53)
A/C.4/78/SR.14
INTERNATIONAL CRIMINAL COURT—REPORTS (Agenda item 74)
A/78/PV.25
TERRORISM (Agenda item 109)
A/C.6/78/SR.5
UN. GENERAL ASSEMBLY (78TH SESS. : 2023-2024). 1ST COMMITTEE—GENERAL DEBATE (Agenda item 8)
A/C.1/78/PV.7; A/C.1/78/PV.8

Banaken Elel, Nelly (Cameroon)

CLIMATE (Agenda item 18d)
A/C.2/78/SR.13
CYBERCRIME (Agenda item 108)
A/C.3/78/SR.5
DEVELOPMENT FINANCE (Agenda item 16b)
A/C.2/78/SR.9
DISPLACED PERSONS (Agenda item 71b)
A/C.3/78/SR.32
FAMILY (Agenda item 24b)
A/C.3/78/SR.2
HUMAN RIGHTS—BURUNDI (Agenda item 71c)
A/C.3/78/SR.36
HUMAN RIGHTS—CENTRAL AFRICAN REPUBLIC (Agenda item 71c)
A/C.3/78/SR.33
HUMAN RIGHTS—DEMOCRATIC PEOPLE'S REPUBLIC OF KOREA (Agenda item 71c)
A/C.3/78/SR.33
HUMAN RIGHTS—ERITREA (Agenda item 71c)
A/C.3/78/SR.36
HUMAN RIGHTS—ETHIOPIA (Agenda item 71c)
A/C.3/78/SR.36

Banaken Elel, Nelly (Cameroon) (continued)

HUMAN RIGHTS—INTERNATIONAL INSTRUMENTS (Agenda item 71a)
A/C.3/78/SR.17; A/C.3/78/SR.25
HUMAN RIGHTS ADVANCEMENT (Agenda item 71b)
A/C.3/78/SR.25
INTERNATIONAL TRADE (Agenda item 16a)
A/C.2/78/SR.9
POVERTY—HUMAN RIGHTS (Agenda item 71b)
A/C.3/78/SR.30
RACIAL DISCRIMINATION—ELIMINATION (Agenda item 69a)
A/C.3/78/SR.40; A/C.3/78/SR.42
RACIAL DISCRIMINATION—PROGRAMMES OF ACTION (Agenda item 69b)
A/C.3/78/SR.40; A/C.3/78/SR.42
RIGHT TO DEVELOPMENT (Agenda item 71b)
A/C.3/78/SR.20
RIGHT TO DRINKING WATER (Agenda item 71b)
A/C.3/78/SR.50
RIGHT TO FOOD (Agenda item 71b)
A/C.3/78/SR.30
RIGHT TO HOUSING (Agenda item 71b)
A/C.3/78/SR.30
RIGHTS OF THE CHILD (Agenda item 67)
A/C.3/78/SR.12; A/C.3/78/SR.55
SOLIDARITY (Agenda item 71b)
A/C.3/78/SR.32
UN. GENERAL ASSEMBLY (78TH SESS. : 2023-2024). 2ND COMMITTEE—GENERAL DEBATE (Agenda item 8)
A/C.2/78/SR.4
UN. HUMAN RIGHTS COMMITTEE—REPORTS (Agenda item 71a)
A/C.3/78/SR.17
UN. HUMAN RIGHTS COUNCIL—REPORTS (Agenda item 66)
A/C.3/78/SR.46
UN HIGH COMMISSIONER FOR REFUGEES—REPORTS (Agenda item 60)
A/C.3/78/SR.44; A/C.3/78/SR.45
UN RESOLUTIONS—IMPLEMENTATION (Agenda item 119)
A/78/PV.103
WOMEN'S ADVANCEMENT (Agenda item 25a)
A/C.3/78/SR.8
WOMEN'S ADVANCEMENT—CONFERENCES (Agenda item 25b)
A/C.3/78/SR.8

Banaken Elel, Nelly (Cameroon) (Economic Community of Central African States)

HUMAN RIGHTS INSTITUTIONS—CENTRAL AFRICA (Agenda item 71b)
A/C.3/78/SR.56

Banaken Elel, Nelly (Cameroon) (UN. Group of African States)

RACIAL DISCRIMINATION—ELIMINATION (Agenda item 69a)
A/78/PV.103
RIGHTS OF THE CHILD (Agenda item 67)
A/C.3/78/SR.55
UN HIGH COMMISSIONER FOR REFUGEES—REPORTS (Agenda item 60)
A/C.3/78/SR.44

Baños Müller, Liliana Verónica (El Salvador)

OUTER SPACE—PEACEFUL USES—INTERNATIONAL COOPERATION (Agenda item 48)
A/C.4/78/SR.16
VETO (Agenda item 63)
A/78/PV.79

Baños Müller, Liliana Verónica (El Salvador) (UN. Committee on Information. Vice-Chair)

INFORMATION (Agenda item 53)
A/C.4/78/SR.12

Banza, Serge Ngoy (Democratic Republic of the Congo) (Groupe des ambassadeurs francophones)

MULTILINGUALISM (Agenda item 124)
A/78/PV.107

Barahona Figueroa, Andrea Alejandra (El Salvador)

FOOD SECURITY (Agenda item 23a)
A/C.2/78/SR.16
POVERTY—INTERNATIONAL DECADES (Agenda item 21a)
A/C.2/78/SR.16
RURAL POVERTY (Agenda item 21b)
A/C.2/78/SR.16

Barahona Figueroa, Andrea Alejandra (El Salvador) (Sistema de la Integración Centroamericana)

SUSTAINABLE DEVELOPMENT (Agenda item 18)
A/C.2/78/SR.22

Barak, Noga (Israel)

SUSTAINABLE DEVELOPMENT (Agenda item 18)
A/C.2/78/SR.24

Barba Bustos, Irina Alexandra (Ecuador)

BIOLOGICAL DIVERSITY—TREATIES (Agenda item 18f)
A/C.2/78/SR.13
CLIMATE (Agenda item 18d)
A/C.2/78/SR.13
DISASTER PREVENTION (Agenda item 18c)
A/C.2/78/SR.13
FOOD SECURITY (Agenda item 23a)
A/C.2/78/SR.17
POVERTY—INTERNATIONAL DECADES (Agenda item 21a)
A/C.2/78/SR.17

Barba Bustos, Irina Alexandra (Ecuador) (continued)

RURAL POVERTY (Agenda item 21b)
A/C.2/78/SR.17

Barbotte, Daphné (European Union)

FOOD SECURITY (Agenda item 23a)
A/C.2/78/SR.25

Bárcena Ibarra, Alicia (Mexico)

UN. GENERAL ASSEMBLY (78TH SESS. : 2023-2024)—GENERAL DEBATE (Agenda item 8)
A/78/PV.12

Baric, Ana (United Kingdom)

INTERNATIONAL TRADE (Agenda item 16a)
A/C.2/78/SR.22
SCIENCE AND TECHNOLOGY—DEVELOPMENT (Agenda item 19a)
A/C.2/78/SR.22
SMALL ISLAND DEVELOPING STATES—PROGRAMMES OF ACTION (Agenda item 18b)
A/C.2/78/SR.22

Barman, Ordell Cedric (Trinidad and Tobago)

CUBA—UNITED STATES (Agenda item 38)
A/78/PV.24

Barnor, Nana Akua (Ghana)

PEACE (Agenda item 14)
A/78/PV.82
RESPONSIBILITY TO PROTECT (Agenda item 129)
A/78/PV.99

Barre, Hamza Abdi (Somalia. Prime Minister)

UN. GENERAL ASSEMBLY (78TH SESS. : 2023-2024)—GENERAL DEBATE (Agenda item 8)
A/78/PV.12
UN. GENERAL ASSEMBLY (78TH SESS. : 2023-2024)—SPECIAL STATEMENTS
A/78/PV.12

Barro, Braima (Burkina Faso)

INFORMATION TECHNOLOGY—DEVELOPMENT (Agenda item 15)
A/C.2/78/SR.10
SCIENCE AND TECHNOLOGY—DEVELOPMENT (Agenda item 19a)
A/C.2/78/SR.10

Barros, Sebastiana (Timor-Leste)

FOOD SECURITY (Agenda item 23a)
A/C.2/78/SR.18
POVERTY—INTERNATIONAL DECADES (Agenda item 21a)
A/C.2/78/SR.18

Bartley, Matilda (Samoa) (Alliance of Small Island States)

DEVELOPMENT FINANCE (Agenda item 16b)
A/C.2/78/SR.8
EXTERNAL DEBT (Agenda item 16c)
A/C.2/78/SR.8
INTERNATIONAL TRADE (Agenda item 16a)
A/C.2/78/SR.8
LANDLOCKED DEVELOPING COUNTRIES—CONFERENCES (Agenda item 20b)
A/C.2/78/SR.7
LAW OF THE SEA (Agenda item 75a)
A/78/PV.43
LEAST DEVELOPED COUNTRIES—CONFERENCES (Agenda item 20a)
A/C.2/78/SR.7
MACROECONOMIC POLICY (Agenda item 16)
A/C.2/78/SR.8
MARINE ECOSYSTEMS—BIOLOGICAL DIVERSITY (Agenda item 75c)
A/78/PV.43; A/78/PV.73
SMALL ISLAND DEVELOPING STATES—PROGRAMMES OF ACTION (Agenda item 18b)
A/C.2/78/SR.22
STRADDLING FISH STOCKS (Agenda item 75b)
A/78/PV.43
UN. GENERAL ASSEMBLY (78TH SESS. : 2023-2024). 2ND COMMITTEE—GENERAL DEBATE (Agenda item 8)
A/C.2/78/SR.2

Bartolini, Natasia (San Marino)

UN. GENERAL ASSEMBLY (78TH SESS. : 2023-2024). 1ST COMMITTEE—GENERAL DEBATE (Agenda item 8)
A/C.1/78/PV.6

Basheer, Manar (Kuwait)

MIDDLE EAST—NUCLEAR-WEAPON-FREE ZONES (Agenda item 95)
A/C.1/78/PV.23

Basinet, Cynthia ((personal capacity))

WESTERN SAHARA QUESTION (Agenda item 58)
A/C.4/78/SR.4

Bastaki, Mohammad Yousuf Abdulla Mohammad (United Arab Emirates)

UN. GENERAL ASSEMBLY (78TH SESS. : 2023-2024). 2ND COMMITTEE—GENERAL DEBATE (Agenda item 8)
A/C.2/78/SR.4

Basu Ray, Deepayan (UN Regional Centre for Peace and Disarmament in Asia and the Pacific. Director)

PEACE—REGIONAL CENTRE—ASIA AND THE PACIFIC (Agenda item 100d)
A/C.1/78/PV.23

Basulto Alvarez, Alejandrina (Mexico)

UN. GENERAL ASSEMBLY—WORK PROGRAMME (Agenda item 120)
A/C.2/78/SR.25

Baur, Lianna Maureen (Canada)

CRIME PREVENTION (Agenda item 107)
A/C.3/78/SR.51
RIGHTS OF THE CHILD (Agenda item 67)
A/C.3/78/SR.55
WOMEN'S ADVANCEMENT (Agenda item 25a)
A/C.3/78/SR.7
WOMEN'S ADVANCEMENT—CONFERENCES (Agenda item 25b)
A/C.3/78/SR.7; A/C.3/78/SR.51

Bauwens, Gilles (Belgium)

DISAPPEARANCE OF PERSONS (Agenda item 71b)
A/C.3/78/SR.22
FREEDOM OF EXPRESSION (Agenda item 71b)
A/C.3/78/SR.19
RACIAL DISCRIMINATION—ELIMINATION (Agenda item 69a)
A/C.3/78/SR.40
RACIAL DISCRIMINATION—PROGRAMMES OF ACTION (Agenda item 69b)
A/C.3/78/SR.40
RELIGIOUS INTOLERANCE (Agenda item 71b)
A/C.3/78/SR.38
RIGHTS OF THE CHILD (Agenda item 67)
A/C.3/78/SR.11
SEXUAL ORIENTATION (Agenda item 71b)
A/C.3/78/SR.39
SUMMARY EXECUTIONS (Agenda item 71b)
A/C.3/78/SR.31
TERRORISM—HUMAN RIGHTS (Agenda item 71b)
A/C.3/78/SR.31
WOMEN'S ADVANCEMENT (Agenda item 25a)
A/C.3/78/SR.7; A/C.3/78/SR.8
WOMEN'S ADVANCEMENT—CONFERENCES (Agenda item 25b)
A/C.3/78/SR.7; A/C.3/78/SR.8

Bayer, Guilherme Marquardt (Brazil)

DEVELOPMENT FINANCE—CONFERENCES (Agenda item 17)
A/78/PV.90

Bayley Angeleri, Roberto (Bolivia (Plurinational State of))

UN—BUDGET (2024) (Agenda item 134)
A/C.5/78/SR.28

Bayley Angeleri, Roberto (Venezuela (Bolivarian Republic of))

UN—BUDGET (2024) (Agenda item 134)
A/C.5/78/SR.34
UN—PROGRAMME PLANNING (Agenda item 135)
A/78/PV.50(Resumption1)

Bayramli-Hamidova, Nigar (Azerbaijan)

CLIMATE (Agenda item 18d)
A/C.2/78/SR.13
MACROECONOMIC POLICY (Agenda item 16)
A/C.2/78/SR.9
SUSTAINABLE DEVELOPMENT (Agenda item 18)
A/C.2/78/SR.13; A/C.2/78/SR.15
SUSTAINABLE ENERGY (Agenda item 18h)
A/C.2/78/SR.13
UN. GENERAL ASSEMBLY (78TH SESS. : 2023-2024). 2ND COMMITTEE—GENERAL DEBATE (Agenda item 8)
A/C.2/78/SR.4; A/C.2/78/SR.5

Bayramov, Jeyhun (Azerbaijan)

UN. GENERAL ASSEMBLY (78TH SESS. : 2023-2024)—GENERAL DEBATE (Agenda item 8)
A/78/PV.12

Bazie, Bassolma (Burkina Faso)

UN. GENERAL ASSEMBLY (78TH SESS. : 2023-2024)—GENERAL DEBATE (Agenda item 8)
A/78/PV.13

Beblavý, Pavol (Slovakia)

AGEING PERSONS (Agenda item 24b)
A/C.3/78/SR.2
RIGHTS OF THE CHILD (Agenda item 67)
A/C.3/78/SR.12
SOCIAL CONDITIONS (Agenda item 24b)
A/C.3/78/SR.2
YOUTH (Agenda item 24b)
A/C.3/78/SR.2

Beckles, Hilary (University of the West Indies)

SLAVERY—MEMORIALS (Agenda item 118)
A/78/PV.64

Bedi, Anmol Sher Singh (India)

ARMS TRANSFERS—TREATIES (Agenda item 99x)
A/C.1/78/PV.28
CONVENTIONAL ARMS—REGIONAL PROGRAMMES (Agenda item 99g)
A/C.1/78/PV.29
DISARMAMENT—UN. GENERAL ASSEMBLY (4TH SPECIAL SESS. ON DISARMAMENT : xxxx) (Agenda item 99h)
A/C.1/78/PV.23
INFORMATION—INTERNATIONAL SECURITY (Agenda item 94)
A/C.1/78/PV.21
LANDMINES—TREATIES (Agenda item 99m)
A/C.1/78/PV.28
SCIENCE AND TECHNOLOGY—INTERNATIONAL SECURITY (Agenda item 98)
A/C.1/78/PV.21
UN. CONFERENCE ON DISARMAMENT—REPORTS (Agenda item 101a)
A/C.1/78/PV.23

Bedi, Anmol Sher Singh (India) (continued)

UN. DISARMAMENT COMMISSION—REPORTS (Agenda item 101b)
A/C.1/78/PV.23

Begaj, Bajram (Albania. President)

UN. GENERAL ASSEMBLY (78TH SESS. : 2023-2024)—GENERAL DEBATE (Agenda item 8)
A/78/PV.9
UN. GENERAL ASSEMBLY (78TH SESS. : 2023-2024)—SPECIAL STATEMENTS
A/78/PV.9

Bekteshi, Etrit (Albania)

UN. GENERAL ASSEMBLY (78TH SESS. : 2023-2024). 1ST COMMITTEE—GENERAL DEBATE (Agenda item 8)
A/C.1/78/PV.6

Belal, Mohammed (Common Fund for Commodities)

COMMODITIES (Agenda item 16d)
A/C.2/78/SR.14
SUSTAINABLE DEVELOPMENT (Agenda item 18)
A/C.2/78/SR.14

Beleffi, Damiano (San Marino)

UN. GENERAL ASSEMBLY (78TH SESS. : 2023-2024)—GENERAL DEBATE (Agenda item 8)
A/78/PV.14
UN. GENERAL ASSEMBLY (78TH SESS. : 2023-2024). 2ND COMMITTEE—GENERAL DEBATE (Agenda item 8)
A/C.2/78/SR.4
UN. SECURITY COUNCIL—MEMBERSHIP (Agenda item 121)
A/78/PV.35
VETO (Agenda item 63)
A/78/PV.61; A/78/PV.75

Bellmont Roldán, Xavier (Spain)

DISPLACED PERSONS (Agenda item 71b)
A/C.3/78/SR.49
HUMAN RIGHTS ACTIVISTS (Agenda item 71b)
A/C.3/78/SR.19
RIGHT TO DRINKING WATER (Agenda item 71b)
A/C.3/78/SR.28; A/C.3/78/SR.50
SELF-DETERMINATION OF PEOPLES (Agenda item 70)
A/C.3/78/SR.56

Bellmont Roldán, Xavier (Spain) (European Union)

HUMAN RIGHTS—DEMOCRATIC PEOPLE'S REPUBLIC OF KOREA (Agenda item 71c)
A/C.3/78/SR.53
HUMAN RIGHTS—IRAN (ISLAMIC REPUBLIC OF) (Agenda item 71c)
A/C.3/78/SR.53
HUMAN RIGHTS—UKRAINE (Agenda item 71c)
A/C.3/78/SR.53

Bellmont Roldán, Xavier (Spain) (European Union) (continued)

HUMAN RIGHTS ACTIVISTS (Agenda item 71b)
A/C.3/78/SR.56
PEACE (Agenda item 14)
A/78/PV.48
RACIAL DISCRIMINATION—ELIMINATION (Agenda item 69a)
A/78/PV.50; A/C.3/78/SR.47
RACIAL DISCRIMINATION—PROGRAMMES OF ACTION (Agenda item 69b)
A/C.3/78/SR.56

Belmeddah, Nor Eddine ((personal capacity))

WESTERN SAHARA QUESTION (Agenda item 58)
A/C.4/78/SR.5

Belousko, Sergey (Russian Federation)

OUTER SPACE—PEACEFUL USES—INTERNATIONAL COOPERATION (Agenda item 48)
A/C.4/78/SR.15; A/C.4/78/SR.16; A/C.4/78/SR.17

Belousov, Andrey I. (Russian Federation)

ARMS TRANSFERS—TREATIES (Agenda item 99x)
A/C.1/78/PV.19
CHEMICAL WEAPONS—TREATIES (Agenda item 99l)
A/C.1/78/PV.26
CLUSTER MUNITIONS (Agenda item 99dd)
A/C.1/78/PV.28
CONVENTIONAL WEAPONS—TREATIES (Agenda item 103)
A/C.1/78/PV.19
DISARMAMENT—GENERAL AND COMPLETE (Agenda item 99)
A/C.1/78/PV.19; A/C.1/78/PV.23; A/C.1/78/PV.24; A/C.1/78/PV.28; A/C.1/78/PV.30
DISARMAMENT AGREEMENTS—OUTER SPACE (Agenda item 97c)
A/C.1/78/PV.27
INFORMATION—INTERNATIONAL SECURITY (Agenda item 94)
A/C.1/78/PV.21; A/C.1/78/PV.28; A/C.1/78/PV.29
LANDMINES—TREATIES (Agenda item 99m)
A/C.1/78/PV.19
MEDITERRANEAN REGION—REGIONAL SECURITY (Agenda item 104)
A/C.1/78/PV.29
MULTILATERALISM—DISARMAMENT (Agenda item 99r)
A/C.1/78/PV.22
NUCLEAR DISARMAMENT—VERIFICATION (Agenda item 99ee)
A/C.1/78/PV.25
NUCLEAR WEAPON TESTS—TREATIES (Agenda item 105)
A/C.1/78/PV.26
NUCLEAR WEAPONS—ELIMINATION (Agenda item 99z)
A/C.1/78/PV.25

Belousov, Andrey I. (Russian Federation) (continued)

OUTER SPACE—CONFIDENCE-BUILDING MEASURES (Agenda item 99v)
A/C.1/78/PV.27
OUTER SPACE—PRINCIPLES (Agenda item 97d)
A/C.1/78/PV.27
SMALL ARMS—ILLICIT TRAFFIC—ASSISTANCE (Agenda item 99n)
A/C.1/78/PV.19
UN. CONFERENCE ON DISARMAMENT—REPORTS (Agenda item 101a)
A/C.1/78/PV.23; A/C.1/78/PV.24; A/C.1/78/PV.29
UN. GENERAL ASSEMBLY (78TH SESS. : 2023-2024). 1ST COMMITTEE—WORK ORGANIZATION (Agenda item 7)
A/C.1/78/PV.27; A/C.1/78/PV.28; A/C.1/78/PV.30
WEAPONS—OUTER SPACE (Agenda item 97b)
A/C.1/78/PV.27

Ben Lagha, Adel (Tunisia)

CRIMES AGAINST HUMANITY (Agenda item 80)
A/C.6/78/SR.10; A/C.6/78/SR.39
RULE OF LAW (Agenda item 83)
A/C.6/78/SR.18
TERRORISM (Agenda item 109)
A/C.6/78/SR.3
VETO (Agenda item 63)
A/78/PV.60

Ben Naftaly, Emil (Israel)

HEALTH (Agenda item 125)
A/78/PV.77
STORMS (Agenda item 18i)
A/C.2/78/SR.22
SUSTAINABLE DEVELOPMENT (Agenda item 18)
A/C.2/78/SR.15; A/C.2/78/SR.21; A/C.2/78/SR.22
TERRITORIES OCCUPIED BY ISRAEL—NATURAL RESOURCES (Agenda item 59)
A/C.2/78/SR.19; A/C.2/78/SR.20; A/C.2/78/SR.21
UN. ECONOMIC AND SOCIAL COUNCIL—REPORTS (Agenda item 9)
A/78/PV.33
UN. GENERAL ASSEMBLY—WORK PROGRAMME (Agenda item 120)
A/78/PV.33
UN RESOLUTIONS—IMPLEMENTATION (Agenda item 119)
A/78/PV.33

Ben Zitun, Esam (Libya)

UN. GENERAL ASSEMBLY (78TH SESS. : 2023-2024). 1ST COMMITTEE—GENERAL DEBATE (Agenda item 8)
A/C.1/78/PV.7

Benard Estrada, Juan Antonio (Guatemala)

FALKLAND ISLANDS (MALVINAS) QUESTION (Agenda item 42)
A/C.4/78/SR.6
PEACEKEEPING OPERATIONS (Agenda item 51)
A/C.4/78/SR.19

Benard Estrada, Juan Antonio (Guatemala) (continued)

WESTERN SAHARA QUESTION (Agenda item 58)
A/C.4/78/SR.6

Bencini, Leonardo (Italy)

ARMS RACE—OUTER SPACE (Agenda item 97a)
A/C.1/78/PV.17
BIOLOGICAL WEAPONS—TREATIES (Agenda item 106)
A/C.1/78/PV.15
CHEMICAL WEAPONS—TREATIES (Agenda item 99l)
A/C.1/78/PV.15
DISARMAMENT AGREEMENTS—OUTER SPACE (Agenda item 97c)
A/C.1/78/PV.17
INFORMATION—INTERNATIONAL SECURITY (Agenda item 94)
A/C.1/78/PV.21
NUCLEAR DISARMAMENT (Agenda item 99b)
A/C.1/78/PV.13
NUCLEAR NON-PROLIFERATION—INTERNATIONAL OBLIGATIONS (Agenda item 99w)
A/C.1/78/PV.13
NUCLEAR WEAPON TESTS—TREATIES (Agenda item 105)
A/C.1/78/PV.13
OUTER SPACE—CONFIDENCE-BUILDING MEASURES (Agenda item 99v)
A/C.1/78/PV.17
OUTER SPACE—PRINCIPLES (Agenda item 97d)
A/C.1/78/PV.17
UN. CONFERENCE ON DISARMAMENT—REPORTS (Agenda item 101a)
A/C.1/78/PV.23
UN. GENERAL ASSEMBLY (78TH SESS. : 2023-2024). 1ST COMMITTEE—GENERAL DEBATE (Agenda item 8)
A/C.1/78/PV.4
WEAPONS OF MASS DESTRUCTION—TERRORISM (Agenda item 99s)
A/C.1/78/PV.15

Bencini, Leonardo (Italy) (Review Conference of the State Parties to the Convention on the Prohibition of the Development, Production and Stockpiling of Bacteriological (Biological) and Toxin Weapons and on Their Destruction. President)

BIOLOGICAL WEAPONS—TREATIES (Agenda item 106)
A/C.1/78/PV.14

Bendjama, Amar (Algeria)

CUBA—UNITED STATES (Agenda item 38)
A/78/PV.24
ECONOMIC SANCTIONS—INTERNATIONAL RELATIONS (Agenda item 28)
A/78/PV.90
IAEA—REPORTS (Agenda item 89)
A/78/PV.30

Bendjama, Amar (Algeria) (continued)
PEACEKEEPING OPERATIONS (Agenda item 51)
A/C.4/78/SR.19
UN. GENERAL ASSEMBLY (78TH SESS. : 2023-2024)—GENERAL DEBATE—RIGHT OF REPLY (Agenda item 8)
A/78/PV.14
UN. SECURITY COUNCIL—MEMBERSHIP (Agenda item 121)
A/78/PV.35
UNRWA—ACTIVITIES (Agenda item 49)
A/C.4/78/SR.22
WESTERN SAHARA QUESTION (Agenda item 58)
A/C.4/78/SR.9

Bendjama, Amar (Algeria) (Coordinating Bureau of the Non-Aligned Countries)
UN. GENERAL ASSEMBLY—WORK PROGRAMME (Agenda item 120)
A/78/PV.32
UN RESOLUTIONS—IMPLEMENTATION (Agenda item 119)
A/78/PV.32

Bendriss, Khalid (Association for the Support of the Moroccan Autonomy Initiative)
WESTERN SAHARA QUESTION (Agenda item 58)
A/C.4/78/SR.6

Bennett, Richard (UN. Human Rights Council. Special Rapporteur on the Situation of Human Rights in Afghanistan)
HUMAN RIGHTS—AFGHANISTAN (Agenda item 71c)
A/C.3/78/SR.34

Benziane, Imane (Morocco)
UN. GENERAL ASSEMBLY—WORK PROGRAMME (Agenda item 120)
A/78/PV.32
UN RESOLUTIONS—IMPLEMENTATION (Agenda item 119)
A/78/PV.32

Berard Cadieux, Xavier (Canada)
INFORMATION—INTERNATIONAL SECURITY (Agenda item 94)
A/C.1/78/PV.20

Berchtold, Aneschka (Switzerland)
SOCIAL CONDITIONS (Agenda item 24b)
A/C.3/78/SR.3
YOUTH (Agenda item 24b)
A/C.3/78/SR.3

Berdimuhamedov, Serdar (Turkmenistan. President)
UN. GENERAL ASSEMBLY (78TH SESS. : 2023-2024)—GENERAL DEBATE (Agenda item 8)
A/78/PV.4
UN. GENERAL ASSEMBLY (78TH SESS. : 2023-2024)—SPECIAL STATEMENTS
A/78/PV.4

Beresford-Hill, Paul (Sovereign Order of Malta)
AGEING PERSONS (Agenda item 24b)
A/C.3/78/SR.1

Beretta Tassano, María Noel (Uruguay)
RESPONSIBILITY TO PROTECT (Agenda item 129)
A/78/PV.97
VETO (Agenda item 63)
A/78/PV.69

Berg, AnneMarie van den (UN. Assistant Secretary-General for Supply Chain Management)
PEACEKEEPING OPERATIONS—FINANCING (Agenda item 146)
A/C.5/78/SR.35
UN—ADMINISTRATION (Agenda item 132)
A/C.5/78/SR.32

Berg, Kristin Soennesyn (Norway)
FREEDOM OF EXPRESSION (Agenda item 71b)
A/C.3/78/SR.19

Beriana, Charlene Aravejo (Philippines)
FOOD SECURITY (Agenda item 23a)
A/C.2/78/SR.16
POVERTY—INTERNATIONAL DECADES (Agenda item 21a)
A/C.2/78/SR.16
RURAL POVERTY (Agenda item 21b)
A/C.2/78/SR.16

Bernandes, Rafael (Brazil)
UN. INTERNATIONAL LAW COMMISSION—REPORTS (Agenda item 79)
A/C.6/78/SR.29; A/C.6/78/SR.31

Berset, Alain (Switzerland. President)
UN. GENERAL ASSEMBLY (78TH SESS. : 2023-2024)—GENERAL DEBATE (Agenda item 8)
A/78/PV.4
UN. GENERAL ASSEMBLY (78TH SESS. : 2023-2024)—SPECIAL STATEMENTS
A/78/PV.4

Beshkova, Krassimira (Bulgaria)
CRIMES AGAINST HUMANITY (Agenda item 80)
A/C.6/78/SR.45
VETO (Agenda item 63)
A/78/PV.68

Besnard, Jérôme (Autonomy for the Sahara Coalition (Organization))

WESTERN SAHARA QUESTION (Agenda item 58)
A/C.4/78/SR.5

Bessadok, Marwa Jabou (Tunisia)

HUMAN RIGHTS—INTERNATIONAL INSTRUMENTS (Agenda item 71a)
A/C.3/78/SR.26
HUMAN RIGHTS—TERRITORIES OCCUPIED BY ISRAEL (Agenda item 71c)
A/C.3/78/SR.35
RACIAL DISCRIMINATION—ELIMINATION (Agenda item 69a)
A/78/PV.103
RIGHTS OF THE CHILD (Agenda item 67)
A/C.3/78/SR.13
UN. GENERAL ASSEMBLY—WORK PROGRAMME (Agenda item 120)
A/C.3/78/SR.56
WOMEN'S ADVANCEMENT (Agenda item 25a)
A/C.3/78/SR.8
WOMEN'S ADVANCEMENT—CONFERENCES (Agenda item 25b)
A/C.3/78/SR.8

Betor, Guensy (Haiti)

UN—BUDGET (2024) (Agenda item 134)
A/C.5/78/SR.4
UN—BUDGET CONTRIBUTIONS (Agenda item 138)
A/C.5/78/SR.1

Bettel, Xavier (Luxembourg. Deputy Prime Minister)

UKRAINE—POLITICAL CONDITIONS (Agenda item 62)
A/78/PV.56
UN. GENERAL ASSEMBLY (78TH SESS. : 2023-2024)—SPECIAL STATEMENTS
A/78/PV.56

Bettel, Xavier (Luxembourg. Prime Minister)

UN. GENERAL ASSEMBLY (78TH SESS. : 2023-2024)—GENERAL DEBATE (Agenda item 8)
A/78/PV.10
UN. GENERAL ASSEMBLY (78TH SESS. : 2023-2024)—SPECIAL STATEMENTS
A/78/PV.10

Beuzit, Léa (Monaco)

RIGHTS OF THE CHILD (Agenda item 67)
A/C.3/78/SR.14

Bhalla, Ashish (India)

PEACEBUILDING (Agenda item 61)
A/78/PV.101
PEACEKEEPING OPERATIONS (Agenda item 51)
A/C.4/78/SR.20

Bhalla, Ashish (India) (continued)

UN. PEACEBUILDING COMMISSION—REPORTS (Agenda item 27)
A/78/PV.101
UN. PEACEBUILDING FUND—REPORTS (Agenda item 111)
A/78/PV.101

Bhat, Kajal (India)

CRIMES AGAINST HUMANITY (Agenda item 80)
A/C.6/78/SR.10; A/C.6/78/SR.11; A/C.6/78/SR.38; A/C.6/78/SR.40; A/C.6/78/SR.42; A/C.6/78/SR.43; A/C.6/78/SR.44; A/C.6/78/SR.47
INTERNATIONAL JURISDICTION (Agenda item 84)
A/C.6/78/SR.13
INTERNATIONAL PARLIAMENTARIANS' CONGRESS—OBSERVER STATUS (Agenda item 170)
A/C.6/78/SR.14
LAW OF THE SEA (Agenda item 75a)
A/78/PV.43
MARINE ECOSYSTEMS—BIOLOGICAL DIVERSITY (Agenda item 75c)
A/78/PV.43
PEACEKEEPING OPERATIONS—CRIMINAL LIABILITY (Agenda item 76)
A/C.6/78/SR.8
RESPONSIBILITY TO PROTECT (Agenda item 129)
A/78/PV.97
RULE OF LAW (Agenda item 83)
A/C.6/78/SR.18
STRADDLING FISH STOCKS (Agenda item 75b)
A/78/PV.43
TERRORISM (Agenda item 109)
A/C.6/78/SR.2; A/C.6/78/SR.4
UN. INTERNATIONAL COURT OF JUSTICE—REPORTS (Agenda item 73)
A/78/PV.27
UN. INTERNATIONAL LAW COMMISSION—REPORTS (Agenda item 79)
A/C.6/78/SR.30; A/C.6/78/SR.32; A/C.6/78/SR.37
UN CHARTER—REPORTS (Agenda item 82)
A/C.6/78/SR.33
UN COMMISSION ON INTERNATIONAL TRADE LAW—REPORTS (Agenda item 77)
A/C.6/78/SR.14

Biang, Michel Xavier (Gabon)

RACIAL DISCRIMINATION—ELIMINATION (Agenda item 69a)
A/C.3/78/SR.42
RACIAL DISCRIMINATION—PROGRAMMES OF ACTION (Agenda item 69b)
A/C.3/78/SR.42
UN HIGH COMMISSIONER FOR REFUGEES—REPORTS (Agenda item 60)
A/C.3/78/SR.45

Biaou, Maurille Firmin (Benin)
WESTERN SAHARA QUESTION (Agenda item 58)
A/C.4/78/SR.8

Biden, Joseph R. (United States. President)
UN. GENERAL ASSEMBLY (78TH SESS. : 2023-2024)—GENERAL DEBATE (Agenda item 8)
A/78/PV.4
UN. GENERAL ASSEMBLY (78TH SESS. : 2023-2024)—SPECIAL STATEMENTS
A/78/PV.4

Bierling, Mirjam (Norway)
CRIMES AGAINST HUMANITY (Agenda item 80)
A/C.6/78/SR.43

Biggs, Ian (Australia)
TERRORISM (Agenda item 109)
A/C.6/78/SR.1

Bilgeri, Andreas (Austria)
ARMS RACE—OUTER SPACE (Agenda item 97a)
A/C.1/78/PV.16
OUTER SPACE—CONFIDENCE-BUILDING MEASURES (Agenda item 99v)
A/C.1/78/PV.16
OUTER SPACE—PRINCIPLES (Agenda item 97d)
A/C.1/78/PV.16

Billingsley, Kelly (United States)
FREEDOM OF EXPRESSION (Agenda item 71b)
A/C.3/78/SR.19
SUMMARY EXECUTIONS (Agenda item 71b)
A/C.3/78/SR.31

Billström, Tobias (Sweden)
UN. GENERAL ASSEMBLY (78TH SESS. : 2023-2024)—GENERAL DEBATE (Agenda item 8)
A/78/PV.11

Bimbaitė, Monika (Lithuania)
HUMAN RIGHTS—BELARUS (Agenda item 71c)
A/C.3/78/SR.37
RELIGIOUS INTOLERANCE (Agenda item 71b)
A/C.3/78/SR.38

Bin Jadid, Faisal Fahad M. (Saudi Arabia)
HUMAN RIGHTS ADVANCEMENT (Agenda item 71b)
A/C.3/78/SR.18
PERSONS WITH DISABILITIES (Agenda item 24b)
A/C.3/78/SR.2
RELIGIOUS INTOLERANCE (Agenda item 71b)
A/C.3/78/SR.38
RIGHT TO DRINKING WATER (Agenda item 71b)
A/C.3/78/SR.50
RIGHTS OF THE CHILD (Agenda item 67)
A/C.3/78/SR.55

Bin Jadid, Faisal Fahad M. (Saudi Arabia) (continued)
SOCIAL DEVELOPMENT (Agenda item 24)
A/C.3/78/SR.2
UN. HUMAN RIGHTS COUNCIL—REPORTS (Agenda item 66)
A/C.3/78/SR.46
YOUTH (Agenda item 24b)
A/C.3/78/SR.2

Bin Shafi, Mohammed (Saudi Arabia)
CONVENTIONAL WEAPONS (Agenda item 99u)
A/C.1/78/PV.19
SMALL ARMS—ILLICIT TRAFFIC (Agenda item 99p)
A/C.1/78/PV.19

Bio, Julius Maada (Sierra Leone. President)
UN. GENERAL ASSEMBLY (78TH SESS. : 2023-2024)—GENERAL DEBATE (Agenda item 8)
A/78/PV.7
UN. GENERAL ASSEMBLY (78TH SESS. : 2023-2024)—SPECIAL STATEMENTS
A/78/PV.7

Birdi, Nitish (India)
DECOLONIZATION (Agenda item 58)
A/C.4/78/SR.7
INFORMATION (Agenda item 53)
A/C.4/78/SR.12
OUTER SPACE—PEACEFUL USES—INTERNATIONAL COOPERATION (Agenda item 48)
A/C.4/78/SR.16
SPECIAL POLITICAL MISSIONS (Agenda item 52)
A/C.4/78/SR.21

Birrer, Jacqueline (Switzerland)
HEALTH (Agenda item 125)
A/78/PV.16; A/78/PV.48; A/78/PV.77
HIV/AIDS—DECLARATIONS (Agenda item 10)
A/78/PV.91

Bisharat, Nadien Isam Fraih (Jordan)
CRIMES AGAINST HUMANITY (Agenda item 80)
A/C.6/78/SR.38; A/C.6/78/SR.40; A/C.6/78/SR.41; A/C.6/78/SR.44; A/C.6/78/SR.45

Bisharat, Nadien Isam Fraih (Jordan) (Group of Arab States)
RULE OF LAW (Agenda item 83)
A/C.6/78/SR.15
UN. INTERNATIONAL COURT OF JUSTICE—REPORTS (Agenda item 73)
A/78/PV.27

Biya, Alain Wilfried (International Renewable Energy Agency)
LANDLOCKED DEVELOPING COUNTRIES—CONFERENCES (Agenda item 20b)
A/C.2/78/SR.7

Biya, Alain Wilfried (International Renewable Energy Agency) (continued)

LEAST DEVELOPED COUNTRIES—CONFERENCES (Agenda item 20a)
A/C.2/78/SR.7
SUSTAINABLE ENERGY (Agenda item 18h)
A/C.2/78/SR.15

Blackstock, Uché (Advancing Health Equity (Organization))

RACIAL DISCRIMINATION—ELIMINATION (Agenda item 69a)
A/78/PV.63

Blanco Conde, José Alfonso (Dominican Republic)

FALKLAND ISLANDS (MALVINAS) QUESTION (Agenda item 42)
A/C.4/78/SR.7
PEACEKEEPING OPERATIONS (Agenda item 51)
A/C.4/78/SR.20
TERRORISM (Agenda item 109)
A/C.6/78/SR.4
UN. GENERAL ASSEMBLY (78TH SESS. : 2023-2024). 2ND COMMITTEE—GENERAL DEBATE (Agenda item 8)
A/C.2/78/SR.3
WESTERN SAHARA QUESTION (Agenda item 58)
A/C.4/78/SR.7
WOMEN'S ADVANCEMENT (Agenda item 25a)
A/78/PV.88; A/C.3/78/SR.7
WOMEN'S ADVANCEMENT—CONFERENCES (Agenda item 25b)
A/C.3/78/SR.7

Blanco Rothe, Lara (UN. Executive Office of the Secretary-General. Sustainable Development Unit. Deputy Director)

PERSONS WITH DISABILITIES—HUMAN RIGHTS (Agenda item 71a)
A/C.3/78/SR.18

Blasius, Jacob (Denmark)

YOUTH (Agenda item 24b)
A/C.3/78/SR.3

Bleeker, Mô (UN. Special Adviser to the Secretary-General on the Responsibility to Protect)

RESPONSIBILITY TO PROTECT (Agenda item 129)
A/78/PV.96

Bless, Adrian (Switzerland)

RIGHT TO THE TRUTH (Agenda item 71b)
A/C.3/78/SR.22
TRANSNATIONAL CORPORATIONS—HUMAN RIGHTS (Agenda item 71b)
A/C.3/78/SR.21

Bobozoda, Amriyo (Tajikistan)

UN. GENERAL ASSEMBLY (78TH SESS. : 2023-2024). 1ST COMMITTEE—GENERAL DEBATE (Agenda item 8)
A/C.1/78/PV.7

Bogaerts, Basiel (Belgium) (European Union)

UN—BUDGET (2024) (Agenda item 134)
A/C.5/78/SR.34
UN INTERIM FORCE IN LEBANON—FINANCING (Agenda item 156b)
A/C.5/78/SR.40

Bokoum, Mahamadou (Burkina Faso)

ECONOMIC COOPERATION AMONG DEVELOPING COUNTRIES (Agenda item 22b)
A/C.2/78/SR.18
EXTERNAL DEBT (Agenda item 16c)
A/C.2/78/SR.9
FOOD SECURITY (Agenda item 23a)
A/C.2/78/SR.16
MACROECONOMIC POLICY (Agenda item 16)
A/C.2/78/SR.9
OPERATIONAL ACTIVITIES—UN SYSTEM (Agenda item 22a)
A/C.2/78/SR.18
POVERTY—INTERNATIONAL DECADES (Agenda item 21a)
A/C.2/78/SR.16
RURAL POVERTY (Agenda item 21b)
A/C.2/78/SR.16

Bologa, Anda (European Union)

INFORMATION TECHNOLOGY—DEVELOPMENT (Agenda item 15)
A/C.2/78/SR.23

Boluarte Zegarra, Dina Ercilia (Peru. President)

UN. GENERAL ASSEMBLY (78TH SESS. : 2023-2024)—GENERAL DEBATE (Agenda item 8)
A/78/PV.5
UN. GENERAL ASSEMBLY (78TH SESS. : 2023-2024)—SPECIAL STATEMENTS
A/78/PV.5

Boluda, Miguel (United States)

NON-SELF-GOVERNING TERRITORIES—REPORTS (Agenda item 54)
A/C.4/78/SR.9

Bolwijn, Richard (UNCTAD)

INVESTMENT PROMOTION (Agenda item 16g)
A/C.2/78/SR.8

Boma, Regina Chama (Zambia)

DEVELOPMENT FINANCE (Agenda item 16b)
A/C.2/78/SR.9
INTERNATIONAL TRADE (Agenda item 16a)
A/C.2/78/SR.9

Boma, Regina Chama (Zambia) (continued)

TAXATION (Agenda item 16h)
A/C.2/78/SR.9
UN. GENERAL ASSEMBLY (78TH SESS. : 2023-2024). 1ST COMMITTEE—GENERAL DEBATE (Agenda item 8)
A/C.1/78/PV.8

Boma, Regina Chama (Zambia) (UN. Group of African States)

AL-SABAH, NAWAF AL-AHMAD AL-JABER (KUWAIT. AMIR)—TRIBUTES
A/78/PV.50(Resumption1)

Bongini, Asia (Hurria - Saharawi Solidarity Association)

WESTERN SAHARA QUESTION (Agenda item 58)
A/C.4/78/SR.5

Boric Font, Gabriel (Chile. President)

UN. GENERAL ASSEMBLY (78TH SESS. : 2023-2024)—GENERAL DEBATE (Agenda item 8)
A/78/PV.7
UN. GENERAL ASSEMBLY (78TH SESS. : 2023-2024)—SPECIAL STATEMENTS
A/78/PV.7

Bosch, Robert in den (Netherlands (Kingdom of the))

ARMS RACE—OUTER SPACE (Agenda item 97a)
A/C.1/78/PV.16
ARMS TRANSFERS—TREATIES (Agenda item 99x)
A/C.1/78/PV.18
BIOLOGICAL WEAPONS—TREATIES (Agenda item 106)
A/C.1/78/PV.14
CHEMICAL WEAPONS—TREATIES (Agenda item 99l)
A/C.1/78/PV.14; A/C.1/78/PV.15
CLUSTER MUNITIONS (Agenda item 99dd)
A/C.1/78/PV.18
DISARMAMENT—GENERAL AND COMPLETE (Agenda item 99)
A/C.1/78/PV.18
DISARMAMENT AGREEMENTS—OUTER SPACE (Agenda item 97c)
A/C.1/78/PV.16
INFORMATION—INTERNATIONAL SECURITY (Agenda item 94)
A/C.1/78/PV.20
LANDMINES—TREATIES (Agenda item 99m)
A/C.1/78/PV.18
NUCLEAR DISARMAMENT (Agenda item 99b)
A/C.1/78/PV.11
NUCLEAR DISARMAMENT—CONFERENCES (Agenda item 99aa)
A/C.1/78/PV.26
NUCLEAR DISARMAMENT—VERIFICATION (Agenda item 99ee)
A/C.1/78/PV.11

Bosch, Robert in den (Netherlands (Kingdom of the)) (continued)

NUCLEAR NON-PROLIFERATION—INTERNATIONAL OBLIGATIONS (Agenda item 99w)
A/C.1/78/PV.11
OUTER SPACE—PRINCIPLES (Agenda item 97d)
A/C.1/78/PV.16
UN. CONFERENCE ON DISARMAMENT—REPORTS (Agenda item 101a)
A/C.1/78/PV.23
UN. GENERAL ASSEMBLY (78TH SESS. : 2023-2024). 1ST COMMITTEE—GENERAL DEBATE (Agenda item 8)
A/C.1/78/PV.3

Botero, Stephanie (Colombia)

INTERNATIONAL LAW—TRAINING PROGRAMMES (Agenda item 78)
A/C.6/78/SR.21
RESPONSIBILITY OF INTERNATIONAL ORGANIZATIONS (Agenda item 85)
A/C.6/78/SR.19
TREATIES (Agenda item 87)
A/C.6/78/SR.20

Botero Martínez, José Leonar (Plataforma Latinoamericana y Caribeña de Solidaridad con el Pueblo Saharaui (Organization))

WESTERN SAHARA QUESTION (Agenda item 58)
A/C.4/78/SR.4

Botto, Florian (Monaco)

LAW OF THE SEA (Agenda item 75a)
A/78/PV.43
MARINE ECOSYSTEMS—BIOLOGICAL DIVERSITY (Agenda item 75c)
A/78/PV.43
STRADDLING FISH STOCKS (Agenda item 75b)
A/78/PV.43

Bouamama, Zoheir (Association algérienne de soutien au peuple sahraoui)

WESTERN SAHARA QUESTION (Agenda item 58)
A/C.4/78/SR.4

Bouaziz, Samir (Algerian Youth Academy (Organization))

WESTERN SAHARA QUESTION (Agenda item 58)
A/C.4/78/SR.5

Bouazzaoui, Chaimae (Morocco)

UN—FINANCIAL SITUATION (Agenda item 136)
A/C.5/78/SR.6

Bouchedoub, Mohamed Faiz (Algeria)

CRIMES AGAINST HUMANITY (Agenda item 80)
A/C.6/78/SR.11; A/C.6/78/SR.39; A/C.6/78/SR.41; A/C.6/78/SR.43; A/C.6/78/SR.45
INTERNATIONAL JURISDICTION (Agenda item 84)
A/C.6/78/SR.13

Bouchedoub, Mohamed Faiz (Algeria) (continued)
RULE OF LAW (Agenda item 83)
A/C.6/78/SR.18
UN. INTERNATIONAL LAW COMMISSION—REPORTS (Agenda item 79)
A/C.6/78/SR.28
UN CHARTER—REPORTS (Agenda item 82)
A/C.6/78/SR.34

Bouchikhi, Hanaa (Morocco)
CRIME PREVENTION (Agenda item 107)
A/C.3/78/SR.6
CYBERCRIME (Agenda item 108)
A/C.3/78/SR.6
DISAPPEARANCE OF PERSONS (Agenda item 71b)
A/C.3/78/SR.22
HUMAN RIGHTS (Agenda item 71)
A/C.3/78/SR.16
RELIGIOUS INTOLERANCE (Agenda item 71b)
A/C.3/78/SR.38
RESPONSIBILITY TO PROTECT (Agenda item 129)
A/78/PV.96
SUMMARY EXECUTIONS (Agenda item 71b)
A/C.3/78/SR.31
TERRORISM—HUMAN RIGHTS (Agenda item 71b)
A/C.3/78/SR.31
TRAFFIC SAFETY (Agenda item 12)
A/78/PV.92
UN. HUMAN RIGHTS COUNCIL—REPORTS (Agenda item 66)
A/C.3/78/SR.46
UN HIGH COMMISSIONER FOR REFUGEES—REPORTS (Agenda item 60)
A/C.3/78/SR.45

Boulon, Malaainin ((personal capacity))
WESTERN SAHARA QUESTION (Agenda item 58)
A/C.4/78/SR.5

Bouquet, André (European Union)
UN. INTERNATIONAL LAW COMMISSION—REPORTS (Agenda item 79)
A/C.6/78/SR.28

Bourdon, Sarah (Canada)
CRIMES AGAINST HUMANITY (Agenda item 80)
A/C.6/78/SR.44

Boussif Hammou, Limam ((personal capacity))
WESTERN SAHARA QUESTION (Agenda item 58)
A/C.4/78/SR.5

Boutaqa, Soufiane (Morocco)
UN—BUDGET (2024) (Agenda item 134)
A/C.5/78/SR.33

Bouthé, Marc Gerard C. (Belgium)
HEALTH (Agenda item 125)
A/78/PV.77
VETO (Agenda item 63)
A/78/PV.67

Bouthé, Marc Gerard C. (Belgium) (European Union)
HEALTH (Agenda item 125)
A/78/PV.77

Boutin, Christophe (Université de Caen)
WESTERN SAHARA QUESTION (Agenda item 58)
A/C.4/78/SR.5

Bouziane, Zineb (Morocco)
RULE OF LAW (Agenda item 83)
A/C.6/78/SR.19
UN COMMISSION ON INTERNATIONAL TRADE LAW—REPORTS (Agenda item 77)
A/C.6/78/SR.14

Boyd, David Richard (UN. Human Rights Council. Special Rapporteur on the Human Right to a Clean, Healthy and Sustainable Environment)
ENVIRONMENT (Agenda item 71b)
A/C.3/78/SR.29

Boyd-Lee, Katherine Suzanne Jenkins (United Kingdom)
DEVELOPMENT FINANCE—CONFERENCES (Agenda item 17)
A/78/PV.90

Brands Kehris, Ilze (UN. Assistant Secretary-General for Human Rights)
DISAPPEARANCE OF PERSONS (Agenda item 71b)
A/C.3/78/SR.18
HUMAN RIGHTS—DEMOCRATIC PEOPLE'S REPUBLIC OF KOREA (Agenda item 71c)
A/C.3/78/SR.18
HUMAN RIGHTS—IRAN (ISLAMIC REPUBLIC OF) (Agenda item 71c)
A/C.3/78/SR.18
HUMAN RIGHTS—MYANMAR (Agenda item 71c)
A/C.3/78/SR.18
HUMAN RIGHTS—UKRAINE (Agenda item 71c)
A/C.3/78/SR.18
HUMAN RIGHTS ADVANCEMENT (Agenda item 71b)
A/C.3/78/SR.18
HUMAN RIGHTS INSTITUTIONS—CENTRAL AFRICA (Agenda item 71b)
A/C.3/78/SR.18
HUMAN RIGHTS INSTITUTIONS—SOUTHWEST ASIA AND ARAB COUNTRIES (Agenda item 71b)
A/C.3/78/SR.18
MIGRANTS—PROTECTION (Agenda item 71b)
A/C.3/78/SR.18

Brands Kehris, Ilze (UN. Assistant Secretary-General for Human Rights) (continued)

MINORITIES (Agenda item 71b)
A/C.3/78/SR.18
NATIONAL INSTITUTIONS—HUMAN RIGHTS (Agenda item 71b)
A/C.3/78/SR.18
RACIAL DISCRIMINATION—ELIMINATION (Agenda item 69a)
A/78/PV.63; A/C.3/78/SR.40
RACIAL DISCRIMINATION—PROGRAMMES OF ACTION (Agenda item 69b)
A/C.3/78/SR.40
RELIGIOUS INTOLERANCE (Agenda item 71b)
A/C.3/78/SR.18
RIGHT TO DEVELOPMENT (Agenda item 71b)
A/C.3/78/SR.18
SELF-DETERMINATION OF PEOPLES (Agenda item 70)
A/C.3/78/SR.40
SLAVERY (Agenda item 71a)
A/C.3/78/SR.18
TERRITORIES OCCUPIED BY ISRAEL—HUMAN RIGHTS (Agenda item 50)
A/C.4/78/SR.24
TERRORISM—HUMAN RIGHTS (Agenda item 71b)
A/C.3/78/SR.18
TORTURE AND OTHER CRUEL TREATMENT (Agenda item 71a)
A/C.3/78/SR.18

Brandt, Yoka (Netherlands (Kingdom of the))

ARMED CONFLICTS PREVENTION (Agenda item 31a)
A/78/PV.72
HUMAN RIGHTS ACTIVISTS (Agenda item 71b)
A/C.3/78/SR.19
INTERNATIONAL CRIMINAL COURT—REPORTS (Agenda item 74)
A/78/PV.21
RESPONSIBILITY TO PROTECT (Agenda item 129)
A/78/PV.96
UNRWA—ACTIVITIES (Agenda item 49)
A/C.4/78/SR.22
VETO (Agenda item 63)
A/78/PV.3

Braoios, Victor Silveira (Brazil)

CRIMES AGAINST HUMANITY (Agenda item 80)
A/C.6/78/SR.9; A/C.6/78/SR.38; A/C.6/78/SR.40; A/C.6/78/SR.43
INTERNATIONAL RESIDUAL MECHANISM FOR CRIMINAL TRIBUNALS (Agenda item 126)
A/78/PV.19
NON-CITIZENS—DEPORTATION (Agenda item 81)
A/C.6/78/SR.34
PEACEKEEPING OPERATIONS—CRIMINAL LIABILITY (Agenda item 76)
A/C.6/78/SR.8
RULE OF LAW (Agenda item 83)
A/C.6/78/SR.16

Braoios, Victor Silveira (Brazil) (continued)

TERRORISM (Agenda item 109)
A/C.6/78/SR.1
UN. INTERNATIONAL COURT OF JUSTICE—REPORTS (Agenda item 73)
A/78/PV.27

Brash, Zoe (Israel)

ADMINISTRATION OF JUSTICE (Agenda item 144)
A/C.5/78/SR.15
PEACEKEEPING OPERATIONS—FINANCING (Agenda item 146)
A/C.5/78/SR.35

Brattested, Merete Fjeld (Norway)

DISARMAMENT—GENERAL AND COMPLETE (Agenda item 99)
A/78/PV.105
HUMAN RIGHTS ACTIVISTS (Agenda item 71b)
A/C.3/78/SR.19
PALESTINE QUESTION (Agenda item 35)
A/78/PV.40
TAXATION (Agenda item 16h)
A/C.2/78/SR.25
UN. GENERAL ASSEMBLY (78TH SESS. : 2023-2024)—OFFICERS (Agenda item 5)
A/C.5/78/SR.1
UN. GENERAL ASSEMBLY (78TH SESS. : 2023-2024). 1ST COMMITTEE—GENERAL DEBATE (Agenda item 8)
A/C.1/78/PV.3
UN. GENERAL ASSEMBLY (78TH SESS. : 2023-2024). 2ND COMMITTEE—GENERAL DEBATE (Agenda item 8)
A/C.2/78/SR.4
VETO (Agenda item 63)
A/78/PV.51; A/78/PV.60
WOMEN'S ADVANCEMENT (Agenda item 25a)
A/C.3/78/SR.8
WOMEN'S ADVANCEMENT—CONFERENCES (Agenda item 25b)
A/C.3/78/SR.8

Bravo, Karina (Ecuador)

CRIME PREVENTION (Agenda item 107)
A/C.3/78/SR.5
CYBERCRIME (Agenda item 108)
A/C.3/78/SR.5

Bredel, Ralf (UNIDO)

SUSTAINABLE ENERGY (Agenda item 18h)
A/C.2/78/SR.15

Breen, Patrick (United States)

JUDICIAL INDEPENDENCE (Agenda item 71b)
A/C.3/78/SR.31
PEACE (Agenda item 14)
A/78/PV.48

Breen, Patrick (United States) (continued)

PERSONS WITH DISABILITIES—HUMAN RIGHTS (Agenda item 71a)
A/C.3/78/SR.38
RACIAL DISCRIMINATION—ELIMINATION (Agenda item 69a)
A/C.3/78/SR.40
RACIAL DISCRIMINATION—PROGRAMMES OF ACTION (Agenda item 69b)
A/C.3/78/SR.40
RIGHT TO HOUSING (Agenda item 71b)
A/C.3/78/SR.30
SOCIAL CONDITIONS (Agenda item 24b)
A/C.3/78/SR.51
UN. HUMAN RIGHTS COMMITTEE—REPORTS (Agenda item 71a)
A/C.3/78/SR.17
UN HIGH COMMISSIONER FOR REFUGEES—REPORTS (Agenda item 60)
A/C.3/78/SR.44
WOMEN'S ADVANCEMENT (Agenda item 25a)
A/C.3/78/SR.7
WOMEN'S ADVANCEMENT—CONFERENCES (Agenda item 25b)
A/C.3/78/SR.7

Bregala, Dennis Borromeo (Philippines)

CULTURE—DEVELOPMENT (Agenda item 19b)
A/C.2/78/SR.11
DEVELOPMENT COOPERATION—MIDDLE-INCOME COUNTRIES (Agenda item 19c)
A/C.2/78/SR.11
SCIENCE AND TECHNOLOGY—DEVELOPMENT (Agenda item 19a)
A/C.2/78/SR.11

Breid Eleil, Hamadi ((personal capacity))

WESTERN SAHARA QUESTION (Agenda item 58)
A/C.4/78/SR.5

Brennen-Haylock, Sharon (UN. Advisory Committee on Administrative and Budgetary Questions. Vice-Chair)

UN—BUDGET (2024) (Agenda item 134)
A/C.5/78/SR.31

Brian Nougrères, Ana (UN. Human Rights Council. Special Rapporteur on the Right to Privacy)

RIGHT TO PRIVACY (Agenda item 71b)
A/C.3/78/SR.21

Brinkman, Henk-Jan (International Development Law Organization)

RULE OF LAW (Agenda item 83)
A/C.6/78/SR.19

Briz Gutiérrez, José Alberto (Guatemala)

UN. INTERNATIONAL LAW COMMISSION—REPORTS (Agenda item 79)
A/C.6/78/SR.27

Broadhurst Estival, Nathalie (France)

LAW OF THE SEA (Agenda item 75a)
A/78/PV.48
SUSTAINABLE DEVELOPMENT (Agenda item 18)
A/78/PV.103

Broderick, Fiona (Ireland)

HUMAN RIGHTS (Agenda item 71)
A/C.3/78/SR.16
HUMAN RIGHTS—AFGHANISTAN (Agenda item 71c)
A/C.3/78/SR.34
HUMAN RIGHTS—IRAN (ISLAMIC REPUBLIC OF) (Agenda item 71c)
A/C.3/78/SR.34
HUMAN RIGHTS—SYRIAN ARAB REPUBLIC (Agenda item 71c)
A/C.3/78/SR.34
YOUTH (Agenda item 24b)
A/C.3/78/SR.55

Brotherson, Moetai (French Polynesia)

FRENCH POLYNESIA QUESTION (Agenda item 58)
A/C.4/78/SR.3

Brown, Tahia (French Polynesia)

FRENCH POLYNESIA QUESTION (Agenda item 58)
A/C.4/78/SR.3

Browne, Gaston Alphonso (Antigua and Barbuda. Prime Minister)

UN. GENERAL ASSEMBLY (78TH SESS. : 2023-2024)—GENERAL DEBATE (Agenda item 8)
A/78/PV.10
UN. GENERAL ASSEMBLY (78TH SESS. : 2023-2024)—SPECIAL STATEMENTS
A/78/PV.10

Bruins Slot, Hanke Gerdina Johannette (Netherlands (Kingdom of the))

UKRAINE—POLITICAL CONDITIONS (Agenda item 62)
A/78/PV.56

Brusbārdis, Reinis (Latvia)

UKRAINE—POLITICAL CONDITIONS (Agenda item 62)
A/78/PV.56

Bryant, Rebecca Suzanne (Australia)

ECONOMIC SANCTIONS—INTERNATIONAL RELATIONS (Agenda item 28)
A/78/PV.89
INFORMATION (Agenda item 53)
A/C.4/78/SR.14
PEACE (Agenda item 14)
A/78/PV.62

Bryant, Rebecca Suzanne (Australia) (continued)

PERSONS WITH DISABILITIES—HUMAN RIGHTS (Agenda item 71a)
A/C.3/78/SR.38
RELIGIOUS INTOLERANCE (Agenda item 71b)
A/C.3/78/SR.38
TERRITORIES OCCUPIED BY ISRAEL—NATURAL RESOURCES (Agenda item 59)
A/C.2/78/SR.19
UN. SECURITY COUNCIL—MEMBERSHIP (Agenda item 121)
A/78/PV.35
VETO (Agenda item 63)
A/78/PV.74

Brzeski, Jessica (United States)

RIGHT OF ASSEMBLY (Agenda item 71b)
A/C.3/78/SR.19
RIGHT TO CULTURE (Agenda item 71b)
A/C.3/78/SR.27
SOCIAL DEVELOPMENT (Agenda item 24)
A/C.3/78/SR.47

Buanahagi, Tarcísio Baltazar (Mozambique)

DECOLONIZATION (Agenda item 58)
A/C.4/78/SR.8
FALKLAND ISLANDS (MALVINAS) QUESTION (Agenda item 42)
A/C.4/78/SR.8
WESTERN SAHARA QUESTION (Agenda item 58)
A/C.4/78/SR.8

Bubanja, Jovana (Montenegro)

ELECTION VERIFICATION—UN (Agenda item 71b)
A/C.3/78/SR.50
HUMAN RIGHTS—RUSSIAN FEDERATION (Agenda item 71c)
A/C.3/78/SR.37
HUMAN RIGHTS—UKRAINE (Agenda item 71c)
A/C.3/78/SR.37

Búcaro Flores, Mario Adolfo (Guatemala)

UN. GENERAL ASSEMBLY (78TH SESS. : 2023-2024)—GENERAL DEBATE—RIGHT OF REPLY (Agenda item 8)
A/78/PV.13
UN. INTERNATIONAL COURT OF JUSTICE—REPORTS (Agenda item 73)
A/78/PV.20

Buckley, James E. (Sovereign Order of Malta)

SOLIDARITY (Agenda item 71b)
A/C.3/78/SR.32
WOMEN'S ADVANCEMENT (Agenda item 25a)
A/C.3/78/SR.7
WOMEN'S ADVANCEMENT—CONFERENCES (Agenda item 25b)
A/C.3/78/SR.7

Buden, Radmila (Serbia)

INTERNATIONAL RESIDUAL MECHANISM FOR CRIMINAL TRIBUNALS (Agenda item 126)
A/78/PV.19

Budhu, Vladamir (Trinidad and Tobago)

DEVELOPMENT FINANCE (Agenda item 16b)
A/C.2/78/SR.9
DEVELOPMENT FINANCE—CONFERENCES (Agenda item 17)
A/C.2/78/SR.9
MACROECONOMIC POLICY (Agenda item 16)
A/C.2/78/SR.9
TAXATION (Agenda item 16h)
A/C.2/78/SR.9
UN. GENERAL ASSEMBLY (78TH SESS. : 2023-2024). 2ND COMMITTEE—GENERAL DEBATE (Agenda item 8)
A/C.2/78/SR.5

Buenrostro Massieu, Alicia (Mexico)

CRIMES AGAINST HUMANITY (Agenda item 80)
A/C.6/78/SR.10; A/C.6/78/SR.45
CUBA—UNITED STATES (Agenda item 38)
A/78/PV.24
DISAPPEARANCE OF PERSONS (Agenda item 71b)
A/C.3/78/SR.22
ECONOMIC SANCTIONS—INTERNATIONAL RELATIONS (Agenda item 28)
A/78/PV.89
HEALTH (Agenda item 125)
A/78/PV.48
IAEA—REPORTS (Agenda item 89)
A/78/PV.29
INDIGENOUS PEOPLES (Agenda item 68a)
A/78/PV.107
INTERNATIONAL CRIMINAL COURT—REPORTS (Agenda item 74)
A/78/PV.22
LAW OF THE SEA (Agenda item 75a)
A/78/PV.44
MARINE ECOSYSTEMS—BIOLOGICAL DIVERSITY (Agenda item 75c)
A/78/PV.44
PERSONS WITH DISABILITIES—HUMAN RIGHTS (Agenda item 71a)
A/C.3/78/SR.51
SPECIAL POLITICAL MISSIONS (Agenda item 52)
A/C.4/78/SR.21
STRADDLING FISH STOCKS (Agenda item 75b)
A/78/PV.44
SUSTAINABLE DEVELOPMENT (Agenda item 18)
A/78/PV.107; A/C.2/78/SR.24
TORTURE AND OTHER CRUEL TREATMENT (Agenda item 71a)
A/C.3/78/SR.18
UKRAINE—POLITICAL CONDITIONS (Agenda item 62)
A/78/PV.57

Buenrostro Massieu, Alicia (Mexico) (continued)
UN—BUDGET (2024) (Agenda item 134)
A/C.5/78/SR.5
UN—PROGRAMME PLANNING (Agenda item 135)
A/C.5/78/SR.5
UN. GENERAL ASSEMBLY—WORK PROGRAMME (Agenda item 120)
A/78/PV.33
UN. GENERAL ASSEMBLY (78TH SESS. : 2023-2024). 1ST COMMITTEE—GENERAL DEBATE (Agenda item 8)
A/C.1/78/PV.2
UN. GENERAL ASSEMBLY (78TH SESS. : 2023-2024). 2ND COMMITTEE—GENERAL DEBATE (Agenda item 8)
A/C.2/78/SR.3
UN. SECURITY COUNCIL—MEMBERSHIP (Agenda item 121)
A/78/PV.34
UN. SECURITY COUNCIL—REPORTS (Agenda item 26)
A/78/PV.93
UN RESOLUTIONS—IMPLEMENTATION (Agenda item 119)
A/78/PV.33
VETO (Agenda item 63)
A/78/PV.71

Buenrostro Massieu, Alicia (Mexico) (Group of Friends of Indigenous Peoples)
INDIGENOUS PEOPLES (Agenda item 68a)
A/C.3/78/SR.15
INDIGENOUS PEOPLES—CONFERENCES (Agenda item 68b)
A/C.3/78/SR.15

Bühler, Konrad G. (Austria)
UN. INTERNATIONAL LAW COMMISSION—REPORTS (Agenda item 79)
A/C.6/78/SR.24

Buist-Catherwood, Emily (New Zealand)
HUMAN RIGHTS ACTIVISTS (Agenda item 71b)
A/C.3/78/SR.56
PERSONS WITH DISABILITIES—HUMAN RIGHTS (Agenda item 71a)
A/C.3/78/SR.18; A/C.3/78/SR.51
RACIAL DISCRIMINATION—ELIMINATION (Agenda item 69a)
A/C.3/78/SR.47
RIGHT TO DEVELOPMENT (Agenda item 71b)
A/C.3/78/SR.48
SOCIAL CONDITIONS (Agenda item 24b)
A/C.3/78/SR.51
UKRAINE—POLITICAL CONDITIONS (Agenda item 62)
A/78/PV.58

Bukele, Nayib Armando (El Salvador. President)
UN. GENERAL ASSEMBLY (78TH SESS. : 2023-2024)—GENERAL DEBATE (Agenda item 8)
A/78/PV.5
UN. GENERAL ASSEMBLY (78TH SESS. : 2023-2024)—SPECIAL STATEMENTS
A/78/PV.5

Bulgaru, Dmitrii I. (Russian Federation)
CENTRAL ASIA—ZONES OF PEACE (Agenda item 64)
A/78/PV.85
CRIME PREVENTION (Agenda item 107)
A/C.3/78/SR.6; A/C.3/78/SR.56
HEALTH (Agenda item 125)
A/78/PV.48

Bulvasová, Kristýna (Czechia)
YOUTH (Agenda item 24b)
A/C.3/78/SR.2

Burbergs, Māris (Latvia)
UN. HUMAN RIGHTS COUNCIL—REPORTS (Agenda item 66)
A/C.3/78/SR.46

Buyanover, Gal (UN. Department for General Assembly and Conference Management)
DEVELOPMENT FINANCE—CONFERENCES (Agenda item 17)
A/78/PV.69

Byth-Visholm, Sebastian (Denmark)
TREATIES (Agenda item 87)
A/C.6/78/SR.20
UN. INTERNATIONAL LAW COMMISSION—REPORTS (Agenda item 79)
A/C.6/78/SR.30

Caccia, Gabriele Giordano (Holy See)
ARMS RACE—OUTER SPACE (Agenda item 97a)
A/C.1/78/PV.17
CRIMES AGAINST HUMANITY (Agenda item 80)
A/C.6/78/SR.11; A/C.6/78/SR.39; A/C.6/78/SR.41; A/C.6/78/SR.45
DEVELOPMENT EDUCATION (Agenda item 18g)
A/C.2/78/SR.15
DISARMAMENT—GENERAL AND COMPLETE (Agenda item 99)
A/78/PV.106
HUMAN RIGHTS (Agenda item 71)
A/C.3/78/SR.27
INDIGENOUS PEOPLES (Agenda item 68a)
A/C.3/78/SR.15
INDIGENOUS PEOPLES—CONFERENCES (Agenda item 68b)
A/C.3/78/SR.15
INFORMATION—INTERNATIONAL SECURITY (Agenda item 94)
A/C.1/78/PV.21

Caccia, Gabriele Giordano (Holy See) (continued)
NON-CITIZENS—DEPORTATION (Agenda item 81)
A/C.6/78/SR.34
NUCLEAR DISARMAMENT (Agenda item 99b)
A/C.1/78/PV.14
NUCLEAR NON-PROLIFERATION—INTERNATIONAL OBLIGATIONS (Agenda item 99w)
A/C.1/78/PV.14
OUTER SPACE—CONFIDENCE-BUILDING MEASURES (Agenda item 99v)
A/C.1/78/PV.17
OUTER SPACE—PEACEFUL USES—INTERNATIONAL COOPERATION (Agenda item 48)
A/C.4/78/SR.17
OUTER SPACE—PRINCIPLES (Agenda item 97d)
A/C.1/78/PV.17
POVERTY—INTERNATIONAL DECADES (Agenda item 21a)
A/C.2/78/SR.18
RACIAL DISCRIMINATION—ELIMINATION (Agenda item 69a)
A/78/PV.63; A/C.3/78/SR.43
RACIAL DISCRIMINATION—PROGRAMMES OF ACTION (Agenda item 69b)
A/C.3/78/SR.43
RADIATION EFFECTS (Agenda item 47)
A/C.4/78/SR.11
RULE OF LAW (Agenda item 83)
A/C.6/78/SR.19
SMALL ARMS—ILLICIT TRAFFIC—ASSISTANCE (Agenda item 99n)
A/C.1/78/PV.20
SUSTAINABLE DEVELOPMENT (Agenda item 18)
A/C.2/78/SR.15
UN. GENERAL ASSEMBLY (78TH SESS. : 2023-2024). 1ST COMMITTEE—GENERAL DEBATE (Agenda item 8)
A/C.1/78/PV.9
UN. INTERNATIONAL LAW COMMISSION—REPORTS (Agenda item 79)
A/C.6/78/SR.28; A/C.6/78/SR.30; A/C.6/78/SR.33
UNRWA—ACTIVITIES (Agenda item 49)
A/C.4/78/SR.23

Caldera Gutiérrez, Fiorella (Bolivia (Plurinational State of))
INDIGENOUS PEOPLES (Agenda item 68a)
A/C.3/78/SR.48
RACIAL DISCRIMINATION—ELIMINATION (Agenda item 69a)
A/C.3/78/SR.42
RACIAL DISCRIMINATION—PROGRAMMES OF ACTION (Agenda item 69b)
A/C.3/78/SR.42
SELF-DETERMINATION OF PEOPLES (Agenda item 70)
A/C.3/78/SR.42
UN. HUMAN RIGHTS COUNCIL—REPORTS (Agenda item 66)
A/78/PV.28

Calem-Sangiorgio, Alyson (Monaco)
YOUTH (Agenda item 24b)
A/C.3/78/SR.3

Cali Tzay, José Francisco (UN. Human Rights Council. Special Rapporteur on Rights of Indigenous Peoples)
INDIGENOUS PEOPLES (Agenda item 68a)
A/C.3/78/SR.15

Callaghan-Pace, Laura Frances (United Kingdom)
HUMAN RIGHTS ADVANCEMENT (Agenda item 71b)
A/C.3/78/SR.52

Camara, Mohamed Nassir (Guinea)
PEACEKEEPING OPERATIONS—CRIMINAL LIABILITY (Agenda item 76)
A/C.6/78/SR.9
RULE OF LAW (Agenda item 83)
A/C.6/78/SR.18

Camelli, Thibault (European Union)
UN—BUDGET (2024) (Agenda item 134)
A/C.5/78/SR.3
UN—FINANCIAL SITUATION (Agenda item 136)
A/C.5/78/SR.38
UN. GENERAL ASSEMBLY (78TH SESS. : 2023-2024). 5TH COMMITTEE—WORK ORGANIZATION (Agenda item 7)
A/C.5/78/SR.27; A/C.5/78/SR.34; A/C.5/78/SR.35

Cameron, David (United Kingdom)
UKRAINE—POLITICAL CONDITIONS (Agenda item 62)
A/78/PV.56

Cameron, Eric (World Action for Refugees (Norway))
WESTERN SAHARA QUESTION (Agenda item 58)
A/C.4/78/SR.5

Camilleri, Darren (Malta)
VETO (Agenda item 63)
A/78/PV.78

Campbell Barr, Epsy (UN. Permanent Forum on People of African Descent. Chair)
RACIAL DISCRIMINATION—PROGRAMMES OF ACTION (Agenda item 69b)
A/C.3/78/SR.42

Campos, Erika Helena (Brazil)
OUTER SPACE—PEACEFUL USES—INTERNATIONAL COOPERATION (Agenda item 48)
A/C.4/78/SR.16
PEACEKEEPING OPERATIONS (Agenda item 51)
A/C.4/78/SR.20

Candia Ibarra, Miguel Ricardo (Paraguay)

RIGHTS OF THE CHILD (Agenda item 67)
A/C.3/78/SR.14
UN. HUMAN RIGHTS COMMITTEE—REPORTS (Agenda item 71a)
A/C.3/78/SR.17

Cano Franco, Zoraya del Carmen (Panama)

PEACE (Agenda item 14)
A/78/PV.82
VETO (Agenda item 63)
A/78/PV.69

Cantero Talavera, Francisco Javier (Spain)

ENVIRONMENT (Agenda item 71b)
A/C.3/78/SR.29

Cao, Liwen (China)

FOOD SECURITY (Agenda item 23a)
A/C.2/78/SR.16
POVERTY—INTERNATIONAL DECADES (Agenda item 21a)
A/C.2/78/SR.16
RURAL POVERTY (Agenda item 21b)
A/C.2/78/SR.16
SUSTAINABLE DEVELOPMENT (Agenda item 18)
A/C.2/78/SR.24
TERRITORIES OCCUPIED BY ISRAEL—NATURAL RESOURCES (Agenda item 59)
A/C.2/78/SR.19

Capek, Hannah Rose (United Kingdom)

UN—BUDGET (2024) (Agenda item 134)
A/C.5/78/SR.26/PartII

Cappon, Noam (Israel)

CRIMES AGAINST HUMANITY (Agenda item 80)
A/C.6/78/SR.10; A/C.6/78/SR.11; A/C.6/78/SR.38
DISASTER VICTIMS (Agenda item 86)
A/C.6/78/SR.5
HEALTH (Agenda item 125)
A/78/PV.41
INTERNATIONAL CRIMINAL COURT—REPORTS (Agenda item 74)
A/78/PV.25
RULE OF LAW (Agenda item 83)
A/C.6/78/SR.19
TERRORISM (Agenda item 109)
A/C.6/78/SR.1; A/C.6/78/SR.5
UN. INTERNATIONAL COURT OF JUSTICE—REPORTS (Agenda item 73)
A/78/PV.28
UN. INTERNATIONAL LAW COMMISSION—REPORTS (Agenda item 79)
A/C.6/78/SR.24
UN INTERIM FORCE IN LEBANON—FINANCING (Agenda item 156b)
A/78/PV.95

Caputová, Zuzana (Slovakia. President)

UN. GENERAL ASSEMBLY (78TH SESS. : 2023-2024)—GENERAL DEBATE (Agenda item 8)
A/78/PV.6
UN. GENERAL ASSEMBLY (78TH SESS. : 2023-2024)—SPECIAL STATEMENTS
A/78/PV.6

Cardon De Lichtbuer, Christophe Alain C. (Belgium)

ARMED CONFLICTS PREVENTION (Agenda item 31a)
A/78/PV.72

Carey, Patrick (UN. Department of Operational Support. Division of Administration. Director)

UN—BUDGET (2024) (Agenda item 134)
A/C.5/78/SR.11

Carlé, Hanne (European Union)

HUMAN RIGHTS (Agenda item 71)
A/C.3/78/SR.16
HUMAN RIGHTS—MYANMAR (Agenda item 71c)
A/C.3/78/SR.33
HUMAN RIGHTS ACTIVISTS (Agenda item 71b)
A/C.3/78/SR.19
HUMAN RIGHTS ADVANCEMENT (Agenda item 71b)
A/C.3/78/SR.18
RIGHT OF ASSEMBLY (Agenda item 71b)
A/C.3/78/SR.19
SUMMARY EXECUTIONS (Agenda item 71b)
A/C.3/78/SR.31
TERRORISM—HUMAN RIGHTS (Agenda item 71b)
A/C.3/78/SR.31
WOMEN'S ADVANCEMENT (Agenda item 25a)
A/C.3/78/SR.7
WOMEN'S ADVANCEMENT—CONFERENCES (Agenda item 25b)
A/C.3/78/SR.7

Carlsson Szlezak, Teresa (European Union)

HUMAN RIGHTS—TERRITORIES OCCUPIED BY ISRAEL (Agenda item 71c)
A/C.3/78/SR.35
RIGHT TO DEVELOPMENT (Agenda item 71b)
A/C.3/78/SR.20

Carmeli, Mor (Israel)

RIGHTS OF THE CHILD (Agenda item 67)
A/C.3/78/SR.12
TERRORISM—HUMAN RIGHTS (Agenda item 71b)
A/C.3/78/SR.26
YOUTH (Agenda item 24b)
A/C.3/78/SR.55

Carmona, Guillermo (Argentina)

FALKLAND ISLANDS (MALVINAS) QUESTION (Agenda item 42)
A/C.4/78/SR.7

Carpenter, Christoph (Switzerland)

TERRITORIES OCCUPIED BY ISRAEL—HUMAN RIGHTS (Agenda item 50)
A/C.4/78/SR.26
UNRWA—ACTIVITIES (Agenda item 49)
A/C.4/78/SR.26

Carr, Michelle (Australia)

ARMS TRANSFERS—TREATIES (Agenda item 99x)
A/C.1/78/PV.19
CLUSTER MUNITIONS (Agenda item 99dd)
A/C.1/78/PV.19
DISARMAMENT—GENERAL AND COMPLETE (Agenda item 99)
A/C.1/78/PV.19; A/C.1/78/PV.28
LANDMINES—TREATIES (Agenda item 99m)
A/C.1/78/PV.19
SMALL ARMS—ILLICIT TRAFFIC—ASSISTANCE (Agenda item 99n)
A/C.1/78/PV.19

Carral Castelo, Arianna (Cuba)

ADMINISTRATION OF JUSTICE (Agenda item 144)
A/C.6/78/SR.9
CRIMES AGAINST HUMANITY (Agenda item 80)
A/C.6/78/SR.39; A/C.6/78/SR.40
DISASTER VICTIMS (Agenda item 86)
A/C.6/78/SR.6
INTERNATIONAL JURISDICTION (Agenda item 84)
A/C.6/78/SR.12
PEACEKEEPING OPERATIONS—CRIMINAL LIABILITY (Agenda item 76)
A/C.6/78/SR.8
UN. INTERNATIONAL COURT OF JUSTICE—REPORTS (Agenda item 73)
A/78/PV.27

Carral Castelo, Arianna (Cuba) (Group of 77)

INTERNATIONAL LAW—TRAINING PROGRAMMES (Agenda item 78)
A/C.6/78/SR.21

Carreiras, Helena (Portugal)

UKRAINE—POLITICAL CONDITIONS (Agenda item 62)
A/78/PV.56

Carrell, Leah (New Zealand)

INDIGENOUS PEOPLES (Agenda item 68a)
A/C.3/78/SR.15
INDIGENOUS PEOPLES—CONFERENCES (Agenda item 68b)
A/C.3/78/SR.15

Carty, Lisa A. (United States)

EMERGENCY ASSISTANCE (Agenda item 72a)
A/78/PV.46

Carty, Lisa A. (United States) (continued)

HEALTH (Agenda item 125)
A/78/PV.16; A/78/PV.48
HUMAN RIGHTS—IRAN (ISLAMIC REPUBLIC OF) (Agenda item 71c)
A/C.3/78/SR.34
HUMAN RIGHTS—SYRIAN ARAB REPUBLIC (Agenda item 71c)
A/C.3/78/SR.54
MILLENNIUM SUMMIT—CONFERENCES (Agenda item 117)
A/78/PV.15
PALESTINIANS—ASSISTANCE (Agenda item 72b)
A/78/PV.46
RACIAL DISCRIMINATION—ELIMINATION (Agenda item 69a)
A/C.3/78/SR.47
SLAVERY—MEMORIALS (Agenda item 118)
A/78/PV.64
UN. GENERAL ASSEMBLY (78TH SESS. : 2023-2024)—VICE-PRESIDENTS (Agenda item 6)
A/78/PV.87
UN. GENERAL ASSEMBLY (78TH SESS. : 2023-2024). 2ND COMMITTEE—GENERAL DEBATE (Agenda item 8)
A/C.2/78/SR.3
UN. GENERAL ASSEMBLY (78TH SESS. : 2023-2024). PRESIDENT (Agenda item 4)
A/78/PV.87
UN CONFERENCES (Agenda item 13)
A/78/PV.15
WOMEN'S ADVANCEMENT (Agenda item 25a)
A/C.3/78/SR.9
WOMEN'S ADVANCEMENT—CONFERENCES (Agenda item 25b)
A/C.3/78/SR.9

Carvalho, Sergio Amaral Alves de (Portugal)

CRIMES AGAINST HUMANITY (Agenda item 80)
A/C.6/78/SR.38; A/C.6/78/SR.40; A/C.6/78/SR.45
PEACEKEEPING OPERATIONS—CRIMINAL LIABILITY (Agenda item 76)
A/C.6/78/SR.8
RESPONSIBILITY OF INTERNATIONAL ORGANIZATIONS (Agenda item 85)
A/C.6/78/SR.19
UN. GENERAL ASSEMBLY—WORK PROGRAMME (Agenda item 120)
A/C.6/78/SR.36
UN. INTERNATIONAL LAW COMMISSION—REPORTS (Agenda item 79)
A/C.6/78/SR.29; A/C.6/78/SR.31

Cassis, Ignazio (Switzerland)

UKRAINE—POLITICAL CONDITIONS (Agenda item 62)
A/78/PV.56

Castillo, William (Venezuela (Bolivarian Republic of)) (Group of Friends in Defence of the Charter of the United Nations)

EMERGENCY ASSISTANCE (Agenda item 72a)
A/78/PV.46
PALESTINIANS—ASSISTANCE (Agenda item 72b)
A/78/PV.46

Castonguay, Marie-Eve (Canada)

HEALTH (Agenda item 125)
A/78/PV.64

Castro Sarmiento, Iris Xiomara (Honduras. President)

UN. GENERAL ASSEMBLY (78TH SESS. : 2023-2024)—GENERAL DEBATE (Agenda item 8)
A/78/PV.6
UN. GENERAL ASSEMBLY (78TH SESS. : 2023-2024)—SPECIAL STATEMENTS
A/78/PV.6

Cedano, Joan Margarita (Dominican Republic)

CRIME PREVENTION (Agenda item 107)
A/C.3/78/SR.6
CYBERCRIME (Agenda item 108)
A/C.3/78/SR.6
HUMAN RIGHTS ADVANCEMENT (Agenda item 71b)
A/C.3/78/SR.26
INFORMATION (Agenda item 53)
A/C.4/78/SR.13
RULE OF LAW (Agenda item 83)
A/C.6/78/SR.18
UN. HUMAN RIGHTS COUNCIL—REPORTS (Agenda item 66)
A/78/PV.28
WOMEN'S ADVANCEMENT (Agenda item 25a)
A/C.3/78/SR.9
WOMEN'S ADVANCEMENT—CONFERENCES (Agenda item 25b)
A/C.3/78/SR.9

Cedano, Joan Margarita (Dominican Republic) (Grupo de Amigos del Español en las Naciones Unidas)

MULTILINGUALISM (Agenda item 124)
A/78/PV.107

Célestin, Miousemine (Haiti)

WOMEN'S ADVANCEMENT (Agenda item 25a)
A/C.3/78/SR.10
WOMEN'S ADVANCEMENT—CONFERENCES (Agenda item 25b)
A/C.3/78/SR.10

Celorio Alcántara, Alexandro (Mexico)

UN. INTERNATIONAL COURT OF JUSTICE—REPORTS (Agenda item 73)
A/78/PV.20

Çetin, Ahmet Erman (Türkiye)

ARMS TRANSFERS—TREATIES (Agenda item 99x)
A/C.1/78/PV.18
CHEMICAL WEAPONS—TREATIES (Agenda item 99l)
A/C.1/78/PV.26
CONVENTIONAL WEAPONS (Agenda item 99u)
A/C.1/78/PV.18
CONVENTIONAL WEAPONS—TREATIES (Agenda item 103)
A/C.1/78/PV.18
DISARMAMENT—GENERAL AND COMPLETE (Agenda item 99)
A/C.1/78/PV.28
DISARMAMENT AGREEMENTS—OUTER SPACE (Agenda item 97c)
A/C.1/78/PV.27
LANDMINES—TREATIES (Agenda item 99m)
A/C.1/78/PV.18
LAW OF THE SEA (Agenda item 75a)
A/78/PV.44
MARINE ECOSYSTEMS—BIOLOGICAL DIVERSITY (Agenda item 75c)
A/78/PV.44
MILLENNIUM SUMMIT—CONFERENCES (Agenda item 117)
A/78/PV.102
NUCLEAR DISARMAMENT (Agenda item 99b)
A/C.1/78/PV.13
NUCLEAR NON-PROLIFERATION—INTERNATIONAL OBLIGATIONS (Agenda item 99w)
A/C.1/78/PV.13
NUCLEAR WEAPON TESTS—TREATIES (Agenda item 105)
A/C.1/78/PV.13
SMALL ARMS—ILLICIT TRAFFIC (Agenda item 99p)
A/C.1/78/PV.18
SMALL ARMS—ILLICIT TRAFFIC—ASSISTANCE (Agenda item 99n)
A/C.1/78/PV.18
STRADDLING FISH STOCKS (Agenda item 75b)
A/78/PV.44
UN. GENERAL ASSEMBLY (78TH SESS. : 2023-2024). 1ST COMMITTEE—GENERAL DEBATE (Agenda item 8)
A/C.1/78/PV.7
UN CONFERENCES (Agenda item 13)
A/78/PV.102

Chabi, Amine (Morocco)

TORTURE AND OTHER CRUEL TREATMENT (Agenda item 71a)
A/C.3/78/SR.18

Chailloux, Steve (France)

FRENCH POLYNESIA QUESTION (Agenda item 58)
A/C.4/78/SR.3

Chaivaivid, Cherdchai (Thailand)
HIV/AIDS—DECLARATIONS (Agenda item 10)
A/78/PV.91

Chak Yong, Mok (Singapore)
EMERGENCY ASSISTANCE (Agenda item 72a)
A/78/PV.46
PALESTINIANS—ASSISTANCE (Agenda item 72b)
A/78/PV.46

Chak Yong, Mok (Singapore) (ASEAN)
UN—BUDGET (2024) (Agenda item 134)
A/C.5/78/SR.12

Chakwera, Lazarus McCarthy (Malawi. President)
UN. GENERAL ASSEMBLY (78TH SESS. : 2023-2024)—GENERAL DEBATE (Agenda item 8)
A/78/PV.8
UN. GENERAL ASSEMBLY (78TH SESS. : 2023-2024)—SPECIAL STATEMENTS
A/78/PV.8

Chala, Samuel Isa (Ethiopia)
HUMAN RIGHTS ADVANCEMENT (Agenda item 71b)
A/C.3/78/SR.25
RIGHTS OF THE CHILD (Agenda item 67)
A/C.3/78/SR.13

Chan Valverde, Maritza (Costa Rica)
AGEING PERSONS (Agenda item 24b)
A/C.3/78/SR.3
ARMED CONFLICTS PREVENTION (Agenda item 31a)
A/78/PV.72
ARMS RACE—OUTER SPACE (Agenda item 97a)
A/C.1/78/PV.16
BIOLOGICAL DIVERSITY—TREATIES (Agenda item 18f)
A/C.2/78/SR.13
CLIMATE (Agenda item 18d)
A/C.2/78/SR.13
CONVENTIONAL WEAPONS (Agenda item 99u)
A/C.1/78/PV.18
CRIMES AGAINST HUMANITY (Agenda item 80)
A/C.6/78/SR.10
DECOLONIZATION (Agenda item 58)
A/C.4/78/SR.7
DISARMAMENT—GENERAL AND COMPLETE (Agenda item 99)
A/C.1/78/PV.18
DISARMAMENT AGREEMENTS—OUTER SPACE (Agenda item 97c)
A/C.1/78/PV.16
DISASTER PREVENTION (Agenda item 18c)
A/C.2/78/SR.13
ENVIRONMENT (Agenda item 71b)
A/C.3/78/SR.26

Chan Valverde, Maritza (Costa Rica) (continued)
FALKLAND ISLANDS (MALVINAS) QUESTION (Agenda item 42)
A/C.4/78/SR.7
FOOD SECURITY (Agenda item 23a)
A/C.2/78/SR.17
HUMAN RIGHTS—INTERNATIONAL INSTRUMENTS (Agenda item 71a)
A/C.3/78/SR.26
IAEA—REPORTS (Agenda item 89)
A/78/PV.29
INFORMATION (Agenda item 53)
A/C.4/78/SR.13
INTERNATIONAL CRIMINAL COURT—REPORTS (Agenda item 74)
A/78/PV.21
LAW OF THE SEA (Agenda item 75a)
A/78/PV.44
MARINE ECOSYSTEMS—BIOLOGICAL DIVERSITY (Agenda item 75c)
A/78/PV.44
MIGRANTS—PROTECTION (Agenda item 71b)
A/C.3/78/SR.26
MILLENNIUM SUMMIT—CONFERENCES (Agenda item 117)
A/78/PV.102
NUCLEAR DISARMAMENT (Agenda item 99b)
A/C.1/78/PV.13
NUCLEAR NON-PROLIFERATION—INTERNATIONAL OBLIGATIONS (Agenda item 99w)
A/C.1/78/PV.13
NUCLEAR WEAPONS—TREATIES (Agenda item 99ff)
A/C.1/78/PV.13
OUTER SPACE—CONFIDENCE-BUILDING MEASURES (Agenda item 99v)
A/C.1/78/PV.16
OUTER SPACE—PEACEFUL USES—INTERNATIONAL COOPERATION (Agenda item 48)
A/C.4/78/SR.16
OUTER SPACE—PRINCIPLES (Agenda item 97d)
A/C.1/78/PV.16
POVERTY—INTERNATIONAL DECADES (Agenda item 21a)
A/C.2/78/SR.17
RACIAL DISCRIMINATION—ELIMINATION (Agenda item 69a)
A/C.3/78/SR.42
RACIAL DISCRIMINATION—PROGRAMMES OF ACTION (Agenda item 69b)
A/C.3/78/SR.42
RESPONSIBILITY TO PROTECT (Agenda item 129)
A/78/PV.96
RULE OF LAW (Agenda item 83)
A/C.6/78/SR.16
RURAL POVERTY (Agenda item 21b)
A/C.2/78/SR.17
SMALL ARMS—ILLICIT TRAFFIC (Agenda item 99p)
A/C.1/78/PV.18

Chan Valverde, Maritza (Costa Rica) (continued)

SMALL ARMS—ILLICIT TRAFFIC—ASSISTANCE (Agenda item 99n)
A/C.1/78/PV.18
SOCIAL CONDITIONS (Agenda item 24b)
A/C.3/78/SR.3
SOCIAL DEVELOPMENT (Agenda item 24)
A/C.3/78/SR.3
SOCIAL DEVELOPMENT—CONFERENCES (Agenda item 24a)
A/C.3/78/SR.3
STRADDLING FISH STOCKS (Agenda item 75b)
A/78/PV.44
UKRAINE—POLITICAL CONDITIONS (Agenda item 62)
A/78/PV.57
UN—BUDGET (2024) (Agenda item 134)
A/C.5/78/SR.5
UN—PROGRAMME PLANNING (Agenda item 135)
A/C.1/78/PV.10; A/C.5/78/SR.5
UN. GENERAL ASSEMBLY—WORK PROGRAMME (Agenda item 120)
A/78/PV.32; A/C.1/78/PV.10; A/C.6/78/SR.36
UN. GENERAL ASSEMBLY (78TH SESS. : 2023-2024)—OFFICERS (Agenda item 5)
A/C.1/78/PV.31
UN. GENERAL ASSEMBLY (78TH SESS. : 2023-2024). 1ST COMMITTEE—GENERAL DEBATE (Agenda item 8)
A/C.1/78/PV.8
UN. HUMAN RIGHTS COUNCIL—REPORTS (Agenda item 66)
A/78/PV.23
UN. INTERNATIONAL COURT OF JUSTICE—REPORTS (Agenda item 73)
A/78/PV.27
UN. SECRETARY-GENERAL—REPORTS (Agenda item 110)
A/78/PV.54
UN. SECURITY COUNCIL—MEMBERSHIP (Agenda item 121)
A/78/PV.34
UN CONFERENCES (Agenda item 13)
A/78/PV.102
UN RESOLUTIONS—IMPLEMENTATION (Agenda item 119)
A/78/PV.32
VETO (Agenda item 63)
A/78/PV.3; A/78/PV.66; A/78/PV.70; A/78/PV.74; A/78/PV.78
WESTERN SAHARA QUESTION (Agenda item 58)
A/C.4/78/SR.7

Chanda, Riccarda (Switzerland)

DISASTER VICTIMS (Agenda item 86)
A/C.6/78/SR.6
INTERNATIONAL CRIMINAL COURT—REPORTS (Agenda item 74)
A/78/PV.22
UN. GENERAL ASSEMBLY (78TH SESS. : 2023-2024)—OFFICERS (Agenda item 5)
A/C.5/78/SR.1

Chanda, Riccarda (Switzerland) (continued)

UN. HUMAN RIGHTS COUNCIL—REPORTS (Agenda item 66)
A/78/PV.23
VETO (Agenda item 63)
A/78/PV.60; A/78/PV.66; A/78/PV.68

Chanda, Theresah Chipulu Luswili (Zambia)

LANDLOCKED DEVELOPING COUNTRIES—CONFERENCES (Agenda item 20b)
A/C.2/78/SR.7
LEAST DEVELOPED COUNTRIES—CONFERENCES (Agenda item 20a)
A/C.2/78/SR.7

Chaouki, Naser-Allah (Morocco)

HAZARDOUS WASTES (Agenda item 71b)
A/C.3/78/SR.29
RIGHT TO FOOD (Agenda item 71b)
A/C.3/78/SR.30

Chaquki, Naser-Allah (Morocco)

YOUTH (Agenda item 24b)
A/C.3/78/SR.3

Charmakar, Ramesh Kumar (Nepal)

PEACEKEEPING OPERATIONS—CRIMINAL LIABILITY (Agenda item 76)
A/C.6/78/SR.8

Chasi, Victoria (International Federation of Red Cross and Red Crescent Societies)

UN HIGH COMMISSIONER FOR REFUGEES—REPORTS (Agenda item 60)
A/C.3/78/SR.45

Chatrnúch, Róbert (Slovakia)

UN. GENERAL ASSEMBLY (78TH SESS. : 2023-2024). 1ST COMMITTEE—GENERAL DEBATE (Agenda item 8)
A/C.1/78/PV.4

Chaves, Joaquim José Costa (Timor-Leste)

PEACEBUILDING (Agenda item 61)
A/78/PV.101
PEACEKEEPING OPERATIONS (Agenda item 51)
A/C.4/78/SR.19
UN. PEACEBUILDING COMMISSION—REPORTS (Agenda item 27)
A/78/PV.101
UN. PEACEBUILDING FUND—REPORTS (Agenda item 111)
A/78/PV.101

Chelbi, Kaouthar (Tunisia)

UN. GENERAL ASSEMBLY (78TH SESS. : 2023-2024). 2ND COMMITTEE—GENERAL DEBATE (Agenda item 8)
A/C.2/78/SR.4

Chen, Jiawen (China)

HUMAN RIGHTS—AFGHANISTAN (Agenda item 71c)
A/C.3/78/SR.34
HUMAN RIGHTS—CENTRAL AFRICAN REPUBLIC (Agenda item 71c)
A/C.3/78/SR.33
HUMAN RIGHTS—DEMOCRATIC PEOPLE'S REPUBLIC OF KOREA (Agenda item 71c)
A/C.3/78/SR.33
HUMAN RIGHTS—IRAN (ISLAMIC REPUBLIC OF) (Agenda item 71c)
A/C.3/78/SR.34
HUMAN RIGHTS—MYANMAR (Agenda item 71c)
A/C.3/78/SR.33
HUMAN RIGHTS—SYRIAN ARAB REPUBLIC (Agenda item 71c)
A/C.3/78/SR.34
HUMAN RIGHTS—UKRAINE (Agenda item 71c)
A/C.3/78/SR.37
PERSONS WITH DISABILITIES—HUMAN RIGHTS (Agenda item 71a)
A/C.3/78/SR.38
RELIGIOUS INTOLERANCE (Agenda item 71b)
A/C.3/78/SR.38

Chen, Jing (Canada) (UN Scientific Committee on the Effects of Atomic Radiation. Chair)

RADIATION EFFECTS (Agenda item 47)
A/C.4/78/SR.11

Chen, Yuanhang (China)

UN—BUDGET (2024) (Agenda item 134)
A/C.5/78/SR.3

Cherif, Ali (Tunisia)

UN. GENERAL ASSEMBLY (78TH SESS. : 2023-2024). 1ST COMMITTEE—GENERAL DEBATE (Agenda item 8)
A/C.1/78/PV.4

Chimbindi, Albert Ranganai (Zimbabwe)

DIAMONDS—FUELLING CONFLICT (Agenda item 30)
A/78/PV.65
ECONOMIC SANCTIONS—INTERNATIONAL RELATIONS (Agenda item 28)
A/78/PV.90
HIV/AIDS—DECLARATIONS (Agenda item 10)
A/78/PV.91
RACIAL DISCRIMINATION—ELIMINATION (Agenda item 69a)
A/78/PV.50

Chimbiri-Molande, Agnes Mary (Malawi)

ALBINISM (Agenda item 71b)
A/C.3/78/SR.47
SOCIAL DEVELOPMENT (Agenda item 24)
A/C.3/78/SR.47

Chimbiri-Molande, Agnes Mary (Malawi) (continued)

UN. GENERAL ASSEMBLY (78TH SESS. : 2023-2024). 2ND COMMITTEE—GENERAL DEBATE (Agenda item 8)
A/C.2/78/SR.6

Chindawongse, Suriya ((personal capacity))

UN. INTERNATIONAL COURT OF JUSTICE—REPORTS (Agenda item 73)
A/C.6/78/SR.26

Chindawongse, Suriya (Thailand)

AFRICA—SUSTAINABLE DEVELOPMENT—PARTNERSHIP (Agenda item 65a)
A/78/PV.18
HEALTH (Agenda item 125)
A/78/PV.41
HUMAN RIGHTS—MYANMAR (Agenda item 71c)
A/C.3/78/SR.33; A/C.3/78/SR.53
HUMAN RIGHTS ADVANCEMENT (Agenda item 71b)
A/C.3/78/SR.25
INTERNATIONAL JURISDICTION (Agenda item 84)
A/C.6/78/SR.12
NUCLEAR DISARMAMENT (Agenda item 99b)
A/C.1/78/PV.13
NUCLEAR NON-PROLIFERATION—INTERNATIONAL OBLIGATIONS (Agenda item 99w)
A/C.1/78/PV.13
NUCLEAR WEAPON TESTS—TREATIES (Agenda item 105)
A/C.1/78/PV.13
NUCLEAR WEAPONS—TREATIES (Agenda item 99ff)
A/C.1/78/PV.13
RIGHT TO HEALTH (Agenda item 71b)
A/C.3/78/SR.25
RULE OF LAW (Agenda item 83)
A/C.6/78/SR.16
SOUTH-EAST ASIA—NUCLEAR-WEAPON-FREE ZONES (Agenda item 99y)
A/C.1/78/PV.13
UKRAINE—POLITICAL CONDITIONS (Agenda item 62)
A/78/PV.58
UN. ECONOMIC AND SOCIAL COUNCIL—REPORTS (Agenda item 9)
A/78/PV.33
UN. GENERAL ASSEMBLY—WORK PROGRAMME (Agenda item 120)
A/78/PV.32
UN. GENERAL ASSEMBLY (78TH SESS. : 2023-2024). 1ST COMMITTEE—GENERAL DEBATE (Agenda item 8)
A/C.1/78/PV.3
UN. GENERAL ASSEMBLY (78TH SESS. : 2023-2024). 2ND COMMITTEE—GENERAL DEBATE (Agenda item 8)
A/C.2/78/SR.3

Chindawongse, Suriya (Thailand) (continued)

UN. SECURITY COUNCIL—MEMBERSHIP (Agenda item 121)
A/78/PV.34
UN CONFERENCES (Agenda item 13)
A/78/PV.33
UN RESOLUTIONS—IMPLEMENTATION (Agenda item 119)
A/78/PV.32
UNRWA—ACTIVITIES (Agenda item 49)
A/C.4/78/SR.22
VETO (Agenda item 63)
A/78/PV.51; A/78/PV.60; A/78/PV.75

Chindawongse, Suriya (Thailand) (ASEAN)

ECONOMIC COOPERATION AMONG DEVELOPING COUNTRIES (Agenda item 22b)
A/C.2/78/SR.18
INFORMATION—INTERNATIONAL SECURITY (Agenda item 94)
A/C.1/78/PV.20
OPERATIONAL ACTIVITIES—UN SYSTEM (Agenda item 22a)
A/C.2/78/SR.18

Ching, Martha (Singapore)

INFORMATION TECHNOLOGY—DEVELOPMENT (Agenda item 15)
A/C.2/78/SR.10
SCIENCE AND TECHNOLOGY—DEVELOPMENT (Agenda item 19a)
A/C.2/78/SR.10

Chivundu, Renata (Malawi)

FOOD SECURITY (Agenda item 23a)
A/C.2/78/SR.17
INFORMATION TECHNOLOGY—DEVELOPMENT (Agenda item 15)
A/C.2/78/SR.10
POVERTY—INTERNATIONAL DECADES (Agenda item 21a)
A/C.2/78/SR.17
RURAL POVERTY (Agenda item 21b)
A/C.2/78/SR.17

Chmielewski, Jakub (UN. Advisory Committee on Administrative and Budgetary Questions. Vice-Chair)

INTERNATIONAL RESIDUAL MECHANISM FOR CRIMINAL TRIBUNALS—FINANCING (Agenda item 145)
A/C.5/78/SR.20
UN—ADMINISTRATION (Agenda item 132)
A/C.5/78/SR.29
UN—BUDGET (2024) (Agenda item 134)
A/C.5/78/SR.3; A/C.5/78/SR.11; A/C.5/78/SR.12
UN MULTIDIMENSIONAL INTEGRATED STABILIZATION MISSION IN MALI—FINANCING (Agenda item 155)
A/C.5/78/SR.20

Cho, Hyunwoo (Republic of Korea)

UN. GENERAL ASSEMBLY (78TH SESS. : 2023-2024). 2ND COMMITTEE—GENERAL DEBATE (Agenda item 8)
A/C.2/78/SR.4
VETO (Agenda item 63)
A/78/PV.70

Cho, Seong-Jun (Republic of Korea)

TAXATION (Agenda item 16h)
A/C.2/78/SR.25

Choi, Taeeun (Republic of Korea)

INTERNATIONAL CRIMINAL COURT—REPORTS (Agenda item 74)
A/78/PV.22
UN COMMISSION ON INTERNATIONAL TRADE LAW—REPORTS (Agenda item 77)
A/C.6/78/SR.14

Chong, Charis (Singapore)

WOMEN'S ADVANCEMENT (Agenda item 25a)
A/C.3/78/SR.8
WOMEN'S ADVANCEMENT—CONFERENCES (Agenda item 25b)
A/C.3/78/SR.8

Chong, Mickaël (Kea Consulting (Organization))

FRENCH POLYNESIA QUESTION (Agenda item 58)
A/C.4/78/SR.3

Choong, Brandon (Singapore)

AGEING PERSONS (Agenda item 24b)
A/C.3/78/SR.2
FAMILY (Agenda item 24b)
A/C.3/78/SR.2
PERSONS WITH DISABILITIES (Agenda item 24b)
A/C.3/78/SR.2
YOUTH (Agenda item 24b)
A/C.3/78/SR.2

Choque Rosario, Dem Mijael (Bolivia (Plurinational State of))

PEACEKEEPING OPERATIONS (Agenda item 51)
A/C.4/78/SR.20

Chrif, Moulay Brahim ((personal capacity))

WESTERN SAHARA QUESTION (Agenda item 58)
A/C.4/78/SR.5

Christodoulides, Nikos (Cyprus. President)

UN. GENERAL ASSEMBLY (78TH SESS. : 2023-2024)—GENERAL DEBATE (Agenda item 8)
A/78/PV.6
UN. GENERAL ASSEMBLY (78TH SESS. : 2023-2024)—SPECIAL STATEMENTS
A/78/PV.6

Christoglou, Konstantinos (Greece)
ARMS TRANSFERS—TREATIES (Agenda item 99x)
A/C.1/78/PV.19
CONVENTIONAL WEAPONS (Agenda item 99u)
A/C.1/78/PV.19
DISARMAMENT—GENERAL AND COMPLETE (Agenda item 99)
A/C.1/78/PV.19
INFORMATION—INTERNATIONAL SECURITY (Agenda item 94)
A/C.1/78/PV.20
MEDITERRANEAN REGION—REGIONAL SECURITY (Agenda item 104)
A/C.1/78/PV.22
MULTILATERALISM—DISARMAMENT (Agenda item 99r)
A/C.1/78/PV.22
SMALL ARMS—ILLICIT TRAFFIC—ASSISTANCE (Agenda item 99n)
A/C.1/78/PV.19

Chua, Li Si Felicia (Singapore) (ASEAN)
UN—BUDGET (2024) (Agenda item 134)
A/C.5/78/SR.33

Chumakov, Dmitry S. (Russian Federation)
AFRICA—DEVELOPMENT (Agenda item 65b)
A/78/PV.57
AFRICA—SUSTAINABLE DEVELOPMENT—PARTNERSHIP (Agenda item 65a)
A/78/PV.57
EMERGENCY ASSISTANCE (Agenda item 72a)
A/78/PV.46; A/78/PV.47
HEALTH (Agenda item 125)
A/78/PV.16; A/78/PV.64; A/78/PV.77
INTERNATIONAL TRADE (Agenda item 16a)
A/C.2/78/SR.24
LANDLOCKED DEVELOPING COUNTRIES—CONFERENCES (Agenda item 20b)
A/78/PV.107
MILLENNIUM SUMMIT—CONFERENCES (Agenda item 117)
A/78/PV.15; A/78/PV.53; A/78/PV.107
PALESTINE QUESTION (Agenda item 35)
A/78/PV.40
SOCIAL CONDITIONS (Agenda item 24b)
A/78/PV.57
SUBSIDIARY ORGANS—APPOINTMENTS (Agenda item 115)
A/78/PV.60
SUSTAINABLE DEVELOPMENT (Agenda item 18)
A/78/PV.107; A/C.2/78/SR.24
TRAFFIC SAFETY (Agenda item 12)
A/78/PV.92
UN—ADMINISTRATION (Agenda item 132)
A/C.5/78/SR.32
UN—BUDGET (2023) (Agenda item 133)
A/C.5/78/SR.26/PartII
UN—BUDGET (2024) (Agenda item 134)
A/C.5/78/SR.5; A/C.5/78/SR.26/PartII;
A/C.5/78/SR.34

Chumakov, Dmitry S. (Russian Federation) (continued)
UN—HUMAN RESOURCES MANAGEMENT (Agenda item 139)
A/C.5/78/SR.34
UN—PROGRAMME PLANNING (Agenda item 135)
A/C.5/78/SR.5; A/C.5/78/SR.24
UN. ECONOMIC AND SOCIAL COUNCIL—REPORTS (Agenda item 9)
A/78/PV.33
UN. GENERAL ASSEMBLY (78TH SESS. : 2023-2024)—OFFICERS (Agenda item 5)
A/C.5/78/SR.1
UN. GENERAL ASSEMBLY (78TH SESS. : 2023-2024). 2ND COMMITTEE—GENERAL DEBATE (Agenda item 8)
A/C.2/78/SR.5
UN CONFERENCES (Agenda item 13)
A/78/PV.15; A/78/PV.33; A/78/PV.53; A/78/PV.107
UN SYSTEM—STRENGTHENING (Agenda item 122)
A/78/PV.98
UNRWA—ACTIVITIES (Agenda item 49)
A/C.4/78/SR.23

Ciobanu, Christian Niculae (Kiribati)
DISARMAMENT—GENERAL AND COMPLETE (Agenda item 99)
A/C.1/78/PV.13
NUCLEAR DISARMAMENT (Agenda item 99b)
A/C.1/78/PV.13
NUCLEAR WEAPONS—HUMANITARIAN CONSEQUENCES (Agenda item 99bb)
A/C.1/78/PV.13

Cisneros Chávez, José de Jesús (Mexico)
DECOLONIZATION (Agenda item 58)
A/C.4/78/SR.2
FALKLAND ISLANDS (MALVINAS) QUESTION (Agenda item 42)
A/C.4/78/SR.2
INFORMATION (Agenda item 53)
A/C.4/78/SR.12
PEACEBUILDING (Agenda item 61)
A/78/PV.100
PEACEKEEPING OPERATIONS (Agenda item 51)
A/C.4/78/SR.18
UN. PEACEBUILDING COMMISSION—REPORTS (Agenda item 27)
A/78/PV.100
UN. PEACEBUILDING FUND—REPORTS (Agenda item 111)
A/78/PV.100
WESTERN SAHARA QUESTION (Agenda item 58)
A/C.4/78/SR.2

Claeys, Carine (European Union)
ARMS RACE—OUTER SPACE (Agenda item 97a)
A/C.1/78/PV.16
BIOLOGICAL WEAPONS—TREATIES (Agenda item 106)
A/C.1/78/PV.14

Claeys, Carine (European Union) (continued)

CHEMICAL WEAPONS—TREATIES (Agenda item 99l)
A/C.1/78/PV.14
OUTER SPACE—CONFIDENCE-BUILDING MEASURES (Agenda item 99v)
A/C.1/78/PV.16
OUTER SPACE—PRINCIPLES (Agenda item 97d)
A/C.1/78/PV.16
WEAPONS—OUTER SPACE (Agenda item 97b)
A/C.1/78/PV.16
WEAPONS OF MASS DESTRUCTION—TERRORISM (Agenda item 99s)
A/C.1/78/PV.14

Clark, Joel (United Kingdom)

TERRORISM (Agenda item 109)
A/C.6/78/SR.1

Clifford, Katarina (European Union)

HUMAN RIGHTS—BELARUS (Agenda item 71c)
A/C.3/78/SR.37
HUMAN RIGHTS—RUSSIAN FEDERATION (Agenda item 71c)
A/C.3/78/SR.37
HUMAN RIGHTS—UKRAINE (Agenda item 71c)
A/C.3/78/SR.37
RIGHTS OF THE CHILD (Agenda item 67)
A/C.3/78/SR.11
UN. HUMAN RIGHTS COUNCIL—REPORTS (Agenda item 66)
A/78/PV.23

Clune, Mary (European Union)

TERRITORIES OCCUPIED BY ISRAEL—HUMAN RIGHTS (Agenda item 50)
A/C.4/78/SR.24
UNRWA—ACTIVITIES (Agenda item 49)
A/C.4/78/SR.22

Clutterbuck, Nicholas (New Zealand)

ARMS RACE—OUTER SPACE (Agenda item 97a)
A/C.1/78/PV.17
DISARMAMENT—GENERAL AND COMPLETE (Agenda item 99)
A/C.1/78/PV.11
DISARMAMENT AGREEMENTS—OUTER SPACE (Agenda item 97c)
A/C.1/78/PV.17
NUCLEAR DISARMAMENT (Agenda item 99b)
A/C.1/78/PV.11
NUCLEAR DISARMAMENT—TREATY COMPLIANCE (Agenda item 99q)
A/C.1/78/PV.11
NUCLEAR NON-PROLIFERATION—INTERNATIONAL OBLIGATIONS (Agenda item 99w)
A/C.1/78/PV.11
NUCLEAR WEAPON TESTS—TREATIES (Agenda item 105)
A/C.1/78/PV.11

Clutterbuck, Nicholas (New Zealand) (continued)

NUCLEAR WEAPONS—HUMANITARIAN CONSEQUENCES (Agenda item 99bb)
A/C.1/78/PV.11
NUCLEAR WEAPONS—TREATIES (Agenda item 99ff)
A/C.1/78/PV.11
NUCLEAR-WEAPON-FREE ZONE—SOUTHERN HEMISPHERE (Agenda item 99i)
A/C.1/78/PV.11
NUCLEAR-WEAPON-FREE ZONES (Agenda item 99cc)
A/C.1/78/PV.11
OUTER SPACE—CONFIDENCE-BUILDING MEASURES (Agenda item 99v)
A/C.1/78/PV.17
OUTER SPACE—PRINCIPLES (Agenda item 97d)
A/C.1/78/PV.17

Colas, Diego (France)

UN. INTERNATIONAL COURT OF JUSTICE—REPORTS (Agenda item 73)
A/78/PV.20
UN. INTERNATIONAL LAW COMMISSION—REPORTS (Agenda item 79)
A/C.6/78/SR.23

Colonna, Catherine (France)

UN. GENERAL ASSEMBLY (78TH SESS. : 2023-2024)—GENERAL DEBATE (Agenda item 8)
A/78/PV.9

Concepción Jaramillo, Markova (Panama)

FOOD SECURITY (Agenda item 23a)
A/C.2/78/SR.16
MIGRANTS—PROTECTION (Agenda item 71b)
A/C.3/78/SR.23
POVERTY—INTERNATIONAL DECADES (Agenda item 21a)
A/C.2/78/SR.16
RURAL POVERTY (Agenda item 21b)
A/C.2/78/SR.16
TAXATION (Agenda item 16h)
A/C.2/78/SR.25
UN. SECURITY COUNCIL—MEMBERSHIP (Agenda item 121)
A/78/PV.36

Condé, N'Nagbé (Guinea)

INTERNATIONAL LAW—TRAINING PROGRAMMES (Agenda item 78)
A/C.6/78/SR.21

Cooper, David (Secretariat of the Convention on Biological Diversity. Deputy Executive Secretary)

BIOLOGICAL DIVERSITY—TREATIES (Agenda item 18f)
A/C.2/78/SR.12

Coppola, Antonio Gaetano (European Union)
PEACEKEEPING OPERATIONS (Agenda item 51)
A/C.4/78/SR.18

Cordero Vargas, Mariana (El Salvador)
YOUTH (Agenda item 24b)
A/C.3/78/SR.55

Córdoba Heredia, Alexandra (Fundación Universitaria Compensa (Colombia))
WESTERN SAHARA QUESTION (Agenda item 58)
A/C.4/78/SR.4

Corquaye, Ama Anima (Ghana)
RIGHTS OF THE CHILD (Agenda item 67)
A/C.3/78/SR.14

Cortizo Cohen, Laurentino (Panama. President)
UN. GENERAL ASSEMBLY (78TH SESS. : 2023-2024)—GENERAL DEBATE (Agenda item 8)
A/78/PV.5
UN. GENERAL ASSEMBLY (78TH SESS. : 2023-2024)—SPECIAL STATEMENTS
A/78/PV.5

Corzo Sosa, Edgar (UN. Committee on the Protection of the Rights of All Migrant Workers and Members of Their Families. Chair)
MIGRANT WORKERS (Agenda item 71a)
A/C.3/78/SR.23

Cosentino, Leandro Carlos (Argentina)
UN—BUDGET (2024) (Agenda item 134)
A/C.5/78/SR.26/PartII; A/C.5/78/SR.33

Costa, Maria (UN. Department of Management Strategy, Policy and Compliance. Office of Programme Planning, Finance and Budget. Finance Division. Director)
INTERNATIONAL RESIDUAL MECHANISM FOR CRIMINAL TRIBUNALS—FINANCING (Agenda item 145)
A/C.5/78/SR.20; A/C.5/78/SR.25
UN—BUDGET (2024) (Agenda item 134)
A/C.5/78/SR.3; A/C.5/78/SR.12; A/C.5/78/SR.14; A/C.5/78/SR.18; A/C.5/78/SR.21; A/C.5/78/SR.22; A/C.5/78/SR.24; A/C.5/78/SR.25; A/C.5/78/SR.31
UN—FINANCIAL REPORTS (Agenda item 131)
A/C.5/78/SR.14
UN MULTIDIMENSIONAL INTEGRATED STABILIZATION MISSION IN MALI—FINANCING (Agenda item 155)
A/C.5/78/SR.20

Cottam, Paul Arthur (United Kingdom)
UN—BUDGET (2024) (Agenda item 134)
A/C.5/78/SR.33
UN—FINANCIAL SITUATION (Agenda item 136)
A/C.5/78/SR.6

Coulibaly, Kanisson (Mali)
FOOD SECURITY (Agenda item 23a)
A/C.2/78/SR.17
POVERTY—INTERNATIONAL DECADES (Agenda item 21a)
A/C.2/78/SR.17
RURAL POVERTY (Agenda item 21b)
A/C.2/78/SR.17

Courtenay, Eamon (Belize)
UN. GENERAL ASSEMBLY (78TH SESS. : 2023-2024)—GENERAL DEBATE (Agenda item 8)
A/78/PV.13

Courtois, Laetitia (International Committee of the Red Cross)
HUMANITARIAN ASSISTANCE (Agenda item 72)
A/78/PV.47

Cowan, Mike (Roberto Gym (Organization))
FRENCH POLYNESIA QUESTION (Agenda item 58)
A/C.4/78/SR.3

Craciunean-Tatu, Laura-Maria (Romania) (UN. Committee on Economic, Social and Cultural Rights. Chair)
HUMAN RIGHTS—INTERNATIONAL INSTRUMENTS (Agenda item 71a)
A/C.3/78/SR.17

Craemer, Cathrine (Germany)
CRIMES AGAINST HUMANITY (Agenda item 80)
A/C.6/78/SR.45

Crespo Aguilar, Juan Ramón (Observatorio de Derechos Humanos de Castilla La Mancha para el Sáhara Occidental (Spain))
WESTERN SAHARA QUESTION (Agenda item 58)
A/C.4/78/SR.4

Croker, Richard (United Kingdom)
HUMAN RIGHTS—RUSSIAN FEDERATION (Agenda item 71c)
A/C.3/78/SR.24
HUMAN RIGHTS—TERRITORIES OCCUPIED BY ISRAEL (Agenda item 71c)
A/C.3/78/SR.24; A/C.3/78/SR.35
HUMAN RIGHTS—UKRAINE (Agenda item 71c)
A/C.3/78/SR.24
HUMAN RIGHTS ADVANCEMENT (Agenda item 71b)
A/C.3/78/SR.18; A/C.3/78/SR.24
OUTER SPACE—PEACEFUL USES—INTERNATIONAL COOPERATION (Agenda item 48)
A/C.4/78/SR.17
SUSTAINABLE DEVELOPMENT (Agenda item 18)
A/C.2/78/SR.24

Croker, Richard (United Kingdom) (continued)

TAXATION (Agenda item 16h)
A/C.2/78/SR.25
TERRITORIES OCCUPIED BY ISRAEL—HUMAN RIGHTS (Agenda item 50)
A/C.4/78/SR.26
UNRWA—ACTIVITIES (Agenda item 49)
A/C.4/78/SR.26

Cronin, Donal (Ireland)

HIV/AIDS—DECLARATIONS (Agenda item 10)
A/78/PV.91

Cronin, Eileen A. (Joint Inspection Unit)

JOINT INSPECTION UNIT (Agenda item 141)
A/C.5/78/SR.27; A/C.5/78/SR.29
UN—ADMINISTRATION (Agenda item 132)
A/C.5/78/SR.29

Cross, Valentina (French Polynesia)

FRENCH POLYNESIA QUESTION (Agenda item 58)
A/C.4/78/SR.3

Cruz, Alice (UN. Human Rights Council. Special Rapporteur on the Elimination of Discrimination against Persons Affected by Leprosy (Hansen's disease) and Their Family Members)

LEPROSY (Agenda item 71b)
A/C.3/78/SR.17

Cruz, Francisco José da (Angola)

AFRICA—DEVELOPMENT (Agenda item 65b)
A/78/PV.18
CUBA—UNITED STATES (Agenda item 38)
A/78/PV.24
DEVELOPMENT FINANCE (Agenda item 16b)
A/C.2/78/SR.9
EXTERNAL DEBT (Agenda item 16c)
A/C.2/78/SR.9
INFORMATION TECHNOLOGY—DEVELOPMENT (Agenda item 15)
A/C.2/78/SR.10
LANDLOCKED DEVELOPING COUNTRIES—CONFERENCES (Agenda item 20b)
A/C.2/78/SR.7
LEAST DEVELOPED COUNTRIES—CONFERENCES (Agenda item 20a)
A/C.2/78/SR.7
SCIENCE AND TECHNOLOGY—DEVELOPMENT (Agenda item 19a)
A/C.2/78/SR.10
SPECIAL POLITICAL MISSIONS (Agenda item 52)
A/C.4/78/SR.21
TRAFFIC SAFETY (Agenda item 12)
A/78/PV.92
UN. ECONOMIC AND SOCIAL COUNCIL—REPORTS (Agenda item 9)
A/78/PV.48

Cruz, Francisco José da (Angola) (continued)

UN. GENERAL ASSEMBLY (78TH SESS. : 2023-2024). 1ST COMMITTEE—GENERAL DEBATE (Agenda item 8)
A/C.1/78/PV.9
UN. GENERAL ASSEMBLY (78TH SESS. : 2023-2024). 2ND COMMITTEE—GENERAL DEBATE (Agenda item 8)
A/C.2/78/SR.3
UN. SECRETARY-GENERAL—REPORTS (Agenda item 110)
A/78/PV.55
UN. SECURITY COUNCIL—REPORTS (Agenda item 26)
A/78/PV.94

Cruz, Francisco José da (Angola) (Comunidade dos Países de Língua Portuguesa)

HUMAN RIGHTS (Agenda item 71)
A/C.3/78/SR.24
HUMAN RIGHTS—INTERNATIONAL INSTRUMENTS (Agenda item 71a)
A/C.3/78/SR.24
INFORMATION (Agenda item 53)
A/C.4/78/SR.12
UN. INTERNATIONAL COURT OF JUSTICE—REPORTS (Agenda item 73)
A/78/PV.27

Cruz, Francisco José da (Angola) (Southern African Development Community)

ECONOMIC SANCTIONS—INTERNATIONAL RELATIONS (Agenda item 28)
A/78/PV.89
RACIAL DISCRIMINATION—ELIMINATION (Agenda item 69a)
A/C.3/78/SR.40
RACIAL DISCRIMINATION—PROGRAMMES OF ACTION (Agenda item 69b)
A/C.3/78/SR.40
RIGHTS OF THE CHILD (Agenda item 67)
A/C.3/78/SR.11
SANCTIONS—INTERNATIONAL RELATIONS (Agenda item 71b)
A/C.3/78/SR.26

Cruz Morataya, Andrea Flor de María (Guatemala)

RACIAL DISCRIMINATION—ELIMINATION (Agenda item 69a)
A/C.3/78/SR.41
RACIAL DISCRIMINATION—PROGRAMMES OF ACTION (Agenda item 69b)
A/C.3/78/SR.41

Csergő, Csongor (Hungary)

UN. INTERNATIONAL LAW COMMISSION—REPORTS (Agenda item 79)
A/C.6/78/SR.24

Cupika-Mavrina, Elvira (Latvia)

CRIMES AGAINST HUMANITY (Agenda item 80)
A/C.6/78/SR.9; A/C.6/78/SR.38; A/C.6/78/SR.39; A/C.6/78/SR.41
TERRORISM (Agenda item 109)
A/C.6/78/SR.1
UN. INTERNATIONAL LAW COMMISSION—REPORTS (Agenda item 79)
A/C.6/78/SR.28

Ćurić Hrvatinić, Hrvoje (Croatia)

ARMED CONFLICTS PREVENTION (Agenda item 31a)
A/78/PV.72
VETO (Agenda item 63)
A/78/PV.69

Curran, Clayton (European Union)

DIAMONDS—FUELLING CONFLICT (Agenda item 30)
A/78/PV.65
SPORTS—OLYMPIC GAMES (Agenda item 11)
A/78/PV.38

Curzio Vila, Elena (Mexico)

CLIMATE (Agenda item 18d)
A/C.2/78/SR.13
COASTAL ZONE MANAGEMENT (Agenda item 18j)
A/C.2/78/SR.23
CULTURE—DEVELOPMENT (Agenda item 19b)
A/C.2/78/SR.10
INFORMATION TECHNOLOGY—DEVELOPMENT (Agenda item 15)
A/C.2/78/SR.10
PEACE (Agenda item 14)
A/78/PV.76
SCIENCE AND TECHNOLOGY—DEVELOPMENT (Agenda item 19a)
A/C.2/78/SR.10
UN CONFERENCES (Agenda item 13)
A/78/PV.63

Dabesa, Kurabachew Tirfesa (Ethiopia)

CRIMES AGAINST HUMANITY (Agenda item 80)
A/C.6/78/SR.39; A/C.6/78/SR.41; A/C.6/78/SR.42
ELECTION VERIFICATION—UN (Agenda item 71b)
A/C.3/78/SR.50

Dabo N'diaye, Djeneba (Mali)

CRIME PREVENTION (Agenda item 107)
A/C.3/78/SR.6
CRIMES AGAINST HUMANITY (Agenda item 80)
A/C.6/78/SR.39; A/C.6/78/SR.42; A/C.6/78/SR.47
ELECTION VERIFICATION—UN (Agenda item 71b)
A/78/PV.50
HUMAN RIGHTS—ERITREA (Agenda item 71c)
A/C.3/78/SR.36
HUMAN RIGHTS—ETHIOPIA (Agenda item 71c)
A/C.3/78/SR.36

Dabo N'diaye, Djeneba (Mali) (continued)

HUMAN RIGHTS ACTIVISTS (Agenda item 71b)
A/C.3/78/SR.56
HUMAN RIGHTS INSTITUTIONS—CENTRAL AFRICA (Agenda item 71b)
A/C.3/78/SR.56
PERSONS WITH DISABILITIES—HUMAN RIGHTS (Agenda item 71a)
A/C.3/78/SR.38; A/C.3/78/SR.51
RIGHT TO CULTURE (Agenda item 71b)
A/C.3/78/SR.27
RIGHT TO DEVELOPMENT (Agenda item 71b)
A/C.3/78/SR.20
RIGHT TO DRINKING WATER (Agenda item 71b)
A/C.3/78/SR.50
RIGHT TO EDUCATION (Agenda item 71b)
A/C.3/78/SR.27
RIGHTS OF THE CHILD (Agenda item 67)
A/C.3/78/SR.14; A/C.3/78/SR.55
SOCIAL CONDITIONS (Agenda item 24b)
A/C.3/78/SR.4
SOCIAL DEVELOPMENT (Agenda item 24)
A/C.3/78/SR.4
UN. HUMAN RIGHTS COUNCIL—REPORTS (Agenda item 66)
A/78/PV.28
WOMEN'S ADVANCEMENT (Agenda item 25a)
A/C.3/78/SR.10
WOMEN'S ADVANCEMENT—CONFERENCES (Agenda item 25b)
A/C.3/78/SR.10
YOUTH (Agenda item 24b)
A/C.3/78/SR.55

DaCosta, Yanique Nissan (Jamaica)

HUMAN RIGHTS ADVANCEMENT (Agenda item 71b)
A/C.3/78/SR.52

Dagari, Rabiu (Nigeria)

ECONOMIC COOPERATION AMONG DEVELOPING COUNTRIES (Agenda item 22b)
A/C.2/78/SR.18
OPERATIONAL ACTIVITIES—UN SYSTEM (Agenda item 22a)
A/C.2/78/SR.18

Dahal, Pushpa Kamal (Nepal. Prime Minister)

UN. GENERAL ASSEMBLY (78TH SESS. : 2023-2024)—GENERAL DEBATE (Agenda item 8)
A/78/PV.9
UN. GENERAL ASSEMBLY (78TH SESS. : 2023-2024)—SPECIAL STATEMENTS
A/78/PV.9

Dahi, Leila (Morocco)

WESTERN SAHARA QUESTION (Agenda item 58)
A/C.4/78/SR.4

Dai, Bing (China)

AFRICA—DEVELOPMENT (Agenda item 65b)
A/78/PV.18
AFRICA—SUSTAINABLE DEVELOPMENT—PARTNERSHIP (Agenda item 65a)
A/78/PV.18
CUBA—UNITED STATES (Agenda item 38)
A/78/PV.24
ECONOMIC COOPERATION AMONG DEVELOPING COUNTRIES (Agenda item 22b)
A/C.2/78/SR.18
EMERGENCY ASSISTANCE (Agenda item 72a)
A/78/PV.46
HEALTH (Agenda item 125)
A/78/PV.48
HUMAN RIGHTS (Agenda item 71)
A/C.3/78/SR.16
HUMAN RIGHTS—REPORTS (Agenda item 71c)
A/C.3/78/SR.25
OPERATIONAL ACTIVITIES—UN SYSTEM (Agenda item 22a)
A/C.2/78/SR.18
PALESTINIANS—ASSISTANCE (Agenda item 72b)
A/78/PV.46
PEACE (Agenda item 14)
A/78/PV.76
RACIAL DISCRIMINATION—ELIMINATION (Agenda item 69a)
A/C.3/78/SR.40
RACIAL DISCRIMINATION—PROGRAMMES OF ACTION (Agenda item 69b)
A/C.3/78/SR.40
SELF-DETERMINATION OF PEOPLES (Agenda item 70)
A/C.3/78/SR.40
SOCIAL DEVELOPMENT (Agenda item 24)
A/C.3/78/SR.2
SPORTS—OLYMPIC GAMES (Agenda item 11)
A/78/PV.38
UN. GENERAL ASSEMBLY (78TH SESS. : 2023-2024)—OFFICERS (Agenda item 5)
A/C.5/78/SR.1
UN. GENERAL ASSEMBLY (78TH SESS. : 2023-2024). 5TH COMMITTEE—WORK ORGANIZATION (Agenda item 7)
A/C.5/78/SR.35
UN. SECURITY COUNCIL—MEMBERSHIP (Agenda item 121)
A/78/PV.104
VETO (Agenda item 63)
A/78/PV.66

Dail, Elizabeth (Classical Conversations Foundation)

WESTERN SAHARA QUESTION (Agenda item 58)
A/C.4/78/SR.4

Dakwak, Gloria (Nigeria)

CRIMES AGAINST HUMANITY (Agenda item 80)
A/C.6/78/SR.38; A/C.6/78/SR.40; A/C.6/78/SR.41; A/C.6/78/SR.44; A/C.6/78/SR.45; A/C.6/78/SR.47

Dakwak, Gloria (Nigeria) (continued)

DISASTER VICTIMS (Agenda item 86)
A/C.6/78/SR.6
PEACEKEEPING OPERATIONS—CRIMINAL LIABILITY (Agenda item 76)
A/C.6/78/SR.9
TERRORISM (Agenda item 109)
A/C.6/78/SR.2
UN CHARTER—REPORTS (Agenda item 82)
A/C.6/78/SR.34
VETO (Agenda item 63)
A/78/PV.70

Dale, Katrine Ørnehaug (Norway)

HUMAN RIGHTS—AFGHANISTAN (Agenda item 71c)
A/C.3/78/SR.34
HUMAN RIGHTS—TERRITORIES OCCUPIED BY ISRAEL (Agenda item 71c)
A/C.3/78/SR.35
HUMAN RIGHTS ACTIVISTS (Agenda item 71b)
A/C.3/78/SR.56
PEACE (Agenda item 14)
A/78/PV.88

Dalin, Inga (Norway)

UN—BUDGET (2024) (Agenda item 134)
A/C.5/78/SR.33

Damdin, Erdenebal Suren (Mongolia)

INTERNATIONAL CRIMINAL COURT—REPORTS (Agenda item 74)
A/78/PV.21

Damico, Flávio Soares (Agency for the Prohibition of Nuclear Weapons in Latin America and the Caribbean)

NUCLEAR-WEAPON-FREE ZONES (Agenda item 99cc)
A/C.1/78/PV.11

Damico, Flávio Soares (Brazil)

ARMS RACE—OUTER SPACE (Agenda item 97a)
A/C.1/78/PV.17
ARMS TRANSFERS—TREATIES (Agenda item 99x)
A/C.1/78/PV.19
BIOLOGICAL WEAPONS—TREATIES (Agenda item 106)
A/C.1/78/PV.15
CHEMICAL WEAPONS—TREATIES (Agenda item 99l)
A/C.1/78/PV.15
DISARMAMENT—GENERAL AND COMPLETE (Agenda item 99)
A/C.1/78/PV.19
INFORMATION—INTERNATIONAL SECURITY (Agenda item 94)
A/C.1/78/PV.21
LANDMINES—TREATIES (Agenda item 99m)
A/C.1/78/PV.19

Damico, Flávio Soares (Brazil) (continued)
MULTILATERALISM—DISARMAMENT (Agenda item 99r)
A/C.1/78/PV.22
NUCLEAR DISARMAMENT (Agenda item 99b)
A/C.1/78/PV.13
NUCLEAR DISARMAMENT—VERIFICATION (Agenda item 99ee)
A/C.1/78/PV.12
NUCLEAR NON-PROLIFERATION—INTERNATIONAL OBLIGATIONS (Agenda item 99w)
A/C.1/78/PV.13
NUCLEAR WEAPONS—TREATIES (Agenda item 99ff)
A/C.1/78/PV.13
OUTER SPACE—CONFIDENCE-BUILDING MEASURES (Agenda item 99v)
A/C.1/78/PV.17
UN. CONFERENCE ON DISARMAMENT—REPORTS (Agenda item 101a)
A/C.1/78/PV.24
UN. GENERAL ASSEMBLY (78TH SESS. : 2023-2024). 1ST COMMITTEE—GENERAL DEBATE (Agenda item 8)
A/C.1/78/PV.9

Danailov Frčkoski, Ljubomir (North Macedonia)
ELECTION VERIFICATION—UN (Agenda item 71b)
A/C.3/78/SR.50
HUMAN RIGHTS—INTERNATIONAL INSTRUMENTS (Agenda item 71a)
A/C.3/78/SR.17
VETO (Agenda item 63)
A/78/PV.69
WOMEN'S ADVANCEMENT (Agenda item 25a)
A/C.3/78/SR.7
WOMEN'S ADVANCEMENT—CONFERENCES (Agenda item 25b)
A/C.3/78/SR.7

Dandy, Alhakam (Syrian Arab Republic)
MIDDLE EAST SITUATION (Agenda item 34)
A/78/PV.40
MILLENNIUM SUMMIT—CONFERENCES (Agenda item 117)
A/78/PV.15
UN CONFERENCES (Agenda item 13)
A/78/PV.15
VETO (Agenda item 63)
A/78/PV.52; A/78/PV.68

Danese, Aurora Maria (Switzerland)
CONFERENCE AND MEETING SERVICES (Agenda item 137)
A/C.5/78/SR.7
JOINT INSPECTION UNIT (Agenda item 141)
A/C.5/78/SR.29
UN—ADMINISTRATION (Agenda item 132)
A/C.5/78/SR.29

Danese, Aurora Maria (Switzerland) (continued)
UN—BUDGET (2024) (Agenda item 134)
A/C.5/78/SR.26/PartII

Danese, Sérgio França (Brazil)
CUBA—UNITED STATES (Agenda item 38)
A/78/PV.26
ECONOMIC SANCTIONS—INTERNATIONAL RELATIONS (Agenda item 28)
A/78/PV.89
HIV/AIDS—DECLARATIONS (Agenda item 10)
A/78/PV.91
ORGANIZATION FOR DEMOCRACY AND ECONOMIC DEVELOPMENT - GUAM (Agenda item 32)
A/78/PV.85
PEACE (Agenda item 14)
A/78/PV.82
UKRAINE—POLITICAL CONDITIONS (Agenda item 62)
A/78/PV.58
UN. SECURITY COUNCIL—REPORTS (Agenda item 26)
A/78/PV.93
VETO (Agenda item 63)
A/78/PV.51; A/78/PV.60; A/78/PV.67; A/78/PV.69; A/78/PV.70; A/78/PV.75; A/78/PV.78

Danese, Sérgio França (Brazil) (Group of Four)
UN. SECURITY COUNCIL—MEMBERSHIP (Agenda item 121)
A/78/PV.104

Danese, Sérgio França (Brazil) (MERCOSUR (Organization))
FALKLAND ISLANDS (MALVINAS) QUESTION (Agenda item 42)
A/C.4/78/SR.2

Danese, Sérgio França (Brazil) (UN. Peacebuilding Commission. Chair)
UN. PEACEBUILDING COMMISSION—REPORTS (Agenda item 27)
A/78/PV.100
UN. SECRETARY-GENERAL—REPORTS (Agenda item 110)
A/78/PV.54

Dang, Hoang Giang (Viet Nam)
CUBA—UNITED STATES (Agenda item 38)
A/78/PV.24
HUMAN RIGHTS ADVANCEMENT (Agenda item 71b)
A/C.3/78/SR.24
IAEA—REPORTS (Agenda item 89)
A/78/PV.30
LAW OF THE SEA (Agenda item 75a)
A/78/PV.43
MARINE ECOSYSTEMS—BIOLOGICAL DIVERSITY (Agenda item 75c)
A/78/PV.43

Dang, Hoang Giang (Viet Nam) (continued)
PALESTINE QUESTION (Agenda item 35)
A/78/PV.40
PEACE (Agenda item 14)
A/78/PV.64; A/78/PV.82
RULE OF LAW (Agenda item 83)
A/C.6/78/SR.16
STRADDLING FISH STOCKS (Agenda item 75b)
A/78/PV.43
UN. GENERAL ASSEMBLY (78TH SESS. : 2023-2024). 1ST COMMITTEE—GENERAL DEBATE (Agenda item 8)
A/C.1/78/PV.6
VETO (Agenda item 63)
A/78/PV.61

Dang, Hoang Giang (Viet Nam) (ASEAN)
AGEING PERSONS (Agenda item 24b)
A/C.3/78/SR.1
FOOD SECURITY (Agenda item 23a)
A/C.2/78/SR.16
NUCLEAR DISARMAMENT (Agenda item 99b)
A/C.1/78/PV.11
NUCLEAR NON-PROLIFERATION (Agenda item 99o)
A/C.1/78/PV.11
NUCLEAR NON-PROLIFERATION—INTERNATIONAL OBLIGATIONS (Agenda item 99w)
A/C.1/78/PV.11
NUCLEAR WEAPON TESTS—TREATIES (Agenda item 105)
A/C.1/78/PV.11
NUCLEAR WEAPONS—TREATIES (Agenda item 99ff)
A/C.1/78/PV.11
PERSONS WITH DISABILITIES (Agenda item 24b)
A/C.3/78/SR.1
POVERTY—INTERNATIONAL DECADES (Agenda item 21a)
A/C.2/78/SR.16
RURAL POVERTY (Agenda item 21b)
A/C.2/78/SR.16
SOCIAL CONDITIONS (Agenda item 24b)
A/C.3/78/SR.1
SOCIAL DEVELOPMENT (Agenda item 24)
A/C.3/78/SR.1
SOUTH-EAST ASIA—NUCLEAR-WEAPON-FREE ZONES (Agenda item 99y)
A/C.1/78/PV.11

Dang, Tran Nam Trung (Viet Nam)
FREEDOM OF EXPRESSION (Agenda item 71b)
A/C.3/78/SR.19
RIGHTS OF THE CHILD (Agenda item 67)
A/C.3/78/SR.12

Darras, Amandine (New Caledonia)
NEW CALEDONIA QUESTION (Agenda item 58)
A/C.4/78/SR.5

Darroux, Kelver Dwight (Dominica)
CUBA—UNITED STATES (Agenda item 38)
A/78/PV.24

Darsalia, Lasha (Georgia)
UKRAINE—POLITICAL CONDITIONS (Agenda item 62)
A/78/PV.56

Davis, Benjamin (FAO)
RURAL POVERTY (Agenda item 21b)
A/C.2/78/SR.16

Daw, Texine Wonda (Guyana)
RULE OF LAW (Agenda item 83)
A/C.6/78/SR.18

Day, Radha (UN. Office for Disarmament Affairs (Mar. 2007-). Regional Disarmament Branch. Chief)
PEACE—REGIONAL CENTRES (Agenda item 100f)
A/C.1/78/PV.23

De Bono Sant Cassia, Andrea (Malta)
RESPONSIBILITY TO PROTECT (Agenda item 129)
A/78/PV.99

De Croo, Alexander (Belgium. Prime Minister)
UN. GENERAL ASSEMBLY (78TH SESS. : 2023-2024)—GENERAL DEBATE (Agenda item 8)
A/78/PV.7
UN. GENERAL ASSEMBLY (78TH SESS. : 2023-2024)—SPECIAL STATEMENTS
A/78/PV.7

De la Gasca LopezDomínguez, José Javier (Ecuador)
UKRAINE—POLITICAL CONDITIONS (Agenda item 62)
A/78/PV.58
VETO (Agenda item 63)
A/78/PV.60; A/78/PV.67; A/78/PV.71; A/78/PV.75; A/78/PV.78

De Schot, Jikita (New Zealand)
ARMS TRANSFERS—TREATIES (Agenda item 99x)
A/C.1/78/PV.19
BIOLOGICAL WEAPONS—TREATIES (Agenda item 106)
A/C.1/78/PV.15
CHEMICAL WEAPONS—TREATIES (Agenda item 99l)
A/C.1/78/PV.15
CLUSTER MUNITIONS (Agenda item 99dd)
A/C.1/78/PV.19
CONVENTIONAL WEAPONS—TREATIES (Agenda item 103)
A/C.1/78/PV.19

De Schot, Jikita (New Zealand) (continued)

DISARMAMENT—GENERAL AND COMPLETE (Agenda item 99)
A/C.1/78/PV.19; A/C.1/78/PV.30
LANDMINES—TREATIES (Agenda item 99m)
A/C.1/78/PV.19

Debataba, Yawa (Togo)

FOOD SECURITY (Agenda item 23a)
A/C.2/78/SR.17
POVERTY—INTERNATIONAL DECADES (Agenda item 21a)
A/C.2/78/SR.17
RURAL POVERTY (Agenda item 21b)
A/C.2/78/SR.17

Debeche, Smail ((personal capacity))

WESTERN SAHARA QUESTION (Agenda item 58)
A/C.4/78/SR.4

DeGregory, Kelli (Bahamas)

EXTERNAL DEBT—HUMAN RIGHTS (Agenda item 71b)
A/C.3/78/SR.32
UN—BUDGET (2024) (Agenda item 134)
A/C.5/78/SR.23
UN. HUMAN RIGHTS COUNCIL—REPORTS (Agenda item 66)
A/C.3/78/SR.46

Del Águila-Castillo, María José (Guatemala)

HEALTH (Agenda item 125)
A/78/PV.16
HUMAN RIGHTS—TERRITORIES OCCUPIED BY ISRAEL (Agenda item 71c)
A/C.3/78/SR.35
VETO (Agenda item 63)
A/78/PV.74; A/78/PV.78

Delgado Fernández, Sergio Emanuel (Mexico)

CRIMES AGAINST HUMANITY (Agenda item 80)
A/C.6/78/SR.44
INTERNATIONAL LAW—TRAINING PROGRAMMES (Agenda item 78)
A/C.6/78/SR.21
RESPONSIBILITY OF INTERNATIONAL ORGANIZATIONS (Agenda item 85)
A/C.6/78/SR.19

Delija, Marsela (Albania)

YOUTH (Agenda item 24b)
A/C.3/78/SR.3

Della-porta, Demi Heather See (Australia)

DISARMAMENT—GENERAL AND COMPLETE (Agenda item 99)
A/C.1/78/PV.30
DISARMAMENT AGREEMENTS—OUTER SPACE (Agenda item 97c)
A/C.1/78/PV.27

Della-porta, Demi Heather See (Australia) (continued)

IAEA—REPORTS (Agenda item 89)
A/78/PV.30
UN—PROGRAMME PLANNING (Agenda item 135)
A/C.1/78/PV.10
UN. CONFERENCE ON DISARMAMENT—REPORTS (Agenda item 101a)
A/C.1/78/PV.24
UN. GENERAL ASSEMBLY—WORK PROGRAMME (Agenda item 120)
A/C.1/78/PV.10
WEAPONS—OUTER SPACE (Agenda item 97b)
A/C.1/78/PV.27

Demchenko, Kyrylo (Ukraine)

YOUTH (Agenda item 24b)
A/C.3/78/SR.3

Demir, İlknur (Türkiye)

COASTAL ZONE MANAGEMENT (Agenda item 18j)
A/C.2/78/SR.23
FOOD SECURITY (Agenda item 23a)
A/C.2/78/SR.17
POVERTY—INTERNATIONAL DECADES (Agenda item 21a)
A/C.2/78/SR.17
RURAL POVERTY (Agenda item 21b)
A/C.2/78/SR.17

Demosthenous, Ioanna (Cyprus)

CRIME PREVENTION (Agenda item 107)
A/C.3/78/SR.5
HUMAN RIGHTS—REPORTS (Agenda item 71c)
A/C.3/78/SR.25
INFORMATION (Agenda item 53)
A/C.4/78/SR.14
SUMMARY EXECUTIONS (Agenda item 71b)
A/C.3/78/SR.31
UN—BUDGET (2024) (Agenda item 134)
A/C.5/78/SR.3
YOUTH (Agenda item 24b)
A/C.3/78/SR.55

Déniz Verona, Palmira ((personal capacity))

WESTERN SAHARA QUESTION (Agenda item 58)
A/C.4/78/SR.4

Denton-Watts, Cyeth Cylonia Allison (Jamaica)

SUSTAINABLE DEVELOPMENT (Agenda item 18)
A/C.2/78/SR.24

Desigis, Lucia Piera Giovanna (Switzerland)

DISPLACED PERSONS (Agenda item 71b)
A/C.3/78/SR.32; A/C.3/78/SR.49
EMERGENCY ASSISTANCE (Agenda item 72a)
A/78/PV.47

Deva, Surya (UN. Human Rights Council. Special Rapporteur on the Right to Development)

RIGHT TO DEVELOPMENT (Agenda item 71b)
A/C.3/78/SR.20

Devereaux, Brendan (United Kingdom)

FREEDOM OF EXPRESSION (Agenda item 71b)
A/C.3/78/SR.19
HUMAN RIGHTS—CENTRAL AFRICAN REPUBLIC (Agenda item 71c)
A/C.3/78/SR.33
HUMAN RIGHTS—DEMOCRATIC PEOPLE'S REPUBLIC OF KOREA (Agenda item 71c)
A/C.3/78/SR.33; A/C.3/78/SR.53
HUMAN RIGHTS—ETHIOPIA (Agenda item 71c)
A/C.3/78/SR.36
HUMAN RIGHTS—MYANMAR (Agenda item 71c)
A/C.3/78/SR.53
HUMAN RIGHTS ACTIVISTS (Agenda item 71b)
A/C.3/78/SR.19
MIGRANTS—PROTECTION (Agenda item 71b)
A/C.3/78/SR.56
RIGHT OF ASSEMBLY (Agenda item 71b)
A/C.3/78/SR.19
SOCIAL DEVELOPMENT (Agenda item 24)
A/C.3/78/SR.47

Devyatkin, Daniil A. (Russian Federation)

CONFERENCE AND MEETING SERVICES (Agenda item 137)
A/C.5/78/SR.7
CRIME PREVENTION (Agenda item 107)
A/78/PV.50(Resumption1)
MULTILINGUALISM (Agenda item 124)
A/78/PV.107
UN—BUDGET (2024) (Agenda item 134)
A/78/PV.50(Resumption1); A/C.5/78/SR.9
UN—PROGRAMME PLANNING (Agenda item 135)
A/78/PV.50(Resumption1)

Dhanutirto, Mariska Dwianti (Indonesia)

DECOLONIZATION (Agenda item 58)
A/C.4/78/SR.7
ELECTION VERIFICATION—UN (Agenda item 71b)
A/C.3/78/SR.50
HUMAN RIGHTS—MYANMAR (Agenda item 71c)
A/C.3/78/SR.53
IAEA—REPORTS (Agenda item 89)
A/78/PV.29
INDIGENOUS PEOPLES (Agenda item 68a)
A/C.3/78/SR.48
PEACE (Agenda item 14)
A/78/PV.76
RACIAL DISCRIMINATION—ELIMINATION (Agenda item 69a)
A/C.3/78/SR.42; A/C.3/78/SR.47
RACIAL DISCRIMINATION—PROGRAMMES OF ACTION (Agenda item 69b)
A/C.3/78/SR.42

Dhanutirto, Mariska Dwianti (Indonesia) (continued)

SELF-DETERMINATION OF PEOPLES (Agenda item 70)
A/C.3/78/SR.42; A/C.3/78/SR.49
TERRITORIES OCCUPIED BY ISRAEL—HUMAN RIGHTS (Agenda item 50)
A/C.4/78/SR.24
UN. HUMAN RIGHTS COUNCIL—REPORTS (Agenda item 66)
A/78/PV.28
UN. SECURITY COUNCIL—REPORTS (Agenda item 26)
A/78/PV.93
UNRWA—ACTIVITIES (Agenda item 49)
A/C.4/78/SR.22
VETO (Agenda item 63)
A/78/PV.70; A/78/PV.78

Dhanutirto, Mariska Dwianti (Indonesia) (Coordinating Bureau of the Non-Aligned Countries)

MIDDLE EAST—NUCLEAR-WEAPON-FREE ZONES (Agenda item 95)
A/C.1/78/PV.11
NUCLEAR DISARMAMENT (Agenda item 99b)
A/C.1/78/PV.11
NUCLEAR DISARMAMENT—CONFERENCES (Agenda item 99aa)
A/C.1/78/PV.11
NUCLEAR NON-PROLIFERATION—INTERNATIONAL OBLIGATIONS (Agenda item 99w)
A/C.1/78/PV.11
NUCLEAR WEAPONS—TREATIES (Agenda item 99ff)
A/C.1/78/PV.11

Dhanutirto, Mariska Dwianti (Indonesia) (UN. General Assembly. Special Political and Decolonization Committee (4th Committee). Rapporteur)

DECOLONIZATION (Agenda item 58)
A/78/PV.45
DECOLONIZATION—UN SYSTEM (Agenda item 56)
A/78/PV.45
INFORMATION (Agenda item 53)
A/78/PV.45
MINE CLEARANCE (Agenda item 46)
A/78/PV.45
NON-SELF-GOVERNING TERRITORIES—ECONOMIC INTERESTS (Agenda item 55)
A/78/PV.45
NON-SELF-GOVERNING TERRITORIES—FELLOWSHIPS (Agenda item 57)
A/78/PV.45
NON-SELF-GOVERNING TERRITORIES—REPORTS (Agenda item 54)
A/78/PV.45
OUTER SPACE—PEACEFUL USES—INTERNATIONAL COOPERATION (Agenda item 48)
A/78/PV.45
PEACEKEEPING OPERATIONS (Agenda item 51)
A/78/PV.45

Dhanutirto, Mariska Dwianti (Indonesia) (UN. General Assembly. Special Political and Decolonization Committee (4th Committee). Rapporteur) (continued)

RADIATION EFFECTS (Agenda item 47)
A/78/PV.45
SPECIAL POLITICAL MISSIONS (Agenda item 52)
A/78/PV.45
TERRITORIES OCCUPIED BY ISRAEL—HUMAN RIGHTS (Agenda item 50)
A/78/PV.45
UN—PROGRAMME PLANNING (Agenda item 135)
A/78/PV.45
UN. GENERAL ASSEMBLY—WORK PROGRAMME (Agenda item 120)
A/78/PV.45
UNRWA—ACTIVITIES (Agenda item 49)
A/78/PV.45

Dhungel, Purushottam (Nepal) (Group of Least Developed Countries)

INFORMATION TECHNOLOGY—DEVELOPMENT (Agenda item 15)
A/C.2/78/SR.10
SCIENCE AND TECHNOLOGY—DEVELOPMENT (Agenda item 19a)
A/C.2/78/SR.10

Di Capua, Giacomo (Italy)

CLIMATE CHANGE (Agenda item 71b)
A/C.3/78/SR.29
RIGHTS OF THE CHILD (Agenda item 67)
A/C.3/78/SR.11
YOUTH (Agenda item 24b)
A/C.3/78/SR.2

Diack, Papa Samba (Senegal)

ARMS TRANSFERS—TREATIES (Agenda item 99x)
A/C.1/78/PV.18
CONVENTIONAL WEAPONS (Agenda item 99u)
A/C.1/78/PV.18
NUCLEAR DISARMAMENT (Agenda item 99b)
A/C.1/78/PV.12

Diallo, Oumou (Guinea)

UN. GENERAL ASSEMBLY (78TH SESS. : 2023-2024). 1ST COMMITTEE—GENERAL DEBATE (Agenda item 8)
A/C.1/78/PV.6

Dias, João Henrique Nascimento (Brazil)

AGEING PERSONS (Agenda item 24b)
A/C.3/78/SR.1
CRIME PREVENTION (Agenda item 107)
A/C.3/78/SR.5
CYBERCRIME (Agenda item 108)
A/C.3/78/SR.5
FAMILY (Agenda item 24b)
A/C.3/78/SR.2
POVERTY—HUMAN RIGHTS (Agenda item 71b)
A/C.3/78/SR.30

Dias, João Henrique Nascimento (Brazil) (continued)

RIGHT TO FOOD (Agenda item 71b)
A/C.3/78/SR.30
RIGHT TO HOUSING (Agenda item 71b)
A/C.3/78/SR.30
RIGHT TO PRIVACY (Agenda item 71b)
A/C.3/78/SR.21
SOCIAL CONDITIONS (Agenda item 24b)
A/C.3/78/SR.2

Díaz Corona, Meigan (Mexico)

WOMEN MIGRANT WORKERS (Agenda item 25a)
A/C.3/78/SR.49

Díaz de la Vega García, Pedro (Banco de Alimentos)

WESTERN SAHARA QUESTION (Agenda item 58)
A/C.4/78/SR.5

Díaz-Canel Bermúdez, Miguel (Cuba. President)

UN. GENERAL ASSEMBLY (78TH SESS. : 2023-2024)—GENERAL DEBATE (Agenda item 8)
A/78/PV.4
UN. GENERAL ASSEMBLY (78TH SESS. : 2023-2024)—SPECIAL STATEMENTS
A/78/PV.4

Dibba, Lamin B. (Gambia)

SUSTAINABLE DEVELOPMENT (Agenda item 18)
A/C.2/78/SR.24

DiCianni, Amanda (Rescue and Relief International (Organization))

WESTERN SAHARA QUESTION (Agenda item 58)
A/C.4/78/SR.4

Diedricks, Meryl Michelle (South Africa)

MIGRANTS—PROTECTION (Agenda item 71b)
A/C.3/78/SR.23

Digney, Leanne (Ireland)

HUMAN RIGHTS—DEMOCRATIC PEOPLE'S REPUBLIC OF KOREA (Agenda item 71c)
A/C.3/78/SR.33
TRAFFICKING IN PERSONS (Agenda item 71b)
A/C.3/78/SR.23

Diloknawarit, Ornwara (Thailand)

WOMEN'S ADVANCEMENT (Agenda item 25a)
A/C.3/78/SR.8
WOMEN'S ADVANCEMENT—CONFERENCES (Agenda item 25b)
A/C.3/78/SR.8

Dime-Labille, Diarra (France)

ARMED CONFLICTS PREVENTION (Agenda item 31a)
A/78/PV.72

Dime-Labille, Diarra (France) (continued)

CRIMES AGAINST HUMANITY (Agenda item 80)
A/C.6/78/SR.38; A/C.6/78/SR.40; A/C.6/78/SR.44
EMERGENCY ASSISTANCE (Agenda item 72a)
A/78/PV.47
HUMAN RIGHTS (Agenda item 71)
A/C.3/78/SR.16
INTERNATIONAL CRIMINAL COURT—REPORTS (Agenda item 74)
A/78/PV.21
INTERNATIONAL LAW—TRAINING PROGRAMMES (Agenda item 78)
A/C.6/78/SR.21
INTERNATIONAL RESIDUAL MECHANISM FOR CRIMINAL TRIBUNALS (Agenda item 126)
A/78/PV.19
LAW OF THE SEA (Agenda item 75a)
A/78/PV.44
MARINE ECOSYSTEMS—BIOLOGICAL DIVERSITY (Agenda item 75c)
A/78/PV.44
PALESTINIANS—ASSISTANCE (Agenda item 72b)
A/78/PV.47
RIGHTS OF THE CHILD (Agenda item 67)
A/C.3/78/SR.13
STRADDLING FISH STOCKS (Agenda item 75b)
A/78/PV.44
UN. GENERAL ASSEMBLY (78TH SESS. : 2023-2024)—AGENDA (Agenda item 7)
A/BUR/78/SR.2
VETO (Agenda item 63)
A/78/PV.70

Dimitrov, Svetozar Angelov (Bulgaria)

HUMAN RIGHTS—RUSSIAN FEDERATION (Agenda item 71c)
A/C.3/78/SR.37
HUMAN RIGHTS—TERRITORIES OCCUPIED BY ISRAEL (Agenda item 71c)
A/C.3/78/SR.35
MIGRANTS—PROTECTION (Agenda item 71b)
A/C.3/78/SR.56

Diome, Diamane (Senegal)

INTERNATIONAL LAW—TRAINING PROGRAMMES (Agenda item 78)
A/C.6/78/SR.21
TERRORISM (Agenda item 109)
A/C.6/78/SR.1
UN. SECURITY COUNCIL—MEMBERSHIP (Agenda item 121)
A/78/PV.35
UNRWA—ACTIVITIES (Agenda item 49)
A/C.4/78/SR.23
WESTERN SAHARA QUESTION (Agenda item 58)
A/C.4/78/SR.7

Diop, Abdoulaye (Mali)

UN. GENERAL ASSEMBLY (78TH SESS. : 2023-2024)—GENERAL DEBATE (Agenda item 8)
A/78/PV.13

Diouf, Aminata (Senegal)

RURAL WOMEN (Agenda item 25a)
A/C.3/78/SR.49
WOMEN MIGRANT WORKERS (Agenda item 25a)
A/C.3/78/SR.49
WOMEN'S ADVANCEMENT (Agenda item 25a)
A/C.3/78/SR.10
WOMEN'S ADVANCEMENT—CONFERENCES (Agenda item 25b)
A/C.3/78/SR.10

Dioum, Assane (Senegal)

FOOD SECURITY (Agenda item 23a)
A/C.2/78/SR.18
TERRITORIES OCCUPIED BY ISRAEL—NATURAL RESOURCES (Agenda item 59)
A/C.2/78/SR.19

Dipama, Abdoul Karim (Burkina Faso)

SUSTAINABLE DEVELOPMENT (Agenda item 18)
A/C.2/78/SR.13

Dix, Laura Gabrielle (United Kingdom)

DEVELOPMENT FINANCE (Agenda item 16b)
A/C.2/78/SR.9
EXTERNAL DEBT (Agenda item 16c)
A/C.2/78/SR.9

Djacta, Larbi (International Civil Service Commission)

PERSONNEL QUESTIONS—UN SYSTEM (Agenda item 142)
A/C.5/78/SR.10

Dodson, Shireen L. (UN Ombudsman)

ADMINISTRATION OF JUSTICE (Agenda item 144)
A/C.5/78/SR.15

Doimen, Tash van (Guyana)

DEVELOPMENT FINANCE (Agenda item 16b)
A/C.2/78/SR.9
DEVELOPMENT FINANCE—CONFERENCES (Agenda item 17)
A/C.2/78/SR.9
INTERNATIONAL TRADE (Agenda item 16a)
A/C.2/78/SR.9

Dolah, Rizzal (Malaysia)

RIGHTS OF THE CHILD (Agenda item 67)
A/C.3/78/SR.11; A/C.3/78/SR.12

Domagała, Przemysław (Poland)

CRIMES AGAINST HUMANITY (Agenda item 80)
A/C.6/78/SR.45

Domańska, Anna (Poland)

RIGHTS OF THE CHILD (Agenda item 67)
A/C.3/78/SR.11

Dongobir, Josie-Ann (Nauru)

HUMAN RIGHTS—TERRITORIES OCCUPIED BY ISRAEL (Agenda item 71c)
A/C.3/78/SR.35

Donoghue, Joan E. (UN. International Court of Justice. President)

UN. INTERNATIONAL COURT OF JUSTICE—REPORTS (Agenda item 73)
A/78/PV.20; A/C.6/78/SR.26

Dorji, Tandi (Bhutan)

UN. GENERAL ASSEMBLY (78TH SESS. : 2023-2024)—GENERAL DEBATE (Agenda item 8)
A/78/PV.14

Dostert, Anne Françoise (Luxembourg)

PERSONS WITH DISABILITIES—HUMAN RIGHTS (Agenda item 71a)
A/C.3/78/SR.38

Douckaga Nzengui, Nicaise Servais (Congo)

PEACEKEEPING OPERATIONS—CRIMINAL LIABILITY (Agenda item 76)
A/C.6/78/SR.9
RULE OF LAW (Agenda item 83)
A/C.6/78/SR.19
UN. GENERAL ASSEMBLY (78TH SESS. : 2023-2024). 1ST COMMITTEE—GENERAL DEBATE (Agenda item 8)
A/C.1/78/PV.7

Douglas, Craig Barrington (Jamaica)

LAW OF THE SEA (Agenda item 75a)
A/78/PV.44
MARINE ECOSYSTEMS—BIOLOGICAL DIVERSITY (Agenda item 75c)
A/78/PV.44
STRADDLING FISH STOCKS (Agenda item 75b)
A/78/PV.44

Douglas, Craig Barrington (Jamaica) (Caribbean Community)

PEACEKEEPING OPERATIONS (Agenda item 51)
A/C.4/78/SR.18
SMALL ARMS—ILLICIT TRAFFIC (Agenda item 99p)
A/C.1/78/PV.18
SMALL ARMS—ILLICIT TRAFFIC—ASSISTANCE (Agenda item 99n)
A/C.1/78/PV.18

Douhan, Alena (UN. Human Rights Council. Special Rapporteur on the Negative Impact of Unilateral Coercive Measures on the Enjoyment of Human Rights)

SANCTIONS—INTERNATIONAL RELATIONS (Agenda item 71b)
A/C.3/78/SR.28

Doumbouya, Mamadi (Guinea. President)

UN. GENERAL ASSEMBLY (78TH SESS. : 2023-2024)—GENERAL DEBATE (Agenda item 8)
A/78/PV.8
UN. GENERAL ASSEMBLY (78TH SESS. : 2023-2024)—SPECIAL STATEMENTS
A/78/PV.8

Dowden, Oliver (United Kingdom. Deputy Prime Minister)

UN. GENERAL ASSEMBLY (78TH SESS. : 2023-2024)—GENERAL DEBATE (Agenda item 8)
A/78/PV.11
UN. GENERAL ASSEMBLY (78TH SESS. : 2023-2024)—SPECIAL STATEMENTS
A/78/PV.11

Doyle, Ciaran James (Ireland)

DISARMAMENT—GENERAL AND COMPLETE (Agenda item 99)
A/C.1/78/PV.22
NUCLEAR WEAPONS—ELIMINATION (Agenda item 99z)
A/C.1/78/PV.26

Drăghia, Alexandru (Romania)

FREEDOM OF EXPRESSION (Agenda item 71b)
A/C.3/78/SR.19
YOUTH (Agenda item 24b)
A/C.3/78/SR.3

Dramova, Dimana (Bulgaria)

UN. INTERNATIONAL LAW COMMISSION—REPORTS (Agenda item 79)
A/C.6/78/SR.28

Drescher, Daniel (Germany)

HUMAN RIGHTS (Agenda item 71)
A/C.3/78/SR.16
HUMAN RIGHTS—AFGHANISTAN (Agenda item 71c)
A/C.3/78/SR.34
HUMAN RIGHTS—IRAN (ISLAMIC REPUBLIC OF) (Agenda item 71c)
A/C.3/78/SR.34
HUMAN RIGHTS—RUSSIAN FEDERATION (Agenda item 71c)
A/C.3/78/SR.37
HUMAN RIGHTS—SYRIAN ARAB REPUBLIC (Agenda item 71c)
A/C.3/78/SR.34
HUMAN RIGHTS—UKRAINE (Agenda item 71c)
A/C.3/78/SR.37
HUMAN RIGHTS ACTIVISTS (Agenda item 71b)
A/C.3/78/SR.19
NATIONAL INSTITUTIONS—HUMAN RIGHTS (Agenda item 71b)
A/C.3/78/SR.49

Drew, Terrance Micheal (Saint Kitts and Nevis. Prime Minister)

UN. GENERAL ASSEMBLY (78TH SESS. : 2023-2024)—GENERAL DEBATE (Agenda item 8)
A/78/PV.12
UN. GENERAL ASSEMBLY (78TH SESS. : 2023-2024)—SPECIAL STATEMENTS
A/78/PV.12

Du Sault, Serena (Monaco)

CLIMATE (Agenda item 18d)
A/C.2/78/SR.15
DISASTER PREVENTION (Agenda item 18c)
A/C.2/78/SR.15
SUSTAINABLE DEVELOPMENT (Agenda item 18)
A/C.2/78/SR.15
SUSTAINABLE ENERGY (Agenda item 18h)
A/C.2/78/SR.15

Dubeux, Rafael (Brazil)

COMMODITIES (Agenda item 16d)
A/C.2/78/SR.14
SUSTAINABLE DEVELOPMENT (Agenda item 18)
A/C.2/78/SR.14

Duda, Andrzej (Poland. President)

UN. GENERAL ASSEMBLY (78TH SESS. : 2023-2024)—GENERAL DEBATE (Agenda item 8)
A/78/PV.4
UN. GENERAL ASSEMBLY (78TH SESS. : 2023-2024)—SPECIAL STATEMENTS
A/78/PV.4

Duffy, Patrick (Ireland)

NUCLEAR DISARMAMENT (Agenda item 99b)
A/C.1/78/PV.12
NUCLEAR NON-PROLIFERATION—INTERNATIONAL OBLIGATIONS (Agenda item 99w)
A/C.1/78/PV.12
NUCLEAR WEAPON TESTS—TREATIES (Agenda item 105)
A/C.1/78/PV.12
NUCLEAR WEAPONS—TREATIES (Agenda item 99ff)
A/C.1/78/PV.12

Dumas, Anouk (France)

DISAPPEARANCE OF PERSONS (Agenda item 71b)
A/C.3/78/SR.22

Dunbar, Ed (Saint Vincent and the Grenadines) (Community of Latin American and Caribbean States)

UN CHARTER—REPORTS (Agenda item 82)
A/C.6/78/SR.22

Dundon, Nick (Australia)

LAW OF THE SEA (Agenda item 75a)
A/78/PV.48

Dussey, Robert (Togo)

UN. GENERAL ASSEMBLY (78TH SESS. : 2023-2024)—GENERAL DEBATE (Agenda item 8)
A/78/PV.9

Dvali, Akaki (Georgia)

MULTILATERALISM—DISARMAMENT (Agenda item 99r)
A/C.1/78/PV.22
UN. GENERAL ASSEMBLY (78TH SESS. : 2023-2024). 1ST COMMITTEE—GENERAL DEBATE (Agenda item 8)
A/C.1/78/PV.8

Dvornyk, Serhii (Ukraine)

HEALTH (Agenda item 125)
A/78/PV.77
UN. SECURITY COUNCIL—MEMBERSHIP (Agenda item 121)
A/78/PV.36
VETO (Agenda item 63)
A/78/PV.71

Dyfan, Isha (UN. Human Rights Council. Independent Expert on the Situation of Human Rights in Somalia)

HUMAN RIGHTS—SOMALIA (Agenda item 71c)
A/C.3/78/SR.35

Dzwonek, Piotr (Poland)

NUCLEAR DISARMAMENT (Agenda item 99b)
A/C.1/78/PV.13
NUCLEAR NON-PROLIFERATION—INTERNATIONAL OBLIGATIONS (Agenda item 99w)
A/C.1/78/PV.13

Eads, Vivian (Capitol Hill Prayer Partners (Organization : United States))

WESTERN SAHARA QUESTION (Agenda item 58)
A/C.4/78/SR.4

Eat, Sophea (Cambodia)

CUBA—UNITED STATES (Agenda item 38)
A/78/PV.24
HUMAN RIGHTS ADVANCEMENT (Agenda item 71b)
A/C.3/78/SR.26
SANCTIONS—INTERNATIONAL RELATIONS (Agenda item 71b)
A/C.3/78/SR.26
UN—BUDGET (2024) (Agenda item 134)
A/C.5/78/SR.16
UN. GENERAL ASSEMBLY (78TH SESS. : 2023-2024). 1ST COMMITTEE—GENERAL DEBATE (Agenda item 8)
A/C.1/78/PV.3
UN. GENERAL ASSEMBLY (78TH SESS. : 2023-2024). 2ND COMMITTEE—GENERAL DEBATE (Agenda item 8)
A/C.2/78/SR.5

Eat, Sophea (Cambodia) (ASEAN)
TERRORISM (Agenda item 109)
A/C.6/78/SR.1

Ebo, Adedeji (UN. Deputy to the High Representative for Disarmament Affairs)
DISARMAMENT—GENERAL AND COMPLETE (Agenda item 99)
A/78/PV.105; A/C.1/78/PV.11

Eckersley, Fergus (United Kingdom)
MIDDLE EAST SITUATION (Agenda item 34)
A/78/PV.40
SELF-DETERMINATION OF PEOPLES (Agenda item 70)
A/C.3/78/SR.49
VETO (Agenda item 63)
A/78/PV.3

Edabadda, Mohamed (Association Rotary International à Boujdour)
WESTERN SAHARA QUESTION (Agenda item 58)
A/C.4/78/SR.5

Edbrooke, Matthew David (Liechtenstein)
SELF-DETERMINATION OF PEOPLES (Agenda item 70)
A/C.3/78/SR.40

Edjo Memba, Juan De Dios (Equatorial Guinea)
DECOLONIZATION (Agenda item 58)
A/C.4/78/SR.7
WESTERN SAHARA QUESTION (Agenda item 58)
A/C.4/78/SR.7

Edokpa, George Ehidiamen (Nigeria)
SUSTAINABLE DEVELOPMENT (Agenda item 18)
A/C.2/78/SR.13

Edtmayer, Matthias (Austria)
DISARMAMENT—GENERAL AND COMPLETE (Agenda item 99)
A/C.1/78/PV.27; A/C.1/78/PV.30
FISSIONABLE MATERIALS—TREATIES (Agenda item 99a)
A/C.1/78/PV.26
NUCLEAR WEAPONS—ELIMINATION (Agenda item 99z)
A/C.1/78/PV.25
NUCLEAR WEAPONS—HUMANITARIAN CONSEQUENCES (Agenda item 99bb)
A/C.1/78/PV.25
NUCLEAR WEAPONS—TREATIES (Agenda item 99ff)
A/C.1/78/PV.25

Edu Mbasogo, Marcial (Equatorial Guinea)
BIOLOGICAL WEAPONS—TREATIES (Agenda item 106)
A/C.1/78/PV.15
CHEMICAL WEAPONS—TREATIES (Agenda item 99l)
A/C.1/78/PV.15
CLUSTER MUNITIONS (Agenda item 99dd)
A/C.1/78/PV.19
CONFIDENCE-BUILDING MEASURES (Agenda item 99t)
A/C.1/78/PV.22
CONFIDENCE-BUILDING MEASURES—REGIONAL PROGRAMMES (Agenda item 100e)
A/C.1/78/PV.29
LANDMINES—TREATIES (Agenda item 99m)
A/C.1/78/PV.19
MULTILATERALISM—DISARMAMENT (Agenda item 99r)
A/C.1/78/PV.22
NUCLEAR WEAPONS—ELIMINATION (Agenda item 99z)
A/C.1/78/PV.25
SMALL ARMS—ILLICIT TRAFFIC (Agenda item 99p)
A/C.1/78/PV.19
WEAPONS OF MASS DESTRUCTION—TERRORISM (Agenda item 99s)
A/C.1/78/PV.15

Edwards, Alice Jill (UN. Human Rights Council. Special Rapporteur on Torture and Other Cruel, Inhuman or Degrading Treatment or Punishment)
TORTURE AND OTHER CRUEL TREATMENT (Agenda item 71a)
A/C.3/78/SR.18

Edwards, Marissa Audra Faith (Guyana)
UN—FINANCIAL SITUATION (Agenda item 136)
A/C.5/78/SR.6

Efson, Gladys Evangelina (Mozambique)
PEACEKEEPING OPERATIONS (Agenda item 51)
A/C.4/78/SR.20

Egmond, Liselot Francesca (Netherlands (Kingdom of the))
UN. INTERNATIONAL LAW COMMISSION—REPORTS (Agenda item 79)
A/C.6/78/SR.31

Ekren, Kemal Onur (Türkiye)
LANDLOCKED DEVELOPING COUNTRIES—CONFERENCES (Agenda item 20b)
A/C.2/78/SR.7
LEAST DEVELOPED COUNTRIES—CONFERENCES (Agenda item 20a)
A/C.2/78/SR.7

Ekren, Kemal Onur (Türkiye) (continued)

TERRITORIES OCCUPIED BY ISRAEL—NATURAL RESOURCES (Agenda item 59)
A/C.2/78/SR.19
TERRORISM (Agenda item 109)
A/C.6/78/SR.3
VETO (Agenda item 63)
A/78/PV.70

El Ahmadi, Brahim ((personal capacity))

WESTERN SAHARA QUESTION (Agenda item 58)
A/C.4/78/SR.6

El Baihi, Hammada (Ligue Sahara pour la démocratie et les droits de l'homme)

WESTERN SAHARA QUESTION (Agenda item 58)
A/C.4/78/SR.6

El Ghazouani, Mohamed Ould Cheikh (Mauritania. President)

UN. GENERAL ASSEMBLY (78TH SESS. : 2023-2024)—GENERAL DEBATE (Agenda item 8)
A/78/PV.7
UN. GENERAL ASSEMBLY (78TH SESS. : 2023-2024)—SPECIAL STATEMENTS
A/78/PV.7

El Hilali, Meriem (Morocco)

COASTAL ZONE MANAGEMENT (Agenda item 18j)
A/C.2/78/SR.23

El Mekaoui, Amina (Mexico)

WESTERN SAHARA QUESTION (Agenda item 58)
A/C.4/78/SR.5

El Mezouaghi, Youssef (Morocco)

INFORMATION (Agenda item 53)
A/C.4/78/SR.13

El Ouali, Zine El Aabidine ((personal capacity))

WESTERN SAHARA QUESTION (Agenda item 58)
A/C.4/78/SR.6

El Ouazzani, Mouna Chahdi (Morocco)

PEACEKEEPING OPERATIONS (Agenda item 51)
A/C.4/78/SR.20
UNRWA—ACTIVITIES (Agenda item 49)
A/C.4/78/SR.22

El Ouazzani, Mouna Chahdi (Morocco) (Coordinating Bureau of the Non-Aligned Countries)

PEACEKEEPING OPERATIONS (Agenda item 51)
A/C.4/78/SR.18
SPECIAL POLITICAL MISSIONS (Agenda item 52)
A/C.4/78/SR.21

El-Sonni, Taher M. (Libya)

SPORTS—OLYMPIC GAMES (Agenda item 11)
A/78/PV.80

Elardja Flitti, Nasria (League of Arab States)

INFORMATION (Agenda item 53)
A/C.4/78/SR.14
TERRITORIES OCCUPIED BY ISRAEL—HUMAN RIGHTS (Agenda item 50)
A/C.4/78/SR.25
UNRWA—ACTIVITIES (Agenda item 49)
A/C.4/78/SR.23

Eldahshan, Wael Mahmoud Abdelaziz (Egypt)

HUMAN RIGHTS—BURUNDI (Agenda item 71c)
A/C.3/78/SR.36
HUMAN RIGHTS—TERRITORIES OCCUPIED BY ISRAEL (Agenda item 71c)
A/C.3/78/SR.35
PEACEKEEPING OPERATIONS (Agenda item 51)
A/C.4/78/SR.18
RIGHT TO DRINKING WATER (Agenda item 71b)
A/C.3/78/SR.28
RIGHTS OF THE CHILD (Agenda item 67)
A/C.3/78/SR.11
SPECIAL POLITICAL MISSIONS (Agenda item 52)
A/C.4/78/SR.21
TERRORISM—HUMAN RIGHTS (Agenda item 71b)
A/C.3/78/SR.31
TORTURE AND OTHER CRUEL TREATMENT (Agenda item 71a)
A/C.3/78/SR.18

Eldahshan, Wael Mahmoud Abdelaziz (Egypt) (UN. Special Committee on Peacekeeping Operations. Rapporteur)

PEACEKEEPING OPERATIONS (Agenda item 51)
A/C.4/78/SR.27

Elhamriti, Soufiane (Morocco)

DISPLACED PERSONS (Agenda item 71b)
A/C.3/78/SR.32
UN HIGH COMMISSIONER FOR REFUGEES—REPORTS (Agenda item 60)
A/C.3/78/SR.44

Elhomosany, Mohamed Kamal Ali (Egypt)

CRIMES AGAINST HUMANITY (Agenda item 80)
A/C.6/78/SR.10
TERRORISM (Agenda item 109)
A/C.6/78/SR.2

Elizondo Belden, Luis Gerardo (Mexico)

HUMAN RIGHTS (Agenda item 71)
A/C.3/78/SR.16
HUMAN RIGHTS ACTIVISTS (Agenda item 71b)
A/C.3/78/SR.19

Elizondo Belden, Luis Gerardo (Mexico) (continued)

HUMAN RIGHTS ADVANCEMENT (Agenda item 71b)
A/C.3/78/SR.24; A/C.3/78/SR.52
PEACE (Agenda item 14)
A/78/PV.62
RACIAL DISCRIMINATION—ELIMINATION (Agenda item 69a)
A/C.3/78/SR.40
RACIAL DISCRIMINATION—PROGRAMMES OF ACTION (Agenda item 69b)
A/C.3/78/SR.40
TERRORISM—HUMAN RIGHTS (Agenda item 71b)
A/C.3/78/SR.31; A/C.3/78/SR.51
UN. HUMAN RIGHTS COUNCIL—REPORTS (Agenda item 66)
A/78/PV.23

Elkon, Nicole (United States)

SPORTS—OLYMPIC GAMES (Agenda item 11)
A/78/PV.38

Elsaeed, Sherine Mohamed Eissa Ahmed (Egypt)

EXTERNAL DEBT (Agenda item 16c)
A/C.2/78/SR.8

Elshandawily, Ahmed (Egypt)

CUBA—UNITED STATES (Agenda item 38)
A/78/PV.26
HEALTH (Agenda item 125)
A/78/PV.16
INFORMATION (Agenda item 53)
A/C.4/78/SR.12
PEACE (Agenda item 14)
A/78/PV.62
TERRITORIES OCCUPIED BY ISRAEL—HUMAN RIGHTS (Agenda item 50)
A/C.4/78/SR.24
UNRWA—ACTIVITIES (Agenda item 49)
A/C.4/78/SR.22

Elsonni, Taher M.T. (Libya)

UN HIGH COMMISSIONER FOR REFUGEES—REPORTS (Agenda item 60)
A/C.3/78/SR.48

Elzuni, Fatalla AF (Libya)

UN. GENERAL ASSEMBLY (78TH SESS. : 2023-2024)—GENERAL DEBATE (Agenda item 8)
A/78/PV.7

Embaló, Úmaro Sissoco (Guinea-Bissau. President)

UN. GENERAL ASSEMBLY (78TH SESS. : 2023-2024)—GENERAL DEBATE (Agenda item 8)
A/78/PV.9
UN. GENERAL ASSEMBLY (78TH SESS. : 2023-2024)—SPECIAL STATEMENTS
A/78/PV.9

Emelina-Sarte, Svetlana (UN. Department for General Assembly and Conference Management)

PEACE (Agenda item 14)
A/78/PV.77

Endoni, Syndoph Paebi (Nigeria)

DISARMAMENT—GENERAL AND COMPLETE (Agenda item 99)
A/78/PV.106
PEACE (Agenda item 14)
A/78/PV.82
RESPONSIBILITY TO PROTECT (Agenda item 129)
A/78/PV.97

Eneström, Anna-Karin (Sweden)

HUMAN RIGHTS—INTERNATIONAL INSTRUMENTS (Agenda item 71a)
A/C.3/78/SR.26
RACIAL DISCRIMINATION—ELIMINATION (Agenda item 69a)
A/C.3/78/SR.47

Ennass, Bahi Larbi (Centre de la paix pour les études politiques et stratégiques)

WESTERN SAHARA QUESTION (Agenda item 58)
A/C.4/78/SR.5

Ensing, Janine (Netherlands (Kingdom of the))

CRIMES AGAINST HUMANITY (Agenda item 80)
A/C.6/78/SR.38; A/C.6/78/SR.40; A/C.6/78/SR.41

Erb, Sherry (Erblaw (Organization))

WESTERN SAHARA QUESTION (Agenda item 58)
A/C.4/78/SR.5

Erdan, Gilad Menashe (Israel)

HUMAN RIGHTS (Agenda item 71)
A/C.3/78/SR.16
HUMAN RIGHTS—TERRITORIES OCCUPIED BY ISRAEL (Agenda item 71c)
A/C.3/78/SR.35
UKRAINE—POLITICAL CONDITIONS (Agenda item 62)
A/78/PV.58
UN. GENERAL ASSEMBLY (78TH SESS. : 2023-2024). 1ST COMMITTEE—GENERAL DEBATE (Agenda item 8)
A/C.1/78/PV.7
VETO (Agenda item 63)
A/78/PV.51; A/78/PV.59; A/78/PV.66; A/78/PV.74

Erdogan, Recep Tayyip (Türkiye. President)

UN. GENERAL ASSEMBLY (78TH SESS. : 2023-2024)—GENERAL DEBATE (Agenda item 8)
A/78/PV.4
UN. GENERAL ASSEMBLY (78TH SESS. : 2023-2024)—SPECIAL STATEMENTS
A/78/PV.4

Eremin, Sergey (Russian Federation)
IAEA—REPORTS (Agenda item 89)
A/78/PV.30

Ershadi, Zahra (Iran (Islamic Republic of))
EMERGENCY ASSISTANCE (Agenda item 72a)
A/78/PV.46
HEALTH (Agenda item 125)
A/78/PV.16
HUMAN RIGHTS—IRAN (ISLAMIC REPUBLIC OF) (Agenda item 71c)
A/C.3/78/SR.53
LAW OF THE SEA (Agenda item 75a)
A/78/PV.43
MARINE ECOSYSTEMS—BIOLOGICAL DIVERSITY (Agenda item 75c)
A/78/PV.43
PALESTINIANS—ASSISTANCE (Agenda item 72b)
A/78/PV.46
STRADDLING FISH STOCKS (Agenda item 75b)
A/78/PV.43
UN. COMMITTEE ON RELATIONS WITH THE HOST COUNTRY—REPORTS (Agenda item 161)
A/C.6/78/SR.35

Ershadi, Zahra (Iran (Islamic Republic of)) (Coordinating Bureau of the Non-Aligned Countries)
TERRORISM (Agenda item 109)
A/C.6/78/SR.1
UN CHARTER—REPORTS (Agenda item 82)
A/C.6/78/SR.22

Escaig, Benjamin (Sweden)
ARMS RACE—OUTER SPACE (Agenda item 97a)
A/C.1/78/PV.16
DISARMAMENT AGREEMENTS—OUTER SPACE (Agenda item 97c)
A/C.1/78/PV.16
NUCLEAR DISARMAMENT (Agenda item 99b)
A/C.1/78/PV.11
NUCLEAR DISARMAMENT—VERIFICATION (Agenda item 99ee)
A/C.1/78/PV.11
NUCLEAR NON-PROLIFERATION—INTERNATIONAL OBLIGATIONS (Agenda item 99w)
A/C.1/78/PV.11
NUCLEAR WEAPON TESTS—TREATIES (Agenda item 105)
A/C.1/78/PV.11
OUTER SPACE—CONFIDENCE-BUILDING MEASURES (Agenda item 99v)
A/C.1/78/PV.16
OUTER SPACE—PRINCIPLES (Agenda item 97d)
A/C.1/78/PV.16

Escobar, Luciano Hernán (Argentina)
HUMAN RIGHTS (Agenda item 71)
A/C.3/78/SR.16
MERCENARIES (Agenda item 70)
A/C.3/78/SR.48

Escobar, Luciano Hernán (Argentina) (continued)
RACIAL DISCRIMINATION—ELIMINATION (Agenda item 69a)
A/78/PV.103
RIGHT TO DEVELOPMENT (Agenda item 71b)
A/C.3/78/SR.48
UN. HUMAN RIGHTS COUNCIL—REPORTS (Agenda item 66)
A/C.3/78/SR.46

Escobar Ullauri, Pablo (Ecuador)
CRIMES AGAINST HUMANITY (Agenda item 80)
A/C.6/78/SR.38
DISASTER VICTIMS (Agenda item 86)
A/C.6/78/SR.6
INTERNATIONAL CRIMINAL COURT—REPORTS (Agenda item 74)
A/78/PV.21
NON-CITIZENS—DEPORTATION (Agenda item 81)
A/C.6/78/SR.34
RULE OF LAW (Agenda item 83)
A/C.6/78/SR.16
TERRORISM (Agenda item 109)
A/C.6/78/SR.1
UN. INTERNATIONAL COURT OF JUSTICE—REPORTS (Agenda item 73)
A/78/PV.27; A/C.6/78/SR.26
UN. INTERNATIONAL LAW COMMISSION—REPORTS (Agenda item 79)
A/C.6/78/SR.24; A/C.6/78/SR.31
UN COMMISSION ON INTERNATIONAL TRADE LAW—REPORTS (Agenda item 77)
A/C.6/78/SR.14

Escobar Vargas, Pamela (Mexico)
WOMEN'S ADVANCEMENT (Agenda item 25a)
A/C.3/78/SR.8
WOMEN'S ADVANCEMENT—CONFERENCES (Agenda item 25b)
A/C.3/78/SR.8

Escopper Zumilla, Michael Jawa (Malaysia)
AGEING PERSONS (Agenda item 24b)
A/C.3/78/SR.49
CLIMATE CHANGE (Agenda item 71b)
A/C.3/78/SR.29
DEMOCRACY (Agenda item 71b)
A/C.3/78/SR.28
ENVIRONMENT (Agenda item 71b)
A/C.3/78/SR.29
HUMAN RIGHTS—AFGHANISTAN (Agenda item 71c)
A/C.3/78/SR.34
HUMAN RIGHTS—INTERNATIONAL INSTRUMENTS (Agenda item 71a)
A/C.3/78/SR.17
HUMAN RIGHTS—MYANMAR (Agenda item 71c)
A/C.3/78/SR.33
HUMAN RIGHTS—TERRITORIES OCCUPIED BY ISRAEL (Agenda item 71c)
A/C.3/78/SR.35

Escopper Zumilla, Michael Jawa (Malaysia) (continued)

INDIGENOUS PEOPLES (Agenda item 68a)
A/C.3/78/SR.48
MIGRANT WORKERS (Agenda item 71a)
A/C.3/78/SR.23
MIGRANTS—PROTECTION (Agenda item 71b)
A/C.3/78/SR.23
MINORITIES (Agenda item 71b)
A/C.3/78/SR.52
PERSONS WITH DISABILITIES—HUMAN RIGHTS (Agenda item 71a)
A/C.3/78/SR.38; A/C.3/78/SR.51
POVERTY—HUMAN RIGHTS (Agenda item 71b)
A/C.3/78/SR.30
RACIAL DISCRIMINATION—PROGRAMMES OF ACTION (Agenda item 69b)
A/C.3/78/SR.40
RIGHT TO CULTURE (Agenda item 71b)
A/C.3/78/SR.27
RIGHT TO DEVELOPMENT (Agenda item 71b)
A/C.3/78/SR.20
RIGHT TO EDUCATION (Agenda item 71b)
A/C.3/78/SR.27
RIGHT TO FOOD (Agenda item 71b)
A/C.3/78/SR.30
RIGHT TO HOUSING (Agenda item 71b)
A/C.3/78/SR.30
RIGHT TO PRIVACY (Agenda item 71b)
A/C.3/78/SR.21
RURAL WOMEN (Agenda item 25a)
A/C.3/78/SR.49
SANCTIONS—INTERNATIONAL RELATIONS (Agenda item 71b)
A/C.3/78/SR.28
SOCIAL CONDITIONS (Agenda item 24b)
A/C.3/78/SR.51
TRAFFICKING IN PERSONS (Agenda item 71b)
A/C.3/78/SR.23
UN HIGH COMMISSIONER FOR REFUGEES—REPORTS (Agenda item 60)
A/C.3/78/SR.44; A/C.3/78/SR.51
WOMEN MIGRANT WORKERS (Agenda item 25a)
A/C.3/78/SR.49
YOUTH (Agenda item 24b)
A/C.3/78/SR.55

Esener, Kaan (Türkiye)

UN. INTERNATIONAL LAW COMMISSION—REPORTS (Agenda item 79)
A/C.6/78/SR.27

Eshkobilov, Oybek (Uzbekistan)

SUSTAINABLE DEVELOPMENT (Agenda item 18)
A/C.2/78/SR.22

Eshragh Jahromi, Asadollah (Iran (Islamic Republic of))

ARMS RACE—OUTER SPACE (Agenda item 97a)
A/C.1/78/PV.17

Eshragh Jahromi, Asadollah (Iran (Islamic Republic of)) (continued)

BIOLOGICAL WEAPONS—TREATIES (Agenda item 106)
A/C.1/78/PV.15
CHEMICAL WEAPONS—TREATIES (Agenda item 99l)
A/C.1/78/PV.15
DISARMAMENT—GENERAL AND COMPLETE (Agenda item 99)
A/C.1/78/PV.19
DISARMAMENT AGREEMENTS—OUTER SPACE (Agenda item 97c)
A/C.1/78/PV.17
OUTER SPACE—PRINCIPLES (Agenda item 97d)
A/C.1/78/PV.17
WEAPONS—OUTER SPACE (Agenda item 97b)
A/C.1/78/PV.17

Esparza Machín, Rafael ((personal capacity))

WESTERN SAHARA QUESTION (Agenda item 58)
A/C.4/78/SR.5

Espinoza Madrid, Noemí Ruth (Honduras)

CRIME PREVENTION (Agenda item 107)
A/78/PV.50(Resumption1)

Espiritu, Michael (Sovereign Order of Malta)

RIGHT TO HEALTH (Agenda item 71b)
A/C.3/78/SR.39
RIGHTS OF THE CHILD (Agenda item 67)
A/C.3/78/SR.14
TERRORISM—HUMAN RIGHTS (Agenda item 71b)
A/C.3/78/SR.31

Esposito, Karin (UN International Civil Servants Federation)

PERSONNEL QUESTIONS—UN SYSTEM (Agenda item 142)
A/C.5/78/SR.10

Espot Zamora, Xavier (Andorra. Head of Government)

UN. GENERAL ASSEMBLY (78TH SESS. : 2023-2024)—GENERAL DEBATE (Agenda item 8)
A/78/PV.10
UN. GENERAL ASSEMBLY (78TH SESS. : 2023-2024)—SPECIAL STATEMENTS
A/78/PV.10

Essaias, Meron Habte (Eritrea)

CRIMES AGAINST HUMANITY (Agenda item 80)
A/C.6/78/SR.10; A/C.6/78/SR.38; A/C.6/78/SR.41; A/C.6/78/SR.45; A/C.6/78/SR.47
INTERNATIONAL JURISDICTION (Agenda item 84)
A/C.6/78/SR.13
INTERNATIONAL LAW—TRAINING PROGRAMMES (Agenda item 78)
A/C.6/78/SR.21

Essaias, Meron Habte (Eritrea) (continued)

UN. INTERNATIONAL COURT OF JUSTICE—REPORTS (Agenda item 73)
A/C.6/78/SR.26
UN. INTERNATIONAL LAW COMMISSION—REPORTS (Agenda item 79)
A/C.6/78/SR.30

Essalek, Hanane (Observatoire du sud pour le développement territorial (Organization))

WESTERN SAHARA QUESTION (Agenda item 58)
A/C.4/78/SR.6

Essig, Ilka (Germany)

YOUTH (Agenda item 24b)
A/C.3/78/SR.3

Estanguet, Tony (France)

SPORTS—OLYMPIC GAMES (Agenda item 11)
A/78/PV.38

Estrada-Tanck, Dorothy (UN. Human Rights Council. Working Group on Discrimination against Women and Girls. Chair)

WOMEN'S ADVANCEMENT (Agenda item 25a)
A/C.3/78/SR.7
WOMEN'S ADVANCEMENT—CONFERENCES (Agenda item 25b)
A/C.3/78/SR.7

Etomzini, Intisar M. KH (Libya) (Group of Arab States)

SUSTAINABLE DEVELOPMENT (Agenda item 18)
A/C.2/78/SR.22

Etoundi Ayissi, Joseph (Cameroon)

FOOD SECURITY (Agenda item 23a)
A/C.2/78/SR.16
OPERATIONAL ACTIVITIES—UN SYSTEM (Agenda item 22a)
A/C.2/78/SR.18
POVERTY—INTERNATIONAL DECADES (Agenda item 21a)
A/C.2/78/SR.16
RURAL POVERTY (Agenda item 21b)
A/C.2/78/SR.16

Eugster, Manuel (Switzerland)

MINORITIES (Agenda item 71b)
A/C.3/78/SR.39

Eustathiou de los Santos, Matías Andrés (Uruguay)

CONVENTIONAL WEAPONS (Agenda item 99u)
A/C.1/78/PV.18
IAEA—REPORTS (Agenda item 89)
A/78/PV.30

Eustathiou de los Santos, Matías Andrés (Uruguay) (continued)

INFORMATION—INTERNATIONAL SECURITY (Agenda item 94)
A/C.1/78/PV.20
MULTILATERALISM—DISARMAMENT (Agenda item 99r)
A/C.1/78/PV.21
NUCLEAR DISARMAMENT (Agenda item 99b)
A/C.1/78/PV.12
SMALL ARMS—ILLICIT TRAFFIC (Agenda item 99p)
A/C.1/78/PV.18
UN—PROGRAMME PLANNING (Agenda item 135)
A/C.1/78/PV.10
UN. GENERAL ASSEMBLY—WORK PROGRAMME (Agenda item 120)
A/C.1/78/PV.10

Evseenko, Pavel (Belarus)

CRIMES AGAINST HUMANITY (Agenda item 80)
A/C.6/78/SR.10
CUBA—UNITED STATES (Agenda item 38)
A/78/PV.24
INTERNATIONAL JURISDICTION (Agenda item 84)
A/C.6/78/SR.12
MILLENNIUM SUMMIT—CONFERENCES (Agenda item 117)
A/78/PV.15
NON-CITIZENS—DEPORTATION (Agenda item 81)
A/C.6/78/SR.34
RESPONSIBILITY OF INTERNATIONAL ORGANIZATIONS (Agenda item 85)
A/C.6/78/SR.19
RULE OF LAW (Agenda item 83)
A/C.6/78/SR.16
TREATIES (Agenda item 87)
A/C.6/78/SR.20
UN—BUDGET (2024) (Agenda item 134)
A/C.5/78/SR.26/PartII; A/C.5/78/SR.34
UN—PROGRAMME PLANNING (Agenda item 135)
A/78/PV.50(Resumption1)
UN. INTERNATIONAL LAW COMMISSION—REPORTS (Agenda item 79)
A/C.6/78/SR.31
UN CHARTER—REPORTS (Agenda item 82)
A/C.6/78/SR.22
UN COMMISSION ON INTERNATIONAL TRADE LAW—REPORTS (Agenda item 77)
A/C.6/78/SR.14
UN CONFERENCES (Agenda item 13)
A/78/PV.15

Evseenko, Pavel (Belarus) (Group of Friends of the Family)

FAMILY (Agenda item 24b)
A/C.3/78/SR.1

Evstigneeva, Anna M. (Russian Federation)

MINE CLEARANCE (Agenda item 46)
A/C.4/78/SR.10

Evstigneeva, Anna M. (Russian Federation) (continued)

PEACEKEEPING OPERATIONS (Agenda item 51)
A/C.4/78/SR.20
SPECIAL POLITICAL MISSIONS (Agenda item 52)
A/C.4/78/SR.21
VETO (Agenda item 63)
A/78/PV.51

Eyeberdiyev, Ata (Turkmenistan)

UN. GENERAL ASSEMBLY (78TH SESS. : 2023-2024). 2ND COMMITTEE—GENERAL DEBATE (Agenda item 8)
A/C.2/78/SR.3

Eyeberdiyev, Ata (Turkmenistan) (UN. Group of Asia-Pacific States)

AL-SABAH, NAWAF AL-AHMAD AL-JABER (KUWAIT. AMIR)—TRIBUTES
A/78/PV.50(Resumption1)

Eyrich, Kara (United States)

CRIME PREVENTION (Agenda item 107)
A/C.3/78/SR.47
HEALTH (Agenda item 125)
A/78/PV.48
HUMAN RIGHTS—DEMOCRATIC PEOPLE'S REPUBLIC OF KOREA (Agenda item 71c)
A/C.3/78/SR.53
HUMAN RIGHTS ACTIVISTS (Agenda item 71b)
A/C.3/78/SR.56
HUMAN RIGHTS ADVANCEMENT (Agenda item 71b)
A/C.3/78/SR.52
PEACE (Agenda item 14)
A/78/PV.62
RELIGIOUS INTOLERANCE (Agenda item 71b)
A/C.3/78/SR.38; A/C.3/78/SR.52
TORTURE AND OTHER CRUEL TREATMENT (Agenda item 71a)
A/C.3/78/SR.18

Ezaoui, Khadija (African Forum for Research and Studies in Human Rights)

WESTERN SAHARA QUESTION (Agenda item 58)
A/C.4/78/SR.5

Faiq, Naseer Ahmed (Afghanistan)

HUMAN RIGHTS (Agenda item 71)
A/C.3/78/SR.16
HUMAN RIGHTS—AFGHANISTAN (Agenda item 71c)
A/C.3/78/SR.26; A/C.3/78/SR.34
UN HIGH COMMISSIONER FOR REFUGEES—REPORTS (Agenda item 60)
A/C.3/78/SR.44; A/C.3/78/SR.45
WOMEN'S ADVANCEMENT (Agenda item 25a)
A/C.3/78/SR.10

Faiq, Naseer Ahmed (Afghanistan) (continued)

WOMEN'S ADVANCEMENT—CONFERENCES (Agenda item 25b)
A/C.3/78/SR.10

Fajon, Tanja (Slovenia. Deputy Prime Minister)

UKRAINE—POLITICAL CONDITIONS (Agenda item 62)
A/78/PV.56
UN. GENERAL ASSEMBLY (78TH SESS. : 2023-2024)—SPECIAL STATEMENTS
A/78/PV.56

Fakhri, Michael (UN. Human Rights Council. Special Rapporteur on the Right to Food)

RIGHT TO FOOD (Agenda item 71b)
A/C.3/78/SR.30

Falaeo, Veylma (New Caledonia)

NEW CALEDONIA QUESTION (Agenda item 58)
A/C.4/78/SR.3

Falconi, Alessandra (Peru)

CRIMES AGAINST HUMANITY (Agenda item 80)
A/C.6/78/SR.10
DISASTER VICTIMS (Agenda item 86)
A/C.6/78/SR.6
RULE OF LAW (Agenda item 83)
A/C.6/78/SR.16
TERRORISM (Agenda item 109)
A/C.6/78/SR.4
UN. INTERNATIONAL LAW COMMISSION—REPORTS (Agenda item 79)
A/C.6/78/SR.25; A/C.6/78/SR.32

Falefou, Tapugao (Tuvalu) (Coalition for Addressing Sea-level Rise and its Existential Threat)

MILLENNIUM SUMMIT—CONFERENCES (Agenda item 117)
A/78/PV.53
UN CONFERENCES (Agenda item 13)
A/78/PV.53

Fall, Ahmed Mohamed (Collective of Saharawi Human Rights Defenders)

WESTERN SAHARA QUESTION (Agenda item 58)
A/C.4/78/SR.5

Fallah Assadi, Mahdad (Iran (Islamic Republic of))

NON-CITIZENS—DEPORTATION (Agenda item 81)
A/C.6/78/SR.34
RESPONSIBILITY OF INTERNATIONAL ORGANIZATIONS (Agenda item 85)
A/C.6/78/SR.37
UN. INTERNATIONAL COURT OF JUSTICE—REPORTS (Agenda item 73)
A/78/PV.28

Fallah Assadi, Mahdad (Iran (Islamic Republic of)) (continued)
UN. INTERNATIONAL LAW COMMISSION—REPORTS (Agenda item 79)
A/C.6/78/SR.29; A/C.6/78/SR.31
UN CHARTER—REPORTS (Agenda item 82)
A/C.6/78/SR.34

Fangco, Maria Roseny Baltazar (Philippines)
AGEING PERSONS (Agenda item 24b)
A/C.3/78/SR.1
EMERGENCY ASSISTANCE (Agenda item 72a)
A/78/PV.46
HUMAN RIGHTS ADVANCEMENT (Agenda item 71b)
A/C.3/78/SR.24
MIGRANTS—PROTECTION (Agenda item 71b)
A/C.3/78/SR.24
RIGHTS OF THE CHILD (Agenda item 67)
A/C.3/78/SR.11

Farhan, Fahmid (Bangladesh)
UN—BUDGET (2024) (Agenda item 134)
A/C.5/78/SR.3
VETO (Agenda item 63)
A/78/PV.61

Fatima, Rabab (UN. High Representative of the Secretary-General for the Least Developed Countries, Landlocked Developing Countries and Small Island Developing States)
LANDLOCKED DEVELOPING COUNTRIES—CONFERENCES (Agenda item 20b)
A/C.2/78/SR.7
LEAST DEVELOPED COUNTRIES—CONFERENCES (Agenda item 20a)
A/C.2/78/SR.7

Fausto, Braulio (Mexico)
ARMS RACE—OUTER SPACE (Agenda item 97a)
A/C.1/78/PV.17
DISARMAMENT AGREEMENTS—OUTER SPACE (Agenda item 97c)
A/C.1/78/PV.17
INFORMATION—INTERNATIONAL SECURITY (Agenda item 94)
A/C.1/78/PV.20

Fefoame, Gertrude Oforiwa (UN. Committee on the Rights of Persons with Disabilities. Chair)
PERSONS WITH DISABILITIES—HUMAN RIGHTS (Agenda item 71a)
A/C.3/78/SR.38

Felemban, Khalid (Saudi Arabia) (Organisation of Islamic Cooperation)
TERRORISM (Agenda item 109)
A/C.6/78/SR.1

Fepuleai, Justin Peter (New Zealand)
EMERGENCY ASSISTANCE (Agenda item 72a)
A/78/PV.46
HUMAN RIGHTS (Agenda item 71)
A/C.3/78/SR.16
INTERNATIONAL CRIMINAL COURT—REPORTS (Agenda item 74)
A/78/PV.22
PALESTINIANS—ASSISTANCE (Agenda item 72b)
A/78/PV.46
PEACE (Agenda item 14)
A/78/PV.62
VETO (Agenda item 63)
A/78/PV.68

Fernandes, Domingos Estêvão (Mozambique)
UN. GENERAL ASSEMBLY (78TH SESS. : 2023-2024). 1ST COMMITTEE—GENERAL DEBATE (Agenda item 8)
A/C.1/78/PV.9

Fernández, Alberto (Argentina. President)
UN. GENERAL ASSEMBLY (78TH SESS. : 2023-2024)—GENERAL DEBATE (Agenda item 8)
A/78/PV.5
UN. GENERAL ASSEMBLY (78TH SESS. : 2023-2024)—SPECIAL STATEMENTS
A/78/PV.5

Fernández Carter, Catalina (Chile)
CLIMATE CHANGE (Agenda item 71b)
A/C.3/78/SR.29
DISAPPEARANCE OF PERSONS (Agenda item 71b)
A/C.3/78/SR.22
ENVIRONMENT (Agenda item 71b)
A/C.3/78/SR.29
HAZARDOUS WASTES (Agenda item 71b)
A/C.3/78/SR.29
HUMAN RIGHTS—INTERNATIONAL INSTRUMENTS (Agenda item 71a)
A/C.3/78/SR.25
HUMAN RIGHTS ACTIVISTS (Agenda item 71b)
A/C.3/78/SR.19
HUMAN RIGHTS ADVANCEMENT (Agenda item 71b)
A/C.3/78/SR.25
JUDICIAL INDEPENDENCE (Agenda item 71b)
A/C.3/78/SR.31
MIGRANTS—PROTECTION (Agenda item 71b)
A/C.3/78/SR.23
RIGHT TO THE TRUTH (Agenda item 71b)
A/C.3/78/SR.22
SLAVERY (Agenda item 71a)
A/C.3/78/SR.21
SUMMARY EXECUTIONS (Agenda item 71b)
A/C.3/78/SR.31
TORTURE AND OTHER CRUEL TREATMENT (Agenda item 71a)
A/C.3/78/SR.18

Fernández Opazo, Carolina María (Joint Inspection Unit. Chair)

JOINT INSPECTION UNIT (Agenda item 141)
A/C.5/78/SR.27

Fernández Palacios, Yumirka (Cuba)

DECOLONIZATION (Agenda item 58)
A/C.4/78/SR.8
OUTER SPACE—PEACEFUL USES—INTERNATIONAL COOPERATION (Agenda item 48)
A/C.4/78/SR.15
TERRITORIES OCCUPIED BY ISRAEL—HUMAN RIGHTS (Agenda item 50)
A/C.4/78/SR.24
UKRAINE—POLITICAL CONDITIONS (Agenda item 62)
A/78/PV.99

Ferrara, Walter (Italy)

UN. INTERNATIONAL LAW COMMISSION—REPORTS (Agenda item 79)
A/C.6/78/SR.29; A/C.6/78/SR.31

Feruţă, Cornel (Romania)

HUMAN RIGHTS (Agenda item 71)
A/C.3/78/SR.16
INTERNATIONAL CRIMINAL COURT—REPORTS (Agenda item 74)
A/78/PV.21
RIGHTS OF THE CHILD (Agenda item 67)
A/C.3/78/SR.13
RULE OF LAW (Agenda item 83)
A/C.6/78/SR.18
UN. GENERAL ASSEMBLY (78TH SESS. : 2023-2024). 1ST COMMITTEE—GENERAL DEBATE (Agenda item 8)
A/C.1/78/PV.5
UN. GENERAL ASSEMBLY (78TH SESS. : 2023-2024). 2ND COMMITTEE—GENERAL DEBATE (Agenda item 8)
A/C.2/78/SR.3
UN HIGH COMMISSIONER FOR REFUGEES—REPORTS (Agenda item 60)
A/C.3/78/SR.44
VETO (Agenda item 63)
A/78/PV.3; A/78/PV.67; A/78/PV.69; A/78/PV.70; A/78/PV.79
WOMEN'S ADVANCEMENT (Agenda item 25a)
A/C.3/78/SR.9
WOMEN'S ADVANCEMENT—CONFERENCES (Agenda item 25b)
A/C.3/78/SR.9

Feruţă, Cornel (Romania) (UN. General Assembly. Ad Hoc Working Group on the Revitalization of the General Assembly. Co-Chair)

UN. GENERAL ASSEMBLY—WORK PROGRAMME (Agenda item 120)
A/78/PV.33

Feruţă, Cornel (Romania) (UN. General Assembly. Ad Hoc Working Group on the Revitalization of the General Assembly. Co-Chair) (continued)

UN RESOLUTIONS—IMPLEMENTATION (Agenda item 119)
A/78/PV.33

Fetz, Thomas (Canada)

DISARMAMENT—GENERAL AND COMPLETE (Agenda item 99)
A/C.1/78/PV.23; A/C.1/78/PV.30
DISARMAMENT AGREEMENTS—OUTER SPACE (Agenda item 97c)
A/C.1/78/PV.27
FISSIONABLE MATERIALS—TREATIES (Agenda item 99a)
A/C.1/78/PV.13; A/C.1/78/PV.25
NUCLEAR DISARMAMENT (Agenda item 99b)
A/C.1/78/PV.13
NUCLEAR DISARMAMENT—TREATY COMPLIANCE (Agenda item 99q)
A/C.1/78/PV.26
NUCLEAR NON-PROLIFERATION—INTERNATIONAL OBLIGATIONS (Agenda item 99w)
A/C.1/78/PV.13
NUCLEAR WEAPON TESTS—TREATIES (Agenda item 105)
A/C.1/78/PV.13
UN. CONFERENCE ON DISARMAMENT—REPORTS (Agenda item 101a)
A/C.1/78/PV.23
WEAPONS—OUTER SPACE (Agenda item 97b)
A/C.1/78/PV.27

Fiallo Karolys, Andrés Fernando (Ecuador)

UN. GENERAL ASSEMBLY—WORK PROGRAMME (Agenda item 120)
A/78/PV.32
UN RESOLUTIONS—IMPLEMENTATION (Agenda item 119)
A/78/PV.32

Fidoe, Nicholas (United Kingdom)

CLIMATE (Agenda item 18d)
A/C.2/78/SR.25
MILLENNIUM SUMMIT—CONFERENCES (Agenda item 117)
A/78/PV.102
SUSTAINABLE ENERGY (Agenda item 18h)
A/C.2/78/SR.23
UN CONFERENCES (Agenda item 13)
A/78/PV.102

Fielding, Julia (Sweden)

CRIMES AGAINST HUMANITY (Agenda item 80)
A/C.6/78/SR.9
INTERNATIONAL JURISDICTION (Agenda item 84)
A/C.6/78/SR.12

Filipsons, Peteris (Latvia)
DISARMAMENT—GENERAL AND COMPLETE (Agenda item 99)
A/C.1/78/PV.30

Fleming, Melissa (UN. Under-Secretary-General for Global Communications)
INFORMATION (Agenda item 53)
A/C.4/78/SR.12

Fleming, Seán (Ireland)
UKRAINE—POLITICAL CONDITIONS (Agenda item 62)
A/78/PV.56

Flores, Bruno (French Polynesia)
FRENCH POLYNESIA QUESTION (Agenda item 58)
A/C.4/78/SR.3

Flores, Mary Elizabeth (Honduras) (Community of Latin American and Caribbean States)
DISARMAMENT—GENERAL AND COMPLETE (Agenda item 99)
A/78/PV.105

Flores, Rachelle (French Polynesia)
FRENCH POLYNESIA QUESTION (Agenda item 58)
A/C.4/78/SR.3

Flores, Ramón Emilio (Honduras)
ECONOMIC SANCTIONS—INTERNATIONAL RELATIONS (Agenda item 28)
A/78/PV.90
IAEA—REPORTS (Agenda item 89)
A/78/PV.29
UN. GENERAL ASSEMBLY (78TH SESS. : 2023-2024). 1ST COMMITTEE—GENERAL DEBATE (Agenda item 8)
A/C.1/78/PV.4
UN. GENERAL ASSEMBLY (78TH SESS. : 2023-2024). 2ND COMMITTEE—GENERAL DEBATE (Agenda item 8)
A/C.2/78/SR.3

Flores Soto, Ligia Lorena (El Salvador)
CRIMES AGAINST HUMANITY (Agenda item 80)
A/C.6/78/SR.10; A/C.6/78/SR.39; A/C.6/78/SR.40; A/C.6/78/SR.42; A/C.6/78/SR.43; A/C.6/78/SR.45
INTERNATIONAL JURISDICTION (Agenda item 84)
A/C.6/78/SR.13
LAW OF THE SEA (Agenda item 75a)
A/78/PV.44
MARINE ECOSYSTEMS—BIOLOGICAL DIVERSITY (Agenda item 75c)
A/78/PV.44

Flores Soto, Ligia Lorena (El Salvador) (continued)
MILLENNIUM SUMMIT—CONFERENCES (Agenda item 117)
A/78/PV.53
NON-CITIZENS—DEPORTATION (Agenda item 81)
A/C.6/78/SR.34; A/C.6/78/SR.37
RESPONSIBILITY OF INTERNATIONAL ORGANIZATIONS (Agenda item 85)
A/C.6/78/SR.19
RULE OF LAW (Agenda item 83)
A/C.6/78/SR.18
STRADDLING FISH STOCKS (Agenda item 75b)
A/78/PV.44
TREATIES (Agenda item 87)
A/C.6/78/SR.20
UN. INTERNATIONAL COURT OF JUSTICE—REPORTS (Agenda item 73)
A/C.6/78/SR.26
UN. INTERNATIONAL LAW COMMISSION—REPORTS (Agenda item 79)
A/C.6/78/SR.28; A/C.6/78/SR.29; A/C.6/78/SR.33
UN CHARTER—REPORTS (Agenda item 82)
A/C.6/78/SR.22
UN COMMISSION ON INTERNATIONAL TRADE LAW—REPORTS (Agenda item 77)
A/C.6/78/SR.14
UN CONFERENCES (Agenda item 13)
A/78/PV.53

Flores Soto, Ligia Lorena (El Salvador) (UN. General Assembly. 6th Committee. Bureau)
UN COMMISSION ON INTERNATIONAL TRADE LAW—REPORTS (Agenda item 77)
A/C.6/78/SR.37

Flores Troche, Manuel (Mexico)
MULTILATERALISM—DISARMAMENT (Agenda item 99r)
A/C.1/78/PV.22

Floyd, Ian (United Kingdom)
BIOLOGICAL WEAPONS—TREATIES (Agenda item 106)
A/C.1/78/PV.15
CHEMICAL WEAPONS—TREATIES (Agenda item 99l)
A/C.1/78/PV.15
DISARMAMENT—GENERAL AND COMPLETE (Agenda item 99)
A/C.1/78/PV.26
DISARMAMENT—UN. GENERAL ASSEMBLY (4TH SPECIAL SESS. ON DISARMAMENT : xxxx) (Agenda item 99h)
A/C.1/78/PV.23
UN. CONFERENCE ON DISARMAMENT—REPORTS (Agenda item 101a)
A/C.1/78/PV.23

Floyd, Robert (Preparatory Commission for the Comprehensive Nuclear Test-Ban Treaty Organization. Executive Secretary)
DISARMAMENT—GENERAL AND COMPLETE (Agenda item 99)
A/78/PV.105

Fogarty, Daniel (United States)
AFRICA—SUSTAINABLE DEVELOPMENT—PARTNERSHIP (Agenda item 65a)
A/78/PV.57
PEACE (Agenda item 14)
A/78/PV.88

Folmer, Sophie (Luxembourg)
HUMAN RIGHTS—BELARUS (Agenda item 71c)
A/C.3/78/SR.37
HUMAN RIGHTS—SYRIAN ARAB REPUBLIC (Agenda item 71c)
A/C.3/78/SR.34
MIGRANTS—PROTECTION (Agenda item 71b)
A/C.3/78/SR.23
TRAFFICKING IN PERSONS (Agenda item 71b)
A/C.3/78/SR.23

Folmsbee, Paul (United States)
CUBA—UNITED STATES (Agenda item 38)
A/78/PV.26

Fondukov, Pavel A. (Russian Federation)
DEVELOPMENT FINANCE—CONFERENCES (Agenda item 17)
A/78/PV.90

Fonina, Svetlana F. (Russian Federation)
UN. ETHICS OFFICE—REPORTS (Agenda item 140)
A/C.5/78/SR.2

Font Vilagines, Meritxell (Andorra)
MULTILINGUALISM (Agenda item 124)
A/78/PV.107
RIGHTS OF THE CHILD (Agenda item 67)
A/C.3/78/SR.14

Fontaine, Manuel (UNICEF)
RIGHTS OF THE CHILD (Agenda item 67)
A/C.3/78/SR.11

Fontana, Barbara (Switzerland)
HUMAN RIGHTS—ETHIOPIA (Agenda item 71c)
A/C.3/78/SR.36
HUMAN RIGHTS—IRAN (ISLAMIC REPUBLIC OF) (Agenda item 71c)
A/C.3/78/SR.34
UN. HUMAN RIGHTS COUNCIL—REPORTS (Agenda item 66)
A/C.3/78/SR.46

Forrest, Mickaël (New Caledonia)
NEW CALEDONIA QUESTION (Agenda item 58)
A/C.4/78/SR.3

Fortea Sevilla, María del Sol (Fundación Canaria de Apoyo a los Trastornos del Neurodesarrollo)
WESTERN SAHARA QUESTION (Agenda item 58)
A/C.4/78/SR.4

Francis, Dennis (Trinidad and Tobago) (UN. General Assembly. President)
AFRICA—DEVELOPMENT (Agenda item 65b)
A/78/PV.18
AFRICA—SUSTAINABLE DEVELOPMENT—PARTNERSHIP (Agenda item 65a)
A/78/PV.18
AL-SABAH, NAWAF AL-AHMAD AL-JABER (KUWAIT. AMIR)—TRIBUTES
A/78/PV.50(Resumption1)
DISARMAMENT—GENERAL AND COMPLETE (Agenda item 99)
A/78/PV.105
GEINGOB, HAGE GOTTFRIED (NAMIBIA. PRESIDENT)—TRIBUTES
A/78/PV.55
INTERNATIONAL CRIMINAL COURT—REPORTS (Agenda item 74)
A/78/PV.21
LAW OF THE SEA (Agenda item 75a)
A/78/PV.43
MARINE ECOSYSTEMS—BIOLOGICAL DIVERSITY (Agenda item 75c)
A/78/PV.43
MILLENNIUM SUMMIT—CONFERENCES (Agenda item 117)
A/78/PV.53; A/78/PV.102
MULTILATERALISM
A/78/PV.81; A/78/PV.84
ORGANIZATION FOR DEMOCRACY AND ECONOMIC DEVELOPMENT - GUAM (Agenda item 32)
A/78/PV.85
PALESTINE QUESTION (Agenda item 35)
A/78/PV.39
RACIAL DISCRIMINATION—ELIMINATION (Agenda item 69a)
A/78/PV.63
RAISI, SEYYED EBRAHIM (IRAN (ISLAMIC REPUBLID OF). PRESIDENT)—TRIBUTES
A/78/PV.83
SLAVERY—MEMORIALS (Agenda item 118)
A/78/PV.64
SMALL ISLAND DEVELOPING STATES—PROGRAMMES OF ACTION (Agenda item 18b)
A/78/PV.103
SPORTS—OLYMPIC GAMES (Agenda item 11)
A/78/PV.93
STRADDLING FISH STOCKS (Agenda item 75b)
A/78/PV.43
UKRAINE—POLITICAL CONDITIONS (Agenda item 62)
A/78/PV.56

Francis, Dennis (Trinidad and Tobago) (UN. General Assembly. President) (continued)

UN. GENERAL ASSEMBLY—WORK PROGRAMME (Agenda item 120)
A/78/PV.32
UN. GENERAL ASSEMBLY (78TH SESS. : 2023-2024)—AGENDA (Agenda item 7)
A/78/PV.1
UN. GENERAL ASSEMBLY (78TH SESS. : 2023-2024)—CLOSING
A/78/PV.109
UN. GENERAL ASSEMBLY (78TH SESS. : 2023-2024)—GENERAL DEBATE (Agenda item 8)
A/78/PV.4; A/78/PV.14
UN. GENERAL ASSEMBLY (78TH SESS. : 2023-2024). 1ST COMMITTEE—GENERAL DEBATE (Agenda item 8)
A/C.1/78/PV.2
UN. GENERAL ASSEMBLY (78TH SESS. : 2023-2024). 2ND COMMITTEE—WORK ORGANIZATION (Agenda item 7)
A/C.2/78/SR.12
UN. GENERAL ASSEMBLY (78TH SESS. : 2023-2024). 3RD COMMITTEE—WORK ORGANIZATION (Agenda item 7)
A/C.3/78/SR.17
UN. GENERAL ASSEMBLY (78TH SESS. : 2023-2024). 4TH COMMITTEE—WORK ORGANIZATION (Agenda item 7)
A/C.4/78/SR.2
UN. GENERAL ASSEMBLY (78TH SESS. : 2023-2024). 5TH COMMITTEE—WORK ORGANIZATION (Agenda item 7)
A/C.5/78/SR.4
UN. GENERAL ASSEMBLY (78TH SESS. : 2023-2024). 6TH COMMITTEE—WORK ORGANIZATION (Agenda item 7)
A/C.6/78/SR.12
UN. GENERAL ASSEMBLY (78TH SESS. : 2023-2024). PRESIDENT (Agenda item 4)
A/78/PV.87
UN. HUMAN RIGHTS COUNCIL—MEMBERS (Agenda item 114c)
A/78/PV.17
UN. HUMAN RIGHTS COUNCIL—REPORTS (Agenda item 66)
A/78/PV.23
UN. INTERNATIONAL COURT OF JUSTICE—REPORTS (Agenda item 73)
A/78/PV.20
UN. SECURITY COUNCIL—MEMBERS (Agenda item 113a)
A/78/PV.86
UN. SECURITY COUNCIL—MEMBERSHIP (Agenda item 121)
A/78/PV.34; A/78/PV.104
UN. SECURITY COUNCIL—REPORTS (Agenda item 26)
A/78/PV.93
UN CONFERENCES (Agenda item 13)
A/78/PV.53; A/78/PV.102

Francis, Dennis (Trinidad and Tobago) (UN. General Assembly. President) (continued)

UN RESOLUTIONS—IMPLEMENTATION (Agenda item 119)
A/78/PV.32
VETO (Agenda item 63)
A/78/PV.3; A/78/PV.59; A/78/PV.66; A/78/PV.68; A/78/PV.70

Frankson-Wallace, Alayne (UN. Office of the Administration of Justice. Executive Director)

ADMINISTRATION OF JUSTICE (Agenda item 144)
A/C.5/78/SR.15

Franz, Silvio (Italy)

CRIME PREVENTION (Agenda item 107)
A/C.3/78/SR.5
CRIMES AGAINST HUMANITY (Agenda item 80)
A/C.6/78/SR.43

Frazier, Vanessa (Malta)

UN. INTERNATIONAL LAW COMMISSION—REPORTS (Agenda item 79)
A/C.6/78/SR.27
UN. SECURITY COUNCIL—MEMBERSHIP (Agenda item 121)
A/78/PV.35
VETO (Agenda item 63)
A/78/PV.3; A/78/PV.51; A/78/PV.59

Freiin von Uslar-Gleichen, Tania (Germany)

LAW OF THE SEA (Agenda item 75a)
A/78/PV.43
MARINE ECOSYSTEMS—BIOLOGICAL DIVERSITY (Agenda item 75c)
A/78/PV.43
STRADDLING FISH STOCKS (Agenda item 75b)
A/78/PV.43
UN. INTERNATIONAL COURT OF JUSTICE—REPORTS (Agenda item 73)
A/78/PV.20
UN. INTERNATIONAL LAW COMMISSION—REPORTS (Agenda item 79)
A/C.6/78/SR.24

Freudenreich, Anne (France)

ELECTION VERIFICATION—UN (Agenda item 71b)
A/C.3/78/SR.50
FREEDOM OF EXPRESSION (Agenda item 71b)
A/C.3/78/SR.19
HUMAN RIGHTS ACTIVISTS (Agenda item 71b)
A/C.3/78/SR.19
RIGHTS OF THE CHILD (Agenda item 67)
A/C.3/78/SR.11
SEXUAL ORIENTATION (Agenda item 71b)
A/C.3/78/SR.39

Frey, Benjamin Jay (Switzerland)

TAXATION (Agenda item 16h)
A/C.2/78/SR.25

Froment, Lucas (France)
HUMAN RIGHTS—AFGHANISTAN (Agenda item 71c)
A/C.3/78/SR.34
HUMAN RIGHTS—MYANMAR (Agenda item 71c)
A/C.3/78/SR.33

Fruean, Tausala (New Zealand)
PERSONS WITH DISABILITIES—HUMAN RIGHTS (Agenda item 71a)
A/C.3/78/SR.38
RURAL WOMEN (Agenda item 25a)
A/C.3/78/SR.49

Fry, Ian (UN. Human Rights Council. Special Rapporteur on the Promotion and Protection of Human Rights in the Context of Climate Change)
CLIMATE CHANGE (Agenda item 71b)
A/C.3/78/SR.29

Fu, Cong (China)
PEACE (Agenda item 14)
A/78/PV.82; A/78/PV.88
UKRAINE—POLITICAL CONDITIONS (Agenda item 62)
A/78/PV.99
UN CONFERENCES (Agenda item 13)
A/78/PV.97
VETO (Agenda item 63)
A/78/PV.75; A/78/PV.78

Fujinuma, Atsuyuki (Japan)
UN—BUDGET (2024) (Agenda item 134)
A/C.5/78/SR.33
UN. GENERAL ASSEMBLY (78TH SESS. : 2023-2024). 5TH COMMITTEE—WORK ORGANIZATION (Agenda item 7)
A/C.5/78/SR.26/PartII

Fuller, Carlos C. (Belize)
CUBA—UNITED STATES (Agenda item 38)
A/78/PV.26
MARINE ECOSYSTEMS—BIOLOGICAL DIVERSITY (Agenda item 75c)
A/78/PV.103
UN. GENERAL ASSEMBLY (78TH SESS. : 2023-2024)—GENERAL DEBATE—RIGHT OF REPLY (Agenda item 8)
A/78/PV.14

Fuller, Carlos C. (Belize) (Caribbean Community)
MARINE ECOSYSTEMS—BIOLOGICAL DIVERSITY (Agenda item 75c)
A/78/PV.73
NUCLEAR DISARMAMENT (Agenda item 99b)
A/C.1/78/PV.11
NUCLEAR NON-PROLIFERATION—INTERNATIONAL OBLIGATIONS (Agenda item 99w)
A/C.1/78/PV.11

Fuller, Carlos C. (Belize) (Caribbean Community) (continued)
NUCLEAR WEAPONS—HUMANITARIAN CONSEQUENCES (Agenda item 99bb)
A/C.1/78/PV.11
NUCLEAR WEAPONS—TREATIES (Agenda item 99ff)
A/C.1/78/PV.11
NUCLEAR-WEAPON-FREE ZONES (Agenda item 99cc)
A/C.1/78/PV.11

Fyneah, Sarah Safyn (Liberia)
WESTERN SAHARA QUESTION (Agenda item 58)
A/C.4/78/SR.8

Gaal, Miklos (Hungary)
HEALTH (Agenda item 125)
A/78/PV.16

Gaal, Miklos (Hungary) (European Union)
HEALTH (Agenda item 125)
A/78/PV.102
SUSTAINABLE DEVELOPMENT (Agenda item 18)
A/78/PV.107

Gaber-Wennholz, Basma (European Union)
UN. GENERAL ASSEMBLY (78TH SESS. : 2023-2024). 5TH COMMITTEE—WORK ORGANIZATION (Agenda item 7)
A/C.5/78/SR.26/PartII

Gabi, Emery (Congo)
CUBA—UNITED STATES (Agenda item 38)
A/78/PV.26
ECONOMIC COOPERATION AMONG DEVELOPING COUNTRIES (Agenda item 22b)
A/C.2/78/SR.18
POVERTY—INTERNATIONAL DECADES (Agenda item 21a)
A/C.2/78/SR.17
RURAL POVERTY (Agenda item 21b)
A/C.2/78/SR.17

Gabriele, Emma de (Malta)
AGEING PERSONS (Agenda item 24b)
A/C.3/78/SR.1
SOCIAL CONDITIONS (Agenda item 24b)
A/C.3/78/SR.3
WOMEN'S ADVANCEMENT (Agenda item 25a)
A/C.3/78/SR.7
WOMEN'S ADVANCEMENT—CONFERENCES (Agenda item 25b)
A/C.3/78/SR.7
YOUTH (Agenda item 24b)
A/C.3/78/SR.3

Gadouri, Hakim (Algeria)
UN—BUDGET (2024) (Agenda item 134)
A/C.5/78/SR.33

Gadouri, Hakim (Algeria) (continued)

UN—HUMAN RESOURCES MANAGEMENT (Agenda item 139)
A/C.5/78/SR.27

Gafoor, Burhan (Singapore)

HUMAN RIGHTS—DEMOCRATIC PEOPLE'S REPUBLIC OF KOREA (Agenda item 71c)
A/C.3/78/SR.53
HUMAN RIGHTS—MYANMAR (Agenda item 71c)
A/C.3/78/SR.53
HUMAN RIGHTS ADVANCEMENT (Agenda item 71b)
A/C.3/78/SR.24
LAW OF THE SEA (Agenda item 75a)
A/78/PV.43
MARINE ECOSYSTEMS—BIOLOGICAL DIVERSITY (Agenda item 75c)
A/78/PV.43
PEACE (Agenda item 14)
A/78/PV.62
SOUTH-EAST ASIA—NUCLEAR-WEAPON-FREE ZONES (Agenda item 99y)
A/C.1/78/PV.30
STRADDLING FISH STOCKS (Agenda item 75b)
A/78/PV.43
TERRORISM (Agenda item 109)
A/C.6/78/SR.1
UKRAINE—POLITICAL CONDITIONS (Agenda item 62)
A/78/PV.57
UN—FINANCIAL SITUATION (Agenda item 136)
A/C.5/78/SR.38
UN. COMMITTEE ON RELATIONS WITH THE HOST COUNTRY—REPORTS (Agenda item 161)
A/C.6/78/SR.35
UN. GENERAL ASSEMBLY (78TH SESS. : 2023-2024). 1ST COMMITTEE—WORK ORGANIZATION (Agenda item 7)
A/C.1/78/PV.30
UN. INTERNATIONAL COURT OF JUSTICE—REPORTS (Agenda item 73)
A/78/PV.27
UN. SECURITY COUNCIL—MEMBERSHIP (Agenda item 121)
A/78/PV.34
UN. SECURITY COUNCIL—REPORTS (Agenda item 26)
A/78/PV.93
VETO (Agenda item 63)
A/78/PV.59; A/78/PV.68

Gafoor, Burhan (Singapore) (ASEAN)

CRIME PREVENTION (Agenda item 107)
A/C.3/78/SR.5
CUBA—UNITED STATES (Agenda item 38)
A/78/PV.24
CYBERCRIME (Agenda item 108)
A/C.3/78/SR.5
UN—FINANCIAL SITUATION (Agenda item 136)
A/C.5/78/SR.38

Gafoor, Burhan (Singapore) (ASEAN) (continued)

UN. GENERAL ASSEMBLY (78TH SESS. : 2023-2024)—OFFICERS (Agenda item 5)
A/C.5/78/SR.1
UN. GENERAL ASSEMBLY (78TH SESS. : 2023-2024). 5TH COMMITTEE—WORK ORGANIZATION (Agenda item 7)
A/C.5/78/SR.27

Gafoor, Burhan (Singapore) (UN. Open-ended Working Group on Security of and in the Use of Information and Communications Technologies 2021-2025. Chair)

INFORMATION—INTERNATIONAL SECURITY (Agenda item 94)
A/C.1/78/PV.21

Gahlot, Petal (India)

CLIMATE (Agenda item 18d)
A/C.2/78/SR.13
COMMODITIES (Agenda item 16d)
A/C.2/78/SR.14
DEVELOPMENT FINANCE—CONFERENCES (Agenda item 17)
A/C.2/78/SR.9
ECONOMIC COOPERATION AMONG DEVELOPING COUNTRIES (Agenda item 22b)
A/C.2/78/SR.18
EXTERNAL DEBT (Agenda item 16c)
A/C.2/78/SR.9
FOOD SECURITY (Agenda item 23a)
A/C.2/78/SR.16
HEALTH (Agenda item 125)
A/78/PV.77
INFORMATION TECHNOLOGY—DEVELOPMENT (Agenda item 15)
A/C.2/78/SR.10
INTERNATIONAL TRADE (Agenda item 16a)
A/C.2/78/SR.9; A/C.2/78/SR.22
LANDLOCKED DEVELOPING COUNTRIES—CONFERENCES (Agenda item 20b)
A/C.2/78/SR.7
LEAST DEVELOPED COUNTRIES—CONFERENCES (Agenda item 20a)
A/C.2/78/SR.7
OPERATIONAL ACTIVITIES—UN SYSTEM (Agenda item 22a)
A/C.2/78/SR.18
POVERTY—INTERNATIONAL DECADES (Agenda item 21a)
A/C.2/78/SR.16
RURAL POVERTY (Agenda item 21b)
A/C.2/78/SR.16
SCIENCE AND TECHNOLOGY—DEVELOPMENT (Agenda item 19a)
A/C.2/78/SR.10
SMALL ISLAND DEVELOPING STATES—PROGRAMMES OF ACTION (Agenda item 18b)
A/C.2/78/SR.13
SUSTAINABLE DEVELOPMENT (Agenda item 18)
A/C.2/78/SR.13; A/C.2/78/SR.14

Gahlot, Petal (India) (continued)

SUSTAINABLE ENERGY (Agenda item 18h)
A/C.2/78/SR.13
UN. GENERAL ASSEMBLY (78TH SESS. : 2023-2024)—GENERAL DEBATE—RIGHT OF REPLY (Agenda item 8)
A/78/PV.11
UN. GENERAL ASSEMBLY (78TH SESS. : 2023-2024). 2ND COMMITTEE—GENERAL DEBATE (Agenda item 8)
A/C.2/78/SR.4

Gai, Elena (Italy)

ARMS TRANSFERS—TREATIES (Agenda item 99x)
A/C.1/78/PV.19
CLUSTER MUNITIONS (Agenda item 99dd)
A/C.1/78/PV.19
CONVENTIONAL WEAPONS—TREATIES (Agenda item 103)
A/C.1/78/PV.19
DISARMAMENT—GENERAL AND COMPLETE (Agenda item 99)
A/C.1/78/PV.19
LANDMINES—TREATIES (Agenda item 99m)
A/C.1/78/PV.19

Gain, Mohammed Ahmed (African Institute for Peacebuilding and Conflict Transformation)

WESTERN SAHARA QUESTION (Agenda item 58)
A/C.4/78/SR.6

Gala López, Yuri (Cuba)

HUMAN RIGHTS (Agenda item 71)
A/C.3/78/SR.16
PEACEBUILDING (Agenda item 61)
A/78/PV.100
UN. COMMITTEE ON RELATIONS WITH THE HOST COUNTRY—REPORTS (Agenda item 161)
A/C.6/78/SR.35
UN. GENERAL ASSEMBLY (78TH SESS. : 2023-2024). 1ST COMMITTEE—GENERAL DEBATE (Agenda item 8)
A/C.1/78/PV.6
UN. PEACEBUILDING COMMISSION—REPORTS (Agenda item 27)
A/78/PV.100
UN. PEACEBUILDING FUND—REPORTS (Agenda item 111)
A/78/PV.100
UN. SECURITY COUNCIL—REPORTS (Agenda item 26)
A/78/PV.93
VETO (Agenda item 63)
A/78/PV.70

Gala López, Yuri (Cuba) (Group of 77)

UN—BUDGET (2024) (Agenda item 134)
A/C.5/78/SR.5
UN—PROGRAMME PLANNING (Agenda item 135)
A/C.5/78/SR.5

Galbavý, Richard (Slovakia)

PEACE (Agenda item 14)
A/78/PV.82
UKRAINE—POLITICAL CONDITIONS (Agenda item 62)
A/78/PV.57

Gallagher, Paul Richard (Holy See)

UN. GENERAL ASSEMBLY (78TH SESS. : 2023-2024)—GENERAL DEBATE (Agenda item 8)
A/78/PV.14

Galstyan, Tigran (Armenia)

CRIMES AGAINST HUMANITY (Agenda item 80)
A/C.6/78/SR.11
IAEA—REPORTS (Agenda item 89)
A/78/PV.29
RULE OF LAW (Agenda item 83)
A/C.6/78/SR.18
TERRORISM (Agenda item 109)
A/C.6/78/SR.5
UN. GENERAL ASSEMBLY (78TH SESS. : 2023-2024)—GENERAL DEBATE—RIGHT OF REPLY (Agenda item 8)
A/78/PV.14
UN. GENERAL ASSEMBLY (78TH SESS. : 2023-2024). 2ND COMMITTEE—GENERAL DEBATE (Agenda item 8)
A/C.2/78/SR.3

Gamba, Virginia (UN. Special Representative of the Secretary-General for Children and Armed Conflict)

RIGHTS OF THE CHILD (Agenda item 67)
A/C.3/78/SR.11

Gambert, Sylvain (European Union)

BIOLOGICAL DIVERSITY—TREATIES (Agenda item 18f)
A/C.2/78/SR.25
COASTAL ZONE MANAGEMENT (Agenda item 18j)
A/C.2/78/SR.23
SUSTAINABLE DEVELOPMENT (Agenda item 18)
A/C.2/78/SR.22

Gana Alkali, Baba (Nigeria)

DEVELOPMENT FINANCE (Agenda item 16b)
A/C.2/78/SR.9
EXTERNAL DEBT (Agenda item 16c)
A/C.2/78/SR.9
TAXATION (Agenda item 16h)
A/C.2/78/SR.9

Ganesh, Vivek (Singapore)

UN. SECURITY COUNCIL—MEMBERSHIP (Agenda item 121)
A/78/PV.104

Ganou, Oumarou (Burkina Faso)
CRIMES AGAINST HUMANITY (Agenda item 80)
A/C.6/78/SR.10
DECOLONIZATION (Agenda item 58)
A/C.4/78/SR.7
IAEA—REPORTS (Agenda item 89)
A/78/PV.30
INTERNATIONAL CRIMINAL COURT—REPORTS (Agenda item 74)
A/78/PV.22
INTERNATIONAL JURISDICTION (Agenda item 84)
A/C.6/78/SR.13
INTERNATIONAL LAW—TRAINING PROGRAMMES (Agenda item 78)
A/C.6/78/SR.21
LANDMINES—TREATIES (Agenda item 99m)
A/C.1/78/PV.18
NUCLEAR DISARMAMENT (Agenda item 99b)
A/C.1/78/PV.12
PEACEKEEPING OPERATIONS—CRIMINAL LIABILITY (Agenda item 76)
A/C.6/78/SR.8
RULE OF LAW (Agenda item 83)
A/C.6/78/SR.17
SMALL ARMS—ILLICIT TRAFFIC (Agenda item 99p)
A/C.1/78/PV.18
UN. GENERAL ASSEMBLY (78TH SESS. : 2023-2024). 1ST COMMITTEE—GENERAL DEBATE (Agenda item 8)
A/C.1/78/PV.6
UN HIGH COMMISSIONER FOR REFUGEES—REPORTS (Agenda item 60)
A/C.3/78/SR.44
WESTERN SAHARA QUESTION (Agenda item 58)
A/C.4/78/SR.7
WOMEN'S ADVANCEMENT (Agenda item 25a)
A/C.3/78/SR.9
WOMEN'S ADVANCEMENT—CONFERENCES (Agenda item 25b)
A/C.3/78/SR.9

Gantana, Audrey Fay (Namibia)
CUBA—UNITED STATES (Agenda item 38)
A/78/PV.24
DEVELOPMENT COOPERATION—MIDDLE-INCOME COUNTRIES (Agenda item 19c)
A/C.2/78/SR.10

Gaouaoui, Nacim (Algeria)
PALESTINE QUESTION (Agenda item 35)
A/78/PV.40
PEACEBUILDING (Agenda item 61)
A/78/PV.100
TERRORISM (Agenda item 109)
A/C.6/78/SR.4
UN. PEACEBUILDING COMMISSION—REPORTS (Agenda item 27)
A/78/PV.100

Gaouaoui, Nacim (Algeria) (continued)
UN. PEACEBUILDING FUND—REPORTS (Agenda item 111)
A/78/PV.100
VETO (Agenda item 63)
A/78/PV.51; A/78/PV.66

Garcia, Joseph (Gibraltar)
GIBRALTAR QUESTION (Agenda item 58)
A/C.4/78/SR.13

García Hernández, Martha (Cuba)
AGEING PERSONS (Agenda item 24b)
A/C.3/78/SR.3
ENVIRONMENT (Agenda item 71b)
A/C.3/78/SR.29
EXTERNAL DEBT—HUMAN RIGHTS (Agenda item 71b)
A/C.3/78/SR.32
PERSONS WITH DISABILITIES (Agenda item 24b)
A/C.3/78/SR.3
RIGHT TO FOOD (Agenda item 71b)
A/C.3/78/SR.30
SOCIAL DEVELOPMENT—CONFERENCES (Agenda item 24a)
A/C.3/78/SR.3
WOMEN'S ADVANCEMENT (Agenda item 25a)
A/C.3/78/SR.7; A/C.3/78/SR.9
WOMEN'S ADVANCEMENT—CONFERENCES (Agenda item 25b)
A/C.3/78/SR.7; A/C.3/78/SR.9
YOUTH (Agenda item 24b)
A/C.3/78/SR.3

Garcia Moré, Yohan Yuniet (Cuba)
ARMS TRANSFERS—TREATIES (Agenda item 99x)
A/C.1/78/PV.28
CONVENTIONAL WEAPONS (Agenda item 99u)
A/C.1/78/PV.28
LANDMINES—TREATIES (Agenda item 99m)
A/C.1/78/PV.28

García Rico, Lucía (Spain) (European Union)
HUMAN RIGHTS—MYANMAR (Agenda item 71c)
A/C.3/78/SR.53
HUMAN RIGHTS—SYRIAN ARAB REPUBLIC (Agenda item 71c)
A/C.3/78/SR.54
UN HIGH COMMISSIONER FOR REFUGEES—REPORTS (Agenda item 60)
A/C.3/78/SR.48

García Toma, Victor Óscar Shiyin (Peru)
INTERNATIONAL CRIMINAL COURT—REPORTS (Agenda item 74)
A/78/PV.21
PEACEBUILDING (Agenda item 61)
A/78/PV.100

García Toma, Victor Óscar Shiyin (Peru) (continued)

UN. PEACEBUILDING COMMISSION—REPORTS (Agenda item 27)
A/78/PV.100
UN. PEACEBUILDING FUND—REPORTS (Agenda item 111)
A/78/PV.100
UN CONFERENCES (Agenda item 13)
A/78/PV.47

Garelova, Tsvetelina (Bulgaria)

YOUTH (Agenda item 24b)
A/C.3/78/SR.2

Garibashvili, Irakli (Georgia. Prime Minister)

UN. GENERAL ASSEMBLY (78TH SESS. : 2023-2024)—GENERAL DEBATE (Agenda item 8)
A/78/PV.11
UN. GENERAL ASSEMBLY (78TH SESS. : 2023-2024)—SPECIAL STATEMENTS
A/78/PV.11

Garrido Melo, Claudio Ernesto (Chile)

UN RESOLUTIONS—IMPLEMENTATION (Agenda item 119)
A/78/PV.103
UNRWA—ACTIVITIES (Agenda item 49)
A/C.4/78/SR.23
VETO (Agenda item 63)
A/78/PV.60; A/78/PV.74
WOMEN'S ADVANCEMENT (Agenda item 25a)
A/C.3/78/SR.8
WOMEN'S ADVANCEMENT—CONFERENCES (Agenda item 25b)
A/C.3/78/SR.8

Gaspard, Fritzner (Haiti)

HIV/AIDS—DECLARATIONS (Agenda item 10)
A/78/PV.91

Gatev, Ivaylo (Bulgaria) (UN. General Assembly. 2nd Committee. Rapporteur)

2030 AGENDA—PROGRAMME IMPLEMENTATION (Agenda item 18a)
A/78/PV.49
BIOLOGICAL DIVERSITY—TREATIES (Agenda item 18f)
A/78/PV.49
CLIMATE (Agenda item 18d)
A/78/PV.49
COASTAL ZONE MANAGEMENT (Agenda item 18j)
A/78/PV.49
COMMODITIES (Agenda item 16d)
A/78/PV.49
CULTURE—DEVELOPMENT (Agenda item 19b)
A/78/PV.49
DESERTIFICATION—TREATIES (Agenda item 18e)
A/78/PV.49

Gatev, Ivaylo (Bulgaria) (UN. General Assembly. 2nd Committee. Rapporteur) (continued)

DEVELOPMENT COOPERATION—MIDDLE-INCOME COUNTRIES (Agenda item 19c)
A/78/PV.49
DEVELOPMENT EDUCATION (Agenda item 18g)
A/78/PV.49
DEVELOPMENT FINANCE (Agenda item 16b)
A/78/PV.49
DEVELOPMENT FINANCE—CONFERENCES (Agenda item 17)
A/78/PV.49
DISASTER PREVENTION (Agenda item 18c)
A/78/PV.49
ECONOMIC COOPERATION AMONG DEVELOPING COUNTRIES (Agenda item 22b)
A/78/PV.49
EXTERNAL DEBT (Agenda item 16c)
A/78/PV.49
FINANCIAL FLOWS (Agenda item 16f)
A/78/PV.49
FINANCIAL INCLUSION (Agenda item 16e)
A/78/PV.49
FOOD SECURITY (Agenda item 23a)
A/78/PV.49
GLOBALIZATION—INTERDEPENDENCE (Agenda item 19)
A/78/PV.49
INFORMATION TECHNOLOGY—DEVELOPMENT (Agenda item 15)
A/78/PV.49
INTERNATIONAL TRADE (Agenda item 16a)
A/78/PV.49
INVESTMENT PROMOTION (Agenda item 16g)
A/78/PV.49
LANDLOCKED DEVELOPING COUNTRIES—CONFERENCES (Agenda item 20b)
A/78/PV.49
LEAST DEVELOPED COUNTRIES—CONFERENCES (Agenda item 20a)
A/78/PV.49
MACROECONOMIC POLICY (Agenda item 16)
A/78/PV.49
NATURAL FIBRES (Agenda item 23b)
A/78/PV.49
OPERATIONAL ACTIVITIES—DEVELOPMENT (Agenda item 22)
A/78/PV.49
OPERATIONAL ACTIVITIES—UN SYSTEM (Agenda item 22a)
A/78/PV.49
POVERTY—INTERNATIONAL DECADES (Agenda item 21a)
A/78/PV.49
POVERTY MITIGATION (Agenda item 21)
A/78/PV.49
RURAL POVERTY (Agenda item 21b)
A/78/PV.49
SCIENCE AND TECHNOLOGY—DEVELOPMENT (Agenda item 19a)
A/78/PV.49

Gatev, Ivaylo (Bulgaria) (UN. General Assembly. 2nd Committee. Rapporteur) (continued)

SMALL ISLAND DEVELOPING STATES—PROGRAMMES OF ACTION (Agenda item 18b)
A/78/PV.49
STORMS (Agenda item 18i)
A/78/PV.49
SUSTAINABLE DEVELOPMENT (Agenda item 18)
A/78/PV.49
SUSTAINABLE ENERGY (Agenda item 18h)
A/78/PV.49
TAXATION (Agenda item 16h)
A/78/PV.49
TERRITORIES OCCUPIED BY ISRAEL—NATURAL RESOURCES (Agenda item 59)
A/78/PV.49
UN—PROGRAMME PLANNING (Agenda item 135)
A/78/PV.49
UN. GENERAL ASSEMBLY—WORK PROGRAMME (Agenda item 120)
A/78/PV.49

Gatt, Francesca Maria (Malta)

UN YOUTH OFFICE—REPORTS (Agenda item 130)
A/78/PV.102

Gatti Santana, Graciela Susana (International Residual Mechanism for Criminal Tribunals. President)

INTERNATIONAL RESIDUAL MECHANISM FOR CRIMINAL TRIBUNALS (Agenda item 126)
A/78/PV.19

Gaviria Betancur, Paula (UN. Human Rights Council. Special Rapporteur on the Human Rights of Internally Displaced Persons)

DISPLACED PERSONS (Agenda item 71b)
A/C.3/78/SR.32

Gazizulina, Zhanna (Kazakhstan)

WOMEN'S ADVANCEMENT (Agenda item 25a)
A/C.3/78/SR.9
WOMEN'S ADVANCEMENT—CONFERENCES (Agenda item 25b)
A/C.3/78/SR.9

Gbai, Tangbae Kortemah (Liberia)

ELECTION VERIFICATION—UN (Agenda item 71b)
A/C.3/78/SR.50

Gebrekidan, Zebib (Eritrea)

CRIME PREVENTION (Agenda item 107)
A/C.3/78/SR.6
CYBERCRIME (Agenda item 108)
A/C.3/78/SR.6
HUMAN RIGHTS (Agenda item 71)
A/C.3/78/SR.28
HUMAN RIGHTS—DEMOCRATIC PEOPLE'S REPUBLIC OF KOREA (Agenda item 71c)
A/C.3/78/SR.33

Gebrekidan, Zebib (Eritrea) (continued)

HUMAN RIGHTS—IRAN (ISLAMIC REPUBLIC OF) (Agenda item 71c)
A/C.3/78/SR.53
HUMAN RIGHTS—RUSSIAN FEDERATION (Agenda item 71c)
A/C.3/78/SR.37
HUMAN RIGHTS—SYRIAN ARAB REPUBLIC (Agenda item 71c)
A/C.3/78/SR.34
RACIAL DISCRIMINATION—ELIMINATION (Agenda item 69a)
A/C.3/78/SR.41; A/C.3/78/SR.43
RACIAL DISCRIMINATION—PROGRAMMES OF ACTION (Agenda item 69b)
A/C.3/78/SR.41; A/C.3/78/SR.43
RIGHT TO CULTURE (Agenda item 71b)
A/C.3/78/SR.27
SANCTIONS—INTERNATIONAL RELATIONS (Agenda item 71b)
A/C.3/78/SR.28
UN. HUMAN RIGHTS COUNCIL—REPORTS (Agenda item 66)
A/C.3/78/SR.51
WOMEN'S ADVANCEMENT (Agenda item 25a)
A/C.3/78/SR.10
WOMEN'S ADVANCEMENT—CONFERENCES (Agenda item 25b)
A/C.3/78/SR.10

Geingob, Hage Gottfried (Namibia. President)

UN. GENERAL ASSEMBLY (78TH SESS. : 2023-2024)—GENERAL DEBATE (Agenda item 8)
A/78/PV.6
UN. GENERAL ASSEMBLY (78TH SESS. : 2023-2024)—SPECIAL STATEMENTS
A/78/PV.6

Geisler, Michael Alexander (Germany)

ARMED CONFLICTS PREVENTION (Agenda item 31a)
A/78/PV.72
HUMAN RIGHTS—MYANMAR (Agenda item 71c)
A/C.3/78/SR.33
PEACEBUILDING (Agenda item 61)
A/78/PV.100
PEACEKEEPING OPERATIONS (Agenda item 51)
A/C.4/78/SR.20
SELF-DETERMINATION OF PEOPLES (Agenda item 70)
A/C.3/78/SR.49
UN. PEACEBUILDING COMMISSION—REPORTS (Agenda item 27)
A/78/PV.100
UN. PEACEBUILDING FUND—REPORTS (Agenda item 111)
A/78/PV.100
VETO (Agenda item 63)
A/78/PV.52

Geiss, Robin (UN Institute for Disarmament Research. Director)
DISARMAMENT—UN. GENERAL ASSEMBLY (12TH SPECIAL SESS. : 1982) (Agenda item 100)
A/C.1/78/PV.24

Geleževičienė, Giedrė (Lithuania)
NUCLEAR DISARMAMENT (Agenda item 99b)
A/C.1/78/PV.13

Geng, Shuang (China)
CRIMES AGAINST HUMANITY (Agenda item 80)
A/C.6/78/SR.10
DECOLONIZATION (Agenda item 58)
A/C.4/78/SR.8
ECONOMIC SANCTIONS—INTERNATIONAL RELATIONS (Agenda item 28)
A/78/PV.89
FALKLAND ISLANDS (MALVINAS) QUESTION (Agenda item 42)
A/C.4/78/SR.8
LAW OF THE SEA (Agenda item 75a)
A/78/PV.43
MARINE ECOSYSTEMS—BIOLOGICAL DIVERSITY (Agenda item 75c)
A/78/PV.43
STRADDLING FISH STOCKS (Agenda item 75b)
A/78/PV.43
TERRITORIES OCCUPIED BY ISRAEL—HUMAN RIGHTS (Agenda item 50)
A/C.4/78/SR.25
TERRORISM (Agenda item 109)
A/C.6/78/SR.3
UN. GENERAL ASSEMBLY (78TH SESS. : 2023-2024). 2ND COMMITTEE—GENERAL DEBATE (Agenda item 8)
A/C.2/78/SR.4
UN CHARTER—REPORTS (Agenda item 82)
A/C.6/78/SR.33
UNRWA—ACTIVITIES (Agenda item 49)
A/C.4/78/SR.23
VETO (Agenda item 63)
A/78/PV.51; A/78/PV.60; A/78/PV.68

Genoversa-Wong, Bridget (United States)
CRIMES AGAINST HUMANITY (Agenda item 80)
A/C.6/78/SR.41; A/C.6/78/SR.43

George, Alan Ebun (Sierra Leone)
FOOD SECURITY (Agenda item 23a)
A/C.2/78/SR.17
POVERTY—INTERNATIONAL DECADES (Agenda item 21a)
A/C.2/78/SR.17
RURAL POVERTY (Agenda item 21b)
A/C.2/78/SR.17
UN. INTERNATIONAL LAW COMMISSION—REPORTS (Agenda item 79)
A/C.6/78/SR.32

Germeaux, Alain (Luxembourg)
INTERNATIONAL CRIMINAL COURT—REPORTS (Agenda item 74)
A/78/PV.21
UN. INTERNATIONAL COURT OF JUSTICE—REPORTS (Agenda item 73)
A/78/PV.27

Géros, Antony (French Polynesia)
FRENCH POLYNESIA QUESTION (Agenda item 58)
A/C.4/78/SR.3

Gertze, Neville Melvin (Namibia)
AFRICA—DEVELOPMENT (Agenda item 65b)
A/78/PV.18
AFRICA—SUSTAINABLE DEVELOPMENT—PARTNERSHIP (Agenda item 65a)
A/78/PV.18
AGEING PERSONS (Agenda item 24b)
A/C.3/78/SR.2
DECOLONIZATION (Agenda item 58)
A/C.4/78/SR.7
FOOD SECURITY (Agenda item 23a)
A/C.2/78/SR.16
GEINGOB, HAGE GOTTFRIED (NAMIBIA. PRESIDENT)—TRIBUTES
A/78/PV.55
HEALTH (Agenda item 125)
A/78/PV.41
IAEA—REPORTS (Agenda item 89)
A/78/PV.30
PALESTINE QUESTION (Agenda item 35)
A/78/PV.39
PEACE (Agenda item 14)
A/78/PV.82
POVERTY—INTERNATIONAL DECADES (Agenda item 21a)
A/C.2/78/SR.16
RURAL POVERTY (Agenda item 21b)
A/C.2/78/SR.16
SOCIAL CONDITIONS (Agenda item 24b)
A/C.3/78/SR.2
SOCIAL DEVELOPMENT (Agenda item 24)
A/C.3/78/SR.2
SUSTAINABLE DEVELOPMENT (Agenda item 18)
A/C.2/78/SR.13
TERRITORIES OCCUPIED BY ISRAEL—HUMAN RIGHTS (Agenda item 50)
A/C.4/78/SR.26
TERRITORIES OCCUPIED BY ISRAEL—NATURAL RESOURCES (Agenda item 59)
A/C.2/78/SR.19
UN. GENERAL ASSEMBLY (78TH SESS. : 2023-2024). 2ND COMMITTEE—GENERAL DEBATE (Agenda item 8)
A/C.2/78/SR.4
VETO (Agenda item 63)
A/78/PV.60
WESTERN SAHARA QUESTION (Agenda item 58)
A/C.4/78/SR.7

Gertze, Neville Melvin (Namibia) (continued)

YOUTH (Agenda item 24b)
A/C.3/78/SR.2

Getahun, Kedir (Ethiopia)

AFRICA—NUCLEAR-WEAPON-FREE ZONES (Agenda item 92)
A/C.1/78/PV.13
INFORMATION—INTERNATIONAL SECURITY (Agenda item 94)
A/C.1/78/PV.20
NUCLEAR DISARMAMENT (Agenda item 99b)
A/C.1/78/PV.13
NUCLEAR NON-PROLIFERATION—INTERNATIONAL OBLIGATIONS (Agenda item 99w)
A/C.1/78/PV.13

Ghadirkhomi, Payman (Iran (Islamic Republic of))

UKRAINE—POLITICAL CONDITIONS (Agenda item 62)
A/78/PV.58
UN. COMMITTEE FOR PROGRAMME AND COORDINATION—MEMBERS (Agenda item 114a)
A/78/PV.37
UN. GENERAL ASSEMBLY (78TH SESS. : 2023-2024)—GENERAL DEBATE—RIGHT OF REPLY (Agenda item 8)
A/78/PV.13
UN. GENERAL ASSEMBLY (78TH SESS. : 2023-2024). CREDENTIALS COMMITTEE—REPORTS (Agenda item 3b)
A/78/PV.48
VETO (Agenda item 63)
A/78/PV.69

Ghafouri, Mojtaba (Iran (Islamic Republic of))

HEALTH (Agenda item 125)
A/78/PV.77
HIV/AIDS—DECLARATIONS (Agenda item 10)
A/78/PV.91
MILLENNIUM SUMMIT—CONFERENCES (Agenda item 117)
A/78/PV.102
RESPONSIBILITY TO PROTECT (Agenda item 129)
A/78/PV.99
SUSTAINABLE DEVELOPMENT (Agenda item 18)
A/C.2/78/SR.24
UKRAINE—POLITICAL CONDITIONS (Agenda item 62)
A/78/PV.99
UN CONFERENCES (Agenda item 13)
A/78/PV.102
UN SYSTEM—STRENGTHENING (Agenda item 122)
A/78/PV.99
WOMEN'S ADVANCEMENT (Agenda item 25a)
A/78/PV.88

Ghanea, Nazila (UN. Human Rights Council. Special Rapporteur on Freedom of Religion or Belief)

RELIGIOUS INTOLERANCE (Agenda item 71b)
A/C.3/78/SR.38

Ghanei, Mohsen (Iran (Islamic Republic of))

HUMAN RIGHTS—ERITREA (Agenda item 71c)
A/C.3/78/SR.36
HUMAN RIGHTS—IRAN (ISLAMIC REPUBLIC OF) (Agenda item 71c)
A/C.3/78/SR.34
HUMAN RIGHTS—REPORTS (Agenda item 71c)
A/C.3/78/SR.37
RACIAL DISCRIMINATION—ELIMINATION (Agenda item 69a)
A/C.3/78/SR.40
RACIAL DISCRIMINATION—PROGRAMMES OF ACTION (Agenda item 69b)
A/C.3/78/SR.40
SELF-DETERMINATION OF PEOPLES (Agenda item 70)
A/C.3/78/SR.40

Ghaus, Hawa (United States)

CRIMES AGAINST HUMANITY (Agenda item 80)
A/C.6/78/SR.40; A/C.6/78/SR.44

Ghawar, Samir (Libya)

TERRITORIES OCCUPIED BY ISRAEL—NATURAL RESOURCES (Agenda item 59)
A/C.2/78/SR.19

Ghelich, Vahid (Iran (Islamic Republic of))

DECOLONIZATION (Agenda item 58)
A/C.4/78/SR.7; A/C.4/78/SR.9
INFORMATION (Agenda item 53)
A/C.4/78/SR.13
TERRITORIES OCCUPIED BY ISRAEL—HUMAN RIGHTS (Agenda item 50)
A/C.4/78/SR.25; A/C.4/78/SR.26
UNRWA—ACTIVITIES (Agenda item 49)
A/C.4/78/SR.22
WESTERN SAHARA QUESTION (Agenda item 58)
A/C.4/78/SR.7

Ghorbanpour Najafabadi, Mohammad (Iran (Islamic Republic of))

ARMS RACE—OUTER SPACE (Agenda item 97a)
A/C.1/78/PV.16; A/C.1/78/PV.17
ARMS TRANSFERS—TREATIES (Agenda item 99x)
A/C.1/78/PV.28
BIOLOGICAL WEAPONS—TREATIES (Agenda item 106)
A/C.1/78/PV.14; A/C.1/78/PV.15
CHEMICAL WEAPONS—TREATIES (Agenda item 99l)
A/C.1/78/PV.14; A/C.1/78/PV.15; A/C.1/78/PV.26
CLUSTER MUNITIONS (Agenda item 99dd)
A/C.1/78/PV.28

Ghorbanpour Najafabadi, Mohammad (Iran (Islamic Republic of)) (continued)

CONVENTIONAL WEAPONS (Agenda item 99u)
A/C.1/78/PV.28
DISARMAMENT—GENERAL AND COMPLETE (Agenda item 99)
A/C.1/78/PV.19; A/C.1/78/PV.21; A/C.1/78/PV.24; A/C.1/78/PV.28; A/C.1/78/PV.30
FISSIONABLE MATERIALS—TREATIES (Agenda item 99a)
A/C.1/78/PV.25; A/C.1/78/PV.26
IAEA—REPORTS (Agenda item 89)
A/78/PV.30
INFORMATION—INTERNATIONAL SECURITY (Agenda item 94)
A/C.1/78/PV.20; A/C.1/78/PV.29
LANDMINES—TREATIES (Agenda item 99m)
A/C.1/78/PV.28
MEDITERRANEAN REGION—REGIONAL SECURITY (Agenda item 104)
A/C.1/78/PV.29
MIDDLE EAST—NUCLEAR PROLIFERATION (Agenda item 102)
A/C.1/78/PV.13; A/C.1/78/PV.26
MIDDLE EAST—NUCLEAR-WEAPON-FREE ZONES (Agenda item 95)
A/C.1/78/PV.12; A/C.1/78/PV.22; A/C.1/78/PV.26
MULTILATERALISM—DISARMAMENT (Agenda item 99r)
A/C.1/78/PV.22
NUCLEAR DISARMAMENT (Agenda item 99b)
A/C.1/78/PV.11; A/C.1/78/PV.12
NUCLEAR DISARMAMENT—TREATY COMPLIANCE (Agenda item 99q)
A/C.1/78/PV.26
NUCLEAR DISARMAMENT—VERIFICATION (Agenda item 99ee)
A/C.1/78/PV.26
NUCLEAR NON-PROLIFERATION—INTERNATIONAL OBLIGATIONS (Agenda item 99w)
A/C.1/78/PV.12
NUCLEAR WEAPON TESTS—TREATIES (Agenda item 105)
A/C.1/78/PV.26
NUCLEAR WEAPONS—ELIMINATION (Agenda item 99z)
A/C.1/78/PV.25
NUCLEAR WEAPONS USE—TREATIES (Agenda item 100a)
A/C.1/78/PV.26
OUTER SPACE—CONFIDENCE-BUILDING MEASURES (Agenda item 99v)
A/C.1/78/PV.27
OUTER SPACE—PRINCIPLES (Agenda item 97d)
A/C.1/78/PV.27
SCIENCE AND TECHNOLOGY—INTERNATIONAL SECURITY (Agenda item 98)
A/C.1/78/PV.29
SMALL ARMS—ILLICIT TRAFFIC—ASSISTANCE (Agenda item 99n)
A/C.1/78/PV.28

Ghorbanpour Najafabadi, Mohammad (Iran (Islamic Republic of)) (continued)

UN. CONFERENCE ON DISARMAMENT—REPORTS (Agenda item 101a)
A/C.1/78/PV.23
UN. GENERAL ASSEMBLY (78TH SESS. : 2023-2024). 1ST COMMITTEE—GENERAL DEBATE (Agenda item 8)
A/C.1/78/PV.2; A/C.1/78/PV.3; A/C.1/78/PV.6; A/C.1/78/PV.7; A/C.1/78/PV.8; A/C.1/78/PV.9
WEAPONS—OUTER SPACE (Agenda item 97b)
A/C.1/78/PV.27

Ghosh, Jayati (University of Massachusetts at Amherst)

UN. GENERAL ASSEMBLY (78TH SESS. : 2023-2024). 2ND COMMITTEE—GENERAL DEBATE (Agenda item 8)
A/C.2/78/SR.2

Giammattei Falla, Alejandro (Guatemala. President)

UN. GENERAL ASSEMBLY (78TH SESS. : 2023-2024)—GENERAL DEBATE (Agenda item 8)
A/78/PV.4
UN. GENERAL ASSEMBLY (78TH SESS. : 2023-2024)—SPECIAL STATEMENTS
A/78/PV.4

Gibbon, James (United Kingdom)

UNRWA—ACTIVITIES (Agenda item 49)
A/C.4/78/SR.23

Gil Pinto, Yvan (Venezuela (Bolivarian Republic of))

ECONOMIC SANCTIONS—INTERNATIONAL RELATIONS (Agenda item 28)
A/78/PV.89
UN. GENERAL ASSEMBLY (78TH SESS. : 2023-2024)—GENERAL DEBATE (Agenda item 8)
A/78/PV.13

Gil Pinto, Yvan (Venezuela (Bolivarian Republic of)) (Group of Friends in Defence of the Charter of the United Nations)

ECONOMIC SANCTIONS—INTERNATIONAL RELATIONS (Agenda item 28)
A/78/PV.89

Gil Rojas, Elia Lizette (Mexico)

MIGRANT WORKERS (Agenda item 71a)
A/C.3/78/SR.23
MIGRANTS—PROTECTION (Agenda item 71b)
A/C.3/78/SR.23

Gilmutdinova, Dina Anisovna (Russian Federation)

UN. GENERAL ASSEMBLY—WORK PROGRAMME (Agenda item 120)
A/78/PV.33

Gilmutdinova, Dina Anisovna (Russian Federation) (continued)

UN RESOLUTIONS—IMPLEMENTATION (Agenda item 119)
A/78/PV.33

Giménez, Francisco Javier (Escuela de Gobierno y Políticas Públicas Norberto Bobbio (Paraguay))

WESTERN SAHARA QUESTION (Agenda item 58)
A/C.4/78/SR.5

Giorgio, Amanuel (Eritrea)

ADMINISTRATION OF JUSTICE (Agenda item 144)
A/C.6/78/SR.9
ARMED CONFLICTS PREVENTION (Agenda item 31a)
A/78/PV.73
RULE OF LAW (Agenda item 83)
A/C.6/78/SR.17
TERRORISM (Agenda item 109)
A/C.6/78/SR.3
UN CHARTER—REPORTS (Agenda item 82)
A/C.6/78/SR.33

Giret Soto, David Antonio (Paraguay)

INTERNATIONAL LAW—TRAINING PROGRAMMES (Agenda item 78)
A/C.6/78/SR.22
RULE OF LAW (Agenda item 83)
A/C.6/78/SR.18
UN. INTERNATIONAL COURT OF JUSTICE—REPORTS (Agenda item 73)
A/78/PV.27

Gisel, Laurent (International Committee of the Red Cross)

UN. GENERAL ASSEMBLY (78TH SESS. : 2023-2024). 1ST COMMITTEE—GENERAL DEBATE (Agenda item 8)
A/C.1/78/PV.9

Glasenhardt, Blanka (Croatia)

LANDMINES—TREATIES (Agenda item 99m)
A/C.1/78/PV.19
UN. GENERAL ASSEMBLY (78TH SESS. : 2023-2024). 1ST COMMITTEE—GENERAL DEBATE (Agenda item 8)
A/C.1/78/PV.7

Glukhov, Dmitry (Russian Federation)

DISARMAMENT—GENERAL AND COMPLETE (Agenda item 99)
A/78/PV.106
UN. GENERAL ASSEMBLY (78TH SESS. : 2023-2024). 1ST COMMITTEE—WORK ORGANIZATION (Agenda item 7)
A/C.1/78/PV.1

Göbel, Thomas (Germany)

ARMS TRANSFERS—TREATIES (Agenda item 99x)
A/C.1/78/PV.18
CONVENTIONAL WEAPONS (Agenda item 99u)
A/C.1/78/PV.18; A/C.1/78/PV.28
DISARMAMENT—GENERAL AND COMPLETE (Agenda item 99)
A/C.1/78/PV.18
LANDMINES—TREATIES (Agenda item 99m)
A/C.1/78/PV.18
SMALL ARMS—ILLICIT TRAFFIC (Agenda item 99p)
A/C.1/78/PV.18
UN. GENERAL ASSEMBLY (78TH SESS. : 2023-2024). 1ST COMMITTEE—GENERAL DEBATE (Agenda item 8)
A/C.1/78/PV.5

Goebel, Suzanne (On Purpose Group (Organization))

WESTERN SAHARA QUESTION (Agenda item 58)
A/C.4/78/SR.4

Gohar, Sarfaraz Ahmed (Pakistan)

BIOLOGICAL WEAPONS—TREATIES (Agenda item 106)
A/C.1/78/PV.15
CHEMICAL WEAPONS—TREATIES (Agenda item 99l)
A/C.1/78/PV.15
DISARMAMENT—GENERAL AND COMPLETE (Agenda item 99)
A/C.1/78/PV.30
DISARMAMENT AGREEMENTS—OUTER SPACE (Agenda item 97c)
A/C.1/78/PV.27
OUTER SPACE—PRINCIPLES (Agenda item 97d)
A/C.1/78/PV.27

Gohiwar Aryal, Indira (Nepal)

BIOLOGICAL WEAPONS—TREATIES (Agenda item 106)
A/C.1/78/PV.15
CHEMICAL WEAPONS—TREATIES (Agenda item 99l)
A/C.1/78/PV.15
NUCLEAR DISARMAMENT (Agenda item 99b)
A/C.1/78/PV.13
NUCLEAR NON-PROLIFERATION—INTERNATIONAL OBLIGATIONS (Agenda item 99w)
A/C.1/78/PV.13
PEACE—REGIONAL CENTRE—ASIA AND THE PACIFIC (Agenda item 100d)
A/C.1/78/PV.23
PEACE—REGIONAL CENTRES (Agenda item 100f)
A/C.1/78/PV.23
UN. CONFERENCE ON DISARMAMENT—REPORTS (Agenda item 101a)
A/C.1/78/PV.23

Gohiwar Aryal, Indira (Nepal) (continued)
UN. DISARMAMENT COMMISSION—REPORTS (Agenda item 101b)
A/C.1/78/PV.23

Gomes, Elaine Cristina Pereira (Brazil)
HEALTH (Agenda item 125)
A/78/PV.102
INDIGENOUS PEOPLES (Agenda item 68a)
A/C.3/78/SR.15
INDIGENOUS PEOPLES—CONFERENCES (Agenda item 68b)
A/C.3/78/SR.15
LEPROSY (Agenda item 71b)
A/C.3/78/SR.17
PEACE (Agenda item 14)
A/78/PV.62
PERSONS WITH DISABILITIES—HUMAN RIGHTS (Agenda item 71a)
A/C.3/78/SR.38
RACIAL DISCRIMINATION—ELIMINATION (Agenda item 69a)
A/C.3/78/SR.40; A/C.3/78/SR.41; A/C.3/78/SR.42
RACIAL DISCRIMINATION—PROGRAMMES OF ACTION (Agenda item 69b)
A/C.3/78/SR.40; A/C.3/78/SR.41; A/C.3/78/SR.42
RIGHTS OF THE CHILD (Agenda item 67)
A/C.3/78/SR.11; A/C.3/78/SR.12
TORTURE AND OTHER CRUEL TREATMENT (Agenda item 71a)
A/C.3/78/SR.18

Gomez, Jan Michael (Philippines)
MULTILATERALISM—DISARMAMENT (Agenda item 99r)
A/C.1/78/PV.22
SOUTH-EAST ASIA—NUCLEAR-WEAPON-FREE ZONES (Agenda item 99y)
A/C.1/78/PV.22
UN. CONFERENCE ON DISARMAMENT—REPORTS (Agenda item 101a)
A/C.1/78/PV.22
UN. DISARMAMENT COMMISSION—REPORTS (Agenda item 101b)
A/C.1/78/PV.22

Gómez Aoiz, Elena (Spain)
GIBRALTAR QUESTION (Agenda item 58)
A/C.4/78/SR.2; A/C.4/78/SR.8

Gómez Aoiz, Elena (Spain) (European Union)
WESTERN SAHARA QUESTION (Agenda item 58)
A/C.4/78/SR.9

Gómez Heredero, Ana (Council of Europe)
UN. INTERNATIONAL LAW COMMISSION—REPORTS (Agenda item 79)
A/C.6/78/SR.28

Gómez Hernández, Héctor José (Spain)
VETO (Agenda item 63)
A/78/PV.60; A/78/PV.67; A/78/PV.69; A/78/PV.75; A/78/PV.79

Gómez Justo, Juan Carlos (Universidad Pablo de Olavide (Spain))
WESTERN SAHARA QUESTION (Agenda item 58)
A/C.4/78/SR.4

Gómez Sardiñas, Yiliam (Cuba)
ARMS RACE—OUTER SPACE (Agenda item 97a)
A/C.1/78/PV.17
ARMS TRANSFERS—TREATIES (Agenda item 99x)
A/C.1/78/PV.19
CONVENTIONAL WEAPONS (Agenda item 99u)
A/C.1/78/PV.19
CONVENTIONAL WEAPONS—TREATIES (Agenda item 103)
A/C.1/78/PV.19
DISARMAMENT—GENERAL AND COMPLETE (Agenda item 99)
A/C.1/78/PV.19
DISARMAMENT AGREEMENTS—OUTER SPACE (Agenda item 97c)
A/C.1/78/PV.17
INFORMATION—INTERNATIONAL SECURITY (Agenda item 94)
A/C.1/78/PV.20
MULTILATERALISM—DISARMAMENT (Agenda item 99r)
A/C.1/78/PV.20; A/C.1/78/PV.21
NON-NUCLEAR-WEAPON STATES—SECURITY (Agenda item 96)
A/C.1/78/PV.25
NUCLEAR DISARMAMENT (Agenda item 99b)
A/C.1/78/PV.25
NUCLEAR DISARMAMENT—CONFERENCES (Agenda item 99aa)
A/C.1/78/PV.25
NUCLEAR NON-PROLIFERATION (Agenda item 99o)
A/C.1/78/PV.25
NUCLEAR WEAPONS—HUMANITARIAN CONSEQUENCES (Agenda item 99bb)
A/C.1/78/PV.25
NUCLEAR WEAPONS—TREATIES (Agenda item 99ff)
A/C.1/78/PV.25
NUCLEAR WEAPONS USE—UN. INTERNATIONAL COURT OF JUSTICE OPINION (Agenda item 99k)
A/C.1/78/PV.25
NUCLEAR-WEAPON-FREE ZONE—SOUTHERN HEMISPHERE (Agenda item 99i)
A/C.1/78/PV.25
NUCLEAR-WEAPON-FREE ZONES (Agenda item 99cc)
A/C.1/78/PV.25
OUTER SPACE—CONFIDENCE-BUILDING MEASURES (Agenda item 99v)
A/C.1/78/PV.17

Gómez Sardiñas, Yiliam (Cuba) (continued)

SMALL ARMS—ILLICIT TRAFFIC (Agenda item 99p)
A/C.1/78/PV.19
SMALL ARMS—ILLICIT TRAFFIC—ASSISTANCE (Agenda item 99n)
A/C.1/78/PV.19

Gonsalves, Ralph E. (Saint Vincent and the Grenadines. Prime Minister)

UN. GENERAL ASSEMBLY (78TH SESS. : 2023-2024)—GENERAL DEBATE (Agenda item 8)
A/78/PV.12
UN. GENERAL ASSEMBLY (78TH SESS. : 2023-2024)—SPECIAL STATEMENTS
A/78/PV.12

González, María Florencia (Argentina)

ELECTION VERIFICATION—UN (Agenda item 71b)
A/C.3/78/SR.50
HUMAN RIGHTS—INTERNATIONAL INSTRUMENTS (Agenda item 71a)
A/C.3/78/SR.24
HUMAN RIGHTS—SYRIAN ARAB REPUBLIC (Agenda item 71c)
A/C.3/78/SR.54
HUMAN RIGHTS ADVANCEMENT (Agenda item 71b)
A/C.3/78/SR.24
RIGHTS OF THE CHILD (Agenda item 67)
A/C.3/78/SR.11
SELF-DETERMINATION OF PEOPLES (Agenda item 70)
A/C.3/78/SR.56
TORTURE AND OTHER CRUEL TREATMENT (Agenda item 71a)
A/C.3/78/SR.18

González Behmaras, Alejandro (Cuba)

AGEING PERSONS (Agenda item 24b)
A/C.3/78/SR.1
ARMED CONFLICTS PREVENTION (Agenda item 31a)
A/78/PV.72
DEMOCRACY (Agenda item 71b)
A/C.3/78/SR.48
DISPLACED PERSONS (Agenda item 71b)
A/78/PV.50; A/C.3/78/SR.49
EMERGENCY ASSISTANCE (Agenda item 72a)
A/78/PV.47
HEALTH (Agenda item 125)
A/78/PV.16; A/78/PV.48; A/78/PV.77
HUMAN RIGHTS (Agenda item 71)
A/C.3/78/SR.25
HUMAN RIGHTS—BURUNDI (Agenda item 71c)
A/C.3/78/SR.36
HUMAN RIGHTS—DEMOCRATIC PEOPLE'S REPUBLIC OF KOREA (Agenda item 71c)
A/78/PV.50; A/C.3/78/SR.53

González Behmaras, Alejandro (Cuba) (continued)

HUMAN RIGHTS—ERITREA (Agenda item 71c)
A/C.3/78/SR.36
HUMAN RIGHTS—ETHIOPIA (Agenda item 71c)
A/C.3/78/SR.36
HUMAN RIGHTS—IRAN (ISLAMIC REPUBLIC OF) (Agenda item 71c)
A/78/PV.50; A/C.3/78/SR.34; A/C.3/78/SR.53
HUMAN RIGHTS—REPORTS (Agenda item 71c)
A/78/PV.50; A/C.3/78/SR.18
HUMAN RIGHTS—SYRIAN ARAB REPUBLIC (Agenda item 71c)
A/78/PV.50; A/C.3/78/SR.34; A/C.3/78/SR.54
HUMAN RIGHTS—TERRITORIES OCCUPIED BY ISRAEL (Agenda item 71c)
A/C.3/78/SR.35
HUMAN RIGHTS ADVANCEMENT (Agenda item 71b)
A/C.3/78/SR.48
MERCENARIES (Agenda item 70)
A/C.3/78/SR.42; A/C.3/78/SR.48
PALESTINIANS—ASSISTANCE (Agenda item 72b)
A/78/PV.47
RACIAL DISCRIMINATION—ELIMINATION (Agenda item 69a)
A/78/PV.50; A/C.3/78/SR.42; A/C.3/78/SR.47
RACIAL DISCRIMINATION—PROGRAMMES OF ACTION (Agenda item 69b)
A/C.3/78/SR.42; A/C.3/78/SR.56
RELIGIOUS INTOLERANCE (Agenda item 71b)
A/C.3/78/SR.38
RIGHT TO DEVELOPMENT (Agenda item 71b)
A/C.3/78/SR.20
RIGHT TO FOOD (Agenda item 71b)
A/C.3/78/SR.48
RIGHTS OF THE CHILD (Agenda item 67)
A/C.3/78/SR.55
SANCTIONS—INTERNATIONAL RELATIONS (Agenda item 71b)
A/C.3/78/SR.48
SELF-DETERMINATION OF PEOPLES (Agenda item 70)
A/78/PV.50; A/C.3/78/SR.42; A/C.3/78/SR.49
TERRORISM—HUMAN RIGHTS (Agenda item 71b)
A/C.3/78/SR.31
UN. HUMAN RIGHTS COUNCIL—REPORTS (Agenda item 66)
A/78/PV.28; A/C.3/78/SR.46; A/C.3/78/SR.51
WOMEN'S ADVANCEMENT (Agenda item 25a)
A/C.3/78/SR.7
WOMEN'S ADVANCEMENT—CONFERENCES (Agenda item 25b)
A/C.3/78/SR.7

González Behmaras, Alejandro (Cuba) (Coordinating Bureau of the Non-Aligned Countries)

HUMAN RIGHTS ADVANCEMENT (Agenda item 71b)
A/C.3/78/SR.48
RIGHT TO DEVELOPMENT (Agenda item 71b)
A/C.3/78/SR.48

González Behmaras, Alejandro (Cuba) (Coordinating Bureau of the Non-Aligned Countries) (continued)

SANCTIONS—INTERNATIONAL RELATIONS (Agenda item 71b)
A/C.3/78/SR.48

González Behmaras, Alejandro (Cuba) (Group of 77)

AGEING PERSONS (Agenda item 24b)
A/C.3/78/SR.1; A/C.3/78/SR.49
EMERGENCY ASSISTANCE (Agenda item 72a)
A/78/PV.46
FAMILY (Agenda item 24b)
A/C.3/78/SR.1; A/C.3/78/SR.49
HEALTH (Agenda item 125)
A/78/PV.16
RACIAL DISCRIMINATION—PROGRAMMES OF ACTION (Agenda item 69b)
A/C.3/78/SR.56
SOCIAL CONDITIONS (Agenda item 24b)
A/C.3/78/SR.1
SOCIAL DEVELOPMENT (Agenda item 24)
A/C.3/78/SR.1
SOCIAL DEVELOPMENT—CONFERENCES (Agenda item 24a)
A/C.3/78/SR.55

González Cabello Maldonado, Stephania Mercedes (Paraguay)

WOMEN'S ADVANCEMENT (Agenda item 25a)
A/C.3/78/SR.9
WOMEN'S ADVANCEMENT—CONFERENCES (Agenda item 25b)
A/C.3/78/SR.9

González Carrillo, Montserrat (Chile)

SUSTAINABLE DEVELOPMENT (Agenda item 18)
A/C.2/78/SR.25
UN. GENERAL ASSEMBLY (78TH SESS. : 2023-2024). 2ND COMMITTEE—GENERAL DEBATE (Agenda item 8)
A/C.2/78/SR.5

González Hernández, Gabriela Lilián (Uruguay)

CRIME PREVENTION (Agenda item 107)
A/C.3/78/SR.6
CYBERCRIME (Agenda item 108)
A/C.3/78/SR.6
UN. GENERAL ASSEMBLY (78TH SESS. : 2023-2024)—OFFICERS (Agenda item 5)
A/C.5/78/SR.1
UN. GENERAL ASSEMBLY (78TH SESS. : 2023-2024). 1ST COMMITTEE—GENERAL DEBATE (Agenda item 8)
A/C.1/78/PV.4
WOMEN'S ADVANCEMENT (Agenda item 25a)
A/C.3/78/SR.10
WOMEN'S ADVANCEMENT—CONFERENCES (Agenda item 25b)
A/C.3/78/SR.10

González López, Egriselda Aracely (El Salvador)

AGEING PERSONS (Agenda item 24b)
A/C.3/78/SR.1
CLIMATE (Agenda item 18d)
A/C.2/78/SR.13
DECOLONIZATION (Agenda item 58)
A/C.4/78/SR.2
DEVELOPMENT FINANCE (Agenda item 16b)
A/C.2/78/SR.8
ECONOMIC COOPERATION AMONG DEVELOPING COUNTRIES (Agenda item 22b)
A/C.2/78/SR.18
FALKLAND ISLANDS (MALVINAS) QUESTION (Agenda item 42)
A/C.4/78/SR.2
IAEA—REPORTS (Agenda item 89)
A/78/PV.29
INFORMATION (Agenda item 53)
A/C.4/78/SR.13
INFORMATION—INTERNATIONAL SECURITY (Agenda item 94)
A/C.1/78/PV.20
INTERNATIONAL CRIMINAL COURT—REPORTS (Agenda item 74)
A/78/PV.25
INTERNATIONAL LAW—TRAINING PROGRAMMES (Agenda item 78)
A/C.6/78/SR.21
MACROECONOMIC POLICY (Agenda item 16)
A/C.2/78/SR.8
MINE CLEARANCE (Agenda item 46)
A/C.4/78/SR.10
OPERATIONAL ACTIVITIES—UN SYSTEM (Agenda item 22a)
A/C.2/78/SR.18
PEACEBUILDING (Agenda item 61)
A/78/PV.100
PEACEKEEPING OPERATIONS (Agenda item 51)
A/C.4/78/SR.19
PEACEKEEPING OPERATIONS—CRIMINAL LIABILITY (Agenda item 76)
A/C.6/78/SR.8
RIGHT TO EDUCATION (Agenda item 71b)
A/C.3/78/SR.27
SPECIAL POLITICAL MISSIONS (Agenda item 52)
A/C.4/78/SR.21
TERRORISM (Agenda item 109)
A/C.6/78/SR.2
UN—BUDGET (2024) (Agenda item 134)
A/C.5/78/SR.5
UN—PROGRAMME PLANNING (Agenda item 135)
A/C.1/78/PV.10; A/C.5/78/SR.5
UN. GENERAL ASSEMBLY—WORK PROGRAMME (Agenda item 120)
A/78/PV.32; A/C.1/78/PV.10
UN. GENERAL ASSEMBLY (78TH SESS. : 2023-2024)—OFFICERS (Agenda item 5)
A/C.5/78/SR.39
UN. HUMAN RIGHTS COUNCIL—REPORTS (Agenda item 66)
A/C.3/78/SR.46

González López, Egriselda Aracely (El Salvador) (continued)

UN. PEACEBUILDING COMMISSION—REPORTS (Agenda item 27)
A/78/PV.100
UN. PEACEBUILDING FUND—REPORTS (Agenda item 111)
A/78/PV.100
UN. SECURITY COUNCIL—REPORTS (Agenda item 26)
A/78/PV.93
UN RESOLUTIONS—IMPLEMENTATION (Agenda item 119)
A/78/PV.32
UNRWA—ACTIVITIES (Agenda item 49)
A/C.4/78/SR.23
VETO (Agenda item 63)
A/78/PV.3; A/78/PV.67
WESTERN SAHARA QUESTION (Agenda item 58)
A/C.4/78/SR.2

González López, Egriselda Aracely (El Salvador) (Sistema de la Integración Centroamericana)

AGEING PERSONS (Agenda item 24b)
A/C.3/78/SR.1
CUBA—UNITED STATES (Agenda item 38)
A/78/PV.24
DECOLONIZATION (Agenda item 58)
A/C.4/78/SR.6
DISASTER VICTIMS (Agenda item 86)
A/C.6/78/SR.5
FALKLAND ISLANDS (MALVINAS) QUESTION (Agenda item 42)
A/C.4/78/SR.6
INDIGENOUS PEOPLES (Agenda item 68a)
A/C.3/78/SR.15
INDIGENOUS PEOPLES—CONFERENCES (Agenda item 68b)
A/C.3/78/SR.15
PERSONS WITH DISABILITIES (Agenda item 24b)
A/C.3/78/SR.1
RACIAL DISCRIMINATION—ELIMINATION (Agenda item 69a)
A/C.3/78/SR.40
RACIAL DISCRIMINATION—PROGRAMMES OF ACTION (Agenda item 69b)
A/C.3/78/SR.40
RIGHTS OF THE CHILD (Agenda item 67)
A/C.3/78/SR.11
SOCIAL CONDITIONS (Agenda item 24b)
A/C.3/78/SR.1
UN. GENERAL ASSEMBLY (78TH SESS. : 2023-2024). 1ST COMMITTEE—GENERAL DEBATE (Agenda item 8)
A/C.1/78/PV.2
WOMEN'S ADVANCEMENT (Agenda item 25a)
A/C.3/78/SR.8
WOMEN'S ADVANCEMENT—CONFERENCES (Agenda item 25b)
A/C.3/78/SR.8
YOUTH (Agenda item 24b)
A/C.3/78/SR.1

González López, Egriselda Aracely (El Salvador) (UN. Group of Latin American and Caribbean States)

GEINGOB, HAGE GOTTFRIED (NAMIBIA. PRESIDENT)—TRIBUTES
A/78/PV.55

González Morales, Felipe (UN. Human Rights Council. Special Rapporteur on the Human Rights of Migrants)

MIGRANTS—PROTECTION (Agenda item 71b)
A/C.3/78/SR.23

González Sánchez, José Luis (International Association of Jurists for Western Sahara)

WESTERN SAHARA QUESTION (Agenda item 58)
A/C.4/78/SR.4

González Sanz, Angel (UNCTAD)

INFORMATION TECHNOLOGY—DEVELOPMENT (Agenda item 15)
A/C.2/78/SR.10
SCIENCE AND TECHNOLOGY—DEVELOPMENT (Agenda item 19a)
A/C.2/78/SR.10

González Sese, José Antonio (Chile)

UN—BUDGET (2024) (Agenda item 134)
A/C.5/78/SR.12

Gordet, Levina Christine Margaux (Luxembourg)

HUMAN RIGHTS—AFGHANISTAN (Agenda item 71c)
A/C.3/78/SR.34
HUMAN RIGHTS—ETHIOPIA (Agenda item 71c)
A/C.3/78/SR.36

Gorely, Amanda Louise (Australia)

NUCLEAR DISARMAMENT (Agenda item 99b)
A/C.1/78/PV.11
NUCLEAR NON-PROLIFERATION—INTERNATIONAL OBLIGATIONS (Agenda item 99w)
A/C.1/78/PV.11
NUCLEAR WEAPON TESTS—TREATIES (Agenda item 105)
A/C.1/78/PV.11

Gorke, Maximilian (Austria)

CRIMES AGAINST HUMANITY (Agenda item 80)
A/C.6/78/SR.9; A/C.6/78/SR.38; A/C.6/78/SR.40; A/C.6/78/SR.41; A/C.6/78/SR.43; A/C.6/78/SR.44; A/C.6/78/SR.45
UN. INTERNATIONAL LAW COMMISSION—REPORTS (Agenda item 79)
A/C.6/78/SR.31
UN COMMISSION ON INTERNATIONAL TRADE LAW—REPORTS (Agenda item 77)
A/C.6/78/SR.14; A/C.6/78/SR.37

Gorke, Maximilian (Austria) (UN. General Assembly. 6th Committee. Bureau)

UN COMMISSION ON INTERNATIONAL TRADE LAW—REPORTS (Agenda item 77)
A/C.6/78/SR.37

Gort, Michael Christian (Canada)

INDIGENOUS PEOPLES (Agenda item 68a)
A/78/PV.107

Górzyńska, Marzena (Poland)

CRIMES AGAINST HUMANITY (Agenda item 80)
A/C.6/78/SR.44

Grandi, Filippo (UN High Commissioner for Refugees)

UN HIGH COMMISSIONER FOR REFUGEES—REPORTS (Agenda item 60)
A/C.3/78/SR.44

Grandjean, Laurence (Belgium)

CRIMES AGAINST HUMANITY (Agenda item 80)
A/C.6/78/SR.9

Gray, Lily (UNESCO)

RIGHT TO EDUCATION (Agenda item 71b)
A/C.3/78/SR.27

Greco, Gianluca (Italy)

CRIME PREVENTION (Agenda item 107)
A/C.3/78/SR.56
HUMAN RIGHTS—INTERNATIONAL INSTRUMENTS (Agenda item 71a)
A/C.3/78/SR.25
HUMAN RIGHTS—TERRITORIES OCCUPIED BY ISRAEL (Agenda item 71c)
A/C.3/78/SR.35
HUMAN RIGHTS ADVANCEMENT (Agenda item 71b)
A/C.3/78/SR.25
UKRAINE—POLITICAL CONDITIONS (Agenda item 62)
A/78/PV.57
VETO (Agenda item 63)
A/78/PV.3

Greenhalgh, Bronwyn (Canada)

RELIGIOUS INTOLERANCE (Agenda item 71b)
A/C.3/78/SR.38

Greenwood, James Harrison (Sovereign Order of Malta)

MIGRANTS—PROTECTION (Agenda item 71b)
A/C.3/78/SR.23
TORTURE AND OTHER CRUEL TREATMENT (Agenda item 71a)
A/C.3/78/SR.18

Greffine, Venise Catherine (European Union)

ALBINISM (Agenda item 71b)
A/C.3/78/SR.27
MINORITIES (Agenda item 71b)
A/C.3/78/SR.39
RACIAL DISCRIMINATION—ELIMINATION (Agenda item 69a)
A/C.3/78/SR.41
RACIAL DISCRIMINATION—PROGRAMMES OF ACTION (Agenda item 69b)
A/C.3/78/SR.41
RIGHT TO CULTURE (Agenda item 71b)
A/C.3/78/SR.27
RIGHT TO HEALTH (Agenda item 71b)
A/C.3/78/SR.39
SEXUAL ORIENTATION (Agenda item 71b)
A/C.3/78/SR.39

Greiver, Bernardo (UN. Committee on Contributions. Chair)

UN—BUDGET CONTRIBUTIONS (Agenda item 138)
A/C.5/78/SR.1

Greve, Silvia (Switzerland)

UN. CONFERENCE ON DISARMAMENT—REPORTS (Agenda item 101a)
A/C.1/78/PV.23

Grigoryan, Andranik (Armenia)

ARMS TRANSFERS—TREATIES (Agenda item 99x)
A/C.1/78/PV.28
DISARMAMENT—GENERAL AND COMPLETE (Agenda item 99)
A/C.1/78/PV.24
DISARMAMENT-DEVELOPMENT LINK (Agenda item 99d)
A/C.1/78/PV.29
LANDMINES—TREATIES (Agenda item 99m)
A/C.1/78/PV.19
MULTILATERALISM—DISARMAMENT (Agenda item 99r)
A/C.1/78/PV.22; A/C.1/78/PV.29
NUCLEAR WEAPONS USE—UN. INTERNATIONAL COURT OF JUSTICE OPINION (Agenda item 99k)
A/C.1/78/PV.29
PEACE—REGIONAL CENTRES (Agenda item 100f)
A/C.1/78/PV.29
UN. GENERAL ASSEMBLY (78TH SESS. : 2023-2024). 1ST COMMITTEE—GENERAL DEBATE (Agenda item 8)
A/C.1/78/PV.7; A/C.1/78/PV.8
WEAPONS OF MASS DESTRUCTION—TERRORISM (Agenda item 99s)
A/C.1/78/PV.29

Grlić-Radman, Gordan (Croatia)

UKRAINE—POLITICAL CONDITIONS (Agenda item 62)
A/78/PV.56

Grossi, Rafael Mariano (IAEA. Director General)
IAEA—REPORTS (Agenda item 89)
A/78/PV.29

Grosso, Elizabeth Maryanne (United States)
DISASTER VICTIMS (Agenda item 86)
A/C.6/78/SR.5
INTERNATIONAL JURISDICTION (Agenda item 84)
A/C.6/78/SR.12
NON-CITIZENS—DEPORTATION (Agenda item 81)
A/C.6/78/SR.34
RESPONSIBILITY OF INTERNATIONAL ORGANIZATIONS (Agenda item 85)
A/C.6/78/SR.19
RULE OF LAW (Agenda item 83)
A/C.6/78/SR.16
UN COMMISSION ON INTERNATIONAL TRADE LAW—REPORTS (Agenda item 77)
A/C.6/78/SR.14

Grünwald, Tomáš (Slovakia)
AGEING PERSONS (Agenda item 24b)
A/C.3/78/SR.1
HUMAN RIGHTS (Agenda item 71)
A/C.3/78/SR.16
HUMAN RIGHTS—BELARUS (Agenda item 71c)
A/C.3/78/SR.24
HUMAN RIGHTS—IRAN (ISLAMIC REPUBLIC OF) (Agenda item 71c)
A/C.3/78/SR.24
HUMAN RIGHTS—RUSSIAN FEDERATION (Agenda item 71c)
A/C.3/78/SR.24
HUMAN RIGHTS—TERRITORIES OCCUPIED BY ISRAEL (Agenda item 71c)
A/C.3/78/SR.24
HUMAN RIGHTS—UKRAINE (Agenda item 71c)
A/C.3/78/SR.24
INDIGENOUS PEOPLES (Agenda item 68a)
A/C.3/78/SR.48
MINORITIES (Agenda item 71b)
A/C.3/78/SR.39
UN YOUTH OFFICE—REPORTS (Agenda item 130)
A/78/PV.102
YOUTH (Agenda item 24b)
A/C.3/78/SR.2

Güç, Eda (Türkiye)
CRIMES AGAINST HUMANITY (Agenda item 80)
A/C.6/78/SR.11
INTERNATIONAL JURISDICTION (Agenda item 84)
A/C.6/78/SR.13
RESPONSIBILITY TO PROTECT (Agenda item 129)
A/78/PV.97
UN. INTERNATIONAL LAW COMMISSION—REPORTS (Agenda item 79)
A/C.6/78/SR.33

Guera, Soueda El (Mauritania)
ELECTION VERIFICATION—UN (Agenda item 71b)
A/78/PV.50
HUMAN RIGHTS—TERRITORIES OCCUPIED BY ISRAEL (Agenda item 71c)
A/C.3/78/SR.35
RURAL WOMEN (Agenda item 25a)
A/C.3/78/SR.49

Guerra, Hugo Emmanuel (Argentina)
ARMS RACE—OUTER SPACE (Agenda item 97a)
A/C.1/78/PV.16
ARMS TRANSFERS—TREATIES (Agenda item 99x)
A/C.1/78/PV.18
CONVENTIONAL WEAPONS (Agenda item 99u)
A/C.1/78/PV.18
CONVENTIONAL WEAPONS—TREATIES (Agenda item 103)
A/C.1/78/PV.18
DISARMAMENT—GENERAL AND COMPLETE (Agenda item 99)
A/C.1/78/PV.18; A/C.1/78/PV.28
DISARMAMENT AGREEMENTS—OUTER SPACE (Agenda item 97c)
A/C.1/78/PV.27
NUCLEAR WEAPONS—ELIMINATION (Agenda item 99z)
A/C.1/78/PV.26
NUCLEAR WEAPONS—TREATIES (Agenda item 99ff)
A/C.1/78/PV.26
OUTER SPACE—PRINCIPLES (Agenda item 97d)
A/C.1/78/PV.16; A/C.1/78/PV.27
SMALL ARMS—ILLICIT TRAFFIC—ASSISTANCE (Agenda item 99n)
A/C.1/78/PV.18
UN. GENERAL ASSEMBLY (78TH SESS. : 2023-2024). 1ST COMMITTEE—GENERAL DEBATE (Agenda item 8)
A/C.1/78/PV.5

Guerra, Stefano Venancio (Portugal)
AGEING PERSONS (Agenda item 24b)
A/C.3/78/SR.1
MIGRANTS—PROTECTION (Agenda item 71b)
A/C.3/78/SR.23
RIGHT TO EDUCATION (Agenda item 71b)
A/C.3/78/SR.27

Guerra Sansonetti, Jhon (Venezuela (Bolivarian Republic of)) (Group of Friends in Defence of the Charter of the United Nations)
UN CHARTER—REPORTS (Agenda item 82)
A/C.6/78/SR.22

Guevara Rodríguez, Adiel (Cuba)
DEVELOPMENT FINANCE (Agenda item 16b)
A/C.2/78/SR.8
EXTERNAL DEBT (Agenda item 16c)
A/C.2/78/SR.8

Guevara Rodríguez, Adiel (Cuba) (continued)
INTERNATIONAL TRADE (Agenda item 16a)
A/C.2/78/SR.8
MACROECONOMIC POLICY (Agenda item 16)
A/C.2/78/SR.8

Guevara Rodríguez, Adiel (Cuba) (Group of 77)
COMMODITIES (Agenda item 16d)
A/C.2/78/SR.14
ECONOMIC COOPERATION AMONG DEVELOPING COUNTRIES (Agenda item 22b)
A/C.2/78/SR.18
FOOD SECURITY (Agenda item 23a)
A/C.2/78/SR.16
GLOBALIZATION—INTERDEPENDENCE (Agenda item 19)
A/C.2/78/SR.10
INFORMATION TECHNOLOGY—DEVELOPMENT (Agenda item 15)
A/C.2/78/SR.10
OPERATIONAL ACTIVITIES—UN SYSTEM (Agenda item 22a)
A/C.2/78/SR.18
POVERTY—INTERNATIONAL DECADES (Agenda item 21a)
A/C.2/78/SR.16
RURAL POVERTY (Agenda item 21b)
A/C.2/78/SR.16
SCIENCE AND TECHNOLOGY—DEVELOPMENT (Agenda item 19a)
A/C.2/78/SR.10
SUSTAINABLE DEVELOPMENT (Agenda item 18)
A/C.2/78/SR.14

Guevara Rodríguez, Carlos Eduardo (Episcopal Church (Colombia))
WESTERN SAHARA QUESTION (Agenda item 58)
A/C.4/78/SR.4

Guevarra-de Dios, Nadine Bobadilla (Philippines)
HUMAN RIGHTS—DEMOCRATIC PEOPLE'S REPUBLIC OF KOREA (Agenda item 71c)
A/C.3/78/SR.53
RIGHTS OF THE CHILD (Agenda item 67)
A/C.3/78/SR.12

Gueye, Cheikh Mohamadou Bamba (Senegal)
PALESTINE QUESTION (Agenda item 35)
A/78/PV.40
UN. INTERNATIONAL LAW COMMISSION—REPORTS (Agenda item 79)
A/C.6/78/SR.29
VETO (Agenda item 63)
A/78/PV.79

Gueye, Mamadou Soule (Senegal)
SUSTAINABLE DEVELOPMENT (Agenda item 18)
A/C.2/78/SR.24

Gulov, Golibjon (Tajikistan)
FAMILY (Agenda item 24b)
A/C.3/78/SR.2
HUMAN RIGHTS—INTERNATIONAL INSTRUMENTS (Agenda item 71a)
A/C.3/78/SR.26
PERSONS WITH DISABILITIES (Agenda item 24b)
A/C.3/78/SR.2
SOCIAL DEVELOPMENT (Agenda item 24)
A/C.3/78/SR.2
YOUTH (Agenda item 24b)
A/C.3/78/SR.2

Gumbi, Mojankunyane (UN. Special Adviser for Addressing Racism in the Workplace)
UN—BUDGET (2024) (Agenda item 134)
A/C.5/78/SR.13

Gunaratna, Pahala Rallage Sanathana Sugeeshwara (Sri Lanka)
ARMS RACE—OUTER SPACE (Agenda item 97a)
A/C.1/78/PV.27
DISARMAMENT AGREEMENTS—OUTER SPACE (Agenda item 97c)
A/C.1/78/PV.27
HUMAN RIGHTS—IRAN (ISLAMIC REPUBLIC OF) (Agenda item 71c)
A/C.3/78/SR.34
HUMAN RIGHTS—RUSSIAN FEDERATION (Agenda item 71c)
A/C.3/78/SR.37
OUTER SPACE—CONFIDENCE-BUILDING MEASURES (Agenda item 99v)
A/C.1/78/PV.27
OUTER SPACE—PRINCIPLES (Agenda item 97d)
A/C.1/78/PV.27
RACIAL DISCRIMINATION—ELIMINATION (Agenda item 69a)
A/C.3/78/SR.47
SCIENCE AND TECHNOLOGY—DEVELOPMENT (Agenda item 19a)
A/C.2/78/SR.11
SOCIAL CONDITIONS (Agenda item 24b)
A/C.3/78/SR.2
SOCIAL DEVELOPMENT (Agenda item 24)
A/C.3/78/SR.2
WEAPONS—OUTER SPACE (Agenda item 97b)
A/C.1/78/PV.27

Gunnarsdóttir, Greta (UNRWA)
UNRWA—ACTIVITIES (Agenda item 49)
A/C.4/78/SR.22

Guo, Jingnan (China)
BIOLOGICAL DIVERSITY—TREATIES (Agenda item 18f)
A/C.2/78/SR.13
CLIMATE (Agenda item 18d)
A/C.2/78/SR.13

Guo, Jingnan (China) (continued)
SUSTAINABLE DEVELOPMENT (Agenda item 18)
A/C.2/78/SR.13
SUSTAINABLE ENERGY (Agenda item 18h)
A/C.2/78/SR.13

Guo, Ke (China)
PERSONNEL QUESTIONS—UN SYSTEM (Agenda item 142)
A/C.5/78/SR.10
UN—HUMAN RESOURCES MANAGEMENT (Agenda item 139)
A/C.5/78/SR.25

Guo, Zhiqi (China)
UN—FINANCIAL REPORTS (Agenda item 131)
A/C.5/78/SR.14
UN—FINANCIAL SITUATION (Agenda item 136)
A/C.5/78/SR.6

Guraisha, Aminath (Maldives)
TERRORISM (Agenda item 109)
A/C.6/78/SR.2
UN. GENERAL ASSEMBLY—WORK PROGRAMME (Agenda item 120)
A/78/PV.32
UN. GENERAL ASSEMBLY (78TH SESS. : 2023-2024). 1ST COMMITTEE—GENERAL DEBATE (Agenda item 8)
A/C.1/78/PV.5
UN RESOLUTIONS—IMPLEMENTATION (Agenda item 119)
A/78/PV.32

Gurbanov, Ilgar (Azerbaijan)
DISARMAMENT—GENERAL AND COMPLETE (Agenda item 99)
A/C.1/78/PV.24
LANDMINES—TREATIES (Agenda item 99m)
A/C.1/78/PV.19
MULTILATERALISM—DISARMAMENT (Agenda item 99r)
A/C.1/78/PV.23
UN. GENERAL ASSEMBLY (78TH SESS. : 2023-2024). 1ST COMMITTEE—GENERAL DEBATE (Agenda item 8)
A/C.1/78/PV.7; A/C.1/78/PV.8

Gurhan, Amina (Uganda)
ELECTION VERIFICATION—UN (Agenda item 71b)
A/C.3/78/SR.50
PEACE (Agenda item 14)
A/78/PV.62
UN HIGH COMMISSIONER FOR REFUGEES—REPORTS (Agenda item 60)
A/C.3/78/SR.45

Gurhan, Amina (Uganda) (UN. Group of African States)
SLAVERY—MEMORIALS (Agenda item 118)
A/78/PV.64

Gusman, Vadim (Azerbaijan)
RESPONSIBILITY TO PROTECT (Agenda item 129)
A/78/PV.97

Guterres, António, 1949- (UN. Secretary-General)
AL-SABAH, NAWAF AL-AHMAD AL-JABER (KUWAIT. AMIR)—TRIBUTES
A/78/PV.50(Resumption1)
GEINGOB, HAGE GOTTFRIED (NAMIBIA. PRESIDENT)—TRIBUTES
A/78/PV.55
MULTILATERALISM
A/78/PV.81
PEACE (Agenda item 14)
A/78/PV.62
RAISI, SEYYED EBRAHIM (IRAN (ISLAMIC REPUBLID OF). PRESIDENT)—TRIBUTES
A/78/PV.83
UN—BUDGET (2024) (Agenda item 134)
A/C.5/78/SR.5
UN—PROGRAMME PLANNING (Agenda item 135)
A/C.5/78/SR.5
UN. GENERAL ASSEMBLY (78TH SESS. : 2023-2024)—CLOSING
A/78/PV.109
UN. GENERAL ASSEMBLY (78TH SESS. : 2023-2024). PRESIDENT (Agenda item 4)
A/78/PV.87
UN. SECRETARY-GENERAL—REPORTS (Agenda item 110)
A/78/PV.4; A/78/PV.54

Gutiérrez Tórrez, Lisandra Marina (Nicaragua)
ECONOMIC COOPERATION AMONG DEVELOPING COUNTRIES (Agenda item 22b)
A/C.2/78/SR.18
POVERTY—INTERNATIONAL DECADES (Agenda item 21a)
A/C.2/78/SR.17
RURAL POVERTY (Agenda item 21b)
A/C.2/78/SR.17

Güven, Fikriye Asli (Türkiye)
AGEING PERSONS (Agenda item 24b)
A/C.3/78/SR.3
PALESTINE QUESTION (Agenda item 35)
A/78/PV.39
PEACE (Agenda item 14)
A/78/PV.62
SOCIAL CONDITIONS (Agenda item 24b)
A/C.3/78/SR.3
SOCIAL DEVELOPMENT (Agenda item 24)
A/C.3/78/SR.3

Güven, Fikriye Asli (Türkiye) (continued)

TAXATION (Agenda item 16h)
A/C.2/78/SR.25
VETO (Agenda item 63)
A/78/PV.51; A/78/PV.60; A/78/PV.67
YOUTH (Agenda item 24b)
A/C.3/78/SR.3

Güven, Fikriye Asli (Türkiye) (UN. Group of Western European and Other States)

GEINGOB, HAGE GOTTFRIED (NAMIBIA. PRESIDENT)—TRIBUTES
A/78/PV.55

Guzik Duno, Aline (Mexico)

INFORMATION (Agenda item 53)
A/C.4/78/SR.14

Gylfadóttir, Thórdís Kolbrún Reykfjörd (Iceland)

UN. GENERAL ASSEMBLY (78TH SESS. : 2023-2024)—GENERAL DEBATE (Agenda item 8)
A/78/PV.12

Habashneh, Ahmad Samir Fahim (Jordan)

CRIME PREVENTION (Agenda item 107)
A/C.3/78/SR.5
CRIMES AGAINST HUMANITY (Agenda item 80)
A/C.6/78/SR.10
CYBERCRIME (Agenda item 108)
A/C.3/78/SR.5
PEACEKEEPING OPERATIONS (Agenda item 51)
A/C.4/78/SR.20
TERRITORIES OCCUPIED BY ISRAEL—HUMAN RIGHTS (Agenda item 50)
A/C.4/78/SR.25
TERRORISM (Agenda item 109)
A/C.6/78/SR.2
UNRWA—ACTIVITIES (Agenda item 49)
A/C.4/78/SR.22
VETO (Agenda item 63)
A/78/PV.61
WESTERN SAHARA QUESTION (Agenda item 58)
A/C.4/78/SR.7

Habet, Orlando (Belize) (Caribbean Community)

SMALL ISLAND DEVELOPING STATES—PROGRAMMES OF ACTION (Agenda item 18b)
A/78/PV.100

Habib, Hanan M.M. (Libya)

PALESTINE QUESTION (Agenda item 35)
A/78/PV.40

Hachem, Hadi (Lebanon)

HUMAN RIGHTS—INTERNATIONAL INSTRUMENTS (Agenda item 71a)
A/C.3/78/SR.24

Hachem, Hadi (Lebanon) (continued)

HUMAN RIGHTS—TERRITORIES OCCUPIED BY ISRAEL (Agenda item 71c)
A/C.3/78/SR.24
MIDDLE EAST SITUATION (Agenda item 34)
A/78/PV.40
PEACEKEEPING OPERATIONS (Agenda item 51)
A/C.4/78/SR.20
SUSTAINABLE DEVELOPMENT (Agenda item 18)
A/C.2/78/SR.21
UN. GENERAL ASSEMBLY (78TH SESS. : 2023-2024). 1ST COMMITTEE—GENERAL DEBATE (Agenda item 8)
A/C.1/78/PV.6
UN HIGH COMMISSIONER FOR REFUGEES—REPORTS (Agenda item 60)
A/C.3/78/SR.44
VETO (Agenda item 63)
A/78/PV.71; A/78/PV.75

Hackman, Khalilah (Ghana)

PEACEKEEPING OPERATIONS—CRIMINAL LIABILITY (Agenda item 76)
A/C.6/78/SR.8
RULE OF LAW (Agenda item 83)
A/C.6/78/SR.17
TERRORISM (Agenda item 109)
A/C.6/78/SR.2

Hackman, Khalilah (Ghana) (UN. General Assembly. 6th Committee. Bureau)

INTERNATIONAL LAW—TRAINING PROGRAMMES (Agenda item 78)
A/C.6/78/SR.37

Hadgu, Daniel Abraham (Eritrea)

UN—BUDGET (2024) (Agenda item 134)
A/C.5/78/SR.26/PartII; A/C.5/78/SR.34
UN—PROGRAMME PLANNING (Agenda item 135)
A/78/PV.50(Resumption1)

Hadjichrysanthou, Andreas (Cyprus)

WOMEN'S ADVANCEMENT (Agenda item 25a)
A/C.3/78/SR.8
WOMEN'S ADVANCEMENT—CONFERENCES (Agenda item 25b)
A/C.3/78/SR.8

Hadjichrysanthou, Andreas (Cyprus) (UN. Committee on Relations with the Host Country)

UN. COMMITTEE ON RELATIONS WITH THE HOST COUNTRY—REPORTS (Agenda item 161)
A/C.6/78/SR.35

Haegen, Laurin van der (Switzerland)

CLUSTER MUNITIONS (Agenda item 99dd)
A/C.1/78/PV.19
CONVENTIONAL WEAPONS (Agenda item 99u)
A/C.1/78/PV.19

Haegen, Laurin van der (Switzerland) (continued)

CONVENTIONAL WEAPONS—TREATIES (Agenda item 103)
A/C.1/78/PV.19
DISARMAMENT—GENERAL AND COMPLETE (Agenda item 99)
A/C.1/78/PV.19
INFORMATION—INTERNATIONAL SECURITY (Agenda item 94)
A/C.1/78/PV.20
LANDMINES—TREATIES (Agenda item 99m)
A/C.1/78/PV.19

Haji Zaini, Hajah Razan Dzafirah Binti (Brunei Darussalam)

SUSTAINABLE DEVELOPMENT (Agenda item 18)
A/C.2/78/SR.13

Hakobyan, Aram (Armenia)

HUMAN RIGHTS (Agenda item 71)
A/C.3/78/SR.16
HUMAN RIGHTS—REPORTS (Agenda item 71c)
A/C.3/78/SR.25
HUMAN RIGHTS ADVANCEMENT (Agenda item 71b)
A/C.3/78/SR.24
MERCENARIES (Agenda item 70)
A/C.3/78/SR.42
RACIAL DISCRIMINATION—ELIMINATION (Agenda item 69a)
A/C.3/78/SR.42
RACIAL DISCRIMINATION—PROGRAMMES OF ACTION (Agenda item 69b)
A/C.3/78/SR.42
RIGHT TO DEVELOPMENT (Agenda item 71b)
A/C.3/78/SR.48
RIGHTS OF THE CHILD (Agenda item 67)
A/C.3/78/SR.11; A/C.3/78/SR.13; A/C.3/78/SR.14
UN HIGH COMMISSIONER FOR REFUGEES—REPORTS (Agenda item 60)
A/C.3/78/SR.44; A/C.3/78/SR.45
WOMEN'S ADVANCEMENT (Agenda item 25a)
A/C.3/78/SR.8; A/C.3/78/SR.10
WOMEN'S ADVANCEMENT—CONFERENCES (Agenda item 25b)
A/C.3/78/SR.8; A/C.3/78/SR.10

Hamamoto, Yukiya (Japan)

PEACEKEEPING OPERATIONS (Agenda item 51)
A/C.4/78/SR.20

Hamblin, Ueva (French Polynesia)

FRENCH POLYNESIA QUESTION (Agenda item 58)
A/C.4/78/SR.3

Hamdouni, Meryem (Morocco)

UN. GENERAL ASSEMBLY (78TH SESS. : 2023-2024). 2ND COMMITTEE—GENERAL DEBATE (Agenda item 8)
A/C.2/78/SR.4

Hamdouni, Meryem (Morocco) (Like-Minded Group of Supporters of Middle-Income Countries)

DEVELOPMENT COOPERATION—MIDDLE-INCOME COUNTRIES (Agenda item 19c)
A/C.2/78/SR.10
DEVELOPMENT FINANCE (Agenda item 16b)
A/C.2/78/SR.8
EXTERNAL DEBT (Agenda item 16c)
A/C.2/78/SR.8

Hamed, Ashraf A.O. (Libya)

ELECTION VERIFICATION—UN (Agenda item 71b)
A/C.3/78/SR.50
HUMAN RIGHTS—TERRITORIES OCCUPIED BY ISRAEL (Agenda item 71c)
A/C.3/78/SR.35
RIGHTS OF THE CHILD (Agenda item 67)
A/C.3/78/SR.55
RURAL WOMEN (Agenda item 25a)
A/C.3/78/SR.49
TERRITORIES OCCUPIED BY ISRAEL—HUMAN RIGHTS (Agenda item 50)
A/C.4/78/SR.25
WOMEN MIGRANT WORKERS (Agenda item 25a)
A/C.3/78/SR.49
YOUTH (Agenda item 24b)
A/C.3/78/SR.55

Hameed, Hala (Maldives)

CLIMATE (Agenda item 18d)
A/C.2/78/SR.13
CLIMATE CHANGE (Agenda item 71b)
A/C.3/78/SR.29
RIGHT TO EDUCATION (Agenda item 71b)
A/C.3/78/SR.27
RIGHTS OF THE CHILD (Agenda item 67)
A/C.3/78/SR.13
SMALL ISLAND DEVELOPING STATES—PROGRAMMES OF ACTION (Agenda item 18b)
A/C.2/78/SR.13
SUSTAINABLE DEVELOPMENT (Agenda item 18)
A/C.2/78/SR.13
TERRITORIES OCCUPIED BY ISRAEL—NATURAL RESOURCES (Agenda item 59)
A/C.2/78/SR.19
UN. HUMAN RIGHTS COUNCIL—REPORTS (Agenda item 66)
A/78/PV.23

Hamer, David (Australia)

ELECTION VERIFICATION—UN (Agenda item 71b)
A/C.3/78/SR.50

Hamer, David (Australia) (continued)
HUMAN RIGHTS—IRAN (ISLAMIC REPUBLIC OF) (Agenda item 71c)
A/C.3/78/SR.53
SEXUAL ORIENTATION (Agenda item 71b)
A/C.3/78/SR.39
SLAVERY (Agenda item 71a)
A/C.3/78/SR.21

Hamilton, Jim (United States)
DEVELOPMENT FINANCE (Agenda item 16b)
A/C.2/78/SR.22
EXTERNAL DEBT (Agenda item 16c)
A/C.2/78/SR.25

Hamudi, Malika ((personal capacity))
WESTERN SAHARA QUESTION (Agenda item 58)
A/C.4/78/SR.5

Hamzah, Fatin Hilyati Haji (Brunei Darussalam)
TERRITORIES OCCUPIED BY ISRAEL—HUMAN RIGHTS (Agenda item 50)
A/C.4/78/SR.24

Han, Jin (China)
UN—BUDGET (2024) (Agenda item 134)
A/C.5/78/SR.28

Han, Zheng (China. Vice-President)
UN. GENERAL ASSEMBLY (78TH SESS. : 2023-2024)—GENERAL DEBATE (Agenda item 8)
A/78/PV.9
UN. GENERAL ASSEMBLY (78TH SESS. : 2023-2024)—SPECIAL STATEMENTS
A/78/PV.9

Hanif, Navid (UN. Assistant Secretary-General for Economic Development)
DEVELOPMENT COOPERATION—MIDDLE-INCOME COUNTRIES (Agenda item 19c)
A/C.2/78/SR.10

Hanlumyuang, Thararut (Thailand)
CRIMES AGAINST HUMANITY (Agenda item 80)
A/C.6/78/SR.10
DISASTER VICTIMS (Agenda item 86)
A/C.6/78/SR.6
INFORMATION—INTERNATIONAL SECURITY (Agenda item 94)
A/C.1/78/PV.20
PEACEKEEPING OPERATIONS (Agenda item 51)
A/C.4/78/SR.18

Hanna, Paul (United States)
UN—FINANCIAL SITUATION (Agenda item 136)
A/C.5/78/SR.6

Hansen, Steen Malthe (European Union)
CHEMICAL WEAPONS—TREATIES (Agenda item 99l)
A/C.1/78/PV.15
DISARMAMENT—GENERAL AND COMPLETE (Agenda item 99)
A/78/PV.105
NUCLEAR DISARMAMENT (Agenda item 99b)
A/C.1/78/PV.11; A/C.1/78/PV.13
NUCLEAR NON-PROLIFERATION—INTERNATIONAL OBLIGATIONS (Agenda item 99w)
A/C.1/78/PV.11
NUCLEAR WEAPON TESTS—TREATIES (Agenda item 105)
A/C.1/78/PV.11
OUTER SPACE—PEACEFUL USES—INTERNATIONAL COOPERATION (Agenda item 48)
A/C.4/78/SR.15
RADIATION EFFECTS (Agenda item 47)
A/C.4/78/SR.11
UN. GENERAL ASSEMBLY (78TH SESS. : 2023-2024). 1ST COMMITTEE—GENERAL DEBATE (Agenda item 8)
A/C.1/78/PV.4

Hardie, Alexandra (New Zealand)
UN—BUDGET (2024) (Agenda item 134)
A/C.5/78/SR.26/PartII

Hardwick, Nicola Ann (Austria)
AGEING PERSONS (Agenda item 24b)
A/C.3/78/SR.1
HUMAN RIGHTS—AFGHANISTAN (Agenda item 71c)
A/C.3/78/SR.34
MIGRANTS—PROTECTION (Agenda item 71b)
A/C.3/78/SR.56
MINORITIES (Agenda item 71b)
A/C.3/78/SR.39; A/C.3/78/SR.52

Hartog, Laurens Thomas den (Netherlands (Kingdom of the)) (UN. General Assembly. 5th Committee. Rapporteur)
ADMINISTRATION OF JUSTICE (Agenda item 144)
A/78/PV.50(Resumption1)
AU-UN HYBRID OPERATION IN DARFUR—FINANCING (Agenda item 159)
A/78/PV.95
CONFERENCE AND MEETING SERVICES (Agenda item 137)
A/78/PV.50(Resumption1)
INTERNATIONAL RESIDUAL MECHANISM FOR CRIMINAL TRIBUNALS—FINANCING (Agenda item 145)
A/78/PV.50(Resumption1)
JOINT INSPECTION UNIT (Agenda item 141)
A/78/PV.73
PEACEKEEPING OPERATIONS—FINANCING (Agenda item 146)
A/78/PV.95

Hartog, Laurens Thomas den (Netherlands (Kingdom of the)) (UN. General Assembly. 5th Committee. Rapporteur) (continued)

UN—ADMINISTRATION (Agenda item 132)
A/78/PV.50(Resumption1); A/78/PV.73; A/78/PV.95
UN—BUDGET (2023) (Agenda item 133)
A/78/PV.50(Resumption1)
UN—BUDGET (2024) (Agenda item 134)
A/78/PV.50(Resumption1); A/78/PV.73
UN—FINANCIAL REPORTS (Agenda item 131)
A/78/PV.50(Resumption1); A/78/PV.95
UN—HUMAN RESOURCES MANAGEMENT (Agenda item 139)
A/78/PV.73; A/78/PV.95
UN—PROGRAMME PLANNING (Agenda item 135)
A/78/PV.50(Resumption1)
UN. ETHICS OFFICE—REPORTS (Agenda item 140)
A/78/PV.50(Resumption1)
UN. OFFICE OF INTERNAL OVERSIGHT SERVICES—REPORTS (Agenda item 143)
A/78/PV.50(Resumption1)
UN. SUPPORT OFFICE IN SOMALIA—FINANCING (Agenda item 160)
A/78/PV.95
UN DISENGAGEMENT OBSERVER FORCE—FINANCING (Agenda item 156a)
A/78/PV.95
UN INTERIM ADMINISTRATION MISSION IN KOSOVO—FINANCING (Agenda item 153)
A/78/PV.95
UN INTERIM FORCE IN LEBANON—FINANCING (Agenda item 156b)
A/78/PV.95
UN MISSION FOR THE REFERENDUM IN WESTERN SAHARA—FINANCING (Agenda item 158)
A/78/PV.95
UN MISSION IN LIBERIA—FINANCING (Agenda item 154)
A/78/PV.95
UN MISSION IN SOUTH SUDAN—FINANCING (Agenda item 157)
A/78/PV.95
UN MULTIDIMENSIONAL INTEGRATED STABILIZATION MISSION IN MALI—FINANCING (Agenda item 155)
A/78/PV.50(Resumption1); A/78/PV.95
UN MULTIDIMENSIONAL INTEGRATED STABILIZATION MISSION IN THE CENTRAL AFRICAN REPUBLIC—FINANCING (Agenda item 148)
A/78/PV.95
UN OPERATION IN CÔTE D'IVOIRE—FINANCING (Agenda item 149)
A/78/PV.95
UN ORGANIZATION STABILIZATION MISSION IN THE DEMOCRATIC REPUBLIC OF THE CONGO—FINANCING (Agenda item 151)
A/78/PV.95
UN PEACEKEEPING FORCE IN CYPRUS—FINANCING (Agenda item 150)
A/78/PV.95
UN SECURITY FORCE FOR ABYEI—FINANCING (Agenda item 147)
A/78/PV.95

Hasanova, Tahmina (Tajikistan)

FOOD SECURITY (Agenda item 23a)
A/C.2/78/SR.17
POVERTY—INTERNATIONAL DECADES (Agenda item 21a)
A/C.2/78/SR.17
RURAL POVERTY (Agenda item 21b)
A/C.2/78/SR.17
SUSTAINABLE DEVELOPMENT (Agenda item 18)
A/C.2/78/SR.15
UN. GENERAL ASSEMBLY (78TH SESS. : 2023-2024). 2ND COMMITTEE—GENERAL DEBATE (Agenda item 8)
A/C.2/78/SR.3

Hasenau, Michael (Germany)

CRIMES AGAINST HUMANITY (Agenda item 80)
A/C.6/78/SR.9; A/C.6/78/SR.38
DISASTER VICTIMS (Agenda item 86)
A/C.6/78/SR.5
INTERNATIONAL CRIMINAL COURT—REPORTS (Agenda item 74)
A/78/PV.22
INTERNATIONAL JURISDICTION (Agenda item 84)
A/C.6/78/SR.12
INTERNATIONAL RESIDUAL MECHANISM FOR CRIMINAL TRIBUNALS (Agenda item 126)
A/78/PV.19
UN. INTERNATIONAL LAW COMMISSION—REPORTS (Agenda item 79)
A/C.6/78/SR.29; A/C.6/78/SR.31
VETO (Agenda item 63)
A/78/PV.70

Hashmi, Khalil Ur Rahman (Pakistan)

UN. GENERAL ASSEMBLY (78TH SESS. : 2023-2024). 1ST COMMITTEE—GENERAL DEBATE (Agenda item 8)
A/C.1/78/PV.6

Hashmi, Khalil Ur Rahman (UNCTAD)

INTERNATIONAL TRADE (Agenda item 16a)
A/C.2/78/SR.8

Hasina, Sheikh (Bangladesh. Prime Minister)

UN. GENERAL ASSEMBLY (78TH SESS. : 2023-2024)—GENERAL DEBATE (Agenda item 8)
A/78/PV.10
UN. GENERAL ASSEMBLY (78TH SESS. : 2023-2024)—SPECIAL STATEMENTS
A/78/PV.10

Hasler, Dominique (Liechtenstein)

UN. GENERAL ASSEMBLY (78TH SESS. : 2023-2024)—GENERAL DEBATE (Agenda item 8)
A/78/PV.9

Hasler, Merhaba (Liechtenstein)
CRIMES AGAINST HUMANITY (Agenda item 80)
A/C.6/78/SR.9; A/C.6/78/SR.40
INTERNATIONAL JURISDICTION (Agenda item 84)
A/C.6/78/SR.12

Hassan, Kadra Ahmed (UN. Human Rights Council. Ad Hoc Committee on the Elaboration of Complementary International Standards. Chair)
RACIAL DISCRIMINATION—ELIMINATION (Agenda item 69a)
A/C.3/78/SR.41

Hassan, Khaled Aly Awadalla (Egypt)
SPORTS—OLYMPIC GAMES (Agenda item 11)
A/78/PV.38

Hassan, Tariq Ahmed (United Arab Emirates)
CLIMATE (Agenda item 18d)
A/C.2/78/SR.13
SUSTAINABLE ENERGY (Agenda item 18h)
A/C.2/78/SR.13

Hassani, Billel (Algeria)
CRIME PREVENTION (Agenda item 107)
A/C.3/78/SR.6
CYBERCRIME (Agenda item 108)
A/C.3/78/SR.6
ELECTION VERIFICATION—UN (Agenda item 71b)
A/C.3/78/SR.50
HEALTH (Agenda item 125)
A/78/PV.41
HUMAN RIGHTS (Agenda item 71)
A/C.3/78/SR.16; A/C.3/78/SR.27
HUMAN RIGHTS—ERITREA (Agenda item 71c)
A/C.3/78/SR.36
HUMAN RIGHTS—INTERNATIONAL INSTRUMENTS (Agenda item 71a)
A/C.3/78/SR.17
HUMAN RIGHTS—TERRITORIES OCCUPIED BY ISRAEL (Agenda item 71c)
A/C.3/78/SR.27
RACIAL DISCRIMINATION—ELIMINATION (Agenda item 69a)
A/C.3/78/SR.42; A/C.3/78/SR.47
RACIAL DISCRIMINATION—PROGRAMMES OF ACTION (Agenda item 69b)
A/C.3/78/SR.42
RIGHT TO DEVELOPMENT (Agenda item 71b)
A/C.3/78/SR.20
SELF-DETERMINATION OF PEOPLES (Agenda item 70)
A/C.3/78/SR.42; A/C.3/78/SR.43
TORTURE AND OTHER CRUEL TREATMENT (Agenda item 71a)
A/C.3/78/SR.18
UN. HUMAN RIGHTS COUNCIL—REPORTS (Agenda item 66)
A/78/PV.28; A/C.3/78/SR.46

Hassen, Demeke Mekonnen (Ethiopia. Deputy Prime Minister)
UN. GENERAL ASSEMBLY (78TH SESS. : 2023-2024)—GENERAL DEBATE (Agenda item 8)
A/78/PV.12
UN. GENERAL ASSEMBLY (78TH SESS. : 2023-2024)—SPECIAL STATEMENTS
A/78/PV.12

Hauata Ah-Min, Maite (French Polynesia)
FRENCH POLYNESIA QUESTION (Agenda item 58)
A/C.4/78/SR.3

Hauri, Adrian (Switzerland)
CENTRAL ASIA—ZONES OF PEACE (Agenda item 64)
A/78/PV.85
SPECIAL POLITICAL MISSIONS (Agenda item 52)
A/C.4/78/SR.21
UN. GENERAL ASSEMBLY (78TH SESS. : 2023-2024). 2ND COMMITTEE—GENERAL DEBATE (Agenda item 8)
A/C.2/78/SR.2
UN HIGH COMMISSIONER FOR REFUGEES—REPORTS (Agenda item 60)
A/C.3/78/SR.44
VETO (Agenda item 63)
A/78/PV.51; A/78/PV.75

Havn, Anne Melangen (Norway)
VETO (Agenda item 63)
A/78/PV.75

Havn, Anne Melangen (Norway) (UN. Working Group on the Financing of the United Nations Relief and Works Agency for Palestine Refugees in the Near East. Rapporteur)
UNRWA—ACTIVITIES (Agenda item 49)
A/C.4/78/SR.22

Hawkins, Penelope (UNCTAD)
EXTERNAL DEBT (Agenda item 16c)
A/C.2/78/SR.8

Hayovyshyn, Khrystyna (Ukraine)
DISARMAMENT—GENERAL AND COMPLETE (Agenda item 99)
A/78/PV.106
EMERGENCY ASSISTANCE (Agenda item 72a)
A/78/PV.47
ORGANIZATION FOR DEMOCRACY AND ECONOMIC DEVELOPMENT - GUAM (Agenda item 32)
A/78/PV.85
UN. GENERAL ASSEMBLY (78TH SESS. : 2023-2024)—AGENDA (Agenda item 7)
A/78/PV.2

Hayovyshyn, Khrystyna (Ukraine) (continued)
UN. GENERAL ASSEMBLY (78TH SESS. : 2023-2024). 1ST COMMITTEE—GENERAL DEBATE (Agenda item 8)
A/C.1/78/PV.4
VETO (Agenda item 63)
A/78/PV.68

Hazlewood, Abosede (Guyana)
INDIGENOUS PEOPLES (Agenda item 68a)
A/C.3/78/SR.15
INDIGENOUS PEOPLES—CONFERENCES (Agenda item 68b)
A/C.3/78/SR.15
RIGHTS OF THE CHILD (Agenda item 67)
A/C.3/78/SR.13

Heartney, Edward (United States)
CYBERCRIME (Agenda item 108)
A/C.3/78/SR.5
DISAPPEARANCE OF PERSONS (Agenda item 71b)
A/C.3/78/SR.22
ECONOMIC SANCTIONS—INTERNATIONAL RELATIONS (Agenda item 28)
A/78/PV.90
HIV/AIDS—DECLARATIONS (Agenda item 10)
A/78/PV.91
HUMAN RIGHTS—REPORTS (Agenda item 71c)
A/C.3/78/SR.18
RACIAL DISCRIMINATION—ELIMINATION (Agenda item 69a)
A/78/PV.103
SMALL ISLAND DEVELOPING STATES—PROGRAMMES OF ACTION (Agenda item 18b)
A/78/PV.103
UN CONFERENCES (Agenda item 13)
A/78/PV.107

Hegazy, Abdelrhman Mohamed Farid (Egypt)
ARMS RACE—OUTER SPACE (Agenda item 97a)
A/C.1/78/PV.16
ARMS TRANSFERS—TREATIES (Agenda item 99x)
A/C.1/78/PV.18; A/C.1/78/PV.28
CLUSTER MUNITIONS (Agenda item 99dd)
A/C.1/78/PV.28
CONVENTIONAL WEAPONS (Agenda item 99u)
A/C.1/78/PV.18; A/C.1/78/PV.28
DISARMAMENT—GENERAL AND COMPLETE (Agenda item 99)
A/C.1/78/PV.18; A/C.1/78/PV.28
DISARMAMENT AGREEMENTS—OUTER SPACE (Agenda item 97c)
A/C.1/78/PV.16; A/C.1/78/PV.27
INFORMATION—INTERNATIONAL SECURITY (Agenda item 94)
A/C.1/78/PV.20; A/C.1/78/PV.29
LANDMINES—TREATIES (Agenda item 99m)
A/C.1/78/PV.28

Hegazy, Abdelrhman Mohamed Farid (Egypt) (continued)
OUTER SPACE—CONFIDENCE-BUILDING MEASURES (Agenda item 99v)
A/C.1/78/PV.16
OUTER SPACE—PRINCIPLES (Agenda item 97d)
A/C.1/78/PV.16; A/C.1/78/PV.27
SMALL ARMS—ILLICIT TRAFFIC (Agenda item 99p)
A/C.1/78/PV.18; A/C.1/78/PV.28
SMALL ARMS—ILLICIT TRAFFIC—ASSISTANCE (Agenda item 99n)
A/C.1/78/PV.18

Heidar, Tomas H. (International Tribunal for the Law of the Sea. President)
LAW OF THE SEA (Agenda item 75a)
A/78/PV.44
MARINE ECOSYSTEMS—BIOLOGICAL DIVERSITY (Agenda item 75c)
A/78/PV.44
STRADDLING FISH STOCKS (Agenda item 75b)
A/78/PV.44

Heidari, Bahram (Iran (Islamic Republic of))
CRIMES AGAINST HUMANITY (Agenda item 80)
A/C.6/78/SR.10
DISASTER VICTIMS (Agenda item 86)
A/C.6/78/SR.5
INTERNATIONAL JURISDICTION (Agenda item 84)
A/C.6/78/SR.12
PEACEKEEPING OPERATIONS—CRIMINAL LIABILITY (Agenda item 76)
A/C.6/78/SR.8
RESPONSIBILITY OF INTERNATIONAL ORGANIZATIONS (Agenda item 85)
A/C.6/78/SR.19
RULE OF LAW (Agenda item 83)
A/C.6/78/SR.16
TERRORISM (Agenda item 109)
A/C.6/78/SR.1
UN COMMISSION ON INTERNATIONAL TRADE LAW—REPORTS (Agenda item 77)
A/C.6/78/SR.14

Heidari, Bahram (Iran (Islamic Republic of)) (Coordinating Bureau of the Non-Aligned Countries)
INTERNATIONAL JURISDICTION (Agenda item 84)
A/C.6/78/SR.12
INTERNATIONAL LAW—TRAINING PROGRAMMES (Agenda item 78)
A/C.6/78/SR.21
RULE OF LAW (Agenda item 83)
A/C.6/78/SR.15

Heller, Claude (UN. Committee against Torture. Chair)

TORTURE AND OTHER CRUEL TREATMENT (Agenda item 71a)
A/C.3/78/SR.18

Hellerová, Zuzana (Czechia)

SOCIAL CONDITIONS (Agenda item 24b)
A/C.3/78/SR.2

Heng, Somoly (Cambodia)

MACROECONOMIC POLICY (Agenda item 16)
A/C.2/78/SR.9
TAXATION (Agenda item 16h)
A/C.2/78/SR.9

Henry, Ariel (Haiti. Prime Minister)

UN. GENERAL ASSEMBLY (78TH SESS. : 2023-2024)—GENERAL DEBATE (Agenda item 8)
A/78/PV.11
UN. GENERAL ASSEMBLY (78TH SESS. : 2023-2024)—SPECIAL STATEMENTS
A/78/PV.11

Henry, Carlton Ronnie (Saint Lucia)

BRITISH VIRGIN ISLANDS QUESTION (Agenda item 58)
A/C.4/78/SR.7
DECOLONIZATION (Agenda item 58)
A/C.4/78/SR.7
FALKLAND ISLANDS (MALVINAS) QUESTION (Agenda item 42)
A/C.4/78/SR.7
WESTERN SAHARA QUESTION (Agenda item 58)
A/C.4/78/SR.7

Henzel, Christopher (United States)

CLIMATE (Agenda item 18d)
A/C.2/78/SR.15
HUMAN RIGHTS—IRAN (ISLAMIC REPUBLIC OF) (Agenda item 71c)
A/C.3/78/SR.53
HUMAN RIGHTS—SYRIAN ARAB REPUBLIC (Agenda item 71c)
A/C.3/78/SR.34
PALESTINE QUESTION (Agenda item 35)
A/78/PV.40
SUSTAINABLE DEVELOPMENT (Agenda item 18)
A/C.2/78/SR.15

Herity, Emer (UN. General Assembly. 2nd Committee. Secretary)

COASTAL ZONE MANAGEMENT (Agenda item 18j)
A/C.2/78/SR.23
SUSTAINABLE DEVELOPMENT (Agenda item 18)
A/C.2/78/SR.24

Hermida Castillo, Jaime (Nicaragua)

CUBA—UNITED STATES (Agenda item 38)
A/78/PV.26

Hermida Castillo, Jaime (Nicaragua) (continued)

DEVELOPMENT FINANCE (Agenda item 16b)
A/C.2/78/SR.9
FALKLAND ISLANDS (MALVINAS) QUESTION (Agenda item 42)
A/C.4/78/SR.6
HUMAN RIGHTS—REPORTS (Agenda item 71c)
A/C.3/78/SR.26
HUMAN RIGHTS ADVANCEMENT (Agenda item 71b)
A/C.3/78/SR.26
INDIGENOUS PEOPLES (Agenda item 68a)
A/C.3/78/SR.15
INDIGENOUS PEOPLES—CONFERENCES (Agenda item 68b)
A/C.3/78/SR.15
INTERNATIONAL TRADE (Agenda item 16a)
A/C.2/78/SR.9
MACROECONOMIC POLICY (Agenda item 16)
A/C.2/78/SR.9
RIGHTS OF THE CHILD (Agenda item 67)
A/C.3/78/SR.13
RULE OF LAW (Agenda item 83)
A/C.6/78/SR.16
SANCTIONS—INTERNATIONAL RELATIONS (Agenda item 71b)
A/C.3/78/SR.26
UN. INTERNATIONAL COURT OF JUSTICE—REPORTS (Agenda item 73)
A/78/PV.28
VETO (Agenda item 63)
A/78/PV.60; A/78/PV.75
WESTERN SAHARA QUESTION (Agenda item 58)
A/C.4/78/SR.6

Hernández Chávez, José Juan (Chile)

CRIMES AGAINST HUMANITY (Agenda item 80)
A/C.6/78/SR.11; A/C.6/78/SR.38; A/C.6/78/SR.41; A/C.6/78/SR.45
INTERNATIONAL LAW—TRAINING PROGRAMMES (Agenda item 78)
A/C.6/78/SR.22
NON-CITIZENS—DEPORTATION (Agenda item 81)
A/C.6/78/SR.34
RULE OF LAW (Agenda item 83)
A/C.6/78/SR.18
UN. INTERNATIONAL COURT OF JUSTICE—REPORTS (Agenda item 73)
A/78/PV.27
UN. INTERNATIONAL LAW COMMISSION—REPORTS (Agenda item 79)
A/C.6/78/SR.29; A/C.6/78/SR.31
UN COMMISSION ON INTERNATIONAL TRADE LAW—REPORTS (Agenda item 77)
A/C.6/78/SR.14

Hernández González, Leticia María (Asociación Canaria de Solidaridad con el Pueblo Saharaui)

WESTERN SAHARA QUESTION (Agenda item 58)
A/C.4/78/SR.4

Hernández Morera, Diosdado de Jesús (Cuba)
UN—PROGRAMME PLANNING (Agenda item 135)
A/C.5/78/SR.24

Hernández Morera, Diosdado de Jesús (Cuba) (Group of 77)
ADMINISTRATION OF JUSTICE (Agenda item 144)
A/C.5/78/SR.15
INTERNATIONAL RESIDUAL MECHANISM FOR CRIMINAL TRIBUNALS—FINANCING (Agenda item 145)
A/C.5/78/SR.20
UN—BUDGET (2024) (Agenda item 134)
A/C.5/78/SR.14; A/C.5/78/SR.16; A/C.5/78/SR.17; A/C.5/78/SR.18; A/C.5/78/SR.19; A/C.5/78/SR.21; A/C.5/78/SR.22
UN—HUMAN RESOURCES MANAGEMENT (Agenda item 139)
A/C.5/78/SR.25

Herrera, Gabriel (Argentina)
UN. INTERNATIONAL COURT OF JUSTICE—REPORTS (Agenda item 73)
A/78/PV.20
UN. INTERNATIONAL LAW COMMISSION—REPORTS (Agenda item 79)
A/C.6/78/SR.28

Herrera García, Edilma America (El Salvador)
UN—BUDGET (2024) (Agenda item 134)
A/C.5/78/SR.18

Heumann, Amit (Israel)
CRIMES AGAINST HUMANITY (Agenda item 80)
A/C.6/78/SR.42; A/C.6/78/SR.44; A/C.6/78/SR.45

Hicuburundi, Alice (UN. Division for Ocean Affairs and the Law of the Sea)
INTERNATIONAL LAW—TRAINING PROGRAMMES (Agenda item 78)
A/C.6/78/SR.21

Hidalgo, Melanie (Dominican Republic)
VETO (Agenda item 63)
A/78/PV.3

Hikmat, Jonibek Ismoil (Tajikistan)
UN CONFERENCES (Agenda item 13)
A/78/PV.77

Hilale, Omar (Morocco)
PEACEBUILDING (Agenda item 61)
A/78/PV.100
SOCIAL CONDITIONS (Agenda item 24b)
A/78/PV.101
SPORTS—OLYMPIC GAMES (Agenda item 11)
A/78/PV.38
UN—BUDGET (2024) (Agenda item 134)
A/C.5/78/SR.5

Hilale, Omar (Morocco) (continued)
UN—PROGRAMME PLANNING (Agenda item 135)
A/C.5/78/SR.5
UN. GENERAL ASSEMBLY (78TH SESS. : 2023-2024)—GENERAL DEBATE (Agenda item 8)
A/78/PV.14
UN. GENERAL ASSEMBLY (78TH SESS. : 2023-2024)—GENERAL DEBATE—RIGHT OF REPLY (Agenda item 8)
A/78/PV.14
UN. PEACEBUILDING COMMISSION—REPORTS (Agenda item 27)
A/78/PV.100
UN. PEACEBUILDING FUND—REPORTS (Agenda item 111)
A/78/PV.100
VETO (Agenda item 63)
A/78/PV.52; A/78/PV.61; A/78/PV.66
WESTERN SAHARA QUESTION (Agenda item 58)
A/C.4/78/SR.9

Hilale, Omar (Morocco) (Like-Minded Group of Supporters of Middle-Income Countries)
UN. GENERAL ASSEMBLY (78TH SESS. : 2023-2024). 2ND COMMITTEE—GENERAL DEBATE (Agenda item 8)
A/C.2/78/SR.2

Hill, Ruth (Australia)
BIOLOGICAL WEAPONS—TREATIES (Agenda item 106)
A/C.1/78/PV.14
CHEMICAL WEAPONS—TREATIES (Agenda item 99l)
A/C.1/78/PV.14
WEAPONS OF MASS DESTRUCTION—TERRORISM (Agenda item 99s)
A/C.1/78/PV.14

Himmler, Benjamin (Germany)
ARMS RACE—OUTER SPACE (Agenda item 97a)
A/C.1/78/PV.16
BIOLOGICAL WEAPONS—TREATIES (Agenda item 106)
A/C.1/78/PV.14
CHEMICAL WEAPONS—TREATIES (Agenda item 99l)
A/C.1/78/PV.14
DISARMAMENT AGREEMENTS—OUTER SPACE (Agenda item 97c)
A/C.1/78/PV.16
NUCLEAR DISARMAMENT (Agenda item 99b)
A/C.1/78/PV.11
NUCLEAR NON-PROLIFERATION—INTERNATIONAL OBLIGATIONS (Agenda item 99w)
A/C.1/78/PV.11
NUCLEAR WEAPON TESTS—TREATIES (Agenda item 105)
A/C.1/78/PV.11

Himmler, Benjamin (Germany) (continued)

OUTER SPACE—CONFIDENCE-BUILDING MEASURES (Agenda item 99v)
A/C.1/78/PV.16
OUTER SPACE—PRINCIPLES (Agenda item 97d)
A/C.1/78/PV.16

Hirji, Hussein (Canada)

PEACE (Agenda item 14)
A/78/PV.62
RADIATION EFFECTS (Agenda item 47)
A/C.4/78/SR.11

Hitti, Youssef (Lebanon)

CRIMES AGAINST HUMANITY (Agenda item 80)
A/C.6/78/SR.11; A/C.6/78/SR.39; A/C.6/78/SR.41; A/C.6/78/SR.43; A/C.6/78/SR.44
DISASTER VICTIMS (Agenda item 86)
A/C.6/78/SR.6
INTERNATIONAL LAW—TRAINING PROGRAMMES (Agenda item 78)
A/C.6/78/SR.22
RULE OF LAW (Agenda item 83)
A/C.6/78/SR.19
TERRORISM (Agenda item 109)
A/C.6/78/SR.2
UN. INTERNATIONAL COURT OF JUSTICE—REPORTS (Agenda item 73)
A/78/PV.27; A/C.6/78/SR.26
UN. INTERNATIONAL LAW COMMISSION—REPORTS (Agenda item 79)
A/C.6/78/SR.28; A/C.6/78/SR.37

Hmoud, Mahmoud Daifallah Mahmoud (Jordan)

PALESTINE QUESTION (Agenda item 35)
A/78/PV.39
UKRAINE—POLITICAL CONDITIONS (Agenda item 62)
A/78/PV.99
VETO (Agenda item 63)
A/78/PV.52; A/78/PV.75

Hmoud, Mahmoud Daifallah Mahmoud (Jordan) (Group of Arab States)

MIDDLE EAST—NUCLEAR PROLIFERATION (Agenda item 102)
A/C.1/78/PV.11
MIDDLE EAST—NUCLEAR-WEAPON-FREE ZONES (Agenda item 95)
A/C.1/78/PV.11
NUCLEAR DISARMAMENT (Agenda item 99b)
A/C.1/78/PV.11
NUCLEAR NON-PROLIFERATION—INTERNATIONAL OBLIGATIONS (Agenda item 99w)
A/C.1/78/PV.11
NUCLEAR WEAPON TESTS—TREATIES (Agenda item 105)
A/C.1/78/PV.11
NUCLEAR WEAPONS—TREATIES (Agenda item 99ff)
A/C.1/78/PV.11

Hmoud, Mahmoud Daifallah Mahmoud (Jordan) (Group of Arab States) (continued)

UN. GENERAL ASSEMBLY (78TH SESS. : 2023-2024). 1ST COMMITTEE—GENERAL DEBATE (Agenda item 8)
A/C.1/78/PV.2

Hmyene, Touria (Association for the Freedom of Women Sequestered in the Tindouf Camps)

WESTERN SAHARA QUESTION (Agenda item 58)
A/C.4/78/SR.6

Hoffmeister, Frank (European Union)

UN. INTERNATIONAL COURT OF JUSTICE—REPORTS (Agenda item 73)
A/78/PV.20
UN. INTERNATIONAL LAW COMMISSION—REPORTS (Agenda item 79)
A/C.6/78/SR.28

Hofmański, Piotr (International Criminal Court. President)

INTERNATIONAL CRIMINAL COURT—REPORTS (Agenda item 74)
A/78/PV.21

Hoiore, Tevaipaea (Centre de jeunes adolescents de Vaiare Moorea (Organization))

FRENCH POLYNESIA QUESTION (Agenda item 58)
A/C.4/78/SR.3

Hollis, Jonathan Samuel (United Kingdom)

CRIMES AGAINST HUMANITY (Agenda item 80)
A/C.6/78/SR.10; A/C.6/78/SR.45
DISASTER VICTIMS (Agenda item 86)
A/C.6/78/SR.6
INTERNATIONAL CRIMINAL COURT—REPORTS (Agenda item 74)
A/78/PV.22
INTERNATIONAL JURISDICTION (Agenda item 84)
A/C.6/78/SR.12
INTERNATIONAL RESIDUAL MECHANISM FOR CRIMINAL TRIBUNALS (Agenda item 126)
A/78/PV.19
PEACEKEEPING OPERATIONS—CRIMINAL LIABILITY (Agenda item 76)
A/C.6/78/SR.8
RESPONSIBILITY OF INTERNATIONAL ORGANIZATIONS (Agenda item 85)
A/C.6/78/SR.19
RESPONSIBILITY TO PROTECT (Agenda item 129)
A/78/PV.97
UN. INTERNATIONAL LAW COMMISSION—REPORTS (Agenda item 79)
A/C.6/78/SR.37

Holm, Tor Tanke (Norway)
PEACEKEEPING OPERATIONS—CRIMINAL LIABILITY (Agenda item 76)
A/C.6/78/SR.8

Holter, Sigrun Stigen (Norway)
HUMAN RIGHTS—IRAN (ISLAMIC REPUBLIC OF) (Agenda item 71c)
A/C.3/78/SR.34

Homai, François (Association Tamariki Teavaroa)
FRENCH POLYNESIA QUESTION (Agenda item 58)
A/C.4/78/SR.3

Homai, Odette (French Polynesia)
FRENCH POLYNESIA QUESTION (Agenda item 58)
A/C.4/78/SR.3

Hong, Daphne Fan Sin (Singapore)
UN. INTERNATIONAL LAW COMMISSION—REPORTS (Agenda item 79)
A/C.6/78/SR.23

Hong, Sung Hun (Republic of Korea)
UKRAINE—POLITICAL CONDITIONS (Agenda item 62)
A/78/PV.58

Horosanu, Gabriela-Cornelia (Romania)
AFRICA—DEVELOPMENT (Agenda item 65b)
A/78/PV.18
AFRICA—SUSTAINABLE DEVELOPMENT—PARTNERSHIP (Agenda item 65a)
A/78/PV.18
UN. SECURITY COUNCIL—REPORTS (Agenda item 26)
A/78/PV.94

Horváth, Zsuzsanna (Hungary)
FREEDOM OF EXPRESSION (Agenda item 71b)
A/C.3/78/SR.19
MILLENNIUM SUMMIT—CONFERENCES (Agenda item 117)
A/78/PV.15
PEACE (Agenda item 14)
A/78/PV.82
SPORTS—OLYMPIC GAMES (Agenda item 11)
A/78/PV.97
UN CONFERENCES (Agenda item 13)
A/78/PV.15

Horváth, Zsuzsanna (Hungary) (European Union)
UN SYSTEM—STRENGTHENING (Agenda item 122)
A/78/PV.98

Hossain, Faruk (Bangladesh)
DEVELOPMENT FINANCE (Agenda item 16b)
A/C.2/78/SR.9
FOOD SECURITY (Agenda item 23a)
A/C.2/78/SR.17
INFORMATION TECHNOLOGY—DEVELOPMENT (Agenda item 15)
A/C.2/78/SR.10
MACROECONOMIC POLICY (Agenda item 16)
A/C.2/78/SR.9
NATURAL FIBRES (Agenda item 23b)
A/C.2/78/SR.23
POVERTY—INTERNATIONAL DECADES (Agenda item 21a)
A/C.2/78/SR.17
RURAL POVERTY (Agenda item 21b)
A/C.2/78/SR.17

Hou, Annemarie (UN Office for Partnerships. Executive Director)
UN—BUDGET (2023) (Agenda item 133)
A/C.5/78/SR.4

Hristea, Traian (Romania)
UKRAINE—POLITICAL CONDITIONS (Agenda item 62)
A/78/PV.56

Hsieh, Nichamon May (Thailand)
CRIME PREVENTION (Agenda item 107)
A/C.3/78/SR.5
CYBERCRIME (Agenda item 108)
A/C.3/78/SR.5

Hu, Xuewen (UN. Board of Auditors. Audit Operations Committee. Chair)
UN—BUDGET (2024) (Agenda item 134)
A/C.5/78/SR.9
UN—FINANCIAL REPORTS (Agenda item 131)
A/C.5/78/SR.35

Hua, Chenghang (China)
EXTERNAL DEBT (Agenda item 16c)
A/C.2/78/SR.9
INTERNATIONAL TRADE (Agenda item 16a)
A/C.2/78/SR.9
MACROECONOMIC POLICY (Agenda item 16)
A/C.2/78/SR.9

Hubatka, Pascal (Switzerland)
CLIMATE CHANGE (Agenda item 71b)
A/C.3/78/SR.29
HUMAN RIGHTS—DEMOCRATIC PEOPLE'S REPUBLIC OF KOREA (Agenda item 71c)
A/C.3/78/SR.33
HUMAN RIGHTS—MYANMAR (Agenda item 71c)
A/C.3/78/SR.33
HUMAN RIGHTS—SYRIAN ARAB REPUBLIC (Agenda item 71c)
A/C.3/78/SR.34

Huber, Marvin (Austria)

YOUTH (Agenda item 24b)
A/C.3/78/SR.2

Huff, Nancy (Teach the Children International (Organization))

WESTERN SAHARA QUESTION (Agenda item 58)
A/C.4/78/SR.4

Huisman, Johannes (UN. Programme Planning and Budget Division. Director)

UN—BUDGET (2024) (Agenda item 134)
A/C.5/78/SR.9; A/C.5/78/SR.23

Hun, Manet (Cambodia. Prime Minister)

UN. GENERAL ASSEMBLY (78TH SESS. : 2023-2024)—GENERAL DEBATE (Agenda item 8)
A/78/PV.11
UN. GENERAL ASSEMBLY (78TH SESS. : 2023-2024)—SPECIAL STATEMENTS
A/78/PV.11

Hunskaar, Maria (Norway)

BIOLOGICAL WEAPONS—TREATIES (Agenda item 106)
A/C.1/78/PV.15
CHEMICAL WEAPONS—TREATIES (Agenda item 99l)
A/C.1/78/PV.15
DISARMAMENT—GENERAL AND COMPLETE (Agenda item 99)
A/C.1/78/PV.15
WEAPONS OF MASS DESTRUCTION—TERRORISM (Agenda item 99s)
A/C.1/78/PV.15

Hussain, Thilmeeza (Maldives)

UN. GENERAL ASSEMBLY (78TH SESS. : 2023-2024). 2ND COMMITTEE—GENERAL DEBATE (Agenda item 8)
A/C.2/78/SR.3

Hutchison, Alexandra (Australia)

ARMED CONFLICTS PREVENTION (Agenda item 31a)
A/78/PV.72
CRIMES AGAINST HUMANITY (Agenda item 80)
A/C.6/78/SR.38; A/C.6/78/SR.41; A/C.6/78/SR.42; A/C.6/78/SR.43; A/C.6/78/SR.44; A/C.6/78/SR.45
DISASTER VICTIMS (Agenda item 86)
A/C.6/78/SR.5
UN. GENERAL ASSEMBLY—WORK PROGRAMME (Agenda item 120)
A/C.6/78/SR.36
UN. INTERNATIONAL COURT OF JUSTICE—REPORTS (Agenda item 73)
A/C.6/78/SR.26

Hwang, Joonkook (Republic of Korea)

HUMAN RIGHTS—DEMOCRATIC PEOPLE'S REPUBLIC OF KOREA (Agenda item 71c)
A/C.3/78/SR.26; A/C.3/78/SR.53
UN. GENERAL ASSEMBLY (78TH SESS. : 2023-2024). 1ST COMMITTEE—GENERAL DEBATE (Agenda item 8)
A/C.1/78/PV.2
UN. SECURITY COUNCIL—MEMBERSHIP (Agenda item 121)
A/78/PV.35
VETO (Agenda item 63)
A/78/PV.3; A/78/PV.68

Hwang, Joonkook (Republic of Korea) (UN. Security Council. President)

UN. SECURITY COUNCIL—REPORTS (Agenda item 26)
A/78/PV.93

Hwang, Won (Republic of Korea)

PEACEKEEPING OPERATIONS (Agenda item 51)
A/C.4/78/SR.20

Hyvärinen, Outi (Finland)

UN. GENERAL ASSEMBLY (78TH SESS. : 2023-2024). 1ST COMMITTEE—GENERAL DEBATE (Agenda item 8)
A/C.1/78/PV.4

Ibrahim, Ahmed Saeed (Eritrea)

LANDLOCKED DEVELOPING COUNTRIES—CONFERENCES (Agenda item 20b)
A/C.2/78/SR.7
LEAST DEVELOPED COUNTRIES—CONFERENCES (Agenda item 20a)
A/C.2/78/SR.7
SUSTAINABLE DEVELOPMENT (Agenda item 18)
A/C.2/78/SR.15

Ibrahim, Anwar (Malaysia. Prime Minister)

UN. GENERAL ASSEMBLY (78TH SESS. : 2023-2024)—GENERAL DEBATE (Agenda item 8)
A/78/PV.10
UN. GENERAL ASSEMBLY (78TH SESS. : 2023-2024)—SPECIAL STATEMENTS
A/78/PV.10

Idres, Nusaiba Hashim Mohamed Ali (Sudan)

ELECTION VERIFICATION—UN (Agenda item 71b)
A/C.3/78/SR.50
HUMAN RIGHTS—INTERNATIONAL INSTRUMENTS (Agenda item 71a)
A/C.3/78/SR.26
HUMAN RIGHTS—TERRITORIES OCCUPIED BY ISRAEL (Agenda item 71c)
A/C.3/78/SR.35

Idres, Nusaiba Hashim Mohamed Ali (Sudan) (continued)

RACIAL DISCRIMINATION—ELIMINATION (Agenda item 69a)
A/C.3/78/SR.47
UN. COMMITTEE ON RELATIONS WITH THE HOST COUNTRY—REPORTS (Agenda item 161)
A/C.6/78/SR.35
UN. HUMAN RIGHTS COUNCIL—REPORTS (Agenda item 66)
A/C.3/78/SR.51
UN HIGH COMMISSIONER FOR REFUGEES—REPORTS (Agenda item 60)
A/C.3/78/SR.44

Iileka, Nekwayahelalia (Namibia)

HUMAN RIGHTS—TERRITORIES OCCUPIED BY ISRAEL (Agenda item 71c)
A/C.3/78/SR.35
RIGHTS OF THE CHILD (Agenda item 67)
A/C.3/78/SR.13

Ijaz, Rabia (Pakistan)

CRIMES AGAINST HUMANITY (Agenda item 80)
A/C.6/78/SR.10; A/C.6/78/SR.11
DISASTER VICTIMS (Agenda item 86)
A/C.6/78/SR.6
PEACEKEEPING OPERATIONS—CRIMINAL LIABILITY (Agenda item 76)
A/C.6/78/SR.8
RACIAL DISCRIMINATION—ELIMINATION (Agenda item 69a)
A/C.3/78/SR.41
RACIAL DISCRIMINATION—PROGRAMMES OF ACTION (Agenda item 69b)
A/C.3/78/SR.41
RELIGIOUS INTOLERANCE (Agenda item 71b)
A/C.3/78/SR.38
RESPONSIBILITY TO PROTECT (Agenda item 129)
A/78/PV.97
RIGHTS OF THE CHILD (Agenda item 67)
A/C.3/78/SR.11
UN CHARTER—REPORTS (Agenda item 82)
A/C.6/78/SR.22

Ikondere, Marvin (Uganda)

CRIMES AGAINST HUMANITY (Agenda item 80)
A/C.6/78/SR.47
INTERNATIONAL JURISDICTION (Agenda item 84)
A/C.6/78/SR.12
INTERNATIONAL LAW—TRAINING PROGRAMMES (Agenda item 78)
A/C.6/78/SR.22
TERRORISM (Agenda item 109)
A/C.6/78/SR.4
UN. INTERNATIONAL LAW COMMISSION—REPORTS (Agenda item 79)
A/C.6/78/SR.27; A/C.6/78/SR.32

Ikondere, Marvin (Uganda) (continued)

UN COMMISSION ON INTERNATIONAL TRADE LAW—REPORTS (Agenda item 77)
A/C.6/78/SR.14

Ikondere, Marvin (Uganda) (Group of 77)

MARINE ECOSYSTEMS—BIOLOGICAL DIVERSITY (Agenda item 75c)
A/78/PV.73

Ikondere, Marvin (Uganda) (UN. Group of African States)

ADMINISTRATION OF JUSTICE (Agenda item 144)
A/C.6/78/SR.9
DISASTER VICTIMS (Agenda item 86)
A/C.6/78/SR.5
INTERNATIONAL JURISDICTION (Agenda item 84)
A/C.6/78/SR.12
INTERNATIONAL LAW—TRAINING PROGRAMMES (Agenda item 78)
A/C.6/78/SR.21
PEACEKEEPING OPERATIONS—CRIMINAL LIABILITY (Agenda item 76)
A/C.6/78/SR.8
RULE OF LAW (Agenda item 83)
A/C.6/78/SR.16
TERRORISM (Agenda item 109)
A/C.6/78/SR.1
UN CHARTER—REPORTS (Agenda item 82)
A/C.6/78/SR.22

Ilgis, Olegs (Latvia)

AFRICA—DEVELOPMENT (Agenda item 65b)
A/78/PV.18
AFRICA—SUSTAINABLE DEVELOPMENT—PARTNERSHIP (Agenda item 65a)
A/78/PV.18
CRIME PREVENTION (Agenda item 107)
A/C.3/78/SR.51
RULE OF LAW (Agenda item 83)
A/C.6/78/SR.15

Ilichev, Petr (Russian Federation)

DECOLONIZATION (Agenda item 58)
A/C.4/78/SR.2
FALKLAND ISLANDS (MALVINAS) QUESTION (Agenda item 42)
A/C.4/78/SR.2

Imanuel, Fnu (Indonesia)

AGEING PERSONS (Agenda item 24b)
A/C.3/78/SR.1
HEALTH (Agenda item 125)
A/78/PV.102
HUMAN RIGHTS ACTIVISTS (Agenda item 71b)
A/C.3/78/SR.56

Imanuel, Fnu (Indonesia) (continued)

PERSONS WITH DISABILITIES (Agenda item 24b)
A/C.3/78/SR.3
PERSONS WITH DISABILITIES—HUMAN RIGHTS (Agenda item 71a)
A/C.3/78/SR.51
RIGHT TO DEVELOPMENT (Agenda item 71b)
A/C.3/78/SR.20
RIGHTS OF THE CHILD (Agenda item 67)
A/C.3/78/SR.55
RURAL WOMEN (Agenda item 25a)
A/C.3/78/SR.49
SOCIAL CONDITIONS (Agenda item 24b)
A/C.3/78/SR.3; A/C.3/78/SR.51
SOCIAL DEVELOPMENT (Agenda item 24)
A/C.3/78/SR.3
SUSTAINABLE DEVELOPMENT (Agenda item 18)
A/C.2/78/SR.24
TAXATION (Agenda item 16h)
A/C.2/78/SR.25
YOUTH (Agenda item 24b)
A/C.3/78/SR.55

Imohe, Uhimwen Robert (Nigeria) (UN. Group of African States)

ECONOMIC SANCTIONS—INTERNATIONAL RELATIONS (Agenda item 28)
A/78/PV.89

Indu, Fiona (Solomon Islands)

CUBA—UNITED STATES (Agenda item 38)
A/78/PV.26

Iohannis, Klaus Werner (Romania. President)

UN. GENERAL ASSEMBLY (78TH SESS. : 2023-2024)—GENERAL DEBATE (Agenda item 8)
A/78/PV.6
UN. GENERAL ASSEMBLY (78TH SESS. : 2023-2024)—SPECIAL STATEMENTS
A/78/PV.6

Ipo, Gbolié Desiré Wulfran (Côte d'Ivoire)

DEVELOPMENT FINANCE (Agenda item 16b)
A/C.2/78/SR.9
INFORMATION (Agenda item 53)
A/C.4/78/SR.13
MACROECONOMIC POLICY (Agenda item 16)
A/C.2/78/SR.9

Iraqui, Abla (Morocco)

WOMEN'S ADVANCEMENT (Agenda item 25a)
A/C.3/78/SR.9
WOMEN'S ADVANCEMENT—CONFERENCES (Agenda item 25b)
A/C.3/78/SR.9

Irawati Mamesah, Febrian (Indonesia)

DEVELOPMENT FINANCE—CONFERENCES (Agenda item 17)
A/78/PV.90
ECONOMIC SANCTIONS—INTERNATIONAL RELATIONS (Agenda item 28)
A/78/PV.90

Iriya, Takayuki (Japan)

HEALTH (Agenda item 125)
A/78/PV.77

Isabirye, Haruna Bazirondere (Uganda)

UN. GENERAL ASSEMBLY (78TH SESS. : 2023-2024). 1ST COMMITTEE—GENERAL DEBATE (Agenda item 8)
A/C.1/78/PV.6

Ishikane, Kimihiro (Japan)

IAEA—REPORTS (Agenda item 89)
A/78/PV.29
SPORTS—OLYMPIC GAMES (Agenda item 11)
A/78/PV.38
UN—BUDGET (2024) (Agenda item 134)
A/C.5/78/SR.5
UN—PROGRAMME PLANNING (Agenda item 135)
A/C.5/78/SR.5
UN. SECURITY COUNCIL—MEMBERSHIP (Agenda item 121)
A/78/PV.35
VETO (Agenda item 63)
A/78/PV.3

Islamuly, Amirbek (Kazakhstan)

HUMAN RIGHTS—INTERNATIONAL INSTRUMENTS (Agenda item 71a)
A/C.3/78/SR.25
HUMAN RIGHTS—IRAN (ISLAMIC REPUBLIC OF) (Agenda item 71c)
A/C.3/78/SR.53
HUMAN RIGHTS ADVANCEMENT (Agenda item 71b)
A/C.3/78/SR.25

Israel Herrera, José (Universidad Autónoma de Campeche (Mexico))

WESTERN SAHARA QUESTION (Agenda item 58)
A/C.4/78/SR.5

İstemil Aydil, Alara (Türkiye)

CLIMATE (Agenda item 18d)
A/C.2/78/SR.15
COASTAL ZONE MANAGEMENT (Agenda item 18j)
A/78/PV.49
DEVELOPMENT FINANCE—CONFERENCES (Agenda item 17)
A/78/PV.90
SMALL ISLAND DEVELOPING STATES—PROGRAMMES OF ACTION (Agenda item 18b)
A/C.2/78/SR.15

İstemil Aydil, Alara (Türkiye) (continued)

STORMS (Agenda item 18i)
A/C.2/78/SR.15
SUSTAINABLE DEVELOPMENT (Agenda item 18)
A/C.2/78/SR.15; A/C.2/78/SR.22
SUSTAINABLE ENERGY (Agenda item 18h)
A/C.2/78/SR.15
UN. GENERAL ASSEMBLY (78TH SESS. : 2023-2024). 2ND COMMITTEE—GENERAL DEBATE (Agenda item 8)
A/C.2/78/SR.6
UN SYSTEM—STRENGTHENING (Agenda item 122)
A/78/PV.99

Ivanyi, Balint (Hungary)

CRIME PREVENTION (Agenda item 107)
A/C.3/78/SR.51
EMERGENCY ASSISTANCE (Agenda item 72a)
A/78/PV.47
UN HIGH COMMISSIONER FOR REFUGEES—REPORTS (Agenda item 60)
A/C.3/78/SR.51; A/C.3/78/SR.54

Jabbour, Suzanne (UN. Subcommittee on Prevention of Torture and Other Cruel, Inhuman or Degrading Treatment or Punishment. Chair)

TORTURE AND OTHER CRUEL TREATMENT (Agenda item 71a)
A/C.3/78/SR.18

Jackman, François (Barbados)

CUBA—UNITED STATES (Agenda item 38)
A/78/PV.26

Jacobs, Mats (Netherlands (Kingdom of the))

INTERNATIONAL JURISDICTION (Agenda item 84)
A/C.6/78/SR.12

Jadoon, Usman Iqbal (Pakistan)

CUBA—UNITED STATES (Agenda item 38)
A/78/PV.26
EMERGENCY ASSISTANCE (Agenda item 72a)
A/78/PV.46
FISSIONABLE MATERIALS—TREATIES (Agenda item 99a)
A/C.1/78/PV.12
HEALTH (Agenda item 125)
A/78/PV.41
INFORMATION (Agenda item 53)
A/C.4/78/SR.12
INTERNATIONAL JURISDICTION (Agenda item 84)
A/C.6/78/SR.12
LAW OF THE SEA (Agenda item 75a)
A/78/PV.44
MARINE ECOSYSTEMS—BIOLOGICAL DIVERSITY (Agenda item 75c)
A/78/PV.44

Jadoon, Usman Iqbal (Pakistan) (continued)

NON-NUCLEAR-WEAPON STATES—SECURITY (Agenda item 96)
A/C.1/78/PV.12
NUCLEAR DISARMAMENT (Agenda item 99b)
A/C.1/78/PV.12
PALESTINE QUESTION (Agenda item 35)
A/78/PV.39
PALESTINIANS—ASSISTANCE (Agenda item 72b)
A/78/PV.46
RIGHT TO DEVELOPMENT (Agenda item 71b)
A/C.3/78/SR.20
STRADDLING FISH STOCKS (Agenda item 75b)
A/78/PV.44
TERRITORIES OCCUPIED BY ISRAEL—NATURAL RESOURCES (Agenda item 59)
A/C.2/78/SR.19; A/C.2/78/SR.21
UN. SECURITY COUNCIL—MEMBERSHIP (Agenda item 121)
A/78/PV.104
UN HIGH COMMISSIONER FOR REFUGEES—REPORTS (Agenda item 60)
A/C.3/78/SR.44
VETO (Agenda item 63)
A/78/PV.51

Jaishankar, Subrahmanyam (India)

UN. GENERAL ASSEMBLY (78TH SESS. : 2023-2024)—GENERAL DEBATE (Agenda item 8)
A/78/PV.14

Jaiteh, Amadou (Gambia)

CRIMES AGAINST HUMANITY (Agenda item 80)
A/C.6/78/SR.45; A/C.6/78/SR.47
RURAL WOMEN (Agenda item 25a)
A/C.3/78/SR.49
WOMEN MIGRANT WORKERS (Agenda item 25a)
A/C.3/78/SR.49

Jaiteh, Amadou (Gambia) (European Union)

CRIMES AGAINST HUMANITY (Agenda item 80)
A/C.6/78/SR.9

Jalil Iravani, Amir Saeid (Iran (Islamic Republic of))

DISARMAMENT—GENERAL AND COMPLETE (Agenda item 99)
A/78/PV.106
IAEA—REPORTS (Agenda item 89)
A/78/PV.29
PALESTINE QUESTION (Agenda item 35)
A/78/PV.40
PEACE (Agenda item 14)
A/78/PV.62; A/78/PV.82
RAISI, SEYYED EBRAHIM (IRAN (ISLAMIC REPUBLID OF). PRESIDENT)—TRIBUTES
A/78/PV.83
VETO (Agenda item 63)
A/78/PV.51; A/78/PV.59; A/78/PV.66; A/78/PV.74

Jalili, Tahereh (Iran (Islamic Republic of))

CLIMATE (Agenda item 18d)
A/C.2/78/SR.13
DESERTIFICATION—TREATIES (Agenda item 18e)
A/C.2/78/SR.13
DISASTER PREVENTION (Agenda item 18c)
A/C.2/78/SR.13
FOOD SECURITY (Agenda item 23a)
A/C.2/78/SR.16
INFORMATION TECHNOLOGY—DEVELOPMENT (Agenda item 15)
A/C.2/78/SR.10
POVERTY—INTERNATIONAL DECADES (Agenda item 21a)
A/C.2/78/SR.16
RURAL POVERTY (Agenda item 21b)
A/C.2/78/SR.16
SCIENCE AND TECHNOLOGY—DEVELOPMENT (Agenda item 19a)
A/C.2/78/SR.10
SUSTAINABLE DEVELOPMENT (Agenda item 18)
A/C.2/78/SR.13
TERRITORIES OCCUPIED BY ISRAEL—NATURAL RESOURCES (Agenda item 59)
A/C.2/78/SR.19

Jalloh, Charles (UN. International Law Commission. Special Rapporteur on Subsidiary Means for the Determination of Rules of International Law)

UN. INTERNATIONAL LAW COMMISSION—REPORTS (Agenda item 79)
A/C.6/78/SR.33

Jallow, Mohammed (Gambia. Vice-President)

UN. GENERAL ASSEMBLY (78TH SESS. : 2023-2024)—GENERAL DEBATE (Agenda item 8)
A/78/PV.9
UN. GENERAL ASSEMBLY (78TH SESS. : 2023-2024)—SPECIAL STATEMENTS
A/78/PV.9

Janah, Naushyn (New Zealand)

CRIMES AGAINST HUMANITY (Agenda item 80)
A/C.6/78/SR.39; A/C.6/78/SR.40; A/C.6/78/SR.42; A/C.6/78/SR.44
TREATIES (Agenda item 87)
A/C.6/78/SR.20
UN. INTERNATIONAL LAW COMMISSION—REPORTS (Agenda item 79)
A/C.6/78/SR.25

Janahi, Balqees (Bahrain)

INFORMATION—INTERNATIONAL SECURITY (Agenda item 94)
A/C.1/78/PV.21
MIDDLE EAST—NUCLEAR-WEAPON-FREE ZONES (Agenda item 95)
A/C.1/78/PV.14
NUCLEAR DISARMAMENT (Agenda item 99b)
A/C.1/78/PV.14

Janahi, Balqees (Bahrain) (continued)

NUCLEAR NON-PROLIFERATION—INTERNATIONAL OBLIGATIONS (Agenda item 99w)
A/C.1/78/PV.14

Janeczko, Frazer (United Kingdom)

UN. INTERNATIONAL LAW COMMISSION—REPORTS (Agenda item 79)
A/C.6/78/SR.29; A/C.6/78/SR.31

Janfalk, Disa (Sweden)

CRIMES AGAINST HUMANITY (Agenda item 80)
A/C.6/78/SR.38

Janina, Suela (Albania)

RESPONSIBILITY TO PROTECT (Agenda item 129)
A/78/PV.96
VETO (Agenda item 63)
A/78/PV.69; A/78/PV.79

Jantarasombat, Panpailin (Thailand)

CRIMES AGAINST HUMANITY (Agenda item 80)
A/C.6/78/SR.42; A/C.6/78/SR.43
UN. INTERNATIONAL LAW COMMISSION—REPORTS (Agenda item 79)
A/C.6/78/SR.30; A/C.6/78/SR.31

Jaraud-Darnault, Isis Marie Doriane (France)

VETO (Agenda item 63)
A/78/PV.66

Jardali, Mohammad Ali (Lebanon)

PEACEKEEPING OPERATIONS (Agenda item 51)
A/C.4/78/SR.20
TERRITORIES OCCUPIED BY ISRAEL—HUMAN RIGHTS (Agenda item 50)
A/C.4/78/SR.25
UNRWA—ACTIVITIES (Agenda item 49)
A/C.4/78/SR.22; A/C.4/78/SR.23

Jasim, Saber Ahmed (Iraq)

CLIMATE (Agenda item 18d)
A/C.2/78/SR.13
DESERTIFICATION—TREATIES (Agenda item 18e)
A/C.2/78/SR.13
STORMS (Agenda item 18i)
A/C.2/78/SR.13
SUSTAINABLE ENERGY (Agenda item 18h)
A/C.2/78/SR.13

Javaid, Hafiza Humaira (Pakistan)

FOOD SECURITY (Agenda item 23a)
A/C.2/78/SR.17
POVERTY—INTERNATIONAL DECADES (Agenda item 21a)
A/C.2/78/SR.17

Javaid, Hafiza Humaira (Pakistan) (continued)

RURAL POVERTY (Agenda item 21b)
A/C.2/78/SR.17
SUSTAINABLE DEVELOPMENT (Agenda item 18)
A/C.2/78/SR.13

Jenca, Miroslav (UN. Assistant Secretary-General for Europe, Central Asia and the Americas)

SPECIAL POLITICAL MISSIONS (Agenda item 52)
A/C.4/78/SR.21

Jenkins, Bonnie D. (United States)

UN. GENERAL ASSEMBLY (78TH SESS. : 2023-2024). 1ST COMMITTEE—GENERAL DEBATE (Agenda item 8)
A/C.1/78/PV.2

Jensen, Jørgen Reymert (Norway)

SOCIAL CONDITIONS (Agenda item 24b)
A/C.3/78/SR.2

Jeranukosol, Natsaran (Thailand)

MINE CLEARANCE (Agenda item 46)
A/C.4/78/SR.10

Jerboui, Hind (Morocco)

TERRITORIES OCCUPIED BY ISRAEL—HUMAN RIGHTS (Agenda item 50)
A/C.4/78/SR.25
UNRWA—ACTIVITIES (Agenda item 49)
A/C.4/78/SR.23

Jerboui, Hind (Morocco) (UN. Committee for Programme and Coordination. Vice-Chair)

UN—PROGRAMME PLANNING (Agenda item 135)
A/C.5/78/SR.5

Jerman, Bostjan (Slovenia)

NUCLEAR DISARMAMENT (Agenda item 99b)
A/C.1/78/PV.14
NUCLEAR DISARMAMENT—VERIFICATION (Agenda item 99ee)
A/C.1/78/PV.14
NUCLEAR NON-PROLIFERATION—INTERNATIONAL OBLIGATIONS (Agenda item 99w)
A/C.1/78/PV.14
NUCLEAR WEAPON TESTS—TREATIES (Agenda item 105)
A/C.1/78/PV.14
UN. CONFERENCE ON DISARMAMENT—REPORTS (Agenda item 101a)
A/C.1/78/PV.23

Jesudason, Joshua E. (Singapore)

CRIME PREVENTION (Agenda item 107)
A/C.3/78/SR.5
CYBERCRIME (Agenda item 108)
A/C.3/78/SR.5

Jiamin, Liu (Singapore)

CLUSTER MUNITIONS (Agenda item 99dd)
A/C.1/78/PV.28
CONVENTIONAL WEAPONS (Agenda item 99u)
A/C.1/78/PV.18
CONVENTIONAL WEAPONS—TREATIES (Agenda item 103)
A/C.1/78/PV.18
LANDMINES—TREATIES (Agenda item 99m)
A/C.1/78/PV.18; A/C.1/78/PV.28
SMALL ARMS—ILLICIT TRAFFIC (Agenda item 99p)
A/C.1/78/PV.18
SMALL ARMS—ILLICIT TRAFFIC—ASSISTANCE (Agenda item 99n)
A/C.1/78/PV.18

Jiang, Hua (China)

MULTILINGUALISM (Agenda item 124)
A/78/PV.108
UN—BUDGET (2024) (Agenda item 134)
A/C.5/78/SR.5; A/C.5/78/SR.33; A/C.5/78/SR.34
UN—PROGRAMME PLANNING (Agenda item 135)
A/C.5/78/SR.5
UN. GENERAL ASSEMBLY (78TH SESS. : 2023-2024). 5TH COMMITTEE—WORK ORGANIZATION (Agenda item 7)
A/C.5/78/SR.26/PartII; A/C.5/78/SR.27; A/C.5/78/SR.34

Jievaltas, Arūnas (Lithuania)

UN. GENERAL ASSEMBLY (78TH SESS. : 2023-2024). 1ST COMMITTEE—GENERAL DEBATE (Agenda item 8)
A/C.1/78/PV.5

Jiménez, Jasser (Nicaragua)

CHEMICAL WEAPONS—TREATIES (Agenda item 99l)
A/C.1/78/PV.26
CLIMATE (Agenda item 18d)
A/C.2/78/SR.13
DISPLACED PERSONS (Agenda item 71b)
A/C.3/78/SR.49
HEALTH (Agenda item 125)
A/78/PV.16
INFORMATION—INTERNATIONAL SECURITY (Agenda item 94)
A/C.1/78/PV.29
MILLENNIUM SUMMIT—CONFERENCES (Agenda item 117)
A/78/PV.15
RURAL WOMEN (Agenda item 25a)
A/C.3/78/SR.49
SUSTAINABLE DEVELOPMENT (Agenda item 18)
A/C.2/78/SR.13
UN. GENERAL ASSEMBLY (78TH SESS. : 2023-2024). 1ST COMMITTEE—GENERAL DEBATE (Agenda item 8)
A/C.1/78/PV.8

Jiménez, Jasser (Nicaragua) (continued)

UN. GENERAL ASSEMBLY (78TH SESS. : 2023-2024). 2ND COMMITTEE—GENERAL DEBATE (Agenda item 8)
A/C.2/78/SR.4
UN. HUMAN RIGHTS COUNCIL—REPORTS (Agenda item 66)
A/78/PV.23
UN CONFERENCES (Agenda item 13)
A/78/PV.15

Jiménez Alegría, Natalia (Mexico)

ADMINISTRATION OF JUSTICE (Agenda item 144)
A/C.6/78/SR.9
CRIMES AGAINST HUMANITY (Agenda item 80)
A/C.6/78/SR.38; A/C.6/78/SR.40; A/C.6/78/SR.47
DISASTER VICTIMS (Agenda item 86)
A/C.6/78/SR.6
NON-CITIZENS—DEPORTATION (Agenda item 81)
A/C.6/78/SR.34
PEACEKEEPING OPERATIONS—CRIMINAL LIABILITY (Agenda item 76)
A/C.6/78/SR.8
RULE OF LAW (Agenda item 83)
A/C.6/78/SR.18
TERRORISM (Agenda item 109)
A/C.6/78/SR.1
UN. INTERNATIONAL LAW COMMISSION—REPORTS (Agenda item 79)
A/78/PV.45; A/C.6/78/SR.32
VETO (Agenda item 63)
A/78/PV.52

Jiménez Alegría, Natalia (Mexico) (UN. General Assembly. 6th Committee. Bureau)

RULE OF LAW (Agenda item 83)
A/C.6/78/SR.37

Jiménez de la Hoz, Ana (Spain)

CRIMES AGAINST HUMANITY (Agenda item 80)
A/C.6/78/SR.45
DEVELOPMENT FINANCE—CONFERENCES (Agenda item 17)
A/C.2/78/SR.25
GIBRALTAR QUESTION (Agenda item 58)
A/C.4/78/SR.2
SOCIAL CONDITIONS (Agenda item 24b)
A/C.3/78/SR.51
UN. GENERAL ASSEMBLY (78TH SESS. : 2023-2024). 1ST COMMITTEE—GENERAL DEBATE (Agenda item 8)
A/C.1/78/PV.8
UN. GENERAL ASSEMBLY (78TH SESS. : 2023-2024). 2ND COMMITTEE—GENERAL DEBATE (Agenda item 8)
A/C.2/78/SR.5
UN. SECURITY COUNCIL—MEMBERSHIP (Agenda item 121)
A/78/PV.36

Jiménez de la Hoz, Ana (Spain) (continued)

VETO (Agenda item 63)
A/78/PV.52; A/78/PV.71

Jiménez de la Hoz, Ana (Spain) (European Union)

CUBA—UNITED STATES (Agenda item 38)
A/78/PV.26
ELECTION VERIFICATION—UN (Agenda item 71b)
A/C.3/78/SR.50
EMERGENCY ASSISTANCE (Agenda item 72a)
A/78/PV.46; A/78/PV.47
HEALTH (Agenda item 125)
A/78/PV.16
MIDDLE EAST SITUATION (Agenda item 34)
A/78/PV.40
MILLENNIUM SUMMIT—CONFERENCES (Agenda item 117)
A/78/PV.15
RELIGIOUS INTOLERANCE (Agenda item 71b)
A/C.3/78/SR.52
UN—BUDGET (2024) (Agenda item 134)
A/C.5/78/SR.26/PartII
UN CONFERENCES (Agenda item 13)
A/78/PV.15

Jiménez Martín, María Inés ((personal capacity))

WESTERN SAHARA QUESTION (Agenda item 58)
A/C.4/78/SR.4

Jo, Tong Hyon (Democratic People's Republic of Korea)

FOOD SECURITY (Agenda item 23a)
A/C.2/78/SR.16
POVERTY—INTERNATIONAL DECADES (Agenda item 21a)
A/C.2/78/SR.16
RURAL POVERTY (Agenda item 21b)
A/C.2/78/SR.16
SUSTAINABLE DEVELOPMENT (Agenda item 18)
A/C.2/78/SR.13

Johnson, Laura (UN Staff Union)

UN—HUMAN RESOURCES MANAGEMENT (Agenda item 139)
A/C.5/78/SR.27

Johnson, Timothy J. (United States)

CRIME PREVENTION (Agenda item 107)
A/C.3/78/SR.56
DISAPPEARANCE OF PERSONS (Agenda item 71b)
A/C.3/78/SR.50
HUMAN RIGHTS—AFGHANISTAN (Agenda item 71c)
A/C.3/78/SR.34
MIGRANTS—PROTECTION (Agenda item 71b)
A/C.3/78/SR.56

Johnson, Timothy J. (United States) (continued)

RACIAL DISCRIMINATION—ELIMINATION (Agenda item 69a)
A/C.3/78/SR.41
RACIAL DISCRIMINATION—PROGRAMMES OF ACTION (Agenda item 69b)
A/C.3/78/SR.41; A/C.3/78/SR.56
RIGHT TO DRINKING WATER (Agenda item 71b)
A/C.3/78/SR.50
SELF-DETERMINATION OF PEOPLES (Agenda item 70)
A/C.3/78/SR.56
TERRORISM—HUMAN RIGHTS (Agenda item 71b)
A/C.3/78/SR.51
UN. HUMAN RIGHTS COUNCIL—REPORTS (Agenda item 66)
A/C.3/78/SR.46; A/C.3/78/SR.51

Johnson Smith, Kamina (Jamaica)

UN. GENERAL ASSEMBLY (78TH SESS. : 2023-2024)—GENERAL DEBATE (Agenda item 8)
A/78/PV.14

Jones, Alexandra (Australia)

UN—ADMINISTRATION (Agenda item 132)
A/C.5/78/SR.26/PartII
UN—BUDGET (2024) (Agenda item 134)
A/C.5/78/SR.26/PartII
UN. GENERAL ASSEMBLY (78TH SESS. : 2023-2024). 5TH COMMITTEE—WORK ORGANIZATION (Agenda item 7)
A/C.5/78/SR.27

Jones, Katherine Sarah (United Kingdom)

IAEA—REPORTS (Agenda item 89)
A/78/PV.30

Joniec, Katarzyna (Poland)

CONVENTIONAL ARMS—REGIONAL PROGRAMMES (Agenda item 99g)
A/C.1/78/PV.29
DISARMAMENT—GENERAL AND COMPLETE (Agenda item 99)
A/C.1/78/PV.28

Jordan, Rudolph (Association de foot ball Otemanu, Bora Bora)

FRENCH POLYNESIA QUESTION (Agenda item 58)
A/C.4/78/SR.3

Jørgensen, Dan (Denmark)

UN. GENERAL ASSEMBLY (78TH SESS. : 2023-2024)—GENERAL DEBATE (Agenda item 8)
A/78/PV.9

Joubin-Bret, Anna (UN Commission on International Trade Law. Secretary)

UN COMMISSION ON INTERNATIONAL TRADE LAW—REPORTS (Agenda item 77)
A/C.6/78/SR.13

Jovanovic, Nikola (Italy)

VETO (Agenda item 63)
A/78/PV.78

Joyini, Mathu (South Africa)

AFRICA—DEVELOPMENT (Agenda item 65b)
A/78/PV.18
AFRICA—SUSTAINABLE DEVELOPMENT—PARTNERSHIP (Agenda item 65a)
A/78/PV.18
CRIMES AGAINST HUMANITY (Agenda item 80)
A/C.6/78/SR.10
CUBA—UNITED STATES (Agenda item 38)
A/78/PV.24
HUMAN RIGHTS—INTERNATIONAL INSTRUMENTS (Agenda item 71a)
A/C.3/78/SR.24
HUMAN RIGHTS—PROGRAMMES OF ACTION (Agenda item 71d)
A/C.3/78/SR.24
IAEA—REPORTS (Agenda item 89)
A/78/PV.29
MILLENNIUM SUMMIT—CONFERENCES (Agenda item 117)
A/78/PV.15
PALESTINE QUESTION (Agenda item 35)
A/78/PV.39
RACIAL DISCRIMINATION—ELIMINATION (Agenda item 69a)
A/C.3/78/SR.40
RACIAL DISCRIMINATION—PROGRAMMES OF ACTION (Agenda item 69b)
A/C.3/78/SR.40
TAXATION (Agenda item 16h)
A/C.2/78/SR.25
UN—BUDGET (2024) (Agenda item 134)
A/C.5/78/SR.5
UN—PROGRAMME PLANNING (Agenda item 135)
A/C.5/78/SR.5
UN. GENERAL ASSEMBLY (78TH SESS. : 2023-2024). 1ST COMMITTEE—GENERAL DEBATE (Agenda item 8)
A/C.1/78/PV.2
UN. SECURITY COUNCIL—REPORTS (Agenda item 26)
A/78/PV.93
UN CONFERENCES (Agenda item 13)
A/78/PV.15
VETO (Agenda item 63)
A/78/PV.60; A/78/PV.67

Joyini, Mathu (South Africa) (UN. General Assembly. Special Political and Decolonization Committee (4th Committee). Chair)

OUTER SPACE—PEACEFUL USES—INTERNATIONAL COOPERATION (Agenda item 48)
A/C.4/78/SR.15
UN. GENERAL ASSEMBLY (78TH SESS. : 2023-2024). 4TH COMMITTEE—WORK ORGANIZATION (Agenda item 7)
A/C.4/78/SR.1
UNRWA—ACTIVITIES (Agenda item 49)
A/C.4/78/SR.22

Jugnauth, Pravind Kumar (Mauritius. Prime Minister)

UN. GENERAL ASSEMBLY (78TH SESS. : 2023-2024)—GENERAL DEBATE (Agenda item 8)
A/78/PV.10
UN. GENERAL ASSEMBLY (78TH SESS. : 2023-2024)—SPECIAL STATEMENTS
A/78/PV.10

Jung, Jae Hyuk (Republic of Korea)

INFORMATION (Agenda item 53)
A/C.4/78/SR.12; A/C.4/78/SR.13

Juntree, Paranut (Thailand)

YOUTH (Agenda item 24b)
A/C.3/78/SR.2

Jurecko, Sasa (Slovenia)

RESPONSIBILITY TO PROTECT (Agenda item 129)
A/78/PV.97
VETO (Agenda item 63)
A/78/PV.70; A/78/PV.79

K.P., Ashwini (UN. Human Rights Council. Special Rapporteur on Contemporary Forms of Racism, Racial Discrimination, Xenophobia and Related Intolerance)

RACIAL DISCRIMINATION—ELIMINATION (Agenda item 69a)
A/C.3/78/SR.41

Kabua, Amatlain Elizabeth (Marshall Islands)

CLIMATE CHANGE (Agenda item 71b)
A/C.3/78/SR.29
DISARMAMENT—GENERAL AND COMPLETE (Agenda item 99)
A/C.1/78/PV.26
HUMAN RIGHTS—DEMOCRATIC PEOPLE'S REPUBLIC OF KOREA (Agenda item 71c)
A/C.3/78/SR.33
HUMAN RIGHTS—MYANMAR (Agenda item 71c)
A/C.3/78/SR.33

Kabua, David (Marshall Islands. President)

UN. GENERAL ASSEMBLY (78TH SESS. : 2023-2024)—GENERAL DEBATE (Agenda item 8)
A/78/PV.7
UN. GENERAL ASSEMBLY (78TH SESS. : 2023-2024)—SPECIAL STATEMENTS
A/78/PV.7

Kadiri, Omar (Morocco)

EMERGENCY ASSISTANCE (Agenda item 72a)
A/78/PV.47
HUMAN RIGHTS—CENTRAL AFRICAN REPUBLIC (Agenda item 71c)
A/C.3/78/SR.33
IAEA—REPORTS (Agenda item 89)
A/78/PV.29
PALESTINE QUESTION (Agenda item 35)
A/78/PV.39
PALESTINIANS—ASSISTANCE (Agenda item 72b)
A/78/PV.47
UN. HUMAN RIGHTS COUNCIL—REPORTS (Agenda item 66)
A/78/PV.28
UN. SECURITY COUNCIL—MEMBERSHIP (Agenda item 121)
A/78/PV.34
VETO (Agenda item 63)
A/78/PV.69
WESTERN SAHARA QUESTION (Agenda item 58)
A/C.4/78/SR.4; A/C.4/78/SR.5

Kadri, Taha (Morocco)

PEACE (Agenda item 14)
A/78/PV.76
VETO (Agenda item 63)
A/78/PV.75

Kadyautumbe, Darlington Mashoko (Zimbabwe)

UN. SECURITY COUNCIL—MEMBERSHIP (Agenda item 121)
A/78/PV.35

Kaeval, Kristel (Estonia)

UN. INTERNATIONAL LAW COMMISSION—REPORTS (Agenda item 79)
A/C.6/78/SR.29; A/C.6/78/SR.33

Kafková, Eva Anna (Czechia)

INTERNATIONAL CRIMINAL COURT—REPORTS (Agenda item 74)
A/78/PV.22

Kagame, Paul (Rwanda. President)

UN. GENERAL ASSEMBLY (78TH SESS. : 2023-2024)—GENERAL DEBATE (Agenda item 8)
A/78/PV.6
UN. GENERAL ASSEMBLY (78TH SESS. : 2023-2024)—SPECIAL STATEMENTS
A/78/PV.6

Kaiser, Annette Karoline (Germany) (European Union)

DEVELOPMENT FINANCE—CONFERENCES (Agenda item 17)
A/78/PV.90

Kakar, Anwaar-ul-Haq (Pakistan. Prime Minister)

UN. GENERAL ASSEMBLY (78TH SESS. : 2023-2024)—GENERAL DEBATE (Agenda item 8)
A/78/PV.10
UN. GENERAL ASSEMBLY (78TH SESS. : 2023-2024)—SPECIAL STATEMENTS
A/78/PV.10

Kakubo, Stanley (Zambia)

UN. GENERAL ASSEMBLY (78TH SESS. : 2023-2024)—GENERAL DEBATE (Agenda item 8)
A/78/PV.14

Kalkku, Elina (Finland)

HUMAN RIGHTS—UKRAINE (Agenda item 71c)
A/C.3/78/SR.37
INTERNATIONAL CRIMINAL COURT—REPORTS (Agenda item 74)
A/78/PV.21
PERSONS WITH DISABILITIES—HUMAN RIGHTS (Agenda item 71a)
A/C.3/78/SR.38
VETO (Agenda item 63)
A/78/PV.68

Kallis Baldrich, Guillem (Andorra)

UN. GENERAL ASSEMBLY (78TH SESS. : 2023-2024). 2ND COMMITTEE—GENERAL DEBATE (Agenda item 8)
A/C.2/78/SR.4

Kalmar, Nimrod (Israel)

ARMS RACE—OUTER SPACE (Agenda item 97a)
A/C.1/78/PV.17
IAEA—REPORTS (Agenda item 89)
A/78/PV.30
ORGANIZATION FOR DEMOCRACY AND ECONOMIC DEVELOPMENT - GUAM (Agenda item 32)
A/78/PV.85

Kamanda, George Shadrack (Sierra Leone)

CRIMES AGAINST HUMANITY (Agenda item 80)
A/C.6/78/SR.44; A/C.6/78/SR.45

Kamara, Abass Salieu (Sierra Leone)

CRIMES AGAINST HUMANITY (Agenda item 80)
A/C.6/78/SR.38; A/C.6/78/SR.41; A/C.6/78/SR.42

Kamboj, Ruchira (India)

BIOLOGICAL WEAPONS—TREATIES (Agenda item 106)
A/C.1/78/PV.15

Kamboj, Ruchira (India) (continued)

CHEMICAL WEAPONS—TREATIES (Agenda item 99l)
A/C.1/78/PV.15
PALESTINE QUESTION (Agenda item 35)
A/78/PV.39
PEACE (Agenda item 14)
A/78/PV.62; A/78/PV.76
SOCIAL CONDITIONS (Agenda item 24b)
A/78/PV.57
UKRAINE—POLITICAL CONDITIONS (Agenda item 62)
A/78/PV.57
UN. SECURITY COUNCIL—MEMBERSHIP (Agenda item 121)
A/78/PV.35
VETO (Agenda item 63)
A/78/PV.52; A/78/PV.59; A/78/PV.67; A/78/PV.70; A/78/PV.74
WEAPONS OF MASS DESTRUCTION—TERRORISM (Agenda item 99s)
A/C.1/78/PV.15

Kaminek, Jan (Czechia)

HUMAN RIGHTS—BELARUS (Agenda item 71c)
A/C.3/78/SR.37
HUMAN RIGHTS—DEMOCRATIC PEOPLE'S REPUBLIC OF KOREA (Agenda item 71c)
A/C.3/78/SR.33
HUMAN RIGHTS—MYANMAR (Agenda item 71c)
A/C.3/78/SR.33
HUMAN RIGHTS—RUSSIAN FEDERATION (Agenda item 71c)
A/C.3/78/SR.37
HUMAN RIGHTS—UKRAINE (Agenda item 71c)
A/C.3/78/SR.37

Kamiya, Masako (Japan)

LEPROSY (Agenda item 71b)
A/C.3/78/SR.17
PERSONS WITH DISABILITIES (Agenda item 24b)
A/C.3/78/SR.3
RIGHTS OF THE CHILD (Agenda item 67)
A/C.3/78/SR.13
SOCIAL DEVELOPMENT (Agenda item 24)
A/C.3/78/SR.3
WOMEN'S ADVANCEMENT (Agenda item 25a)
A/C.3/78/SR.10
WOMEN'S ADVANCEMENT—CONFERENCES (Agenda item 25b)
A/C.3/78/SR.10

Kane, Imogen (Australia)

YOUTH (Agenda item 24b)
A/C.3/78/SR.3

Kanu, Michael Imran (Sierra Leone)

AFRICA—DEVELOPMENT (Agenda item 65b)
A/78/PV.18

Kanu, Michael Imran (Sierra Leone) (continued)

AFRICA—SUSTAINABLE DEVELOPMENT—PARTNERSHIP (Agenda item 65a)
A/78/PV.18
HUMAN RIGHTS ADVANCEMENT (Agenda item 71b)
A/C.3/78/SR.25
INTERNATIONAL JURISDICTION (Agenda item 84)
A/C.6/78/SR.13
PEACE (Agenda item 14)
A/78/PV.82
TERRORISM (Agenda item 109)
A/C.6/78/SR.3
UN. GENERAL ASSEMBLY (78TH SESS. : 2023-2024). 2ND COMMITTEE—GENERAL DEBATE (Agenda item 8)
A/C.2/78/SR.3
UNRWA—ACTIVITIES (Agenda item 49)
A/C.4/78/SR.23
VETO (Agenda item 63)
A/78/PV.3

Kanu, Michael Imran (Sierra Leone) (UN. Group of African States)

UN. INTERNATIONAL LAW COMMISSION—REPORTS (Agenda item 79)
A/C.6/78/SR.23

Kanwal, Tehreem (Pakistan)

HUMAN RIGHTS ACTIVISTS (Agenda item 71b)
A/C.3/78/SR.19
RIGHT OF ASSEMBLY (Agenda item 71b)
A/C.3/78/SR.19
TORTURE AND OTHER CRUEL TREATMENT (Agenda item 71a)
A/C.3/78/SR.18
WOMEN'S ADVANCEMENT (Agenda item 25a)
A/C.3/78/SR.7
WOMEN'S ADVANCEMENT—CONFERENCES (Agenda item 25b)
A/C.3/78/SR.7

Kapisyzi, Arb (Albania)

UN. GENERAL ASSEMBLY (78TH SESS. : 2023-2024). 2ND COMMITTEE—GENERAL DEBATE (Agenda item 8)
A/C.2/78/SR.5

Kara, Kamel (Algeria)

UN—BUDGET (2024) (Agenda item 134)
A/C.5/78/SR.5
UN—PROGRAMME PLANNING (Agenda item 135)
A/C.5/78/SR.5

Karatepe, Merve (Türkiye)

SMALL ISLAND DEVELOPING STATES—PROGRAMMES OF ACTION (Agenda item 18b)
A/78/PV.100

Karczmarz, Michał (European Union)

ARMS TRANSFERS—TREATIES (Agenda item 99x)
A/C.1/78/PV.18; A/C.1/78/PV.19
CONVENTIONAL WEAPONS—TREATIES (Agenda item 103)
A/C.1/78/PV.18
DISARMAMENT—GENERAL AND COMPLETE (Agenda item 99)
A/C.1/78/PV.18; A/C.1/78/PV.21
INFORMATION—INTERNATIONAL SECURITY (Agenda item 94)
A/C.1/78/PV.20
LANDMINES—TREATIES (Agenda item 99m)
A/C.1/78/PV.18
MULTILATERALISM—DISARMAMENT (Agenda item 99r)
A/C.1/78/PV.22
SMALL ARMS—ILLICIT TRAFFIC (Agenda item 99p)
A/C.1/78/PV.18
SMALL ARMS—ILLICIT TRAFFIC—ASSISTANCE (Agenda item 99n)
A/C.1/78/PV.18
UN. CONFERENCE ON DISARMAMENT—REPORTS (Agenda item 101a)
A/C.1/78/PV.22
UN. DISARMAMENT COMMISSION—REPORTS (Agenda item 101b)
A/C.1/78/PV.22

Kardash, Viktoriia E. (Russian Federation)

DEVELOPMENT FINANCE (Agenda item 16b)
A/C.2/78/SR.9
HEALTH (Agenda item 125)
A/78/PV.102
INTERNATIONAL TRADE (Agenda item 16a)
A/C.2/78/SR.9
LANDLOCKED DEVELOPING COUNTRIES—CONFERENCES (Agenda item 20b)
A/C.2/78/SR.7
LEAST DEVELOPED COUNTRIES—CONFERENCES (Agenda item 20a)
A/C.2/78/SR.7
MACROECONOMIC POLICY (Agenda item 16)
A/C.2/78/SR.25
MILLENNIUM SUMMIT—CONFERENCES (Agenda item 117)
A/78/PV.102
TAXATION (Agenda item 16h)
A/C.2/78/SR.9
UN CONFERENCES (Agenda item 13)
A/78/PV.102

Karimi Magham, Ali (Iran (Islamic Republic of))

UN. GENERAL ASSEMBLY (78TH SESS. : 2023-2024)—GENERAL DEBATE—RIGHT OF REPLY (Agenda item 8)
A/78/PV.11
UN. SECURITY COUNCIL—MEMBERSHIP (Agenda item 121)
A/78/PV.35

Karis, Alar (Estonia. President)
UN. GENERAL ASSEMBLY (78TH SESS. : 2023-2024)—GENERAL DEBATE (Agenda item 8)
A/78/PV.7
UN. GENERAL ASSEMBLY (78TH SESS. : 2023-2024)—SPECIAL STATEMENTS
A/78/PV.7

Kariuki, James (United Kingdom)
EMERGENCY ASSISTANCE (Agenda item 72a)
A/78/PV.46
HUMAN RIGHTS—REPORTS (Agenda item 71c)
A/C.3/78/SR.26
PEACE (Agenda item 14)
A/78/PV.62
UN. GENERAL ASSEMBLY (78TH SESS. : 2023-2024)—OFFICERS (Agenda item 5)
A/C.5/78/SR.1
UN. GENERAL ASSEMBLY (78TH SESS. : 2023-2024). 2ND COMMITTEE—GENERAL DEBATE (Agenda item 8)
A/C.2/78/SR.5
UN. GENERAL ASSEMBLY (78TH SESS. : 2023-2024). 5TH COMMITTEE—WORK ORGANIZATION (Agenda item 7)
A/C.5/78/SR.35
UN. SECURITY COUNCIL—MEMBERSHIP (Agenda item 121)
A/78/PV.34
VETO (Agenda item 63)
A/78/PV.75

Kariuki, Kamau (Kenya)
RIGHT TO EDUCATION (Agenda item 71b)
A/C.3/78/SR.27

Karlsdóttir, Helga Hronn (Iceland)
CRIMES AGAINST HUMANITY (Agenda item 80)
A/C.6/78/SR.44; A/C.6/78/SR.45

Kasabri, Qais Z.F. (State of Palestine)
ARMS RACE—OUTER SPACE (Agenda item 97a)
A/C.1/78/PV.16
BIOLOGICAL WEAPONS—TREATIES (Agenda item 106)
A/C.1/78/PV.14
CHEMICAL WEAPONS—TREATIES (Agenda item 99l)
A/C.1/78/PV.14
DISARMAMENT—GENERAL AND COMPLETE (Agenda item 99)
A/C.1/78/PV.23; A/C.1/78/PV.24
UN. GENERAL ASSEMBLY (78TH SESS. : 2023-2024). 1ST COMMITTEE—GENERAL DEBATE (Agenda item 8)
A/C.1/78/PV.9

Kashaev, Roman G. (Russian Federation)
AGEING PERSONS (Agenda item 24b)
A/C.3/78/SR.2; A/C.3/78/SR.49

Kashaev, Roman G. (Russian Federation) (continued)
CRIME PREVENTION (Agenda item 107)
A/C.3/78/SR.51
DISPLACED PERSONS (Agenda item 71b)
A/C.3/78/SR.49
ELECTION VERIFICATION—UN (Agenda item 71b)
A/C.3/78/SR.50
FAMILY (Agenda item 24b)
A/C.3/78/SR.2
HUMAN RIGHTS—MYANMAR (Agenda item 71c)
A/C.3/78/SR.33
RIGHTS OF THE CHILD (Agenda item 67)
A/C.3/78/SR.55
SOCIAL CONDITIONS (Agenda item 24b)
A/C.3/78/SR.2
SOCIAL DEVELOPMENT (Agenda item 24)
A/C.3/78/SR.2
UN HIGH COMMISSIONER FOR REFUGEES—REPORTS (Agenda item 60)
A/C.3/78/SR.48
YOUTH (Agenda item 24b)
A/C.3/78/SR.2

Kasmi, Aldi (Albania)
YOUTH (Agenda item 24b)
A/C.3/78/SR.3

Kaspar, Martin (European Union)
CLIMATE (Agenda item 18d)
A/C.2/78/SR.25
OPERATIONAL ACTIVITIES—UN SYSTEM (Agenda item 22a)
A/C.2/78/SR.22
SMALL ISLAND DEVELOPING STATES—PROGRAMMES OF ACTION (Agenda item 18b)
A/C.2/78/SR.22
SUSTAINABLE ENERGY (Agenda item 18h)
A/C.2/78/SR.23

Kassaye, Yoseph (Ethiopia)
DECOLONIZATION (Agenda item 58)
A/C.4/78/SR.8
INFORMATION (Agenda item 53)
A/C.4/78/SR.8
OUTER SPACE—PEACEFUL USES—INTERNATIONAL COOPERATION (Agenda item 48)
A/C.4/78/SR.8
PEACEKEEPING OPERATIONS (Agenda item 51)
A/C.4/78/SR.8
SPECIAL POLITICAL MISSIONS (Agenda item 52)
A/C.4/78/SR.8
WESTERN SAHARA QUESTION (Agenda item 58)
A/C.4/78/SR.8

Kastanas, Elias (Greece)
CLIMATE CHANGE (Agenda item 71b)
A/C.3/78/SR.29
TRAFFICKING IN PERSONS (Agenda item 71b)
A/C.3/78/SR.23

Kasymalieva, Aida (Kyrgyzstan)

PERSONS WITH DISABILITIES (Agenda item 24b)
A/C.3/78/SR.3
SOCIAL CONDITIONS (Agenda item 24b)
A/C.3/78/SR.3
SOCIAL DEVELOPMENT (Agenda item 24)
A/C.3/78/SR.3
UN. GENERAL ASSEMBLY (78TH SESS. : 2023-2024). 2ND COMMITTEE—GENERAL DEBATE (Agenda item 8)
A/C.2/78/SR.6
WOMEN'S ADVANCEMENT (Agenda item 25a)
A/C.3/78/SR.9
WOMEN'S ADVANCEMENT—CONFERENCES (Agenda item 25b)
A/C.3/78/SR.9

Kattanga, Hussein A. (United Republic of Tanzania)

DIAMONDS—FUELLING CONFLICT (Agenda item 30)
A/78/PV.65
FOOD SECURITY (Agenda item 23a)
A/C.2/78/SR.17
INTERNATIONAL JURISDICTION (Agenda item 84)
A/C.6/78/SR.13
PEACE (Agenda item 14)
A/78/PV.82
POVERTY—INTERNATIONAL DECADES (Agenda item 21a)
A/C.2/78/SR.17
RURAL POVERTY (Agenda item 21b)
A/C.2/78/SR.17
SOCIAL CONDITIONS (Agenda item 24b)
A/C.3/78/SR.3
SOCIAL DEVELOPMENT (Agenda item 24)
A/C.3/78/SR.3
SUSTAINABLE DEVELOPMENT (Agenda item 18)
A/C.2/78/SR.15
SUSTAINABLE ENERGY (Agenda item 18h)
A/C.2/78/SR.15
UN. GENERAL ASSEMBLY (78TH SESS. : 2023-2024). 1ST COMMITTEE—GENERAL DEBATE (Agenda item 8)
A/C.1/78/PV.5
UN. GENERAL ASSEMBLY (78TH SESS. : 2023-2024). 2ND COMMITTEE—GENERAL DEBATE (Agenda item 8)
A/C.2/78/SR.5
WOMEN'S ADVANCEMENT (Agenda item 25a)
A/C.3/78/SR.10
WOMEN'S ADVANCEMENT—CONFERENCES (Agenda item 25b)
A/C.3/78/SR.10
YOUTH (Agenda item 24b)
A/C.3/78/SR.3

Kattanga, Hussein A. (United Republic of Tanzania) (UN. Group of African States)

MULTILINGUALISM (Agenda item 124)
A/78/PV.97

Katz Pavlotzky, Alejandro Leonel (Uruguay)

CRIMES AGAINST HUMANITY (Agenda item 80)
A/C.6/78/SR.11; A/C.6/78/SR.45
RULE OF LAW (Agenda item 83)
A/C.6/78/SR.18
TERRORISM (Agenda item 109)
A/C.6/78/SR.4

Katzarova, Mariana (UN. Human Rights Council. Special Rapporteur on the Situation of Human Rights in the Russian Federation)

HUMAN RIGHTS—RUSSIAN FEDERATION (Agenda item 71c)
A/C.3/78/SR.37

Kavaleuskaya, Alena (Belarus)

DEVELOPMENT COOPERATION—MIDDLE-INCOME COUNTRIES (Agenda item 19c)
A/C.2/78/SR.10
EMERGENCY ASSISTANCE (Agenda item 72a)
A/78/PV.47
FOOD SECURITY (Agenda item 23a)
A/C.2/78/SR.25
IAEA—REPORTS (Agenda item 89)
A/78/PV.29; A/78/PV.30
INTERNATIONAL TRADE (Agenda item 16a)
A/C.2/78/SR.9; A/C.2/78/SR.22; A/C.2/78/SR.24

Kawasaki, Yuta (Japan)

PERSONNEL QUESTIONS—UN SYSTEM (Agenda item 142)
A/C.5/78/SR.10
UN. GENERAL ASSEMBLY (78TH SESS. : 2023-2024). 5TH COMMITTEE—WORK ORGANIZATION (Agenda item 7)
A/C.5/78/SR.34

Kayinamura, Robert (Rwanda)

INTERNATIONAL RESIDUAL MECHANISM FOR CRIMINAL TRIBUNALS (Agenda item 126)
A/78/PV.19

Keane, Shane (United States)

SUSTAINABLE DEVELOPMENT (Agenda item 18)
A/C.2/78/SR.22

Kebe, Hawanatu (Sierra Leone)

CRIMES AGAINST HUMANITY (Agenda item 80)
A/C.6/78/SR.43
DISASTER VICTIMS (Agenda item 86)
A/C.6/78/SR.6
RULE OF LAW (Agenda item 83)
A/C.6/78/SR.19

Kebe, Hawanatu (Sierra Leone) (continued)
UN. INTERNATIONAL LAW COMMISSION—REPORTS (Agenda item 79)
A/C.6/78/SR.27

Kedar, Gershon (Israel)
OUTER SPACE—PEACEFUL USES—INTERNATIONAL COOPERATION (Agenda item 48)
A/C.4/78/SR.16
PEACEKEEPING OPERATIONS (Agenda item 51)
A/C.4/78/SR.19; A/C.4/78/SR.20
TERRITORIES OCCUPIED BY ISRAEL—HUMAN RIGHTS (Agenda item 50)
A/C.4/78/SR.25
UNRWA—ACTIVITIES (Agenda item 49)
A/C.4/78/SR.23; A/C.4/78/SR.26

Keller, Janet (United States)
RIGHTS OF THE CHILD (Agenda item 67)
A/C.3/78/SR.12
WOMEN'S ADVANCEMENT (Agenda item 25a)
A/C.3/78/SR.7
WOMEN'S ADVANCEMENT—CONFERENCES (Agenda item 25b)
A/C.3/78/SR.7

Kelley, John (United States)
TERRITORIES OCCUPIED BY ISRAEL—HUMAN RIGHTS (Agenda item 50)
A/C.4/78/SR.26
UNRWA—ACTIVITIES (Agenda item 49)
A/C.4/78/SR.26

Kelsey, Alistair Robert Steven (United Kingdom)
FOOD SECURITY (Agenda item 23a)
A/C.2/78/SR.25
INFORMATION TECHNOLOGY—DEVELOPMENT (Agenda item 15)
A/C.2/78/SR.23
INTERNATIONAL TRADE (Agenda item 16a)
A/C.2/78/SR.24
SUSTAINABLE DEVELOPMENT (Agenda item 18)
A/C.2/78/SR.24
TERRITORIES OCCUPIED BY ISRAEL—NATURAL RESOURCES (Agenda item 59)
A/C.2/78/SR.21

Kelson, Matthew (Australia)
RIGHTS OF THE CHILD (Agenda item 67)
A/C.3/78/SR.55
TRAFFICKING IN PERSONS (Agenda item 71b)
A/C.3/78/SR.23

Kenga, Emmanuel Kingi (Kenya)
BIOLOGICAL DIVERSITY—TREATIES (Agenda item 18f)
A/C.2/78/SR.13
CLIMATE (Agenda item 18d)
A/C.2/78/SR.13

Kenga, Emmanuel Kingi (Kenya) (continued)
DISASTER PREVENTION (Agenda item 18c)
A/C.2/78/SR.13
SUSTAINABLE ENERGY (Agenda item 18h)
A/C.2/78/SR.13

Keogh, Briana (European Union)
HUMAN RIGHTS—INTERNATIONAL INSTRUMENTS (Agenda item 71a)
A/C.3/78/SR.17
JUDICIAL INDEPENDENCE (Agenda item 71b)
A/C.3/78/SR.31
LEPROSY (Agenda item 71b)
A/C.3/78/SR.17
RIGHT TO EDUCATION (Agenda item 71b)
A/C.3/78/SR.27
RIGHTS OF THE CHILD (Agenda item 67)
A/C.3/78/SR.12
UN. HUMAN RIGHTS COMMITTEE—REPORTS (Agenda item 71a)
A/C.3/78/SR.17

Kerimkulov, Bauyrzhan (Kazakhstan)
LANDLOCKED DEVELOPING COUNTRIES—CONFERENCES (Agenda item 20b)
A/C.2/78/SR.7
LEAST DEVELOPED COUNTRIES—CONFERENCES (Agenda item 20a)
A/C.2/78/SR.7
SUSTAINABLE DEVELOPMENT (Agenda item 18)
A/C.2/78/SR.21
UN. GENERAL ASSEMBLY (78TH SESS. : 2023-2024). 2ND COMMITTEE—GENERAL DEBATE (Agenda item 8)
A/C.2/78/SR.5

Kesse Antwi, Linda (Ghana)
DISARMAMENT—GENERAL AND COMPLETE (Agenda item 99)
A/78/PV.106; A/C.1/78/PV.30
FISSIONABLE MATERIALS—TREATIES (Agenda item 99a)
A/C.1/78/PV.12
NUCLEAR DISARMAMENT (Agenda item 99b)
A/C.1/78/PV.12
NUCLEAR NON-PROLIFERATION—INTERNATIONAL OBLIGATIONS (Agenda item 99w)
A/C.1/78/PV.12
UKRAINE—POLITICAL CONDITIONS (Agenda item 62)
A/78/PV.99
UN. GENERAL ASSEMBLY (78TH SESS. : 2023-2024). 1ST COMMITTEE—GENERAL DEBATE (Agenda item 8)
A/C.1/78/PV.5

Kessel, Alan (Canada)
LAW OF THE SEA (Agenda item 75a)
A/78/PV.43

Kessel, Alan (Canada) (continued)

MARINE ECOSYSTEMS—BIOLOGICAL DIVERSITY (Agenda item 75c)
A/78/PV.43
STRADDLING FISH STOCKS (Agenda item 75b)
A/78/PV.43
UN. INTERNATIONAL LAW COMMISSION—REPORTS (Agenda item 79)
A/C.6/78/SR.25

Khaddour, Mhd. Riyad (Syrian Arab Republic)

ARMED CONFLICTS PREVENTION (Agenda item 31a)
A/78/PV.73
CRIMES AGAINST HUMANITY (Agenda item 80)
A/C.6/78/SR.11; A/C.6/78/SR.39; A/C.6/78/SR.40; A/C.6/78/SR.41; A/C.6/78/SR.42; A/C.6/78/SR.46
DISASTER VICTIMS (Agenda item 86)
A/C.6/78/SR.6
INTERNATIONAL CRIMINAL COURT—REPORTS (Agenda item 74)
A/78/PV.21; A/78/PV.25
INTERNATIONAL JURISDICTION (Agenda item 84)
A/C.6/78/SR.12; A/C.6/78/SR.13
LAW OF THE SEA (Agenda item 75a)
A/78/PV.44
MARINE ECOSYSTEMS—BIOLOGICAL DIVERSITY (Agenda item 75c)
A/78/PV.44
RULE OF LAW (Agenda item 83)
A/C.6/78/SR.18; A/C.6/78/SR.37
STRADDLING FISH STOCKS (Agenda item 75b)
A/78/PV.44
TERRORISM (Agenda item 109)
A/C.6/78/SR.3
UN. COMMITTEE ON RELATIONS WITH THE HOST COUNTRY—REPORTS (Agenda item 161)
A/C.6/78/SR.35
UN. SECURITY COUNCIL—MEMBERSHIP (Agenda item 121)
A/78/PV.36
UN CHARTER—REPORTS (Agenda item 82)
A/C.6/78/SR.22

Khadeeja, Aufiyau (Maldives)

EMERGENCY ASSISTANCE (Agenda item 72a)
A/78/PV.46
PALESTINIANS—ASSISTANCE (Agenda item 72b)
A/78/PV.46
PERSONS WITH DISABILITIES—HUMAN RIGHTS (Agenda item 71a)
A/C.3/78/SR.38
RIGHT TO HEALTH (Agenda item 71b)
A/C.3/78/SR.39
SOCIAL CONDITIONS (Agenda item 24b)
A/C.3/78/SR.3
SOCIAL DEVELOPMENT (Agenda item 24)
A/C.3/78/SR.3
WOMEN'S ADVANCEMENT (Agenda item 25a)
A/C.3/78/SR.9

Khadeeja, Aufiyau (Maldives) (continued)

WOMEN'S ADVANCEMENT—CONFERENCES (Agenda item 25b)
A/C.3/78/SR.9
YOUTH (Agenda item 24b)
A/C.3/78/SR.3

Khairunsyah, Aidil (Indonesia)

DISPLACED PERSONS (Agenda item 71b)
A/C.3/78/SR.32
HUMAN RIGHTS—AFGHANISTAN (Agenda item 71c)
A/C.3/78/SR.34
HUMAN RIGHTS—MYANMAR (Agenda item 71c)
A/C.3/78/SR.33
HUMAN RIGHTS—TERRITORIES OCCUPIED BY ISRAEL (Agenda item 71c)
A/C.3/78/SR.35
RELIGIOUS INTOLERANCE (Agenda item 71b)
A/C.3/78/SR.38
UN HIGH COMMISSIONER FOR REFUGEES—REPORTS (Agenda item 60)
A/C.3/78/SR.44

Khaleel, Ahmed (Maldives)

UN. GENERAL ASSEMBLY (78TH SESS. : 2023-2024)—GENERAL DEBATE (Agenda item 8)
A/78/PV.14

Khan, Irene (UN. Human Rights Council. Special Rapporteur on the Promotion and Protection of the Right to Freedom of Opinion and Expression)

FREEDOM OF EXPRESSION (Agenda item 71b)
A/C.3/78/SR.19

Khan, Mohammad Aamir (Pakistan)

CRIME PREVENTION (Agenda item 107)
A/C.3/78/SR.5
CYBERCRIME (Agenda item 108)
A/C.3/78/SR.5
HUMAN RIGHTS (Agenda item 71)
A/C.3/78/SR.16

Khan, Naeem Sabir (Pakistan)

DECOLONIZATION (Agenda item 58)
A/C.4/78/SR.7
OUTER SPACE—PEACEFUL USES—INTERNATIONAL COOPERATION (Agenda item 48)
A/C.4/78/SR.15
RADIATION EFFECTS (Agenda item 47)
A/C.4/78/SR.11

Khare, Atul (UN. Under-Secretary-General for Operational Support)

PEACEKEEPING OPERATIONS (Agenda item 51)
A/C.4/78/SR.18
SPECIAL POLITICAL MISSIONS (Agenda item 52)
A/C.4/78/SR.21

Khare, Atul (UN. Under-Secretary-General for Operational Support) (continued)

UN—BUDGET (2024) (Agenda item 134)
A/C.5/78/SR.17

Khiari, Mohamed Khaled (UN. Assistant Secretary-General for Middle East, Asia and the Pacific)

ELECTION VERIFICATION—UN (Agenda item 71b)
A/C.3/78/SR.18
HUMAN RIGHTS—MYANMAR (Agenda item 71c)
A/C.3/78/SR.33

Khng, Nathaniel (Singapore)

CRIMES AGAINST HUMANITY (Agenda item 80)
A/C.6/78/SR.9; A/C.6/78/SR.39; A/C.6/78/SR.41; A/C.6/78/SR.42; A/C.6/78/SR.43; A/C.6/78/SR.44; A/C.6/78/SR.45; A/C.6/78/SR.47
PEACE (Agenda item 14)
A/78/PV.82
RESPONSIBILITY OF INTERNATIONAL ORGANIZATIONS (Agenda item 85)
A/C.6/78/SR.19
TREATIES (Agenda item 87)
A/C.6/78/SR.20
UN. INTERNATIONAL LAW COMMISSION—REPORTS (Agenda item 79)
A/C.6/78/SR.37

Khng, Nathaniel (Singapore) (UN. General Assembly. 6th Committee. Bureau)

TREATIES (Agenda item 87)
A/C.6/78/SR.37
UN COMMISSION ON INTERNATIONAL TRADE LAW—REPORTS (Agenda item 77)
A/C.6/78/SR.37

Khokhar, Adeel Mumtaz (Pakistan)

INTERNATIONAL LAW—TRAINING PROGRAMMES (Agenda item 78)
A/C.6/78/SR.21
UN COMMISSION ON INTERNATIONAL TRADE LAW—REPORTS (Agenda item 77)
A/C.6/78/SR.14

Khousakoun, Phetvanxay (Lao People's Democratic Republic)

UN. SECURITY COUNCIL—MEMBERSHIP (Agenda item 121)
A/78/PV.36

Khundee, Wichayaporn (Thailand)

AFRICA—NUCLEAR-WEAPON-FREE ZONES (Agenda item 92)
A/C.1/78/PV.26
BIOLOGICAL WEAPONS—TREATIES (Agenda item 106)
A/C.1/78/PV.15
CHEMICAL WEAPONS—TREATIES (Agenda item 99l)
A/C.1/78/PV.15

Khundee, Wichayaporn (Thailand) (continued)

CONVENTIONAL WEAPONS (Agenda item 99u)
A/C.1/78/PV.18
DISARMAMENT—GENERAL AND COMPLETE (Agenda item 99)
A/C.1/78/PV.26
LANDMINES—TREATIES (Agenda item 99m)
A/C.1/78/PV.18
NUCLEAR WEAPONS USE—TREATIES (Agenda item 100a)
A/C.1/78/PV.26

Khurelsukh, Ukhnaa (Mongolia. President)

UN. GENERAL ASSEMBLY (78TH SESS. : 2023-2024)—GENERAL DEBATE (Agenda item 8)
A/78/PV.7
UN. GENERAL ASSEMBLY (78TH SESS. : 2023-2024)—SPECIAL STATEMENTS
A/78/PV.7

Kiboino, Michael Kapkiai (Kenya)

PEACEBUILDING (Agenda item 61)
A/78/PV.100
PEACEKEEPING OPERATIONS (Agenda item 51)
A/C.4/78/SR.20
TERRORISM (Agenda item 109)
A/C.6/78/SR.4
UN. GENERAL ASSEMBLY (78TH SESS. : 2023-2024). 1ST COMMITTEE—GENERAL DEBATE (Agenda item 8)
A/C.1/78/PV.8
UN. PEACEBUILDING COMMISSION—REPORTS (Agenda item 27)
A/78/PV.100
UN. PEACEBUILDING FUND—REPORTS (Agenda item 111)
A/78/PV.100
UN. SECURITY COUNCIL—MEMBERSHIP (Agenda item 121)
A/78/PV.36
VETO (Agenda item 63)
A/78/PV.3; A/78/PV.52

Kiir Mayardit, Slava (South Sudan. President)

UN. GENERAL ASSEMBLY (78TH SESS. : 2023-2024)—GENERAL DEBATE (Agenda item 8)
A/78/PV.8
UN. GENERAL ASSEMBLY (78TH SESS. : 2023-2024)—SPECIAL STATEMENTS
A/78/PV.8

Kim, Hyunsoo (Republic of Korea)

RESPONSIBILITY TO PROTECT (Agenda item 129)
A/78/PV.97
RULE OF LAW (Agenda item 83)
A/C.6/78/SR.18
TERRORISM (Agenda item 109)
A/C.6/78/SR.4
UN CHARTER—REPORTS (Agenda item 82)
A/C.6/78/SR.33; A/C.6/78/SR.34

Kim, In Chol (Democratic People's Republic of Korea)

ARMS RACE—OUTER SPACE (Agenda item 97a)
A/C.1/78/PV.17
DISARMAMENT—GENERAL AND COMPLETE (Agenda item 99)
A/C.1/78/PV.19; A/C.1/78/PV.21
INFORMATION (Agenda item 53)
A/C.4/78/SR.12
MULTILATERALISM—DISARMAMENT (Agenda item 99r)
A/C.1/78/PV.22; A/C.1/78/PV.23
NUCLEAR DISARMAMENT (Agenda item 99b)
A/C.1/78/PV.13
NUCLEAR DISARMAMENT—TREATY COMPLIANCE (Agenda item 99q)
A/C.1/78/PV.26
NUCLEAR WEAPON TESTS—TREATIES (Agenda item 105)
A/C.1/78/PV.26
NUCLEAR WEAPONS—ELIMINATION (Agenda item 99z)
A/C.1/78/PV.25; A/C.1/78/PV.26
OUTER SPACE—PEACEFUL USES—INTERNATIONAL COOPERATION (Agenda item 48)
A/C.4/78/SR.17
PEACEKEEPING OPERATIONS (Agenda item 51)
A/C.4/78/SR.19
TERRITORIES OCCUPIED BY ISRAEL—HUMAN RIGHTS (Agenda item 50)
A/C.4/78/SR.24; A/C.4/78/SR.26
UN—PROGRAMME PLANNING (Agenda item 135)
A/C.5/78/SR.24
UN. GENERAL ASSEMBLY (78TH SESS. : 2023-2024). 1ST COMMITTEE—GENERAL DEBATE (Agenda item 8)
A/C.1/78/PV.2; A/C.1/78/PV.4; A/C.1/78/PV.5; A/C.1/78/PV.7; A/C.1/78/PV.8
UN CHARTER—REPORTS (Agenda item 82)
A/C.6/78/SR.33; A/C.6/78/SR.34

Kim, Nam Hyok (Democratic People's Republic of Korea)

DISAPPEARANCE OF PERSONS (Agenda item 71b)
A/C.3/78/SR.22
HUMAN RIGHTS (Agenda item 71)
A/C.3/78/SR.16
HUMAN RIGHTS—BURUNDI (Agenda item 71c)
A/C.3/78/SR.36
HUMAN RIGHTS—DEMOCRATIC PEOPLE'S REPUBLIC OF KOREA (Agenda item 71c)
A/78/PV.50; A/C.3/78/SR.18; A/C.3/78/SR.27
HUMAN RIGHTS—ERITREA (Agenda item 71c)
A/C.3/78/SR.36
HUMAN RIGHTS—IRAN (ISLAMIC REPUBLIC OF) (Agenda item 71c)
A/C.3/78/SR.34; A/C.3/78/SR.53
HUMAN RIGHTS—REPORTS (Agenda item 71c)
A/C.3/78/SR.25

Kim, Nam Hyok (Democratic People's Republic of Korea) (continued)

HUMAN RIGHTS—RUSSIAN FEDERATION (Agenda item 71c)
A/C.3/78/SR.37
HUMAN RIGHTS—SYRIAN ARAB REPUBLIC (Agenda item 71c)
A/C.3/78/SR.34; A/C.3/78/SR.54
HUMAN RIGHTS—TERRITORIES OCCUPIED BY ISRAEL (Agenda item 71c)
A/C.3/78/SR.35
HUMAN RIGHTS—UKRAINE (Agenda item 71c)
A/C.3/78/SR.53
RACIAL DISCRIMINATION—ELIMINATION (Agenda item 69a)
A/78/PV.50; A/C.3/78/SR.47
RIGHT TO THE TRUTH (Agenda item 71b)
A/C.3/78/SR.22
RIGHTS OF THE CHILD (Agenda item 67)
A/C.3/78/SR.13
UKRAINE—POLITICAL CONDITIONS (Agenda item 62)
A/78/PV.56; A/78/PV.58
UN—BUDGET (2024) (Agenda item 134)
A/78/PV.73; A/C.5/78/SR.26/PartII; A/C.5/78/SR.34
UN—PROGRAMME PLANNING (Agenda item 135)
A/78/PV.50(Resumption1)
UN. HUMAN RIGHTS COUNCIL—REPORTS (Agenda item 66)
A/C.3/78/SR.46
UN HIGH COMMISSIONER FOR REFUGEES—REPORTS (Agenda item 60)
A/C.3/78/SR.45

Kim, Sangjin (Republic of Korea)

NUCLEAR WEAPONS—ELIMINATION (Agenda item 99z)
A/C.1/78/PV.26
UKRAINE—POLITICAL CONDITIONS (Agenda item 62)
A/78/PV.58
UN. GENERAL ASSEMBLY (78TH SESS. : 2023-2024)—GENERAL DEBATE—RIGHT OF REPLY (Agenda item 8)
A/78/PV.14
UN HIGH COMMISSIONER FOR REFUGEES—REPORTS (Agenda item 60)
A/C.3/78/SR.45
VETO (Agenda item 63)
A/78/PV.51; A/78/PV.60; A/78/PV.66; A/78/PV.75

Kim, Song (Democratic People's Republic of Korea)

ARMED CONFLICTS PREVENTION (Agenda item 31a)
A/78/PV.72
CUBA—UNITED STATES (Agenda item 38)
A/78/PV.24
HUMAN RIGHTS—DEMOCRATIC PEOPLE'S REPUBLIC OF KOREA (Agenda item 71c)
A/C.3/78/SR.53

Kim, Song (Democratic People's Republic of Korea) (continued)

HUMAN RIGHTS—REPORTS (Agenda item 71c)
A/C.3/78/SR.25
IAEA—REPORTS (Agenda item 89)
A/78/PV.29
NUCLEAR DISARMAMENT (Agenda item 99b)
A/C.1/78/PV.11
OUTER SPACE—PEACEFUL USES—INTERNATIONAL COOPERATION (Agenda item 48)
A/C.4/78/SR.15
RESPONSIBILITY TO PROTECT (Agenda item 129)
A/78/PV.96
TERRORISM (Agenda item 109)
A/C.6/78/SR.3
UN. GENERAL ASSEMBLY (78TH SESS. : 2023-2024)—GENERAL DEBATE (Agenda item 8)
A/78/PV.14
UN. GENERAL ASSEMBLY (78TH SESS. : 2023-2024)—GENERAL DEBATE—RIGHT OF REPLY (Agenda item 8)
A/78/PV.14
UN. GENERAL ASSEMBLY (78TH SESS. : 2023-2024). 1ST COMMITTEE—GENERAL DEBATE (Agenda item 8)
A/C.1/78/PV.7
UN. GENERAL ASSEMBLY (78TH SESS. : 2023-2024). 2ND COMMITTEE—GENERAL DEBATE (Agenda item 8)
A/C.2/78/SR.3
UN. SECURITY COUNCIL—MEMBERSHIP (Agenda item 121)
A/78/PV.36
VETO (Agenda item 63)
A/78/PV.3; A/78/PV.51; A/78/PV.60; A/78/PV.67; A/78/PV.68; A/78/PV.71; A/78/PV.75
WOMEN'S ADVANCEMENT (Agenda item 25a)
A/C.3/78/SR.9
WOMEN'S ADVANCEMENT—CONFERENCES (Agenda item 25b)
A/C.3/78/SR.9

Kim, Sunghoon (Republic of Korea)

ARMS RACE—OUTER SPACE (Agenda item 97a)
A/C.1/78/PV.17
DISARMAMENT—GENERAL AND COMPLETE (Agenda item 99)
A/C.1/78/PV.28
DISARMAMENT-DEVELOPMENT LINK (Agenda item 99d)
A/C.1/78/PV.28
IAEA—REPORTS (Agenda item 89)
A/78/PV.30
LANDMINES—TREATIES (Agenda item 99m)
A/C.1/78/PV.28
NUCLEAR DISARMAMENT (Agenda item 99b)
A/C.1/78/PV.12; A/C.1/78/PV.13
NUCLEAR NON-PROLIFERATION—INTERNATIONAL OBLIGATIONS (Agenda item 99w)
A/C.1/78/PV.12

Kim, Sunghoon (Republic of Korea) (continued)

NUCLEAR WEAPON TESTS—TREATIES (Agenda item 105)
A/C.1/78/PV.12
UN. GENERAL ASSEMBLY (78TH SESS. : 2023-2024). 1ST COMMITTEE—GENERAL DEBATE (Agenda item 8)
A/C.1/78/PV.2; A/C.1/78/PV.7
VETO (Agenda item 63)
A/78/PV.68

Kim, Yong Yi (Republic of Korea)

HUMAN RIGHTS—MYANMAR (Agenda item 71c)
A/C.3/78/SR.33

Kim, Yunei (Australia)

CLIMATE CHANGE (Agenda item 71b)
A/C.3/78/SR.29
HEALTH (Agenda item 125)
A/78/PV.48
HUMAN RIGHTS (Agenda item 71)
A/C.3/78/SR.16
HUMAN RIGHTS—DEMOCRATIC PEOPLE'S REPUBLIC OF KOREA (Agenda item 71c)
A/C.3/78/SR.33
HUMAN RIGHTS—IRAN (ISLAMIC REPUBLIC OF) (Agenda item 71c)
A/C.3/78/SR.34
HUMAN RIGHTS—RUSSIAN FEDERATION (Agenda item 71c)
A/C.3/78/SR.37
HUMAN RIGHTS—UKRAINE (Agenda item 71c)
A/C.3/78/SR.37
PEACE (Agenda item 14)
A/78/PV.88
RACIAL DISCRIMINATION—ELIMINATION (Agenda item 69a)
A/C.3/78/SR.47
RURAL WOMEN (Agenda item 25a)
A/C.3/78/SR.49

Kimani, Martin (Kenya)

UKRAINE—POLITICAL CONDITIONS (Agenda item 62)
A/78/PV.57
VETO (Agenda item 63)
A/78/PV.60; A/78/PV.69; A/78/PV.70; A/78/PV.75

Kindeya, Tsigabu Girmay (Ethiopia)

FOOD SECURITY (Agenda item 23a)
A/C.2/78/SR.17
POVERTY—INTERNATIONAL DECADES (Agenda item 21a)
A/C.2/78/SR.17
RURAL POVERTY (Agenda item 21b)
A/C.2/78/SR.17

King, Inga Rhonda (Saint Vincent and the Grenadines)

CUBA—UNITED STATES (Agenda item 38)
A/78/PV.24
ECONOMIC SANCTIONS—INTERNATIONAL RELATIONS (Agenda item 28)
A/78/PV.90

King, Inga Rhonda (Saint Vincent and the Grenadines) (Community of Latin American and Caribbean States)

DECOLONIZATION (Agenda item 58)
A/C.4/78/SR.7
FALKLAND ISLANDS (MALVINAS) QUESTION (Agenda item 42)
A/C.4/78/SR.7
NON-SELF-GOVERNING TERRITORIES—REPORTS (Agenda item 54)
A/C.4/78/SR.7
TURKS AND CAICOS ISLANDS QUESTION (Agenda item 58)
A/C.4/78/SR.7
WESTERN SAHARA QUESTION (Agenda item 58)
A/C.4/78/SR.7

King, Inga Rhonda (Saint Vincent and the Grenadines) (L.69 Group)

UN. SECURITY COUNCIL—MEMBERSHIP (Agenda item 121)
A/78/PV.104

King, Yolanda ((personal capacity))

SLAVERY—MEMORIALS (Agenda item 118)
A/78/PV.64

Kinyungu, Njambi (Kenya)

CUBA—UNITED STATES (Agenda item 38)
A/78/PV.24
RACIAL DISCRIMINATION—ELIMINATION (Agenda item 69a)
A/C.3/78/SR.40
RACIAL DISCRIMINATION—PROGRAMMES OF ACTION (Agenda item 69b)
A/C.3/78/SR.40
UN—BUDGET (2024) (Agenda item 134)
A/C.5/78/SR.5; A/C.5/78/SR.11
UN—PROGRAMME PLANNING (Agenda item 135)
A/C.5/78/SR.5

Kirk, James (Ireland)

ARMED CONFLICTS PREVENTION (Agenda item 31a)
A/78/PV.72
CRIMES AGAINST HUMANITY (Agenda item 80)
A/C.6/78/SR.10; A/C.6/78/SR.38; A/C.6/78/SR.39; A/C.6/78/SR.42; A/C.6/78/SR.43; A/C.6/78/SR.45
DISASTER VICTIMS (Agenda item 86)
A/C.6/78/SR.6

Kirk, James (Ireland) (continued)

INTERNATIONAL CRIMINAL COURT—REPORTS (Agenda item 74)
A/78/PV.22
INTERNATIONAL JURISDICTION (Agenda item 84)
A/C.6/78/SR.12
INTERNATIONAL LAW—TRAINING PROGRAMMES (Agenda item 78)
A/C.6/78/SR.22
UN. INTERNATIONAL COURT OF JUSTICE—REPORTS (Agenda item 73)
A/78/PV.27
UN. INTERNATIONAL LAW COMMISSION—REPORTS (Agenda item 79)
A/C.6/78/SR.29; A/C.6/78/SR.31

Kishida, Fumio (Japan. Prime Minister)

UN. GENERAL ASSEMBLY (78TH SESS. : 2023-2024)—GENERAL DEBATE (Agenda item 8)
A/78/PV.5
UN. GENERAL ASSEMBLY (78TH SESS. : 2023-2024)—SPECIAL STATEMENTS
A/78/PV.5

Kita, Yosuke (Japan)

HEALTH (Agenda item 125)
A/78/PV.48

Kitada, Tetsuo (Japan)

HIV/AIDS—DECLARATIONS (Agenda item 10)
A/78/PV.91

Klaise, Inara (Canada)

RIGHTS OF THE CHILD (Agenda item 67)
A/C.3/78/SR.55
TORTURE AND OTHER CRUEL TREATMENT (Agenda item 71a)
A/C.3/78/SR.18
UN HIGH COMMISSIONER FOR REFUGEES—REPORTS (Agenda item 60)
A/C.3/78/SR.51

Klanduch, Peter (Slovakia)

INTERNATIONAL CRIMINAL COURT—REPORTS (Agenda item 74)
A/78/PV.21
UN. INTERNATIONAL LAW COMMISSION—REPORTS (Agenda item 79)
A/C.6/78/SR.25; A/C.6/78/SR.29

Klose, Christoph (UNIDO)

DEVELOPMENT FINANCE (Agenda item 16b)
A/C.2/78/SR.11
MACROECONOMIC POLICY (Agenda item 16)
A/C.2/78/SR.11

Kloss, Emerson Coraiola Yinde (Brazil)

BIOLOGICAL DIVERSITY—TREATIES (Agenda item 18f)
A/C.2/78/SR.13
CLIMATE (Agenda item 18d)
A/C.2/78/SR.13
SUSTAINABLE ENERGY (Agenda item 18h)
A/C.2/78/SR.13

Kmentt, Alexander (Austria)

CLUSTER MUNITIONS (Agenda item 99dd)
A/C.1/78/PV.18
CONVENTIONAL WEAPONS—TREATIES (Agenda item 103)
A/C.1/78/PV.18
DISARMAMENT—GENERAL AND COMPLETE (Agenda item 99)
A/C.1/78/PV.18
LANDMINES—TREATIES (Agenda item 99m)
A/C.1/78/PV.18
NUCLEAR DISARMAMENT (Agenda item 99b)
A/C.1/78/PV.12
NUCLEAR NON-PROLIFERATION—INTERNATIONAL OBLIGATIONS (Agenda item 99w)
A/C.1/78/PV.12
NUCLEAR WEAPON TESTS—TREATIES (Agenda item 105)
A/C.1/78/PV.12
NUCLEAR WEAPONS—HUMANITARIAN CONSEQUENCES (Agenda item 99bb)
A/C.1/78/PV.12
NUCLEAR WEAPONS—TREATIES (Agenda item 99ff)
A/C.1/78/PV.12
SMALL ARMS—ILLICIT TRAFFIC (Agenda item 99p)
A/C.1/78/PV.18
SMALL ARMS—ILLICIT TRAFFIC—ASSISTANCE (Agenda item 99n)
A/C.1/78/PV.18
UN. CONFERENCE ON DISARMAMENT—REPORTS (Agenda item 101a)
A/C.1/78/PV.23

Knight, Stephen B. (United States)

UN. GENERAL ASSEMBLY (78TH SESS. : 2023-2024). 1ST COMMITTEE—WORK ORGANIZATION (Agenda item 7)
A/C.1/78/PV.1

Kohumoetini, Hina (French Polynesia)

FRENCH POLYNESIA QUESTION (Agenda item 58)
A/C.4/78/SR.3

Kohumoetini, Marielle (French Polynesia)

FRENCH POLYNESIA QUESTION (Agenda item 58)
A/C.4/78/SR.3

Kókai, Anita (Hungary)

HUMAN RIGHTS—TERRITORIES OCCUPIED BY ISRAEL (Agenda item 71c)
A/C.3/78/SR.35
VETO (Agenda item 63)
A/78/PV.52

Kókai, Anita (Hungary) (European Union)

SOCIAL CONDITIONS (Agenda item 24b)
A/78/PV.101

Kolsöe, Ragnheidur (Iceland)

HUMAN RIGHTS—AFGHANISTAN (Agenda item 71c)
A/C.3/78/SR.34
HUMAN RIGHTS—ETHIOPIA (Agenda item 71c)
A/C.3/78/SR.36
HUMAN RIGHTS—IRAN (ISLAMIC REPUBLIC OF) (Agenda item 71c)
A/C.3/78/SR.34
HUMAN RIGHTS—MYANMAR (Agenda item 71c)
A/C.3/78/SR.33

Kommasith, Saleumxay (Lao People's Democratic Republic. Deputy Prime Minister)

UN. GENERAL ASSEMBLY (78TH SESS. : 2023-2024)—GENERAL DEBATE (Agenda item 8)
A/78/PV.12
UN. GENERAL ASSEMBLY (78TH SESS. : 2023-2024)—SPECIAL STATEMENTS
A/78/PV.12

Komsic, Zeljko (Bosnia and Herzegovina. Presidency. Chair)

UN. GENERAL ASSEMBLY (78TH SESS. : 2023-2024)—GENERAL DEBATE (Agenda item 8)
A/78/PV.6
UN. GENERAL ASSEMBLY (78TH SESS. : 2023-2024)—SPECIAL STATEMENTS
A/78/PV.6

Konaté, Sékou (Guinea)

RIGHTS OF THE CHILD (Agenda item 67)
A/C.3/78/SR.13

Koncul, Ivana (Croatia)

HUMAN RIGHTS—AFGHANISTAN (Agenda item 71c)
A/C.3/78/SR.34
HUMAN RIGHTS—SYRIAN ARAB REPUBLIC (Agenda item 71c)
A/C.3/78/SR.34
WOMEN'S ADVANCEMENT (Agenda item 25a)
A/C.3/78/SR.7
WOMEN'S ADVANCEMENT—CONFERENCES (Agenda item 25b)
A/C.3/78/SR.7

Kondratev, Sergei V. (Russian Federation)

HUMAN RIGHTS—BURUNDI (Agenda item 71c)
A/C.3/78/SR.36
HUMAN RIGHTS—ERITREA (Agenda item 71c)
A/C.3/78/SR.36
HUMAN RIGHTS—ETHIOPIA (Agenda item 71c)
A/C.3/78/SR.36
PERSONS WITH DISABILITIES—HUMAN RIGHTS (Agenda item 71a)
A/C.3/78/SR.38
RACIAL DISCRIMINATION—ELIMINATION (Agenda item 69a)
A/C.3/78/SR.41
RACIAL DISCRIMINATION—PROGRAMMES OF ACTION (Agenda item 69b)
A/C.3/78/SR.41
RELIGIOUS INTOLERANCE (Agenda item 71b)
A/C.3/78/SR.38
SPORTS—OLYMPIC GAMES (Agenda item 11)
A/78/PV.97
UN. HUMAN RIGHTS COUNCIL—REPORTS (Agenda item 66)
A/C.3/78/SR.46

Kone, Tiémoko Meyliet (Côte d'Ivoire. Vice-President)

UN. GENERAL ASSEMBLY (78TH SESS. : 2023-2024)—GENERAL DEBATE (Agenda item 8)
A/78/PV.9
UN. GENERAL ASSEMBLY (78TH SESS. : 2023-2024)—SPECIAL STATEMENTS
A/78/PV.9

Konfourou, Issa (Mali)

CRIMES AGAINST HUMANITY (Agenda item 80)
A/C.6/78/SR.11
INTERNATIONAL CRIMINAL COURT—REPORTS (Agenda item 74)
A/78/PV.22
INTERNATIONAL JURISDICTION (Agenda item 84)
A/C.6/78/SR.13
TERRORISM (Agenda item 109)
A/C.6/78/SR.4
VETO (Agenda item 63)
A/78/PV.3; A/78/PV.69

Kontoleontos, Ifigeneia (Organisation internationale de la Francophonie)

PEACEKEEPING OPERATIONS (Agenda item 51)
A/C.4/78/SR.20

Koonjul, Jagdish (Mauritius)

VETO (Agenda item 63)
A/78/PV.61

Korac, Sofija (United States)

ELECTION VERIFICATION—UN (Agenda item 71b)
A/78/PV.50

Korac, Sofija (United States) (continued)

HEALTH (Agenda item 125)
A/78/PV.77
HUMAN RIGHTS—INTERNATIONAL INSTRUMENTS (Agenda item 71a)
A/C.3/78/SR.47
RACIAL DISCRIMINATION—ELIMINATION (Agenda item 69a)
A/78/PV.50
RIGHT TO DEVELOPMENT (Agenda item 71b)
A/C.3/78/SR.47
RIGHT TO EDUCATION (Agenda item 71b)
A/C.3/78/SR.47
RURAL WOMEN (Agenda item 25a)
A/C.3/78/SR.49
SUSTAINABLE DEVELOPMENT (Agenda item 18)
A/C.3/78/SR.47

Korac, Sofija (United States) (European Union)

HEALTH (Agenda item 125)
A/78/PV.77

Korbieh, Solomon (Ghana)

CRIMES AGAINST HUMANITY (Agenda item 80)
A/C.6/78/SR.45

Korithiwada, Sunitha (UN. Enterprise Resource Planning Solution Division. Director)

UN—BUDGET (2024) (Agenda item 134)
A/C.5/78/SR.19

Korteweg, Chantal (Netherlands (Kingdom of the))

WOMEN'S ADVANCEMENT (Agenda item 25a)
A/C.3/78/SR.9
WOMEN'S ADVANCEMENT—CONFERENCES (Agenda item 25b)
A/C.3/78/SR.9

Korynevych, Anton (Ukraine)

UN. INTERNATIONAL COURT OF JUSTICE—REPORTS (Agenda item 73)
A/78/PV.20
UN. INTERNATIONAL LAW COMMISSION—REPORTS (Agenda item 79)
A/C.6/78/SR.25

Košuth, Matus (Slovakia)

ARMED CONFLICTS PREVENTION (Agenda item 31a)
A/78/PV.72
CRIMES AGAINST HUMANITY (Agenda item 80)
A/C.6/78/SR.10; A/C.6/78/SR.39; A/C.6/78/SR.40; A/C.6/78/SR.42; A/C.6/78/SR.45
FREEDOM OF EXPRESSION (Agenda item 71b)
A/C.3/78/SR.19
UN. INTERNATIONAL LAW COMMISSION—REPORTS (Agenda item 79)
A/C.6/78/SR.31

Košuth, Matus (Slovakia) (UN. General Assembly. 6th Committee. Bureau)

UN. INTERNATIONAL LAW COMMISSION—REPORTS (Agenda item 79)
A/C.6/78/SR.37

Kouakou, Kouadjo Michel (Côte d'Ivoire)

HUMAN RIGHTS ACTIVISTS (Agenda item 71b)
A/C.3/78/SR.19
RIGHTS OF THE CHILD (Agenda item 67)
A/C.3/78/SR.11

Koudri, Toufik Laid (Algeria)

WESTERN SAHARA QUESTION (Agenda item 58)
A/C.4/78/SR.5

Koumba Pambo, Aurélie Flore (Gabon)

CUBA—UNITED STATES (Agenda item 38)
A/78/PV.26
UN. GENERAL ASSEMBLY (78TH SESS. : 2023-2024). 1ST COMMITTEE—GENERAL DEBATE (Agenda item 8)
A/C.1/78/PV.9

Koumjian, Nicholas (UN. Independent Investigative Mechanism for Myanmar. Head)

HUMAN RIGHTS—MYANMAR (Agenda item 71c)
A/C.3/78/SR.33

Kowalski, Mateus (Portugal)

CRIMES AGAINST HUMANITY (Agenda item 80)
A/C.6/78/SR.42; A/C.6/78/SR.43; A/C.6/78/SR.44
UN. INTERNATIONAL LAW COMMISSION—REPORTS (Agenda item 79)
A/C.6/78/SR.24

Kpukumu, Sulay-Manah J. (Sierra Leone) (African Union)

UN. SECURITY COUNCIL—MEMBERSHIP (Agenda item 121)
A/78/PV.34

Krabatsch, Ann-Jasmin (Germany)

SEXUAL ORIENTATION (Agenda item 71b)
A/C.3/78/SR.39

Kridelka, Philippe (Belgium)

HUMAN RIGHTS—INTERNATIONAL INSTRUMENTS (Agenda item 71a)
A/C.3/78/SR.25
NATIONAL INSTITUTIONS—HUMAN RIGHTS (Agenda item 71b)
A/C.3/78/SR.25
PALESTINIANS—ASSISTANCE (Agenda item 72b)
A/78/PV.46
RIGHT OF ASSEMBLY (Agenda item 71b)
A/C.3/78/SR.19
SOCIAL CONDITIONS (Agenda item 24b)
A/78/PV.101

Kridelka, Philippe (Belgium) (continued)

UN. GENERAL ASSEMBLY (78TH SESS. : 2023-2024). 1ST COMMITTEE—GENERAL DEBATE (Agenda item 8)
A/C.1/78/PV.8
VETO (Agenda item 63)
A/78/PV.59; A/78/PV.68

Kridelka, Philippe (Belgium) (European Union)

RACIAL DISCRIMINATION—ELIMINATION (Agenda item 69a)
A/78/PV.63

Kris, Robert (United States)

AMERICAN SAMOA QUESTION (Agenda item 58)
A/C.4/78/SR.7
DECOLONIZATION (Agenda item 58)
A/C.4/78/SR.7
GUAM QUESTION (Agenda item 58)
A/C.4/78/SR.7
TERRITORIES OCCUPIED BY ISRAEL—HUMAN RIGHTS (Agenda item 50)
A/C.4/78/SR.26
UNITED STATES VIRGIN ISLANDS QUESTION (Agenda item 58)
A/C.4/78/SR.7

Kriss, Benjamin (United Kingdom)

DIAMONDS—FUELLING CONFLICT (Agenda item 30)
A/78/PV.65

Kristanti, Maria Benedicta Diah (Indonesia)

BIOLOGICAL WEAPONS—TREATIES (Agenda item 106)
A/C.1/78/PV.14
CHEMICAL WEAPONS—TREATIES (Agenda item 99l)
A/C.1/78/PV.14
DISARMAMENT—GENERAL AND COMPLETE (Agenda item 99)
A/C.1/78/PV.30
DISARMAMENT AGREEMENTS—OUTER SPACE (Agenda item 97c)
A/C.1/78/PV.27
FISSIONABLE MATERIALS—TREATIES (Agenda item 99a)
A/C.1/78/PV.26
NUCLEAR WEAPONS—ELIMINATION (Agenda item 99z)
A/C.1/78/PV.26
OUTER SPACE—PRINCIPLES (Agenda item 97d)
A/C.1/78/PV.27

Kristanti, Maria Benedicta Diah (Indonesia) (Coordinating Bureau of the Non-Aligned Countries)

ARMS TRANSFERS—TREATIES (Agenda item 99x)
A/C.1/78/PV.17
CONVENTIONAL WEAPONS (Agenda item 99u)
A/C.1/78/PV.17

Kristanti, Maria Benedicta Diah (Indonesia) (Coordinating Bureau of the Non-Aligned Countries) (continued)

CONVENTIONAL WEAPONS—TREATIES (Agenda item 103)
A/C.1/78/PV.17
DISARMAMENT—GENERAL AND COMPLETE (Agenda item 99)
A/C.1/78/PV.17
LANDMINES—TREATIES (Agenda item 99m)
A/C.1/78/PV.17
SMALL ARMS—ILLICIT TRAFFIC (Agenda item 99p)
A/C.1/78/PV.17
SMALL ARMS—ILLICIT TRAFFIC—ASSISTANCE (Agenda item 99n)
A/C.1/78/PV.17

Kristmoen, Rina Lise (Norway)

SUSTAINABLE DEVELOPMENT (Agenda item 18)
A/C.2/78/SR.24

Kroeker-Maus, Faith (United States)

COASTAL ZONE MANAGEMENT (Agenda item 18j)
A/C.2/78/SR.23
CULTURE—DEVELOPMENT (Agenda item 19b)
A/C.2/78/SR.23
DESERTIFICATION—TREATIES (Agenda item 18e)
A/C.2/78/SR.23
DEVELOPMENT COOPERATION—MIDDLE-INCOME COUNTRIES (Agenda item 19c)
A/C.2/78/SR.23
DISASTER PREVENTION (Agenda item 18c)
A/C.2/78/SR.23
FOOD SECURITY (Agenda item 23a)
A/C.2/78/SR.25
LANDLOCKED DEVELOPING COUNTRIES—CONFERENCES (Agenda item 20b)
A/C.2/78/SR.23
LEAST DEVELOPED COUNTRIES—CONFERENCES (Agenda item 20a)
A/C.2/78/SR.23
NATURAL FIBRES (Agenda item 23b)
A/C.2/78/SR.23
SUSTAINABLE ENERGY (Agenda item 18h)
A/C.2/78/SR.23

Kryvaltsevich, Aliaksei (Belarus)

HUMAN RIGHTS—REPORTS (Agenda item 71c)
A/C.3/78/SR.24
HUMAN RIGHTS ADVANCEMENT (Agenda item 71b)
A/C.3/78/SR.24
RIGHT TO FOOD (Agenda item 71b)
A/C.3/78/SR.30
SANCTIONS—INTERNATIONAL RELATIONS (Agenda item 71b)
A/C.3/78/SR.28
TRAFFICKING IN PERSONS (Agenda item 71b)
A/C.3/78/SR.23

Kuleba, Dmytro (Ukraine)

UKRAINE—POLITICAL CONDITIONS (Agenda item 62)
A/78/PV.56

Kulhánek, Jakub (Czechia)

ARMED CONFLICTS PREVENTION (Agenda item 31a)
A/78/PV.72
FREEDOM OF EXPRESSION (Agenda item 71b)
A/C.3/78/SR.19
HUMAN RIGHTS—AFGHANISTAN (Agenda item 71c)
A/C.3/78/SR.24
HUMAN RIGHTS—REPORTS (Agenda item 71c)
A/C.3/78/SR.24
HUMAN RIGHTS—TERRITORIES OCCUPIED BY ISRAEL (Agenda item 71c)
A/C.3/78/SR.35
HUMAN RIGHTS—UKRAINE (Agenda item 71c)
A/C.3/78/SR.24
HUMAN RIGHTS ACTIVISTS (Agenda item 71b)
A/C.3/78/SR.19
HUMAN RIGHTS ADVANCEMENT (Agenda item 71b)
A/C.3/78/SR.52
RIGHT OF ASSEMBLY (Agenda item 71b)
A/C.3/78/SR.19
VETO (Agenda item 63)
A/78/PV.3; A/78/PV.67; A/78/PV.69; A/78/PV.78

Kulkarni, Maitrey (India)

DISARMAMENT—GENERAL AND COMPLETE (Agenda item 99)
A/C.1/78/PV.30
DISARMAMENT AGREEMENTS—OUTER SPACE (Agenda item 97c)
A/C.1/78/PV.27
FISSIONABLE MATERIALS—TREATIES (Agenda item 99a)
A/C.1/78/PV.25
MIDDLE EAST—NUCLEAR PROLIFERATION (Agenda item 102)
A/C.1/78/PV.25
NUCLEAR WEAPONS—HUMANITARIAN CONSEQUENCES (Agenda item 99bb)
A/C.1/78/PV.25
NUCLEAR WEAPONS—TREATIES (Agenda item 99ff)
A/C.1/78/PV.25
NUCLEAR WEAPONS USE—UN. INTERNATIONAL COURT OF JUSTICE OPINION (Agenda item 99k)
A/C.1/78/PV.25
OUTER SPACE—PRINCIPLES (Agenda item 97d)
A/C.1/78/PV.27
SOUTH-EAST ASIA—NUCLEAR-WEAPON-FREE ZONES (Agenda item 99y)
A/C.1/78/PV.30
WEAPONS—OUTER SPACE (Agenda item 97b)
A/C.1/78/PV.27

Kumanga, Martins Mariano (Mozambique)
UN—BUDGET (2024) (Agenda item 134)
A/C.5/78/SR.5
UN—PROGRAMME PLANNING (Agenda item 135)
A/C.5/78/SR.5

Kumaria, Sacha (United Kingdom)
MERCENARIES (Agenda item 70)
A/C.3/78/SR.48
RIGHT TO FOOD (Agenda item 71b)
A/C.3/78/SR.48

Kun, Russ (Nauru. President)
UN. GENERAL ASSEMBLY (78TH SESS. : 2023-2024)—GENERAL DEBATE (Agenda item 8)
A/78/PV.9
UN. GENERAL ASSEMBLY (78TH SESS. : 2023-2024)—SPECIAL STATEMENTS
A/78/PV.9

Kupradze, Sopio (Georgia)
RULE OF LAW (Agenda item 83)
A/C.6/78/SR.18
TERRORISM (Agenda item 109)
A/C.6/78/SR.4
UN CHARTER—REPORTS (Agenda item 82)
A/C.6/78/SR.22

Kuramitsu, Shizuka (Arms Control Association (Washington, D.C.))
DISARMAMENT—GENERAL AND COMPLETE (Agenda item 99)
A/78/PV.105

Kusano, Yuta (Japan)
IAEA—REPORTS (Agenda item 89)
A/78/PV.30
OUTER SPACE—PEACEFUL USES—INTERNATIONAL COOPERATION (Agenda item 48)
A/C.4/78/SR.16
UN—PROGRAMME PLANNING (Agenda item 135)
A/C.1/78/PV.10
UN. GENERAL ASSEMBLY—WORK PROGRAMME (Agenda item 120)
A/C.1/78/PV.10

Kuymizakis, Adam (Malta)
CRIMES AGAINST HUMANITY (Agenda item 80)
A/C.6/78/SR.40
INTERNATIONAL CRIMINAL COURT—REPORTS (Agenda item 74)
A/78/PV.22
INTERNATIONAL RESIDUAL MECHANISM FOR CRIMINAL TRIBUNALS (Agenda item 126)
A/78/PV.19
RIGHTS OF THE CHILD (Agenda item 67)
A/C.3/78/SR.11
SEXUAL ORIENTATION (Agenda item 71b)
A/C.3/78/SR.39

Kuymizakis, Adam (Malta) (continued)
UKRAINE—POLITICAL CONDITIONS (Agenda item 62)
A/78/PV.58
UN. GENERAL ASSEMBLY (78TH SESS. : 2023-2024). 1ST COMMITTEE—GENERAL DEBATE (Agenda item 8)
A/C.1/78/PV.3
UN. GENERAL ASSEMBLY (78TH SESS. : 2023-2024). 2ND COMMITTEE—GENERAL DEBATE (Agenda item 8)
A/C.2/78/SR.3
UN. INTERNATIONAL COURT OF JUSTICE—REPORTS (Agenda item 73)
A/78/PV.27
VETO (Agenda item 63)
A/78/PV.66; A/78/PV.68; A/78/PV.70; A/78/PV.75

Kuzee, Helena Ndapewa (Namibia)
HEALTH (Agenda item 125)
A/78/PV.16
HIV/AIDS—DECLARATIONS (Agenda item 10)
A/78/PV.91
INFORMATION (Agenda item 53)
A/C.4/78/SR.14
NUCLEAR DISARMAMENT (Agenda item 99b)
A/C.1/78/PV.14
UN. GENERAL ASSEMBLY (78TH SESS. : 2023-2024). 1ST COMMITTEE—GENERAL DEBATE (Agenda item 8)
A/C.1/78/PV.8
VETO (Agenda item 63)
A/78/PV.52
WOMEN'S ADVANCEMENT (Agenda item 25a)
A/C.3/78/SR.9
WOMEN'S ADVANCEMENT—CONFERENCES (Agenda item 25b)
A/C.3/78/SR.9

Kuzmenkov, Stepan Y. (Russian Federation)
AGEING PERSONS (Agenda item 24b)
A/C.3/78/SR.1
CLIMATE CHANGE (Agenda item 71b)
A/C.3/78/SR.29
CRIME PREVENTION (Agenda item 107)
A/78/PV.50
DEMOCRACY (Agenda item 71b)
A/C.3/78/SR.28
DISPLACED PERSONS (Agenda item 71b)
A/C.3/78/SR.32
ENVIRONMENT (Agenda item 71b)
A/C.3/78/SR.29
EXTERNAL DEBT—HUMAN RIGHTS (Agenda item 71b)
A/C.3/78/SR.32
FREEDOM OF EXPRESSION (Agenda item 71b)
A/C.3/78/SR.19
HUMAN RIGHTS—AFGHANISTAN (Agenda item 71c)
A/C.3/78/SR.34

Kuzmenkov, Stepan Y. (Russian Federation) (continued)

HUMAN RIGHTS—CENTRAL AFRICAN REPUBLIC (Agenda item 71c)
A/C.3/78/SR.33
HUMAN RIGHTS—DEMOCRATIC PEOPLE'S REPUBLIC OF KOREA (Agenda item 71c)
A/C.3/78/SR.33; A/C.3/78/SR.53
HUMAN RIGHTS—INTERNATIONAL INSTRUMENTS (Agenda item 71a)
A/C.3/78/SR.17; A/C.3/78/SR.25
HUMAN RIGHTS—IRAN (ISLAMIC REPUBLIC OF) (Agenda item 71c)
A/C.3/78/SR.34; A/C.3/78/SR.53
HUMAN RIGHTS—MYANMAR (Agenda item 71c)
A/C.3/78/SR.53
HUMAN RIGHTS—SOMALIA (Agenda item 71c)
A/C.3/78/SR.35
HUMAN RIGHTS—SYRIAN ARAB REPUBLIC (Agenda item 71c)
A/C.3/78/SR.34; A/C.3/78/SR.54
HUMAN RIGHTS—TERRITORIES OCCUPIED BY ISRAEL (Agenda item 71c)
A/C.3/78/SR.27; A/C.3/78/SR.35
INDIGENOUS PEOPLES (Agenda item 68a)
A/C.3/78/SR.15
INDIGENOUS PEOPLES—CONFERENCES (Agenda item 68b)
A/C.3/78/SR.15
JUDICIAL INDEPENDENCE (Agenda item 71b)
A/C.3/78/SR.31
MIGRANTS—PROTECTION (Agenda item 71b)
A/C.3/78/SR.23
MINORITIES (Agenda item 71b)
A/C.3/78/SR.39
POVERTY—HUMAN RIGHTS (Agenda item 71b)
A/C.3/78/SR.30
RACIAL DISCRIMINATION—ELIMINATION (Agenda item 69a)
A/C.3/78/SR.40; A/C.3/78/SR.42
RACIAL DISCRIMINATION—PROGRAMMES OF ACTION (Agenda item 69b)
A/C.3/78/SR.40; A/C.3/78/SR.42
RIGHT OF ASSEMBLY (Agenda item 71b)
A/C.3/78/SR.19
RIGHT TO CULTURE (Agenda item 71b)
A/C.3/78/SR.27
RIGHT TO DRINKING WATER (Agenda item 71b)
A/C.3/78/SR.28
RIGHT TO EDUCATION (Agenda item 71b)
A/C.3/78/SR.27
RIGHT TO FOOD (Agenda item 71b)
A/C.3/78/SR.30
RIGHT TO HEALTH (Agenda item 71b)
A/C.3/78/SR.39
RIGHT TO HOUSING (Agenda item 71b)
A/C.3/78/SR.30
RIGHT TO PRIVACY (Agenda item 71b)
A/C.3/78/SR.21
RIGHTS OF THE CHILD (Agenda item 67)
A/C.3/78/SR.11; A/C.3/78/SR.12

Kuzmenkov, Stepan Y. (Russian Federation) (continued)

SANCTIONS—INTERNATIONAL RELATIONS (Agenda item 71b)
A/C.3/78/SR.28
SELF-DETERMINATION OF PEOPLES (Agenda item 70)
A/C.3/78/SR.40
SLAVERY (Agenda item 71a)
A/C.3/78/SR.21
SOLIDARITY (Agenda item 71b)
A/C.3/78/SR.32
SUMMARY EXECUTIONS (Agenda item 71b)
A/C.3/78/SR.31
TERRORISM—HUMAN RIGHTS (Agenda item 71b)
A/C.3/78/SR.31
TORTURE AND OTHER CRUEL TREATMENT (Agenda item 71a)
A/C.3/78/SR.18
TRAFFICKING IN PERSONS (Agenda item 71b)
A/C.3/78/SR.23
TRANSNATIONAL CORPORATIONS—HUMAN RIGHTS (Agenda item 71b)
A/C.3/78/SR.21
UN. HUMAN RIGHTS COMMITTEE—REPORTS (Agenda item 71a)
A/C.3/78/SR.17
WOMEN'S ADVANCEMENT (Agenda item 25a)
A/C.3/78/SR.7; A/C.3/78/SR.8
WOMEN'S ADVANCEMENT—CONFERENCES (Agenda item 25b)
A/C.3/78/SR.7; A/C.3/78/SR.8

Kwarra, Nasir Isa (Nigeria)

WOMEN'S ADVANCEMENT (Agenda item 25a)
A/C.3/78/SR.9
WOMEN'S ADVANCEMENT—CONFERENCES (Agenda item 25b)
A/C.3/78/SR.9

Kwoba, Godfrey (Uganda)

DECOLONIZATION (Agenda item 58)
A/C.4/78/SR.8
HUMAN RIGHTS (Agenda item 71)
A/C.3/78/SR.28
RIGHT TO DEVELOPMENT (Agenda item 71b)
A/C.3/78/SR.28

Kwoba, Godfrey (Uganda) (Coordinating Bureau of the Non-Aligned Countries)

ECONOMIC SANCTIONS—INTERNATIONAL RELATIONS (Agenda item 28)
A/78/PV.89
RAISI, SEYYED EBRAHIM (IRAN (ISLAMIC REPUBLID OF). PRESIDENT)—TRIBUTES
A/78/PV.83
VETO (Agenda item 63)
A/78/PV.74

Kwoba, Godfrey (Uganda) (Group of 77)

AFRICA—DEVELOPMENT (Agenda item 65b)
A/78/PV.57

Kwoba, Godfrey (Uganda) (Group of 77) (continued)
AFRICA—SUSTAINABLE DEVELOPMENT—PARTNERSHIP (Agenda item 65a)
A/78/PV.57
CUBA—UNITED STATES (Agenda item 38)
A/78/PV.24
ECONOMIC SANCTIONS—INTERNATIONAL RELATIONS (Agenda item 28)
A/78/PV.89
LANDLOCKED DEVELOPING COUNTRIES—CONFERENCES (Agenda item 20b)
A/78/PV.98
SMALL ISLAND DEVELOPING STATES—PROGRAMMES OF ACTION (Agenda item 18b)
A/78/PV.100
STORMS (Agenda item 18i)
A/78/PV.98

Kyslytsya, Sergiy (Ukraine)
ARMED CONFLICTS PREVENTION (Agenda item 31a)
A/78/PV.72
HUMAN RIGHTS—UKRAINE (Agenda item 71c)
A/78/PV.50; A/C.3/78/SR.53
RESPONSIBILITY TO PROTECT (Agenda item 129)
A/78/PV.99
UKRAINE—POLITICAL CONDITIONS (Agenda item 62)
A/78/PV.58; A/78/PV.99
UN. SECURITY COUNCIL—REPORTS (Agenda item 26)
A/78/PV.93
UN HIGH COMMISSIONER FOR REFUGEES—REPORTS (Agenda item 60)
A/C.3/78/SR.48

La, Haozhao (China)
HUMAN RIGHTS—INTERNATIONAL INSTRUMENTS (Agenda item 71a)
A/C.3/78/SR.17
LEPROSY (Agenda item 71b)
A/C.3/78/SR.17
RIGHTS OF THE CHILD (Agenda item 67)
A/C.3/78/SR.11; A/C.3/78/SR.12
TORTURE AND OTHER CRUEL TREATMENT (Agenda item 71a)
A/C.3/78/SR.18

Laariche, Hayat (Morocco)
WESTERN SAHARA QUESTION (Agenda item 58)
A/C.4/78/SR.4

Laboti, Shkëlqim (Albania)
CRIMES AGAINST HUMANITY (Agenda item 80)
A/C.6/78/SR.11; A/C.6/78/SR.45

Labrousse, Lou (Amazones Pacific (Organization))
FRENCH POLYNESIA QUESTION (Agenda item 58)
A/C.4/78/SR.3

Lacalle Pou, Luis (Uruguay. President)
UN. GENERAL ASSEMBLY (78TH SESS. : 2023-2024)—GENERAL DEBATE (Agenda item 8)
A/78/PV.5
UN. GENERAL ASSEMBLY (78TH SESS. : 2023-2024)—SPECIAL STATEMENTS
A/78/PV.5

Ladeb, Tarek (Tunisia)
PALESTINE QUESTION (Agenda item 35)
A/78/PV.40
PEACE (Agenda item 14)
A/78/PV.62; A/78/PV.82
VETO (Agenda item 63)
A/78/PV.67; A/78/PV.74

Ladeb, Tarek (Tunisia) (Group of Arab States)
UN. SECRETARY-GENERAL—REPORTS (Agenda item 110)
A/78/PV.55

Ladeb, Tarek (Tunisia) (UN. Group of African States)
2030 AGENDA—PROGRAMME IMPLEMENTATION (Agenda item 18a)
A/C.2/78/SR.12
AFRICA—DEVELOPMENT (Agenda item 65b)
A/78/PV.18
AFRICA—SUSTAINABLE DEVELOPMENT—PARTNERSHIP (Agenda item 65a)
A/78/PV.18
EXTERNAL DEBT (Agenda item 16c)
A/C.2/78/SR.9
FINANCIAL FLOWS (Agenda item 16f)
A/C.2/78/SR.9
INTERNATIONAL TRADE (Agenda item 16a)
A/C.2/78/SR.9
MACROECONOMIC POLICY (Agenda item 16)
A/C.2/78/SR.9
RACIAL DISCRIMINATION—ELIMINATION (Agenda item 69a)
A/C.3/78/SR.40
RACIAL DISCRIMINATION—PROGRAMMES OF ACTION (Agenda item 69b)
A/C.3/78/SR.40
RIGHT TO DEVELOPMENT (Agenda item 71b)
A/C.3/78/SR.20
RIGHTS OF THE CHILD (Agenda item 67)
A/C.3/78/SR.12
SOCIAL CONDITIONS (Agenda item 24b)
A/C.3/78/SR.2
SUSTAINABLE DEVELOPMENT (Agenda item 18)
A/C.2/78/SR.12
TAXATION (Agenda item 16h)
A/C.2/78/SR.9

Ladeb, Tarek (Tunisia) (UN. Group of African States) (continued)

UN. GENERAL ASSEMBLY (78TH SESS. : 2023-2024)—OFFICERS (Agenda item 5)
A/C.5/78/SR.1

Ladois, Jean-Noël (European Union)

INFORMATION (Agenda item 53)
A/C.4/78/SR.12

Lagardien, Yaseen (South Africa)

ARMS TRANSFERS—TREATIES (Agenda item 99x)
A/C.1/78/PV.18
CONVENTIONAL WEAPONS (Agenda item 99u)
A/C.1/78/PV.18
DISARMAMENT—GENERAL AND COMPLETE (Agenda item 99)
A/C.1/78/PV.28
INFORMATION—INTERNATIONAL SECURITY (Agenda item 94)
A/C.1/78/PV.20; A/C.1/78/PV.29
SMALL ARMS—ILLICIT TRAFFIC (Agenda item 99p)
A/C.1/78/PV.18
SMALL ARMS—ILLICIT TRAFFIC—ASSISTANCE (Agenda item 99n)
A/C.1/78/PV.18
UN. SECRETARY-GENERAL—REPORTS (Agenda item 110)
A/78/PV.55

Lagatie, Karl (Belgium)

INTERNATIONAL CRIMINAL COURT—REPORTS (Agenda item 74)
A/78/PV.22
LAW OF THE SEA (Agenda item 75a)
A/78/PV.43
MARINE ECOSYSTEMS—BIOLOGICAL DIVERSITY (Agenda item 75c)
A/78/PV.43; A/78/PV.103
STRADDLING FISH STOCKS (Agenda item 75b)
A/78/PV.43
VETO (Agenda item 63)
A/78/PV.51; A/78/PV.75

Lagatie, Karl (Belgium) (European Union)

CENTRAL ASIA—ZONES OF PEACE (Agenda item 64)
A/78/PV.85
PEACE (Agenda item 14)
A/78/PV.62

Lagdameo, Antonio Manuel Revilla (Philippines)

CUBA—UNITED STATES (Agenda item 38)
A/78/PV.26
DISASTER VICTIMS (Agenda item 86)
A/C.6/78/SR.5
HIV/AIDS—DECLARATIONS (Agenda item 10)
A/78/PV.91
IAEA—REPORTS (Agenda item 89)
A/78/PV.30

Lagdameo, Antonio Manuel Revilla (Philippines) (continued)

INTERNATIONAL CRIMINAL COURT—REPORTS (Agenda item 74)
A/78/PV.22
PEACE (Agenda item 14)
A/78/PV.76
SOCIAL CONDITIONS (Agenda item 24b)
A/C.3/78/SR.2
UN. GENERAL ASSEMBLY—WORK PROGRAMME (Agenda item 120)
A/78/PV.32
UN. INTERNATIONAL COURT OF JUSTICE—REPORTS (Agenda item 73)
A/78/PV.28
UN. SECURITY COUNCIL—MEMBERSHIP (Agenda item 121)
A/78/PV.35
UN RESOLUTIONS—IMPLEMENTATION (Agenda item 119)
A/78/PV.32
VETO (Agenda item 63)
A/78/PV.70
WOMEN MIGRANT WORKERS (Agenda item 25a)
A/C.3/78/SR.49

Lagdameo, Antonio Manuel Revilla (Philippines) (ASEAN)

UN—BUDGET (2024) (Agenda item 134)
A/C.5/78/SR.13

Lagdameo, Antonio Manuel Revilla (Philippines) (UN. General Assembly. 6th Committee. Working Group on Protection of Persons in the Event of Disasters. Chair)

DISASTER VICTIMS (Agenda item 86)
A/C.6/78/SR.36

Lages, Afonso (Portugal)

SMALL ISLAND DEVELOPING STATES—PROGRAMMES OF ACTION (Agenda item 18b)
A/78/PV.103

Laghdaf, Sidi Mohamed (Mauritania)

DISARMAMENT—GENERAL AND COMPLETE (Agenda item 99)
A/78/PV.105
PEACE (Agenda item 14)
A/78/PV.76
TERRITORIES OCCUPIED BY ISRAEL—NATURAL RESOURCES (Agenda item 59)
A/C.2/78/SR.19

Laghdaf, Sidi Mohamed (Mauritania) (Organisation of Islamic Cooperation)

CUBA—UNITED STATES (Agenda item 38)
A/78/PV.24
UN. INTERNATIONAL COURT OF JUSTICE—REPORTS (Agenda item 73)
A/78/PV.27

Lagorio, Ricardo E. (Argentina)
RESPONSIBILITY TO PROTECT (Agenda item 129)
A/78/PV.96
UN. SECURITY COUNCIL—REPORTS (Agenda item 26)
A/78/PV.93
VETO (Agenda item 63)
A/78/PV.67; A/78/PV.69; A/78/PV.71; A/78/PV.78

Lahsaini, Khalid (Morocco)
CRIMES AGAINST HUMANITY (Agenda item 80)
A/C.6/78/SR.39; A/C.6/78/SR.41
INTERNATIONAL JURISDICTION (Agenda item 84)
A/C.6/78/SR.13
UN. INTERNATIONAL LAW COMMISSION—REPORTS (Agenda item 79)
A/C.6/78/SR.37

Lai, Haiyang (China)
DISARMAMENT—GENERAL AND COMPLETE (Agenda item 99)
A/C.1/78/PV.21

Lambrinidis, Stavros (European Union)
ORGANIZATION FOR DEMOCRACY AND ECONOMIC DEVELOPMENT - GUAM (Agenda item 32)
A/78/PV.85
UKRAINE—POLITICAL CONDITIONS (Agenda item 62)
A/78/PV.57
VETO (Agenda item 63)
A/78/PV.59; A/78/PV.66; A/78/PV.68

Lamce, Enian (Albania)
ELECTION VERIFICATION—UN (Agenda item 71b)
A/C.3/78/SR.50
HUMAN RIGHTS—AFGHANISTAN (Agenda item 71c)
A/C.3/78/SR.26; A/C.3/78/SR.34
HUMAN RIGHTS—RUSSIAN FEDERATION (Agenda item 71c)
A/C.3/78/SR.37
HUMAN RIGHTS—TERRITORIES OCCUPIED BY ISRAEL (Agenda item 71c)
A/C.3/78/SR.35
HUMAN RIGHTS—UKRAINE (Agenda item 71c)
A/C.3/78/SR.26; A/C.3/78/SR.37
HUMAN RIGHTS ACTIVISTS (Agenda item 71b)
A/C.3/78/SR.26
MINORITIES (Agenda item 71b)
A/C.3/78/SR.39
RACIAL DISCRIMINATION—ELIMINATION (Agenda item 69a)
A/C.3/78/SR.47
RIGHTS OF THE CHILD (Agenda item 67)
A/C.3/78/SR.11
WOMEN'S ADVANCEMENT (Agenda item 25a)
A/C.3/78/SR.9

Lamce, Enian (Albania) (continued)
WOMEN'S ADVANCEMENT—CONFERENCES (Agenda item 25b)
A/C.3/78/SR.9

Lamigueiro Cañedo, Ivette (Cuba)
DEMOCRACY (Agenda item 71b)
A/C.3/78/SR.28
INDIGENOUS PEOPLES (Agenda item 68a)
A/C.3/78/SR.15
INDIGENOUS PEOPLES—CONFERENCES (Agenda item 68b)
A/C.3/78/SR.15
POVERTY—HUMAN RIGHTS (Agenda item 71b)
A/C.3/78/SR.30
SANCTIONS—INTERNATIONAL RELATIONS (Agenda item 71b)
A/C.3/78/SR.28
SOLIDARITY (Agenda item 71b)
A/C.3/78/SR.32

Lampridis, Spyridon (Greece)
UKRAINE—POLITICAL CONDITIONS (Agenda item 62)
A/78/PV.56

Lamuwa, Adamu Ibrahim (Nigeria)
UN. SECURITY COUNCIL—MEMBERSHIP (Agenda item 121)
A/78/PV.36

Lamuwa, Adamu Ibrahim (Nigeria) (UN. Group of African States)
UN—BUDGET (2024) (Agenda item 134)
A/C.5/78/SR.13

Lamy, Jean (France)
HUMAN RIGHTS—UKRAINE (Agenda item 71c)
A/C.3/78/SR.37
TRANSNATIONAL CORPORATIONS—HUMAN RIGHTS (Agenda item 71b)
A/C.3/78/SR.21

Landsbergis, Gabrielius (Lithuania)
UKRAINE—POLITICAL CONDITIONS (Agenda item 62)
A/78/PV.56

Landy, Caoimhe (Ireland)
FREEDOM OF EXPRESSION (Agenda item 71b)
A/C.3/78/SR.19
RELIGIOUS INTOLERANCE (Agenda item 71b)
A/C.3/78/SR.38

Lang, Dylan (United States)
AGEING PERSONS (Agenda item 24b)
A/C.3/78/SR.1
ENVIRONMENT (Agenda item 71b)
A/C.3/78/SR.29

Lang, Dylan (United States) (continued)

FAMILY (Agenda item 24b)
A/C.3/78/SR.49
HUMAN RIGHTS INSTITUTIONS—CENTRAL AFRICA (Agenda item 71b)
A/C.3/78/SR.56
MINORITIES (Agenda item 71b)
A/C.3/78/SR.39
PERSONS WITH DISABILITIES—HUMAN RIGHTS (Agenda item 71a)
A/C.3/78/SR.51
RACIAL DISCRIMINATION—ELIMINATION (Agenda item 69a)
A/C.3/78/SR.42
RACIAL DISCRIMINATION—PROGRAMMES OF ACTION (Agenda item 69b)
A/C.3/78/SR.42
RIGHT TO EDUCATION (Agenda item 71b)
A/C.3/78/SR.27
RIGHT TO HEALTH (Agenda item 71b)
A/C.3/78/SR.39
RIGHTS OF THE CHILD (Agenda item 67)
A/C.3/78/SR.11; A/C.3/78/SR.55
SEXUAL ORIENTATION (Agenda item 71b)
A/C.3/78/SR.39
SOCIAL DEVELOPMENT—CONFERENCES (Agenda item 24a)
A/C.3/78/SR.55
WOMEN'S ADVANCEMENT—CONFERENCES (Agenda item 25b)
A/C.3/78/SR.51
YOUTH (Agenda item 24b)
A/C.3/78/SR.55

Langrish, Sally (United Kingdom)

UN. INTERNATIONAL COURT OF JUSTICE—REPORTS (Agenda item 73)
A/78/PV.20
UN. INTERNATIONAL LAW COMMISSION—REPORTS (Agenda item 79)
A/C.6/78/SR.23

Lapasov, Ulugbek (Uzbekistan)

CENTRAL ASIA—ZONES OF PEACE (Agenda item 64)
A/78/PV.85
SUSTAINABLE DEVELOPMENT (Agenda item 18)
A/78/PV.57; A/78/PV.103
UN. GENERAL ASSEMBLY (78TH SESS. : 2023-2024). 2ND COMMITTEE—GENERAL DEBATE (Agenda item 8)
A/C.2/78/SR.6

Laputin, Vadim (Russian Federation)

UN—ADMINISTRATION (Agenda item 132)
A/C.5/78/SR.2
UN—BUDGET (2024) (Agenda item 134)
A/78/PV.73; A/C.5/78/SR.23; A/C.5/78/SR.28
UN—BUDGET CONTRIBUTIONS (Agenda item 138)
A/C.5/78/SR.1

Laputin, Vadim (Russian Federation) (continued)

UN—HUMAN RESOURCES MANAGEMENT (Agenda item 139)
A/C.5/78/SR.27
UN. GENERAL ASSEMBLY (78TH SESS. : 2023-2024). 5TH COMMITTEE—WORK ORGANIZATION (Agenda item 7)
A/C.5/78/SR.27; A/C.5/78/SR.35
UN. OFFICE OF INTERNAL OVERSIGHT SERVICES—REPORTS (Agenda item 143)
A/C.5/78/SR.2

Larsen, James (Australia)

CLIMATE (Agenda item 18d)
A/C.2/78/SR.15
DISARMAMENT—GENERAL AND COMPLETE (Agenda item 99)
A/78/PV.106
EMERGENCY ASSISTANCE (Agenda item 72a)
A/78/PV.46
HEALTH (Agenda item 125)
A/78/PV.16
HIV/AIDS—DECLARATIONS (Agenda item 10)
A/78/PV.91
HUMAN RIGHTS—AFGHANISTAN (Agenda item 71c)
A/C.3/78/SR.34
HUMAN RIGHTS—INTERNATIONAL INSTRUMENTS (Agenda item 71a)
A/C.3/78/SR.25
HUMAN RIGHTS—REPORTS (Agenda item 71c)
A/C.3/78/SR.25
HUMAN RIGHTS—SYRIAN ARAB REPUBLIC (Agenda item 71c)
A/C.3/78/SR.34
INDIGENOUS PEOPLES (Agenda item 68a)
A/78/PV.107; A/C.3/78/SR.15
INDIGENOUS PEOPLES—CONFERENCES (Agenda item 68b)
A/C.3/78/SR.15
INTERNATIONAL CRIMINAL COURT—REPORTS (Agenda item 74)
A/78/PV.22
LAW OF THE SEA (Agenda item 75a)
A/78/PV.43
MARINE ECOSYSTEMS—BIOLOGICAL DIVERSITY (Agenda item 75c)
A/78/PV.43
MILLENNIUM SUMMIT—CONFERENCES (Agenda item 117)
A/78/PV.15
MINE CLEARANCE (Agenda item 46)
A/C.4/78/SR.10
NUCLEAR DISARMAMENT (Agenda item 99b)
A/C.1/78/PV.12
NUCLEAR DISARMAMENT—VERIFICATION (Agenda item 99ee)
A/C.1/78/PV.12
NUCLEAR NON-PROLIFERATION—INTERNATIONAL OBLIGATIONS (Agenda item 99w)
A/C.1/78/PV.12

Larsen, James (Australia) (continued)

NUCLEAR WEAPON TESTS—TREATIES (Agenda item 105)
A/C.1/78/PV.12
ORGANIZATION FOR DEMOCRACY AND ECONOMIC DEVELOPMENT - GUAM (Agenda item 32)
A/78/PV.85
PEACEKEEPING OPERATIONS (Agenda item 51)
A/C.4/78/SR.18
RACIAL DISCRIMINATION—ELIMINATION (Agenda item 69a)
A/C.3/78/SR.47
RESPONSIBILITY TO PROTECT (Agenda item 129)
A/78/PV.96
SMALL ISLAND DEVELOPING STATES—PROGRAMMES OF ACTION (Agenda item 18b)
A/C.2/78/SR.15
STRADDLING FISH STOCKS (Agenda item 75b)
A/78/PV.43
SUSTAINABLE DEVELOPMENT (Agenda item 18)
A/78/PV.107; A/C.2/78/SR.15
UKRAINE—POLITICAL CONDITIONS (Agenda item 62)
A/78/PV.57
UN. GENERAL ASSEMBLY (78TH SESS. : 2023-2024)—OFFICERS (Agenda item 5)
A/C.5/78/SR.1
UN. GENERAL ASSEMBLY (78TH SESS. : 2023-2024). 2ND COMMITTEE—GENERAL DEBATE (Agenda item 8)
A/C.2/78/SR.2
UN CONFERENCES (Agenda item 13)
A/78/PV.15
VETO (Agenda item 63)
A/78/PV.51; A/78/PV.59; A/78/PV.68; A/78/PV.78

LaRue, Claudia M. (Dominican Republic)

UN. GENERAL ASSEMBLY (78TH SESS. : 2023-2024). 2ND COMMITTEE—GENERAL DEBATE (Agenda item 8)
A/C.2/78/SR.2

Lasota, Josephine (Germany)

UN HIGH COMMISSIONER FOR REFUGEES—REPORTS (Agenda item 60)
A/C.3/78/SR.45

Lasri, El Hassan (Morocco)

DISASTER VICTIMS (Agenda item 86)
A/C.6/78/SR.6
TERRORISM (Agenda item 109)
A/C.6/78/SR.4

Lassen, Christina Markus (Denmark)

INDIGENOUS PEOPLES (Agenda item 68a)
A/C.3/78/SR.15
INDIGENOUS PEOPLES—CONFERENCES (Agenda item 68b)
A/C.3/78/SR.15

Lassen, Christina Markus (Denmark) (continued)

TORTURE AND OTHER CRUEL TREATMENT (Agenda item 71a)
A/C.3/78/SR.18
UN HIGH COMMISSIONER FOR REFUGEES—REPORTS (Agenda item 60)
A/C.3/78/SR.44
UNRWA—ACTIVITIES (Agenda item 49)
A/C.4/78/SR.22
VETO (Agenda item 63)
A/78/PV.3; A/78/PV.78

Lasseur, Katja (Netherlands (Kingdom of the))

HUMAN RIGHTS (Agenda item 71)
A/C.3/78/SR.16
HUMAN RIGHTS—RUSSIAN FEDERATION (Agenda item 71c)
A/C.3/78/SR.37
HUMAN RIGHTS—UKRAINE (Agenda item 71c)
A/C.3/78/SR.37
UN. HUMAN RIGHTS COUNCIL—REPORTS (Agenda item 66)
A/C.3/78/SR.46
YOUTH (Agenda item 24b)
A/C.3/78/SR.55

Lasso Mendoza, Guillermo (Ecuador. President)

UN. GENERAL ASSEMBLY (78TH SESS. : 2023-2024)—GENERAL DEBATE (Agenda item 8)
A/78/PV.6
UN. GENERAL ASSEMBLY (78TH SESS. : 2023-2024)—SPECIAL STATEMENTS
A/78/PV.6

Latrous, Mohamed-Esseghir (Algeria)

COMMODITIES (Agenda item 16d)
A/C.2/78/SR.14
FOOD SECURITY (Agenda item 23a)
A/C.2/78/SR.17
POVERTY—INTERNATIONAL DECADES (Agenda item 21a)
A/C.2/78/SR.17
RURAL POVERTY (Agenda item 21b)
A/C.2/78/SR.17
SUSTAINABLE DEVELOPMENT (Agenda item 18)
A/C.2/78/SR.14
UN. GENERAL ASSEMBLY (78TH SESS. : 2023-2024). 2ND COMMITTEE—GENERAL DEBATE (Agenda item 8)
A/C.2/78/SR.6

Laukkanen, Virpi (Finland)

RESPONSIBILITY OF INTERNATIONAL ORGANIZATIONS (Agenda item 85)
A/C.6/78/SR.19

Laursen, Erik (Denmark)

CRIMES AGAINST HUMANITY (Agenda item 80)
A/C.6/78/SR.41

Laursen, Erik (Denmark) (continued)

DISASTER VICTIMS (Agenda item 86)
A/C.6/78/SR.5
INTERNATIONAL LAW—TRAINING PROGRAMMES (Agenda item 78)
A/C.6/78/SR.21
PEACEBUILDING (Agenda item 61)
A/78/PV.100
RULE OF LAW (Agenda item 83)
A/C.6/78/SR.15
TERRORISM (Agenda item 109)
A/C.6/78/SR.1
UN. GENERAL ASSEMBLY (78TH SESS. : 2023-2024). 1ST COMMITTEE—GENERAL DEBATE (Agenda item 8)
A/C.1/78/PV.2
UN. INTERNATIONAL LAW COMMISSION—REPORTS (Agenda item 79)
A/C.6/78/SR.29
UN. PEACEBUILDING COMMISSION—REPORTS (Agenda item 27)
A/78/PV.100
UN. PEACEBUILDING FUND—REPORTS (Agenda item 111)
A/78/PV.100
UN. SECURITY COUNCIL—MEMBERSHIP (Agenda item 121)
A/78/PV.34
UN HIGH COMMISSIONER FOR REFUGEES—REPORTS (Agenda item 60)
A/C.3/78/SR.51
VETO (Agenda item 63)
A/78/PV.70

Lautasi, Isaia (Samoa) (Alliance of Small Island States)

2030 AGENDA—PROGRAMME IMPLEMENTATION (Agenda item 18a)
A/C.2/78/SR.12
CLIMATE (Agenda item 18d)
A/C.2/78/SR.12
DISASTER PREVENTION (Agenda item 18c)
A/C.2/78/SR.12
FOOD SECURITY (Agenda item 23a)
A/C.2/78/SR.16
MILLENNIUM SUMMIT—CONFERENCES (Agenda item 117)
A/78/PV.102
POVERTY—INTERNATIONAL DECADES (Agenda item 21a)
A/C.2/78/SR.16
RURAL POVERTY (Agenda item 21b)
A/C.2/78/SR.16
SUSTAINABLE DEVELOPMENT (Agenda item 18)
A/C.2/78/SR.12
UN CONFERENCES (Agenda item 13)
A/78/PV.102

Lavalle Merchán, Jesús María (Spain) (European Union)

TERRITORIES OCCUPIED BY ISRAEL—NATURAL RESOURCES (Agenda item 59)
A/C.2/78/SR.21

Lavrov, Sergei Viktorovich (Russian Federation)

UN. GENERAL ASSEMBLY (78TH SESS. : 2023-2024)—GENERAL DEBATE (Agenda item 8)
A/78/PV.12

Lawlor, Mary (UN. Human Rights Council. Special Rapporteur on the Situation of Human Rights Defenders)

HUMAN RIGHTS ACTIVISTS (Agenda item 71b)
A/C.3/78/SR.19

Lawrence, Jason N. (United States)

BIOLOGICAL DIVERSITY—TREATIES (Agenda item 18f)
A/C.2/78/SR.25
CLIMATE (Agenda item 18d)
A/C.2/78/SR.25
COMMODITIES (Agenda item 16d)
A/C.2/78/SR.23
FINANCIAL FLOWS (Agenda item 16f)
A/C.2/78/SR.23
INFORMATION TECHNOLOGY—DEVELOPMENT (Agenda item 15)
A/C.2/78/SR.23
INTERNATIONAL TRADE (Agenda item 16a)
A/C.2/78/SR.22; A/C.2/78/SR.24
INVESTMENT PROMOTION (Agenda item 16g)
A/C.2/78/SR.23
RURAL POVERTY (Agenda item 21b)
A/C.2/78/SR.22
SCIENCE AND TECHNOLOGY—DEVELOPMENT (Agenda item 19a)
A/C.2/78/SR.22

Lázár, Lilla (Hungary) (European Union)

UN CONFERENCES (Agenda item 13)
A/78/PV.107

Lazaruc, Ana Maria (Romania)

SOCIAL DEVELOPMENT (Agenda item 24)
A/C.3/78/SR.3

Le, Duc Hanh (Viet Nam)

UN. INTERNATIONAL LAW COMMISSION—REPORTS (Agenda item 79)
A/C.6/78/SR.25; A/C.6/78/SR.28

Le, Shuang (China)

WOMEN'S ADVANCEMENT (Agenda item 25a)
A/C.3/78/SR.7
WOMEN'S ADVANCEMENT—CONFERENCES (Agenda item 25b)
A/C.3/78/SR.7

Le Gayic, Tematai (France)
FRENCH POLYNESIA QUESTION (Agenda item 58)
A/C.4/78/SR.3

Le Son, Daphné Brigitte Marie (Monaco)
SPORTS—OLYMPIC GAMES (Agenda item 11)
A/78/PV.38

Leal Matta, Edgar Daniel (Guatemala)
CRIMES AGAINST HUMANITY (Agenda item 80)
A/C.6/78/SR.45; A/C.6/78/SR.46
PEACE (Agenda item 14)
A/78/PV.82
UN. GENERAL ASSEMBLY (78TH SESS. : 2023-2024)—GENERAL DEBATE—RIGHT OF REPLY (Agenda item 8)
A/78/PV.14
UN. INTERNATIONAL LAW COMMISSION—REPORTS (Agenda item 79)
A/C.6/78/SR.30; A/C.6/78/SR.32

Lebbaz, Larbi Abdelfattah (Algeria)
ARMS RACE—OUTER SPACE (Agenda item 97a)
A/C.1/78/PV.17
BIOLOGICAL WEAPONS—TREATIES (Agenda item 106)
A/C.1/78/PV.15
CHEMICAL WEAPONS—TREATIES (Agenda item 99l)
A/C.1/78/PV.15
CONVENTIONAL WEAPONS—TREATIES (Agenda item 103)
A/C.1/78/PV.19
DISARMAMENT—GENERAL AND COMPLETE (Agenda item 99)
A/C.1/78/PV.19; A/C.1/78/PV.30
DISARMAMENT AGREEMENTS—OUTER SPACE (Agenda item 97c)
A/C.1/78/PV.17
INFORMATION—INTERNATIONAL SECURITY (Agenda item 94)
A/C.1/78/PV.21
LANDMINES—TREATIES (Agenda item 99m)
A/C.1/78/PV.19
MEDITERRANEAN REGION—REGIONAL SECURITY (Agenda item 104)
A/C.1/78/PV.22
MIDDLE EAST—NUCLEAR-WEAPON-FREE ZONES (Agenda item 95)
A/C.1/78/PV.14; A/C.1/78/PV.22
MULTILATERALISM—DISARMAMENT (Agenda item 99r)
A/C.1/78/PV.22
NUCLEAR DISARMAMENT (Agenda item 99b)
A/C.1/78/PV.14
NUCLEAR NON-PROLIFERATION—INTERNATIONAL OBLIGATIONS (Agenda item 99w)
A/C.1/78/PV.14

Lebbaz, Larbi Abdelfattah (Algeria) (continued)
NUCLEAR WEAPON TESTS—TREATIES (Agenda item 105)
A/C.1/78/PV.14
OUTER SPACE—CONFIDENCE-BUILDING MEASURES (Agenda item 99v)
A/C.1/78/PV.17
OUTER SPACE—PRINCIPLES (Agenda item 97d)
A/C.1/78/PV.17
PEACE—REGIONAL CENTRE—AFRICA (Agenda item 100b)
A/C.1/78/PV.23
SMALL ARMS—ILLICIT TRAFFIC (Agenda item 99p)
A/C.1/78/PV.19
SMALL ARMS—ILLICIT TRAFFIC—ASSISTANCE (Agenda item 99n)
A/C.1/78/PV.19
UN. GENERAL ASSEMBLY (78TH SESS. : 2023-2024). 1ST COMMITTEE—GENERAL DEBATE (Agenda item 8)
A/C.1/78/PV.8
WEAPONS—OUTER SPACE (Agenda item 97b)
A/C.1/78/PV.17

Lebdioui, Amir (University of Oxford)
COMMODITIES (Agenda item 16d)
A/C.2/78/SR.14
SUSTAINABLE DEVELOPMENT (Agenda item 18)
A/C.2/78/SR.14

Lebédel-Delumeau, Eric (France)
HUMAN RIGHTS—AFGHANISTAN (Agenda item 71c)
A/C.3/78/SR.25
HUMAN RIGHTS—REPORTS (Agenda item 71c)
A/C.3/78/SR.25
HUMAN RIGHTS—SYRIAN ARAB REPUBLIC (Agenda item 71c)
A/C.3/78/SR.25
HUMAN RIGHTS—UKRAINE (Agenda item 71c)
A/C.3/78/SR.25
POVERTY—HUMAN RIGHTS (Agenda item 71b)
A/C.3/78/SR.30

LeClerc, Emmanuel (France)
WOMEN'S ADVANCEMENT (Agenda item 25a)
A/C.3/78/SR.9
WOMEN'S ADVANCEMENT—CONFERENCES (Agenda item 25b)
A/C.3/78/SR.9

Lee, Hyun Goo (Republic of Korea)
DISARMAMENT—YOUTH (Agenda item 99gg)
A/C.1/78/PV.21; A/C.1/78/PV.28
INFORMATION—INTERNATIONAL SECURITY (Agenda item 94)
A/C.1/78/PV.21; A/C.1/78/PV.29
OUTER SPACE—PEACEFUL USES—INTERNATIONAL COOPERATION (Agenda item 48)
A/C.4/78/SR.17

Lee, Hyun Goo (Republic of Korea) (continued)
VETO (Agenda item 63)
A/78/PV.79

Lee, Kok Ting (Brunei Darussalam)
EMERGENCY ASSISTANCE (Agenda item 72a)
A/78/PV.47
PALESTINIANS—ASSISTANCE (Agenda item 72b)
A/78/PV.47

Lee, Shin-wha (Republic of Korea)
HUMAN RIGHTS—DEMOCRATIC PEOPLE'S REPUBLIC OF KOREA (Agenda item 71c)
A/C.3/78/SR.33

Lee, Yeseung (Republic of Korea)
PERSONS WITH DISABILITIES—HUMAN RIGHTS (Agenda item 71a)
A/C.3/78/SR.38
TERRORISM—HUMAN RIGHTS (Agenda item 71b)
A/C.3/78/SR.31

Lee, Young Ju (Republic of Korea)
UN. INTERNATIONAL LAW COMMISSION—REPORTS (Agenda item 79)
A/C.6/78/SR.28; A/C.6/78/SR.30; A/C.6/78/SR.31

Leede, Iris Mariken de (Netherlands (Kingdom of the))
HUMAN RIGHTS—ETHIOPIA (Agenda item 71c)
A/C.3/78/SR.36

Leendertse, Antje (Germany)
HUMAN RIGHTS ADVANCEMENT (Agenda item 71b)
A/C.3/78/SR.26
PEACE (Agenda item 14)
A/78/PV.82
VETO (Agenda item 63)
A/78/PV.68; A/78/PV.78

Leendertse, Antje (Germany) (Group of Four)
UN. SECURITY COUNCIL—MEMBERSHIP (Agenda item 121)
A/78/PV.34

Leendertse, Antje (Germany) (UN. Group of Western European and Other States)
RACIAL DISCRIMINATION—ELIMINATION (Agenda item 69a)
A/78/PV.63

Lefeber, René (Netherlands (Kingdom of the))
UN. INTERNATIONAL COURT OF JUSTICE—REPORTS (Agenda item 73)
A/78/PV.20; A/C.6/78/SR.26
UN. INTERNATIONAL LAW COMMISSION—REPORTS (Agenda item 79)
A/C.6/78/SR.24

Leite, Patricia Soares (Brazil)
RIGHT TO HEALTH (Agenda item 71b)
A/C.3/78/SR.39
SEXUAL ORIENTATION (Agenda item 71b)
A/C.3/78/SR.39
WOMEN'S ADVANCEMENT (Agenda item 25a)
A/C.3/78/SR.7
WOMEN'S ADVANCEMENT—CONFERENCES (Agenda item 25b)
A/C.3/78/SR.7

Lelek, Julia (United States)
DIAMONDS—FUELLING CONFLICT (Agenda item 30)
A/78/PV.65

Lelisa, Nthabiseng Matlhohonolofatso (Lesotho)
HUMAN RIGHTS (Agenda item 71)
A/C.3/78/SR.28
HUMAN RIGHTS—INTERNATIONAL INSTRUMENTS (Agenda item 71a)
A/C.3/78/SR.28
JUDICIAL INDEPENDENCE (Agenda item 71b)
A/C.3/78/SR.31
PERSONS WITH DISABILITIES—HUMAN RIGHTS (Agenda item 71a)
A/C.3/78/SR.38
RACIAL DISCRIMINATION—ELIMINATION (Agenda item 69a)
A/C.3/78/SR.40
RACIAL DISCRIMINATION—PROGRAMMES OF ACTION (Agenda item 69b)
A/C.3/78/SR.40
RIGHT TO HEALTH (Agenda item 71b)
A/C.3/78/SR.39

Lemmetty, Elina (Finland)
CRIMES AGAINST HUMANITY (Agenda item 80)
A/C.6/78/SR.39

Lenanguy Brinz, Yannick-Michel (Central African Republic)
RIGHTS OF THE CHILD (Agenda item 67)
A/C.3/78/SR.13
WOMEN'S ADVANCEMENT (Agenda item 25a)
A/C.3/78/SR.9
WOMEN'S ADVANCEMENT—CONFERENCES (Agenda item 25b)
A/C.3/78/SR.9
YOUTH (Agenda item 24b)
A/C.3/78/SR.3

Lenz, Janet ((personal capacity))
WESTERN SAHARA QUESTION (Agenda item 58)
A/C.4/78/SR.5

Leonard, Mary Beth (United States)
FOOD SECURITY (Agenda item 23a)
A/C.2/78/SR.17

Leonard, Mary Beth (United States) (continued)
HUMAN RIGHTS—BURUNDI (Agenda item 71c)
A/C.3/78/SR.36
HUMAN RIGHTS—CENTRAL AFRICAN REPUBLIC (Agenda item 71c)
A/C.3/78/SR.33
HUMAN RIGHTS—ERITREA (Agenda item 71c)
A/C.3/78/SR.36
HUMAN RIGHTS—ETHIOPIA (Agenda item 71c)
A/C.3/78/SR.36
HUMAN RIGHTS—SOMALIA (Agenda item 71c)
A/C.3/78/SR.35
POVERTY—INTERNATIONAL DECADES (Agenda item 21a)
A/C.2/78/SR.17
RURAL POVERTY (Agenda item 21b)
A/C.2/78/SR.17

Leonard, Roisin (Ireland)
HUMAN RIGHTS ADVANCEMENT (Agenda item 71b)
A/C.3/78/SR.18
RIGHTS OF THE CHILD (Agenda item 67)
A/C.3/78/SR.13
TERRORISM—HUMAN RIGHTS (Agenda item 71b)
A/C.3/78/SR.18; A/C.3/78/SR.31
TRANSNATIONAL CORPORATIONS—HUMAN RIGHTS (Agenda item 71b)
A/C.3/78/SR.21

Leonidchenko, Sergey A. (Russian Federation)
CRIME PREVENTION (Agenda item 107)
A/C.3/78/SR.5
CYBERCRIME (Agenda item 108)
A/C.3/78/SR.5
RESPONSIBILITY TO PROTECT (Agenda item 129)
A/78/PV.97; A/78/PV.99
UN. GENERAL ASSEMBLY (78TH SESS. : 2023-2024)—AGENDA (Agenda item 7)
A/BUR/78/SR.2

Lepage, Natasha (Luxembourg)
RIGHTS OF THE CHILD (Agenda item 67)
A/C.3/78/SR.12
TORTURE AND OTHER CRUEL TREATMENT (Agenda item 71a)
A/C.3/78/SR.18
WOMEN'S ADVANCEMENT (Agenda item 25a)
A/C.3/78/SR.8
WOMEN'S ADVANCEMENT—CONFERENCES (Agenda item 25b)
A/C.3/78/SR.8

Leschenko, Volodymyr (Ukraine)
CLIMATE (Agenda item 18d)
A/C.2/78/SR.13
FOOD SECURITY (Agenda item 23a)
A/C.2/78/SR.16; A/C.2/78/SR.25

Leschenko, Volodymyr (Ukraine) (continued)
POVERTY—INTERNATIONAL DECADES (Agenda item 21a)
A/C.2/78/SR.16
RURAL POVERTY (Agenda item 21b)
A/C.2/78/SR.16
SUSTAINABLE DEVELOPMENT (Agenda item 18)
A/C.2/78/SR.13
TRAFFIC SAFETY (Agenda item 12)
A/78/PV.92
UN. GENERAL ASSEMBLY (78TH SESS. : 2023-2024). 2ND COMMITTEE—GENERAL DEBATE (Agenda item 8)
A/C.2/78/SR.3

Leuca, Gheorghe (Republic of Moldova)
HUMAN RIGHTS (Agenda item 71)
A/C.3/78/SR.25
SANCTIONS—INTERNATIONAL RELATIONS (Agenda item 71b)
A/C.3/78/SR.25
UKRAINE—POLITICAL CONDITIONS (Agenda item 62)
A/78/PV.57

Li, Hong (Organisation for the Prohibition of Chemical Weapons)
CHEMICAL WEAPONS—TREATIES (Agenda item 99l)
A/C.1/78/PV.16

Li, Junhua (UN. Under-Secretary-General for Economic and Social Affairs)
SOCIAL DEVELOPMENT (Agenda item 24)
A/C.3/78/SR.1
UN. GENERAL ASSEMBLY (78TH SESS. : 2023-2024). 2ND COMMITTEE—GENERAL DEBATE (Agenda item 8)
A/C.2/78/SR.2
UN. GENERAL ASSEMBLY (78TH SESS. : 2023-2024). 2ND COMMITTEE—WORK ORGANIZATION (Agenda item 7)
A/C.2/78/SR.25

Li, Lifeng (FAO)
STORMS (Agenda item 18i)
A/C.2/78/SR.12

Li, Linlin (China)
CRIMES AGAINST HUMANITY (Agenda item 80)
A/C.6/78/SR.38; A/C.6/78/SR.40
INTERNATIONAL JURISDICTION (Agenda item 84)
A/C.6/78/SR.12
LAW OF THE SEA (Agenda item 75a)
A/78/PV.44
MARINE ECOSYSTEMS—BIOLOGICAL DIVERSITY (Agenda item 75c)
A/78/PV.44

Li, Linlin (China) (continued)

RULE OF LAW (Agenda item 83)
A/C.6/78/SR.16
STRADDLING FISH STOCKS (Agenda item 75b)
A/78/PV.44
UN. COMMITTEE ON RELATIONS WITH THE HOST COUNTRY—REPORTS (Agenda item 161)
A/C.6/78/SR.35
UN. GENERAL ASSEMBLY (78TH SESS. : 2023-2024)—GENERAL DEBATE—RIGHT OF REPLY (Agenda item 8)
A/78/PV.13
UN. INTERNATIONAL LAW COMMISSION—REPORTS (Agenda item 79)
A/C.6/78/SR.37

Li, Nan (China)

HIV/AIDS—DECLARATIONS (Agenda item 10)
A/78/PV.91
INFORMATION—INTERNATIONAL SECURITY (Agenda item 94)
A/C.1/78/PV.29
UN. GENERAL ASSEMBLY (78TH SESS. : 2023-2024). 1ST COMMITTEE—GENERAL DEBATE (Agenda item 8)
A/C.1/78/PV.6

Lia, Alex (Australia)

ARMS RACE—OUTER SPACE (Agenda item 97a)
A/C.1/78/PV.16
OUTER SPACE—PRINCIPLES (Agenda item 97d)
A/C.1/78/PV.16

Liang, Hengzhu (China)

UN. GENERAL ASSEMBLY (78TH SESS. : 2023-2024)—AGENDA (Agenda item 7)
A/BUR/78/SR.2

Liddle, Aidan Thomas (United Kingdom)

ARMS RACE—OUTER SPACE (Agenda item 97a)
A/C.1/78/PV.16
MULTILATERALISM—DISARMAMENT (Agenda item 99r)
A/C.1/78/PV.21
NUCLEAR DISARMAMENT (Agenda item 99b)
A/C.1/78/PV.13
NUCLEAR DISARMAMENT—VERIFICATION (Agenda item 99ee)
A/C.1/78/PV.13
NUCLEAR NON-PROLIFERATION—INTERNATIONAL OBLIGATIONS (Agenda item 99w)
A/C.1/78/PV.13
NUCLEAR WEAPON TESTS—TREATIES (Agenda item 105)
A/C.1/78/PV.13
OUTER SPACE—PRINCIPLES (Agenda item 97d)
A/C.1/78/PV.16; A/C.1/78/PV.27
UN—PROGRAMME PLANNING (Agenda item 135)
A/C.1/78/PV.10

Liddle, Aidan Thomas (United Kingdom) (continued)

UN. GENERAL ASSEMBLY—WORK PROGRAMME (Agenda item 120)
A/C.1/78/PV.10
UN. GENERAL ASSEMBLY (78TH SESS. : 2023-2024). 1ST COMMITTEE—GENERAL DEBATE (Agenda item 8)
A/C.1/78/PV.4
WEAPONS—OUTER SPACE (Agenda item 97b)
A/C.1/78/PV.16

Lim, Jessie (Singapore)

IAEA—REPORTS (Agenda item 89)
A/78/PV.29
NUCLEAR DISARMAMENT (Agenda item 99b)
A/C.1/78/PV.12
NUCLEAR NON-PROLIFERATION—INTERNATIONAL OBLIGATIONS (Agenda item 99w)
A/C.1/78/PV.12
NUCLEAR WEAPON TESTS—TREATIES (Agenda item 105)
A/C.1/78/PV.12
SOUTH-EAST ASIA—NUCLEAR-WEAPON-FREE ZONES (Agenda item 99y)
A/C.1/78/PV.12

Lim, Luo You Clarice (Singapore)

OUTER SPACE—PEACEFUL USES—INTERNATIONAL COOPERATION (Agenda item 48)
A/C.4/78/SR.16

Ling, Feng (China)

RADIATION EFFECTS (Agenda item 47)
A/C.4/78/SR.11

Linton, Sarah Joy (Australia)

SUSTAINABLE DEVELOPMENT (Agenda item 18)
A/C.2/78/SR.24

Linton, Sarah Joy (Australia) (European Union)

UN. GENERAL ASSEMBLY—WORK PROGRAMME (Agenda item 120)
A/C.2/78/SR.25

Liolocha, Victoria Lieta (Democratic Republic of the Congo)

NUCLEAR NON-PROLIFERATION—INTERNATIONAL OBLIGATIONS (Agenda item 99w)
A/C.1/78/PV.13
NUCLEAR WEAPONS—HUMANITARIAN CONSEQUENCES (Agenda item 99bb)
A/C.1/78/PV.13
NUCLEAR WEAPONS—TREATIES (Agenda item 99ff)
A/C.1/78/PV.13

Lipana, Diane Shayne Dela Fuente (Philippines)

ARMS RACE—OUTER SPACE (Agenda item 97a)
A/C.1/78/PV.16

Lipana, Diane Shayne Dela Fuente (Philippines) (continued)

BIOLOGICAL WEAPONS—TREATIES (Agenda item 106)
A/C.1/78/PV.14
CHEMICAL WEAPONS—TREATIES (Agenda item 99l)
A/C.1/78/PV.14
DISARMAMENT—GENERAL AND COMPLETE (Agenda item 99)
A/78/PV.105; A/C.1/78/PV.20
DISARMAMENT AGREEMENTS—ENVIRONMENT (Agenda item 99j)
A/C.1/78/PV.20
DISARMAMENT AGREEMENTS—OUTER SPACE (Agenda item 97c)
A/C.1/78/PV.27
DISARMAMENT-DEVELOPMENT LINK (Agenda item 99d)
A/C.1/78/PV.20
INFORMATION—INTERNATIONAL SECURITY (Agenda item 94)
A/C.1/78/PV.20; A/C.1/78/PV.29
OUTER SPACE—CONFIDENCE-BUILDING MEASURES (Agenda item 99v)
A/C.1/78/PV.16
OUTER SPACE—PRINCIPLES (Agenda item 97d)
A/C.1/78/PV.16; A/C.1/78/PV.27
UN. CONFERENCE ON DISARMAMENT—REPORTS (Agenda item 101a)
A/C.1/78/PV.29
UN. GENERAL ASSEMBLY (78TH SESS. : 2023-2024). 1ST COMMITTEE—WORK ORGANIZATION (Agenda item 7)
A/C.1/78/PV.29
WEAPONS OF MASS DESTRUCTION—TERRORISM (Agenda item 99s)
A/C.1/78/PV.14

Lippwe, Jeem (Micronesia (Federated States of))

DISASTER VICTIMS (Agenda item 86)
A/C.6/78/SR.6
LAW OF THE SEA (Agenda item 75a)
A/78/PV.44
MARINE ECOSYSTEMS—BIOLOGICAL DIVERSITY (Agenda item 75c)
A/78/PV.44
RIGHTS OF THE CHILD (Agenda item 67)
A/C.3/78/SR.13
STRADDLING FISH STOCKS (Agenda item 75b)
A/78/PV.44
UN. INTERNATIONAL LAW COMMISSION—REPORTS (Agenda item 79)
A/C.6/78/SR.27
WOMEN'S ADVANCEMENT (Agenda item 25a)
A/C.3/78/SR.10
WOMEN'S ADVANCEMENT—CONFERENCES (Agenda item 25b)
A/C.3/78/SR.10

Lito, Melina (United Kingdom)

ADMINISTRATION OF JUSTICE (Agenda item 144)
A/C.6/78/SR.9
INTERNATIONAL LAW—TRAINING PROGRAMMES (Agenda item 78)
A/C.6/78/SR.21
NON-CITIZENS—DEPORTATION (Agenda item 81)
A/C.6/78/SR.34
RULE OF LAW (Agenda item 83)
A/C.6/78/SR.16
TREATIES (Agenda item 87)
A/C.6/78/SR.20
UN CHARTER—REPORTS (Agenda item 82)
A/C.6/78/SR.22
UN COMMISSION ON INTERNATIONAL TRADE LAW—REPORTS (Agenda item 77)
A/C.6/78/SR.14

Liu, Han (China)

CRIME PREVENTION (Agenda item 107)
A/C.3/78/SR.5
CYBERCRIME (Agenda item 108)
A/C.3/78/SR.5

Liu, Liqun (China)

BIOLOGICAL DIVERSITY—TREATIES (Agenda item 18f)
A/C.2/78/SR.25
CLIMATE (Agenda item 18d)
A/C.2/78/SR.25
RURAL POVERTY (Agenda item 21b)
A/C.2/78/SR.22

Liu, Lu (Singapore)

NUCLEAR WEAPONS—TREATIES (Agenda item 99ff)
A/C.1/78/PV.26

Liu, Luoge (China)

CLIMATE CHANGE (Agenda item 71b)
A/C.3/78/SR.29
ENVIRONMENT (Agenda item 71b)
A/C.3/78/SR.29
HUMAN RIGHTS—BURUNDI (Agenda item 71c)
A/C.3/78/SR.36
HUMAN RIGHTS—ERITREA (Agenda item 71c)
A/C.3/78/SR.36
MINORITIES (Agenda item 71b)
A/C.3/78/SR.39
POVERTY—HUMAN RIGHTS (Agenda item 71b)
A/C.3/78/SR.30
RACIAL DISCRIMINATION—ELIMINATION (Agenda item 69a)
A/C.3/78/SR.41
RACIAL DISCRIMINATION—PROGRAMMES OF ACTION (Agenda item 69b)
A/C.3/78/SR.40; A/C.3/78/SR.41
RIGHT TO FOOD (Agenda item 71b)
A/C.3/78/SR.30

Liu, Luoge (China) (continued)

RIGHT TO HEALTH (Agenda item 71b)
A/C.3/78/SR.39
RIGHT TO HOUSING (Agenda item 71b)
A/C.3/78/SR.30
TRAFFICKING IN PERSONS (Agenda item 71b)
A/C.3/78/SR.23

Liu, Zhao (China)

IAEA—REPORTS (Agenda item 89)
A/78/PV.30

Llano, Alina J. (Nicaragua)

CRIMES AGAINST HUMANITY (Agenda item 80)
A/C.6/78/SR.45
HEALTH (Agenda item 125)
A/78/PV.48
MARINE ECOSYSTEMS—BIOLOGICAL DIVERSITY (Agenda item 75c)
A/78/PV.73
TERRORISM (Agenda item 109)
A/C.6/78/SR.5
UN—BUDGET (2024) (Agenda item 134)
A/78/PV.73; A/C.5/78/SR.28; A/C.5/78/SR.34
UN CHARTER—REPORTS (Agenda item 82)
A/C.6/78/SR.34

Llewellyn, Huw (UN. Office of Legal Affairs. Codification Division. Director)

UN CHARTER—REPORTS (Agenda item 82)
A/C.6/78/SR.22

Llosa, Luis Felipe (Peru)

PEACEKEEPING OPERATIONS (Agenda item 51)
A/C.4/78/SR.19

Lodge, Michael (International Seabed Authority. Secretary-General)

LAW OF THE SEA (Agenda item 75a)
A/78/PV.44
MARINE ECOSYSTEMS—BIOLOGICAL DIVERSITY (Agenda item 75c)
A/78/PV.44
STRADDLING FISH STOCKS (Agenda item 75b)
A/78/PV.44

Lompo, Boulmonli Léonard (Burkina Faso)

DISASTER VICTIMS (Agenda item 86)
A/C.6/78/SR.6

López, Martha Helena (UN. Assistant Secretary-General for Human Resources Management)

PERSONNEL QUESTIONS—UN SYSTEM (Agenda item 142)
A/C.5/78/SR.27
UN—HUMAN RESOURCES MANAGEMENT (Agenda item 139)
A/C.5/78/SR.25; A/C.5/78/SR.27

López Ferrucci, Mariano Javier (Argentina)

CRIMES AGAINST HUMANITY (Agenda item 80)
A/C.6/78/SR.38

Lora-Santos, Leila Castillon (Philippines)

CRIMES AGAINST HUMANITY (Agenda item 80)
A/C.6/78/SR.38
HEALTH (Agenda item 125)
A/78/PV.48
UN. GENERAL ASSEMBLY (78TH SESS. : 2023-2024). 2ND COMMITTEE—GENERAL DEBATE (Agenda item 8)
A/C.2/78/SR.3

Lora-Santos, Leila Castillon (Philippines) (ASEAN)

2030 AGENDA—PROGRAMME IMPLEMENTATION (Agenda item 18a)
A/C.2/78/SR.12
BIOLOGICAL DIVERSITY—TREATIES (Agenda item 18f)
A/C.2/78/SR.12
DISASTER PREVENTION (Agenda item 18c)
A/C.2/78/SR.12
SUSTAINABLE DEVELOPMENT (Agenda item 18)
A/C.2/78/SR.12
UN—HUMAN RESOURCES MANAGEMENT (Agenda item 139)
A/C.5/78/SR.27

Lorenzen, Emma Siemens (Denmark) (European Union)

SMALL ISLAND DEVELOPING STATES—PROGRAMMES OF ACTION (Agenda item 18b)
A/78/PV.103

Lortkipanidze, Ekaterine (Georgia)

CRIME PREVENTION (Agenda item 107)
A/C.3/78/SR.6
DISPLACED PERSONS (Agenda item 71b)
A/C.3/78/SR.32
HUMAN RIGHTS (Agenda item 71)
A/C.3/78/SR.16
HUMAN RIGHTS—RUSSIAN FEDERATION (Agenda item 71c)
A/C.3/78/SR.37
HUMAN RIGHTS—UKRAINE (Agenda item 71c)
A/C.3/78/SR.37
HUMAN RIGHTS ACTIVISTS (Agenda item 71b)
A/C.3/78/SR.19
PERSONS WITH DISABILITIES—HUMAN RIGHTS (Agenda item 71a)
A/C.3/78/SR.38
RACIAL DISCRIMINATION—ELIMINATION (Agenda item 69a)
A/C.3/78/SR.42
RACIAL DISCRIMINATION—PROGRAMMES OF ACTION (Agenda item 69b)
A/C.3/78/SR.42
RIGHTS OF THE CHILD (Agenda item 67)
A/C.3/78/SR.11; A/C.3/78/SR.13

Lortkipanidze, Ekaterine (Georgia) (continued)

SEXUAL ORIENTATION (Agenda item 71b)
A/C.3/78/SR.39
TORTURE AND OTHER CRUEL TREATMENT (Agenda item 71a)
A/C.3/78/SR.18
WOMEN'S ADVANCEMENT (Agenda item 25a)
A/C.3/78/SR.9
WOMEN'S ADVANCEMENT—CONFERENCES (Agenda item 25b)
A/C.3/78/SR.9

Lourenço, João Manuel Gonçalves (Angola. President)

UN. GENERAL ASSEMBLY (78TH SESS. : 2023-2024)—GENERAL DEBATE (Agenda item 8)
A/78/PV.6
UN. GENERAL ASSEMBLY (78TH SESS. : 2023-2024)—SPECIAL STATEMENTS
A/78/PV.6

Loussan, Cliff (French Polynesia)

FRENCH POLYNESIA QUESTION (Agenda item 58)
A/C.4/78/SR.3

Lovold, Andreas (Norway)

DEVELOPMENT FINANCE (Agenda item 16b)
A/C.2/78/SR.11
EMERGENCY ASSISTANCE (Agenda item 72a)
A/78/PV.46
FINANCIAL FLOWS (Agenda item 16f)
A/C.2/78/SR.11
HUMAN RIGHTS—INTERNATIONAL INSTRUMENTS (Agenda item 71a)
A/C.3/78/SR.24
HUMAN RIGHTS ACTIVISTS (Agenda item 71b)
A/C.3/78/SR.24
LAW OF THE SEA (Agenda item 75a)
A/78/PV.43
MARINE ECOSYSTEMS—BIOLOGICAL DIVERSITY (Agenda item 75c)
A/78/PV.43
PEACEKEEPING OPERATIONS (Agenda item 51)
A/C.4/78/SR.19
STRADDLING FISH STOCKS (Agenda item 75b)
A/78/PV.43
TAXATION (Agenda item 16h)
A/C.2/78/SR.11
UN. SECURITY COUNCIL—REPORTS (Agenda item 26)
A/78/PV.93
UNRWA—ACTIVITIES (Agenda item 49)
A/C.4/78/SR.22
VETO (Agenda item 63)
A/78/PV.67; A/78/PV.68

Low, Si Tong Berenice (Singapore)

DISARMAMENT AGREEMENTS—OUTER SPACE (Agenda item 97c)
A/C.1/78/PV.27

Low, Si Tong Berenice (Singapore) (continued)

OUTER SPACE—PRINCIPLES (Agenda item 97d)
A/C.1/78/PV.27
UN. GENERAL ASSEMBLY (78TH SESS. : 2023-2024). 1ST COMMITTEE—GENERAL DEBATE (Agenda item 8)
A/C.1/78/PV.3

Lu, Christopher P. (United States)

AL-SABAH, NAWAF AL-AHMAD AL-JABER (KUWAIT. AMIR)—TRIBUTES
A/78/PV.50(Resumption1)
INTERNATIONAL RESIDUAL MECHANISM FOR CRIMINAL TRIBUNALS (Agenda item 126)
A/78/PV.19
UN—BUDGET (2024) (Agenda item 134)
A/C.5/78/SR.5; A/C.5/78/SR.26/PartII
UN—PROGRAMME PLANNING (Agenda item 135)
A/C.5/78/SR.5
UN. GENERAL ASSEMBLY (78TH SESS. : 2023-2024)—OFFICERS (Agenda item 5)
A/C.5/78/SR.1
UN. GENERAL ASSEMBLY (78TH SESS. : 2023-2024). 5TH COMMITTEE—WORK ORGANIZATION (Agenda item 7)
A/C.5/78/SR.26/PartII; A/C.5/78/SR.27; A/C.5/78/SR.34; A/C.5/78/SR.35; A/C.5/78/SR.40
UN INTERIM FORCE IN LEBANON—FINANCING (Agenda item 156b)
A/C.5/78/SR.40
UNRWA—ACTIVITIES (Agenda item 49)
A/C.4/78/SR.23

Lucii, Costanza (Sovereign Order of Malta)

RIGHT TO DRINKING WATER (Agenda item 71b)
A/C.3/78/SR.28
RIGHT TO HOUSING (Agenda item 71b)
A/C.3/78/SR.30
RURAL WOMEN (Agenda item 25a)
A/C.3/78/SR.10
WOMEN'S ADVANCEMENT (Agenda item 25a)
A/C.3/78/SR.7; A/C.3/78/SR.10
WOMEN'S ADVANCEMENT—CONFERENCES (Agenda item 25b)
A/C.3/78/SR.7; A/C.3/78/SR.10

Ludwig, Annette (Germany)

RACIAL DISCRIMINATION—ELIMINATION (Agenda item 69a)
A/C.3/78/SR.41
RACIAL DISCRIMINATION—PROGRAMMES OF ACTION (Agenda item 69b)
A/C.3/78/SR.41
WOMEN'S ADVANCEMENT (Agenda item 25a)
A/C.3/78/SR.8
WOMEN'S ADVANCEMENT—CONFERENCES (Agenda item 25b)
A/C.3/78/SR.8

Luemba, Mateus Pedro (Angola)

CHEMICAL WEAPONS—TREATIES (Agenda item 99l)
A/C.1/78/PV.15
CLIMATE (Agenda item 18d)
A/C.2/78/SR.13
DECOLONIZATION (Agenda item 58)
A/C.4/78/SR.6
DISASTER PREVENTION (Agenda item 18c)
A/C.2/78/SR.13
FALKLAND ISLANDS (MALVINAS) QUESTION (Agenda item 42)
A/C.4/78/SR.6
FOOD SECURITY (Agenda item 23a)
A/C.2/78/SR.16
HUMAN RIGHTS (Agenda item 71)
A/C.3/78/SR.28
LANDMINES—TREATIES (Agenda item 99m)
A/C.1/78/PV.19
MINE CLEARANCE (Agenda item 46)
A/C.4/78/SR.10
PEACE (Agenda item 14)
A/78/PV.82
POVERTY—INTERNATIONAL DECADES (Agenda item 21a)
A/C.2/78/SR.16
RACIAL DISCRIMINATION—ELIMINATION (Agenda item 69a)
A/78/PV.50
RULE OF LAW (Agenda item 83)
A/C.6/78/SR.19
RURAL POVERTY (Agenda item 21b)
A/C.2/78/SR.16
UN—BUDGET (2024) (Agenda item 134)
A/C.5/78/SR.5; A/C.5/78/SR.33
UN—PROGRAMME PLANNING (Agenda item 135)
A/C.5/78/SR.5
UN. SECURITY COUNCIL—MEMBERSHIP (Agenda item 121)
A/78/PV.36
WEAPONS OF MASS DESTRUCTION—TERRORISM (Agenda item 99s)
A/C.1/78/PV.15
WESTERN SAHARA QUESTION (Agenda item 58)
A/C.4/78/SR.6

Luemba, Mateus Pedro (Angola) (Southern African Development Community)

RIGHTS OF THE CHILD (Agenda item 67)
A/C.3/78/SR.55

Lukabyo, Emma Jane Mutesi (Australia)

CRIME PREVENTION (Agenda item 107)
A/C.3/78/SR.56
INFORMATION—INTERNATIONAL SECURITY (Agenda item 94)
A/C.1/78/PV.20; A/C.1/78/PV.29

Lukiantsev, Grigory Y. (Russian Federation)

RACIAL DISCRIMINATION—ELIMINATION (Agenda item 69a)
A/C.3/78/SR.47

Lula, Iwona Anna (Poland)

PERSONS WITH DISABILITIES—HUMAN RIGHTS (Agenda item 71a)
A/C.3/78/SR.38
RIGHTS OF THE CHILD (Agenda item 67)
A/C.3/78/SR.11
SOCIAL DEVELOPMENT (Agenda item 24)
A/C.3/78/SR.1
WOMEN'S ADVANCEMENT (Agenda item 25a)
A/C.3/78/SR.7
WOMEN'S ADVANCEMENT—CONFERENCES (Agenda item 25b)
A/C.3/78/SR.7
YOUTH (Agenda item 24b)
A/C.3/78/SR.55

Luna, Madelin Esther (Dominican Republic)

UN. GENERAL ASSEMBLY (78TH SESS. : 2023-2024). 1ST COMMITTEE—GENERAL DEBATE (Agenda item 8)
A/C.1/78/PV.9

Lundy, Phoebe (United Kingdom)

HUMAN RIGHTS—MYANMAR (Agenda item 71c)
A/C.3/78/SR.33
HUMAN RIGHTS—SOMALIA (Agenda item 71c)
A/C.3/78/SR.35
HUMAN RIGHTS INSTITUTIONS—CENTRAL AFRICA (Agenda item 71b)
A/C.3/78/SR.56
RACIAL DISCRIMINATION—PROGRAMMES OF ACTION (Agenda item 69b)
A/C.3/78/SR.56
RIGHT TO DEVELOPMENT (Agenda item 71b)
A/C.3/78/SR.48
SANCTIONS—INTERNATIONAL RELATIONS (Agenda item 71b)
A/C.3/78/SR.48

Lungu, Alis (Romania)

CRIMES AGAINST HUMANITY (Agenda item 80)
A/C.6/78/SR.11; A/C.6/78/SR.38; A/C.6/78/SR.42; A/C.6/78/SR.43; A/C.6/78/SR.44; A/C.6/78/SR.45; A/C.6/78/SR.47

Luo, Phoebe (Singapore)

SUSTAINABLE DEVELOPMENT (Agenda item 18)
A/C.2/78/SR.24
TAXATION (Agenda item 16h)
A/C.2/78/SR.25

Luque Nuñez, Linda del Carmen (Panama)

INDIGENOUS PEOPLES (Agenda item 68a)
A/C.3/78/SR.15

Luque Nuñez, Linda del Carmen (Panama) (continued)

INDIGENOUS PEOPLES—CONFERENCES (Agenda item 68b)
A/C.3/78/SR.15
WOMEN'S ADVANCEMENT (Agenda item 25a)
A/C.3/78/SR.10
WOMEN'S ADVANCEMENT—CONFERENCES (Agenda item 25b)
A/C.3/78/SR.10

Luteru, Fatumanava-o-Upolu III Pa'olelei (Samoa) (Alliance of Small Island States)

MARINE ECOSYSTEMS—BIOLOGICAL DIVERSITY (Agenda item 75c)
A/78/PV.103
MILLENNIUM SUMMIT—CONFERENCES (Agenda item 117)
A/78/PV.53
SMALL ISLAND DEVELOPING STATES—PROGRAMMES OF ACTION (Agenda item 18b)
A/78/PV.100; A/78/PV.103
UN. INTERNATIONAL LAW COMMISSION—REPORTS (Agenda item 79)
A/C.6/78/SR.27
UN CONFERENCES (Agenda item 13)
A/78/PV.53

Lyazidi, Naima (Morocco)

RIGHTS OF THE CHILD (Agenda item 67)
A/C.3/78/SR.14

Lygeros, Nikos ((personal capacity))

WESTERN SAHARA QUESTION (Agenda item 58)
A/C.4/78/SR.5

Lysikov, Andrei (Russian Federation)

UN—FINANCIAL SITUATION (Agenda item 136)
A/C.5/78/SR.38

Ma, Xinmin (China)

INTERNATIONAL CRIMINAL COURT—REPORTS (Agenda item 74)
A/78/PV.21
UN. INTERNATIONAL COURT OF JUSTICE—REPORTS (Agenda item 73)
A/78/PV.20
UN. INTERNATIONAL LAW COMMISSION—REPORTS (Agenda item 79)
A/C.6/78/SR.27; A/C.6/78/SR.29

Ma, Yanbo (China)

ADMINISTRATION OF JUSTICE (Agenda item 144)
A/C.6/78/SR.9
CRIMES AGAINST HUMANITY (Agenda item 80)
A/C.6/78/SR.42; A/C.6/78/SR.43; A/C.6/78/SR.44; A/C.6/78/SR.45
INTERNATIONAL LAW—TRAINING PROGRAMMES (Agenda item 78)
A/C.6/78/SR.21

Ma, Yuanchun (China)

OUTER SPACE—PEACEFUL USES—INTERNATIONAL COOPERATION (Agenda item 48)
A/C.4/78/SR.16

Maalla M'jid, Najat (UN. Special Representative of the Secretary-General on Violence against Children)

RIGHTS OF THE CHILD (Agenda item 67)
A/C.3/78/SR.11

Maamaatuaiahutapu, Maurea (French Polynesia)

FRENCH POLYNESIA QUESTION (Agenda item 58)
A/C.4/78/SR.3

Maamau, Taneti (Kiribati. President)

UN. GENERAL ASSEMBLY (78TH SESS. : 2023-2024)—GENERAL DEBATE (Agenda item 8)
A/78/PV.8
UN. GENERAL ASSEMBLY (78TH SESS. : 2023-2024)—SPECIAL STATEMENTS
A/78/PV.8

Maayan, Michal (Israel)

ARMS RACE—OUTER SPACE (Agenda item 97a)
A/C.1/78/PV.16
BIOLOGICAL WEAPONS—TREATIES (Agenda item 106)
A/C.1/78/PV.15
CHEMICAL WEAPONS—TREATIES (Agenda item 99l)
A/C.1/78/PV.15
INFORMATION (Agenda item 53)
A/C.4/78/SR.13
MIDDLE EAST—NUCLEAR-WEAPON-FREE ZONES (Agenda item 95)
A/C.1/78/PV.12
NUCLEAR DISARMAMENT (Agenda item 99b)
A/C.1/78/PV.11; A/C.1/78/PV.12; A/C.1/78/PV.13; A/C.1/78/PV.14
NUCLEAR NON-PROLIFERATION—INTERNATIONAL OBLIGATIONS (Agenda item 99w)
A/C.1/78/PV.12
UN. GENERAL ASSEMBLY (78TH SESS. : 2023-2024). 1ST COMMITTEE—GENERAL DEBATE (Agenda item 8)
A/C.1/78/PV.6; A/C.1/78/PV.7; A/C.1/78/PV.8; A/C.1/78/PV.9

Mabe, Brady Michael (International Committee of the Red Cross)

TORTURE AND OTHER CRUEL TREATMENT (Agenda item 71a)
A/C.3/78/SR.18

Mabeba, Bernard (South Africa)

OUTER SPACE—PEACEFUL USES—INTERNATIONAL COOPERATION (Agenda item 48)
A/C.4/78/SR.16

Mabeba, Bernard (South Africa) (continued)
PEACEKEEPING OPERATIONS (Agenda item 51)
A/C.4/78/SR.20

Macarena Apud, Maria (United States)
FINANCIAL INCLUSION (Agenda item 16e)
A/C.2/78/SR.22

Macchiavello, Julissa (Peru) (Group of Friends for Disaster Risk Reduction)
2030 AGENDA—PROGRAMME IMPLEMENTATION (Agenda item 18a)
A/C.2/78/SR.12
DISASTER PREVENTION (Agenda item 18c)
A/C.2/78/SR.12
SUSTAINABLE DEVELOPMENT (Agenda item 18)
A/C.2/78/SR.12

Macchiavello, Julissa (Peru) (Group of Friends of the United Nations Voluntary Fund for Victims of Torture)
TORTURE AND OTHER CRUEL TREATMENT (Agenda item 71a)
A/C.3/78/SR.24

Machado Mouriño, Felipe (Uruguay)
ADMINISTRATION OF JUSTICE—HUMAN RIGHTS (Agenda item 71b)
A/C.3/78/SR.28
CAPITAL PUNISHMENT (Agenda item 71b)
A/C.3/78/SR.28
HUMAN RIGHTS (Agenda item 71)
A/C.3/78/SR.28
SUMMARY EXECUTIONS (Agenda item 71b)
A/C.3/78/SR.28
UN—BUDGET (2024) (Agenda item 134)
A/C.5/78/SR.21
UN. GENERAL ASSEMBLY (78TH SESS. : 2023-2024). 5TH COMMITTEE—WORK ORGANIZATION (Agenda item 7)
A/C.5/78/SR.27; A/C.5/78/SR.35; A/C.5/78/SR.40

MacLeod, Sorcha (UN. Human Rights Council. Working Group on the Use of Mercenaries as a Means of Violating Human Rights and Impeding the Exercise of the Right of Peoples to Self-Determination)
MERCENARIES (Agenda item 70)
A/C.3/78/SR.42

Made, Angelique van der (Netherlands (Kingdom of the))
ADMINISTRATION OF JUSTICE (Agenda item 144)
A/C.6/78/SR.9
CRIMES AGAINST HUMANITY (Agenda item 80)
A/C.6/78/SR.10
PEACEKEEPING OPERATIONS—CRIMINAL LIABILITY (Agenda item 76)
A/C.6/78/SR.8

Madeleine, Ian Dereck Joseph (Seychelles)
SMALL ISLAND DEVELOPING STATES—PROGRAMMES OF ACTION (Agenda item 18b)
A/78/PV.103

Madinger, Sean (United States)
CENTRAL ASIA—ZONES OF PEACE (Agenda item 64)
A/78/PV.85

Madrigal-Borloz, Victor (UN. Human Rights Council. Independent Expert on Protection against Violence and Discrimination based on Sexual Orientation and Gender Identity)
SEXUAL ORIENTATION (Agenda item 71b)
A/C.3/78/SR.39

Maeda, Gensaku (Japan)
UN. INTERNATIONAL LAW COMMISSION—REPORTS (Agenda item 79)
A/C.6/78/SR.30; A/C.6/78/SR.32

Maenpaa, Conor C. (Sovereign Order of Malta)
CRIME PREVENTION (Agenda item 107)
A/C.3/78/SR.6
CYBERCRIME (Agenda item 108)
A/C.3/78/SR.6

Maes, Olivier (Luxembourg)
ARMED CONFLICTS PREVENTION (Agenda item 31a)
A/78/PV.72
HUMAN RIGHTS—RUSSIAN FEDERATION (Agenda item 71c)
A/C.3/78/SR.37
RIGHTS OF THE CHILD (Agenda item 67)
A/C.3/78/SR.11
UN. SECURITY COUNCIL—MEMBERSHIP (Agenda item 121)
A/78/PV.34
VETO (Agenda item 63)
A/78/PV.52; A/78/PV.60; A/78/PV.67; A/78/PV.70; A/78/PV.78

Maes, Olivier (Luxembourg) (LGBTI Core Group)
SEXUAL ORIENTATION (Agenda item 71b)
A/C.3/78/SR.24

Maesschalck, Filip de (Belgium)
UKRAINE—POLITICAL CONDITIONS (Agenda item 62)
A/78/PV.57

Maesschalck, Filip de (Belgium) (European Union)
AFRICA—SUSTAINABLE DEVELOPMENT—PARTNERSHIP (Agenda item 65a)
A/78/PV.57
HEALTH (Agenda item 125)
A/78/PV.64

Mahidi, Mourad (Austria)

HUMAN RIGHTS ACTIVISTS (Agenda item 71b)
A/C.3/78/SR.19
RIGHT OF ASSEMBLY (Agenda item 71b)
A/C.3/78/SR.19

Mahler, Claudia (UN. Human Rights Council. Independent Expert on the Enjoyment of All Human Rights by Older Persons)

AGEING PERSONS (Agenda item 24b)
A/C.3/78/SR.1

Mahmassani, Ziad (UN. General Assembly. 3rd Committee. Secretary)

CRIME PREVENTION (Agenda item 107)
A/C.3/78/SR.47
WOMEN'S ADVANCEMENT—CONFERENCES (Agenda item 25b)
A/C.3/78/SR.51

Mahmud, Mohammed Lawal (Nigeria)

ARMS RACE—OUTER SPACE (Agenda item 97a)
A/C.1/78/PV.17
ARMS TRANSFERS—TREATIES (Agenda item 99x)
A/C.1/78/PV.19
IAEA—REPORTS (Agenda item 89)
A/78/PV.30
OUTER SPACE—PRINCIPLES (Agenda item 97d)
A/C.1/78/PV.17
SMALL ARMS—ILLICIT TRAFFIC (Agenda item 99p)
A/C.1/78/PV.19
UN. GENERAL ASSEMBLY (78TH SESS. : 2023-2024). 1ST COMMITTEE—GENERAL DEBATE (Agenda item 8)
A/C.1/78/PV.8
WEAPONS—OUTER SPACE (Agenda item 97b)
A/C.1/78/PV.17

Mahmud, Mohammed Lawal (Nigeria) (UN. Group of African States)

AFRICA—NUCLEAR-WEAPON-FREE ZONES (Agenda item 92)
A/C.1/78/PV.11
ARMS RACE—OUTER SPACE (Agenda item 97a)
A/C.1/78/PV.16
CONVENTIONAL WEAPONS (Agenda item 99u)
A/C.1/78/PV.17
DISARMAMENT AGREEMENTS—OUTER SPACE (Agenda item 97c)
A/C.1/78/PV.16
MIDDLE EAST—NUCLEAR-WEAPON-FREE ZONES (Agenda item 95)
A/C.1/78/PV.11
NUCLEAR DISARMAMENT (Agenda item 99b)
A/C.1/78/PV.11
NUCLEAR NON-PROLIFERATION—INTERNATIONAL OBLIGATIONS (Agenda item 99w)
A/C.1/78/PV.11

Mahmud, Mohammed Lawal (Nigeria) (UN. Group of African States) (continued)

NUCLEAR WEAPON TESTS—TREATIES (Agenda item 105)
A/C.1/78/PV.11
NUCLEAR WEAPONS—HUMANITARIAN CONSEQUENCES (Agenda item 99bb)
A/C.1/78/PV.11
NUCLEAR WEAPONS—TREATIES (Agenda item 99ff)
A/C.1/78/PV.11
OUTER SPACE—CONFIDENCE-BUILDING MEASURES (Agenda item 99v)
A/C.1/78/PV.16
SMALL ARMS—ILLICIT TRAFFIC (Agenda item 99p)
A/C.1/78/PV.17
SMALL ARMS—ILLICIT TRAFFIC—ASSISTANCE (Agenda item 99n)
A/C.1/78/PV.17
WEAPONS—OUTER SPACE (Agenda item 97b)
A/C.1/78/PV.16

Mahomed, Shuaib (South Africa)

BIOLOGICAL WEAPONS—TREATIES (Agenda item 106)
A/C.1/78/PV.14
CHEMICAL WEAPONS—TREATIES (Agenda item 99l)
A/C.1/78/PV.14
UN. CONFERENCE ON DISARMAMENT—REPORTS (Agenda item 101a)
A/C.1/78/PV.22
UN. DISARMAMENT COMMISSION—REPORTS (Agenda item 101b)
A/C.1/78/PV.22

Mahuta, Nanaia (New Zealand)

UN. GENERAL ASSEMBLY (78TH SESS. : 2023-2024)—GENERAL DEBATE (Agenda item 8)
A/78/PV.12

Mai, Ngan Ha (Viet Nam)

CONVENTIONAL WEAPONS (Agenda item 99u)
A/C.1/78/PV.18
INFORMATION—INTERNATIONAL SECURITY (Agenda item 94)
A/C.1/78/PV.29
LANDMINES—TREATIES (Agenda item 99m)
A/C.1/78/PV.18
SMALL ARMS—ILLICIT TRAFFIC—ASSISTANCE (Agenda item 99n)
A/C.1/78/PV.18

Maiga, Aissata Ibrahim (Mali)

HUMAN RIGHTS—BURUNDI (Agenda item 71c)
A/C.3/78/SR.36
HUMAN RIGHTS—INTERNATIONAL INSTRUMENTS (Agenda item 71a)
A/C.3/78/SR.26

Maiga, Aissata Ibrahim (Mali) (continued)
SANCTIONS—INTERNATIONAL RELATIONS (Agenda item 71b)
A/C.3/78/SR.26

Maillé, Béatrice (Canada)
DEVELOPMENT FINANCE—CONFERENCES (Agenda item 17)
A/C.2/78/SR.25
HUMAN RIGHTS—AFGHANISTAN (Agenda item 71c)
A/C.3/78/SR.34
INTERNATIONAL CRIMINAL COURT—REPORTS (Agenda item 74)
A/78/PV.21

Maillé, Béatrice (Canada) (UN. General Assembly. 6th Committee. Bureau)
TERRORISM (Agenda item 109)
A/C.6/78/SR.37

Mainero, Martín Juan (Argentina)
CRIMES AGAINST HUMANITY (Agenda item 80)
A/C.6/78/SR.10; A/C.6/78/SR.40; A/C.6/78/SR.41; A/C.6/78/SR.43; A/C.6/78/SR.44; A/C.6/78/SR.45
INTERNATIONAL JURISDICTION (Agenda item 84)
A/C.6/78/SR.12
LAW OF THE SEA (Agenda item 75a)
A/78/PV.44
MARINE ECOSYSTEMS—BIOLOGICAL DIVERSITY (Agenda item 75c)
A/78/PV.44
ORGANIZATION OF IBERO-AMERICAN STATES FOR EDUCATION, SCIENCE AND CULTURE—OBSERVER STATUS (Agenda item 171)
A/C.6/78/SR.36
RULE OF LAW (Agenda item 83)
A/C.6/78/SR.16
STRADDLING FISH STOCKS (Agenda item 75b)
A/78/PV.44
TERRORISM (Agenda item 109)
A/C.6/78/SR.1
TREATIES (Agenda item 87)
A/C.6/78/SR.20
UKRAINE—POLITICAL CONDITIONS (Agenda item 62)
A/78/PV.58
UN. INTERNATIONAL LAW COMMISSION—REPORTS (Agenda item 79)
A/C.6/78/SR.30; A/C.6/78/SR.37

Maitafsir, Musa Garba (Nigeria)
FOOD SECURITY (Agenda item 23a)
A/C.2/78/SR.17
POVERTY—INTERNATIONAL DECADES (Agenda item 21a)
A/C.2/78/SR.17
RURAL POVERTY (Agenda item 21b)
A/C.2/78/SR.17

Majeed, Aleena (Pakistan)
SOCIAL CONDITIONS (Agenda item 24b)
A/78/PV.57
UN. GENERAL ASSEMBLY (78TH SESS. : 2023-2024). 2ND COMMITTEE—GENERAL DEBATE (Agenda item 8)
A/C.2/78/SR.2

Majszyk, Slawomir (Poland)
UN. INTERNATIONAL LAW COMMISSION—REPORTS (Agenda item 79)
A/C.6/78/SR.24

Makarevich, Siarhei (Belarus)
BIOLOGICAL WEAPONS—TREATIES (Agenda item 106)
A/C.1/78/PV.15
CHEMICAL WEAPONS—TREATIES (Agenda item 99l)
A/C.1/78/PV.15
UN. SECURITY COUNCIL—MEMBERSHIP (Agenda item 121)
A/78/PV.36
WEAPONS OF MASS DESTRUCTION (Agenda item 93)
A/C.1/78/PV.29

Makayat-Safouesse, Lazare (Congo)
TERRORISM (Agenda item 109)
A/C.6/78/SR.4
UN. GENERAL ASSEMBLY (78TH SESS. : 2023-2024). 2ND COMMITTEE—GENERAL DEBATE (Agenda item 8)
A/C.2/78/SR.4

Makgati, Penelope Ramatsobane (South Africa)
AGEING PERSONS (Agenda item 24b)
A/C.3/78/SR.2
SOCIAL CONDITIONS (Agenda item 24b)
A/C.3/78/SR.2
SOCIAL DEVELOPMENT (Agenda item 24)
A/C.3/78/SR.2
UN YOUTH OFFICE—REPORTS (Agenda item 130)
A/78/PV.102

Makiza, Maurice Gatien (Congo) (UN. Group of African States)
DISARMAMENT—GENERAL AND COMPLETE (Agenda item 99)
A/78/PV.105

Makwati, Babalwa (South Africa)
RIGHTS OF THE CHILD (Agenda item 67)
A/C.3/78/SR.12

Malebo, Hamisi (United Republic of Tanzania)
INDIGENOUS PEOPLES (Agenda item 68a)
A/C.3/78/SR.15

Malebo, Hamisi (United Republic of Tanzania) (continued)

INDIGENOUS PEOPLES—CONFERENCES (Agenda item 68b)
A/C.3/78/SR.15

Malinauskas, Andrius (Lithuania)

INTERNATIONAL TRADE (Agenda item 16a)
A/C.2/78/SR.24

Malovrh, Bostjan (Slovenia)

AGEING PERSONS (Agenda item 24b)
A/C.3/78/SR.1
INTERNATIONAL CRIMINAL COURT—REPORTS (Agenda item 74)
A/78/PV.22
UN. GENERAL ASSEMBLY—WORK PROGRAMME (Agenda item 120)
A/78/PV.33
UN. GENERAL ASSEMBLY (78TH SESS. : 2023-2024). 1ST COMMITTEE—GENERAL DEBATE (Agenda item 8)
A/C.1/78/PV.6
UN. SECURITY COUNCIL—MEMBERSHIP (Agenda item 121)
A/78/PV.35
UN RESOLUTIONS—IMPLEMENTATION (Agenda item 119)
A/78/PV.33
UNRWA—ACTIVITIES (Agenda item 49)
A/C.4/78/SR.22
VETO (Agenda item 63)
A/78/PV.3; A/78/PV.51; A/78/PV.60; A/78/PV.67; A/78/PV.69; A/78/PV.74

Manalo, Enrique A. (Philippines)

UN. GENERAL ASSEMBLY (78TH SESS. : 2023-2024)—GENERAL DEBATE (Agenda item 8)
A/78/PV.12

Mandla, Bulelani (South Africa)

DISASTER PREVENTION (Agenda item 18c)
A/C.2/78/SR.15
ECONOMIC COOPERATION AMONG DEVELOPING COUNTRIES (Agenda item 22b)
A/C.2/78/SR.18
FOOD SECURITY (Agenda item 23a)
A/C.2/78/SR.17
OPERATIONAL ACTIVITIES—UN SYSTEM (Agenda item 22a)
A/C.2/78/SR.18
POVERTY—INTERNATIONAL DECADES (Agenda item 21a)
A/C.2/78/SR.17
RURAL POVERTY (Agenda item 21b)
A/C.2/78/SR.17

Mangue, Victoriana Mbasogo (Equatorial Guinea)

HUMAN RIGHTS (Agenda item 71)
A/C.3/78/SR.28

Maniratanga, Zéphyrin (Burundi)

DISARMAMENT—GENERAL AND COMPLETE (Agenda item 99)
A/78/PV.105
HUMAN RIGHTS—BURUNDI (Agenda item 71c)
A/C.3/78/SR.36

Maniratanga, Zéphyrin (Burundi) (UN. Group of African States)

RAISI, SEYYED EBRAHIM (IRAN (ISLAMIC REPUBLID OF). PRESIDENT)—TRIBUTES
A/78/PV.83

Maniratanga, Zéphyrin (Burundi) (UN. Special Committee on the Charter of the United Nations and on the Strengthening of the Role of the Organization. Chair)

UN CHARTER—REPORTS (Agenda item 82)
A/C.6/78/SR.22

Mansour, Riyad H. (State of Palestine)

PALESTINE QUESTION (Agenda item 35)
A/78/PV.39
TERRITORIES OCCUPIED BY ISRAEL—HUMAN RIGHTS (Agenda item 50)
A/C.4/78/SR.26
UN. INTERNATIONAL COURT OF JUSTICE—REPORTS (Agenda item 73)
A/78/PV.28
UNRWA—ACTIVITIES (Agenda item 49)
A/C.4/78/SR.26
VETO (Agenda item 63)
A/78/PV.51; A/78/PV.59; A/78/PV.66; A/78/PV.74

Manyanga, Garikai (Zimbabwe)

HEALTH (Agenda item 125)
A/78/PV.16
HUMAN RIGHTS (Agenda item 71)
A/C.3/78/SR.27
HUMAN RIGHTS—DEMOCRATIC PEOPLE'S REPUBLIC OF KOREA (Agenda item 71c)
A/C.3/78/SR.33
HUMAN RIGHTS—ETHIOPIA (Agenda item 71c)
A/C.3/78/SR.36
HUMAN RIGHTS—REPORTS (Agenda item 71c)
A/C.3/78/SR.27
RIGHT TO DEVELOPMENT (Agenda item 71b)
A/C.3/78/SR.20
SANCTIONS—INTERNATIONAL RELATIONS (Agenda item 71b)
A/C.3/78/SR.28

Manzare, Max (United Kingdom)

RELIGIOUS INTOLERANCE (Agenda item 71b)
A/C.3/78/SR.38
SLAVERY (Agenda item 71a)
A/C.3/78/SR.21
UN. HUMAN RIGHTS COUNCIL—REPORTS (Agenda item 66)
A/C.3/78/SR.46

Manzeri Ngondo, Jean Claude (Congo)
DECOLONIZATION (Agenda item 58)
A/C.4/78/SR.7
INFORMATION (Agenda item 53)
A/C.4/78/SR.13

Mao, Tithiarun (Cambodia)
PEACE (Agenda item 14)
A/78/PV.76
PEACEKEEPING OPERATIONS (Agenda item 51)
A/C.4/78/SR.20
UN. SECURITY COUNCIL—MEMBERSHIP (Agenda item 121)
A/78/PV.36
VETO (Agenda item 63)
A/78/PV.75

Mao, Tithiarun (Cambodia) (ASEAN)
ARMS TRANSFERS—TREATIES (Agenda item 99x)
A/C.1/78/PV.17
CONVENTIONAL WEAPONS (Agenda item 99u)
A/C.1/78/PV.17
CONVENTIONAL WEAPONS—TREATIES (Agenda item 103)
A/C.1/78/PV.17
LANDMINES—TREATIES (Agenda item 99m)
A/C.1/78/PV.17
SMALL ARMS—ILLICIT TRAFFIC (Agenda item 99p)
A/C.1/78/PV.17
SMALL ARMS—ILLICIT TRAFFIC—ASSISTANCE (Agenda item 99n)
A/C.1/78/PV.17

Mao, Yizong (China)
HUMAN RIGHTS—ETHIOPIA (Agenda item 71c)
A/C.3/78/SR.36
RACIAL DISCRIMINATION—ELIMINATION (Agenda item 69a)
A/C.3/78/SR.41
RACIAL DISCRIMINATION—PROGRAMMES OF ACTION (Agenda item 69b)
A/C.3/78/SR.41

Marchi-Uhel, Catherine (International, Impartial and Independent Mechanism to Assist in the Investigation and Prosecution of Persons Responsible for the Most Serious Crimes under International Law Committed in the Syrian Arab Republic since March 2011)
ARMED CONFLICTS PREVENTION (Agenda item 31a)
A/78/PV.72

Margaris, Pantelis (Greece)
NUCLEAR DISARMAMENT (Agenda item 99b)
A/C.1/78/PV.11
NUCLEAR NON-PROLIFERATION—INTERNATIONAL OBLIGATIONS (Agenda item 99w)
A/C.1/78/PV.11

Margaris, Pantelis (Greece) (continued)
NUCLEAR WEAPON TESTS—TREATIES (Agenda item 105)
A/C.1/78/PV.11

Margaryan, Mher (Armenia)
CRIMES AGAINST HUMANITY (Agenda item 80)
A/C.6/78/SR.11
ORGANIZATION FOR DEMOCRACY AND ECONOMIC DEVELOPMENT - GUAM (Agenda item 32)
A/78/PV.85
PEACE (Agenda item 14)
A/78/PV.82
RESPONSIBILITY TO PROTECT (Agenda item 129)
A/78/PV.96
UN. GENERAL ASSEMBLY (78TH SESS. : 2023-2024). 1ST COMMITTEE—GENERAL DEBATE (Agenda item 8)
A/C.1/78/PV.4
UN. INTERNATIONAL COURT OF JUSTICE—REPORTS (Agenda item 73)
A/78/PV.28
UN. SECRETARY-GENERAL—REPORTS (Agenda item 110)
A/78/PV.54

Marian, Jan (Czechia)
UKRAINE—POLITICAL CONDITIONS (Agenda item 62)
A/78/PV.56

Maric, Martina (Switzerland)
RACIAL DISCRIMINATION—ELIMINATION (Agenda item 69a)
A/C.3/78/SR.47
TERRORISM—HUMAN RIGHTS (Agenda item 71b)
A/C.3/78/SR.51
WOMEN'S ADVANCEMENT (Agenda item 25a)
A/C.3/78/SR.7
WOMEN'S ADVANCEMENT—CONFERENCES (Agenda item 25b)
A/C.3/78/SR.7

Marin, Anaïs (UN. Human Rights Council. Special Rapporteur on the Situation of Human Rights in Belarus)
HUMAN RIGHTS—BELARUS (Agenda item 71c)
A/C.3/78/SR.37

Marín Sevilla, Asbina (Venezuela (Bolivarian Republic of))
COASTAL ZONE MANAGEMENT (Agenda item 18j)
A/78/PV.49; A/C.2/78/SR.23
INTERNATIONAL TRADE (Agenda item 16a)
A/C.2/78/SR.9; A/C.2/78/SR.24
MACROECONOMIC POLICY (Agenda item 16)
A/C.2/78/SR.9

Marín Sevilla, Asbina (Venezuela (Bolivarian Republic of)) (continued)

TERRITORIES OCCUPIED BY ISRAEL—NATURAL RESOURCES (Agenda item 59)
A/C.2/78/SR.19
UN. GENERAL ASSEMBLY (78TH SESS. : 2023-2024). 2ND COMMITTEE—GENERAL DEBATE (Agenda item 8)
A/C.2/78/SR.5

Marín Sevilla, Asbina (Venezuela (Bolivarian Republic of)) (Group of Friends in Defence of the Charter of the United Nations)

FOOD SECURITY (Agenda item 23a)
A/C.2/78/SR.16
POVERTY—INTERNATIONAL DECADES (Agenda item 21a)
A/C.2/78/SR.16
RURAL POVERTY (Agenda item 21b)
A/C.2/78/SR.16
VETO (Agenda item 63)
A/78/PV.66

Marinho, Joana Almeida (Portugal)

HUMAN RIGHTS (Agenda item 71)
A/C.3/78/SR.25
RACIAL DISCRIMINATION—ELIMINATION (Agenda item 69a)
A/C.3/78/SR.41
RACIAL DISCRIMINATION—PROGRAMMES OF ACTION (Agenda item 69b)
A/C.3/78/SR.41
RIGHTS OF THE CHILD (Agenda item 67)
A/C.3/78/SR.11
SEXUAL ORIENTATION (Agenda item 71b)
A/C.3/78/SR.39
UN HIGH COMMISSIONER FOR REFUGEES—REPORTS (Agenda item 60)
A/C.3/78/SR.44

Marjanović, Tamara (Serbia)

YOUTH (Agenda item 24b)
A/C.3/78/SR.3

Mark, Hayley-Ann (Saint Vincent and the Grenadines) (Community of Latin American and Caribbean States)

DISASTER VICTIMS (Agenda item 86)
A/C.6/78/SR.5
INTERNATIONAL JURISDICTION (Agenda item 84)
A/C.6/78/SR.12
INTERNATIONAL LAW—TRAINING PROGRAMMES (Agenda item 78)
A/C.6/78/SR.21
PEACEKEEPING OPERATIONS—CRIMINAL LIABILITY (Agenda item 76)
A/C.6/78/SR.8
TERRORISM (Agenda item 109)
A/C.6/78/SR.2

Mark, Hayley-Ann (Saint Vincent and the Grenadines) (Community of Latin American and Caribbean States) (continued)

TREATIES (Agenda item 87)
A/C.6/78/SR.20

Marks, Rose Ann (United States)

DEVELOPMENT FINANCE—CONFERENCES (Agenda item 17)
A/78/PV.90; A/C.2/78/SR.25
ECONOMIC COOPERATION AMONG DEVELOPING COUNTRIES (Agenda item 22b)
A/C.2/78/SR.25
POVERTY—INTERNATIONAL DECADES (Agenda item 21a)
A/C.2/78/SR.25
SMALL ISLAND DEVELOPING STATES—PROGRAMMES OF ACTION (Agenda item 18b)
A/C.2/78/SR.22
SUSTAINABLE DEVELOPMENT (Agenda item 18)
A/C.2/78/SR.22
TAXATION (Agenda item 16h)
A/C.2/78/SR.25

Marquardt, Stephan (European Union)

INTERNATIONAL CRIMINAL COURT—REPORTS (Agenda item 74)
A/78/PV.21
UN. INTERNATIONAL LAW COMMISSION—REPORTS (Agenda item 79)
A/C.6/78/SR.23

Márquez Mina, Francia (Colombia. Vice-President)

RACIAL DISCRIMINATION—ELIMINATION (Agenda item 69a)
A/78/PV.103
UN. GENERAL ASSEMBLY (78TH SESS. : 2023-2024)—SPECIAL STATEMENTS
A/78/PV.103

Marschik, Alexander (Austria)

PEACEKEEPING OPERATIONS (Agenda item 51)
A/C.4/78/SR.19
UN. GENERAL ASSEMBLY (78TH SESS. : 2023-2024). 1ST COMMITTEE—GENERAL DEBATE (Agenda item 8)
A/C.1/78/PV.4
VETO (Agenda item 63)
A/78/PV.51; A/78/PV.69; A/78/PV.70; A/78/PV.79

Marschik, Alexander (Austria) (Group of Friends of the Rule of Law)

RULE OF LAW (Agenda item 83)
A/C.6/78/SR.15

Marschik, Alexander (Austria) (UN. General Assembly. 3rd Committee. Chair)

UN. GENERAL ASSEMBLY (78TH SESS. : 2023-2024)—OFFICERS (Agenda item 5)
A/C.3/78/SR.57

Marschik, Alexander (Austria) (UN. Group of Western European and Other States)
UN. GENERAL ASSEMBLY (78TH SESS. : 2023-2024). PRESIDENT (Agenda item 4)
A/78/PV.87

Marschik, Nikolaus (Austria)
UKRAINE—POLITICAL CONDITIONS (Agenda item 62)
A/78/PV.56

Marsudi, Retno Lestari Priansari (Indonesia)
PALESTINE QUESTION (Agenda item 35)
A/78/PV.39
UN. GENERAL ASSEMBLY (78TH SESS. : 2023-2024)—GENERAL DEBATE (Agenda item 8)
A/78/PV.12

Mart, Saša (Serbia)
FOOD SECURITY (Agenda item 23a)
A/C.2/78/SR.17
INVESTMENT PROMOTION (Agenda item 16g)
A/C.2/78/SR.9
MACROECONOMIC POLICY (Agenda item 16)
A/C.2/78/SR.9
POVERTY—INTERNATIONAL DECADES (Agenda item 21a)
A/C.2/78/SR.17
RURAL POVERTY (Agenda item 21b)
A/C.2/78/SR.17
SCIENCE AND TECHNOLOGY—DEVELOPMENT (Agenda item 19a)
A/C.2/78/SR.11

Martín Couce, Adrián (Spain)
DEVELOPMENT FINANCE (Agenda item 16b)
A/C.2/78/SR.9
EXTERNAL DEBT (Agenda item 16c)
A/C.2/78/SR.9

Martín Couce, Adrián (Spain) (European Union)
INTERNATIONAL TRADE (Agenda item 16a)
A/C.2/78/SR.22; A/C.2/78/SR.24
RURAL POVERTY (Agenda item 21b)
A/C.2/78/SR.22
SUSTAINABLE DEVELOPMENT (Agenda item 18)
A/C.2/78/SR.24
TAXATION (Agenda item 16h)
A/C.2/78/SR.25

Martin Topranin, Pietro de (Italy)
PEACEBUILDING (Agenda item 61)
A/78/PV.100
UN. PEACEBUILDING COMMISSION—REPORTS (Agenda item 27)
A/78/PV.100
UN. PEACEBUILDING FUND—REPORTS (Agenda item 111)
A/78/PV.100

Martinet, Philippe (France)
HUMAN RIGHTS—RUSSIAN FEDERATION (Agenda item 71c)
A/C.3/78/SR.37

Martínez Badillo, Juan José (UNCTAD)
COMMODITIES (Agenda item 16d)
A/C.2/78/SR.14
SUSTAINABLE DEVELOPMENT (Agenda item 18)
A/C.2/78/SR.14

Marwa, Mohammed Buba (Nigeria)
CRIME PREVENTION (Agenda item 107)
A/C.3/78/SR.5

Marzooq, Mohammed Sahib (Iraq)
IAEA—REPORTS (Agenda item 89)
A/78/PV.29

Masisi, Mokgweetsi Eric Keabetswe (Botswana. President)
UN. GENERAL ASSEMBLY (78TH SESS. : 2023-2024)—GENERAL DEBATE (Agenda item 8)
A/78/PV.7
UN. GENERAL ASSEMBLY (78TH SESS. : 2023-2024)—SPECIAL STATEMENTS
A/78/PV.7

Masmejean, Laurent (Switzerland)
ARMS RACE—OUTER SPACE (Agenda item 97a)
A/C.1/78/PV.17
OUTER SPACE—PRINCIPLES (Agenda item 97d)
A/C.1/78/PV.17
WEAPONS—OUTER SPACE (Agenda item 97b)
A/C.1/78/PV.17

Mason, Michelle (Safety and Security Instructional Services)
WESTERN SAHARA QUESTION (Agenda item 58)
A/C.4/78/SR.4

Mason, Naomi (Australia)
UN. INTERNATIONAL LAW COMMISSION—REPORTS (Agenda item 79)
A/C.6/78/SR.29

Massari, Maurizio (Italy)
CRIME PREVENTION (Agenda item 107)
A/78/PV.63
DISASTER VICTIMS (Agenda item 86)
A/C.6/78/SR.5
FOOD SECURITY (Agenda item 23a)
A/C.2/78/SR.16
INTERNATIONAL CRIMINAL COURT—REPORTS (Agenda item 74)
A/78/PV.22
POVERTY—INTERNATIONAL DECADES (Agenda item 21a)
A/C.2/78/SR.16

Massari, Maurizio (Italy) (continued)

RURAL POVERTY (Agenda item 21b)
A/C.2/78/SR.16
UN. GENERAL ASSEMBLY (78TH SESS. : 2023-2024). 2ND COMMITTEE—GENERAL DEBATE (Agenda item 8)
A/C.2/78/SR.6
VETO (Agenda item 63)
A/78/PV.52; A/78/PV.68; A/78/PV.71

Massari, Maurizio (Italy) (Uniting for Consensus Group)

UN. SECURITY COUNCIL—MEMBERSHIP (Agenda item 121)
A/78/PV.34; A/78/PV.104

Mataafa, Fiame Naomi (Samoa. Prime Minister)

UN. GENERAL ASSEMBLY (78TH SESS. : 2023-2024)—GENERAL DEBATE (Agenda item 8)
A/78/PV.12
UN. GENERAL ASSEMBLY (78TH SESS. : 2023-2024)—SPECIAL STATEMENTS
A/78/PV.12

Matar, Shahd Jamal Yousuf (United Arab Emirates)

DECOLONIZATION (Agenda item 58)
A/C.4/78/SR.8
UN. GENERAL ASSEMBLY (78TH SESS. : 2023-2024)—GENERAL DEBATE—RIGHT OF REPLY (Agenda item 8)
A/78/PV.13
VETO (Agenda item 63)
A/78/PV.69

Matekane, Ntsokoane Samuel (Lesotho. Prime Minister)

UN. GENERAL ASSEMBLY (78TH SESS. : 2023-2024)—GENERAL DEBATE (Agenda item 8)
A/78/PV.11
UN. GENERAL ASSEMBLY (78TH SESS. : 2023-2024)—SPECIAL STATEMENTS
A/78/PV.11

Mathur, Pratik (India)

UN. GENERAL ASSEMBLY—WORK PROGRAMME (Agenda item 120)
A/78/PV.33
UN. SECURITY COUNCIL—REPORTS (Agenda item 26)
A/78/PV.94
UN RESOLUTIONS—IMPLEMENTATION (Agenda item 119)
A/78/PV.33

Matković, Mihajlo (Serbia)

YOUTH (Agenda item 24b)
A/C.3/78/SR.3

Matos, Ines (Portugal)

DISASTER VICTIMS (Agenda item 86)
A/C.6/78/SR.5
INTERNATIONAL LAW—TRAINING PROGRAMMES (Agenda item 78)
A/C.6/78/SR.21

Matos Menéndez, Gala (Dominican Republic)

HEALTH (Agenda item 125)
A/78/PV.16
PERSONS WITH DISABILITIES—HUMAN RIGHTS (Agenda item 71a)
A/C.3/78/SR.38
RIGHT TO EDUCATION (Agenda item 71b)
A/C.3/78/SR.27
RIGHT TO HEALTH (Agenda item 71b)
A/C.3/78/SR.39
RIGHTS OF THE CHILD (Agenda item 67)
A/C.3/78/SR.11; A/C.3/78/SR.13
SOCIAL CONDITIONS (Agenda item 24b)
A/C.3/78/SR.51

Mattarella, Sergio (Italy. President)

MULTILATERALISM
A/78/PV.81
UN. GENERAL ASSEMBLY (78TH SESS. : 2023-2024)—SPECIAL STATEMENTS
A/78/PV.81

Maure, Adnito (Mozambique)

FOOD SECURITY (Agenda item 23a)
A/C.2/78/SR.17
POVERTY—INTERNATIONAL DECADES (Agenda item 21a)
A/C.2/78/SR.17
RURAL POVERTY (Agenda item 21b)
A/C.2/78/SR.17

Mawire, Tirivavi (Zimbabwe)

WESTERN SAHARA QUESTION (Agenda item 58)
A/C.4/78/SR.8

May, Vueti Kosoniu (Fiji)

MILLENNIUM SUMMIT—CONFERENCES (Agenda item 117)
A/78/PV.102
SMALL ISLAND DEVELOPING STATES—PROGRAMMES OF ACTION (Agenda item 18b)
A/78/PV.103
UN CONFERENCES (Agenda item 13)
A/78/PV.102

May, Vueti Kosoniu (Fiji) (Pacific Islands Forum)

MILLENNIUM SUMMIT—CONFERENCES (Agenda item 117)
A/78/PV.102
UN CONFERENCES (Agenda item 13)
A/78/PV.102

Mazaeva, Viktoriia (Russian Federation)
PERSONS WITH DISABILITIES—HUMAN RIGHTS (Agenda item 71a)
A/C.3/78/SR.51
SOCIAL CONDITIONS (Agenda item 24b)
A/78/PV.101
UN RESOLUTIONS—IMPLEMENTATION (Agenda item 119)
A/78/PV.103
UN YOUTH OFFICE—REPORTS (Agenda item 130)
A/78/PV.102
YOUTH (Agenda item 24b)
A/C.3/78/SR.55

Mbella Mbella, Lejeune (Cameroon)
UN. GENERAL ASSEMBLY (78TH SESS. : 2023-2024)—GENERAL DEBATE (Agenda item 8)
A/78/PV.14

Mbingo, Mduduzi Kieth Kenneth (Eswatini)
UN. GENERAL ASSEMBLY (78TH SESS. : 2023-2024). 1ST COMMITTEE—GENERAL DEBATE (Agenda item 8)
A/C.1/78/PV.8

Mc Bean, Keith (Ireland)
HUMAN RIGHTS—RUSSIAN FEDERATION (Agenda item 71c)
A/C.3/78/SR.37
HUMAN RIGHTS—SYRIAN ARAB REPUBLIC (Agenda item 71c)
A/C.3/78/SR.54
HUMAN RIGHTS—TERRITORIES OCCUPIED BY ISRAEL (Agenda item 71c)
A/C.3/78/SR.35
HUMAN RIGHTS—UKRAINE (Agenda item 71c)
A/C.3/78/SR.37
VETO (Agenda item 63)
A/78/PV.59
WOMEN'S ADVANCEMENT (Agenda item 25a)
A/C.3/78/SR.9
WOMEN'S ADVANCEMENT—CONFERENCES (Agenda item 25b)
A/C.3/78/SR.9

McCarthy, Adam (Australia)
UN. INTERNATIONAL COURT OF JUSTICE—REPORTS (Agenda item 73)
A/78/PV.20
UN. INTERNATIONAL LAW COMMISSION—REPORTS (Agenda item 79)
A/C.6/78/SR.23

McCauley, Natalie (European Union)
DISPLACED PERSONS (Agenda item 71b)
A/C.3/78/SR.32

McGlothlin, Cameron (United States)
DISPLACED PERSONS (Agenda item 71b)
A/C.3/78/SR.32

McGlothlin, Cameron (United States) (continued)
MIGRANTS—PROTECTION (Agenda item 71b)
A/C.3/78/SR.23
TRAFFICKING IN PERSONS (Agenda item 71b)
A/C.3/78/SR.23

McGuire, Peter Davidson (Sovereign Order of Malta)
FREEDOM OF EXPRESSION (Agenda item 71b)
A/C.3/78/SR.19
MIGRANT WORKERS (Agenda item 71a)
A/C.3/78/SR.23
SUMMARY EXECUTIONS (Agenda item 71b)
A/C.3/78/SR.31

McIntyre, Colin Roger (United Kingdom)
CRIMES AGAINST HUMANITY (Agenda item 80)
A/C.6/78/SR.39

Mead, Kevin Timothy (Canada)
ADMINISTRATION OF JUSTICE (Agenda item 144)
A/C.6/78/SR.9
CENTRAL ASIA—ZONES OF PEACE (Agenda item 64)
A/78/PV.85
CRIMES AGAINST HUMANITY (Agenda item 80)
A/C.6/78/SR.38; A/C.6/78/SR.40; A/C.6/78/SR.42; A/C.6/78/SR.43
UN. INTERNATIONAL LAW COMMISSION—REPORTS (Agenda item 79)
A/C.6/78/SR.30
UN COMMISSION ON INTERNATIONAL TRADE LAW—REPORTS (Agenda item 77)
A/C.6/78/SR.14

Mead, Kevin Timothy (Canada) (European Union)
PEACEKEEPING OPERATIONS—CRIMINAL LIABILITY (Agenda item 76)
A/C.6/78/SR.37

Medzinyuie, Edem Kodzovi (Togo)
PEACEKEEPING OPERATIONS (Agenda item 51)
A/C.4/78/SR.18

Megally, Hanny (Independent International Commission of Inquiry on the Syrian Arab Republic)
HUMAN RIGHTS—SYRIAN ARAB REPUBLIC (Agenda item 71c)
A/C.3/78/SR.34

Meidert, Michael Sebastian (Liechtenstein)
HUMAN RIGHTS—UKRAINE (Agenda item 71c)
A/C.3/78/SR.37

Meizura, Novia (Indonesia)
ENVIRONMENT (Agenda item 71b)
A/C.3/78/SR.29

Meizura, Novia (Indonesia) (continued)

POVERTY—HUMAN RIGHTS (Agenda item 71b)
A/C.3/78/SR.30
RIGHT TO EDUCATION (Agenda item 71b)
A/C.3/78/SR.27
RIGHT TO THE TRUTH (Agenda item 71b)
A/C.3/78/SR.22

Melchionna, Luca (European Public Law Organization)

RULE OF LAW (Agenda item 83)
A/C.6/78/SR.19

Melikbekyan, Elena A. (Russian Federation)

UN. INTERNATIONAL LAW COMMISSION—REPORTS (Agenda item 79)
A/C.6/78/SR.30

Melikyan, Varduhi (Armenia)

CRIMES AGAINST HUMANITY (Agenda item 80)
A/C.6/78/SR.41

Meloni, Giorgia (Italy. Council of Ministers. President)

UN. GENERAL ASSEMBLY (78TH SESS. : 2023-2024)—GENERAL DEBATE (Agenda item 8)
A/78/PV.7
UN. GENERAL ASSEMBLY (78TH SESS. : 2023-2024)—SPECIAL STATEMENTS
A/78/PV.7

Mendes, Francisco (Guinea-Bissau)

WESTERN SAHARA QUESTION (Agenda item 58)
A/C.4/78/SR.8

Méndez Bocanegra, Rodrigo Andrés (Colombia)

HIV/AIDS—DECLARATIONS (Agenda item 10)
A/78/PV.91
INDIGENOUS PEOPLES (Agenda item 68a)
A/C.3/78/SR.15
INDIGENOUS PEOPLES—CONFERENCES (Agenda item 68b)
A/C.3/78/SR.15
YOUTH (Agenda item 24b)
A/C.3/78/SR.55

Méndez Gruezo, Elizabeth (Ecuador)

AGEING PERSONS (Agenda item 24b)
A/C.3/78/SR.2
RIGHTS OF THE CHILD (Agenda item 67)
A/C.3/78/SR.13
SOCIAL CONDITIONS (Agenda item 24b)
A/C.3/78/SR.2
UN. HUMAN RIGHTS COUNCIL—REPORTS (Agenda item 66)
A/C.3/78/SR.46
WOMEN'S ADVANCEMENT (Agenda item 25a)
A/C.3/78/SR.9

Méndez Gruezo, Elizabeth (Ecuador) (continued)

WOMEN'S ADVANCEMENT—CONFERENCES (Agenda item 25b)
A/C.3/78/SR.9
YOUTH (Agenda item 24b)
A/C.3/78/SR.2

Mendoza Elguea, Sylvia Paola (Mexico)

DEVELOPMENT FINANCE—CONFERENCES (Agenda item 17)
A/78/PV.90
HEALTH (Agenda item 125)
A/78/PV.64
HIV/AIDS—DECLARATIONS (Agenda item 10)
A/78/PV.91
HUMAN RIGHTS—UKRAINE (Agenda item 71c)
A/C.3/78/SR.53
MIGRANTS—PROTECTION (Agenda item 71b)
A/C.3/78/SR.56
RACIAL DISCRIMINATION—ELIMINATION (Agenda item 69a)
A/78/PV.103
RIGHT TO HEALTH (Agenda item 71b)
A/C.3/78/SR.39
RURAL POVERTY (Agenda item 21b)
A/C.2/78/SR.22
UN. GENERAL ASSEMBLY (78TH SESS. : 2023-2024). 2ND COMMITTEE—GENERAL DEBATE (Agenda item 8)
A/C.2/78/SR.2
UN HIGH COMMISSIONER FOR REFUGEES—REPORTS (Agenda item 60)
A/C.3/78/SR.44
UN SYSTEM—STRENGTHENING (Agenda item 122)
A/78/PV.99

Merabet, Ismaïl (Algeria)

INFORMATION (Agenda item 53)
A/C.4/78/SR.13
PEACE (Agenda item 14)
A/78/PV.82
SUSTAINABLE DEVELOPMENT (Agenda item 18)
A/C.2/78/SR.15; A/C.2/78/SR.25
TERRITORIES OCCUPIED BY ISRAEL—NATURAL RESOURCES (Agenda item 59)
A/C.2/78/SR.19

Merron, Eric (United States)

CRIME PREVENTION (Agenda item 107)
A/C.3/78/SR.5
CYBERCRIME (Agenda item 108)
A/C.3/78/SR.5
DEMOCRACY (Agenda item 71b)
A/C.3/78/SR.48
HUMAN RIGHTS ADVANCEMENT (Agenda item 71b)
A/C.3/78/SR.48
MERCENARIES (Agenda item 70)
A/C.3/78/SR.48
RIGHT TO DEVELOPMENT (Agenda item 71b)
A/C.3/78/SR.48

Merron, Eric (United States) (continued)

RIGHT TO FOOD (Agenda item 71b)
A/C.3/78/SR.48
RIGHT TO PRIVACY (Agenda item 71b)
A/C.3/78/SR.21
SANCTIONS—INTERNATIONAL RELATIONS (Agenda item 71b)
A/C.3/78/SR.48
TORTURE AND OTHER CRUEL TREATMENT (Agenda item 71a)
A/C.3/78/SR.18

Mesarek, Gordana Vidovic (Croatia)

UN. INTERNATIONAL LAW COMMISSION—REPORTS (Agenda item 79)
A/C.6/78/SR.27

Meschchanov, Boris A. (Russian Federation)

AFRICA—DEVELOPMENT (Agenda item 65b)
A/78/PV.18
AFRICA—SUSTAINABLE DEVELOPMENT—PARTNERSHIP (Agenda item 65a)
A/78/PV.18
CLIMATE (Agenda item 18d)
A/C.2/78/SR.25
ECONOMIC COOPERATION AMONG DEVELOPING COUNTRIES (Agenda item 22b)
A/C.2/78/SR.18
FOOD SECURITY (Agenda item 23a)
A/C.2/78/SR.25
HEALTH (Agenda item 125)
A/78/PV.41
INTERNATIONAL TRADE (Agenda item 16a)
A/C.2/78/SR.22; A/C.2/78/SR.24
OPERATIONAL ACTIVITIES—UN SYSTEM (Agenda item 22a)
A/C.2/78/SR.18
SMALL ISLAND DEVELOPING STATES—PROGRAMMES OF ACTION (Agenda item 18b)
A/78/PV.100
SUSTAINABLE ENERGY (Agenda item 18h)
A/C.2/78/SR.23
TAXATION (Agenda item 16h)
A/C.2/78/SR.25
TERRITORIES OCCUPIED BY ISRAEL—NATURAL RESOURCES (Agenda item 59)
A/C.2/78/SR.20
UN. GENERAL ASSEMBLY (78TH SESS. : 2023-2024). 2ND COMMITTEE—GENERAL DEBATE (Agenda item 8)
A/C.2/78/SR.2
UN SYSTEM—STRENGTHENING (Agenda item 122)
A/78/PV.99

Meunluang, Veomanee (Lao People's Democratic Republic)

MIGRANT WORKERS (Agenda item 71a)
A/C.3/78/SR.23
RELIGIOUS INTOLERANCE (Agenda item 71b)
A/C.3/78/SR.38

Meunluang, Veomanee (Lao People's Democratic Republic) (continued)

RIGHTS OF THE CHILD (Agenda item 67)
A/C.3/78/SR.13

Meynet, Nathalie (Coordinating Committee for International Staff Unions and Associations of the United Nations System)

PERSONNEL QUESTIONS—UN SYSTEM (Agenda item 142)
A/C.5/78/SR.10

Meyrick, Phoebe (United Kingdom)

DECOLONIZATION (Agenda item 58)
A/C.4/78/SR.9
DECOLONIZATION—UN SYSTEM (Agenda item 56)
A/C.4/78/SR.9
FALKLAND ISLANDS (MALVINAS) QUESTION (Agenda item 42)
A/C.4/78/SR.2; A/C.4/78/SR.6; A/C.4/78/SR.7; A/C.4/78/SR.8; A/C.4/78/SR.9
GIBRALTAR QUESTION (Agenda item 58)
A/C.4/78/SR.2
NON-SELF-GOVERNING TERRITORIES—ECONOMIC INTERESTS (Agenda item 55)
A/C.4/78/SR.9
NON-SELF-GOVERNING TERRITORIES—REPORTS (Agenda item 54)
A/C.4/78/SR.9

Meza Murillo, Andrea (Secretariat of the Convention to Combat Desertification. Deputy Executive Secretary)

DESERTIFICATION—TREATIES (Agenda item 18e)
A/C.2/78/SR.12

Mezang Akamba, Serge Pamphile (Cameroon)

RACIAL DISCRIMINATION—ELIMINATION (Agenda item 69a)
A/C.3/78/SR.41
RACIAL DISCRIMINATION—PROGRAMMES OF ACTION (Agenda item 69b)
A/C.3/78/SR.41
SUSTAINABLE DEVELOPMENT (Agenda item 18)
A/C.2/78/SR.24; A/C.2/78/SR.25
TAXATION (Agenda item 16h)
A/C.2/78/SR.25

Mezzetti, Andrea (Rete Saharawi (Organization))

WESTERN SAHARA QUESTION (Agenda item 58)
A/C.4/78/SR.5

Micallef, Justine (Malta)

CLIMATE CHANGE (Agenda item 71b)
A/C.3/78/SR.29
HUMAN RIGHTS—AFGHANISTAN (Agenda item 71c)
A/C.3/78/SR.34

Micallef, Justine (Malta) (continued)

HUMAN RIGHTS—SYRIAN ARAB REPUBLIC (Agenda item 71c)
A/C.3/78/SR.34
TRAFFICKING IN PERSONS (Agenda item 71b)
A/C.3/78/SR.23
YOUTH (Agenda item 24b)
A/C.3/78/SR.55

Michaelidou, Gabriella (Cyprus)

HUMAN RIGHTS (Agenda item 71)
A/C.3/78/SR.24

Michel, Charles (European Council. President)

UN. GENERAL ASSEMBLY (78TH SESS. : 2023-2024)—GENERAL DEBATE (Agenda item 8)
A/78/PV.8

Miguel, Nedra P. (Saint Vincent and the Grenadines) (Community of Latin American and Caribbean States)

UN. GENERAL ASSEMBLY (78TH SESS. : 2023-2024). 1ST COMMITTEE—GENERAL DEBATE (Agenda item 8)
A/C.1/78/PV.3

Miguel, Nedra P. (Saint Vincent and the Grenadines) (L.69 Group)

UN. SECURITY COUNCIL—MEMBERSHIP (Agenda item 121)
A/78/PV.34

Mihail, Ioana-Cristina (Romania)

HUMAN RIGHTS—INTERNATIONAL INSTRUMENTS (Agenda item 71a)
A/C.3/78/SR.25
HUMAN RIGHTS—UKRAINE (Agenda item 71c)
A/C.3/78/SR.25; A/C.3/78/SR.37
HUMAN RIGHTS ADVANCEMENT (Agenda item 71b)
A/C.3/78/SR.18
RACIAL DISCRIMINATION—ELIMINATION (Agenda item 69a)
A/C.3/78/SR.41
RACIAL DISCRIMINATION—PROGRAMMES OF ACTION (Agenda item 69b)
A/C.3/78/SR.41
RIGHT TO EDUCATION (Agenda item 71b)
A/C.3/78/SR.27
RIGHT TO FOOD (Agenda item 71b)
A/C.3/78/SR.30
RIGHTS OF THE CHILD (Agenda item 67)
A/C.3/78/SR.11
RURAL WOMEN (Agenda item 25a)
A/C.3/78/SR.7
TRAFFICKING IN PERSONS (Agenda item 71b)
A/C.3/78/SR.23
UN HIGH COMMISSIONER FOR REFUGEES—REPORTS (Agenda item 60)
A/C.3/78/SR.45

Mikanagi, Tomohiro (Japan)

UN. INTERNATIONAL COURT OF JUSTICE—REPORTS (Agenda item 73)
A/78/PV.20

Mikhaylov, Oleg O. (Russian Federation)

TERRORISM (Agenda item 109)
A/C.6/78/SR.2

Milambo, Chola (Zambia)

CLIMATE (Agenda item 18d)
A/C.2/78/SR.15
COMMODITIES (Agenda item 16d)
A/C.2/78/SR.14
HUMAN RIGHTS—INTERNATIONAL INSTRUMENTS (Agenda item 71a)
A/C.3/78/SR.26
HUMAN RIGHTS ADVANCEMENT (Agenda item 71b)
A/C.3/78/SR.26
INFORMATION TECHNOLOGY—DEVELOPMENT (Agenda item 15)
A/C.2/78/SR.11
NUCLEAR DISARMAMENT (Agenda item 99b)
A/C.1/78/PV.14
RIGHTS OF THE CHILD (Agenda item 67)
A/C.3/78/SR.13
SCIENCE AND TECHNOLOGY—DEVELOPMENT (Agenda item 19a)
A/C.2/78/SR.11
SUSTAINABLE DEVELOPMENT (Agenda item 18)
A/C.2/78/SR.14; A/C.2/78/SR.15
SUSTAINABLE ENERGY (Agenda item 18h)
A/C.2/78/SR.15
UN. GENERAL ASSEMBLY (78TH SESS. : 2023-2024). 2ND COMMITTEE—GENERAL DEBATE (Agenda item 8)
A/C.2/78/SR.6
UN. INTERNATIONAL COURT OF JUSTICE—REPORTS (Agenda item 73)
A/78/PV.28
WOMEN'S ADVANCEMENT (Agenda item 25a)
A/C.3/78/SR.10
WOMEN'S ADVANCEMENT—CONFERENCES (Agenda item 25b)
A/C.3/78/SR.10

Milambo, Chola (Zambia) (UN. Group of African States)

CUBA—UNITED STATES (Agenda item 38)
A/78/PV.24
HUMAN RIGHTS—BURUNDI (Agenda item 71c)
A/C.3/78/SR.36
HUMAN RIGHTS—ERITREA (Agenda item 71c)
A/C.3/78/SR.36
HUMAN RIGHTS—ETHIOPIA (Agenda item 71c)
A/C.3/78/SR.36
UN. HUMAN RIGHTS COUNCIL—REPORTS (Agenda item 66)
A/C.3/78/SR.51

Milambo, Chola (Zambia) (UN. Group of African States) (continued)

UN CONFERENCES (Agenda item 13)
A/78/PV.33

Milano, Enrico (Italy)

CRIMES AGAINST HUMANITY (Agenda item 80)
A/C.6/78/SR.11; A/C.6/78/SR.38; A/C.6/78/SR.40; A/C.6/78/SR.41; A/C.6/78/SR.44; A/C.6/78/SR.45
UN COMMISSION ON INTERNATIONAL TRADE LAW—REPORTS (Agenda item 77)
A/C.6/78/SR.14

Milanovic, Zoran (Croatia. President)

UN. GENERAL ASSEMBLY (78TH SESS. : 2023-2024)—GENERAL DEBATE (Agenda item 8)
A/78/PV.6
UN. GENERAL ASSEMBLY (78TH SESS. : 2023-2024)—SPECIAL STATEMENTS
A/78/PV.6

Milatović, Jakov (Montenegro. President)

UN. GENERAL ASSEMBLY (78TH SESS. : 2023-2024)—GENERAL DEBATE (Agenda item 8)
A/78/PV.8
UN. GENERAL ASSEMBLY (78TH SESS. : 2023-2024)—SPECIAL STATEMENTS
A/78/PV.8

Miljkovicova, Adriana (UNIDO)

FOOD SECURITY (Agenda item 23a)
A/C.2/78/SR.18
POVERTY—INTERNATIONAL DECADES (Agenda item 21a)
A/C.2/78/SR.18

Millard, Elisabeth I. (United States)

ELECTION VERIFICATION—UN (Agenda item 71b)
A/C.3/78/SR.50
HUMAN RIGHTS—BELARUS (Agenda item 71c)
A/C.3/78/SR.37
HUMAN RIGHTS—RUSSIAN FEDERATION (Agenda item 71c)
A/C.3/78/SR.37
HUMAN RIGHTS—UKRAINE (Agenda item 71c)
A/C.3/78/SR.37
WOMEN'S ADVANCEMENT (Agenda item 25a)
A/C.3/78/SR.7
WOMEN'S ADVANCEMENT—CONFERENCES (Agenda item 25b)
A/C.3/78/SR.7

Miller, Brett Jonathan (Israel)

UN. GENERAL ASSEMBLY (78TH SESS. : 2023-2024). 2ND COMMITTEE—GENERAL DEBATE (Agenda item 8)
A/C.2/78/SR.3
VETO (Agenda item 63)
A/78/PV.69; A/78/PV.79

Milligan, Ashlyn (Canada)

ARMS RACE—OUTER SPACE (Agenda item 97a)
A/C.1/78/PV.17
DISARMAMENT AGREEMENTS—OUTER SPACE (Agenda item 97c)
A/C.1/78/PV.17
OUTER SPACE—CONFIDENCE-BUILDING MEASURES (Agenda item 99v)
A/C.1/78/PV.17
OUTER SPACE—PRINCIPLES (Agenda item 97d)
A/C.1/78/PV.17

Mimran Rosenberg, Avital (Israel)

CRIME PREVENTION (Agenda item 107)
A/C.3/78/SR.5
HUMAN RIGHTS (Agenda item 71)
A/C.3/78/SR.25
HUMAN RIGHTS—IRAN (ISLAMIC REPUBLIC OF) (Agenda item 71c)
A/C.3/78/SR.53
HUMAN RIGHTS—UKRAINE (Agenda item 71c)
A/C.3/78/SR.37
HUMAN RIGHTS ACTIVISTS (Agenda item 71b)
A/C.3/78/SR.19
HUMAN RIGHTS ADVANCEMENT (Agenda item 71b)
A/C.3/78/SR.52
INDIGENOUS PEOPLES (Agenda item 68a)
A/C.3/78/SR.17
PEACE (Agenda item 14)
A/78/PV.77
RACIAL DISCRIMINATION—ELIMINATION (Agenda item 69a)
A/C.3/78/SR.41; A/C.3/78/SR.47
RACIAL DISCRIMINATION—PROGRAMMES OF ACTION (Agenda item 69b)
A/C.3/78/SR.41; A/C.3/78/SR.56
RELIGIOUS INTOLERANCE (Agenda item 71b)
A/C.3/78/SR.38
RIGHT TO FOOD (Agenda item 71b)
A/C.3/78/SR.30
RIGHT TO HOUSING (Agenda item 71b)
A/C.3/78/SR.30
RIGHTS OF THE CHILD (Agenda item 67)
A/C.3/78/SR.11; A/C.3/78/SR.55
SELF-DETERMINATION OF PEOPLES (Agenda item 70)
A/C.3/78/SR.42; A/C.3/78/SR.49
UN. HUMAN RIGHTS COUNCIL—REPORTS (Agenda item 66)
A/C.3/78/SR.51

Min, Yongyi (UN. Statistics Division. Director)

SUSTAINABLE DEVELOPMENT (Agenda item 18)
A/C.2/78/SR.12

Minale, Lemlem Fiseha (Ethiopia)

CRIMES AGAINST HUMANITY (Agenda item 80)
A/C.6/78/SR.11

Minale, Lemlem Fiseha (Ethiopia) (UN. Group of African States)

INTERNATIONAL RESIDUAL MECHANISM FOR CRIMINAL TRIBUNALS—FINANCING (Agenda item 145)
A/C.5/78/SR.20
PEACEKEEPING OPERATIONS—FINANCING (Agenda item 146)
A/C.5/78/SR.36
UN—BUDGET (2024) (Agenda item 134)
A/C.5/78/SR.3; A/C.5/78/SR.11; A/C.5/78/SR.12; A/C.5/78/SR.22; A/C.5/78/SR.23; A/C.5/78/SR.33
UN—HUMAN RESOURCES MANAGEMENT (Agenda item 139)
A/C.5/78/SR.27
UN. GENERAL ASSEMBLY (78TH SESS. : 2023-2024). 5TH COMMITTEE—WORK ORGANIZATION (Agenda item 7)
A/C.5/78/SR.26/PartII; A/C.5/78/SR.34; A/C.5/78/SR.35; A/C.5/78/SR.40

Minchenberg, Eliot (UNESCO)

CULTURE—DEVELOPMENT (Agenda item 19b)
A/C.2/78/SR.10
DEVELOPMENT EDUCATION (Agenda item 18g)
A/C.2/78/SR.12

Minegishi, Shunsuke (Japan)

MULTILINGUALISM (Agenda item 124)
A/78/PV.108

Mira Ramírez, Walter José (El Salvador)

SCIENCE AND TECHNOLOGY—DEVELOPMENT (Agenda item 19a)
A/C.2/78/SR.10

Miranda, Ruth de (UN. Department for General Assembly and Conference Management)

LANDLOCKED DEVELOPING COUNTRIES—CONFERENCES (Agenda item 20b)
A/78/PV.80
MILLENNIUM SUMMIT—CONFERENCES (Agenda item 117)
A/78/PV.102
UN CONFERENCES (Agenda item 13)
A/78/PV.102

Mirziyoyev, Shavkat (Uzbekistan. President)

UN. GENERAL ASSEMBLY (78TH SESS. : 2023-2024)—GENERAL DEBATE (Agenda item 8)
A/78/PV.4
UN. GENERAL ASSEMBLY (78TH SESS. : 2023-2024)—SPECIAL STATEMENTS
A/78/PV.4

Mirzoyan, Ararat (Armenia)

UN. GENERAL ASSEMBLY (78TH SESS. : 2023-2024)—GENERAL DEBATE (Agenda item 8)
A/78/PV.13

Mitchell, Dickon (Grenada. Prime Minister)

UN. GENERAL ASSEMBLY (78TH SESS. : 2023-2024)—GENERAL DEBATE (Agenda item 8)
A/78/PV.11
UN. GENERAL ASSEMBLY (78TH SESS. : 2023-2024)—SPECIAL STATEMENTS
A/78/PV.11

Mitchell, Frederick A. (Bahamas)

UN. GENERAL ASSEMBLY (78TH SESS. : 2023-2024)—GENERAL DEBATE (Agenda item 8)
A/78/PV.11

Mitchell, Rob (Australia)

RIGHTS OF THE CHILD (Agenda item 67)
A/C.3/78/SR.13
WOMEN'S ADVANCEMENT (Agenda item 25a)
A/C.3/78/SR.7
WOMEN'S ADVANCEMENT—CONFERENCES (Agenda item 25b)
A/C.3/78/SR.7

Miti-Drummond, Muluka-Anne (UN. Human Rights Council. Independent Expert on the Enjoyment of Human Rights by Persons with Albinism)

ALBINISM (Agenda item 71b)
A/C.3/78/SR.27

Mitsotakis, Kyriakos (Greece. Prime Minister)

UN. GENERAL ASSEMBLY (78TH SESS. : 2023-2024)—GENERAL DEBATE (Agenda item 8)
A/78/PV.9
UN. GENERAL ASSEMBLY (78TH SESS. : 2023-2024)—SPECIAL STATEMENTS
A/78/PV.9

Miyamoto, Sogaku (Japan)

DISAPPEARANCE OF PERSONS (Agenda item 71b)
A/C.3/78/SR.22
EMERGENCY ASSISTANCE (Agenda item 72a)
A/78/PV.46
PALESTINIANS—ASSISTANCE (Agenda item 72b)
A/78/PV.46
RIGHT TO THE TRUTH (Agenda item 71b)
A/C.3/78/SR.22
UN HIGH COMMISSIONER FOR REFUGEES—REPORTS (Agenda item 60)
A/C.3/78/SR.45

Mizutori, Mami (UN. Special Representative of the Secretary-General for Disaster Risk Reduction)

DISASTER PREVENTION (Agenda item 18c)
A/C.2/78/SR.12

Mmalane, Katlego Boase (Botswana) (Group of Landlocked Developing Countries)
COMMODITIES (Agenda item 16d)
A/C.2/78/SR.8
DEVELOPMENT FINANCE (Agenda item 16b)
A/C.2/78/SR.8
INVESTMENT PROMOTION (Agenda item 16g)
A/C.2/78/SR.8
MACROECONOMIC POLICY (Agenda item 16)
A/C.2/78/SR.8

Mnangagwa, Emmerson Dambudzo (Zimbabwe. President)
UN. GENERAL ASSEMBLY (78TH SESS. : 2023-2024)—GENERAL DEBATE (Agenda item 8)
A/78/PV.8
UN. GENERAL ASSEMBLY (78TH SESS. : 2023-2024)—SPECIAL STATEMENTS
A/78/PV.8

Mngomezulu, Portia Lindiwe (South Africa)
UN. HUMAN RIGHTS COUNCIL—REPORTS (Agenda item 66)
A/C.3/78/SR.46

Mocanu, Andreea (Romania)
ARMS TRANSFERS—TREATIES (Agenda item 99x)
A/C.1/78/PV.19
CRIMES AGAINST HUMANITY (Agenda item 80)
A/C.6/78/SR.40
HUMAN RIGHTS—TERRITORIES OCCUPIED BY ISRAEL (Agenda item 71c)
A/C.3/78/SR.35
INFORMATION (Agenda item 53)
A/C.4/78/SR.12; A/C.4/78/SR.13
PEACEKEEPING OPERATIONS (Agenda item 51)
A/C.4/78/SR.19
UN. GENERAL ASSEMBLY (78TH SESS. : 2023-2024)—AGENDA (Agenda item 7)
A/BUR/78/SR.2

Moctar, El Hadji (Fédération mondiale des amis du Sahara marocain)
WESTERN SAHARA QUESTION (Agenda item 58)
A/C.4/78/SR.5

Mofokeng, Tlaleng (UN. Human Rights Council. Special Rapporteur on the Right of Everyone to the Enjoyment of the Highest Attainable Standard of Physical and Mental Health)
RIGHT TO HEALTH (Agenda item 71b)
A/C.3/78/SR.39

Mogyorósi, Bálint (Hungary)
ELECTION VERIFICATION—UN (Agenda item 71b)
A/C.3/78/SR.50
INDIGENOUS PEOPLES (Agenda item 68a)
A/C.3/78/SR.48

Mogyorósi, Bálint (Hungary) (continued)
MINORITIES (Agenda item 71b)
A/C.3/78/SR.39
RACIAL DISCRIMINATION—ELIMINATION (Agenda item 69a)
A/78/PV.103
RELIGIOUS INTOLERANCE (Agenda item 71b)
A/C.3/78/SR.38

Mogyorósi, Bálint (Hungary) (European Union)
SOCIAL CONDITIONS (Agenda item 24b)
A/78/PV.57

Mohamed, Abuzied Shamseldin Ahmed (Sudan)
ARMED CONFLICTS PREVENTION (Agenda item 31a)
A/78/PV.72
ECONOMIC SANCTIONS—INTERNATIONAL RELATIONS (Agenda item 28)
A/78/PV.90
INFORMATION (Agenda item 53)
A/C.4/78/SR.13
MINE CLEARANCE (Agenda item 46)
A/C.4/78/SR.10
PEACEKEEPING OPERATIONS (Agenda item 51)
A/C.4/78/SR.19
SPECIAL POLITICAL MISSIONS (Agenda item 52)
A/C.4/78/SR.21
TERRITORIES OCCUPIED BY ISRAEL—HUMAN RIGHTS (Agenda item 50)
A/C.4/78/SR.24
UNRWA—ACTIVITIES (Agenda item 49)
A/C.4/78/SR.23
VETO (Agenda item 63)
A/78/PV.79

Mohamed, Al-Harith Idriss al-Harith (Sudan)
UN. INTERNATIONAL COURT OF JUSTICE—REPORTS (Agenda item 73)
A/78/PV.28

Mohamed, Ali Naseer (Maldives)
SMALL ISLAND DEVELOPING STATES—PROGRAMMES OF ACTION (Agenda item 18b)
A/78/PV.100
VETO (Agenda item 63)
A/78/PV.60

Mohamed, El Fadel Bua Da ((personal capacity))
WESTERN SAHARA QUESTION (Agenda item 58)
A/C.4/78/SR.6

Mohamed, Faisal Abdelazim Salim (Sudan)
UN. GENERAL ASSEMBLY (78TH SESS. : 2023-2024). 1ST COMMITTEE—GENERAL DEBATE (Agenda item 8)
A/C.1/78/PV.5

Mohamed, Mahfud ((personal capacity))
WESTERN SAHARA QUESTION (Agenda item 58)
A/C.4/78/SR.6

Mohamed, Mohamed Omar Elfarouk Hassan (Egypt)
HEALTH (Agenda item 125)
A/78/PV.41; A/78/PV.77
MIGRANTS—PROTECTION (Agenda item 71b)
A/C.3/78/SR.23; A/C.3/78/SR.56
RIGHT TO EDUCATION (Agenda item 71b)
A/C.3/78/SR.27
RIGHT TO HEALTH (Agenda item 71b)
A/C.3/78/SR.39
RIGHTS OF THE CHILD (Agenda item 67)
A/C.3/78/SR.11; A/C.3/78/SR.12; A/C.3/78/SR.55
SOCIAL CONDITIONS (Agenda item 24b)
A/C.3/78/SR.51
TRAFFICKING IN PERSONS (Agenda item 71b)
A/C.3/78/SR.23
UN HIGH COMMISSIONER FOR REFUGEES—REPORTS (Agenda item 60)
A/C.3/78/SR.44
UN RESOLUTIONS—IMPLEMENTATION (Agenda item 119)
A/78/PV.108
UN YOUTH OFFICE—REPORTS (Agenda item 130)
A/78/PV.102
WOMEN MIGRANT WORKERS (Agenda item 25a)
A/C.3/78/SR.49
YOUTH (Agenda item 24b)
A/C.3/78/SR.55

Mohamedou, El Hadj Lehbib (Mauritania)
CONVENTIONAL WEAPONS (Agenda item 99u)
A/C.1/78/PV.19
LANDMINES—TREATIES (Agenda item 99m)
A/C.1/78/PV.19
SMALL ARMS—ILLICIT TRAFFIC (Agenda item 99p)
A/C.1/78/PV.19
SMALL ARMS—ILLICIT TRAFFIC—ASSISTANCE (Agenda item 99n)
A/C.1/78/PV.19

Mohamedou, Mohamed Mahmoud Ould (Mauritania)
UN. GENERAL ASSEMBLY (78TH SESS. : 2023-2024). 1ST COMMITTEE—GENERAL DEBATE (Agenda item 8)
A/C.1/78/PV.8

Mohammad, Fatema Yousuf Ibrahim (United Arab Emirates)
DECOLONIZATION (Agenda item 58)
A/C.4/78/SR.7; A/C.4/78/SR.9

Mohammed, Amina J. (UN. Deputy Secretary-General)
HIV/AIDS—DECLARATIONS (Agenda item 10)
A/78/PV.91

Mohammed, Amina J. (UN. Deputy Secretary-General) (continued)
RULE OF LAW (Agenda item 83)
A/C.6/78/SR.16
UN SYSTEM—STRENGTHENING (Agenda item 122)
A/78/PV.1

Mohammed, Ammar Mohammed Mahmoud (Sudan)
CRIMES AGAINST HUMANITY (Agenda item 80)
A/C.6/78/SR.39
INTERNATIONAL JURISDICTION (Agenda item 84)
A/C.6/78/SR.12
INTERNATIONAL LAW—TRAINING PROGRAMMES (Agenda item 78)
A/C.6/78/SR.21
PEACEKEEPING OPERATIONS—CRIMINAL LIABILITY (Agenda item 76)
A/C.6/78/SR.8
RESPONSIBILITY TO PROTECT (Agenda item 129)
A/78/PV.99
RULE OF LAW (Agenda item 83)
A/C.6/78/SR.16
TERRORISM (Agenda item 109)
A/C.6/78/SR.2
UN CHARTER—REPORTS (Agenda item 82)
A/C.6/78/SR.22

Mohammed, Osman Saleh (Eritrea)
UN. GENERAL ASSEMBLY (78TH SESS. : 2023-2024)—GENERAL DEBATE (Agenda item 8)
A/78/PV.13

Moharram, Wajdi Hassan M. (Saudi Arabia)
ARMS RACE—OUTER SPACE (Agenda item 97a)
A/C.1/78/PV.16
CONVENTIONAL WEAPONS (Agenda item 99u)
A/C.1/78/PV.28
DISARMAMENT—GENERAL AND COMPLETE (Agenda item 99)
A/C.1/78/PV.21; A/C.1/78/PV.23; A/C.1/78/PV.30
MULTILATERALISM—DISARMAMENT (Agenda item 99r)
A/C.1/78/PV.21
OUTER SPACE—CONFIDENCE-BUILDING MEASURES (Agenda item 99v)
A/C.1/78/PV.16
UN. GENERAL ASSEMBLY (78TH SESS. : 2023-2024). 1ST COMMITTEE—GENERAL DEBATE (Agenda item 8)
A/C.1/78/PV.6

Mokhawa, Gladys (Botswana)
DECOLONIZATION (Agenda item 58)
A/C.4/78/SR.8
RULE OF LAW (Agenda item 83)
A/C.6/78/SR.18
UN—BUDGET (2024) (Agenda item 134)
A/C.5/78/SR.5
UN—PROGRAMME PLANNING (Agenda item 135)
A/C.5/78/SR.5

Mokhawa, Gladys (Botswana) (continued)

UN. GENERAL ASSEMBLY (78TH SESS. : 2023-2024). 1ST COMMITTEE—GENERAL DEBATE (Agenda item 8)
A/C.1/78/PV.7
UN. GENERAL ASSEMBLY (78TH SESS. : 2023-2024). 2ND COMMITTEE—GENERAL DEBATE (Agenda item 8)
A/C.2/78/SR.5
UN. GENERAL ASSEMBLY (78TH SESS. : 2023-2024). 5TH COMMITTEE—WORK ORGANIZATION (Agenda item 7)
A/C.5/78/SR.40
WESTERN SAHARA QUESTION (Agenda item 58)
A/C.4/78/SR.8

Mokhawa, Gladys (Botswana) (Group of Landlocked Developing Countries)

COMMODITIES (Agenda item 16d)
A/C.2/78/SR.14
FOOD SECURITY (Agenda item 23a)
A/C.2/78/SR.16
LANDLOCKED DEVELOPING COUNTRIES—CONFERENCES (Agenda item 20b)
A/C.2/78/SR.7
LEAST DEVELOPED COUNTRIES—CONFERENCES (Agenda item 20a)
A/C.2/78/SR.7
POVERTY—INTERNATIONAL DECADES (Agenda item 21a)
A/C.2/78/SR.16
RURAL POVERTY (Agenda item 21b)
A/C.2/78/SR.16
SUSTAINABLE DEVELOPMENT (Agenda item 18)
A/C.2/78/SR.14
UN. GENERAL ASSEMBLY (78TH SESS. : 2023-2024). 2ND COMMITTEE—GENERAL DEBATE (Agenda item 8)
A/C.2/78/SR.2

Mokhawa, Gladys (Botswana) (UN. Group of African States)

AFRICA—DEVELOPMENT (Agenda item 65b)
A/78/PV.57
AFRICA—SUSTAINABLE DEVELOPMENT—PARTNERSHIP (Agenda item 65a)
A/78/PV.57
GEINGOB, HAGE GOTTFRIED (NAMIBIA. PRESIDENT)—TRIBUTES
A/78/PV.55

Mokono, Anna Konara (Papua New Guinea)

RIGHTS OF THE CHILD (Agenda item 67)
A/C.3/78/SR.14

Molina García Alcañiz, Mar ((personal capacity))

WESTERN SAHARA QUESTION (Agenda item 58)
A/C.4/78/SR.4

Molla, Md Rafiqul Alam (Bangladesh)

LANDLOCKED DEVELOPING COUNTRIES—CONFERENCES (Agenda item 20b)
A/C.2/78/SR.7
LEAST DEVELOPED COUNTRIES—CONFERENCES (Agenda item 20a)
A/C.2/78/SR.7
MULTILATERALISM—DISARMAMENT (Agenda item 99r)
A/C.1/78/PV.21
NUCLEAR DISARMAMENT (Agenda item 99b)
A/C.1/78/PV.12
NUCLEAR NON-PROLIFERATION—INTERNATIONAL OBLIGATIONS (Agenda item 99w)
A/C.1/78/PV.12
NUCLEAR WEAPONS—TREATIES (Agenda item 99ff)
A/C.1/78/PV.12
RADIATION EFFECTS (Agenda item 47)
A/C.4/78/SR.11
UN. CONFERENCE ON DISARMAMENT—REPORTS (Agenda item 101a)
A/C.1/78/PV.23
UN. DISARMAMENT COMMISSION—REPORTS (Agenda item 101b)
A/C.1/78/PV.23
UN. GENERAL ASSEMBLY—WORK PROGRAMME (Agenda item 120)
A/78/PV.33
UN. SECURITY COUNCIL—MEMBERSHIP (Agenda item 121)
A/78/PV.35
UN RESOLUTIONS—IMPLEMENTATION (Agenda item 119)
A/78/PV.33

Momeni, Javad (Iran (Islamic Republic of))

COASTAL ZONE MANAGEMENT (Agenda item 18j)
A/C.2/78/SR.23
MILLENNIUM SUMMIT—CONFERENCES (Agenda item 117)
A/78/PV.15
STORMS (Agenda item 18i)
A/C.2/78/SR.22
SUSTAINABLE DEVELOPMENT (Agenda item 18)
A/C.2/78/SR.21; A/C.2/78/SR.22
TERRITORIES OCCUPIED BY ISRAEL—NATURAL RESOURCES (Agenda item 59)
A/C.2/78/SR.21
UN. GENERAL ASSEMBLY (78TH SESS. : 2023-2024). 2ND COMMITTEE—GENERAL DEBATE (Agenda item 8)
A/C.2/78/SR.2; A/C.2/78/SR.3
UN CONFERENCES (Agenda item 13)
A/78/PV.15

Moncada Acosta, Samuel R. (Venezuela (Bolivarian Republic of))

PALESTINE QUESTION (Agenda item 35)
A/78/PV.39

Moncada Acosta, Samuel R. (Venezuela (Bolivarian Republic of)) (continued)

VETO (Agenda item 63)
A/78/PV.75

Moncada Acosta, Samuel R. (Venezuela (Bolivarian Republic of)) (Group of Friends in Defence of the Charter of the United Nations)

PEACE (Agenda item 14)
A/78/PV.76

Moncada Colindres, Denis Ronaldo (Nicaragua)

UN. GENERAL ASSEMBLY (78TH SESS. : 2023-2024)—GENERAL DEBATE (Agenda item 8)
A/78/PV.14

Monica, Mosammat Shahanara (Bangladesh)

FREEDOM OF EXPRESSION (Agenda item 71b)
A/C.3/78/SR.19
HUMAN RIGHTS (Agenda item 71)
A/C.3/78/SR.16
HUMAN RIGHTS—MYANMAR (Agenda item 71c)
A/C.3/78/SR.33; A/C.3/78/SR.53
HUMAN RIGHTS—TERRITORIES OCCUPIED BY ISRAEL (Agenda item 71c)
A/C.3/78/SR.35
HUMAN RIGHTS ACTIVISTS (Agenda item 71b)
A/C.3/78/SR.19
PERSONS WITH DISABILITIES—HUMAN RIGHTS (Agenda item 71a)
A/C.3/78/SR.38
RELIGIOUS INTOLERANCE (Agenda item 71b)
A/C.3/78/SR.38
RIGHT OF ASSEMBLY (Agenda item 71b)
A/C.3/78/SR.19
RIGHT TO DEVELOPMENT (Agenda item 71b)
A/C.3/78/SR.20
RIGHTS OF THE CHILD (Agenda item 67)
A/C.3/78/SR.11; A/C.3/78/SR.12
SELF-DETERMINATION OF PEOPLES (Agenda item 70)
A/C.3/78/SR.49
UN. HUMAN RIGHTS COUNCIL—REPORTS (Agenda item 66)
A/C.3/78/SR.46
UN HIGH COMMISSIONER FOR REFUGEES—REPORTS (Agenda item 60)
A/C.3/78/SR.44; A/C.3/78/SR.45
WOMEN'S ADVANCEMENT (Agenda item 25a)
A/C.3/78/SR.7; A/C.3/78/SR.10
WOMEN'S ADVANCEMENT—CONFERENCES (Agenda item 25b)
A/C.3/78/SR.7; A/C.3/78/SR.10

Montalvo Sosa, Andrés Efren (Ecuador)

DECOLONIZATION (Agenda item 58)
A/C.4/78/SR.7
FALKLAND ISLANDS (MALVINAS) QUESTION (Agenda item 42)
A/C.4/78/SR.7

Montalvo Sosa, Andrés Efren (Ecuador) (continued)

HUMAN RIGHTS—INTERNATIONAL INSTRUMENTS (Agenda item 71a)
A/C.3/78/SR.26
IAEA—REPORTS (Agenda item 89)
A/78/PV.29
MIGRANTS—PROTECTION (Agenda item 71b)
A/C.3/78/SR.26
PEACE (Agenda item 14)
A/78/PV.77
UN. GENERAL ASSEMBLY (78TH SESS. : 2023-2024). 1ST COMMITTEE—GENERAL DEBATE (Agenda item 8)
A/C.1/78/PV.5
UN. GENERAL ASSEMBLY (78TH SESS. : 2023-2024). 2ND COMMITTEE—GENERAL DEBATE (Agenda item 8)
A/C.2/78/SR.5
UN. SECURITY COUNCIL—MEMBERSHIP (Agenda item 121)
A/78/PV.36
WESTERN SAHARA QUESTION (Agenda item 58)
A/C.4/78/SR.7

Montejo, Blanca (UN. Security Council Practices and Charter Research Branch)

UN CHARTER—REPORTS (Agenda item 82)
A/C.6/78/SR.22

Monyane, Nkopane Raseeng (Lesotho)

LANDLOCKED DEVELOPING COUNTRIES—CONFERENCES (Agenda item 20b)
A/C.2/78/SR.7
LEAST DEVELOPED COUNTRIES—CONFERENCES (Agenda item 20a)
A/C.2/78/SR.7

Mora Fonseca, Vladimir (Cuba)

NON-CITIZENS—DEPORTATION (Agenda item 81)
A/C.6/78/SR.34
RESPONSIBILITY OF INTERNATIONAL ORGANIZATIONS (Agenda item 85)
A/C.6/78/SR.19
RULE OF LAW (Agenda item 83)
A/C.6/78/SR.16
TREATIES (Agenda item 87)
A/C.6/78/SR.20
UN. INTERNATIONAL LAW COMMISSION—REPORTS (Agenda item 79)
A/C.6/78/SR.25
UN CHARTER—REPORTS (Agenda item 82)
A/C.6/78/SR.22
UN COMMISSION ON INTERNATIONAL TRADE LAW—REPORTS (Agenda item 77)
A/C.6/78/SR.14

Moraga Duque, Juan Carlos (Derechos Humanos sin Fronteras (Organization : Peru))

WESTERN SAHARA QUESTION (Agenda item 58)
A/C.4/78/SR.5

Moretti, Norberto (Brazil)

HUMAN RIGHTS—SYRIAN ARAB REPUBLIC (Agenda item 71c)
A/C.3/78/SR.34
RACIAL DISCRIMINATION—ELIMINATION (Agenda item 69a)
A/78/PV.103
UN. GENERAL ASSEMBLY (78TH SESS. : 2023-2024). 1ST COMMITTEE—GENERAL DEBATE (Agenda item 8)
A/C.1/78/PV.8
UN. GENERAL ASSEMBLY (78TH SESS. : 2023-2024). 2ND COMMITTEE—GENERAL DEBATE (Agenda item 8)
A/C.2/78/SR.4
UN. SECURITY COUNCIL—MEMBERSHIP (Agenda item 121)
A/78/PV.35
VETO (Agenda item 63)
A/78/PV.3

Morgant-Cross, Hinamoeura (ICAN France (Organization))

FRENCH POLYNESIA QUESTION (Agenda item 58)
A/C.4/78/SR.3

Moriko, Tiémoko (Côte d'Ivoire)

ARMS TRANSFERS—TREATIES (Agenda item 99x)
A/C.1/78/PV.18
CLIMATE (Agenda item 18d)
A/C.2/78/SR.15
CONVENTIONAL WEAPONS (Agenda item 99u)
A/C.1/78/PV.18
CONVENTIONAL WEAPONS—TREATIES (Agenda item 103)
A/C.1/78/PV.18
DECOLONIZATION (Agenda item 58)
A/C.4/78/SR.2
DESERTIFICATION—TREATIES (Agenda item 18e)
A/C.2/78/SR.15
HUMAN RIGHTS—INTERNATIONAL INSTRUMENTS (Agenda item 71a)
A/C.3/78/SR.26
INFORMATION—INTERNATIONAL SECURITY (Agenda item 94)
A/C.1/78/PV.20
INTERNATIONAL JURISDICTION (Agenda item 84)
A/C.6/78/SR.13
NATIONAL INSTITUTIONS—HUMAN RIGHTS (Agenda item 71b)
A/C.3/78/SR.26
NUCLEAR DISARMAMENT (Agenda item 99b)
A/C.1/78/PV.12
NUCLEAR NON-PROLIFERATION—INTERNATIONAL OBLIGATIONS (Agenda item 99w)
A/C.1/78/PV.12

Moriko, Tiémoko (Côte d'Ivoire) (continued)

NUCLEAR WEAPON TESTS—TREATIES (Agenda item 105)
A/C.1/78/PV.12
NUCLEAR WEAPONS—HUMANITARIAN CONSEQUENCES (Agenda item 99bb)
A/C.1/78/PV.12
NUCLEAR WEAPONS—TREATIES (Agenda item 99ff)
A/C.1/78/PV.12
PEACEKEEPING OPERATIONS (Agenda item 51)
A/C.4/78/SR.19
RACIAL DISCRIMINATION—ELIMINATION (Agenda item 69a)
A/C.3/78/SR.42
RACIAL DISCRIMINATION—PROGRAMMES OF ACTION (Agenda item 69b)
A/C.3/78/SR.42
RESPONSIBILITY TO PROTECT (Agenda item 129)
A/78/PV.97
RIGHTS OF THE CHILD (Agenda item 67)
A/C.3/78/SR.14
SMALL ARMS—ILLICIT TRAFFIC—ASSISTANCE (Agenda item 99n)
A/C.1/78/PV.18
SOCIAL DEVELOPMENT (Agenda item 24)
A/C.3/78/SR.3
SUSTAINABLE DEVELOPMENT (Agenda item 18)
A/C.2/78/SR.15
TERRORISM (Agenda item 109)
A/C.6/78/SR.3
UN. GENERAL ASSEMBLY (78TH SESS. : 2023-2024). 1ST COMMITTEE—GENERAL DEBATE (Agenda item 8)
A/C.1/78/PV.4
UN. GENERAL ASSEMBLY (78TH SESS. : 2023-2024). 2ND COMMITTEE—GENERAL DEBATE (Agenda item 8)
A/C.2/78/SR.4
UN. INTERNATIONAL LAW COMMISSION—REPORTS (Agenda item 79)
A/C.6/78/SR.28; A/C.6/78/SR.30
WEAPONS OF MASS DESTRUCTION—TERRORISM (Agenda item 99s)
A/C.1/78/PV.12
WESTERN SAHARA QUESTION (Agenda item 58)
A/C.4/78/SR.2
WOMEN'S ADVANCEMENT (Agenda item 25a)
A/C.3/78/SR.10
WOMEN'S ADVANCEMENT—CONFERENCES (Agenda item 25b)
A/C.3/78/SR.10

Morin, Cassandra (Canada)

HUMAN RIGHTS ADVANCEMENT (Agenda item 71b)
A/C.3/78/SR.48
INDIGENOUS PEOPLES (Agenda item 68a)
A/C.3/78/SR.48

Morin, Cassandra (Canada) (continued)

SEXUAL ORIENTATION (Agenda item 71b)
A/C.3/78/SR.39

Moruke, Cathy (South Africa)

UN HIGH COMMISSIONER FOR REFUGEES—REPORTS (Agenda item 60)
A/C.3/78/SR.44

Møse, Erik (UN. Human Rights Council. Independent International Commission of Inquiry to Investigate All Alleged Violations of Human Rights in the Context of the Russian Federation's Aggression against Ukraine. Chair)

HUMAN RIGHTS—UKRAINE (Agenda item 71c)
A/C.3/78/SR.37

Mostafa Rizk, Heba (Egypt)

AGEING PERSONS (Agenda item 24b)
A/C.3/78/SR.2
CRIME PREVENTION (Agenda item 107)
A/C.3/78/SR.6; A/C.3/78/SR.56
CYBERCRIME (Agenda item 108)
A/C.3/78/SR.6
ELECTION VERIFICATION—UN (Agenda item 71b)
A/78/PV.50; A/C.3/78/SR.50
FAMILY (Agenda item 24b)
A/C.3/78/SR.2
FREEDOM OF EXPRESSION (Agenda item 71b)
A/C.3/78/SR.19
HEALTH (Agenda item 125)
A/78/PV.48
HUMAN RIGHTS (Agenda item 71)
A/C.3/78/SR.16
HUMAN RIGHTS—REPORTS (Agenda item 71c)
A/C.3/78/SR.26
HUMAN RIGHTS ACTIVISTS (Agenda item 71b)
A/C.3/78/SR.56
HUMAN RIGHTS ADVANCEMENT (Agenda item 71b)
A/C.3/78/SR.52
RACIAL DISCRIMINATION—ELIMINATION (Agenda item 69a)
A/78/PV.50; A/78/PV.103; A/C.3/78/SR.43; A/C.3/78/SR.47
RACIAL DISCRIMINATION—PROGRAMMES OF ACTION (Agenda item 69b)
A/C.3/78/SR.43
RELIGIOUS INTOLERANCE (Agenda item 71b)
A/C.3/78/SR.18; A/C.3/78/SR.26
RESPONSIBILITY TO PROTECT (Agenda item 129)
A/78/PV.97
RIGHT TO DEVELOPMENT (Agenda item 71b)
A/C.3/78/SR.20; A/C.3/78/SR.26; A/C.3/78/SR.48
RURAL WOMEN (Agenda item 25a)
A/C.3/78/SR.10; A/C.3/78/SR.49
SELF-DETERMINATION OF PEOPLES (Agenda item 70)
A/78/PV.50; A/C.3/78/SR.43

Mostafa Rizk, Heba (Egypt) (continued)

SOCIAL CONDITIONS (Agenda item 24b)
A/78/PV.57; A/C.3/78/SR.2
UN. HUMAN RIGHTS COUNCIL—REPORTS (Agenda item 66)
A/78/PV.28; A/C.3/78/SR.46
WOMEN'S ADVANCEMENT (Agenda item 25a)
A/C.3/78/SR.10
WOMEN'S ADVANCEMENT—CONFERENCES (Agenda item 25b)
A/C.3/78/SR.10

Mostafa Rizk, Heba (Egypt) (Organisation of Islamic Cooperation)

RELIGIOUS INTOLERANCE (Agenda item 71b)
A/C.3/78/SR.52
SELF-DETERMINATION OF PEOPLES (Agenda item 70)
A/C.3/78/SR.49

Motsepe, Keke Mantsho (South Africa)

CRIMES AGAINST HUMANITY (Agenda item 80)
A/C.6/78/SR.39; A/C.6/78/SR.40; A/C.6/78/SR.42; A/C.6/78/SR.45
DISASTER VICTIMS (Agenda item 86)
A/C.6/78/SR.6
INTERNATIONAL LAW—TRAINING PROGRAMMES (Agenda item 78)
A/C.6/78/SR.21
NON-CITIZENS—DEPORTATION (Agenda item 81)
A/C.6/78/SR.34
PEACEKEEPING OPERATIONS—CRIMINAL LIABILITY (Agenda item 76)
A/C.6/78/SR.8
RULE OF LAW (Agenda item 83)
A/C.6/78/SR.16
TERRORISM (Agenda item 109)
A/C.6/78/SR.2
TREATIES (Agenda item 87)
A/C.6/78/SR.20
UN. INTERNATIONAL LAW COMMISSION—REPORTS (Agenda item 79)
A/C.6/78/SR.25; A/C.6/78/SR.29; A/C.6/78/SR.31
UN COMMISSION ON INTERNATIONAL TRADE LAW—REPORTS (Agenda item 77)
A/C.6/78/SR.14

Motsumi, Lorato (Botswana) (Group of Landlocked Developing Countries)

2030 AGENDA—PROGRAMME IMPLEMENTATION (Agenda item 18a)
A/C.2/78/SR.12
ECONOMIC COOPERATION AMONG DEVELOPING COUNTRIES (Agenda item 22b)
A/C.2/78/SR.18
INFORMATION TECHNOLOGY—DEVELOPMENT (Agenda item 15)
A/C.2/78/SR.10
OPERATIONAL ACTIVITIES—UN SYSTEM (Agenda item 22a)
A/C.2/78/SR.18

Motsumi, Lorato (Botswana) (Group of Landlocked Developing Countries) (continued)
SCIENCE AND TECHNOLOGY—DEVELOPMENT (Agenda item 19a)
A/C.2/78/SR.10
SUSTAINABLE DEVELOPMENT (Agenda item 18)
A/C.2/78/SR.12

Mott, T'Sean (Bahamas)
DEVELOPMENT FINANCE (Agenda item 16b)
A/C.2/78/SR.11
EXTERNAL DEBT (Agenda item 16c)
A/C.2/78/SR.11
SMALL ISLAND DEVELOPING STATES—PROGRAMMES OF ACTION (Agenda item 18b)
A/78/PV.100
TAXATION (Agenda item 16h)
A/C.2/78/SR.11; A/C.2/78/SR.25

Mottley, Mia Amor (Barbados. Prime Minister)
UN. GENERAL ASSEMBLY (78TH SESS. : 2023-2024)—GENERAL DEBATE (Agenda item 8)
A/78/PV.10
UN. GENERAL ASSEMBLY (78TH SESS. : 2023-2024)—SPECIAL STATEMENTS
A/78/PV.10

Mousa, Sulafa (Saudi Arabia)
HEALTH (Agenda item 125)
A/78/PV.41
HUMAN RIGHTS (Agenda item 71)
A/C.3/78/SR.16
HUMAN RIGHTS—MYANMAR (Agenda item 71c)
A/C.3/78/SR.33
HUMAN RIGHTS—TERRITORIES OCCUPIED BY ISRAEL (Agenda item 71c)
A/C.3/78/SR.35
RIGHTS OF THE CHILD (Agenda item 67)
A/C.3/78/SR.11
WOMEN'S ADVANCEMENT (Agenda item 25a)
A/C.3/78/SR.8
WOMEN'S ADVANCEMENT—CONFERENCES (Agenda item 25b)
A/C.3/78/SR.8
YOUTH (Agenda item 24b)
A/C.3/78/SR.55

Mousavi, Seyed Ali (Iran (Islamic Republic of))
INTERNATIONAL CRIMINAL COURT—REPORTS (Agenda item 74)
A/78/PV.21
UN. INTERNATIONAL COURT OF JUSTICE—REPORTS (Agenda item 73)
A/78/PV.20; A/C.6/78/SR.26
UN. INTERNATIONAL LAW COMMISSION—REPORTS (Agenda item 79)
A/C.6/78/SR.24

Moussa, Mahaman (Niger)
FOOD SECURITY (Agenda item 23a)
A/C.2/78/SR.17

Moussa, Mahaman (Niger) (continued)
POVERTY—INTERNATIONAL DECADES (Agenda item 21a)
A/C.2/78/SR.17
RURAL POVERTY (Agenda item 21b)
A/C.2/78/SR.17
SUSTAINABLE DEVELOPMENT (Agenda item 18)
A/C.2/78/SR.24

Moussa, Moussa Mohamed (Djibouti)
CRIMES AGAINST HUMANITY (Agenda item 80)
A/C.6/78/SR.11
RULE OF LAW (Agenda item 83)
A/C.6/78/SR.17
TERRORISM (Agenda item 109)
A/C.6/78/SR.4
UN. INTERNATIONAL LAW COMMISSION—REPORTS (Agenda item 79)
A/C.6/78/SR.30

Moussa, Moussa Mohamed (Djibouti) (UN. General Assembly. 6th Committee. Rapporteur)
BOAO FORUM FOR ASIA—OBSERVER STATUS (Agenda item 169)
A/78/PV.45
COMMUNITY OF DEMOCRACIES—OBSERVER STATUS (Agenda item 164)
A/78/PV.45
COOPERATION COUNCIL OF TURKIC-SPEAKING STATES—OBSERVER STATUS (Agenda item 162)
A/78/PV.45
DISASTER VICTIMS (Agenda item 86)
A/78/PV.45
EURASIAN ECONOMIC UNION—OBSERVER STATUS (Agenda item 163)
A/78/PV.45
GLOBAL ENVIRONMENT FACILITY—OBSERVER STATUS (Agenda item 166)
A/78/PV.45
INTERNATIONAL JURISDICTION (Agenda item 84)
A/78/PV.45
INTERNATIONAL LAW—TRAINING PROGRAMMES (Agenda item 78)
A/78/PV.45
INTERNATIONAL ORGANIZATION OF EMPLOYERS—OBSERVER STATUS (Agenda item 167)
A/78/PV.45
INTERNATIONAL PARLIAMENTARIANS' CONGRESS—OBSERVER STATUS (Agenda item 170)
A/78/PV.45
INTERNATIONAL TRADE UNION CONFEDERATION—OBSERVER STATUS (Agenda item 168)
A/78/PV.45
NON-CITIZENS—DEPORTATION (Agenda item 81)
A/78/PV.45
ORGANIZATION OF IBERO-AMERICAN STATES FOR EDUCATION, SCIENCE AND CULTURE—OBSERVER STATUS (Agenda item 171)
A/78/PV.45

Moussa, Moussa Mohamed (Djibouti) (UN. General Assembly. 6th Committee. Rapporteur) (continued)

PEACEKEEPING OPERATIONS—CRIMINAL LIABILITY (Agenda item 76)
A/78/PV.45
RAMSAR CONVENTION SECRETARIAT—OBSERVER STATUS (Agenda item 165)
A/78/PV.45
RESPONSIBILITY OF INTERNATIONAL ORGANIZATIONS (Agenda item 85)
A/78/PV.45
RULE OF LAW (Agenda item 83)
A/78/PV.45
TERRORISM (Agenda item 109)
A/78/PV.45
TREATIES (Agenda item 87)
A/78/PV.45
UN—PROGRAMME PLANNING (Agenda item 135)
A/78/PV.45
UN. COMMITTEE ON RELATIONS WITH THE HOST COUNTRY—REPORTS (Agenda item 161)
A/78/PV.45
UN. GENERAL ASSEMBLY—WORK PROGRAMME (Agenda item 120)
A/78/PV.45
UN. INTERNATIONAL LAW COMMISSION—REPORTS (Agenda item 79)
A/78/PV.45
UN CHARTER—REPORTS (Agenda item 82)
A/78/PV.45
UN COMMISSION ON INTERNATIONAL TRADE LAW—REPORTS (Agenda item 77)
A/78/PV.45

Moussa, Youssouf Aden (Djibouti)

ELECTION VERIFICATION—UN (Agenda item 71b)
A/78/PV.50
HUMAN RIGHTS INSTITUTIONS—CENTRAL AFRICA (Agenda item 71b)
A/C.3/78/SR.56
SOCIAL CONDITIONS (Agenda item 24b)
A/78/PV.101
UN. GENERAL ASSEMBLY (78TH SESS. : 2023-2024)—AGENDA (Agenda item 7)
A/BUR/78/SR.2
WESTERN SAHARA QUESTION (Agenda item 58)
A/C.4/78/SR.8
WOMEN'S ADVANCEMENT—CONFERENCES (Agenda item 25b)
A/C.3/78/SR.51
YOUTH (Agenda item 24b)
A/C.3/78/SR.55

Moutchou, Majda (Morocco)

AGEING PERSONS (Agenda item 24b)
A/C.3/78/SR.1
HUMAN RIGHTS—INTERNATIONAL INSTRUMENTS (Agenda item 71a)
A/C.3/78/SR.27

Moutchou, Majda (Morocco) (continued)

HUMAN RIGHTS—TERRITORIES OCCUPIED BY ISRAEL (Agenda item 71c)
A/C.3/78/SR.27
RIGHTS OF THE CHILD (Agenda item 67)
A/C.3/78/SR.11; A/C.3/78/SR.12
SELF-DETERMINATION OF PEOPLES (Agenda item 70)
A/C.3/78/SR.43
SOCIAL DEVELOPMENT (Agenda item 24)
A/C.3/78/SR.1

Moxey, Matthew (Bahamas) (Caribbean Community)

PEACE—REGIONAL CENTRE—LATIN AMERICA AND THE CARIBBEAN (Agenda item 100c)
A/C.1/78/PV.22
UN. CONFERENCE ON DISARMAMENT—REPORTS (Agenda item 101a)
A/C.1/78/PV.22
UN. DISARMAMENT COMMISSION—REPORTS (Agenda item 101b)
A/C.1/78/PV.22

Mozgovaya, Ekaterina (Belarus)

AGEING PERSONS (Agenda item 24b)
A/C.3/78/SR.2
ELECTION VERIFICATION—UN (Agenda item 71b)
A/78/PV.50; A/C.3/78/SR.50
FAMILY (Agenda item 24b)
A/C.3/78/SR.49
HEALTH (Agenda item 125)
A/78/PV.16
HIV/AIDS—DECLARATIONS (Agenda item 10)
A/78/PV.91
HUMAN RIGHTS—RUSSIAN FEDERATION (Agenda item 71c)
A/C.3/78/SR.37
PERSONS WITH DISABILITIES (Agenda item 24b)
A/C.3/78/SR.2
SOCIAL CONDITIONS (Agenda item 24b)
A/78/PV.57; A/C.3/78/SR.2
SOCIAL DEVELOPMENT—CONFERENCES (Agenda item 24a)
A/C.3/78/SR.2
SPORTS—OLYMPIC GAMES (Agenda item 11)
A/78/PV.38
UN. SECRETARY-GENERAL—REPORTS (Agenda item 110)
A/78/PV.55

Mpama, Sibusiso Qetello (South Africa)

INFORMATION TECHNOLOGY—DEVELOPMENT (Agenda item 15)
A/C.2/78/SR.11
SCIENCE AND TECHNOLOGY—DEVELOPMENT (Agenda item 19a)
A/C.2/78/SR.11

Mpango, Philip Isdor (United Republic of Tanzania. Vice-President)

UN. GENERAL ASSEMBLY (78TH SESS. : 2023-2024)—GENERAL DEBATE (Agenda item 8)
A/78/PV.9
UN. GENERAL ASSEMBLY (78TH SESS. : 2023-2024)—SPECIAL STATEMENTS
A/78/PV.9

Mswati III, King of Eswatini, 1968- (Eswatini)

UN. GENERAL ASSEMBLY (78TH SESS. : 2023-2024)—GENERAL DEBATE (Agenda item 8)
A/78/PV.7
UN. GENERAL ASSEMBLY (78TH SESS. : 2023-2024)—SPECIAL STATEMENTS
A/78/PV.7

Muaku, Samuel (Belgium)

YOUTH (Agenda item 24b)
A/C.3/78/SR.3

Mudrenko, Nataliia (Ukraine)

DISAPPEARANCE OF PERSONS (Agenda item 71b)
A/C.3/78/SR.22
HUMAN RIGHTS (Agenda item 71)
A/C.3/78/SR.16
HUMAN RIGHTS—BELARUS (Agenda item 71c)
A/C.3/78/SR.37
HUMAN RIGHTS—INTERNATIONAL INSTRUMENTS (Agenda item 71a)
A/C.3/78/SR.25
HUMAN RIGHTS—RUSSIAN FEDERATION (Agenda item 71c)
A/C.3/78/SR.37
HUMAN RIGHTS—UKRAINE (Agenda item 71c)
A/C.3/78/SR.18; A/C.3/78/SR.25; A/C.3/78/SR.37
JUDICIAL INDEPENDENCE (Agenda item 71b)
A/C.3/78/SR.31
RACIAL DISCRIMINATION—ELIMINATION (Agenda item 69a)
A/78/PV.50; A/C.3/78/SR.41; A/C.3/78/SR.47
RACIAL DISCRIMINATION—PROGRAMMES OF ACTION (Agenda item 69b)
A/C.3/78/SR.41
RELIGIOUS INTOLERANCE (Agenda item 71b)
A/78/PV.50
RIGHT TO THE TRUTH (Agenda item 71b)
A/C.3/78/SR.22
RIGHTS OF THE CHILD (Agenda item 67)
A/C.3/78/SR.11; A/C.3/78/SR.12
TERRORISM—HUMAN RIGHTS (Agenda item 71b)
A/C.3/78/SR.31
TORTURE AND OTHER CRUEL TREATMENT (Agenda item 71a)
A/C.3/78/SR.18
UN. HUMAN RIGHTS COUNCIL—REPORTS (Agenda item 66)
A/C.3/78/SR.46

Mudrenko, Nataliia (Ukraine) (continued)

UN HIGH COMMISSIONER FOR REFUGEES—REPORTS (Agenda item 60)
A/78/PV.50; A/C.3/78/SR.44; A/C.3/78/SR.45

Muhamad, Ahmad Faisal (Malaysia)

AGEING PERSONS (Agenda item 24b)
A/C.3/78/SR.2
ARMS RACE—OUTER SPACE (Agenda item 97a)
A/C.1/78/PV.16
HUMAN RIGHTS (Agenda item 71)
A/C.3/78/SR.16
IAEA—REPORTS (Agenda item 89)
A/78/PV.29
NUCLEAR DISARMAMENT (Agenda item 99b)
A/C.1/78/PV.11
NUCLEAR NON-PROLIFERATION—INTERNATIONAL OBLIGATIONS (Agenda item 99w)
A/C.1/78/PV.11
NUCLEAR WEAPON TESTS—TREATIES (Agenda item 105)
A/C.1/78/PV.11
NUCLEAR WEAPONS—TREATIES (Agenda item 99ff)
A/C.1/78/PV.11
NUCLEAR WEAPONS USE—UN. INTERNATIONAL COURT OF JUSTICE OPINION (Agenda item 99k)
A/C.1/78/PV.11
OUTER SPACE—CONFIDENCE-BUILDING MEASURES (Agenda item 99v)
A/C.1/78/PV.16
OUTER SPACE—PRINCIPLES (Agenda item 97d)
A/C.1/78/PV.16
PEACE (Agenda item 14)
A/78/PV.62
SOCIAL CONDITIONS (Agenda item 24b)
A/C.3/78/SR.2
SOUTH-EAST ASIA—NUCLEAR-WEAPON-FREE ZONES (Agenda item 99y)
A/C.1/78/PV.11
TERRITORIES OCCUPIED BY ISRAEL—HUMAN RIGHTS (Agenda item 50)
A/C.4/78/SR.24
UN. GENERAL ASSEMBLY (78TH SESS. : 2023-2024). 1ST COMMITTEE—GENERAL DEBATE (Agenda item 8)
A/C.1/78/PV.4
VETO (Agenda item 63)
A/78/PV.59; A/78/PV.70; A/78/PV.74

Muhamad, Ahmad Faisal (Malaysia) (ASEAN)

ARMS RACE—OUTER SPACE (Agenda item 97a)
A/C.1/78/PV.16
DISARMAMENT AGREEMENTS—OUTER SPACE (Agenda item 97c)
A/C.1/78/PV.16
HUMAN RIGHTS—INTERNATIONAL INSTRUMENTS (Agenda item 71a)
A/C.3/78/SR.24

Muhamad, Ahmad Faisal (Malaysia) (ASEAN) (continued)

HUMAN RIGHTS ADVANCEMENT (Agenda item 71b)
A/C.3/78/SR.24
OUTER SPACE—CONFIDENCE-BUILDING MEASURES (Agenda item 99v)
A/C.1/78/PV.16
OUTER SPACE—PRINCIPLES (Agenda item 97d)
A/C.1/78/PV.16
SCIENCE AND TECHNOLOGY—DEVELOPMENT (Agenda item 19a)
A/C.2/78/SR.10
WEAPONS—OUTER SPACE (Agenda item 97b)
A/C.1/78/PV.16

Muhamad, Ahmad Faisal (Malaysia) (UN. Committee on the Exercise of the Inalienable Rights of the Palestinian People. Vice-Chair)

PALESTINE QUESTION (Agenda item 35)
A/78/PV.39

Muhamad, Ahmad Faisal (Malaysia) (UN. General Assembly. Vice-President)

VETO (Agenda item 63)
A/78/PV.78

Muhammad Bande, Tijjani (Nigeria)

TAXATION (Agenda item 16h)
A/C.2/78/SR.25
UN. GENERAL ASSEMBLY (78TH SESS. : 2023-2024). 2ND COMMITTEE—GENERAL DEBATE (Agenda item 8)
A/C.2/78/SR.2

Muhammad Bande, Tijjani (Nigeria) (UN. Group of African States)

TAXATION (Agenda item 16h)
A/C.2/78/SR.25
UN. GENERAL ASSEMBLY (78TH SESS. : 2023-2024). 1ST COMMITTEE—GENERAL DEBATE (Agenda item 8)
A/C.1/78/PV.3
UN. GENERAL ASSEMBLY (78TH SESS. : 2023-2024). 2ND COMMITTEE—GENERAL DEBATE (Agenda item 8)
A/C.2/78/SR.2

Muhith, Muhammad A. (Bangladesh)

ARMS RACE—OUTER SPACE (Agenda item 97a)
A/C.1/78/PV.16
BIOLOGICAL WEAPONS—TREATIES (Agenda item 106)
A/C.1/78/PV.15
CHEMICAL WEAPONS—TREATIES (Agenda item 99l)
A/C.1/78/PV.15
CRIMES AGAINST HUMANITY (Agenda item 80)
A/C.6/78/SR.10

Muhith, Muhammad A. (Bangladesh) (continued)

HUMAN RIGHTS—INTERNATIONAL INSTRUMENTS (Agenda item 71a)
A/C.3/78/SR.25
HUMAN RIGHTS—MYANMAR (Agenda item 71c)
A/C.3/78/SR.25
INFORMATION (Agenda item 53)
A/C.4/78/SR.13
INFORMATION—INTERNATIONAL SECURITY (Agenda item 94)
A/C.1/78/PV.20
INTERNATIONAL CRIMINAL COURT—REPORTS (Agenda item 74)
A/78/PV.21
OUTER SPACE—PRINCIPLES (Agenda item 97d)
A/C.1/78/PV.16
PALESTINE QUESTION (Agenda item 35)
A/78/PV.40
PEACE (Agenda item 14)
A/78/PV.76
PEACEKEEPING OPERATIONS (Agenda item 51)
A/C.4/78/SR.19
PEACEKEEPING OPERATIONS—CRIMINAL LIABILITY (Agenda item 76)
A/C.6/78/SR.8
RACIAL DISCRIMINATION—ELIMINATION (Agenda item 69a)
A/C.3/78/SR.43
RACIAL DISCRIMINATION—PROGRAMMES OF ACTION (Agenda item 69b)
A/C.3/78/SR.43
SELF-DETERMINATION OF PEOPLES (Agenda item 70)
A/C.3/78/SR.43
SUSTAINABLE DEVELOPMENT (Agenda item 18)
A/C.2/78/SR.15
UN—BUDGET (2024) (Agenda item 134)
A/C.5/78/SR.5
UN—PROGRAMME PLANNING (Agenda item 135)
A/C.5/78/SR.5
UN. GENERAL ASSEMBLY (78TH SESS. : 2023-2024)—OFFICERS (Agenda item 5)
A/C.2/78/SR.26
UN. GENERAL ASSEMBLY (78TH SESS. : 2023-2024). 5TH COMMITTEE—WORK ORGANIZATION (Agenda item 7)
A/C.5/78/SR.35
UN. INTERNATIONAL COURT OF JUSTICE—REPORTS (Agenda item 73)
A/78/PV.27
UN CONFERENCES (Agenda item 13)
A/78/PV.107
UNRWA—ACTIVITIES (Agenda item 49)
A/C.4/78/SR.23
VETO (Agenda item 63)
A/78/PV.52; A/78/PV.67; A/78/PV.71; A/78/PV.75
WEAPONS OF MASS DESTRUCTION—TERRORISM (Agenda item 99s)
A/C.1/78/PV.15

Muhumuza, Duncan Laki (Uganda)
ADMINISTRATION OF JUSTICE (Agenda item 144)
A/C.6/78/SR.9
HIV/AIDS—DECLARATIONS (Agenda item 10)
A/78/PV.91
INTERNATIONAL CRIMINAL COURT—REPORTS (Agenda item 74)
A/78/PV.21
RULE OF LAW (Agenda item 83)
A/C.6/78/SR.18
UN. INTERNATIONAL COURT OF JUSTICE—MEMBERS (Agenda item 113c)
A/78/PV.31
VETO (Agenda item 63)
A/78/PV.60

Muhumuza, Duncan Laki (Uganda) (Group of 77)
HEALTH (Agenda item 125)
A/78/PV.77

Muhumuza, Duncan Laki (Uganda) (UN. Group of African States)
CRIMES AGAINST HUMANITY (Agenda item 80)
A/C.6/78/SR.9; A/C.6/78/SR.38

Muigai, Stephanie Ngonyo (Kenya)
INFORMATION—INTERNATIONAL SECURITY (Agenda item 94)
A/C.1/78/PV.20

Mukherjee, Shantanu (UN. Department of Economic and Social Affairs. Development Policy Analysis Division. Director)
INTERNATIONAL TRADE (Agenda item 16a)
A/C.2/78/SR.8

Mukongo Ngay, Zénon (Democratic Republic of the Congo)
DECOLONIZATION (Agenda item 58)
A/C.4/78/SR.9
INTERNATIONAL CRIMINAL COURT—REPORTS (Agenda item 74)
A/78/PV.22
PEACE (Agenda item 14)
A/78/PV.82
PEACEKEEPING OPERATIONS (Agenda item 51)
A/C.4/78/SR.20
UN. INTERNATIONAL COURT OF JUSTICE—REPORTS (Agenda item 73)
A/78/PV.28
WESTERN SAHARA QUESTION (Agenda item 58)
A/C.4/78/SR.9

Muktar, Anwar (Ethiopia)
DEVELOPMENT FINANCE (Agenda item 16b)
A/C.2/78/SR.11
INFORMATION TECHNOLOGY—DEVELOPMENT (Agenda item 15)
A/C.2/78/SR.11

Muktar, Anwar (Ethiopia) (continued)
INTERNATIONAL TRADE (Agenda item 16a)
A/C.2/78/SR.11
SCIENCE AND TECHNOLOGY—DEVELOPMENT (Agenda item 19a)
A/C.2/78/SR.11

Mullally, Siobhán (UN. Human Rights Council. Special Rapporteur on Trafficking in Persons, Especially in Women and Children)
TRAFFICKING IN PERSONS (Agenda item 71b)
A/C.3/78/SR.23

Mungandi, Lubasi (Zambia)
FOOD SECURITY (Agenda item 23a)
A/C.2/78/SR.17
OUTER SPACE—PEACEFUL USES—INTERNATIONAL COOPERATION (Agenda item 48)
A/C.4/78/SR.16
POVERTY—INTERNATIONAL DECADES (Agenda item 21a)
A/C.2/78/SR.17
RURAL POVERTY (Agenda item 21b)
A/C.2/78/SR.17

Muñoz, Zachary N. (Sovereign Order of Malta)
HUMAN RIGHTS (Agenda item 71)
A/C.3/78/SR.28
JUDICIAL INDEPENDENCE (Agenda item 71b)
A/C.3/78/SR.31
LEPROSY (Agenda item 71b)
A/C.3/78/SR.17
RELIGIOUS INTOLERANCE (Agenda item 71b)
A/C.3/78/SR.38
RIGHTS OF THE CHILD (Agenda item 67)
A/C.3/78/SR.11
SANCTIONS—INTERNATIONAL RELATIONS (Agenda item 71b)
A/C.3/78/SR.28

Muñoz Ponce, Tatiana Bárbara (Bolivia (Plurinational State of))
ARMS RACE—OUTER SPACE (Agenda item 97a)
A/C.1/78/PV.17
DISARMAMENT AGREEMENTS—OUTER SPACE (Agenda item 97c)
A/C.1/78/PV.17
NUCLEAR DISARMAMENT (Agenda item 99b)
A/C.1/78/PV.13
NUCLEAR NON-PROLIFERATION—INTERNATIONAL OBLIGATIONS (Agenda item 99w)
A/C.1/78/PV.13
NUCLEAR WEAPON TESTS—TREATIES (Agenda item 105)
A/C.1/78/PV.13
OUTER SPACE—CONFIDENCE-BUILDING MEASURES (Agenda item 99v)
A/C.1/78/PV.17
TAXATION (Agenda item 16h)
A/C.2/78/SR.25

Muñoz Ponce, Tatiana Bárbara (Bolivia (Plurinational State of)) (continued)
UN—BUDGET (2024) (Agenda item 134)
A/C.5/78/SR.26/PartII
UN—PROGRAMME PLANNING (Agenda item 135)
A/78/PV.50(Resumption1); A/C.5/78/SR.24
UN CONFERENCES (Agenda item 13)
A/78/PV.107
WEAPONS—OUTER SPACE (Agenda item 97b)
A/C.1/78/PV.17

Murillo Ferrer, Jorge Adrián (Colombia)
DEVELOPMENT COOPERATION—MIDDLE-INCOME COUNTRIES (Agenda item 19c)
A/C.2/78/SR.23
EXTERNAL DEBT (Agenda item 16c)
A/C.2/78/SR.25
INTERNATIONAL TRADE (Agenda item 16a)
A/C.2/78/SR.22
INVESTMENT PROMOTION (Agenda item 16g)
A/C.2/78/SR.23
SMALL ISLAND DEVELOPING STATES—PROGRAMMES OF ACTION (Agenda item 18b)
A/C.2/78/SR.22
TAXATION (Agenda item 16h)
A/C.2/78/SR.25

Murphy, Daniel (United States)
HUMAN RIGHTS ACTIVISTS (Agenda item 71b)
A/C.3/78/SR.19
INDIGENOUS PEOPLES (Agenda item 68a)
A/C.3/78/SR.15
INDIGENOUS PEOPLES—CONFERENCES (Agenda item 68b)
A/C.3/78/SR.15
RACIAL DISCRIMINATION—ELIMINATION (Agenda item 69a)
A/C.3/78/SR.41; A/C.3/78/SR.42
RACIAL DISCRIMINATION—PROGRAMMES OF ACTION (Agenda item 69b)
A/C.3/78/SR.41
TERRORISM—HUMAN RIGHTS (Agenda item 71b)
A/C.3/78/SR.31

Murphy, Robert David (Holy See)
CRIME PREVENTION (Agenda item 107)
A/C.3/78/SR.6
CRIMES AGAINST HUMANITY (Agenda item 80)
A/C.6/78/SR.43; A/C.6/78/SR.44
CYBERCRIME (Agenda item 108)
A/C.3/78/SR.6
ELECTION VERIFICATION—UN (Agenda item 71b)
A/C.3/78/SR.50
FAMILY (Agenda item 24b)
A/C.3/78/SR.4
HEALTH (Agenda item 125)
A/78/PV.48
HUMAN RIGHTS ACTIVISTS (Agenda item 71b)
A/C.3/78/SR.56

Murphy, Robert David (Holy See) (continued)
HUMAN RIGHTS ADVANCEMENT (Agenda item 71b)
A/C.3/78/SR.52
INDIGENOUS PEOPLES (Agenda item 68a)
A/C.3/78/SR.48
LANDLOCKED DEVELOPING COUNTRIES—CONFERENCES (Agenda item 20b)
A/C.2/78/SR.7
LEAST DEVELOPED COUNTRIES—CONFERENCES (Agenda item 20a)
A/C.2/78/SR.7
MIGRANTS—PROTECTION (Agenda item 71b)
A/C.3/78/SR.56
PERSONS WITH DISABILITIES—HUMAN RIGHTS (Agenda item 71a)
A/C.3/78/SR.51
RIGHTS OF THE CHILD (Agenda item 67)
A/C.3/78/SR.14; A/C.3/78/SR.55
SOCIAL CONDITIONS (Agenda item 24b)
A/C.3/78/SR.4
SOCIAL DEVELOPMENT (Agenda item 24)
A/C.3/78/SR.4
SUSTAINABLE DEVELOPMENT (Agenda item 18)
A/C.2/78/SR.25
TERRORISM (Agenda item 109)
A/C.6/78/SR.5
UN. GENERAL ASSEMBLY (78TH SESS. : 2023-2024). 2ND COMMITTEE—GENERAL DEBATE (Agenda item 8)
A/C.2/78/SR.6
UN HIGH COMMISSIONER FOR REFUGEES—REPORTS (Agenda item 60)
A/C.3/78/SR.51
WOMEN'S ADVANCEMENT (Agenda item 25a)
A/C.3/78/SR.10
WOMEN'S ADVANCEMENT—CONFERENCES (Agenda item 25b)
A/C.3/78/SR.10
YOUTH (Agenda item 24b)
A/C.3/78/SR.4; A/C.3/78/SR.55

Musayev, Tofig (Azerbaijan)
CRIMES AGAINST HUMANITY (Agenda item 80)
A/C.6/78/SR.11
PEACE (Agenda item 14)
A/78/PV.82
RULE OF LAW (Agenda item 83)
A/C.6/78/SR.19
TERRORISM (Agenda item 109)
A/C.6/78/SR.4; A/C.6/78/SR.5
UN. GENERAL ASSEMBLY (78TH SESS. : 2023-2024)—GENERAL DEBATE—RIGHT OF REPLY (Agenda item 8)
A/78/PV.14
UN. GENERAL ASSEMBLY (78TH SESS. : 2023-2024). 1ST COMMITTEE—GENERAL DEBATE (Agenda item 8)
A/C.1/78/PV.7
UN. INTERNATIONAL COURT OF JUSTICE—REPORTS (Agenda item 73)
A/78/PV.27; A/78/PV.28

Musayev, Tofig (Azerbaijan) (Coordinating Bureau of the Non-Aligned Countries)

UN. INTERNATIONAL COURT OF JUSTICE—REPORTS (Agenda item 73)
A/78/PV.27

Musikhin, Maxim V. (Russian Federation)

UN. INTERNATIONAL LAW COMMISSION—REPORTS (Agenda item 79)
A/C.6/78/SR.26

Musonda, Oliver (Zambia)

ARMS RACE—OUTER SPACE (Agenda item 97a)
A/C.1/78/PV.17
WEAPONS—OUTER SPACE (Agenda item 97b)
A/C.1/78/PV.17

Mustafa, Marah (Syrian Arab Republic)

CHEMICAL WEAPONS—TREATIES (Agenda item 99l)
A/C.1/78/PV.26
MINE CLEARANCE (Agenda item 46)
A/C.4/78/SR.10
SPORTS—OLYMPIC GAMES (Agenda item 11)
A/78/PV.38
UKRAINE—POLITICAL CONDITIONS (Agenda item 62)
A/78/PV.99

Mutabazi, Deo (Rwanda)

PEACEKEEPING OPERATIONS (Agenda item 51)
A/C.4/78/SR.20

Mutasah, Tawanda (Oxfam America)

COMMODITIES (Agenda item 16d)
A/C.2/78/SR.14
SUSTAINABLE DEVELOPMENT (Agenda item 18)
A/C.2/78/SR.14

Muzumbwe-Katongo, Miyoba (Zambia)

RULE OF LAW (Agenda item 83)
A/C.6/78/SR.18

Mwasota, Joseph Aron (United Republic of Tanzania)

CUBA—UNITED STATES (Agenda item 38)
A/78/PV.24
INTERNATIONAL LAW—TRAINING PROGRAMMES (Agenda item 78)
A/C.6/78/SR.22
INTERNATIONAL RESIDUAL MECHANISM FOR CRIMINAL TRIBUNALS (Agenda item 126)
A/78/PV.19

Mwasota, Joseph Aron (United Republic of Tanzania) (UN. Group of African States)

PERSONNEL QUESTIONS—UN SYSTEM (Agenda item 142)
A/C.5/78/SR.10

Mythen, Fergal Tomas (Ireland)

UN. SECURITY COUNCIL—MEMBERSHIP (Agenda item 121)
A/78/PV.35
VETO (Agenda item 63)
A/78/PV.3; A/78/PV.51; A/78/PV.67; A/78/PV.74; A/78/PV.78

Mythen, Fergal Tomas (Ireland) (European Union)

HUMAN RIGHTS ADVANCEMENT (Agenda item 71b)
A/C.3/78/SR.24

Naanda, Anne (Namibia)

DEVELOPMENT FINANCE (Agenda item 16b)
A/C.2/78/SR.9
INTERNATIONAL TRADE (Agenda item 16a)
A/C.2/78/SR.9
MACROECONOMIC POLICY (Agenda item 16)
A/C.2/78/SR.9

Nabeta, Celia Kafureka (Uganda)

INDIGENOUS PEOPLES (Agenda item 68a)
A/C.3/78/SR.17
RIGHTS OF THE CHILD (Agenda item 67)
A/C.3/78/SR.13
SEXUAL ORIENTATION (Agenda item 71b)
A/C.3/78/SR.27
WOMEN'S ADVANCEMENT (Agenda item 25a)
A/C.3/78/SR.9
WOMEN'S ADVANCEMENT—CONFERENCES (Agenda item 25b)
A/C.3/78/SR.9

Nabeta, Celia Kafureka (Uganda) (Group of 77)

SOCIAL CONDITIONS (Agenda item 24b)
A/78/PV.101

Nabeta, Celia Kafureka (Uganda) (UN. Group of African States)

RACIAL DISCRIMINATION—ELIMINATION (Agenda item 69a)
A/78/PV.63

Nachom, Yaninee (Thailand)

UN COMMISSION ON INTERNATIONAL TRADE LAW—REPORTS (Agenda item 77)
A/C.6/78/SR.14

Nadarajah, Vicnesh (Singapore)

PEACEKEEPING OPERATIONS (Agenda item 51)
A/C.4/78/SR.20

Naeem, Mohammad (Ireland)

YOUTH (Agenda item 24b)
A/C.3/78/SR.2

Nagai, Nana (Japan)
SMALL ARMS—ILLICIT TRAFFIC (Agenda item 99p)
A/C.1/78/PV.27

Nagano, Shunsuke (Japan)
INTERNATIONAL RESIDUAL MECHANISM FOR CRIMINAL TRIBUNALS (Agenda item 126)
A/78/PV.19
LAW OF THE SEA (Agenda item 75a)
A/78/PV.44
MARINE ECOSYSTEMS—BIOLOGICAL DIVERSITY (Agenda item 75c)
A/78/PV.44
RULE OF LAW (Agenda item 83)
A/C.6/78/SR.18
STRADDLING FISH STOCKS (Agenda item 75b)
A/78/PV.44
UN. INTERNATIONAL LAW COMMISSION—REPORTS (Agenda item 79)
A/C.6/78/SR.28
UN. SECURITY COUNCIL—MEMBERSHIP (Agenda item 121)
A/78/PV.36
UN COMMISSION ON INTERNATIONAL TRADE LAW—REPORTS (Agenda item 77)
A/C.6/78/SR.14

Najafi, Reza (Iran (Islamic Republic of))
ECONOMIC SANCTIONS—INTERNATIONAL RELATIONS (Agenda item 28)
A/78/PV.89

Najib Azmi Mikati, Mohammad (Lebanon. Prime Minister)
UN. GENERAL ASSEMBLY (78TH SESS. : 2023-2024)—GENERAL DEBATE (Agenda item 8)
A/78/PV.7
UN. GENERAL ASSEMBLY (78TH SESS. : 2023-2024)—SPECIAL STATEMENTS
A/78/PV.7

Nakagawa, Shu (Japan)
HEALTH (Agenda item 125)
A/78/PV.16

Nakamitsu, Izumi (UN. High Representative for Disarmament Affairs)
UN. GENERAL ASSEMBLY (78TH SESS. : 2023-2024). 1ST COMMITTEE—GENERAL DEBATE (Agenda item 8)
A/C.1/78/PV.2

Nakano, Kenji (UN. Department for General Assembly and Conference Management)
AFRICA—DEVELOPMENT (Agenda item 65b)
A/78/PV.57
LAW OF THE SEA (Agenda item 75a)
A/78/PV.44

Nakano, Kenji (UN. Department for General Assembly and Conference Management) (continued)
MARINE ECOSYSTEMS—BIOLOGICAL DIVERSITY (Agenda item 75c)
A/78/PV.44; A/78/PV.103
MULTILINGUALISM (Agenda item 124)
A/78/PV.107
PEACE (Agenda item 14)
A/78/PV.82
SMALL ISLAND DEVELOPING STATES—PROGRAMMES OF ACTION (Agenda item 18b)
A/78/PV.103
STRADDLING FISH STOCKS (Agenda item 75b)
A/78/PV.44

Nam, Christine (New Zealand)
DISARMAMENT AGREEMENTS—OUTER SPACE (Agenda item 97c)
A/C.1/78/PV.27
FISSIONABLE MATERIALS—TREATIES (Agenda item 99a)
A/C.1/78/PV.26
IAEA—REPORTS (Agenda item 89)
A/78/PV.30
INFORMATION—INTERNATIONAL SECURITY (Agenda item 94)
A/C.1/78/PV.20
NUCLEAR DISARMAMENT—TREATY COMPLIANCE (Agenda item 99q)
A/C.1/78/PV.25
NUCLEAR WEAPONS—ELIMINATION (Agenda item 99z)
A/C.1/78/PV.26
NUCLEAR-WEAPON-FREE ZONE—SOUTHERN HEMISPHERE (Agenda item 99i)
A/C.1/78/PV.25
WEAPONS—OUTER SPACE (Agenda item 97b)
A/C.1/78/PV.27

Namangale, Clement Amamai Dima (Malawi)
TERRORISM (Agenda item 109)
A/C.6/78/SR.5

Namekawa, Hirochika (Japan)
DISARMAMENT—GENERAL AND COMPLETE (Agenda item 99)
A/C.1/78/PV.28; A/C.1/78/PV.30
DISARMAMENT AGREEMENTS—OUTER SPACE (Agenda item 97c)
A/C.1/78/PV.27
INFORMATION—INTERNATIONAL SECURITY (Agenda item 94)
A/C.1/78/PV.29

Napolitano, Annarita (Italy)
RIGHT TO EDUCATION (Agenda item 71b)
A/C.3/78/SR.27
RURAL WOMEN (Agenda item 25a)
A/C.3/78/SR.7
WOMEN'S ADVANCEMENT (Agenda item 25a)
A/C.3/78/SR.9

Napolitano, Annarita (Italy) (continued)
WOMEN'S ADVANCEMENT—CONFERENCES (Agenda item 25b)
A/C.3/78/SR.9

Napurí Pita, Andrés (Peru)
FOOD SECURITY (Agenda item 23a)
A/C.2/78/SR.17
POVERTY—INTERNATIONAL DECADES (Agenda item 21a)
A/C.2/78/SR.17
RURAL POVERTY (Agenda item 21b)
A/C.2/78/SR.17
SUSTAINABLE DEVELOPMENT (Agenda item 18)
A/C.2/78/SR.24
UN. GENERAL ASSEMBLY (78TH SESS. : 2023-2024). 2ND COMMITTEE—GENERAL DEBATE (Agenda item 8)
A/C.2/78/SR.5

Naranjo Lizano, Verónica Elizabeth (Universidad de la Tierra (Mexico))
WESTERN SAHARA QUESTION (Agenda item 58)
A/C.4/78/SR.5

Narváez Ojeda, Paula (Chile)
CUBA—UNITED STATES (Agenda item 38)
A/78/PV.26
IAEA—REPORTS (Agenda item 89)
A/78/PV.29
INTERNATIONAL CRIMINAL COURT—REPORTS (Agenda item 74)
A/78/PV.21
LAW OF THE SEA (Agenda item 75a)
A/78/PV.43
MARINE ECOSYSTEMS—BIOLOGICAL DIVERSITY (Agenda item 75c)
A/78/PV.43
MILLENNIUM SUMMIT—CONFERENCES (Agenda item 117)
A/78/PV.15
PALESTINE QUESTION (Agenda item 35)
A/78/PV.40
STRADDLING FISH STOCKS (Agenda item 75b)
A/78/PV.43
UKRAINE—POLITICAL CONDITIONS (Agenda item 62)
A/78/PV.57
UN CONFERENCES (Agenda item 13)
A/78/PV.15
VETO (Agenda item 63)
A/78/PV.51; A/78/PV.66; A/78/PV.68

Narváez Ojeda, Paula (Chile) (Group of Friends of Older Persons)
AGEING PERSONS (Agenda item 24b)
A/C.3/78/SR.1

Narváez Ojeda, Paula (Chile) (UN. Economic and Social Council. President)
COMMODITIES (Agenda item 16d)
A/C.2/78/SR.14
SUSTAINABLE DEVELOPMENT (Agenda item 18)
A/C.2/78/SR.14

Nashwa, Fathimath (Maldives)
FOOD SECURITY (Agenda item 23a)
A/C.2/78/SR.16
POVERTY—INTERNATIONAL DECADES (Agenda item 21a)
A/C.2/78/SR.16
RURAL POVERTY (Agenda item 21b)
A/C.2/78/SR.16
UN. ECONOMIC AND SOCIAL COUNCIL—REPORTS (Agenda item 9)
A/78/PV.33

Nasir, Arrmanatha Christiawan (Indonesia)
CUBA—UNITED STATES (Agenda item 38)
A/78/PV.26
PEACE (Agenda item 14)
A/78/PV.62
UN. GENERAL ASSEMBLY (78TH SESS. : 2023-2024). 1ST COMMITTEE—GENERAL DEBATE (Agenda item 8)
A/C.1/78/PV.3
UN. INTERNATIONAL COURT OF JUSTICE—REPORTS (Agenda item 73)
A/78/PV.28
UN. SECRETARY-GENERAL—REPORTS (Agenda item 110)
A/78/PV.54
UN. SECURITY COUNCIL—MEMBERSHIP (Agenda item 121)
A/78/PV.35
UNRWA—ACTIVITIES (Agenda item 49)
A/C.4/78/SR.26
VETO (Agenda item 63)
A/78/PV.52

Nasir, Arrmanatha Christiawan (Indonesia) (ASEAN)
DEVELOPMENT FINANCE (Agenda item 16b)
A/C.2/78/SR.8
EMERGENCY ASSISTANCE (Agenda item 72a)
A/78/PV.46
HUMANITARIAN ASSISTANCE (Agenda item 72)
A/78/PV.46
INTERNATIONAL TRADE (Agenda item 16a)
A/C.2/78/SR.8
INVESTMENT PROMOTION (Agenda item 16g)
A/C.2/78/SR.8
MACROECONOMIC POLICY (Agenda item 16)
A/C.2/78/SR.8
PALESTINIANS—ASSISTANCE (Agenda item 72b)
A/78/PV.46
PEACEKEEPING OPERATIONS (Agenda item 51)
A/C.4/78/SR.18

Nasir, Arrmanatha Christiawan (Indonesia) (ASEAN) (continued)

SOUTH-EAST ASIA—NUCLEAR-WEAPON-FREE ZONES (Agenda item 99y)
A/C.1/78/PV.30
SPECIAL POLITICAL MISSIONS (Agenda item 52)
A/C.4/78/SR.21

Nasir, Arrmanatha Christiawan (Indonesia) (Coordinating Bureau of the Non-Aligned Countries)

UN. GENERAL ASSEMBLY (78TH SESS. : 2023-2024). 1ST COMMITTEE—GENERAL DEBATE (Agenda item 8)
A/C.1/78/PV.2

Nasir, Arrmanatha Christiawan (Indonesia) (UN. Special Committee of 24. Vice-Chair)

DECOLONIZATION (Agenda item 58)
A/C.4/78/SR.2
DECOLONIZATION—UN SYSTEM (Agenda item 56)
A/C.4/78/SR.2
NON-SELF-GOVERNING TERRITORIES—ECONOMIC INTERESTS (Agenda item 55)
A/C.4/78/SR.2
NON-SELF-GOVERNING TERRITORIES—FELLOWSHIPS (Agenda item 57)
A/C.4/78/SR.2
NON-SELF-GOVERNING TERRITORIES—REPORTS (Agenda item 54)
A/C.4/78/SR.2

Nasser-Abushawesh, Sahar (State of Palestine)

SUSTAINABLE DEVELOPMENT (Agenda item 18)
A/C.2/78/SR.15
TERRITORIES OCCUPIED BY ISRAEL—NATURAL RESOURCES (Agenda item 59)
A/C.2/78/SR.19; A/C.2/78/SR.20

Nastav, Bojan (UNCTAD)

FINANCIAL FLOWS (Agenda item 16f)
A/C.2/78/SR.8

Natale, Giuliana (Canada)

BIOLOGICAL DIVERSITY—TREATIES (Agenda item 18f)
A/C.2/78/SR.15
CLIMATE (Agenda item 18d)
A/C.2/78/SR.15
SUSTAINABLE DEVELOPMENT (Agenda item 18)
A/C.2/78/SR.15

Natano, Kausea (Tuvalu. Prime Minister)

UN. GENERAL ASSEMBLY (78TH SESS. : 2023-2024)—GENERAL DEBATE (Agenda item 8)
A/78/PV.11
UN. GENERAL ASSEMBLY (78TH SESS. : 2023-2024)—SPECIAL STATEMENTS
A/78/PV.11

Nausėda, Gitanas (Lithuania. President)

UN. GENERAL ASSEMBLY (78TH SESS. : 2023-2024)—GENERAL DEBATE (Agenda item 8)
A/78/PV.6
UN. GENERAL ASSEMBLY (78TH SESS. : 2023-2024)—SPECIAL STATEMENTS
A/78/PV.6

Navarrete, Angelica Saldivar (Philippines)

INDIGENOUS PEOPLES (Agenda item 68a)
A/C.3/78/SR.15
INDIGENOUS PEOPLES—CONFERENCES (Agenda item 68b)
A/C.3/78/SR.15

Navarro Barro, Nadieska (Cuba) (Group of 77)

RACIAL DISCRIMINATION—ELIMINATION (Agenda item 69a)
A/C.3/78/SR.40
RACIAL DISCRIMINATION—PROGRAMMES OF ACTION (Agenda item 69b)
A/C.3/78/SR.40

Navoti, Selema K. (Tuvalu)

MILLENNIUM SUMMIT—CONFERENCES (Agenda item 117)
A/78/PV.102
UN CONFERENCES (Agenda item 13)
A/78/PV.102

Nayyal, Mhd. Majd (Syrian Arab Republic)

HEALTH (Agenda item 125)
A/78/PV.48

Ndayishimiye, Évariste (Burundi. President)

UN. GENERAL ASSEMBLY (78TH SESS. : 2023-2024)—GENERAL DEBATE (Agenda item 8)
A/78/PV.8
UN. GENERAL ASSEMBLY (78TH SESS. : 2023-2024)—SPECIAL STATEMENTS
A/78/PV.8

Ndiaye, Fatoumata (UN. Under-Secretary-General for Internal Oversight Services)

UN—ADMINISTRATION (Agenda item 132)
A/C.5/78/SR.2; A/C.5/78/SR.32
UN—BUDGET (2024) (Agenda item 134)
A/C.5/78/SR.11
UN. OFFICE OF INTERNAL OVERSIGHT SERVICES—REPORTS (Agenda item 143)
A/C.5/78/SR.2

Ndiaye, Joseph Dominique Ngor (Senegal)

PEACEKEEPING OPERATIONS (Agenda item 51)
A/C.4/78/SR.19

Ndiaye, Mamadou Mounsir (Senegal)

INDIGENOUS PEOPLES (Agenda item 68a)
A/C.3/78/SR.48

Ndiaye, Mamadou Mounsir (Senegal) (continued)

RACIAL DISCRIMINATION—ELIMINATION (Agenda item 69a)
A/C.3/78/SR.47

Ndiaye, Ndeye Fatou (Senegal)

UN. GENERAL ASSEMBLY (78TH SESS. : 2023-2024). 1ST COMMITTEE—GENERAL DEBATE (Agenda item 8)
A/C.1/78/PV.8

Ndong Mba, Anatolio (Equatorial Guinea)

ECONOMIC SANCTIONS—INTERNATIONAL RELATIONS (Agenda item 28)
A/78/PV.90
RACIAL DISCRIMINATION—ELIMINATION (Agenda item 69a)
A/78/PV.63
RESPONSIBILITY TO PROTECT (Agenda item 129)
A/78/PV.97
SLAVERY—MEMORIALS (Agenda item 118)
A/78/PV.64
TERRORISM (Agenda item 109)
A/C.6/78/SR.2
UN. GENERAL ASSEMBLY (78TH SESS. : 2023-2024). 1ST COMMITTEE—GENERAL DEBATE (Agenda item 8)
A/C.1/78/PV.9

Ndong Sima, Raymond (Gabon. Prime Minister)

UN. GENERAL ASSEMBLY (78TH SESS. : 2023-2024)—GENERAL DEBATE (Agenda item 8)
A/78/PV.10
UN. GENERAL ASSEMBLY (78TH SESS. : 2023-2024)—SPECIAL STATEMENTS
A/78/PV.10

Ndoye, Abdou (Senegal)

CRIMES AGAINST HUMANITY (Agenda item 80)
A/C.6/78/SR.10
INTERNATIONAL JURISDICTION (Agenda item 84)
A/C.6/78/SR.12
PEACEKEEPING OPERATIONS—CRIMINAL LIABILITY (Agenda item 76)
A/C.6/78/SR.8
RULE OF LAW (Agenda item 83)
A/C.6/78/SR.18
UN. GENERAL ASSEMBLY (78TH SESS. : 2023-2024). 2ND COMMITTEE—GENERAL DEBATE (Agenda item 8)
A/C.2/78/SR.3
UN. INTERNATIONAL COURT OF JUSTICE—REPORTS (Agenda item 73)
A/78/PV.27
VETO (Agenda item 63)
A/78/PV.61; A/78/PV.67

Ndung'u, Gideon Kinuthia (Kenya)

NUCLEAR DISARMAMENT (Agenda item 99b)
A/C.1/78/PV.12

Nebenzia, Vasilii (Russian Federation)

CUBA—UNITED STATES (Agenda item 38)
A/78/PV.24
ECONOMIC SANCTIONS—INTERNATIONAL RELATIONS (Agenda item 28)
A/78/PV.89
PEACE (Agenda item 14)
A/78/PV.82
UKRAINE—POLITICAL CONDITIONS (Agenda item 62)
A/78/PV.56
VETO (Agenda item 63)
A/78/PV.3; A/78/PV.68; A/78/PV.75; A/78/PV.78

Nena, Matete (Lesotho)

ARMS TRANSFERS—TREATIES (Agenda item 99x)
A/C.1/78/PV.19
DECOLONIZATION (Agenda item 58)
A/C.4/78/SR.8
DISARMAMENT—GENERAL AND COMPLETE (Agenda item 99)
A/C.1/78/PV.19
DISPLACED PERSONS (Agenda item 71b)
A/C.3/78/SR.32
EXTERNAL DEBT—HUMAN RIGHTS (Agenda item 71b)
A/C.3/78/SR.32
FOOD SECURITY (Agenda item 23a)
A/C.2/78/SR.17
POVERTY—INTERNATIONAL DECADES (Agenda item 21a)
A/C.2/78/SR.17
RIGHT TO FOOD (Agenda item 71b)
A/C.3/78/SR.30
RIGHTS OF THE CHILD (Agenda item 67)
A/C.3/78/SR.13
RURAL POVERTY (Agenda item 21b)
A/C.2/78/SR.17
SMALL ARMS—ILLICIT TRAFFIC (Agenda item 99p)
A/C.1/78/PV.19
SMALL ARMS—ILLICIT TRAFFIC—ASSISTANCE (Agenda item 99n)
A/C.1/78/PV.19
SOLIDARITY (Agenda item 71b)
A/C.3/78/SR.32
UN—BUDGET (2024) (Agenda item 134)
A/C.5/78/SR.5
UN—PROGRAMME PLANNING (Agenda item 135)
A/C.5/78/SR.5
UN. GENERAL ASSEMBLY (78TH SESS. : 2023-2024). 1ST COMMITTEE—GENERAL DEBATE (Agenda item 8)
A/C.1/78/PV.6

Nena, Matete (Lesotho) (continued)

UN. GENERAL ASSEMBLY (78TH SESS. : 2023-2024). 2ND COMMITTEE—GENERAL DEBATE (Agenda item 8)
A/C.2/78/SR.3
WESTERN SAHARA QUESTION (Agenda item 58)
A/C.4/78/SR.8
WOMEN'S ADVANCEMENT (Agenda item 25a)
A/C.3/78/SR.10
WOMEN'S ADVANCEMENT—CONFERENCES (Agenda item 25b)
A/C.3/78/SR.10

Netanyahu, Benjamin (Israel. Prime Minister)

UN. GENERAL ASSEMBLY (78TH SESS. : 2023-2024)—GENERAL DEBATE (Agenda item 8)
A/78/PV.10
UN. GENERAL ASSEMBLY (78TH SESS. : 2023-2024)—SPECIAL STATEMENTS
A/78/PV.10

Neuffer, Philippe (Maohi Protestant Church (French Polynesia))

FRENCH POLYNESIA QUESTION (Agenda item 58)
A/C.4/78/SR.3

Neuffer, Tetuanuiahuuraiterai (Maohi Protestant Church (French Polynesia))

FRENCH POLYNESIA QUESTION (Agenda item 58)
A/C.4/78/SR.3

Ngirwa-Mpesha, Doris (FAO)

RURAL WOMEN (Agenda item 25a)
A/C.3/78/SR.10
WOMEN'S ADVANCEMENT (Agenda item 25a)
A/C.3/78/SR.10
WOMEN'S ADVANCEMENT—CONFERENCES (Agenda item 25b)
A/C.3/78/SR.10

Ngouambe Wouaga, Jean Luc (Cameroon)

INFORMATION (Agenda item 53)
A/C.4/78/SR.14

Nguema Obiang Mangue, Teodoro (Equatorial Guinea. Vice-President)

UN. GENERAL ASSEMBLY (78TH SESS. : 2023-2024)—GENERAL DEBATE (Agenda item 8)
A/78/PV.9
UN. GENERAL ASSEMBLY (78TH SESS. : 2023-2024)—SPECIAL STATEMENTS
A/78/PV.9

Ngungu, Edith Kaki (Kenya)

PEACEKEEPING OPERATIONS—CRIMINAL LIABILITY (Agenda item 76)
A/C.6/78/SR.9

Nguyen, Hoang Nguyen (Viet Nam)

DECOLONIZATION (Agenda item 58)
A/C.4/78/SR.2
DEVELOPMENT FINANCE—CONFERENCES (Agenda item 17)
A/78/PV.90
FOOD SECURITY (Agenda item 23a)
A/C.2/78/SR.16
OPERATIONAL ACTIVITIES—UN SYSTEM (Agenda item 22a)
A/C.2/78/SR.18
PEACEKEEPING OPERATIONS (Agenda item 51)
A/C.4/78/SR.19
POVERTY—INTERNATIONAL DECADES (Agenda item 21a)
A/C.2/78/SR.16
RURAL POVERTY (Agenda item 21b)
A/C.2/78/SR.16
SUSTAINABLE DEVELOPMENT (Agenda item 18)
A/C.2/78/SR.13
SUSTAINABLE ENERGY (Agenda item 18h)
A/C.2/78/SR.13
UN. GENERAL ASSEMBLY (78TH SESS. : 2023-2024). 2ND COMMITTEE—GENERAL DEBATE (Agenda item 8)
A/C.2/78/SR.4
UN. SECURITY COUNCIL—MEMBERSHIP (Agenda item 121)
A/78/PV.35
UN SYSTEM—STRENGTHENING (Agenda item 122)
A/78/PV.99
UNRWA—ACTIVITIES (Agenda item 49)
A/C.4/78/SR.23

Nguyen, Hoang Nguyen (Viet Nam) (ASEAN)

INFORMATION (Agenda item 53)
A/C.4/78/SR.12
OUTER SPACE—PEACEFUL USES—INTERNATIONAL COOPERATION (Agenda item 48)
A/C.4/78/SR.15

Nguyen, Hong Nhat (Viet Nam)

TERRORISM (Agenda item 109)
A/C.6/78/SR.2

Nguyen, Thi Hong Quyen (Viet Nam)

DISASTER VICTIMS (Agenda item 86)
A/C.6/78/SR.6

Nguyen, Thi Ngoc Ha (Viet Nam)

CRIMES AGAINST HUMANITY (Agenda item 80)
A/C.6/78/SR.10
PEACEKEEPING OPERATIONS—CRIMINAL LIABILITY (Agenda item 76)
A/C.6/78/SR.9

Ní Aoláin, Fionnuala (UN. Human Rights Council. Special Rapporteur on the Promotion and Protection of Human Rights and Fundamental Freedoms while Countering Terrorism)

TERRORISM—HUMAN RIGHTS (Agenda item 71b)
A/C.3/78/SR.31

Niamba Congo, Salamata Odette (Burkina Faso)

RURAL WOMEN (Agenda item 25a)
A/C.3/78/SR.49
SOCIAL CONDITIONS (Agenda item 24b)
A/C.3/78/SR.2

Niane, Adja Binta (Senegal)

INFORMATION (Agenda item 53)
A/C.4/78/SR.12

Niang, Cheikh (Senegal)

INTERNATIONAL CRIMINAL COURT—REPORTS (Agenda item 74)
A/78/PV.22
TERRITORIES OCCUPIED BY ISRAEL—HUMAN RIGHTS (Agenda item 50)
A/C.4/78/SR.24
UN. GENERAL ASSEMBLY (78TH SESS. : 2023-2024)—AGENDA (Agenda item 7)
A/BUR/78/SR.1

Niang, Cheikh (Senegal) (UN. General Assembly. Vice-President)

VETO (Agenda item 63)
A/78/PV.51

Niasse, Samba Thiam (Senegal)

ELECTION VERIFICATION—UN (Agenda item 71b)
A/C.3/78/SR.50
HUMAN RIGHTS ACTIVISTS (Agenda item 71b)
A/C.3/78/SR.56
HUMAN RIGHTS ADVANCEMENT (Agenda item 71b)
A/C.3/78/SR.52
PERSONS WITH DISABILITIES—HUMAN RIGHTS (Agenda item 71a)
A/C.3/78/SR.51
RIGHT TO DRINKING WATER (Agenda item 71b)
A/C.3/78/SR.50
RIGHTS OF THE CHILD (Agenda item 67)
A/C.3/78/SR.14; A/C.3/78/SR.55
SOCIAL CONDITIONS (Agenda item 24b)
A/C.3/78/SR.51
SPORTS—OLYMPIC GAMES (Agenda item 11)
A/78/PV.38
YOUTH (Agenda item 24b)
A/C.3/78/SR.55

Nicolino, Sebastián Lucas (Argentina)

COMMODITIES (Agenda item 16d)
A/C.2/78/SR.14

Nicolino, Sebastián Lucas (Argentina) (continued)

HEALTH (Agenda item 125)
A/78/PV.16
SUSTAINABLE DEVELOPMENT (Agenda item 18)
A/C.2/78/SR.14; A/C.2/78/SR.25
UN. GENERAL ASSEMBLY (78TH SESS. : 2023-2024). 2ND COMMITTEE—GENERAL DEBATE (Agenda item 8)
A/C.2/78/SR.2

Nidup, Dorji (Bhutan)

UN. ECONOMIC AND SOCIAL COUNCIL—REPORTS (Agenda item 9)
A/78/PV.48

Nidup, Dorji (Bhutan) (Group of 77)

UN. ECONOMIC AND SOCIAL COUNCIL—REPORTS (Agenda item 9)
A/78/PV.48

Niinistö, Sauli (Finland. President)

UN. GENERAL ASSEMBLY (78TH SESS. : 2023-2024)—GENERAL DEBATE (Agenda item 8)
A/78/PV.6
UN. GENERAL ASSEMBLY (78TH SESS. : 2023-2024)—SPECIAL STATEMENTS
A/78/PV.6

Nilsson, Ann-Sofie (Sweden)

UN. GENERAL ASSEMBLY (78TH SESS. : 2023-2024). 1ST COMMITTEE—GENERAL DEBATE (Agenda item 8)
A/C.1/78/PV.4

Nipomici, Galina (Republic of Moldova)

SUSTAINABLE DEVELOPMENT (Agenda item 18)
A/C.2/78/SR.24
UN. GENERAL ASSEMBLY (78TH SESS. : 2023-2024). 1ST COMMITTEE—GENERAL DEBATE (Agenda item 8)
A/C.1/78/PV.6
UN. GENERAL ASSEMBLY (78TH SESS. : 2023-2024). 2ND COMMITTEE—GENERAL DEBATE (Agenda item 8)
A/C.2/78/SR.4

Nishigori, Naofumi (Japan)

COASTAL ZONE MANAGEMENT (Agenda item 18j)
A/C.2/78/SR.23
TAXATION (Agenda item 16h)
A/C.2/78/SR.8; A/C.2/78/SR.25

Nishihara, Carmen (Chile)

ELECTION VERIFICATION—UN (Agenda item 71b)
A/C.3/78/SR.50
HUMAN RIGHTS—TERRITORIES OCCUPIED BY ISRAEL (Agenda item 71c)
A/C.3/78/SR.35

Nishihara, Carmen (Chile) (continued)

MERCENARIES (Agenda item 70)
A/C.3/78/SR.48
POVERTY—HUMAN RIGHTS (Agenda item 71b)
A/C.3/78/SR.30
RIGHT TO DEVELOPMENT (Agenda item 71b)
A/C.3/78/SR.48
RIGHT TO HOUSING (Agenda item 71b)
A/C.3/78/SR.30
SANCTIONS—INTERNATIONAL RELATIONS (Agenda item 71b)
A/C.3/78/SR.48
UN. HUMAN RIGHTS COUNCIL—REPORTS (Agenda item 66)
A/C.3/78/SR.46

Nishiyama, Akira (Japan)

TERRITORIES OCCUPIED BY ISRAEL—HUMAN RIGHTS (Agenda item 50)
A/C.4/78/SR.25
UNRWA—ACTIVITIES (Agenda item 49)
A/C.4/78/SR.23

Niu, Xiaoqiang (China)

ARMED CONFLICTS PREVENTION (Agenda item 31a)
A/78/PV.72

Njapau-Efrati, Grace (Women Investment Network (Zambia))

WESTERN SAHARA QUESTION (Agenda item 58)
A/C.4/78/SR.5

Nkalwo, Joseph Léa (Organisation internationale de la Francophonie)

INFORMATION (Agenda item 53)
A/C.4/78/SR.14

Noordin, Shamsuri (Malaysia)

ARMS TRANSFERS—TREATIES (Agenda item 99x)
A/C.1/78/PV.18
CONVENTIONAL WEAPONS (Agenda item 99u)
A/C.1/78/PV.18
PEACEKEEPING OPERATIONS (Agenda item 51)
A/C.4/78/SR.19
SMALL ARMS—ILLICIT TRAFFIC (Agenda item 99p)
A/C.1/78/PV.18
SMALL ARMS—ILLICIT TRAFFIC—ASSISTANCE (Agenda item 99n)
A/C.1/78/PV.18

Norapoompipat, Sorawut (Thailand)

INFORMATION (Agenda item 53)
A/C.4/78/SR.12

Nordin, Hana Binti (Malaysia)

OUTER SPACE—PEACEFUL USES—INTERNATIONAL COOPERATION (Agenda item 48)
A/C.4/78/SR.15

Normand, Lena (Association 193 (French Polynesia))

FRENCH POLYNESIA QUESTION (Agenda item 58)
A/C.4/78/SR.3

Noronha, Ligia (UNEP)

COASTAL ZONE MANAGEMENT (Agenda item 18j)
A/C.2/78/SR.12

Norton, Leslie (Canada)

UN. GENERAL ASSEMBLY (78TH SESS. : 2023-2024). 1ST COMMITTEE—GENERAL DEBATE (Agenda item 8)
A/C.1/78/PV.3

Nouh, Amr Mohamed Mosaad (Egypt)

CRIMES AGAINST HUMANITY (Agenda item 80)
A/C.6/78/SR.43; A/C.6/78/SR.47
DISASTER VICTIMS (Agenda item 86)
A/C.6/78/SR.6
INTERNATIONAL LAW—TRAINING PROGRAMMES (Agenda item 78)
A/C.6/78/SR.21
PEACEKEEPING OPERATIONS—CRIMINAL LIABILITY (Agenda item 76)
A/C.6/78/SR.8
RULE OF LAW (Agenda item 83)
A/C.6/78/SR.16
UN. GENERAL ASSEMBLY—WORK PROGRAMME (Agenda item 120)
A/C.6/78/SR.36

Nouh, Amr Mohamed Mosaad (Egypt) (UN. General Assembly. 6th Committee. Bureau)

UN CHARTER—REPORTS (Agenda item 82)
A/C.6/78/SR.37

Novák, Katalin (Hungary. President)

UN. GENERAL ASSEMBLY (78TH SESS. : 2023-2024)—GENERAL DEBATE (Agenda item 8)
A/78/PV.4
UN. GENERAL ASSEMBLY (78TH SESS. : 2023-2024)—SPECIAL STATEMENTS
A/78/PV.4

Novicio, Noel Mangaoang (Philippines)

OUTER SPACE—PEACEFUL USES—INTERNATIONAL COOPERATION (Agenda item 48)
A/C.4/78/SR.17
PEACEKEEPING OPERATIONS (Agenda item 51)
A/C.4/78/SR.20
UNRWA—ACTIVITIES (Agenda item 49)
A/C.4/78/SR.23

Novruz, Leyla (Azerbaijan) (Coordinating Bureau of the Non-Aligned Countries)

DEMOCRACY (Agenda item 71b)
A/C.3/78/SR.28

Novruz, Leyla (Azerbaijan) (Coordinating Bureau of the Non-Aligned Countries) (continued)

HUMAN RIGHTS—INTERNATIONAL INSTRUMENTS (Agenda item 71a)
A/C.3/78/SR.33
HUMAN RIGHTS—REPORTS (Agenda item 71c)
A/C.3/78/SR.53
HUMAN RIGHTS—TERRITORIES OCCUPIED BY ISRAEL (Agenda item 71c)
A/C.3/78/SR.35
RACIAL DISCRIMINATION—ELIMINATION (Agenda item 69a)
A/C.3/78/SR.41
RACIAL DISCRIMINATION—PROGRAMMES OF ACTION (Agenda item 69b)
A/C.3/78/SR.41
RIGHT TO DEVELOPMENT (Agenda item 71b)
A/C.3/78/SR.20
RIGHT TO FOOD (Agenda item 71b)
A/C.3/78/SR.30
SANCTIONS—INTERNATIONAL RELATIONS (Agenda item 71b)
A/C.3/78/SR.28
SOLIDARITY (Agenda item 71b)
A/C.3/78/SR.32

Nunes, Karlito (Timor-Leste)

BIOLOGICAL DIVERSITY—TREATIES (Agenda item 18f)
A/C.2/78/SR.15
CUBA—UNITED STATES (Agenda item 38)
A/78/PV.26
DECOLONIZATION (Agenda item 58)
A/C.4/78/SR.2
FALKLAND ISLANDS (MALVINAS) QUESTION (Agenda item 42)
A/C.4/78/SR.2
GIBRALTAR QUESTION (Agenda item 58)
A/C.4/78/SR.2
HUMAN RIGHTS—MYANMAR (Agenda item 71c)
A/C.3/78/SR.25
HUMAN RIGHTS ADVANCEMENT (Agenda item 71b)
A/C.3/78/SR.25
LANDLOCKED DEVELOPING COUNTRIES—CONFERENCES (Agenda item 20b)
A/C.2/78/SR.7
LEAST DEVELOPED COUNTRIES—CONFERENCES (Agenda item 20a)
A/C.2/78/SR.7
RIGHTS OF THE CHILD (Agenda item 67)
A/C.3/78/SR.13
SUSTAINABLE DEVELOPMENT (Agenda item 18)
A/C.2/78/SR.15
UN. GENERAL ASSEMBLY (78TH SESS. : 2023-2024). 2ND COMMITTEE—GENERAL DEBATE (Agenda item 8)
A/C.2/78/SR.4
WESTERN SAHARA QUESTION (Agenda item 58)
A/C.4/78/SR.2
WOMEN'S ADVANCEMENT (Agenda item 25a)
A/C.3/78/SR.10

Nunes, Karlito (Timor-Leste) (continued)

WOMEN'S ADVANCEMENT—CONFERENCES (Agenda item 25b)
A/C.3/78/SR.10

Nurken, Azat (Kazakhstan)

REGIONAL DISARMAMENT (Agenda item 99f)
A/C.1/78/PV.21

Nusseibeh, Lana Zaki (United Arab Emirates)

VETO (Agenda item 63)
A/78/PV.52
WOMEN'S ADVANCEMENT (Agenda item 25a)
A/C.3/78/SR.8
WOMEN'S ADVANCEMENT—CONFERENCES (Agenda item 25b)
A/C.3/78/SR.8

Nyagura, Petronella (Zimbabwe)

MILLENNIUM SUMMIT—CONFERENCES (Agenda item 117)
A/78/PV.15
UN CONFERENCES (Agenda item 13)
A/78/PV.15

Nyakoe, Catherine Nyaboke (Kenya)

CRIMES AGAINST HUMANITY (Agenda item 80)
A/C.6/78/SR.11; A/C.6/78/SR.43; A/C.6/78/SR.44; A/C.6/78/SR.47
DISASTER VICTIMS (Agenda item 86)
A/C.6/78/SR.6
INTERNATIONAL JURISDICTION (Agenda item 84)
A/C.6/78/SR.13
INTERNATIONAL LAW—TRAINING PROGRAMMES (Agenda item 78)
A/C.6/78/SR.22
RULE OF LAW (Agenda item 83)
A/C.6/78/SR.18

Nyanid, Zacharie Serge Raoul (Cameroon)

ADMINISTRATION OF JUSTICE (Agenda item 144)
A/C.6/78/SR.9
CRIMES AGAINST HUMANITY (Agenda item 80)
A/C.6/78/SR.10; A/C.6/78/SR.39; A/C.6/78/SR.40; A/C.6/78/SR.41; A/C.6/78/SR.42; A/C.6/78/SR.43; A/C.6/78/SR.44; A/C.6/78/SR.47
DISARMAMENT—GENERAL AND COMPLETE (Agenda item 99)
A/C.1/78/PV.30
DISASTER VICTIMS (Agenda item 86)
A/C.6/78/SR.6
INTERNATIONAL JURISDICTION (Agenda item 84)
A/C.6/78/SR.12; A/C.6/78/SR.37
INTERNATIONAL LAW—TRAINING PROGRAMMES (Agenda item 78)
A/C.6/78/SR.21
NON-CITIZENS—DEPORTATION (Agenda item 81)
A/C.6/78/SR.34

Nyanid, Zacharie Serge Raoul (Cameroon) (continued)

PEACEKEEPING OPERATIONS—CRIMINAL LIABILITY (Agenda item 76)
A/C.6/78/SR.9
RESPONSIBILITY OF INTERNATIONAL ORGANIZATIONS (Agenda item 85)
A/C.6/78/SR.19
RULE OF LAW (Agenda item 83)
A/C.6/78/SR.16
TERRORISM (Agenda item 109)
A/C.6/78/SR.2
TREATIES (Agenda item 87)
A/C.6/78/SR.20
UN. INTERNATIONAL LAW COMMISSION—REPORTS (Agenda item 79)
A/C.6/78/SR.25; A/C.6/78/SR.30; A/C.6/78/SR.33; A/C.6/78/SR.37

Nyarku, Felix Akom (Ghana)

DECOLONIZATION (Agenda item 58)
A/C.4/78/SR.8

Nyirongo, Bertha Mkaka (Malawi)

RIGHTS OF THE CHILD (Agenda item 67)
A/C.3/78/SR.13

Nyman, Klas (European Union)

FREEDOM OF EXPRESSION (Agenda item 71b)
A/C.3/78/SR.19
HUMAN RIGHTS—BURUNDI (Agenda item 71c)
A/C.3/78/SR.36
HUMAN RIGHTS—CENTRAL AFRICAN REPUBLIC (Agenda item 71c)
A/C.3/78/SR.33
HUMAN RIGHTS—DEMOCRATIC PEOPLE'S REPUBLIC OF KOREA (Agenda item 71c)
A/C.3/78/SR.33
HUMAN RIGHTS—ERITREA (Agenda item 71c)
A/C.3/78/SR.36
HUMAN RIGHTS—ETHIOPIA (Agenda item 71c)
A/C.3/78/SR.36
HUMAN RIGHTS—SOMALIA (Agenda item 71c)
A/C.3/78/SR.35
INDIGENOUS PEOPLES (Agenda item 68a)
A/C.3/78/SR.15
INDIGENOUS PEOPLES—CONFERENCES (Agenda item 68b)
A/C.3/78/SR.15
MERCENARIES (Agenda item 70)
A/C.3/78/SR.42
PERSONS WITH DISABILITIES—HUMAN RIGHTS (Agenda item 71a)
A/C.3/78/SR.38
RACIAL DISCRIMINATION—ELIMINATION (Agenda item 69a)
A/C.3/78/SR.40; A/C.3/78/SR.42
RACIAL DISCRIMINATION—PROGRAMMES OF ACTION (Agenda item 69b)
A/C.3/78/SR.40; A/C.3/78/SR.42
RELIGIOUS INTOLERANCE (Agenda item 71b)
A/C.3/78/SR.38

Nyman, Klas (European Union) (continued)

TORTURE AND OTHER CRUEL TREATMENT (Agenda item 71a)
A/C.3/78/SR.18

Nyusi, Filipe Jacinto (Mozambique. President)

UN. GENERAL ASSEMBLY (78TH SESS. : 2023-2024)—GENERAL DEBATE (Agenda item 8)
A/78/PV.5
UN. GENERAL ASSEMBLY (78TH SESS. : 2023-2024)—SPECIAL STATEMENTS
A/78/PV.5

Nze Mansogo, Estela Mercedes (Equatorial Guinea)

CRIMES AGAINST HUMANITY (Agenda item 80)
A/C.6/78/SR.45
DISASTER VICTIMS (Agenda item 86)
A/C.6/78/SR.6
INTERNATIONAL LAW—TRAINING PROGRAMMES (Agenda item 78)
A/C.6/78/SR.22
RESPONSIBILITY OF INTERNATIONAL ORGANIZATIONS (Agenda item 85)
A/C.6/78/SR.19
RULE OF LAW (Agenda item 83)
A/C.6/78/SR.18
UN. INTERNATIONAL COURT OF JUSTICE—REPORTS (Agenda item 73)
A/78/PV.28
UN CHARTER—REPORTS (Agenda item 82)
A/C.6/78/SR.33

Nzessioue, Marius Aristide Hoja (Central African Republic)

HUMAN RIGHTS—CENTRAL AFRICAN REPUBLIC (Agenda item 71c)
A/C.3/78/SR.33

Nzumbu, Christine (Kenya)

DEVELOPMENT FINANCE (Agenda item 16b)
A/C.2/78/SR.9
EXTERNAL DEBT (Agenda item 16c)
A/C.2/78/SR.9
FOOD SECURITY (Agenda item 23a)
A/C.2/78/SR.16
POVERTY—INTERNATIONAL DECADES (Agenda item 21a)
A/C.2/78/SR.16
RURAL POVERTY (Agenda item 21b)
A/C.2/78/SR.16
TAXATION (Agenda item 16h)
A/C.2/78/SR.9

O'Hara Rusckowski, Deborah (Sovereign Order of Malta)

DISAPPEARANCE OF PERSONS (Agenda item 71b)
A/C.3/78/SR.22

O'Hara Rusckowski, Deborah (Sovereign Order of Malta) (continued)

TRAFFICKING IN PERSONS (Agenda item 71b)
A/C.3/78/SR.23

O'Sullivan, Alicia (Ireland)

SOCIAL DEVELOPMENT (Agenda item 24)
A/C.3/78/SR.2

Obokata, Tomoya (UN. Human Rights Council. Special Rapporteur on Contemporary Forms of Slavery)

SLAVERY (Agenda item 71a)
A/C.3/78/SR.21

Ochoa Espinales, Olimpia Raquel (Nicaragua)

EMERGENCY ASSISTANCE (Agenda item 72a)
A/78/PV.47
HUMAN RIGHTS—DEMOCRATIC PEOPLE'S REPUBLIC OF KOREA (Agenda item 71c)
A/78/PV.50
HUMAN RIGHTS—REPORTS (Agenda item 71c)
A/78/PV.50
RACIAL DISCRIMINATION—ELIMINATION (Agenda item 69a)
A/78/PV.50
UN—BUDGET (2024) (Agenda item 134)
A/C.5/78/SR.26/PartII
UN—PROGRAMME PLANNING (Agenda item 135)
A/78/PV.50(Resumption1); A/C.5/78/SR.24

Ochoa Martínez, Enrique Javier (Mexico)

PALESTINE QUESTION (Agenda item 35)
A/78/PV.40
VETO (Agenda item 63)
A/78/PV.3

Oddone, Fabián (Argentina)

DISAPPEARANCE OF PERSONS (Agenda item 71b)
A/C.3/78/SR.22
PEACE (Agenda item 14)
A/78/PV.62; A/78/PV.82
RIGHT TO THE TRUTH (Agenda item 71b)
A/C.3/78/SR.22
UN. GENERAL ASSEMBLY (78TH SESS. : 2023-2024). 2ND COMMITTEE—GENERAL DEBATE (Agenda item 8)
A/C.2/78/SR.3
UN. SECURITY COUNCIL—MEMBERSHIP (Agenda item 121)
A/78/PV.35
WOMEN'S ADVANCEMENT (Agenda item 25a)
A/C.3/78/SR.8
WOMEN'S ADVANCEMENT—CONFERENCES (Agenda item 25b)
A/C.3/78/SR.8

Oehri, Myriam (Liechtenstein)

HUMAN RIGHTS—MYANMAR (Agenda item 71c)
A/C.3/78/SR.53

Oehri, Myriam (Liechtenstein) (continued)

RULE OF LAW (Agenda item 83)
A/C.6/78/SR.15
TERRITORIES OCCUPIED BY ISRAEL—HUMAN RIGHTS (Agenda item 50)
A/C.4/78/SR.26
UKRAINE—POLITICAL CONDITIONS (Agenda item 62)
A/78/PV.57
UN. GENERAL ASSEMBLY (78TH SESS. : 2023-2024). 1ST COMMITTEE—GENERAL DEBATE (Agenda item 8)
A/C.1/78/PV.3
UN. HUMAN RIGHTS COUNCIL—REPORTS (Agenda item 66)
A/78/PV.23
UN. INTERNATIONAL COURT OF JUSTICE—REPORTS (Agenda item 73)
A/78/PV.27
UNRWA—ACTIVITIES (Agenda item 49)
A/C.4/78/SR.26
VETO (Agenda item 63)
A/78/PV.51; A/78/PV.66; A/78/PV.75

Oehri, Noah (Liechtenstein)

ELECTION VERIFICATION—UN (Agenda item 71b)
A/C.3/78/SR.50
ENVIRONMENT (Agenda item 71b)
A/C.3/78/SR.24
HIV/AIDS—DECLARATIONS (Agenda item 10)
A/78/PV.91
HUMAN RIGHTS—AFGHANISTAN (Agenda item 71c)
A/C.3/78/SR.34
HUMAN RIGHTS—BELARUS (Agenda item 71c)
A/C.3/78/SR.37
HUMAN RIGHTS—INTERNATIONAL INSTRUMENTS (Agenda item 71a)
A/C.3/78/SR.24
HUMAN RIGHTS—MYANMAR (Agenda item 71c)
A/C.3/78/SR.33
HUMAN RIGHTS—RUSSIAN FEDERATION (Agenda item 71c)
A/C.3/78/SR.37
JUDICIAL INDEPENDENCE (Agenda item 71b)
A/C.3/78/SR.31
RACIAL DISCRIMINATION—ELIMINATION (Agenda item 69a)
A/C.3/78/SR.47
RIGHT TO DEVELOPMENT (Agenda item 71b)
A/C.3/78/SR.48
RIGHTS OF THE CHILD (Agenda item 67)
A/C.3/78/SR.11
SLAVERY (Agenda item 71a)
A/C.3/78/SR.21
TAXATION (Agenda item 16h)
A/C.2/78/SR.25
UN. HUMAN RIGHTS COUNCIL—REPORTS (Agenda item 66)
A/C.3/78/SR.51

Oehri, Noah (Liechtenstein) (continued)

WOMEN'S ADVANCEMENT (Agenda item 25a)
A/C.3/78/SR.8
WOMEN'S ADVANCEMENT—CONFERENCES (Agenda item 25b)
A/C.3/78/SR.8

Offenbächer, Csenge (Hungary)

YOUTH (Agenda item 24b)
A/C.3/78/SR.3

Ogasawara, Ichiro (Japan)

ARMS RACE—OUTER SPACE (Agenda item 97a)
A/C.1/78/PV.17
BIOLOGICAL WEAPONS—TREATIES (Agenda item 106)
A/C.1/78/PV.15
CHEMICAL WEAPONS—TREATIES (Agenda item 99l)
A/C.1/78/PV.15
CLUSTER MUNITIONS (Agenda item 99dd)
A/C.1/78/PV.18
CONVENTIONAL WEAPONS (Agenda item 99u)
A/C.1/78/PV.18
CONVENTIONAL WEAPONS—TREATIES (Agenda item 103)
A/C.1/78/PV.18
DISARMAMENT—GENERAL AND COMPLETE (Agenda item 99)
A/C.1/78/PV.18
DISARMAMENT AGREEMENTS—OUTER SPACE (Agenda item 97c)
A/C.1/78/PV.17
INFORMATION—INTERNATIONAL SECURITY (Agenda item 94)
A/C.1/78/PV.20
LANDMINES—TREATIES (Agenda item 99m)
A/C.1/78/PV.18
NUCLEAR DISARMAMENT (Agenda item 99b)
A/C.1/78/PV.12
NUCLEAR NON-PROLIFERATION—INTERNATIONAL OBLIGATIONS (Agenda item 99w)
A/C.1/78/PV.12
NUCLEAR WEAPONS—ELIMINATION (Agenda item 99z)
A/C.1/78/PV.12; A/C.1/78/PV.25; A/C.1/78/PV.26
NUCLEAR WEAPONS—HUMANITARIAN CONSEQUENCES (Agenda item 99bb)
A/C.1/78/PV.26
NUCLEAR WEAPONS—TREATIES (Agenda item 99ff)
A/C.1/78/PV.26
OUTER SPACE—CONFIDENCE-BUILDING MEASURES (Agenda item 99v)
A/C.1/78/PV.17
OUTER SPACE—PRINCIPLES (Agenda item 97d)
A/C.1/78/PV.17
SMALL ARMS—ILLICIT TRAFFIC (Agenda item 99p)
A/C.1/78/PV.18

Ogasawara, Ichiro (Japan) (continued)

UN. GENERAL ASSEMBLY (78TH SESS. : 2023-2024). 1ST COMMITTEE—GENERAL DEBATE (Agenda item 8)
A/C.1/78/PV.5; A/C.1/78/PV.6; A/C.1/78/PV.7

Okafor, Obiora Chinedu (UN. Human Rights Council. Independent Expert on Human Rights and International Solidarity)

SOLIDARITY (Agenda item 71b)
A/C.3/78/SR.32

Okeke, Vivian Nwunaku Rose (IAEA)

DISARMAMENT—GENERAL AND COMPLETE (Agenda item 99)
A/78/PV.105
NUCLEAR DISARMAMENT (Agenda item 99b)
A/C.1/78/PV.13

Olawuyi, Damilola (UN. Human Rights Council. Working Group on the Issue of Human Rights and Transnational Corporations and Other Business Enterprises. Chair)

TRANSNATIONAL CORPORATIONS—HUMAN RIGHTS (Agenda item 71b)
A/C.3/78/SR.21

Olisa, Janet (Nigeria)

INTERNATIONAL LAW—TRAINING PROGRAMMES (Agenda item 78)
A/C.6/78/SR.22

Oliveira, Sasha (Canada)

SPECIAL POLITICAL MISSIONS (Agenda item 52)
A/C.4/78/SR.21

Oliveira, Vitorino Alberto Melo Gomes (Portugal)

SMALL ISLAND DEVELOPING STATES—PROGRAMMES OF ACTION (Agenda item 18b)
A/78/PV.100

Omar, Khairi (Malaysia)

CUBA—UNITED STATES (Agenda item 38)
A/78/PV.24
TERRORISM (Agenda item 109)
A/C.6/78/SR.4
UN. INTERNATIONAL COURT OF JUSTICE—REPORTS (Agenda item 73)
A/78/PV.27
UN. INTERNATIONAL LAW COMMISSION—REPORTS (Agenda item 79)
A/C.6/78/SR.27

Omar, Khairi (Malaysia) (ASEAN)

UN. GENERAL ASSEMBLY—WORK PROGRAMME (Agenda item 120)
A/78/PV.32

Omar, Khairi (Malaysia) (ASEAN) (continued)

UN RESOLUTIONS—IMPLEMENTATION (Agenda item 119)
A/78/PV.32

Omar, Sidi (Frente Polisario)

WESTERN SAHARA QUESTION (Agenda item 58)
A/C.4/78/SR.4

Omarov, Arsen (Kazakhstan)

BIOLOGICAL WEAPONS—TREATIES (Agenda item 106)
A/C.1/78/PV.15
CHEMICAL WEAPONS—TREATIES (Agenda item 99l)
A/C.1/78/PV.15

Önal, Sedat (Türkiye)

UKRAINE—POLITICAL CONDITIONS (Agenda item 62)
A/78/PV.57
UN. SECURITY COUNCIL—MEMBERSHIP (Agenda item 121)
A/78/PV.35

Ondo Ebang, William (Cameroon)

MINE CLEARANCE (Agenda item 46)
A/C.4/78/SR.10
RADIATION EFFECTS (Agenda item 47)
A/C.4/78/SR.11

Ong, Shirley (Canada)

DEVELOPMENT FINANCE (Agenda item 16b)
A/C.2/78/SR.8
DEVELOPMENT FINANCE—CONFERENCES (Agenda item 17)
A/78/PV.90
EMERGENCY ASSISTANCE (Agenda item 72a)
A/78/PV.46; A/78/PV.47
TAXATION (Agenda item 16h)
A/C.2/78/SR.8

Ono, Sho (Japan)

CRIME PREVENTION (Agenda item 107)
A/C.3/78/SR.6
CYBERCRIME (Agenda item 108)
A/C.3/78/SR.6
ELECTION VERIFICATION—UN (Agenda item 71b)
A/C.3/78/SR.50
ENVIRONMENT (Agenda item 71b)
A/C.3/78/SR.29
HUMAN RIGHTS (Agenda item 71)
A/C.3/78/SR.27
HUMAN RIGHTS—AFGHANISTAN (Agenda item 71c)
A/C.3/78/SR.26
HUMAN RIGHTS—DEMOCRATIC PEOPLE'S REPUBLIC OF KOREA (Agenda item 71c)
A/C.3/78/SR.53

Ono, Sho (Japan) (continued)

HUMAN RIGHTS—MYANMAR (Agenda item 71c)
A/C.3/78/SR.26
HUMAN RIGHTS—UKRAINE (Agenda item 71c)
A/C.3/78/SR.26; A/C.3/78/SR.37
HUMAN RIGHTS ADVANCEMENT (Agenda item 71b)
A/C.3/78/SR.18
HUMAN RIGHTS INSTITUTIONS—CENTRAL AFRICA (Agenda item 71b)
A/C.3/78/SR.56
MINE CLEARANCE (Agenda item 46)
A/C.4/78/SR.10
PEACE (Agenda item 14)
A/78/PV.88
RACIAL DISCRIMINATION—ELIMINATION (Agenda item 69a)
A/C.3/78/SR.47
RACIAL DISCRIMINATION—PROGRAMMES OF ACTION (Agenda item 69b)
A/C.3/78/SR.56
RIGHT TO DRINKING WATER (Agenda item 71b)
A/C.3/78/SR.28
RIGHT TO FOOD (Agenda item 71b)
A/C.3/78/SR.30; A/C.3/78/SR.48
RIGHTS OF THE CHILD (Agenda item 67)
A/C.3/78/SR.11
SOCIAL DEVELOPMENT (Agenda item 24)
A/C.3/78/SR.47
YOUTH (Agenda item 24b)
A/C.3/78/SR.55

Onyoni-Mogaka, Catherine Bonareri (Kenya)

UN. GENERAL ASSEMBLY (78TH SESS. : 2023-2024). 2ND COMMITTEE—GENERAL DEBATE (Agenda item 8)
A/C.2/78/SR.4
WOMEN'S ADVANCEMENT (Agenda item 25a)
A/C.3/78/SR.8
WOMEN'S ADVANCEMENT—CONFERENCES (Agenda item 25b)
A/C.3/78/SR.8

Oppong-Ntiri, Carolyn (Ghana)

SUSTAINABLE DEVELOPMENT (Agenda item 18)
A/78/PV.88

Oral, Nilufer (UN. International Law Commission. Chair)

UN. INTERNATIONAL LAW COMMISSION—REPORTS (Agenda item 79)
A/C.6/78/SR.23; A/C.6/78/SR.33

Ordóñez, Andrés (Universidad Nacional Autónoma de México)

WESTERN SAHARA QUESTION (Agenda item 58)
A/C.4/78/SR.5

Orduz Durán, Jessica Beatriz (Colombia)
CLIMATE CHANGE (Agenda item 71b)
A/C.3/78/SR.29
ENVIRONMENT (Agenda item 71b)
A/C.3/78/SR.29
HUMAN RIGHTS—INTERNATIONAL INSTRUMENTS (Agenda item 71a)
A/C.3/78/SR.24
RACIAL DISCRIMINATION—ELIMINATION (Agenda item 69a)
A/C.3/78/SR.42
RACIAL DISCRIMINATION—PROGRAMMES OF ACTION (Agenda item 69b)
A/C.3/78/SR.42
RELIGIOUS INTOLERANCE (Agenda item 71b)
A/C.3/78/SR.38
RIGHTS OF THE CHILD (Agenda item 67)
A/C.3/78/SR.11

Orellana, Marcos (UN. Human Rights Council. Special Rapporteur on the Implications for Human Rights of the Environmentally Sound Management and Disposal of Hazardous Substances and Wastes)
HAZARDOUS WASTES (Agenda item 71b)
A/C.3/78/SR.29

Orosan, Alina (Romania)
INTERNATIONAL CRIMINAL COURT—REPORTS (Agenda item 74)
A/78/PV.21
UN. INTERNATIONAL COURT OF JUSTICE—REPORTS (Agenda item 73)
A/78/PV.20
UN. INTERNATIONAL LAW COMMISSION—REPORTS (Agenda item 79)
A/C.6/78/SR.25; A/C.6/78/SR.29; A/C.6/78/SR.31

Ortiz Palacio, Ignacio (Forum Canario-Saharaui)
WESTERN SAHARA QUESTION (Agenda item 58)
A/C.4/78/SR.4

Osei, Rita (Ghana) (UN. Group of African States)
UN—FINANCIAL SITUATION (Agenda item 136)
A/C.5/78/SR.6

Óskarsson, Thórdur Aegir (Iceland)
SEXUAL ORIENTATION (Agenda item 71b)
A/C.3/78/SR.39

Osmani, Bujar (North Macedonia)
UKRAINE—POLITICAL CONDITIONS (Agenda item 62)
A/78/PV.56

Osmundsen, Jorn (Norway)
NUCLEAR DISARMAMENT (Agenda item 99b)
A/C.1/78/PV.13

Osmundsen, Jorn (Norway) (continued)
NUCLEAR DISARMAMENT—VERIFICATION (Agenda item 99ee)
A/C.1/78/PV.12; A/C.1/78/PV.13
NUCLEAR NON-PROLIFERATION—INTERNATIONAL OBLIGATIONS (Agenda item 99w)
A/C.1/78/PV.13
NUCLEAR WEAPON TESTS—TREATIES (Agenda item 105)
A/C.1/78/PV.13

Ossebi Iyolo, Isis (Congo) (UN. Group of African States)
UN HIGH COMMISSIONER FOR REFUGEES—REPORTS (Agenda item 60)
A/C.3/78/SR.54

Othman, Mohamed Chande (UN. International Commission of Human Rights Experts on Ethiopia. Chair)
HUMAN RIGHTS—ETHIOPIA (Agenda item 71c)
A/C.3/78/SR.36

Ouafi, Sara (Morocco)
MIGRANTS—PROTECTION (Agenda item 71b)
A/C.3/78/SR.23

Ouakli, Mohamed ((personal capacity))
WESTERN SAHARA QUESTION (Agenda item 58)
A/C.4/78/SR.5

Ouatiki, Assia (Morocco)
CLIMATE (Agenda item 18d)
A/C.2/78/SR.13
ECONOMIC COOPERATION AMONG DEVELOPING COUNTRIES (Agenda item 22b)
A/C.2/78/SR.18
OPERATIONAL ACTIVITIES—UN SYSTEM (Agenda item 22a)
A/C.2/78/SR.18
SUSTAINABLE DEVELOPMENT (Agenda item 18)
A/C.2/78/SR.13
SUSTAINABLE ENERGY (Agenda item 18h)
A/C.2/78/SR.13

Ouattara, Isaac Alassane (Burkina Faso)
RIGHTS OF THE CHILD (Agenda item 67)
A/C.3/78/SR.13

Ouattara Cisse, Aminata (Burkina Faso)
HUMAN RIGHTS—INTERNATIONAL INSTRUMENTS (Agenda item 71a)
A/C.3/78/SR.25
INFORMATION (Agenda item 53)
A/C.4/78/SR.13
TERRORISM (Agenda item 109)
A/C.6/78/SR.2
TERRORISM—HUMAN RIGHTS (Agenda item 71b)
A/C.3/78/SR.25

Ouro-bodi, Tchakpide (Togo)
INTERNATIONAL JURISDICTION (Agenda item 84)
A/C.6/78/SR.13
TERRORISM (Agenda item 109)
A/C.6/78/SR.4

Ouro-Tagba, Tawfic (Togo)
NUCLEAR DISARMAMENT (Agenda item 99b)
A/C.1/78/PV.12
NUCLEAR NON-PROLIFERATION—INTERNATIONAL OBLIGATIONS (Agenda item 99w)
A/C.1/78/PV.12
NUCLEAR WEAPON TESTS—TREATIES (Agenda item 105)
A/C.1/78/PV.12

Ousman, Samadou (Niger)
TERRORISM (Agenda item 109)
A/C.6/78/SR.4

Oussein, Kadim (Comoros)
DECOLONIZATION (Agenda item 58)
A/C.4/78/SR.9
NUCLEAR DISARMAMENT (Agenda item 99b)
A/C.1/78/PV.13
NUCLEAR WEAPONS—TREATIES (Agenda item 99ff)
A/C.1/78/PV.13
WESTERN SAHARA QUESTION (Agenda item 58)
A/C.4/78/SR.9

Özgür, Ceren Hande (Türkiye)
ARMED CONFLICTS PREVENTION (Agenda item 31a)
A/78/PV.72
TERRITORIES OCCUPIED BY ISRAEL—NATURAL RESOURCES (Agenda item 59)
A/C.2/78/SR.21
UNRWA—ACTIVITIES (Agenda item 49)
A/C.4/78/SR.22

Pace, Giulia ((personal capacity))
WESTERN SAHARA QUESTION (Agenda item 58)
A/C.4/78/SR.4

Pacey-Parker, Sarah (Canada)
OUTER SPACE—PEACEFUL USES—INTERNATIONAL COOPERATION (Agenda item 48)
A/C.4/78/SR.16

Padilla González, Cristian (Cuba)
RACIAL DISCRIMINATION—ELIMINATION (Agenda item 69a)
A/78/PV.103
UN RESOLUTIONS—IMPLEMENTATION (Agenda item 119)
A/78/PV.103
UN SYSTEM—STRENGTHENING (Agenda item 122)
A/78/PV.99

Padło-Pękala, Katarzyna (Poland)
UN. INTERNATIONAL LAW COMMISSION—REPORTS (Agenda item 79)
A/C.6/78/SR.29; A/C.6/78/SR.31

Page, Elizabeth Louise (United Kingdom)
INFORMATION—INTERNATIONAL SECURITY (Agenda item 94)
A/C.1/78/PV.20

Palacios, Iván Lara (Nicaragua)
ECONOMIC SANCTIONS—INTERNATIONAL RELATIONS (Agenda item 28)
A/78/PV.89

Pallek, Markus (Advisory Committee on the United Nations Programme of Assistance in the Teaching, Study, Dissemination and Wider Appreciation of International Law. Secretary)
INTERNATIONAL LAW—TRAINING PROGRAMMES (Agenda item 78)
A/C.6/78/SR.21

Panier, Wisnique (Haiti)
CRIMES AGAINST HUMANITY (Agenda item 80)
A/C.6/78/SR.11; A/C.6/78/SR.45
DISASTER VICTIMS (Agenda item 86)
A/C.6/78/SR.6
INTERNATIONAL LAW—TRAINING PROGRAMMES (Agenda item 78)
A/C.6/78/SR.22
PEACEKEEPING OPERATIONS—CRIMINAL LIABILITY (Agenda item 76)
A/C.6/78/SR.9
TERRORISM (Agenda item 109)
A/C.6/78/SR.4

Panier, Wisnique (Haiti) (UN. General Assembly. 6th Committee. Bureau)
NON-CITIZENS—DEPORTATION (Agenda item 81)
A/C.6/78/SR.37

Panteli, Rona Marie (Cyprus)
PEACEKEEPING OPERATIONS (Agenda item 51)
A/C.4/78/SR.20

Papac, Kristijan (Croatia)
DISASTER VICTIMS (Agenda item 86)
A/C.6/78/SR.6

Papathanasiou, Artemis (Greece)
ARMS RACE—OUTER SPACE (Agenda item 97a)
A/C.1/78/PV.17
OUTER SPACE—PRINCIPLES (Agenda item 97d)
A/C.1/78/PV.17

Paranhos, Pedro Barreto Da Rocha (Brazil)
FREEDOM OF EXPRESSION (Agenda item 71b)
A/C.3/78/SR.19

Paranhos, Pedro Barreto Da Rocha (Brazil) (continued)

HUMAN RIGHTS—TERRITORIES OCCUPIED BY ISRAEL (Agenda item 71c)
A/C.3/78/SR.35
HUMAN RIGHTS ACTIVISTS (Agenda item 71b)
A/C.3/78/SR.19
RIGHT TO DEVELOPMENT (Agenda item 71b)
A/C.3/78/SR.20

Paredes Campaña, Jairo Andrés (Colombia)

CRIME PREVENTION (Agenda item 107)
A/C.3/78/SR.56
DISAPPEARANCE OF PERSONS (Agenda item 71b)
A/C.3/78/SR.22
RIGHT TO THE TRUTH (Agenda item 71b)
A/C.3/78/SR.22

Parihar, Rajesh (India)

AFRICA—DEVELOPMENT (Agenda item 65b)
A/78/PV.18
AFRICA—SUSTAINABLE DEVELOPMENT—PARTNERSHIP (Agenda item 65a)
A/78/PV.18
CONVENTIONAL WEAPONS (Agenda item 99u)
A/C.1/78/PV.19
CONVENTIONAL WEAPONS—TREATIES (Agenda item 103)
A/C.1/78/PV.19
DISARMAMENT—GENERAL AND COMPLETE (Agenda item 99)
A/C.1/78/PV.19
HUMAN RIGHTS—REPORTS (Agenda item 71c)
A/C.3/78/SR.25
INFORMATION—INTERNATIONAL SECURITY (Agenda item 94)
A/C.1/78/PV.29
LANDMINES—TREATIES (Agenda item 99m)
A/C.1/78/PV.19
TRAFFICKING IN PERSONS (Agenda item 71b)
A/C.3/78/SR.23

Park, Jeewon (Republic of Korea)

PEACEBUILDING (Agenda item 61)
A/78/PV.101
UN. PEACEBUILDING COMMISSION—REPORTS (Agenda item 27)
A/78/PV.101
UN. PEACEBUILDING FUND—REPORTS (Agenda item 111)
A/78/PV.101

Parmanand, Sosheena Foranda (Guyana)

UN YOUTH OFFICE—REPORTS (Agenda item 130)
A/78/PV.102

Parra-Lancourt, Mariangela (UN. Department of Economic and Social Affairs. Financing for Sustainable Development Office. Strategic Engagement and Policy Integration Branch. Chief)

COMMODITIES (Agenda item 16d)
A/C.2/78/SR.14
SUSTAINABLE DEVELOPMENT (Agenda item 18)
A/C.2/78/SR.14

Pary Rodríguez, Diego (Bolivia (Plurinational State of))

BIOLOGICAL DIVERSITY—TREATIES (Agenda item 18f)
A/C.2/78/SR.13
CLIMATE (Agenda item 18d)
A/C.2/78/SR.13
CUBA—UNITED STATES (Agenda item 38)
A/78/PV.26
DECOLONIZATION (Agenda item 58)
A/C.4/78/SR.2
ECONOMIC SANCTIONS—INTERNATIONAL RELATIONS (Agenda item 28)
A/78/PV.90
FALKLAND ISLANDS (MALVINAS) QUESTION (Agenda item 42)
A/C.4/78/SR.2
HUMAN RIGHTS—INTERNATIONAL INSTRUMENTS (Agenda item 71a)
A/C.3/78/SR.26
INDIGENOUS PEOPLES (Agenda item 68a)
A/C.3/78/SR.15
INDIGENOUS PEOPLES—CONFERENCES (Agenda item 68b)
A/C.3/78/SR.15
INFORMATION TECHNOLOGY—DEVELOPMENT (Agenda item 15)
A/C.2/78/SR.11
MILLENNIUM SUMMIT—CONFERENCES (Agenda item 117)
A/78/PV.15
SUSTAINABLE DEVELOPMENT (Agenda item 18)
A/C.2/78/SR.13
SUSTAINABLE ENERGY (Agenda item 18h)
A/C.2/78/SR.13
TERRITORIES OCCUPIED BY ISRAEL—NATURAL RESOURCES (Agenda item 59)
A/C.2/78/SR.19
TERRORISM (Agenda item 109)
A/C.6/78/SR.3
UN. GENERAL ASSEMBLY (78TH SESS. : 2023-2024). 1ST COMMITTEE—GENERAL DEBATE (Agenda item 8)
A/C.1/78/PV.4
UN. GENERAL ASSEMBLY (78TH SESS. : 2023-2024). 2ND COMMITTEE—GENERAL DEBATE (Agenda item 8)
A/C.2/78/SR.4
UN. SECURITY COUNCIL—MEMBERSHIP (Agenda item 121)
A/78/PV.36

Pary Rodríguez, Diego (Bolivia (Plurinational State of)) (continued)
UN. SECURITY COUNCIL—REPORTS (Agenda item 26)
A/78/PV.94
UN CONFERENCES (Agenda item 13)
A/78/PV.15
VETO (Agenda item 63)
A/78/PV.60
WESTERN SAHARA QUESTION (Agenda item 58)
A/C.4/78/SR.2

Passmoor, Jonathan David (South Africa)
ELECTION VERIFICATION—UN (Agenda item 71b)
A/C.3/78/SR.50
HEALTH (Agenda item 125)
A/78/PV.41
HUMAN RIGHTS—TERRITORIES OCCUPIED BY ISRAEL (Agenda item 71c)
A/C.3/78/SR.35
RACIAL DISCRIMINATION—ELIMINATION (Agenda item 69a)
A/C.3/78/SR.47
RACIAL DISCRIMINATION—PROGRAMMES OF ACTION (Agenda item 69b)
A/C.3/78/SR.40; A/C.3/78/SR.56
RESPONSIBILITY TO PROTECT (Agenda item 129)
A/78/PV.96
RIGHT TO DEVELOPMENT (Agenda item 71b)
A/C.3/78/SR.20
SANCTIONS—INTERNATIONAL RELATIONS (Agenda item 71b)
A/C.3/78/SR.28
SELF-DETERMINATION OF PEOPLES (Agenda item 70)
A/C.3/78/SR.43; A/C.3/78/SR.49
SEXUAL ORIENTATION (Agenda item 71b)
A/C.3/78/SR.39
TERRORISM—HUMAN RIGHTS (Agenda item 71b)
A/C.3/78/SR.31
UN. SECURITY COUNCIL—MEMBERSHIP (Agenda item 121)
A/78/PV.34
WOMEN'S ADVANCEMENT (Agenda item 25a)
A/C.3/78/SR.8
WOMEN'S ADVANCEMENT—CONFERENCES (Agenda item 25b)
A/C.3/78/SR.8

Pasternak Jørgensen, Vibeke (Denmark)
UN. INTERNATIONAL COURT OF JUSTICE—REPORTS (Agenda item 73)
A/78/PV.20
UN. INTERNATIONAL LAW COMMISSION—REPORTS (Agenda item 79)
A/C.6/78/SR.23

Patel, Yojna (India)
HIV/AIDS—DECLARATIONS (Agenda item 10)
A/78/PV.91

Patel, Yojna (India) (continued)
UN. SECURITY COUNCIL—MEMBERSHIP (Agenda item 121)
A/78/PV.104
UN YOUTH OFFICE—REPORTS (Agenda item 130)
A/78/PV.102

Pättikangas, Paula (Finland)
YOUTH (Agenda item 24b)
A/C.3/78/SR.3

Patton, Dorothy (United States)
ADMINISTRATION OF JUSTICE (Agenda item 144)
A/C.6/78/SR.9
INTERNATIONAL LAW—TRAINING PROGRAMMES (Agenda item 78)
A/C.6/78/SR.21
INTERNATIONAL PARLIAMENTARIANS' CONGRESS—OBSERVER STATUS (Agenda item 170)
A/C.6/78/SR.14
PEACEKEEPING OPERATIONS—CRIMINAL LIABILITY (Agenda item 76)
A/C.6/78/SR.8
TERRORISM (Agenda item 109)
A/C.6/78/SR.1
TREATIES (Agenda item 87)
A/C.6/78/SR.20
UN. COMMITTEE ON RELATIONS WITH THE HOST COUNTRY—REPORTS (Agenda item 161)
A/C.6/78/SR.35
UN CHARTER—REPORTS (Agenda item 82)
A/C.6/78/SR.22

Paulauskas, Rytis (Lithuania)
INTERNATIONAL JURISDICTION (Agenda item 84)
A/C.6/78/SR.12
ORGANIZATION FOR DEMOCRACY AND ECONOMIC DEVELOPMENT - GUAM (Agenda item 32)
A/78/PV.85
SUSTAINABLE DEVELOPMENT (Agenda item 18)
A/C.2/78/SR.15; A/C.2/78/SR.22
UN. INTERNATIONAL COURT OF JUSTICE—REPORTS (Agenda item 73)
A/78/PV.27
VETO (Agenda item 63)
A/78/PV.68

Paulauskas, Rytis (Lithuania) (UN. General Assembly. 1st Committee. Chair)
UN. GENERAL ASSEMBLY (78TH SESS. : 2023-2024). 1ST COMMITTEE—GENERAL DEBATE (Agenda item 8)
A/C.1/78/PV.2; A/C.1/78/PV.7
UN. GENERAL ASSEMBLY (78TH SESS. : 2023-2024). 1ST COMMITTEE—WORK ORGANIZATION (Agenda item 7)
A/C.1/78/PV.1; A/C.1/78/PV.30

Pauli, Aurore N'zassa Julianne (Switzerland)
FINANCIAL FLOWS (Agenda item 16f)
A/C.2/78/SR.23

Pavel, Petr (Czechia. President)
UN. GENERAL ASSEMBLY (78TH SESS. : 2023-2024)—GENERAL DEBATE (Agenda item 8)
A/78/PV.5
UN. GENERAL ASSEMBLY (78TH SESS. : 2023-2024)—SPECIAL STATEMENTS
A/78/PV.5

Pavlov, Vasiliy (Belarus)
UN. GENERAL ASSEMBLY (78TH SESS. : 2023-2024). 1ST COMMITTEE—GENERAL DEBATE (Agenda item 8)
A/C.1/78/PV.5

Pavļuta-Deslandes, Sanita (Latvia)
ARMED CONFLICTS PREVENTION (Agenda item 31a)
A/78/PV.72
HUMAN RIGHTS ADVANCEMENT (Agenda item 71b)
A/C.3/78/SR.18
INFORMATION (Agenda item 53)
A/C.4/78/SR.13
INTERNATIONAL RESIDUAL MECHANISM FOR CRIMINAL TRIBUNALS (Agenda item 126)
A/78/PV.19
RESPONSIBILITY TO PROTECT (Agenda item 129)
A/78/PV.96
RIGHT OF ASSEMBLY (Agenda item 71b)
A/C.3/78/SR.19
UN. GENERAL ASSEMBLY (78TH SESS. : 2023-2024)—OFFICERS (Agenda item 5)
A/C.4/78/SR.28
UN. GENERAL ASSEMBLY (78TH SESS. : 2023-2024). 1ST COMMITTEE—GENERAL DEBATE (Agenda item 8)
A/C.1/78/PV.3
WOMEN'S ADVANCEMENT (Agenda item 25a)
A/C.3/78/SR.7
WOMEN'S ADVANCEMENT—CONFERENCES (Agenda item 25b)
A/C.3/78/SR.7

Pedraza Calleja, Rodrigo (Mexico)
SEXUAL ORIENTATION (Agenda item 71b)
A/C.3/78/SR.39

Pedroso Cuesta, Pedro Luis (Cuba)
UN CONFERENCES (Agenda item 13)
A/78/PV.52

Pedroza, David (Peru)
POVERTY—HUMAN RIGHTS (Agenda item 71b)
A/C.3/78/SR.30

Pedroza, David (Peru) (continued)
SEXUAL ORIENTATION (Agenda item 71b)
A/C.3/78/SR.39
UN. HUMAN RIGHTS COUNCIL—REPORTS (Agenda item 66)
A/C.3/78/SR.46

Peláez Narváez, Ana (UN. Committee on the Elimination of Discrimination against Women. Chair)
WOMEN'S ADVANCEMENT (Agenda item 25a)
A/C.3/78/SR.7
WOMEN'S ADVANCEMENT—CONFERENCES (Agenda item 25b)
A/C.3/78/SR.7

Pell, Herbert (United States)
MILLENNIUM SUMMIT—CONFERENCES (Agenda item 117)
A/78/PV.102
UN CONFERENCES (Agenda item 13)
A/78/PV.102

Pella, Blandina Ruth Viditha Adeleide (Indonesia)
CLIMATE CHANGE (Agenda item 71b)
A/C.3/78/SR.29
CRIME PREVENTION (Agenda item 107)
A/C.3/78/SR.6; A/C.3/78/SR.56
CYBERCRIME (Agenda item 108)
A/C.3/78/SR.6
HEALTH (Agenda item 125)
A/78/PV.48
HUMAN RIGHTS ACTIVISTS (Agenda item 71b)
A/C.3/78/SR.19
HUMAN RIGHTS ADVANCEMENT (Agenda item 71b)
A/C.3/78/SR.52
INDIGENOUS PEOPLES (Agenda item 68a)
A/C.3/78/SR.17

Peña Palacios, Santiago (Paraguay. President)
UN. GENERAL ASSEMBLY (78TH SESS. : 2023-2024)—GENERAL DEBATE (Agenda item 8)
A/78/PV.5
UN. GENERAL ASSEMBLY (78TH SESS. : 2023-2024)—SPECIAL STATEMENTS
A/78/PV.5

Peñalver Portal, Gerardo (Cuba)
CRIMES AGAINST HUMANITY (Agenda item 80)
A/C.6/78/SR.10
HEALTH (Agenda item 125)
A/78/PV.41
IAEA—REPORTS (Agenda item 89)
A/78/PV.30
MIDDLE EAST—NUCLEAR-WEAPON-FREE ZONES (Agenda item 95)
A/C.1/78/PV.11

Peñalver Portal, Gerardo (Cuba) (continued)

MILLENNIUM SUMMIT—CONFERENCES (Agenda item 117)
A/78/PV.15
NUCLEAR DISARMAMENT (Agenda item 99b)
A/C.1/78/PV.11
NUCLEAR NON-PROLIFERATION—INTERNATIONAL OBLIGATIONS (Agenda item 99w)
A/C.1/78/PV.11
NUCLEAR WEAPONS—TREATIES (Agenda item 99ff)
A/C.1/78/PV.11
TERRITORIES OCCUPIED BY ISRAEL—NATURAL RESOURCES (Agenda item 59)
A/C.2/78/SR.19
TERRORISM (Agenda item 109)
A/C.6/78/SR.2
UN CONFERENCES (Agenda item 13)
A/78/PV.15
VETO (Agenda item 63)
A/78/PV.51; A/78/PV.60

Peñalver Portal, Gerardo (Cuba) (Group of 77)

INFORMATION (Agenda item 53)
A/C.4/78/SR.13
LAW OF THE SEA (Agenda item 75a)
A/78/PV.43
MARINE ECOSYSTEMS—BIOLOGICAL DIVERSITY (Agenda item 75c)
A/78/PV.43
MILLENNIUM SUMMIT—CONFERENCES (Agenda item 117)
A/78/PV.15
STRADDLING FISH STOCKS (Agenda item 75b)
A/78/PV.43
UN CONFERENCES (Agenda item 13)
A/78/PV.15

Peñaranda, Ariel Rodelas (Philippines)

LAW OF THE SEA (Agenda item 75a)
A/78/PV.43
MARINE ECOSYSTEMS—BIOLOGICAL DIVERSITY (Agenda item 75c)
A/78/PV.43
PALESTINE QUESTION (Agenda item 35)
A/78/PV.39
STRADDLING FISH STOCKS (Agenda item 75b)
A/78/PV.43
TERRORISM (Agenda item 109)
A/C.6/78/SR.2
UN. GENERAL ASSEMBLY (78TH SESS. : 2023-2024)—OFFICERS (Agenda item 5)
A/C.5/78/SR.1
UN. GENERAL ASSEMBLY (78TH SESS. : 2023-2024). 1ST COMMITTEE—GENERAL DEBATE (Agenda item 8)
A/C.1/78/PV.3
UN. INTERNATIONAL LAW COMMISSION—REPORTS (Agenda item 79)
A/C.6/78/SR.32

Peñaranda, Ariel Rodelas (Philippines) (continued)

WOMEN'S ADVANCEMENT (Agenda item 25a)
A/C.3/78/SR.8
WOMEN'S ADVANCEMENT—CONFERENCES (Agenda item 25b)
A/C.3/78/SR.8

Peñaranda, Ariel Rodelas (Philippines) (ASEAN)

UN. GENERAL ASSEMBLY (78TH SESS. : 2023-2024). 1ST COMMITTEE—GENERAL DEBATE (Agenda item 8)
A/C.1/78/PV.2

Pendarovski, Stevo (North Macedonia. President)

UN. GENERAL ASSEMBLY (78TH SESS. : 2023-2024)—GENERAL DEBATE (Agenda item 8)
A/78/PV.10
UN. GENERAL ASSEMBLY (78TH SESS. : 2023-2024)—SPECIAL STATEMENTS
A/78/PV.10

Perdomo, María Paula (Chile)

HUMAN RIGHTS (Agenda item 71)
A/C.3/78/SR.16
RIGHTS OF THE CHILD (Agenda item 67)
A/C.3/78/SR.55
SOCIAL DEVELOPMENT—CONFERENCES (Agenda item 24a)
A/C.3/78/SR.4
WOMEN'S ADVANCEMENT (Agenda item 25a)
A/C.3/78/SR.7
WOMEN'S ADVANCEMENT—CONFERENCES (Agenda item 25b)
A/C.3/78/SR.7

Pereira Sosa, José Eduardo (Paraguay)

DECOLONIZATION (Agenda item 58)
A/C.4/78/SR.7
FALKLAND ISLANDS (MALVINAS) QUESTION (Agenda item 42)
A/C.4/78/SR.7
INDIGENOUS PEOPLES (Agenda item 68a)
A/C.3/78/SR.15
INDIGENOUS PEOPLES—CONFERENCES (Agenda item 68b)
A/C.3/78/SR.15
INTERNATIONAL CRIMINAL COURT—REPORTS (Agenda item 74)
A/78/PV.22
LANDLOCKED DEVELOPING COUNTRIES—CONFERENCES (Agenda item 20b)
A/C.2/78/SR.7
LEAST DEVELOPED COUNTRIES—CONFERENCES (Agenda item 20a)
A/C.2/78/SR.7
SOCIAL CONDITIONS (Agenda item 24b)
A/C.3/78/SR.3
SOCIAL DEVELOPMENT (Agenda item 24)
A/C.3/78/SR.3
TERRORISM (Agenda item 109)
A/C.6/78/SR.5

Pereira Sosa, José Eduardo (Paraguay) (continued)

UKRAINE—POLITICAL CONDITIONS (Agenda item 62)
A/78/PV.58
UN. GENERAL ASSEMBLY (78TH SESS. : 2023-2024). 1ST COMMITTEE—GENERAL DEBATE (Agenda item 8)
A/C.1/78/PV.9
UN. GENERAL ASSEMBLY (78TH SESS. : 2023-2024). 2ND COMMITTEE—GENERAL DEBATE (Agenda item 8)
A/C.2/78/SR.3
WESTERN SAHARA QUESTION (Agenda item 58)
A/C.4/78/SR.7

Perera, Amrith Rohan (Sri Lanka) (UN. General Assembly. 6th Committee. Working Group on Measures to Eliminate International Terrorism. Chair)

TERRORISM (Agenda item 109)
A/C.6/78/SR.36

Pérez Ayestarán, Joaquín Alberto (Venezuela (Bolivarian Republic of))

AFRICA—DEVELOPMENT (Agenda item 65b)
A/78/PV.18
AFRICA—SUSTAINABLE DEVELOPMENT—PARTNERSHIP (Agenda item 65a)
A/78/PV.18
CUBA—UNITED STATES (Agenda item 38)
A/78/PV.24
DECOLONIZATION (Agenda item 58)
A/C.4/78/SR.2
FALKLAND ISLANDS (MALVINAS) QUESTION (Agenda item 42)
A/C.4/78/SR.2
FRENCH POLYNESIA QUESTION (Agenda item 58)
A/C.4/78/SR.2
INTERNATIONAL CRIMINAL COURT—REPORTS (Agenda item 74)
A/78/PV.25
LAW OF THE SEA (Agenda item 75a)
A/78/PV.44
MARINE ECOSYSTEMS—BIOLOGICAL DIVERSITY (Agenda item 75c)
A/78/PV.44
NEW CALEDONIA QUESTION (Agenda item 58)
A/C.4/78/SR.2
STRADDLING FISH STOCKS (Agenda item 75b)
A/78/PV.44
TERRITORIES OCCUPIED BY ISRAEL—HUMAN RIGHTS (Agenda item 50)
A/C.4/78/SR.24
UKRAINE—POLITICAL CONDITIONS (Agenda item 62)
A/78/PV.58
UN. GENERAL ASSEMBLY (78TH SESS. : 2023-2024). 1ST COMMITTEE—GENERAL DEBATE (Agenda item 8)
A/C.1/78/PV.7

Pérez Ayestarán, Joaquín Alberto (Venezuela (Bolivarian Republic of)) (continued)

UN. SECURITY COUNCIL—MEMBERSHIP (Agenda item 121)
A/78/PV.35
UN SYSTEM—STRENGTHENING (Agenda item 122)
A/78/PV.107
VETO (Agenda item 63)
A/78/PV.59
WESTERN SAHARA QUESTION (Agenda item 58)
A/C.4/78/SR.2

Pérez Ayestarán, Joaquín Alberto (Venezuela (Bolivarian Republic of)) (Group of Friends in Defence of the Charter of the United Nations)

2030 AGENDA—PROGRAMME IMPLEMENTATION (Agenda item 18a)
A/C.2/78/SR.12
CLIMATE (Agenda item 18d)
A/C.2/78/SR.12
DECOLONIZATION (Agenda item 58)
A/C.4/78/SR.2
DEVELOPMENT FINANCE (Agenda item 16b)
A/C.2/78/SR.8
GLOBALIZATION—INTERDEPENDENCE (Agenda item 19)
A/C.2/78/SR.10
HEALTH (Agenda item 125)
A/78/PV.16; A/78/PV.41
HUMAN RIGHTS (Agenda item 71)
A/C.3/78/SR.24
HUMAN RIGHTS—REPORTS (Agenda item 71c)
A/C.3/78/SR.24
INFORMATION (Agenda item 53)
A/C.4/78/SR.12
INTERNATIONAL TRADE (Agenda item 16a)
A/C.2/78/SR.8
INVESTMENT PROMOTION (Agenda item 16g)
A/C.2/78/SR.8
MACROECONOMIC POLICY (Agenda item 16)
A/C.2/78/SR.8
MILLENNIUM SUMMIT—CONFERENCES (Agenda item 117)
A/78/PV.15
RIGHT TO DEVELOPMENT (Agenda item 71b)
A/C.3/78/SR.20
RULE OF LAW (Agenda item 83)
A/C.6/78/SR.15
SUSTAINABLE DEVELOPMENT (Agenda item 18)
A/C.2/78/SR.12
TERRORISM (Agenda item 109)
A/C.6/78/SR.2
UN. COMMITTEE ON RELATIONS WITH THE HOST COUNTRY—REPORTS (Agenda item 161)
A/C.6/78/SR.35
UN. HUMAN RIGHTS COUNCIL—REPORTS (Agenda item 66)
A/78/PV.23
UN. SECRETARY-GENERAL—REPORTS (Agenda item 110)
A/78/PV.55
UN CONFERENCES (Agenda item 13)
A/78/PV.15

Pérez Ayestarán, Joaquín Alberto (Venezuela (Bolivarian Republic of)) (Group of Friends in Defence of the Charter of the United Nations) (continued)

UNRWA—ACTIVITIES (Agenda item 49)
A/C.4/78/SR.23
VETO (Agenda item 63)
A/78/PV.3; A/78/PV.59

Pérez Loose, Hernán (Ecuador)

INDIGENOUS PEOPLES (Agenda item 68a)
A/C.3/78/SR.15
INDIGENOUS PEOPLES—CONFERENCES (Agenda item 68b)
A/C.3/78/SR.15
VETO (Agenda item 63)
A/78/PV.3

Pérez Manríquez, Alfredo Uriel (Mexico)

CRIMES AGAINST HUMANITY (Agenda item 80)
A/C.6/78/SR.41; A/C.6/78/SR.43

Perino, Romina ((personal capacity))

WESTERN SAHARA QUESTION (Agenda item 58)
A/C.4/78/SR.6

Perrez, Franz (Switzerland)

UN. INTERNATIONAL COURT OF JUSTICE—REPORTS (Agenda item 73)
A/78/PV.20

Persaud, Trishala Simantini (Guyana)

VETO (Agenda item 63)
A/78/PV.75

Peters, Winston (New Zealand. Deputy Prime Minister)

UN. GENERAL ASSEMBLY (78TH SESS. : 2023-2024)—SPECIAL STATEMENTS
A/78/PV.66
VETO (Agenda item 63)
A/78/PV.66

Petit, Camille (France)

ARMS RACE—OUTER SPACE (Agenda item 97a)
A/C.1/78/PV.17
ARMS TRANSFERS—TREATIES (Agenda item 99x)
A/C.1/78/PV.18
BIOLOGICAL WEAPONS—TREATIES (Agenda item 106)
A/C.1/78/PV.15
CHEMICAL WEAPONS—TREATIES (Agenda item 99l)
A/C.1/78/PV.15
CLUSTER MUNITIONS (Agenda item 99dd)
A/C.1/78/PV.18
CONVENTIONAL WEAPONS (Agenda item 99u)
A/C.1/78/PV.18
CONVENTIONAL WEAPONS—TREATIES (Agenda item 103)
A/C.1/78/PV.18

Petit, Camille (France) (continued)

DISARMAMENT—GENERAL AND COMPLETE (Agenda item 99)
A/C.1/78/PV.18; A/C.1/78/PV.26; A/C.1/78/PV.30
DISARMAMENT AGREEMENTS—OUTER SPACE (Agenda item 97c)
A/C.1/78/PV.17
INFORMATION—INTERNATIONAL SECURITY (Agenda item 94)
A/C.1/78/PV.21; A/C.1/78/PV.28
LANDMINES—TREATIES (Agenda item 99m)
A/C.1/78/PV.18; A/C.1/78/PV.19
MEDITERRANEAN REGION—REGIONAL SECURITY (Agenda item 104)
A/C.1/78/PV.25
MIDDLE EAST—NUCLEAR-WEAPON-FREE ZONES (Agenda item 95)
A/C.1/78/PV.25
MULTILATERALISM—DISARMAMENT (Agenda item 99r)
A/C.1/78/PV.22
NUCLEAR DISARMAMENT (Agenda item 99b)
A/C.1/78/PV.11
NUCLEAR NON-PROLIFERATION—INTERNATIONAL OBLIGATIONS (Agenda item 99w)
A/C.1/78/PV.11
NUCLEAR WEAPONS—ELIMINATION (Agenda item 99z)
A/C.1/78/PV.26
OUTER SPACE—CONFIDENCE-BUILDING MEASURES (Agenda item 99v)
A/C.1/78/PV.17
OUTER SPACE—PRINCIPLES (Agenda item 97d)
A/C.1/78/PV.17
SMALL ARMS—ILLICIT TRAFFIC (Agenda item 99p)
A/C.1/78/PV.18
SMALL ARMS—ILLICIT TRAFFIC—ASSISTANCE (Agenda item 99n)
A/C.1/78/PV.18
UN. CONFERENCE ON DISARMAMENT—REPORTS (Agenda item 101a)
A/C.1/78/PV.22
UN. GENERAL ASSEMBLY (78TH SESS. : 2023-2024). 1ST COMMITTEE—GENERAL DEBATE (Agenda item 8)
A/C.1/78/PV.8

Petro Urrego, Gustavo (Colombia. President)

UN. GENERAL ASSEMBLY (78TH SESS. : 2023-2024)—GENERAL DEBATE (Agenda item 8)
A/78/PV.4
UN. GENERAL ASSEMBLY (78TH SESS. : 2023-2024)—SPECIAL STATEMENTS
A/78/PV.4

Pg Ibrahim, Dk Nur Maseleiana Rahimah (Brunei Darussalam)

INFORMATION TECHNOLOGY—DEVELOPMENT (Agenda item 15)
A/C.2/78/SR.10

Pham, Cao Cuong (Viet Nam)

UN. GENERAL ASSEMBLY (78TH SESS. : 2023-2024). 5TH COMMITTEE—WORK ORGANIZATION (Agenda item 7)
A/C.5/78/SR.26/PartII; A/C.5/78/SR.40

Pham, Minh Chinh (Viet Nam. Prime Minister)

UN. GENERAL ASSEMBLY (78TH SESS. : 2023-2024)—GENERAL DEBATE (Agenda item 8)
A/78/PV.11
UN. GENERAL ASSEMBLY (78TH SESS. : 2023-2024)—SPECIAL STATEMENTS
A/78/PV.11

Pham, Nha (Viet Nam)

INTERNATIONAL JURISDICTION (Agenda item 84)
A/C.6/78/SR.13

Philakone, Khamphinh (Lao People's Democratic Republic) (ASEAN)

DISARMAMENT—GENERAL AND COMPLETE (Agenda item 99)
A/78/PV.105

Phuaknuem, Kanok (Thailand)

CLIMATE (Agenda item 18d)
A/C.2/78/SR.13
DISASTER PREVENTION (Agenda item 18c)
A/C.2/78/SR.13

Pichardo Urbina, Eleane Yaoska (Nicaragua)

AGEING PERSONS (Agenda item 24b)
A/C.3/78/SR.4
ARMED CONFLICTS PREVENTION (Agenda item 31a)
A/78/PV.72
CRIME PREVENTION (Agenda item 107)
A/C.3/78/SR.6
CYBERCRIME (Agenda item 108)
A/C.3/78/SR.6
HUMAN RIGHTS—BURUNDI (Agenda item 71c)
A/C.3/78/SR.36
HUMAN RIGHTS—DEMOCRATIC PEOPLE'S REPUBLIC OF KOREA (Agenda item 71c)
A/C.3/78/SR.33; A/C.3/78/SR.53
HUMAN RIGHTS—ERITREA (Agenda item 71c)
A/C.3/78/SR.36
HUMAN RIGHTS—ETHIOPIA (Agenda item 71c)
A/C.3/78/SR.36
HUMAN RIGHTS—IRAN (ISLAMIC REPUBLIC OF) (Agenda item 71c)
A/C.3/78/SR.34; A/C.3/78/SR.53
HUMAN RIGHTS—RUSSIAN FEDERATION (Agenda item 71c)
A/C.3/78/SR.37
HUMAN RIGHTS—SYRIAN ARAB REPUBLIC (Agenda item 71c)
A/C.3/78/SR.34; A/C.3/78/SR.54

Pichardo Urbina, Eleane Yaoska (Nicaragua) (continued)

PALESTINE QUESTION (Agenda item 35)
A/78/PV.40
PEACE (Agenda item 14)
A/78/PV.76; A/78/PV.82
PERSONS WITH DISABILITIES (Agenda item 24b)
A/C.3/78/SR.4
RACIAL DISCRIMINATION—ELIMINATION (Agenda item 69a)
A/C.3/78/SR.42; A/C.3/78/SR.47
RACIAL DISCRIMINATION—PROGRAMMES OF ACTION (Agenda item 69b)
A/C.3/78/SR.42
RESPONSIBILITY TO PROTECT (Agenda item 129)
A/78/PV.96
RIGHT TO DEVELOPMENT (Agenda item 71b)
A/C.3/78/SR.20
SANCTIONS—INTERNATIONAL RELATIONS (Agenda item 71b)
A/C.3/78/SR.28
SELF-DETERMINATION OF PEOPLES (Agenda item 70)
A/C.3/78/SR.42
SOCIAL CONDITIONS (Agenda item 24b)
A/C.3/78/SR.4
SOCIAL DEVELOPMENT (Agenda item 24)
A/C.3/78/SR.4
TORTURE AND OTHER CRUEL TREATMENT (Agenda item 71a)
A/C.3/78/SR.18
UN. HUMAN RIGHTS COUNCIL—REPORTS (Agenda item 66)
A/C.3/78/SR.46; A/C.3/78/SR.51
VETO (Agenda item 63)
A/78/PV.69
WOMEN'S ADVANCEMENT (Agenda item 25a)
A/C.3/78/SR.9
WOMEN'S ADVANCEMENT—CONFERENCES (Agenda item 25b)
A/C.3/78/SR.9
YOUTH (Agenda item 24b)
A/C.3/78/SR.4

Pickbourn, Lynda (University of Massachusetts at Amherst)

COMMODITIES (Agenda item 16d)
A/C.2/78/SR.14
SUSTAINABLE DEVELOPMENT (Agenda item 18)
A/C.2/78/SR.14

Pickens, Andrew (United Kingdom)

LAW OF THE SEA (Agenda item 75a)
A/78/PV.48

Pieris, Peter Mohan Maithri (Sri Lanka)

ARMS RACE—OUTER SPACE (Agenda item 97a)
A/C.1/78/PV.16

Pieris, Peter Mohan Maithri (Sri Lanka) (continued)

BIOLOGICAL WEAPONS—TREATIES (Agenda item 106)
A/C.1/78/PV.14
CHEMICAL WEAPONS—TREATIES (Agenda item 99l)
A/C.1/78/PV.14
CONVENTIONAL WEAPONS (Agenda item 99u)
A/C.1/78/PV.18
CRIMES AGAINST HUMANITY (Agenda item 80)
A/C.6/78/SR.10; A/C.6/78/SR.39; A/C.6/78/SR.42; A/C.6/78/SR.43; A/C.6/78/SR.44; A/C.6/78/SR.47
CUBA—UNITED STATES (Agenda item 38)
A/78/PV.26
DISARMAMENT—GENERAL AND COMPLETE (Agenda item 99)
A/78/PV.105
DISASTER VICTIMS (Agenda item 86)
A/C.6/78/SR.5
ECONOMIC COOPERATION AMONG DEVELOPING COUNTRIES (Agenda item 22b)
A/C.2/78/SR.18
IAEA—REPORTS (Agenda item 89)
A/78/PV.30
INFORMATION (Agenda item 53)
A/C.4/78/SR.13
INFORMATION—INTERNATIONAL SECURITY (Agenda item 94)
A/C.1/78/PV.20
INTERNATIONAL JURISDICTION (Agenda item 84)
A/C.6/78/SR.12
MINE CLEARANCE (Agenda item 46)
A/C.4/78/SR.10
NUCLEAR DISARMAMENT (Agenda item 99b)
A/C.1/78/PV.11
NUCLEAR NON-PROLIFERATION—INTERNATIONAL OBLIGATIONS (Agenda item 99w)
A/C.1/78/PV.11
NUCLEAR WEAPONS—TREATIES (Agenda item 99ff)
A/C.1/78/PV.11
OUTER SPACE—CONFIDENCE-BUILDING MEASURES (Agenda item 99v)
A/C.1/78/PV.16
OUTER SPACE—PEACEFUL USES—INTERNATIONAL COOPERATION (Agenda item 48)
A/C.4/78/SR.15
PEACE (Agenda item 14)
A/78/PV.76
PEACEKEEPING OPERATIONS (Agenda item 51)
A/C.4/78/SR.18
RACIAL DISCRIMINATION—ELIMINATION (Agenda item 69a)
A/C.3/78/SR.42
RACIAL DISCRIMINATION—PROGRAMMES OF ACTION (Agenda item 69b)
A/C.3/78/SR.42
RADIATION EFFECTS (Agenda item 47)
A/C.4/78/SR.11
RIGHTS OF THE CHILD (Agenda item 67)
A/C.3/78/SR.13

Pieris, Peter Mohan Maithri (Sri Lanka) (continued)

RULE OF LAW (Agenda item 83)
A/C.6/78/SR.16
SMALL ARMS—ILLICIT TRAFFIC (Agenda item 99p)
A/C.1/78/PV.18
SMALL ARMS—ILLICIT TRAFFIC—ASSISTANCE (Agenda item 99n)
A/C.1/78/PV.18
TERRORISM (Agenda item 109)
A/C.6/78/SR.1
UN. GENERAL ASSEMBLY—WORK PROGRAMME (Agenda item 120)
A/78/PV.33
UN. GENERAL ASSEMBLY (78TH SESS. : 2023-2024)—AGENDA (Agenda item 7)
A/78/PV.2
UN. GENERAL ASSEMBLY (78TH SESS. : 2023-2024). 1ST COMMITTEE—GENERAL DEBATE (Agenda item 8)
A/C.1/78/PV.4
UN. GENERAL ASSEMBLY (78TH SESS. : 2023-2024). 2ND COMMITTEE—GENERAL DEBATE (Agenda item 8)
A/C.2/78/SR.4
UN. SECURITY COUNCIL—MEMBERSHIP (Agenda item 121)
A/78/PV.104
UN RESOLUTIONS—IMPLEMENTATION (Agenda item 119)
A/78/PV.33
UNRWA—ACTIVITIES (Agenda item 49)
A/C.4/78/SR.22
VETO (Agenda item 63)
A/78/PV.61; A/78/PV.71
WEAPONS OF MASS DESTRUCTION—TERRORISM (Agenda item 99s)
A/C.1/78/PV.14
WOMEN'S ADVANCEMENT (Agenda item 25a)
A/C.3/78/SR.9
WOMEN'S ADVANCEMENT—CONFERENCES (Agenda item 25b)
A/C.3/78/SR.9

Pieris, Peter Mohan Maithri (Sri Lanka) (UN. General Assembly. Vice-President)

SPORTS—OLYMPIC GAMES (Agenda item 11)
A/78/PV.38

Pieris, Peter Mohan Maithri (Sri Lanka) (UN. Special Committee to Investigate Israeli Practices affecting the Human Rights of the Palestinian People and Other Arabs of the Occupied Territories. Chair)

TERRITORIES OCCUPIED BY ISRAEL—HUMAN RIGHTS (Agenda item 50)
A/C.4/78/SR.24

Pierre, Christopher (Haiti)

INFORMATION (Agenda item 53)
A/C.4/78/SR.13

Pierre, Christopher (Haiti) (continued)

PEACEKEEPING OPERATIONS (Agenda item 51)
A/C.4/78/SR.20
SPECIAL POLITICAL MISSIONS (Agenda item 52)
A/C.4/78/SR.21

Pierre, Neil (UN. Department of Economic and Social Affairs. Office of Intergovernmental Support and Coordination for Sustainable Development. Director)

OPERATIONAL ACTIVITIES—UN SYSTEM (Agenda item 22a)
A/C.2/78/SR.18

Pierre, Philip Joseph (Saint Lucia. Prime Minister)

UN. GENERAL ASSEMBLY (78TH SESS. : 2023-2024)—GENERAL DEBATE (Agenda item 8)
A/78/PV.10
UN. GENERAL ASSEMBLY (78TH SESS. : 2023-2024)—SPECIAL STATEMENTS
A/78/PV.10

Pierre, Wislyne (Haiti)

UN. GENERAL ASSEMBLY (78TH SESS. : 2023-2024). 1ST COMMITTEE—GENERAL DEBATE (Agenda item 8)
A/C.1/78/PV.8

Pierre Fabre, Celine (Haiti)

RIGHTS OF THE CHILD (Agenda item 67)
A/C.3/78/SR.14
SOCIAL DEVELOPMENT (Agenda item 24)
A/C.3/78/SR.4

Pietracci, Federica (UN System Chief Executives Board for Coordination)

JOINT INSPECTION UNIT (Agenda item 141)
A/C.5/78/SR.27; A/C.5/78/SR.29
UN—ADMINISTRATION (Agenda item 132)
A/C.5/78/SR.29

Pihaatae, François (Maohi Protestant Church (French Polynesia))

FRENCH POLYNESIA QUESTION (Agenda item 58)
A/C.4/78/SR.3

Pilipenko, Igor (Belarus)

CRIME PREVENTION (Agenda item 107)
A/C.3/78/SR.50
HEALTH (Agenda item 125)
A/78/PV.48
HUMAN RIGHTS (Agenda item 71)
A/C.3/78/SR.16
HUMAN RIGHTS—DEMOCRATIC PEOPLE'S REPUBLIC OF KOREA (Agenda item 71c)
A/78/PV.50; A/C.3/78/SR.53

Pilipenko, Igor (Belarus) (continued)

HUMAN RIGHTS—IRAN (ISLAMIC REPUBLIC OF) (Agenda item 71c)
A/78/PV.50; A/C.3/78/SR.53
HUMAN RIGHTS—MYANMAR (Agenda item 71c)
A/78/PV.50; A/C.3/78/SR.53
HUMAN RIGHTS—REPORTS (Agenda item 71c)
A/78/PV.50
HUMAN RIGHTS—SYRIAN ARAB REPUBLIC (Agenda item 71c)
A/78/PV.50; A/C.3/78/SR.54
HUMAN RIGHTS—UKRAINE (Agenda item 71c)
A/78/PV.50
RACIAL DISCRIMINATION—ELIMINATION (Agenda item 69a)
A/78/PV.50
RIGHT TO FOOD (Agenda item 71b)
A/C.3/78/SR.48
SANCTIONS—INTERNATIONAL RELATIONS (Agenda item 71b)
A/C.3/78/SR.48
UN. HUMAN RIGHTS COUNCIL—REPORTS (Agenda item 66)
A/78/PV.23
UN HIGH COMMISSIONER FOR REFUGEES—REPORTS (Agenda item 60)
A/C.3/78/SR.44

Pilipenko, Igor (Belarus) (Collective Security Treaty Organization)

RACIAL DISCRIMINATION—ELIMINATION (Agenda item 69a)
A/C.3/78/SR.47

Pillay, Navanethem (UN. Human Rights Council. Independent International Commission of Inquiry on the Occupied Palestinian Territory, including East Jerusalem, and Israel. Chair)

HUMAN RIGHTS—TERRITORIES OCCUPIED BY ISRAEL (Agenda item 71c)
A/C.3/78/SR.35

Pinheiro, Paulo Sérgio de M.S. (Independent International Commission of Inquiry on the Syrian Arab Republic)

HUMAN RIGHTS—SYRIAN ARAB REPUBLIC (Agenda item 71c)
A/C.3/78/SR.34

Pinto, Alessandro De Rezende (Brazil)

INTERNATIONAL CRIMINAL COURT—REPORTS (Agenda item 74)
A/78/PV.22; A/78/PV.25

Pinto Berrío, Harry Eduardo (Panama)

FALKLAND ISLANDS (MALVINAS) QUESTION (Agenda item 42)
A/C.4/78/SR.7

Pipia, Temur (Georgia)

RESPONSIBILITY TO PROTECT (Agenda item 129)
A/78/PV.97; A/78/PV.99

Pirc Musar, Nataša (Slovenia. President)

UN. GENERAL ASSEMBLY (78TH SESS. : 2023-2024)—GENERAL DEBATE (Agenda item 8)
A/78/PV.4
UN. GENERAL ASSEMBLY (78TH SESS. : 2023-2024)—SPECIAL STATEMENTS
A/78/PV.4

Pisarevich, Vadim (Belarus)

2030 AGENDA—PROGRAMME IMPLEMENTATION (Agenda item 18a)
A/C.2/78/SR.13
FOOD SECURITY (Agenda item 23a)
A/C.2/78/SR.16
OPERATIONAL ACTIVITIES—UN SYSTEM (Agenda item 22a)
A/C.2/78/SR.18
POVERTY—INTERNATIONAL DECADES (Agenda item 21a)
A/C.2/78/SR.16
RIGHT TO DEVELOPMENT (Agenda item 71b)
A/C.3/78/SR.20
RURAL POVERTY (Agenda item 21b)
A/C.2/78/SR.16
SUSTAINABLE DEVELOPMENT (Agenda item 18)
A/C.2/78/SR.13

Pittakis, Theodoulos (Cyprus)

CRIMES AGAINST HUMANITY (Agenda item 80)
A/C.6/78/SR.39; A/C.6/78/SR.41; A/C.6/78/SR.45
INTERNATIONAL CRIMINAL COURT—REPORTS (Agenda item 74)
A/78/PV.22
UN. COMMITTEE ON RELATIONS WITH THE HOST COUNTRY—REPORTS (Agenda item 161)
A/C.6/78/SR.37
UN. INTERNATIONAL COURT OF JUSTICE—REPORTS (Agenda item 73)
A/78/PV.28
UN. INTERNATIONAL LAW COMMISSION—REPORTS (Agenda item 79)
A/C.6/78/SR.28

Pizarro-Viales, Laura Raquel (Costa Rica)

COMMODITIES (Agenda item 16d)
A/C.2/78/SR.14
ELECTION VERIFICATION—UN (Agenda item 71b)
A/C.3/78/SR.50
RIGHT TO DEVELOPMENT (Agenda item 71b)
A/C.3/78/SR.48
SUSTAINABLE DEVELOPMENT (Agenda item 18)
A/C.2/78/SR.14

Poblete Troncoso, Moisés (Chile)

UN. INTERNATIONAL COURT OF JUSTICE—REPORTS (Agenda item 73)
A/78/PV.20

Poling, Caitlin (United States)

OUTER SPACE—PEACEFUL USES—INTERNATIONAL COOPERATION (Agenda item 48)
A/C.4/78/SR.16

Pollard, Catherine (UN. Under-Secretary-General for Management Strategy, Policy and Compliance)

PERSONNEL QUESTIONS—UN SYSTEM (Agenda item 142)
A/C.5/78/SR.10
UN—BUDGET (2024) (Agenda item 134)
A/C.5/78/SR.5; A/C.5/78/SR.13; A/C.5/78/SR.33
UN—FINANCIAL SITUATION (Agenda item 136)
A/C.5/78/SR.4; A/C.5/78/SR.6; A/C.5/78/SR.37; A/C.5/78/SR.38
UN—PROGRAMME PLANNING (Agenda item 135)
A/C.5/78/SR.5

Polyanskiy, Dmitry A. (Russian Federation)

TERRITORIES OCCUPIED BY ISRAEL—HUMAN RIGHTS (Agenda item 50)
A/C.4/78/SR.25
UKRAINE—POLITICAL CONDITIONS (Agenda item 62)
A/78/PV.99
UN. SECURITY COUNCIL—MEMBERSHIP (Agenda item 121)
A/78/PV.36; A/78/PV.104
VETO (Agenda item 63)
A/78/PV.61; A/78/PV.66; A/78/PV.70

Pongor, Magdolna (Hungary)

MIGRANTS—PROTECTION (Agenda item 71b)
A/C.3/78/SR.56
PERSONS WITH DISABILITIES—HUMAN RIGHTS (Agenda item 71a)
A/C.3/78/SR.38
WOMEN MIGRANT WORKERS (Agenda item 25a)
A/C.3/78/SR.49
WOMEN'S ADVANCEMENT (Agenda item 25a)
A/C.3/78/SR.10
WOMEN'S ADVANCEMENT—CONFERENCES (Agenda item 25b)
A/C.3/78/SR.10
YOUTH (Agenda item 24b)
A/C.3/78/SR.55

Ponikvar, Ursa (Slovenia)

WOMEN'S ADVANCEMENT (Agenda item 25a)
A/C.3/78/SR.7
WOMEN'S ADVANCEMENT—CONFERENCES (Agenda item 25b)
A/C.3/78/SR.7

Ponikvar Velázquez, Jasna (Slovenia)
ARMS TRANSFERS—TREATIES (Agenda item 99x)
A/C.1/78/PV.19
CLUSTER MUNITIONS (Agenda item 99dd)
A/C.1/78/PV.19
DISARMAMENT—GENERAL AND COMPLETE (Agenda item 99)
A/C.1/78/PV.19
LANDMINES—TREATIES (Agenda item 99m)
A/C.1/78/PV.19

Popadiuk, Mykola (Ukraine)
SOCIAL CONDITIONS (Agenda item 24b)
A/C.3/78/SR.3
YOUTH (Agenda item 24b)
A/C.3/78/SR.3

Popan, Simona (European Union)
ADMINISTRATION OF JUSTICE (Agenda item 144)
A/C.6/78/SR.9
CRIMES AGAINST HUMANITY (Agenda item 80)
A/C.6/78/SR.9; A/C.6/78/SR.38; A/C.6/78/SR.39; A/C.6/78/SR.41; A/C.6/78/SR.43; A/C.6/78/SR.44; A/C.6/78/SR.45
ECONOMIC SANCTIONS—INTERNATIONAL RELATIONS (Agenda item 28)
A/78/PV.89
INTERNATIONAL JURISDICTION (Agenda item 84)
A/C.6/78/SR.12
INTERNATIONAL LAW—TRAINING PROGRAMMES (Agenda item 78)
A/C.6/78/SR.21
INTERNATIONAL RESIDUAL MECHANISM FOR CRIMINAL TRIBUNALS (Agenda item 126)
A/78/PV.19
RESPONSIBILITY OF INTERNATIONAL ORGANIZATIONS (Agenda item 85)
A/C.6/78/SR.19
RULE OF LAW (Agenda item 83)
A/C.6/78/SR.15
UN. COMMITTEE ON RELATIONS WITH THE HOST COUNTRY—REPORTS (Agenda item 161)
A/C.6/78/SR.35
UN CHARTER—REPORTS (Agenda item 82)
A/C.6/78/SR.22

Popkov, Andrei N. (Belarus)
UN. INTERNATIONAL LAW COMMISSION—REPORTS (Agenda item 79)
A/C.6/78/SR.24; A/C.6/78/SR.28

Popowski, Maciej (European Union)
HUMANITARIAN ASSISTANCE (Agenda item 72)
A/78/PV.46

Pougin de La Maisonneuve, Axel (European Union)
COMMODITIES (Agenda item 16d)
A/C.2/78/SR.14

Pougin de La Maisonneuve, Axel (European Union) (continued)
DEVELOPMENT FINANCE—CONFERENCES (Agenda item 17)
A/C.2/78/SR.25
SUSTAINABLE DEVELOPMENT (Agenda item 18)
A/C.2/78/SR.14

Poveda Brito, Robert Alexander (Venezuela (Bolivarian Republic of))
ARMED CONFLICTS PREVENTION (Agenda item 31a)
A/78/PV.72
CRIME PREVENTION (Agenda item 107)
A/C.3/78/SR.6
CYBERCRIME (Agenda item 108)
A/C.3/78/SR.6
HUMAN RIGHTS—BURUNDI (Agenda item 71c)
A/C.3/78/SR.36
HUMAN RIGHTS—DEMOCRATIC PEOPLE'S REPUBLIC OF KOREA (Agenda item 71c)
A/78/PV.50; A/C.3/78/SR.33; A/C.3/78/SR.53
HUMAN RIGHTS—ERITREA (Agenda item 71c)
A/C.3/78/SR.36
HUMAN RIGHTS—ETHIOPIA (Agenda item 71c)
A/C.3/78/SR.36
HUMAN RIGHTS—IRAN (ISLAMIC REPUBLIC OF) (Agenda item 71c)
A/C.3/78/SR.34
HUMAN RIGHTS—REPORTS (Agenda item 71c)
A/78/PV.50; A/C.3/78/SR.25; A/C.3/78/SR.37
HUMAN RIGHTS—SYRIAN ARAB REPUBLIC (Agenda item 71c)
A/C.3/78/SR.34
HUMAN RIGHTS—TERRITORIES OCCUPIED BY ISRAEL (Agenda item 71c)
A/C.3/78/SR.35
INDIGENOUS PEOPLES (Agenda item 68a)
A/C.3/78/SR.17
MIGRANTS—PROTECTION (Agenda item 71b)
A/C.3/78/SR.23
RACIAL DISCRIMINATION—ELIMINATION (Agenda item 69a)
A/78/PV.50; A/C.3/78/SR.47
SANCTIONS—INTERNATIONAL RELATIONS (Agenda item 71b)
A/C.3/78/SR.28
SOLIDARITY (Agenda item 71b)
A/C.3/78/SR.32

Poveda Brito, Robert Alexander (Venezuela (Bolivarian Republic of)) (Group of Friends in Defence of the Charter of the United Nations)
CRIME PREVENTION (Agenda item 107)
A/C.3/78/SR.50
HUMAN RIGHTS (Agenda item 71)
A/C.3/78/SR.16
HUMAN RIGHTS—DEMOCRATIC PEOPLE'S REPUBLIC OF KOREA (Agenda item 71c)
A/C.3/78/SR.53

Poveda Brito, Robert Alexander (Venezuela (Bolivarian Republic of)) (Group of Friends in Defence of the Charter of the United Nations) (continued)

HUMAN RIGHTS—IRAN (ISLAMIC REPUBLIC OF) (Agenda item 71c)
A/C.3/78/SR.53
HUMAN RIGHTS—SYRIAN ARAB REPUBLIC (Agenda item 71c)
A/C.3/78/SR.54
HUMAN RIGHTS—UKRAINE (Agenda item 71c)
A/C.3/78/SR.53
SANCTIONS—INTERNATIONAL RELATIONS (Agenda item 71b)
A/C.3/78/SR.28; A/C.3/78/SR.48
UN HIGH COMMISSIONER FOR REFUGEES—REPORTS (Agenda item 60)
A/C.3/78/SR.44

Poveda Brito, Robert Alexander (Venezuela (Bolivarian Republic of)) (UN. General Assembly. 3rd Committee. Rapporteur)

CRIME PREVENTION (Agenda item 107)
A/78/PV.50
CYBERCRIME (Agenda item 108)
A/78/PV.50
HUMAN RIGHTS (Agenda item 71)
A/78/PV.50
HUMAN RIGHTS—INTERNATIONAL INSTRUMENTS (Agenda item 71a)
A/78/PV.50
HUMAN RIGHTS—PROGRAMMES OF ACTION (Agenda item 71d)
A/78/PV.50
HUMAN RIGHTS—REPORTS (Agenda item 71c)
A/78/PV.50
HUMAN RIGHTS ADVANCEMENT (Agenda item 71b)
A/78/PV.50
INDIGENOUS PEOPLES (Agenda item 68a)
A/78/PV.50
INDIGENOUS PEOPLES—CONFERENCES (Agenda item 68b)
A/78/PV.50
RACIAL DISCRIMINATION—ELIMINATION (Agenda item 69a)
A/78/PV.50
RACIAL DISCRIMINATION—PROGRAMMES OF ACTION (Agenda item 69b)
A/78/PV.50
RIGHTS OF THE CHILD (Agenda item 67)
A/78/PV.50
SELF-DETERMINATION OF PEOPLES (Agenda item 70)
A/78/PV.50
SOCIAL CONDITIONS (Agenda item 24b)
A/78/PV.50
SOCIAL DEVELOPMENT (Agenda item 24)
A/78/PV.50
SOCIAL DEVELOPMENT—CONFERENCES (Agenda item 24a)
A/78/PV.50
UN—PROGRAMME PLANNING (Agenda item 135)
A/78/PV.50

Poveda Brito, Robert Alexander (Venezuela (Bolivarian Republic of)) (UN. General Assembly. 3rd Committee. Rapporteur) (continued)

UN. GENERAL ASSEMBLY—WORK PROGRAMME (Agenda item 120)
A/78/PV.50
UN. HUMAN RIGHTS COUNCIL—REPORTS (Agenda item 66)
A/78/PV.50
UN HIGH COMMISSIONER FOR REFUGEES—REPORTS (Agenda item 60)
A/78/PV.50
WOMEN'S ADVANCEMENT (Agenda item 25a)
A/78/PV.50
WOMEN'S ADVANCEMENT—CONFERENCES (Agenda item 25b)
A/78/PV.50

Prabowo, Hari (Indonesia)

CLIMATE (Agenda item 18d)
A/C.2/78/SR.15
DEVELOPMENT COOPERATION—MIDDLE-INCOME COUNTRIES (Agenda item 19c)
A/C.2/78/SR.11
DEVELOPMENT FINANCE (Agenda item 16b)
A/C.2/78/SR.9
DISASTER PREVENTION (Agenda item 18c)
A/C.2/78/SR.15
ECONOMIC COOPERATION AMONG DEVELOPING COUNTRIES (Agenda item 22b)
A/C.2/78/SR.18
FOOD SECURITY (Agenda item 23a)
A/C.2/78/SR.17
HEALTH (Agenda item 125)
A/78/PV.16; A/78/PV.41
INFORMATION TECHNOLOGY—DEVELOPMENT (Agenda item 15)
A/C.2/78/SR.11
INVESTMENT PROMOTION (Agenda item 16g)
A/C.2/78/SR.9
LAW OF THE SEA (Agenda item 75a)
A/78/PV.44
MACROECONOMIC POLICY (Agenda item 16)
A/C.2/78/SR.9; A/C.2/78/SR.25
MARINE ECOSYSTEMS—BIOLOGICAL DIVERSITY (Agenda item 75c)
A/78/PV.44
OPERATIONAL ACTIVITIES—UN SYSTEM (Agenda item 22a)
A/C.2/78/SR.18
PEACE (Agenda item 14)
A/78/PV.82
POVERTY—INTERNATIONAL DECADES (Agenda item 21a)
A/C.2/78/SR.17
RESPONSIBILITY TO PROTECT (Agenda item 129)
A/78/PV.96
RURAL POVERTY (Agenda item 21b)
A/C.2/78/SR.17
STRADDLING FISH STOCKS (Agenda item 75b)
A/78/PV.44
SUSTAINABLE DEVELOPMENT (Agenda item 18)
A/C.2/78/SR.15

Prabowo, Hari (Indonesia) (continued)

TAXATION (Agenda item 16h)
A/C.2/78/SR.9
TERRITORIES OCCUPIED BY ISRAEL—NATURAL RESOURCES (Agenda item 59)
A/C.2/78/SR.19
TERRORISM (Agenda item 109)
A/C.6/78/SR.2
UKRAINE—POLITICAL CONDITIONS (Agenda item 62)
A/78/PV.57
VETO (Agenda item 63)
A/78/PV.60; A/78/PV.67; A/78/PV.75
WOMEN'S ADVANCEMENT (Agenda item 25a)
A/C.3/78/SR.10
WOMEN'S ADVANCEMENT—CONFERENCES (Agenda item 25b)
A/C.3/78/SR.10

Prabowo, Hari (Indonesia) (ASEAN)

RIGHTS OF THE CHILD (Agenda item 67)
A/C.3/78/SR.11
UN. GENERAL ASSEMBLY (78TH SESS. : 2023-2024). 2ND COMMITTEE—GENERAL DEBATE (Agenda item 8)
A/C.2/78/SR.2

Pretterhofer, Stefan (Austria)

ARMED CONFLICTS PREVENTION (Agenda item 31a)
A/78/PV.72
DISARMAMENT—GENERAL AND COMPLETE (Agenda item 99)
A/78/PV.105
HUMAN RIGHTS (Agenda item 71)
A/C.3/78/SR.16
HUMAN RIGHTS—INTERNATIONAL INSTRUMENTS (Agenda item 71a)
A/C.3/78/SR.24
HUMAN RIGHTS—PROGRAMMES OF ACTION (Agenda item 71d)
A/C.3/78/SR.24
HUMAN RIGHTS—TERRITORIES OCCUPIED BY ISRAEL (Agenda item 71c)
A/C.3/78/SR.35
IAEA—REPORTS (Agenda item 89)
A/78/PV.30
RACIAL DISCRIMINATION—ELIMINATION (Agenda item 69a)
A/C.3/78/SR.47
UN. INTERNATIONAL LAW COMMISSION—REPORTS (Agenda item 79)
A/C.6/78/SR.29
UN. SECURITY COUNCIL—REPORTS (Agenda item 26)
A/78/PV.93
VETO (Agenda item 63)
A/78/PV.3

Prince, Gomar Faruk Khandakar (Bangladesh)

TERRITORIES OCCUPIED BY ISRAEL—NATURAL RESOURCES (Agenda item 59)
A/C.2/78/SR.19

Pringle, Rachael (New Zealand)

ARMED CONFLICTS PREVENTION (Agenda item 31a)
A/78/PV.72
TAXATION (Agenda item 16h)
A/C.2/78/SR.25

Prizreni, Ingrit (Albania)

UN—BUDGET (2024) (Agenda item 134)
A/C.5/78/SR.34

Proskuryakov, Alexander S. (Russian Federation)

INTERNATIONAL JURISDICTION (Agenda item 84)
A/C.6/78/SR.12
LAW OF THE SEA (Agenda item 75a)
A/78/PV.44
MARINE ECOSYSTEMS—BIOLOGICAL DIVERSITY (Agenda item 75c)
A/78/PV.44
RULE OF LAW (Agenda item 83)
A/C.6/78/SR.17; A/C.6/78/SR.19
STRADDLING FISH STOCKS (Agenda item 75b)
A/78/PV.44
UN. COMMITTEE ON RELATIONS WITH THE HOST COUNTRY—REPORTS (Agenda item 161)
A/C.6/78/SR.35

Prosser, Amy (Australia)

DISASTER PREVENTION (Agenda item 18c)
A/C.2/78/SR.23

Prytula, Mykola (Ukraine)

CRIMES AGAINST HUMANITY (Agenda item 80)
A/C.6/78/SR.45
INTERNATIONAL CRIMINAL COURT—REPORTS (Agenda item 74)
A/78/PV.22
RIGHT TO EDUCATION (Agenda item 71b)
A/C.3/78/SR.27
TERRORISM (Agenda item 109)
A/C.6/78/SR.1
UN. GENERAL ASSEMBLY—WORK PROGRAMME (Agenda item 120)
A/78/PV.33
UN RESOLUTIONS—IMPLEMENTATION (Agenda item 119)
A/78/PV.33

Puarai, Tevaearai (Association Moruroa e Tatou (French Polynesia))

FRENCH POLYNESIA QUESTION (Agenda item 58)
A/C.4/78/SR.3

Pulchérie, Mayel Camille Asnayde (Congo)
WOMEN'S ADVANCEMENT (Agenda item 25a)
A/C.3/78/SR.9
WOMEN'S ADVANCEMENT—CONFERENCES (Agenda item 25b)
A/C.3/78/SR.9

Pullela, Shilpa Kadambari (Australia)
HEALTH (Agenda item 125)
A/78/PV.41
HUMAN RIGHTS—MYANMAR (Agenda item 71c)
A/C.3/78/SR.33
HUMAN RIGHTS—TERRITORIES OCCUPIED BY ISRAEL (Agenda item 71c)
A/C.3/78/SR.35
UN. HUMAN RIGHTS COUNCIL—REPORTS (Agenda item 66)
A/C.3/78/SR.46

Pureza, José Manuel (Portugal)
WESTERN SAHARA QUESTION (Agenda item 58)
A/C.4/78/SR.5

Quinet, Manon (Belgium)
YOUTH (Agenda item 24b)
A/C.3/78/SR.3

Quinn, Gerard (UN. Human Rights Council. Special Rapporteur on the Rights of Persons with Disabilities)
PERSONS WITH DISABILITIES—HUMAN RIGHTS (Agenda item 71a)
A/C.3/78/SR.38

Quinn-Maguire, Tanya (Federation of International Civil Servants' Associations)
PERSONNEL QUESTIONS—UN SYSTEM (Agenda item 142)
A/C.5/78/SR.10

Quintero Correa, Nohra María (Colombia)
BIOLOGICAL WEAPONS—TREATIES (Agenda item 106)
A/C.1/78/PV.16
CHEMICAL WEAPONS—TREATIES (Agenda item 99l)
A/C.1/78/PV.16
CONVENTIONAL WEAPONS (Agenda item 99u)
A/C.1/78/PV.18
DISARMAMENT—GENERAL AND COMPLETE (Agenda item 99)
A/C.1/78/PV.18
INFORMATION—INTERNATIONAL SECURITY (Agenda item 94)
A/C.1/78/PV.21
LANDMINES—TREATIES (Agenda item 99m)
A/C.1/78/PV.18; A/C.1/78/PV.28
NUCLEAR DISARMAMENT (Agenda item 99b)
A/C.1/78/PV.14

Quintero Correa, Nohra María (Colombia) (continued)
NUCLEAR NON-PROLIFERATION—INTERNATIONAL OBLIGATIONS (Agenda item 99w)
A/C.1/78/PV.14
NUCLEAR WEAPONS—ELIMINATION (Agenda item 99z)
A/C.1/78/PV.26
SMALL ARMS—ILLICIT TRAFFIC (Agenda item 99p)
A/C.1/78/PV.18; A/C.1/78/PV.28
SMALL ARMS—ILLICIT TRAFFIC—ASSISTANCE (Agenda item 99n)
A/C.1/78/PV.18
UN—PROGRAMME PLANNING (Agenda item 135)
A/C.1/78/PV.10
UN. GENERAL ASSEMBLY—WORK PROGRAMME (Agenda item 120)
A/C.1/78/PV.10
UN. GENERAL ASSEMBLY (78TH SESS. : 2023-2024). 1ST COMMITTEE—WORK ORGANIZATION (Agenda item 7)
A/C.1/78/PV.28; A/C.1/78/PV.30

Quinto González, Jatnael (Mexico)
HEALTH (Agenda item 125)
A/78/PV.102

Quirighetti, Giuseppe (Holy See)
PEACEKEEPING OPERATIONS (Agenda item 51)
A/C.4/78/SR.20

Qureshi, Hadeeqa (Pakistan)
DISAPPEARANCE OF PERSONS (Agenda item 71b)
A/C.3/78/SR.22
ELECTION VERIFICATION—UN (Agenda item 71b)
A/C.3/78/SR.50
FREEDOM OF EXPRESSION (Agenda item 71b)
A/C.3/78/SR.19
HUMAN RIGHTS—ERITREA (Agenda item 71c)
A/C.3/78/SR.36
HUMAN RIGHTS—IRAN (ISLAMIC REPUBLIC OF) (Agenda item 71c)
A/C.3/78/SR.53
HUMAN RIGHTS—TERRITORIES OCCUPIED BY ISRAEL (Agenda item 71c)
A/C.3/78/SR.35
MIGRANTS—PROTECTION (Agenda item 71b)
A/C.3/78/SR.23
MINORITIES (Agenda item 71b)
A/C.3/78/SR.39
POVERTY—HUMAN RIGHTS (Agenda item 71b)
A/C.3/78/SR.30
RACIAL DISCRIMINATION—ELIMINATION (Agenda item 69a)
A/C.3/78/SR.41
RACIAL DISCRIMINATION—PROGRAMMES OF ACTION (Agenda item 69b)
A/C.3/78/SR.41

Qureshi, Hadeeqa (Pakistan) (continued)

RIGHT TO FOOD (Agenda item 71b)
A/C.3/78/SR.30
RIGHTS OF THE CHILD (Agenda item 67)
A/C.3/78/SR.11; A/C.3/78/SR.14
SUMMARY EXECUTIONS (Agenda item 71b)
A/C.3/78/SR.31
TERRORISM—HUMAN RIGHTS (Agenda item 71b)
A/C.3/78/SR.31
TRAFFICKING IN PERSONS (Agenda item 71b)
A/C.3/78/SR.23
TRANSNATIONAL CORPORATIONS—HUMAN RIGHTS (Agenda item 71b)
A/C.3/78/SR.21
UN. HUMAN RIGHTS COUNCIL—REPORTS (Agenda item 66)
A/78/PV.28
UN HIGH COMMISSIONER FOR REFUGEES—REPORTS (Agenda item 60)
A/C.3/78/SR.44

Rabuka, Sitiveni Ligamamada (Fiji. Prime Minister)

UN. GENERAL ASSEMBLY (78TH SESS. : 2023-2024)—GENERAL DEBATE (Agenda item 8)
A/78/PV.10
UN. GENERAL ASSEMBLY (78TH SESS. : 2023-2024)—SPECIAL STATEMENTS
A/78/PV.10

Radev, Rumen (Bulgaria. President)

UN. GENERAL ASSEMBLY (78TH SESS. : 2023-2024)—GENERAL DEBATE (Agenda item 8)
A/78/PV.6
UN. GENERAL ASSEMBLY (78TH SESS. : 2023-2024)—SPECIAL STATEMENTS
A/78/PV.6

Radović, Branislav (Serbia)

HUMAN RIGHTS—INTERNATIONAL INSTRUMENTS (Agenda item 71a)
A/C.3/78/SR.27
MIGRANTS—PROTECTION (Agenda item 71b)
A/C.3/78/SR.27
PEACEKEEPING OPERATIONS (Agenda item 51)
A/C.4/78/SR.20
UN HIGH COMMISSIONER FOR REFUGEES—REPORTS (Agenda item 60)
A/C.3/78/SR.45

Rae, Robert (Canada)

ARMED CONFLICTS PREVENTION (Agenda item 31a)
A/78/PV.72
HUMAN RIGHTS—IRAN (ISLAMIC REPUBLIC OF) (Agenda item 71c)
A/C.3/78/SR.34
HUMAN RIGHTS—MYANMAR (Agenda item 71c)
A/C.3/78/SR.33
HUMAN RIGHTS—UKRAINE (Agenda item 71c)
A/C.3/78/SR.37

Rae, Robert (Canada) (continued)

INDIGENOUS PEOPLES (Agenda item 68a)
A/C.3/78/SR.15
INDIGENOUS PEOPLES—CONFERENCES (Agenda item 68b)
A/C.3/78/SR.15
INTERNATIONAL CRIMINAL COURT—REPORTS (Agenda item 74)
A/78/PV.22
TERRITORIES OCCUPIED BY ISRAEL—HUMAN RIGHTS (Agenda item 50)
A/78/PV.45
UKRAINE—POLITICAL CONDITIONS (Agenda item 62)
A/78/PV.57
UN. GENERAL ASSEMBLY (78TH SESS. : 2023-2024)—GENERAL DEBATE (Agenda item 8)
A/78/PV.14
UN HIGH COMMISSIONER FOR REFUGEES—REPORTS (Agenda item 60)
A/C.3/78/SR.44
VETO (Agenda item 63)
A/78/PV.66; A/78/PV.69; A/78/PV.79

Raed Dawood Al-Saadi, Amna (Iraq)

HUMAN RIGHTS ADVANCEMENT (Agenda item 71b)
A/C.3/78/SR.18
WOMEN'S ADVANCEMENT (Agenda item 25a)
A/C.3/78/SR.9
WOMEN'S ADVANCEMENT—CONFERENCES (Agenda item 25b)
A/C.3/78/SR.9

Raes, Elisa de (Belgium)

CRIMES AGAINST HUMANITY (Agenda item 80)
A/C.6/78/SR.38; A/C.6/78/SR.45
TREATIES (Agenda item 87)
A/C.6/78/SR.20
UN. INTERNATIONAL COURT OF JUSTICE—REPORTS (Agenda item 73)
A/78/PV.27

Raes, Elisa de (Belgium) (European Union)

MARINE ECOSYSTEMS—BIOLOGICAL DIVERSITY (Agenda item 75c)
A/78/PV.73

Rahimi Majd, Hassan (Iran (Islamic Republic of))

DISARMAMENT—GENERAL AND COMPLETE (Agenda item 99)
A/78/PV.106
VETO (Agenda item 63)
A/78/PV.78

Rahman, Siti Adibah Abdul (Malaysia)

AGEING PERSONS (Agenda item 24b)
A/C.3/78/SR.1

Rahman, Siti Adibah Abdul (Malaysia) (continued)
INDIGENOUS PEOPLES (Agenda item 68a)
A/C.3/78/SR.15
INDIGENOUS PEOPLES—CONFERENCES (Agenda item 68b)
A/C.3/78/SR.15
WOMEN'S ADVANCEMENT (Agenda item 25a)
A/C.3/78/SR.7
WOMEN'S ADVANCEMENT—CONFERENCES (Agenda item 25b)
A/C.3/78/SR.7

Rahmon, Emomali (Tajikistan. President)
UN. GENERAL ASSEMBLY (78TH SESS. : 2023-2024)—GENERAL DEBATE (Agenda item 8)
A/78/PV.6
UN. GENERAL ASSEMBLY (78TH SESS. : 2023-2024)—SPECIAL STATEMENTS
A/78/PV.6

Rai, Max (Papua New Guinea)
WOMEN'S ADVANCEMENT (Agenda item 25a)
A/C.3/78/SR.10
WOMEN'S ADVANCEMENT—CONFERENCES (Agenda item 25b)
A/C.3/78/SR.10

Rai, Pratigya (Nepal)
INDIGENOUS PEOPLES (Agenda item 68a)
A/C.3/78/SR.15
INDIGENOUS PEOPLES—CONFERENCES (Agenda item 68b)
A/C.3/78/SR.15

Raisi, Seyyed Ebrahim (Iran (Islamic Republic of). President)
UN. GENERAL ASSEMBLY (78TH SESS. : 2023-2024)—GENERAL DEBATE (Agenda item 8)
A/78/PV.5
UN. GENERAL ASSEMBLY (78TH SESS. : 2023-2024)—SPECIAL STATEMENTS
A/78/PV.5

Raivoso, Ilda (Mozambique)
RIGHT TO DEVELOPMENT (Agenda item 71b)
A/C.3/78/SR.26

Rajagopal, Balakrishnan (UN. Human Rights Council. Special Rapporteur on Adequate Housing as a Component of the Right to an Adequate Standard of Living)
RIGHT TO HOUSING (Agenda item 71b)
A/C.3/78/SR.30

Rajandran, Dhivya (Singapore)
CENTRAL ASIA—ZONES OF PEACE (Agenda item 64)
A/78/PV.85

Rajandran, Dhivya (Singapore) (continued)
ELECTION VERIFICATION—UN (Agenda item 71b)
A/C.3/78/SR.50
HEALTH (Agenda item 125)
A/78/PV.48
HUMAN RIGHTS—IRAN (ISLAMIC REPUBLIC OF) (Agenda item 71c)
A/C.3/78/SR.53
HUMAN RIGHTS—SYRIAN ARAB REPUBLIC (Agenda item 71c)
A/C.3/78/SR.54
HUMAN RIGHTS—UKRAINE (Agenda item 71c)
A/C.3/78/SR.53
HUMAN RIGHTS ADVANCEMENT (Agenda item 71b)
A/C.3/78/SR.52
RACIAL DISCRIMINATION—ELIMINATION (Agenda item 69a)
A/C.3/78/SR.47
RIGHTS OF THE CHILD (Agenda item 67)
A/C.3/78/SR.55
UN HIGH COMMISSIONER FOR REFUGEES—REPORTS (Agenda item 60)
A/C.3/78/SR.51

Rakhmetullin, Akan (Kazakhstan)
ARMS RACE—OUTER SPACE (Agenda item 97a)
A/C.1/78/PV.16
OUTER SPACE—CONFIDENCE-BUILDING MEASURES (Agenda item 99v)
A/C.1/78/PV.16
UN CONFERENCES (Agenda item 13)
A/78/PV.48

Rakhmetullin, Akan (Kazakhstan) (UN. Disarmament Commission. Chair)
UN. DISARMAMENT COMMISSION—REPORTS (Agenda item 101b)
A/C.1/78/PV.24

Rakovec, Marko (Slovenia)
UN. INTERNATIONAL COURT OF JUSTICE—REPORTS (Agenda item 73)
A/78/PV.20
UN. INTERNATIONAL LAW COMMISSION—REPORTS (Agenda item 79)
A/C.6/78/SR.27

Ramanathan, Chandramouli (UN. Controller)
AU-UN HYBRID OPERATION IN DARFUR—FINANCING (Agenda item 159)
A/C.5/78/SR.35
PEACEKEEPING OPERATIONS—FINANCING (Agenda item 146)
A/C.5/78/SR.35; A/C.5/78/SR.36
UN—BUDGET (2023) (Agenda item 133)
A/C.5/78/SR.9

Ramanathan, Chandramouli (UN. Controller) (continued)

UN—BUDGET (2024) (Agenda item 134)
A/C.5/78/SR.2; A/C.5/78/SR.4; A/C.5/78/SR.11; A/C.5/78/SR.16; A/C.5/78/SR.26/PartII; A/C.5/78/SR.28; A/C.5/78/SR.30; A/C.5/78/SR.33
UN—BUDGET CONTRIBUTIONS (Agenda item 138)
A/C.5/78/SR.1
UN—FINANCIAL REPORTS (Agenda item 131)
A/C.5/78/SR.35
UN—FINANCIAL SITUATION (Agenda item 136)
A/C.5/78/SR.6
UN. GENERAL ASSEMBLY (78TH SESS. : 2023-2024). 5TH COMMITTEE—WORK ORGANIZATION (Agenda item 7)
A/C.5/78/SR.26/PartII; A/C.5/78/SR.40
UN. SUPPORT OFFICE IN SOMALIA—FINANCING (Agenda item 160)
A/C.5/78/SR.35
UN DISENGAGEMENT OBSERVER FORCE—FINANCING (Agenda item 156a)
A/C.5/78/SR.35
UN INTERIM ADMINISTRATION MISSION IN KOSOVO—FINANCING (Agenda item 153)
A/C.5/78/SR.35
UN INTERIM FORCE IN LEBANON—FINANCING (Agenda item 156b)
A/C.5/78/SR.35
UN MISSION FOR THE REFERENDUM IN WESTERN SAHARA—FINANCING (Agenda item 158)
A/C.5/78/SR.35
UN MISSION IN SOUTH SUDAN—FINANCING (Agenda item 157)
A/C.5/78/SR.36
UN MULTIDIMENSIONAL INTEGRATED STABILIZATION MISSION IN MALI—FINANCING (Agenda item 155)
A/C.5/78/SR.36
UN MULTIDIMENSIONAL INTEGRATED STABILIZATION MISSION IN THE CENTRAL AFRICAN REPUBLIC—FINANCING (Agenda item 148)
A/C.5/78/SR.35
UN ORGANIZATION STABILIZATION MISSION IN THE DEMOCRATIC REPUBLIC OF THE CONGO—FINANCING (Agenda item 151)
A/C.5/78/SR.35
UN PEACEKEEPING FORCE IN CYPRUS—FINANCING (Agenda item 150)
A/C.5/78/SR.35
UN SECURITY FORCE FOR ABYEI—FINANCING (Agenda item 147)
A/C.5/78/SR.36

Ramaphosa, Matamela Cyril (South Africa. President)

UN. GENERAL ASSEMBLY (78TH SESS. : 2023-2024)—GENERAL DEBATE (Agenda item 8)
A/78/PV.4
UN. GENERAL ASSEMBLY (78TH SESS. : 2023-2024)—SPECIAL STATEMENTS
A/78/PV.4

Rambally, Menissa (Saint Lucia)

CUBA—UNITED STATES (Agenda item 38)
A/78/PV.24

Rambally, Menissa (Saint Lucia) (Caribbean Community)

CUBA—UNITED STATES (Agenda item 38)
A/78/PV.24
UN. SECURITY COUNCIL—MEMBERSHIP (Agenda item 121)
A/78/PV.34

Rambally, Menissa (Saint Lucia) (UN. Special Committee of 24. Chair)

DECOLONIZATION (Agenda item 58)
A/C.4/78/SR.2
DECOLONIZATION—UN SYSTEM (Agenda item 56)
A/C.4/78/SR.2
NON-SELF-GOVERNING TERRITORIES—ECONOMIC INTERESTS (Agenda item 55)
A/C.4/78/SR.2
NON-SELF-GOVERNING TERRITORIES—FELLOWSHIPS (Agenda item 57)
A/C.4/78/SR.2
NON-SELF-GOVERNING TERRITORIES—REPORTS (Agenda item 54)
A/C.4/78/SR.2

Ramboll, Unni (Norway)

DISPLACED PERSONS (Agenda item 71b)
A/C.3/78/SR.32; A/C.3/78/SR.49
MINE CLEARANCE (Agenda item 46)
A/C.4/78/SR.10

Ramírez Baca, Gustavo Adolfo (Costa Rica)

INTERNATIONAL JURISDICTION (Agenda item 84)
A/C.6/78/SR.12
TERRORISM (Agenda item 109)
A/C.6/78/SR.2

Ramírez Galindo, Sergio (Asociación Siembra Canaria)

WESTERN SAHARA QUESTION (Agenda item 58)
A/C.4/78/SR.4

Ramírez Marrero, Carmelo ((personal capacity))

WESTERN SAHARA QUESTION (Agenda item 58)
A/C.4/78/SR.4

Ramírez Soler, Henry (Fondazione Proclade Internazionale - Onlus)

WESTERN SAHARA QUESTION (Agenda item 58)
A/C.4/78/SR.4

Ramkalawan, Wavel (Seychelles. President)

UN. GENERAL ASSEMBLY (78TH SESS. : 2023-2024)—GENERAL DEBATE (Agenda item 8)
A/78/PV.6

Ramkalawan, Wavel (Seychelles. President) (continued)

UN. GENERAL ASSEMBLY (78TH SESS. : 2023-2024)—SPECIAL STATEMENTS
A/78/PV.6

Ramopoulos, Thomas (European Union)

DISASTER VICTIMS (Agenda item 86)
A/C.6/78/SR.5
LAW OF THE SEA (Agenda item 75a)
A/78/PV.43
MARINE ECOSYSTEMS—BIOLOGICAL DIVERSITY (Agenda item 75c)
A/78/PV.43
PEACEKEEPING OPERATIONS—CRIMINAL LIABILITY (Agenda item 76)
A/C.6/78/SR.8
STRADDLING FISH STOCKS (Agenda item 75b)
A/78/PV.43
TERRORISM (Agenda item 109)
A/C.6/78/SR.1
UN. INTERNATIONAL LAW COMMISSION—REPORTS (Agenda item 79)
A/C.6/78/SR.23; A/C.6/78/SR.30
UN COMMISSION ON INTERNATIONAL TRADE LAW—REPORTS (Agenda item 77)
A/C.6/78/SR.14

Ramos, Vanessa (American Association of Jurists)

WESTERN SAHARA QUESTION (Agenda item 58)
A/C.4/78/SR.5

Ramos-Horta, José (Timor-Leste. President)

UN. GENERAL ASSEMBLY (78TH SESS. : 2023-2024)—GENERAL DEBATE (Agenda item 8)
A/78/PV.8
UN. GENERAL ASSEMBLY (78TH SESS. : 2023-2024)—SPECIAL STATEMENTS
A/78/PV.8

Rando Ibáñez, Alicia (International Youth Organization for Ibero-America)

RIGHT TO CULTURE (Agenda item 71b)
A/C.3/78/SR.27

Raojee, Vreeshini (Mauritius) (UN. General Assembly. 6th Committee. Bureau)

INTERNATIONAL JURISDICTION (Agenda item 84)
A/C.6/78/SR.37

Rasmussen, Lea (Denmark)

UN HIGH COMMISSIONER FOR REFUGEES—REPORTS (Agenda item 60)
A/C.3/78/SR.44

Rathe, Fanny Elizabeth (Switzerland)

ADMINISTRATION OF JUSTICE (Agenda item 144)
A/C.6/78/SR.9
CRIMES AGAINST HUMANITY (Agenda item 80)
A/C.6/78/SR.10; A/C.6/78/SR.38; A/C.6/78/SR.40; A/C.6/78/SR.42; A/C.6/78/SR.43; A/C.6/78/SR.44; A/C.6/78/SR.45
TREATIES (Agenda item 87)
A/C.6/78/SR.20
UN. INTERNATIONAL LAW COMMISSION—REPORTS (Agenda item 79)
A/C.6/78/SR.24

Ratnamurti, Karina (Indonesia)

UN. GENERAL ASSEMBLY (78TH SESS. : 2023-2024). 5TH COMMITTEE—WORK ORGANIZATION (Agenda item 7)
A/C.5/78/SR.35

Ratner, Steven R. (UN. International Commission of Human Rights Experts on Ethiopia)

HUMAN RIGHTS—ETHIOPIA (Agenda item 71c)
A/C.3/78/SR.36

Rattray, Courtenay (UN. Under-Secretary-General and Chef de Cabinet)

RACIAL DISCRIMINATION—ELIMINATION (Agenda item 69a)
A/78/PV.63
SLAVERY—MEMORIALS (Agenda item 118)
A/78/PV.64

Ray, Anupam (India)

CHEMICAL WEAPONS—TREATIES (Agenda item 99l)
A/C.1/78/PV.26
DISARMAMENT—GENERAL AND COMPLETE (Agenda item 99)
A/C.1/78/PV.26; A/C.1/78/PV.28
NUCLEAR DISARMAMENT (Agenda item 99b)
A/C.1/78/PV.13
NUCLEAR NON-PROLIFERATION (Agenda item 99o)
A/C.1/78/PV.13
NUCLEAR WEAPONS—ELIMINATION (Agenda item 99z)
A/C.1/78/PV.26
NUCLEAR WEAPONS USE—TREATIES (Agenda item 100a)
A/C.1/78/PV.13
UN. GENERAL ASSEMBLY (78TH SESS. : 2023-2024). 1ST COMMITTEE—GENERAL DEBATE (Agenda item 8)
A/C.1/78/PV.6

Ray, Kaushal Kishor (Nepal)

DECOLONIZATION (Agenda item 58)
A/C.4/78/SR.6

Ray, Kaushal Kishor (Nepal) (continued)

FALKLAND ISLANDS (MALVINAS) QUESTION (Agenda item 42)
A/C.4/78/SR.6
HUMAN RIGHTS—INTERNATIONAL INSTRUMENTS (Agenda item 71a)
A/C.3/78/SR.25
HUMAN RIGHTS ADVANCEMENT (Agenda item 71b)
A/C.3/78/SR.25
INFORMATION (Agenda item 53)
A/C.4/78/SR.13
LANDLOCKED DEVELOPING COUNTRIES—CONFERENCES (Agenda item 20b)
A/C.2/78/SR.7
LEAST DEVELOPED COUNTRIES—CONFERENCES (Agenda item 20a)
A/C.2/78/SR.7
PEACEKEEPING OPERATIONS (Agenda item 51)
A/C.4/78/SR.19
RULE OF LAW (Agenda item 83)
A/C.6/78/SR.17
TERRITORIES OCCUPIED BY ISRAEL—HUMAN RIGHTS (Agenda item 50)
A/78/PV.45
WESTERN SAHARA QUESTION (Agenda item 58)
A/C.4/78/SR.6

Ray, Kaushal Kishor (Nepal) (Group of Least Developed Countries)

DEVELOPMENT FINANCE (Agenda item 16b)
A/C.2/78/SR.8
ECONOMIC COOPERATION AMONG DEVELOPING COUNTRIES (Agenda item 22b)
A/C.2/78/SR.18
INTERNATIONAL TRADE (Agenda item 16a)
A/C.2/78/SR.8
INVESTMENT PROMOTION (Agenda item 16g)
A/C.2/78/SR.8
LANDLOCKED DEVELOPING COUNTRIES—CONFERENCES (Agenda item 20b)
A/C.2/78/SR.7
LEAST DEVELOPED COUNTRIES—CONFERENCES (Agenda item 20a)
A/C.2/78/SR.7
OPERATIONAL ACTIVITIES—UN SYSTEM (Agenda item 22a)
A/C.2/78/SR.18

Rehman, Javaid (UN. Human Rights Council. Special Rapporteur on the Situation of Human Rights in the Islamic Republic of Iran)

HUMAN RIGHTS—IRAN (ISLAMIC REPUBLIC OF) (Agenda item 71c)
A/C.3/78/SR.34

Reichwein, Mark (Netherlands (Kingdom of the))

ELECTION VERIFICATION—UN (Agenda item 71b)
A/78/PV.50; A/C.3/78/SR.50

Reichwein, Mark (Netherlands (Kingdom of the)) (continued)

FREEDOM OF EXPRESSION (Agenda item 71b)
A/C.3/78/SR.19
SEXUAL ORIENTATION (Agenda item 71b)
A/C.3/78/SR.39

Ren, Hongyan (China)

DISARMAMENT—GENERAL AND COMPLETE (Agenda item 99)
A/78/PV.105

Rendtorff-Smith, Sara (Denmark)

HUMAN RIGHTS ADVANCEMENT (Agenda item 71b)
A/C.3/78/SR.52

Repkin, Alexander V. (Russian Federation)

DIAMONDS—FUELLING CONFLICT (Agenda item 30)
A/78/PV.65

Reta Haddad, Rodolfo (Mexico)

COMMODITIES (Agenda item 16d)
A/C.2/78/SR.9
DEVELOPMENT FINANCE (Agenda item 16b)
A/C.2/78/SR.9
EXTERNAL DEBT (Agenda item 16c)
A/C.2/78/SR.9

Retalis, Michail (Greece)

PERSONS WITH DISABILITIES—HUMAN RIGHTS (Agenda item 71a)
A/C.3/78/SR.38
RELIGIOUS INTOLERANCE (Agenda item 71b)
A/C.3/78/SR.38
UN HIGH COMMISSIONER FOR REFUGEES—REPORTS (Agenda item 60)
A/C.3/78/SR.44

Reyes, Gaia (United Kingdom)

CRIME PREVENTION (Agenda item 107)
A/C.3/78/SR.51
HEALTH (Agenda item 125)
A/78/PV.102
RIGHTS OF THE CHILD (Agenda item 67)
A/C.3/78/SR.55
UN SYSTEM—STRENGTHENING (Agenda item 122)
A/78/PV.99
WOMEN'S ADVANCEMENT—CONFERENCES (Agenda item 25b)
A/C.3/78/SR.51

Reyes, Narciso (Philippines)

CONVENTIONAL WEAPONS (Agenda item 99u)
A/C.1/78/PV.18
FISSIONABLE MATERIALS—TREATIES (Agenda item 99a)
A/C.1/78/PV.12
NUCLEAR DISARMAMENT (Agenda item 99b)
A/C.1/78/PV.12

Reyes, Narciso (Philippines) (continued)

NUCLEAR NON-PROLIFERATION—INTERNATIONAL OBLIGATIONS (Agenda item 99w)
A/C.1/78/PV.12
NUCLEAR WEAPON TESTS—TREATIES (Agenda item 105)
A/C.1/78/PV.12
NUCLEAR WEAPONS—TREATIES (Agenda item 99ff)
A/C.1/78/PV.12
SMALL ARMS—ILLICIT TRAFFIC (Agenda item 99p)
A/C.1/78/PV.18
SMALL ARMS—ILLICIT TRAFFIC—ASSISTANCE (Agenda item 99n)
A/C.1/78/PV.18
SOUTH-EAST ASIA—NUCLEAR-WEAPON-FREE ZONES (Agenda item 99y)
A/C.1/78/PV.12

Reyes Hernández, Jorge Arturo (Venezuela (Bolivarian Republic of))

PEACE (Agenda item 14)
A/78/PV.82

Reyes Hernández, Jorge Arturo (Venezuela (Bolivarian Republic of)) (Group of Friends in Defence of the Charter of the United Nations)

RESPONSIBILITY TO PROTECT (Agenda item 129)
A/78/PV.96

Reyes Moncayo, Miguel Ángel (Mexico)

UN. INTERNATIONAL LAW COMMISSION—REPORTS (Agenda item 79)
A/C.6/78/SR.25

Reyna Barrón, María Fernanda (Mexico)

FAMILY (Agenda item 24b)
A/C.3/78/SR.49
UN RESOLUTIONS—IMPLEMENTATION (Agenda item 119)
A/78/PV.108

Reynolds, Barbara G. (UN. Human Rights Council. Working Group of Experts on People of African Descent. Chair)

RACIAL DISCRIMINATION—ELIMINATION (Agenda item 69a)
A/C.3/78/SR.42

Reynolds, Gregory Edward Ivor (Australia)

SMALL ISLAND DEVELOPING STATES—PROGRAMMES OF ACTION (Agenda item 18b)
A/78/PV.103

Reza Bautista, Mauricio (Mexico)

CENTRAL ASIA—ZONES OF PEACE (Agenda item 64)
A/78/PV.85
CRIME PREVENTION (Agenda item 107)
A/C.3/78/SR.5
CYBERCRIME (Agenda item 108)
A/C.3/78/SR.5
PERSONS WITH DISABILITIES—HUMAN RIGHTS (Agenda item 71a)
A/C.3/78/SR.38
RIGHTS OF THE CHILD (Agenda item 67)
A/C.3/78/SR.11; A/C.3/78/SR.12

Richard, Olivier-Gabriel (France)

SPORTS—OLYMPIC GAMES (Agenda item 11)
A/78/PV.38

Riep, Elisabeth (Netherlands (Kingdom of the))

CRIMES AGAINST HUMANITY (Agenda item 80)
A/C.6/78/SR.43; A/C.6/78/SR.44

Rinkevics, Edgars (Latvia. President)

UN. GENERAL ASSEMBLY (78TH SESS. : 2023-2024)—GENERAL DEBATE (Agenda item 8)
A/78/PV.6
UN. GENERAL ASSEMBLY (78TH SESS. : 2023-2024)—SPECIAL STATEMENTS
A/78/PV.6

Ríos, Carmen Rosa (Bolivia (Plurinational State of))

CRIMES AGAINST HUMANITY (Agenda item 80)
A/C.6/78/SR.10; A/C.6/78/SR.45
INFORMATION (Agenda item 53)
A/C.4/78/SR.14
INTERNATIONAL LAW—TRAINING PROGRAMMES (Agenda item 78)
A/C.6/78/SR.22
RULE OF LAW (Agenda item 83)
A/C.6/78/SR.17
TERRITORIES OCCUPIED BY ISRAEL—HUMAN RIGHTS (Agenda item 50)
A/C.4/78/SR.25
UN. INTERNATIONAL COURT OF JUSTICE—REPORTS (Agenda item 73)
A/78/PV.27
UN CHARTER—REPORTS (Agenda item 82)
A/C.6/78/SR.34
VETO (Agenda item 63)
A/78/PV.79

Ríos Serna, Manuela (Colombia)

2030 AGENDA—PROGRAMME IMPLEMENTATION (Agenda item 18a)
A/C.2/78/SR.12
CLIMATE (Agenda item 18d)
A/C.2/78/SR.12
COASTAL ZONE MANAGEMENT (Agenda item 18j)
A/C.2/78/SR.23

Ríos Serna, Manuela (Colombia) (continued)

DEVELOPMENT COOPERATION—MIDDLE-INCOME COUNTRIES (Agenda item 19c)
A/C.2/78/SR.10
DISASTER PREVENTION (Agenda item 18c)
A/C.2/78/SR.12
SCIENCE AND TECHNOLOGY—DEVELOPMENT (Agenda item 19a)
A/C.2/78/SR.10
SUSTAINABLE DEVELOPMENT (Agenda item 18)
A/C.2/78/SR.12; A/C.2/78/SR.22; A/C.2/78/SR.24
SUSTAINABLE ENERGY (Agenda item 18h)
A/C.2/78/SR.23

Riva Grela, Juan José (Uruguay)

FAMILY (Agenda item 24b)
A/C.3/78/SR.49
HUMAN RIGHTS ADVANCEMENT (Agenda item 71b)
A/C.3/78/SR.52
SEXUAL ORIENTATION (Agenda item 71b)
A/C.3/78/SR.39
YOUTH (Agenda item 24b)
A/C.3/78/SR.55

Riva Grela, Juan José (Uruguay) (UN. Group of Latin American and Caribbean States)

RIGHTS OF THE CHILD (Agenda item 67)
A/C.3/78/SR.55

Rivera Reyes, Isabella Regina (Honduras)

DECOLONIZATION (Agenda item 58)
A/C.4/78/SR.2
FALKLAND ISLANDS (MALVINAS) QUESTION (Agenda item 42)
A/C.4/78/SR.2
SOCIAL CONDITIONS (Agenda item 24b)
A/C.3/78/SR.2
SOCIAL DEVELOPMENT (Agenda item 24)
A/C.3/78/SR.2
TERRORISM (Agenda item 109)
A/C.6/78/SR.2
UN. INTERNATIONAL COURT OF JUSTICE—REPORTS (Agenda item 73)
A/78/PV.27

Riveroll Usabiaga, Renata (Mexico)

ENVIRONMENT (Agenda item 71b)
A/C.3/78/SR.29
FREEDOM OF EXPRESSION (Agenda item 71b)
A/C.3/78/SR.19
RACIAL DISCRIMINATION—ELIMINATION (Agenda item 69a)
A/C.3/78/SR.42
RACIAL DISCRIMINATION—PROGRAMMES OF ACTION (Agenda item 69b)
A/C.3/78/SR.42
SUMMARY EXECUTIONS (Agenda item 71b)
A/C.3/78/SR.31

Riveroll Usabiaga, Renata (Mexico) (continued)

UN. HUMAN RIGHTS COMMITTEE—REPORTS (Agenda item 71a)
A/C.3/78/SR.17

Rivière, Nicolas de (France)

FRENCH POLYNESIA QUESTION (Agenda item 58)
A/C.4/78/SR.3
NEW CALEDONIA QUESTION (Agenda item 58)
A/C.4/78/SR.7
UN. SECURITY COUNCIL—MEMBERSHIP (Agenda item 121)
A/78/PV.35
VETO (Agenda item 63)
A/78/PV.51; A/78/PV.60; A/78/PV.68; A/78/PV.74; A/78/PV.78

Rizal, Nizhan Faraz Bin (Malaysia)

CRIME PREVENTION (Agenda item 107)
A/C.3/78/SR.5
CRIMES AGAINST HUMANITY (Agenda item 80)
A/C.6/78/SR.46
CYBERCRIME (Agenda item 108)
A/C.3/78/SR.5
ELECTION VERIFICATION—UN (Agenda item 71b)
A/78/PV.50; A/C.3/78/SR.50
HUMAN RIGHTS—INTERNATIONAL INSTRUMENTS (Agenda item 71a)
A/C.3/78/SR.24
HUMAN RIGHTS—MYANMAR (Agenda item 71c)
A/C.3/78/SR.24; A/C.3/78/SR.53
HUMAN RIGHTS—PROGRAMMES OF ACTION (Agenda item 71d)
A/C.3/78/SR.24
HUMAN RIGHTS ACTIVISTS (Agenda item 71b)
A/C.3/78/SR.56
HUMAN RIGHTS ADVANCEMENT (Agenda item 71b)
A/C.3/78/SR.24
RACIAL DISCRIMINATION—ELIMINATION (Agenda item 69a)
A/C.3/78/SR.41; A/C.3/78/SR.47
RACIAL DISCRIMINATION—PROGRAMMES OF ACTION (Agenda item 69b)
A/C.3/78/SR.41
RIGHTS OF THE CHILD (Agenda item 67)
A/C.3/78/SR.11; A/C.3/78/SR.55
SELF-DETERMINATION OF PEOPLES (Agenda item 70)
A/C.3/78/SR.49
UN. HUMAN RIGHTS COUNCIL—REPORTS (Agenda item 66)
A/78/PV.23
VETO (Agenda item 63)
A/78/PV.66

Robinson, Jason (Ireland)

ARMS RACE—OUTER SPACE (Agenda item 97a)
A/C.1/78/PV.17

Robinson, Jason (Ireland) (continued)

DISARMAMENT AGREEMENTS—OUTER SPACE (Agenda item 97c)
A/C.1/78/PV.17
OUTER SPACE—CONFIDENCE-BUILDING MEASURES (Agenda item 99v)
A/C.1/78/PV.17
OUTER SPACE—PRINCIPLES (Agenda item 97d)
A/C.1/78/PV.17

Robledo López, Carmen (Mexico)

COMMODITIES (Agenda item 16d)
A/C.2/78/SR.14
ECONOMIC COOPERATION AMONG DEVELOPING COUNTRIES (Agenda item 22b)
A/C.2/78/SR.18
OPERATIONAL ACTIVITIES—UN SYSTEM (Agenda item 22a)
A/C.2/78/SR.18
SUSTAINABLE DEVELOPMENT (Agenda item 18)
A/C.2/78/SR.14
UNRWA—ACTIVITIES (Agenda item 49)
A/C.4/78/SR.22

Rodkin, Boaz (Israel)

RIGHTS OF THE CHILD (Agenda item 67)
A/C.3/78/SR.13

Rodrigue, Antonio (Haiti)

SLAVERY—MEMORIALS (Agenda item 118)
A/78/PV.64
UN—BUDGET (2024) (Agenda item 134)
A/C.5/78/SR.18

Rodrigue, Antonio (Haiti) (Caribbean Community)

RACIAL DISCRIMINATION—ELIMINATION (Agenda item 69a)
A/78/PV.63
SLAVERY—MEMORIALS (Agenda item 118)
A/78/PV.64

Rodrigue, Antonio (Haiti) (UN. Group of Latin American and Caribbean States)

RAISI, SEYYED EBRAHIM (IRAN (ISLAMIC REPUBLID OF). PRESIDENT)—TRIBUTES
A/78/PV.83

Rodrigues-Birkett, Carolyn (Guyana)

CUBA—UNITED STATES (Agenda item 38)
A/78/PV.24
DECOLONIZATION (Agenda item 58)
A/C.4/78/SR.7
GLOBALIZATION—INTERDEPENDENCE (Agenda item 19)
A/C.2/78/SR.10
NON-SELF-GOVERNING TERRITORIES—REPORTS (Agenda item 54)
A/C.4/78/SR.7
PALESTINE QUESTION (Agenda item 35)
A/78/PV.39

Rodrigues-Birkett, Carolyn (Guyana) (continued)

RURAL WOMEN (Agenda item 25a)
A/C.3/78/SR.10
SCIENCE AND TECHNOLOGY—DEVELOPMENT (Agenda item 19a)
A/C.2/78/SR.10
TERRITORIES OCCUPIED BY ISRAEL—NATURAL RESOURCES (Agenda item 59)
A/C.2/78/SR.19
UKRAINE—POLITICAL CONDITIONS (Agenda item 62)
A/78/PV.58
UN. GENERAL ASSEMBLY (78TH SESS. : 2023-2024)—GENERAL DEBATE—RIGHT OF REPLY (Agenda item 8)
A/78/PV.14
UN. GENERAL ASSEMBLY (78TH SESS. : 2023-2024). 1ST COMMITTEE—GENERAL DEBATE (Agenda item 8)
A/C.1/78/PV.3
UN. GENERAL ASSEMBLY (78TH SESS. : 2023-2024). 2ND COMMITTEE—GENERAL DEBATE (Agenda item 8)
A/C.2/78/SR.5
UN. INTERNATIONAL COURT OF JUSTICE—REPORTS (Agenda item 73)
A/78/PV.28
UN. SECURITY COUNCIL—MEMBERSHIP (Agenda item 121)
A/78/PV.36
VETO (Agenda item 63)
A/78/PV.61
WESTERN SAHARA QUESTION (Agenda item 58)
A/C.4/78/SR.7
WOMEN'S ADVANCEMENT (Agenda item 25a)
A/C.3/78/SR.10
WOMEN'S ADVANCEMENT—CONFERENCES (Agenda item 25b)
A/C.3/78/SR.10

Rodríguez Acosta, Julia Elizabeth (El Salvador)

CONVENTIONAL WEAPONS (Agenda item 99u)
A/C.1/78/PV.18
DISARMAMENT—GENERAL AND COMPLETE (Agenda item 99)
A/C.1/78/PV.18
DISARMAMENT AGREEMENTS—OUTER SPACE (Agenda item 97c)
A/C.1/78/PV.27
OUTER SPACE—PRINCIPLES (Agenda item 97d)
A/C.1/78/PV.27
SMALL ARMS—ILLICIT TRAFFIC (Agenda item 99p)
A/C.1/78/PV.18
SMALL ARMS—ILLICIT TRAFFIC—ASSISTANCE (Agenda item 99n)
A/C.1/78/PV.18
VETO (Agenda item 63)
A/78/PV.68

Rodríguez Gómez-Aller, Juan (Spain)
INFORMATION (Agenda item 53)
A/C.4/78/SR.12

Rodríguez Mackay, Miguel Ángel (Sociedad Peruana de Derecho Internacional)
WESTERN SAHARA QUESTION (Agenda item 58)
A/C.4/78/SR.4

Rodríguez Mancia, Carla María (Guatemala)
AGEING PERSONS (Agenda item 24b)
A/C.3/78/SR.1
ARMS TRANSFERS—TREATIES (Agenda item 99x)
A/C.1/78/PV.18
COMMODITIES (Agenda item 16d)
A/C.2/78/SR.14
CONVENTIONAL WEAPONS (Agenda item 99u)
A/C.1/78/PV.18
CRIME PREVENTION (Agenda item 107)
A/C.3/78/SR.5
CRIMES AGAINST HUMANITY (Agenda item 80)
A/C.6/78/SR.9
CYBERCRIME (Agenda item 108)
A/C.3/78/SR.5
DISASTER VICTIMS (Agenda item 86)
A/C.6/78/SR.5
FOOD SECURITY (Agenda item 23a)
A/C.2/78/SR.17
IAEA—REPORTS (Agenda item 89)
A/78/PV.29
INDIGENOUS PEOPLES (Agenda item 68a)
A/78/PV.107; A/C.3/78/SR.15
INDIGENOUS PEOPLES—CONFERENCES (Agenda item 68b)
A/C.3/78/SR.15
INFORMATION—INTERNATIONAL SECURITY (Agenda item 94)
A/C.1/78/PV.20
INTERNATIONAL CRIMINAL COURT—REPORTS (Agenda item 74)
A/78/PV.21
LANDMINES—TREATIES (Agenda item 99m)
A/C.1/78/PV.18
LAW OF THE SEA (Agenda item 75a)
A/78/PV.43
MARINE ECOSYSTEMS—BIOLOGICAL DIVERSITY (Agenda item 75c)
A/78/PV.43
MULTILINGUALISM (Agenda item 124)
A/78/PV.107
PERSONS WITH DISABILITIES (Agenda item 24b)
A/C.3/78/SR.1
POVERTY—INTERNATIONAL DECADES (Agenda item 21a)
A/C.2/78/SR.17
RESPONSIBILITY TO PROTECT (Agenda item 129)
A/78/PV.96
RIGHTS OF THE CHILD (Agenda item 67)
A/C.3/78/SR.11

Rodríguez Mancia, Carla María (Guatemala) (continued)
RULE OF LAW (Agenda item 83)
A/C.6/78/SR.15
RURAL POVERTY (Agenda item 21b)
A/C.2/78/SR.17
SMALL ARMS—ILLICIT TRAFFIC (Agenda item 99p)
A/C.1/78/PV.18
SOCIAL CONDITIONS (Agenda item 24b)
A/C.3/78/SR.1
STRADDLING FISH STOCKS (Agenda item 75b)
A/78/PV.43
SUSTAINABLE DEVELOPMENT (Agenda item 18)
A/C.2/78/SR.14
TERRORISM (Agenda item 109)
A/C.6/78/SR.1
UKRAINE—POLITICAL CONDITIONS (Agenda item 62)
A/78/PV.58
UN. GENERAL ASSEMBLY (78TH SESS. : 2023-2024). 1ST COMMITTEE—GENERAL DEBATE (Agenda item 8)
A/C.1/78/PV.5
UN. GENERAL ASSEMBLY (78TH SESS. : 2023-2024). 2ND COMMITTEE—GENERAL DEBATE (Agenda item 8)
A/C.2/78/SR.5
UN HIGH COMMISSIONER FOR REFUGEES—REPORTS (Agenda item 60)
A/C.3/78/SR.48
VETO (Agenda item 63)
A/78/PV.3; A/78/PV.68; A/78/PV.70
WOMEN'S ADVANCEMENT (Agenda item 25a)
A/C.3/78/SR.8
WOMEN'S ADVANCEMENT—CONFERENCES (Agenda item 25b)
A/C.3/78/SR.8
YOUTH (Agenda item 24b)
A/C.3/78/SR.1

Rodríguez Mancia, Carla María (Guatemala) (Group of Friends of the Responsibility to Protect)
UN. SECRETARY-GENERAL—REPORTS (Agenda item 110)
A/78/PV.54

Rodríguez Mancia, Carla María (Guatemala) (UN. Group of Latin American and Caribbean States)
RACIAL DISCRIMINATION—ELIMINATION (Agenda item 69a)
A/78/PV.63
SLAVERY—MEMORIALS (Agenda item 118)
A/78/PV.64

Rodríguez Parrilla, Bruno Eduardo (Cuba)
CUBA—UNITED STATES (Agenda item 38)
A/78/PV.26

Rodríguez Perdomo, Elio (Cuba)
ECONOMIC SANCTIONS—INTERNATIONAL RELATIONS (Agenda item 28)
A/78/PV.89

Rodríguez Torres, Radhafil (Dominican Republic)
CRIMES AGAINST HUMANITY (Agenda item 80)
A/C.6/78/SR.11

Roeder-Messell, Ernst Heinrich (Germany)
TERRITORIES OCCUPIED BY ISRAEL—NATURAL RESOURCES (Agenda item 59)
A/C.2/78/SR.21

Roios, Ana ((personal capacity))
WESTERN SAHARA QUESTION (Agenda item 58)
A/C.4/78/SR.4

Rojas, Eder (Peru)
ELECTION VERIFICATION—UN (Agenda item 71b)
A/C.3/78/SR.50
HUMAN RIGHTS—DEMOCRATIC PEOPLE'S REPUBLIC OF KOREA (Agenda item 71c)
A/C.3/78/SR.33
HUMAN RIGHTS—SYRIAN ARAB REPUBLIC (Agenda item 71c)
A/C.3/78/SR.54
INDIGENOUS PEOPLES (Agenda item 68a)
A/C.3/78/SR.15
INDIGENOUS PEOPLES—CONFERENCES (Agenda item 68b)
A/C.3/78/SR.15
PEACE (Agenda item 14)
A/78/PV.62
PERSONS WITH DISABILITIES (Agenda item 24b)
A/C.3/78/SR.4
SOCIAL CONDITIONS (Agenda item 24b)
A/C.3/78/SR.4
SOCIAL DEVELOPMENT (Agenda item 24)
A/C.3/78/SR.4

Rolle Hernández, Gretel (Cuba)
RADIATION EFFECTS (Agenda item 47)
A/C.4/78/SR.11

Romero López, Rosanis (Cuba)
ARMS RACE—OUTER SPACE (Agenda item 97a)
A/C.1/78/PV.27
CHEMICAL WEAPONS—TREATIES (Agenda item 99l)
A/C.1/78/PV.26
DISARMAMENT—GENERAL AND COMPLETE (Agenda item 99)
A/C.1/78/PV.30
DISARMAMENT AGREEMENTS—ENVIRONMENT (Agenda item 99j)
A/C.1/78/PV.28

Romero López, Rosanis (Cuba) (continued)
DISARMAMENT AGREEMENTS—OUTER SPACE (Agenda item 97c)
A/C.1/78/PV.27
DISARMAMENT-DEVELOPMENT LINK (Agenda item 99d)
A/C.1/78/PV.28
FISSIONABLE MATERIALS—TREATIES (Agenda item 99a)
A/C.1/78/PV.26
INFORMATION—INTERNATIONAL SECURITY (Agenda item 94)
A/C.1/78/PV.28; A/C.1/78/PV.29
MULTILATERALISM—DISARMAMENT (Agenda item 99r)
A/C.1/78/PV.28
OUTER SPACE—CONFIDENCE-BUILDING MEASURES (Agenda item 99v)
A/C.1/78/PV.27
OUTER SPACE—PRINCIPLES (Agenda item 97d)
A/C.1/78/PV.27
UN—PROGRAMME PLANNING (Agenda item 135)
A/C.1/78/PV.10
UN. GENERAL ASSEMBLY—WORK PROGRAMME (Agenda item 120)
A/C.1/78/PV.10
WEAPONS—OUTER SPACE (Agenda item 97b)
A/C.1/78/PV.27

Romero Puentes, Yusnier (Cuba)
CUBA—UNITED STATES (Agenda item 38)
A/78/PV.26
DECOLONIZATION (Agenda item 58)
A/C.4/78/SR.2
FALKLAND ISLANDS (MALVINAS) QUESTION (Agenda item 42)
A/C.4/78/SR.2
HIV/AIDS—DECLARATIONS (Agenda item 10)
A/78/PV.91
HUMAN RIGHTS—INTERNATIONAL INSTRUMENTS (Agenda item 71a)
A/C.3/78/SR.25
INTERNATIONAL TRADE (Agenda item 16a)
A/C.2/78/SR.24
PALESTINE QUESTION (Agenda item 35)
A/78/PV.40
RESPONSIBILITY TO PROTECT (Agenda item 129)
A/78/PV.96
SANCTIONS—INTERNATIONAL RELATIONS (Agenda item 71b)
A/C.3/78/SR.25
TERRITORIES OCCUPIED BY ISRAEL—HUMAN RIGHTS (Agenda item 50)
A/C.4/78/SR.26
UN. SECRETARY-GENERAL—REPORTS (Agenda item 110)
A/78/PV.55
UN. SECURITY COUNCIL—MEMBERSHIP (Agenda item 121)
A/78/PV.36

Romero Puentes, Yusnier (Cuba) (continued)

UNRWA—ACTIVITIES (Agenda item 49)
A/C.4/78/SR.23; A/C.4/78/SR.26
WESTERN SAHARA QUESTION (Agenda item 58)
A/C.4/78/SR.2

Romero Puentes, Yusnier (Cuba) (Group of 77)

INFORMATION (Agenda item 53)
A/C.4/78/SR.12
TERRITORIES OCCUPIED BY ISRAEL—NATURAL RESOURCES (Agenda item 59)
A/C.2/78/SR.19

Romero Veiga, Stefany (Uruguay)

SUSTAINABLE DEVELOPMENT (Agenda item 18)
A/C.2/78/SR.25
UN. GENERAL ASSEMBLY (78TH SESS. : 2023-2024). 2ND COMMITTEE—GENERAL DEBATE (Agenda item 8)
A/C.2/78/SR.5

Romualdo, Tania Serafim Yvonne (Cabo Verde)

DISARMAMENT—GENERAL AND COMPLETE (Agenda item 99)
A/78/PV.106
FOOD SECURITY (Agenda item 23a)
A/C.2/78/SR.17
HIV/AIDS—DECLARATIONS (Agenda item 10)
A/78/PV.91
POVERTY—INTERNATIONAL DECADES (Agenda item 21a)
A/C.2/78/SR.17
RURAL POVERTY (Agenda item 21b)
A/C.2/78/SR.17
TERRORISM (Agenda item 109)
A/C.6/78/SR.5
UN. GENERAL ASSEMBLY (78TH SESS. : 2023-2024). 1ST COMMITTEE—GENERAL DEBATE (Agenda item 8)
A/C.1/78/PV.9
WOMEN'S ADVANCEMENT (Agenda item 25a)
A/C.3/78/SR.9
WOMEN'S ADVANCEMENT—CONFERENCES (Agenda item 25b)
A/C.3/78/SR.9
YOUTH (Agenda item 24b)
A/C.3/78/SR.55

Romualdo, Tania Serafim Yvonne (Cabo Verde) (Comunidade dos Países de Língua Portuguesa)

MULTILINGUALISM (Agenda item 124)
A/78/PV.107

Ron Martínez, Carlos (Venezuela (Bolivarian Republic of))

ECONOMIC SANCTIONS—INTERNATIONAL RELATIONS (Agenda item 28)
A/78/PV.90

Rosario Vela, Manuel Jesús del (Spain)

ARMS RACE—OUTER SPACE (Agenda item 97a)
A/C.1/78/PV.17
ARMS TRANSFERS—TREATIES (Agenda item 99x)
A/C.1/78/PV.19
BIOLOGICAL WEAPONS—TREATIES (Agenda item 106)
A/C.1/78/PV.15
CHEMICAL WEAPONS—TREATIES (Agenda item 99l)
A/C.1/78/PV.15
CLUSTER MUNITIONS (Agenda item 99dd)
A/C.1/78/PV.19
CONVENTIONAL WEAPONS (Agenda item 99u)
A/C.1/78/PV.19
DISARMAMENT—GENERAL AND COMPLETE (Agenda item 99)
A/C.1/78/PV.19
LANDMINES—TREATIES (Agenda item 99m)
A/C.1/78/PV.19
NUCLEAR DISARMAMENT (Agenda item 99b)
A/C.1/78/PV.12
NUCLEAR NON-PROLIFERATION—INTERNATIONAL OBLIGATIONS (Agenda item 99w)
A/C.1/78/PV.12
NUCLEAR WEAPON TESTS—TREATIES (Agenda item 105)
A/C.1/78/PV.12
OUTER SPACE—CONFIDENCE-BUILDING MEASURES (Agenda item 99v)
A/C.1/78/PV.17
OUTER SPACE—PRINCIPLES (Agenda item 97d)
A/C.1/78/PV.17
WEAPONS OF MASS DESTRUCTION—TERRORISM (Agenda item 99s)
A/C.1/78/PV.15

Rosario-Blackett, Marissa del (Sovereign Order of Malta)

ENVIRONMENT (Agenda item 71b)
A/C.3/78/SR.29
INDIGENOUS PEOPLES (Agenda item 68a)
A/C.3/78/SR.17
MINORITIES (Agenda item 71b)
A/C.3/78/SR.39
RIGHT TO FOOD (Agenda item 71b)
A/C.3/78/SR.30
UN HIGH COMMISSIONER FOR REFUGEES—REPORTS (Agenda item 60)
A/C.3/78/SR.44

Rosemarine, Andrew M. (International Law Chambers (United Kingdom))

WESTERN SAHARA QUESTION (Agenda item 58)
A/C.4/78/SR.5

Rosemberg Guerrero, José (Preparatory Commission for the Comprehensive Nuclear Test-Ban Treaty Organization)

NUCLEAR WEAPON TESTS—TREATIES (Agenda item 105)
A/C.1/78/PV.13

Rosen, Katie (United Kingdom)

HUMAN RIGHTS—BELARUS (Agenda item 71c)
A/C.3/78/SR.37

Roshdy, Hussein Ossama Hussein Abdelrhman (Egypt)

ADMINISTRATION OF JUSTICE (Agenda item 144)
A/C.5/78/SR.15
CRIMES AGAINST HUMANITY (Agenda item 80)
A/C.6/78/SR.39; A/C.6/78/SR.41; A/C.6/78/SR.42; A/C.6/78/SR.44
INTERNATIONAL JURISDICTION (Agenda item 84)
A/C.6/78/SR.12
RESPONSIBILITY OF INTERNATIONAL ORGANIZATIONS (Agenda item 85)
A/C.6/78/SR.19
UN. GENERAL ASSEMBLY (78TH SESS. : 2023-2024). 5TH COMMITTEE—WORK ORGANIZATION (Agenda item 7)
A/C.5/78/SR.26/PartII; A/C.5/78/SR.40
UN. INTERNATIONAL COURT OF JUSTICE—REPORTS (Agenda item 73)
A/78/PV.28

Rosinas, Robertas (Lithuania)

IAEA—REPORTS (Agenda item 89)
A/78/PV.30

Rosso, John (Papua New Guinea. Deputy Prime Minister)

UN. GENERAL ASSEMBLY (78TH SESS. : 2023-2024)—GENERAL DEBATE (Agenda item 8)
A/78/PV.12
UN. GENERAL ASSEMBLY (78TH SESS. : 2023-2024)—SPECIAL STATEMENTS
A/78/PV.12

Rowley, Keith (Trinidad and Tobago. Prime Minister)

UN. GENERAL ASSEMBLY (78TH SESS. : 2023-2024)—GENERAL DEBATE (Agenda item 8)
A/78/PV.9
UN. GENERAL ASSEMBLY (78TH SESS. : 2023-2024)—SPECIAL STATEMENTS
A/78/PV.9

Ruas, Juliana Gaspar (UN. Advisory Committee on Administrative and Budgetary Questions. Vice-Chair)

ADMINISTRATION OF JUSTICE (Agenda item 144)
A/C.5/78/SR.15
INTERNATIONAL RESIDUAL MECHANISM FOR CRIMINAL TRIBUNALS—FINANCING (Agenda item 145)
A/C.5/78/SR.25
UN—BUDGET (2024) (Agenda item 134)
A/C.5/78/SR.2; A/C.5/78/SR.18; A/C.5/78/SR.25

Ruas, Juliana Gaspar (UN. Advisory Committee on Administrative and Budgetary Questions. Vice-Chair) (continued)

UN—HUMAN RESOURCES MANAGEMENT (Agenda item 139)
A/C.5/78/SR.25

Rubinshtein, Yarden (Israel)

DISASTER VICTIMS (Agenda item 86)
A/C.6/78/SR.7
INTERNATIONAL JURISDICTION (Agenda item 84)
A/C.6/78/SR.12; A/C.6/78/SR.13
UN. INTERNATIONAL LAW COMMISSION—REPORTS (Agenda item 79)
A/C.6/78/SR.28; A/C.6/78/SR.31; A/C.6/78/SR.33

Rubio, Celina (Dominican Republic)

INFORMATION TECHNOLOGY—DEVELOPMENT (Agenda item 15)
A/C.2/78/SR.10

Ruffer, Emil (Czechia) (Visegrad Group)

UN. INTERNATIONAL COURT OF JUSTICE—REPORTS (Agenda item 73)
A/78/PV.20

Ruidíaz, René (Chile)

FALKLAND ISLANDS (MALVINAS) QUESTION (Agenda item 42)
A/C.4/78/SR.7
RIGHT TO HEALTH (Agenda item 71b)
A/C.3/78/SR.39
SEXUAL ORIENTATION (Agenda item 71b)
A/C.3/78/SR.39
TAXATION (Agenda item 16h)
A/C.2/78/SR.25

Rupende, Tapiwa Roy (Zimbabwe)

CLIMATE (Agenda item 18d)
A/C.2/78/SR.13
COMMODITIES (Agenda item 16d)
A/C.2/78/SR.14
CUBA—UNITED STATES (Agenda item 38)
A/78/PV.24
EXTERNAL DEBT (Agenda item 16c)
A/C.2/78/SR.9
INTERNATIONAL TRADE (Agenda item 16a)
A/C.2/78/SR.9; A/C.2/78/SR.24
LANDLOCKED DEVELOPING COUNTRIES—CONFERENCES (Agenda item 20b)
A/C.2/78/SR.7
LEAST DEVELOPED COUNTRIES—CONFERENCES (Agenda item 20a)
A/C.2/78/SR.7
MACROECONOMIC POLICY (Agenda item 16)
A/C.2/78/SR.9
SUSTAINABLE DEVELOPMENT (Agenda item 18)
A/C.2/78/SR.13; A/C.2/78/SR.14

Rupende, Tapiwa Roy (Zimbabwe) (continued)
UN. GENERAL ASSEMBLY (78TH SESS. : 2023-2024). 2ND COMMITTEE—GENERAL DEBATE (Agenda item 8)
A/C.2/78/SR.5

Ruslan, Muhammad Ammar Rafiq (Malaysia)
RIGHTS OF THE CHILD (Agenda item 67)
A/C.3/78/SR.11
WOMEN'S ADVANCEMENT (Agenda item 25a)
A/C.3/78/SR.8
WOMEN'S ADVANCEMENT—CONFERENCES (Agenda item 25b)
A/C.3/78/SR.8

Russell, Zoe (New Zealand)
CRIMES AGAINST HUMANITY (Agenda item 80)
A/C.6/78/SR.9
PEACEKEEPING OPERATIONS—CRIMINAL LIABILITY (Agenda item 76)
A/C.6/78/SR.8

Ruto, William Samoei (Kenya. President)
UN. GENERAL ASSEMBLY (78TH SESS. : 2023-2024)—GENERAL DEBATE (Agenda item 8)
A/78/PV.8
UN. GENERAL ASSEMBLY (78TH SESS. : 2023-2024)—SPECIAL STATEMENTS
A/78/PV.8

Rutte, Mark (Netherlands (Kingdom of the). Prime Minister)
UN. GENERAL ASSEMBLY (78TH SESS. : 2023-2024)—GENERAL DEBATE (Agenda item 8)
A/78/PV.10
UN. GENERAL ASSEMBLY (78TH SESS. : 2023-2024)—SPECIAL STATEMENTS
A/78/PV.10

Rwakazina, Marie Chantal (UN. Human Rights Council. Intergovernmental Working Group on the Effective Implementation of the Durban Declaration and Programme of Action. Chair)
RACIAL DISCRIMINATION—PROGRAMMES OF ACTION (Agenda item 69b)
A/C.3/78/SR.40

Rwamucyo, Ernest (Rwanda)
PEACE (Agenda item 14)
A/78/PV.82

Rybakov, Valentin (Belarus)
ECONOMIC SANCTIONS—INTERNATIONAL RELATIONS (Agenda item 28)
A/78/PV.89

Saadi, Abu Alhakam Adnan Sadek (Iraq)
INFORMATION—INTERNATIONAL SECURITY (Agenda item 94)
A/C.1/78/PV.20

Saadi, Samy Sofian (Germany)
VETO (Agenda item 63)
A/78/PV.3

Sabanovic, Damir (Montenegro)
PEACE (Agenda item 14)
A/78/PV.82
UKRAINE—POLITICAL CONDITIONS (Agenda item 62)
A/78/PV.58

Sabarudin, Mohamad Shahir (Malaysia)
INFORMATION (Agenda item 53)
A/C.4/78/SR.13
UNRWA—ACTIVITIES (Agenda item 49)
A/C.4/78/SR.22

Sabbagh, Bassam (Syrian Arab Republic)
UN. GENERAL ASSEMBLY (78TH SESS. : 2023-2024)—GENERAL DEBATE (Agenda item 8)
A/78/PV.14

Sabo, Kathryn (UN Commission on International Trade Law. Chair)
UN COMMISSION ON INTERNATIONAL TRADE LAW—REPORTS (Agenda item 77)
A/C.6/78/SR.13; A/C.6/78/SR.14

Sabo, Tesfaye Yilma (Ethiopia)
HUMAN RIGHTS—ETHIOPIA (Agenda item 71c)
A/C.3/78/SR.36
UN. GENERAL ASSEMBLY (78TH SESS. : 2023-2024). 2ND COMMITTEE—GENERAL DEBATE (Agenda item 8)
A/C.2/78/SR.2

Sabo, Tesfaye Yilma (Ethiopia) (UN. Group of African States)
UN—BUDGET (2024) (Agenda item 134)
A/C.5/78/SR.5; A/C.5/78/SR.14
UN—PROGRAMME PLANNING (Agenda item 135)
A/C.5/78/SR.5

Sæter, William (Norway)
ARMS RACE—OUTER SPACE (Agenda item 97a)
A/C.1/78/PV.17
OUTER SPACE—CONFIDENCE-BUILDING MEASURES (Agenda item 99v)
A/C.1/78/PV.17
OUTER SPACE—PRINCIPLES (Agenda item 97d)
A/C.1/78/PV.17

Saggese, Eleonora (United Kingdom)
ARMS TRANSFERS—TREATIES (Agenda item 99x)
A/C.1/78/PV.19
CLUSTER MUNITIONS (Agenda item 99dd)
A/C.1/78/PV.19
DISARMAMENT—GENERAL AND COMPLETE (Agenda item 99)
A/C.1/78/PV.19
LANDMINES—TREATIES (Agenda item 99m)
A/C.1/78/PV.19

Sah, Hermy Ahmad (Brunei Darussalam)
UN. GENERAL ASSEMBLY (78TH SESS. : 2023-2024). 1ST COMMITTEE—GENERAL DEBATE (Agenda item 8)
A/C.1/78/PV.7

Sahel, Makhlouf (Algeria)
WESTERN SAHARA QUESTION (Agenda item 58)
A/C.4/78/SR.5

Sahraei, Mohammad Reza (Iran (Islamic Republic of))
CUBA—UNITED STATES (Agenda item 38)
A/78/PV.26
DECOLONIZATION (Agenda item 58)
A/C.4/78/SR.8
INFORMATION (Agenda item 53)
A/C.4/78/SR.13
MINE CLEARANCE (Agenda item 46)
A/C.4/78/SR.10
OUTER SPACE—PEACEFUL USES—INTERNATIONAL COOPERATION (Agenda item 48)
A/C.4/78/SR.15
PEACEKEEPING OPERATIONS (Agenda item 51)
A/C.4/78/SR.20
RADIATION EFFECTS (Agenda item 47)
A/C.4/78/SR.11

Sahraoui, Ahmed (Algeria)
DISPLACED PERSONS (Agenda item 71b)
A/C.3/78/SR.49
HEALTH (Agenda item 125)
A/78/PV.16
TERRITORIES OCCUPIED BY ISRAEL—HUMAN RIGHTS (Agenda item 50)
A/C.4/78/SR.24
UN HIGH COMMISSIONER FOR REFUGEES—REPORTS (Agenda item 60)
A/C.3/78/SR.45
UNRWA—ACTIVITIES (Agenda item 49)
A/C.4/78/SR.23
VETO (Agenda item 63)
A/78/PV.59; A/78/PV.74

Sahrip, Nazihah Mohd (Brunei Darussalam)
RULE OF LAW (Agenda item 83)
A/C.6/78/SR.18

Sakala, Rose (Zambia)
UN—FINANCIAL SITUATION (Agenda item 136)
A/C.5/78/SR.6

Sakowicz, Mateusz (Poland)
AFRICA—DEVELOPMENT (Agenda item 65b)
A/78/PV.18
AFRICA—SUSTAINABLE DEVELOPMENT—PARTNERSHIP (Agenda item 65a)
A/78/PV.18
PEACEKEEPING OPERATIONS (Agenda item 51)
A/C.4/78/SR.19
UN. GENERAL ASSEMBLY (78TH SESS. : 2023-2024). 2ND COMMITTEE—GENERAL DEBATE (Agenda item 8)
A/C.2/78/SR.4

Salah, Yassine (Tunisia)
PEACEKEEPING OPERATIONS (Agenda item 51)
A/C.4/78/SR.19
TERRITORIES OCCUPIED BY ISRAEL—HUMAN RIGHTS (Agenda item 50)
A/C.4/78/SR.24
UNRWA—ACTIVITIES (Agenda item 49)
A/C.4/78/SR.22

Salas de los Ríos, Javier Leonardo (Peru)
UN. GENERAL ASSEMBLY (78TH SESS. : 2023-2024). 1ST COMMITTEE—GENERAL DEBATE (Agenda item 8)
A/C.1/78/PV.7

Saleem, Saima (Pakistan)
ELECTION VERIFICATION—UN (Agenda item 71b)
A/78/PV.50
HUMAN RIGHTS—IRAN (ISLAMIC REPUBLIC OF) (Agenda item 71c)
A/C.3/78/SR.34
HUMAN RIGHTS—REPORTS (Agenda item 71c)
A/C.3/78/SR.25
RIGHTS OF THE CHILD (Agenda item 67)
A/C.3/78/SR.13
UN. GENERAL ASSEMBLY (78TH SESS. : 2023-2024)—GENERAL DEBATE—RIGHT OF REPLY (Agenda item 8)
A/78/PV.11
UN HIGH COMMISSIONER FOR REFUGEES—REPORTS (Agenda item 60)
A/C.3/78/SR.45

Salem, Sahar K.H. (State of Palestine)
HUMAN RIGHTS (Agenda item 71)
A/C.3/78/SR.26
HUMAN RIGHTS—TERRITORIES OCCUPIED BY ISRAEL (Agenda item 71c)
A/C.3/78/SR.35
POVERTY—HUMAN RIGHTS (Agenda item 71b)
A/C.3/78/SR.30

Salem, Sahar K.H. (State of Palestine) (continued)
RIGHTS OF THE CHILD (Agenda item 67)
A/C.3/78/SR.11; A/C.3/78/SR.14
SELF-DETERMINATION OF PEOPLES (Agenda item 70)
A/C.3/78/SR.49
SOLIDARITY (Agenda item 71b)
A/C.3/78/SR.32

Salerno Vega, James Azel (Panama)
RACIAL DISCRIMINATION—ELIMINATION (Agenda item 69a)
A/C.3/78/SR.40
RACIAL DISCRIMINATION—PROGRAMMES OF ACTION (Agenda item 69b)
A/C.3/78/SR.40
SPORTS—OLYMPIC GAMES (Agenda item 11)
A/78/PV.38

Salih, Muthanna (Iraq)
NUCLEAR DISARMAMENT (Agenda item 99b)
A/C.1/78/PV.12
NUCLEAR NON-PROLIFERATION—INTERNATIONAL OBLIGATIONS (Agenda item 99w)
A/C.1/78/PV.12

Sall, Macky (Senegal. President)
UN. GENERAL ASSEMBLY (78TH SESS. : 2023-2024)—GENERAL DEBATE (Agenda item 8)
A/78/PV.5
UN. GENERAL ASSEMBLY (78TH SESS. : 2023-2024)—SPECIAL STATEMENTS
A/78/PV.5

Salmon, Allen (French Polynesia)
FRENCH POLYNESIA QUESTION (Agenda item 58)
A/C.4/78/SR.3

Salmón, Elizabeth (UN. Human Rights Council. Special Rapporteur on the Situation of Human Rights in the Democratic People's Republic of Korea)
HUMAN RIGHTS—DEMOCRATIC PEOPLE'S REPUBLIC OF KOREA (Agenda item 71c)
A/C.3/78/SR.33

Salvia, Fabio (European Conference of Support and Solidarity with the Saharawi People)
WESTERN SAHARA QUESTION (Agenda item 58)
A/C.4/78/SR.4

Salvioli, Fabián (UN. Human Rights Council. Special Rapporteur on the Promotion of Truth, Justice, Reparation and Guarantees of Non-Recurrence)
RIGHT TO THE TRUTH (Agenda item 71b)
A/C.3/78/SR.22

Samai, Rahma (Algeria)
AGEING PERSONS (Agenda item 24b)
A/C.3/78/SR.3
EMERGENCY ASSISTANCE (Agenda item 72a)
A/78/PV.47
PALESTINIANS—ASSISTANCE (Agenda item 72b)
A/78/PV.47
PERSONS WITH DISABILITIES—HUMAN RIGHTS (Agenda item 71a)
A/C.3/78/SR.38; A/C.3/78/SR.51
RIGHTS OF THE CHILD (Agenda item 67)
A/C.3/78/SR.11; A/C.3/78/SR.12; A/C.3/78/SR.14
RURAL WOMEN (Agenda item 25a)
A/C.3/78/SR.9; A/C.3/78/SR.49
SOCIAL CONDITIONS (Agenda item 24b)
A/C.3/78/SR.3
SOCIAL DEVELOPMENT (Agenda item 24)
A/C.3/78/SR.3
UN. HUMAN RIGHTS COUNCIL—REPORTS (Agenda item 66)
A/C.3/78/SR.46
UN HIGH COMMISSIONER FOR REFUGEES—REPORTS (Agenda item 60)
A/C.3/78/SR.44
WOMEN'S ADVANCEMENT (Agenda item 25a)
A/C.3/78/SR.7; A/C.3/78/SR.9
WOMEN'S ADVANCEMENT—CONFERENCES (Agenda item 25b)
A/C.3/78/SR.7; A/C.3/78/SR.9; A/C.3/78/SR.51

Samson, Hedda (European Union)
AFRICA—DEVELOPMENT (Agenda item 65b)
A/78/PV.18
AFRICA—SUSTAINABLE DEVELOPMENT—PARTNERSHIP (Agenda item 65a)
A/78/PV.18
ARMED CONFLICTS PREVENTION (Agenda item 31a)
A/78/PV.72
CRIME PREVENTION (Agenda item 107)
A/C.3/78/SR.5
IAEA—REPORTS (Agenda item 89)
A/78/PV.29
INDIGENOUS PEOPLES (Agenda item 68a)
A/C.3/78/SR.15
INDIGENOUS PEOPLES—CONFERENCES (Agenda item 68b)
A/C.3/78/SR.15
MILLENNIUM SUMMIT—CONFERENCES (Agenda item 117)
A/78/PV.102
MINE CLEARANCE (Agenda item 46)
A/C.4/78/SR.10
PEACE (Agenda item 14)
A/78/PV.76
RESPONSIBILITY TO PROTECT (Agenda item 129)
A/78/PV.96
UN—BUDGET (2024) (Agenda item 134)
A/C.5/78/SR.5
UN—PROGRAMME PLANNING (Agenda item 135)
A/C.5/78/SR.5

Samson, Hedda (European Union) (continued)

UN. GENERAL ASSEMBLY—WORK PROGRAMME (Agenda item 120)
A/78/PV.32
UN. GENERAL ASSEMBLY (78TH SESS. : 2023-2024)—OFFICERS (Agenda item 5)
A/C.5/78/SR.1
UN. GENERAL ASSEMBLY (78TH SESS. : 2023-2024). 5TH COMMITTEE—WORK ORGANIZATION (Agenda item 7)
A/C.5/78/SR.40
UN CONFERENCES (Agenda item 13)
A/78/PV.102
UN RESOLUTIONS—IMPLEMENTATION (Agenda item 119)
A/78/PV.32
UN YOUTH OFFICE—REPORTS (Agenda item 130)
A/78/PV.102
VETO (Agenda item 63)
A/78/PV.78
WOMEN'S ADVANCEMENT (Agenda item 25a)
A/C.3/78/SR.7
WOMEN'S ADVANCEMENT—CONFERENCES (Agenda item 25b)
A/C.3/78/SR.7

San Román Valdés, Jorge (Cuba)

UN. GENERAL ASSEMBLY—WORK PROGRAMME (Agenda item 120)
A/78/PV.32
UN RESOLUTIONS—IMPLEMENTATION (Agenda item 119)
A/78/PV.32

Sanabria de Montiel, María Gloria Beatriz (Paraguay)

IAEA—REPORTS (Agenda item 89)
A/78/PV.30

Sanabria Duarte, Viviana Rocio (Paraguay)

ARMS RACE—OUTER SPACE (Agenda item 97a)
A/C.1/78/PV.17
OUTER SPACE—CONFIDENCE-BUILDING MEASURES (Agenda item 99v)
A/C.1/78/PV.17

Sánchez, Pedro (Spain. President)

UN. GENERAL ASSEMBLY (78TH SESS. : 2023-2024)—GENERAL DEBATE (Agenda item 8)
A/78/PV.7
UN. GENERAL ASSEMBLY (78TH SESS. : 2023-2024)—SPECIAL STATEMENTS
A/78/PV.7

Sánchez Cordero Dávila, Jorge A. (Mexico)

UN COMMISSION ON INTERNATIONAL TRADE LAW—REPORTS (Agenda item 77)
A/C.6/78/SR.14

Sánchez de Lerín García-Ovies, Ignacio (Spain)

AFRICA—NUCLEAR-WEAPON-FREE ZONES (Agenda item 92)
A/C.1/78/PV.25

Sánchez de Lerín García-Ovies, Ignacio (Spain) (European Union)

DISARMAMENT—GENERAL AND COMPLETE (Agenda item 99)
A/C.1/78/PV.30
DISARMAMENT AGREEMENTS—OUTER SPACE (Agenda item 97c)
A/C.1/78/PV.27
INFORMATION—INTERNATIONAL SECURITY (Agenda item 94)
A/C.1/78/PV.29
MEDITERRANEAN REGION—REGIONAL SECURITY (Agenda item 104)
A/C.1/78/PV.29
MIDDLE EAST—NUCLEAR-WEAPON-FREE ZONES (Agenda item 95)
A/C.1/78/PV.26
UN. CONFERENCE ON DISARMAMENT—REPORTS (Agenda item 101a)
A/C.1/78/PV.29
WEAPONS—OUTER SPACE (Agenda item 97b)
A/C.1/78/PV.27

Sánchez Fuentes, Jorge Sain (Cuba)

PEACEKEEPING OPERATIONS (Agenda item 51)
A/C.4/78/SR.18

Sánchez García, Nathalia (Colombia)

ELECTION VERIFICATION—UN (Agenda item 71b)
A/C.3/78/SR.50
HUMAN RIGHTS (Agenda item 71)
A/C.3/78/SR.16
HUMAN RIGHTS ACTIVISTS (Agenda item 71b)
A/C.3/78/SR.19
JUDICIAL INDEPENDENCE (Agenda item 71b)
A/C.3/78/SR.31
PALESTINIANS—ASSISTANCE (Agenda item 72b)
A/78/PV.46
PERSONS WITH DISABILITIES—HUMAN RIGHTS (Agenda item 71a)
A/C.3/78/SR.51
RURAL WOMEN (Agenda item 25a)
A/C.3/78/SR.7; A/C.3/78/SR.49
SUMMARY EXECUTIONS (Agenda item 71b)
A/C.3/78/SR.31
UN. HUMAN RIGHTS COUNCIL—REPORTS (Agenda item 66)
A/78/PV.28
UN HIGH COMMISSIONER FOR REFUGEES—REPORTS (Agenda item 60)
A/C.3/78/SR.44
WOMEN MIGRANT WORKERS (Agenda item 25a)
A/C.3/78/SR.7; A/C.3/78/SR.49
WOMEN'S ADVANCEMENT (Agenda item 25a)
A/C.3/78/SR.7

Sánchez García, Nathalia (Colombia) (continued)

WOMEN'S ADVANCEMENT—CONFERENCES (Agenda item 25b)
A/C.3/78/SR.7

Sánchez Izquierdo, Mónica (Ecuador)

VETO (Agenda item 63)
A/78/PV.68

Sánchez Kiesslich, Eduardo Alcibiades (Mexico)

CLUSTER MUNITIONS (Agenda item 99dd)
A/C.1/78/PV.18
CONVENTIONAL WEAPONS (Agenda item 99u)
A/C.1/78/PV.18
DISARMAMENT—GENERAL AND COMPLETE (Agenda item 99)
A/C.1/78/PV.18; A/C.1/78/PV.30
DISARMAMENT AGREEMENTS—OUTER SPACE (Agenda item 97c)
A/C.1/78/PV.27
FISSIONABLE MATERIALS—TREATIES (Agenda item 99a)
A/C.1/78/PV.26
INFORMATION—INTERNATIONAL SECURITY (Agenda item 94)
A/C.1/78/PV.29
NUCLEAR DISARMAMENT (Agenda item 99b)
A/C.1/78/PV.12
NUCLEAR DISARMAMENT—TREATY COMPLIANCE (Agenda item 99q)
A/C.1/78/PV.12
NUCLEAR NON-PROLIFERATION—INTERNATIONAL OBLIGATIONS (Agenda item 99w)
A/C.1/78/PV.12
NUCLEAR WEAPON TESTS—TREATIES (Agenda item 105)
A/C.1/78/PV.12; A/C.1/78/PV.25
NUCLEAR WEAPONS—ELIMINATION (Agenda item 99z)
A/C.1/78/PV.26
NUCLEAR WEAPONS—TREATIES (Agenda item 99ff)
A/C.1/78/PV.11; A/C.1/78/PV.12
NUCLEAR WEAPONS USE—TREATIES (Agenda item 100a)
A/C.1/78/PV.25
OUTER SPACE—PRINCIPLES (Agenda item 97d)
A/C.1/78/PV.27
SMALL ARMS—ILLICIT TRAFFIC—ASSISTANCE (Agenda item 99n)
A/C.1/78/PV.18
UN—PROGRAMME PLANNING (Agenda item 135)
A/C.1/78/PV.10
UN. CONFERENCE ON DISARMAMENT—REPORTS (Agenda item 101a)
A/C.1/78/PV.22; A/C.1/78/PV.29
UN. DISARMAMENT COMMISSION—REPORTS (Agenda item 101b)
A/C.1/78/PV.22

Sánchez Kiesslich, Eduardo Alcibiades (Mexico) (continued)

UN. GENERAL ASSEMBLY—WORK PROGRAMME (Agenda item 120)
A/C.1/78/PV.10
WEAPONS—OUTER SPACE (Agenda item 97b)
A/C.1/78/PV.27

Sánchez Kiesslich, Eduardo Alcibiades (Mexico) (New Agenda Coalition)

UN. GENERAL ASSEMBLY (78TH SESS. : 2023-2024). 1ST COMMITTEE—GENERAL DEBATE (Agenda item 8)
A/C.1/78/PV.4

Sánchez Serra, Ricardo (Federación de Periodistas del Perú)

WESTERN SAHARA QUESTION (Agenda item 58)
A/C.4/78/SR.4

Sandiori, Sherley Mega (Indonesia)

CRIMES AGAINST HUMANITY (Agenda item 80)
A/C.6/78/SR.44; A/C.6/78/SR.45
JUDICIAL INDEPENDENCE (Agenda item 71b)
A/C.3/78/SR.31
UN. INTERNATIONAL LAW COMMISSION—REPORTS (Agenda item 79)
A/C.6/78/SR.27

Sandström Jaffe, Sofie (International Union for Conservation of Nature and Natural Resources)

ENVIRONMENT (Agenda item 71b)
A/C.3/78/SR.29

Sandu, Maia (Republic of Moldova. President)

UN. GENERAL ASSEMBLY (78TH SESS. : 2023-2024)—GENERAL DEBATE (Agenda item 8)
A/78/PV.7
UN. GENERAL ASSEMBLY (78TH SESS. : 2023-2024)—SPECIAL STATEMENTS
A/78/PV.7

Sangkhapreecha, Kantapon (Thailand)

FOOD SECURITY (Agenda item 23a)
A/C.2/78/SR.16
POVERTY—INTERNATIONAL DECADES (Agenda item 21a)
A/C.2/78/SR.16
RURAL POVERTY (Agenda item 21b)
A/C.2/78/SR.16

Santa Ana Vara, Alma Esperanza (Mexico)

AGEING PERSONS (Agenda item 24b)
A/C.3/78/SR.1; A/C.3/78/SR.2
ELECTION VERIFICATION—UN (Agenda item 71b)
A/C.3/78/SR.50
RIGHT TO DEVELOPMENT (Agenda item 71b)
A/C.3/78/SR.48
RURAL WOMEN (Agenda item 25a)
A/C.3/78/SR.49

Santa Ana Vara, Alma Esperanza (Mexico) (continued)

SOCIAL CONDITIONS (Agenda item 24b)
A/C.3/78/SR.2; A/C.3/78/SR.47
SOCIAL DEVELOPMENT—CONFERENCES (Agenda item 24a)
A/C.3/78/SR.55
WOMEN'S ADVANCEMENT (Agenda item 25a)
A/C.3/78/SR.7
WOMEN'S ADVANCEMENT—CONFERENCES (Agenda item 25b)
A/C.3/78/SR.7; A/C.3/78/SR.51
YOUTH (Agenda item 24b)
A/C.3/78/SR.2

Santokhi, Chandrikapersad (Suriname. President)

UN. GENERAL ASSEMBLY (78TH SESS. : 2023-2024)—GENERAL DEBATE (Agenda item 8)
A/78/PV.6
UN. GENERAL ASSEMBLY (78TH SESS. : 2023-2024)—SPECIAL STATEMENTS
A/78/PV.6

Santos, Luiz Felipe Rosa dos (Brazil)

FOOD SECURITY (Agenda item 23a)
A/C.2/78/SR.17
POVERTY—INTERNATIONAL DECADES (Agenda item 21a)
A/C.2/78/SR.17
RURAL POVERTY (Agenda item 21b)
A/C.2/78/SR.17

Santosa, Teguh (RMOL Network (Organization))

WESTERN SAHARA QUESTION (Agenda item 58)
A/C.4/78/SR.4

Sanusi, Zainu-Deen (Sierra Leone)

LANDLOCKED DEVELOPING COUNTRIES—CONFERENCES (Agenda item 20b)
A/C.2/78/SR.7
LEAST DEVELOPED COUNTRIES—CONFERENCES (Agenda item 20a)
A/C.2/78/SR.7

Sao, Mariam (Mauritania)

INTERNATIONAL LAW—TRAINING PROGRAMMES (Agenda item 78)
A/C.6/78/SR.22
RULE OF LAW (Agenda item 83)
A/C.6/78/SR.16
TERRORISM (Agenda item 109)
A/C.6/78/SR.5

Sapkul, Louismongkol (Thailand)

DEVELOPMENT FINANCE (Agenda item 16b)
A/C.2/78/SR.9
INTERNATIONAL TRADE (Agenda item 16a)
A/C.2/78/SR.9

Sar, Minke van der (Netherlands (Kingdom of the))

UN YOUTH OFFICE—REPORTS (Agenda item 130)
A/78/PV.102

Saran, Sherina (South Africa)

NUCLEAR DISARMAMENT (Agenda item 99b)
A/C.1/78/PV.11
NUCLEAR NON-PROLIFERATION—INTERNATIONAL OBLIGATIONS (Agenda item 99w)
A/C.1/78/PV.11
NUCLEAR WEAPON TESTS—TREATIES (Agenda item 105)
A/C.1/78/PV.11
NUCLEAR WEAPONS—TREATIES (Agenda item 99ff)
A/C.1/78/PV.11
NUCLEAR-WEAPON-FREE ZONES (Agenda item 99cc)
A/C.1/78/PV.11

Saranga, Geraldo (Mozambique)

ADMINISTRATION OF JUSTICE (Agenda item 144)
A/C.6/78/SR.9
CRIMES AGAINST HUMANITY (Agenda item 80)
A/C.6/78/SR.11
INTERNATIONAL JURISDICTION (Agenda item 84)
A/C.6/78/SR.13
RULE OF LAW (Agenda item 83)
A/C.6/78/SR.18
TERRORISM (Agenda item 109)
A/C.6/78/SR.4

Sarufa, Fred (Papua New Guinea)

FRENCH POLYNESIA QUESTION (Agenda item 58)
A/C.4/78/SR.6
NEW CALEDONIA QUESTION (Agenda item 58)
A/C.4/78/SR.3
UN. INTERNATIONAL LAW COMMISSION—REPORTS (Agenda item 79)
A/C.6/78/SR.27
WESTERN SAHARA QUESTION (Agenda item 58)
A/C.4/78/SR.6

Sarufa, Fred (Papua New Guinea) (Melanesian Spearhead Group)

DECOLONIZATION (Agenda item 58)
A/C.4/78/SR.6
NEW CALEDONIA QUESTION (Agenda item 58)
A/C.4/78/SR.6

Sarvarian, Arman (Armenia)

CRIMES AGAINST HUMANITY (Agenda item 80)
A/C.6/78/SR.39
UN. INTERNATIONAL LAW COMMISSION—REPORTS (Agenda item 79)
A/C.6/78/SR.27; A/C.6/78/SR.30

Sarwani, Gul Qaiser (Pakistan)

ARMS RACE—OUTER SPACE (Agenda item 97a)
A/C.1/78/PV.16
CLUSTER MUNITIONS (Agenda item 99dd)
A/C.1/78/PV.28
DISARMAMENT—GENERAL AND COMPLETE (Agenda item 99)
A/C.1/78/PV.26; A/C.1/78/PV.28
DISARMAMENT—UN. GENERAL ASSEMBLY (4TH SPECIAL SESS. ON DISARMAMENT : xxxx) (Agenda item 99h)
A/C.1/78/PV.23
INFORMATION—INTERNATIONAL SECURITY (Agenda item 94)
A/C.1/78/PV.29
LANDMINES—TREATIES (Agenda item 99m)
A/C.1/78/PV.28
MIDDLE EAST—NUCLEAR PROLIFERATION (Agenda item 102)
A/C.1/78/PV.26
NUCLEAR DISARMAMENT (Agenda item 99b)
A/C.1/78/PV.26
NUCLEAR DISARMAMENT—TREATY COMPLIANCE (Agenda item 99q)
A/C.1/78/PV.26
NUCLEAR NON-PROLIFERATION—INTERNATIONAL OBLIGATIONS (Agenda item 99w)
A/C.1/78/PV.26
NUCLEAR WEAPON TESTS—TREATIES (Agenda item 105)
A/C.1/78/PV.26
NUCLEAR WEAPONS—ELIMINATION (Agenda item 99z)
A/C.1/78/PV.26
NUCLEAR WEAPONS—TREATIES (Agenda item 99ff)
A/C.1/78/PV.26
NUCLEAR WEAPONS USE—UN. INTERNATIONAL COURT OF JUSTICE OPINION (Agenda item 99k)
A/C.1/78/PV.26
OUTER SPACE—CONFIDENCE-BUILDING MEASURES (Agenda item 99v)
A/C.1/78/PV.16
OUTER SPACE—PRINCIPLES (Agenda item 97d)
A/C.1/78/PV.16
UN. CONFERENCE ON DISARMAMENT—REPORTS (Agenda item 101a)
A/C.1/78/PV.23

Sassou N'Guesso, Denis (Congo. President)

UN. GENERAL ASSEMBLY (78TH SESS. : 2023-2024)—GENERAL DEBATE (Agenda item 8)
A/78/PV.8
UN. GENERAL ASSEMBLY (78TH SESS. : 2023-2024)—SPECIAL STATEMENTS
A/78/PV.8

Satterthwaite, Margaret L. (UN. Human Rights Council. Special Rapporteur on the Independence of Judges and Lawyers)

JUDICIAL INDEPENDENCE (Agenda item 71b)
A/C.3/78/SR.31

Satuli, Tiina (European Union)

HEALTH (Agenda item 125)
A/78/PV.41

Savadogo, Halidou (Burkina Faso)

PEACEKEEPING OPERATIONS (Agenda item 51)
A/C.4/78/SR.20

Savarin, Charles Angelo (Dominica. President)

UN. GENERAL ASSEMBLY (78TH SESS. : 2023-2024)—GENERAL DEBATE (Agenda item 8)
A/78/PV.8
UN. GENERAL ASSEMBLY (78TH SESS. : 2023-2024)—SPECIAL STATEMENTS
A/78/PV.8

Savova, Victoria (Bulgaria)

YOUTH (Agenda item 24b)
A/C.3/78/SR.2

Sawicz, Jacek (Poland)

UN. GENERAL ASSEMBLY (78TH SESS. : 2023-2024). 1ST COMMITTEE—GENERAL DEBATE (Agenda item 8)
A/C.1/78/PV.5

Sayej, Loureen O.A. (State of Palestine)

CRIMES AGAINST HUMANITY (Agenda item 80)
A/C.6/78/SR.39; A/C.6/78/SR.41; A/C.6/78/SR.43; A/C.6/78/SR.44; A/C.6/78/SR.45
DISASTER VICTIMS (Agenda item 86)
A/C.6/78/SR.7
INTERNATIONAL JURISDICTION (Agenda item 84)
A/C.6/78/SR.13
RULE OF LAW (Agenda item 83)
A/C.6/78/SR.19
UN. INTERNATIONAL LAW COMMISSION—REPORTS (Agenda item 79)
A/C.6/78/SR.28; A/C.6/78/SR.33
UN CHARTER—REPORTS (Agenda item 82)
A/C.6/78/SR.34

Scalabrini-McKellar, Tobias (Sovereign Order of Malta)

DEMOCRACY (Agenda item 71b)
A/C.3/78/SR.28
HUMAN RIGHTS (Agenda item 71)
A/C.3/78/SR.16
POVERTY—HUMAN RIGHTS (Agenda item 71b)
A/C.3/78/SR.30

Schaare, Ben (New Zealand)

HEALTH (Agenda item 125)
A/78/PV.77

Schalkwyk, Marthinus van (South Africa)

ECONOMIC SANCTIONS—INTERNATIONAL RELATIONS (Agenda item 28)
A/78/PV.89
HEALTH (Agenda item 125)
A/78/PV.16
HIV/AIDS—DECLARATIONS (Agenda item 10)
A/78/PV.91
INFORMATION (Agenda item 53)
A/C.4/78/SR.14
NUCLEAR WEAPONS—ELIMINATION (Agenda item 99z)
A/C.1/78/PV.25
PEACEBUILDING (Agenda item 61)
A/78/PV.100
RACIAL DISCRIMINATION—ELIMINATION (Agenda item 69a)
A/78/PV.63; A/78/PV.103
RIGHTS OF THE CHILD (Agenda item 67)
A/C.3/78/SR.12
SPECIAL POLITICAL MISSIONS (Agenda item 52)
A/C.4/78/SR.21
TERRITORIES OCCUPIED BY ISRAEL—HUMAN RIGHTS (Agenda item 50)
A/C.4/78/SR.25
TERRITORIES OCCUPIED BY ISRAEL—NATURAL RESOURCES (Agenda item 59)
A/C.2/78/SR.19
UKRAINE—POLITICAL CONDITIONS (Agenda item 62)
A/78/PV.99
UN. GENERAL ASSEMBLY—WORK PROGRAMME (Agenda item 120)
A/78/PV.32
UN. GENERAL ASSEMBLY (78TH SESS. : 2023-2024). 2ND COMMITTEE—GENERAL DEBATE (Agenda item 8)
A/C.2/78/SR.3
UN. HUMAN RIGHTS COUNCIL—REPORTS (Agenda item 66)
A/78/PV.28
UN. PEACEBUILDING COMMISSION—REPORTS (Agenda item 27)
A/78/PV.100
UN. PEACEBUILDING FUND—REPORTS (Agenda item 111)
A/78/PV.100
UN RESOLUTIONS—IMPLEMENTATION (Agenda item 119)
A/78/PV.32
UNRWA—ACTIVITIES (Agenda item 49)
A/C.4/78/SR.22; A/C.4/78/SR.23; A/C.4/78/SR.26
VETO (Agenda item 63)
A/78/PV.3; A/78/PV.51; A/78/PV.68; A/78/PV.70; A/78/PV.74
WESTERN SAHARA QUESTION (Agenda item 58)
A/C.4/78/SR.6

Schalkwyk, Marthinus van (South Africa) (Foreign Policy and Global Health Initiative)

HEALTH (Agenda item 125)
A/78/PV.77

Schallenberg, Alexander (Austria)

UN. GENERAL ASSEMBLY (78TH SESS. : 2023-2024)—GENERAL DEBATE (Agenda item 8)
A/78/PV.9

Schantz, Delphine (UN Office on Drugs and Crime. New York Office)

CRIME PREVENTION (Agenda item 107)
A/C.3/78/SR.5
CYBERCRIME (Agenda item 108)
A/C.3/78/SR.5

Scheuer, Emil Fischer-Nielsen (Denmark)

ELECTION VERIFICATION—UN (Agenda item 71b)
A/C.3/78/SR.50

Schlaepfer, Christian (Switzerland)

INFORMATION TECHNOLOGY—DEVELOPMENT (Agenda item 15)
A/C.2/78/SR.23
INTERNATIONAL TRADE (Agenda item 16a)
A/C.2/78/SR.24
SUSTAINABLE DEVELOPMENT (Agenda item 18)
A/C.2/78/SR.24

Schlyter, Charlotta (Sweden)

FREEDOM OF EXPRESSION (Agenda item 71b)
A/C.3/78/SR.19

Schmied, Gina Andrea (Switzerland)

ADMINISTRATION OF JUSTICE (Agenda item 144)
A/C.5/78/SR.15
PEACEKEEPING OPERATIONS—FINANCING (Agenda item 146)
A/C.5/78/SR.35
PERSONNEL QUESTIONS—UN SYSTEM (Agenda item 142)
A/C.5/78/SR.10
UN—ADMINISTRATION (Agenda item 132)
A/C.5/78/SR.2
UN—BUDGET (2024) (Agenda item 134)
A/C.5/78/SR.26/PartII; A/C.5/78/SR.28; A/C.5/78/SR.33
UN—FINANCIAL SITUATION (Agenda item 136)
A/C.5/78/SR.6
UN—HUMAN RESOURCES MANAGEMENT (Agenda item 139)
A/C.5/78/SR.27
UN—PROGRAMME PLANNING (Agenda item 135)
A/C.5/78/SR.24
UN. OFFICE OF INTERNAL OVERSIGHT SERVICES—REPORTS (Agenda item 143)
A/C.5/78/SR.2

Scholz, Olaf (Germany. Chancellor)

UN. GENERAL ASSEMBLY (78TH SESS. : 2023-2024)—GENERAL DEBATE (Agenda item 8)
A/78/PV.5
UN. GENERAL ASSEMBLY (78TH SESS. : 2023-2024)—SPECIAL STATEMENTS
A/78/PV.5

Schönburg, Laetitia (Sovereign Order of Malta)

SOCIAL CONDITIONS (Agenda item 24b)
A/C.3/78/SR.4
SOCIAL DEVELOPMENT (Agenda item 24)
A/C.3/78/SR.4

Schuller, Simone (European Union)

AGEING PERSONS (Agenda item 24b)
A/C.3/78/SR.1
CRIME PREVENTION (Agenda item 107)
A/C.3/78/SR.5
CYBERCRIME (Agenda item 108)
A/C.3/78/SR.5
HUMAN RIGHTS—AFGHANISTAN (Agenda item 71c)
A/C.3/78/SR.34
HUMAN RIGHTS—IRAN (ISLAMIC REPUBLIC OF) (Agenda item 71c)
A/C.3/78/SR.34
HUMAN RIGHTS—SYRIAN ARAB REPUBLIC (Agenda item 71c)
A/C.3/78/SR.34
PERSONS WITH DISABILITIES—HUMAN RIGHTS (Agenda item 71a)
A/C.3/78/SR.18
RIGHTS OF THE CHILD (Agenda item 67)
A/C.3/78/SR.11; A/C.3/78/SR.12

Schutter, Olivier de (UN. Human Rights Council. Special Rapporteur on Extreme Poverty and Human Rights)

POVERTY—HUMAN RIGHTS (Agenda item 71b)
A/C.3/78/SR.30

Schwalger, Carolyn (New Zealand)

INTERNATIONAL RESIDUAL MECHANISM FOR CRIMINAL TRIBUNALS (Agenda item 126)
A/78/PV.19
UN. GENERAL ASSEMBLY (78TH SESS. : 2023-2024). 1ST COMMITTEE—GENERAL DEBATE (Agenda item 8)
A/C.1/78/PV.3
VETO (Agenda item 63)
A/78/PV.51; A/78/PV.60; A/78/PV.70; A/78/PV.75; A/78/PV.78

Seah, Mark (Singapore)

INTERNATIONAL LAW—TRAINING PROGRAMMES (Agenda item 78)
A/C.6/78/SR.21
MARINE ECOSYSTEMS—BIOLOGICAL DIVERSITY (Agenda item 75c)
A/78/PV.73

Seah, Mark (Singapore) (continued)

RESPONSIBILITY TO PROTECT (Agenda item 129)
A/78/PV.97
RULE OF LAW (Agenda item 83)
A/C.6/78/SR.15
UN. GENERAL ASSEMBLY—WORK PROGRAMME (Agenda item 120)
A/78/PV.32
UN RESOLUTIONS—IMPLEMENTATION (Agenda item 119)
A/78/PV.32
VETO (Agenda item 63)
A/78/PV.70

Seah, Mark (Singapore) (ASEAN)

INTERNATIONAL LAW—TRAINING PROGRAMMES (Agenda item 78)
A/C.6/78/SR.21
UN—BUDGET (2024) (Agenda item 134)
A/C.5/78/SR.3
UN—FINANCIAL SITUATION (Agenda item 136)
A/C.5/78/SR.6
UN. CONFERENCE ON DISARMAMENT—REPORTS (Agenda item 101a)
A/C.1/78/PV.22
UN. DISARMAMENT COMMISSION—REPORTS (Agenda item 101b)
A/C.1/78/PV.22

Šebenik, Nataša (Slovenia)

CRIMES AGAINST HUMANITY (Agenda item 80)
A/C.6/78/SR.10
INTERNATIONAL JURISDICTION (Agenda item 84)
A/C.6/78/SR.12
RULE OF LAW (Agenda item 83)
A/C.6/78/SR.16

Seedat, Ahmed Hoosen (South Africa)

DEVELOPMENT FINANCE (Agenda item 16b)
A/C.2/78/SR.11
FINANCIAL FLOWS (Agenda item 16f)
A/C.2/78/SR.11
INTERNATIONAL TRADE (Agenda item 16a)
A/C.2/78/SR.11
MACROECONOMIC POLICY (Agenda item 16)
A/C.2/78/SR.11

Segessemann, Tim (Switzerland)

HUMAN RIGHTS—BELARUS (Agenda item 71c)
A/C.3/78/SR.37
HUMAN RIGHTS—RUSSIAN FEDERATION (Agenda item 71c)
A/C.3/78/SR.37
HUMAN RIGHTS—SOMALIA (Agenda item 71c)
A/C.3/78/SR.35
HUMAN RIGHTS—UKRAINE (Agenda item 71c)
A/C.3/78/SR.37

Segobin Maulloo, Vandana (Mauritius)

VETO (Agenda item 63)
A/78/PV.67; A/78/PV.75

Segovia, Lisa Isabelle (France)

CLIMATE (Agenda item 18d)
A/C.2/78/SR.25

Segura Aragón, Carlos Efraín (El Salvador)

MIGRANTS—PROTECTION (Agenda item 71b)
A/C.3/78/SR.23
NUCLEAR DISARMAMENT (Agenda item 99b)
A/C.1/78/PV.12
NUCLEAR NON-PROLIFERATION—INTERNATIONAL OBLIGATIONS (Agenda item 99w)
A/C.1/78/PV.12
NUCLEAR WEAPONS—TREATIES (Agenda item 99ff)
A/C.1/78/PV.12
NUCLEAR-WEAPON-FREE ZONES (Agenda item 99cc)
A/C.1/78/PV.12
PERSONS WITH DISABILITIES—HUMAN RIGHTS (Agenda item 71a)
A/C.3/78/SR.38
RIGHT TO HEALTH (Agenda item 71b)
A/C.3/78/SR.39
RIGHTS OF THE CHILD (Agenda item 67)
A/C.3/78/SR.12
SUSTAINABLE DEVELOPMENT (Agenda item 18)
A/C.2/78/SR.22
UN. SECURITY COUNCIL—MEMBERSHIP (Agenda item 121)
A/78/PV.36
VETO (Agenda item 63)
A/78/PV.61

Seid, Ilana Victorya (Palau)

SMALL ISLAND DEVELOPING STATES—PROGRAMMES OF ACTION (Agenda item 18b)
A/78/PV.100

Seillan, Hubert (Fondation France Maroc)

WESTERN SAHARA QUESTION (Agenda item 58)
A/C.4/78/SR.5

Séjourné, Stéphane (France)

UKRAINE—POLITICAL CONDITIONS (Agenda item 62)
A/78/PV.56

Sekeris, Evangelos C. (Greece)

HUMAN RIGHTS—INTERNATIONAL INSTRUMENTS (Agenda item 71a)
A/C.3/78/SR.25
HUMAN RIGHTS ADVANCEMENT (Agenda item 71b)
A/C.3/78/SR.52
INFORMATION (Agenda item 53)
A/C.4/78/SR.13

Sekeris, Evangelos C. (Greece) (continued)

PEACE (Agenda item 14)
A/78/PV.82
RESPONSIBILITY TO PROTECT (Agenda item 129)
A/78/PV.97
SPORTS—OLYMPIC GAMES (Agenda item 11)
A/78/PV.38
UN. GENERAL ASSEMBLY (78TH SESS. : 2023-2024). 1ST COMMITTEE—GENERAL DEBATE (Agenda item 8)
A/C.1/78/PV.4
UN. GENERAL ASSEMBLY (78TH SESS. : 2023-2024). 2ND COMMITTEE—GENERAL DEBATE (Agenda item 8)
A/C.2/78/SR.4
VETO (Agenda item 63)
A/78/PV.52; A/78/PV.69

Sekhar, Uma (India)

UN. INTERNATIONAL LAW COMMISSION—REPORTS (Agenda item 79)
A/C.6/78/SR.25

Sekonyana, Ngako Elphus (South Africa)

CRIME PREVENTION (Agenda item 107)
A/C.3/78/SR.5
CYBERCRIME (Agenda item 108)
A/C.3/78/SR.5
RIGHT TO HEALTH (Agenda item 71b)
A/C.3/78/SR.39

Selim, Sameh Hassan Shokry (Egypt)

UN. GENERAL ASSEMBLY (78TH SESS. : 2023-2024)—GENERAL DEBATE (Agenda item 8)
A/78/PV.12

Semon, Alizée (France)

UN—PROGRAMME PLANNING (Agenda item 135)
A/C.1/78/PV.10
UN. GENERAL ASSEMBLY—WORK PROGRAMME (Agenda item 120)
A/C.1/78/PV.10

Seneduangdeth, Vilayluck (Lao People's Democratic Republic)

TERRORISM (Agenda item 109)
A/C.6/78/SR.4
WOMEN'S ADVANCEMENT (Agenda item 25a)
A/C.3/78/SR.9
WOMEN'S ADVANCEMENT—CONFERENCES (Agenda item 25b)
A/C.3/78/SR.9

Senesi, Roselynn Finda (Sierra Leone)

WOMEN'S ADVANCEMENT (Agenda item 25a)
A/C.3/78/SR.9
WOMEN'S ADVANCEMENT—CONFERENCES (Agenda item 25b)
A/C.3/78/SR.9

Sengdara, Xayfhong (Lao People's Democratic Republic)

HUMAN RIGHTS—DEMOCRATIC PEOPLE'S REPUBLIC OF KOREA (Agenda item 71c)
A/C.3/78/SR.33
HUMAN RIGHTS—INTERNATIONAL INSTRUMENTS (Agenda item 71a)
A/C.3/78/SR.25
HUMAN RIGHTS ADVANCEMENT (Agenda item 71b)
A/C.3/78/SR.25

Seong, Woong (Republic of Korea)

UN. GENERAL ASSEMBLY (78TH SESS. : 2023-2024)—OFFICERS (Agenda item 5)
A/C.5/78/SR.1
UN. GENERAL ASSEMBLY (78TH SESS. : 2023-2024). 5TH COMMITTEE—WORK ORGANIZATION (Agenda item 7)
A/C.5/78/SR.27; A/C.5/78/SR.35

Sepe, Tobie (Central African Republic)

WESTERN SAHARA QUESTION (Agenda item 58)
A/C.4/78/SR.6

Serage, Bruno Bernardo (Mozambique)

SELF-DETERMINATION OF PEOPLES (Agenda item 70)
A/C.3/78/SR.42
UN HIGH COMMISSIONER FOR REFUGEES—REPORTS (Agenda item 60)
A/C.3/78/SR.45

Sesonga, Fred (Rwanda)

RESPONSIBILITY TO PROTECT (Agenda item 129)
A/78/PV.99

Sewanyana, Livingstone (UN. Human Rights Council. Independent Expert on the Promotion of a Democratic and Equitable International Order)

DEMOCRACY (Agenda item 71b)
A/C.3/78/SR.28

Seydou, Abdoul Fadh Mahamadou (Niger)

ELECTION VERIFICATION—UN (Agenda item 71b)
A/78/PV.50; A/C.3/78/SR.50
HUMAN RIGHTS ACTIVISTS (Agenda item 71b)
A/C.3/78/SR.56
HUMAN RIGHTS ADVANCEMENT (Agenda item 71b)
A/C.3/78/SR.52
MINORITIES (Agenda item 71b)
A/C.3/78/SR.52
PERSONS WITH DISABILITIES—HUMAN RIGHTS (Agenda item 71a)
A/C.3/78/SR.51
RIGHTS OF THE CHILD (Agenda item 67)
A/C.3/78/SR.55

Seydou, Abdoul Fadh Mahamadou (Niger) (continued)

RURAL WOMEN (Agenda item 25a)
A/C.3/78/SR.49
SANCTIONS—INTERNATIONAL RELATIONS (Agenda item 71b)
A/C.3/78/SR.48
WOMEN MIGRANT WORKERS (Agenda item 25a)
A/C.3/78/SR.49
WOMEN'S ADVANCEMENT—CONFERENCES (Agenda item 25b)
A/C.3/78/SR.51
YOUTH (Agenda item 24b)
A/C.3/78/SR.55

Seymenoğlu, Melek Dilsen (Türkiye)

CRIMES AGAINST HUMANITY (Agenda item 80)
A/C.6/78/SR.39; A/C.6/78/SR.41

Seymour, Daniel (UN-Women)

RURAL WOMEN (Agenda item 25a)
A/C.3/78/SR.7
WOMEN MIGRANT WORKERS (Agenda item 25a)
A/C.3/78/SR.7
WOMEN'S ADVANCEMENT—CONFERENCES (Agenda item 25b)
A/C.3/78/SR.7

Sezer, Alper (Türkiye)

TERRITORIES OCCUPIED BY ISRAEL—HUMAN RIGHTS (Agenda item 50)
A/C.4/78/SR.24

Shaev, Evgeny (Belarus)

UN. COMMITTEE ON RELATIONS WITH THE HOST COUNTRY—REPORTS (Agenda item 161)
A/C.6/78/SR.35

Shafique, Umar (Pakistan)

DEVELOPMENT FINANCE (Agenda item 16b)
A/C.2/78/SR.9
EXTERNAL DEBT (Agenda item 16c)
A/C.2/78/SR.9
FINANCIAL FLOWS (Agenda item 16f)
A/C.2/78/SR.9
INFORMATION TECHNOLOGY—DEVELOPMENT (Agenda item 15)
A/C.2/78/SR.10
SCIENCE AND TECHNOLOGY—DEVELOPMENT (Agenda item 19a)
A/C.2/78/SR.10

Shaheed, Farida (UN. Human Rights Council. Special Rapporteur on the Right to Education)

RIGHT TO EDUCATION (Agenda item 71b)
A/C.3/78/SR.27

Shaheen, Ghasaq Yousif (United Arab Emirates)

UN. GENERAL ASSEMBLY (78TH SESS. : 2023-2024). 1ST COMMITTEE—GENERAL DEBATE (Agenda item 8)
A/C.1/78/PV.4
UN. SECURITY COUNCIL—REPORTS (Agenda item 26)
A/78/PV.93
VETO (Agenda item 63)
A/78/PV.3

Shaibata, Mrabih Rabou ((personal capacity))

WESTERN SAHARA QUESTION (Agenda item 58)
A/C.4/78/SR.5

Shaked, Or (Israel)

AGEING PERSONS (Agenda item 24b)
A/C.3/78/SR.1
HUMAN RIGHTS—SYRIAN ARAB REPUBLIC (Agenda item 71c)
A/C.3/78/SR.54
HUMAN RIGHTS—TERRITORIES OCCUPIED BY ISRAEL (Agenda item 71c)
A/C.3/78/SR.27
PERSONS WITH DISABILITIES—HUMAN RIGHTS (Agenda item 71a)
A/C.3/78/SR.38
POVERTY—HUMAN RIGHTS (Agenda item 71b)
A/C.3/78/SR.30
RIGHT TO EDUCATION (Agenda item 71b)
A/C.3/78/SR.27

Shaker, Mohammed Amin (Saudi Arabia)

CYBERCRIME (Agenda item 108)
A/C.3/78/SR.5
DEVELOPMENT COOPERATION—MIDDLE-INCOME COUNTRIES (Agenda item 19c)
A/C.2/78/SR.10
INFORMATION TECHNOLOGY—DEVELOPMENT (Agenda item 15)
A/C.2/78/SR.10

Shaman, Ali (Saudi Arabia)

UN HIGH COMMISSIONER FOR REFUGEES—REPORTS (Agenda item 60)
A/C.3/78/SR.44

Shamun, Amr Danyal (Maldives)

LANDLOCKED DEVELOPING COUNTRIES—CONFERENCES (Agenda item 20b)
A/C.2/78/SR.7
LAW OF THE SEA (Agenda item 75a)
A/78/PV.43
LEAST DEVELOPED COUNTRIES—CONFERENCES (Agenda item 20a)
A/C.2/78/SR.7
MARINE ECOSYSTEMS—BIOLOGICAL DIVERSITY (Agenda item 75c)
A/78/PV.43

Shamun, Amr Danyal (Maldives) (continued)

STRADDLING FISH STOCKS (Agenda item 75b)
A/78/PV.43

Shapir Ben Naftaly, Reut (Israel)

DECOLONIZATION (Agenda item 58)
A/C.4/78/SR.7; A/C.4/78/SR.8
DISARMAMENT—GENERAL AND COMPLETE (Agenda item 99)
A/78/PV.106
INFORMATION (Agenda item 53)
A/C.4/78/SR.14
PALESTINE QUESTION (Agenda item 35)
A/78/PV.39
RACIAL DISCRIMINATION—ELIMINATION (Agenda item 69a)
A/78/PV.103
UNRWA—ACTIVITIES (Agenda item 49)
A/C.4/78/SR.22

Sharaf, Omran (United Arab Emirates) (UN. Committee on the Peaceful Uses of Outer Space. Chair)

OUTER SPACE—PEACEFUL USES—INTERNATIONAL COOPERATION (Agenda item 48)
A/C.4/78/SR.15

Sharaf, Omran (United Arab Emirates) (UN. General Assembly. Special Political and Decolonization Committee (4th Committee). Working Group on International Cooperation in the Peaceful Uses of Outer Space. Chair)

OUTER SPACE—PEACEFUL USES—INTERNATIONAL COOPERATION (Agenda item 48)
A/C.4/78/SR.17

Sharif, Shahsawar (Pakistan)

ECONOMIC COOPERATION AMONG DEVELOPING COUNTRIES (Agenda item 22b)
A/C.2/78/SR.18
OPERATIONAL ACTIVITIES—UN SYSTEM (Agenda item 22a)
A/C.2/78/SR.18

Sharma, Deeksha (United States)

DEVELOPMENT EDUCATION (Agenda item 18g)
A/C.2/78/SR.22

Sharma, Sangeeta (UN. Department for General Assembly and Conference Management)

HEALTH (Agenda item 125)
A/78/PV.16
PEACE (Agenda item 14)
A/78/PV.62
SMALL ISLAND DEVELOPING STATES—PROGRAMMES OF ACTION (Agenda item 18b)
A/78/PV.100
SOCIAL CONDITIONS (Agenda item 24b)
A/78/PV.101

Sharoni, Benjamin (Israel)

ARMS RACE—OUTER SPACE (Agenda item 97a)
A/C.1/78/PV.27
ARMS TRANSFERS—TREATIES (Agenda item 99x)
A/C.1/78/PV.19; A/C.1/78/PV.28
CHEMICAL WEAPONS—TREATIES (Agenda item 99l)
A/C.1/78/PV.26
CONVENTIONAL WEAPONS—TREATIES (Agenda item 103)
A/C.1/78/PV.19
DISARMAMENT—GENERAL AND COMPLETE (Agenda item 99)
A/C.1/78/PV.19; A/C.1/78/PV.24; A/C.1/78/PV.28
FISSIONABLE MATERIALS—TREATIES (Agenda item 99a)
A/C.1/78/PV.26
INFORMATION—INTERNATIONAL SECURITY (Agenda item 94)
A/C.1/78/PV.21; A/C.1/78/PV.29
MEDITERRANEAN REGION—REGIONAL SECURITY (Agenda item 104)
A/C.1/78/PV.29
MIDDLE EAST—NUCLEAR PROLIFERATION (Agenda item 102)
A/C.1/78/PV.26
MIDDLE EAST—NUCLEAR-WEAPON-FREE ZONES (Agenda item 95)
A/C.1/78/PV.26
MULTILATERALISM—DISARMAMENT (Agenda item 99r)
A/C.1/78/PV.23
NUCLEAR WEAPONS—TREATIES (Agenda item 99ff)
A/C.1/78/PV.26
OUTER SPACE—CONFIDENCE-BUILDING MEASURES (Agenda item 99v)
A/C.1/78/PV.27
SMALL ARMS—ILLICIT TRAFFIC (Agenda item 99p)
A/C.1/78/PV.28

Sharp, Matthew (United States)

DISARMAMENT—GENERAL AND COMPLETE (Agenda item 99)
A/78/PV.105

Shatil, Toufiq Islam (Bangladesh)

ARMS TRANSFERS—TREATIES (Agenda item 99x)
A/C.1/78/PV.18
DECOLONIZATION (Agenda item 58)
A/C.4/78/SR.2
LANDMINES—TREATIES (Agenda item 99m)
A/C.1/78/PV.18
MINE CLEARANCE (Agenda item 46)
A/C.4/78/SR.10
OUTER SPACE—PEACEFUL USES—INTERNATIONAL COOPERATION (Agenda item 48)
A/C.4/78/SR.15

Shatil, Toufiq Islam (Bangladesh) (continued)

RESPONSIBILITY TO PROTECT (Agenda item 129)
A/78/PV.99
SMALL ARMS—ILLICIT TRAFFIC (Agenda item 99p)
A/C.1/78/PV.18
SMALL ARMS—ILLICIT TRAFFIC—ASSISTANCE (Agenda item 99n)
A/C.1/78/PV.18
SOCIAL CONDITIONS (Agenda item 24b)
A/C.3/78/SR.3
SOCIAL DEVELOPMENT (Agenda item 24)
A/C.3/78/SR.3
SPECIAL POLITICAL MISSIONS (Agenda item 52)
A/C.4/78/SR.21
TERRITORIES OCCUPIED BY ISRAEL—HUMAN RIGHTS (Agenda item 50)
A/C.4/78/SR.24
TERRORISM (Agenda item 109)
A/C.6/78/SR.1
UN. GENERAL ASSEMBLY (78TH SESS. : 2023-2024)—OFFICERS (Agenda item 5)
A/C.5/78/SR.1
UN. GENERAL ASSEMBLY (78TH SESS. : 2023-2024). 1ST COMMITTEE—GENERAL DEBATE (Agenda item 8)
A/C.1/78/PV.3
UN. GENERAL ASSEMBLY (78TH SESS. : 2023-2024). 2ND COMMITTEE—GENERAL DEBATE (Agenda item 8)
A/C.2/78/SR.6

Shehata, Kyrollos (Rwanda)

CRIMES AGAINST HUMANITY (Agenda item 80)
A/C.6/78/SR.39

Shehu, Muktar (Nigeria)

UN—BUDGET (2024) (Agenda item 134)
A/C.5/78/SR.33

Shen, Jian (China)

ARMS RACE—OUTER SPACE (Agenda item 97a)
A/C.1/78/PV.17; A/C.1/78/PV.27
DISARMAMENT—GENERAL AND COMPLETE (Agenda item 99)
A/C.1/78/PV.19; A/C.1/78/PV.20; A/C.1/78/PV.23; A/C.1/78/PV.30
DISARMAMENT AGREEMENTS—OUTER SPACE (Agenda item 97c)
A/C.1/78/PV.17; A/C.1/78/PV.27
INFORMATION—INTERNATIONAL SECURITY (Agenda item 94)
A/C.1/78/PV.20
LANDMINES—TREATIES (Agenda item 99m)
A/C.1/78/PV.19
OUTER SPACE—CONFIDENCE-BUILDING MEASURES (Agenda item 99v)
A/C.1/78/PV.17; A/C.1/78/PV.27

Shen, Jian (China) (continued)

OUTER SPACE—PRINCIPLES (Agenda item 97d)
A/C.1/78/PV.17; A/C.1/78/PV.27
SMALL ARMS—ILLICIT TRAFFIC (Agenda item 99p)
A/C.1/78/PV.19
SMALL ARMS—ILLICIT TRAFFIC—ASSISTANCE (Agenda item 99n)
A/C.1/78/PV.19
SOUTH-EAST ASIA—NUCLEAR-WEAPON-FREE ZONES (Agenda item 99y)
A/C.1/78/PV.30
UN. CONFERENCE ON DISARMAMENT—REPORTS (Agenda item 101a)
A/C.1/78/PV.23
WEAPONS—OUTER SPACE (Agenda item 97b)
A/C.1/78/PV.17

Shepherd, Verene (UN. Committee on the Elimination of Racial Discrimination. Chair)

RACIAL DISCRIMINATION—ELIMINATION (Agenda item 69a)
A/78/PV.63; A/C.3/78/SR.41

Shibl, Maruan Naserdien Ali (Libya)

CRIMES AGAINST HUMANITY (Agenda item 80)
A/C.6/78/SR.11

Shiferaw, Girum Getachew (Ethiopia)

CLIMATE (Agenda item 18d)
A/C.2/78/SR.15
DESERTIFICATION—TREATIES (Agenda item 18e)
A/C.2/78/SR.15
DISASTER PREVENTION (Agenda item 18c)
A/C.2/78/SR.15
SUSTAINABLE ENERGY (Agenda item 18h)
A/C.2/78/SR.15

Shino, Mitsuko (Japan)

ARMED CONFLICTS PREVENTION (Agenda item 31a)
A/78/PV.72
HUMAN RIGHTS—TERRITORIES OCCUPIED BY ISRAEL (Agenda item 71c)
A/C.3/78/SR.35
ORGANIZATION FOR DEMOCRACY AND ECONOMIC DEVELOPMENT - GUAM (Agenda item 32)
A/78/PV.85
PEACEBUILDING (Agenda item 61)
A/78/PV.100
UN. GENERAL ASSEMBLY (78TH SESS. : 2023-2024)—GENERAL DEBATE—RIGHT OF REPLY (Agenda item 8)
A/78/PV.11; A/78/PV.14
UN. PEACEBUILDING COMMISSION—REPORTS (Agenda item 27)
A/78/PV.100

Shino, Mitsuko (Japan) (continued)

UN. PEACEBUILDING FUND—REPORTS (Agenda item 111)
A/78/PV.100
UN. SECURITY COUNCIL—MEMBERSHIP (Agenda item 121)
A/78/PV.104
VETO (Agenda item 63)
A/78/PV.52; A/78/PV.67; A/78/PV.70

Shirotori, Miho (UNCTAD)

COMMODITIES (Agenda item 16d)
A/C.2/78/SR.8; A/C.2/78/SR.14
INTERNATIONAL TRADE (Agenda item 16a)
A/C.2/78/SR.8
SUSTAINABLE DEVELOPMENT (Agenda item 18)
A/C.2/78/SR.14

Shrier, Jonathan (United States)

HEALTH (Agenda item 125)
A/78/PV.102
HUMAN RIGHTS (Agenda item 71)
A/C.3/78/SR.16
HUMAN RIGHTS—AFGHANISTAN (Agenda item 71c)
A/C.3/78/SR.25
HUMAN RIGHTS—BELARUS (Agenda item 71c)
A/C.3/78/SR.25
HUMAN RIGHTS—DEMOCRATIC PEOPLE'S REPUBLIC OF KOREA (Agenda item 71c)
A/C.3/78/SR.25
HUMAN RIGHTS—REPORTS (Agenda item 71c)
A/C.3/78/SR.25
HUMAN RIGHTS—RUSSIAN FEDERATION (Agenda item 71c)
A/C.3/78/SR.25
HUMAN RIGHTS—SYRIAN ARAB REPUBLIC (Agenda item 71c)
A/C.3/78/SR.25
HUMAN RIGHTS—TERRITORIES OCCUPIED BY ISRAEL (Agenda item 71c)
A/C.3/78/SR.35
INDIGENOUS PEOPLES (Agenda item 68a)
A/78/PV.107; A/C.3/78/SR.15
INDIGENOUS PEOPLES—CONFERENCES (Agenda item 68b)
A/C.3/78/SR.15
PEACEBUILDING (Agenda item 61)
A/78/PV.101
RESPONSIBILITY TO PROTECT (Agenda item 129)
A/78/PV.97
RIGHTS OF THE CHILD (Agenda item 67)
A/C.3/78/SR.13
SELF-DETERMINATION OF PEOPLES (Agenda item 70)
A/C.3/78/SR.49
SUSTAINABLE DEVELOPMENT (Agenda item 18)
A/78/PV.107

Shrier, Jonathan (United States) (continued)

UN. PEACEBUILDING COMMISSION—REPORTS (Agenda item 27)
A/78/PV.101
UN. PEACEBUILDING FUND—REPORTS (Agenda item 111)
A/78/PV.101
UN HIGH COMMISSIONER FOR REFUGEES—REPORTS (Agenda item 60)
A/C.3/78/SR.45

Shuang, Le (China)

WOMEN'S ADVANCEMENT (Agenda item 25a)
A/C.3/78/SR.8
WOMEN'S ADVANCEMENT—CONFERENCES (Agenda item 25b)
A/C.3/78/SR.8

Shulgin, Egor S. (Russian Federation)

UN. GENERAL ASSEMBLY (78TH SESS. : 2023-2024)—OFFICERS (Agenda item 5)
A/C.4/78/SR.28

Siamalambwa, Bentry (Zambia)

YOUTH (Agenda item 24b)
A/C.3/78/SR.55

Sibomana, Landry (Burundi)

DISPLACED PERSONS (Agenda item 71b)
A/C.3/78/SR.49
HUMAN RIGHTS—DEMOCRATIC PEOPLE'S REPUBLIC OF KOREA (Agenda item 71c)
A/C.3/78/SR.33
HUMAN RIGHTS—ERITREA (Agenda item 71c)
A/C.3/78/SR.36
HUMAN RIGHTS—REPORTS (Agenda item 71c)
A/C.3/78/SR.37
HUMAN RIGHTS—SYRIAN ARAB REPUBLIC (Agenda item 71c)
A/C.3/78/SR.54
WESTERN SAHARA QUESTION (Agenda item 58)
A/C.4/78/SR.8

Sibomana, Landry (Burundi) (UN. Group of African States)

PEACEKEEPING OPERATIONS—FINANCING (Agenda item 146)
A/C.5/78/SR.35

Sid Ahmed, Mula Ihfid (Sahrawi Association in the USA)

WESTERN SAHARA QUESTION (Agenda item 58)
A/C.4/78/SR.5

Siddique, Umer (Pakistan)

UN. GENERAL ASSEMBLY (78TH SESS. : 2023-2024). 1ST COMMITTEE—GENERAL DEBATE (Agenda item 8)
A/C.1/78/PV.6

Sidibe, Souleymane Satigui (Institut sahélien de recherche et d'analyse pour la transformation des conflits)

WESTERN SAHARA QUESTION (Agenda item 58)
A/C.4/78/SR.5

Sigley, Andrew (United Kingdom)

HUMAN RIGHTS ADVANCEMENT (Agenda item 71b)
A/C.3/78/SR.52
MULTILINGUALISM (Agenda item 124)
A/78/PV.108

Sikorski, Radoslaw (Poland)

UKRAINE—POLITICAL CONDITIONS (Agenda item 62)
A/78/PV.56

Silk, John M. (Marshall Islands)

DISARMAMENT—GENERAL AND COMPLETE (Agenda item 99)
A/78/PV.105
RESPONSIBILITY TO PROTECT (Agenda item 129)
A/78/PV.97

Sillah, Aminata (Gambia)

INDIGENOUS PEOPLES (Agenda item 68a)
A/C.3/78/SR.48

Silva, José Ulisses Correia e (Cabo Verde. Prime Minister)

UN. GENERAL ASSEMBLY (78TH SESS. : 2023-2024)—GENERAL DEBATE (Agenda item 8)
A/78/PV.12
UN. GENERAL ASSEMBLY (78TH SESS. : 2023-2024)—SPECIAL STATEMENTS
A/78/PV.12

Silva, Luiz Inácio Lula da (Brazil. President)

UN. GENERAL ASSEMBLY (78TH SESS. : 2023-2024)—GENERAL DEBATE (Agenda item 8)
A/78/PV.4
UN. GENERAL ASSEMBLY (78TH SESS. : 2023-2024)—SPECIAL STATEMENTS
A/78/PV.4

Silva, Miguel Alegre (Portugal)

HUMAN RIGHTS—INTERNATIONAL INSTRUMENTS (Agenda item 71a)
A/C.3/78/SR.17

Silva Walker, Eva Yelina (Cuba)

INTERNATIONAL CRIMINAL COURT—REPORTS (Agenda item 74)
A/78/PV.22
UN. INTERNATIONAL LAW COMMISSION—REPORTS (Agenda item 79)
A/C.6/78/SR.29; A/C.6/78/SR.32

Silverberg, Peter Andrew (Israel)
TAXATION (Agenda item 16h)
A/C.2/78/SR.25

Siman, Augustina (Malta)
CRIMES AGAINST HUMANITY (Agenda item 80)
A/C.6/78/SR.10; A/C.6/78/SR.47

Simina, Wesley (Micronesia (Federated States of). President)
UN. GENERAL ASSEMBLY (78TH SESS. : 2023-2024)—GENERAL DEBATE (Agenda item 8)
A/78/PV.8
UN. GENERAL ASSEMBLY (78TH SESS. : 2023-2024)—SPECIAL STATEMENTS
A/78/PV.8

Simonoff, Mark (United States)
CRIMES AGAINST HUMANITY (Agenda item 80)
A/C.6/78/SR.9; A/C.6/78/SR.38; A/C.6/78/SR.45

Simonovic, Ivan (Croatia)
RESPONSIBILITY TO PROTECT (Agenda item 129)
A/78/PV.96
UN. HUMAN RIGHTS COUNCIL—REPORTS (Agenda item 66)
A/78/PV.28
UN. PEACEBUILDING COMMISSION—REPORTS (Agenda item 27)
A/78/PV.100
UN. SECRETARY-GENERAL—REPORTS (Agenda item 110)
A/78/PV.55

Simonovic, Ivan (Croatia) (Group of Friends of the Responsibility to Protect)
RESPONSIBILITY TO PROTECT (Agenda item 129)
A/78/PV.96

Sinaga, Liandra Jean (Indonesia)
ARMS RACE—OUTER SPACE (Agenda item 97a)
A/C.1/78/PV.16
DISARMAMENT AGREEMENTS—OUTER SPACE (Agenda item 97c)
A/C.1/78/PV.16
OUTER SPACE—CONFIDENCE-BUILDING MEASURES (Agenda item 99v)
A/C.1/78/PV.16
OUTER SPACE—PRINCIPLES (Agenda item 97d)
A/C.1/78/PV.16
WEAPONS—OUTER SPACE (Agenda item 97b)
A/C.1/78/PV.16

Singhateh, Mama Fatima (UN. Human Rights Council. Special Rapporteur on the Sale, Sexual Exploitation and Sexual Abuse of Children)
RIGHTS OF THE CHILD (Agenda item 67)
A/C.3/78/SR.12

Šinigoj, Miha (Slovenia)
UN. INTERNATIONAL LAW COMMISSION—REPORTS (Agenda item 79)
A/C.6/78/SR.29; A/C.6/78/SR.31

Sirie, Mochammad Iqbal (Indonesia)
ARMS TRANSFERS—TREATIES (Agenda item 99x)
A/C.1/78/PV.28
CONVENTIONAL WEAPONS (Agenda item 99u)
A/C.1/78/PV.18; A/C.1/78/PV.28
DISARMAMENT—GENERAL AND COMPLETE (Agenda item 99)
A/C.1/78/PV.28
DISARMAMENT—UN. GENERAL ASSEMBLY (4TH SPECIAL SESS. ON DISARMAMENT : xxxx) (Agenda item 99h)
A/C.1/78/PV.22
INFORMATION—INTERNATIONAL SECURITY (Agenda item 94)
A/C.1/78/PV.20; A/C.1/78/PV.29
SMALL ARMS—ILLICIT TRAFFIC (Agenda item 99p)
A/C.1/78/PV.18
SMALL ARMS—ILLICIT TRAFFIC—ASSISTANCE (Agenda item 99n)
A/C.1/78/PV.18
SOUTH-EAST ASIA—NUCLEAR-WEAPON-FREE ZONES (Agenda item 99y)
A/C.1/78/PV.21
UN. DISARMAMENT COMMISSION—REPORTS (Agenda item 101b)
A/C.1/78/PV.22

Sirie, Mochammad Iqbal (Indonesia) (Coordinating Bureau of the Non-Aligned Countries)
ARMS RACE—OUTER SPACE (Agenda item 97a)
A/C.1/78/PV.16
DISARMAMENT—UN. GENERAL ASSEMBLY (4TH SPECIAL SESS. ON DISARMAMENT : xxxx) (Agenda item 99h)
A/C.1/78/PV.22
DISARMAMENT AGREEMENTS—ENVIRONMENT (Agenda item 99j)
A/C.1/78/PV.20
DISARMAMENT-DEVELOPMENT LINK (Agenda item 99d)
A/C.1/78/PV.20
INDIAN OCEAN—ZONES OF PEACE (Agenda item 91)
A/C.1/78/PV.21
INFORMATION—INTERNATIONAL SECURITY (Agenda item 94)
A/C.1/78/PV.20

Sirie, Mochammad Iqbal (Indonesia) (Coordinating Bureau of the Non-Aligned Countries) (continued)
MIDDLE EAST—NUCLEAR-WEAPON-FREE ZONES (Agenda item 95)
A/C.1/78/PV.21
MULTILATERALISM—DISARMAMENT (Agenda item 99r)
A/C.1/78/PV.20
OUTER SPACE—CONFIDENCE-BUILDING MEASURES (Agenda item 99v)
A/C.1/78/PV.16
PEACE—REGIONAL CENTRES (Agenda item 100f)
A/C.1/78/PV.22
UN. DISARMAMENT COMMISSION—REPORTS (Agenda item 101b)
A/C.1/78/PV.22
WEAPONS—OUTER SPACE (Agenda item 97b)
A/C.1/78/PV.16

Sirmen, Vedia (Türkiye)
CRIMES AGAINST HUMANITY (Agenda item 80)
A/C.6/78/SR.44

Sisior, Gwendalyn (Palau)
MILLENNIUM SUMMIT—CONFERENCES (Agenda item 117)
A/78/PV.102
UN CONFERENCES (Agenda item 13)
A/78/PV.102

Sissoko, Aboubacar (Mali)
UN MULTIDIMENSIONAL INTEGRATED STABILIZATION MISSION IN MALI—FINANCING (Agenda item 155)
A/C.5/78/SR.36

Sitaldin, Sunil A. (Suriname)
PEACE (Agenda item 14)
A/78/PV.76

Sithole, Tiyani Raymond (South Africa)
UN CONFERENCES (Agenda item 13)
A/78/PV.33

Sivamohan, Shivanand (Malaysia)
BIOLOGICAL WEAPONS—TREATIES (Agenda item 106)
A/C.1/78/PV.14
CHEMICAL WEAPONS—TREATIES (Agenda item 99l)
A/C.1/78/PV.14; A/C.1/78/PV.26
DISARMAMENT AGREEMENTS—OUTER SPACE (Agenda item 97c)
A/C.1/78/PV.27
INFORMATION—INTERNATIONAL SECURITY (Agenda item 94)
A/C.1/78/PV.20; A/C.1/78/PV.29
MIDDLE EAST—NUCLEAR-WEAPON-FREE ZONES (Agenda item 95)
A/C.1/78/PV.22

Sivamohan, Shivanand (Malaysia) (continued)
MULTILATERALISM—DISARMAMENT (Agenda item 99r)
A/C.1/78/PV.22
NUCLEAR WEAPONS—ELIMINATION (Agenda item 99z)
A/C.1/78/PV.25
NUCLEAR WEAPONS USE—UN. INTERNATIONAL COURT OF JUSTICE OPINION (Agenda item 99k)
A/C.1/78/PV.25
OUTER SPACE—PRINCIPLES (Agenda item 97d)
A/C.1/78/PV.27
SOUTH-EAST ASIA—NUCLEAR-WEAPON-FREE ZONES (Agenda item 99y)
A/C.1/78/PV.22; A/C.1/78/PV.30
UN. CONFERENCE ON DISARMAMENT—REPORTS (Agenda item 101a)
A/C.1/78/PV.23
UN. DISARMAMENT COMMISSION—REPORTS (Agenda item 101b)
A/C.1/78/PV.23
VETO (Agenda item 63)
A/78/PV.69

Skachkov, Evgeny A. (Russian Federation)
ARMED CONFLICTS PREVENTION (Agenda item 31a)
A/78/PV.73
CRIMES AGAINST HUMANITY (Agenda item 80)
A/C.6/78/SR.11; A/C.6/78/SR.39; A/C.6/78/SR.41; A/C.6/78/SR.42; A/C.6/78/SR.43; A/C.6/78/SR.44; A/C.6/78/SR.45; A/C.6/78/SR.47
INTERNATIONAL LAW—TRAINING PROGRAMMES (Agenda item 78)
A/C.6/78/SR.21
UN. INTERNATIONAL LAW COMMISSION—REPORTS (Agenda item 79)
A/C.6/78/SR.32
UN CHARTER—REPORTS (Agenda item 82)
A/C.6/78/SR.22
UN COMMISSION ON INTERNATIONAL TRADE LAW—REPORTS (Agenda item 77)
A/C.6/78/SR.14

Skali, Abla (Morocco)
YOUTH (Agenda item 24b)
A/C.3/78/SR.3

Skelton, Ann Marie (South Africa) (UN. Committee on the Rights of the Child. Chair)
RIGHTS OF THE CHILD (Agenda item 67)
A/C.3/78/SR.12

Skoczek, Joanna Sylwia (Poland)
COMMODITIES (Agenda item 16d)
A/C.2/78/SR.14
CRIME PREVENTION (Agenda item 107)
A/C.3/78/SR.50
EMERGENCY ASSISTANCE (Agenda item 72a)
A/78/PV.46

Skoczek, Joanna Sylwia (Poland) (continued)

FREEDOM OF EXPRESSION (Agenda item 71b)
A/C.3/78/SR.19
HUMAN RIGHTS—UKRAINE (Agenda item 71c)
A/C.3/78/SR.37
HUMAN RIGHTS ACTIVISTS (Agenda item 71b)
A/C.3/78/SR.19
PALESTINIANS—ASSISTANCE (Agenda item 72b)
A/78/PV.46
PERSONS WITH DISABILITIES—HUMAN RIGHTS (Agenda item 71a)
A/C.3/78/SR.18; A/C.3/78/SR.51
RELIGIOUS INTOLERANCE (Agenda item 71b)
A/C.3/78/SR.38
SUSTAINABLE DEVELOPMENT (Agenda item 18)
A/C.2/78/SR.14
UN HIGH COMMISSIONER FOR REFUGEES—REPORTS (Agenda item 60)
A/C.3/78/SR.44

Skoog, Olof (European Union)

HUMAN RIGHTS—AFGHANISTAN (Agenda item 71c)
A/C.3/78/SR.24
HUMAN RIGHTS—BELARUS (Agenda item 71c)
A/C.3/78/SR.24
HUMAN RIGHTS—DEMOCRATIC PEOPLE'S REPUBLIC OF KOREA (Agenda item 71c)
A/C.3/78/SR.24
HUMAN RIGHTS—INTERNATIONAL INSTRUMENTS (Agenda item 71a)
A/C.3/78/SR.24
HUMAN RIGHTS—MYANMAR (Agenda item 71c)
A/C.3/78/SR.24
HUMAN RIGHTS—RUSSIAN FEDERATION (Agenda item 71c)
A/C.3/78/SR.24
HUMAN RIGHTS—SYRIAN ARAB REPUBLIC (Agenda item 71c)
A/C.3/78/SR.24
HUMAN RIGHTS—UKRAINE (Agenda item 71c)
A/C.3/78/SR.24
HUMAN RIGHTS ADVANCEMENT (Agenda item 71b)
A/C.3/78/SR.24
RIGHT TO FOOD (Agenda item 71b)
A/C.3/78/SR.24
UN. GENERAL ASSEMBLY (78TH SESS. : 2023-2024). 1ST COMMITTEE—GENERAL DEBATE (Agenda item 8)
A/C.1/78/PV.2
UN. GENERAL ASSEMBLY (78TH SESS. : 2023-2024). 2ND COMMITTEE—GENERAL DEBATE (Agenda item 8)
A/C.2/78/SR.2
UN HIGH COMMISSIONER FOR REFUGEES—REPORTS (Agenda item 60)
A/C.3/78/SR.44
VETO (Agenda item 63)
A/78/PV.3

Sloboda, Pedro Muniz Pinto (Brazil)

CRIMES AGAINST HUMANITY (Agenda item 80)
A/C.6/78/SR.41; A/C.6/78/SR.44; A/C.6/78/SR.45
DISASTER VICTIMS (Agenda item 86)
A/C.6/78/SR.5
INTERNATIONAL JURISDICTION (Agenda item 84)
A/C.6/78/SR.12
RESPONSIBILITY TO PROTECT (Agenda item 129)
A/78/PV.96
UN. INTERNATIONAL LAW COMMISSION—REPORTS (Agenda item 79)
A/C.6/78/SR.23

Sloboda, Pedro Muniz Pinto (Brazil) (UN. General Assembly. 6th Committee. Bureau)

RESPONSIBILITY OF INTERNATIONAL ORGANIZATIONS (Agenda item 85)
A/C.6/78/SR.37

Šmidt, Arina (Slovenia)

RIGHTS OF THE CHILD (Agenda item 67)
A/C.3/78/SR.11
YOUTH (Agenda item 24b)
A/C.3/78/SR.1

Smolek, Martin (Czechia)

UN. INTERNATIONAL LAW COMMISSION—REPORTS (Agenda item 79)
A/C.6/78/SR.25

Smyre, Calvin (United States)

INTERNATIONAL CRIMINAL COURT—REPORTS (Agenda item 74)
A/78/PV.22
RACIAL DISCRIMINATION—ELIMINATION (Agenda item 69a)
A/C.3/78/SR.41
RACIAL DISCRIMINATION—PROGRAMMES OF ACTION (Agenda item 69b)
A/C.3/78/SR.41
SLAVERY (Agenda item 71a)
A/C.3/78/SR.21

Smyth, Declan (Ireland)

UN. INTERNATIONAL LAW COMMISSION—REPORTS (Agenda item 79)
A/C.6/78/SR.25

Soares, Dionísio Da Costa Babo (Timor-Leste)

DEVELOPMENT FINANCE—CONFERENCES (Agenda item 17)
A/78/PV.90
ECONOMIC SANCTIONS—INTERNATIONAL RELATIONS (Agenda item 28)
A/78/PV.90
MILLENNIUM SUMMIT—CONFERENCES (Agenda item 117)
A/78/PV.102

Soares, Dionísio Da Costa Babo (Timor-Leste) (continued)
PEACE (Agenda item 14)
A/78/PV.77
RESPONSIBILITY TO PROTECT (Agenda item 129)
A/78/PV.96
UN. SECURITY COUNCIL—REPORTS (Agenda item 26)
A/78/PV.94
UN CONFERENCES (Agenda item 13)
A/78/PV.102
VETO (Agenda item 63)
A/78/PV.67

Soares, Dionísio Da Costa Babo (Timor-Leste) (Comunidade dos Países de Língua Portuguesa)
CRIMES AGAINST HUMANITY (Agenda item 80)
A/C.6/78/SR.45

Soares, João Miguel Ferreira de Serpa (UN. Legal Counsel)
INTERNATIONAL LAW—TRAINING PROGRAMMES (Agenda item 78)
A/C.6/78/SR.21

Soberón Guzmán, Ernesto (Cuba)
PEACE (Agenda item 14)
A/78/PV.76; A/78/PV.82
VETO (Agenda item 63)
A/78/PV.67; A/78/PV.69; A/78/PV.74

Sogavare, Manasseh (Solomon Islands. Prime Minister)
UN. GENERAL ASSEMBLY (78TH SESS. : 2023-2024)—GENERAL DEBATE (Agenda item 8)
A/78/PV.11
UN. GENERAL ASSEMBLY (78TH SESS. : 2023-2024)—SPECIAL STATEMENTS
A/78/PV.11

Solà Pardell, Oriol (Spain)
UN. INTERNATIONAL LAW COMMISSION—REPORTS (Agenda item 79)
A/C.6/78/SR.27

Solano Ramírez, Lucía Teresa (Colombia)
CENTRAL ASIA—ZONES OF PEACE (Agenda item 64)
A/78/PV.85
CLIMATE (Agenda item 18d)
A/C.2/78/SR.25
CRIMES AGAINST HUMANITY (Agenda item 80)
A/C.6/78/SR.10; A/C.6/78/SR.39; A/C.6/78/SR.40; A/C.6/78/SR.41; A/C.6/78/SR.42; A/C.6/78/SR.43; A/C.6/78/SR.44; A/C.6/78/SR.45
DISASTER VICTIMS (Agenda item 86)
A/C.6/78/SR.5
INTERNATIONAL CRIMINAL COURT—REPORTS (Agenda item 74)
A/78/PV.21

Solano Ramírez, Lucía Teresa (Colombia) (continued)
NON-CITIZENS—DEPORTATION (Agenda item 81)
A/C.6/78/SR.34
RULE OF LAW (Agenda item 83)
A/C.6/78/SR.16
UN. INTERNATIONAL COURT OF JUSTICE—REPORTS (Agenda item 73)
A/C.6/78/SR.26
UN. INTERNATIONAL LAW COMMISSION—REPORTS (Agenda item 79)
A/C.6/78/SR.27; A/C.6/78/SR.30; A/C.6/78/SR.33

Solano Ramírez, Lucía Teresa (Colombia) (UN. General Assembly. 6th Committee. Bureau)
UN. INTERNATIONAL LAW COMMISSION—REPORTS (Agenda item 79)
A/C.6/78/SR.37

Solorzano Cavalieri, Isis Amahl Gabriela (Venezuela (Bolivarian Republic of))
CENTRAL ASIA—ZONES OF PEACE (Agenda item 64)
A/78/PV.85

Song, Hye-ryoung (Republic of Korea)
HUMAN RIGHTS (Agenda item 71)
A/C.3/78/SR.27
HUMAN RIGHTS—AFGHANISTAN (Agenda item 71c)
A/C.3/78/SR.34
HUMAN RIGHTS—DEMOCRATIC PEOPLE'S REPUBLIC OF KOREA (Agenda item 71c)
A/C.3/78/SR.27
UN. HUMAN RIGHTS COUNCIL—REPORTS (Agenda item 66)
A/C.3/78/SR.46
UN HIGH COMMISSIONER FOR REFUGEES—REPORTS (Agenda item 60)
A/C.3/78/SR.45

Song, Miyoung (Republic of Korea)
CRIMES AGAINST HUMANITY (Agenda item 80)
A/C.6/78/SR.38; A/C.6/78/SR.39; A/C.6/78/SR.41; A/C.6/78/SR.43; A/C.6/78/SR.44

Sonkar, Suman (India)
AGEING PERSONS (Agenda item 24b)
A/C.3/78/SR.1
FREEDOM OF EXPRESSION (Agenda item 71b)
A/C.3/78/SR.19
HUMAN RIGHTS (Agenda item 71)
A/C.3/78/SR.16
HUMAN RIGHTS—INTERNATIONAL INSTRUMENTS (Agenda item 71a)
A/C.3/78/SR.26
HUMAN RIGHTS ACTIVISTS (Agenda item 71b)
A/C.3/78/SR.19
HUMAN RIGHTS ADVANCEMENT (Agenda item 71b)
A/C.3/78/SR.26

Sonkar, Suman (India) (continued)

INDIGENOUS PEOPLES (Agenda item 68a)
A/C.3/78/SR.15
INDIGENOUS PEOPLES—CONFERENCES (Agenda item 68b)
A/C.3/78/SR.15
MINORITIES (Agenda item 71b)
A/C.3/78/SR.39
NATIONAL INSTITUTIONS—HUMAN RIGHTS (Agenda item 71b)
A/C.3/78/SR.26
RACIAL DISCRIMINATION—ELIMINATION (Agenda item 69a)
A/C.3/78/SR.41
RACIAL DISCRIMINATION—PROGRAMMES OF ACTION (Agenda item 69b)
A/C.3/78/SR.41
RELIGIOUS INTOLERANCE (Agenda item 71b)
A/C.3/78/SR.38
RIGHT TO CULTURE (Agenda item 71b)
A/C.3/78/SR.27
RIGHTS OF THE CHILD (Agenda item 67)
A/C.3/78/SR.11; A/C.3/78/SR.13
SELF-DETERMINATION OF PEOPLES (Agenda item 70)
A/C.3/78/SR.41; A/C.3/78/SR.56
SOCIAL CONDITIONS (Agenda item 24b)
A/C.3/78/SR.3
SOCIAL DEVELOPMENT (Agenda item 24)
A/C.3/78/SR.3
SUMMARY EXECUTIONS (Agenda item 71b)
A/C.3/78/SR.31
TERRORISM—HUMAN RIGHTS (Agenda item 71b)
A/C.3/78/SR.31
TORTURE AND OTHER CRUEL TREATMENT (Agenda item 71a)
A/C.3/78/SR.18
UN. HUMAN RIGHTS COUNCIL—REPORTS (Agenda item 66)
A/78/PV.28
UN HIGH COMMISSIONER FOR REFUGEES—REPORTS (Agenda item 60)
A/C.3/78/SR.45
WOMEN'S ADVANCEMENT (Agenda item 25a)
A/C.3/78/SR.7; A/C.3/78/SR.9
WOMEN'S ADVANCEMENT—CONFERENCES (Agenda item 25b)
A/C.3/78/SR.7; A/C.3/78/SR.9

Soomer, June (UN. Permanent Forum on People of African Descent)

RACIAL DISCRIMINATION—ELIMINATION (Agenda item 69a)
A/78/PV.63

Soomro, Tara (United Kingdom)

SMALL ISLAND DEVELOPING STATES—PROGRAMMES OF ACTION (Agenda item 18b)
A/78/PV.103
SUSTAINABLE DEVELOPMENT (Agenda item 18)
A/78/PV.107

Sorimachi, Masayuki (Japan)

LAW OF THE SEA (Agenda item 75a)
A/78/PV.44
MARINE ECOSYSTEMS—BIOLOGICAL DIVERSITY (Agenda item 75c)
A/78/PV.44
STRADDLING FISH STOCKS (Agenda item 75b)
A/78/PV.44

Sorto Rosales, Mayra Lisseth (El Salvador)

HUMAN RIGHTS—INTERNATIONAL INSTRUMENTS (Agenda item 71a)
A/C.3/78/SR.17
MIGRANT WORKERS (Agenda item 71a)
A/C.3/78/SR.23
MIGRANTS—PROTECTION (Agenda item 71b)
A/C.3/78/SR.56
RIGHTS OF THE CHILD (Agenda item 67)
A/C.3/78/SR.55
UN. GENERAL ASSEMBLY—WORK PROGRAMME (Agenda item 120)
A/C.3/78/SR.56

Sorto Rosales, Mayra Lisseth (El Salvador) (Sistema de la Integración Centroamericana)

MIGRANTS—PROTECTION (Agenda item 71b)
A/C.3/78/SR.24

Sosa Guerra, Sibisse (Federación Estatal de Instituciones Solidarias con el Pueblo Saharaui)

WESTERN SAHARA QUESTION (Agenda item 58)
A/C.4/78/SR.4

Souliyong, So Inxay (Lao People's Democratic Republic)

CLUSTER MUNITIONS (Agenda item 99dd)
A/C.1/78/PV.19
LANDMINES—TREATIES (Agenda item 99m)
A/C.1/78/PV.19
MINE CLEARANCE (Agenda item 46)
A/C.4/78/SR.10
SMALL ARMS—ILLICIT TRAFFIC (Agenda item 99p)
A/C.1/78/PV.19
SMALL ARMS—ILLICIT TRAFFIC—ASSISTANCE (Agenda item 99n)
A/C.1/78/PV.19

Soumaré, Boukary (Mauritania)

CLIMATE (Agenda item 18d)
A/C.2/78/SR.15
SUSTAINABLE DEVELOPMENT (Agenda item 18)
A/C.2/78/SR.15

Sourek, Amanda Pirutti (International Institute for Democracy and Electoral Assistance)

HUMAN RIGHTS—MYANMAR (Agenda item 71c)
A/C.3/78/SR.33

Sousa, Ivens Gusmao de (Timor-Leste)
INFORMATION—INTERNATIONAL SECURITY (Agenda item 94)
A/C.1/78/PV.20
NUCLEAR DISARMAMENT (Agenda item 99b)
A/C.1/78/PV.13
NUCLEAR NON-PROLIFERATION—INTERNATIONAL OBLIGATIONS (Agenda item 99w)
A/C.1/78/PV.13
NUCLEAR WEAPONS—TREATIES (Agenda item 99ff)
A/C.1/78/PV.13
UN. GENERAL ASSEMBLY (78TH SESS. : 2023-2024). 1ST COMMITTEE—GENERAL DEBATE (Agenda item 8)
A/C.1/78/PV.5

Sousa, Marcelo Rebelo de (Portugal. President)
UN. GENERAL ASSEMBLY (78TH SESS. : 2023-2024)—GENERAL DEBATE (Agenda item 8)
A/78/PV.4
UN. GENERAL ASSEMBLY (78TH SESS. : 2023-2024)—SPECIAL STATEMENTS
A/78/PV.4

Sousa, Maria Lourdes de (Timor-Leste)
PERSONS WITH DISABILITIES—HUMAN RIGHTS (Agenda item 71a)
A/C.3/78/SR.38
RACIAL DISCRIMINATION—PROGRAMMES OF ACTION (Agenda item 69b)
A/C.3/78/SR.40

Souvi, Mouhidine ((personal capacity))
WESTERN SAHARA QUESTION (Agenda item 58)
A/C.4/78/SR.5

Sovaleni, Siaosi 'Ofakivahafolau (Tonga. Prime Minister)
UN. GENERAL ASSEMBLY (78TH SESS. : 2023-2024)—GENERAL DEBATE (Agenda item 8)
A/78/PV.11
UN. GENERAL ASSEMBLY (78TH SESS. : 2023-2024)—SPECIAL STATEMENTS
A/78/PV.11

Sowa, Amara Sheikh Mohammed (Sierra Leone)
CRIMES AGAINST HUMANITY (Agenda item 80)
A/C.6/78/SR.11
EXTERNAL DEBT (Agenda item 16c)
A/C.2/78/SR.9
FINANCIAL FLOWS (Agenda item 16f)
A/C.2/78/SR.9
MACROECONOMIC POLICY (Agenda item 16)
A/C.2/78/SR.9
PEACEKEEPING OPERATIONS (Agenda item 51)
A/C.4/78/SR.19
PEACEKEEPING OPERATIONS—CRIMINAL LIABILITY (Agenda item 76)
A/C.6/78/SR.8

Sowa, Amara Sheikh Mohammed (Sierra Leone) (continued)
RACIAL DISCRIMINATION—ELIMINATION (Agenda item 69a)
A/C.3/78/SR.42
RACIAL DISCRIMINATION—PROGRAMMES OF ACTION (Agenda item 69b)
A/C.3/78/SR.42
SUSTAINABLE DEVELOPMENT (Agenda item 18)
A/C.2/78/SR.13
VETO (Agenda item 63)
A/78/PV.52; A/78/PV.67; A/78/PV.75

Sowa, Amara Sheikh Mohammed (Sierra Leone) (African Union)
UN. SECURITY COUNCIL—MEMBERSHIP (Agenda item 121)
A/78/PV.104

Sowah, Malcolm (United Kingdom)
COMMODITIES (Agenda item 16d)
A/C.2/78/SR.23
HEALTH (Agenda item 125)
A/78/PV.48; A/78/PV.77
HIV/AIDS—DECLARATIONS (Agenda item 10)
A/78/PV.91
INVESTMENT PROMOTION (Agenda item 16g)
A/C.2/78/SR.23

Soyka, Juliane (Austria)
FREEDOM OF EXPRESSION (Agenda item 71b)
A/C.3/78/SR.19
HUMAN RIGHTS ADVANCEMENT (Agenda item 71b)
A/C.3/78/SR.52
RIGHT TO PRIVACY (Agenda item 71b)
A/C.3/78/SR.21

Spasse, Arian (Albania)
TERRORISM (Agenda item 109)
A/C.6/78/SR.4
UKRAINE—POLITICAL CONDITIONS (Agenda item 62)
A/78/PV.57
VETO (Agenda item 63)
A/78/PV.3

Spiegel, Shari (UN. Department of Economic and Social Affairs. Financing for Sustainable Development Office. Policy Analysis and Development Branch. Chief)
DEVELOPMENT FINANCE (Agenda item 16b)
A/C.2/78/SR.8
DEVELOPMENT FINANCE—CONFERENCES (Agenda item 17)
A/C.2/78/SR.8
FINANCIAL FLOWS (Agenda item 16f)
A/C.2/78/SR.8
TAXATION (Agenda item 16h)
A/C.2/78/SR.8

Squassoni, Sharon A. (George Washington University (Washington, D.C.))
DISARMAMENT—GENERAL AND COMPLETE (Agenda item 99)
A/78/PV.105

Squeff, María del Carmen (Argentina)
AGEING PERSONS (Agenda item 24b)
A/C.3/78/SR.1; A/C.3/78/SR.2; A/C.3/78/SR.49
CUBA—UNITED STATES (Agenda item 38)
A/78/PV.24
DISAPPEARANCE OF PERSONS (Agenda item 71b)
A/C.3/78/SR.50
FAMILY (Agenda item 24b)
A/C.3/78/SR.2
IAEA—REPORTS (Agenda item 89)
A/78/PV.29
INTERNATIONAL CRIMINAL COURT—REPORTS (Agenda item 74)
A/78/PV.22
LAW OF THE SEA (Agenda item 75a)
A/78/PV.44
MARINE ECOSYSTEMS—BIOLOGICAL DIVERSITY (Agenda item 75c)
A/78/PV.44
MIDDLE EAST SITUATION (Agenda item 34)
A/78/PV.40
MILLENNIUM SUMMIT—CONFERENCES (Agenda item 117)
A/78/PV.15
NON-NUCLEAR-WEAPON STATES—SECURITY (Agenda item 96)
A/C.1/78/PV.13
NUCLEAR DISARMAMENT (Agenda item 99b)
A/C.1/78/PV.13
NUCLEAR DISARMAMENT—VERIFICATION (Agenda item 99ee)
A/C.1/78/PV.13
NUCLEAR WEAPON TESTS—TREATIES (Agenda item 105)
A/C.1/78/PV.13
ORGANIZATION OF IBERO-AMERICAN STATES FOR EDUCATION, SCIENCE AND CULTURE—OBSERVER STATUS (Agenda item 171)
A/C.6/78/SR.14
PALESTINE QUESTION (Agenda item 35)
A/78/PV.39
SOCIAL DEVELOPMENT (Agenda item 24)
A/C.3/78/SR.2
STRADDLING FISH STOCKS (Agenda item 75b)
A/78/PV.44
UN. GENERAL ASSEMBLY—WORK PROGRAMME (Agenda item 120)
A/78/PV.33
UN. HUMAN RIGHTS COUNCIL—REPORTS (Agenda item 66)
A/78/PV.23
UN CONFERENCES (Agenda item 13)
A/78/PV.15

Squeff, María del Carmen (Argentina) (continued)
UN RESOLUTIONS—IMPLEMENTATION (Agenda item 119)
A/78/PV.33
UNRWA—ACTIVITIES (Agenda item 49)
A/C.4/78/SR.23

Squeff, María del Carmen (Argentina) (LGBTI Core Group)
SEXUAL ORIENTATION (Agenda item 71b)
A/C.3/78/SR.39

Sresthabutr, Hataipat (Thailand)
INTERNATIONAL LAW—TRAINING PROGRAMMES (Agenda item 78)
A/C.6/78/SR.21

Stadnicka, Małgorzata (Poland)
CYBERCRIME (Agenda item 108)
A/C.3/78/SR.5
RIGHTS OF THE CHILD (Agenda item 67)
A/C.3/78/SR.11
SOCIAL CONDITIONS (Agenda item 24b)
A/C.3/78/SR.2
YOUTH (Agenda item 24b)
A/C.3/78/SR.2

Stame Cervone, Anna Maria (Cenacolo (Organization))
WESTERN SAHARA QUESTION (Agenda item 58)
A/C.4/78/SR.4

Staples, James (United Kingdom)
UN—BUDGET (2024) (Agenda item 134)
A/C.5/78/SR.5
UN—PROGRAMME PLANNING (Agenda item 135)
A/C.5/78/SR.5
UN. GENERAL ASSEMBLY (78TH SESS. : 2023-2024). 5TH COMMITTEE—WORK ORGANIZATION (Agenda item 7)
A/C.5/78/SR.26/PartII

Stastoli, Andris (Albania)
INTERNATIONAL RESIDUAL MECHANISM FOR CRIMINAL TRIBUNALS (Agenda item 126)
A/78/PV.19

Stavridi, Zinovia Chaido (Greece)
INTERNATIONAL CRIMINAL COURT—REPORTS (Agenda item 74)
A/78/PV.21
UN. INTERNATIONAL LAW COMMISSION—REPORTS (Agenda item 79)
A/C.6/78/SR.27

Stellakatos-Loverdos, Michael (Greece)
UN. INTERNATIONAL COURT OF JUSTICE—REPORTS (Agenda item 73)
A/78/PV.28

Stellakatos-Loverdos, Michael (Greece) (continued)

UN. INTERNATIONAL LAW COMMISSION—REPORTS (Agenda item 79)
A/C.6/78/SR.30; A/C.6/78/SR.32

Štěpánek, Jaroslav (Czechia)

ARMS RACE—OUTER SPACE (Agenda item 97a)
A/C.1/78/PV.16
BIOLOGICAL WEAPONS—TREATIES (Agenda item 106)
A/C.1/78/PV.14
CHEMICAL WEAPONS—TREATIES (Agenda item 99l)
A/C.1/78/PV.14
FISSIONABLE MATERIALS—TREATIES (Agenda item 99a)
A/C.1/78/PV.12
NUCLEAR DISARMAMENT (Agenda item 99b)
A/C.1/78/PV.12
NUCLEAR NON-PROLIFERATION—INTERNATIONAL OBLIGATIONS (Agenda item 99w)
A/C.1/78/PV.12
NUCLEAR WEAPON TESTS—TREATIES (Agenda item 105)
A/C.1/78/PV.12
OUTER SPACE—PRINCIPLES (Agenda item 97d)
A/C.1/78/PV.16

Stetter, Elizabeth (United States)

MULTILINGUALISM (Agenda item 124)
A/78/PV.108

Stewart, Mallory (United States)

UN. GENERAL ASSEMBLY (78TH SESS. : 2023-2024). 1ST COMMITTEE—GENERAL DEBATE (Agenda item 8)
A/C.1/78/PV.4

Stiglitz, Joseph E. (Columbia University (New York))

COMMODITIES (Agenda item 16d)
A/C.2/78/SR.14
SUSTAINABLE DEVELOPMENT (Agenda item 18)
A/C.2/78/SR.14

Stillhart, Dominik (Switzerland)

EMERGENCY ASSISTANCE (Agenda item 72a)
A/78/PV.46

Stoeva, Lachezara (Bulgaria)

ARMED CONFLICTS PREVENTION (Agenda item 31a)
A/78/PV.72
FISSIONABLE MATERIALS—TREATIES (Agenda item 99a)
A/C.1/78/PV.12
NUCLEAR DISARMAMENT (Agenda item 99b)
A/C.1/78/PV.12

Stoeva, Lachezara (Bulgaria) (continued)

NUCLEAR NON-PROLIFERATION—INTERNATIONAL OBLIGATIONS (Agenda item 99w)
A/C.1/78/PV.12
NUCLEAR WEAPON TESTS—TREATIES (Agenda item 105)
A/C.1/78/PV.12
RIGHTS OF THE CHILD (Agenda item 67)
A/C.3/78/SR.12
UKRAINE—POLITICAL CONDITIONS (Agenda item 62)
A/78/PV.57
UN. GENERAL ASSEMBLY (78TH SESS. : 2023-2024). 1ST COMMITTEE—GENERAL DEBATE (Agenda item 8)
A/C.1/78/PV.5
VETO (Agenda item 63)
A/78/PV.3; A/78/PV.70; A/78/PV.78
WOMEN'S ADVANCEMENT (Agenda item 25a)
A/C.3/78/SR.9
WOMEN'S ADVANCEMENT—CONFERENCES (Agenda item 25b)
A/C.3/78/SR.9

Stoeva, Lachezara (Bulgaria) (UN. Economic and Social Council. President)

UN. ECONOMIC AND SOCIAL COUNCIL—REPORTS (Agenda item 9)
A/78/PV.33

Stokke, Kristine Meek (Norway)

YOUTH (Agenda item 24b)
A/C.3/78/SR.2

Storsve, Alison (United States)

CONVENTIONAL WEAPONS (Agenda item 99u)
A/C.1/78/PV.19; A/C.1/78/PV.28
DISARMAMENT—GENERAL AND COMPLETE (Agenda item 99)
A/C.1/78/PV.19; A/C.1/78/PV.28
NUCLEAR WEAPONS—ELIMINATION (Agenda item 99z)
A/C.1/78/PV.25
UN—PROGRAMME PLANNING (Agenda item 135)
A/C.1/78/PV.10
UN. GENERAL ASSEMBLY—WORK PROGRAMME (Agenda item 120)
A/C.1/78/PV.10
UN. GENERAL ASSEMBLY (78TH SESS. : 2023-2024). 1ST COMMITTEE—WORK ORGANIZATION (Agenda item 7)
A/C.1/78/PV.27

Stricker, Julia (Switzerland)

RIGHTS OF THE CHILD (Agenda item 67)
A/C.3/78/SR.11

Stritt, Marc-Alain (Switzerland)

PEACEKEEPING OPERATIONS (Agenda item 51)
A/C.4/78/SR.19

Stromsiková, Veronika (Czechia)
UN. GENERAL ASSEMBLY (78TH SESS. : 2023-2024). 1ST COMMITTEE—GENERAL DEBATE (Agenda item 8)
A/C.1/78/PV.3

Strzhizhovskiy, Fedor K. (Russian Federation)
INFORMATION (Agenda item 53)
A/C.4/78/SR.12; A/C.4/78/SR.13; A/C.4/78/SR.14

Suárez Moreno, Sergio Agustín (Juntos por Guía (Firm : Spain))
WESTERN SAHARA QUESTION (Agenda item 58)
A/C.4/78/SR.4

Suchocka, Hanna (UN. Human Rights Council. Group of Independent Eminent Experts on the Implementation of the Durban Declaration and Programme of Action. Chair)
RACIAL DISCRIMINATION—PROGRAMMES OF ACTION (Agenda item 69b)
A/C.3/78/SR.40

Šukurica, Alen (Croatia)
CLIMATE CHANGE (Agenda item 71b)
A/C.3/78/SR.29
ENVIRONMENT (Agenda item 71b)
A/C.3/78/SR.29
RIGHT TO DRINKING WATER (Agenda item 71b)
A/C.3/78/SR.28
RIGHT TO HOUSING (Agenda item 71b)
A/C.3/78/SR.30

Sulaiman, Muhamad Syukri (Brunei Darussalam)
RIGHTS OF THE CHILD (Agenda item 67)
A/C.3/78/SR.13

Sulaiman, Noor Qamar (Brunei Darussalam)
VETO (Agenda item 63)
A/78/PV.60

Sulaiman, Noor Qamar (Brunei Darussalam) (ASEAN)
PEACE (Agenda item 14)
A/78/PV.76

Suleiman, Suleiman Haji (United Republic of Tanzania)
INTERNATIONAL RESIDUAL MECHANISM FOR CRIMINAL TRIBUNALS—FINANCING (Agenda item 145)
A/C.5/78/SR.20

Sullivan, Stephanie (United States)
ARMED CONFLICTS PREVENTION (Agenda item 31a)
A/78/PV.72

Summersgill, Kevin (UN. Department of Management Strategy, Policy and Compliance. Business Transformation and Accountability Division)
UN—ADMINISTRATION (Agenda item 132)
A/C.5/78/SR.29

Sun, Xiaobo (China)
UN. GENERAL ASSEMBLY (78TH SESS. : 2023-2024). 1ST COMMITTEE—GENERAL DEBATE (Agenda item 8)
A/C.1/78/PV.5

Sun, Yiliang (China)
BIOLOGICAL WEAPONS—TREATIES (Agenda item 106)
A/C.1/78/PV.15
CHEMICAL WEAPONS—TREATIES (Agenda item 99l)
A/C.1/78/PV.15
DISARMAMENT—GENERAL AND COMPLETE (Agenda item 99)
A/C.1/78/PV.26
FISSIONABLE MATERIALS—TREATIES (Agenda item 99a)
A/C.1/78/PV.13; A/C.1/78/PV.26
NUCLEAR DISARMAMENT (Agenda item 99b)
A/C.1/78/PV.11; A/C.1/78/PV.13
NUCLEAR NON-PROLIFERATION (Agenda item 99o)
A/C.1/78/PV.13
NUCLEAR WEAPON TESTS—TREATIES (Agenda item 105)
A/C.1/78/PV.26
NUCLEAR WEAPONS—ELIMINATION (Agenda item 99z)
A/C.1/78/PV.26
NUCLEAR WEAPONS—TREATIES (Agenda item 99ff)
A/C.1/78/PV.26
UN. GENERAL ASSEMBLY (78TH SESS. : 2023-2024). 1ST COMMITTEE—GENERAL DEBATE (Agenda item 8)
A/C.1/78/PV.5

Sun, Zhiqiang (China)
RESPONSIBILITY TO PROTECT (Agenda item 129)
A/78/PV.97

Surkov, Vladimir (Russian Federation)
UN HIGH COMMISSIONER FOR REFUGEES—REPORTS (Agenda item 60)
A/C.3/78/SR.44

Suwantra, Maes (Thailand)
ECONOMIC COOPERATION AMONG DEVELOPING COUNTRIES (Agenda item 22b)
A/C.2/78/SR.18

Suwantra, Maes (Thailand) (continued)
OPERATIONAL ACTIVITIES—UN SYSTEM (Agenda item 22a)
A/C.2/78/SR.18

Suweed, Mohamed (Libya)
AFRICA—DEVELOPMENT (Agenda item 65b)
A/78/PV.18
AFRICA—SUSTAINABLE DEVELOPMENT—PARTNERSHIP (Agenda item 65a)
A/78/PV.18

Suwwannikha, Surat (Thailand)
UN—BUDGET (2024) (Agenda item 134)
A/C.5/78/SR.12

Svadjian, Méliné (Canada)
ARMS TRANSFERS—TREATIES (Agenda item 99x)
A/C.1/78/PV.19
CLUSTER MUNITIONS (Agenda item 99dd)
A/C.1/78/PV.19
DISARMAMENT—GENERAL AND COMPLETE (Agenda item 99)
A/C.1/78/PV.19
LANDMINES—TREATIES (Agenda item 99m)
A/C.1/78/PV.19

Svana, Lukas (European Union)
YOUTH (Agenda item 24b)
A/C.3/78/SR.1

Svercsok, Szabolcs (Hungary)
ARMED CONFLICTS PREVENTION (Agenda item 31a)
A/78/PV.72
DISARMAMENT—GENERAL AND COMPLETE (Agenda item 99)
A/C.1/78/PV.26
VETO (Agenda item 63)
A/78/PV.79

Sverrisdóttir, Anna Pála (Iceland)
CRIMES AGAINST HUMANITY (Agenda item 80)
A/C.6/78/SR.41; A/C.6/78/SR.46; A/C.6/78/SR.47

Swan, Ellen (Ireland)
HUMAN RIGHTS—MYANMAR (Agenda item 71c)
A/C.3/78/SR.33
HUMAN RIGHTS ACTIVISTS (Agenda item 71b)
A/C.3/78/SR.19
PERSONS WITH DISABILITIES—HUMAN RIGHTS (Agenda item 71a)
A/C.3/78/SR.38
RACIAL DISCRIMINATION—ELIMINATION (Agenda item 69a)
A/C.3/78/SR.41
RACIAL DISCRIMINATION—PROGRAMMES OF ACTION (Agenda item 69b)
A/C.3/78/SR.41

Swan, Ellen (Ireland) (continued)
SEXUAL ORIENTATION (Agenda item 71b)
A/C.3/78/SR.39

Swanson, Benjamin Gordon Robert (UN. Assistant Secretary-General for Internal Oversight Services)
PEACEKEEPING OPERATIONS—FINANCING (Agenda item 146)
A/C.5/78/SR.35
UN MISSION IN SOUTH SUDAN—FINANCING (Agenda item 157)
A/C.5/78/SR.36

Syed, Ansar Hussain Shah (Pakistan)
CRIMES AGAINST HUMANITY (Agenda item 80)
A/C.6/78/SR.39; A/C.6/78/SR.41; A/C.6/78/SR.42; A/C.6/78/SR.44

Syedibrahim, Abdul Basith Pattinathar K. (World Humanitarian Drive (Organization : United Kingdom))
WESTERN SAHARA QUESTION (Agenda item 58)
A/C.4/78/SR.5

Sylvester, Timothy James (United Kingdom)
ARMED CONFLICTS PREVENTION (Agenda item 31a)
A/78/PV.72
HUMAN RIGHTS (Agenda item 71)
A/C.3/78/SR.16
HUMAN RIGHTS—IRAN (ISLAMIC REPUBLIC OF) (Agenda item 71c)
A/C.3/78/SR.34
HUMAN RIGHTS—RUSSIAN FEDERATION (Agenda item 71c)
A/C.3/78/SR.37
HUMAN RIGHTS—SYRIAN ARAB REPUBLIC (Agenda item 71c)
A/C.3/78/SR.54
HUMAN RIGHTS—UKRAINE (Agenda item 71c)
A/C.3/78/SR.37; A/C.3/78/SR.53
INDIGENOUS PEOPLES (Agenda item 68a)
A/C.3/78/SR.48
SUMMARY EXECUTIONS (Agenda item 71b)
A/C.3/78/SR.31

Syrymbet, Zhangeldy (Kazakhstan)
DISARMAMENT—GENERAL AND COMPLETE (Agenda item 99)
A/C.1/78/PV.12
IAEA—REPORTS (Agenda item 89)
A/78/PV.30
NUCLEAR DISARMAMENT (Agenda item 99b)
A/C.1/78/PV.12
NUCLEAR NON-PROLIFERATION—INTERNATIONAL OBLIGATIONS (Agenda item 99w)
A/C.1/78/PV.12

Syrymbet, Zhangeldy (Kazakhstan) (continued)

NUCLEAR WEAPON TESTS—TREATIES (Agenda item 105)
A/C.1/78/PV.12

Szatmari, Roberto Wazima (Brazil)

ARMS RACE—OUTER SPACE (Agenda item 97a)
A/C.1/78/PV.27
CLUSTER MUNITIONS (Agenda item 99dd)
A/C.1/78/PV.28
DISARMAMENT—GENERAL AND COMPLETE (Agenda item 99)
A/C.1/78/PV.28; A/C.1/78/PV.30
DISARMAMENT AGREEMENTS—OUTER SPACE (Agenda item 97c)
A/C.1/78/PV.27
FISSIONABLE MATERIALS—TREATIES (Agenda item 99a)
A/C.1/78/PV.26
INFORMATION—INTERNATIONAL SECURITY (Agenda item 94)
A/C.1/78/PV.29
NUCLEAR WEAPONS—ELIMINATION (Agenda item 99z)
A/C.1/78/PV.26
OUTER SPACE—CONFIDENCE-BUILDING MEASURES (Agenda item 99v)
A/C.1/78/PV.27
OUTER SPACE—PRINCIPLES (Agenda item 97d)
A/C.1/78/PV.27
WEAPONS—OUTER SPACE (Agenda item 97b)
A/C.1/78/PV.27

Szczerski, Krzysztof (Poland)

CHEMICAL WEAPONS—TREATIES (Agenda item 99l)
A/C.1/78/PV.26
CRIMES AGAINST HUMANITY (Agenda item 80)
A/C.6/78/SR.10
HIV/AIDS—DECLARATIONS (Agenda item 10)
A/78/PV.91
HUMAN RIGHTS—BELARUS (Agenda item 71c)
A/C.3/78/SR.37
HUMAN RIGHTS—RUSSIAN FEDERATION (Agenda item 71c)
A/C.3/78/SR.37
INTERNATIONAL CRIMINAL COURT—REPORTS (Agenda item 74)
A/78/PV.22
MINE CLEARANCE (Agenda item 46)
A/C.4/78/SR.10
PEACEBUILDING (Agenda item 61)
A/78/PV.100
RESPONSIBILITY TO PROTECT (Agenda item 129)
A/78/PV.96
RIGHTS OF THE CHILD (Agenda item 67)
A/C.3/78/SR.11
TERRITORIES OCCUPIED BY ISRAEL—HUMAN RIGHTS (Agenda item 50)
A/C.4/78/SR.26

Szczerski, Krzysztof (Poland) (continued)

UN. PEACEBUILDING COMMISSION—REPORTS (Agenda item 27)
A/78/PV.100
UN. PEACEBUILDING FUND—REPORTS (Agenda item 111)
A/78/PV.100
UN. SECURITY COUNCIL—REPORTS (Agenda item 26)
A/78/PV.93
VETO (Agenda item 63)
A/78/PV.68; A/78/PV.78
WESTERN SAHARA QUESTION (Agenda item 58)
A/C.4/78/SR.6

Szczerski, Krzysztof (Poland) (European Union)

MINE CLEARANCE (Agenda item 46)
A/C.4/78/SR.10

Szelivanov, Julia (European Union)

CLIMATE CHANGE (Agenda item 71b)
A/C.3/78/SR.29
DISAPPEARANCE OF PERSONS (Agenda item 71b)
A/C.3/78/SR.22
ENVIRONMENT (Agenda item 71b)
A/C.3/78/SR.29
MIGRANT WORKERS (Agenda item 71a)
A/C.3/78/SR.23
MIGRANTS—PROTECTION (Agenda item 71b)
A/C.3/78/SR.23
POVERTY—HUMAN RIGHTS (Agenda item 71b)
A/C.3/78/SR.30
RIGHT TO DRINKING WATER (Agenda item 71b)
A/C.3/78/SR.28
RIGHT TO FOOD (Agenda item 71b)
A/C.3/78/SR.30
RIGHT TO HOUSING (Agenda item 71b)
A/C.3/78/SR.30
RIGHT TO PRIVACY (Agenda item 71b)
A/C.3/78/SR.21
SLAVERY (Agenda item 71a)
A/C.3/78/SR.21
TRAFFICKING IN PERSONS (Agenda item 71b)
A/C.3/78/SR.23
TRANSNATIONAL CORPORATIONS—HUMAN RIGHTS (Agenda item 71b)
A/C.3/78/SR.21

Szijjártó, Péter (Hungary)

VETO (Agenda item 63)
A/78/PV.59

Szűcs, Margit (Hungary) (UN. Conference on Disarmament. President)

UN. CONFERENCE ON DISARMAMENT—REPORTS (Agenda item 101a)
A/C.1/78/PV.24

Tabuteau-Mangels, Aurélie (France)
UN COMMISSION ON INTERNATIONAL TRADE LAW—REPORTS (Agenda item 77)
A/C.6/78/SR.14

Tahtinen, Lotta (UN. Department of Economic and Social Affairs. Division for Sustainable Development Goals. Officer-in-Charge)
2030 AGENDA—PROGRAMME IMPLEMENTATION (Agenda item 18a)
A/C.2/78/SR.12
SMALL ISLAND DEVELOPING STATES—PROGRAMMES OF ACTION (Agenda item 18b)
A/C.2/78/SR.12
SUSTAINABLE DEVELOPMENT (Agenda item 18)
A/C.2/78/SR.12
SUSTAINABLE ENERGY (Agenda item 18h)
A/C.2/78/SR.12

Tahzib-Lie, Bahia (Netherlands (Kingdom of the))
HIV/AIDS—DECLARATIONS (Agenda item 10)
A/78/PV.91
HUMAN RIGHTS—IRAN (ISLAMIC REPUBLIC OF) (Agenda item 71c)
A/C.3/78/SR.34
IAEA—REPORTS (Agenda item 89)
A/78/PV.30
VETO (Agenda item 63)
A/78/PV.70
WOMEN'S ADVANCEMENT (Agenda item 25a)
A/C.3/78/SR.7
WOMEN'S ADVANCEMENT—CONFERENCES (Agenda item 25b)
A/C.3/78/SR.7

Tahzib-Lie, Bahia (Netherlands (Kingdom of the)) (Justice Action Coalition)
RULE OF LAW (Agenda item 83)
A/C.6/78/SR.15

Tairua, Tiare Maohi (Union chrétienne des jeunes gens de Polynésie)
FRENCH POLYNESIA QUESTION (Agenda item 58)
A/C.4/78/SR.3

Tak, Minsoo (Republic of Korea)
VETO (Agenda item 63)
A/78/PV.71

Taleb Aomar, Boullah ((personal capacity))
WESTERN SAHARA QUESTION (Agenda item 58)
A/C.4/78/SR.5

Talpai, Tamás (Hungary)
BIOLOGICAL WEAPONS—TREATIES (Agenda item 106)
A/C.1/78/PV.15

Talpai, Tamás (Hungary) (continued)
FISSIONABLE MATERIALS—TREATIES (Agenda item 99a)
A/C.1/78/PV.13
NUCLEAR DISARMAMENT (Agenda item 99b)
A/C.1/78/PV.13
NUCLEAR DISARMAMENT—VERIFICATION (Agenda item 99ee)
A/C.1/78/PV.13
NUCLEAR NON-PROLIFERATION—INTERNATIONAL OBLIGATIONS (Agenda item 99w)
A/C.1/78/PV.13

Tam, Noelle (Singapore)
SPORTS—OLYMPIC GAMES (Agenda item 11)
A/78/PV.38

Tam, Noelle (Singapore) (ASEAN)
UN—BUDGET (2024) (Agenda item 134)
A/C.5/78/SR.11

Tambwe, Zuleikha Rutha (United Republic of Tanzania)
ALBINISM (Agenda item 71b)
A/C.3/78/SR.27
ELECTION VERIFICATION—UN (Agenda item 71b)
A/C.3/78/SR.50
HUMAN RIGHTS—REPORTS (Agenda item 71c)
A/C.3/78/SR.26
RIGHTS OF THE CHILD (Agenda item 67)
A/C.3/78/SR.14

Tamekamta, Zozime Alphonse (Centre Africain de recherche pour la paix et le développement durable (Organization))
WESTERN SAHARA QUESTION (Agenda item 58)
A/C.4/78/SR.4

Tammsaar, Rein (Estonia)
FREEDOM OF EXPRESSION (Agenda item 71b)
A/C.3/78/SR.26
HUMAN RIGHTS—REPORTS (Agenda item 71c)
A/C.3/78/SR.26
HUMAN RIGHTS—UKRAINE (Agenda item 71c)
A/C.3/78/SR.26
INTERNATIONAL CRIMINAL COURT—REPORTS (Agenda item 74)
A/78/PV.21
RIGHTS OF THE CHILD (Agenda item 67)
A/C.3/78/SR.11
SEXUAL ORIENTATION (Agenda item 71b)
A/C.3/78/SR.26
UKRAINE—POLITICAL CONDITIONS (Agenda item 62)
A/78/PV.58
UN. GENERAL ASSEMBLY (78TH SESS. : 2023-2024). 1ST COMMITTEE—GENERAL DEBATE (Agenda item 8)
A/C.1/78/PV.6

Tammsaar, Rein (Estonia) (continued)
UN. SECURITY COUNCIL—MEMBERSHIP (Agenda item 121)
A/78/PV.36
UN CONFERENCES (Agenda item 13)
A/78/PV.47
VETO (Agenda item 63)
A/78/PV.70; A/78/PV.78
WOMEN'S ADVANCEMENT (Agenda item 25a)
A/C.3/78/SR.7
WOMEN'S ADVANCEMENT—CONFERENCES (Agenda item 25b)
A/C.3/78/SR.7

Tammsaar, Rein (Estonia) (Accountability, Coherence and Transparency (ACT) Group)
UN. GENERAL ASSEMBLY—WORK PROGRAMME (Agenda item 120)
A/78/PV.32
UN RESOLUTIONS—IMPLEMENTATION (Agenda item 119)
A/78/PV.32

Tan, Jason Han Wei (Singapore)
INTERNATIONAL TRADE (Agenda item 16a)
A/C.2/78/SR.24
PEACE (Agenda item 14)
A/78/PV.76
UN. GENERAL ASSEMBLY (78TH SESS. : 2023-2024). 2ND COMMITTEE—GENERAL DEBATE (Agenda item 8)
A/C.2/78/SR.4

Tan, Jonathan Necaster (Canada)
UN—BUDGET (2024) (Agenda item 134)
A/C.5/78/SR.26/PartII

Tan, Scott (Singapore)
DISASTER VICTIMS (Agenda item 86)
A/C.6/78/SR.6
INTERNATIONAL JURISDICTION (Agenda item 84)
A/C.6/78/SR.13
NON-CITIZENS—DEPORTATION (Agenda item 81)
A/C.6/78/SR.34
UN. INTERNATIONAL LAW COMMISSION—REPORTS (Agenda item 79)
A/C.6/78/SR.29; A/C.6/78/SR.31
UN COMMISSION ON INTERNATIONAL TRADE LAW—REPORTS (Agenda item 77)
A/C.6/78/SR.14

Tang, Suphanvasa Chotikajan (Thailand)
UN. INTERNATIONAL COURT OF JUSTICE—REPORTS (Agenda item 73)
A/C.6/78/SR.26
UN. INTERNATIONAL LAW COMMISSION—REPORTS (Agenda item 79)
A/C.6/78/SR.25

Tanriöven, Enes (Türkiye)
TORTURE AND OTHER CRUEL TREATMENT (Agenda item 71a)
A/C.3/78/SR.18

Tanriöver, Emre (Türkiye)
CENTRAL ASIA—ZONES OF PEACE (Agenda item 64)
A/78/PV.85

Tansu-Seckin, Cagla (Türkiye)
UN. INTERNATIONAL LAW COMMISSION—REPORTS (Agenda item 79)
A/C.6/78/SR.30

Tantawy, Myan Medhat Anwar (United Arab Emirates)
CRIMES AGAINST HUMANITY (Agenda item 80)
A/C.6/78/SR.41

Tapati, Tafai (French Polynesia)
FRENCH POLYNESIA QUESTION (Agenda item 58)
A/C.4/78/SR.3

Tarahu, Frangelica (Association Te Utuafare No Mahaena)
FRENCH POLYNESIA QUESTION (Agenda item 58)
A/C.4/78/SR.3

Tarakinikini, Filipo (Fiji)
FRENCH POLYNESIA QUESTION (Agenda item 58)
A/C.4/78/SR.3

Tariello, Giulia (European Union)
SOCIAL DEVELOPMENT (Agenda item 24)
A/C.3/78/SR.1
YOUTH (Agenda item 24b)
A/C.3/78/SR.1

Tate, El Moustapha ((personal capacity))
WESTERN SAHARA QUESTION (Agenda item 58)
A/C.4/78/SR.5

Taualumru, Chejuna ((personal capacity))
WESTERN SAHARA QUESTION (Agenda item 58)
A/C.4/78/SR.5

Taylor Jay, Elizabeth (Colombia)
VETO (Agenda item 63)
A/78/PV.74

Tchalare, Abd-el Kader Yasmin (Togo)
ARMS TRANSFERS—TREATIES (Agenda item 99x)
A/C.1/78/PV.19

Tchalare, Abd-el Kader Yasmin (Togo) (continued)

INFORMATION—INTERNATIONAL SECURITY (Agenda item 94)
A/C.1/78/PV.21
RACIAL DISCRIMINATION—ELIMINATION (Agenda item 69a)
A/78/PV.103
SMALL ARMS—ILLICIT TRAFFIC (Agenda item 99p)
A/C.1/78/PV.19
SMALL ARMS—ILLICIT TRAFFIC—ASSISTANCE (Agenda item 99n)
A/C.1/78/PV.19

Teatin Rosas, Alfa Maritza (Corporación Líderes Unidos para Servir (Organization))

WESTERN SAHARA QUESTION (Agenda item 58)
A/C.4/78/SR.4

Tebboune, Abdelmadjid (Algeria. President)

UN. GENERAL ASSEMBLY (78TH SESS. : 2023-2024)—GENERAL DEBATE (Agenda item 8)
A/78/PV.5
UN. GENERAL ASSEMBLY (78TH SESS. : 2023-2024)—SPECIAL STATEMENTS
A/78/PV.5

Tegoni, Nicola (Sovereign Order of Malta)

RACIAL DISCRIMINATION—ELIMINATION (Agenda item 69a)
A/C.3/78/SR.40

Teles, Patricia Galvao (UN. International Law Commission. Chair)

UN. INTERNATIONAL LAW COMMISSION—REPORTS (Agenda item 79)
A/C.6/78/SR.23; A/C.6/78/SR.33

Téllez Alonso, Frank (Cuba) (Group of 77)

2030 AGENDA—PROGRAMME IMPLEMENTATION (Agenda item 18a)
A/C.2/78/SR.12
CLIMATE (Agenda item 18d)
A/C.2/78/SR.12
LANDLOCKED DEVELOPING COUNTRIES—CONFERENCES (Agenda item 20b)
A/C.2/78/SR.7
LEAST DEVELOPED COUNTRIES—CONFERENCES (Agenda item 20a)
A/C.2/78/SR.7
SMALL ISLAND DEVELOPING STATES—PROGRAMMES OF ACTION (Agenda item 18b)
A/C.2/78/SR.12
SUSTAINABLE DEVELOPMENT (Agenda item 18)
A/C.2/78/SR.12; A/C.2/78/SR.21
TERRITORIES OCCUPIED BY ISRAEL—NATURAL RESOURCES (Agenda item 59)
A/C.2/78/SR.21

Téllez Alonso, Frank (Cuba) (Group of 77) (continued)

UN. GENERAL ASSEMBLY (78TH SESS. : 2023-2024). 2ND COMMITTEE—GENERAL DEBATE (Agenda item 8)
A/C.2/78/SR.2

Temaru, Oscar Manutahi (French Polynesia)

FRENCH POLYNESIA QUESTION (Agenda item 58)
A/C.4/78/SR.3

Temauri, Vainui (Association Na Papa e Vaù (French Polynesia))

FRENCH POLYNESIA QUESTION (Agenda item 58)
A/C.4/78/SR.3

Temesgen, Tenna Misgana (Ethiopia)

OUTER SPACE—PEACEFUL USES—INTERNATIONAL COOPERATION (Agenda item 48)
A/C.4/78/SR.16

Teo, Bernice Yi Lin (Singapore)

RIGHTS OF THE CHILD (Agenda item 67)
A/C.3/78/SR.13

Teremate, Ruben (French Polynesia)

FRENCH POLYNESIA QUESTION (Agenda item 58)
A/C.4/78/SR.3

Terou, Pierre (French Polynesia)

FRENCH POLYNESIA QUESTION (Agenda item 58)
A/C.4/78/SR.3

Tesfamariam, Sophia (Eritrea)

ECONOMIC SANCTIONS—INTERNATIONAL RELATIONS (Agenda item 28)
A/78/PV.90
HUMAN RIGHTS—BURUNDI (Agenda item 71c)
A/C.3/78/SR.36
HUMAN RIGHTS—ERITREA (Agenda item 71c)
A/C.3/78/SR.36
UN. GENERAL ASSEMBLY (78TH SESS. : 2023-2024). 1ST COMMITTEE—GENERAL DEBATE (Agenda item 8)
A/C.1/78/PV.9
UN. GENERAL ASSEMBLY (78TH SESS. : 2023-2024). 2ND COMMITTEE—GENERAL DEBATE (Agenda item 8)
A/C.2/78/SR.4

Tesfamariam, Sophia (Eritrea) (Group of Friends in Defence of the Charter of the United Nations)

CUBA—UNITED STATES (Agenda item 38)
A/78/PV.24

Tessouh, Miloud ((personal capacity))
WESTERN SAHARA QUESTION (Agenda item 58)
A/C.4/78/SR.5

Tevi, Odo (Vanuatu)
UN. GENERAL ASSEMBLY (78TH SESS. : 2023-2024)—GENERAL DEBATE (Agenda item 8)
A/78/PV.14

Teymourpour, Nooshin (Iran (Islamic Republic of))
DEVELOPMENT FINANCE (Agenda item 16b)
A/C.2/78/SR.8
INTERNATIONAL TRADE (Agenda item 16a)
A/C.2/78/SR.8

Thanabalasingam, Aruna (UN. Department of Management Strategy, Policy and Compliance. Office of Human Resources. Administrative Law Division. Director)
PEACEKEEPING OPERATIONS (Agenda item 51)
A/C.4/78/SR.18

Thapa, Lok Bahadur (Nepal)
DISASTER VICTIMS (Agenda item 86)
A/C.6/78/SR.6
SOCIAL CONDITIONS (Agenda item 24b)
A/C.3/78/SR.2
TERRORISM (Agenda item 109)
A/C.6/78/SR.2
UN. GENERAL ASSEMBLY (78TH SESS. : 2023-2024). 1ST COMMITTEE—GENERAL DEBATE (Agenda item 8)
A/C.1/78/PV.5
UN. GENERAL ASSEMBLY (78TH SESS. : 2023-2024). 2ND COMMITTEE—GENERAL DEBATE (Agenda item 8)
A/C.2/78/SR.2
YOUTH (Agenda item 24b)
A/C.3/78/SR.2

Thapa, Lok Bahadur (Nepal) (Group of Least Developed Countries)
UN. GENERAL ASSEMBLY (78TH SESS. : 2023-2024). 2ND COMMITTEE—GENERAL DEBATE (Agenda item 8)
A/C.2/78/SR.2

Thaphanya, Natthakith (Lao People's Democratic Republic)
OPERATIONAL ACTIVITIES—UN SYSTEM (Agenda item 22a)
A/C.2/78/SR.18

Tharyat, Tri (Indonesia)
COMMODITIES (Agenda item 16d)
A/C.2/78/SR.14
SUSTAINABLE DEVELOPMENT (Agenda item 18)
A/C.2/78/SR.14

Thavisin, Srettha (Thailand. Prime Minister)
UN. GENERAL ASSEMBLY (78TH SESS. : 2023-2024)—GENERAL DEBATE (Agenda item 8)
A/78/PV.10
UN. GENERAL ASSEMBLY (78TH SESS. : 2023-2024)—SPECIAL STATEMENTS
A/78/PV.10

Theeuwen, Wieteke Elisabeth Christina (Netherlands (Kingdom of the))
CRIMES AGAINST HUMANITY (Agenda item 80)
A/C.6/78/SR.41
DISASTER VICTIMS (Agenda item 86)
A/C.6/78/SR.5
NON-CITIZENS—DEPORTATION (Agenda item 81)
A/C.6/78/SR.34
RESPONSIBILITY OF INTERNATIONAL ORGANIZATIONS (Agenda item 85)
A/C.6/78/SR.19
UN. INTERNATIONAL LAW COMMISSION—REPORTS (Agenda item 79)
A/C.6/78/SR.28

Thiéry, Charline (France)
UN. INTERNATIONAL LAW COMMISSION—REPORTS (Agenda item 79)
A/C.6/78/SR.29; A/C.6/78/SR.31

Thoa Le, Thi Minh (Viet Nam)
SOCIAL DEVELOPMENT (Agenda item 24)
A/C.3/78/SR.3
UN. GENERAL ASSEMBLY—WORK PROGRAMME (Agenda item 120)
A/78/PV.32
UN. INTERNATIONAL COURT OF JUSTICE—REPORTS (Agenda item 73)
A/78/PV.27
UN RESOLUTIONS—IMPLEMENTATION (Agenda item 119)
A/78/PV.32
WOMEN'S ADVANCEMENT (Agenda item 25a)
A/C.3/78/SR.8
WOMEN'S ADVANCEMENT—CONFERENCES (Agenda item 25b)
A/C.3/78/SR.8

Thoeni, Julien (Switzerland)
BIOLOGICAL WEAPONS—TREATIES (Agenda item 106)
A/C.1/78/PV.15
CHEMICAL WEAPONS—TREATIES (Agenda item 99l)
A/C.1/78/PV.15
NUCLEAR DISARMAMENT (Agenda item 99b)
A/C.1/78/PV.12
NUCLEAR NON-PROLIFERATION—INTERNATIONAL OBLIGATIONS (Agenda item 99w)
A/C.1/78/PV.12

Thoeni, Julien (Switzerland) (continued)

NUCLEAR WEAPON TESTS—TREATIES (Agenda item 105)
A/C.1/78/PV.12
UN—PROGRAMME PLANNING (Agenda item 135)
A/C.1/78/PV.10
UN. GENERAL ASSEMBLY—WORK PROGRAMME (Agenda item 120)
A/C.1/78/PV.10
UN. GENERAL ASSEMBLY (78TH SESS. : 2023-2024). 1ST COMMITTEE—GENERAL DEBATE (Agenda item 8)
A/C.1/78/PV.3

Tholin, Isadora Jahanfar (Sweden) (European Union)

SUSTAINABLE DEVELOPMENT (Agenda item 18)
A/C.2/78/SR.24

Thomas, Glentis (Antigua and Barbuda)

BRITISH VIRGIN ISLANDS QUESTION (Agenda item 58)
A/C.4/78/SR.9
WESTERN SAHARA QUESTION (Agenda item 58)
A/C.4/78/SR.9

Thomas, Kathleen (Global Directives (Organization))

WESTERN SAHARA QUESTION (Agenda item 58)
A/C.4/78/SR.5

Thomas Ramírez, Vilma (Cuba)

BIOLOGICAL WEAPONS—TREATIES (Agenda item 106)
A/C.1/78/PV.15
CHEMICAL WEAPONS—TREATIES (Agenda item 99l)
A/C.1/78/PV.15
UN. CONFERENCE ON DISARMAMENT—REPORTS (Agenda item 101a)
A/C.1/78/PV.23
UN. DISARMAMENT COMMISSION—REPORTS (Agenda item 101b)
A/C.1/78/PV.23

Thomas Ramírez, Vilma (Cuba) (Grupo de Amigos del Español en las Naciones Unidas)

INFORMATION (Agenda item 53)
A/C.4/78/SR.12

Thomas-Greenfield, Linda (United States)

GEINGOB, HAGE GOTTFRIED (NAMIBIA. PRESIDENT)—TRIBUTES
A/78/PV.55
RACIAL DISCRIMINATION—ELIMINATION (Agenda item 69a)
A/78/PV.63
UKRAINE—POLITICAL CONDITIONS (Agenda item 62)
A/78/PV.56

Thomas-Greenfield, Linda (United States) (continued)

UN. SECURITY COUNCIL—MEMBERSHIP (Agenda item 121)
A/78/PV.34
UN CONFERENCES (Agenda item 13)
A/78/PV.63

Thompson Ramírez, Marilyn del Carmen (Panama)

CLIMATE (Agenda item 18d)
A/C.2/78/SR.13
SUSTAINABLE ENERGY (Agenda item 18h)
A/C.2/78/SR.13
UN. GENERAL ASSEMBLY (78TH SESS. : 2023-2024). 2ND COMMITTEE—GENERAL DEBATE (Agenda item 8)
A/C.2/78/SR.3

Thorbjörnsdóttir, Guðrún (Iceland)

UN—BUDGET (2024) (Agenda item 134)
A/C.5/78/SR.26/PartII

Thornton, Nicole (United States)

UN. INTERNATIONAL LAW COMMISSION—REPORTS (Agenda item 79)
A/C.6/78/SR.29; A/C.6/78/SR.31

Tiatoa, Sylvana (Association Tumu Ra'i Fenua)

FRENCH POLYNESIA QUESTION (Agenda item 58)
A/C.4/78/SR.3

Tickner, Arlene Beth (Colombia)

COMMODITIES (Agenda item 16d)
A/C.2/78/SR.14
DEVELOPMENT FINANCE (Agenda item 16b)
A/C.2/78/SR.8
DISPLACED PERSONS (Agenda item 71b)
A/C.3/78/SR.32
EXTERNAL DEBT (Agenda item 16c)
A/C.2/78/SR.8
FREEDOM OF EXPRESSION (Agenda item 71b)
A/C.3/78/SR.19
HEALTH (Agenda item 125)
A/78/PV.48
RIGHT OF ASSEMBLY (Agenda item 71b)
A/C.3/78/SR.19
SUSTAINABLE DEVELOPMENT (Agenda item 18)
A/C.2/78/SR.14
TAXATION (Agenda item 16h)
A/C.2/78/SR.8

Tidball-Binz, Morris (UN. Human Rights Council. Special Rapporteur on Extrajudicial, Summary or Arbitrary Executions)

SUMMARY EXECUTIONS (Agenda item 71b)
A/C.3/78/SR.31

Tieman, Connor (New Zealand)

WOMEN'S ADVANCEMENT (Agenda item 25a)
A/C.3/78/SR.8

Tieman, Connor (New Zealand) (continued)
WOMEN'S ADVANCEMENT—CONFERENCES (Agenda item 25b)
A/C.3/78/SR.8

Tierala, Lauri (Finland)
UKRAINE—POLITICAL CONDITIONS (Agenda item 62)
A/78/PV.56

Tingal, Magalie (Front de libération nationale kanak et socialiste (New Caledonia))
NEW CALEDONIA QUESTION (Agenda item 58)
A/C.4/78/SR.5

Tinubu, Bola Ahmed (Nigeria. President)
UN. GENERAL ASSEMBLY (78TH SESS. : 2023-2024)—GENERAL DEBATE (Agenda item 8)
A/78/PV.5
UN. GENERAL ASSEMBLY (78TH SESS. : 2023-2024)—SPECIAL STATEMENTS
A/78/PV.5

Tito, Teburoro (Kiribati)
DECOLONIZATION (Agenda item 58)
A/C.4/78/SR.8
DISARMAMENT—GENERAL AND COMPLETE (Agenda item 99)
A/78/PV.106; A/C.1/78/PV.25
RESPONSIBILITY TO PROTECT (Agenda item 129)
A/78/PV.97
UN. GENERAL ASSEMBLY (78TH SESS. : 2023-2024). 1ST COMMITTEE—GENERAL DEBATE (Agenda item 8)
A/C.1/78/PV.8
WESTERN SAHARA QUESTION (Agenda item 58)
A/C.4/78/SR.8

Tokarska, Anastasiia (Ukraine)
CRIME PREVENTION (Agenda item 107)
A/C.3/78/SR.51
FREEDOM OF EXPRESSION (Agenda item 71b)
A/C.3/78/SR.19
HUMAN RIGHTS—UKRAINE (Agenda item 71c)
A/C.3/78/SR.27
INDIGENOUS PEOPLES (Agenda item 68a)
A/C.3/78/SR.15
INDIGENOUS PEOPLES—CONFERENCES (Agenda item 68b)
A/C.3/78/SR.15
INFORMATION (Agenda item 53)
A/C.4/78/SR.14
PEACE (Agenda item 14)
A/78/PV.48
PERSONS WITH DISABILITIES—HUMAN RIGHTS (Agenda item 71a)
A/C.3/78/SR.38

Tokarska, Anastasiia (Ukraine) (continued)
RACIAL DISCRIMINATION—ELIMINATION (Agenda item 69a)
A/C.3/78/SR.41
RACIAL DISCRIMINATION—PROGRAMMES OF ACTION (Agenda item 69b)
A/C.3/78/SR.41
RIGHT TO CULTURE (Agenda item 71b)
A/C.3/78/SR.27
RIGHT TO FOOD (Agenda item 71b)
A/C.3/78/SR.30
RIGHT TO HOUSING (Agenda item 71b)
A/C.3/78/SR.30
SEXUAL ORIENTATION (Agenda item 71b)
A/C.3/78/SR.39
SPORTS—OLYMPIC GAMES (Agenda item 11)
A/78/PV.38
SUMMARY EXECUTIONS (Agenda item 71b)
A/C.3/78/SR.31
TRAFFICKING IN PERSONS (Agenda item 71b)
A/C.3/78/SR.23
WOMEN'S ADVANCEMENT (Agenda item 25a)
A/C.3/78/SR.9
WOMEN'S ADVANCEMENT—CONFERENCES (Agenda item 25b)
A/C.3/78/SR.9

Tokayev, Kassym-Jomart (Kazakhstan. President)
UN. GENERAL ASSEMBLY (78TH SESS. : 2023-2024)—GENERAL DEBATE (Agenda item 8)
A/78/PV.5
UN. GENERAL ASSEMBLY (78TH SESS. : 2023-2024)—SPECIAL STATEMENTS
A/78/PV.5

Tokoragi, Ella (Baku Initiative Group)
FRENCH POLYNESIA QUESTION (Agenda item 58)
A/C.4/78/SR.3

Tokunaga, Fumie (Japan)
INTERNATIONAL CRIMINAL COURT—REPORTS (Agenda item 74)
A/78/PV.22

Tolstoi, Natalie (European Union)
PEACEBUILDING (Agenda item 61)
A/78/PV.100
UN. PEACEBUILDING COMMISSION—REPORTS (Agenda item 27)
A/78/PV.100
UN. PEACEBUILDING FUND—REPORTS (Agenda item 111)
A/78/PV.100

Tomlinson, Bryan (Canada)
BIOLOGICAL WEAPONS—TREATIES (Agenda item 106)
A/C.1/78/PV.15

Tomlinson, Bryan (Canada) (continued)

CHEMICAL WEAPONS—TREATIES (Agenda item 99l)
A/C.1/78/PV.15
DISARMAMENT—GENERAL AND COMPLETE (Agenda item 99)
A/C.1/78/PV.15

Tommo Monthe, Michel (Cameroon)

AFRICA—DEVELOPMENT (Agenda item 65b)
A/78/PV.18
AFRICA—SUSTAINABLE DEVELOPMENT—PARTNERSHIP (Agenda item 65a)
A/78/PV.18
HUMAN RIGHTS INSTITUTIONS—CENTRAL AFRICA (Agenda item 71b)
A/C.3/78/SR.56
LAW OF THE SEA (Agenda item 75a)
A/78/PV.44
MARINE ECOSYSTEMS—BIOLOGICAL DIVERSITY (Agenda item 75c)
A/78/PV.44
PEACEKEEPING OPERATIONS (Agenda item 51)
A/C.4/78/SR.20
STRADDLING FISH STOCKS (Agenda item 75b)
A/78/PV.44
UN—BUDGET (2024) (Agenda item 134)
A/C.5/78/SR.22
UN. HUMAN RIGHTS COUNCIL—REPORTS (Agenda item 66)
A/78/PV.23
WESTERN SAHARA QUESTION (Agenda item 58)
A/C.4/78/SR.8

Tommo Monthe, Michel (Cameroon) (UN. Group of African States)

UN. GENERAL ASSEMBLY (78TH SESS. : 2023-2024). PRESIDENT (Agenda item 4)
A/78/PV.87

Tonai, Akihiro (Japan)

HUMAN RIGHTS—AFGHANISTAN (Agenda item 71c)
A/C.3/78/SR.34
SLAVERY (Agenda item 71a)
A/C.3/78/SR.21

Tonon, Daniela (Italy)

HUMAN RIGHTS (Agenda item 71)
A/C.3/78/SR.16
PERSONS WITH DISABILITIES (Agenda item 24b)
A/C.3/78/SR.2
RIGHTS OF THE CHILD (Agenda item 67)
A/C.3/78/SR.13
SOCIAL CONDITIONS (Agenda item 24b)
A/C.3/78/SR.2
WOMEN'S ADVANCEMENT (Agenda item 25a)
A/C.3/78/SR.9

Tonon, Daniela (Italy) (continued)

WOMEN'S ADVANCEMENT—CONFERENCES (Agenda item 25b)
A/C.3/78/SR.9
YOUTH (Agenda item 24b)
A/C.3/78/SR.2

Töpfer, Lew (Germany)

YOUTH (Agenda item 24b)
A/C.3/78/SR.3

Tornius, Hanna-Stiina (Estonia)

YOUTH (Agenda item 24b)
A/C.3/78/SR.2

Torres Seara, Dalia Marlen (Cuba) (Group of 77)

2030 AGENDA—PROGRAMME IMPLEMENTATION (Agenda item 18a)
A/C.2/78/SR.21
BIOLOGICAL DIVERSITY—TREATIES (Agenda item 18f)
A/C.2/78/SR.21
CLIMATE (Agenda item 18d)
A/C.2/78/SR.21
COMMODITIES (Agenda item 16d)
A/C.2/78/SR.21
CULTURE—DEVELOPMENT (Agenda item 19b)
A/C.2/78/SR.21
DESERTIFICATION—TREATIES (Agenda item 18e)
A/C.2/78/SR.21
DEVELOPMENT COOPERATION—MIDDLE-INCOME COUNTRIES (Agenda item 19c)
A/C.2/78/SR.21
DEVELOPMENT EDUCATION (Agenda item 18g)
A/C.2/78/SR.21
DEVELOPMENT FINANCE (Agenda item 16b)
A/C.2/78/SR.8; A/C.2/78/SR.21
DEVELOPMENT FINANCE—CONFERENCES (Agenda item 17)
A/C.2/78/SR.21
DISASTER PREVENTION (Agenda item 18c)
A/C.2/78/SR.21
ECONOMIC COOPERATION AMONG DEVELOPING COUNTRIES (Agenda item 22b)
A/C.2/78/SR.21
EXTERNAL DEBT (Agenda item 16c)
A/C.2/78/SR.8; A/C.2/78/SR.21
FINANCIAL FLOWS (Agenda item 16f)
A/C.2/78/SR.21
FINANCIAL INCLUSION (Agenda item 16e)
A/C.2/78/SR.21
FOOD SECURITY (Agenda item 23a)
A/C.2/78/SR.21
INFORMATION TECHNOLOGY—DEVELOPMENT (Agenda item 15)
A/C.2/78/SR.21
INTERNATIONAL TRADE (Agenda item 16a)
A/C.2/78/SR.8; A/C.2/78/SR.21
INVESTMENT PROMOTION (Agenda item 16g)
A/C.2/78/SR.21

Torres Seara, Dalia Marlen (Cuba) (Group of 77) (continued)

LANDLOCKED DEVELOPING COUNTRIES—CONFERENCES (Agenda item 20b)
A/C.2/78/SR.21
LEAST DEVELOPED COUNTRIES—CONFERENCES (Agenda item 20a)
A/C.2/78/SR.21
OPERATIONAL ACTIVITIES—UN SYSTEM (Agenda item 22a)
A/C.2/78/SR.21
POVERTY—INTERNATIONAL DECADES (Agenda item 21a)
A/C.2/78/SR.21
RURAL POVERTY (Agenda item 21b)
A/C.2/78/SR.21
SCIENCE AND TECHNOLOGY—DEVELOPMENT (Agenda item 19a)
A/C.2/78/SR.21
SMALL ISLAND DEVELOPING STATES—PROGRAMMES OF ACTION (Agenda item 18b)
A/C.2/78/SR.21
STORMS (Agenda item 18i)
A/C.2/78/SR.21
SUSTAINABLE ENERGY (Agenda item 18h)
A/C.2/78/SR.21

Torres Small, Xochitl (United States)

FOOD SECURITY (Agenda item 23a)
A/78/PV.77

Toschi, Stéphanie (Luxembourg)

FREEDOM OF EXPRESSION (Agenda item 71b)
A/C.3/78/SR.19
HUMAN RIGHTS—MYANMAR (Agenda item 71c)
A/C.3/78/SR.33
SEXUAL ORIENTATION (Agenda item 71b)
A/C.3/78/SR.39

Touadera, Faustin Archange (Central African Republic. President)

UN. GENERAL ASSEMBLY (78TH SESS. : 2023-2024)—GENERAL DEBATE (Agenda item 8)
A/78/PV.8
UN. GENERAL ASSEMBLY (78TH SESS. : 2023-2024)—SPECIAL STATEMENTS
A/78/PV.8

Tozik, Artsiom (Belarus)

HUMAN RIGHTS—BURUNDI (Agenda item 71c)
A/C.3/78/SR.36
HUMAN RIGHTS—DEMOCRATIC PEOPLE'S REPUBLIC OF KOREA (Agenda item 71c)
A/C.3/78/SR.33
HUMAN RIGHTS—ERITREA (Agenda item 71c)
A/C.3/78/SR.36
HUMAN RIGHTS—ETHIOPIA (Agenda item 71c)
A/C.3/78/SR.36
HUMAN RIGHTS—IRAN (ISLAMIC REPUBLIC OF) (Agenda item 71c)
A/C.3/78/SR.34

Tozik, Artsiom (Belarus) (continued)

HUMAN RIGHTS—MYANMAR (Agenda item 71c)
A/C.3/78/SR.33
HUMAN RIGHTS—SYRIAN ARAB REPUBLIC (Agenda item 71c)
A/C.3/78/SR.34
PERSONS WITH DISABILITIES—HUMAN RIGHTS (Agenda item 71a)
A/C.3/78/SR.38
RACIAL DISCRIMINATION—ELIMINATION (Agenda item 69a)
A/C.3/78/SR.40
RACIAL DISCRIMINATION—PROGRAMMES OF ACTION (Agenda item 69b)
A/C.3/78/SR.40
RIGHT TO HEALTH (Agenda item 71b)
A/C.3/78/SR.39

Tran, Thi Phuong Ha (Viet Nam)

INTERNATIONAL LAW—TRAINING PROGRAMMES (Agenda item 78)
A/C.6/78/SR.21
RESPONSIBILITY OF INTERNATIONAL ORGANIZATIONS (Agenda item 85)
A/C.6/78/SR.19
UN COMMISSION ON INTERNATIONAL TRADE LAW—REPORTS (Agenda item 77)
A/C.6/78/SR.14

Tran, Thi Thanh Hai (Viet Nam)

NUCLEAR DISARMAMENT (Agenda item 99b)
A/C.1/78/PV.13
NUCLEAR NON-PROLIFERATION—INTERNATIONAL OBLIGATIONS (Agenda item 99w)
A/C.1/78/PV.13
NUCLEAR WEAPON TESTS—TREATIES (Agenda item 105)
A/C.1/78/PV.13
SOUTH-EAST ASIA—NUCLEAR-WEAPON-FREE ZONES (Agenda item 99y)
A/C.1/78/PV.13

Travieso Darias, María Dolores (Asociación Canaria de Juristas por la Paz y los Derechos Humanos)

WESTERN SAHARA QUESTION (Agenda item 58)
A/C.4/78/SR.4

Travieso Hernández, Victoria (Asociación Canaria de Mujeres Tejiendo Futuro)

WESTERN SAHARA QUESTION (Agenda item 58)
A/C.4/78/SR.4

Treedara, Jakarin (Thailand)

RIGHTS OF THE CHILD (Agenda item 67)
A/C.3/78/SR.11

Trenyiwa, Karyl (New Caledonia)

NEW CALEDONIA QUESTION (Agenda item 58)
A/C.4/78/SR.5

Tripptrap, Ravi Christian (Sovereign Order of Malta)

CLIMATE CHANGE (Agenda item 71b)
A/C.3/78/SR.29

Troch, Harald (Austria)

WESTERN SAHARA QUESTION (Agenda item 58)
A/C.4/78/SR.5

Troncoso, Claudio (Chile)

UN. INTERNATIONAL LAW COMMISSION—REPORTS (Agenda item 79)
A/C.6/78/SR.24

Trovoada, Patrice Emery (Sao Tome and Principe. Prime Minister)

UN. GENERAL ASSEMBLY (78TH SESS. : 2023-2024)—GENERAL DEBATE (Agenda item 8)
A/78/PV.7
UN. GENERAL ASSEMBLY (78TH SESS. : 2023-2024)—SPECIAL STATEMENTS
A/78/PV.7

Tshisekedi Tshilombo, Félix Antoine (Democratic Republic of the Congo. President)

UN. GENERAL ASSEMBLY (78TH SESS. : 2023-2024)—GENERAL DEBATE (Agenda item 8)
A/78/PV.7
UN. GENERAL ASSEMBLY (78TH SESS. : 2023-2024)—SPECIAL STATEMENTS
A/78/PV.7

Tsiode, Branessa (Nauru)

UN. GENERAL ASSEMBLY (78TH SESS. : 2023-2024). 2ND COMMITTEE—GENERAL DEBATE (Agenda item 8)
A/C.2/78/SR.6

Tsuji, Kiyoto (Japan)

UKRAINE—POLITICAL CONDITIONS (Agenda item 62)
A/78/PV.56

Tudor-Bezies, Elizabeth (Canada)

PERSONS WITH DISABILITIES—HUMAN RIGHTS (Agenda item 71a)
A/C.3/78/SR.38; A/C.3/78/SR.51
RACIAL DISCRIMINATION—ELIMINATION (Agenda item 69a)
A/C.3/78/SR.42
RACIAL DISCRIMINATION—PROGRAMMES OF ACTION (Agenda item 69b)
A/C.3/78/SR.42
YOUTH (Agenda item 24b)
A/C.3/78/SR.55

Tuheiava, Richard Ariihau (French Polynesia)

FRENCH POLYNESIA QUESTION (Agenda item 58)
A/C.4/78/SR.3

Tun, Kyaw Moe (Myanmar)

BIOLOGICAL WEAPONS—TREATIES (Agenda item 106)
A/C.1/78/PV.16
CHEMICAL WEAPONS—TREATIES (Agenda item 99l)
A/C.1/78/PV.16
CRIME PREVENTION (Agenda item 107)
A/C.3/78/SR.6
CRIMES AGAINST HUMANITY (Agenda item 80)
A/C.6/78/SR.11
DISAPPEARANCE OF PERSONS (Agenda item 71b)
A/C.3/78/SR.22
DISPLACED PERSONS (Agenda item 71b)
A/C.3/78/SR.32
EMERGENCY ASSISTANCE (Agenda item 72a)
A/78/PV.47
FOOD SECURITY (Agenda item 23a)
A/C.2/78/SR.17
FREEDOM OF EXPRESSION (Agenda item 71b)
A/C.3/78/SR.19
HUMAN RIGHTS (Agenda item 71)
A/C.3/78/SR.16
HUMAN RIGHTS—MYANMAR (Agenda item 71c)
A/C.3/78/SR.27; A/C.3/78/SR.33; A/C.3/78/SR.53
HUMAN RIGHTS ACTIVISTS (Agenda item 71b)
A/C.3/78/SR.19
IAEA—REPORTS (Agenda item 89)
A/78/PV.29
INFORMATION (Agenda item 53)
A/C.4/78/SR.14
INTERNATIONAL CRIMINAL COURT—REPORTS (Agenda item 74)
A/78/PV.22
INTERNATIONAL JURISDICTION (Agenda item 84)
A/C.6/78/SR.13
LANDLOCKED DEVELOPING COUNTRIES—CONFERENCES (Agenda item 20b)
A/C.2/78/SR.7
LEAST DEVELOPED COUNTRIES—CONFERENCES (Agenda item 20a)
A/C.2/78/SR.7
MACROECONOMIC POLICY (Agenda item 16)
A/C.2/78/SR.9
MINE CLEARANCE (Agenda item 46)
A/C.4/78/SR.10
NUCLEAR DISARMAMENT (Agenda item 99b)
A/C.1/78/PV.14
NUCLEAR NON-PROLIFERATION—INTERNATIONAL OBLIGATIONS (Agenda item 99w)
A/C.1/78/PV.14
NUCLEAR WEAPON TESTS—TREATIES (Agenda item 105)
A/C.1/78/PV.14

Tun, Kyaw Moe (Myanmar) (continued)

PEACE (Agenda item 14)
A/78/PV.76
PERSONS WITH DISABILITIES—HUMAN RIGHTS (Agenda item 71a)
A/C.3/78/SR.38
POVERTY—INTERNATIONAL DECADES (Agenda item 21a)
A/C.2/78/SR.17
RESPONSIBILITY TO PROTECT (Agenda item 129)
A/78/PV.96
RIGHTS OF THE CHILD (Agenda item 67)
A/C.3/78/SR.14
RULE OF LAW (Agenda item 83)
A/C.6/78/SR.18
RURAL POVERTY (Agenda item 21b)
A/C.2/78/SR.17
SOCIAL CONDITIONS (Agenda item 24b)
A/C.3/78/SR.3
SUMMARY EXECUTIONS (Agenda item 71b)
A/C.3/78/SR.31
SUSTAINABLE DEVELOPMENT (Agenda item 18)
A/C.2/78/SR.15
TORTURE AND OTHER CRUEL TREATMENT (Agenda item 71a)
A/C.3/78/SR.18
UN—BUDGET (2024) (Agenda item 134)
A/C.5/78/SR.5
UN—PROGRAMME PLANNING (Agenda item 135)
A/C.5/78/SR.5
UN. GENERAL ASSEMBLY (78TH SESS. : 2023-2024). 1ST COMMITTEE—GENERAL DEBATE (Agenda item 8)
A/C.1/78/PV.7
UN. GENERAL ASSEMBLY (78TH SESS. : 2023-2024). 2ND COMMITTEE—GENERAL DEBATE (Agenda item 8)
A/C.2/78/SR.5
UN. HUMAN RIGHTS COUNCIL—REPORTS (Agenda item 66)
A/78/PV.23; A/C.3/78/SR.46
UN. INTERNATIONAL COURT OF JUSTICE—REPORTS (Agenda item 73)
A/78/PV.28
UN. SECRETARY-GENERAL—REPORTS (Agenda item 110)
A/78/PV.55
UN. SECURITY COUNCIL—REPORTS (Agenda item 26)
A/78/PV.93
UN HIGH COMMISSIONER FOR REFUGEES—REPORTS (Agenda item 60)
A/C.3/78/SR.45
WOMEN'S ADVANCEMENT (Agenda item 25a)
A/C.3/78/SR.10
WOMEN'S ADVANCEMENT—CONFERENCES (Agenda item 25b)
A/C.3/78/SR.10

Tunen, Maarten van (Netherlands (Kingdom of the))

HUMAN RIGHTS—BELARUS (Agenda item 71c)
A/C.3/78/SR.37
HUMAN RIGHTS—MYANMAR (Agenda item 71c)
A/C.3/78/SR.33

Tur de la Concepción, Richard (Cuba)

UN—BUDGET (2024) (Agenda item 134)
A/78/PV.50(Resumption1); A/C.5/78/SR.3; A/C.5/78/SR.26/PartII; A/C.5/78/SR.34
UN—PROGRAMME PLANNING (Agenda item 135)
A/78/PV.50(Resumption1)

Tur de la Concepción, Richard (Cuba) (Group of 77)

CONFERENCE AND MEETING SERVICES (Agenda item 137)
A/C.5/78/SR.7
PERSONNEL QUESTIONS—UN SYSTEM (Agenda item 142)
A/C.5/78/SR.10
UN—ADMINISTRATION (Agenda item 132)
A/C.5/78/SR.2
UN—BUDGET (2023) (Agenda item 133)
A/C.5/78/SR.4; A/C.5/78/SR.9
UN—BUDGET (2024) (Agenda item 134)
A/C.5/78/SR.2; A/C.5/78/SR.9; A/C.5/78/SR.11; A/C.5/78/SR.12; A/C.5/78/SR.13; A/C.5/78/SR.26/PartII
UN—BUDGET CONTRIBUTIONS (Agenda item 138)
A/C.5/78/SR.1
UN—FINANCIAL REPORTS (Agenda item 131)
A/C.5/78/SR.14
UN—FINANCIAL SITUATION (Agenda item 136)
A/C.5/78/SR.6
UN. ETHICS OFFICE—REPORTS (Agenda item 140)
A/C.5/78/SR.2
UN. GENERAL ASSEMBLY (78TH SESS. : 2023-2024)—OFFICERS (Agenda item 5)
A/C.5/78/SR.1
UN. GENERAL ASSEMBLY (78TH SESS. : 2023-2024). 5TH COMMITTEE—WORK ORGANIZATION (Agenda item 7)
A/C.5/78/SR.26/PartII
UN. OFFICE OF INTERNAL OVERSIGHT SERVICES—REPORTS (Agenda item 143)
A/C.5/78/SR.2

Türk, Volker (UN High Commissioner for Human Rights)

HUMAN RIGHTS (Agenda item 71)
A/C.3/78/SR.16

Turnbull, Andrea Megan (Canada)

INFORMATION (Agenda item 53)
A/C.4/78/SR.14

Turner, Bruce (United States)

ARMS RACE—OUTER SPACE (Agenda item 97a)
A/C.1/78/PV.17
BIOLOGICAL WEAPONS—TREATIES (Agenda item 106)
A/C.1/78/PV.15; A/C.1/78/PV.16
CHEMICAL WEAPONS—TREATIES (Agenda item 99l)
A/C.1/78/PV.15; A/C.1/78/PV.26
CLUSTER MUNITIONS (Agenda item 99dd)
A/C.1/78/PV.28
CONVENTIONAL ARMS—REGIONAL PROGRAMMES (Agenda item 99g)
A/C.1/78/PV.29
DISARMAMENT—GENERAL AND COMPLETE (Agenda item 99)
A/C.1/78/PV.15; A/C.1/78/PV.26; A/C.1/78/PV.30
DISARMAMENT AGREEMENTS—ENVIRONMENT (Agenda item 99j)
A/C.1/78/PV.29
DISARMAMENT AGREEMENTS—OUTER SPACE (Agenda item 97c)
A/C.1/78/PV.17; A/C.1/78/PV.27
DISARMAMENT-DEVELOPMENT LINK (Agenda item 99d)
A/C.1/78/PV.29
FISSIONABLE MATERIALS—TREATIES (Agenda item 99a)
A/C.1/78/PV.25
INFORMATION—INTERNATIONAL SECURITY (Agenda item 94)
A/C.1/78/PV.21
MEDITERRANEAN REGION—REGIONAL SECURITY (Agenda item 104)
A/C.1/78/PV.29
MIDDLE EAST—NUCLEAR PROLIFERATION (Agenda item 102)
A/C.1/78/PV.26
MIDDLE EAST—NUCLEAR-WEAPON-FREE ZONES (Agenda item 95)
A/C.1/78/PV.25
NUCLEAR DISARMAMENT (Agenda item 99b)
A/C.1/78/PV.13
NUCLEAR DISARMAMENT—TREATY COMPLIANCE (Agenda item 99q)
A/C.1/78/PV.25
NUCLEAR NON-PROLIFERATION—INTERNATIONAL OBLIGATIONS (Agenda item 99w)
A/C.1/78/PV.13
NUCLEAR WEAPONS—HUMANITARIAN CONSEQUENCES (Agenda item 99bb)
A/C.1/78/PV.25
NUCLEAR-WEAPON-FREE ZONE—SOUTHERN HEMISPHERE (Agenda item 99i)
A/C.1/78/PV.25; A/C.1/78/PV.26
NUCLEAR-WEAPON-FREE ZONES (Agenda item 99cc)
A/C.1/78/PV.25
OUTER SPACE—CONFIDENCE-BUILDING MEASURES (Agenda item 99v)
A/C.1/78/PV.17

Turner, Bruce (United States) (continued)

OUTER SPACE—PRINCIPLES (Agenda item 97d)
A/C.1/78/PV.17; A/C.1/78/PV.27
REGIONAL DISARMAMENT (Agenda item 99f)
A/C.1/78/PV.22
SCIENCE AND TECHNOLOGY—INTERNATIONAL SECURITY (Agenda item 98)
A/C.1/78/PV.29
SOUTH-EAST ASIA—NUCLEAR-WEAPON-FREE ZONES (Agenda item 99y)
A/C.1/78/PV.30
UN. CONFERENCE ON DISARMAMENT—REPORTS (Agenda item 101a)
A/C.1/78/PV.23
UN. GENERAL ASSEMBLY (78TH SESS. : 2023-2024). 1ST COMMITTEE—GENERAL DEBATE (Agenda item 8)
A/C.1/78/PV.5; A/C.1/78/PV.6; A/C.1/78/PV.7
UN. GENERAL ASSEMBLY (78TH SESS. : 2023-2024). 1ST COMMITTEE—WORK ORGANIZATION (Agenda item 7)
A/C.1/78/PV.30
WEAPONS—OUTER SPACE (Agenda item 97b)
A/C.1/78/PV.17; A/C.1/78/PV.27
WEAPONS OF MASS DESTRUCTION (Agenda item 93)
A/C.1/78/PV.29

Tusscher, Berendina ten (Netherlands (Kingdom of the))

RELIGIOUS INTOLERANCE (Agenda item 71b)
A/C.3/78/SR.38

Tvinnereim, Anne Beathe (Norway)

UN. GENERAL ASSEMBLY (78TH SESS. : 2023-2024)—GENERAL DEBATE (Agenda item 8)
A/78/PV.13

Uddin, Nasir (Bangladesh)

DISASTER VICTIMS (Agenda item 86)
A/C.6/78/SR.6
LAW OF THE SEA (Agenda item 75a)
A/78/PV.43
MARINE ECOSYSTEMS—BIOLOGICAL DIVERSITY (Agenda item 75c)
A/78/PV.43
STRADDLING FISH STOCKS (Agenda item 75b)
A/78/PV.43
UN. INTERNATIONAL LAW COMMISSION—REPORTS (Agenda item 79)
A/C.6/78/SR.24

Uddin, Nasir (Bangladesh) (UN. General Assembly. 6th Committee. Bureau)

PEACEKEEPING OPERATIONS—CRIMINAL LIABILITY (Agenda item 76)
A/C.6/78/SR.37

Udell, Isabel (United States)

SUSTAINABLE DEVELOPMENT (Agenda item 18)
A/C.2/78/SR.22; A/C.2/78/SR.24

Udom, Caoimhe (Ireland)

ARMS TRANSFERS—TREATIES (Agenda item 99x)
A/C.1/78/PV.18
BIOLOGICAL WEAPONS—TREATIES (Agenda item 106)
A/C.1/78/PV.15
CHEMICAL WEAPONS—TREATIES (Agenda item 99l)
A/C.1/78/PV.15
CLUSTER MUNITIONS (Agenda item 99dd)
A/C.1/78/PV.18
CONVENTIONAL WEAPONS (Agenda item 99u)
A/C.1/78/PV.18
CONVENTIONAL WEAPONS—TREATIES (Agenda item 103)
A/C.1/78/PV.18
LANDMINES—TREATIES (Agenda item 99m)
A/C.1/78/PV.18

Uexküll, Andreas von (Sweden)

EMERGENCY ASSISTANCE (Agenda item 72a)
A/78/PV.46
HUMAN RIGHTS—RUSSIAN FEDERATION (Agenda item 71c)
A/C.3/78/SR.37
SUMMARY EXECUTIONS (Agenda item 71b)
A/C.3/78/SR.31

Uexküll, Andreas von (Sweden) (UN. Group of Western European and Other States)

AL-SABAH, NAWAF AL-AHMAD AL-JABER (KUWAIT. AMIR)—TRIBUTES
A/78/PV.50(Resumption1)

Ugarelli, Luis F. (Peru)

CUBA—UNITED STATES (Agenda item 38)
A/78/PV.26
DECOLONIZATION (Agenda item 58)
A/C.4/78/SR.7
FALKLAND ISLANDS (MALVINAS) QUESTION (Agenda item 42)
A/C.4/78/SR.7
SOCIAL CONDITIONS (Agenda item 24b)
A/C.3/78/SR.51
SPECIAL POLITICAL MISSIONS (Agenda item 52)
A/C.4/78/SR.21
UKRAINE—POLITICAL CONDITIONS (Agenda item 62)
A/78/PV.58
UN. INTERNATIONAL COURT OF JUSTICE—REPORTS (Agenda item 73)
A/78/PV.27
WESTERN SAHARA QUESTION (Agenda item 58)
A/C.4/78/SR.7

Ulziibayar, Vangansuren (Mongolia)

LANDLOCKED DEVELOPING COUNTRIES—CONFERENCES (Agenda item 20b)
A/C.2/78/SR.7
LEAST DEVELOPED COUNTRIES—CONFERENCES (Agenda item 20a)
A/C.2/78/SR.7
SOCIAL CONDITIONS (Agenda item 24b)
A/C.3/78/SR.47
UN CONFERENCES (Agenda item 13)
A/78/PV.91

Umar, Mujahid Ahmed (Nigeria)

UN HIGH COMMISSIONER FOR REFUGEES—REPORTS (Agenda item 60)
A/C.3/78/SR.45

Umarov, Kairat (Kazakhstan)

DISARMAMENT—GENERAL AND COMPLETE (Agenda item 99)
A/78/PV.105

Umulisa, Flavia (Rwanda)

HUMAN RIGHTS (Agenda item 71)
A/C.3/78/SR.16
HUMAN RIGHTS INSTITUTIONS—CENTRAL AFRICA (Agenda item 71b)
A/C.3/78/SR.56
SOCIAL CONDITIONS (Agenda item 24b)
A/C.3/78/SR.2
WOMEN'S ADVANCEMENT (Agenda item 25a)
A/C.3/78/SR.8
WOMEN'S ADVANCEMENT—CONFERENCES (Agenda item 25b)
A/C.3/78/SR.8
YOUTH (Agenda item 24b)
A/C.3/78/SR.2

Uprety, Prathma (Nepal)

WOMEN'S ADVANCEMENT (Agenda item 25a)
A/C.3/78/SR.9
WOMEN'S ADVANCEMENT—CONFERENCES (Agenda item 25b)
A/C.3/78/SR.9

Urano, Hibiki (Japan)

CRIMES AGAINST HUMANITY (Agenda item 80)
A/C.6/78/SR.44

Uraz, Onur (Türkiye)

CRIMES AGAINST HUMANITY (Agenda item 80)
A/C.6/78/SR.42; A/C.6/78/SR.43

Urosevic, Zoritsa (World Tourism Organization)

CLIMATE (Agenda item 18d)
A/C.2/78/SR.12

Urruela Arenales, María Soledad (UN Regional Centre for Peace, Disarmament and Development in Latin America and the Caribbean. Director)

PEACE—REGIONAL CENTRE—LATIN AMERICA AND THE CARIBBEAN (Agenda item 100c)
A/C.1/78/PV.23

Uskov, Vladimir (Russian Federation)

CLIMATE (Agenda item 18d)
A/C.2/78/SR.15
SUSTAINABLE DEVELOPMENT (Agenda item 18)
A/C.2/78/SR.15
SUSTAINABLE ENERGY (Agenda item 18h)
A/C.2/78/SR.15

Utebaev, Meder (Kyrgyzstan)

UN. GENERAL ASSEMBLY (78TH SESS. : 2023-2024). 1ST COMMITTEE—GENERAL DEBATE (Agenda item 8)
A/C.1/78/PV.9

Uzabumwana Tona, Yannick (Rwanda)

INTERNATIONAL RESIDUAL MECHANISM FOR CRIMINAL TRIBUNALS—FINANCING (Agenda item 145)
A/C.5/78/SR.20

Uzunovski, Dushko (North Macedonia)

VETO (Agenda item 63)
A/78/PV.79

Va'inga Tone, Viliami (Tonga)

SMALL ISLAND DEVELOPING STATES—PROGRAMMES OF ACTION (Agenda item 18b)
A/78/PV.100
UN. INTERNATIONAL LAW COMMISSION—REPORTS (Agenda item 79)
A/C.6/78/SR.28

Va'inga Tone, Viliami (Tonga) (Pacific Islands Forum)

MILLENNIUM SUMMIT—CONFERENCES (Agenda item 117)
A/78/PV.53
UN CONFERENCES (Agenda item 13)
A/78/PV.53

Vaea, Darlene Atuamua Hakeifalehaakili (Tonga) (Pacific Islands Forum)

LAW OF THE SEA (Agenda item 75a)
A/78/PV.43
MARINE ECOSYSTEMS—BIOLOGICAL DIVERSITY (Agenda item 75c)
A/78/PV.43
SMALL ISLAND DEVELOPING STATES—PROGRAMMES OF ACTION (Agenda item 18b)
A/C.2/78/SR.22
STRADDLING FISH STOCKS (Agenda item 75b)
A/78/PV.43

Vaeroyvik, Vilde (Norway)

WOMEN'S ADVANCEMENT (Agenda item 25a)
A/C.3/78/SR.7
WOMEN'S ADVANCEMENT—CONFERENCES (Agenda item 25b)
A/C.3/78/SR.7

Vaianui, Jeanne (French Polynesia)

FRENCH POLYNESIA QUESTION (Agenda item 58)
A/C.4/78/SR.3

Vaianui, Marania (Association Vaihau)

FRENCH POLYNESIA QUESTION (Agenda item 58)
A/C.4/78/SR.3

Valido Martínez, Yoangel (Cuba)

CRIME PREVENTION (Agenda item 107)
A/C.3/78/SR.5
CYBERCRIME (Agenda item 108)
A/C.3/78/SR.5
DEMOCRACY (Agenda item 71b)
A/C.3/78/SR.28
HEALTH (Agenda item 125)
A/78/PV.102
HUMAN RIGHTS—DEMOCRATIC PEOPLE'S REPUBLIC OF KOREA (Agenda item 71c)
A/C.3/78/SR.33
MIGRANTS—PROTECTION (Agenda item 71b)
A/C.3/78/SR.23
RACIAL DISCRIMINATION—ELIMINATION (Agenda item 69a)
A/C.3/78/SR.41
RACIAL DISCRIMINATION—PROGRAMMES OF ACTION (Agenda item 69b)
A/C.3/78/SR.41
RIGHT TO CULTURE (Agenda item 71b)
A/C.3/78/SR.27
RIGHT TO EDUCATION (Agenda item 71b)
A/C.3/78/SR.27
RIGHT TO HEALTH (Agenda item 71b)
A/C.3/78/SR.39
SEXUAL ORIENTATION (Agenda item 71b)
A/C.3/78/SR.39

Valiña, Liliana (UN. Human Rights Council. Expert Mechanism on the Right to Development. Chair)

RIGHT TO DEVELOPMENT (Agenda item 71b)
A/C.3/78/SR.20

Valle Blanco, Daniel del (International Youth Organization for Ibero-America)

HUMAN RIGHTS (Agenda item 71)
A/C.3/78/SR.28
RIGHT TO EDUCATION (Agenda item 71b)
A/C.3/78/SR.27

Valles, Marivil Villa (Philippines)
UN—BUDGET (2024) (Agenda item 134)
A/C.5/78/SR.33

Valles, Marivil Villa (Philippines) (ASEAN)
UN—BUDGET (2024) (Agenda item 134)
A/C.5/78/SR.5
UN—PROGRAMME PLANNING (Agenda item 135)
A/C.5/78/SR.5

Valtýsson, Jörundur (Iceland)
HUMAN RIGHTS ACTIVISTS (Agenda item 71b)
A/C.3/78/SR.26
LAW OF THE SEA (Agenda item 75a)
A/78/PV.44
MARINE ECOSYSTEMS—BIOLOGICAL DIVERSITY (Agenda item 75c)
A/78/PV.44
PEACE (Agenda item 14)
A/78/PV.62
RIGHTS OF THE CHILD (Agenda item 67)
A/C.3/78/SR.14
SEXUAL ORIENTATION (Agenda item 71b)
A/C.3/78/SR.26
STRADDLING FISH STOCKS (Agenda item 75b)
A/78/PV.44
UN. GENERAL ASSEMBLY (78TH SESS. : 2023-2024). 1ST COMMITTEE—GENERAL DEBATE (Agenda item 8)
A/C.1/78/PV.7
UN. HUMAN RIGHTS COUNCIL—REPORTS (Agenda item 66)
A/78/PV.23
UN COMMISSION ON INTERNATIONAL TRADE LAW—REPORTS (Agenda item 77)
A/C.6/78/SR.14
VETO (Agenda item 63)
A/78/PV.61
WOMEN'S ADVANCEMENT (Agenda item 25a)
A/C.3/78/SR.10
WOMEN'S ADVANCEMENT—CONFERENCES (Agenda item 25b)
A/C.3/78/SR.10

Valtýsson, Jörundur (Iceland) (UN. General Assembly. Vice-President)
HIV/AIDS—DECLARATIONS (Agenda item 10)
A/78/PV.91

Van Bronswijk, Sarah (Australia)
UN. GENERAL ASSEMBLY—WORK PROGRAMME (Agenda item 120)
A/78/PV.32
UN RESOLUTIONS—IMPLEMENTATION (Agenda item 119)
A/78/PV.32

Van Houtte, Annick (UN Joint Staff Pension Board. Chair)
UN—BUDGET (2024) (Agenda item 134)
A/C.5/78/SR.9

Vanaa, Elise (French Polynesia)
FRENCH POLYNESIA QUESTION (Agenda item 58)
A/C.4/78/SR.3

Vanker, Imran (UN. Independent Audit Advisory Committee. Chair)
UN—ADMINISTRATION (Agenda item 132)
A/C.5/78/SR.2

Vannasin, Soudchai (Lao People's Democratic Republic)
RULE OF LAW (Agenda item 83)
A/C.6/78/SR.18

Varadkar, Leo (Ireland. Prime Minister)
UN. GENERAL ASSEMBLY (78TH SESS. : 2023-2024)—GENERAL DEBATE (Agenda item 8)
A/78/PV.11
UN. GENERAL ASSEMBLY (78TH SESS. : 2023-2024)—SPECIAL STATEMENTS
A/78/PV.11

Varem, Mattias (Estonia)
INFORMATION—INTERNATIONAL SECURITY (Agenda item 94)
A/C.1/78/PV.20
REGIONAL DISARMAMENT (Agenda item 99f)
A/C.1/78/PV.22

Varennes, Fernand de (UN. Human Rights Council. Special Rapporteur on Minority Issues)
MINORITIES (Agenda item 71b)
A/C.3/78/SR.39

Vasconcelos y Cruz, Héctor Enrique (Mexico)
DISARMAMENT—GENERAL AND COMPLETE (Agenda item 99)
A/78/PV.105
PEACE (Agenda item 14)
A/78/PV.82
RESPONSIBILITY TO PROTECT (Agenda item 129)
A/78/PV.96
UKRAINE—POLITICAL CONDITIONS (Agenda item 62)
A/78/PV.99
VETO (Agenda item 63)
A/78/PV.60; A/78/PV.67; A/78/PV.68; A/78/PV.75; A/78/PV.78

Vasović, Angela (United States)
HUMAN RIGHTS ADVANCEMENT (Agenda item 71b)
A/C.3/78/SR.52

Vásquez Solano, Leonel (Mexico)

FOOD SECURITY (Agenda item 23a)
A/C.2/78/SR.16
INDIGENOUS PEOPLES (Agenda item 68a)
A/C.3/78/SR.15
INDIGENOUS PEOPLES—CONFERENCES (Agenda item 68b)
A/C.3/78/SR.15
POVERTY—INTERNATIONAL DECADES (Agenda item 21a)
A/C.2/78/SR.16
RURAL POVERTY (Agenda item 21b)
A/C.2/78/SR.16

Vázquez-Bermúdez, Marcelo (UN. International Law Commission. Special Rapporteur on General Principles of Law)

UN. INTERNATIONAL LAW COMMISSION—REPORTS (Agenda item 79)
A/C.6/78/SR.28

Vea, Jeanett (Tonga)

DISASTER VICTIMS (Agenda item 86)
A/C.6/78/SR.6
UN. GENERAL ASSEMBLY (78TH SESS. : 2023-2024). 2ND COMMITTEE—GENERAL DEBATE (Agenda item 8)
A/C.2/78/SR.6

Vea, Jeanett (Tonga) (Pacific Islands Forum)

MARINE ECOSYSTEMS—BIOLOGICAL DIVERSITY (Agenda item 75c)
A/78/PV.103

Vega, Pablo de la (Asociación Ecuatoriana de Amistad con el Pueblo Saharaui)

WESTERN SAHARA QUESTION (Agenda item 58)
A/C.4/78/SR.4

Vegas Torres, Juan Pablo (Peru)

PEACE (Agenda item 14)
A/78/PV.82

Velázquez Castillo, Jesús (Mexico)

PERSONNEL QUESTIONS—UN SYSTEM (Agenda item 142)
A/C.5/78/SR.10
UN—BUDGET (2024) (Agenda item 134)
A/C.5/78/SR.3; A/C.5/78/SR.33
UN. GENERAL ASSEMBLY (78TH SESS. : 2023-2024)—OFFICERS (Agenda item 5)
A/C.5/78/SR.1
UN. GENERAL ASSEMBLY (78TH SESS. : 2023-2024). 5TH COMMITTEE—WORK ORGANIZATION (Agenda item 7)
A/C.5/78/SR.27; A/C.5/78/SR.35

Velichko, Irina (Belarus)

CRIME PREVENTION (Agenda item 107)
A/C.3/78/SR.5
CYBERCRIME (Agenda item 108)
A/C.3/78/SR.5
RIGHTS OF THE CHILD (Agenda item 67)
A/C.3/78/SR.11; A/C.3/78/SR.12
WOMEN'S ADVANCEMENT (Agenda item 25a)
A/C.3/78/SR.8
WOMEN'S ADVANCEMENT—CONFERENCES (Agenda item 25b)
A/C.3/78/SR.8

Veliz Rodríguez, Aris Anel (Panama)

NUCLEAR WEAPON TESTS—TREATIES (Agenda item 105)
A/C.1/78/PV.25
NUCLEAR WEAPONS—ELIMINATION (Agenda item 99z)
A/C.1/78/PV.25
NUCLEAR WEAPONS—TREATIES (Agenda item 99ff)
A/C.1/78/PV.25
NUCLEAR-WEAPON-FREE ZONES (Agenda item 99cc)
A/C.1/78/PV.25
UN. GENERAL ASSEMBLY (78TH SESS. : 2023-2024). 1ST COMMITTEE—GENERAL DEBATE (Agenda item 8)
A/C.1/78/PV.7

Veski, Kerli (Estonia)

UN. INTERNATIONAL LAW COMMISSION—REPORTS (Agenda item 79)
A/C.6/78/SR.24

Vest, Dangirutė (Lithuania)

CRIME PREVENTION (Agenda item 107)
A/C.3/78/SR.51

Vichankaiyakij, Vathayudh (Thailand)

OUTER SPACE—PEACEFUL USES—INTERNATIONAL COOPERATION (Agenda item 48)
A/C.4/78/SR.15
PEACE (Agenda item 14)
A/78/PV.76; A/78/PV.82
TERRORISM (Agenda item 109)
A/C.6/78/SR.2
UN. GENERAL ASSEMBLY (78TH SESS. : 2023-2024)—OFFICERS (Agenda item 5)
A/C.5/78/SR.1
UN HIGH COMMISSIONER FOR REFUGEES—REPORTS (Agenda item 60)
A/C.3/78/SR.44
VETO (Agenda item 63)
A/78/PV.67

Vichankaiyakij, Vathayudh (Thailand) (ASEAN)

WOMEN'S ADVANCEMENT (Agenda item 25a)
A/C.3/78/SR.8

Vichankaiyakij, Vathayudh (Thailand) (ASEAN) (continued)

WOMEN'S ADVANCEMENT—CONFERENCES (Agenda item 25b)
A/C.3/78/SR.8

Vidal Garrido, Manuel (University of Las Palmas)

WESTERN SAHARA QUESTION (Agenda item 58)
A/C.4/78/SR.4

Vidal Mercado, Jorge Andrés (Chile)

ARMS RACE—OUTER SPACE (Agenda item 97a)
A/C.1/78/PV.16
BIOLOGICAL WEAPONS—TREATIES (Agenda item 106)
A/C.1/78/PV.14
CHEMICAL WEAPONS—TREATIES (Agenda item 99l)
A/C.1/78/PV.14
CONVENTIONAL WEAPONS (Agenda item 99u)
A/C.1/78/PV.18
DISARMAMENT—GENERAL AND COMPLETE (Agenda item 99)
A/C.1/78/PV.18; A/C.1/78/PV.23
DISARMAMENT—YOUTH (Agenda item 99gg)
A/C.1/78/PV.20
INFORMATION—INTERNATIONAL SECURITY (Agenda item 94)
A/C.1/78/PV.20
NUCLEAR DISARMAMENT (Agenda item 99b)
A/C.1/78/PV.12
NUCLEAR NON-PROLIFERATION—INTERNATIONAL OBLIGATIONS (Agenda item 99w)
A/C.1/78/PV.12
NUCLEAR WEAPON TESTS—TREATIES (Agenda item 105)
A/C.1/78/PV.12
NUCLEAR WEAPONS—TREATIES (Agenda item 99ff)
A/C.1/78/PV.12
OUTER SPACE—PRINCIPLES (Agenda item 97d)
A/C.1/78/PV.16
SMALL ARMS—ILLICIT TRAFFIC (Agenda item 99p)
A/C.1/78/PV.18
UN—PROGRAMME PLANNING (Agenda item 135)
A/C.1/78/PV.10
UN. GENERAL ASSEMBLY—WORK PROGRAMME (Agenda item 120)
A/C.1/78/PV.10
UN. GENERAL ASSEMBLY (78TH SESS. : 2023-2024). 1ST COMMITTEE—GENERAL DEBATE (Agenda item 8)
A/C.1/78/PV.5
UN. SECURITY COUNCIL—MEMBERSHIP (Agenda item 121)
A/78/PV.35
UN. SECURITY COUNCIL—REPORTS (Agenda item 26)
A/78/PV.93

Vidal Mercado, Jorge Andrés (Chile) (continued)

VETO (Agenda item 63)
A/78/PV.70; A/78/PV.78

Videche Guevara, Carlos Manuel (Costa Rica)

UN—BUDGET (2024) (Agenda item 134)
A/C.5/78/SR.23
UN. GENERAL ASSEMBLY (78TH SESS. : 2023-2024). 5TH COMMITTEE—WORK ORGANIZATION (Agenda item 7)
A/C.5/78/SR.27
UN. SECURITY COUNCIL—REPORTS (Agenda item 26)
A/78/PV.94
VETO (Agenda item 63)
A/78/PV.59; A/78/PV.68

Viinanen, Jarmo Veli Tapio (Finland)

NUCLEAR DISARMAMENT (Agenda item 99b)
A/C.1/78/PV.12
NUCLEAR NON-PROLIFERATION—INTERNATIONAL OBLIGATIONS (Agenda item 99w)
A/C.1/78/PV.12

Viktorov, Evgeny (Russian Federation)

HUMAN RIGHTS (Agenda item 71)
A/C.3/78/SR.16

Villarreal, Marcela (FAO)

FOOD SECURITY (Agenda item 23a)
A/C.2/78/SR.16

Vilmenay Joseph, Linouse (Haiti)

FOOD SECURITY (Agenda item 23a)
A/C.2/78/SR.17
POVERTY—INTERNATIONAL DECADES (Agenda item 21a)
A/C.2/78/SR.17
RURAL POVERTY (Agenda item 21b)
A/C.2/78/SR.17
UN. GENERAL ASSEMBLY (78TH SESS. : 2023-2024). 2ND COMMITTEE—GENERAL DEBATE (Agenda item 8)
A/C.2/78/SR.5

Viñayo Fernández, Sofía (Spain) (European Union)

UN—PROGRAMME PLANNING (Agenda item 135)
A/C.5/78/SR.24

Vinhas, Rui (Portugal) (Accountability, Coherence and Transparency (ACT) Group)

UN. SECURITY COUNCIL—REPORTS (Agenda item 26)
A/78/PV.93

Violetti, Daniele (Secretariat of the United Nations Framework Convention on Climate Change. Technology and Capacity-Building Programme. Director)

CLIMATE (Agenda item 18d)
A/C.2/78/SR.12

Visek, Richard (United States)

UN. INTERNATIONAL COURT OF JUSTICE—REPORTS (Agenda item 73)
A/78/PV.20
UN. INTERNATIONAL LAW COMMISSION—REPORTS (Agenda item 79)
A/C.6/78/SR.24

Vittay, Melinda (Hungary)

CRIMES AGAINST HUMANITY (Agenda item 80)
A/C.6/78/SR.9; A/C.6/78/SR.38; A/C.6/78/SR.40; A/C.6/78/SR.45
INTERNATIONAL JURISDICTION (Agenda item 84)
A/C.6/78/SR.12
RESPONSIBILITY TO PROTECT (Agenda item 129)
A/78/PV.96
UN. INTERNATIONAL LAW COMMISSION—REPORTS (Agenda item 79)
A/C.6/78/SR.31

Vittay, Melinda (Hungary) (European Union)

MARINE ECOSYSTEMS—BIOLOGICAL DIVERSITY (Agenda item 75c)
A/78/PV.103

Vittay, Melinda (Hungary) (UN. General Assembly. 6th Committee. Bureau)

ADMINISTRATION OF JUSTICE (Agenda item 144)
A/C.6/78/SR.37

Vives Balmaña, Elisenda (Andorra)

VETO (Agenda item 63)
A/78/PV.75
WOMEN'S ADVANCEMENT (Agenda item 25a)
A/C.3/78/SR.10
WOMEN'S ADVANCEMENT—CONFERENCES (Agenda item 25b)
A/C.3/78/SR.10

Vlokhoven, Flore van (Luxembourg)

ENVIRONMENT (Agenda item 71b)
A/C.3/78/SR.29
RIGHT TO EDUCATION (Agenda item 71b)
A/C.3/78/SR.27

Vmulisa, Flavia (Rwanda)

HUMAN RIGHTS—REPORTS (Agenda item 71c)
A/C.3/78/SR.24
RIGHTS OF THE CHILD (Agenda item 67)
A/C.3/78/SR.11

Vogel, Robin Maria de (Netherlands (Kingdom of the))

HUMAN RIGHTS—AFGHANISTAN (Agenda item 71c)
A/C.3/78/SR.34
HUMAN RIGHTS—SYRIAN ARAB REPUBLIC (Agenda item 71c)
A/C.3/78/SR.34

Voionmaa, Lauri (Finland)

ARMS TRANSFERS—TREATIES (Agenda item 99x)
A/C.1/78/PV.19
DISARMAMENT—GENERAL AND COMPLETE (Agenda item 99)
A/C.1/78/PV.19
LANDMINES—TREATIES (Agenda item 99m)
A/C.1/78/PV.19
WOMEN'S ADVANCEMENT (Agenda item 25a)
A/C.3/78/SR.10
WOMEN'S ADVANCEMENT—CONFERENCES (Agenda item 25b)
A/C.3/78/SR.10

Volkov, Alice (Australia)

DECOLONIZATION—UN SYSTEM (Agenda item 56)
A/C.4/78/SR.9

Vongnorkeo, Anouparb (Lao People's Democratic Republic)

CUBA—UNITED STATES (Agenda item 38)
A/78/PV.24
ECONOMIC SANCTIONS—INTERNATIONAL RELATIONS (Agenda item 28)
A/78/PV.90
NUCLEAR DISARMAMENT (Agenda item 99b)
A/C.1/78/PV.13
NUCLEAR NON-PROLIFERATION—INTERNATIONAL OBLIGATIONS (Agenda item 99w)
A/C.1/78/PV.13
NUCLEAR WEAPON TESTS—TREATIES (Agenda item 105)
A/C.1/78/PV.13
PALESTINE QUESTION (Agenda item 35)
A/78/PV.40
PERSONS WITH DISABILITIES (Agenda item 24b)
A/C.3/78/SR.4
REGIONAL DISARMAMENT (Agenda item 99f)
A/C.1/78/PV.13
SOCIAL DEVELOPMENT (Agenda item 24)
A/C.3/78/SR.4
SOUTH-EAST ASIA—NUCLEAR-WEAPON-FREE ZONES (Agenda item 99y)
A/C.1/78/PV.13
UN. GENERAL ASSEMBLY (78TH SESS. : 2023-2024). 1ST COMMITTEE—GENERAL DEBATE (Agenda item 8)
A/C.1/78/PV.6

Vongnorkeo, Anouparb (Lao People's Democratic Republic) (continued)

UN. GENERAL ASSEMBLY (78TH SESS. : 2023-2024). 2ND COMMITTEE—GENERAL DEBATE (Agenda item 8)
A/C.2/78/SR.6

Vongnorkeo, Anouparb (Lao People's Democratic Republic) (ASEAN)

BIOLOGICAL WEAPONS—TREATIES (Agenda item 106)
A/C.1/78/PV.14
CHEMICAL WEAPONS—TREATIES (Agenda item 99l)
A/C.1/78/PV.14
DISARMAMENT—GENERAL AND COMPLETE (Agenda item 99)
A/C.1/78/PV.14
LANDLOCKED DEVELOPING COUNTRIES—CONFERENCES (Agenda item 20b)
A/C.2/78/SR.7
LEAST DEVELOPED COUNTRIES—CONFERENCES (Agenda item 20a)
A/C.2/78/SR.7

Vorobiev, Dmitry V. (Russian Federation)

WOMEN'S ADVANCEMENT—CONFERENCES (Agenda item 25b)
A/C.3/78/SR.51

Vorontsov, Konstantin (Russian Federation)

ARMS RACE—OUTER SPACE (Agenda item 97a)
A/C.1/78/PV.16
BIOLOGICAL WEAPONS—TREATIES (Agenda item 106)
A/C.1/78/PV.14; A/C.1/78/PV.15; A/C.1/78/PV.16
CHEMICAL WEAPONS—TREATIES (Agenda item 99l)
A/C.1/78/PV.14; A/C.1/78/PV.15
DISARMAMENT AGREEMENTS—OUTER SPACE (Agenda item 97c)
A/C.1/78/PV.16; A/C.1/78/PV.17
NUCLEAR DISARMAMENT (Agenda item 99b)
A/C.1/78/PV.11; A/C.1/78/PV.12; A/C.1/78/PV.13
NUCLEAR NON-PROLIFERATION—INTERNATIONAL OBLIGATIONS (Agenda item 99w)
A/C.1/78/PV.12
NUCLEAR WEAPON TESTS—TREATIES (Agenda item 105)
A/C.1/78/PV.12
OUTER SPACE—CONFIDENCE-BUILDING MEASURES (Agenda item 99v)
A/C.1/78/PV.16; A/C.1/78/PV.17
UN—PROGRAMME PLANNING (Agenda item 135)
A/C.1/78/PV.10
UN. GENERAL ASSEMBLY—WORK PROGRAMME (Agenda item 120)
A/C.1/78/PV.10

Vorontsov, Konstantin (Russian Federation) (continued)

UN. GENERAL ASSEMBLY (78TH SESS. : 2023-2024). 1ST COMMITTEE—GENERAL DEBATE (Agenda item 8)
A/C.1/78/PV.2; A/C.1/78/PV.3; A/C.1/78/PV.4; A/C.1/78/PV.5; A/C.1/78/PV.6; A/C.1/78/PV.7; A/C.1/78/PV.8
WEAPONS—OUTER SPACE (Agenda item 97b)
A/C.1/78/PV.16; A/C.1/78/PV.17
WEAPONS OF MASS DESTRUCTION—TERRORISM (Agenda item 99s)
A/C.1/78/PV.15

Vorshilov, Enkhbold (Mongolia)

AGEING PERSONS (Agenda item 24b)
A/C.3/78/SR.2
CLIMATE (Agenda item 18d)
A/C.2/78/SR.13
DESERTIFICATION—TREATIES (Agenda item 18e)
A/C.2/78/SR.13
EXTERNAL DEBT (Agenda item 16c)
A/C.2/78/SR.9
PEACEKEEPING OPERATIONS (Agenda item 51)
A/C.4/78/SR.19
RURAL WOMEN (Agenda item 25a)
A/C.3/78/SR.49
SOCIAL CONDITIONS (Agenda item 24b)
A/C.3/78/SR.2
TERRORISM (Agenda item 109)
A/C.6/78/SR.2
UN. GENERAL ASSEMBLY—WORK PROGRAMME (Agenda item 120)
A/78/PV.32
UN. GENERAL ASSEMBLY (78TH SESS. : 2023-2024). 1ST COMMITTEE—GENERAL DEBATE (Agenda item 8)
A/C.1/78/PV.6
UN. GENERAL ASSEMBLY (78TH SESS. : 2023-2024). 2ND COMMITTEE—GENERAL DEBATE (Agenda item 8)
A/C.2/78/SR.3
UN. SECURITY COUNCIL—MEMBERSHIP (Agenda item 121)
A/78/PV.35
UN RESOLUTIONS—IMPLEMENTATION (Agenda item 119)
A/78/PV.32
YOUTH (Agenda item 24b)
A/C.3/78/SR.2

Voulé, Clément Nyaletsossi (UN. Human Rights Council. Special Rapporteur on the Rights to Freedom of Peaceful Assembly and of Association)

RIGHT OF ASSEMBLY (Agenda item 71b)
A/C.3/78/SR.19

Vučić, Aleksandar (Serbia. President)

PEACE (Agenda item 14)
A/78/PV.82

Vučić, Aleksandar (Serbia. President) (continued)

UN. GENERAL ASSEMBLY (78TH SESS. : 2023-2024)—GENERAL DEBATE (Agenda item 8)
A/78/PV.8
UN. GENERAL ASSEMBLY (78TH SESS. : 2023-2024)—SPECIAL STATEMENTS
A/78/PV.8; A/78/PV.82

Vucic, Mihajlo ((personal capacity))

WESTERN SAHARA QUESTION (Agenda item 58)
A/C.4/78/SR.4

Vujačić, Dušan (Serbia)

DECOLONIZATION (Agenda item 58)
A/C.4/78/SR.8
FALKLAND ISLANDS (MALVINAS) QUESTION (Agenda item 42)
A/C.4/78/SR.8
UN. GENERAL ASSEMBLY (78TH SESS. : 2023-2024). 2ND COMMITTEE—GENERAL DEBATE (Agenda item 8)
A/C.2/78/SR.5

Waetara, Jane Mugafalu Kabui (Solomon Islands)

FRENCH POLYNESIA QUESTION (Agenda item 58)
A/C.4/78/SR.3

Waetara, Jane Mugafalu Kabui (Solomon Islands) (UN. General Assembly. Credentials Committee. Chair)

UN. GENERAL ASSEMBLY (78TH SESS. : 2023-2024). CREDENTIALS COMMITTEE—REPORTS (Agenda item 3b)
A/78/PV.48

Wafiuddin, Illyana (Brunei Darussalam)

RIGHT TO HEALTH (Agenda item 71b)
A/C.3/78/SR.26

Wägli, Christian (Switzerland)

TERRORISM—HUMAN RIGHTS (Agenda item 71b)
A/C.3/78/SR.31

Wagner, Julie (France)

RACIAL DISCRIMINATION—ELIMINATION (Agenda item 69a)
A/C.3/78/SR.41
RACIAL DISCRIMINATION—PROGRAMMES OF ACTION (Agenda item 69b)
A/C.3/78/SR.41
YOUTH (Agenda item 24b)
A/C.3/78/SR.55

Wagner, Valérie (Switzerland)

ENVIRONMENT (Agenda item 71b)
A/C.3/78/SR.29
FREEDOM OF EXPRESSION (Agenda item 71b)
A/C.3/78/SR.19

Wagner, Valérie (Switzerland) (continued)

HUMAN RIGHTS—AFGHANISTAN (Agenda item 71c)
A/C.3/78/SR.34
HUMAN RIGHTS—INTERNATIONAL INSTRUMENTS (Agenda item 71a)
A/C.3/78/SR.24
HUMAN RIGHTS ACTIVISTS (Agenda item 71b)
A/C.3/78/SR.19
HUMAN RIGHTS ADVANCEMENT (Agenda item 71b)
A/C.3/78/SR.24
PEACE (Agenda item 14)
A/78/PV.62; A/78/PV.88
RIGHT OF ASSEMBLY (Agenda item 71b)
A/C.3/78/SR.19
RIGHTS OF THE CHILD (Agenda item 67)
A/C.3/78/SR.12
SOCIAL DEVELOPMENT (Agenda item 24)
A/C.3/78/SR.3
TRAFFICKING IN PERSONS (Agenda item 71b)
A/C.3/78/SR.23
WOMEN'S ADVANCEMENT (Agenda item 25a)
A/C.3/78/SR.8
WOMEN'S ADVANCEMENT—CONFERENCES (Agenda item 25b)
A/C.3/78/SR.8

Wainwel, Gwedji Doris (Cameroon)

DEMOCRACY (Agenda item 71b)
A/C.3/78/SR.28
HUMAN RIGHTS (Agenda item 71)
A/C.3/78/SR.16
INDIGENOUS PEOPLES (Agenda item 68a)
A/C.3/78/SR.15
INDIGENOUS PEOPLES—CONFERENCES (Agenda item 68b)
A/C.3/78/SR.15
MIGRANTS—PROTECTION (Agenda item 71b)
A/C.3/78/SR.23
RIGHT TO CULTURE (Agenda item 71b)
A/C.3/78/SR.27
RIGHT TO EDUCATION (Agenda item 71b)
A/C.3/78/SR.27
TRANSNATIONAL CORPORATIONS—HUMAN RIGHTS (Agenda item 71b)
A/C.3/78/SR.21

Wakabayashi, Sato (Japan)

UN—BUDGET CONTRIBUTIONS (Agenda item 138)
A/C.5/78/SR.1

Wald, Julien (Luxembourg)

CRIME PREVENTION (Agenda item 107)
A/C.3/78/SR.6
CYBERCRIME (Agenda item 108)
A/C.3/78/SR.6
RIGHT TO PRIVACY (Agenda item 71b)
A/C.3/78/SR.21
RIGHTS OF THE CHILD (Agenda item 67)
A/C.3/78/SR.11; A/C.3/78/SR.12

Wallace, Brian Christopher Manley (Jamaica)

CUBA—UNITED STATES (Agenda item 38)
A/78/PV.26

Wallace, Brian Christopher Manley (Jamaica) (Caribbean Community)

2030 AGENDA—PROGRAMME IMPLEMENTATION (Agenda item 18a)
A/C.2/78/SR.12
BIOLOGICAL WEAPONS—TREATIES (Agenda item 106)
A/C.1/78/PV.14
CHEMICAL WEAPONS—TREATIES (Agenda item 99l)
A/C.1/78/PV.14
CLIMATE (Agenda item 18d)
A/C.2/78/SR.12
CRIME PREVENTION (Agenda item 107)
A/C.3/78/SR.5
CYBERCRIME (Agenda item 108)
A/C.3/78/SR.5
DEVELOPMENT FINANCE (Agenda item 16b)
A/C.2/78/SR.8
DISARMAMENT-DEVELOPMENT LINK (Agenda item 99d)
A/C.1/78/PV.21
DISASTER VICTIMS (Agenda item 86)
A/C.6/78/SR.5
FOOD SECURITY (Agenda item 23a)
A/C.2/78/SR.16
GLOBALIZATION—INTERDEPENDENCE (Agenda item 19)
A/C.2/78/SR.10
HUMAN RIGHTS—PROGRAMMES OF ACTION (Agenda item 71d)
A/C.3/78/SR.24
HUMAN RIGHTS ADVANCEMENT (Agenda item 71b)
A/C.3/78/SR.24
INDIGENOUS PEOPLES (Agenda item 68a)
A/C.3/78/SR.15
INDIGENOUS PEOPLES—CONFERENCES (Agenda item 68b)
A/C.3/78/SR.15
INFORMATION (Agenda item 53)
A/C.4/78/SR.12
INFORMATION—INTERNATIONAL SECURITY (Agenda item 94)
A/C.1/78/PV.21
INFORMATION TECHNOLOGY—DEVELOPMENT (Agenda item 15)
A/C.2/78/SR.10
INTERNATIONAL TRADE (Agenda item 16a)
A/C.2/78/SR.8
MACROECONOMIC POLICY (Agenda item 16)
A/C.2/78/SR.8
OPERATIONAL ACTIVITIES—UN SYSTEM (Agenda item 22a)
A/C.2/78/SR.18
PALESTINE QUESTION (Agenda item 35)
A/78/PV.39

Wallace, Brian Christopher Manley (Jamaica) (Caribbean Community) (continued)

POVERTY—INTERNATIONAL DECADES (Agenda item 21a)
A/C.2/78/SR.16
RACIAL DISCRIMINATION—ELIMINATION (Agenda item 69a)
A/C.3/78/SR.40
RACIAL DISCRIMINATION—PROGRAMMES OF ACTION (Agenda item 69b)
A/C.3/78/SR.40
RIGHTS OF THE CHILD (Agenda item 67)
A/C.3/78/SR.12
RURAL POVERTY (Agenda item 21b)
A/C.2/78/SR.16
SCIENCE AND TECHNOLOGY—DEVELOPMENT (Agenda item 19a)
A/C.2/78/SR.10
SMALL ISLAND DEVELOPING STATES—PROGRAMMES OF ACTION (Agenda item 18b)
A/C.2/78/SR.12
SOCIAL CONDITIONS (Agenda item 24b)
A/C.3/78/SR.1
SUSTAINABLE DEVELOPMENT (Agenda item 18)
A/C.2/78/SR.12
UN—BUDGET (2024) (Agenda item 134)
A/C.5/78/SR.13
UN. GENERAL ASSEMBLY (78TH SESS. : 2023-2024). 1ST COMMITTEE—GENERAL DEBATE (Agenda item 8)
A/C.1/78/PV.2
UN. GENERAL ASSEMBLY (78TH SESS. : 2023-2024). 2ND COMMITTEE—GENERAL DEBATE (Agenda item 8)
A/C.2/78/SR.2
WEAPONS OF MASS DESTRUCTION—TERRORISM (Agenda item 99s)
A/C.1/78/PV.14
WOMEN'S ADVANCEMENT (Agenda item 25a)
A/C.3/78/SR.8
WOMEN'S ADVANCEMENT—CONFERENCES (Agenda item 25b)
A/C.3/78/SR.8

Wallenius, Devyn Lyn (Canada)

FREEDOM OF EXPRESSION (Agenda item 71b)
A/C.3/78/SR.19
HEALTH (Agenda item 125)
A/78/PV.48
HUMAN RIGHTS—SYRIAN ARAB REPUBLIC (Agenda item 71c)
A/C.3/78/SR.54
HUMAN RIGHTS ACTIVISTS (Agenda item 71b)
A/C.3/78/SR.19
HUMAN RIGHTS INSTITUTIONS—CENTRAL AFRICA (Agenda item 71b)
A/C.3/78/SR.56
RACIAL DISCRIMINATION—ELIMINATION (Agenda item 69a)
A/C.3/78/SR.47
RIGHT TO DEVELOPMENT (Agenda item 71b)
A/C.3/78/SR.48

Wallenius, Devyn Lyn (Canada) (continued)

SOCIAL DEVELOPMENT (Agenda item 24)
A/C.3/78/SR.47

Walters, Iyeeka Latoy (Jamaica) (Caribbean Community)

UN—BUDGET (2024) (Agenda item 134)
A/C.5/78/SR.18

Wamytan, Roch (New Caledonia)

NEW CALEDONIA QUESTION (Agenda item 58)
A/C.4/78/SR.5

Wang, Hongbo (China)

LANDLOCKED DEVELOPING COUNTRIES—CONFERENCES (Agenda item 20b)
A/C.2/78/SR.7
LEAST DEVELOPED COUNTRIES—CONFERENCES (Agenda item 20a)
A/C.2/78/SR.7

Wang, Xiaojun Grace (UN Office for South-South Cooperation. Director)

ECONOMIC COOPERATION AMONG DEVELOPING COUNTRIES (Agenda item 22b)
A/C.2/78/SR.18

Wang, Yuanjie (China)

PEACEKEEPING OPERATIONS—CRIMINAL LIABILITY (Agenda item 76)
A/C.6/78/SR.8

Wang, Zhenjiang (China)

MINE CLEARANCE (Agenda item 46)
A/C.4/78/SR.10

Wang, Zixu (China)

ALBINISM (Agenda item 71b)
A/C.3/78/SR.27
CENTRAL ASIA—ZONES OF PEACE (Agenda item 64)
A/78/PV.85
ELECTION VERIFICATION—UN (Agenda item 71b)
A/C.3/78/SR.50
RIGHT TO CULTURE (Agenda item 71b)
A/C.3/78/SR.27
RIGHT TO DEVELOPMENT (Agenda item 71b)
A/C.3/78/SR.20
RIGHT TO EDUCATION (Agenda item 71b)
A/C.3/78/SR.27

Wardhana, Yochpy Ihsan (Indonesia)

UN. GENERAL ASSEMBLY (78TH SESS. : 2023-2024). 5TH COMMITTEE—WORK ORGANIZATION (Agenda item 7)
A/C.5/78/SR.26/PartII

Waris, Attiya (UN. Human Rights Council. Independent Expert on the Effects of Foreign Debt and Other Related International Financial Obligations of States on the Full Enjoyment of All Human Rights, particularly Economic, Social and Cultural Rights)

EXTERNAL DEBT—HUMAN RIGHTS (Agenda item 71b)
A/C.3/78/SR.32

Washino, Yurie (Japan)

RADIATION EFFECTS (Agenda item 47)
A/C.4/78/SR.11
SPECIAL POLITICAL MISSIONS (Agenda item 52)
A/C.4/78/SR.21

Wateou, Naïa ((personal capacity))

NEW CALEDONIA QUESTION (Agenda item 58)
A/C.4/78/SR.5

Wavrin, Hugo (France)

CRIMES AGAINST HUMANITY (Agenda item 80)
A/C.6/78/SR.11; A/C.6/78/SR.42; A/C.6/78/SR.43
UN. GENERAL ASSEMBLY—WORK PROGRAMME (Agenda item 120)
A/78/PV.33
UN RESOLUTIONS—IMPLEMENTATION (Agenda item 119)
A/78/PV.33

Waweru, James Ndiragu (Kenya)

INTERNATIONAL CRIMINAL COURT—REPORTS (Agenda item 74)
A/78/PV.21
UN. INTERNATIONAL LAW COMMISSION—REPORTS (Agenda item 79)
A/C.6/78/SR.33

Weah, George Manneh (Liberia. President)

UN. GENERAL ASSEMBLY (78TH SESS. : 2023-2024)—GENERAL DEBATE (Agenda item 8)
A/78/PV.7
UN. GENERAL ASSEMBLY (78TH SESS. : 2023-2024)—SPECIAL STATEMENTS
A/78/PV.7

Webson, Walton Alfonso (Antigua and Barbuda)

SMALL ISLAND DEVELOPING STATES—PROGRAMMES OF ACTION (Agenda item 18b)
A/78/PV.100; A/78/PV.103

Weerasekara, Weerasekarage Chathura Ramyajith (Sri Lanka)

HEALTH (Agenda item 125)
A/78/PV.48

Weinstein, Andrew (United States)

TERRITORIES OCCUPIED BY ISRAEL—NATURAL RESOURCES (Agenda item 59)
A/C.2/78/SR.19
TRANSNATIONAL CORPORATIONS—HUMAN RIGHTS (Agenda item 71b)
A/C.3/78/SR.21

Weld-Blundell, Stacy John (United Kingdom)

PEACEBUILDING (Agenda item 61)
A/78/PV.101
UN. PEACEBUILDING COMMISSION—REPORTS (Agenda item 27)
A/78/PV.101
UN. PEACEBUILDING FUND—REPORTS (Agenda item 111)
A/78/PV.101

Welles, Kenneth (Micronesia (Federated States of))

BIOLOGICAL DIVERSITY—TREATIES (Agenda item 18f)
A/C.2/78/SR.15
DISASTER PREVENTION (Agenda item 18c)
A/C.2/78/SR.15
ELECTION VERIFICATION—UN (Agenda item 71b)
A/C.3/78/SR.50
HUMAN RIGHTS—TERRITORIES OCCUPIED BY ISRAEL (Agenda item 71c)
A/C.3/78/SR.35
INDIGENOUS PEOPLES (Agenda item 68a)
A/C.3/78/SR.15
INDIGENOUS PEOPLES—CONFERENCES (Agenda item 68b)
A/C.3/78/SR.15
SMALL ISLAND DEVELOPING STATES—PROGRAMMES OF ACTION (Agenda item 18b)
A/C.2/78/SR.15

Wells, Majorie May (Vanuatu) (Pacific Small Island Developing States)

MARINE ECOSYSTEMS—BIOLOGICAL DIVERSITY (Agenda item 75c)
A/78/PV.103

Wells, Majorie May (Vanuatu) (UN. Group of Asia-Pacific States)

RAISI, SEYYED EBRAHIM (IRAN (ISLAMIC REPUBLID OF). PRESIDENT)—TRIBUTES
A/78/PV.83

Wenaweser, Christian (Liechtenstein)

ARMED CONFLICTS PREVENTION (Agenda item 31a)
A/78/PV.72
HUMAN RIGHTS (Agenda item 71)
A/C.3/78/SR.16

Wenaweser, Christian (Liechtenstein) (continued)

INTERNATIONAL CRIMINAL COURT—REPORTS (Agenda item 74)
A/78/PV.22
UN. SECURITY COUNCIL—MEMBERSHIP (Agenda item 121)
A/78/PV.34
UN. SECURITY COUNCIL—REPORTS (Agenda item 26)
A/78/PV.93
VETO (Agenda item 63)
A/78/PV.3; A/78/PV.59; A/78/PV.70

Wennholz, Philipp Alexander (Germany)

CLIMATE CHANGE (Agenda item 71b)
A/C.3/78/SR.29
RESPONSIBILITY TO PROTECT (Agenda item 129)
A/78/PV.97
RIGHT TO DRINKING WATER (Agenda item 71b)
A/C.3/78/SR.28

Wheatley, Natalio (British Virgin Islands)

BRITISH VIRGIN ISLANDS QUESTION (Agenda item 58)
A/C.4/78/SR.3

Whipps, Surangel S. (Palau. President)

UN. GENERAL ASSEMBLY (78TH SESS. : 2023-2024)—GENERAL DEBATE (Agenda item 8)
A/78/PV.5
UN. GENERAL ASSEMBLY (78TH SESS. : 2023-2024)—SPECIAL STATEMENTS
A/78/PV.5

White, Megan Marie (United Kingdom)

ELECTION VERIFICATION—UN (Agenda item 71b)
A/C.3/78/SR.50
FAMILY (Agenda item 24b)
A/C.3/78/SR.49
HUMAN RIGHTS—AFGHANISTAN (Agenda item 71c)
A/C.3/78/SR.34
HUMAN RIGHTS—SYRIAN ARAB REPUBLIC (Agenda item 71c)
A/C.3/78/SR.34
SEXUAL ORIENTATION (Agenda item 71b)
A/C.3/78/SR.39
WOMEN'S ADVANCEMENT (Agenda item 25a)
A/C.3/78/SR.8
WOMEN'S ADVANCEMENT—CONFERENCES (Agenda item 25b)
A/C.3/78/SR.8

White, Noel (Ireland)

UN. GENERAL ASSEMBLY (78TH SESS. : 2023-2024). 1ST COMMITTEE—GENERAL DEBATE (Agenda item 8)
A/C.1/78/PV.6

Wickremesinghe, Ranil (Sri Lanka. President)
UN. GENERAL ASSEMBLY (78TH SESS. : 2023-2024)—GENERAL DEBATE (Agenda item 8)
A/78/PV.8
UN. GENERAL ASSEMBLY (78TH SESS. : 2023-2024)—SPECIAL STATEMENTS
A/78/PV.8

Willekens, Vincent (Belgium)
RACIAL DISCRIMINATION—ELIMINATION (Agenda item 69a)
A/C.3/78/SR.41
RACIAL DISCRIMINATION—PROGRAMMES OF ACTION (Agenda item 69b)
A/C.3/78/SR.41

William, Sanlan (Vanuatu)
UN. GENERAL ASSEMBLY (78TH SESS. : 2023-2024). 1ST COMMITTEE—GENERAL DEBATE (Agenda item 8)
A/C.1/78/PV.8

William, Sanlan (Vanuatu) (Pacific Small Island Developing States)
MARINE ECOSYSTEMS—BIOLOGICAL DIVERSITY (Agenda item 75c)
A/78/PV.73

Williams, Christopher (UN-HABITAT)
SOCIAL DEVELOPMENT (Agenda item 24)
A/C.3/78/SR.1

Williams, Edna Stephanie (Ghana)
HUMAN RIGHTS—INTERNATIONAL INSTRUMENTS (Agenda item 71a)
A/C.3/78/SR.26
NATIONAL INSTITUTIONS—HUMAN RIGHTS (Agenda item 71b)
A/C.3/78/SR.26

Williams, Ian (United Kingdom)
UN—FINANCIAL SITUATION (Agenda item 136)
A/C.5/78/SR.38

Williams, Mutryce (Saint Kitts and Nevis) (Caribbean Community)
MARINE ECOSYSTEMS—BIOLOGICAL DIVERSITY (Agenda item 75c)
A/78/PV.103
SMALL ISLAND DEVELOPING STATES—PROGRAMMES OF ACTION (Agenda item 18b)
A/78/PV.103

Wilmoth, John (UN. Department of Economic and Social Affairs. Division for Inclusive Social Development. Officer-in-Charge)
AGEING PERSONS (Agenda item 24b)
A/C.3/78/SR.1

Wilmoth, John (UN. Department of Economic and Social Affairs. Division for Inclusive Social Development. Officer-in-Charge) (continued)
FAMILY (Agenda item 24b)
A/C.3/78/SR.1
PERSONS WITH DISABILITIES (Agenda item 24b)
A/C.3/78/SR.1
POVERTY—INTERNATIONAL DECADES (Agenda item 21a)
A/C.2/78/SR.16
SOCIAL CONDITIONS (Agenda item 24b)
A/C.3/78/SR.1
SOCIAL DEVELOPMENT—CONFERENCES (Agenda item 24a)
A/C.3/78/SR.1
YOUTH (Agenda item 24b)
A/C.3/78/SR.1

Wittke, Albrecht von (Germany) (UN. Open-ended Working Group on Conventional Ammunition. Chair)
CONVENTIONAL WEAPONS (Agenda item 99u)
A/C.1/78/PV.18

Woergoetter, Caroline (Austria)
BIOLOGICAL WEAPONS—TREATIES (Agenda item 106)
A/C.1/78/PV.15
CHEMICAL WEAPONS—TREATIES (Agenda item 99l)
A/C.1/78/PV.15

Won Pat-Borja, Melvin (Guam)
GUAM QUESTION (Agenda item 58)
A/C.4/78/SR.3

Wong, Penny (Australia)
UN. GENERAL ASSEMBLY (78TH SESS. : 2023-2024)—GENERAL DEBATE (Agenda item 8)
A/78/PV.11

Wood, Grace Louise (United Kingdom)
TERRITORIES OCCUPIED BY ISRAEL—NATURAL RESOURCES (Agenda item 59)
A/C.2/78/SR.19

Wood, Robert A. (United States)
TERRITORIES OCCUPIED BY ISRAEL—HUMAN RIGHTS (Agenda item 50)
A/C.4/78/SR.25
VETO (Agenda item 63)
A/78/PV.3; A/78/PV.51; A/78/PV.59; A/78/PV.66; A/78/PV.69; A/78/PV.70; A/78/PV.74; A/78/PV.78

Wood, Vanessa (Australia)
UN. GENERAL ASSEMBLY (78TH SESS. : 2023-2024). 1ST COMMITTEE—GENERAL DEBATE (Agenda item 8)
A/C.1/78/PV.3; A/C.1/78/PV.5

Woodifield, Mungo (United Kingdom)
CRIMES AGAINST HUMANITY (Agenda item 80)
A/C.6/78/SR.40; A/C.6/78/SR.42; A/C.6/78/SR.43; A/C.6/78/SR.44
DECOLONIZATION (Agenda item 58)
A/C.4/78/SR.8
FALKLAND ISLANDS (MALVINAS) QUESTION (Agenda item 42)
A/C.4/78/SR.8
GIBRALTAR QUESTION (Agenda item 58)
A/C.4/78/SR.8
INFORMATION (Agenda item 53)
A/C.4/78/SR.14

Woodroffe, Tom (United Kingdom)
HEALTH (Agenda item 125)
A/78/PV.16
MILLENNIUM SUMMIT—CONFERENCES (Agenda item 117)
A/78/PV.15
UN CONFERENCES (Agenda item 13)
A/78/PV.15

Woodward, Barbara (United Kingdom)
LAW OF THE SEA (Agenda item 75a)
A/78/PV.44
MARINE ECOSYSTEMS—BIOLOGICAL DIVERSITY (Agenda item 75c)
A/78/PV.44
STRADDLING FISH STOCKS (Agenda item 75b)
A/78/PV.44
VETO (Agenda item 63)
A/78/PV.59; A/78/PV.67; A/78/PV.68; A/78/PV.78

Worku, Hirut Habtamu (Ethiopia)
UN HIGH COMMISSIONER FOR REFUGEES—REPORTS (Agenda item 60)
A/C.3/78/SR.45

Worthe, Jeffrey (United States)
CLIMATE CHANGE (Agenda item 71b)
A/C.3/78/SR.29
RIGHT TO DRINKING WATER (Agenda item 71b)
A/C.3/78/SR.28

Woźniak, Agata Magdalena (European Union)
POVERTY—INTERNATIONAL DECADES (Agenda item 21a)
A/C.2/78/SR.25

Wu, Jianjian (China)
NUCLEAR DISARMAMENT (Agenda item 99b)
A/C.1/78/PV.13

Wynhoven, Ursula (ITU)
INFORMATION TECHNOLOGY—DEVELOPMENT (Agenda item 15)
A/C.2/78/SR.11

Xaiyavong, Thanouphet (Lao People's Democratic Republic)
SCIENCE AND TECHNOLOGY—DEVELOPMENT (Agenda item 19a)
A/C.2/78/SR.11
SUSTAINABLE DEVELOPMENT (Agenda item 18)
A/C.2/78/SR.15

Xanthaki, Alexandra (UN. Human Rights Council. Special Rapporteur in the Field of Cultural Rights)
RIGHT TO CULTURE (Agenda item 71b)
A/C.3/78/SR.27

Xing, Jisheng (China)
RACIAL DISCRIMINATION—ELIMINATION (Agenda item 69a)
A/C.3/78/SR.47

Yabouri, Anselme (UN Regional Centre for Peace and Disarmament in Africa. Director)
PEACE—REGIONAL CENTRE—AFRICA (Agenda item 100b)
A/C.1/78/PV.23

Yahiaoui, Dahmane (Algeria)
HUMAN RIGHTS—TERRITORIES OCCUPIED BY ISRAEL (Agenda item 71c)
A/C.3/78/SR.35

Yahya, Alamine (Hispafrica Aprican (Organization))
WESTERN SAHARA QUESTION (Agenda item 58)
A/C.4/78/SR.6

Yajah, Christian Fayia (Sierra Leone)
CRIME PREVENTION (Agenda item 107)
A/C.3/78/SR.6
CYBERCRIME (Agenda item 108)
A/C.3/78/SR.6
UN—BUDGET (2024) (Agenda item 134)
A/C.5/78/SR.33

Yamanaka, Osamu (Japan)
HUMAN RIGHTS (Agenda item 71)
A/C.3/78/SR.16
HUMAN RIGHTS—DEMOCRATIC PEOPLE'S REPUBLIC OF KOREA (Agenda item 71c)
A/C.3/78/SR.33
HUMAN RIGHTS—MYANMAR (Agenda item 71c)
A/C.3/78/SR.33
MILLENNIUM SUMMIT—CONFERENCES (Agenda item 117)
A/78/PV.15
UN. GENERAL ASSEMBLY (78TH SESS. : 2023-2024)—OFFICERS (Agenda item 5)
A/C.5/78/SR.1

Yamanaka, Osamu (Japan) (continued)

UN. GENERAL ASSEMBLY (78TH SESS. : 2023-2024). 2ND COMMITTEE—GENERAL DEBATE (Agenda item 8)
A/C.2/78/SR.4
UN. GENERAL ASSEMBLY (78TH SESS. : 2023-2024). 5TH COMMITTEE—WORK ORGANIZATION (Agenda item 7)
A/C.5/78/SR.27; A/C.5/78/SR.35
UN CONFERENCES (Agenda item 13)
A/78/PV.15

Yamashita, Yuhei (Japan)

CRIMES AGAINST HUMANITY (Agenda item 80)
A/C.6/78/SR.39; A/C.6/78/SR.40; A/C.6/78/SR.42; A/C.6/78/SR.43

Yamazaki, Kazuyuki (Japan)

VETO (Agenda item 63)
A/78/PV.68; A/78/PV.75; A/78/PV.78

Yamazaki, Kazuyuki (Japan) (Friends of the Comprehensive Nuclear Test-Ban Treaty)

DISARMAMENT—GENERAL AND COMPLETE (Agenda item 99)
A/78/PV.105

Yang, Fan (China)

DEMOCRACY (Agenda item 71b)
A/C.3/78/SR.28
DISPLACED PERSONS (Agenda item 71b)
A/C.3/78/SR.32
EXTERNAL DEBT—HUMAN RIGHTS (Agenda item 71b)
A/C.3/78/SR.32
HUMAN RIGHTS—SOMALIA (Agenda item 71c)
A/C.3/78/SR.35
SOLIDARITY (Agenda item 71b)
A/C.3/78/SR.32

Yang, Philémon (Cameroon)

UN. GENERAL ASSEMBLY (78TH SESS. : 2023-2024). PRESIDENT (Agenda item 4)
A/78/PV.87

Yang, Philémon (Cameroon) (UN. General Assembly. President)

UN. GENERAL ASSEMBLY—PRESIDENT-ELECT—OATH OF OFFICE
A/78/PV.109

Yang, Xiaokun (China)

HUMAN RIGHTS (Agenda item 71)
A/C.3/78/SR.27
HUMAN RIGHTS—RUSSIAN FEDERATION (Agenda item 71c)
A/C.3/78/SR.37
HUMAN RIGHTS—TERRITORIES OCCUPIED BY ISRAEL (Agenda item 71c)
A/C.3/78/SR.35

Yang, Xiaokun (China) (continued)

RIGHT TO DRINKING WATER (Agenda item 71b)
A/C.3/78/SR.28
SANCTIONS—INTERNATIONAL RELATIONS (Agenda item 71b)
A/C.3/78/SR.28

Yankssar, Ahlam (Saudi Arabia)

CRIMES AGAINST HUMANITY (Agenda item 80)
A/C.6/78/SR.38
DISASTER VICTIMS (Agenda item 86)
A/C.6/78/SR.6
UN. INTERNATIONAL LAW COMMISSION—REPORTS (Agenda item 79)
A/C.6/78/SR.37

Yarahuán Dodero, Santiago (Mexico)

BIOLOGICAL WEAPONS—TREATIES (Agenda item 106)
A/C.1/78/PV.14
CHEMICAL WEAPONS—TREATIES (Agenda item 99l)
A/C.1/78/PV.14
RIGHTS OF THE CHILD (Agenda item 67)
A/C.3/78/SR.12

Yaseen, Safaa (Iraq)

DISPLACED PERSONS (Agenda item 71b)
A/C.3/78/SR.32
MINORITIES (Agenda item 71b)
A/C.3/78/SR.39
RACIAL DISCRIMINATION—ELIMINATION (Agenda item 69a)
A/C.3/78/SR.41
RACIAL DISCRIMINATION—PROGRAMMES OF ACTION (Agenda item 69b)
A/C.3/78/SR.41
SELF-DETERMINATION OF PEOPLES (Agenda item 70)
A/C.3/78/SR.41

Yildiz, Ahmet (Türkiye)

VETO (Agenda item 63)
A/78/PV.74

Yoon, Seong-mee (Republic of Korea)

ARMS RACE—OUTER SPACE (Agenda item 97a)
A/C.1/78/PV.17
ARMS TRANSFERS—TREATIES (Agenda item 99x)
A/C.1/78/PV.18
BIOLOGICAL WEAPONS—TREATIES (Agenda item 106)
A/C.1/78/PV.15
CHEMICAL WEAPONS—TREATIES (Agenda item 99l)
A/C.1/78/PV.15
CONVENTIONAL WEAPONS (Agenda item 99u)
A/C.1/78/PV.18

Yoon, Seong-mee (Republic of Korea) (continued)

CONVENTIONAL WEAPONS—TREATIES (Agenda item 103)
A/C.1/78/PV.18
DISARMAMENT—GENERAL AND COMPLETE (Agenda item 99)
A/C.1/78/PV.18; A/C.1/78/PV.19
DISARMAMENT AGREEMENTS—OUTER SPACE (Agenda item 97c)
A/C.1/78/PV.17
OUTER SPACE—CONFIDENCE-BUILDING MEASURES (Agenda item 99v)
A/C.1/78/PV.17
OUTER SPACE—PRINCIPLES (Agenda item 97d)
A/C.1/78/PV.17
SMALL ARMS—ILLICIT TRAFFIC (Agenda item 99p)
A/C.1/78/PV.18
SMALL ARMS—ILLICIT TRAFFIC—ASSISTANCE (Agenda item 99n)
A/C.1/78/PV.18
UN. CONFERENCE ON DISARMAMENT—REPORTS (Agenda item 101a)
A/C.1/78/PV.23
UN. DISARMAMENT COMMISSION—REPORTS (Agenda item 101b)
A/C.1/78/PV.23

Yoon, Suk Yeol (Republic of Korea. President)

UN. GENERAL ASSEMBLY (78TH SESS. : 2023-2024)—GENERAL DEBATE (Agenda item 8)
A/78/PV.6
UN. GENERAL ASSEMBLY (78TH SESS. : 2023-2024)—SPECIAL STATEMENTS
A/78/PV.6

Yoshida, Aya (Japan)

INFORMATION (Agenda item 53)
A/C.4/78/SR.13
UN. GENERAL ASSEMBLY—WORK PROGRAMME (Agenda item 120)
A/78/PV.32
UN RESOLUTIONS—IMPLEMENTATION (Agenda item 119)
A/78/PV.32

Young, Archie (United Kingdom)

AFRICA—DEVELOPMENT (Agenda item 65b)
A/78/PV.57
AFRICA—SUSTAINABLE DEVELOPMENT—PARTNERSHIP (Agenda item 65a)
A/78/PV.57
ECONOMIC SANCTIONS—INTERNATIONAL RELATIONS (Agenda item 28)
A/78/PV.90
UN. GENERAL ASSEMBLY (78TH SESS. : 2023-2024). 5TH COMMITTEE—WORK ORGANIZATION (Agenda item 7)
A/C.5/78/SR.27; A/C.5/78/SR.34; A/C.5/78/SR.40
VETO (Agenda item 63)
A/78/PV.51; A/78/PV.71

Yousfi, Salim (Morocco)

UN. GENERAL ASSEMBLY (78TH SESS. : 2023-2024). 1ST COMMITTEE—GENERAL DEBATE (Agenda item 8)
A/C.1/78/PV.3
VETO (Agenda item 63)
A/78/PV.79

Youssouf, Mahamoud Ali (Djibouti)

UN. GENERAL ASSEMBLY (78TH SESS. : 2023-2024)—GENERAL DEBATE (Agenda item 8)
A/78/PV.13

Yuan Fang, Yeo (Singapore)

CLIMATE (Agenda item 18d)
A/C.2/78/SR.13
SUSTAINABLE ENERGY (Agenda item 18h)
A/C.2/78/SR.13

Yusof, Dato Erywan Pehin (Brunei Darussalam)

UN. GENERAL ASSEMBLY (78TH SESS. : 2023-2024)—GENERAL DEBATE (Agenda item 8)
A/78/PV.13

Zabolotskaya, Maria V. (Russian Federation)

HEALTH (Agenda item 125)
A/78/PV.48
HUMAN RIGHTS—DEMOCRATIC PEOPLE'S REPUBLIC OF KOREA (Agenda item 71c)
A/78/PV.50
HUMAN RIGHTS—IRAN (ISLAMIC REPUBLIC OF) (Agenda item 71c)
A/78/PV.50
HUMAN RIGHTS—MYANMAR (Agenda item 71c)
A/78/PV.50
HUMAN RIGHTS—REPORTS (Agenda item 71c)
A/78/PV.50
HUMAN RIGHTS—SYRIAN ARAB REPUBLIC (Agenda item 71c)
A/78/PV.50
HUMAN RIGHTS—UKRAINE (Agenda item 71c)
A/78/PV.50; A/C.3/78/SR.53
INTERNATIONAL CRIMINAL COURT—REPORTS (Agenda item 74)
A/78/PV.21; A/78/PV.25
INTERNATIONAL RESIDUAL MECHANISM FOR CRIMINAL TRIBUNALS (Agenda item 126)
A/78/PV.19
ORGANIZATION FOR DEMOCRACY AND ECONOMIC DEVELOPMENT - GUAM (Agenda item 32)
A/78/PV.85
PEACE (Agenda item 14)
A/78/PV.48; A/78/PV.62; A/78/PV.76
RACIAL DISCRIMINATION—ELIMINATION (Agenda item 69a)
A/78/PV.50
RIGHT TO DEVELOPMENT (Agenda item 71b)
A/C.3/78/SR.20
SPORTS—OLYMPIC GAMES (Agenda item 11)
A/78/PV.38

Zabolotskaya, Maria V. (Russian Federation) (continued)

UN. GENERAL ASSEMBLY (78TH SESS. : 2023-2024)—AGENDA (Agenda item 7)
A/78/PV.2; A/BUR/78/SR.1
UN. INTERNATIONAL COURT OF JUSTICE—REPORTS (Agenda item 73)
A/78/PV.28

Zacarias, Ana Paula (Portugal)

AGEING PERSONS (Agenda item 24b)
A/C.3/78/SR.2
CRIMES AGAINST HUMANITY (Agenda item 80)
A/C.6/78/SR.10
HUMAN RIGHTS (Agenda item 71)
A/C.3/78/SR.16
LEPROSY (Agenda item 71b)
A/C.3/78/SR.17
PEACEKEEPING OPERATIONS (Agenda item 51)
A/C.4/78/SR.19
SOCIAL CONDITIONS (Agenda item 24b)
A/78/PV.57; A/C.3/78/SR.2
SOCIAL DEVELOPMENT (Agenda item 24)
A/C.3/78/SR.2
UN. GENERAL ASSEMBLY (78TH SESS. : 2023-2024). 1ST COMMITTEE—GENERAL DEBATE (Agenda item 8)
A/C.1/78/PV.4
UN. GENERAL ASSEMBLY (78TH SESS. : 2023-2024). 2ND COMMITTEE—GENERAL DEBATE (Agenda item 8)
A/C.2/78/SR.4
VETO (Agenda item 63)
A/78/PV.3; A/78/PV.61; A/78/PV.67; A/78/PV.74; A/78/PV.78
YOUTH (Agenda item 24b)
A/C.3/78/SR.2

Zade Iseni, Cecilia (Denmark)

YOUTH (Agenda item 24b)
A/C.3/78/SR.3

Zadra, Estelle (UNESCO)

RIGHT TO CULTURE (Agenda item 71b)
A/C.3/78/SR.27

Zahneisen, Thomas (Germany)

HUMAN RIGHTS—TERRITORIES OCCUPIED BY ISRAEL (Agenda item 71c)
A/C.3/78/SR.35

Zahneisen, Thomas (Germany) (Coalition for Addressing Sea-level Rise and its Existential Threat)

MILLENNIUM SUMMIT—CONFERENCES (Agenda item 117)
A/78/PV.102
UN CONFERENCES (Agenda item 13)
A/78/PV.102

Zahneisen, Thomas (Germany) (UN. Group of Western European and Other States)

SLAVERY—MEMORIALS (Agenda item 118)
A/78/PV.64

Zakaria, Izzat Hayati (Brunei Darussalam) (ASEAN)

SOUTH-EAST ASIA—NUCLEAR-WEAPON-FREE ZONES (Agenda item 99y)
A/C.1/78/PV.22

Zalabata Torres, Leonor (Colombia)

CRIME PREVENTION (Agenda item 107)
A/C.3/78/SR.5
CUBA—UNITED STATES (Agenda item 38)
A/78/PV.24
CYBERCRIME (Agenda item 108)
A/C.3/78/SR.5
DISASTER VICTIMS (Agenda item 86)
A/C.6/78/SR.5
ECONOMIC SANCTIONS—INTERNATIONAL RELATIONS (Agenda item 28)
A/78/PV.90
FALKLAND ISLANDS (MALVINAS) QUESTION (Agenda item 42)
A/C.4/78/SR.7
IAEA—REPORTS (Agenda item 89)
A/78/PV.29
INDIGENOUS PEOPLES (Agenda item 68a)
A/C.3/78/SR.15; A/C.3/78/SR.48
INDIGENOUS PEOPLES—CONFERENCES (Agenda item 68b)
A/C.3/78/SR.15
MILLENNIUM SUMMIT—CONFERENCES (Agenda item 117)
A/78/PV.15
PALESTINE QUESTION (Agenda item 35)
A/78/PV.40
PEACEBUILDING (Agenda item 61)
A/78/PV.100
RACIAL DISCRIMINATION—ELIMINATION (Agenda item 69a)
A/78/PV.103; A/C.3/78/SR.41
RACIAL DISCRIMINATION—PROGRAMMES OF ACTION (Agenda item 69b)
A/C.3/78/SR.41
RIGHTS OF THE CHILD (Agenda item 67)
A/C.3/78/SR.12
SMALL ISLAND DEVELOPING STATES—PROGRAMMES OF ACTION (Agenda item 18b)
A/78/PV.103
SOCIAL DEVELOPMENT (Agenda item 24)
A/C.3/78/SR.2
SPECIAL POLITICAL MISSIONS (Agenda item 52)
A/C.4/78/SR.21
UN—BUDGET (2024) (Agenda item 134)
A/C.5/78/SR.4; A/C.5/78/SR.18

Zalabata Torres, Leonor (Colombia) (continued)

UN. GENERAL ASSEMBLY (78TH SESS. : 2023-2024). 1ST COMMITTEE—GENERAL DEBATE (Agenda item 8)
A/C.1/78/PV.7
UN. GENERAL ASSEMBLY (78TH SESS. : 2023-2024). 2ND COMMITTEE—GENERAL DEBATE (Agenda item 8)
A/C.2/78/SR.3
UN. PEACEBUILDING COMMISSION—REPORTS (Agenda item 27)
A/78/PV.100
UN. PEACEBUILDING FUND—REPORTS (Agenda item 111)
A/78/PV.100
UN. SECURITY COUNCIL—MEMBERSHIP (Agenda item 121)
A/78/PV.34
UN. SECURITY COUNCIL—REPORTS (Agenda item 26)
A/78/PV.93
UN CONFERENCES (Agenda item 13)
A/78/PV.15
UNRWA—ACTIVITIES (Agenda item 49)
A/C.4/78/SR.23
VETO (Agenda item 63)
A/78/PV.61; A/78/PV.67; A/78/PV.68; A/78/PV.71; A/78/PV.79
WOMEN'S ADVANCEMENT (Agenda item 25a)
A/C.3/78/SR.8
WOMEN'S ADVANCEMENT—CONFERENCES (Agenda item 25b)
A/C.3/78/SR.8

Zalaquett, Ignacia (Chile)

PERSONS WITH DISABILITIES—HUMAN RIGHTS (Agenda item 71a)
A/C.3/78/SR.38

Zambrana Flores, Carlos Iván (Bolivia (Plurinational State of))

FOOD SECURITY (Agenda item 23a)
A/C.2/78/SR.16
PALESTINIANS—ASSISTANCE (Agenda item 72b)
A/78/PV.47
POVERTY—INTERNATIONAL DECADES (Agenda item 21a)
A/C.2/78/SR.16
RURAL POVERTY (Agenda item 21b)
A/C.2/78/SR.16

Zamora Zumbado, Leticia María (Costa Rica)

CLIMATE (Agenda item 18d)
A/C.2/78/SR.25
DEVELOPMENT COOPERATION—MIDDLE-INCOME COUNTRIES (Agenda item 19c)
A/C.2/78/SR.11
DEVELOPMENT FINANCE (Agenda item 16b)
A/C.2/78/SR.9
EXTERNAL DEBT (Agenda item 16c)
A/C.2/78/SR.9

Zamora Zumbado, Leticia María (Costa Rica) (continued)

INFORMATION TECHNOLOGY—DEVELOPMENT (Agenda item 15)
A/C.2/78/SR.11
SCIENCE AND TECHNOLOGY—DEVELOPMENT (Agenda item 19a)
A/C.2/78/SR.11
UN. GENERAL ASSEMBLY (78TH SESS. : 2023-2024). 2ND COMMITTEE—GENERAL DEBATE (Agenda item 8)
A/C.2/78/SR.2; A/C.2/78/SR.5

Zanini, Stefano (Italy)

UN. INTERNATIONAL COURT OF JUSTICE—REPORTS (Agenda item 73)
A/78/PV.20
UN. INTERNATIONAL LAW COMMISSION—REPORTS (Agenda item 79)
A/C.6/78/SR.23

Zavala Porras, Daniel Andrés (Costa Rica)

CLIMATE CHANGE (Agenda item 71b)
A/C.3/78/SR.29
CRIME PREVENTION (Agenda item 107)
A/C.3/78/SR.6
CYBERCRIME (Agenda item 108)
A/C.3/78/SR.6
ENVIRONMENT (Agenda item 71b)
A/C.3/78/SR.29
RIGHTS OF THE CHILD (Agenda item 67)
A/C.3/78/SR.14
UN. HUMAN RIGHTS COMMITTEE—REPORTS (Agenda item 71a)
A/C.3/78/SR.17
UN. HUMAN RIGHTS COUNCIL—REPORTS (Agenda item 66)
A/C.3/78/SR.46
WOMEN'S ADVANCEMENT (Agenda item 25a)
A/C.3/78/SR.7; A/C.3/78/SR.10
WOMEN'S ADVANCEMENT—CONFERENCES (Agenda item 25b)
A/C.3/78/SR.7; A/C.3/78/SR.10
YOUTH (Agenda item 24b)
A/C.3/78/SR.55

Zelenskyy, Volodymyr (Ukraine. President)

UN. GENERAL ASSEMBLY (78TH SESS. : 2023-2024)—GENERAL DEBATE (Agenda item 8)
A/78/PV.4
UN. GENERAL ASSEMBLY (78TH SESS. : 2023-2024)—SPECIAL STATEMENTS
A/78/PV.4

Zerbe, Yannick (Switzerland)

RULE OF LAW (Agenda item 83)
A/C.6/78/SR.16

Zhang, Jun (China)

HUMAN RIGHTS—REPORTS (Agenda item 71c)
A/C.3/78/SR.24; A/C.3/78/SR.27

Zhang, Jun (China) (continued)

HUMAN RIGHTS—TERRITORIES OCCUPIED BY ISRAEL (Agenda item 71c)
A/C.3/78/SR.24
HUMAN RIGHTS ADVANCEMENT (Agenda item 71b)
A/C.3/78/SR.24
SANCTIONS—INTERNATIONAL RELATIONS (Agenda item 71b)
A/C.3/78/SR.24
UN. SECURITY COUNCIL—MEMBERSHIP (Agenda item 121)
A/78/PV.35

Zhang, Junjie (China)

DISARMAMENT—GENERAL AND COMPLETE (Agenda item 99)
A/C.1/78/PV.28
DISARMAMENT AGREEMENTS—OUTER SPACE (Agenda item 97c)
A/C.1/78/PV.27
OUTER SPACE—PRINCIPLES (Agenda item 97d)
A/C.1/78/PV.27

Zhang, Qian (China)

CHEMICAL WEAPONS—TREATIES (Agenda item 99l)
A/C.1/78/PV.26

Zhang, Qiuruo (China)

DISAPPEARANCE OF PERSONS (Agenda item 71b)
A/C.3/78/SR.22
JUDICIAL INDEPENDENCE (Agenda item 71b)
A/C.3/78/SR.31
MIGRANTS—PROTECTION (Agenda item 71b)
A/C.3/78/SR.23
SUMMARY EXECUTIONS (Agenda item 71b)
A/C.3/78/SR.31
TERRORISM—HUMAN RIGHTS (Agenda item 71b)
A/C.3/78/SR.31

Zhang, Sisi (China)

HEALTH (Agenda item 125)
A/78/PV.41
HUMAN RIGHTS—DEMOCRATIC PEOPLE'S REPUBLIC OF KOREA (Agenda item 71c)
A/78/PV.50; A/C.3/78/SR.53
HUMAN RIGHTS—IRAN (ISLAMIC REPUBLIC OF) (Agenda item 71c)
A/78/PV.50; A/C.3/78/SR.53
HUMAN RIGHTS—MYANMAR (Agenda item 71c)
A/78/PV.50; A/C.3/78/SR.53
HUMAN RIGHTS—REPORTS (Agenda item 71c)
A/78/PV.50; A/C.3/78/SR.18
HUMAN RIGHTS—SYRIAN ARAB REPUBLIC (Agenda item 71c)
A/78/PV.50; A/C.3/78/SR.54
HUMAN RIGHTS—UKRAINE (Agenda item 71c)
A/78/PV.50; A/C.3/78/SR.53

Zhang, Sisi (China) (continued)

HUMAN RIGHTS ACTIVISTS (Agenda item 71b)
A/C.3/78/SR.56
HUMAN RIGHTS ADVANCEMENT (Agenda item 71b)
A/C.3/78/SR.18
INDIGENOUS PEOPLES (Agenda item 68a)
A/C.3/78/SR.15
INDIGENOUS PEOPLES—CONFERENCES (Agenda item 68b)
A/C.3/78/SR.15
RACIAL DISCRIMINATION—ELIMINATION (Agenda item 69a)
A/78/PV.50; A/C.3/78/SR.41; A/C.3/78/SR.42
RACIAL DISCRIMINATION—PROGRAMMES OF ACTION (Agenda item 69b)
A/C.3/78/SR.41; A/C.3/78/SR.42
UN—PROGRAMME PLANNING (Agenda item 135)
A/78/PV.50(Resumption1)
UN. HUMAN RIGHTS COUNCIL—REPORTS (Agenda item 66)
A/C.3/78/SR.46
UN HIGH COMMISSIONER FOR REFUGEES—REPORTS (Agenda item 60)
A/C.3/78/SR.44

Zhang, Tianhao (China)

FREEDOM OF EXPRESSION (Agenda item 71b)
A/C.3/78/SR.19
HEALTH (Agenda item 125)
A/78/PV.16
RIGHT OF ASSEMBLY (Agenda item 71b)
A/C.3/78/SR.19
RIGHT TO PRIVACY (Agenda item 71b)
A/C.3/78/SR.21
SLAVERY (Agenda item 71a)
A/C.3/78/SR.21
TRANSNATIONAL CORPORATIONS—HUMAN RIGHTS (Agenda item 71b)
A/C.3/78/SR.21

Zhangarayev, Nurmukhamed (Kazakhstan)

UN. DISARMAMENT COMMISSION—REPORTS (Agenda item 101b)
A/C.1/78/PV.29

Zhao, Haibo (China)

INFORMATION TECHNOLOGY—DEVELOPMENT (Agenda item 15)
A/C.2/78/SR.10
SCIENCE AND TECHNOLOGY—DEVELOPMENT (Agenda item 19a)
A/C.2/78/SR.10

Zhao, Yanrui (China)

DISASTER VICTIMS (Agenda item 86)
A/C.6/78/SR.6
TREATIES (Agenda item 87)
A/C.6/78/SR.20

Zhao, Yanrui (China) (continued)

UN COMMISSION ON INTERNATIONAL TRADE LAW—REPORTS (Agenda item 77)
A/C.6/78/SR.14

Zhaparov, Sadyr (Kyrgyzstan. President)

UN. GENERAL ASSEMBLY (78TH SESS. : 2023-2024)—GENERAL DEBATE (Agenda item 8)
A/78/PV.5
UN. GENERAL ASSEMBLY (78TH SESS. : 2023-2024)—SPECIAL STATEMENTS
A/78/PV.5

Zilbergeld, Sherry (Israel)

UN—BUDGET (2024) (Agenda item 134)
A/78/PV.50(Resumption1); A/C.5/78/SR.5; A/C.5/78/SR.26/PartII
UN—PROGRAMME PLANNING (Agenda item 135)
A/C.5/78/SR.5
UN. GENERAL ASSEMBLY (78TH SESS. : 2023-2024)—OFFICERS (Agenda item 5)
A/C.5/78/SR.1
UN INTERIM FORCE IN LEBANON—FINANCING (Agenda item 156b)
A/C.5/78/SR.40

Zilmer-Johns, Lisbet (Denmark)

UKRAINE—POLITICAL CONDITIONS (Agenda item 62)
A/78/PV.56

Zin Zawawi, Nordiana Binti (Malaysia)

HEALTH (Agenda item 125)
A/78/PV.77
PEACE (Agenda item 14)
A/78/PV.77
UN. SECRETARY-GENERAL—REPORTS (Agenda item 110)
A/78/PV.55
UN. SECURITY COUNCIL—REPORTS (Agenda item 26)
A/78/PV.93

Zitko, Andrej (Slovenia)

ENVIRONMENT (Agenda item 71b)
A/C.3/78/SR.29
HUMAN RIGHTS (Agenda item 71)
A/C.3/78/SR.16
HUMAN RIGHTS ACTIVISTS (Agenda item 71b)
A/C.3/78/SR.19
RACIAL DISCRIMINATION—ELIMINATION (Agenda item 69a)
A/C.3/78/SR.47

Živković, Ivana (UNDP)

SUSTAINABLE DEVELOPMENT (Agenda item 18)
A/C.2/78/SR.12

Zlenko, Anatoli M. (Ukraine)

BIOLOGICAL WEAPONS—TREATIES (Agenda item 106)
A/C.1/78/PV.15
CHEMICAL WEAPONS—TREATIES (Agenda item 99l)
A/C.1/78/PV.14; A/C.1/78/PV.15
DISARMAMENT—GENERAL AND COMPLETE (Agenda item 99)
A/C.1/78/PV.15
DISPLACED PERSONS (Agenda item 71b)
A/C.3/78/SR.32
NUCLEAR DISARMAMENT (Agenda item 99b)
A/C.1/78/PV.12; A/C.1/78/PV.13
NUCLEAR NON-PROLIFERATION—INTERNATIONAL OBLIGATIONS (Agenda item 99w)
A/C.1/78/PV.12
NUCLEAR WEAPON TESTS—TREATIES (Agenda item 105)
A/C.1/78/PV.12
VETO (Agenda item 63)
A/78/PV.79

Zlenko, Anatolii (Ukraine)

IAEA—REPORTS (Agenda item 89)
A/78/PV.30
MINE CLEARANCE (Agenda item 46)
A/C.4/78/SR.10
UN. GENERAL ASSEMBLY (78TH SESS. : 2023-2024). 1ST COMMITTEE—GENERAL DEBATE (Agenda item 8)
A/C.1/78/PV.3
VETO (Agenda item 63)
A/78/PV.3

Zoghbi, Rawa (Lebanon)

DISPLACED PERSONS (Agenda item 71b)
A/C.3/78/SR.32
HUMAN RIGHTS—TERRITORIES OCCUPIED BY ISRAEL (Agenda item 71c)
A/C.3/78/SR.35
HUMAN RIGHTS ADVANCEMENT (Agenda item 71b)
A/C.3/78/SR.52
RIGHTS OF THE CHILD (Agenda item 67)
A/C.3/78/SR.11
UN. GENERAL ASSEMBLY—WORK PROGRAMME (Agenda item 120)
A/C.3/78/SR.56
UN. GENERAL ASSEMBLY (78TH SESS. : 2023-2024). 2ND COMMITTEE—GENERAL DEBATE (Agenda item 8)
A/C.2/78/SR.5
WOMEN'S ADVANCEMENT (Agenda item 25a)
A/C.3/78/SR.8
WOMEN'S ADVANCEMENT—CONFERENCES (Agenda item 25b)
A/C.3/78/SR.8

Zongo, Fortuné Gaétan (UN. Human Rights Council. Special Rapporteur on the Situation of Human Rights in Burundi)

HUMAN RIGHTS—BURUNDI (Agenda item 71c)
A/C.3/78/SR.36

Zouev, Alexandre (UN. Assistant Secretary-General for Rule of Law and Security Institutions)

MINE CLEARANCE (Agenda item 46)
A/C.4/78/SR.10
PEACEKEEPING OPERATIONS (Agenda item 51)
A/C.4/78/SR.18

Zoumanigui, Paul Goa (Guinea)

ECONOMIC COOPERATION AMONG DEVELOPING COUNTRIES (Agenda item 22b)
A/C.2/78/SR.18
OPERATIONAL ACTIVITIES—UN SYSTEM (Agenda item 22a)
A/C.2/78/SR.18
WESTERN SAHARA QUESTION (Agenda item 58)
A/C.4/78/SR.8

Zrug, Lemaadla Mohamed Salem (Association sahraouie contre l'impunité dans les camps de Tindouf)

WESTERN SAHARA QUESTION (Agenda item 58)
A/C.4/78/SR.6

Zuhuree, Ibrahim (Maldives)

EXTERNAL DEBT (Agenda item 16c)
A/C.2/78/SR.9
HUMAN RIGHTS ADVANCEMENT (Agenda item 71b)
A/C.3/78/SR.25
INTERNATIONAL TRADE (Agenda item 16a)
A/C.2/78/SR.9
PALESTINE QUESTION (Agenda item 35)
A/78/PV.39
RULE OF LAW (Agenda item 83)
A/C.6/78/SR.17
UN. SECURITY COUNCIL—MEMBERSHIP (Agenda item 121)
A/78/PV.34
UNRWA—ACTIVITIES (Agenda item 49)
A/C.4/78/SR.22
VETO (Agenda item 63)
A/78/PV.52

Zukal, Marek (Czechia)

INTERNATIONAL JURISDICTION (Agenda item 84)
A/C.6/78/SR.12
UN. INTERNATIONAL LAW COMMISSION—REPORTS (Agenda item 79)
A/C.6/78/SR.29; A/C.6/78/SR.31

Zulasri Bin Rosdi, Muhammad (Malaysia)

BIOLOGICAL DIVERSITY—TREATIES (Agenda item 18f)
A/C.2/78/SR.15
CLIMATE (Agenda item 18d)
A/C.2/78/SR.15
DISASTER PREVENTION (Agenda item 18c)
A/C.2/78/SR.15
FOOD SECURITY (Agenda item 23a)
A/C.2/78/SR.17
LANDLOCKED DEVELOPING COUNTRIES—CONFERENCES (Agenda item 20b)
A/C.2/78/SR.7
LEAST DEVELOPED COUNTRIES—CONFERENCES (Agenda item 20a)
A/C.2/78/SR.7
OPERATIONAL ACTIVITIES—UN SYSTEM (Agenda item 22a)
A/C.2/78/SR.18
POVERTY—INTERNATIONAL DECADES (Agenda item 21a)
A/C.2/78/SR.17
RURAL POVERTY (Agenda item 21b)
A/C.2/78/SR.17

Zvachula, Martin (Micronesia (Federated States of))

UN. GENERAL ASSEMBLY (78TH SESS. : 2023-2024). 1ST COMMITTEE—WORK ORGANIZATION (Agenda item 7)
A/C.1/78/PV.30

2030 AGENDA—PROGRAMME IMPLEMENTATION (Agenda item 18a)

Alliance of Small Island States
Lautasi, Isaia (Samoa) - A/C.2/78/SR.12
ASEAN
Lora-Santos, Leila Castillon (Philippines) - A/C.2/78/SR.12
Belarus
Pisarevich, Vadim - A/C.2/78/SR.13
Caribbean Community
Wallace, Brian Christopher Manley (Jamaica) - A/C.2/78/SR.12
Colombia
Ríos Serna, Manuela - A/C.2/78/SR.12
Egypt
Abdelaal, Ahmed Magdy Mohamed Rashad - A/C.2/78/SR.12
Group of 77
Téllez Alonso, Frank (Cuba) - A/C.2/78/SR.12
Torres Seara, Dalia Marlen (Cuba) - A/C.2/78/SR.21
Group of Friends for Disaster Risk Reduction
Macchiavello, Julissa (Peru) - A/C.2/78/SR.12
Group of Friends in Defence of the Charter of the United Nations
Pérez Ayestarán, Joaquín Alberto (Venezuela (Bolivarian Republic of)) - A/C.2/78/SR.12
Group of Landlocked Developing Countries
Motsumi, Lorato (Botswana) - A/C.2/78/SR.12
Group of Least Developed Countries
Adhikari, Pramita (Nepal) - A/C.2/78/SR.12
Qatar
Al-Kuwari, Shaheen - A/C.2/78/SR.12
Switzerland
Allet, Alexandra - A/C.2/78/SR.22
UN. Department of Economic and Social Affairs. Division for Sustainable Development Goals. Officer-in-Charge
Tahtinen, Lotta - A/C.2/78/SR.12
UN. General Assembly. 2nd Committee. Rapporteur
Gatev, Ivaylo (Bulgaria) - A/78/PV.49
UN. Group of African States
Ladeb, Tarek (Tunisia) - A/C.2/78/SR.12

ADMINISTRATION OF JUSTICE (Agenda item 144)

Cameroon
Nyanid, Zacharie Serge Raoul - A/C.6/78/SR.9
Canada
Mead, Kevin Timothy - A/C.6/78/SR.9
China
Ma, Yanbo - A/C.6/78/SR.9
Cuba
Carral Castelo, Arianna - A/C.6/78/SR.9
Egypt
Roshdy, Hussein Ossama Hussein Abdelrhman - A/C.5/78/SR.15
Eritrea
Giorgio, Amanuel - A/C.6/78/SR.9

ADMINISTRATION OF JUSTICE (Agenda item 144) (continued)

European Union
Popan, Simona - A/C.6/78/SR.9
Group of 77
Hernández Morera, Diosdado de Jesús (Cuba) - A/C.5/78/SR.15
Israel
Brash, Zoe - A/C.5/78/SR.15
Mexico
Jiménez Alegría, Natalia - A/C.6/78/SR.9
Mozambique
Saranga, Geraldo - A/C.6/78/SR.9
Netherlands (Kingdom of the)
Made, Angelique van der - A/C.6/78/SR.9
Switzerland
Rathe, Fanny Elizabeth - A/C.6/78/SR.9
Schmied, Gina Andrea - A/C.5/78/SR.15
Uganda
Muhumuza, Duncan Laki - A/C.6/78/SR.9
UN. Advisory Committee on Administrative and Budgetary Questions. Vice-Chair
Ruas, Juliana Gaspar - A/C.5/78/SR.15
UN. General Assembly. 5th Committee. Rapporteur
Hartog, Laurens Thomas den (Netherlands (Kingdom of the)) - A/78/PV.50(Resumption1)
UN. General Assembly. 6th Committee. Bureau
Vittay, Melinda (Hungary) - A/C.6/78/SR.37
UN. Group of African States
Ikondere, Marvin (Uganda) - A/C.6/78/SR.9
UN. Office of the Administration of Justice. Executive Director
Frankson-Wallace, Alayne - A/C.5/78/SR.15
UN Ombudsman
Dodson, Shireen L. - A/C.5/78/SR.15
United Kingdom
Lito, Melina - A/C.6/78/SR.9
United States
Patton, Dorothy - A/C.6/78/SR.9

ADMINISTRATION OF JUSTICE—HUMAN RIGHTS (Agenda item 71b)

Bahrain
Alhammadi, Hessa - A/C.3/78/SR.25
Uruguay
Machado Mouriño, Felipe - A/C.3/78/SR.28

AFRICA—DEVELOPMENT (Agenda item 65b)

Angola
Cruz, Francisco José da - A/78/PV.18
Cameroon
Tommo Monthe, Michel - A/78/PV.18
China
Dai, Bing - A/78/PV.18
European Union
Samson, Hedda - A/78/PV.18
Group of 77
Kwoba, Godfrey (Uganda) - A/78/PV.57
Hungary
Atanaszov, Anna Mária - A/78/PV.57

AFRICA—DEVELOPMENT (Agenda item 65b) (continued)

India
Parihar, Rajesh - A/78/PV.18
Latvia
Ilgis, Olegs - A/78/PV.18
Libya
Suweed, Mohamed - A/78/PV.18
Namibia
Gertze, Neville Melvin - A/78/PV.18
Poland
Sakowicz, Mateusz - A/78/PV.18
Romania
Horosanu, Gabriela-Cornelia - A/78/PV.18
Russian Federation
Chumakov, Dmitry S. - A/78/PV.57
Meschchanov, Boris A. - A/78/PV.18
Sierra Leone
Kanu, Michael Imran - A/78/PV.18
South Africa
Joyini, Mathu - A/78/PV.18
UN. Department for General Assembly and Conference Management
Nakano, Kenji - A/78/PV.57
UN. General Assembly. President
Francis, Dennis (Trinidad and Tobago) - A/78/PV.18
UN. Group of African States
Ladeb, Tarek (Tunisia) - A/78/PV.18
Mokhawa, Gladys (Botswana) - A/78/PV.57
United Kingdom
Young, Archie - A/78/PV.57
Venezuela (Bolivarian Republic of)
Pérez Ayestarán, Joaquín Alberto - A/78/PV.18

AFRICA—NUCLEAR-WEAPON-FREE ZONES (Agenda item 92)

Egypt
Ahmed, Amr Essameldin Sadek - A/C.1/78/PV.25
Ethiopia
Getahun, Kedir - A/C.1/78/PV.13
Spain
Sánchez de Lerín García-Ovies, Ignacio - A/C.1/78/PV.25
Thailand
Khundee, Wichayaporn - A/C.1/78/PV.26
UN. General Assembly. 1st Committee. Rapporteur
Balouji, Heidar Ali (Iran (Islamic Republic of)) - A/78/PV.42
UN. Group of African States
Mahmud, Mohammed Lawal (Nigeria) - A/C.1/78/PV.11

AFRICA—SUSTAINABLE DEVELOPMENT—PARTNERSHIP (Agenda item 65a)

Cameroon
Tommo Monthe, Michel - A/78/PV.18
China
Dai, Bing - A/78/PV.18
European Union
Maesschalck, Filip de (Belgium) - A/78/PV.57
Samson, Hedda - A/78/PV.18

AFRICA—SUSTAINABLE DEVELOPMENT—PARTNERSHIP (Agenda item 65a) (continued)

Group of 77
Kwoba, Godfrey (Uganda) - A/78/PV.57
Hungary
Atanaszov, Anna Mária - A/78/PV.57
India
Parihar, Rajesh - A/78/PV.18
Latvia
Ilgis, Olegs - A/78/PV.18
Libya
Suweed, Mohamed - A/78/PV.18
Namibia
Gertze, Neville Melvin - A/78/PV.18
Poland
Sakowicz, Mateusz - A/78/PV.18
Romania
Horosanu, Gabriela-Cornelia - A/78/PV.18
Russian Federation
Chumakov, Dmitry S. - A/78/PV.57
Meschchanov, Boris A. - A/78/PV.18
Sierra Leone
Kanu, Michael Imran - A/78/PV.18
South Africa
Joyini, Mathu - A/78/PV.18
Thailand
Chindawongse, Suriya - A/78/PV.18
UN. General Assembly. President
Francis, Dennis (Trinidad and Tobago) - A/78/PV.18
UN. Group of African States
Ladeb, Tarek (Tunisia) - A/78/PV.18
Mokhawa, Gladys (Botswana) - A/78/PV.57
United Kingdom
Young, Archie - A/78/PV.57
United States
Fogarty, Daniel - A/78/PV.57
Venezuela (Bolivarian Republic of)
Pérez Ayestarán, Joaquín Alberto - A/78/PV.18

AGEING PERSONS (Agenda item 24b)

Algeria
Samai, Rahma - A/C.3/78/SR.3
Argentina
Squeff, María del Carmen - A/C.3/78/SR.1; A/C.3/78/SR.2; A/C.3/78/SR.49
ASEAN
Dang, Hoang Giang (Viet Nam) - A/C.3/78/SR.1
Austria
Hardwick, Nicola Ann - A/C.3/78/SR.1
Bahrain
Alhammadi, Hessa - A/C.3/78/SR.3
Bangladesh
Abdullah, Md Showeb - A/C.3/78/SR.1
Belarus
Mozgovaya, Ekaterina - A/C.3/78/SR.2
Brazil
Dias, João Henrique Nascimento - A/C.3/78/SR.1
Costa Rica
Chan Valverde, Maritza - A/C.3/78/SR.3

AGEING PERSONS (Agenda item 24b) (continued)
Cuba
García Hernández, Martha - A/C.3/78/SR.3
González Behmaras, Alejandro - A/C.3/78/SR.1
Dominican Republic
Andújar, Luz del Carmen - A/C.3/78/SR.1; A/C.3/78/SR.3
Ecuador
Méndez Gruezo, Elizabeth - A/C.3/78/SR.2
Egypt
Mostafa Rizk, Heba - A/C.3/78/SR.2
El Salvador
González López, Egriselda Aracely - A/C.3/78/SR.1
European Union
Schuller, Simone - A/C.3/78/SR.1
Group of 77
González Behmaras, Alejandro (Cuba) - A/C.3/78/SR.1; A/C.3/78/SR.49
Group of Friends of Older Persons
Narváez Ojeda, Paula (Chile) - A/C.3/78/SR.1
Guatemala
Rodríguez Mancia, Carla María - A/C.3/78/SR.1
India
Sonkar, Suman - A/C.3/78/SR.1
Indonesia
Imanuel, Fnu - A/C.3/78/SR.1
Iran (Islamic Republic of)
Arab Bafrani, Fatemeh - A/C.3/78/SR.2
Israel
Aviel, Shir - A/C.3/78/SR.2
Shaked, Or - A/C.3/78/SR.1
Kazakhstan
Bakytbekkyzy, Anel - A/C.3/78/SR.2
Kuwait
Al Mulla, Wafiqah - A/C.3/78/SR.3
Malaysia
Escopper Zumilla, Michael Jawa - A/C.3/78/SR.49
Muhamad, Ahmad Faisal - A/C.3/78/SR.2
Rahman, Siti Adibah Abdul - A/C.3/78/SR.1
Malta
Gabriele, Emma de - A/C.3/78/SR.1
Mexico
Santa Ana Vara, Alma Esperanza - A/C.3/78/SR.1; A/C.3/78/SR.2
Mongolia
Vorshilov, Enkhbold - A/C.3/78/SR.2
Morocco
Moutchou, Majda - A/C.3/78/SR.1
Namibia
Gertze, Neville Melvin - A/C.3/78/SR.2
Nicaragua
Pichardo Urbina, Eleane Yaoska - A/C.3/78/SR.4
Nigeria
Asaju, Bola - A/C.3/78/SR.1
Philippines
Fangco, Maria Roseny Baltazar - A/C.3/78/SR.1
Portugal
Guerra, Stefano Venancio - A/C.3/78/SR.1
Zacarias, Ana Paula - A/C.3/78/SR.2

AGEING PERSONS (Agenda item 24b) (continued)
Russian Federation
Kashaev, Roman G. - A/C.3/78/SR.2; A/C.3/78/SR.49
Kuzmenkov, Stepan Y. - A/C.3/78/SR.1
Singapore
Choong, Brandon - A/C.3/78/SR.2
Sistema de la Integración Centroamericana
González López, Egriselda Aracely (El Salvador) - A/C.3/78/SR.1
Slovakia
Beblavý, Pavol - A/C.3/78/SR.2
Grünwald, Tomáš - A/C.3/78/SR.1
Slovenia
Malovrh, Bostjan - A/C.3/78/SR.1
South Africa
Makgati, Penelope Ramatsobane - A/C.3/78/SR.2
Sovereign Order of Malta
Beresford-Hill, Paul - A/C.3/78/SR.1
Syrian Arab Republic
Altarsha, Elie - A/C.3/78/SR.1
Türkiye
Güven, Fikriye Asli - A/C.3/78/SR.3
UN. Department of Economic and Social Affairs. Division for Inclusive Social Development. Officer-in-Charge
Wilmoth, John - A/C.3/78/SR.1
UN. Human Rights Council. Independent Expert on the Enjoyment of All Human Rights by Older Persons
Mahler, Claudia - A/C.3/78/SR.1
United States
Lang, Dylan - A/C.3/78/SR.1

AL-SABAH, NAWAF AL-AHMAD AL-JABER (KUWAIT. AMIR)—TRIBUTES
Group of Arab States
Abdelkhalek, Osama Mahmoud (Egypt) - A/78/PV.50(Resumption1)
Gulf Cooperation Council
Al-Thani, Alya Ahmed S.A. (Qatar) - A/78/PV.50(Resumption1)
Kuwait
Albanai, Tareq M.A.M. - A/78/PV.50(Resumption1)
UN. General Assembly. President
Francis, Dennis (Trinidad and Tobago) - A/78/PV.50(Resumption1)
UN. Group of African States
Boma, Regina Chama (Zambia) - A/78/PV.50(Resumption1)
UN. Group of Asia-Pacific States
Eyeberdiyev, Ata (Turkmenistan) - A/78/PV.50(Resumption1)
UN. Group of Western European and Other States
Uexküll, Andreas von (Sweden) - A/78/PV.50(Resumption1)
UN. Secretary-General
Guterres, António, 1949- - A/78/PV.50(Resumption1)

AL-SABAH, NAWAF AL-AHMAD AL-JABER (KUWAIT. AMIR)—TRIBUTES (continued)

United States
Lu, Christopher P. - A/78/PV.50(Resumption1)

ALBINISM (Agenda item 71b)

China
Wang, Zixu - A/C.3/78/SR.27
European Union
Greffine, Venise Catherine - A/C.3/78/SR.27
Malawi
Chimbiri-Molande, Agnes Mary - A/C.3/78/SR.47
Syrian Arab Republic
Altarsha, Elie - A/C.3/78/SR.27
UN. Human Rights Council. Independent Expert on the Enjoyment of Human Rights by Persons with Albinism
Miti-Drummond, Muluka-Anne - A/C.3/78/SR.27
United Republic of Tanzania
Tambwe, Zuleikha Rutha - A/C.3/78/SR.27

AMERICAN SAMOA QUESTION (Agenda item 58)

United States
Kris, Robert - A/C.4/78/SR.7

ARMED CONFLICTS PREVENTION (Agenda item 31a)

Australia
Hutchison, Alexandra - A/78/PV.72
Austria
Pretterhofer, Stefan - A/78/PV.72
Belgium
Cardon De Lichtbuer, Christophe Alain C. - A/78/PV.72
Bulgaria
Stoeva, Lachezara - A/78/PV.72
Canada
Rae, Robert - A/78/PV.72
China
Niu, Xiaoqiang - A/78/PV.72
Costa Rica
Chan Valverde, Maritza - A/78/PV.72
Croatia
Ćurić Hrvatinić, Hrvoje - A/78/PV.72
Cuba
González Behmaras, Alejandro - A/78/PV.72
Czechia
Kulhánek, Jakub - A/78/PV.72
Democratic People's Republic of Korea
Kim, Song - A/78/PV.72
Eritrea
Giorgio, Amanuel - A/78/PV.73
European Union
Samson, Hedda - A/78/PV.72
France
Dime-Labille, Diarra - A/78/PV.72
Georgia
Abesadze, David - A/78/PV.72

ARMED CONFLICTS PREVENTION (Agenda item 31a) (continued)

Germany
Geisler, Michael Alexander - A/78/PV.72
Hungary
Svercsok, Szabolcs - A/78/PV.72
International, Impartial and Independent Mechanism to Assist in the Investigation and Prosecution of Persons Responsible for the Most Serious Crimes under International Law Committed in the Syrian Arab Republic since March 2011
Marchi-Uhel, Catherine - A/78/PV.72
Iran (Islamic Republic of)
Aref, Yahya - A/78/PV.72
Ireland
Kirk, James - A/78/PV.72
Japan
Shino, Mitsuko - A/78/PV.72
Latvia
Pavļuta-Deslandes, Sanita - A/78/PV.72
Liechtenstein
Wenaweser, Christian - A/78/PV.72
Luxembourg
Maes, Olivier - A/78/PV.72
Netherlands (Kingdom of the)
Brandt, Yoka - A/78/PV.72
New Zealand
Pringle, Rachael - A/78/PV.72
Nicaragua
Pichardo Urbina, Eleane Yaoska - A/78/PV.72
Qatar
Alnesf, Sharifa Yousef A.S. - A/78/PV.72
Russian Federation
Skachkov, Evgeny A. - A/78/PV.73
Slovakia
Košuth, Matus - A/78/PV.72
Sudan
Mohamed, Abuzied Shamseldin Ahmed - A/78/PV.72
Switzerland
Baeriswyl, Pascale - A/78/PV.72
Syrian Arab Republic
Khaddour, Mhd. Riyad - A/78/PV.73
Türkiye
Özgür, Ceren Hande - A/78/PV.72
Ukraine
Kyslytsya, Sergiy - A/78/PV.72
United Kingdom
Sylvester, Timothy James - A/78/PV.72
United States
Sullivan, Stephanie - A/78/PV.72
Venezuela (Bolivarian Republic of)
Poveda Brito, Robert Alexander - A/78/PV.72

ARMS RACE—OUTER SPACE (Agenda item 97a)

Algeria
Lebbaz, Larbi Abdelfattah - A/C.1/78/PV.17
Argentina
Guerra, Hugo Emmanuel - A/C.1/78/PV.16
ASEAN
Muhamad, Ahmad Faisal (Malaysia) - A/C.1/78/PV.16

ARMS RACE—OUTER SPACE (Agenda item 97a) (continued)

Australia
Lia, Alex - A/C.1/78/PV.16
Austria
Bilgeri, Andreas - A/C.1/78/PV.16
Bangladesh
Muhith, Muhammad A. - A/C.1/78/PV.16
Bolivia (Plurinational State of)
Muñoz Ponce, Tatiana Bárbara - A/C.1/78/PV.17
Brazil
Damico, Flávio Soares - A/C.1/78/PV.17
Szatmari, Roberto Wazima - A/C.1/78/PV.27
Canada
Milligan, Ashlyn - A/C.1/78/PV.17
Chile
Vidal Mercado, Jorge Andrés - A/C.1/78/PV.16
China
Shen, Jian - A/C.1/78/PV.17; A/C.1/78/PV.27
Coordinating Bureau of the Non-Aligned Countries
Sirie, Mochammad Iqbal (Indonesia) - A/C.1/78/PV.16
Costa Rica
Chan Valverde, Maritza - A/C.1/78/PV.16
Cuba
Gómez Sardiñas, Yiliam - A/C.1/78/PV.17
Romero López, Rosanis - A/C.1/78/PV.27
Czechia
Štěpánek, Jaroslav - A/C.1/78/PV.16
Democratic People's Republic of Korea
Kim, In Chol - A/C.1/78/PV.17
Egypt
Hegazy, Abdelrhman Mohamed Farid - A/C.1/78/PV.16
European Union
Claeys, Carine - A/C.1/78/PV.16
France
Petit, Camille - A/C.1/78/PV.17
Germany
Himmler, Benjamin - A/C.1/78/PV.16
Greece
Papathanasiou, Artemis - A/C.1/78/PV.17
Group of Arab States
Alqaisi, Sultan Natheir Mustafa (Jordan) - A/C.1/78/PV.16; A/C.1/78/PV.17
Holy See
Caccia, Gabriele Giordano - A/C.1/78/PV.17
Indonesia
Sinaga, Liandra Jean - A/C.1/78/PV.16
Iran (Islamic Republic of)
Eshragh Jahromi, Asadollah - A/C.1/78/PV.17
Ghorbanpour Najafabadi, Mohammad - A/C.1/78/PV.16; A/C.1/78/PV.17
Ireland
Robinson, Jason - A/C.1/78/PV.17
Israel
Kalmar, Nimrod - A/C.1/78/PV.17
Maayan, Michal - A/C.1/78/PV.16
Sharoni, Benjamin - A/C.1/78/PV.27
Italy
Bencini, Leonardo - A/C.1/78/PV.17

ARMS RACE—OUTER SPACE (Agenda item 97a) (continued)

Japan
Ogasawara, Ichiro - A/C.1/78/PV.17
Kazakhstan
Rakhmetullin, Akan - A/C.1/78/PV.16
Malaysia
Muhamad, Ahmad Faisal - A/C.1/78/PV.16
Mexico
Fausto, Braulio - A/C.1/78/PV.17
Netherlands (Kingdom of the)
Bosch, Robert in den - A/C.1/78/PV.16
New Zealand
Clutterbuck, Nicholas - A/C.1/78/PV.17
Nigeria
Mahmud, Mohammed Lawal - A/C.1/78/PV.17
Norway
Sæter, William - A/C.1/78/PV.17
Pakistan
Sarwani, Gul Qaiser - A/C.1/78/PV.16
Paraguay
Sanabria Duarte, Viviana Rocio - A/C.1/78/PV.17
Philippines
Lipana, Diane Shayne Dela Fuente - A/C.1/78/PV.16
Republic of Korea
Kim, Sunghoon - A/C.1/78/PV.17
Yoon, Seong-mee - A/C.1/78/PV.17
Russian Federation
Vorontsov, Konstantin - A/C.1/78/PV.16
Saudi Arabia
Moharram, Wajdi Hassan M. - A/C.1/78/PV.16
Spain
Rosario Vela, Manuel Jesús del - A/C.1/78/PV.17
Sri Lanka
Gunaratna, Pahala Rallage Sanathana Sugeeshwara - A/C.1/78/PV.27
Pieris, Peter Mohan Maithri - A/C.1/78/PV.16
State of Palestine
Kasabri, Qais Z.F. - A/C.1/78/PV.16
Sweden
Escaig, Benjamin - A/C.1/78/PV.16
Switzerland
Masmejean, Laurent - A/C.1/78/PV.17
Syrian Arab Republic
Al Ashkar, Adib - A/C.1/78/PV.17
UN. General Assembly. 1st Committee. Rapporteur
Balouji, Heidar Ali (Iran (Islamic Republic of)) - A/78/PV.42
UN. Group of African States
Mahmud, Mohammed Lawal (Nigeria) - A/C.1/78/PV.16
United Kingdom
Liddle, Aidan Thomas - A/C.1/78/PV.16
United States
Turner, Bruce - A/C.1/78/PV.17
Yemen
Al-Dobhany, Marwan Ali Noman - A/C.1/78/PV.16
Zambia
Musonda, Oliver - A/C.1/78/PV.17

ARMS TRANSFERS—TREATIES (Agenda item 99x)

Argentina
Guerra, Hugo Emmanuel - A/C.1/78/PV.18
Armenia
Grigoryan, Andranik - A/C.1/78/PV.28
ASEAN
Mao, Tithiarun (Cambodia) - A/C.1/78/PV.17
Australia
Carr, Michelle - A/C.1/78/PV.19
Bangladesh
Shatil, Toufiq Islam - A/C.1/78/PV.18
Brazil
Damico, Flávio Soares - A/C.1/78/PV.19
Canada
Svadjian, Méliné - A/C.1/78/PV.19
Coordinating Bureau of the Non-Aligned Countries
Kristanti, Maria Benedicta Diah (Indonesia) - A/C.1/78/PV.17
Côte d'Ivoire
Moriko, Tiémoko - A/C.1/78/PV.18
Cuba
Garcia Moré, Yohan Yuniet - A/C.1/78/PV.28
Gómez Sardiñas, Yiliam - A/C.1/78/PV.19
Egypt
Hegazy, Abdelrhman Mohamed Farid - A/C.1/78/PV.18; A/C.1/78/PV.28
European Union
Karczmarz, Michał - A/C.1/78/PV.18; A/C.1/78/PV.19
Finland
Voionmaa, Lauri - A/C.1/78/PV.19
France
Petit, Camille - A/C.1/78/PV.18
Germany
Göbel, Thomas - A/C.1/78/PV.18
Greece
Christoglou, Konstantinos - A/C.1/78/PV.19
Guatemala
Rodríguez Mancia, Carla María - A/C.1/78/PV.18
India
Bedi, Anmol Sher Singh - A/C.1/78/PV.28
Indonesia
Sirie, Mochammad Iqbal - A/C.1/78/PV.28
Iran (Islamic Republic of)
Ghorbanpour Najafabadi, Mohammad - A/C.1/78/PV.28
Ireland
Udom, Caoimhe - A/C.1/78/PV.18
Israel
Sharoni, Benjamin - A/C.1/78/PV.19; A/C.1/78/PV.28
Italy
Gai, Elena - A/C.1/78/PV.19
Lesotho
Nena, Matete - A/C.1/78/PV.19
Malaysia
Noordin, Shamsuri - A/C.1/78/PV.18
Netherlands (Kingdom of the)
Bosch, Robert in den - A/C.1/78/PV.18

ARMS TRANSFERS—TREATIES (Agenda item 99x) (continued)

New Zealand
De Schot, Jikita - A/C.1/78/PV.19
Nigeria
Mahmud, Mohammed Lawal - A/C.1/78/PV.19
Norway
Andersen, Tor Henrik - A/C.1/78/PV.19
Pakistan
Ahmed, Husham - A/C.1/78/PV.19
Republic of Korea
Yoon, Seong-mee - A/C.1/78/PV.18
Romania
Mocanu, Andreea - A/C.1/78/PV.19
Russian Federation
Belousov, Andrey I. - A/C.1/78/PV.19
Senegal
Diack, Papa Samba - A/C.1/78/PV.18
Slovenia
Ponikvar Velázquez, Jasna - A/C.1/78/PV.19
South Africa
Lagardien, Yaseen - A/C.1/78/PV.18
Spain
Rosario Vela, Manuel Jesús del - A/C.1/78/PV.19
Syrian Arab Republic
Al Ashkar, Adib - A/C.1/78/PV.28
Togo
Tchalare, Abd-el Kader Yasmin - A/C.1/78/PV.19
Türkiye
Çetin, Ahmet Erman - A/C.1/78/PV.18
United Kingdom
Saggese, Eleonora - A/C.1/78/PV.19

AU-UN HYBRID OPERATION IN DARFUR—FINANCING (Agenda item 159)

UN. Controller
Ramanathan, Chandramouli - A/C.5/78/SR.35
UN. General Assembly. 5th Committee. Rapporteur
Hartog, Laurens Thomas den (Netherlands (Kingdom of the)) - A/78/PV.95

BIOLOGICAL DIVERSITY—TREATIES (Agenda item 18f)

ASEAN
Lora-Santos, Leila Castillon (Philippines) - A/C.2/78/SR.12
Bolivia (Plurinational State of)
Pary Rodríguez, Diego - A/C.2/78/SR.13
Brazil
Kloss, Emerson Coraiola Yinde - A/C.2/78/SR.13
Canada
Natale, Giuliana - A/C.2/78/SR.15
China
Guo, Jingnan - A/C.2/78/SR.13
Liu, Liqun - A/C.2/78/SR.25
Costa Rica
Chan Valverde, Maritza - A/C.2/78/SR.13
Ecuador
Barba Bustos, Irina Alexandra - A/C.2/78/SR.13

BIOLOGICAL DIVERSITY—TREATIES (Agenda item 18f) (continued)

Egypt
Abdelaal, Ahmed Magdy Mohamed Rashad - A/C.2/78/SR.12
European Union
Gambert, Sylvain - A/C.2/78/SR.25
Group of 77
Torres Seara, Dalia Marlen (Cuba) - A/C.2/78/SR.21
Kenya
Kenga, Emmanuel Kingi - A/C.2/78/SR.13
Malaysia
Zulasri Bin Rosdi, Muhammad - A/C.2/78/SR.15
Micronesia (Federated States of)
Welles, Kenneth - A/C.2/78/SR.15
Secretariat of the Convention on Biological Diversity. Deputy Executive Secretary
Cooper, David - A/C.2/78/SR.12
Switzerland
Allet, Alexandra - A/C.2/78/SR.25
Timor-Leste
Nunes, Karlito - A/C.2/78/SR.15
UN. General Assembly. 2nd Committee. Rapporteur
Gatev, Ivaylo (Bulgaria) - A/78/PV.49
United States
Lawrence, Jason N. - A/C.2/78/SR.25

BIOLOGICAL WEAPONS—TREATIES (Agenda item 106)

Algeria
Lebbaz, Larbi Abdelfattah - A/C.1/78/PV.15
ASEAN
Vongnorkeo, Anouparb (Lao People's Democratic Republic) - A/C.1/78/PV.14
Australia
Hill, Ruth - A/C.1/78/PV.14
Austria
Woergoetter, Caroline - A/C.1/78/PV.15
Bangladesh
Muhith, Muhammad A. - A/C.1/78/PV.15
Belarus
Makarevich, Siarhei - A/C.1/78/PV.15
Brazil
Damico, Flávio Soares - A/C.1/78/PV.15
Canada
Tomlinson, Bryan - A/C.1/78/PV.15
Caribbean Community
Wallace, Brian Christopher Manley (Jamaica) - A/C.1/78/PV.14
Chile
Vidal Mercado, Jorge Andrés - A/C.1/78/PV.14
China
Sun, Yiliang - A/C.1/78/PV.15
Colombia
Quintero Correa, Nohra María - A/C.1/78/PV.16
Coordinating Bureau of the Non-Aligned Countries
Aron, Andy (Indonesia) - A/C.1/78/PV.14
Cuba
Thomas Ramírez, Vilma - A/C.1/78/PV.15

BIOLOGICAL WEAPONS—TREATIES (Agenda item 106) (continued)

Czechia
Štěpánek, Jaroslav - A/C.1/78/PV.14
Egypt
Ahmed, Amr Essameldin Sadek - A/C.1/78/PV.14
Equatorial Guinea
Edu Mbasogo, Marcial - A/C.1/78/PV.15
European Union
Claeys, Carine - A/C.1/78/PV.14
France
Petit, Camille - A/C.1/78/PV.15
Germany
Himmler, Benjamin - A/C.1/78/PV.14
Group of Arab States
Alqaisi, Sultan Natheir Mustafa (Jordan) - A/C.1/78/PV.14
Hungary
Talpai, Tamás - A/C.1/78/PV.15
India
Kamboj, Ruchira - A/C.1/78/PV.15
Indonesia
Kristanti, Maria Benedicta Diah - A/C.1/78/PV.14
Iran (Islamic Republic of)
Eshragh Jahromi, Asadollah - A/C.1/78/PV.15
Ghorbanpour Najafabadi, Mohammad - A/C.1/78/PV.14; A/C.1/78/PV.15
Ireland
Udom, Caoimhe - A/C.1/78/PV.15
Israel
Maayan, Michal - A/C.1/78/PV.15
Italy
Bencini, Leonardo - A/C.1/78/PV.15
Japan
Ogasawara, Ichiro - A/C.1/78/PV.15
Kazakhstan
Omarov, Arsen - A/C.1/78/PV.15
Malaysia
Sivamohan, Shivanand - A/C.1/78/PV.14
Mexico
Yarahuán Dodero, Santiago - A/C.1/78/PV.14
Myanmar
Tun, Kyaw Moe - A/C.1/78/PV.16
Nepal
Gohiwar Aryal, Indira - A/C.1/78/PV.15
Netherlands (Kingdom of the)
Bosch, Robert in den - A/C.1/78/PV.14
New Zealand
De Schot, Jikita - A/C.1/78/PV.15
Norway
Hunskaar, Maria - A/C.1/78/PV.15
Pakistan
Gohar, Sarfaraz Ahmed - A/C.1/78/PV.15
Philippines
Lipana, Diane Shayne Dela Fuente - A/C.1/78/PV.14
Qatar
Al-Mehaizza, Essa Abdulla - A/C.1/78/PV.15
Republic of Korea
Yoon, Seong-mee - A/C.1/78/PV.15

BIOLOGICAL WEAPONS—TREATIES (Agenda item 106) (continued)

Review Conference of the State Parties to the Convention on the Prohibition of the Development, Production and Stockpiling of Bacteriological (Biological) and Toxin Weapons and on Their Destruction. President
Bencini, Leonardo (Italy) - A/C.1/78/PV.14
Russian Federation
Vorontsov, Konstantin - A/C.1/78/PV.14; A/C.1/78/PV.15; A/C.1/78/PV.16
South Africa
Mahomed, Shuaib - A/C.1/78/PV.14
Spain
Rosario Vela, Manuel Jesús del - A/C.1/78/PV.15
Sri Lanka
Pieris, Peter Mohan Maithri - A/C.1/78/PV.14
State of Palestine
Kasabri, Qais Z.F. - A/C.1/78/PV.14
Switzerland
Thoeni, Julien - A/C.1/78/PV.15
Syrian Arab Republic
Al Ashkar, Adib - A/C.1/78/PV.15
Thailand
Khundee, Wichayaporn - A/C.1/78/PV.15
Ukraine
Zlenko, Anatoli M. - A/C.1/78/PV.15
UN. General Assembly. 1st Committee. Rapporteur
Balouji, Heidar Ali (Iran (Islamic Republic of)) - A/78/PV.42
United Kingdom
Floyd, Ian - A/C.1/78/PV.15
United States
Turner, Bruce - A/C.1/78/PV.15; A/C.1/78/PV.16

BOAO FORUM FOR ASIA—OBSERVER STATUS (Agenda item 169)

UN. General Assembly. 6th Committee. Rapporteur
Moussa, Moussa Mohamed (Djibouti) - A/78/PV.45

BRITISH VIRGIN ISLANDS QUESTION (Agenda item 58)

Antigua and Barbuda
Thomas, Glentis - A/C.4/78/SR.9
British Virgin Islands
Wheatley, Natalio - A/C.4/78/SR.3
Saint Lucia
Henry, Carlton Ronnie - A/C.4/78/SR.7

CAPITAL PUNISHMENT (Agenda item 71b)

Uruguay
Machado Mouriño, Felipe - A/C.3/78/SR.28

CENTRAL ASIA—ZONES OF PEACE (Agenda item 64)

Azerbaijan
Ahangari, Narmin - A/78/PV.85
Canada
Mead, Kevin Timothy - A/78/PV.85

CENTRAL ASIA—ZONES OF PEACE (Agenda item 64) (continued)

China
Wang, Zixu - A/78/PV.85
Colombia
Solano Ramírez, Lucía Teresa - A/78/PV.85
European Union
Lagatie, Karl (Belgium) - A/78/PV.85
Mexico
Reza Bautista, Mauricio - A/78/PV.85
Russian Federation
Bulgaru, Dmitrii I. - A/78/PV.85
Saudi Arabia
Alomair, Reem Fahad O. - A/78/PV.85
Singapore
Rajandran, Dhivya - A/78/PV.85
Switzerland
Hauri, Adrian - A/78/PV.85
Türkiye
Tanriöver, Emre - A/78/PV.85
United States
Madinger, Sean - A/78/PV.85
Uzbekistan
Lapasov, Ulugbek - A/78/PV.85
Venezuela (Bolivarian Republic of)
Solorzano Cavalieri, Isis Amahl Gabriela - A/78/PV.85

CHEMICAL WEAPONS—TREATIES (Agenda item 99l)

Algeria
Lebbaz, Larbi Abdelfattah - A/C.1/78/PV.15
Angola
Luemba, Mateus Pedro - A/C.1/78/PV.15
ASEAN
Vongnorkeo, Anouparb (Lao People's Democratic Republic) - A/C.1/78/PV.14
Australia
Hill, Ruth - A/C.1/78/PV.14
Austria
Woergoetter, Caroline - A/C.1/78/PV.15
Bangladesh
Muhith, Muhammad A. - A/C.1/78/PV.15
Belarus
Makarevich, Siarhei - A/C.1/78/PV.15
Brazil
Damico, Flávio Soares - A/C.1/78/PV.15
Canada
Tomlinson, Bryan - A/C.1/78/PV.15
Caribbean Community
Wallace, Brian Christopher Manley (Jamaica) - A/C.1/78/PV.14
Chile
Vidal Mercado, Jorge Andrés - A/C.1/78/PV.14
China
Sun, Yiliang - A/C.1/78/PV.15
Zhang, Qian - A/C.1/78/PV.26
Colombia
Quintero Correa, Nohra María - A/C.1/78/PV.16

CHEMICAL WEAPONS—TREATIES (Agenda item 99l) (continued)

Coordinating Bureau of the Non-Aligned Countries
Aron, Andy (Indonesia) - A/C.1/78/PV.14
Cuba
Romero López, Rosanis - A/C.1/78/PV.26
Thomas Ramírez, Vilma - A/C.1/78/PV.15
Czechia
Štěpánek, Jaroslav - A/C.1/78/PV.14
Egypt
Ahmed, Amr Essameldin Sadek - A/C.1/78/PV.14; A/C.1/78/PV.26
Equatorial Guinea
Edu Mbasogo, Marcial - A/C.1/78/PV.15
European Union
Claeys, Carine - A/C.1/78/PV.14
Hansen, Steen Malthe - A/C.1/78/PV.15
France
Petit, Camille - A/C.1/78/PV.15
Germany
Himmler, Benjamin - A/C.1/78/PV.14
Group of Arab States
Alqaisi, Sultan Natheir Mustafa (Jordan) - A/C.1/78/PV.14
India
Kamboj, Ruchira - A/C.1/78/PV.15
Ray, Anupam - A/C.1/78/PV.26
Indonesia
Kristanti, Maria Benedicta Diah - A/C.1/78/PV.14
Iran (Islamic Republic of)
Eshragh Jahromi, Asadollah - A/C.1/78/PV.15
Ghorbanpour Najafabadi, Mohammad - A/C.1/78/PV.14; A/C.1/78/PV.15; A/C.1/78/PV.26
Ireland
Udom, Caoimhe - A/C.1/78/PV.15
Israel
Maayan, Michal - A/C.1/78/PV.15
Sharoni, Benjamin - A/C.1/78/PV.26
Italy
Bencini, Leonardo - A/C.1/78/PV.15
Japan
Ogasawara, Ichiro - A/C.1/78/PV.15
Kazakhstan
Omarov, Arsen - A/C.1/78/PV.15
Malaysia
Sivamohan, Shivanand - A/C.1/78/PV.14; A/C.1/78/PV.26
Mexico
Yarahuán Dodero, Santiago - A/C.1/78/PV.14
Myanmar
Tun, Kyaw Moe - A/C.1/78/PV.16
Nepal
Gohiwar Aryal, Indira - A/C.1/78/PV.15
Netherlands (Kingdom of the)
Bosch, Robert in den - A/C.1/78/PV.14; A/C.1/78/PV.15
New Zealand
De Schot, Jikita - A/C.1/78/PV.15
Nicaragua
Jiménez, Jasser - A/C.1/78/PV.26

CHEMICAL WEAPONS—TREATIES (Agenda item 99l) (continued)

Norway
Hunskaar, Maria - A/C.1/78/PV.15
Organisation for the Prohibition of Chemical Weapons
Li, Hong - A/C.1/78/PV.16
Pakistan
Gohar, Sarfaraz Ahmed - A/C.1/78/PV.15
Philippines
Lipana, Diane Shayne Dela Fuente - A/C.1/78/PV.14
Poland
Szczerski, Krzysztof - A/C.1/78/PV.26
Qatar
Al-Mehaizza, Essa Abdulla - A/C.1/78/PV.15
Republic of Korea
Yoon, Seong-mee - A/C.1/78/PV.15
Russian Federation
Belousov, Andrey I. - A/C.1/78/PV.26
Vorontsov, Konstantin - A/C.1/78/PV.14; A/C.1/78/PV.15
South Africa
Mahomed, Shuaib - A/C.1/78/PV.14
Spain
Rosario Vela, Manuel Jesús del - A/C.1/78/PV.15
Sri Lanka
Pieris, Peter Mohan Maithri - A/C.1/78/PV.14
State of Palestine
Kasabri, Qais Z.F. - A/C.1/78/PV.14
Switzerland
Thoeni, Julien - A/C.1/78/PV.15
Syrian Arab Republic
Al Ashkar, Adib - A/C.1/78/PV.14; A/C.1/78/PV.15
Mustafa, Marah - A/C.1/78/PV.26
Thailand
Khundee, Wichayaporn - A/C.1/78/PV.15
Türkiye
Çetin, Ahmet Erman - A/C.1/78/PV.26
Ukraine
Zlenko, Anatoli M. - A/C.1/78/PV.14; A/C.1/78/PV.15
United Kingdom
Floyd, Ian - A/C.1/78/PV.15
United States
Turner, Bruce - A/C.1/78/PV.15; A/C.1/78/PV.26

CLIMATE (Agenda item 18d)

Alliance of Small Island States
Lautasi, Isaia (Samoa) - A/C.2/78/SR.12
Angola
Luemba, Mateus Pedro - A/C.2/78/SR.13
Armenia
Babikyan, Araksya - A/C.2/78/SR.15
Australia
Larsen, James - A/C.2/78/SR.15
Azerbaijan
Bayramli-Hamidova, Nigar - A/C.2/78/SR.13
Bolivia (Plurinational State of)
Pary Rodríguez, Diego - A/C.2/78/SR.13

CLIMATE (Agenda item 18d) (continued)

Brazil
Kloss, Emerson Coraiola Yinde - A/C.2/78/SR.13
Cameroon
Banaken Elel, Nelly - A/C.2/78/SR.13
Canada
Natale, Giuliana - A/C.2/78/SR.15
Caribbean Community
Wallace, Brian Christopher Manley (Jamaica) - A/C.2/78/SR.12
China
Guo, Jingnan - A/C.2/78/SR.13
Liu, Liqun - A/C.2/78/SR.25
Colombia
Ríos Serna, Manuela - A/C.2/78/SR.12
Solano Ramírez, Lucía Teresa - A/C.2/78/SR.25
Costa Rica
Chan Valverde, Maritza - A/C.2/78/SR.13
Zamora Zumbado, Leticia María - A/C.2/78/SR.25
Côte d'Ivoire
Moriko, Tiémoko - A/C.2/78/SR.15
Ecuador
Barba Bustos, Irina Alexandra - A/C.2/78/SR.13
Egypt
Abdelaal, Ahmed Magdy Mohamed Rashad - A/C.2/78/SR.12
El Salvador
González López, Egriselda Aracely - A/C.2/78/SR.13
Ethiopia
Shiferaw, Girum Getachew - A/C.2/78/SR.15
European Union
Kaspar, Martin - A/C.2/78/SR.25
France
Segovia, Lisa Isabelle - A/C.2/78/SR.25
Group of 77
Téllez Alonso, Frank (Cuba) - A/C.2/78/SR.12
Torres Seara, Dalia Marlen (Cuba) - A/C.2/78/SR.21
Group of Friends in Defence of the Charter of the United Nations
Pérez Ayestarán, Joaquín Alberto (Venezuela (Bolivarian Republic of)) - A/C.2/78/SR.12
Guyana
Alkins, Royston - A/C.2/78/SR.15
India
Gahlot, Petal - A/C.2/78/SR.13
Indonesia
Prabowo, Hari - A/C.2/78/SR.15
Iran (Islamic Republic of)
Jalili, Tahereh - A/C.2/78/SR.13
Iraq
Jasim, Saber Ahmed - A/C.2/78/SR.13
Kenya
Kenga, Emmanuel Kingi - A/C.2/78/SR.13
Malaysia
Zulasri Bin Rosdi, Muhammad - A/C.2/78/SR.15
Maldives
Hameed, Hala - A/C.2/78/SR.13
Mauritania
Soumaré, Boukary - A/C.2/78/SR.15

CLIMATE (Agenda item 18d) (continued)

Mexico
Curzio Vila, Elena - A/C.2/78/SR.13
Monaco
Du Sault, Serena - A/C.2/78/SR.15
Mongolia
Vorshilov, Enkhbold - A/C.2/78/SR.13
Morocco
Ouatiki, Assia - A/C.2/78/SR.13
Nicaragua
Jiménez, Jasser - A/C.2/78/SR.13
Panama
Thompson Ramírez, Marilyn del Carmen - A/C.2/78/SR.13
Russian Federation
Meschchanov, Boris A. - A/C.2/78/SR.25
Uskov, Vladimir - A/C.2/78/SR.15
Secretariat of the United Nations Framework Convention on Climate Change. Technology and Capacity-Building Programme. Director
Violetti, Daniele - A/C.2/78/SR.12
Singapore
Yuan Fang, Yeo - A/C.2/78/SR.13
Thailand
Phuaknuem, Kanok - A/C.2/78/SR.13
Türkiye
İstemil Aydil, Alara - A/C.2/78/SR.15
Ukraine
Leschenko, Volodymyr - A/C.2/78/SR.13
UN. General Assembly. 2nd Committee. Rapporteur
Gatev, Ivaylo (Bulgaria) - A/78/PV.49
United Arab Emirates
Hassan, Tariq Ahmed - A/C.2/78/SR.13
United Kingdom
Fidoe, Nicholas - A/C.2/78/SR.25
United States
Henzel, Christopher - A/C.2/78/SR.15
Lawrence, Jason N. - A/C.2/78/SR.25
World Tourism Organization
Urosevic, Zoritsa - A/C.2/78/SR.12
Zambia
Milambo, Chola - A/C.2/78/SR.15
Zimbabwe
Rupende, Tapiwa Roy - A/C.2/78/SR.13

CLIMATE CHANGE (Agenda item 71b)

Australia
Kim, Yunei - A/C.3/78/SR.29
Bangladesh
Abdullah, Md Showeb - A/C.3/78/SR.29
Chile
Fernández Carter, Catalina - A/C.3/78/SR.29
China
Liu, Luoge - A/C.3/78/SR.29
Colombia
Orduz Durán, Jessica Beatriz - A/C.3/78/SR.29
Costa Rica
Zavala Porras, Daniel Andrés - A/C.3/78/SR.29
Croatia
Šukurica, Alen - A/C.3/78/SR.29

CLIMATE CHANGE (Agenda item 71b) (continued)
Dominican Republic
Andújar, Luz del Carmen - A/C.3/78/SR.29
European Union
Szelivanov, Julia - A/C.3/78/SR.29
Germany
Wennholz, Philipp Alexander - A/C.3/78/SR.29
Greece
Kastanas, Elias - A/C.3/78/SR.29
Indonesia
Pella, Blandina Ruth Viditha Adeleide - A/C.3/78/SR.29
Italy
Di Capua, Giacomo - A/C.3/78/SR.29
Liechtenstein
Alcaraz Romero De Tejada, Leticia - A/C.3/78/SR.29
Malaysia
Escopper Zumilla, Michael Jawa - A/C.3/78/SR.29
Maldives
Hameed, Hala - A/C.3/78/SR.29
Malta
Micallef, Justine - A/C.3/78/SR.29
Marshall Islands
Kabua, Amatlain Elizabeth - A/C.3/78/SR.29
Morocco
Alaoui, Rabia - A/C.3/78/SR.29
Russian Federation
Kuzmenkov, Stepan Y. - A/C.3/78/SR.29
Sovereign Order of Malta
Tripptrap, Ravi Christian - A/C.3/78/SR.29
Switzerland
Hubatka, Pascal - A/C.3/78/SR.29
UN. Human Rights Council. Special Rapporteur on the Promotion and Protection of Human Rights in the Context of Climate Change
Fry, Ian - A/C.3/78/SR.29
United States
Worthe, Jeffrey - A/C.3/78/SR.29

CLUSTER MUNITIONS (Agenda item 99dd)
Australia
Carr, Michelle - A/C.1/78/PV.19
Austria
Kmentt, Alexander - A/C.1/78/PV.18
Brazil
Szatmari, Roberto Wazima - A/C.1/78/PV.28
Canada
Svadjian, Méliné - A/C.1/78/PV.19
Egypt
Hegazy, Abdelrhman Mohamed Farid - A/C.1/78/PV.28
Equatorial Guinea
Edu Mbasogo, Marcial - A/C.1/78/PV.19
France
Petit, Camille - A/C.1/78/PV.18
Iran (Islamic Republic of)
Ghorbanpour Najafabadi, Mohammad - A/C.1/78/PV.28
Iraq
Al-Sadar, Hamzah - A/C.1/78/PV.18

CLUSTER MUNITIONS (Agenda item 99dd) (continued)
Ireland
Udom, Caoimhe - A/C.1/78/PV.18
Italy
Gai, Elena - A/C.1/78/PV.19
Japan
Ogasawara, Ichiro - A/C.1/78/PV.18
Lao People's Democratic Republic
Souliyong, So Inxay - A/C.1/78/PV.19
Mexico
Sánchez Kiesslich, Eduardo Alcibiades - A/C.1/78/PV.18
Netherlands (Kingdom of the)
Bosch, Robert in den - A/C.1/78/PV.18
New Zealand
De Schot, Jikita - A/C.1/78/PV.19
Norway
Andersen, Tor Henrik - A/C.1/78/PV.19
Pakistan
Sarwani, Gul Qaiser - A/C.1/78/PV.28
Russian Federation
Belousov, Andrey I. - A/C.1/78/PV.28
Singapore
Jiamin, Liu - A/C.1/78/PV.28
Slovenia
Ponikvar Velázquez, Jasna - A/C.1/78/PV.19
Spain
Rosario Vela, Manuel Jesús del - A/C.1/78/PV.19
Switzerland
Haegen, Laurin van der - A/C.1/78/PV.19
United Kingdom
Saggese, Eleonora - A/C.1/78/PV.19
United States
Turner, Bruce - A/C.1/78/PV.28

COASTAL ZONE MANAGEMENT (Agenda item 18j)
Colombia
Ríos Serna, Manuela - A/C.2/78/SR.23
European Union
Gambert, Sylvain - A/C.2/78/SR.23
Iran (Islamic Republic of)
Momeni, Javad - A/C.2/78/SR.23
Japan
Nishigori, Naofumi - A/C.2/78/SR.23
Mexico
Curzio Vila, Elena - A/C.2/78/SR.23
Morocco
El Hilali, Meriem - A/C.2/78/SR.23
Türkiye
Demir, İlknur - A/C.2/78/SR.23
İstemil Aydil, Alara - A/78/PV.49
UN. General Assembly. 2nd Committee. Rapporteur
Gatev, Ivaylo (Bulgaria) - A/78/PV.49
UN. General Assembly. 2nd Committee. Secretary
Herity, Emer - A/C.2/78/SR.23
UNEP
Noronha, Ligia - A/C.2/78/SR.12

COASTAL ZONE MANAGEMENT (Agenda item 18j) (continued)

United States
Kroeker-Maus, Faith - A/C.2/78/SR.23
Venezuela (Bolivarian Republic of)
Marín Sevilla, Asbina - A/78/PV.49; A/C.2/78/SR.23

COMMODITIES (Agenda item 16d)

Algeria
Latrous, Mohamed-Esseghir - A/C.2/78/SR.14
Argentina
Nicolino, Sebastián Lucas - A/C.2/78/SR.14
Brazil
Dubeux, Rafael - A/C.2/78/SR.14
Colombia
Tickner, Arlene Beth - A/C.2/78/SR.14
Columbia University (New York)
Stiglitz, Joseph E. - A/C.2/78/SR.14
Common Fund for Commodities
Belal, Mohammed - A/C.2/78/SR.14
Costa Rica
Pizarro-Viales, Laura Raquel - A/C.2/78/SR.14
European Union
Pougin de La Maisonneuve, Axel - A/C.2/78/SR.14
Group of 77
Guevara Rodríguez, Adiel (Cuba) - A/C.2/78/SR.14
Torres Seara, Dalia Marlen (Cuba) - A/C.2/78/SR.21
Group of Landlocked Developing Countries
Mmalane, Katlego Boase (Botswana) - A/C.2/78/SR.8
Mokhawa, Gladys (Botswana) - A/C.2/78/SR.14
Guatemala
Rodríguez Mancia, Carla María - A/C.2/78/SR.14
India
Gahlot, Petal - A/C.2/78/SR.14
Indonesia
Tharyat, Tri - A/C.2/78/SR.14
Iraq
Al-Niami, Mustafa - A/C.2/78/SR.9
Malaysia
Adnan, Yang Aishah Binti - A/C.2/78/SR.14
Mexico
Reta Haddad, Rodolfo - A/C.2/78/SR.9
Robledo López, Carmen - A/C.2/78/SR.14
Oxfam America
Mutasah, Tawanda - A/C.2/78/SR.14
Poland
Skoczek, Joanna Sylwia - A/C.2/78/SR.14
UN. Department of Economic and Social Affairs. Financing for Sustainable Development Office. Strategic Engagement and Policy Integration Branch. Chief
Parra-Lancourt, Mariangela - A/C.2/78/SR.14
UN. Economic and Social Council. President
Narváez Ojeda, Paula (Chile) - A/C.2/78/SR.14
UN. General Assembly. 2nd Committee. Chair
Amorín, Carlos Daniel (Uruguay) - A/C.2/78/SR.14
UN. General Assembly. 2nd Committee. Rapporteur
Gatev, Ivaylo (Bulgaria) - A/78/PV.49

COMMODITIES (Agenda item 16d) (continued)

UNCTAD
Martínez Badillo, Juan José - A/C.2/78/SR.14
Shirotori, Miho - A/C.2/78/SR.8; A/C.2/78/SR.14
United Kingdom
Sowah, Malcolm - A/C.2/78/SR.23
United States
Lawrence, Jason N. - A/C.2/78/SR.23
University of Massachusetts at Amherst
Pickbourn, Lynda - A/C.2/78/SR.14
University of Oxford
Lebdioui, Amir - A/C.2/78/SR.14
Zambia
Milambo, Chola - A/C.2/78/SR.14
Zimbabwe
Rupende, Tapiwa Roy - A/C.2/78/SR.14

COMMUNITY OF DEMOCRACIES—OBSERVER STATUS (Agenda item 164)

UN. General Assembly. 6th Committee. Rapporteur
Moussa, Moussa Mohamed (Djibouti) - A/78/PV.45

CONFERENCE AND MEETING SERVICES (Agenda item 137)

Group of 77
Tur de la Concepción, Richard (Cuba) - A/C.5/78/SR.7
Qatar
Alnasr, Mohammed Khalifa H. - A/C.5/78/SR.7
Russian Federation
Devyatkin, Daniil A. - A/C.5/78/SR.7
Switzerland
Danese, Aurora Maria - A/C.5/78/SR.7
UN. Advisory Committee on Administrative and Budgetary Questions. Chair
Bachar Bong, Abdallah - A/C.5/78/SR.7
UN. Committee on Conferences. Chair
Abo, Ai (Japan) - A/C.5/78/SR.7
UN. General Assembly. 5th Committee. Rapporteur
Hartog, Laurens Thomas den (Netherlands (Kingdom of the)) - A/78/PV.50(Resumption1)
UN. Under-Secretary-General for General Assembly and Conference Management
Abelian, Movses - A/C.5/78/SR.7

CONFIDENCE-BUILDING MEASURES (Agenda item 99t)

Equatorial Guinea
Edu Mbasogo, Marcial - A/C.1/78/PV.22
Pakistan
Ahmed, Husham - A/C.1/78/PV.21

CONFIDENCE-BUILDING MEASURES—REGIONAL PROGRAMMES (Agenda item 100e)

Equatorial Guinea
Edu Mbasogo, Marcial - A/C.1/78/PV.29

CONVENTIONAL ARMS—REGIONAL PROGRAMMES (Agenda item 99g)

India
Bedi, Anmol Sher Singh - A/C.1/78/PV.29
Pakistan
Ahmed, Husham - A/C.1/78/PV.21
Poland
Joniec, Katarzyna - A/C.1/78/PV.29
United States
Turner, Bruce - A/C.1/78/PV.29

CONVENTIONAL WEAPONS (Agenda item 99u)

Argentina
Guerra, Hugo Emmanuel - A/C.1/78/PV.18
ASEAN
Mao, Tithiarun (Cambodia) - A/C.1/78/PV.17
Chile
Vidal Mercado, Jorge Andrés - A/C.1/78/PV.18
Colombia
Quintero Correa, Nohra María - A/C.1/78/PV.18
Coordinating Bureau of the Non-Aligned Countries
Kristanti, Maria Benedicta Diah (Indonesia) - A/C.1/78/PV.17
Costa Rica
Chan Valverde, Maritza - A/C.1/78/PV.18
Côte d'Ivoire
Moriko, Tiémoko - A/C.1/78/PV.18
Cuba
Garcia Moré, Yohan Yuniet - A/C.1/78/PV.28
Gómez Sardiñas, Yiliam - A/C.1/78/PV.19
Egypt
Hegazy, Abdelrhman Mohamed Farid - A/C.1/78/PV.18; A/C.1/78/PV.28
El Salvador
Rodríguez Acosta, Julia Elizabeth - A/C.1/78/PV.18
France
Petit, Camille - A/C.1/78/PV.18
Germany
Göbel, Thomas - A/C.1/78/PV.18; A/C.1/78/PV.28
Greece
Christoglou, Konstantinos - A/C.1/78/PV.19
Group of Arab States
Alqaisi, Sultan Natheir Mustafa (Jordan) - A/C.1/78/PV.28
Guatemala
Rodríguez Mancia, Carla María - A/C.1/78/PV.18
India
Parihar, Rajesh - A/C.1/78/PV.19
Indonesia
Sirie, Mochammad Iqbal - A/C.1/78/PV.18; A/C.1/78/PV.28
Iran (Islamic Republic of)
Ghorbanpour Najafabadi, Mohammad - A/C.1/78/PV.28
Iraq
Al-Sadar, Hamzah - A/C.1/78/PV.18
Ireland
Udom, Caoimhe - A/C.1/78/PV.18

CONVENTIONAL WEAPONS (Agenda item 99u) (continued)

Japan
Ogasawara, Ichiro - A/C.1/78/PV.18
Malaysia
Noordin, Shamsuri - A/C.1/78/PV.18
Mauritania
Mohamedou, El Hadj Lehbib - A/C.1/78/PV.19
Mexico
Sánchez Kiesslich, Eduardo Alcibiades - A/C.1/78/PV.18
Philippines
Reyes, Narciso - A/C.1/78/PV.18
Republic of Korea
Yoon, Seong-mee - A/C.1/78/PV.18
Saudi Arabia
Bin Shafi, Mohammed - A/C.1/78/PV.19
Moharram, Wajdi Hassan M. - A/C.1/78/PV.28
Senegal
Diack, Papa Samba - A/C.1/78/PV.18
Singapore
Jiamin, Liu - A/C.1/78/PV.18
South Africa
Lagardien, Yaseen - A/C.1/78/PV.18
Spain
Rosario Vela, Manuel Jesús del - A/C.1/78/PV.19
Sri Lanka
Pieris, Peter Mohan Maithri - A/C.1/78/PV.18
Switzerland
Haegen, Laurin van der - A/C.1/78/PV.19
Syrian Arab Republic
Al Ashkar, Adib - A/C.1/78/PV.28
Thailand
Khundee, Wichayaporn - A/C.1/78/PV.18
Türkiye
Çetin, Ahmet Erman - A/C.1/78/PV.18
UN. Group of African States
Mahmud, Mohammed Lawal (Nigeria) - A/C.1/78/PV.17
UN. Open-ended Working Group on Conventional Ammunition. Chair
Wittke, Albrecht von (Germany) - A/C.1/78/PV.18
United States
Storsve, Alison - A/C.1/78/PV.19; A/C.1/78/PV.28
Uruguay
Eustathiou de los Santos, Matías Andrés - A/C.1/78/PV.18
Viet Nam
Mai, Ngan Ha - A/C.1/78/PV.18

CONVENTIONAL WEAPONS—TREATIES (Agenda item 103)

Algeria
Lebbaz, Larbi Abdelfattah - A/C.1/78/PV.19
Argentina
Guerra, Hugo Emmanuel - A/C.1/78/PV.18
ASEAN
Mao, Tithiarun (Cambodia) - A/C.1/78/PV.17
Austria
Kmentt, Alexander - A/C.1/78/PV.18

CONVENTIONAL WEAPONS—TREATIES (Agenda item 103) (continued)

Coordinating Bureau of the Non-Aligned Countries
Kristanti, Maria Benedicta Diah (Indonesia) - A/C.1/78/PV.17
Côte d'Ivoire
Moriko, Tiémoko - A/C.1/78/PV.18
Cuba
Gómez Sardiñas, Yiliam - A/C.1/78/PV.19
European Union
Karczmarz, Michał - A/C.1/78/PV.18
France
Petit, Camille - A/C.1/78/PV.18
India
Parihar, Rajesh - A/C.1/78/PV.19
Ireland
Udom, Caoimhe - A/C.1/78/PV.18
Israel
Sharoni, Benjamin - A/C.1/78/PV.19
Italy
Gai, Elena - A/C.1/78/PV.19
Japan
Ogasawara, Ichiro - A/C.1/78/PV.18
New Zealand
De Schot, Jikita - A/C.1/78/PV.19
Pakistan
Ahmed, Husham - A/C.1/78/PV.19
Republic of Korea
Yoon, Seong-mee - A/C.1/78/PV.18
Russian Federation
Belousov, Andrey I. - A/C.1/78/PV.19
Singapore
Jiamin, Liu - A/C.1/78/PV.18
Switzerland
Haegen, Laurin van der - A/C.1/78/PV.19
Türkiye
Çetin, Ahmet Erman - A/C.1/78/PV.18
UN. General Assembly. 1st Committee. Rapporteur
Balouji, Heidar Ali (Iran (Islamic Republic of)) - A/78/PV.42

COOPERATION COUNCIL OF TURKIC-SPEAKING STATES—OBSERVER STATUS (Agenda item 162)

UN. General Assembly. 6th Committee. Rapporteur
Moussa, Moussa Mohamed (Djibouti) - A/78/PV.45

CRIME PREVENTION (Agenda item 107)

Algeria
Hassani, Billel - A/C.3/78/SR.6
ASEAN
Gafoor, Burhan (Singapore) - A/C.3/78/SR.5
Australia
Lukabyo, Emma Jane Mutesi - A/C.3/78/SR.56
Belarus
Pilipenko, Igor - A/C.3/78/SR.50
Velichko, Irina - A/C.3/78/SR.5
Brazil
Dias, João Henrique Nascimento - A/C.3/78/SR.5

CRIME PREVENTION (Agenda item 107) (continued)

Canada
Baur, Lianna Maureen - A/C.3/78/SR.51
Caribbean Community
Wallace, Brian Christopher Manley (Jamaica) - A/C.3/78/SR.5
China
Liu, Han - A/C.3/78/SR.5
Colombia
Paredes Campaña, Jairo Andrés - A/C.3/78/SR.56
Zalabata Torres, Leonor - A/C.3/78/SR.5
Costa Rica
Zavala Porras, Daniel Andrés - A/C.3/78/SR.6
Cuba
Valido Martínez, Yoangel - A/C.3/78/SR.5
Cyprus
Demosthenous, Ioanna - A/C.3/78/SR.5
Dominican Republic
Cedano, Joan Margarita - A/C.3/78/SR.6
Ecuador
Bravo, Karina - A/C.3/78/SR.5
Egypt
Mostafa Rizk, Heba - A/C.3/78/SR.6; A/C.3/78/SR.56
Eritrea
Gebrekidan, Zebib - A/C.3/78/SR.6
European Union
Alonso Giganto, Ana María (Spain) - A/C.3/78/SR.50
Samson, Hedda - A/C.3/78/SR.5
Schuller, Simone - A/C.3/78/SR.5
Georgia
Lortkipanidze, Ekaterine - A/C.3/78/SR.6
Ghana
Anyanah, Bismark - A/C.3/78/SR.6
Group of Friends in Defence of the Charter of the United Nations
Poveda Brito, Robert Alexander (Venezuela (Bolivarian Republic of)) - A/C.3/78/SR.50
Guatemala
Rodríguez Mancia, Carla María - A/C.3/78/SR.5
Holy See
Murphy, Robert David - A/C.3/78/SR.6
Honduras
Espinoza Madrid, Noemí Ruth - A/78/PV.50(Resumption1)
Hungary
Ivanyi, Balint - A/C.3/78/SR.51
Indonesia
Pella, Blandina Ruth Viditha Adeleide - A/C.3/78/SR.6; A/C.3/78/SR.56
Iran (Islamic Republic of)
Arab Bafrani, Fatemeh - A/C.3/78/SR.5; A/C.3/78/SR.51; A/C.3/78/SR.56
Israel
Mimran Rosenberg, Avital - A/C.3/78/SR.5
Italy
Franz, Silvio - A/C.3/78/SR.5
Greco, Gianluca - A/C.3/78/SR.56
Massari, Maurizio - A/78/PV.63

CRIME PREVENTION (Agenda item 107) (continued)

Japan
Ono, Sho - A/C.3/78/SR.6
Jordan
Habashneh, Ahmad Samir Fahim - A/C.3/78/SR.5
Latvia
Ilgis, Olegs - A/C.3/78/SR.51
Lithuania
Vest, Dangiruté - A/C.3/78/SR.51
Luxembourg
Wald, Julien - A/C.3/78/SR.6
Malaysia
Rizal, Nizhan Faraz Bin - A/C.3/78/SR.5
Mali
Dabo N'diaye, Djeneba - A/C.3/78/SR.6
Mexico
Reza Bautista, Mauricio - A/C.3/78/SR.5
Morocco
Bouchikhi, Hanaa - A/C.3/78/SR.6
Myanmar
Tun, Kyaw Moe - A/C.3/78/SR.6
Nicaragua
Pichardo Urbina, Eleane Yaoska - A/C.3/78/SR.6
Nigeria
Marwa, Mohammed Buba - A/C.3/78/SR.5
Oman
Al-Sinani, Nashwa Hilal - A/C.3/78/SR.6
Pakistan
Khan, Mohammad Aamir - A/C.3/78/SR.5
Poland
Skoczek, Joanna Sylwia - A/C.3/78/SR.50
Russian Federation
Bulgaru, Dmitrii I. - A/C.3/78/SR.6; A/C.3/78/SR.56
Devyatkin, Daniil A. - A/78/PV.50(Resumption1)
Kashaev, Roman G. - A/C.3/78/SR.51
Kuzmenkov, Stepan Y. - A/78/PV.50
Leonidchenko, Sergey A. - A/C.3/78/SR.5
Sierra Leone
Yajah, Christian Fayia - A/C.3/78/SR.6
Singapore
Jesudason, Joshua E. - A/C.3/78/SR.5
South Africa
Sekonyana, Ngako Elphus - A/C.3/78/SR.5
Sovereign Order of Malta
Maenpaa, Conor C. - A/C.3/78/SR.6
Syrian Arab Republic
Altarsha, Elie - A/C.3/78/SR.6; A/C.3/78/SR.51
Thailand
Hsieh, Nichamon May - A/C.3/78/SR.5
Türkiye
Aydil, İsmail - A/C.3/78/SR.6
Ukraine
Tokarska, Anastasiia - A/C.3/78/SR.51
UN. General Assembly. 3rd Committee. Rapporteur
Poveda Brito, Robert Alexander (Venezuela (Bolivarian Republic of)) - A/78/PV.50
UN. General Assembly. 3rd Committee. Secretary
Mahmassani, Ziad - A/C.3/78/SR.47

CRIME PREVENTION (Agenda item 107) (continued)

UN Office on Drugs and Crime. New York Office
Schantz, Delphine - A/C.3/78/SR.5
United Kingdom
Reyes, Gaia - A/C.3/78/SR.51
United States
Eyrich, Kara - A/C.3/78/SR.47
Johnson, Timothy J. - A/C.3/78/SR.56
Merron, Eric - A/C.3/78/SR.5
Uruguay
González Hernández, Gabriela Lilián - A/C.3/78/SR.6
Venezuela (Bolivarian Republic of)
Poveda Brito, Robert Alexander - A/C.3/78/SR.6

CRIMES AGAINST HUMANITY (Agenda item 80)

Albania
Laboti, Shkëlqim - A/C.6/78/SR.11; A/C.6/78/SR.45
Algeria
Bouchedoub, Mohamed Faiz - A/C.6/78/SR.11; A/C.6/78/SR.39; A/C.6/78/SR.41; A/C.6/78/SR.43; A/C.6/78/SR.45
Argentina
López Ferrucci, Mariano Javier - A/C.6/78/SR.38
Mainero, Martín Juan - A/C.6/78/SR.10; A/C.6/78/SR.40; A/C.6/78/SR.41; A/C.6/78/SR.43; A/C.6/78/SR.44; A/C.6/78/SR.45
Armenia
Galstyan, Tigran - A/C.6/78/SR.11
Margaryan, Mher - A/C.6/78/SR.11
Melikyan, Varduhi - A/C.6/78/SR.41
Sarvarian, Arman - A/C.6/78/SR.39
Australia
Hutchison, Alexandra - A/C.6/78/SR.38; A/C.6/78/SR.41; A/C.6/78/SR.42; A/C.6/78/SR.43; A/C.6/78/SR.44; A/C.6/78/SR.45
Austria
Gorke, Maximilian - A/C.6/78/SR.9; A/C.6/78/SR.38; A/C.6/78/SR.40; A/C.6/78/SR.41; A/C.6/78/SR.43; A/C.6/78/SR.44; A/C.6/78/SR.45
Azerbaijan
Musayev, Tofig - A/C.6/78/SR.11
Bangladesh
Muhith, Muhammad A. - A/C.6/78/SR.10
Belarus
Evseenko, Pavel - A/C.6/78/SR.10
Belgium
Grandjean, Laurence - A/C.6/78/SR.9
Raes, Elisa de - A/C.6/78/SR.38; A/C.6/78/SR.45
Bolivia (Plurinational State of)
Ríos, Carmen Rosa - A/C.6/78/SR.10; A/C.6/78/SR.45
Brazil
Braoios, Victor Silveira - A/C.6/78/SR.9; A/C.6/78/SR.38; A/C.6/78/SR.40; A/C.6/78/SR.43
Sloboda, Pedro Muniz Pinto - A/C.6/78/SR.41; A/C.6/78/SR.44; A/C.6/78/SR.45

CRIMES AGAINST HUMANITY (Agenda item 80) (continued)

Bulgaria
Beshkova, Krassimira - A/C.6/78/SR.45
Burkina Faso
Ganou, Oumarou - A/C.6/78/SR.10
Cameroon
Nyanid, Zacharie Serge Raoul - A/C.6/78/SR.10; A/C.6/78/SR.39; A/C.6/78/SR.40; A/C.6/78/SR.41; A/C.6/78/SR.42; A/C.6/78/SR.43; A/C.6/78/SR.44; A/C.6/78/SR.47
Canada
Bourdon, Sarah - A/C.6/78/SR.44
Mead, Kevin Timothy - A/C.6/78/SR.38; A/C.6/78/SR.40; A/C.6/78/SR.42; A/C.6/78/SR.43
Chile
Hernández Chávez, José Juan - A/C.6/78/SR.11; A/C.6/78/SR.38; A/C.6/78/SR.41; A/C.6/78/SR.45
China
Geng, Shuang - A/C.6/78/SR.10
Li, Linlin - A/C.6/78/SR.38; A/C.6/78/SR.40
Ma, Yanbo - A/C.6/78/SR.42; A/C.6/78/SR.43; A/C.6/78/SR.44; A/C.6/78/SR.45
Colombia
Solano Ramírez, Lucía Teresa - A/C.6/78/SR.10; A/C.6/78/SR.39; A/C.6/78/SR.40; A/C.6/78/SR.41; A/C.6/78/SR.42; A/C.6/78/SR.43; A/C.6/78/SR.44; A/C.6/78/SR.45
Comunidade dos Países de Língua Portuguesa
Soares, Dionísio Da Costa Babo (Timor-Leste) - A/C.6/78/SR.45
Costa Rica
Chan Valverde, Maritza - A/C.6/78/SR.10
Cuba
Carral Castelo, Arianna - A/C.6/78/SR.39; A/C.6/78/SR.40
Peñalver Portal, Gerardo - A/C.6/78/SR.10
Cyprus
Pittakis, Theodoulos - A/C.6/78/SR.39; A/C.6/78/SR.41; A/C.6/78/SR.45
Denmark
Laursen, Erik - A/C.6/78/SR.41
Djibouti
Moussa, Moussa Mohamed - A/C.6/78/SR.11
Dominican Republic
Rodríguez Torres, Radhafil - A/C.6/78/SR.11
Ecuador
Escobar Ullauri, Pablo - A/C.6/78/SR.38
Egypt
Elhomosany, Mohamed Kamal Ali - A/C.6/78/SR.10
Nouh, Amr Mohamed Mosaad - A/C.6/78/SR.43; A/C.6/78/SR.47
Roshdy, Hussein Ossama Hussein Abdelrhman - A/C.6/78/SR.39; A/C.6/78/SR.41; A/C.6/78/SR.42; A/C.6/78/SR.44

CRIMES AGAINST HUMANITY (Agenda item 80) (continued)

El Salvador
Flores Soto, Ligia Lorena - A/C.6/78/SR.10; A/C.6/78/SR.39; A/C.6/78/SR.40; A/C.6/78/SR.42; A/C.6/78/SR.43; A/C.6/78/SR.45
Equatorial Guinea
Nze Mansogo, Estela Mercedes - A/C.6/78/SR.45
Eritrea
Essaias, Meron Habte - A/C.6/78/SR.10; A/C.6/78/SR.38; A/C.6/78/SR.41; A/C.6/78/SR.45; A/C.6/78/SR.47
Ethiopia
Dabesa, Kurabachew Tirfesa - A/C.6/78/SR.39; A/C.6/78/SR.41; A/C.6/78/SR.42
Minale, Lemlem Fiseha - A/C.6/78/SR.11
European Union
Jaiteh, Amadou (Gambia) - A/C.6/78/SR.9
Popan, Simona - A/C.6/78/SR.9; A/C.6/78/SR.38; A/C.6/78/SR.39; A/C.6/78/SR.41; A/C.6/78/SR.43; A/C.6/78/SR.44; A/C.6/78/SR.45
Finland
Lemmetty, Elina - A/C.6/78/SR.39
France
Dime-Labille, Diarra - A/C.6/78/SR.38; A/C.6/78/SR.40; A/C.6/78/SR.44
Wavrin, Hugo - A/C.6/78/SR.11; A/C.6/78/SR.42; A/C.6/78/SR.43
Gambia
Jaiteh, Amadou - A/C.6/78/SR.45; A/C.6/78/SR.47
Georgia
Abesadze, David - A/C.6/78/SR.44
Germany
Craemer, Cathrine - A/C.6/78/SR.45
Hasenau, Michael - A/C.6/78/SR.9; A/C.6/78/SR.38
Ghana
Korbieh, Solomon - A/C.6/78/SR.45
Group of Arab States
Alwasil, Abdulaziz M.O. (Saudi Arabia) - A/C.6/78/SR.38
Guatemala
Leal Matta, Edgar Daniel - A/C.6/78/SR.45; A/C.6/78/SR.46
Rodríguez Mancia, Carla María - A/C.6/78/SR.9
Haiti
Panier, Wisnique - A/C.6/78/SR.11; A/C.6/78/SR.45
Holy See
Caccia, Gabriele Giordano - A/C.6/78/SR.11; A/C.6/78/SR.39; A/C.6/78/SR.41; A/C.6/78/SR.45
Murphy, Robert David - A/C.6/78/SR.43; A/C.6/78/SR.44
Hungary
Vittay, Melinda - A/C.6/78/SR.9; A/C.6/78/SR.38; A/C.6/78/SR.40; A/C.6/78/SR.45
Iceland
Karlsdóttir, Helga Hronn - A/C.6/78/SR.44; A/C.6/78/SR.45
Sverrisdóttir, Anna Pála - A/C.6/78/SR.41; A/C.6/78/SR.46; A/C.6/78/SR.47

CRIMES AGAINST HUMANITY (Agenda item 80) (continued)

India
Bhat, Kajal - A/C.6/78/SR.10; A/C.6/78/SR.11; A/C.6/78/SR.38; A/C.6/78/SR.40; A/C.6/78/SR.42; A/C.6/78/SR.43; A/C.6/78/SR.44; A/C.6/78/SR.47
Indonesia
Aron, Andy - A/C.6/78/SR.11; A/C.6/78/SR.38; A/C.6/78/SR.39; A/C.6/78/SR.42
Sandiori, Sherley Mega - A/C.6/78/SR.44; A/C.6/78/SR.45
Iran (Islamic Republic of)
Aref, Yahya - A/C.6/78/SR.38; A/C.6/78/SR.40; A/C.6/78/SR.42; A/C.6/78/SR.43; A/C.6/78/SR.44; A/C.6/78/SR.45; A/C.6/78/SR.47
Heidari, Bahram - A/C.6/78/SR.10
Iraq
Al-Fatlawi, Abbas Kadhom Obaid - A/C.6/78/SR.38
Al-Hasani, Haider - A/C.6/78/SR.11
Ireland
Kirk, James - A/C.6/78/SR.10; A/C.6/78/SR.38; A/C.6/78/SR.39; A/C.6/78/SR.42; A/C.6/78/SR.43; A/C.6/78/SR.45
Israel
Cappon, Noam - A/C.6/78/SR.10; A/C.6/78/SR.11; A/C.6/78/SR.38
Heumann, Amit - A/C.6/78/SR.42; A/C.6/78/SR.44; A/C.6/78/SR.45
Italy
Franz, Silvio - A/C.6/78/SR.43
Milano, Enrico - A/C.6/78/SR.11; A/C.6/78/SR.38; A/C.6/78/SR.40; A/C.6/78/SR.41; A/C.6/78/SR.44; A/C.6/78/SR.45
Japan
Urano, Hibiki - A/C.6/78/SR.44
Yamashita, Yuhei - A/C.6/78/SR.39; A/C.6/78/SR.40; A/C.6/78/SR.42; A/C.6/78/SR.43
Jordan
Bisharat, Nadien Isam Fraih - A/C.6/78/SR.38; A/C.6/78/SR.40; A/C.6/78/SR.41; A/C.6/78/SR.44; A/C.6/78/SR.45
Habashneh, Ahmad Samir Fahim - A/C.6/78/SR.10
Kenya
Nyakoe, Catherine Nyaboke - A/C.6/78/SR.11; A/C.6/78/SR.43; A/C.6/78/SR.44; A/C.6/78/SR.47
Kuwait
Alenezi, Faisal G. - A/C.6/78/SR.11
Latvia
Cupika-Mavrina, Elvira - A/C.6/78/SR.9; A/C.6/78/SR.38; A/C.6/78/SR.39; A/C.6/78/SR.41
Lebanon
Hitti, Youssef - A/C.6/78/SR.11; A/C.6/78/SR.39; A/C.6/78/SR.41; A/C.6/78/SR.43; A/C.6/78/SR.44
Libya
Shibl, Maruan Naserdien Ali - A/C.6/78/SR.11
Liechtenstein
Hasler, Merhaba - A/C.6/78/SR.9; A/C.6/78/SR.40

CRIMES AGAINST HUMANITY (Agenda item 80) (continued)

Malaysia
Abd Karim, Nur Azura Binti - A/C.6/78/SR.10
Rizal, Nizhan Faraz Bin - A/C.6/78/SR.46
Mali
Dabo N'diaye, Djeneba - A/C.6/78/SR.39; A/C.6/78/SR.42; A/C.6/78/SR.47
Konfourou, Issa - A/C.6/78/SR.11
Malta
Kuymizakis, Adam - A/C.6/78/SR.40
Siman, Augustina - A/C.6/78/SR.10; A/C.6/78/SR.47
Mexico
Buenrostro Massieu, Alicia - A/C.6/78/SR.10; A/C.6/78/SR.45
Delgado Fernández, Sergio Emanuel - A/C.6/78/SR.44
Jiménez Alegría, Natalia - A/C.6/78/SR.38; A/C.6/78/SR.40; A/C.6/78/SR.47
Pérez Manríquez, Alfredo Uriel - A/C.6/78/SR.41; A/C.6/78/SR.43
Morocco
Lahsaini, Khalid - A/C.6/78/SR.39; A/C.6/78/SR.41
Mozambique
Saranga, Geraldo - A/C.6/78/SR.11
Myanmar
Tun, Kyaw Moe - A/C.6/78/SR.11
Netherlands (Kingdom of the)
Ensing, Janine - A/C.6/78/SR.38; A/C.6/78/SR.40; A/C.6/78/SR.41
Made, Angelique van der - A/C.6/78/SR.10
Riep, Elisabeth - A/C.6/78/SR.43; A/C.6/78/SR.44
Theeuwen, Wieteke Elisabeth Christina - A/C.6/78/SR.41
New Zealand
Janah, Naushyn - A/C.6/78/SR.39; A/C.6/78/SR.40; A/C.6/78/SR.42; A/C.6/78/SR.44
Russell, Zoe - A/C.6/78/SR.9
Nicaragua
Llano, Alina J. - A/C.6/78/SR.45
Nigeria
Ajayi, Eniola Olaitan - A/C.6/78/SR.11
Dakwak, Gloria - A/C.6/78/SR.38; A/C.6/78/SR.40; A/C.6/78/SR.41; A/C.6/78/SR.44; A/C.6/78/SR.45; A/C.6/78/SR.47
Norway
Bierling, Mirjam - A/C.6/78/SR.43
Pakistan
Ijaz, Rabia - A/C.6/78/SR.10; A/C.6/78/SR.11
Syed, Ansar Hussain Shah - A/C.6/78/SR.39; A/C.6/78/SR.41; A/C.6/78/SR.42; A/C.6/78/SR.44
Peru
Falconi, Alessandra - A/C.6/78/SR.10
Philippines
Arumpac-Marte, Azela Guerrero - A/C.6/78/SR.11; A/C.6/78/SR.40; A/C.6/78/SR.42
Lora-Santos, Leila Castillon - A/C.6/78/SR.38
Poland
Domagała, Przemysław - A/C.6/78/SR.45
Górzyńska, Marzena - A/C.6/78/SR.44
Szczerski, Krzysztof - A/C.6/78/SR.10

CRIMES AGAINST HUMANITY (Agenda item 80) (continued)

Portugal
Carvalho, Sergio Amaral Alves de - A/C.6/78/SR.38; A/C.6/78/SR.40; A/C.6/78/SR.45
Kowalski, Mateus - A/C.6/78/SR.42; A/C.6/78/SR.43; A/C.6/78/SR.44
Zacarias, Ana Paula - A/C.6/78/SR.10
Qatar
Al-Kaabi, Soud Abdulaziz - A/C.6/78/SR.10; A/C.6/78/SR.39
Al-Marri, Rashid Ali - A/C.6/78/SR.40; A/C.6/78/SR.43
Republic of Korea
Song, Miyoung - A/C.6/78/SR.38; A/C.6/78/SR.39; A/C.6/78/SR.41; A/C.6/78/SR.43; A/C.6/78/SR.44
Romania
Lungu, Alis - A/C.6/78/SR.11; A/C.6/78/SR.38; A/C.6/78/SR.42; A/C.6/78/SR.43; A/C.6/78/SR.44; A/C.6/78/SR.45; A/C.6/78/SR.47
Mocanu, Andreea - A/C.6/78/SR.40
Russian Federation
Skachkov, Evgeny A. - A/C.6/78/SR.11; A/C.6/78/SR.39; A/C.6/78/SR.41; A/C.6/78/SR.42; A/C.6/78/SR.43; A/C.6/78/SR.44; A/C.6/78/SR.45; A/C.6/78/SR.47
Rwanda
Shehata, Kyrollos - A/C.6/78/SR.39
Saudi Arabia
Alabdali, Ali - A/C.6/78/SR.42
Alamri, Hassan Mohammed A. - A/C.6/78/SR.11
Yankssar, Ahlam - A/C.6/78/SR.38
Senegal
Ndoye, Abdou - A/C.6/78/SR.10
Sierra Leone
Kamanda, George Shadrack - A/C.6/78/SR.44; A/C.6/78/SR.45
Kamara, Abass Salieu - A/C.6/78/SR.38; A/C.6/78/SR.41; A/C.6/78/SR.42
Kebe, Hawanatu - A/C.6/78/SR.43
Sowa, Amara Sheikh Mohammed - A/C.6/78/SR.11
Singapore
Khng, Nathaniel - A/C.6/78/SR.9; A/C.6/78/SR.39; A/C.6/78/SR.41; A/C.6/78/SR.42; A/C.6/78/SR.43; A/C.6/78/SR.44; A/C.6/78/SR.45; A/C.6/78/SR.47
Slovakia
Košuth, Matus - A/C.6/78/SR.10; A/C.6/78/SR.39; A/C.6/78/SR.40; A/C.6/78/SR.42; A/C.6/78/SR.45
Slovenia
Šebenik, Nataša - A/C.6/78/SR.10
South Africa
Joyini, Mathu - A/C.6/78/SR.10
Motsepe, Keke Mantsho - A/C.6/78/SR.39; A/C.6/78/SR.40; A/C.6/78/SR.42; A/C.6/78/SR.45
Spain
Jiménez de la Hoz, Ana - A/C.6/78/SR.45

CRIMES AGAINST HUMANITY (Agenda item 80) (continued)

Sri Lanka
Pieris, Peter Mohan Maithri - A/C.6/78/SR.10; A/C.6/78/SR.39; A/C.6/78/SR.42; A/C.6/78/SR.43; A/C.6/78/SR.44; A/C.6/78/SR.47
State of Palestine
Bamya, Majed - A/C.6/78/SR.11
Sayej, Loureen O.A. - A/C.6/78/SR.39; A/C.6/78/SR.41; A/C.6/78/SR.43; A/C.6/78/SR.44; A/C.6/78/SR.45
Sudan
Mohammed, Ammar Mohammed Mahmoud - A/C.6/78/SR.39
Sweden
Fielding, Julia - A/C.6/78/SR.9
Janfalk, Disa - A/C.6/78/SR.38
Switzerland
Rathe, Fanny Elizabeth - A/C.6/78/SR.10; A/C.6/78/SR.38; A/C.6/78/SR.40; A/C.6/78/SR.42; A/C.6/78/SR.43; A/C.6/78/SR.44; A/C.6/78/SR.45
Syrian Arab Republic
Khaddour, Mhd. Riyad - A/C.6/78/SR.11; A/C.6/78/SR.39; A/C.6/78/SR.40; A/C.6/78/SR.41; A/C.6/78/SR.42; A/C.6/78/SR.46
Thailand
Hanlumyuang, Thararut - A/C.6/78/SR.10
Jantarasombat, Panpailin - A/C.6/78/SR.42; A/C.6/78/SR.43
Tunisia
Ben Lagha, Adel - A/C.6/78/SR.10; A/C.6/78/SR.39
Türkiye
Güç, Eda - A/C.6/78/SR.11
Seymenoğlu, Melek Dilsen - A/C.6/78/SR.39; A/C.6/78/SR.41
Sirmen, Vedia - A/C.6/78/SR.44
Uraz, Onur - A/C.6/78/SR.42; A/C.6/78/SR.43
Uganda
Ikondere, Marvin - A/C.6/78/SR.47
Ukraine
Prytula, Mykola - A/C.6/78/SR.45
UN. Group of African States
Muhumuza, Duncan Laki (Uganda) - A/C.6/78/SR.9; A/C.6/78/SR.38
United Arab Emirates
Tantawy, Myan Medhat Anwar - A/C.6/78/SR.41
United Kingdom
Hollis, Jonathan Samuel - A/C.6/78/SR.10; A/C.6/78/SR.45
McIntyre, Colin Roger - A/C.6/78/SR.39
Woodifield, Mungo - A/C.6/78/SR.40; A/C.6/78/SR.42; A/C.6/78/SR.43; A/C.6/78/SR.44
United States
Genoversa-Wong, Bridget - A/C.6/78/SR.41; A/C.6/78/SR.43
Ghaus, Hawa - A/C.6/78/SR.40; A/C.6/78/SR.44
Simonoff, Mark - A/C.6/78/SR.9; A/C.6/78/SR.38; A/C.6/78/SR.45

CRIMES AGAINST HUMANITY (Agenda item 80) (continued)

Uruguay
Katz Pavlotzky, Alejandro Leonel - A/C.6/78/SR.11; A/C.6/78/SR.45
Viet Nam
Nguyen, Thi Ngoc Ha - A/C.6/78/SR.10
Yemen
Balobaid, Ali Mabkhot Salem - A/C.6/78/SR.11

CUBA—UNITED STATES (Agenda item 38)

Algeria
Bendjama, Amar - A/78/PV.24
Angola
Cruz, Francisco José da - A/78/PV.24
Argentina
Squeff, María del Carmen - A/78/PV.24
ASEAN
Gafoor, Burhan (Singapore) - A/78/PV.24
Barbados
Jackman, François - A/78/PV.26
Belarus
Evseenko, Pavel - A/78/PV.24
Belize
Fuller, Carlos C. - A/78/PV.26
Bolivia (Plurinational State of)
Pary Rodríguez, Diego - A/78/PV.26
Brazil
Danese, Sérgio França - A/78/PV.26
Cambodia
Eat, Sophea - A/78/PV.24
Caribbean Community
Rambally, Menissa (Saint Lucia) - A/78/PV.24
Chile
Narváez Ojeda, Paula - A/78/PV.26
China
Dai, Bing - A/78/PV.24
Colombia
Zalabata Torres, Leonor - A/78/PV.24
Congo
Gabi, Emery - A/78/PV.26
Coordinating Bureau of the Non-Aligned Countries
Aliyev, Yashar T. (Azerbaijan) - A/78/PV.24
Cuba
Rodríguez Parrilla, Bruno Eduardo - A/78/PV.26
Romero Puentes, Yusnier - A/78/PV.26
Democratic People's Republic of Korea
Kim, Song - A/78/PV.24
Dominica
Darroux, Kelver Dwight - A/78/PV.24
Egypt
Elshandawily, Ahmed - A/78/PV.26
Ethiopia
Anulo, Semalign Kebede - A/78/PV.24
European Union
Jiménez de la Hoz, Ana (Spain) - A/78/PV.26
Gabon
Koumba Pambo, Aurélie Flore - A/78/PV.26
Group of 77
Kwoba, Godfrey (Uganda) - A/78/PV.24

CUBA—UNITED STATES (Agenda item 38) (continued)

Group of Friends in Defence of the Charter of the United Nations
Tesfamariam, Sophia (Eritrea) - A/78/PV.24
Guyana
Rodrigues-Birkett, Carolyn - A/78/PV.24
Indonesia
Nasir, Arrmanatha Christiawan - A/78/PV.26
Iran (Islamic Republic of)
Sahraei, Mohammad Reza - A/78/PV.26
Jamaica
Wallace, Brian Christopher Manley - A/78/PV.26
Kenya
Kinyungu, Njambi - A/78/PV.24
Lao People's Democratic Republic
Vongnorkeo, Anouparb - A/78/PV.24
Malaysia
Omar, Khairi - A/78/PV.24
Mexico
Buenrostro Massieu, Alicia - A/78/PV.24
Namibia
Gantana, Audrey Fay - A/78/PV.24
Nicaragua
Hermida Castillo, Jaime - A/78/PV.26
Organisation of Islamic Cooperation
Laghdaf, Sidi Mohamed (Mauritania) - A/78/PV.24
Pakistan
Jadoon, Usman Iqbal - A/78/PV.26
Peru
Ugarelli, Luis F. - A/78/PV.26
Philippines
Lagdameo, Antonio Manuel Revilla - A/78/PV.26
Russian Federation
Nebenzia, Vasilii - A/78/PV.24
Saint Lucia
Rambally, Menissa - A/78/PV.24
Saint Vincent and the Grenadines
King, Inga Rhonda - A/78/PV.24
Sistema de la Integración Centroamericana
González López, Egriselda Aracely (El Salvador) - A/78/PV.24
Solomon Islands
Indu, Fiona - A/78/PV.26
South Africa
Joyini, Mathu - A/78/PV.24
Sri Lanka
Pieris, Peter Mohan Maithri - A/78/PV.26
Syrian Arab Republic
Altarsha, Elie - A/78/PV.24
Timor-Leste
Nunes, Karlito - A/78/PV.26
Trinidad and Tobago
Barman, Ordell Cedric - A/78/PV.24
UN. Group of African States
Milambo, Chola (Zambia) - A/78/PV.24
United Republic of Tanzania
Mwasota, Joseph Aron - A/78/PV.24
United States
Folmsbee, Paul - A/78/PV.26

CUBA—UNITED STATES (Agenda item 38) (continued)

Venezuela (Bolivarian Republic of)
Pérez Ayestarán, Joaquín Alberto - A/78/PV.24
Viet Nam
Dang, Hoang Giang - A/78/PV.24
Zimbabwe
Rupende, Tapiwa Roy - A/78/PV.24

CULTURE—DEVELOPMENT (Agenda item 19b)

Azerbaijan
Ahmadova, Billur - A/C.2/78/SR.11
Group of 77
Torres Seara, Dalia Marlen (Cuba) - A/C.2/78/SR.21
Mexico
Curzio Vila, Elena - A/C.2/78/SR.10
Philippines
Bregala, Dennis Borromeo - A/C.2/78/SR.11
UN. General Assembly. 2nd Committee. Rapporteur
Gatev, Ivaylo (Bulgaria) - A/78/PV.49
UNESCO
Minchenberg, Eliot - A/C.2/78/SR.10
United States
Kroeker-Maus, Faith - A/C.2/78/SR.23

CYBERCRIME (Agenda item 108)

Algeria
Hassani, Billel - A/C.3/78/SR.6
ASEAN
Gafoor, Burhan (Singapore) - A/C.3/78/SR.5
Belarus
Velichko, Irina - A/C.3/78/SR.5
Brazil
Dias, João Henrique Nascimento - A/C.3/78/SR.5
Cameroon
Banaken Elel, Nelly - A/C.3/78/SR.5
Caribbean Community
Wallace, Brian Christopher Manley (Jamaica) - A/C.3/78/SR.5
China
Liu, Han - A/C.3/78/SR.5
Colombia
Zalabata Torres, Leonor - A/C.3/78/SR.5
Costa Rica
Zavala Porras, Daniel Andrés - A/C.3/78/SR.6
Cuba
Valido Martínez, Yoangel - A/C.3/78/SR.5
Dominican Republic
Cedano, Joan Margarita - A/C.3/78/SR.6
Ecuador
Bravo, Karina - A/C.3/78/SR.5
Egypt
Mostafa Rizk, Heba - A/C.3/78/SR.6
Eritrea
Gebrekidan, Zebib - A/C.3/78/SR.6
European Union
Schuller, Simone - A/C.3/78/SR.5
Ghana
Anyanah, Bismark - A/C.3/78/SR.6
Guatemala
Rodríguez Mancia, Carla María - A/C.3/78/SR.5
Holy See
Murphy, Robert David - A/C.3/78/SR.6
Indonesia
Pella, Blandina Ruth Viditha Adeleide - A/C.3/78/SR.6
Iran (Islamic Republic of)
Arab Bafrani, Fatemeh - A/C.3/78/SR.5

CYBERCRIME (Agenda item 108) (continued)

Japan
Ono, Sho - A/C.3/78/SR.6
Jordan
Habashneh, Ahmad Samir Fahim - A/C.3/78/SR.5
Luxembourg
Wald, Julien - A/C.3/78/SR.6
Malaysia
Rizal, Nizhan Faraz Bin - A/C.3/78/SR.5
Mexico
Reza Bautista, Mauricio - A/C.3/78/SR.5
Morocco
Bouchikhi, Hanaa - A/C.3/78/SR.6
Nicaragua
Pichardo Urbina, Eleane Yaoska - A/C.3/78/SR.6
Pakistan
Khan, Mohammad Aamir - A/C.3/78/SR.5
Poland
Stadnicka, Małgorzata - A/C.3/78/SR.5
Russian Federation
Leonidchenko, Sergey A. - A/C.3/78/SR.5
Saudi Arabia
Shaker, Mohammed Amin - A/C.3/78/SR.5
Sierra Leone
Yajah, Christian Fayia - A/C.3/78/SR.6
Singapore
Jesudason, Joshua E. - A/C.3/78/SR.5
South Africa
Sekonyana, Ngako Elphus - A/C.3/78/SR.5
Sovereign Order of Malta
Maenpaa, Conor C. - A/C.3/78/SR.6
Thailand
Hsieh, Nichamon May - A/C.3/78/SR.5
Türkiye
Aydil, İsmail - A/C.3/78/SR.6
UN. General Assembly. 3rd Committee. Rapporteur
Poveda Brito, Robert Alexander (Venezuela (Bolivarian Republic of)) - A/78/PV.50
UN Office on Drugs and Crime. New York Office
Schantz, Delphine - A/C.3/78/SR.5
United States
Heartney, Edward - A/C.3/78/SR.5
Merron, Eric - A/C.3/78/SR.5
Uruguay
González Hernández, Gabriela Lilián - A/C.3/78/SR.6
Venezuela (Bolivarian Republic of)
Poveda Brito, Robert Alexander - A/C.3/78/SR.6

DECOLONIZATION (Agenda item 58)

Angola
Luemba, Mateus Pedro - A/C.4/78/SR.6
Argentina
Alvarez, Maximiliano Javier - A/C.4/78/SR.9
Bahrain
Aljalahma, Shaikha - A/C.4/78/SR.7
Bangladesh
Shatil, Toufiq Islam - A/C.4/78/SR.2

DECOLONIZATION (Agenda item 58) (continued)

Bolivia (Plurinational State of)
Pary Rodríguez, Diego - A/C.4/78/SR.2
Botswana
Mokhawa, Gladys - A/C.4/78/SR.8
Burkina Faso
Ganou, Oumarou - A/C.4/78/SR.7
China
Geng, Shuang - A/C.4/78/SR.8
Community of Latin American and Caribbean States
King, Inga Rhonda (Saint Vincent and the Grenadines) - A/C.4/78/SR.7
Comoros
Oussein, Kadim - A/C.4/78/SR.9
Congo
Manzeri Ngondo, Jean Claude - A/C.4/78/SR.7
Costa Rica
Chan Valverde, Maritza - A/C.4/78/SR.7
Côte d'Ivoire
Moriko, Tiémoko - A/C.4/78/SR.2
Cuba
Fernández Palacios, Yumirka - A/C.4/78/SR.8
Romero Puentes, Yusnier - A/C.4/78/SR.2
Democratic Republic of the Congo
Mukongo Ngay, Zénon - A/C.4/78/SR.9
Ecuador
Montalvo Sosa, Andrés Efren - A/C.4/78/SR.7
El Salvador
González López, Egriselda Aracely - A/C.4/78/SR.2
Equatorial Guinea
Edjo Memba, Juan De Dios - A/C.4/78/SR.7
Ethiopia
Kassaye, Yoseph - A/C.4/78/SR.8
Gabon
Ayoune, Lia Berthiana Bouanga - A/C.4/78/SR.9
Ghana
Nyarku, Felix Akom - A/C.4/78/SR.8
Group of Friends in Defence of the Charter of the United Nations
Pérez Ayestarán, Joaquín Alberto (Venezuela (Bolivarian Republic of)) - A/C.4/78/SR.2
Guyana
Rodrigues-Birkett, Carolyn - A/C.4/78/SR.7
Honduras
Rivera Reyes, Isabella Regina - A/C.4/78/SR.2
India
Birdi, Nitish - A/C.4/78/SR.7
Indonesia
Dhanutirto, Mariska Dwianti - A/C.4/78/SR.7
Iran (Islamic Republic of)
Ghelich, Vahid - A/C.4/78/SR.7; A/C.4/78/SR.9
Sahraei, Mohammad Reza - A/C.4/78/SR.8
Iraq
Al-Fatlawi, Abbas Kadhom Obaid - A/C.4/78/SR.8
Israel
Shapir Ben Naftaly, Reut - A/C.4/78/SR.7; A/C.4/78/SR.8
Kiribati
Tito, Teburoro - A/C.4/78/SR.8

DECOLONIZATION (Agenda item 58) (continued)
Kuwait
Alenezi, Faisal G. - A/C.4/78/SR.8
Lesotho
Nena, Matete - A/C.4/78/SR.8
Melanesian Spearhead Group
Sarufa, Fred (Papua New Guinea) - A/C.4/78/SR.6
Mexico
Cisneros Chávez, José de Jesús - A/C.4/78/SR.2
Mozambique
Buanahagi, Tarcísio Baltazar - A/C.4/78/SR.8
Namibia
Gertze, Neville Melvin - A/C.4/78/SR.7
Nepal
Ray, Kaushal Kishor - A/C.4/78/SR.6
Pakistan
Akram, Munir - A/C.4/78/SR.2
Khan, Naeem Sabir - A/C.4/78/SR.7
Paraguay
Pereira Sosa, José Eduardo - A/C.4/78/SR.7
Peru
Ugarelli, Luis F. - A/C.4/78/SR.7
Qatar
Al-thani, Jassim Abdulaziz J.A. - A/C.4/78/SR.2
Russian Federation
Ilichev, Petr - A/C.4/78/SR.2
Saint Lucia
Henry, Carlton Ronnie - A/C.4/78/SR.7
Saint Vincent and the Grenadines
Andrews, Lasana - A/C.4/78/SR.8
Saudi Arabia
Alamri, Hassan Mohammed A. - A/C.4/78/SR.7
Serbia
Vujačić, Dušan - A/C.4/78/SR.8
Sierra Leone
Alghali, Francess Piagie - A/C.4/78/SR.7
Sistema de la Integración Centroamericana
González López, Egriselda Aracely (El Salvador) - A/C.4/78/SR.6
Syrian Arab Republic
Baghdadi, Mohannad - A/C.4/78/SR.7
Timor-Leste
Nunes, Karlito - A/C.4/78/SR.2
Uganda
Kwoba, Godfrey - A/C.4/78/SR.8
UN. General Assembly. Special Political and Decolonization Committee (4th Committee). Rapporteur
Dhanutirto, Mariska Dwianti (Indonesia) - A/78/PV.45
UN. Special Committee of 24. Chair
Rambally, Menissa (Saint Lucia) - A/C.4/78/SR.2
UN. Special Committee of 24. Vice-Chair
Nasir, Arrmanatha Christiawan (Indonesia) - A/C.4/78/SR.2
United Arab Emirates
Al-Ali, Maryam - A/C.4/78/SR.7
Matar, Shahd Jamal Yousuf - A/C.4/78/SR.8
Mohammad, Fatema Yousuf Ibrahim - A/C.4/78/SR.7; A/C.4/78/SR.9

DECOLONIZATION (Agenda item 58) (continued)
United Kingdom
Meyrick, Phoebe - A/C.4/78/SR.9
Woodifield, Mungo - A/C.4/78/SR.8
United States
Kris, Robert - A/C.4/78/SR.7
Uruguay
Amorín, Carlos Daniel - A/C.4/78/SR.2
Venezuela (Bolivarian Republic of)
Pérez Ayestarán, Joaquín Alberto - A/C.4/78/SR.2
Viet Nam
Nguyen, Hoang Nguyen - A/C.4/78/SR.2

DECOLONIZATION—UN SYSTEM (Agenda item 56)
Argentina
Alvarez, Maximiliano Javier - A/C.4/78/SR.9
Australia
Volkov, Alice - A/C.4/78/SR.9
UN. General Assembly. Special Political and Decolonization Committee (4th Committee). Rapporteur
Dhanutirto, Mariska Dwianti (Indonesia) - A/78/PV.45
UN. Special Committee of 24. Chair
Rambally, Menissa (Saint Lucia) - A/C.4/78/SR.2
UN. Special Committee of 24. Vice-Chair
Nasir, Arrmanatha Christiawan (Indonesia) - A/C.4/78/SR.2
United Kingdom
Meyrick, Phoebe - A/C.4/78/SR.9

DEMOCRACY (Agenda item 71b)
Cameroon
Wainwel, Gwedji Doris - A/C.3/78/SR.28
China
Yang, Fan - A/C.3/78/SR.28
Coordinating Bureau of the Non-Aligned Countries
Novruz, Leyla (Azerbaijan) - A/C.3/78/SR.28
Cuba
González Behmaras, Alejandro - A/C.3/78/SR.48
Lamigueiro Cañedo, Ivette - A/C.3/78/SR.28
Valido Martínez, Yoangel - A/C.3/78/SR.28
Iran (Islamic Republic of)
Arab Bafrani, Fatemeh - A/C.3/78/SR.28
Malaysia
Escopper Zumilla, Michael Jawa - A/C.3/78/SR.28
Russian Federation
Kuzmenkov, Stepan Y. - A/C.3/78/SR.28
Sovereign Order of Malta
Scalabrini-McKellar, Tobias - A/C.3/78/SR.28
UN. Human Rights Council. Independent Expert on the Promotion of a Democratic and Equitable International Order
Sewanyana, Livingstone - A/C.3/78/SR.28
United States
Merron, Eric - A/C.3/78/SR.48

DESERTIFICATION—TREATIES (Agenda item 18e)

Côte d'Ivoire
Moriko, Tiémoko - A/C.2/78/SR.15
Ethiopia
Shiferaw, Girum Getachew - A/C.2/78/SR.15
Group of 77
Torres Seara, Dalia Marlen (Cuba) - A/C.2/78/SR.21
Iran (Islamic Republic of)
Jalili, Tahereh - A/C.2/78/SR.13
Iraq
Jasim, Saber Ahmed - A/C.2/78/SR.13
Mongolia
Vorshilov, Enkhbold - A/C.2/78/SR.13
Secretariat of the Convention to Combat Desertification. Deputy Executive Secretary
Meza Murillo, Andrea - A/C.2/78/SR.12
UN. General Assembly. 2nd Committee. Rapporteur
Gatev, Ivaylo (Bulgaria) - A/78/PV.49
United States
Kroeker-Maus, Faith - A/C.2/78/SR.23

DEVELOPMENT COOPERATION—MIDDLE-INCOME COUNTRIES (Agenda item 19c)

Belarus
Kavaleuskaya, Alena - A/C.2/78/SR.10
Colombia
Murillo Ferrer, Jorge Adrián - A/C.2/78/SR.23
Ríos Serna, Manuela - A/C.2/78/SR.10
Costa Rica
Zamora Zumbado, Leticia María - A/C.2/78/SR.11
Group of 77
Torres Seara, Dalia Marlen (Cuba) - A/C.2/78/SR.21
Indonesia
Prabowo, Hari - A/C.2/78/SR.11
Like-Minded Group of Supporters of Middle-Income Countries
Hamdouni, Meryem (Morocco) - A/C.2/78/SR.10
Namibia
Gantana, Audrey Fay - A/C.2/78/SR.10
Philippines
Bregala, Dennis Borromeo - A/C.2/78/SR.11
Russian Federation
Aristov, Dmitry S. - A/C.2/78/SR.10
Saudi Arabia
Shaker, Mohammed Amin - A/C.2/78/SR.10
UN. Assistant Secretary-General for Economic Development
Hanif, Navid - A/C.2/78/SR.10
UN. General Assembly. 2nd Committee. Rapporteur
Gatev, Ivaylo (Bulgaria) - A/78/PV.49
United States
Kroeker-Maus, Faith - A/C.2/78/SR.23

DEVELOPMENT EDUCATION (Agenda item 18g)

Group of 77
Torres Seara, Dalia Marlen (Cuba) - A/C.2/78/SR.21
Holy See
Caccia, Gabriele Giordano - A/C.2/78/SR.15
UN. General Assembly. 2nd Committee. Rapporteur
Gatev, Ivaylo (Bulgaria) - A/78/PV.49
UNESCO
Minchenberg, Eliot - A/C.2/78/SR.12
United States
Sharma, Deeksha - A/C.2/78/SR.22

DEVELOPMENT FINANCE (Agenda item 16b)

Alliance of Small Island States
Bartley, Matilda (Samoa) - A/C.2/78/SR.8
Angola
Cruz, Francisco José da - A/C.2/78/SR.9
ASEAN
Nasir, Arrmanatha Christiawan (Indonesia) - A/C.2/78/SR.8
Bahamas
Mott, T'Sean - A/C.2/78/SR.11
Bangladesh
Hossain, Faruk - A/C.2/78/SR.9
Cameroon
Banaken Elel, Nelly - A/C.2/78/SR.9
Canada
Ong, Shirley - A/C.2/78/SR.8
Caribbean Community
Wallace, Brian Christopher Manley (Jamaica) - A/C.2/78/SR.8
Colombia
Tickner, Arlene Beth - A/C.2/78/SR.8
Costa Rica
Zamora Zumbado, Leticia María - A/C.2/78/SR.9
Côte d'Ivoire
Ipo, Gbolié Desiré Wulfran - A/C.2/78/SR.9
Cuba
Guevara Rodríguez, Adiel - A/C.2/78/SR.8
Egypt
Abdelaal, Ahmed Magdy Mohamed Rashad - A/C.2/78/SR.9
El Salvador
González López, Egriselda Aracely - A/C.2/78/SR.8
Ethiopia
Muktar, Anwar - A/C.2/78/SR.11
Group of 77
Torres Seara, Dalia Marlen (Cuba) - A/C.2/78/SR.8; A/C.2/78/SR.21
Group of Friends in Defence of the Charter of the United Nations
Pérez Ayestarán, Joaquín Alberto (Venezuela (Bolivarian Republic of)) - A/C.2/78/SR.8
Group of Landlocked Developing Countries
Mmalane, Katlego Boase (Botswana) - A/C.2/78/SR.8
Group of Least Developed Countries
Ray, Kaushal Kishor (Nepal) - A/C.2/78/SR.8

DEVELOPMENT FINANCE (Agenda item 16b) (continued)

Guyana
Doimen, Tash van - A/C.2/78/SR.9
Indonesia
Prabowo, Hari - A/C.2/78/SR.9
Iran (Islamic Republic of)
Teymourpour, Nooshin - A/C.2/78/SR.8
Kenya
Nzumbu, Christine - A/C.2/78/SR.9
Like-Minded Group of Supporters of Middle-Income Countries
Hamdouni, Meryem (Morocco) - A/C.2/78/SR.8
Malaysia
Adnan, Yang Aishah Binti - A/C.2/78/SR.9
Mexico
Reta Haddad, Rodolfo - A/C.2/78/SR.9
Namibia
Naanda, Anne - A/C.2/78/SR.9
Nicaragua
Hermida Castillo, Jaime - A/C.2/78/SR.9
Nigeria
Gana Alkali, Baba - A/C.2/78/SR.9
Norway
Lovold, Andreas - A/C.2/78/SR.11
Pakistan
Shafique, Umar - A/C.2/78/SR.9
Russian Federation
Kardash, Viktoriia E. - A/C.2/78/SR.9
South Africa
Seedat, Ahmed Hoosen - A/C.2/78/SR.11
Spain
Martín Couce, Adrián - A/C.2/78/SR.9
Thailand
Sapkul, Louismongkol - A/C.2/78/SR.9
Trinidad and Tobago
Budhu, Vladamir - A/C.2/78/SR.9
UN. Department of Economic and Social Affairs. Financing for Sustainable Development Office. Policy Analysis and Development Branch. Chief
Spiegel, Shari - A/C.2/78/SR.8
UN. General Assembly. 2nd Committee. Rapporteur
Gatev, Ivaylo (Bulgaria) - A/78/PV.49
UNIDO
Klose, Christoph - A/C.2/78/SR.11
United Kingdom
Dix, Laura Gabrielle - A/C.2/78/SR.9
United States
Armbruster, Thomas - A/C.2/78/SR.21
Hamilton, Jim - A/C.2/78/SR.22
Zambia
Boma, Regina Chama - A/C.2/78/SR.9

DEVELOPMENT FINANCE—CONFERENCES (Agenda item 17)

Brazil
Bayer, Guilherme Marquardt - A/78/PV.90
Canada
Maillé, Béatrice - A/C.2/78/SR.25
Ong, Shirley - A/78/PV.90

DEVELOPMENT FINANCE—CONFERENCES (Agenda item 17) (continued)

European Union
Kaiser, Annette Karoline (Germany) - A/78/PV.90
Pougin de La Maisonneuve, Axel - A/C.2/78/SR.25
Group of 77
Torres Seara, Dalia Marlen (Cuba) - A/C.2/78/SR.21
Guyana
Doimen, Tash van - A/C.2/78/SR.9
India
Gahlot, Petal - A/C.2/78/SR.9
Indonesia
Irawati Mamesah, Febrian - A/78/PV.90
Mexico
Mendoza Elguea, Sylvia Paola - A/78/PV.90
Russian Federation
Fondukov, Pavel A. - A/78/PV.90
Spain
Jiménez de la Hoz, Ana - A/C.2/78/SR.25
Timor-Leste
Soares, Dionísio Da Costa Babo - A/78/PV.90
Trinidad and Tobago
Budhu, Vladamir - A/C.2/78/SR.9
Türkiye
İstemil Aydil, Alara - A/78/PV.90
UN. Department for General Assembly and Conference Management
Buyanover, Gal - A/78/PV.69
UN. Department of Economic and Social Affairs. Financing for Sustainable Development Office. Policy Analysis and Development Branch. Chief
Spiegel, Shari - A/C.2/78/SR.8
UN. General Assembly. 2nd Committee. Rapporteur
Gatev, Ivaylo (Bulgaria) - A/78/PV.49
United Kingdom
Boyd-Lee, Katherine Suzanne Jenkins - A/78/PV.90
United States
Marks, Rose Ann - A/78/PV.90; A/C.2/78/SR.25
Viet Nam
Nguyen, Hoang Nguyen - A/78/PV.90

DIAMONDS—FUELLING CONFLICT (Agenda item 30)

Botswana
Badubi, Ronald Seabo - A/78/PV.65
European Union
Curran, Clayton - A/78/PV.65
Russian Federation
Repkin, Alexander V. - A/78/PV.65
United Arab Emirates
Abushahab, Mohamed Issa - A/78/PV.65
United Kingdom
Kriss, Benjamin - A/78/PV.65
United Republic of Tanzania
Kattanga, Hussein A. - A/78/PV.65
United States
Lelek, Julia - A/78/PV.65
Zimbabwe
Chimbindi, Albert Ranganai - A/78/PV.65

DISAPPEARANCE OF PERSONS (Agenda item 71b)

Argentina
  Oddone, Fabián - A/C.3/78/SR.22
  Squeff, María del Carmen - A/C.3/78/SR.50
Belgium
  Bauwens, Gilles - A/C.3/78/SR.22
Chile
  Fernández Carter, Catalina - A/C.3/78/SR.22
China
  Zhang, Qiuruo - A/C.3/78/SR.22
Colombia
  Paredes Campaña, Jairo Andrés - A/C.3/78/SR.22
Croatia
  Andrić, Katarina - A/C.3/78/SR.22
Democratic People's Republic of Korea
  Kim, Nam Hyok - A/C.3/78/SR.22
European Union
  Szelivanov, Julia - A/C.3/78/SR.22
France
  Dumas, Anouk - A/C.3/78/SR.22
Iraq
  Al-Khaqani, Hassan Jabbar - A/C.3/78/SR.22
Japan
  Miyamoto, Sogaku - A/C.3/78/SR.22
Mexico
  Buenrostro Massieu, Alicia - A/C.3/78/SR.22
Morocco
  Bouchikhi, Hanaa - A/C.3/78/SR.22
Myanmar
  Tun, Kyaw Moe - A/C.3/78/SR.22
Pakistan
  Qureshi, Hadeeqa - A/C.3/78/SR.22
Sovereign Order of Malta
  O'Hara Rusckowski, Deborah - A/C.3/78/SR.22
Syrian Arab Republic
  Altarsha, Elie - A/C.3/78/SR.22
Ukraine
  Mudrenko, Nataliia - A/C.3/78/SR.22
UN. Assistant Secretary-General for Human Rights
  Brands Kehris, Ilze - A/C.3/78/SR.18
UN. Committee on Enforced Disappearances. Rapporteur
  Albán Alencastro, Juan Pablo - A/C.3/78/SR.22
UN. Human Rights Council. Working Group on Enforced or Involuntary Disappearances. Chair
  Baldé, Aua - A/C.3/78/SR.22
United States
  Heartney, Edward - A/C.3/78/SR.22
  Johnson, Timothy J. - A/C.3/78/SR.50

DISARMAMENT—GENERAL AND COMPLETE (Agenda item 99)

Algeria
  Lebbaz, Larbi Abdelfattah - A/C.1/78/PV.19; A/C.1/78/PV.30
Argentina
  Guerra, Hugo Emmanuel - A/C.1/78/PV.18; A/C.1/78/PV.28

DISARMAMENT—GENERAL AND COMPLETE (Agenda item 99) (continued)

Armenia
  Grigoryan, Andranik - A/C.1/78/PV.24
Arms Control Association (Washington, D.C.)
  Kuramitsu, Shizuka - A/78/PV.105
ASEAN
  Philakone, Khamphinh (Lao People's Democratic Republic) - A/78/PV.105
  Vongnorkeo, Anouparb (Lao People's Democratic Republic) - A/C.1/78/PV.14
Australia
  Carr, Michelle - A/C.1/78/PV.19; A/C.1/78/PV.28
  Della-porta, Demi Heather See - A/C.1/78/PV.30
  Larsen, James - A/78/PV.106
Austria
  Edtmayer, Matthias - A/C.1/78/PV.27; A/C.1/78/PV.30
  Kmentt, Alexander - A/C.1/78/PV.18
  Pretterhofer, Stefan - A/78/PV.105
Azerbaijan
  Gurbanov, Ilgar - A/C.1/78/PV.24
Brazil
  Damico, Flávio Soares - A/C.1/78/PV.19
  Szatmari, Roberto Wazima - A/C.1/78/PV.28; A/C.1/78/PV.30
Burundi
  Maniratanga, Zéphyrin - A/78/PV.105
Cabo Verde
  Romualdo, Tania Serafim Yvonne - A/78/PV.106
Cameroon
  Nyanid, Zacharie Serge Raoul - A/C.1/78/PV.30
Canada
  Fetz, Thomas - A/C.1/78/PV.23; A/C.1/78/PV.30
  Svadjian, Méliné - A/C.1/78/PV.19
  Tomlinson, Bryan - A/C.1/78/PV.15
Chile
  Vidal Mercado, Jorge Andrés - A/C.1/78/PV.18; A/C.1/78/PV.23
China
  Lai, Haiyang - A/C.1/78/PV.21
  Ren, Hongyan - A/78/PV.105
  Shen, Jian - A/C.1/78/PV.19; A/C.1/78/PV.20; A/C.1/78/PV.23; A/C.1/78/PV.30
  Sun, Yiliang - A/C.1/78/PV.26
  Zhang, Junjie - A/C.1/78/PV.28
Colombia
  Quintero Correa, Nohra María - A/C.1/78/PV.18
Community of Latin American and Caribbean States
  Flores, Mary Elizabeth (Honduras) - A/78/PV.105
Coordinating Bureau of the Non-Aligned Countries
  Kristanti, Maria Benedicta Diah (Indonesia) - A/C.1/78/PV.17
Costa Rica
  Chan Valverde, Maritza - A/C.1/78/PV.18
Cuba
  Gómez Sardiñas, Yiliam - A/C.1/78/PV.19
  Romero López, Rosanis - A/C.1/78/PV.30
Democratic People's Republic of Korea
  Kim, In Chol - A/C.1/78/PV.19; A/C.1/78/PV.21

DISARMAMENT—GENERAL AND COMPLETE (Agenda item 99) (continued)

Egypt
Ahmed, Amr Essameldin Sadek - A/C.1/78/PV.23; A/C.1/78/PV.30
Hegazy, Abdelrhman Mohamed Farid - A/C.1/78/PV.18; A/C.1/78/PV.28
El Salvador
Rodríguez Acosta, Julia Elizabeth - A/C.1/78/PV.18
European Union
Hansen, Steen Malthe - A/78/PV.105
Karczmarz, Michał - A/C.1/78/PV.18; A/C.1/78/PV.21
Sánchez de Lerín García-Ovies, Ignacio (Spain) - A/C.1/78/PV.30
Finland
Voionmaa, Lauri - A/C.1/78/PV.19
France
Petit, Camille - A/C.1/78/PV.18; A/C.1/78/PV.26; A/C.1/78/PV.30
Friends of the Comprehensive Nuclear Test-Ban Treaty
Yamazaki, Kazuyuki (Japan) - A/78/PV.105
George Washington University (Washington, D.C.)
Squassoni, Sharon A. - A/78/PV.105
Germany
Göbel, Thomas - A/C.1/78/PV.18
Ghana
Kesse Antwi, Linda - A/78/PV.106; A/C.1/78/PV.30
Greece
Christoglou, Konstantinos - A/C.1/78/PV.19
Group of Arab States
Aldahhak, Koussay Abduljabbar (Syrian Arab Republic) - A/78/PV.105
Alqaisi, Sultan Natheir Mustafa (Jordan) - A/C.1/78/PV.19; A/C.1/78/PV.21; A/C.1/78/PV.23
Holy See
Caccia, Gabriele Giordano - A/78/PV.106
Hungary
Svercsok, Szabolcs - A/C.1/78/PV.26
IAEA
Okeke, Vivian Nwunaku Rose - A/78/PV.105
India
Kulkarni, Maitrey - A/C.1/78/PV.30
Parihar, Rajesh - A/C.1/78/PV.19
Ray, Anupam - A/C.1/78/PV.26; A/C.1/78/PV.28
Indonesia
Kristanti, Maria Benedicta Diah - A/C.1/78/PV.30
Sirie, Mochammad Iqbal - A/C.1/78/PV.28
Iran (Islamic Republic of)
Eshragh Jahromi, Asadollah - A/C.1/78/PV.19
Ghorbanpour Najafabadi, Mohammad - A/C.1/78/PV.19; A/C.1/78/PV.21; A/C.1/78/PV.24; A/C.1/78/PV.28; A/C.1/78/PV.30
Jalil Iravani, Amir Saeid - A/78/PV.106
Rahimi Majd, Hassan - A/78/PV.106
Iraq
Al-Sadar, Hamzah - A/C.1/78/PV.19
Al-Taie, Sarmad Muwafaq Mohammed - A/C.1/78/PV.24; A/C.1/78/PV.30

DISARMAMENT—GENERAL AND COMPLETE (Agenda item 99) (continued)

Ireland
Doyle, Ciaran James - A/C.1/78/PV.22
Israel
Shapir Ben Naftaly, Reut - A/78/PV.106
Sharoni, Benjamin - A/C.1/78/PV.19; A/C.1/78/PV.24; A/C.1/78/PV.28
Italy
Gai, Elena - A/C.1/78/PV.19
Japan
Namekawa, Hirochika - A/C.1/78/PV.28; A/C.1/78/PV.30
Ogasawara, Ichiro - A/C.1/78/PV.18
Jordan
Alqaisi, Sultan Natheir Mustafa - A/C.1/78/PV.19; A/C.1/78/PV.23
Kazakhstan
Syrymbet, Zhangeldy - A/C.1/78/PV.12
Umarov, Kairat - A/78/PV.105
Kiribati
Ciobanu, Christian Niculae - A/C.1/78/PV.13
Tito, Teburoro - A/78/PV.106; A/C.1/78/PV.25
Kuwait
Alsharhan, Reem - A/C.1/78/PV.24
Latvia
Filipsons, Peteris - A/C.1/78/PV.30
Lesotho
Nena, Matete - A/C.1/78/PV.19
Marshall Islands
Kabua, Amatlain Elizabeth - A/C.1/78/PV.26
Silk, John M. - A/78/PV.105
Mauritania
Laghdaf, Sidi Mohamed - A/78/PV.105
Mexico
Sánchez Kiesslich, Eduardo Alcibiades - A/C.1/78/PV.18; A/C.1/78/PV.30
Vasconcelos y Cruz, Héctor Enrique - A/78/PV.105
Netherlands (Kingdom of the)
Bosch, Robert in den - A/C.1/78/PV.18
New Zealand
Clutterbuck, Nicholas - A/C.1/78/PV.11
De Schot, Jikita - A/C.1/78/PV.19; A/C.1/78/PV.30
Nigeria
Endoni, Syndoph Paebi - A/78/PV.106
Norway
Andersen, Tor Henrik - A/C.1/78/PV.19; A/C.1/78/PV.30
Brattested, Merete Fjeld - A/78/PV.105
Hunskaar, Maria - A/C.1/78/PV.15
Pakistan
Ahmed, Husham - A/C.1/78/PV.19; A/C.1/78/PV.20
Gohar, Sarfaraz Ahmed - A/C.1/78/PV.30
Sarwani, Gul Qaiser - A/C.1/78/PV.26; A/C.1/78/PV.28
Philippines
Lipana, Diane Shayne Dela Fuente - A/78/PV.105; A/C.1/78/PV.20
Poland
Joniec, Katarzyna - A/C.1/78/PV.28

DISARMAMENT—GENERAL AND COMPLETE (Agenda item 99) (continued)

Preparatory Commission for the Comprehensive Nuclear Test-Ban Treaty Organization. Executive Secretary
Floyd, Robert - A/78/PV.105
Republic of Korea
Kim, Sunghoon - A/C.1/78/PV.28
Yoon, Seong-mee - A/C.1/78/PV.18; A/C.1/78/PV.19
Russian Federation
Belousov, Andrey I. - A/C.1/78/PV.19; A/C.1/78/PV.23; A/C.1/78/PV.24; A/C.1/78/PV.28; A/C.1/78/PV.30
Glukhov, Dmitry - A/78/PV.106
Saudi Arabia
Moharram, Wajdi Hassan M. - A/C.1/78/PV.21; A/C.1/78/PV.23; A/C.1/78/PV.30
Slovenia
Ponikvar Velázquez, Jasna - A/C.1/78/PV.19
South Africa
Lagardien, Yaseen - A/C.1/78/PV.28
Spain
Rosario Vela, Manuel Jesús del - A/C.1/78/PV.19
Sri Lanka
Pieris, Peter Mohan Maithri - A/78/PV.105
State of Palestine
Kasabri, Qais Z.F. - A/C.1/78/PV.23; A/C.1/78/PV.24
Switzerland
Haegen, Laurin van der - A/C.1/78/PV.19
Syrian Arab Republic
Al Ashkar, Adib - A/C.1/78/PV.23; A/C.1/78/PV.30
Thailand
Khundee, Wichayaporn - A/C.1/78/PV.26
Türkiye
Çetin, Ahmet Erman - A/C.1/78/PV.28
Ukraine
Hayovyshyn, Khrystyna - A/78/PV.106
Zlenko, Anatoli M. - A/C.1/78/PV.15
UN. Deputy to the High Representative for Disarmament Affairs
Ebo, Adedeji - A/78/PV.105; A/C.1/78/PV.11
UN. General Assembly. 1st Committee. Rapporteur
Balouji, Heidar Ali (Iran (Islamic Republic of)) - A/78/PV.42
UN. General Assembly. President
Francis, Dennis (Trinidad and Tobago) - A/78/PV.105
UN. Group of African States
Makiza, Maurice Gatien (Congo) - A/78/PV.105
United Kingdom
Floyd, Ian - A/C.1/78/PV.26
Saggese, Eleonora - A/C.1/78/PV.19
United States
Sharp, Matthew - A/78/PV.105
Storsve, Alison - A/C.1/78/PV.19; A/C.1/78/PV.28
Turner, Bruce - A/C.1/78/PV.15; A/C.1/78/PV.26; A/C.1/78/PV.30

DISARMAMENT—UN. GENERAL ASSEMBLY (4TH SPECIAL SESS. ON DISARMAMENT : xxxx) (Agenda item 99h)

Coordinating Bureau of the Non-Aligned Countries
Sirie, Mochammad Iqbal (Indonesia) - A/C.1/78/PV.22
Egypt
Ahmed, Amr Essameldin Sadek - A/C.1/78/PV.23
Group of Arab States
Alqaisi, Sultan Natheir Mustafa (Jordan) - A/C.1/78/PV.22
India
Bedi, Anmol Sher Singh - A/C.1/78/PV.23
Indonesia
Sirie, Mochammad Iqbal - A/C.1/78/PV.22
Pakistan
Sarwani, Gul Qaiser - A/C.1/78/PV.23
United Kingdom
Floyd, Ian - A/C.1/78/PV.23

DISARMAMENT—UN. GENERAL ASSEMBLY (10TH SPECIAL SESS. : 1978) (Agenda item 101)

UN. General Assembly. 1st Committee. Rapporteur
Balouji, Heidar Ali (Iran (Islamic Republic of)) - A/78/PV.42

DISARMAMENT—UN. GENERAL ASSEMBLY (12TH SPECIAL SESS. : 1982) (Agenda item 100)

UN. General Assembly. 1st Committee. Rapporteur
Balouji, Heidar Ali (Iran (Islamic Republic of)) - A/78/PV.42
UN Institute for Disarmament Research. Director
Geiss, Robin - A/C.1/78/PV.24

DISARMAMENT—YOUTH (Agenda item 99gg)

Chile
Vidal Mercado, Jorge Andrés - A/C.1/78/PV.20
Republic of Korea
Lee, Hyun Goo - A/C.1/78/PV.21; A/C.1/78/PV.28

DISARMAMENT AGREEMENTS—ENVIRONMENT (Agenda item 99j)

Coordinating Bureau of the Non-Aligned Countries
Sirie, Mochammad Iqbal (Indonesia) - A/C.1/78/PV.20
Cuba
Romero López, Rosanis - A/C.1/78/PV.28
Philippines
Lipana, Diane Shayne Dela Fuente - A/C.1/78/PV.20
United States
Turner, Bruce - A/C.1/78/PV.29

DISARMAMENT AGREEMENTS—OUTER SPACE (Agenda item 97c)

Algeria
Lebbaz, Larbi Abdelfattah - A/C.1/78/PV.17

DISARMAMENT AGREEMENTS—OUTER SPACE (Agenda item 97c) (continued)

Argentina
Guerra, Hugo Emmanuel - A/C.1/78/PV.27
ASEAN
Muhamad, Ahmad Faisal (Malaysia) - A/C.1/78/PV.16
Australia
Della-porta, Demi Heather See - A/C.1/78/PV.27
Bolivia (Plurinational State of)
Muñoz Ponce, Tatiana Bárbara - A/C.1/78/PV.17
Brazil
Szatmari, Roberto Wazima - A/C.1/78/PV.27
Canada
Fetz, Thomas - A/C.1/78/PV.27
Milligan, Ashlyn - A/C.1/78/PV.17
China
Shen, Jian - A/C.1/78/PV.17; A/C.1/78/PV.27
Zhang, Junjie - A/C.1/78/PV.27
Costa Rica
Ávila Becerril, Ana Maricela - A/C.1/78/PV.27
Chan Valverde, Maritza - A/C.1/78/PV.16
Cuba
Gómez Sardiñas, Yiliam - A/C.1/78/PV.17
Romero López, Rosanis - A/C.1/78/PV.27
Egypt
Hegazy, Abdelrhman Mohamed Farid - A/C.1/78/PV.16; A/C.1/78/PV.27
El Salvador
Rodríguez Acosta, Julia Elizabeth - A/C.1/78/PV.27
European Union
Sánchez de Lerín García-Ovies, Ignacio (Spain) - A/C.1/78/PV.27
France
Petit, Camille - A/C.1/78/PV.17
Germany
Himmler, Benjamin - A/C.1/78/PV.16
Group of Arab States
Alqaisi, Sultan Natheir Mustafa (Jordan) - A/C.1/78/PV.16
India
Kulkarni, Maitrey - A/C.1/78/PV.27
Indonesia
Kristanti, Maria Benedicta Diah - A/C.1/78/PV.27
Sinaga, Liandra Jean - A/C.1/78/PV.16
Iran (Islamic Republic of)
Eshragh Jahromi, Asadollah - A/C.1/78/PV.17
Ireland
Robinson, Jason - A/C.1/78/PV.17
Italy
Bencini, Leonardo - A/C.1/78/PV.17
Japan
Namekawa, Hirochika - A/C.1/78/PV.27
Ogasawara, Ichiro - A/C.1/78/PV.17
Malaysia
Sivamohan, Shivanand - A/C.1/78/PV.27
Mexico
Fausto, Braulio - A/C.1/78/PV.17
Sánchez Kiesslich, Eduardo Alcibiades - A/C.1/78/PV.27

DISARMAMENT AGREEMENTS—OUTER SPACE (Agenda item 97c) (continued)

Netherlands (Kingdom of the)
Bosch, Robert in den - A/C.1/78/PV.16
New Zealand
Clutterbuck, Nicholas - A/C.1/78/PV.17
Nam, Christine - A/C.1/78/PV.27
Pakistan
Gohar, Sarfaraz Ahmed - A/C.1/78/PV.27
Philippines
Lipana, Diane Shayne Dela Fuente - A/C.1/78/PV.27
Republic of Korea
Yoon, Seong-mee - A/C.1/78/PV.17
Russian Federation
Belousov, Andrey I. - A/C.1/78/PV.27
Vorontsov, Konstantin - A/C.1/78/PV.16; A/C.1/78/PV.17
Singapore
Low, Si Tong Berenice - A/C.1/78/PV.27
Sri Lanka
Gunaratna, Pahala Rallage Sanathana Sugeeshwara - A/C.1/78/PV.27
Sweden
Escaig, Benjamin - A/C.1/78/PV.16
Switzerland
Anderegg, Julius - A/C.1/78/PV.27
Türkiye
Çetin, Ahmet Erman - A/C.1/78/PV.27
UN. General Assembly. 1st Committee. Rapporteur
Balouji, Heidar Ali (Iran (Islamic Republic of)) - A/78/PV.42
UN. Group of African States
Mahmud, Mohammed Lawal (Nigeria) - A/C.1/78/PV.16
United States
Turner, Bruce - A/C.1/78/PV.17; A/C.1/78/PV.27

DISARMAMENT-DEVELOPMENT LINK (Agenda item 99d)

Armenia
Grigoryan, Andranik - A/C.1/78/PV.29
Caribbean Community
Wallace, Brian Christopher Manley (Jamaica) - A/C.1/78/PV.21
Coordinating Bureau of the Non-Aligned Countries
Sirie, Mochammad Iqbal (Indonesia) - A/C.1/78/PV.20
Cuba
Romero López, Rosanis - A/C.1/78/PV.28
Group of Arab States
Alqaisi, Sultan Natheir Mustafa (Jordan) - A/C.1/78/PV.20
Philippines
Lipana, Diane Shayne Dela Fuente - A/C.1/78/PV.20
Republic of Korea
Kim, Sunghoon - A/C.1/78/PV.28
United States
Turner, Bruce - A/C.1/78/PV.29

DISASTER PREVENTION (Agenda item 18c)

Alliance of Small Island States
Lautasi, Isaia (Samoa) - A/C.2/78/SR.12

DISASTER PREVENTION (Agenda item 18c) (continued)

Angola
Luemba, Mateus Pedro - A/C.2/78/SR.13
ASEAN
Lora-Santos, Leila Castillon (Philippines) - A/C.2/78/SR.12
Australia
Prosser, Amy - A/C.2/78/SR.23
Colombia
Ríos Serna, Manuela - A/C.2/78/SR.12
Costa Rica
Chan Valverde, Maritza - A/C.2/78/SR.13
Ecuador
Barba Bustos, Irina Alexandra - A/C.2/78/SR.13
Ethiopia
Shiferaw, Girum Getachew - A/C.2/78/SR.15
Group of 77
Torres Seara, Dalia Marlen (Cuba) - A/C.2/78/SR.21
Group of Friends for Disaster Risk Reduction
Macchiavello, Julissa (Peru) - A/C.2/78/SR.12
Guyana
Alkins, Royston - A/C.2/78/SR.15
Indonesia
Prabowo, Hari - A/C.2/78/SR.15
International Federation of Red Cross and Red Crescent Societies
Aultman, Kallie - A/C.2/78/SR.15
Iran (Islamic Republic of)
Jalili, Tahereh - A/C.2/78/SR.13
Kenya
Kenga, Emmanuel Kingi - A/C.2/78/SR.13
Malaysia
Zulasri Bin Rosdi, Muhammad - A/C.2/78/SR.15
Micronesia (Federated States of)
Welles, Kenneth - A/C.2/78/SR.15
Monaco
Du Sault, Serena - A/C.2/78/SR.15
Mozambique
Abdala, Paulina Feliciano Francisco - A/C.2/78/SR.15
South Africa
Mandla, Bulelani - A/C.2/78/SR.15
Thailand
Phuaknuem, Kanok - A/C.2/78/SR.13
UN. General Assembly. 2nd Committee. Rapporteur
Gatev, Ivaylo (Bulgaria) - A/78/PV.49
UN. Special Representative of the Secretary-General for Disaster Risk Reduction
Mizutori, Mami - A/C.2/78/SR.12
United States
Armbruster, Thomas - A/C.2/78/SR.21
Kroeker-Maus, Faith - A/C.2/78/SR.23

DISASTER VICTIMS (Agenda item 86)

Australia
Hutchison, Alexandra - A/C.6/78/SR.5
Bangladesh
Uddin, Nasir - A/C.6/78/SR.6

DISASTER VICTIMS (Agenda item 86) (continued)

Brazil
Sloboda, Pedro Muniz Pinto - A/C.6/78/SR.5
Burkina Faso
Lompo, Boulmonli Léonard - A/C.6/78/SR.6
Cameroon
Nyanid, Zacharie Serge Raoul - A/C.6/78/SR.6
Caribbean Community
Wallace, Brian Christopher Manley (Jamaica) - A/C.6/78/SR.5
China
Zhao, Yanrui - A/C.6/78/SR.6
Colombia
Solano Ramírez, Lucía Teresa - A/C.6/78/SR.5
Zalabata Torres, Leonor - A/C.6/78/SR.5
Community of Latin American and Caribbean States
Mark, Hayley-Ann (Saint Vincent and the Grenadines) - A/C.6/78/SR.5
Croatia
Papac, Kristijan - A/C.6/78/SR.6
Cuba
Carral Castelo, Arianna - A/C.6/78/SR.6
Denmark
Laursen, Erik - A/C.6/78/SR.5
Ecuador
Escobar Ullauri, Pablo - A/C.6/78/SR.6
Egypt
Nouh, Amr Mohamed Mosaad - A/C.6/78/SR.6
Equatorial Guinea
Nze Mansogo, Estela Mercedes - A/C.6/78/SR.6
Ethiopia
Alemayehu, Betelihem Taye - A/C.6/78/SR.6
European Union
Ramopoulos, Thomas - A/C.6/78/SR.5
Germany
Hasenau, Michael - A/C.6/78/SR.5
Guatemala
Rodríguez Mancia, Carla María - A/C.6/78/SR.5
Haiti
Panier, Wisnique - A/C.6/78/SR.6
Indonesia
Aron, Andy - A/C.6/78/SR.5; A/C.6/78/SR.36
International Federation of Red Cross and Red Crescent Societies
Aultman, Kallie - A/C.6/78/SR.7
Iran (Islamic Republic of)
Heidari, Bahram - A/C.6/78/SR.5
Ireland
Kirk, James - A/C.6/78/SR.6
Israel
Cappon, Noam - A/C.6/78/SR.5
Rubinshtein, Yarden - A/C.6/78/SR.7
Italy
Massari, Maurizio - A/C.6/78/SR.5
Kenya
Nyakoe, Catherine Nyaboke - A/C.6/78/SR.6
Lebanon
Hitti, Youssef - A/C.6/78/SR.6
Malaysia
Abd Karim, Nur Azura Binti - A/C.6/78/SR.6

DISASTER VICTIMS (Agenda item 86) (continued)
Mexico
Jiménez Alegría, Natalia - A/C.6/78/SR.6
Micronesia (Federated States of)
Lippwe, Jeem - A/C.6/78/SR.6
Morocco
Lasri, El Hassan - A/C.6/78/SR.6
Nepal
Thapa, Lok Bahadur - A/C.6/78/SR.6
Netherlands (Kingdom of the)
Theeuwen, Wieteke Elisabeth Christina - A/C.6/78/SR.5
Nigeria
Dakwak, Gloria - A/C.6/78/SR.6
Pakistan
Ijaz, Rabia - A/C.6/78/SR.6
Peru
Falconi, Alessandra - A/C.6/78/SR.6
Philippines
Lagdameo, Antonio Manuel Revilla - A/C.6/78/SR.5
Portugal
Matos, Ines - A/C.6/78/SR.5
Russian Federation
Antonova, Anna V. - A/C.6/78/SR.6
Saudi Arabia
Yankssar, Ahlam - A/C.6/78/SR.6
Sierra Leone
Kebe, Hawanatu - A/C.6/78/SR.6
Singapore
Tan, Scott - A/C.6/78/SR.6
Sistema de la Integración Centroamericana
González López, Egriselda Aracely (El Salvador) - A/C.6/78/SR.5
South Africa
Motsepe, Keke Mantsho - A/C.6/78/SR.6
Sri Lanka
Pieris, Peter Mohan Maithri - A/C.6/78/SR.5
State of Palestine
Sayej, Loureen O.A. - A/C.6/78/SR.7
Switzerland
Chanda, Riccarda - A/C.6/78/SR.6
Syrian Arab Republic
Khaddour, Mhd. Riyad - A/C.6/78/SR.6
Thailand
Hanlumyuang, Thararut - A/C.6/78/SR.6
Tonga
Vea, Jeanett - A/C.6/78/SR.6
UN. General Assembly. 6th Committee. Rapporteur
Moussa, Moussa Mohamed (Djibouti) - A/78/PV.45
UN. General Assembly. 6th Committee. Working Group on Protection of Persons in the Event of Disasters. Chair
Lagdameo, Antonio Manuel Revilla (Philippines) - A/C.6/78/SR.36
UN. Group of African States
Ikondere, Marvin (Uganda) - A/C.6/78/SR.5
United Arab Emirates
Al Blooshi, Ahmed Ali - A/C.6/78/SR.7
United Kingdom
Hollis, Jonathan Samuel - A/C.6/78/SR.6

DISASTER VICTIMS (Agenda item 86) (continued)
United States
Grosso, Elizabeth Maryanne - A/C.6/78/SR.5
Viet Nam
Nguyen, Thi Hong Quyen - A/C.6/78/SR.6

DISPLACED PERSONS (Agenda item 71b)
Algeria
Sahraoui, Ahmed - A/C.3/78/SR.49
Bangladesh
Abdullah, Md Showeb - A/C.3/78/SR.32
Burundi
Sibomana, Landry - A/C.3/78/SR.49
Cameroon
Banaken Elel, Nelly - A/C.3/78/SR.32
China
Yang, Fan - A/C.3/78/SR.32
Colombia
Tickner, Arlene Beth - A/C.3/78/SR.32
Cuba
González Behmaras, Alejandro - A/78/PV.50; A/C.3/78/SR.49
European Union
McCauley, Natalie - A/C.3/78/SR.32
Georgia
Lortkipanidze, Ekaterine - A/C.3/78/SR.32
Indonesia
Khairunsyah, Aidil - A/C.3/78/SR.32
Iraq
Yaseen, Safaa - A/C.3/78/SR.32
Lebanon
Zoghbi, Rawa - A/C.3/78/SR.32
Lesotho
Nena, Matete - A/C.3/78/SR.32
Morocco
Elhamriti, Soufiane - A/C.3/78/SR.32
Myanmar
Tun, Kyaw Moe - A/C.3/78/SR.32
Nicaragua
Jiménez, Jasser - A/C.3/78/SR.49
Norway
Ramboll, Unni - A/C.3/78/SR.32; A/C.3/78/SR.49
Russian Federation
Kashaev, Roman G. - A/C.3/78/SR.49
Kuzmenkov, Stepan Y. - A/C.3/78/SR.32
Spain
Bellmont Roldán, Xavier - A/C.3/78/SR.49
Switzerland
Desigis, Lucia Piera Giovanna - A/C.3/78/SR.32; A/C.3/78/SR.49
Syrian Arab Republic
Altarsha, Elie - A/C.3/78/SR.49
Ukraine
Zlenko, Anatoli M. - A/C.3/78/SR.32
UN. Human Rights Council. Special Rapporteur on the Human Rights of Internally Displaced Persons
Gaviria Betancur, Paula - A/C.3/78/SR.32
United States
McGlothlin, Cameron - A/C.3/78/SR.32

DISPLACED PERSONS (Agenda item 71b) (continued)

Yemen
Al-mashehari, Sarah Ahmed Ahmed - A/C.3/78/SR.32

ECONOMIC COOPERATION AMONG DEVELOPING COUNTRIES (Agenda item 22b)

ASEAN
Chindawongse, Suriya (Thailand) - A/C.2/78/SR.18
Burkina Faso
Bokoum, Mahamadou - A/C.2/78/SR.18
China
Dai, Bing - A/C.2/78/SR.18
Congo
Gabi, Emery - A/C.2/78/SR.18
El Salvador
González López, Egriselda Aracely - A/C.2/78/SR.18
Group of 77
Guevara Rodríguez, Adiel (Cuba) - A/C.2/78/SR.18
Torres Seara, Dalia Marlen (Cuba) - A/C.2/78/SR.21
Group of Landlocked Developing Countries
Motsumi, Lorato (Botswana) - A/C.2/78/SR.18
Group of Least Developed Countries
Ray, Kaushal Kishor (Nepal) - A/C.2/78/SR.18
Guinea
Zoumanigui, Paul Goa - A/C.2/78/SR.18
India
Gahlot, Petal - A/C.2/78/SR.18
Indonesia
Prabowo, Hari - A/C.2/78/SR.18
Kenya
Abbas, Swabri Ali - A/C.2/78/SR.18
Mexico
Robledo López, Carmen - A/C.2/78/SR.18
Morocco
Ouatiki, Assia - A/C.2/78/SR.18
Mozambique
Abdala, Paulina Feliciano Francisco - A/C.2/78/SR.18
Nicaragua
Gutiérrez Tórrez, Lisandra Marina - A/C.2/78/SR.18
Nigeria
Dagari, Rabiu - A/C.2/78/SR.18
Pakistan
Sharif, Shahsawar - A/C.2/78/SR.18
Russian Federation
Meschchanov, Boris A. - A/C.2/78/SR.18
South Africa
Mandla, Bulelani - A/C.2/78/SR.18
Sri Lanka
Pieris, Peter Mohan Maithri - A/C.2/78/SR.18
Thailand
Suwantra, Maes - A/C.2/78/SR.18
UN. General Assembly. 2nd Committee. Rapporteur
Gatev, Ivaylo (Bulgaria) - A/78/PV.49
UN Office for South-South Cooperation. Director
Wang, Xiaojun Grace - A/C.2/78/SR.18

ECONOMIC COOPERATION AMONG DEVELOPING COUNTRIES (Agenda item 22b) (continued)

United States
Armbruster, Thomas - A/C.2/78/SR.21
Marks, Rose Ann - A/C.2/78/SR.25

ECONOMIC SANCTIONS—INTERNATIONAL RELATIONS (Agenda item 28)

Algeria
Bendjama, Amar - A/78/PV.90
Australia
Bryant, Rebecca Suzanne - A/78/PV.89
Belarus
Rybakov, Valentin - A/78/PV.89
Bolivia (Plurinational State of)
Pary Rodríguez, Diego - A/78/PV.90
Brazil
Danese, Sérgio França - A/78/PV.89
China
Geng, Shuang - A/78/PV.89
Colombia
Zalabata Torres, Leonor - A/78/PV.90
Coordinating Bureau of the Non-Aligned Countries
Kwoba, Godfrey (Uganda) - A/78/PV.89
Cuba
Rodríguez Perdomo, Elio - A/78/PV.89
Equatorial Guinea
Ndong Mba, Anatolio - A/78/PV.90
Eritrea
Tesfamariam, Sophia - A/78/PV.90
European Union
Popan, Simona - A/78/PV.89
Group of 77
Kwoba, Godfrey (Uganda) - A/78/PV.89
Group of Friends in Defence of the Charter of the United Nations
Gil Pinto, Yvan (Venezuela (Bolivarian Republic of)) - A/78/PV.89
Honduras
Flores, Ramón Emilio - A/78/PV.90
Indonesia
Irawati Mamesah, Febrian - A/78/PV.90
Iran (Islamic Republic of)
Najafi, Reza - A/78/PV.89
Lao People's Democratic Republic
Vongnorkeo, Anouparb - A/78/PV.90
Malaysia
Abd Karim, Sofian Akmal Bin - A/78/PV.89
Mexico
Buenrostro Massieu, Alicia - A/78/PV.89
Nicaragua
Palacios, Iván Lara - A/78/PV.89
Russian Federation
Nebenzia, Vasilii - A/78/PV.89
Saint Vincent and the Grenadines
King, Inga Rhonda - A/78/PV.90
South Africa
Schalkwyk, Marthinus van - A/78/PV.89

ECONOMIC SANCTIONS—INTERNATIONAL RELATIONS (Agenda item 28) (continued)

Southern African Development Community
Cruz, Francisco José da (Angola) - A/78/PV.89
State of Palestine
Abdelhady-Nasser, Feda - A/78/PV.90
Sudan
Mohamed, Abuzied Shamseldin Ahmed - A/78/PV.90
Syrian Arab Republic
Aldahhak, Koussay Abduljabbar - A/78/PV.89
Timor-Leste
Soares, Dionísio Da Costa Babo - A/78/PV.90
UN. Group of African States
Imohe, Uhimwen Robert (Nigeria) - A/78/PV.89
United Kingdom
Young, Archie - A/78/PV.90
United States
Heartney, Edward - A/78/PV.90
Venezuela (Bolivarian Republic of)
Gil Pinto, Yvan - A/78/PV.89
Ron Martínez, Carlos - A/78/PV.90
Zimbabwe
Chimbindi, Albert Ranganai - A/78/PV.90

ELECTION VERIFICATION—UN (Agenda item 71b)

Albania
Lamce, Enian - A/C.3/78/SR.50
Algeria
Hassani, Billel - A/C.3/78/SR.50
Argentina
González, María Florencia - A/C.3/78/SR.50
Australia
Hamer, David - A/C.3/78/SR.50
Belarus
Mozgovaya, Ekaterina - A/78/PV.50; A/C.3/78/SR.50
Brazil
Balbino, Viviane Rios - A/C.3/78/SR.50
Chile
Nishihara, Carmen - A/C.3/78/SR.50
China
Wang, Zixu - A/C.3/78/SR.50
Colombia
Sánchez García, Nathalia - A/C.3/78/SR.50
Costa Rica
Pizarro-Viales, Laura Raquel - A/C.3/78/SR.50
Denmark
Scheuer, Emil Fischer-Nielsen - A/C.3/78/SR.50
Djibouti
Moussa, Youssouf Aden - A/78/PV.50
Dominican Republic
Andújar, Luz del Carmen - A/C.3/78/SR.50
Egypt
Mostafa Rizk, Heba - A/78/PV.50; A/C.3/78/SR.50
Ethiopia
Dabesa, Kurabachew Tirfesa - A/C.3/78/SR.50
European Union
Jiménez de la Hoz, Ana (Spain) - A/C.3/78/SR.50

ELECTION VERIFICATION—UN (Agenda item 71b) (continued)

France
Freudenreich, Anne - A/C.3/78/SR.50
Gulf Cooperation Council
Al Rawahi, Abdulhalim Mubarak Saloom (Oman) - A/C.3/78/SR.50
Al-thani, Almaha Mubarak F.J. (Qatar) - A/78/PV.50
Holy See
Murphy, Robert David - A/C.3/78/SR.50
Hungary
Mogyorósi, Bálint - A/C.3/78/SR.50
Indonesia
Dhanutirto, Mariska Dwianti - A/C.3/78/SR.50
Iran (Islamic Republic of)
Arab Bafrani, Fatemeh - A/C.3/78/SR.50
Japan
Ono, Sho - A/C.3/78/SR.50
Liberia
Gbai, Tangbae Kortemah - A/C.3/78/SR.50
Libya
Hamed, Ashraf A.O. - A/C.3/78/SR.50
Liechtenstein
Oehri, Noah - A/C.3/78/SR.50
Malaysia
Rizal, Nizhan Faraz Bin - A/78/PV.50; A/C.3/78/SR.50
Mali
Dabo N'diaye, Djeneba - A/78/PV.50
Mauritania
Guera, Soueda El - A/78/PV.50
Mexico
Santa Ana Vara, Alma Esperanza - A/C.3/78/SR.50
Micronesia (Federated States of)
Welles, Kenneth - A/C.3/78/SR.50
Montenegro
Bubanja, Jovana - A/C.3/78/SR.50
Netherlands (Kingdom of the)
Reichwein, Mark - A/78/PV.50; A/C.3/78/SR.50
Niger
Seydou, Abdoul Fadh Mahamadou - A/78/PV.50; A/C.3/78/SR.50
Nigeria
Asaju, Bola - A/78/PV.50; A/C.3/78/SR.50
North Macedonia
Danailov Frčkoski, Ljubomir - A/C.3/78/SR.50
Pakistan
Qureshi, Hadeeqa - A/C.3/78/SR.50
Saleem, Saima - A/78/PV.50
Peru
Rojas, Eder - A/C.3/78/SR.50
Russian Federation
Kashaev, Roman G. - A/C.3/78/SR.50
Senegal
Niasse, Samba Thiam - A/C.3/78/SR.50
Singapore
Rajandran, Dhivya - A/C.3/78/SR.50
South Africa
Passmoor, Jonathan David - A/C.3/78/SR.50

ELECTION VERIFICATION—UN (Agenda item 71b) (continued)

Sudan
Idres, Nusaiba Hashim Mohamed Ali - A/C.3/78/SR.50
Syrian Arab Republic
Altarsha, Elie - A/C.3/78/SR.50
Uganda
Gurhan, Amina - A/C.3/78/SR.50
UN. Assistant Secretary-General for Middle East, Asia and the Pacific
Khiari, Mohamed Khaled - A/C.3/78/SR.18
United Kingdom
White, Megan Marie - A/C.3/78/SR.50
United Republic of Tanzania
Tambwe, Zuleikha Rutha - A/C.3/78/SR.50
United States
Korac, Sofija - A/78/PV.50
Millard, Elisabeth I. - A/C.3/78/SR.50
Yemen
Al-mashehari, Sarah Ahmed Ahmed - A/78/PV.50; A/C.3/78/SR.50

EMERGENCY ASSISTANCE (Agenda item 72a)

Algeria
Samai, Rahma - A/78/PV.47
ASEAN
Nasir, Arrmanatha Christiawan (Indonesia) - A/78/PV.46
Australia
Larsen, James - A/78/PV.46
Belarus
Kavaleuskaya, Alena - A/78/PV.47
Brunei Darussalam
Lee, Kok Ting - A/78/PV.47
Canada
Ong, Shirley - A/78/PV.46; A/78/PV.47
China
Dai, Bing - A/78/PV.46
Cuba
González Behmaras, Alejandro - A/78/PV.47
European Union
Jiménez de la Hoz, Ana (Spain) - A/78/PV.46; A/78/PV.47
France
Dime-Labille, Diarra - A/78/PV.47
Group of 77
González Behmaras, Alejandro (Cuba) - A/78/PV.46
Group of Arab States
Abdelkhalek, Osama Mahmoud (Egypt) - A/78/PV.46
Group of Friends in Defence of the Charter of the United Nations
Castillo, William (Venezuela (Bolivarian Republic of)) - A/78/PV.46
Gulf Cooperation Council
Al-Thani, Abdulrahman Abdulaziz F.A. (Qatar) - A/78/PV.47
Hungary
Ivanyi, Balint - A/78/PV.47

EMERGENCY ASSISTANCE (Agenda item 72a) (continued)

Iran (Islamic Republic of)
Ershadi, Zahra - A/78/PV.46
Japan
Miyamoto, Sogaku - A/78/PV.46
Kuwait
Alajmi, Fahad M. - A/78/PV.47
Maldives
Khadeeja, Aufiyau - A/78/PV.46
Morocco
Kadiri, Omar - A/78/PV.47
Myanmar
Tun, Kyaw Moe - A/78/PV.47
New Zealand
Fepuleai, Justin Peter - A/78/PV.46
Nicaragua
Ochoa Espinales, Olimpia Raquel - A/78/PV.47
Norway
Lovold, Andreas - A/78/PV.46
Pakistan
Jadoon, Usman Iqbal - A/78/PV.46
Philippines
Fangco, Maria Roseny Baltazar - A/78/PV.46
Poland
Skoczek, Joanna Sylwia - A/78/PV.46
Russian Federation
Chumakov, Dmitry S. - A/78/PV.46; A/78/PV.47
Saudi Arabia
Alwasil, Abdulaziz M.O. - A/78/PV.46
Singapore
Chak Yong, Mok - A/78/PV.46
State of Palestine
Abushawesh, Sahar - A/78/PV.47
Sweden
Uexküll, Andreas von - A/78/PV.46
Switzerland
Desigis, Lucia Piera Giovanna - A/78/PV.47
Stillhart, Dominik - A/78/PV.46
Türkiye
Akbulut, Mustafa Kemal - A/78/PV.46
Ukraine
Hayovyshyn, Khrystyna - A/78/PV.47
United Arab Emirates
Alolama, Mohd Abdulrahman Mohamed Jalil Sultan - A/78/PV.47
United Kingdom
Kariuki, James - A/78/PV.46
United States
Carty, Lisa A. - A/78/PV.46

ENVIRONMENT (Agenda item 71b)

Chile
Fernández Carter, Catalina - A/C.3/78/SR.29
China
Liu, Luoge - A/C.3/78/SR.29
Colombia
Orduz Durán, Jessica Beatriz - A/C.3/78/SR.29
Costa Rica
Chan Valverde, Maritza - A/C.3/78/SR.26
Zavala Porras, Daniel Andrés - A/C.3/78/SR.29

ENVIRONMENT (Agenda item 71b) (continued)

Croatia
Šukurica, Alen - A/C.3/78/SR.29
Cuba
García Hernández, Martha - A/C.3/78/SR.29
Dominican Republic
Andújar, Luz del Carmen - A/C.3/78/SR.29
European Union
Szelivanov, Julia - A/C.3/78/SR.29
Indonesia
Meizura, Novia - A/C.3/78/SR.29
International Union for Conservation of Nature and Natural Resources
Sandström Jaffe, Sofie - A/C.3/78/SR.29
Japan
Ono, Sho - A/C.3/78/SR.29
Liechtenstein
Oehri, Noah - A/C.3/78/SR.24
Luxembourg
Vlokhoven, Flore van - A/C.3/78/SR.29
Malaysia
Escopper Zumilla, Michael Jawa - A/C.3/78/SR.29
Mexico
Riveroll Usabiaga, Renata - A/C.3/78/SR.29
Russian Federation
Kuzmenkov, Stepan Y. - A/C.3/78/SR.29
Slovenia
Zitko, Andrej - A/C.3/78/SR.29
Sovereign Order of Malta
Rosario-Blackett, Marissa del - A/C.3/78/SR.29
Spain
Cantero Talavera, Francisco Javier - A/C.3/78/SR.29
Switzerland
Wagner, Valérie - A/C.3/78/SR.29
UN. Human Rights Council. Special Rapporteur on the Human Right to a Clean, Healthy and Sustainable Environment
Boyd, David Richard - A/C.3/78/SR.29
United States
Lang, Dylan - A/C.3/78/SR.29

EURASIAN ECONOMIC UNION—OBSERVER STATUS (Agenda item 163)

UN. General Assembly. 6th Committee. Rapporteur
Moussa, Moussa Mohamed (Djibouti) - A/78/PV.45

EXTERNAL DEBT (Agenda item 16c)

Alliance of Small Island States
Bartley, Matilda (Samoa) - A/C.2/78/SR.8
Angola
Cruz, Francisco José da - A/C.2/78/SR.9
Bahamas
Mott, T'Sean - A/C.2/78/SR.11
Burkina Faso
Bokoum, Mahamadou - A/C.2/78/SR.9
China
Hua, Chenghang - A/C.2/78/SR.9

EXTERNAL DEBT (Agenda item 16c) (continued)

Colombia
Murillo Ferrer, Jorge Adrián - A/C.2/78/SR.25
Tickner, Arlene Beth - A/C.2/78/SR.8
Costa Rica
Zamora Zumbado, Leticia María - A/C.2/78/SR.9
Cuba
Guevara Rodríguez, Adiel - A/C.2/78/SR.8
Egypt
Abdelaal, Ahmed Magdy Mohamed Rashad - A/C.2/78/SR.9
Elsaeed, Sherine Mohamed Eissa Ahmed - A/C.2/78/SR.8
Group of 77
Torres Seara, Dalia Marlen (Cuba) - A/C.2/78/SR.8; A/C.2/78/SR.21
India
Gahlot, Petal - A/C.2/78/SR.9
Kenya
Nzumbu, Christine - A/C.2/78/SR.9
Like-Minded Group of Supporters of Middle-Income Countries
Hamdouni, Meryem (Morocco) - A/C.2/78/SR.8
Malaysia
Adnan, Yang Aishah Binti - A/C.2/78/SR.9
Maldives
Zuhuree, Ibrahim - A/C.2/78/SR.9
Mexico
Reta Haddad, Rodolfo - A/C.2/78/SR.9
Mongolia
Vorshilov, Enkhbold - A/C.2/78/SR.9
Nigeria
Gana Alkali, Baba - A/C.2/78/SR.9
Pakistan
Shafique, Umar - A/C.2/78/SR.9
Sierra Leone
Sowa, Amara Sheikh Mohammed - A/C.2/78/SR.9
Spain
Martín Couce, Adrián - A/C.2/78/SR.9
UN. General Assembly. 2nd Committee. Rapporteur
Gatev, Ivaylo (Bulgaria) - A/78/PV.49
UN. Group of African States
Ladeb, Tarek (Tunisia) - A/C.2/78/SR.9
UNCTAD
Hawkins, Penelope - A/C.2/78/SR.8
United Kingdom
Dix, Laura Gabrielle - A/C.2/78/SR.9
United States
Hamilton, Jim - A/C.2/78/SR.25
Zimbabwe
Rupende, Tapiwa Roy - A/C.2/78/SR.9

EXTERNAL DEBT—HUMAN RIGHTS (Agenda item 71b)

Bahamas
DeGregory, Kelli - A/C.3/78/SR.32
China
Yang, Fan - A/C.3/78/SR.32
Cuba
García Hernández, Martha - A/C.3/78/SR.32

EXTERNAL DEBT—HUMAN RIGHTS (Agenda item 71b) (continued)

Lesotho
Nena, Matete - A/C.3/78/SR.32
Russian Federation
Kuzmenkov, Stepan Y. - A/C.3/78/SR.32
Syrian Arab Republic
Altarsha, Elie - A/C.3/78/SR.32
UN. Human Rights Council. Independent Expert on the Effects of Foreign Debt and Other Related International Financial Obligations of States on the Full Enjoyment of All Human Rights, particularly Economic, Social and Cultural Rights
Waris, Attiya - A/C.3/78/SR.32

FALKLAND ISLANDS (MALVINAS) QUESTION (Agenda item 42)

Angola
Luemba, Mateus Pedro - A/C.4/78/SR.6
Argentina
Alvarez, Maximiliano Javier - A/C.4/78/SR.2; A/C.4/78/SR.6; A/C.4/78/SR.7; A/C.4/78/SR.8; A/C.4/78/SR.9
Carmona, Guillermo - A/C.4/78/SR.7
Bolivia (Plurinational State of)
Pary Rodríguez, Diego - A/C.4/78/SR.2
Chile
Ruidíaz, René - A/C.4/78/SR.7
China
Geng, Shuang - A/C.4/78/SR.8
Colombia
Zalabata Torres, Leonor - A/C.4/78/SR.7
Community of Latin American and Caribbean States
King, Inga Rhonda (Saint Vincent and the Grenadines) - A/C.4/78/SR.7
Costa Rica
Chan Valverde, Maritza - A/C.4/78/SR.7
Cuba
Romero Puentes, Yusnier - A/C.4/78/SR.2
Dominican Republic
Blanco Conde, José Alfonso - A/C.4/78/SR.7
Ecuador
Montalvo Sosa, Andrés Efren - A/C.4/78/SR.7
El Salvador
González López, Egriselda Aracely - A/C.4/78/SR.2
Guatemala
Benard Estrada, Juan Antonio - A/C.4/78/SR.6
Honduras
Rivera Reyes, Isabella Regina - A/C.4/78/SR.2
MERCOSUR (Organization)
Danese, Sérgio França (Brazil) - A/C.4/78/SR.2
Mexico
Cisneros Chávez, José de Jesús - A/C.4/78/SR.2
Mozambique
Buanahagi, Tarcísio Baltazar - A/C.4/78/SR.8
Nepal
Ray, Kaushal Kishor - A/C.4/78/SR.6
Nicaragua
Hermida Castillo, Jaime - A/C.4/78/SR.6

FALKLAND ISLANDS (MALVINAS) QUESTION (Agenda item 42) (continued)

Panama
Pinto Berrío, Harry Eduardo - A/C.4/78/SR.7
Paraguay
Pereira Sosa, José Eduardo - A/C.4/78/SR.7
Peru
Ugarelli, Luis F. - A/C.4/78/SR.7
Russian Federation
Ilichev, Petr - A/C.4/78/SR.2
Saint Lucia
Henry, Carlton Ronnie - A/C.4/78/SR.7
Saint Vincent and the Grenadines
Andrews, Lasana - A/C.4/78/SR.8
Serbia
Vujačić, Dušan - A/C.4/78/SR.8
Sistema de la Integración Centroamericana
González López, Egriselda Aracely (El Salvador) - A/C.4/78/SR.6
Timor-Leste
Nunes, Karlito - A/C.4/78/SR.2
United Kingdom
Meyrick, Phoebe - A/C.4/78/SR.2; A/C.4/78/SR.6; A/C.4/78/SR.7; A/C.4/78/SR.8; A/C.4/78/SR.9
Woodifield, Mungo - A/C.4/78/SR.8
Uruguay
Amorín, Carlos Daniel - A/C.4/78/SR.2
Venezuela (Bolivarian Republic of)
Pérez Ayestarán, Joaquín Alberto - A/C.4/78/SR.2

FAMILY (Agenda item 24b)

Argentina
Squeff, María del Carmen - A/C.3/78/SR.2
Belarus
Mozgovaya, Ekaterina - A/C.3/78/SR.49
Brazil
Dias, João Henrique Nascimento - A/C.3/78/SR.2
Cameroon
Banaken Elel, Nelly - A/C.3/78/SR.2
Egypt
Mostafa Rizk, Heba - A/C.3/78/SR.2
European Union
Alonso Giganto, Ana María (Spain) - A/C.3/78/SR.49
Group of 77
González Behmaras, Alejandro (Cuba) - A/C.3/78/SR.1; A/C.3/78/SR.49
Group of Friends of the Family
Evseenko, Pavel (Belarus) - A/C.3/78/SR.1
Holy See
Murphy, Robert David - A/C.3/78/SR.4
Iran (Islamic Republic of)
Arab Bafrani, Fatemeh - A/C.3/78/SR.2
Iraq
Al-Khaqani, Hassan Jabbar - A/C.3/78/SR.4
Kuwait
Al Mulla, Wafiqah - A/C.3/78/SR.3
Mexico
Reyna Barrón, María Fernanda - A/C.3/78/SR.49

FAMILY (Agenda item 24b) (continued)

Qatar
Al-Thani, Alya Ahmed S.A. - A/C.3/78/SR.3
Russian Federation
Kashaev, Roman G. - A/C.3/78/SR.2
Singapore
Choong, Brandon - A/C.3/78/SR.2
Tajikistan
Gulov, Golibjon - A/C.3/78/SR.2
UN. Department of Economic and Social Affairs. Division for Inclusive Social Development. Officer-in-Charge
Wilmoth, John - A/C.3/78/SR.1
United Kingdom
White, Megan Marie - A/C.3/78/SR.49
United States
Lang, Dylan - A/C.3/78/SR.49
Uruguay
Riva Grela, Juan José - A/C.3/78/SR.49
Yemen
Al-mashehari, Sarah Ahmed Ahmed - A/C.3/78/SR.2

FINANCIAL FLOWS (Agenda item 16f)

Group of 77
Torres Seara, Dalia Marlen (Cuba) - A/C.2/78/SR.21
Iraq
Al-Niami, Mustafa - A/C.2/78/SR.9
Norway
Lovold, Andreas - A/C.2/78/SR.11
Pakistan
Shafique, Umar - A/C.2/78/SR.9
Saudi Arabia
Alomair, Reem Fahad O. - A/C.2/78/SR.9
Sierra Leone
Sowa, Amara Sheikh Mohammed - A/C.2/78/SR.9
South Africa
Seedat, Ahmed Hoosen - A/C.2/78/SR.11
Switzerland
Pauli, Aurore N'zassa Julianne - A/C.2/78/SR.23
UN. Department of Economic and Social Affairs. Financing for Sustainable Development Office. Policy Analysis and Development Branch. Chief
Spiegel, Shari - A/C.2/78/SR.8
UN. General Assembly. 2nd Committee. Rapporteur
Gatev, Ivaylo (Bulgaria) - A/78/PV.49
UN. Group of African States
Ladeb, Tarek (Tunisia) - A/C.2/78/SR.9
UNCTAD
Nastav, Bojan - A/C.2/78/SR.8
United States
Armbruster, Thomas - A/C.2/78/SR.21
Lawrence, Jason N. - A/C.2/78/SR.23

FINANCIAL INCLUSION (Agenda item 16e)

Group of 77
Torres Seara, Dalia Marlen (Cuba) - A/C.2/78/SR.21
UN. General Assembly. 2nd Committee. Rapporteur
Gatev, Ivaylo (Bulgaria) - A/78/PV.49

FINANCIAL INCLUSION (Agenda item 16e) (continued)

United States
Macarena Apud, Maria - A/C.2/78/SR.22

FISSIONABLE MATERIALS—TREATIES (Agenda item 99a)

Austria
Edtmayer, Matthias - A/C.1/78/PV.26
Brazil
Szatmari, Roberto Wazima - A/C.1/78/PV.26
Bulgaria
Stoeva, Lachezara - A/C.1/78/PV.12
Canada
Fetz, Thomas - A/C.1/78/PV.13; A/C.1/78/PV.25
China
Sun, Yiliang - A/C.1/78/PV.13; A/C.1/78/PV.26
Cuba
Romero López, Rosanis - A/C.1/78/PV.26
Czechia
Štěpánek, Jaroslav - A/C.1/78/PV.12
Egypt
Ahmed, Amr Essameldin Sadek - A/C.1/78/PV.25; A/C.1/78/PV.26
Ghana
Kesse Antwi, Linda - A/C.1/78/PV.12
Hungary
Talpai, Tamás - A/C.1/78/PV.13
India
Kulkarni, Maitrey - A/C.1/78/PV.25
Indonesia
Kristanti, Maria Benedicta Diah - A/C.1/78/PV.26
Iran (Islamic Republic of)
Ghorbanpour Najafabadi, Mohammad - A/C.1/78/PV.25; A/C.1/78/PV.26
Israel
Sharoni, Benjamin - A/C.1/78/PV.26
Mexico
Sánchez Kiesslich, Eduardo Alcibiades - A/C.1/78/PV.26
New Zealand
Nam, Christine - A/C.1/78/PV.26
Pakistan
Ahmed, Husham - A/C.1/78/PV.25
Jadoon, Usman Iqbal - A/C.1/78/PV.12
Philippines
Reyes, Narciso - A/C.1/78/PV.12
United States
Turner, Bruce - A/C.1/78/PV.25

FOOD SECURITY (Agenda item 23a)

Algeria
Latrous, Mohamed-Esseghir - A/C.2/78/SR.17
Alliance of Small Island States
Lautasi, Isaia (Samoa) - A/C.2/78/SR.16
Angola
Luemba, Mateus Pedro - A/C.2/78/SR.16
ASEAN
Dang, Hoang Giang (Viet Nam) - A/C.2/78/SR.16
Bahrain
Alsindi, Yusuf Khaled - A/C.2/78/SR.17

FOOD SECURITY (Agenda item 23a) (continued)

Bangladesh
Hossain, Faruk - A/C.2/78/SR.17
Belarus
Kavaleuskaya, Alena - A/C.2/78/SR.25
Pisarevich, Vadim - A/C.2/78/SR.16
Bolivia (Plurinational State of)
Zambrana Flores, Carlos Iván - A/C.2/78/SR.16
Brazil
Santos, Luiz Felipe Rosa dos - A/C.2/78/SR.17
Burkina Faso
Bokoum, Mahamadou - A/C.2/78/SR.16
Cabo Verde
Romualdo, Tania Serafim Yvonne - A/C.2/78/SR.17
Cameroon
Etoundi Ayissi, Joseph - A/C.2/78/SR.16
Caribbean Community
Wallace, Brian Christopher Manley (Jamaica) - A/C.2/78/SR.16
China
Cao, Liwen - A/C.2/78/SR.16
Costa Rica
Chan Valverde, Maritza - A/C.2/78/SR.17
Democratic People's Republic of Korea
Jo, Tong Hyon - A/C.2/78/SR.16
Ecuador
Barba Bustos, Irina Alexandra - A/C.2/78/SR.17
El Salvador
Barahona Figueroa, Andrea Alejandra - A/C.2/78/SR.16
Ethiopia
Kindeya, Tsigabu Girmay - A/C.2/78/SR.17
European Union
Barbotte, Daphné - A/C.2/78/SR.25
FAO
Villarreal, Marcela - A/C.2/78/SR.16
Group of 77
Guevara Rodríguez, Adiel (Cuba) - A/C.2/78/SR.16
Torres Seara, Dalia Marlen (Cuba) - A/C.2/78/SR.21
Group of Friends in Defence of the Charter of the United Nations
Marín Sevilla, Asbina (Venezuela (Bolivarian Republic of)) - A/C.2/78/SR.16
Group of Landlocked Developing Countries
Mokhawa, Gladys (Botswana) - A/C.2/78/SR.16
Group of Least Developed Countries
Adhikari, Pramita (Nepal) - A/C.2/78/SR.16
Guatemala
Rodríguez Mancia, Carla María - A/C.2/78/SR.17
Guyana
Alkins, Royston - A/C.2/78/SR.17
Haiti
Vilmenay Joseph, Linouse - A/C.2/78/SR.17
India
Gahlot, Petal - A/C.2/78/SR.16
Indonesia
Prabowo, Hari - A/C.2/78/SR.17
Iran (Islamic Republic of)
Jalili, Tahereh - A/C.2/78/SR.16

FOOD SECURITY (Agenda item 23a) (continued)

Italy
Massari, Maurizio - A/C.2/78/SR.16
Kenya
Nzumbu, Christine - A/C.2/78/SR.16
Kuwait
Almezyad, Fatma - A/C.2/78/SR.17
Lesotho
Nena, Matete - A/C.2/78/SR.17
Malawi
Chivundu, Renata - A/C.2/78/SR.17
Malaysia
Zulasri Bin Rosdi, Muhammad - A/C.2/78/SR.17
Maldives
Nashwa, Fathimath - A/C.2/78/SR.16
Mali
Coulibaly, Kanisson - A/C.2/78/SR.17
Mexico
Vásquez Solano, Leonel - A/C.2/78/SR.16
Mozambique
Maure, Adnito - A/C.2/78/SR.17
Myanmar
Tun, Kyaw Moe - A/C.2/78/SR.17
Namibia
Gertze, Neville Melvin - A/C.2/78/SR.16
Niger
Moussa, Mahaman - A/C.2/78/SR.17
Nigeria
Maitafsir, Musa Garba - A/C.2/78/SR.17
Pakistan
Javaid, Hafiza Humaira - A/C.2/78/SR.17
Panama
Concepción Jaramillo, Markova - A/C.2/78/SR.16
Peru
Napurí Pita, Andrés - A/C.2/78/SR.17
Philippines
Beriana, Charlene Aravejo - A/C.2/78/SR.16
Qatar
Al-Khayareen, Abdulla Ghanim - A/C.2/78/SR.16
Russian Federation
Aristov, Dmitry S. - A/C.2/78/SR.17
Meschchanov, Boris A. - A/C.2/78/SR.25
Saudi Arabia
Bakhsh, Khalid - A/C.2/78/SR.17
Senegal
Dioum, Assane - A/C.2/78/SR.18
Serbia
Mart, Saša - A/C.2/78/SR.17
Sierra Leone
George, Alan Ebun - A/C.2/78/SR.17
South Africa
Mandla, Bulelani - A/C.2/78/SR.17
Tajikistan
Hasanova, Tahmina - A/C.2/78/SR.17
Thailand
Sangkhapreecha, Kantapon - A/C.2/78/SR.16
Timor-Leste
Barros, Sebastiana - A/C.2/78/SR.18
Togo
Debataba, Yawa - A/C.2/78/SR.17

FOOD SECURITY (Agenda item 23a) (continued)

Türkiye
Demir, İlknur - A/C.2/78/SR.17
Ukraine
Leschenko, Volodymyr - A/C.2/78/SR.16; A/C.2/78/SR.25
UN. General Assembly. 2nd Committee. Rapporteur
Gatev, Ivaylo (Bulgaria) - A/78/PV.49
UNIDO
Miljkovicova, Adriana - A/C.2/78/SR.18
United Arab Emirates
Almahmoud, Ahmed Abdelrahman Ahmed - A/C.2/78/SR.16
United Kingdom
Kelsey, Alistair Robert Steven - A/C.2/78/SR.25
United Republic of Tanzania
Kattanga, Hussein A. - A/C.2/78/SR.17
United States
Armbruster, Thomas - A/C.2/78/SR.21
Kroeker-Maus, Faith - A/C.2/78/SR.25
Leonard, Mary Beth - A/C.2/78/SR.17
Torres Small, Xochitl - A/78/PV.77
Viet Nam
Nguyen, Hoang Nguyen - A/C.2/78/SR.16
Yemen
Al-barati, Abdulrahman Hasan Yahya - A/C.2/78/SR.17
Zambia
Mungandi, Lubasi - A/C.2/78/SR.17

FREEDOM OF EXPRESSION (Agenda item 71b)

Austria
Soyka, Juliane - A/C.3/78/SR.19
Bangladesh
Monica, Mosammat Shahanara - A/C.3/78/SR.19
Belgium
Bauwens, Gilles - A/C.3/78/SR.19
Brazil
Paranhos, Pedro Barreto Da Rocha - A/C.3/78/SR.19
Canada
Wallenius, Devyn Lyn - A/C.3/78/SR.19
China
Zhang, Tianhao - A/C.3/78/SR.19
Colombia
Tickner, Arlene Beth - A/C.3/78/SR.19
Czechia
Kulhánek, Jakub - A/C.3/78/SR.19
Egypt
Mostafa Rizk, Heba - A/C.3/78/SR.19
Estonia
Tammsaar, Rein - A/C.3/78/SR.26
European Union
Nyman, Klas - A/C.3/78/SR.19
France
Freudenreich, Anne - A/C.3/78/SR.19
Greece
Alexandridou, Alexandra - A/C.3/78/SR.19

FREEDOM OF EXPRESSION (Agenda item 71b) (continued)

Hungary
Horváth, Zsuzsanna - A/C.3/78/SR.19
India
Sonkar, Suman - A/C.3/78/SR.19
Iran (Islamic Republic of)
Arab Bafrani, Fatemeh - A/C.3/78/SR.19
Ireland
Landy, Caoimhe - A/C.3/78/SR.19
Luxembourg
Toschi, Stéphanie - A/C.3/78/SR.19
Mexico
Riveroll Usabiaga, Renata - A/C.3/78/SR.19
Myanmar
Tun, Kyaw Moe - A/C.3/78/SR.19
Netherlands (Kingdom of the)
Reichwein, Mark - A/C.3/78/SR.19
Norway
Berg, Kristin Soennesyn - A/C.3/78/SR.19
Pakistan
Qureshi, Hadeeqa - A/C.3/78/SR.19
Poland
Skoczek, Joanna Sylwia - A/C.3/78/SR.19
Romania
Drăghia, Alexandru - A/C.3/78/SR.19
Russian Federation
Kuzmenkov, Stepan Y. - A/C.3/78/SR.19
Slovakia
Košuth, Matus - A/C.3/78/SR.19
Sovereign Order of Malta
McGuire, Peter Davidson - A/C.3/78/SR.19
Sweden
Schlyter, Charlotta - A/C.3/78/SR.19
Switzerland
Wagner, Valérie - A/C.3/78/SR.19
Syrian Arab Republic
Altarsha, Elie - A/C.3/78/SR.19
Ukraine
Tokarska, Anastasiia - A/C.3/78/SR.19
UN. Human Rights Council. Special Rapporteur on the Promotion and Protection of the Right to Freedom of Opinion and Expression
Khan, Irene - A/C.3/78/SR.19
United Kingdom
Devereaux, Brendan - A/C.3/78/SR.19
United States
Billingsley, Kelly - A/C.3/78/SR.19
Viet Nam
Dang, Tran Nam Trung - A/C.3/78/SR.19

FRENCH POLYNESIA QUESTION (Agenda item 58)

Amazones Pacific (Organization)
Labrousse, Lou - A/C.4/78/SR.3
Association 193 (French Polynesia)
Normand, Lena - A/C.4/78/SR.3
Association de foot ball Otemanu, Bora Bora
Jordan, Rudolph - A/C.4/78/SR.3
Association Moruroa e Tatou (French Polynesia)
Puarai, Tevaearai - A/C.4/78/SR.3

FRENCH POLYNESIA QUESTION (Agenda item 58) (continued)

Association Na Papa e Vaù (French Polynesia)
Temauri, Vainui - A/C.4/78/SR.3
Association Tamariki Teavaroa
Homai, François - A/C.4/78/SR.3
Association Te Utuafare No Mahaena
Tarahu, Frangelica - A/C.4/78/SR.3
Association Tumu Ra'i Fenua
Tiatoa, Sylvana - A/C.4/78/SR.3
Association Vaihau
Vaianui, Marania - A/C.4/78/SR.3
Baku Initiative Group
Tokoragi, Ella - A/C.4/78/SR.3
Centre de jeunes adolescents de Vaiare Moorea (Organization)
Hoiore, Tevaipaea - A/C.4/78/SR.3
Fiji
Tarakinikini, Filipo - A/C.4/78/SR.3
France
Chailloux, Steve - A/C.4/78/SR.3
Le Gayic, Tematai - A/C.4/78/SR.3
Rivière, Nicolas de - A/C.4/78/SR.3
French Polynesia
Brotherson, Moetai - A/C.4/78/SR.3
Brown, Tahia - A/C.4/78/SR.3
Cross, Valentina - A/C.4/78/SR.3
Flores, Bruno - A/C.4/78/SR.3
Flores, Rachelle - A/C.4/78/SR.3
Géros, Antony - A/C.4/78/SR.3
Hamblin, Ueva - A/C.4/78/SR.3
Hauata Ah-Min, Maite - A/C.4/78/SR.3
Homai, Odette - A/C.4/78/SR.3
Kohumoetini, Hina - A/C.4/78/SR.3
Kohumoetini, Marielle - A/C.4/78/SR.3
Loussan, Cliff - A/C.4/78/SR.3
Maamaatuaiahutapu, Maurea - A/C.4/78/SR.3
Salmon, Allen - A/C.4/78/SR.3
Tapati, Tafai - A/C.4/78/SR.3
Temaru, Oscar Manutahi - A/C.4/78/SR.3
Teremate, Ruben - A/C.4/78/SR.3
Terou, Pierre - A/C.4/78/SR.3
Tuheiava, Richard Ariihau - A/C.4/78/SR.3
Vaianui, Jeanne - A/C.4/78/SR.3
Vanaa, Elise - A/C.4/78/SR.3
ICAN France (Organization)
Morgant-Cross, Hinamoeura - A/C.4/78/SR.3
Kea Consulting (Organization)
Chong, Mickaël - A/C.4/78/SR.3
Maohi Protestant Church (French Polynesia)
Neuffer, Philippe - A/C.4/78/SR.3
Neuffer, Tetuanuiahuuraiterai - A/C.4/78/SR.3
Pihaatae, François - A/C.4/78/SR.3
Papua New Guinea
Sarufa, Fred - A/C.4/78/SR.6
Roberto Gym (Organization)
Cowan, Mike - A/C.4/78/SR.3
Solomon Islands
Waetara, Jane Mugafalu Kabui - A/C.4/78/SR.3
Union chrétienne des jeunes gens de Polynésie
Tairua, Tiare Maohi - A/C.4/78/SR.3

FRENCH POLYNESIA QUESTION (Agenda item 58) (continued)

Venezuela (Bolivarian Republic of)
Pérez Ayestarán, Joaquín Alberto - A/C.4/78/SR.2

GEINGOB, HAGE GOTTFRIED (NAMIBIA. PRESIDENT)—TRIBUTES

Namibia
Gertze, Neville Melvin - A/78/PV.55
UN. General Assembly. President
Francis, Dennis (Trinidad and Tobago) - A/78/PV.55
UN. Group of African States
Mokhawa, Gladys (Botswana) - A/78/PV.55
UN. Group of Asia-Pacific States
Abushahab, Mohamed Issa (United Arab Emirates) - A/78/PV.55
UN. Group of Latin American and Caribbean States
González López, Egriselda Aracely (El Salvador) - A/78/PV.55
UN. Group of Western European and Other States
Güven, Fikriye Asli (Türkiye) - A/78/PV.55
UN. Secretary-General
Guterres, António, 1949- - A/78/PV.55
United States
Thomas-Greenfield, Linda - A/78/PV.55

GIBRALTAR QUESTION (Agenda item 58)

Gibraltar
Garcia, Joseph - A/C.4/78/SR.13
Spain
Gómez Aoiz, Elena - A/C.4/78/SR.2; A/C.4/78/SR.8
Jiménez de la Hoz, Ana - A/C.4/78/SR.2
Timor-Leste
Nunes, Karlito - A/C.4/78/SR.2
United Kingdom
Meyrick, Phoebe - A/C.4/78/SR.2
Woodifield, Mungo - A/C.4/78/SR.8

GLOBAL ENVIRONMENT FACILITY—OBSERVER STATUS (Agenda item 166)

UN. General Assembly. 6th Committee. Rapporteur
Moussa, Moussa Mohamed (Djibouti) - A/78/PV.45

GLOBALIZATION—INTERDEPENDENCE (Agenda item 19)

Caribbean Community
Wallace, Brian Christopher Manley (Jamaica) - A/C.2/78/SR.10
Group of 77
Guevara Rodríguez, Adiel (Cuba) - A/C.2/78/SR.10
Group of Friends in Defence of the Charter of the United Nations
Pérez Ayestarán, Joaquín Alberto (Venezuela (Bolivarian Republic of)) - A/C.2/78/SR.10
Guyana
Rodrigues-Birkett, Carolyn - A/C.2/78/SR.10
Nigeria
Adenopo, Adeyinka A. - A/C.2/78/SR.10

GLOBALIZATION—INTERDEPENDENCE (Agenda item 19) (continued)

UN. General Assembly. 2nd Committee. Rapporteur
Gatev, Ivaylo (Bulgaria) - A/78/PV.49

GUAM QUESTION (Agenda item 58)

Guam
Won Pat-Borja, Melvin - A/C.4/78/SR.3
United States
Kris, Robert - A/C.4/78/SR.7

HAZARDOUS WASTES (Agenda item 71b)

Chile
Fernández Carter, Catalina - A/C.3/78/SR.29
Morocco
Chaouki, Naser-Allah - A/C.3/78/SR.29
UN. Human Rights Council. Special Rapporteur on the Implications for Human Rights of the Environmentally Sound Management and Disposal of Hazardous Substances and Wastes
Orellana, Marcos - A/C.3/78/SR.29

HEALTH (Agenda item 125)

Algeria
Hassani, Billel - A/78/PV.41
Sahraoui, Ahmed - A/78/PV.16
Argentina
Nicolino, Sebastián Lucas - A/78/PV.16
Australia
Kim, Yunei - A/78/PV.48
Larsen, James - A/78/PV.16
Pullela, Shilpa Kadambari - A/78/PV.41
Belarus
Mozgovaya, Ekaterina - A/78/PV.16
Pilipenko, Igor - A/78/PV.48
Belgium
Bouthé, Marc Gerard C. - A/78/PV.77
Brazil
Gomes, Elaine Cristina Pereira - A/78/PV.102
Canada
Castonguay, Marie-Eve - A/78/PV.64
Wallenius, Devyn Lyn - A/78/PV.48
China
Dai, Bing - A/78/PV.48
Zhang, Sisi - A/78/PV.41
Zhang, Tianhao - A/78/PV.16
Colombia
Tickner, Arlene Beth - A/78/PV.48
Cuba
González Behmaras, Alejandro - A/78/PV.16; A/78/PV.48; A/78/PV.77
Peñalver Portal, Gerardo - A/78/PV.41
Valido Martínez, Yoangel - A/78/PV.102
Dominican Republic
Matos Menéndez, Gala - A/78/PV.16

HEALTH (Agenda item 125) (continued)

Egypt
Elshandawily, Ahmed - A/78/PV.16
Mohamed, Mohamed Omar Elfarouk Hassan - A/78/PV.41; A/78/PV.77
Mostafa Rizk, Heba - A/78/PV.48
European Union
Alonso Giganto, Ana María (Spain) - A/78/PV.48
Bouthé, Marc Gerard C. (Belgium) - A/78/PV.77
Gaal, Miklos (Hungary) - A/78/PV.102
Jiménez de la Hoz, Ana (Spain) - A/78/PV.16
Korac, Sofija (United States) - A/78/PV.77
Maesschalck, Filip de (Belgium) - A/78/PV.64
Satuli, Tiina - A/78/PV.41
Foreign Policy and Global Health Initiative
Schalkwyk, Marthinus van (South Africa) - A/78/PV.77
Group of 77
González Behmaras, Alejandro (Cuba) - A/78/PV.16
Muhumuza, Duncan Laki (Uganda) - A/78/PV.77
Group of Friends in Defence of the Charter of the United Nations
Pérez Ayestarán, Joaquín Alberto (Venezuela (Bolivarian Republic of)) - A/78/PV.16; A/78/PV.41
Guatemala
Del Águila-Castillo, María José - A/78/PV.16
Gulf Cooperation Council
Al Rubkhi, Khalid Saleh Said (Oman) - A/78/PV.16
Al-thani, Almaha Mubarak F.J. (Qatar) - A/78/PV.48
Holy See
Murphy, Robert David - A/78/PV.48
Hungary
Gaal, Miklos - A/78/PV.16
India
Gahlot, Petal - A/78/PV.77
Indonesia
Imanuel, Fnu - A/78/PV.102
Pella, Blandina Ruth Viditha Adeleide - A/78/PV.48
Prabowo, Hari - A/78/PV.16; A/78/PV.41
Iran (Islamic Republic of)
Arab Bafrani, Fatemeh - A/78/PV.48
Ershadi, Zahra - A/78/PV.16
Ghafouri, Mojtaba - A/78/PV.77
Iraq
Al-Musawi, Ali Rida Abdulmohsin Hasan - A/78/PV.48
Israel
Ben Naftaly, Emil - A/78/PV.77
Cappon, Noam - A/78/PV.41
Japan
Iriya, Takayuki - A/78/PV.77
Kita, Yosuke - A/78/PV.48
Nakagawa, Shu - A/78/PV.16
Kuwait
Albanai, Tareq M.A.M. - A/78/PV.41
Malaysia
Zin Zawawi, Nordiana Binti - A/78/PV.77

HEALTH (Agenda item 125) (continued)

Mexico
Buenrostro Massieu, Alicia - A/78/PV.48
Mendoza Elguea, Sylvia Paola - A/78/PV.64
Quinto González, Jatnael - A/78/PV.102
Namibia
Gertze, Neville Melvin - A/78/PV.41
Kuzee, Helena Ndapewa - A/78/PV.16
New Zealand
Schaare, Ben - A/78/PV.77
Nicaragua
Jiménez, Jasser - A/78/PV.16
Llano, Alina J. - A/78/PV.48
Pakistan
Jadoon, Usman Iqbal - A/78/PV.41
Philippines
Lora-Santos, Leila Castillon - A/78/PV.48
Russian Federation
Bulgaru, Dmitrii I. - A/78/PV.48
Chumakov, Dmitry S. - A/78/PV.16; A/78/PV.64; A/78/PV.77
Kardash, Viktoriia E. - A/78/PV.102
Meschchanov, Boris A. - A/78/PV.41
Zabolotskaya, Maria V. - A/78/PV.48
Saudi Arabia
Alwasil, Abdulaziz M.O. - A/78/PV.97
Mousa, Sulafa - A/78/PV.41
Singapore
Rajandran, Dhivya - A/78/PV.48
South Africa
Passmoor, Jonathan David - A/78/PV.41
Schalkwyk, Marthinus van - A/78/PV.16
Sri Lanka
Weerasekara, Weerasekarage Chathura Ramyajith - A/78/PV.48
Switzerland
Birrer, Jacqueline - A/78/PV.16; A/78/PV.48; A/78/PV.77
Syrian Arab Republic
Al Nahhas, Wissam - A/78/PV.77
Altarsha, Elie - A/78/PV.41
Baghdadi, Mohannad - A/78/PV.16
Nayyal, Mhd. Majd - A/78/PV.48
Thailand
Chindawongse, Suriya - A/78/PV.41
Ukraine
Dvornyk, Serhii - A/78/PV.77
UN. Department for General Assembly and Conference Management
Sharma, Sangeeta - A/78/PV.16
United Kingdom
Reyes, Gaia - A/78/PV.102
Sowah, Malcolm - A/78/PV.48; A/78/PV.77
Woodroffe, Tom - A/78/PV.16
United States
Carty, Lisa A. - A/78/PV.16; A/78/PV.48
Eyrich, Kara - A/78/PV.48
Korac, Sofija - A/78/PV.77
Shrier, Jonathan - A/78/PV.102
Zimbabwe
Manyanga, Garikai - A/78/PV.16

HIV/AIDS—DECLARATIONS (Agenda item 10)

Australia
Larsen, James - A/78/PV.91
Belarus
Mozgovaya, Ekaterina - A/78/PV.91
Brazil
Danese, Sérgio França - A/78/PV.91
Cabo Verde
Romualdo, Tania Serafim Yvonne - A/78/PV.91
China
Li, Nan - A/78/PV.91
Colombia
Méndez Bocanegra, Rodrigo Andrés - A/78/PV.91
Cuba
Romero Puentes, Yusnier - A/78/PV.91
Georgia
Abesadze, David - A/78/PV.91
Haiti
Gaspard, Fritzner - A/78/PV.91
India
Patel, Yojna - A/78/PV.91
Iran (Islamic Republic of)
Ghafouri, Mojtaba - A/78/PV.91
Ireland
Cronin, Donal - A/78/PV.91
Japan
Kitada, Tetsuo - A/78/PV.91
Liechtenstein
Oehri, Noah - A/78/PV.91
Mexico
Mendoza Elguea, Sylvia Paola - A/78/PV.91
Namibia
Kuzee, Helena Ndapewa - A/78/PV.91
Netherlands (Kingdom of the)
Tahzib-Lie, Bahia - A/78/PV.91
Panama
Abad Garcia, Jienevit Juset - A/78/PV.91
Philippines
Lagdameo, Antonio Manuel Revilla - A/78/PV.91
Poland
Szczerski, Krzysztof - A/78/PV.91
Russian Federation
Aristov, Dmitry S. - A/78/PV.91
South Africa
Schalkwyk, Marthinus van - A/78/PV.91
Switzerland
Birrer, Jacqueline - A/78/PV.91
Thailand
Chaivaivid, Cherdchai - A/78/PV.91
Uganda
Muhumuza, Duncan Laki - A/78/PV.91
UN. Deputy Secretary-General
Mohammed, Amina J. - A/78/PV.91
UN. General Assembly. Vice-President
Valtýsson, Jörundur (Iceland) - A/78/PV.91
United Kingdom
Sowah, Malcolm - A/78/PV.91
United States
Heartney, Edward - A/78/PV.91

HIV/AIDS—DECLARATIONS (Agenda item 10) (continued)

Zimbabwe
Chimbindi, Albert Ranganai - A/78/PV.91

HUMAN RIGHTS (Agenda item 71)

Afghanistan
Faiq, Naseer Ahmed - A/C.3/78/SR.16
Algeria
Hassani, Billel - A/C.3/78/SR.16; A/C.3/78/SR.27
Angola
Luemba, Mateus Pedro - A/C.3/78/SR.28
Argentina
Escobar, Luciano Hernán - A/C.3/78/SR.16
Armenia
Hakobyan, Aram - A/C.3/78/SR.16
Australia
Kim, Yunei - A/C.3/78/SR.16
Austria
Pretterhofer, Stefan - A/C.3/78/SR.16
Azerbaijan
Ahangari, Narmin - A/C.3/78/SR.25
Bangladesh
Monica, Mosammat Shahanara - A/C.3/78/SR.16
Belarus
Pilipenko, Igor - A/C.3/78/SR.16
Cameroon
Wainwel, Gwedji Doris - A/C.3/78/SR.16
Canada
Arbeiter, Richard - A/C.3/78/SR.16
Chile
Perdomo, María Paula - A/C.3/78/SR.16
China
Dai, Bing - A/C.3/78/SR.16
Yang, Xiaokun - A/C.3/78/SR.27
Colombia
Sánchez García, Nathalia - A/C.3/78/SR.16
Comunidade dos Países de Língua Portuguesa
Cruz, Francisco José da (Angola) - A/C.3/78/SR.24
Cuba
Gala López, Yuri - A/C.3/78/SR.16
González Behmaras, Alejandro - A/C.3/78/SR.25
Cyprus
Michaelidou, Gabriella - A/C.3/78/SR.24
Democratic People's Republic of Korea
Kim, Nam Hyok - A/C.3/78/SR.16
Egypt
Mostafa Rizk, Heba - A/C.3/78/SR.16
Equatorial Guinea
Mangue, Victoriana Mbasogo - A/C.3/78/SR.28
Eritrea
Gebrekidan, Zebib - A/C.3/78/SR.28
European Union
Carlé, Hanne - A/C.3/78/SR.16
France
Dime-Labille, Diarra - A/C.3/78/SR.16
Georgia
Lortkipanidze, Ekaterine - A/C.3/78/SR.16
Germany
Drescher, Daniel - A/C.3/78/SR.16

HUMAN RIGHTS (Agenda item 71) (continued)

Greece
Alexandridou, Alexandra - A/C.3/78/SR.16
Group of Friends in Defence of the Charter of the United Nations
Pérez Ayestarán, Joaquín Alberto (Venezuela (Bolivarian Republic of)) - A/C.3/78/SR.24
Poveda Brito, Robert Alexander (Venezuela (Bolivarian Republic of)) - A/C.3/78/SR.16
Holy See
Caccia, Gabriele Giordano - A/C.3/78/SR.27
India
Sonkar, Suman - A/C.3/78/SR.16
International Federation of Red Cross and Red Crescent Societies
Aultman, Kallie - A/C.3/78/SR.28
International Youth Organization for Ibero-America
Valle Blanco, Daniel del - A/C.3/78/SR.28
Iran (Islamic Republic of)
Arab Bafrani, Fatemeh - A/C.3/78/SR.16
Iraq
Al-Khaqani, Hassan Jabbar - A/C.3/78/SR.16
Ireland
Broderick, Fiona - A/C.3/78/SR.16
Israel
Erdan, Gilad Menashe - A/C.3/78/SR.16
Mimran Rosenberg, Avital - A/C.3/78/SR.25
Italy
Tonon, Daniela - A/C.3/78/SR.16
Japan
Ono, Sho - A/C.3/78/SR.27
Yamanaka, Osamu - A/C.3/78/SR.16
Lesotho
Lelisa, Nthabiseng Matlhohonolofatso - A/C.3/78/SR.28
Liechtenstein
Wenaweser, Christian - A/C.3/78/SR.16
Malaysia
Muhamad, Ahmad Faisal - A/C.3/78/SR.16
Mexico
Elizondo Belden, Luis Gerardo - A/C.3/78/SR.16
Morocco
Bouchikhi, Hanaa - A/C.3/78/SR.16
Myanmar
Tun, Kyaw Moe - A/C.3/78/SR.16
Netherlands (Kingdom of the)
Lasseur, Katja - A/C.3/78/SR.16
New Zealand
Fepuleai, Justin Peter - A/C.3/78/SR.16
Oman
Al Jaradi, Heba Khalid - A/C.3/78/SR.27
Pakistan
Khan, Mohammad Aamir - A/C.3/78/SR.16
Portugal
Marinho, Joana Almeida - A/C.3/78/SR.25
Zacarias, Ana Paula - A/C.3/78/SR.16
Qatar
Al-Buainain, Hemyan Hassan Nasser - A/C.3/78/SR.16

HUMAN RIGHTS (Agenda item 71) (continued)

Republic of Korea
Song, Hye-ryoung - A/C.3/78/SR.27
Republic of Moldova
Leuca, Gheorghe - A/C.3/78/SR.25
Romania
Feruță, Cornel - A/C.3/78/SR.16
Russian Federation
Viktorov, Evgeny - A/C.3/78/SR.16
Rwanda
Umulisa, Flavia - A/C.3/78/SR.16
Saudi Arabia
Mousa, Sulafa - A/C.3/78/SR.16
Slovakia
Grünwald, Tomáš - A/C.3/78/SR.16
Slovenia
Zitko, Andrej - A/C.3/78/SR.16
Sovereign Order of Malta
Muñoz, Zachary N. - A/C.3/78/SR.28
Scalabrini-McKellar, Tobias - A/C.3/78/SR.16
State of Palestine
Bamya, Majed - A/C.3/78/SR.16
Salem, Sahar K.H. - A/C.3/78/SR.26
Switzerland
Baeriswyl, Pascale - A/C.3/78/SR.16
Syrian Arab Republic
Altarsha, Elie - A/C.3/78/SR.16; A/C.3/78/SR.25
Uganda
Kwoba, Godfrey - A/C.3/78/SR.28
Ukraine
Mudrenko, Nataliia - A/C.3/78/SR.16
UN. General Assembly. 3rd Committee. Rapporteur
Poveda Brito, Robert Alexander (Venezuela (Bolivarian Republic of)) - A/78/PV.50
UN High Commissioner for Human Rights
Türk, Volker - A/C.3/78/SR.16
United Arab Emirates
Alameri, Reem Mohamed - A/C.3/78/SR.16
United Kingdom
Sylvester, Timothy James - A/C.3/78/SR.16
United States
Shrier, Jonathan - A/C.3/78/SR.16
Uruguay
Machado Mouriño, Felipe - A/C.3/78/SR.28
Zimbabwe
Manyanga, Garikai - A/C.3/78/SR.27

HUMAN RIGHTS—AFGHANISTAN (Agenda item 71c)

Afghanistan
Faiq, Naseer Ahmed - A/C.3/78/SR.26; A/C.3/78/SR.34
Albania
Lamce, Enian - A/C.3/78/SR.26; A/C.3/78/SR.34
Australia
Larsen, James - A/C.3/78/SR.34
Austria
Hardwick, Nicola Ann - A/C.3/78/SR.34

HUMAN RIGHTS—AFGHANISTAN (Agenda item 71c) (continued)

Canada
Arbeiter, Richard - A/C.3/78/SR.26
Maillé, Béatrice - A/C.3/78/SR.34
China
Chen, Jiawen - A/C.3/78/SR.34
Croatia
Koncul, Ivana - A/C.3/78/SR.34
Czechia
Kulhánek, Jakub - A/C.3/78/SR.24
Dominican Republic
Andújar, Luz del Carmen - A/C.3/78/SR.34
European Union
Schuller, Simone - A/C.3/78/SR.34
Skoog, Olof - A/C.3/78/SR.24
France
Froment, Lucas - A/C.3/78/SR.34
Lebédel-Delumeau, Eric - A/C.3/78/SR.25
Germany
Drescher, Daniel - A/C.3/78/SR.34
Iceland
Kolsöe, Ragnheidur - A/C.3/78/SR.34
Indonesia
Khairunsyah, Aidil - A/C.3/78/SR.34
Ireland
Broderick, Fiona - A/C.3/78/SR.34
Japan
Ono, Sho - A/C.3/78/SR.26
Tonai, Akihiro - A/C.3/78/SR.34
Liechtenstein
Oehri, Noah - A/C.3/78/SR.34
Luxembourg
Gordet, Levina Christine Margaux - A/C.3/78/SR.34
Malaysia
Escopper Zumilla, Michael Jawa - A/C.3/78/SR.34
Malta
Micallef, Justine - A/C.3/78/SR.34
Netherlands (Kingdom of the)
Vogel, Robin Maria de - A/C.3/78/SR.34
Norway
Dale, Katrine Ørnehaug - A/C.3/78/SR.34
Pakistan
Ajmal, Muhammad Jawad - A/C.3/78/SR.34
Republic of Korea
Song, Hye-ryoung - A/C.3/78/SR.34
Russian Federation
Kuzmenkov, Stepan Y. - A/C.3/78/SR.34
Spain
Alonso Giganto, Ana María - A/C.3/78/SR.34
Switzerland
Wagner, Valérie - A/C.3/78/SR.34
Türkiye
Aydil, İsmail - A/C.3/78/SR.26
UN. Human Rights Council. Special Rapporteur on the Situation of Human Rights in Afghanistan
Bennett, Richard - A/C.3/78/SR.34
United Kingdom
White, Megan Marie - A/C.3/78/SR.34

HUMAN RIGHTS—AFGHANISTAN (Agenda item 71c) (continued)

United States
Johnson, Timothy J. - A/C.3/78/SR.34
Shrier, Jonathan - A/C.3/78/SR.25

HUMAN RIGHTS—BELARUS (Agenda item 71c)

Czechia
Kaminek, Jan - A/C.3/78/SR.37
European Union
Clifford, Katarina - A/C.3/78/SR.37
Skoog, Olof - A/C.3/78/SR.24
Liechtenstein
Oehri, Noah - A/C.3/78/SR.37
Lithuania
Bimbaitė, Monika - A/C.3/78/SR.37
Luxembourg
Folmer, Sophie - A/C.3/78/SR.37
Netherlands (Kingdom of the)
Tunen, Maarten van - A/C.3/78/SR.37
Poland
Szczerski, Krzysztof - A/C.3/78/SR.37
Slovakia
Grünwald, Tomáš - A/C.3/78/SR.24
Switzerland
Segessemann, Tim - A/C.3/78/SR.37
Ukraine
Mudrenko, Nataliia - A/C.3/78/SR.37
UN. Human Rights Council. Special Rapporteur on the Situation of Human Rights in Belarus
Marin, Anaïs - A/C.3/78/SR.37
United Kingdom
Rosen, Katie - A/C.3/78/SR.37
United States
Millard, Elisabeth I. - A/C.3/78/SR.37
Shrier, Jonathan - A/C.3/78/SR.25

HUMAN RIGHTS—BURUNDI (Agenda item 71c)

Belarus
Tozik, Artsiom - A/C.3/78/SR.36
Burundi
Maniratanga, Zéphyrin - A/C.3/78/SR.36
Cameroon
Banaken Elel, Nelly - A/C.3/78/SR.36
China
Liu, Luoge - A/C.3/78/SR.36
Cuba
González Behmaras, Alejandro - A/C.3/78/SR.36
Democratic People's Republic of Korea
Kim, Nam Hyok - A/C.3/78/SR.36
Egypt
Eldahshan, Wael Mahmoud Abdelaziz - A/C.3/78/SR.36
Eritrea
Tesfamariam, Sophia - A/C.3/78/SR.36
European Union
Nyman, Klas - A/C.3/78/SR.36

HUMAN RIGHTS—BURUNDI (Agenda item 71c) (continued)

Mali
Maiga, Aissata Ibrahim - A/C.3/78/SR.36
Nicaragua
Pichardo Urbina, Eleane Yaoska - A/C.3/78/SR.36
Russian Federation
Kondratev, Sergei V. - A/C.3/78/SR.36
UN. Group of African States
Milambo, Chola (Zambia) - A/C.3/78/SR.36
UN. Human Rights Council. Special Rapporteur on the Situation of Human Rights in Burundi
Zongo, Fortuné Gaétan - A/C.3/78/SR.36
United States
Leonard, Mary Beth - A/C.3/78/SR.36
Venezuela (Bolivarian Republic of)
Poveda Brito, Robert Alexander - A/C.3/78/SR.36

HUMAN RIGHTS—CENTRAL AFRICAN REPUBLIC (Agenda item 71c)

Cameroon
Banaken Elel, Nelly - A/C.3/78/SR.33
Central African Republic
Nzessioue, Marius Aristide Hoja - A/C.3/78/SR.33
China
Chen, Jiawen - A/C.3/78/SR.33
European Union
Nyman, Klas - A/C.3/78/SR.33
Morocco
Kadiri, Omar - A/C.3/78/SR.33
Russian Federation
Kuzmenkov, Stepan Y. - A/C.3/78/SR.33
UN. Human Rights Council. Independent Expert on the Situation of Human Rights in the Central African Republic
Agbetse, Yao - A/C.3/78/SR.33
United Kingdom
Devereaux, Brendan - A/C.3/78/SR.33
United States
Leonard, Mary Beth - A/C.3/78/SR.33

HUMAN RIGHTS—DEMOCRATIC PEOPLE'S REPUBLIC OF KOREA (Agenda item 71c)

Australia
Kim, Yunei - A/C.3/78/SR.33
Belarus
Pilipenko, Igor - A/78/PV.50; A/C.3/78/SR.53
Tozik, Artsiom - A/C.3/78/SR.33
Burundi
Sibomana, Landry - A/C.3/78/SR.33
Cameroon
Banaken Elel, Nelly - A/C.3/78/SR.33
China
Chen, Jiawen - A/C.3/78/SR.33
Zhang, Sisi - A/78/PV.50; A/C.3/78/SR.53
Cuba
González Behmaras, Alejandro - A/78/PV.50; A/C.3/78/SR.53
Valido Martínez, Yoangel - A/C.3/78/SR.33

HUMAN RIGHTS—DEMOCRATIC PEOPLE'S REPUBLIC OF KOREA (Agenda item 71c) (continued)

Czechia
Kaminek, Jan - A/C.3/78/SR.33
Democratic People's Republic of Korea
Kim, Nam Hyok - A/78/PV.50; A/C.3/78/SR.18; A/C.3/78/SR.27
Kim, Song - A/C.3/78/SR.53
Eritrea
Gebrekidan, Zebib - A/C.3/78/SR.33
European Union
Bellmont Roldán, Xavier (Spain) - A/C.3/78/SR.53
Nyman, Klas - A/C.3/78/SR.33
Skoog, Olof - A/C.3/78/SR.24
Group of Friends in Defence of the Charter of the United Nations
Poveda Brito, Robert Alexander (Venezuela (Bolivarian Republic of)) - A/C.3/78/SR.53
Iran (Islamic Republic of)
Arab Bafrani, Fatemeh - A/C.3/78/SR.33; A/C.3/78/SR.53
Ireland
Digney, Leanne - A/C.3/78/SR.33
Japan
Ono, Sho - A/C.3/78/SR.53
Yamanaka, Osamu - A/C.3/78/SR.33
Lao People's Democratic Republic
Sengdara, Xayfhong - A/C.3/78/SR.33
Marshall Islands
Kabua, Amatlain Elizabeth - A/C.3/78/SR.33
Nicaragua
Ochoa Espinales, Olimpia Raquel - A/78/PV.50
Pichardo Urbina, Eleane Yaoska - A/C.3/78/SR.33; A/C.3/78/SR.53
Peru
Rojas, Eder - A/C.3/78/SR.33
Philippines
Guevarra-de Dios, Nadine Bobadilla - A/C.3/78/SR.53
Republic of Korea
Hwang, Joonkook - A/C.3/78/SR.26; A/C.3/78/SR.53
Lee, Shin-wha - A/C.3/78/SR.33
Song, Hye-ryoung - A/C.3/78/SR.27
Russian Federation
Kuzmenkov, Stepan Y. - A/C.3/78/SR.33; A/C.3/78/SR.53
Zabolotskaya, Maria V. - A/78/PV.50
Singapore
Gafoor, Burhan - A/C.3/78/SR.53
Switzerland
Hubatka, Pascal - A/C.3/78/SR.33
Syrian Arab Republic
Al Nahhas, Wissam - A/78/PV.50
Altarsha, Elie - A/C.3/78/SR.33; A/C.3/78/SR.53
UN. Assistant Secretary-General for Human Rights
Brands Kehris, Ilze - A/C.3/78/SR.18
UN. Human Rights Council. Special Rapporteur on the Situation of Human Rights in the Democratic People's Republic of Korea
Salmón, Elizabeth - A/C.3/78/SR.33
United Kingdom
Devereaux, Brendan - A/C.3/78/SR.33; A/C.3/78/SR.53
United States
Armbruster, Thomas - A/C.3/78/SR.33
Eyrich, Kara - A/C.3/78/SR.53
Shrier, Jonathan - A/C.3/78/SR.25
Venezuela (Bolivarian Republic of)
Poveda Brito, Robert Alexander - A/78/PV.50; A/C.3/78/SR.33; A/C.3/78/SR.53
Zimbabwe
Manyanga, Garikai - A/C.3/78/SR.33

HUMAN RIGHTS—ERITREA (Agenda item 71c)

Algeria
Hassani, Billel - A/C.3/78/SR.36
Belarus
Tozik, Artsiom - A/C.3/78/SR.36
Burundi
Sibomana, Landry - A/C.3/78/SR.36
Cameroon
Banaken Elel, Nelly - A/C.3/78/SR.36
China
Liu, Luoge - A/C.3/78/SR.36
Cuba
González Behmaras, Alejandro - A/C.3/78/SR.36
Democratic People's Republic of Korea
Kim, Nam Hyok - A/C.3/78/SR.36
Eritrea
Tesfamariam, Sophia - A/C.3/78/SR.36
European Union
Nyman, Klas - A/C.3/78/SR.36
Iran (Islamic Republic of)
Ghanei, Mohsen - A/C.3/78/SR.36
Mali
Dabo N'diaye, Djeneba - A/C.3/78/SR.36
Nicaragua
Pichardo Urbina, Eleane Yaoska - A/C.3/78/SR.36
Nigeria
Asaju, Bola - A/C.3/78/SR.36
Pakistan
Qureshi, Hadeeqa - A/C.3/78/SR.36
Russian Federation
Kondratev, Sergei V. - A/C.3/78/SR.36
South Sudan
Adeng, Cecilia A.M. - A/C.3/78/SR.36
Sudan
Bakhit, Badreldeen Bakhit Musa - A/C.3/78/SR.36
Syrian Arab Republic
Altarsha, Elie - A/C.3/78/SR.36
UN. Group of African States
Milambo, Chola (Zambia) - A/C.3/78/SR.36
UN. Human Rights Council. Special Rapporteur on the Situation of Human Rights in Eritrea
Babiker, Mohamed Abdelsalam - A/C.3/78/SR.36

HUMAN RIGHTS—ERITREA (Agenda item 71c) (continued)

United States
Leonard, Mary Beth - A/C.3/78/SR.36
Venezuela (Bolivarian Republic of)
Poveda Brito, Robert Alexander - A/C.3/78/SR.36

HUMAN RIGHTS—ETHIOPIA (Agenda item 71c)

Belarus
Tozik, Artsiom - A/C.3/78/SR.36
Cameroon
Banaken Elel, Nelly - A/C.3/78/SR.36
China
Mao, Yizong - A/C.3/78/SR.36
Cuba
González Behmaras, Alejandro - A/C.3/78/SR.36
Ethiopia
Sabo, Tesfaye Yilma - A/C.3/78/SR.36
European Union
Nyman, Klas - A/C.3/78/SR.36
Iceland
Kolsöe, Ragnheidur - A/C.3/78/SR.36
Luxembourg
Gordet, Levina Christine Margaux - A/C.3/78/SR.36
Mali
Dabo N'diaye, Djeneba - A/C.3/78/SR.36
Netherlands (Kingdom of the)
Leede, Iris Mariken de - A/C.3/78/SR.36
Nicaragua
Pichardo Urbina, Eleane Yaoska - A/C.3/78/SR.36
Russian Federation
Kondratev, Sergei V. - A/C.3/78/SR.36
Switzerland
Fontana, Barbara - A/C.3/78/SR.36
UN. Group of African States
Milambo, Chola (Zambia) - A/C.3/78/SR.36
UN. International Commission of Human Rights Experts on Ethiopia
Ratner, Steven R. - A/C.3/78/SR.36
UN. International Commission of Human Rights Experts on Ethiopia. Chair
Othman, Mohamed Chande - A/C.3/78/SR.36
United Kingdom
Devereaux, Brendan - A/C.3/78/SR.36
United States
Leonard, Mary Beth - A/C.3/78/SR.36
Venezuela (Bolivarian Republic of)
Poveda Brito, Robert Alexander - A/C.3/78/SR.36
Zimbabwe
Manyanga, Garikai - A/C.3/78/SR.36

HUMAN RIGHTS—INTERNATIONAL INSTRUMENTS (Agenda item 71a)

Algeria
Hassani, Billel - A/C.3/78/SR.17
Argentina
González, María Florencia - A/C.3/78/SR.24
ASEAN
Muhamad, Ahmad Faisal (Malaysia) - A/C.3/78/SR.24

HUMAN RIGHTS—INTERNATIONAL INSTRUMENTS (Agenda item 71a) (continued)

Australia
Larsen, James - A/C.3/78/SR.25
Austria
Pretterhofer, Stefan - A/C.3/78/SR.24
Azerbaijan
Ahangari, Narmin - A/C.3/78/SR.25
Bangladesh
Muhith, Muhammad A. - A/C.3/78/SR.25
Belgium
Kridelka, Philippe - A/C.3/78/SR.25
Bolivia (Plurinational State of)
Pary Rodríguez, Diego - A/C.3/78/SR.26
Burkina Faso
Ouattara Cisse, Aminata - A/C.3/78/SR.25
Cameroon
Banaken Elel, Nelly - A/C.3/78/SR.17; A/C.3/78/SR.25
Chile
Fernández Carter, Catalina - A/C.3/78/SR.25
China
La, Haozhao - A/C.3/78/SR.17
Colombia
Orduz Durán, Jessica Beatriz - A/C.3/78/SR.24
Comunidade dos Países de Língua Portuguesa
Cruz, Francisco José da (Angola) - A/C.3/78/SR.24
Coordinating Bureau of the Non-Aligned Countries
Novruz, Leyla (Azerbaijan) - A/C.3/78/SR.33
Costa Rica
Chan Valverde, Maritza - A/C.3/78/SR.26
Côte d'Ivoire
Moriko, Tiémoko - A/C.3/78/SR.26
Cuba
Romero Puentes, Yusnier - A/C.3/78/SR.25
Ecuador
Montalvo Sosa, Andrés Efren - A/C.3/78/SR.26
El Salvador
Sorto Rosales, Mayra Lisseth - A/C.3/78/SR.17
European Union
Keogh, Briana - A/C.3/78/SR.17
Skoog, Olof - A/C.3/78/SR.24
Ghana
Williams, Edna Stephanie - A/C.3/78/SR.26
Greece
Sekeris, Evangelos C. - A/C.3/78/SR.25
Group of Arab States
Al-halique, Katherine Anas Ahmad (Jordan) - A/C.3/78/SR.24
India
Sonkar, Suman - A/C.3/78/SR.26
Indonesia
Aron, Andy - A/C.3/78/SR.26
Iran (Islamic Republic of)
Arab Bafrani, Fatemeh - A/C.3/78/SR.25
Italy
Greco, Gianluca - A/C.3/78/SR.25
Kazakhstan
Islamuly, Amirbek - A/C.3/78/SR.25
Lao People's Democratic Republic
Sengdara, Xayfhong - A/C.3/78/SR.25

HUMAN RIGHTS—INTERNATIONAL INSTRUMENTS (Agenda item 71a) (continued)

Lebanon
Hachem, Hadi - A/C.3/78/SR.24
Lesotho
Lelisa, Nthabiseng Matlhohonolofatso - A/C.3/78/SR.28
Liechtenstein
Oehri, Noah - A/C.3/78/SR.24
Malaysia
Escopper Zumilla, Michael Jawa - A/C.3/78/SR.17
Rizal, Nizhan Faraz Bin - A/C.3/78/SR.24
Mali
Maiga, Aissata Ibrahim - A/C.3/78/SR.26
Morocco
Moutchou, Majda - A/C.3/78/SR.27
Nepal
Ray, Kaushal Kishor - A/C.3/78/SR.25
Nigeria
Asaju, Bola - A/C.3/78/SR.25
North Macedonia
Danailov Frčkoski, Ljubomir - A/C.3/78/SR.17
Norway
Lovold, Andreas - A/C.3/78/SR.24
Organisation of Islamic Cooperation
Abdelkhalek, Osama Mahmoud (Egypt) - A/C.3/78/SR.24
Portugal
Silva, Miguel Alegre - A/C.3/78/SR.17
Romania
Mihail, Ioana-Cristina - A/C.3/78/SR.25
Russian Federation
Kuzmenkov, Stepan Y. - A/C.3/78/SR.17; A/C.3/78/SR.25
Saudi Arabia
Alwasil, Abdulaziz M.O. - A/C.3/78/SR.26
Serbia
Radović, Branislav - A/C.3/78/SR.27
South Africa
Joyini, Mathu - A/C.3/78/SR.24
Sudan
Idres, Nusaiba Hashim Mohamed Ali - A/C.3/78/SR.26
Sweden
Eneström, Anna-Karin - A/C.3/78/SR.26
Switzerland
Wagner, Valérie - A/C.3/78/SR.24
Tajikistan
Gulov, Golibjon - A/C.3/78/SR.26
Togo
Baka, Sondou - A/C.3/78/SR.26
Tunisia
Bessadok, Marwa Jabou - A/C.3/78/SR.26
Türkiye
Aydil, İsmail - A/C.3/78/SR.26
Ukraine
Mudrenko, Nataliia - A/C.3/78/SR.25
UN. Committee on Economic, Social and Cultural Rights. Chair
Craciunean-Tatu, Laura-Maria (Romania) - A/C.3/78/SR.17

HUMAN RIGHTS—INTERNATIONAL INSTRUMENTS (Agenda item 71a) (continued)

UN. General Assembly. 3rd Committee. Rapporteur
Poveda Brito, Robert Alexander (Venezuela (Bolivarian Republic of)) - A/78/PV.50
United Arab Emirates
Alameri, Reem Mohamed - A/C.3/78/SR.25
United States
Korac, Sofija - A/C.3/78/SR.47
Yemen
Balobaid, Ali Mabkhot Salem - A/C.3/78/SR.28
Zambia
Milambo, Chola - A/C.3/78/SR.26

HUMAN RIGHTS—IRAN (ISLAMIC REPUBLIC OF) (Agenda item 71c)

Australia
Hamer, David - A/C.3/78/SR.53
Kim, Yunei - A/C.3/78/SR.34
Belarus
Pilipenko, Igor - A/78/PV.50; A/C.3/78/SR.53
Tozik, Artsiom - A/C.3/78/SR.34
Brazil
Balbino, Viviane Rios - A/C.3/78/SR.53
Canada
Arbeiter, Richard - A/C.3/78/SR.26; A/C.3/78/SR.53; A/C.3/78/SR.54
Rae, Robert - A/C.3/78/SR.34
China
Chen, Jiawen - A/C.3/78/SR.34
Zhang, Sisi - A/78/PV.50; A/C.3/78/SR.53
Cuba
González Behmaras, Alejandro - A/78/PV.50; A/C.3/78/SR.34; A/C.3/78/SR.53
Democratic People's Republic of Korea
Kim, Nam Hyok - A/C.3/78/SR.34; A/C.3/78/SR.53
Eritrea
Gebrekidan, Zebib - A/C.3/78/SR.53
European Union
Bellmont Roldán, Xavier (Spain) - A/C.3/78/SR.53
Schuller, Simone - A/C.3/78/SR.34
Germany
Drescher, Daniel - A/C.3/78/SR.34
Group of Friends in Defence of the Charter of the United Nations
Poveda Brito, Robert Alexander (Venezuela (Bolivarian Republic of)) - A/C.3/78/SR.53
Iceland
Kolsöe, Ragnheidur - A/C.3/78/SR.34
Iran (Islamic Republic of)
Arab Bafrani, Fatemeh - A/78/PV.50; A/C.3/78/SR.18; A/C.3/78/SR.27; A/C.3/78/SR.34; A/C.3/78/SR.54
Ershadi, Zahra - A/C.3/78/SR.53
Ghanei, Mohsen - A/C.3/78/SR.34
Ireland
Broderick, Fiona - A/C.3/78/SR.34
Israel
Aviel, Shir - A/C.3/78/SR.34
Mimran Rosenberg, Avital - A/C.3/78/SR.53

HUMAN RIGHTS—IRAN (ISLAMIC REPUBLIC OF) (Agenda item 71c) (continued)

Kazakhstan
Islamuly, Amirbek - A/C.3/78/SR.53
Netherlands (Kingdom of the)
Tahzib-Lie, Bahia - A/C.3/78/SR.34
Nicaragua
Pichardo Urbina, Eleane Yaoska - A/C.3/78/SR.34; A/C.3/78/SR.53
Norway
Holter, Sigrun Stigen - A/C.3/78/SR.34
Pakistan
Qureshi, Hadeeqa - A/C.3/78/SR.53
Saleem, Saima - A/C.3/78/SR.34
Russian Federation
Kuzmenkov, Stepan Y. - A/C.3/78/SR.34; A/C.3/78/SR.53
Zabolotskaya, Maria V. - A/78/PV.50
Singapore
Rajandran, Dhivya - A/C.3/78/SR.53
Slovakia
Grünwald, Tomáš - A/C.3/78/SR.24
Sri Lanka
Gunaratna, Pahala Rallage Sanathana Sugeeshwara - A/C.3/78/SR.34
Switzerland
Fontana, Barbara - A/C.3/78/SR.34
Syrian Arab Republic
Altarsha, Elie - A/C.3/78/SR.34; A/C.3/78/SR.53
UN. Assistant Secretary-General for Human Rights
Brands Kehris, Ilze - A/C.3/78/SR.18
UN. Human Rights Council. Special Rapporteur on the Situation of Human Rights in the Islamic Republic of Iran
Rehman, Javaid - A/C.3/78/SR.34
United Kingdom
Sylvester, Timothy James - A/C.3/78/SR.34
United States
Carty, Lisa A. - A/C.3/78/SR.34
Henzel, Christopher - A/C.3/78/SR.53
Venezuela (Bolivarian Republic of)
Poveda Brito, Robert Alexander - A/C.3/78/SR.34

HUMAN RIGHTS—MYANMAR (Agenda item 71c)

Australia
Pullela, Shilpa Kadambari - A/C.3/78/SR.33
Bangladesh
Monica, Mosammat Shahanara - A/C.3/78/SR.33; A/C.3/78/SR.53
Muhith, Muhammad A. - A/C.3/78/SR.25
Belarus
Pilipenko, Igor - A/78/PV.50; A/C.3/78/SR.53
Tozik, Artsiom - A/C.3/78/SR.33
Canada
Rae, Robert - A/C.3/78/SR.33
China
Chen, Jiawen - A/C.3/78/SR.33
Zhang, Sisi - A/78/PV.50; A/C.3/78/SR.53

HUMAN RIGHTS—MYANMAR (Agenda item 71c) (continued)

Czechia
Kaminek, Jan - A/C.3/78/SR.33
European Union
Alwasil, Abdulaziz M.O. (Saudi Arabia) - A/C.3/78/SR.53
Carlé, Hanne - A/C.3/78/SR.33
García Rico, Lucía (Spain) - A/C.3/78/SR.53
Skoog, Olof - A/C.3/78/SR.24
France
Froment, Lucas - A/C.3/78/SR.33
Germany
Geisler, Michael Alexander - A/C.3/78/SR.33
Iceland
Kolsöe, Ragnheidur - A/C.3/78/SR.33
Indonesia
Dhanutirto, Mariska Dwianti - A/C.3/78/SR.53
Khairunsyah, Aidil - A/C.3/78/SR.33
International Institute for Democracy and Electoral Assistance
Sourek, Amanda Pirutti - A/C.3/78/SR.33
Iran (Islamic Republic of)
Arab Bafrani, Fatemeh - A/C.3/78/SR.33
Ireland
Swan, Ellen - A/C.3/78/SR.33
Japan
Ono, Sho - A/C.3/78/SR.26
Yamanaka, Osamu - A/C.3/78/SR.33
Liechtenstein
Oehri, Myriam - A/C.3/78/SR.53
Oehri, Noah - A/C.3/78/SR.33
Luxembourg
Toschi, Stéphanie - A/C.3/78/SR.33
Malaysia
Escopper Zumilla, Michael Jawa - A/C.3/78/SR.33
Rizal, Nizhan Faraz Bin - A/C.3/78/SR.24; A/C.3/78/SR.53
Marshall Islands
Kabua, Amatlain Elizabeth - A/C.3/78/SR.33
Myanmar
Tun, Kyaw Moe - A/C.3/78/SR.27; A/C.3/78/SR.33; A/C.3/78/SR.53
Netherlands (Kingdom of the)
Tunen, Maarten van - A/C.3/78/SR.33
Organisation of Islamic Cooperation
Alwasil, Abdulaziz M.O. (Saudi Arabia) - A/C.3/78/SR.53
Republic of Korea
Kim, Yong Yi - A/C.3/78/SR.33
Russian Federation
Kashaev, Roman G. - A/C.3/78/SR.33
Kuzmenkov, Stepan Y. - A/C.3/78/SR.53
Zabolotskaya, Maria V. - A/78/PV.50
Saudi Arabia
Mousa, Sulafa - A/C.3/78/SR.33
Singapore
Gafoor, Burhan - A/C.3/78/SR.53
Switzerland
Hubatka, Pascal - A/C.3/78/SR.33

HUMAN RIGHTS—MYANMAR (Agenda item 71c) (continued)

Thailand
Chindawongse, Suriya - A/C.3/78/SR.33; A/C.3/78/SR.53
Timor-Leste
Nunes, Karlito - A/C.3/78/SR.25
UN. Assistant Secretary-General for Human Rights
Brands Kehris, Ilze - A/C.3/78/SR.18
UN. Assistant Secretary-General for Middle East, Asia and the Pacific
Khiari, Mohamed Khaled - A/C.3/78/SR.33
UN. Human Rights Council. Special Rapporteur on the Situation of Human Rights in Myanmar
Andrews, Thomas H. - A/C.3/78/SR.33
UN. Independent Investigative Mechanism for Myanmar. Head
Koumjian, Nicholas - A/C.3/78/SR.33
United Kingdom
Devereaux, Brendan - A/C.3/78/SR.53
Lundy, Phoebe - A/C.3/78/SR.33
United States
Armbruster, Thomas - A/C.3/78/SR.33

HUMAN RIGHTS—PROGRAMMES OF ACTION (Agenda item 71d)

Austria
Pretterhofer, Stefan - A/C.3/78/SR.24
Caribbean Community
Wallace, Brian Christopher Manley (Jamaica) - A/C.3/78/SR.24
Malaysia
Rizal, Nizhan Faraz Bin - A/C.3/78/SR.24
South Africa
Joyini, Mathu - A/C.3/78/SR.24
UN. General Assembly. 3rd Committee. Rapporteur
Poveda Brito, Robert Alexander (Venezuela (Bolivarian Republic of)) - A/78/PV.50

HUMAN RIGHTS—REPORTS (Agenda item 71c)

Armenia
Hakobyan, Aram - A/C.3/78/SR.25
Australia
Larsen, James - A/C.3/78/SR.25
Belarus
Kryvaltsevich, Aliaksei - A/C.3/78/SR.24
Pilipenko, Igor - A/78/PV.50
Burundi
Sibomana, Landry - A/C.3/78/SR.37
China
Dai, Bing - A/C.3/78/SR.25
Zhang, Jun - A/C.3/78/SR.24; A/C.3/78/SR.27
Zhang, Sisi - A/78/PV.50; A/C.3/78/SR.18
Coordinating Bureau of the Non-Aligned Countries
Novruz, Leyla (Azerbaijan) - A/C.3/78/SR.53
Cuba
González Behmaras, Alejandro - A/78/PV.50; A/C.3/78/SR.18

HUMAN RIGHTS—REPORTS (Agenda item 71c) (continued)

Cyprus
Demosthenous, Ioanna - A/C.3/78/SR.25
Czechia
Kulhánek, Jakub - A/C.3/78/SR.24
Democratic People's Republic of Korea
Kim, Nam Hyok - A/C.3/78/SR.25
Kim, Song - A/C.3/78/SR.25
Egypt
Mostafa Rizk, Heba - A/C.3/78/SR.26
Estonia
Tammsaar, Rein - A/C.3/78/SR.26
France
Lebédel-Delumeau, Eric - A/C.3/78/SR.25
Group of Friends in Defence of the Charter of the United Nations
Pérez Ayestarán, Joaquín Alberto (Venezuela (Bolivarian Republic of)) - A/C.3/78/SR.24
India
Parihar, Rajesh - A/C.3/78/SR.25
Iran (Islamic Republic of)
Arab Bafrani, Fatemeh - A/C.3/78/SR.18; A/C.3/78/SR.25
Ghanei, Mohsen - A/C.3/78/SR.37
Nicaragua
Hermida Castillo, Jaime - A/C.3/78/SR.26
Ochoa Espinales, Olimpia Raquel - A/78/PV.50
Pakistan
Akram, Munir - A/C.3/78/SR.24
Saleem, Saima - A/C.3/78/SR.25
Russian Federation
Zabolotskaya, Maria V. - A/78/PV.50
Rwanda
Vmulisa, Flavia - A/C.3/78/SR.24
Saudi Arabia
Alwasil, Abdulaziz M.O. - A/C.3/78/SR.26
Syrian Arab Republic
Altarsha, Elie - A/C.3/78/SR.25
Türkiye
Aydil, İsmail - A/C.3/78/SR.25
UN. General Assembly. 3rd Committee. Rapporteur
Poveda Brito, Robert Alexander (Venezuela (Bolivarian Republic of)) - A/78/PV.50
United Kingdom
Kariuki, James - A/C.3/78/SR.26
United Republic of Tanzania
Tambwe, Zuleikha Rutha - A/C.3/78/SR.26
United States
Heartney, Edward - A/C.3/78/SR.18
Shrier, Jonathan - A/C.3/78/SR.25
Venezuela (Bolivarian Republic of)
Poveda Brito, Robert Alexander - A/78/PV.50; A/C.3/78/SR.25; A/C.3/78/SR.37
Zimbabwe
Manyanga, Garikai - A/C.3/78/SR.27

HUMAN RIGHTS—RUSSIAN FEDERATION (Agenda item 71c)

Albania
Lamce, Enian - A/C.3/78/SR.37

HUMAN RIGHTS—RUSSIAN FEDERATION (Agenda item 71c) (continued)

Australia
Kim, Yunei - A/C.3/78/SR.37
Belarus
Mozgovaya, Ekaterina - A/C.3/78/SR.37
Bulgaria
Dimitrov, Svetozar Angelov - A/C.3/78/SR.37
China
Yang, Xiaokun - A/C.3/78/SR.37
Czechia
Kaminek, Jan - A/C.3/78/SR.37
Democratic People's Republic of Korea
Kim, Nam Hyok - A/C.3/78/SR.37
Eritrea
Gebrekidan, Zebib - A/C.3/78/SR.37
European Union
Clifford, Katarina - A/C.3/78/SR.37
Skoog, Olof - A/C.3/78/SR.24
France
Martinet, Philippe - A/C.3/78/SR.37
Georgia
Lortkipanidze, Ekaterine - A/C.3/78/SR.37
Germany
Drescher, Daniel - A/C.3/78/SR.37
Ireland
Mc Bean, Keith - A/C.3/78/SR.37
Liechtenstein
Oehri, Noah - A/C.3/78/SR.37
Luxembourg
Maes, Olivier - A/C.3/78/SR.37
Montenegro
Bubanja, Jovana - A/C.3/78/SR.37
Netherlands (Kingdom of the)
Lasseur, Katja - A/C.3/78/SR.37
Nicaragua
Pichardo Urbina, Eleane Yaoska - A/C.3/78/SR.37
Poland
Szczerski, Krzysztof - A/C.3/78/SR.37
Slovakia
Grünwald, Tomáš - A/C.3/78/SR.24
Sri Lanka
Gunaratna, Pahala Rallage Sanathana Sugeeshwara - A/C.3/78/SR.37
Sweden
Uexküll, Andreas von - A/C.3/78/SR.37
Switzerland
Segessemann, Tim - A/C.3/78/SR.37
Syrian Arab Republic
Altarsha, Elie - A/C.3/78/SR.37
Ukraine
Mudrenko, Nataliia - A/C.3/78/SR.37
UN. Human Rights Council. Special Rapporteur on the Situation of Human Rights in the Russian Federation
Katzarova, Mariana - A/C.3/78/SR.37
United Kingdom
Croker, Richard - A/C.3/78/SR.24
Sylvester, Timothy James - A/C.3/78/SR.37

HUMAN RIGHTS—RUSSIAN FEDERATION (Agenda item 71c) (continued)

United States
Millard, Elisabeth I. - A/C.3/78/SR.37
Shrier, Jonathan - A/C.3/78/SR.25

HUMAN RIGHTS—SOMALIA (Agenda item 71c)

China
Yang, Fan - A/C.3/78/SR.35
European Union
Nyman, Klas - A/C.3/78/SR.35
Russian Federation
Kuzmenkov, Stepan Y. - A/C.3/78/SR.35
Switzerland
Segessemann, Tim - A/C.3/78/SR.35
UN. Human Rights Council. Independent Expert on the Situation of Human Rights in Somalia
Dyfan, Isha - A/C.3/78/SR.35
United Kingdom
Lundy, Phoebe - A/C.3/78/SR.35
United States
Leonard, Mary Beth - A/C.3/78/SR.35

HUMAN RIGHTS—SYRIAN ARAB REPUBLIC (Agenda item 71c)

Argentina
González, María Florencia - A/C.3/78/SR.54
Australia
Larsen, James - A/C.3/78/SR.34
Belarus
Pilipenko, Igor - A/78/PV.50; A/C.3/78/SR.54
Tozik, Artsiom - A/C.3/78/SR.34
Brazil
Balbino, Viviane Rios - A/C.3/78/SR.54
Moretti, Norberto - A/C.3/78/SR.34
Burundi
Sibomana, Landry - A/C.3/78/SR.54
Canada
Wallenius, Devyn Lyn - A/C.3/78/SR.54
China
Chen, Jiawen - A/C.3/78/SR.34
Zhang, Sisi - A/78/PV.50; A/C.3/78/SR.54
Croatia
Koncul, Ivana - A/C.3/78/SR.34
Cuba
González Behmaras, Alejandro - A/78/PV.50; A/C.3/78/SR.34; A/C.3/78/SR.54
Democratic People's Republic of Korea
Kim, Nam Hyok - A/C.3/78/SR.34; A/C.3/78/SR.54
Eritrea
Gebrekidan, Zebib - A/C.3/78/SR.34
European Union
García Rico, Lucía (Spain) - A/C.3/78/SR.54
Schuller, Simone - A/C.3/78/SR.34
Skoog, Olof - A/C.3/78/SR.24
France
Lebédel-Delumeau, Eric - A/C.3/78/SR.25
Germany
Drescher, Daniel - A/C.3/78/SR.34

HUMAN RIGHTS—SYRIAN ARAB REPUBLIC (Agenda item 71c) (continued)

Group of Friends in Defence of the Charter of the United Nations
Poveda Brito, Robert Alexander (Venezuela (Bolivarian Republic of)) - A/C.3/78/SR.54
Independent International Commission of Inquiry on the Syrian Arab Republic
Megally, Hanny - A/C.3/78/SR.34
Pinheiro, Paulo Sérgio de M.S. - A/C.3/78/SR.34
Iran (Islamic Republic of)
Arab Bafrani, Fatemeh - A/C.3/78/SR.34; A/C.3/78/SR.54
Ireland
Broderick, Fiona - A/C.3/78/SR.34
Mc Bean, Keith - A/C.3/78/SR.54
Israel
Aviel, Shir - A/C.3/78/SR.34
Shaked, Or - A/C.3/78/SR.54
Luxembourg
Folmer, Sophie - A/C.3/78/SR.34
Malta
Micallef, Justine - A/C.3/78/SR.34
Netherlands (Kingdom of the)
Vogel, Robin Maria de - A/C.3/78/SR.34
Nicaragua
Pichardo Urbina, Eleane Yaoska - A/C.3/78/SR.34; A/C.3/78/SR.54
Peru
Rojas, Eder - A/C.3/78/SR.54
Qatar
Al-Maawda, Jassim Sayyar - A/C.3/78/SR.54
Russian Federation
Kuzmenkov, Stepan Y. - A/C.3/78/SR.34; A/C.3/78/SR.54
Zabolotskaya, Maria V. - A/78/PV.50
Singapore
Rajandran, Dhivya - A/C.3/78/SR.54
Switzerland
Hubatka, Pascal - A/C.3/78/SR.34
Syrian Arab Republic
Al Nahhas, Wissam - A/78/PV.50
Altarsha, Elie - A/C.3/78/SR.34; A/C.3/78/SR.54
Türkiye
Aydil, İsmail - A/C.3/78/SR.26; A/C.3/78/SR.54
United Kingdom
Sylvester, Timothy James - A/C.3/78/SR.54
White, Megan Marie - A/C.3/78/SR.34
United States
Carty, Lisa A. - A/C.3/78/SR.54
Henzel, Christopher - A/C.3/78/SR.34
Shrier, Jonathan - A/C.3/78/SR.25
Venezuela (Bolivarian Republic of)
Poveda Brito, Robert Alexander - A/C.3/78/SR.34

HUMAN RIGHTS—TERRITORIES OCCUPIED BY ISRAEL (Agenda item 71c)

Albania
Lamce, Enian - A/C.3/78/SR.35

HUMAN RIGHTS—TERRITORIES OCCUPIED BY ISRAEL (Agenda item 71c) (continued)

Algeria
Hassani, Billel - A/C.3/78/SR.27
Yahiaoui, Dahmane - A/C.3/78/SR.35
Australia
Pullela, Shilpa Kadambari - A/C.3/78/SR.35
Austria
Pretterhofer, Stefan - A/C.3/78/SR.35
Bangladesh
Abdullah, Md Showeb - A/C.3/78/SR.35
Monica, Mosammat Shahanara - A/C.3/78/SR.35
Brazil
Paranhos, Pedro Barreto Da Rocha - A/C.3/78/SR.35
Bulgaria
Dimitrov, Svetozar Angelov - A/C.3/78/SR.35
Chile
Nishihara, Carmen - A/C.3/78/SR.35
China
Yang, Xiaokun - A/C.3/78/SR.35
Zhang, Jun - A/C.3/78/SR.24
Coordinating Bureau of the Non-Aligned Countries
Novruz, Leyla (Azerbaijan) - A/C.3/78/SR.35
Cuba
González Behmaras, Alejandro - A/C.3/78/SR.35
Czechia
Kulhánek, Jakub - A/C.3/78/SR.35
Democratic People's Republic of Korea
Kim, Nam Hyok - A/C.3/78/SR.35
Egypt
Eldahshan, Wael Mahmoud Abdelaziz - A/C.3/78/SR.35
European Union
Carlsson Szlezak, Teresa - A/C.3/78/SR.35
Germany
Zahneisen, Thomas - A/C.3/78/SR.35
Group of Arab States
Al-halique, Katherine Anas Ahmad (Jordan) - A/C.3/78/SR.24
Guatemala
Del Águila-Castillo, María José - A/C.3/78/SR.35
Gulf Cooperation Council
Al Jaradi, Heba Khalid (Oman) - A/C.3/78/SR.35
Hungary
Kókai, Anita - A/C.3/78/SR.35
Indonesia
Khairunsyah, Aidil - A/C.3/78/SR.35
Iran (Islamic Republic of)
Arab Bafrani, Fatemeh - A/C.3/78/SR.27; A/C.3/78/SR.35
Iraq
Abdullateef, Mohammed Ayad - A/C.3/78/SR.35
Al-Khaqani, Hassan Jabbar - A/C.3/78/SR.35
Ireland
Mc Bean, Keith - A/C.3/78/SR.35
Israel
Erdan, Gilad Menashe - A/C.3/78/SR.35
Shaked, Or - A/C.3/78/SR.27
Italy
Greco, Gianluca - A/C.3/78/SR.35

HUMAN RIGHTS—TERRITORIES OCCUPIED BY ISRAEL (Agenda item 71c) (continued)

Japan
Shino, Mitsuko - A/C.3/78/SR.35
Jordan
Al-halique, Katherine Anas Ahmad - A/C.3/78/SR.35
Kuwait
Al Mulla, Wafiqah - A/C.3/78/SR.35
Lebanon
Hachem, Hadi - A/C.3/78/SR.24
Zoghbi, Rawa - A/C.3/78/SR.35
Libya
Hamed, Ashraf A.O. - A/C.3/78/SR.35
Malaysia
Escopper Zumilla, Michael Jawa - A/C.3/78/SR.35
Mauritania
Guera, Soueda El - A/C.3/78/SR.35
Micronesia (Federated States of)
Welles, Kenneth - A/C.3/78/SR.35
Morocco
Moutchou, Majda - A/C.3/78/SR.27
Namibia
Iileka, Nekwayahelalia - A/C.3/78/SR.35
Nauru
Dongobir, Josie-Ann - A/C.3/78/SR.35
Norway
Dale, Katrine Ørnehaug - A/C.3/78/SR.35
Oman
Al Jaradi, Heba Khalid - A/C.3/78/SR.27
Organisation of Islamic Cooperation
Abdelkhalek, Osama Mahmoud (Egypt) - A/C.3/78/SR.24
Pakistan
Akram, Munir - A/C.3/78/SR.24
Qureshi, Hadeeqa - A/C.3/78/SR.35
Qatar
Al-thani, Almaha Mubarak F.J. - A/C.3/78/SR.24
Romania
Mocanu, Andreea - A/C.3/78/SR.35
Russian Federation
Kuzmenkov, Stepan Y. - A/C.3/78/SR.27; A/C.3/78/SR.35
Saudi Arabia
Mousa, Sulafa - A/C.3/78/SR.35
Slovakia
Grünwald, Tomáš - A/C.3/78/SR.24
South Africa
Passmoor, Jonathan David - A/C.3/78/SR.35
State of Palestine
Salem, Sahar K.H. - A/C.3/78/SR.35
Sudan
Idres, Nusaiba Hashim Mohamed Ali - A/C.3/78/SR.35
Syrian Arab Republic
Altarsha, Elie - A/C.3/78/SR.35
Tunisia
Bessadok, Marwa Jabou - A/C.3/78/SR.35
Türkiye
Aydil, İsmail - A/C.3/78/SR.35

HUMAN RIGHTS—TERRITORIES OCCUPIED BY ISRAEL (Agenda item 71c) (continued)

UN. Human Rights Council. Independent International Commission of Inquiry on the Occupied Palestinian Territory, including East Jerusalem, and Israel. Chair
Pillay, Navanethem - A/C.3/78/SR.35
UN. Human Rights Council. Special Rapporteur on the Human Right to Safe Drinking Water and Sanitation
Arrojo Agudo, Pedro - A/C.3/78/SR.28
UN. Human Rights Council. Special Rapporteur on the Situation of Human Rights in the Palestinian Territories Occupied since 1967
Albanese, Francesca - A/C.3/78/SR.35
United Kingdom
Croker, Richard - A/C.3/78/SR.24; A/C.3/78/SR.35
United States
Shrier, Jonathan - A/C.3/78/SR.35
Venezuela (Bolivarian Republic of)
Poveda Brito, Robert Alexander - A/C.3/78/SR.35
Yemen
Al-mashehari, Sarah Ahmed Ahmed - A/C.3/78/SR.35

HUMAN RIGHTS—UKRAINE (Agenda item 71c)

Albania
Lamce, Enian - A/C.3/78/SR.26; A/C.3/78/SR.37
Australia
Kim, Yunei - A/C.3/78/SR.37
Azerbaijan
Ahangari, Narmin - A/C.3/78/SR.53
Belarus
Pilipenko, Igor - A/78/PV.50
Canada
Rae, Robert - A/C.3/78/SR.37
China
Chen, Jiawen - A/C.3/78/SR.37
Zhang, Sisi - A/78/PV.50; A/C.3/78/SR.53
Czechia
Kaminek, Jan - A/C.3/78/SR.37
Kulhánek, Jakub - A/C.3/78/SR.24
Democratic People's Republic of Korea
Kim, Nam Hyok - A/C.3/78/SR.53
Estonia
Tammsaar, Rein - A/C.3/78/SR.26
European Union
Bellmont Roldán, Xavier (Spain) - A/C.3/78/SR.53
Clifford, Katarina - A/C.3/78/SR.37
Skoog, Olof - A/C.3/78/SR.24
Finland
Kalkku, Elina - A/C.3/78/SR.37
France
Lamy, Jean - A/C.3/78/SR.37
Lebédel-Delumeau, Eric - A/C.3/78/SR.25
Georgia
Abesadze, David - A/C.3/78/SR.53
Lortkipanidze, Ekaterine - A/C.3/78/SR.37
Germany
Drescher, Daniel - A/C.3/78/SR.37

HUMAN RIGHTS—UKRAINE (Agenda item 71c) (continued)

Group of Friends in Defence of the Charter of the United Nations
Poveda Brito, Robert Alexander (Venezuela (Bolivarian Republic of)) - A/C.3/78/SR.53
Iran (Islamic Republic of)
Arab Bafrani, Fatemeh - A/C.3/78/SR.53
Ireland
Mc Bean, Keith - A/C.3/78/SR.37
Israel
Mimran Rosenberg, Avital - A/C.3/78/SR.37
Japan
Ono, Sho - A/C.3/78/SR.26; A/C.3/78/SR.37
Liechtenstein
Meidert, Michael Sebastian - A/C.3/78/SR.37
Mexico
Mendoza Elguea, Sylvia Paola - A/C.3/78/SR.53
Montenegro
Bubanja, Jovana - A/C.3/78/SR.37
Netherlands (Kingdom of the)
Lasseur, Katja - A/C.3/78/SR.37
Poland
Skoczek, Joanna Sylwia - A/C.3/78/SR.37
Qatar
Al-thani, Almaha Mubarak F.J. - A/C.3/78/SR.53
Romania
Mihail, Ioana-Cristina - A/C.3/78/SR.25; A/C.3/78/SR.37
Russian Federation
Zabolotskaya, Maria V. - A/78/PV.50; A/C.3/78/SR.53
Singapore
Rajandran, Dhivya - A/C.3/78/SR.53
Slovakia
Grünwald, Tomáš - A/C.3/78/SR.24
Switzerland
Segessemann, Tim - A/C.3/78/SR.37
Syrian Arab Republic
Altarsha, Elie - A/C.3/78/SR.53
Türkiye
Aydil, İsmail - A/C.3/78/SR.26
Ukraine
Kyslytsya, Sergiy - A/78/PV.50; A/C.3/78/SR.53
Mudrenko, Nataliia - A/C.3/78/SR.18; A/C.3/78/SR.25; A/C.3/78/SR.37
Tokarska, Anastasiia - A/C.3/78/SR.27
UN. Assistant Secretary-General for Human Rights
Brands Kehris, Ilze - A/C.3/78/SR.18
UN. Human Rights Council. Independent International Commission of Inquiry to Investigate All Alleged Violations of Human Rights in the Context of the Russian Federation's Aggression against Ukraine. Chair
Møse, Erik - A/C.3/78/SR.37
United Kingdom
Croker, Richard - A/C.3/78/SR.24
Sylvester, Timothy James - A/C.3/78/SR.37; A/C.3/78/SR.53
United States
Millard, Elisabeth I. - A/C.3/78/SR.37

HUMAN RIGHTS ACTIVISTS (Agenda item 71b)

Albania
Lamce, Enian - A/C.3/78/SR.26
Austria
Mahidi, Mourad - A/C.3/78/SR.19
Bangladesh
Monica, Mosammat Shahanara - A/C.3/78/SR.19
Brazil
Paranhos, Pedro Barreto Da Rocha - A/C.3/78/SR.19
Canada
Wallenius, Devyn Lyn - A/C.3/78/SR.19
Chile
Fernández Carter, Catalina - A/C.3/78/SR.19
China
Zhang, Sisi - A/C.3/78/SR.56
Colombia
Sánchez García, Nathalia - A/C.3/78/SR.19
Côte d'Ivoire
Kouakou, Kouadjo Michel - A/C.3/78/SR.19
Czechia
Kulhánek, Jakub - A/C.3/78/SR.19
Egypt
Mostafa Rizk, Heba - A/C.3/78/SR.56
European Union
Bellmont Roldán, Xavier (Spain) - A/C.3/78/SR.56
Carlé, Hanne - A/C.3/78/SR.19
France
Freudenreich, Anne - A/C.3/78/SR.19
Georgia
Lortkipanidze, Ekaterine - A/C.3/78/SR.19
Germany
Drescher, Daniel - A/C.3/78/SR.19
Gulf Cooperation Council
Al Jaradi, Heba Khalid (Oman) - A/C.3/78/SR.19
Holy See
Murphy, Robert David - A/C.3/78/SR.56
Iceland
Valtýsson, Jörundur - A/C.3/78/SR.26
India
Sonkar, Suman - A/C.3/78/SR.19
Indonesia
Imanuel, Fnu - A/C.3/78/SR.56
Pella, Blandina Ruth Viditha Adeleide - A/C.3/78/SR.19
Iran (Islamic Republic of)
Arab Bafrani, Fatemeh - A/C.3/78/SR.56
Iraq
Abdullateef, Mohammed Ayad - A/C.3/78/SR.56
Ireland
Swan, Ellen - A/C.3/78/SR.19
Israel
Mimran Rosenberg, Avital - A/C.3/78/SR.19
Malaysia
Rizal, Nizhan Faraz Bin - A/C.3/78/SR.56
Mali
Dabo N'diaye, Djeneba - A/C.3/78/SR.56
Mexico
Elizondo Belden, Luis Gerardo - A/C.3/78/SR.19

HUMAN RIGHTS ACTIVISTS (Agenda item 71b) (continued)

Myanmar
Tun, Kyaw Moe - A/C.3/78/SR.19
Netherlands (Kingdom of the)
Brandt, Yoka - A/C.3/78/SR.19
New Zealand
Buist-Catherwood, Emily - A/C.3/78/SR.56
Niger
Seydou, Abdoul Fadh Mahamadou - A/C.3/78/SR.56
Nigeria
Asaju, Bola - A/C.3/78/SR.56
Norway
Brattested, Merete Fjeld - A/C.3/78/SR.19
Dale, Katrine Ørnehaug - A/C.3/78/SR.56
Lovold, Andreas - A/C.3/78/SR.24
Pakistan
Kanwal, Tehreem - A/C.3/78/SR.19
Poland
Skoczek, Joanna Sylwia - A/C.3/78/SR.19
Senegal
Niasse, Samba Thiam - A/C.3/78/SR.56
Slovenia
Zitko, Andrej - A/C.3/78/SR.19
Spain
Bellmont Roldán, Xavier - A/C.3/78/SR.19
Switzerland
Wagner, Valérie - A/C.3/78/SR.19
Syrian Arab Republic
Altarsha, Elie - A/C.3/78/SR.56
UN. Human Rights Council. Special Rapporteur on the Situation of Human Rights Defenders
Lawlor, Mary - A/C.3/78/SR.19
United Arab Emirates
Alameri, Reem Mohamed - A/C.3/78/SR.19
United Kingdom
Devereaux, Brendan - A/C.3/78/SR.19
United States
Eyrich, Kara - A/C.3/78/SR.56
Murphy, Daniel - A/C.3/78/SR.19
Yemen
Al-mashehari, Sarah Ahmed Ahmed - A/C.3/78/SR.19

HUMAN RIGHTS ADVANCEMENT (Agenda item 71b)

Argentina
González, María Florencia - A/C.3/78/SR.24
Armenia
Hakobyan, Aram - A/C.3/78/SR.24
ASEAN
Muhamad, Ahmad Faisal (Malaysia) - A/C.3/78/SR.24
Austria
Soyka, Juliane - A/C.3/78/SR.52
Azerbaijan
Ahangari, Narmin - A/C.3/78/SR.25
Belarus
Kryvaltsevich, Aliaksei - A/C.3/78/SR.24
Cambodia
Eat, Sophea - A/C.3/78/SR.26

HUMAN RIGHTS ADVANCEMENT (Agenda item 71b) (continued)

Cameroon
Banaken Elel, Nelly - A/C.3/78/SR.25
Canada
Morin, Cassandra - A/C.3/78/SR.48
Caribbean Community
Wallace, Brian Christopher Manley (Jamaica) - A/C.3/78/SR.24
Chile
Fernández Carter, Catalina - A/C.3/78/SR.25
China
Zhang, Jun - A/C.3/78/SR.24
Zhang, Sisi - A/C.3/78/SR.18
Coordinating Bureau of the Non-Aligned Countries
González Behmaras, Alejandro (Cuba) - A/C.3/78/SR.48
Cuba
González Behmaras, Alejandro - A/C.3/78/SR.48
Czechia
Kulhánek, Jakub - A/C.3/78/SR.52
Denmark
Rendtorff-Smith, Sara - A/C.3/78/SR.52
Dominican Republic
Cedano, Joan Margarita - A/C.3/78/SR.26
Egypt
Mostafa Rizk, Heba - A/C.3/78/SR.52
Ethiopia
Chala, Samuel Isa - A/C.3/78/SR.25
European Union
Carlé, Hanne - A/C.3/78/SR.18
Mythen, Fergal Tomas (Ireland) - A/C.3/78/SR.24
Skoog, Olof - A/C.3/78/SR.24
Germany
Leendertse, Antje - A/C.3/78/SR.26
Greece
Sekeris, Evangelos C. - A/C.3/78/SR.52
Holy See
Murphy, Robert David - A/C.3/78/SR.52
India
Sonkar, Suman - A/C.3/78/SR.26
Indonesia
Pella, Blandina Ruth Viditha Adeleide - A/C.3/78/SR.52
Iran (Islamic Republic of)
Arab Bafrani, Fatemeh - A/C.3/78/SR.52
Iraq
Raed Dawood Al-Saadi, Amna - A/C.3/78/SR.18
Ireland
Leonard, Roisin - A/C.3/78/SR.18
Israel
Mimran Rosenberg, Avital - A/C.3/78/SR.52
Italy
Greco, Gianluca - A/C.3/78/SR.25
Jamaica
DaCosta, Yanique Nissan - A/C.3/78/SR.52
Japan
Ono, Sho - A/C.3/78/SR.18
Kazakhstan
Islamuly, Amirbek - A/C.3/78/SR.25

HUMAN RIGHTS ADVANCEMENT (Agenda item 71b) (continued)

Kuwait
Al-Dikaan, Ahmed Khaled Ghanem - A/C.3/78/SR.26
Lao People's Democratic Republic
Sengdara, Xayfhong - A/C.3/78/SR.25
Latvia
Pavļuta-Deslandes, Sanita - A/C.3/78/SR.18
Lebanon
Zoghbi, Rawa - A/C.3/78/SR.52
Malaysia
Rizal, Nizhan Faraz Bin - A/C.3/78/SR.24
Maldives
Zuhuree, Ibrahim - A/C.3/78/SR.25
Mexico
Elizondo Belden, Luis Gerardo - A/C.3/78/SR.24; A/C.3/78/SR.52
Nepal
Ray, Kaushal Kishor - A/C.3/78/SR.25
Nicaragua
Hermida Castillo, Jaime - A/C.3/78/SR.26
Niger
Seydou, Abdoul Fadh Mahamadou - A/C.3/78/SR.52
Nigeria
Asaju, Bola - A/C.3/78/SR.52
Philippines
Fangco, Maria Roseny Baltazar - A/C.3/78/SR.24
Qatar
Al-thani, Almaha Mubarak F.J. - A/C.3/78/SR.24
Romania
Mihail, Ioana-Cristina - A/C.3/78/SR.18
Saudi Arabia
Bin Jadid, Faisal Fahad M. - A/C.3/78/SR.18
Senegal
Niasse, Samba Thiam - A/C.3/78/SR.52
Sierra Leone
Kanu, Michael Imran - A/C.3/78/SR.25
Singapore
Gafoor, Burhan - A/C.3/78/SR.24
Rajandran, Dhivya - A/C.3/78/SR.52
Switzerland
Wagner, Valérie - A/C.3/78/SR.24
Syrian Arab Republic
Altarsha, Elie - A/C.3/78/SR.52
Thailand
Chindawongse, Suriya - A/C.3/78/SR.25
Timor-Leste
Nunes, Karlito - A/C.3/78/SR.25
Togo
Baka, Sondou - A/C.3/78/SR.26
UN. Assistant Secretary-General for Human Rights
Brands Kehris, Ilze - A/C.3/78/SR.18
UN. General Assembly. 3rd Committee. Rapporteur
Poveda Brito, Robert Alexander (Venezuela (Bolivarian Republic of)) - A/78/PV.50
United Arab Emirates
Alameri, Reem Mohamed - A/C.3/78/SR.25
United Kingdom
Callaghan-Pace, Laura Frances - A/C.3/78/SR.52
Croker, Richard - A/C.3/78/SR.18; A/C.3/78/SR.24
Sigley, Andrew - A/C.3/78/SR.52

HUMAN RIGHTS ADVANCEMENT (Agenda item 71b) (continued)

United States
Eyrich, Kara - A/C.3/78/SR.52
Merron, Eric - A/C.3/78/SR.48
Vasović, Angela - A/C.3/78/SR.52
Uruguay
Riva Grela, Juan José - A/C.3/78/SR.52
Viet Nam
Dang, Hoang Giang - A/C.3/78/SR.24
Zambia
Milambo, Chola - A/C.3/78/SR.26

HUMAN RIGHTS INSTITUTIONS—CENTRAL AFRICA (Agenda item 71b)

Cameroon
Tommo Monthe, Michel - A/C.3/78/SR.56
Canada
Wallenius, Devyn Lyn - A/C.3/78/SR.56
Congo
Ahoue Itoua Lekegny, Patience - A/C.3/78/SR.56
Djibouti
Moussa, Youssouf Aden - A/C.3/78/SR.56
Economic Community of Central African States
Banaken Elel, Nelly (Cameroon) - A/C.3/78/SR.56
European Union
Alonso Giganto, Ana María (Spain) - A/C.3/78/SR.56
Japan
Ono, Sho - A/C.3/78/SR.56
Mali
Dabo N'diaye, Djeneba - A/C.3/78/SR.56
Nigeria
Asaju, Bola - A/C.3/78/SR.56
Rwanda
Umulisa, Flavia - A/C.3/78/SR.56
UN. Assistant Secretary-General for Human Rights
Brands Kehris, Ilze - A/C.3/78/SR.18
United Kingdom
Lundy, Phoebe - A/C.3/78/SR.56
United States
Lang, Dylan - A/C.3/78/SR.56

HUMAN RIGHTS INSTITUTIONS—SOUTHWEST ASIA AND ARAB COUNTRIES (Agenda item 71b)

Qatar
Al-Thani, Alya Ahmed S.A. - A/C.3/78/SR.50
UN. Assistant Secretary-General for Human Rights
Brands Kehris, Ilze - A/C.3/78/SR.18

HUMANITARIAN ASSISTANCE (Agenda item 72)

ASEAN
Nasir, Arrmanatha Christiawan (Indonesia) - A/78/PV.46
European Union
Popowski, Maciej - A/78/PV.46
International Committee of the Red Cross
Courtois, Laetitia - A/78/PV.47

HUMANITARIAN ASSISTANCE (Agenda item 72) (continued)

International Federation of Red Cross and Red Crescent Societies
Aultman, Kallie - A/78/PV.47

IAEA—REPORTS (Agenda item 89)

Algeria
Bendjama, Amar - A/78/PV.30
Argentina
Squeff, María del Carmen - A/78/PV.29
Armenia
Galstyan, Tigran - A/78/PV.29
Australia
Della-porta, Demi Heather See - A/78/PV.30
Austria
Pretterhofer, Stefan - A/78/PV.30
Bangladesh
Abdullah, Md Showeb - A/78/PV.29
Belarus
Kavaleuskaya, Alena - A/78/PV.29; A/78/PV.30
Burkina Faso
Ganou, Oumarou - A/78/PV.30
Chile
Narváez Ojeda, Paula - A/78/PV.29
China
Liu, Zhao - A/78/PV.30
Colombia
Zalabata Torres, Leonor - A/78/PV.29
Costa Rica
Chan Valverde, Maritza - A/78/PV.29
Cuba
Peñalver Portal, Gerardo - A/78/PV.30
Democratic People's Republic of Korea
Kim, Song - A/78/PV.29
Ecuador
Montalvo Sosa, Andrés Efren - A/78/PV.29
Egypt
Ahmed, Amr Essameldin Sadek - A/78/PV.30
El Salvador
González López, Egriselda Aracely - A/78/PV.29
European Union
Samson, Hedda - A/78/PV.29
Guatemala
Rodríguez Mancia, Carla María - A/78/PV.29
Honduras
Flores, Ramón Emilio - A/78/PV.29
IAEA. Director General
Grossi, Rafael Mariano - A/78/PV.29
Indonesia
Dhanutirto, Mariska Dwianti - A/78/PV.29
Iran (Islamic Republic of)
Ghorbanpour Najafabadi, Mohammad - A/78/PV.30
Jalil Iravani, Amir Saeid - A/78/PV.29
Iraq
Marzooq, Mohammed Sahib - A/78/PV.29
Israel
Kalmar, Nimrod - A/78/PV.30

IAEA—REPORTS (Agenda item 89) (continued)

Japan
Ishikane, Kimihiro - A/78/PV.29
Kusano, Yuta - A/78/PV.30
Kazakhstan
Syrymbet, Zhangeldy - A/78/PV.30
Kuwait
Alsaeedi, Abdulaziz - A/78/PV.29
Lithuania
Rosinas, Robertas - A/78/PV.30
Malaysia
Muhamad, Ahmad Faisal - A/78/PV.29
Mexico
Buenrostro Massieu, Alicia - A/78/PV.29
Morocco
Kadiri, Omar - A/78/PV.29
Myanmar
Tun, Kyaw Moe - A/78/PV.29
Namibia
Gertze, Neville Melvin - A/78/PV.30
Netherlands (Kingdom of the)
Tahzib-Lie, Bahia - A/78/PV.30
New Zealand
Nam, Christine - A/78/PV.30
Nigeria
Mahmud, Mohammed Lawal - A/78/PV.30
Oman
Al Rubkhi, Khalid Saleh Said - A/78/PV.30
Pakistan
Akram, Munir - A/78/PV.29
Paraguay
Sanabria de Montiel, María Gloria Beatriz - A/78/PV.30
Philippines
Lagdameo, Antonio Manuel Revilla - A/78/PV.30
Republic of Korea
Kim, Sunghoon - A/78/PV.30
Russian Federation
Eremin, Sergey - A/78/PV.30
Singapore
Lim, Jessie - A/78/PV.29
South Africa
Joyini, Mathu - A/78/PV.29
Sri Lanka
Pieris, Peter Mohan Maithri - A/78/PV.30
Syrian Arab Republic
Al Ashkar, Adib - A/78/PV.29; A/78/PV.30
Ukraine
Zlenko, Anatolii - A/78/PV.30
United Kingdom
Jones, Katherine Sarah - A/78/PV.30
Uruguay
Eustathiou de los Santos, Matías Andrés - A/78/PV.30
Viet Nam
Dang, Hoang Giang - A/78/PV.30

INDIAN OCEAN—ZONES OF PEACE (Agenda item 91)

Coordinating Bureau of the Non-Aligned Countries
Sirie, Mochammad Iqbal (Indonesia) - A/C.1/78/PV.21
UN. General Assembly. 1st Committee. Rapporteur
Balouji, Heidar Ali (Iran (Islamic Republic of)) - A/78/PV.42

INDIGENOUS PEOPLES (Agenda item 68a)

Australia
Larsen, James - A/78/PV.107; A/C.3/78/SR.15
Bangladesh
Abdullah, Md Showeb - A/C.3/78/SR.15
Bolivia (Plurinational State of)
Caldera Gutiérrez, Fiorella - A/C.3/78/SR.48
Pary Rodríguez, Diego - A/C.3/78/SR.15
Brazil
Balbino, Viviane Rios - A/C.3/78/SR.48
Gomes, Elaine Cristina Pereira - A/C.3/78/SR.15
Cameroon
Wainwel, Gwedji Doris - A/C.3/78/SR.15
Canada
Gort, Michael Christian - A/78/PV.107
Morin, Cassandra - A/C.3/78/SR.48
Rae, Robert - A/C.3/78/SR.15
Caribbean Community
Wallace, Brian Christopher Manley (Jamaica) - A/C.3/78/SR.15
China
Zhang, Sisi - A/C.3/78/SR.15
Colombia
Méndez Bocanegra, Rodrigo Andrés - A/C.3/78/SR.15
Zalabata Torres, Leonor - A/C.3/78/SR.15; A/C.3/78/SR.48
Cuba
Lamigueiro Cañedo, Ivette - A/C.3/78/SR.15
Denmark
Lassen, Christina Markus - A/C.3/78/SR.15
Ecuador
Pérez Loose, Hernán - A/C.3/78/SR.15
European Union
Nyman, Klas - A/C.3/78/SR.15
Samson, Hedda - A/C.3/78/SR.15
Gambia
Sillah, Aminata - A/C.3/78/SR.48
Group of Friends of Indigenous Peoples
Buenrostro Massieu, Alicia (Mexico) - A/C.3/78/SR.15
Guatemala
Rodríguez Mancia, Carla María - A/78/PV.107; A/C.3/78/SR.15
Guyana
Hazlewood, Abosede - A/C.3/78/SR.15
Holy See
Caccia, Gabriele Giordano - A/C.3/78/SR.15
Murphy, Robert David - A/C.3/78/SR.48
Hungary
Mogyorósi, Bálint - A/C.3/78/SR.48

INDIGENOUS PEOPLES (Agenda item 68a) (continued)

India
Sonkar, Suman - A/C.3/78/SR.15
Indonesia
Dhanutirto, Mariska Dwianti - A/C.3/78/SR.48
Pella, Blandina Ruth Viditha Adeleide - A/C.3/78/SR.17
Iran (Islamic Republic of)
Arab Bafrani, Fatemeh - A/C.3/78/SR.15; A/C.3/78/SR.48
Israel
Mimran Rosenberg, Avital - A/C.3/78/SR.17
Malaysia
Escopper Zumilla, Michael Jawa - A/C.3/78/SR.48
Rahman, Siti Adibah Abdul - A/C.3/78/SR.15
Mexico
Buenrostro Massieu, Alicia - A/78/PV.107
Vásquez Solano, Leonel - A/C.3/78/SR.15
Micronesia (Federated States of)
Welles, Kenneth - A/C.3/78/SR.15
Nepal
Rai, Pratigya - A/C.3/78/SR.15
New Zealand
Carrell, Leah - A/C.3/78/SR.15
Nicaragua
Hermida Castillo, Jaime - A/C.3/78/SR.15
Panama
Luque Nuñez, Linda del Carmen - A/C.3/78/SR.15
Paraguay
Pereira Sosa, José Eduardo - A/C.3/78/SR.15
Peru
Rojas, Eder - A/C.3/78/SR.15
Philippines
Navarrete, Angelica Saldivar - A/C.3/78/SR.15
Russian Federation
Kuzmenkov, Stepan Y. - A/C.3/78/SR.15
Senegal
Ndiaye, Mamadou Mounsir - A/C.3/78/SR.48
Sistema de la Integración Centroamericana
González López, Egriselda Aracely (El Salvador) - A/C.3/78/SR.15
Slovakia
Grünwald, Tomáš - A/C.3/78/SR.48
Sovereign Order of Malta
Rosario-Blackett, Marissa del - A/C.3/78/SR.17
Syrian Arab Republic
Altarsha, Elie - A/C.3/78/SR.15
Uganda
Nabeta, Celia Kafureka - A/C.3/78/SR.17
Ukraine
Tokarska, Anastasiia - A/C.3/78/SR.15
UN. General Assembly. 3rd Committee. Rapporteur
Poveda Brito, Robert Alexander (Venezuela (Bolivarian Republic of)) - A/78/PV.50
UN. Human Rights Council. Special Rapporteur on Rights of Indigenous Peoples
Cali Tzay, José Francisco - A/C.3/78/SR.15
United Kingdom
Sylvester, Timothy James - A/C.3/78/SR.48

INDIGENOUS PEOPLES (Agenda item 68a) (continued)

United Republic of Tanzania
Malebo, Hamisi - A/C.3/78/SR.15
United States
Murphy, Daniel - A/C.3/78/SR.15
Shrier, Jonathan - A/78/PV.107; A/C.3/78/SR.15
Venezuela (Bolivarian Republic of)
Poveda Brito, Robert Alexander - A/C.3/78/SR.17

INDIGENOUS PEOPLES—CONFERENCES (Agenda item 68b)

Australia
Larsen, James - A/C.3/78/SR.15
Bangladesh
Abdullah, Md Showeb - A/C.3/78/SR.15
Bolivia (Plurinational State of)
Pary Rodríguez, Diego - A/C.3/78/SR.15
Brazil
Gomes, Elaine Cristina Pereira - A/C.3/78/SR.15
Cameroon
Wainwel, Gwedji Doris - A/C.3/78/SR.15
Canada
Rae, Robert - A/C.3/78/SR.15
Caribbean Community
Wallace, Brian Christopher Manley (Jamaica) - A/C.3/78/SR.15
China
Zhang, Sisi - A/C.3/78/SR.15
Colombia
Méndez Bocanegra, Rodrigo Andrés - A/C.3/78/SR.15
Zalabata Torres, Leonor - A/C.3/78/SR.15
Cuba
Lamigueiro Cañedo, Ivette - A/C.3/78/SR.15
Denmark
Lassen, Christina Markus - A/C.3/78/SR.15
Ecuador
Pérez Loose, Hernán - A/C.3/78/SR.15
European Union
Nyman, Klas - A/C.3/78/SR.15
Samson, Hedda - A/C.3/78/SR.15
Group of Friends of Indigenous Peoples
Buenrostro Massieu, Alicia (Mexico) - A/C.3/78/SR.15
Guatemala
Rodríguez Mancia, Carla María - A/C.3/78/SR.15
Guyana
Hazlewood, Abosede - A/C.3/78/SR.15
Holy See
Caccia, Gabriele Giordano - A/C.3/78/SR.15
India
Sonkar, Suman - A/C.3/78/SR.15
Iran (Islamic Republic of)
Arab Bafrani, Fatemeh - A/C.3/78/SR.15
Malaysia
Rahman, Siti Adibah Abdul - A/C.3/78/SR.15
Mexico
Vásquez Solano, Leonel - A/C.3/78/SR.15
Micronesia (Federated States of)
Welles, Kenneth - A/C.3/78/SR.15

INDIGENOUS PEOPLES—CONFERENCES (Agenda item 68b) (continued)

Nepal
Rai, Pratigya - A/C.3/78/SR.15
New Zealand
Carrell, Leah - A/C.3/78/SR.15
Nicaragua
Hermida Castillo, Jaime - A/C.3/78/SR.15
Panama
Luque Nuñez, Linda del Carmen - A/C.3/78/SR.15
Paraguay
Pereira Sosa, José Eduardo - A/C.3/78/SR.15
Peru
Rojas, Eder - A/C.3/78/SR.15
Philippines
Navarrete, Angelica Saldivar - A/C.3/78/SR.15
Russian Federation
Kuzmenkov, Stepan Y. - A/C.3/78/SR.15
Sistema de la Integración Centroamericana
González López, Egriselda Aracely (El Salvador) - A/C.3/78/SR.15
Syrian Arab Republic
Altarsha, Elie - A/C.3/78/SR.15
Ukraine
Tokarska, Anastasiia - A/C.3/78/SR.15
UN. General Assembly. 3rd Committee. Rapporteur
Poveda Brito, Robert Alexander (Venezuela (Bolivarian Republic of)) - A/78/PV.50
United Republic of Tanzania
Malebo, Hamisi - A/C.3/78/SR.15
United States
Murphy, Daniel - A/C.3/78/SR.15
Shrier, Jonathan - A/C.3/78/SR.15

INFORMATION (Agenda item 53)

Algeria
Merabet, Ismaïl - A/C.4/78/SR.13
Argentina
Alvarez, Maximiliano Javier - A/C.4/78/SR.13
ASEAN
Nguyen, Hoang Nguyen (Viet Nam) - A/C.4/78/SR.12
Australia
Bryant, Rebecca Suzanne - A/C.4/78/SR.14
Bangladesh
Muhith, Muhammad A. - A/C.4/78/SR.13
Bolivia (Plurinational State of)
Ríos, Carmen Rosa - A/C.4/78/SR.14
Burkina Faso
Ouattara Cisse, Aminata - A/C.4/78/SR.13
Cameroon
Ngouambe Wouaga, Jean Luc - A/C.4/78/SR.14
Canada
Turnbull, Andrea Megan - A/C.4/78/SR.14
Caribbean Community
Wallace, Brian Christopher Manley (Jamaica) - A/C.4/78/SR.12
Comunidade dos Países de Língua Portuguesa
Cruz, Francisco José da (Angola) - A/C.4/78/SR.12
Congo
Manzeri Ngondo, Jean Claude - A/C.4/78/SR.13

INFORMATION (Agenda item 53) (continued)
Costa Rica
Chan Valverde, Maritza - A/C.4/78/SR.13
Côte d'Ivoire
Ipo, Gbolié Desiré Wulfran - A/C.4/78/SR.13
Cyprus
Demosthenous, Ioanna - A/C.4/78/SR.14
Democratic People's Republic of Korea
Kim, In Chol - A/C.4/78/SR.12
Dominican Republic
Cedano, Joan Margarita - A/C.4/78/SR.13
Egypt
Elshandawily, Ahmed - A/C.4/78/SR.12
El Salvador
González López, Egriselda Aracely - A/C.4/78/SR.13
Ethiopia
Kassaye, Yoseph - A/C.4/78/SR.8
European Union
Ladois, Jean-Noël - A/C.4/78/SR.12
Greece
Sekeris, Evangelos C. - A/C.4/78/SR.13
Group of 77
Peñalver Portal, Gerardo (Cuba) - A/C.4/78/SR.13
Romero Puentes, Yusnier (Cuba) - A/C.4/78/SR.12
Group of Friends in Defence of the Charter of the United Nations
Pérez Ayestarán, Joaquín Alberto (Venezuela (Bolivarian Republic of)) - A/C.4/78/SR.12
Grupo de Amigos del Español en las Naciones Unidas
Thomas Ramírez, Vilma (Cuba) - A/C.4/78/SR.12
Haiti
Pierre, Christopher - A/C.4/78/SR.13
India
Birdi, Nitish - A/C.4/78/SR.12
Iran (Islamic Republic of)
Ghelich, Vahid - A/C.4/78/SR.13
Sahraei, Mohammad Reza - A/C.4/78/SR.13
Iraq
Alsammak, Uday Qais Mahdi - A/C.4/78/SR.13
Israel
Maayan, Michal - A/C.4/78/SR.13
Shapir Ben Naftaly, Reut - A/C.4/78/SR.14
Japan
Yoshida, Aya - A/C.4/78/SR.13
Latvia
Pavļuta-Deslandes, Sanita - A/C.4/78/SR.13
League of Arab States
Elardja Flitti, Nasria - A/C.4/78/SR.14
Malaysia
Sabarudin, Mohamad Shahir - A/C.4/78/SR.13
Mexico
Cisneros Chávez, José de Jesús - A/C.4/78/SR.12
Guzik Duno, Aline - A/C.4/78/SR.14
Morocco
El Mezouaghi, Youssef - A/C.4/78/SR.13
Myanmar
Tun, Kyaw Moe - A/C.4/78/SR.14

INFORMATION (Agenda item 53) (continued)
Namibia
Kuzee, Helena Ndapewa - A/C.4/78/SR.14
Nepal
Ray, Kaushal Kishor - A/C.4/78/SR.13
Oman
Al Rashdi, Amal - A/C.4/78/SR.13
Organisation internationale de la Francophonie
Nkalwo, Joseph Léa - A/C.4/78/SR.14
Pakistan
Jadoon, Usman Iqbal - A/C.4/78/SR.12
Portugal
Aranda, Jorge Eduardo Ferreira Silva - A/C.4/78/SR.13
Qatar
Al-Thani, Alya Ahmed S.A. - A/C.4/78/SR.14
Republic of Korea
Jung, Jae Hyuk - A/C.4/78/SR.12; A/C.4/78/SR.13
Romania
Mocanu, Andreea - A/C.4/78/SR.12; A/C.4/78/SR.13
Russian Federation
Strzhizhovskiy, Fedor K. - A/C.4/78/SR.12; A/C.4/78/SR.13; A/C.4/78/SR.14
Saudi Arabia
Alaklabi, Faisal Saeed M. - A/C.4/78/SR.13
Senegal
Niane, Adja Binta - A/C.4/78/SR.12
South Africa
Schalkwyk, Marthinus van - A/C.4/78/SR.14
Spain
Rodríguez Gómez-Aller, Juan - A/C.4/78/SR.12
Sri Lanka
Pieris, Peter Mohan Maithri - A/C.4/78/SR.13
State of Palestine
Bamya, Majed - A/C.4/78/SR.14
Sudan
Mohamed, Abuzied Shamseldin Ahmed - A/C.4/78/SR.13
Thailand
Norapoompipat, Sorawut - A/C.4/78/SR.12
Ukraine
Tokarska, Anastasiia - A/C.4/78/SR.14
UN. Committee on Information. Vice-Chair
Baños Müller, Liliana Verónica (El Salvador) - A/C.4/78/SR.12
UN. General Assembly. Special Political and Decolonization Committee (4th Committee). Rapporteur
Dhanutirto, Mariska Dwianti (Indonesia) - A/78/PV.45
UN. Under-Secretary-General for Global Communications
Fleming, Melissa - A/C.4/78/SR.12
United Kingdom
Woodifield, Mungo - A/C.4/78/SR.14
Yemen
Al-mashehari, Sarah Ahmed Ahmed - A/C.4/78/SR.14

INFORMATION—INTERNATIONAL SECURITY (Agenda item 94)

Algeria
Lebbaz, Larbi Abdelfattah - A/C.1/78/PV.21
ASEAN
Chindawongse, Suriya (Thailand) - A/C.1/78/PV.20
Australia
Lukabyo, Emma Jane Mutesi - A/C.1/78/PV.20; A/C.1/78/PV.29
Bahrain
Janahi, Balqees - A/C.1/78/PV.21
Bangladesh
Muhith, Muhammad A. - A/C.1/78/PV.20
Brazil
Damico, Flávio Soares - A/C.1/78/PV.21
Szatmari, Roberto Wazima - A/C.1/78/PV.29
Canada
Berard Cadieux, Xavier - A/C.1/78/PV.20
Caribbean Community
Wallace, Brian Christopher Manley (Jamaica) - A/C.1/78/PV.21
Chile
Vidal Mercado, Jorge Andrés - A/C.1/78/PV.20
China
Li, Nan - A/C.1/78/PV.29
Shen, Jian - A/C.1/78/PV.20
Colombia
Quintero Correa, Nohra María - A/C.1/78/PV.21
Coordinating Bureau of the Non-Aligned Countries
Sirie, Mochammad Iqbal (Indonesia) - A/C.1/78/PV.20
Costa Rica
Ávila Becerril, Ana Maricela - A/C.1/78/PV.21
Côte d'Ivoire
Moriko, Tiémoko - A/C.1/78/PV.20
Cuba
Gómez Sardiñas, Yiliam - A/C.1/78/PV.20
Romero López, Rosanis - A/C.1/78/PV.28; A/C.1/78/PV.29
Djibouti
Assoweh, Zeinab Ismaël - A/C.1/78/PV.29
Egypt
Hegazy, Abdelrhman Mohamed Farid - A/C.1/78/PV.20; A/C.1/78/PV.29
El Salvador
González López, Egriselda Aracely - A/C.1/78/PV.20
Estonia
Varem, Mattias - A/C.1/78/PV.20
Ethiopia
Getahun, Kedir - A/C.1/78/PV.20
European Union
Karczmarz, Michał - A/C.1/78/PV.20
Sánchez de Lerín García-Ovies, Ignacio (Spain) - A/C.1/78/PV.29
France
Petit, Camille - A/C.1/78/PV.21; A/C.1/78/PV.28
Greece
Christoglou, Konstantinos - A/C.1/78/PV.20

INFORMATION—INTERNATIONAL SECURITY (Agenda item 94) (continued)

Group of Arab States
Alqaisi, Sultan Natheir Mustafa (Jordan) - A/C.1/78/PV.20
Guatemala
Rodríguez Mancia, Carla María - A/C.1/78/PV.20
Holy See
Caccia, Gabriele Giordano - A/C.1/78/PV.21
India
Bedi, Anmol Sher Singh - A/C.1/78/PV.21
Parihar, Rajesh - A/C.1/78/PV.29
Indonesia
Sirie, Mochammad Iqbal - A/C.1/78/PV.20; A/C.1/78/PV.29
Iran (Islamic Republic of)
Ghorbanpour Najafabadi, Mohammad - A/C.1/78/PV.20; A/C.1/78/PV.29
Iraq
Saadi, Abu Alhakam Adnan Sadek - A/C.1/78/PV.20
Israel
Sharoni, Benjamin - A/C.1/78/PV.21; A/C.1/78/PV.29
Italy
Bencini, Leonardo - A/C.1/78/PV.21
Japan
Namekawa, Hirochika - A/C.1/78/PV.29
Ogasawara, Ichiro - A/C.1/78/PV.20
Kenya
Muigai, Stephanie Ngonyo - A/C.1/78/PV.20
Malaysia
Sivamohan, Shivanand - A/C.1/78/PV.20; A/C.1/78/PV.29
Mexico
Fausto, Braulio - A/C.1/78/PV.20
Sánchez Kiesslich, Eduardo Alcibiades - A/C.1/78/PV.29
Netherlands (Kingdom of the)
Bosch, Robert in den - A/C.1/78/PV.20
New Zealand
Nam, Christine - A/C.1/78/PV.20
Nicaragua
Jiménez, Jasser - A/C.1/78/PV.29
Pakistan
Ahmed, Husham - A/C.1/78/PV.20
Sarwani, Gul Qaiser - A/C.1/78/PV.29
Philippines
Lipana, Diane Shayne Dela Fuente - A/C.1/78/PV.20; A/C.1/78/PV.29
Republic of Korea
Lee, Hyun Goo - A/C.1/78/PV.21; A/C.1/78/PV.29
Russian Federation
Belousov, Andrey I. - A/C.1/78/PV.21; A/C.1/78/PV.28; A/C.1/78/PV.29
South Africa
Lagardien, Yaseen - A/C.1/78/PV.20; A/C.1/78/PV.29
Sri Lanka
Pieris, Peter Mohan Maithri - A/C.1/78/PV.20

INFORMATION—INTERNATIONAL SECURITY (Agenda item 94) (continued)

Switzerland
Anderegg, Julius - A/C.1/78/PV.29
Haegen, Laurin van der - A/C.1/78/PV.20
Syrian Arab Republic
Al Ashkar, Adib - A/C.1/78/PV.29
Thailand
Hanlumyuang, Thararut - A/C.1/78/PV.20
Timor-Leste
Sousa, Ivens Gusmao de - A/C.1/78/PV.20
Togo
Tchalare, Abd-el Kader Yasmin - A/C.1/78/PV.21
UN. General Assembly. 1st Committee. Rapporteur
Balouji, Heidar Ali (Iran (Islamic Republic of)) - A/78/PV.42
UN. Open-ended Working Group on Security of and in the Use of Information and Communications Technologies 2021-2025. Chair
Gafoor, Burhan (Singapore) - A/C.1/78/PV.21
United Kingdom
Page, Elizabeth Louise - A/C.1/78/PV.20
United States
Turner, Bruce - A/C.1/78/PV.21
Uruguay
Eustathiou de los Santos, Matías Andrés - A/C.1/78/PV.20
Viet Nam
Mai, Ngan Ha - A/C.1/78/PV.29

INFORMATION TECHNOLOGY—DEVELOPMENT (Agenda item 15)

Angola
Cruz, Francisco José da - A/C.2/78/SR.10
Armenia
Babikyan, Araksya - A/C.2/78/SR.10
Azerbaijan
Ahmadova, Billur - A/C.2/78/SR.11
Bahrain
Alatawi, Innas Abdulrahman - A/C.2/78/SR.10
Bangladesh
Hossain, Faruk - A/C.2/78/SR.10
Bolivia (Plurinational State of)
Pary Rodríguez, Diego - A/C.2/78/SR.11
Brunei Darussalam
Pg Ibrahim, Dk Nur Maseleiana Rahimah - A/C.2/78/SR.10
Burkina Faso
Barro, Braima - A/C.2/78/SR.10
Caribbean Community
Wallace, Brian Christopher Manley (Jamaica) - A/C.2/78/SR.10
China
Zhao, Haibo - A/C.2/78/SR.10
Costa Rica
Zamora Zumbado, Leticia María - A/C.2/78/SR.11
Dominican Republic
Rubio, Celina - A/C.2/78/SR.10
Ethiopia
Muktar, Anwar - A/C.2/78/SR.11

INFORMATION TECHNOLOGY—DEVELOPMENT (Agenda item 15) (continued)

European Union
Bologa, Anda - A/C.2/78/SR.23
Group of 77
Guevara Rodríguez, Adiel (Cuba) - A/C.2/78/SR.10
Torres Seara, Dalia Marlen (Cuba) - A/C.2/78/SR.21
Group of Landlocked Developing Countries
Motsumi, Lorato (Botswana) - A/C.2/78/SR.10
Group of Least Developed Countries
Dhungel, Purushottam (Nepal) - A/C.2/78/SR.10
India
Gahlot, Petal - A/C.2/78/SR.10
Indonesia
Prabowo, Hari - A/C.2/78/SR.11
Iran (Islamic Republic of)
Jalili, Tahereh - A/C.2/78/SR.10
ITU
Wynhoven, Ursula - A/C.2/78/SR.11
Kuwait
Alkhuraibet, Ali - A/C.2/78/SR.10
Malawi
Chivundu, Renata - A/C.2/78/SR.10
Mexico
Curzio Vila, Elena - A/C.2/78/SR.10
Pakistan
Shafique, Umar - A/C.2/78/SR.10
Russian Federation
Aristov, Dmitry S. - A/C.2/78/SR.10
Saudi Arabia
Shaker, Mohammed Amin - A/C.2/78/SR.10
Sierra Leone
Alghali, Francess Piagie - A/C.2/78/SR.11
Singapore
Ching, Martha - A/C.2/78/SR.10
South Africa
Mpama, Sibusiso Qetello - A/C.2/78/SR.11
Switzerland
Schlaepfer, Christian - A/C.2/78/SR.23
UN. General Assembly. 2nd Committee. Rapporteur
Gatev, Ivaylo (Bulgaria) - A/78/PV.49
UNCTAD
González Sanz, Angel - A/C.2/78/SR.10
United Kingdom
Kelsey, Alistair Robert Steven - A/C.2/78/SR.23
United States
Lawrence, Jason N. - A/C.2/78/SR.23
Zambia
Milambo, Chola - A/C.2/78/SR.11

INTERNATIONAL CRIMINAL COURT—REPORTS (Agenda item 74)

Argentina
Squeff, María del Carmen - A/78/PV.22
Australia
Larsen, James - A/78/PV.22
Bangladesh
Muhith, Muhammad A. - A/78/PV.21
Belgium
Lagatie, Karl - A/78/PV.22

INTERNATIONAL CRIMINAL COURT—REPORTS (Agenda item 74) (continued)

Brazil
Pinto, Alessandro De Rezende - A/78/PV.22; A/78/PV.25
Burkina Faso
Ganou, Oumarou - A/78/PV.22
Canada
Maillé, Béatrice - A/78/PV.21
Rae, Robert - A/78/PV.22
Chile
Narváez Ojeda, Paula - A/78/PV.21
China
Ma, Xinmin - A/78/PV.21
Colombia
Solano Ramírez, Lucía Teresa - A/78/PV.21
Costa Rica
Chan Valverde, Maritza - A/78/PV.21
Cuba
Silva Walker, Eva Yelina - A/78/PV.22
Cyprus
Pittakis, Theodoulos - A/78/PV.22
Czechia
Kafková, Eva Anna - A/78/PV.22
Democratic Republic of the Congo
Mukongo Ngay, Zénon - A/78/PV.22
Ecuador
Escobar Ullauri, Pablo - A/78/PV.21
El Salvador
González López, Egriselda Aracely - A/78/PV.25
Estonia
Tammsaar, Rein - A/78/PV.21
European Union
Marquardt, Stephan - A/78/PV.21
Finland
Kalkku, Elina - A/78/PV.21
France
Dime-Labille, Diarra - A/78/PV.21
Georgia
Abesadze, David - A/78/PV.22
Germany
Hasenau, Michael - A/78/PV.22
Greece
Stavridi, Zinovia Chaido - A/78/PV.21
Guatemala
Rodríguez Mancia, Carla María - A/78/PV.21
International Criminal Court. President
Hofmański, Piotr - A/78/PV.21
Iran (Islamic Republic of)
Mousavi, Seyed Ali - A/78/PV.21
Ireland
Kirk, James - A/78/PV.22
Israel
Cappon, Noam - A/78/PV.25
Italy
Massari, Maurizio - A/78/PV.22
Japan
Tokunaga, Fumie - A/78/PV.22
Kenya
Waweru, James Ndiragu - A/78/PV.21

INTERNATIONAL CRIMINAL COURT—REPORTS (Agenda item 74) (continued)

Liechtenstein
Wenaweser, Christian - A/78/PV.22
Luxembourg
Germeaux, Alain - A/78/PV.21
Mali
Konfourou, Issa - A/78/PV.22
Malta
Kuymizakis, Adam - A/78/PV.22
Mexico
Buenrostro Massieu, Alicia - A/78/PV.22
Mongolia
Damdin, Erdenebal Suren - A/78/PV.21
Myanmar
Tun, Kyaw Moe - A/78/PV.22
Netherlands (Kingdom of the)
Brandt, Yoka - A/78/PV.21
New Zealand
Fepuleai, Justin Peter - A/78/PV.22
Paraguay
Pereira Sosa, José Eduardo - A/78/PV.22
Peru
García Toma, Victor Óscar Shiyin - A/78/PV.21
Philippines
Lagdameo, Antonio Manuel Revilla - A/78/PV.22
Poland
Szczerski, Krzysztof - A/78/PV.22
Republic of Korea
Choi, Taeeun - A/78/PV.22
Romania
Feruță, Cornel - A/78/PV.21
Orosan, Alina - A/78/PV.21
Russian Federation
Zabolotskaya, Maria V. - A/78/PV.21; A/78/PV.25
Senegal
Niang, Cheikh - A/78/PV.22
Slovakia
Klanduch, Peter - A/78/PV.21
Slovenia
Malovrh, Bostjan - A/78/PV.22
State of Palestine
Bamya, Majed - A/78/PV.25
Switzerland
Chanda, Riccarda - A/78/PV.22
Syrian Arab Republic
Khaddour, Mhd. Riyad - A/78/PV.21; A/78/PV.25
Trinidad and Tobago
Abraham, Devita - A/78/PV.22
Uganda
Muhumuza, Duncan Laki - A/78/PV.21
Ukraine
Prytula, Mykola - A/78/PV.22
UN. General Assembly. President
Francis, Dennis (Trinidad and Tobago) - A/78/PV.21
United Kingdom
Hollis, Jonathan Samuel - A/78/PV.22
United States
Smyre, Calvin - A/78/PV.22

INTERNATIONAL CRIMINAL COURT—REPORTS (Agenda item 74) (continued)

Venezuela (Bolivarian Republic of)
Pérez Ayestarán, Joaquín Alberto - A/78/PV.25

INTERNATIONAL JURISDICTION (Agenda item 84)

Algeria
Bouchedoub, Mohamed Faiz - A/C.6/78/SR.13
Argentina
Mainero, Martín Juan - A/C.6/78/SR.12
Belarus
Evseenko, Pavel - A/C.6/78/SR.12
Brazil
Sloboda, Pedro Muniz Pinto - A/C.6/78/SR.12
Burkina Faso
Ganou, Oumarou - A/C.6/78/SR.13
Cameroon
Nyanid, Zacharie Serge Raoul - A/C.6/78/SR.12; A/C.6/78/SR.37
Canada
Agnello, Alexander - A/C.6/78/SR.12
China
Li, Linlin - A/C.6/78/SR.12
Community of Latin American and Caribbean States
Mark, Hayley-Ann (Saint Vincent and the Grenadines) - A/C.6/78/SR.12
Coordinating Bureau of the Non-Aligned Countries
Heidari, Bahram (Iran (Islamic Republic of)) - A/C.6/78/SR.12
Costa Rica
Ramírez Baca, Gustavo Adolfo - A/C.6/78/SR.12
Côte d'Ivoire
Moriko, Tiémoko - A/C.6/78/SR.13
Cuba
Carral Castelo, Arianna - A/C.6/78/SR.12
Czechia
Zukal, Marek - A/C.6/78/SR.12
Egypt
Roshdy, Hussein Ossama Hussein Abdelrhman - A/C.6/78/SR.12
El Salvador
Flores Soto, Ligia Lorena - A/C.6/78/SR.13
Eritrea
Essaias, Meron Habte - A/C.6/78/SR.13
Ethiopia
Alemayehu, Betelihem Taye - A/C.6/78/SR.13
European Union
Popan, Simona - A/C.6/78/SR.12
Germany
Hasenau, Michael - A/C.6/78/SR.12
Hungary
Vittay, Melinda - A/C.6/78/SR.12
India
Bhat, Kajal - A/C.6/78/SR.13
International Committee of the Red Cross
Apraxine, Pierre - A/C.6/78/SR.13
Iran (Islamic Republic of)
Heidari, Bahram - A/C.6/78/SR.12

INTERNATIONAL JURISDICTION (Agenda item 84) (continued)

Ireland
Kirk, James - A/C.6/78/SR.12
Israel
Rubinshtein, Yarden - A/C.6/78/SR.12; A/C.6/78/SR.13
Kenya
Nyakoe, Catherine Nyaboke - A/C.6/78/SR.13
Liechtenstein
Hasler, Merhaba - A/C.6/78/SR.12
Lithuania
Paulauskas, Rytis - A/C.6/78/SR.12
Mali
Konfourou, Issa - A/C.6/78/SR.13
Mexico
Arrocha Olabuenaga, Pablo Adrián - A/C.6/78/SR.12
Morocco
Lahsaini, Khalid - A/C.6/78/SR.13
Mozambique
Saranga, Geraldo - A/C.6/78/SR.13
Myanmar
Tun, Kyaw Moe - A/C.6/78/SR.13
Netherlands (Kingdom of the)
Jacobs, Mats - A/C.6/78/SR.12
Nigeria
Ajayi, Eniola Olaitan - A/C.6/78/SR.13
Pakistan
Jadoon, Usman Iqbal - A/C.6/78/SR.12
Philippines
Arumpac-Marte, Azela Guerrero - A/C.6/78/SR.13
Russian Federation
Proskuryakov, Alexander S. - A/C.6/78/SR.12
Saudi Arabia
Alwasil, Abdulaziz M.O. - A/C.6/78/SR.13
Senegal
Ndoye, Abdou - A/C.6/78/SR.12
Sierra Leone
Kanu, Michael Imran - A/C.6/78/SR.13
Singapore
Tan, Scott - A/C.6/78/SR.13
Slovenia
Šebenik, Nataša - A/C.6/78/SR.12
Sri Lanka
Pieris, Peter Mohan Maithri - A/C.6/78/SR.12
State of Palestine
Sayej, Loureen O.A. - A/C.6/78/SR.13
Sudan
Mohammed, Ammar Mohammed Mahmoud - A/C.6/78/SR.12
Sweden
Fielding, Julia - A/C.6/78/SR.12
Syrian Arab Republic
Khaddour, Mhd. Riyad - A/C.6/78/SR.12; A/C.6/78/SR.13
Thailand
Chindawongse, Suriya - A/C.6/78/SR.12
Togo
Ouro-bodi, Tchakpide - A/C.6/78/SR.13
Türkiye
Güç, Eda - A/C.6/78/SR.13

INTERNATIONAL JURISDICTION (Agenda item 84) (continued)

Uganda
Ikondere, Marvin - A/C.6/78/SR.12
UN. General Assembly. 6th Committee. Bureau
Raojee, Vreeshini (Mauritius) - A/C.6/78/SR.37
UN. General Assembly. 6th Committee. Rapporteur
Moussa, Moussa Mohamed (Djibouti) - A/78/PV.45
UN. Group of African States
Ikondere, Marvin (Uganda) - A/C.6/78/SR.12
United Arab Emirates
Al Blooshi, Ahmed Ali - A/C.6/78/SR.13
United Kingdom
Hollis, Jonathan Samuel - A/C.6/78/SR.12
United Republic of Tanzania
Kattanga, Hussein A. - A/C.6/78/SR.13
United States
Grosso, Elizabeth Maryanne - A/C.6/78/SR.12
Viet Nam
Pham, Nha - A/C.6/78/SR.13

INTERNATIONAL LAW—TRAINING PROGRAMMES (Agenda item 78)

Advisory Committee on the United Nations Programme of Assistance in the Teaching, Study, Dissemination and Wider Appreciation of International Law. Chair
Agyeman, Harold Adlai (Ghana) - A/C.6/78/SR.21
Advisory Committee on the United Nations Programme of Assistance in the Teaching, Study, Dissemination and Wider Appreciation of International Law. Secretary
Pallek, Markus - A/C.6/78/SR.21
ASEAN
Seah, Mark (Singapore) - A/C.6/78/SR.21
Bolivia (Plurinational State of)
Ríos, Carmen Rosa - A/C.6/78/SR.22
Burkina Faso
Ganou, Oumarou - A/C.6/78/SR.21
Cameroon
Nyanid, Zacharie Serge Raoul - A/C.6/78/SR.21
Chile
Hernández Chávez, José Juan - A/C.6/78/SR.22
China
Ma, Yanbo - A/C.6/78/SR.21
Colombia
Botero, Stephanie - A/C.6/78/SR.21
Community of Latin American and Caribbean States
Mark, Hayley-Ann (Saint Vincent and the Grenadines) - A/C.6/78/SR.21
Coordinating Bureau of the Non-Aligned Countries
Heidari, Bahram (Iran (Islamic Republic of)) - A/C.6/78/SR.21
Denmark
Laursen, Erik - A/C.6/78/SR.21
Egypt
Nouh, Amr Mohamed Mosaad - A/C.6/78/SR.21
El Salvador
González López, Egriselda Aracely - A/C.6/78/SR.21

INTERNATIONAL LAW—TRAINING PROGRAMMES (Agenda item 78) (continued)

Equatorial Guinea
Nze Mansogo, Estela Mercedes - A/C.6/78/SR.22
Eritrea
Essaias, Meron Habte - A/C.6/78/SR.21
Ethiopia
Alemayehu, Betelihem Taye - A/C.6/78/SR.21
European Union
Popan, Simona - A/C.6/78/SR.21
France
Dime-Labille, Diarra - A/C.6/78/SR.21
Group of 77
Carral Castelo, Arianna (Cuba) - A/C.6/78/SR.21
Guinea
Condé, N'Nagbé - A/C.6/78/SR.21
Haiti
Panier, Wisnique - A/C.6/78/SR.22
Ireland
Kirk, James - A/C.6/78/SR.22
Kenya
Nyakoe, Catherine Nyaboke - A/C.6/78/SR.22
Lebanon
Hitti, Youssef - A/C.6/78/SR.22
Malaysia
Abd Karim, Nur Azura Binti - A/C.6/78/SR.21
Mauritania
Sao, Mariam - A/C.6/78/SR.22
Mexico
Delgado Fernández, Sergio Emanuel - A/C.6/78/SR.21
Nigeria
Olisa, Janet - A/C.6/78/SR.22
Pakistan
Khokhar, Adeel Mumtaz - A/C.6/78/SR.21
Paraguay
Giret Soto, David Antonio - A/C.6/78/SR.22
Philippines
Arumpac-Marte, Azela Guerrero - A/C.6/78/SR.21
Portugal
Matos, Ines - A/C.6/78/SR.21
Russian Federation
Skachkov, Evgeny A. - A/C.6/78/SR.21
Senegal
Diome, Diamane - A/C.6/78/SR.21
Singapore
Seah, Mark - A/C.6/78/SR.21
South Africa
Motsepe, Keke Mantsho - A/C.6/78/SR.21
Sudan
Mohammed, Ammar Mohammed Mahmoud - A/C.6/78/SR.21
Thailand
Sresthabutr, Hataipat - A/C.6/78/SR.21
Uganda
Ikondere, Marvin - A/C.6/78/SR.22
UN. Division for Ocean Affairs and the Law of the Sea
Hicuburundi, Alice - A/C.6/78/SR.21
UN. General Assembly. 6th Committee. Bureau
Hackman, Khalilah (Ghana) - A/C.6/78/SR.37

INTERNATIONAL LAW—TRAINING PROGRAMMES (Agenda item 78) (continued)

UN. General Assembly. 6th Committee. Rapporteur
Moussa, Moussa Mohamed (Djibouti) - A/78/PV.45
UN. Group of African States
Ikondere, Marvin (Uganda) - A/C.6/78/SR.21
UN. Legal Counsel
Soares, João Miguel Ferreira de Serpa - A/C.6/78/SR.21
United Kingdom
Lito, Melina - A/C.6/78/SR.21
United Republic of Tanzania
Mwasota, Joseph Aron - A/C.6/78/SR.22
United States
Patton, Dorothy - A/C.6/78/SR.21
Viet Nam
Tran, Thi Phuong Ha - A/C.6/78/SR.21

INTERNATIONAL ORGANIZATION OF EMPLOYERS—OBSERVER STATUS (Agenda item 167)

UN. General Assembly. 6th Committee. Rapporteur
Moussa, Moussa Mohamed (Djibouti) - A/78/PV.45

INTERNATIONAL PARLIAMENTARIANS' CONGRESS—OBSERVER STATUS (Agenda item 170)

India
Bhat, Kajal - A/C.6/78/SR.14
Pakistan
Akram, Munir - A/C.6/78/SR.14
UN. General Assembly. 6th Committee. Rapporteur
Moussa, Moussa Mohamed (Djibouti) - A/78/PV.45
United States
Patton, Dorothy - A/C.6/78/SR.14

INTERNATIONAL RESIDUAL MECHANISM FOR CRIMINAL TRIBUNALS (Agenda item 126)

Albania
Stastoli, Andris - A/78/PV.19
Brazil
Braoios, Victor Silveira - A/78/PV.19
European Union
Popan, Simona - A/78/PV.19
France
Dime-Labille, Diarra - A/78/PV.19
Germany
Hasenau, Michael - A/78/PV.19
International Residual Mechanism for Criminal Tribunals. President
Gatti Santana, Graciela Susana - A/78/PV.19
Japan
Nagano, Shunsuke - A/78/PV.19
Latvia
Pavļuta-Deslandes, Sanita - A/78/PV.19
Malta
Kuymizakis, Adam - A/78/PV.19
New Zealand
Schwalger, Carolyn - A/78/PV.19
Russian Federation
Zabolotskaya, Maria V. - A/78/PV.19

INTERNATIONAL RESIDUAL MECHANISM FOR CRIMINAL TRIBUNALS (Agenda item 126) (continued)

Rwanda
Kayinamura, Robert - A/78/PV.19
Serbia
Buden, Radmila - A/78/PV.19
United Kingdom
Hollis, Jonathan Samuel - A/78/PV.19
United Republic of Tanzania
Mwasota, Joseph Aron - A/78/PV.19
United States
Lu, Christopher P. - A/78/PV.19

INTERNATIONAL RESIDUAL MECHANISM FOR CRIMINAL TRIBUNALS—FINANCING (Agenda item 145)

Group of 77
Hernández Morera, Diosdado de Jesús (Cuba) - A/C.5/78/SR.20
Rwanda
Uzabumwana Tona, Yannick - A/C.5/78/SR.20
UN. Advisory Committee on Administrative and Budgetary Questions. Vice-Chair
Chmielewski, Jakub - A/C.5/78/SR.20
Ruas, Juliana Gaspar - A/C.5/78/SR.25
UN. Department of Management Strategy, Policy and Compliance. Office of Programme Planning, Finance and Budget. Finance Division. Director
Costa, Maria - A/C.5/78/SR.20; A/C.5/78/SR.25
UN. General Assembly. 5th Committee. Rapporteur
Hartog, Laurens Thomas den (Netherlands (Kingdom of the)) - A/78/PV.50(Resumption1)
UN. Group of African States
Minale, Lemlem Fiseha (Ethiopia) - A/C.5/78/SR.20
United Republic of Tanzania
Suleiman, Suleiman Haji - A/C.5/78/SR.20

INTERNATIONAL TRADE (Agenda item 16a)

Alliance of Small Island States
Bartley, Matilda (Samoa) - A/C.2/78/SR.8
ASEAN
Nasir, Arrmanatha Christiawan (Indonesia) - A/C.2/78/SR.8
Belarus
Kavaleuskaya, Alena - A/C.2/78/SR.9; A/C.2/78/SR.22; A/C.2/78/SR.24
Cameroon
Banaken Elel, Nelly - A/C.2/78/SR.9
Caribbean Community
Wallace, Brian Christopher Manley (Jamaica) - A/C.2/78/SR.8
China
Hua, Chenghang - A/C.2/78/SR.9
Colombia
Murillo Ferrer, Jorge Adrián - A/C.2/78/SR.22
Cuba
Guevara Rodríguez, Adiel - A/C.2/78/SR.8
Romero Puentes, Yusnier - A/C.2/78/SR.24

INTERNATIONAL TRADE (Agenda item 16a) (continued)

Ethiopia
Muktar, Anwar - A/C.2/78/SR.11
European Union
Martín Couce, Adrián (Spain) - A/C.2/78/SR.22; A/C.2/78/SR.24
Group of 77
Torres Seara, Dalia Marlen (Cuba) - A/C.2/78/SR.8; A/C.2/78/SR.21
Group of Friends in Defence of the Charter of the United Nations
Pérez Ayestarán, Joaquín Alberto (Venezuela (Bolivarian Republic of)) - A/C.2/78/SR.8
Group of Least Developed Countries
Ray, Kaushal Kishor (Nepal) - A/C.2/78/SR.8
Guyana
Doimen, Tash van - A/C.2/78/SR.9
India
Gahlot, Petal - A/C.2/78/SR.9; A/C.2/78/SR.22
Iran (Islamic Republic of)
Teymourpour, Nooshin - A/C.2/78/SR.8
Iraq
Al-Niami, Mustafa - A/C.2/78/SR.9
Lithuania
Malinauskas, Andrius - A/C.2/78/SR.24
Malaysia
Adnan, Yang Aishah Binti - A/C.2/78/SR.9
Maldives
Zuhuree, Ibrahim - A/C.2/78/SR.9
Namibia
Naanda, Anne - A/C.2/78/SR.9
Nicaragua
Hermida Castillo, Jaime - A/C.2/78/SR.9
Russian Federation
Chumakov, Dmitry S. - A/C.2/78/SR.24
Kardash, Viktoriia E. - A/C.2/78/SR.9
Meschchanov, Boris A. - A/C.2/78/SR.22; A/C.2/78/SR.24
Saudi Arabia
Alomair, Reem Fahad O. - A/C.2/78/SR.9
Singapore
Tan, Jason Han Wei - A/C.2/78/SR.24
South Africa
Seedat, Ahmed Hoosen - A/C.2/78/SR.11
Switzerland
Schlaepfer, Christian - A/C.2/78/SR.24
Syrian Arab Republic
Al Nahhas, Wissam - A/C.2/78/SR.8
Altarsha, Elie - A/C.2/78/SR.24
Thailand
Sapkul, Louismongkol - A/C.2/78/SR.9
UN. Department of Economic and Social Affairs. Development Policy Analysis Division. Director
Mukherjee, Shantanu - A/C.2/78/SR.8
UN. General Assembly. 2nd Committee. Rapporteur
Gatev, Ivaylo (Bulgaria) - A/78/PV.49
UN. Group of African States
Ladeb, Tarek (Tunisia) - A/C.2/78/SR.9

INTERNATIONAL TRADE (Agenda item 16a) (continued)

UNCTAD
Hashmi, Khalil Ur Rahman - A/C.2/78/SR.8
Shirotori, Miho - A/C.2/78/SR.8
United Kingdom
Baric, Ana - A/C.2/78/SR.22
Kelsey, Alistair Robert Steven - A/C.2/78/SR.24
United States
Armbruster, Thomas - A/C.2/78/SR.21
Lawrence, Jason N. - A/C.2/78/SR.22; A/C.2/78/SR.24
Venezuela (Bolivarian Republic of)
Marín Sevilla, Asbina - A/C.2/78/SR.9; A/C.2/78/SR.24
Zambia
Boma, Regina Chama - A/C.2/78/SR.9
Zimbabwe
Rupende, Tapiwa Roy - A/C.2/78/SR.9; A/C.2/78/SR.24

INTERNATIONAL TRADE UNION CONFEDERATION—OBSERVER STATUS (Agenda item 168)

UN. General Assembly. 6th Committee. Rapporteur
Moussa, Moussa Mohamed (Djibouti) - A/78/PV.45

INVESTMENT PROMOTION (Agenda item 16g)

ASEAN
Nasir, Arrmanatha Christiawan (Indonesia) - A/C.2/78/SR.8
Colombia
Murillo Ferrer, Jorge Adrián - A/C.2/78/SR.23
Group of 77
Torres Seara, Dalia Marlen (Cuba) - A/C.2/78/SR.21
Group of Friends in Defence of the Charter of the United Nations
Pérez Ayestarán, Joaquín Alberto (Venezuela (Bolivarian Republic of)) - A/C.2/78/SR.8
Group of Landlocked Developing Countries
Mmalane, Katlego Boase (Botswana) - A/C.2/78/SR.8
Group of Least Developed Countries
Ray, Kaushal Kishor (Nepal) - A/C.2/78/SR.8
Indonesia
Prabowo, Hari - A/C.2/78/SR.9
Malaysia
Adnan, Yang Aishah Binti - A/C.2/78/SR.9
Serbia
Mart, Saša - A/C.2/78/SR.9
UN. General Assembly. 2nd Committee. Rapporteur
Gatev, Ivaylo (Bulgaria) - A/78/PV.49
UNCTAD
Bolwijn, Richard - A/C.2/78/SR.8
United Kingdom
Sowah, Malcolm - A/C.2/78/SR.23
United States
Lawrence, Jason N. - A/C.2/78/SR.23

JOINT INSPECTION UNIT (Agenda item 141)

Group of 77
Ainomuhisha, Medard (Uganda) - A/C.5/78/SR.29
Joint Inspection Unit
Cronin, Eileen A. - A/C.5/78/SR.27; A/C.5/78/SR.29
Joint Inspection Unit. Chair
Fernández Opazo, Carolina María - A/C.5/78/SR.27
Switzerland
Danese, Aurora Maria - A/C.5/78/SR.29
UN. General Assembly. 5th Committee. Rapporteur
Hartog, Laurens Thomas den (Netherlands (Kingdom of the)) - A/78/PV.73
UN System Chief Executives Board for Coordination
Pietracci, Federica - A/C.5/78/SR.27; A/C.5/78/SR.29

JUDICIAL INDEPENDENCE (Agenda item 71b)

Chile
Fernández Carter, Catalina - A/C.3/78/SR.31
China
Zhang, Qiuruo - A/C.3/78/SR.31
Colombia
Sánchez García, Nathalia - A/C.3/78/SR.31
European Union
Keogh, Briana - A/C.3/78/SR.31
Indonesia
Sandiori, Sherley Mega - A/C.3/78/SR.31
Lesotho
Lelisa, Nthabiseng Matlhohonolofatso - A/C.3/78/SR.31
Liechtenstein
Oehri, Noah - A/C.3/78/SR.31
Russian Federation
Kuzmenkov, Stepan Y. - A/C.3/78/SR.31
Sovereign Order of Malta
Muñoz, Zachary N. - A/C.3/78/SR.31
Ukraine
Mudrenko, Nataliia - A/C.3/78/SR.31
UN. Human Rights Council. Special Rapporteur on the Independence of Judges and Lawyers
Satterthwaite, Margaret L. - A/C.3/78/SR.31
United States
Breen, Patrick - A/C.3/78/SR.31

LANDLOCKED DEVELOPING COUNTRIES—CONFERENCES (Agenda item 20b)

Alliance of Small Island States
Bartley, Matilda (Samoa) - A/C.2/78/SR.7
Angola
Cruz, Francisco José da - A/C.2/78/SR.7
Armenia
Babikyan, Araksya - A/C.2/78/SR.7
ASEAN
Vongnorkeo, Anouparb (Lao People's Democratic Republic) - A/C.2/78/SR.7

LANDLOCKED DEVELOPING COUNTRIES—CONFERENCES (Agenda item 20b) (continued)

Azerbaijan
Ahmadova, Billur - A/C.2/78/SR.7
Bangladesh
Molla, Md Rafiqul Alam - A/C.2/78/SR.7
China
Wang, Hongbo - A/C.2/78/SR.7
Eritrea
Ibrahim, Ahmed Saeed - A/C.2/78/SR.7
Ethiopia
Abebe, Leulseged Tadese - A/C.2/78/SR.7
Group of 77
Kwoba, Godfrey (Uganda) - A/78/PV.98
Téllez Alonso, Frank (Cuba) - A/C.2/78/SR.7
Torres Seara, Dalia Marlen (Cuba) - A/C.2/78/SR.21
Group of Landlocked Developing Countries
Mokhawa, Gladys (Botswana) - A/C.2/78/SR.7
Group of Least Developed Countries
Ray, Kaushal Kishor (Nepal) - A/C.2/78/SR.7
Holy See
Murphy, Robert David - A/C.2/78/SR.7
India
Gahlot, Petal - A/C.2/78/SR.7
International Renewable Energy Agency
Biya, Alain Wilfried - A/C.2/78/SR.7
Kazakhstan
Kerimkulov, Bauyrzhan - A/C.2/78/SR.7
Lesotho
Monyane, Nkopane Raseeng - A/C.2/78/SR.7
Malaysia
Zulasri Bin Rosdi, Muhammad - A/C.2/78/SR.7
Maldives
Shamun, Amr Danyal - A/C.2/78/SR.7
Mongolia
Ulziibayar, Vangansuren - A/C.2/78/SR.7
Myanmar
Tun, Kyaw Moe - A/C.2/78/SR.7
Nepal
Ray, Kaushal Kishor - A/C.2/78/SR.7
Paraguay
Pereira Sosa, José Eduardo - A/C.2/78/SR.7
Qatar
Al-naama, Talal Abdulaziz - A/C.2/78/SR.7
Russian Federation
Chumakov, Dmitry S. - A/78/PV.107
Kardash, Viktoriia E. - A/C.2/78/SR.7
Sierra Leone
Sanusi, Zainu-Deen - A/C.2/78/SR.7
Timor-Leste
Nunes, Karlito - A/C.2/78/SR.7
Türkiye
Ekren, Kemal Onur - A/C.2/78/SR.7
UN. Department for General Assembly and Conference Management
Miranda, Ruth de - A/78/PV.80
UN. General Assembly. 2nd Committee. Rapporteur
Gatev, Ivaylo (Bulgaria) - A/78/PV.49

LANDLOCKED DEVELOPING COUNTRIES—CONFERENCES (Agenda item 20b) (continued)

UN. High Representative of the Secretary-General for the Least Developed Countries, Landlocked Developing Countries and Small Island Developing States
Fatima, Rabab - A/C.2/78/SR.7
United States
Armbruster, Thomas - A/C.2/78/SR.7
Kroeker-Maus, Faith - A/C.2/78/SR.23
Zambia
Chanda, Theresah Chipulu Luswili - A/C.2/78/SR.7
Zimbabwe
Rupende, Tapiwa Roy - A/C.2/78/SR.7

LANDMINES—TREATIES (Agenda item 99m)

Algeria
Lebbaz, Larbi Abdelfattah - A/C.1/78/PV.19
Angola
Luemba, Mateus Pedro - A/C.1/78/PV.19
Armenia
Grigoryan, Andranik - A/C.1/78/PV.19
ASEAN
Mao, Tithiarun (Cambodia) - A/C.1/78/PV.17
Australia
Carr, Michelle - A/C.1/78/PV.19
Austria
Kmentt, Alexander - A/C.1/78/PV.18
Azerbaijan
Gurbanov, Ilgar - A/C.1/78/PV.19
Bangladesh
Shatil, Toufiq Islam - A/C.1/78/PV.18
Brazil
Damico, Flávio Soares - A/C.1/78/PV.19
Burkina Faso
Ganou, Oumarou - A/C.1/78/PV.18
Canada
Svadjian, Méliné - A/C.1/78/PV.19
China
Shen, Jian - A/C.1/78/PV.19
Colombia
Quintero Correa, Nohra María - A/C.1/78/PV.18; A/C.1/78/PV.28
Coordinating Bureau of the Non-Aligned Countries
Kristanti, Maria Benedicta Diah (Indonesia) - A/C.1/78/PV.17
Croatia
Glasenhardt, Blanka - A/C.1/78/PV.19
Cuba
Garcia Moré, Yohan Yuniet - A/C.1/78/PV.28
Egypt
Hegazy, Abdelrhman Mohamed Farid - A/C.1/78/PV.28
Equatorial Guinea
Edu Mbasogo, Marcial - A/C.1/78/PV.19
European Union
Karczmarz, Michał - A/C.1/78/PV.18
Finland
Voionmaa, Lauri - A/C.1/78/PV.19
France
Petit, Camille - A/C.1/78/PV.18; A/C.1/78/PV.19

LANDMINES—TREATIES (Agenda item 99m) (continued)

Germany
Göbel, Thomas - A/C.1/78/PV.18
Guatemala
Rodríguez Mancia, Carla María - A/C.1/78/PV.18
India
Bedi, Anmol Sher Singh - A/C.1/78/PV.28
Parihar, Rajesh - A/C.1/78/PV.19
Iran (Islamic Republic of)
Ghorbanpour Najafabadi, Mohammad - A/C.1/78/PV.28
Iraq
Al-Sadar, Hamzah - A/C.1/78/PV.18
Ireland
Udom, Caoimhe - A/C.1/78/PV.18
Italy
Gai, Elena - A/C.1/78/PV.19
Japan
Ogasawara, Ichiro - A/C.1/78/PV.18
Lao People's Democratic Republic
Souliyong, So Inxay - A/C.1/78/PV.19
Mauritania
Mohamedou, El Hadj Lehbib - A/C.1/78/PV.19
Netherlands (Kingdom of the)
Bosch, Robert in den - A/C.1/78/PV.18
New Zealand
De Schot, Jikita - A/C.1/78/PV.19
Norway
Andersen, Tor Henrik - A/C.1/78/PV.19
Pakistan
Sarwani, Gul Qaiser - A/C.1/78/PV.28
Republic of Korea
Kim, Sunghoon - A/C.1/78/PV.28
Russian Federation
Belousov, Andrey I. - A/C.1/78/PV.19
Singapore
Jiamin, Liu - A/C.1/78/PV.18; A/C.1/78/PV.28
Slovenia
Ponikvar Velázquez, Jasna - A/C.1/78/PV.19
Spain
Rosario Vela, Manuel Jesús del - A/C.1/78/PV.19
Switzerland
Haegen, Laurin van der - A/C.1/78/PV.19
Thailand
Khundee, Wichayaporn - A/C.1/78/PV.18
Türkiye
Çetin, Ahmet Erman - A/C.1/78/PV.18
United Kingdom
Saggese, Eleonora - A/C.1/78/PV.19
Viet Nam
Mai, Ngan Ha - A/C.1/78/PV.18

LAW OF THE SEA (Agenda item 75a)

Alliance of Small Island States
Bartley, Matilda (Samoa) - A/78/PV.43
Argentina
Mainero, Martín Juan - A/78/PV.44
Squeff, María del Carmen - A/78/PV.44
Australia
Dundon, Nick - A/78/PV.48
Larsen, James - A/78/PV.43

LAW OF THE SEA (Agenda item 75a) (continued)
Bangladesh
Uddin, Nasir - A/78/PV.43
Belgium
Lagatie, Karl - A/78/PV.43
Cameroon
Tommo Monthe, Michel - A/78/PV.44
Canada
Kessel, Alan - A/78/PV.43
Chile
Narváez Ojeda, Paula - A/78/PV.43
China
Geng, Shuang - A/78/PV.43
Li, Linlin - A/78/PV.44
Costa Rica
Chan Valverde, Maritza - A/78/PV.44
El Salvador
Flores Soto, Ligia Lorena - A/78/PV.44
European Union
Ramopoulos, Thomas - A/78/PV.43
France
Broadhurst Estival, Nathalie - A/78/PV.48
Dime-Labille, Diarra - A/78/PV.44
Germany
Freiin von Uslar-Gleichen, Tania - A/78/PV.43
Group of 77
Peñalver Portal, Gerardo (Cuba) - A/78/PV.43
Guatemala
Rodríguez Mancia, Carla María - A/78/PV.43
Iceland
Valtýsson, Jörundur - A/78/PV.44
India
Bhat, Kajal - A/78/PV.43
Indonesia
Prabowo, Hari - A/78/PV.44
International Seabed Authority. Secretary-General
Lodge, Michael - A/78/PV.44
International Tribunal for the Law of the Sea. President
Heidar, Tomas H. - A/78/PV.44
Iran (Islamic Republic of)
Aref, Yahya - A/78/PV.44
Ershadi, Zahra - A/78/PV.43
Jamaica
Douglas, Craig Barrington - A/78/PV.44
Japan
Nagano, Shunsuke - A/78/PV.44
Sorimachi, Masayuki - A/78/PV.44
Kuwait
Alajmi, Fahad M. - A/78/PV.44
Maldives
Shamun, Amr Danyal - A/78/PV.43
Mexico
Buenrostro Massieu, Alicia - A/78/PV.44
Micronesia (Federated States of)
Lippwe, Jeem - A/78/PV.44
Monaco
Botto, Florian - A/78/PV.43
Nauru
Adire, Anastasia Francilia - A/78/PV.44

LAW OF THE SEA (Agenda item 75a) (continued)
Norway
Lovold, Andreas - A/78/PV.43
Pacific Islands Forum
Vaea, Darlene Atuamua Hakeifalehaakili (Tonga) - A/78/PV.43
Pakistan
Jadoon, Usman Iqbal - A/78/PV.44
Philippines
Arumpac-Marte, Azela Guerrero - A/78/PV.44
Peñaranda, Ariel Rodelas - A/78/PV.43
Russian Federation
Proskuryakov, Alexander S. - A/78/PV.44
Singapore
Gafoor, Burhan - A/78/PV.43
Syrian Arab Republic
Khaddour, Mhd. Riyad - A/78/PV.44
Türkiye
Çetin, Ahmet Erman - A/78/PV.44
UN. Department for General Assembly and Conference Management
Nakano, Kenji - A/78/PV.44
UN. General Assembly. President
Francis, Dennis (Trinidad and Tobago) - A/78/PV.43
United Arab Emirates
Azzam, Rashed Jamal Ibrahim Ibrahim - A/78/PV.44
United Kingdom
Pickens, Andrew - A/78/PV.48
Woodward, Barbara - A/78/PV.44
United States
Armbruster, Thomas - A/78/PV.44
Venezuela (Bolivarian Republic of)
Pérez Ayestarán, Joaquín Alberto - A/78/PV.44
Viet Nam
Dang, Hoang Giang - A/78/PV.43

LEAST DEVELOPED COUNTRIES—CONFERENCES (Agenda item 20a)
Alliance of Small Island States
Bartley, Matilda (Samoa) - A/C.2/78/SR.7
Angola
Cruz, Francisco José da - A/C.2/78/SR.7
Armenia
Babikyan, Araksya - A/C.2/78/SR.7
ASEAN
Vongnorkeo, Anouparb (Lao People's Democratic Republic) - A/C.2/78/SR.7
Azerbaijan
Ahmadova, Billur - A/C.2/78/SR.7
Bangladesh
Molla, Md Rafiqul Alam - A/C.2/78/SR.7
China
Wang, Hongbo - A/C.2/78/SR.7
Eritrea
Ibrahim, Ahmed Saeed - A/C.2/78/SR.7
Ethiopia
Abebe, Leulseged Tadese - A/C.2/78/SR.7

LEAST DEVELOPED COUNTRIES—CONFERENCES (Agenda item 20a) (continued)

Group of 77
Téllez Alonso, Frank (Cuba) - A/C.2/78/SR.7
Torres Seara, Dalia Marlen (Cuba) - A/C.2/78/SR.21
Group of Landlocked Developing Countries
Mokhawa, Gladys (Botswana) - A/C.2/78/SR.7
Group of Least Developed Countries
Ray, Kaushal Kishor (Nepal) - A/C.2/78/SR.7
Holy See
Murphy, Robert David - A/C.2/78/SR.7
India
Gahlot, Petal - A/C.2/78/SR.7
International Renewable Energy Agency
Biya, Alain Wilfried - A/C.2/78/SR.7
Kazakhstan
Kerimkulov, Bauyrzhan - A/C.2/78/SR.7
Lesotho
Monyane, Nkopane Raseeng - A/C.2/78/SR.7
Malaysia
Zulasri Bin Rosdi, Muhammad - A/C.2/78/SR.7
Maldives
Shamun, Amr Danyal - A/C.2/78/SR.7
Mongolia
Ulziibayar, Vangansuren - A/C.2/78/SR.7
Myanmar
Tun, Kyaw Moe - A/C.2/78/SR.7
Nepal
Ray, Kaushal Kishor - A/C.2/78/SR.7
Paraguay
Pereira Sosa, José Eduardo - A/C.2/78/SR.7
Qatar
Al-naama, Talal Abdulaziz - A/C.2/78/SR.7
Russian Federation
Kardash, Viktoriia E. - A/C.2/78/SR.7
Sierra Leone
Sanusi, Zainu-Deen - A/C.2/78/SR.7
Timor-Leste
Nunes, Karlito - A/C.2/78/SR.7
Türkiye
Ekren, Kemal Onur - A/C.2/78/SR.7
UN. General Assembly. 2nd Committee. Rapporteur
Gatev, Ivaylo (Bulgaria) - A/78/PV.49
UN. High Representative of the Secretary-General for the Least Developed Countries, Landlocked Developing Countries and Small Island Developing States
Fatima, Rabab - A/C.2/78/SR.7
United States
Armbruster, Thomas - A/C.2/78/SR.7
Kroeker-Maus, Faith - A/C.2/78/SR.23
Zambia
Chanda, Theresah Chipulu Luswili - A/C.2/78/SR.7
Zimbabwe
Rupende, Tapiwa Roy - A/C.2/78/SR.7

LEPROSY (Agenda item 71b)

Brazil
Gomes, Elaine Cristina Pereira - A/C.3/78/SR.17

LEPROSY (Agenda item 71b) (continued)

China
La, Haozhao - A/C.3/78/SR.17
European Union
Keogh, Briana - A/C.3/78/SR.17
Japan
Kamiya, Masako - A/C.3/78/SR.17
Portugal
Zacarias, Ana Paula - A/C.3/78/SR.17
Sovereign Order of Malta
Muñoz, Zachary N. - A/C.3/78/SR.17
UN. Human Rights Council. Special Rapporteur on the Elimination of Discrimination against Persons Affected by Leprosy (Hansen's disease) and Their Family Members
Cruz, Alice - A/C.3/78/SR.17

MACROECONOMIC POLICY (Agenda item 16)

Alliance of Small Island States
Bartley, Matilda (Samoa) - A/C.2/78/SR.8
ASEAN
Nasir, Arrmanatha Christiawan (Indonesia) - A/C.2/78/SR.8
Azerbaijan
Bayramli-Hamidova, Nigar - A/C.2/78/SR.9
Bangladesh
Hossain, Faruk - A/C.2/78/SR.9
Burkina Faso
Bokoum, Mahamadou - A/C.2/78/SR.9
Cambodia
Heng, Somoly - A/C.2/78/SR.9
Caribbean Community
Wallace, Brian Christopher Manley (Jamaica) - A/C.2/78/SR.8
China
Hua, Chenghang - A/C.2/78/SR.9
Côte d'Ivoire
Ipo, Gbolié Desiré Wulfran - A/C.2/78/SR.9
Cuba
Guevara Rodríguez, Adiel - A/C.2/78/SR.8
El Salvador
González López, Egriselda Aracely - A/C.2/78/SR.8
Group of Friends in Defence of the Charter of the United Nations
Pérez Ayestarán, Joaquín Alberto (Venezuela (Bolivarian Republic of)) - A/C.2/78/SR.8
Group of Landlocked Developing Countries
Mmalane, Katlego Boase (Botswana) - A/C.2/78/SR.8
Indonesia
Prabowo, Hari - A/C.2/78/SR.9; A/C.2/78/SR.25
Iraq
Al-Niami, Mustafa - A/C.2/78/SR.9
Myanmar
Tun, Kyaw Moe - A/C.2/78/SR.9
Namibia
Naanda, Anne - A/C.2/78/SR.9
Nicaragua
Hermida Castillo, Jaime - A/C.2/78/SR.9
Russian Federation
Kardash, Viktoriia E. - A/C.2/78/SR.25

MACROECONOMIC POLICY (Agenda item 16) (continued)

Saudi Arabia
Alomair, Reem Fahad O. - A/C.2/78/SR.9
Serbia
Mart, Saša - A/C.2/78/SR.9
Sierra Leone
Sowa, Amara Sheikh Mohammed - A/C.2/78/SR.9
South Africa
Seedat, Ahmed Hoosen - A/C.2/78/SR.11
Trinidad and Tobago
Budhu, Vladamir - A/C.2/78/SR.9
UN. General Assembly. 2nd Committee. Rapporteur
Gatev, Ivaylo (Bulgaria) - A/78/PV.49
UN. Group of African States
Ladeb, Tarek (Tunisia) - A/C.2/78/SR.9
UNIDO
Klose, Christoph - A/C.2/78/SR.11
Venezuela (Bolivarian Republic of)
Marín Sevilla, Asbina - A/C.2/78/SR.9
Zimbabwe
Rupende, Tapiwa Roy - A/C.2/78/SR.9

MARINE ECOSYSTEMS—BIOLOGICAL DIVERSITY (Agenda item 75c)

Alliance of Small Island States
Bartley, Matilda (Samoa) - A/78/PV.43; A/78/PV.73
Luteru, Fatumanava-o-Upolu III Pa'olelei (Samoa) - A/78/PV.103
Argentina
Mainero, Martín Juan - A/78/PV.44
Squeff, María del Carmen - A/78/PV.44
Australia
Larsen, James - A/78/PV.43
Bangladesh
Uddin, Nasir - A/78/PV.43
Belgium
Lagatie, Karl - A/78/PV.43; A/78/PV.103
Belize
Fuller, Carlos C. - A/78/PV.103
Cameroon
Tommo Monthe, Michel - A/78/PV.44
Canada
Kessel, Alan - A/78/PV.43
Caribbean Community
Fuller, Carlos C. (Belize) - A/78/PV.73
Williams, Mutryce (Saint Kitts and Nevis) - A/78/PV.103
Chile
Narváez Ojeda, Paula - A/78/PV.43
China
Geng, Shuang - A/78/PV.43
Li, Linlin - A/78/PV.44
Costa Rica
Chan Valverde, Maritza - A/78/PV.44
El Salvador
Flores Soto, Ligia Lorena - A/78/PV.44

MARINE ECOSYSTEMS—BIOLOGICAL DIVERSITY (Agenda item 75c) (continued)

European Union
Raes, Elisa de (Belgium) - A/78/PV.73
Ramopoulos, Thomas - A/78/PV.43
Vittay, Melinda (Hungary) - A/78/PV.103
France
Dime-Labille, Diarra - A/78/PV.44
Germany
Freiin von Uslar-Gleichen, Tania - A/78/PV.43
Group of 77
Ikondere, Marvin (Uganda) - A/78/PV.73
Peñalver Portal, Gerardo (Cuba) - A/78/PV.43
Guatemala
Rodríguez Mancia, Carla María - A/78/PV.43
Iceland
Valtýsson, Jörundur - A/78/PV.44
India
Bhat, Kajal - A/78/PV.43
Indonesia
Prabowo, Hari - A/78/PV.44
International Seabed Authority. Secretary-General
Lodge, Michael - A/78/PV.44
International Tribunal for the Law of the Sea. President
Heidar, Tomas H. - A/78/PV.44
Iran (Islamic Republic of)
Aref, Yahya - A/78/PV.44
Ershadi, Zahra - A/78/PV.43
Jamaica
Douglas, Craig Barrington - A/78/PV.44
Japan
Nagano, Shunsuke - A/78/PV.44
Sorimachi, Masayuki - A/78/PV.44
Kuwait
Alajmi, Fahad M. - A/78/PV.44
Maldives
Shamun, Amr Danyal - A/78/PV.43
Mexico
Buenrostro Massieu, Alicia - A/78/PV.44
Micronesia (Federated States of)
Lippwe, Jeem - A/78/PV.44
Monaco
Botto, Florian - A/78/PV.43
Nauru
Adire, Anastasia Francilia - A/78/PV.44
Nicaragua
Llano, Alina J. - A/78/PV.73
Norway
Lovold, Andreas - A/78/PV.43
Pacific Islands Forum
Vaea, Darlene Atuamua Hakeifalehaakili (Tonga) - A/78/PV.43
Vea, Jeanett (Tonga) - A/78/PV.103
Pacific Small Island Developing States
Wells, Majorie May (Vanuatu) - A/78/PV.103
William, Sanlan (Vanuatu) - A/78/PV.73
Pakistan
Jadoon, Usman Iqbal - A/78/PV.44

MARINE ECOSYSTEMS—BIOLOGICAL DIVERSITY (Agenda item 75c) (continued)

Philippines
Arumpac-Marte, Azela Guerrero - A/78/PV.44
Peñaranda, Ariel Rodelas - A/78/PV.43
Russian Federation
Antonova, Anna V. - A/78/PV.73; A/78/PV.103
Proskuryakov, Alexander S. - A/78/PV.44
Singapore
Gafoor, Burhan - A/78/PV.43
Seah, Mark - A/78/PV.73
Syrian Arab Republic
Khaddour, Mhd. Riyad - A/78/PV.44
Türkiye
Çetin, Ahmet Erman - A/78/PV.44
UN. Department for General Assembly and Conference Management
Nakano, Kenji - A/78/PV.44; A/78/PV.103
UN. General Assembly. President
Francis, Dennis (Trinidad and Tobago) - A/78/PV.43
United Arab Emirates
Azzam, Rashed Jamal Ibrahim Ibrahim - A/78/PV.44
United Kingdom
Woodward, Barbara - A/78/PV.44
United States
Armbruster, Thomas - A/78/PV.44
Venezuela (Bolivarian Republic of)
Pérez Ayestarán, Joaquín Alberto - A/78/PV.44
Viet Nam
Dang, Hoang Giang - A/78/PV.43

MEDITERRANEAN REGION—REGIONAL SECURITY (Agenda item 104)

Algeria
Lebbaz, Larbi Abdelfattah - A/C.1/78/PV.22
European Union
Sánchez de Lerín García-Ovies, Ignacio (Spain) - A/C.1/78/PV.29
France
Petit, Camille - A/C.1/78/PV.25
Greece
Christoglou, Konstantinos - A/C.1/78/PV.22
Iran (Islamic Republic of)
Ghorbanpour Najafabadi, Mohammad - A/C.1/78/PV.29
Israel
Sharoni, Benjamin - A/C.1/78/PV.29
Russian Federation
Belousov, Andrey I. - A/C.1/78/PV.29
Syrian Arab Republic
Al Ashkar, Adib - A/C.1/78/PV.29
UN. General Assembly. 1st Committee. Rapporteur
Balouji, Heidar Ali (Iran (Islamic Republic of)) - A/78/PV.42
United States
Turner, Bruce - A/C.1/78/PV.29

MERCENARIES (Agenda item 70)

Argentina
Escobar, Luciano Hernán - A/C.3/78/SR.48

MERCENARIES (Agenda item 70) (continued)

Armenia
Hakobyan, Aram - A/C.3/78/SR.42
Chile
Nishihara, Carmen - A/C.3/78/SR.48
Cuba
González Behmaras, Alejandro - A/C.3/78/SR.42; A/C.3/78/SR.48
European Union
Nyman, Klas - A/C.3/78/SR.42
Iraq
Abdullateef, Mohammed Ayad - A/C.3/78/SR.42
UN. Human Rights Council. Working Group on the Use of Mercenaries as a Means of Violating Human Rights and Impeding the Exercise of the Right of Peoples to Self-Determination
MacLeod, Sorcha - A/C.3/78/SR.42
United Kingdom
Kumaria, Sacha - A/C.3/78/SR.48
United States
Merron, Eric - A/C.3/78/SR.48

MIDDLE EAST—NUCLEAR PROLIFERATION (Agenda item 102)

Egypt
Ahmed, Amr Essameldin Sadek - A/C.1/78/PV.11; A/C.1/78/PV.25
Group of Arab States
Hmoud, Mahmoud Daifallah Mahmoud (Jordan) - A/C.1/78/PV.11
India
Kulkarni, Maitrey - A/C.1/78/PV.25
Iran (Islamic Republic of)
Ghorbanpour Najafabadi, Mohammad - A/C.1/78/PV.13; A/C.1/78/PV.26
Israel
Sharoni, Benjamin - A/C.1/78/PV.26
Pakistan
Sarwani, Gul Qaiser - A/C.1/78/PV.26
Switzerland
Anderegg, Julius - A/C.1/78/PV.26
Syrian Arab Republic
Al Ashkar, Adib - A/C.1/78/PV.13; A/C.1/78/PV.26
UN. General Assembly. 1st Committee. Rapporteur
Balouji, Heidar Ali (Iran (Islamic Republic of)) - A/78/PV.42
United States
Turner, Bruce - A/C.1/78/PV.26

MIDDLE EAST—NUCLEAR-WEAPON-FREE ZONES (Agenda item 95)

Algeria
Lebbaz, Larbi Abdelfattah - A/C.1/78/PV.14; A/C.1/78/PV.22
Bahrain
Janahi, Balqees - A/C.1/78/PV.14

MIDDLE EAST—NUCLEAR-WEAPON-FREE ZONES (Agenda item 95) (continued)

Coordinating Bureau of the Non-Aligned Countries
Dhanutirto, Mariska Dwianti (Indonesia) - A/C.1/78/PV.11
Sirie, Mochammad Iqbal (Indonesia) - A/C.1/78/PV.21
Cuba
Peñalver Portal, Gerardo - A/C.1/78/PV.11
Egypt
Ahmed, Amr Essameldin Sadek - A/C.1/78/PV.11; A/C.1/78/PV.14; A/C.1/78/PV.21; A/C.1/78/PV.25
European Union
Sánchez de Lerín García-Ovies, Ignacio (Spain) - A/C.1/78/PV.26
France
Petit, Camille - A/C.1/78/PV.25
Group of Arab States
Alqaisi, Sultan Natheir Mustafa (Jordan) - A/C.1/78/PV.14; A/C.1/78/PV.21
Hmoud, Mahmoud Daifallah Mahmoud (Jordan) - A/C.1/78/PV.11
Iran (Islamic Republic of)
Ghorbanpour Najafabadi, Mohammad - A/C.1/78/PV.12; A/C.1/78/PV.22; A/C.1/78/PV.26
Iraq
Al-Taie, Sarmad Muwafaq Mohammed - A/C.1/78/PV.22
Israel
Maayan, Michal - A/C.1/78/PV.12
Sharoni, Benjamin - A/C.1/78/PV.26
Kuwait
Basheer, Manar - A/C.1/78/PV.23
Malaysia
Sivamohan, Shivanand - A/C.1/78/PV.22
Qatar
Al-Safran, Hussain Mohammed - A/C.1/78/PV.12
Syrian Arab Republic
Al Ashkar, Adib - A/C.1/78/PV.15; A/C.1/78/PV.21; A/C.1/78/PV.22; A/C.1/78/PV.26
UN. General Assembly. 1st Committee. Rapporteur
Balouji, Heidar Ali (Iran (Islamic Republic of)) - A/78/PV.42
UN. Group of African States
Mahmud, Mohammed Lawal (Nigeria) - A/C.1/78/PV.11
United Arab Emirates
Alemad, Ahmed - A/C.1/78/PV.22
United States
Turner, Bruce - A/C.1/78/PV.25

MIDDLE EAST SITUATION (Agenda item 34)

Argentina
Squeff, María del Carmen - A/78/PV.40
Egypt
Abdelkhalek, Osama Mahmoud - A/78/PV.40
European Union
Jiménez de la Hoz, Ana (Spain) - A/78/PV.40
Lebanon
Hachem, Hadi - A/78/PV.40

MIDDLE EAST SITUATION (Agenda item 34) (continued)

Syrian Arab Republic
Dandy, Alhakam - A/78/PV.40
United Kingdom
Eckersley, Fergus - A/78/PV.40

MIGRANT WORKERS (Agenda item 71a)

Bangladesh
Abdullah, Md Showeb - A/C.3/78/SR.23
El Salvador
Sorto Rosales, Mayra Lisseth - A/C.3/78/SR.23
European Union
Szelivanov, Julia - A/C.3/78/SR.23
Lao People's Democratic Republic
Meunluang, Veomanee - A/C.3/78/SR.23
Malaysia
Escopper Zumilla, Michael Jawa - A/C.3/78/SR.23
Mexico
Gil Rojas, Elia Lizette - A/C.3/78/SR.23
Sovereign Order of Malta
McGuire, Peter Davidson - A/C.3/78/SR.23
UN. Committee on the Protection of the Rights of All Migrant Workers and Members of Their Families. Chair
Corzo Sosa, Edgar - A/C.3/78/SR.23

MIGRANTS—PROTECTION (Agenda item 71b)

Austria
Hardwick, Nicola Ann - A/C.3/78/SR.56
Bangladesh
Abdullah, Md Showeb - A/C.3/78/SR.23
Bulgaria
Dimitrov, Svetozar Angelov - A/C.3/78/SR.56
Cameroon
Wainwel, Gwedji Doris - A/C.3/78/SR.23
Chile
Fernández Carter, Catalina - A/C.3/78/SR.23
China
Zhang, Qiuruo - A/C.3/78/SR.23
Costa Rica
Chan Valverde, Maritza - A/C.3/78/SR.26
Cuba
Valido Martínez, Yoangel - A/C.3/78/SR.23
Ecuador
Montalvo Sosa, Andrés Efren - A/C.3/78/SR.26
Egypt
Mohamed, Mohamed Omar Elfarouk Hassan - A/C.3/78/SR.23; A/C.3/78/SR.56
El Salvador
Segura Aragón, Carlos Efraín - A/C.3/78/SR.23
Sorto Rosales, Mayra Lisseth - A/C.3/78/SR.56
European Union
Alonso Giganto, Ana María (Spain) - A/C.3/78/SR.56
Szelivanov, Julia - A/C.3/78/SR.23
Gulf Cooperation Council
Al-Sinani, Nashwa Hilal (Oman) - A/C.3/78/SR.23
Holy See
Murphy, Robert David - A/C.3/78/SR.56

MIGRANTS—PROTECTION (Agenda item 71b) (continued)

Hungary
Pongor, Magdolna - A/C.3/78/SR.56
Luxembourg
Folmer, Sophie - A/C.3/78/SR.23
Malaysia
Escopper Zumilla, Michael Jawa - A/C.3/78/SR.23
Mexico
Gil Rojas, Elia Lizette - A/C.3/78/SR.23
Mendoza Elguea, Sylvia Paola - A/C.3/78/SR.56
Morocco
Ouafi, Sara - A/C.3/78/SR.23
Pakistan
Qureshi, Hadeeqa - A/C.3/78/SR.23
Panama
Concepción Jaramillo, Markova - A/C.3/78/SR.23
Philippines
Fangco, Maria Roseny Baltazar - A/C.3/78/SR.24
Portugal
Guerra, Stefano Venancio - A/C.3/78/SR.23
Russian Federation
Kuzmenkov, Stepan Y. - A/C.3/78/SR.23
Serbia
Radović, Branislav - A/C.3/78/SR.27
Sistema de la Integración Centroamericana
Sorto Rosales, Mayra Lisseth (El Salvador) - A/C.3/78/SR.24
South Africa
Diedricks, Meryl Michelle - A/C.3/78/SR.23
Sovereign Order of Malta
Greenwood, James Harrison - A/C.3/78/SR.23
Switzerland
Allet, Alexandra - A/C.3/78/SR.23
Syrian Arab Republic
Altarsha, Elie - A/C.3/78/SR.23
UN. Assistant Secretary-General for Human Rights
Brands Kehris, Ilze - A/C.3/78/SR.18
UN. Human Rights Council. Special Rapporteur on the Human Rights of Migrants
González Morales, Felipe - A/C.3/78/SR.23
United Kingdom
Devereaux, Brendan - A/C.3/78/SR.56
United States
Johnson, Timothy J. - A/C.3/78/SR.56
McGlothlin, Cameron - A/C.3/78/SR.23
Venezuela (Bolivarian Republic of)
Poveda Brito, Robert Alexander - A/C.3/78/SR.23

MILITARY BUDGETS (Agenda item 90)

UN. General Assembly. 1st Committee. Rapporteur
Balouji, Heidar Ali (Iran (Islamic Republic of)) - A/78/PV.42

MILLENNIUM SUMMIT—CONFERENCES (Agenda item 117)

Alliance of Small Island States
Lautasi, Isaia (Samoa) - A/78/PV.102
Luteru, Fatumanava-o-Upolu III Pa'olelei (Samoa) - A/78/PV.53

MILLENNIUM SUMMIT—CONFERENCES (Agenda item 117) (continued)

Argentina
Squeff, María del Carmen - A/78/PV.15
Australia
Larsen, James - A/78/PV.15
Belarus
Evseenko, Pavel - A/78/PV.15
Bolivia (Plurinational State of)
Pary Rodríguez, Diego - A/78/PV.15
Chile
Narváez Ojeda, Paula - A/78/PV.15
Coalition for Addressing Sea-level Rise and its Existential Threat
Falefou, Tapugao (Tuvalu) - A/78/PV.53
Zahneisen, Thomas (Germany) - A/78/PV.102
Colombia
Zalabata Torres, Leonor - A/78/PV.15
Costa Rica
Chan Valverde, Maritza - A/78/PV.102
Cuba
Peñalver Portal, Gerardo - A/78/PV.15
Egypt
Abdelkhalek, Osama Mahmoud - A/78/PV.15
El Salvador
Flores Soto, Ligia Lorena - A/78/PV.53
European Union
Jiménez de la Hoz, Ana (Spain) - A/78/PV.15
Samson, Hedda - A/78/PV.102
Fiji
May, Vueti Kosoniu - A/78/PV.102
Group of 77
Peñalver Portal, Gerardo (Cuba) - A/78/PV.15
Group of Friends in Defence of the Charter of the United Nations
Pérez Ayestarán, Joaquín Alberto (Venezuela (Bolivarian Republic of)) - A/78/PV.15
Gulf Cooperation Council
Al-Hassan, Mohamed (Oman) - A/78/PV.15
Hungary
Horváth, Zsuzsanna - A/78/PV.15
Iran (Islamic Republic of)
Ghafouri, Mojtaba - A/78/PV.102
Momeni, Javad - A/78/PV.15
Japan
Yamanaka, Osamu - A/78/PV.15
Nicaragua
Jiménez, Jasser - A/78/PV.15
Pacific Islands Forum
May, Vueti Kosoniu (Fiji) - A/78/PV.102
Va'inga Tone, Viliami (Tonga) - A/78/PV.53
Pakistan
Akram, Munir - A/78/PV.15
Palau
Sisior, Gwendalyn - A/78/PV.102
Russian Federation
Chumakov, Dmitry S. - A/78/PV.15; A/78/PV.53; A/78/PV.107
Kardash, Viktoriia E. - A/78/PV.102
South Africa
Joyini, Mathu - A/78/PV.15

MILLENNIUM SUMMIT—CONFERENCES (Agenda item 117) (continued)

Syrian Arab Republic
Dandy, Alhakam - A/78/PV.15
Timor-Leste
Soares, Dionísio Da Costa Babo - A/78/PV.102
Türkiye
Çetin, Ahmet Erman - A/78/PV.102
Tuvalu
Navoti, Selema K. - A/78/PV.102
UN. Department for General Assembly and Conference Management
Miranda, Ruth de - A/78/PV.102
UN. General Assembly. President
Francis, Dennis (Trinidad and Tobago) - A/78/PV.53; A/78/PV.102
United Kingdom
Fidoe, Nicholas - A/78/PV.102
Woodroffe, Tom - A/78/PV.15
United States
Carty, Lisa A. - A/78/PV.15
Pell, Herbert - A/78/PV.102
Zimbabwe
Nyagura, Petronella - A/78/PV.15

MINE CLEARANCE (Agenda item 46)

Angola
Luemba, Mateus Pedro - A/C.4/78/SR.10
Australia
Larsen, James - A/C.4/78/SR.10
Bangladesh
Shatil, Toufiq Islam - A/C.4/78/SR.10
Cameroon
Ondo Ebang, William - A/C.4/78/SR.10
China
Wang, Zhenjiang - A/C.4/78/SR.10
El Salvador
González López, Egriselda Aracely - A/C.4/78/SR.10
European Union
Samson, Hedda - A/C.4/78/SR.10
Szczerski, Krzysztof (Poland) - A/C.4/78/SR.10
Iran (Islamic Republic of)
Sahraei, Mohammad Reza - A/C.4/78/SR.10
Iraq
Al-Saed, Saadoon - A/C.4/78/SR.10
Japan
Ono, Sho - A/C.4/78/SR.10
Lao People's Democratic Republic
Souliyong, So Inxay - A/C.4/78/SR.10
Myanmar
Tun, Kyaw Moe - A/C.4/78/SR.10
Norway
Ramboll, Unni - A/C.4/78/SR.10
Poland
Szczerski, Krzysztof - A/C.4/78/SR.10
Russian Federation
Evstigneeva, Anna M. - A/C.4/78/SR.10
Saudi Arabia
Abaalala, Majed - A/C.4/78/SR.10

MINE CLEARANCE (Agenda item 46) (continued)

Sri Lanka
Pieris, Peter Mohan Maithri - A/C.4/78/SR.10
Sudan
Mohamed, Abuzied Shamseldin Ahmed - A/C.4/78/SR.10
Syrian Arab Republic
Mustafa, Marah - A/C.4/78/SR.10
Thailand
Jeranukosol, Natsaran - A/C.4/78/SR.10
Ukraine
Zlenko, Anatolii - A/C.4/78/SR.10
UN. Assistant Secretary-General for Rule of Law and Security Institutions
Zouev, Alexandre - A/C.4/78/SR.10
UN. General Assembly. Special Political and Decolonization Committee (4th Committee). Rapporteur
Dhanutirto, Mariska Dwianti (Indonesia) - A/78/PV.45
Yemen
Al-mashehari, Sarah Ahmed Ahmed - A/C.4/78/SR.10

MINORITIES (Agenda item 71b)

Albania
Lamce, Enian - A/C.3/78/SR.39
Austria
Hardwick, Nicola Ann - A/C.3/78/SR.39; A/C.3/78/SR.52
Azerbaijan
Ahangari, Narmin - A/C.3/78/SR.25
Cameroon
Ahidjo, Ahidjo - A/C.3/78/SR.39
China
Liu, Luoge - A/C.3/78/SR.39
European Union
Greffine, Venise Catherine - A/C.3/78/SR.39
Hungary
Mogyorósi, Bálint - A/C.3/78/SR.39
India
Sonkar, Suman - A/C.3/78/SR.39
Iraq
Yaseen, Safaa - A/C.3/78/SR.39
Israel
Aviel, Shir - A/C.3/78/SR.39
Japan
Akita, Mio - A/C.3/78/SR.39
Malaysia
Escopper Zumilla, Michael Jawa - A/C.3/78/SR.52
Niger
Seydou, Abdoul Fadh Mahamadou - A/C.3/78/SR.52
Pakistan
Qureshi, Hadeeqa - A/C.3/78/SR.39
Russian Federation
Kuzmenkov, Stepan Y. - A/C.3/78/SR.39
Slovakia
Grünwald, Tomáš - A/C.3/78/SR.39
Sovereign Order of Malta
Rosario-Blackett, Marissa del - A/C.3/78/SR.39

MINORITIES (Agenda item 71b) (continued)
Switzerland
Eugster, Manuel - A/C.3/78/SR.39
Türkiye
Aydil, İsmail - A/C.3/78/SR.39; A/C.3/78/SR.52
UN. Assistant Secretary-General for Human Rights
Brands Kehris, Ilze - A/C.3/78/SR.18
UN. Human Rights Council. Special Rapporteur on Minority Issues
Varennes, Fernand de - A/C.3/78/SR.39
United States
Lang, Dylan - A/C.3/78/SR.39

MULTILATERALISM
Guatemala. President
Arévalo de León, César Bernardo - A/78/PV.84
Italy. President
Mattarella, Sergio - A/78/PV.81
UN. General Assembly. President
Francis, Dennis (Trinidad and Tobago) - A/78/PV.81; A/78/PV.84
UN. Secretary-General
Guterres, António, 1949- - A/78/PV.81

MULTILATERALISM—DISARMAMENT (Agenda item 99r)
Algeria
Lebbaz, Larbi Abdelfattah - A/C.1/78/PV.22
Armenia
Grigoryan, Andranik - A/C.1/78/PV.22; A/C.1/78/PV.29
Azerbaijan
Gurbanov, Ilgar - A/C.1/78/PV.23
Bangladesh
Molla, Md Rafiqul Alam - A/C.1/78/PV.21
Brazil
Damico, Flávio Soares - A/C.1/78/PV.22
Coordinating Bureau of the Non-Aligned Countries
Sirie, Mochammad Iqbal (Indonesia) - A/C.1/78/PV.20
Cuba
Gómez Sardiñas, Yiliam - A/C.1/78/PV.20; A/C.1/78/PV.21
Romero López, Rosanis - A/C.1/78/PV.28
Democratic People's Republic of Korea
Kim, In Chol - A/C.1/78/PV.22; A/C.1/78/PV.23
Equatorial Guinea
Edu Mbasogo, Marcial - A/C.1/78/PV.22
European Union
Karczmarz, Michał - A/C.1/78/PV.22
France
Petit, Camille - A/C.1/78/PV.22
Georgia
Dvali, Akaki - A/C.1/78/PV.22
Greece
Christoglou, Konstantinos - A/C.1/78/PV.22
Group of Arab States
Alqaisi, Sultan Natheir Mustafa (Jordan) - A/C.1/78/PV.20; A/C.1/78/PV.21

MULTILATERALISM—DISARMAMENT (Agenda item 99r) (continued)
Iran (Islamic Republic of)
Ghorbanpour Najafabadi, Mohammad - A/C.1/78/PV.22
Iraq
Al-Taie, Sarmad Muwafaq Mohammed - A/C.1/78/PV.22
Israel
Sharoni, Benjamin - A/C.1/78/PV.23
Kuwait
Al-Murad, Mariam - A/C.1/78/PV.21
Malaysia
Sivamohan, Shivanand - A/C.1/78/PV.22
Mexico
Flores Troche, Manuel - A/C.1/78/PV.22
Philippines
Gomez, Jan Michael - A/C.1/78/PV.22
Russian Federation
Belousov, Andrey I. - A/C.1/78/PV.22
Saudi Arabia
Moharram, Wajdi Hassan M. - A/C.1/78/PV.21
United Arab Emirates
Alemad, Ahmed - A/C.1/78/PV.22
United Kingdom
Liddle, Aidan Thomas - A/C.1/78/PV.21
Uruguay
Eustathiou de los Santos, Matías Andrés - A/C.1/78/PV.21

MULTILINGUALISM (Agenda item 124)
Andorra
Font Vilagines, Meritxell - A/78/PV.107
China
Jiang, Hua - A/78/PV.108
Comunidade dos Países de Língua Portuguesa
Romualdo, Tania Serafim Yvonne (Cabo Verde) - A/78/PV.107
Groupe des ambassadeurs francophones
Banza, Serge Ngoy (Democratic Republic of the Congo) - A/78/PV.107
Grupo de Amigos del Español en las Naciones Unidas
Cedano, Joan Margarita (Dominican Republic) - A/78/PV.107
Guatemala
Rodríguez Mancia, Carla María - A/78/PV.107
Japan
Minegishi, Shunsuke - A/78/PV.108
Russian Federation
Devyatkin, Daniil A. - A/78/PV.107
UN. Department for General Assembly and Conference Management
Nakano, Kenji - A/78/PV.107
UN. Group of African States
Kattanga, Hussein A. (United Republic of Tanzania) - A/78/PV.97
United Kingdom
Sigley, Andrew - A/78/PV.108
United States
Stetter, Elizabeth - A/78/PV.108

NATIONAL INSTITUTIONS—HUMAN RIGHTS (Agenda item 71b)

Bahrain
Alhammadi, Hessa - A/C.3/78/SR.25
Belgium
Kridelka, Philippe - A/C.3/78/SR.25
Côte d'Ivoire
Moriko, Tiémoko - A/C.3/78/SR.26
Germany
Drescher, Daniel - A/C.3/78/SR.49
Ghana
Williams, Edna Stephanie - A/C.3/78/SR.26
India
Sonkar, Suman - A/C.3/78/SR.26
UN. Assistant Secretary-General for Human Rights
Brands Kehris, Ilze - A/C.3/78/SR.18

NATURAL FIBRES (Agenda item 23b)

Bangladesh
Hossain, Faruk - A/C.2/78/SR.23
UN. General Assembly. 2nd Committee. Rapporteur
Gatev, Ivaylo (Bulgaria) - A/78/PV.49
United States
Kroeker-Maus, Faith - A/C.2/78/SR.23

NEW CALEDONIA QUESTION (Agenda item 58)

(personal capacity)
Wateou, Naïa - A/C.4/78/SR.5
France
Rivière, Nicolas de - A/C.4/78/SR.7
Front de libération nationale kanak et socialiste (New Caledonia)
Tingal, Magalie - A/C.4/78/SR.5
Melanesian Spearhead Group
Sarufa, Fred (Papua New Guinea) - A/C.4/78/SR.6
New Caledonia
Darras, Amandine - A/C.4/78/SR.5
Falaeo, Veylma - A/C.4/78/SR.3
Forrest, Mickaël - A/C.4/78/SR.3
Trenyiwa, Karyl - A/C.4/78/SR.5
Wamytan, Roch - A/C.4/78/SR.5
Papua New Guinea
Sarufa, Fred - A/C.4/78/SR.3
Venezuela (Bolivarian Republic of)
Pérez Ayestarán, Joaquín Alberto - A/C.4/78/SR.2

NON-CITIZENS—DEPORTATION (Agenda item 81)

Belarus
Evseenko, Pavel - A/C.6/78/SR.34
Brazil
Braoios, Victor Silveira - A/C.6/78/SR.34
Cameroon
Nyanid, Zacharie Serge Raoul - A/C.6/78/SR.34
Chile
Hernández Chávez, José Juan - A/C.6/78/SR.34

NON-CITIZENS—DEPORTATION (Agenda item 81) (continued)

Colombia
Solano Ramírez, Lucía Teresa - A/C.6/78/SR.34
Cuba
Mora Fonseca, Vladimir - A/C.6/78/SR.34
Ecuador
Escobar Ullauri, Pablo - A/C.6/78/SR.34
El Salvador
Flores Soto, Ligia Lorena - A/C.6/78/SR.34; A/C.6/78/SR.37
Holy See
Caccia, Gabriele Giordano - A/C.6/78/SR.34
Iran (Islamic Republic of)
Fallah Assadi, Mahdad - A/C.6/78/SR.34
Malaysia
Abd Karim, Nur Azura Binti - A/C.6/78/SR.34
Mexico
Jiménez Alegría, Natalia - A/C.6/78/SR.34
Netherlands (Kingdom of the)
Theeuwen, Wieteke Elisabeth Christina - A/C.6/78/SR.34
Philippines
Arumpac-Marte, Azela Guerrero - A/C.6/78/SR.34
Russian Federation
Antonova, Anna V. - A/C.6/78/SR.34
Singapore
Tan, Scott - A/C.6/78/SR.34
South Africa
Motsepe, Keke Mantsho - A/C.6/78/SR.34
UN. General Assembly. 6th Committee. Bureau
Panier, Wisnique (Haiti) - A/C.6/78/SR.37
UN. General Assembly. 6th Committee. Rapporteur
Moussa, Moussa Mohamed (Djibouti) - A/78/PV.45
United Kingdom
Lito, Melina - A/C.6/78/SR.34
United States
Grosso, Elizabeth Maryanne - A/C.6/78/SR.34

NON-NUCLEAR-WEAPON STATES—SECURITY (Agenda item 96)

Argentina
Squeff, María del Carmen - A/C.1/78/PV.13
Cuba
Gómez Sardiñas, Yiliam - A/C.1/78/PV.25
Pakistan
Jadoon, Usman Iqbal - A/C.1/78/PV.12
UN. General Assembly. 1st Committee. Rapporteur
Balouji, Heidar Ali (Iran (Islamic Republic of)) - A/78/PV.42

NON-SELF-GOVERNING TERRITORIES—ECONOMIC INTERESTS (Agenda item 55)

Argentina
Alvarez, Maximiliano Javier - A/C.4/78/SR.9
UN. General Assembly. Special Political and Decolonization Committee (4th Committee). Rapporteur
Dhanutirto, Mariska Dwianti (Indonesia) - A/78/PV.45
UN. Special Committee of 24. Chair
Rambally, Menissa (Saint Lucia) - A/C.4/78/SR.2

NON-SELF-GOVERNING TERRITORIES—ECONOMIC INTERESTS (Agenda item 55) (continued)

UN. Special Committee of 24. Vice-Chair
Nasir, Arrmanatha Christiawan (Indonesia) - A/C.4/78/SR.2
United Kingdom
Meyrick, Phoebe - A/C.4/78/SR.9

NON-SELF-GOVERNING TERRITORIES—FELLOWSHIPS (Agenda item 57)

UN. General Assembly. Special Political and Decolonization Committee (4th Committee). Rapporteur
Dhanutirto, Mariska Dwianti (Indonesia) - A/78/PV.45
UN. Special Committee of 24. Chair
Rambally, Menissa (Saint Lucia) - A/C.4/78/SR.2
UN. Special Committee of 24. Vice-Chair
Nasir, Arrmanatha Christiawan (Indonesia) - A/C.4/78/SR.2

NON-SELF-GOVERNING TERRITORIES—REPORTS (Agenda item 54)

Community of Latin American and Caribbean States
King, Inga Rhonda (Saint Vincent and the Grenadines) - A/C.4/78/SR.7
Guyana
Rodrigues-Birkett, Carolyn - A/C.4/78/SR.7
UN. General Assembly. Special Political and Decolonization Committee (4th Committee). Rapporteur
Dhanutirto, Mariska Dwianti (Indonesia) - A/78/PV.45
UN. Special Committee of 24. Chair
Rambally, Menissa (Saint Lucia) - A/C.4/78/SR.2
UN. Special Committee of 24. Vice-Chair
Nasir, Arrmanatha Christiawan (Indonesia) - A/C.4/78/SR.2
United Kingdom
Meyrick, Phoebe - A/C.4/78/SR.9
United States
Boluda, Miguel - A/C.4/78/SR.9

NUCLEAR DISARMAMENT (Agenda item 99b)

Algeria
Lebbaz, Larbi Abdelfattah - A/C.1/78/PV.14
Argentina
Squeff, María del Carmen - A/C.1/78/PV.13
ASEAN
Dang, Hoang Giang (Viet Nam) - A/C.1/78/PV.11
Australia
Gorely, Amanda Louise - A/C.1/78/PV.11
Larsen, James - A/C.1/78/PV.12
Austria
Kmentt, Alexander - A/C.1/78/PV.12
Bahrain
Janahi, Balqees - A/C.1/78/PV.14
Bangladesh
Molla, Md Rafiqul Alam - A/C.1/78/PV.12

NUCLEAR DISARMAMENT (Agenda item 99b) (continued)

Bolivia (Plurinational State of)
Muñoz Ponce, Tatiana Bárbara - A/C.1/78/PV.13
Brazil
Damico, Flávio Soares - A/C.1/78/PV.13
Bulgaria
Stoeva, Lachezara - A/C.1/78/PV.12
Burkina Faso
Ganou, Oumarou - A/C.1/78/PV.12
Canada
Fetz, Thomas - A/C.1/78/PV.13
Caribbean Community
Fuller, Carlos C. (Belize) - A/C.1/78/PV.11
Chile
Vidal Mercado, Jorge Andrés - A/C.1/78/PV.12
China
Sun, Yiliang - A/C.1/78/PV.11; A/C.1/78/PV.13
Wu, Jianjian - A/C.1/78/PV.13
Colombia
Quintero Correa, Nohra María - A/C.1/78/PV.14
Comoros
Oussein, Kadim - A/C.1/78/PV.13
Coordinating Bureau of the Non-Aligned Countries
Dhanutirto, Mariska Dwianti (Indonesia) - A/C.1/78/PV.11
Costa Rica
Chan Valverde, Maritza - A/C.1/78/PV.13
Côte d'Ivoire
Moriko, Tiémoko - A/C.1/78/PV.12
Cuba
Gómez Sardiñas, Yiliam - A/C.1/78/PV.25
Peñalver Portal, Gerardo - A/C.1/78/PV.11
Czechia
Štěpánek, Jaroslav - A/C.1/78/PV.12
Democratic People's Republic of Korea
Kim, In Chol - A/C.1/78/PV.13
Kim, Song - A/C.1/78/PV.11
Egypt
Ahmed, Amr Essameldin Sadek - A/C.1/78/PV.11
El Salvador
Segura Aragón, Carlos Efraín - A/C.1/78/PV.12
Ethiopia
Getahun, Kedir - A/C.1/78/PV.13
European Union
Hansen, Steen Malthe - A/C.1/78/PV.11; A/C.1/78/PV.13
Finland
Viinanen, Jarmo Veli Tapio - A/C.1/78/PV.12
France
Petit, Camille - A/C.1/78/PV.11
Germany
Himmler, Benjamin - A/C.1/78/PV.11
Ghana
Kesse Antwi, Linda - A/C.1/78/PV.12
Greece
Margaris, Pantelis - A/C.1/78/PV.11
Group of Arab States
Hmoud, Mahmoud Daifallah Mahmoud (Jordan) - A/C.1/78/PV.11

NUCLEAR DISARMAMENT (Agenda item 99b) (continued)

Holy See
Caccia, Gabriele Giordano - A/C.1/78/PV.14
Hungary
Talpai, Tamás - A/C.1/78/PV.13
IAEA
Okeke, Vivian Nwunaku Rose - A/C.1/78/PV.13
India
Ray, Anupam - A/C.1/78/PV.13
Indonesia
Aron, Andy - A/C.1/78/PV.11
Iran (Islamic Republic of)
Ghorbanpour Najafabadi, Mohammad - A/C.1/78/PV.11; A/C.1/78/PV.12
Iraq
Salih, Muthanna - A/C.1/78/PV.12
Ireland
Duffy, Patrick - A/C.1/78/PV.12
Israel
Maayan, Michal - A/C.1/78/PV.11; A/C.1/78/PV.12; A/C.1/78/PV.13; A/C.1/78/PV.14
Italy
Bencini, Leonardo - A/C.1/78/PV.13
Japan
Ogasawara, Ichiro - A/C.1/78/PV.12
Kazakhstan
Syrymbet, Zhangeldy - A/C.1/78/PV.12
Kenya
Ndung'u, Gideon Kinuthia - A/C.1/78/PV.12
Kiribati
Ciobanu, Christian Niculae - A/C.1/78/PV.13
Lao People's Democratic Republic
Vongnorkeo, Anouparb - A/C.1/78/PV.13
Lithuania
Geleževičienė, Giedrė - A/C.1/78/PV.13
Malaysia
Muhamad, Ahmad Faisal - A/C.1/78/PV.11
Mexico
Sánchez Kiesslich, Eduardo Alcibiades - A/C.1/78/PV.12
Myanmar
Tun, Kyaw Moe - A/C.1/78/PV.14
Namibia
Kuzee, Helena Ndapewa - A/C.1/78/PV.14
Nepal
Gohiwar Aryal, Indira - A/C.1/78/PV.13
Netherlands (Kingdom of the)
Bosch, Robert in den - A/C.1/78/PV.11
New Zealand
Clutterbuck, Nicholas - A/C.1/78/PV.11
Nigeria
Ajayi, Eniola Olaitan - A/C.1/78/PV.13
Norway
Osmundsen, Jorn - A/C.1/78/PV.13
Pakistan
Jadoon, Usman Iqbal - A/C.1/78/PV.12
Sarwani, Gul Qaiser - A/C.1/78/PV.26
Philippines
Reyes, Narciso - A/C.1/78/PV.12

NUCLEAR DISARMAMENT (Agenda item 99b) (continued)

Poland
Dzwonek, Piotr - A/C.1/78/PV.13
Qatar
Al-Safran, Hussain Mohammed - A/C.1/78/PV.12
Republic of Korea
Kim, Sunghoon - A/C.1/78/PV.12; A/C.1/78/PV.13
Russian Federation
Vorontsov, Konstantin - A/C.1/78/PV.11; A/C.1/78/PV.12; A/C.1/78/PV.13
Saudi Arabia
Alibrahim, Faisal - A/C.1/78/PV.13
Senegal
Diack, Papa Samba - A/C.1/78/PV.12
Singapore
Lim, Jessie - A/C.1/78/PV.12
Slovenia
Jerman, Bostjan - A/C.1/78/PV.14
South Africa
Saran, Sherina - A/C.1/78/PV.11
Spain
Rosario Vela, Manuel Jesús del - A/C.1/78/PV.12
Sri Lanka
Pieris, Peter Mohan Maithri - A/C.1/78/PV.11
Sweden
Escaig, Benjamin - A/C.1/78/PV.11
Switzerland
Thoeni, Julien - A/C.1/78/PV.12
Syrian Arab Republic
Al Ashkar, Adib - A/C.1/78/PV.11; A/C.1/78/PV.14
Thailand
Chindawongse, Suriya - A/C.1/78/PV.13
Timor-Leste
Sousa, Ivens Gusmao de - A/C.1/78/PV.13
Togo
Ouro-Tagba, Tawfic - A/C.1/78/PV.12
Türkiye
Çetin, Ahmet Erman - A/C.1/78/PV.13
Ukraine
Zlenko, Anatoli M. - A/C.1/78/PV.12; A/C.1/78/PV.13
UN. Group of African States
Mahmud, Mohammed Lawal (Nigeria) - A/C.1/78/PV.11
United Arab Emirates
Alnuaimi, Hessa - A/C.1/78/PV.14
United Kingdom
Liddle, Aidan Thomas - A/C.1/78/PV.13
United States
Turner, Bruce - A/C.1/78/PV.13
Uruguay
Eustathiou de los Santos, Matías Andrés - A/C.1/78/PV.12
Viet Nam
Tran, Thi Thanh Hai - A/C.1/78/PV.13
Zambia
Milambo, Chola - A/C.1/78/PV.14

NUCLEAR DISARMAMENT—CONFERENCES (Agenda item 99aa)

Coordinating Bureau of the Non-Aligned Countries
Dhanutirto, Mariska Dwianti (Indonesia) - A/C.1/78/PV.11
Cuba
Gómez Sardiñas, Yiliam - A/C.1/78/PV.25
Egypt
Ahmed, Amr Essameldin Sadek - A/C.1/78/PV.25
Netherlands (Kingdom of the)
Bosch, Robert in den - A/C.1/78/PV.26
Switzerland
Anderegg, Julius - A/C.1/78/PV.26

NUCLEAR DISARMAMENT—TREATY COMPLIANCE (Agenda item 99q)

Canada
Fetz, Thomas - A/C.1/78/PV.26
Democratic People's Republic of Korea
Kim, In Chol - A/C.1/78/PV.26
Egypt
Ahmed, Amr Essameldin Sadek - A/C.1/78/PV.11; A/C.1/78/PV.25
Iran (Islamic Republic of)
Ghorbanpour Najafabadi, Mohammad - A/C.1/78/PV.26
Mexico
Sánchez Kiesslich, Eduardo Alcibiades - A/C.1/78/PV.12
New Zealand
Clutterbuck, Nicholas - A/C.1/78/PV.11
Nam, Christine - A/C.1/78/PV.25
Pakistan
Sarwani, Gul Qaiser - A/C.1/78/PV.26
Switzerland
Anderegg, Julius - A/C.1/78/PV.26
United States
Turner, Bruce - A/C.1/78/PV.25

NUCLEAR DISARMAMENT—VERIFICATION (Agenda item 99ee)

Argentina
Squeff, María del Carmen - A/C.1/78/PV.13
Australia
Larsen, James - A/C.1/78/PV.12
Brazil
Damico, Flávio Soares - A/C.1/78/PV.12
Hungary
Talpai, Tamás - A/C.1/78/PV.13
Iran (Islamic Republic of)
Ghorbanpour Najafabadi, Mohammad - A/C.1/78/PV.26
Netherlands (Kingdom of the)
Bosch, Robert in den - A/C.1/78/PV.11
Norway
Osmundsen, Jorn - A/C.1/78/PV.12; A/C.1/78/PV.13
Russian Federation
Belousov, Andrey I. - A/C.1/78/PV.25
Slovenia
Jerman, Bostjan - A/C.1/78/PV.14

NUCLEAR DISARMAMENT—VERIFICATION (Agenda item 99ee) (continued)

Sweden
Escaig, Benjamin - A/C.1/78/PV.11
United Kingdom
Liddle, Aidan Thomas - A/C.1/78/PV.13

NUCLEAR NON-PROLIFERATION (Agenda item 99o)

ASEAN
Dang, Hoang Giang (Viet Nam) - A/C.1/78/PV.11
China
Sun, Yiliang - A/C.1/78/PV.13
Cuba
Gómez Sardiñas, Yiliam - A/C.1/78/PV.25
India
Ray, Anupam - A/C.1/78/PV.13
Pakistan
Ahmed, Husham - A/C.1/78/PV.25

NUCLEAR NON-PROLIFERATION—INTERNATIONAL OBLIGATIONS (Agenda item 99w)

Algeria
Lebbaz, Larbi Abdelfattah - A/C.1/78/PV.14
ASEAN
Dang, Hoang Giang (Viet Nam) - A/C.1/78/PV.11
Australia
Gorely, Amanda Louise - A/C.1/78/PV.11
Larsen, James - A/C.1/78/PV.12
Austria
Kmentt, Alexander - A/C.1/78/PV.12
Bahrain
Janahi, Balqees - A/C.1/78/PV.14
Bangladesh
Molla, Md Rafiqul Alam - A/C.1/78/PV.12
Bolivia (Plurinational State of)
Muñoz Ponce, Tatiana Bárbara - A/C.1/78/PV.13
Brazil
Damico, Flávio Soares - A/C.1/78/PV.13
Bulgaria
Stoeva, Lachezara - A/C.1/78/PV.12
Canada
Fetz, Thomas - A/C.1/78/PV.13
Caribbean Community
Fuller, Carlos C. (Belize) - A/C.1/78/PV.11
Chile
Vidal Mercado, Jorge Andrés - A/C.1/78/PV.12
Colombia
Quintero Correa, Nohra María - A/C.1/78/PV.14
Coordinating Bureau of the Non-Aligned Countries
Dhanutirto, Mariska Dwianti (Indonesia) - A/C.1/78/PV.11
Costa Rica
Chan Valverde, Maritza - A/C.1/78/PV.13
Côte d'Ivoire
Moriko, Tiémoko - A/C.1/78/PV.12
Cuba
Peñalver Portal, Gerardo - A/C.1/78/PV.11
Czechia
Štěpánek, Jaroslav - A/C.1/78/PV.12

NUCLEAR NON-PROLIFERATION—INTERNATIONAL OBLIGATIONS (Agenda item 99w) (continued)

Democratic Republic of the Congo
Liolocha, Victoria Lieta - A/C.1/78/PV.13
Egypt
Ahmed, Amr Essameldin Sadek - A/C.1/78/PV.11
El Salvador
Segura Aragón, Carlos Efraín - A/C.1/78/PV.12
Ethiopia
Getahun, Kedir - A/C.1/78/PV.13
European Union
Hansen, Steen Malthe - A/C.1/78/PV.11
Finland
Viinanen, Jarmo Veli Tapio - A/C.1/78/PV.12
France
Petit, Camille - A/C.1/78/PV.11
Germany
Himmler, Benjamin - A/C.1/78/PV.11
Ghana
Kesse Antwi, Linda - A/C.1/78/PV.12
Greece
Margaris, Pantelis - A/C.1/78/PV.11
Group of Arab States
Hmoud, Mahmoud Daifallah Mahmoud (Jordan) - A/C.1/78/PV.11
Holy See
Caccia, Gabriele Giordano - A/C.1/78/PV.14
Hungary
Talpai, Tamás - A/C.1/78/PV.13
Indonesia
Aron, Andy - A/C.1/78/PV.11
Iran (Islamic Republic of)
Ghorbanpour Najafabadi, Mohammad - A/C.1/78/PV.12
Iraq
Salih, Muthanna - A/C.1/78/PV.12
Ireland
Duffy, Patrick - A/C.1/78/PV.12
Israel
Maayan, Michal - A/C.1/78/PV.12
Italy
Bencini, Leonardo - A/C.1/78/PV.13
Japan
Ogasawara, Ichiro - A/C.1/78/PV.12
Kazakhstan
Syrymbet, Zhangeldy - A/C.1/78/PV.12
Lao People's Democratic Republic
Vongnorkeo, Anouparb - A/C.1/78/PV.13
Malaysia
Muhamad, Ahmad Faisal - A/C.1/78/PV.11
Mexico
Sánchez Kiesslich, Eduardo Alcibiades - A/C.1/78/PV.12
Myanmar
Tun, Kyaw Moe - A/C.1/78/PV.14
Nepal
Gohiwar Aryal, Indira - A/C.1/78/PV.13
Netherlands (Kingdom of the)
Bosch, Robert in den - A/C.1/78/PV.11
New Zealand
Clutterbuck, Nicholas - A/C.1/78/PV.11
Nigeria
Ajayi, Eniola Olaitan - A/C.1/78/PV.13
Norway
Osmundsen, Jorn - A/C.1/78/PV.13
Pakistan
Sarwani, Gul Qaiser - A/C.1/78/PV.26
Philippines
Reyes, Narciso - A/C.1/78/PV.12
Poland
Dzwonek, Piotr - A/C.1/78/PV.13
Qatar
Al-Safran, Hussain Mohammed - A/C.1/78/PV.12
Republic of Korea
Kim, Sunghoon - A/C.1/78/PV.12
Russian Federation
Vorontsov, Konstantin - A/C.1/78/PV.12
Singapore
Lim, Jessie - A/C.1/78/PV.12
Slovenia
Jerman, Bostjan - A/C.1/78/PV.14
South Africa
Saran, Sherina - A/C.1/78/PV.11
Spain
Rosario Vela, Manuel Jesús del - A/C.1/78/PV.12
Sri Lanka
Pieris, Peter Mohan Maithri - A/C.1/78/PV.11
Sweden
Escaig, Benjamin - A/C.1/78/PV.11
Switzerland
Thoeni, Julien - A/C.1/78/PV.12
Thailand
Chindawongse, Suriya - A/C.1/78/PV.13
Timor-Leste
Sousa, Ivens Gusmao de - A/C.1/78/PV.13
Togo
Ouro-Tagba, Tawfic - A/C.1/78/PV.12
Türkiye
Çetin, Ahmet Erman - A/C.1/78/PV.13
Ukraine
Zlenko, Anatoli M. - A/C.1/78/PV.12
UN. Group of African States
Mahmud, Mohammed Lawal (Nigeria) - A/C.1/78/PV.11
United Arab Emirates
Alnuaimi, Hessa - A/C.1/78/PV.14
United Kingdom
Liddle, Aidan Thomas - A/C.1/78/PV.13
United States
Turner, Bruce - A/C.1/78/PV.13
Viet Nam
Tran, Thi Thanh Hai - A/C.1/78/PV.13

NUCLEAR WEAPON TESTS—TREATIES (Agenda item 105)

Algeria
Lebbaz, Larbi Abdelfattah - A/C.1/78/PV.14
Argentina
Squeff, María del Carmen - A/C.1/78/PV.13

NUCLEAR WEAPON TESTS—TREATIES (Agenda item 105) (continued)

ASEAN
Dang, Hoang Giang (Viet Nam) - A/C.1/78/PV.11
Australia
Gorely, Amanda Louise - A/C.1/78/PV.11
Larsen, James - A/C.1/78/PV.12
Austria
Kmentt, Alexander - A/C.1/78/PV.12
Bolivia (Plurinational State of)
Muñoz Ponce, Tatiana Bárbara - A/C.1/78/PV.13
Bulgaria
Stoeva, Lachezara - A/C.1/78/PV.12
Canada
Fetz, Thomas - A/C.1/78/PV.13
Chile
Vidal Mercado, Jorge Andrés - A/C.1/78/PV.12
China
Sun, Yiliang - A/C.1/78/PV.26
Côte d'Ivoire
Moriko, Tiémoko - A/C.1/78/PV.12
Czechia
Štěpánek, Jaroslav - A/C.1/78/PV.12
Democratic People's Republic of Korea
Kim, In Chol - A/C.1/78/PV.26
Egypt
Ahmed, Amr Essameldin Sadek - A/C.1/78/PV.26
European Union
Hansen, Steen Malthe - A/C.1/78/PV.11
Germany
Himmler, Benjamin - A/C.1/78/PV.11
Greece
Margaris, Pantelis - A/C.1/78/PV.11
Group of Arab States
Hmoud, Mahmoud Daifallah Mahmoud (Jordan) - A/C.1/78/PV.11
Indonesia
Aron, Andy - A/C.1/78/PV.11
Iran (Islamic Republic of)
Ghorbanpour Najafabadi, Mohammad - A/C.1/78/PV.26
Ireland
Duffy, Patrick - A/C.1/78/PV.12
Italy
Bencini, Leonardo - A/C.1/78/PV.13
Kazakhstan
Syrymbet, Zhangeldy - A/C.1/78/PV.12
Lao People's Democratic Republic
Vongnorkeo, Anouparb - A/C.1/78/PV.13
Malaysia
Muhamad, Ahmad Faisal - A/C.1/78/PV.11
Mexico
Sánchez Kiesslich, Eduardo Alcibiades - A/C.1/78/PV.12; A/C.1/78/PV.25
Myanmar
Tun, Kyaw Moe - A/C.1/78/PV.14
New Zealand
Clutterbuck, Nicholas - A/C.1/78/PV.11

NUCLEAR WEAPON TESTS—TREATIES (Agenda item 105) (continued)

Norway
Osmundsen, Jorn - A/C.1/78/PV.13
Pakistan
Sarwani, Gul Qaiser - A/C.1/78/PV.26
Panama
Veliz Rodríguez, Aris Anel - A/C.1/78/PV.25
Philippines
Reyes, Narciso - A/C.1/78/PV.12
Preparatory Commission for the Comprehensive Nuclear Test-Ban Treaty Organization
Rosemberg Guerrero, José - A/C.1/78/PV.13
Republic of Korea
Kim, Sunghoon - A/C.1/78/PV.12
Russian Federation
Belousov, Andrey I. - A/C.1/78/PV.26
Vorontsov, Konstantin - A/C.1/78/PV.12
Singapore
Lim, Jessie - A/C.1/78/PV.12
Slovenia
Jerman, Bostjan - A/C.1/78/PV.14
South Africa
Saran, Sherina - A/C.1/78/PV.11
Spain
Rosario Vela, Manuel Jesús del - A/C.1/78/PV.12
Sweden
Escaig, Benjamin - A/C.1/78/PV.11
Switzerland
Thoeni, Julien - A/C.1/78/PV.12
Thailand
Chindawongse, Suriya - A/C.1/78/PV.13
Togo
Ouro-Tagba, Tawfic - A/C.1/78/PV.12
Türkiye
Çetin, Ahmet Erman - A/C.1/78/PV.13
Ukraine
Zlenko, Anatoli M. - A/C.1/78/PV.12
UN. General Assembly. 1st Committee. Rapporteur
Balouji, Heidar Ali (Iran (Islamic Republic of)) - A/78/PV.42
UN. Group of African States
Mahmud, Mohammed Lawal (Nigeria) - A/C.1/78/PV.11
United Kingdom
Liddle, Aidan Thomas - A/C.1/78/PV.13
Viet Nam
Tran, Thi Thanh Hai - A/C.1/78/PV.13

NUCLEAR WEAPONS—ELIMINATION (Agenda item 99z)

Argentina
Guerra, Hugo Emmanuel - A/C.1/78/PV.26
Austria
Edtmayer, Matthias - A/C.1/78/PV.25
Brazil
Szatmari, Roberto Wazima - A/C.1/78/PV.26
China
Sun, Yiliang - A/C.1/78/PV.26
Colombia
Quintero Correa, Nohra María - A/C.1/78/PV.26
Costa Rica
Ávila Becerril, Ana Maricela - A/C.1/78/PV.26

NUCLEAR WEAPONS—ELIMINATION (Agenda item 99z) (continued)

Democratic People's Republic of Korea
Kim, In Chol - A/C.1/78/PV.25; A/C.1/78/PV.26
Equatorial Guinea
Edu Mbasogo, Marcial - A/C.1/78/PV.25
France
Petit, Camille - A/C.1/78/PV.26
India
Ray, Anupam - A/C.1/78/PV.26
Indonesia
Kristanti, Maria Benedicta Diah - A/C.1/78/PV.26
Iran (Islamic Republic of)
Ghorbanpour Najafabadi, Mohammad - A/C.1/78/PV.25
Ireland
Doyle, Ciaran James - A/C.1/78/PV.26
Japan
Ogasawara, Ichiro - A/C.1/78/PV.12; A/C.1/78/PV.25; A/C.1/78/PV.26
Malaysia
Sivamohan, Shivanand - A/C.1/78/PV.25
Mexico
Sánchez Kiesslich, Eduardo Alcibiades - A/C.1/78/PV.26
New Zealand
Nam, Christine - A/C.1/78/PV.26
Pakistan
Sarwani, Gul Qaiser - A/C.1/78/PV.26
Panama
Veliz Rodríguez, Aris Anel - A/C.1/78/PV.25
Republic of Korea
Kim, Sangjin - A/C.1/78/PV.26
Russian Federation
Belousov, Andrey I. - A/C.1/78/PV.25
South Africa
Schalkwyk, Marthinus van - A/C.1/78/PV.25
Switzerland
Anderegg, Julius - A/C.1/78/PV.26
United States
Storsve, Alison - A/C.1/78/PV.25

NUCLEAR WEAPONS—HUMANITARIAN CONSEQUENCES (Agenda item 99bb)

Austria
Edtmayer, Matthias - A/C.1/78/PV.25
Kmentt, Alexander - A/C.1/78/PV.12
Caribbean Community
Fuller, Carlos C. (Belize) - A/C.1/78/PV.11
Côte d'Ivoire
Moriko, Tiémoko - A/C.1/78/PV.12
Cuba
Gómez Sardiñas, Yiliam - A/C.1/78/PV.25
Democratic Republic of the Congo
Liolocha, Victoria Lieta - A/C.1/78/PV.13
India
Kulkarni, Maitrey - A/C.1/78/PV.25
Japan
Ogasawara, Ichiro - A/C.1/78/PV.26
Kiribati
Ciobanu, Christian Niculae - A/C.1/78/PV.13

NUCLEAR WEAPONS—HUMANITARIAN CONSEQUENCES (Agenda item 99bb) (continued)

New Zealand
Clutterbuck, Nicholas - A/C.1/78/PV.11
Pakistan
Ahmed, Husham - A/C.1/78/PV.25
UN. Group of African States
Mahmud, Mohammed Lawal (Nigeria) - A/C.1/78/PV.11
United States
Turner, Bruce - A/C.1/78/PV.25

NUCLEAR WEAPONS—TREATIES (Agenda item 99ff)

Argentina
Guerra, Hugo Emmanuel - A/C.1/78/PV.26
ASEAN
Dang, Hoang Giang (Viet Nam) - A/C.1/78/PV.11
Austria
Edtmayer, Matthias - A/C.1/78/PV.25
Kmentt, Alexander - A/C.1/78/PV.12
Bangladesh
Molla, Md Rafiqul Alam - A/C.1/78/PV.12
Brazil
Damico, Flávio Soares - A/C.1/78/PV.13
Caribbean Community
Fuller, Carlos C. (Belize) - A/C.1/78/PV.11
Chile
Vidal Mercado, Jorge Andrés - A/C.1/78/PV.12
China
Sun, Yiliang - A/C.1/78/PV.26
Comoros
Oussein, Kadim - A/C.1/78/PV.13
Coordinating Bureau of the Non-Aligned Countries
Dhanutirto, Mariska Dwianti (Indonesia) - A/C.1/78/PV.11
Costa Rica
Chan Valverde, Maritza - A/C.1/78/PV.13
Côte d'Ivoire
Moriko, Tiémoko - A/C.1/78/PV.12
Cuba
Gómez Sardiñas, Yiliam - A/C.1/78/PV.25
Peñalver Portal, Gerardo - A/C.1/78/PV.11
Democratic Republic of the Congo
Liolocha, Victoria Lieta - A/C.1/78/PV.13
El Salvador
Segura Aragón, Carlos Efraín - A/C.1/78/PV.12
Group of Arab States
Hmoud, Mahmoud Daifallah Mahmoud (Jordan) - A/C.1/78/PV.11
India
Kulkarni, Maitrey - A/C.1/78/PV.25
Indonesia
Aron, Andy - A/C.1/78/PV.11
Ireland
Duffy, Patrick - A/C.1/78/PV.12
Israel
Sharoni, Benjamin - A/C.1/78/PV.26
Japan
Ogasawara, Ichiro - A/C.1/78/PV.26

NUCLEAR WEAPONS—TREATIES (Agenda item 99ff) (continued)

Malaysia
Muhamad, Ahmad Faisal - A/C.1/78/PV.11
Mexico
Sánchez Kiesslich, Eduardo Alcibiades - A/C.1/78/PV.11; A/C.1/78/PV.12
New Zealand
Clutterbuck, Nicholas - A/C.1/78/PV.11
Nigeria
Ajayi, Eniola Olaitan - A/C.1/78/PV.13
Pakistan
Sarwani, Gul Qaiser - A/C.1/78/PV.26
Panama
Veliz Rodríguez, Aris Anel - A/C.1/78/PV.25
Philippines
Reyes, Narciso - A/C.1/78/PV.12
Singapore
Liu, Lu - A/C.1/78/PV.26
South Africa
Saran, Sherina - A/C.1/78/PV.11
Sri Lanka
Pieris, Peter Mohan Maithri - A/C.1/78/PV.11
Switzerland
Anderegg, Julius - A/C.1/78/PV.26
Thailand
Chindawongse, Suriya - A/C.1/78/PV.13
Timor-Leste
Sousa, Ivens Gusmao de - A/C.1/78/PV.13
UN. Group of African States
Mahmud, Mohammed Lawal (Nigeria) - A/C.1/78/PV.11

NUCLEAR WEAPONS USE—TREATIES (Agenda item 100a)

India
Ray, Anupam - A/C.1/78/PV.13
Iran (Islamic Republic of)
Ghorbanpour Najafabadi, Mohammad - A/C.1/78/PV.26
Mexico
Sánchez Kiesslich, Eduardo Alcibiades - A/C.1/78/PV.25
Pakistan
Ahmed, Husham - A/C.1/78/PV.25
Thailand
Khundee, Wichayaporn - A/C.1/78/PV.26

NUCLEAR WEAPONS USE—UN. INTERNATIONAL COURT OF JUSTICE OPINION (Agenda item 99k)

Armenia
Grigoryan, Andranik - A/C.1/78/PV.29
Cuba
Gómez Sardiñas, Yiliam - A/C.1/78/PV.25
India
Kulkarni, Maitrey - A/C.1/78/PV.25
Malaysia
Muhamad, Ahmad Faisal - A/C.1/78/PV.11
Sivamohan, Shivanand - A/C.1/78/PV.25
Pakistan
Sarwani, Gul Qaiser - A/C.1/78/PV.26

NUCLEAR-WEAPON-FREE ZONE—SOUTHERN HEMISPHERE (Agenda item 99i)

Cuba
Gómez Sardiñas, Yiliam - A/C.1/78/PV.25
New Zealand
Clutterbuck, Nicholas - A/C.1/78/PV.11
Nam, Christine - A/C.1/78/PV.25
United States
Turner, Bruce - A/C.1/78/PV.25; A/C.1/78/PV.26

NUCLEAR-WEAPON-FREE ZONES (Agenda item 99cc)

Agency for the Prohibition of Nuclear Weapons in Latin America and the Caribbean
Damico, Flávio Soares - A/C.1/78/PV.11
Caribbean Community
Fuller, Carlos C. (Belize) - A/C.1/78/PV.11
Cuba
Gómez Sardiñas, Yiliam - A/C.1/78/PV.25
El Salvador
Segura Aragón, Carlos Efraín - A/C.1/78/PV.12
New Zealand
Clutterbuck, Nicholas - A/C.1/78/PV.11
Pakistan
Ahmed, Husham - A/C.1/78/PV.25
Panama
Veliz Rodríguez, Aris Anel - A/C.1/78/PV.25
South Africa
Saran, Sherina - A/C.1/78/PV.11
United States
Turner, Bruce - A/C.1/78/PV.25

OPERATIONAL ACTIVITIES—DEVELOPMENT (Agenda item 22)

UN. General Assembly. 2nd Committee. Rapporteur
Gatev, Ivaylo (Bulgaria) - A/78/PV.49

OPERATIONAL ACTIVITIES—UN SYSTEM (Agenda item 22a)

ASEAN
Chindawongse, Suriya (Thailand) - A/C.2/78/SR.18
Belarus
Pisarevich, Vadim - A/C.2/78/SR.18
Burkina Faso
Bokoum, Mahamadou - A/C.2/78/SR.18
Cameroon
Etoundi Ayissi, Joseph - A/C.2/78/SR.18
Caribbean Community
Wallace, Brian Christopher Manley (Jamaica) - A/C.2/78/SR.18
China
Dai, Bing - A/C.2/78/SR.18
El Salvador
González López, Egriselda Aracely - A/C.2/78/SR.18
European Union
Kaspar, Martin - A/C.2/78/SR.22

OPERATIONAL ACTIVITIES—UN SYSTEM (Agenda item 22a) (continued)

Group of 77
  Guevara Rodríguez, Adiel (Cuba) - A/C.2/78/SR.18
  Torres Seara, Dalia Marlen (Cuba) - A/C.2/78/SR.21
Group of Landlocked Developing Countries
  Motsumi, Lorato (Botswana) - A/C.2/78/SR.18
Group of Least Developed Countries
  Ray, Kaushal Kishor (Nepal) - A/C.2/78/SR.18
Guinea
  Zoumanigui, Paul Goa - A/C.2/78/SR.18
India
  Gahlot, Petal - A/C.2/78/SR.18
Indonesia
  Prabowo, Hari - A/C.2/78/SR.18
Kenya
  Abbas, Swabri Ali - A/C.2/78/SR.18
Lao People's Democratic Republic
  Thaphanya, Natthakith - A/C.2/78/SR.18
Malaysia
  Zulasri Bin Rosdi, Muhammad - A/C.2/78/SR.18
Mexico
  Robledo López, Carmen - A/C.2/78/SR.18
Morocco
  Ouatiki, Assia - A/C.2/78/SR.18
Nigeria
  Dagari, Rabiu - A/C.2/78/SR.18
Pakistan
  Sharif, Shahsawar - A/C.2/78/SR.18
Russian Federation
  Meschchanov, Boris A. - A/C.2/78/SR.18
South Africa
  Mandla, Bulelani - A/C.2/78/SR.18
Thailand
  Suwantra, Maes - A/C.2/78/SR.18
UN. Department of Economic and Social Affairs. Office of Intergovernmental Support and Coordination for Sustainable Development. Director
  Pierre, Neil - A/C.2/78/SR.18
UN. General Assembly. 2nd Committee. Rapporteur
  Gatev, Ivaylo (Bulgaria) - A/78/PV.49
Viet Nam
  Nguyen, Hoang Nguyen - A/C.2/78/SR.18

ORGANIZATION FOR DEMOCRACY AND ECONOMIC DEVELOPMENT - GUAM (Agenda item 32)

Armenia
  Margaryan, Mher - A/78/PV.85
Australia
  Larsen, James - A/78/PV.85
Brazil
  Danese, Sérgio França - A/78/PV.85
European Union
  Lambrinidis, Stavros - A/78/PV.85
Georgia
  Bakradze, David - A/78/PV.85
Israel
  Kalmar, Nimrod - A/78/PV.85

ORGANIZATION FOR DEMOCRACY AND ECONOMIC DEVELOPMENT - GUAM (Agenda item 32) (continued)

Japan
  Shino, Mitsuko - A/78/PV.85
Lithuania
  Paulauskas, Rytis - A/78/PV.85
Russian Federation
  Zabolotskaya, Maria V. - A/78/PV.85
Ukraine
  Hayovyshyn, Khrystyna - A/78/PV.85
UN. General Assembly. President
  Francis, Dennis (Trinidad and Tobago) - A/78/PV.85
United Kingdom
  Alldridge, Rebecca - A/78/PV.85

ORGANIZATION OF IBERO-AMERICAN STATES FOR EDUCATION, SCIENCE AND CULTURE—OBSERVER STATUS (Agenda item 171)

Argentina
  Mainero, Martín Juan - A/C.6/78/SR.36
  Squeff, María del Carmen - A/C.6/78/SR.14
UN. General Assembly. 6th Committee. Rapporteur
  Moussa, Moussa Mohamed (Djibouti) - A/78/PV.45

OUTER SPACE—CONFIDENCE-BUILDING MEASURES (Agenda item 99v)

Algeria
  Lebbaz, Larbi Abdelfattah - A/C.1/78/PV.17
ASEAN
  Muhamad, Ahmad Faisal (Malaysia) - A/C.1/78/PV.16
Austria
  Bilgeri, Andreas - A/C.1/78/PV.16
Bolivia (Plurinational State of)
  Muñoz Ponce, Tatiana Bárbara - A/C.1/78/PV.17
Brazil
  Damico, Flávio Soares - A/C.1/78/PV.17
  Szatmari, Roberto Wazima - A/C.1/78/PV.27
Canada
  Milligan, Ashlyn - A/C.1/78/PV.17
China
  Shen, Jian - A/C.1/78/PV.17; A/C.1/78/PV.27
Coordinating Bureau of the Non-Aligned Countries
  Sirie, Mochammad Iqbal (Indonesia) - A/C.1/78/PV.16
Costa Rica
  Chan Valverde, Maritza - A/C.1/78/PV.16
Cuba
  Gómez Sardiñas, Yiliam - A/C.1/78/PV.17
  Romero López, Rosanis - A/C.1/78/PV.27
Egypt
  Hegazy, Abdelrhman Mohamed Farid - A/C.1/78/PV.16
European Union
  Claeys, Carine - A/C.1/78/PV.16
France
  Petit, Camille - A/C.1/78/PV.17
Germany
  Himmler, Benjamin - A/C.1/78/PV.16

OUTER SPACE—CONFIDENCE-BUILDING MEASURES (Agenda item 99v) (continued)

Group of Arab States
Alqaisi, Sultan Natheir Mustafa (Jordan) - A/C.1/78/PV.16
Holy See
Caccia, Gabriele Giordano - A/C.1/78/PV.17
Indonesia
Sinaga, Liandra Jean - A/C.1/78/PV.16
Iran (Islamic Republic of)
Ghorbanpour Najafabadi, Mohammad - A/C.1/78/PV.27
Ireland
Robinson, Jason - A/C.1/78/PV.17
Israel
Sharoni, Benjamin - A/C.1/78/PV.27
Italy
Bencini, Leonardo - A/C.1/78/PV.17
Japan
Ogasawara, Ichiro - A/C.1/78/PV.17
Kazakhstan
Rakhmetullin, Akan - A/C.1/78/PV.16
Malaysia
Muhamad, Ahmad Faisal - A/C.1/78/PV.16
New Zealand
Clutterbuck, Nicholas - A/C.1/78/PV.17
Norway
Sæter, William - A/C.1/78/PV.17
Pakistan
Sarwani, Gul Qaiser - A/C.1/78/PV.16
Paraguay
Sanabria Duarte, Viviana Rocio - A/C.1/78/PV.17
Philippines
Lipana, Diane Shayne Dela Fuente - A/C.1/78/PV.16
Republic of Korea
Yoon, Seong-mee - A/C.1/78/PV.17
Russian Federation
Belousov, Andrey I. - A/C.1/78/PV.27
Vorontsov, Konstantin - A/C.1/78/PV.16; A/C.1/78/PV.17
Saudi Arabia
Moharram, Wajdi Hassan M. - A/C.1/78/PV.16
Spain
Rosario Vela, Manuel Jesús del - A/C.1/78/PV.17
Sri Lanka
Gunaratna, Pahala Rallage Sanathana Sugeeshwara - A/C.1/78/PV.27
Pieris, Peter Mohan Maithri - A/C.1/78/PV.16
Sweden
Escaig, Benjamin - A/C.1/78/PV.16
UN. Group of African States
Mahmud, Mohammed Lawal (Nigeria) - A/C.1/78/PV.16
United States
Turner, Bruce - A/C.1/78/PV.17

OUTER SPACE—PEACEFUL USES—INTERNATIONAL COOPERATION (Agenda item 48)

Argentina
Alvarez, Maximiliano Javier - A/C.4/78/SR.15
ASEAN
Nguyen, Hoang Nguyen (Viet Nam) - A/C.4/78/SR.15
Bahrain
Aljalahma, Shaikha - A/C.4/78/SR.17
Bangladesh
Shatil, Toufiq Islam - A/C.4/78/SR.15
Brazil
Campos, Erika Helena - A/C.4/78/SR.16
Cameroon
Ahidjo, Ahidjo - A/C.4/78/SR.16
Canada
Pacey-Parker, Sarah - A/C.4/78/SR.16
China
Ma, Yuanchun - A/C.4/78/SR.16
Costa Rica
Chan Valverde, Maritza - A/C.4/78/SR.16
Cuba
Fernández Palacios, Yumirka - A/C.4/78/SR.15
Democratic People's Republic of Korea
Kim, In Chol - A/C.4/78/SR.17
Kim, Song - A/C.4/78/SR.15
El Salvador
Baños Müller, Liliana Verónica - A/C.4/78/SR.16
Ethiopia
Kassaye, Yoseph - A/C.4/78/SR.8
Temesgen, Tenna Misgana - A/C.4/78/SR.16
European Union
Hansen, Steen Malthe - A/C.4/78/SR.15
Holy See
Caccia, Gabriele Giordano - A/C.4/78/SR.17
India
Birdi, Nitish - A/C.4/78/SR.16
Iran (Islamic Republic of)
Sahraei, Mohammad Reza - A/C.4/78/SR.15
Iraq
Alsammak, Uday Qais Mahdi - A/C.4/78/SR.15
Israel
Kedar, Gershon - A/C.4/78/SR.16
Japan
Kusano, Yuta - A/C.4/78/SR.16
Malaysia
Nordin, Hana Binti - A/C.4/78/SR.15
Oman
Al Rashdi, Amal - A/C.4/78/SR.16
Pakistan
Khan, Naeem Sabir - A/C.4/78/SR.15
Philippines
Novicio, Noel Mangaoang - A/C.4/78/SR.17
Republic of Korea
Lee, Hyun Goo - A/C.4/78/SR.17
Russian Federation
Belousko, Sergey - A/C.4/78/SR.15; A/C.4/78/SR.16; A/C.4/78/SR.17

OUTER SPACE—PEACEFUL USES—INTERNATIONAL COOPERATION (Agenda item 48) (continued)

Saudi Arabia
  Al Kahtani, Fayee Fahad M. - A/C.4/78/SR.16
Singapore
  Lim, Luo You Clarice - A/C.4/78/SR.16
South Africa
  Mabeba, Bernard - A/C.4/78/SR.16
Sri Lanka
  Pieris, Peter Mohan Maithri - A/C.4/78/SR.15
Switzerland
  Archinard, Natália - A/C.4/78/SR.16
Thailand
  Vichankaiyakij, Vathayudh - A/C.4/78/SR.15
UN. Committee on the Peaceful Uses of Outer Space. Chair
  Sharaf, Omran (United Arab Emirates) - A/C.4/78/SR.15
UN. General Assembly. Special Political and Decolonization Committee (4th Committee). Chair
  Joyini, Mathu (South Africa) - A/C.4/78/SR.15
UN. General Assembly. Special Political and Decolonization Committee (4th Committee). Rapporteur
  Dhanutirto, Mariska Dwianti (Indonesia) - A/78/PV.45
UN. General Assembly. Special Political and Decolonization Committee (4th Committee). Working Group on International Cooperation in the Peaceful Uses of Outer Space. Chair
  Sharaf, Omran (United Arab Emirates) - A/C.4/78/SR.17
United Arab Emirates
  Al Qasim, Ibrahim - A/C.4/78/SR.16
United Kingdom
  Croker, Richard - A/C.4/78/SR.17
United States
  Poling, Caitlin - A/C.4/78/SR.16
Zambia
  Mungandi, Lubasi - A/C.4/78/SR.16

OUTER SPACE—PRINCIPLES (Agenda item 97d)

Algeria
  Lebbaz, Larbi Abdelfattah - A/C.1/78/PV.17
Argentina
  Guerra, Hugo Emmanuel - A/C.1/78/PV.16; A/C.1/78/PV.27
ASEAN
  Muhamad, Ahmad Faisal (Malaysia) - A/C.1/78/PV.16
Australia
  Lia, Alex - A/C.1/78/PV.16
Austria
  Bilgeri, Andreas - A/C.1/78/PV.16
Bangladesh
  Muhith, Muhammad A. - A/C.1/78/PV.16
Brazil
  Szatmari, Roberto Wazima - A/C.1/78/PV.27
Canada
  Milligan, Ashlyn - A/C.1/78/PV.17
Chile
  Vidal Mercado, Jorge Andrés - A/C.1/78/PV.16
China
  Shen, Jian - A/C.1/78/PV.17; A/C.1/78/PV.27
Zhang, Junjie - A/C.1/78/PV.27
Costa Rica
  Ávila Becerril, Ana Maricela - A/C.1/78/PV.27
  Chan Valverde, Maritza - A/C.1/78/PV.16
Cuba
  Romero López, Rosanis - A/C.1/78/PV.27
Czechia
  Štěpánek, Jaroslav - A/C.1/78/PV.16
Egypt
  Hegazy, Abdelrhman Mohamed Farid - A/C.1/78/PV.16; A/C.1/78/PV.27
El Salvador
  Rodríguez Acosta, Julia Elizabeth - A/C.1/78/PV.27
European Union
  Claeys, Carine - A/C.1/78/PV.16
France
  Petit, Camille - A/C.1/78/PV.17
Germany
  Himmler, Benjamin - A/C.1/78/PV.16
Greece
  Papathanasiou, Artemis - A/C.1/78/PV.17
Group of Arab States
  Alqaisi, Sultan Natheir Mustafa (Jordan) - A/C.1/78/PV.16
Holy See
  Caccia, Gabriele Giordano - A/C.1/78/PV.17
India
  Kulkarni, Maitrey - A/C.1/78/PV.27
Indonesia
  Kristanti, Maria Benedicta Diah - A/C.1/78/PV.27
  Sinaga, Liandra Jean - A/C.1/78/PV.16
Iran (Islamic Republic of)
  Eshragh Jahromi, Asadollah - A/C.1/78/PV.17
  Ghorbanpour Najafabadi, Mohammad - A/C.1/78/PV.27

OUTER SPACE—PRINCIPLES (Agenda item 97d) (continued)

Ireland
Robinson, Jason - A/C.1/78/PV.17
Italy
Bencini, Leonardo - A/C.1/78/PV.17
Japan
Ogasawara, Ichiro - A/C.1/78/PV.17
Malaysia
Muhamad, Ahmad Faisal - A/C.1/78/PV.16
Sivamohan, Shivanand - A/C.1/78/PV.27
Mexico
Sánchez Kiesslich, Eduardo Alcibiades - A/C.1/78/PV.27
Netherlands (Kingdom of the)
Bosch, Robert in den - A/C.1/78/PV.16
New Zealand
Clutterbuck, Nicholas - A/C.1/78/PV.17
Nigeria
Mahmud, Mohammed Lawal - A/C.1/78/PV.17
Norway
Sæter, William - A/C.1/78/PV.17
Pakistan
Gohar, Sarfaraz Ahmed - A/C.1/78/PV.27
Sarwani, Gul Qaiser - A/C.1/78/PV.16
Philippines
Lipana, Diane Shayne Dela Fuente - A/C.1/78/PV.16; A/C.1/78/PV.27
Republic of Korea
Yoon, Seong-mee - A/C.1/78/PV.17
Russian Federation
Belousov, Andrey I. - A/C.1/78/PV.27
Singapore
Low, Si Tong Berenice - A/C.1/78/PV.27
Spain
Rosario Vela, Manuel Jesús del - A/C.1/78/PV.17
Sri Lanka
Gunaratna, Pahala Rallage Sanathana Sugeeshwara - A/C.1/78/PV.27
Sweden
Escaig, Benjamin - A/C.1/78/PV.16
Switzerland
Masmejean, Laurent - A/C.1/78/PV.17
UN. General Assembly. 1st Committee. Rapporteur
Balouji, Heidar Ali (Iran (Islamic Republic of)) - A/78/PV.42
United Kingdom
Liddle, Aidan Thomas - A/C.1/78/PV.16; A/C.1/78/PV.27
United States
Turner, Bruce - A/C.1/78/PV.17; A/C.1/78/PV.27

PALESTINE QUESTION (Agenda item 35)

Algeria
Gaouaoui, Nacim - A/78/PV.40
Argentina
Squeff, María del Carmen - A/78/PV.39
Bahrain
Alrowaiei, Jamal Fares - A/78/PV.40
Bangladesh
Muhith, Muhammad A. - A/78/PV.40
Caribbean Community
Wallace, Brian Christopher Manley (Jamaica) - A/78/PV.39
Chile
Narváez Ojeda, Paula - A/78/PV.40
Colombia
Zalabata Torres, Leonor - A/78/PV.40
Cuba
Romero Puentes, Yusnier - A/78/PV.40
Egypt
Abdelkhalek, Osama Mahmoud - A/78/PV.39
Gulf Cooperation Council
Al Rubkhi, Khalid Saleh Said (Oman) - A/78/PV.39
Guyana
Rodrigues-Birkett, Carolyn - A/78/PV.39
India
Kamboj, Ruchira - A/78/PV.39
Indonesia
Marsudi, Retno Lestari Priansari - A/78/PV.39
Iran (Islamic Republic of)
Jalil Iravani, Amir Saeid - A/78/PV.40
Israel
Shapir Ben Naftaly, Reut - A/78/PV.39
Jordan
Hmoud, Mahmoud Daifallah Mahmoud - A/78/PV.39
Kuwait
Alenezi, Faisal G. - A/78/PV.40
Lao People's Democratic Republic
Vongnorkeo, Anouparb - A/78/PV.40
Libya
Habib, Hanan M.M. - A/78/PV.40
Malaysia
Abdul Kadir, Zambry - A/78/PV.39

PALESTINE QUESTION (Agenda item 35) (continued)

Maldives
Zuhuree, Ibrahim - A/78/PV.39
Mexico
Ochoa Martínez, Enrique Javier - A/78/PV.40
Morocco
Kadiri, Omar - A/78/PV.39
Namibia
Gertze, Neville Melvin - A/78/PV.39
Nicaragua
Pichardo Urbina, Eleane Yaoska - A/78/PV.40
Norway
Brattested, Merete Fjeld - A/78/PV.40
Pakistan
Jadoon, Usman Iqbal - A/78/PV.39
Philippines
Peñaranda, Ariel Rodelas - A/78/PV.39
Qatar
Al-Thani, Alya Ahmed S.A. - A/78/PV.39
Russian Federation
Chumakov, Dmitry S. - A/78/PV.40
Saudi Arabia
Alwasil, Abdulaziz M.O. - A/78/PV.40
Senegal
Gueye, Cheikh Mohamadou Bamba - A/78/PV.40
Sierra Leone
Baimarro, Karen Jean - A/78/PV.40
South Africa
Joyini, Mathu - A/78/PV.39
State of Palestine
Mansour, Riyad H. - A/78/PV.39
Tunisia
Ladeb, Tarek - A/78/PV.40
Türkiye
Güven, Fikriye Asli - A/78/PV.39
UN. Committee on the Exercise of the Inalienable Rights of the Palestinian People. Vice-Chair
Muhamad, Ahmad Faisal (Malaysia) - A/78/PV.39
UN. General Assembly. President
Francis, Dennis (Trinidad and Tobago) - A/78/PV.39
United Arab Emirates
Abushahab, Mohamed Issa - A/78/PV.40
United States
Henzel, Christopher - A/78/PV.40
Venezuela (Bolivarian Republic of)
Moncada Acosta, Samuel R. - A/78/PV.39
Viet Nam
Dang, Hoang Giang - A/78/PV.40
Yemen
Al-Saadi, Abdullah Ali Fadhel - A/78/PV.40

PALESTINIANS—ASSISTANCE (Agenda item 72b)

Algeria
Samai, Rahma - A/78/PV.47
ASEAN
Nasir, Arrmanatha Christiawan (Indonesia) - A/78/PV.46
Belgium
Kridelka, Philippe - A/78/PV.46
Bolivia (Plurinational State of)
Zambrana Flores, Carlos Iván - A/78/PV.47
Brunei Darussalam
Lee, Kok Ting - A/78/PV.47
China
Dai, Bing - A/78/PV.46
Colombia
Sánchez García, Nathalia - A/78/PV.46
Cuba
González Behmaras, Alejandro - A/78/PV.47
France
Dime-Labille, Diarra - A/78/PV.47
Group of Arab States
Abdelkhalek, Osama Mahmoud (Egypt) - A/78/PV.46
Group of Friends in Defence of the Charter of the United Nations
Castillo, William (Venezuela (Bolivarian Republic of)) - A/78/PV.46
Iran (Islamic Republic of)
Ershadi, Zahra - A/78/PV.46
Iraq
Al-Khaqani, Hassan Jabbar - A/78/PV.47
Japan
Miyamoto, Sogaku - A/78/PV.46
Kuwait
Alajmi, Fahad M. - A/78/PV.47
Maldives
Khadeeja, Aufiyau - A/78/PV.46
Morocco
Kadiri, Omar - A/78/PV.47
New Zealand
Fepuleai, Justin Peter - A/78/PV.46
Pakistan
Jadoon, Usman Iqbal - A/78/PV.46
Poland
Skoczek, Joanna Sylwia - A/78/PV.46
Saudi Arabia
Alwasil, Abdulaziz M.O. - A/78/PV.46
Singapore
Chak Yong, Mok - A/78/PV.46
State of Palestine
Abushawesh, Sahar - A/78/PV.47
Türkiye
Akbulut, Mustafa Kemal - A/78/PV.46

PALESTINIANS—ASSISTANCE (Agenda item 72b) (continued)

United Arab Emirates
Alolama, Mohd Abdulrahman Mohamed Jalil Sultan - A/78/PV.47
United States
Carty, Lisa A. - A/78/PV.46

PEACE (Agenda item 14)

Algeria
Alem, Mohammed Walid - A/78/PV.77
Merabet, Ismaïl - A/78/PV.82
Angola
Luemba, Mateus Pedro - A/78/PV.82
Argentina
Oddone, Fabián - A/78/PV.62; A/78/PV.82
Armenia
Margaryan, Mher - A/78/PV.82
ASEAN
Sulaiman, Noor Qamar (Brunei Darussalam) - A/78/PV.76
Australia
Bryant, Rebecca Suzanne - A/78/PV.62
Kim, Yunei - A/78/PV.88
Azerbaijan
Musayev, Tofig - A/78/PV.82
Bahrain
Alrowaiei, Jamal Fares - A/78/PV.76
Bangladesh
Muhith, Muhammad A. - A/78/PV.76
Brazil
Danese, Sérgio França - A/78/PV.82
Gomes, Elaine Cristina Pereira - A/78/PV.62
Cambodia
Mao, Tithiarun - A/78/PV.76
Canada
Hirji, Hussein - A/78/PV.62
China
Dai, Bing - A/78/PV.76
Fu, Cong - A/78/PV.82; A/78/PV.88
Cuba
Soberón Guzmán, Ernesto - A/78/PV.76; A/78/PV.82
Democratic Republic of the Congo
Mukongo Ngay, Zénon - A/78/PV.82
Ecuador
Montalvo Sosa, Andrés Efren - A/78/PV.77
Egypt
Abdelkhalek, Osama Mahmoud - A/78/PV.76; A/78/PV.82
Elshandawily, Ahmed - A/78/PV.62
European Union
Bellmont Roldán, Xavier (Spain) - A/78/PV.48
Lagatie, Karl (Belgium) - A/78/PV.62
Samson, Hedda - A/78/PV.76
Germany
Leendertse, Antje - A/78/PV.82
Ghana
Barnor, Nana Akua - A/78/PV.82
Greece
Sekeris, Evangelos C. - A/78/PV.82

PEACE (Agenda item 14) (continued)

Group of Friends in Defence of the Charter of the United Nations
Moncada Acosta, Samuel R. (Venezuela (Bolivarian Republic of)) - A/78/PV.76
Guatemala
Leal Matta, Edgar Daniel - A/78/PV.82
Hungary
Horváth, Zsuzsanna - A/78/PV.82
Iceland
Valtýsson, Jörundur - A/78/PV.62
India
Kamboj, Ruchira - A/78/PV.62; A/78/PV.76
Indonesia
Dhanutirto, Mariska Dwianti - A/78/PV.76
Nasir, Arrmanatha Christiawan - A/78/PV.62
Prabowo, Hari - A/78/PV.82
Iran (Islamic Republic of)
Jalil Iravani, Amir Saeid - A/78/PV.62; A/78/PV.82
Iraq
Al-Fatlawi, Abbas Kadhom Obaid - A/78/PV.62
Israel
Mimran Rosenberg, Avital - A/78/PV.77
Japan
Ono, Sho - A/78/PV.88
Kuwait
Albanai, Tareq M.A.M. - A/78/PV.62
Malaysia
Muhamad, Ahmad Faisal - A/78/PV.62
Zin Zawawi, Nordiana Binti - A/78/PV.77
Mauritania
Laghdaf, Sidi Mohamed - A/78/PV.76
Mexico
Curzio Vila, Elena - A/78/PV.76
Elizondo Belden, Luis Gerardo - A/78/PV.62
Vasconcelos y Cruz, Héctor Enrique - A/78/PV.82
Montenegro
Sabanovic, Damir - A/78/PV.82
Morocco
Kadri, Taha - A/78/PV.76
Myanmar
Tun, Kyaw Moe - A/78/PV.76
Namibia
Gertze, Neville Melvin - A/78/PV.82
New Zealand
Fepuleai, Justin Peter - A/78/PV.62
Nicaragua
Pichardo Urbina, Eleane Yaoska - A/78/PV.76; A/78/PV.82
Nigeria
Endoni, Syndoph Paebi - A/78/PV.82
Norway
Dale, Katrine Ørnehaug - A/78/PV.88
Oman
Al Rubkhi, Khalid Saleh Said - A/78/PV.62; A/78/PV.82
Organisation of Islamic Cooperation
Akram, Munir (Pakistan) - A/78/PV.62

PEACE (Agenda item 14) (continued)
Pakistan
Akram, Munir - A/78/PV.48; A/78/PV.76; A/78/PV.82
Panama
Cano Franco, Zoraya del Carmen - A/78/PV.82
Peru
Rojas, Eder - A/78/PV.62
Vegas Torres, Juan Pablo - A/78/PV.82
Philippines
Lagdameo, Antonio Manuel Revilla - A/78/PV.76
Qatar
Al-thani, Almaha Mubarak F.J. - A/78/PV.76
Russian Federation
Nebenzia, Vasilii - A/78/PV.82
Zabolotskaya, Maria V. - A/78/PV.48; A/78/PV.62; A/78/PV.76
Rwanda
Rwamucyo, Ernest - A/78/PV.82
Saint Vincent and the Grenadines
Andrews, Lasana - A/78/PV.82
Saudi Arabia
Alwasil, Abdulaziz M.O. - A/78/PV.62; A/78/PV.77; A/78/PV.82
Serbia. President
Vučić, Aleksandar - A/78/PV.82
Sierra Leone
Kanu, Michael Imran - A/78/PV.82
Singapore
Gafoor, Burhan - A/78/PV.62
Khng, Nathaniel - A/78/PV.82
Tan, Jason Han Wei - A/78/PV.76
Slovakia
Galbavý, Richard - A/78/PV.82
Sri Lanka
Pieris, Peter Mohan Maithri - A/78/PV.76
Suriname
Sitaldin, Sunil A. - A/78/PV.76
Switzerland
Wagner, Valérie - A/78/PV.62; A/78/PV.88
Syrian Arab Republic
Aldahhak, Koussay Abduljabbar - A/78/PV.82
Alnwelati, Mohammad Feras - A/78/PV.62
Thailand
Vichankaiyakij, Vathayudh - A/78/PV.76; A/78/PV.82
Timor-Leste
Soares, Dionísio Da Costa Babo - A/78/PV.77
Togo
Akakpo, Koffi - A/78/PV.76
Tunisia
Ladeb, Tarek - A/78/PV.62; A/78/PV.82
Türkiye
Güven, Fikriye Asli - A/78/PV.62
Turkmenistan
Ataeva, Aksoltan T. - A/78/PV.63
Uganda
Gurhan, Amina - A/78/PV.62
Ukraine
Tokarska, Anastasiia - A/78/PV.48

PEACE (Agenda item 14) (continued)
UN. Department for General Assembly and Conference Management
Emelina-Sarte, Svetlana - A/78/PV.77
Nakano, Kenji - A/78/PV.82
Sharma, Sangeeta - A/78/PV.62
UN. Secretary-General
Guterres, António, 1949- - A/78/PV.62
United Arab Emirates
Abushahab, Mohamed Issa - A/78/PV.76; A/78/PV.82
United Kingdom
Kariuki, James - A/78/PV.62
United Republic of Tanzania
Kattanga, Hussein A. - A/78/PV.82
United States
Breen, Patrick - A/78/PV.48
Eyrich, Kara - A/78/PV.62
Fogarty, Daniel - A/78/PV.88
Venezuela (Bolivarian Republic of)
Reyes Hernández, Jorge Arturo - A/78/PV.82
Viet Nam
Dang, Hoang Giang - A/78/PV.64; A/78/PV.82

PEACE—REGIONAL CENTRE—AFRICA (Agenda item 100b)
Algeria
Lebbaz, Larbi Abdelfattah - A/C.1/78/PV.23
UN Regional Centre for Peace and Disarmament in Africa. Director
Yabouri, Anselme - A/C.1/78/PV.23

PEACE—REGIONAL CENTRE—ASIA AND THE PACIFIC (Agenda item 100d)
Nepal
Gohiwar Aryal, Indira - A/C.1/78/PV.23
UN Regional Centre for Peace and Disarmament in Asia and the Pacific. Director
Basu Ray, Deepayan - A/C.1/78/PV.23

PEACE—REGIONAL CENTRE—LATIN AMERICA AND THE CARIBBEAN (Agenda item 100c)
Caribbean Community
Moxey, Matthew (Bahamas) - A/C.1/78/PV.22
UN Regional Centre for Peace, Disarmament and Development in Latin America and the Caribbean. Director
Urruela Arenales, María Soledad - A/C.1/78/PV.23

PEACE—REGIONAL CENTRES (Agenda item 100f)
Armenia
Grigoryan, Andranik - A/C.1/78/PV.29
Coordinating Bureau of the Non-Aligned Countries
Sirie, Mochammad Iqbal (Indonesia) - A/C.1/78/PV.22
Nepal
Gohiwar Aryal, Indira - A/C.1/78/PV.23

PEACE—REGIONAL CENTRES (Agenda item 100f) (continued)

UN. Office for Disarmament Affairs (Mar. 2007-). Regional Disarmament Branch. Chief
Day, Radha - A/C.1/78/PV.23

PEACEBUILDING (Agenda item 61)

Algeria
Gaouaoui, Nacim - A/78/PV.100
Colombia
Zalabata Torres, Leonor - A/78/PV.100
Cuba
Gala López, Yuri - A/78/PV.100
Denmark
Laursen, Erik - A/78/PV.100
Egypt
Abdelkhalek, Osama Mahmoud - A/78/PV.100
El Salvador
González López, Egriselda Aracely - A/78/PV.100
European Union
Tolstoi, Natalie - A/78/PV.100
Germany
Geisler, Michael Alexander - A/78/PV.100
India
Bhalla, Ashish - A/78/PV.101
Italy
Martin Topranin, Pietro de - A/78/PV.100
Japan
Shino, Mitsuko - A/78/PV.100
Kenya
Kiboino, Michael Kapkiai - A/78/PV.100
Mexico
Cisneros Chávez, José de Jesús - A/78/PV.100
Morocco
Hilale, Omar - A/78/PV.100
Peru
García Toma, Victor Óscar Shiyin - A/78/PV.100
Poland
Szczerski, Krzysztof - A/78/PV.100
Republic of Korea
Park, Jeewon - A/78/PV.101
Russian Federation
Agaronova, Gloriya A. - A/78/PV.101
South Africa
Schalkwyk, Marthinus van - A/78/PV.100
Timor-Leste
Chaves, Joaquim José Costa - A/78/PV.101
United Kingdom
Weld-Blundell, Stacy John - A/78/PV.101
United States
Shrier, Jonathan - A/78/PV.101

PEACEKEEPING OPERATIONS (Agenda item 51)

Algeria
Bendjama, Amar - A/C.4/78/SR.19
ASEAN
Nasir, Arrmanatha Christiawan (Indonesia) - A/C.4/78/SR.18
Australia
Larsen, James - A/C.4/78/SR.18

PEACEKEEPING OPERATIONS (Agenda item 51) (continued)

Austria
Marschik, Alexander - A/C.4/78/SR.19
Bangladesh
Muhith, Muhammad A. - A/C.4/78/SR.19
Bolivia (Plurinational State of)
Choque Rosario, Dem Mijael - A/C.4/78/SR.20
Brazil
Campos, Erika Helena - A/C.4/78/SR.20
Burkina Faso
Savadogo, Halidou - A/C.4/78/SR.20
Cambodia
Mao, Tithiarun - A/C.4/78/SR.20
Cameroon
Tommo Monthe, Michel - A/C.4/78/SR.20
Caribbean Community
Douglas, Craig Barrington (Jamaica) - A/C.4/78/SR.18
Coordinating Bureau of the Non-Aligned Countries
El Ouazzani, Mouna Chahdi (Morocco) - A/C.4/78/SR.18
Côte d'Ivoire
Moriko, Tiémoko - A/C.4/78/SR.19
Cuba
Sánchez Fuentes, Jorge Sain - A/C.4/78/SR.18
Cyprus
Panteli, Rona Marie - A/C.4/78/SR.20
Democratic People's Republic of Korea
Kim, In Chol - A/C.4/78/SR.19
Democratic Republic of the Congo
Mukongo Ngay, Zénon - A/C.4/78/SR.20
Dominican Republic
Blanco Conde, José Alfonso - A/C.4/78/SR.20
Egypt
Eldahshan, Wael Mahmoud Abdelaziz - A/C.4/78/SR.18
El Salvador
González López, Egriselda Aracely - A/C.4/78/SR.19
Ethiopia
Kassaye, Yoseph - A/C.4/78/SR.8
European Union
Coppola, Antonio Gaetano - A/C.4/78/SR.18
Gambia
Badjie, Isatou - A/C.4/78/SR.19
Germany
Geisler, Michael Alexander - A/C.4/78/SR.20
Groupe des ambassadeurs francophones
Abdillahi, Elaye Yacin (Djibouti) - A/C.4/78/SR.18
Guatemala
Benard Estrada, Juan Antonio - A/C.4/78/SR.19
Haiti
Pierre, Christopher - A/C.4/78/SR.20
Holy See
Quirighetti, Giuseppe - A/C.4/78/SR.20
India
Bhalla, Ashish - A/C.4/78/SR.20
Iran (Islamic Republic of)
Sahraei, Mohammad Reza - A/C.4/78/SR.20

PEACEKEEPING OPERATIONS (Agenda item 51) (continued)

Iraq
Al-Dahlaki, Hasanain Hadi Hasan - A/C.4/78/SR.20
Israel
Kedar, Gershon - A/C.4/78/SR.19; A/C.4/78/SR.20
Japan
Hamamoto, Yukiya - A/C.4/78/SR.20
Jordan
Habashneh, Ahmad Samir Fahim - A/C.4/78/SR.20
Kenya
Kiboino, Michael Kapkiai - A/C.4/78/SR.20
Lebanon
Hachem, Hadi - A/C.4/78/SR.20
Jardali, Mohammad Ali - A/C.4/78/SR.20
Malaysia
Noordin, Shamsuri - A/C.4/78/SR.19
Mexico
Cisneros Chávez, José de Jesús - A/C.4/78/SR.18
Mongolia
Vorshilov, Enkhbold - A/C.4/78/SR.19
Morocco
El Ouazzani, Mouna Chahdi - A/C.4/78/SR.20
Mozambique
Efson, Gladys Evangelina - A/C.4/78/SR.20
Nepal
Ray, Kaushal Kishor - A/C.4/78/SR.19
Norway
Lovold, Andreas - A/C.4/78/SR.19
Organisation internationale de la Francophonie
Kontoleontos, Ifigeneia - A/C.4/78/SR.20
Pakistan
Akram, Munir - A/C.4/78/SR.18
Peru
Llosa, Luis Felipe - A/C.4/78/SR.19
Philippines
Novicio, Noel Mangaoang - A/C.4/78/SR.20
Poland
Sakowicz, Mateusz - A/C.4/78/SR.19
Portugal
Zacarias, Ana Paula - A/C.4/78/SR.19
Republic of Korea
Hwang, Won - A/C.4/78/SR.20
Romania
Mocanu, Andreea - A/C.4/78/SR.19
Russian Federation
Evstigneeva, Anna M. - A/C.4/78/SR.20
Rwanda
Mutabazi, Deo - A/C.4/78/SR.20
Senegal
Ndiaye, Joseph Dominique Ngor - A/C.4/78/SR.19
Serbia
Radović, Branislav - A/C.4/78/SR.20
Sierra Leone
Sowa, Amara Sheikh Mohammed - A/C.4/78/SR.19
Singapore
Nadarajah, Vicnesh - A/C.4/78/SR.20
South Africa
Mabeba, Bernard - A/C.4/78/SR.20
Sri Lanka
Pieris, Peter Mohan Maithri - A/C.4/78/SR.18

PEACEKEEPING OPERATIONS (Agenda item 51) (continued)

Sudan
Mohamed, Abuzied Shamseldin Ahmed - A/C.4/78/SR.19
Switzerland
Stritt, Marc-Alain - A/C.4/78/SR.19
Syrian Arab Republic
Baghdadi, Mohannad - A/C.4/78/SR.19
Thailand
Hanlumyuang, Thararut - A/C.4/78/SR.18
Timor-Leste
Chaves, Joaquim José Costa - A/C.4/78/SR.19
Togo
Medzinyuie, Edem Kodzovi - A/C.4/78/SR.18
Tunisia
Salah, Yassine - A/C.4/78/SR.19
UN. Assistant Secretary-General for Rule of Law and Security Institutions
Zouev, Alexandre - A/C.4/78/SR.18
UN. Department of Management Strategy, Policy and Compliance. Office of Human Resources. Administrative Law Division. Director
Thanabalasingam, Aruna - A/C.4/78/SR.18
UN. General Assembly. Special Political and Decolonization Committee (4th Committee). Rapporteur
Dhanutirto, Mariska Dwianti (Indonesia) - A/78/PV.45
UN. Special Committee on Peacekeeping Operations. Rapporteur
Eldahshan, Wael Mahmoud Abdelaziz (Egypt) - A/C.4/78/SR.27
UN. Under-Secretary-General for Operational Support
Khare, Atul - A/C.4/78/SR.18
Uruguay
Amorín, Carlos Daniel - A/C.4/78/SR.19
Viet Nam
Nguyen, Hoang Nguyen - A/C.4/78/SR.19

PEACEKEEPING OPERATIONS—CRIMINAL LIABILITY (Agenda item 76)

Bangladesh
Muhith, Muhammad A. - A/C.6/78/SR.8
Brazil
Braoios, Victor Silveira - A/C.6/78/SR.8
Burkina Faso
Ganou, Oumarou - A/C.6/78/SR.8
Cameroon
Nyanid, Zacharie Serge Raoul - A/C.6/78/SR.9
China
Wang, Yuanjie - A/C.6/78/SR.8
Community of Latin American and Caribbean States
Mark, Hayley-Ann (Saint Vincent and the Grenadines) - A/C.6/78/SR.8
Congo
Douckaga Nzengui, Nicaise Servais - A/C.6/78/SR.9
Coordinating Bureau of the Non-Aligned Countries
Aref, Yahya (Iran (Islamic Republic of)) - A/C.6/78/SR.8

PEACEKEEPING OPERATIONS—CRIMINAL LIABILITY (Agenda item 76) (continued)

Cuba
Carral Castelo, Arianna - A/C.6/78/SR.8
Egypt
Nouh, Amr Mohamed Mosaad - A/C.6/78/SR.8
El Salvador
González López, Egriselda Aracely - A/C.6/78/SR.8
Ethiopia
Alemayehu, Betelihem Taye - A/C.6/78/SR.9
European Union
Mead, Kevin Timothy (Canada) - A/C.6/78/SR.37
Ramopoulos, Thomas - A/C.6/78/SR.8
Ghana
Hackman, Khalilah - A/C.6/78/SR.8
Guinea
Camara, Mohamed Nassir - A/C.6/78/SR.9
Haiti
Panier, Wisnique - A/C.6/78/SR.9
India
Bhat, Kajal - A/C.6/78/SR.8
Iran (Islamic Republic of)
Heidari, Bahram - A/C.6/78/SR.8
Iraq
Al-Hasani, Haider - A/C.6/78/SR.9
Kenya
Ngungu, Edith Kaki - A/C.6/78/SR.9
Malaysia
Abd Karim, Nur Azura Binti - A/C.6/78/SR.8
Mexico
Jiménez Alegría, Natalia - A/C.6/78/SR.8
Nepal
Charmakar, Ramesh Kumar - A/C.6/78/SR.8
Netherlands (Kingdom of the)
Made, Angelique van der - A/C.6/78/SR.8
New Zealand
Russell, Zoe - A/C.6/78/SR.8
Nigeria
Dakwak, Gloria - A/C.6/78/SR.9
Norway
Holm, Tor Tanke - A/C.6/78/SR.8
Pakistan
Ijaz, Rabia - A/C.6/78/SR.8
Portugal
Carvalho, Sergio Amaral Alves de - A/C.6/78/SR.8
Russian Federation
Antonova, Anna V. - A/C.6/78/SR.8
Senegal
Ndoye, Abdou - A/C.6/78/SR.8
Sierra Leone
Sowa, Amara Sheikh Mohammed - A/C.6/78/SR.8
South Africa
Motsepe, Keke Mantsho - A/C.6/78/SR.8
Sudan
Mohammed, Ammar Mohammed Mahmoud - A/C.6/78/SR.8
UN. General Assembly. 6th Committee. Bureau
Uddin, Nasir (Bangladesh) - A/C.6/78/SR.37
UN. General Assembly. 6th Committee. Rapporteur
Moussa, Moussa Mohamed (Djibouti) - A/78/PV.45
UN. Group of African States
Ikondere, Marvin (Uganda) - A/C.6/78/SR.8

PEACEKEEPING OPERATIONS—CRIMINAL LIABILITY (Agenda item 76) (continued)

United Kingdom
Hollis, Jonathan Samuel - A/C.6/78/SR.8
United States
Patton, Dorothy - A/C.6/78/SR.8
Viet Nam
Nguyen, Thi Ngoc Ha - A/C.6/78/SR.9

PEACEKEEPING OPERATIONS—FINANCING (Agenda item 146)

Group of 77
Ainomuhisha, Medard (Uganda) - A/C.5/78/SR.35; A/C.5/78/SR.36
Israel
Brash, Zoe - A/C.5/78/SR.35
Switzerland
Schmied, Gina Andrea - A/C.5/78/SR.35
UN. Assistant Secretary-General for Internal Oversight Services
Swanson, Benjamin Gordon Robert - A/C.5/78/SR.35
UN. Assistant Secretary-General for Supply Chain Management
Berg, AnneMarie van den - A/C.5/78/SR.35
UN. Controller
Ramanathan, Chandramouli - A/C.5/78/SR.35; A/C.5/78/SR.36
UN. General Assembly. 5th Committee. Rapporteur
Hartog, Laurens Thomas den (Netherlands (Kingdom of the)) - A/78/PV.95
UN. Group of African States
Minale, Lemlem Fiseha (Ethiopia) - A/C.5/78/SR.36
Sibomana, Landry (Burundi) - A/C.5/78/SR.35

PERSONNEL QUESTIONS—UN SYSTEM (Agenda item 142)

China
Guo, Ke - A/C.5/78/SR.10
Coordinating Committee for International Staff Unions and Associations of the United Nations System
Meynet, Nathalie - A/C.5/78/SR.10
Federation of International Civil Servants' Associations
Quinn-Maguire, Tanya - A/C.5/78/SR.10
Group of 77
Tur de la Concepción, Richard (Cuba) - A/C.5/78/SR.10
International Civil Service Commission
Djacta, Larbi - A/C.5/78/SR.10
Japan
Kawasaki, Yuta - A/C.5/78/SR.10
Mexico
Velázquez Castillo, Jesús - A/C.5/78/SR.10
Switzerland
Schmied, Gina Andrea - A/C.5/78/SR.10
UN. Advisory Committee on Administrative and Budgetary Questions. Chair
Bachar Bong, Abdallah - A/C.5/78/SR.10

PERSONNEL QUESTIONS—UN SYSTEM (Agenda item 142) (continued)

UN. Advisory Committee on Administrative and Budgetary Questions. Vice-Chair
Al-Kumaim, Amjad Qaid Ahmed - A/C.5/78/SR.27
UN. Assistant Secretary-General for Human Resources Management
López, Martha Helena - A/C.5/78/SR.27
UN. Group of African States
Mwasota, Joseph Aron (United Republic of Tanzania) - A/C.5/78/SR.10
UN. Under-Secretary-General for Management Strategy, Policy and Compliance
Pollard, Catherine - A/C.5/78/SR.10
UN International Civil Servants Federation
Esposito, Karin - A/C.5/78/SR.10

PERSONS WITH DISABILITIES (Agenda item 24b)

ASEAN
Dang, Hoang Giang (Viet Nam) - A/C.3/78/SR.1
Bahrain
Alhammadi, Hessa - A/C.3/78/SR.3
Belarus
Mozgovaya, Ekaterina - A/C.3/78/SR.2
Cuba
García Hernández, Martha - A/C.3/78/SR.3
Dominican Republic
Andújar, Luz del Carmen - A/C.3/78/SR.3
Guatemala
Rodríguez Mancia, Carla María - A/C.3/78/SR.1
Indonesia
Imanuel, Fnu - A/C.3/78/SR.3
Israel
Aviel, Shir - A/C.3/78/SR.2
Italy
Tonon, Daniela - A/C.3/78/SR.2
Japan
Kamiya, Masako - A/C.3/78/SR.3
Kyrgyzstan
Kasymalieva, Aida - A/C.3/78/SR.3
Lao People's Democratic Republic
Vongnorkeo, Anouparb - A/C.3/78/SR.4
Nicaragua
Pichardo Urbina, Eleane Yaoska - A/C.3/78/SR.4
Peru
Rojas, Eder - A/C.3/78/SR.4
Qatar
Al-Thani, Alya Ahmed S.A. - A/C.3/78/SR.3
Saudi Arabia
Bin Jadid, Faisal Fahad M. - A/C.3/78/SR.2
Singapore
Choong, Brandon - A/C.3/78/SR.2
Sistema de la Integración Centroamericana
González López, Egriselda Aracely (El Salvador) - A/C.3/78/SR.1
Tajikistan
Gulov, Golibjon - A/C.3/78/SR.2

PERSONS WITH DISABILITIES (Agenda item 24b) (continued)

UN. Department of Economic and Social Affairs. Division for Inclusive Social Development. Officer-in-Charge
Wilmoth, John - A/C.3/78/SR.1
United Arab Emirates
Alseyabi, Eman - A/C.3/78/SR.3

PERSONS WITH DISABILITIES—HUMAN RIGHTS (Agenda item 71a)

Algeria
Samai, Rahma - A/C.3/78/SR.38; A/C.3/78/SR.51
Australia
Bryant, Rebecca Suzanne - A/C.3/78/SR.38
Bangladesh
Monica, Mosammat Shahanara - A/C.3/78/SR.38
Belarus
Tozik, Artsiom - A/C.3/78/SR.38
Brazil
Gomes, Elaine Cristina Pereira - A/C.3/78/SR.38
Canada
Tudor-Bezies, Elizabeth - A/C.3/78/SR.38; A/C.3/78/SR.51
Chile
Zalaquett, Ignacia - A/C.3/78/SR.38
China
Chen, Jiawen - A/C.3/78/SR.38
Colombia
Sánchez García, Nathalia - A/C.3/78/SR.51
Dominican Republic
Matos Menéndez, Gala - A/C.3/78/SR.38
El Salvador
Segura Aragón, Carlos Efraín - A/C.3/78/SR.38
European Union
Nyman, Klas - A/C.3/78/SR.38
Schuller, Simone - A/C.3/78/SR.18
Finland
Kalkku, Elina - A/C.3/78/SR.38
Georgia
Lortkipanidze, Ekaterine - A/C.3/78/SR.38
Greece
Retalis, Michail - A/C.3/78/SR.38
Gulf Cooperation Council
Al Rawahi, Abdulhalim Mubarak Saloom (Oman) - A/C.3/78/SR.51
Holy See
Murphy, Robert David - A/C.3/78/SR.51
Hungary
Pongor, Magdolna - A/C.3/78/SR.38
Indonesia
Imanuel, Fnu - A/C.3/78/SR.51
Iran (Islamic Republic of)
Arab Bafrani, Fatemeh - A/C.3/78/SR.38; A/C.3/78/SR.51
Iraq
Al-Khaqani, Hassan Jabbar - A/C.3/78/SR.51
Ireland
Swan, Ellen - A/C.3/78/SR.38

PERSONS WITH DISABILITIES—HUMAN RIGHTS (Agenda item 71a) (continued)

Israel
Shaked, Or - A/C.3/78/SR.38
Kuwait
Al Mulla, Wafiqah - A/C.3/78/SR.51
Lesotho
Lelisa, Nthabiseng Matlhohonolofatso - A/C.3/78/SR.38
Luxembourg
Dostert, Anne Françoise - A/C.3/78/SR.38
Malaysia
Escopper Zumilla, Michael Jawa - A/C.3/78/SR.38; A/C.3/78/SR.51
Maldives
Khadeeja, Aufiyau - A/C.3/78/SR.38
Mali
Dabo N'diaye, Djeneba - A/C.3/78/SR.38; A/C.3/78/SR.51
Malta
Aquilina, Cara Borg - A/C.3/78/SR.38
Mexico
Buenrostro Massieu, Alicia - A/C.3/78/SR.51
Reza Bautista, Mauricio - A/C.3/78/SR.38
Myanmar
Tun, Kyaw Moe - A/C.3/78/SR.38
New Zealand
Buist-Catherwood, Emily - A/C.3/78/SR.18; A/C.3/78/SR.51
Fruean, Tausala - A/C.3/78/SR.38
Niger
Seydou, Abdoul Fadh Mahamadou - A/C.3/78/SR.51
Nigeria
Asaju, Bola - A/C.3/78/SR.51
Poland
Lula, Iwona Anna - A/C.3/78/SR.38
Skoczek, Joanna Sylwia - A/C.3/78/SR.18; A/C.3/78/SR.51
Qatar
Al Khayarin, Saleh Mohammed - A/C.3/78/SR.51
Al-thani, Almaha Mubarak F.J. - A/C.3/78/SR.24
Republic of Korea
Lee, Yeseung - A/C.3/78/SR.38
Russian Federation
Kondratev, Sergei V. - A/C.3/78/SR.38
Mazaeva, Viktoriia - A/C.3/78/SR.51
Senegal
Niasse, Samba Thiam - A/C.3/78/SR.51
Sovereign Order of Malta
Arditi di Castelvetere Manzo, Fiamma - A/C.3/78/SR.38
Syrian Arab Republic
Altarsha, Elie - A/C.3/78/SR.38; A/C.3/78/SR.51
Timor-Leste
Sousa, Maria Lourdes de - A/C.3/78/SR.38
Ukraine
Tokarska, Anastasiia - A/C.3/78/SR.38
UN. Committee on the Rights of Persons with Disabilities. Chair
Fefoame, Gertrude Oforiwa - A/C.3/78/SR.38
UN. Executive Office of the Secretary-General. Sustainable Development Unit. Deputy Director
Blanco Rothe, Lara - A/C.3/78/SR.18
UN. Human Rights Council. Special Rapporteur on the Rights of Persons with Disabilities
Quinn, Gerard - A/C.3/78/SR.38
United States
Breen, Patrick - A/C.3/78/SR.38
Lang, Dylan - A/C.3/78/SR.51
Yemen
Al-mashehari, Sarah Ahmed Ahmed - A/C.3/78/SR.51

POVERTY—HUMAN RIGHTS (Agenda item 71b)

Bangladesh
Abdullah, Md Showeb - A/C.3/78/SR.30
Brazil
Dias, João Henrique Nascimento - A/C.3/78/SR.30
Cameroon
Banaken Elel, Nelly - A/C.3/78/SR.30
Chile
Nishihara, Carmen - A/C.3/78/SR.30
China
Liu, Luoge - A/C.3/78/SR.30
Cuba
Lamigueiro Cañedo, Ivette - A/C.3/78/SR.30
European Union
Szelivanov, Julia - A/C.3/78/SR.30
France
Lebédel-Delumeau, Eric - A/C.3/78/SR.30
Indonesia
Meizura, Novia - A/C.3/78/SR.30
Israel
Shaked, Or - A/C.3/78/SR.30
Malaysia
Escopper Zumilla, Michael Jawa - A/C.3/78/SR.30
Pakistan
Qureshi, Hadeeqa - A/C.3/78/SR.30
Peru
Pedroza, David - A/C.3/78/SR.30
Russian Federation
Kuzmenkov, Stepan Y. - A/C.3/78/SR.30
Sovereign Order of Malta
Scalabrini-McKellar, Tobias - A/C.3/78/SR.30
State of Palestine
Salem, Sahar K.H. - A/C.3/78/SR.30
Syrian Arab Republic
Altarsha, Elie - A/C.3/78/SR.30
UN. Human Rights Council. Special Rapporteur on Extreme Poverty and Human Rights
Schutter, Olivier de - A/C.3/78/SR.30

POVERTY—INTERNATIONAL DECADES (Agenda item 21a)

Algeria
Latrous, Mohamed-Esseghir - A/C.2/78/SR.17
Alliance of Small Island States
Lautasi, Isaia (Samoa) - A/C.2/78/SR.16

POVERTY—INTERNATIONAL DECADES (Agenda item 21a) (continued)

Angola
Luemba, Mateus Pedro - A/C.2/78/SR.16
ASEAN
Dang, Hoang Giang (Viet Nam) - A/C.2/78/SR.16
Bahrain
Alsindi, Yusuf Khaled - A/C.2/78/SR.17
Bangladesh
Hossain, Faruk - A/C.2/78/SR.17
Belarus
Pisarevich, Vadim - A/C.2/78/SR.16
Bolivia (Plurinational State of)
Zambrana Flores, Carlos Iván - A/C.2/78/SR.16
Brazil
Santos, Luiz Felipe Rosa dos - A/C.2/78/SR.17
Burkina Faso
Bokoum, Mahamadou - A/C.2/78/SR.16
Cabo Verde
Romualdo, Tania Serafim Yvonne - A/C.2/78/SR.17
Cameroon
Etoundi Ayissi, Joseph - A/C.2/78/SR.16
Caribbean Community
Wallace, Brian Christopher Manley (Jamaica) - A/C.2/78/SR.16
China
Cao, Liwen - A/C.2/78/SR.16
Congo
Gabi, Emery - A/C.2/78/SR.17
Costa Rica
Chan Valverde, Maritza - A/C.2/78/SR.17
Democratic People's Republic of Korea
Jo, Tong Hyon - A/C.2/78/SR.16
Ecuador
Barba Bustos, Irina Alexandra - A/C.2/78/SR.17
El Salvador
Barahona Figueroa, Andrea Alejandra - A/C.2/78/SR.16
Ethiopia
Kindeya, Tsigabu Girmay - A/C.2/78/SR.17
European Union
Woźniak, Agata Magdalena - A/C.2/78/SR.25
Group of 77
Guevara Rodríguez, Adiel (Cuba) - A/C.2/78/SR.16
Torres Seara, Dalia Marlen (Cuba) - A/C.2/78/SR.21
Group of Friends in Defence of the Charter of the United Nations
Marín Sevilla, Asbina (Venezuela (Bolivarian Republic of)) - A/C.2/78/SR.16
Group of Landlocked Developing Countries
Mokhawa, Gladys (Botswana) - A/C.2/78/SR.16
Group of Least Developed Countries
Adhikari, Pramita (Nepal) - A/C.2/78/SR.16
Guatemala
Rodríguez Mancia, Carla María - A/C.2/78/SR.17
Guyana
Alkins, Royston - A/C.2/78/SR.17
Haiti
Vilmenay Joseph, Linouse - A/C.2/78/SR.17

POVERTY—INTERNATIONAL DECADES (Agenda item 21a) (continued)

Holy See
Caccia, Gabriele Giordano - A/C.2/78/SR.18
India
Gahlot, Petal - A/C.2/78/SR.16
Indonesia
Prabowo, Hari - A/C.2/78/SR.17
Iran (Islamic Republic of)
Jalili, Tahereh - A/C.2/78/SR.16
Italy
Massari, Maurizio - A/C.2/78/SR.16
Kenya
Nzumbu, Christine - A/C.2/78/SR.16
Kuwait
Almezyad, Fatma - A/C.2/78/SR.17
Lesotho
Nena, Matete - A/C.2/78/SR.17
Malawi
Chivundu, Renata - A/C.2/78/SR.17
Malaysia
Zulasri Bin Rosdi, Muhammad - A/C.2/78/SR.17
Maldives
Nashwa, Fathimath - A/C.2/78/SR.16
Mali
Coulibaly, Kanisson - A/C.2/78/SR.17
Mexico
Vásquez Solano, Leonel - A/C.2/78/SR.16
Mozambique
Maure, Adnito - A/C.2/78/SR.17
Myanmar
Tun, Kyaw Moe - A/C.2/78/SR.17
Namibia
Gertze, Neville Melvin - A/C.2/78/SR.16
Nicaragua
Gutiérrez Tórrez, Lisandra Marina - A/C.2/78/SR.17
Niger
Moussa, Mahaman - A/C.2/78/SR.17
Nigeria
Maitafsir, Musa Garba - A/C.2/78/SR.17
Pakistan
Javaid, Hafiza Humaira - A/C.2/78/SR.17
Panama
Concepción Jaramillo, Markova - A/C.2/78/SR.16
Peru
Napurí Pita, Andrés - A/C.2/78/SR.17
Philippines
Beriana, Charlene Aravejo - A/C.2/78/SR.16
Qatar
Al-Khayareen, Abdulla Ghanim - A/C.2/78/SR.16
Russian Federation
Aristov, Dmitry S. - A/C.2/78/SR.17
Saudi Arabia
Bakhsh, Khalid - A/C.2/78/SR.17
Serbia
Mart, Saša - A/C.2/78/SR.17
Sierra Leone
George, Alan Ebun - A/C.2/78/SR.17
South Africa
Mandla, Bulelani - A/C.2/78/SR.17

POVERTY—INTERNATIONAL DECADES (Agenda item 21a) (continued)

Tajikistan
Hasanova, Tahmina - A/C.2/78/SR.17
Thailand
Sangkhapreecha, Kantapon - A/C.2/78/SR.16
Timor-Leste
Barros, Sebastiana - A/C.2/78/SR.18
Togo
Debataba, Yawa - A/C.2/78/SR.17
Türkiye
Demir, İlknur - A/C.2/78/SR.17
Ukraine
Leschenko, Volodymyr - A/C.2/78/SR.16
UN. Department of Economic and Social Affairs. Division for Inclusive Social Development. Officer-in-Charge
Wilmoth, John - A/C.2/78/SR.16
UN. General Assembly. 2nd Committee. Rapporteur
Gatev, Ivaylo (Bulgaria) - A/78/PV.49
UNIDO
Miljkovicova, Adriana - A/C.2/78/SR.18
United Arab Emirates
Almahmoud, Ahmed Abdelrahman Ahmed - A/C.2/78/SR.16
United Republic of Tanzania
Kattanga, Hussein A. - A/C.2/78/SR.17
United States
Leonard, Mary Beth - A/C.2/78/SR.17
Marks, Rose Ann - A/C.2/78/SR.25
Viet Nam
Nguyen, Hoang Nguyen - A/C.2/78/SR.16
Yemen
Al-barati, Abdulrahman Hasan Yahya - A/C.2/78/SR.17
Zambia
Mungandi, Lubasi - A/C.2/78/SR.17

POVERTY MITIGATION (Agenda item 21)

UN. General Assembly. 2nd Committee. Rapporteur
Gatev, Ivaylo (Bulgaria) - A/78/PV.49

RACIAL DISCRIMINATION—ELIMINATION (Agenda item 69a)

Advancing Health Equity (Organization)
Blackstock, Uché - A/78/PV.63
Albania
Lamce, Enian - A/C.3/78/SR.47
Algeria
Hassani, Billel - A/C.3/78/SR.42; A/C.3/78/SR.47
Angola
Luemba, Mateus Pedro - A/78/PV.50
Argentina
Escobar, Luciano Hernán - A/78/PV.103
Armenia
Hakobyan, Aram - A/C.3/78/SR.42
Australia
Kim, Yunei - A/C.3/78/SR.47
Larsen, James - A/C.3/78/SR.47

RACIAL DISCRIMINATION—ELIMINATION (Agenda item 69a) (continued)

Austria
Pretterhofer, Stefan - A/C.3/78/SR.47
Azerbaijan
Ahangari, Narmin - A/C.3/78/SR.41; A/C.3/78/SR.43
Bangladesh
Muhith, Muhammad A. - A/C.3/78/SR.43
Belarus
Pilipenko, Igor - A/78/PV.50
Tozik, Artsiom - A/C.3/78/SR.40
Belgium
Bauwens, Gilles - A/C.3/78/SR.40
Willekens, Vincent - A/C.3/78/SR.41
Bolivia (Plurinational State of)
Caldera Gutiérrez, Fiorella - A/C.3/78/SR.42
Brazil
Gomes, Elaine Cristina Pereira - A/C.3/78/SR.40; A/C.3/78/SR.41; A/C.3/78/SR.42
Moretti, Norberto - A/78/PV.103
Cameroon
Banaken Elel, Nelly - A/C.3/78/SR.40; A/C.3/78/SR.42
Mezang Akamba, Serge Pamphile - A/C.3/78/SR.41
Canada
Tudor-Bezies, Elizabeth - A/C.3/78/SR.42
Wallenius, Devyn Lyn - A/C.3/78/SR.47
Caribbean Community
Rodrigue, Antonio (Haiti) - A/78/PV.63
Wallace, Brian Christopher Manley (Jamaica) - A/C.3/78/SR.40
China
Dai, Bing - A/C.3/78/SR.40
Liu, Luoge - A/C.3/78/SR.41
Mao, Yizong - A/C.3/78/SR.41
Xing, Jisheng - A/C.3/78/SR.47
Zhang, Sisi - A/78/PV.50; A/C.3/78/SR.41; A/C.3/78/SR.42
Collective Security Treaty Organization
Pilipenko, Igor (Belarus) - A/C.3/78/SR.47
Colombia
Orduz Durán, Jessica Beatriz - A/C.3/78/SR.42
Zalabata Torres, Leonor - A/78/PV.103; A/C.3/78/SR.41
Colombia. Vice-President
Márquez Mina, Francia - A/78/PV.103
Coordinating Bureau of the Non-Aligned Countries
Novruz, Leyla (Azerbaijan) - A/C.3/78/SR.41
Costa Rica
Chan Valverde, Maritza - A/C.3/78/SR.42
Côte d'Ivoire
Moriko, Tiémoko - A/C.3/78/SR.42
Cuba
González Behmaras, Alejandro - A/78/PV.50; A/C.3/78/SR.42; A/C.3/78/SR.47
Padilla González, Cristian - A/78/PV.103
Valido Martínez, Yoangel - A/C.3/78/SR.41
Democratic People's Republic of Korea
Kim, Nam Hyok - A/78/PV.50; A/C.3/78/SR.47

RACIAL DISCRIMINATION—ELIMINATION (Agenda item 69a) (continued)

Egypt
Mostafa Rizk, Heba - A/78/PV.50; A/78/PV.103; A/C.3/78/SR.43; A/C.3/78/SR.47
Equatorial Guinea
Ndong Mba, Anatolio - A/78/PV.63
Eritrea
Gebrekidan, Zebib - A/C.3/78/SR.41; A/C.3/78/SR.43
European Union
Bellmont Roldán, Xavier (Spain) - A/78/PV.50; A/C.3/78/SR.47
Greffine, Venise Catherine - A/C.3/78/SR.41
Kridelka, Philippe (Belgium) - A/78/PV.63
Nyman, Klas - A/C.3/78/SR.40; A/C.3/78/SR.42
France
Wagner, Julie - A/C.3/78/SR.41
Gabon
Biang, Michel Xavier - A/C.3/78/SR.42
Georgia
Lortkipanidze, Ekaterine - A/C.3/78/SR.42
Germany
Ludwig, Annette - A/C.3/78/SR.41
Group of 77
Navarro Barro, Nadieska (Cuba) - A/C.3/78/SR.40
Group of Friends in Defence of the Charter of the United Nations
Altarsha, Elie (Syrian Arab Republic) - A/C.3/78/SR.40
Guatemala
Cruz Morataya, Andrea Flor de María - A/C.3/78/SR.41
Holy See
Caccia, Gabriele Giordano - A/78/PV.63; A/C.3/78/SR.43
Hungary
Mogyorósi, Bálint - A/78/PV.103
India
Sonkar, Suman - A/C.3/78/SR.41
Indonesia
Dhanutirto, Mariska Dwianti - A/C.3/78/SR.42; A/C.3/78/SR.47
Iran (Islamic Republic of)
Arab Bafrani, Fatemeh - A/78/PV.103; A/C.3/78/SR.41
Ghanei, Mohsen - A/C.3/78/SR.40
Iraq
Yaseen, Safaa - A/C.3/78/SR.41
Ireland
Swan, Ellen - A/C.3/78/SR.41
Israel
Mimran Rosenberg, Avital - A/C.3/78/SR.41; A/C.3/78/SR.47
Shapir Ben Naftaly, Reut - A/78/PV.103
Japan
Ono, Sho - A/C.3/78/SR.47
Jordan
Al-halique, Katherine Anas Ahmad - A/C.3/78/SR.42
Kenya
Kinyungu, Njambi - A/C.3/78/SR.40

RACIAL DISCRIMINATION—ELIMINATION (Agenda item 69a) (continued)

Kuwait
Al Munaifi, Shahad - A/C.3/78/SR.41
Lesotho
Lelisa, Nthabiseng Matlhohonolofatso - A/C.3/78/SR.40
Liechtenstein
Oehri, Noah - A/C.3/78/SR.47
Malaysia
Rizal, Nizhan Faraz Bin - A/C.3/78/SR.41; A/C.3/78/SR.47
Malta
Aquilina, Cara Borg - A/C.3/78/SR.41
Mexico
Elizondo Belden, Luis Gerardo - A/C.3/78/SR.40
Mendoza Elguea, Sylvia Paola - A/78/PV.103
Riveroll Usabiaga, Renata - A/C.3/78/SR.42
Namibia
Ashipala, Sevelina - A/C.3/78/SR.40
New Zealand
Buist-Catherwood, Emily - A/C.3/78/SR.47
Nicaragua
Ochoa Espinales, Olimpia Raquel - A/78/PV.50
Pichardo Urbina, Eleane Yaoska - A/C.3/78/SR.42; A/C.3/78/SR.47
Nigeria
Asaju, Bola - A/78/PV.63; A/78/PV.103; A/C.3/78/SR.41; A/C.3/78/SR.47
Pakistan
Ijaz, Rabia - A/C.3/78/SR.41
Qureshi, Hadeeqa - A/C.3/78/SR.41
Panama
Salerno Vega, James Azel - A/C.3/78/SR.40
Portugal
Marinho, Joana Almeida - A/C.3/78/SR.41
Romania
Mihail, Ioana-Cristina - A/C.3/78/SR.41
Russian Federation
Kondratev, Sergei V. - A/C.3/78/SR.41
Kuzmenkov, Stepan Y. - A/C.3/78/SR.40; A/C.3/78/SR.42
Lukiantsev, Grigory Y. - A/C.3/78/SR.47
Zabolotskaya, Maria V. - A/78/PV.50
Saudi Arabia
Albadr, Saleh - A/C.3/78/SR.41
Senegal
Ndiaye, Mamadou Mounsir - A/C.3/78/SR.47
Sierra Leone
Sowa, Amara Sheikh Mohammed - A/C.3/78/SR.42
Singapore
Rajandran, Dhivya - A/C.3/78/SR.47
Sistema de la Integración Centroamericana
González López, Egriselda Aracely (El Salvador) - A/C.3/78/SR.40
Slovenia
Zitko, Andrej - A/C.3/78/SR.47

RACIAL DISCRIMINATION—ELIMINATION (Agenda item 69a) (continued)

South Africa
Joyini, Mathu - A/C.3/78/SR.40
Passmoor, Jonathan David - A/C.3/78/SR.47
Schalkwyk, Marthinus van - A/78/PV.63; A/78/PV.103
Southern African Development Community
Cruz, Francisco José da (Angola) - A/C.3/78/SR.40
Sovereign Order of Malta
Tegoni, Nicola - A/C.3/78/SR.40
Sri Lanka
Gunaratna, Pahala Rallage Sanathana Sugeeshwara - A/C.3/78/SR.47
Pieris, Peter Mohan Maithri - A/C.3/78/SR.42
Sudan
Idres, Nusaiba Hashim Mohamed Ali - A/C.3/78/SR.47
Sweden
Eneström, Anna-Karin - A/C.3/78/SR.47
Switzerland
Maric, Martina - A/C.3/78/SR.47
Syrian Arab Republic
Al Nahhas, Wissam - A/78/PV.50
Altarsha, Elie - A/78/PV.103; A/C.3/78/SR.47
Togo
Tchalare, Abd-el Kader Yasmin - A/78/PV.103
Tunisia
Bessadok, Marwa Jabou - A/78/PV.103
Türkiye
Aydil, İsmail - A/C.3/78/SR.42
Ukraine
Mudrenko, Nataliia - A/78/PV.50; A/C.3/78/SR.41; A/C.3/78/SR.47
Tokarska, Anastasiia - A/C.3/78/SR.41
UN. Assistant Secretary-General for Human Rights
Brands Kehris, Ilze - A/78/PV.63; A/C.3/78/SR.40
UN. Committee on the Elimination of Racial Discrimination. Chair
Shepherd, Verene - A/78/PV.63; A/C.3/78/SR.41
UN. General Assembly. 3rd Committee. Rapporteur
Poveda Brito, Robert Alexander (Venezuela (Bolivarian Republic of)) - A/78/PV.50
UN. General Assembly. President
Francis, Dennis (Trinidad and Tobago) - A/78/PV.63
UN. Group of African States
Banaken Elel, Nelly (Cameroon) - A/78/PV.103
Ladeb, Tarek (Tunisia) - A/C.3/78/SR.40
Nabeta, Celia Kafureka (Uganda) - A/78/PV.63
UN. Group of Asia-Pacific States
Alrowaiei, Jamal Fares (Bahrain) - A/78/PV.63
UN. Group of Latin American and Caribbean States
Rodríguez Mancia, Carla María (Guatemala) - A/78/PV.63
UN. Group of Western European and Other States
Leendertse, Antje (Germany) - A/78/PV.63
UN. Human Rights Council. Ad Hoc Committee on the Elaboration of Complementary International Standards. Chair
Hassan, Kadra Ahmed - A/C.3/78/SR.41

RACIAL DISCRIMINATION—ELIMINATION (Agenda item 69a) (continued)

UN. Human Rights Council. Special Rapporteur on Contemporary Forms of Racism, Racial Discrimination, Xenophobia and Related Intolerance
K.P., Ashwini - A/C.3/78/SR.41
UN. Human Rights Council. Working Group of Experts on People of African Descent. Chair
Reynolds, Barbara G. - A/C.3/78/SR.42
UN. Permanent Forum on People of African Descent
Soomer, June - A/78/PV.63
UN. Under-Secretary-General and Chef de Cabinet
Rattray, Courtenay - A/78/PV.63
United Arab Emirates
Al Dhanani, Nouf Abdulla - A/C.3/78/SR.41
United States
Breen, Patrick - A/C.3/78/SR.40
Carty, Lisa A. - A/C.3/78/SR.47
Heartney, Edward - A/78/PV.103
Johnson, Timothy J. - A/C.3/78/SR.41
Korac, Sofija - A/78/PV.50
Lang, Dylan - A/C.3/78/SR.42
Murphy, Daniel - A/C.3/78/SR.41; A/C.3/78/SR.42
Smyre, Calvin - A/C.3/78/SR.41
Thomas-Greenfield, Linda - A/78/PV.63
Venezuela (Bolivarian Republic of)
Poveda Brito, Robert Alexander - A/78/PV.50; A/C.3/78/SR.47
Zimbabwe
Chimbindi, Albert Ranganai - A/78/PV.50

RACIAL DISCRIMINATION—PROGRAMMES OF ACTION (Agenda item 69b)

Algeria
Hassani, Billel - A/C.3/78/SR.42
Armenia
Hakobyan, Aram - A/C.3/78/SR.42
Azerbaijan
Ahangari, Narmin - A/C.3/78/SR.41; A/C.3/78/SR.43
Bangladesh
Muhith, Muhammad A. - A/C.3/78/SR.43
Belarus
Tozik, Artsiom - A/C.3/78/SR.40
Belgium
Bauwens, Gilles - A/C.3/78/SR.40
Willekens, Vincent - A/C.3/78/SR.41
Bolivia (Plurinational State of)
Caldera Gutiérrez, Fiorella - A/C.3/78/SR.42
Brazil
Balbino, Viviane Rios - A/C.3/78/SR.56
Gomes, Elaine Cristina Pereira - A/C.3/78/SR.40; A/C.3/78/SR.41; A/C.3/78/SR.42
Cameroon
Banaken Elel, Nelly - A/C.3/78/SR.40; A/C.3/78/SR.42
Mezang Akamba, Serge Pamphile - A/C.3/78/SR.41
Canada
Tudor-Bezies, Elizabeth - A/C.3/78/SR.42

RACIAL DISCRIMINATION—PROGRAMMES OF ACTION (Agenda item 69b) (continued)

Caribbean Community
Wallace, Brian Christopher Manley (Jamaica) - A/C.3/78/SR.40
China
Dai, Bing - A/C.3/78/SR.40
Liu, Luoge - A/C.3/78/SR.40; A/C.3/78/SR.41
Mao, Yizong - A/C.3/78/SR.41
Zhang, Sisi - A/C.3/78/SR.41; A/C.3/78/SR.42
Colombia
Orduz Durán, Jessica Beatriz - A/C.3/78/SR.42
Zalabata Torres, Leonor - A/C.3/78/SR.41
Coordinating Bureau of the Non-Aligned Countries
Novruz, Leyla (Azerbaijan) - A/C.3/78/SR.41
Costa Rica
Chan Valverde, Maritza - A/C.3/78/SR.42
Côte d'Ivoire
Moriko, Tiémoko - A/C.3/78/SR.42
Cuba
González Behmaras, Alejandro - A/C.3/78/SR.42; A/C.3/78/SR.56
Valido Martínez, Yoangel - A/C.3/78/SR.41
Egypt
Mostafa Rizk, Heba - A/C.3/78/SR.43
Eritrea
Gebrekidan, Zebib - A/C.3/78/SR.41; A/C.3/78/SR.43
European Union
Bellmont Roldán, Xavier (Spain) - A/C.3/78/SR.56
Greffine, Venise Catherine - A/C.3/78/SR.41
Nyman, Klas - A/C.3/78/SR.40; A/C.3/78/SR.42
France
Wagner, Julie - A/C.3/78/SR.41
Gabon
Biang, Michel Xavier - A/C.3/78/SR.42
Georgia
Lortkipanidze, Ekaterine - A/C.3/78/SR.42
Germany
Ludwig, Annette - A/C.3/78/SR.41
Group of 77
González Behmaras, Alejandro (Cuba) - A/C.3/78/SR.56
Navarro Barro, Nadieska (Cuba) - A/C.3/78/SR.40
Group of Friends in Defence of the Charter of the United Nations
Altarsha, Elie (Syrian Arab Republic) - A/C.3/78/SR.40
Guatemala
Cruz Morataya, Andrea Flor de María - A/C.3/78/SR.41
Holy See
Caccia, Gabriele Giordano - A/C.3/78/SR.43
India
Sonkar, Suman - A/C.3/78/SR.41
Indonesia
Dhanutirto, Mariska Dwianti - A/C.3/78/SR.42
Iran (Islamic Republic of)
Arab Bafrani, Fatemeh - A/C.3/78/SR.41
Ghanei, Mohsen - A/C.3/78/SR.40

RACIAL DISCRIMINATION—PROGRAMMES OF ACTION (Agenda item 69b) (continued)

Iraq
Yaseen, Safaa - A/C.3/78/SR.41
Ireland
Swan, Ellen - A/C.3/78/SR.41
Israel
Mimran Rosenberg, Avital - A/C.3/78/SR.41; A/C.3/78/SR.56
Japan
Ono, Sho - A/C.3/78/SR.56
Jordan
Al-halique, Katherine Anas Ahmad - A/C.3/78/SR.42
Kenya
Kinyungu, Njambi - A/C.3/78/SR.40
Kuwait
Al Munaifi, Shahad - A/C.3/78/SR.41
Lesotho
Lelisa, Nthabiseng Matlhohonolofatso - A/C.3/78/SR.40
Malaysia
Escopper Zumilla, Michael Jawa - A/C.3/78/SR.40
Rizal, Nizhan Faraz Bin - A/C.3/78/SR.41
Malta
Aquilina, Cara Borg - A/C.3/78/SR.41
Mexico
Elizondo Belden, Luis Gerardo - A/C.3/78/SR.40
Riveroll Usabiaga, Renata - A/C.3/78/SR.42
Namibia
Ashipala, Sevelina - A/C.3/78/SR.40
Nicaragua
Pichardo Urbina, Eleane Yaoska - A/C.3/78/SR.42
Nigeria
Asaju, Bola - A/C.3/78/SR.41
Pakistan
Ijaz, Rabia - A/C.3/78/SR.41
Qureshi, Hadeeqa - A/C.3/78/SR.41
Panama
Salerno Vega, James Azel - A/C.3/78/SR.40
Portugal
Marinho, Joana Almeida - A/C.3/78/SR.41
Romania
Mihail, Ioana-Cristina - A/C.3/78/SR.41
Russian Federation
Kondratev, Sergei V. - A/C.3/78/SR.41
Kuzmenkov, Stepan Y. - A/C.3/78/SR.40; A/C.3/78/SR.42
Saudi Arabia
Albadr, Saleh - A/C.3/78/SR.41
Sierra Leone
Sowa, Amara Sheikh Mohammed - A/C.3/78/SR.42
Sistema de la Integración Centroamericana
González López, Egriselda Aracely (El Salvador) - A/C.3/78/SR.40
South Africa
Joyini, Mathu - A/C.3/78/SR.40
Passmoor, Jonathan David - A/C.3/78/SR.40; A/C.3/78/SR.56
Southern African Development Community
Cruz, Francisco José da (Angola) - A/C.3/78/SR.40

RACIAL DISCRIMINATION—PROGRAMMES OF ACTION (Agenda item 69b) (continued)

Sri Lanka
Pieris, Peter Mohan Maithri - A/C.3/78/SR.42
Timor-Leste
Sousa, Maria Lourdes de - A/C.3/78/SR.40
Türkiye
Aydil, İsmail - A/C.3/78/SR.42
Ukraine
Mudrenko, Nataliia - A/C.3/78/SR.41
Tokarska, Anastasiia - A/C.3/78/SR.41
UN. Assistant Secretary-General for Human Rights
Brands Kehris, Ilze - A/C.3/78/SR.40
UN. General Assembly. 3rd Committee. Rapporteur
Poveda Brito, Robert Alexander (Venezuela (Bolivarian Republic of)) - A/78/PV.50
UN. Group of African States
Ladeb, Tarek (Tunisia) - A/C.3/78/SR.40
UN. Human Rights Council. Group of Independent Eminent Experts on the Implementation of the Durban Declaration and Programme of Action. Chair
Suchocka, Hanna - A/C.3/78/SR.40
UN. Human Rights Council. Intergovernmental Working Group on the Effective Implementation of the Durban Declaration and Programme of Action. Chair
Rwakazina, Marie Chantal - A/C.3/78/SR.40
UN. Permanent Forum on People of African Descent. Chair
Campbell Barr, Epsy - A/C.3/78/SR.42
United Arab Emirates
Al Dhanani, Nouf Abdulla - A/C.3/78/SR.41
United Kingdom
Lundy, Phoebe - A/C.3/78/SR.56
United States
Breen, Patrick - A/C.3/78/SR.40
Johnson, Timothy J. - A/C.3/78/SR.41; A/C.3/78/SR.56
Lang, Dylan - A/C.3/78/SR.42
Murphy, Daniel - A/C.3/78/SR.41
Smyre, Calvin - A/C.3/78/SR.41

RADIATION EFFECTS (Agenda item 47)

Argentina
Alvarez, Maximiliano Javier - A/C.4/78/SR.11
Bangladesh
Molla, Md Rafiqul Alam - A/C.4/78/SR.11
Cameroon
Ondo Ebang, William - A/C.4/78/SR.11
Canada
Hirji, Hussein - A/C.4/78/SR.11
China
Ling, Feng - A/C.4/78/SR.11
Cuba
Rolle Hernández, Gretel - A/C.4/78/SR.11
European Union
Hansen, Steen Malthe - A/C.4/78/SR.11
Holy See
Caccia, Gabriele Giordano - A/C.4/78/SR.11
Iran (Islamic Republic of)
Sahraei, Mohammad Reza - A/C.4/78/SR.11

RADIATION EFFECTS (Agenda item 47) (continued)

Iraq
Al-Saed, Saadoon - A/C.4/78/SR.11
Japan
Washino, Yurie - A/C.4/78/SR.11
Pakistan
Khan, Naeem Sabir - A/C.4/78/SR.11
Sri Lanka
Pieris, Peter Mohan Maithri - A/C.4/78/SR.11
UN. General Assembly. Special Political and Decolonization Committee (4th Committee). Rapporteur
Dhanutirto, Mariska Dwianti (Indonesia) - A/78/PV.45
UN Scientific Committee on the Effects of Atomic Radiation. Chair
Chen, Jing (Canada) - A/C.4/78/SR.11

RADIOACTIVE WASTES MANAGEMENT (Agenda item 99e)

Egypt
Ahmed, Amr Essameldin Sadek - A/C.1/78/PV.25

RAISI, SEYYED EBRAHIM (IRAN (ISLAMIC REPUBLID OF). PRESIDENT)—TRIBUTES

Coordinating Bureau of the Non-Aligned Countries
Kwoba, Godfrey (Uganda) - A/78/PV.83
Gulf Cooperation Council
Al-Thani, Alya Ahmed S.A. (Qatar) - A/78/PV.83
Iran (Islamic Republic of)
Jalil Iravani, Amir Saeid - A/78/PV.83
Organisation of Islamic Cooperation
Akram, Munir (Pakistan) - A/78/PV.83
UN. General Assembly. President
Francis, Dennis (Trinidad and Tobago) - A/78/PV.83
UN. Group of African States
Maniratanga, Zéphyrin (Burundi) - A/78/PV.83
UN. Group of Asia-Pacific States
Wells, Majorie May (Vanuatu) - A/78/PV.83
UN. Group of Latin American and Caribbean States
Rodrigue, Antonio (Haiti) - A/78/PV.83
UN. Secretary-General
Guterres, António, 1949- - A/78/PV.83

RAMSAR CONVENTION SECRETARIAT—OBSERVER STATUS (Agenda item 165)

UN. General Assembly. 6th Committee. Rapporteur
Moussa, Moussa Mohamed (Djibouti) - A/78/PV.45

REGIONAL DISARMAMENT (Agenda item 99f)

Estonia
Varem, Mattias - A/C.1/78/PV.22
Kazakhstan
Nurken, Azat - A/C.1/78/PV.21
Lao People's Democratic Republic
Vongnorkeo, Anouparb - A/C.1/78/PV.13

REGIONAL DISARMAMENT (Agenda item 99f) (continued)

Pakistan
Ahmed, Husham - A/C.1/78/PV.21
United States
Turner, Bruce - A/C.1/78/PV.22

RELIGIOUS INTOLERANCE (Agenda item 71b)

Australia
Bryant, Rebecca Suzanne - A/C.3/78/SR.38
Bahrain
Alhammadi, Hessa - A/C.3/78/SR.25
Bangladesh
Monica, Mosammat Shahanara - A/C.3/78/SR.38
Belgium
Bauwens, Gilles - A/C.3/78/SR.38
Canada
Greenhalgh, Bronwyn - A/C.3/78/SR.38
China
Chen, Jiawen - A/C.3/78/SR.38
Colombia
Orduz Durán, Jessica Beatriz - A/C.3/78/SR.38
Cuba
González Behmaras, Alejandro - A/C.3/78/SR.38
Egypt
Mostafa Rizk, Heba - A/C.3/78/SR.18; A/C.3/78/SR.26
European Union
Jiménez de la Hoz, Ana (Spain) - A/C.3/78/SR.52
Nyman, Klas - A/C.3/78/SR.38
Greece
Retalis, Michail - A/C.3/78/SR.38
Gulf Cooperation Council
Al Rubkhi, Khalid Saleh Said (Oman) - A/C.3/78/SR.26
Hungary
Mogyorósi, Bálint - A/C.3/78/SR.38
India
Sonkar, Suman - A/C.3/78/SR.38
Indonesia
Khairunsyah, Aidil - A/C.3/78/SR.38
Iran (Islamic Republic of)
Arab Bafrani, Fatemeh - A/C.3/78/SR.38
Iraq
Abdullateef, Mohammed Ayad - A/C.3/78/SR.38
Ireland
Landy, Caoimhe - A/C.3/78/SR.38
Israel
Mimran Rosenberg, Avital - A/C.3/78/SR.38
Lao People's Democratic Republic
Meunluang, Veomanee - A/C.3/78/SR.38
Lithuania
Bimbaitė, Monika - A/C.3/78/SR.38
Morocco
Bouchikhi, Hanaa - A/C.3/78/SR.38
Netherlands (Kingdom of the)
Tusscher, Berendina ten - A/C.3/78/SR.38

RELIGIOUS INTOLERANCE (Agenda item 71b) (continued)

Organisation of Islamic Cooperation
Abdelkhalek, Osama Mahmoud (Egypt) - A/C.3/78/SR.24
Mostafa Rizk, Heba (Egypt) - A/C.3/78/SR.52
Pakistan
Akram, Munir - A/C.3/78/SR.24
Ijaz, Rabia - A/C.3/78/SR.38
Poland
Skoczek, Joanna Sylwia - A/C.3/78/SR.38
Russian Federation
Kondratev, Sergei V. - A/C.3/78/SR.38
Saudi Arabia
Bin Jadid, Faisal Fahad M. - A/C.3/78/SR.38
Sovereign Order of Malta
Muñoz, Zachary N. - A/C.3/78/SR.38
Ukraine
Mudrenko, Nataliia - A/78/PV.50
UN. Assistant Secretary-General for Human Rights
Brands Kehris, Ilze - A/C.3/78/SR.18
UN. Human Rights Council. Special Rapporteur on Freedom of Religion or Belief
Ghanea, Nazila - A/C.3/78/SR.38
United Kingdom
Manzare, Max - A/C.3/78/SR.38
United States
Eyrich, Kara - A/C.3/78/SR.38; A/C.3/78/SR.52

RESPONSIBILITY OF INTERNATIONAL ORGANIZATIONS (Agenda item 85)

Belarus
Evseenko, Pavel - A/C.6/78/SR.19
Cameroon
Nyanid, Zacharie Serge Raoul - A/C.6/78/SR.19
Colombia
Botero, Stephanie - A/C.6/78/SR.19
Cuba
Mora Fonseca, Vladimir - A/C.6/78/SR.19
Egypt
Roshdy, Hussein Ossama Hussein Abdelrhman - A/C.6/78/SR.19
El Salvador
Flores Soto, Ligia Lorena - A/C.6/78/SR.19
Equatorial Guinea
Nze Mansogo, Estela Mercedes - A/C.6/78/SR.19
Ethiopia
Alemayehu, Betelihem Taye - A/C.6/78/SR.19
European Union
Popan, Simona - A/C.6/78/SR.19
Finland
Laukkanen, Virpi - A/C.6/78/SR.19
Iran (Islamic Republic of)
Fallah Assadi, Mahdad - A/C.6/78/SR.37
Heidari, Bahram - A/C.6/78/SR.19
Mexico
Delgado Fernández, Sergio Emanuel - A/C.6/78/SR.19

RESPONSIBILITY OF INTERNATIONAL ORGANIZATIONS (Agenda item 85) (continued)

Netherlands (Kingdom of the)
Theeuwen, Wieteke Elisabeth Christina - A/C.6/78/SR.19
Portugal
Carvalho, Sergio Amaral Alves de - A/C.6/78/SR.19
Russian Federation
Antonova, Anna V. - A/C.6/78/SR.19
Singapore
Khng, Nathaniel - A/C.6/78/SR.19
UN. General Assembly. 6th Committee. Bureau
Sloboda, Pedro Muniz Pinto (Brazil) - A/C.6/78/SR.37
UN. General Assembly. 6th Committee. Rapporteur
Moussa, Moussa Mohamed (Djibouti) - A/78/PV.45
United Kingdom
Hollis, Jonathan Samuel - A/C.6/78/SR.19
United States
Grosso, Elizabeth Maryanne - A/C.6/78/SR.19
Viet Nam
Tran, Thi Phuong Ha - A/C.6/78/SR.19

RESPONSIBILITY TO PROTECT (Agenda item 129)

Albania
Janina, Suela - A/78/PV.96
Argentina
Lagorio, Ricardo E. - A/78/PV.96
Armenia
Margaryan, Mher - A/78/PV.96
Australia
Larsen, James - A/78/PV.96
Azerbaijan
Gusman, Vadim - A/78/PV.97
Bangladesh
Shatil, Toufiq Islam - A/78/PV.99
Brazil
Sloboda, Pedro Muniz Pinto - A/78/PV.96
China
Sun, Zhiqiang - A/78/PV.97
Costa Rica
Chan Valverde, Maritza - A/78/PV.96
Côte d'Ivoire
Moriko, Tiémoko - A/78/PV.97
Croatia
Simonovic, Ivan - A/78/PV.96
Cuba
Romero Puentes, Yusnier - A/78/PV.96
Democratic People's Republic of Korea
Kim, Song - A/78/PV.96
Egypt
Mostafa Rizk, Heba - A/78/PV.97
Equatorial Guinea
Ndong Mba, Anatolio - A/78/PV.97
European Union
Samson, Hedda - A/78/PV.96
Georgia
Pipia, Temur - A/78/PV.97; A/78/PV.99

RESPONSIBILITY TO PROTECT (Agenda item 129) (continued)

Germany
Wennholz, Philipp Alexander - A/78/PV.97
Ghana
Barnor, Nana Akua - A/78/PV.99
Greece
Sekeris, Evangelos C. - A/78/PV.97
Group of Friends in Defence of the Charter of the United Nations
Reyes Hernández, Jorge Arturo (Venezuela (Bolivarian Republic of)) - A/78/PV.96
Group of Friends of the Responsibility to Protect
Simonovic, Ivan (Croatia) - A/78/PV.96
Guatemala
Rodríguez Mancia, Carla María - A/78/PV.96
Hungary
Vittay, Melinda - A/78/PV.96
India
Bhat, Kajal - A/78/PV.97
Indonesia
Prabowo, Hari - A/78/PV.96
Iran (Islamic Republic of)
Ghafouri, Mojtaba - A/78/PV.99
Jordan
Alqaisi, Sultan Natheir Mustafa - A/78/PV.96
Kiribati
Tito, Teburoro - A/78/PV.97
Latvia
Pavļuta-Deslandes, Sanita - A/78/PV.96
Malta
De Bono Sant Cassia, Andrea - A/78/PV.99
Marshall Islands
Silk, John M. - A/78/PV.97
Mexico
Vasconcelos y Cruz, Héctor Enrique - A/78/PV.96
Morocco
Bouchikhi, Hanaa - A/78/PV.96
Myanmar
Tun, Kyaw Moe - A/78/PV.96
Netherlands (Kingdom of the)
Brandt, Yoka - A/78/PV.96
Nicaragua
Pichardo Urbina, Eleane Yaoska - A/78/PV.96
Nigeria
Endoni, Syndoph Paebi - A/78/PV.97
Pakistan
Akram, Munir - A/78/PV.97
Ijaz, Rabia - A/78/PV.97
Philippines
Arumpac-Marte, Azela Guerrero - A/78/PV.99
Poland
Szczerski, Krzysztof - A/78/PV.96
Republic of Korea
Kim, Hyunsoo - A/78/PV.97
Russian Federation
Leonidchenko, Sergey A. - A/78/PV.97; A/78/PV.99
Rwanda
Sesonga, Fred - A/78/PV.99
Singapore
Seah, Mark - A/78/PV.97

RESPONSIBILITY TO PROTECT (Agenda item 129) (continued)

Slovenia
Jurecko, Sasa - A/78/PV.97
South Africa
Passmoor, Jonathan David - A/78/PV.96
Sudan
Mohammed, Ammar Mohammed Mahmoud - A/78/PV.99
Switzerland
Baeriswyl, Pascale - A/78/PV.96
Syrian Arab Republic
Alshahin, Essam - A/78/PV.99
Timor-Leste
Soares, Dionísio Da Costa Babo - A/78/PV.96
Türkiye
Güç, Eda - A/78/PV.97
Ukraine
Kyslytsya, Sergiy - A/78/PV.99
UN. Special Adviser to the Secretary-General on the Responsibility to Protect
Bleeker, Mô - A/78/PV.96
United Arab Emirates
Abushahab, Mohamed Issa - A/78/PV.97
United Kingdom
Hollis, Jonathan Samuel - A/78/PV.97
United States
Shrier, Jonathan - A/78/PV.97
Uruguay
Beretta Tassano, María Noel - A/78/PV.97

RIGHT OF ASSEMBLY (Agenda item 71b)

Austria
Mahidi, Mourad - A/C.3/78/SR.19
Bangladesh
Monica, Mosammat Shahanara - A/C.3/78/SR.19
Belgium
Kridelka, Philippe - A/C.3/78/SR.19
China
Zhang, Tianhao - A/C.3/78/SR.19
Colombia
Tickner, Arlene Beth - A/C.3/78/SR.19
Czechia
Kulhánek, Jakub - A/C.3/78/SR.19
European Union
Carlé, Hanne - A/C.3/78/SR.19
Latvia
Pavļuta-Deslandes, Sanita - A/C.3/78/SR.19
Pakistan
Kanwal, Tehreem - A/C.3/78/SR.19
Russian Federation
Kuzmenkov, Stepan Y. - A/C.3/78/SR.19
Switzerland
Wagner, Valérie - A/C.3/78/SR.19
UN. Human Rights Council. Special Rapporteur on the Rights to Freedom of Peaceful Assembly and of Association
Voulé, Clément Nyaletsossi - A/C.3/78/SR.19
United Kingdom
Devereaux, Brendan - A/C.3/78/SR.19

RIGHT OF ASSEMBLY (Agenda item 71b) (continued)

United States
Brzeski, Jessica - A/C.3/78/SR.19

RIGHT TO CULTURE (Agenda item 71b)

Cameroon
Wainwel, Gwedji Doris - A/C.3/78/SR.27
China
Wang, Zixu - A/C.3/78/SR.27
Cuba
Valido Martínez, Yoangel - A/C.3/78/SR.27
Eritrea
Gebrekidan, Zebib - A/C.3/78/SR.27
European Union
Greffine, Venise Catherine - A/C.3/78/SR.27
India
Sonkar, Suman - A/C.3/78/SR.27
International Youth Organization for Ibero-America
Rando Ibáñez, Alicia - A/C.3/78/SR.27
Malaysia
Escopper Zumilla, Michael Jawa - A/C.3/78/SR.27
Mali
Dabo N'diaye, Djeneba - A/C.3/78/SR.27
Russian Federation
Kuzmenkov, Stepan Y. - A/C.3/78/SR.27
Ukraine
Tokarska, Anastasiia - A/C.3/78/SR.27
UN. Human Rights Council. Special Rapporteur in the Field of Cultural Rights
Xanthaki, Alexandra - A/C.3/78/SR.27
UNESCO
Zadra, Estelle - A/C.3/78/SR.27
United States
Brzeski, Jessica - A/C.3/78/SR.27

RIGHT TO DEVELOPMENT (Agenda item 71b)

Algeria
Hassani, Billel - A/C.3/78/SR.20
Argentina
Escobar, Luciano Hernán - A/C.3/78/SR.48
Armenia
Hakobyan, Aram - A/C.3/78/SR.48
Bangladesh
Monica, Mosammat Shahanara - A/C.3/78/SR.20
Belarus
Pisarevich, Vadim - A/C.3/78/SR.20
Brazil
Paranhos, Pedro Barreto Da Rocha - A/C.3/78/SR.20
Cameroon
Banaken Elel, Nelly - A/C.3/78/SR.20
Canada
Wallenius, Devyn Lyn - A/C.3/78/SR.48
Chile
Nishihara, Carmen - A/C.3/78/SR.48
China
Wang, Zixu - A/C.3/78/SR.20

RIGHT TO DEVELOPMENT (Agenda item 71b) (continued)

Coordinating Bureau of the Non-Aligned Countries
González Behmaras, Alejandro (Cuba) - A/C.3/78/SR.48
Novruz, Leyla (Azerbaijan) - A/C.3/78/SR.20
Costa Rica
Pizarro-Viales, Laura Raquel - A/C.3/78/SR.48
Cuba
González Behmaras, Alejandro - A/C.3/78/SR.20
Egypt
Mostafa Rizk, Heba - A/C.3/78/SR.20; A/C.3/78/SR.26; A/C.3/78/SR.48
European Union
Alonso Giganto, Ana María (Spain) - A/C.3/78/SR.48
Carlsson Szlezak, Teresa - A/C.3/78/SR.20
Group of Friends in Defence of the Charter of the United Nations
Pérez Ayestarán, Joaquín Alberto (Venezuela (Bolivarian Republic of)) - A/C.3/78/SR.20
Gulf Cooperation Council
Al Rubkhi, Khalid Saleh Said (Oman) - A/C.3/78/SR.26
Indonesia
Imanuel, Fnu - A/C.3/78/SR.20
Iran (Islamic Republic of)
Arab Bafrani, Fatemeh - A/C.3/78/SR.20
Liechtenstein
Oehri, Noah - A/C.3/78/SR.48
Malaysia
Escopper Zumilla, Michael Jawa - A/C.3/78/SR.20
Mali
Dabo N'diaye, Djeneba - A/C.3/78/SR.20
Mexico
Santa Ana Vara, Alma Esperanza - A/C.3/78/SR.48
Mozambique
Raivoso, Ilda - A/C.3/78/SR.26
New Zealand
Buist-Catherwood, Emily - A/C.3/78/SR.48
Nicaragua
Pichardo Urbina, Eleane Yaoska - A/C.3/78/SR.20
Pakistan
Jadoon, Usman Iqbal - A/C.3/78/SR.20
Russian Federation
Zabolotskaya, Maria V. - A/C.3/78/SR.20
Saudi Arabia
Al Mandil, Mishal - A/C.3/78/SR.20
Alwasil, Abdulaziz M.O. - A/C.3/78/SR.26
South Africa
Passmoor, Jonathan David - A/C.3/78/SR.20
Syrian Arab Republic
Altarsha, Elie - A/C.3/78/SR.20
Uganda
Kwoba, Godfrey - A/C.3/78/SR.28
UN. Assistant Secretary-General for Human Rights
Brands Kehris, Ilze - A/C.3/78/SR.18
UN. Group of African States
Ladeb, Tarek (Tunisia) - A/C.3/78/SR.20

RIGHT TO DEVELOPMENT (Agenda item 71b) (continued)

UN. Human Rights Council. Expert Mechanism on the Right to Development. Chair
Valiña, Liliana - A/C.3/78/SR.20
UN. Human Rights Council. Special Rapporteur on the Right to Development
Deva, Surya - A/C.3/78/SR.20
UN. Human Rights Council. Working Group on the Right to Development. Chair
Akram, Zamir - A/C.3/78/SR.20
United Kingdom
Lundy, Phoebe - A/C.3/78/SR.48
United States
Korac, Sofija - A/C.3/78/SR.47
Merron, Eric - A/C.3/78/SR.48
Zimbabwe
Manyanga, Garikai - A/C.3/78/SR.20

RIGHT TO DRINKING WATER (Agenda item 71b)

Bangladesh
Abdullah, Md Showeb - A/C.3/78/SR.28
Cameroon
Banaken Elel, Nelly - A/C.3/78/SR.50
China
Yang, Xiaokun - A/C.3/78/SR.28
Croatia
Šukurica, Alen - A/C.3/78/SR.28
Egypt
Eldahshan, Wael Mahmoud Abdelaziz - A/C.3/78/SR.28
European Union
Szelivanov, Julia - A/C.3/78/SR.28
Germany
Wennholz, Philipp Alexander - A/C.3/78/SR.28
Iraq
Al-Khaqani, Hassan Jabbar - A/C.3/78/SR.28
Japan
Ono, Sho - A/C.3/78/SR.28
Mali
Dabo N'diaye, Djeneba - A/C.3/78/SR.50
Morocco
Alaoui, Rabia - A/C.3/78/SR.28
Russian Federation
Kuzmenkov, Stepan Y. - A/C.3/78/SR.28
Saudi Arabia
Bin Jadid, Faisal Fahad M. - A/C.3/78/SR.50
Senegal
Niasse, Samba Thiam - A/C.3/78/SR.50
Sovereign Order of Malta
Lucii, Costanza - A/C.3/78/SR.28
Spain
Bellmont Roldán, Xavier - A/C.3/78/SR.28; A/C.3/78/SR.50
Türkiye
Aydil, İsmail - A/C.3/78/SR.28; A/C.3/78/SR.50

RIGHT TO DRINKING WATER (Agenda item 71b) (continued)

UN. Human Rights Council. Special Rapporteur on the Human Right to Safe Drinking Water and Sanitation
Arrojo Agudo, Pedro - A/C.3/78/SR.28
United States
Johnson, Timothy J. - A/C.3/78/SR.50
Worthe, Jeffrey - A/C.3/78/SR.28

RIGHT TO EDUCATION (Agenda item 71b)

Bangladesh
Abdullah, Md Showeb - A/C.3/78/SR.27
Cameroon
Wainwel, Gwedji Doris - A/C.3/78/SR.27
China
Wang, Zixu - A/C.3/78/SR.27
Cuba
Valido Martínez, Yoangel - A/C.3/78/SR.27
Dominican Republic
Matos Menéndez, Gala - A/C.3/78/SR.27
Egypt
Mohamed, Mohamed Omar Elfarouk Hassan - A/C.3/78/SR.27
El Salvador
González López, Egriselda Aracely - A/C.3/78/SR.27
European Union
Keogh, Briana - A/C.3/78/SR.27
Indonesia
Meizura, Novia - A/C.3/78/SR.27
International Youth Organization for Ibero-America
Valle Blanco, Daniel del - A/C.3/78/SR.27
Israel
Shaked, Or - A/C.3/78/SR.27
Italy
Napolitano, Annarita - A/C.3/78/SR.27
Kenya
Kariuki, Kamau - A/C.3/78/SR.27
Luxembourg
Vlokhoven, Flore van - A/C.3/78/SR.27
Malaysia
Escopper Zumilla, Michael Jawa - A/C.3/78/SR.27
Maldives
Hameed, Hala - A/C.3/78/SR.27
Mali
Dabo N'diaye, Djeneba - A/C.3/78/SR.27
Morocco
Alaoui, Rabia - A/C.3/78/SR.27
Portugal
Guerra, Stefano Venancio - A/C.3/78/SR.27
Romania
Mihail, Ioana-Cristina - A/C.3/78/SR.27
Russian Federation
Kuzmenkov, Stepan Y. - A/C.3/78/SR.27
Syrian Arab Republic
Altarsha, Elie - A/C.3/78/SR.27
Ukraine
Prytula, Mykola - A/C.3/78/SR.27

RIGHT TO EDUCATION (Agenda item 71b) (continued)

UN. Human Rights Council. Special Rapporteur on the Right to Education
Shaheed, Farida - A/C.3/78/SR.27
UNESCO
Gray, Lily - A/C.3/78/SR.27
United States
Korac, Sofija - A/C.3/78/SR.47
Lang, Dylan - A/C.3/78/SR.27

RIGHT TO FOOD (Agenda item 71b)

Belarus
Kryvaltsevich, Aliaksei - A/C.3/78/SR.30
Pilipenko, Igor - A/C.3/78/SR.48
Brazil
Dias, João Henrique Nascimento - A/C.3/78/SR.30
Cameroon
Banaken Elel, Nelly - A/C.3/78/SR.30
China
Liu, Luoge - A/C.3/78/SR.30
Coordinating Bureau of the Non-Aligned Countries
Novruz, Leyla (Azerbaijan) - A/C.3/78/SR.30
Cuba
García Hernández, Martha - A/C.3/78/SR.30
González Behmaras, Alejandro - A/C.3/78/SR.48
Dominican Republic
Andújar, Luz del Carmen - A/C.3/78/SR.30
El Salvador
Amaya Garay, Sofía Alejandra - A/C.3/78/SR.30
European Union
Skoog, Olof - A/C.3/78/SR.24
Szelivanov, Julia - A/C.3/78/SR.30
Iran (Islamic Republic of)
Arab Bafrani, Fatemeh - A/C.3/78/SR.30
Israel
Mimran Rosenberg, Avital - A/C.3/78/SR.30
Japan
Ono, Sho - A/C.3/78/SR.30; A/C.3/78/SR.48
Lesotho
Nena, Matete - A/C.3/78/SR.30
Malaysia
Escopper Zumilla, Michael Jawa - A/C.3/78/SR.30
Morocco
Chaouki, Naser-Allah - A/C.3/78/SR.30
Pakistan
Qureshi, Hadeeqa - A/C.3/78/SR.30
Romania
Mihail, Ioana-Cristina - A/C.3/78/SR.30
Russian Federation
Kuzmenkov, Stepan Y. - A/C.3/78/SR.30
Sovereign Order of Malta
Rosario-Blackett, Marissa del - A/C.3/78/SR.30
Syrian Arab Republic
Altarsha, Elie - A/C.3/78/SR.30
Ukraine
Tokarska, Anastasiia - A/C.3/78/SR.30
UN. Human Rights Council. Special Rapporteur on the Right to Food
Fakhri, Michael - A/C.3/78/SR.30

RIGHT TO FOOD (Agenda item 71b) (continued)

United Kingdom
Kumaria, Sacha - A/C.3/78/SR.48
United States
Merron, Eric - A/C.3/78/SR.48

RIGHT TO HEALTH (Agenda item 71b)

Bangladesh
Abdullah, Md Showeb - A/C.3/78/SR.39
Belarus
Tozik, Artsiom - A/C.3/78/SR.39
Brazil
Leite, Patricia Soares - A/C.3/78/SR.39
Brunei Darussalam
Wafiuddin, Illyana - A/C.3/78/SR.26
Cameroon
Ahidjo, Ahidjo - A/C.3/78/SR.39
Chile
Ruidíaz, René - A/C.3/78/SR.39
China
Liu, Luoge - A/C.3/78/SR.39
Cuba
Valido Martínez, Yoangel - A/C.3/78/SR.39
Dominican Republic
Matos Menéndez, Gala - A/C.3/78/SR.39
Egypt
Mohamed, Mohamed Omar Elfarouk Hassan - A/C.3/78/SR.39
El Salvador
Segura Aragón, Carlos Efraín - A/C.3/78/SR.39
European Union
Greffine, Venise Catherine - A/C.3/78/SR.39
Lesotho
Lelisa, Nthabiseng Matlhohonolofatso - A/C.3/78/SR.39
Maldives
Khadeeja, Aufiyau - A/C.3/78/SR.39
Mexico
Mendoza Elguea, Sylvia Paola - A/C.3/78/SR.39
Russian Federation
Kuzmenkov, Stepan Y. - A/C.3/78/SR.39
South Africa
Sekonyana, Ngako Elphus - A/C.3/78/SR.39
Sovereign Order of Malta
Espiritu, Michael - A/C.3/78/SR.39
Syrian Arab Republic
Altarsha, Elie - A/C.3/78/SR.39
Thailand
Chindawongse, Suriya - A/C.3/78/SR.25
UN. Human Rights Council. Special Rapporteur on the Right of Everyone to the Enjoyment of the Highest Attainable Standard of Physical and Mental Health
Mofokeng, Tlaleng - A/C.3/78/SR.39
United States
Lang, Dylan - A/C.3/78/SR.39

RIGHT TO HOUSING (Agenda item 71b)

Bangladesh
Abdullah, Md Showeb - A/C.3/78/SR.30

RIGHT TO HOUSING (Agenda item 71b) (continued)

Brazil
Dias, João Henrique Nascimento - A/C.3/78/SR.30
Cameroon
Banaken Elel, Nelly - A/C.3/78/SR.30
Chile
Nishihara, Carmen - A/C.3/78/SR.30
China
Liu, Luoge - A/C.3/78/SR.30
Croatia
Šukurica, Alen - A/C.3/78/SR.30
El Salvador
Amaya Garay, Sofía Alejandra - A/C.3/78/SR.30
European Union
Szelivanov, Julia - A/C.3/78/SR.30
Israel
Mimran Rosenberg, Avital - A/C.3/78/SR.30
Malaysia
Escopper Zumilla, Michael Jawa - A/C.3/78/SR.30
Russian Federation
Kuzmenkov, Stepan Y. - A/C.3/78/SR.30
Sovereign Order of Malta
Lucii, Costanza - A/C.3/78/SR.30
Ukraine
Tokarska, Anastasiia - A/C.3/78/SR.30
UN. Human Rights Council. Special Rapporteur on Adequate Housing as a Component of the Right to an Adequate Standard of Living
Rajagopal, Balakrishnan - A/C.3/78/SR.30
United States
Breen, Patrick - A/C.3/78/SR.30

RIGHT TO PRIVACY (Agenda item 71b)

Austria
Soyka, Juliane - A/C.3/78/SR.21
Brazil
Dias, João Henrique Nascimento - A/C.3/78/SR.21
China
Zhang, Tianhao - A/C.3/78/SR.21
European Union
Szelivanov, Julia - A/C.3/78/SR.21
Luxembourg
Wald, Julien - A/C.3/78/SR.21
Malaysia
Escopper Zumilla, Michael Jawa - A/C.3/78/SR.21
Russian Federation
Kuzmenkov, Stepan Y. - A/C.3/78/SR.21
Syrian Arab Republic
Altarsha, Elie - A/C.3/78/SR.21
UN. Human Rights Council. Special Rapporteur on the Right to Privacy
Brian Nougrères, Ana - A/C.3/78/SR.21
United States
Merron, Eric - A/C.3/78/SR.21

RIGHT TO THE TRUTH (Agenda item 71b)

Argentina
Oddone, Fabián - A/C.3/78/SR.22
Chile
Fernández Carter, Catalina - A/C.3/78/SR.22

RIGHT TO THE TRUTH (Agenda item 71b) (continued)

Colombia
Paredes Campaña, Jairo Andrés - A/C.3/78/SR.22
Democratic People's Republic of Korea
Kim, Nam Hyok - A/C.3/78/SR.22
Indonesia
Meizura, Novia - A/C.3/78/SR.22
Japan
Miyamoto, Sogaku - A/C.3/78/SR.22
Switzerland
Bless, Adrian - A/C.3/78/SR.22
Ukraine
Mudrenko, Nataliia - A/C.3/78/SR.22
UN. Human Rights Council. Special Rapporteur on the Promotion of Truth, Justice, Reparation and Guarantees of Non-Recurrence
Salvioli, Fabián - A/C.3/78/SR.22

RIGHTS OF THE CHILD (Agenda item 67)

Albania
Lamce, Enian - A/C.3/78/SR.11
Algeria
Samai, Rahma - A/C.3/78/SR.11; A/C.3/78/SR.12; A/C.3/78/SR.14
Andorra
Font Vilagines, Meritxell - A/C.3/78/SR.14
Argentina
González, María Florencia - A/C.3/78/SR.11
Armenia
Hakobyan, Aram - A/C.3/78/SR.11; A/C.3/78/SR.13; A/C.3/78/SR.14
ASEAN
Prabowo, Hari (Indonesia) - A/C.3/78/SR.11
Australia
Kelson, Matthew - A/C.3/78/SR.55
Mitchell, Rob - A/C.3/78/SR.13
Azerbaijan
Ahangari, Narmin - A/C.3/78/SR.11; A/C.3/78/SR.13; A/C.3/78/SR.14
Bahrain
Alabbasi, Amina Abdulaziz - A/C.3/78/SR.14
Bangladesh
Abdullah, Md Showeb - A/C.3/78/SR.13
Monica, Mosammat Shahanara - A/C.3/78/SR.11; A/C.3/78/SR.12
Belarus
Velichko, Irina - A/C.3/78/SR.11; A/C.3/78/SR.12
Belgium
Bauwens, Gilles - A/C.3/78/SR.11
Brazil
Gomes, Elaine Cristina Pereira - A/C.3/78/SR.11; A/C.3/78/SR.12
Brunei Darussalam
Sulaiman, Muhamad Syukri - A/C.3/78/SR.13
Bulgaria
Stoeva, Lachezara - A/C.3/78/SR.12
Burkina Faso
Ouattara, Isaac Alassane - A/C.3/78/SR.13

RIGHTS OF THE CHILD (Agenda item 67) (continued)

Cameroon
Banaken Elel, Nelly - A/C.3/78/SR.12; A/C.3/78/SR.55
Canada
Baur, Lianna Maureen - A/C.3/78/SR.55
Klaise, Inara - A/C.3/78/SR.55
Caribbean Community
Wallace, Brian Christopher Manley (Jamaica) - A/C.3/78/SR.12
Central African Republic
Lenanguy Brinz, Yannick-Michel - A/C.3/78/SR.13
Chile
Perdomo, María Paula - A/C.3/78/SR.55
China
La, Haozhao - A/C.3/78/SR.11; A/C.3/78/SR.12
Colombia
Orduz Durán, Jessica Beatriz - A/C.3/78/SR.11
Zalabata Torres, Leonor - A/C.3/78/SR.12
Congo
Ahoue Itoua Lekegny, Patience - A/C.3/78/SR.13
Costa Rica
Zavala Porras, Daniel Andrés - A/C.3/78/SR.14
Côte d'Ivoire
Kouakou, Kouadjo Michel - A/C.3/78/SR.11
Moriko, Tiémoko - A/C.3/78/SR.14
Croatia
Andrić, Katarina - A/C.3/78/SR.11
Cuba
Armas García, Mercedes de - A/C.3/78/SR.12
González Behmaras, Alejandro - A/C.3/78/SR.55
Democratic People's Republic of Korea
Kim, Nam Hyok - A/C.3/78/SR.13
Democratic Republic of the Congo
Ahuka Lutundul, Claudy - A/C.3/78/SR.14
Dominican Republic
Matos Menéndez, Gala - A/C.3/78/SR.11; A/C.3/78/SR.13
Ecuador
Méndez Gruezo, Elizabeth - A/C.3/78/SR.13
Egypt
Eldahshan, Wael Mahmoud Abdelaziz - A/C.3/78/SR.11
Mohamed, Mohamed Omar Elfarouk Hassan - A/C.3/78/SR.11; A/C.3/78/SR.12; A/C.3/78/SR.55
El Salvador
Segura Aragón, Carlos Efraín - A/C.3/78/SR.12
Sorto Rosales, Mayra Lisseth - A/C.3/78/SR.55
Estonia
Tammsaar, Rein - A/C.3/78/SR.11
Ethiopia
Chala, Samuel Isa - A/C.3/78/SR.13
European Union
Alonso Giganto, Ana María (Spain) - A/C.3/78/SR.55
Clifford, Katarina - A/C.3/78/SR.11
Keogh, Briana - A/C.3/78/SR.12
Schuller, Simone - A/C.3/78/SR.11; A/C.3/78/SR.12

RIGHTS OF THE CHILD (Agenda item 67) (continued)

France
Dime-Labille, Diarra - A/C.3/78/SR.13
Freudenreich, Anne - A/C.3/78/SR.11
Georgia
Lortkipanidze, Ekaterine - A/C.3/78/SR.11; A/C.3/78/SR.13
Ghana
Corquaye, Ama Anima - A/C.3/78/SR.14
Greece
Alexandridou, Alexandra - A/C.3/78/SR.11
Guatemala
Rodríguez Mancia, Carla María - A/C.3/78/SR.11
Guinea
Konaté, Sékou - A/C.3/78/SR.13
Guyana
Hazlewood, Abosede - A/C.3/78/SR.13
Haiti
Pierre Fabre, Celine - A/C.3/78/SR.14
Holy See
Murphy, Robert David - A/C.3/78/SR.14; A/C.3/78/SR.55
Iceland
Valtýsson, Jörundur - A/C.3/78/SR.14
India
Sonkar, Suman - A/C.3/78/SR.11; A/C.3/78/SR.13
Indonesia
Imanuel, Fnu - A/C.3/78/SR.55
Iran (Islamic Republic of)
Arab Bafrani, Fatemeh - A/C.3/78/SR.11; A/C.3/78/SR.12; A/C.3/78/SR.55
Iraq
Abdullateef, Mohammed Ayad - A/C.3/78/SR.55
Ireland
Leonard, Roisin - A/C.3/78/SR.13
Israel
Carmeli, Mor - A/C.3/78/SR.12
Mimran Rosenberg, Avital - A/C.3/78/SR.11; A/C.3/78/SR.55
Rodkin, Boaz - A/C.3/78/SR.13
Italy
Di Capua, Giacomo - A/C.3/78/SR.11
Tonon, Daniela - A/C.3/78/SR.13
Japan
Kamiya, Masako - A/C.3/78/SR.13
Ono, Sho - A/C.3/78/SR.11
Kazakhstan
Bakytbekkyzy, Anel - A/C.3/78/SR.13
Kuwait
Al Munaifi, Shahad - A/C.3/78/SR.12
Lao People's Democratic Republic
Meunluang, Veomanee - A/C.3/78/SR.13
Lebanon
Zoghbi, Rawa - A/C.3/78/SR.11
Lesotho
Nena, Matete - A/C.3/78/SR.13
Libya
Hamed, Ashraf A.O. - A/C.3/78/SR.55
Liechtenstein
Oehri, Noah - A/C.3/78/SR.11

RIGHTS OF THE CHILD (Agenda item 67) (continued)

Luxembourg
Lepage, Natasha - A/C.3/78/SR.12
Maes, Olivier - A/C.3/78/SR.11
Wald, Julien - A/C.3/78/SR.11; A/C.3/78/SR.12
Malawi
Nyirongo, Bertha Mkaka - A/C.3/78/SR.13
Malaysia
Dolah, Rizzal - A/C.3/78/SR.11; A/C.3/78/SR.12
Rizal, Nizhan Faraz Bin - A/C.3/78/SR.11; A/C.3/78/SR.55
Ruslan, Muhammad Ammar Rafiq - A/C.3/78/SR.11
Maldives
Hameed, Hala - A/C.3/78/SR.13
Mali
Dabo N'diaye, Djeneba - A/C.3/78/SR.14; A/C.3/78/SR.55
Malta
Kuymizakis, Adam - A/C.3/78/SR.11
Mexico
Reza Bautista, Mauricio - A/C.3/78/SR.11; A/C.3/78/SR.12
Yarahuán Dodero, Santiago - A/C.3/78/SR.12
Micronesia (Federated States of)
Lippwe, Jeem - A/C.3/78/SR.13
Monaco
Beuzit, Léa - A/C.3/78/SR.14
Morocco
Lyazidi, Naima - A/C.3/78/SR.14
Moutchou, Majda - A/C.3/78/SR.11; A/C.3/78/SR.12
Myanmar
Tun, Kyaw Moe - A/C.3/78/SR.14
Namibia
Iileka, Nekwayahelalia - A/C.3/78/SR.13
Nepal
Aryal, Krishna - A/C.3/78/SR.12
Nicaragua
Hermida Castillo, Jaime - A/C.3/78/SR.13
Niger
Seydou, Abdoul Fadh Mahamadou - A/C.3/78/SR.55
Nigeria
Asaju, Bola - A/C.3/78/SR.11; A/C.3/78/SR.13; A/C.3/78/SR.55
Oman
Al Jaradi, Heba Khalid - A/C.3/78/SR.14
Al Rawahi, Abdulhalim Mubarak Saloom - A/C.3/78/SR.55
Pakistan
Ijaz, Rabia - A/C.3/78/SR.11
Qureshi, Hadeeqa - A/C.3/78/SR.11; A/C.3/78/SR.14
Saleem, Saima - A/C.3/78/SR.13
Papua New Guinea
Mokono, Anna Konara - A/C.3/78/SR.14
Paraguay
Candia Ibarra, Miguel Ricardo - A/C.3/78/SR.14
Philippines
Fangco, Maria Roseny Baltazar - A/C.3/78/SR.11
Guevarra-de Dios, Nadine Bobadilla - A/C.3/78/SR.12

RIGHTS OF THE CHILD (Agenda item 67) (continued)

Poland
Domańska, Anna - A/C.3/78/SR.11
Lula, Iwona Anna - A/C.3/78/SR.11
Stadnicka, Małgorzata - A/C.3/78/SR.11
Szczerski, Krzysztof - A/C.3/78/SR.11
Portugal
Marinho, Joana Almeida - A/C.3/78/SR.11
Qatar
Al-Buainain, Hemyan Hassan Nasser - A/C.3/78/SR.11
Al-thani, Almaha Mubarak F.J. - A/C.3/78/SR.12
Romania
Feruță, Cornel - A/C.3/78/SR.13
Mihail, Ioana-Cristina - A/C.3/78/SR.11
Russian Federation
Kashaev, Roman G. - A/C.3/78/SR.55
Kuzmenkov, Stepan Y. - A/C.3/78/SR.11; A/C.3/78/SR.12
Rwanda
Vmulisa, Flavia - A/C.3/78/SR.11
San Marino
Arona, Sofia - A/C.3/78/SR.14
Saudi Arabia
Al Mandil, Mishal - A/C.3/78/SR.12
Bin Jadid, Faisal Fahad M. - A/C.3/78/SR.55
Mousa, Sulafa - A/C.3/78/SR.11
Senegal
Niasse, Samba Thiam - A/C.3/78/SR.14; A/C.3/78/SR.55
Sierra Leone
Alghali, Francess Piagie - A/C.3/78/SR.13
Singapore
Rajandran, Dhivya - A/C.3/78/SR.55
Teo, Bernice Yi Lin - A/C.3/78/SR.13
Sistema de la Integración Centroamericana
González López, Egriselda Aracely (El Salvador) - A/C.3/78/SR.11
Slovakia
Beblavý, Pavol - A/C.3/78/SR.12
Slovenia
Šmidt, Arina - A/C.3/78/SR.11
South Africa
Makwati, Babalwa - A/C.3/78/SR.12
Schalkwyk, Marthinus van - A/C.3/78/SR.12
Southern African Development Community
Cruz, Francisco José da (Angola) - A/C.3/78/SR.11
Luemba, Mateus Pedro (Angola) - A/C.3/78/SR.55
Sovereign Order of Malta
Espiritu, Michael - A/C.3/78/SR.14
Muñoz, Zachary N. - A/C.3/78/SR.11
Sri Lanka
Pieris, Peter Mohan Maithri - A/C.3/78/SR.13
State of Palestine
Salem, Sahar K.H. - A/C.3/78/SR.11; A/C.3/78/SR.14
Switzerland
Stricker, Julia - A/C.3/78/SR.11
Wagner, Valérie - A/C.3/78/SR.12

RIGHTS OF THE CHILD (Agenda item 67) (continued)

Syrian Arab Republic
Altarsha, Elie - A/C.3/78/SR.11; A/C.3/78/SR.12; A/C.3/78/SR.13; A/C.3/78/SR.55
Thailand
Treedara, Jakarin - A/C.3/78/SR.11
Timor-Leste
Nunes, Karlito - A/C.3/78/SR.13
Tunisia
Bessadok, Marwa Jabou - A/C.3/78/SR.13
Türkiye
Aydil, İsmail - A/C.3/78/SR.14
Uganda
Nabeta, Celia Kafureka - A/C.3/78/SR.13
Ukraine
Mudrenko, Nataliia - A/C.3/78/SR.11; A/C.3/78/SR.12
UN. Committee on the Rights of the Child. Chair
Skelton, Ann Marie (South Africa) - A/C.3/78/SR.12
UN. General Assembly. 3rd Committee. Rapporteur
Poveda Brito, Robert Alexander (Venezuela (Bolivarian Republic of)) - A/78/PV.50
UN. Group of African States
Banaken Elel, Nelly (Cameroon) - A/C.3/78/SR.55
Ladeb, Tarek (Tunisia) - A/C.3/78/SR.12
UN. Group of Latin American and Caribbean States
Alonso Giganto, Ana María (Spain) - A/C.3/78/SR.55
Riva Grela, Juan José (Uruguay) - A/C.3/78/SR.55
UN. Human Rights Council. Special Rapporteur on the Sale, Sexual Exploitation and Sexual Abuse of Children
Singhateh, Mama Fatima - A/C.3/78/SR.12
UN. Special Representative of the Secretary-General for Children and Armed Conflict
Gamba, Virginia - A/C.3/78/SR.11
UN. Special Representative of the Secretary-General on Violence against Children
Maalla M'jid, Najat - A/C.3/78/SR.11
UNICEF
Fontaine, Manuel - A/C.3/78/SR.11
United Arab Emirates
Abdalrhman, Fatma Mohammad - A/C.3/78/SR.13
United Kingdom
Reyes, Gaia - A/C.3/78/SR.55
United Republic of Tanzania
Tambwe, Zuleikha Rutha - A/C.3/78/SR.14
United States
Keller, Janet - A/C.3/78/SR.12
Lang, Dylan - A/C.3/78/SR.11; A/C.3/78/SR.55
Shrier, Jonathan - A/C.3/78/SR.13
Uruguay
Amorín, Carlos Daniel - A/C.3/78/SR.13
Viet Nam
Dang, Tran Nam Trung - A/C.3/78/SR.12
Yemen
Al-mashehari, Sarah Ahmed Ahmed - A/C.3/78/SR.55
Balobaid, Ali Mabkhot Salem - A/C.3/78/SR.11; A/C.3/78/SR.14

RIGHTS OF THE CHILD (Agenda item 67) (continued)

Zambia
Milambo, Chola - A/C.3/78/SR.13

RULE OF LAW (Agenda item 83)

Algeria
Bouchedoub, Mohamed Faiz - A/C.6/78/SR.18
Angola
Luemba, Mateus Pedro - A/C.6/78/SR.19
Argentina
Mainero, Martín Juan - A/C.6/78/SR.16
Armenia
Galstyan, Tigran - A/C.6/78/SR.18
ASEAN
Arumpac-Marte, Azela Guerrero (Philippines) - A/C.6/78/SR.15
Azerbaijan
Musayev, Tofig - A/C.6/78/SR.19
Belarus
Evseenko, Pavel - A/C.6/78/SR.16
Bolivia (Plurinational State of)
Ríos, Carmen Rosa - A/C.6/78/SR.17
Botswana
Mokhawa, Gladys - A/C.6/78/SR.18
Brazil
Braoios, Victor Silveira - A/C.6/78/SR.16
Brunei Darussalam
Sahrip, Nazihah Mohd - A/C.6/78/SR.18
Burkina Faso
Ganou, Oumarou - A/C.6/78/SR.17
Cameroon
Nyanid, Zacharie Serge Raoul - A/C.6/78/SR.16
Canada
Agnello, Alexander - A/C.6/78/SR.15
Chile
Hernández Chávez, José Juan - A/C.6/78/SR.18
China
Li, Linlin - A/C.6/78/SR.16
Colombia
Solano Ramírez, Lucía Teresa - A/C.6/78/SR.16
Congo
Douckaga Nzengui, Nicaise Servais - A/C.6/78/SR.19
Coordinating Bureau of the Non-Aligned Countries
Heidari, Bahram (Iran (Islamic Republic of)) - A/C.6/78/SR.15
Costa Rica
Chan Valverde, Maritza - A/C.6/78/SR.16
Cuba
Mora Fonseca, Vladimir - A/C.6/78/SR.16
Denmark
Laursen, Erik - A/C.6/78/SR.15
Djibouti
Moussa, Moussa Mohamed - A/C.6/78/SR.17
Dominican Republic
Cedano, Joan Margarita - A/C.6/78/SR.18
Ecuador
Escobar Ullauri, Pablo - A/C.6/78/SR.16

RULE OF LAW (Agenda item 83) (continued)

Egypt
Nouh, Amr Mohamed Mosaad - A/C.6/78/SR.16
El Salvador
Flores Soto, Ligia Lorena - A/C.6/78/SR.18
Equatorial Guinea
Nze Mansogo, Estela Mercedes - A/C.6/78/SR.18
Eritrea
Giorgio, Amanuel - A/C.6/78/SR.17
Ethiopia
Alemayehu, Betelihem Taye - A/C.6/78/SR.18
European Public Law Organization
Melchionna, Luca - A/C.6/78/SR.19
European Union
Popan, Simona - A/C.6/78/SR.15
Georgia
Kupradze, Sopio - A/C.6/78/SR.18
Ghana
Hackman, Khalilah - A/C.6/78/SR.17
Group of Arab States
Bisharat, Nadien Isam Fraih (Jordan) - A/C.6/78/SR.15
Group of Friends in Defence of the Charter of the United Nations
Pérez Ayestarán, Joaquín Alberto (Venezuela (Bolivarian Republic of)) - A/C.6/78/SR.15
Group of Friends of the Rule of Law
Marschik, Alexander (Austria) - A/C.6/78/SR.15
Guatemala
Rodríguez Mancia, Carla María - A/C.6/78/SR.15
Guinea
Camara, Mohamed Nassir - A/C.6/78/SR.18
Guyana
Daw, Texine Wonda - A/C.6/78/SR.18
Holy See
Caccia, Gabriele Giordano - A/C.6/78/SR.19
India
Bhat, Kajal - A/C.6/78/SR.18
Indonesia
Aron, Andy - A/C.6/78/SR.18
International Development Law Organization
Brinkman, Henk-Jan - A/C.6/78/SR.19
Iran (Islamic Republic of)
Heidari, Bahram - A/C.6/78/SR.16
Israel
Cappon, Noam - A/C.6/78/SR.19
Japan
Nagano, Shunsuke - A/C.6/78/SR.18
Justice Action Coalition
Tahzib-Lie, Bahia (Netherlands (Kingdom of the)) - A/C.6/78/SR.15
Kenya
Nyakoe, Catherine Nyaboke - A/C.6/78/SR.18
Kuwait
Alharbi, Saoud Abdullah - A/C.6/78/SR.19
Lao People's Democratic Republic
Vannasin, Soudchai - A/C.6/78/SR.18
Latvia
Ilgis, Olegs - A/C.6/78/SR.15

RULE OF LAW (Agenda item 83) (continued)

Lebanon
Hitti, Youssef - A/C.6/78/SR.19
Liechtenstein
Oehri, Myriam - A/C.6/78/SR.15
Malaysia
Abd Karim, Nur Azura Binti - A/C.6/78/SR.19
Maldives
Zuhuree, Ibrahim - A/C.6/78/SR.17
Mauritania
Sao, Mariam - A/C.6/78/SR.16
Mexico
Jiménez Alegría, Natalia - A/C.6/78/SR.18
Morocco
Bouziane, Zineb - A/C.6/78/SR.19
Mozambique
Saranga, Geraldo - A/C.6/78/SR.18
Myanmar
Tun, Kyaw Moe - A/C.6/78/SR.18
Nepal
Ray, Kaushal Kishor - A/C.6/78/SR.17
Nicaragua
Hermida Castillo, Jaime - A/C.6/78/SR.16
Nigeria
Ajayi, Eniola Olaitan - A/C.6/78/SR.17
Oman
Al-Ajmi, Mohammed - A/C.6/78/SR.18
Pakistan
Akram, Munir - A/C.6/78/SR.16
Paraguay
Giret Soto, David Antonio - A/C.6/78/SR.18
Peru
Falconi, Alessandra - A/C.6/78/SR.16
Philippines
Arumpac-Marte, Azela Guerrero - A/C.6/78/SR.16
Qatar
Al-Kaabi, Soud Abdulaziz - A/C.6/78/SR.16
Republic of Korea
Kim, Hyunsoo - A/C.6/78/SR.18
Romania
Feruţă, Cornel - A/C.6/78/SR.18
Russian Federation
Proskuryakov, Alexander S. - A/C.6/78/SR.17; A/C.6/78/SR.19
Saudi Arabia
Almhawas, Ibtihal - A/C.6/78/SR.18
Senegal
Ndoye, Abdou - A/C.6/78/SR.18
Sierra Leone
Kebe, Hawanatu - A/C.6/78/SR.19
Singapore
Seah, Mark - A/C.6/78/SR.15
Slovenia
Šebenik, Nataša - A/C.6/78/SR.16
South Africa
Motsepe, Keke Mantsho - A/C.6/78/SR.16
Sri Lanka
Pieris, Peter Mohan Maithri - A/C.6/78/SR.16
State of Palestine
Sayej, Loureen O.A. - A/C.6/78/SR.19

RULE OF LAW (Agenda item 83) (continued)

Sudan
Mohammed, Ammar Mohammed Mahmoud - A/C.6/78/SR.16
Switzerland
Zerbe, Yannick - A/C.6/78/SR.16
Syrian Arab Republic
Khaddour, Mhd. Riyad - A/C.6/78/SR.18; A/C.6/78/SR.37
Thailand
Chindawongse, Suriya - A/C.6/78/SR.16
Tunisia
Ben Lagha, Adel - A/C.6/78/SR.18
Uganda
Muhumuza, Duncan Laki - A/C.6/78/SR.18
UN. Deputy Secretary-General
Mohammed, Amina J. - A/C.6/78/SR.16
UN. General Assembly. 6th Committee. Bureau
Jiménez Alegría, Natalia (Mexico) - A/C.6/78/SR.37
UN. General Assembly. 6th Committee. Rapporteur
Moussa, Moussa Mohamed (Djibouti) - A/78/PV.45
UN. Group of African States
Ikondere, Marvin (Uganda) - A/C.6/78/SR.16
United Arab Emirates
Al Marzooqi, Tahreer - A/C.6/78/SR.19
United Kingdom
Lito, Melina - A/C.6/78/SR.16
United States
Grosso, Elizabeth Maryanne - A/C.6/78/SR.16
Uruguay
Katz Pavlotzky, Alejandro Leonel - A/C.6/78/SR.18
Viet Nam
Dang, Hoang Giang - A/C.6/78/SR.16
Zambia
Muzumbwe-Katongo, Miyoba - A/C.6/78/SR.18

RURAL POVERTY (Agenda item 21b)

Algeria
Latrous, Mohamed-Esseghir - A/C.2/78/SR.17
Alliance of Small Island States
Lautasi, Isaia (Samoa) - A/C.2/78/SR.16
Angola
Luemba, Mateus Pedro - A/C.2/78/SR.16
ASEAN
Dang, Hoang Giang (Viet Nam) - A/C.2/78/SR.16
Bahrain
Alsindi, Yusuf Khaled - A/C.2/78/SR.17
Bangladesh
Hossain, Faruk - A/C.2/78/SR.17
Belarus
Pisarevich, Vadim - A/C.2/78/SR.16
Bolivia (Plurinational State of)
Zambrana Flores, Carlos Iván - A/C.2/78/SR.16
Brazil
Santos, Luiz Felipe Rosa dos - A/C.2/78/SR.17
Burkina Faso
Bokoum, Mahamadou - A/C.2/78/SR.16
Cabo Verde
Romualdo, Tania Serafim Yvonne - A/C.2/78/SR.17

RURAL POVERTY (Agenda item 21b) (continued)

Cameroon
Etoundi Ayissi, Joseph - A/C.2/78/SR.16
Caribbean Community
Wallace, Brian Christopher Manley (Jamaica) - A/C.2/78/SR.16
China
Cao, Liwen - A/C.2/78/SR.16
Liu, Liqun - A/C.2/78/SR.22
Congo
Gabi, Emery - A/C.2/78/SR.17
Costa Rica
Chan Valverde, Maritza - A/C.2/78/SR.17
Democratic People's Republic of Korea
Jo, Tong Hyon - A/C.2/78/SR.16
Ecuador
Barba Bustos, Irina Alexandra - A/C.2/78/SR.17
El Salvador
Barahona Figueroa, Andrea Alejandra - A/C.2/78/SR.16
Ethiopia
Kindeya, Tsigabu Girmay - A/C.2/78/SR.17
European Union
Martín Couce, Adrián (Spain) - A/C.2/78/SR.22
FAO
Davis, Benjamin - A/C.2/78/SR.16
Group of 77
Guevara Rodríguez, Adiel (Cuba) - A/C.2/78/SR.16
Torres Seara, Dalia Marlen (Cuba) - A/C.2/78/SR.21
Group of Friends in Defence of the Charter of the United Nations
Marín Sevilla, Asbina (Venezuela (Bolivarian Republic of)) - A/C.2/78/SR.16
Group of Landlocked Developing Countries
Mokhawa, Gladys (Botswana) - A/C.2/78/SR.16
Group of Least Developed Countries
Adhikari, Pramita (Nepal) - A/C.2/78/SR.16
Guatemala
Rodríguez Mancia, Carla María - A/C.2/78/SR.17
Guyana
Alkins, Royston - A/C.2/78/SR.17
Haiti
Vilmenay Joseph, Linouse - A/C.2/78/SR.17
India
Gahlot, Petal - A/C.2/78/SR.16
Indonesia
Prabowo, Hari - A/C.2/78/SR.17
Iran (Islamic Republic of)
Jalili, Tahereh - A/C.2/78/SR.16
Italy
Massari, Maurizio - A/C.2/78/SR.16
Kenya
Nzumbu, Christine - A/C.2/78/SR.16
Kuwait
Almezyad, Fatma - A/C.2/78/SR.17
Lesotho
Nena, Matete - A/C.2/78/SR.17
Malawi
Chivundu, Renata - A/C.2/78/SR.17

RURAL POVERTY (Agenda item 21b) (continued)

Malaysia
Zulasri Bin Rosdi, Muhammad - A/C.2/78/SR.17
Maldives
Nashwa, Fathimath - A/C.2/78/SR.16
Mali
Coulibaly, Kanisson - A/C.2/78/SR.17
Mexico
Mendoza Elguea, Sylvia Paola - A/C.2/78/SR.22
Vásquez Solano, Leonel - A/C.2/78/SR.16
Mozambique
Maure, Adnito - A/C.2/78/SR.17
Myanmar
Tun, Kyaw Moe - A/C.2/78/SR.17
Namibia
Gertze, Neville Melvin - A/C.2/78/SR.16
Nicaragua
Gutiérrez Tórrez, Lisandra Marina - A/C.2/78/SR.17
Niger
Moussa, Mahaman - A/C.2/78/SR.17
Nigeria
Maitafsir, Musa Garba - A/C.2/78/SR.17
Pakistan
Javaid, Hafiza Humaira - A/C.2/78/SR.17
Panama
Concepción Jaramillo, Markova - A/C.2/78/SR.16
Peru
Napurí Pita, Andrés - A/C.2/78/SR.17
Philippines
Beriana, Charlene Aravejo - A/C.2/78/SR.16
Qatar
Al-Khayareen, Abdulla Ghanim - A/C.2/78/SR.16
Russian Federation
Aristov, Dmitry S. - A/C.2/78/SR.17
Saudi Arabia
Bakhsh, Khalid - A/C.2/78/SR.17
Serbia
Mart, Saša - A/C.2/78/SR.17
Sierra Leone
George, Alan Ebun - A/C.2/78/SR.17
South Africa
Mandla, Bulelani - A/C.2/78/SR.17
Tajikistan
Hasanova, Tahmina - A/C.2/78/SR.17
Thailand
Sangkhapreecha, Kantapon - A/C.2/78/SR.16
Togo
Debataba, Yawa - A/C.2/78/SR.17
Türkiye
Demir, İlknur - A/C.2/78/SR.17
Ukraine
Leschenko, Volodymyr - A/C.2/78/SR.16
UN. General Assembly. 2nd Committee. Rapporteur
Gatev, Ivaylo (Bulgaria) - A/78/PV.49
United Arab Emirates
Almahmoud, Ahmed Abdelrahman Ahmed - A/C.2/78/SR.16
United Republic of Tanzania
Kattanga, Hussein A. - A/C.2/78/SR.17

RURAL POVERTY (Agenda item 21b) (continued)

United States
Lawrence, Jason N. - A/C.2/78/SR.22
Leonard, Mary Beth - A/C.2/78/SR.17
Viet Nam
Nguyen, Hoang Nguyen - A/C.2/78/SR.16
Yemen
Al-barati, Abdulrahman Hasan Yahya - A/C.2/78/SR.17
Zambia
Mungandi, Lubasi - A/C.2/78/SR.17

RURAL WOMEN (Agenda item 25a)

Algeria
Samai, Rahma - A/C.3/78/SR.9; A/C.3/78/SR.49
Australia
Kim, Yunei - A/C.3/78/SR.49
Azerbaijan
Ahangari, Narmin - A/C.3/78/SR.10
Burkina Faso
Niamba Congo, Salamata Odette - A/C.3/78/SR.49
Colombia
Sánchez García, Nathalia - A/C.3/78/SR.7; A/C.3/78/SR.49
Egypt
Mostafa Rizk, Heba - A/C.3/78/SR.10; A/C.3/78/SR.49
Ethiopia
Arega, Elleni Henok - A/C.3/78/SR.10
European Union
Alonso Giganto, Ana María (Spain) - A/C.3/78/SR.49
FAO
Ngirwa-Mpesha, Doris - A/C.3/78/SR.10
Gambia
Jaiteh, Amadou - A/C.3/78/SR.49
Gulf Cooperation Council
Al Rawahi, Abdulhalim Mubarak Saloom (Oman) - A/C.3/78/SR.49
Guyana
Rodrigues-Birkett, Carolyn - A/C.3/78/SR.10
Indonesia
Imanuel, Fnu - A/C.3/78/SR.49
Iran (Islamic Republic of)
Arab Bafrani, Fatemeh - A/C.3/78/SR.49
Iraq
Al-Khaqani, Hassan Jabbar - A/C.3/78/SR.49
Italy
Napolitano, Annarita - A/C.3/78/SR.7
Libya
Hamed, Ashraf A.O. - A/C.3/78/SR.49
Malaysia
Escopper Zumilla, Michael Jawa - A/C.3/78/SR.49
Mauritania
Guera, Soueda El - A/C.3/78/SR.49
Mexico
Santa Ana Vara, Alma Esperanza - A/C.3/78/SR.49
Mongolia
Vorshilov, Enkhbold - A/C.3/78/SR.49

RURAL WOMEN (Agenda item 25a) (continued)

New Zealand
Fruean, Tausala - A/C.3/78/SR.49
Nicaragua
Jiménez, Jasser - A/C.3/78/SR.49
Niger
Seydou, Abdoul Fadh Mahamadou - A/C.3/78/SR.49
Nigeria
Asaju, Bola - A/C.3/78/SR.49
Romania
Mihail, Ioana-Cristina - A/C.3/78/SR.7
Senegal
Diouf, Aminata - A/C.3/78/SR.49
Sovereign Order of Malta
Lucii, Costanza - A/C.3/78/SR.10
Syrian Arab Republic
Altarsha, Elie - A/C.3/78/SR.49
UN-Women
Seymour, Daniel - A/C.3/78/SR.7
United States
Korac, Sofija - A/C.3/78/SR.49
Yemen
Al-mashehari, Sarah Ahmed Ahmed - A/C.3/78/SR.49

SANCTIONS—INTERNATIONAL RELATIONS (Agenda item 71b)

Belarus
Kryvaltsevich, Aliaksei - A/C.3/78/SR.28
Pilipenko, Igor - A/C.3/78/SR.48
Cambodia
Eat, Sophea - A/C.3/78/SR.26
Chile
Nishihara, Carmen - A/C.3/78/SR.48
China
Yang, Xiaokun - A/C.3/78/SR.28
Zhang, Jun - A/C.3/78/SR.24
Coordinating Bureau of the Non-Aligned Countries
González Behmaras, Alejandro (Cuba) - A/C.3/78/SR.48
Novruz, Leyla (Azerbaijan) - A/C.3/78/SR.28
Cuba
González Behmaras, Alejandro - A/C.3/78/SR.48
Lamigueiro Cañedo, Ivette - A/C.3/78/SR.28
Romero Puentes, Yusnier - A/C.3/78/SR.25
Eritrea
Gebrekidan, Zebib - A/C.3/78/SR.28
European Union
Alonso Giganto, Ana María (Spain) - A/C.3/78/SR.48
Group of Friends in Defence of the Charter of the United Nations
Poveda Brito, Robert Alexander (Venezuela (Bolivarian Republic of)) - A/C.3/78/SR.28; A/C.3/78/SR.48
Iran (Islamic Republic of)
Arab Bafrani, Fatemeh - A/C.3/78/SR.25; A/C.3/78/SR.28
Malaysia
Escopper Zumilla, Michael Jawa - A/C.3/78/SR.28

SANCTIONS—INTERNATIONAL RELATIONS (Agenda item 71b) (continued)

Mali
Maiga, Aissata Ibrahim - A/C.3/78/SR.26
Nicaragua
Hermida Castillo, Jaime - A/C.3/78/SR.26
Pichardo Urbina, Eleane Yaoska - A/C.3/78/SR.28
Niger
Seydou, Abdoul Fadh Mahamadou - A/C.3/78/SR.48
Republic of Moldova
Leuca, Gheorghe - A/C.3/78/SR.25
Russian Federation
Kuzmenkov, Stepan Y. - A/C.3/78/SR.28
South Africa
Passmoor, Jonathan David - A/C.3/78/SR.28
Southern African Development Community
Cruz, Francisco José da (Angola) - A/C.3/78/SR.26
Sovereign Order of Malta
Muñoz, Zachary N. - A/C.3/78/SR.28
Syrian Arab Republic
Alnwelati, Mohammad Feras - A/C.3/78/SR.28
UN. Human Rights Council. Special Rapporteur on the Negative Impact of Unilateral Coercive Measures on the Enjoyment of Human Rights
Douhan, Alena - A/C.3/78/SR.28
United Kingdom
Lundy, Phoebe - A/C.3/78/SR.48
United States
Merron, Eric - A/C.3/78/SR.48
Venezuela (Bolivarian Republic of)
Poveda Brito, Robert Alexander - A/C.3/78/SR.28
Zimbabwe
Manyanga, Garikai - A/C.3/78/SR.28

SCIENCE AND TECHNOLOGY—DEVELOPMENT (Agenda item 19a)

Angola
Cruz, Francisco José da - A/C.2/78/SR.10
Armenia
Babikyan, Araksya - A/C.2/78/SR.10
ASEAN
Muhamad, Ahmad Faisal (Malaysia) - A/C.2/78/SR.10
Burkina Faso
Barro, Braima - A/C.2/78/SR.10
Caribbean Community
Wallace, Brian Christopher Manley (Jamaica) - A/C.2/78/SR.10
China
Zhao, Haibo - A/C.2/78/SR.10
Colombia
Ríos Serna, Manuela - A/C.2/78/SR.10
Costa Rica
Zamora Zumbado, Leticia María - A/C.2/78/SR.11
El Salvador
Mira Ramírez, Walter José - A/C.2/78/SR.10
Ethiopia
Muktar, Anwar - A/C.2/78/SR.11

SCIENCE AND TECHNOLOGY—DEVELOPMENT (Agenda item 19a) (continued)

Group of 77
Guevara Rodríguez, Adiel (Cuba) - A/C.2/78/SR.10
Torres Seara, Dalia Marlen (Cuba) - A/C.2/78/SR.21
Group of Landlocked Developing Countries
Motsumi, Lorato (Botswana) - A/C.2/78/SR.10
Group of Least Developed Countries
Dhungel, Purushottam (Nepal) - A/C.2/78/SR.10
Guyana
Rodrigues-Birkett, Carolyn - A/C.2/78/SR.10
India
Gahlot, Petal - A/C.2/78/SR.10
Iran (Islamic Republic of)
Jalili, Tahereh - A/C.2/78/SR.10
Lao People's Democratic Republic
Xaiyavong, Thanouphet - A/C.2/78/SR.11
Mexico
Curzio Vila, Elena - A/C.2/78/SR.10
Nigeria
Adenopo, Adeyinka A. - A/C.2/78/SR.10
Pakistan
Shafique, Umar - A/C.2/78/SR.10
Philippines
Bregala, Dennis Borromeo - A/C.2/78/SR.11
Russian Federation
Aristov, Dmitry S. - A/C.2/78/SR.10
Serbia
Mart, Saša - A/C.2/78/SR.11
Sierra Leone
Alghali, Francess Piagie - A/C.2/78/SR.11
Singapore
Ching, Martha - A/C.2/78/SR.10
South Africa
Mpama, Sibusiso Qetello - A/C.2/78/SR.11
Sri Lanka
Gunaratna, Pahala Rallage Sanathana Sugeeshwara - A/C.2/78/SR.11
UN. General Assembly. 2nd Committee. Rapporteur
Gatev, Ivaylo (Bulgaria) - A/78/PV.49
UNCTAD
González Sanz, Angel - A/C.2/78/SR.10
United Kingdom
Baric, Ana - A/C.2/78/SR.22
United States
Lawrence, Jason N. - A/C.2/78/SR.22
Zambia
Milambo, Chola - A/C.2/78/SR.11

SCIENCE AND TECHNOLOGY—INTERNATIONAL SECURITY (Agenda item 98)

India
Bedi, Anmol Sher Singh - A/C.1/78/PV.21
Iran (Islamic Republic of)
Ghorbanpour Najafabadi, Mohammad - A/C.1/78/PV.29
UN. General Assembly. 1st Committee. Rapporteur
Balouji, Heidar Ali (Iran (Islamic Republic of)) - A/78/PV.42

SCIENCE AND TECHNOLOGY—INTERNATIONAL SECURITY (Agenda item 98) (continued)

United States
Turner, Bruce - A/C.1/78/PV.29

SELF-DETERMINATION OF PEOPLES (Agenda item 70)

Algeria
Hassani, Billel - A/C.3/78/SR.42; A/C.3/78/SR.43
Argentina
Alvarez, Maximiliano Javier - A/C.3/78/SR.49
González, María Florencia - A/C.3/78/SR.56
Bangladesh
Monica, Mosammat Shahanara - A/C.3/78/SR.49
Muhith, Muhammad A. - A/C.3/78/SR.43
Bolivia (Plurinational State of)
Caldera Gutiérrez, Fiorella - A/C.3/78/SR.42
China
Dai, Bing - A/C.3/78/SR.40
Cuba
González Behmaras, Alejandro - A/78/PV.50; A/C.3/78/SR.42; A/C.3/78/SR.49
Egypt
Mostafa Rizk, Heba - A/78/PV.50; A/C.3/78/SR.43
Germany
Geisler, Michael Alexander - A/C.3/78/SR.49
India
Sonkar, Suman - A/C.3/78/SR.41; A/C.3/78/SR.56
Indonesia
Dhanutirto, Mariska Dwianti - A/C.3/78/SR.42; A/C.3/78/SR.49
Iran (Islamic Republic of)
Arab Bafrani, Fatemeh - A/C.3/78/SR.49
Ghanei, Mohsen - A/C.3/78/SR.40
Iraq
Yaseen, Safaa - A/C.3/78/SR.41
Israel
Mimran Rosenberg, Avital - A/C.3/78/SR.42; A/C.3/78/SR.49
Kuwait
Al Munaifi, Shahad - A/C.3/78/SR.41
League of Arab States
Abdallah, Amina Mohamed - A/C.3/78/SR.43
Liechtenstein
Edbrooke, Matthew David - A/C.3/78/SR.40
Malaysia
Rizal, Nizhan Faraz Bin - A/C.3/78/SR.49
Morocco
Moutchou, Majda - A/C.3/78/SR.43
Mozambique
Serage, Bruno Bernardo - A/C.3/78/SR.42
Namibia
Ashipala, Sevelina - A/C.3/78/SR.40
Nicaragua
Pichardo Urbina, Eleane Yaoska - A/C.3/78/SR.42
Organisation of Islamic Cooperation
Mostafa Rizk, Heba (Egypt) - A/C.3/78/SR.49
Pakistan
Akram, Munir - A/C.3/78/SR.40; A/C.3/78/SR.56

SELF-DETERMINATION OF PEOPLES (Agenda item 70) (continued)

Russian Federation
Kuzmenkov, Stepan Y. - A/C.3/78/SR.40
Saudi Arabia
Albadr, Saleh - A/C.3/78/SR.41
South Africa
Passmoor, Jonathan David - A/C.3/78/SR.43; A/C.3/78/SR.49
Spain
Bellmont Roldán, Xavier - A/C.3/78/SR.56
State of Palestine
Salem, Sahar K.H. - A/C.3/78/SR.49
Syrian Arab Republic
Altarsha, Elie - A/C.3/78/SR.42; A/C.3/78/SR.49
UN. Assistant Secretary-General for Human Rights
Brands Kehris, Ilze - A/C.3/78/SR.40
UN. General Assembly. 3rd Committee. Rapporteur
Poveda Brito, Robert Alexander (Venezuela (Bolivarian Republic of)) - A/78/PV.50
United Kingdom
Eckersley, Fergus - A/C.3/78/SR.49
United States
Johnson, Timothy J. - A/C.3/78/SR.56
Shrier, Jonathan - A/C.3/78/SR.49
Yemen
Balobaid, Ali Mabkhot Salem - A/C.3/78/SR.43

SEXUAL ORIENTATION (Agenda item 71b)

Australia
Hamer, David - A/C.3/78/SR.39
Belgium
Bauwens, Gilles - A/C.3/78/SR.39
Brazil
Leite, Patricia Soares - A/C.3/78/SR.39
Canada
Arbeiter, Richard - A/C.3/78/SR.26
Morin, Cassandra - A/C.3/78/SR.39
Chile
Ruidíaz, René - A/C.3/78/SR.39
Cuba
Valido Martínez, Yoangel - A/C.3/78/SR.39
Estonia
Tammsaar, Rein - A/C.3/78/SR.26
European Union
Greffine, Venise Catherine - A/C.3/78/SR.39
France
Freudenreich, Anne - A/C.3/78/SR.39
Georgia
Lortkipanidze, Ekaterine - A/C.3/78/SR.39
Germany
Krabatsch, Ann-Jasmin - A/C.3/78/SR.39
Iceland
Óskarsson, Thórdur Aegir - A/C.3/78/SR.39
Valtýsson, Jörundur - A/C.3/78/SR.26
Ireland
Swan, Ellen - A/C.3/78/SR.39
Japan
Akita, Mio - A/C.3/78/SR.39

SEXUAL ORIENTATION (Agenda item 71b) (continued)

LGBTI Core Group
Maes, Olivier (Luxembourg) - A/C.3/78/SR.24
Squeff, María del Carmen (Argentina) - A/C.3/78/SR.39
Luxembourg
Toschi, Stéphanie - A/C.3/78/SR.39
Malta
Kuymizakis, Adam - A/C.3/78/SR.39
Mexico
Pedraza Calleja, Rodrigo - A/C.3/78/SR.39
Netherlands (Kingdom of the)
Reichwein, Mark - A/C.3/78/SR.39
Peru
Pedroza, David - A/C.3/78/SR.39
Portugal
Marinho, Joana Almeida - A/C.3/78/SR.39
South Africa
Passmoor, Jonathan David - A/C.3/78/SR.39
Spain
Alonso Giganto, Ana María - A/C.3/78/SR.39
Uganda
Nabeta, Celia Kafureka - A/C.3/78/SR.27
Ukraine
Tokarska, Anastasiia - A/C.3/78/SR.39
UN. Human Rights Council. Independent Expert on Protection against Violence and Discrimination based on Sexual Orientation and Gender Identity
Madrigal-Borloz, Victor - A/C.3/78/SR.39
United Kingdom
White, Megan Marie - A/C.3/78/SR.39
United States
Lang, Dylan - A/C.3/78/SR.39
Uruguay
Riva Grela, Juan José - A/C.3/78/SR.39

SLAVERY (Agenda item 71a)

Australia
Hamer, David - A/C.3/78/SR.21
Chile
Fernández Carter, Catalina - A/C.3/78/SR.21
China
Zhang, Tianhao - A/C.3/78/SR.21
European Union
Szelivanov, Julia - A/C.3/78/SR.21
Japan
Tonai, Akihiro - A/C.3/78/SR.21
Liechtenstein
Oehri, Noah - A/C.3/78/SR.21
Russian Federation
Kuzmenkov, Stepan Y. - A/C.3/78/SR.21
UN. Assistant Secretary-General for Human Rights
Brands Kehris, Ilze - A/C.3/78/SR.18
UN. Human Rights Council. Special Rapporteur on Contemporary Forms of Slavery
Obokata, Tomoya - A/C.3/78/SR.21
United Kingdom
Manzare, Max - A/C.3/78/SR.21

SLAVERY (Agenda item 71a) (continued)

United States
Smyre, Calvin - A/C.3/78/SR.21

SLAVERY—MEMORIALS (Agenda item 118)

(personal capacity)
King, Yolanda - A/78/PV.64
Caribbean Community
Rodrigue, Antonio (Haiti) - A/78/PV.64
Equatorial Guinea
Ndong Mba, Anatolio - A/78/PV.64
Haiti
Rodrigue, Antonio - A/78/PV.64
Nigeria
Asaju, Bola - A/78/PV.64
UN. General Assembly. President
Francis, Dennis (Trinidad and Tobago) - A/78/PV.64
UN. Group of African States
Gurhan, Amina (Uganda) - A/78/PV.64
UN. Group of Asia-Pacific States
Alalaiwat, Suma Sameer (Bahrain) - A/78/PV.64
UN. Group of Latin American and Caribbean States
Rodríguez Mancia, Carla María (Guatemala) - A/78/PV.64
UN. Group of Western European and Other States
Zahneisen, Thomas (Germany) - A/78/PV.64
UN. Under-Secretary-General and Chef de Cabinet
Rattray, Courtenay - A/78/PV.64
United States
Carty, Lisa A. - A/78/PV.64
University of the West Indies
Beckles, Hilary - A/78/PV.64

SMALL ARMS—ILLICIT TRAFFIC (Agenda item 99p)

Algeria
Lebbaz, Larbi Abdelfattah - A/C.1/78/PV.19
ASEAN
Mao, Tithiarun (Cambodia) - A/C.1/78/PV.17
Austria
Kmentt, Alexander - A/C.1/78/PV.18
Bangladesh
Shatil, Toufiq Islam - A/C.1/78/PV.18
Burkina Faso
Ganou, Oumarou - A/C.1/78/PV.18
Caribbean Community
Douglas, Craig Barrington (Jamaica) - A/C.1/78/PV.18
Chile
Vidal Mercado, Jorge Andrés - A/C.1/78/PV.18
China
Shen, Jian - A/C.1/78/PV.19
Colombia
Quintero Correa, Nohra María - A/C.1/78/PV.18; A/C.1/78/PV.28
Coordinating Bureau of the Non-Aligned Countries
Kristanti, Maria Benedicta Diah (Indonesia) - A/C.1/78/PV.17

SMALL ARMS—ILLICIT TRAFFIC (Agenda item 99p) (continued)

Costa Rica
Chan Valverde, Maritza - A/C.1/78/PV.18
Cuba
Gómez Sardiñas, Yiliam - A/C.1/78/PV.19
Egypt
Hegazy, Abdelrhman Mohamed Farid - A/C.1/78/PV.18; A/C.1/78/PV.28
El Salvador
Rodríguez Acosta, Julia Elizabeth - A/C.1/78/PV.18
Equatorial Guinea
Edu Mbasogo, Marcial - A/C.1/78/PV.19
European Union
Karczmarz, Michał - A/C.1/78/PV.18
France
Petit, Camille - A/C.1/78/PV.18
Germany
Göbel, Thomas - A/C.1/78/PV.18
Group of Arab States
Alqaisi, Sultan Natheir Mustafa (Jordan) - A/C.1/78/PV.28
Guatemala
Rodríguez Mancia, Carla María - A/C.1/78/PV.18
Indonesia
Sirie, Mochammad Iqbal - A/C.1/78/PV.18
Israel
Sharoni, Benjamin - A/C.1/78/PV.28
Japan
Nagai, Nana - A/C.1/78/PV.27
Ogasawara, Ichiro - A/C.1/78/PV.18
Lao People's Democratic Republic
Souliyong, So Inxay - A/C.1/78/PV.19
Lesotho
Nena, Matete - A/C.1/78/PV.19
Malaysia
Noordin, Shamsuri - A/C.1/78/PV.18
Mauritania
Mohamedou, El Hadj Lehbib - A/C.1/78/PV.19
Nigeria
Mahmud, Mohammed Lawal - A/C.1/78/PV.19
Philippines
Reyes, Narciso - A/C.1/78/PV.18
Republic of Korea
Yoon, Seong-mee - A/C.1/78/PV.18
Saudi Arabia
Bin Shafi, Mohammed - A/C.1/78/PV.19
Singapore
Jiamin, Liu - A/C.1/78/PV.18
South Africa
Lagardien, Yaseen - A/C.1/78/PV.18
Sri Lanka
Pieris, Peter Mohan Maithri - A/C.1/78/PV.18
Timor-Leste
Alves, Nuno Moniz - A/C.1/78/PV.18
Togo
Tchalare, Abd-el Kader Yasmin - A/C.1/78/PV.19
Türkiye
Çetin, Ahmet Erman - A/C.1/78/PV.18

SMALL ARMS—ILLICIT TRAFFIC (Agenda item 99p) (continued)

UN. Group of African States
Mahmud, Mohammed Lawal (Nigeria) - A/C.1/78/PV.17
Uruguay
Eustathiou de los Santos, Matías Andrés - A/C.1/78/PV.18

SMALL ARMS—ILLICIT TRAFFIC—ASSISTANCE (Agenda item 99n)

Algeria
Lebbaz, Larbi Abdelfattah - A/C.1/78/PV.19
Argentina
Guerra, Hugo Emmanuel - A/C.1/78/PV.18
ASEAN
Mao, Tithiarun (Cambodia) - A/C.1/78/PV.17
Australia
Carr, Michelle - A/C.1/78/PV.19
Austria
Kmentt, Alexander - A/C.1/78/PV.18
Bangladesh
Shatil, Toufiq Islam - A/C.1/78/PV.18
Caribbean Community
Douglas, Craig Barrington (Jamaica) - A/C.1/78/PV.18
China
Shen, Jian - A/C.1/78/PV.19
Colombia
Quintero Correa, Nohra María - A/C.1/78/PV.18
Coordinating Bureau of the Non-Aligned Countries
Kristanti, Maria Benedicta Diah (Indonesia) - A/C.1/78/PV.17
Costa Rica
Chan Valverde, Maritza - A/C.1/78/PV.18
Côte d'Ivoire
Moriko, Tiémoko - A/C.1/78/PV.18
Cuba
Gómez Sardiñas, Yiliam - A/C.1/78/PV.19
Egypt
Hegazy, Abdelrhman Mohamed Farid - A/C.1/78/PV.18
El Salvador
Rodríguez Acosta, Julia Elizabeth - A/C.1/78/PV.18
European Union
Karczmarz, Michał - A/C.1/78/PV.18
France
Petit, Camille - A/C.1/78/PV.18
Greece
Christoglou, Konstantinos - A/C.1/78/PV.19
Holy See
Caccia, Gabriele Giordano - A/C.1/78/PV.20
Indonesia
Sirie, Mochammad Iqbal - A/C.1/78/PV.18
Iran (Islamic Republic of)
Ghorbanpour Najafabadi, Mohammad - A/C.1/78/PV.28
Lao People's Democratic Republic
Souliyong, So Inxay - A/C.1/78/PV.19
Lesotho
Nena, Matete - A/C.1/78/PV.19

SMALL ARMS—ILLICIT TRAFFIC—ASSISTANCE (Agenda item 99n) (continued)

Malaysia
Noordin, Shamsuri - A/C.1/78/PV.18
Mauritania
Mohamedou, El Hadj Lehbib - A/C.1/78/PV.19
Mexico
Sánchez Kiesslich, Eduardo Alcibiades - A/C.1/78/PV.18
Philippines
Reyes, Narciso - A/C.1/78/PV.18
Republic of Korea
Yoon, Seong-mee - A/C.1/78/PV.18
Russian Federation
Belousov, Andrey I. - A/C.1/78/PV.19
Singapore
Jiamin, Liu - A/C.1/78/PV.18
South Africa
Lagardien, Yaseen - A/C.1/78/PV.18
Sri Lanka
Pieris, Peter Mohan Maithri - A/C.1/78/PV.18
Timor-Leste
Alves, Nuno Moniz - A/C.1/78/PV.18
Togo
Tchalare, Abd-el Kader Yasmin - A/C.1/78/PV.19
Türkiye
Çetin, Ahmet Erman - A/C.1/78/PV.18
UN. Group of African States
Mahmud, Mohammed Lawal (Nigeria) - A/C.1/78/PV.17
Viet Nam
Mai, Ngan Ha - A/C.1/78/PV.18

SMALL ISLAND DEVELOPING STATES—PROGRAMMES OF ACTION (Agenda item 18b)

Alliance of Small Island States
Bartley, Matilda (Samoa) - A/C.2/78/SR.22
Luteru, Fatumanava-o-Upolu III Pa'olelei (Samoa) - A/78/PV.100; A/78/PV.103
Antigua and Barbuda
Webson, Walton Alfonso - A/78/PV.100; A/78/PV.103
Australia
Larsen, James - A/C.2/78/SR.15
Reynolds, Gregory Edward Ivor - A/78/PV.103
Bahamas
Mott, T'Sean - A/78/PV.100
Caribbean Community
Habet, Orlando (Belize) - A/78/PV.100
Wallace, Brian Christopher Manley (Jamaica) - A/C.2/78/SR.12
Williams, Mutryce (Saint Kitts and Nevis) - A/78/PV.103
Colombia
Murillo Ferrer, Jorge Adrián - A/C.2/78/SR.22
Zalabata Torres, Leonor - A/78/PV.103
European Union
Kaspar, Martin - A/C.2/78/SR.22
Lorenzen, Emma Siemens (Denmark) - A/78/PV.103
Fiji
May, Vueti Kosoniu - A/78/PV.103

SMALL ISLAND DEVELOPING STATES—PROGRAMMES OF ACTION (Agenda item 18b) (continued)

Group of 77
Kwoba, Godfrey (Uganda) - A/78/PV.100
Téllez Alonso, Frank (Cuba) - A/C.2/78/SR.12
Torres Seara, Dalia Marlen (Cuba) - A/C.2/78/SR.21
Guyana
Alkins, Royston - A/C.2/78/SR.15
India
Gahlot, Petal - A/C.2/78/SR.13
Maldives
Hameed, Hala - A/C.2/78/SR.13
Mohamed, Ali Naseer - A/78/PV.100
Micronesia (Federated States of)
Welles, Kenneth - A/C.2/78/SR.15
Pacific Islands Forum
Vaea, Darlene Atuamua Hakeifalehaakili (Tonga) - A/C.2/78/SR.22
Palau
Seid, Ilana Victorya - A/78/PV.100
Portugal
Lages, Afonso - A/78/PV.103
Oliveira, Vitorino Alberto Melo Gomes - A/78/PV.100
Russian Federation
Meschchanov, Boris A. - A/78/PV.100
Seychelles
Madeleine, Ian Dereck Joseph - A/78/PV.103
Tonga
Va'inga Tone, Viliami - A/78/PV.100
Türkiye
İstemil Aydil, Alara - A/C.2/78/SR.15
Karatepe, Merve - A/78/PV.100
UN. Department for General Assembly and Conference Management
Nakano, Kenji - A/78/PV.103
Sharma, Sangeeta - A/78/PV.100
UN. Department of Economic and Social Affairs. Division for Sustainable Development Goals. Officer-in-Charge
Tahtinen, Lotta - A/C.2/78/SR.12
UN. General Assembly. 2nd Committee. Rapporteur
Gatev, Ivaylo (Bulgaria) - A/78/PV.49
UN. General Assembly. President
Francis, Dennis (Trinidad and Tobago) - A/78/PV.103
United Kingdom
Baric, Ana - A/C.2/78/SR.22
Soomro, Tara - A/78/PV.103
United States
Aiello, Jack - A/78/PV.100
Heartney, Edward - A/78/PV.103
Marks, Rose Ann - A/C.2/78/SR.22

SOCIAL CONDITIONS (Agenda item 24b)

Algeria
Samai, Rahma - A/C.3/78/SR.3
ASEAN
Dang, Hoang Giang (Viet Nam) - A/C.3/78/SR.1

SOCIAL CONDITIONS (Agenda item 24b) (continued)

Bangladesh
Shatil, Toufiq Islam - A/C.3/78/SR.3
Belarus
Mozgovaya, Ekaterina - A/78/PV.57; A/C.3/78/SR.2
Belgium
Kridelka, Philippe - A/78/PV.101
Brazil
Dias, João Henrique Nascimento - A/C.3/78/SR.2
Burkina Faso
Niamba Congo, Salamata Odette - A/C.3/78/SR.2
Caribbean Community
Wallace, Brian Christopher Manley (Jamaica) - A/C.3/78/SR.1
Costa Rica
Chan Valverde, Maritza - A/C.3/78/SR.3
Czechia
Hellerová, Zuzana - A/C.3/78/SR.2
Djibouti
Moussa, Youssouf Aden - A/78/PV.101
Dominican Republic
Matos Menéndez, Gala - A/C.3/78/SR.51
Ecuador
Méndez Gruezo, Elizabeth - A/C.3/78/SR.2
Egypt
Mohamed, Mohamed Omar Elfarouk Hassan - A/C.3/78/SR.51
Mostafa Rizk, Heba - A/78/PV.57; A/C.3/78/SR.2
European Union
Kókai, Anita (Hungary) - A/78/PV.101
Mogyorósi, Bálint (Hungary) - A/78/PV.57
Group of 77
González Behmaras, Alejandro (Cuba) - A/C.3/78/SR.1
Nabeta, Celia Kafureka (Uganda) - A/78/PV.101
Guatemala
Rodríguez Mancia, Carla María - A/C.3/78/SR.1
Holy See
Murphy, Robert David - A/C.3/78/SR.4
Honduras
Rivera Reyes, Isabella Regina - A/C.3/78/SR.2
India
Kamboj, Ruchira - A/78/PV.57
Sonkar, Suman - A/C.3/78/SR.3
Indonesia
Imanuel, Fnu - A/C.3/78/SR.3; A/C.3/78/SR.51
Iran (Islamic Republic of)
Arab Bafrani, Fatemeh - A/C.3/78/SR.51
Italy
Tonon, Daniela - A/C.3/78/SR.2
Kyrgyzstan
Kasymalieva, Aida - A/C.3/78/SR.3
Malaysia
Escopper Zumilla, Michael Jawa - A/C.3/78/SR.51
Muhamad, Ahmad Faisal - A/C.3/78/SR.2
Maldives
Khadeeja, Aufiyau - A/C.3/78/SR.3
Mali
Dabo N'diaye, Djeneba - A/C.3/78/SR.4

SOCIAL CONDITIONS (Agenda item 24b) (continued)

Malta
Gabriele, Emma de - A/C.3/78/SR.3
Mexico
Santa Ana Vara, Alma Esperanza - A/C.3/78/SR.2; A/C.3/78/SR.47
Mongolia
Ulziibayar, Vangansuren - A/C.3/78/SR.47
Vorshilov, Enkhbold - A/C.3/78/SR.2
Morocco
Hilale, Omar - A/78/PV.101
Myanmar
Tun, Kyaw Moe - A/C.3/78/SR.3
Namibia
Gertze, Neville Melvin - A/C.3/78/SR.2
Nepal
Thapa, Lok Bahadur - A/C.3/78/SR.2
New Zealand
Buist-Catherwood, Emily - A/C.3/78/SR.51
Nicaragua
Pichardo Urbina, Eleane Yaoska - A/C.3/78/SR.4
Nigeria
Asaju, Bola - A/C.3/78/SR.3; A/C.3/78/SR.51
Norway
Jensen, Jørgen Reymert - A/C.3/78/SR.2
Pakistan
Akram, Munir - A/C.3/78/SR.2
Majeed, Aleena - A/78/PV.57
Paraguay
Pereira Sosa, José Eduardo - A/C.3/78/SR.3
Peru
Rojas, Eder - A/C.3/78/SR.4
Ugarelli, Luis F. - A/C.3/78/SR.51
Philippines
Lagdameo, Antonio Manuel Revilla - A/C.3/78/SR.2
Poland
Stadnicka, Małgorzata - A/C.3/78/SR.2
Portugal
Zacarias, Ana Paula - A/78/PV.57; A/C.3/78/SR.2
Russian Federation
Chumakov, Dmitry S. - A/78/PV.57
Kashaev, Roman G. - A/C.3/78/SR.2
Mazaeva, Viktoriia - A/78/PV.101
Rwanda
Umulisa, Flavia - A/C.3/78/SR.2
Senegal
Niasse, Samba Thiam - A/C.3/78/SR.51
Sistema de la Integración Centroamericana
González López, Egriselda Aracely (El Salvador) - A/C.3/78/SR.1
Slovakia
Beblavý, Pavol - A/C.3/78/SR.2
South Africa
Makgati, Penelope Ramatsobane - A/C.3/78/SR.2
Sovereign Order of Malta
Schönburg, Laetitia - A/C.3/78/SR.4
Spain
Alonso Giganto, Ana María - A/C.3/78/SR.3
Jiménez de la Hoz, Ana - A/C.3/78/SR.51

SOCIAL CONDITIONS (Agenda item 24b) (continued)

Sri Lanka
Gunaratna, Pahala Rallage Sanathana Sugeeshwara - A/C.3/78/SR.2
Switzerland
Berchtold, Aneschka - A/C.3/78/SR.3
Türkiye
Aydil, İsmail - A/78/PV.101
Güven, Fikriye Asli - A/C.3/78/SR.3
Ukraine
Popadiuk, Mykola - A/C.3/78/SR.3
UN. Department for General Assembly and Conference Management
Sharma, Sangeeta - A/78/PV.101
UN. Department of Economic and Social Affairs. Division for Inclusive Social Development. Officer-in-Charge
Wilmoth, John - A/C.3/78/SR.1
UN. General Assembly. 3rd Committee. Rapporteur
Poveda Brito, Robert Alexander (Venezuela (Bolivarian Republic of)) - A/78/PV.50
UN. Group of African States
Ladeb, Tarek (Tunisia) - A/C.3/78/SR.2
United Arab Emirates
Alseyabi, Eman - A/C.3/78/SR.3
United Republic of Tanzania
Kattanga, Hussein A. - A/C.3/78/SR.3
United States
Breen, Patrick - A/C.3/78/SR.51

SOCIAL DEVELOPMENT (Agenda item 24)

Algeria
Samai, Rahma - A/C.3/78/SR.3
Argentina
Squeff, María del Carmen - A/C.3/78/SR.2
ASEAN
Dang, Hoang Giang (Viet Nam) - A/C.3/78/SR.1
Bahrain
Alhammadi, Hessa - A/C.3/78/SR.3
Bangladesh
Shatil, Toufiq Islam - A/C.3/78/SR.3
Canada
Wallenius, Devyn Lyn - A/C.3/78/SR.47
China
Dai, Bing - A/C.3/78/SR.2
Colombia
Zalabata Torres, Leonor - A/C.3/78/SR.2
Costa Rica
Chan Valverde, Maritza - A/C.3/78/SR.3
Côte d'Ivoire
Moriko, Tiémoko - A/C.3/78/SR.3
Dominican Republic
Andújar, Luz del Carmen - A/C.3/78/SR.3
European Union
Tariello, Giulia - A/C.3/78/SR.1
Group of 77
González Behmaras, Alejandro (Cuba) - A/C.3/78/SR.1

SOCIAL DEVELOPMENT (Agenda item 24) (continued)

Haiti
Pierre Fabre, Celine - A/C.3/78/SR.4
Holy See
Murphy, Robert David - A/C.3/78/SR.4
Honduras
Rivera Reyes, Isabella Regina - A/C.3/78/SR.2
India
Sonkar, Suman - A/C.3/78/SR.3
Indonesia
Imanuel, Fnu - A/C.3/78/SR.3
Iraq
Al-Khaqani, Hassan Jabbar - A/C.3/78/SR.4
Ireland
O'Sullivan, Alicia - A/C.3/78/SR.2
Japan
Kamiya, Masako - A/C.3/78/SR.3
Ono, Sho - A/C.3/78/SR.47
Kazakhstan
Bakytbekkyzy, Anel - A/C.3/78/SR.2
Kuwait
Al Mulla, Wafiqah - A/C.3/78/SR.3
Kyrgyzstan
Kasymalieva, Aida - A/C.3/78/SR.3
Lao People's Democratic Republic
Vongnorkeo, Anouparb - A/C.3/78/SR.4
Malawi
Chimbiri-Molande, Agnes Mary - A/C.3/78/SR.47
Maldives
Khadeeja, Aufiyau - A/C.3/78/SR.3
Mali
Dabo N'diaye, Djeneba - A/C.3/78/SR.4
Morocco
Moutchou, Majda - A/C.3/78/SR.1
Namibia
Gertze, Neville Melvin - A/C.3/78/SR.2
Nicaragua
Pichardo Urbina, Eleane Yaoska - A/C.3/78/SR.4
Nigeria
Asaju, Bola - A/C.3/78/SR.3
Pakistan
Akram, Munir - A/C.3/78/SR.2
Paraguay
Pereira Sosa, José Eduardo - A/C.3/78/SR.3
Peru
Rojas, Eder - A/C.3/78/SR.4
Poland
Lula, Iwona Anna - A/C.3/78/SR.1
Portugal
Zacarias, Ana Paula - A/C.3/78/SR.2
Romania
Lazaruc, Ana Maria - A/C.3/78/SR.3
Russian Federation
Kashaev, Roman G. - A/C.3/78/SR.2
Saudi Arabia
Bin Jadid, Faisal Fahad M. - A/C.3/78/SR.2
South Africa
Makgati, Penelope Ramatsobane - A/C.3/78/SR.2
Sovereign Order of Malta
Schönburg, Laetitia - A/C.3/78/SR.4

SOCIAL DEVELOPMENT (Agenda item 24) (continued)

Spain
Alonso Giganto, Ana María - A/C.3/78/SR.3
Sri Lanka
Gunaratna, Pahala Rallage Sanathana Sugeeshwara - A/C.3/78/SR.2
Switzerland
Wagner, Valérie - A/C.3/78/SR.3
Syrian Arab Republic
Altarsha, Elie - A/C.3/78/SR.3
Tajikistan
Gulov, Golibjon - A/C.3/78/SR.2
Türkiye
Güven, Fikriye Asli - A/C.3/78/SR.3
UN. General Assembly. 3rd Committee. Rapporteur
Poveda Brito, Robert Alexander (Venezuela (Bolivarian Republic of)) - A/78/PV.50
UN. Group of African States
Andriamiarisoa, Vero Henintsoa (Madagascar) - A/C.3/78/SR.47
UN. Under-Secretary-General for Economic and Social Affairs
Li, Junhua - A/C.3/78/SR.1
UN-HABITAT
Williams, Christopher - A/C.3/78/SR.1
United Arab Emirates
Alseyabi, Eman - A/C.3/78/SR.3
United Kingdom
Devereaux, Brendan - A/C.3/78/SR.47
United Republic of Tanzania
Kattanga, Hussein A. - A/C.3/78/SR.3
United States
Brzeski, Jessica - A/C.3/78/SR.47
Viet Nam
Thoa Le, Thi Minh - A/C.3/78/SR.3

SOCIAL DEVELOPMENT—CONFERENCES (Agenda item 24a)

Belarus
Mozgovaya, Ekaterina - A/C.3/78/SR.2
Chile
Perdomo, María Paula - A/C.3/78/SR.4
Costa Rica
Chan Valverde, Maritza - A/C.3/78/SR.3
Cuba
García Hernández, Martha - A/C.3/78/SR.3
European Union
Alonso Giganto, Ana María (Spain) - A/C.3/78/SR.55
Group of 77
González Behmaras, Alejandro (Cuba) - A/C.3/78/SR.55
Mexico
Santa Ana Vara, Alma Esperanza - A/C.3/78/SR.55
Nigeria
Asaju, Bola - A/C.3/78/SR.3

SOCIAL DEVELOPMENT—CONFERENCES (Agenda item 24a) (continued)

UN. Department of Economic and Social Affairs. Division for Inclusive Social Development. Officer-in-Charge
Wilmoth, John - A/C.3/78/SR.1
UN. General Assembly. 3rd Committee. Rapporteur
Poveda Brito, Robert Alexander (Venezuela (Bolivarian Republic of)) - A/78/PV.50
United States
Lang, Dylan - A/C.3/78/SR.55

SOLIDARITY (Agenda item 71b)

Cameroon
Banaken Elel, Nelly - A/C.3/78/SR.32
China
Yang, Fan - A/C.3/78/SR.32
Coordinating Bureau of the Non-Aligned Countries
Novruz, Leyla (Azerbaijan) - A/C.3/78/SR.32
Cuba
Lamigueiro Cañedo, Ivette - A/C.3/78/SR.32
Lesotho
Nena, Matete - A/C.3/78/SR.32
Russian Federation
Kuzmenkov, Stepan Y. - A/C.3/78/SR.32
Sovereign Order of Malta
Buckley, James E. - A/C.3/78/SR.32
State of Palestine
Salem, Sahar K.H. - A/C.3/78/SR.32
UN. Human Rights Council. Independent Expert on Human Rights and International Solidarity
Okafor, Obiora Chinedu - A/C.3/78/SR.32
Venezuela (Bolivarian Republic of)
Poveda Brito, Robert Alexander - A/C.3/78/SR.32

SOUTH-EAST ASIA—NUCLEAR-WEAPON-FREE ZONES (Agenda item 99y)

ASEAN
Dang, Hoang Giang (Viet Nam) - A/C.1/78/PV.11
Nasir, Arrmanatha Christiawan (Indonesia) - A/C.1/78/PV.30
Zakaria, Izzat Hayati (Brunei Darussalam) - A/C.1/78/PV.22
China
Shen, Jian - A/C.1/78/PV.30
India
Kulkarni, Maitrey - A/C.1/78/PV.30
Indonesia
Sirie, Mochammad Iqbal - A/C.1/78/PV.21
Lao People's Democratic Republic
Vongnorkeo, Anouparb - A/C.1/78/PV.13
Malaysia
Muhamad, Ahmad Faisal - A/C.1/78/PV.11
Sivamohan, Shivanand - A/C.1/78/PV.22; A/C.1/78/PV.30
Philippines
Gomez, Jan Michael - A/C.1/78/PV.22
Reyes, Narciso - A/C.1/78/PV.12

SOUTH-EAST ASIA—NUCLEAR-WEAPON-FREE ZONES (Agenda item 99y) (continued)

Singapore
Gafoor, Burhan - A/C.1/78/PV.30
Lim, Jessie - A/C.1/78/PV.12
Thailand
Chindawongse, Suriya - A/C.1/78/PV.13
United States
Turner, Bruce - A/C.1/78/PV.30
Viet Nam
Tran, Thi Thanh Hai - A/C.1/78/PV.13

SPECIAL POLITICAL MISSIONS (Agenda item 52)

Algeria
Alem, Mohammed Walid - A/C.4/78/SR.21
Angola
Cruz, Francisco José da - A/C.4/78/SR.21
ASEAN
Nasir, Arrmanatha Christiawan (Indonesia) - A/C.4/78/SR.21
Bangladesh
Shatil, Toufiq Islam - A/C.4/78/SR.21
Canada
Oliveira, Sasha - A/C.4/78/SR.21
Colombia
Zalabata Torres, Leonor - A/C.4/78/SR.21
Coordinating Bureau of the Non-Aligned Countries
El Ouazzani, Mouna Chahdi (Morocco) - A/C.4/78/SR.21
Egypt
Eldahshan, Wael Mahmoud Abdelaziz - A/C.4/78/SR.21
El Salvador
González López, Egriselda Aracely - A/C.4/78/SR.21
Ethiopia
Kassaye, Yoseph - A/C.4/78/SR.8
Haiti
Pierre, Christopher - A/C.4/78/SR.21
India
Birdi, Nitish - A/C.4/78/SR.21
Iraq
Al-Dahlaki, Hasanain Hadi Hasan - A/C.4/78/SR.21
Japan
Washino, Yurie - A/C.4/78/SR.21
Mexico
Buenrostro Massieu, Alicia - A/C.4/78/SR.21
Peru
Ugarelli, Luis F. - A/C.4/78/SR.21
Russian Federation
Evstigneeva, Anna M. - A/C.4/78/SR.21
Sierra Leone
Baimarro, Karen Jean - A/C.4/78/SR.21
South Africa
Schalkwyk, Marthinus van - A/C.4/78/SR.21
Sudan
Mohamed, Abuzied Shamseldin Ahmed - A/C.4/78/SR.21

SPECIAL POLITICAL MISSIONS (Agenda item 52) (continued)

Switzerland
Hauri, Adrian - A/C.4/78/SR.21
UN. Assistant Secretary-General for Europe, Central Asia and the Americas
Jenca, Miroslav - A/C.4/78/SR.21
UN. General Assembly. Special Political and Decolonization Committee (4th Committee). Rapporteur
Dhanutirto, Mariska Dwianti (Indonesia) - A/78/PV.45
UN. Under-Secretary-General for Operational Support
Khare, Atul - A/C.4/78/SR.21
United Arab Emirates
Al-Ali, Maryam - A/C.4/78/SR.21
Yemen
Al-mashehari, Sarah Ahmed Ahmed - A/C.4/78/SR.21

SPORTS—OLYMPIC GAMES (Agenda item 11)

Bahrain
Alrowaiei, Jamal Fares - A/78/PV.38
Belarus
Mozgovaya, Ekaterina - A/78/PV.38
China
Dai, Bing - A/78/PV.38
Egypt
Hassan, Khaled Aly Awadalla - A/78/PV.38
European Union
Curran, Clayton - A/78/PV.38
France
Estanguet, Tony - A/78/PV.38
Richard, Olivier-Gabriel - A/78/PV.38
Greece
Sekeris, Evangelos C. - A/78/PV.38
Guyana
Alkins, Royston - A/78/PV.38
Hungary
Horváth, Zsuzsanna - A/78/PV.97
International Olympic Committee
Bach, Thomas - A/78/PV.38
Japan
Ishikane, Kimihiro - A/78/PV.38
Libya
El-Sonni, Taher M. - A/78/PV.80
Monaco
Le Son, Daphné Brigitte Marie - A/78/PV.38
Morocco
Hilale, Omar - A/78/PV.38
Panama
Salerno Vega, James Azel - A/78/PV.38
Qatar
Alnesf, Sharifa Yousef A.S. - A/78/PV.38
Russian Federation
Kondratev, Sergei V. - A/78/PV.97
Zabolotskaya, Maria V. - A/78/PV.38
Senegal
Niasse, Samba Thiam - A/78/PV.38
Singapore
Tam, Noelle - A/78/PV.38

SPORTS—OLYMPIC GAMES (Agenda item 11) (continued)

Syrian Arab Republic
Mustafa, Marah - A/78/PV.38
Turkmenistan
Ataeva, Aksoltan T. - A/78/PV.107
Ukraine
Tokarska, Anastasiia - A/78/PV.38
UN. General Assembly. President
Francis, Dennis (Trinidad and Tobago) - A/78/PV.93
UN. General Assembly. Vice-President
Pieris, Peter Mohan Maithri (Sri Lanka) - A/78/PV.38
United Arab Emirates
Alawadhi, Sarah Ebrahim Abdulla Beddah - A/78/PV.38
United States
Elkon, Nicole - A/78/PV.38

STORMS (Agenda item 18i)

FAO
Li, Lifeng - A/C.2/78/SR.12
Group of 77
Kwoba, Godfrey (Uganda) - A/78/PV.98
Torres Seara, Dalia Marlen (Cuba) - A/C.2/78/SR.21
Iran (Islamic Republic of)
Momeni, Javad - A/C.2/78/SR.22
Iraq
Jasim, Saber Ahmed - A/C.2/78/SR.13
Israel
Ben Naftaly, Emil - A/C.2/78/SR.22
Türkiye
İstemil Aydil, Alara - A/C.2/78/SR.15
UN. General Assembly. 2nd Committee. Rapporteur
Gatev, Ivaylo (Bulgaria) - A/78/PV.49

STRADDLING FISH STOCKS (Agenda item 75b)

Alliance of Small Island States
Bartley, Matilda (Samoa) - A/78/PV.43
Argentina
Mainero, Martín Juan - A/78/PV.44
Squeff, María del Carmen - A/78/PV.44
Australia
Larsen, James - A/78/PV.43
Bangladesh
Uddin, Nasir - A/78/PV.43
Belgium
Lagatie, Karl - A/78/PV.43
Cameroon
Tommo Monthe, Michel - A/78/PV.44
Canada
Kessel, Alan - A/78/PV.43
Chile
Narváez Ojeda, Paula - A/78/PV.43
China
Geng, Shuang - A/78/PV.43
Li, Linlin - A/78/PV.44

STRADDLING FISH STOCKS (Agenda item 75b) (continued)

Costa Rica
Chan Valverde, Maritza - A/78/PV.44
El Salvador
Flores Soto, Ligia Lorena - A/78/PV.44
European Union
Ramopoulos, Thomas - A/78/PV.43
France
Dime-Labille, Diarra - A/78/PV.44
Germany
Freiin von Uslar-Gleichen, Tania - A/78/PV.43
Group of 77
Peñalver Portal, Gerardo (Cuba) - A/78/PV.43
Guatemala
Rodríguez Mancia, Carla María - A/78/PV.43
Iceland
Valtýsson, Jörundur - A/78/PV.44
India
Bhat, Kajal - A/78/PV.43
Indonesia
Prabowo, Hari - A/78/PV.44
International Seabed Authority. Secretary-General
Lodge, Michael - A/78/PV.44
International Tribunal for the Law of the Sea. President
Heidar, Tomas H. - A/78/PV.44
Iran (Islamic Republic of)
Aref, Yahya - A/78/PV.44
Ershadi, Zahra - A/78/PV.43
Jamaica
Douglas, Craig Barrington - A/78/PV.44
Japan
Nagano, Shunsuke - A/78/PV.44
Sorimachi, Masayuki - A/78/PV.44
Kuwait
Alajmi, Fahad M. - A/78/PV.44
Maldives
Shamun, Amr Danyal - A/78/PV.43
Mexico
Buenrostro Massieu, Alicia - A/78/PV.44
Micronesia (Federated States of)
Lippwe, Jeem - A/78/PV.44
Monaco
Botto, Florian - A/78/PV.43
Nauru
Adire, Anastasia Francilia - A/78/PV.44
Norway
Lovold, Andreas - A/78/PV.43
Pacific Islands Forum
Vaea, Darlene Atuamua Hakeifalehaakili (Tonga) - A/78/PV.43
Pakistan
Jadoon, Usman Iqbal - A/78/PV.44
Philippines
Arumpac-Marte, Azela Guerrero - A/78/PV.44
Peñaranda, Ariel Rodelas - A/78/PV.43
Russian Federation
Proskuryakov, Alexander S. - A/78/PV.44
Singapore
Gafoor, Burhan - A/78/PV.43

STRADDLING FISH STOCKS (Agenda item 75b) (continued)

Syrian Arab Republic
Khaddour, Mhd. Riyad - A/78/PV.44
Türkiye
Çetin, Ahmet Erman - A/78/PV.44
UN. Department for General Assembly and Conference Management
Nakano, Kenji - A/78/PV.44
UN. General Assembly. President
Francis, Dennis (Trinidad and Tobago) - A/78/PV.43
United Arab Emirates
Azzam, Rashed Jamal Ibrahim Ibrahim - A/78/PV.44
United Kingdom
Woodward, Barbara - A/78/PV.44
United States
Armbruster, Thomas - A/78/PV.44
Venezuela (Bolivarian Republic of)
Pérez Ayestarán, Joaquín Alberto - A/78/PV.44
Viet Nam
Dang, Hoang Giang - A/78/PV.43

SUBSIDIARY ORGANS—APPOINTMENTS (Agenda item 115)

Russian Federation
Chumakov, Dmitry S. - A/78/PV.60
UN. General Assembly. 5th Committee. Chair
Abdelkhalek, Osama Mahmoud (Egypt) - A/C.5/78/SR.8

SUMMARY EXECUTIONS (Agenda item 71b)

Belgium
Bauwens, Gilles - A/C.3/78/SR.31
Chile
Fernández Carter, Catalina - A/C.3/78/SR.31
China
Zhang, Qiuruo - A/C.3/78/SR.31
Colombia
Sánchez García, Nathalia - A/C.3/78/SR.31
Cyprus
Demosthenous, Ioanna - A/C.3/78/SR.31
European Union
Carlé, Hanne - A/C.3/78/SR.31
India
Sonkar, Suman - A/C.3/78/SR.31
Mexico
Riveroll Usabiaga, Renata - A/C.3/78/SR.31
Morocco
Bouchikhi, Hanaa - A/C.3/78/SR.31
Myanmar
Tun, Kyaw Moe - A/C.3/78/SR.31
Pakistan
Qureshi, Hadeeqa - A/C.3/78/SR.31
Russian Federation
Kuzmenkov, Stepan Y. - A/C.3/78/SR.31
Sovereign Order of Malta
McGuire, Peter Davidson - A/C.3/78/SR.31
Sweden
Uexküll, Andreas von - A/C.3/78/SR.31

SUMMARY EXECUTIONS (Agenda item 71b) (continued)

Ukraine
Tokarska, Anastasiia - A/C.3/78/SR.31
UN. Human Rights Council. Special Rapporteur on Extrajudicial, Summary or Arbitrary Executions
Tidball-Binz, Morris - A/C.3/78/SR.31
United Kingdom
Sylvester, Timothy James - A/C.3/78/SR.31
United States
Billingsley, Kelly - A/C.3/78/SR.31
Uruguay
Machado Mouriño, Felipe - A/C.3/78/SR.28

SUSTAINABLE DEVELOPMENT (Agenda item 18)

Algeria
Latrous, Mohamed-Esseghir - A/C.2/78/SR.14
Merabet, Ismaïl - A/C.2/78/SR.15; A/C.2/78/SR.25
Alliance of Small Island States
Lautasi, Isaia (Samoa) - A/C.2/78/SR.12
Argentina
Nicolino, Sebastián Lucas - A/C.2/78/SR.14; A/C.2/78/SR.25
Armenia
Babikyan, Araksya - A/C.2/78/SR.15
ASEAN
Lora-Santos, Leila Castillon (Philippines) - A/C.2/78/SR.12
Australia
Larsen, James - A/78/PV.107; A/C.2/78/SR.15
Linton, Sarah Joy - A/C.2/78/SR.24
Azerbaijan
Bayramli-Hamidova, Nigar - A/C.2/78/SR.13; A/C.2/78/SR.15
Bahrain
Al Fadhel, Noura Abdul Rahman - A/C.2/78/SR.13
Bangladesh
Muhith, Muhammad A. - A/C.2/78/SR.15
Belarus
Pisarevich, Vadim - A/C.2/78/SR.13
Bolivia (Plurinational State of)
Pary Rodríguez, Diego - A/C.2/78/SR.13
Brazil
Dubeux, Rafael - A/C.2/78/SR.14
Brunei Darussalam
Haji Zaini, Hajah Razan Dzafirah Binti - A/C.2/78/SR.13
Burkina Faso
Dipama, Abdoul Karim - A/C.2/78/SR.13
Cameroon
Mezang Akamba, Serge Pamphile - A/C.2/78/SR.24; A/C.2/78/SR.25
Canada
Natale, Giuliana - A/C.2/78/SR.15
Caribbean Community
Wallace, Brian Christopher Manley (Jamaica) - A/C.2/78/SR.12
Chile
González Carrillo, Montserrat - A/C.2/78/SR.25

SUSTAINABLE DEVELOPMENT (Agenda item 18) (continued)

China
Cao, Liwen - A/C.2/78/SR.24
Guo, Jingnan - A/C.2/78/SR.13
Colombia
Ríos Serna, Manuela - A/C.2/78/SR.12; A/C.2/78/SR.22; A/C.2/78/SR.24
Tickner, Arlene Beth - A/C.2/78/SR.14
Columbia University (New York)
Stiglitz, Joseph E. - A/C.2/78/SR.14
Common Fund for Commodities
Belal, Mohammed - A/C.2/78/SR.14
Costa Rica
Pizarro-Viales, Laura Raquel - A/C.2/78/SR.14
Côte d'Ivoire
Moriko, Tiémoko - A/C.2/78/SR.15
Democratic People's Republic of Korea
Jo, Tong Hyon - A/C.2/78/SR.13
Egypt
Abdelaal, Ahmed Magdy Mohamed Rashad - A/C.2/78/SR.12; A/C.2/78/SR.24
El Salvador
Segura Aragón, Carlos Efraín - A/C.2/78/SR.22
Eritrea
Ibrahim, Ahmed Saeed - A/C.2/78/SR.15
European Union
Gaal, Miklos (Hungary) - A/78/PV.107
Gambert, Sylvain - A/C.2/78/SR.22
Martín Couce, Adrián (Spain) - A/C.2/78/SR.24
Pougin de La Maisonneuve, Axel - A/C.2/78/SR.14
Tholin, Isadora Jahanfar (Sweden) - A/C.2/78/SR.24
France
Broadhurst Estival, Nathalie - A/78/PV.103
Gambia
Dibba, Lamin B. - A/C.2/78/SR.24
Ghana
Oppong-Ntiri, Carolyn - A/78/PV.88
Group of 77
Guevara Rodríguez, Adiel (Cuba) - A/C.2/78/SR.14
Téllez Alonso, Frank (Cuba) - A/C.2/78/SR.12; A/C.2/78/SR.21
Group of Arab States
Etomzini, Intisar M. KH (Libya) - A/C.2/78/SR.22
Group of Friends for Disaster Risk Reduction
Macchiavello, Julissa (Peru) - A/C.2/78/SR.12
Group of Friends in Defence of the Charter of the United Nations
Pérez Ayestarán, Joaquín Alberto (Venezuela (Bolivarian Republic of)) - A/C.2/78/SR.12
Group of Landlocked Developing Countries
Mokhawa, Gladys (Botswana) - A/C.2/78/SR.14
Motsumi, Lorato (Botswana) - A/C.2/78/SR.12
Group of Least Developed Countries
Adhikari, Pramita (Nepal) - A/C.2/78/SR.12
Guatemala
Rodríguez Mancia, Carla María - A/C.2/78/SR.14
Guyana
Alkins, Royston - A/C.2/78/SR.15

SUSTAINABLE DEVELOPMENT (Agenda item 18) (continued)

Holy See
Caccia, Gabriele Giordano - A/C.2/78/SR.15
Murphy, Robert David - A/C.2/78/SR.25
India
Gahlot, Petal - A/C.2/78/SR.13; A/C.2/78/SR.14
Indonesia
Imanuel, Fnu - A/C.2/78/SR.24
Prabowo, Hari - A/C.2/78/SR.15
Tharyat, Tri - A/C.2/78/SR.14
Iran (Islamic Republic of)
Ghafouri, Mojtaba - A/C.2/78/SR.24
Jalili, Tahereh - A/C.2/78/SR.13
Momeni, Javad - A/C.2/78/SR.21; A/C.2/78/SR.22
Iraq
Al-khalidi, Hasan Badri Mhalhal - A/C.2/78/SR.15; A/C.2/78/SR.24
Israel
Barak, Noga - A/C.2/78/SR.24
Ben Naftaly, Emil - A/C.2/78/SR.15; A/C.2/78/SR.21; A/C.2/78/SR.22
Jamaica
Denton-Watts, Cyeth Cylonia Allison - A/C.2/78/SR.24
Jordan
Alqudah, Mohammad Abdel Rahman Hasan - A/C.2/78/SR.24
Kazakhstan
Kerimkulov, Bauyrzhan - A/C.2/78/SR.21
Kuwait
Alkhuraibet, Ali - A/C.2/78/SR.13
Lao People's Democratic Republic
Xaiyavong, Thanouphet - A/C.2/78/SR.15
Lebanon
Hachem, Hadi - A/C.2/78/SR.21
Lithuania
Paulauskas, Rytis - A/C.2/78/SR.15; A/C.2/78/SR.22
Malaysia
Adnan, Yang Aishah Binti - A/C.2/78/SR.14
Maldives
Hameed, Hala - A/C.2/78/SR.13
Mauritania
Soumaré, Boukary - A/C.2/78/SR.15
Mexico
Buenrostro Massieu, Alicia - A/78/PV.107; A/C.2/78/SR.24
Robledo López, Carmen - A/C.2/78/SR.14
Monaco
Du Sault, Serena - A/C.2/78/SR.15
Morocco
Ouatiki, Assia - A/C.2/78/SR.13
Myanmar
Tun, Kyaw Moe - A/C.2/78/SR.15
Namibia
Gertze, Neville Melvin - A/C.2/78/SR.13
Nicaragua
Jiménez, Jasser - A/C.2/78/SR.13
Niger
Moussa, Mahaman - A/C.2/78/SR.24

SUSTAINABLE DEVELOPMENT (Agenda item 18) (continued)

Nigeria
Anyaegbu, Ezekwesiri David - A/C.2/78/SR.24
Edokpa, George Ehidiamen - A/C.2/78/SR.13
Norway
Kristmoen, Rina Lise - A/C.2/78/SR.24
Oman
Al Haddabi, Alya Nasser Saif - A/C.2/78/SR.15
Oxfam America
Mutasah, Tawanda - A/C.2/78/SR.14
Pakistan
Javaid, Hafiza Humaira - A/C.2/78/SR.13
Peru
Napurí Pita, Andrés - A/C.2/78/SR.24
Poland
Skoczek, Joanna Sylwia - A/C.2/78/SR.14
Qatar
Al-Kuwari, Shaheen - A/C.2/78/SR.12
Al-naama, Talal Abdulaziz - A/C.2/78/SR.24
Republic of Moldova
Nipomici, Galina - A/C.2/78/SR.24
Russian Federation
Chumakov, Dmitry S. - A/78/PV.107; A/C.2/78/SR.24
Uskov, Vladimir - A/C.2/78/SR.15
Saudi Arabia
Al Shehri, Muhammad - A/C.2/78/SR.15
Alomair, Reem Fahad O. - A/C.2/78/SR.24
Senegal
Gueye, Mamadou Soule - A/C.2/78/SR.24
Sierra Leone
Sowa, Amara Sheikh Mohammed - A/C.2/78/SR.13
Singapore
Luo, Phoebe - A/C.2/78/SR.24
Sistema de la Integración Centroamericana
Barahona Figueroa, Andrea Alejandra (El Salvador) - A/C.2/78/SR.22
State of Palestine
Abushawesh, Sahar - A/C.2/78/SR.22
Nasser-Abushawesh, Sahar - A/C.2/78/SR.15
Switzerland
Schlaepfer, Christian - A/C.2/78/SR.24
Syrian Arab Republic
Al Nahhas, Wissam - A/C.2/78/SR.13; A/C.2/78/SR.22; A/C.2/78/SR.24
Tajikistan
Hasanova, Tahmina - A/C.2/78/SR.15
Timor-Leste
Nunes, Karlito - A/C.2/78/SR.15
Türkiye
Aydil, İsmail - A/78/PV.107
İstemil Aydil, Alara - A/C.2/78/SR.15; A/C.2/78/SR.22
Turkmenistan
Ataeva, Aksoltan T. - A/C.2/78/SR.22; A/C.2/78/SR.23
Ukraine
Leschenko, Volodymyr - A/C.2/78/SR.13

SUSTAINABLE DEVELOPMENT (Agenda item 18) (continued)

UN. Department of Economic and Social Affairs. Division for Sustainable Development Goals. Officer-in-Charge
Tahtinen, Lotta - A/C.2/78/SR.12
UN. Department of Economic and Social Affairs. Financing for Sustainable Development Office. Strategic Engagement and Policy Integration Branch. Chief
Parra-Lancourt, Mariangela - A/C.2/78/SR.14
UN. Economic and Social Council. President
Narváez Ojeda, Paula (Chile) - A/C.2/78/SR.14
UN. General Assembly. 2nd Committee. Chair
Amorín, Carlos Daniel (Uruguay) - A/C.2/78/SR.14
UN. General Assembly. 2nd Committee. Rapporteur
Gatev, Ivaylo (Bulgaria) - A/78/PV.49
UN. General Assembly. 2nd Committee. Secretary
Herity, Emer - A/C.2/78/SR.24
UN. Group of African States
Ladeb, Tarek (Tunisia) - A/C.2/78/SR.12
UN. Statistics Division. Director
Min, Yongyi - A/C.2/78/SR.12
UNCTAD
Martínez Badillo, Juan José - A/C.2/78/SR.14
Shirotori, Miho - A/C.2/78/SR.14
UNDP
Al-Hammal, Ahmad - A/C.2/78/SR.12
Živković, Ivana - A/C.2/78/SR.12
United Arab Emirates
Abushahab, Mohamed Issa - A/78/PV.107
United Kingdom
Croker, Richard - A/C.2/78/SR.24
Kelsey, Alistair Robert Steven - A/C.2/78/SR.24
Soomro, Tara - A/78/PV.107
United Republic of Tanzania
Kattanga, Hussein A. - A/C.2/78/SR.15
United States
Armbruster, Thomas - A/C.2/78/SR.21
Henzel, Christopher - A/C.2/78/SR.15
Keane, Shane - A/C.2/78/SR.22
Korac, Sofija - A/C.3/78/SR.47
Marks, Rose Ann - A/C.2/78/SR.22
Shrier, Jonathan - A/78/PV.107
Udell, Isabel - A/C.2/78/SR.22; A/C.2/78/SR.24
University of Massachusetts at Amherst
Pickbourn, Lynda - A/C.2/78/SR.14
University of Oxford
Lebdioui, Amir - A/C.2/78/SR.14
Uruguay
Romero Veiga, Stefany - A/C.2/78/SR.25
Uzbekistan
Eshkobilov, Oybek - A/C.2/78/SR.22
Lapasov, Ulugbek - A/78/PV.57; A/78/PV.103
Viet Nam
Nguyen, Hoang Nguyen - A/C.2/78/SR.13
Yemen
Al-barati, Abdulrahman Hasan Yahya - A/C.2/78/SR.24; A/C.2/78/SR.25
Zambia
Milambo, Chola - A/C.2/78/SR.14; A/C.2/78/SR.15

SUSTAINABLE DEVELOPMENT (Agenda item 18) (continued)

Zimbabwe
    Rupende, Tapiwa Roy - A/C.2/78/SR.13; A/C.2/78/SR.14

SUSTAINABLE ENERGY (Agenda item 18h)

Azerbaijan
    Bayramli-Hamidova, Nigar - A/C.2/78/SR.13
Bolivia (Plurinational State of)
    Pary Rodríguez, Diego - A/C.2/78/SR.13
Brazil
    Kloss, Emerson Coraiola Yinde - A/C.2/78/SR.13
China
    Guo, Jingnan - A/C.2/78/SR.13
Colombia
    Ríos Serna, Manuela - A/C.2/78/SR.23
Ethiopia
    Shiferaw, Girum Getachew - A/C.2/78/SR.15
European Union
    Kaspar, Martin - A/C.2/78/SR.23
Group of 77
    Torres Seara, Dalia Marlen (Cuba) - A/C.2/78/SR.21
Guyana
    Alkins, Royston - A/C.2/78/SR.15
India
    Gahlot, Petal - A/C.2/78/SR.13
International Renewable Energy Agency
    Biya, Alain Wilfried - A/C.2/78/SR.15
Iraq
    Jasim, Saber Ahmed - A/C.2/78/SR.13
Kenya
    Kenga, Emmanuel Kingi - A/C.2/78/SR.13
Monaco
    Du Sault, Serena - A/C.2/78/SR.15
Morocco
    Ouatiki, Assia - A/C.2/78/SR.13
Panama
    Thompson Ramírez, Marilyn del Carmen - A/C.2/78/SR.13
Russian Federation
    Meschchanov, Boris A. - A/C.2/78/SR.23
    Uskov, Vladimir - A/C.2/78/SR.15
Singapore
    Yuan Fang, Yeo - A/C.2/78/SR.13
Türkiye
    İstemil Aydil, Alara - A/C.2/78/SR.15
UN. Department of Economic and Social Affairs. Division for Sustainable Development Goals. Officer-in-Charge
    Tahtinen, Lotta - A/C.2/78/SR.12
UN. General Assembly. 2nd Committee. Rapporteur
    Gatev, Ivaylo (Bulgaria) - A/78/PV.49
UNIDO
    Bredel, Ralf - A/C.2/78/SR.15
United Arab Emirates
    Hassan, Tariq Ahmed - A/C.2/78/SR.13
United Kingdom
    Fidoe, Nicholas - A/C.2/78/SR.23

SUSTAINABLE ENERGY (Agenda item 18h) (continued)

United Republic of Tanzania
    Kattanga, Hussein A. - A/C.2/78/SR.15
United States
    Kroeker-Maus, Faith - A/C.2/78/SR.23
Viet Nam
    Nguyen, Hoang Nguyen - A/C.2/78/SR.13
Zambia
    Milambo, Chola - A/C.2/78/SR.15

TAXATION (Agenda item 16h)

Bahamas
    Mott, T'Sean - A/C.2/78/SR.11; A/C.2/78/SR.25
Bolivia (Plurinational State of)
    Muñoz Ponce, Tatiana Bárbara - A/C.2/78/SR.25
Cambodia
    Heng, Somoly - A/C.2/78/SR.9
Cameroon
    Mezang Akamba, Serge Pamphile - A/C.2/78/SR.25
Canada
    Ong, Shirley - A/C.2/78/SR.8
Chile
    Ruidíaz, René - A/C.2/78/SR.25
Colombia
    Murillo Ferrer, Jorge Adrián - A/C.2/78/SR.25
    Tickner, Arlene Beth - A/C.2/78/SR.8
European Union
    Martín Couce, Adrián (Spain) - A/C.2/78/SR.25
Indonesia
    Imanuel, Fnu - A/C.2/78/SR.25
    Prabowo, Hari - A/C.2/78/SR.9
Israel
    Silverberg, Peter Andrew - A/C.2/78/SR.25
Japan
    Nishigori, Naofumi - A/C.2/78/SR.8; A/C.2/78/SR.25
Kenya
    Nzumbu, Christine - A/C.2/78/SR.9
Liechtenstein
    Oehri, Noah - A/C.2/78/SR.25
New Zealand
    Pringle, Rachael - A/C.2/78/SR.25
Nigeria
    Gana Alkali, Baba - A/C.2/78/SR.9
    Muhammad Bande, Tijjani - A/C.2/78/SR.25
Norway
    Brattested, Merete Fjeld - A/C.2/78/SR.25
    Lovold, Andreas - A/C.2/78/SR.11
Panama
    Concepción Jaramillo, Markova - A/C.2/78/SR.25
Republic of Korea
    Cho, Seong-Jun - A/C.2/78/SR.25
Russian Federation
    Kardash, Viktoriia E. - A/C.2/78/SR.9
    Meschchanov, Boris A. - A/C.2/78/SR.25
Singapore
    Luo, Phoebe - A/C.2/78/SR.25
South Africa
    Joyini, Mathu - A/C.2/78/SR.25

TAXATION (Agenda item 16h) (continued)

Switzerland
Frey, Benjamin Jay - A/C.2/78/SR.25
Trinidad and Tobago
Budhu, Vladamir - A/C.2/78/SR.9
Türkiye
Güven, Fikriye Asli - A/C.2/78/SR.25
UN. Department of Economic and Social Affairs. Financing for Sustainable Development Office. Policy Analysis and Development Branch. Chief
Spiegel, Shari - A/C.2/78/SR.8
UN. General Assembly. 2nd Committee. Rapporteur
Gatev, Ivaylo (Bulgaria) - A/78/PV.49
UN. Group of African States
Ladeb, Tarek (Tunisia) - A/C.2/78/SR.9
Muhammad Bande, Tijjani (Nigeria) - A/C.2/78/SR.25
United Kingdom
Croker, Richard - A/C.2/78/SR.25
United States
Aiello, Jack - A/C.2/78/SR.9
Marks, Rose Ann - A/C.2/78/SR.25
Zambia
Boma, Regina Chama - A/C.2/78/SR.9

TERRITORIES OCCUPIED BY ISRAEL—HUMAN RIGHTS (Agenda item 50)

Algeria
Sahraoui, Ahmed - A/C.4/78/SR.24
Bahrain
Aljalahma, Shaikha - A/C.4/78/SR.25
Bangladesh
Shatil, Toufiq Islam - A/C.4/78/SR.24
Bolivia (Plurinational State of)
Ríos, Carmen Rosa - A/C.4/78/SR.25
Brunei Darussalam
Hamzah, Fatin Hilyati Haji - A/C.4/78/SR.24
Canada
Rae, Robert - A/78/PV.45
China
Geng, Shuang - A/C.4/78/SR.25
Cuba
Fernández Palacios, Yumirka - A/C.4/78/SR.24
Romero Puentes, Yusnier - A/C.4/78/SR.26
Democratic People's Republic of Korea
Kim, In Chol - A/C.4/78/SR.24; A/C.4/78/SR.26
Egypt
Elshandawily, Ahmed - A/C.4/78/SR.24
European Union
Angarón Bolea, María del Mar (Spain) - A/C.4/78/SR.26
Clune, Mary - A/C.4/78/SR.24
Group of Arab States
Alwasil, Abdulaziz M.O. (Saudi Arabia) - A/C.4/78/SR.24
Gulf Cooperation Council
Al Rashdi, Amal (Oman) - A/C.4/78/SR.24
Indonesia
Dhanutirto, Mariska Dwianti - A/C.4/78/SR.24

TERRITORIES OCCUPIED BY ISRAEL—HUMAN RIGHTS (Agenda item 50) (continued)

Iran (Islamic Republic of)
Baghaei Hamaneh, Esmaeil - A/C.4/78/SR.25
Ghelich, Vahid - A/C.4/78/SR.25; A/C.4/78/SR.26
Iraq
Al-Dahlaki, Hasanain Hadi Hasan - A/C.4/78/SR.25
Israel
Kedar, Gershon - A/C.4/78/SR.25
Japan
Nishiyama, Akira - A/C.4/78/SR.25
Jordan
Habashneh, Ahmad Samir Fahim - A/C.4/78/SR.25
Kuwait
Alajmi, Fahad M. - A/C.4/78/SR.25
League of Arab States
Elardja Flitti, Nasria - A/C.4/78/SR.25
Lebanon
Jardali, Mohammad Ali - A/C.4/78/SR.25
Libya
Hamed, Ashraf A.O. - A/C.4/78/SR.25
Liechtenstein
Oehri, Myriam - A/C.4/78/SR.26
Malaysia
Muhamad, Ahmad Faisal - A/C.4/78/SR.24
Morocco
Jerboui, Hind - A/C.4/78/SR.25
Namibia
Gertze, Neville Melvin - A/C.4/78/SR.26
Nepal
Ray, Kaushal Kishor - A/78/PV.45
Poland
Szczerski, Krzysztof - A/C.4/78/SR.26
Qatar
Al-thani, Jassim Abdulaziz J.A. - A/C.4/78/SR.25
Russian Federation
Polyanskiy, Dmitry A. - A/C.4/78/SR.25
Saudi Arabia
Al Kahtani, Fayee Fahad M. - A/C.4/78/SR.25
Senegal
Niang, Cheikh - A/C.4/78/SR.24
South Africa
Schalkwyk, Marthinus van - A/C.4/78/SR.25
State of Palestine
Abdelhady-Nasser, Feda - A/C.4/78/SR.24; A/C.4/78/SR.25
Mansour, Riyad H. - A/C.4/78/SR.26
Sudan
Mohamed, Abuzied Shamseldin Ahmed - A/C.4/78/SR.24
Switzerland
Carpenter, Christoph - A/C.4/78/SR.26
Syrian Arab Republic
Baghdadi, Mohannad - A/C.4/78/SR.25; A/C.4/78/SR.26
Tunisia
Salah, Yassine - A/C.4/78/SR.24
Türkiye
Sezer, Alper - A/C.4/78/SR.24
UN. Assistant Secretary-General for Human Rights
Brands Kehris, Ilze - A/C.4/78/SR.24

TERRITORIES OCCUPIED BY ISRAEL—HUMAN RIGHTS (Agenda item 50) (continued)

UN. General Assembly. Special Political and Decolonization Committee (4th Committee). Rapporteur
Dhanutirto, Mariska Dwianti (Indonesia) - A/78/PV.45
UN. Special Committee to Investigate Israeli Practices affecting the Human Rights of the Palestinian People and Other Arabs of the Occupied Territories. Chair
Pieris, Peter Mohan Maithri (Sri Lanka) - A/C.4/78/SR.24
United Arab Emirates
Al-Ali, Maryam - A/C.4/78/SR.25
United Kingdom
Croker, Richard - A/C.4/78/SR.26
United States
Kelley, John - A/C.4/78/SR.26
Kris, Robert - A/C.4/78/SR.26
Wood, Robert A. - A/C.4/78/SR.25
Venezuela (Bolivarian Republic of)
Pérez Ayestarán, Joaquín Alberto - A/C.4/78/SR.24
Yemen
Al-mashehari, Sarah Ahmed Ahmed - A/C.4/78/SR.24

TERRITORIES OCCUPIED BY ISRAEL—NATURAL RESOURCES (Agenda item 59)

Algeria
Merabet, Ismaïl - A/C.2/78/SR.19
Australia
Bryant, Rebecca Suzanne - A/C.2/78/SR.19
Bahrain
Al Bin Khalil, Maryam - A/C.2/78/SR.19
Bangladesh
Prince, Gomar Faruk Khandakar - A/C.2/78/SR.19
Bolivia (Plurinational State of)
Pary Rodríguez, Diego - A/C.2/78/SR.19
Canada
Arbeiter, Richard - A/C.2/78/SR.20
China
Cao, Liwen - A/C.2/78/SR.19
Cuba
Peñalver Portal, Gerardo - A/C.2/78/SR.19
Egypt
Abdelaal, Ahmed Magdy Mohamed Rashad - A/C.2/78/SR.19
European Union
Lavalle Merchán, Jesús María (Spain) - A/C.2/78/SR.21
Germany
Roeder-Messell, Ernst Heinrich - A/C.2/78/SR.21
Group of 77
Romero Puentes, Yusnier (Cuba) - A/C.2/78/SR.19
Téllez Alonso, Frank (Cuba) - A/C.2/78/SR.21
Group of Arab States
Al-halique, Katherine Anas Ahmad (Jordan) - A/C.2/78/SR.19
Gulf Cooperation Council
Al Rubkhi, Khalid Saleh Said (Oman) - A/C.2/78/SR.19

TERRITORIES OCCUPIED BY ISRAEL—NATURAL RESOURCES (Agenda item 59) (continued)

Guyana
Rodrigues-Birkett, Carolyn - A/C.2/78/SR.19
Indonesia
Prabowo, Hari - A/C.2/78/SR.19
Iran (Islamic Republic of)
Jalili, Tahereh - A/C.2/78/SR.19
Momeni, Javad - A/C.2/78/SR.21
Iraq
Al-khalidi, Hasan Badri Mhalhal - A/C.2/78/SR.19
Israel
Ben Naftaly, Emil - A/C.2/78/SR.19; A/C.2/78/SR.20; A/C.2/78/SR.21
Kuwait
Almezyad, Fatma - A/C.2/78/SR.19
League of Arab States
Al-Amri, Islam Abdullah Hassan - A/C.2/78/SR.20
Libya
Ghawar, Samir - A/C.2/78/SR.19
Malaysia
Adnan, Yang Aishah Binti - A/C.2/78/SR.19
Maldives
Hameed, Hala - A/C.2/78/SR.19
Mauritania
Laghdaf, Sidi Mohamed - A/C.2/78/SR.19
Namibia
Gertze, Neville Melvin - A/C.2/78/SR.19
Pakistan
Jadoon, Usman Iqbal - A/C.2/78/SR.19; A/C.2/78/SR.21
Qatar
Al-naama, Talal Abdulaziz - A/C.2/78/SR.19
Russian Federation
Meschchanov, Boris A. - A/C.2/78/SR.20
Saudi Arabia
Al-Saud, Prince of Saudi Arabia - A/C.2/78/SR.19
Senegal
Dioum, Assane - A/C.2/78/SR.19
South Africa
Schalkwyk, Marthinus van - A/C.2/78/SR.19
State of Palestine
Abushawesh, Sahar - A/C.2/78/SR.21
Nasser-Abushawesh, Sahar - A/C.2/78/SR.19; A/C.2/78/SR.20
Syrian Arab Republic
Al Nahhas, Wissam - A/C.2/78/SR.19; A/C.2/78/SR.21
Türkiye
Ekren, Kemal Onur - A/C.2/78/SR.19
Özgür, Ceren Hande - A/C.2/78/SR.21
UN. ESCWA. Division for Emerging and Conflict-related Issues. Director
Alami, Tarik - A/C.2/78/SR.19
UN. General Assembly. 2nd Committee. Rapporteur
Gatev, Ivaylo (Bulgaria) - A/78/PV.49
United Arab Emirates
Al Hammadi, Asma Hassan Mohamed - A/C.2/78/SR.19

TERRITORIES OCCUPIED BY ISRAEL—NATURAL RESOURCES (Agenda item 59) (continued)

United Kingdom
Kelsey, Alistair Robert Steven - A/C.2/78/SR.21
Wood, Grace Louise - A/C.2/78/SR.19
United States
Armbruster, Thomas - A/C.2/78/SR.21
Weinstein, Andrew - A/C.2/78/SR.19
Venezuela (Bolivarian Republic of)
Marín Sevilla, Asbina - A/C.2/78/SR.19
Yemen
Al-barati, Abdulrahman Hasan Yahya - A/C.2/78/SR.19

TERRORISM (Agenda item 109)

Albania
Spasse, Arian - A/C.6/78/SR.4
Algeria
Gaouaoui, Nacim - A/C.6/78/SR.4
Argentina
Mainero, Martín Juan - A/C.6/78/SR.1
Armenia
Galstyan, Tigran - A/C.6/78/SR.5
ASEAN
Eat, Sophea (Cambodia) - A/C.6/78/SR.1
Australia
Biggs, Ian - A/C.6/78/SR.1
Azerbaijan
Musayev, Tofig - A/C.6/78/SR.4; A/C.6/78/SR.5
Bahrain
Almarzooqi, Hazem Abdulqader Khalifa Abdulla - A/C.6/78/SR.4
Bangladesh
Shatil, Toufiq Islam - A/C.6/78/SR.1
Bolivia (Plurinational State of)
Pary Rodríguez, Diego - A/C.6/78/SR.3
Brazil
Braoios, Victor Silveira - A/C.6/78/SR.1
Burkina Faso
Ouattara Cisse, Aminata - A/C.6/78/SR.2
Cabo Verde
Romualdo, Tania Serafim Yvonne - A/C.6/78/SR.5
Cameroon
Nyanid, Zacharie Serge Raoul - A/C.6/78/SR.2
China
Geng, Shuang - A/C.6/78/SR.3
Community of Latin American and Caribbean States
Mark, Hayley-Ann (Saint Vincent and the Grenadines) - A/C.6/78/SR.2
Congo
Makayat-Safouesse, Lazare - A/C.6/78/SR.4
Coordinating Bureau of the Non-Aligned Countries
Ershadi, Zahra (Iran (Islamic Republic of)) - A/C.6/78/SR.1
Costa Rica
Ramírez Baca, Gustavo Adolfo - A/C.6/78/SR.2
Côte d'Ivoire
Moriko, Tiémoko - A/C.6/78/SR.3

TERRORISM (Agenda item 109) (continued)

Cuba
Peñalver Portal, Gerardo - A/C.6/78/SR.2
Democratic People's Republic of Korea
Kim, Song - A/C.6/78/SR.3
Denmark
Laursen, Erik - A/C.6/78/SR.1
Djibouti
Moussa, Moussa Mohamed - A/C.6/78/SR.4
Dominican Republic
Blanco Conde, José Alfonso - A/C.6/78/SR.4
Ecuador
Escobar Ullauri, Pablo - A/C.6/78/SR.1
Egypt
Elhomosany, Mohamed Kamal Ali - A/C.6/78/SR.2
El Salvador
González López, Egriselda Aracely - A/C.6/78/SR.2
Equatorial Guinea
Ndong Mba, Anatolio - A/C.6/78/SR.2
Eritrea
Giorgio, Amanuel - A/C.6/78/SR.3
Ethiopia
Alemayehu, Betelihem Taye - A/C.6/78/SR.4
European Union
Ramopoulos, Thomas - A/C.6/78/SR.1
Georgia
Kupradze, Sopio - A/C.6/78/SR.4
Ghana
Hackman, Khalilah - A/C.6/78/SR.2
Group of Friends in Defence of the Charter of the United Nations
Pérez Ayestarán, Joaquín Alberto (Venezuela (Bolivarian Republic of)) - A/C.6/78/SR.2
Guatemala
Rodríguez Mancia, Carla María - A/C.6/78/SR.1
Haiti
Panier, Wisnique - A/C.6/78/SR.4
Holy See
Murphy, Robert David - A/C.6/78/SR.5
Honduras
Rivera Reyes, Isabella Regina - A/C.6/78/SR.2
India
Bhat, Kajal - A/C.6/78/SR.2; A/C.6/78/SR.4
Indonesia
Prabowo, Hari - A/C.6/78/SR.2
International Committee of the Red Cross
Apraxine, Pierre - A/C.6/78/SR.5
Iran (Islamic Republic of)
Heidari, Bahram - A/C.6/78/SR.1
Iraq
Al-Zubaidi, Zaid Mohammed Hussein Abed - A/C.6/78/SR.4
Israel
Cappon, Noam - A/C.6/78/SR.1; A/C.6/78/SR.5
Jordan
Habashneh, Ahmad Samir Fahim - A/C.6/78/SR.2
Kenya
Kiboino, Michael Kapkiai - A/C.6/78/SR.4
Lao People's Democratic Republic
Seneduangdeth, Vilayluck - A/C.6/78/SR.4

TERRORISM (Agenda item 109) (continued)

Latvia
Cupika-Mavrina, Elvira - A/C.6/78/SR.1
Lebanon
Hitti, Youssef - A/C.6/78/SR.2
Malawi
Namangale, Clement Amamai Dima - A/C.6/78/SR.5
Malaysia
Omar, Khairi - A/C.6/78/SR.4
Maldives
Guraisha, Aminath - A/C.6/78/SR.2
Mali
Konfourou, Issa - A/C.6/78/SR.4
Mauritania
Sao, Mariam - A/C.6/78/SR.5
Mexico
Jiménez Alegría, Natalia - A/C.6/78/SR.1
Mongolia
Vorshilov, Enkhbold - A/C.6/78/SR.2
Morocco
Lasri, El Hassan - A/C.6/78/SR.4
Mozambique
Saranga, Geraldo - A/C.6/78/SR.4
Nepal
Thapa, Lok Bahadur - A/C.6/78/SR.2
Nicaragua
Llano, Alina J. - A/C.6/78/SR.5
Niger
Ousman, Samadou - A/C.6/78/SR.4
Nigeria
Dakwak, Gloria - A/C.6/78/SR.2
Oman
Al Shehhi, Mohammed Ali Ahmed - A/C.6/78/SR.2
Organisation of Islamic Cooperation
Felemban, Khalid (Saudi Arabia) - A/C.6/78/SR.1
Pakistan
Ajmal, Muhammad Jawad - A/C.6/78/SR.4
Akram, Munir - A/C.6/78/SR.2
Paraguay
Pereira Sosa, José Eduardo - A/C.6/78/SR.5
Peru
Falconi, Alessandra - A/C.6/78/SR.4
Philippines
Peñaranda, Ariel Rodelas - A/C.6/78/SR.2
Qatar
Almansouri, Ali Ahmad M.A. - A/C.6/78/SR.2
Republic of Korea
Kim, Hyunsoo - A/C.6/78/SR.4
Russian Federation
Mikhaylov, Oleg O. - A/C.6/78/SR.2
Saudi Arabia
Alodaib, Khalid Nasser A. - A/C.6/78/SR.4
Senegal
Diome, Diamane - A/C.6/78/SR.1
Sierra Leone
Kanu, Michael Imran - A/C.6/78/SR.3
Singapore
Gafoor, Burhan - A/C.6/78/SR.1
South Africa
Motsepe, Keke Mantsho - A/C.6/78/SR.2

TERRORISM (Agenda item 109) (continued)

Sri Lanka
Pieris, Peter Mohan Maithri - A/C.6/78/SR.1
State of Palestine
Bamya, Majed - A/C.6/78/SR.5
Sudan
Mohammed, Ammar Mohammed Mahmoud - A/C.6/78/SR.2
Syrian Arab Republic
Khaddour, Mhd. Riyad - A/C.6/78/SR.3
Thailand
Vichankaiyakij, Vathayudh - A/C.6/78/SR.2
Togo
Ouro-bodi, Tchakpide - A/C.6/78/SR.4
Tunisia
Ben Lagha, Adel - A/C.6/78/SR.3
Türkiye
Ekren, Kemal Onur - A/C.6/78/SR.3
Uganda
Ikondere, Marvin - A/C.6/78/SR.4
Ukraine
Prytula, Mykola - A/C.6/78/SR.1
UN. General Assembly. 6th Committee. Bureau
Maillé, Béatrice (Canada) - A/C.6/78/SR.37
UN. General Assembly. 6th Committee. Rapporteur
Moussa, Moussa Mohamed (Djibouti) - A/78/PV.45
UN. General Assembly. 6th Committee. Working Group on Measures to Eliminate International Terrorism. Chair
Perera, Amrith Rohan (Sri Lanka) - A/C.6/78/SR.36
UN. Group of African States
Ikondere, Marvin (Uganda) - A/C.6/78/SR.1
United Arab Emirates
Al Marzooqi, Tahreer - A/C.6/78/SR.4
United Kingdom
Clark, Joel - A/C.6/78/SR.1
United States
Patton, Dorothy - A/C.6/78/SR.1
Uruguay
Katz Pavlotzky, Alejandro Leonel - A/C.6/78/SR.4
Viet Nam
Nguyen, Hong Nhat - A/C.6/78/SR.2
Yemen
Balobaid, Ali Mabkhot Salem - A/C.6/78/SR.4

TERRORISM—HUMAN RIGHTS (Agenda item 71b)

Belgium
Bauwens, Gilles - A/C.3/78/SR.31
Burkina Faso
Ouattara Cisse, Aminata - A/C.3/78/SR.25
China
Zhang, Qiuruo - A/C.3/78/SR.31
Cuba
González Behmaras, Alejandro - A/C.3/78/SR.31
Egypt
Eldahshan, Wael Mahmoud Abdelaziz - A/C.3/78/SR.31
European Union
Carlé, Hanne - A/C.3/78/SR.31

TERRORISM—HUMAN RIGHTS (Agenda item 71b) (continued)

Gulf Cooperation Council
Al Rubkhi, Khalid Saleh Said (Oman) - A/C.3/78/SR.26
India
Sonkar, Suman - A/C.3/78/SR.31
Ireland
Leonard, Roisin - A/C.3/78/SR.18; A/C.3/78/SR.31
Israel
Carmeli, Mor - A/C.3/78/SR.26
Mexico
Elizondo Belden, Luis Gerardo - A/C.3/78/SR.31; A/C.3/78/SR.51
Morocco
Bouchikhi, Hanaa - A/C.3/78/SR.31
Pakistan
Qureshi, Hadeeqa - A/C.3/78/SR.31
Republic of Korea
Lee, Yeseung - A/C.3/78/SR.31
Russian Federation
Kuzmenkov, Stepan Y. - A/C.3/78/SR.31
South Africa
Passmoor, Jonathan David - A/C.3/78/SR.31
Sovereign Order of Malta
Espiritu, Michael - A/C.3/78/SR.31
Switzerland
Maric, Martina - A/C.3/78/SR.51
Wägli, Christian - A/C.3/78/SR.31
Syrian Arab Republic
Altarsha, Elie - A/C.3/78/SR.31
Ukraine
Mudrenko, Nataliia - A/C.3/78/SR.31
UN. Assistant Secretary-General for Human Rights
Brands Kehris, Ilze - A/C.3/78/SR.18
UN. Human Rights Council. Special Rapporteur on the Promotion and Protection of Human Rights and Fundamental Freedoms while Countering Terrorism
Ní Aoláin, Fionnuala - A/C.3/78/SR.31
United States
Johnson, Timothy J. - A/C.3/78/SR.51
Murphy, Daniel - A/C.3/78/SR.31

TORTURE AND OTHER CRUEL TREATMENT (Agenda item 71a)

Algeria
Hassani, Billel - A/C.3/78/SR.18
Argentina
González, María Florencia - A/C.3/78/SR.18
Brazil
Gomes, Elaine Cristina Pereira - A/C.3/78/SR.18
Canada
Klaise, Inara - A/C.3/78/SR.18
Chile
Fernández Carter, Catalina - A/C.3/78/SR.18
China
La, Haozhao - A/C.3/78/SR.18
Denmark
Lassen, Christina Markus - A/C.3/78/SR.18

TORTURE AND OTHER CRUEL TREATMENT (Agenda item 71a) (continued)

Dominican Republic
Andújar, Luz del Carmen - A/C.3/78/SR.18
Egypt
Eldahshan, Wael Mahmoud Abdelaziz - A/C.3/78/SR.18
European Union
Nyman, Klas - A/C.3/78/SR.18
Georgia
Lortkipanidze, Ekaterine - A/C.3/78/SR.18
Group of Friends of the United Nations Voluntary Fund for Victims of Torture
Macchiavello, Julissa (Peru) - A/C.3/78/SR.24
India
Sonkar, Suman - A/C.3/78/SR.18
International Committee of the Red Cross
Mabe, Brady Michael - A/C.3/78/SR.18
Iran (Islamic Republic of)
Arab Bafrani, Fatemeh - A/C.3/78/SR.18
Israel
Aviel, Shir - A/C.3/78/SR.18
Luxembourg
Lepage, Natasha - A/C.3/78/SR.18
Mexico
Buenrostro Massieu, Alicia - A/C.3/78/SR.18
Morocco
Chabi, Amine - A/C.3/78/SR.18
Myanmar
Tun, Kyaw Moe - A/C.3/78/SR.18
Nicaragua
Pichardo Urbina, Eleane Yaoska - A/C.3/78/SR.18
Pakistan
Kanwal, Tehreem - A/C.3/78/SR.18
Russian Federation
Kuzmenkov, Stepan Y. - A/C.3/78/SR.18
Saudi Arabia
Albadr, Saleh - A/C.3/78/SR.18
Sovereign Order of Malta
Greenwood, James Harrison - A/C.3/78/SR.18
Syrian Arab Republic
Altarsha, Elie - A/C.3/78/SR.18
Türkiye
Tanriöven, Enes - A/C.3/78/SR.18
Ukraine
Mudrenko, Nataliia - A/C.3/78/SR.18
UN. Assistant Secretary-General for Human Rights
Brands Kehris, Ilze - A/C.3/78/SR.18
UN. Committee against Torture. Chair
Heller, Claude - A/C.3/78/SR.18
UN. Human Rights Council. Special Rapporteur on Torture and Other Cruel, Inhuman or Degrading Treatment or Punishment
Edwards, Alice Jill - A/C.3/78/SR.18
UN. Subcommittee on Prevention of Torture and Other Cruel, Inhuman or Degrading Treatment or Punishment. Chair
Jabbour, Suzanne - A/C.3/78/SR.18
United States
Eyrich, Kara - A/C.3/78/SR.18
Merron, Eric - A/C.3/78/SR.18

TRAFFIC SAFETY (Agenda item 12)
Angola
Cruz, Francisco José da - A/78/PV.92
Morocco
Bouchikhi, Hanaa - A/78/PV.92
Russian Federation
Chumakov, Dmitry S. - A/78/PV.92
Ukraine
Leschenko, Volodymyr - A/78/PV.92

TRAFFICKING IN PERSONS (Agenda item 71b)
Australia
Kelson, Matthew - A/C.3/78/SR.23
Belarus
Kryvaltsevich, Aliaksei - A/C.3/78/SR.23
China
Liu, Luoge - A/C.3/78/SR.23
Dominican Republic
Andújar, Luz del Carmen - A/C.3/78/SR.23
Egypt
Mohamed, Mohamed Omar Elfarouk Hassan - A/C.3/78/SR.23
European Union
Szelivanov, Julia - A/C.3/78/SR.23
Greece
Kastanas, Elias - A/C.3/78/SR.23
India
Parihar, Rajesh - A/C.3/78/SR.23
Ireland
Digney, Leanne - A/C.3/78/SR.23
Luxembourg
Folmer, Sophie - A/C.3/78/SR.23
Malaysia
Escopper Zumilla, Michael Jawa - A/C.3/78/SR.23
Malta
Micallef, Justine - A/C.3/78/SR.23
Morocco
Alaoui, Rabia - A/C.3/78/SR.23
Pakistan
Qureshi, Hadeeqa - A/C.3/78/SR.23
Romania
Mihail, Ioana-Cristina - A/C.3/78/SR.23
Russian Federation
Kuzmenkov, Stepan Y. - A/C.3/78/SR.23
Sovereign Order of Malta
O'Hara Rusckowski, Deborah - A/C.3/78/SR.23
Switzerland
Wagner, Valérie - A/C.3/78/SR.23
Syrian Arab Republic
Altarsha, Elie - A/C.3/78/SR.23
Ukraine
Tokarska, Anastasiia - A/C.3/78/SR.23
UN. Human Rights Council. Special Rapporteur on Trafficking in Persons, Especially in Women and Children
Mullally, Siobhán - A/C.3/78/SR.23
United States
McGlothlin, Cameron - A/C.3/78/SR.23

TRANSNATIONAL CORPORATIONS—HUMAN RIGHTS (Agenda item 71b)
Cameroon
Wainwel, Gwedji Doris - A/C.3/78/SR.21
China
Zhang, Tianhao - A/C.3/78/SR.21
European Union
Szelivanov, Julia - A/C.3/78/SR.21
France
Lamy, Jean - A/C.3/78/SR.21
Ireland
Leonard, Roisin - A/C.3/78/SR.21
Pakistan
Qureshi, Hadeeqa - A/C.3/78/SR.21
Russian Federation
Kuzmenkov, Stepan Y. - A/C.3/78/SR.21
Switzerland
Bless, Adrian - A/C.3/78/SR.21
UN. Human Rights Council. Working Group on the Issue of Human Rights and Transnational Corporations and Other Business Enterprises. Chair
Olawuyi, Damilola - A/C.3/78/SR.21
United States
Weinstein, Andrew - A/C.3/78/SR.21

TREATIES (Agenda item 87)
Argentina
Mainero, Martín Juan - A/C.6/78/SR.20
Belarus
Evseenko, Pavel - A/C.6/78/SR.20
Belgium
Raes, Elisa de - A/C.6/78/SR.20
Cameroon
Nyanid, Zacharie Serge Raoul - A/C.6/78/SR.20
China
Zhao, Yanrui - A/C.6/78/SR.20
Colombia
Botero, Stephanie - A/C.6/78/SR.20
Community of Latin American and Caribbean States
Mark, Hayley-Ann (Saint Vincent and the Grenadines) - A/C.6/78/SR.20
Cuba
Mora Fonseca, Vladimir - A/C.6/78/SR.20
Denmark
Byth-Visholm, Sebastian - A/C.6/78/SR.20
El Salvador
Flores Soto, Ligia Lorena - A/C.6/78/SR.20
Malaysia
Abd Karim, Nur Azura Binti - A/C.6/78/SR.20
Mexico
Arrocha Olabuenaga, Pablo Adrián - A/C.6/78/SR.20
New Zealand
Janah, Naushyn - A/C.6/78/SR.20
Nigeria
Ajileye, Abimbola - A/C.6/78/SR.20
Philippines
Arumpac-Marte, Azela Guerrero - A/C.6/78/SR.20
Singapore
Khng, Nathaniel - A/C.6/78/SR.20

TREATIES (Agenda item 87) (continued)

South Africa
Motsepe, Keke Mantsho - A/C.6/78/SR.20
Switzerland
Rathe, Fanny Elizabeth - A/C.6/78/SR.20
UN. General Assembly. 6th Committee. Bureau
Khng, Nathaniel (Singapore) - A/C.6/78/SR.37
UN. General Assembly. 6th Committee. Rapporteur
Moussa, Moussa Mohamed (Djibouti) - A/78/PV.45
United Kingdom
Lito, Melina - A/C.6/78/SR.20
United States
Patton, Dorothy - A/C.6/78/SR.20

TURKS AND CAICOS ISLANDS QUESTION (Agenda item 58)

Community of Latin American and Caribbean States
King, Inga Rhonda (Saint Vincent and the Grenadines) - A/C.4/78/SR.7

UKRAINE—POLITICAL CONDITIONS (Agenda item 62)

Albania
Spasse, Arian - A/78/PV.57
Argentina
Mainero, Martín Juan - A/78/PV.58
Australia
Larsen, James - A/78/PV.57
Austria
Marschik, Nikolaus - A/78/PV.56
Belgium
Maesschalck, Filip de - A/78/PV.57
Brazil
Danese, Sérgio França - A/78/PV.58
Bulgaria
Stoeva, Lachezara - A/78/PV.57
Canada
Rae, Robert - A/78/PV.57
Chile
Narváez Ojeda, Paula - A/78/PV.57
China
Fu, Cong - A/78/PV.99
Costa Rica
Chan Valverde, Maritza - A/78/PV.57
Croatia
Grlić-Radman, Gordan - A/78/PV.56
Cuba
Fernández Palacios, Yumirka - A/78/PV.99
Czechia
Marian, Jan - A/78/PV.56
Democratic People's Republic of Korea
Kim, Nam Hyok - A/78/PV.56; A/78/PV.58
Denmark
Zilmer-Johns, Lisbet - A/78/PV.56
Ecuador
De la Gasca LopezDomínguez, José Javier - A/78/PV.58
Estonia
Tammsaar, Rein - A/78/PV.58

UKRAINE—POLITICAL CONDITIONS (Agenda item 62) (continued)

European Union
Lambrinidis, Stavros - A/78/PV.57
Finland
Tierala, Lauri - A/78/PV.56
France
Séjourné, Stéphane - A/78/PV.56
Georgia
Darsalia, Lasha - A/78/PV.56
Germany
Baerbock, Annalena - A/78/PV.56
Ghana
Kesse Antwi, Linda - A/78/PV.99
Greece
Lampridis, Spyridon - A/78/PV.56
Guatemala
Rodríguez Mancia, Carla María - A/78/PV.58
Gulf Cooperation Council
Al-Thani, Alya Ahmed S.A. (Qatar) - A/78/PV.57
Guyana
Rodrigues-Birkett, Carolyn - A/78/PV.58
India
Kamboj, Ruchira - A/78/PV.57
Indonesia
Prabowo, Hari - A/78/PV.57
Iran (Islamic Republic of)
Ghadirkhomi, Payman - A/78/PV.58
Ghafouri, Mojtaba - A/78/PV.99
Ireland
Fleming, Seán - A/78/PV.56
Israel
Erdan, Gilad Menashe - A/78/PV.58
Italy
Greco, Gianluca - A/78/PV.57
Japan
Tsuji, Kiyoto - A/78/PV.56
Jordan
Hmoud, Mahmoud Daifallah Mahmoud - A/78/PV.99
Kenya
Kimani, Martin - A/78/PV.57
Latvia
Brusbārdis, Reinis - A/78/PV.56
Liechtenstein
Oehri, Myriam - A/78/PV.57
Lithuania
Landsbergis, Gabrielius - A/78/PV.56
Luxembourg. Deputy Prime Minister
Bettel, Xavier - A/78/PV.56
Malta
Kuymizakis, Adam - A/78/PV.58
Mexico
Buenrostro Massieu, Alicia - A/78/PV.57
Vasconcelos y Cruz, Héctor Enrique - A/78/PV.99
Montenegro
Sabanovic, Damir - A/78/PV.58
Netherlands (Kingdom of the)
Bruins Slot, Hanke Gerdina Johannette - A/78/PV.56
New Zealand
Buist-Catherwood, Emily - A/78/PV.58

UKRAINE—POLITICAL CONDITIONS (Agenda item 62) (continued)

North Macedonia
Osmani, Bujar - A/78/PV.56
Paraguay
Pereira Sosa, José Eduardo - A/78/PV.58
Peru
Ugarelli, Luis F. - A/78/PV.58
Poland
Sikorski, Radoslaw - A/78/PV.56
Portugal
Carreiras, Helena - A/78/PV.56
Qatar
Al-Thani, Abdulrahman Abdulaziz F.A. - A/78/PV.99
Republic of Korea
Hong, Sung Hun - A/78/PV.58
Kim, Sangjin - A/78/PV.58
Republic of Moldova
Leuca, Gheorghe - A/78/PV.57
Romania
Hristea, Traian - A/78/PV.56
Russian Federation
Nebenzia, Vasilii - A/78/PV.56
Polyanskiy, Dmitry A. - A/78/PV.99
Singapore
Gafoor, Burhan - A/78/PV.57
Slovakia
Galbavý, Richard - A/78/PV.57
Slovenia. Deputy Prime Minister
Fajon, Tanja - A/78/PV.56
South Africa
Schalkwyk, Marthinus van - A/78/PV.99
Spain
Albares Bueno, José Manuel - A/78/PV.56
Switzerland
Cassis, Ignazio - A/78/PV.56
Syrian Arab Republic
Aldahhak, Koussay Abduljabbar - A/78/PV.58
Mustafa, Marah - A/78/PV.99
Thailand
Chindawongse, Suriya - A/78/PV.58
Türkiye
Önal, Sedat - A/78/PV.57
Ukraine
Kuleba, Dmytro - A/78/PV.56
Kyslytsya, Sergiy - A/78/PV.58; A/78/PV.99
UN. General Assembly. President
Francis, Dennis (Trinidad and Tobago) - A/78/PV.56
United Kingdom
Cameron, David - A/78/PV.56
United States
Thomas-Greenfield, Linda - A/78/PV.56
Venezuela (Bolivarian Republic of)
Pérez Ayestarán, Joaquín Alberto - A/78/PV.58

UN—ADMINISTRATION (Agenda item 132)

Australia
Jones, Alexandra - A/C.5/78/SR.26/PartII

UN—ADMINISTRATION (Agenda item 132) (continued)

Group of 77
Ainomuhisha, Medard (Uganda) - A/C.5/78/SR.29; A/C.5/78/SR.32
Tur de la Concepción, Richard (Cuba) - A/C.5/78/SR.2
Joint Inspection Unit
Cronin, Eileen A. - A/C.5/78/SR.29
Russian Federation
Chumakov, Dmitry S. - A/C.5/78/SR.32
Laputin, Vadim - A/C.5/78/SR.2
Switzerland
Danese, Aurora Maria - A/C.5/78/SR.29
Schmied, Gina Andrea - A/C.5/78/SR.2
UN. Advisory Committee on Administrative and Budgetary Questions. Chair
Bachar Bong, Abdallah - A/C.5/78/SR.32
UN. Advisory Committee on Administrative and Budgetary Questions. Vice-Chair
Chmielewski, Jakub - A/C.5/78/SR.29
UN. Assistant Secretary-General for Supply Chain Management
Berg, AnneMarie van den - A/C.5/78/SR.32
UN. Department of Management Strategy, Policy and Compliance. Business Transformation and Accountability Division
Summersgill, Kevin - A/C.5/78/SR.29
UN. General Assembly. 5th Committee. Rapporteur
Hartog, Laurens Thomas den (Netherlands (Kingdom of the)) - A/78/PV.50(Resumption1); A/78/PV.73; A/78/PV.95
UN. Independent Audit Advisory Committee. Chair
Vanker, Imran - A/C.5/78/SR.2
UN. Under-Secretary-General for Internal Oversight Services
Ndiaye, Fatoumata - A/C.5/78/SR.2; A/C.5/78/SR.32
UN System Chief Executives Board for Coordination
Pietracci, Federica - A/C.5/78/SR.29

UN—BUDGET (2023) (Agenda item 133)

Group of 77
Tur de la Concepción, Richard (Cuba) - A/C.5/78/SR.4; A/C.5/78/SR.9
Russian Federation
Chumakov, Dmitry S. - A/C.5/78/SR.26/PartII
UN. Advisory Committee on Administrative and Budgetary Questions. Chair
Bachar Bong, Abdallah - A/C.5/78/SR.9
UN. Controller
Ramanathan, Chandramouli - A/C.5/78/SR.9
UN. General Assembly. 5th Committee. Rapporteur
Hartog, Laurens Thomas den (Netherlands (Kingdom of the)) - A/78/PV.50(Resumption1)
UN Office for Partnerships. Executive Director
Hou, Annemarie - A/C.5/78/SR.4

UN—BUDGET (2024) (Agenda item 134)

Albania
Prizreni, Ingrit - A/C.5/78/SR.34

UN—BUDGET (2024) (Agenda item 134) (continued)
Algeria
Gadouri, Hakim - A/C.5/78/SR.33
Kara, Kamel - A/C.5/78/SR.5
Angola
Luemba, Mateus Pedro - A/C.5/78/SR.5; A/C.5/78/SR.33
Argentina
Cosentino, Leandro Carlos - A/C.5/78/SR.26/PartII; A/C.5/78/SR.33
ASEAN
Chak Yong, Mok (Singapore) - A/C.5/78/SR.12
Chua, Li Si Felicia (Singapore) - A/C.5/78/SR.33
Lagdameo, Antonio Manuel Revilla (Philippines) - A/C.5/78/SR.13
Seah, Mark (Singapore) - A/C.5/78/SR.3
Tam, Noelle (Singapore) - A/C.5/78/SR.11
Valles, Marivil Villa (Philippines) - A/C.5/78/SR.5
Australia
Jones, Alexandra - A/C.5/78/SR.26/PartII
Bahamas
DeGregory, Kelli - A/C.5/78/SR.23
Bangladesh
Farhan, Fahmid - A/C.5/78/SR.3
Muhith, Muhammad A. - A/C.5/78/SR.5
Belarus
Evseenko, Pavel - A/C.5/78/SR.26/PartII; A/C.5/78/SR.34
Bolivia (Plurinational State of)
Bayley Angeleri, Roberto - A/C.5/78/SR.28
Muñoz Ponce, Tatiana Bárbara - A/C.5/78/SR.26/PartII
Botswana
Mokhawa, Gladys - A/C.5/78/SR.5
Cambodia
Eat, Sophea - A/C.5/78/SR.16
Cameroon
Tommo Monthe, Michel - A/C.5/78/SR.22
Canada
Tan, Jonathan Necaster - A/C.5/78/SR.26/PartII
Caribbean Community
Wallace, Brian Christopher Manley (Jamaica) - A/C.5/78/SR.13
Walters, Iyeeka Latoy (Jamaica) - A/C.5/78/SR.18
Chile
González Sese, José Antonio - A/C.5/78/SR.12
China
Chen, Yuanhang - A/C.5/78/SR.3
Han, Jin - A/C.5/78/SR.28
Jiang, Hua - A/C.5/78/SR.5; A/C.5/78/SR.33; A/C.5/78/SR.34
Colombia
Zalabata Torres, Leonor - A/C.5/78/SR.4; A/C.5/78/SR.18
Costa Rica
Chan Valverde, Maritza - A/C.5/78/SR.5
Videche Guevara, Carlos Manuel - A/C.5/78/SR.23

UN—BUDGET (2024) (Agenda item 134) (continued)
Cuba
Tur de la Concepción, Richard - A/78/PV.50(Resumption1); A/C.5/78/SR.3; A/C.5/78/SR.26/PartII; A/C.5/78/SR.34
Cyprus
Demosthenous, Ioanna - A/C.5/78/SR.3
Democratic People's Republic of Korea
Kim, Nam Hyok - A/78/PV.73; A/C.5/78/SR.26/PartII; A/C.5/78/SR.34
El Salvador
González López, Egriselda Aracely - A/C.5/78/SR.5
Herrera García, Edilma America - A/C.5/78/SR.18
Eritrea
Hadgu, Daniel Abraham - A/C.5/78/SR.26/PartII; A/C.5/78/SR.34
European Union
Bogaerts, Basiel (Belgium) - A/C.5/78/SR.34
Camelli, Thibault - A/C.5/78/SR.3
Jiménez de la Hoz, Ana (Spain) - A/C.5/78/SR.26/PartII
Samson, Hedda - A/C.5/78/SR.5
Group of 77
Ainomuhisha, Medard (Uganda) - A/C.5/78/SR.33
Gala López, Yuri (Cuba) - A/C.5/78/SR.5
Hernández Morera, Diosdado de Jesús (Cuba) - A/C.5/78/SR.14; A/C.5/78/SR.16; A/C.5/78/SR.17; A/C.5/78/SR.18; A/C.5/78/SR.19; A/C.5/78/SR.21; A/C.5/78/SR.22
Tur de la Concepción, Richard (Cuba) - A/C.5/78/SR.2; A/C.5/78/SR.9; A/C.5/78/SR.11; A/C.5/78/SR.12; A/C.5/78/SR.13; A/C.5/78/SR.26/PartII
Gulf Cooperation Council
Al-Sharji, Saud (Oman) - A/C.5/78/SR.13
Haiti
Betor, Guensy - A/C.5/78/SR.4
Rodrigue, Antonio - A/C.5/78/SR.18
Iceland
Thorbjörnsdóttir, Guðrún - A/C.5/78/SR.26/PartII
Iran (Islamic Republic of)
Amrollahi, Mohammad Taghi - A/78/PV.73; A/C.5/78/SR.3; A/C.5/78/SR.26/PartII; A/C.5/78/SR.28; A/C.5/78/SR.34
Iraq
Al-Fatlawi, Abbas Kadhom Obaid - A/C.5/78/SR.3
Israel
Zilbergeld, Sherry - A/78/PV.50(Resumption1); A/C.5/78/SR.5; A/C.5/78/SR.26/PartII
Japan
Abo, Ai - A/C.5/78/SR.3
Fujinuma, Atsuyuki - A/C.5/78/SR.33
Ishikane, Kimihiro - A/C.5/78/SR.5
Kenya
Kinyungu, Njambi - A/C.5/78/SR.5; A/C.5/78/SR.11
Kuwait
Alenezi, Faisal G. - A/C.5/78/SR.3
Lesotho
Nena, Matete - A/C.5/78/SR.5

UN—BUDGET (2024) (Agenda item 134) (continued)

Mexico
Buenrostro Massieu, Alicia - A/C.5/78/SR.5
Velázquez Castillo, Jesús - A/C.5/78/SR.3; A/C.5/78/SR.33
Morocco
Boutaqa, Soufiane - A/C.5/78/SR.33
Hilale, Omar - A/C.5/78/SR.5
Mozambique
Kumanga, Martins Mariano - A/C.5/78/SR.5
Myanmar
Tun, Kyaw Moe - A/C.5/78/SR.5
New Zealand
Hardie, Alexandra - A/C.5/78/SR.26/PartII
Nicaragua
Llano, Alina J. - A/78/PV.73; A/C.5/78/SR.28; A/C.5/78/SR.34
Ochoa Espinales, Olimpia Raquel - A/C.5/78/SR.26/PartII
Nigeria
Shehu, Muktar - A/C.5/78/SR.33
Norway
Dalin, Inga - A/C.5/78/SR.33
Philippines
Valles, Marivil Villa - A/C.5/78/SR.33
Qatar
Al-Thani, Alya Ahmed S.A. - A/C.5/78/SR.5
Alnasr, Mohammed Khalifa H. - A/C.5/78/SR.26/PartII
Russian Federation
Chumakov, Dmitry S. - A/C.5/78/SR.5; A/C.5/78/SR.26/PartII; A/C.5/78/SR.34
Devyatkin, Daniil A. - A/78/PV.50(Resumption1); A/C.5/78/SR.9
Laputin, Vadim - A/78/PV.73; A/C.5/78/SR.23; A/C.5/78/SR.28
Saudi Arabia
AlRasheed, Mohammed Abdullah - A/C.5/78/SR.13
Alwasil, Abdulaziz M.O. - A/C.5/78/SR.5
Sierra Leone
Yajah, Christian Fayia - A/C.5/78/SR.33
South Africa
Joyini, Mathu - A/C.5/78/SR.5
Sudan
Bakhit, Badreldeen Bakhit Musa - A/78/PV.50(Resumption1); A/C.5/78/SR.4; A/C.5/78/SR.23; A/C.5/78/SR.26/PartII
Switzerland
Baeriswyl, Pascale - A/C.5/78/SR.5; A/C.5/78/SR.14
Danese, Aurora Maria - A/C.5/78/SR.26/PartII
Schmied, Gina Andrea - A/C.5/78/SR.26/PartII; A/C.5/78/SR.28; A/C.5/78/SR.33
Syrian Arab Republic
Al-mansour, Osama - A/78/PV.73; A/C.5/78/SR.3; A/C.5/78/SR.5; A/C.5/78/SR.26/PartII; A/C.5/78/SR.28; A/C.5/78/SR.34
Thailand
Suwwannikha, Surat - A/C.5/78/SR.12

UN—BUDGET (2024) (Agenda item 134) (continued)

Türkiye
Aras, Nisan Su - A/C.5/78/SR.3; A/C.5/78/SR.5
Uganda
Ainomuhisha, Medard - A/C.5/78/SR.33
UN. Advisory Committee on Administrative and Budgetary Questions. Chair
Bachar Bong, Abdallah - A/C.5/78/SR.5; A/C.5/78/SR.9; A/C.5/78/SR.14; A/C.5/78/SR.16; A/C.5/78/SR.17; A/C.5/78/SR.19; A/C.5/78/SR.21; A/C.5/78/SR.23; A/C.5/78/SR.24; A/C.5/78/SR.28; A/C.5/78/SR.30; A/C.5/78/SR.33
UN. Advisory Committee on Administrative and Budgetary Questions. Vice-Chair
Al-Kumaim, Amjad Qaid Ahmed - A/C.5/78/SR.4; A/C.5/78/SR.13; A/C.5/78/SR.22
Brennen-Haylock, Sharon - A/C.5/78/SR.31
Chmielewski, Jakub - A/C.5/78/SR.3; A/C.5/78/SR.11; A/C.5/78/SR.12
Ruas, Juliana Gaspar - A/C.5/78/SR.2; A/C.5/78/SR.18; A/C.5/78/SR.25
UN. Board of Auditors. Audit Operations Committee. Chair
Hu, Xuewen - A/C.5/78/SR.9
UN. Controller
Ramanathan, Chandramouli - A/C.5/78/SR.2; A/C.5/78/SR.4; A/C.5/78/SR.11; A/C.5/78/SR.16; A/C.5/78/SR.26/PartII; A/C.5/78/SR.28; A/C.5/78/SR.30; A/C.5/78/SR.33
UN. Department of Management Strategy, Policy and Compliance. Office of Programme Planning, Finance and Budget. Finance Division. Director
Costa, Maria - A/C.5/78/SR.3; A/C.5/78/SR.12; A/C.5/78/SR.14; A/C.5/78/SR.18; A/C.5/78/SR.21; A/C.5/78/SR.22; A/C.5/78/SR.24; A/C.5/78/SR.25; A/C.5/78/SR.31
UN. Department of Operational Support. Division of Administration. Director
Carey, Patrick - A/C.5/78/SR.11
UN. Enterprise Resource Planning Solution Division. Director
Korithiwada, Sunitha - A/C.5/78/SR.19
UN. General Assembly. 5th Committee. Rapporteur
Hartog, Laurens Thomas den (Netherlands (Kingdom of the)) - A/78/PV.50(Resumption1); A/78/PV.73
UN. Group of African States
Lamuwa, Adamu Ibrahim (Nigeria) - A/C.5/78/SR.13
Minale, Lemlem Fiseha (Ethiopia) - A/C.5/78/SR.3; A/C.5/78/SR.11; A/C.5/78/SR.12; A/C.5/78/SR.22; A/C.5/78/SR.23; A/C.5/78/SR.33
Sabo, Tesfaye Yilma (Ethiopia) - A/C.5/78/SR.5; A/C.5/78/SR.14
UN. Programme Planning and Budget Division. Director
Huisman, Johannes - A/C.5/78/SR.9; A/C.5/78/SR.23
UN. Secretary-General
Guterres, António, 1949- - A/C.5/78/SR.5

UN—BUDGET (2024) (Agenda item 134) (continued)

UN. Special Adviser for Addressing Racism in the Workplace
Gumbi, Mojankunyane - A/C.5/78/SR.13
UN. Under-Secretary-General for Internal Oversight Services
Ndiaye, Fatoumata - A/C.5/78/SR.11
UN. Under-Secretary-General for Management Strategy, Policy and Compliance
Pollard, Catherine - A/C.5/78/SR.5; A/C.5/78/SR.13; A/C.5/78/SR.33
UN. Under-Secretary-General for Operational Support
Khare, Atul - A/C.5/78/SR.17
UN Joint Staff Pension Board. Chair
Van Houtte, Annick - A/C.5/78/SR.9
United Kingdom
Capek, Hannah Rose - A/C.5/78/SR.26/PartII
Cottam, Paul Arthur - A/C.5/78/SR.33
Staples, James - A/C.5/78/SR.5
United States
Lu, Christopher P. - A/C.5/78/SR.5; A/C.5/78/SR.26/PartII
Uruguay
Machado Mouriño, Felipe - A/C.5/78/SR.21
Venezuela (Bolivarian Republic of)
Bayley Angeleri, Roberto - A/C.5/78/SR.34

UN—BUDGET CONTRIBUTIONS (Agenda item 138)

Group of 77
Tur de la Concepción, Richard (Cuba) - A/C.5/78/SR.1
Haiti
Betor, Guensy - A/C.5/78/SR.1
Japan
Wakabayashi, Sato - A/C.5/78/SR.1
Russian Federation
Alyakin, Dmitry S. - A/78/PV.16; A/C.5/78/SR.2
Laputin, Vadim - A/C.5/78/SR.1
UN. Committee on Contributions. Chair
Greiver, Bernardo - A/C.5/78/SR.1
UN. Controller
Ramanathan, Chandramouli - A/C.5/78/SR.1

UN—FINANCIAL REPORTS (Agenda item 131)

China
Guo, Zhiqi - A/C.5/78/SR.14
Group of 77
Ainomuhisha, Medard (Uganda) - A/C.5/78/SR.35
Tur de la Concepción, Richard (Cuba) - A/C.5/78/SR.14
UN. Advisory Committee on Administrative and Budgetary Questions. Chair
Bachar Bong, Abdallah - A/C.5/78/SR.14
UN. Board of Auditors. Audit Operations Committee. Chair
Hu, Xuewen - A/C.5/78/SR.35

UN—FINANCIAL REPORTS (Agenda item 131) (continued)

UN. Controller
Ramanathan, Chandramouli - A/C.5/78/SR.35
UN. Department of Management Strategy, Policy and Compliance. Office of Programme Planning, Finance and Budget. Finance Division. Director
Costa, Maria - A/C.5/78/SR.14
UN. General Assembly. 5th Committee. Rapporteur
Hartog, Laurens Thomas den (Netherlands (Kingdom of the)) - A/78/PV.50(Resumption1); A/78/PV.95

UN—FINANCIAL SITUATION (Agenda item 136)

ASEAN
Gafoor, Burhan (Singapore) - A/C.5/78/SR.38
Seah, Mark (Singapore) - A/C.5/78/SR.6
China
Guo, Zhiqi - A/C.5/78/SR.6
European Union
Camelli, Thibault - A/C.5/78/SR.38
Group of 77
Ainomuhisha, Medard (Uganda) - A/C.5/78/SR.38
Tur de la Concepción, Richard (Cuba) - A/C.5/78/SR.6
Guyana
Edwards, Marissa Audra Faith - A/C.5/78/SR.6
Japan
Abo, Ai - A/C.5/78/SR.6
Morocco
Bouazzaoui, Chaimae - A/C.5/78/SR.6
Russian Federation
Lysikov, Andrei - A/C.5/78/SR.38
Saudi Arabia
Alshaikh, Hayfaa Abdullatif A. - A/C.5/78/SR.38
Singapore
Gafoor, Burhan - A/C.5/78/SR.38
Switzerland
Schmied, Gina Andrea - A/C.5/78/SR.6
UN. Controller
Ramanathan, Chandramouli - A/C.5/78/SR.6
UN. General Assembly. 5th Committee. Chair
Abdelkhalek, Osama Mahmoud (Egypt) - A/C.5/78/SR.38
UN. Group of African States
Osei, Rita (Ghana) - A/C.5/78/SR.6
UN. Under-Secretary-General for Management Strategy, Policy and Compliance
Pollard, Catherine - A/C.5/78/SR.4; A/C.5/78/SR.6; A/C.5/78/SR.37; A/C.5/78/SR.38
United Kingdom
Cottam, Paul Arthur - A/C.5/78/SR.6
Williams, Ian - A/C.5/78/SR.38
United States
Hanna, Paul - A/C.5/78/SR.6
Zambia
Sakala, Rose - A/C.5/78/SR.6

UN—HUMAN RESOURCES MANAGEMENT (Agenda item 139)

Algeria
Gadouri, Hakim - A/C.5/78/SR.27
ASEAN
Lora-Santos, Leila Castillon (Philippines) - A/C.5/78/SR.27
China
Guo, Ke - A/C.5/78/SR.25
Group of 77
Ainomuhisha, Medard (Uganda) - A/C.5/78/SR.27
Hernández Morera, Diosdado de Jesús (Cuba) - A/C.5/78/SR.25
Gulf Cooperation Council
Alnasr, Mohammed Khalifa H. (Qatar) - A/C.5/78/SR.27
Russian Federation
Chumakov, Dmitry S. - A/C.5/78/SR.34
Laputin, Vadim - A/C.5/78/SR.27
Switzerland
Schmied, Gina Andrea - A/C.5/78/SR.27
UN. Advisory Committee on Administrative and Budgetary Questions. Vice-Chair
Al-Kumaim, Amjad Qaid Ahmed - A/C.5/78/SR.27
Ruas, Juliana Gaspar - A/C.5/78/SR.25
UN. Assistant Secretary-General for Human Resources Management
López, Martha Helena - A/C.5/78/SR.25; A/C.5/78/SR.27
UN. General Assembly. 5th Committee. Rapporteur
Hartog, Laurens Thomas den (Netherlands (Kingdom of the)) - A/78/PV.73; A/78/PV.95
UN. Group of African States
Minale, Lemlem Fiseha (Ethiopia) - A/C.5/78/SR.27
UN Staff Union
Johnson, Laura - A/C.5/78/SR.27

UN—PROGRAMME PLANNING (Agenda item 135)

Algeria
Kara, Kamel - A/C.5/78/SR.5
Angola
Luemba, Mateus Pedro - A/C.5/78/SR.5
ASEAN
Valles, Marivil Villa (Philippines) - A/C.5/78/SR.5
Australia
Della-porta, Demi Heather See - A/C.1/78/PV.10
Bangladesh
Muhith, Muhammad A. - A/C.5/78/SR.5
Belarus
Evseenko, Pavel - A/78/PV.50(Resumption1)
Bolivia (Plurinational State of)
Muñoz Ponce, Tatiana Bárbara - A/78/PV.50(Resumption1); A/C.5/78/SR.24
Botswana
Mokhawa, Gladys - A/C.5/78/SR.5
Chile
Vidal Mercado, Jorge Andrés - A/C.1/78/PV.10

UN—PROGRAMME PLANNING (Agenda item 135) (continued)

China
Jiang, Hua - A/C.5/78/SR.5
Zhang, Sisi - A/78/PV.50(Resumption1)
Colombia
Quintero Correa, Nohra María - A/C.1/78/PV.10
Costa Rica
Chan Valverde, Maritza - A/C.1/78/PV.10; A/C.5/78/SR.5
Cuba
Hernández Morera, Diosdado de Jesús - A/C.5/78/SR.24
Romero López, Rosanis - A/C.1/78/PV.10
Tur de la Concepción, Richard - A/78/PV.50(Resumption1)
Democratic People's Republic of Korea
Kim, In Chol - A/C.5/78/SR.24
Kim, Nam Hyok - A/78/PV.50(Resumption1)
El Salvador
González López, Egriselda Aracely - A/C.1/78/PV.10; A/C.5/78/SR.5
Eritrea
Hadgu, Daniel Abraham - A/78/PV.50(Resumption1)
European Union
Samson, Hedda - A/C.5/78/SR.5
Viñayo Fernández, Sofía (Spain) - A/C.5/78/SR.24
France
Semon, Alizée - A/C.1/78/PV.10
Group of 77
Gala López, Yuri (Cuba) - A/C.5/78/SR.5
Iran (Islamic Republic of)
Amrollahi, Mohammad Taghi - A/78/PV.50(Resumption1); A/C.5/78/SR.24
Israel
Zilbergeld, Sherry - A/C.5/78/SR.5
Japan
Ishikane, Kimihiro - A/C.5/78/SR.5
Kusano, Yuta - A/C.1/78/PV.10
Kenya
Kinyungu, Njambi - A/C.5/78/SR.5
Lesotho
Nena, Matete - A/C.5/78/SR.5
Mexico
Buenrostro Massieu, Alicia - A/C.5/78/SR.5
Sánchez Kiesslich, Eduardo Alcibiades - A/C.1/78/PV.10
Morocco
Hilale, Omar - A/C.5/78/SR.5
Mozambique
Kumanga, Martins Mariano - A/C.5/78/SR.5
Myanmar
Tun, Kyaw Moe - A/C.5/78/SR.5
Nicaragua
Ochoa Espinales, Olimpia Raquel - A/78/PV.50(Resumption1); A/C.5/78/SR.24
Qatar
Al-Thani, Alya Ahmed S.A. - A/C.5/78/SR.5
Alnasr, Mohammed Khalifa H. - A/C.5/78/SR.24

UN—PROGRAMME PLANNING (Agenda item 135) (continued)

Russian Federation
Chumakov, Dmitry S. - A/C.5/78/SR.5; A/C.5/78/SR.24
Devyatkin, Daniil A. - A/78/PV.50(Resumption1)
Vorontsov, Konstantin - A/C.1/78/PV.10
Saudi Arabia
Alwasil, Abdulaziz M.O. - A/C.5/78/SR.5
South Africa
Joyini, Mathu - A/C.5/78/SR.5
Switzerland
Baeriswyl, Pascale - A/C.5/78/SR.5
Schmied, Gina Andrea - A/C.5/78/SR.24
Thoeni, Julien - A/C.1/78/PV.10
Syrian Arab Republic
Al-mansour, Osama - A/78/PV.50(Resumption1); A/C.5/78/SR.5; A/C.5/78/SR.24
Türkiye
Aras, Nisan Su - A/C.5/78/SR.5
UN. Committee for Programme and Coordination. Vice-Chair
Jerboui, Hind (Morocco) - A/C.5/78/SR.5
UN. General Assembly. 1st Committee. Rapporteur
Balouji, Heidar Ali (Iran (Islamic Republic of)) - A/78/PV.42
UN. General Assembly. 2nd Committee. Chair
Amorín, Carlos Daniel (Uruguay) - A/C.2/78/SR.1
UN. General Assembly. 2nd Committee. Rapporteur
Gatev, Ivaylo (Bulgaria) - A/78/PV.49
UN. General Assembly. 3rd Committee. Rapporteur
Poveda Brito, Robert Alexander (Venezuela (Bolivarian Republic of)) - A/78/PV.50
UN. General Assembly. 5th Committee. Rapporteur
Hartog, Laurens Thomas den (Netherlands (Kingdom of the)) - A/78/PV.50(Resumption1)
UN. General Assembly. 6th Committee. Rapporteur
Moussa, Moussa Mohamed (Djibouti) - A/78/PV.45
UN. General Assembly. Special Political and Decolonization Committee (4th Committee). Rapporteur
Dhanutirto, Mariska Dwianti (Indonesia) - A/78/PV.45
UN. Group of African States
Sabo, Tesfaye Yilma (Ethiopia) - A/C.5/78/SR.5
UN. Secretary-General
Guterres, António, 1949- - A/C.5/78/SR.5
UN. Under-Secretary-General for Management Strategy, Policy and Compliance
Pollard, Catherine - A/C.5/78/SR.5
United Kingdom
Liddle, Aidan Thomas - A/C.1/78/PV.10
Staples, James - A/C.5/78/SR.5
United States
Lu, Christopher P. - A/C.5/78/SR.5
Storsve, Alison - A/C.1/78/PV.10
Uruguay
Eustathiou de los Santos, Matías Andrés - A/C.1/78/PV.10
Venezuela (Bolivarian Republic of)
Bayley Angeleri, Roberto - A/78/PV.50(Resumption1)

UN. ADVISORY COMMITTEE ON ADMINISTRATIVE AND BUDGETARY QUESTIONS—MEMBERS (Agenda item 115a)

UN. General Assembly. 5th Committee. Chair
Abdelkhalek, Osama Mahmoud (Egypt) - A/C.5/78/SR.8

UN. BOARD OF AUDITORS—MEMBERS (Agenda item 115d)

UN. General Assembly. 5th Committee. Chair
Abdelkhalek, Osama Mahmoud (Egypt) - A/C.5/78/SR.8

UN. COMMITTEE FOR PROGRAMME AND COORDINATION—MEMBERS (Agenda item 114a)

Iran (Islamic Republic of)
Alshahin, Essam - A/78/PV.37
Ghadirkhomi, Payman - A/78/PV.37

UN. COMMITTEE ON CONTRIBUTIONS—MEMBERS (Agenda item 115b)

UN. General Assembly. 5th Committee. Chair
Abdelkhalek, Osama Mahmoud (Egypt) - A/C.5/78/SR.8

UN. COMMITTEE ON RELATIONS WITH THE HOST COUNTRY—REPORTS (Agenda item 161)

Belarus
Shaev, Evgeny - A/C.6/78/SR.35
China
Li, Linlin - A/C.6/78/SR.35
Coordinating Bureau of the Non-Aligned Countries
Aref, Yahya (Iran (Islamic Republic of)) - A/C.6/78/SR.35
Cuba
Gala López, Yuri - A/C.6/78/SR.35
Cyprus
Pittakis, Theodoulos - A/C.6/78/SR.37
European Union
Popan, Simona - A/C.6/78/SR.35
Group of Friends in Defence of the Charter of the United Nations
Pérez Ayestarán, Joaquín Alberto (Venezuela (Bolivarian Republic of)) - A/C.6/78/SR.35
Iran (Islamic Republic of)
Ershadi, Zahra - A/C.6/78/SR.35
Russian Federation
Proskuryakov, Alexander S. - A/C.6/78/SR.35
Singapore
Gafoor, Burhan - A/C.6/78/SR.35
Sudan
Idres, Nusaiba Hashim Mohamed Ali - A/C.6/78/SR.35
Syrian Arab Republic
Khaddour, Mhd. Riyad - A/C.6/78/SR.35

UN. COMMITTEE ON RELATIONS WITH THE HOST COUNTRY—REPORTS (Agenda item 161) (continued)

UN. Committee on Relations with the Host Country
Hadjichrysanthou, Andreas (Cyprus) - A/C.6/78/SR.35
UN. General Assembly. 6th Committee. Rapporteur
Moussa, Moussa Mohamed (Djibouti) - A/78/PV.45
United States
Patton, Dorothy - A/C.6/78/SR.35

UN. CONFERENCE ON DISARMAMENT—REPORTS (Agenda item 101a)

ASEAN
Seah, Mark (Singapore) - A/C.1/78/PV.22
Australia
Della-porta, Demi Heather See - A/C.1/78/PV.24
Austria
Kmentt, Alexander - A/C.1/78/PV.23
Bangladesh
Molla, Md Rafiqul Alam - A/C.1/78/PV.23
Brazil
Damico, Flávio Soares - A/C.1/78/PV.24
Canada
Fetz, Thomas - A/C.1/78/PV.23
Caribbean Community
Moxey, Matthew (Bahamas) - A/C.1/78/PV.22
China
Shen, Jian - A/C.1/78/PV.23
Cuba
Thomas Ramírez, Vilma - A/C.1/78/PV.23
Egypt
Ahmed, Amr Essameldin Sadek - A/C.1/78/PV.23
European Union
Karczmarz, Michał - A/C.1/78/PV.22
Sánchez de Lerín García-Ovies, Ignacio (Spain) - A/C.1/78/PV.29
France
Petit, Camille - A/C.1/78/PV.22
Group of Arab States
Alqaisi, Sultan Natheir Mustafa (Jordan) - A/C.1/78/PV.22
India
Bedi, Anmol Sher Singh - A/C.1/78/PV.23
Iran (Islamic Republic of)
Ghorbanpour Najafabadi, Mohammad - A/C.1/78/PV.23
Italy
Bencini, Leonardo - A/C.1/78/PV.23
Malaysia
Sivamohan, Shivanand - A/C.1/78/PV.23
Mexico
Sánchez Kiesslich, Eduardo Alcibiades - A/C.1/78/PV.22; A/C.1/78/PV.29
Nepal
Gohiwar Aryal, Indira - A/C.1/78/PV.23
Netherlands (Kingdom of the)
Bosch, Robert in den - A/C.1/78/PV.23
Pakistan
Sarwani, Gul Qaiser - A/C.1/78/PV.23

UN. CONFERENCE ON DISARMAMENT—REPORTS (Agenda item 101a) (continued)

Philippines
Gomez, Jan Michael - A/C.1/78/PV.22
Lipana, Diane Shayne Dela Fuente - A/C.1/78/PV.29
Republic of Korea
Yoon, Seong-mee - A/C.1/78/PV.23
Russian Federation
Belousov, Andrey I. - A/C.1/78/PV.23; A/C.1/78/PV.24; A/C.1/78/PV.29
Slovenia
Jerman, Bostjan - A/C.1/78/PV.23
South Africa
Mahomed, Shuaib - A/C.1/78/PV.22
Switzerland
Greve, Silvia - A/C.1/78/PV.23
UN. Conference on Disarmament. President
Szűcs, Margit (Hungary) - A/C.1/78/PV.24
United Kingdom
Floyd, Ian - A/C.1/78/PV.23
United States
Turner, Bruce - A/C.1/78/PV.23

UN. DISARMAMENT COMMISSION—REPORTS (Agenda item 101b)

ASEAN
Seah, Mark (Singapore) - A/C.1/78/PV.22
Bangladesh
Molla, Md Rafiqul Alam - A/C.1/78/PV.23
Caribbean Community
Moxey, Matthew (Bahamas) - A/C.1/78/PV.22
Coordinating Bureau of the Non-Aligned Countries
Sirie, Mochammad Iqbal (Indonesia) - A/C.1/78/PV.22
Cuba
Thomas Ramírez, Vilma - A/C.1/78/PV.23
Egypt
Ahmed, Amr Essameldin Sadek - A/C.1/78/PV.23
European Union
Karczmarz, Michał - A/C.1/78/PV.22
Group of Arab States
Alqaisi, Sultan Natheir Mustafa (Jordan) - A/C.1/78/PV.22
India
Bedi, Anmol Sher Singh - A/C.1/78/PV.23
Indonesia
Sirie, Mochammad Iqbal - A/C.1/78/PV.22
Kazakhstan
Zhangarayev, Nurmukhamed - A/C.1/78/PV.29
Malaysia
Sivamohan, Shivanand - A/C.1/78/PV.23
Mexico
Sánchez Kiesslich, Eduardo Alcibiades - A/C.1/78/PV.22
Nepal
Gohiwar Aryal, Indira - A/C.1/78/PV.23
Philippines
Gomez, Jan Michael - A/C.1/78/PV.22
Republic of Korea
Yoon, Seong-mee - A/C.1/78/PV.23

UN. DISARMAMENT COMMISSION—REPORTS (Agenda item 101b) (continued)

South Africa
Mahomed, Shuaib - A/C.1/78/PV.22
UN. Disarmament Commission. Chair
Rakhmetullin, Akan (Kazakhstan) - A/C.1/78/PV.24

UN. ECONOMIC AND SOCIAL COUNCIL—REPORTS (Agenda item 9)

Angola
Cruz, Francisco José da - A/78/PV.48
Bhutan
Nidup, Dorji - A/78/PV.48
Group of 77
Nidup, Dorji (Bhutan) - A/78/PV.48
Israel
Ben Naftaly, Emil - A/78/PV.33
Kuwait
Al-Kandari, Ismail Abdullah - A/78/PV.33
Maldives
Nashwa, Fathimath - A/78/PV.33
Russian Federation
Chumakov, Dmitry S. - A/78/PV.33
Thailand
Chindawongse, Suriya - A/78/PV.33
UN. Economic and Social Council. President
Stoeva, Lachezara (Bulgaria) - A/78/PV.33

UN. ETHICS OFFICE—REPORTS (Agenda item 140)

Group of 77
Tur de la Concepción, Richard (Cuba) - A/C.5/78/SR.2
Russian Federation
Fonina, Svetlana F. - A/C.5/78/SR.2
UN. Ethics Office. Director
Armstrong, Elia Yi - A/C.5/78/SR.2
UN. General Assembly. 5th Committee. Rapporteur
Hartog, Laurens Thomas den (Netherlands (Kingdom of the)) - A/78/PV.50(Resumption1)

UN. GENERAL ASSEMBLY—PRESIDENT-ELECT—OATH OF OFFICE

UN. General Assembly. President
Yang, Philémon (Cameroon) - A/78/PV.109

UN. GENERAL ASSEMBLY—WORK PROGRAMME (Agenda item 120)

Accountability, Coherence and Transparency (ACT) Group
Tammsaar, Rein (Estonia) - A/78/PV.32
Argentina
Squeff, María del Carmen - A/78/PV.33
ASEAN
Omar, Khairi (Malaysia) - A/78/PV.32

UN. GENERAL ASSEMBLY—WORK PROGRAMME (Agenda item 120) (continued)

Australia
Della-porta, Demi Heather See - A/C.1/78/PV.10
Hutchison, Alexandra - A/C.6/78/SR.36
Van Bronswijk, Sarah - A/78/PV.32
Bangladesh
Molla, Md Rafiqul Alam - A/78/PV.33
Chile
Vidal Mercado, Jorge Andrés - A/C.1/78/PV.10
Colombia
Quintero Correa, Nohra María - A/C.1/78/PV.10
Coordinating Bureau of the Non-Aligned Countries
Bendjama, Amar (Algeria) - A/78/PV.32
Costa Rica
Chan Valverde, Maritza - A/78/PV.32; A/C.1/78/PV.10; A/C.6/78/SR.36
Cuba
Romero López, Rosanis - A/C.1/78/PV.10
San Román Valdés, Jorge - A/78/PV.32
Ecuador
Fiallo Karolys, Andrés Fernando - A/78/PV.32
Egypt
Abdelkhalek, Osama Mahmoud - A/78/PV.32
Nouh, Amr Mohamed Mosaad - A/C.6/78/SR.36
El Salvador
González López, Egriselda Aracely - A/78/PV.32; A/C.1/78/PV.10
Sorto Rosales, Mayra Lisseth - A/C.3/78/SR.56
European Union
Linton, Sarah Joy (Australia) - A/C.2/78/SR.25
Samson, Hedda - A/78/PV.32
France
Semon, Alizée - A/C.1/78/PV.10
Wavrin, Hugo - A/78/PV.33
India
Mathur, Pratik - A/78/PV.33
Indonesia
Aron, Andy - A/78/PV.32
Israel
Ben Naftaly, Emil - A/78/PV.33
Japan
Kusano, Yuta - A/C.1/78/PV.10
Yoshida, Aya - A/78/PV.32
Lebanon
Zoghbi, Rawa - A/C.3/78/SR.56
Maldives
Guraisha, Aminath - A/78/PV.32
Mexico
Basulto Alvarez, Alejandrina - A/C.2/78/SR.25
Buenrostro Massieu, Alicia - A/78/PV.33
Sánchez Kiesslich, Eduardo Alcibiades - A/C.1/78/PV.10
Mongolia
Vorshilov, Enkhbold - A/78/PV.32
Morocco
Benziane, Imane - A/78/PV.32
Pakistan
Akram, Munir - A/78/PV.32
Philippines
Lagdameo, Antonio Manuel Revilla - A/78/PV.32

UN. GENERAL ASSEMBLY—WORK PROGRAMME (Agenda item 120) (continued)

Portugal
Aranda, Jorge Eduardo Ferreira Silva - A/78/PV.33
Carvalho, Sergio Amaral Alves de - A/C.6/78/SR.36
Qatar
Al-Thani, Hamad bin Abdulrahman - A/78/PV.33
Russian Federation
Antonova, Anna V. - A/C.6/78/SR.36
Gilmutdinova, Dina Anisovna - A/78/PV.33
Vorontsov, Konstantin - A/C.1/78/PV.10
Singapore
Seah, Mark - A/78/PV.32
Slovenia
Malovrh, Bostjan - A/78/PV.33
South Africa
Schalkwyk, Marthinus van - A/78/PV.32
Sri Lanka
Pieris, Peter Mohan Maithri - A/78/PV.33
Switzerland
Thoeni, Julien - A/C.1/78/PV.10
Thailand
Chindawongse, Suriya - A/78/PV.32
Tunisia
Bessadok, Marwa Jabou - A/C.3/78/SR.56
Ukraine
Prytula, Mykola - A/78/PV.33
UN. General Assembly. 1st Committee. Rapporteur
Balouji, Heidar Ali (Iran (Islamic Republic of)) - A/78/PV.42
UN. General Assembly. 2nd Committee. Rapporteur
Gatev, Ivaylo (Bulgaria) - A/78/PV.49
UN. General Assembly. 3rd Committee. Rapporteur
Poveda Brito, Robert Alexander (Venezuela (Bolivarian Republic of)) - A/78/PV.50
UN. General Assembly. 6th Committee. Rapporteur
Moussa, Moussa Mohamed (Djibouti) - A/78/PV.45
UN. General Assembly. Ad Hoc Working Group on the Revitalization of the General Assembly. Co-Chair
Feruță, Cornel (Romania) - A/78/PV.33
UN. General Assembly. President
Francis, Dennis (Trinidad and Tobago) - A/78/PV.32
UN. General Assembly. Special Political and Decolonization Committee (4th Committee). Rapporteur
Dhanutirto, Mariska Dwianti (Indonesia) - A/78/PV.45
United Kingdom
Liddle, Aidan Thomas - A/C.1/78/PV.10
United States
Adelman, Dylan - A/78/PV.33
Storsve, Alison - A/C.1/78/PV.10
Uruguay
Eustathiou de los Santos, Matías Andrés - A/C.1/78/PV.10
Viet Nam
Thoa Le, Thi Minh - A/78/PV.32

UN. GENERAL ASSEMBLY (78TH SESS. : 2023-2024)—AGENDA (Agenda item 7)

China
Liang, Hengzhu - A/BUR/78/SR.2
Djibouti
Moussa, Youssouf Aden - A/BUR/78/SR.2
France
Dime-Labille, Diarra - A/BUR/78/SR.2
Romania
Mocanu, Andreea - A/BUR/78/SR.2
Russian Federation
Leonidchenko, Sergey A. - A/BUR/78/SR.2
Zabolotskaya, Maria V. - A/78/PV.2; A/BUR/78/SR.1
Senegal
Niang, Cheikh - A/BUR/78/SR.1
Sri Lanka
Pieris, Peter Mohan Maithri - A/78/PV.2
Ukraine
Hayovyshyn, Khrystyna - A/78/PV.2
UN. General Assembly. President
Francis, Dennis (Trinidad and Tobago) - A/78/PV.1

UN. GENERAL ASSEMBLY (78TH SESS. : 2023-2024)—CLOSING

UN. General Assembly. President
Francis, Dennis (Trinidad and Tobago) - A/78/PV.109
UN. Secretary-General
Guterres, António, 1949- - A/78/PV.109

UN. GENERAL ASSEMBLY (78TH SESS. : 2023-2024)—GENERAL DEBATE (Agenda item 8)

Albania. President
Begaj, Bajram - A/78/PV.9
Algeria. President
Tebboune, Abdelmadjid - A/78/PV.5
Andorra. Head of Government
Espot Zamora, Xavier - A/78/PV.10
Angola. President
Lourenço, João Manuel Gonçalves - A/78/PV.6
Antigua and Barbuda. Prime Minister
Browne, Gaston Alphonso - A/78/PV.10
Argentina. President
Fernández, Alberto - A/78/PV.5
Armenia
Mirzoyan, Ararat - A/78/PV.13
Australia
Wong, Penny - A/78/PV.11
Austria
Schallenberg, Alexander - A/78/PV.9
Azerbaijan
Bayramov, Jeyhun - A/78/PV.12
Bahamas
Mitchell, Frederick A. - A/78/PV.11
Bahrain
Al Zayani, Abdul Latif bin Rashid - A/78/PV.11

UN. GENERAL ASSEMBLY (78TH SESS. : 2023-2024)—GENERAL DEBATE (Agenda item 8) (continued)

Bangladesh. Prime Minister
Hasina, Sheikh - A/78/PV.10
Barbados. Prime Minister
Mottley, Mia Amor - A/78/PV.10
Belarus
Aleinik, Sergei - A/78/PV.13
Belgium. Prime Minister
De Croo, Alexander - A/78/PV.7
Belize
Courtenay, Eamon - A/78/PV.13
Benin
Araba, Marc Hermanne Gninadoou - A/78/PV.14
Bhutan
Dorji, Tandi - A/78/PV.14
Bolivia (Plurinational State of). President
Arce Catacora, Luis Alberto - A/78/PV.5
Bosnia and Herzegovina. Presidency. Chair
Komsic, Zeljko - A/78/PV.6
Botswana. President
Masisi, Mokgweetsi Eric Keabetswe - A/78/PV.7
Brazil. President
Silva, Luiz Inácio Lula da - A/78/PV.4
Brunei Darussalam
Yusof, Dato Erywan Pehin - A/78/PV.13
Bulgaria. President
Radev, Rumen - A/78/PV.6
Burkina Faso
Bazie, Bassolma - A/78/PV.13
Burundi. President
Ndayishimiye, Évariste - A/78/PV.8
Cabo Verde. Prime Minister
Silva, José Ulisses Correia e - A/78/PV.12
Cambodia. Prime Minister
Hun, Manet - A/78/PV.11
Cameroon
Mbella Mbella, Lejeune - A/78/PV.14
Canada
Rae, Robert - A/78/PV.14
Central African Republic. President
Touadera, Faustin Archange - A/78/PV.8
Chad
Annadif, Mahamat Saleh - A/78/PV.9
Chile. President
Boric Font, Gabriel - A/78/PV.7
China. Vice-President
Han, Zheng - A/78/PV.9
Colombia. President
Petro Urrego, Gustavo - A/78/PV.4
Comoros. President
Assoumani, Azali - A/78/PV.7
Congo. President
Sassou N'Guesso, Denis - A/78/PV.8
Costa Rica
André Tinoco, Arnoldo - A/78/PV.11
Côte d'Ivoire. Vice-President
Kone, Tiémoko Meyliet - A/78/PV.9
Croatia. President
Milanovic, Zoran - A/78/PV.6

UN. GENERAL ASSEMBLY (78TH SESS. : 2023-2024)—GENERAL DEBATE (Agenda item 8) (continued)

Cuba. President
Díaz-Canel Bermúdez, Miguel - A/78/PV.4
Cyprus. President
Christodoulides, Nikos - A/78/PV.6
Czechia. President
Pavel, Petr - A/78/PV.5
Democratic People's Republic of Korea
Kim, Song - A/78/PV.14
Democratic Republic of the Congo. President
Tshisekedi Tshilombo, Félix Antoine - A/78/PV.7
Denmark
Jørgensen, Dan - A/78/PV.9
Djibouti
Youssouf, Mahamoud Ali - A/78/PV.13
Dominica. President
Savarin, Charles Angelo - A/78/PV.8
Dominican Republic. President
Abinader Corona, Luis Rodolfo - A/78/PV.7
Ecuador. President
Lasso Mendoza, Guillermo - A/78/PV.6
Egypt
Selim, Sameh Hassan Shokry - A/78/PV.12
El Salvador. President
Bukele, Nayib Armando - A/78/PV.5
Equatorial Guinea. Vice-President
Nguema Obiang Mangue, Teodoro - A/78/PV.9
Eritrea
Mohammed, Osman Saleh - A/78/PV.13
Estonia. President
Karis, Alar - A/78/PV.7
Eswatini
Mswati III, King of Eswatini, 1968- - A/78/PV.7
Ethiopia. Deputy Prime Minister
Hassen, Demeke Mekonnen - A/78/PV.12
European Council. President
Michel, Charles - A/78/PV.8
Fiji. Prime Minister
Rabuka, Sitiveni Ligamamada - A/78/PV.10
Finland. President
Niinistö, Sauli - A/78/PV.6
France
Colonna, Catherine - A/78/PV.9
Gabon. Prime Minister
Ndong Sima, Raymond - A/78/PV.10
Gambia. Vice-President
Jallow, Mohammed - A/78/PV.9
Georgia. Prime Minister
Garibashvili, Irakli - A/78/PV.11
Germany. Chancellor
Scholz, Olaf - A/78/PV.5
Ghana. President
Akufo-Addo, Nana Addo Dankwa - A/78/PV.6
Greece. Prime Minister
Mitsotakis, Kyriakos - A/78/PV.9
Grenada. Prime Minister
Mitchell, Dickon - A/78/PV.11
Guatemala. President
Giammattei Falla, Alejandro - A/78/PV.4

UN. GENERAL ASSEMBLY (78TH SESS. : 2023-2024)—GENERAL DEBATE (Agenda item 8) (continued)

Guinea. President
    Doumbouya, Mamadi - A/78/PV.8
Guinea-Bissau. President
    Embaló, Úmaro Sissoco - A/78/PV.9
Guyana. President
    Ali, Mohamed Irfaan - A/78/PV.6
Haiti. Prime Minister
    Henry, Ariel - A/78/PV.11
Holy See
    Gallagher, Paul Richard - A/78/PV.14
Honduras. President
    Castro Sarmiento, Iris Xiomara - A/78/PV.6
Hungary. President
    Novák, Katalin - A/78/PV.4
Iceland
    Gylfadóttir, Thórdís Kolbrún Reykfjörd - A/78/PV.12
India
    Jaishankar, Subrahmanyam - A/78/PV.14
Indonesia
    Marsudi, Retno Lestari Priansari - A/78/PV.12
Iran (Islamic Republic of). President
    Raisi, Seyyed Ebrahim - A/78/PV.5
Iraq. Prime Minister
    Al Sudani, Mohammed Shia' - A/78/PV.10
Ireland. Prime Minister
    Varadkar, Leo - A/78/PV.11
Israel. Prime Minister
    Netanyahu, Benjamin - A/78/PV.10
Italy. Council of Ministers. President
    Meloni, Giorgia - A/78/PV.7
Jamaica
    Johnson Smith, Kamina - A/78/PV.14
Japan. Prime Minister
    Kishida, Fumio - A/78/PV.5
Jordan
    Abdullah II, King of Jordan, 1962- - A/78/PV.4
Kazakhstan. President
    Tokayev, Kassym-Jomart - A/78/PV.5
Kenya. President
    Ruto, William Samoei - A/78/PV.8
Kiribati. President
    Maamau, Taneti - A/78/PV.8
Kuwait. Prime Minister
    Al-Sabah, Ahmad Nawaf Al-Ahmad - A/78/PV.9
Kyrgyzstan. President
    Zhaparov, Sadyr - A/78/PV.5
Lao People's Democratic Republic. Deputy Prime Minister
    Kommasith, Saleumxay - A/78/PV.12
Latvia. President
    Rinkevics, Edgars - A/78/PV.6
Lebanon. Prime Minister
    Najib Azmi Mikati, Mohammad - A/78/PV.7
Lesotho. Prime Minister
    Matekane, Ntsokoane Samuel - A/78/PV.11
Liberia. President
    Weah, George Manneh - A/78/PV.7

UN. GENERAL ASSEMBLY (78TH SESS. : 2023-2024)—GENERAL DEBATE (Agenda item 8) (continued)

Libya
    Elzuni, Fatalla AF - A/78/PV.7
Liechtenstein
    Hasler, Dominique - A/78/PV.9
Lithuania. President
    Nausėda, Gitanas - A/78/PV.6
Luxembourg. Prime Minister
    Bettel, Xavier - A/78/PV.10
Malawi. President
    Chakwera, Lazarus McCarthy - A/78/PV.8
Malaysia. Prime Minister
    Ibrahim, Anwar - A/78/PV.10
Maldives
    Khaleel, Ahmed - A/78/PV.14
Mali
    Diop, Abdoulaye - A/78/PV.13
Malta. Prime Minister
    Abela, Robert - A/78/PV.10
Marshall Islands. President
    Kabua, David - A/78/PV.7
Mauritania. President
    El Ghazouani, Mohamed Ould Cheikh - A/78/PV.7
Mauritius. Prime Minister
    Jugnauth, Pravind Kumar - A/78/PV.10
Mexico
    Bárcena Ibarra, Alicia - A/78/PV.12
Micronesia (Federated States of). President
    Simina, Wesley - A/78/PV.8
Monaco
    Albert II, Prince of Monaco, 1958- - A/78/PV.7
Mongolia. President
    Khurelsukh, Ukhnaa - A/78/PV.7
Montenegro. President
    Milatović, Jakov - A/78/PV.8
Morocco
    Hilale, Omar - A/78/PV.14
Mozambique. President
    Nyusi, Filipe Jacinto - A/78/PV.5
Namibia. President
    Geingob, Hage Gottfried - A/78/PV.6
Nauru. President
    Kun, Russ - A/78/PV.9
Nepal. Prime Minister
    Dahal, Pushpa Kamal - A/78/PV.9
Netherlands (Kingdom of the). Prime Minister
    Rutte, Mark - A/78/PV.10
New Zealand
    Mahuta, Nanaia - A/78/PV.12
Nicaragua
    Moncada Colindres, Denis Ronaldo - A/78/PV.14
Nigeria. President
    Tinubu, Bola Ahmed - A/78/PV.5
North Macedonia. President
    Pendarovski, Stevo - A/78/PV.10
Norway
    Tvinnereim, Anne Beathe - A/78/PV.13

UN. GENERAL ASSEMBLY (78TH SESS. : 2023-2024)—GENERAL DEBATE (Agenda item 8) (continued)

Oman
AlBusaidi, Sayyid Badr Bin Hamad bin Hamood - A/78/PV.13
Pakistan. Prime Minister
Kakar, Anwaar-ul-Haq - A/78/PV.10
Palau. President
Whipps, Surangel S. - A/78/PV.5
Panama. President
Cortizo Cohen, Laurentino - A/78/PV.5
Papua New Guinea. Deputy Prime Minister
Rosso, John - A/78/PV.12
Paraguay. President
Peña Palacios, Santiago - A/78/PV.5
Peru. President
Boluarte Zegarra, Dina Ercilia - A/78/PV.5
Philippines
Manalo, Enrique A. - A/78/PV.12
Poland. President
Duda, Andrzej - A/78/PV.4
Portugal. President
Sousa, Marcelo Rebelo de - A/78/PV.4
Qatar. Amir
Al-Thani, Sheikh Tamim bin Hamad - A/78/PV.4
Republic of Korea. President
Yoon, Suk Yeol - A/78/PV.6
Republic of Moldova. President
Sandu, Maia - A/78/PV.7
Romania. President
Iohannis, Klaus Werner - A/78/PV.6
Russian Federation
Lavrov, Sergei Viktorovich - A/78/PV.12
Rwanda. President
Kagame, Paul - A/78/PV.6
Saint Kitts and Nevis. Prime Minister
Drew, Terrance Micheal - A/78/PV.12
Saint Lucia. Prime Minister
Pierre, Philip Joseph - A/78/PV.10
Saint Vincent and the Grenadines. Prime Minister
Gonsalves, Ralph E. - A/78/PV.12
Samoa. Prime Minister
Mataafa, Fiame Naomi - A/78/PV.12
San Marino
Beleffi, Damiano - A/78/PV.14
Sao Tome and Principe. Prime Minister
Trovoada, Patrice Emery - A/78/PV.7
Saudi Arabia
Al-Saud, Prince of Saudi Arabia - A/78/PV.13
Senegal. President
Sall, Macky - A/78/PV.5
Serbia. President
Vučić, Aleksandar - A/78/PV.8
Seychelles. President
Ramkalawan, Wavel - A/78/PV.6
Sierra Leone. President
Bio, Julius Maada - A/78/PV.7
Singapore
Balakrishnan, Vivian - A/78/PV.11

UN. GENERAL ASSEMBLY (78TH SESS. : 2023-2024)—GENERAL DEBATE (Agenda item 8) (continued)

Slovakia. President
Caputová, Zuzana - A/78/PV.6
Slovenia. President
Pirc Musar, Nataša - A/78/PV.4
Solomon Islands. Prime Minister
Sogavare, Manasseh - A/78/PV.11
Somalia. Prime Minister
Barre, Hamza Abdi - A/78/PV.12
South Africa. President
Ramaphosa, Matamela Cyril - A/78/PV.4
South Sudan. President
Kiir Mayardit, Slava - A/78/PV.8
Spain. President
Sánchez, Pedro - A/78/PV.7
Sri Lanka. President
Wickremesinghe, Ranil - A/78/PV.8
State of Palestine. President
Abbas, Mahmoud - A/78/PV.8
Sudan. President
Al-Burhan, Abdel-Fattah Al-Burhan Abdelrahman - A/78/PV.9
Suriname. President
Santokhi, Chandrikapersad - A/78/PV.6
Sweden
Billström, Tobias - A/78/PV.11
Switzerland. President
Berset, Alain - A/78/PV.4
Syrian Arab Republic
Sabbagh, Bassam - A/78/PV.14
Tajikistan. President
Rahmon, Emomali - A/78/PV.6
Thailand. Prime Minister
Thavisin, Srettha - A/78/PV.10
Timor-Leste. President
Ramos-Horta, José - A/78/PV.8
Togo
Dussey, Robert - A/78/PV.9
Tonga. Prime Minister
Sovaleni, Siaosi 'Ofakivahafolau - A/78/PV.11
Trinidad and Tobago. Prime Minister
Rowley, Keith - A/78/PV.9
Tunisia
Ammar, Nabil - A/78/PV.12
Türkiye. President
Erdogan, Recep Tayyip - A/78/PV.4
Turkmenistan. President
Berdimuhamedov, Serdar - A/78/PV.4
Tuvalu. Prime Minister
Natano, Kausea - A/78/PV.11
Uganda. Vice-President
Alupo, Jessica - A/78/PV.9
Ukraine. President
Zelenskyy, Volodymyr - A/78/PV.4
UN. General Assembly. President
Francis, Dennis (Trinidad and Tobago) - A/78/PV.4; A/78/PV.14
United Arab Emirates
Al Hashimy, Reem Ebrahim - A/78/PV.13

UN. GENERAL ASSEMBLY (78TH SESS. : 2023-2024)—GENERAL DEBATE (Agenda item 8) (continued)

United Kingdom. Deputy Prime Minister
Dowden, Oliver - A/78/PV.11
United Republic of Tanzania. Vice-President
Mpango, Philip Isdor - A/78/PV.9
United States. President
Biden, Joseph R. - A/78/PV.4
Uruguay. President
Lacalle Pou, Luis - A/78/PV.5
Uzbekistan. President
Mirziyoyev, Shavkat - A/78/PV.4
Vanuatu
Tevi, Odo - A/78/PV.14
Venezuela (Bolivarian Republic of)
Gil Pinto, Yvan - A/78/PV.13
Viet Nam. Prime Minister
Pham, Minh Chinh - A/78/PV.11
Yemen. Presidential Leadership Council. President
Al-Alimi, Rashad Mohammed - A/78/PV.8
Zambia
Kakubo, Stanley - A/78/PV.14
Zimbabwe. President
Mnangagwa, Emmerson Dambudzo - A/78/PV.8

UN. GENERAL ASSEMBLY (78TH SESS. : 2023-2024)—GENERAL DEBATE—RIGHT OF REPLY (Agenda item 8)

Algeria
Bendjama, Amar - A/78/PV.14
Armenia
Galstyan, Tigran - A/78/PV.14
Azerbaijan
Musayev, Tofig - A/78/PV.14
Belize
Fuller, Carlos C. - A/78/PV.14
China
Li, Linlin - A/78/PV.13
Democratic People's Republic of Korea
Kim, Song - A/78/PV.14
Guatemala
Búcaro Flores, Mario Adolfo - A/78/PV.13
Leal Matta, Edgar Daniel - A/78/PV.14
Guyana
Rodrigues-Birkett, Carolyn - A/78/PV.14
India
Gahlot, Petal - A/78/PV.11
Iran (Islamic Republic of)
Ghadirkhomi, Payman - A/78/PV.13
Karimi Magham, Ali - A/78/PV.11
Japan
Shino, Mitsuko - A/78/PV.11; A/78/PV.14
Morocco
Hilale, Omar - A/78/PV.14
Pakistan
Saleem, Saima - A/78/PV.11
Republic of Korea
Kim, Sangjin - A/78/PV.14

UN. GENERAL ASSEMBLY (78TH SESS. : 2023-2024)—GENERAL DEBATE—RIGHT OF REPLY (Agenda item 8) (continued)

United Arab Emirates
Matar, Shahd Jamal Yousuf - A/78/PV.13

UN. GENERAL ASSEMBLY (78TH SESS. : 2023-2024)—OFFICERS (Agenda item 5)

ASEAN
Gafoor, Burhan (Singapore) - A/C.5/78/SR.1
Australia
Larsen, James - A/C.5/78/SR.1
Bangladesh
Muhith, Muhammad A. - A/C.2/78/SR.26
Shatil, Toufiq Islam - A/C.5/78/SR.1
China
Dai, Bing - A/C.5/78/SR.1
Costa Rica
Chan Valverde, Maritza - A/C.1/78/PV.31
El Salvador
González López, Egriselda Aracely - A/C.5/78/SR.39
European Union
Samson, Hedda - A/C.5/78/SR.1
Group of 77
Tur de la Concepción, Richard (Cuba) - A/C.5/78/SR.1
Gulf Cooperation Council
Al-Hassan, Mohamed (Oman) - A/C.5/78/SR.1
Iraq
Albu-Mohammed, Ahmed Kamil Rahif - A/C.5/78/SR.1
Israel
Zilbergeld, Sherry - A/C.5/78/SR.1
Japan
Yamanaka, Osamu - A/C.5/78/SR.1
Latvia
Pavļuta-Deslandes, Sanita - A/C.4/78/SR.28
Mexico
Velázquez Castillo, Jesús - A/C.5/78/SR.1
Norway
Brattested, Merete Fjeld - A/C.5/78/SR.1
Philippines
Peñaranda, Ariel Rodelas - A/C.5/78/SR.1
Portugal
Aranda, Jorge Eduardo Ferreira Silva - A/C.6/78/SR.48
Republic of Korea
Seong, Woong - A/C.5/78/SR.1
Russian Federation
Chumakov, Dmitry S. - A/C.5/78/SR.1
Shulgin, Egor S. - A/C.4/78/SR.28
Switzerland
Chanda, Riccarda - A/C.5/78/SR.1
Thailand
Vichankaiyakij, Vathayudh - A/C.5/78/SR.1
UN. General Assembly. 3rd Committee. Chair
Marschik, Alexander (Austria) - A/C.3/78/SR.57
UN. Group of African States
Ladeb, Tarek (Tunisia) - A/C.5/78/SR.1

UN. GENERAL ASSEMBLY (78TH SESS. : 2023-2024)—OFFICERS (Agenda item 5) (continued)

United Arab Emirates
Al-Khaabi, Najla - A/C.5/78/SR.1
United Kingdom
Kariuki, James - A/C.5/78/SR.1
United States
Lu, Christopher P. - A/C.5/78/SR.1
Uruguay
González Hernández, Gabriela Lilián - A/C.5/78/SR.1

UN. GENERAL ASSEMBLY (78TH SESS. : 2023-2024)—SPECIAL STATEMENTS

Albania. President
Begaj, Bajram - A/78/PV.9
Algeria. President
Tebboune, Abdelmadjid - A/78/PV.5
Andorra. Head of Government
Espot Zamora, Xavier - A/78/PV.10
Angola. President
Lourenço, João Manuel Gonçalves - A/78/PV.6
Antigua and Barbuda. Prime Minister
Browne, Gaston Alphonso - A/78/PV.10
Argentina. President
Fernández, Alberto - A/78/PV.5
Bangladesh. Prime Minister
Hasina, Sheikh - A/78/PV.10
Barbados. Prime Minister
Mottley, Mia Amor - A/78/PV.10
Belgium. Prime Minister
De Croo, Alexander - A/78/PV.7
Bolivia (Plurinational State of). President
Arce Catacora, Luis Alberto - A/78/PV.5
Bosnia and Herzegovina. Presidency. Chair
Komsic, Zeljko - A/78/PV.6
Botswana. President
Masisi, Mokgweetsi Eric Keabetswe - A/78/PV.7
Brazil. President
Silva, Luiz Inácio Lula da - A/78/PV.4
Bulgaria. President
Radev, Rumen - A/78/PV.6
Burundi. President
Ndayishimiye, Évariste - A/78/PV.8
Cabo Verde. Prime Minister
Silva, José Ulisses Correia e - A/78/PV.12
Cambodia. Prime Minister
Hun, Manet - A/78/PV.11
Central African Republic. President
Touadera, Faustin Archange - A/78/PV.8
Chile. President
Boric Font, Gabriel - A/78/PV.7
China. Vice-President
Han, Zheng - A/78/PV.9
Colombia. President
Petro Urrego, Gustavo - A/78/PV.4
Colombia. Vice-President
Márquez Mina, Francia - A/78/PV.103

UN. GENERAL ASSEMBLY (78TH SESS. : 2023-2024)—SPECIAL STATEMENTS (continued)

Comoros. President
Assoumani, Azali - A/78/PV.7
Congo. President
Sassou N'Guesso, Denis - A/78/PV.8
Côte d'Ivoire. Vice-President
Kone, Tiémoko Meyliet - A/78/PV.9
Croatia. President
Milanovic, Zoran - A/78/PV.6
Cuba. President
Díaz-Canel Bermúdez, Miguel - A/78/PV.4
Cyprus. President
Christodoulides, Nikos - A/78/PV.6
Czechia. President
Pavel, Petr - A/78/PV.5
Democratic Republic of the Congo. President
Tshisekedi Tshilombo, Félix Antoine - A/78/PV.7
Dominica. President
Savarin, Charles Angelo - A/78/PV.8
Dominican Republic. President
Abinader Corona, Luis Rodolfo - A/78/PV.7
Ecuador. President
Lasso Mendoza, Guillermo - A/78/PV.6
El Salvador. President
Bukele, Nayib Armando - A/78/PV.5
Equatorial Guinea. Vice-President
Nguema Obiang Mangue, Teodoro - A/78/PV.9
Estonia. President
Karis, Alar - A/78/PV.7
Eswatini
Mswati III, King of Eswatini, 1968- - A/78/PV.7
Ethiopia. Deputy Prime Minister
Hassen, Demeke Mekonnen - A/78/PV.12
Fiji. Prime Minister
Rabuka, Sitiveni Ligamamada - A/78/PV.10
Finland. President
Niinistö, Sauli - A/78/PV.6
Gabon. Prime Minister
Ndong Sima, Raymond - A/78/PV.10
Gambia. Vice-President
Jallow, Mohammed - A/78/PV.9
Georgia. Prime Minister
Garibashvili, Irakli - A/78/PV.11
Germany. Chancellor
Scholz, Olaf - A/78/PV.5
Ghana. President
Akufo-Addo, Nana Addo Dankwa - A/78/PV.6
Greece. Prime Minister
Mitsotakis, Kyriakos - A/78/PV.9
Grenada. Prime Minister
Mitchell, Dickon - A/78/PV.11
Guatemala. President
Arévalo de León, César Bernardo - A/78/PV.84
Giammattei Falla, Alejandro - A/78/PV.4
Guinea. President
Doumbouya, Mamadi - A/78/PV.8
Guinea-Bissau. President
Embaló, Úmaro Sissoco - A/78/PV.9
Guyana. President
Ali, Mohamed Irfaan - A/78/PV.6

UN. GENERAL ASSEMBLY (78TH SESS. : 2023-2024)—SPECIAL STATEMENTS (continued)

Haiti. Prime Minister
Henry, Ariel - A/78/PV.11
Honduras. President
Castro Sarmiento, Iris Xiomara - A/78/PV.6
Hungary. President
Novák, Katalin - A/78/PV.4
Iran (Islamic Republic of). President
Raisi, Seyyed Ebrahim - A/78/PV.5
Iraq. Prime Minister
Al Sudani, Mohammed Shia' - A/78/PV.10
Ireland. Prime Minister
Varadkar, Leo - A/78/PV.11
Israel. Prime Minister
Netanyahu, Benjamin - A/78/PV.10
Italy. Council of Ministers. President
Meloni, Giorgia - A/78/PV.7
Italy. President
Mattarella, Sergio - A/78/PV.81
Japan. Prime Minister
Kishida, Fumio - A/78/PV.5
Jordan
Abdullah II, King of Jordan, 1962- - A/78/PV.4
Kazakhstan. President
Tokayev, Kassym-Jomart - A/78/PV.5
Kenya. President
Ruto, William Samoei - A/78/PV.8
Kiribati. President
Maamau, Taneti - A/78/PV.8
Kuwait. Prime Minister
Al-Sabah, Ahmad Nawaf Al-Ahmad - A/78/PV.9
Kyrgyzstan. President
Zhaparov, Sadyr - A/78/PV.5
Lao People's Democratic Republic. Deputy Prime Minister
Kommasith, Saleumxay - A/78/PV.12
Latvia. President
Rinkevics, Edgars - A/78/PV.6
Lebanon. Prime Minister
Najib Azmi Mikati, Mohammad - A/78/PV.7
Lesotho. Prime Minister
Matekane, Ntsokoane Samuel - A/78/PV.11
Liberia. President
Weah, George Manneh - A/78/PV.7
Lithuania. President
Nausėda, Gitanas - A/78/PV.6
Luxembourg. Deputy Prime Minister
Bettel, Xavier - A/78/PV.56
Luxembourg. Prime Minister
Bettel, Xavier - A/78/PV.10
Malawi. President
Chakwera, Lazarus McCarthy - A/78/PV.8
Malaysia. Prime Minister
Ibrahim, Anwar - A/78/PV.10
Malta. Prime Minister
Abela, Robert - A/78/PV.10
Marshall Islands. President
Kabua, David - A/78/PV.7
Mauritania. President
El Ghazouani, Mohamed Ould Cheikh - A/78/PV.7

UN. GENERAL ASSEMBLY (78TH SESS. : 2023-2024)—SPECIAL STATEMENTS (continued)

Mauritius. Prime Minister
Jugnauth, Pravind Kumar - A/78/PV.10
Micronesia (Federated States of). President
Simina, Wesley - A/78/PV.8
Monaco
Albert II, Prince of Monaco, 1958- - A/78/PV.7
Mongolia. President
Khurelsukh, Ukhnaa - A/78/PV.7
Montenegro. President
Milatović, Jakov - A/78/PV.8
Mozambique. President
Nyusi, Filipe Jacinto - A/78/PV.5
Namibia. President
Geingob, Hage Gottfried - A/78/PV.6
Nauru. President
Kun, Russ - A/78/PV.9
Nepal. Prime Minister
Dahal, Pushpa Kamal - A/78/PV.9
Netherlands (Kingdom of the). Prime Minister
Rutte, Mark - A/78/PV.10
New Zealand. Deputy Prime Minister
Peters, Winston - A/78/PV.66
Nigeria. President
Tinubu, Bola Ahmed - A/78/PV.5
North Macedonia. President
Pendarovski, Stevo - A/78/PV.10
Pakistan. Prime Minister
Kakar, Anwaar-ul-Haq - A/78/PV.10
Palau. President
Whipps, Surangel S. - A/78/PV.5
Panama. President
Cortizo Cohen, Laurentino - A/78/PV.5
Papua New Guinea. Deputy Prime Minister
Rosso, John - A/78/PV.12
Paraguay. President
Peña Palacios, Santiago - A/78/PV.5
Peru. President
Boluarte Zegarra, Dina Ercilia - A/78/PV.5
Poland. President
Duda, Andrzej - A/78/PV.4
Portugal. President
Sousa, Marcelo Rebelo de - A/78/PV.4
Qatar. Amir
Al-Thani, Sheikh Tamim bin Hamad - A/78/PV.4
Republic of Korea. President
Yoon, Suk Yeol - A/78/PV.6
Republic of Moldova. President
Sandu, Maia - A/78/PV.7
Romania. President
Iohannis, Klaus Werner - A/78/PV.6
Rwanda. President
Kagame, Paul - A/78/PV.6
Saint Kitts and Nevis. Prime Minister
Drew, Terrance Micheal - A/78/PV.12
Saint Lucia. Prime Minister
Pierre, Philip Joseph - A/78/PV.10
Saint Vincent and the Grenadines. Prime Minister
Gonsalves, Ralph E. - A/78/PV.12

UN. GENERAL ASSEMBLY (78TH SESS. : 2023-2024)—SPECIAL STATEMENTS (continued)

Samoa. President
Mataafa, Fiame Naomi - A/78/PV.12
Sao Tome and Principe. Prime Minister
Trovoada, Patrice Emery - A/78/PV.7
Saudi Arabia
Al-Saud, Prince of Saudi Arabia - A/78/PV.13
Senegal. President
Sall, Macky - A/78/PV.5
Serbia. President
Vučić, Aleksandar - A/78/PV.8; A/78/PV.82
Seychelles. President
Ramkalawan, Wavel - A/78/PV.6
Sierra Leone. President
Bio, Julius Maada - A/78/PV.7
Slovakia. President
Caputová, Zuzana - A/78/PV.6
Slovenia. Deputy Prime Minister
Fajon, Tanja - A/78/PV.56
Slovenia. President
Pirc Musar, Nataša - A/78/PV.4
Solomon Islands. Prime Minister
Sogavare, Manasseh - A/78/PV.11
Somalia. Prime Minister
Barre, Hamza Abdi - A/78/PV.12
South Africa. President
Ramaphosa, Matamela Cyril - A/78/PV.4
South Sudan. President
Kiir Mayardit, Slava - A/78/PV.8
Spain. President
Sánchez, Pedro - A/78/PV.7
Sri Lanka. President
Wickremesinghe, Ranil - A/78/PV.8
State of Palestine. President
Abbas, Mahmoud - A/78/PV.8
Sudan. President
Al-Burhan, Abdel-Fattah Al-Burhan Abdelrahman - A/78/PV.9
Suriname. President
Santokhi, Chandrikapersad - A/78/PV.6
Switzerland. President
Berset, Alain - A/78/PV.4
Tajikistan. President
Rahmon, Emomali - A/78/PV.6
Thailand. Prime Minister
Thavisin, Srettha - A/78/PV.10
Timor-Leste. President
Ramos-Horta, José - A/78/PV.8
Tonga. Prime Minister
Sovaleni, Siaosi 'Ofakivahafolau - A/78/PV.11
Trinidad and Tobago. Prime Minister
Rowley, Keith - A/78/PV.9
Türkiye. President
Erdogan, Recep Tayyip - A/78/PV.4
Turkmenistan. President
Berdimuhamedov, Serdar - A/78/PV.4
Tuvalu. Prime Minister
Natano, Kausea - A/78/PV.11
Uganda. Vice-President
Alupo, Jessica - A/78/PV.9

UN. GENERAL ASSEMBLY (78TH SESS. : 2023-2024)—SPECIAL STATEMENTS (continued)

Ukraine. President
Zelenskyy, Volodymyr - A/78/PV.4
United Kingdom. Deputy Prime Minister
Dowden, Oliver - A/78/PV.11
United Republic of Tanzania. Vice-President
Mpango, Philip Isdor - A/78/PV.9
United States. President
Biden, Joseph R. - A/78/PV.4
Uruguay. President
Lacalle Pou, Luis - A/78/PV.5
Uzbekistan. President
Mirziyoyev, Shavkat - A/78/PV.4
Viet Nam. Prime Minister
Pham, Minh Chinh - A/78/PV.11
Yemen. Presidential Leadership Council. President
Al-Alimi, Rashad Mohammed - A/78/PV.8
Zimbabwe. President
Mnangagwa, Emmerson Dambudzo - A/78/PV.8

UN. GENERAL ASSEMBLY (78TH SESS. : 2023-2024)—VICE-PRESIDENTS (Agenda item 6)

United States
Carty, Lisa A. - A/78/PV.87

UN. GENERAL ASSEMBLY (78TH SESS. : 2023-2024). 1ST COMMITTEE—GENERAL DEBATE (Agenda item 8)

Albania
Bekteshi, Etrit - A/C.1/78/PV.6
Algeria
Lebbaz, Larbi Abdelfattah - A/C.1/78/PV.8
Angola
Cruz, Francisco José da - A/C.1/78/PV.9
Argentina
Guerra, Hugo Emmanuel - A/C.1/78/PV.5
Armenia
Grigoryan, Andranik - A/C.1/78/PV.7; A/C.1/78/PV.8
Margaryan, Mher - A/C.1/78/PV.4
ASEAN
Peñaranda, Ariel Rodelas (Philippines) - A/C.1/78/PV.2
Australia
Wood, Vanessa - A/C.1/78/PV.3; A/C.1/78/PV.5
Austria
Marschik, Alexander - A/C.1/78/PV.4
Azerbaijan
Gurbanov, Ilgar - A/C.1/78/PV.7; A/C.1/78/PV.8
Musayev, Tofig - A/C.1/78/PV.7
Bahrain
Alrowaiei, Jamal Fares - A/C.1/78/PV.9
Bangladesh
Shatil, Toufiq Islam - A/C.1/78/PV.3
Belarus
Pavlov, Vasiliy - A/C.1/78/PV.5

UN. GENERAL ASSEMBLY (78TH SESS. : 2023-2024). 1ST COMMITTEE—GENERAL DEBATE (Agenda item 8) (continued)

Belgium
Kridelka, Philippe - A/C.1/78/PV.8
Bolivia (Plurinational State of)
Pary Rodríguez, Diego - A/C.1/78/PV.4
Botswana
Mokhawa, Gladys - A/C.1/78/PV.7
Brazil
Damico, Flávio Soares - A/C.1/78/PV.9
Moretti, Norberto - A/C.1/78/PV.8
Brunei Darussalam
Sah, Hermy Ahmad - A/C.1/78/PV.7
Bulgaria
Stoeva, Lachezara - A/C.1/78/PV.5
Burkina Faso
Ganou, Oumarou - A/C.1/78/PV.6
Cabo Verde
Romualdo, Tania Serafim Yvonne - A/C.1/78/PV.9
Cambodia
Eat, Sophea - A/C.1/78/PV.3
Cameroon
Babo, Paul David - A/C.1/78/PV.8
Canada
Norton, Leslie - A/C.1/78/PV.3
Caribbean Community
Wallace, Brian Christopher Manley (Jamaica) - A/C.1/78/PV.2
Chile
Vidal Mercado, Jorge Andrés - A/C.1/78/PV.5
China
Li, Nan - A/C.1/78/PV.6
Sun, Xiaobo - A/C.1/78/PV.5
Sun, Yiliang - A/C.1/78/PV.5
Colombia
Zalabata Torres, Leonor - A/C.1/78/PV.7
Community of Latin American and Caribbean States
Miguel, Nedra P. (Saint Vincent and the Grenadines) - A/C.1/78/PV.3
Congo
Douckaga Nzengui, Nicaise Servais - A/C.1/78/PV.7
Coordinating Bureau of the Non-Aligned Countries
Nasir, Arrmanatha Christiawan (Indonesia) - A/C.1/78/PV.2
Costa Rica
Chan Valverde, Maritza - A/C.1/78/PV.8
Côte d'Ivoire
Moriko, Tiémoko - A/C.1/78/PV.4
Croatia
Glasenhardt, Blanka - A/C.1/78/PV.7
Cuba
Gala López, Yuri - A/C.1/78/PV.6
Czechia
Stromsiková, Veronika - A/C.1/78/PV.3
Democratic People's Republic of Korea
Kim, In Chol - A/C.1/78/PV.2; A/C.1/78/PV.4; A/C.1/78/PV.5; A/C.1/78/PV.7; A/C.1/78/PV.8
Kim, Song - A/C.1/78/PV.7
Denmark
Laursen, Erik - A/C.1/78/PV.2

UN. GENERAL ASSEMBLY (78TH SESS. : 2023-2024). 1ST COMMITTEE—GENERAL DEBATE (Agenda item 8) (continued)

Djibouti
Assoweh, Zeinab Ismaël - A/C.1/78/PV.8
Dominican Republic
Luna, Madelin Esther - A/C.1/78/PV.9
Ecuador
Montalvo Sosa, Andrés Efren - A/C.1/78/PV.5
Egypt
Ahmed, Amr Essameldin Sadek - A/C.1/78/PV.3
Equatorial Guinea
Ndong Mba, Anatolio - A/C.1/78/PV.9
Eritrea
Tesfamariam, Sophia - A/C.1/78/PV.9
Estonia
Tammsaar, Rein - A/C.1/78/PV.6
Eswatini
Mbingo, Mduduzi Kieth Kenneth - A/C.1/78/PV.8
Ethiopia
Abebe, Leulseged Tadese - A/C.1/78/PV.8
European Union
Hansen, Steen Malthe - A/C.1/78/PV.4
Skoog, Olof - A/C.1/78/PV.2
Finland
Hyvärinen, Outi - A/C.1/78/PV.4
France
Petit, Camille - A/C.1/78/PV.8
Gabon
Koumba Pambo, Aurélie Flore - A/C.1/78/PV.9
Georgia
Bakradze, David - A/C.1/78/PV.7
Dvali, Akaki - A/C.1/78/PV.8
Germany
Göbel, Thomas - A/C.1/78/PV.5
Ghana
Kesse Antwi, Linda - A/C.1/78/PV.5
Greece
Sekeris, Evangelos C. - A/C.1/78/PV.4
Group of Arab States
Hmoud, Mahmoud Daifallah Mahmoud (Jordan) - A/C.1/78/PV.2
Guatemala
Rodríguez Mancia, Carla María - A/C.1/78/PV.5
Guinea
Diallo, Oumou - A/C.1/78/PV.6
Guyana
Rodrigues-Birkett, Carolyn - A/C.1/78/PV.3
Haiti
Pierre, Wislyne - A/C.1/78/PV.8
Holy See
Caccia, Gabriele Giordano - A/C.1/78/PV.9
Honduras
Flores, Ramón Emilio - A/C.1/78/PV.4
Hungary
Balázs, Szilvia - A/C.1/78/PV.5
Iceland
Valtýsson, Jörundur - A/C.1/78/PV.7
India
Ray, Anupam - A/C.1/78/PV.6

UN. GENERAL ASSEMBLY (78TH SESS. : 2023-2024). 1ST COMMITTEE—GENERAL DEBATE (Agenda item 8) (continued)

Indonesia
  Nasir, Arrmanatha Christiawan - A/C.1/78/PV.3
International Committee of the Red Cross
  Gisel, Laurent - A/C.1/78/PV.9
Iran (Islamic Republic of)
  Ghorbanpour Najafabadi, Mohammad - A/C.1/78/PV.2; A/C.1/78/PV.3; A/C.1/78/PV.6; A/C.1/78/PV.7; A/C.1/78/PV.8; A/C.1/78/PV.9
Iraq
  Al-Fatlawi, Abbas Kadhom Obaid - A/C.1/78/PV.6
Ireland
  White, Noel - A/C.1/78/PV.6
Israel
  Erdan, Gilad Menashe - A/C.1/78/PV.7
  Maayan, Michal - A/C.1/78/PV.6; A/C.1/78/PV.7; A/C.1/78/PV.8; A/C.1/78/PV.9
Italy
  Bencini, Leonardo - A/C.1/78/PV.4
Japan
  Ogasawara, Ichiro - A/C.1/78/PV.5; A/C.1/78/PV.6; A/C.1/78/PV.7
Jordan
  Alqaisi, Sultan Natheir Mustafa - A/C.1/78/PV.5
Kazakhstan
  Baissuanov, Arman - A/C.1/78/PV.5
Kenya
  Kiboino, Michael Kapkiai - A/C.1/78/PV.8
Kiribati
  Tito, Teburoro - A/C.1/78/PV.8
Kuwait
  Alajmi, Fahad M. - A/C.1/78/PV.9
Kyrgyzstan
  Utebaev, Meder - A/C.1/78/PV.9
Lao People's Democratic Republic
  Vongnorkeo, Anouparb - A/C.1/78/PV.6
Latvia
  Pavļuta-Deslandes, Sanita - A/C.1/78/PV.3
League of Arab States
  Abdelaziz, Maged Abdelfattah - A/C.1/78/PV.9
Lebanon
  Hachem, Hadi - A/C.1/78/PV.6
Lesotho
  Nena, Matete - A/C.1/78/PV.6
Libya
  Ben Zitun, Esam - A/C.1/78/PV.7
Liechtenstein
  Oehri, Myriam - A/C.1/78/PV.3
Lithuania
  Jievaltas, Arūnas - A/C.1/78/PV.5
Malaysia
  Muhamad, Ahmad Faisal - A/C.1/78/PV.4
Maldives
  Guraisha, Aminath - A/C.1/78/PV.5
Malta
  Kuymizakis, Adam - A/C.1/78/PV.3
Mauritania
  Mohamedou, Mohamed Mahmoud Ould - A/C.1/78/PV.8

UN. GENERAL ASSEMBLY (78TH SESS. : 2023-2024). 1ST COMMITTEE—GENERAL DEBATE (Agenda item 8) (continued)

Mexico
  Buenrostro Massieu, Alicia - A/C.1/78/PV.2
Mongolia
  Vorshilov, Enkhbold - A/C.1/78/PV.6
Morocco
  Yousfi, Salim - A/C.1/78/PV.3
Mozambique
  Fernandes, Domingos Estêvão - A/C.1/78/PV.9
Myanmar
  Tun, Kyaw Moe - A/C.1/78/PV.7
Namibia
  Kuzee, Helena Ndapewa - A/C.1/78/PV.8
Nepal
  Thapa, Lok Bahadur - A/C.1/78/PV.5
Netherlands (Kingdom of the)
  Bosch, Robert in den - A/C.1/78/PV.3
New Agenda Coalition
  Sánchez Kiesslich, Eduardo Alcibiades (Mexico) - A/C.1/78/PV.4
New Zealand
  Schwalger, Carolyn - A/C.1/78/PV.3
Nicaragua
  Jiménez, Jasser - A/C.1/78/PV.8
Nigeria
  Mahmud, Mohammed Lawal - A/C.1/78/PV.8
Norway
  Brattested, Merete Fjeld - A/C.1/78/PV.3
Oman
  Al Rubkhi, Khalid Saleh Said - A/C.1/78/PV.6
Pakistan
  Hashmi, Khalil Ur Rahman - A/C.1/78/PV.6
  Siddique, Umer - A/C.1/78/PV.6
Panama
  Veliz Rodríguez, Aris Anel - A/C.1/78/PV.7
Paraguay
  Pereira Sosa, José Eduardo - A/C.1/78/PV.9
Peru
  Salas de los Ríos, Javier Leonardo - A/C.1/78/PV.7
Philippines
  Peñaranda, Ariel Rodelas - A/C.1/78/PV.3
Poland
  Sawicz, Jacek - A/C.1/78/PV.5
Portugal
  Zacarias, Ana Paula - A/C.1/78/PV.4
Qatar
  Al-Thani, Abdulrahman Abdulaziz F.A. - A/C.1/78/PV.3
Republic of Korea
  Hwang, Joonkook - A/C.1/78/PV.2
  Kim, Sunghoon - A/C.1/78/PV.2; A/C.1/78/PV.7
Republic of Moldova
  Nipomici, Galina - A/C.1/78/PV.6
Romania
  Feruță, Cornel - A/C.1/78/PV.5

UN. GENERAL ASSEMBLY (78TH SESS. : 2023-2024). 1ST COMMITTEE—GENERAL DEBATE (Agenda item 8) (continued)

Russian Federation
Vorontsov, Konstantin - A/C.1/78/PV.2; A/C.1/78/PV.3; A/C.1/78/PV.4; A/C.1/78/PV.5; A/C.1/78/PV.6; A/C.1/78/PV.7; A/C.1/78/PV.8
San Marino
Bartolini, Natasia - A/C.1/78/PV.6
Saudi Arabia
Moharram, Wajdi Hassan M. - A/C.1/78/PV.6
Senegal
Ndiaye, Ndeye Fatou - A/C.1/78/PV.8
Sierra Leone
Alghali, Francess Piagie - A/C.1/78/PV.7
Singapore
Low, Si Tong Berenice - A/C.1/78/PV.3
Sistema de la Integración Centroamericana
González López, Egriselda Aracely (El Salvador) - A/C.1/78/PV.2
Slovakia
Chatrnúch, Róbert - A/C.1/78/PV.4
Slovenia
Malovrh, Bostjan - A/C.1/78/PV.6
South Africa
Joyini, Mathu - A/C.1/78/PV.2
Spain
Jiménez de la Hoz, Ana - A/C.1/78/PV.8
Sri Lanka
Pieris, Peter Mohan Maithri - A/C.1/78/PV.4
State of Palestine
Bamya, Majed - A/C.1/78/PV.7; A/C.1/78/PV.8
Kasabri, Qais Z.F. - A/C.1/78/PV.9
Sudan
Mohamed, Faisal Abdelazim Salim - A/C.1/78/PV.5
Sweden
Nilsson, Ann-Sofie - A/C.1/78/PV.4
Switzerland
Thoeni, Julien - A/C.1/78/PV.3
Syrian Arab Republic
Al Ashkar, Adib - A/C.1/78/PV.3; A/C.1/78/PV.4; A/C.1/78/PV.5; A/C.1/78/PV.6; A/C.1/78/PV.7; A/C.1/78/PV.8
Tajikistan
Bobozoda, Amriyo - A/C.1/78/PV.7
Thailand
Chindawongse, Suriya - A/C.1/78/PV.3
Timor-Leste
Sousa, Ivens Gusmao de - A/C.1/78/PV.5
Tunisia
Cherif, Ali - A/C.1/78/PV.4
Türkiye
Çetin, Ahmet Erman - A/C.1/78/PV.7
Uganda
Isabirye, Haruna Bazirondere - A/C.1/78/PV.6
Ukraine
Hayovyshyn, Khrystyna - A/C.1/78/PV.4
Zlenko, Anatolii - A/C.1/78/PV.3
UN. General Assembly. 1st Committee. Chair
Paulauskas, Rytis (Lithuania) - A/C.1/78/PV.2; A/C.1/78/PV.7

UN. GENERAL ASSEMBLY (78TH SESS. : 2023-2024). 1ST COMMITTEE—GENERAL DEBATE (Agenda item 8) (continued)

UN. General Assembly. President
Francis, Dennis (Trinidad and Tobago) - A/C.1/78/PV.2
UN. Group of African States
Muhammad Bande, Tijjani (Nigeria) - A/C.1/78/PV.3
UN. High Representative for Disarmament Affairs
Nakamitsu, Izumi - A/C.1/78/PV.2
United Arab Emirates
Shaheen, Ghasaq Yousif - A/C.1/78/PV.4
United Kingdom
Liddle, Aidan Thomas - A/C.1/78/PV.4
United Republic of Tanzania
Kattanga, Hussein A. - A/C.1/78/PV.5
United States
Jenkins, Bonnie D. - A/C.1/78/PV.2
Stewart, Mallory - A/C.1/78/PV.4
Turner, Bruce - A/C.1/78/PV.5; A/C.1/78/PV.6; A/C.1/78/PV.7
Uruguay
González Hernández, Gabriela Lilián - A/C.1/78/PV.4
Vanuatu
William, Sanlan - A/C.1/78/PV.8
Venezuela (Bolivarian Republic of)
Pérez Ayestarán, Joaquín Alberto - A/C.1/78/PV.7
Viet Nam
Dang, Hoang Giang - A/C.1/78/PV.6
Yemen
Al-Dobhany, Marwan Ali Noman - A/C.1/78/PV.4
Zambia
Boma, Regina Chama - A/C.1/78/PV.8

UN. GENERAL ASSEMBLY (78TH SESS. : 2023-2024). 1ST COMMITTEE—WORK ORGANIZATION (Agenda item 7)

Colombia
Quintero Correa, Nohra María - A/C.1/78/PV.28; A/C.1/78/PV.30
Egypt
Ahmed, Amr Essameldin Sadek - A/C.1/78/PV.26; A/C.1/78/PV.30
Micronesia (Federated States of)
Zvachula, Martin - A/C.1/78/PV.30
Philippines
Lipana, Diane Shayne Dela Fuente - A/C.1/78/PV.29
Russian Federation
Belousov, Andrey I. - A/C.1/78/PV.27; A/C.1/78/PV.28; A/C.1/78/PV.30
Glukhov, Dmitry - A/C.1/78/PV.1
Singapore
Gafoor, Burhan - A/C.1/78/PV.30
UN. General Assembly. 1st Committee. Chair
Paulauskas, Rytis (Lithuania) - A/C.1/78/PV.1; A/C.1/78/PV.30

UN. GENERAL ASSEMBLY (78TH SESS. : 2023-2024). 1ST COMMITTEE—WORK ORGANIZATION (Agenda item 7) (continued)

United States
Knight, Stephen B. - A/C.1/78/PV.1
Storsve, Alison - A/C.1/78/PV.27
Turner, Bruce - A/C.1/78/PV.30

UN. GENERAL ASSEMBLY (78TH SESS. : 2023-2024). 2ND COMMITTEE—GENERAL DEBATE (Agenda item 8)

Albania
Kapisyzi, Arb - A/C.2/78/SR.5
Algeria
Latrous, Mohamed-Esseghir - A/C.2/78/SR.6
Alliance of Small Island States
Bartley, Matilda (Samoa) - A/C.2/78/SR.2
Andorra
Kallis Baldrich, Guillem - A/C.2/78/SR.4
Angola
Cruz, Francisco José da - A/C.2/78/SR.3
Argentina
Nicolino, Sebastián Lucas - A/C.2/78/SR.2
Oddone, Fabián - A/C.2/78/SR.3
Armenia
Babikyan, Araksya - A/C.2/78/SR.5
Galstyan, Tigran - A/C.2/78/SR.3
ASEAN
Prabowo, Hari (Indonesia) - A/C.2/78/SR.2
Australia
Larsen, James - A/C.2/78/SR.2
Azerbaijan
Bayramli-Hamidova, Nigar - A/C.2/78/SR.4; A/C.2/78/SR.5
Bahrain
Alatawi, Innas Abdulrahman - A/C.2/78/SR.5
Bangladesh
Shatil, Toufiq Islam - A/C.2/78/SR.6
Bolivia (Plurinational State of)
Pary Rodríguez, Diego - A/C.2/78/SR.4
Botswana
Mokhawa, Gladys - A/C.2/78/SR.5
Brazil
Moretti, Norberto - A/C.2/78/SR.4
Cambodia
Eat, Sophea - A/C.2/78/SR.5
Cameroon
Banaken Elel, Nelly - A/C.2/78/SR.4
Caribbean Community
Wallace, Brian Christopher Manley (Jamaica) - A/C.2/78/SR.2
Chile
González Carrillo, Montserrat - A/C.2/78/SR.5
China
Geng, Shuang - A/C.2/78/SR.4
Colombia
Zalabata Torres, Leonor - A/C.2/78/SR.3
Congo
Makayat-Safouesse, Lazare - A/C.2/78/SR.4

UN. GENERAL ASSEMBLY (78TH SESS. : 2023-2024). 2ND COMMITTEE—GENERAL DEBATE (Agenda item 8) (continued)

Costa Rica
Zamora Zumbado, Leticia María - A/C.2/78/SR.2; A/C.2/78/SR.5
Côte d'Ivoire
Moriko, Tiémoko - A/C.2/78/SR.4
Democratic People's Republic of Korea
Kim, Song - A/C.2/78/SR.3
Dominican Republic
Blanco Conde, José Alfonso - A/C.2/78/SR.3
LaRue, Claudia M. - A/C.2/78/SR.2
Ecuador
Montalvo Sosa, Andrés Efren - A/C.2/78/SR.5
Egypt
Abdelkhalek, Osama Mahmoud - A/C.2/78/SR.2
Eritrea
Tesfamariam, Sophia - A/C.2/78/SR.4
Ethiopia
Abebe, Leulseged Tadese - A/C.2/78/SR.2
Sabo, Tesfaye Yilma - A/C.2/78/SR.2
European Union
Skoog, Olof - A/C.2/78/SR.2
Georgia
Abesadze, David - A/C.2/78/SR.3
Ghana
Abudu-Birresborn, Jeswuni - A/C.2/78/SR.3
Greece
Sekeris, Evangelos C. - A/C.2/78/SR.4
Group of 77
Téllez Alonso, Frank (Cuba) - A/C.2/78/SR.2
Group of Landlocked Developing Countries
Mokhawa, Gladys (Botswana) - A/C.2/78/SR.2
Group of Least Developed Countries
Thapa, Lok Bahadur (Nepal) - A/C.2/78/SR.2
Guatemala
Rodríguez Mancia, Carla María - A/C.2/78/SR.5
Guyana
Rodrigues-Birkett, Carolyn - A/C.2/78/SR.5
Haiti
Vilmenay Joseph, Linouse - A/C.2/78/SR.5
Holy See
Murphy, Robert David - A/C.2/78/SR.6
Honduras
Flores, Ramón Emilio - A/C.2/78/SR.3
India
Gahlot, Petal - A/C.2/78/SR.4
Iran (Islamic Republic of)
Momeni, Javad - A/C.2/78/SR.2; A/C.2/78/SR.3
Iraq
Al-khalidi, Hasan Badri Mhalhal - A/C.2/78/SR.3
Israel
Miller, Brett Jonathan - A/C.2/78/SR.3
Italy
Massari, Maurizio - A/C.2/78/SR.6
Japan
Yamanaka, Osamu - A/C.2/78/SR.4
Jordan
Al-halique, Katherine Anas Ahmad - A/C.2/78/SR.3

UN. GENERAL ASSEMBLY (78TH SESS. : 2023-2024). 2ND COMMITTEE—GENERAL DEBATE (Agenda item 8) (continued)

Kazakhstan
Kerimkulov, Bauyrzhan - A/C.2/78/SR.5
Kenya
Onyoni-Mogaka, Catherine Bonareri - A/C.2/78/SR.4
Kuwait
Aldehani, Bader A. - A/C.2/78/SR.5
Kyrgyzstan
Kasymalieva, Aida - A/C.2/78/SR.6
Lao People's Democratic Republic
Vongnorkeo, Anouparb - A/C.2/78/SR.6
Lebanon
Zoghbi, Rawa - A/C.2/78/SR.5
Lesotho
Nena, Matete - A/C.2/78/SR.3
Like-Minded Group of Supporters of Middle-Income Countries
Hilale, Omar (Morocco) - A/C.2/78/SR.2
Malawi
Chimbiri-Molande, Agnes Mary - A/C.2/78/SR.6
Malaysia
Adnan, Yang Aishah Binti - A/C.2/78/SR.5
Maldives
Hussain, Thilmeeza - A/C.2/78/SR.3
Malta
Kuymizakis, Adam - A/C.2/78/SR.3
Mexico
Buenrostro Massieu, Alicia - A/C.2/78/SR.3
Mendoza Elguea, Sylvia Paola - A/C.2/78/SR.2
Mongolia
Vorshilov, Enkhbold - A/C.2/78/SR.3
Morocco
Hamdouni, Meryem - A/C.2/78/SR.4
Myanmar
Tun, Kyaw Moe - A/C.2/78/SR.5
Namibia
Gertze, Neville Melvin - A/C.2/78/SR.4
Nauru
Tsiode, Branessa - A/C.2/78/SR.6
Nepal
Thapa, Lok Bahadur - A/C.2/78/SR.2
Nicaragua
Jiménez, Jasser - A/C.2/78/SR.4
Nigeria
Muhammad Bande, Tijjani - A/C.2/78/SR.2
Norway
Brattested, Merete Fjeld - A/C.2/78/SR.4
Oman
Al Rawahi, Abdulhalim Mubarak Saloom - A/C.2/78/SR.6
Pakistan
Akram, Munir - A/C.2/78/SR.2
Majeed, Aleena - A/C.2/78/SR.2
Panama
Thompson Ramírez, Marilyn del Carmen - A/C.2/78/SR.3
Paraguay
Pereira Sosa, José Eduardo - A/C.2/78/SR.3

UN. GENERAL ASSEMBLY (78TH SESS. : 2023-2024). 2ND COMMITTEE—GENERAL DEBATE (Agenda item 8) (continued)

Peru
Napurí Pita, Andrés - A/C.2/78/SR.5
Philippines
Lora-Santos, Leila Castillon - A/C.2/78/SR.3
Poland
Sakowicz, Mateusz - A/C.2/78/SR.4
Portugal
Zacarias, Ana Paula - A/C.2/78/SR.4
Qatar
Al-naama, Talal Abdulaziz - A/C.2/78/SR.2
Republic of Korea
Cho, Hyunwoo - A/C.2/78/SR.4
Republic of Moldova
Nipomici, Galina - A/C.2/78/SR.4
Romania
Feruță, Cornel - A/C.2/78/SR.3
Russian Federation
Chumakov, Dmitry S. - A/C.2/78/SR.5
Meschchanov, Boris A. - A/C.2/78/SR.2
San Marino
Beleffi, Damiano - A/C.2/78/SR.4
Saudi Arabia
Alomair, Reem Fahad O. - A/C.2/78/SR.4
Senegal
Ndoye, Abdou - A/C.2/78/SR.3
Serbia
Vujačić, Dušan - A/C.2/78/SR.5
Sierra Leone
Kanu, Michael Imran - A/C.2/78/SR.3
Singapore
Tan, Jason Han Wei - A/C.2/78/SR.4
South Africa
Schalkwyk, Marthinus van - A/C.2/78/SR.3
Spain
Jiménez de la Hoz, Ana - A/C.2/78/SR.5
Sri Lanka
Pieris, Peter Mohan Maithri - A/C.2/78/SR.4
Sudan
Abuhaj, Hiba Jafaar Abubakr - A/C.2/78/SR.5
Switzerland
Hauri, Adrian - A/C.2/78/SR.2
Syrian Arab Republic
Al Nahhas, Wissam - A/C.2/78/SR.3
Tajikistan
Hasanova, Tahmina - A/C.2/78/SR.3
Thailand
Chindawongse, Suriya - A/C.2/78/SR.3
Timor-Leste
Nunes, Karlito - A/C.2/78/SR.4
Tonga
Vea, Jeanett - A/C.2/78/SR.6
Trinidad and Tobago
Budhu, Vladamir - A/C.2/78/SR.5
Tunisia
Chelbi, Kaouthar - A/C.2/78/SR.4
Türkiye
İstemil Aydil, Alara - A/C.2/78/SR.6

UN. GENERAL ASSEMBLY (78TH SESS. : 2023-2024). 2ND COMMITTEE—GENERAL DEBATE (Agenda item 8) (continued)

Turkmenistan
Eyeberdiyev, Ata - A/C.2/78/SR.3
Ukraine
Leschenko, Volodymyr - A/C.2/78/SR.3
UN. General Assembly. 2nd Committee. Chair
Amorín, Carlos Daniel (Uruguay) - A/C.2/78/SR.2
UN. Group of African States
Muhammad Bande, Tijjani (Nigeria) - A/C.2/78/SR.2
UN. Under-Secretary-General for Economic and Social Affairs
Li, Junhua - A/C.2/78/SR.2
United Arab Emirates
Bastaki, Mohammad Yousuf Abdulla Mohammad - A/C.2/78/SR.4
United Kingdom
Kariuki, James - A/C.2/78/SR.5
United Republic of Tanzania
Kattanga, Hussein A. - A/C.2/78/SR.5
United States
Carty, Lisa A. - A/C.2/78/SR.3
University of Massachusetts at Amherst
Ghosh, Jayati - A/C.2/78/SR.2
Uruguay
Romero Veiga, Stefany - A/C.2/78/SR.5
Uzbekistan
Lapasov, Ulugbek - A/C.2/78/SR.6
Venezuela (Bolivarian Republic of)
Marín Sevilla, Asbina - A/C.2/78/SR.5
Viet Nam
Nguyen, Hoang Nguyen - A/C.2/78/SR.4
Yemen
Al-barati, Abdulrahman Hasan Yahya - A/C.2/78/SR.6
Zambia
Milambo, Chola - A/C.2/78/SR.6
Zimbabwe
Rupende, Tapiwa Roy - A/C.2/78/SR.5

UN. GENERAL ASSEMBLY (78TH SESS. : 2023-2024). 2ND COMMITTEE—WORK ORGANIZATION (Agenda item 7)

UN. General Assembly. 2nd Committee. Chair
Amorín, Carlos Daniel (Uruguay) - A/C.2/78/SR.1; A/C.2/78/SR.25
UN. General Assembly. President
Francis, Dennis (Trinidad and Tobago) - A/C.2/78/SR.12
UN. Under-Secretary-General for Economic and Social Affairs
Li, Junhua - A/C.2/78/SR.25

UN. GENERAL ASSEMBLY (78TH SESS. : 2023-2024). 3RD COMMITTEE—WORK ORGANIZATION (Agenda item 7)

UN. General Assembly. President
Francis, Dennis (Trinidad and Tobago) - A/C.3/78/SR.17

UN. GENERAL ASSEMBLY (78TH SESS. : 2023-2024). 4TH COMMITTEE—WORK ORGANIZATION (Agenda item 7)

UN. General Assembly. President
Francis, Dennis (Trinidad and Tobago) - A/C.4/78/SR.2
UN. General Assembly. Special Political and Decolonization Committee (4th Committee). Chair
Joyini, Mathu (South Africa) - A/C.4/78/SR.1

UN. GENERAL ASSEMBLY (78TH SESS. : 2023-2024). 5TH COMMITTEE—WORK ORGANIZATION (Agenda item 7)

ASEAN
Gafoor, Burhan (Singapore) - A/C.5/78/SR.27
Australia
Jones, Alexandra - A/C.5/78/SR.27
Bangladesh
Muhith, Muhammad A. - A/C.5/78/SR.35
Botswana
Mokhawa, Gladys - A/C.5/78/SR.40
Canada
Arbeiter, Richard - A/C.5/78/SR.35
China
Dai, Bing - A/C.5/78/SR.35
Jiang, Hua - A/C.5/78/SR.26/PartII; A/C.5/78/SR.27; A/C.5/78/SR.34
Costa Rica
Videche Guevara, Carlos Manuel - A/C.5/78/SR.27
Egypt
Roshdy, Hussein Ossama Hussein Abdelrhman - A/C.5/78/SR.26/PartII; A/C.5/78/SR.40
European Union
Camelli, Thibault - A/C.5/78/SR.27; A/C.5/78/SR.34; A/C.5/78/SR.35
Gaber-Wennholz, Basma - A/C.5/78/SR.26/PartII
Samson, Hedda - A/C.5/78/SR.40
Group of 77
Ainomuhisha, Medard (Uganda) - A/C.5/78/SR.27; A/C.5/78/SR.34; A/C.5/78/SR.35; A/C.5/78/SR.40
Tur de la Concepción, Richard (Cuba) - A/C.5/78/SR.26/PartII
Gulf Cooperation Council
Alnasr, Mohammed Khalifa H. (Qatar) - A/C.5/78/SR.27
Indonesia
Ratnamurti, Karina - A/C.5/78/SR.35
Wardhana, Yochpy Ihsan - A/C.5/78/SR.26/PartII
Japan
Abo, Ai - A/C.5/78/SR.40
Fujinuma, Atsuyuki - A/C.5/78/SR.26/PartII
Kawasaki, Yuta - A/C.5/78/SR.34
Yamanaka, Osamu - A/C.5/78/SR.27; A/C.5/78/SR.35
Mexico
Velázquez Castillo, Jesús - A/C.5/78/SR.27; A/C.5/78/SR.35
Republic of Korea
Seong, Woong - A/C.5/78/SR.27; A/C.5/78/SR.35

UN. GENERAL ASSEMBLY (78TH SESS. : 2023-2024). 5TH COMMITTEE—WORK ORGANIZATION (Agenda item 7) (continued)

Russian Federation
Laputin, Vadim - A/C.5/78/SR.27; A/C.5/78/SR.35
UN. Controller
Ramanathan, Chandramouli - A/C.5/78/SR.26/PartII; A/C.5/78/SR.40
UN. General Assembly. 5th Committee. Chair
Abdelkhalek, Osama Mahmoud (Egypt) - A/C.5/78/SR.35
UN. General Assembly. President
Francis, Dennis (Trinidad and Tobago) - A/C.5/78/SR.4
UN. Group of African States
Minale, Lemlem Fiseha (Ethiopia) - A/C.5/78/SR.26/PartII; A/C.5/78/SR.34; A/C.5/78/SR.35; A/C.5/78/SR.40
United Kingdom
Kariuki, James - A/C.5/78/SR.35
Staples, James - A/C.5/78/SR.26/PartII
Young, Archie - A/C.5/78/SR.27; A/C.5/78/SR.34; A/C.5/78/SR.40
United States
Lu, Christopher P. - A/C.5/78/SR.26/PartII; A/C.5/78/SR.27; A/C.5/78/SR.34; A/C.5/78/SR.35; A/C.5/78/SR.40
Uruguay
Machado Mouriño, Felipe - A/C.5/78/SR.27; A/C.5/78/SR.35; A/C.5/78/SR.40
Viet Nam
Pham, Cao Cuong - A/C.5/78/SR.26/PartII; A/C.5/78/SR.40

UN. GENERAL ASSEMBLY (78TH SESS. : 2023-2024). 6TH COMMITTEE—WORK ORGANIZATION (Agenda item 7)

UN. General Assembly. President
Francis, Dennis (Trinidad and Tobago) - A/C.6/78/SR.12

UN. GENERAL ASSEMBLY (78TH SESS. : 2023-2024). CREDENTIALS COMMITTEE—REPORTS (Agenda item 3b)

Iran (Islamic Republic of)
Ghadirkhomi, Payman - A/78/PV.48
UN. General Assembly. Credentials Committee. Chair
Waetara, Jane Mugafalu Kabui (Solomon Islands) - A/78/PV.48

UN. GENERAL ASSEMBLY (78TH SESS. : 2023-2024). PRESIDENT (Agenda item 4)

Cameroon
Yang, Philémon - A/78/PV.87
UN. General Assembly. President
Francis, Dennis (Trinidad and Tobago) - A/78/PV.87
UN. Group of African States
Tommo Monthe, Michel (Cameroon) - A/78/PV.87

UN. GENERAL ASSEMBLY (78TH SESS. : 2023-2024). PRESIDENT (Agenda item 4) (continued)

UN. Group of Asia-Pacific States
Al-Saadi, Abdullah Ali Fadhel (Yemen) - A/78/PV.87
UN. Group of Western European and Other States
Marschik, Alexander (Austria) - A/78/PV.87
UN. Secretary-General
Guterres, António, 1949- - A/78/PV.87
United States
Carty, Lisa A. - A/78/PV.87

UN. HUMAN RIGHTS COMMITTEE—REPORTS (Agenda item 71a)

Cameroon
Banaken Elel, Nelly - A/C.3/78/SR.17
Costa Rica
Zavala Porras, Daniel Andrés - A/C.3/78/SR.17
European Union
Keogh, Briana - A/C.3/78/SR.17
Mexico
Riveroll Usabiaga, Renata - A/C.3/78/SR.17
Paraguay
Candia Ibarra, Miguel Ricardo - A/C.3/78/SR.17
Russian Federation
Kuzmenkov, Stepan Y. - A/C.3/78/SR.17
UN. Human Rights Committee. Chair
Abdo Rocholl, Tania María (Paraguay) - A/C.3/78/SR.17
United States
Breen, Patrick - A/C.3/78/SR.17

UN. HUMAN RIGHTS COUNCIL—MEMBERS (Agenda item 114c)

UN. General Assembly. President
Francis, Dennis (Trinidad and Tobago) - A/78/PV.17

UN. HUMAN RIGHTS COUNCIL—REPORTS (Agenda item 66)

Algeria
Hassani, Billel - A/78/PV.28; A/C.3/78/SR.46
Samai, Rahma - A/C.3/78/SR.46
Argentina
Escobar, Luciano Hernán - A/C.3/78/SR.46
Squeff, María del Carmen - A/78/PV.23
Australia
Pullela, Shilpa Kadambari - A/C.3/78/SR.46
Bahamas
DeGregory, Kelli - A/C.3/78/SR.46
Bangladesh
Monica, Mosammat Shahanara - A/C.3/78/SR.46
Belarus
Pilipenko, Igor - A/78/PV.23
Bolivia (Plurinational State of)
Caldera Gutiérrez, Fiorella - A/78/PV.28

UN. HUMAN RIGHTS COUNCIL—REPORTS (Agenda item 66) (continued)

Cameroon
Banaken Elel, Nelly - A/C.3/78/SR.46
Tommo Monthe, Michel - A/78/PV.23
Chile
Nishihara, Carmen - A/C.3/78/SR.46
China
Zhang, Sisi - A/C.3/78/SR.46
Colombia
Sánchez García, Nathalia - A/78/PV.28
Costa Rica
Chan Valverde, Maritza - A/78/PV.23
Zavala Porras, Daniel Andrés - A/C.3/78/SR.46
Croatia
Simonovic, Ivan - A/78/PV.28
Cuba
González Behmaras, Alejandro - A/78/PV.28; A/C.3/78/SR.46; A/C.3/78/SR.51
Democratic People's Republic of Korea
Kim, Nam Hyok - A/C.3/78/SR.46
Dominican Republic
Andújar, Luz del Carmen - A/C.3/78/SR.46
Cedano, Joan Margarita - A/78/PV.28
Ecuador
Méndez Gruezo, Elizabeth - A/C.3/78/SR.46
Egypt
Mostafa Rizk, Heba - A/78/PV.28; A/C.3/78/SR.46
El Salvador
González López, Egriselda Aracely - A/C.3/78/SR.46
Eritrea
Gebrekidan, Zebib - A/C.3/78/SR.51
European Union
Alonso Giganto, Ana María (Spain) - A/C.3/78/SR.51
Clifford, Katarina - A/78/PV.23
Georgia
Abesadze, David - A/78/PV.23
Group of Friends in Defence of the Charter of the United Nations
Pérez Ayestarán, Joaquín Alberto (Venezuela (Bolivarian Republic of)) - A/78/PV.23
Iceland
Valtýsson, Jörundur - A/78/PV.23
India
Sonkar, Suman - A/78/PV.28
Indonesia
Dhanutirto, Mariska Dwianti - A/78/PV.28
Iran (Islamic Republic of)
Arab Bafrani, Fatemeh - A/78/PV.23; A/C.3/78/SR.46; A/C.3/78/SR.51
Iraq
Abdullateef, Mohammed Ayad - A/C.3/78/SR.46
Israel
Mimran Rosenberg, Avital - A/C.3/78/SR.51
Kuwait
AlSabah, Khaled S. - A/78/PV.23
Latvia
Burbergs, Māris - A/C.3/78/SR.46

UN. HUMAN RIGHTS COUNCIL—REPORTS (Agenda item 66) (continued)

Liechtenstein
Oehri, Myriam - A/78/PV.23
Oehri, Noah - A/C.3/78/SR.51
Malaysia
Rizal, Nizhan Faraz Bin - A/78/PV.23
Maldives
Hameed, Hala - A/78/PV.23
Mali
Dabo N'diaye, Djeneba - A/78/PV.28
Mexico
Elizondo Belden, Luis Gerardo - A/78/PV.23
Morocco
Bouchikhi, Hanaa - A/C.3/78/SR.46
Kadiri, Omar - A/78/PV.28
Myanmar
Tun, Kyaw Moe - A/78/PV.23; A/C.3/78/SR.46
Netherlands (Kingdom of the)
Lasseur, Katja - A/C.3/78/SR.46
Nicaragua
Jiménez, Jasser - A/78/PV.23
Pichardo Urbina, Eleane Yaoska - A/C.3/78/SR.46; A/C.3/78/SR.51
Nigeria
Asaju, Bola - A/C.3/78/SR.46
Pakistan
Akram, Munir - A/78/PV.23
Qureshi, Hadeeqa - A/78/PV.28
Peru
Pedroza, David - A/C.3/78/SR.46
Qatar
Al-thani, Almaha Mubarak F.J. - A/78/PV.23
Republic of Korea
Song, Hye-ryoung - A/C.3/78/SR.46
Russian Federation
Kondratev, Sergei V. - A/C.3/78/SR.46
Saudi Arabia
Alwasil, Abdulaziz M.O. - A/78/PV.23
Bin Jadid, Faisal Fahad M. - A/C.3/78/SR.46
South Africa
Mngomezulu, Portia Lindiwe - A/C.3/78/SR.46
Schalkwyk, Marthinus van - A/78/PV.28
Sudan
Idres, Nusaiba Hashim Mohamed Ali - A/C.3/78/SR.51
Switzerland
Chanda, Riccarda - A/78/PV.23
Fontana, Barbara - A/C.3/78/SR.46
Syrian Arab Republic
Altarsha, Elie - A/C.3/78/SR.46; A/C.3/78/SR.51
Ukraine
Mudrenko, Nataliia - A/C.3/78/SR.46
UN. General Assembly. 3rd Committee. Rapporteur
Poveda Brito, Robert Alexander (Venezuela (Bolivarian Republic of)) - A/78/PV.50
UN. General Assembly. President
Francis, Dennis (Trinidad and Tobago) - A/78/PV.23
UN. Group of African States
Milambo, Chola (Zambia) - A/C.3/78/SR.51

UN. HUMAN RIGHTS COUNCIL—REPORTS (Agenda item 66) (continued)

UN. Human Rights Council. President
Bálek, Václav (Czechia) - A/78/PV.23; A/C.3/78/SR.46
United Kingdom
Manzare, Max - A/C.3/78/SR.46
United States
Johnson, Timothy J. - A/C.3/78/SR.46; A/C.3/78/SR.51

UN. INDEPENDENT AUDIT ADVISORY COMMITTEE—MEMBERS (Agenda item 115e)

UN. General Assembly. 5th Committee. Chair
Abdelkhalek, Osama Mahmoud (Egypt) - A/C.5/78/SR.8

UN. INTERNATIONAL COURT OF JUSTICE—MEMBERS (Agenda item 113c)

Uganda
Muhumuza, Duncan Laki - A/78/PV.31

UN. INTERNATIONAL COURT OF JUSTICE—REPORTS (Agenda item 73)

(personal capacity)
Chindawongse, Suriya - A/C.6/78/SR.26
Argentina
Herrera, Gabriel - A/78/PV.20
Armenia
Margaryan, Mher - A/78/PV.28
Australia
Hutchison, Alexandra - A/C.6/78/SR.26
McCarthy, Adam - A/78/PV.20
Azerbaijan
Musayev, Tofig - A/78/PV.27; A/78/PV.28
Bangladesh
Muhith, Muhammad A. - A/78/PV.27
Belgium
Raes, Elisa de - A/78/PV.27
Bolivia (Plurinational State of)
Ríos, Carmen Rosa - A/78/PV.27
Brazil
Braoios, Victor Silveira - A/78/PV.27
Chile
Hernández Chávez, José Juan - A/78/PV.27
Poblete Troncoso, Moisés - A/78/PV.20
China
Ma, Xinmin - A/78/PV.20
Colombia
Solano Ramírez, Lucía Teresa - A/C.6/78/SR.26
Comunidade dos Países de Língua Portuguesa
Cruz, Francisco José da (Angola) - A/78/PV.27
Coordinating Bureau of the Non-Aligned Countries
Musayev, Tofig (Azerbaijan) - A/78/PV.27
Costa Rica
Chan Valverde, Maritza - A/78/PV.27
Cuba
Carral Castelo, Arianna - A/78/PV.27

UN. INTERNATIONAL COURT OF JUSTICE—REPORTS (Agenda item 73) (continued)

Cyprus
Pittakis, Theodoulos - A/78/PV.28
Democratic Republic of the Congo
Mukongo Ngay, Zénon - A/78/PV.28
Denmark
Pasternak Jørgensen, Vibeke - A/78/PV.20
Ecuador
Escobar Ullauri, Pablo - A/78/PV.27; A/C.6/78/SR.26
Egypt
Roshdy, Hussein Ossama Hussein Abdelrhman - A/78/PV.28
El Salvador
Flores Soto, Ligia Lorena - A/C.6/78/SR.26
Equatorial Guinea
Nze Mansogo, Estela Mercedes - A/78/PV.28
Eritrea
Essaias, Meron Habte - A/C.6/78/SR.26
European Union
Hoffmeister, Frank - A/78/PV.20
France
Colas, Diego - A/78/PV.20
Georgia
Bakradze, David - A/78/PV.28
Germany
Freiin von Uslar-Gleichen, Tania - A/78/PV.20
Greece
Stellakatos-Loverdos, Michael - A/78/PV.28
Group of Arab States
Bisharat, Nadien Isam Fraih (Jordan) - A/78/PV.27
Guatemala
Búcaro Flores, Mario Adolfo - A/78/PV.20
Guyana
Rodrigues-Birkett, Carolyn - A/78/PV.28
Honduras
Rivera Reyes, Isabella Regina - A/78/PV.27
India
Bhat, Kajal - A/78/PV.27
Indonesia
Nasir, Arrmanatha Christiawan - A/78/PV.28
Iran (Islamic Republic of)
Fallah Assadi, Mahdad - A/78/PV.28
Mousavi, Seyed Ali - A/78/PV.20; A/C.6/78/SR.26
Ireland
Kirk, James - A/78/PV.27
Israel
Cappon, Noam - A/78/PV.28
Italy
Zanini, Stefano - A/78/PV.20
Japan
Mikanagi, Tomohiro - A/78/PV.20
Lebanon
Hitti, Youssef - A/78/PV.27; A/C.6/78/SR.26
Liechtenstein
Oehri, Myriam - A/78/PV.27
Lithuania
Paulauskas, Rytis - A/78/PV.27
Luxembourg
Germeaux, Alain - A/78/PV.27

UN. INTERNATIONAL COURT OF JUSTICE—REPORTS (Agenda item 73) (continued)

Malaysia
Omar, Khairi - A/78/PV.27
Malta
Kuymizakis, Adam - A/78/PV.27
Mexico
Celorio Alcántara, Alexandro - A/78/PV.20
Myanmar
Tun, Kyaw Moe - A/78/PV.28
Netherlands (Kingdom of the)
Lefeber, René - A/78/PV.20; A/C.6/78/SR.26
Nicaragua
Hermida Castillo, Jaime - A/78/PV.28
Oman
Al Shehhi, Mohammed Ali Ahmed - A/78/PV.27
Organisation of Islamic Cooperation
Laghdaf, Sidi Mohamed (Mauritania) - A/78/PV.27
Pakistan
Akram, Munir - A/78/PV.27
Paraguay
Giret Soto, David Antonio - A/78/PV.27
Peru
Ugarelli, Luis F. - A/78/PV.27
Philippines
Lagdameo, Antonio Manuel Revilla - A/78/PV.28
Romania
Orosan, Alina - A/78/PV.20
Russian Federation
Zabolotskaya, Maria V. - A/78/PV.28
Senegal
Ndoye, Abdou - A/78/PV.27
Singapore
Gafoor, Burhan - A/78/PV.27
Slovenia
Rakovec, Marko - A/78/PV.20
State of Palestine
Mansour, Riyad H. - A/78/PV.28
Sudan
Mohamed, Al-Harith Idriss al-Harith - A/78/PV.28
Switzerland
Perrez, Franz - A/78/PV.20
Thailand
Tang, Suphanvasa Chotikajan - A/C.6/78/SR.26
Ukraine
Korynevych, Anton - A/78/PV.20
UN. General Assembly. President
Francis, Dennis (Trinidad and Tobago) - A/78/PV.20
UN. International Court of Justice. President
Donoghue, Joan E. - A/78/PV.20; A/C.6/78/SR.26
United Arab Emirates
Alshamsi, Khaula Ali Khamis Obaid - A/78/PV.28
United Kingdom
Langrish, Sally - A/78/PV.20
United States
Visek, Richard - A/78/PV.20
Viet Nam
Thoa Le, Thi Minh - A/78/PV.27
Visegrad Group
Ruffer, Emil (Czechia) - A/78/PV.20

UN. INTERNATIONAL COURT OF JUSTICE—REPORTS (Agenda item 73) (continued)

Zambia
Milambo, Chola - A/78/PV.28

UN. INTERNATIONAL LAW COMMISSION—REPORTS (Agenda item 79)

Algeria
Bouchedoub, Mohamed Faiz - A/C.6/78/SR.28
Alliance of Small Island States
Luteru, Fatumanava-o-Upolu III Pa'olelei (Samoa) - A/C.6/78/SR.27
Argentina
Herrera, Gabriel - A/C.6/78/SR.28
Mainero, Martín Juan - A/C.6/78/SR.30; A/C.6/78/SR.37
Armenia
Sarvarian, Arman - A/C.6/78/SR.27; A/C.6/78/SR.30
Australia
Mason, Naomi - A/C.6/78/SR.29
McCarthy, Adam - A/C.6/78/SR.23
Austria
Bühler, Konrad G. - A/C.6/78/SR.24
Gorke, Maximilian - A/C.6/78/SR.31
Pretterhofer, Stefan - A/C.6/78/SR.29
Bangladesh
Uddin, Nasir - A/C.6/78/SR.24
Belarus
Evseenko, Pavel - A/C.6/78/SR.31
Popkov, Andrei N. - A/C.6/78/SR.24; A/C.6/78/SR.28
Brazil
Bernandes, Rafael - A/C.6/78/SR.29; A/C.6/78/SR.31
Sloboda, Pedro Muniz Pinto - A/C.6/78/SR.23
Bulgaria
Dramova, Dimana - A/C.6/78/SR.28
Cameroon
Nyanid, Zacharie Serge Raoul - A/C.6/78/SR.25; A/C.6/78/SR.30; A/C.6/78/SR.33; A/C.6/78/SR.37
Canada
Kessel, Alan - A/C.6/78/SR.25
Mead, Kevin Timothy - A/C.6/78/SR.30
Chile
Hernández Chávez, José Juan - A/C.6/78/SR.29; A/C.6/78/SR.31
Troncoso, Claudio - A/C.6/78/SR.24
China
Li, Linlin - A/C.6/78/SR.37
Ma, Xinmin - A/C.6/78/SR.27; A/C.6/78/SR.29
Colombia
Solano Ramírez, Lucía Teresa - A/C.6/78/SR.27; A/C.6/78/SR.30; A/C.6/78/SR.33
Côte d'Ivoire
Moriko, Tiémoko - A/C.6/78/SR.28; A/C.6/78/SR.30
Council of Europe
Gómez Heredero, Ana - A/C.6/78/SR.28
Croatia
Mesarek, Gordana Vidovic - A/C.6/78/SR.27

UN. OFFICE OF INTERNAL OVERSIGHT SERVICES—REPORTS (Agenda item 143) (continued)

Switzerland
Schmied, Gina Andrea - A/C.5/78/SR.2
UN. General Assembly. 5th Committee. Rapporteur
Hartog, Laurens Thomas den (Netherlands (Kingdom of the)) - A/78/PV.50(Resumption1)
UN. Under-Secretary-General for Internal Oversight Services
Ndiaye, Fatoumata - A/C.5/78/SR.2

UN. PEACEBUILDING COMMISSION—REPORTS (Agenda item 27)

Algeria
Gaouaoui, Nacim - A/78/PV.100
Colombia
Zalabata Torres, Leonor - A/78/PV.100
Croatia
Simonovic, Ivan - A/78/PV.100
Cuba
Gala López, Yuri - A/78/PV.100
Denmark
Laursen, Erik - A/78/PV.100
Egypt
Abdelkhalek, Osama Mahmoud - A/78/PV.100
El Salvador
González López, Egriselda Aracely - A/78/PV.100
European Union
Tolstoi, Natalie - A/78/PV.100
Germany
Geisler, Michael Alexander - A/78/PV.100
India
Bhalla, Ashish - A/78/PV.101
Italy
Martin Topranin, Pietro de - A/78/PV.100
Japan
Shino, Mitsuko - A/78/PV.100
Kenya
Kiboino, Michael Kapkiai - A/78/PV.100
Mexico
Cisneros Chávez, José de Jesús - A/78/PV.100
Morocco
Hilale, Omar - A/78/PV.100
Peru
García Toma, Victor Óscar Shiyin - A/78/PV.100
Poland
Szczerski, Krzysztof - A/78/PV.100
Republic of Korea
Park, Jeewon - A/78/PV.101
Russian Federation
Agaronova, Gloriya A. - A/78/PV.101
South Africa
Schalkwyk, Marthinus van - A/78/PV.100
Timor-Leste
Chaves, Joaquim José Costa - A/78/PV.101
UN. Peacebuilding Commission. Chair
Danese, Sérgio França (Brazil) - A/78/PV.100
United Kingdom
Weld-Blundell, Stacy John - A/78/PV.101

UN. PEACEBUILDING COMMISSION—REPORTS (Agenda item 27) (continued)

United States
Shrier, Jonathan - A/78/PV.101

UN. PEACEBUILDING FUND—REPORTS (Agenda item 111)

Algeria
Gaouaoui, Nacim - A/78/PV.100
Colombia
Zalabata Torres, Leonor - A/78/PV.100
Cuba
Gala López, Yuri - A/78/PV.100
Denmark
Laursen, Erik - A/78/PV.100
Egypt
Abdelkhalek, Osama Mahmoud - A/78/PV.100
El Salvador
González López, Egriselda Aracely - A/78/PV.100
European Union
Tolstoi, Natalie - A/78/PV.100
Germany
Geisler, Michael Alexander - A/78/PV.100
India
Bhalla, Ashish - A/78/PV.101
Italy
Martin Topranin, Pietro de - A/78/PV.100
Japan
Shino, Mitsuko - A/78/PV.100
Kenya
Kiboino, Michael Kapkiai - A/78/PV.100
Mexico
Cisneros Chávez, José de Jesús - A/78/PV.100
Morocco
Hilale, Omar - A/78/PV.100
Peru
García Toma, Victor Óscar Shiyin - A/78/PV.100
Poland
Szczerski, Krzysztof - A/78/PV.100
Republic of Korea
Park, Jeewon - A/78/PV.101
Russian Federation
Agaronova, Gloriya A. - A/78/PV.101
South Africa
Schalkwyk, Marthinus van - A/78/PV.100
Timor-Leste
Chaves, Joaquim José Costa - A/78/PV.101
United Kingdom
Weld-Blundell, Stacy John - A/78/PV.101
United States
Shrier, Jonathan - A/78/PV.101

UN. SECRETARY-GENERAL—REPORTS (Agenda item 110)

Angola
Cruz, Francisco José da - A/78/PV.55
Armenia
Margaryan, Mher - A/78/PV.54
Belarus
Mozgovaya, Ekaterina - A/78/PV.55

UN. SECRETARY-GENERAL—REPORTS (Agenda item 110) (continued)

Costa Rica
Chan Valverde, Maritza - A/78/PV.54
Croatia
Simonovic, Ivan - A/78/PV.55
Cuba
Romero Puentes, Yusnier - A/78/PV.55
Group of Arab States
Ladeb, Tarek (Tunisia) - A/78/PV.55
Group of Friends in Defence of the Charter of the United Nations
Pérez Ayestarán, Joaquín Alberto (Venezuela (Bolivarian Republic of)) - A/78/PV.55
Group of Friends of the Responsibility to Protect
Rodríguez Mancia, Carla María (Guatemala) - A/78/PV.54
Indonesia
Nasir, Arrmanatha Christiawan - A/78/PV.54
Malaysia
Zin Zawawi, Nordiana Binti - A/78/PV.55
Myanmar
Tun, Kyaw Moe - A/78/PV.55
Pakistan
Akram, Munir - A/78/PV.55
South Africa
Lagardien, Yaseen - A/78/PV.55
UN. Peacebuilding Commission. Chair
Danese, Sérgio França (Brazil) - A/78/PV.54
UN. Secretary-General
Guterres, António, 1949- - A/78/PV.4; A/78/PV.54

UN. SECURITY COUNCIL—MEMBERS (Agenda item 113a)

UN. General Assembly. President
Francis, Dennis (Trinidad and Tobago) - A/78/PV.86

UN. SECURITY COUNCIL—MEMBERSHIP (Agenda item 121)

African Union
Kpukumu, Sulay-Manah J. (Sierra Leone) - A/78/PV.34
Sowa, Amara Sheikh Mohammed (Sierra Leone) - A/78/PV.104
Algeria
Bendjama, Amar - A/78/PV.35
Angola
Luemba, Mateus Pedro - A/78/PV.36
Argentina
Oddone, Fabián - A/78/PV.35
Australia
Bryant, Rebecca Suzanne - A/78/PV.35
Bangladesh
Molla, Md Rafiqul Alam - A/78/PV.35
Belarus
Makarevich, Siarhei - A/78/PV.36
Bolivia (Plurinational State of)
Pary Rodríguez, Diego - A/78/PV.36

UN. SECURITY COUNCIL—MEMBERSHIP (Agenda item 121) (continued)

Brazil
Moretti, Norberto - A/78/PV.35
Cambodia
Mao, Tithiarun - A/78/PV.36
Caribbean Community
Rambally, Menissa (Saint Lucia) - A/78/PV.34
Chile
Vidal Mercado, Jorge Andrés - A/78/PV.35
China
Dai, Bing - A/78/PV.104
Zhang, Jun - A/78/PV.35
Colombia
Zalabata Torres, Leonor - A/78/PV.34
Costa Rica
Chan Valverde, Maritza - A/78/PV.34
Cuba
Romero Puentes, Yusnier - A/78/PV.36
Democratic People's Republic of Korea
Kim, Song - A/78/PV.36
Denmark
Laursen, Erik - A/78/PV.34
Ecuador
Montalvo Sosa, Andrés Efren - A/78/PV.36
Egypt
Abdelkhalek, Osama Mahmoud - A/78/PV.35
El Salvador
Segura Aragón, Carlos Efraín - A/78/PV.36
Estonia
Tammsaar, Rein - A/78/PV.36
Ethiopia
Anulo, Semalign Kebede - A/78/PV.36
France
Rivière, Nicolas de - A/78/PV.35
Group of Arab States
Alrowaiei, Jamal Fares (Bahrain) - A/78/PV.34; A/78/PV.104
Group of Four
Danese, Sérgio França (Brazil) - A/78/PV.104
Leendertse, Antje (Germany) - A/78/PV.34
Guyana
Rodrigues-Birkett, Carolyn - A/78/PV.36
India
Kamboj, Ruchira - A/78/PV.35
Patel, Yojna - A/78/PV.104
Indonesia
Nasir, Arrmanatha Christiawan - A/78/PV.35
Iran (Islamic Republic of)
Karimi Magham, Ali - A/78/PV.35
Ireland
Mythen, Fergal Tomas - A/78/PV.35
Japan
Ishikane, Kimihiro - A/78/PV.35
Nagano, Shunsuke - A/78/PV.36
Shino, Mitsuko - A/78/PV.104
Kenya
Kiboino, Michael Kapkiai - A/78/PV.36

UN. SECURITY COUNCIL—MEMBERSHIP (Agenda item 121) (continued)

L.69 Group
King, Inga Rhonda (Saint Vincent and the Grenadines) - A/78/PV.104
Miguel, Nedra P. (Saint Vincent and the Grenadines) - A/78/PV.34
Lao People's Democratic Republic
Khousakoun, Phetvanxay - A/78/PV.36
Liechtenstein
Wenaweser, Christian - A/78/PV.34
Luxembourg
Maes, Olivier - A/78/PV.34
Malaysia
Abd Karim, Sofian Akmal Bin - A/78/PV.35
Maldives
Zuhuree, Ibrahim - A/78/PV.34
Malta
Frazier, Vanessa - A/78/PV.35
Mexico
Buenrostro Massieu, Alicia - A/78/PV.34
Mongolia
Vorshilov, Enkhbold - A/78/PV.35
Morocco
Kadiri, Omar - A/78/PV.34
Nigeria
Lamuwa, Adamu Ibrahim - A/78/PV.36
Pakistan
Akram, Munir - A/78/PV.35
Jadoon, Usman Iqbal - A/78/PV.104
Panama
Concepción Jaramillo, Markova - A/78/PV.36
Philippines
Lagdameo, Antonio Manuel Revilla - A/78/PV.35
Qatar
Alnesf, Sharifa Yousef A.S. - A/78/PV.36
Republic of Korea
Hwang, Joonkook - A/78/PV.35
Russian Federation
Polyanskiy, Dmitry A. - A/78/PV.36; A/78/PV.104
San Marino
Beleffi, Damiano - A/78/PV.35
Saudi Arabia
Alwasil, Abdulaziz M.O. - A/78/PV.36
Senegal
Diome, Diamane - A/78/PV.35
Singapore
Gafoor, Burhan - A/78/PV.34
Ganesh, Vivek - A/78/PV.104
Slovenia
Malovrh, Bostjan - A/78/PV.35
South Africa
Passmoor, Jonathan David - A/78/PV.34
Spain
Jiménez de la Hoz, Ana - A/78/PV.36
Sri Lanka
Pieris, Peter Mohan Maithri - A/78/PV.104
Switzerland
Baeriswyl, Pascale - A/78/PV.34
Syrian Arab Republic
Khaddour, Mhd. Riyad - A/78/PV.36

UN. SECURITY COUNCIL—MEMBERSHIP (Agenda item 121) (continued)

Thailand
Chindawongse, Suriya - A/78/PV.34
Türkiye
Önal, Sedat - A/78/PV.35
Ukraine
Dvornyk, Serhii - A/78/PV.36
UN. General Assembly. President
Francis, Dennis (Trinidad and Tobago) - A/78/PV.34; A/78/PV.104
United Kingdom
Kariuki, James - A/78/PV.34
United States
Thomas-Greenfield, Linda - A/78/PV.34
Uniting for Consensus Group
Massari, Maurizio (Italy) - A/78/PV.34; A/78/PV.104
Venezuela (Bolivarian Republic of)
Pérez Ayestarán, Joaquín Alberto - A/78/PV.35
Viet Nam
Nguyen, Hoang Nguyen - A/78/PV.35
Zimbabwe
Kadyautumbe, Darlington Mashoko - A/78/PV.35

UN. SECURITY COUNCIL—REPORTS (Agenda item 26)

Accountability, Coherence and Transparency (ACT) Group
Vinhas, Rui (Portugal) - A/78/PV.93
Angola
Cruz, Francisco José da - A/78/PV.94
Argentina
Lagorio, Ricardo E. - A/78/PV.93
Austria
Pretterhofer, Stefan - A/78/PV.93
Bolivia (Plurinational State of)
Pary Rodríguez, Diego - A/78/PV.94
Brazil
Danese, Sérgio França - A/78/PV.93
Chile
Vidal Mercado, Jorge Andrés - A/78/PV.93
Colombia
Zalabata Torres, Leonor - A/78/PV.93
Costa Rica
Videche Guevara, Carlos Manuel - A/78/PV.94
Cuba
Gala López, Yuri - A/78/PV.93
El Salvador
González López, Egriselda Aracely - A/78/PV.93
Germany
Alscher, Daniel Friedrich - A/78/PV.93
India
Mathur, Pratik - A/78/PV.94
Indonesia
Dhanutirto, Mariska Dwianti - A/78/PV.93
Liechtenstein
Wenaweser, Christian - A/78/PV.93
Malaysia
Zin Zawawi, Nordiana Binti - A/78/PV.93

UN. SECURITY COUNCIL—REPORTS (Agenda item 26) (continued)

Mexico
Buenrostro Massieu, Alicia - A/78/PV.93
Mozambique
Afonso, Pedro Comissário - A/78/PV.94
Myanmar
Tun, Kyaw Moe - A/78/PV.93
Norway
Lovold, Andreas - A/78/PV.93
Oman
Al Shehhi, Mohammed Ali Ahmed - A/78/PV.94
Pakistan
Akram, Munir - A/78/PV.93
Poland
Szczerski, Krzysztof - A/78/PV.93
Romania
Horosanu, Gabriela-Cornelia - A/78/PV.94
Singapore
Gafoor, Burhan - A/78/PV.93
South Africa
Joyini, Mathu - A/78/PV.93
Syrian Arab Republic
Alshahin, Essam - A/78/PV.93
Timor-Leste
Soares, Dionísio Da Costa Babo - A/78/PV.94
Ukraine
Kyslytsya, Sergiy - A/78/PV.93
UN. General Assembly. President
Francis, Dennis (Trinidad and Tobago) - A/78/PV.93
UN. Security Council. President
Hwang, Joonkook (Republic of Korea) - A/78/PV.93
United Arab Emirates
Shaheen, Ghasaq Yousif - A/78/PV.93

UN. SUPPORT OFFICE IN SOMALIA—FINANCING (Agenda item 160)

UN. Controller
Ramanathan, Chandramouli - A/C.5/78/SR.35
UN. General Assembly. 5th Committee. Rapporteur
Hartog, Laurens Thomas den (Netherlands (Kingdom of the)) - A/78/PV.95

UN CHARTER—REPORTS (Agenda item 82)

Algeria
Bouchedoub, Mohamed Faiz - A/C.6/78/SR.34
Belarus
Evseenko, Pavel - A/C.6/78/SR.22
Bolivia (Plurinational State of)
Ríos, Carmen Rosa - A/C.6/78/SR.34
China
Geng, Shuang - A/C.6/78/SR.33
Community of Latin American and Caribbean States
Dunbar, Ed (Saint Vincent and the Grenadines) - A/C.6/78/SR.22
Coordinating Bureau of the Non-Aligned Countries
Ershadi, Zahra (Iran (Islamic Republic of)) - A/C.6/78/SR.22

UN CHARTER—REPORTS (Agenda item 82) (continued)

Cuba
Mora Fonseca, Vladimir - A/C.6/78/SR.22
Democratic People's Republic of Korea
Kim, In Chol - A/C.6/78/SR.33; A/C.6/78/SR.34
Egypt
Attelb, Abdullah Ibrahim Abdelhamud Alsayed - A/C.6/78/SR.34
El Salvador
Flores Soto, Ligia Lorena - A/C.6/78/SR.22
Equatorial Guinea
Nze Mansogo, Estela Mercedes - A/C.6/78/SR.33
Eritrea
Giorgio, Amanuel - A/C.6/78/SR.33
European Union
Popan, Simona - A/C.6/78/SR.22
Georgia
Kupradze, Sopio - A/C.6/78/SR.22
Group of Friends in Defence of the Charter of the United Nations
Guerra Sansonetti, Jhon (Venezuela (Bolivarian Republic of)) - A/C.6/78/SR.22
India
Bhat, Kajal - A/C.6/78/SR.33
Iran (Islamic Republic of)
Fallah Assadi, Mahdad - A/C.6/78/SR.34
Mexico
Arrocha Olabuenaga, Pablo Adrián - A/C.6/78/SR.22
Nicaragua
Llano, Alina J. - A/C.6/78/SR.34
Nigeria
Dakwak, Gloria - A/C.6/78/SR.34
Pakistan
Ijaz, Rabia - A/C.6/78/SR.22
Philippines
Arumpac-Marte, Azela Guerrero - A/C.6/78/SR.33
Qatar
Al-Marri, Rashid Ali - A/C.6/78/SR.22
Republic of Korea
Kim, Hyunsoo - A/C.6/78/SR.33; A/C.6/78/SR.34
Russian Federation
Skachkov, Evgeny A. - A/C.6/78/SR.22
Saudi Arabia
Almuaithir, Nouf - A/C.6/78/SR.33
State of Palestine
Sayej, Loureen O.A. - A/C.6/78/SR.34
Sudan
Mohammed, Ammar Mohammed Mahmoud - A/C.6/78/SR.22
Syrian Arab Republic
Khaddour, Mhd. Riyad - A/C.6/78/SR.22
UN. General Assembly. 6th Committee. Bureau
Nouh, Amr Mohamed Mosaad (Egypt) - A/C.6/78/SR.37
UN. General Assembly. 6th Committee. Rapporteur
Moussa, Moussa Mohamed (Djibouti) - A/78/PV.45
UN. Group of African States
Ikondere, Marvin (Uganda) - A/C.6/78/SR.22
UN. Office of Legal Affairs. Codification Division. Director
Llewellyn, Huw - A/C.6/78/SR.22

UN CHARTER—REPORTS (Agenda item 82) (continued)

UN. Security Council Practices and Charter Research Branch
Montejo, Blanca - A/C.6/78/SR.22
UN. Special Committee on the Charter of the United Nations and on the Strengthening of the Role of the Organization. Chair
Maniratanga, Zéphyrin (Burundi) - A/C.6/78/SR.22
United Kingdom
Lito, Melina - A/C.6/78/SR.22
United States
Patton, Dorothy - A/C.6/78/SR.22

UN COMMISSION ON INTERNATIONAL TRADE LAW—REPORTS (Agenda item 77)

Austria
Gorke, Maximilian - A/C.6/78/SR.14; A/C.6/78/SR.37
Belarus
Evseenko, Pavel - A/C.6/78/SR.14
Canada
Mead, Kevin Timothy - A/C.6/78/SR.14
Chile
Hernández Chávez, José Juan - A/C.6/78/SR.14
China
Zhao, Yanrui - A/C.6/78/SR.14
Cuba
Mora Fonseca, Vladimir - A/C.6/78/SR.14
Ecuador
Escobar Ullauri, Pablo - A/C.6/78/SR.14
Egypt
Attelb, Abdullah Ibrahim Abdelhamud Alsayed - A/C.6/78/SR.14
El Salvador
Flores Soto, Ligia Lorena - A/C.6/78/SR.14
European Union
Ramopoulos, Thomas - A/C.6/78/SR.14
France
Tabuteau-Mangels, Aurélie - A/C.6/78/SR.14
Iceland
Valtýsson, Jörundur - A/C.6/78/SR.14
India
Bhat, Kajal - A/C.6/78/SR.14
Iran (Islamic Republic of)
Heidari, Bahram - A/C.6/78/SR.14
Italy
Milano, Enrico - A/C.6/78/SR.14
Japan
Nagano, Shunsuke - A/C.6/78/SR.14
Kuwait
Alenezi, Faisal G. - A/C.6/78/SR.14
Malaysia
Abd Karim, Nur Azura Binti - A/C.6/78/SR.14
Mexico
Sánchez Cordero Dávila, Jorge A. - A/C.6/78/SR.14
Morocco
Bouziane, Zineb - A/C.6/78/SR.14
Pakistan
Khokhar, Adeel Mumtaz - A/C.6/78/SR.14

UN COMMISSION ON INTERNATIONAL TRADE LAW—REPORTS (Agenda item 77) (continued)

Philippines
Arumpac-Marte, Azela Guerrero - A/C.6/78/SR.14
Republic of Korea
Choi, Taeeun - A/C.6/78/SR.14
Russian Federation
Skachkov, Evgeny A. - A/C.6/78/SR.14
Singapore
Tan, Scott - A/C.6/78/SR.14
South Africa
Motsepe, Keke Mantsho - A/C.6/78/SR.14
Thailand
Nachom, Yaninee - A/C.6/78/SR.14
Uganda
Ikondere, Marvin - A/C.6/78/SR.14
UN. General Assembly. 6th Committee. Bureau
Flores Soto, Ligia Lorena (El Salvador) - A/C.6/78/SR.37
Gorke, Maximilian (Austria) - A/C.6/78/SR.37
Khng, Nathaniel (Singapore) - A/C.6/78/SR.37
UN. General Assembly. 6th Committee. Rapporteur
Moussa, Moussa Mohamed (Djibouti) - A/78/PV.45
UN Commission on International Trade Law. Chair
Sabo, Kathryn - A/C.6/78/SR.13; A/C.6/78/SR.14
UN Commission on International Trade Law. Secretary
Joubin-Bret, Anna - A/C.6/78/SR.13
United Kingdom
Lito, Melina - A/C.6/78/SR.14
United States
Grosso, Elizabeth Maryanne - A/C.6/78/SR.14
Viet Nam
Tran, Thi Phuong Ha - A/C.6/78/SR.14

UN CONFERENCES (Agenda item 13)

Alliance of Small Island States
Lautasi, Isaia (Samoa) - A/78/PV.102
Luteru, Fatumanava-o-Upolu III Pa'olelei (Samoa) - A/78/PV.53
Argentina
Squeff, María del Carmen - A/78/PV.15
Australia
Larsen, James - A/78/PV.15
Azerbaijan
Aliyev, Yashar T. - A/78/PV.37
Bangladesh
Muhith, Muhammad A. - A/78/PV.107
Belarus
Evseenko, Pavel - A/78/PV.15
Bolivia (Plurinational State of)
Muñoz Ponce, Tatiana Bárbara - A/78/PV.107
Pary Rodríguez, Diego - A/78/PV.15
Chile
Narváez Ojeda, Paula - A/78/PV.15
China
Fu, Cong - A/78/PV.97

UN CONFERENCES (Agenda item 13) (continued)

Coalition for Addressing Sea-level Rise and its Existential Threat
Falefou, Tapugao (Tuvalu) - A/78/PV.53
Zahneisen, Thomas (Germany) - A/78/PV.102
Colombia
Zalabata Torres, Leonor - A/78/PV.15
Costa Rica
Chan Valverde, Maritza - A/78/PV.102
Cuba
Pedroso Cuesta, Pedro Luis - A/78/PV.52
Peñalver Portal, Gerardo - A/78/PV.15
Egypt
Abdelkhalek, Osama Mahmoud - A/78/PV.15
El Salvador
Flores Soto, Ligia Lorena - A/78/PV.53
Estonia
Tammsaar, Rein - A/78/PV.47
European Union
Jiménez de la Hoz, Ana (Spain) - A/78/PV.15
Lázár, Lilla (Hungary) - A/78/PV.107
Samson, Hedda - A/78/PV.102
Fiji
May, Vueti Kosoniu - A/78/PV.102
Group of 77
Peñalver Portal, Gerardo (Cuba) - A/78/PV.15
Group of Friends in Defence of the Charter of the United Nations
Pérez Ayestarán, Joaquín Alberto (Venezuela (Bolivarian Republic of)) - A/78/PV.15
Gulf Cooperation Council
Al-Hassan, Mohamed (Oman) - A/78/PV.15
Hungary
Horváth, Zsuzsanna - A/78/PV.15
Iran (Islamic Republic of)
Ghafouri, Mojtaba - A/78/PV.102
Momeni, Javad - A/78/PV.15
Japan
Yamanaka, Osamu - A/78/PV.15
Kazakhstan
Rakhmetullin, Akan - A/78/PV.48
Mexico
Curzio Vila, Elena - A/78/PV.63
Mongolia
Ulziibayar, Vangansuren - A/78/PV.91
Nicaragua
Jiménez, Jasser - A/78/PV.15
Pacific Islands Forum
May, Vueti Kosoniu (Fiji) - A/78/PV.102
Va'inga Tone, Viliami (Tonga) - A/78/PV.53
Pakistan
Akram, Munir - A/78/PV.15
Palau
Sisior, Gwendalyn - A/78/PV.102
Peru
García Toma, Victor Óscar Shiyin - A/78/PV.47
Russian Federation
Chumakov, Dmitry S. - A/78/PV.15; A/78/PV.33; A/78/PV.53; A/78/PV.107
Kardash, Viktoriia E. - A/78/PV.102

UN CONFERENCES (Agenda item 13) (continued)

South Africa
Joyini, Mathu - A/78/PV.15
Sithole, Tiyani Raymond - A/78/PV.33
Syrian Arab Republic
Dandy, Alhakam - A/78/PV.15
Tajikistan
Hikmat, Jonibek Ismoil - A/78/PV.77
Thailand
Chindawongse, Suriya - A/78/PV.33
Timor-Leste
Soares, Dionísio Da Costa Babo - A/78/PV.102
Türkiye
Çetin, Ahmet Erman - A/78/PV.102
Tuvalu
Navoti, Selema K. - A/78/PV.102
UN. Department for General Assembly and Conference Management
Miranda, Ruth de - A/78/PV.102
UN. General Assembly. President
Francis, Dennis (Trinidad and Tobago) - A/78/PV.53; A/78/PV.102
UN. Group of African States
Milambo, Chola (Zambia) - A/78/PV.33
United Kingdom
Fidoe, Nicholas - A/78/PV.102
Woodroffe, Tom - A/78/PV.15
United States
Carty, Lisa A. - A/78/PV.15
Heartney, Edward - A/78/PV.107
Pell, Herbert - A/78/PV.102
Thomas-Greenfield, Linda - A/78/PV.63
Zimbabwe
Nyagura, Petronella - A/78/PV.15

UN DISENGAGEMENT OBSERVER FORCE—FINANCING (Agenda item 156a)

Syrian Arab Republic
Al-mansour, Osama - A/C.5/78/SR.35
UN. Controller
Ramanathan, Chandramouli - A/C.5/78/SR.35
UN. General Assembly. 5th Committee. Rapporteur
Hartog, Laurens Thomas den (Netherlands (Kingdom of the)) - A/78/PV.95

UN HIGH COMMISSIONER FOR REFUGEES—REPORTS (Agenda item 60)

Afghanistan
Faiq, Naseer Ahmed - A/C.3/78/SR.44; A/C.3/78/SR.45
Algeria
Sahraoui, Ahmed - A/C.3/78/SR.45
Samai, Rahma - A/C.3/78/SR.44
Armenia
Hakobyan, Aram - A/C.3/78/SR.44; A/C.3/78/SR.45
Azerbaijan
Ahangari, Narmin - A/C.3/78/SR.44; A/C.3/78/SR.45

UN HIGH COMMISSIONER FOR REFUGEES—REPORTS (Agenda item 60) (continued)

Bangladesh
Monica, Mosammat Shahanara - A/C.3/78/SR.44; A/C.3/78/SR.45
Belarus
Pilipenko, Igor - A/C.3/78/SR.44
Burkina Faso
Ganou, Oumarou - A/C.3/78/SR.44
Cameroon
Banaken Elel, Nelly - A/C.3/78/SR.44; A/C.3/78/SR.45
Canada
Klaise, Inara - A/C.3/78/SR.51
Rae, Robert - A/C.3/78/SR.44
China
Zhang, Sisi - A/C.3/78/SR.44
Colombia
Sánchez García, Nathalia - A/C.3/78/SR.44
Democratic People's Republic of Korea
Kim, Nam Hyok - A/C.3/78/SR.45
Denmark
Lassen, Christina Markus - A/C.3/78/SR.44
Laursen, Erik - A/C.3/78/SR.51
Rasmussen, Lea - A/C.3/78/SR.44
Egypt
Mohamed, Mohamed Omar Elfarouk Hassan - A/C.3/78/SR.44
Ethiopia
Worku, Hirut Habtamu - A/C.3/78/SR.45
European Union
García Rico, Lucía (Spain) - A/C.3/78/SR.48
Skoog, Olof - A/C.3/78/SR.44
Gabon
Biang, Michel Xavier - A/C.3/78/SR.45
Georgia
Abesadze, David - A/C.3/78/SR.45
Germany
Lasota, Josephine - A/C.3/78/SR.45
Greece
Retalis, Michail - A/C.3/78/SR.44
Group of Friends in Defence of the Charter of the United Nations
Poveda Brito, Robert Alexander (Venezuela (Bolivarian Republic of)) - A/C.3/78/SR.44
Guatemala
Rodríguez Mancia, Carla María - A/C.3/78/SR.48
Gulf Cooperation Council
Al Jaradi, Heba Khalid (Oman) - A/C.3/78/SR.44
Al Rawahi, Abdulhalim Mubarak Saloom (Oman) - A/C.3/78/SR.51
Holy See
Murphy, Robert David - A/C.3/78/SR.51
Hungary
Ivanyi, Balint - A/C.3/78/SR.51; A/C.3/78/SR.54
India
Sonkar, Suman - A/C.3/78/SR.45
Indonesia
Khairunsyah, Aidil - A/C.3/78/SR.44

UN HIGH COMMISSIONER FOR REFUGEES—REPORTS (Agenda item 60) (continued)

International Federation of Red Cross and Red Crescent Societies
Chasi, Victoria - A/C.3/78/SR.45
Iran (Islamic Republic of)
Arab Bafrani, Fatemeh - A/C.3/78/SR.44; A/C.3/78/SR.51
Iraq
Al-Musawi, Ali Rida Abdulmohsin Hasan - A/C.3/78/SR.45
Japan
Miyamoto, Sogaku - A/C.3/78/SR.45
Jordan
Al-halique, Katherine Anas Ahmad - A/C.3/78/SR.44
Kuwait
Al-Dikaan, Ahmed Khaled Ghanem - A/C.3/78/SR.45
Lebanon
Hachem, Hadi - A/C.3/78/SR.44
Libya
Elsonni, Taher M.T. - A/C.3/78/SR.48
Malaysia
Escopper Zumilla, Michael Jawa - A/C.3/78/SR.44; A/C.3/78/SR.51
Mexico
Mendoza Elguea, Sylvia Paola - A/C.3/78/SR.44
Morocco
Bouchikhi, Hanaa - A/C.3/78/SR.45
Elhamriti, Soufiane - A/C.3/78/SR.44
Mozambique
Serage, Bruno Bernardo - A/C.3/78/SR.45
Myanmar
Tun, Kyaw Moe - A/C.3/78/SR.45
Nigeria
Asaju, Bola - A/C.3/78/SR.44
Umar, Mujahid Ahmed - A/C.3/78/SR.45
Pakistan
Jadoon, Usman Iqbal - A/C.3/78/SR.44
Qureshi, Hadeeqa - A/C.3/78/SR.44
Saleem, Saima - A/C.3/78/SR.45
Poland
Skoczek, Joanna Sylwia - A/C.3/78/SR.44
Portugal
Marinho, Joana Almeida - A/C.3/78/SR.44
Qatar
Al Khayarin, Saleh Mohammed - A/C.3/78/SR.45
Republic of Korea
Kim, Sangjin - A/C.3/78/SR.45
Song, Hye-ryoung - A/C.3/78/SR.45
Romania
Feruță, Cornel - A/C.3/78/SR.44
Mihail, Ioana-Cristina - A/C.3/78/SR.45
Russian Federation
Kashaev, Roman G. - A/C.3/78/SR.48
Surkov, Vladimir - A/C.3/78/SR.44
Saudi Arabia
Shaman, Ali - A/C.3/78/SR.44
Serbia
Radović, Branislav - A/C.3/78/SR.45
Singapore
Rajandran, Dhivya - A/C.3/78/SR.51

UN HIGH COMMISSIONER FOR REFUGEES—REPORTS (Agenda item 60) (continued)

South Africa
Moruke, Cathy - A/C.3/78/SR.44
Sovereign Order of Malta
Rosario-Blackett, Marissa del - A/C.3/78/SR.44
Sudan
Idres, Nusaiba Hashim Mohamed Ali - A/C.3/78/SR.44
Switzerland
Hauri, Adrian - A/C.3/78/SR.44
Syrian Arab Republic
Alnwelati, Mohammad Feras - A/C.3/78/SR.45
Altarsha, Elie - A/C.3/78/SR.44
Thailand
Vichankaiyakij, Vathayudh - A/C.3/78/SR.44
Türkiye
Aydil, İsmail - A/C.3/78/SR.45
Uganda
Gurhan, Amina - A/C.3/78/SR.45
Ukraine
Kyslytsya, Sergiy - A/C.3/78/SR.48
Mudrenko, Nataliia - A/78/PV.50; A/C.3/78/SR.44; A/C.3/78/SR.45
UN. General Assembly. 3rd Committee. Rapporteur
Poveda Brito, Robert Alexander (Venezuela (Bolivarian Republic of)) - A/78/PV.50
UN. Group of African States
Banaken Elel, Nelly (Cameroon) - A/C.3/78/SR.44
Ossebi Iyolo, Isis (Congo) - A/C.3/78/SR.54
UN High Commissioner for Refugees
Grandi, Filippo - A/C.3/78/SR.44
United States
Breen, Patrick - A/C.3/78/SR.44
Shrier, Jonathan - A/C.3/78/SR.45
Yemen
Balobaid, Ali Mabkhot Salem - A/C.3/78/SR.45

UN INTERIM ADMINISTRATION MISSION IN KOSOVO—FINANCING (Agenda item 153)

UN. Controller
Ramanathan, Chandramouli - A/C.5/78/SR.35
UN. General Assembly. 5th Committee. Rapporteur
Hartog, Laurens Thomas den (Netherlands (Kingdom of the)) - A/78/PV.95

UN INTERIM FORCE IN LEBANON—FINANCING (Agenda item 156b)

European Union
Bogaerts, Basiel (Belgium) - A/C.5/78/SR.40
Group of 77
Ainomuhisha, Medard (Uganda) - A/C.5/78/SR.40
Israel
Cappon, Noam - A/78/PV.95
Zilbergeld, Sherry - A/C.5/78/SR.40
UN. Controller
Ramanathan, Chandramouli - A/C.5/78/SR.35
UN. General Assembly. 5th Committee. Rapporteur
Hartog, Laurens Thomas den (Netherlands (Kingdom of the)) - A/78/PV.95

UN INTERIM FORCE IN LEBANON—FINANCING (Agenda item 156b) (continued)

United States
Lu, Christopher P. - A/C.5/78/SR.40

UN MISSION FOR THE REFERENDUM IN WESTERN SAHARA—FINANCING (Agenda item 158)

UN. Controller
Ramanathan, Chandramouli - A/C.5/78/SR.35
UN. General Assembly. 5th Committee. Rapporteur
Hartog, Laurens Thomas den (Netherlands (Kingdom of the)) - A/78/PV.95

UN MISSION IN LIBERIA—FINANCING (Agenda item 154)

UN. General Assembly. 5th Committee. Rapporteur
Hartog, Laurens Thomas den (Netherlands (Kingdom of the)) - A/78/PV.95

UN MISSION IN SOUTH SUDAN—FINANCING (Agenda item 157)

UN. Assistant Secretary-General for Internal Oversight Services
Swanson, Benjamin Gordon Robert - A/C.5/78/SR.36
UN. Controller
Ramanathan, Chandramouli - A/C.5/78/SR.36
UN. General Assembly. 5th Committee. Rapporteur
Hartog, Laurens Thomas den (Netherlands (Kingdom of the)) - A/78/PV.95

UN MULTIDIMENSIONAL INTEGRATED STABILIZATION MISSION IN MALI—FINANCING (Agenda item 155)

Mali
Sissoko, Aboubacar - A/C.5/78/SR.36
UN. Advisory Committee on Administrative and Budgetary Questions. Vice-Chair
Chmielewski, Jakub - A/C.5/78/SR.20
UN. Controller
Ramanathan, Chandramouli - A/C.5/78/SR.36
UN. Department of Management Strategy, Policy and Compliance. Office of Programme Planning, Finance and Budget. Finance Division. Director
Costa, Maria - A/C.5/78/SR.20
UN. General Assembly. 5th Committee. Rapporteur
Hartog, Laurens Thomas den (Netherlands (Kingdom of the)) - A/78/PV.50(Resumption1); A/78/PV.95

UN MULTIDIMENSIONAL INTEGRATED STABILIZATION MISSION IN THE CENTRAL AFRICAN REPUBLIC—FINANCING (Agenda item 148)

UN. Controller
Ramanathan, Chandramouli - A/C.5/78/SR.35
UN. General Assembly. 5th Committee. Rapporteur
Hartog, Laurens Thomas den (Netherlands (Kingdom of the)) - A/78/PV.95

UN OPERATION IN CÔTE D'IVOIRE—FINANCING (Agenda item 149)

UN. General Assembly. 5th Committee. Rapporteur
Hartog, Laurens Thomas den (Netherlands (Kingdom of the)) - A/78/PV.95

UN ORGANIZATION STABILIZATION MISSION IN THE DEMOCRATIC REPUBLIC OF THE CONGO—FINANCING (Agenda item 151)

UN. Controller
Ramanathan, Chandramouli - A/C.5/78/SR.35
UN. General Assembly. 5th Committee. Rapporteur
Hartog, Laurens Thomas den (Netherlands (Kingdom of the)) - A/78/PV.95

UN PEACEKEEPING FORCE IN CYPRUS—FINANCING (Agenda item 150)

UN. Controller
Ramanathan, Chandramouli - A/C.5/78/SR.35
UN. General Assembly. 5th Committee. Rapporteur
Hartog, Laurens Thomas den (Netherlands (Kingdom of the)) - A/78/PV.95

UN RESOLUTIONS—IMPLEMENTATION (Agenda item 119)

Accountability, Coherence and Transparency (ACT) Group
Tammsaar, Rein (Estonia) - A/78/PV.32
Argentina
Squeff, María del Carmen - A/78/PV.33
ASEAN
Omar, Khairi (Malaysia) - A/78/PV.32
Australia
Van Bronswijk, Sarah - A/78/PV.32
Bangladesh
Molla, Md Rafiqul Alam - A/78/PV.33
Cameroon
Banaken Elel, Nelly - A/78/PV.103
Chile
Garrido Melo, Claudio Ernesto - A/78/PV.103
Coordinating Bureau of the Non-Aligned Countries
Bendjama, Amar (Algeria) - A/78/PV.32
Costa Rica
Chan Valverde, Maritza - A/78/PV.32
Cuba
Padilla González, Cristian - A/78/PV.103
San Román Valdés, Jorge - A/78/PV.32
Ecuador
Fiallo Karolys, Andrés Fernando - A/78/PV.32
Egypt
Abdelkhalek, Osama Mahmoud - A/78/PV.32
Mohamed, Mohamed Omar Elfarouk Hassan - A/78/PV.108
El Salvador
González López, Egriselda Aracely - A/78/PV.32
European Union
Samson, Hedda - A/78/PV.32

UN RESOLUTIONS—IMPLEMENTATION (Agenda item 119) (continued)

France
Wavrin, Hugo - A/78/PV.33
India
Mathur, Pratik - A/78/PV.33
Indonesia
Aron, Andy - A/78/PV.32
Iran (Islamic Republic of)
Arab Bafrani, Fatemeh - A/78/PV.103
Israel
Ben Naftaly, Emil - A/78/PV.33
Japan
Yoshida, Aya - A/78/PV.32
Malaysia
Abd Karim, Sofian Akmal Bin - A/78/PV.108
Maldives
Guraisha, Aminath - A/78/PV.32
Mexico
Buenrostro Massieu, Alicia - A/78/PV.33
Reyna Barrón, María Fernanda - A/78/PV.108
Mongolia
Vorshilov, Enkhbold - A/78/PV.32
Morocco
Benziane, Imane - A/78/PV.32
Pakistan
Akram, Munir - A/78/PV.32
Philippines
Lagdameo, Antonio Manuel Revilla - A/78/PV.32
Portugal
Aranda, Jorge Eduardo Ferreira Silva - A/78/PV.33
Qatar
Al-Thani, Hamad bin Abdulrahman - A/78/PV.33
Russian Federation
Gilmutdinova, Dina Anisovna - A/78/PV.33
Mazaeva, Viktoriia - A/78/PV.103
Singapore
Seah, Mark - A/78/PV.32
Slovenia
Malovrh, Bostjan - A/78/PV.33
South Africa
Schalkwyk, Marthinus van - A/78/PV.32
Sri Lanka
Pieris, Peter Mohan Maithri - A/78/PV.33
Thailand
Chindawongse, Suriya - A/78/PV.32
Ukraine
Prytula, Mykola - A/78/PV.33
UN. General Assembly. Ad Hoc Working Group on the Revitalization of the General Assembly. Co-Chair
Feruță, Cornel (Romania) - A/78/PV.33
UN. General Assembly. President
Francis, Dennis (Trinidad and Tobago) - A/78/PV.32
United States
Adelman, Dylan - A/78/PV.33
Viet Nam
Thoa Le, Thi Minh - A/78/PV.32

UN SECURITY FORCE FOR ABYEI—FINANCING (Agenda item 147)

UN. Controller
Ramanathan, Chandramouli - A/C.5/78/SR.36
UN. General Assembly. 5th Committee. Rapporteur
Hartog, Laurens Thomas den (Netherlands (Kingdom of the)) - A/78/PV.95

UN SYSTEM—STRENGTHENING (Agenda item 122)

Cuba
Padilla González, Cristian - A/78/PV.99
European Union
Horváth, Zsuzsanna (Hungary) - A/78/PV.98
Iran (Islamic Republic of)
Ghafouri, Mojtaba - A/78/PV.99
Mexico
Mendoza Elguea, Sylvia Paola - A/78/PV.99
Russian Federation
Chumakov, Dmitry S. - A/78/PV.98
Meschchanov, Boris A. - A/78/PV.99
Saudi Arabia
Alamri, Hassan Mohammed A. - A/78/PV.99
Togo
Akakpo, Koffi - A/78/PV.99
Türkiye
İstemil Aydil, Alara - A/78/PV.99
UN. Deputy Secretary-General
Mohammed, Amina J. - A/78/PV.1
United Kingdom
Reyes, Gaia - A/78/PV.99
United States
Adelman, Dylan - A/78/PV.99
Venezuela (Bolivarian Republic of)
Pérez Ayestarán, Joaquín Alberto - A/78/PV.107
Viet Nam
Nguyen, Hoang Nguyen - A/78/PV.99
Yemen
Al-Dobhany, Marwan Ali Noman - A/78/PV.99

UN YOUTH OFFICE—REPORTS (Agenda item 130)

Egypt
Mohamed, Mohamed Omar Elfarouk Hassan - A/78/PV.102
European Union
Samson, Hedda - A/78/PV.102
Guyana
Parmanand, Sosheena Foranda - A/78/PV.102
India
Patel, Yojna - A/78/PV.102
Malta
Gatt, Francesca Maria - A/78/PV.102
Netherlands (Kingdom of the)
Sar, Minke van der - A/78/PV.102
Portugal
Aranda, Jorge Eduardo Ferreira Silva - A/78/PV.102

UN YOUTH OFFICE—REPORTS (Agenda item 130) (continued)

Russian Federation
Mazaeva, Viktoriia - A/78/PV.102
Slovakia
Grünwald, Tomáš - A/78/PV.102
South Africa
Makgati, Penelope Ramatsobane - A/78/PV.102

UNITED STATES VIRGIN ISLANDS QUESTION (Agenda item 58)

United States
Kris, Robert - A/C.4/78/SR.7

UNRWA—ACTIVITIES (Agenda item 49)

Algeria
Bendjama, Amar - A/C.4/78/SR.22
Sahraoui, Ahmed - A/C.4/78/SR.23
Argentina
Squeff, María del Carmen - A/C.4/78/SR.23
Bangladesh
Muhith, Muhammad A. - A/C.4/78/SR.23
Canada
Arbeiter, Richard - A/C.4/78/SR.26
Chile
Garrido Melo, Claudio Ernesto - A/C.4/78/SR.23
China
Geng, Shuang - A/C.4/78/SR.23
Colombia
Zalabata Torres, Leonor - A/C.4/78/SR.23
Coordinating Bureau of the Non-Aligned Countries
Alizada, Kamal (Azerbaijan) - A/C.4/78/SR.23
Cuba
Romero Puentes, Yusnier - A/C.4/78/SR.23; A/C.4/78/SR.26
Denmark
Lassen, Christina Markus - A/C.4/78/SR.22
Egypt
Elshandawily, Ahmed - A/C.4/78/SR.22
El Salvador
González López, Egriselda Aracely - A/C.4/78/SR.23
European Union
Clune, Mary - A/C.4/78/SR.22
Group of Arab States
Alwasil, Abdulaziz M.O. (Saudi Arabia) - A/C.4/78/SR.22
Group of Friends in Defence of the Charter of the United Nations
Pérez Ayestarán, Joaquín Alberto (Venezuela (Bolivarian Republic of)) - A/C.4/78/SR.23
Gulf Cooperation Council
Al Busaidi, Ahmed Hamood Faisal (Oman) - A/C.4/78/SR.22
Holy See
Caccia, Gabriele Giordano - A/C.4/78/SR.23
Indonesia
Dhanutirto, Mariska Dwianti - A/C.4/78/SR.22
Nasir, Arrmanatha Christiawan - A/C.4/78/SR.26

UNRWA—ACTIVITIES (Agenda item 49) (continued)

Iran (Islamic Republic of)
Ghelich, Vahid - A/C.4/78/SR.22
Iraq
Al-Dahlaki, Hasanain Hadi Hasan - A/C.4/78/SR.23
Israel
Kedar, Gershon - A/C.4/78/SR.23; A/C.4/78/SR.26
Shapir Ben Naftaly, Reut - A/C.4/78/SR.22
Japan
Nishiyama, Akira - A/C.4/78/SR.23
Jordan
Habashneh, Ahmad Samir Fahim - A/C.4/78/SR.22
Kuwait
Abushaibah, Shayea - A/C.4/78/SR.22
League of Arab States
Elardja Flitti, Nasria - A/C.4/78/SR.23
Lebanon
Jardali, Mohammad Ali - A/C.4/78/SR.22; A/C.4/78/SR.23
Liechtenstein
Oehri, Myriam - A/C.4/78/SR.26
Malaysia
Sabarudin, Mohamad Shahir - A/C.4/78/SR.22
Maldives
Zuhuree, Ibrahim - A/C.4/78/SR.22
Mexico
Robledo López, Carmen - A/C.4/78/SR.22
Morocco
El Ouazzani, Mouna Chahdi - A/C.4/78/SR.22
Jerboui, Hind - A/C.4/78/SR.23
Netherlands (Kingdom of the)
Brandt, Yoka - A/C.4/78/SR.22
Norway
Lovold, Andreas - A/C.4/78/SR.22
Pakistan
Akram, Munir - A/C.4/78/SR.22
Philippines
Novicio, Noel Mangaoang - A/C.4/78/SR.23
Qatar
Al-thani, Jassim Abdulaziz J.A. - A/C.4/78/SR.22
Russian Federation
Chumakov, Dmitry S. - A/C.4/78/SR.23
Saudi Arabia
Alamri, Hassan Mohammed A. - A/C.4/78/SR.23
Senegal
Diome, Diamane - A/C.4/78/SR.23
Sierra Leone
Kanu, Michael Imran - A/C.4/78/SR.23
Slovenia
Malovrh, Bostjan - A/C.4/78/SR.22
South Africa
Schalkwyk, Marthinus van - A/C.4/78/SR.22; A/C.4/78/SR.23; A/C.4/78/SR.26
Sri Lanka
Pieris, Peter Mohan Maithri - A/C.4/78/SR.22
State of Palestine
Abdelhady-Nasser, Feda - A/C.4/78/SR.22
Mansour, Riyad H. - A/C.4/78/SR.26
Sudan
Mohamed, Abuzied Shamseldin Ahmed - A/C.4/78/SR.23
Switzerland
Carpenter, Christoph - A/C.4/78/SR.26
Syrian Arab Republic
Baghdadi, Mohannad - A/C.4/78/SR.23; A/C.4/78/SR.26
Thailand
Chindawongse, Suriya - A/C.4/78/SR.22
Tunisia
Salah, Yassine - A/C.4/78/SR.22
Türkiye
Özgür, Ceren Hande - A/C.4/78/SR.22
UN. General Assembly. Special Political and Decolonization Committee (4th Committee). Chair
Joyini, Mathu (South Africa) - A/C.4/78/SR.22
UN. General Assembly. Special Political and Decolonization Committee (4th Committee). Rapporteur
Dhanutirto, Mariska Dwianti (Indonesia) - A/78/PV.45
UN. Working Group on the Financing of the United Nations Relief and Works Agency for Palestine Refugees in the Near East. Rapporteur
Havn, Anne Melangen (Norway) - A/C.4/78/SR.22
United Arab Emirates
Al Nahyan, Zayed bin Sultan - A/C.4/78/SR.23
United Kingdom
Croker, Richard - A/C.4/78/SR.26
Gibbon, James - A/C.4/78/SR.23
United States
Kelley, John - A/C.4/78/SR.26
Lu, Christopher P. - A/C.4/78/SR.23
UNRWA
Gunnarsdóttir, Greta - A/C.4/78/SR.22
Viet Nam
Nguyen, Hoang Nguyen - A/C.4/78/SR.23
Yemen
Al-mashehari, Sarah Ahmed Ahmed - A/C.4/78/SR.23

VETO (Agenda item 63)

Albania
Janina, Suela - A/78/PV.69; A/78/PV.79
Spasse, Arian - A/78/PV.3
Algeria
Gaouaoui, Nacim - A/78/PV.51; A/78/PV.66
Sahraoui, Ahmed - A/78/PV.59; A/78/PV.74
Andorra
Vives Balmaña, Elisenda - A/78/PV.75
Argentina
Lagorio, Ricardo E. - A/78/PV.67; A/78/PV.69; A/78/PV.71; A/78/PV.78
Australia
Bryant, Rebecca Suzanne - A/78/PV.74
Larsen, James - A/78/PV.51; A/78/PV.59; A/78/PV.68; A/78/PV.78

VETO (Agenda item 63) (continued)

Austria
Marschik, Alexander - A/78/PV.51; A/78/PV.69; A/78/PV.70; A/78/PV.79
Pretterhofer, Stefan - A/78/PV.3
Bahrain
Alrowaiei, Jamal Fares - A/78/PV.67; A/78/PV.75
Bangladesh
Farhan, Fahmid - A/78/PV.61
Muhith, Muhammad A. - A/78/PV.52; A/78/PV.67; A/78/PV.71; A/78/PV.75
Belgium
Bouthé, Marc Gerard C. - A/78/PV.67
Kridelka, Philippe - A/78/PV.59; A/78/PV.68
Lagatie, Karl - A/78/PV.51; A/78/PV.75
Bolivia (Plurinational State of)
Pary Rodríguez, Diego - A/78/PV.60
Ríos, Carmen Rosa - A/78/PV.79
Brazil
Danese, Sérgio França - A/78/PV.51; A/78/PV.60; A/78/PV.67; A/78/PV.69; A/78/PV.70; A/78/PV.75; A/78/PV.78
Moretti, Norberto - A/78/PV.3
Brunei Darussalam
Sulaiman, Noor Qamar - A/78/PV.60
Bulgaria
Beshkova, Krassimira - A/78/PV.68
Stoeva, Lachezara - A/78/PV.3; A/78/PV.70; A/78/PV.78
Cambodia
Mao, Tithiarun - A/78/PV.75
Canada
Arbeiter, Richard - A/78/PV.3; A/78/PV.52
Rae, Robert - A/78/PV.66; A/78/PV.69; A/78/PV.79
Chile
Garrido Melo, Claudio Ernesto - A/78/PV.60; A/78/PV.74
Narváez Ojeda, Paula - A/78/PV.51; A/78/PV.66; A/78/PV.68
Vidal Mercado, Jorge Andrés - A/78/PV.70; A/78/PV.78
China
Dai, Bing - A/78/PV.66
Fu, Cong - A/78/PV.75; A/78/PV.78
Geng, Shuang - A/78/PV.51; A/78/PV.60; A/78/PV.68
Colombia
Taylor Jay, Elizabeth - A/78/PV.74
Zalabata Torres, Leonor - A/78/PV.61; A/78/PV.67; A/78/PV.68; A/78/PV.71; A/78/PV.79
Coordinating Bureau of the Non-Aligned Countries
Kwoba, Godfrey (Uganda) - A/78/PV.74
Costa Rica
Chan Valverde, Maritza - A/78/PV.3; A/78/PV.66; A/78/PV.70; A/78/PV.74; A/78/PV.78
Videche Guevara, Carlos Manuel - A/78/PV.59; A/78/PV.68
Croatia
Ćurić Hrvatinić, Hrvoje - A/78/PV.69

VETO (Agenda item 63) (continued)

Cuba
Gala López, Yuri - A/78/PV.70
Peñalver Portal, Gerardo - A/78/PV.51; A/78/PV.60
Soberón Guzmán, Ernesto - A/78/PV.67; A/78/PV.69; A/78/PV.74
Czechia
Kulhánek, Jakub - A/78/PV.3; A/78/PV.67; A/78/PV.69; A/78/PV.78
Democratic People's Republic of Korea
Kim, Song - A/78/PV.3; A/78/PV.51; A/78/PV.60; A/78/PV.67; A/78/PV.68; A/78/PV.71; A/78/PV.75
Denmark
Lassen, Christina Markus - A/78/PV.3; A/78/PV.78
Laursen, Erik - A/78/PV.70
Dominican Republic
Hidalgo, Melanie - A/78/PV.3
Ecuador
De la Gasca LopezDomínguez, José Javier - A/78/PV.60; A/78/PV.67; A/78/PV.71; A/78/PV.75; A/78/PV.78
Pérez Loose, Hernán - A/78/PV.3
Sánchez Izquierdo, Mónica - A/78/PV.68
Egypt
Abdelkhalek, Osama Mahmoud - A/78/PV.52; A/78/PV.60; A/78/PV.66; A/78/PV.70; A/78/PV.74
El Salvador
Baños Müller, Liliana Verónica - A/78/PV.79
González López, Egriselda Aracely - A/78/PV.3; A/78/PV.67
Rodríguez Acosta, Julia Elizabeth - A/78/PV.68
Segura Aragón, Carlos Efraín - A/78/PV.61
Estonia
Tammsaar, Rein - A/78/PV.70; A/78/PV.78
European Union
Lambrinidis, Stavros - A/78/PV.59; A/78/PV.66; A/78/PV.68
Samson, Hedda - A/78/PV.78
Skoog, Olof - A/78/PV.3
Finland
Kalkku, Elina - A/78/PV.68
France
Dime-Labille, Diarra - A/78/PV.70
Jaraud-Darnault, Isis Marie Doriane - A/78/PV.66
Rivière, Nicolas de - A/78/PV.51; A/78/PV.60; A/78/PV.68; A/78/PV.74; A/78/PV.78
Georgia
Abesadze, David - A/78/PV.71
Germany
Geisler, Michael Alexander - A/78/PV.52
Hasenau, Michael - A/78/PV.70
Leendertse, Antje - A/78/PV.68; A/78/PV.78
Saadi, Samy Sofian - A/78/PV.3
Ghana
Agyeman, Harold Adlai - A/78/PV.75; A/78/PV.78
Greece
Sekeris, Evangelos C. - A/78/PV.52; A/78/PV.69

VETO (Agenda item 63) (continued)

Group of Arab States
Abushahab, Mohamed Issa (United Arab Emirates) - A/78/PV.74
Al-Saadi, Abdullah Ali Fadhel (Yemen) - A/78/PV.59
Alrowaiei, Jamal Fares (Bahrain) - A/78/PV.51
Alwasil, Abdulaziz M.O. (Saudi Arabia) - A/78/PV.66
Group of Friends in Defence of the Charter of the United Nations
Marín Sevilla, Asbina (Venezuela (Bolivarian Republic of)) - A/78/PV.66
Pérez Ayestarán, Joaquín Alberto (Venezuela (Bolivarian Republic of)) - A/78/PV.3; A/78/PV.59
Guatemala
Del Águila-Castillo, María José - A/78/PV.74; A/78/PV.78
Rodríguez Mancia, Carla María - A/78/PV.3; A/78/PV.68; A/78/PV.70
Gulf Cooperation Council
Al-Thani, Alya Ahmed S.A. (Qatar) - A/78/PV.59
Guyana
Persaud, Trishala Simantini - A/78/PV.75
Rodrigues-Birkett, Carolyn - A/78/PV.61
Hungary
Kókai, Anita - A/78/PV.52
Svercsok, Szabolcs - A/78/PV.79
Szijjártó, Péter - A/78/PV.59
Iceland
Valtýsson, Jörundur - A/78/PV.61
India
Kamboj, Ruchira - A/78/PV.52; A/78/PV.59; A/78/PV.67; A/78/PV.70; A/78/PV.74
Indonesia
Dhanutirto, Mariska Dwianti - A/78/PV.70; A/78/PV.78
Nasir, Arrmanatha Christiawan - A/78/PV.52
Prabowo, Hari - A/78/PV.60; A/78/PV.67; A/78/PV.75
Iran (Islamic Republic of)
Ghadirkhomi, Payman - A/78/PV.69
Jalil Iravani, Amir Saeid - A/78/PV.51; A/78/PV.59; A/78/PV.66; A/78/PV.74
Rahimi Majd, Hassan - A/78/PV.78
Iraq
Al-Fatlawi, Abbas Kadhom Obaid - A/78/PV.61
Al-Khaqani, Hassan Jabbar - A/78/PV.67
Ireland
Mc Bean, Keith - A/78/PV.59
Mythen, Fergal Tomas - A/78/PV.3; A/78/PV.51; A/78/PV.67; A/78/PV.74; A/78/PV.78
Israel
Erdan, Gilad Menashe - A/78/PV.51; A/78/PV.59; A/78/PV.66; A/78/PV.74
Miller, Brett Jonathan - A/78/PV.69; A/78/PV.79
Italy
Greco, Gianluca - A/78/PV.3
Jovanovic, Nikola - A/78/PV.78
Massari, Maurizio - A/78/PV.52; A/78/PV.68; A/78/PV.71

VETO (Agenda item 63) (continued)

Japan
Ishikane, Kimihiro - A/78/PV.3
Shino, Mitsuko - A/78/PV.52; A/78/PV.67; A/78/PV.70
Yamazaki, Kazuyuki - A/78/PV.68; A/78/PV.75; A/78/PV.78
Jordan
Alqaisi, Sultan Natheir Mustafa - A/78/PV.67
Habashneh, Ahmad Samir Fahim - A/78/PV.61
Hmoud, Mahmoud Daifallah Mahmoud - A/78/PV.52; A/78/PV.75
Kenya
Kiboino, Michael Kapkiai - A/78/PV.3; A/78/PV.52
Kimani, Martin - A/78/PV.60; A/78/PV.69; A/78/PV.70; A/78/PV.75
League of Arab States
Abdelaziz, Maged Abdelfattah - A/78/PV.61
Lebanon
Hachem, Hadi - A/78/PV.71; A/78/PV.75
Liechtenstein
Oehri, Myriam - A/78/PV.51; A/78/PV.66; A/78/PV.75
Wenaweser, Christian - A/78/PV.3; A/78/PV.59; A/78/PV.70
Lithuania
Paulauskas, Rytis - A/78/PV.68
Luxembourg
Maes, Olivier - A/78/PV.52; A/78/PV.60; A/78/PV.67; A/78/PV.70; A/78/PV.78
Malaysia
Abd Karim, Sofian Akmal Bin - A/78/PV.51
Muhamad, Ahmad Faisal - A/78/PV.59; A/78/PV.70; A/78/PV.74
Rizal, Nizhan Faraz Bin - A/78/PV.66
Sivamohan, Shivanand - A/78/PV.69
Maldives
Ahmed, Ali Haidar - A/78/PV.74
Mohamed, Ali Naseer - A/78/PV.60
Zuhuree, Ibrahim - A/78/PV.52
Mali
Konfourou, Issa - A/78/PV.3; A/78/PV.69
Malta
Camilleri, Darren - A/78/PV.78
Frazier, Vanessa - A/78/PV.3; A/78/PV.51; A/78/PV.59
Kuymizakis, Adam - A/78/PV.66; A/78/PV.68; A/78/PV.70; A/78/PV.75
Mauritius
Koonjul, Jagdish - A/78/PV.61
Segobin Maulloo, Vandana - A/78/PV.67; A/78/PV.75
Mexico
Buenrostro Massieu, Alicia - A/78/PV.71
Jiménez Alegría, Natalia - A/78/PV.52
Ochoa Martínez, Enrique Javier - A/78/PV.3
Vasconcelos y Cruz, Héctor Enrique - A/78/PV.60; A/78/PV.67; A/78/PV.68; A/78/PV.75; A/78/PV.78

VETO (Agenda item 63) (continued)
Morocco
Hilale, Omar - A/78/PV.52; A/78/PV.61; A/78/PV.66
Kadiri, Omar - A/78/PV.69
Kadri, Taha - A/78/PV.75
Yousfi, Salim - A/78/PV.79
Mozambique
Afonso, Pedro Comissário - A/78/PV.75
Namibia
Gertze, Neville Melvin - A/78/PV.60
Kuzee, Helena Ndapewa - A/78/PV.52
Netherlands (Kingdom of the)
Brandt, Yoka - A/78/PV.3
Tahzib-Lie, Bahia - A/78/PV.70
New Zealand
Fepuleai, Justin Peter - A/78/PV.68
Schwalger, Carolyn - A/78/PV.51; A/78/PV.60; A/78/PV.70; A/78/PV.75; A/78/PV.78
New Zealand. Deputy Prime Minister
Peters, Winston - A/78/PV.66
Nicaragua
Hermida Castillo, Jaime - A/78/PV.60; A/78/PV.75
Pichardo Urbina, Eleane Yaoska - A/78/PV.69
Nigeria
Asaju, Bola - A/78/PV.67
Dakwak, Gloria - A/78/PV.70
North Macedonia
Danailov Frčkoski, Ljubomir - A/78/PV.69
Uzunovski, Dushko - A/78/PV.79
Norway
Brattested, Merete Fjeld - A/78/PV.51; A/78/PV.60
Havn, Anne Melangen - A/78/PV.75
Lovold, Andreas - A/78/PV.67; A/78/PV.68
Oman
Al-Hassan, Mohamed - A/78/PV.74
Organisation of Islamic Cooperation
Akram, Munir (Pakistan) - A/78/PV.59
Pakistan
Akram, Munir - A/78/PV.67; A/78/PV.74; A/78/PV.78
Jadoon, Usman Iqbal - A/78/PV.51
Panama
Cano Franco, Zoraya del Carmen - A/78/PV.69
Philippines
Lagdameo, Antonio Manuel Revilla - A/78/PV.70
Poland
Szczerski, Krzysztof - A/78/PV.68; A/78/PV.78
Portugal
Aranda, Jorge Eduardo Ferreira Silva - A/78/PV.52; A/78/PV.68; A/78/PV.70
Zacarias, Ana Paula - A/78/PV.3; A/78/PV.61; A/78/PV.67; A/78/PV.74; A/78/PV.78
Qatar
Al-Maawda, Jassim Sayyar - A/78/PV.70
Al-Thani, Alya Ahmed S.A. - A/78/PV.66; A/78/PV.75

VETO (Agenda item 63) (continued)
Republic of Korea
Cho, Hyunwoo - A/78/PV.70
Hwang, Joonkook - A/78/PV.3; A/78/PV.68
Kim, Sangjin - A/78/PV.51; A/78/PV.60; A/78/PV.66; A/78/PV.75
Kim, Sunghoon - A/78/PV.68
Lee, Hyun Goo - A/78/PV.79
Tak, Minsoo - A/78/PV.71
Romania
Feruță, Cornel - A/78/PV.3; A/78/PV.67; A/78/PV.69; A/78/PV.70; A/78/PV.79
Russian Federation
Evstigneeva, Anna M. - A/78/PV.51
Nebenzia, Vasilii - A/78/PV.3; A/78/PV.68; A/78/PV.75; A/78/PV.78
Polyanskiy, Dmitry A. - A/78/PV.61; A/78/PV.66; A/78/PV.70
San Marino
Beleffi, Damiano - A/78/PV.61; A/78/PV.75
Saudi Arabia
Alwasil, Abdulaziz M.O. - A/78/PV.60; A/78/PV.75
Senegal
Gueye, Cheikh Mohamadou Bamba - A/78/PV.79
Ndoye, Abdou - A/78/PV.61; A/78/PV.67
Sierra Leone
Baimarro, Karen Jean - A/78/PV.61
Kanu, Michael Imran - A/78/PV.3
Sowa, Amara Sheikh Mohammed - A/78/PV.52; A/78/PV.67; A/78/PV.75
Singapore
Gafoor, Burhan - A/78/PV.59; A/78/PV.68
Seah, Mark - A/78/PV.70
Slovenia
Jurecko, Sasa - A/78/PV.70; A/78/PV.79
Malovrh, Bostjan - A/78/PV.3; A/78/PV.51; A/78/PV.60; A/78/PV.67; A/78/PV.69; A/78/PV.74
South Africa
Joyini, Mathu - A/78/PV.60; A/78/PV.67
Schalkwyk, Marthinus van - A/78/PV.3; A/78/PV.51; A/78/PV.68; A/78/PV.70; A/78/PV.74
Spain
Gómez Hernández, Héctor José - A/78/PV.60; A/78/PV.67; A/78/PV.69; A/78/PV.75; A/78/PV.79
Jiménez de la Hoz, Ana - A/78/PV.52; A/78/PV.71
Sri Lanka
Pieris, Peter Mohan Maithri - A/78/PV.61; A/78/PV.71
State of Palestine
Mansour, Riyad H. - A/78/PV.51; A/78/PV.59; A/78/PV.66; A/78/PV.74
Sudan
Mohamed, Abuzied Shamseldin Ahmed - A/78/PV.79
Switzerland
Baeriswyl, Pascale - A/78/PV.3; A/78/PV.70; A/78/PV.78
Chanda, Riccarda - A/78/PV.60; A/78/PV.66; A/78/PV.68
Hauri, Adrian - A/78/PV.51; A/78/PV.75

VETO (Agenda item 63) (continued)

Syrian Arab Republic
Al Ashkar, Adib - A/78/PV.78
Aldahhak, Koussay Abduljabbar - A/78/PV.60; A/78/PV.67; A/78/PV.75
Dandy, Alhakam - A/78/PV.52; A/78/PV.68
Thailand
Chindawongse, Suriya - A/78/PV.51; A/78/PV.60; A/78/PV.75
Vichankaiyakij, Vathayudh - A/78/PV.67
Timor-Leste
Soares, Dionísio Da Costa Babo - A/78/PV.67
Tunisia
Ben Lagha, Adel - A/78/PV.60
Ladeb, Tarek - A/78/PV.67; A/78/PV.74
Türkiye
Ekren, Kemal Onur - A/78/PV.70
Güven, Fikriye Asli - A/78/PV.51; A/78/PV.60; A/78/PV.67
Yildiz, Ahmet - A/78/PV.74
Uganda
Muhumuza, Duncan Laki - A/78/PV.60
Ukraine
Dvornyk, Serhii - A/78/PV.71
Hayovyshyn, Khrystyna - A/78/PV.68
Zlenko, Anatoli M. - A/78/PV.79
Zlenko, Anatolii - A/78/PV.3
UN. General Assembly. President
Francis, Dennis (Trinidad and Tobago) - A/78/PV.3; A/78/PV.59; A/78/PV.66; A/78/PV.68; A/78/PV.70
UN. General Assembly. Vice-President
Muhamad, Ahmad Faisal (Malaysia) - A/78/PV.78
Niang, Cheikh (Senegal) - A/78/PV.51
United Arab Emirates
Abushahab, Mohamed Issa - A/78/PV.61; A/78/PV.67; A/78/PV.78
Al-Ali, Mohamed Essa Saif Boausaibah - A/78/PV.71
Matar, Shahd Jamal Yousuf - A/78/PV.69
Nusseibeh, Lana Zaki - A/78/PV.52
Shaheen, Ghasaq Yousif - A/78/PV.3
United Kingdom
Eckersley, Fergus - A/78/PV.3
Kariuki, James - A/78/PV.75
Woodward, Barbara - A/78/PV.59; A/78/PV.67; A/78/PV.68; A/78/PV.78
Young, Archie - A/78/PV.51; A/78/PV.71
United States
Wood, Robert A. - A/78/PV.3; A/78/PV.51; A/78/PV.59; A/78/PV.66; A/78/PV.69; A/78/PV.70; A/78/PV.74; A/78/PV.78
Uruguay
Amorín, Carlos Daniel - A/78/PV.61; A/78/PV.75; A/78/PV.78
Beretta Tassano, María Noel - A/78/PV.69
Venezuela (Bolivarian Republic of)
Moncada Acosta, Samuel R. - A/78/PV.75
Pérez Ayestarán, Joaquín Alberto - A/78/PV.59
Viet Nam
Dang, Hoang Giang - A/78/PV.61

VETO (Agenda item 63) (continued)

Yemen
Al-Dobhany, Marwan Ali Noman - A/78/PV.75

WEAPONS—OUTER SPACE (Agenda item 97b)

Algeria
Lebbaz, Larbi Abdelfattah - A/C.1/78/PV.17
ASEAN
Muhamad, Ahmad Faisal (Malaysia) - A/C.1/78/PV.16
Australia
Della-porta, Demi Heather See - A/C.1/78/PV.27
Bolivia (Plurinational State of)
Muñoz Ponce, Tatiana Bárbara - A/C.1/78/PV.17
Brazil
Szatmari, Roberto Wazima - A/C.1/78/PV.27
Canada
Fetz, Thomas - A/C.1/78/PV.27
China
Shen, Jian - A/C.1/78/PV.17
Coordinating Bureau of the Non-Aligned Countries
Sirie, Mochammad Iqbal (Indonesia) - A/C.1/78/PV.16
Costa Rica
Ávila Becerril, Ana Maricela - A/C.1/78/PV.27
Cuba
Romero López, Rosanis - A/C.1/78/PV.27
European Union
Claeys, Carine - A/C.1/78/PV.16
Sánchez de Lerín García-Ovies, Ignacio (Spain) - A/C.1/78/PV.27
India
Kulkarni, Maitrey - A/C.1/78/PV.27
Indonesia
Sinaga, Liandra Jean - A/C.1/78/PV.16
Iran (Islamic Republic of)
Eshragh Jahromi, Asadollah - A/C.1/78/PV.17
Ghorbanpour Najafabadi, Mohammad - A/C.1/78/PV.27
Mexico
Sánchez Kiesslich, Eduardo Alcibiades - A/C.1/78/PV.27
New Zealand
Nam, Christine - A/C.1/78/PV.27
Nigeria
Mahmud, Mohammed Lawal - A/C.1/78/PV.17
Russian Federation
Belousov, Andrey I. - A/C.1/78/PV.27
Vorontsov, Konstantin - A/C.1/78/PV.16; A/C.1/78/PV.17
Sri Lanka
Gunaratna, Pahala Rallage Sanathana Sugeeshwara - A/C.1/78/PV.27
Switzerland
Anderegg, Julius - A/C.1/78/PV.27
Masmejean, Laurent - A/C.1/78/PV.17
UN. General Assembly. 1st Committee. Rapporteur
Balouji, Heidar Ali (Iran (Islamic Republic of)) - A/78/PV.42
UN. Group of African States
Mahmud, Mohammed Lawal (Nigeria) - A/C.1/78/PV.16
United Kingdom
Liddle, Aidan Thomas - A/C.1/78/PV.16

WEAPONS—OUTER SPACE (Agenda item 97b) (continued)

United States
Turner, Bruce - A/C.1/78/PV.17; A/C.1/78/PV.27
Zambia
Musonda, Oliver - A/C.1/78/PV.17

WEAPONS OF MASS DESTRUCTION (Agenda item 93)

Belarus
Makarevich, Siarhei - A/C.1/78/PV.29
UN. General Assembly. 1st Committee. Rapporteur
Balouji, Heidar Ali (Iran (Islamic Republic of)) - A/78/PV.42
United States
Turner, Bruce - A/C.1/78/PV.29

WEAPONS OF MASS DESTRUCTION—TERRORISM (Agenda item 99s)

Angola
Luemba, Mateus Pedro - A/C.1/78/PV.15
Armenia
Grigoryan, Andranik - A/C.1/78/PV.29
Australia
Hill, Ruth - A/C.1/78/PV.14
Bangladesh
Muhith, Muhammad A. - A/C.1/78/PV.15
Caribbean Community
Wallace, Brian Christopher Manley (Jamaica) - A/C.1/78/PV.14
Coordinating Bureau of the Non-Aligned Countries
Aron, Andy (Indonesia) - A/C.1/78/PV.14
Côte d'Ivoire
Moriko, Tiémoko - A/C.1/78/PV.12
Egypt
Ahmed, Amr Essameldin Sadek - A/C.1/78/PV.14
Equatorial Guinea
Edu Mbasogo, Marcial - A/C.1/78/PV.15
European Union
Claeys, Carine - A/C.1/78/PV.14
India
Kamboj, Ruchira - A/C.1/78/PV.15
Italy
Bencini, Leonardo - A/C.1/78/PV.15
Norway
Hunskaar, Maria - A/C.1/78/PV.15
Philippines
Lipana, Diane Shayne Dela Fuente - A/C.1/78/PV.14
Qatar
Al-Mehaizza, Essa Abdulla - A/C.1/78/PV.15
Russian Federation
Vorontsov, Konstantin - A/C.1/78/PV.15
Spain
Rosario Vela, Manuel Jesús del - A/C.1/78/PV.15
Sri Lanka
Pieris, Peter Mohan Maithri - A/C.1/78/PV.14
Syrian Arab Republic
Al Ashkar, Adib - A/C.1/78/PV.15

WESTERN SAHARA QUESTION (Agenda item 58)

(personal capacity)
Adda, M'Rabih - A/C.4/78/SR.5
Adjissa, Youcef - A/C.4/78/SR.5
Aly, Ahmed - A/C.4/78/SR.4
Assor Sydney, Solomon - A/C.4/78/SR.6
Basinet, Cynthia - A/C.4/78/SR.4
Belmeddah, Nor Eddine - A/C.4/78/SR.5
Boulon, Malaainin - A/C.4/78/SR.5
Boussif Hammou, Limam - A/C.4/78/SR.5
Breid Eleil, Hamadi - A/C.4/78/SR.5
Chrif, Moulay Brahim - A/C.4/78/SR.5
Debeche, Smail - A/C.4/78/SR.4
Déniz Verona, Palmira - A/C.4/78/SR.4
El Ahmadi, Brahim - A/C.4/78/SR.6
El Ouali, Zine El Aabidine - A/C.4/78/SR.6
Esparza Machín, Rafael - A/C.4/78/SR.5
Hamudi, Malika - A/C.4/78/SR.5
Jiménez Martín, María Inés - A/C.4/78/SR.4
Lenz, Janet - A/C.4/78/SR.5
Lygeros, Nikos - A/C.4/78/SR.5
Mohamed, El Fadel Bua Da - A/C.4/78/SR.6
Mohamed, Mahfud - A/C.4/78/SR.6
Molina García Alcañiz, Mar - A/C.4/78/SR.4
Ouakli, Mohamed - A/C.4/78/SR.5
Pace, Giulia - A/C.4/78/SR.4
Perino, Romina - A/C.4/78/SR.6
Ramírez Marrero, Carmelo - A/C.4/78/SR.4
Roios, Ana - A/C.4/78/SR.4
Shaibata, Mrabih Rabou - A/C.4/78/SR.5
Souvi, Mouhidine - A/C.4/78/SR.5
Taleb Aomar, Boullah - A/C.4/78/SR.5
Tate, El Moustapha - A/C.4/78/SR.5
Taualumru, Chejuna - A/C.4/78/SR.5
Tessouh, Miloud - A/C.4/78/SR.5
Vucic, Mihajlo - A/C.4/78/SR.4
Africa Centre for Strategic Intelligence (Senegal)
Aidara, Abdoul Latif - A/C.4/78/SR.5
African Forum for Research and Studies in Human Rights
Ezaoui, Khadija - A/C.4/78/SR.5
African Institute for Peacebuilding and Conflict Transformation
Gain, Mohammed Ahmed - A/C.4/78/SR.6
Algeria
Bendjama, Amar - A/C.4/78/SR.9
Koudri, Toufik Laid - A/C.4/78/SR.5
Sahel, Makhlouf - A/C.4/78/SR.5
Algerian Youth Academy (Organization)
Bouaziz, Samir - A/C.4/78/SR.5
American Association of Jurists
Ramos, Vanessa - A/C.4/78/SR.5
Angola
Luemba, Mateus Pedro - A/C.4/78/SR.6
Antigua and Barbuda
Thomas, Glentis - A/C.4/78/SR.9

WESTERN SAHARA QUESTION (Agenda item 58) (continued)

Asociación Canaria de Juristas por la Paz y los Derechos Humanos
Travieso Darias, María Dolores - A/C.4/78/SR.4
Asociación Canaria de Mujeres Tejiendo Futuro
Travieso Hernández, Victoria - A/C.4/78/SR.4
Asociación Canaria de Solidaridad con el Pueblo Saharaui
Hernández González, Leticia María - A/C.4/78/SR.4
Asociación Colombiana de Amistad con el Pueblo Saharaui
Angola Mejía, Nassoli Bibiana - A/C.4/78/SR.4
Asociación Ecuatoriana de Amistad con el Pueblo Saharaui
Vega, Pablo de la - A/C.4/78/SR.4
Asociación Siembra Canaria
Ramírez Galindo, Sergio - A/C.4/78/SR.4
Association algérienne de soutien au peuple sahraoui
Bouamama, Zoheir - A/C.4/78/SR.4
Association for the Freedom of Women Sequestered in the Tindouf Camps
Hmyene, Touria - A/C.4/78/SR.6
Association for the Support of the Moroccan Autonomy Initiative
Bendriss, Khalid - A/C.4/78/SR.6
Association Rotary International à Boujdour
Edabadda, Mohamed - A/C.4/78/SR.5
Association sahraouie contre l'impunité dans les camps de Tindouf
Zrug, Lemaadla Mohamed Salem - A/C.4/78/SR.6
Austria
Troch, Harald - A/C.4/78/SR.5
Autonomy for the Sahara Coalition (Organization)
Abugamel, Firas - A/C.4/78/SR.4
Besnard, Jérôme - A/C.4/78/SR.5
Bahrain
Aljalahma, Shaikha - A/C.4/78/SR.7
Banco de Alimentos
Díaz de la Vega García, Pedro - A/C.4/78/SR.5
Benin
Biaou, Maurille Firmin - A/C.4/78/SR.8
Bolivia (Plurinational State of)
Pary Rodríguez, Diego - A/C.4/78/SR.2
Botswana
Mokhawa, Gladys - A/C.4/78/SR.8
Burkina Faso
Ganou, Oumarou - A/C.4/78/SR.7
Burundi
Sibomana, Landry - A/C.4/78/SR.8
Cameroon
Tommo Monthe, Michel - A/C.4/78/SR.8
Capitol Hill Prayer Partners (Organization : United States)
Eads, Vivian - A/C.4/78/SR.4
Cenacolo (Organization)
Stame Cervone, Anna Maria - A/C.4/78/SR.4
Central African Republic
Sepe, Tobie - A/C.4/78/SR.6

WESTERN SAHARA QUESTION (Agenda item 58) (continued)

Centre Africain de recherche pour la paix et le développement durable (Organization)
Tamekamta, Zozime Alphonse - A/C.4/78/SR.4
Centre de la paix pour les études politiques et stratégiques
Ennass, Bahi Larbi - A/C.4/78/SR.5
Classical Conversations Foundation
Dail, Elizabeth - A/C.4/78/SR.4
Collective of Saharawi Human Rights Defenders
Fall, Ahmed Mohamed - A/C.4/78/SR.5
Community of Latin American and Caribbean States
King, Inga Rhonda (Saint Vincent and the Grenadines) - A/C.4/78/SR.7
Comoros
Oussein, Kadim - A/C.4/78/SR.9
Corporación Líderes Unidos para Servir (Organization)
Teatin Rosas, Alfa Maritza - A/C.4/78/SR.4
Costa Rica
Chan Valverde, Maritza - A/C.4/78/SR.7
Côte d'Ivoire
Moriko, Tiémoko - A/C.4/78/SR.2
Cuba
Romero Puentes, Yusnier - A/C.4/78/SR.2
Democratic Republic of the Congo
Mukongo Ngay, Zénon - A/C.4/78/SR.9
Derechos Humanos sin Fronteras (Organization : Peru)
Moraga Duque, Juan Carlos - A/C.4/78/SR.5
Djibouti
Moussa, Youssouf Aden - A/C.4/78/SR.8
Dominican Republic
Blanco Conde, José Alfonso - A/C.4/78/SR.7
Ecuador
Montalvo Sosa, Andrés Efren - A/C.4/78/SR.7
El Salvador
González López, Egriselda Aracely - A/C.4/78/SR.2
Episcopal Church (Colombia)
Guevara Rodríguez, Carlos Eduardo - A/C.4/78/SR.4
Equatorial Guinea
Edjo Memba, Juan De Dios - A/C.4/78/SR.7
Erblaw (Organization)
Erb, Sherry - A/C.4/78/SR.5
Escuela de Gobierno y Políticas Públicas Norberto Bobbio (Paraguay)
Giménez, Francisco Javier - A/C.4/78/SR.5
Ethiopia
Kassaye, Yoseph - A/C.4/78/SR.8
European Conference of Support and Solidarity with the Saharawi People
Salvia, Fabio - A/C.4/78/SR.4
European Union
Gómez Aoiz, Elena (Spain) - A/C.4/78/SR.9
Federación de Periodistas del Perú
Sánchez Serra, Ricardo - A/C.4/78/SR.4
Federación Estatal de Instituciones Solidarias con el Pueblo Saharaui
Sosa Guerra, Sibisse - A/C.4/78/SR.4

WESTERN SAHARA QUESTION (Agenda item 58) (continued)

Fédération mondiale des amis du Sahara marocain
Moctar, El Hadji - A/C.4/78/SR.5
Fondation France Maroc
Seillan, Hubert - A/C.4/78/SR.5
Fondazione Proclade Internazionale - Onlus
Ramírez Soler, Henry - A/C.4/78/SR.4
Forum Canario-Saharaui
Ortiz Palacio, Ignacio - A/C.4/78/SR.4
Frente Polisario
Omar, Sidi - A/C.4/78/SR.4
Fundación Canaria de Apoyo a los Trastornos del Neurodesarrollo
Fortea Sevilla, María del Sol - A/C.4/78/SR.4
Fundación Universitaria Compensa (Colombia)
Córdoba Heredia, Alexandra - A/C.4/78/SR.4
Gabon
Ayoune, Lia Berthiana Bouanga - A/C.4/78/SR.9
Gambia
Badjie, Isatou - A/C.4/78/SR.6
Global Directives (Organization)
Thomas, Kathleen - A/C.4/78/SR.5
Guatemala
Benard Estrada, Juan Antonio - A/C.4/78/SR.6
Guinea
Zoumanigui, Paul Goa - A/C.4/78/SR.8
Guinea-Bissau
Mendes, Francisco - A/C.4/78/SR.8
Guyana
Rodrigues-Birkett, Carolyn - A/C.4/78/SR.7
Hispafrica Aprican (Organization)
Yahya, Alamine - A/C.4/78/SR.6
Hurria - Saharawi Solidarity Association
Bongini, Asia - A/C.4/78/SR.5
Institut sahélien de recherche et d'analyse pour la transformation des conflits
Sidibe, Souleymane Satigui - A/C.4/78/SR.5
International Association of Jurists for Western Sahara
González Sánchez, José Luis - A/C.4/78/SR.4
International Law Chambers (United Kingdom)
Rosemarine, Andrew M. - A/C.4/78/SR.5
Iran (Islamic Republic of)
Ghelich, Vahid - A/C.4/78/SR.7
Jordan
Habashneh, Ahmad Samir Fahim - A/C.4/78/SR.7
Juntos por Guía (Firm : Spain)
Suárez Moreno, Sergio Agustín - A/C.4/78/SR.4
Kiribati
Tito, Teburoro - A/C.4/78/SR.8
Kuwait
Alenezi, Faisal G. - A/C.4/78/SR.8
Lesotho
Nena, Matete - A/C.4/78/SR.8
Liberia
Fyneah, Sarah Safyn - A/C.4/78/SR.8
Ligue Sahara pour la démocratie et les droits de l'homme
El Baihi, Hammada - A/C.4/78/SR.6

WESTERN SAHARA QUESTION (Agenda item 58) (continued)

Mexico
Cisneros Chávez, José de Jesús - A/C.4/78/SR.2
El Mekaoui, Amina - A/C.4/78/SR.5
Moroccan Jordanian Friendship Association
Alkhalaileh, Fawaz - A/C.4/78/SR.4
Morocco
Dahi, Leila - A/C.4/78/SR.4
Hilale, Omar - A/C.4/78/SR.9
Kadiri, Omar - A/C.4/78/SR.4; A/C.4/78/SR.5
Laariche, Hayat - A/C.4/78/SR.4
Mozambique
Buanahagi, Tarcísio Baltazar - A/C.4/78/SR.8
Namibia
Gertze, Neville Melvin - A/C.4/78/SR.7
Nepal
Ray, Kaushal Kishor - A/C.4/78/SR.6
Nicaragua
Hermida Castillo, Jaime - A/C.4/78/SR.6
Observatoire du sud pour le développement territorial (Organization)
Essalek, Hanane - A/C.4/78/SR.6
Observatorio Asturiano de Derechos Humanos para el Sáhara Occidental (Spain)
Arbesu Sancho, Gemma - A/C.4/78/SR.4
Observatorio de Derechos Humanos de Castilla La Mancha para el Sáhara Occidental (Spain)
Crespo Aguilar, Juan Ramón - A/C.4/78/SR.4
On Purpose Group (Organization)
Goebel, Suzanne - A/C.4/78/SR.4
Palestinian Moroccan Friendship Society
Aljabari, Ziad - A/C.4/78/SR.4
Papua New Guinea
Sarufa, Fred - A/C.4/78/SR.6
Paraguay
Pereira Sosa, José Eduardo - A/C.4/78/SR.7
Peru
Ugarelli, Luis F. - A/C.4/78/SR.7
Plataforma Latinoamericana y Caribeña de Solidaridad con el Pueblo Saharaui (Organization)
Botero Martínez, José Leonar - A/C.4/78/SR.4
Poland
Szczerski, Krzysztof - A/C.4/78/SR.6
Portugal
Pureza, José Manuel - A/C.4/78/SR.5
Qatar
Al-thani, Jassim Abdulaziz J.A. - A/C.4/78/SR.2
Rescue and Relief International (Organization)
DiCianni, Amanda - A/C.4/78/SR.4
Rete Saharawi (Organization)
Mezzetti, Andrea - A/C.4/78/SR.5
RMOL Network (Organization)
Santosa, Teguh - A/C.4/78/SR.4
Safety and Security Instructional Services
Mason, Michelle - A/C.4/78/SR.4
Sahrawi Association in the USA
Sid Ahmed, Mula Ihfid - A/C.4/78/SR.5
Saint Lucia
Henry, Carlton Ronnie - A/C.4/78/SR.7

WESTERN SAHARA QUESTION (Agenda item 58) (continued)

Saint Vincent and the Grenadines
Andrews, Lasana - A/C.4/78/SR.8
Saudi Arabia
Alamri, Hassan Mohammed A. - A/C.4/78/SR.7
Senegal
Diome, Diamane - A/C.4/78/SR.7
Sierra Leone
Alghali, Francess Piagie - A/C.4/78/SR.7
Sociedad Peruana de Derecho Internacional
Rodríguez Mackay, Miguel Ángel - A/C.4/78/SR.4
South Africa
Schalkwyk, Marthinus van - A/C.4/78/SR.6
Syrian Arab Republic
Baghdadi, Mohannad - A/C.4/78/SR.7
Teach the Children International (Organization)
Huff, Nancy - A/C.4/78/SR.4
Timor-Leste
Nunes, Karlito - A/C.4/78/SR.2
Togo
Akakpo, Koffi - A/C.4/78/SR.6
United Arab Emirates
Al-Ali, Maryam - A/C.4/78/SR.7
Universidad Autónoma de Campeche (Mexico)
Israel Herrera, José - A/C.4/78/SR.5
Universidad de la Tierra (Mexico)
Naranjo Lizano, Verónica Elizabeth - A/C.4/78/SR.5
Universidad Nacional Autónoma de México
Ordóñez, Andrés - A/C.4/78/SR.5
Universidad Pablo de Olavide (Spain)
Gómez Justo, Juan Carlos - A/C.4/78/SR.4
Université de Caen
Boutin, Christophe - A/C.4/78/SR.5
Université nationale du Rwanda
Aboui, Ismael Buchanan - A/C.4/78/SR.4
University of Las Palmas
Vidal Garrido, Manuel - A/C.4/78/SR.4
Venezuela (Bolivarian Republic of)
Pérez Ayestarán, Joaquín Alberto - A/C.4/78/SR.2
Women Investment Network (Zambia)
Njapau-Efrati, Grace - A/C.4/78/SR.5
World Action for Refugees (Norway)
Cameron, Eric - A/C.4/78/SR.5
World Humanitarian Drive (Organization : United Kingdom)
Syedibrahim, Abdul Basith Pattinathar K. - A/C.4/78/SR.5
Zimbabwe
Mawire, Tirivavi - A/C.4/78/SR.8

WOMEN MIGRANT WORKERS (Agenda item 25a)

Colombia
Sánchez García, Nathalia - A/C.3/78/SR.7; A/C.3/78/SR.49
Egypt
Mohamed, Mohamed Omar Elfarouk Hassan - A/C.3/78/SR.49

WOMEN MIGRANT WORKERS (Agenda item 25a) (continued)

European Union
Alonso Giganto, Ana María (Spain) - A/C.3/78/SR.49
Gambia
Jaiteh, Amadou - A/C.3/78/SR.49
Hungary
Pongor, Magdolna - A/C.3/78/SR.49
Iran (Islamic Republic of)
Arab Bafrani, Fatemeh - A/C.3/78/SR.49
Iraq
Al-Khaqani, Hassan Jabbar - A/C.3/78/SR.49
Libya
Hamed, Ashraf A.O. - A/C.3/78/SR.49
Malaysia
Escopper Zumilla, Michael Jawa - A/C.3/78/SR.49
Mexico
Díaz Corona, Meigan - A/C.3/78/SR.49
Niger
Seydou, Abdoul Fadh Mahamadou - A/C.3/78/SR.49
Philippines
Lagdameo, Antonio Manuel Revilla - A/C.3/78/SR.49
Senegal
Diouf, Aminata - A/C.3/78/SR.49
UN-Women
Seymour, Daniel - A/C.3/78/SR.7

WOMEN'S ADVANCEMENT (Agenda item 25a)

Afghanistan
Faiq, Naseer Ahmed - A/C.3/78/SR.10
Albania
Lamce, Enian - A/C.3/78/SR.9
Algeria
Samai, Rahma - A/C.3/78/SR.7; A/C.3/78/SR.9
Andorra
Vives Balmaña, Elisenda - A/C.3/78/SR.10
Argentina
Oddone, Fabián - A/C.3/78/SR.8
Armenia
Hakobyan, Aram - A/C.3/78/SR.8; A/C.3/78/SR.10
ASEAN
Vichankaiyakij, Vathayudh (Thailand) - A/C.3/78/SR.8
Australia
Mitchell, Rob - A/C.3/78/SR.7
Azerbaijan
Ahangari, Narmin - A/C.3/78/SR.10
Bahrain
Alabbasi, Amina Abdulaziz - A/C.3/78/SR.9
Bangladesh
Monica, Mosammat Shahanara - A/C.3/78/SR.7; A/C.3/78/SR.10
Belarus
Velichko, Irina - A/C.3/78/SR.8
Belgium
Bauwens, Gilles - A/C.3/78/SR.7; A/C.3/78/SR.8
Brazil
Balbino, Viviane Rios - A/C.3/78/SR.9
Leite, Patricia Soares - A/C.3/78/SR.7

WOMEN'S ADVANCEMENT (Agenda item 25a) (continued)

Bulgaria
Stoeva, Lachezara - A/C.3/78/SR.9
Burkina Faso
Ganou, Oumarou - A/C.3/78/SR.9
Cabo Verde
Romualdo, Tania Serafim Yvonne - A/C.3/78/SR.9
Cameroon
Banaken Elel, Nelly - A/C.3/78/SR.8
Canada
Arbeiter, Richard - A/C.3/78/SR.8
Baur, Lianna Maureen - A/C.3/78/SR.7
Caribbean Community
Wallace, Brian Christopher Manley (Jamaica) - A/C.3/78/SR.8
Central African Republic
Lenanguy Brinz, Yannick-Michel - A/C.3/78/SR.9
Chile
Garrido Melo, Claudio Ernesto - A/C.3/78/SR.8
Perdomo, María Paula - A/C.3/78/SR.7
China
Le, Shuang - A/C.3/78/SR.7
Shuang, Le - A/C.3/78/SR.8
Colombia
Sánchez García, Nathalia - A/C.3/78/SR.7
Zalabata Torres, Leonor - A/C.3/78/SR.8
Congo
Pulchérie, Mayel Camille Asnayde - A/C.3/78/SR.9
Costa Rica
Zavala Porras, Daniel Andrés - A/C.3/78/SR.7; A/C.3/78/SR.10
Côte d'Ivoire
Moriko, Tiémoko - A/C.3/78/SR.10
Croatia
Koncul, Ivana - A/C.3/78/SR.7
Cuba
García Hernández, Martha - A/C.3/78/SR.7; A/C.3/78/SR.9
González Behmaras, Alejandro - A/C.3/78/SR.7
Cyprus
Hadjichrysanthou, Andreas - A/C.3/78/SR.8
Democratic People's Republic of Korea
Kim, Song - A/C.3/78/SR.9
Dominican Republic
Blanco Conde, José Alfonso - A/78/PV.88; A/C.3/78/SR.7
Cedano, Joan Margarita - A/C.3/78/SR.9
Ecuador
Méndez Gruezo, Elizabeth - A/C.3/78/SR.9
Egypt
Mostafa Rizk, Heba - A/C.3/78/SR.10
Eritrea
Gebrekidan, Zebib - A/C.3/78/SR.10
Estonia
Tammsaar, Rein - A/C.3/78/SR.7
Ethiopia
Arega, Elleni Henok - A/C.3/78/SR.10
European Union
Carlé, Hanne - A/C.3/78/SR.7
Samson, Hedda - A/C.3/78/SR.7

WOMEN'S ADVANCEMENT (Agenda item 25a) (continued)

FAO
Ngirwa-Mpesha, Doris - A/C.3/78/SR.10
Finland
Voionmaa, Lauri - A/C.3/78/SR.10
France
LeClerc, Emmanuel - A/C.3/78/SR.9
Georgia
Lortkipanidze, Ekaterine - A/C.3/78/SR.9
Germany
Ludwig, Annette - A/C.3/78/SR.8
Greece
Alexandridou, Alexandra - A/C.3/78/SR.7
Guatemala
Rodríguez Mancia, Carla María - A/C.3/78/SR.8
Gulf Cooperation Council
Al Jaradi, Heba Khalid (Oman) - A/C.3/78/SR.7
Guyana
Rodrigues-Birkett, Carolyn - A/C.3/78/SR.10
Haiti
Célestin, Miousemine - A/C.3/78/SR.10
Holy See
Murphy, Robert David - A/C.3/78/SR.10
Hungary
Pongor, Magdolna - A/C.3/78/SR.10
Iceland
Valtýsson, Jörundur - A/C.3/78/SR.10
India
Sonkar, Suman - A/C.3/78/SR.7; A/C.3/78/SR.9
Indonesia
Prabowo, Hari - A/C.3/78/SR.10
Iran (Islamic Republic of)
Arab Bafrani, Fatemeh - A/C.3/78/SR.8
Azad, Farzaneh Baniasad - A/C.3/78/SR.10
Ghafouri, Mojtaba - A/78/PV.88
Iraq
Raed Dawood Al-Saadi, Amna - A/C.3/78/SR.9
Ireland
Mc Bean, Keith - A/C.3/78/SR.9
Israel
Aviel, Shir - A/C.3/78/SR.8
Italy
Napolitano, Annarita - A/C.3/78/SR.9
Tonon, Daniela - A/C.3/78/SR.9
Japan
Akita, Mio - A/C.3/78/SR.7
Kamiya, Masako - A/C.3/78/SR.10
Kazakhstan
Gazizulina, Zhanna - A/C.3/78/SR.9
Kenya
Onyoni-Mogaka, Catherine Bonareri - A/C.3/78/SR.8
Kuwait
Al Mulla, Wafiqah - A/C.3/78/SR.7; A/C.3/78/SR.8
Kyrgyzstan
Kasymalieva, Aida - A/C.3/78/SR.9
Lao People's Democratic Republic
Seneduangdeth, Vilayluck - A/C.3/78/SR.9
Latvia
Pavļuta-Deslandes, Sanita - A/C.3/78/SR.7

WOMEN'S ADVANCEMENT (Agenda item 25a) (continued)

Lebanon
Zoghbi, Rawa - A/C.3/78/SR.8
Lesotho
Nena, Matete - A/C.3/78/SR.10
Liechtenstein
Oehri, Noah - A/C.3/78/SR.8
Luxembourg
Lepage, Natasha - A/C.3/78/SR.8
Malaysia
Rahman, Siti Adibah Abdul - A/C.3/78/SR.7
Ruslan, Muhammad Ammar Rafiq - A/C.3/78/SR.8
Maldives
Khadeeja, Aufiyau - A/C.3/78/SR.9
Mali
Dabo N'diaye, Djeneba - A/C.3/78/SR.10
Malta
Gabriele, Emma de - A/C.3/78/SR.7
Mexico
Escobar Vargas, Pamela - A/C.3/78/SR.8
Santa Ana Vara, Alma Esperanza - A/C.3/78/SR.7
Micronesia (Federated States of)
Lippwe, Jeem - A/C.3/78/SR.10
Morocco
Iraqui, Abla - A/C.3/78/SR.9
Myanmar
Tun, Kyaw Moe - A/C.3/78/SR.10
Namibia
Kuzee, Helena Ndapewa - A/C.3/78/SR.9
Nepal
Aryal, Krishna - A/C.3/78/SR.7
Uprety, Prathma - A/C.3/78/SR.9
Netherlands (Kingdom of the)
Korteweg, Chantal - A/C.3/78/SR.9
Tahzib-Lie, Bahia - A/C.3/78/SR.7
New Zealand
Tieman, Connor - A/C.3/78/SR.8
Nicaragua
Pichardo Urbina, Eleane Yaoska - A/C.3/78/SR.9
Nigeria
Kwarra, Nasir Isa - A/C.3/78/SR.9
North Macedonia
Danailov Frčkoski, Ljubomir - A/C.3/78/SR.7
Norway
Brattested, Merete Fjeld - A/C.3/78/SR.8
Vaeroyvik, Vilde - A/C.3/78/SR.7
Oman
Al Rubkhi, Khalid Saleh Said - A/C.3/78/SR.10
Pakistan
Akram, Munir - A/C.3/78/SR.8
Kanwal, Tehreem - A/C.3/78/SR.7
Panama
Luque Nuñez, Linda del Carmen - A/C.3/78/SR.10
Papua New Guinea
Rai, Max - A/C.3/78/SR.10
Paraguay
González Cabello Maldonado, Stephania Mercedes - A/C.3/78/SR.9
Philippines
Peñaranda, Ariel Rodelas - A/C.3/78/SR.8

WOMEN'S ADVANCEMENT (Agenda item 25a) (continued)

Poland
Lula, Iwona Anna - A/C.3/78/SR.7
Qatar
Al-Buainain, Hemyan Hassan Nasser - A/C.3/78/SR.7
Al-Thani, Alya Ahmed S.A. - A/C.3/78/SR.8
Romania
Feruță, Cornel - A/C.3/78/SR.9
Russian Federation
Kuzmenkov, Stepan Y. - A/C.3/78/SR.7; A/C.3/78/SR.8
Rwanda
Umulisa, Flavia - A/C.3/78/SR.8
Saudi Arabia
Mousa, Sulafa - A/C.3/78/SR.8
Senegal
Diouf, Aminata - A/C.3/78/SR.10
Sierra Leone
Senesi, Roselynn Finda - A/C.3/78/SR.9
Singapore
Chong, Charis - A/C.3/78/SR.8
Sistema de la Integración Centroamericana
González López, Egriselda Aracely (El Salvador) - A/C.3/78/SR.8
Slovenia
Ponikvar, Ursa - A/C.3/78/SR.7
South Africa
Passmoor, Jonathan David - A/C.3/78/SR.8
Sovereign Order of Malta
Buckley, James E. - A/C.3/78/SR.7
Lucii, Costanza - A/C.3/78/SR.7; A/C.3/78/SR.10
Spain
Alonso Giganto, Ana María - A/C.3/78/SR.7; A/C.3/78/SR.9
Sri Lanka
Pieris, Peter Mohan Maithri - A/C.3/78/SR.9
Switzerland
Maric, Martina - A/C.3/78/SR.7
Wagner, Valérie - A/C.3/78/SR.8
Syrian Arab Republic
Altarsha, Elie - A/C.3/78/SR.7; A/C.3/78/SR.9
Thailand
Diloknawarit, Ornwara - A/C.3/78/SR.8
Timor-Leste
Nunes, Karlito - A/C.3/78/SR.10
Tunisia
Bessadok, Marwa Jabou - A/C.3/78/SR.8
Türkiye
Aydil, İsmail - A/C.3/78/SR.10
Uganda
Nabeta, Celia Kafureka - A/C.3/78/SR.9
Ukraine
Tokarska, Anastasiia - A/C.3/78/SR.9
UN. Committee on the Elimination of Discrimination against Women. Chair
Peláez Narváez, Ana - A/C.3/78/SR.7
UN. General Assembly. 3rd Committee. Rapporteur
Poveda Brito, Robert Alexander (Venezuela (Bolivarian Republic of)) - A/78/PV.50

WOMEN'S ADVANCEMENT—CONFERENCES (Agenda item 25b) (continued)

Eritrea
Gebrekidan, Zebib - A/C.3/78/SR.10
Estonia
Tammsaar, Rein - A/C.3/78/SR.7
Ethiopia
Arega, Elleni Henok - A/C.3/78/SR.10
European Union
Carlé, Hanne - A/C.3/78/SR.7
Samson, Hedda - A/C.3/78/SR.7
FAO
Ngirwa-Mpesha, Doris - A/C.3/78/SR.10
Finland
Voionmaa, Lauri - A/C.3/78/SR.10
France
LeClerc, Emmanuel - A/C.3/78/SR.9
Georgia
Lortkipanidze, Ekaterine - A/C.3/78/SR.9
Germany
Ludwig, Annette - A/C.3/78/SR.8
Greece
Alexandridou, Alexandra - A/C.3/78/SR.7
Guatemala
Rodríguez Mancia, Carla María - A/C.3/78/SR.8
Gulf Cooperation Council
Al Jaradi, Heba Khalid (Oman) - A/C.3/78/SR.7
Guyana
Rodrigues-Birkett, Carolyn - A/C.3/78/SR.10
Haiti
Célestin, Miousemine - A/C.3/78/SR.10
Holy See
Murphy, Robert David - A/C.3/78/SR.10
Hungary
Pongor, Magdolna - A/C.3/78/SR.10
Iceland
Valtýsson, Jörundur - A/C.3/78/SR.10
India
Sonkar, Suman - A/C.3/78/SR.7; A/C.3/78/SR.9
Indonesia
Prabowo, Hari - A/C.3/78/SR.10
Iran (Islamic Republic of)
Arab Bafrani, Fatemeh - A/C.3/78/SR.8; A/C.3/78/SR.51
Azad, Farzaneh Baniasad - A/C.3/78/SR.10
Iraq
Al-Khaqani, Hassan Jabbar - A/C.3/78/SR.51
Raed Dawood Al-Saadi, Amna - A/C.3/78/SR.9
Ireland
Mc Bean, Keith - A/C.3/78/SR.9
Israel
Aviel, Shir - A/C.3/78/SR.8
Italy
Napolitano, Annarita - A/C.3/78/SR.9
Tonon, Daniela - A/C.3/78/SR.9
Japan
Akita, Mio - A/C.3/78/SR.7
Kamiya, Masako - A/C.3/78/SR.10
Kazakhstan
Gazizulina, Zhanna - A/C.3/78/SR.9

WOMEN'S ADVANCEMENT—CONFERENCES (Agenda item 25b) (continued)

Kenya
Onyoni-Mogaka, Catherine Bonareri - A/C.3/78/SR.8
Kuwait
Al Mulla, Wafiqah - A/C.3/78/SR.7; A/C.3/78/SR.8
Kyrgyzstan
Kasymalieva, Aida - A/C.3/78/SR.9
Lao People's Democratic Republic
Seneduangdeth, Vilayluck - A/C.3/78/SR.9
Latvia
Pavļuta-Deslandes, Sanita - A/C.3/78/SR.7
Lebanon
Zoghbi, Rawa - A/C.3/78/SR.8
Lesotho
Nena, Matete - A/C.3/78/SR.10
Liechtenstein
Oehri, Noah - A/C.3/78/SR.8
Luxembourg
Lepage, Natasha - A/C.3/78/SR.8
Malaysia
Rahman, Siti Adibah Abdul - A/C.3/78/SR.7
Ruslan, Muhammad Ammar Rafiq - A/C.3/78/SR.8
Maldives
Khadeeja, Aufiyau - A/C.3/78/SR.9
Mali
Dabo N'diaye, Djeneba - A/C.3/78/SR.10
Malta
Gabriele, Emma de - A/C.3/78/SR.7
Mexico
Escobar Vargas, Pamela - A/C.3/78/SR.8
Santa Ana Vara, Alma Esperanza - A/C.3/78/SR.7; A/C.3/78/SR.51
Micronesia (Federated States of)
Lippwe, Jeem - A/C.3/78/SR.10
Morocco
Iraqui, Abla - A/C.3/78/SR.9
Myanmar
Tun, Kyaw Moe - A/C.3/78/SR.10
Namibia
Kuzee, Helena Ndapewa - A/C.3/78/SR.9
Nepal
Aryal, Krishna - A/C.3/78/SR.7
Uprety, Prathma - A/C.3/78/SR.9
Netherlands (Kingdom of the)
Korteweg, Chantal - A/C.3/78/SR.9
Tahzib-Lie, Bahia - A/C.3/78/SR.7
New Zealand
Tieman, Connor - A/C.3/78/SR.8
Nicaragua
Pichardo Urbina, Eleane Yaoska - A/C.3/78/SR.9
Niger
Seydou, Abdoul Fadh Mahamadou - A/C.3/78/SR.51
Nigeria
Kwarra, Nasir Isa - A/C.3/78/SR.9
North Macedonia
Danailov Frčkoski, Ljubomir - A/C.3/78/SR.7
Norway
Brattested, Merete Fjeld - A/C.3/78/SR.8
Vaeroyvik, Vilde - A/C.3/78/SR.7

WOMEN'S ADVANCEMENT—CONFERENCES (Agenda item 25b) (continued)

Oman
Al Rubkhi, Khalid Saleh Said - A/C.3/78/SR.10
Pakistan
Akram, Munir - A/C.3/78/SR.8
Kanwal, Tehreem - A/C.3/78/SR.7
Panama
Luque Nuñez, Linda del Carmen - A/C.3/78/SR.10
Papua New Guinea
Rai, Max - A/C.3/78/SR.10
Paraguay
González Cabello Maldonado, Stephania Mercedes - A/C.3/78/SR.9
Philippines
Peñaranda, Ariel Rodelas - A/C.3/78/SR.8
Poland
Lula, Iwona Anna - A/C.3/78/SR.7
Qatar
Al-Buainain, Hemyan Hassan Nasser - A/C.3/78/SR.7
Al-Thani, Alya Ahmed S.A. - A/C.3/78/SR.8
Romania
Feruță, Cornel - A/C.3/78/SR.9
Russian Federation
Kuzmenkov, Stepan Y. - A/C.3/78/SR.7; A/C.3/78/SR.8
Vorobiev, Dmitry V. - A/C.3/78/SR.51
Rwanda
Umulisa, Flavia - A/C.3/78/SR.8
Saudi Arabia
Mousa, Sulafa - A/C.3/78/SR.8
Senegal
Diouf, Aminata - A/C.3/78/SR.10
Sierra Leone
Senesi, Roselynn Finda - A/C.3/78/SR.9
Singapore
Chong, Charis - A/C.3/78/SR.8
Sistema de la Integración Centroamericana
González López, Egriselda Aracely (El Salvador) - A/C.3/78/SR.8
Slovenia
Ponikvar, Ursa - A/C.3/78/SR.7
South Africa
Passmoor, Jonathan David - A/C.3/78/SR.8
Sovereign Order of Malta
Buckley, James E. - A/C.3/78/SR.7
Lucii, Costanza - A/C.3/78/SR.7; A/C.3/78/SR.10
Spain
Alonso Giganto, Ana María - A/C.3/78/SR.7; A/C.3/78/SR.9
Sri Lanka
Pieris, Peter Mohan Maithri - A/C.3/78/SR.9
Switzerland
Maric, Martina - A/C.3/78/SR.7
Wagner, Valérie - A/C.3/78/SR.8
Syrian Arab Republic
Altarsha, Elie - A/C.3/78/SR.7; A/C.3/78/SR.9
Thailand
Diloknawarit, Ornwara - A/C.3/78/SR.8
Timor-Leste
Nunes, Karlito - A/C.3/78/SR.10

WOMEN'S ADVANCEMENT—CONFERENCES (Agenda item 25b) (continued)

Tunisia
Bessadok, Marwa Jabou - A/C.3/78/SR.8
Türkiye
Aydil, İsmail - A/C.3/78/SR.10
Uganda
Nabeta, Celia Kafureka - A/C.3/78/SR.9
Ukraine
Tokarska, Anastasiia - A/C.3/78/SR.9
UN. Committee on the Elimination of Discrimination against Women. Chair
Peláez Narváez, Ana - A/C.3/78/SR.7
UN. General Assembly. 3rd Committee. Rapporteur
Poveda Brito, Robert Alexander (Venezuela (Bolivarian Republic of)) - A/78/PV.50
UN. General Assembly. 3rd Committee. Secretary
Mahmassani, Ziad - A/C.3/78/SR.51
UN. Group of African States
Arega, Elleni Henok (Ethiopia) - A/C.3/78/SR.7
UN. Human Rights Council. Special Rapporteur on Violence against Women and Girls, its Causes and its Consequences
Alsalem, Reem - A/C.3/78/SR.7
UN. Human Rights Council. Working Group on Discrimination against Women and Girls. Chair
Estrada-Tanck, Dorothy - A/C.3/78/SR.7
UN-Women
Seymour, Daniel - A/C.3/78/SR.7
United Arab Emirates
Al Hebsi, Jawaher Abdulla - A/C.3/78/SR.9
Nusseibeh, Lana Zaki - A/C.3/78/SR.8
United Kingdom
Reyes, Gaia - A/C.3/78/SR.51
White, Megan Marie - A/C.3/78/SR.8
United Republic of Tanzania
Kattanga, Hussein A. - A/C.3/78/SR.10
United States
Breen, Patrick - A/C.3/78/SR.7
Carty, Lisa A. - A/C.3/78/SR.9
Keller, Janet - A/C.3/78/SR.7
Lang, Dylan - A/C.3/78/SR.51
Millard, Elisabeth I. - A/C.3/78/SR.7
Uruguay
González Hernández, Gabriela Lilián - A/C.3/78/SR.10
Viet Nam
Thoa Le, Thi Minh - A/C.3/78/SR.8
Yemen
Al-mashehari, Sarah Ahmed Ahmed - A/C.3/78/SR.8
Zambia
Milambo, Chola - A/C.3/78/SR.10

YOUTH (Agenda item 24b)

Albania
Delija, Marsela - A/C.3/78/SR.3
Kasmi, Aldi - A/C.3/78/SR.3
Australia
Kane, Imogen - A/C.3/78/SR.3
Austria
Huber, Marvin - A/C.3/78/SR.2

YOUTH (Agenda item 24b) (continued)

Bahrain
Alhammadi, Hessa - A/C.3/78/SR.3
Belgium
Muaku, Samuel - A/C.3/78/SR.3
Quinet, Manon - A/C.3/78/SR.3
Bulgaria
Garelova, Tsvetelina - A/C.3/78/SR.2
Savova, Victoria - A/C.3/78/SR.2
Cabo Verde
Romualdo, Tania Serafim Yvonne - A/C.3/78/SR.55
Canada
Tudor-Bezies, Elizabeth - A/C.3/78/SR.55
Central African Republic
Lenanguy Brinz, Yannick-Michel - A/C.3/78/SR.3
Colombia
Méndez Bocanegra, Rodrigo Andrés - A/C.3/78/SR.55
Costa Rica
Zavala Porras, Daniel Andrés - A/C.3/78/SR.55
Cuba
García Hernández, Martha - A/C.3/78/SR.3
Cyprus
Demosthenous, Ioanna - A/C.3/78/SR.55
Czechia
Bulvasová, Kristýna - A/C.3/78/SR.2
Denmark
Andersen, Julie Juel - A/C.3/78/SR.55
Blasius, Jacob - A/C.3/78/SR.3
Zade Iseni, Cecilia - A/C.3/78/SR.3
Djibouti
Moussa, Youssouf Aden - A/C.3/78/SR.55
Dominican Republic
Andújar, Luz del Carmen - A/C.3/78/SR.3; A/C.3/78/SR.55
Ecuador
Méndez Gruezo, Elizabeth - A/C.3/78/SR.2
Egypt
Mohamed, Mohamed Omar Elfarouk Hassan - A/C.3/78/SR.55
El Salvador
Cordero Vargas, Mariana - A/C.3/78/SR.55
Estonia
Tornius, Hanna-Stiina - A/C.3/78/SR.2
European Union
Svana, Lukas - A/C.3/78/SR.1
Tariello, Giulia - A/C.3/78/SR.1
Finland
Pättikangas, Paula - A/C.3/78/SR.3
France
Wagner, Julie - A/C.3/78/SR.55
Germany
Essig, Ilka - A/C.3/78/SR.3
Töpfer, Lew - A/C.3/78/SR.3
Guatemala
Rodríguez Mancia, Carla María - A/C.3/78/SR.1
Holy See
Murphy, Robert David - A/C.3/78/SR.4; A/C.3/78/SR.55
Hungary
Offenbächer, Csenge - A/C.3/78/SR.3
Pongor, Magdolna - A/C.3/78/SR.55

YOUTH (Agenda item 24b) (continued)

Indonesia
Imanuel, Fnu - A/C.3/78/SR.55
Iran (Islamic Republic of)
Arab Bafrani, Fatemeh - A/C.3/78/SR.2; A/C.3/78/SR.55
Iraq
Abdullateef, Mohammed Ayad - A/C.3/78/SR.55
Al-Khaqani, Hassan Jabbar - A/C.3/78/SR.4
Ireland
Broderick, Fiona - A/C.3/78/SR.55
Naeem, Mohammad - A/C.3/78/SR.2
Israel
Aviel, Shir - A/C.3/78/SR.2
Carmeli, Mor - A/C.3/78/SR.55
Italy
Di Capua, Giacomo - A/C.3/78/SR.2
Tonon, Daniela - A/C.3/78/SR.2
Japan
Ono, Sho - A/C.3/78/SR.55
Kazakhstan
Bakytbekkyzy, Anel - A/C.3/78/SR.2
Libya
Hamed, Ashraf A.O. - A/C.3/78/SR.55
Malaysia
Escopper Zumilla, Michael Jawa - A/C.3/78/SR.55
Maldives
Khadeeja, Aufiyau - A/C.3/78/SR.3
Mali
Dabo N'diaye, Djeneba - A/C.3/78/SR.55
Malta
Gabriele, Emma de - A/C.3/78/SR.3
Micallef, Justine - A/C.3/78/SR.55
Mexico
Santa Ana Vara, Alma Esperanza - A/C.3/78/SR.2
Monaco
Calem-Sangiorgio, Alyson - A/C.3/78/SR.3
Mongolia
Vorshilov, Enkhbold - A/C.3/78/SR.2
Morocco
Chaquki, Naser-Allah - A/C.3/78/SR.3
Skali, Abla - A/C.3/78/SR.3
Namibia
Gertze, Neville Melvin - A/C.3/78/SR.2
Nepal
Thapa, Lok Bahadur - A/C.3/78/SR.2
Netherlands (Kingdom of the)
Lasseur, Katja - A/C.3/78/SR.55
Nicaragua
Pichardo Urbina, Eleane Yaoska - A/C.3/78/SR.4
Niger
Seydou, Abdoul Fadh Mahamadou - A/C.3/78/SR.55
Nigeria
Asaju, Bola - A/C.3/78/SR.55
Norway
Stokke, Kristine Meek - A/C.3/78/SR.2
Oman
Al Rawahi, Abdulhalim Mubarak Saloom - A/C.3/78/SR.55

YOUTH (Agenda item 24b) (continued)

Poland
Lula, Iwona Anna - A/C.3/78/SR.55
Stadnicka, Małgorzata - A/C.3/78/SR.2
Portugal
Zacarias, Ana Paula - A/C.3/78/SR.2
Qatar
Al-Thani, Alya Ahmed S.A. - A/C.3/78/SR.3
Romania
Drăghia, Alexandru - A/C.3/78/SR.3
Russian Federation
Kashaev, Roman G. - A/C.3/78/SR.2
Mazaeva, Viktoriia - A/C.3/78/SR.55
Rwanda
Umulisa, Flavia - A/C.3/78/SR.2
Saudi Arabia
Bin Jadid, Faisal Fahad M. - A/C.3/78/SR.2
Mousa, Sulafa - A/C.3/78/SR.55
Senegal
Niasse, Samba Thiam - A/C.3/78/SR.55
Serbia
Marjanović, Tamara - A/C.3/78/SR.3
Matković, Mihajlo - A/C.3/78/SR.3
Singapore
Choong, Brandon - A/C.3/78/SR.2
Sistema de la Integración Centroamericana
González López, Egriselda Aracely (El Salvador) - A/C.3/78/SR.1
Slovakia
Beblavý, Pavol - A/C.3/78/SR.2
Grünwald, Tomáš - A/C.3/78/SR.2
Slovenia
Šmidt, Arina - A/C.3/78/SR.1
Switzerland
Berchtold, Aneschka - A/C.3/78/SR.3
Tajikistan
Gulov, Golibjon - A/C.3/78/SR.2
Thailand
Akanitvong, Pataschol - A/C.3/78/SR.2
Juntree, Paranut - A/C.3/78/SR.2
Türkiye
Güven, Fikriye Asli - A/C.3/78/SR.3
Ukraine
Demchenko, Kyrylo - A/C.3/78/SR.3
Popadiuk, Mykola - A/C.3/78/SR.3
UN. Department of Economic and Social Affairs. Division for Inclusive Social Development. Officer-in-Charge
Wilmoth, John - A/C.3/78/SR.1
United Arab Emirates
Alshamsi, Mohamed - A/C.3/78/SR.3
United Republic of Tanzania
Kattanga, Hussein A. - A/C.3/78/SR.3
United States
Lang, Dylan - A/C.3/78/SR.55
Uruguay
Riva Grela, Juan José - A/C.3/78/SR.55
Yemen
Al-mashehari, Sarah Ahmed Ahmed - A/C.3/78/SR.2; A/C.3/78/SR.55

YOUTH (Agenda item 24b) (continued)

Zambia
Siamalambwa, Bentry - A/C.3/78/SR.55